THE PLANT FINDER

THE PLANT FINDER

The Right Plants for Every Garden

Senior Consultants **TONY RODD** and **GEOFF BRYANT**

FIREFLY BOOKS

49.95

RJ
SB
407
P595
2007

MANAGING DIRECTOR
Cheryl Perry

PUBLISHING MANAGER
Sarah Anderson

ART DIRECTOR
Kylie Mulquin

PROJECT MANAGER
Dannielle Doggett

SENIOR CONSULTANTS
Geoff Bryant, Tony Rodd

CONTRIBUTORS
David Austin, David Banks, Matthew Biggs,
Don Blaxell, David Bond, Peter Brownless,
Geoff Bryant, Kate Bryant, Derek Butcher,
Jerry Coleby-Williams, Ian Connor, Peter
Cundall, Penny Dunn, Jane Edmanson,
Jude Fanton, Lorraine Flanigan, Richard
Francis, Jo Ann Gardner, William Grant,
Ken Grapes, Sarah Guest, Keith Hammett,
Ian Hay, Terry Hewitt, Geoff Hodge, Sean
Hogan, Melanie Kinsey, Folko Kullmann,
Isobyl la Croix, Todd Lasseigne, Marilyn S.
Light, Tony Lord, David Mabberley, Ross
McKinnon, Judyth McLeod, Tim Marshall,
Lawrie Metcalf, Leonie Norrington, Andrew
O'Sullivan, Valda Paddison, Ron Parsons,
Neville Passmore, John Patrick, Lee Reich,
Tony Rodd, Nick Romanowski, Stephen Ryan,
Donald Schnell, Patrick Seymour, Julie Silk,
Shirley Stackhouse, Geoff Stebbings, Angus
Stewart, Wendy Thomas, R. G. Turner, Jr.,
Marion Tyree, Ben-Erik van Wyk, Rachel
Vogan, Scott Williams

EDITORS
Loretta Barnard, Kate Etherington,
Janet Parker, Marie-Louise Taylor

PHOTO LIBRARY
Alan Edwards

COVER DESIGN
Stan Lamond

DESIGNERS
Stan Lamond, Jacqueline Richards

INDEX
Sarah Plant

PRODUCTION
Ian Coles

CONTRACTS
Alan Edwards

FOREIGN RIGHTS
Dee Rogers

PUBLISHING ASSISTANT
Katie Holmes

A FIREFLY BOOK

Published by Firefly Books Ltd. 2007

Copyright © 2007 Global Book Publishing
Pty Ltd

Photographs © Global Book Publishing
Photo Library 2007

Text © Global Book Publishing Pty Ltd 2007

First printing

Publisher Cataloging-in-Publication Data (U.S.)
 The plant finder : the right plants for every
 garden / senior consultant Tony Rodd ;
 Geoff Bryant.
 [992] p. : col. photos. ; cm.
 Includes index.
 ISBN-13: 978-1-55407-265-1
 ISBN-10: 1-55407-265-4
 1. Plants, Ornamental. 2. Gardening. 3.
 Landscape plants I. Rodd, Tony. II. Bryant,
 Geoff. III. Title.
635.9/03 dc22   SB407.P536   2007

Library and Archives Canada Cataloguing in
Publication
 The plant finder : the right plants for every
 garden / senior consultants, Tony Rodd &
 Geoff Bryant.
 Includes index.
 ISBN-13: 978-1-55407-265-1
 ISBN-10: 1-55407-265-4
 1. Plants, Ornamental. 2. Plants,
Ornamental–Selection. 3. Plant selection.
4. Landscape gardening. I. Rodd, Tony II.
Bryant, Geoff
SB407.P62 2007   635.9   C2006-906030-4

Published in the United States by
Firefly Books (U.S.) Inc.
P.O. Box 1338, Ellicott Station
Buffalo, New York 14205

Published in Canada by
Firefly Books Ltd.
66 Leek Crescent
Richmond Hill, Ontario L4B 1H1

Printed in China by C & C Offset Printing
Co. Ltd.
Color separation Pica Digital Pte Ltd,
Singapore

Captions
Page 1 (left to right) Prunus mume *'Geisha';* Dahlia, *Cactus, 'Border Princess';* Pellaea falcata
Page 2 Echinacea purpurea
Page 3 (left to right) Echinopsis, *HC, 'Arizona';* Coreopsis lanceolata *'Sterntaler';* Agave attenuata
Pages 4–5 Pyrus communis

Contents

How This Book Works

Stunningly illustrated with hundreds of full-color photographs, this book provides a wealth of up-to-date information on over 5,000 plants suitable for gardens of all sizes from all parts of the world. Because the great majority of garden enthusiasts live in the temperate zones, there is a more complete coverage of temperate plants than of tropical or alpine species.

The book is divided into ten chapters: Trees and Shrubs; Annuals and Perennials; Bulbs, Corms, and Tubers; Grasses, Sedges, and Bamboos; Fruit Trees, Nut Trees, and Other Fruits; Vegetables and Herbs; Climbers and Creepers; Cacti and Succulents; Orchids; and Ferns, Palms, and Cycads. Each chapter begins with a short introduction to the plant group, followed by a comprehensive table of all the species in the chapter, with at-a-glance information on height, spread, plant type, climate, frost tolerance, aspect, and more. Directly after the table are the extensive individual plant entries, arranged alphabetically by genus name.

The symbol × before a genus or species name usually indicates a hybrid genus or species. This convention is not followed for orchid genera. The genus entries give the family to which the plant belongs, as well as geographical range, number of species, distinguishing features, commercial uses, and propagation and cultivation requirements of the genus as a whole.

Under every genus entry are a number of species entries (which include synonyms and common names, if applicable), each containing information such as the growth habit, flowering season, flower color, forms, and hardiness zones, with symbols denoting aspect, frost hardiness, spread, and height. The spread and height given apply to a mature plant in cultivation. The hardiness zones show the climatic areas in which plants can be grown. However, for annuals the minimum zone is that in which the plant can be raised and planted out over the spring to autumn period, disregarding winter hardiness.

Page heading
The heading on the left-hand page names the first genus or species entry on that page; the right-hand page heading names the last entry on that page.

Family name
The name of the group to which the genus belongs; related plant genera are placed in the same family.

Genus entry
Contains information about the genus as a whole, including geographical range, and cultivation and propagation requirements.

Cultivation
General information on growing and propagating the members of the genus as a whole.

Species entry
Contains detailed information on particular species and forms, and includes hardiness rating by zones.

Common names
The non-botanical names by which the plant is generally known, usually in its native region.

Place of origin
The particular countries or regions of the world where the plant is naturally found.

Hardiness zones
The regions in which the plant can be successfully cultivated. See page 7 for more information.

Synonyms
Incorrect botanical names by which the plant may have been known in the past.

Symbols
At-a-glance information about the plant—see the list of symbols on page 7 for their meaning.

Forms
Includes well-known or award-winning subspecies, varieties, forms, and cultivars of the species.

---

710   Macadamia

Macadamia integrifolia

MACADAMIA
This genus from the protea (Proteaceae) family contains 8 species of evergreen rainforest trees, 7 from coastal eastern Australia; one from Sulawesi, Indonesia. In warm frost-free climates they grow into compact trees with large glossy leaves and long pendulous sprays of creamy white or pale pink blossoms. Self-pollinating, the round hard-shelled nuts ripen in late summer to autumn. Two species are cultivated commercially in Australia, Hawaii and California, USA.
CULTIVATION: Grow in a humus-rich well-drained soil in full sun or partial shade. They require an ample supply of water in dry periods. Propagate from seed, but trees will not bear fruit until at least 6 years old. Selected clones are commonly grafted or budded.

Macadamia integrifolia
SMOOTH-SHELLED MACADAMIA NUT
○/◐ ❀ ↔20 ft (6 m) ↑50 ft (15 m)
From southeastern Queensland, Australia. Glossy oblong leaves, in whorls of 3, smooth, slightly wavy edges. Creamy white to pinkish flowers. Creamy white nut. Zones 9–11.

Macadamia tetraphylla
BOPPLE NUT, MACADAMIA NUT, QUEENSLAND NUT
○/◐ ❀ ↔20 ft (6 m) ↑40 ft (12 m)
From subtropical rainforests of coastal eastern Australia. Whorls of dark green oblong leaves, prickly teeth. Long pendulous racemes of white or pinkish flowers, in winter–spring. Zones 9–11.

MALUS (see page 214)

Malus pumila
syns *Malus × domestica, Pyrus malus*
APPLE, CRABAPPLE, ORCHARD APPLE
○ ✳ ↔20 ft (6 m) ↑50 ft (15 m)
The origins of eating apples were uncertain, but recent intensive botanical studies have virtually solved this puzzle and helped to

establish correct botanical names. It was believed that apples were of ancient hybrid origin, so the name *M. × domestica* was used to distinguish them from wild species. But now DNA and other evidence has shown that only one wild species is involved, *M. pumila*, and fieldwork has revealed a large range of variation in wild populations. The wild range of *M. pumila* is from western China through mountain regions of Central Asia to Europe. Young leaves, flower stalks, and calyces vary in downiness. Flower buds open to white flowers suffused with pink. Fruits over 2 in (5 cm) in diameter. *M. p.* 'Niedzwetzkyana', the most significant parent of hybrid crabapples, has young leaves, buds, blossoms, fruit, bark, branches all purple-red.

Orchard apples run to many thousands of cultivars, some still popular after 200 years. Some can be eaten raw, some are better cooked, and a number are suitable only for cider. Apples often need a pollinator of a different cultivar to set good crops. 'Bramley's Seedling', late red fruit, best cooked; 'Cox's Orange Pippin', small, strong-flavored, orange to red fruit; 'Fuji' ★, white-fleshed red fruit with yellowish markings; 'Gala', good flavor, long-keeping, yellow-marked red fruit; 'Golden Delicious', golden yellow fruit; 'Honey Crisp', very juicy, yellow-marked red fruit, cold tolerant; 'James Grieve', yellow-fleshed red fruit, quite acidic; 'Red Delicious', deep red to black-red, strong-flavored; 'Scarlet Gala', red fruit. Recent varieties, such as 'Pacific Rose', are patent-protected. Zones 3–9.

Malus pumila 'Scarlet Gala'

MANGIFERA
Best known for the mango, *M. indica*. This genus is from the cashew (Anacardiaceae) family and consists of around 40 to 60 species originally from the tropical rainforests of India, Southeast Asia, and the Solomon Islands. Simple, leathery, smooth-edged leaves are reddish when young. Panicles of small bisexual and male flowers are produced on the same plant. The fruit is a large, fleshy, hanging drupe with a flat fibrous seed. Grown in tropical and warm-temperate countries for their handsome foliage and fruit. The timber of some species is used for floorboards and tea chests. The sap and plant parts may cause dermatitis.
CULTIVATION: They need deep well-drained soil with regular fertilizing, a warm frost-free climate, and warm dry weather to set fruit; regions with low rainfall during flowering must be selected for fruit production. Propagate from seed or by grafting.

Mangifera indica
MANGO
○ ✛ ↔25 ft (8 m) ↑80 ft (24 m)
From Southeast Asia, especially Myanmar and eastern India. Young leaves red, ageing to shiny dark green. Yellowish or reddish flowers, in dense panicles. Fruit irregularly egg-shaped fleshy drupe. May be "alternate-bearing," fruiting heavily every 2 to 4 years. 'Campeche', deep yellow fruit with reddish pink tinge; 'Edward', medium to large fruit; 'Kensington Pride' (syn. 'Pride of Bowen'), Australian cultivar, propagated as seedling. Zones 11–12.

Symbols

Each species entry in this book features symbols that provide at-a-glance information about the species.

★ Flora Award—the plant is recommended by
our consultants as outstanding in its group

↔ Spread—the width of the mature plant in cultivation

↑ Height—the height of the mature plant in cultivation

☼ Full Sun—the plant thrives in sunny conditions

◐ Half Sun—the plant thrives in dappled sunlight
or part-shade

☀ Shade—the plant thrives in shady conditions

❄ Frost Tolerance—the plant is fully hardy

❄ Frost Tolerance—the plant is frost hardy (for orchids,
the plant tolerates moderate levels of frost)

⦚ Frost Tolerance—the plant is half-hardy

✈ Frost Tolerance—the plant is frost tender

♧ Epiphyte—the orchid plant grows naturally
on the trunks or branches of trees

⋀ Lithophyte—the orchid plant grows naturally on rocks

⚘ Terrestrial—the orchid plant grows naturally in the soil

World Hardiness Zones

This world map is divided into Plant Hardiness Zones, which indicate how well cultivated plants survive the minimum winter temperature expected for each zone. The system was developed by the U.S.
Department of Agriculture, originally for North America, but it now includes other geographical areas.
Zone 1 applies to the cold subarctic climates of Alaska and Siberia, for example, whereas Zone 12 covers
the warmest areas around the equator.

Both a minimum and maximum zone is given for every plant species listed in this book. A European
native, *Rosa canina* will withstand the winter frosts occurring in parts of Zone 3, in which temperatures
fall below −30°F (−34°C); it will also thrive up to Zone 10, where the minimum winter temperatures are
above 30°F (−1°C). It is important to note that maximum temperatures also have an effect, and plants
that can survive the cold of Zone 3 are unlikely to succeed in the heat of Zones 10 and 11.

Other climatic factors also affect plant growth. Humidity, day length, season length, wind, soil
temperature, and rainfall all need to be considered.

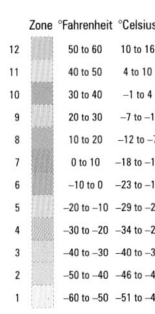

Zone	°Fahrenheit	°Celsius
12	50 to 60	10 to 16
11	40 to 50	4 to 10
10	30 to 40	−1 to 4
9	20 to 30	−7 to −1
8	10 to 20	−12 to −7
7	0 to 10	−18 to −12
6	−10 to 0	−23 to −18
5	−20 to −10	−29 to −23
4	−30 to −20	−34 to −29
3	−40 to −30	−40 to −34
2	−50 to −40	−46 to −40
1	−60 to −50	−51 to −46

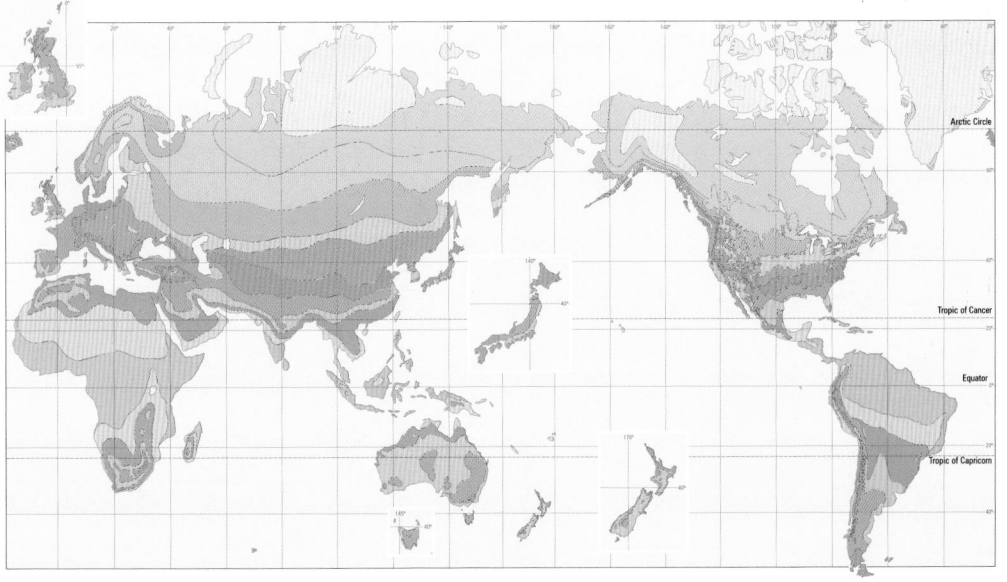

Trees and Shrubs

Trees are defined as woody perennial plants that are distinguished from other woody plants such as shrubs by the presence of usually, but not always, a single woody stem—the trunk. Shrubs are defined as woody perennial plants that possess multiple stems arising from a common point known as the crown. Both trees and shrubs inhabit virtually all climates and soil types, with a large variation in form, adaptability, and stress tolerance from species to species.

Most trees are long lived, with some living for many centuries, such as the bristlecone pine *(Pinus longaeva)* of California that reaches ages of 4,500 years or more. Some trees can attain a great height—reaching over 320 ft (96 m) tall—such as the Australian mountain ash *(Eucalyptus regnans);* other trees might grow to only 3 ft (0.9 m) tall due to the harsh climate in which they live.

Not merely existing as miniature trees, shrubs instead display completely different growth habits— some can creep or sucker, such as *Deutzia* species and *Viburnum tinus,* while others rarely or never spread in this fashion. Many shrubs, such as *Choisya* species, are very tolerant of hard pruning, wherein the entire crown can be cut back to ground level—this is a natural adaptation to fire or browsing by animals.

The oriental photinia *(Photinia villosa)* is native to China, Korea, and Japan. Its dark green leaves take on attractive shades of yellow, orange, and red in autumn.

Tree and Shrub Finder

The following cultivation table features at-a-glance information for every species or hybrid with an individual entry in the Trees and Shrubs chapter of this book. Simply find the plant you wish to know more about, and run your eye along the row to discover its height and spread, whether it is frost tolerant or not, the aspect it prefers, and more.

The type of plant is abbreviated to **T**, **S**, or **C**:
T – the plant is a tree.
S – the plant is a shrub.
C – the plant is a conifer.

The climate(s) that each plant needs to thrive in the outdoors are given (some plants will grow in more than one climate), abbreviated to **C**, **W**, or **T**:
C – the plant prefers a cool climate.
W – the plant prefers a warm-temperate or subtropical climate.
T – the plant prefers a tropical climate.

The flowering season is abbreviated to **A**, **W**, **Sp**, or **Su**:
A – the plant bears flowers in autumn.
W – the plant bears flowers in winter.
Sp – the plant bears flowers in spring.
Su – the plant bears flowers in summer.

Plant name	Height	Spread	Type	Climate	Deciduous	Evergreen	Showy flowers	Showy foliage	Scented flowers	Flowering season	Grow in pot/tub	Indoor use	Frost tolerant	Full sun	Half sun	Heavy shade
Abelia floribunda	6 ft (1.8 m)	6 ft (1.8 m)	S	W		♦	♦			Su/A				♦		
Abelia × grandiflora	6 ft (1.8 m)	6 ft (1.8 m)	S	C/W		♦	♦	♦	♦	Su/A				♦	♦	
Abelia schumannii	4 ft (1.2 m)	8 ft (2.4 m)	S	C/W		♦	♦			Su/A				♦	♦	
Abeliophyllum distichum	3 ft (0.9 m)	6 ft (1.8 m)	S	C/W	♦		♦		♦	W/Sp				♦	♦	
Abies balsamea	50 ft (15 m)	15 ft (4.5 m)	C	C		♦		♦		Sp				♦	♦	
Abies cephalonica	100 ft (30 m)	25 ft (8 m)	C	C/W		♦		♦		Sp				♦	♦	
Abies concolor	120 ft (36 m)	25 ft (8 m)	C	C		♦		♦		Sp				♦	♦	
Abies fargesii	60 ft (18 m)	12 ft (3.5 m)	C	C		♦		♦		Sp				♦	♦	
Abies fraseri	60 ft (18 m)	20 ft (6 m)	C	C		♦		♦		Sp				♦	♦	
Abies grandis	300 ft (90 m)	25 ft (8 m)	C	C		♦		♦		Sp				♦	♦	
Abies homolepis	80 ft (24 m)	25 ft (8 m)	C	C		♦		♦		Sp				♦	♦	
Abies koreana	50 ft (15 m)	5 ft (1.5 m)	C	C		♦		♦		Sp				♦	♦	
Abies pinsapo	80 ft (24 m)	15 ft (4.5 m)	C	C		♦		♦		Sp				♦	♦	
Abies procera	150 ft (45 m)	30 ft (9 m)	C	C		♦		♦		Sp				♦	♦	
Abutilon × hybridum	6–15 ft (1.8–4.5 m)	5–10 ft (1.5–3 m)	S	W		♦	♦			Sp–A	♦		♦	♦	♦	♦
Abutilon megapotamicum	8 ft (2.4 m)	8 ft (2.4 m)	S	W		♦	♦			Sp–A	♦			♦	♦	
Abutilon × suntense	12 ft (3.5 m)	8 ft (2.4 m)	S	W	♦		♦			Sp/Su				♦	♦	
Abutilon vitifolium	15 ft (4.5 m)	8 ft (2.4 m)	S	W	♦		♦			Sp/Su				♦	♦	
Acacia adunca	20 ft (6 m)	12 ft (3.5 m)	S	W		♦	♦		♦	W/Sp				♦		
Acacia baileyana	6–20 ft (1.8–6 m)	20 ft (6 m)	T	W		♦	♦	♦		W/Sp				♦		
Acacia binervia	50 ft (15 m)	35 ft (10 m)	T	W		♦	♦	♦		Sp				♦		

Plant name	Height	Spread	Type	Climate	Deciduous	Evergreen	Showy flowers	Showy foliage	Scented flowers	Flowering season	Grow in pot/tub	Indoor use	Frost tolerant	Full sun	Half sun	Heavy shade
Acacia cardiophylla	3–10 ft (0.9–3 m)	5–8 ft (1.5–2.4 m)	T	W		♦	♦	♦	♦	W/Sp			♦	♦		
Acacia cultriformis	6–10 ft (1.8–3 m)	6–10 ft (1.8–3 m)	S	W		♦	♦	♦	♦	Sp			♦	♦		
Acacia cyclops	7–15 ft (2–4.5 m)	7–15 ft (2–4.5 m)	S	W		♦	♦			Sp–A			♦	♦		
Acacia dealbata	50 ft (15 m)	25 ft (8 m)	T	W		♦	♦		♦	W/Sp			♦	♦		
Acacia elata	100 ft (30 m)	40 ft (12 m)	T	W		♦	♦	♦		Su				♦		
Acacia farnesiana	15 ft (4.5 m)	15 ft (4.5 m)	S	W/T		♦	♦		♦	W/Sp				♦		
Acacia giraffae	40–60 ft (12–18 m)	40 ft (12 m)	T	W		♦	♦		♦	W/Sp				♦		
Acacia howittii	25 ft (8 m)	10 ft (3 m)	T	W		♦	♦		♦	Sp				♦		
Acacia karroo	25 ft (8 m)	25 ft (8 m)	T	W	♦		♦		♦	Su/A				♦		
Acacia longifolia	6–25 ft (1.8–8 m)	15 ft (4.5 m)	T	W		♦	♦			W/Sp				♦		
Acacia melanoxylon	100 ft (30 m)	20 ft (6 m)	T	W		♦	♦			W/Sp			♦	♦		
Acacia podalyriifolia	10–15 ft (3–4.5 m)	15 ft (4.5 m)	S	W		♦	♦	♦	♦	W/Sp				♦		
Acacia pravissima	10–25 ft (3–8 m)	10 ft (3 m)	S	W		♦	♦	♦		Sp			♦	♦		
Acacia pycnantha	10–25 ft (3–8 m)	15 ft (4.5 m)	S	W					♦	W/Sp				♦		
Acacia riceana	10–20 ft (3–6 m)	10 ft (3 m)	S	W		♦	♦			Sp			♦	♦		
Acacia verticillata	10 ft (3 m)	7 ft (2 m)	S	W		♦	♦			W/Sp						♦
Acacia vestita	6–15 ft (1.8–4.5 m)	6–15 ft (1.8–4.5 m)	S	W		♦	♦	♦		Sp				♦		
Acacia xanthophloea	50 ft (15 m)	20–40 ft (6–12 m)	T	W	♦		♦	♦	♦	Sp				♦		
Acalypha amentacea subsp. *wilkesiana*	10 ft (3 m)	10 ft (3 m)	S	W/T	♦			♦		Su/A	♦		♦			
Acalypha hispida	12 ft (3.5 m)	5 ft (1.5 m)	S	W/T		♦	♦			Su	♦	♦				♦
Acalypha reptans	12 in (30 cm)	12 in (30 cm)	S	W/T		♦	♦			Su	♦	♦				♦
Acca sellowiana	10 ft (3 m)	10 ft (3 m)	S	W		♦	♦			Su			♦	♦		
Acer buergerianum	30 ft (9 m)	25 ft (8 m)	T	C/W	♦			♦		Sp			♦	♦		
Acer campestre	30 ft (9 m)	12 ft (3.5 m)	T	C	♦			♦		Sp			♦	♦	♦	
Acer capillipes	40 ft (12 m)	35 ft (10 m)	T	C	♦			♦		Sp			♦	♦		
Acer cappadocicum	60 ft (18 m)	50 ft (15 m)	T	C	♦			♦		Sp			♦	♦		
Acer circinnatum	15 ft (4.5 m)	15 ft (4.5 m)	T	C	♦			♦		Sp			♦	♦		
Acer davidii	30 ft (9 m)	25 ft (8 m)	T	C	♦			♦		Sp			♦	♦		
Acer forrestii	25–40 ft (8–12 m)	20–30 ft (6–9 m)	T	C	♦			♦		Sp			♦	♦		
Acer griseum	40 ft (12 m)	35 ft (10 m)	T	C	♦			♦		Sp			♦	♦		

Plant name	Height	Spread	Type	Climate	Deciduous	Evergreen	Showy flowers	Showy foliage	Scented flowers	Flowering season	Grow in pot/tub	Indoor use	Frost tolerant	Full sun	Half sun	Heavy shade
Acer japonicum	30 ft (9 m)	30 ft (9 m)	T	C	◆			◆		Sp			◆	◆		
Acer macrophyllum	80 ft (24 m)	80 ft (24 m)	T	C	◆			◆		Sp			◆	◆		
Acer maximowiczianum	60 ft (18 m)	40 ft (12 m)	T	C	◆			◆		Sp			◆	◆		
Acer negundo	60 ft (18 m)	30 ft (9 m)	T	C/W	◆		◆	◆		Sp			◆	◆		
Acer palmatum	20 ft (6 m)	25 ft (8 m)	T	C	◆			◆		Sp	◆		◆	◆		◆
Acer pensylvanicum	30 ft (9 m)	35 ft (10 m)	T	C	◆			◆		Sp			◆	◆		◆
Acer platanoides	80 ft (24 m)	50 ft (15 m)	T	C	◆			◆		Sp			◆	◆		
Acer pseudoplatanus	100 ft (30 m)	80 ft (24 m)	T	C	◆			◆		Sp			◆	◆		
Acer rubrum	100 ft (30 m)	35 ft (10 m)	T	C	◆		◆	◆		Sp			◆	◆		
Acer saccharinum	100 ft (30 m)	80 ft (24 m)	T	C	◆			◆		Sp			◆	◆		
Acer saccharum	100 ft (30 m)	40 ft (12 m)	T	C	◆			◆		Sp			◆	◆		
Acmena ingens	100 ft (30 m)	15–30 ft (4.5–9 m)	T	W		◆	◆			Su			◆			
Acmena smithii	60 ft (18 m)	35 ft (10 m)	T	W/T		◆	◆			Su			◆			
Acokanthera oblongifolia	10 ft (3 m)	5–8 ft (1.5–2.4 m)	S	W		◆	◆	◆	◆	Sp/Su			◆			
Adenium obesum	5 ft (1.5 m)	5 ft (1.5 m)	S	W/T		◆	◆			Su/A	◆	◆	◆			
Aesculus californica	15 ft (4.5 m)	30 ft (9 m)	S	C/W	◆		◆			Su			◆	◆		
Aesculus × carnea	30 ft (9 m)	15 ft (4.5 m)	T	C/W	◆		◆			Sp			◆	◆		
Aesculus hippocastanum	100 ft (30 m)	70 ft (21 m)	T	C	◆		◆			Sp			◆	◆		
Aesculus parviflora	10 ft (3 m)	15 ft (4.5 m)	S	C/W	◆		◆			Su			◆	◆		
Aesculus pavia	15 ft (4.5 m)	10 ft (3 m)	T	C/W	◆		◆			Su			◆	◆		
Afrocarpus falcatus	60–200 ft (18–60 m)	25–50 ft (8–15 m)	C	W		◆		◆		Su/A			◆			
Agathis australis	150 ft (45 m)	50 ft (15 m)	C	W		◆		◆		Sp			◆	◆		
Agathis robusta	180 ft (55 m)	40 ft (12 m)	C	W/T		◆		◆		Sp			◆			
Agonis flexuosa	30 ft (9 m)	15 ft (4.5 m)	T	W		◆	◆	◆		Sp/Su			◆			
Ailanthus altissima	40 ft (12 m)	40 ft (12 m)	T	C/W	◆			◆		Su			◆	◆		
Albizia julibrissin	20–40 ft (6–12 m)	15–20 ft (4.5–6 m)	T	C/W/T	◆		◆	◆		Su			◆	◆		
Albizia saman	100 ft (30 m)	50–100 ft (15–30 m)	T	W/T		◆		◆		Su				◆	◆	
Aleurites fordii	25 ft (8 m)	10 ft (3 m)	T	W	◆		◆			Sp			◆	◆		
Aleurites moluccana	80 ft (24 m)	35 ft (10 m)	T	W/T		◆		◆		Sp			◆			
Allamanda schottii	6 ft (1.8 m)	6 ft (1.8 m)	S	W/T		◆	◆	◆		Su	◆		◆			
Allocasuarina torulosa	40–80 ft (12–24 m)	20 ft (6 m)	T	W		◆		◆		A			◆	◆	◆	

Plant name	Height	Spread	Type	Climate	Deciduous	Evergreen	Showy flowers	Showy foliage	Scented flowers	Flowering season	Grow in pot/tub	Indoor use	Frost tolerant	Full sun	Half sun	Heavy shade
Alloxylon flammeum	60 ft (18 m)	20 ft (6 m)	T	W		♦	♦		♦	W/Sp				♦		
Alnus acuminata	40 ft (12 m)	20 ft (6 m)	T	W		♦		♦		W/Sp			♦	♦		
Alnus glutinosa	60 ft (18 m)	35 ft (10 m)	T	C	♦			♦		W/Sp			♦	♦		
Alnus incana	70 ft (21 m)	30 ft (9 m)	T	C	♦			♦		W/Sp			♦	♦		
Alnus rubra	50 ft (15 m)	30 ft (9 m)	T	C	♦			♦		W/Sp			♦	♦		
Alyogyne huegelii	3–6 ft (0.9–1.8 m)	3–6 ft (0.9–1.8 m)	S	W		♦	♦			Sp/Su	♦			♦		
Amelanchier alnifolia	3–6 ft (0.9–1.8 m)	12 ft (3.5 m)	S	C	♦		♦			Sp/Su			♦			♦
Amelanchier arborea	60 ft (18 m)	30 ft (9 m)	T	C	♦		♦			Sp			♦	♦		
Amelanchier canadensis	25 ft (8 m)	10 ft (3 m)	T	C	♦		♦			Sp			♦			♦
Amelanchier laevis	25 ft (8 m)	25 ft (8 m)	T	C	♦		♦			Sp			♦			♦
Amelanchier lamarckii	30 ft (9 m)	35 ft (10 m)	T	C	♦		♦			Sp			♦			♦
Amherstia nobilis	40 ft (12 m)	50 ft (15 m)	T	T		♦	♦		♦	Sp/Su				♦		
Andromeda polifolia	4–18 in (10–45 cm)	22 in (55 cm)	S	C		♦	♦			Sp/Su			♦			♦
Angophora costata	100 ft (30 m)	80 ft (24 m)	T	W		♦	♦	♦		Sp/Su				♦		
Angophora hispida	10 ft (3 m)	12 ft (3.5 m)	S/T	W		♦	♦	♦		Sp/Su				♦		
Anisodontea capensis	3 ft (0.9 m)	30 in (75 cm)	S	W		♦	♦			Sp–A				♦		
Aphelandra sinclairiana	15 ft (4.5 m)	10 ft (3 m)	S	W/T		♦	♦			Sp–A	♦	♦				♦
Aphelandra squarrosa	6 ft (1.8 m)	5 ft (1.5 m)	S	W/T		♦	♦	♦		Sp–A	♦	♦				♦
Aralia elata	40 ft (12 m)	30 ft (9 m)	S	C	♦		♦	♦		Su/A			♦		♦	
Aralia spinosa	20 ft (6 m)	15 ft (4.5 m)	S	C	♦		♦	♦		Su			♦		♦	
Araucaria araucana	80 ft (24 m)	35 ft (10 m)	C	C/W		♦		♦		Sp			♦	♦		
Araucaria bidwillii	150 ft (45 m)	35 ft (10 m)	C	W		♦		♦		Sp				♦		
Araucaria cunninghamii	150 ft (45 m)	12 ft (3.5 m)	C	W		♦		♦		Sp				♦		
Araucaria heterophylla	200 ft (60 m)	25 ft (8 m)	C	W		♦		♦		Sp	♦	♦		♦		
Arbutus andrachne	20 ft (6 m)	20 ft (6 m)	T	C/W		♦	♦			Sp			♦	♦		
Arbutus 'Marina'	25–50 ft (8–15 m)	20–40 ft (6–12 m)	T	C/W		♦	♦			All			♦	♦		
Arbutus menziesii	30 ft (9 m)	30 ft (9 m)	T	C/W		♦	♦			Su			♦	♦		
Arbutus unedo	25 ft (8 m)	20 ft (6 m)	T	C/W		♦	♦			A/W			♦	♦		
Arctostaphylos densiflora	5 ft (1.5 m)	6 ft (1.8 m)	S	W		♦	♦			Sp				♦	♦	♦
Arctostaphylos hookeri	6–48 in (15–120 cm)	4–15 ft (1.2–4.5 m)	S	W		♦	♦			W/Sp				♦	♦	
Arctostaphylos manzanita	15 ft (4.5 m)	10 ft (3 m)	S	W		♦	♦			Sp				♦	♦	

Plant name	Height	Spread	Type	Climate	Deciduous	Evergreen	Showy flowers	Showy foliage	Scented flowers	Flowering season	Grow in pot/tub	Indoor use	Frost tolerant	Full sun	Half sun	Heavy shade
Arctostaphylos pumila	1–5 ft (0.3–1.5 m)	3–10 ft (0.9–3 m)	S	W		◆	◆			W/Sp			◆	◆		
Arctostaphylos uva-ursi	4 in (10 cm)	20 in (50 cm)	S	C		◆	◆			Sp			◆	◆		
Arctostaphylos Hybrid Cultivars	6 in–10 ft (15 cm–3 m)	5–15 ft (1.5–4.5 m)	S	W		◆	◆	◆		Sp			◆	◆	◆	
Ardisia crenata	6 ft (1.8 m)	18 in (45 cm)	S	W		◆	◆			Sp/Su			◆			◆
Ardisia japonica	12 in (30 cm)	unlimited	S	W		◆	◆			Su			◆			
Argyranthemum frutescens	3 ft (0.9 m)	3 ft (0.9 m)	S	W		◆	◆			All	◆			◆		
Argyranthemum maderense	18 in (45 cm)	20 in (50 cm)	S	W		◆	◆			All	◆			◆		
Argyranthemum Hybrid Cultivars	12–30 in (30–75 cm)	18–36 in (45–90 cm)	S	W		◆	◆			All	◆			◆	◆	
Argyrocytisus battandieri	12 ft (3.5 m)	12 ft (3.5 m)	S	C/W		◆	◆	◆	◆	Sp/Su			◆	◆		
Aronia arbutifolia	6 ft (1.8 m)	5 ft (1.5 m)	S	C	◆		◆	◆		Sp			◆		◆	
Artemisia abrotanum	4 ft (1.2 m)	4 ft (1.2 m)	S	C/W		◆		◆		Su			◆	◆		
Artemisia arborescens	5 ft (1.5 m)	5 ft (1.5 m)	S	W		◆		◆		Su			◆	◆		
Atherosperma moschatum	100 ft (30 m)	15 ft (4.5 m)	T	W		◆	◆			Sp				◆		
Atriplex canescens	5 ft (1.5 m)	5 ft (1.5 m)	S	C/W		◆		◆		Su			◆	◆		
Atriplex halimus	6 ft (1.8 m)	10 ft (3 m)	S	W		◆		◆		Su			◆	◆		
Aucuba japonica	6 ft (1.8 m)	6 ft (1.8 m)	S	C/W		◆		◆		Sp/Su	◆		◆			◆
Auranticarpa rhombifolia	20–60 ft (6–18 m)	10–20 ft (3–6 m)	T	W		◆	◆		◆	Su				◆		
Azara microphylla	25 ft (8 m)	15 ft (4.5 m)	T	W		◆	◆		◆	Sp				◆		
Azara serrata	12 ft (3.5 m)	8 ft (2.4 m)	S	W		◆	◆			Sp			◆		◆	
Baccharis 'Centennial'	3 ft (0.9 m)	5 ft (1.5 m)	S	W		◆		◆		W/Sp			◆	◆		
Baccharis pilularis	20 in (50 cm)	20 in (50 cm)	S	W		◆				Sp			◆	◆		
Backhousia citriodora	20–25 ft (6–8 m)	10–15 ft (3–4.5 m)	T	W		◆	◆		◆	Su				◆		
Banksia ericifolia	8–20 ft (2.4–6 m)	15 ft (4.5 m)	S	W		◆	◆			A/W			◆	◆		
Banksia 'Giant Candles'	15 ft (4.5 m)	12 ft (3.5 m)	S	W		◆	◆			A/W			◆	◆		
Banksia integrifolia	20–80 ft (6–24 m)	20 ft (6 m)	T	W		◆	◆			Su–W			◆	◆		
Banksia marginata	8–30 ft (2.4–9 m)	15–20 ft (4.5–6 m)	S/T	W		◆	◆			Su–W			◆	◆		
Banksia menziesii	50 ft (15 m)	15 ft (4.5 m)	T	W		◆	◆			A/W				◆		
Banksia robur	10 ft (3 m)	7 ft (2 m)	S	W		◆	◆			Su–W				◆		
Banksia serrata	15–30 ft (4.5–9 m)	5–10 ft (1.5–3 m)	T	W		◆	◆			Su–W			◆	◆		
Banksia spinulosa	3 ft (0.9 m)	5 ft (1.5 m)	S	W		◆	◆			A/W				◆	◆	
Barleria albostellata	5 ft (1.5 m)	5 ft (1.5 m)	S	W/T		◆	◆	◆		Sp/Su				◆		

Plant name	Height	Spread	Type	Climate	Deciduous	Evergreen	Showy flowers	Showy foliage	Scented flowers	Flowering season	Grow in pot/tub	Indoor use	Frost tolerant	Full sun	Half sun	Heavy shade
Barleria cristata	3 ft (0.9 m)	5 ft (1.5 m)	S	W/T		♦	♦			All						♦
Barleria obtusa	3 ft (0.9 m)	3 ft (0.9 m)	S	W		♦	♦			A					♦	
Bartlettina sordida	10 ft (3 m)	7 ft (2 m)	S	W/T		♦	♦		♦	Su–W					♦	
Bauera rubioides	2–6 ft (0.6–1.8 m)	7 ft (2 m)	S	W		♦	♦			W/Sp						♦
Bauera sessiliflora	6 ft (1.8 m)	6 ft (1.8 m)	S	W		♦	♦			Sp/Su						♦
Bauhinia × blakeana	30 ft (9 m)	15 ft (4.5 m)	T	W/T		♦	♦			A/W					♦	
Bauhinia galpinii	10–20 ft (3–6 m)	8 ft (2.4 m)	S	W/T		♦	♦			Su/A					♦	
Bauhinia tomentosa	15 ft (4.5 m)	10 ft (3 m)	S	W/T		♦	♦			All					♦	
Bauhinia variegata	25 ft (8 m)	25 ft (8 m)	T	W/T	♦		♦			W–Su					♦	
Berberis buxifolia	8 ft (2.4 m)	10 ft (3 m)	S	C		♦	♦			Sp				♦	♦	
Berberis × carminea	5 ft (1.5 m)	8 ft (2.4 m)	S	C	♦		♦			Sp/Su				♦	♦	
Berberis darwinii	10 ft (3 m)	10 ft (3 m)	S	C		♦	♦			Sp				♦	♦	
Berberis julianae	10 ft (3 m)	10 ft (3 m)	S	C		♦	♦			Sp				♦	♦	
Berberis × macracantha	12 ft (3.5 m)	12 ft (3.5 m)	S	C	♦					Sp				♦	♦	
Berberis × ottawensis	8 ft (2.4 m)	8 ft (2.4 m)	S	C	♦		♦	♦		Sp				♦	♦	
Berberis × rubrostilla	5 ft (1.5 m)	8 ft (2.4 m)	S	C	♦			♦		Sp/Su				♦	♦	
Berberis × stenophylla	10 ft (3 m)	15 ft (4.5 m)	S	C		♦	♦			Sp				♦	♦	
Berberis thunbergii	3 ft (0.9 m)	8 ft (2.4 m)	S	C	♦			♦	♦	Sp				♦	♦	
Berberis valdiviana	15 ft (4.5 m)	15 ft (4.5 m)	S	C/W		♦	♦			Sp/Su				♦	♦	
Berberis wilsoniae	3 ft (0.9 m)	6 ft (1.8 m)	S	C	♦			♦	♦	Su				♦	♦	
Betula albosinensis	80 ft (24 m)	30 ft (9 m)	T	C	♦			♦	♦	Sp				♦	♦	
Betula ermanii	70 ft (21 m)	40 ft (12 m)	T	C	♦				♦	Sp				♦	♦	
Betula lenta	50 ft (15 m)	40 ft (12 m)	T	C	♦		♦		♦	Sp				♦	♦	
Betula mandschurica	70 ft (21 m)	30 ft (9 m)	T	C	♦				♦	Sp				♦	♦	
Betula nigra	30 ft (9 m)	15 ft (4.5 m)	T	C/W	♦				♦	Sp				♦	♦	
Betula papyrifera	60 ft (18 m)	30 ft (9 m)	T	C	♦				♦	Sp				♦	♦	
Betula pendula	80 ft (24 m)	35 ft (10 m)	T	C	♦				♦	Sp				♦	♦	
Betula platyphylla	70 ft (21 m)	40 ft (12 m)	T	C	♦			♦	♦	Sp				♦	♦	
Bixa orellana	30 ft (9 m)	10–15 ft (3–4.5 m)	T	W/T		♦	♦			Sp					♦	
Bocconia arborea	25 ft (8 m)	15 ft (4.5 m)	T	W/T		♦	♦			Su				♦	♦	
Bombax ceiba	60 ft (18 m)	30–40 ft (9–12 m)	T	W/T	♦		♦			Sp					♦	

Plant name	Height	Spread	Type	Climate	Deciduous	Evergreen	Showy flowers	Showy foliage	Scented flowers	Flowering season	Grow in pot/tub	Indoor use	Frost tolerant	Full sun	Half sun	Heavy shade
Boronia heterophylla	6 ft (1.8 m)	4 ft (1.2 m)	S	W		♦	♦		♦	W/Sp	♦				♦	
Boronia megastigma	3 ft (0.9 m)	3 ft (0.9 m)	S	W		♦	♦		♦	W/Sp	♦				♦	
Boronia pinnata	5 ft (1.5 m)	5 ft (1.5 m)	S	W		♦	♦			W/Sp					♦	
Bouvardia longiflora	3 ft (0.9 m)	3 ft (0.9 m)	S	W		♦	♦		♦	A/W	♦				♦	
Bouvardia ternifolia	3 ft (0.9 m)	3 ft (0.9 m)	S	W		♦	♦			Su/A	♦				♦	
Brachychiton acerifolius	40 ft (12 m)	20 ft (6 m)	T	W		♦				Sp/Su				♦		
Brachychiton discolor	80 ft (24 m)	30 ft (9 m)	T	W		♦				Su				♦		
Brachychiton populneus	30 ft (9 m)	15 ft (4.5 m)	T	W		♦				Sp/Su			♦	♦		
Brachyglottis greyi	5 ft (1.5 m)	10 fr (3 m)	S	W		♦	♦	♦		Su			♦	♦		
Brachyglottis laxifolia	3 ft (0.9 m)	7 ft (2 m)	S	W		♦	♦	♦		Su			♦	♦		
Breynia disticha	4 ft (1.2 m)	3 ft (0.9 m)	S	W/T		♦		♦		Su					♦	
Broussonetia papyrifera	50 ft (15 m)	30 ft (9 m)	S	W/T	♦			♦		Su			♦	♦		
Brugmansia arborea	15 ft (4.5 m)	5–8 ft (1.5–2.4 m)	S	W/T		♦	♦			Su/A				♦		
Brugmansia × candida	10 ft (3 m)	6 ft (1.8 m)	S	W/T		♦	♦		♦	Su/A	♦				♦	
Brugmansia 'Charles Grimaldi'	6 ft (1.8 m)	4 ft (1.2 m)	S	W/T		♦	♦		♦	A–Sp	♦			♦		
Brugmansia × insignis	12 ft (3.5 m)	8–10 ft (2.4–3 m)	S	W/T		♦	♦			Su/A	♦			♦		
Brugmansia sanguinea	12 ft (3.5 m)	12 ft (3.5 m)	S	W/T		♦	♦			Su/A				♦		
Brugmansia suaveolens	15 ft (4.5 m)	10 ft (3 m)	S	W/T		♦	♦		♦	Su/A				♦		
Brunfelsia americana	15 ft (4.5 m)	4–7 ft (1.2–2 m)	S	W/T		♦	♦		♦	Su	♦				♦	
Brunfelsia pauciflora	8 ft (2.4 m)	5 ft (1.5 m)	S	W/T		♦	♦			Su	♦			♦	♦	
Buckinghamia celsissima	30 ft (9 m)	12 ft (3.5 m)	T	W/T		♦	♦			A				♦		
Buddleja alternifolia	15 ft (4.5 m)	15 ft (4.5 m)	S	C	♦		♦		♦	Sp/Su			♦	♦		
Buddleja colvilei	20 ft (6 m)	20 ft (6 m)	S	C	♦		♦	♦		Sp			♦	♦		
Buddleja davidii	10–17 ft (3–5 m)	17 ft (5 m)	S	C	♦		♦		♦	Sp/Su			♦	♦		
Buddleja globosa	10–20 ft (3–6 m)	10 ft (3 m)	S	C		♦	♦		♦	Sp/Su			♦	♦		
Buddleja salviifolia	12–25 ft (3.5–8 m)	15 ft (4.5 m)	S	C		♦	♦		♦	A/W			♦	♦		
Buddleja × weyeriana	15 ft (4.5 m)	12 ft (3.5 m)	S	C		♦	♦		♦	Sp/Su				♦		
Burchellia bubalina	10 ft (3 m)	8 ft (2.4 m)	S	W		♦	♦			Sp/Su				♦		
Buxus microphylla	8 ft (2.4 m)	7 ft (2 m)	S	C/W		♦		♦		Sp			♦	♦	♦	
Buxus sempervirens	5–30 ft (1.5–9 m)	5–15 ft (1.5–4.5 m)	S	C/W		♦		♦		Sp			♦	♦	♦	
Buxus, Sheridan Hybrids	18–24 in (45–60 cm)	18–24 in (45–60 cm)	S	C/W		♦		♦		Sp				♦	♦	

Plant name	Height	Spread	Type	Climate	Deciduous	Evergreen	Showy flowers	Showy foliage	Scented flowers	Flowering season	Grow in pot/tub	Indoor use	Frost tolerant	Full sun	Half sun	Heavy shade
Buxus sinica	3–20 ft (0.9–6 m)	2–12 ft (0.6–3.5 m)	S	C/W		◆		◆	◆	Sp			◆	◆	◆	
Caesalpinia ferrea	50 ft (15 m)	20 ft (6 m)	T	W/T	◆		◆			Su				◆		
Caesalpinia gilliesii	10 ft (3 m)	4–8 ft (1.2–2.4 m)	S	W		◆	◆	◆		Su				◆		
Caesalpinia pulcherrima	10 ft (3 m)	6–12 ft (1.8–3.5 m)	S	W		◆	◆	◆		All				◆		
Calliandra haematocephala	10 ft (3 m)	20 ft (6 m)	S	W/T		◆	◆			A/W				◆	◆	
Calliandra surinamensis	10 ft (3 m)	10 ft (3 m)	S	W/T		◆	◆			All				◆		
Calliandra tweedii	6 ft (1.8 m)	6 ft (1.8 m)	S	W		◆	◆			Sp–A				◆		
Callicarpa americana	10 ft (3 m)	7 ft (2 m)	S	C/W			◆	◆		Sp			◆	◆	◆	
Callicarpa bodinieri	10 ft (3 m)	8 ft (2.4 m)	S	C/W	◆			◆		Sp			◆	◆	◆	
Callicarpa japonica	6 ft (1.8 m)	5 ft (1.5 m)	S	W	◆			◆		Sp			◆	◆		
Callicoma serratifolia	12–30 ft (3.5–9 m)	10 ft (3 m)	S	W		◆	◆	◆		Sp/Su				◆		
Callistemon citrinus	10 ft (3 m)	10 ft (3 m)	S	W		◆	◆			Sp/Su			◆	◆		
Callistemon phoeniceus	10 ft (3 m)	5 ft (1.5 m)	S	W		◆	◆			Sp/Su				◆		
Callistemon salignus	15–30 ft (4.5–9 m)	15–20 ft (4.5–6 m)	S	W		◆	◆			Sp/Su				◆		
Callistemon viminalis	25 ft (8 m)	7–10 ft (2–3 m)	S	W		◆	◆			Sp/Su				◆		
Callistemon Hybrid Cultivars	6–20 ft (1.8–6 m)	5–10 ft (1.5–3 m)	S	W		◆	◆			Sp/Su				◆		
Callitris rhomboidea	50 ft (15 m)	10–15 ft (3–4.5 m)	C	W		◆		◆		Sp			◆	◆		
Calluna vulgaris	24 in (60 cm)	30 in (75 cm)	S	C		◆	◆	◆		Su/A	◆		◆	◆		
Calocedrus decurrens	120 ft (36 m)	30 ft (9 m)	C	C		◆		◆		Sp			◆	◆		
Calodendrum capense	30 ft (9 m)	30 ft (9 m)	T	W		◆	◆			Sp/Su				◆		
Calothamnus quadrifidus	8 ft (2.4 m)	8 ft (2.4 m)	S	W		◆	◆			W/Sp				◆		
Calothamnus validus	8 ft (2.4 m)	8 ft (2.4 m)	S	W		◆	◆			W/Sp				◆		
Calycanthus floridus	10 ft (3 m)	7 ft (2 m)	S	C/W	◆		◆		◆	Sp/Su			◆	◆	◆	◆
Calycanthus occidentalis	10 ft (3 m)	7 ft (2 m)	S	C/W	◆		◆		◆	Sp/Su			◆	◆	◆	◆
Camellia grijsii	10 ft (3 m)	8 ft (2.4 m)	S	C/W		◆	◆			W/SP			◆	◆	◆	
Camellia japonica	30 ft (9 m)	25 ft (8 m)	S/T	C/W		◆	◆			W/SP			◆	◆	◆	
Camellia nitidissima	10 ft (3 m)	8 ft (2.4 m)	S	W		◆	◆			W/SP				◆	◆	
Camellia pitardii	20 ft (6 m)	12 ft (3.5 m)	S	C/W		◆	◆			W/SP			◆	◆	◆	
Camellia reticulata	30 ft (9 m)	15 ft (4.5 m)	S/T	W		◆	◆			W/SP				◆		
Camellia saluenensis	4–15 ft (1.2–4.5 m)	4–15 ft (1.2–4.5 m)	S	C/W		◆	◆			W/SP	◆		◆	◆	◆	
Camellia sasanqua	10–25 ft (3–8 m)	5 ft (1.5 m)	S	C/W		◆	◆		◆	A	◆		◆		◆	

Plant name	Height	Spread	Type	Climate	Deciduous	Evergreen	Showy flowers	Showy foliage	Scented flowers	Flowering season	Grow in pot/tub	Indoor use	Frost tolerant	Full sun	Half sun	Heavy shade
Camellia sinensis	8–20 ft (2.4–6 m)	10 ft (3 m)	S	C/W/T		◆	◆			W/SP	◆		◆		◆	
Camellia × williamsii	7–15 ft (2–4.5 m)	4–10 ft (1.2–3 m)	S/T	C/W		◆	◆			W/SP			◆		◆	
Camellia Hybrid Cultivars	3–20 ft (0.9–6 m)	3–20 ft (0.9–6 m)	S	C/W		◆	◆			W/SP	◆		◆		◆	
Cantua buxifolia	12 ft (3.5 m)	8 ft (2.4 m)	S	W		◆	◆			Sp/Su	◆			◆		
Caragana arborescens	10 ft (3 m)	4 ft (1.2 m)	S	C	◆		◆			Sp			◆	◆		
Caragana frutex	10 ft (3 m)	8 ft (2.4 m)	S	C	◆		◆			Sp			◆	◆		
Carica × heilbornii	6–12 ft (1.8–3.5 m)	10 ft (3 m)	S	W		◆		◆		Su	◆			◆		
Carissa edulis	5 ft (1.5 m)	5 ft (1.5 m)	S	W		◆	◆		◆	Sp/Su	◆	◆		◆		
Carissa macrocarpa	7–10 ft (2–3 m)	10 ft (3 m)	S	W/T		◆	◆		◆	Sp/Su	◆	◆		◆		
Carmichaelia odorata	6 ft (1.8 m)	6 ft (1.8 m)	S	C/W		◆	◆		◆	Sp/Su				◆	◆	
Carmichaelia stevensonii	12 ft (3.5 m)	10 ft (3 m)	S	C/W		◆	◆			Sp/Su				◆	◆	
Carpenteria californica	8 ft (2.4 m)	8 ft (2.4 m)	S	W/T		◆	◆			Su				◆	◆	
Carpinus betulus	80 ft (24 m)	60 ft (18 m)	T	C	◆			◆		Sp				◆	◆	
Carpinus caroliniana	40 ft (12 m)	40 ft (12 m)	T	C	◆			◆		Sp				◆	◆	
Carya cordiformis	80 ft (24 m)	50 ft (15 m)	T	C	◆			◆		Sp				◆	◆	
Caryopteris × clandonensis	5 ft (1.5 m)	5 ft (1.5 m)	S	C/W	◆		◆			Su				◆	◆	
Caryopteris incana	5 ft (1.5 m)	5 ft (1.5 m)	S	C/W	◆		◆			Su				◆	◆	
Cassia fistula	60 ft (18 m)	20 ft (6 m)	T	W/T	◆		◆		◆	Su				◆		
Cassia javanica	50 ft (15 m)	10 ft (3 m)	T	W/T	◆		◆			Su				◆		
Cassia × nealiae	25–50 ft (8–15 m)	20–30 ft (6–9 m)	T	W/T	◆		◆		◆	Sp/Su				◆		
Cassiope lycopodioides	3 in (8 cm)	10 in (25 cm)	S	C		◆	◆			Sp/Su	◆		◆	◆		
Cassiope mertensiana	6–12 in (15–30 cm)	10 in (25 cm)	S	C		◆	◆			Sp	◆		◆	◆		
Castanospermum australe	40 ft (12 m)	40 ft (12 m)	T	W/T		◆	◆			Su				◆		
Casuarina cunninghamiana	100 ft (30 m)	25 ft (8 m)	T	W		◆		◆		Su				◆		
Casuarina equisetifolia	60 ft (18 m)	20 ft (6 m)	T	W/T		◆		◆		Su				◆		
Casuarina glauca	70 ft (21 m)	20 ft (6 m)	T	W/T		◆		◆		Su				◆		
Catalpa bignonioides	50 ft (15 m)	40 ft (12 m)	T	C/W	◆		◆	◆		Su				◆	◆	
Catalpa bungei	30 ft (9 m)	25 ft (8 m)	T	C/W	◆			◆		Su				◆	◆	
Catalpa speciosa	120 ft (36 m)	90 ft (27 m)	T	C/W	◆		◆	◆		Su				◆	◆	
Ceanothus arboreus	20 ft (6 m)	12 ft (3.5 m)	S	C		◆	◆			Sp				◆	◆	
Ceanothus × delileanus	5 ft (1.5 m)	5 ft (1.5 m)	S	C	◆		◆			Su				◆	◆	

Plant name	Height	Spread	Type	Climate	Deciduous	Evergreen	Showy flowers	Showy foliage	Scented flowers	Flowering season	Grow in pot/tub	Indoor use	Frost tolerant	Full sun	Half sun	Heavy shade
Ceanothus diversifolius	4–12 in (10–30 cm)	3–6 ft (0.9–1.8 m)	S	C		◆	◆			Sp/Su			◆	◆		
Ceanothus gloriosus	12 in (30 cm)	12 ft (3.5 m)	S	C		◆	◆			Sp			◆	◆		
Ceanothus griseus	10 ft (3 m)	10 ft (3 m)	S	C		◆	◆			Sp			◆	◆		
Ceanothus hearstiorum	12 in (30 cm)	6 ft (1.8 m)	S	C		◆	◆			Sp/Su			◆	◆		
Ceanothus impressus	10 ft (3 m)	10 ft (3 m)	S	C		◆	◆			Sp			◆	◆		
Ceanothus prostratus	3 in (8 cm)	8 ft (2.4 m)	S	C		◆	◆			Sp			◆	◆		
Cedrus atlantica	80 ft (24 m)	30 ft (9 m)	C	C/W		◆		◆		A			◆	◆		
Cedrus deodara	200 ft (60 m)	30 ft (9 m)	C	C/W		◆		◆		A			◆	◆		
Cedrus libani	150 ft (45 m)	90 ft (27 m)	C	C/W		◆		◆		A			◆	◆		
Ceiba insignis	60 ft (18 m)	40 ft (12 m)	T	W/T	◆		◆			Su–W				◆		
Ceiba pentandra	230 ft (70 m)	80 ft (24 m)	T	W/T	◆		◆			Su–W				◆		
Celtis australis	60 ft (18 m)	60 ft (18 m)	S	W	◆			◆		Sp			◆	◆		
Celtis laevigata	80 ft (24 m)	60 ft (18 m)	S	C/W	◆			◆		Sp			◆	◆		
Celtis occidentalis	60 ft (18 m)	60 ft (18 m)	S	C/W	◆			◆		Sp			◆	◆		
Celtis reticulata	25 ft (8 m)	25 ft (8 m)	S	C/W	◆			◆		Sp			◆	◆		
Cephalotaxus fortunei	20 ft (6 m)	10 ft (3 m)	C	C/W		◆		◆		Sp			◆	◆		
Cephalotaxus harringtonia	15 ft (4.5 m)	10 ft (3 m)	C	C/W		◆		◆		Sp			◆	◆		
Ceratonia siliqua	40 ft (12 m)	25 ft (8 m)	T	W		◆	◆	◆		A				◆		
Ceratopetalum gummiferum	15 ft (4.5 m)	6 ft (1.8 m)	S	W		◆	◆			Su				◆	◆	
Ceratostigma plumbaginoides	18 in (45 cm)	12 in (30 cm)	S	C	◆		◆			Su/A			◆	◆		
Ceratostigma willmottianum	3 ft (0.9 m)	5 ft (1.5 m)	S	C/W	◆		◆			Su/A			◆	◆		
Cercidiphyllum japonicum	60 ft (18 m)	35 ft (10 m)	T	C/W	◆			◆		Sp			◆	◆		
Cercis canadensis	30 ft (9 m)	30 ft (9 m)	T	C	◆		◆	◆		Sp			◆	◆		
Cercis siliquastrum	35 ft (10 m)	35 ft (10 m)	T	C/W	◆		◆			Sp			◆	◆		
Cestrum aurantiacum	10 ft (3 m)	6 ft (1.8 m)	S	W		◆	◆			Sp/Su				◆	◆	
Cestrum × cultum	10 ft (3 m)	6 ft (1.8 m)	S	W		◆	◆			Sp/Su				◆	◆	
Cestrum elegans	10 ft (3 m)	8 ft (2.4 m)	S	W		◆	◆			Su/A				◆	◆	
Cestrum 'Newellii'	10 ft (3 m)	10 ft (3 m)	S	W		◆	◆			All	◆			◆	◆	
Cestrum nocturnum	10 ft (3 m)	10 ft (3 m)	S	W		◆	◆		◆	Su/A	◆			◆	◆	
Chaenomeles × californica	6 ft (1.8 m)	5 ft (1.5 m)	S	C/W	◆		◆			Sp			◆	◆	◆	
Chaenomeles japonica	3 ft (0.9 m)	6 ft (1.8 m)	S	C	◆		◆			W/Sp			◆	◆	◆	

Plant name	Height	Spread	Type	Climate	Deciduous	Evergreen	Showy flowers	Showy foliage	Scented flowers	Flowering season	Grow in pot/tub	Indoor use	Frost tolerant	Full sun	Half sun	Heavy shade
Chaenomeles speciosa	10 ft (3 m)	15 ft (4.5 m)	S	C	◆		◆			W/Sp			◆	◆	◆	
Chaenomeles × superba	5 ft (1.5 m)	6 ft (1.8 m)	S	C/W	◆		◆			Sp			◆	◆	◆	
Chamaecyparis lawsoniana	100 ft (30 m)	10–15 ft (3–4.5 m)	C	C		◆		◆		Sp			◆	◆		
Chamaecyparis obtusa	60 ft (18 m)	20 ft (6 m)	C	C/W		◆		◆		Sp			◆	◆		
Chamaecyparis pisifera	75 ft (23 m)	15 ft (4.5 m)	C	C/W		◆		◆		Sp			◆	◆		
Chamaecyparis thyoides	50 ft (15 m)	12 ft (3.5 m)	C	C		◆		◆		Sp			◆	◆		
Chamaecytisus purpureus	18 in (45 cm)	24 in (60 cm)	S	C/W	◆		◆			Su			◆	◆	◆	
Chamelaucium uncinatum	8 ft (2.4 m)	8 ft (2.4 m)	S	W		◆	◆			W	◆			◆		
Chilopsis linearis	10–20 ft (3–6 m)	8 ft (2.4 m)	S	W		◆	◆			Sp/Su			◆	◆		
Chimonanthus praecox	12 ft (3.5 m)	10 ft (3 m)	S	C/W	◆		◆		◆	W			◆	◆		
Chionanthus retusus	15–30 ft (4.5–9 m)	10 ft (3 m)	T	C/W	◆		◆		◆	Su			◆	◆		
Chionanthus virginicus	12–25 ft (3.5–8 m)	10 ft (3 m)	T	C/W	◆		◆		◆	Su			◆	◆		
Choisya 'Aztec Pearl'	8 ft (2.4 m)	8 ft (2.4 m)	S	W		◆	◆		◆	Sp/Su	◆			◆	◆	
Choisya ternata	6 ft (1.8 m)	6 ft (1.8 m)	S	W		◆	◆		◆	Sp/Su	◆			◆	◆	
Chorizema cordatum	4 ft (1.2 m)	4 ft (1.2 m)	S	W		◆	◆			Su–W	◆			◆	◆	
Chrysophyllum cainito	50 ft (15 m)	15 ft (4.5 m)	T	W/T		◆	◆	◆		Su						
Cinnamomum camphora	60 ft (18 m)	30 ft (9 m)	T	W		◆		◆		Sp				◆		
Cistus albidus	3 ft (0.9 m)	4 ft (1.2 m)	S	W		◆	◆			Sp/Su				◆	◆	
Cistus creticus	3 ft (0.9 m)	3 ft (0.9 m)	S	W		◆	◆			Sp/Su				◆	◆	
Cistus ladanifer	5 ft (1.5 m)	5 ft (1.5 m)	S	W		◆	◆			Sp/Su				◆	◆	
Cistus × pulverulentus	2 ft (0.6 m)	6 ft (1.8 m)	S	W		◆	◆			Sp/Su				◆	◆	
Cistus × purpureus	4 ft (1.2 m)	5 ft (1.5 m)	S	W		◆	◆			Su				◆	◆	
Cistus salviifolius	30 in (75 cm)	30 in (75 cm)	S	W		◆	◆			Sp/Su				◆	◆	
Cistus Hybrid Cultivars	2–5 ft (0.6–1.5 m)	3–6 ft (0.9–1.8 m)	S	W		◆	◆			Sp/Su				◆	◆	
Citrus trifoliata	15 ft (4.5 m)	15 ft (4.5 m)	S	C/W	◆		◆		◆	Sp/Su				◆	◆	
Cladrastis kentukea	25–40 ft (8–12 m)	30 ft (9 m)	T	C	◆		◆		◆	Su				◆	◆	
Clematis heracleifolia	3–6 ft (0.9–1.8 m)	2–5 ft (0.6–1.5 m)	S	C	◆		◆		◆	Su/A			◆	◆	◆	
Clerodendrum bungei	8 ft (2.4 m)	8 ft (2.4 m)	S	W		◆	◆	◆	◆	Su				◆	◆	
Clerodendrum speciosissimum	6 ft (1.8 m)	4 ft (1.2 m)	S	W/T		◆	◆			Su					◆	
Clerodendrum trichotomum	15 ft (4.5 m)	15 ft (4.5 m)	S	W	◆		◆	◆		Su				◆		◆
Clethra acuminata	12 ft (3.5 m)	12 ft (3.5 m)	S	C/W	◆		◆	◆	◆	Su				◆	◆	

Plant name	Height	Spread	Type	Climate	Deciduous	Evergreen	Showy flowers	Showy foliage	Scented flowers	Flowering season	Grow in pot/tub	Indoor use	Frost tolerant	Full sun	Half sun	Heavy shade
Clethra alnifolia	6 ft (1.8 m)	6 ft (1.8 m)	S	C/W	◆		◆		◆	Su			◆		◆	
Clethra arborea	25 ft (8 m)	20 ft (6 m)	S	W		◆	◆		◆	Su					◆	
Clethra barbinervis	10 ft (3 m)	10 ft (3 m)	S	C/W	◆		◆		◆	Su/A			◆		◆	
Clianthus puniceus	6 ft (1.8 m)	6 ft (1.8 m)	S	W		◆	◆			Sp/Su	◆		◆	◆	◆	
Clusia major	50 ft (15 m)	50 ft (15 m)	T	W/T		◆	◆			Su				◆		
Coccoloba uvifera	20 ft (6 m)	10 ft (3 m)	T	W		◆			◆	Su				◆		
Codiaeum variegatum	3–12 ft (0.9–3.5 m)	2–4 ft (0.6–1.2 m)	S	W/T		◆		◆		Su	◆	◆			◆	◆
Coffea arabica	10 ft (3 m)	10 ft (3 m)	S	W/T		◆	◆	◆	◆	A	◆	◆			◆	◆
Coleonema pulchellum	2–5 ft (0.6–1.5 m)	3–4 ft (0.9–1.2 m)	S	W		◆			◆	W/Sp	◆			◆	◆	
Colletia hystrix	10–15 ft (3–4.5 m)	10–15 ft (3–4.5 m)	S	C/W		◆	◆		◆	Su/A				◆	◆	
Colletia paradoxa	6 ft (1.8 m)	8 ft (2.4 m)	S	C/W		◆	◆		◆	Su/A				◆	◆	
Colutea arborescens	15 ft (4.5 m)	10 ft (3 m)	S	C/W	◆		◆	◆		Sp				◆	◆	
Combretum kraussii	40 ft (12 m)	15 ft (4.5 m)	T	W		◆	◆	◆		W/Sp				◆	◆	
Coprosma 'Coppershine'	3–5 ft (0.9–1.5 m)	3–4 ft (0.9–1.2 m)	S	W		◆		◆		Sp	◆			◆	◆	
Coprosma × *kirkii*	3 ft (0.9 m)	7 ft (2 m)	S	W		◆		◆		Sp					◆	
Coprosma repens	20 ft (6 m)	12 ft (3.5 m)	S	W		◆		◆		Sp					◆	
Coprosma rugosa	6 ft (1.8 m)	6 ft (1.8 m)	S	W		◆		◆		Sp					◆	
Cordia boissieri	8 ft (2.4 m)	8 ft (2.4 m)	S	W		◆	◆			Su				◆	◆	
Cordyline australis	20 ft (6 m)	8 ft (2.4 m)	T	C/W		◆	◆	◆	◆	Su	◆		◆	◆	◆	
Cordyline fruticosa	10 ft (3 m)	4 ft (1.2 m)	S	W/T		◆		◆		Su	◆	◆			◆	
Cordyline rubra	10–15 ft (3–4.5 m)	3–7 ft (0.9–2 m)	S	W		◆		◆		Su	◆				◆	
Cordyline stricta	15 ft (4.5 m)	3 ft (0.9 m)	S	W/T		◆		◆		Sp/Su	◆	◆				◆
Cornus alba	10 ft (3 m)	10 ft (3 m)	S	C	◆			◆		Sp			◆	◆	◆	
Cornus capitata	30 ft (9 m)	30 ft (9 m)	T	C/W		◆	◆			Sp/Su			◆	◆	◆	
Cornus controversa	60 ft (18 m)	50 ft (15 m)	T	C	◆		◆			Sp			◆	◆		
Cornus 'Eddie's White Wonder'	15 ft (4.5 m)	15 ft (4.5 m)	S	C	◆		◆	◆		Sp			◆	◆		
Cornus florida	30 ft (9 m)	25 ft (8 m)	T	C	◆		◆	◆		Sp			◆	◆	◆	
Cornus kousa	25 ft (8 m)	15 ft (4.5 m)	T	C	◆		◆	◆		Su			◆	◆		
Cornus mas	25 ft (8 m)	20 ft (6 m)	T	C	◆		◆	◆		W/Sp			◆	◆		
Cornus nuttallii	60 ft (18 m)	40 ft (12 m)	T	C	◆		◆	◆		Sp/Su			◆	◆		
Cornus sanguinea	15 ft (4.5 m)	10 ft (3 m)	T	C	◆			◆		Sp			◆	◆		

Plant name	Height	Spread	Type	Climate	Deciduous	Evergreen	Showy flowers	Showy foliage	Scented flowers	Flowering season	Grow in pot/tub	Indoor use	Frost tolerant	Full sun	Half sun	Heavy shade
Corokia buddlejoides	10 ft (3 m)	7 ft (2 m)	S	C/W		♦	♦			Sp			♦	♦	♦	
Corokia cotoneaster	10 ft (3 m)	10 ft (3 m)	S	C/W		♦	♦			Sp			♦	♦	♦	
Corokia × virgata	6 ft (1.8 m)	6 ft (1.8 m)	S	C/W		♦	♦			Sp			♦	♦		
Correa alba	3 ft (0.9 m)	6 ft (1.8 m)	S	W		♦	♦			W/Sp	♦		♦	♦	♦	
Correa backhouseana	6 ft (1.8 m)	6 ft (1.8 m)	S	W		♦	♦			W/Sp	♦		♦	♦		
Correa pulchella	3 ft (0.9 m)	3 ft (0.9 m)	S	W		♦	♦			W/Sp	♦		♦	♦	♦	
Correa reflexa	2–6 ft (0.6–1.8 m)	1–7 ft (0.3–2 m)	S	W		♦	♦			W/Sp	♦		♦	♦	♦	
Correa Hybrid Cultivars	18 in–6 ft (45 cm–1.8 m)	2–4 ft (0.6–1.2 m)	S	W		♦	♦			W/Sp	♦				♦	
Corylopsis sinensis	15 ft (4.5 m)	15 ft (4.5 m)	S	C	♦		♦			Sp/Su			♦		♦	
Corylopsis spicata	6 ft (1.8 m)	10 ft (3 m)	S	C	♦		♦			Sp			♦		♦	
Corymbia citriodora	100 ft (30 m)	35 ft (10 m)	T	W/T		♦	♦			Su/A				♦		
Corymbia ficifolia	30 ft (9 m)	15 ft (4.5 m)	T	W		♦	♦	♦		Su				♦		
Corynocarpus laevigata	50 ft (15 m)	25 ft (8 m)	T	W		♦	♦			Sp	♦					
Cotinus coggygria	15 ft (4.5 m)	15 ft (4.5 m)	S	C/W	♦		♦	♦		Su			♦	♦		
Cotinus 'Grace'	20 ft (6 m)	15 ft (4.5 m)	S	C/W	♦		♦	♦		Su			♦	♦		
Cotinus obovatus	30 ft (9 m)	20 ft (6 m)	T	C/W	♦		♦	♦		Su			♦	♦		
Cotoneaster dammeri	8 in (20 cm)	6 ft (1.8 m)	S	C/W		♦	♦			Su			♦	♦		
Cotoneaster franchetii	10 ft (3 m)	10 ft (3 m)	S	C/W		♦	♦			Su			♦	♦		
Cotoneaster frigidus	30 ft (9 m)	30 ft (9 m)	S	C/W	♦		♦			Su			♦	♦		
Cotoneaster horizontalis	3 ft (0.9 m)	5 ft (1.5 m)	S	C/W	♦		♦			Sp			♦	♦		
Cotoneaster lacteus	12 ft (3.5 m)	12 ft (3.5 m)	S	C/W		♦	♦			Su			♦	♦		
Cotoneaster microphyllus	3 ft (0.9 m)	3 ft (0.9 m)	S	C/W		♦	♦			Sp/Su			♦	♦		
Cotoneaster salicifolius	15 ft (4.5 m)	15 ft (4.5 m)	S	C/W		♦	♦			Su			♦	♦		
Cotoneaster simonsii	8 ft (2.4 m)	6 ft (1.8 m)	S	C/W	♦		♦			Su			♦	♦		
Cotoneaster × watereri	15 ft (4.5 m)	15 ft (4.5 m)	S	C/W		♦	♦			Su			♦	♦		
Couroupita guianensis	100 ft (30 m)	15 ft (4.5 m)	T	W/T		♦	♦			Sp				♦		
Crataegus 'Autumn Glory'	10 ft (3 m)	10 ft (3 m)	S	C/W	♦		♦			Su			♦	♦		
Crataegus crus-galli	30 ft (9 m)	35 ft (10 m)	T	C/W	♦			♦	♦	Sp			♦	♦		
Crataegus laciniata	20 ft (6 m)	20 ft (6 m)	T	C	♦		♦			Su			♦	♦		
Crataegus laevigata	25 ft (8 m)	25 ft (8 m)	T	C	♦		♦			Sp			♦	♦		
Crataegus × lavalleei	20 ft (6 m)	20 ft (6 m)	T	C/W	♦		♦			Su				♦	♦	

Plant name	Height	Spread	Type	Climate	Deciduous	Evergreen	Showy flowers	Showy foliage	Scented flowers	Flowering season	Grow in pot/tub	Indoor use	Frost tolerant	Full sun	Half sun	Heavy shade
Crataegus monogyna	25 ft (8 m)	25 ft (8 m)	T	C	♦		♦			W/Sp			♦	♦		
Crataegus persimilis 'Prunifolia'	20 ft (6 m)	25 ft (8 m)	T	C	♦		♦			Sp/Su			♦	♦		
Crataegus phaenopyrum	30 ft (9 m)	30 ft (9 m)	T	C	♦		♦		♦	Su			♦	♦		
Crataegus punctata	30 ft (9 m)	30 ft (9 m)	T	C	♦		♦			Su			♦	♦		
Crescentia cujete	30 ft (9 m)	20 ft (6 m)	T	W/T	♦		♦	♦		Sp				♦		♦
Crowea exalata	18–36 in (45–90 cm)	12–60 in (30–150 cm)	S	W		♦	♦			All	♦					♦
Crowea saligna	3 ft (0.9 m)	3 ft (0.9 m)	S	W		♦	♦			A/W	♦					♦
Cryptomeria japonica	90 ft (27 m)	20 ft (6 m)	C	C/W		♦		♦		Sp			♦	♦		
Cunninghamia lanceolata	70 ft (21 m)	20 ft (6 m)	C	C/W		♦		♦		Sp				♦		
Cunonia capensis	50 ft (15 m)	15 ft (4.5 m)	S	W		♦	♦		♦	Su/A				♦		
Cupaniopsis anacardioides	50 ft (15 m)	15–30 ft (4.5–9 m)	S	W		♦	♦	♦		Sp/Su				♦		
Cuphea hyssopifolia	18 in (45 cm)	15 in (38 cm)	S	W/T		♦	♦			Sp–A	♦	♦		♦		
Cuphea ignea	24 in (60 cm)	30 in (75 cm)	S	W/T		♦	♦			Sp–A	♦	♦		♦		
Cuphea micropetala	30 in (75 cm)	30 in (75 cm)	S	W/T		♦	♦			Su/A	♦			♦		
Cuphea × purpurea	18 in (45 cm)	18 in (45 cm)	S	W		♦	♦			Sp/Su	♦	♦		♦		
Cupressus arizonica	40 ft (12 m)	15 ft (4.5 m)	C	C/W		♦		♦		Sp			♦	♦		
Cupressus cashmeriana	30 ft (9 m)	20 ft (6 m)	C	C/W		♦		♦		Sp				♦		
Cupressus funebris	70–80 ft (21–24 m)	25–30 ft (8–9 m)	C	C/W		♦		♦		Sp			♦	♦		
Cupressus lusitanica	40 ft (12 m)	20 ft (6 m)	C	C/W		♦		♦		Sp			♦	♦		
Cupressus macrocarpa	100 ft (30 m)	35 ft (10 m)	C	C/W		♦		♦		Sp				♦		
Cupressus sempervirens	50 ft (15 m)	15 ft (4.5 m)	C	C/W		♦		♦		Sp	♦			♦		
Cupressus torulosa	60 ft (18 m)	15 ft (4.5 m)	C	C/W		♦		♦		Sp				♦		
× Cuprocyparis leylandii	120 ft (36 m)	15 ft (4.5 m)	C	C/W		♦		♦		Sp				♦		
Cussonia spicata	30 ft (9 m)	12 ft (3.5 m)	T	W		♦		♦		Sp/Su				♦		
Cytisus ardoinoi	10–24 in (25–60 cm)	10–24 in (25–60 cm)	S	C	♦		♦			Sp/Su	♦		♦	♦		
Cytisus × kewensis	18 in (45 cm)	5 ft (1.5 m)	S	C	♦		♦			Sp/Su			♦	♦		
Cytisus multiflorus	10 ft (3 m)	8 ft (2.4 m)	S	C	♦		♦			Su			♦	♦		
Cytisus × praecox	5 ft (1.5 m)	5 ft (1.5 m)	S	C/W	♦		♦		♦	Sp/Su			♦	♦		
Cytisus scoparius	7 ft (2 m)	7 ft (2 m)	S	C	♦		♦			Su			♦	♦		
Cytisus Hybrid Cultivars	3–8 ft (0.9–2.4 m)	3–6 ft (0.9–1.8 m)	S	C/W	♦	♦	♦		♦	Sp/Su	♦		♦	♦		
Daboecia cantabrica	15 in (38 cm)	26 in (65 cm)	S	C		♦	♦			Su/A	♦		♦	♦		

Plant name	Height	Spread	Type	Climate	Deciduous	Evergreen	Showy flowers	Showy foliage	Scented flowers	Flowering season	Grow in pot/tub	Indoor use	Frost tolerant	Full sun	Half sun	Heavy shade
Dacrydium cupressinum	90–200 ft (27–60 m)	30 ft (9 m)	C	W		◆		◆		Sp			◆	◆		
Dais cotinifolia	10 ft (3 m)	10 ft (3 m)	S	W		◆	◆			Su				◆		
Daphne bholua	10 ft (3 m)	4 ft (1.2 m)	S	C/W		◆	◆		◆	W/Sp			◆		◆	
Daphne cneorum	8 in (20 cm)	24 in (60 cm)	S	C/W		◆	◆		◆	Sp	◆		◆		◆	
Daphne genkwa	5 ft (1.5 m)	5 ft (1.5 m)	S	C/W	◆		◆		◆	Sp			◆		◆	
Daphne gnidium	6 ft (1.8 m)	4 ft (1.2 m)	S	W		◆	◆		◆	Sp/Su	◆		◆		◆	
Daphne laureola	5 ft (1.5 m)	5 ft (1.5 m)	S	C/W		◆	◆		◆	W/Sp			◆		◆	
Daphne mezereum	4 ft (1.2 m)	3 ft (0.9 m)	S	C/W	◆		◆		◆	W/Sp			◆		◆	
Daphne odora	5 ft (1.5 m)	5 ft (1.5 m)	S	W		◆	◆		◆	W/Sp			◆		◆	
Daphne pontica	5 ft (1.5 m)	5 ft (1.5 m)	S	C/W		◆	◆		◆	Sp			◆		◆	
Daphne tangutica	6 ft (1.8 m)	5 ft (1.5 m)	S	C/W		◆	◆		◆	Sp/Su			◆		◆	
Darwinia citriodora	5 ft (1.5 m)	5 ft (1.5 m)	S	W		◆	◆	◆		W–Su	◆				◆	
Davidia involucrata	60 ft (18 m)	30 ft (9 m)	T	C	◆		◆			Sp			◆	◆		
Delonix regia	30 ft (9 m)	30 ft (9 m)	T	W/T	◆		◆	◆		Su				◆		
Dendromecon rigida	10 ft (3 m)	10 ft (3 m)	S	W		◆	◆			Su			◆	◆		
Desfontainia spinosa	10 ft (3 m)	10 ft (3 m)	S	C/W		◆	◆			Su/A	◆				◆	
Deutzia × *elegantissima*	5 ft (1.5 m)	5 ft (1.5 m)	S	C	◆		◆			Su			◆	◆		
Deutzia gracilis	3–6 ft (0.9–1.8 m)	3–6 ft (0.9–1.8 m)	S	C	◆		◆			Sp/Su			◆	◆		
Deutzia × *kalmiiflora*	5 ft (1.5 m)	5 ft (1.5 m)	S	C	◆		◆			Su			◆	◆		
Deutzia × *magnifica*	6 ft (1.8 m)	7 ft (2 m)	S	C	◆		◆			Su			◆	◆		
Deutzia × *rosea*	3 ft (0.9 m)	3 ft (0.9 m)	S	C	◆		◆			Su			◆	◆		
Deutzia scabra	10 ft (3 m)	7 ft (2 m)	S	C	◆		◆			Su			◆	◆		
Dillenia alata	25 ft (8 m)	12 ft (3.5 m)	T	W/T		◆	◆	◆		Sp/Su				◆		
Dillenia indica	30–50 ft (9–15 m)	12 ft (3.5 m)	T	W/T		◆	◆	◆		Sp/Su					◆	
Dimocarpus longan	40 ft (12 m)	20 ft (6 m)	T	W/T		◆	◆	◆		Sp					◆	
Disanthus cercidifolius	20 ft (6 m)	10 ft (3 m)	S	C	◆			◆		A			◆	◆		
Dodonaea viscosa	10 ft (3 m)	5 ft (1.5 m)	S	W		◆		◆		Sp				◆	◆	
Dombeya cacuminum	40 ft (12 m)	20 ft (6 m)	T	W/T		◆	◆	◆		Su/A				◆		
Dombeya tiliacea	25 ft (8 m)	12 ft (3.5 m)	T	W/T		◆	◆	◆		Su/A				◆		
Dracaena draco	30 ft (9 m)	12 ft (3.5 m)	T	W/T		◆		◆		Su		◆		◆		
Dracaena fragrans	10–30 ft (3–9 m)	6 ft (1.8 m)	T	W/T		◆	◆	◆	◆	Su		◆		◆	◆	

Plant name	Height	Spread	Type	Climate	Deciduous	Evergreen	Showy flowers	Showy foliage	Scented flowers	Flowering season	Grow in pot/tub	Indoor use	Frost tolerant	Full sun	Half sun	Heavy shade
Dracaena marginata	7–17 ft (2–5 m)	3–10 ft (0.9–3 m)	T	W/T		◆		◆		Su	◆			◆	◆	◆
Dracaena reflexa	8 ft (2.4 m)	3 ft (0.9 m)	T	W/T		◆	◆	◆	◆	Sp	◆			◆		
Dracaena sanderiana	5 ft (1.5 m)	16–32 in (40–80 cm)	T	W/T		◆		◆		Su	◆			◆		
Drimys winteri	50 ft (15 m)	30 ft (9 m)	T	W		◆	◆		◆	Sp/Su			◆	◆	◆	
Dryandra formosa	10 ft (3 m)	7 ft (2 m)	S	W		◆	◆	◆		W/Sp				◆		
Dryandra quercifolia	10 ft (3 m)	10 ft (3 m)	S	W		◆		◆		W/Sp				◆		
Duranta erecta	15 ft (4.5 m)	8 ft (2.4 m)	T	W/T		◆	◆			A				◆		
Duranta stenostachya	4–6 ft (1.2–1.8 m)	4–5 ft (1.2–1.5 m)	S	W/T		◆	◆		◆	Su	◆			◆		
Edgeworthia chrysantha	8 ft (2.4 m)	6 ft (1.8 m)	S	C/W	◆		◆		◆	W/Sp			◆		◆	
Elaeagnus × ebbingei	12 ft (3.5 m)	12 ft (3.5 m)	S	C		◆	◆	◆	◆	A			◆	◆		
Elaeagnus macrophylla	10 ft (3 m)	12 ft (3.5 m)	S	C/W		◆		◆	◆	A			◆	◆		
Elaeagnus multiflora	10 ft (3 m)	10 ft (3 m)	S	C	◆		◆	◆	◆	Sp				◆		
Elaeagnus pungens	15 ft (4.5 m)	20 ft (6 m)	S	C/W		◆		◆	◆	A			◆	◆		
Elaeagnus umbellata	30 ft (9 m)	30 ft (9 m)	S	C	◆		◆	◆	◆	Sp/Su			◆	◆		
Elaeocarpus hookerianus	40–80 ft (12–24 m)	15–30 ft (4.5–9 m)	T	W		◆	◆			Sp/Su					◆	
Elaeocarpus reticulatus	15–30 ft (4.5–9 m)	15 ft (4.5 m)	S	W		◆	◆			Sp/Su					◆	
Embothrium coccineum	40 ft (12 m)	20 ft (6 m)	T	W		◆	◆			Sp/Su				◆		
Empetrum nigrum	12 in (30 cm)	15 in (38 cm)	S	C		◆		◆		Sp/Su	◆			◆		
Enkianthus campanulatus	15 ft (4.5 m)	15 ft (4.5 m)	S	C	◆		◆	◆		Sp/Su				◆	◆	
Enkianthus cernuus	8 ft (2.4 m)	8 ft (2.4 m)	S	C	◆		◆	◆		Sp/Su				◆	◆	
Enkianthus perulatus	7 ft (2 m)	7 ft (2 m)	S	C	◆		◆	◆		Sp			◆	◆	◆	
Epacris impressa	3 ft (0.9 m)	30 in (75 cm)	S	W		◆	◆			W/Sp	◆		◆		◆	
Epacris longiflora	3 ft (0.9 m)	3 ft (0.9 m)	S	W		◆	◆			W/Sp	◆			◆		
Ephedra distachya	3 ft (0.9 m)	3 ft (0.9 m)	S	C		◆		◆		Sp				◆	◆	
Ephedra viridis	4 ft (1.2 m)	3 ft (0.9 m)	S	C/W		◆		◆		Sp				◆	◆	
Epigaea repens	4–8 in (10–20 cm)	12–24 in (30–60 cm)	S	C		◆	◆		◆	Sp			◆		◆	
Eranthemum pulchellum	4 ft (1.2 m)	3 ft (0.9 m)	S	W/T		◆	◆			Sp					◆	
Eremophila maculata	3–8 ft (0.9–2.4 m)	3–10 ft (0.9–3 m)	S	W		◆	◆			A–Sp	◆			◆		
Eremophila nivea	5 ft (1.5 m)	5 ft (1.5 m)	S	W		◆	◆			W/Sp	◆			◆		
Erica arborea	15 ft (4.5 m)	10 ft (3 m)	S	C/W		◆	◆		◆	Sp				◆	◆	
Erica canaliculata	6 ft (1.8 m)	4 ft (1.2 m)	S	W		◆	◆			W/Sp				◆	◆	

Plant name	Height	Spread	Type	Climate	Deciduous	Evergreen	Showy flowers	Showy foliage	Scented flowers	Flowering season	Grow in pot/tub	Indoor use	Frost tolerant	Full sun	Half sun	Heavy shade
Erica carnea	12 in (30 cm)	22 in (55 cm)	S	C/W		◆	◆	◆		W/Sp			◆	◆	◆	
Erica cerinthoides	2–5 ft (0.6–1.5 m)	3 ft (0.9 m)	S	W		◆	◆			W/Sp	◆			◆		
Erica cinerea	24 in (60 cm)	30 in (75 cm)	S	C/W		◆	◆	◆		Su/A				◆	◆	
Erica × darleyensis	12 in (30 cm)	24 in (60 cm)	S	C/W		◆	◆	◆		W/Sp				◆	◆	
Erica erigena	8 ft (2.4 m)	3 ft (0.9 m)	S	C/W		◆	◆	◆	◆	W/Sp				◆	◆	
Erica lusitanica	5–10 ft (1.5–3 m)	3 ft (0.9 m)	S	W		◆	◆			W/Sp				◆	◆	
Erica mammosa	5 ft (1.5 m)	6 ft (1.8 m)	S	W		◆	◆			Sp/Su	◆			◆		
Erica manipuliflora	3 ft (0.9 m)	3 ft (0.9 m)	S	W		◆	◆			Su/A				◆	◆	
Erica melanthera	24 in (60 cm)	18 in (45 cm)	S	W		◆	◆			Sp/Su	◆			◆	◆	
Erica regia	3 ft (0.9 m)	3 ft (0.9 m)	S	W		◆	◆			Sp	◆			◆		
Erica scoparia	6 ft (1.8 m)	3 ft (0.9 m)	S	W		◆	◆			Su				◆	◆	
Erica tetralix	12 in (30 cm)	20 in (50 cm)	S	C		◆	◆	◆		Su/A				◆	◆	
Erica vagans	30 in (75 cm)	30 in (75 cm)	S	C		◆	◆	◆		Su/A				◆	◆	
Erica ventricosa	20 in (50 cm)	20 in (50 cm)	S	W		◆	◆			Sp	◆			◆		
Erica × williamsii	30 in (75 cm)	18 in (45 cm)	S	C		◆	◆			Su/A				◆	◆	
Eriostemon australasius	6 ft (1.8 m)	3 ft (0.9 m)	S	W		◆	◆			W/Sp					◆	◆
Erythrina acanthocarpa	6 ft (1.8 m)	6 ft (1.8 m)	S	W	◆		◆			Sp/Su				◆		
Erythrina × bidwillii	12 ft (3.5 m)	10 ft (3 m)	S	W/T	◆		◆			Sp/Su				◆		
Erythrina crista-galli	30 ft (9 m)	12–40 ft (3.5–12 m)	T	W	◆		◆			Sp/Su				◆		
Erythrina humeana	12 ft (3.5 m)	7 ft (2 m)	S	W	◆		◆			Su				◆		
Erythrina × sykesii	50 ft (15 m)	30 ft (9 m)	T	W	◆		◆			W/Sp				◆		
Erythrina variegata	30–60 ft (9–18 m)	30 ft (9 m)	T	T	◆		◆			W				◆		
Escallonia bifida	15–30 ft (4.5–9 m)	10–20 ft (3–6 m)	T	W		◆	◆		◆	A			◆	◆		
Escallonia × exoniensis	15–20 ft (4.5–6 m)	12 ft (3.5 m)	T	W		◆	◆			Sp–A			◆	◆		
Escallonia rubra	15 ft (4.5 m)	15 ft (4.5 m)	S	W		◆	◆			Su			◆	◆		
Escallonia Hybrid Cultivars	5–10 ft (1.5–3 m)	6–12 ft (1.8–3.5 m)	S	W		◆	◆			Su/A			◆	◆		
Eucalyptus bicostata	120 ft (36 m)	25–50 ft (8–15 m)	T	W		◆		◆		Sp/Su				◆		
Eucalyptus caesia	20 ft (6 m)	15 ft (4.5 m)	T	W/T		◆	◆			Sp–A				◆		
Eucalyptus camaldulensis	150 ft (45 m)	50 ft (15 m)	T	W/T		◆	◆			Sp/Su				◆		
Eucalyptus cinerea	50 ft (15 m)	30 ft (9 m)	T	W/T		◆		◆		Su			◆	◆		
Eucalyptus erythrocorys	25 ft (8 m)	10 ft (3 m)	T	W/T		◆	◆			Su/A				◆		

Plant name	Height	Spread	Type	Climate	Deciduous	Evergreen	Showy flowers	Showy foliage	Scented flowers	Flowering season	Grow in pot/tub	Indoor use	Frost tolerant	Full sun	Half sun	Heavy shade
Eucalyptus forrestiana	15 ft (4.5 m)	12 ft (3.5 m)	T	W/T		♦	♦	♦		Su/A				♦		
Eucalyptus glaucescens	20–70 ft (6–21 m)	20 ft (6 m)	T	W		♦		♦		A			♦	♦		
Eucalyptus globulus	180 ft (55 m)	40 ft (12 m)	T	W/T		♦		♦		Sp				♦		
Eucalyptus grandis	200 ft (60 m)	30–50 ft (9–15 m)	T	W/T		♦		♦		W				♦		
Eucalyptus gunnii	80 ft (24 m)	25 ft (8 m)	T	C/W		♦		♦		Sp/Su			♦	♦		
Eucalyptus leucoxylon	100 ft (30 m)	20–40 ft (6–12 m)	T	W		♦	♦	♦		A–Sp						
Eucalyptus macrocarpa	6–12 ft (1.8–3.5 m)	12 ft (3.5 m)	S	W		♦	♦			W/Sp						
Eucalyptus mannifera	70 ft (21 m)	30 ft (9 m)	T	W		♦		♦		Su/A				♦	♦	
Eucalyptus microcorys	60–180 ft (18–55 m)	40 ft (12 m)	T	W/T		♦	♦	♦		W–Su				♦	♦	
Eucalyptus nicholii	50 ft (15 m)	20–40 ft (6–12 m)	T	W/T		♦		♦		A				♦	♦	
Eucalyptus pauciflora	60 ft (18 m)	20 ft (6 m)	T	C/W		♦	♦	♦		Sp/Su				♦	♦	
Eucalyptus perriniana	20–40 ft (6–12 m)	10–20 ft (3–6 m)	T	C/W		♦	♦	♦		Su				♦	♦	
Eucalyptus polyanthemos	25–80 ft (8–24 m)	20 ft (6 m)	T	W/T		♦		♦		Sp				♦	♦	
Eucalyptus pulverulenta	15–30 ft (4.5–9 m)	12 ft (3.5 m)	T	W		♦		♦		Sp				♦	♦	
Eucalyptus regnans	320 ft (96 m)	30–60 ft (9–18 m)	T	W		♦		♦		Su				♦	♦	
Eucalyptus rhodantha	10 ft (3 m)	10 ft (3 m)	S	W/T		♦	♦	♦		Sp/A				♦	♦	
Eucalyptus urnigera	40 ft (12 m)	15–30 ft (4.5–9 m)	T	C/W		♦	♦			Su/A			♦	♦		
Eucalyptus viminalis	80–180 ft (24–55 m)	35 ft (10 m)	T	W		♦		♦		Su				♦	♦	
Eucryphia glutinosa	30 ft (9 m)	20 ft (6 m)	T	W		♦	♦			Su				♦	♦	
Eucryphia × intermedia	30 ft (9 m)	15 ft (4.5 m)	T	W		♦	♦			Sp–A				♦	♦	
Eucryphia lucida	25 ft (8 m)	15 ft (4.5 m)	T	W		♦	♦			Su				♦	♦	
Eucryphia × nymansensis	30 ft (9 m)	15 ft (4.5 m)	T	W		♦	♦			Sp–A				♦	♦	
Eugenia uniflora	10–30 ft (3–9 m)	8 ft (2.4 m)	S	W/T		♦	♦		♦	Su						♦
Euonymus alatus	6 ft (1.8 m)	10 ft (3 m)	S	C/W	♦			♦		Su				♦	♦	
Euonymus americanus	8 ft (2.4 m)	6 ft (1.8 m)	S	C/W	♦			♦		Su				♦	♦	
Euonymus europaeus	20 ft (6 m)	8 ft (2.4 m)	S	C/W	♦			♦		Sp				♦	♦	
Euonymus fortunei	1–10 ft (0.3–3 m)	3–10 ft (0.9–3 m)	S	C/W		♦		♦		Su				♦	♦	
Euonymus japonicus	12 ft (3.5 m)	6–12 ft (1.8–3.5 m)	S	C/W		♦		♦		Su				♦	♦	
Euonymus planipes	10 ft (3 m)	10 ft (3 m)	S	C/W	♦			♦		Su				♦	♦	
Euphorbia fulgens	5 ft (1.5 m)	30 in (75 cm)	S	W		♦	♦	♦		W	♦	♦		♦		
Euphorbia leucocephala	6–10 ft (1.8–3 m)	6–10 ft (1.8–3 m)	S	W/T		♦	♦	♦		A/W	♦			♦		

Plant name	Height	Spread	Type	Climate	Deciduous	Evergreen	Showy flowers	Showy foliage	Scented flowers	Flowering season	Grow in pot/tub	Indoor use	Frost tolerant	Full sun	Half sun	Heavy shade
Euphorbia pulcherrima	10 ft (3 m)	7 ft (2 m)	S	W/T	◆		◆	◆		W	◆	◆		◆		
Euptelea pleiosperma	15–30 ft (4.5–9 m)	15 ft (4.5 m)	T	C	◆			◆		Sp				◆	◆	
Euryops acraeus	12–36 in (30–90 cm)	36 in (90 cm)	S	W		◆	◆	◆		Sp/Su	◆			◆	◆	
Euryops chrysanthemoides	4 ft (1.2 m)	5 ft (1.5 m)	S	W/T		◆	◆			W/Sp				◆		
Euryops pectinatus	4 ft (1.2 m)	5 ft (1.5 m)	S	W/T		◆	◆	◆		All	◆			◆		
Exochorda giraldii	10 ft (3 m)	10 ft (3 m)	S	C	◆		◆			Sp				◆	◆	
Exochorda × macrantha	7 ft (2 m)	10 ft (3 m)	S	C	◆		◆			Sp				◆	◆	
Exochorda racemosa	10 ft (3 m)	10 ft (3 m)	S	C	◆		◆		◆	Sp				◆	◆	
Fabiana imbricata	8 ft (2.4 m)	7 ft (2 m)	S	W		◆	◆			Su				◆	◆	
Fagus crenata	30 ft (9 m)	20 ft (6 m)	T	C	◆			◆		Sp				◆	◆	
Fagus grandifolia	80 ft (24 m)	35 ft (10 m)	T	C	◆			◆		Sp				◆	◆	
Fagus japonica	80 ft (24 m)	25 ft (8 m)	T	C	◆			◆		Sp				◆	◆	
Fagus sylvatica	100 ft (30 m)	50 ft (15 m)	T	C	◆			◆		Sp				◆	◆	
× Fatshedera lizei	6 ft (1.8 m)	8 ft (2.4 m)	S	C/W/T		◆		◆		A	◆	◆	◆		◆	◆
Fatsia japonica	6–12 ft (1.8–3.5 m)	6–12 ft (1.8–3.5 m)	S	C/W		◆	◆	◆		Su/A	◆			◆	◆	◆
Ficus benghalensis	30–40 ft (9–12 m)	75–400 ft (23–120 m)	T	T		◆		◆		Sp				◆		
Ficus benjamina	80 ft (24 m)	50 ft (15 m)	T	W/T		◆		◆		Sp	◆	◆		◆		
Ficus elastica	40–100 ft (12–30 m)	40–100 ft (12–30 m)	T	T		◆		◆		Sp	◆	◆		◆		
Ficus lyrata	30 ft (9 m)	30 ft (9 m)	T	W/T		◆		◆		Sp	◆	◆		◆		
Ficus macrophylla	80–100 ft (24–30 m)	130 ft (40 m)	T	W/T		◆		◆		Sp				◆		
Ficus microcarpa	40–70 ft (12–21 m)	20–50 ft (6–15 m)	T	W/T		◆		◆		Sp				◆		
Ficus religiosa	30–40 ft (9–12 m)	25 ft (8 m)	T	W/T	◆			◆		Sp				◆		
Ficus rubiginosa	30–80 ft (9–24 m)	35–70 ft (10–21 m)	T	W/T		◆		◆		Sp				◆		
Firmiana simplex	60 ft (18 m)	35 ft (10 m)	T	C/W	◆		◆	◆		Sp				◆	◆	
Forsythia × intermedia	15 ft (4.5 m)	7 ft (2 m)	S	C	◆		◆			Sp				◆	◆	
Forsythia ovata	5 ft (1.5 m)	8 ft (2.4 m)	S	C	◆		◆			Sp				◆	◆	
Forsythia suspensa	12 ft (3.5 m)	10 ft (3 m)	S	C	◆		◆			Sp				◆	◆	
Forsythia viridissima	10 ft (3 m)	10 ft (3 m)	S	C	◆		◆			Sp				◆	◆	
Forsythia Hybrid Cultivars	5–10 ft (1.5–3 m)	10 ft (3 m)	S	C	◆		◆			Sp				◆	◆	
Fothergilla gardenii	3 ft (0.9 m)	3 ft (0.9 m)	S	C	◆		◆		◆	Sp				◆	◆	
Fothergilla major	5–10 ft (1.5–3 m)	6 ft (1.8 m)	S	C	◆		◆		◆	Sp/Su				◆	◆	

Plant name	Height	Spread	Type	Climate	Deciduous	Evergreen	Showy flowers	Showy foliage	Scented flowers	Flowering season	Grow in pot/tub	Indoor use	Frost tolerant	Full sun	Half sun	Heavy shade
Franklinia alatamaha	20 ft (6 m)	12 ft (3.5 m)	T	C/W	♦		♦	♦		Su/A			♦		♦	
Fraxinus americana	80 ft (24 m)	50 ft (15 m)	T	C/W	♦			♦		Sp			♦	♦		
Fraxinus angustifolia	80 ft (24 m)	40 ft (12 m)	T	C/W	♦			♦		Sp			♦	♦		
Fraxinus chinensis	80 ft (24 m)	25 ft (8 m)	T	C	♦		♦	♦		Sp			♦	♦		
Fraxinus excelsior	100 ft (30 m)	60 ft (18 m)	T	C/W	♦		♦	♦		Sp			♦	♦		
Fraxinus nigra	50 ft (15 m)	25 ft (8 m)	T	C/W	♦			♦		Sp			♦	♦		
Fraxinus ornus	50 ft (15 m)	40 ft (12 m)	T	C/W	♦		♦	♦		Sp			♦	♦		
Fraxinus pennsylvanica	70 ft (21 m)	70 ft (21 m)	T	C/W	♦		♦	♦		Sp			♦	♦		
Fraxinus uhdei	25 ft (8 m)	15 ft (4.5 m)	T	W		♦	♦	♦		Sp			♦	♦		
Fraxinus velutina	30 ft (9 m)	30 ft (9 m)	T	C/W	♦		♦	♦		Sp			♦	♦		
Fremontodendron californicum	12–25 ft (3.5–8 m)	15 ft (4.5 m)	S	W		♦	♦			Sp/Su			♦	♦		
Fremontodendron mexicanum	20 ft (6 m)	12 ft (3.5 m)	S	W/T		♦	♦			Sp-A				♦		
Fremontodendron Hybrid Cultivars	12–20 ft (3.5–6 m)	10–15 ft (3–4.5 m)	S	W		♦	♦			Sp/Su			♦	♦		
Fuchsia arborescens	6 ft (1.8 m)	5 ft (1.5 m)	S	W/T		♦	♦			Su	♦			♦	♦	
Fuchsia boliviana	12 ft (3.5 m)	3–4 ft (0.9–1.2 m)	S	W/T		♦	♦		♦	Su/A	♦				♦	
Fuchsia coccinea	5–20 ft (1.6–6 m)	4 ft (1.2 m)	S	W/T		♦	♦			Su	♦			♦	♦	♦
Fuchsia fulgens	5 ft (1.5 m)	30 in (75 cm)	S	T		♦	♦	♦		Su/A	♦			♦	♦	
Fuchsia magellanica	10 ft (3 m)	6 ft (1.8 m)	S	C/W	♦		♦	♦		Su/A			♦	♦	♦	♦
Fuchsia procumbens	6 in (15 cm)	3 ft (0.9 m)	S	W/T		♦	♦			Su	♦	♦		♦	♦	
Fuchsia splendens	8 ft (2.4 m)	3 ft (0.9 m)	S	W/T		♦	♦			Su	♦			♦	♦	
Fuchsia thymifolia	36 in 90 cm)	20 in (50 cm)	S	W/T		♦	♦			Su/A	♦			♦	♦	
Fuchsia triphylla	6 ft (1.8 m)	2 ft (0.6 m)	S	T		♦	♦	♦		Su/A	♦	♦		♦	♦	
Fuchsia Hybrid Cultivars	1–7 ft (0.3–2 m)	18–36 in (45–90 cm)	S	C/W	♦	♦	♦	♦		Su/A	♦	♦		♦	♦	
Garcinia mangostana	50 ft (15 m)	15 ft (4.5 m)	T	T		♦		♦		Sp				♦		
Gardenia augusta	5–8 ft (1.5–2.4 m)	5 ft (1.5 m)	S	W/T		♦	♦	♦	♦	Su	♦	♦		♦	♦	
Gardenia thunbergia	12 ft (3.5 m)	7 ft (2 m)	S	W/T		♦	♦	♦	♦	Su				♦		
Garrya elliptica	8–12 ft (2.4–3.5 m)	6 ft (1.8 m)	S	W		♦	♦			W/Sp			♦	♦		
Garrya fremontii	7–10 ft (2–3 m)	6 ft (1.8 m)	S	W		♦	♦			Su/A			♦	♦		
Gaultheria depressa	4 in (10 cm)	10 in (25 cm)	S	C/W		♦	♦			Su			♦	♦	♦	
Gaultheria mucronata	18–60 in (45–150 cm)	48 in (120 cm)	S	C/W		♦	♦			Sp			♦	♦	♦	
Gaultheria procumbens	6 in (15 cm)	36 in (90 cm)	S	C/W		♦	♦			Su			♦	♦	♦	

Plant name	Height	Spread	Type	Climate	Deciduous	Evergreen	Showy flowers	Showy foliage	Scented flowers	Flowering season	Grow in pot/tub	Indoor use	Frost tolerant	Full sun	Half sun	Heavy shade
Gaultheria shallon	5 ft (1.5 m)	5 ft (1.5 m)	S	C/W		◆	◆			Sp				◆	◆	◆
Gaultheria × wisleyensis	3 ft (0.9 m)	3 ft (0.9 m)	S	C/W		◆	◆			Su				◆	◆	◆
Geijera parviflora	40 ft (12 m)	35 ft (10 m)	T	W/T		◆	◆			Sp				◆	◆	
Genista aetnensis	25 ft (8 m)	25 ft (8 m)	S	W		◆	◆		◆	Su/A				◆	◆	
Genista lydia	24 in (60 cm)	36 in (90 cm)	S	C/W	◆		◆			Sp/Su				◆	◆	
Genista sagittalis	6 in (15 cm)	36 in (90 cm)	S	C/W	◆		◆			Sp/Su				◆	◆	
Genista × spachiana	10–20 ft (3–6 m)	17 ft (5 m)	S	W/T		◆	◆			W/Sp	◆	◆			◆	
Genista tinctoria	3 ft (0.9 m)	3 ft (0.9 m)	S	C/W	◆		◆			Su				◆	◆	
Ginkgo biloba	100 ft (30 m)	25 ft (8 m)	T	C/W	◆			◆		Sp				◆	◆	
Gleditsia triacanthos	150 ft (45 m)	70 ft (21 m)	T	C/W	◆			◆		Sp				◆	◆	
Glyptostrobus pensilis	80 ft (24 m)	20 ft (6 m)	C	W	◆			◆		Sp				◆	◆	
Gordonia axillaris	12–20 ft (3.5–6 m)	12 ft (3.5 m)	S	W		◆	◆			W/Sp	◆			◆		◆
Gordonia lasianthus	50 ft (15 m)	30 ft (9 m)	S	W		◆	◆			Su						◆
Graptophyllum pictum	6 ft (1.8 m)	30 in (75 cm)	S	W/T		◆	◆			Su	◆				◆	
Grevillea aquifolium	6 ft (1.8 m)	6 ft (1.8 m)	S	W		◆	◆			W–Su				◆	◆	
Grevillea banksii	10–30 ft (3–9 m)	7 ft (2 m)	S/T	W/T		◆	◆			Sp					◆	
Grevillea curviloba	6 ft (1.8 m)	4 ft (1.2 m)	S	W		◆	◆		◆	Sp				◆	◆	
Grevillea × gaudichaudii	4 in (10 cm)	10 ft (3 m)	S	W		◆	◆	◆		Sp/Su				◆	◆	
Grevillea juniperina	8 ft (2.4 m)	7 ft (2 m)	S	W		◆	◆			Sp/Su				◆	◆	
Grevillea lanigera	5 ft (1.5 m)	4 ft (1.2 m)	S	C/W		◆	◆			W/Sp				◆	◆	
Grevillea lavandulacea	3 ft (0.9 m)	3 ft (0.9 m)	S	W		◆	◆			Sp/Su				◆	◆	
Grevillea robusta	60 ft (18 m)	30 ft (9 m)	T	W/T		◆	◆	◆		Sp/Su	◆				◆	
Grevillea rosmarinifolia	6 ft (1.8 m)	6 ft (1.8 m)	S	W		◆	◆			W–Su				◆	◆	
Grevillea thelemanniana	3 ft (0.9 m)	6 ft (1.8 m)	S	W/T		◆	◆			W/Sp				◆	◆	
Grevillea victoriae	6 ft (1.8 m)	6 ft (1.8 m)	S	W		◆	◆			Sp/Su				◆	◆	
Grevillea Hybrid Cultivars	6 in–20 ft (15 cm–6 m)	4–15 ft (1.2–4.5 m)	S	W		◆	◆	◆		W–Su					◆	◆
Grewia occidentalis	10 ft (3 m)	10 ft (3 m)	S	W/T		◆	◆			Sp/Su	◆				◆	
Greyia sutherlandii	15 ft (4.5 m)	7 ft (2 m)	S	W/T	◆		◆	◆		W/Sp					◆	
Griselinia littoralis	25 ft (8 m)	15 ft (4.5 m)	S	W/T		◆		◆		Sp	◆			◆	◆	
Gymnocladus dioica	75 ft (23 m)	12 ft (3.5 m)	T	C	◆			◆		Su				◆	◆	
Hakea bucculenta	8 ft (2.4 m)	7 ft (2 m)	S	W		◆	◆			W/Sp					◆	
Hakea cristata	12 ft (3.5 m)	8 ft (2.4 m)	S	W/T		◆	◆			W					◆	

Plant name	Height	Spread	Type	Climate	Deciduous	Evergreen	Showy flowers	Showy foliage	Scented flowers	Flowering season	Grow in pot/tub	Indoor use	Frost tolerant	Full sun	Half sun	Heavy shade
Hakea laurina	25 ft (8 m)	8 ft (2.4 m)	S	W/T		◆	◆			A/W				◆		
Hakea microcarpa	6 ft (1.8 m)	6 ft (1.8 m)	S	C/W		◆	◆			W/Sp			◆	◆		
Hakea myrtoides	18 in (45 cm)	15 in (38 cm)	S	W/T		◆	◆			W/Sp				◆		
Hakea purpurea	6–10 ft (1.8–3 m)	6–10 ft (1.8–3 m)	S	W/T		◆	◆			W/Sp				◆		
Hakea salicifolia	20 ft (6 m)	12 ft (3.5 m)	S	C/W		◆	◆			Sp			◆	◆		
Halesia carolina	25 ft (8 m)	25–30 ft (8–10 m)	T	C	◆		◆			Sp			◆	◆		
Halesia monticola	30 ft (9 m)	20 ft (6 m)	T	C	◆		◆			Sp			◆	◆		
× *Halimiocistus wintonensis*	24 in (60 cm)	30 in (75 cm)	S	C/W		◆	◆			Su	◆		◆	◆		
Halimium halimifolium	3 ft (0.9 m)	3 ft (0.9 m)	S	C/W		◆	◆			Sp/Su	◆		◆	◆		
Halimium lasianthum	3 ft (0.9 m)	4 ft (1.2 m)	S	W		◆	◆			Sp/Su	◆		◆	◆		
Halimium Hybrid Cultivars	3 ft (0.9 m)	3 ft (0.9 m)	S	W		◆	◆			Su	◆			◆		
Halleria lucida	35 ft (10 m)	12 ft (3.5 m)	T	W		◆	◆			W/Sp			◆	◆		
Hamamelis × *intermedia*	12 ft (3.5 m)	12 ft (3.5 m)	S	C	◆		◆	◆	◆	W/Sp			◆	◆		◆
Hamamelis japonica	15 ft (4.5 m)	12 ft (3.5 m)	S	C/W	◆		◆		◆	W/Sp			◆			◆
Hamamelis mollis	15 ft (4.5 m)	12 ft (3.5 m)	S	C	◆		◆	◆	◆	W/Sp			◆			◆
Hamamelis virginiana	12–15 ft (3.5–4.5 m)	8–12 ft (2.4–3.5 m)	S	C	◆		◆		◆	A			◆			◆
Harpephyllum caffrum	30 ft (9 m)	25 ft (8 m)	T	W/T		◆		◆		Sp				◆		
Hebe albicans	18–24 in (45–60 cm)	27 in (70 cm)	S	W		◆	◆	◆		Su/A	◆		◆	◆		
Hebe × *andersonii*	3–7 ft (0.9–2 m)	4 ft (1.2 m)	S	W/T		◆	◆	◆		Su/A	◆			◆		
Hebe armstrongii	3 ft (0.9 m)	3 ft (0.9 m)	S	C/W		◆		◆		Su			◆	◆		
Hebe cupressoides	3 ft (0.9 m)	3 ft (0.9 m)	S	C/W		◆		◆		Su			◆	◆		
Hebe diosmifolia	36 in (90 cm)	24 in (60 cm)	S	W/T		◆	◆			Sp	◆			◆		
Hebe elliptica	3–7 ft (0.9–2 m)	4 ft (1.2 m)	S	W/T		◆	◆	◆		Su/A			◆	◆		
Hebe × *franciscana*	3 ft (0.9 m)	4 ft (1.2 m)	S	W/T		◆	◆	◆		Su/A				◆		
Hebe odora	3 ft (0.9 m)	4 ft (1.2 m)	S	C/W		◆		◆		Sp/Su			◆	◆		
Hebe pinguifolia	10 in (25 cm)	30 in (75 cm)	S	C/W		◆	◆	◆		Sp–A	◆		◆	◆		
Hebe salicifolia	8 ft (2.4 m)	7 ft (2 m)	S	C/W		◆	◆			Su			◆	◆		
Hebe speciosa	3 ft (0.9 m)	3 ft (0.9 m)	S	W/T		◆	◆			Su/A	◆			◆		
Hebe topiaria	3 ft (0.9 m)	3 ft (0.9 m)	S	W/T		◆		◆		Su			◆	◆		
Hebe Hybrid Cultivars	12 in–5 ft (30 cm–1.5 m)	12 in–5 ft (30 cm–1.5 m)	S	W/T		◆	◆	◆		Sp–A			◆	◆		
Helianthemum croceum	12–14 in (30–35 cm)	16–20 in (40–50 cm)	S	C/W		◆	◆			Sp/Su	◆		◆	◆		
Helianthemum nummularium	20 in (50 cm)	24 in (60 cm)	S	C/W		◆	◆			Sp/Su	◆		◆	◆		

Plant name	Height	Spread	Type	Climate	Deciduous	Evergreen	Showy flowers	Showy foliage	Scented flowers	Flowering season	Grow in pot/tub	Indoor use	Frost tolerant	Full sun	Half sun	Heavy shade
Helianthemum Hybrid Cultivars	6–12 in (15–30 cm)	18–36 in (45–90 cm)	S	C/W		◆	◆	◆		Sp/Su	◆		◆	◆		
Heptacodium miconioides	10–15 ft (3–4.5 m)	7–10 ft (2–3 m)	S	C	◆		◆		◆	Su/A			◆		◆	
Heteromeles arbutifolia	12 ft (3.5 m)	12 ft (3.5 m)	S	W	◆		◆		◆	Su			◆	◆		
Hibbertia miniata	15 in (38 cm)	8 in (20 cm)	S	W/T		◆	◆			Sp/Su	◆					◆
Hibbertia stellaris	30 in (75 cm)	30 in (75 cm)	S	W/T		◆	◆			Sp–A	◆					◆
Hibiscus coccineus	7 ft (2 m)	2–3 ft (0.6–0.9 m)	S	W/T	◆		◆			Su				◆	◆	
Hibiscus heterophyllus	10–20 ft (3–6 m)	6–10 ft (1.8–3 m)	S	W/T		◆	◆			All				◆		
Hibiscus moscheutos	8 ft (2.4 m)	40 in (100 cm)	S	C/W	◆		◆			Sp/Su				◆	◆	
Hibiscus mutabilis	10–15 ft (3–4.5 m)	6–8 ft (1.8–2.4 m)	S	W	◆		◆			Su/A				◆	◆	
Hibiscus pedunculatus	4–6 ft (1.2–1.8 m)	5 ft (1.5 m)	S	W/T		◆	◆			All				◆		
Hibiscus rosa-sinensis	8–30 ft (2.4–9 m)	5 ft (1.5 m)	S	W/T		◆	◆			Su–W	◆			◆		
Hibiscus schizopetalus	10 ft (3 m)	6 ft (1.8 m)	S	W/T		◆	◆			Su/A				◆		
Hibiscus syriacus	8–20 ft (2.4–6 m)	6–10 ft (1.8–3 m)	S	C/W	◆		◆			Su/A				◆		
Hibiscus tiliaceus	25 ft (8 m)	10–20 ft (3–6 m)	S	W/T		◆	◆			Su				◆		
Hibiscus trionum	12–24 in (30–60 cm)	12 in (30 cm)	S	W/T	◆		◆			Su/A				◆		
Hoheria lyallii	7–12 (2–3.5 m)	10 ft (3 m)	T	W	◆		◆			Su/A				◆	◆	
Hoheria sexstylosa	15–25 ft (4.5–8 m)	20 ft (6 m)	T	W/T		◆	◆		◆	Su/A				◆	◆	
Holmskioldia sanguinea	3–6 ft (0.9–1.8 m)	6 ft (1.8 m)	S	W/T		◆	◆			Sp–A	◆			◆	◆	
Holodiscus discolor	12 ft (3.5 m)	12 ft (3.5 m)	S	C/W	◆		◆			Su			◆	◆	◆	
Homalocladium platycladum	6–10 ft (1.8–3 m)	6 ft (1.8 m)	S	W/T		◆		◆		Sp				◆		
Hydrangea arborescens	3–12 ft (0.9–3.5 m)	8 ft (2.4 m)	S	C/W	◆		◆			Su			◆	◆	◆	
Hydrangea aspera	10 ft (3 m)	10 ft (3 m)	S	C/W	◆		◆		◆	Su/A			◆	◆	◆	
Hydrangea heteromalla	10–15 ft (3–4.5 m)	10 ft (3 m)	S	C/W	◆		◆			Su				◆	◆	
Hydrangea macrophylla	10 ft (3 m)	8 ft (2.4 m)	S	C/W	◆		◆			Su/A			◆	◆	◆	
Hydrangea paniculata	6–20 ft (1.8–6 m)	10 ft (3 m)	S	C/W	◆		◆			Su/A				◆	◆	
Hydrangea 'Preziosa'	5 ft (1.5 m)	5 ft (1.5 m)	S	C/W	◆		◆	◆		Su	◆			◆	◆	
Hydrangea quercifolia	3–8 ft (0.9–2.4 m)	8 ft (2.4 m)	S	C/W	◆		◆	◆		Su				◆	◆	
Hydrangea serrata	3–6 ft (0.9–1.8 m)	5 ft (1.5 m)	S	C/W	◆		◆			Su			◆	◆	◆	
Hymenosporum flavum	30 ft (9 m)	12 ft (3.5 m)	T	W/T		◆	◆			Sp				◆		
Hypericum balearicum	10 in (25 cm)	10 in (25 cm)	S	C/W		◆	◆			Su	◆			◆	◆	
Hypericum beanii	2–6 ft (0.6–1.8 m)	6 ft (1.8 m)	S	C/W		◆	◆			Su				◆	◆	
Hypericum calycinum	8–24 in (20–60 cm	5 ft (1.5 m)	S	C/W		◆	◆			Su/A	◆			◆		◆

Plant name	Height	Spread	Type	Climate	Deciduous	Evergreen	Showy flowers	Showy foliage	Scented flowers	Flowering season	Grow in pot/tub	Indoor use	Frost tolerant	Full sun	Half sun	Heavy shade
Hypericum empetrifolium	2 ft (0.6 m)	3 ft (0.9 m)	S	C/W		♦	♦	♦		Su			♦	♦		
Hypericum 'Hidcote'	4 ft (1.2 m)	4 ft (1.2 m)	S	C/W		♦	♦			Su/A			♦	♦		
Hypericum lancasteri	3 ft (0.9 m)	3 ft (0.9 m)	S	C/W	♦		♦			Su			♦	♦		
Hypericum × *moserianum*	12–16 in (30–40 cm)	24–32 in (60–80 cm)	S	C/W		♦	♦	♦		Su/A			♦	♦		
Hypericum olympicum	10 in (25 cm)	15 in (38 cm)	S	C/W	♦		♦			Su			♦	♦		
Hypericum prolificum	6 ft (1.8 m)	5 ft (1.5 m)	S	C/W		♦	♦			Su			♦	♦		
Hypericum 'Rowallane'	6 ft (1.8 m)	4 ft (1.2 m)	S	C/W		♦	♦			Su/A			♦	♦		
Hypoestes aristata	3 ft (0.9 m)	26 in (65 cm)	S	W/T		♦	♦			A						♦
Hypoestes phyllostachya	3 ft (0.9 m)	30 in (75 cm)	S	W/T		♦		♦		A	♦	♦				♦
Idesia polycarpa	50 ft (15 m)	35 ft (10 m)	T	C/W	♦		♦		♦	Su			♦	♦		
Ilex × *altaclerensis*	70 ft 921 m)	20 ft (6 m)	T	C/W		♦	♦	♦		Sp/Su			♦	♦		
Ilex aquifolium	40–80 ft (12–24 m)	25 ft (8 m)	T	C/W		♦	♦	♦		Sp/Su			♦	♦		
Ilex × *aquipernyi*	20 ft (6 m)	12 ft (3.5 m)	T	C/W		♦	♦			Sp/Su			♦	♦		
Ilex cassine	40 ft (12 m)	15 ft (4.5 m)	T	C/W		♦	♦	♦		Sp/Su			♦	♦		
Ilex cornuta	6–12 ft (1.8–3.5 m)	6–12 ft (1.8–3.5 m)	S	C/W		♦	♦			Sp/Su			♦	♦		
Ilex crenata	15 ft (4.5 m)	12 ft (3.5 m)	S	C/W		♦	♦			Sp/Su			♦	♦		
Ilex decidua	6–20 ft (1.8–6 m)	6–15 ft (1.8–4.5 m)	S	C/W	♦		♦			Sp/Su			♦	♦		
Ilex glabra	10 ft (3 m)	10 ft (3 m)	S	C/W		♦	♦			Sp/Su			♦	♦		
Ilex × *koehneana*	20 ft (6 m)	12 ft (3.5 m)	T	C/W		♦	♦	♦		Sp			♦	♦		
Ilex × *meserveae*	6–15 ft (1.8–4.5 m)	10 ft (3 m)	S	C/W		♦	♦	♦		Sp/Su			♦	♦		
Ilex mitis	30 ft (9 m)	20 ft (6 m)	T	W/T		♦	♦	♦		Sp/Su				♦	♦	
Ilex opaca	50 ft (15 m)	35 ft (10 m)	T	C/W		♦	♦	♦		Sp/Su			♦	♦		
Ilex pedunculosa	30 ft (9 m)	20 ft (6 m)	T	C/W		♦	♦	♦		Sp/Su			♦	♦		
Ilex pernyi	30 ft (9 m)	12 ft (3.5 m)	S	C/W		♦	♦	♦		Sp/Su			♦	♦		
Ilex serrata	15 ft (4.5 m)	10 ft (3 m)	S	C/W	♦		♦	♦		Sp/Su			♦	♦		
Ilex verticillata	15 ft (4.5 m)	15 ft (4.5 m)	S	C/W	♦		♦	♦		Sp/Su			♦	♦		
Ilex vomitoria	20 ft (6 m)	12 ft (3.5 m)	S	C/W		♦	♦			Sp/Su			♦	♦	♦	
Ilex Hybrid Cultivars	8–20 ft (2.4–6 m)	5–15 ft (1.5–4.5 m)	S/T	C/W	♦	♦	♦			Sp/Su	♦		♦	♦		
Illicium anisatum	25 ft (8 m)	20 ft (6 m)	S	W/T		♦	♦		♦	Sp			♦	♦		
Illicium floridanum	10 ft (3 m)	8 ft (2.4 m)	S	W/T		♦	♦		♦	Sp/Su			♦	♦		
Indigofera australis	6 ft (1.8 m)	6 ft (1.8 m)	S	W/T		♦	♦	♦		Su				♦		
Indigofera decora	30 in (75 cm)	4 ft (1.2 m)	S	C/W	♦		♦	♦		Su	♦		♦	♦		

Plant name	Height	Spread	Type	Climate	Deciduous	Evergreen	Showy flowers	Showy foliage	Scented flowers	Flowering season	Grow in pot/tub	Indoor use	Frost tolerant	Full sun	Half sun	Heavy shade
Indigofera heterantha	8 ft (2.4 m)	8 ft (2.4 m)	S	C/W	◆		◆			Su			◆	◆		
Indigofera kirilowii	2–5 ft (0.6–1.5 m)	3–6 ft (0.9–1.8 m)	S	C/W	◆		◆			Su			◆	◆		
Indigofera potaninii	3–5 ft (0.9–1.5 m)	4 ft (1.2 m)	S	C/W	◆		◆		◆	Su/A			◆	◆		
Iochroma coccineum	10 ft (3 m)	6 ft (1.8 m)	S	W/T		◆	◆			Su				◆		
Iochroma cyaneum	10 ft (3 m)	5 ft (1.5 m)	S	W/T		◆	◆		◆	Su				◆	◆	
Iochroma grandiflorum	8 ft (2.4 m)	6 ft (1.8 m)	S	W/T		◆	◆			Su/A				◆		
Isopogon anemonifolius	6 ft (1.8 m)	6 ft (1.8 m)	S	W/T		◆	◆			Sp/Su				◆		
Isopogon dubius	5 ft (1.5 m)	5 ft (1.5 m)	S	W/T		◆	◆			W/Sp				◆		
Isopogon formosus	6 ft (1.8 m)	6 ft (1.8 m)	S	W/T		◆	◆			W/Sp				◆		
Itea ilicifolia	15 ft (4.5 m)	10 ft (3 m)	S	C/W		◆	◆		◆	Su			◆	◆		
Itea virginica	4–10 ft (1.2–3 m)	5 ft (1.5 m)	S	C	◆		◆	◆	◆	Sp/Su			◆	◆		
Ixora casei	12 ft (3.5 m)	8 ft (2.4 m)	S	W/T		◆	◆			Su				◆		
Ixora chinensis	6 ft (1.8 m)	5 ft (1.5 m)	S	W/T		◆	◆			Sp–A	◆	◆		◆		
Ixora coccinea	8 ft (2.4 m)	8 ft (2.4 m)	S	T		◆	◆			All	◆	◆		◆		
Ixora Hybrid Cultivars	1–6 ft (0.3–1.8 m)	1–3 ft (0.3–0.9 m)	S	T		◆	◆			All	◆	◆		◆		
Jacaranda cuspidifolia	15–40 ft (4.5–12 m)	30 ft (9 m)	T	W/T	◆		◆	◆		Sp/Su				◆		
Jacaranda mimosifolia	25–50 ft (8–15 m)	20–35 ft (6–10 m)	T	W/T	◆		◆	◆		Sp/Su				◆		
Jasminum humile	12 ft (3.5 m)	12 ft (3.5 m)	S	W		◆	◆		◆	Su			◆	◆	◆	
Jasminum mesnyi	10 ft (3 m)	10 ft (3 m)	S	W		◆	◆			Su			◆	◆	◆	
Jasminum nudiflorum	10 ft (3 m)	10 ft (3 m)	S	C/W	◆		◆		◆	W			◆	◆	◆	
Jatropha integerrima	10–20 ft (3–6 m)	4–8 ft (1.2–2.4 m)	S	W/T		◆	◆	◆		Sp–A	◆			◆		
Jatropha multifida	12 ft (3.5 m)	10 ft (3 m)	S	W/T		◆	◆	◆		Su	◆			◆		
Juglans ailanthifolia	50 ft (15 m)	40 ft (12 m)	T	C/W	◆			◆		Sp			◆	◆		
Juglans californica	30 ft (9 m)	30 ft (9 m)	T	C/W	◆			◆		Sp			◆	◆		
Juglans cinerea	60 ft (18 m)	50 ft (15 m)	T	C/W	◆			◆		Sp			◆	◆		
Juniperus chinensis	30 ft (9 m)	15 ft (4.5 m)	C	C/W		◆		◆		Sp	◆		◆	◆		
Juniperus communis	20 ft (6 m)	3–15 ft (0.9–4.5 m)	C	C		◆		◆		Sp			◆	◆		
Juniperus conferta	2 ft (0.6 m)	5–8 ft (1.5–2.4 m)	C	C		◆		◆		Sp			◆	◆		
Juniperus deppeana	20 ft (6 m)	7 ft (2 m)	C	C		◆		◆		Sp				◆		
Juniperus horizontalis	18 in (45 cm)	12 ft (3.5 m)	C	C/W		◆		◆		Sp			◆	◆		
Juniperus osteosperma	12–20 ft (3.5–6 m)	20 ft (6 m)	C	C		◆		◆		Sp			◆	◆		
Juniperus × pfitzeriana	4–10 ft (1.2–3 m)	5–15 ft (1.5–4.5 m)	C	C/W		◆		◆		Sp	◆		◆	◆		

Plant name	Height	Spread	Type	Climate	Deciduous	Evergreen	Showy flowers	Showy foliage	Scented flowers	Flowering season	Grow in pot/tub	Indoor use	Frost tolerant	Full sun	Half sun	Heavy shade
Juniperus procumbens	30 in (75 cm)	12 ft (3.5 m)	C	C		◆		◆		Sp			◆	◆		
Juniperus recurva	30 ft (9 m)	15 ft (4.5 m)	C	C		◆		◆		Sp			◆	◆		
Juniperus sabina	12 ft (3.5 m)	15 ft (4.5 m)	C	C/W		◆		◆		Sp			◆	◆		
Juniperus scopulorum	30 ft (9 m)	15 ft (4.5 m)	C	C		◆		◆		Sp	◆		◆	◆		
Juniperus squamata	2–20 ft (0.6–6 m)	15 ft (4.5 m)	C	C		◆		◆		Sp			◆	◆		
Juniperus virginiana	40 ft (12 m)	12–20 ft (3.5–6 m)	T	C/W		◆		◆		Sp			◆	◆		
Justicia adhatoda	6–8 ft (1.8–2.4 m)	3–5 ft (0.9–1.5 m)	S	W/T		◆	◆			Su				◆	◆	
Justicia aurea	3–5 ft (0.9–1.5 m)	3 ft (0.9 m)	S	W/T		◆	◆	◆		Su/A	◆	◆			◆	
Justicia brandegeeana	36 in (90 cm)	26 in (65 cm)	S	W/T		◆	◆			Sp–A	◆	◆		◆	◆	
Justicia carnea	3–6 ft (0.9–1.8 m)	3 ft (0.9 m)	S	W/T		◆	◆			Su/A	◆	◆		◆	◆	
Justicia rizzinii	10–22 in (25–55 cm)	10–22 in (25–55 cm)	S	W/T		◆	◆			W/Sp	◆	◆		◆	◆	
Justicia spicigera	6 ft (1.8 m)	5 ft (1.5 m)	S	W/T		◆	◆			Sp–A	◆			◆	◆	
Kalmia angustifolia	3 ft (0.9 m)	5 ft (1.5 m)	S	C		◆	◆			Su				◆	◆	
Kalmia latifolia	10 ft (3 m)	10 ft (3 m)	S	C		◆	◆			Sp/Su	◆			◆	◆	
Kalmia polifolia	2 ft (0.6 m)	3 ft (0.9 m)	S	C		◆	◆			Sp				◆	◆	
Kalopanax septemlobus	20–60 ft (6–18 m)	10–30 ft (3–9 m)	T	C/W	◆		◆	◆		Su				◆	◆	
Kerria japonica	6 ft (1.8 m)	5 ft (1.5 m)	S	C/W	◆		◆			Sp				◆	◆	◆
Kigelia africana	40 ft (12 m)	12 ft (3.5 m)	T	W/T		◆	◆	◆	◆	Su				◆		
Koelreuteria bipinnata	30 ft (9 m)	25 ft (8 m)	T	W/T	◆		◆			Su/A				◆	◆	
Koelreuteria paniculata	30 ft (9 m)	30 ft (9 m)	T	C/W	◆		◆			Su				◆	◆	
Kolkwitzia amabilis	12 ft (3.5 m)	12 ft (3.5 m)	S	C/W	◆		◆			Sp/Su				◆	◆	
Kunzea ambigua	12 ft (3.5 m)	12 ft (3.5 m)	S	W/T		◆	◆			Sp/Su				◆		
Kunzea baxteri	8 ft (2.4 m)	8 ft (2.4 m)	S	W/T		◆	◆			W/Sp				◆		
Kunzea parvifolia	5 ft (1.5 m)	5 ft (1.5 m)	S	W		◆	◆			Sp/Su				◆	◆	
Kunzea pulchella	6 ft (1.8 m)	6 ft (1.8 m)	S	W/T		◆	◆			W/Sp				◆		
+ *Laburnocytisus adamii*	25 ft (8 m)	15 ft (4.5 m)	T	C	◆		◆			Sp				◆	◆	
Laburnum alpinum	25 ft (8 m)	25 ft (8 m)	T	C	◆		◆			Su				◆	◆	
Laburnum anagyroides	25 ft (8 m)	25 ft (8 m)	T	C	◆		◆			Sp/Su				◆	◆	
Laburnum × watereri	25 ft (8 m)	25 ft (8 m)	T	C	◆		◆			Sp/Su				◆	◆	
Lagerstroemia floribunda	40 ft (12 m)	15 ft (4.5 m)	T	T		◆	◆			Su/A				◆		
Lagerstroemia indica	20 ft (6 m)	20 ft (6 m)	T	W/T	◆		◆	◆		Su/A				◆	◆	
Lagerstroemia speciosa	30–50 ft (9–15 m)	30 ft (9 m)	T	W/T	◆		◆	◆		Su/A				◆		

Plant name	Height	Spread	Type	Climate	Deciduous	Evergreen	Showy flowers	Showy foliage	Scented flowers	Flowering season	Grow in pot/tub	Indoor use	Frost tolerant	Full sun	Half sun	Heavy shade
Lagerstroemia Hybrid Cultivars	15–25 ft (4.5–8 m)	8–25 ft (2.4–8 m)	T	W/T	♦		♦	♦		Su/A	♦		♦	♦		
Lagunaria patersonia	25–50 ft (8–15 m)	15 ft (4.5 m)	T	W/T		♦	♦			Su	♦		♦	♦		
Lantana camara	4–12 ft (1.2–3.5 m)	8–30 ft (2.4–9 m)	S	W/T		♦	♦			All	♦		♦	♦		
Lantana montevidensis	3 ft (0.9 m)	10 ft (3 m)	S	W/T		♦	♦		♦	All	♦		♦	♦		
Larix decidua	165 ft (50 m)	12–20 ft (3.5–6 m)	C	C	♦			♦		Sp			♦	♦	♦	
Larix kaempferi	100 ft (30 m)	12–20 ft (3.5–6 m)	C	C	♦			♦		Sp			♦	♦	♦	
Larix laricina	60 ft 918 m)	12–20 ft (3.5–6 m)	C	C	♦			♦		Sp			♦	♦	♦	
Larix × *marschlinsii*	90 ft (27 m)	20 ft (6 m)	C	C	♦			♦		Sp			♦	♦	♦	
Larix occidentalis	180 ft (55 m)	15 ft (4.5 m)	C	C	♦			♦		Sp			♦	♦	♦	
Lavandula × *allardii*	3 ft (0.9 m)	3 ft (0.9 m)	S	W/T		♦	♦	♦	♦	Su			♦	♦		
Lavandula angustifolia	2–3 ft (0.6–0.9 m)	4 ft (1.2 m)	S	C/W		♦	♦	♦	♦	Sp/Su			♦	♦		
Lavandula dentata	3–5 ft (0.9–1.5 m)	5 ft (1.5 m)	S	W/T		♦	♦	♦	♦	Sp/Su			♦	♦		
Lavandula × *intermedia*	3 ft (0.9 m)	3 ft (0.9 m)	S	C/W		♦	♦	♦	♦	Sp/Su			♦	♦		
Lavandula lanata	3 ft (0.9 m)	3 ft (0.9 m)	S	C/W		♦	♦	♦	♦	Su			♦	♦		
Lavandula latifolia	3 ft (0.9 m)	4 ft (1.2 m)	S	C/W		♦	♦	♦	♦	Su			♦	♦		
Lavandula pinnata	3 ft (0.9 m)	3 ft (0.9 m)	S	W/T		♦	♦	♦	♦	Sp–A				♦		
Lavandula stoechas	24 in (60 cm)	24 in (60 cm)	S	W/T		♦	♦	♦	♦	Su			♦	♦		
Lavandula viridis	36 in (90 cm)	30 in (75 cm)	S	W/T		♦	♦	♦	♦	Su			♦	♦	♦	
Lavatera olbia	6 ft (1.8 m)	5 ft (1.5 m)	S	W		♦	♦			Su				♦		
Leptospermum laevigatum	10–20 ft (3–6 m)	10–15 ft (3–4.5 m)	S	W/T		♦	♦			Sp				♦		
Leptospermum nitidum	8 ft (2.4 m)	6 ft (1.8 m)	S	W		♦	♦			Su			♦	♦		
Leptospermum petersonii	20 ft (6 m)	10 ft (3 m)	S	W/T		♦	♦			Su				♦		
Leptospermum rotundifolium	6 ft (1.8 m)	10 ft (3 m)	S	W		♦	♦			Sp			♦	♦		
Leptospermum scoparium	6 ft (1.8 m)	6 ft (1.8 m)	S	W		♦	♦			Sp/Su			♦	♦		
Leptospermum spectabile	10 ft (3 m)	6 ft (1.8 m)	S	W/T		♦	♦			Sp			♦	♦		
Leptospermum squarrosum	6 ft (1.8 m)	5 ft (1.5 m)	S	W/T		♦	♦			A			♦	♦		
Leschenaultia biloba	24 in (60 cm)	24 in (60 cm)	S	W/T		♦	♦			W	♦			♦		
Leschenaultia formosa	12 in (30 cm)	24 in (60 cm)	S	W/T		♦	♦			W	♦			♦		
Leucadendron argenteum	20–30 ft (6–9 m)	6–12 ft (1.8–6 m)	T	W		♦		♦		Su				♦		
Leucadendron eucalyptifolium	20 ft (6 m)	8 ft (2.4 m)	S	W		♦	♦	♦		W/Sp			♦	♦		
Leucadendron salicifolium	10 ft (3 m)	6 ft (1.8 m)	S	W		♦	♦			W/Sp			♦	♦		
Leucadendron sessile	5 ft (1.5 m)	3 ft (0.9 m)	S	W		♦	♦	♦		W				♦	♦	

Plant name	Height	Spread	Type	Climate	Deciduous	Evergreen	Showy flowers	Showy foliage	Scented flowers	Flowering season	Grow in pot/tub	Indoor use	Frost tolerant	Full sun	Half sun	Heavy shade
Leucadendron tinctum	4 ft (1.2 m)	4 ft (1.2 m)	S	W		♦	♦	♦	♦	W			♦	♦		
Leucadendron Hybrid Cultivars	4–8 ft (1.2–2.4 m)	4–8 ft (1.2–2.4 m)	S	W/T		♦	♦	♦		A–Sp	♦			♦		
Leucaena leucocephala	30 ft (9 m)	15 ft (4.5 m)	T	W/T		♦	♦		♦	Sp				♦		
Leucophyta brownii	3 ft (0.9 m)	3 ft (0.9 m)	S	W/T		♦		♦		Su/A				♦		
Leucospermum bolusii	5–6 ft (1.5–1.8 m)	5–6 ft (1.5–1.8 m)	S	W		♦	♦			Sp			♦	♦		
Leucospermum cordifolium	6 ft (1.8 m)	6 ft (1.8 m)	S	W		♦	♦			Sp			♦	♦		
Leucospermum tottum	5 ft (1.5 m)	5 ft (1.5 m)	S	W		♦	♦			Sp/Su			♦	♦		
Leucospermum 'Veldfire'	5 ft (1.5 m)	5 ft (1.5 m)	S	W		♦	♦			Sp/Su	♦		♦	♦		
Leucothoe fontanesiana	6 ft (1.8 m)	7 ft (2 m)	S	C/W		♦	♦		♦	Sp			♦			♦
Leucothoe racemosa	3–8 ft (0.9–2.4 m)	5 ft (1.5 m)	S	C/W	♦		♦			Sp/Su			♦			♦
Leycesteria formosa	6 ft (1.8 m)	6 ft (1.8 m)	S	C/W		♦	♦			Su/A			♦	♦		
Libocedrus plumosa	40 ft (12 m)	10 ft (3 m)	T	W/T		♦		♦		Sp	♦		♦	♦		
Ligustrum japonicum	10 ft (3 m)	8 ft (2.4 m)	S	C/W		♦	♦		♦	Su/A			♦	♦		
Ligustrum lucidum	30 ft (9 m)	30 ft (9 m)	S	W/T		♦	♦	♦	♦	A			♦	♦		
Ligustrum ovalifolium	12 ft (3.5 m)	12 ft (3.5 m)	S	C/W		♦	♦	♦	♦	Su			♦	♦		
Lindera obtusiloba	30 ft (9 m)	25 ft (9 m)	T	C/W	♦			♦		Sp			♦	♦		
Liquidambar formosana	60 ft (18 m)	30 ft (9 m)	T	W/T	♦			♦		Sp			♦	♦		
Liquidambar orientalis	25–50 ft (8–15 m)	15 ft (4.5 m)	T	W/T	♦			♦		Sp			♦	♦		
Liquidambar styraciflua	70 ft (21 m)	35 ft (10 m)	T	C/W/T	♦			♦		Sp			♦	♦		
Liriodendron tulipifera	100 ft (30 m)	40 ft (12 m)	T	C/W	♦		♦	♦		Sp			♦	♦		
Lithocarpus densiflorus	100 ft (30 m)	40 ft (12 m)	T	C/W		♦		♦		Sp			♦	♦		
Lithodora diffusa	6–12 in (15–30 cm)	24–36 in (60–90 cm)	S	C/W		♦	♦			Sp/Su			♦	♦	♦	
Lomatia ferruginea	30 ft (9 m)	15 ft (4.5 m)	T	W		♦	♦	♦		Su				♦		
Lomatia polymorpha	6–12 ft (1.8–3.5 m)	5 ft (1.5 m)	T	W		♦	♦	♦		Sp/Su				♦		
Lonicera fragrantissima	6 ft (1.8 m)	8 ft (2.4 m)	S	C/W	♦		♦		♦	W/Sp			♦	♦		
Lonicera involucrata	3 ft (0.9 m)	3 ft (0.9 m)	S	C/W	♦		♦			Sp			♦	♦		
Lonicera maackii	15 ft (4.5 m)	15 ft (4.5 m)	S	C/W	♦		♦		♦	Sp/Su			♦	♦		
Lonicera nitida	12 ft (3.5 m)	10 ft (3 m)	S	C/W	♦			♦		Sp			♦	♦		
Lonicera × purpusii	10 ft (3 m)	8 ft (2.4 m)	S	C/W	♦		♦		♦	W/Sp			♦	♦		
Lonicera syringantha	10 ft (3 m)	7 ft (2 m)	S	C/W	♦		♦		♦	Sp/Su			♦	♦		
Lonicera tatarica	10 ft (3 m)	7 ft (2 m)	S	C/W	♦		♦			Sp/Su			♦	♦		
Lophomyrtus bullata	8–12 ft (2.4–3.5 m)	8 ft (2.4 m)	S	W		♦		♦		Su				♦		

Plant name	Height	Spread	Type	Climate	Deciduous	Evergreen	Showy flowers	Showy foliage	Scented flowers	Flowering season	Grow in pot/tub	Indoor use	Frost tolerant	Full sun	Half sun	Heavy shade
Lophomyrtus × ralphii	6 ft (1.8 m)	5 ft (1.5 m)	S	W/T		♦		♦		Su				♦		
Lophostemon confertus	130 ft (40 m)	30 ft (9 m)	T	W/T		♦	♦			Su				♦		
Loropetalum chinense	6–15 ft (1.8–4.5 m)	8 ft (2.4 m)	S	W/T		♦	♦	♦		Sp	♦			♦	♦	
Luculia grandifolia	12–20 ft (3.5–6 m)	7 ft (2 m)	S	W		♦	♦		♦	Su	♦			♦	♦	
Luculia gratissima	10–20 ft (3–6 m)	10–15 ft (3–4.5 m)	S	W		♦	♦		♦	A/W	♦			♦	♦	
Luma apiculata	20 ft (6 m)	20 ft (6 m)	T	W		♦	♦			Sp/Su				♦	♦	
Lupinus arboreus	3–7 ft (0.9–2 m)	4–8 ft (1.2–2.4 m)	S	W		♦	♦			Sp/Su			♦	♦	♦	
Mackaya bella	8 ft (2.4 m)	4 ft (1.2 m)	S	W/T		♦	♦			Sp–A	♦			♦	♦	
Maclura pomifera	50 ft (15 m)	30 ft (9 m)	T	C/W	♦			♦		Su			♦	♦	♦	
Maclura tricuspidata	25 ft (8 m)	15 ft (4.5 m)	T	C/W	♦					Su				♦	♦	
Magnolia acuminata	100 ft (30 m)	30 ft (9 m)	T	C/W	♦		♦			Su				♦	♦	
Magnolia campbellii	100 ft (30 m)	30 ft (9 m)	T	C/W	♦		♦			W/Sp				♦	♦	
Magnolia delavayi	35 ft (10 m)	30 ft (9 m)	T	W		♦	♦			Su				♦	♦	
Magnolia denudata	30 ft (9 m)	30 ft (9 m)	T	C/W	♦		♦		♦	Su				♦	♦	
Magnolia fraseri	40 ft (12 m)	30 ft (9 m)	T	C/W	♦		♦		♦	Sp/Su				♦	♦	
Magnolia grandiflora	35 ft (10 m)	35 ft (10 m)	T	C/W		♦	♦	♦	♦	Su				♦		♦
Magnolia kobus	40 ft (12 m)	30 ft (9 m)	T	C	♦		♦			Sp				♦	♦	
Magnolia liliiflora	10 ft (3 m)	15 ft (4.5 m)	S	C/W/T	♦		♦		♦	Sp/Su	♦			♦	♦	
Magnolia × loebneri	30 ft (9 m)	20 ft (6 m)	T	C	♦		♦			Sp/Su				♦	♦	
Magnolia macrophylla	50 ft (15 m)	30 ft (9 m)	T	C	♦		♦			Su				♦		♦
Magnolia salicifolia	40 ft (12 m)	20 ft (6 m)	T	C/W	♦		♦		♦	Sp				♦	♦	
Magnolia sargentiana	60 ft (18 m)	25 ft (8 m)	T	C/W	♦		♦	♦		Sp				♦	♦	
Magnolia sieboldii	20 ft (6 m)	25 ft (8 m)	S	C/W	♦		♦		♦	Sp/Su				♦	♦	
Magnolia × soulangeana	20 ft (6 m)	20 ft (6 m)	S	C/W	♦		♦			Sp/Su				♦	♦	
Magnolia sprengeri	40 ft (12 m)	25 ft (8 m)	T	C/W	♦		♦			Sp				♦	♦	
Magnolia stellata	15 ft (4.5 m)	10 ft (3 m)	S	C/W	♦		♦		♦	W/Sp	♦			♦	♦	
Magnolia × veitchii	100 ft (30 m)	15 ft (4.5 m)	T	C/W	♦		♦			Sp	♦			♦	♦	
Magnolia virginiana	30 ft (9 m)	20 ft (6 m)	T	C/W	♦	♦	♦	♦	♦	Su				♦	♦	
Magnolia wilsonii	20 ft (6 m)	20 ft (6 m)	S	C/W	♦		♦		♦	Sp/Su				♦	♦	
Magnolia Hybrid Cultivars	20–40 ft (6–12 m)	20–30 ft (6–9 m)	S/T	C/W	♦		♦			W–Su	♦		♦	♦		
Mahonia aquifolium	6 ft (1.8 m)	8 ft (2.4 m)	S	C/W		♦	♦	♦		W				♦		♦
Mahonia fortunei	7 ft (2 m)	3 ft (0.9 m)	S	C/W		♦	♦		♦	A				♦		♦

Plant name	Height	Spread	Type	Climate	Deciduous	Evergreen	Showy flowers	Showy foliage	Scented flowers	Flowering season	Grow in pot/tub	Indoor use	Frost tolerant	Full sun	Half sun	Heavy shade
Mahonia fremontii	12 ft (3.5 m)	7 ft (2 m)	S	W/T		◆	◆	◆		Su				◆		◆
Mahonia 'Golden Abundance'	6–8 ft (1.8–2.4 m)	3 ft (0.9 m)	S	C/W		◆	◆	◆		Su	◆			◆	◆	
Mahonia japonica	6 ft (1.8 m)	10 ft (3 m)	S	C/W		◆	◆	◆	◆	W				◆		◆
Mahonia lomariifolia	10 ft (3 m)	8 ft (2.4 m)	S	C/W		◆	◆	◆	◆	A–Sp	◆			◆		◆
Mahonia × media	15 ft (4.5 m)	12 ft (3.5 m)	S	C/W		◆	◆		◆	Su	◆			◆		◆
Mahonia repens	18 in (45 cm)	36 in (90 cm)	S	C/W		◆	◆		◆	Sp				◆		◆
Malpighia coccigera	30 in (75 cm)	30 in (75 cm)	S	W/T		◆	◆			Su	◆	◆				◆
Malpighia glabra	10 ft (3 m)	4 ft (1.2 m)	S	W/T		◆	◆			Su	◆	◆				◆
Malus baccata	40 ft (12 m)	40 ft (12 m)	T	C/W	◆		◆		◆	Sp				◆	◆	
Malus coronaria	30 ft (9 m)	30 ft (9 m)	T	C/W	◆		◆		◆	Sp				◆	◆	
Malus floribunda	12 ft (3.5 m)	20 ft (6 m)	T	C/W	◆		◆			Sp				◆	◆	
Malus × gloriosa	10 ft (3 m)	8–10 ft (2–3 m)	T	C/W	◆		◆	◆		Sp				◆	◆	
Malus halliana	15 ft (4.5 m)	10 ft (3 m)	T	C/W	◆		◆			Sp				◆	◆	
Malus hupehensis	15 ft (4.5 m)	25 ft (8 m)	T	C/W	◆		◆		◆	Sp				◆	◆	
Malus ioensis	20 ft (6 m)	20 ft (6 m)	T	C	◆		◆		◆	Sp				◆	◆	
Malus × micromalus	15 ft (4.5 m)	15 ft (4.5 m)	T	C/W	◆		◆			Sp				◆	◆	
Malus × purpurea	20 ft (6 m)	25 ft (8 m)	T	C/W	◆		◆	◆		Sp				◆	◆	
Malus sargentii	6 ft (1.8 m)	15 ft (4.5 m)	T	C/W	◆		◆			Sp				◆	◆	
Malus × scheideckeri	15 ft (4.5 m)	8 ft (2.4 m)	T	C/W	◆		◆			Sp				◆	◆	
Malus sieboldii	15 ft (4.5 m)	10 ft (3 m)	T	C/W	◆		◆		◆	Sp				◆	◆	
Malus sylvestris	30 ft (9 m)	10 ft (3 m)	T	C	◆		◆			Sp				◆	◆	
Malus tschonoskii	40 ft (12 m)	20 ft (6 m)	T	C/W	◆		◆			Sp				◆	◆	
Malus × zumi	15 ft (4.5 m)	10 ft (3 m)	T	C	◆		◆			Sp				◆	◆	
Malus Hybrid Cultivars	10–40 ft (3–12 m)	5–25 ft (1.5–8 m)	T	C	◆		◆		◆	Sp				◆	◆	
Malvaviscus arboreus	12–15 ft (3.5–4.5 m)	10 ft (3 m)	S	W/T		◆	◆			Su/A				◆		
Malvaviscus penduliflorus	12–15 ft (3.5–4.5 m)	10 ft (3 m)	S	W/T		◆	◆			Su				◆		
Maytenus boaria	70 ft (21 m)	30 ft (9 m)	T	W/T		◆		◆		Sp				◆	◆	
Megaskepasma erythrochlamys	10 ft (3 m)	4 ft (1.2 m)	S	W/T		◆	◆	◆		All	◆					◆
Melaleuca armillaris	25 ft (8 m)	12 ft (3.5 m)	T	W/T		◆	◆			Sp/Su				◆		
Melaleuca bracteata	30 ft (9 m)	20 ft (6 m)	S	W/T		◆	◆			Sp				◆		
Melaleuca fulgens	10 ft (3 m)	6 ft (1.8 m)	S	W/T		◆	◆			Sp/Su	◆			◆	◆	
Melaleuca hypericifolia	15 ft (4.5 m)	15 ft (4.5 m)	S	W/T		◆	◆			Sp/Su				◆		

Plant name	Height	Spread	Type	Climate	Deciduous	Evergreen	Showy flowers	Showy foliage	Scented flowers	Flowering season	Grow in pot/tub	Indoor use	Frost tolerant	Full sun	Half sun	Heavy shade
Melaleuca incana	10 ft (3 m)	10 ft (3 m)	S	W/T		◆	◆	◆		Sp/Su				◆		
Melaleuca lateritia	6 ft (1.8 m)	3 ft (0.9 m)	S	W/T		◆	◆			Sp/Su				◆		
Melaleuca leucadendra	90 ft (27 m)	30 ft (9 m)	T	W/T		◆	◆		◆	A/W				◆		
Melaleuca linariifolia	20 ft (6 m)	10 ft (3 m)	T	W/T		◆	◆			Su			◆	◆		
Melaleuca pulchella	6 ft (1.8 m)	6 ft (1.8 m)	S	W/T		◆	◆			Sp/Su				◆	◆	
Melaleuca quinquenervia	30–50 ft (9–15 m)	20 ft (6 m)	T	W/T		◆	◆		◆	Sp				◆		
Melaleuca radula	6 ft (1.8 m)	6 ft (1.8 m)	S	W/T		◆	◆			W/Sp				◆	◆	
Melaleuca thymifolia	3 ft (0.9 m)	3 ft (0.9 m)	S	W/T		◆	◆			All				◆	◆	
Melastoma malabathricum	6–8 ft (1.8–2.4 m)	5 ft (1.5 m)	S	W/T		◆	◆		◆	All				◆		
Melia azederach	20–80 ft (6–24 m)	25 ft (8 m)	T	W/T	◆		◆			Su				◆	◆	
Melianthus major	6–10 ft (1.8–3 m)	3 ft (0.9 m)	S	W/T		◆	◆	◆		Sp/Su				◆	◆	◆
Metasequoia glyptostroboides	70 ft (21 m)	20 ft (6 m)	T	C/W	◆			◆		Sp				◆		
Metrosideros excelsa	15–50 ft (4.5–15 m)	25 ft (8 m)	T	W/T		◆	◆			Su	◆			◆		
Metrosideros kermadecensis	20 ft (6 m)	15 ft (4.5 m)	T	W/T		◆	◆			Any	◆			◆		
Metrosideros polymorpha	20–50 ft (6–15 m)	20 ft (6 m)	T	T		◆	◆			Sp/Su				◆		
Michelia champaca	100 ft (30 m)	10 ft (3 m)	T	W/T		◆	◆		◆	Su/A				◆		
Michelia doltsopa	30 ft (9 m)	20 ft (6 m)	T	W/T		◆	◆		◆	W/Sp				◆		
Michelia figo	15 ft (4.5 m)	10 ft (3 m)	S	W/T		◆	◆		◆	Sp/Su	◆			◆		
Michelia yunnanensis	15 ft (4.5 m)	7 ft (2 m)	S	W/T		◆	◆			W/Sp	◆			◆		
Microbiota decussata	2 ft (0.6 m)	5 ft (1.5 m)	C	C		◆				Sp	◆		◆	◆		
Millettia grandis	20–40 ft (6–12 m)	30 ft (9 m)	T	W/T	◆		◆			Su				◆		
Mimosa pudica	3 ft (0.9 m)	3 ft (0.9 m)	S	W/T		◆	◆			Su	◆	◆		◆		
Montanoa bipinnatifida	10–20 ft (3–6 m)	7 ft (2 m)	S	W/T		◆	◆			A				◆		
Morella cerifera	30 ft (9 m)	15 ft (4.5 m)	T	C/W		◆		◆		Su				◆		◆
Morella pensylvanica	6–10 ft (1.8–3 m)	4 ft (1.2 m)	S	C	◆			◆		Su				◆	◆	
Murraya paniculata	10 ft (3 m)	10 ft (3 m)	S	W/T		◆	◆	◆	◆	Sp	◆	◆		◆		
Mussaenda erythrophylla	10 ft (3 m)	5 ft (1.5 m)	S	T		◆	◆	◆		Sp				◆		
Mussaenda Hybrid Cultivars	10 ft (3 m)	5–7 ft (1.5–2 m)	S	T		◆	◆	◆		Sp	◆			◆		
Myoporum floribundum	10 ft (3 m)	8 ft (2.4 m)	S	W		◆	◆		◆	W–Su				◆		
Myoporum laetum	15–30 ft (4.5–9 m)	10 ft (3 m)	S	W		◆		◆		Su				◆		
Myrica gale	3–6 ft (0.9–1.8 m)	4 ft (1.2 m)	S	C	◆		◆	◆		Su			◆	◆	◆	
Myrtus communis	10 ft (3 m)	10 ft (3 m)	S	W/T		◆	◆		◆	Sp	◆			◆	◆	

Plant name	Height	Spread	Type	Climate	Deciduous	Evergreen	Showy flowers	Showy foliage	Scented flowers	Flowering season	Grow in pot/tub	Indoor use	Frost tolerant	Full sun	Half sun	Heavy shade
Nageia nagi	70 ft (21 m)	15 ft (4.5 m)	C	W		♦		♦		Sp			♦		♦	
Nandina domestica	7 ft (2 m)	4 ft (1.2 m)	S	C/W		♦		♦		Su	♦		♦	♦		
Neillia sinensis	10 ft (3 m)	7 ft (2 m)	S	C/W	♦		♦			Sp/Su			♦	♦		
Neillia thibetica	6 ft (1.8 m)	6 ft (1.8 m)	S	C/W	♦		♦			Su			♦	♦		
Nerium oleander	10 ft (3 m)	8 ft (2.4 m)	S	W/T		♦	♦			Sp–A	♦		♦	♦		
Neviusia alabamensis	5 ft (1.5 m)	5 ft (1.5 m)	S	C/W	♦		♦			Sp			♦	♦	♦	
Nothofagus antarctica	40 ft (12 m)	20 ft (6 m)	T	C/W	♦			♦		Sp			♦	♦		
Nothofagus cunninghamii	5–100 ft (1.5–30 m)	8–30 ft (2.4–9 m)	T	C/W		♦		♦		Sp			♦	♦		
Nothofagus fusca	100 ft (30 m)	25 ft (8 m)	T	C/W		♦		♦		Sp			♦	♦		
Nothofagus menziesii	60 ft (18 m)	30 ft (9 m)	T	C/W		♦		♦		Sp			♦	♦		
Nothofagus solanderi	60 ft (18 m)	25 ft (8 m)	T	C/W		♦		♦		Sp			♦	♦		
Nyssa aquatica	50 ft (15 m)	15 ft (4.5 m)	T	C/W	♦			♦		Su			♦	♦		
Nyssa sinensis	40 ft (12 m)	30 ft (9 m)	T	C/W		♦		♦		Su			♦	♦		
Nyssa sylvatica	50 ft (15 m)	30 ft (9 m)	T	C/W	♦			♦		Su			♦	♦		
Ochna kirkii	10 ft (3 m)	7 ft (2 m)	S	W/T		♦	♦			Sp				♦		
Ochna serrulata	12 ft (3.5 m)	7 ft (2 m)	S	W/T		♦	♦		♦	Sp/Su				♦		
Odontonema callistachyum	6 ft (1.8 m)	3–6 ft (0.9–1.8 m)	S	W/T		♦	♦			All	♦	♦		♦		
Odontonema schomburgkianum	6 ft (1.8 m)	2 ft (0.6 m)	S	W/T		♦	♦			Sp	♦	♦		♦		
Olea capensis	50 ft (15 m)	15 ft (4.5 m)	T	W/T		♦		♦		Sp				♦		
Olearia albida	10 ft (3 m)	7 ft (2 m)	S	W		♦	♦			Su/A			♦	♦		
Olearia furfuracea	8–15 ft (2.4–4.5 m)	7 ft (2 m)	S	W/T		♦	♦			Su			♦	♦		
Olearia insignis	3–7 ft (0.9–2 m)	3–7 ft (0.9–2 m)	S	W/T		♦	♦			Su				♦		
Olearia macrodonta	7 ft (2 m)	7 ft (2 m)	S	W/T		♦	♦			Su			♦	♦		
Olearia phlogopappa	8 ft (2.4 m)	7 ft (2 m)	S	W		♦	♦			Sp	♦			♦		
Olearia × scilloniensis	10 ft (3 m)	8 ft (2.4 m)	S	W		♦	♦			Sp			♦	♦		
Olearia traversii	15 ft (4.5 m)	10 ft (3 m)	S	W/T		♦		♦		Su			♦	♦		
Oncoba spinosa	6–10 ft (1.8–3 m)	6 ft (1.8 m)	S	W/T		♦	♦		♦	Sp–A				♦		
Oplopanax horridus	3–10 ft (0.9–3 m)	5 ft (1.5 m)	S	C/W	♦			♦		Sp/Su			♦		♦	♦
Orphium frutescens	24 in (60 cm)	18 in (45 cm)	S	W/T		♦	♦			Su				♦		
Osmanthus × burkwoodii	10 ft (3 m)	10 ft (3 m)	S	C/W		♦	♦		♦	Sp			♦	♦		
Osmanthus delavayi	8 ft (2.4 m)	8 ft (2.4 m)	S	C/W		♦	♦		♦	W/Sp			♦	♦		
Osmanthus × fortunei	10 ft (3 m)	10 ft (3 m)	S	C/W		♦	♦		♦	A			♦	♦		

Plant name	Height	Spread	Type	Climate	Deciduous	Evergreen	Showy flowers	Showy foliage	Scented flowers	Flowering season	Grow in pot/tub	Indoor use	Frost tolerant	Full sun	Half sun	Heavy shade
Osmanthus fragrans	20 ft (6 m)	20 ft (6 m)	S	C/W		♦	♦		♦	W/Sp/A			♦	♦		
Osmanthus heterophyllus	12 ft (3.5 m)	12 ft (3.5 m)	S	C/W		♦	♦	♦	♦	A/W			♦	♦		
Ostrya carpinifolia	70 ft (21 m)	70 ft (21 m)	T	C/W	♦		♦	♦		Sp			♦	♦		
Ostrya virginiana	50 ft (15 m)	35 ft (10 m)	T	C/W	♦		♦	♦		Sp			♦	♦		
Oxydendrum arboreum	6–10 ft (1.8–3 m)	10 ft (3 m)	T	C/W	♦		♦	♦		Su			♦	♦		
Pachira aquatica	20 ft (6 m)	10 ft (3 m)	T	W/T		♦		♦		Su				♦		
Pachystachys lutea	36 in (90 cm)	20 in (50 cm)	S	W/T		♦	♦			Sp–A	♦	♦				♦
Paeonia delavayi	7 ft (2 m)	5 ft (1.5 m)	S	C	♦		♦			Sp			♦	♦	♦	
Paeonia × lemoinei	6 ft (1.8 m)	6 ft (1.8 m)	S	C	♦		♦			Sp/Su			♦	♦	♦	
Paeonia rockii	7 ft (2 m)	3 ft (0.9 m)	S	C/W	♦		♦			Sp/Su			♦	♦		
Paeonia suffruticosa	7 ft (2 m)	7 ft (2 m)	S	C	♦		♦			Sp			♦	♦	♦	
Pandanus tectorius	12–25 ft (3.5–8 m)	10–20 ft (3–6 m)	T	W/T		♦	♦	♦		Sp				♦		
Paraserianthes lophantha	25 ft (8 m)	10 ft (3 m)	T	W		♦	♦	♦		Sp				♦		
Parkinsonia aculeata	30 ft (9 m)	20 ft (6 m)	S	W/T		♦	♦			Sp				♦	♦	
Parmentiera cereifera	20 ft (6 m)	10 ft (3 m)	T	W/T		♦	♦			Sp				♦		
Parrotia persica	25–40 ft (8–12 m)	20 ft (6 m)	T	C/W	♦			♦		W/Sp			♦	♦		
Paulownia fortunei	60 ft (18 m)	40 ft (12 m)	T	C/W	♦		♦	♦		Sp			♦	♦		
Paulownia tomentosa	50 ft (15 m)	30 ft (9 m)	T	C/W	♦		♦	♦		Sp			♦	♦		
Pavonia × gledhillii	5 ft (1.5 m)	3 ft (0.9 m)	S	W/T		♦	♦			Sp–A	♦	♦				
Pavonia hastata	36 in (90 cm)	24 in (60 cm)	S	W/T		♦	♦			Sp–A	♦	♦				
Peltophorum pterocarpum	50 ft (15 m)	30 ft (9 m)	T	T		♦	♦		♦	Su				♦		
Persoonia pinifolia	10–15 ft (3–4.5 m)	10 ft (3 m)	S	W/T		♦	♦			Su/A						♦
Phellodendron amurense	50 ft (15 m)	40 ft (12 m)	T	C	♦			♦		Su			♦	♦		
Philadelphus coronarius	10 ft (3 m)	8 ft (2.4 m)	S	C/W	♦		♦		♦	Su			♦	♦		
Philadelphus incanus	12 ft (3.5 m)	6 ft (1.8 m)	S	C/W	♦		♦			Su			♦	♦		
Philadelphus inodorus	10 ft (3 m)	4 ft (1.2 m)	S	C/W	♦		♦			Su			♦	♦		
Philadelphus lewisii	10 ft (3 m)	10 ft (3 m)	S	C/W	♦		♦			Su			♦	♦		
Philadelphus mexicanus	15 ft (4.5 m)	8 ft (2.4 m)	S	C/W	♦		♦		♦	Su				♦		
Philadelphus Hybrid Cultivars	30 in–10 ft (75 cm–3 m)	6–8 ft (1.8–2.4 m)	S	C/W	♦		♦		♦	Su			♦	♦		
Philodendron bipinnatifidum	10 ft (3 m)	10 ft (3 m)	S	W/T		♦		♦		Su	♦	♦				♦
Phlomis chrysophylla	4 ft (1.2 m)	3 ft (0.9 m)	S	W		♦	♦	♦		Su			♦	♦		
Phlomis fruticosa	30 in (75 cm)	30 in (75 cm)	S	C/W		♦	♦	♦		Su			♦	♦		

Plant name	Height	Spread	Type	Climate	Deciduous	Evergreen	Showy flowers	Showy foliage	Scented flowers	Flowering season	Grow in pot/tub	Indoor use	Frost tolerant	Full sun	Half sun	Heavy shade
Phlomis italica	12 in (30 cm)	12 in (30 cm)	S	W		♦	♦	♦		Su/A			♦	♦		
Photinia davidiana	25 ft (8 m)	20 ft (6 m)	S	W		♦	♦	♦		Su			♦	♦		
Photinia × fraseri	15 ft (4.5 m)	15 ft (4.5 m)	S	C/W		♦	♦	♦		Sp			♦	♦		
Photinia glabra	15 ft (4.5 m)	12 ft (3.5 m)	T	C/W		♦	♦	♦		Su			♦	♦		
Photinia serratifolia	30 ft (9 m)	25 ft (8 m)	T	C/W		♦		♦		Sp			♦	♦		
Photinia villosa	15 ft (4.5 m)	15 ft (4.5 m)	T	C	♦			♦		Sp			♦	♦		
Phygelius aequalis	3 ft (0.9 m)	3 ft (0.9 m)	S	W		♦	♦			Su				♦		♦
Phygelius capensis	6 ft (1.8 m)	22 in (55 cm)	S	W		♦	♦			Su				♦		
Phygelius × rectus	4 ft (1.2 m)	4 ft (1.2 m)	S	W		♦	♦			Su				♦		♦
Phylica plumosa	3–6 ft (0.9–1.8 m)	3 ft (0.9 m)	S	W/T		♦	♦	♦		W				♦		
Phyllocladus glaucus	35–50 ft (10–15 m)	10–15 ft (3–4.5 m)	C	W/T		♦		♦		Sp				♦	♦	
Phyllocladus trichomanoides	70 ft (21 m)	20 ft (6 m)	C	W		♦		♦		Sp				♦		
Physocarpus monogynus	4 ft (1.2 m)	4 ft (1.2 m)	S	C	♦					Sp/Su			♦	♦		
Physocarpus opulifolius	10 ft (3 m)	15 ft (4.5 m)	S	C	♦		♦	♦		Sp/Su			♦	♦		
Phytolacca dioica	50 ft (15 m)	30 ft (9 m)	T	W/T		♦		♦		Sp/Su				♦		
Picea abies	200 ft (60 m)	20 ft (6 m)	C	C		♦		♦		Sp			♦	♦		
Picea engelmannii	150 ft (45 m)	15 ft (4.5 m)	C	C		♦		♦		Sp			♦	♦		
Picea glauca	80 ft (24 m)	12–20 ft (3.5–6 m)	C	C		♦		♦		Sp			♦	♦		
Picea jezoensis	120 ft (36 m)	25 ft (8 m)	C	C/W		♦		♦		Sp			♦	♦		
Picea mariana	60 ft (18 m)	10 ft (3 m)	C	C		♦		♦		Sp			♦	♦		
Picea omorika	100 ft (30 m)	20 ft (6 m)	C	C		♦		♦		Sp			♦	♦		
Picea orientalis	100 ft (30 m)	20 ft (6 m)	C	C		♦		♦		Sp			♦	♦		
Picea pungens	100 ft (30 m)	20 ft (6 m)	C	C		♦		♦		Sp				♦		
Picea sitchensis	100 ft (30 m)	25 ft (8 m)	C	C		♦		♦		Sp			♦	♦		
Picea smithiana	75 ft (23 m)	20 ft (6 m)	C	C		♦		♦		Sp			♦	♦		
Pieris floribunda	6 ft (1.8 m)	7 ft (2 m)	S	C/W		♦	♦	♦		Sp			♦	♦		
Pieris 'Forest Flame'	12 ft (3.5 m)	6 ft (1.8 m)	S	C/W		♦	♦	♦		Sp			♦	♦		
Pieris formosa	10–20 ft (3–6 m)	7 ft (2 m)	S	C/W		♦	♦	♦		Sp			♦	♦		
Pieris japonica	8–10 ft (2.4–3 m)	8 ft (2.4 m)	S	C/W		♦	♦	♦		Sp	♦		♦	♦		
Pimelea ferruginea	3 ft (0.9 m)	3 ft (0.9 m)	S	W		♦	♦			Sp	♦		♦	♦		
Pimelea nivea	6 ft (1.8 m)	3 ft (0.9 m)	S	W		♦	♦			Su				♦		♦
Pimelea physodes	3 ft (0.9 m)	2 ft (0.6 m)	S	W		♦	♦			Sp				♦		

Plant name	Height	Spread	Type	Climate	Deciduous	Evergreen	Showy flowers	Showy foliage	Scented flowers	Flowering season	Grow in pot/tub	Indoor use	Frost tolerant	Full sun	Half sun	Heavy shade
Pimelea prostrata	6 in (15 cm)	36 in (90 cm)	S	W		♦	♦			Su			♦	♦		
Pinus banksiana	60 ft (18 m)	20 ft (6 m)	C	C		♦		♦		Sp			♦	♦		
Pinus bungeana	60 ft (18 m)	20 ft (6 m)	C	C		♦		♦		Sp			♦	♦		
Pinus canariensis	130 ft (40 m)	25 ft (8 m)	C	W/T		♦		♦		Sp			♦	♦		
Pinus cembra	30 ft (9 m)	15 ft (4.5 m)	C	C		♦		♦		Sp			♦	♦		
Pinus contorta	75 ft (23 m)	25 ft (8 m)	C	C		♦		♦		Sp			♦	♦		
Pinus coulteri	100 ft (30 m)	30 ft (9 m)	C	C/W		♦		♦		Sp			♦	♦		
Pinus densiflora	70 ft (21 m)	20 ft (6 m)	C	C		♦		♦		Sp			♦	♦		
Pinus halepensis	60 ft (18 m)	20 ft (6 m)	C	C/W		♦		♦		Sp			♦	♦		
Pinus heldreichii	60 ft (18 m)	20 ft (6 m)	C	C		♦		♦		Sp			♦	♦		
Pinus lambertiana	150 ft (45 m)	20 ft (6 m)	C	C/W		♦		♦		Sp			♦	♦		
Pinus longaeva	60 ft (18 m)	15 ft (4.5 m)	C	C		♦		♦		Sp			♦	♦		
Pinus merkusii	150 ft (45 m)	20 ft (6 m)	C	W/T		♦		♦		Sp				♦		
Pinus monticola	100 ft (30 m)	20 ft (6 m)	C	C		♦		♦		Sp			♦	♦		
Pinus mugo	25 ft (8 m)	12 ft (3.5 m)	C	C		♦		♦		Sp	♦		♦	♦		
Pinus nigra	120 ft (36 m)	25 ft (8 m)	C	C		♦		♦		Sp			♦	♦		
Pinus palustris	100 ft (30 m)	15 ft (4.5 m)	C	C/W		♦		♦		Sp			♦	♦		
Pinus parviflora	80 ft (24 m)	20 ft (6 m)	C	C		♦		♦		Sp			♦	♦		
Pinus patula	50 ft (15 m)	30 ft (9 m)	C	W		♦		♦		Sp			♦	♦		
Pinus pinaster	100 ft (30 m)	30 ft (9 m)	C	C/W		♦		♦		Sp			♦	♦		
Pinus pinea	80 ft (24 m)	20 ft (6 m)	C	C/W		♦		♦		Sp			♦	♦		
Pinus ponderosa	130 ft (40 m)	20 ft (6 m)	C	C		♦		♦		Sp			♦	♦		
Pinus radiata	100 ft (30 m)	25 ft (8 m)	C	C/W		♦		♦		Sp			♦	♦		
Pinus resinosa	100 ft (30 m)	20 ft (6 m)	C	C		♦		♦		Sp			♦	♦		
Pinus roxburghii	100 ft (30 m)	15 ft (4.5 m)	C	W		♦		♦		Sp			♦	♦		
Pinus strobus	165 ft (50 m)	20 ft (6 m)	C	C		♦		♦		Sp			♦	♦		
Pinus sylvestris	100 ft (30 m)	20 ft (6 m)	C	C		♦		♦		Sp			♦	♦		
Pinus taeda	100 ft (30 m)	25 ft (8 m)	C	C/W		♦		♦		Sp			♦	♦		
Pinus thunbergii	130 ft (40 m)	20 ft (6 m)	C	C		♦		♦		Sp			♦	♦		
Pinus wallichiana	150 ft (45 m)	20 ft (6 m)	C	C		♦		♦		Sp			♦	♦		
Piper aduncum	17–25 ft (5–8 m)	8–17 ft (2.4–5 m)	S	W/T		♦		♦		Sp–A				♦		
Pistacia chinensis	25–50 ft (8–15 m)	15 ft (4.5 m)	T	C/W	♦			♦		Su			♦	♦		

Plant name	Height	Spread	Type	Climate	Deciduous	Evergreen	Showy flowers	Showy foliage	Scented flowers	Flowering season	Grow in pot/tub	Indoor use	Frost tolerant	Full sun	Half sun	Heavy shade
Pistacia lentiscus	12 ft (3.5 m)	12 ft (3.5 m)	S	W/T		◆		◆		Sp			◆	◆		
Pittosporum crassifolium	10–20 ft (3–6 m)	8 ft (2.4 m)	S	W/T		◆		◆	◆	Sp/Su				◆		
Pittosporum eugenioides	40 ft (12 m)	12 ft (3.5 m)	T	W/T		◆		◆	◆	Sp/Su			◆	◆		
Pittosporum 'Garnettii'	7–10 ft (2–3 m)	7 ft (2 m)	S	W/T		◆		◆	◆	Sp			◆	◆		
Pittosporum tenuifolium	15–20 ft (4.5–6 m)	15 ft (4.5 m)	S	W/T		◆		◆		Sp			◆	◆		
Pittosporum tobira	20 ft (6 m)	7 ft (2 m)	S	W/T		◆	◆	◆	◆	Sp/Su	◆			◆		
Pittosporum undulatum	15–40 ft (4.5–12 m)	20 ft (6 m)	T	W/T		◆	◆	◆	◆	Sp				◆		
Platanus × *hispanica*	100 ft (30 m)	60 ft (18 m)	T	C	◆			◆		Sp			◆	◆		
Platanus occidentalis	150 ft (45 m)	70 ft (21 m)	T	C	◆			◆		Sp			◆	◆		
Platanus orientalis	100 ft (30 m)	70 ft (21 m)	T	C	◆			◆		Sp			◆	◆		
Platanus racemosa	100 ft (30 m)	75 ft (23 m)	T	C/W	◆			◆		Sp				◆		
Platycladus orientalis	40 ft (12 m)	15 ft (4.5 m)	C	C/W		◆		◆		Sp	◆		◆	◆		
Plumbago auriculata	15 ft (4.5 m)	7 ft (2 m)	S	W/T		◆	◆			Sp–A				◆		
Plumbago indica	5 ft (1.5 m)	3 ft (0.9 m)	S	W/T		◆	◆			Sp–A					◆	
Plumeria obtusa	25 ft (8 m)	12 ft (3.5 m)	T	W/T		◆	◆	◆	◆	Sp–A				◆		
Plumeria rubra	25 ft (8 m)	15 ft (4.5 m)	T	W/T	◆		◆	◆	◆	Su/A	◆			◆		
Podalyria calyptrata	12 ft (3.5 m)	12 ft (3.5 m)	S	W		◆	◆	◆		Sp/Su						
Podocarpus elatus	50 ft (15 m)	20 ft (6 m)	C	W/T		◆		◆		Sp	◆			◆		
Podocarpus latifolius	90 ft (27 m)	15 ft (4.5 m)	C	W/T		◆		◆		Sp				◆		
Podocarpus lawrencei	12 ft (3.5 m)	4 ft (1.2 m)	C	C/W		◆		◆		Sp			◆	◆		
Podocarpus macrophyllus	60 ft (18 m)	20 ft (6 m)	C	W/T		◆		◆		Sp				◆		
Podocarpus totara	80 ft (24 m)	25 ft (8 m)	C	W/T		◆		◆		Sp				◆		
Polyalthia longifolia	50 ft (15 m)	3–10 ft (0.9–3 m)	T	W/T		◆	◆	◆		Su				◆		
Polygala × *dalmaisiana*	3–10 ft (0.9–3 m)	3 ft (0.9 m)	S	W/T		◆	◆			All				◆		
Polygala myrtifolia	6 ft (1.8 m)	3–6 ft (0.9–1.8 m)	S	W/T		◆	◆			All				◆		
Polyscias elegans	100 ft (30 m)	15 ft (4.5 m)	T	W/T		◆	◆	◆		A/W					◆	
Polyscias filicifolia	15 ft (4.5 m)	4 ft (1.2 m)	T	W/T		◆	◆	◆		Su					◆	
Polyscias guilfoylei	20 ft (6 m)	8 ft (2.4 m)	T	W/T		◆		◆		Su					◆	
Populus alba	80 ft (24 m)	40 ft (12 m)	T	C/W	◆			◆		Sp			◆	◆		
Populus balsamifera	80 ft (24 m)	25 ft (8 m)	T	C	◆			◆		Sp			◆	◆		
Populus × *canadensis*	80 ft (24 m)	35 ft (10 m)	T	C	◆			◆		Sp			◆	◆		
Populus × *canescens*	100 ft (30 m)	40 ft (12 m)	T	C	◆			◆		Sp			◆	◆		

Plant name	Height	Spread	Type	Climate	Deciduous	Evergreen	Showy flowers	Showy foliage	Scented flowers	Flowering season	Grow in pot/tub	Indoor use	Frost tolerant	Full sun	Half sun	Heavy shade
Populus deltoides	100 ft (30 m)	60 ft (18 m)	T	C/W	◆			◆		Sp			◆	◆		
Populus fremontii	100 ft (30 m)	40 ft (12 m)	T	C/W	◆			◆		Sp			◆	◆		
Populus grandidentata	60 ft (18 m)	30 ft (9 m)	T	C	◆			◆		Sp			◆	◆		
Populus lasiocarpa	50–80 ft (15–24 m)	35 ft (10 m)	T	C/W	◆			◆		Sp			◆	◆		
Populus nigra	100 ft (30 m)	60 ft (18 m)	T	C/W	◆			◆		Sp			◆	◆		
Populus simonii	80–100 ft (24–30 m)	25 ft (8 m)	T	C	◆			◆		Sp			◆	◆		
Populus tremula	50 ft (15 m)	35 ft (10 m)	T	C	◆			◆		Sp			◆	◆		
Populus tremuloides	50 ft (15 m)	30 ft (9 m)	T	C	◆			◆		Sp			◆	◆		
Populus trichocarpa	80–120 ft (24–36 m)	35 ft (10 m)	T	C/W	◆			◆		Sp			◆	◆		
Posoqueria latifolia	6–20 ft (1.8–6 m)	15 ft (4.5 m)	T	W/T		◆	◆	◆	◆	Sp						
Potentilla fruticosa	5 ft (1.5 m)	5 ft (1.5 m)	S	C	◆		◆			Su/A			◆	◆		
Pouteria cainito	35 ft (10 m)	15 ft (4.5 m)	T	W/T		◆		◆		Sp				◆		
Pouteria campechiana	60 ft (18 m)	25 ft (8 m)	T	W/T		◆		◆		Sp				◆		
Prinsepia sinensis	6 ft (1.8 m)	6 ft (1.8 m)	S	C	◆		◆		◆	Sp			◆	◆		
Prinsepia uniflora	5 ft (1.5 m)	6 ft (1.8 m)	S	C	◆		◆		◆	Sp			◆	◆		
Prosopis glandulosa	30 ft (9 m)	25 ft (8 m)	T	W/T	◆		◆			Sp/Su			◆	◆		
Prosopis velutina	15–40 ft (4.5–12 m)	15–40 ft (4.5–12 m)	T	W/T	◆		◆			Sp/Su			◆	◆		
Prostanthera cuneata	3 ft (0.9 m)	5 ft (1.5 m)	S	W		◆	◆			Su	◆		◆	◆	◆	◆
Prostanthera lasianthos	15 ft (4.5 m)	12 ft (3.5 m)	S	W		◆	◆			Su			◆			◆
Prostanthera nivea	12 ft (3.5 m)	7 ft (2 m)	S	W/T		◆	◆			Sp				◆	◆	
Prostanthera ovalifolia	6 ft (1.8 m)	6 ft (1.8 m)	S	W/T		◆	◆			Sp						◆
Protea aurea	10 ft (3 m)	10 ft (3 m)	S	W		◆	◆	◆		A/W			◆	◆		
Protea cynaroides	7 ft (2 m)	7 ft (2 m)	S	W		◆	◆	◆		W–Su				◆		
Protea eximia	10 ft (3 m)	10 ft (3 m)	S	W		◆	◆	◆		Any			◆	◆		
Protea grandiceps	5 ft (1.5 m)	5 ft (1.5 m)	S	W		◆	◆	◆		W–Su			◆	◆		
Protea lacticolor	7–15 ft (2–4.5 m)	7 ft (2 m)	S	W		◆	◆	◆		A/W			◆	◆		
Protea magnifica	5 ft (1.5 m)	5 ft (1.5 m)	S	W		◆	◆	◆		Sp/Su			◆	◆		
Protea neriifolia	7 ft (2 m)	7 ft (2 m)	S	W		◆	◆	◆		A–Sp			◆	◆		
Protea repens	8 ft (2.4 m)	7 ft (2 m)	S	W		◆	◆	◆		A/W			◆	◆		
Protea scolymocephala	3 ft (0.9 m)	3 ft (0.9 m)	S	W		◆	◆	◆		W/Sp			◆	◆		
Protea speciosa	3 ft (0.9 m)	3 ft (0.9 m)	S	W		◆	◆	◆		Su/A			◆	◆		
Protea venusta	30 in (75 cm)	8 ft (2.4 m)	S	W		◆	◆	◆		Su/A			◆	◆		

Plant name	Height	Spread	Type	Climate	Deciduous	Evergreen	Showy flowers	Showy foliage	Scented flowers	Flowering season	Grow in pot/tub	Indoor use	Frost tolerant	Full sun	Half sun	Heavy shade
Protea Hybrid Cultivars	5–8 ft (1.5–2.4 m)	10 ft (3 m)	S	W		♦	♦		♦	Any				♦	♦	
Prunus × *amygdalo-persica*	20 ft (6 m)	20 ft (6 m)	T	C	♦		♦			W/Sp			♦	♦		
Prunus × *blireana*	15 ft (4.5 m)	15 ft (4.5 m)	T	C/W	♦		♦			Sp			♦	♦		
Prunus campanulata	30 ft (9 m)	25 ft (8 m)	T	C/W	♦		♦			W/Sp			♦	♦		
Prunus caroliniana	40 ft (12 m)	20 ft (6 m)	T	C/W	♦		♦			Sp			♦	♦		
Prunus cerasifera	30 ft (9 m)	30 ft (9 m)	T	C/W	♦		♦	♦		Sp			♦	♦		
Prunus glandulosa	5 ft (1.5 m)	5 ft (1.5 m)	S	C	♦		♦			Sp			♦	♦		
Prunus ilicifolia	25 ft (8 m)	20 ft (6 m)	S	W/T		♦	♦			Sp				♦		
Prunus incisa	15–20 ft (4.5–6 m)	15 ft (4.5 m)	T	C	♦		♦	♦		Sp			♦	♦		
Prunus laurocerasus	20 ft (6 m)	30 ft (9 m)	T	C/W		♦	♦		♦	Sp			♦	♦		
Prunus lusitanica	20 ft (6 m)	30 ft (9 m)	T	C/W		♦	♦			Sp			♦	♦		
Prunus maackii	50 ft (15 m)	25 ft (8 m)	T	C	♦		♦			Sp			♦	♦		
Prunus padus	30–50 ft (9–15 m)	25 ft (8 m)	T	C	♦		♦			Sp			♦	♦		
Prunus pensylvanica	30 ft (9 m)	30 ft (9 m)	T	C	♦		♦			Sp			♦	♦		
Prunus sargentii	50 ft (15 m)	35 ft (10 m)	T	C	♦		♦			Sp			♦	♦		
Prunus, Sato-zakura Group	20–40 ft (6–12 m)	30 ft (9 m)	T	C	♦		♦	♦		Sp			♦	♦		
Prunus serotina	100 ft (30 m)	30 ft (9 m)	T	C	♦		♦			Sp			♦	♦		
Prunus spinosa	20 ft (6 m)	15 ft (4.5 m)	S	C/W	♦		♦			Sp			♦	♦		
Prunus × *subhirtella*	50 ft (15 m)	25 ft (8 m)	T	C	♦		♦			Sp			♦	♦		
Prunus tenella	5 ft (1.5 m)	5 ft (1.5 m)	S	C	♦		♦			Sp			♦	♦		
Prunus triloba	12 ft (3.5 m)	12 ft (3.5 m)	S	C	♦		♦			Sp			♦	♦		
Prunus × *yedoensis*	40 ft (12 m)	30 ft (9 m)	T	C	♦		♦		♦	Sp			♦	♦		
Pseuderanthemum atropurpureum	4 ft (1.2 m)	3 ft (0.9 m)	S	W/T		♦	♦	♦		Su	♦					♦
Pseuderanthemum reticulatum	3 ft (0.9 m)	3 ft (0.9 m)	S	W/T		♦	♦	♦		Su	♦					♦
Pseudolarix amabilis	100 ft (30 m)	25 ft (8 m)	T	C	♦			♦		Sp			♦	♦		
Pseudopanax arboreus	10–20 ft (3–6 m)	15 ft (4.5 m)	T	W/T		♦		♦		W				♦		
Pseudopanax ferox	15 ft (4.5 m)	7 ft (2 m)	S	W/T		♦		♦		Sp				♦		
Pseudopanax lessonii	12 ft (3.5 m)	7 ft (2 m)	T	W/T		♦		♦		Sp				♦		
Pseudotsuga menziesii	80–150 ft (24–45 m)	15–30 ft (4.5–9 m)	T	C/W		♦		♦		Sp			♦	♦		
Psidium cattleianum	10–20 ft (3–6 m)	8 ft (2.4 m)	T	W/T		♦	♦			Sp				♦	♦	
Psoralea pinnata	6–10 ft (1.8–3 m)	7 ft (2 m)	S	W/T		♦	♦			Sp/Su				♦		
Ptelea angustifolia	12 ft (3.5 m)	12 ft (3.5 m)	S	W	♦			♦	♦	Su			♦	♦		

Plant name	Height	Spread	Type	Climate	Deciduous	Evergreen	Showy flowers	Showy foliage	Scented flowers	Flowering season	Grow in pot/tub	Indoor use	Frost tolerant	Full sun	Half sun	Heavy shade
Ptelea trifoliata	25 ft (8 m)	12 ft (3.5 m)	S	C/W	◆			◆	◆	Su			◆	◆		
Pterocarpus indicus	80 ft (24 m)	35 ft (10 m)	T	W/T		◆	◆		◆	Sp				◆		
Pterocarya fraxinifolia	80 ft (24 m)	60 ft (18 m)	T	C	◆		◆	◆		Su			◆	◆		
Pterocarya stenoptera	70 ft (21 m)	40 ft (12 m)	T	C	◆		◆	◆		Sp			◆	◆		
Pterostyrax corymbosa	40 ft (12 m)	20 ft (6 m)	T	C/W	◆		◆		◆	Sp			◆	◆		
Pterostyrax hispida	25 ft (8 m)	20 ft (6 m)	T	C/W	◆		◆		◆	Sp			◆	◆		
Pycnostachys urticifolia	8 ft (2.4 m)	4 ft (1.2 m)	S	W/T		◆	◆			Su/A				◆		
Pyracantha angustifolia	12 ft (3.5 m)	12 ft (3.5 m)	S	C/W		◆	◆			Su			◆	◆		
Pyracantha coccinea	15 ft (4.5 m)	15 ft (4.5 m)	S	C/W		◆	◆			Su			◆	◆		
Pyracantha crenulata	15 ft (4.5 m)	12 ft (3.5 m)	S	C/W		◆	◆			Su			◆	◆		
Pyracantha koidzumii	12–15 ft (3.5–4.5 m)	12 ft (3.5 m)	S	C/W		◆	◆			Su			◆	◆		
Pyracantha rogersiana	12 ft (3.5 m)	12 ft (3.5 m)	S	W		◆	◆			Sp			◆	◆		
Pyracantha Hybrid Cultivars	5–10 ft (1.5–3 m)	6–10 ft (1.8–3 m)	S	C/W		◆	◆	◆		Su			◆	◆		
Pyrus calleryana	40 ft (12 m)	40 ft (12 m)	T	C/W	◆		◆	◆	◆	Sp			◆	◆		
Pyrus nivalis	30 ft (9 m)	20 ft (6 m)	T	C	◆		◆		◆	Sp			◆	◆		
Pyrus salicifolia	25 ft (8 m)	15 ft (4.5 m)	T	C	◆		◆	◆	◆	Sp			◆	◆		
Pyrus ussuriensis	50 ft (15 m)	20 ft (6 m)	T	C	◆		◆	◆	◆	Sp			◆	◆		
Quercus acutissima	80 ft (24 m)	40 ft (12 m)	T	C/W	◆			◆		Sp			◆	◆		
Quercus agrifolia	40 ft (12 m)	35 ft (10 m)	T	W		◆		◆		Sp			◆	◆		
Quercus alba	100 ft (30 m)	100 ft (30 m)	T	C	◆			◆		Sp			◆	◆		
Quercus bicolor	80 ft (24 m)	40 ft (12 m)	T	C/W	◆			◆		Sp			◆	◆		
Quercus canariensis	80 ft (24 m)	40 ft (12 m)	T	W	◆			◆		Sp			◆	◆		
Quercus castaneifolia	100 ft (30 m)	60 ft (18 m)	T	C/W	◆			◆		Sp			◆	◆		
Quercus cerris	100 ft (30 m)	75 ft (23 m)	T	C/W	◆			◆		Sp			◆	◆		
Quercus chrysolepis	70 ft (21 m)	30 ft (9 m)	T	W		◆		◆		Sp			◆	◆		
Quercus coccinea	70 ft (21 m)	40 ft (12 m)	T	C	◆			◆		Sp			◆	◆		
Quercus dentata	50 ft (15 m)	30 ft (9 m)	T	C	◆			◆		Sp			◆	◆		
Quercus douglasii	70 ft (21 m)	20 ft (6 m)	T	C/W	◆			◆		Sp			◆	◆		
Quercus falcata	80 ft (24 m)	35 ft (10 m)	T	W	◆			◆		Sp				◆		
Quercus frainetto	100 ft (30 m)	60 ft (18 m)	T	C/W	◆			◆		Sp			◆	◆		
Quercus gambelii	30 ft (9 m)	25 ft (8 m)	T	C	◆			◆		Sp			◆	◆		
Quercus garryana	15 ft (4.5 m)	15 ft (4.5 m)	T	C/W	◆			◆		Sp			◆	◆		

Plant name	Height	Spread	Type	Climate	Deciduous	Evergreen	Showy flowers	Showy foliage	Scented flowers	Flowering season	Grow in pot/tub	Indoor use	Frost tolerant	Full sun	Half sun	Heavy shade
Quercus × hispanica	100 ft (30 m)	25 ft (8 m)	T	C/W	◆			◆		Sp			◆	◆		
Quercus ilex	70 ft (21 m)	60 ft (18 m)	T	W		◆		◆		Sp			◆	◆		
Quercus kelloggii	60–90 ft (18–27 m)	40 ft (12 m)	T	C/W	◆			◆		Sp			◆	◆		
Quercus laurifolia	60 ft (18 m)	60 ft (18 m)	T	C/W		◆		◆		Sp			◆	◆		
Quercus lyrata	60 ft (18 m)	30 ft (9 m)	T	W	◆			◆		Sp			◆	◆		
Quercus macrocarpa	120 ft (36 m)	40 ft (12 m)	T	C	◆			◆		Sp			◆	◆		
Quercus mongolica	100 ft (30 m)	40 ft (12 m)	T	C	◆			◆		Sp			◆	◆		
Quercus muehlenbergii	100 ft (30 m)	40 ft (12 m)	T	C	◆			◆		Sp			◆	◆		
Quercus nigra	50 ft (15 m)	40 ft (12 m)	T	C/W	◆			◆		Sp			◆	◆		
Quercus palustris	100 ft (30 m)	60 ft (18 m)	T	C/W	◆			◆		Sp			◆	◆		
Quercus petraea	150 ft (45 m)	75 ft (23 m)	T	C/W	◆			◆		Sp			◆	◆		
Quercus phellos	100 ft (30 m)	40 ft (12 m)	T	C/W	◆			◆		Sp			◆	◆		
Quercus robur	100 ft (30 m)	70 ft (21 m)	T	C/W	◆			◆		Sp			◆	◆		
Quercus rubra	100 ft (30 m)	70 ft (21 m)	T	C/W	◆			◆		Sp			◆	◆		
Quercus shumardii	100 ft (30 m)	40 ft (12 m)	T	C/W	◆			◆		Sp			◆	◆		
Quercus suber	70 ft (21 m)	70 ft (21 m)	T	W		◆		◆		Sp			◆	◆		
Quercus texana	50–70 ft (15–21 m)	50–70 ft (15–21 m)	T	C/W	◆			◆		Sp			◆	◆		
Quercus velutina	100 ft (30 m)	75 ft (23 m)	T	C/W	◆			◆		Sp			◆	◆		
Quercus virginiana	70 ft (21 m)	35 ft (10 m)	T	C/W		◆		◆		Sp			◆	◆		
Quercus wislizeni	80 ft (24 m)	35 ft (10 m)	T	W		◆		◆		Sp			◆	◆		
Quillaja saponaria	50–60 ft (15–18 m)	15–25 ft (4.5–8 m)	T	W		◆	◆			Sp			◆			◆
Radermachera sinica	30 ft (9 m)	15 ft (4.5 m)	T	W/T		◆	◆	◆	◆	Sp/Su				◆		
Rehderodendron macrocarpum	25–35 ft (8–10 m)	15–17 ft (4.5–5 m)	T	W	◆		◆	◆	◆	Sp			◆			◆
Reinwardtia indica	3 ft (0.9 m)	2 ft (0.6 m)	S	W		◆	◆			A/W/Sp				◆		
Retama monosperma	10 ft (3 m)	10 ft (3 m)	S	W		◆			◆	Sp				◆		
Rhamnus alaternus	15 ft (4.5 m)	12 ft (3.5 m)	S	C/W		◆		◆		Sp/Su			◆	◆		
Rhamnus californica	12 ft (3.5 m)	10 ft (3 m)	S	C/W		◆		◆		Sp/Su			◆	◆		
Rhamnus cathartica	20 ft (6 m)	15 ft (4.5 m)	S	C	◆			◆		Sp/Su			◆	◆		
Rhamnus crocea	6 ft (1.8 m)	7 ft (2 m)	S	C/W		◆		◆		Sp/Su			◆	◆		
Rhamnus frangula	15 ft (4.5 m)	15 ft (4.5 m)	S	C	◆			◆		Sp/Su			◆	◆		
Rhamnus imeretina	10 ft (3 m)	15 ft (4.5 m)	S	C	◆			◆		Sp/Su			◆	◆		
Rhamnus prinoides	25 ft (8 m)	15 ft (4.5 m)	S	C/W		◆		◆		Sp/Su				◆		

Plant name	Height	Spread	Type	Climate	Deciduous	Evergreen	Showy flowers	Showy foliage	Scented flowers	Flowering season	Grow in pot/tub	Indoor use	Frost tolerant	Full sun	Half sun	Heavy shade
Rhaphiolepis × delacourii	6 ft (1.8 m)	8 ft (2.4 m)	S	W/T		◆	◆	◆		Sp/Su			◆	◆		
Rhaphiolepis indica	8 ft (2.4 m)	8 ft (2.4 m)	S	W/T		◆	◆	◆		Sp			◆	◆		
Rhaphiolepis umbellata	6 ft (1.8 m)	7 ft (2 m)	S	W/T		◆	◆	◆		Sp/Su			◆	◆		
Rhododendron aberconwayi	6 ft (1.8 m)	4 ft (1.2 m)	S	C/W		◆	◆			Sp/Su			◆		◆	
Rhododendron albrechtii	7 ft (2 m)	4 ft (1.2 m)	S	C	◆		◆			Sp			◆		◆	
Rhododendron alutaceum	7–15 ft (2–4.5 m)	5–12 ft (1.5–3.5 m)	S	C/W		◆	◆			Sp			◆		◆	
Rhododendron arborescens	10 ft (3 m)	8 ft (2.4 m)	S	C	◆		◆		◆	Sp/Su			◆		◆	
Rhododendron arboreum	60 ft (18 m)	15 ft (4.5 m)	T	C/W		◆	◆			Sp			◆		◆	
Rhododendron arizelum	6–25 ft (1.8–8 m)	6–25 ft (1.8–8 m)	S	C/W		◆	◆	◆		Sp/Su			◆		◆	
Rhododendron augustinii	3–20 ft (0.9–6 m)	2–10 ft (0.6–3 m)	S	C/W		◆	◆			Sp/Su			◆		◆	
Rhododendron austrinum	10 ft (3 m)	10 ft (3 m)	S	C	◆		◆			Sp			◆		◆	
Rhododendron calophytum	15 ft (4.5 m)	20 ft (6 m)	T	C/W		◆	◆	◆		Sp			◆		◆	
Rhododendron campanulatum	15 ft (4.5 m)	15 ft (4.5 m)	S	C		◆	◆			Sp			◆		◆	
Rhododendron campylogynum	18 in (45 cm)	30 in (75 cm)	S	C/W		◆	◆			Sp/Su	◆		◆		◆	
Rhododendron canescens	15 ft (4.5 m)	8 ft (2.4 m)	S	C/W	◆		◆		◆	Sp			◆		◆	
Rhododendron catawbiense	10 ft (3 m)	10 ft (3 m)	S	C/W		◆	◆			Sp/Su			◆		◆	
Rhododendron ciliatum	6 ft (1.8 m)	6 ft (1.8 m)	S	W		◆	◆			Sp					◆	
Rhododendron cinnabarinum	10 ft (3 m)	7 ft (2 m)	S	C/W		◆	◆	◆		Sp/Su			◆		◆	
Rhododendron concinnum	6–20 ft (1.8–6 m)	6–10 ft (1.8–3 m)	S	C/W		◆	◆			Sp			◆		◆	
Rhododendron dauricum	8 ft (2.4 m)	8 ft (2.4 m)	S	C/W		◆	◆			W/Sp			◆		◆	
Rhododendron decorum	20 ft (6 m)	8 ft (2.4 m)	S	C/W		◆	◆	◆	◆	Su			◆		◆	
Rhododendron degronianum	8 ft (2.4 m)	7 ft (2 m)	S	C/W		◆	◆			Sp/Su	◆		◆		◆	
Rhododendron edgeworthii	6 ft (1.8 m)	6 ft (1.8 m)	S	W		◆	◆	◆	◆	Sp			◆		◆	
Rhododendron falconeri	40 ft (12 m)	30 ft (9 m)	T	W		◆	◆	◆	◆	Sp/Su					◆	
Rhododendron flammeum	6 ft (1.8 m)	3 ft (0.9 m)	S	W/T	◆		◆			Sp/Su					◆	
Rhododendron forrestii	4 in (10 cm)	48 in (120 cm)	S	W		◆	◆	◆		Sp/Su	◆		◆		◆	
Rhododendron fortunei	15 ft (4.5 m)	8 ft (2.4 m)	S	C/W		◆	◆		◆	Su			◆		◆	
Rhododendron griffithianum	60 ft (18 m)	10 ft (3 m)	T	W		◆	◆		◆	Sp/Su					◆	
Rhododendron haematodes	5 ft (1.5 m)	5 ft (1.5 m)	S	C/W		◆	◆	◆		Sp/Su			◆		◆	
Rhododendron impeditum	12 in (30 cm)	12 in (30 cm)	S	C/W		◆	◆			Sp	◆		◆		◆	
Rhododendron indicum	3 ft (0.9 m)	2 ft (0.6 m)	S	C/W		◆	◆			Sp			◆		◆	
Rhododendron intricatum	5 ft (1.5 m)	5 ft (1.5 m)	S	C		◆	◆			Sp/Su			◆		◆	

Plant name	Height	Spread	Type	Climate	Deciduous	Evergreen	Showy flowers	Showy foliage	Scented flowers	Flowering season	Grow in pot/tub	Indoor use	Frost tolerant	Full sun	Half sun	Heavy shade
Rhododendron jasminiflorum	22 in (55 cm)	22 in (55 cm)	S	W/T		◆	◆		◆	W	◆	◆			◆	
Rhododendron kaempferi	4 ft (1.2 m)	4 ft (1.2 m)	S	C	◆	◆	◆			Sp				◆	◆	
Rhododendron kiusianum	3 ft (0.9 m)	3 ft (0.9 m)	S	C/W		◆	◆			Sp	◆				◆	
Rhododendron konori	12 ft (3.5 m)	6 ft (1.8 m)	S	W/T		◆	◆			W	◆	◆			◆	
Rhododendron lacteum	12 ft (3.5 m)	12 ft (3.5 m)	S	C/W		◆	◆			Sp				◆	◆	
Rhododendron laetum	10 ft (3 m)	4 ft (1.2 m)	S	W/T		◆	◆			A–Sp	◆	◆			◆	
Rhododendron leucaspis	4 ft (1.2 m)	4 ft (1.2 m)	S	C/W		◆	◆	◆		W/Sp					◆	
Rhododendron lochiae	3 ft (0.9 m)	2 ft (0.6 m)	S	W/T		◆	◆			W	◆	◆			◆	
Rhododendron luteiflorum	12–36 in (30–90 cm)	18–32 in (45–80 cm)	S	C/W		◆	◆			Sp	◆		◆	◆	◆	
Rhododendron lutescens	20 ft (6 m)	15 ft (4.5 m)	S	C/W		◆	◆			W/Sp					◆	
Rhododendron luteum	12 ft (3.5 m)	8 ft (2.4 m)	S	C/W	◆		◆	◆		Sp				◆	◆	
Rhododendron macgregoriae	15 ft (4.5 m)	7 ft (2 m)	S	W/T		◆	◆			W	◆				◆	
Rhododendron macrophyllum	12 ft (3.5 m)	12 ft (3.5 m)	S	C/W		◆	◆			Su					◆	
Rhododendron maddenii	25 ft (8 m)	8 ft (2.4 m)	T	W		◆	◆		◆	Sp					◆	
Rhododendron mallotum	20 ft (6 m)	12 ft (3.5 m)	S	C/W		◆	◆			Sp					◆	
Rhododendron maximum	6 ft (1.8 m)	7 ft (2 m)	S	C		◆	◆			Sp/Su					◆	
Rhododendron megeratum	15–30 in (38–75 cm)	15 in (38 cm)	S	W		◆	◆			W/Sp	◆					
Rhododendron minus	3–5 ft (0.9–1.5 m)	3–5 ft (0.9–1.5 m)	S	C		◆	◆			Sp/Su					◆	
Rhododendron molle	4 ft (1.2 m)	4 ft (1.2 m)	S	C/W	◆		◆			Sp					◆	
Rhododendron mucronulatum	6 ft (1.8 m)	3 ft (0.9 m)	S	C	◆		◆			Sp					◆	
Rhododendron neriifolium	10–20 ft (3–6 m)	6–12 ft (1.8–3.5 m)	S	C/W		◆	◆	◆		Sp/Su			◆	◆	◆	
Rhododendron nuttallii	35 ft (10 m)	20 ft (6 m)	T	W		◆	◆	◆	◆	Su					◆	
Rhododendron × obtusum	3 ft (0.9 m)	3 ft (0.9 m)	S	C/W		◆	◆			Sp	◆				◆	
Rhododendron occidentale	5 ft (1.5 m)	5 ft (1.5 m)	S	C/W	◆		◆	◆		Sp					◆	
Rhododendron orbiculare	10 ft (3 m)	10 ft (3 m)	S	C/W		◆	◆	◆		Sp					◆	
Rhododendron orbiculatum	3 ft (0.9 m)	3 ft (0.9 m)	S	W/T		◆	◆			A–Sp	◆	◆			◆	
Rhododendron pachysanthum	4 ft (1.2 m)	3 ft (0.9 m)	S	C/W		◆	◆	◆		Sp					◆	
Rhododendron periclymenoides	10 ft (3 m)	8 ft (2.4 m)	S	C/W	◆		◆			Sp					◆	
Rhododendron ponticum	25 ft (8 m)	20 ft (6 m)	S	C/W		◆	◆			Sp				◆	◆	
Rhododendron protistum	100 ft (30 m)	15 ft (4.5 m)	T	W		◆	◆	◆		W/Sp					◆	
Rhododendron quinquefolium	8–25 ft (2.4–8 m)	4–8 ft (1.2–2.4 m)	S	C/W	◆		◆	◆		Sp					◆	
Rhododendron racemosum	5 ft (1.5 m)	5 ft (1.5 m)	S	C		◆	◆			Sp				◆	◆	

Plant name	Height	Spread	Type	Climate	Deciduous	Evergreen	Showy flowers	Showy foliage	Scented flowers	Flowering season	Grow in pot/tub	Indoor use	Frost tolerant	Full sun	Half sun	Heavy shade
Rhododendron reticulatum	4 ft (1.2 m)	4 ft (1.2 m)	S	C/W		♦	♦			Sp			♦		♦	
Rhododendron rubiginosum	30 ft (9 m)	20 ft (6 m)	S	C/W		♦	♦			Sp			♦		♦	
Rhododendron schlippenbachii	15 ft (4.5 m)	15 ft (4.5 m)	S	C	♦		♦	♦		Sp			♦		♦	
Rhododendron scopulorum	15 ft (4.5 m)	8 ft (2.4 m)	S	W		♦	♦		♦	Sp/Su					♦	
Rhododendron sinogrande	50 ft (15 m)	30 ft (9 m)	S	W		♦	♦	♦		Sp			♦		♦	
Rhododendron spinuliferum	10 ft (3 m)	8 ft (2.4 m)	S	W		♦	♦			Sp			♦		♦	
Rhododendron stamineum	10 ft (3 m)	10 ft (3 m)	S	W		♦	♦			Sp					♦	
Rhododendron thomsonii	2–20 ft (0.6–6 m)	2–20 ft (0.6–6 m)	S	C/W		♦	♦	♦		Sp			♦		♦	
Rhododendron tomentosum	1–4 ft (0.3–1.2 m)	3 ft (0.9 m)	S	C		♦	♦			Sp/Su			♦		♦	♦
Rhododendron trichostomum	5 ft (1.5 m)	3 ft (0.9 m)	S	C/W		♦	♦			Sp			♦		♦	
Rhododendron veitchianum	8 ft (2.4 m)	8 ft (2.4 m)	S	W		♦	♦		♦	Sp/Su					♦	
Rhododendron viscosum	8 ft (2.4 m)	8 ft (2.4 m)	S	C/W	♦		♦		♦	Sp/Su			♦		♦	
Rhododendron wardii	25 ft (8 m)	15 ft (4.5 m)	S	C/W		♦	♦			Sp			♦		♦	
Rhododendron williamsianum	5 ft (1.5 m)	4 ft (1.2 m)	S	C/W		♦	♦	♦		Sp			♦		♦	
Rhododendron yedoense	3 ft (0.9 m)	3 ft (0.9 m)	S	C	♦		♦	♦	♦	Sp			♦		♦	
Rhododendron zoelleri	6 ft (1.8 m)	3 ft (0.9 m)	S	W/T		♦	♦			A–Sp	♦	♦			♦	
Rhododendron, Hardy Small Hybrids	12–40 in (30–100 cm)	12–40 in (30–100 cm)	S	C/W		♦	♦	♦		Sp/Su	♦		♦		♦	
Rhododendron, Hardy Medium Hybrids	3–6 ft (0.9–1.8 m)	2–6 ft (0.6–1.8 m)	S	C/W		♦	♦	♦		Sp/Su			♦		♦	
Rhododendron, Hardy Tall Hybrids	6–35 ft (1.8–10 m)	5–17 ft (1.5–5 m)	S	C/W		♦	♦	♦		Sp/Su			♦		♦	
Rhododendron, Tender Hybrids	3–17 ft (0.9–5 m)	3–10 ft (0.9–3 m)	S	W		♦	♦	♦	♦	Sp/Su				♦	♦	
Rhododendron, Vireya Hybrids	18–72 in (45–180 cm)	12–60 in (30–150 cm)	S	W/T		♦	♦			A–Sp	♦	♦			♦	♦
Rhododendron, Yak Hybrids	1–6 ft (0.3–1.8 m)	2–5 ft (0.6–1.5 m)	S	C/W		♦	♦	♦		Sp/Su	♦		♦		♦	
Rhododendron, Ghent Hybrids	5–8 ft (1.5–2.4 m)	3–6 ft (0.9–1.8 m)	S	C/W	♦		♦			Sp/Su				♦	♦	
Rhododendron, Ilam and Melford Hybrids	4–10 ft (1.2–3 m)	4–7 ft (1.2–2 m)	S	C/W	♦		♦			Sp/Su			♦	♦	♦	
Rhododendron, Knap Hill and Exbury Hybrids	4–10 ft (1.2–3 m)	4–7 ft (1.2–2 m)	S	C/W	♦		♦			Sp/Su			♦	♦	♦	
Rhododendron, Mollis Hybrids	5–8 ft (1.5–2.4 m)	5–7 ft (1.5–2 m)	S	C/W	♦		♦			Sp/Su			♦	♦	♦	
Rhododendron, Occidentale Hybrids	6–10 ft (1.8–3 m)	6–10 ft (1.8–3 m)	S	C/W	♦		♦		♦	Sp				♦	♦	
Rhododendron, Belgian Indica Hybrids	2–5 ft (0.6–1.5 m)	3–6 ft (0.9–1.8 m)	S	W		♦	♦			W/Sp	♦	♦	♦	♦	♦	

Plant name	Height	Spread	Type	Climate	Deciduous	Evergreen	Showy flowers	Showy foliage	Scented flowers	Flowering season	Grow in pot/tub	Indoor use	Frost tolerant	Full sun	Half sun	Heavy shade
Rhododendron, Rutherford Indica Hybrids	3–8 ft (0.9–2.4 m)	4–8 ft (1.2–2.4 m)	S	W		◆	◆			W/Sp	◆	◆		◆	◆	
Rhododendron, Southern Indica Hybrids	5–10 ft (1.5–3 m)	6–12 ft (1.8–3.5 m)	S	W		◆	◆			Sp			◆	◆	◆	
Rhododendron, Kaempferi or Malvatica Hybrids	2–8 ft (0.6–2.4 m)	3–7 ft (0.9–2 m)	S	C/W		◆	◆			Sp			◆	◆	◆	
Rhododendron, Vuyk Hybrids	2–8 ft (0.6–2.4 m)	3–7 ft (0.9–2 m)	S	C/W		◆	◆			Sp	◆		◆	◆	◆	
Rhododendron, Kurume Hybrids	2–4 ft (0.6–1.2 m)	2–4 ft (0.6–1.2 m)	S	C/W		◆	◆			Sp	◆		◆	◆	◆	
Rhododendron, Satsuki Hybrids	12–36 in (30–90 cm)	24–48 in (60–120 cm)	S	C/W		◆	◆			Sp/Su	◆		◆	◆	◆	
Rhododendron, Azaleodendron Hybrids	2–8 ft (0.6–2.4 m)	2–7 ft (0.6–2 m)	S	C/W	◆	◆	◆		◆	Sp/Su	◆		◆	◆	◆	
Rhodoleia championii	20 ft (6 m)	12 ft (3.5 m)	T	W		◆	◆			W/Sp			◆		◆	
Rhus aromatica	3–5 ft (0.9–1.5 m)	5 ft (1.5 m)	S	C	◆			◆	◆	Sp				◆	◆	
Rhus chinensis	20 ft (6 m)	15 ft (4.5 m)	T	W/T	◆		◆	◆		Su/A				◆	◆	
Rhus copallina	5 ft (1.5 m)	5 ft (1.5 m)	S	C/W	◆			◆		Su				◆	◆	
Rhus glabra	8 ft (2.4 m)	8 ft (2.4 m)	S	C/W	◆			◆		Su				◆	◆	
Rhus lancea	25 ft (8 m)	25 ft (8 m)	T	W/T		◆		◆		Su					◆	
Rhus lucida	12 ft (3.5 m)	12 ft (3.5 m)	S/T	W		◆		◆		Sp				◆	◆	
Rhus microphylla	6–10 ft (1.8–3 m)	4–6 ft (1.2–1.8 m)	S	W	◆			◆	◆	Sp				◆	◆	
Rhus pendulina	15 ft (4.5 m)	15 ft (4.5 m)	T	W	◆			◆		Su					◆	
Rhus typhina	15 ft (4.5 m)	15 ft (4.5 m)	T	C	◆			◆		Su				◆	◆	
Ribes alpinum	3–6 ft (0.9–1.8 m)	3 ft (0.9 m)	S	C	◆		◆			Sp				◆	◆	
Ribes aureum	6 ft (1.8 m)	6 ft (1.8 m)	S	C/W	◆		◆			Sp				◆	◆	
Ribes fasciculatum	5 ft (1.5 m)	4 ft (1.2 m)	S	C/W	◆		◆			Sp					◆	
Ribes magellanicum	6–8 ft (1.8–2.4 m)	6 ft (1.8 m)	S	C/W	◆		◆			Sp				◆	◆	
Ribes sanguineum	10 ft (3 m)	10 ft (3 m)	S	C/W	◆		◆			Sp				◆	◆	
Ribes speciosum	12 ft (3.5 m)	10 ft (3 m)	S	W		◆	◆	◆		Su				◆	◆	
Ricinocarpos pinifolius	3 ft (0.9 m)	3 ft (0.9 m)	S	W/T		◆	◆			Sp						◆
Ricinus communis	5–15 ft (1.5–4.5 m)	3 ft (0.9 m)	S	W/T		◆		◆		Su					◆	
Robinia hispida	10 ft (3 m)	10 ft (3 m)	T	C/W	◆		◆			Sp				◆	◆	
Robinia pseudoacacia	50 ft (15 m)	35 ft (10 m)	T	C/W	◆		◆		◆	Sp				◆	◆	
Robinia × slavinii	15 ft (4.5 m)	10 ft (3 m)	S	C/W	◆		◆			Sp				◆	◆	
Robinia viscosa	30 ft (9 m)	20 ft (6 m)	T	C/W	◆		◆			Sp				◆	◆	

Plant name	Height	Spread	Type	Climate	Deciduous	Evergreen	Showy flowers	Showy foliage	Scented flowers	Flowering season	Grow in pot/tub	Indoor use	Frost tolerant	Full sun	Half sun	Heavy shade
Roella ciliata	3 ft (0.9 m)	2 ft (0.6 m)	S	W		♦	♦			Sp/Su				♦		
Roldana petasitis	6–10 ft (1.8–3 m)	6–10 ft (1.8–3 m)	S	W/T		♦	♦	♦		W				♦		
Rondeletia amoena	10 ft (3 m)	8 ft (2.4 m)	S	W/T		♦	♦		♦	Sp				♦		
Rondeletia odorata	5 ft (1.5 m)	3 ft (0.9 m)	S	W/T		♦	♦		♦	Su/A	♦			♦		
Rosa acicularis	6 ft (1.8 m)	4 ft (1.2 m)	S	C/W	♦		♦		♦	Su			♦	♦		
Rosa beggeriana	8 ft (2.4 m)	8 ft (2.4 m)	S	C	♦		♦		♦	Su			♦	♦		
Rosa blanda	3–7 ft (0.9–2 m)	3 ft (0.9 m)	S	C/W	♦		♦		♦	Su			♦	♦		
Rosa californica	7 ft (2 m)	6 ft (1.8 m)	S	C/W	♦		♦		♦	Su			♦	♦		
Rosa canina	10 ft (3 m)	10 ft (3 m)	S	C/W	♦		♦		♦	Su			♦	♦		
Rosa chinensis	20 ft (6 m)	8 ft (2.4 m)	S	W	♦		♦			Su				♦		
Rosa cinnamomea plena	6 ft (1.8 m)	5 ft (1.5 m)	S	C/W	♦		♦			Su			♦	♦		
Rosa davurica	3–5 ft (0.9–1.5 m)	4 ft (1.2 m)	S	C/W	♦		♦			Su			♦	♦		
Rosa ecae	4 ft (1.2 m)	4 ft (1.2 m)	S	C/W	♦		♦			Sp			♦	♦		
Rosa eglanteria	10 ft (3 m)	10 ft (3 m)	S	C/W	♦		♦		♦	Su			♦	♦		
Rosa elegantula	3–7 ft (0.9–2 m)	8 ft (2.4 m)	S	C/W	♦		♦			Su			♦	♦		
Rosa foetida	3–10 ft (0.9–3 m)	6 ft (1.8 m)	S	C/W	♦		♦			Su				♦		
Rosa gallica	4 ft (1.2 m)	4 ft (1.2 m)	S	C/W	♦		♦			Su			♦	♦		
Rosa gigantea	30–60 ft (9–18 m)	20–40 ft (6–12 m)	S	C/W	♦		♦		♦	Su			♦	♦		
Rosa glauca	6 ft (1.8 m)	6 ft (1.8 m)	S	C/W	♦		♦	♦		Su			♦	♦		
Rosa hemisphaerica	7 ft (2 m)	7 ft (2 m)	S	C/W	♦		♦			Su			♦	♦		
Rosa hugonis	7 ft (2 m)	6 ft (1.8 m)	S	C/W	♦		♦		♦	Sp/Su			♦	♦		
Rosa laxa	7–8 ft (2–2.4 m)	5–10 ft (1.5–3 m)	S	C/W	♦		♦			Su			♦	♦	♦	
Rosa macrophylla	10 ft (3 m)	10 ft (3 m)	S	C/W	♦		♦		♦	Su			♦	♦		
Rosa marginata	3–8 ft (0.9–2.4 m)	8 ft (2.4 m)	S	C/W	♦		♦			Su			♦	♦		
Rosa minutifolia	4 ft (1.2 m)	4 ft (1.2 m)	S	W		♦	♦			Su				♦		♦
Rosa moyesii	10 ft (3 m)	10 ft (3 m)	S	C/W	♦		♦			Su			♦	♦		
Rosa multiflora	10–15 ft (3–4.5 m)	10 ft (3 m)	S	C/W	♦		♦			Su			♦	♦	♦	
Rosa nitida	3 ft (0.9 m)	4 ft (1.2 m)	S	C/W	♦		♦	♦	♦	Su			♦	♦		
Rosa nutkana	6–10 ft (1.8–3 m)	7 ft (2 m)	S	C/W	♦		♦		♦	Su			♦	♦		
Rosa pendulina	2–7 ft (0.6–2 m)	5 ft (1.5 m)	S	C/W	♦		♦			Su			♦	♦		
Rosa pisocarpa	3–7 ft (0.9–2 m)	4 ft (1.2 m)	S	C/W	♦		♦			Su			♦	♦		
Rosa primula	5–10 ft (1.5–3 m)	5 ft (1.5 m)	S	C/W	♦		♦		♦	Su			♦	♦		

Plant name	Height	Spread	Type	Climate	Deciduous	Evergreen	Showy flowers	Showy foliage	Scented flowers	Flowering season	Grow in pot/tub	Indoor use	Frost tolerant	Full sun	Half sun	Heavy shade
Rosa roxburghii	7 ft (2 m)	7 ft (2 m)	S	C/W	◆		◆		◆	Su			◆	◆		
Rosa rugosa	5–8 ft (1.5–2.4 m)	5–8 ft (1.5–2.4 m)	S	C/W	◆		◆		◆	Su/A			◆	◆		
Rosa sempervirens	1–6 ft (0.3–1.8 m)	20–35 ft (6–10 m)	S	C/W		◆	◆		◆	Su			◆	◆		
Rosa sericea	10 ft (3 m)	8 ft (2.4 m)	S	C/W	◆		◆			Sp			◆	◆		
Rosa setipoda	8 ft (2.4 m)	5 ft (1.5 m)	S	C/W	◆		◆			Su			◆	◆		
Rosa spinosissima	3–7 ft (0.9–2 m)	4 ft (1.2 m)	S	C/W	◆		◆			Sp			◆	◆		
Rosa stellata	3 ft (0.9 m)	3 ft (0.9 m)	S	C/W	◆		◆			Su			◆	◆		
Rosa sweginzowii	12 ft (3.5 m)	15 ft (4.5 m)	S	C/W	◆		◆			Su			◆	◆		
Rosa virginiana	5 ft (1.5 m)	5 ft (1.5 m)	S	C/W	◆		◆			Su			◆	◆		
Rosa wichurana	6 ft (1.8 m)	20 ft (6 m)	S	C/W	◆		◆		◆	Su			◆	◆		
Rosa willmottiae	6 ft (1.8 m)	5 ft (1.5 m)	S	C/W	◆		◆			Su			◆	◆		
Rosa woodsii	3–7 ft (0.9–2 m)	5 ft (1.5 m)	S	C/W	◆		◆			Su			◆	◆		
Rosa, Cluster-flowered (Floribunda) Roses	4–7 ft (1.2–2 m)	3–6 ft (0.9–1.8 m)	S	C/W	◆		◆		◆	Su/A			◆	◆		
Rosa, Large-flowered (Hybrid Tea) Roses	5–8 ft (1.5–2.4 m)	3–6 ft (0.9–1.8 m)	S	C/W	◆		◆		◆	Su/A			◆	◆		
Rosa, Patio (Dwarf Cluster-flowered) Roses	18–30 in (45–75 cm)	18–36 in (45–90 cm)	S	C/W	◆		◆		◆	Su/A	◆		◆	◆		
Rosa, Polyantha Roses	2–4 ft (0.6–1.2 m)	2–3 ft (0.6–0.9 m)	S	C/W	◆		◆		◆	Su			◆	◆		
Rosa, Hybrid Rugosa Roses	2–7 ft (0.6–2 m)	5–10 ft (1.5–3 m)	S	C/W	◆		◆	◆	◆	Su			◆	◆		
Rosa, Modern Shrub Roses	4–8 ft (1.2–2.4 m)	4–8 ft (1.2–2.4 m)	S	C/W	◆		◆		◆	Su			◆	◆		
Rosa, Miniature Roses	8–24 in (20–60 cm)	12–18 in (30–45 cm)	S	C/W	◆		◆		◆	Su		◆	◆	◆		
Rosa, Alba Roses	2–8 ft (0.6–2.4 m)	6–10 ft (1.8–3 m)	S	C/W	◆		◆			Su			◆	◆		
Rosa, Bourbon Roses	4–7 ft (1.2–2 m)	5–8 ft (1.5–2.4 m)	S	C/W	◆		◆		◆	Su/A			◆	◆		
Rosa, Centifolia Roses	2–8 ft (0.6–2.4 m)	4–8 ft (1.2–2.4 m)	S	C/W	◆		◆		◆	Su			◆	◆		
Rosa, China Roses	3–6 ft (0.9–1.8 m)	3–6 ft (0.9–1.8 m)	S	C/W	◆		◆		◆	Su/A			◆	◆		
Rosa, Damask Roses	3–7 ft (0.9–2 m)	5–8 ft (1.5–2.4 m)	S	C/W	◆		◆		◆	Su			◆	◆		
Rosa, Gallica Roses	4–6 ft (1.2–1.8 m)	4–6 ft (1.2–1.8 m)	S	C/W	◆		◆		◆	Su			◆	◆		
Rosa, Hybrid Perpetual Roses	4–7 ft (1.2–2 m)	3–6 ft (0.9–1.8 m)	S	C/W	◆		◆		◆	Su/A			◆	◆		
Rosa, Moss Roses	3–7 ft (0.9–2 m)	5–8 ft (1.5–2.4 m)	S	C/W	◆		◆		◆	Su			◆	◆		
Rosa, Portland Roses	2–4 ft (0.6–1.2 m)	3–5 ft (0.9–1.5 m)	S	C/W	◆		◆		◆	Su			◆	◆		
Rosa, Scots Roses	3–7 ft (0.9–2 m)	5–8 ft (1.5–2.4 m)	S	C/W	◆		◆	◆	◆	Su			◆	◆		
Rosa, Sweet Briar Roses	4–8 ft (1.2–2.4 m)	5–10 ft (1.5–3 m)	S	C/W	◆		◆		◆	Su			◆	◆		

Plant name	Height	Spread	Type	Climate	Deciduous	Evergreen	Showy flowers	Showy foliage	Scented flowers	Flowering season	Grow in pot/tub	Indoor use	Frost tolerant	Full sun	Half sun	Heavy shade
Rosa, Tea Roses	3–7 ft (0.9–2 m)	3–6 ft (0.9–1.8 m)	S	C/W	♦		♦			Su/A			♦	♦		
Rosa, Miscellaneous Old Garden Roses	2–6 ft (0.6–1.8 m)	20–48 in (50–120 cm)	S	C/W	♦		♦		♦	Su			♦	♦	♦	
Rothmannia globosa	12–20 ft (3.5–6 m)	6–10 ft (1.8–3 m)	S	W		♦	♦	♦	♦	Sp				♦		
Rubus biflorus	10 ft (3 m)	10 ft (3 m)	S	C/W	♦			♦		Su			♦	♦		
Rubus cockburnianus	8 ft (2.4 m)	8 ft (2.4 m)	S	C/W	♦		♦	♦		Su			♦	♦		
Rubus crataegifolius	8 ft (2.4 m)	5 ft (1.5 m)	S	C/W	♦		♦	♦		Su			♦	♦		
Rubus fruticosus	3–6 ft (0.9–1.8 m)	10–25 ft (3–8 m)	S	C	♦		♦			Sp/Su			♦	♦		
Rubus odoratus	8 ft (2.4 m)	8 ft (2.4 m)	S	C/W	♦				♦	Su/A			♦	♦		
Rubus pentalobus	4 in (10 cm)	3–7 ft (0.9–2 m)	S	W		♦	♦	♦		Su			♦	♦		
Rubus spectabilis	6 ft (1.8 m)	6 ft (1.8 m)	S	C/W	♦		♦			Sp			♦	♦		
Rubus thibetanus	6–8 ft (1.8–2.4 m)	6–8 ft (1.8–2.4 m)	S	C/W	♦			♦		Su			♦	♦		
Rubus tricolor	2 ft (0.6 m)	8–15 ft (2.4–4.5 m)	S	C/W		♦	♦	♦		Su			♦	♦		
Rubus ursinus	20–36 in (50–90 cm)	3–10 ft (0.9–3 m)	S	C/W	♦		♦			Sp/Su			♦	♦		
Ruellia macrantha	6 ft (1.8 m)	20 in (50 cm)	S	W/T		♦	♦			W	♦				♦	
Ruspolia hypocrateriformis	3 ft (0.9 m)	3 ft (0.9 m)	S	W/T		♦	♦			Sp–A	♦				♦	
Russelia equisetiformis	5 ft (1.5 m)	8 ft (2.4 m)	S	W/T		♦	♦			All				♦		
Ruttya fruticosa	12 ft (3.5 m)	5 ft (1.5 m)	S	W/T		♦	♦			Sp–A				♦		
Salix alba	80 ft (24 m)	30 ft (9 m)	T	C/W	♦			♦		Sp			♦	♦		
Salix amygdaloides	70 ft (21 m)	25 ft (8 m)	T	C/W	♦			♦		Sp			♦	♦		
Salix arctica	4 in (10 cm)	24–48 in (60–120 cm)	S	C	♦		♦	♦		Sp			♦	♦		
Salix babylonica	40 ft (12 m)	35 ft (10 m)	T	C/W	♦			♦		Sp			♦	♦		
Salix 'Boydii'	3 ft (0.9 m)	2 ft (0.6 m)	S	C	♦			♦		Sp			♦	♦		
Salix caprea	15–35 ft (4.5–10 m)	10–20 ft (3–6 m)	T	C/W	♦		♦			Sp			♦	♦		
Salix cinerea	10 ft (3 m)	8 ft (2.4 m)	S	C	♦				♦	W/Sp			♦	♦		
Salix daphnoides	35 ft (10 m)	20 ft (6 m)	T	C/W	♦		♦	♦		W/Sp			♦	♦		
Salix discolor	25 ft (8 m)	15 ft (4.5 m)	T	C	♦		♦			W/Sp			♦	♦		
Salix elaeagnos	20 ft (6 m)	20 ft (6 m)	T	C/W	♦			♦		W/Sp			♦	♦		
Salix fargesii	10 ft (3 m)	10 ft (3 m)	S	C/W	♦			♦		Sp				♦	♦	
Salix 'Flame'	20 ft (6 m)	20 ft (6 m)	T	C	♦			♦		Sp			♦	♦		
Salix fragilis	50 ft (15 m)	35 ft (10 m)	T	C/W	♦					Sp			♦	♦		
Salix gracilistyla	10–15 ft (3–4.5 m)	10–15 ft (3–4.5 m)	S	C/W	♦		♦			W/Sp			♦	♦		

Plant name	Height	Spread	Type	Climate	Deciduous	Evergreen	Showy flowers	Showy foliage	Scented flowers	Flowering season	Grow in pot/tub	Indoor use	Frost tolerant	Full sun	Half sun	Heavy shade
Salix hastata	5 ft (1.5 m)	7 ft (2 m)	S	C/W	◆		◆			Sp			◆	◆		
Salix helvetica	2–5 ft (0.6–1.5 m)	3 ft (0.9 m)	S	C	◆		◆			Sp			◆	◆		
Salix integra	10–15 ft (3–4.5 m)	12 ft (3.5 m)	S	C/W	◆			◆		W/Sp			◆	◆		
Salix lanata	2–4 ft (0.6–1.2 m)	6 ft (1.8 m)	S	C/W	◆		◆	◆		Sp			◆	◆		
Salix lindleyana	2 in (5 cm)	30 in (75 cm)	S	C/W	◆			◆		Sp			◆	◆		
Salix magnifica	20 ft (6 m)	10 ft (3 m)	T	C/W	◆		◆	◆		Sp			◆	◆		
Salix nakamurana	12 in (30 cm)	36 in (90 cm)	S	C/W	◆			◆		Sp			◆	◆		
Salix nigra	10–30 ft (3–9 m)	15 ft (4.5 m)	T	C/W	◆					Sp			◆	◆		
Salix purpurea	15 ft (4.5 m)	15 ft (4.5 m)	S	C/W	◆			◆		Sp			◆	◆		
Salix repens	8 in–5 ft (20 cm–1.5 m)	5 ft (1.5 m)	S	C/W	◆			◆		Sp			◆	◆		
Salix reptans	2 in (5 cm)	18–36 in (45–90 cm)	S	C	◆		◆	◆		Sp			◆	◆		
Salix reticulata	6 in (15 cm)	15 in (38 cm)	S	C/W	◆			◆		Sp			◆	◆		
Salix × rubens	35 ft (10 m)	25 ft (8 m)	T	C/W	◆			◆		Sp			◆	◆		
Salix × sepulcralis	40 ft (12 m)	40 ft (12 m)	T	C/W	◆			◆		Sp			◆	◆		
Salix taxifolia	10–15 ft (3–4.5 m)	7–10 ft (2–3 m)	S	W	◆			◆		Sp			◆	◆		
Salix viminalis	8–20 ft (2.4–6 m)	15 ft (4.5 m)	S	C/W	◆					Sp			◆	◆		
Salvia apiana	4 ft (1.2 m)	3 ft (0.9 m)	S	W/T		◆	◆	◆		Sp				◆		
Salvia aurea	3–5 ft (0.9–1.5 m)	3 ft (0.9 m)	S	W/T		◆	◆	◆		Su/A				◆		
Salvia canariensis	4–7 ft (1.2–2 m)	3 ft (0.9 m)	S	W/T		◆	◆			Sp/Su				◆		
Salvia clevelandii	24–48 in (60–120 cm)	15–26 in (38–65 cm)	S	W		◆	◆		◆	Su				◆		
Salvia fruticosa	3 ft (0.9 m)	2 ft (0.6 m)	S	W		◆	◆			Su				◆		
Salvia × jamensis	27–40 in (70–100 cm)	27–40 in (70–100 cm)	S	W/T		◆	◆			Su/A				◆		
Salvia karwinskii	8 ft (2.4 m)	4 ft (1.2 m)	S	W/T		◆	◆	◆		W				◆		
Salvia leucophylla	5 ft (1.5 m)	3 ft (0.9 m)	S	W/T		◆	◆	◆		A				◆		
Salvia mexicana	10 ft (3 m)	7 ft (2 m)	S	W/T		◆	◆			A				◆		
Salvia regla	4 ft (1.2 m)	3 ft (0.9 m)	S	W		◆	◆			A				◆		
Sambucus canadensis	8–12 ft (2.4–3.5 m)	12 ft (3.5 m)	S	C	◆		◆	◆		Su			◆	◆		
Sambucus ebulus	5–7 ft (1.5–2 m)	3–7 ft (0.9–2 m)	S	C/W	◆		◆			Su			◆	◆		
Sambucus nigra	8–30 ft (2.4–9 m)	10–20 ft (2–6 m)	S	C/W	◆		◆	◆	◆	Sp/Su			◆	◆		
Sambucus racemosa	12 ft (3.5 m)	12 ft (3.5 m)	S	C/W	◆			◆		Sp/Su			◆	◆		
Sanchezia speciosa	5 ft (1.5 m)	5 ft (1.5 m)	S	W/T		◆	◆	◆		Su	◆			◆		
Santalum acuminatum	20 ft (6 m)	12 ft (3.5 m)	S	W/T		◆	◆			Any				◆		

Plant name	Height	Spread	Type	Climate	Deciduous	Evergreen	Showy flowers	Showy foliage	Scented flowers	Flowering season	Grow in pot/tub	Indoor use	Frost tolerant	Full sun	Half sun	Heavy shade
Santalum lanceolatum	20 ft (6 m)	15 ft (4.5 m)	S	W/T		♦	♦			Sp/Su				♦		
Santolina rosmarinifolia	12–24 in (30–60 cm)	36 in (90 cm)	S	W		♦	♦	♦		Su			♦	♦		
Sapindus drummondii	50 ft (15 m)	30 ft (9 m)	T	W	♦				♦	Su			♦	♦		
Sapindus mukorossi	40–80 ft (12–24 m)	20 ft (6 m)	T	W	♦				♦	Su			♦	♦		
Sapindus saponaria	30 ft (9 m)	20 ft (6 m)	T	W/T		♦	♦			Su				♦		
Sapium integerrinum	10–20 ft (3–6 m)	20 ft (6 m)	T	W/T	♦			♦	♦	Sp/Su				♦		
Saraca cauliflora	30 ft (9 m)	25 ft (8 m)	T	W/T		♦	♦		♦	Su/A						♦
Sarcobatus vermiculatus	6 ft (1.8 m)	7 ft (2 m)	S	C/W	♦			♦		Su			♦	♦		
Sarcococca confusa	7 ft (2 m)	7 ft (2 m)	S	C/W		♦	♦	♦	♦	W			♦			♦
Sarcococca hookeriana	5 ft (1.5 m)	6 ft (1.8 m)	S	C/W		♦	♦	♦	♦	A/W			♦			♦
Sarcococca ruscifolia	3 ft (0.9 m)	3 ft (0.9 m)	S	W		♦	♦	♦	♦	W	♦		♦			♦
Sarcococca saligna	3 ft (0.9 m)	3 ft (0.9 m)	S	C/W		♦	♦	♦	♦	W/Sp	♦		♦			♦
Sassafras albidum	50 ft (15 m)	30 ft (9 m)	T	C/W	♦			♦		Sp			♦	♦		
Schefflera actinophylla	30 ft (9 m)	12 ft (3.5 m)	T	W/T		♦		♦		A–Sp				♦		
Schefflera arboricola	3–5 ft (0.9–1.5 m)	3 ft (0.9 m)	T	W/T		♦		♦		Sp/Su	♦	♦		♦		
Schefflera elegantissima	50 ft (15 m)	10 ft (3 m)	T	W/T		♦				Sp/Su	♦	♦		♦		
Schefflera umbellifera	30 ft (9 m)	25 ft (8 m)	T	W/T		♦				Sp/Su				♦		
Schima wallichii	25 ft (8 m)	20 ft (6 m)	T	W		♦	♦	♦	♦	Su	♦	♦		♦		
Schinus molle	50–60 ft (15–18 m)	50 ft (15 m)	T	W/T		♦				Sp				♦		
Schinus terebinthifolius	20 ft (6 m)	15 ft (4.5 m)	T	W/T		♦				Sp				♦		
Schotia brachypetala	50 ft (15 m)	15–25 ft (4.5–8 m)	S	W/T	♦		♦		♦	Su				♦		
Schotia latifolia	50 ft (15 m)	25 ft (8 m)	S	W/T	♦		♦			Su				♦		
Sciadopitys verticillata	70 ft (21 m)	20 ft (6 m)	C	C/W		♦		♦		Sp	♦		♦	♦		
Senna alata	30 ft (9 m)	15 ft (4.5 m)	T	W/T		♦	♦			Su/A				♦		
Senna artemisioides	7 ft (2 m)	7 ft (2 m)	S	W/T		♦	♦			Sp–A				♦		
Senna corymbosa	10 ft (3 m)	8 ft (2.4 m)	S	W/T		♦	♦			Sp–A			♦	♦		
Senna didymobotrya	10 ft (3 m)	10 ft (3 m)	S	W/T		♦	♦			Sp–A				♦		
Senna multijuga	25 ft (8 m)	20 ft (6 m)	T	W/T		♦	♦			Su/A				♦		
Senna polyphylla	25 ft (8 m)	12 ft (3.5 m)	T	W/T		♦	♦			Any				♦		
Senna siamea	40 ft (12 m)	35 ft (10 m)	T	W		♦	♦			Sp/Su				♦		
Senna splendida	10–15 ft (3–4.5 m)	8–12 ft (2.4–3.5 m)	T	W/T		♦	♦			A				♦		
Sequoia sempervirens	150 ft (45 m)	15–25 ft (4.5–8 m)	C	W		♦		♦		Sp			♦	♦		

Plant name	Height	Spread	Type	Climate	Deciduous	Evergreen	Showy flowers	Showy foliage	Scented flowers	Flowering season	Grow in pot/tub	Indoor use	Frost tolerant	Full sun	Half sun	Heavy shade
Sequoiadendron giganteum	150–165 ft (45–50 m)	20–35 ft (6–9 m)	C	C/W		◆		◆		Sp			◆	◆		
Serruria 'Sugar 'n' Spice'	4 ft (1.2 m)	4 ft (1.2 m)	S	W		◆	◆			W/Sp				◆		
Sesbania punicea	6 ft (1.8 m)	4 ft (1.2 m)	S	W/T		◆	◆			Su				◆		
Shepherdia argentea	12 ft (3.5 m)	12 ft (3.5 m)	S	C	◆			◆		Sp			◆	◆		
Shepherdia canadensis	8 ft (2.4 m)	8 ft (2.4 m)	S	C	◆		◆			Su			◆	◆		
Simmondsia chinensis	8 ft (2.4 m)	6 ft (1.8 m)	S	W/T		◆	◆			Su				◆		
Skimmia × confusa	2–10 ft (0.6–3 m)	4 ft (1.2 m)	S	C/W		◆	◆	◆	◆	W	◆		◆	◆	◆	◆
Skimmia japonica	20 ft (6 m)	20 ft (6 m)	S	C/W		◆	◆	◆	◆	Sp	◆		◆	◆		
Skimmia laureola	2–40 ft (0.6–12 m)	3–10 ft (0.9–3 m)	S	C/W		◆	◆	◆	◆	Sp			◆	◆	◆	
Solanum aviculare	3–12 ft (0.9–3.5 m)	3–12 ft (0.9–3.5 m)	S	W/T		◆	◆			Su/A						◆
Solanum capsicastrum	12–24 in (30–60 cm)	24 in (60 cm)	S	W/T		◆		◆		Su/A	◆	◆		◆		
Solanum giganteum	12 ft (3.5 m)	10 ft (3 m)	S	W/T		◆	◆	◆		Su/A				◆		
Solanum mammosum	5 ft (1.5 m)	3 ft (0.9 m)	S	W/T		◆	◆	◆		Su/A	◆	◆		◆		
Solanum pseudocapsicum	3–6 ft (0.9–1.8 m)	4 ft (1.2 m)	S	W/T		◆		◆		Su/A				◆		
Solanum pyracanthum	3–6 ft (0.9–1.8 m)	2–3 ft (0.6–0.9 m)	S	W/T		◆	◆	◆		Su			◆	◆		
Solanum rantonnetii	6 ft (1.8 m)	7 ft (2 m)	S	W/T		◆	◆		◆	Su			◆	◆		
Sophora arizonica	10–15 ft (3–4.5 m)	8–10 ft (2.4–3 m)	S	W		◆	◆		◆	Sp			◆	◆		
Sophora davidii	10 ft (3 m)	10 ft (3 m)	S	C/W	◆		◆			Su			◆	◆		
Sophora japonica	50 ft (15 m)	35 ft (10 m)	T	C/W	◆		◆			Su			◆	◆		
Sophora microphylla	20–30 ft (6–9 m)	20 ft (6 m)	T	W		◆	◆			Sp			◆	◆		
Sophora prostrata	6 ft (1.8 m)	7 ft (2 m)	S	W		◆	◆	◆		W/Sp			◆	◆		
Sophora secundiflora	30 ft (9 m)	15 ft (4.5 m)	T	W/T		◆	◆		◆	Sp			◆	◆		
Sophora tetraptera	15–40 ft (4.5–12 m)	15 ft (4.5 m)	T	W		◆	◆			Sp			◆	◆		
Sophora tomentosa	30 ft (9 m)	8 ft (2.4 m)	T	W/T		◆	◆			Sp/Su			◆	◆		
Sorbaria kirilowii	17 ft (5 m)	20 ft (6 m)	S	C	◆		◆		◆	Su			◆	◆		
Sorbaria sorbifolia	10 ft (3 m)	10 ft (3 m)	S	C/W	◆		◆	◆		Su			◆	◆		
Sorbaria tomentosa	20 ft (6 m)	15 ft (4.5 m)	S	C/W	◆		◆			Su			◆	◆		
Sorbus alnifolia	50 ft (15 m)	25 ft (8 m)	T	C	◆		◆	◆		Sp			◆	◆		
Sorbus americana	20–30 ft (6–9 m)	20 ft (6 m)	T	C	◆		◆			Sp			◆	◆		
Sorbus aria	20–40 ft (6–12 m)	25 ft (8 m)	T	C	◆		◆	◆		Sp			◆	◆		
Sorbus × arnoldiana	15–40 ft (4.5–12 m)	20 ft (6 m)	T	C	◆		◆			Sp			◆	◆		
Sorbus aucuparia	15–40 ft (4.5–12 m)	20 ft (6 m)	T	C	◆		◆		◆	Sp			◆	◆		

Plant name	Height	Spread	Type	Climate	Deciduous	Evergreen	Showy flowers	Showy foliage	Scented flowers	Flowering season	Grow in pot/tub	Indoor use	Frost tolerant	Full sun	Half sun	Heavy shade
Sorbus cashmiriana	30 ft (9 m)	20 ft (6 m)	T	C/W	◆		◆	◆		Sp			◆	◆		
Sorbus chamaemespilus	3–6 ft (0.9–1.8 m)	3–6 ft (0.9–1.8 m)	T	C/W	◆		◆			Sp			◆	◆		
Sorbus commixta	20–30 ft (6–9 m)	20 ft (6 m)	T	C/W	◆		◆	◆		Sp			◆	◆		
Sorbus decora	30 ft (9 m)	15 ft (4.5 m)	T	C	◆		◆			Sp			◆	◆		
Sorbus esserteauiana	50 ft (15 m)	35 ft (10 m)	T	C/W	◆		◆	◆		Sp			◆	◆		
Sorbus forrestii	25 ft (8 m)	20 ft (6 m)	T	C/W	◆		◆			Sp			◆	◆		
Sorbus × *hostii*	12–15 ft (3.5–4.5 m)	10 ft (3 m)	T	C/W	◆		◆			Sp			◆	◆		
Sorbus hupehensis	30 ft (9 m)	20 ft (6 m)	T	C/W	◆		◆	◆		Sp			◆	◆		
Sorbus intermedia	20–30 ft (6–9 m)	20 ft (6 m)	T	C	◆		◆	◆		Sp			◆	◆		
Sorbus latifolia	30–50 ft (9–15 m)	20 ft (6 m)	T	C	◆		◆			Sp			◆	◆		
Sorbus megalocarpa	30 ft (9 m)	8 ft (2.4 m)	T	C/W	◆		◆			Sp			◆	◆		
Sorbus mougeotii	40 ft (12 m)	15 ft (4.5 m)	T	C/W	◆		◆			Sp			◆	◆		
Sorbus pohuashanensis	70 ft (21 m)	20 ft (6 m)	T	C	◆		◆			Sp			◆	◆		
Sorbus reducta	15 in (38 cm)	6 ft (1.8 m)	S	C/W	◆			◆		Sp			◆	◆		
Sorbus sargentiana	20–30 ft (6–9 m)	20 ft (6 m)	T	C/W	◆		◆			Sp			◆	◆		
Sorbus thibetica	50 ft (15 m)	30 ft (9 m)	T	W	◆		◆	◆		Sp			◆	◆		
Sorbus × *thuringiaca*	30–40 ft (9–12 m)	25 ft (8 m)	T	C/W	◆		◆			Sp			◆	◆		
Sorbus torminalis	30–50 ft (9–15 m)	25 ft (8 m)	T	C/W	◆		◆	◆		Sp			◆	◆		
Sorbus vilmorinii	20 ft (6 m)	15 ft (4.5 m)	T	C/W	◆		◆	◆		Sp			◆	◆		
Sorbus Hybrid Cultivars	10–25 ft (3–8 m)	7–15 ft (2–4.5 m)	T	C/W	◆		◆			Sp			◆	◆		
Sparmannia africana	20 ft (6 m)	10 ft (3 m)	T	W/T		◆	◆	◆		Sp/Su				◆		
Spartium junceum	10 ft (3 m)	10 ft (3 m)	S	W	◆		◆		◆	Sp/Su			◆	◆		
Spathodea campanulata	25–35 ft (8–10 m)	25 ft (8 m)	T	W/T	◆		◆			Sp/Su				◆		
Spiraea 'Arguta'	5–7 ft (1.5–2 m)	4 ft (1.2 m)	S	C/W	◆		◆			Sp			◆	◆		
Spiraea betulifolia	3 ft (0.9 m)	3 ft (0.9 m)	S	C/W	◆		◆			Su			◆	◆		
Spiraea × *billardii*	7 ft (2 m)	7 ft (2 m)	S	C/W	◆		◆			Su			◆	◆		
Spiraea × *brachybotrys*	8 ft (2.4 m)	6 ft (1.8 m)	S	C/W	◆		◆			Su			◆	◆		
Spiraea cantoniensis	6 ft (1.8 m)	8 ft (2.4 m)	S	C/W	◆		◆			Su			◆	◆		
Spiraea × *cinerea*	5 ft (1.5 m)	5 ft (1.5 m)	S	C/W	◆		◆			Sp			◆	◆		
Spiraea douglasii	6 ft (1.8 m)	6 ft (1.8 m)	S	C/W	◆		◆			Su			◆	◆		
Spiraea fritschiana	3 ft (0.9 m)	5 ft (1.5 m)	S	C/W	◆		◆			Su			◆	◆		
Spiraea japonica	6 ft (1.8 m)	4 ft (1.2 m)	S	C/W	◆		◆	◆		Su			◆	◆		

Plant name	Height	Spread	Type	Climate	Deciduous	Evergreen	Showy flowers	Showy foliage	Scented flowers	Flowering season	Grow in pot/tub	Indoor use	Frost tolerant	Full sun	Half sun	Heavy shade
Spiraea nipponica	6 ft (1.8 m)	6 ft (1.8 m)	S	C/W	◆		◆			Su			◆	◆		
Spiraea prunifolia	7 ft (2 m)	7 ft (2 m)	S	C/W	◆		◆			Sp			◆	◆		
Spiraea thunbergii	5 ft (1.5 m)	7 ft (2 m)	S	C/W	◆		◆			Sp			◆	◆		
Spiraea tomentosa	7 ft (2 m)	7 ft (2 m)	S	C/W	◆		◆			Su			◆	◆		
Spiraea trichocarpa	6 ft (1.8 m)	4 ft (1.2 m)	S	C/W	◆		◆			Su			◆	◆		
Spiraea × vanhouttei	6 ft (1.8 m)	4 ft (1.2 m)	S	C/W	◆		◆			Su			◆	◆		
Stachyurus chinensis	8 ft (2.4 m)	8 ft (2.4 m)	S	C/W	◆		◆		◆	Sp			◆	◆		
Stachyurus praecox	6–12 ft (1.8–3.5 m)	6–12 ft (1.8–3.5 m)	S	C/W	◆		◆			W/Sp			◆	◆		
Staphylea bumalda	7 ft (2 m)	6 ft (1.8 m)	S	C/W	◆		◆			Sp			◆	◆		
Staphylea colchica	10–15 ft (3–4.5 m)	10 ft (3 m)	S	C/W	◆		◆		◆	Sp			◆	◆		
Staphylea holocarpa	15 ft (4.5 m)	10 ft (3 m)	S	C/W	◆		◆			Sp			◆	◆		
Staphylea pinnata	15 ft (4.5 m)	15 ft (4.5 m)	S	C/W	◆		◆			Sp			◆	◆		
Staphylea trifolia	15 ft (4.5 m)	15 ft (4.5 m)	S	C/W	◆		◆	◆	◆	Sp			◆	◆		
Stenocarpus salignus	100 ft (30 m)	10–15 ft (3–4.5 m)	T	W/T		◆	◆			Sp/Su				◆		
Stenocarpus sinuatus	120 ft (36 m)	15 ft (4.5 m)	T	W/T		◆	◆			Sp/Su				◆		
Stephanandra incisa	6 ft (1.8 m)	10 ft (3 m)	S	C/W	◆		◆	◆		Su			◆	◆		
Stephanandra tanakae	10 ft (3 m)	8 ft (2.4 m)	S	C/W	◆			◆		Su				◆		
Sterculia murex	20–40 ft (6–12 m)	10–20 ft (3–6 m)	T	W	◆		◆			Sp				◆		
Sterculia quadrifida	40 ft (12 m)	20 ft (6 m)	T	W/T	◆		◆	◆	◆	Su				◆		
Stewartia malacodendron	15–30 ft (4.5–9 m)	10 ft (3 m)	T	C/W	◆		◆			Su			◆	◆		
Stewartia monadelpha	50 ft (15 m)	20 ft (6 m)	T	C/W	◆		◆			Su			◆	◆		
Stewartia ovata	15–20 ft (4.5–6 m)	15 ft (4.5 m)	T	C/W	◆		◆			Su			◆	◆		
Stewartia pseudocamellia	20–50 ft (6–15 m)	15 ft (4.5 m)	T	C/W	◆		◆			Sp			◆	◆		
Stewartia pteropetiolata	20 ft (6 m)	12 ft (3.5 m)	T	C/W	◆		◆			Su			◆	◆		
Stewartia sinensis	15–30 ft (4.5–9 m)	20 ft (6 m)	T	C/W	◆		◆		◆	Su			◆	◆		
Strelitzia nicolai	30 ft (9 m)	15 ft (4.5 m)	T	W/T		◆	◆	◆		Sp/Su				◆		
Streptosolen jamesonii	7 ft (2 m)	5 ft (1.5 m)	S	W/T		◆	◆			Sp	◆			◆		
Strychnos decussata	30 ft (9 m)	15 ft (4.5 m)	T	W/T		◆	◆			Sp/Su						◆
Strychnos spinosa	20 ft (6 m)	12 ft (3.5 m)	T	W/T		◆	◆			Sp				◆		
Styphelia tubiflora	24 in (60 cm)	30 in (75 cm)	S	W		◆	◆			W			◆		◆	
Styrax americanus	10 ft (3 m)	8 ft (2.4 m)	S	C/W	◆		◆		◆	Sp			◆	◆		
Styrax benzoin	20 ft (6 m)	10–20 ft (3–6 m)	T	W/T		◆	◆		◆	Sp						

Plant name	Height	Spread	Type	Climate	Deciduous	Evergreen	Showy flowers	Showy foliage	Scented flowers	Flowering season	Grow in pot/tub	Indoor use	Frost tolerant	Full sun	Half sun	Heavy shade
Styrax grandifolius	15 ft (4.5 m)	15 ft (4.5 m)	S	W	◆		◆	◆	◆	Sp			◆	◆		
Styrax japonicus	20–30 ft (6–9 m)	15 ft (4.5 m)	S	C/W	◆		◆	◆		Sp/Su			◆	◆		
Styrax obassia	35 ft (10 m)	20 ft (6 m)	S	C/W	◆		◆	◆		Sp			◆	◆		
Sutherlandia frutescens	5 ft (1.5 m)	5 ft (1.5 m)	S	W/T		◆	◆			W/Sp				◆		
Swietenia macrophylla	150 ft (45 m)	25 ft (8 m)	T	W/T		◆		◆		Sp				◆		
Swietenia mahogani	80 ft (24 m)	15 ft (4.5 m)	T	W/T		◆		◆		Sp				◆		
Symphoricarpos albus	4–6 ft (1.2–1.8 m)	4–6 ft (1.2–1.8 m)	S	C/W	◆		◆			Sp			◆	◆		
Symphoricarpos × chenaultii	6–8 ft (1.8–2.4 m)	5 ft (1.5 m)	S	C/W	◆		◆			Su			◆	◆		
Symphoricarpos mollis	3 ft (0.9 m)	3 ft (0.9 m)	S	C/W						Sp			◆	◆		
Symphoricarpos orbiculatus	6 ft (1.8 m)	6 ft (1.8 m)	S	C/W	◆		◆			Su			◆	◆		
Symplocos paniculata	15 ft (4.5 m)	15 ft (4.5 m)	S	C/W	◆		◆		◆	Sp/Su			◆	◆		
Syncarpha vestita	12–20 in (30–50 cm)	12–20 in (30–50 cm)	S	W		◆	◆	◆		Sp/Su				◆		
Syncarpia glomulifera	100 ft (30 m)	25 ft (8 m)	T	W/T		◆	◆			Sp/Su				◆		
Syringa × chinensis	12 ft (3.5 m)	12 ft (3.5 m)	S	C/W	◆		◆		◆	Sp			◆	◆		
Syringa emodi	15 ft (4.5 m)	12 ft (3.5 m)	S	C/W	◆		◆	◆	◆	Su			◆	◆		
Syringa × hyacinthiflora	15 ft (4.5 m)	15 ft (4.5 m)	S	C/W	◆		◆		◆	Sp			◆	◆		
Syringa × josiflexa	8–10 ft (2.4–3 m)	7 ft (2 m)	S	C/W	◆		◆		◆	Su			◆	◆		
Syringa josikaea	12 ft (3.5 m)	10 ft (3 m)	S	C/W	◆		◆	◆	◆	Su			◆	◆		
Syringa laciniata	12 ft (3.5 m)	10 ft (3 m)	S	C/W	◆		◆	◆	◆	Sp			◆	◆		
Syringa meyeri	5 ft (1.5 m)	4 ft (1.2 m)	S	C/W	◆		◆		◆	Sp–A			◆	◆		
Syringa oblata	12 ft (3.5 m)	10 ft (3 m)	S	C/W	◆		◆		◆	Sp			◆	◆		
Syringa pekinensis	15 ft (4.5 m)	12 ft (3.5 m)	S	C/W	◆		◆		◆	Su			◆	◆		
Syringa potaninii	6–8 ft (1.8–2.4 m)	6 ft (1.8 m)	S	C/W	◆		◆		◆	Sp			◆	◆		
Syringa × prestoniae	12 ft (3.5 m)	12 ft (3.5 m)	S	C/W	◆		◆		◆	Su			◆	◆		
Syringa pubescens	12 ft (3.5 m)	12 ft (3.5 m)	S	C/W	◆		◆		◆	Sp/Su			◆	◆		
Syringa reflexa	12 ft (3.5 m)	12 ft (3.5 m)	S	C/W	◆		◆			Su			◆	◆		
Syringa reticulata	30 ft (9 m)	15 ft (4.5 m)	S	C/W	◆		◆		◆	Su			◆	◆		
Syringa × swegiflexa	10 ft (3 m)	5 ft (1.5 m)	S	C/W	◆		◆		◆	Sp			◆	◆		
Syringa sweginzowii	10 ft (3 m)	6 ft (1.8 m)	S	C/W	◆		◆		◆	Sp/Su			◆	◆		
Syringa tigerstedtii	8 ft (2.4 m)	8 ft (2.4 m)	S	C/W	◆		◆			Su			◆	◆		
Syringa tomentella	10 ft (3 m)	10 ft (3 m)	S	C/W	◆		◆		◆	Su			◆	◆		
Syringa vulgaris	20 ft (6 m)	20 ft (6 m)	S	C/W	◆		◆		◆	Sp/Su			◆	◆		

Plant name	Height	Spread	Type	Climate	Deciduous	Evergreen	Showy flowers	Showy foliage	Scented flowers	Flowering season	Grow in pot/tub	Indoor use	Frost tolerant	Full sun	Half sun	Heavy shade
Syringa wolfii	15 ft (4.5 m)	12 ft (3.5 m)	S	C/W	◆		◆		◆	Sp			◆	◆		
Syzygium australe	25 ft (8 m)	20 ft (6 m)	T	W/T		◆	◆			Su				◆		
Syzygium francisii	80 ft (24 m)	70 ft (21 m)	T	W/T		◆	◆			Su				◆		
Syzygium jambos	20 ft (6 m)	15 ft (4.5 m)	T	W/T		◆	◆		◆	Su				◆		
Syzygium luehmannii	50 ft (15 m)	30 ft (9 m)	T	W/T		◆	◆	◆		Su				◆		
Syzygium paniculatum	25 ft (8 m)	20 ft (6 m)	T	W/T		◆	◆	◆		Su				◆		
Syzygium wilsonii	6 ft (1.8 m)	7 ft (2 m)	S	W/T		◆	◆	◆		Sp/Su				◆		
Tabebuia chrysantha	20–50 ft (6–15 m)	20 ft (6 m)	T	W/T	◆		◆			Sp				◆		
Tabebuia rosea	90 ft (27 m)	30 ft (9 m)	T	W/T		◆	◆			Sp				◆		
Tabernaemontana divaricata	6 ft (1.8 m)	5 ft (1.5 m)	S	W/T		◆	◆	◆	◆	Su	◆	◆		◆		
Tabernaemontana elegans	10–20 ft (3–6 m)	10 ft (3 m)	S	W/T	◆		◆	◆	◆	Sp/Su				◆		
Taiwania cryptomerioides	180 ft (55 m)	35 ft (10 m)	C	W		◆		◆		Sp			◆	◆		
Tamarindus indica	90 ft (27 m)	35 ft (10 m)	T	W/T		◆	◆	◆		Su				◆		
Tamarix chinensis	15 ft (4.5 m)	10 ft (3 m)	S	C/W	◆		◆			Su			◆	◆		
Tamarix gallica	12 ft (3.5 m)	10 ft (3 m)	S	C/W	◆		◆			Su			◆	◆		
Tamarix parviflora	15 ft (4.5 m)	20 ft (6 m)	T	C/W	◆		◆			Sp			◆	◆		
Tamarix ramosissima	15 ft (4.5 m)	15 ft (4.5 m)	S	C/W	◆		◆			Su/A			◆	◆		
Taxodium distichum	75 ft (23 m)	20 ft (6 m)	C	C/W	◆			◆		Sp			◆	◆		
Taxodium mucronatum	100 ft (30 m)	50 ft (15 m)	C	W	◆	◆		◆		Sp			◆	◆		
Taxus baccata	50 ft (15 m)	25 ft (8 m)	C	C/W		◆		◆		Su			◆	◆		
Taxus chinensis	20 ft (6 m)	15 ft (4.5 m)	C	C/W		◆		◆		Su			◆	◆		
Taxus cuspidata	50 ft (15 m)	20 ft (6 m)	C	C/W		◆		◆		Sp			◆	◆		
Taxus × media	25 ft (8 m)	20 ft (6 m)	C	C/W		◆		◆		Sp			◆	◆		
Tecoma capensis	10 ft (3 m)	7 ft (2 m)	S	W/T		◆	◆			Sp–A				◆		
Tecoma castaneifolia	15–25 ft (4.5–8 m)	8–12 ft (2.4–3.5 m)	T	W/T		◆	◆			Sp–A				◆		
Tecoma stans	15–30 ft (4.5–9 m)	10 ft (3 m)	T	W/T		◆	◆			W–Su				◆		
Telanthophora grandifolia	20 ft (6 m)	12 ft (3.5 m)	S	W/T		◆	◆			Sp/Su				◆		
Telopea mongaensis	10 ft (3 m)	10 ft (3 m)	S	W		◆	◆			Sp/Su			◆	◆		
Telopea oreades	10–30 ft (3–9 m)	10 ft (3 m)	S	W		◆	◆			Su				◆		
Telopea speciosissima	10 ft (3 m)	5 ft (1.5 m)	S	W		◆	◆			Sp				◆		
Telopea truncata	10 ft (3 m)	10 ft (3 m)	S	W		◆	◆			Sp			◆	◆		
Tephrosia grandiflora	2–5 ft (0.6–1.5 m)	3 ft (0.9 m)	S	W		◆	◆			Sp/Su				◆		

Plant name	Height	Spread	Type	Climate	Deciduous	Evergreen	Showy flowers	Showy foliage	Scented flowers	Flowering season	Grow in pot/tub	Indoor use	Frost tolerant	Full sun	Half sun	Heavy shade
Terminalia arostrata	17–35 ft (5–10 m)	6–10 ft (1.8–3 m)	T	W	◆			◆		Su				◆		
Ternstroemia japonica	12 ft (3.5 m)	10 ft (3 m)	T	W	◆		◆	◆	◆	Su			◆		◆	
Tetraclinis articulata	50 ft (15 m)	25 ft (8 m)	C	W/T		◆		◆		Sp				◆		
Tetradenia riparia	8–10 ft (2.4–3 m)	8 ft (2.4 m)	S	W/T	◆		◆		◆	W/Sp				◆		
Tetradium daniellii	50 ft (15 m)	40 ft (12 m)	T	W	◆		◆	◆	◆	Su/A			◆	◆		
Tetradium ruticarpum	30 ft (9 m)	15 ft (4.5 m)	T	W	◆		◆		◆	Su				◆		
Tetratheca thymifolia	2 ft (0.6 m)	2 ft (0.6 m)	S	W		◆	◆			Sp						◆
Teucrium fruticans	4 ft (1.2 m)	6 ft (1.8 m)	S	W		◆	◆	◆		Su			◆	◆		
Thevetia peruviana	15 ft (4.5 m)	8 ft (2.4 m)	S	W/T		◆	◆		◆	Su				◆		
Thryptomene calycina	4–6 ft (1.2–1.8 m)	8 ft (2.4 m)	S	W		◆	◆			W/Sp				◆		
Thryptomene saxicola	3–5 ft (0.9–1.5 m)	5 ft (1.5 m)	S	W		◆	◆			W/Sp				◆		
Thuja occidentalis	30–70 ft (9–21 m)	15 ft (4.5 m)	C	C/W		◆		◆		Sp			◆	◆		
Thuja plicata	70–120 ft (21–36 m)	15 ft (4.5 m)	C	C/W		◆		◆		Sp			◆	◆		
Thuja standishii	100 ft (30 m)	20 ft (6 m)	C	C/W		◆		◆		Sp			◆	◆		
Thujopsis dolabrata	100 ft (30 m)	20 ft (6 m)	C	C/W		◆		◆		Sp			◆	◆		
Thunbergia erecta	6–8 ft (1.8–2.4 m)	7 ft (2 m)	S	W/T		◆	◆			Su	◆			◆		
Tibouchina granulosa	12–35 ft (3.5–10 m)	10 ft (3 m)	S	W/T		◆	◆	◆		A	◆			◆		
Tibouchina heteromalla	3 ft (0.9 m)	4 ft (1.2 m)	S	W/T		◆	◆	◆		Su/A	◆			◆		
Tibouchina lepidota	12 ft (3.5 m)	10 ft (3 m)	S	W/T		◆	◆	◆		Su/W				◆		
Tibouchina macrantha	10 ft (3 m)	8 ft (2.4 m)	S	W/T		◆	◆	◆		A–Sp	◆			◆		
Tibouchina urvilleana	15 ft (4.5 m)	10 ft (3 m)	S	W/T		◆	◆	◆		Su				◆		
Tilia americana	100 ft (30 m)	40 ft (12 m)	T	C/W	◆			◆	◆	Su			◆	◆		
Tilia cordata	80–100 ft (24–30 m)	40 ft (12 m)	T	C/W	◆			◆	◆	Su			◆	◆		
Tilia × euchlora	70 ft (21 m)	40 ft (12 m)	T	C/W	◆			◆	◆	Su			◆	◆		
Tilia × europaea	100 ft (30 m)	40 ft (12 m)	T	C/W	◆			◆		Su			◆	◆		
Tilia japonica	50 ft (15 m)	20 ft (6 m)	T	C/W	◆			◆	◆	Su				◆		
Tilia oliveri	100 ft (30 m)	30 ft (9 m)	T	C/W	◆		◆		◆	Su				◆		
Tilia platyphyllos	100 ft (30 m)	50 ft (15 m)	T	C/W	◆			◆	◆	Su			◆	◆		
Tilia tomentosa	80–100 ft (24–30 m)	50 ft (15 m)	T	C/W	◆			◆	◆	Su				◆		
Tipuana tipu	100 ft (30 m)	25 ft (8 m)	T	W/T		◆	◆			Sp				◆		
Toona ciliata	120 ft (36 m)	20 ft (6 m)	T	W/T	◆		◆	◆	◆	Sp				◆		
Toona sinensis	40 ft (12 m)	30 ft (9 m)	T	W	◆		◆	◆	◆	Sp			◆	◆		

Plant name	Height	Spread	Type	Climate	Deciduous	Evergreen	Showy flowers	Showy foliage	Scented flowers	Flowering season	Grow in pot/tub	Indoor use	Frost tolerant	Full sun	Half sun	Heavy shade
Torreya californica	80 ft (24 m)	25 ft (8 m)	C	C/W		◆		◆		Su			◆	◆		
Torreya nucifera	50–80 ft (15–24 m)	25 ft (8 m)	C	C/W		◆		◆		Su			◆	◆		
Toxicodendron diversilobum	8 ft (2.4 m)	7 ft (2 m)	S	C/W	◆			◆		Su			◆	◆		
Toxicodendron succedaneum	30 ft (9 m)	20 ft (6 m)	S	C/W	◆			◆		Su			◆	◆		
Toxicodendron vernix	10 ft (3 m)	10 ft (3 m)	S	C/W	◆			◆		Su			◆	◆		
Trevesia palmata	30 ft (9 m)	12 ft (3.5 m)	S	C/W			◆	◆		Su						◆
Triadica sebifera	20–30 ft (6–9 m)	15–20 ft (4.5–6 m)	T	W/T	◆			◆		Sp/Su			◆	◆		
Tristania neriifolia	15 ft (4.5 m)	7 ft (2 m)	S/T	W			◆			Su				◆		
Tristaniopsis laurina	60 ft (18 m)	20 ft (6 m)	T	W/T		◆	◆	◆		Su				◆		
Trochodendron aralioides	70 ft (21 m)	25 ft (8 m)	T	W		◆		◆		Sp			◆			◆
Tsuga canadensis	80–120 ft (24–36 m)	30 ft (9 m)	C	C		◆		◆		Sp			◆	◆		
Tsuga heterophylla	60–120 ft (18–36 m)	20–30 ft (6–9 m)	C	C/W		◆		◆		Sp			◆	◆		
Tsuga mertensiana	50 ft (15 m)	20 ft (6 m)	C	C		◆		◆		Sp			◆	◆		
Tsuga sieboldii	50–100 ft (15–30 m)	25 ft (8 m)	C	C/W		◆		◆		Sp			◆	◆		
Ulex europaeus	8 ft (2.4 m)	7 ft (2 m)	S	C/W		◆	◆		◆	W/Sp			◆	◆		
Ulmus americana	100 ft (30 m)	100 ft (30 m)	T	C	◆			◆		Sp			◆	◆		
Ulmus carpinifolia	50–70 ft (15–21 m)	70 ft (21 m)	T	C/W	◆		◆	◆		Sp			◆	◆		
Ulmus crassifolia	70–100 ft (21–30 m)	40 ft (12 m)	T	C/W	◆			◆		Sp			◆	◆		
Ulmus glabra	100 ft (30 m)	70 ft (21 m)	T	C	◆		◆	◆		Sp			◆	◆		
Ulmus × hollandica	100 ft (30 m)	80 ft (24 m)	T	C/W	◆		◆	◆		Sp			◆	◆		
Ulmus japonica	100 ft (30 m)	60 ft (18 m)	T	C/W	◆		◆	◆		Sp			◆	◆		
Ulmus laevis	70 ft (21 m)	30 ft (9 m)	T	C/W	◆			◆		Sp			◆	◆		
Ulmus parvifolia	70 ft (21 m)	30 ft (9 m)	T	C/W	◆			◆		Sp			◆	◆		
Ulmus procera	70–100 ft (21–30 m)	50 ft (15 m)	T	C/W	◆		◆	◆		Sp			◆	◆		
Ulmus pumila	20–35 m (6–10 m)	20–30 ft (6–9 m)	T	C/W	◆			◆		Sp			◆	◆		
Ulmus 'Sapporo Autumn Gold'	50 ft (15 m)	35 ft (10 m)	T	C/W	◆			◆		Sp			◆	◆		
Ulmus 'Sarniensis'	75–80 ft (23–24 m)	23–25 ft (7–8 m)	T	C/W	◆		◆	◆		Sp			◆	◆		
Ulmus thomasii	100 ft (30 m)	40 ft (12 m)	T	C	◆			◆		Sp			◆	◆		
Umbellularia californica	50–70 ft (15–21 m)	35 ft (10 m)	T	W		◆	◆	◆		Sp				◆		
Vaccinium crassifolium	15 in (38 cm)	3 ft (0.9 m)	S	C/W		◆	◆			Sp			◆	◆		
Vaccinium nummularia	12–15 in (30–38 cm)	12–15 in (30–38 cm)	S	C/W		◆	◆			Sp			◆	◆		
Vaccinium stamineum	5 ft (1.5 m)	3 ft (0.9 m)	S	C/W	◆		◆			Sp			◆	◆		

Plant name	Height	Spread	Type	Climate	Deciduous	Evergreen	Showy flowers	Showy foliage	Scented flowers	Flowering season	Grow in pot/tub	Indoor use	Frost tolerant	Full sun	Half sun	Heavy shade
Vaccinium vitis-idaea	6 in (15 cm)	2–4 ft (0.6–1.2 m)	S	C		◆	◆			Sp			◆	◆		
Verticordia chrysantha	2 ft (0.6 m)	2 ft (0.6 m)	S	W		◆	◆			Sp			◆	◆		
Verticordia grandis	7 ft (2 m)	3 ft (0.9 m)	S	W		◆	◆			Sp			◆	◆		
Verticordia plumosa	20 in (50 cm)	20 in (50 cm)	S	W		◆	◆			Sp			◆	◆		
Vestia foetida	6 ft (1.8 m)	5 ft (1.5 m)	S	W		◆	◆			Sp/Su						◆
Viburnum betulifolium	10 ft (3 m)	10 ft (3 m)	S	C/W	◆			◆		Su			◆	◆		
Viburnum × bodnantense	10 ft (3 m)	7 ft (2 m)	S	C/W	◆		◆		◆	A–Sp			◆	◆		
Viburnum × burkwoodii	8 ft (2.4 m)	8 ft (2.4 m)	S	C/W	◆		◆		◆	Sp			◆	◆		
Viburnum × carlcephalum	8 ft (2.4 m)	8 ft (2.4 m)	S	C/W	◆		◆	◆	◆	Sp			◆	◆		
Viburnum carlesii	8 ft (2.4 m)	7 ft (2 m)	S	C/W	◆		◆	◆	◆	Sp			◆	◆		
Viburnum 'Cayuga'	6 ft (1.8 m)	6 ft (1.8 m)	S	C/W	◆		◆		◆	Sp			◆	◆		
Viburnum davidii	4 ft (1.2 m)	4 ft (1.2 m)	S	C/W		◆	◆	◆		Sp			◆	◆		
Viburnum dentatum	10 ft (3 m)	10 ft (3 m)	S	C	◆		◆	◆		Sp/Su			◆	◆		
Viburnum dilatatum	10 ft (3 m)	8 ft (2.4 m)	S	C	◆		◆	◆		Sp/Su			◆	◆		
Viburnum erubescens	20 ft (6 m)	10 ft (3 m)	S	C/W	◆		◆			Su			◆	◆		
Viburnum farreri	10 ft (3 m)	8 ft (2.4 m)	S	C/W	◆		◆	◆	◆	A–Sp			◆	◆		
Viburnum × globosum	3–4 ft (0.9–1.2 m)	3–4 ft (0.9–1.2 m)	S	C/W		◆	◆			Sp			◆	◆		
Viburnum × hillieri	6–8 ft (1.8–2.4 m)	7 ft (2 m)	S	C/W		◆	◆	◆		Su			◆	◆		
Viburnum japonicum	8 ft (2.4 m)	8 ft (2.4 m)	S	C/W		◆	◆	◆	◆	Su			◆	◆		
Viburnum × juddii	6 ft (1.8 m)	7 ft (2 m)	S	C/W	◆		◆		◆	Sp			◆	◆		
Viburnum lantana	15 ft (4.5 m)	12 ft (3.5 m)	S	C	◆		◆	◆		Sp/Su			◆	◆		
Viburnum lantanoides	15 ft (4.5 m)	15 ft (4.5 m)	S	C	◆		◆	◆		Sp/Su			◆	◆		
Viburnum lentago	20 ft (6 m)	10 ft (3 m)	S	C	◆		◆	◆		Sp/Su			◆	◆		
Viburnum macrocephalum	15 ft (4.5 m)	15 ft (4.5 m)	S	C/W	◆		◆			Sp			◆	◆		
Viburnum nudum	10 ft (3 m)	6 ft (1.8 m)	S	C/W	◆		◆	◆		Su			◆	◆		
Viburnum opulus	15 ft (4.5 m)	15 ft (4.5 m)	S	C/W	◆		◆	◆		Sp/Su			◆	◆		
Viburnum plicatum	8 ft (2.4 m)	10 ft (3 m)	S	C/W	◆		◆	◆		Sp/Su			◆	◆		
Viburnum prunifolium	20 ft (6 m)	12 ft (3.5 m)	S	C/W	◆		◆	◆		Sp/Su			◆	◆		
Viburnum rhytidophyllum	10 ft (3 m)	8 ft (2.4 m)	S	C		◆	◆	◆		Su			◆	◆		
Viburnum sieboldii	10 ft (3 m)	15 ft (4.5 m)	S	C	◆		◆	◆		Sp/Su			◆	◆		
Viburnum tinus	8–10 ft (2.4–3 m)	8–10 ft (2.4–3 m)	S	C/W		◆	◆	◆	◆	W/Sp			◆	◆		
Viburnum trilobum	10 ft (3 m)	10 ft (3 m)	S	C	◆		◆	◆		Su			◆	◆		

Plant name	Height	Spread	Type	Climate	Deciduous	Evergreen	Showy flowers	Showy foliage	Scented flowers	Flowering season	Grow in pot/tub	Indoor use	Frost tolerant	Full sun	Half sun	Heavy shade
Viburnum utile	6 ft (1.8 m)	5 ft (1.5 m)	S	C/W		♦	♦			Sp			♦	♦		
Viburnum veitchii	5 ft (1.5 m)	5 ft (1.5 m)	S	C/W	♦		♦		♦	Sp/Su			♦	♦		
Virgilia oroboides	30 ft (9 m)	15 ft (4.5 m)	T	W		♦	♦		♦	Sp/Su				♦		
Vitex agnus-castus	15 ft (4.5 m)	15 ft (4.5 m)	S	C/W	♦		♦		♦	Su/A			♦	♦		
Vitex lucens	30–50 ft (9–15 m)	10–15 ft (3–4.5 m)	T	W		♦	♦		♦	A/W				♦		
Warszewiczia coccinea	15 ft (4.5 m)	10 ft (3 m)	S	W/T		♦	♦			All				♦		
Weigela decora	10–15 ft (3–4.5 m)	5–7 ft (1.5–2 m)	S	C/W	♦		♦			Sp/Su			♦	♦		
Weigela floribunda	10 ft (3 m)	8 ft (2.4 m)	S	C/W	♦		♦			Sp/Su			♦	♦		
Weigela florida	8 ft (2.4 m)	8 ft (2.4 m)	S	C/W	♦		♦			Sp/Su			♦	♦		
Weigela japonica	10 ft (3 m)	10 ft (3 m)	S	C/W	♦		♦			Sp			♦	♦		
Weigela middendorffiana	5 ft (1.5 m)	5 ft (1.5 m)	S	C/W	♦		♦			Su			♦	♦		♦
Weigela praecox	8 ft (2.4 m)	7 ft (2 m)	S	C/W	♦		♦		♦	Sp/Su			♦	♦		
Weigela Hybrid Cultivars	5–12 ft (1.5–3.5 m)	5–8 ft (1.5–2.4 m)	S	C/W	♦		♦			Sp/Su			♦	♦		
Weinmannia racemosa	30 ft (9 m)	8–15 ft (2.4–4.5 m)	T	W		♦	♦		♦	Su				♦		
Weinmannia trichosperma	70 ft (21 m)	5–12 ft (1.5–3.5 m)	T	W		♦	♦			Su				♦		
Westringia fruticosa	6 ft (1.8 m)	7 ft (2 m)	S	W		♦	♦			Any				♦		
Westringia 'Wynyabbie Gem'	4 ft (1.2 m)	5 ft (1.5 m)	S	W		♦	♦			Any	♦			♦		
Widdringtonia nodiflora	40 ft (12 m)	6–12 ft (1.8–3.5 m)	C	W		♦		♦		Sp				♦		
Widdringtonia schwarzii	120 ft (36 m)	15–30 ft (4.5–9 m)	C	W		♦		♦		Sp			♦	♦		
Wigandia caracasana	15 ft (4.5 m)	12 ft (3.5 m)	T	W/T		♦	♦		♦	Sp/Su	♦	♦		♦		
Wollemia nobilis	120 ft (36 m)	4–10 ft (1.2–3 m)	C	W		♦		♦		Sp				♦		
Xanthoceras sorbifolium	25 ft (8 m)	10 ft (3 m)	T	C/W	♦		♦		♦	Sp/Su				♦		
Zanthoxylum americanum	25 ft (8 m)	15 ft (4.5 m)	T	C/W	♦			♦		Sp				♦		
Zanthoxylum piperitum	20 ft (6 m)	10 ft (3 m)	T	C/W	♦			♦		Sp				♦		
Zanthoxylum planispinum	12 ft (3.5 m)	8 ft (2.4 m)	T	C/W	♦			♦		Sp				♦		
Zanthoxylum simulans	7–25 ft (2–8 m)	7–25 ft (2–8 m)	T	C	♦			♦		Su			♦	♦		
Zelkova carpinifolia	100 ft (30 m)	25 ft (8 m)	T	C/W	♦			♦	♦	Sp			♦	♦		
Zelkova serrata	60–100 ft (18–30 m)	50 ft (15 m)	T	C/W	♦			♦		Sp				♦		
Zenobia pulverulenta	3–10 ft (0.9–3 m)	4 ft (1.2 m)	S	C/W	♦		♦		♦	Sp/Su				♦		♦
Ziziphus mucronata	17–35 ft (5–10 m)	10–20 ft (3–6 m)	T	W	♦		♦			Sp			♦	♦		

Abelia × grandiflora

ABELIA

This decorative genus from the woodbine (Caprifoliaceae) family has about 30 ornamental shrubs, both evergreen and deciduous, and occurs in eastern Asia and Mexico. The leaves are glossy and opposite or whorled, while the funnelform or tubular flowers, white or pinkish, sometimes with orange blotches, appear in summer. Some species have persistent reddish sepals that provide an additional ornamental feature after the flowers have faded.
CULTIVATION: *Abelia* species are moderately frost hardy, and perform best when planted in a sunny spot in any well-drained, moderately fertile soil. Pruning should be carried out in winter, removing some of the basal shoots to make room for new growth, plus the cane ends. Care should be taken to preserve the plant's naturally arching habit. Propagate from soft-tip cuttings in spring or summer, or half-hardened cuttings in late autumn or winter.

Abelia floribunda
☀ ⚘ ↔ 6 ft (1.8 m) ↕ 6 ft (1.8 m)
From Mexico. Generally evergreen with an open habit. Leaves smaller and less glossy than *A. × grandiflora*. Pendulous clusters of pale rose to deep red flowers in summer–autumn. Persistent sepals. Zones 9–11.

Abelia × grandiflora ★
GLOSSY ABELIA
☀ ❋ ↔ 6 ft (1.8 m) ↕ 6 ft (1.8 m)
Evergreen shrub with arching canes, hybrid between *A. chinensis* and *A. uniflora*. Reddish brown stems. Leaves dark green, turning red to orange in winter. Perfumed flowers flushed mauve-pink.

'Francis Mason', leaves heavily margined and suffused with yellow; 'Prostrata', low growing, to 24 in (60 cm) high; 'Sherwoodii', compact habit, to 3–4 ft (0.9–1.2 m) high; 'Sunrise', to 6 ft (1.8 m) tall, attractive autumn foliage color. Zones 7–10.

Abelia schumannii
syn. *Abelia longituba*
SCHUMANN'S ABELIA
☀ ❋ ↔ 8 ft (2.4 m) ↕ 4 ft (1.2 m)
From China. Nearly evergreen shrub with pale green to dull green leaves. Pale rosy mauve flowers in clusters, with broad white stripe and some orange spots on lower lobe, in summer–autumn. Zones 7–10.

ABELIOPHYLLUM

The name of this genus, of the olive (Oleaceae) family, is derived from *Abelia*, which it is said to resemble. It contains just one species of small deciduous shrub, closely related to *Forsythia*, bearing similar flowers in white. The shrub is native to the mountains of Korea, where it is becoming scarce.
CULTIVATION: The species will grow in a range of soil conditions but in cool temperate climates should be given a warm site. It can be trained against a wall if desired. Less vigorous old canes should be cut out. Prune every 2 to 3 years to maintain shape. Propagation is usually by half-hardened cuttings taken in summer or by layering in spring or autumn.

Abeliophyllum distichum
WHITE FORSYTHIA
☀ ❋ ↔ 6 ft (1.8 m) ↕ 3 ft (0.9 m)
Arching, straggly, deciduous shrub from Korea. In late winter, bare branches are smothered in fragrant, white, forsythia-like flowers that burst from pink-tinged buds. In some forms buds are deeper shade with flowers emerging pale pink. Zones 5–10.

ABIES

This genus in the pine (Pinaceae) family consists of about 50 species occurring in the northern temperate zones of Europe, North Africa, Asia, and North America. Mostly long lived and medium to very tall, these evergreen conifers have narrow smooth leaves. The leaves are mid- to dark green, often with a grayish white band. The female

Abies homolepis

cones are carried erect on upper branches, while the hanging male cones grow throughout the crown. *Abies* species are fully hardy, although frost damage can occur on juvenile foliage.
CULTIVATION: They do best in neutral to acid, moist, fertile soil with good drainage in full sun; most tolerate some shade. Some, including *A. pinsapo*, tolerate alkaline soils. Some juvenile trees need shelter from cold winds. Adelgids and honey fungus can be a problem. Sow seed as it ripens, but it needs to be stratified for 3 weeks for better germination. Graft cultivars in winter.

Abies balsamea

BALSAM FIR, DWARF BALSAM FIR

☀ ❄ ↔ 15 ft (4.5 m) ↑ 50 ft (15 m)

Conical tree from northeastern USA, east and central Canada. Sleek gray bark, fragrant resin. Leaves dark green, whitish beneath. Cones cylindrical, purplish blue. Fairly short lived in gardens. Dwarf cultivars include 'Nana' and Hudsonia Group. Zones 3–8.

Abies cephalonica

syn. *Abies apollinis*

GREEK FIR

☀ ❄ ↔ 25 ft (8 m) ↑ 100 ft (30 m)

Pyramidal tree, native to central and southern Greece. Dark green, rigid, slightly curved leaves, greenish white beneath. Cylindrical greenish brown cones are resinous. 'Meyer's Dwarf', with shorter leaves, forms mound only 20 in (50 cm) high, with diameter of 10 ft (3 m). Zones 7–10.

Abies concolor

BLUE FIR, COLORADO WHITE FIR, SILVER FIR, WHITE FIR

☀ ❄ ↔ 25 ft (8 m) ↑ 120 ft (36 m)

Grows in western USA down to northern Mexico. Statuesque tree with pyramidal crown, dull greenish gray leaves, mid-green to brown cylindrical cones. Cultivars include 'Compacta', 'Masonic Broom', and Violacea Group ★. Dwarf cultivars grow no more than 30 in (75 cm) in height and spread. Zones 5–9.

Abies fargesii

syn. *Abies sutchuenensis*

☀ ❄ ↔ 12 ft (3.5 m) ↑ 60 ft (18 m)

Statuesque tree from central China. Leaves dark green with silver-striped undersides. Egg-shaped cones violet-purple in color, with protruding, slightly resinous bracts. Zones 7–9.

Abies fraseri

☀ ❄ ↔ 20 ft (6 m) ↑ 60 ft (18 m)

Pyramidal tree, native to southwestern Virginia, western North Carolina, and eastern Tennessee, USA. Leaves 1 in (25 mm) long, mid- to dark green with silvery to greenish white band on underside. Cylindrical cones green to dark purple, ripening to brown; pronounced bracts. Zones 6–9.

Abies grandis

GIANT FIR

☀ ❄ ↔ 25 ft (8 m) ↑ 300 ft (90 m)

Giant conical to columnar tree from western North America. Dark green, soft, shiny leaves, with whitish banding on undersides. Cones smallish, ripening to gray-brown. 'Johnsonii', reaches height of 60–70 ft (18–21 m). Zones 6–9.

Abies homolepis

syn. *Abies brachyphylla*

MANCHURIAN FIR, NIKKO FIR

☀ ❄ ↔ 25 ft (8 m) ↑ 80 ft (24 m)

Conical tree native to southern and central Japan. Leaves dull grayish green with silver banding. Branches tiered up trunk. Cones cylindrical and violet-blue, turning brown with age. Zones 5–9.

Abies koreana ★

KOREAN FIR

☀ ❄ ↔ 5 ft (1.5 m) ↑ 50 ft (15 m)

From mountains of South Korea. Narrow, pyramid-shaped, slow-growing tree; striking purple cones. Leaves dark green above, shiny white beneath. Cultivars include 'Compact Dwarf', 'Flava', and 'Silberlocke' (syn. 'Horstmann's Silberlocke'). Zones 5–8.

Abies pinsapo

SPANISH FIR

☀ ❄ ↔ 15 ft (4.5 m) ↑ 80 ft (24 m)

From dry mountain slopes of southern Spain. Rigid, short, linear, dark green leaves. Purplish brown cylindrical cones. Cultivars include 'Glauca', with gray-blue leaves; and 'Kelleriis', robust dwarf. Zones 6–8.

Abies procera

syn. *Abies nobilis*

NOBLE FIR

☀ ❄ ↔ 30 ft (9 m) ↑ 150 ft (45 m)

Native to high-rainfall areas of western USA. Pyramidal tree becomes broader with age. Leaves gray-green to blue-silver, banded gray underneath. Barrel-shaped green cones ripen to brown. Glauca Group features cultivars (including 'Glauca Prostrata') with blue leaves. Zones 4–9.

Abies koreana

Abies pinsapo

Abies procera, Glauca Group cultivar

ABUTILON

CHINESE LANTERN

This genus of the mallow (Malvaceae) family is represented in warmer parts of South or Central America, Australia, and Africa. Most are shrubs with slender tough-barked twigs but a few are annuals, perennials, or even small trees. Leaves vary from heart-shaped to jaggedly lobed with toothed margins. The common name alludes to the pendent bell-shaped flowers of some species with 5 petals. Colors range from white to pink, and from yellow and orange to deep bronzy red. Fruit is a capsule. In mild climates they flower almost throughout the year, in cooler climates from spring to autumn.
CULTIVATION: Plant Chinese lanterns in well-drained moderately fertile soil, in light shade or bright sun. Extra water is needed if they are planted in an exposed position. In cool climates keep indoors until the worst frosts are past, then plant out for summer display; newer dwarf cultivars are suitable for this purpose. Prune leading shoots in late winter for a compact form, although some cultivars display their blooms best on long arching branches. Propagate from tip cuttings in late summer.

Abutilon vitifolium

Abutilon × *hybridum*

CHINESE LANTERN, GARDEN ABUTILON

☼/◑ ❄ ↔ 5–10 ft (1.5–3 m) ↑ 6–15 ft (1.8–4.5 m)
Wide-ranging group of hybrids with unclear origins, although most show *A. pictum* influence. Leaves usually dark green, smooth, 3–6 in (8–15 cm) long, toothed or with up to 5 lobes. Flowers to 3 in (8 cm) wide, one per leaf axil, mainly yellow, orange, and red shades, appear most of the year. Popular hybrids include 'Apricot', 'Ashford Red', 'Bartley Schwartz', 'Boule de Neige', 'Canary Bird', 'Cannington Carol', 'Cannington Skies', 'Cerise Queen', 'Clementine', 'Crimson Belle', 'Dwarf Red', 'Kentish Belle', 'Linda Vista Peach', 'Mobile Pink', 'Moonchimes', 'Moritz', 'Nabob' ★, 'Souvenir de Bonn', and 'Summer Sherbet'. Zones 9–11.

Abutilon × *hybridum*
'Cannington Skies'

Abutilon megapotamicum

Abutilon megapotamicum

syn. *Abutilon vexillarium*

CHINESE LANTERN, TRAILING ABUTILON

☼ ❄ ↔ 8 ft (2.4 m) ↑ 8 ft (2.4 m)
From southern Brazil. Has several forms, from an erect shrub with arching branches to an almost prostrate form. Bell-shaped flowers, red calyx, pale yellow petals. 'Marianne', tangerine flowers; 'Variegatum', yellow mottled leaves; 'Victory' ★, smaller, with darker yellow leaves. Zones 8–10.

Abutilon × *suntense*

☼ ❄ ↔ 8 ft (2.4 m) ↑ 12 ft (3.5 m)
Deciduous shrub with bright green leaves and violet flowers. Dislikes hot/humid summer areas. Cultivars include 'Gorer's White', large pure white flowers; and 'Jermyns', clear mauve-purple flowers. Zones 8–10.

Abutilon vitifolium

syn. *Corynabutilon vitifolium*

☼ ❄ ↔ 8 ft (2.4 m) ↑ 15 ft (4.5 m)
Weak-branched deciduous shrub from Chile. Maple-like toothed leaves. Flowers saucer-shaped, white to violet-purple, in spring–summer. Dislikes hot/humid summer areas. 'Veronica Tennant', slightly larger pale mauve-pink flowers. Zones 8–10.

ACACIA

From the mimosa subfamily of the legume (Fabaceae) family, *Acacia* consists of at least 1,200 species. It comes mainly from Australia, but is also found in Africa, the tropical Americas, Asia, and islands of the Pacific and Indian Oceans. There are shrubs, small to medium-sized trees, a few large forest trees, and a few climbers. Flowers are very small, but densely crowded into spikes or globular heads in colors of yellow, cream, or white. Leaf structure is bipinnate—but in many species the leaves change to phyllodes. The acacia fruit is a typical legume pod, splitting open when ripe to reveal a row of hard seeds. Fast-growing acacias enrich the soil by converting nitrogen from the air into soil nitrogen.
CULTIVATION: Most acacias require well-drained soil and full sun. In mild climates they can become environmental weeds. They are often short lived. Propagate from seeds, treated to soften the hard case. Give a light prune after flowering.

Acacia adunca

WALLANGARRA WATTLE

☼ ❂ ↔ 12 ft (3.5 m) ↑ 20 ft (6 m)
Bushy shrub or small tree from southeastern Australia. Phyllodes narrow, light green. Long sprays of ball-shaped, sweetly scented, golden yellow flowers in late winter and spring. Zones 9–11.

Acacia baileyana

COOTAMUNDRA WATTLE

☼ ❂ ↔ 20 ft (6 m) ↑ 6–20 ft (1.8–6 m)
Widely naturalized in most Australian States. Small elegant tree occurs naturally around Cootamundra, New South Wales. Leaves

Acacia adunca

Acacia cyclops
ROOIKRANS, WESTERN COASTAL WATTLE

☀ ❄ ↔ 7–15 ft (2–4.5 m) ↑7–15 ft (2–4.5 m)

Occurs along coastal fringe of southern and southwestern Australia. Dense shrub, spreading, branching near ground level. Thick, slightly curved phyllodes, 1½–4 in (3.5–10 cm) long, with 3 to 5 prominent veins. Heads of about 40 lemon yellow flowers during spring–autumn. Grayish brown leathery pods. Has naturalized in southern Africa and is serious environmental weed. Zones 9–11.

Acacia dealbata
MIMOSA, SILVER WATTLE

☀ ❄ ↔ 25 ft (8 m) ↑50 ft (15 m)

From southeastern Australia. Trunk dark gray to black bark. Silvery branchlets, gray-green bipinnate leaves. Pale lemon to bright yellow globular flowers on extended racemes in late winter–spring. Known in Europe as mimosa. '**Gaulois Astier**', deep green foliage; '**Kambah Karpet**', dense, prostrate habit. Drought tolerant. Zones 8–10.

Acacia elata
CEDAR WATTLE

☀ ❧ ↔ 40 ft (12 m) ↑100 ft (30 m)

From moist sheltered forests in coastal eastern Australia. Dark green bipinnate leaves, long individual leaflets. Clusters of fluffy, pale yellow, ball-shaped flowers in summer. Zones 9–11.

Acacia farnesiana
MIMOSA BUSH

☀ ⚘ ↔ 15 ft (4.5 m) ↑15 ft (4.5 m)

Can be spreading shrub or small tree, native to tropical zones of Americas. Bipinnate leaves with strong spines in leaf axils. Golden, sweetly scented, globular flowers in winter–spring. Zones 11–12.

Acacia farnesiana

Acacia giraffae
syn. *Acacia erioloba*
CAMEL THORN

☀ ❧ ↔ 40 ft (12 m) ↑40–60 ft (12–18 m)

Shapely tree with wide-spreading crown, widespread in southern Africa. Straight thorns, bipinnate leaves. Sweetly scented, yellow, ball-shaped flowers in late winter–early spring. Sickle-shaped pod. Good shade. Zones 9–11.

Acacia howittii
HOWITT'S WATTLE

☀ ❧ ↔ 10 ft (3 m) ↑25 ft (8 m)

From southeastern Australia. Small tree with dense weeping habit. Sticky dark green phyllodes; displays masses of scented lemon flower balls in spring. Makes very good hedge plant. Low-spreading form is in cultivation. Zones 9–11.

feathery silver-gray. Flowers bright yellow, globular, in racemes, in winter–spring. '**Purpurea**', attractive purplish foliage and new growth. Zones 9–10.

Acacia binervia
syn. *Acacia glaucescens*
COAST MYALL

☀ ❧ ↔ 35 ft (10 m) ↑50 ft (15 m)

From tablelands and coast of New South Wales, Australia. Handsome tree; large compact crown of silvery gray curved phyllodes. Masses of bright yellow flower spikes in early spring. Young foliage may be poisonous to stock. Zones 9–11.

Acacia cardiophylla
WYALONG WATTLE

☀ ❄ ↔ 5–8 ft (1.5–2.4 m) ↑3–10 ft (0.9–3 m)

Beautiful free-flowering shrub from mallee country of inland New South Wales, Australia. Leaves bipinnate with tiny heart-shaped leaflets on long arching branches. Panicles of small, sweetly scented, bright yellow, ball-shaped flowers. '**Gold Lace**' (syn. 'Kuranga Gold Lace') differs from species by its prostrate and trailing habit and earlier flowering time (late winter–early spring). Stems become twisted with age. Zones 8–11.

Acacia cultriformis
KNIFE-LEAF WATTLE, PLOUGHSHARE WATTLE

☀ ❄ ↔ 6–10 ft (1.8–3 m) ↑6–10 ft (1.8–3 m)

Widely cultivated tall shrub from eastern Australia. Drooping branches with blue-gray almost triangular phyllodes. Perfumed, bright yellow, globular flowers, on long sprays, in spring. Excellent plant for hedging. '**Cascade**' (syn. 'Austraflora Cascade'), prostrate habit, with flowers similar in size and color to species. Zones 8–11.

Acacia karroo

KARROO THORN, SWEET THORN

☼ ⚘ ↔25 ft (8 m) ↑25 ft (8 m)

Common and widespread tree from southern Africa. Spreading rounded crown of deciduous, dark green, bipinnate leaves. Smooth brownish gray bark, paired straight thorns. Dark yellow, sweetly scented, globular flowers in summer–autumn. Zones 9–11.

Acacia longifolia

SYDNEY GOLDEN WATTLE

☼ ⚘ ↔15 ft (4.5 m) ↑6–25 ft (1.8–8 m)

From eastern Australia. Small bushy tree, low spreading branches. Bright green thick phyllodes. Bright yellow flower spikes along branches in winter–spring. Useful as hedge. Zones 9–11.

Acacia melanoxylon

BLACKWOOD

☼ ❋ ↔20 ft (6 m) ↑100 ft (30 m)

From mainland eastern Australia and Tasmania. Spreading bushy crown of dull green phyllodes with longitudinal veins. Clusters of pale yellow globular flowers in late winter–early spring. Best in moist sheltered situation. Weed in South Africa. Zones 8–11.

Acacia podalyriifolia

QUEENSLAND WATTLE

☼ ⚘ ↔15 ft (4.5 m) ↑10–15 ft (3–4.5 m)

Native to coastal southern Queensland, Australia. Large shrub or slender small tree. Rounded silvery phyllodes and profuse, fragrant, golden flower balls, in clusters, in early winter–spring. Zones 9–11.

Acacia longifolia

Acacia podalyriifolia

Acacia melanoxylon

Acacia pravissima

OVENS WATTLE, WEDGE-LEAFED WATTLE

☼ ❋ ↔10 ft (3 m) ↑10–25 ft (3–8 m)

Native to hilly country in southeastern Australia. Spreading shrub or small tree, drooping branches and small, roughly triangular, olive green phyllodes. Profuse, golden yellow, globular flowers, in extended racemes, in spring. Prostrate form, '**Golden Carpet**', spreads to 15 ft (4.5 m). Zones 8–10.

Acacia pycnantha

GOLDEN WATTLE

☼ ⚘ ↔15 ft (4.5 m) ↑10–25 ft (3–8 m)

Tall shrub or small open-branched tree; Australia's national floral emblem. Pendulous branches, bright green phyllodes. Racemes of large, perfumed, golden yellow, ball-shaped flowers in late winter–spring. Zones 9–11.

Acacia riceana ★

RICE'S WATTLE

☼ ❋ ↔10 ft (3 m) ↑10–20 ft (3–6 m)

Native to Tasmania, Australia. Prickly shrub or small tree, often with drooping branches. Narrow, dark green, sharply pointed phyllodes. Profuse pale yellow flower balls, in loose sprays, in early spring. Zones 8–10.

Acacia verticillata

PRICKLY MOSES

◑ ⚘ ↔7 ft (2 m) ↑10 ft (3 m)

Shrub from southeastern mainland Australia and Tasmania. May be low and spreading or upright with arching branches. Very sharp needle-like phyllodes in whorls. Bright yellow flower spikes in late winter–spring. *A. v.* **var.** *latifolia* covers a range of forms with broader, flatter, and often blunt-tipped phyllodes. Zones 9–11.

Acacia vestita

WEEPING BOREE

☼ ⚘ ↔6–15 ft (1.8–4.5 m) ↑6–15 ft (1.8–4.5 m)

From eastern Australia. Dense shrub, widely cultivated, attractive pendulous branches, green phyllodes. Masses of golden yellow ball-shaped flowers, in clusters, in spring. Good screen, hedge, or low windbreak. Prune after flowering to maintain shape. Zones 9–11.

Acacia xanthophloea
FEVER TREE
☼ ⚘ ↔ 20–40 ft (6–12 m) ↑ 50 ft (15 m)
Native to southeastern Africa. Deciduous tree with somewhat sparse wide-spreading crown. Bark smooth, powdery, yellow-green; straight sharp thorns and small bipinnate leaves. Fragrant, golden yellow, rounded flowers in spring. This is fever tree of Rudyard Kipling's story, "The Elephant's Child." Zones 9–11.

ACALYPHA
This pantropical genus of the spurge or euphorbia (Euphorbiaceae) family contains over 400 species of perennials, shrubs, and trees best known for their long catkins or spikes of flowers, often bright magenta to red shades. Their leaves are simple, fairly large, and oval-shaped with toothed edges. Individually the flowers are minute, but those of the female plants form densely packed catkins that in some species can be as much as 18 in (45 cm) long.
CULTIVATION: Warm, almost frost-free conditions are essential as is plenty of moisture during the growing season. Plant in moist, humus-rich, well-drained soil, and feed well to keep the foliage lush and the plants flowering freely. Pinch back the young shoots and deadhead the flowers to keep the growth compact; otherwise little pruning is required. Propagate from cuttings and, if growing indoors, watch for mealybugs and white flies.

Acalypha amentacea subsp. *wilkesiana*
syn. *Acalypha wilkesiana*
COPPERLEAF, FIJIAN FIRE PLANT, JACOB'S COAT
☼ ⚘ ↔ 10 ft (3 m) ↑ 10 ft (3 m)
From Fiji and nearby Pacific islands. Shrub with striking foliage colors and patterns. Colors range from green to bronze, and in tapestries of pink, rosy red, cream, or yellow, sometimes with contrasting margins that are coarsely serrated. Flowers in summer–autumn are upstaged by foliage. '**Ceylon**', bronze-purple leaves, edged in pink or white; '**Marginata**', coppery leaves edged in red. Zones 10–12.

Acalypha hispida
CHENILLE PLANT, RED-HOT CAT-TAIL
☀ ✿ ↔ 5 ft (1.5 m) ↑ 12 ft (3.5 m)
Famed for its long tassels of blood red flowers, this species is most likely a native of tropical East Asia. Leaves bright green, with toothed edges, and covered in fine hairs. Excellent in hanging baskets where the tassels can be seen from below. Zones 11–12.

Acalypha reptans
RED CAT-TAILS
☀ ⚘ ↔ 12 in (30 cm) ↑ 12 in (30 cm)
Native of Florida, USA, and nearby Caribbean islands, often grown as hanging basket plant. Soft light to mid-green leaves.

Acalypha reptans

Flower catkins deep pink to pale red in summer, spot flowering at other times. Zones 10–12.

ACCA
syn. *Feijoa*
This South American genus of the myrtle (Myrtaceae) family consists of 6 species of evergreen shrubs and small trees that bear a guava-like fruit. Simple, smooth-edged leaves are paler on the underside. The attractive single flowers have fleshy petals and conspicuous stamens. Only one species, *A. sellowiana* (syn. *Feijoa sellowiana*), is commonly cultivated, for its tasty fruit or for ornament, and is grown in the same kinds of warm-temperate climates that suit oranges.

CULTIVATION: The feijoa likes a sunny position and well-drained soil of moderate fertility. It is tolerant of exposure and even salt-laden winds, and can be clipped to form a dense hedge. Mature plants tolerate moderate winter frosts but in cooler climates will thrive better against a wall that traps the sun's heat. Cross-pollination, preferably by another plant not of the same clone, is needed for good fruit production. Named varieties are propagated from cuttings or grafting, but seed-raised plants are just as ornamental, if lacking fruit quality, and are more reliable pollinators.

Acca sellowiana

Acca sellowiana ★
syn. *Feijoa sellowiana*
FEIJOA, PINEAPPLE GUAVA
☼ ❄ ↔ 10 ft (3 m) ↑ 10 ft (3 m)
Native from southern Brazil to northern Argentina. Leathery, oval, glossy green leaves, whitish beneath. Flowers have cupped petals, pale carmine, with dark crimson stamens. Fruit elliptical with sweet, aromatic, cream flesh. '**Beechwood**', smooth-skinned fruit; '**Coolidge**', abundant fruit; '**Mammoth**', bearing large wrinkled-skinned fruit; '**Nazemetz**', bearing large fruit to 4 in (10 cm) long; and '**Trask**', thick-skinned fruit. Zones 8–11.

ACER

MAPLE

This genus of mostly deciduous trees was formerly treated as a family of its own, but is now included in the soapberry (Sapindaceae) family. It consists of around 120 species, most from the Northern Hemisphere. Maples are forest or woodland trees of moist climates. The majority have simple leaves, mostly toothed or lobed, borne on slender leaf stalks attached to the twigs in opposite pairs. A small number have compound leaves with 3, 5, or 7 leaflets. Flowers are small, in clusters or dense spikes. Fruits consist of two small nuts (samaras), joined where attached to the flower stalk, each terminating in an elongated wing. CULTIVATION: Maples thrive best in cooler temperate climates with adequate rainfall, aided by warm humid summers and sharply demarcated winters. They are best in deep well-drained soil with permanent subsoil moisture. Some need dappled shade to preserve their foliage from summer scorching, but some can tolerate exposure to drying winds. Propagation of species is from seed, cultivars by grafting.

Acer buergerianum

TRIDENT MAPLE

☀ ❄ ↔ 25 ft (8 m) ↑ 30 ft (9 m)

From eastern China and Korea. Usually seen as sturdy small tree; popular bonsai subject. Leaves have 3 short lobes, turning yellowish often flushed with red in autumn. Bark flaky, pale gray. Winged fruits persist through winter. Zones 6–10.

Acer campestre

FIELD MAPLE, HEDGE MAPLE

☀ ❄ ↔ 12 ft (3.5 m) ↑ 30 ft (9 m)

Spreading tree from western Asia, Europe, and North Africa. Leaves turn clear golden yellow in autumn; bark becomes thick and furrowed with age. *A. c.* subsp. *tauricum,* smaller leaves with downy undersides. *A. c.* 'Carnival', slow-growing to 10 ft (3 m) high and wide, leaves heavily margined white; 'Elsrijk', rich dark green foliage, conical habit; 'Queen Elizabeth' ★, erect habit, lustrous foliage; and 'Schwerinii', reddish foliage, turning purple. Zones 3–9.

Acer capillipes

RED SNAKEBARK MAPLE

☀ ❄ ↔ 35 ft (10 m) ↑ 40 ft (12 m)

From Japan. Young stems bright pinkish red ageing to white-striped green-brown bark. Leaves dark green with serrated edges and prominent red stalks. Zones 5–9.

Acer cappadocicum

CAPPADOCIAN MAPLE

☀ ❄ ↔ 50 ft (15 m) ↑ 60 ft (18 m)

Fast-growing species from highlands of Turkey and southwest Asia to Himalayas. Leaves with 5 or 7 very regular, triangular lobes and flat base. Unfolding leaves may be reddish, and turn

Acer japonicum

butter yellow in autumn. *A. c.* subsp. *lobelii,* columnar form; *A. c.* subsp. *sinicum,* more sharply pointed leaf lobes and rougher bark. *A. c.* 'Aureum', golden new foliage in spring; 'Rubrum', deep red young foliage. Zones 5–9.

Acer circinnatum

VINE MAPLE

☀ ❄ ↔ 15 ft (4.5 m) ↑ 15 ft (4.5 m)

Shrub or low-branching tree from western North America. Leaves rounded, 7 to 9 lobes, turn orange-scarlet to deep red in autumn. Purple flowers. Red horizontal winged fruits. 'Monroe', deeply cut leaves. Zones 4–9.

Acer davidii ★

PERE DAVID'S MAPLE

☀ ❄ ↔ 25 ft (8 m) ↑ 30 ft (9 m)

Elegant fast-growing tree from central and western China. Open habit with arching branches, striped greenish bark. Leaves pointed, toothed, some with small lobes near base. Small reddish fruits in long pendent spikes. 'Ernest Wilson', compact tree, narrow orange leaves; 'George Forrest', dark red young foliage, almost unlobed leaves; and 'Serpentine', smaller-leafed than species. Zones 5–9.

Acer forrestii

syn. *Acer pectinatum* subsp. *forrestii*

☀ ❄ ↔ 20–30 ft (6–9 m) ↑ 25–40 ft (8–12 m)

Medium-sized tree with spreading branches from western China. Bark reddish or purplish on young branches, striped with white. Leaves dull dark green, long-pointed, 2 to 4 lateral lobes. 'Alice', large strong-veined leaves variegated pink in summer. Zones 5–9.

Acer griseum

CHINESE PAPERBARK MAPLE, PAPERBARK MAPLE

☀ ❄ ↔ 35 ft (10 m) ↑ 40 ft (12 m)

Slender tree from central and western China. Outstanding bark texture and color. Leaves turn orange, scarlet, and crimson in autumn. Winged fruits with large seeds. Zones 4–9.

Acer japonicum

FULL-MOON MAPLE

☀ ❄ ↔ 30 ft (9 m) ↑ 30 ft (9 m)

Broadly spreading small tree from mostly dry and sunny mountain forests of Japan. Leaves rounded; 7 to 11 sharp-toothed, pointed lobes turn yellow, orange, and crimson in autumn. 'Aconitifolium', leaves deeply dissected and toothed turning crimson in autumn; 'Vitifolium', large leaves, bronzy when young. Zones 6–9.

Acer macrophyllum

OREGON MAPLE

☀ ❄ ↔ 80 ft (24 m) ↑ 80 ft (24 m)

Tall broadly columnar tree from western North America. Leaves largest of all maples, 5-lobed, dark green, glossy, turning bright orange in autumn. Large pendulous fruit clusters. Zones 6–9.

Acer maximowiczianum ★

syn. *Acer nikoense*

NIKKO MAPLE

☼ ❄ ↔40 ft (12 m) ↑60 ft (18 m)

Broadly spreading tree from China and Japan; 3-part dark green leaves, brilliant red in autumn. Green winged fruits in spreading pairs. Zones 4–9.

Acer negundo

BOX ELDER, BOX ELDER MAPLE, MANITOBA MAPLE

☼ ❄ ↔30 ft (9 m) ↑60 ft (18 m)

Fast-growing hardy tree from North America with several popular variegated forms. Green species is rounded to broadly columnar tree. Colored forms are smaller and less vigorous. All have compound leaves with 3 to 5 or 7 large leaflets. *A. n.* var. *violaceum*, red to purple flowers on dark branches. *A. n.* 'Aureovariegatum', gold-edged leaflets; 'Elegans', broad gold margin, male clone; 'Flamingo', pink-margined in early spring, fading to white; 'Sensation', rich pink autumn color; and 'Variegatum' ★, white-margined, sterile, female clone. Zones 5–10.

Acer palmatum

GREENLEAF JAPANESE MAPLE, JAPANESE MAPLE

☼ ❄ ↔25 ft (8 m) ↑20 ft (6 m)

Tree from Japan, Korea, and China with more than 1,000 cultivars. The 5- to 7-lobed leaves turn yellow, amber, crimson, and purple. Cultivars must be propagated by grafting or cuttings to be true to type. *A. p.* var. *coreanum* 'Korean Gem' has black bark and spectacular autumn foliage.

Many cultivars belong to *A. p.* **Dissectum Group**, which consists of shrubs with narrow

Acer platanoides 'Drummondii'

leaf lobes, which themselves are strongly lobed. Most are low growing with cascading branches, giving mature plants an umbrella-like or dome-like form. Further subdivisions include the **Dissectum Viride Group** and the **Dissectum Atropurpureum Group**; 'Crimson Queen', vigorous growth, bright red autumn foliage; 'Dissectum Nigrum' (syn. 'Ever Red'), bright red in autumn; 'Inabe-shidare', burgundy foliage; 'Ornatum', deeply dissected leaves, turning red, amber, and gold in autumn.

A. p. 'Akaji-nishiki' (syn. 'Bonfire'), pinkish foliage in spring and autumn; 'Butterfly', vase-shaped with cream-white margined 5-lobed leaves; 'Garnet', deep red spring foliage turning fiery red in autumn; 'Higasayama', cream and pink variegated leaves; 'Kotohime', dwarf to 5 ft (1.5 m) high, green-brown leaves turning golden in autumn; 'Nigrum', dark purple shrub with light green winged fruits; 'Osakazuki', 7-lobed brown-green leaves, turning russet in autumn; 'Red Dragon', rich purple foliage; 'Red Filigree Lace', the most finely divided leaves of all maples of this type; 'Sango-kaku', remarkable for its glowing red bark in winter; 'Seiryu', distinctive vigorous growth and upright habit; 'Shishigashira', the "lion's head maple," good for seaside gardens; 'Trompenburg', unique among maples for its mature foliage; and 'Waterfall', a classic, cascading, dome-shaped shrub. Other cultivars include 'Atrolineare' (syns 'Filiferum Purpureum', 'Linearilobium Rubrum'), 'Atropurpureum', 'Bloodgood', 'Burgundy Lace', 'Chishio', 'Chitoseyama', 'Heptalobum Rubrum', 'Katsura', 'Linearilobum', 'Moonfire', 'Nicholsonii', 'Red Pygmy', 'Shigitatsu-sawa', 'Shindeshojo', 'Suminagashi', and 'Villa Taranto'. Zones 6–10.

Acer pensylvanicum

GOOSEFOOT MAPLE, MOOSEWOOD, STRIPED MAPLE

☼ ❄ ↔35 ft (10 m) ↑30 ft (9 m)

Only North American snakebark maple, with branches marked like markings found on garter snake. Broadly columnar tree from moist woodlands. White and red-brown stripes pattern green bark. 'Erythrocladum', winter bark coral to salmon red, striped white. Leaves turn golden amber. Zones 4–9.

Acer platanoides

NORWAY MAPLE

☼ ❄ ↔50 ft (15 m) ↑80 ft (24 m)

Fast-growing broadly columnar tree. Leaves 5-lobed, bright green, on long slender stalks, color clear yellow in autumn. Yellow-green flower clusters. Large winged fruits. Cultivars include 'Cavalier', 'Cleveland', 'Columnare', 'Crimson King', 'Deborah', 'Drummondii', 'Emerald Queen', 'Faassen's Black', 'Globe', 'Goldsworth Purple', 'Green Lace', 'Jade Gem', 'Laciniatum', 'Palmatifidum', 'Schwedleri', 'Undulatum', and 'Walderseei'. Zones 4–8.

Acer palmatum

Acer pseudoplatanus

SYCAMORE MAPLE

☼ ❋ ↔ 80 ft (24 m) ↑ 100 ft (30 m)

Large-domed tree native to central and southern Europe. Leaves mid-green, 5 rounded lobes, turn burnt yellow in autumn. Greenish yellow flowers. Large winged fruit. Seeds prolifically. '**Atropurpureum**', leaves dark green above and reddish purple underneath; '**Brilliantissimum**', striking salmon pink spring foliage; '**Erectum**', upright branches; '**Leopoldii**', gold-flecked leaves; and '**Prinz Handjery**', similar to 'Brilliantissimum', with purplish reverse to leaves. Zones 4–8.

Acer rubrum

CANADIAN MAPLE, RED MAPLE, SCARLET MAPLE, SWAMP MAPLE

☼ ❋ ↔ 35 ft (10 m) ↑ 100 ft (30 m)

Acer saccharinum 'Beebe's Cutleaf Weeping'

Large tree native to eastern North America. Appreciated for its fast growth, spectacular autumn color, and tolerance of wet soils and atmospheric pollution. Leaves 3- to 5-lobed, dark green, bluish beneath, changing to yellow, amber, or fiery red. Dense red flower clusters. Red winged fruit. *A. r.* var. *drummondii,* larger flowers and thicker leaves, whitish beneath. *A. r.* '**Autumn Flame**', dense rounded crown, crimson autumn foliage; '**Gerling**', broad conical shape, fiery red autumn color; '**October Glory**', spectacular "Lipstick" tree; '**Scanlon**', leaves turn gold-orange and speckled crimson in autumn; '**Scarsen**', upright habit, yellow-orange to vivid red color in autumn; and '**Sunshine**', popular cultivar. Zones 4–8.

Acer saccharinum

RIVER MAPLE, SILVER MAPLE, SOFT MAPLE, WHITE MAPLE

☼ ❋ ↔ 80 ft (24 m) ↑ 100 ft (30 m)

Large tree found on moist riverbanks in eastern North America. Fast growing but can be short lived, easily damaged by wind. Deep angularly lobed leaves, silvery beneath, turn clear yellow in autumn. Coppery green winged fruits fall early. *A. s.* f. *lutescens*, yellow spring foliage turns light green then yellow in autumn; *A. s.* f. *pyramidale*, narrower form with deeply cut leaves, ideal street tree. Cultivars include *A. s.* '**Beebe's Cutleaf Weeping**' and '**Skinneri**'. Zones 4–9.

Acer saccharum

HARD MAPLE, ROCK MAPLE, SUGAR MAPLE

☼ ❋ ↔ 40 ft (12 m) ↑ 100 ft (30 m)

This North American species produces the best sap, extracted to make maple syrup. Tree and foliage resemble *A. platanoides*. Leaves turn yellow-orange and crimson in autumn. Stylized interpretation of leaf is national symbol of Canada. *A. s.* **subsp.** *grandidentatum* (syn. *A. grandidentatum*) grows 35–40 ft (10–12 m) high; *A. s.* **subsp.** *leucoderme* (syn. *A. leucoderme*) grows to 25 ft (8 m) high; and *A. s.* **subsp.** *nigrum* (syn. *A. nigrum*) is known as the black maple for its black bark; '**Green Column**', light green foliage turning yellow to apricot orange in autumn; '**Temple's Upright**', narrow upright form. Cultivars include *A. s.* '**Flax Hill Majesty**', '**Green Mountain**', '**Legacy**', and '**Seneca Chief**'. Zones 4–9.

ACMENA

Fifteen species make up this genus from the myrtle (Myrtaceae) family of evergreen rainforest trees, native to eastern Australia and New Guinea. All *Acmena* species were once included in *Eugenia*, but that name is now restricted almost entirely to the

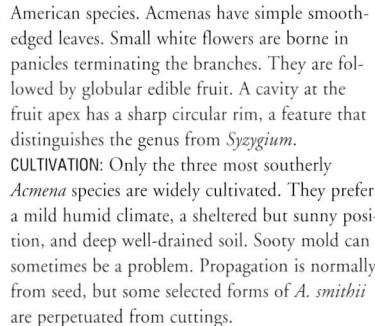

American species. Acmenas have simple smooth-edged leaves. Small white flowers are borne in panicles terminating the branches. They are followed by globular edible fruit. A cavity at the fruit apex has a sharp circular rim, a feature that distinguishes the genus from *Syzygium*.

CULTIVATION: Only the three most southerly *Acmena* species are widely cultivated. They prefer a mild humid climate, a sheltered but sunny position, and deep well-drained soil. Sooty mold can sometimes be a problem. Propagation is normally from seed, but some selected forms of *A. smithii* are perpetuated from cuttings.

Acmena ingens

syns *Acmena australis, Eugenia brachyandra*

RED APPLE

☼ ◗ ↔ 15–30 ft (4.5–9 m) ↑ 100 ft (30 m)

Tree from northeastern New South Wales to southeastern Queensland, Australia. Narrow pointed leaves. White flowers in summer. Large magenta or crimson fruit. Zones 9–11.

Acmena smithii

syn. *Eugenia smithii*

LILLYPILLY

☼ ◗ ↔ 35 ft (10 m) ↑ 60 ft (18 m)

Found along whole length of east Australian coast and ranges. Medium-sized tree with dense bushy crown, glossy green leaves, and tiny white flowers in summer. White to dull mauve fruit, edible, ripen in winter. Zones 9–12.

Acmena smithii

ACOKANTHERA

There are 7 species in this genus of evergreen shrubs and small trees, generally occurring in open forest and scrub from south-eastern Africa to southern Arabia. The genus belongs to the dog-bane (Apocynaceae) family and has similar poisonous properties. However, *Acokanthera* has been widely cultivated for ornament, with accidental poisoning being rare. Leaves are smooth, leathery, in opposite pairs or whorls of three. Sweet-scented, tubular, white flowers in the leaf axils are followed by fruit the shape and size of olives. Fruit, leaves, and bark all bleed a thick white sap.
CULTIVATION: These are tough shrubs and trees that are adapted to growing in exposed positions, and they are fairly drought and salt tolerant. In the garden they tolerate neglect as long as they are not too shaded by other trees or shrubs. Heavy pruning results in vigorous resprouting. Propagate from seed or soft tip cuttings.

Acokanthera oblongifolia

Acokanthera oblongifolia
syn. *Carissa spectabilis*
DUNE POISON BUSH, WINTERSWEET
☼ ❁ ↔ 5–8 ft (1.5–2.4 m) ↑ 10 ft (3 m)
Shrub native to coastal zone of eastern South Africa and adjacent Mozambique. Foliage often tinged purple, coloring more deeply in winter. Clusters of sweet-scented flowers, pink in bud, opening white. Fruit reddish, ripening black. 'Variegata', leaves marbled in white and gray-green, flushed pink. Zones 9–11.

ADENIUM

The current view is that this genus, which belongs to the dog-bane (Apocynaceae) family, consists of a single variable species ranging from southern Arabia through eastern and central Africa to northeastern South Africa. There are a number of subspecies, some with swollen succulent stems. Less succulent forms are popular ornamentals in tropical gardens around the world, dis-playing their striking trumpet-shaped blooms. The milky sap is believed to be poisonous. The fleshy leaves, widest toward the apex, are spirally arranged rather than opposite or whorled.
CULTIVATION: Drought and heat tolerant, adeniums are grown outdoors in the tropics, in containers or well-drained garden beds. In warm-temperate climates they can be grown against a hot sunny wall but in cool climates they require a greenhouse or conservatory with high light levels. Watering through summer and autumn promotes leaf growth and prolongs flowering. Propagation is from seed (if obtainable) or cuttings allowed to callus before planting.

Adenium obesum
syn. *Adenium multiflorum*
DESERT ROSE, IMPALA LILY, SABI STAR
☼ ❁ ↔ 5 ft (1.5 m) ↑ 5 ft (1.5 m)
Usually a shrub, branching into multiple stems with age, but can be more tree-like, reaching 15 ft (4.5 m) or more. Growing on sunny rock outcrops, roots are swollen and succulent, as are stem bases. Forms grown for showy flowers all belong to *A. o.* subsp. *obesum* ★; flower color of cultivars varies from pink to deep crim-son, commonly with white or paler zone, late summer–autumn.

Adenium obesum subsp. *swazicum*

A. o. subsp. *oleifolium*, tuberous and largely underground; *A. o.* subsp. *somaliense*, small tree, smooth hairless leaves; *A. o.* subsp. *swazicum*, also largely underground. Zones 10–12.

AESCULUS
BUCKEYE, HORSE CHESTNUT
There are about 15 species of deciduous shrubs to tall trees in this genus of the soap-berry (Sapindaceae) family. Half are native to North America, commonly called buck-eye; the remainder spread from Asia to south-eastern Europe. Growing in sheltered valleys, they have large compound leaves of 5 to 11 leaflets palmately arranged, and in spring–summer showy upright panicles of cream to reddish flowers are borne. Inedible fruits are held in big smooth to spiny seed capsules, and give rise to the other common name, horse chestnut.
CULTIVATION: These trees do best in cool-temperate climates with marked differences in summer and winter temperatures. The larger species suit parks and open landscapes where their pyramidal crowns can develop fully. They need a deep, fertile, and moisture-retentive soil. Propagation is from seed, which is best sown fresh, and cultivars are grafted in late winter.

Aesculus californica
CALIFORNIA BUCKEYE
☼ ❁ ↔ 30 ft (9 m) ↑ 15 ft (4.5 m)
From California and Oregon, USA. Spreading shrub with grayish green leaves. Cylindrical panicles of creamy white flowers, pink tinged, in summer, followed by fig-shaped fruit. Can stand hot dry summers. Deciduous in summer in dry areas. Zones 7–10.

Aesculus × carnea
syn. *Aesculus rubicunda*
RED HORSE CHESTNUT
☼ ❁ ↔ 15 ft (4.5 m) ↑ 30 ft (9 m)
Hybrid of *A. hippocastanum* and *A. pavia*. Erect panicles of deep reddish pink flowers with yellow blotches in spring. 'Briotii' (syn. *A. hippocastanum* 'Briotii'), bigger and darker flowers. Zones 6–9.

Aesculus hippocastanum

COMMON HORSE CHESTNUT, EUROPEAN HORSE CHESTNUT, HORSE CHESTNUT

☼ ❋ ↔ 70 ft (21 m) ↑ 100 ft (30 m)

Spreading tree from Greece, Albania, and Bulgaria. Best suited to large gardens. Erect panicles of white flowers with yellow to red basal blotches in late spring, followed by round prickly fruits commonly known as conkers. '**Baumannii**', rounded crown and showy, white, double flowers; '**Pyramidalis**', pyramidal growth habit. Zones 6–9.

Aesculus parviflora

BOTTLEBRUSH BUCKEYE

☼ ❋ ↔ 15 ft (4.5 m) ↑ 10 ft (3 m)

Shrub growing in woodland areas of southeastern USA. Leaves downy beneath, buff-colored when young. Slender panicles of white summer flowers with protruding pink stamens. *A. p. f. serotina*, leaves less downy, bluish green. Zones 6–10.

Aesculus parviflora

Aesculus pavia

syn. *Aesculus splendens*

RED BUCKEYE

☼ ❋ ↔ 10 ft (3 m) ↑ 15 ft (4.5 m)

From woodlands on coastal plains of eastern USA. Shrub or small tree. Leaves reddish in autumn. Crimson flowers on short erect panicles in early summer. '**Atrosanguinea**', deep red flowers. Zones 6–10.

AFROCARPUS

The 6 or so species of this African genus of conifers, of the podocarp or plum-pine (Podocarpaceae) family, were formerly included in *Podocarpus*. In their native habitats they are tall forest trees with massive trunks, seen in mountainous regions of central, eastern, and southern Africa. All have attractive bark that peels off in flakes or strips. Leaves are leathery and narrow. Male (pollen) and female (seed) organs are on different trees; female cones have a thin stalk with a single, usually larger seed with a thick juicy outer layer. CULTIVATION: These slow-growing trees suit parks and avenues in warm-temperate and subtropical climates with adequate rainfall. Plant in deep, well-drained, reasonably fertile soil. They are affected by few pests or diseases and require little shaping. Propagate from seed, sown fresh after removing the fleshy coating.

Afrocarpus falcatus

syns *Nageia falcata*, *Podocarpus falcatus*

OUTENIQUA YELLOWWOOD

☼ ◖ ↔ 25–50 ft (8–15 m) ↑ 60–200 ft (18–60 m)

One of South Africa's largest trees. In cultivation reaches 30–50 ft (9–15 m). Peeling and flaky bark, purplish brown to paler red-brown. Fine dense foliage, drab green. Female trees covered in pale yellow "fruit" in summer–autumn. Zones 9–11.

AGATHIS

KAURI

These conifers, which grow into massive trees, are from the araucaria (Araucariaceae) family. This genus is of great evolutionary interest because it dates back to the temperate rainforests that covered much of the southern supercontinent of Gondwana. The species are scattered from Sumatra in the northwest to New Zealand and Fiji in the southeast. Kauri trees have a straight smooth trunk, developing massive ascending limbs with age. Peeling bark produces distinctive patterns. Broad leathery leaves, with no midrib, are arranged in almost opposite pairs. Cones are almost globular with tightly packed scales. CULTIVATION: *Agathis* grow readily in the wet tropics and in warmer temperate climates. They prefer deep soil with reliable subsoil moisture. Height growth may be quite fast, but a large trunk diameter takes many decades to achieve. Propagate only from seed, gathered as soon as it falls and sown immediately.

Agathis australis

NEW ZEALAND KAURI

☼ ❋ ↔ 50 ft (15 m) ↑ 150 ft (45 m)

New Zealand's largest native tree. Found in swampy lowland forests in North Island. Small leaves, 1½ in (35 mm) long, closely crowded on adult branches. Slow growing, dense conical or columnar form. Bark dappled gray and brown with small thick scales detaching. Bluish cones in summer. Zones 8–10.

Agathis robusta

QUEENSLAND KAURI

☼ ◖ ↔ 40 ft (12 m) ↑ 180 ft (55 m)

Huge tree with orange-tan bark finely dappled with gray, becoming flaky with age. Fast growing in cultivation, with pole-like trunk and short side branches. At full size stem diameter increases rapidly. Zones 9–12.

AGONIS

This small genus consists of 12 evergreen species growing naturally in temperate regions of southwest Western Australia. All have white or pink flowers. Like other members of the myrtle (Myrtaceae) family, the leaves contain aromatic oil, released when the leaves are crushed. The fibrous bark is a feature of the genus.

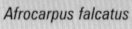

Afrocarpus falcatus

Agathis robusta

CULTIVATION: An adaptable, almost pest-free genus, suited to full sun in a range of well-drained soils and climates. Some species can be damaged by frost. Tip prune at any time for bushier growth; trees also respond to pruning after flowering. Propagate species from seed or cuttings, cultivars from cuttings only.

Agonis flexuosa ★
PEPPERMINT TREE, WILLOW MYRTLE
☼ ❄ ↔ 15 ft (4.5 m) ↑ 30 ft (9 m)
Dome shape and weeping habit when mature. White flowers resemble tea-tree. '**Nana**', to 10 ft (3 m); dwarf form '**Weeping Wonder**', to 3 ft (0.9 m); '**Belbra Gold**' and '**Variegata**', dainty variegated foliage forms. Zones 9–11.

Albizia saman

AILANTHUS
There are 5 or 6 species of medium-sized to large trees in this genus, in the quassia (Simaroubaceae) family, occurring from India to northern China and Australia. They include both evergreen tropical and deciduous cold-hardy species. Leaves are pinnate, mostly with a long midrib and many leaflets arranged in 2 regular rows. Flowers, of different sexes on different trees, are small and greenish yellow, in large stalked clusters in leaf axils toward tips of branches, followed by clusters of flat elongated fruits.
CULTIVATION: Easily cultivated if their respective climatic requirements are met, they make fast growth when young. Propagate from seed (may need cold stratification) or root cuttings.

Ailanthus altissima
syn. *Ailanthus glandulosa*
TREE OF HEAVEN
☼ ❄ ↔ 40 ft (12 m) ↑ 40 ft (12 m)
Deciduous tree from China. Long pinnate leaves with unpleasant smell. Female trees flower in mid-summer, fruit in early autumn. Profuse suckers; a weed in many areas. Zones 5–10.

ALBIZIA
This genus contains trees, shrubs, and vines in the mimosa subfamily of the legumes. Most have feathery foliage of bipinnate compound leaves and showy flowerheads of prominent stamens in pink, cream, or white followed by flattened pods.
CULTIVATION: Tolerant of poor soils, they perform best on well-drained loam in a sheltered position, requiring moisture and warmth in summer. As seeds have impermeable coats, soak in sulfuric acid for half an hour, then wash thoroughly prior to sowing. In early spring, root cuttings of at least ½ in (12 mm) diameter planted immediately are also successful.

Albizia julibrissin
PERSIAN SILK TREE, PINK SIRIS, SILK TREE
☼ ❄ ↔ 15–20 ft (4.5–6 m) ↑ 20–40 ft (6–12 m)
Deciduous tree from Japan and western Asia. Pinkish inflorescences with silky stamens in summer. Feathery compound leaves dark green, paler beneath, yellowish in autumn. Zones 6–12.

Albizia saman
syn. *Samanea saman*
MONKEY POD, RAIN TREE, SAMAN
☼/◑ ❄ ↔ 50–100 ft (15–30 m) ↑ 100 ft (30 m)
Evergreen or briefly deciduous tree found from Caribbean and Central America to Brazil. Broad spreading crown of pinnate leaves with fine leaflets. Pink flowerheads, clustered, followed by edible black-brown seed pods. Zones 10–12.

ALEURITES
This genus in the spurge (Euphorbiaceae) family includes 5 evergreen and deciduous Asian–Australasian species, 3 of which are important for the oils obtained from their large seeds. They are medium-sized to large trees with a straight central trunk and tiered branches. Leaves are large and heart-shaped. Flowers are mostly funnel-shaped with 5 white or cream petals, in large clusters at branch tips. Fruits are globular, the husk enclosing 2 to 5 large nut-like seeds, which may cause violent vomiting if eaten.
CULTIVATION: Best in climates with long humid summers, they thrive in deep fertile soils but will grow in poorer soils. Deciduous species tolerate moderate winter frosts. Propagate from fresh seed in autumn, or from hardwood cuttings for deciduous species.

Aleurites fordii
syn. *Vernicia fordii*
TUNG-OIL TREE
☼ ❄ ↔ 10 ft (3 m) ↑ 25 ft (8 m)
Deciduous tree from China, cultivated for seed oil. Compact crown, broad heart-shaped leaves. White flowers with red centers in spring. Fruit green, ripening black, in summer. Zones 8–11.

Aleurites moluccana
syn. *Aleurites triloba*
CANDLENUT TREE
☼ ❄ ↔ 35 ft (10 m) ↑ 80 ft (24 m)
Evergreen forest tree from tropical Asia to islands of western Pacific. Glossy heart-shaped leaves. Small cream flowers in spring. Green fruit in summer. Zones 10–12.

ALLAMANDA

This genus, a member of the dogbane (Apocynaceae) family, consists of around 12 evergreen shrubs, including both upright and semi-climbing species. They are tropical American natives and are lush, colorful, and flamboyant. The large, glossy, deep green leaves are the perfect foil to the flowers, usually a deep golden yellow. The flowers appear mainly in summer and autumn and are trumpet-shaped with a widely flared throat and 5 large, overlapping petals. CULTIVATION: Protection from frost is paramount, and a moist subtropical to tropical climate is best, though it is possible to grow allamandas in sheltered areas in cooler zones. For a prolific flower display give them rich well-drained soil and plenty of summer moisture. They also do well in conservatories but watch out for insects. Propagation is usually from half-hardened cuttings.

Allamanda schottii
syn. *Allamanda neriifolia*
BUSH ALLAMANDA

☼ ✦ ↔ 6 ft (1.8 m) ↕ 6 ft (1.8 m)

South American species, kept neat with regular pinching back and annual spring trim. Glossy deep green leaves, bright golden yellow flowers streaked light orange, large green seed pods. Zones 11–12.

ALLOCASUARINA
SHE-OAK

Allocasuarina, part of the she-oak (Casuarinaceae) family, has 59 species entirely confined to Australia, all trees or shrubs with a pine-like appearance. The fine twigs appear leafless, but in fact have whorls of narrow leaves fused flat against their surfaces, with only tips remaining free and appearing as rings of minute teeth at regular intervals along the twig. The number of teeth per ring is a characteristic feature of each species. Flowers are mostly of different sexes on different plants. Fruits are fused into a cone-like spike, splitting apart to release the "seeds." CULTIVATION: Most species are adapted to poor sandy or stony soils, low in essential nutrients; however taller tree species adapt to more fertile soils. Propagation is from seed, which quickly falls out of gathered cones and germinates readily.

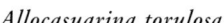
Alnus glutinosa

Allocasuarina torulosa
syn. *Casuarina torulosa*
FOREST OAK, FOREST SHE-OAK

☼/◑ ❋ ↔ 20 ft (6 m) ↕ 40–80 ft (12–24 m)

Native to eastern Australian coast. Coppery drooping branches and branchlets in winter. Corky light brown bark. Male flowers golden orange in autumn. Rounded warty cones. Zones 8–11.

ALLOXYLON

Belonging to the protea (Proteaceae) family, *Alloxylon* comprises 4 species of evergreen rainforest trees native to tropical and subtropical eastern Australia and New Guinea. Conspicuous red or pinkish flowers in large terminal clusters attract nectar-feeding birds. The leaves are irregularly lobed or pinnate, though tending

Alloxylon flammeum

to become unlobed and simple on flowering branches. The fruit is a large follicle that splits to release winged seeds. CULTIVATION: They are demanding, requiring a subtropical climate with year-round rainfall, or tropical hill conditions with a not too severe dry season. Soil must be well drained and moderately fertile, and the trees sheltered from strong winds. Young plants less than 10–15 ft (3–4.5 m) tall are prone to sudden wilting and death. Propagation is from seed, sown as soon as collected.

Alloxylon flammeum
syn. *Oreocallis wickhamii* of gardens
WARATAH TREE

☼ ❈ ↔ 20 ft (6 m) ↕ 60 ft (18 m)

From Atherton Tableland of far northeastern Queensland, Australia. Dark green sapling leaves to 18 in (45 cm) long with 3 to 7 large lobes, smaller on flowering shoots. Bright scarlet flower clusters in late winter–spring. Zones 10–11.

ALNUS
ALDER

Alnus, of the birch (Betulaceae) family, is an essentially Northern Hemisphere genus. Of the 25 alder species only 2 extend across the equator. All are deciduous or semi-evergreen. In the wild, alders are fast-growing pioneer trees of disturbed ground. Alders mostly have darker brownish or blackish bark, with leaves usually larger and slightly thicker than birches; leaf margins vary from smooth and wavy to jaggedly toothed, winter buds sticky and aromatic. The flowers are tiny and arranged in catkins; the male is long and thin, while the female is short and barrel-shaped. CULTIVATION: These plants are easily grown in their appropriate climate. Sapling growth is often very fast but they mature early and are sometimes not very long lived. Many are able to thrive in soils of low fertility and poor drainage, aided by nitrogen-fixing fungi in the roots. Propagation is normally from seed, which may need stratification over winter and should not be covered, as germination is stimulated by light. Some cultivars require grafting.

Alnus acuminata

syn. *Alnus jorullensis* of gardens

EVERGREEN ALDER, MEXICAN ALDER

☼ ❀ ↔ 20 ft (6 m) ↑ 40 ft (12 m)

Often misidentified as *A. jorullensis,* a close relation. Evergreen broad-crowned tree in warm climates. Narrow drooping leaves tapering to long points, jaggedly toothed. Brownish yellow male catkins. *A. a.* subsp. *glabrata* is the form in cultivation. Zones 8–11.

Alnus glutinosa

BLACK ALDER, COMMON ALDER

☼ ❀ ↔ 35 ft (10 m) ↑ 60 ft (18 m)

From Europe to Siberia and North Africa. Deciduous tree, may reach 30 ft (9 m) in cultivation. Leaves dark green, rounded, shallowly toothed. Buds and twigs sticky. Male catkins dull purple to yellow. Female catkins purple to burgundy to green to brown. 'Imperialis', open habit; 'Laciniata', dissected leaves. Zones 4–8.

Alnus incana

GRAY ALDER

☼ ❀ ↔ 30 ft (9 m) ↑ 70 ft (21 m)

Found in Caucasus and mountains of Europe. Bark smooth gray. Gray down on young shoots and undersides of leaves. *A. i.* subsp. *tenuifolia* (syn. *A. tenuifolia*), smaller with red downy young shoots that are soon smooth. *A. i.* 'Aurea', yellowish foliage; 'Laciniata', narrow-lobed leaves; and 'Pendula', weeping form. Zones 3–9.

Alnus rubra

syn. *Alnus oregona*

OREGON ALDER, RED ALDER

☼ ❀ ↔ 30 ft (9 m) ↑ 50 ft (15 m)

From canyons and riverbanks of North America. Fast growing tree, pyramidal crown, somewhat pendulous habit. Young shoots dark red; reddish brown down on new leaves, turning dark green above and blue-gray beneath. Zones 4–9.

ALYOGYNE

Once included within the genus *Hibiscus*, the 4 species that make up this genus, of the mallow (Malvaceae) family, are distinctive, evergreen, Australian shrubs which, despite their delicate silky blooms, are native to the drier regions of the western half of the continent. Leaves are variable; in some species they are smooth-edged, in others palmately lobed. They are fast growing and, as though to make up for their short-lived single blooms, usually in pinks or mauves, they flower profusely over a long period. CULTIVATION: These are hardy plants for non-humid areas. Most are able to survive frost. They do best planted in full sun and can survive in all soil types but appreciate good drainage. Pruning is sometimes necessary. Propagate from cuttings or seed.

Alyogyne huegelii ★

BLUE HIBISCUS

☼ ⚬ ↔ 3–6 ft (0.9–1.8 m) ↑ 3–6 ft (0.9–1.8 m)

Fast growing. Flowers pale mauve to purplish with overlapping petals set against pale green, slightly felty, deeply lobed leaves. 'Monterey Bay' and 'Santa Cruz' are popular cultivars. Zones 9–10.

AMELANCHIER

SERVICEBERRY

Amelanchier, a member of the rose (Rosaceae) family, consists of 30 or so species of deciduous shrubs and small trees from North America and Mexico, with one species in China, and another in Europe and Turkey. All have smallish oval or elliptical leaves with finely toothed margins. Flowers, each with 5 white narrow petals, are borne in small sprays; the small hawthorn-like fruit has sepals at the apex. The fruit ripens to blue-black and is edible. CULTIVATION: These are mostly woodland plants preferring moist sheltered sites, while some species do well at the edge of a pond or stream. They are prone to the same pests and diseases as apples, pears, and hawthorns, including fireblight. Propagation is normally from seed, germination being aided by cold stratification, or by layering of low branches or suckers. Cultivars are often grafted.

Amelanchier alnifolia

syn. *Amelanchier florida*

ALDERLEAF SERVICEBERRY, JUNEBERRY, SASKATOON SERVICEBERRY

◐ ❀ ↔ 12 ft (3.5 m) ↑ 3–6 ft (0.9–1.8 m)

North American species found on banks of rivulets or on sheltered mountainsides. Leaves rounded, toothed mainly in upper half, 1 in (25 mm) long. Flowers in late spring–early summer, dark purple edible fruit. *A. a.* var. *semiintegrifolia* (syn. *A. florida*), from southern Alaska to northern California. Zones 3–9.

Amelanchier arborea

syn. *Amelanchier canadensis* of gardens

DOWNY SERVICEBERRY

☼ ❀ ↔ 30 ft (9 m) ↑ 60 ft (18 m)

From eastern USA. Narrow rounded crown. Silver-gray smooth bark, rough with age. Leaves abruptly pointed, turn red or yellow in autumn. Flowers early spring. Small purple-black fruit. Zones 4–9.

Amelanchier canadensis

syn. *Amelanchier oblongifolia*

JUNEBERRY, SERVICEBERRY, SHADBLOW SERVICEBERRY

◐ ❀ ↔ 10 ft (3 m) ↑ 25 ft (8 m)

Upright suckering shrub or small tree mainly from boggy ground in eastern North America. Woolly new leaves, spring flowers in upright sprays, juicy blue-black fruit about ½ in (12 mm) wide. Cultivars include 'Glenn Form' and 'Sprizam'. Zones 5–9.

Alyogyne huegelii

Angophora costata, in the wild, New South Wales, Australia

Amelanchier laevis
syn. *Amelanchier canadensis* of gardens
ALLEGHENY SERVICEBERRY, SARVIS TREE
☀ ❋ ↔ 25 ft (8 m) ↕ 25 ft (8 m)
Found mainly in Appalachian mountains of eastern USA, extending into Canada. Bronzy purple slightly downy new leaves; sweet, juicy, blue-black fruit. Flowers as leaves unfold in late spring. Zones 4–9.

Amelanchier lamarckii
LAMARCK SERVICEBERRY
☀ ❋ ↔ 35 ft (10 m) ↕ 30 ft (9 m)
Probable hybrid origin. Small tree with spreading branches, leaves silky-haired, bronzy red when new. Loose sprays of flowers open with new leaves. Fruit purple-black. Zones 4–9.

AMHERSTIA
The 1 species of this genus, of the cassia sub-family of legumes (Fabaceae), is from the lowlands of southern Myanmar, and almost unknown in the wild. It has long pinnate leaves with glossy leaflets and may be briefly deciduous. At the start of the wet season pale bronzy pink new leaves emerge, changing through brown to green. On long stalks, flowers are orchid-like with a pair of large pink bracts at the base, up to 4 in (10 cm) across, pinkish red with darker red and yellow markings. Rarely produced are the curved woody pods.
CULTIVATION: *Amherstia* has been successfully cultivated only in the lowland wet tropics. Its growth is fairly slow, and it needs a sheltered but sunny situation and deep moist soil. Propagate from seed if it can be obtained; an alternative is layering of low branches.

Amherstia nobilis
PRIDE OF BURMA
☀ ✦ ↔ 50 ft (15 m) ↕ 40 ft (12 m)
Lovely tree with broad low-branching canopy of foliage. Mature specimens may flower for much of year, but flowering season is spring–early summer. Red orchid-like flowers. Zone 12.

Amelanchier lamarckii

ANDROMEDA
Two fully hardy, low-growing, evergreen shrub species make up this genus of the heath (Ericaceae) family, found growing in the acid peat bogs of the Northern Hemisphere. The somewhat leathery, smooth-edged, small oblong leaves form a deep green background to the tiny, white or pink, bell-like flowers held in terminal clusters during spring.
CULTIVATION: *Andromeda* species require an acid soil where constant moisture is assured, and are best grown in peat beds, shady woodlands, or rock gardens. They can be propagated from suckers, by layering, or from softwood cuttings.

Andromeda polifolia
BOG ROSEMARY, MARSH ANDROMEDA
☀ ❋ ↔ 22 in (55 cm) ↕ 4–18 in (10–45 cm)
Variable growing shrub, either erect or prostrate. Small, pointed, oblong leaves with clusters of bell-like flowers in spring or early summer. 'Alba', low-growing prostrate shrub with pure white flowers; 'Compacta', compact growth habit, pink flowers; and 'Macrophylla', larger leaves and pink flowers. Zones 2–9.

ANGOPHORA
This eastern Australian genus of the myrtle (Myrtaceae) family is closely allied to *Eucalyptus* and *Corymbia*. Its 15 species of evergreen trees have separate sepals and petals enclosing the buds. Most are medium to large trees of open forest, woodland, and heath. Bark is usually rough, rather corky or flaky, though smooth in some species. Leaves, in opposite pairs, vary from narrow pointed to broad heart-shaped. Flowers have masses of white to cream stamens, in terminal clusters at the branch tips. Blooms are followed by ribbed woody capsules.
CULTIVATION: These trees are light-loving and fast growing, preferring sandy moderately fertile soils and shelter from strong winds. Most tolerate a degree or two of overnight frost as long as days are warm and sunny. Propagate from seed, to be collected just as capsules discharge.

Angophora costata
syn. *Angophora lanceolata*
ANGOPHORA, RUSTY GUM, SYDNEY RED GUM
☀ ✦ ↔ 80 ft (24 m) ↕ 100 ft (30 m)
From sandy forest country of coastal New South Wales, Australia. Pinkish gray bark sheds in early summer to reveal bright orange-brown bark. Deep wine red new foliage. Clusters of white flowers in spring–early summer. Zones 9–11.

Angophora hispida
syn. *Angophora cordifolia*
DWARF APPLE
☀ ✦ ↔ 12 ft (3.5 m) ↕ 10 ft (3 m)
Localized to sandstone ridges around Sydney, Australia. Broad, harsh-textured leaves. Flowers in large heads, in mid-spring–summer. New shoots and flower buds have deep red bristles. Zones 10–11.

ANISODONTEA

This genus of 20 species of shrubs and subshrubs in the mallow (Malvaceae) family is native to South Africa. They are half-hardy evergreen species with toothed leaves that can be palmately lobed or elliptic and toothed. Flowers are 5-petalled with shallow cups. CULTIVATION: Plants do best in loam-based gritty compost. Grown indoors, they need maximum light. Outdoors they need full sun and should be fed in spring. Pot-grown specimens should receive a balanced fertilizer once a month. In winter, watering should be reduced and feeding stopped. New plants can be tip pruned for bushiness, pruning old wood in spring. Pot plants are prone to red spider mite and white fly. Seeds should be sown in spring. Take half-hardened cuttings in summer, but they need bottom heat.

Anisodontea capensis

syn. *Malvastrum capensis*

↔30 in (75 cm) ↑3 ft (0.9 m)

Erect shrub with hairy stems and ovate to triangular leaves. Flowers pale red to deep red-purple, up to 1 in (25 mm) across, most of year in warm climates, all summer in cool-temperate. Zones 9–11.

APHELANDRA

This genus, a member of the acanthus (Acanthaceae) family, consists of about 170 species of shrubs and subshrubs. Short-lived red and yellow flowers appear year-round. Native to tropical North, Central, and South America, all species are frost tender and live in the wild as understory plants in moist woodland. CULTIVATION: To grow in pots, combine loam-based compost in the ratio 2:1, with one part of leaf mold. These plants thrive when watered with rainwater (soft water). They should be fed regularly through the growing season, with food and water reduced throughout dormancy. Avoid drafts and direct sun. After flowering, cut back plants to encourage side shoots, which can be used for propagation. Spider mites, aphids, and scale insects can be a problem under glass.

Aphelandra sinclairiana

↔10 ft (3 m) ↑15 ft (4.5 m)

Central America species, often grown as house plant. Deep pink flowers open from candle-like, orange-pink-bracted flower spikes. Leaves bright mid-green, covering of fine hairs. Zones 10–12.

Aphelandra squarrosa

SAFFRON SPIKE, ZEBRA PLANT

↔5 ft (1.5 m) ↑6 ft (1.8 m)

Native to Brazil. Leaves 12 in (30 cm) long, heavy cream veining, pronounced midrib. Flower spikes of generally yellow flowers with cream, yellow, or maroon bracts. **'Claire'**, broad cream zones along leaf veins; **'Leopoldii'**, yellow or orange flowers; **'Louisae'**, white veins against dark green background; and **'Snow Queen'**, silvery white veins and lemon flowers. Zones 11–12.

ARALIA

From the ivy (Araliaceae) family, this genus of trees, shrubs, and herbaceous perennials consists of around 40 species mostly from Southeast Asia and North, Central, and South America. Most are deciduous and nearly all have large compound leaves. Flowers are small, numerous, usually cream, carried in umbels arranged in panicles terminating the branches, followed by black fruits. Some species have prickly stems, and suckering can occur. Roots and bark of several species are used in traditional medicine. CULTIVATION: All species known in cultivation will tolerate at least light frosts, but most need a warm humid summer for best growth. They prefer deep reasonably fertile soil and shelter from strong winds. Though shade tolerant, they grow and flower better in sun. Propagate from seed, which for tree species may need cold stratification, or from root cuttings or basal suckers.

Aralia elata

JAPANESE ANGELICA TREE

↔30 ft (9 m) ↑40 ft (12 m)

Native to Japan, shrub spread by root suckers, with prickly corky trunk. Bipinnate leaves, to 4 ft (1.2 m) long, yellow-purplish in autumn. Large panicles of near-white flowers in late summer. **'Aureomarginata'**, yellow leaf margins, turning to creamy white; **'Variegata'** ★ (syn. 'Albomarginata'), white leaf margins. Zones 4–9.

Aralia spinosa

AMERICAN ANGELICA TREE, DEVIL'S WALKING-STICK, HERCULES CLUB

↔15 ft (4.5 m) ↑20 ft (6 m)

Occurring wild in damp woodland from Pennsylvania, USA, southward. Bipinnate leaves, up to 3 ft (0.9 m) long, turning yellow in autumn. Panicles of flowers in mid- to late summer. Zones 5–9.

Anisodontea capensis

Aphelandra sinclairiana

Aralia spinosa

ARAUCARIA

This ancient conifer genus from the araucaria (Araucariaceae) family consists of 19 species—13 from New Caledonia, 2 from South America, 2 from Australia, 2 from New Guinea (1 also in Australia), and 1 from Norfolk Island. Araucarias have a distinctive growth habit with a straight trunk and usually whorled branches; the spirally arranged leaves are densely crowded and often overlapping on flexible branchlets. Male and female organs are on the same tree, the tassel-like pollen cones on the side branches, and egg-shaped seed cones with spine-tipped scales near the top of the crown. The seeds, which may be quite large and nut-like, are embedded in the tough cone scales, a feature unique to this genus. CULTIVATION: Cold tolerance varies, and these plants cannot be grown outdoors in severe climates. They are best grown as conservatory plants and may be kept in tubs for many years. In warmer climates araucarias are grown in large gardens, parks, and avenues. Propagation is from fresh seed, which germinates readily; cuttings tend to retain sideways growth if taken from lower branches.

Arbutus unedo

Araucaria araucana
syn. Araucaria imbricata
MONKEY PUZZLE TREE
☼ ❄ ↔ 35 ft (10 m) ↑ 80 ft (24 m)
From Andean slopes of south-central Chile. Young trees have tangle of upcurved branches, developing broad crown with age. Leaves densely overlapping, rigid, sharp pointed. Globular seed cones 3–6 in (8–15 cm) in diameter. Zones 7–9.

Araucaria araucana, in the wild, Chile

Araucaria bidwillii
BUNYA BUNYA, BUNYA PINE
☼ ❄ ↔ 35 ft (10 m) ↑ 150 ft (45 m)
From Queensland, Australia. Sharp-pointed leaves, up to 2 in (5 cm) long, glossy dark green, arranged on branchlets that are soon shed. Large seed cones up to 12 in (30 cm) in diameter. Zones 9–11.

Araucaria cunninghamii
HOOP PINE
☼ ❄ ↔ 12 ft (3.5 m) ↑ 150 ft (45 m)
Native to eastern Australia. Dark gray bark often furrowed into "hoops" encircling trunk. Juvenile foliage prickly. Adult leaves small, densely overlapping, very dark green. Bluish-leafed forms are known. A. c. var. papuana, from New Guinea. Zones 9–12.

Araucaria heterophylla
syn. Araucaria excelsa
NORFOLK ISLAND PINE
☼ ❄ ↔ 25 ft (8 m) ↑ 200 ft (60 m)
From Norfolk Island. Very symmetrical form, with regularly whorled branches on which branchlets form 2 neat rows with V-shaped trough between. Best near seashores in subtropical regions; not pollution tolerant. Zones 10–11.

ARBUTUS

This small genus contains about 8 to 10 species of small evergreen trees belonging to the heath or erica (Ericaceae) family, which are known as strawberry trees due to their strawberry-like fruit. They occur in the Mediterranean region, western Asia, and southwestern USA, with a few species in Central America and Mexico. All have attractive bell-shaped flowers and red or yellow fruit, and in some cases have red or cinnamon-colored, stringy, peeling bark. CULTIVATION: Arbutus like a well-drained soil, preferably free of lime, and an open sunny position protected from cold winds. Most species are tolerant of sustained cold winters. Little pruning is required. Propagation is from half-hardened cuttings taken in autumn or winter; scions can also be top-grafted on seedling understocks. Seeds can be sown in spring.

Arbutus andrachne
GRECIAN STRAWBERRY TREE
☼ ❄ ↔ 20 ft (6 m) ↑ 20 ft (6 m)
From eastern Mediterranean. Cinnamon brown bark flakes away to reveal greenish cream bark beneath. White pitcher-shaped flowers, in upright clusters, in spring, followed by orange-red fruit. Protect from frost when young. Zones 7–10.

Arbutus 'Marina'
☼ ❄ ↔ 20–40 ft (6–12 m) ↑ 25–50 ft (8–15 m)
Possibly clone of A. × andrachnoides or with some hybrid influence of A. canariensis. First noticed in a San Francisco garden in 1984. Smooth reddish bark, bronze new leaves, pink-flushed flowers nearly all year, yellow fruit ageing red, edible. Zones 8–10.

Arbutus menziesii ★
MADRONA, MADRONE, PACIFIC MADRONE

☼ ❄ ↔ 30 ft (9 m) ↥ 30 ft (9 m)

From Pacific coast of northern USA. Spreading, shrubby. Bright brick red bark peels to reveal green new layer. White flowers, in drooping clusters. Fruit orange-red. Zones 7–10.

Arbutus unedo
IRISH STRAWBERRY TREE, STRAWBERRY TREE

☼ ❄ ↔ 20 ft (6 m) ↥ 25 ft (8 m)

Occurring in Mediterranean region and Ireland. Red stringy bark, often arranged in spiral fashion. Flowers white, flushed with pink, in autumn–winter. Fruit ripening green to orange-red to bright red, edible though bland. Tolerant of pollution. *A. u.* f. *rubra,* 4–6 ft (1.2–1.5 m) tall. *A. u.* 'Compacta', smaller form; '**Elfin King**', bushy form; and '**Oktoberfest**', pink-flowered form. Zones 7–10.

Arctostaphylos pumila   Arctostaphylos uva-ursi

ARCTOSTAPHYLOS
There are about 50 species in this genus of mostly evergreen small shrubs and trees in the heath or erica (Ericaceae) family. The genus is found only in North America, except for 2 species from the alpine-arctic regions of the Northern Hemisphere. They have reddish brown ornamental bark, smooth or peeling in flakes. Leaves are alternate, smooth or toothed. White or pink bell- or urn-shaped flowers are in terminal racemes or panicles. Fruits are spherical. In the UK, leaves of *A. uva-ursi* have been used as a urinary antiseptic since the thirteenth century.
CULTIVATION: They need lime-free soil, and are mostly disease-free except for leaf spot. In pots water freely and feed in the growing season. Withhold water and fertilizer from western North American species in summer. Put seed in boiling water for 15–20 seconds before sowing in autumn with protection against frosts. Layer prostrate species in autumn. Plant half-hardened cuttings in summer.

Arctostaphylos densiflora
☼/◐ ❄ ↔ 6 ft (1.8 m) ↥ 5 ft (1.5 m)

Native to Sonoma County, California, USA. Procumbent shrub with dark red to nearly black, smooth bark. Flowers in small short panicles, white with tinge of pink. Leaves glossy, mid-green, elliptical. '**Emerald Carpet**', dense ground cover up to 12 in (30 cm) high; '**Howard McMinn**', denser than species. Zones 8–10.

Arctostaphylos hookeri
MONTEREY MANZANITA

☼ ❄ ↔ 4–15 ft (1.2–4.5 m) ↥ 6–48 in (15–120 cm)

Coastal species found from San Francisco Bay to near Monterey, California, USA, often on dunes. Forms extensive dense mat, mounding with age. Leaves small, shiny green. Flowers white to pink, in winter–spring. Fruit shiny red, in summer. *A. h.* subsp. *franciscana* (Franciscan manzanita), mat-forming, from San Francisco Peninsula, extinct in wild but preserved in cultivation; *A. h.* subsp. *hearstiorum* (Hearsts' manzanita), quite prostrate, rooting along stems, leaves under ½ in (12 mm) long; *A. h.* subsp. *montana* (Tamalpais manzanita), more erect or mounding form, sometimes to 6 ft (1.8 m) high. *A. h.* '**Monterey Carpet**', compact cultivar. Zones 8–10.

Arctostaphylos manzanita
MANZANITA

☼ ❄ ↔ 10 ft (3 m) ↥ 15 ft (4.5 m)

From California and Oregon, USA. Bark red to brown, tending to peel. Leaves leathery, hairy, oval, green to gray-green. Deep pink flowers in early spring. White fruit, ripening to red-brown, in autumn. '**Doctor Hurd**', upright cultivar. Zones 8–10.

Arctostaphylos pumila
DUNE MANZANITA, SANDMAT MANZANITA

☼ ❄ ↔ 3–10 ft (0.9–3 m) ↥ 1–5 ft (0.3–1.5 m)

From coastal dunes around Monterey Bay, California, USA. Prostrate to mound-forming shrub, ascending branches. Dull green leaves. Small groups of white, sometimes pale pink, flowers in late winter–early spring. Pea-sized, brown fruit in summer. Zones 8–10.

Arctostaphylos uva-ursi
BEARBERRY, KINNIKINICK

☼ ❄ ↔ 20 in (50 cm) ↥ 4 in (10 cm)

Native of cool-temperate regions of Northern Hemisphere. White flowers flushed pink, followed by red fruit. Leaves are traditionally smoked in North America and used for herbal tea in Europe. '**Massachusetts**', vigorous mat-former, to 12 in (30 cm) high and 15 ft (4.5 m) wide; '**Vancouver Jade**', glossy leaves, vigorous habit, ability to resist diseases; and '**Wood's Red**', dwarf cultivar with pink flowers, large shiny red fruit, red young shoots. Zones 4–9.

Arctostaphylos Hybrid Cultivars
☼/◐ ❄ ↔ 5–15 ft (1.5–4.5 m) ↥ 6 in–10 ft (15 cm–3 m)

Nearly all these hybrids originated in wild or as accidental crosses in gardens. They range from low mat-forming plants to tall shrubs. '**Indian Hill**', possible form of *A. edmundsii*, extensive mat of glossy bright green foliage, new shoots attractive bronze, white flowers in winter; '**John Dourley**' ★, of uncertain classification, mound-forming shrub, dense bluish green foliage, bronze new growths, pale pink flowers; '**Pacific Mist**', mat-forming to mound-forming shrub, pink young branches, narrow gray-green leaves, white flowers; '**Sunset**', densely mounding shrub, dark red branches, deep gray-green foliage, bright new growths, pink flowers. Zones 8–10.

ARDISIA

Over 250 species of evergreen shrubs and small trees make up this Myrsinaceae family genus, occurring in the tropics and subtropics of all continents except Africa. They occur mainly in high-rainfall mountain areas. Leaves are simple with margins sometimes toothed or crinkled, crowded at the ends of branchlets. A common feature is translucent brownish spots or streaks in the leaves, more easily seen in thinner leaves. The small flowers are mostly star-shaped, borne in stalked umbels among the outer leaves; the 5 petals are often patterned with tiny spots. Fruits are small one-seeded berries. CULTIVATION: Most are shade-loving plants and prefer humid conditions protected from the wind. Soil should be well drained, humus rich, and moisture retentive. Indoor plants should be kept away from hot sunny positions. They can be cut back near the base, resulting in renewal by vigorous shoots. Propagation is usually from seed; cuttings can also be used.

Argyranthemum, Hybrid Cultivar, Butterfly/'Ulyssis'

Argyranthemum, Hybrid Cultivar, 'Petite Pink'

Ardisia crenata

CORAL ARDISIA, CORALBERRY

☀ ❄ ↔ 18 in (45 cm) ↑ 6 ft (1.8 m)

From southern Japan, China, and eastern Himalayas. Side branches in tiers form bushy dark green foliage. White starry flowers in umbels, in spring–summer. Coral red fruits persist into winter. Zones 8–11.

Ardisia japonica

☀ ❄ ↔ unlimited ↑ 12 in (30 cm)

Native to Japan and China. Leaves in whorls of 3 in (8 cm), glossy, dark green, saw-toothed margins. White to pale pink flowers in summer. Fruit pink to red. 'Nishiki', variegated with irregular cream margins, translucent pink on new leaves. Zones 7–10.

ARGYRANTHEMUM

From the Canary Islands and Madeira and often treated as perennials, the 24 members of this genus, of the daisy (Asteraceae) family, are evergreen shrubs. There are numerous cultivars, most with "double" or "semi-double" flowerheads over a long season. All branch low, with brittle stems and crowded leaves from coarsely toothed to deeply dissected. Leaves have a slightly aromatic, bitter smell when bruised. Long-stalked flowerheads are borne in groups of 2 to 5. CULTIVATION: Marginally frost hardy, in cold climates these shrubs need to be brought under shelter in winter. They prefer a temperate climate with a distinct cool winter. Soil should be very well drained and not too rich; a sunny position is needed. Pinch out young plants to shape. Propagate from tip cuttings at any time, preferably in autumn for spring–summer display.

Ardisia crenata

Argyranthemum frutescens

syn. Chrysanthemum frutescens

MARGUERITE, MARGUERITE DAISY

☀ ❄ ↔ 3 ft (0.9 m) ↑ 3 ft (0.9 m)

Original wild form of this Canary Islands native is low spreading shrub with leaves dissected into few narrow segments. Single

white flowerheads, golden yellow centers, for much of year. Most recent cultivars have generally been included in this species, but are in fact of hybrid origin, with other species in parentage. Zones 9–10.

Argyranthemum maderense

YELLOW MARGUERITE

☀ ❄ ↔ 20 in (50 cm) ↑ 18 in (45 cm)

Native of Canary Islands. Leaves broad, soft, deep green, mostly with coarse blunt teeth toward tip rather than lobed. Flowerheads broad pale golden yellow rays, disc slightly deeper color. Zones 9–11.

Argyranthemum Hybrid Cultivars

☀/☀ ❄ ↔ 18–36 in (45–90 cm) ↑ 12–30 in (30–75 cm)

Though many references have included all Argyranthemum cultivars under A. frutescens, most present-day cultivars are of hybrid origin. Apart from A. frutescens, likely parent species include A. foeniculaceum and A. maderense. Single cultivars include Butterfly/'Ulyssis', compact, rich yellow flowers; 'California Gold' ★, dwarf habit, large golden yellow blooms, leaf segments few and broad; 'Cornish Gold', yellow flowers, darker centers; 'Donnington Hero', low and spreading, coarsely lobed leaves, neat white flowers; 'Gill's Pink', pale pink rays, deeper at base, and broad leaf lobes; 'Jamaica Primrose', pale to mid-yellow blooms; and 'Petite Pink', pink flowers. Doubles include 'Blizzard', rather tangled white rays and some disc florets showing. Anemone-form or semi-double group includes 'Mary Wootton', older cultivar with pale pink center; 'Tauranga Star', white rays, slightly quilled, white "button" grading with pale gold center; and 'Vancouver', similar to 'Mary Wootton' but with bright pink domed central "button" and paler rays like the spokes of a wheel. Zones 9–10.

ARGYROCYTISUS

A monotypic genus of the pea-flower subfamily of legumes (Fabaceae), its sole species is an evergreen shrub native to the Rif and Atlas Mountains of Morocco. The name is a combination of

argyros (silver) and *Cytisus* (the plant's former genus). It refers to the silvery foliage, which derives its color from a dense covering of fine, silvery, reflective hairs that give the plant a metallic sheen. Spikes of bright golden yellow flowers open in late spring–early summer.
CULTIVATION: Left alone, this species can become rather spindly, though it bushes up if trimmed regularly. It is quite hardy and prefers a gritty well-drained soil in full sun. Propagate from seed or half-hardened late summer and autumn cuttings.

Argyrocytisus battandieri
syn. *Cytisus battandieri*
SILVER BROOM
☼ ❋ ↔ 12 ft (3.5 m) ↑ 12 ft (3.5 m)
Shrub with silvery trifoliate foliage. Bright yellow flowers, scented. Pea-pod-like seed capsules, covered with fine silvery hair. '**Yellow Tail**', richer yellow flowers. Zones 7–10.

ARONIA
CHOKEBERRY
This genus of deciduous shrubs from woodlands of eastern USA contains 2 species and a naturally occurring hybrid. In the rose (Rosaceae) family, it is closely allied to *Photinia*—in fact current opinion suggests it should be in that genus, though this has not gained wide acceptance. The shrubs are of compact size bearing white or pale pink spring blossoms that are followed by small berry-like fruits of red, purple, or black. The foliage colors attractively in autumn in shades of red and crimson.
CULTIVATION: These shrubs are well suited to informal plantings and woodland edges. They need deep, moist, well-drained soil and will grow in part-shade or sun. Sunnier sites encourage better fruiting and autumn coloring. The shiny black cherry and pear slug can cause unsightly damage to the foliage but can be controlled with a carbaryl or pyrethrin preparation. Propagate from half-hardened cuttings, layering, removal of suckers, or seed sown in autumn.

Aronia arbutifolia
syn. *Photinia pyrifolia*
AMELANCHIER, RED CHOKEBERRY
◑ ❋ ↔ 5 ft (1.5 m) ↑ 6 ft (1.8 m)
Downy young branches. Clusters of small white to pale pink flowers in spring. Bright red berries, persisting into winter. '**Brilliantissima**', vivid red autumn leaves. Zones 4–9.

ARTEMISIA *(see page 413)*

Artemisia abrotanum
LAD'S LOVE, OLD MAN, SOUTHERNWOOD
☼ ❋ ↔ 4 ft (1.2 m) ↑ 4 ft (1.2 m)
Soft-stemmed shrub of uncertain origin. Aromatic, gray, filigree leaves. Insignificant heads of yellow flowers in summer. Zones 3–10.

Argyrocytisus battandieri

Artemisia arborescens
SHRUB WORMWOOD
☼ ❋ ↔ 5 ft (1.5 m) ↑ 5 ft (1.5 m)
Attractive Mediterranean species that grows into rounded shrub. Finely divided silver foliage, aromatic. More frost tender than most species in genus but its cultivar '**Faith Raven**' is much hardier. Zones 8–11.

ATHEROSPERMA
The sole species in this genus is a large evergreen tree native to the States of New South Wales, Victoria, and Tasmania in Australia. It is a member of the family Monimiaceae. Although not closely related to the true sassafras *(Sassafras albidum),* the tree yields similar oils, most intensely from the bark. It has dark green, aromatic, lance-shaped leaves. Dainty white flowers are produced during spring, with male and female flowers borne on separate plants.
CULTIVATION: Although a little tender when young, *Atherosperma* adapts well to cultivation and seems happy in any well-drained soil with at least a half-day of sun. For the best results grow it in a moist climate with rich soil. Seedlings are slow to develop but are usually more reliable than cuttings.

Atherosperma moschatum ★
BLACK SASSAFRAS, SOUTHERN SASSAFRAS
☼ ❋ ↔ 15 ft (4.5 m) ↑ 100 ft (30 m)
Under cultivation this species rarely reaches 50 ft (15 m) tall. Leathery foliage, deep green above with pale hairs below. Pendulous white flowers open in spring. Female flowers have a covering of silky hairs. Zones 8–10.

Atherosperma moschatum, in the wild, Tasmania, Australia

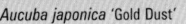
Aucuba japonica 'Gold Dust'

Auranticarpa rhombifolia

ATRIPLEX

SALTBUSH

From all continents except Antarctica, there are around 300 species included in this genus in the goosefoot or saltbush (Chenopodiaceae) family. *Atriplex* includes many shrubs, as well as annuals and perennials, that are multi-branched with wiry crooked twigs. The leaves are fleshy, and may be covered in fine whitish scales giving the foliage a silvery or pale bluish cast. They frequently grow in saline soils and the leaf sap is then salty. Flowers are small, of different sexes often on different plants.
CULTIVATION: These plants are suited to hot, dry, or saline environments, including exposed seashores. All require full sun and do best in a well-drained soil of moderate fertility. They can be cut back hard, responding with thicker foliage, and trained into hedges. Propagate from softwood cuttings or seed. Soak seed to simulate the effect of rain needed for these plants to germinate.

Atriplex canescens

CHAMIZO, FOUR-WING SALTBUSH

☼ ❄ ↔ 5 ft (1.5 m) ↑ 5 ft (1.5 m)
From western USA and Mexico. Densely massed stems. Narrow blunt-tipped leaves of mealy whitish appearance. Tiny yellowish flowers give way to 4-winged papery fruit bracts crowded onto short spikes, in late summer. Zones 6–10.

Atriplex halimus ★

TREE PURSLANE

☼ ❄ ↔ 10 ft (3 m) ↑ 6 ft (1.8 m)
Shrub from saltmarshes of southern Europe. Slightly larger, more silvery leaves than other species. Irregular spikes of greenish white flowers in late summer. Zones 8–10.

AUCUBA

This genus of dioecious plants in the silk-tassel (Garryaceae) family originates from the Himalayas and eastern Asia. It contains 3 or 4 species of evergreen shrubs or small trees, frequently used in garden situations, as they tolerate deep shade. Spotted forms are most popular. The glossy leaves are lance-shaped, smooth or serrate, and grow in an alternate arrangement along the branches. Flowers, either green or maroon, are in leaf axils or at the ends of terminal shoots and are of different sexes on different plants. Fruit are red, orange, or whitish yellow.
CULTIVATION: *Aucuba* grows best in moist soil. The spotted forms require partial shade—in sun they can scorch, while in deep shade the spotting fades. Both male and female plants are required to ensure berries. Cut back in spring. If grown in containers, use loam-based compost, and feed monthly when in growth. Sow seed in spring. Take half-hardened cuttings in summer.

Aucuba japonica

JAPANESE AUCUBA, JAPANESE LAUREL

☀ ❄ ↔ 6 ft (1.8 m) ↑ 6 ft (1.8 m)
Evergreen shrub from Japan. Purplish flowers and red berries. 'Crotonifolia', strongly gold-variegated cultivar; 'Gold Dust', female, variegated leaves; 'Rozannie', self-fruiting form; 'Salicifolia', female, narrow long-pointed leaves; and 'Variegata' ★, gold variegated, preferring deep shade. Zones 7–10.

AURANTICARPA

Close study of the large genus *Pittosporum* by some Australian botanists revealed that a group of northern Australian species is not closely related to the remainder of the species. As a result they named it as a new genus, *Auranticarpa* ("gold fruit"), though it is still in the pittosporum (Pittosporaceae) family. It is distinguished by a much-branched inflorescence with small bright orange fruit with blackish seeds. It consists of 6 species of evergreen trees, 3 transferred from *Pittosporum* and 3 new to science. Five of them are confined to the tropical north, while one extends from north Queensland to northeastern New South Wales.
CULTIVATION: Only *A. rhombifolia* is widely cultivated, popular as a street and park tree and adapting well to drier and cooler regions. It prefers moderately fertile, moist but well-drained soil and tolerates exposure to strong winds as well as part-shade, but full sun is required for a good display of its fruit. Propagate from seed.

Auranticarpa rhombifolia

syn. *Pittosporum rhombifolium*

DIAMOND-LEAF LAUREL, HOLLY WOOD

☼ ⚘ ↔ 10–20 ft (3–6 m) ↑ 20–60 ft (6–18 m)
Eastern Australian native, young growth covered in dense rusty hairs. Glossy green leaves, roughly diamond-shaped. Small, sweetly scented, white flowers in summer. Showy orange seed capsules. Zones 9–11.

AZARA

One of temperate South America's gifts to horticulture, this genus in the governor's plum (Flacourtiaceae) family contains 10 species of evergreen trees and shrubs with attractive foliage, graceful growth habits, and easy culture. Mostly native to Chile, their foliage varies in size but is generally glossy and leathery. Each main leaf is appended with one or two smaller "accessory leaves." Flowers tend to be golden yellow, small, fluffy pompons without petals. Fleshy fruits follow.
CULTIVATION: Most species will tolerate repeated light frosts but are damaged by severe cold. They do not tolerate extreme heat

and generally prefer a temperate climate with cool moist soil. Otherwise, they are easy-care plants that can be kept compact with routine trimming. Propagate from seed or half-hardened cuttings.

Azara microphylla
VANILLA TREE

☀ ❄ ↔ 15 ft (4.5 m) ↑ 25 ft (8 m)

Tree from Chile and Argentina. Small leaves on frond-like branches in ferny spray. Vanilla-scented, tiny, dull yellow flowers in spring, red fruit. 'Variegata', golden variegated foliage. Zones 8–10.

Azara serrata ★

☀ ❄ ↔ 8 ft (2.4 m) ↑ 12 ft (3.5 m)

Shrub from Chile. Sharply toothed foliage. Golden flowers open later than other azaras. With age can become rather sparse. Zones 8–10.

BACCHARIS
Of the daisy (Asteraceae) family, this genus of about 350 species is native to North, Central, and South America. These shrub or herb perennials are deciduous or evergreen and bear male and female flowers on separate plants. Some species have no leaves, so photosynthesis takes place in the green stems. The flowers are carried in panicles or corymbs.
CULTIVATION: Fully frost hardy to frost tender, these plants do best in good soil in full sun. Softwood cuttings can be taken in summer, while seed can be sown in spring. In colder areas plants may behave as perennials.

Azara microphylla

Baccharis 'Centennial'
COYOTE BRUSH, DESERT BROOM

☀ ❄ ↔ 5 ft (1.5 m) ↑ 3 ft (0.9 m)

Female cross between *B. pilularis* and *B. sarothroides* from USA. Evergreen sprawling shrub, narrow leaves. Inconspicuous white flowers in winter–spring. Tan seed pods, white fluffy seeds. Zones 8–10.

Banksia 'Giant Candles'

Baccharis pilularis
CHAPARRAL BROOM

☀ ❄ ↔ 20 in (50 cm) ↑ 20 in (50 cm)

Evergreen shrub native to western coast of USA. Leaves broad to ovate, hairless. Flowers white with green spot, found at branch tips. Cultivars include 'Pigeon Point' and 'Twin Peaks' ★. Zones 8–10.

BACKHOUSIA
This genus, a member of the myrtle (Myrtaceae) family, consists of 7 evergreen species of both shrubs and trees, all of which occur in the subtropical and tropical rainforests of east coast Australia. All species have a neat habit, white or cream flowers that have prominent stamens, and smooth-edged leaves in opposite pairs.
CULTIVATION: These rainforest plants do best in rich well-composted soil, in which sufficient moisture is retained. Although partial shade is best while young, plants often flower more profusely in full sun. Propagate from cuttings or fresh seed.

Backhousia citriodora
LEMON-SCENTED MYRTLE, SWEET VERBENA TREE

☀ ◗ ↔ 10–15 ft (3–4.5 m) ↑ 20–25 ft (6–8 m)

Neat small tree with foliage from ground level. Dense dull green leaves scented lemon when crushed. Oil contained in leaves used for food flavoring. Flowers strongly lemon scented, creamy white, in summer. Zones 9–11.

BANKSIA
From the protea (Proteaceae) family, the 75 or so species are endemic to Australia, with just one, *B. dentata*, extending to New Guinea. They vary from prostrate shrubs to low-branching trees. Thick leathery leaves are variously toothed. Large cylindrical or globular flower spikes are rich in nectar and are followed by woody cones. Species from southwest Western Australia are not always easy to cultivate, especially in summer-rainfall areas. Species from eastern Australia are more adaptable.
CULTIVATION: Most species prefer an open sunny position and well-drained sandy soil low in phosphorus. Some are moderately frost tolerant and, once established, most will withstand dry conditions. Harvest flowers to encourage flower production. To propagate, extract seed from the cone after it has been heated in a hot oven.

Banksia ericifolia
HEATH BANKSIA, HEATH-LEAFED BANKSIA

☀ ❄ ↔ 15 ft (4.5 m) ↑ 8–20 ft (2.4–6 m)

Australian east coast shrub. Narrow leaves, bright green above, furry beneath. Flower spikes to 10 in (25 cm) long, pale yellow to orange-red, yellow or orange-brown styles, in autumn–winter. Zones 8–10.

Banksia 'Giant Candles' ★
HYBRID BANKSIA

☀ ◗ ↔ 12 ft (3.5 m) ↑ 15 ft (4.5 m)

Shrub from eastern Australia. *B. ericifolia* and *B. spinulosa* hybrid, branching to near ground level. Bright green foliage. Orange flower spikes to 15 in (38 cm) long, in autumn–winter. Zones 9–10.

Banksia integrifolia ★

COAST BANKSIA

☼ ❄ ↔ 20 ft (6 m) ↕ 20–80 ft (6–24 m)

Fast-growing tree from east coast of Australia. Bark has roughly square pattern. Leaves dull green above, silvery woolly beneath. Flowers pale yellow-green, in summer–winter. Persistent fruits. Tolerates clay soils. 'Roller Coaster', prostrate form. Zones 8–11.

Banksia marginata ★

SILVER BANKSIA

☼ ❄ ↔ 15–20 ft (4.5–6 m) ↕ 8–30 ft (2.4–9 m)

From southeast Australia, variable banksia species found as shrub, tree, or prostrate form. Leaves narrow, silvery furry beneath. Flowers in short, pale yellow, cylindrical spikes, in late summer– winter. Hard prune plants with underground stems, others only lightly shape. Zones 8–10.

Banksia menziesii

FIREWOOD BANKSIA

☼ ۚ ↔ 15 ft (4.5 m) ↕ 50 ft (15 m)

Gnarled tree from Western Australia, much smaller and more compact in cultivation. Leaves long and toothed. Flowers silvery pink and gold, in acorn-shaped spikes, in autumn–winter. Patterned seed cones. Best in areas with dry summer. Zones 10–11.

Banksia robur

LARGE-LEAF BANKSIA, SWAMP BANKSIA

☼ ۚ ↔ 7 ft (2 m) ↕ 10 ft (3 m)

Found on east coast of Australia, usually in swampy woodlands. Leaves large, stiff, coarsely serrated, smooth above, furry beneath. Persistent golden flowers in summer–winter. Zones 9–10.

Banksia menziesii

Banksia serrata ★

OLD MAN BANKSIA, SAW BANKSIA

☼ ۚ ↔ 5–10 ft (1.5–3 m) ↕ 15–30 ft (4.5–9 m)

From Australian east coast. Gnarled trunk and branches. Leaves stiff, coarsely serrated. Large, cylindrical, creamy flower spikes in summer–winter. Persistent woody fruits, immortalized by children's author May Gibbs as "big bad Banksia Men." Fire tolerant. 'Pygmy Possum', ground cover to 2 ft (0.6 m) tall and 8 ft (2.4 m) wide; 'Superman', to 20 ft (6 m) in height. Zones 9–10.

Banksia spinulosa

HAIRPIN BANKSIA

☼/◗ ۚ ↔ 5 ft (1.5 m) ↕ 3 ft (0.9 m)

From east coast of Australia. Branchlets furry. Leaves linear, woolly undersides. Flower spikes cylindrical to 5 in (12 cm), golden yellow with gold, red, or orange styles, in autumn–winter. Fire tolerant. *B. s.* var. *collina* (syn. *B. collina*), bright yellow flowers, yellow to red styles. *B. s.* var. *cunninghamii*, large yellow spikes; 'Lemon Glow', pale yellow-flowered form. *B. s.* 'Honeypots', open-branched shrub, flowers golden, red styles, in summer–winter. Zones 9–10.

Barleria albostellata

BARLERIA

Barleria belongs to the acanthus (Acanthaceae) family, and consists of around 250 species of shrubs, subshrubs, and scrambling climbers. From tropical continents, except Australia, many occur in dry rocky habitats. Leaves are simple and smooth edged, arranged in opposite pairs on the stems. Flowers are more or less trumpet-shaped but distinctly 2-lipped, in shades from white through yellow, orange, pink, mauve, and violet. They emerge from between stiff bracts that are often edged by spiny teeth. Flowers appear over a long season, followed by club-shaped seed capsules. CULTIVATION: Easily cultivated in warm climates, these plants are fast growing but short lived. Grow in fertile well-drained soil, in a sunny but sheltered position. In cool climates they make good conservatory plants, but need strong light. They can be trimmed as hedges or cut back hard, responding to this treatment with denser, more vigorous foliage. Propagate from cuttings.

Barleria albostellata

GRAY BARLERIA

☼ ۚ ↔ 5 ft (1.5 m) ↕ 5 ft (1.5 m)

Evergreen shrub from northeastern South Africa, Zimbabwe, and Mozambique. Gray foliage due to dense coating of hairs on 2–3 in (5–8 cm) long oval leaves. Flowers white, 1 in (25 mm) wide, at branch tips, in spring–summer. Zones 9–12.

Barleria cristata

PHILIPPINE VIOLET

☼ ۚ ↔ 5 ft (1.5 m) ↕ 3 ft (0.9 m)

Widely grown ornamental species from Myanmar. Densely branching from ground level with soft deep green foliage. Flowers white, mauve, or violet from bristly edged green bracts, most of year. Tip prune to encourage denser growth. Zones 10–12.

Bartlettina sordida

Bauera rubioides

Bauhinia × *blakeana*

Barleria obtusa
BUSH VIOLET

↔3 ft (0.9 m) ↕3 ft (0.9 m)

Native to southern Africa. Spreading shrub, twiggy habit, small silky-haired leaves. Profuse white-pink or violet flowers, 1 in (25 mm) wide, from small furry bracts, in autumn. **Zones 9–11.**

BARTLETTINA

Found in tropical and Central America and Mexico, this daisy (Asteraceae) family genus comprises 23 species of evergreen shrubs and small trees. They form a dense, many-branched crown with young stems that are usually covered with fine hairs. The leaves are lance-shaped to oval, often with toothed edges; the corymbs or panicles of crowded small flowerheads occur in a variety of shades. **CULTIVATION:** Most species grow extremely freely and may be somewhat invasive. Plant in moist well-drained soil with a position in full sun or partial shade. If necessary, trim to shape after flowering. Propagate from seed or half-hardened cuttings.

Bartlettina sordida
syns *Bartlettina megalophylla, Eupatorium megalophyllum, E. sordidum*

↔7 ft (2 m) ↕10 ft (3 m)

Very vigorous shrub from Mexico. Young stems covered with red hairs; leaves oval with toothed edges, to 4 in (10 cm) long. Fragrant violet flowers in corymbs in warmer months. **Zones 10–11.**

BAUERA

Bauera is an eastern Australian genus of just 4 species. Once included in the saxifrage (Saxifragaceae) family, these evergreen wiry-stemmed shrubs are now included in the spoonbush (Cunoniaceae) family. The small leaves, borne in opposite pairs, are trifoliate but stalkless, their leaflets appearing like a whorl of 6 small leaves at each node. Bowl-shaped flowers arise from leaf axils in spring and early summer. **CULTIVATION:** Apart from being fairly frost tender, *Bauera* plants are easily grown and undemanding. They do best in well-drained, light, sandy soil with added humus. They prefer to avoid extremes of heat and cold, so some shade from the hottest sun is appreciated, as is winter shelter. Occasional trimming will keep the bushes compact. Propagate from seed or half-hardened cuttings.

Bauera rubioides ★
DOG ROSE, RIVER ROSE

↔7 ft (2 m) ↕2–6 ft (0.6–1.8 m)

Shrub from moister regions of southeastern Australia. Leaves ½ in (12 mm) long, often covered in fine hairs. Flowers white or pink, to 1 in (25 mm) wide, with 6 to 8 radiating petals, in late winter–spring. '**Luina Gem**', pale pink double flowers. **Zones 9–11.**

Bauera sessiliflora
GRAMPIANS BAUERA

↔6 ft (1.8 m) ↕6 ft (1.8 m)

Native to the Grampians, a mountain range in western Victoria, Australia. Flowers rosy pink to magenta, in late spring–early summer. Various cultivars are available. **Zones 9–10.**

BAUHINIA

This genus of around 300 species, many confined to the tropics, occurs in all continents except Europe, and on larger tropical islands. They belong to the caesalpinia subfamily of the legume (Fabaceae) family and include shrubs, climbers, and small to medium-sized trees, many deciduous. A characteristic feature is the compound leaf consisting of only 2 broad leaflets, their inner edges often fused. Flowers have 5 petals, borne in the leaf axils or in terminal sprays. Seed pods are slightly woody and flattened. Bauhinias are ornamental trees and shrubs, but some are used in traditional medicine or as a source of fiber; a few species have seeds that can be eaten. **CULTIVATION:** These plants are easily cultivated in warm climates, though often slow growing. Species from tropical climates with a long dry season do not grow or flower well in wetter climates. Deep rooted, they do not like being transplanted, but will often tolerate hot exposed positions and hard dry soils. Few grow well in shade. Propagate from seed; half-hardened cuttings can also be taken.

Bauhinia × *blakeana*
HONG KONG ORCHID TREE

↔15 ft (4.5 m) ↕30 ft (9 m)

This hybrid, probably between *B. purpurea* and *B. variegata*, is floral emblem of Hong Kong. Leaves broad, reliably evergreen. Flowers purple-red, slightly scented, 4–6 in (10–15 cm) wide, in autumn–winter. **Zones 10–12.**

Berberis buxifolia

Berberis × macracantha

Berberis × ottawensis f. purpurea

Bauhinia galpinii

syn. *Bauhinia punctata*

PRIDE OF DE KAAP, SOUTH AFRICAN ORCHID-BUSH

↔ 8 ft (2.4 m) ↑ 10–20 ft (3–6 m)

Horizontally branching evergreen shrub or scrambling climber from South Africa. Leaves rounded with 2 distinct lobes, paler undersides. Flowers light to brick red, in summer–autumn. Fruits woody, persistent, flattened, green-brown pods. Zones 9–11.

Bauhinia tomentosa

YELLOW BELL BAUHINIA

↔ 10 ft (3 m) ↑ 15 ft (4.5 m)

From tropical Africa and Asia, usually a multi-stemmed evergreen shrub. Leaves light green, 3 in (8 cm) long, hairy beneath. Flowers bell-shaped, cream to pale yellow, throughout year. Zones 10–12.

Bauhinia variegata

BUTTERFLY BUSH, ORCHID TREE

↔ 25 ft (8 m) ↑ 25 ft (8 m)

From tropical foothills of Himalayas through to Malay Peninsula, small tree with short trunk and spreading canopy. Semi-deciduous in warm areas, fully in cool areas. Orchid-like flowers, pale to deep pink. White form also seen. Zones 9–10.

BERBERIS

BARBERRY

This Berberidaceae family genus consists of more than 450 species of evergreen and deciduous shrubs, mainly seen across the Northern Hemisphere, with a smaller group in the South American Andes. They are variable in size, with spines on their branches, and are generally cultivated for the ornamental value of their leaves, flowers, and berries. All of the plant parts are supposed to cause mild stomach upsets if eaten. *B.* × *stenophylla* has become a serious pest in New Zealand. Many North American botanists now include all of the *Mahonia* species in *Berberis*.
CULTIVATION: *Berberis* will grow in most well-drained to fairly heavy soils. Tropical African species prefer rocky soil in mountainous areas. Plants can be grown in full sun or partial shade but autumn color is better in full sun. Propagate from softwood cuttings in early summer, or half-hardened cuttings later in summer. Site with care as branch spines can be hazardous.

Berberis buxifolia

☼ ❈ ↔ 10 ft (3 m) ↑ 8 ft (2.4 m)

Native to Chile and Argentina. Erect evergreen or semi-evergreen species with arching branches. Leaves leathery, dark green, spiny tips. Flowers deep orange-yellow in upper leaf axils, in mid- to late spring. Dark purple fruits. '**Pygmaea**' (syn. 'Nana'), dwarf form to 3 ft (0.9 m) tall. Zones 6–9.

Berberis × carminea

☼ ❈ ↔ 8 ft (2.4 m) ↑ 5 ft (1.5 m)

Hybrid of *B. aggregata* and *B. wilsoniae*. Leaves egg-shaped, dull gray-green. Flowers yellow, arranged in clusters of 10 to 16 blooms per panicle, in late spring–early summer. Fruits red or orange, in dense clusters. '**Barbarossa**', showy bright red fruits; '**Pirate King**', dense foliage. Zones 6–9.

Berberis darwinii

DARWIN BARBERRY

☼ ❈ ↔ 10 ft (3 m) ↑ 10 ft (3 m)

Evergreen shrub native to Chile and Argentina. Leaves dark green, toothed, with spines, pale green beneath. Flowers deep yellow or orange in pendulous racemes. Oblong purplish black fruits with bloom. '**Flame**', grows to half the height of the species. Zones 7–10.

Berberis julianae

WINTERGREEN BARBERRY

☼ ❈ ↔ 10 ft (3 m) ↑ 10 ft (3 m)

Evergreen shrub found in western Hubei Province, China. Spiny stems, leaves oval shaped with narrow end at base, serrated margins, dark green above, paler undersurface. Juvenile foliage with copper tints. Flowers yellow or tinged red, in clusters, in early spring. Fruits black with white bloom. '**Lombarts Red**', leaves tinged red underneath. Zones 5–9.

Berberis × macracantha

☼ ❈ ↔ 12 ft (3.5 m) ↑ 12 ft (3.5 m)

Garden hybrid between *B. aristata* and *B. vulgaris*; deciduous shrub. Stems well protected by thorns more than 1 in (25 mm) long. Long racemes of bright yellow flowers in spring, followed by deep purple-red berries in autumn. Zones 5–9.

Berberis × *ottawensis*

HYBRID PURPLE BARBERRY

☼ ❄ ↔ 8 ft (2.4 m) ↕ 8 ft (2.4 m)

Cross between *B. thunbergii* and *B. vulgaris*. Leaves mid-green, egg-shaped. Flowers pale yellow, in clusters, in spring. Fruits egg-shaped red berries. *B.* × *o.* f. *purpurea*, purple-red foliage; '**Superba**' (syn. 'Purpurea'), new growth almost bronze. *B.* × *o.* '**Silver Miles**', dark purplish red leaves marked silvery gray. Zones 5–10.

Berberis × *rubrostilla*

☼ ❄ ↔ 8 ft (2.4 m) ↕ 5 ft (1.5 m)

Deciduous hybrid, possibly cross of *B. aggregata* and *B. wilsoniae*. Leaves narrow, egg-shaped, mid-green above, gray undersides, 1¼ in (30 mm) long, with marginal spines. Pale yellow flowers. Egg-shaped, translucent, red fruits. Zones 6–9.

Berberis × *stenophylla*

☼ ❄ ↔ 15 ft (4.5 m) ↕ 10 ft (3 m)

Hybrid of *B. darwinii* and *B. empetrifolia*. Leaves narrow, elliptical, ¾ in (18 mm) long, dark green above, bluish green beneath. Flowers deep yellow, in late spring. Fruits black with blue bloom. Cultivars include '**Corallina Compacta**', '**Crawley Gem**', '**Irwinii**', and '**Lemon Queen**' (syn. 'Cornish Cream'). Zones 6–9.

Berberis thunbergii

JAPANESE BARBERRY

☼ ❄ ↔ 8 ft (2.4 m) ↕ 3 ft (0.9 m)

Deciduous shrub native to Japan. Compact foliage and rounded shape. Leaves egg-shaped, smooth, fresh green above, bluish green beneath. Flowers pale yellow, can be tinged red, in racemes, in mid-spring. Fruits glossy red. *B. t.* f. *atropurpurea*, purple-red stems and leaves. *B. t.* '**Helmond Pillar**', to 5 ft (1.5 m) tall, dark red foliage; '**Red Chief**, to 6 ft (1.8 m) tall, pink-variegated leaves; '**Rose Glow**' ★, red-purple foliage flecked with white; '**Sparkle**', persistent bright red fruit. Zones 4–9.

Berberis thunbergii 'Sparkle'

Berberis valdiviana

☼ ❄ ↔ 15 ft (4.5 m) ↕ 15 ft (4.5 m)

Native to Chile. Leaves 2 in (5 cm) long, elliptical, smooth, dark green above, yellow-green beneath. Saffron yellow flowers in drooping racemes in late spring. Fruits black with blue bloom. Zones 8–10.

Berberis wilsoniae

WILSON BARBERRY

☼ ❄ ↔ 6 ft (1.8 m) ↕ 3 ft (0.9 m)

Betula albosinensis

Deciduous or semi-evergreen shrub from western Sichuan and Yunnan Provinces, China. Branches dense, spiny, arching. Leaves gray-green, oval to linear, orange-red in autumn. Pale yellow flowers in summer. Pink to red fruits. Zones 5–10.

BETULA

BIRCH

This genus gives its name to the birch family, Betulaceae, and consists of about 60 deciduous small shrubs or tall trees occurring throughout temperate and arctic zones of the Northern Hemisphere. Tree trunks are often marked in different shades; in many species the outer layer of bark peels off. Pendulous male catkins and erect female catkins are carried on the same tree in early spring. Leaves are mid- to dark green, ovate in shape, with indented margins.

CULTIVATION: Birches are hardy trees, withstanding extreme cold and exposure to wind. They are best in well-drained fertile soil, with some moisture and full sun or light shade. Take softwood cuttings in summer, or half-hardened cuttings in autumn. Birches are susceptible to fungi such as *Armillaria melea* and *Piptoporus betulinus*; the latter, specific to the birch family, will destroy the tree.

Betula albosinensis

CHINESE RED BIRCH

☼ ❄ ↔ 30 ft (9 m) ↕ 80 ft (24 m)

Native to Provinces of Sichuan, Gansu, and Shaanxi, southwestern China. New bark gray-cream turning orange or red-brown. Leaves glossy, green above, paler beneath, to 2½ in (6 cm) long, turn yellow in autumn. Showy male catkins. Zones 6–9.

Betula ermanii

ERMAN'S BIRCH, GOLD BIRCH, RUSSIAN ROCK-BIRCH

☼ ❄ ↔ 40 ft (12 m) ↕ 70 ft (21 m)

Native to Japan and mainland Asia. Bark pink or creamy white turning pinkish. Tapered oval leaves, dark green, margins serrated. Male catkins in groups of 3. Zones 2–8.

Betula lenta

BLACK BIRCH, CHERRY BIRCH, SWEET BIRCH

☼ ❄ ↔ 40 ft (12 m) ↕ 50 ft (15 m)

Native to eastern North America. Bark crimson, becomes scaly and gray ageing to black. Leaves egg-shaped, chartreuse, 4 in (10 cm) long, autumn color. Male catkins pendulous, 3 in (8 cm) long. Female catkins erect. Zones 3–9.

Betula papyrifera, in the wild, USA

Betula mandschurica

syn. *Betula platyphylla* var. *japonica*
MANCHURIAN BIRCH
☼ ❋ ↔ 30 ft (9 m) ↑ 70 ft (21 m)
Native to northeastern China and southeastern Siberia. Bark
dusty milky white. Leaves mid-green, egg-shaped, to 3 in (8 cm)
long, deeply indented, heavily veined. Male and
female catkins pendulous, 1 in (25 mm) long. *B.
m.* var. *japonica*, with white bark, to 80 ft (24 m)
tall; 'Whitespire' (syn. *B. platyphylla* 'Whitespire'),
narrowly conical habit. Zones 2–9.

Betula nigra

RIVER BIRCH, TROPICAL BIRCH
☼ ❋ ↔ 15 ft (4.5 m) ↑ 30 ft (9 m)
Deciduous tree from along rivers in eastern USA.
Bark white, smooth then thin flaking plates of
cream, salmon, and pale brown. Dark and fur-
rowed with age. Tolerates heat and dryness.
'Heritage', peeling cream to pale brown bark;
'Little King', dwarf cultivar, to 10 ft (3 m) tall. Zones 4–9.

Betula papyrifera

CANOE BIRCH, PAPER BIRCH, WHITE BIRCH
☼ ❋ ↔ 30 ft (9 m) ↑ 60 ft (18 m)
Deciduous North American tree. White papery bark peeling to
orange-brown. Light canopy allows sunlight through. Tolerates
cold and drought. Zones 2–8.

Betula pendula

EUROPEAN SILVER BIRCH, EUROPEAN WHITE BIRCH
☼ ❋ ↔ 35 ft (10 m) ↑ 80 ft (24 m)
Deciduous tree from northern Europe, commonly found on poor
soils. Foliage turns clear yellow in autumn. Arching habit, white
bark. Trunk blackens with age. 'Dalecarlica' (weeping birch), dissected foliage; 'Fastigiata', erect tree to 70 ft (21 m); 'Laciniata',
loses leaves earlier in autumn than species; 'Purpurea', with thin

pendulous branches; 'Tristis', narrowly
conical habit; 'Youngii' ★, usually sold
as grafted tree with strongly weeping head.
Zones 2–8.

Betula platyphylla

☼ ❋ ↔ 40 ft (12 m) ↑ 70 ft (21 m)
Native to Siberia, northeastern China, Korea,
and Japan. Bark pure white. Leaves chartreuse,
4 in (10 cm) long, egg-shaped with serrated
margins. Male catkins to 3 in (8 cm) long;
female catkins to 1¼ in (3 cm) long. Zones 4–9.

BIXA

This genus of a single species gives its name
to the family Bixaceae. The sole member is a
small tree from tropical South America. Cultivated as an ornamental, it is also commercially grown for an orange food and fabric
dye, annatto, obtained from its seeds. It features pretty flowers,
lush foliage, and distinctive bristly red seed pods.
CULTIVATION: Most at home in moist humid tropics, *Bixa* can
be grown in a frost-free temperate climate if sheltered from cool
winds. It prefers year-round moisture, good drainage, and moderately fertile soil in full sun or partial shade. Cutting-grown
plants flower at a younger age than seedlings.

Bixa orellana

ANNATTO, LIPSTICK PLANT
☼ ❧ ↔ 10–15 ft (3–4.5 m) ↑ 30 ft (9 m)
Large shrub or small tree. Leaves oval, leathery,
bright green. Pink or pinkish white flowers in
panicles. Clusters of red to red-brown spiny seed
pods persist after seeds released. Zones 10–12.

Bixa orellana

BOCCONIA

This genus of 9 species from subtropical and
tropical America is part of the poppy (Papaveraceae) family. The leaves, while very large, are at
least reminiscent of garden poppies, but the flowers are not what
would commonly be thought of as poppy-like. They lack petals
and are carried in large plume-like terminal racemes. The
plants normally start as a single trunk topped with a head of leaves, but
with age, side shoots and suckers develop to form multiple trunks.
All parts release a yellow latex if cut.
CULTIVATION: *Bocconia* plants can tolerate light frosts but need
a mild climate to thrive. They grow best in moist, well-drained,
humus-rich soil with a sunny or partly shaded exposure. They are
very vigorous plants and care should be taken to plant them only
where their seeding and suckering can be controlled.

Bocconia arborea

☼/◐ ❧ ↔ 15 ft (4.5 m) ↑ 25 ft (8 m)
Found in Central America. Leaves deeply cut and divided, 18 in
(45 cm) long, 12 in (30 cm) wide, toothed, often downy beneath.
Flowers in racemes, up to 8 in (20 cm) long, in summer. Zones 10–12.

BOMBAX

This genus of large tropical deciduous trees, a member of the mallow (Malvaceae) family, consists of around 20 species from tropical Africa, southern Asia, and northern Australia. They grow around rock outcrops or along river valleys. Trunks are thick and straight, with tiered branches, often buttressed at the base. Bark is often armed with conical prickles. Leaves are compound with 5 or more leaflets attached to a common stalk. Appearing on leafless branches in the dry season, the large flowers have 5 tongue-shaped red, white, or yellow petals and a central mass of stamens. Large fruits split when ripe to release oily seeds embedded in white hairs.
CULTIVATION: Easily grown in the tropics, plants prefer a sheltered site; deep, fertile, well-drained soil; and subsoil moisture. Fast growing when young, they can be short lived if attacked by insects. Propagate from fresh seed or tip cuttings, planted in the wet season.

Bombax ceiba

syn. *Bombax malabaricum*
SILK COTTON TREE
☼ ❄ ↔ 30–40 ft (9–12 m) ↑ 60 ft (18 m)
Broadly spreading, heavy-limbed tree from Asia. Trunk prickly when young. Flowers profuse, deep scarlet, appear in tropical dry season (spring). In Asia, fiber obtained from bark. Zones 10–12.

BORONIA

Noted for its sweet fragrance, early spring blooms, and aromatic foliage, this genus is a member of the rue (Rutaceae) family and consists of approximately 100 species of small to medium-sized, compact, evergreen shrubs, nearly all from Australia. They have simple or pinnate leaves and small 4-petalled flowers that may be open and star-shaped or bell-like with overlapping petals. Flowers come in a range of colors from white, pink, and bluish mauve to red, yellow, yellow-green, and brown.
CULTIVATION: Locate boronias in sheltered positions with the protection of other plants in sun or part-shade. The soil should be well drained with a fairly high organic content; avoid drying out. If growing in pots, ensure that the potting mix does not contain added fertilizers with high phosphorus levels. The flowers generally last well when picked. After flowering, up to half of the plant can be removed to prolong life and improve bushiness. Propagate from half-hardened tip-cuttings. Some species can be short lived.

Boronia heterophylla

KALGAN BORONIA, RED BORONIA
◑ ❄ ↔ 4 ft (1.2 m) ↑ 6 ft (1.8 m)
Evergreen shrub native to southern Western Australia. Leaves bright green, aromatic. Flowers fragrant, deep pink, bell-shaped, in late winter–early spring. Zones 9–10.

Boronia megastigma ★

BROWN BORONIA
◑ ❄ ↔ 3 ft (0.9 m) ↑ 3 ft (0.9 m)
From southwest Western Australia. Popular species with light green foliage, slender stems, spicy aromatic leaves. Flowers reddish brown outside, yellow inside, pendent, bell-like, highly fragrant, in late winter–early spring. Often short lived; best in well-drained moist

soil. '**Harlequin**', yellow and brown flowers; '**Heaven Scent**', compact dwarf, brown flowers; '**Jack Maguire's Red**', scarlet flowers; '**Lutea**', clear greenish yellow flowers, foliage lighter green than species; '**Virtuoso**', near-black petals. Zones 9–11.

Boronia pinnata

PINNATE BORONIA
◑ ❄ ↔ 5 ft (1.5 m) ↑ 5 ft (1.5 m)
Erect shrub from temperate east coast Australia. Pinnate leaves, strongly aromatic. Fragrant, pink to mauve, starry flowers, in loose sprays, in late winter–spring. Best in sheltered partially shaded position. '**Spring White**', profuse white flowers. Zones 9–11.

BOUVARDIA

This genus, reaching from southern North America to northern South America, includes several evergreen shrubs among its 30 or so species, and belongs to the madder (Rubiaceae) family. *Bouvardia* tend to be rather sprawling, weak-stemmed plants that need support to keep them upright. Their leaves are not large but they are a pleasant shade of deep green and are usually glossy. The long-tubed flowers are the main attraction. The brighter colors are visually striking, while those in lighter shades or white are fragrant.
CULTIVATION: *Bouvardia* species tolerate light frost only and need a mild climate with rich well-drained soil to flower well. They are best in partial shade and also perform well as greenhouse plants. Light trimming helps to keep them compact and bushy.

Bouvardia longiflora

SCENTED BOUVARDIA
◑ ❄ ↔ 3 ft (0.9 m) ↑ 3 ft (0.9 m)
Shrub from Mexico. Weak stems, easily damaged. Highly fragrant, waxy white, long-tubed, 4-petalled flowers, in autumn–winter. '**Albatross**' (syn. *B. humboldtii* 'Albatross'), larger flowers. Zones 10–11.

Bouvardia ternifolia

◑ ❄ ↔ 3 ft (0.9 m) ↑ 3 ft (0.9 m)
Soft-stemmed evergreen shrub native to Arizona and Texas, USA, and Mexico. Flowers vivid red, tubular, in corymbs. Cultivars available with flowers in various pink and red shades. Zones 9–11.

Boronia megastigma

Bouvardia ternifolia

BRACHYCHITON

This genus in the mallow (Malvaceae) family contains around 30 species of evergreen or partially deciduous trees, mostly native to Australia, and found chiefly in northern tropical and subtropical regions with a few extending to arid regions. They have large smooth or lobed leaves and showy sprays or clusters of colorful flowers often appearing just ahead of the new foliage in spring and summer. All species have shapely, sometimes swollen trunks and large, boat-shaped, woody seed follicles.
CULTIVATION: Although moderately frost hardy when established, most species are relatively slow growing in the initial stages and require a warm climate to bring out their best display of flowers. They do best in a well-drained acidic soil in full sun. Propagate from fresh seed in spring, or by grafting in the case of hybrids.

Brachychiton acerifolius
syn. *Sterculia acerifolia*
FLAME KURRAJONG, ILLAWARRA FLAME TREE
☼ ⁑ ↔ 20 ft (6 m) ↑ 40 ft (12 m)
Deciduous tree from Australian east coast. Flowers crimson, on bare branches. For gardens, grafted trees desirable because seedlings take many years to flower. Very drought tolerant. Zones 9–10.

Brachychiton discolor
syn. *Sterculia discolor*
LACEBARK KURRAJONG
☼ ⁑ ↔ 30 ft (9 m) ↑ 80 ft (24 m)
Conical deciduous tree from eastern Australian rainforests. Leaves dark green, lobed, paler beneath. Bark very green. Flowers pink, velvety, on leafless branches, in early summer. Zones 9–11.

Brachychiton populneus
syn. *Sterculia diversifolia*
KURRAJONG
☼ ❈ ↔ 15 ft (4.5 m) ↑ 30 ft (9 m)
Semi-deciduous, with greenish bark. Glossy, ovate, deeply 3-lobed leaves. Flowers white, bell-shaped, in spring–early summer. Woody boat-shaped fruits. Zones 8–11.

Brachychiton populneus   Brachyglottis laxifolia

BRACHYGLOTTIS

This genus of about 30 evergreen trees, shrubs, climbers, and perennials is part of the large daisy (Asteraceae) family. They are found in New Zealand and Tasmania, Australia, in habitats ranging from coastal to alpine. Most were previously included in the genus *Senecio*. They are usually grown for their attractive gray foliage which is covered in white or buff down in varying degrees. Generally the yellow or white daisies are of little significance but in a small number of species they are quite showy.
CULTIVATION: Most species prefer a well-drained soil and a sunny site, and many tolerate harsh coastal conditions. In cool-temperate climates the more tender species are cultivated in the greenhouse and the hardier species against a sunny wall. Prune to maintain a compact bushy shape. Species are propagated from seed or half-hardened cuttings in autumn, and cultivars from cuttings only.

Brachyglottis greyi
syn. *Senecio greyi*
☼ ❈ ↔ 10 ft (3 m) ↑ 5 ft (1.5 m)
From Wellington on New Zealand's North Island. Leaves oblong, grayish green, wavy margins, white down beneath. Flowers bright yellow, in summer. Suitable for hedging. Zones 8–10.

Brachyglottis laxifolia
syn. *Senecio laxifolius*
☼ ❈ ↔ 7 ft (2 m) ↑ 3 ft (0.9 m)
Found in mountains of northern South Island of New Zealand. Lax habit. Leaves narrow, oblong, close set, slightly leathery, covered with dense gray down beneath. Zones 8–10.

BREYNIA

Part of the spurge (Euphorbiaceae) family, the 25 or so species in this genus of evergreen shrubs and small trees range from Australia and the Pacific Islands northward to Southeast and East Asia. Often suckering from the roots, they have delicate twigs and small oval leaves arranged alternately and tending to form 2 rows. Leaves often turn black before falling. Inconspicuous greenish flowers, both male and female on the same plant, appear in the leaf axils followed by small, flattened, white, red, or black berries.

Brachychiton discolor

CULTIVATION: Use as border shrubs in tropical and subtropical gardens; in cooler climates, grow indoors in pots or plant out for summer in bedding schemes or patio tubs. Species prefer a sunny but sheltered spot and well-drained soil. Propagate from cuttings.

Breynia disticha
syns *Breynia nivosa, Phyllanthus nivosus*
SNOW BUSH
☀ 🌓 ↔ 3 ft (0.9 m) ↑ 4 ft (1.2 m)
From islands of western Pacific. Ovate leaves, 1 in (25 mm) long, spotted white or cream, or some all green, others all white. 'Roseopicta', pink new growth, many leaves pink-flushed, has largely replaced white-spotted form in gardens. Zones 10–12.

BROUSSONETIA
From the mulberry (Moraceae) family, *Broussonetia* consists of 8 species of deciduous trees and shrubs with milky sap, from tropical and eastern Asia; 1 species is endemic to Madagascar. Deeply lobed leaves are broad, heart-shaped, with toothed edges. Small male and female flowers are borne on separate trees, males in long catkins, females in globular heads. Male flowers expel pollen explosively, visible as tiny spurts of white dust. Small fleshy fruits are clustered on a globular fruiting head.
CULTIVATION: Only the more cold-hardy species from East Asia are known in cultivation. Moderately frost tolerant, they prefer hot humid summers. Heavy pruning creates vigorous resprouting. Propagate from cuttings of short shoots taken in summer; seed can be used if available.

Broussonetia papyrifera
PAPER MULBERRY
☀ ✳ ↔ 30 ft (9 m) ↑ 50 ft (15 m)
From China and Japan. Young branches softly hairy. Leaves variably lobed or unlobed to 8 in (20 cm). Male catkins whitish, female purplish. Fruiting heads red. Zones 6–12.

Breynia disticha

BRUGMANSIA
This genus in the Solanaceae family contains 5 species of small trees or shrubs native to South America, particularly the Andes. They are grown for their drooping tubular or funnelform flowers, which are fragrant, with a 2- to 5-lobed cylindrical calyx. Fruits are ovoid or elliptical. All plant parts are poisonous; seeds are hallucinogenic.
CULTIVATION: Brugmansias need a sunny protected position with no more than light frost. Moderately fertile, free-draining soil is suitable. Plants are best trained to a single trunk by removing any competing leaders; branchlets should be shortened annually in late winter or early spring. Propagation is from soft-tip cuttings taken in spring or summer, or hardwood cuttings in autumn or winter.

Brugmansia arborea
syn. *Brugmansia cornigera*
☀ 🌓 ↔ 5–8 ft (1.5–2.4 m) ↑ 15 ft (4.5 m)
Small evergreen tree from Ecuador and northern Chile. Leaves irregularly alternate. Flowers white, solitary, with extended green tip, in summer–autumn. Fruits green, ovoid, with numerous

seeds. 'Knightii' (syn. *B.* × *candida* 'Double White'), off-white double flowers, gray-green leaves. Zones 10–12.

Brugmansia × candida
ANGEL'S TRUMPET
☀ 🌓 ↔ 6 ft (1.8 m) ↑ 10 ft (3 m)
Hybrid of *B. aurea* and *B. versicolor*, sometimes labelled *B. knightii*. Small evergreen tree from Ecuador. Leaves bright green, paler below. Flowers greenish white, fragrant at night, in summer–autumn. Fruit green capsule. 'Grand Marnier', peach flowers. Zones 10–12.

Brugmansia 'Charles Grimaldi'
☀ 🌓 ↔ 4 ft (1.2 m) ↑ 6 ft (1.8 m)
Cross between 'Doctor Seuss' and 'Frosty Pink'. Leaves large. Flowers long, widely flared, fragrant, salmon pink to yellow-orange, in autumn–spring. Compact plant, flowers heavily. Zones 10–12.

Brugmansia × insignis
syn. *Brugmania sanguinea* 'Rosea'
☀ 🌓 ↔ 8–10 ft (2.4–3 m) ↑ 12 ft (3.5 m)
Hybrid of *B. suaveolens* and *B. versicolor*, a multi-stemmed shrub. Flowers slender, tubular, flared petals, white ageing to pink or apricot. 'Betty Marshall', compact growth habit, white flowers; 'Jamaica Yellow', pale yellow blooms. Zones 9–10.

Brugmansia sanguinea ★
RED ANGEL'S TRUMPET
☀ 🌓 ↔ 12 ft (3.5 m) ↑ 12 ft (3.5 m)
Small tree or shrub native to Colombia, Ecuador, and Peru. Leaves long. Flowers solitary, persistent calyx. Corolla yellowish, turning orange-scarlet. Fruits ovoid, smooth skinned. Zones 9–11.

Brugmansia sanguinea

Brugmansia suaveolens

ANGEL'S TRUMPET

☼ ❄ ↔ 10 ft (3 m) ↑ 15 ft (4.5 m)

From southeastern Brazil. Leaves soft, dark green. Single flowers, calyx green, corolla white, narrowly funnelform, with 3 pale green ribs. Fruits narrowly ellipsoidal, green, smooth. Zones 10–12.

BRUNFELSIA

Found from Central America to subtropical South America, this genus in the nightshade (Solanaceae) family includes some 40 species of mainly evergreen shrubs and trees. Most have fragrant, large, simple, long-tubed, 5-petalled flowers, notable for their progression of color changes. White, mauve, and purple are the usual colors. The leaves are usually simple pointed ovals in lush, deep green tones. All species contain potent toxic alkaloids. CULTIVATION: While very frost tender, *Brunfelsia* presents no cultivation difficulties in mild climates. Any sunny or partly shaded position with moist well-drained soil will do. They are not drought tolerant but grow well in containers if watered routinely. Indoor potted specimens are prone to mites and mealybugs. Propagate from soft or half-hardened tip cuttings.

Brunfelsia americana

LADY OF THE NIGHT

☽ ❄ ↔ 4–7 ft (1.2–2 m) ↑ 15 ft (4.5 m)

Large shrub or small tree from Central America and West Indies. Flowers scented at night. White when first open, with hint of purple, ageing through cream to yellow, in summer. Zones 10–12.

Brunfelsia pauciflora

syn. *Brunfelsia calycina*

☼/☽ ❄ ↔ 5 ft (1.5 m) ↑ 8 ft (2.4 m)

Heavy-flowering semi-deciduous shrub from Brazil and Venezuela. Large flowers purple-blue then age through pale mauve to white. Cultivars include 'Floribunda' ★ and 'Macrantha'. Zones 10–12.

Brunfelsia pauciflora

BUCKINGHAMIA

There are 2 species of this genus in the protea (Proteaceae) family, both from Queensland, Australia. They are fast-growing, tropical rainforest trees that resemble grevilleas in foliage and flower. *B. celsissima* is frequently grown as a street tree and is appreciated for its abundant flowers.

CULTIVATION: These plants prefer warm sheltered spots but they will also tolerate cool frost-free conditions. They prefer moist well-drained loam in either full sun or partial shade. Initial directional pruning can be beneficial, but pruning is not required once the tree's framework is established. They are propagated from ripe seed in autumn.

Buckinghamia celsissima

Buckinghamia celsissima

IVORY CURL TREE

☼ ❄ ↔ 12 ft (3.5 m) ↑ 30 ft (9 m)

Evergreen tree from northeastern Queensland, Australia. Leaves dark green, shiny, pale below, lobed when juvenile. Creamy flowers on long recurved inflorescences on short stems in autumn. Woody fruits follow. Zones 10–12.

BUDDLEJA

The name of this genus of deciduous, semi-deciduous, and evergreen plants from the Americas, Asia, and South Africa can be spelt buddleja or buddleia. The genus, a member of the foxglove (Scrophulariaceae) family, consists of about 100 species, of which a few shrubby or tree-like ones are garden grown. There are also some decorative cultivars that are grown for their profuse, small, fragrant flowers that are held in large panicles. The leaves are, with the exception of *B. alternifolia*, paired and opposite. The plants are tough, undemanding, quick growing, and salt tolerant. They are also sun loving and vigorous and, if given shelter, can be grown in climates considerably cooler than those found in their native habitats. CULTIVATION: Basic requirements include sunlight, good drainage, fertile soil, and, from the gardener's point of view, regular pruning. Some plants show a mild preference for chalky and limy soils. Propagate from half-hardened cuttings in summer.

Buddleja alternifolia ★

FOUNTAIN BUDDLEJA

☼ ✳ ↔ 15 ft (4.5 m) ↑ 15 ft (4.5 m)

Deciduous shrub native to northwest China. Leaves small, green above, whitish beneath. Flowers fragrant, misty mauve, attract butterflies, in late spring–early-summer. 'Argentea', mauve flowers, fine growth of silvery hairs on leaves. Zones 5–9.

Buddleja colvilei

SUMMER LILAC

☼ ✳ ↔ 20 ft (6 m) ↑ 20 ft (6 m)

Large upright shrub from eastern Asia. Branches arching. Leaves dark gray-green, long, pointed, heavily veined, white woolly beneath. Flowers large, bell-like, cherry pink to rosy red, in spring. 'Kewensis', rich raspberry red flowers. Zones 8–11.

Buddleja davidii 'Black Knight'

Buddleja × *weyeriana*

Buddleja davidii

BUTTERFLY BUSH

☼ ❄ ↔ 17 ft (5 m) ↑ 10–17 ft (3–5 m)

Tough deciduous plant native to rocky riversides in central and western China. Quick vigorous growth, bushy habit, arching stems. Long pointed leaves, dark green above, woolly white beneath. Fragrant mauve flowers in panicles. Can be invasive. *B. d.* var. *nanhoensis*, to 5 ft (1.5 m) tall and wide. *B. d.* 'Black Knight', royal purple flowers; 'Dartmoor', red-purple flowers on fan-like stems; 'Empire Blue', steely violet-blue flowers, orange eye; 'Harlequin', cream-edged leaves; 'Nanho Blue', lavender-purple flowers; 'Nanho Purple', rich purple flowers; 'Royal Red', purple-red flowers; White Profusion', white flowers, golden eye. Zones 4–10.

Buddleja globosa

ORANGE BALL TREE

☼ ❄ ↔ 10 ft (3 m) ↑ 10–20 ft (3–6 m)

Semi-evergreen tree native to Argentina and Chile. Leaves dark green above, wrinkled, woolly white beneath; young stems silvery white. Flowers scented, orange-yellow, in clusters, in late spring– early summer. Zones 7–9.

Buddleja salviifolia

SOUTH AFRICAN SAGEWOOD, WINTER BUDDLEJA

☼ ❄ ↔ 15 ft (4.5 m) ↑ 12–25 ft (3.5–8 m)

Dense shrub or small tree from South Africa. Leaves long, narrow, pointed, felted, sage gray, lightly crinkled, on short stalks. Flowers in heavy plumes, scented, smoky mauve, in late autumn–winter. Zones 8–10.

Buddleja × *weyeriana*

☼ ❄ ↔ 12 ft (3.5 m) ↑ 15 ft (4.5 m)

Deciduous hybrid between *B. davidii* and *B. globosa*. Leaves dark, lance-shaped. Flowers bobble-like clusters, scented, orange-yellow shaded with lilac. 'Golden Glow', soft purple buds, apricot flowers in open panicles; 'Honeycomb', pale yellow flowers; 'Sungold', dense heads of bright yellow flowers with orange centers. Zones 6–9.

BURCHELLIA

This genus from South Africa contains a single species in the madder (Rubiaceae) family. It is named for William Burchell, a botanical explorer in South Africa. Not often seen in gardens, despite its attractive foliage and bright flowers.

CULTIVATION: *Burchellia* prefers a light, fertile, and well-drained soil with plenty of summer moisture, in a warm area not subject to heavy frosts. It tolerates full sun and filtered shade. Trim occasionally to maintain shape. Propagate from seed sown in late winter or spring or from half-hardened cuttings in late summer or autumn.

Burchellia bubalina

syn. *Burchellia capensis*

SOUTH AFRICAN POMEGRANATE

☼ ❄ ↔ 8 ft (2.4 m) ↑ 10 ft (3 m)

Evergreen shrub found from Cape of Good Hope to Tropic of Capricorn. Leaves simple, dark green and shiny above, bright green beneath. Inflorescence is terminal head of 10 to 12 flowers, bright orange-red to scarlet, in spring–summer. Zones 9–11.

BUXUS

BOX

A member of the family Buxaceae, this genus has most of its 50 or so species in the West Indies and Central America; there are also species through eastern Asia, the Himalayas, Africa, and Europe. All are evergreen shrubs or trees with simple smooth-edged leaves arranged in opposite pairs. Small greenish or yellowish flowers are borne in the leaf axils. Fruits are small capsules. The leaves and twigs are poisonous to livestock.

CULTIVATION: The smaller-leafed species are pop-

Burchellia bubalina

ular in cool-climate gardens. They are valued for their dense fine-textured foliage, hardiness, and ability to take frequent trimming and shaping. They grow in most soil types, including chalk, as long as there is reasonable drainage. Propagate from cuttings, but seed also germinates readily.

Buxus microphylla

CHINESE BOX, JAPANESE BOX, KOREAN BOX

☼ ❄ ↔ 7 ft (2 m) ↑ 8 ft (2.4 m)

East Asian species with many forms and cultivars differing in frost tolerance. Wild forms have slightly brownish green leaves, ¾ in (18 mm) long. Flowers greenish yellow, in spring. *B. m.* var. *japonica*, dense upright shrub, slow growing to 8 ft (2.4 m) high; 'Green Beauty', deep green foliage; 'Morris Midget', low-growing with yellow-green leaves. Other popular cultivars include *B. m.* 'Compacta', 'Curly Locks', 'Faulkner', 'Green Jade', and 'Green Pillow'. Zones 6–10.

Buxus sempervirens

COMMON BOX, ENGLISH BOX

☼ ❊ ↔ 5–15 ft (1.5–4.5 m) ↕ 5–30 ft (1.5–9 m)
Widespread in Europe, western Asia, and
northwestern Africa. Native to British Isles.
Leaves to 1 in (25 mm) long; leaf apex pointed,
blunt, or slightly notched. Greenish cream
flower clusters in late spring. **'Argenteovariegata'**
(syn. 'Argentea'), delicate gray-green leaves
with narrow cream margin; **'Elegantissima'**,
mid-green leaves with creamy white margins;
'Graham Blandy', narrow columnar growth
habit; **'Handsworthiensis'**, unusually large
leaves; **'Latifolia Maculata'**, pale gold juvenile leaves, yellow-variegated when mature;
'Marginata', misshapen leaves with yellowish
band around upper margin; **'Memorial'**, symmetrical form, grows to 2 ft (0.6 m); **'Suffruti-
cosa'**, dense erect habit, small leaves; **'Vardar Valley'** ★, dense
mound-forming shrub, mid- to dark green leaves. Zones 5–10.

Buxus, Sheridan Hybrid, 'Green Mountain'

Buxus, Sheridan Hybrids

☼ ❊ ↔ 18–24 in (45–60 cm) ↕ 18–24 in (45–60 cm)
From North America, cultivars from crosses between *B. semper-
virens* and *B. microphylla* var. *koreana*. Dense compact shrubs.
'Green Gem', globular form, rich green foliage;
'Green Mountain', darker foliage. Zones 5–10.

Buxus sinica

CHINESE BOX, KOREAN BOXWOOD

☼/◑ ❊ ↔ 2–12 ft (0.6–3.5 m) ↕ 3–20 ft (0.9–6 m)
Shrub or small tree from eastern China and
Korea, once regarded as variety of *B. microphylla*.
Occurs in many varieties covering wide size
range. Glossy light green leaves to 1¼ in (30 mm)
long. **B. s. var. *insularis*** (syn. *B. microphylla* var.
koreana), slow growing, with small but fragrant
green-yellow flowers; **'Justin Brouwers'**, dense
mound with small, narrow, deep green leaves;
'Pincushion' (syn. *B. microphylla* 'Cushion'),
dwarf cushion-forming shrub with dull green
rounded leaves; **'Tide Hill'**, dwarf to 12 in (30 cm)
tall; **'Winter Gem'** (syn. *B. microphylla* 'Winter
Gem'), hardy, foliage remains green during winter. Zones 6–10.

Caesalpinia ferrea

CAESALPINIA

Occurring in the tropics and many warm-temperate regions (mainly
in the Americas), *Caesalpinia* belongs to the cassia subfamily of
the legume (Fabaceae) family, and consists of around 150 species
of evergreen and deciduous trees, shrubs, and scrambling climbers.
Caesalpinia species all have bipinnate leaves, with numerous leaflets. Hooked prickles on branches and leaves are common, mainly
on the climbers. Flowers are in spikes, terminating the branches.
Many species have yellow flowers; most have 5 petals, and protruding stamens of often contrasting color. The pods can be flattened and smooth, or swollen and spiny, containing hard seeds.

CULTIVATION: These plants are readily cultivated in warm climates.
Many caesalpinias tolerate exposed seashores, arid climates, or
poorly drained soil. Some of the ornamental shrub and tree species prefer deeper well-drained soils and a sunny but sheltered
position. Propagation is usually from the seed, pre-treated to
penetrate the hard coat. *C. gilliesii* can be grown from cuttings.

Caesalpinia ferrea

BRAZILIAN IRONWOOD, LEOPARD TREE

☼ ❊ ↔ 20 ft (6 m) ↕ 50 ft (15 m)
Long-lived tree native to eastern Brazil. Deciduous, smooth creamy bark dappled with gray.
Foliage bright green. Flowers pale gold panicles
in summer. Zones 10–12.

Caesalpinia gilliesii

syn. *Poinciana gilliesii*

BIRD-OF-PARADISE SHRUB

☼ ❊ ↔ 4–8 ft (1.2–2.4 m) ↕ 10 ft (3 m)
From northern Argentina and Uruguay. Evergreen or may be deciduous in dry winter climate. Ferny leaves, numerous small leaflets.
Flowers pale yellow, in erect spikes. Showy red
stamens to 3 in (8 cm) long. Zones 9–11.

Caesalpinia pulcherrima

syn. *Poinciana pulcherrima*

BARBADOS PRIDE, PEACOCK FLOWER

☼ ✿ ↔ 6–12 ft (1.8–3.5 m) ↕ 10 ft (3 m)
Of uncertain origin, from tropical America or Asia. Long-stalked
showy flowers, bright scarlet to pink, gold or pale yellow, or may
be red and gold, all year. Stamens like cat's whiskers. Zones 11–12.

CALLIANDRA

This genus in the mimosa subfamily of the legume (Fabaceae)
family consists of around 200 species, the majority occurring in
South and Central America and the West Indies. Mostly shrubs
or small trees, they have bipinnate leaves, and long-stamened

flowers in globular heads or elongated spikes. Flower colors range from white and pink to crimson. Seed pods are rigid and flattened.
CULTIVATION: Most calliandras come from regions that are warm but dry, or have a pronounced dry season. Many species are frost tender. Where the climate is suitable, they tolerate hard dry soils and moderately exposed positions. Most species adapt well to clipping and can be used for hedges. Propagate from seed, or from cuttings taken in winter from short lateral branches.

Calliandra haematocephala
BLOOD-RED TASSEL FLOWER, POWDERPUFF TREE
☼/◑ ∗ ↔ 20 ft (6 m) ↑ 10 ft (3 m)
From northern South America. Flowers pink to scarlet or deep red, densely crowded into globular heads at branch tips, most of year, autumn–winter in cooler areas. Zones 10–12.

Calliandra surinamensis
PINK-AND-WHITE POWDERPUFF
☼ ∗ ↔ 10 ft (3 m) ↑ 10 ft (3 m)
From northern South America. Showy powderpuff flowerheads, white to pale mauve, most of year. Vase-shaped habit, with arching branches, and small clustered leaves. Drought tolerant. Zones 10–12.

Calliandra tweedii ★
syn. *Inga pulcherrima*
RED TASSEL FLOWER
☼ ∗ ↔ 6 ft (1.8 m) ↑ 6 ft (1.8 m)
Native to Uruguay and southern Brazil. Multi-stemmed fresh green foliage has tiny crowded leaflets. Deep scarlet flowerheads in spring–autumn. Can be trimmed to dense hedge. Zones 9–11.

CALLICARPA
BEAUTY BUSH
This genus has about 140 species of trees and shrubs, both deciduous and evergreen, in the mint (Lamiaceae) family. They occur from the tropics to warm-temperate regions around much of the globe. They have simple, conspicuously veined, and toothed leaves, and spring-borne heads of tiny flowers. Individual drupes that ripen in late summer and autumn are often small but distinctively colored; massed together they create a long-lasting display.
CULTIVATION: Hardiness varies with the species; some tolerate little or no frost, while others are very tough. They thrive in any moist

well-drained soil in sun or partial shade. Prune the plants after the fruit has fallen, and propagate from half-hardened cuttings.

Callicarpa americana
AMERICAN BEAUTY BERRY, AMERICAN BEAUTY BUSH
☼/◑ ∗ ↔ 7 ft (2 m) ↑ 10 ft (3 m)
Found in southern USA and parts of West Indies. Leaves to 8 in (20 cm) long, downy below. Violet flowers. Densely clustered magenta drupes last well into winter. Zones 5–10.

Callicarpa bodinieri
☼/◑ ∗ ↔ 8 ft (2.4 m) ↑ 10 ft (3 m)
From central and western China. Deciduous. Toothed leaves to 8 in (20 cm) long, turn golden in autumn. Lilac flowers. Drupes violet-purple, small but profuse. *C. b.* var. *giraldii* and its cultivar, '**Profusion**' ★, are more commonly cultivated. Zones 6–9.

Callicarpa japonica
JAPANESE BEAUTY BERRY, JAPANESE BEAUTY BUSH
☼ ∗ ↔ 5 ft (1.5 m) ↑ 6 ft (1.8 m)
Deciduous shrub native to China and Japan. Leaves to 8 in (20 cm) long, finely toothed margins, tapering to point. Flowers pale pink, fruit pink to violet-purple. '**Leucocarpa**', white fruit. Zones 7–10.

CALLICOMA
Found in coastal eastern Australia, usually near streams or rivers, the single species in this genus is a large evergreen tree in the Cunoniaceae family. Although the name wattle has become synonymous with Australian acacias, the early European settlers first gave the name to this tree in a completely different plant family but sharing similar fluffy flowerheads.
CULTIVATION: Apart from intolerance of heavy frosts, black wattle is easily cultivated. It prefers a cool root run with moist, humus-enriched, well-drained soil. Prune to shape when young and thin out any weak branches as the tree matures. Propagate from seed.

Callicoma serratifolia
BLACK WATTLE
☼ ∗ ↔ 10 ft (3 m) ↑ 12–30 ft (3.5–9 m)
Leaves glossy, heavily veined, serrated edges, downy beneath, to 5 in (12 cm) long. Young stems downy. Round heads of filamentous creamy white flowers at branch tips, in spring–summer. Zones 9–11.

Calliandra surinamensis

Callicarpa americana

Callicoma serratifolia

CALLISTEMON

BOTTLEBRUSH

This Australian genus of about 30 species of evergreen shrubs and small trees in the myrtle (Myrtaceae) family has a large range of hybrids and cultivars. The leathery, linear or lanceolate leaves are arranged spirally around the stem. Often new growth is richly colored, usually pink or bronze. Blooming in spring, summer, and autumn, the showy long-stemmed flowers, massed together in terminal spikes, form cylindrical bottlebrush-like heads. Round woody seed capsules crowd into a cylindrical group along the stem. Nectar-feeding birds are attracted to the flowers.
CULTIVATION: Most callistemons prefer moist, well-drained, slightly acid soil in a sunny position; some are only marginally frost tolerant. All respond well to pruning in the final days of flowering to promote bushier growth. Propagate species from seed. Selected forms and cultivars are grown from half-hardened tip cuttings.

Callistemon citrinus

syn. *Callistemon lanceolatus*

SCARLET BOTTLEBRUSH

☼ ❄ ↔ 10 ft (3 m) ↑ 10 ft (3 m)

From eastern Australia. Shoots pink and silky. Bright red flowers in spring–autumn. Tolerates moderate coastal exposure and poor drainage. 'Burgundy', dark red bottlebrush flowers; 'Jeffersii', dwarf to 6 ft (1.8 m) tall, red-purple flowers, lemon-scented leaves; 'Splendens' (syn. 'Endeavour'), broader leaves, masses of large, brilliant red flowers; 'White Anzac', white bottlebrush flowers. Zones 8–11.

Callistemon phoeniceus

LESSER BOTTLEBRUSH

☼ ❄ ↔ 5 ft (1.5 m) ↑ 10 ft (3 m)

From southern Western Australia. Sturdy, slightly weeping shrub. Leaves narrow, thick, gray-green. Flower spikes bright scarlet in early spring–summer. 'Pink Ice', pink flowers. Zones 9–11.

Callistemon viminalis 'Wild River'

Callistemon salignus

PINK TIPS, WHITE BOTTLEBRUSH

☼ ❄ ↔ 15–20 ft (4.5–6 m) ↑ 15–30 ft (4.5–9 m)

From moist locations of coastal eastern Australia. Small tree, weeping habit, white papery bark. Bright pink silky new foliage. Flower spikes creamy white, in spring–early summer. 'Eureka' ★, bushy form, purplish red new shoots, vivid pink flowers. Zones 9–11.

Callistemon viminalis

WEEPING BOTTLEBRUSH

☼ ❄ ↔ 7–10 ft (2–3 m) ↑ 25 ft (8 m)

Tall shrub or small tree from coastal eastern Australia. Heavily weeping crown of light green narrow leaves, brilliant red bottlebrush flowers in spring–summer. Cultivars include 'Captain Cook', 'Dawson River Weeper', 'Hannah Ray', and 'Wild River'. Zones 9–12.

Callitris rhomboidea

Callistemon Hybrid Cultivars

☼ ❄ ↔ 5–10 ft (1.5–3 m) ↑ 6–20 ft (1.8–6 m)

Propagate callistemon hybrids from tip cuttings to retain characteristics of selected clone. 'Harkness', light green leaves, brilliant red flowers; 'Injune', gray-green leaves, light pink flowers; 'Little John' ★, dwarf to 3 ft (0.9 m) high, blue-green leaves, dark red flowers; 'Mauve Mist', narrow leaves, spikes of mauve-pink flowers; 'Reeve's Pink', to 10 ft (3 m) high, with pink flowers. Zones 9–11.

CALLITRIS

AUSTRALIAN CYPRESS PINE

This Southern Hemisphere conifer genus of the cypress (Cupressaceae) family consists of 19 species of small to medium-sized trees, 2 found only in New Caledonia, the 17 remaining species in Australia. The fine thread-like twigs are clothed in tiny scale-like leaves, arranged in whorls of 3 rather than in opposite pairs as in *Cupressus*. The cones likewise have scales arranged in whorls of three. The pollen cones are tiny, while the seed cones, borne on the same tree, are more or less globular, their gray outer surfaces smooth or dotted with warty resin blisters.
CULTIVATION: *Callitris* species are light-loving, and occur on sandy or stony soils. Most species adapt very readily to being cultivated in warm-temperate climates; species from semi-arid regions prefer a warm dry summer. Grow in deep well-drained soils. They tolerate trimming and can be grown effectively in groups or closely spaced as hedges. They should be propagated from seed.

Callitris rhomboidea

syns *Callitris cupressiformis, C. tasmanica*

OYSTER BAY PINE, PORT JACKSON CYPRESS PINE

☼ ❄ ↔ 10–15 ft (3–4.5 m) ↑ 50 ft (15 m)

Native to mainland southeastern Australia, Tasmania, and central Queensland. Variable, sometimes broadly conical, sometimes columnar. Leaves fine, olive green; turn brownish in cold winters. Cones small and woody, in tight clusters beneath leaves. Useful for screens and hedges. Zones 8–11.

CALLUNA

There is only one species in this genus belonging to the erica (Ericaceae) family. It is found from north and western Europe to Siberia, Turkey, Morocco, and the Azores. The height of this small shrub is 24 in (60 cm) on average, but this can vary greatly in some of the 500 or more cultivars. The leaves grow in overlapping pairs, arranged oppositely, along the stems, and look more like scales. The leaves are dark green, usually turning reddish or tinged with purple in winter. *Calluna* differs from *Erica* in that the corolla is hidden by the calyx.
CULTIVATION: This plant prefers acid soil in an open well-drained position in full sun. Layer stems in spring and detach once rooted, or take cuttings of half-hardened wood in mid-summer.

Calluna vulgaris

syn. *Erica vulgaris*
HEATHER, LING
☼ ❋ ↔30 in (75 cm) ↕24 in (60 cm)
Native to acid heathland. Flowers are tubular or bell-shaped racemes, single or double, ranging from white to pink to purple in mid-summer–late autumn. '**Beoley Gold**', yellow foliage, single white flowers on shorter racemes; '**Blazeaway**' ★, red foliage in winter; '**Dark Beauty**', double dark crimson-red flowers; '**Firefly**', rust-colored summer foliage, turning dull dark red in winter; '**Gold Haze**', light gold foliage, white flowers; and '**Silver Queen**', silver-gray foliage, pale mauve-tinted white flowers. Other cultivars include '**Con Brio**', '**County Wicklow**', '**Darkness**', '**Kinlochruel**', '**Multicolor**', '**Radnor**', and '**Wickwar Flame**'. Zones 4–9.

CALOCEDRUS

This genus of 2 or 3 evergreen species, in the cypress (Cupressaceae) family, is native to Thailand, Vietnam, Myanmar, southwest China, and western North America. The overlapping leaves are arranged in crossed pairs in 2 rows along the stems. Male cones are borne singly and female cones are up to 1 in (25 mm) long, and have 6, sometimes 8, scales in pairs; only the center pair is fertile. The crown shape varies with climatic conditions. The timber is used for shingle tiles.
CULTIVATION: These plants are best suited to moderately fertile soil in full sun, although they will tolerate partial shade. Half-hardened cuttings can be taken in summer, and seed should be grown in containers with protection from winter frosts.

Calocedrus decurrens

INCENSE CEDAR
☼ ❋ ↔30 ft (9 m) ↕120 ft (36 m)
Native to western North America. Bark flakes off as it ages. Leaves glossy dark green with triangular tip, closely pressed to stem. Cylindrical cones ripen to red-brown. '**Aureovariegata**', smaller than other cultivars of species, foliage marked with yellow blotches; '**Compacta**' ★, globe-shaped, sometimes columnar, and very densely branched. In winter its branches turn brown. Zones 5–9.

Calluna vulgaris 'Con Brio'

CALODENDRUM

This genus comprising a single evergreen species in the rue (Rutaceae) family is from the coastal region of South Africa. It has a spreading crown and is often used in parks and large gardens or as a street tree in the more temperate regions of the Southern Hemisphere and warmer regions of North America.
CULTIVATION: *Calodendrum* prefers an open full-sun position where its crown can develop unhindered. Grow in a fertile, well-composted, and well-drained position where water is assured, especially in its initial growth period. Hardy to light frost when mature, it requires protection in early years when grown in marginal areas.

Calodendrum capense

CAPE CHESTNUT
☼ ❁ ↔30 ft (9 m) ↕30 ft (9 m)

Bright mid-green leaves dotted with oil glands. Flowers in pink clusters, protruding stamens, recurved petals dotted with oil glands, in spring–summer. Zones 9–11.

Calodendrum capense

CALOTHAMNUS

CLAW FLOWER, NET BUSH
One of the many Australian myrtle (Myrtaceae) family genera, these 40 species of evergreen shrubs are native to Western Australia. They are notable for their one-sided flower spikes and flowers with stamen filaments fused into broad straps. The flowers usually occur in late winter and spring. The leaves are needle-like, varying in length with the species.
CULTIVATION: Net bushes need a light, gritty, well-drained soil. They are drought tolerant and hardy to light frosts once established, needing moisture and shelter when young. Propagate from seed or soft to half-hardened tip cuttings, preferably from non-flowering stems.

Calothamnus quadrifidus

COMMON NET BUSH, ONE-SIDED BOTTLEBRUSH
☼ ❁ ↔8 ft (2.4 m) ↕8 ft (2.4 m)
Upright, heavily branched shrub. Flattened needle-like leaves to 1¼ in (30 mm) long. Flower spikes bright red, with stamens in bundles of 4, to 8 in (20 cm) long. Zones 9–10.

Calothamnus validus
BARRENS CLAW FLOWER

☼ ❧ ↔ 8 ft (2.4 m) ↑ 8 ft (2.4 m)

Easily grown, vigorous, upright or rounded shrub; can become a weed. Leaves narrow, aromatic; essential oils used in homeopathy and aromatherapy. Flowers large, crimson, in small clusters below leaves. Zones 9–11.

CALYCANTHUS

Resembling magnolias, but in the allspice (Calycanthaceae) family, the aromatic deciduous shrubs of this temperate East Asian and North American genus of up to 6 species have similar characteristics. They grow to around 10 ft (3 m) tall with a considerable spread, and have large elliptical leaves and strappy, many-petalled flowers in late spring and summer. Although the flowers are sometimes small and have rather dull colors, they are borne on the new growth and stand out well. CULTIVATION: Although difficult to propagate from cuttings (layering or seed being preferred), allspices are not difficult to grow. They prefer cool moist soil with ample summer water in sun or half-sun. The flowers do not last well in low humidity.

Calothamnus validus

Calycanthus floridus
CAROLINA ALLSPICE, STRAWBERRY SHRUB

☼/◗ ❄ ↔ 7 ft (2 m) ↑ 10 ft (3 m)

Native to southeastern USA. Leaves large, oval, dull mid-green. Bright red to dark red-brown fragrant flowers, up to 2 in (5 cm) wide, in spring–summer. Zones 5–9.

Calycanthus occidentalis ★
CALIFORNIAN ALLSPICE, SPICE BUSH

☼/◗ ❄ ↔ 7 ft (2 m) ↑ 10 ft (3 m)

From California. Reddish flowers fade to yellow with age. Large-flowered forms, with blooms up to 3 in (8 cm) wide, most often seen in garden centers. Zones 7–10.

Camellia japonica 'Elegans'

CAMELLIA

A member of the Theaceae family, this genus has nearly 300 species, native to the coast and mountain regions of east Asia. They are evergreen shrubs or small trees, bearing short-stalked flowers that bloom during the colder months. A number of flower forms, sizes, and subtle and more flamboyant petal markings are recognized. Petal colors range between shades of white, yellow, pink, rose red, dark red, scarlet, purple-red, and puce. Camellias are suitable for planting in formal or woodland settings, and for hedging, edging, topiary, and espalier. CULTIVATION: While it is usual to choose and plant camellias in late autumn and winter, it is important to withhold nutrition and additional water during this time. Acid to neutral well-drained soils, shaded or semi-shaded positions, plus dry winters and wet summers suit the majority. Propagation is by grafting, or from cuttings in late summer to winter.

Camellia grijsii

◗ ❄ ↔ 8 ft (2.4 m) ↑ 10 ft (3 m)

From eastern and central China. Leaves oval, dark green, finely toothed. Flowers fragrant, small, white, lobed petals, yellow stamens. Resembles *C. sasanqua*, but flowers in winter and early spring. Zones 8–10.

Camellia japonica
COMMON CAMELLIA

◗ ❄ ↔ 25 ft (8 m) ↑ 30 ft (9 m)

Shrub or small tree found on several Chinese, Korean, Taiwanese, and Japanese islands. Single flowers, red or puce-pink, mildly scented. Leaves broadly oval, pointed, very glossy above; paler, duller, lightly spotted beneath. Variable-sized fruit. Appearance and tolerance variable in wild. Well-known variation is apple camellia, *C. j.* var. *macrocarpa*, with large, red, apple-like fruit.

Cultivars of *C. japonica* are most popular; over 2,000 display different flower forms, colors, petal markings, growth habits, preferences, and tolerances. Leaves glossy, neat, and elliptical. Most grow into neat dense shrubs and, ultimately, small trees. They flourish in suitable climates and soils, in shaded or semi-shaded positions, and sheltered in cold climates. Well-draining neutral to acid soil is essential. 'Adolphe Audusson', semi-double dark red flowers; 'Alba Plena', double with snow white, symmetrical, overlapping petals; 'Akashigata' (syn. 'Lady Clare'), semi-double rich rose pink flowers; 'Alexander Hunter', rich crimson flowers; 'Berenice Boddy', large, semi-double, pink flowers; 'Bob Hope', dark red semi-double flowers with yellow stamens; 'Bob's Tinsie', small, bright red, anemone-form flowers; 'Bokuhan' (syn. 'Tinsie'), miniature anemone-form flowers, red outer petals, dense boss of white petaloids, moderately sun tolerant; 'Brushfield's Yellow', anemone-form, pale creamish white flowers; 'Coquettii', formal double, or incomplete double, red flowers; 'Debutante', large, pale rose, informal double flowers; 'Dona Herzilia de Freitas Magalhaes', purple-violet flowers; 'Elegans' (syn. 'Chandleri Elegans'), pink flowers; 'Elegans Champagne', big creamy petals; 'Elegans Supreme', deep pink ruffled flowers; 'Elegans Variegated', pink flowers with white blotches; 'Gloire de Nantes', semi-double to

Camellia japonica 'Alba Plena'

Camellia nitidissima

Camellia pitardii

incomplete double mid-pink flowers; **'Grand Prix'**, semi-double vivid red flowers; **'Janet Waterhouse'**, white, double, symmetrical flowers; **'Jupiter'**, formal double red flowers; **'Lady Loch'**, veined, whitish pink, peony-form flowers; **'Lavinia Maggi'**, white petals, streaked light and dark pinkish red; **'Masayoshi'** (syn. 'Donckelaeri'), rich pinkish red double flowers, whitish blotches on petals; **'Miss Charleston'**, intense red flowers; **'Mrs D. W. Davis Descanso'**, semi-double flowers of softest pink; **'Nuccio's Cameo'**, coral pink flowers; **'Nuccio's Carousel'**, medium-sized, semi-double, pink flowers; **'Nuccio's Gem'**, early blooming; **'Nuccio's Jewel'**, formal double, star-shaped flowers, shaded pink petals; **'Nuccio's Pearl'**, blush white petals tipped in shades of orchid pink; **'Roma Risorta'**, pink and red striped petals; **'Rubescens Major'**, glowing rose red, veined petals, dark glossy leaves; **'Tama-no-ura'**, dark red, petals edged in white, upright yellow stamens; **'Tomorrow'**, prize-winning early blooming American plant with large informal double flowers, pink petals and petaloids with deeper pink markings; **'Tricolor'**, with semi-double flowers, white petals with rose-red markings; and **'Twilight'**, with large light blush pink flowers that fade to silvery white. The **Higo Group** camellias, a popular Japanese form of *C. japonica*, are not a separate species; they have flat flowers, with profuse flared stamens, gold, pink, or red, and come in single and semi-double forms. Petals solid, blotched, or striped. Zones 8–10.

Camellia nitidissima
syn. *Camellia chrysantha*
GOLDEN CAMELLIA
☀ ❄ ↔ 8 ft (2.4 m) ↑ 10 ft (3 m)
From northern Vietnam and southwestern China. Pale bark; leaves leathery, large, conspicuously veined, pale green, with bronze new growth. Flowers golden yellow, in winter–spring. Zones 9–11.

Camellia pitardii
☀ ❄ ↔ 12 ft (3.5 m) ↑ 20 ft (6 m)
Native to southern China. Leaves lance-shaped, saw-toothed. Flowers in shades of delicate pale pink, rose pink, or white, with conspicuous bright red-pink stamens that fade to white. Cultivars include **'Fairy Bouquet'**, soft pink flowers; **'Gay Pixie'**, rich pink

flowers; **'Moonbeam'**, upright habit, pink flowers; **'Snippet'**, pale pink notched petals, used as an edging plant or bonsai specimen; **'Sprite'**, attractive flowers with soft salmon pink petals. Zones 8–10.

Camellia reticulata
☀ ❄ ↔ 15 ft (4.5 m) ↑ 30 ft (9 m)
Tough open species, originating in western China. Flowers rose pink, in noticeably velvety bracts. Leaves net-veined and toothed, and duller, darker, and narrower than those of *C. japonica*. This long-lived plant can adopt tree-like form and grow to 30 ft (9 m), but is usually shorter in cultivation. Many cultivars carry distinctive leaves of parent plant and can develop parent's tree-like stance, size, and open habit. Today cultivars of *C. reticulata* sometimes referred to as Yunnan camellias. *C. r. f. simplex* is wild form. *C. r.* **'Arch of Triumph'**, huge, peony-form, loose flowers, rose red petals, glowing yellow stamens; **'Bright Beauty'**, soft light red blooms; **'Captain Rawes'**, irregular, semi-double, carmine flowers; **'Change of Day'**, semi-double pale pink flowers, yellow stamens; **'Cornelian'**, large white-blotched red flowers, leaves can be variegated; **'Dark Jewel'**, rich red peony-form flowers; **'Dayinhong'** (syn. 'Shot Silk'), prolific, large, peony-form flowers with wavy ruby pink petals; **'Highlight'**, semi-double scarlet blooms, yellow stamens; **'Ida Cossom'**, attractive pink blooms; **'Mandalay Queen'**, dark green foliage, pinkish red flowers; Narrow-leafed Shot Silk/**'Liuye Yinhong'** somewhat willowy appearance and narrower leaves; **'Nuccio's Ruby'**, semi-double flowers of ruby red; **'Otto Hopfer'**, dark pink flowers, stamens tipped with gold; **'Red Crystal'**, scarlet flowers, golden stamens; **'Zipao'** (syn. 'Purple Gown'), old Chinese cultivar, bears deep purple buds, opening into large wine red flowers, pin-striped in red. Zones 9–11.

Camellia reticulata 'Bright Beauty'

Camellia saluenensis
☀ ❄ ↔ 4–15 ft (1.2–4.5 m) ↑ 4–15 ft (1.2–4.5 m)
Native to southwestern China. Open, branching. Crowded, elongate, oval leaves, dark green with blunt tips. Flowers single; white, sugar pink, or red, wavy lightly lobed petals, in late winter–early spring. Zones 7–10.

Camellia sasanqua 'Mikunikô'

Camellia sasanqua

☀ ❄ ↔ 5 ft (1.5 m) ↑ 10–25 ft (3–8 m)

Straggling, woodland, tree-like shrub from Japan. Leaves very shiny, dark green. Flowers scented, single, white or pale pink, in autumn. 'Cotton Candy', tall, spreading, free-flowering plant with soft, clear pink, semi-double flowers and ruffled petals; 'Crimson King', blooms early, deep pink-red semi-double flowers; 'Jean May', upright habit, double pink flowers; 'Mikunikô', early bloomer, single rose pink flowers with mauve tonings; 'Mine-no-yuki', early bloomer, snow white flowers; 'Misty Moon', upright habit, large, wavy, rounded petals of pale lavender-pink; 'Narumigata', white petals with curled pinkish red edges. Australia has produced **Paradise Series** of sasanqua camellias, with profuse, fluffy, small to medium-sized informal double flowers. Zones 8–11.

Camellia sinensis

syn. *Thea sinensis*

TEA

☀ ❄ ↔ 10 ft (3 m) ↑ 8–20 ft (2.4–6 m)

Probably originating in China, grown commercially for tea production for centuries. Flowers small, single, long-stalked, often in pairs, pronounced yellow stamens, usually rounded white petals. Most tea drunk in Western world made from *C. s.* var. *assamica* (Assam tea), with smooth-edged, thin, tapering leaves. *C. s.* var. *sinensis* (Chinese tea), from which unfermented green teas are made, has long, narrow, crinkly leaves and bushy appearance to about 20 ft (6 m). *C. s.* 'Blushing Bride' is attractive cultivar. Zones 7–12.

Camellia × williamsii

☀ ❄ ↔ 4–10 ft (1.2–3 m) ↑ 7–15 ft (2–4.5 m)

These hybrids of *C. japonica* and *C. saluenensis* first developed in UK in 1930s. Said to be the most easily grown and free flowering of all camellias. Leaves duller, paler than *C. japonica*. Flowers occur mostly in shades of silvery sugary pink. Award-winner 'Anticipation', deep pink flowers to 4 in (10 cm) across; 'Brigadoon', semi-double

pink flowers; 'Donation', light pink with darker pink-veined petals; 'Elsie Jury', created in New Zealand, large frilly pale pink blooms to 5 in (12 cm) in diameter; 'Francis Hanger', single white flowers; 'George Blandford', early flowering, with semi-double flowers of lavender-pink; 'Golden Spangles', single red flowers, variegated leaves; 'J. C. Williams', pink flowers over long flowering season; 'Joan Treharne', mid-pink double flowers; 'Jubilation', informal double pink flowers with long golden stamens; 'Jury's Yellow', white outer petals around dense boss of creamy yellow petaloids; 'Margaret Waterhouse', vigorous plant with well-formed, sugar pink, semi-double flowers that have rounded petals; 'Mary Christian', rich pink petals surrounding mass of golden stamens; 'Saint Ewe', single vivid pink flowers, lustrous leaves; 'Shocking Pink', tall bushy shrub, with bright pink, irregular, ruffled petals in irregular semi-double formation; 'Water Lily', upright shrub, formal double rose pink flowers with pointed petals. Zones 8–10.

Camellia Hybrid Cultivars

☀ ❄ ↔ 3–20 ft (0.9–6 m) ↑ 3–20 ft (0.9 m–6 m)

Most popular hybrids bred to withstand particular conditions, notably cold wet winters, exposure to sunlight, or marginal soil conditions, as well as for attractive appearance. 'Adorable', upright habit, formal double pink flowers; 'Fragrant Pink Improved', miniature, deep pink, fragrant flowers, open spreading habit, long flowering season, red new growth; 'Francie L', semi-double pink to red flowers; 'Freedom Bell', upright habit, semi-double red flowers; 'Inspiration', abundant semi-double pink flowers, petals sometimes with ruffled edges; 'Ole', dark pink buds open to salmon pink flowers; 'Salutation', notched silvery pink petals, long yellow stamens, large semi-double flower formation. 'Satan's Robe', upright glossy shrub, flowers large, semi-double carmine petals, golden stamens; 'Snow Drop', small distinctive gray-green leaves, with miniature white flowers occasionally flushed with pale pink. **Winter Series**, blooming during colder months, bred in Maryland, USA, to withstand cold conditions. 'Winter's Charm', upright shrub, medium-sized semi-double flowers with orchid pink petals and petaloids; 'Winter's Fire', single, open, puce-pink petals surrounding pronounced yellow stamens; 'Winter's Rose', palest of pink serrated petals arranged in semi-double fluffy-looking formation. Australian-bred **Wirlinga Series** produces amazing number of miniature, often

Camellia × williamsii 'Francis Hanger'

clustered flowers over prolonged periods. 'Wirlinga Belle', single, soft pink, medium-sized flowers, and open growth habit; 'Wirlinga Cascade', seedling from 'Wirlinga Belle', bears single pink flowers; 'Wirlinga Gem', abundant tiny pale pink flowers. Zones 8–10.

CANTUA

This South American genus, of the phlox (Polemoniaceae) family, is mainly Peruvian. It includes about 6 species of evergreen or semi-deciduous shrubs; all have, at one time or another, been used as garden plants. The flowers are long tubes with widely flared throats, carried in pendulous clusters, usually at branch tips.

CULTIVATION: *Cantua* is best grown in moist, humus-enriched, well-drained soil. A position in full sun will yield the best flower display, though if necessary the shrub will tolerate light shade and still flower satisfactorily. Regular pruning will result in more compact growth and also encourages heavier flowering and better foliage cover next season. Propagate from tip cuttings or fresh seed, which germinates well at around 65°F (18°C).

Cantua buxifolia ★

MAGIC FLOWER, SACRED FLOWER OF THE INCAS

☼ ⚘ ↔ 8 ft (2.4 m) ↑ 12 ft (3.5 m)

From mountains of Peru, Bolivia, and northern Chile. Flowers 3 in (8 cm) long, deep pink to purple, in early spring or in warm areas year round. 'Hot Pants', North American cultivar. Zones 9–11.

CARAGANA

PEA SHRUB, PEA TREE

This genus of around 80 species of often hardy deciduous trees and shrubs from central and eastern Asia belongs to the pea-flower subfamily of the legume (Fabaceae) family. They are wiry branched, and sometimes thorny. The pinnate leaves are made up of several tiny leaflets. The small pea-flowers are nearly always yellow, borne singly or in small clusters in spring and summer. They are followed by small brownish seed pods. CULTIVATION: Naturally adapted to a temperate continental climate with cool to cold winters and hot summers, these are tough, easily grown plants that adapt to most temperate climates with distinct seasons. They generally perform best on neutral to slightly alkaline soils. Trim to shape but avoid hard pruning because the old wood can be slow to reshoot. Propagation is usually from seed; cultivars are cutting-grown or grafted depending on the growth form.

Caragana arborescens

SIBERIAN PEA SHRUB, SIBERIAN PEA TREE

☼ ❋ ↔ 4 ft (1.2 m) ↑ 10 ft (3 m)

Widely cultivated tree from Siberia and northeastern China. Leaves have bristle-tipped leaflets; young stems covered with very fine

Camellia, Hybrid Cultivar, 'Wirlinga Gem'

hairs. Clusters of light yellow flowers in spring. 'Nana', dwarf form, short twisted branches; 'Pendula' ★, weeping growth; 'Sericea', covering of fine silky hairs. Zones 2–9.

Caragana frutex

RUSSIAN PEA SHRUB

☼ ❋ ↔ 8 ft (2.4 m) ↑ 10 ft (3 m)

Found from southern Russia to Siberia. Suckering shrub, thicket-forming with age. Leaves comprise 4 deep green leaflets on thorny rachis. Yellow flowers, in clusters of 1–3 blooms. 'Globosa', rounded form; 'Macrantha', large flowers. Zones 2–9.

CARICA

The 22 species in this South American and southern Central American genus are thick-stemmed shrubs and trees with large deeply lobed leaves and long, pulpy-fleshed, usually edible fruits; the best known is the common papaya. Leaves commonly have a snowflake shape with a long stalk. Separate male and female flowers are white or cream to green. Larger female flowers quickly develop into fruit once fertilized. CULTIVATION: These plants need steady warm temperatures, not necessarily tropical, for the fruit to ripen well. Species from higher altitudes can even withstand very light frosts. They are best in rich, moist, well-drained soil with ample humus, in a position that receives at least a half-day of sun. The plants fruit heavily from a very young age, but often lose their fruiting vigor just as quickly, so keep a stock of strong young plants to ensure a steady supply of fruit. Propagate from seed, cuttings, or grafts.

Carica × heilbornii

syn. *Carica pentagona*

BABACO, MOUNTAIN PAPAYA

☼ ⚘ ↔ 10 ft (3 m) ↑ 6–12 ft (1.8–3.5 m)

Natural self-fertile hybrid between *C. pubescens* and *C. stipulata*. Leaves 18 in (45 cm) wide. Fruit to 12 in (30 cm) long. Fruits sterile; new plants raised from cuttings. Zones 10–11.

Camellia, Hybrid Cultivar, 'Ole'

Caragana arborescens

Carica × *heilbornii*

CARISSA

This genus of around 20 species of evergreen shrubs and small trees, in the dogbane (Apocynaceae) family, is found throughout tropical and subtropical Africa, Asia, and Australia. Many are densely branched and spiny; they have glossy green foliage, and clusters of fragrant, pure white, 5-petalled, long-tubed flowers. Fruit is edible.
CULTIVATION: Usually drought tolerant once established, most species prefer to be moist throughout the growing season. They thrive in warm frost-free areas in a position with well-drained soil and full sun. Prune to shape as necessary, or shear hedges after flowering or after fruiting if the fruit is required. Propagate from seed or cuttings. The stems yield a milky sap when cut, and cuttings should be allowed to dry before inserting in the soil mix.

Carissa edulis
SMALL NUM-NUM
☼ ❀ ↔ 5 ft (1.5 m) ↑ 5 ft (1.5 m)
Spreading spiny shrub found in Africa and Middle East. Leaves rounded, dark green on red stems. Fruit tasty, round, purple-red to black. Excellent cascading container plant. Zones 10–11.

Carissa macrocarpa
AMATUNGULA, NATAL PLUM
☼ ❀ ↔ 10 ft (3 m) ↑ 7–10 ft (2–3 m)
Widely cultivated species from South Africa, with forked spines. Leaves rounded, deep glossy green, leathery, redden in bright light. Flowers white, to 2 in (5 cm) wide. Red to purple-red fruit. 'Boxwood Beauty' ★, compact habit. Zones 10–12.

CARMICHAELIA
syns *Chordospartium*, *Notospartium*
Part of the pea-flower subfamily of the legume (Fabaceae) family, this genus of about 23 almost leafless small trees and shrubs is native to New Zealand, with a species from Lord Howe Island, Australia. They grow in a wide range of habitats, from shaded river valleys to coastal and alpine areas, varying in form from tall to prostrate. Juvenile plants have very small leaves, generally absent in mature specimens. Leafless branchlets are flattened or very slender and reed-like. Many small pea-flowers, often fragrant, are carried on short racemes in shades of pinkish mauve to purple and white in spring or summer.
CULTIVATION: Most species are only half-hardy, needing greenhouse protection in cool-temperate areas. They prefer sunny well-drained situations, tolerating dry and poor soils but repaying better conditions with profuse flowering. Propagate from seed; half-hardened cuttings can be taken in summer.

Carissa edulis

Carmichaelia odorata ★
NEW ZEALAND SCENTED BROOM, SCENTED BROOM
☼ ❀ ↔ 6 ft (1.8 m) ↑ 6 ft (1.8 m)
Found along streamsides and forest edges in New Zealand's North Island. Bushy shrub, with slightly weeping branchlets. White and mauve flowers, lightly scented, in spring–summer. Zones 8–10.

Carpenteria californica

Carmichaelia stevensonii
syn. *Chordospartium stevensonii*
☼ ❀ ↔ 10 ft (3 m) ↑ 12 ft (3.5 m)
From New Zealand's South Island. Graceful weeping branches but can look straw-like and lifeless for several years when young as it has no juvenile leaves. Flowers in summer. Zones 8–10.

CARPENTERIA
This genus contains a single species of evergreen shrub from the hydrangea (Hydrangeaceae) family, which has a very limited natural range in central California on rocky mountain slopes. It has narrow glossy green leaves, lightly felted beneath. The fragrant white flowers resemble those of *Philadelphus*.
CULTIVATION: It requires a sunny site and a light, moisture-retentive, well-drained soil. It can be pruned to maintain a more compact form. Propagate from seed in spring or autumn, or cuttings that can be difficult to root.

Carpenteria californica
TREE ANEMONE
☼ ❀ ↔ 8 ft (2.4 m) ↑ 8 ft (2.4 m)
Flowers pure white with 5 to 7 overlapping petals, prominent yellow stamens, to 2½ in (6 cm) across, in early summer. Zones 6–10.

CARPINUS
HORNBEAM
This genus in the birch (Betulaceae) family contains about 35 deciduous trees and shrubs found throughout the temperate regions of the Northern Hemisphere. Commonly known as hornbeams, they are appealing trees at all times of year. The leaves have prominent parallel veining and color well in autumn. In spring they bear pendulous yellow male catkins and separate female catkins, which are erect at first. The fruiting clusters in autumn are surrounded by leafy bracts and in winter an attractive branch pattern is revealed.

CULTIVATION: Hornbeams will grow in most soils. *C. betulus* is a popular species for pleaching and hedging. Hornbeams are propagated from seed sown in autumn; cultivars are grafted.

Carpinus betulus
COMMON HORNBEAM, EUROPEAN HORNBEAM

☼ ❄ ↔ 60 ft (18 m) ↑ 80 ft (24 m)

From Turkey to southeastern England. Trunk gray, fluted. Pointed oval leaves, serrated margins, prominent veins, turn orange in autumn. 'Fielder's Tabular', light green leaves. Zones 5–9.

Carpinus caroliniana
AMERICAN HORNBEAM, BLUE BEECH, IRONWOOD, MUSCLEWOOD

☼ ❄ ↔ 40 ft (12 m) ↑ 40 ft (12 m)

Native to moist woods and riverbanks in eastern North America. Similar to *C. betulus* but often shrubby. Leaves turn to deep shades of orange and scarlet in autumn. Zones 5–9.

CARYA (see page 702)

Carya cordiformis
syns *Carya amara, Juglans cordiformis*
BITTERNUT HICKORY, SWAMP HICKORY

☼ ❄ ↔ 50 ft (15 m) ↑ 80 ft (24 m)

From eastern North America. Smooth pale gray bark; narrow, deep, scaly ridges with age. Buds yellow, flattened, hairy, in winter. Leaves have up to 9 pinnate leaflets, 5 large terminal leaflets. Zones 4–9.

CARYOPTERIS

This genus in the mint (Lamiaceae) family occurs in eastern Asia, from the Himalayas to Japan, and contains 6 species of deciduous flowering shrubs with slender cane-like stems. Most species have opposite, simple, toothed leaves, often aromatic and grayish. The flowers, borne in late summer, are mainly blue, mauve, or white in axillary or terminal panicles. The fruit is winged and nut-like.
CULTIVATION: Species prefer an open sunny position and thrive in cool-temperate regions, ideally in a fibrous loamy soil with free drainage. They flower on the current season's growth and should be pruned moderately in late winter or early spring. Propagate from soft-tip or firm leafy cuttings between spring and early autumn; dormant hardwood cuttings from winter prunings can also be used.

Caryopteris × clandonensis
BLUE MIST SHRUB, BLUE SPIRAEA

☼ ❄ ↔ 5 ft (1.5 m) ↑ 5 ft (1.5 m)

Hybrid of *C. incana* and *C. mongolica*. Slender vase-shaped shrub. Leaves downy, serrated. Deep blue to violet flowers, in dense cymes, in late summer. 'Arthur Simmonds', purple-blue flowers. Zones 5–9.

Caryopteris incana
syn. *Caryopteris mastacanthus*
BLUE SPIRAEA, BLUEBEARD

☼ ❄ ↔ 5 ft (1.5 m) ↑ 5 ft (1.5 m)

Small shrub native to China and Japan. Grayish, serrated, pointed leaves, slender arching stems. Heads of spiraea-like powder-blue flowers in tiers along stems in late summer. Zones 7–10.

CASSIA

Once a very large genus, *Cassia* has been revised and is now a far more consistent group of over 100 species in the cassia subfamily of the legume (Fabaceae) family. Found in tropical areas of the world, the mainly evergreen shrubs and trees have pinnate, sometimes hairy leaves, and yellow or pink flowers, borne singly, in small clusters or in panicles. Flowers are followed by bean-like seed pods.
CULTIVATION: Few species tolerate repeated frosts. They prefer a mild climate, moist well-drained soil, and full or half-sun. Propagate from seed, which should be soaked in warm water prior to sowing; some cassias will grow from half-hardened cuttings.

Cassia fistula
GOLDEN SHOWER TREE, INDIAN SENNA

☼ ❄ ↔ 20 ft (6 m) ↑ 60 ft (18 m)

Native to tropical Asia. Deciduous to semi-evergreen. Smooth gray bark. Leaves pinnate, leaflets in 3–8 pairs. Flowers yellow, scented, pendulous racemes, in summer. Dark brown seed pods. Zones 10–12.

Cassia javanica
syn. *Cassia nodosa*
PINK SHOWER, RAINBOW SHOWER

☼ ✿ ↔ 10 ft (3 m) ↑ 50 ft (15 m)

From Southeast Asia. Pinnate leaves composed of up to 34 long, narrow, drooping leaflets. Flowers over 2 in (5 cm) wide in racemes, color variable, buff through pink to crimson. Zones 11–12.

Carpinus betulus 'Fielder's Tabular'

Caryopteris × *clandonensis* 'Arthur Simmonds'

Cassia fistula

Cassia × *nealiae* ★

RAINBOW SHOWER

☼ ⚘ ↔ 20–30 ft (6–9 m) ↑ 25–50 ft (8–15 m)

Deciduous flowering tree, hybrid between yellow-flowered *C. fistula* and pink-flowered *C. javanica*. Flowers vary from cream to orange and red. Most common cultivars are pale yellow-white 'Queen's Hospital White' and 'Wilhelmina Tenney', odorless yellow flowers. 'Lunalilo Yellow', fragrant yellow flowers. Zones 10–12.

CASSIOPE

This genus of 12 species of small evergreen shrubs is closely related to the heaths and heathers (Ericaceae). Found mainly in northern Europe and northern Asia with outliers in the Himalayas and western North America, they are very much cool-temperate to cold climate plants, with a few species ranging into the Arctic. They seldom exceed 8 in (20 cm) high and have tiny leaves arranged in 4 distinct rows on wiry whipcord stems. The flowers, which appear mainly in spring, are small, usually bell-shaped, and carried singly, though often in large numbers, on fine stems.
CULTIVATION: Cassiopes prefer moist well-drained soil that is rich in humus and slightly acidic. They are not drought tolerant plants and need ample summer moisture. Very frost hardy, they prefer a climate with distinct seasons with a cool moist summer. They are best shaded from the hot summer sun. Trim lightly if necessary. Propagate from self-layered stems or by taking cuttings.

Cassiope lycopodioides

☼ ❄ ↔ 10 in (25 cm) ↑ 3 in (8 cm)

Native to mountains of Japan, northeastern Asia, and Alaska. Flat sprawling habit, minute leaves. Flowers, nodding, around ¼ in (6 mm) wide, carried on 1 in (25 mm) long stems. Zones 3–8.

Cassiope lycopodioides

Cassiope mertensiana

☼ ❄ ↔ 10 in (25 cm) ↑ 6–12 in (15–30 cm)

Upright or spreading shrub from mountainous regions of western North America. Leaves tightly pressed to stem. Small, white, bell-shaped flowers in spring. 'Gracilis', mound-forming. Zones 5–9.

CASTANOSPERMUM

The sole species in this genus in the pea-flower subfamily of the legume (Fabaceae) family is a rainforest tree from northeastern Australia and New Caledonia. Developing slowly into a beautifully shaped tree with a dense rounded crown of lush deep green foliage, it is prized not only as a specimen tree, but also for its timber, which is a warm deep brown color. The summer floral display is also attractive, though the flowers are often largely hidden within the foliage. Very large seed pods follow the flowers in autumn.
CULTIVATION: Considering its origins, *C. australe* is surprisingly hardy. Although best grown in

warm areas, it does well in any reasonably mild, frost-free garden and will even tolerate light frosts—with some foliage loss. The soil should be humus rich, moist, and free draining. Young trees will tolerate light shade. Propagation is from seed.

Castanospermum australe

MORETON BAY CHESTNUT, QUEENSLAND BLACK BEAN

☼ ⚘ ↔ 40 ft (12 m) ↑ 40 ft (12 m)

Deep green pinnate leaves made up of 11 to 15 leaflets. Flowers pea-like, in racemes, yellow, ageing orange-red. Seed pods to 12 in (30 cm) long, containing 1 to 5 large black seeds. Zones 10–12.

CASUARINA

This is a small genus in the she-oak (Casuarinaceae) family of shapely evergreen trees containing approximately 17 species from Australia and the Pacific Islands. In 1982 the genus was subdivided into 4 genera, with most Australian species now classified as *Allocasuarina*. All *Casuarina* species have distinctive, dark green or gray-green, slender, wiry branchlets, modified to function as leaves. The true leaves are reduced to tiny teeth-like scales in whorls at regular intervals along the branchlets. The minute, pollen-bearing, rusty red, male flowers form at the tips of branchlets. Female flowers, small and tassel-like, produce the next season's fruiting cones. Casuarinas are fast growing and may be planted singly or grouped for shade, shelter, and screening purposes. As they will withstand harsh windy conditions they are ideal for wind protection.
CULTIVATION: Grow casuarinas in full sun in any soil as long as it is well drained. Water well during the establishment period and dry hot weather. Propagate from seed.

Castanospermum australe

Casuarina cunninghamiana
RIVER OAK, RIVER SHE-OAK

☼ ⇥ ↔25 ft (8 m) ↑100 ft (30 m)

Stately tree, common on riverbanks in eastern Australia. Upright trunk. Dark green, slightly drooping branchlets near ground level. Useful for windbreaks. Prefers open moist position. Zones 9–11.

Casuarina equisetifolia
AUSTRALIAN PINE, BEACH SHE-OAK

☼ ⇥ ↔20 ft (6 m) ↑60 ft (18 m)

From subtropical and tropical eastern Australia, Pacific Islands, and Malaysia. Spreading tree, open branching crown, weeping branchlets. *C. e.* subsp. *incana*, weeping silvery green branchlets. Zones 10–12.

Casuarina glauca
SWAMP OAK, SWAMP SHE-OAK

☼ ⇥ ↔20 ft (6 m) ↑70 ft (21 m)

Native to east coast Australia. Upright tree, weeping dark green branchlets with waxy coating. Forms dense thickets in saline swamps. Withstands quite dry conditions. Zones 9–12.

CATALPA

This genus of 11 species of small to medium deciduous trees, belonging to the trumpet-vine (Bignoniaceae) family, occurs in North America, the West Indies, and southwestern China. They are attractive trees, with a tropical appearance from their large long-stalked leaves. They bear upright panicles of 2 in (5 cm) long, bell-shaped flowers, followed by hanging bean-like seed capsules up to 30 in (75 cm) in length.

CULTIVATION: *Catalpa* make excellent specimen trees and are good for street planting. They should be sheltered from wind to protect the large leaves. A sunny site with rich, moist, well-drained soil provides the most suitable conditions. Young trees may require protection from late frosts and should be trained to a single trunk. The species are propagated from seed sown in autumn and the cultivars from softwood cuttings taken in late spring or early summer.

Catalpa bignonioides
BEAN TREE, INDIAN BEAN TREE, SOUTHERN CATALPA

☼ ❋ ↔40 ft (12 m) ↑50 ft (15 m)

Found at streamsides and in low woods in south-eastern USA. Leaves large, heart-shaped bases, unpleasant smell when crushed. Large erect panicles of bell-shaped white flowers, marked with yellow and purple, in summer. Large bean-like pods. 'Aurea' ★, fine form with velvety golden leaves; 'Nana', small shrub to 6 ft (1.8 m) high, seldom bears flowers. Zones 5–10.

Catalpa bungei

☼ ❋ ↔25 ft (8 m) ↑30 ft (9 m)

Small tree native to northern China. Leaves triangular, with long central tip. Flowers rosy pink to white with purple spots, in summer. Seed capsule up to 20 in (50 cm) in length. Zones 5–10.

Casuarina equisetifolia subsp. *incana*

Catalpa speciosa
NORTHERN CATALPA, SHAWNEE WOOD, WESTERN CATALPA

☼ ❋ ↔90 ft (27 m) ↑120 ft (36 m)

From riverbanks, damp woods, and swamps of central southern USA. Like *C. bignonioides*, but has larger leaves. White flowers are larger, less dense, appearing a few weeks earlier. Zones 5–10.

CEANOTHUS
CALIFORNIAN LILAC

This genus of about 50 species of mostly evergreen, ornamental, flowering shrubs is a member of the buckthorn (Rhamnaceae) family. Mainly native to western North America, some are found in eastern USA, and from Mexico south to Guatemala. They range from low, spreading, ground-cover plants to tall shrubs. Most are quick growing but they may also be short lived. The flowers range from powder blue to deep purple, some having white or cream flowers, and appear mainly in early summer.

CULTIVATION: *Ceanothus* will grow in most soils, preferring a position in sun. They tolerate drought, heat, and cold if the soil is free draining. Most prefer dry-summer climates and are quite wind-tolerant. Tip prune young plants; adult plants require little pruning apart from removing spent flowerheads and wayward shoots. *Ceanothus* resent disturbance. Species can be propagated from the seed, and soft tip or firm hardwood cuttings can be taken between spring and early autumn.

Catalpa speciosa

Ceanothus arboreus
CATALINA MOUNTAIN LILAC, TREE CEANOTHUS

☼ ❋ ↔12 ft (3.5 m) ↑20 ft (6 m)

From southern Californian coast. Vigorous, wide-spreading, smaller in cultivation. Leaves ovate, downy beneath, larger than in other species. Flowers pale blue, fragrant, in abundant panicles, in spring. 'Mist' ★, paler gray-blue flowers; 'Trewithen Blue', large panicles of fragrant deep blue flowers. Zones 7–9.

Ceanothus × delileanus 'Gloire de Versailles'

Ceanothus × delileanus

☼ ❋ ↔ 5 ft (1.5 m) ↑ 5 ft (1.5 m)

Strong-growing, deciduous shrub, hybrid between *C. americanus* and *C. coeruleus*. Broadly oval bright green leaves. Panicles of soft blue flowers throughout summer. Cultivars include '**Gloire de Versailles**' and '**Topaze**'. Zones 6–9.

Ceanothus diversifolius

PINE-MAT

☼ ❋ ↔ 3–6 ft (0.9–1.8 m) ↑ 4–12 in (10–30 cm)

Evergreen shrub from California. Long flexible branches form low clumps. Small pale bluish green leaves, hairy beneath. Tiny heads of white to pale blue flowers in spring–early summer. Zones 8–10.

Ceanothus gloriosus

POINT REYES CREEPER

☼ ❋ ↔ 12 ft (3.5 m) ↑ 12 in (30 cm)

Occurs naturally on central Californian coast. Prostrate shrub with dark green, glossy, toothed leaves. Clusters of lavender-blue flowers in spring. *C. g.* var. *exaltatus*, erect shrub to 6 ft (1.8 m) high. *C. g.* '**Anchor Bay**', very dense foliage, mauve-blue flowers. Zones 7–9.

Ceanothus griseus

CARMEL CEANOTHUS

☼ ❋ ↔ 10 ft (3 m) ↑ 10 ft (3 m)

Shrub native to hills of central California. Dark green leaves, gray beneath. Pale lilac-blue flowers in spring. New growth arching. *C. g.* var. *horizontalis,* low-growing form with spreading habit; '**Diamond Heights**', produces golden leaves blotched with dark green; '**Hurricane Point**', fast growing, light blue flowers; '**Yankee Point**' ★, bright blue flowers. Another form, *C. g.* '**Kurt Zalnik**', discovered clinging precariously to eroding cliff face, has extremely dark blue blooms, height to 3 ft (0.9 m), spread of 15 ft (4.5 m). '**Santa Ana**', spreading habit, deep blue flowers. Zones 8–10.

Ceanothus hearstiorum

☼ ❋ ↔ 6 ft (1.8 m) ↑ 12 in (30 cm)

Prostrate, spreading, evergreen shrub from California. Previously called a hybrid, now a species. Small puckered leaves. Mid- to violet-blue flowers in small clusters in late spring–early summer. Zones 8–10.

Ceanothus impressus

SANTA BARBARA CEANOTHUS

☼ ❋ ↔ 10 ft (3 m) ↑ 10 ft (3 m)

Spreading, hardy, evergreen shrub. Leaves small, deeply veined. Flowers deep blue, in small thin clusters, in spring. Zones 8–10.

Ceanothus prostratus

MAHALA MATS, SQUAW CARPET

☼ ❋ ↔ 8 ft (2.4 m) ↑ 3 in (8 cm)

From mountainous areas of Oregon and California, USA, differing from other ceanothus in being subalpine. Creeping evergreen shrub makes dense mat, stems often rooting as they grow. Leaves toothed, dark green; flowers pale lavender-blue, in spring. *C. p.* var. *occidentalis,* wavy-edged wedge-shaped leaves. Zones 8–10.

CEDRUS

TRUE CEDAR

Cedrus species come from widely separated regions in northwest Africa, Cyprus, Turkey, Lebanon, and the western Himalayas. They are large long-lived trees from the pine (Pinaceae) family, with needle-like leaves arranged spirally on the leading shoots at the branch tip, crowding on the short lateral shoots to form neat rosettes. Both the male and female cones are large and conspicuous; the seeds have papery wings. All the cedars are somewhat similar in appearance, and are sometimes treated as varieties or subspecies of a single species, or as 2 or 4 separate species. CULTIVATION: Cedars are fairly frost hardy but cannot be grown in the more severe northern climates. They adapt to a range of soil types, if the soil is of moderate depth and fertility, and there is subsoil moisture available. These trees do not normally require pruning. Planting out is best done when still at a small size. Propagate from seed except for the cultivars, which must be grafted.

Cedrus atlantica

syn. *Cedrus libani* subsp. *atlantica*

ATLANTIC CEDAR, ATLAS CEDAR

☼ ❋ ↔ 30 ft (9 m) ↑ 80 ft (24 m)

From Atlas and Rif Mountains of Morocco and Algeria. Young trees conical with stiff erect leading shoots, ageing to broad-headed. Needles crowded on short shoots into tight neat rosettes. Foliage

Cedrus atlantica

Cedrus deodara

varies from rather bluish to green. '**Aurea**', distinctive golden yellow-tipped foliage. '**Glauca Pendula**' ★, requires support of long branches from which foliage sweeps to ground. '**Pendula**', all growths completely pendulous, forming curtain of bluish gray foliage, hanging down to 10 ft (3 m) or more. Zones 6–10.

Cedrus deodara
DEODAR, DEODAR CEDAR

☼ ❋ ↔ 30 ft (9 m) ↕ 200 ft (60 m)

Native to western Himalayas from Afghanistan to western Nepal. Largest of cedars. Spire-like crown with lower branches resting on ground. Leading shoots drooping with soft green needles. Seed cones barrel-shaped. '**Aurea**', pale yellowish new growth, changing to darker lime green. Zones 7–10.

Cedrus libani
CEDAR OF LEBANON

☼ ❋ ↔ 90 ft (27 m) ↕ 150 ft (45 m)

From Mt Lebanon in Lebanon. Young trees narrowly conical, with stiff leading shoots and grayish green leaves. Old trees massive horizontally spreading limbs. '**Golden Dwarf**' (syn. '**Aurea-Prostrata**'), dwarf form. Zones 5–10.

CEIBA
syn. *Chorisia*

About 10 species of tropical American deciduous trees make up this genus in the mallow (Malvaceae) family. They are tall stout-trunked trees with smooth bark often armed with large conical prickles. Leaves are compound with leaflets radiating from the end of the leaf stalk. Flowers are cream to yellow, pink, or red, and carried in loose panicles toward branch tips. The fruit is a large green capsule enclosing seeds buried in cottonwool-like hairs called kapok.
CULTIVATION: They thrive in lowland tropics or in subtropical regions; they are best in climates with a summer rainfall and a distinct dry season, in deep, well-drained, alluvial soils and a reasonably sheltered position. Early growth is fast, with the full height attained in only 10 to 20 years. Propagate from freshly gathered seed or half-hardened cuttings in summer.

Ceiba insignis
PINK FLOSS-SILK TREE

☼ ❂ ↔ 40 ft (12 m) ↕ 60 ft (18 m)

Widespread in tropical South America. Ornamental yellowish green trunk, thickest near ground; crown of broadly spreading limbs. Pink to reddish pink flowers in late summer–early winter. Zones 9–11.

Ceiba pentandra
syn. *Eriodendron anfractuosum*
KAPOK TREE

☼ ❂ ↔ 80 ft (24 m) ↕ 230 ft (70 m)

From South America. High open canopy. Cream to dull yellow or pink flowers on pendent stalks from bare branch tips before new leaves. Elongated pods about 6 in (15 cm) long. Zones 11–12.

CELTIS

Occurring in all continents and many larger islands, the large, mainly tropical and mainly evergreen genus *Celtis* consists of over 100 species. Belonging to the hemp (Cannabaceae) family, the genus has the characteristic leaf shape with usually toothed edges and an asymmetric base. Flowers are greenish and inconspicuous, with male and female separate on the one tree. Small berry-like fruit has thin but sugary flesh that conceals a hard stone; in most species they ripen to black or dark brown, and are greedily eaten by birds. Some species become troublesome weed trees when cultivated outside their native lands.
CULTIVATION: Vigorous growers, they adapt well to tough environments such as urban streets and parks, tolerating a wide range of soil conditions. The deciduous species make excellent shade trees. Propagate from seed, which in the case of temperate species should be cold-stratified for 2 to 3 months before sowing in spring; germination is often erratic.

Celtis australis

Celtis australis
EUROPEAN NETTLE-TREE

☼ ❋ ↔ 60 ft (18 m) ↕ 60 ft (18 m)

Found throughout southern Europe, northwest Africa, and eastern Mediterranean region. Deciduous, rounded canopy, smooth gray-barked trunk. Leaves have saw-toothed edges with slender point, dense short hairs beneath. Berries ripen bright orange to dark brown in summer. Can be invasive. Zones 8–11.

Celtis laevigata
syn. *Celtis mississippiensis*
SUGAR HACKBERRY, SUGARBERRY

☼ ❋ ↔ 60 ft (18 m) ↕ 80 ft (24 m)

Native to southeastern USA. Deciduous species with smooth dark gray bark. Leaves thin, hairless, very one-sided at base, finely tapered at apex, with teeth in upper part. Fruit orange, ripening to purple-black, in autumn. Zones 6–11.

Ceiba insignis

Celtis occidentalis
AMERICAN HACKBERRY

☼ ❋ ↔ 60 ft (18 m) ↑ 60 ft (18 m)

From northern USA. Deciduous, low-branching; smooth, gray, bark, develops rows of corky pustules, becomes dark and furrowed with age. Leaves broad, toothed, pale yellow in autumn. Fruit ripens red to dark purple in autumn. 'Prairie Pride', dense bushy crown. Zones 3–10.

Celtis reticulata
syn. *Celtis douglasii*

NETLEAF HACKBERRY

☼ ❋ ↔ 25 ft (8 m) ↑ 25 ft (8 m)

Deciduous species from mountains of western USA and Mexico, similar to *C. occidentalis*. Pea-sized orange-red fruits. Zones 6–10.

CEPHALOTAXUS
PLUM YEW

This interesting genus of conifers consists of 6 or more species, mostly found in China. In foliage features they resemble the yews *(Taxus)* but on female plants the ovules and the plum-like seeds that develop from them are crowded onto stalked head-like cones. On male plants the pollen cones are likewise crowded into small knob-like heads. The genus is now placed in a separate family, Cephalotaxaceae. All species are shrubs or small trees with flaky brown or reddish bark, often multi-stemmed and suckering from ground level.
CULTIVATION: Tough flexible plants that adapt to a wide range of soils and climates, they tolerate exposed positions as well as partial shade, preferring a climate with adequate steady rainfall throughout the year. They are excellent for hedging as they withstand frequent trimming. Propagate from cuttings, preferably taken from leading shoots. Cold stratification is used to germinate seed.

Cephalotaxus fortunei
FORTUNE'S PLUM YEW

☼ ❋ ↔ 10 ft (3 m) ↑ 20 ft (6 m)

Whorled branches; linear, gently curved, finely pointed leaves, 2 white bands beneath, arranged in 2 rows. Oval seeds ripen to glossy purplish brown. Zones 7–10.

Celtis occidentalis

Cephalotaxus harringtonia
JAPANESE PLUM YEW

☼ ❋ ↔ 10 ft (3 m) ↑ 15 ft (4.5 m)

Spreading shrub, sometimes small tree. Branches occur alternately. Olive green leaves, arranged in 2 rows, narrowed at tip. *C. h.* var. *drupacea* ★, short stiff leaves, rows arranged in neat V-shape. *C. h.* 'Fastigiata', erect branches densely crowded into column. Zones 6–10.

CERATONIA
This genus of the cassia subfamily of the legume (Fabaceae) family consists of 2 species of evergreen tree native to the Arabian Peninsula and Somalia. The leaves are pinnate with large leathery leaflets; the flowers are small and arranged in dense branched spikes emerging from the trunk and branches. The sexes are variably distributed on each tree. The fruits are plump brownish pods with shiny seeds embedded in a sweet, floury, edible pulp.
CULTIVATION: Only *C. siliqua* (carob) is known in cultivation. It prefers a hot dry summer, moderately wet winter, and permanent deep soil moisture. It likes a position in full sun, though it will tolerate part-shade. If only one tree can be grown it should be a variety that bears male and female flowers together. Propagate from seed, or from green branch cuttings in late summer.

Ceratonia siliqua
CAROB, ST JOHN'S BREAD

☼ ⬥ ↔ 25 ft (8 m) ↑ 40 ft (12 m)

Thick gnarled trunk, broad low canopy. Flowers pale greenish purple, with rank smell, in autumn. Abundant curved pods mature in early winter. Pulp used as chocolate substitute. Zones 9–12.

CERATOPETALUM
This genus of 5 evergreen species, in the Cunoniaceae family, is from east-coastal Australia and New Guinea. Small white flowers are followed by swollen reddened calyces lasting for weeks. Leaf size differs with the species: some are open lightly foliaged shrubs, others are tall densely clothed trees. Most grow in moist forests or rainforest habitats along the eastern coastline.

Cephalotaxus fortunei

Ceratopetalum gummiferum

Ceratostigma willmottianum

CULTIVATION: All species are easy to grow, but require adequate water and well-drained soil. Organic fertilizers like mulch or compost are preferred over chemical fertilizers. Partial shade will suit but better coloring will occur in full sun. Propagate from seed.

Ceratopetalum gummiferum
NEW SOUTH WALES CHRISTMAS BUSH

☼/◑ ❅ ↔6 ft (1.8 m) ↑15 ft (4.5 m)

Erect growing shrub, dainty trifoliate leaves, shallow toothed edges. Bright red calyces follow small white flowers in summer. Popular with florists at Christmas in New South Wales, Australia. Zones 9–11.

CERATOSTIGMA
From the leadwort (Plumbaginaceae) family, this is a genus of 8 species of herbaceous perennials or small evergreen or deciduous shrubs, all but one native to the Himalayas or China. They are grown for their intense blue, 5-petalled, flat flowers, borne in terminal clusters during summer into autumn, when the small-leafed foliage becomes red or bronze depending on the intensity of the colder weather.
CULTIVATION: These low-growing frost-tender plants are best grown in moist well-drained soil in full sun. Lightly prune to promote a dense compact bush—but remember, they flower on the current season's growth. They will re-shoot if killed back by winter frosts.

Ceratostigma plumbaginoides ★
syn. *Plumbago larpentiae*

☼ ❅ ↔12 in (30 cm) ↑18 in (45 cm)

Slender upright stem. Spreads from rhizomes. Cornflower blue flowers at ends of red stems, in summer–autumn. Leaves turn red with colder weather. Zones 6–9.

Ceratostigma willmottianum
CHINESE PLUMBAGO

☼ ❅ ↔5 ft (1.5 m) ↑3 ft (0.9 m)

Deciduous shrub with open low-branching habit. Mid-green leaves. Pale to bright blue flowers throughout summer–autumn. Foliage turns rich bronze tones in autumn. Forest Blue/'Lice', elliptical leaves, deep blue flowers. Zones 7–10.

CERCIDIPHYLLUM
The sole member of the Cercidiphyllaceae family, and closely allied to the magnolia family, this genus is represented by 2 species, and includes the largest deciduous native tree species in China and Japan. A distinctive elegant habit of horizontally held branches and heart-shaped leaves that color well—red, pink, and yellow—in autumn are the most notable characteristics of the species. Commonly it is found with the trunks forked low to the ground, which makes it vulnerable to damage in strong winds.
CULTIVATION: A sheltered position is essential to avoid disfigurement from drying winds and late spring frosts. Regular summer moisture is required and preferably rich soils. Propagate from seed after first subjecting to cold. Cuttings are readily struck in late spring to early summer in cool and moist conditions.

Cercis canadensis

Cercidiphyllum japonicum
KATSURA TREE

☼ ❅ ↔35 ft (10 m) ↑60 ft (18 m)

Elegant horizontal branch structure, vibrant autumn foliage. Leaves bluish green (reddish when unfolding), change to smoky pink, yellow, red in autumn, exude pungent aroma reminiscent of burnt sugar. *C. j.* var. *sinense,* velvety hairs beneath leaves. *C. j.* f. *pendulum* ★, weeping branches. Zones 6–9.

CERCIS
This small genus of 6 or 7 deciduous trees and shrubs in the cassia subfamily of the legume (Fabaceae) family, found in North America, eastern Asia, and Europe, is grown for the showy spring flowers. Leaves are alternate and mostly broadly ovate; flowers are pea-flower-like, with 5 petals in a squat calyx, usually borne on bare stems before or with the early leaves. The fruit is a flat legume with a shallow wing.
CULTIVATION: Frost hardy, plants prefer a moderately fertile soil that drains well, and exposure to the sun for most of the day. Shape to select a main leader but little regular pruning is required after that. Propagate from pre-soaked fresh seed. Take half-hardened cuttings in summer or autumn.

Cercidiphyllum japonicum

Cercis canadensis
EASTERN REDBUD, REDBUD

☼ ❅ ↔30 ft (9 m) ↑30 ft (9 m)

From USA. Variable with short main trunk, or multi-stemmed, rounded crown. Flowers dark red-brown sepals, rose pink petals, in late winter–early spring. Fruits reddish brown, in summer. 'Alba,' white flowers. 'Forest Pansy', burgundy foliage. Zones 5–9.

Cercis siliquastrum
JUDAS TREE

☼ ❅ ↔35 ft (10 m) ↑35 ft (10 m)

Native to Mediterranean region. Heart-shaped to kidney-shaped leaves. Flowers rosy purple, on bare branches, in early spring. *C. s.* f. *albida*, white flowers; 'Bodnant', deep purple-red flowers. Zones 6–9.

CESTRUM

This genus, belonging to the nightshade (Solanaceae) family, consists of around 180 species all from tropical America. They are evergreen or deciduous woody shrubs or small trees, and have mostly simple alternate leaves, usually narrow with smooth margins. The tubular to funnel-shaped flowers are borne in clusters; and they are often very fragrant and in some species are night-scented. The flowers are followed by small mostly blackish or reddish berries. All parts of the plant are poisonous. Some species have been classified as weeds. CULTIVATION: Most grow easily in full or half-sun and moderately fertile soil with adequate watering in summer. Where frosts occur, grow these plants against a sunny wall for protection. In colder areas they may be grown in a greenhouse. Plants respond well to pruning; pinch back to encourage bushy growth. Propagate from soft-tip cuttings.

Chaenomeles japonica

Cestrum aurantiacum
ORANGE CESTRUM
☼ ❋ ↔ 6 ft (1.8 m) ↑ 10 ft (3 m)
Evergreen or semi-deciduous rambling shrub native to tropical America. Requires regular pruning. Smooth light green leaves, slightly hairy new growth, unpleasant smell when crushed. Flowers orange, in clusters at ends of stems, in spring–summer. Fleshy white berries. Zones 8–12.

Cestrum × cultum
PURPLE CESTRUM
☼ ❋ ↔ 6 ft (1.8 m) ↑ 10 ft (3 m)
Cross between *C. elegans* and *C. parqui*. Ovate to lance-shaped leaves. Densely flowering terminal panicles, similar to *C. elegans*; single tubular flowers resemble *C. parqui*, although pink to violet in color. Zones 8–12.

Cestrum elegans
syn. *Cestrum purpureum*
☼ ❋ ↔ 8 ft (2.4 m) ↑ 10 ft (3 m)
Strong-growing shrub from Mexico. Arching branches. Ovate-oblong to lance-shaped, hairy, olive green leaves give off disagreeable odor when crushed. Tubular-shaped red to purple flowers, in dense panicles, in summer–autumn. Succulent, globular, purple-red berries. 'Smithii', orange-red flowers. Can be invasive. Zones 8–12.

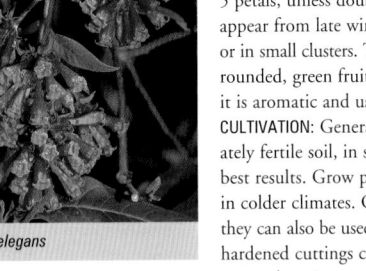

Cestrum elegans

Cestrum 'Newellii'
RED CESTRUM
☼ ❋ ↔ 10 ft (3 m) ↑ 10 ft (3 m)
Arching branches. Dark green leaves, narrowly ovate to elliptical, hairy, unpleasant smell when crushed. Rich crimson unscented flowers most of year. Berries small, round, dark red. Zones 8–11.

Cestrum nocturnum
NIGHT-SCENTED JESSAMINE
☼ ❋ ↔ 10 ft (3 m) ↑ 10 ft (3 m)
Evergreen shrub from West Indies. Pale greenish yellow tubular flowers give off strong night fragrance in summer–late autumn. No scent in daylight. Ovoid berries ripen green to white. Leaves somewhat succulent, bright green, paler on reverse. Zones 9–12.

CHAENOMELES
FLOWERING QUINCE, JAPANESE QUINCE, JAPONICA
This genus, which belongs to the rose (Rosaceae) family, has 3 species of spiny deciduous shrubs native to the high-altitude woodlands of Japan and China. Their early red, pink, or white flowers appear before the leaves on last year's wood. The leaves are alternate, serrate, oval, and deep green. The flowers, which usually have 5 petals, unless double, are cup-shaped and appear from late winter to late spring, singly or in small clusters. The roughly apple-shaped, rounded, green fruit turns yellow when ripe; it is aromatic and used in jams and jellies. CULTIVATION: Generally, well-drained moderately fertile soil, in sun or half-sun, will give best results. Grow plants against a south wall in colder climates. Good ornamental plants, they can also be used as hedging plants. Half-hardened cuttings can be obtained in summer or later in autumn. Seed can be sown in autumn in containers with protection from winter frosts or in a seed bed in the open ground.

Chaenomeles × californica
☼/◐ ❋ ↔ 5 ft (1.5 m) ↑ 6 ft (1.8 m)
Hybrid between *C. cathayensis* and *C. × superba*. Leaves mid-green, lance-shaped, 3 in (8 cm) long. Flowers 2 in (5 cm) in diameter, pink to pale red, in spring. Fruit 2½ in (6 cm) long. Zones 5–10.

Chaenomeles japonica

JAPANESE FLOWERING QUINCE

☼/◐ ❈ ↔ 6 ft (1.8 m) ↑ 3 ft (0.9 m)

From Japan. Open twiggy habit with spiny branchlets. Flowers orange-scarlet, prominent cream stamens, in late winter–early spring. Fruit fragrant, ripens green to dull yellow. Zones 6–9.

Chaenomeles speciosa

syns *Chaenomeles lagenaria, Cydonia speciosa*

CHINESE FLOWERING QUINCE, FLOWERING QUINCE, JAPONICA

☼/◐ ❈ ↔ 15 ft (4.5 m) ↑ 10 ft (3 m)

Native to China. Thicket forming, spiny suckering stems. Showy flowers in winter. Aromatic fruit ripens to green-yellow. '**Geisha Girl**', apricot double-flowered form. Some cultivars are hybrids with *C. japonica*, including '**Nivalis**', snow white flowers; '**Phylis Moore**', pale pink flowers; '**Toyo-nishiki**', pink and white flowers on same branch, sometimes produces branch of red flowers. Zones 6–9.

Chaenomeles × superba

☼/◐ ❈ ↔ 6 ft (1.8 m) ↑ 5 ft (1.5 m)

Hybrid of *C. japonica* and *C. speciosa*, garden origin. Leaves 2½ in (6 cm) long, oval to oblong-shape, lustrous mid-green. Spring flowers, white, pink, orange to orange-scarlet. Fruit to 3 in (8 cm) long, aromatic when ripe. '**Cameo**' ★, fleshy pink flowers; '**Glowing Embers**', orange-red blooms; '**Nicoline**', large dark red flowers, '**Rowallane**', bright red with yellow anthers. Zones 6–10.

CHAMAECYPARIS

This genus in the cypress (Cupressaceae) family consists of some 8 species from North America and eastern Asia. It is distinguished from true *Cupressus* by its small cones and short branches which have small leaves arranged in pairs and flattened to the stems of the branchlets. Leaves become more scale-like as it ages. Pollen and seed cones are borne on the same tree. Rice-grain-sized pollen cones appear in huge numbers; seed cones ⅓ in (8 mm) or less in diameter release small winged seeds as soon as they mature (in contrast to *Cupressus*, in which unopened seed cones may persist for years). Contact with the foliage can cause skin allergies. CULTIVATION: This genus is lime and air-pollution tolerant but will grow better in neutral to acid soil. Propagate from half-hardened cuttings taken in summer or seed sown in autumn or spring. Early trimming is necessary. Named cultivars should be grafted in late winter or early spring.

Chamaecyparis lawsoniana

LAWSON CYPRESS, OREGON CEDAR, PORT ORFORD CEDAR

☼ ❈ ↔ 10–15 ft (3–4.5 m) ↑ 100 ft (30 m)

Native to western North America. Foliage bright green to blue-green; some cultivars have yellow foliage. Red male flowers in early spring. Grayish cones ripen to rusty brown. '**Chilworth Silver**', slow growing, bluish gray juvenile foliage; '**Columnaris**', narrow pale gray leaves, grows to 30 ft (9 m) high; '**Intertexta**', slightly weeping branches, gray-green foliage; '**Nana**', yellow foliage, grows to 6 ft (1.8 m); '**Pembury Blue**', silver-blue foliage; '**Stardust**', medium-sized slow-growing conical tree. Other cultivars include '**Ellwoodii**' ★, '**Gnome**', '**Lanei Aurea**', and '**Stewartii**'. Zones 4–9.

Chamaecyparis obtusa

syn. *Cupressus obtusa*

HINOKI CYPRESS

☼ ❈ ↔ 20 ft (6 m) ↑ 60 ft (18 m)

Slow-growing tree native to Japan. Bark thick, rusty colored. Leaves opposite, deep green above, striped silvery white beneath. Foliage aromatic when crushed. Male cones yellow in spring. Rounded seed cones ripen to orange-brown. '**Crippsii**' (syn. 'Crippsii Aurea'), golden yellow foliage; '**Coralliformis**', to 8 ft (2.4 m) tall, dark green leaves; '**Nana Aurea**', golden foliage; '**Nana Gracilis**', to 10 ft (3 m) high; '**Spiralis**', lush bright green foliage. Zones 5–10.

Chamaecyparis pisifera

syn. *Cupressus pisifera*

SAWARA CYPRESS

☼ ❈ ↔ 15 ft (4.5 m) ↑ 75 ft (23 m)

Native to southern Japan. Rusty brown bark. Foliage mid-green, white markings beneath. Male cones very small, tawny; seed cones round, black-brown. '**Boulevard**', to 30 ft (9 m) tall, blue-green foliage; '**Filifera Aurea**', golden yellow leaves; '**Filifera Aurea Nana**', dwarf form; '**Squarrosa**' (syn. 'Squarrosa Veitchii'), soft young foliage, deep green to blue-green. Other cultivars include '**Gold Spangle**', '**Golden Mop**', '**Nana Variegata**', '**Plumosa Aurea Nana**', '**Plumosa Juniperoides**', and '**Squarrosa Sulphurea**'. Zones 5–10.

Chamaecyparis thyoides

ATLANTIC WHITE CEDAR, COAST WHITE CEDAR, WHITE CYPRESS

☼ ❈ ↔ 12 ft (3.5 m) ↑ 50 ft (15 m)

From east coast USA. Bark gray-brown. Leaves pointed, dark green, fan-shaped sprays. Small yellow male cones; seed cones purplish black. '**Andelyensis**', blue-green foliage; '**Ericoides**', purplish brown winter foliage; '**Heatherbun**' ★, dwarf form. Zones 4–9.

Chamaecyparis lawsoniana, in the wild, Oregon, USA

CHAMAECYTISUS

This genus includes some 30 species of trees, shrubs, and subshrubs from Eurasia and the Canary Islands in the pea-flower subfamily of the legume (Fabaceae) family. Some are ornamental, others are cultivated as quick-growing shelter and fodder. All have trifoliate leaves and pea-like flowers, usually in white, yellow, or pink shades. CULTIVATION: Though often short lived, species tolerate nitrogen-poor soils. Good drainage is important, and most prefer to be kept on the dry side except when in flower. A full-sun position is best. Propagate from seed or half-hardened cuttings.

Chamaecytisus purpureus ★

☼ ❄ ↔ 24 in (60 cm) ↑ 18 in (45 cm)
Native to southeast Europe and Balkans. Deciduous species, densely branched. Flowers pale pink to crimson, with dark central blotch, in late summer–spring. *C. p.* f. *albus,* white flowers. Zones 6–10.

CHAMELAUCIUM

One of Australia's best-known cut flowers, this genus, which belongs to the myrtle (Myrtaceae) family, comprises 23 species, all from the southwestern regions of the continent where they grow in well-drained gravelly soil in somewhat dry conditions. They are tough evergreen shrubs with fine needle-like leaves and masses of white or pink flowers with a wax-like texture that bloom during winter. CULTIVATION: Chamelauciums have a reputation for being finicky. However, when grown in well-drained soil in a sunny situation where water and humidity can be controlled, they do well, though they can be short lived. Propagate from seed or half-hardened cuttings.

Chamelaucium uncinatum

GERALDTON WAX
☼ ⚘ ↔ 8 ft (2.4 m) ↑ 8 ft (2.4 m)
From West Australian coast. Grown in gardens and for florists' trade. Flowers pink, purple, or red. Prune to keep compact. 'University', purple-red flowers; 'Vista' ★, pink flowers. Zones 10–11.

CHILOPSIS

Belonging to the trumpet-flower (Bignoniaceae) family, this genus consists of a single species of evergreen shrub or small tree native to arid regions of southwestern USA and western Mexico. It has brittle cane-like branches and narrow leaves. Short sprays of showy trumpet-shaped flowers terminate the branches, each flower 2-lipped at its mouth. Fruits are thin pendulous capsules packed with winged seeds. CULTIVATION: *Chilopsis* comes from a warm climate with a very hot dry atmosphere and although fairly frost hardy, will not thrive in cool humid climates. A warm sunny position and deep, well-drained, sandy soil suit it best. Propagate from cuttings or seed.

Chilopsis linearis

Chilopsis linearis

DESERT WILLOW
☼ ❄ ↔ 8 ft (2.4 m) ↑ 10–20 ft (3–6 m)
Downy twigs, grayish green leaves to 4 in (10 cm) or longer. Flowers 1½ in (35 mm) long, almost as wide, deep rose pink to white, darker spots in throat. 'Burgundy' ★, red-purple flowers; 'Hope', white flowers with light yellow center. Zones 8–11.

CHIMONANTHUS

There are 6 species in this deciduous or evergreen genus from China within the allspice (Calycanthaceae) family. Their scented flowers can be used dried, like lavender. Leaves are arranged opposite in pairs and appear after the flowers in spring. CULTIVATION: In colder areas they benefit from a sheltered position, which protects early flowers from frost damage. In less cold areas they can be grown in the open garden, needing full sun in fertile free-draining soil. Propagate from cuttings in summer. Sow seed in a position protected from winter frost as soon as it is ripe, but seed-raised plants will take 5 to 10 years or more to flower.

Chimonanthus praecox

syns *Chimonanthus fragrans, Meratia praecox*
JAPANESE ALLSPICE, WINTERSWEET
☼ ❄ ↔ 10 ft (3 m) ↑ 12 ft (3.5 m)
Deciduous shrub native to China. Lance-shaped leaves, glossy green, rough surface, turn pale yellow in autumn. Fragrant flowers on second-year bare wood, sulfur yellow to pale yellow, purple or brown stain on inner petals, in winter. 'Grandiflorus' ★, flowers to 2 in (5 cm) wide; 'Parviflorus', small flowers. Zones 6–10.

CHIONANTHUS

This genus in the olive (Oleaceae) family includes over 100 species of evergreen and deciduous trees and shrubs mostly from tropical regions of the world but with a few in eastern Asia and eastern USA. Leaves are smooth-edged and opposite each other on the branches. The white 4-petalled flowers are borne in terminal panicles, and are followed in autumn by a purple-blue fruit with a single seed.

Chimonanthus praecox

Choisya ternata

CULTIVATION: Some species tolerate alkaline soil; others prefer a neutral or acid soil and a position in full sun. Wood must be ripened by the sun for a good flower set. Sow seed when ripe in autumn, protecting it from frosts. Germination takes up to 18 months.

Chionanthus retusus ★
CHINESE FRINGE TREE
☀ ❄ ↔ 10 ft (3 m) ↑ 15–30 ft (4.5–9 m)
Native to China and Taiwan. Bark deeply grooved or peeling. Glossy, bright green, egg-shaped leaves, white downy undersides. Panicles of fragrant white flowers in summer. Blue-black fruit. Zones 6–10.

Chionanthus virginicus
FRINGE TREE
☀ ❄ ↔ 10 ft (3 m) ↑ 12–25 ft (3.5–8 m)
Native to eastern USA. Leaves egg-shaped, dark green, glossy, to 8 in (20 cm) long. Fragrant white flowers in pendent panicles. Blue-black fruit. 'Angustifolius' ★, narrower leaves. Zones 4–10.

CHOISYA
This genus within the rue (Rutaceae) family has about 8 species of evergreen shrubs that are native to southwest USA and Mexico. These are attractive ornamental shrubs with aromatic palmate leaves and scented, white, star-shaped flowers.
CULTIVATION: Most grow well in full sun in fertile well-drained soil. Propagation is from half-hardened cuttings rooted in summer.

Choisya 'Aztec Pearl'
☀ ❄ ↔ 8 ft (2.4 m) ↑ 8 ft (2.4 m)
Hybrid of *C. arizonica* and *C. ternata*. Strongly aromatic shrub, lush dark green foliage, fine narrow leaflets. Abundant white flowers open from pale pink buds in spring–early summer. Zones 8–10.

Choisya ternata
MEXICAN ORANGE, MEXICAN ORANGE BLOSSOM
☀ ❄ ↔ 6 ft (1.8 m) ↑ 6 ft (1.8 m)
Evergreen Mexican shrub. Glossy 3-lobed leaves. White, starry, fragrant flower clusters in spring; second flush in late summer.

Good drainage essential. Sundance/'Lich' ★, pale gold foliage, becoming more greenish on ageing, needs light shade. Zones 8–10.

CHORIZEMA
A genus of 18 species, all but one native to southwest Australia, *Chorizema* consists of evergreen shrubs or twiners. They are part of the pea-flower subfamily of the legume (Fabaceae) family, with massed short racemes of pea-flowers, often in contrasting colors. Leaves are heart-shaped, narrow, or lobed, and sometimes aromatic.
CULTIVATION: *Chorizema* species generally prefer light well-drained soil and a position in full sun or partial shade. While prolonged wet conditions are not tolerated, these plants will appreciate an occasional deep watering in summer. Propagate from seed, which needs to be soaked before sowing, or from half-hardened cuttings.

Chorizema cordatum ★
HEART-LEAFED FLAME PEA
☀/◐ ❄ ↔ 4 ft (1.2 m) ↑ 4 ft (1.2 m)
From southern Western Australia. Foliage heart-shaped, with small teeth. Flowers orange and yellow standard, deep pink to red keel. Best in well-drained soil, with a little shade. Zones 9–11.

CHRYSOPHYLLUM
This tropical genus from the sapodilla (Sapotaceae) family includes some 80 species of evergreen shrubs and trees. It is widespread in the tropics, particularly the Americas. They have medium to large-sized smooth-edged leaves, often with brown or golden yellow hair on the undersides. Flowers are small, white to cream with purple markings, in small clusters. The large fleshy berries are edible.
CULTIVATION: These trees need a warm humid climate free of frosts and cold winds. They prefer fertile, moist, well-drained, humus-enriched soil and regular feeding. Any pruning or trimming can be carried out as the fruit is harvested or, if the fruit is not required, after flowering. Propagate from seed or grafting. Seedlings take 8 to 12 years to fruit; grafted plants will crop well in 4 to 5 years.

Chrysophyllum cainito
STAR APPLE
☀ ✿ ↔ 15 ft (4.5 m) ↑ 50 ft (15 m)
Native to Central America. Leaves deep green, elliptical, yellow-brown felting beneath. Small, starry, creamy white flowers. Rounded, 4 in (10 cm) wide fruit ripens to purple. Zones 11–12.

Chorizema cordatum

Chrysophyllum cainito

Cistus albidus

Cistus ladanifer

Cistus × pulverulentus

CINNAMOMUM

This is a genus of about 250 usually evergreen trees and shrubs in the family Lauraceae, with aromatic leaves, wood, and bark. They are native to warm-temperate to subtropical regions from eastern and southeastern Asia to Australia. Panicles of inconspicuous flowers appear in summer. The fleshy berry-like fruit is grown for its spicy flavoring and for use in traditional medicine. The timber is used for making utensils and furniture, for building construction, and as fuel. Ornamentally, *Cinnamomum* species are valued both for the appearance of their foliage and as shade trees. Cinnamon is derived from the bark of *C. verum*, which is grown commercially. CULTIVATION: These plants are best grown in full sun or part-shade, in well-drained fertile soil, preferably in a sandy loam medium. They tolerate regular pruning. Propagation is from seed sown in autumn or from cuttings of half-hardened softwood taken in spring.

Cinnamomum camphora

CAMPHOR LAUREL, CAMPHOR TREE

↔ 30 ft (9 m) ↑ 60 ft (18 m)

Evergreen shade and screen tree from China, Taiwan, and Japan. Leaves aromatic, shiny, pink-red at first, turning light green. Cream flower clusters in spring. Oval, shiny, black berries. Camphor extracted from timber. Weed in subtropical Australia. Zones 9–11.

CISTUS

A genus of about 20 species in the rock-rose (Cistaceae) family, all are small to medium-sized, evergreen, flowering shrubs found throughout the Mediterranean region. They grow on sun-baked stony hillsides. In cultivation they become very adaptable long-flowering ornamentals, ideal for difficult dry sites. The leaves are opposite, mostly dark green or whitish, and in some species they exude a sticky resin called ladanum or labdanum, which is used in incense and perfume. The flowers, which are individually short lived, have 5 broad petals in either white, pink, mauve, or reddish purple, often blotched, and with prominent yellow stamens. CULTIVATION: All *Cistus* species revel in a hot sunny position and will grow in most soils provided drainage is good. They thrive in all climates of the Mediterranean type. Young plants should be tip pruned; pinch back older plants after the flowering period. Seeds can be sown in spring. Short cuttings from non-flowering sideshoots can be taken in autumn.

Cistus albidus

↔ 4 ft (1.2 m) ↑ 3 ft (0.9 m)

Widely distributed through southwestern Europe and North Africa. Dense shrub. Leaves whitish, white downy twigs. Flowers pale rose-lilac with yellow center. Zones 7–9.

Cistus creticus

syn. *Cistus incanus* subsp. *creticus*

HAIRY ROCK ROSE, ROCK ROSE

↔ 3 ft (0.9 m) ↑ 3 ft (0.9 m)

Found in eastern Mediterranean region from Corsica and Italy eastward. Stems hairy; leaves whitish green beneath. Flowers purple, flushed yellow at petal base. *C. c.* subsp. *incanus* (syn. *C. incanus*), less wavy margins, no yellow on petal bases. Zones 7–9.

Cistus ladanifer

GUM CISTUS

↔ 5 ft (1.5 m) ↑ 5 ft (1.5 m)

Native to North Africa and southwestern Mediterranean region. Leaves dark green, whitish, furry beneath, exuding ladanum. Flowers up to 4 in (10 cm) wide, white with brownish crimson blotch, bright yellow stamens. *C. l.* subsp. *sulcatus*, previously called *C. palhinhae*, low-growing, compact, shiny sticky leaves, white flowers. *C. l.* 'Blanche', deep green glossy leaves, grayish beneath, white flowers; 'Paladin', glossy green leaves, paler beneath, large white flowers with dark red basal blotches; 'Pat', large flowers, to 5 in (12 cm) across, white with maroon basal blotches. Zones 8–10.

Cistus × pulverulentus

↔ 6 ft (1.8 m) ↑ 2 ft (0.6 m)

Hybrid between *C. albidus* and *C. crispus*, often sold as 'Sunset' ★. Dwarf compact shrub bearing gray-green leaves with undulating margins. Bright pink flowers in spring–early autumn. Zones 8–10.

Cistus × purpureus

↔ 5 ft (1.5 m) ↑ 4 ft (1.2 m)

Hybrid between *C. ladanifer* and *C. creticus*. Sticky young stems, dark green leaves, grayish hairs beneath. Flowers to 2 in (5 cm) wide, pink to magenta, dark red basal spots, in summer. *C. × p.* f. *holorhodos*, pink unblotched flowers. *C. × p.* f. *stictus*, pale pink flowers with blotches. *C. × p.* 'Alan Fradd', albino sport. Zones 7–10.

Cistus salviifolius

SAGE-LEAFED ROCK ROSE

☼ ✳ ↔ 30 in (75 cm) ↑ 30 in (75 cm)

Leaves slightly aromatic, wrinkled, rough, downy, dark gray-green upper surface, whitish gray undersurface. Flowers borne singly or in groups of 2 or 3, with crepe-like white petals, suffused with yellow at their base. 'Prostratus', prostrate form. Zones 7–10.

Cistus Hybrid Cultivars

☼ ✳ ↔ 3–6 ft (0.9–1.8 m) ↑ 2–5 ft (0.6–1.5 m)

Hybrid cultivars that cannot readily be assigned names such as C. × dansereaui, C. × pulverulentus, and C. × purpureus include 'Grayswood Pink', with pink flowers; and 'Snow Fire', vigorous and hardy, with white flowers bearing deep red blotches. Zones 7–9.

CITRUS (see page 704)

Citrus trifoliata

syn. Poncirus trifoliata

TRIFOLIATE ORANGE

☼ ✳ ↔ 15 ft (4.5 m) ↑ 15 ft (4.5 m)

Dense fast-growing shrub from north China and Korea. Deciduous; dark green trifoliate leaves turn yellow in autumn; branches deep green in winter. Solitary fragrant white flowers, on second-year wood, in late spring–early summer. Fruit green, ripens to orange. Zones 5–11.

Clerodendrum bungei

CLADRASTIS

Native to China, Japan, and eastern USA, these 5 species of deciduous trees in the pea-flower subfamily of the legume (Fabaceae) family are cultivated mainly for their flowers, which are carried in wisteria-like racemes from early summer, followed by flat seed pods. The pinnate leaves have fine hairs on the undersides of the leaflets. CULTIVATION: Species tolerate a wide range of soils provided drainage is good. They will not withstand drought or waterlogging, but are otherwise easily grown in any sunny position protected from strong winds. Propagate from seed or winter hardwood cuttings.

Cladrastis kentukea

Cladrastis kentukea

syn. Cladastris lutea

YELLOWWOOD

☼ ✳ ↔ 30 ft (9 m) ↑ 25–40 ft (8–12 m)

Native to eastern USA. Bright green leaves, 7 to 11 oval leaflets, golden yellow in autumn. Fragrant white flowers, 12 in (30 cm) long racemes, in early summer. Narrow, 3 in (8 cm) long, brown seed pods. Zones 3–9.

CLEMATIS (see page 772)

Clematis heracleifolia

☼/◐ ✳ ↔ 2–5 ft (0.6–1.5 m) ↑ 3–6 ft (0.9–1.8 m)

Woody-based species from central and northern China. Lightly downy trifoliate leaves, irregularly toothed leaflets, to 2½ in (6 cm) long. Clusters of dusky, purple-blue, tubular flowers, with 4 flared and reflexed sepals, in summer–autumn. 'New Love', dark purple-blue flowers, lighter inside, fragrant. Zones 3–9.

CLERODENDRUM

GLORY BOWER

This genus of about 400 evergreen and deciduous small trees, shrubs, and climbers is in the mint (Lamiaceae) family. They are found mostly in tropical and subtropical regions of Asia and Africa. Their simple leaves are opposite or whorled. They are grown for their summer terminal panicles of showy violet or red flowers. The fruit is a drupe or berry. CULTIVATION: They prefer light to medium well-drained soils, rich in humus, in a protected partly shaded to sunny position. Water freely in the growing season. The stems of young plants may require support, and sucking insects such as mites, mealybugs, or whitefly can pose a problem. Propagate from seed in spring or half-hardened cuttings in winter or summer.

Clerodendrum bungei

GLORY FLOWER

☼/◐ ✳ ↔ 8 ft (2.4 m) ↑ 8 ft (2.4 m)

Evergreen aromatic shrub from south China and north India. Leaves triangular, toothed-edged, dark green, purple overtones. Flowers strongly scented, pale pink to purple-red, in summer. Zones 8–10.

Clerodendrum speciosissimum

JAVA GLORY BEAN, MATA AJAM

◐ ◑ ↔ 4 ft (1.2 m) ↑ 6 ft (1.8 m)

Erect shrub native to Java. Large oval leaves to 12 in (30 cm) long. Vivid red flowers, in panicles to 8 in (20 cm) long, in summer. Purplish blue fruit. Ideal container plant. Zones 10–12.

Clerodendrum trichotomum

◐ ✳ ↔ 15 ft (4.5 m) ↑ 15 ft (4.5 m)

From China and Japan. Downy leaves. Heads of long-tubed, white, scented flowers in late summer. Flowers backed by pink calyces, darkening as fruit matures. Purplish blue drupes. Zones 8–10.

Clethra barbinervis

Clianthus puniceus

CLETHRA

This genus of about 60 species of deciduous small trees or shrubs in the family Clethraceae is widely distributed from southern USA to Central and South America and Asia, with one species native to Madeira. They are grown for their white fragrant flowers, often borne in long racemes or panicles, which resemble lily-of-the-valley flowers. Some of the species have attractive peeling bark, and the flowers are followed by numerous tiny seed capsules.
CULTIVATION: Being closely related to the erica family, clethras like a lime-free soil and a moist sheltered spot, with some shade from taller trees. They can be propagated from seed, cuttings, or layers.

Clethra acuminata
CINNAMON CLETHRA, WHITE ALDER
◑ ❄ ↔ 12 ft (3.5 m) ↑ 12 ft (3.5 m)
Large shrub from southeastern USA. Racemes of scented creamy white flowers in late summer. Mid-green elliptical leaves have attractive golden tones in autumn. Zones 6–9.

Clethra alnifolia
SUMMERSWEET CLETHRA, SWEET PEPPER BUSH
◑ ❄ ↔ 6 ft (1.8 m) ↑ 6 ft (1.8 m)
Native to eastern North America. Fragrant white flowers, in erect terminal racemes to 6 in (15 cm) long, in late summer. 'Rosea' ★, buds and flowers tinged with pink. Zones 4–9.

Clethra arborea
LILY-OF-THE-VALLEY TREE
◑ ❅ ↔ 20 ft (6 m) ↑ 25 ft (8 m)
From Madeira, densely foliaged. Long terminal panicles of scented white flowers. Needs mild conditions to thrive. 'Flora Plena', double flowers. Zones 9–10.

Clethra barbinervis
JAPANESE CLETHRA
◑ ❄ ↔ 10 ft (3 m) ↑ 10 ft (3 m)
From mountainous woodlands of Japan. Peeling rusty brown bark. Dark green leaves, veined, attractive autumn color. Scented white flowers in terminal racemes in summer–autumn. Zones 8–9.

CLIANTHUS

This genus consists of just one (or possibly two) New Zealand species. *Clianthus*, a member of the pea-flower subfamily of the legume (Fabaceae) family, grows into a sprawling evergreen shrub, with pinnate leaves and large red flowers in early summer.
CULTIVATION: When grown in cool-temperate climates it needs the protection of a sunny wall or greenhouse to prosper. In warmer areas it should be grown in sun or partial shade where protection is available from strong winds and heavy frosts. It requires well-drained soil and should be watered during dry periods. Light pruning will encourage bushier growth. Snails and slugs find the foliage very appealing and are serious pests. Propagation is from seed sown in spring or half-hardened cuttings taken in summer.

Clianthus puniceus ★
KAKA BEAK, PARROT'S BILL
◑/◐ ❄ ↔ 6 ft (1.8 m) ↑ 6 ft (1.8 m)
Rare in native habitat, northern North Island of New Zealand. Branches clothed with attractive fern-like leaves. Red flowers, shape reminiscent of beak of kaka (native parrot). Easy to propagate, fast growing, can be short lived. 'Albus', attractive white-flowering form that grows true from seed. Zones 8–11.

CLUSIA

This genus of over 140 species from the rainforests of the American tropics and subtropics belongs to the St John's wort (Clusiaceae) family. They often start life as epiphytes, but form such a thicket of aerial roots that they eventually swamp or strangle their host tree, grow down to the ground, and form a trunk of their own. Most species have thick, leathery, deep green leaves that are roughly oval in shape. Although both male and female flowers appear on the same plant, they are separate. Both occur in 3-flowered clusters and have 4 to 9 rounded petals, but the males are larger and have numerous stamens. Near-spherical leathery seed capsules follow.
CULTIVATION: Most *Clusia* species require tropical warmth. They also need moist, well-drained, humus-rich soil and will not

Clusia major

withstand drought, frost, or even prolonged cool conditions. Prune to shape when young. Propagate from cuttings or aerial layers.

Clusia major

syn. *Clusia rosea*

COPEY

☼ ↔ 50 ft (15 m) ↑ 50 ft (15 m)

Shrub or tree with spreading, densely foliaged crown. Several trunks from thickened aerial roots. Flowers 3 in (8 cm) wide, pale pink with darker markings, in summer. Pale green fruit. Zones 11–12.

COCCOLOBA

A genus of about 150 mostly evergreen trees, shrubs, or vines in the knotweed (Polygonaceae) family from tropical and subtropical America, they have alternate, smooth-edged, leathery leaves, often quite large. The immature leaves are normally a different shape to the mature leaves. Spikes or racemes of small greenish white flowers are followed by a fleshy grape-like fruit, which is technically a small nut enclosed in the swollen floral remains.

CULTIVATION: Light or sandy well-drained soils are preferable, in an open sunny position, with ample watering, particularly in dry weather. Pruning is unnecessary except to maintain shape. Propagation is from seed, cuttings of ripe wood in spring, or of half-hardened wood in autumn, or by layering.

Coccoloba uvifera

JAMAICAN KING, PLATTER LEAF, SEA GRAPE

☼ ↔ 10 ft (3 m) ↑ 20 ft (6 m)

Native of tropical America. Erect, branching, evergreen tree. Leaves mid-green, leathery, heart-shaped, with reddish veins. Racemes of fragrant white flowers in summer, followed by edible fruit. Zones 10–12.

CODIAEUM

This genus belonging to the euphorbia (Euphorbiaceae) family consists of 6 species of evergreen perennials, shrubs, and small trees, native to tropical Asia and the western Pacific region. The leathery leaves are often variegated or marked and are the main ornamental attraction. Small, star-shaped, usually yellow flowers, carried in axillary racemes, appear in spring. They make good indoor plants.

CULTIVATION: They do best in fertile, well-drained, moist soil, but need to be fed and misted regularly throughout the growing season. In tropical areas they can be grown in shade. In cool climates, where they are grown under cover, they need maximum light but can suffer scorching in direct sunlight through glass. Propagate by air layering in spring or taking softwood cuttings in summer. Contact dermatitis may occur as a result of handling these plants.

Codiaeum variegatum

CROTON

◐/☀ ↔ 2–4 ft (0.6–1.2 m) ↑ 3–12 ft (0.9–3.5 m)

Native to tropical Asia and Australia. Small tree with numerous cultivars, varying quite widely in leaf color and pattern. Leaves may be smooth-edged, lobed, or twisted into a spiral, and are linear or egg-shaped, sometimes deeply cut to midrib, variegated red, white, and yellow on green. **'Elaine'**, stiff erect leaves; **'Grusonii'**, narrow greenish yellow leaves, flushed red on edges; **'Petra'** ★, leaves variously colored yellow, green, and orange; **'Philip Geduldig'**, leaves turn rich orange to purple with pinkish veins. **'Evelyn Chilcot'** and **'Lady Balfour'** are also popular. Zones 11–12.

Coffea arabica

Codiaeum variegatum 'Philip Geduldig'

COFFEA

COFFEE

Renowned as the source of coffee beans, this tropical African and Asian genus in the madder (Rubiaceae) family includes some 40 species of evergreen shrubs and small trees. The species most often grown for commercial coffee production is *C. arabica*, though *C. canephora* is also popular. These are quite ornamental plants with lush deep green foliage. They bear clusters of attractive, white, fragrant flowers in the leaf axils. The flowers are followed by colorful berries, in which is found the coffee bean.

CULTIVATION: Coffee requires warm temperatures to crop well, but when grown as an ornamental it will survive in most frost-free gardens. It also adapts well to container cultivation and life as a house plant. The soil should be moist, humus enriched, and well drained. A position in light shade is best. Commercial crops are subject to attack by several pests and diseases, but these are seldom a problem in gardens. Propagate from seed, which should be fresh.

Coffea arabica ★

ARABIAN COFFEE

◐/☀ ↔ 10 ft (3 m) ↑ 10 ft (3 m)

Widely cultivated commercially, originally from Ethiopia. Large shrub or small tree. Lustrous, wavy-edged, glossy, deep green leaves. Clusters of small, fragrant, funnel-shaped, white flowers in autumn. Round berries ½ in (12 mm) in diameter, ripen to yellow, red, or purple. Zones 10–11.

COLEONEMA

All of these 8 species of evergreen shrubs in the rue (Rutaceae) family are native to South Africa, most of them confined to Western Cape Province. All have small heath-like leaves on fine twigs and small starry flowers in winter and spring, sometimes repeating in summer. The foliage is slightly aromatic. They make useful small hedges if pruned regularly after flowering when young and brought slowly to the required height. They are often referred to as *Diosma*, which is a separate but related genus.
CULTIVATION: A position in full sun is preferred, with a free-draining rather sandy soil. Avoid exposure to strong winds, as they tend to dislodge the surface roots and blow the plants over. These species are not recommended for cold climates. Seeds germinate freely, but may result in plants of uncertain flowering quality; soft-tip cuttings taken in late summer or autumn give true results.

Coleonema pulchellum
syn. *Coleonema pulchrum* of gardens
🌣 ❄ ↔ 3–4 ft (0.9–1.2 m) ↑ 2–5 ft (0.6–1.5 m)
From South Africa. Well-foliaged shrub, slender branches. Soft, needle-like, aromatic leaves. Masses of tiny, starry, pink flowers in late winter–spring. Number of dwarf forms. 'Pinkie', compact, very floriferous, dark pink flowers, darker pink center stripes on petals; 'Sunset Gold' ★, pale yellow foliage intensifies to deep golden yellow in late summer–autumn if grown in semi-exposed position. Other cultivars include 'Compactum' and 'Nanum'. Zones 9–11.

COLLETIA
ANCHOR PLANT
This genus of 17 thorny shrubs in the buckthorn (Rhamnaceae) family, covered in spines and often with thickened and flattened branches, is native to temperate regions of South America. They are cultivated for their ornamental value, their spines making them particularly useful for boundary planting. Leaves are non-existent or very small and short-lived, while the small, scented, bell-shaped or tubular, usually yellowish or white flowers appear singly or in clusters, normally from summer to early autumn. The fruit is a leathery 3-lobed capsule.
CULTIVATION: They prefer light to medium, sandy, well-drained soil in a protected but sunny position. Propagation is from seed or from cuttings of half-hardened wood taken in autumn.

Colletia hystrix
syn. *Colletia armata*
🌣 ❄ ↔ 10–15 ft (3–4.5 m) ↑ 10–15 ft (3–4.5 m)
Large prickly shrub from Chile and Argentina. Leaves tiny, inconspicuous, deciduous; gray-green, rounded, spine-tipped stems perform most photosynthesis. Produces tiny, scented, tubular, white flowers in late summer–autumn. Zones 8–11.

Colletia paradoxa
syn. *Colletia cruciata*
ANCHOR BUSH
🌣 ❄ ↔ 8 ft (2.4 m) ↑ 6 ft (1.8 m)
Slow-growing deciduous shrub from Uruguay and southern Brazil. Flattened triangular spines instead of leaves. All parts bluish green. Fragrant yellowish white flowers in summer–early autumn. Zones 8–9.

COLUTEA
The 30-odd species of leguminous deciduous shrubs and small trees in this genus in the pea-flower subfamily of the legume (Fabaceae) family occur naturally in Africa and Europe eastward to Central Asia. They are wiry-stemmed, sometimes spiny, and have pinnate or trifoliate leaves, usually composed of very small leaflets. The small racemes of yellow to orange pea-like flowers appear from spring to autumn and are quite attractive. The pods become very inflated and balloon-like and may be colored, translucent, glossy, or hairy. They are worth growing as novelties; children love the pods because of the noise they make when burst by squeezing.
CULTIVATION: Most *Colutea* species are moderately to very frost hardy and grow in a wide range of soils with good drainage. They thrive in inland gardens and grow well near the coast. Plant in full sun for the best flower and pod production. Regular tip pinching and thinning will help to keep plants compact. Propagate from seed or from cuttings taken in summer.

Colutea arborescens
BLADDER SENNA
🌣 ❄ ↔ 10 ft (3 m) ↑ 15 ft (4.5 m)
Native to southern Europe. Leaves 6 in (15 cm) long, 5 to 7 pairs of leaflets. Small yellow and orange-red flowers in late spring. Pods to 3 in (8 cm) long, bright green, developing red tints, translucent when mature. 'Bullata', compact form. Zones 5–10.

Coleonema pulchellum

Colletia paradoxa

Colutea arborescens

COMBRETUM

Widespread in the tropics, with the exception of Australia, this genus in the family Combretaceae consists of around 250 species of mainly evergreen and a few deciduous trees and shrubs, some of which are scrambling climbers. The paired leaves are usually a simple, pointed, oval to lance shape. The deciduous species, from South Africa, may have bright foliage in autumn. The flowers are small and may be petal-less, but are brightly colored and carried in racemes or panicles at the stem tips and in the leaf axils. Long-lasting 4- or 5-winged seed pods follow the flowers.
CULTIVATION: Primarily a genus of the seasonal rainfall tropics, most of these species prefer constantly warm conditions. Some of the South African species will tolerate light frosts provided the soil is dry in winter. Soil must be well-drained. Plant in full sun and propagate from seed or half-hardened cuttings.

Coprosma repens 'Variegata'

Combretum kraussii
☼ ⬍ ↔ 15 ft (4.5 m) ↑ 40 ft (12 m)
Deciduous tree from eastern South Africa. Leaves elliptical, dark glossy green, silvery white beneath. New leaves change color from green-white in spring to green-red by autumn. Creamy white flowers with new leaves in late winter–late spring. **Zones 9–11.**

COPROSMA

This genus belongs to the large family Rubiaceae. It comprises about 90 species of evergreen shrubs and small trees from Australia, New Zealand, and the Pacific region. There is a wide variation in habit from erect to creeping; leaves range from minute to large. Inconspicuous male and female flowers grow on separate plants. The berries on the female can give a pretty display in summer and autumn.
CULTIVATION: Adaptable plants tolerating a wide range of situations and soils, *Coprosma* species are usually best in full sun and well-drained conditions. Some are suited to harsh coastal conditions; others are useful for ground cover, hedging, and shelter. In cool-temperate climates they are barely hardy and require overwintering in the greenhouse. If a display of berries is required, male and female plants must be grown together. Propagation is from seed, which is best sown fresh, or from half-hardened cuttings taken in autumn.

Combretum kraussii

Coprosma 'Coppershine'
☼ ❋ ↔ 3–4 ft (0.9–1.2 m) ↑ 3–5 ft (0.9–1.5 m)
New Zealand raised hybrid. Compact shrub, densely foliaged, with small very glossy leaves, green with bronze overtones. **Zones 8–10.**

Coprosma × *kirkii*
☼ ⬍ ↔ 7 ft (2 m) ↑ 3 ft (0.9 m)
May be natural hybrid between *C. acerosa* and *C. repens*. Variable plant, mounding or prostrate. Small, narrow, glossy leaves, inconspicuous flowers. Erratic crop of red-flecked, translucent, cream to white berries. Tolerates coastal gardens. 'Variegata', popular cultivar with silvery, cream-edged, sage green leaves. **Zones 9–10.**

Coprosma repens
MIRROR BUSH, TAUPATA
☼ ⬍ ↔ 12 ft (3.5 m) ↑ 20 ft (6 m)
From New Zealand coastal areas. Very glossy, thick, dark green, oblong leaves. Berries orangey red. Excellent plant for warm coastal gardens. 'Marble Queen' ★, leaves speckled white; 'Painter's Palette', very glossy leaves of red, cream, yellow, green, and chocolate brown; 'Picturata', glossy leaves variegated cream; 'Variegata', cream-edged, shiny green leaves; 'Yvonne', glossy dark green and chocolate brown leaves, intensifying color in winter. **Zones 9–11.**

Coprosma rugosa
☼ ❋ ↔ 6 ft (1.8 m) ↑ 6 ft (1.8 m)
From New Zealand. Reddish brown branches, needle-like leaves. Berries range from pale to dark blue. 'Clearwater Gold', selected male form, attractive golden coloring. **Zones 8–10.**

CORDIA

This genus in the family Boraginaceae comprises about 300 deciduous or evergreen trees or shrubs that are native to tropical regions of Central and South America, Africa, and Asia. They have terminal flowerheads or spikes of bell-shaped or tubular white or orange flowers, and alternate simple leaves; the fruit is a drupe.
CULTIVATION: They like moist, well-drained, peaty soils, in an open sunny position. Pruning is not usually needed. Propagate in winter to spring from ripe seed, or from cuttings.

Cordia boissieri
TEXAS OLIVE
☼ ❋ ↔ 8 ft (2.4 m) ↑ 8 ft (2.4 m)
Found in Texas and New Mexico, USA, and nearby parts of Mexico. Evergreen shrub, with leaves elliptical to ovate, dull green on upper surface, downy on underside. Large, white, yellow-centered flowers in summer. Will not tolerate prolonged wet, cold conditions. **Zones 8–11.**

Cordyline australis, in the wild, New Zealand

CORDYLINE

This small group of about 15 species of erect, palm-like, evergreen shrubs in the family Rusca-ceae is found in Australasia, the Pacific region, and one in tropical America. They are usually sparingly branched or suckering with fibrous stems tipped with a tuft of strap-like pointed leaves. Masses of small flowers with 6 spreading segments are produced in large panicles, followed by red, black, or whitish berry-like fruit. CULTIVATION: In warmer areas grow in well-drained organically rich soil with regular water during the warmer months. Most prefer a protected partially shaded position, although *C. australis* will thrive in full sun. If multiple trunks and a clumping effect are required, cut the main stem at any height. Propagate from seed, stem cuttings, or by division.

Cordyline fruticosa 'Kiwi'

Cordyline australis
syn. *Dracaena australis*
NEW ZEALAND CABBAGE TREE
◐/◑ ❄ ↔ 8 ft (2.4 m) ↑ 20 ft (6 m)
Erect palm-like tree from New Zealand. Usually an unbranched stem, developing broad crown of spreading, sword-like, pointed leaves. In late spring–summer, mature trees bear broad panicles of sweet-scented, creamy white, starry flowers. Clusters of white or bluish berries. 'Albertii', smaller variegated form; Purpurea Group ★, leaves suffused bronze to purple. Zones 8–11.

Cordyline fruticosa
syn. *Cordyline terminalis*
TI PLANT
◑ ¾ ↔ 4 ft (1.2 m) ↑ 10 ft (3 m)
From Southeast Asia, northern Australia, and many Pacific islands. Erect sparingly branched species, with thin-textured, distinctly stalked, lance-shaped leaves. White, mauve, or purplish flowers; clusters of bright red berries. 'Glauca', slender green leaves, blackish reverse, hint of purple on new growth, small starry flowers in spring. Colorful foliage forms include 'Kiwi' and 'Rubra'. Zones 10–12.

Cordyline rubra
PALM LILY
◑ ¾ ↔ 3–7 ft (0.9–2 m) ↑ 10–15 ft (3–4.5 m)
From subtropical eastern Australia. Leaves 6–20 in (15–50 cm) long. Lilac flowers in summer, followed by scarlet-red berries. Zones 10–11.

Cordyline stricta ★
SLENDER PALM LILY
☀ ¾ ↔ 3 ft (0.9 m) ↑ 15 ft (4.5 m)
From subtropical forests of eastern Australia. Erect multi-stemmed clumps. Leaves narrow, drooping, toothed margins. Small purple or violet flowers in spring–summer. Glossy black berries. Zones 10–12.

CORNUS
DOGWOOD
There are about 65 species of deciduous and evergreen trees, shrubs, and herbs in this genus of the family Cornaceae, nearly all from eastern Asia, North America, and Europe. A few are ornamental, garden-grown for their autumn leaf color, colored winter stems, or their branches covered in blankets of "flowers," composed of large petals or wide decorative bracts surrounding small insignificant flowers. Other species are bractless. The simple oval leaves are usually opposite. The fleshy fruits have stones. CULTIVATION: They need sun or part-shade, good drainage, and a fertile neutral to acid soil. Those grown for their winter stem color are best grown in full sun and cut back in early spring. Propagate the multi-stemmed species by layering of sucker growths, from hardwood cuttings taken in summer or autumn, or from seed cleaned and cold-stratified for at least 3 months. The large-bracted species can be raised from seed (also stratified), from half-hardened cuttings in summer, or by grafting.

Cornus alba
RED-BARKED DOGWOOD, TARTARIAN DOGWOOD
◐/◑ ❄ ↔ 10 ft (3 m) ↑ 10 ft (3 m)
Deciduous spreading shrub, native to eastern Asia. Forms dense thickets. Blood red young stems in winter. Dark green oval leaves, colorful autumn tones. Clusters of creamy flowers in late spring. Small, white, blue-tinted fruits. 'Argenteomarginata', cream- to white-edged leaves; 'Aurea', light greenish gold foliage; 'Gouchaltii', white and red variegations; 'Kesselringii', black-purple stems, red-and-purple autumn leaves; 'Sibirica' ★, glowing coral red stems; 'Sibirica Variegata', deep green leaves edged with creamy white. Zones 4–9.

Cornus capitata
BENTHAM'S CORNEL, HIMALAYAN DOGWOOD
◐/◑ ❄ ↔ 30 ft (9 m) ↑ 30 ft (9 m)
Bushy evergreen or semi-evergreen tree from China and Himalayas. Leathery, oval, gray-green leaves, paler underneath. Minute flowers, cream to lemon yellow sky-facing bracts in late spring–early summer. Pendent, rose to apricot, pink-tinted fruits. Zones 8–10.

Cornus controversa
GIANT DOGWOOD, TABLETOP DOGWOOD
☼ ✿ ↔ 50 ft (15 m) ↑ 60 ft (18 m)
Large deciduous tree native to Japan and China. Horizontally spreading branches, well-separated tiers. Oval pointed leaves, glossy dark green above, downy beneath, turn red and purple in autumn. White, upturned, flattish flowerheads. Fruits blue-black. Zones 5–8.

Cornus 'Eddie's White Wonder'
☼ ✿ ↔ 15 ft (4.5 m) ↑ 15 ft (4.5 m)
Hybrid between *C. florida* and *C. nuttallii*. Deciduous upright tree or shrub, pendulous outer branches. Large white flowers in spring. Autumn foliage brilliant orange, red, and purple. Zones 5–9.

Cornus florida
FLOWERING DOGWOOD
☼/◑ ✿ ↔ 25 ft (8 m) ↑ 30 ft (9 m)
Tree native to eastern and central USA. Leaves slightly twisted, oval, pointed, dark green, paler undersides; orange, red, yellow, and purple in autumn. Bracts white to pink in late spring–early summer. Berries red, persist through winter. Zones 5–9.

Cornus kousa
CHINESE DOGWOOD, JAPANESE FLOWERING DOGWOOD, KOUSA DOGWOOD
☼ ✿ ↔ 15 ft (4.5 m) ↑ 25 ft (8 m)
From Japan, China, and Korea. Deciduous. Glossy wavy-edged leaves, pointed oval, turn bronze-crimson in autumn. Profuse green flowers in summer. Creamy white bracts, edged red. Pink- or red-tinted fruits. *C. k.* var. *chinensis* ★, paler leaves. Zones 5–8.

Cornus mas
CORNELIAN CHERRY
☼ ✿ ↔ 20 ft (6 m) ↑ 25 ft (8 m)
Native to southern Europe. Short-stemmed leaves, oval, pointed, shiny, deeply veined, mid-green, turn reddish purple in autumn. Flowers yellow, on previous year's bare wood, from mid-winter to early spring. Kidney-shaped fruit. Zones 5–9.

Cornus nuttallii
CANADIAN DOGWOOD, MOUNTAIN DOGWOOD
☼ ✿ ↔ 40 ft (12 m) ↑ 60 ft (18 m)
From northwestern USA and adjacent Canada. Oval leaves, dark green, turn yellow and scarlet in autumn. Flowers small; large, flat, irregular, white bracts, flushed pink, in late spring–early autumn. Orange-red fruits. 'Gold Spot', yellow splotched leaves. Zones 7–9.

Cornus capitata

Corokia buddlejoides

Cornus controversa

Cornus sanguinea
BLOODWING DOGWOOD, COMMON DOGWOOD, EUROPEAN DOGWOOD
☼ ✿ ↔ 10 ft (3 m) ↑ 15 ft (4.5 m)
Deciduous shrub native to Europe. Red-green shoots. White scented flowers in loose clusters; blue-black fruit. Red-purple autumn foliage. 'Winter Beauty' ★, red shoots in winter. Zones 6–9.

COROKIA
This is a small genus of 4 evergreen shrubs in the family Grossulariaceae. Three are native to New Zealand; the fourth is a rare Australian species. The species are variable, but all bear small starry flowers in early summer, followed by orange, yellow, or red berries. CULTIVATION: These shrubs will grow in sun or part-shade and in soils with a reasonable level of fertility. The site should be well drained. *C. cotoneaster* tolerates dry conditions. Light pruning will maintain a compact shape. Propagate species from fresh seed, or from half-hardened spring cuttings, cultivars from cuttings only.

Corokia buddlejoides
KOROKIO
☼/◑ ✿ ↔ 7 ft (2 m) ↑ 10 ft (3 m)
From northern North Island of New Zealand. Erect slender habit. Leaves lance-shaped, leathery, olive green above, silvery gray below. Small yellow flowers. Berries bright red to almost black. Zones 8–10.

Corokia cotoneaster
WIRE NETTING BUSH
☼/◑ ✿ ↔ 10 ft (3 m) ↑ 10 ft (3 m)
From New Zealand. Tangled wiry branches, silvery when young. Sparse foliage. Starry yellow flowers. Red to yellow berries. Zones 8–11.

Corokia × virgata
☼ ✿ ↔ 6 ft (1.8 m) ↑ 6 ft (1.8 m)
Natural hybrid of *C. buddlejoides* and *C. cotoneaster*. Cultivars form well-branched shrubs, with different leaf colors, more showy displays of berries. 'Bronze King', bronze foliage; 'Frosted Chocolate', chocolate brown leaves; 'Red Wonder' ★ and 'Yellow Wonder', starry yellow flowers and red or yellow berries. Zones 8–10.

Correa, Hybrid Cultivar, 'Mannii'

Corylopsis spicata

CORREA

A member of the rue (Rutaceae) family, this is an Australian genus of 11 species, all of which hybridize readily. Handsome evergreen shrubs, *Correa* species respond well to cultivation. Most species flower from winter to spring. Some have bell-shaped flowers; others are tubular with protruding stamens.

CULTIVATION: Often found in cool, moist, shaded positions, some species are also able to tolerate coastal situations in full sun. They prefer friable, well-drained, fertile loams, and are not recommended for hot humid summer climates. Tip pruning immediately after flowering will improve plant form and density.

Correa alba

☼/◐ ❄ ↔6 ft (1.8 m) ↑3 ft (0.9 m)
From coastal southern Australia. Vigorous evergreen shrub. Leaves green, round, fragrant, furry undersurface. Small, white, starry flowers in winter–spring. Zones 8–10.

Correa backhouseana

☼ ❄ ↔6 ft (1.8 m) ↑6 ft (1.8 m)
Dense evergreen shrub from Tasmania, Australia. Leaves oval, dark green. Cream-green flowers with golden brown edges, in winter–spring. Zones 8–9.

Correa pulchella ★

☼/◐ ❄ ↔3 ft (0.9 m) ↑3 ft (0.9 m)
Small evergreen shrub from South Australia. Leaves smooth, elliptical to lance-shaped. Tubular red, salmon pink, or pink flowers in autumn–spring. Zones 8–10.

Correa reflexa

NATIVE FUCHSIA
☼/◐ ❄ ↔1–7 ft (0.3–2 m) ↑2–6 ft (0.6–1.8 m)
Tidy but variable shrub from Queensland and southern Australia. Leaves oval, narrow, or heart-shaped; smooth to hairy. Flowers tubular, pendulous, red with green or yellow tips, in spring. 'Fat Fred' ★, inflated red flowers with greenish yellow tips. Zones 8–10.

Correa Hybrid Cultivars

☼ ◑ ↔2–4 ft (0.6–1.2 m) ↑18 in–6 ft (45 cm–1.8 m)
Several cultivars and hybrids of uncertain origin have become popular with gardeners. Compact and heavy flowering. 'Dusky Bells' ★, deep dusky pink to soft red flowers; 'Ivory Bells', white to cream flowers; 'Mannii', long, tubular, red flowers; 'Marian's Marvel', pendulous clusters of pink flowers, green base. Zones 9–10.

CORYLOPSIS

Native to the eastern Himalayas, China, Taiwan, and Japan, this genus in the family Hamamelidaceae contains about 10 species of deciduous shrubs and small trees. The young branches are downy; the egg-shaped blunt-toothed leaves are light to dark green and appear in spring after the fragrant yellow flowers. The fruit, a woody capsule about ½ in (12 mm) wide, contains 2 shiny black seeds.

CULTIVATION: All species prefer acid soil and need moist, fertile, well-drained woodland conditions. Propagate from freshly ripened seed in autumn, protected against winter frosts, or take softwood cuttings in summer.

Corylopsis sinensis ★

syn. *Corylopsis willmottiae*
CHINESE WINTER-HAZEL
☼ ❄ ↔15 ft (4.5 m) ↑15 ft (4.5 m)
Erect spreading shrub native to China. Oblong or slightly egg-shaped leaves, green above, blue-green below, to 5 in (12 cm) long. Pendent racemes of yellow flowers, velvety bracts, in mid-spring–early summer. *C. s.* var. *clavescens* f. *veitchiana* (syn. *C. veitchiana*), more upright, smooth leaf stems, broader pale lemon flowers. Zones 6–9.

Corylopsis spicata

SPIKE WINTER-HAZEL
☼ ❄ ↔10 ft (3 m) ↑6 ft (1.8 m)
Spreading shrub native to Japan. Egg-shaped tapering leaves, dark green above, grayish below. Pendent racemes of bright yellow flowers, red anthers, felted floral bracts, in spring. Zones 6–9.

Corymbia ficifolia

CORYMBIA

This newly named genus of 110 or more species of evergreen trees belongs to the myrtle (Myrtaceae) family. It contains many of the eucalypts (*Eucalyptus* species) traditionally known as bloodwoods and ghost gums. Many outstanding flowering species belong to this group, including the red-flowering gum (*C. ficifolia*). They are grown for their fine straight trunks and attractive bark. The urn-shaped fruiting capsules are fairly large and often very ornamental. The genus occurs mostly across the northern half of Australia, as well as in temperate eastern Australia and southwest Western Australia. A few species occur in New Guinea.

CULTIVATION: Most species are fast growing and long lived, and many are grown as specimen plants. They are easy to grow provided the correct species is chosen for a given area. They prefer full sun; frost hardiness varies, as does the preference for moist

Corymbia citriodora

are arranged alternately on the branches, and they bear tiny flowers in terminal panicles followed by smooth-skinned plum-like fruits.
CULTIVATION: The New Zealand species, *C. laevigata*, is the one that is usually seen in cultivation. It requires a warm site in a rich soil with adequate moisture, particularly when it is young. It should be propagated from seed, which is best sown fresh.

Corynocarpus laevigata
KARAKA

☼ ᛃ ↔ 25 ft (8 m) ↑ 50 ft (15 m)

Forest tree found on both islands of New Zealand. Densely foliaged. Leaves large, leathery, oblong, glossy, dark green. Oval orange fruits ripen in autumn. Kernels of fruits poisonous. Zones 9–11.

COTINUS
SMOKE BUSH

This genus contains 3 species of deciduous trees or shrubs found in North America and across southern Europe to central China. It belongs to the same family (Anacardiaceae) as *Rhus* and, like members of that genus, has been known to cause contact dermatitis. *Cotinus* are valuable garden plants, and have a long season of interest. In summer many tiny flowers are borne on long panicles, giving a hazy effect to the plant; hence the common name of smoke bush. In autumn their broadly oval leaves deepen in color to shades of red, yellow, and orange.
CULTIVATION: Smoke bushes will grow in a wide range of soils and climatic conditions but are best in a well-drained site in full sun. As with many trees from cool-temperate climates, richer autumn colors are achieved in areas where winters are cold. Prune to remove dead wood or to shorten long straggly branches. Propage from seed sown in autumn or from hardwood cuttings taken in late summer.

or dry conditions. Propagation is from seed, which germinates readily. Flower color may not always come true from seed.

Corymbia citriodora
syn. *Eucalyptus citriodora*
LEMON-SCENTED GUM

☼ ᛃ ↔ 35 ft (10 m) ↑ 100 ft (30 m)

Deciduous tree native to tropical Queensland, Australia. Slender straight trunk, smooth powdery white to gray bark. Long narrow leaves exude lemon fragrance. White flowers in summer–autumn. More southern *C. c.* subsp. *variegata* characterized by variegated foliage and lack of lemon scent. Zones 9–12.

Corymbia ficifolia
syn. *Eucalyptus ficifolia*
RED-FLOWERING GUM

☼ ᛃ ↔ 15 ft (4.5 m) ↑ 30 ft (9 m)

Native to southwestern corner of Western Australia. Large densely foliaged crown, short trunk, dark rough bark. Flowers scarlet, crimson, pink, or orange, in terminal clusters, in summer. Urn-shaped fruit to 1½ in (35 mm) long. Zones 9–10.

CORYNOCARPUS
The 4 species of this genus in the family Corynocarpaceae are tall, evergreen, forest trees. They are found on some western Pacific islands and in New Zealand and Australia. Their simple leathery leaves

Cotinus coggygria
syn. *Rhus cotinus*
EURASIAN SMOKEBUSH, SMOKE BUSH, VENETIAN SUMACH

☼ ❄ ↔ 15 ft (4.5 m) ↑ 15 ft (4.5 m)

Rounded bush from southern Europe to central China. Broadly oval leaves. Numerous plume-like panicles, tiny bronze-pink flowers, fading to grayish purple in summer. 'Royal Purple' ★, dark red-purple leaves; 'Velvet Cloak', deep reddish purple leaves, turning entirely red in autumn. Zones 6–10.

Cotinus 'Grace'

☼ ❄ ↔ 15 ft (4.5 m) ↑ 20 ft (6 m)

Hybrid of *C. coggygria* 'Velvet Cloak' and *C. obovatus*. Reddish purple leaves, flower plumes grayish, enhancing hazy smoke-like effect. Zones 5–10.

Cotinus obovatus
syns *Cotinus americanus, C. cotinoides, Rhus cotinoides*
AMERICAN SMOKE TREE, CHITTAMWOOD

☼ ❄ ↔ 20 ft (6 m) ↑ 30 ft (9 m)

Native to central and southern USA. Foliage colors brilliantly in autumn. Similar to *C. coggygria*. Tree-like, broad conical form. Zones 5–10.

Cotinus 'Grace'

COTONEASTER

From the rose (Rosaceae) family, a genus of about 200 species of evergreen, semi-evergreen, or deciduous shrubs and trees from the northern temperate areas. Leaves are rounded to lance-shaped, simple, smooth-edged, and arranged alternately. Small flowers are white, sometimes flushed pink or red, with 5 petals, and are borne singly or in cymes. They are followed by red-black or red fruits with rather dry flesh and 2 to 5 nutlets. Grown for their profuse flowers and fruit, they can also be used as hedging plants and as attractive specimens.

CULTIVATION: Cotoneasters grow well in moderately fertile well-drained soil. Dwarf evergreens and deciduous plants fruit better in full sun, while taller evergreens grow well in part-shade. In exposed situations they may need protection from cold drying winds. Propagate by taking half-hardened cuttings of evergreen species in late summer, and of deciduous species in early summer.

Cotoneaster dammeri
syn. *Cotoneaster humifusus*
☼ ❈ ↔ 6 ft (1.8 m) ↑ 8 in (20 cm)
Prostrate evergreen shrub native to Hubei region of China. Leaves shiny green, oblong, strongly veined. White flowers, solitary or grouped in cymes, in early summer, followed by scarlet fruit in autumn. Zones 5–10.

Cotoneaster franchetii
☼ ❈ ↔ 10 ft (3 m) ↑ 10 ft (3 m)
Evergreen, sometimes semi-evergreen, erect shrub native to western China. Lustrous, bright green, oval leaves with felty undersides. Generous cymes of pink-tinted white flowers in summer. Egg-shaped orange-red fruit. Zones 6–10.

Cotoneaster frigidus
HIMALAYAN TREE COTONEASTER
☼ ❈ ↔ 30 ft (9 m) ↑ 30 ft (9 m)
Deciduous large shrub or small tree native to Himalayas. Peeling bark. Egg-shaped dull green leaves, wavy edges. Sprays of profuse white flowers in summer. Red fruit. 'Cornubia' (syn. *C.* × *watereri* 'Cornubia'), dark green lance-shaped leaves turn rich bronze in winter; 'Fructu Luteo', creamy yellow fruit; 'Notcutt's Variety', large dark green leaves. Zones 6–9.

Cotoneaster horizontalis
ROCK COTONEASTER, ROCKSPRAY COTONEASTER
☼ ❈ ↔ 5 ft (1.5 m) ↑ 3 ft (0.9 m)
From western China. Deciduous, herringbone-like branching. Elliptical to rounded tiny leaves, dark green, glossy, color in autumn. Flesh pink flowers in late spring. Scarlet fruit. Zones 4–9.

Cotoneaster lacteus
syn. *Cotoneaster parneyi*
☼ ❈ ↔ 12 ft (3.5 m) ↑ 12 ft (3.5 m)
Evergreen shrub from China. Arching branches. Leathery oval leaves, dark green above, felty beneath, deep veins. Creamy white flowers in summer. Red fruit persist in winter. Zones 6–11.

Cotoneaster microphyllus
☼ ❈ ↔ 3 ft (0.9 m) ↑ 3 ft (0.9 m)
Native to Himalayas. Prostrate evergreen shrub, dense mound. Thick leaves, egg-shaped, glossy deep green, hairy coating beneath when young. Tiny white flowers in spring–summer. Crimson fruit. Zones 5–10.

Cotoneaster salicifolius
syn. *Cotoneaster floccosus* of gardens
☼ ❈ ↔ 15 ft (4.5 m) ↑ 15 ft (4.5 m)
Naturally occurring in China. Variable species with slim, graceful, bowed branches. Lance-shaped deeply veined leaves, pointed, white felty undersides. Large corymbs in summer. Round, red, persistent fruit. 'Exburyensis', white flowers in early summer, followed by pinkish yellow fruit in winter; 'Herbstfeuer' (syn. 'Autumn Fire'), low spreading habit, red fruit; 'Repens', prostrate form; 'Rothschildianus' (syn. *C.* × *watereri* 'Rothschildianus'), vigorous, evergreen, spreading shrub, clusters of white flowers in summer, followed by lemon yellow fruit. Zones 6–10.

Cotoneaster simonsii
☼ ❈ ↔ 6 ft (1.8 m) ↑ 8 ft (2.4 m)
Deciduous or semi-evergreen shrub found naturally in northern India and eastern Himalayas. Egg-shaped deep green leaves, paler with bristly hair on undersurfaces. Pink-tinged white flowers, single or in cymes, borne throughout summer. Orange-red fruit follow flowers. Zones 5–9.

Cotoneaster franchetii

Cotoneaster horizontalis

Cotoneaster lacteus

Cotoneaster × watereri

☀ ❄ ↔ 15 ft (4.5 m) ↑ 15 ft (4.5 m)

Of garden origin, 3-way cross between *C. frigidus, C. salicifolius,* and *C. rugosus.* Evergreen shrub or small tree, bowed branches. Leaves egg-shaped, dark green, veined upper surface, felty underside. White flowers in cymes in summer. Round, red, persistent fruit. '**John Waterer**', original clone with numerous cultivars. Zones 6–10.

COUROUPITA

From the jungles of tropical South America comes this genus of 4 species of large evergreen trees belonging to the brazilnut (Lecythidaceae) family. Although these trees are fairly rare in cultivation, one species—the cannonball tree, *C. guianensis*—is grown in tropical gardens and parks for its spectacular and remarkable fruits, which emerge and dangle on long stems directly from the tree trunk. The pincushion-like flowers are large and complex in structure, usually with 6 fleshy petals.
CULTIVATION: In subtropical and tropical areas *Couroupita* species are grown in well-drained organically rich soil in a sunny position. Propagation is from seed.

Couroupita guianensis

CANNONBALL TREE

☀ ✿ ↔ 15 ft (4.5 m) ↑ 100 ft (30 m)

Evergreen tree from tropical South America. Rosettes of large elliptical leaves at branch tips. Large flowers, 6 in (15 cm) across, on long drooping branches that emerge directly from trunk, with red spreading petals and hundreds of yellow stamens. Brownish ball-like capsules mature to red pulp; they have disagreeable odor. Zones 11–12.

Couroupita guianensis

CRATAEGUS

HAWTHORN

This genus within the rose (Rosaceae) family contains around 200 species from temperate Eurasia and North America. Most are large thorny shrubs or small trees. The deep green leaves are alternate, simple or lobed, and some are toothed. The white or pink flowers, carried singly or in corymbs, have 5 sepals and/or petals. Nutlets with a fleshy edible covering follow the flowers. These fruit can be black, yellow, or bluish green, but the majority are red. *C. laevigata* and *C. monogyna* have both been used as hedging plants for centuries.
CULTIVATION: Grow species in sun or partial shade in any soil. Bud cultivars in summer or graft them in winter. Sow seed when ripe in a position that is protected from winter frosts. Germination may take up to 18 months.

Crataegus 'Autumn Glory'

☀ ❄ ↔ 10 ft (3 m) ↑ 10 ft (3 m)

Possible hybrid of *C. laevigata.* Deciduous shrub. Glossy leaves with 3 to 5 rounded blunt-toothed lobes. Produces clusters of large white flowers in early summer, followed by oval red fruit in autumn, persisting into winter. Zones 5–10.

Crataegus crus-galli

Crataegus crus-galli

COCKSPUR THORN

☀ ❄ ↔ 35 ft (10 m) ↑ 30 ft (9 m)

Native to eastern USA. Small flat-topped tree with long curved thorns. Shiny, dark green, egg-shaped leaves. Foliage turns red in autumn. Large corymbs of small white flowers in spring. Deep red fruit persist throughout winter. *C. c.* var. *salicifolia,* narrow leaves. Zones 5–9.

Crataegus laciniata

syn. *Crataegus orientalis*

☀ ❄ ↔ 20 ft (6 m) ↑ 20 ft (6 m)

Thorny shrub or tree native to southeastern Europe and western Asia. Leaves deeply lobed, dark green, to 2 in (5 cm) long, with covering of silvery white hairs. Clusters of white flowers in summer, followed by large red fruit. Zones 6–9.

Crataegus laevigata

syn. *Crataegus oxyacantha* of gardens
ENGLISH HAWTHORN, MAY, WHITE THORN

☀ ❄ ↔ 25 ft (8 m) ↑ 25 ft (8 m)

Thorny tree native to most of Europe and far northwest of Africa. Leaves egg-shaped, glossy mid-green, lobed, toothed, paler green undersides. White or pink flowers in corymbs in spring, followed by red fruit. Often grown as hedge. '**Paul's Scarlet**' ★, double deep pink flowers; '**Plena**,' double white flowers, becoming pink-tinged with age; '**Rosea Flore Pleno**', double pink flowers. Zones 5–9.

Crataegus × lavalleei

syn. *Crataegus carrierei*
LAVALLEE HAWTHORN

☀ ❄ ↔ 20 ft (6 m) ↑ 20 ft (6 m)

Of garden origin, from France. Cross between *C. crus-galli* and *C. pubescens.* Semi-evergreen in warmer climates. Leaves elliptical to oval in shape, toothed, glossy green; develop good autumn color. White flowers, red stamens, in early summer. Long-lasting red fruit. Zones 6–10.

Crataegus monogyna

HAWTHORN, MAY, QUICKTHORN

☼ ❄ ↔ 25 ft (8 m) ↑ 25 ft (8 m)

Native to Europe. Leaves broadly egg-shaped, dark green upper surface, paler green downy underside. Small clusters of white flowers, pink-tinged. Dark red, single-seeded fruit. 'Biflora', Glastonbury thorn, flowers in mid-winter, second time in spring; 'Stricta', columnar habit, spreads to 12 ft (3.5 m). Zones 4–9.

Crataegus persimilis 'Prunifolia'

syn. *Crataegus × prunifolia*

☼ ❄ ↔ 25 ft (8 m) ↑ 20 ft (6 m)

Large deciduous shrub or small tree. Dense foliage, thorny branches. Serrated-edged oval leaves to 3 in (8 cm) long, bright red tones in autumn. Flowers white, pink anthers, in corymbs. Red fruit. 'Prunifolia Splendens', larger leaves and flower clusters. Zones 5–9.

Crataegus phaenopyrum

syn. *Crataegus cordata*

WASHINGTON HAWTHORN

☼ ❄ ↔ 30 ft (9 m) ↑ 30 ft (9 m)

Thorny tree from southeast USA. Leaves sharply toothed, broadly egg-shaped, lobed, shiny green, autumn color. White flowers in summer; red fruit in spring. 'Fastigiata', narrow, upright. Zones 5–10.

Crataegus punctata

DOTTED HAWTHORN

☼ ❄ ↔ 30 ft (9 m) ↑ 30 ft (9 m)

Thorny tree native to eastern USA. Broadly egg-shaped, dark green leaves, toothed, downy underside. White flowers, pale pink anthers, in hairy corymbs. Red fruit with pale speckles. 'Ohio Pioneer' ★, brick red fruit. Zones 4–9.

CRESCENTIA

This genus in the trumpet-vine (Bignoniaceae) family has 6 species of evergreen trees and vines. They are found in the Americas from Mexico to Brazil, including the West Indies. They have simple oval to paddle-shaped or trifoliate leaves and tubular flowers with widely flared lobes, usually in shades of yellow to tan. The bat-pollinated flowers grow straight out of the branches, rather than forming in the leaf axils or stem tips. The spherical to ovoid fruit can be very large, with a hard woody shell and a pulpy flesh. CULTIVATION: These plants demand a warm, humid, tropical climate with ample moisture during the fruiting period. They thrive in moist, humus-enriched, well-drained soil in full sun or partial shade, but will tolerate drought. Pruning or trimming is seldom necessary. Propagate from seed or half-hardened cuttings.

Crescentia cujete

CALABASH TREE

☼/◐ ✦ ↔ 20 ft (6 m) ↑ 30 ft (9 m)

Found in Mexico and Central America. Paddle-shaped, deep green leaves to 10 in (25 cm) long. Flowers single, on old wood, light

Crataegus persimilis 'Prunifolia Splendens'

Crescentia cujete

yellow-brown, purple interior. Yellow-green fruit, to 12 in (30 cm) long, tough shell, often hollowed and used as gourd. Zones 11–12.

CROWEA

This small Australian genus in the rue (Rutaceae) family is closely related to the genus *Eriostemon*. Of its 3 evergreen shrubs, the 2 species from southeastern Australia are the showiest and are the parents of several cultivars. These small rounded shrubs have linear gray-green leaves and star-shaped flowers in white or shades of pink. CULTIVATION: *Crowea* species grow naturally as understory shrubs in light dappled shade, but can withstand full sun provided they are planted in reasonably moist, well-drained, open soil with a mulch of leaf litter or similar organic matter. A light tip prune after flowering will ensure compact growth.

Crowea exalata ★

◑ ⋇ ↔ 12–60 in (30–150 cm) ↑ 18–36 in (45–90 cm)

Extended flowering period, from spring into winter. Starry 5-petalled flowers, white to deep pink. Many forms selected, hybrids bred for cultivation, including prostrate or low spreading varieties. Zones 9–10.

Crowea saligna

◑ ⋇ ↔ 3 ft (0.9 m) ↑ 3 ft (0.9 m)

Rounded shrub. Leaves small, linear, slightly recurved margins, prominent midrib. Flowers star-like, pink, to 1½ in (35 mm) across, in autumn–winter. Good cut flower. Zones 9–10.

CRYPTOMERIA

This single-species genus belonging to the cypress (Cupressaceae) family has numerous attractive cultivars, which are also prized as garden plants. An evergreen species from Japan and China, it is a densely clothed conifer with reddish brown fibrous bark and a straight trunk that forms buttresses as it matures. The pollen-bearing male cones, held in clusters at the tips of the branches, release their pollen in spring, while the persistent female seed-bearing cones, held further along the branches, can take up to 10 months to ripen.

Cryptomeria japonica 'Nana'

CULTIVATION: This long-lived species prefers deep, moist, rich soil in a full-sun position. It can be propagated from fresh seed, but cultivars need to be grown from cuttings.

Cryptomeria japonica
JAPANESE CEDAR, SUGI

☀ ❄ ↔ 20 ft (6 m) ↑ 90 ft (27 m)

Narrow, conical shape. Dense adult foliage in forward-growing spirals. Branches tiered, outer branchlets slightly pendulous. 'Compressa', dwarf form with purple-brown winter foliage; 'Elegans' ★, purplish winter foliage; 'Nana', low growing; 'Yoshino', to 50 ft (15 m) high. Zones 7–11.

CUNNINGHAMIA
This genus belonging to the cypress (Cupressaceae) family includes just 2 species, one from central China, the other from Taiwan. They are evergreen conifers that can grow to 150 ft (45 m) tall, though they seldom reach that height in cultivation. The narrow leaves are flattened and sharply pointed, deep green above but with bluish white bands on the undersides, and arranged in double rows along the branchlets. The bark is fibrous and red-brown.

CULTIVATION: Both species are rather frost tender for conifers, *C. lanceolata* being the hardier. They are not fussy about soil type as long as it is reasonably fertile and the drainage is good. Young plants will tolerate light shade and eventually grow to see the sun. Propagate from seed or cuttings.

Cunninghamia lanceolata

Cunninghamia lanceolata
CHINA FIR, CHINESE CEDAR

☀ ❄ ↔ 20 ft (6 m) ↑ 70 ft (21 m)

From central to southern China. Spirally arranged deep green leaves, to 3 in (8 cm) long. Cones sticky while green, to 1½ in (35 mm) in diameter, at branch tips. 'Glauca' ★, blue-tinted foliage. Zones 7–10.

CUNONIA
This genus of the family Cunoniaceae contains 15 species of evergreen shrubs and trees from New Caledonia, and one species in South Africa. They have lustrous, deep green, pinnate leaves in opposite pairs, with striking spoon-shaped stipules sheathing the growing tips. The bottlebrush-like racemes of fragrant white to cream or red flowers can turn an unsightly brown as they die, and are best removed at this time.

CULTIVATION: Although most species are frost tender, they are not difficult to grow. They prefer moist, fertile, well-drained soil and a position in full sun. If necessary they will tolerate poor soil and, once established, can withstand considerable periods of drought. Prune young plants to a single trunk to make them tree-like; otherwise, a light trim after flowering will keep them compact. Propagate from seed or half-hardened tip cuttings.

Cunonia capensis
BUTTERKNIFE BUSH, SPOON BUSH

☀ ☁ ↔ 15 ft (4.5 m) ↑ 50 ft (15 m)

South African species. Often large shrub. Foliage deep green, bronze-tipped new growth, pinnate leaves of 5 to 7 leaflets, each up to 4 in (10 cm) long. Racemes of cream flowers in late summer–autumn. Zones 9–11.

CUPANIOPSIS
From Australia, New Guinea, and some Pacific islands, this genus in the soapberry (Sapindaceae) family consists of some 60 species of tropical and subtropical evergreen trees. All have divided leathery leaves, small yellow or greenish flower clusters on the branch ends, and fruit capsules that split into 3 compartments, each with a large seed and a bright fleshy attachment.

CULTIVATION: Many species adapt to difficult sites with poor soils and polluted air. Training to a single stem and early removal of side shoots is desirable. Summer mulching is useful, especially on sandy soils. Regular application of fertilizer promotes vigorous growth. Propagate from fresh seed.

Cupaniopsis anacardioides
TUCKEROO

☀ ☁ ↔ 15–30 ft (4.5–9 m) ↑ 50 ft (15 m)

Occurs along eastern and northern coasts of Australia. Leathery, shiny, divided leaves. Large clusters of small yellow flowers. In summer, yellow-orange, 3-part, capsular fruit ripen. Regarded as threatening weed in Florida, USA. Zones 9–11.

Cunonia capensis

CUPHEA

This large genus in the loosestrife (Lythraceae) family consists of about 250 species of annuals, evergreen perennials, and low-growing shrubs from Central and South America. They have flexible leafy stems and small opposite or whorled leaves. They are grown for their masses of irregularly shaped tubular flowers, produced over a long period—almost the whole year.
CULTIVATION: Species are fairly frost tender, but in warm climates they are easy to grow in average garden conditions. They do best in full sun or light shade, in well-drained moist soil, with protection from strong winds. Occasional tip pruning from an early age will encourage compact growth. Propagate from seed or from tip cuttings.

Cuphea hyssopifolia
FALSE HEATHER, MEXICAN HEATHER
☼ ❄ ↔ 15 in (38 cm) ↑ 18 in (45 cm)
Small rounded shrub native to Mexico and Guatemala. Small, dark green, narrow, pointed leaves, on thin stems with soft hairs. Purplish pink or white 6-petalled flowers, in small axillary racemes, in late spring–summer. Can be invasive. Zones 9–12.

Cuphea ignea
CIGAR FLOWER, CIGARETTE PLANT, FIRECRACKER PLANT
☼ ❄ ↔ 30 in (75 cm) ↑ 24 in (60 cm)
Bushy subshrub from Mexico and Jamaica. Leaves bright green, oval, pointed. Thin, orange-red, tubular flowers, tipped white, touch of black, almost year-round, peak in late spring–autumn. Zones 10–12.

Cuphea micropetala
☼ ❄ ↔ 30 in (75 cm) ↑ 30 in (75 cm)
Rounded shrub from Mexico. Bright green lance-shaped leaves. Terminal racemes of narrow tubular flowers, golden yellow to orange-red, tipped with greenish yellow, in summer–autumn. Zones 9–11.

Cuphea × purpurea
☼ ❄ ↔ 18 in (45 cm) ↑ 18 in (45 cm)
Bushy subshrub, garden hybrid of C. llavea and C. procumbens. Dark green, lance-shaped, pointed leaves. Narrow, tubular, deep pink to purplish red flowers, in late spring–autumn. Zones 9–11.

CUPRESSUS
CYPRESS

Originating in the warmer temperate regions of the Northern Hemisphere, this genus in the cypress (Cupressaceae) family comprises about 13 species of evergreen coniferous trees or shrubs. They are cultivated in mild climates for their dense compact crowns and bold symmetrical outlines. The tiny, scale-like, closely overlapping leaves vary in character and color; they may be soft to the touch or rather coarse, and are often aromatic. The small female cones have woody scales, are rarely over 1¾ in (4 cm) long, and are persistent.
CULTIVATION: These plants grow well in any well-drained fertile soil, preferably in full sun. Place each in a well-spaced position to enable it to develop its symmetrical shape and to avoid fungal disease. Propagate from seed in spring or from cuttings in late summer.

Cupressus arizonica
ARIZONA CYPRESS
☼ ❄ ↔ 15 ft (4.5 m) ↑ 40 ft (12 m)
Evergreen conifer from Arizona, USA, and Mexico. Densely conical at first, becomes broadly columnar. Bark gray-brown and stringy. Blue-green foliage, white markings beneath. Cones up to 1 in (25 mm) in diameter. Drought tolerant. *C. a.* var. *glabra,* smooth bark; 'Blue Ice' ★, silvery blue foliage. *C. a.* var. *stephensonii,* smooth, reddish, peeling bark, blue-green foliage. Zones 7–9.

Cupressus cashmeriana
BHUTAN CYPRESS, KASHMIR CYPRESS
☼ ❄ ↔ 20 ft (6 m) ↑ 30 ft (9 m)
From Bhutan. Narrowly conical habit, ascending branches, long pendulous sprays of aromatic blue-gray branchlets. Unstable, prone to wind damage. Prefers warm sheltered site, regular moisture. *C. c.* var. *darjeelingensis,* soft silvery green foliage. Zones 9–11.

Cupressus funebris
syn. *Chamaecyparis funebris*
CHINESE WEEPING CYPRESS, COFFIN CYPRESS
☼ ❄ ↔ 25–30 ft (8–9 m) ↑ 70–80 ft (21–24 m)
Conical tree from China, timber used to make coffins. Gray-green foliage, pendulous branchlets, shoots all in one plane. Zones 8–10.

Cuphea micropetala

Cupressus cashmeriana var. darjeelingensis

Cupressus sempervirens 'Swane's Gold'

Cupressus lusitanica

CEDAR OF GOA, MEXICAN CYPRESS

☼ ❄ ↔ 20 ft (6 m) ↑ 40 ft (12 m)

From mountains of western Mexico. Vigorous conifer with spreading habit. Red-brown bark, peeling in strips. Broad crown of pendulous deep green foliage. Good tree for windbreaks. Cones round, blue-gray. 'Brice's Weeping', attractive cultivar with weeping branches. Zones 8–10.

Cupressus macrocarpa

MONTEREY CYPRESS

☼ ❄ ↔ 35 ft (10 m) ↑ 100 ft (30 m)

Fast-growing evergreen conifer from Monterey, California, USA. Rare in wild. Spreading open habit. Thick red to brown or gray bark. Leaves small, scaly, yellowish green, aromatic. Tolerates strong winds and salt-laden air. 'Brunniana Aurea', upright conical tree, golden foliage, lemon verbena scent; 'Coneybearii Aurea', fine, drooping, golden leaves; 'Donard Gold', upright, conical tree, gold-tipped leaves; 'Greenstead Magnificent', dense, low, almost prostrate mound of blue-gray foliage becomes even bluer in shade; 'Horizontalis', large horizontally spreading tree, grown for hedging, especially gold form 'Horizontalis Aurea'. Zones 7–9.

Cupressus sempervirens

MEDITERRANEAN CYPRESS, PENCIL PINE

☼ ❄ ↔ 15 ft (4.5 m) ↑ 50 ft (15 m)

From Mediterranean region and southern Europe. Strongly upright habit. Fast growing when young, forming attractive spires of dark green. Persistent cones shining green, ripening red-brown to dull gray with age. **Stricta Group**, very narrow form; 'Swane's Gold' ★, Australian cultivar, golden foliage. Zones 8–10.

Cupressus torulosa

BHUTAN CYPRESS, HIMALAYAN CYPRESS

☼ ❄ ↔ 15 ft (4.5 m) ↑ 60 ft (18 m)

From below 9,000 ft (2,700 m) in Himalayas. Strongly upright conical habit, broadly spreading at base in cool climates, narrower in warm areas. Cones small, purplish, marble-like. Suited for windbreak. 'Nana', dwarf form, bright green foliage. Zones 8–9.

× CUPROCYPARIS

This group of hybrids between *Xanthocyparis* and *Cupressus* within the cypress (Cupressaceae) family are fast-growing, evergreen, coniferous trees. Fine dark green branchlets are arranged in flattened sprays. Egg-shaped male cones are yellow, the round female cones at first green, turning brown as they ripen. The crosses were made in the late nineteenth century, and 5 of the 6 have been named. They are probably the most frequently planted shelter belt trees in Britain and northern Europe, and will grow to a height of 70 ft (21 m) or so over a period of 25 years.

CULTIVATION: They are best grown in deeply dug, fertile, well-drained soil in full sun, but can be grown in partial shade. As hedging,

Cussonia spicata

trim back early in establishment, ideally 2 or 3 times a year. Propagate by taking cuttings in late summer from half-hardened wood.

× Cuprocyparis leylandii

syns × *Cupressocyparis leylandii*, *Cupressus leylandii*

☼ ❄ ↔ 15 ft (4.5 m) ↑ 120 ft (36 m)

Cross between *Cupressus macrocarpa* and *Xanthocyparis nootkatensis* features flattened, slightly drooping sprays of dark green leaves with gray sheen. '**Castlewellan**' ★ (syn. 'Galway Gold'), young foliage golden yellow, bronze-green with age; '**Harlequin**' (syn. 'Variegata'), creamy white variegations on leaves; '**Naylor's Blue**,' blue-gray foliage; '**Stapehill**', dense columnar tree. Zones 5–10.

CUSSONIA

Found in tropical and southern Africa and the Comoros Islands, this genus in the ivy (Araliaceae) family has 20 species of evergreen and deciduous shrubs and trees. They are characterized by large snowflake-shaped compound leaves, in spiral rosettes at the branch tips. They produce large candelabra-like heads of small white to yellow blooms and small, soft, red to black drupes.

CULTIVATION: Most species need a warm frost-free climate and ample moisture in summer. Plant in a sheltered position in full sun in moist well-drained soil. *Cussonia* species also grow well in containers, but can be very top-heavy, and are inclined to tip over. Propagate from seed.

Cussonia spicata

COMMON CABBAGE TREE

☼ ❄ ↔ 12 ft (3.5 m) ↑ 30 ft (9 m)

Native to southern and eastern Africa and Comoros Islands. Widely grown species. Thickened rather succulent trunk, develops multiple trunks with age. Much-divided leaves, carried on heavy stems. Large flowerheads in spring–summer. Zones 9–11.

× Cuprocyparis leylandii

CYTISUS

BROOM

This genus of about 50 species from the pea-flower subfamily of the legume (Fabaceae) family consists of mainly evergreen shrubs. They are native to Europe, with a few in western Asia and North Africa. All *Cytisus* species have typical pea-flowers; the main flowering season is late spring or summer. The plant's broom-like twiggy growths are sometimes almost leafless. The fruit is a flattened legume with small hard-coated seeds.

CULTIVATION: Brooms need a free-draining soil that is slightly acidic and fairly low in fertility. A sunny position gives the best flowers. Spent flowers and shoots should be removed after flowering, plus some of the older shoots, to encourage new growth from the base. The typical arching habit of the plant should be maintained. Most *Cytisus* species can be propagated from short-tip cuttings of ripened current year's growth, taken in late autumn or early winter.

Cytisus ardoinoi

☼ ❄ ↔ 10–24 in (25–60 cm) ↑ 10–24 in (25–60 cm)
Native to maritime Alps in southern France. Low, mat-forming, alpine shrub, arching stems, leaves deciduous, trifoliate. Bright yellow flowers in leaf axils in spring–summer. Zones 6–9.

Cytisus × kewensis

☼ ❄ ↔ 5 ft (1.5 m) ↑ 18 in (45 cm)
Hybrid between *C. ardoinoi* and *C. multiflorus*. Semi-prostrate habit, trailing stems. Masses of creamy yellow flowers in early summer. Zones 6–9.

Cytisus multiflorus

syn. *Cytisus albus*

PORTUGUESE BROOM, WHITE SPANISH BROOM

☼ ❄ ↔ 8 ft (2.4 m) ↑ 10 ft (3 m)
Erect shrub native to Spain, Portugal, and parts of North Africa. Leaves simple, narrow in upper part of plant, trifoliate lower down. Clusters of white flowers in early to mid-summer. Zones 6–10.

Cytisus × kewensis

Cytisus × praecox

☼ ❄ ↔ 5 ft (1.5 m) ↑ 5 ft (1.5 m)
Group of hybrids between *C. multiflorus* and *C. purgans*. Compact habit, profusion of flowers. 'Albus', white flowers; 'Warminster', to 5 ft (1.5 m) tall, deciduous, stems arching outward, flowers held in long sprays on outer stems, heavily perfumed. Zones 6–9.

Cytisus scoparius

COMMON BROOM, SCOTCH BROOM

☼ ❄ ↔ 7 ft (2 m) ↑ 7 ft (2 m)
Medium-sized shrub. Almost leafless. Golden yellow flowers, mostly solitary, in upper leaf axils in early summer. Brownish streaks on standards, keels yellow, anthers orange-red. Can be invasive. 'Cornish Cream', creamy white flowers. Zones 5–9.

Cytisus Hybrid Cultivars

☼ ❄ ↔ 3–6 ft (0.9–1.8 m) ↑ 3–8 ft (0.9–2.4 m)
Usually originating from *C.* × *praecox* or *C. scoparius*. Many sizes and flower colors. 'Boskoop Ruby', small rounded shrub, abundant red flowers; 'Burkwoodii' ★, vigorous, pink flowers, crimson wings yellow-edged; 'Firefly', yellow standards, wings stained bronze; 'Fulgens', late flowering, orange-yellow flowers, deep crimson wings; 'Hollandia', cream flowers, backs of standards and wings pink, late spring–mid-summer; 'Lena', compact free-flowering shrub, red standards, red wings yellow-edged, pale yellow keels; 'Luna', creamy yellow red-tinted flowers, wings yellow, keels lemon yellow; 'Minstead', mauve-tinged white flowers, wings flushed deeper mauve; 'Porlock', racemes of fragrant creamy yellow flowers in spring. Zones 5–9.

DABOECIA

There is only 1 species of evergreen, low-growing, spreading shrub in this genus within the heath (Ericaceae) family. Native to western Europe and the Azores, its habitat covers heathland from coastal cliffs to mountains. The roughly ovate leaves are green on the upper surface and silver on the underside. The small urn-shaped flowers are carried in racemes clear of the foliage.

CULTIVATION: Plants grow well in full sun in lime-free or neutral soil; some cultivars tolerate part-shade. Cut back after flowering. If grown indoors, feed and water freely during the growing season; these plants need good light but in direct sun young growth can be scorched. Propagate by sowing seed in spring or take half-hardened cuttings, especially of cultivars, in summer.

Daboecia cantabrica

syn. *Daboecia polifolia*

ST DABEOC'S HEATH

☼ ❄ ↔ 26 in (65 cm) ↑ 15 in (38 cm)
Native to western Europe. Variable habit, erect to very prostrate and straggling. Narrowly elliptic leaves, dark green, shiny. Flowers pale to pinkish violet in mid-summer–mid-autumn. *D. c.* subsp. *azorica* (syn. *D. azorica*), from Azores, flowers pale to deep ruby red, not frost tolerant. *D. c.* subsp. *scotica*, compact, flowers white to pink and crimson; 'Jack Drake', rich red flowers; 'Silverwells',

Daboecia cantabrica

Dacrydium cupressinum, in the wild, New Zealand

white flowers, light green foliage; **'William Buchanan'** ★, floriferous with purple-red flowers. **D. c. 'Alba'**, white flowers; **'Atropurpurea'**, deep red-purple flowers; **'Bicolor'**, mid-green leaves, dark red, pink, and white flowers, sometimes striped, on same plant or raceme; **'Creeping White'**, low-growing spreading habit, white flowers; **'Praegerae'**, mid-green leaves, pinkish red flowers; **'Purpurea'**, bright purple-pink flowers; **'Snowdrift'**, white flowers; **'Waley's Red'** (syn. 'Whally'), deep magenta flowers. Zones 6–9.

DACRYDIUM

Native to Southeast Asia, the western Pacific, and New Zealand, this genus within the plum-pine (Podocarpaceae) family contains around 30 species of evergreen coniferous shrubs and trees with scale-like leaves. The small cones consist of a fleshy receptacle from which 1 to 3 seeds project. They are valued for their timber. CULTIVATION: They like cool, moist, deep, rich peaty soils with plenty of moisture, in a protected sunny position. They resent root disturbance caused by transplanting. Propagate from cuttings or from seed sown in autumn.

Dacrydium cupressinum
NEW ZEALAND RED PINE, RIMU

☼ ❀ ↔ 30 ft (9 m) ↑ 90–200 ft (27–60 m)
Slow-growing evergreen tree native to New Zealand. Tiny leaves on pendulous bronzy green branchlets. Resents transplanting. Its growth slow, up to 12 in (30 cm) per year,

with nursery stock often collected from bush. Drought tender, and producing tiny nut-like seeds. Zones 8–10.

DAIS

This genus consists of 2 species of evergreen or semi-deciduous shrubs or small trees belonging to the daphne (Thymelaeaceae) family. They are found in South Africa and on the island of Madagascar where they grow in the moist frost-free margins of wooded regions. One species is widely grown in warmer climate gardens as an evergreen; it is commonly known as the pompon tree for its showy clusters of small pink flowers. CULTIVATION: Mature plants can withstand light frost, but are best planted in a sunny position with some protection from surrounding shrubs. They thrive in well-drained fertile loam covered with an organic mulch to retain moisture during the summer months. Propagate from seed in spring or from half-hardened cuttings.

Dais cotinifolia ★
POMPON TREE

☼ ❀ ↔ 10 ft (3 m) ↑ 10 ft (3 m)
Found in South Africa and Madagascar. Compact, rounded, evergreen shrub. Deciduous in cooler situations. Reddish bark, slightly scented pink flowerheads on tips of branches in summer. Blue-green foliage. Zones 9–11.

DAPHNE

Renowned for its fragrance, this popular genus in the daphne (Thymelaeaceae) family includes 50 or so evergreen and deciduous shrubs, extending from Europe and North Africa to temperate and subtropical Asia. Forming neat compact bushes, many of them make excellent rockery plants. The leaves are usually simple, smooth-edged, blunt-tipped, elongated ovals, either thin and dull green or thick, leathery, and slightly glossy. Individually flowers are small, usually in shades of white, cream, yellow, or pink, but they are carried in showy rounded heads that are sometimes highly scented. Drupes follow the flowers and are sometimes colorful. CULTIVATION: *Daphne* species generally prefer moist, cool, humus-rich, well-drained, slightly acid soil. If camellias and rhododendrons do well in your garden, so should daphnes. Once they are established, daphnes resent disturbance, so avoid damaging the surface roots by cultivation. Use mulch to suppress weeds. Small-leafed species prefer bright conditions; those with larger leaves are happier shaded from the hottest sun. Propagate from seed, cuttings, or layers.

Dais cotinifolia

Daphne bholua
PAPER DAPHNE

☼ ❀ ↔ 4 ft (1.2 m) ↑ 10 ft (3 m)
Native to eastern Himalayas. Deciduous and evergreen forms available. Strongly scented white flowers, tinged with pink, develop from deep pink buds, in winter–spring. Drupes ripen to black. Known as paper daphnes as paper and ropes were once made from bark. **'Gurkha'**, both hardy and deciduous. Zones 7–10.

Daphne genkwa

Daphne cneorum

GARLAND DAPHNE, GARLAND FLOWER, ROCK DAPHNE, ROSE DAPHNE

◐ ❋ ↔ 24 in (60 cm) ↕ 8 in (20 cm)

Near-evergreen, dense, twiggy, Eurasian shrub. Massed heads of small, fragrant, bright pink flowers in spring. Requires excellent drainage, shelter from hot sun, some winter chilling. 'Eximia' ★, sturdier than species; 'Ruby Glow', rich red flowers. Zones 4–9.

Daphne genkwa

LILAC DAPHNE

◐ ❋ ↔ 5 ft (1.5 m) ↕ 5 ft (1.5 m)

Deciduous shrub from China. Young foliage coppery, new stems covered in fine down. Large, lavender, slightly fragrant, delicate flowers in spring. Zones 5–9.

Daphne gnidium

◐ ❋ ↔ 4 ft (1.2 m) ↕ 6 ft (1.8 m)

Evergreen shrub from Eurasia, North Africa, and Canary Islands. Sparse glossy leaves. Small, fragrant, creamy white to pale pink flowers, densely clustered in panicles, in late spring–early summer. Red drupes. Zones 8–10.

Daphne laureola

SPURGE LAUREL

◐ ❋ ↔ 5 ft (1.5 m) ↕ 5 ft (1.5 m)

Tough, adaptable, Eurasian native. Dark green evergreen foliage. Flowers fragrant, small, pale green, in late winter–spring. Zones 7–10.

Daphne mezereum

FEBRUARY DAPHNE, MEZEREON

◐ ❋ ↔ 3 ft (0.9 m) ↕ 4 ft (1.2 m)

European species, most common of deciduous daphnes, similar to D. × burkwoodii. Flowers on bare wood, in late winter–early spring. White- and pink-flowered fragrant forms, singles and doubles available. D. m. f. alba, white flowers, yellow fruit. Zones 4–9.

Daphne odora

WINTER DAPHNE

◐ ❋ ↔ 5 ft (1.5 m) ↕ 5 ft (1.5 m)

Evergreen shrub native to China and Japan. Deep green leaves. Fragrant clusters of fleshy, pale pink flowers from mid-winter. Not long lived. D. o. f. rosacea, white and pink flowers; 'Rubra', dark red-pink flowers, less fragrance. D. o. var. variegata 'Aureomarginata', yellow-edged leaves, hardier and easier to grow than species. Zones 8–10.

Daphne pontica

◐ ❋ ↔ 5 ft (1.5 m) ↕ 5 ft (1.5 m)

Evergreen shrub native to Balkans and western Asia. Glossy, deep green, leathery leaves. Flowers fragrant, sometimes very pale pink to white, but usually light green. Zones 6–10.

Daphne tangutica

◐ ❋ ↔ 5 ft (1.5 m) ↕ 6 ft (1.8 m)

Evergreen shrub native to northwestern China. Small gray-haired leaves. Densely crowded clusters of small, fragrant, rosy purple flowers, reminiscent of lilac (Syringa), in spring–summer. Small red fruit. Retusa Group, dark green leaves. Zones 6–9.

DARWINIA

This genus of around 45 species in the myrtle (Myrtaceae) family is endemic to Australia; many are from Western Australia. Most are small evergreen shrubs, with small crowded leaves often marked with numerous oil glands. The tiny tubular flowerheads have long protruding styles and fall roughly into 2 groups: those clustered into pincushion-like flowers and those enclosed by large colorful bracts giving the flowerhead a bell-like appearance. The flowers of most species are rich in nectar and will attract birds.

CULTIVATION: They are suited to growing in containers, and this is recommended in frost-prone areas. They require a light well-drained soil with some moisture and a little dappled shade. Good mulch around the root area will conserve soil moisture during summer. Prune lightly after flowering to maintain a compact shape. Propagate from half-hardened tip cuttings at the end of summer.

Darwinia citriodora

LEMON-SCENTED DARWINIA

◐ ❋ ↔ 5 ft (1.5 m) ↕ 5 ft (1.5 m)

Widely cultivated, compact, rounded shrub from far southwestern Western Australia. Small, neatly arranged, blue-green, oblong leaves, sometimes with reddish tints, in autumn–winter, aromatic when crushed. Small clusters of flowers, prominent orange and green leaf-like bracts, in winter–summer. Zones 9–11.

DAVIDIA

The only species in this genus of the dogwood (Cornaceae) family, a deciduous tree, was introduced from China by the French missionary Armand David in the 1890s and the genus was subsequently named after him. D. involucrata is native to southwestern China

where it grows in damp mountain woods. It has a broadly conical outline and attractive foliage, flowering bracts, and fruit.
CULTIVATION: *D. involucrata* makes an excellent specimen tree although it does have a tendency to branch at a low level so corrective pruning should be carried out to ensure a good straight trunk develops. It requires deep, rich, moist soil and a sheltered site. It flowers when the tree is about 10 years old. Propagate from fresh seed, as dry seed has a much-reduced germination rate.

Davidia involucrata ★
DOVE TREE, GHOST TREE, HANDKERCHIEF TREE
☼ ❈ ↔ 30 ft (9 m) ↑ 60 ft (18 m)
Leaves aromatic, toothed margins, heart-shaped bases, downy beneath, taper to long point. Spherical heads of tiny true flowers surrounded by 2 large, white, ornamental bracts of unequal size, in late spring, with new leaves. Plum-like fruit ripens to purple-brown. *D. i.* var. *vilmoriniana*, leaves smooth beneath. Zones 6–9.

DELONIX
This small genus comprising 10 species of tropical deciduous, semi-evergreen, or evergreen trees in the cassia subfamily of the legume (Fabaceae) family includes the spectacular poinciana, *D. regia*. The wide umbrella-like canopies provide good summer shade. Large, terminal, orchid-like flower clusters smother the tree crown, and appear after deciduous and semi-evergreen species shed their leaves.
CULTIVATION: For the first few years, vigorous growth should be promoted in a humus-enriched well-watered soil. A sturdy trunk should be encouraged by removing the side shoots, thus lifting the canopy above head height. These trees require ample space to spread and are tolerant of all soil types except for heavy clay. They are easily propagated from seed or cuttings, but the seedlings take 10 years or longer to flower. The flower color from the seedlings may be disappointing.

Delonix regia
FLAMBOYANT TREE, ROYAL POINCIANA
☼ ⚘ ↔ 30 ft (9 m) ↑ 30 ft (9 m)
Deciduous shade tree from Madagascar. Bright green feathery leaves mature to deep green; shed prior to flowering. Large orange-scarlet flower clusters form in profusion on branch ends in summer. Huge flattened pods harden in autumn. Zones 11–12.

DENDROMECON
This genus contains just one species of evergreen shrub, native to California in the USA, and Mexico where it grows on the dry rocky chaparral. It belongs to the poppy (Papaveraceae) family, and the relationship can be seen in the single yellow flowers borne in summer.
CULTIVATION: These plants require winter protection in climates with severe frosts. When grown outdoors, they will not survive severe winters and must be given a warm sheltered site in a well-drained, gritty soil that is not too rich. The shrub dislikes root disturbance and care should be taken at planting time to reduce transplant shock. Propagation is from half-hardened cuttings taken in summer, but these can be quite difficult to strike.

Dendromecon rigida
TREE POPPY
☼ ❈ ↔ 10 ft (3 m) ↑ 10 ft (3 m)
Stiff gray-green leaves. Pure yellow, 4-petalled poppy flowers of simple beauty, in summer. *D. r.* subsp. *harfordii*, thicker stems and leaves than species, and slightly smaller yellow flowers. Zones 8–10.

Dendromecon rigida

DESFONTAINIA
This genus, belonging to its own family, Desfontainiaceae, comprises a single species of evergreen shrub, found growing throughout the Andes from Colombia to Tierra del Fuego. In the north it grows in cool mountain forests, while further south it is found at sea level. It has brilliant orange and yellow flowers that stand out against dark glossy foliage.
CULTIVATION: *Desfontainia* needs a cool moist climate and an acid soil that is moisture retentive and rich in humus. It should have a partially shaded, sheltered position; water well in dry spells. Propagate from seed or half-hardened cuttings in summer.

Desfontainia spinosa ★
☀ ❈ ↔ 10 ft (3 m) ↑ 10 ft (3 m)
Bushy slow-growing shrub. Tubular flowers scarlet to orange with yellow tips, in summer–autumn. Cherry-sized fruit. Zones 8–9.

Davidia involucrata

Delonix regia

DEUTZIA

Widely cultivated for its ornamental members, this genus of the hydrangea (Hydrangeaceae) family contains 60 species of deciduous and evergreen shrubs, mainly from temperate Asia with a toehold in Central America. Most commonly grown deutzias are spring flowering and deciduous. They have pointed oval to lance-shaped leaves in opposite pairs, often with serrated edges, and heads of small, starry, 5-petalled, white, cream, or pink flowers usually held clear of the foliage.
CULTIVATION: Most species are very frost hardy, and are the mainstay of temperate gardens. Shelter from strong winds. Prune and thin after flowering to maintain a framework of strong branches. Propagate from seed or half-hardened summer cuttings.

Deutzia × elegantissima
☀ ❄ ↔ 5 ft (1.5 m) ↑ 5 ft (1.5 m)
Derived from *D. purpurascens* and *D. sieboldiana,* of garden origin. Ovate to oblong-ovate leaves, uneven sharp teeth. Cymes of pink flowers in early summer. 'Fasciculata', white to pale pink flowers, deep pink in bud; 'Rosealind' ★, compact white flowers with pink tinge. Zones 5–9.

Deutzia gracilis
SLENDER DEUTZIA
☀ ❄ ↔ 3–6 ft (0.9–1.8 m) ↑ 3–6 ft (0.9–1.8 m)
One of main parents of hybrid deutzias, from Japan. Spreading shrub, mounded form. Slender erect shoots arch at ends. Narrow leaves bright green, ovate to lance-shaped, pointed at ends. Narrow panicles of white flowers in mid-spring–early summer. Zones 5–9.

Deutzia × kalmiiflora
☀ ❄ ↔ 5 ft (1.5 m) ↑ 5 ft (1.5 m)
Hybrid between *D. parviflora* and *D. purpurascens,* of garden origin. Open shrub with arching branches. Finely toothed, mid-green, narrowly oval leaves. Upright panicles of cup-shaped flowers, deep pink outside, paler inside, in early to mid-summer. Zones 5–9.

Deutzia × magnifica
☀ ❄ ↔ 7 ft (2 m) ↑ 6 ft (1.8 m)
Of uncertain parents, possibly *D. crenata* and *D. longifolia,* hybrid shrub with strong upright growth. Ovate to oblong-shaped leaves, finely toothed margins, gray and felt-like beneath. Dense panicles of single or double white flowers in early summer. Zones 5–9.

Deutzia × rosea
☀ ❄ ↔ 3 ft (0.9 m) ↑ 3 ft (0.9 m)
Dwarf shrub, hybrid of *D. gracilis* and *D. purpurascens.* Ovate to oblong, lance-shaped, finely serrated, dark green leaves. Short terminal panicles of flowers, pale pink inside, purplish outside. 'Campanulata', white flowers in dense panicles. Zones 5–9.

Deutzia scabra
FUZZY DEUTZIA
☀ ❄ 7 ft (2 m) ↑ 10 ft (3 m)
Native to Japan and China. Arching shoots; broadly ovate, rough, dark green leaves. Dense cylindrical panicles of honey-scented, white or pink-tinged, bell-shaped flowers terminate branches, in early to mid-summer. Peeling brown to orange bark. 'Candidissima', white double flowers; 'Pride of Rochester', very large, double white flowers tinged pinkish purple. Zones 5–9.

DILLENIA

This genus of about 60 evergreen trees and shrubs of the family Dilleniaceae is distributed throughout tropical Asia, the islands of the Indian Ocean, and tropical Australia. Leaves are large, lustrous, and simple; flowers are borne in terminal panicles, in spring and summer. Fleshy star-shaped fruit comprises 5 to 8 segments.
CULTIVATION: Drought and frost tender, *Dillenia* species prefer well-drained soils with heavy mulching and watering, and a protected sunny position. Propagate from seed or cuttings.

Dillenia alata
QUEENSLAND RED BEECH
☀ ✦ ↔ 12 ft (3.5 m) ↑ 25 ft (8 m)
Broadly spreading tree from Queensland and Northern Territory, Australia. Loose, bright reddish brown, papery bark. Thick, glossy, egg-shaped leaves. Large, showy, yellow flowers in spring–summer. Red fruit, fleshy part edible, used by Aboriginal Australians to stop swelling. Zones 10–12.

Dillenia indica
CHULTA, ELEPHANT APPLE, INDIAN DILLENIA
☀ ✦ ↔ 12 ft (3.5 m) ↑ 30–50 ft (9–15 m)
Evergreen shrub or tree from India to Java. Erect stems, roughly textured bark. Large leaves, deeply ribbed. White magnolia-like flowers. Fruit up to 4 in (10 cm) across. Zones 10–12.

Deutzia × magnifica

Dimocarpus longan

Disanthus cercidifolius

DIMOCARPUS

syn. *Euphoria*

This is a small genus of 5 species in the soapberry (Sapindaceae) family closely allied to *Litchi* (lychee), occurring from Southeast Asia to Australia. All are trees with large pinnate leaves, a heavy crown, and small flowers borne in large dense terminal panicles. A characteristic is the fleshy edible aril surrounding the seeds inside the almost leathery skin of the fruit, which is smooth.

CULTIVATION: Rich sandy loams and protection from frost are preferred. Propagation is from seed sown soon after hardening since the seeds lose viability quite quickly.

Dimocarpus longan

syn. *Euphoria longan*

LONGAN

◐ ✦ ↔ 20 ft (6 m) ↑ 40 ft (12 m)

Native to Southeast Asia. Cultivated for its fruit. Heavily foliaged branches, alternate pinnate leaves. Flowering in spring, fruit ripens in summer. *D. l.* subsp. *malesianus* varies little from species. Zones 11–12.

DISANTHUS

This genus belonging to the witchhazel (Hamamelidaceae) family contains a single deciduous shrub, with alternate leaves and inconspicuous flowers, that is native to China and Japan. The fruit is a dehiscent capsule.

CULTIVATION: Frost resistant but drought tender, *Disanthus* prefers a cool, moist, rich, acid or peaty soil in a protected sunny position, in conditions similar to rhododendrons and azaleas. Propagate from seed, which takes 2 years to germinate, or from cuttings taken in summer and struck under glass, or by layering.

Disanthus cercidifolius ★

◐ ❄ ↔ 10 ft (3 m) ↑ 20 ft (6 m)

From mountainous areas of China and Japan. Long leaf stalks; luxuriant, heart-shaped, bluish green leaves, turning maroon, red,

and orange in autumn. Curious, inconspicuous, deep purple flowers, spidery petals, in late autumn. Zones 7–9.

DODONAEA

A genus in the soapberry (Sapindaceae) family, it has about 70 species of evergreen shrubs or small trees found in tropical and temperate regions, mostly in Australia, quite often in arid and semi-arid areas. It is commonly known as hopbush, as early European settlers substituted fruits of some species for hops in brewing. Male and female flowers are mostly on separate plants. Flowers are small and insignificant; it is the highly colored, inflated, winged capsules that form the attraction of these plants.

CULTIVATION: Frost tender, they do best in a moderately fertile well-drained soil in full sun. Some species withstand extended dry periods. Tip pruning will maintain bushy growth. Propagate from tip cuttings taken in summer.

Dodonaea viscosa

HOPBUSH

◐/◐ ⌾ ↔ 5 ft (1.5 m) ↑ 10 ft (3 m)

Fast-growing evergreen tree from Australia, New Zealand, Pacific islands, tropical America, and southern Africa. Shiny, light green, sticky foliage. Masses of green winged fruit capsules in summer, hardening to papery light brown. 'Purpurea' ★, sought-after form distinguished by its purple-red foliage and capsules. Zones 9–11.

DOMBEYA

This is a large genus of about 225 species occurring from Africa to the Mascarene Islands, with 190 species in Madagascar alone. It is a member of the mallow (Malvaceae) family. All are evergreen, deciduous, or semi-deciduous shrubs or trees with simple, alternate, broad, often lobed leaves, and often with conspicuous stipules at the base of the leaf stalk. Flowers, in axillary or terminal panicles, often densely packed, are 5-petalled, white, pink, or red in color. The fruit is a small and often hairy capsule.

CULTIVATION: Only a few species from southern Africa are cultivated, in warm-temperate and subtropical areas with adequate moisture in summer. A well-drained, fertile soil in full sun or part-shade is required. Some species are only just frost hardy for short periods. Propagate from seed in spring, or cuttings in summer.

Dombeya cacuminum

Dombeya cacuminum

◐ ✦ ↔ 20 ft (6 m) ↑ 40 ft (12 m)

Upright, evergreen tree native to open woodlands of Madagascar. Large leaves, maple-like, shiny. Flowers large, in pendent clusters, deep pink to red. Zones 10–12.

Dombeya tiliacea

FOREST DOMBEYA, NATAL WEDDING FLOWER

◐ ⌾ ↔ 12 ft (3.5 m) ↑ 25 ft (8 m)

Small evergreen tree from Eastern Cape and KwaZulu Natal in South Africa. Flowers white, in few-flowered pendulous clusters, in late summer–autumn; fruit in autumn–winter. Zones 9–11.

Dracaena draco

DRACAENA

This genus in the family Ruscaceae contains about 60 evergreen perennials, shrubs, or trees, mostly from Africa but with species in most tropical regions, plus 2 endemic to the Canary Islands. Leaves are smooth, glossy, sword-like, and often variegated; terminal panicles of flowers are short lived. Some species have a spiky growth habit, others are softer and more shrubby. The fruit is a berry.
CULTIVATION: In gardens, species prefer rich, moist, well-drained soil in a protected sunny position, or a standard potting mix in diffused sunlight or full shade. Propagate from stem or tip cuttings, or root cuttings, preferably with bottom heat, or from seed sown in spring.

Dracaena draco ★

DRAGON'S-BLOOD TREE, DRAGON TREE
☼ ❄ ↔ 12 ft (3.5 m) ↕ 30 ft (9 m)
Slow-growing palm-like tree from Canary Islands. Trunk upright, many branched. Canopy of stiff gray leaves bunched at branch ends. Insignificant flowers, orange berries, in summer. Requires free-draining soil, warmth, sun. Suitable for containers. Zones 10–12.

Dracaena fragrans

syn. *Pleomele fragrans*
HAPPY PLANT
☼/❋ ❄ ↔ 6 ft (1.8 m) ↕ 10–30 ft (3–9 m)
Variable species from tropical West Africa to Malawi. Glossy, sword-like, pale green leaves. Clusters of fragrant yellow flowers. **Deremensis Group** (syn. *D. deremensis*) cultivars have dark red flowers: '**Longii**', leaves with broad white central stripe; '**Warn-eckei**', leaves greenish white with bright green edging. *D. f.* '**Massangeana**', bright green leaves striped with cream to yellow down center. Zones 9–11.

Dracaena marginata ★

☼/❋ ❄ ↔ 3–10 ft (0.9–3 m) ↕ 7–17 ft (2–5 m)
Upright branching shrub or small tree from Réunion and Mauritius. Good structural upright form. Long, lance-shaped, green leaves cover tips of thin erect branches. Adapts well to indoor and out-door cultivation. Prefers fertile moist soils. Zones 9–12.

Dracaena reflexa

☼ ❄ ↔ 3 ft (0.9 m) ↕ 8 ft (2.4 m)
Native of Madagascar and Mauritius, but now linked with plants from tropical Africa, merged as *D. reflexa*. Tangle of wiry stems, lance-shaped dark green leaves. Flowers cream, sweet-smelling at night, in spring. Bright red berries, in early summer. '**Song of India**', variegated, broad creamy white marginal stripes. Zones 10–12.

Dracaena sanderiana

RIBBON PLANT
☼ ❄ ↔ 16–32 in (40–80 cm) ↕ 5 ft (1.5 m)
From Cameroun. Upright narrow shrub, only few branches from base. Rich dark green, lance-shaped leaves edged in white. Zones 9–11.

Dracaena reflexa 'Song of India'

DRIMYS

This genus is one of 5 that make up the small family Winteraceae, the origins of which date back to the earliest evolution of flowering plants in the age of dinosaurs. It consists of 6 species of ever-green shrubs and small trees occurring in South America and higher mountains of Mexico and Central America. Another 20 to 40 species from Australasia and Southeast Asia have often been included in *Drimys*, but most recent evidence supports their being separated into the separate genus *Tasmannia*. Simple leathery leaves, without teeth or lobes, are arranged spirally and clustered toward the end of the season's growth, with new leaves often red. Star-shaped white or cream flowers are carried in umbel-like clusters in spring. The bark is aromatic, with a hot pepper-like taste. From its first discovery by Europeans it was believed to be an effective treatment for scurvy.
CULTIVATION: Most species are not fully frost hardy and at best tolerate down to 14°F (–10°C) for short spells. They thrive in a sheltered position; grow them in sun or partial shade in moist but well-drained fertile soil. Propagate by taking half-hardened cuttings in summer or sowing seed into pots as soon as it is ripe in autumn, with protection against winter frosts.

Drimys winteri ★

syn. *Wintera aromatica*
WINTER'S BARK
☼/❋ ❄ ↔ 30 ft (9 m) ↕ 50 ft (15 m)
Aromatic tree from Mexico, Chile, and Argentina. Lustrous, dark green, lance-shaped leaves, pale blue-white beneath. Fragrant flowers, creamy white, in umbels of 20 individual blossoms, in spring–early summer. Zones 8–9.

DRYANDRA

These beautiful flowering evergreen shrubs, numbering about 60 species, are native to Western Australia. They belong to the protea (Proteaceae) family and are related to banksias, and in many respects closely resemble that genus. They are grown for their decorative lobed or toothed leaves and richly colored, yellow, gold, or bronze, rounded flowerheads. Some species flower during the winter months. The flowers are most attractive to nectar-feeding birds.

CULTIVATION: Dryandras come from warm regions with winter rainfall and a pronounced dry summer season, and are frost tender. Many species will grow well in containers. Excellent drainage is essential, in full sun or part-shade. They prefer dry neutral or acid soil and low levels of nitrates or phosphates. Tip prune while young, and lightly after flowering to promote compact growth. Propagate from seed in spring.

Dryandra formosa
SHOWY DRYANDRA

☼ ⊰ ↔ 7 ft (2 m) ↑ 10 ft (3 m)

From far southern coastal regions of Western Australia. Prized for its cut flowers. Slender dark green leaves, with prickly triangular lobes, whitish underside. Rounded, almost metallic, golden flowerheads, in winter–spring. Zones 9–11.

Dryandra quercifolia
OAK-LEAF DRYANDRA

☼ ⊰ ↔ 10 ft (3 m) ↑ 10 ft (3 m)

From Esperance, far southern Western Australia. Felty new growth, dark green leaves prickly lobed. Flowerheads iridescent yellow and green, in winter–spring. Zones 9–11.

DURANTA

A genus in the vervain (Verbenaceae) family, it comprises 30 or so species of hard-wooded shrubs from southern USA to Mexico and Brazil. Evergreen, except in cold climates, they have blue, white, or violet flowers, in racemes or panicles, in summer, followed by decorative but poisonous fruit in autumn and winter. CULTIVATION: They will grow in most subtropical and frost-free temperate areas in fertile well-drained soil and full sun. They can be grown as small trees on a single trunk. Propagate from soft-tip cuttings in spring, or from firm-wood leafy cuttings in autumn.

Duranta erecta
syns *Duranta plumieri*, *D. repens*
GOLDEN BEAD TREE, GOLDEN DEW DROP, PIGEON BERRY

☼ ⊰ ↔ 8 ft (2.4 m) ↑ 15 ft (4.5 m)

Small evergreen species from tropical America. Drooping branches, sharp spines. Inflorescence 5–12 racemes, up to 30 lavender-blue

Drimys winteri

flowers, purplish calyx, in mid-autumn. Fruit enclosed in persistent calyx, hardens glossy yellow in early autumn. 'Alba', white flowers; 'Variegata', leaf margins creamy yellow. Zones 9–12.

Duranta stenostachya
BRAZILIAN SKY FLOWER

☼ ⊰ ↔ 4–5 ft (1.2–1.5 m) ↑ 4–6 ft (1.2–1.8 m)

Evergreen shrub from tropical Brazil. Oblong to sword-shaped leaves, slightly toothed. Clusters of fragrant, tubular, medium, blue-lilac to purple flowers in summer. Contrasting orange-yellow berries. Zones 9–11.

EDGEWORTHIA

This genus of 2 or 3 rather similar species in the daphne (Thymelaeaceae) family is named for Michael Pakenham Edgeworth (1812–81), a part-time botanist, plant collector, and employee of the East India Company. They are heavily wooded shrubs with large, elongated oval, mid-green leaves; when young the leaves have prominent midribs and a felty coating. The bark contains a very strong fiber and is naturally papery, and has been used for the production of paper pulp. The structure and fragrance of the flowerheads, which open in late winter to spring, reveal the close relationship between this genus and *Daphne*. CULTIVATION: *Edgeworthia* are best suited to moist, well-drained, humus-enriched soil in part-shade. They are moderately frost hardy plants, but are likely to be severely damaged if struck by a late frost after the young foliage has started to develop. Propagate from half-hardened cuttings, by air-layering, or from seed.

Edgeworthia chrysantha ★
PAPER BUSH

◑ ❄ ↔ 6 ft (1.8 m) ↑ 8 ft (2.4 m)

Native to China. Deciduous shrub with sparse growth and very heavy branches, which produces attractive new foliage. Globose heads of short, fragrant, tubular flowers are bright yellow, ageing to creamy white, at end of winter, and are followed by dry drupes. Some botanists regard *E. papyrifera* and *E. chrysantha* as the one species. Zones 8–10.

Dryandra quercifolia

Duranta erecta

Edgeworthia chrysantha

ELAEAGNUS

This genus of 30 to 40 species of deciduous and evergreen shrubs or small trees
belonging to the oleaster (Elaeagnaceae)
family is from Asia and southern Europe;
North America has a single species. Valuable as hedges and windbreaks, especially
in coastal areas, some species have spiny
branches. Leaves may be simple or alternate, green or variegated, often covered
beneath and sometimes above with silvery or brown scales. Tubular or bell-
shaped flowers are borne on the lower

Elaeagnus pungens 'Aurea'

side of the upper twigs. Flowers are small, whitish or cream, sometimes strongly fragrant. The red, brown, or yellowish fruit is edible.
CULTIVATION: These plants tolerate a wide range of soil types, the
exception is shallow chalk soils, and they like adequate summer
water and a position in full sun. They should be pruned lightly to
promote a dense leafy habit; hedges should not be close-clipped.
Propagate from seed sown as soon as ripe, or from soft-tip or semi-
hardwood cuttings; cultivars should be grown from cuttings.

Elaeagnus × ebbingei

☼ ❊ ↔ 12 ft (3.5 m) ↑ 12 ft (3.5 m)

Hybrid of garden origin between *E. macrophylla* and *E. pungens*.
Dense, fast-growing, hardy, evergreen shrub. Glossy dark green
leaves, silvery beneath, to 4 in (10 cm) long. Silver-scaled, fragrant,
creamy white flowers in autumn. Orange-red fruit with silver
freckles follow in spring. 'Gilt Edge' ★, deep green leaves with
bright golden yellow margin; 'Limelight', silvery young leaves
becoming light green with golden yellow variegation in center,
though many revert as plant grows older. Zones 6–9.

Elaeagnus macrophylla

☼ ❊ ↔ 12 ft (3.5 m) ↑ 10 ft (3 m)

Large spreading shrub from Korea and Japan. Broadly ovate leaves
covered in silvery scales on both surfaces, upper surface becoming
green. Fragrant silvery flowers in autumn. Red scaly fruit. Zones 7–10.

Elaeagnus umbellata

Elaeagnus multiflora

☼ ❊ ↔ 10 ft (3 m) ↑ 10 ft (3 m)

Evergreen wide-spreading shrub from
China and Japan. Leaves green on upper
surface, silvery beneath. Fragrant creamy
white flowers, on red-brown new shoots,
in spring. Most attractive in mid- to late
summer when covered with oblong,
oxblood red, edible fruit. Zones 5–9.

Elaeagnus pungens

SILVERBERRY

☼ ❊ ↔ 20 ft (6 m) ↑ 15 ft (4.5 m)

Evergreen shrub, suitable for hedging, from Japan. Main branches
spiny and horizontal. Leaves oval, glossy green above, silvery white
beneath, with scattered, brown, glandular dots. Small clusters of
creamy white flowers with brown dots in autumn. Fruit reddish
brown with silvery white spots. 'Aurea', leaves with bright yellow
margin of irregular width; 'Goldrim', deep glossy leaves with bright
yellow margin; 'Maculata', large, yellow, central patch on each
leaf and dark green margin, though it can revert; 'Variegata',
large shrub, leaves with thin creamy yellow margin. Zones 7–10.

Elaeagnus umbellata

syn. *Elaeagnus crispa*

AUTUMN OLIVE

☼ ❊ ↔ 30 ft (9 m) ↑ 30 ft (9 m)

Strong-growing shrub from China, Korea, and Japan. New shoots
golden brown, thorny. Leaves soft green, wavy-edged, silvery beneath. Fragrant yellow-white flowers in late spring–early summer.
Small, rounded, silvery bronze fruit ripens to pale red speckled
with white in autumn. Zones 3–9.

ELAEOCARPUS

Species in this genus of about 60 evergreen shrubs and trees, in
the family Elaeocarpaceae, occur throughout the Indo-Pacific
region, from tropical East Asia and India to New Zealand. The
leaves are usually simple, deep green, elongated ovals, often with
markedly serrated edges. The flowers are small, often white and
fragrant, with fringed edges. They are carried in small, sometimes
rather pendulous, racemes, and followed by unusually colored drupes.
CULTIVATION: Hardiness varies, but most species tolerate only light
frosts, if any. They prefer moist, well-drained, fairly fertile soil
with a position in sun or part-shade; they are not drought tolerant. Unless complete rejuvenation is required, restrict pruning
to trimming to shape. Propagate from half-hardened cuttings
or from seed that has been soaked before sowing.

Elaeocarpus hookerianus

POKAKA

☼ ❊ ↔ 15–30 ft (4.5–9 m) ↑ 40–80 ft (12–24 m)

Evergreen tree from New Zealand. Densely interwoven branches.
Leaves usually narrow and irregularly lobed when young, become
broader with toothed edges and more clearly defined pointed tip
with age. Small sprays of pale green to greenish white flowers in
spring–summer. Purple-red drupes. Zones 9–10.

Embothrium coccineum

Elaeocarpus reticulatus
BLUEBERRY ASH
☀ ❄ ↔ 15 ft (4.5 m) ↑ 15–30 ft (4.5–9 m)
From Australia. Pruned to shrub in cultivation. Leaves to 6 in (15 cm) long, with toothed edges. Short racemes of creamy white to pale pink flowers in spring–summer. Deep blue drupes. Zones 9–11.

EMBOTHRIUM
This genus in the protea (Proteaceae) family is represented by a single species, with regional forms, from Chile and the adjacent Andean region of Argentina. The rather upright tree is spectacular when in flower in late spring and early summer; its profusion of orange-scarlet tubular flowers are best appreciated from above.
CULTIVATION: An open sunny position with free-draining soil will reduce this plant's inclination to legginess. Protect from frost. With plentiful moisture, it grows quickly, producing flowers within a decade, but its life expectancy may not exceed 25 years. It can be propagated from seed, cuttings, or basal suckers.

Embothrium coccineum
CHILEAN FIRE BUSH
☀ ❄ ↔ 20 ft (6 m) ↑ 40 ft (12 m)
Upright evergreen tree native to Chile. Glossy leathery leaves. Orange-scarlet flowers. In cultivation, treat as tall shrub. 'Norquinco' ★, hardy; flower clusters crowded on branches. Zones 9–10.

EMPETRUM
Exposed windswept sites across the cool-temperate regions of the Northern Hemisphere (and also the southern Andes and the Falkland Islands in the South Atlantic) are home to this genus of 2 heath-like, intricately branched, evergreen shrubs belonging to the family Ericaceae, low growing and carpeting in habit. Very small solitary flowers appear in the leaf axils, and the fruit is a small, juicy, edible, berry-like drupe containing up to 9 hard white seeds.

CULTIVATION: They prefer moist lime-free soil in an open sunny position, and are ideal for the rock garden in cooler climates. Propagate from seed sown in spring or from cuttings.

Empetrum nigrum
BLACK CROWBERRY, CRAKE BERRY, CURLEW BERRY, MONOX
☀ ❄ ↔ 15 in (38 cm) ↑ 12 in (30 cm)
From USA, northern Europe, and Asia. Spreading, heath-like, evergreen shrub resembling miniature fir tree. Decumbent branches. Short needle-like leaves on stems with long woolly hairs. Loose clusters of purplish red flowers in late spring–early summer. Edible fruit, glossy, blackish purple. Zones 3–8.

ENKIANTHUS
This genus from the heath (Ericaceae) family consists of about 10 species of mainly deciduous, rarely evergreen, shrubs found from the Himalayas to Japan. The leaves are elliptical or ovate. The plants flower from mid-spring through to early summer, producing umbels or racemes of white, pink, or red urn- or bell-shaped flowers at the ends of the branches.
CULTIVATION: These shrubs grow on the edge of woodlands or in woodland conditions, preferring full sun or light shade and moist, well-drained, humus-rich, acid to neutral soil. Propagate from half-hardened cuttings taken in summer, by air-layering in autumn, or from seed sown in winter or early spring. The best propagation medium is peat with lime-free sharp sand.

Enkianthus campanulatus

Enkianthus campanulatus
REDVEIN ENKIANTHUS
☀ ❄ ↔ 15 ft (4.5 m) ↑ 15 ft (4.5 m)
From mountains of Honshu in Japan. Deciduous species with whorled branches. Leaves dull green and elliptic with sharp tip and toothed margins, turning deep red in autumn. Flowers in drooping corymb-like racemes of creamy bells with red or pink veining in late spring–early summer. *E. c.* var. *palibinii*, dark red flowers. *E. c.* 'Albiflorus', cream flowers; 'Donardensis', larger red flowers than species; 'Red Bells' ★, to 10 in (25 cm) tall, red autumn leaves, red flowers in pendent clusters. Zones 6–9.

Enkianthus cernuus
☀ ❄ ↔ 8 ft (2.4 m) ↑ 8 ft (2.4 m)
Deciduous shrub from Honshu in Japan. Bright green leaves, ovate to elliptic, with toothed margins, pointed tips, and brown downy veins beneath. Good autumn color. Pendent racemes of white flowers in late spring–summer. *E. c.* f. *rubens,* deep red flowers. Zones 6–9.

Enkianthus perulatus
☀ ❄ ↔ 7 ft (2 m) ↑ 7 ft (2 m)
From Japan. Produces attractive shiny red young shoots. Oval toothed leaves with downy midribs beneath, mid-green, turning bright red in autumn. Small drooping umbels of white flowers in mid-spring. Zones 6–9.

EPACRIS

From the heath (Ericaceae) family, this genus comprises approximately 40 species of shrubs or subshrubs. The majority are native to heathland or sandy soils in southeastern Australia, including Tasmania, where they do not dry out because of the moisture from creeks. Foliage is mostly prickly, gray-green to deep green, with a coarse texture. Many flower for months or in regular flushes all year, but their lifespan is short to medium, even under ideal conditions. CULTIVATION: They prefer filtered light. To maintain density and improve longevity, trim lightly after flowering. Mulch to retain moisture; gravels are ideal. Propagate from half-hardened cuttings in summer. Their fine root systems make transplanting difficult.

Epacris impressa
COMMON HEATH, PINK HEATH

☀ ❄ ↔ 30 in (75 cm) ↑ 3 ft (0.9 m)

Floral emblem of State of Victoria, Australia. Straggly shrub. Tubular pendulous flowers from white through pink to red. Spot flowers throughout year, with winter–spring flush. Zones 8–10.

Epacris longiflora
FUCHSIA HEATH

☀ ⚘ ↔ 3 ft (0.9 m) ↑ 3 ft (0.9 m)

Straggly but adaptable shrub found on poor sandstone-derived soil in New South Wales and Queensland, Australia. Flowers sporadically with flushes of tubular flowers, red with white tips, producing major flush in spring. Zones 9–10.

EPHEDRA
JOINT FIR, JOINT PINE, MEXICAN TEA

The 40 or so curious shrubs or climbing plants in this genus, the only one of the joint-fir (Ephedraceae) family, have slender, rush-like, jointed, green branches resembling horsetails, becoming woody with age, and very reduced, opposite, scale-like leaves. Small yellow flowers, to ½ in (12 mm) across, appear in cone-like clusters, followed by fleshy, red, berry-like fruit. Species are native to dry or desert regions across southern Europe, North Africa, Asia, and the mountains of both North and South America. CULTIVATION: These plants prefer sandy soil in a sunny position; they are ideal rock-garden plants in drier areas. Propagate by dividing clumps, separating suckers, or air-layering, or from seed.

Ephedra distachya
EUROPEAN JOINT PINE

☀ ❄ ↔ 3 ft (0.9 m) ↑ 3 ft (0.9 m)

From southern Europe to Siberia; cultivated from sixteenth century. Low evergreen shrub with creeping stems forming mats. Slender erect branches. Scale-like leaves. Red fruit in summer. Zones 4–9.

Ephedra viridis
GREEN JOINT FIR, MORMON TEA

☀ ❄ ↔ 3 ft (0.9 m) ↑ 4 ft (1.2 m)

From western USA. Erect evergreen shrub. Thin vivid green branches and awl-like leaves. Zones 6–10.

EPIGAEA

A genus of 3 small, prostrate, evergreen shrubs in the heath (Ericaceae) family, their distribution is interesting, with one species each from North America, Japan, and Turkey. They make great additions to a rockery in a cool-temperate climate. The leaves are pointed ovals with a heart-shaped base, usually deep green and glossy, sometimes red-tinted in winter. Clusters of tiny, bell-shaped, erica-like flowers appear in spring at the branch tips and in the leaf axils. CULTIVATION: Although requiring some sunlight to flower well, these cool-climate plants need shade from the hottest sun. Plant in cool, moist, humus-rich soil in dappled sunlight and water well in summer. Unless seed is required, remove spent flowers and trim lanky shoots to keep the plant tidy. Propagation can be from seed, which is very fine, or from small tip cuttings, and also by air-layering.

Epigaea repens
MAYFLOWER, TRAILING ARBUTUS

☀ ❄ ↔ 12–24 in (30–60 cm) ↑ 4–8 in (10–20 cm)

Native to North America, with low spreading habit. Leaves 1–3 in (2.5–8 cm) long and half as wide. Racemes, ½ in (12 mm) long, of 4 to 6 sweetly scented white to pale pink flowers. Zones 2–9.

ERANTHEMUM

Native to tropical regions in Asia and within the acanthus (Acanthaceae) family, this genus consists of about 30 shrubby perennial herbs and evergreen shrubs with opposite simple leaves. They produce dense branched spikes or panicles of flowers with slender tubular corollas in spring.

Epacris longiflora

Ephedra viridis

Eranthemum pulchellum

CULTIVATION: All species thrive in light, rich, medium loams in a part-shaded or protected position provided they have ample moisture. Propagate from cuttings of younger wood taken in spring.

Eranthemum pulchellum
syn. *Eranthemum nervosum*
BLUE SAGE
☀ ✦ ↔ 3 ft (0.9 m) ↕ 4 ft (1.2 m)
Evergreen shrub from India. Slightly toothed, prominently veined, glossy, green leaves, 4–8 in (10–20 cm) long. Feathery flower spikes, about 3 in (8 cm) long, bear tubular vivid blue flowers, with deep purple throats and green, papery, pointed bracts. Zones 10–12.

EREMOPHILA
This genus of about 200 species belongs to the boobialla (Myoporaceae) family and is native to mainland Australia, with most species occurring in semi-arid and arid areas. They are evergreen shrubs or small trees, often with felted or resinous leaves, stems, and floral parts. The 2-lipped tubular flowers, on short to long stalks emerging from the leaf axils, are variously lobed and may be white, yellow, violet, purple, pink, or red, and sometimes have a spotted interior. The fruit is a berry-like drupe, the seed enclosed in a tough corky or fibrous layer.
CULTIVATION: Marginally frost hardy, most species do not like moist humid conditions. They prefer a position with excellent drainage in an open sunny area with plenty of air movement. Regular light pruning encourages vigorous growth. These plants are propagated most readily from half-hardened cuttings.

Eremophila maculata
SPOTTED EMU BUSH
☀ ⊰ ↔ 3–10 ft (0.9–3 m) ↕ 3–8 ft (0.9–2.4 m)
Occurs across mainland Australia. Compact dense shrub, gray-green leaves to 2 in (5 cm) long; young leaves often downy. Red, purple, pink, or yellow flowers, often spotted with darker blotches, in autumn–spring. 'Aurea', compact habit to about 3 ft (0.9 m), with light green leaves, yellow flowers; 'Carmine Star', low shrub, to 20 in (50 cm) high, purplish young branches, carmine flowers, insides paler with prominent carmine spots; 'Pink Beauty', 10–12 ft (3–3.5 m) tall, profuse bluish pink flowers, 1½ in (35 mm) across, in late winter. Zones 9–11.

Eremophila nivea
☀ ⊰ ↔ 5 ft (1.5 m) ↕ 5 ft (1.5 m)
Silvery gray shrub from Western Australia's "wheatbelt," east of Perth. Erect stems covered in dense white hairs. Small, velvety gray, linear leaves. Tubular lilac flowers, in upper leaf axils, in winter–spring. Dislikes humidity; excellent container plant. Zones 9–11.

ERICA
HEATH, HEATHER
This large genus gives its name to the heath (Ericaceae) family. It consists of about 750 evergreen species, ranging from small

Eremophila maculata

subshrubs to shrubs and trees, the great majority endemic to the Cape region of South Africa, the remainder scattered throughout East Africa, Madagascar, the Atlantic Islands, the Mediterranean region, and Europe. Habitats include wet and dry heathland and moorland. Most are only half-hardy; the European species are more frost hardy. The small leaves are linear with rolled edges, whorled, rarely opposite. The flowers are bell-shaped or tubular, in all colors except blue. Briar pipes are made from the woody root burls of *E. arborea*. Some species yield a yellow dye.
CULTIVATION: The winter-flowering heathers are lime tolerant and will grow in neutral and alkaline soil, while the summer-flowering ones like acid soil; both grow in neutral soil. Feed container-grown plants monthly during the growing season and give them plenty of water, reducing both feed and water during the dormant season. Propagation is from half-hardened cuttings taken from mid- to late summer or by air-layering in spring. The successful germination of some of the South African Cape heaths is helped by smoke treatment.

Erica canaliculata

Erica arborea
BRUYERE, TREE HEATH
☀ ❋ ↔ 10 ft (3 m) ↕ 15 ft (4.5 m)
Upright shrub native to southwest Europe, through Mediterranean region, and in higher mountains of east Africa. Dark green leaves, grooved beneath. Pyramidal racemes of gray-white, scented, bell-shaped flowers in late spring. *E. a.* var. *alpina*, smaller, dense cylindrical racemes of white flowers; *E. a.* 'Albert's Gold', golden leaves year round, white flowers; 'Estrella Gold', young growth bright yellow, white flowers. Zones 7–10.

Erica canaliculata
☀ ❋ ↔ 4 ft (1.2 m) ↕ 6 ft (1.8 m)
Erect shrub from Western and Eastern Cape in South Africa. Mid-green linear leaves in whorls; undersurface paler green, hairy. Whorls of 3 white to pale pink flowers at ends of branchlets in winter–spring. Zones 8–10.

Erica cerinthoides

Erica lusitanica

Erica regia

Erica carnea
syn. *Erica herbacea*
ALPINE HEATH, SNOW HEATH, WINTER HEATH

☼/◐ ❄ ↔ 22 in (55 cm) ↕ 12 in (30 cm)

Low-spreading shrub from Alps, northwest Italy, northwest Balkans, and eastern Europe. Dark green linear leaves in whorls of 4. Purple-pink flowers in winter–spring. 'Ann Sparkes', rose pink flowers, golden foliage with bronze tips; 'Challenger', green foliage, magenta flowers; 'December Red', deep pink flowers turn red; 'Foxhollow', lime green leaves, pinkish white flowers; 'Kramer's Rubin', blackish green foliage, dull deep pink flowers; 'March Seedling', flowers into late spring; 'Myretoun Ruby' (syn. 'Myreton Ruby'), pink flowers deepening to crimson; 'Pink Spangles', deep pink flowers; 'Pirbright Rose', rose pink flowers; 'R. B. Cooke', pink flowers turn mauve; 'Springwood White', bright green foliage, abundant white flowers; 'Winter Beauty', deep pink flowers. Zones 5–9.

Erica cerinthoides
☼ ❀ ↔ 3 ft (0.9 m) ↕ 2–5 ft (0.6–1.5 m)

From Limpopo to Eastern Cape in South Africa, also Swaziland and Lesotho. Whorls of erect, hairy, gray-green leaves. Small umbels of tubular flowers, to 1½ in (35 mm) long, bright scarlet, occasionally pink or white, at branch tips, in winter–spring. Zones 9–10.

Erica cinerea
BELL HEATHER

☼ ❄ ↔ 30 in (75 cm) ↕ 24 in (60 cm)

Compact low-growing shrub from western Europe. Bottle green leaves with rolled-under edges in whorls of 3. Racemes of urn-shaped flowers, white to pink to purple, at stem tips, in summer–early autumn. 'Alba Major', mid-green foliage, white flowers; 'Alba Minor', dense habit, profuse white blooms; 'Alice Ann Davies', vigorous spreader, long spikes of dark pink blooms; 'Altadena', chartreuse foliage; 'Atrorubens', profuse bright rose purple flowers; 'Atrosanguinea', bright reddish purple flowers; 'C. D. Eason', broadly spreading low shrub, erect sprays of rose purple flowers; 'Cindy', dwarf, almost prostrate, tight clusters of rose purple flowers; 'Fiddler's Gold', leaves turn from gold to red in winter, lilac-pink flowers; 'Flamingo', bright rose pink flowers; 'Golden Drop', mat-like, lilac-pink flowers; 'Katinka', dark green foliage, black-purple flowers; 'Mrs E. A. Mitchell', fine dark green foliage, dark red

flowers; 'Pink Ice', dwarf, soft rose pink flowers; 'Plummer's Seedling', mound-forming, deep pinkish red flowers; 'Prostrate Lavender', semi-prostrate, lavender-pink flowers fade to white; 'Purple Beauty', dwarf, rose-purple flowers; 'Startler', bright rose flowers; 'Vivienne Patricia', lax spreader, mauve-pink flowers; 'Wine', spreading, dense spikes of rose pink blooms. Zones 5–9.

Erica × darleyensis
DARLEY DALE HEATH

☼ ❄ ↔ 24 in (60 cm) ↕ 12 in (30 cm)

Cross between *E. carnea* and *E. erigena*, of garden origin. Vigorous bushy shrub. Mid-green lance-shaped leaves. Racemes of various-colored flowers, in winter–early spring. 'Darley Dale', pink flowers and cream-tipped leaves in spring; 'Ghost Hills', light green cream-tipped leaves; 'Jenny Porter', pinkish white flowers, pale cream-tipped foliage; 'Kramers Rote', bronze-green foliage, magenta flowers; 'Margaret Porter', lilac-pink flowers, long season; 'Silberschmelze', silver-white flowers, foliage tinged red in winter. Zones 6–9.

Erica erigena
syns *Erica hibernica, E. mediterranea*
IRISH HEATHER

☼ ❄ ↔ 3 ft (0.9 m) ↕ 8 ft (2.4 m)

An upright shrub with brittle stems found in Ireland, southwest France, Spain, Portugal, and Tangiers in northwest Africa. Dark green linear leaves. Racemes of urn-shaped, honey-scented, lilac-pink flowers in winter–spring. 'Golden Lady', golden yellow foliage, white flowers; 'Irish Dusk', gray-green foliage, rose pink flowers in late autumn–spring; 'Superba' ★ (syn. 'Mediterranea Superba'), mid-green foliage, strongly scented pale pink flowers; 'W. T. Rackliff', mid-green foliage, white flowers in spring. Zones 7–9.

Erica lusitanica
syn. *Erica codonodes*
PORTUGUESE HEATH, SPANISH HEATH

☼ ❄ ↔ 3 ft (0.9 m) ↕ 5–10 ft (1.5–3 m)

Found from west of Iberian Peninsula to southwest France. Naturalized in southern England, New Zealand, and Australia. Whorls of 3 or 4 mid-green linear leaves. Racemes of tubular flowers, pink in bud, opening to white, in winter–spring. Can be invasive. 'George Hunt', yellow leaves, white flowers. Zones 8–10.

Erica mammosa

❋ ⚘ ↔ 6 ft (1.8 m) ↑ 5 ft (1.5 m)

From Western Cape, South Africa. Dark green lance-shaped leaves in whorls of 4. Tubular flowers, white or green through to pink and dark red, in spring–summer. 'Jubilee', pink flowers. Zones 9–10.

Erica manipuliflora

syn. *Erica verticillata* of gardens

❋ ❊ ↔ 3 ft (0.9 m) ↑ 3 ft (0.9 m)

Found in southeastern Italy and Balkans. Mid-green, linear, pointed leaves in whorls of 3. Rose pink flowers, in irregular racemes on previous year's wood, in summer–autumn. 'Aldeburgh', scented lilac-pink flowers; 'Korcula', pink-tinged white flowers. Zones 8–10.

Erica melanthera

❋ ❊ ↔ 18 in (45 cm) ↑ 24 in (60 cm)

Erect shrub from Western Cape, South Africa. Tiny dark green leaves in whorls of 3. Pendent pale pink to deep red blooms, black anthers extend outside cup, in spring–early summer. Zones 8–10.

Erica regia

ELIM HEATH

❋ ⚘ ↔ 3 ft (0.9 m) ↑ 3 ft (0.9 m)

Erect much-branched shrub from Western Cape, South Africa. Gray-green leaves in whorls of 6 on hairy branches. Smooth, tubular, waxy flowers, small spreading lobes, in spring. Color: upper red part separated from lower white part by purple band. Zones 9–10.

Erica scoparia

BESOM HEATH

❋ ❊ ↔ 3 ft (0.9 m) ↑ 6 ft (1.8 m)

Erect shrub from southwest France, Spain, Canary Islands, north Africa. Dark green linear leaves in whorls of 3 or 4. Racemes of bell-shaped flowers, brown-red tinged green, in summer. Zones 8–10.

Erica tetralix

CROSS-LEAFED HEATH

❋ ❊ ↔ 20 in (50 cm) ↑ 12 in (30 cm)

From UK, France, and Iberian Peninsula. Gray-green lance-shaped to linear leaves, silver below, whorls of 4. Umbels of pale pink urn-shaped flowers, at stem tips, in summer–autumn. 'Alba Mollis', silvery foliage, white flowers; 'Con Underwood', gray-green leaves, purple-red flowers; 'Pink Star', dark pink flowers. Zones 3–9.

Erica vagans

CORNISH HEATH, WANDERING HEATH

❋ ❊ ↔ 30 in (75 cm) ↑ 30 in (75 cm)

From UK, Ireland, western France, and Spain. Dark to mid-green linear leaves in whorls of 4 or 5. Racemes of cylindrical or bell-shaped flowers, white to pink and mauve, in mid-summer–mid-autumn. 'Lyonesse', white flowers with light brown anthers, bright green foliage; 'Mrs D. F. Maxwell', compact habit, vivid

rose pink flowers; 'Saint Keverne', bright pink flowers; 'Valerie Proudley', yellow foliage, white flowers. Zones 5–9.

Erica ventricosa

❋ ⚘ ↔ 20 in (50 cm) ↑ 20 in (50 cm)

Compact shrub from Western Cape, South Africa. Dark green leaves, dark green hairy margins, in whorls of 4. Clusters of pinkish red, waxy, tubular flowers, at branch tips, in spring. 'Grandiflora', larger than species, with pink-mauve flowers. Zones 9–11.

Erica × williamsii

❋ ❊ ↔ 18 in (45 cm) ↑ 30 in (75 cm)

Cross between *E. tetralix* and *E. vagans* that occurred in wild in Cornwall, UK. Racemes of rose pink bell-shaped flowers in summer–late autumn. 'P. D. Williams', yellow-tipped new growth, pink flowers. Zones 5–9.

ERIOSTEMON

As now understood, following a recent revision, this genus of evergreen shrubs in the rue (Rutaceae) family consists of only 2 species from coastal eastern Australia. Other species formerly included in *Eriostemon* have now been reclassified under *Philotheca*. Growing in stunted forest heathland in poor sandy soil, they have simple spirally arranged leaves and rather conspicuous flowers with 5 waxy pink petals, borne singly in leaf axils, in late winter to spring, giving massed displays for long periods.
CULTIVATION: Species prefer light to medium, well-drained, slightly acid to neutral soil in an open position in sun or part-shade. Prune lightly to preserve shape. Propagate from tip cuttings; seed is difficult to germinate.

Eriostemon australasius

syn. *Eriostemon lanceolatus*

PINK WAX FLOWER, WAX PLANT

❋/❋ ⚘ ↔ 3 ft (0.9 m) ↑ 6 ft (1.8 m)

Erect shrub from eastern New South Wales and southeastern Queensland, Australia. Leaves narrow-elliptical. Massed, shell pink, mauve, or white flowers, to 1½ in (35 mm) across. Zones 9–10.

Eriostemon australasius, New South Wales, Australia

ERYTHRINA
CORAL TREE

A member of the pea-flower subfamily of the legume (Fabaceae) family, this genus of over 100 mainly tropical deciduous or semi-evergreen trees, perennials, and shrubs is distributed globally in warm-temperate to tropical regions. Stems, branches, and even the leaflet midribs may be armed with conical or curved prickles. The compound leaves have 3 broad leaflets and inflorescences are erect to drooping racemes of showy tubular to bell-shaped flowers with the upper petal longer than the other petals. Flowers in deciduous species usually precede leaves. The fruits are elongated pods, narrowed between the seeds. Some species have medicinal properties; others may be poisonous.

CULTIVATION: Species of *Erythrina* prefer a warm dry climate and thrive in sandy, moist, but well-drained soils in sunny exposed positions in coastal environments. They are easily propagated from seed sown in spring and summer, and from cuttings of growing wood; the rootstock of herbaceous species may be divided. While fairly free of pests, mites can be a problem in drier weather.

Erythrina crista-galli

Erythrina acanthocarpa
TAMBOOKIE THORN

☼ ⚬ ↔ 6 ft (1.8 m) ↑ 6 ft (1.8 m)

Deciduous stiff shrub with many thorny stems from Cape region of South Africa. Bluish green leaflets from large underground root. Clusters of showy, pea-flower-like, scarlet blooms, tipped green, in late spring–early summer. Prickly bean-like pods. Zones 9–11.

Erythrina × bidwillii ★
HYBRID CORAL TREE

☼ ⚬ ↔ 10 ft (3 m) ↑ 12 ft (3.5 m)

Originated in Australia as garden hybrid between *E. crista-galli* and *E. herbacea*. Deciduous shrub suited to drier gardens. Pale to mid-green trifoliate leaves, to 4 in (10 cm) long, on prickly stems. Striking dark red flowers with upper petal to 2 in (5 cm) long, in 3s, in spring–early summer. Zones 9–11.

Erythrina crista-galli
COCKSPUR CORAL TREE, COMMON CORAL TREE

☼ ⚬ ↔ 12–40 ft (3.5–12 m) ↑ 30 ft (9 m)

Native to Brazil. Deciduous species sometimes found as gnarled old tree with considerable character. If lopped annually, very large red flower clusters appear in spring–summer. Can be grown as potted greenhouse plant in cooler climates; it should be pruned heavily in late autumn. Zones 9–11.

Erythrina humeana
DWARF ERYTHRINA, NATAL CORAL TREE

☼ ⚬ ↔ 7 ft (2 m) ↑ 12 ft (3.5 m)

Native to eastern South Africa and Mozambique. Deciduous shrub or small tree with light gray prickly bark and dark green shiny leaflets. Slender dense racemes, to 20 in (50 cm) long, of scarlet-red, tubular, pea-flower-like blooms, borne at branch tips, in summer. Bean pods black or purple. Zones 9–11.

Erythrina × sykesii
syn. *Erythrina indica* of gardens
CORAL TREE

☼ ⚬ ↔ 30 ft (9 m) ↑ 50 ft (15 m)

Deciduous tree of uncertain origin, first appearing in Australia and New Zealand. Squat trunk with ascending branches armed with hooked prickles. Large scarlet pea-flowers in winter–spring. Very brittle; sheds limbs when windy. Tolerates poor soil and salt-laden air. Easily grown from branches or even wood chips. Zones 9–11.

Erythrina variegata
syn. *Erythrina indica*
CORAL TREE, INDIAN CORAL BEAN, TIGER'S CLAW

☼ ✦ ↔ 30 ft (9 m) ↑ 30–60 ft (9–18 m)

Widespread along coastlines of tropical Asia, Indian Ocean, and western Pacific. Deciduous tree with thick large-prickled branches, grayish green furrowed bark. Large heart-shaped leaflets. Dense clusters of scarlet or crimson pea-flowers, occasionally white, at branch tips, in winter. '**Parcellii**', leaves variegated with light green and yellow. Zones 11–12.

ESCALLONIA

A genus of about 60 species of mostly evergreen shrubs and small trees in the gooseberry (Grossulariaceae) family, they are native to temperate regions of South America, and found mainly on hill slopes or exposed coasts in the Andes region. Free flowering over a long season, they bear panicles or racemes of small white to pink or red flowers with 5 separate petals, though these are usually pressed together in the lower half to form an apparent tube. Leaves are usually small and toothed, sometimes glandular and aromatic. The fruits are small globular capsules that shed fine seed.

Erythrina acanthocarpa

CULTIVATION: Not all species are hardy in cold inland areas but most can be grown successfully in exposed coastal gardens. These plants are lime tolerant and drought resistant, and they thrive in almost any well-drained soil in full sun. Prune immediately after flowering, but in cold climates delay this until early spring. Propagate from soft-tip cuttings in spring or semi-hardwood tips in autumn.

Escallonia bifida
syn. *Escallonia montevidensis*
WHITE ESCALLONIA
☀ ❈ ↕ 10–20 ft (3–6 m) ↑ 15–30 ft (4.5–9 m)
Small tree from Uruguay and southern Brazil. Leaves finely toothed, larger than most species; whitish midrib, dark green and slightly shiny on upper surface, paler beneath. Panicles of honey-scented white flowers, at branch tips, in early–mid-autumn. Zones 8–10.

Escallonia × exoniensis
☀ ❈ ↔ 12 ft (3.5 m) ↑ 15–20 ft (4.5–6 m)
Hybrid of Chilean species *E. rosea* and *E. rubra*. Strong erect shoots from base. Glandular young stems. Leaves dark lustrous green above, paler beneath. Loose panicles of blush pink to white flowers at branch tips in mid-spring–late autumn. 'Frades', crimson flowers. Zones 8–10.

Escallonia rubra
syns *Escallonia microphylla, E. punctata*
☀ ❈ ↔ 15 ft (4.5 m) ↑ 15 ft (4.5 m)
Variable shrub from Chile. Aromatic leaves. Loose panicles of deep pink to red flowers in mid-summer. *E. r.* var. **macrantha**, rose-crimson flowers, glossy aromatic leaves; 'C. F. Ball', grows to 10 ft (3 m) tall, large aromatic leaves, crimson flowers. *E. r.* 'Crimson Spire' ★, erect habit, bright crimson flowers; 'Woodside', low-growing, small leaves, good rock-garden plant. Zones 8–10.

Escallonia Hybrid Cultivars
☀ ❈ ↔ 6–12 ft (1.8–3.5 m) ↑ 5–10 ft (1.5–3 m)
Most popular hybrids derived from *E. rubra* and *E. virgata;* originated in UK and Ireland in first half of twentieth century. Most raised in Slieve Donard Nursery in County Down, Ireland. 'Apple Blossom', suitable for hedging, to 8 ft (2.4 m), short racemes of pink and white flowers; 'Donard Beauty', rich rose red flowers, free flowering, large leaves aromatic when crushed; 'Donard Radiance', bushy plant, rounded, glossy, dark green leaves to 1¾ in (40 mm) long, clusters of rich pink tubular flowers in summer; 'Donard Seedling', vigorous, slightly arching, with oval, deep green, glossy leaves to 1 in (25 mm) long, clusters of pink-stained white flowers in summer; 'Iveyi', upright shrub, good for hedging, very dark green glossy leaves to 2½ in (6 cm) long, dense clusters of white flowers in summer; 'Langleyensis', large spreading shrub, oval dark green leaves to 1 in (25 mm) long, masses of almost flat bright cerise flowers in summer; 'Peach Blossom', medium-sized, similar in habit to 'Apple Blossom', clear peach pink flowers; 'Pride of Donard', racemes of brilliantly rose-colored, somewhat bell-shaped flowers, larger than those of most other species, borne at branch tips, from mid-summer onward; and 'Slieve Donard', medium-sized, compact, very hardy, with small leaves and panicles of apple-blossom-pink flowers. Zones 8–10.

Escallonia, Hybrid Cultivar, 'Pride of Donard'

EUCALYPTUS

Most of the approximately 800 species of this large genus of evergreen trees are endemic to Australia; a few are found in New Guinea and southeastern Indonesia, with one *(E. deglupta)* restricted to the southern Philippines and eastern New Guinea. This genus belongs to the myrtle (Myrtaceae) family and is noted for its aromatic leaves dotted with oil glands. Species vary in size from immense forest trees to the small multi-stemmed shrubs collectively called mallees. The distinctive bark types of these plants give rise to many of the common names. Most species have 2 distinctive types of foliage: opposite juvenile leaves and alternate adult leaves. The flowers have numerous fluffy stamens, which may be white, cream, yellow, pink, or red; in bud the stamens are enclosed in a cap known as an operculum, which is composed of the fused sepals or petals or both. As the stamens expand, the operculum is forced off, splitting away from the cup-like base of the flower; this is one of the main features that unites the genus. The fruit is a woody capsule. Eucalypt flowers are rich in nectar; some species are among the world's finest honey plants. In a recent reclassification over 100 species have been split off from *Eucalyptus* to form the genus *Corymbia,* including the Western Australian red-flowering gum and the lemon-scented gum.
CULTIVATION: The great majority of species are fast growing and long lived, and once established require very little artificial watering or fertilizer. They are best suited to semi-arid or warm-temperate regions. Frost hardiness varies between species, as does the need for moist or dry conditions. Some of the Western Australian mallees dislike summer humidity. Most species can be shaped by pruning or cut back heavily if desired. Propagation is from seed, which germinates readily.

Eucalyptus bicostata
syn. *Eucalyptus globulus* subsp. *bicostata*
EURABBIE
☀ ❈ ↔ 25–50 ft (8–15 m) ↑ 120 ft (36 m)
From southeastern Australia. Smooth white or blue-gray bark, shedding in long ribbons. Juvenile leaves silvery blue, heart-shaped; adult, deep glossy green, to 24 in (60 cm) long. Creamy white flowers in spring–summer. Fruit ribbed and bell-shaped. Zones 8–10.

Eucalyptus caesia
GUNGURRU
☼ ✤ ↔15 ft (4.5 m) ↑20 ft (6 m)
From Western Australia. Mallee or small tree with weeping branches and fairly open crown. Stems, buds, and capsules have powdery white appearance. Smooth reddish brown bark, shedding in long curling strips. Pendent clusters of large red or pink flowers in late spring–early autumn. Urn-shaped capsules. *E. c.* **subsp.** *magna,* red bell-shaped flowers, waxy, white, bell-shaped fruit. Zones 9–11.

Eucalyptus camaldulensis
RIVER RED GUM
☼ ✤ ↔50 ft (15 m) ↑150 ft (45 m)
Found along watercourses of inland Australia. Single or multiple, often massive, trunk with smooth attractively mottled bark. Rich green pendent leaves. Profuse white flowers in late spring–summer. Grown worldwide for its timber, and as fuel wood. Zones 9–12.

Eucalyptus cinerea
ARGYLE APPLE, SILVER DOLLAR TREE
☼ ✤ ↔30 ft (9 m) ↑50 ft (15 m)
From southeastern Australia. Fairly short trunk. Dense spreading crown. Juvenile leaves circular, silvery gray; adult leaves often absent. Small white flowers in early summer. Moderately fast growing; retains lower branches to near ground level. Zones 8–11.

Eucalyptus erythrocorys ★
ILLYARRIE, RED-CAP GUM
☼ ✤ ↔10 ft (3 m) ↑25 ft (8 m)
From Western Australia. Mallee shrub or small tree with smooth, gray to white, deciduous bark. Bright green leathery leaves. Unusual, large, 4-lobed, scarlet bud caps open to reveal bright yellow flowers in summer–autumn. Flowers followed by attractive, broad, bell-shaped, woody seed capsules, to 1½ in (35 mm) long. Zones 9–11.

Eucalyptus forrestiana
FUCHSIA GUM
☼ ✤ ↔12 ft (3.5 m) ↑15 ft (4.5 m)
From Western Australia. Dense dark green canopy. Smooth gray bark peels in long strips in late summer. Bright red 4-sided flower buds, to 2 in (5 cm) long, open to reveal short yellow stamens in summer–autumn. Conspicuous red fruit. Zones 9–11.

Eucalyptus glaucescens
TINGIRINGI GUM
☼ ✤ ↔20 ft (6 m) ↑20–70 ft (6–21 m)
From mountains in southeastern Australia. Short stocking of fibrous bark at trunk's base; smooth white, gray, or greenish bark above, peeling in short ribbons. Adult leaves narrow, gray-green; juvenile broader, glaucous. White flowers in autumn. Zones 8–9.

Eucalyptus globulus
BLUE GUM, TASMANIAN BLUE GUM
☼ ✤ ↔40 ft (12 m) ↑180 ft (55 m)
Large forest tree mostly from Tasmania, Australia. Straight trunk. Smooth dark gray bark, shed in summer–autumn. Young leaves blue-gray, rounded; adult deep green, leathery, sickle-shaped. Single, creamy white, stalkless flowers in spring. Zones 9–11.

Eucalyptus grandis
FLOODED GUM
☼ ✤ ↔30–50 ft (9–15 m) ↑200 ft (60 m)
From coastal districts of eastern Australia. Straight shaft-like trunk, short stocking of persistent fibrous bark at base, smooth powdery white bark above. Adult leaves narrow, dark green. Clusters of small white flowers in winter. Fast-growing tree. Zones 9–12.

Eucalyptus gunnii
CIDER GUM
☼ ✤ ↔25 ft (8 m) ↑80 ft (24 m)
Found in highlands of Tasmania, Australia. Smooth gray-pink to reddish brown bark shed in late summer. Juvenile leaves glaucous, gray-green, rounded, stem-clasping. Adult leaves narrow, stalked. Small creamy white flowers in spring–summer. Zones 7–9.

Eucalyptus leucoxylon
SOUTH AUSTRALIAN BLUE GUM, YELLOW GUM
☼ ✤ ↔20–40 ft (6–12 m) ↑100 ft (30 m)
Woodland tree from southeastern South Australia and western Victoria. Single straight trunk with smooth creamy yellow or bluish gray bark, shedding in irregular flakes. Narrow gray-green adult leaves hang vertically. Profusion of white, cream, pink, or red flowers, hang in pendulous clusters of 3, in late autumn–spring; attractive to nectar-feeding birds. Pink- and red-flowered forms often sold under name '**Rosea**'. Zones 9–11.

Eucalyptus caesia subsp. *magna*

Eucalyptus cinerea

Eucalyptus forrestiana

Eucalyptus pauciflora, in the wild, Victoria, Australia

Eucalyptus macrocarpa

MOTTLECAH

☼ ❄ ↔ 12 ft (3.5 m) ↑ 6–12 ft (1.8–3.5 m)

Mallee shrub from Western Australia. Stems, new bark, and buds powdery gray. Leaves broadly ovate, silvery gray, thick-textured, stem-clasping. Showy deep pink to red flowers in late winter–spring. Woody seed capsules, to 4 in (10 cm) wide. Zones 9–10.

Eucalyptus mannifera

BRITTLE GUM

☼ ❄ ↔ 30 ft (9 m) ↑ 70 ft (21 m)

Widespread in southeastern Australia. Powdery white, cream, or gray bark, smooth to ground level, turning reddish before shedding in patches. Open canopy of narrow, gray-green, drooping leaves. Clusters of small white flowers in summer–autumn. Zones 8–10.

Eucalyptus microcorys

TALLOWWOOD

☼/◐ ❄ ↔ 40 ft (12 m) ↑ 60–180 ft (18–55 m)

From eastern Australia. Distinctive soft, fibrous, reddish brown bark. Dense spreading crown. Thin-textured dark green leaves. Showy clusters of creamy white flowers in winter–early summer. Excellent shade and shelter tree. Zones 10–12.

Eucalyptus nicholii

NARROW-LEAFED BLACK PEPPERMINT

☼ ❄ ↔ 20–40 ft (6–12 m) ↑ 50 ft (15 m)

From eastern Australia. Fast growing. Relatively short trunk, fibrous brown bark. Compact crown. Pendulous, fine, sickle-shaped, blue-green leaves. Small white flowers in autumn. Zones 8–11.

Eucalyptus pauciflora

SNOW GUM, WHITE SALLY

☼ ❄ ↔ 20 ft (6 m) ↑ 60 ft (18 m)

From mountains of southeastern Australia. Short trunk with smooth, mottled, light gray, white, or yellowish bark, shedding in irregular patches. Adult leaves shiny, leathery, blue-green, to 8 in (20 cm) long. Profuse, nectar-rich, white blossoms in spring–summer. *E. p.* subsp. *niphophila* (syn. *E. niphophila*), commonly known as alpine snow gum; occurring at elevations above 5,000 ft (1,500 m) in Snowy Mountains of New South Wales and Victoria; low-branching habit; attractive bark that sheds to leave smooth white or gray surface with patches of orange, red, yellow, and olive green; shiny blue-green leaves; glaucous buds and fruit. Zones 7–9.

Eucalyptus perriniana

SPINNING GUM

☼ ❄ ↔ 10–20 ft (3–6 m) ↑ 20–40 ft (6–12 m)

Mallee-like small tree from subalpine areas of southeastern Australia. Bark sheds to leave smooth whitish gray surface with pale brown and green patches. Juvenile leaves powdery gray, fused into disk around twig; adult leaves dull gray-green, lance-shaped. Profuse creamy white flowers in summer. Juvenile leaves popular as cut foliage for floral arrangements. Zones 7–9.

Eucalyptus polyanthemos

RED BOX

☼ ❄ ↔ 20 ft (6 m) ↑ 25–80 ft (8–24 m)

From southeastern Australia. Short trunk. Large, often irregular crown. Oval to almost circular bluish gray leaves, pendent on slender stalks. Bark variable: may be rough, gray, and persistent on smaller branches or may shed annually, leaving tree smooth-barked. Small white flowers in spring. Zones 8–11.

Eucalyptus leucoxylon 'Rosea'

Eucalyptus pulverulenta

☼ ❄ ↔ 12 ft (3.5 m) ↑ 15–30 ft (4.5–9 m)

Small tree or mallee shrub from mountains of southeastern New South Wales, Australia. Circular silvery blue juvenile leaves; rarely produces adult leaves. Attractive smooth bark, often pale brown or coppery, peels in long strips. Buds and fruit both have silvery waxy bloom. Small white flowers produced in spring. Used by florists for cut foliage. Zones 8–10.

Eucalyptus regnans

MOUNTAIN ASH

☼ ❄ ↔ 30–60 ft (9–18 m) ↑ 320 ft (96 m)

From cool mountain forests in southeastern Australia. Straight trunk with fibrous persistent bark on lower part; rest of bark sheds to reveal smooth whitish or gray-green surface. Narrow open crown. Lance-shaped leaves. Produces small white flowers in summer. *E. regnans* is recognized as tallest hardwood species in world. Zones 8–9.

Eucalyptus rhodantha

ROSE MALLEE

☼ ⧫ ↔ 10 ft (3 m) ↑ 10 ft (3 m)

Spreading mallee from southwestern Australia. Smooth pale brown bark. Powdery whitish gray branchlets. Juvenile and adult leaves rounded to heart-shaped, thick-textured, powdery gray. Solitary red flowers, on pendent stalks, in spring–autumn. Zones 9–11.

Eucalyptus urnigera

URN GUM

☼ ❄ ↔ 15–30 ft (4.5–9 m) ↑ 40 ft (12 m)

From Tasmania, Australia. Smooth-barked. Olive green leaves, to 4 in (10 cm) long. Creamy white flowers, in clusters of 3, in late summer–autumn. Urn-shaped seed capsules. Zones 8–9.

Eucalyptus viminalis

CANDLEBARK, MANNA GUM, RIBBON GUM

☼ ❄ ↔ 35 ft (10 m) ↑ 80–180 ft (24–55 m)

Forest tree from eastern Australia. Bark smooth or with stocking of rough bark on lower trunk; upper bark sheds, revealing smooth white bark. Many small white flowers in summer. Zones 8–10.

EUCRYPHIA

Found in Chile, eastern mainland Australia, and Tasmania, this genus includes 7 species of evergreen or semi-evergreen shrubs and trees, 2 of them recently discovered in Queensland, Australia. Although previously placed in a family (Eucryphiaceae) of its own, *Eucryphia* is now regarded as a member of the family Cunoniaceae. The leaves are simple or pinnate, with oblong to elliptical leaflets, and are dark green above and much lighter below, usually with a fine downy covering that wears away from the upper surfaces. The flowers, which resemble small single roses, have 4 or 5 petals that are white, cream, or occasionally pale pink. They open from late spring to autumn, and are often slightly scented.
CULTIVATION: These plants tolerate only light to moderate frost but are easily cultivated in a mild climate. The general preference is for a relatively humid atmosphere; a moist, humus-enriched, well-drained soil; and a position in sun or partial shade. In areas with hot dry summers, provide shade from the hottest sun.

Eucryphia glutinosa

HARDY EUCRYPHIA, NIRRHE

☼ ❄ ↔ 20 ft (6 m) ↑ 30 ft (9 m)

From dry mountainous areas in central Chile. May drop foliage in cold winters. Leaves pinnate, 2 in (5 cm) long, composed of elliptical leaflets, serrated edges. Large white flowers, 2½ in (6 cm) across, with red-brown anthers, in summer. **Plena Group** cultivars have semi-double or double flowers. Zones 8–9.

Eucryphia × intermedia

☼ ❄ ↔ 15 ft (4.5 m) ↑ 30 ft (9 m)

Hybrid between *E. glutinosa* from Chile and *E. lucida* from Tasmania, Australia. Simple and trifoliate leaves, also a few pinnate

Eucryphia × intermedia

Eucalyptus urnigera

leaves. Although evergreen, may drop some foliage over winter. Leaves light green with hint of blue on undersides. Pure white flowers. 'Rostrevor' ★, named after Irish garden where cross originated, most common form. Zones 8–9.

Eucryphia lucida

PINKWOOD, TASMANIAN LEATHERWOOD

☼ ❄ ↔ 15 ft (4.5 m) ↑ 25 ft (8 m)

Upright tree from Tasmania, Australia. Trifoliate leaves of young plants change to simple, narrow, oblong leaves with age. Pendulous, usually white flowers, to 2 in (5 cm) across, in summer. 'Ballerina', flowers 1¼ in (30 mm) across, pale pink petals edged darker pink, red stamens; 'Leatherwood Cream', cream-edged leaves. Zones 8–9.

Eucryphia × nymansensis

☼ ❄ ↔ 15 ft (4.5 m) ↑ 30 ft (9 m)

Hybrid between 2 Chilean species—*E. cordifolia* and *E. glutinosa*—appeared around 1914 at Nymans in Sussex, England. 'Mount Usher', semi-double flowers. Most commonly grown form, 'Nymansay', is densely foliaged, strongly upright, and evergreen, bearing both simple, glossy, elliptical leaves and compound leaves with 3 serrated-edged leaflets. White flowers, to 3 in (8 cm) across, with clearly separated petals. Zones 8–9.

EUGENIA

STOPPER

This genus in the myrtle (Myrtaceae) family has about 550 species of evergreen trees or shrubs widely spread across tropical to subtropical regions in the Americas, with scattered species in Africa, Asia, and the Pacific Islands. They have firm, opposite, glossy, simple leaves. Conspicuous flowers, with numerous stamens, may be solitary, in panicles, or in racemes, and usually appear in spring or summer. The fruit is a drupe-like yellow, purple, red, or black berry and is sometimes edible. This genus is grown for the ornamental value of its flowers, fruit, and foliage; for hedging and screening; and some species for their edible fruit.

CULTIVATION: Easily grown in tropical and subtropical areas in sun or part-shade, they do best in well-drained sandy loam. Propagate from seed in summer or from half-hardened cuttings in autumn.

Eugenia uniflora
BRAZILIAN CHERRY, FLORIDA CHERRY, PITANGA, SURINAM CHERRY

☀ ✦ ↔ 8 ft (2.4 m) ↕ 10–30 ft (3–9 m)

Shrub or small tree from Brazil. Dull green narrow leaves, to 2½ in (6 cm) long. Fragrant, fluffy, white flowers, ½ in (12 mm) across, solitary or in groups, in summer. Red, 8-ribbed, edible fruit, 1¼ in (30 mm) in diameter. Can be invasive. Zones 10–12.

EUONYMUS
This genus belonging to the spindle-tree (Celastraceae) family consists of over 175 species of evergreen, semi-evergreen, or deciduous shrubs, trees, and climbers native to Asia, Europe, North and Central America, and the island of Madagascar; there is also a single Australian species. Not all are frost hardy. Stems and branches are often 4-sided. The leaves may be toothed or smooth-edged. The small flowers may be yellow, green, white, or red-brown, and are borne singly or in cymes in the leaf axils from late spring to early summer. The fruit is a distinctive capsule with 3, 4, or 5 compartments, each containing one large seed surrounded by a usually red or orange aril. The capsule splits open to reveal a paler, often pink, interior that contrasts with the brightly colored aril. Parts of the plant can cause stomach upsets or even poisoning if they are eaten. CULTIVATION: They tolerate all types of soil, but *E. alatus* is especially good in alkaline soil. Grow in well-drained soil in sun or part-shade. Evergreen species need shelter from drying cold winds and slightly more moisture in the soil. Variegated forms perform better in full sun. Propagation is from seed, or from nodal cuttings taken from deciduous plants in summer or from evergreen plants in early summer to mid-autumn.

Euonymus alatus
BURNING BUSH, CORKBUSH, WINGED SPINDLE TREE

☀ ❄ ↔ 10 ft (3 m) ↕ 6 ft (1.8 m)

Dense, deciduous, bushy shrub found from northeastern Asia to central China and Japan. Corky wings on branches. Leaves ovate to elliptical, dark green, toothed margins, turn brilliant red in autumn. Pale green flowers in summer. Fruit pale red, 4-lobed, bright orange seeds. 'Compactus', dwarf compact shrub, winged corky branches, scarlet to purple foliage in winter; 'Nordine', large orange leaves in winter, abundant fruit; 'Timber Creek', vigorous, with arching branches and broad recurving leaves that color brilliant scarlet in autumn. Zones 3–9.

Euonymus americanus
STRAWBERRY BUSH, WAHOO

☀ ❄ ↔ 6 ft (1.8 m) ↕ 8 ft (2.4 m)

Deciduous upright shrub from eastern USA. Leaves deep green, ovate to lance-shaped, scalloped margins, somewhat wrinkly, last well into late autumn. Red-tinged green flowers in summer. Pink 3- to 5-lobed fruit with yellow-tinged white seeds. Zones 6–9.

Euonymus europaeus
EUROPEAN EUONYMUS, EUROPEAN SPINDLE TREE, SPINDLE TREE

☀ ❄ ↔ 8 ft (2.4 m) ↕ 20 ft (6 m)

Deciduous shrub or small tree found from Europe to western Asia. Green branches. Leaves elliptic, scalloped, pointed tips. Small cymes of 5 to 7 yellow to green flowers in spring. Pink to red 4-lobed fruit with white seeds and orange arils. *E. e.* f. *albus*, white fruit. *E. e.* 'Aucubifolius', white variegated foliage; 'Red Cap', bright red fruit, persisting on bare winter branches; 'Red Cascade' ★, often small tree, good autumn color, persistent orange-red fruit. Zones 3–9.

Euonymus fortunei
syn. *Euonymus radicans*
WINTERCREEPER EUONYMUS

☀ ❄ ↔ 3–10 ft (0.9–3 m) ↕ 1–10 ft (0.3–3 m)

From China. Evergreen ground-cover shrub or root-clinging climber; as climber, can reach 15 ft (4.5 m) high. Green branches with fine warts. Leaves oval or elliptic, toothed, pointed tips. Greenish yellow flowers in summer. White fruit, orange arils. *E. f.* var. *vegetus*, spreading, bushy, stiff branches, thick dull green leaves. *E. f.* 'Canadale Gold', marginal bands of yellow on leaves; 'Coloratus', green foliage turns purple-red in winter; 'E.T.', prostrate form, rounded leaves with pinkish cream margins; 'Emerald Gaiety', green leaves with white margins tinged pink in winter; 'Emerald 'n' Gold', leaves with yellow margins

Euonymus fortunei 'Emerald Gaiety'

tinged pink in winter; 'Harlequin', leaves grayish green, streaked and marbled with cream or white, frequently throwing entirely cream leaves; 'Kewensis', prostrate form, tiny leaves; 'Minims', procumbent, rooting along branches, 2 in (5 cm) high; 'Niagara Green', deep green leaves, new growth lime green; 'Sheridan Gold', yellowish green young foliage; 'Silver Queen', bushy shrub or spreading climber, leaves with broad white margins tinged pink in winter; 'Sunspot', semiprostrate, weak arching branches, leaves with large cream or yellow blotch mainly on basal half; 'Variegatus' older variegated cultivar. Zones 5–10.

Euonymus alatus 'Timber Creek'

Euonymus japonicus
EVERGREEN EUONYMUS

☼ ❄ ↔6–12 ft (1.8–3.5 m) ↑12 ft (3.5 m)

Found in Korea, China, and Japan. Evergreen, dense, bushy shrub or small tree, grows larger in wild than in cultivation. Leaves dark green, oval to oblong, tough, leathery. Flattened cymes of green flowers in summer. Rounded pink fruit contain white seeds and orange arils. 'Albomarginatus', dark green leaves with narrow white margins; 'Bravo', leaves deep green streaked gray-green with broad yellow margins; 'Emerald 'n' Gold', dwarf form with compact foliage, pale yellow leaves with green central zone; 'Microphyllus Aureovariegatus', deep green leaves with narrow yellow margins; 'Ovatus Aureus', leaves blotched and streaked yellow. Zones 7–10.

Euonymus planipes
syn. *Euonymus sachalinensis* of gardens

☼ ❄ ↔10 ft (3 m) ↑10 ft (3 m)

Deciduous upright shrub or small tree from northeastern China to Japan and far eastern Russia. Leaves mid-green, elliptic, coarsely toothed, turn red in autumn. Small greenish flowers. Fruit red, almost spherical, 4 or 5 lobes, red seeds with orange arils. Zones 4–9.

EUPHORBIA (see page 462)

Euphorbia fulgens ★
SCARLET PLUME

☼ ⚘ ↔30 in (75 cm) ↑5 ft (1.5 m)

Arching well-branched shrub from Mexico. Leaves deciduous, lance-shaped, on long stalks. Rounded bright red floral bracts in winter. 'Alba', cream bracts; 'Albatross', bluish green leaves, pure white bracts; 'Purple Leaf', burgundy foliage, bright orange bracts. Zones 10–11.

Euphorbia leucocephala
PASCUITA, SNOWS OF KILIMANJARO

☼ ⚘ ↔6–10 ft (1.8–3 m) ↑6–10 ft (1.8–3 m)

Deciduous shrub from Central America (despite common name snows of Kilimanjaro). Erect habit; widely spaced whorls of up to 10 long-stalked pale green leaves. Profuse panicles of blooms like miniature poinsettia *(E. pulcherrima)*; white floral bracts in autumn–winter. Zones 9–11.

Euphorbia pulcherrima ★
syn. *Poinsettia pulcherrima*
POINSETTIA

☼ ⚘ ↔7 ft (2 m) ↑10 ft (3 m)

Straggly deciduous shrub from Mexico. Inconspicuous yellow flowers surrounded by large brilliant red floral bracts in winter–spring. Potted poinsettias have huge commercial market. 'Henrietta Ecke', double form; 'Rosea', one of a number of named pink varieties. Other forms have cream, white, or marbled floral bracts. Zones 9–11.

EUPTELEA

Native to Japan, China, and the eastern Himalayas, this genus consists of only 2 species of smallish deciduous trees, valued in temperate-climate gardens for their sharply toothed leaves, which quiver gracefully on slender stalks in slight breezes and take on pretty tints in autumn. Small bisexual flowers appear in globular clusters along the twigs just before the leaves, followed by small winged fruit. *Euptelea*, the only genus in the family Eupteleaceae, is one of a group of rather primitive flowering plant families that includes the planes and the beeches. CULTIVATION: A cool moist climate, a sheltered but sunny position, and deep, moderately fertile soil produce the best growth. *Euptelea* are useful small trees for overplanting of rhododendrons, azaleas, and other such shrubs. Little maintenance is required, apart from trimming away basal suckers from time to time. Propagate from freshly collected seed or by air-layering of suckers or low branches.

Euryops pectinatus

Euptelea pleiosperma

☼ ❄ ↔15 ft (4.5 m) ↑15–30 ft (4.5–9 m)

Occurs wild from central and western China to far northeastern India and Bhutan. Leaves shallowly toothed, underside somewhat whitish, turning red in autumn. Pinkish green flowers with red anthers in spring. Small brown fruit, usually containing more than one seed. Zones 6–9.

EURYOPS

There are about 100 species of evergreen shrubs, perennials, and annuals in this genus, a member of the large daisy (Asteraceae) family. The majority are native to South Africa. They are attractive plants with lobed or finely divided green to grayish green leaves and bright yellow daisy flowers borne over a long period. CULTIVATION: Easily grown in a wide range of conditions, *Euryops* species can withstand some frost, are drought tolerant, and are suitable for planting in coastal gardens. Deep free-draining soil in full sun is best. Grow against a warm wall or in a greenhouse or conservatory in cool-temperate climates. Prune after flowering to maintain a compact form. Propagate from seed or half-hardened or softwood cuttings.

Euphorbia pulcherrima

Euptelea pleiosperma

Euryops acraeus

syn. *Euryops evansii*

☼ ❊ ↔ 36 in (90 cm) ↑ 12–36 in (30–90 cm)

Compact plant with small, narrow, silvery gray leaves. Bright yellow daisies, to 1½ in (35 mm) across, in spring–summer. Short-lived plant in damp climates; requires perfect drainage. Zones 7–10.

Euryops chrysanthemoides

syn. *Gamolepis chrysanthemoides*

PARIS DAISY

☼ ❊ ↔ 5 ft (1.5 m) ↑ 4 ft (1.2 m)

Easily grown, particularly in warm climates. Well foliaged with deeply lobed dark green leaves. Yellow daisies, 2 in (5 cm) across, on slender stalks above foliage, in winter–spring. Zones 9–11.

Euryops pectinatus

GOLDEN DAISY BUSH, GRAY-HAIRED EURYOPS

☼ ❊ ↔ 5 ft (1.5 m) ↑ 4 ft (1.2 m)

Fern-like foliage, deeply cut, downy, gray leaves. Bright yellow daisies held well above foliage, in spring–summer. Seldom without flowers in warm climates. Zones 8–11.

EXOCHORDA

PEARL BUSH

This genus consists of 4 or 5 species of deciduous shrubs, within the rose (Rosaceae) family, native to northeast and central Asia. Some botanists now prefer to combine these into a single variable species, for which the name *E. racemosa* takes priority. They are all attractive spring-flowering shrubs, many with arching branches that become festooned with waxy white flowers, which are borne in racemes in the leaf axils or at the branch tips. The leaves are simple and alternate.

CULTIVATION: They prefer moderately fertile well-drained soil in a cool-temperate climate with well-defined seasons, and a sheltered position in full sun. They may become chlorotic in chalk soils. Prune basal shoots by one-third in late winter; remove spent flower clusters after flowering. Seeds germinate readily when sown in spring in a warm humid atmosphere. Soft-tip or half-hardened cuttings taken in summer or autumn can be rooted under cover; or use hardwood cuttings from winter pruning.

Fabiana imbricata

Exochorda giraldii

☼ ❊ ↔ 10 ft (3 m) ↑ 10 ft (3 m)

Large free-flowering shrub from northwestern China. Arching, spreading habit. Green leaves, red veins. White flowers in late spring. *E. g.* var. *wilsonii*, more upright. Zones 5–9.

Exochorda × macrantha

PEARL BUSH

☼ ❊ ↔ 10 ft (3 m) ↑ 7 ft (2 m)

Strong-growing hybrid of *E. korolkowii* and *E. racemosa* closely resembles *E. racemosa*. Abundant racemes of pure white flowers

Exochorda racemosa

in late spring. **'The Bride'** ★, compact shrub, to 6 ft (1.8 m) high, with slightly weeping habit and arching branches covered with large white flowers in spring. Zones 5–9.

Exochorda racemosa

syn. *Exochorda grandiflora*

COMMON PEARL BUSH, PEARL BUSH

☼ ❊ ↔ 10 ft (3 m) ↑ 10 ft (3 m)

Shrub of northeastern China. Dense spherical shape when mature, with many erect arching shoots from base. Flower buds like miniature white pearls, open to pure white, waxy, slightly fragrant flowers. Zones 4–9.

FABIANA

This genus belongs to the nightshade (Solanaceae) family and contains about 25 shrubs from warm-temperate parts of South America, especially Chile and Argentina. They have small, overlapping, needle-like to narrow, triangular leaves, usually deep green. The light-colored flowers are tubular, like those of some ericas. They open in summer, and are usually white to pale pink.

CULTIVATION: Most species tolerate light to moderate frosts but prefer mild winters. They are not fussy about soil requirements, provided the winter drainage is good. These shrubs are easily propagated from half-hardened cuttings.

Fabiana imbricata

PICHI

☼ ❊ ↔ 7 ft (2 m) ↑ 8 ft (2.4 m)

Chilean species. Leaves dark green, covered with fine down when young. Upper third of stems smothered with tubular, white to pale pink flowers in summer. *F. i.* f. *violacea*, mauve to light purple flowers. *F. i.* 'Prostrata', low-growing cultivar. Zones 8–10.

Fagus grandifolia

× Fatshedera lizei

FAGUS
BEECH

This genus gives its name to the family Fagaceae, which also includes oaks and chestnuts. The genus consists of about 10 species of deciduous trees, native to Europe and the British Isles, and also found through temperate Asia and North America, China, and Japan, with branches to ground level and smooth light green leaves. Horizontally held limbs produce layers of foliage that protect the smooth silvery gray trunks from sunburn. In late autumn to winter, leaves turn golden brown or coppery red before falling. Buds are distinctly sharp-pointed, held at an angle to the stem. Prickly fruits release 2 triangular nuts.
CULTIVATION: Grow in well-drained reasonably fertile soil in wind-sheltered gardens. Summer moisture is necessary until trees become established. They handle moderate air pollution. Propagate from seed sown when fresh, or use grafted cultivars.

Fagus crenata
JAPANESE BEECH

☼ ✳ ↔ 20 ft (6 m) ↑ 30 ft (9 m)
From Japan, important deciduous tree of temperate areas. Bark gray. Leaves oval, pale green on underside, wavy furry margins when young. Veins beneath, also furry. Zones 6–9.

Fagus grandifolia
AMERICAN BEECH

☼ ✳ ↔ 35 ft (10 m) ↑ 80 ft (24 m)
From eastern USA and Canada. Deciduous straight-trunked tree, develops spreading crown when grown in open. Does not perform well in cooler summers. Often produces suckers. Zones 4–8.

Fagus japonica
JAPANESE BLUE BEECH

☼ ✳ ↔ 25 ft (8 m) ↑ 80 ft (24 m)
Deciduous tree from mountains of Honshu, Shikoku, and Kyushu in Japan. Persistent soft hairs on underside of oval leaves. Both surfaces furry on young leaves. Zones 6–8.

Fagus sylvatica
COMMON BEECH, EUROPEAN BEECH

☼ ✳ ↔ 50 ft (15 m) ↑ 100 ft (30 m)
Deciduous tree from Europe and southern England. Strongly veined foliage, provides dense shade. Trunk straight, smooth gray bark. Autumn foliage gold to orange to brown. Prickly fruits. *F. s. f fastigiata*, leaves deep green with gold; *F. s. f. heterophylla* 'Aspleniifolia', narrow long-pointed leaves; *F. s. f. pendula*, weeping beech, pendulous thick branches; *F. s. f. tortuosa*, twisted branches. *F. s.* 'Albomarginata', variegated leaves; **Cuprea Group**, copper colored; 'Dawyck', upright tree resembling Lombardy poplar; 'Dawyck Gold', gold-tipped foliage; 'Dawyck Purple', purplish foliage; **Purpurea Group** ★, soft green turning purple; 'Purpurea Pendula', weeping foliage; 'Quercina', prickly pale copper nuts; 'Riversii' ★, color intensifies to almost black; 'Tricolor', slow growing, pink margins, white-blotched green leaves. Zones 5–9.

× FATSHEDERA

Originating in France, this is a cross between Atlantic ivy (*Hedera hibernica*) and Japanese fatsia (*Fatsia japonica*) and belongs to the ivy (Araliaceae) family. It is an unusual, sprawling, evergreen shrub, sometimes climbing. Flowers are insignificant and sterile.
CULTIVATION: It is easily grown in moist well-drained soil in partial or full shade, and tolerates neglect provided the plant remains moist. With a somewhat rangy habit, × *Fatshedera* needs regular pinching back to keep it compact and a support to keep it upright. As it is sterile it must be propagated from cuttings, though it sometimes self-layers.

× Fatshedera lizei

☼/◐ ✳ ↔ 8 ft (2.4 m) ↑ 6 ft (1.8 m)
Multi-stemmed shrub. Leaves deeply lobed, hand-shaped, bright glossy green. Small heads of greenish white flowers in autumn. 'Annemeike', yellow leaves; 'Variegata', cream-edged leaves. Zones 7–11.

FATSIA

This genus within the ivy (Araliaceae) family contains only 3 evergreen species of large-leafed small trees and shrubs from moist coastal woodlands of South Korea, Japan, and Taiwan. They tend to sucker from the base, producing a fuller shrub; unwanted stems can be removed. They are good indoor and conservatory plants with ornamental leaves, and

Fatsia japonica

good specimen plants for courtyards and terraces.
CULTIVATION: They are tolerant of pollution and salt spray, and are moderately frost hardy; variegated cultivars are less frost tolerant. They like moisture-retentive soil in sun or part-shade. In warm climates they can be grown under trees. In shade, they tolerate dry nutrient-deficient soil, but do better in more fertile soil. In colder areas, they need the protection of a wall or similar shelter. Under glass and in pots, they need a loam-based compost, regular feeding, and watering during the growing season. Propagate from seed sown in autumn, from cuttings, or by air-layering.

Fatsia japonica

syns *Aralia japonica, A. sieboldii*

FATSIA, JAPANESE ARALIA

☼/◑ ❄ ↔6–12 ft (1.8–3.5 m) ↑6–12 ft (1.8–3.5 m)

Native to South Korea and Japan. Leaves dark green, glossy, 7 to 11 lobes, mostly toothed, palmately lobed. Rounded flowerheads of creamy white flowers in late summer–autumn. Fruit green, ripening black by spring. Cultivars include '**Aurea**', '**Marginata**', '**Moseri**' ★, and '**Variegata**'. Zones 8–11.

FICUS

FIG

Although this genus is in the mulberry (Moraceae) family, its flower and fruiting stages differ from those of the rest of this family. Fig species come in many variations, from climbers and creepers to large shrubs and very large trees. Many fig species of tropical forests display the "strangler" growth habit, some also develop "curtains" of aerial roots, or even the "banyan" growth form. *Ficus* species have a milky sap, and a large stipule enclosing the tip of each twig and leaving a ring-like scar when it falls. Leaves vary from tiny to huge, with variable shape. Many species shed their leaves in the tropical dry season. The variable-sized "fruits" (figs) are edible. CULTIVATION: Some species tolerate light frosts only if protected when small. Figs are vigorous, and will quickly outgrow a small garden. Propagate from seed, from cuttings, or by air-layering. *F. carica*, the edible fig, is the most easily propagated species.

Ficus benghalensis

BANYAN

☼ ✦ ↔75–400 ft (23–120 m) ↑30–40 ft (9–12 m)

Southern Asian fig, widespread in India. Vastly spreading; single tree may produce hundreds, sometimes thousands, of trunks, creating its own mini forest. Broad, stiff leaves, shiny deep green; stalkless figs, ripen to orange. Sacred tree of Hinduism. '**Krishnae**', similar proportions, inrolled cup-shaped leaves. Zones 11–12.

Ficus benjamina

BENJAMIN FIG, BENJAMIN TREE, WEEPING FIG

☼ ⬥ ↔50 ft (15 m) ↑80 ft (24 m)

Tropical Asian species. Small glossy leaves, pointing downward, narrowing abruptly at apex. Figs deep reddish tan. *F. b.* **var.** *nuda* (syn. *F. b.* var. *comosa*), broad-spreading limbs, non-drooping branchlets, leaves narrowed at tip, orange figs. *F. b.* '**Exotica**' ★, thinner, more finely pointed leaves; '**Golden Princess**', leaves tinged lemon yellow; '**Pandora**', small thin leaves, wavy margins; '**Starlight**', leaves cream-edged, gray-green flecked. Zones 10–12.

Ficus elastica

INDIA-RUBBER TREE, RUBBER TREE

☼ ✦ ↔40–100 ft (12–30 m) ↑40–100 ft (12–30 m)

Tropical Asian fig. Large tree, numerous aerial roots draped from branches. '**Decora**' ★, broad, glossy, bronze-tinted leaves, large reddish buds at apex; '**Doescheri**', leaves irregularly edged cream, center marbled gray; '**Schrüveriana**', leaves peppered dark green, new leaves flushed red; '**Variegata**', variegated leaves. Zones 11–12.

Ficus lyrata

FIDDLE-LEAF FIG

☼ ⬥ ↔30 ft (9 m) ↑30 ft (9 m)

From rainforests of central Africa and tropical west Africa. Bushy-crowned erect tree; large stiff leaves resemble violin body. Green figs, hidden under leaves. Popular pot plant. Zones 9–12.

Ficus macrophylla

MORETON BAY FIG

☼ ⬥ ↔130 ft (40 m) ↑80–100 ft (24–30 m)

From Australia's east coast. Rapid growth, dramatic trunk buttresses, large canopy. Large dark green leaves, glossy, thick. Purple figs. *F. m* **subsp.** *columnaris*, from Lord Howe Island, forms spreading canopy over endemic palm, *Howea forsteriana*. Zones 9–11.

Ficus microcarpa

syns *Ficus nitida, F. retusa*

BANYAN FIG, INDIAN LAUREL FIG

☼ ⬥ ↔20–50 ft (6–15 m) ↑40–70 ft (12–21 m)

Native to southern China, Southeast Asia to northern Australia.

Evergreen tree, upright branchlets, often forms aerial roots. Gray to reddish bark, small horizontal flecks. Dense foliage; small, oval, dark green leaves alternate along stems. *F. m.* **var.** *hillii* (syn. *F. hillii*) (Hill's weeping fig), popular park tree, open habit, high sweeping limbs, drooping branchlets. Zones 10–12.

Ficus religiosa

BO TREE, PEEPUL TREE, SACRED FIG

☼ ⬥ ↔25 ft (8 m) ↑30–40 ft (9–12 m)

Native to mountains of Southeast Asia and Himalayan foothills. Strangling fig, normally deciduous in monsoonal climates. Pale gray-barked trunk, spreading branches. Leaves heart-shaped, apex drawn out into long slender point. Zones 9–12.

Ficus macrophylla subsp. *columnaris*, in the wild, Lord Howe Island, Australia

Ficus benghalensis

Ficus rubiginosa

PORT JACKSON FIG, RUSTY FIG

↔ 35–70 ft (10–21 m) ↑ 30–80 ft (9–24 m)

From east coast of Australia. Evergreen tree, forms broad dome. Massive buttressed trunk, smooth gray limbs, sprouting aerial roots. Thick, leathery, oval leaves, dark green with rusty or pale olive felted reverse. Figs yellowish green, warty, ripen in autumn. Gold-variegated form available. Zones 9–11.

FIRMIANA

A genus of 9 mostly deciduous trees or shrubs in the mallow (Malvaceae) family, it is found in tropical Southeast Asia, with one species from eastern Africa. They have smooth-edged or palmate leaves and racemes or panicles of stalk-like flowers, with no petals but a colored calyx. The curious fruit consists of 4 or 5 papery, leaf-like follicles, each containing round wrinkled seeds on its margins. CULTIVATION: Adaptable to most soil types and easily transplanted, they prefer some protection from wind. Propagate from seed in warmer months, or from cuttings of lateral shoots in early spring.

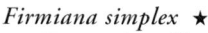

Firmiana simplex

Firmiana simplex ★

syn. *Firmiana platanifolia*

CHINESE PARASOL TREE, JAPANESE VARNISH TREE

↔ 35 ft (10 m) ↑ 60 ft (18 m)

Deciduous tree native to China and eastern Asia, from Ryukyu Islands to Vietnam. Smooth green bark; large, maple-like, palmate leaves divided into 3 to 7 lobes. Calyx lemon yellow, seed follicles hairy. '**Variegata**', green leaves mottled with white. Zones 7–10.

FORSYTHIA

This small genus of about 7 species of deciduous shrubs is a member of the olive (Oleaceae) family. They occur mainly in eastern Asia, with one in southeastern Europe. Simple opposite leaves color in autumn. Yellow flowers appear before, or with, the new leaves in spring. Semi-pendulous species can be trained over a support.

Forsythia ovata 'Tetragold'

CULTIVATION: They are frost hardy and easy to cultivate in well-drained fertile soil in an open sunny position, with adequate water in summer, and winter temperatures below freezing to induce flowering. Flowers are borne on overwintered year-old shoots; remove older shoots after flowering to make room for new shoots from the base of the plant. Propagate from soft-tip cuttings in summer, or hardwood cuttings in winter. Some species are self-layering and can be increased in this way in late winter.

Forsythia × intermedia

BORDER FORSYTHIA

↔ 7 ft (2 m) ↑ 15 ft (4.5 m)

Shrub with erect spreading habit; hybrid between *F. suspensa* var. *sieboldii* and *F. viridissima*. Single basal trunk, ascending arching branches. Leaves oval, sharply toothed on upper half, with reddish stalks. Flowers lemon yellow, solitary or in 2- to 6-flowered racemes, on 1- and 2-year-old branches, in spring. '**Arnold Giant**', large, nodding, rich yellow flowers; '**Goldzauber**', brilliant yellow flowers before leaves; '**Lynwood**', prolific large flowers, broad petals; '**Spectabilis**', upright, outwardly arching shrub, flowers large, golden yellow. Zones 5–9.

Forsythia ovata

EARLY FORSYTHIA, KOREAN FORSYTHIA

↔ 8 ft (2.4 m) ↑ 5 ft (1.5 m)

Compact, bushy, early-flowering species from Korea. Leaves dark green, ovate. Golden yellow flowers in early spring. '**Tetragold**', raised in Holland, dense habit, earlier larger flowers. Zones 5–9.

Forsythia suspensa

GOLDENBELLS, WEEPING FORSYTHIA

↔ 10 ft (3 m) ↑ 12 ft (3.5 m)

From China. Slender drooping branches. Autumn foliage dull yellow. Flowers solitary or in small clusters, golden yellow, in spring. *F. s.* var. *fortunei*, vigorous form, more upright habit; *F. s.* var. *sieboldii*, almost prostrate, rarely taller than 3 ft (0.9 m). Zones 4–9.

Forsythia viridissima

GOLDEN BELLS, GREEN STEM FORSYTHIA

↔ 10 ft (3 m) ↑ 10 ft (3 m)

From China. Cane-like branches grow from base into hemispherical bush. Leaves long, narrow, smooth, dark green, rather shiny, maroon in autumn. Clusters of yellow flowers in leaf axils before leaves, calyx purple shaded. '**Bronxensis**', dwarf form. Zones 5–9.

Forsythia Hybrid Cultivars

↔ 10 ft (3 m) ↑ 5–10 ft (1.5–3 m)

Hardy and colorful. '**Arnold Dwarf**' ★, light green foliage; '**Happy Centennial**', bright yellow flowers; '**Maluch**', profuse flowers with new leaves; Marée d'Or/'**Courtasol**', heavily branched dwarf, prolific yellow-gold flowers; '**Meadow Lark**', heavy flowering, hardy buds; '**New Hampshire Gold**', yellow flowers in early spring; '**Northern Gold**', shiny bright green leaves, golden yellow flowers; '**Northern Sun**', strong-growing shrub. Zones 4–9.

Fothergilla major

FOTHERGILLA

Mainly from southeastern USA, this genus of 2 deciduous shrubs belongs to the witchhazel (Hamamelidaceae) family. Spikes of petal-less flowers appear in spring before the leaves, their long white stamens creating a bottlebrush effect. Autumn foliage is colorful. CULTIVATION: Slow growing, they need moist, well-drained, humus-rich soil. Full sun gives best autumn color. Propagate from seed, best sown fresh, from softwood cuttings in summer, or by layering.

Fothergilla gardenii ★
DWARF FOTHERGILLA
☼ ❋ ↔ 3 ft (0.9 m) ↕ 3 ft (0.9 m)
Southeastern USA, from North Carolina to Alabama. Spreading shrub, oval leaves, irregularly toothed, fragrant white flowers. 'Blue Mist', glaucous blue foliage. Zones 5–9.

Fothergilla major
LARGE FOTHERGILLA
☼ ❋ ↔ 6 ft (1.8 m) ↕ 5–10 ft (1.5–3 m)
From Allegheny Mountains of eastern USA. Slow-growing. Leaves dark green above, glaucous beneath. Good autumn color. Fragrant white flower spikes, pinkish tinge, in late spring–early summer. 'Mount Airy', scented white flowers, red autumn foliage. Zones 5–9.

FRANKLINIA

This is a monotypic genus in the camellia (Theaceae) family. The species has not been seen in the wild for over 200 years. *Franklinia* is closely related to *Gordonia*, with which it is sometimes merged, but differs in being deciduous, and having almost stalkless flowers. The fruit is a large woody capsule containing two flattened seeds.
CULTIVATION: *Franklinia* will tolerate a slightly alkaline soil, but likes plenty of organic material; a sheltered aspect with some morning sun is preferred. Propagate from fresh seed.

Franklinia alatamaha ★
FRANKLIN TREE, FRANKLINIA
◑ ❋ ↔ 12 ft (3.5 m) ↕ 20 ft (6 m)
From Altahama River region in Georgia, USA. Attractive, small, upright, deciduous tree. Glossy bright green leaves color scarlet in autumn. Single camellia-like flowers, pure white with central bunch of yellow stamens, in late summer–autumn. Zones 7–10.

FRAXINUS
ASH
This genus in the olive (Oleaceae) family consists of 65 species. Most *Fraxinus* species are deciduous trees, but the genus also includes a few evergreens. They are mainly from temperate Europe, Asia, and North America, although a few species are found in the tropics. Their leaves are opposite and pinnate. Racemes of small, usually insignificant flowers are borne terminally or in the leaf axils, appearing before the leaves, in spring; flowers are unisexual or bisexual. They harden into single-seeded winged fruits.
CULTIVATION: Most grow well in moist loam and make good specimen trees in large gardens. They tolerate coastal salt air, exposed positions, urban pollution, alkaline soil, and heavy clay. Most species prefer alkaline soil. Propagate by sowing seed after stratifying. Cultivars can be grafted in spring, or they may be budded onto seedling stock of the same species in summer.

Fraxinus americana
WHITE ASH
☼ ❋ ↔ 50 ft (15 m) ↕ 80 ft (24 m)
Columnar tree with spreading crown native to eastern North America. Leaves pinnate, dark green, with 5 to 9 lance-shaped leaflets. 'Autumn Blaze', purple color in autumn; 'Autumn Purple' ★, autumn foliage colored red to deep crimson; 'Rose Hill', dark green leaves, turning bronze-red in autumn. Zones 4–10.

Fraxinus americana 'Autumn Purple'

Fraxinus angustifolia
syn. *Fraxinus rotundifolia*
NARROW-LEAFED ASH
☼ ❋ ↔ 40 ft (12 m) ↕ 80 ft (24 m)
Closely allied to *F. excelsior*, occurs wild in Mediterranean region and western Asia. Typical race (*F. a.* subsp. *angustifolia*) is restricted to southern Europe and northwestern Africa. Vigorous tree, ascending branches, darkish furrowed bark. Leaves have 7 to 13 rather narrow leaflets, arranged in whorls of 3. Winter buds large and dark brown. *F. a.* subsp. *oxycarpa* (syn. *F. oxycarpa*) occurs in southeastern Europe and Caucasus region, only 5 to 7 leaflets per leaf, bands of hairs on underside; *F. a.* subsp. *syriaca* (syn. *F. syriaca* 'Desert Ash'), occurs in Turkey, Syria, and Iran, smaller bushier tree, blackish bark, very thick knobbly twigs, leaves in whorls of 3 or 4, grows well in semi-arid climates. *F. a.* 'Elegantissima', small tree, light green leaves; 'Lentiscifolia', leaflets more widely spaced on longer common stalk; 'Raywood', dark wine red autumn foliage. Zones 6–10.

Fraxinus chinensis   Fraxinus uhdei

Fraxinus chinensis

☼ ❋ ↔ 25 ft (8 m) ↕ 80 ft (24 m)

Native to Korea and China. Yellow hairless young growth. Leaves with 8 leaflets, invertly egg-shaped, dark green above, slightly downy underneath. Flowers on new growth in terminal panicles. Winged fruits in summer. Zones 6–9.

Fraxinus excelsior

COMMON ASH, EUROPEAN ASH

☼ ❋ ↔ 60 ft (18 m) ↕ 100 ft (30 m)

Native to Europe. Gray branches, prominent black buds in winter. Dark green leaves with 11 pairs of leaflets, turn bright yellow in autumn. Flower panicles before leaves in spring. Fruits winged, pendent, remaining after leaves fall. *F. e.* f. *diversifolia*, leaves usually single large leaflet. *F. e.* 'Aurea Pendula', pendulous golden branches; 'Eureka', bright green leaves, serrated edges; 'Jaspidea', yellow shoots in winter; 'Pendula', weeping branches. Zones 4–10.

Fraxinus nigra

BLACK ASH, SWAMP ASH

☼ ❋ ↔ 25 ft (8 m) ↕ 50 ft (15 m)

Upright deciduous tree native to North America. Leaves dark green, 11 stalkless leaflets, lance-shaped, small-toothed edges, curved upward, downy brown veins, underside paler green. Fruit oblong, winged. 'Fallgold', non-fruiting, yellow autumn color. Zones 7–10.

Fraxinus ornus

FLOWERING ASH, MANNA ASH

☼ ❋ ↔ 40 ft (12 m) ↕ 50 ft (15 m)

Native to southern Europe and southwestern Asia. Leaves with 7 leaflets, paler beneath, hairy midribs. Dense panicles of fragrant white flowers in late spring. Fruit narrow, winged. Damaged bark secretes sugary substance. 'Arie Peters', creamy flowers. Zones 6–10.

Fraxinus pennsylvanica

GREEN ASH, RED ASH

☼ ❋ ↔ 70 ft (21 m) ↕ 70 ft (21 m)

Robust tree from North America. Olive green leaves, 9 lance-shaped leaflets, smooth or toothed edges, pointed tip, sunken midrib.

Flowers on old wood, followed by winged fruit. 'Marshall's Seedless', non-fruiting, dark green leaves; 'Patmore', strongly erect, glossy leaves, oval crown, does not fruit; 'Summit' ★, pyramidal when young, becoming upright, autumn leaves deep yellow. Zones 4–10.

Fraxinus uhdei

EVERGREEN ASH, SHAMEL ASH

☼ ❋ ↔ 15 ft (4.5 m) ↕ 25 ft (8 m)

Semi-evergreen to evergreen upright tree from Mexico and Central America. Leaves dark green, lance-shaped to oblong, toothed, hairless, 7 leaflets. Flowers in dense panicles. 'Tomlinson', small upright tree, reaches 12 ft (3.5 m) in 10 years. Zones 8–11.

Fraxinus velutina

ARIZONA ASH, DESERT ASH, VELVET ASH

☼ ❋ ↔ 30 ft (9 m) ↕ 30 ft (9 m)

Native to southwestern USA and northwestern Mexico. Dull green leaves, 7 lance-shaped to oval, toothed leaflets, leathery, hairy felting beneath. *F. v.* var. *coriacea,* leaves thicker and almost hairless; *F. v.* var. *glabra*, doubtfully distinct from *F. v.* var. *coriacea*; *F. v.* var. *toumeyi*, longer-stalked, narrower leaflets, gray-green upper surface stays velvety until late summer. *F. v.* 'Fan-Tex', handsome tree, larger dark green leaves, non-fruiting. Zones 7–10.

FREMONTODENDRON

FLANNEL BUSH

There are 3 species of evergreen shrubs in this genus from southwestern North America, which is a member of the cacao (Sterculiaceae) family. Flannel bushes have showy golden yellow to orange blooms of 5 petal-like sepals. The stems, flower buds, and seed capsules, and the underside of the leaves, are covered with fine bronze bristles that give rise to the common name of flannel bush. CULTIVATION: These shrubs require a warm, sunny, sheltered site, and in cool-temperate climates should be grown under the protection of a wall, although they will withstand some frost. Poor dry soils suit them best, as rich soils produce an excess of foliage rather than flowers and can be a factor in reducing the plant's life span. Too much moisture and root disturbance are other reasons why flannel bush plants are fairly short lived. Propagate from seed, or from softwood or half-hardened cuttings.

Fremontodendron californicum

FLANNEL BUSH, FREMONTIA

☼ ❋ ↔ 15 ft (4.5 m) ↕ 12–25 ft (3.5–8 m)

Found in Sierra Nevada range of California, USA. Leaves variable, almost round to pointed oval shape, dull green, roughened by tiny hairs. Flowers in flushes in spring–summer, bright yellow, often with orange tones on their backs. Zones 8–10.

Fremontodendron mexicanum

MEXICAN FLANNEL BUSH, MEXICAN FREMONTIA, SOUTHERN FLANNEL BUSH

☼ ❂ ↔ 12 ft (3.5 m) ↕ 20 ft (6 m)

Native to Mexico's Baja California Peninsula and San Diego area, USA. Grows in chaparral and woodland. More tender than *F. californicum*. Golden yellow flowers, partly hidden by foliage, over many months, from spring. Zones 9–11.

Fremontodendron Hybrid Cultivars

☼ ❈ ↔ 10–15 ft (3–4.5 m) ↕ 12–20 ft (3.5–6 m)

Hybrids between *F. californicum* and *F. mexicanum* have largely proved superior to either of their parents, being more vigorous, with heavier crop of larger flowers. '**California Glory**', vigorous shrub, large yellow flowers; '**Ken Taylor**' low grower, bright orange-yellow flowers; '**Pacific Sunset**', vigorous, almost tree-like, bright yellow flowers with elongated petal tips. Zones 8–10.

FUCHSIA

There are about 100 species of small or medium-sized trees and spreading or climbing shrubs in this genus, which is a member of the evening primrose (Onagraceae) family. Almost all species are from South and Central America, but a few are native to New Zealand and Tahiti. They are evergreen or deciduous, with foliage growing in whorls, alternate or opposite. Flowers bloom in terminal clusters or from leaf axils and are usually tubular and pendent, often bicolored. The flowers are followed by edible berries, usually with many seeds. In their native habitat, the American species are pollinated by hummingbirds.

CULTIVATION: Most fuchsias are frost tender, and even the few fully hardy forms may die down to ground level in a severe winter. Fuchsias planted in the garden do best in fairly fertile moist soil with good drainage in full sun or partial shade. Feed regularly during flowering. Propagate species from seed and cuttings; raise cultivars from cuttings only, using softwood cuttings in spring or half-hardened cuttings in late summer.

Fremontodendron, Hybrid Cultivar, 'California Glory'

Fuchsia arborescens

TREE FUCHSIA

☼/❂ ❋ ↔ 5 ft (1.5 m) ↕ 6 ft (1.8 m)

Native to Mexico and Central America. Leaves opposite or in whorls of 3 or 4, elliptical with pointed tip, shiny, dark green upper surface, paler green underneath. Flowers in panicles of pink-purple sepals and tubes with pale mauve corolla, in summer. Fruit purple, becomes wrinkled when ripe. Zones 10–12.

Fuchsia boliviana

☼ ❋ ↔ 3–4 ft (0.9–1.2 m) ↕ 12 ft (3.5 m)

Erect shrub or small tree occurring naturally in South America from northern Argentina to Peru; has become naturalized in Colombia and Venezuela. Dark green leaves in whorls of 3, pale gray felty veining on underside. Terminal flowers, tubes pale to dark pink, sepals pale pink to red, scarlet petals, in summer–autumn. Fruit small, red-purple, edible, sweetly flavored. *F. b.* var. *alba* ★, white tubes, sepals with light red marks at base. Zones 9–11.

Fuchsia coccinea

☼/❂ ❈ ↔ 4 ft (1.2 m) ↕ 5–20 ft (1.5–6 m)

Climber or erect shrub native to Brazil. Older branches lose bark in long strips. Leaves in groups of 2, 3, or 4, egg-shaped, pointed tip, matt light green above, paler underneath, hairless or slightly hairy. Deep pink to red flowers grow from leaf axils in summer. Zones 8–11.

Fuchsia fulgens ★

☼/❂ ❋ ↔ 30 in (75 cm) ↕ 5 ft (1.5 m)

Native to Mexico. Toothed heart-shaped leaves, red above, underside paler, flushed with red. Small flowers with red sepals tinged yellow-green toward tips and bright red corolla. Fruit oblong, deep purple. Zones 11–12.

Fuchsia magellanica

LADIES' EARDROPS

☼/❂ ❈ ↔ 6 ft (1.8 m) ↕ 10 ft (3 m)

Originating in Chile and Argentina, naturalized elsewhere. Erect vigorous shrub; older branches have flaking bark. Leaves elliptical to egg-shaped and tinted red underneath. Flowers red tubes, dark red sepals, purple corolla, in summer–late autumn. Fruit oblong, crimson in color. Makes colorful hedge in mild winter areas. *F. m.* var. *gracilis* (syn. *F. m.* var. *macrostemma*), small leaves, abundant, very pendent, small flowers, deep scarlet calyx, purple petals; *F. m.* var. *molinae*, name used for pale pink-flowered variants in cultivation; *F. m.* var. *pumila*, to 12 in (30 cm) high, red and blue flowers. *F. m.* '**Riccartonii**', commonly used for hedging in Ireland and islands around Britain; '**Versicolor**', gray-green leaves, tinted silver, small deep red flowers. Zones 7–10.

Fuchsia arborescens

Fuchsia procumbens
TRAILING FUCHSIA

☼/◐ ❋ ↔ 3 ft (0.9 m) ↑ 6 in (15 cm)

Evergreen, prostrate, spreading shrub native to New Zealand. Leaves small, heart-shaped. Small upward-facing flowers, greenish to pale orange tubes, purple-tipped green sepals, no petals, in summer. Fruit bright red, persistent. Good rock-garden plant. Zones 9–11.

Fuchsia splendens
☼/◐ ❋ ↔ 3 ft (0.9 m) ↑ 8 ft (2.4 m)

Terrestrial or epiphytic shrub from Mexico to Costa Rica. Leaves heart-shaped, toothed edges, green above; paler, flushed red, and veined beneath. Flower tube rose pink, sepals green with red base, petals olive green. Fruit green to purple, warty. Zones 8–11.

Fuchsia thymifolia
☼/◐ ❋ ↔ 20 in (50 cm) ↑ 36 in (90 cm)

From Mexico to northern Guatemala. Leaves oval to egg-shaped, sometimes with toothed edge, finely hairy both above and underneath. Flowers solitary, tube green-white to pink, sepals and petals same color, ageing to dark purple, in summer–autumn. Zones 8–11.

Fuchsia triphylla
HONEYSUCKLE FUCHSIA

☼/◐ ✿ ↔ 2 ft (0.6 m) ↑ 6 ft (1.8 m)

Native to West Indies. Leaves opposite, in whorls of 3 or 4; oval or lance-shaped, sometimes finely toothed, dull dark green upper surface, paler undersurface often tinged silvery purple. Flowers orange to coral red; fruit shiny reddish purple. 'Billy Green', rose pink flowers, light green leaves. Zones 11–12.

Fuchsia Hybrid Cultivars
☼/◐ ❋ ↔ 18–36 in (45–90 cm) ↑ 1–7 ft (0.3–2 m)

Over 8,000 fuchsia cultivars have been recorded, with about 2,000 still in cultivation. Most are derived from *F. magellanica, F. fulgens,* and *F. triphylla.*

"Hardy" types withstand winter in Zone 7, and include 'Abbé Farges', semi-double flowers, cherry red tube and sepal, rose-lilac corolla; 'Constance', tube and sepals pale pink, green-tipped corolla; 'Hawkshead', tube and sepals white with green, corolla white; 'White Pixie', red tube and sepal, corolla white, veined deep pink.

Other hybrids include 'Brookwood Belle', prolific, double medium-sized flowers, deep cerise tube, sepals and corolla white, flushed pale pink; 'Coachman', coral pink sepals, reddish orange corolla; 'Display', large flowers, pink-red calyx, corolla deeper rose pink, long stamens; 'Golden Marinka', later flowering form, trailing habit, variegated red-veined leaves, medium-sized single blooms, rich red tube and sepals, darker red corolla; 'La Campanella', semi-double, white tube, white sepals tinted pink, corolla imperial purple; 'Marcus Graham', trailing habit, large double pink flowers; 'Prosperity', medium-sized double flowers, crimson tube, crimson sepals, pink corolla, veined rose red; 'Rading's Inge', tiny flowers, rose pink tube, cream sepals, orange corolla; and 'Ri Mia', pale lilac tube, sepals, corolla. Zones 9–11.

GARCINIA

This genus in the St John's-wort (Clusiaceae) family containing 200 tropical species is found mostly in Asia and Africa. They are densely foliaged evergreen trees and shrubs with highly scented flowers that open at night. The fleshy fruits of some are edible, notably those of *G. mangostana*. Male and female flowers are separate, usually on different plants, sometimes on the same plant. Damaged branches and twigs secrete a yellow sap reputed to have medicinal qualities. CULTIVATION: Plants require a rich soil and plenty of water and are very frost sensitive, being suitable only for tropical and warmest subtropical regions. Propagation is generally from fresh seed, although some species have been successful using cuttings and air-layering.

Garcinia mangostana
MANGOSTEEN

☼ ✿ ↔ 15 ft (4.5 m) ↑ 50 ft (15 m)

Native to Malaysia and Indonesia, slow-growing (15 years before fruit), evergreen tree cultivated for delicious fruit. Large glossy leaves, heavy crown. Male and female flowers on separate trees, females generally produce seedless fruit, to 4 in (10 cm) in diameter, thick skin, rich purple color when ripe. Zones 11–12.

GARDENIA

This genus from the madder (Rubiaceae) family consists of around 250 species from tropical Africa, Asia, and Australasia. Mostly evergreen shrubs or small trees, they have opposite or whorled, shiny, simple, deep green leaves. Fragrant large flowers, tubular

Fuchsia procumbens

Fuchsia, Hybrid Cultivar, 'Marcus Graham'

Garcinia mangostana

to funnel-shaped, white or yellow, are produced singly or in few-flowered cymes. The fruit is a leathery or fleshy berry.
CULTIVATION: Most are fairly adaptable plants tolerant of sun or part-shade, and do best in a well-drained, humus-rich, acidic soil. Gardenias are surface rooted, responding well to regular mulching with good-quality compost, fertilizer, and adequate summer watering. In cool climates grow in a heated greenhouse. Propagate from seed or leafy tip or half-hardened cuttings in late spring and summer.

Gardenia augusta
syn. *Gardenia jasminoides*
CAPE JASMINE, COMMON GARDENIA
☼/◐ ❀ ✦ ↔ 5 ft (1.5 m) ↕ 5–8 ft (1.5–2.4 m)
Native to southeastern China and Japan. Bushy habit; elliptic to obovate, glossy, dark green leaves. Flowers strongly fragrant, white, wheel-shaped, in summer. Double-flowered cultivars include 'August Beauty', lush green foliage, white flowers; 'Florida' ★, to 3 ft (0.9 m) tall, white flowers; 'Grandiflora', larger leaves and pure white flowers; 'Magnifica', semi-double creamy white flowers; 'Radicans', spreading low growth, smaller leaves, plentiful semi-double white flowers; and 'Veitchii', upright yet compact shrub with small, highly scented, double white flowers. Zones 10–11.

Gardenia thunbergia
STARRY GARDENIA
☼ ❀ ↔ 7 ft (2 m) ↕ 12 ft (3.5 m)
Occurs in humid forests of South Africa. Upright shrub or small tree. Smooth gray bark. Glossy dark green leaves with wavy margins. Fragrant, white or cream, solitary flowers, spoke-like petals at end of long tube, in summer. Zones 9–11.

GARRYA
This genus of about 18 evergreen trees or shrubs belongs to the silk-tassel (Garryaceae) family. They are grown for their tough leathery leaves and distinctive pendulous catkins of inconspicuous flowers without petals. Male and female flowers are borne on separate plants from winter to early summer, while the fruit of the female plant consists of clusters of round, dry, dark, 2-seeded berries, borne from summer to autumn. Native to western North America and the West Indies, they are valued for their durability in warmer climates.
CULTIVATION: Well suited to salty coastal environments and tolerant of pollution, *Garrya* species prefer a sunny sheltered position but can cope with a wide range of soil types. Most dislike humid summers. Avoid transplanting. They are propagated from cuttings of half-hardened wood, or by layering, and from seed.

Garrya elliptica ★
CATKIN BUSH, COAST SILKTASSEL, SILKTASSEL BUSH
☼ ❀ ↔ 6 ft (1.8 m) ↕ 8–12 ft (2.4–3.5 m)
Native to southwestern USA, from Oregon to California. Glossy, oval, gray-green to matt green leaves, undulating margins, dense woolly coating beneath. Long grayish green male catkins in winter–spring. Smaller female catkins, abundant clusters of oval-shaped

Gardenia augusta 'Magnifica'

Garrya elliptica

dark purple fruit. 'Evie', catkins to 12 in (30 cm) long; 'James Roof', male form, larger leaves and catkins than species. Zones 8–10.

Garrya fremontii
FEVER BUSH, FREMONT SILKTASSEL, QUININE BUSH, SKUNK BUSH
☼ ❀ ↔ 6 ft (1.8 m) ↕ 7–10 ft (2–3 m)
Native to western USA, from California to Oregon. Leathery, glossy, hairy, dark green leaves, smooth above, woolly underneath. Terminal clusters of male catkins, to 8 in (20 cm) long, in spring. Woolly female catkins, to 2 in (5 cm) long, in late summer–autumn. Dark purple oval-shaped fruit. Zones 7–10.

GAULTHERIA
SNOWBERRY, WINTERGREEN
This genus contains some 170 species of evergreen shrubs, ranging from the Americas to Japan and Australasia. Belonging to the heath (Ericaceae) family, these tough bushes have leathery foliage and prefer temperate to cool climates. They are often found in mountainous areas, where their bright, relatively large fruits stand out among the short alpine vegetation. Flowers tend to be bell-shaped and pendulous. Fruit may be small and fairly dry or a fleshy berry. Many species are quite aromatic, often highly so, especially the fruit.
CULTIVATION: Frost hardiness varies with the species, the toughest being among the large broadleafed evergreens. They prefer moist, well-drained, humus-rich, slightly acidic soil with ample summer moisture. The exposure preference also varies with the species, though few do well in full shade. Propagate from seed, or from half-hardened cuttings or layers, which will often form naturally where the stems remain in contact with the ground.

Gaultheria depressa
☼/◐ ❀ ↔ 10 in (25 cm) ↕ 4 in (10 cm)
Near-prostrate, wiry-stemmed shrub from rocky or boggy ground in mountains of New Zealand. Tiny, leathery, serrated leaves, reddish stems. Small white to pale pink flowers, carried singly, in summer. White to deep pink berries. Zones 8–9.

Gaultheria mucronata

syn. *Pernettya mucronata*

/ ❀ ↔ 48 in (120 cm) ↕ 18–60 in (45–150 cm)

Native to Argentina and Chile. Strongly branched suckering shrub, young stems often bright pinkish red, densely covered with small deep green leaves, sharp pointed tips. White or pale pink flowers in late spring. Fruit large, white, shades of pink and red. '**Alba**', white fruit; '**Bell's Seedling**', crimson fruit; '**Coccinea**', scarlet fruit; '**Crimsonia**', crimson fruit; '**Mulberry Wine**', maroon to purple fruit; Snow White/ '**Sneeuwwitje**', red-speckled white fruit; '**Wintertime**', long-lasting white fruit. Zones 6–10.

Gaultheria procumbens

CHECKERBERRY, TEABERRY, WINTERGREEN

/ ❀ ↔ 36 in (90 cm) ↕ 6 in (15 cm)

Attractive shrub from eastern North America. Deep green glossy leaves to 2 in (5 cm) long. Racemes of white to pale pink flowers in summer. Red fruit, to ½ in (12 mm) wide; source of pungent liniment used for muscle or joint problems. '**Macrocarpa**', compact form, abundant fruit. Zones 4–9.

Gaultheria × wisleyensis

Gaultheria shallon

SALAL, SHALLON

/ ❀ ↔ 5 ft (1.5 m) ↕ 5 ft (1.5 m)

Found in western North America, from California to Alaska. Spreading shrub takes root along prostrate branches. Broad oval leaves to 4 in (10 cm) long. Tiny white to deep pink flowers, in conspicuous red-stemmed racemes near stem tips, in late spring. Red fruit ripens to black. Zones 5–9.

Gaultheria × wisleyensis

syn. × *Gaulnettya wisleyensis*

/ ❀ ↔ 3 ft (0.9 m) ↕ 3 ft (0.9 m)

Hybrid between North American *G. shallon* and *G. mucronata* of South America. Low spreading shrub forms small thickets of suckering stems. Several cultivars with leaves of varying sizes, up to 1½ in (35 mm) long. Flowers white or various shades of pink to light purple. Purplish red fruit. Zones 6–9.

GEIJERA

A member of the rue (Rutaceae) family, this genus contains 8 species from New Guinea, eastern Australia, and New Caledonia. Of the 5 endemic Australian species, 2 occur in rainforests and the other 3 in various habitats, even relatively arid regions. All are small to medium trees reaching 80 ft (24 m) tall when growing in rainforests. The flowers are small, no more than ¼ in (6 mm) across, and they are borne in terminal panicles. They are followed by small brown fruits of 2 to 4 compartments, each containing a glossy black seed. CULTIVATION: The different species come from natural habitats ranging from semi-arid inland plains to drier types of coastal rainforest, but the inland species adapt well to moister climates. All prefer reasonably fertile soil. Propagation is from fresh seed, which may germinate quite erratically.

Geijera parviflora ★

WILGA

❀ ↔ 35 ft (10 m) ↕ 40 ft (12 m)

Small tree occurring in drier inland regions of all Australian States except Tasmania and Western Australia. Pendulous narrow leaves. Creamy white flowers in spring. Propagation not easy, as seed often difficult to obtain. Zones 8–11.

GENISTA

syns *Chamaespartium, Echinospartium*

About 90 species belong to this genus within the pea-flower subfamily of the legume (Fabaceae) family. Most are deciduous but some appear evergreen because of their flat green branchlets. Native to Europe and the Mediterranean to western Asia, these shrubs or small trees mostly grow on rocky hillsides. Leaves are alternate, simple, or consist of 3 leaflets; branches can be nearly leafless. CULTIVATION: Full sun is necessary and not all plants are fully frost hardy. Grow half-hardy plants in a well-ventilated greenhouse. They tolerate all soils but need a light well-drained soil to flower well. Propagate from ripe seed in autumn or spring, and protect from winter frosts, or half-hardened cuttings in summer.

Genista aetnensis

MOUNT ETNA BROOM

❀ ↔ 25 ft (8 m) ↕ 25 ft (8 m)

Shrub native to Sardinia and Sicily. Weeping branches; narrow leaves only on young shoots, fall off as branches age. Fragrant, yellow, pea-like flowers on pendent shoots in summer–autumn. Zones 8–10.

Genista lydia

DWARF GENISTA, GENISTA

❀ ↔ 36 in (90 cm) ↕ 24 in (60 cm)

Native to eastern Balkans. Deciduous prostrate shrub, smaller in wild. Blue-green leaves, long and narrow or elliptic in shape.

Genista sagittalis

Short racemes of golden yellow flowers appear in late spring–early summer. Flat non-hairy fruit. Zones 7–9.

Genista sagittalis
WINGED BROOM
☼ ❋ ↔ 36 in (90 cm) ↑ 6 in (15 cm)

Prostrate shrub native to southern and central Europe. Winged branchlets. Leaves lance-shaped, hairy below. Golden flowers in terminal racemes in late spring–early summer. Silky fruit. Zones 4–9.

Genista × *spachiana*
syns *Cytisus fragrans*, *C.* × *spachiana*, *Genista fragrans*
☼ ⚘ ↔ 17 ft (5 m) ↑ 10–20 ft (3–6 m)

Vigorous, evergreen, arching shrub, cross of *G. stenopetala* and *G. canariensis*. Dark green leaves with 3 oval leaflets, ¼–¾ in (6–18 mm) long, silky underneath. Long slender clusters of fragrant golden yellow flowers, ½ in (12 mm) across, in winter–early spring. Zones 9–11.

Genista tinctoria
COMMON WOADWAXEN, DYER'S GREENWEED
☼ ❋ ↔ 3 ft (0.9 m) ↑ 3 ft (0.9 m)

Deciduous spineless shrub native to Europe and western Asia. Bright green leaves, elliptic or lance-shaped. Golden flowers on upright racemes in summer. 'Flore Pleno', dwarf, double flowers; 'Golden Plate', clear yellow flowers, spreading compact shape, weeping branches; 'Royal Gold', more erect, flowers carried in panicles. Zones 2–9.

GINKGO

A primitive genus containing a single species and given its own family, Ginkgoaceae, *Ginkgo* is different from all other conifers. Fossil records show it to be ancient. Now unknown in the wild, it was certainly grown in China in the eleventh century; some specimens are believed to be well over 1,000 years old. The foliage resembles that of the maidenhair fern. Pollination is achieved by motile spores, a feature unknown among the higher plants, but normal among ferns. Male and female organs are carried on separate trees. The fruit is edible and nutritious. CULTIVATION: This tree prefers hot summers but tolerates a range of conditions, including air pollution. Plant in well-drained soil in full sun. Propagate from seed or half-hardened summer cuttings.

Ginkgo biloba
GINKGO, MAIDENHAIR TREE
☼ ❋ ↔ 25 ft (8 m) ↑ 100 ft (30 m)

Deciduous, very long lived, crown only developing fully after first 100 years. Fronds fan-shaped, parallel veins spreading out from stalk. Male flowers pendulous short-stalked catkins. Fruit yellow-green, unpleasant odor when decaying. Foliage turns golden yellow in autumn. 'Aurea', yellow leaves in summer; 'Autumn Gold' ★, broadly conical, leaves turn gold in autumn; 'Fastigiata', grows to 30 ft (9 m) in height; Pendula Group members have nodding branches; 'Princeton Sentry', narrow growth habit, yellow autumn coloring; 'Saratoga', dense rounded form, with deeply cut leaves;

Ginkgo biloba

Gleditsia triacanthos f. *inermis* 'Halka'

'Tremonia', strongly erect form, very narrow crown; Variegata Group members have bold streaks of whitish yellow on leaves. Zones 3–10.

GLEDITSIA
LOCUST

There are 14 species of deciduous trees in this genus from the cassia subfamily of the legume (Fabaceae) family, native to North and South America, central and eastern Asia, Iran, and parts of Africa. All have fern-like, pinnately or bipinnately arranged leaves, and stout, sometimes branching, thorns on the trunk and branches. Flowers are insignificant and followed by seed pods that sometimes contain a sweet pulp. CULTIVATION: Plants grow best in sun, in moderately fertile soil that is moisture retentive, and may require frost protection when young. However, they are generally very tough, tolerating a range of soils and climates and are pollution resistant. Species are propagated from seed sown in autumn, while cultivars are grafted or budded.

Gleditsia triacanthos
HONEY LOCUST, THORNLESS HONEY LOCUST
☼ ❋ ↔ 70 ft (21 m) ↑ 150 ft (45 m)

Native to central and eastern USA. Fern-like foliage bright green, turning bright yellow in autumn. Thorns up to 12 in (30 cm). *G. t.* f. *inermis* is thornless—nearly all cultivars of honey locust derived from it. 'Elegantissima', very compact, almost shrub-like, fine foliage, very slow growing, rarely exceeds 15 ft (4.5 m) tall; 'Emerald Cascade', weeping tree, dark emerald green foliage turns bright yellow in autumn; 'Halka', fast-growing selection, narrow crown; fine foliage color in autumn; 'Marando', dwarf with spreading twisted branches; 'Moraine' ★, tall, shapely, thornless tree, broadly spreading lower branches, dense ferny foliage; 'Rubylace', dark red young foliage, bronzing as it ages; 'Shademaster', broad-crowned upright tree, deep green leaves persisting late in autumn; 'Skyline', symmetrical outline, broadly conical crown, dark green leaves, golden yellow in autumn; 'Sunburst', bright yellow young leaves become lime green as season progresses. Zones 3–10.

GLYPTOSTROBUS

There is just a single species in this genus, allied to *Taxodium*, within the cypress (Cupressaceae) family. This tree is grown in China and northern Vietnam at the edges of riverbanks and rice paddies to stabilize the banks.
CULTIVATION: Ideal for planting in wet sites, beside water features, and riverbank planting, *Glyptostrobus* needs moist marshy soil and will even grow in shallow water. When green wood is damaged by frost, multiple stems can be produced. In moist warm climates with long, hot, humid summers it can be grown from seed. In acid soil, cuttings can be taken or it should be grafted onto *Taxodium*. The graft should be below water or soil level to encourage root growth.

Glyptostrobus pensilis
CHINESE SWAMP CYPRESS
☀ ❄ ↔ 20 ft (6 m) ↕ 80 ft (24 m)
Deciduous tree originally native to southeastern China and northern Vietnam, probably extinct in wild. Conical or columnar in shape, with irregular open canopy. Gray bark. Fine, pale green, new spring leaves, turn red-brown in autumn. Male cones form clusters of tassels; female cones erect, pear-shaped. Zones 8–11.

GORDONIA

Found in East Asia and the warmer temperate parts of North America, this genus of some 70 species of evergreen trees and shrubs is from the camellia (Theaceae) family. They are impressive plants with lush deep green foliage and beautiful flowers. Some species provide the added bonus of flowering in winter, though frost may destroy the flowers. Their flowers are usually white or cream with golden stamens, resembling the blooms of a single-flowered camellia.
CULTIVATION: The large deep green leaves suggest a preference for shade, but, as with camellias and rhododendrons, they need some sun to flower well. Shade from the midday summer sun is best. The soil should be humus-rich, friable, slightly acidic, and well drained—in other words, a woodland soil. Gordonias are not drought tolerant and need ample summer moisture. Prune lightly or tip-pinch after flowering. Propagate from seed or half-hardened cuttings.

Gordonia axillaris ★
☀ ❄ ↔ 12 ft (3.5 m) ↕ 12–20 ft (3.5–6 m)
Large shrub or small tree. Leaves leathery, dark green, to 6 in (15 cm) long, smooth-edged, slightly lobed or shallowly toothed. Creamy white flowers, conspicuous stamens, 5 or 6 petals, 4 in (10 cm) wide, from mid-winter to spring. Feed regularly. Zones 8–10.

Gordonia lasianthus
LOBLOLLY BAY
☀ ❄ ↔ 30 ft (9 m) ↕ 50 ft (15 m)
Native to southeastern USA. More commonly grows to around 25 ft (8 m) tall in cultivation. Narrow upright habit and shallowly serrated, deep green, glossy leaves. Although technically evergreen,

Gordonia axillaris

Glyptostrobus pensilis

older leaves develop red tones before finally falling. Flowers white, to 3 in (8 cm) wide, in summer. Zones 9–11.

GRAPTOPHYLLUM

Occurring in Australia, New Guinea, and the southwestern Pacific, this is a genus of 10 species of tall shrubs or small trees in the acanthus (Acanthaceae) family, several of which are popular as house plants. It has a tropical and subtropical distribution in a range of habitats from rainforest margins to rocky hillsides. All have curved tubular flowers in shades of red, as well as opposite glossy leaves; some species have unfriendly spines on the stems or leaves.
CULTIVATION: These plants will grow in sun or part-shade on a range of well-drained soils, but flower better in full sun. They are mostly frost tender and need a warm climate if grown outdoors. Propagate from fresh seed, if obtainable, or from cuttings of 2- to 3-year-old shoots.

Graptophyllum pictum
CARICATURE PLANT
☀ ➤ ↔ 30 in (75 cm) ↕ 6 ft (1.8 m)
From New Guinea. Leaves elliptical, glossy, deep green. Flowers red to purple, in terminal spikes, in summer. Various color forms include leaves all purple-bronze, others green marked with white, yellow, pink, or purple, in blotches or stripes of many shapes and sizes. Propagate cultivars from cuttings to ensure color. Zones 10–12.

GREVILLEA

This genus in the protea (Proteaceae) family is represented by around 340 species. Most are native to Australia, with some from New Guinea, New Caledonia, Vanuatu, and Sulawesi. Naturally occurring Australian forms have been selected and hybrid cultivars developed with huge horticultural potential. They range from prostrate ground covers to tall trees. Distinctive colorful flower clusters come in 3 basic forms—spider-like, toothbrush-like, and large brushes. Many are rich in nectar, which makes them attractive to insects, birds, and animals (especially Australian marsupials), all of which are pollinators. They are found in a wide climatic range and are tolerant of extremes. Some are short lived but spectacular, others have unique flower clusters, and some have flowers with a strong sweet fragrance.

CULTIVATION: Most grevilleas prefer an open sunny position and free-draining loams, and many perform best in phosphorus-deficient soils. Propagate from half-hardened cuttings; seed also germinates well but is often difficult to obtain. Some of the species that are difficult to grow have responded well to grafting onto stocks of vigorous species such as *G. robusta*; this technique has also been used to produce weeping standard specimens.

Grevillea aquifolium
HOLLY GREVILLEA

☼ ❈ ↔ 6 ft (1.8 m) ↑ 6 ft (1.8 m)

From southeastern Australia. Variable habit, prostrate and suckering, or rounded dense shrub. Holly-like leaves, thick sharp-pointed lobes, hairy underside. Toothbrush flowers, red, pink, or dull orange, in winter–summer. Zones 8–10.

Graptophyllum pictum

Grevillea banksii
BANKS'S GREVILLEA, RED SILKY OAK

☼ ❈ ↔ 7 ft (2 m) ↑ 10–30 ft (3–9 m)

Variable dense shrub or slender tree native to coastal Queensland, Australia. Long leaves, very deeply divided, smooth, silky both sides, prominent midvein. Large nectar-rich brush flowers, red or white, with pink and apricot forms, long flowering period, spring peak. Annual light pruning, avoid old wood. **G. b. var. forsteri**, silvery leafed shrub to 10 ft (3 m), red or cream flowers over long period. Zones 9–11.

Grevillea curviloba
syn. *Grevillea biternata* of gardens

☼ ❈ ↔ 4 ft (1.2 m) ↑ 6 ft (1.8 m)

Spreading informal shrub native to southwest Western Australia. Leaves rich bright green, deeply lobed. Fragrant white flower clusters in spring. Long-lived dense ground cover. **G. c. subsp. incurva**, form most widely grown, much narrower, slightly curved leaf lobes. Prostrate to more erect, often grown under wrong name, *G. biternata*. Zones 8–10.

Grevillea × gaudichaudii

☼ ❈ ↔ 10 ft (3 m) ↑ 4 in (10 cm)

Vigorous naturally occurring hybrid between *G. acanthifolia* and *G. laurifolia*. Handsome divided leaves, reddish at tips. Clusters of burgundy toothbrush flowers in spring–summer. Zones 8–10.

Grevillea juniperina
JUNIPER-LEAF GREVILLEA, PRICKLY SPIDER FLOWER

☼ ❈ ↔ 7 ft (2 m) ↑ 8 ft (2.4 m)

Dense spreading shrub found in eastern New South Wales, Australia. Leaves dark green, needle-like. Spider flower clusters, commonly red, but can be yellow, apricot, or orange, in spring–summer. Long-lived hardy plants, excellent shelter for small birds. '**Lunar Light**' (syn. *G.* 'Australflora Lunar Light'), yellow leaf-margin variegation; '**Molonglo**', spreading habit, pale apricot flowers. Zones 8–10.

Grevillea lanigera ★
WOOLLY GREVILLEA

☼ ❈ ↔ 4 ft (1.2 m) ↑ 5 ft (1.5 m)

Native to southeastern Australia. Variable shrub, sometimes prostrate and suckering. Narrow, occasionally fleshy leaves, soft silvery felting. Flowers all year, with flush of spider clusters of pink, red, orange, or yellow in winter–spring. Zones 7–10.

Grevillea lavandulacea
LAVENDER GREVILLEA

☼ ❈ ↔ 3 ft (0.9 m) ↑ 3 ft (0.9 m)

Compact shrub from southern Australia, parent of several hybrid cultivars. Gray-green needle-like leaves, plentiful spider flower clusters of pink-red. Variations in leaf texture, habit, and flower color common. Do not crowd, avoid summer watering. Zones 8–10.

Grevillea robusta
SILK OAK, SILKY OAK

☼ ❈ ↔ 30 ft (9 m) ↑ 60 ft (18 m)

Largest of all grevilleas, semi-deciduous. Valued timber and shade tree from southeastern Queensland, Australia. Large, golden, nectar-laden flower brushes in spring–summer; fern-like foliage. Rapid growing; prefers rich, well-drained, heavy loam. Zones 8–12.

Grevillea banksii

Grevillea lavandulacea

Grevillea robusta

Grevillea rosmarinifolia

Grevillea, Hybrid Cultivar, Banksii Group, 'Misty Pink'

Grevillea, Hybrid Cultivar, Rosmarinifolia Group, 'Canberra Gem'

Grevillea rosmarinifolia
ROSEMARY GREVILLEA

☼ ❄ ↔ 6 ft (1.8 m) ↑ 6 ft (1.8 m)

Variable, dense or open shrub from southeastern Australia. Dark green needle-like leaves. Abundant spider flower clusters, cream to pale or deep pink, in winter–summer. Zones 8–10.

Grevillea thelemanniana
HUMMINGBIRD BUSH, SPIDER-NET GREVILLEA

☼ ❄ ↔ 6 ft (1.8 m) ↑ 3 ft (0.9 m)

Dense shrub from southwestern Western Australia. Leaves linear or divided, dark green. Red spider flower clusters in winter–spring. Prefers moist but well-drained sandy loam. Zones 9–11.

Grevillea victoriae
ROYAL GREVILLEA

☼ ❄ ↔ 6 ft (1.8 m) ↑ 6 ft (1.8 m)

Hardy adaptable shrub from southern Australia. Leaves simple, oval or narrowly so, leathery texture, shiny above, silky below. Pendent spider-like flower clusters of red, orange, yellow, or pink in spring–summer. Reliable feature or screen plant. Zones 8–10.

Grevillea Hybrid Cultivars

☼/❂ ❄ ↔ 4–15 ft (1.2–4.5 m) ↑ 6 in–20 ft (15 cm–6 m)

Most hybrids fall into one of 3 groups, each derived from a limited range of parent species but with none shared between the groups. A few hybrids can be placed in a "miscellaneous" group.

BANKSII GROUP

Main parent is *G. banksii* from east coast of Australia, but cultivars can be subdivided into 2 groups: those whose other parent is *G. bipinnatifida*, and those bred from taller-growing tropical and subtropical species such as *G. pteridifolia* and *G. sessilis*. All have leaves dissected into narrow segments and dense bottlebrush-like spikes of flowers, crowded toward upper side of spike. 'Coconut Ice', shrub to 7 ft (2 m) tall, bright green foliage, red-pink flowers; 'Honey Gem', shrub to 15 ft (4.5 m) tall, dark green fern-like leaves, prolific orange or yellow flower clusters; 'Mason's Hybrid' (syn. 'Ned Kelly'), fast-growing hardy shrub to 6 ft (1.8 m), ferny light green foliage, orange-red flower clusters all year; 'Misty Pink', silvery shrub to 10 ft (3 m) tall, long pink flower clusters with cream tips; 'Moonlight', upright shrub to 10 ft (3 m) tall, ferny olive green foliage, long creamy flower clusters; 'Parfait Crème',

dense shrub to 10 ft (3 m) high and wide, creamy yellow to caramel flowers; 'Robyn Gordon'—most widely planted grevillea—shrub to 6 ft (1.8 m) tall, ferny foliage, clusters of bright pinkish red flowers; 'Sandra Gordon', shrub to 15 ft (4.5 m) tall, bright yellow flowers; 'Superb', apricot-pink tint to flowers; 'Sylvia', shrub to 10 ft (3 m) tall, rosy pink flower clusters with cream tips; 'Winter Sparkles', winter-flowering shrub to 20 ft (6 m) tall. Zones 9–12.

ROSMARINIFOLIA GROUP

Most of earliest hybrids belonged to this group, derived from *G. rosmarinifolia*, *G. juniperina*, and allies with small smooth-edged leaves and flowers in characteristic spider flower clusters. Includes most Clearview and Poorinda hybrids. Some cultivars in this group hybridize freely and may become invasive. 'Canberra Gem', 6 ft (1.8 m) tall shrub, dark green needle leaves, cerise flowers; 'Clearview David', dense shrub to 8 ft (2.4 m) tall, prickly leaves, bright red spider flowers; 'Clearview Robyn', shrub to 6 ft (1.8 m) tall, blue-green needle leaves, vibrant cerise spider flowers; 'Crosbie Morrison', dense shrub to 5 ft (1.5 m) tall, gray-green leaves, pink-red spider flowers; 'Evelyn's Coronet', erect shrub to 6 ft (1.8 m) tall, silvery, woolly, pink spider flowers; 'Noellii', may be compact form of *G. rosmarinifolia*, neat bushy growth habit; 'Penola', gray leaves, abundance of red and cream blooms; 'Poorinda Beauty', 3 ft (0.9 m) tall shrub, needle leaves, dense clusters of orange-red flowers; 'Poorinda Constance', dense shrub 8 ft (2.4 m) high, soft foliage, red flowers; 'Poorinda Firebird', shrub to 6 ft (1.8 m) high, abundant scarlet spider flower clusters; 'Poorinda Leane', dense soft-foliaged shrub to 8 ft (2.4 m) tall, orange flowers; 'Poorinda Rachel', shrub to 3 ft (0.9 m) tall, oval leaves, orange-red flowers; 'Poorinda Stephen', shrub to 3 ft (0.9 m) tall, silvery oval leaves, large dark red spider flower clusters; and 'Poorinda Vivacity', shrub to 3 ft (0.9 m) tall, broad oval leaves, tight orange-red spider flower clusters. Other cultivars include 'Poorinda Queen', 'Poorinda Rondeau', 'Poorinda Tranquillity', and 'Scarlet Sprite'. Zones 8–12.

TOOTHBRUSH GROUP

These hybrid cultivars derived from large group of species, mainly from southeastern Australian, with "toothbrush" type of flower spike: flowers densely crowded and all turned upward to form elongated brush; often bent sharply backward as well. Leaves range from simple and smooth-edged to toothed, lobed, or dissected into narrow segments. Plants range from prostrate to tall and erect. 'Boongala Spinebill' ★, adaptable spreading shrub to 8 ft (2.4 m) tall, cascading branches, new ferny foliage coppery red, deep crimson toothbrush flower clusters; '**Bronze Rambler**', vigorous, spread of 15 ft (4.5 m), dissected leaves, bronze tint on new growth, purplish flowers; '**Brookvale Letitia**', tall shrub to 15 ft (4.5 m) high, orange and red hairy flowers; '**Fanfare**' (syn. 'Australflora Fanfare'), prostrate, spreading to 17 ft (5 m), spring to summer inflorescences dark red, pink styles; '**Ivanhoe**' ★, dense foliage, vigorous growth to 10 ft (3 m) tall and 15 ft (4.5 m) wide, red flowers. Zones 9–12.

MISCELLANEOUS GROUP

This group includes '**Granya Glory**', to 2 ft (0.6 m) high, creamy and rosy flowers; '**Long John**', shrub to 10 ft (3 m) tall, red and pink flowers; '**Merinda Gordon**', to 10 ft (3 m) tall, deep pink to red flowers; '**Orange Marmalade**', to 8 ft (2.4 m) tall, leaves smooth-edged and silky hairy on undersurface, flowers orange; '**Pendant Clusters**' (syn. 'Australflora Pendant Clusters'), creamy yellow flowers, deep red styles; '**Poorinda Ensign**', less than 3 ft (0.9 m) tall, leaves smooth edged, densely clustered bright pink flowers; '**Sid Reynolds**', shrub to 8 ft (2.4 m) tall, pale reddish pink flowers; and '**Winpara Gem**', shrub to 7 ft (2 m) tall, reddish flowers. Zones 9–12.

GREWIA

This genus from the mallow (Malvaceae) family includes about 150 species of shrubs, trees, and climbers found in Africa, Asia, and Australia. Although often attractive plants, very few are cultivated and only one species, *G. occidentalis*, is at all common. Most species have oval leaves with finely toothed edges. The flowers are starry, with 5 narrow petals and a conspicuous group of stamens at the center; they are followed by small drupes.

CULTIVATION: Best suited to warm-temperate and subtropical climates, few species will tolerate any but the lightest frosts. They prefer a sunny position with moist well-drained soil and should be pinched back to keep the growth compact. If necessary, old overgrown plants can often be rejuvenated by heavy pruning. Propagate from seed or half-hardened cuttings.

Grewia occidentalis

FOUR CORNERS

☼ ❄ ↔ 10 ft (3 m) ↑ 10 ft (3 m)

Southern African shrub. Bright green foliage. Flowers around 1½ in (35 mm) wide, mauve to pale purple, sepals same length as petals, creating double-flowered effect, in spring–summer. Purple-red 4-lobed fruit. Zones 9–11.

GREYIA

This South African genus of 3 species of deciduous shrubs gives its name to the family Greyiaceae. The leaves resemble those of a regal pelargonium, being rounded, lobed, and around 3 in (8 cm) wide. They occur mainly at the tips of heavily wooded branches and redden before dropping in autumn. Flowers are bright red and comprise 5 petals fused to a fleshy central disc, with 10 long stamens. They are clustered in racemes up to 6 in (15 cm) wide.

CULTIVATION: Best grown in a hot sunny position, *Greyia* species prefer mild climates but will tolerate light frosts. Soil should be fairly fertile and well drained. Water well in summer but allow plants to dry off as they approach winter dormancy. Propagate from seed or half-hardened cuttings in late spring or summer.

Greyia sutherlandii

NATAL BOTTLEBRUSH

☼ ❄ ↔ 7 ft (2 m) ↑ 15 ft (4.5 m)

Large shrub; branches very heavy at base. Bright red flowerheads at tips of bare branches in late winter–early spring. Deeply lobed leaves follow in summer, coloring in autumn. Zones 9–11.

GRISELINIA

This is a genus of 7 evergreen trees and shrubs from the dogwood (Cornaceae) family, 5 of which are native to Chile and southeastern Brazil and 2 to New Zealand. Generally plants of coastal areas, they have large, glossy, leathery leaves. The tiny yellow-green flowers are unisexual, with male and female flowers borne on separate trees.

Griselinia littoralis

CULTIVATION: *Griselinia* species are grown for their shiny foliage and are useful for providing screens, shelter, and hedging. They are invaluable in coastal areas, being very tolerant of salt winds, and will grow in most well-drained soils in sun or part-shade. In very cold areas they are best given a warm sheltered site or grown in a conservatory. Pruning should be carried out in summer. Propagation is easiest from half-hardened cuttings in autumn, as seed can be difficult to germinate.

Griselinia littoralis

BROADLEAF, KAPUKA, PAPAUMA

☼ ✲ ↔ 15 ft (4.5 m) ↑ 25 ft (8 m)

Found in New Zealand. Leathery oval leaves, very glossy, bright green. Panicles of tiny flowers in spring. Small purplish fruits on female trees. Attractive cultivars with foliage variegated creamy yellow include '**Dixon's Cream**' and '**Variegata**'. Zones 8–11.

Greyia sutherlandii

GYMNOCLADUS

A member of the cassia subfamily of the legume (Fabaceae) family, this genus of 2 to 5 deciduous trees allied to *Gleditsia* occurs across warm-temperate regions of North America and eastern Asia. They have bipinnate leaves and separate male and female plants with flowers in short terminal panicles. The fruit is a large woody pod containing flat, hard, glossy seeds. The fruit of *G. dioica* was used by early American settlers as a substitute for coffee.
CULTIVATION: Adaptable to most soil types in an open sunny position, these trees are drought and frost tolerant. Propagation is from seed.

Hakea laurina

Gymnocladus dioica ★
CHICOT, KENTUCKY COFFEE TREE
☼ ❄ ↔ 12 ft (3.5 m) ↑ 75 ft (23 m)
Native to central and eastern North America. Coarsely textured bark, thick branchlets, young twigs light gray, almost white. Large bipinnate leaves, 8 to 14 oval leaflets, pink, turning yellow in autumn. Dull greenish white flowers, in racemes, in summer. Thick, succulent, reddish brown or maroon fruit. *G. d.* var. *folio-variegata*, variegated foliage. *G. d.* 'Variegata', variegated cream foliage. Zones 4–8.

HAKEA

There are about 140 species in this genus of evergreen Australian plants of the protea (Proteaceae) family, mostly shrubs or small trees. Many are grown for their ornamental foliage, particularly the silky new growth. Leaves vary in shape. The nectar-rich bird-attracting flowers are borne in short axillary clusters, tight pincushion-like heads, or showy spike-like racemes. Large and decorative woody fruit usually persist on the plant until dried or burnt and then split open into 2 valves to release 2 winged seeds.
CULTIVATION: Most species are frost tender, especially when young. Hakeas prefer full sun and good drainage and dislike high-phosphorus fertilizers. Many are from Western Australia and can usually tolerate periods of dryness during the summer months. Light or moderate pruning will stimulate a compact shape, healthy regrowth, and plant vigor. Some prickly species will trim into a fine impenetrable hedge. Propagation is usually from seed.

Gymnocladus dioica

Hakea bucculenta
RED POKERS
☼ ❄ ↔ 7 ft (2 m) ↑ 8 ft (2.4 m)
From Western Australia. Shrub with erect open habit. Flat, leathery, narrow-linear leaves to 8 in (20 cm) long. Red flowers, in spike-like racemes to 6 in (15 cm) long, in late winter–spring. Ornamental, bird-attracting species. Does best away from summer humidity. Zones 9–10.

Hakea cristata
☼ ❄ ↔ 8 ft (2.4 m) ↑ 12 ft (3.5 m)
Medium upright shrub from Western Australia. Gray-green leaves, prickly toothed edges. White flowers in small clusters, in upper leaf axils, in winter. Dislikes excessive humidity. Zones 9–11.

Hakea laurina
PINCUSHION HAKEA, PINCUSHION TREE, SEA URCHIN
☼ ❄ ↔ 8 ft (2.4 m) ↑ 25 ft (8 m)
Ornamental shrub or small tree from southern sandplains of Western Australia. Long, narrow, leathery, prominently veined leaves. Nectar-rich creamy white and bright crimson flowers, in ball-like clusters, in autumn–winter. Dislikes strong winds, excessive humidity. Zones 9–11.

Hakea microcarpa
SMALL-FRUITED HAKEA
☼ ❄ ↔ 6 ft (1.8 m) ↑ 6 ft (1.8 m)
Shrub found at higher altitudes of southeastern Australia. Leathery needle-like leaves. Creamy white flowers, in small clusters, in late winter–spring. Small leathery fruit. Zones 8–10.

Hakea myrtoides
MYRTLE HAKEA
☼ ❄ ↔ 15 in (38 cm) ↑ 18 in (45 cm)
Low spreading shrub from Western Australia. Leaves crowded, small, broad, with long points. Small clusters of deep pink flowers toward branch ends in winter–early spring. Zones 9–11.

Hakea purpurea
☼ ❄ ↔ 6–10 ft (1.8–3 m) ↑ 6–10 ft (1.8–3 m)
East Australian shrub. Dark green cylindrical leaves, prickly segments. Red flowers in clusters along stems in winter–spring. Zones 9–11.

Hakea salicifolia

syn. *Hakea saligna*

WILLOW HAKEA

☀ ❄ ↔ 12 ft (3.5 m) ↑ 20 ft (6 m)

Eastern Australian shrub or small tree. Flat deep green leaves, may be bronze-colored when young. Masses of creamy white scented flowers in axillary clusters in spring. Small woody fruit. Zones 8–9.

HALESIA

SILVERBELL

This is a genus of 4 or 5 species of deciduous shrubs or small trees in the storax (Styracaceae) family, indigenous to China and eastern North America. Predominantly found in moist deciduous woodlands, these plants have graceful and attractive spring flowers. Individually the flowers are simple, small, white bells, but massed together, moving on the breeze, they have an instant appeal. The leaf is usually a simple mid-green ellipse, to 5 in (12 cm) long. Winged fruit appear in autumn.

CULTIVATION: At home in a moist humid environment sheltered from strong winds, they are cool-climate plants but need a hot summer for the best display of flowers. Soil should be well drained and slightly acidic. Confine pruning to trimming the plant to shape. Propagate from seed or summer cuttings.

Halesia carolina

syn. *Halesia tetraptera*

CAROLINA SILVERBELL, SILVERBELL, SNOWDROP TREE

☀ ❄ ↔ 25–30 ft (8–10 m) ↑ 25 ft (8 m)

From southeastern USA. Spreading crown. Most commonly cultivated species. Heavy flowering, in spring, with tree smothered in pendulous clusters of white or pink-flushed bells which, by autumn, develop into 4-winged fruit. Foliage develops yellow tones in autumn. Zones 3–9.

Halesia monticola

MOUNTAIN SILVERBELL, MOUNTAIN SNOWDROP TREE

☀ ❄ ↔ 20 ft (6 m) ↑ 30 ft (9 m)

From southern Appalachian mountains of eastern USA. Larger in wild. Wide-spreading crown. White flowers in clusters of 2 to 5 blooms, followed by 4-winged fruit. *H. m.* f. *rosea*, pale pink flowers. Some botanists now treat this species as subspecies of *H. carolina*. Zones 4–9.

× HALIMIOCISTUS

This grouping of intergeneric hybrids between *Halimium* and *Cistus* includes some that occur naturally in their Mediterranean homelands and others of garden origin. These members of the rock-rose (Cistaceae) family are small evergreen shrubs intermediate in form between the parent genera, with small downy leaves, often gray-green to slightly glaucous, and flowers similar to *Cistus* but smaller and with the addition of yellow to their palette. Most flower in summer.

CULTIVATION: Tolerating hardy to moderate frosts and easily grown in any sunny position with light well-drained soil, these are vigorous shrubs well suited to large rock gardens or general planting with other sun-lovers. They can be trimmed after flowering, though tidying is often best left until spring, when winter damage can be removed. Propagate from half-hardened tip cuttings in late summer or autumn.

× *Halimiocistus wintonensis*

☀ ❄ ↔ 30 in (75 cm) ↑ 24 in (60 cm)

Originating in Hillier's Nursery, chance hybrid between *Halimium ocymoides* and *Cistus salviifolius*. Grayish leaves. Large, 2 in (5 cm) wide flowers, pearly white, feathered zone of crimson-maroon, contrasting with yellow stains at petal base. 'Merrist Wood Cream', flowers pale milky yellow, maroon basal spot. Zones 8–9.

HALIMIUM

There are about 12 species of evergreen shrubs and subshrubs in this genus of the rock-rose (Cistaceae) family. They are native to the Mediterranean region and western Asia in dry open forest thickets and sandy and rocky scrubland. These gray-leafed plants resemble *Cistus* (rock rose), for which they are often mistaken.

CULTIVATION: Mild winters and warm summers are the ideal conditions for cultivation. *Halimium* species grow in full sun in sandy, moderately fertile soil with protection from cold and drying winds. For best results, grow in pots or a rock-garden border. In areas with wet winters, extra sharp drainage needs to be provided or the plants need to be protected from over-saturation. Grow from seed in spring in a heated tray or take half-hardened cuttings in late summer.

Halimium halimifolium

☀ ❄ ↔ 3 ft (0.9 m) ↑ 3 ft (0.9 m)

From southwestern Europe and North Africa. Leaves oblong to lance-shaped, gray-green, silver scales. Cymes of yellow flowers, red-brown blotch at petal base, in late spring–early summer. Zones 8–9.

Halesia carolina

× Halimiocistus wintonensis 'Merrist Wood Cream'

Halimium lasianthum ★

syn. *Halimium formosum*

☼ ❅ ↔ 4 ft (1.2 m) ↕ 3 ft (0.9 m)

Bushy erect shrub from Spain and Portugal. Gray foliage. Clusters of yellow flowers, dark red basal spot, from leaf axils, in spring–early summer. *H. l.* subsp. *alyssoides*, egg- to lance-shaped leaves, dark green above, white hairy underside. *H. l.* subsp. *formosum*, slightly larger flowers with rust red basal spot. *H. l.* 'Concolor', no basal spot; 'Sandling', bright maroon basal spot. Zones 8–9.

Halimium Hybrid Cultivars

☼ ❅ ↔ 3 ft (0.9 m) ↕ 3 ft (0.9 m)

Shrubs with spreading habit. 'Sarah', bright yellow blooms with brown center; 'Susan', compact habit, broader leaves, semi-double yellow flowers in summer. Zones 8–9.

HALLERIA

Belonging to the foxglove (Scrophulariaceae) family, this genus contains 4 species from southern Africa and Madagascar. All are evergreen trees or shrubs with curved, tubular, nectar-rich flowers that attract many birds, particularly sunbirds. Fruits are fleshy and black when ripe; long style persists at maturity.
CULTIVATION: These plants are frost hardy and drought resistant and prefer a fertile light soil and full sun in a warm climate. Propagate from seed or cuttings. Fruit contain a germination inhibitor so the flesh must be removed and the seeds air-dried in shade before sowing. Seedlings take 4 to 8 weeks to appear.

Halleria lucida

TREE FUCHSIA

☼ ❅ ↔ 12 ft (3.5 m) ↕ 35 ft (10 m)

Evergreen tree, larger in wild, from Ethiopia to southern tip of Africa. Leaves glossy green above, paler below, broadly lance-shaped

Halimium lasianthum

to oval, tapering tip, finely toothed edges. Flowers tubular, orangey red, in clusters in leaf axils or borne on branches or trunk or stems, in winter–spring. Edible fleshy black fruit. Zones 8–10.

HAMAMELIS

This small genus of 5 or 6 species of deciduous winter-flowering shrubs or small trees in the witch hazel (Hamamelidaceae) family is found in eastern North America and eastern Asia. They are characterized by spider-like, yellow or reddish, perfumed flowers with crinkled strap-shaped petals, clustered on the bare branches from mid-winter to early spring. Foliage often provides attractive autumn color. Fruit is a horned capsule containing 2 shiny black seeds.
CULTIVATION: They grow mainly in the shade of light woodland, prefer some shade from the midday sun, and like a cool moist climate. The best flowers are borne on strong, young, 1- to 3-year-old shoots that have not been shortened. Cutting for indoor decoration makes way for new shoots. Seeds can be collected before they are discharged and sown at once, but germination may take a year or more. Layers can be put down in winter and lifted the following winter.

Hamamelis × intermedia

HYBRID WITCH HAZEL

☼ ❅ ↔ 12 ft (3.5 m) ↕ 12 ft (3.5 m)

Hybrid between *H. japonica* and *H. mollis*, large shrub. Leaves to 6 in (15 cm) long, turn yellow in autumn. Flowers creamy, red, and apricot crimped petals. 'Arnold Promise' ★, dense clusters of dark yellow flowers; 'Diane', red flowers, leaves color well in autumn; 'Jelena', vigorous spreading habit, large broad leaves, flowers yellow suffused copper red, foliage turns orange, red, and scarlet; 'Pallida', clear sulfur or lemon yellow flowers with no trace of other colors. Zones 4–9.

Hamamelis japonica

JAPANESE WITCH HAZEL

☼ ❅ ↔ 12 ft (3.5 m) ↕ 15 ft (4.5 m)

Large spreading shrub or small tree. Short stout trunk, rigid branches. Leaves shiny and smooth when mature. Flowers small to medium, with crimpled petals. 'Sulphurea', large spreading shrub, ascending branches, flowers small to medium, pale sulfur yellow. Zones 4–9.

Hamamelis mollis

CHINESE WITCH HAZEL, WITCH HAZEL

☼ ❅ ↔ 12 ft (3.5 m) ↕ 15 ft (4.5 m)

Native of central and eastern China. Leaves mid-green, downy above, gray-green beneath, turn deep golden yellow in autumn. Perfumed flowers in axillary clusters, golden yellow straight petals, calyx yellow-brown, 4 spreading sepals chocolate brown inside. Zones 4–9.

Hamamelis virginiana ★

syn. *Hamamelis macrophylla*

COMMON WITCH HAZEL, WITCH HAZEL

☼ ❅ ↔ 8–12 ft (2.4–3.5 m) ↕ 12–15 ft (3.5–4.5 m)

Native to northeastern USA down to Lawrence Valley and into Virginia. Leaves dark green, shiny above, paler beneath. Flowers

Hamamelis japonica

borne in small clusters in upper axils, yellow in color, in autumn before leaves fall, sometimes partly obscured. Zones 7–9.

HARPEPHYLLUM

One species makes up this genus from South Africa which, though its common name suggests it is a type of plum, is a member of the cashew (Anacardiaceae) family. An evergreen, it is widely planted as a street or park tree in warmer climates or on the west side of houses for shade. However, in a garden situation it may be difficult to grow plants under it due to the dense shade it provides.
CULTIVATION: Although tolerant of a wide range of soils, it needs a frost-free situation where its low branching habit has room to form a dense crown. Propagation is from seed, which is only produced by the female tree if a male tree is nearby.

Harpephyllum caffrum
SOUTH AFRICAN WILD PLUM, WILDEPRUIM
☼ ⚘ ↔ 25 ft (8 m) ↑ 30 ft (9 m)
Densely foliaged tree, broad crown deep green, shiny compound leaves. White flowers insignificant. Plum-sized fruit follows, ripening to orange-red, used for jam. Zones 9–11.

HEBE

There are about 100 species of evergreen shrubs in this genus allied to *Veronica* in the figwort or foxglove (Scrophulariaceae) family, mostly native to New Zealand, with a handful from southern South America and New Guinea. They grow in a wide range of habitats from coastal to alpine regions. There are 2 distinct foliage groups: those with oval or lance-shaped leaves, and the "whipcord" hebes, which have compressed scale-like leaves resembling conifers. Flower spikes of small tubular flowers range in color from white through pink to deep purple and crimson.
CULTIVATION: Most hebes prefer a sunny situation, tolerating a wide range of soil conditions. They vary in degree of frost hardiness, bigger-leafed species being more tender. Whipcord species dislike heat and humidity, requiring a gritty well-drained soil. Some are suitable for coastal planting. Leaf spot and downy mildew can be a problem in humid areas. Prune after flowering to maintain a compact shape. Propagation is from seed or half-hardened cuttings in late summer, cultivars from cuttings only.

Hebe albicans
☼ ⚘ ↔ 27 in (70 cm) ↑ 18–24 in (45–60 cm)
Compact shrub found in rocky mountain areas of northern South Island, New Zealand. Attractive glaucous leaves, closely packed on stout branchlets. Small white flowers, crowded on short racemes, in summer–autumn. 'Red Edge', dark red margins around grayish green leaves, in winter becoming suffused with maroon; 'Sussex Carpet', opposite pairs of blue-green leaves. Zones 8–10.

Hebe × *andersonii* ★
☼ ⚘ ↔ 4 ft (1.2 m) ↑ 3–7 ft (0.9–2 m)
Hybrid of *H. speciosa* and *H. stricta*. Well-branched shrub, broadly lance-shaped leaves to 4 in (10 cm) long. Violet flowers on spikes to 4 in (10 cm) long, in summer–autumn. 'Andersonii Variegata', leaves dark green, grayish green, and creamy white. Zones 9–11.

Hebe × *andersonii* 'Andersonii Variegata'

Hebe armstrongii
☼ ❀ ↔ 3 ft (0.9 m) ↑ 3 ft (0.9 m)
Whipcord species, erect well-branched shrub. Very rare in wild, found in few mountain areas of central South Island, New Zealand. Yellowish green color of branches intensifies in winter. Small white flowers, secondary to foliage effect. Zones 8–10.

Hebe cupressoides
WHIPCORD HEBE
☼ ❀ ↔ 3 ft (0.9 m) ↑ 3 ft (0.9 m)
Whipcord species native to subalpine regions of South Island, New Zealand. Attractive conifer-like appearance, densely branched. Well-spaced scale-like leaves, branchlets bright green. Pale blue flowers, borne sparingly, of secondary importance. 'Boughton Dome', to 30 in (75 cm) tall, gray-green branchlets covered in small scale-like leaves. Zones 8–10.

Hebe diosmifolia
☼ ❀ ↔ 24 in (60 cm) ↑ 36 in (90 cm)
Variable species from northern North Island, New Zealand. Well-branched shrub, narrow glossy green leaves. Covered with small flowerheads of tiny white to lavender flowers in spring. Zones 8–11.

Harpephyllum caffrum

Hebe pinguifolia 'Pagei'

Hebe speciosa

Hebe, Hybrid Cultivar, 'Marjorie'

Hebe elliptica

☼ ❄ ↔ 4 ft (1.2 m) ↑ 3–7 ft (0.9–2 m)

Found in southern South America as well as New Zealand. Well-branched; small, leathery, dark green leaves. White to lavender flowers, bigger than most species, in late spring–autumn. Tolerant of salt spray, suitable for seaside gardens. Zones 8–11.

Hebe × *franciscana*

☼ ❄ ↔ 4 ft (1.2 m) ↑ 3 ft (0.9 m)

Older hybrid, cross between *H. elliptica* and *H. speciosa*. Rounded habit, dark green leaves. Pinkish purple flowers, on spikes to 3 in (8 cm) long, in summer–autumn. '**Blue Gem**', bluish purple flowers, often seen, useful for coastal areas; '**Variegata**' (syn. *H.* 'Waireka'), mottled leaves with yellow margins. Zones 7–11.

Hebe odora

syn. *Hebe buxifolia*

☼ ❄ ↔ 4 ft (1.2 m) ↑ 3 ft (0.9 m)

Variable in wild, rounded bush in cultivation. Small dark green box-like leaves. Conical heads of white flowers, at branch tips, in spring–late summer. '**Patty's Purple**', popular American cultivar; '**New Zealand Gold**', strong grower, new leaves can be bright yellow. Zones 7–10.

Hebe pinguifolia

VERONICA

☼ ❄ ↔ 30 in (75 cm) ↑ 10 in (25 cm)

From drier eastern ranges of South Island of New Zealand. Variable habit in wild. Cultivated plants usually low growing. Stout branches, small thick bluish gray leaves with red margins. Small white flowers, in dense heads near branch tips, in spring–autumn. '**Pagei**', excellent rock-garden plant, spreading to 3 ft (0.9 m) wide, with very glaucous leaves and dark purplish branch-lets. Zones 6–10.

Hebe salicifolia

KOROMIKO

☼ ❄ ↔ 7 ft (2 m) ↑ 8 ft (2.4 m)

Found throughout South Island of New Zealand and also in Chile. Well-branched spreading shrub. Attractive willow-like leaves. Drooping racemes of white to pale lilac flowers in summer. Zones 7–10.

Hebe speciosa

SHOWY HEBE

☼ ❅ ↔ 3 ft (0.9 m) ↑ 3 ft (0.9 m)

Rare in wild, in some coastal areas of North Island, New Zealand. Rounded shrub. Glossy dark green leaves, oval, reddish margins, red midrib. Racemes of purplish red flowers in summer–autumn. '**Variegata**', leaves with yellow variegation, red margins. Zones 9–11.

Hebe topiaria

☼ ❄ ↔ 3 ft (0.9 m) ↑ 3 ft (0.9 m)

Compact, ball-shaped. Good for foliage contrast. Small, almost overlapping, bluish green leaves. Small white flowers between leaves in summer. Zones 8–11.

Hebe Hybrid Cultivars

☼ ❄ ↔ 12 in–5 ft (30 cm–1.5 m) ↑ 12 in–5 ft (30 cm–1.5 m)

Many attractive *Hebe* cultivars available. '**Alicia Amherst**', to 5 ft (1.5 m) tall, deep purple flowers densely packed on spikes up to 2½ in (6 cm) long, in autumn; '**Amy**', rounded compact shrub 3–5 ft (0.9–1.5 m) tall, leaves deep purplish bronze when young, erect spikes of purple flowers in late summer; '**Autumn Glory**' ★, low bushy shrub to 24 in (60 cm) tall, violet flowers on short crowded spikes in mid-summer–autumn; '**Carnea**', dense spreading shrub to 5 ft (1.5 m) tall, rosy purple summer flowers on racemes to 3 in (8 cm) long; '**Edinensis**', to 12 in (30 cm) high, 18 in (45 cm) wide, tiny vivid green leaves, white flowers slightly tinted mauve; '**Emerald Green**' (syns 'Emerald Gem', 'Green Globe'), fresh green compact bun shape 8–12 in (20–30 cm) high, small white flowers in summer; '**Fragrant Jewel**', 5 ft (1.5 m) high, masses of large, fragrant, lavender-purple flowers; '**Inspiration**', 3 ft (0.9 m) high, deep purple flowers for long periods, main flush in summer; '**Loganioides**' (syn. *H. selaginoides*), to 10 in (25 cm) tall, white flowers; '**Margret**', 16 in (40 cm) tall, sky blue flowers fade to white in late spring–early summer; '**Marjorie**', to 5 ft (1.5 m) tall, large mauve-blue flowers fade to white; '**Midsummer Beauty**' (syn. *H.* × *andersonii* 'Midsummer Beauty'), to 6 ft (1.8 m) tall, plum-colored new growth, lilac-purple flowers fade to white; '**Mrs Winder**' (syns 'Waikiki', 'Warleyensis'), to 3 ft (0.9 m) high, leaves flushed red at base, reddish purple in winter, violet flowers in summer; '**Orphan Annie**', to 3 ft (0.9 m) tall, narrow cream and green variegated leaves, pink early summer flowers; '**Pink Elephant**', 2 ft (0.6 m) tall, yellow-edged pink-tinged new growth, white summer flowers; 'Temptation', to 12 in (30 cm) tall, pink flowers fade to white; 'Wardiensis', to 8 in (20 cm) tall, white summer flowers; 'Wiri Charm', 30 in (75 cm) high, rosy purple flowers in summer; 'Wiri Dawn', to 18 in (45 cm) high, light olive green leaves, pale pinkish white flowers; 'Wiri Grace', to 5 ft (1.5 m), long spikes of light purple flowers in summer; 'Wiri Image', vigorous, to 3 ft (0.9 m) tall, long racemes of violet flowers in early summer; 'Youngii' (syn. 'Carl Teschner'), 8 in (20 cm) tall, branchlets purplish, deep violet flowers on short spikes in summer. Zones 8–11.

HELIANTHEMUM

ROCK ROSE, SUN ROSE

Related to *Cistus*, the 110 or so evergreen and semi-evergreen shrubs and subshrubs in this genus, in the rock-rose (Cistaceae) family, are less widely grown but have a wider natural range: Eurasia, North Africa, and the Americas. Relatively low-mounding, short-lived plants, foliage is often hairy, giving it a gray-green color. Flowers resemble tiny roses, and are individually short lived but appear through late spring and summer. They are in shades of yellow, orange, red, or pink, with bright yellow stamens massed at the center. CULTIVATION: They need full sun for their flowers to develop, and suit sunny borders, rock gardens, or large containers. Soil should be rather gritty and free draining. Keep moist in summer, dry in winter. Trim lightly after flowering to shape and encourage vigor. Propagation is from seed; hybrids and cultivars should be propagated from cuttings or by removing rooted pieces from established plants.

Heptacodium miconioides

Helianthemum croceum

☀ ❋ ↔ 16–20 in (40–50 cm) ↕ 12–14 in (30–35 cm)
From southern Europe and northern Africa. Slightly fleshy leaves to ¾ in (18 mm) long. Flowers up to ¾ in (18 mm) wide in shades of yellow, white, or apricot. Zones 7–10.

Helianthemum, Hybrid Cultivar, 'Rhodanthe Carneum'

Helianthemum nummularium

syn. *Helianthemum chamaecistus*
COMMON SUN ROSE, SUN ROSE

☀ ❋ ↔ 24 in (60 cm) ↕ 20 in (50 cm)
Leaves dark green above, gray-green, felted below. Flowers bright yellow, orange, or red shades, any color except purple or blue, in late spring–summer. *H. n.* subsp. *glabrum* (syn. *H. nitidum*), from central and southwest Europe, fewer leaf hairs, slightly downy margins, orange-yellow flowers. Zones 5–10.

Helianthemum Hybrid Cultivars

☀ ❋ ↔ 18–36 in (45–90 cm) ↕ 6–12 in (15–30 cm)
Alpine and rock-garden enthusiasts have produced many hybrids in broad color spectrum. Most have *H. nummularium* in background. 'Ben Heckla', bronze-gold flowers; 'Ben Hope', light foliage, red flowers with orange center; 'Ben Ledi', dark green leaves, deep rose flowers; 'Ben Vane', terracotta flowers; 'Ben Vorlich', orange flowers; 'Butter and Eggs', creamy yellow; 'Dazzler', dark green foliage, deep red flowers; 'Fire Dragon', gray-green leaves, orange-red flowers; 'Golden Queen', large bright yellow flowers; 'Henfield Brilliant' ★, gray-green leaves, dark red flowers; 'Jubilee', double primrose yellow flowers; 'Mrs C. W. Earle', double scarlet flowers; 'Orange Surprise', orange flowers; 'Raspberry Ripple', deep reddish pink flowers tipped white; 'Rhodanthe Carneum', silvery gray leaves, orange-centered pink flowers; 'Rose Queen', rose pink flowers; 'Sudbury Gem', grayish green leaves, deep pink flowers with red center; 'The Bride', silver-gray foliage, white flowers; 'Wisley Pink', silver-gray foliage, light pink flowers; 'Wisley Primrose', gray-green foliage, primrose yellow flowers; 'Wisley White', gray foliage, white flowers. Zones 6–10.

HEPTACODIUM

This genus, in the woodbine (Caprifoliaceae) family and allied to *Abelia* and *Kolkwitzia*, consists of 1 species of deciduous shrub from central and eastern China. It has large glossy leaves with 3 longitudinal veins, in opposite pairs on the twigs. Small white flowers are borne in large panicles at branch ends. As the small dry fruits develop, the sepals, inconspicuous in flower, enlarge and turn deep pink, making a display that lasts several months. CULTIVATION: This plant likes woodland conditions with moist acid soil and shelter, though not too much shade. Lower twiggy growth should be thinned out in winter. Propagation should be from hardwood cuttings in autumn or half-hardened tip cuttings in summer, from basal suckers, or from seed.

Heptacodium miconioides ★

syn. *Heptacodium jasminoides*
CHINESE HEPTACODIUM, SEVEN SON FLOWER

☀ ❋ ↔ 7–10 ft (2–3 m) ↕ 10–15 ft (3–4.5 m)
Chinese deciduous shrub or small tree, dark green elliptical leaves. Heads of fragrant white flowers, from late summer to first frosts. Calyces of flowers turn rosy red to purple in autumn. Zones 5–9.

HETEROMELES
CALIFORNIA HOLLY, CHRISTMAS BERRY, TOLLON, TOYON

This genus comprises a single species, a native of California that is an evergreen shrub closely related to *Photinia*. Fruit, which may be red or yellow, small or large, develop from heads of small creamy white flowers and, as the name "Christmas berry" suggests, it ripens around Christmas, or mid-winter, in its home range.
CULTIVATION: Any well-drained soil with a sunny or partly shaded aspect will do. Heat and drought resistant, this species will tolerate poor soils. The bush is usually a neat grower and needs trimming to shape only occasionally. It may be propagated from half-hardened cuttings or seed.

Heteromeles arbutifolia
☼ ❅ ↔ 12 ft (3.5 m) ↑ 12 ft (3.5 m)

Native to Sierra Nevada foothills of coastal California, USA, to Baja California, Mexico. Simple, oval, mid-green leaves, finely serrated edges. Flowerheads nectar-rich, with honey-like scent, in summer. Compact tough plant. Zones 8–10.

HIBBERTIA
GOLDEN GUINEA FLOWER

This mostly Australian genus in the Dilleniaceae family contains around 120 species of small, evergreen, shrubby plants or climbers grown for their profuse, usually bright yellow or sometimes orange flowers. Flowering is mostly during spring and early summer, though with some species it also occurs sporadically throughout most of the year. Though there is variation in growth habit, it is mostly the low spreading species and climbers that have become well known to horticulture. These are ideal rock-garden, container, and ground cover plants.
CULTIVATION: Easy to grow, they enjoy moderately fertile well-drained soil that does not dry out too quickly. In hotter areas partial shade is best. Marginally frost hardy, they

Hibbertia miniata

need protection in colder regions, especially when young. To keep their shape, prune tips from an early age and after flowering. Propagate from half-hardened tip cuttings taken in late summer.

Hibbertia miniata
☼ ❅ ↔ 8 in (20 cm) ↑ 15 in (38 cm)

Small erect shrub, rare in wild, confined to jarrah forests of Western Australia. Broad gray-green linear leaves. Showy orange flowers, dark purple anthers, in spring–summer. Zones 9–11.

Hibbertia stellaris
ORANGE STARS
☼ ❅ ↔ 30 in (75 cm) ↑ 30 in (75 cm)

Small dense shrub from coastal areas of Western Australia, growing at edges of swamps. Soft fine green foliage, red stems. Small starry apricot flowers in spring–autumn. Often difficult to grow, and is short lived. Zones 9–11.

HIBISCUS
GIANT MALLOW, MALLOW, ROSE MALLOW

This genus of over 200 annual or perennial herbs, shrubs, or trees in the mallow (Malvaceae) family is widely distributed throughout warm-temperate, subtropical, and tropical regions of the world. They are grown mostly for their large dramatic flowers, borne singly or in terminal clusters, usually lasting for just a day. The open bell-shaped flowers appear in a wide variety of colors, and are characterized by a prominent staminal column and a darker coloring in the center. The alternate simple leaves are usually palmate. The fruit is a capsule.
CULTIVATION: Most species of *Hibiscus* are drought tender and rather frost tender, and prefer a position in full sun in a rich and moist soil. Many will tolerate hard pruning after flowering to maintain shape. Perennials are propagated from seed or by division, while annuals are best grown from seed in the growing position. Shrub types can be propagated from cuttings, by grafting, or from seed sown in containers for later transplanting.

Hibiscus coccineus
SCARLET HIBISCUS, SCARLET ROSE MALLOW, SWAMP HIBISCUS
☼ ❅ ↔ 2–3 ft (0.6–0.9 m) ↑ 7 ft (2 m)

From southern USA. Shrub-like herbaceous species with 5-petalled crimson flowers, 6–8 in (15–20 cm) across, in early to mid-summer, followed by attractive papery green fruit. Vigorous grower in good conditions. 'Davis Creek', robust cultivar. Zones 7–11.

Hibiscus heterophyllus
AUSTRALIAN NATIVE ROSELLA, SCRUB KURRAJONG
☼ ❅ ↔ 6–10 ft (1.8–3 m) ↑ 10–20 ft (3–6 m)

Evergreen shrub or small tree native to eastern Australia. Prickly branches, narrow pointed leaves, deeply lobed. Flowers white with purple eye. *H. h.* subsp. *luteus*, yellow flowers usual in northern parts of range. Zones 10–12.

Heteromeles arbutifolia

Hibiscus moscheutos

COMMON ROSE MALLOW, SWAMP ROSE MALLOW

☼ ❋ ↔ 40 in (100 cm) ↑ 8 ft (2.4 m)

Woody perennial shrub from eastern North America. Lobed leaves 2–6 in (5–15 cm) long. Flowers large, trumpet-shaped, pink and white, in spring–summer. 'Lord Baltimore', large, single, crimson red flowers, to 12 in (30 cm) across; 'Southern Belle', compact, to 40 in (100 cm), deep pink flowers. Zones 5–9.

Hibiscus mutabilis

CONFEDERATE ROSE, COTTON ROSE

☼ ❋ ↔ 6–8 ft (1.8–2.4 m) ↑ 10–15 ft (3–4.5 m)

Small, spreading, deciduous shrub, or erect, branching, small tree native to China. Large palm-shaped leaves, 7 serrated lobes. Double or single flowers, white or pink with darker base and staminal column. 'Plena', rounded double flowers. Zones 8–9.

Hibiscus pedunculatus

DWARF PINK HIBISCUS

☼ ❊ ↔ 5 ft (1.5 m) ↑ 4–6 ft (1.2–1.8 m)

Native from Mozambique to South Africa. Leaves have 3 to 5 rounded lobes. Nodding solitary flowers, staminal column and 2 in (5 cm) long petals, pale or deep rose purple or lilac. Zones 10–12.

Hibiscus rosa-sinensis

CHINA ROSE, CHINESE HIBISCUS, HAWAIIAN HIBISCUS, ROSE OF CHINA, SHOE BLACK

☼ ❊ ↔ 5 ft (1.5 m) ↑ 8–30 ft (2.4–9 m)

Erect, branching, evergreen shrub, or small tree to 30 ft (9 m) high. Solitary flowers, variable in color, normally red to dark red, in summer–winter. Oval-shaped, serrated, glossy, deep green leaves. Hybrid cultivars include 'Agnes Galt' ★, tall vigorous shrub, large rose pink flowers; 'Aurora', blush pink pompon-shaped flowers; 'Bridal Veil', large pure white flowers with crape texture; 'Cooperi', small, rose pink, single flowers, narrow variegated leaves, olive green marbled with red, pink, and white, good container plant; 'Crown of Bohemia', bushy shrub, medium double flowers, gold with bright orange throat; 'D. J. O'Brien', medium, double, orange-apricot flowers; 'Eileen McMullen', large deep yellow flowers heavily flushed with crimson; 'Moon Beam', bright yellow flowers, crimson throat, strongly reflexed petals. Zones 9–11.

Hibiscus heterophyllus subsp. *luteus*

Hibiscus schizopetalus

CORAL HIBISCUS, FRINGED HIBISCUS, JAPANESE HIBISCUS, JAPANESE LANTERN

☼ ❊ ↔ 6 ft (1.8 m) ↑ 10 ft (3 m)

Evergreen to semi-deciduous shrub native to tropical east Africa. Arching, slender, weeping habit, clusters of small, oval, serrated leaves. Flowers ragged, fringed margins, petals pink or brilliant red, long staminal column, in summer–autumn. Zones 10–12.

Hibiscus syriacus

BLUE HIBISCUS, ROSE OF SHARON, SHRUB ALTHEA, SYRIAN HIBISCUS

☼ ❋ ↔ 6–10 ft (1.8–3 m) ↑ 8–20 ft (2.4–6 m)

Shrub or small tree native to warm-temperate areas of China. Smooth gray branches; leaves with 3 narrow, coarsely toothed, triangular lobes. Single or double flowers, petals white, reddish purple, or bluish lavender with crimson base and staminal column. Blue Bird/'Oiseau Bleu', gentian blue flowers, lilac-purple center, grows to 5 ft (1.5 m); 'Diana', single pure white flowers, grows to 5 ft (1.5 m); 'Hamabo', large, light pink, single flowers with red center that radiates at edges into fine red streaks; 'White Supreme', semi-double white flowers with crimson center, rose pink on outside of petals; 'Woodbridge', wine red flowers with darker center, grows to 6 ft (1.8 m). Other cultivars include 'Aphrodite', 'Boule de Feu', 'Lady Stanley', 'Lohengrin', 'Minerva', and 'Red Heart'. Zones 5–9.

Hibiscus tiliaceus

COAST COTTONWOOD, MAHOE, MANGROVE HIBISCUS, MAU

☼ ❊ ↔ 10–20 ft (3–6 m) ↑ 25 ft (8 m)

Evergreen shrub or small tree widespread across tropical regions of world. Smooth gray bark, gnarled picturesque trunk. Rounded, smooth, leathery green leaves, hairy beneath. Solitary yellow or white flowers, with red to brown throat and staminal column, in summer. Salt tolerant and drought resistant. Zones 10–12.

Hibiscus trionum

FLOWER-OF-AN-HOUR

☼ ❊ ↔ 12 in (30 cm) ↑ 12–24 in (30–60 cm)

From warmer regions of Africa, Asia, and Australia. Hairy stems and lobed leaves. Yellow flowers, crimson-black eye. Zones 10–12.

Hibiscus moscheutos 'Lord Baltimore'

Hibiscus schizopetalus

Hibiscus trionum

Hoheria lyallii

HOHERIA

LACEBARK, RIBBONWOOD

This New Zealand genus of 5 species of deciduous and evergreen trees is in the mallow (Malvaceae) family. Leaves usually have pointed tips and serrated margins. White 5-petalled flowers are profuse in summer or autumn. The name "lacebark" is due to the lace-like fibrous layer under the surface bark.

CULTIVATION: These trees are suitable for specimen or woodland planting. They are fast growing and most will tolerate a wide range of conditions in sun or part-shade. In cold climates they need the protection of a warm wall, and in such areas the deciduous species are more hardy. Plants can be pruned if necessary. Propagation is from seed sown in autumn, or half-hardened cuttings.

Hoheria lyallii

MOUNTAIN RIBBONWOOD, NEW ZEALAND LACEBARK

☀ ❄ ↔ 10 ft (3 m) ↑ 7–12 ft (2–3.5 m)

Found on drier east coast of New Zealand's South Island. Leaves bright green, often turn yellow in autumn. White flowers. Zones 8–10.

Hoheria sexstylosa

RIBBONWOOD

☀ ❄ ↔ 20 ft (6 m) ↑ 15–25 ft (4.5–8 m)

Variable species. Leaves toothed leaves, long, narrow. Flowers small, scented. Branches tend to weep, with graceful appearance. Zones 8–11.

HOLMSKIOLDIA

This mint (Lamiaceae) family genus from the Himalayan region contains a single variable species of sprawling evergreen shrub. Leaves are opposite, simple, and oval, with a variable covering of fine hairs, and finely serrated edges. The flowers occur in small panicles or racemes and are very interestingly shaped, with a narrow tubular corolla backed by a flattened, widely flared calyx.

CULTIVATION: Quite frost tender, these shrubs are best grown in a light well-drained soil that stays moist through the warmer months. Plant in full sun or partial shade and provide a trellis or other support to keep the growth upright. Regular pinching back will prevent the stems becoming too elongated. Propagate from seed or half-hardened cuttings.

Holmskioldia sanguinea

CHINESE HAT PLANT, CUP AND SAUCER PLANT

☀/◐ ❄ ↔ 6 ft (1.8 m) ↑ 3–6 ft (0.9–1.8 m)

Found in Himalayan lowlands. Shallowly serrated leaves to 3 in (8 cm) long. Flowers orange to scarlet with brick red calyces, in dense clusters, in warmest months. Zones 10–11.

HOLODISCUS

This genus in the rose (Rosaceae) family consists of 8 species of deciduous shrubs. Growing in dry woodland, they are found in western North America and as far south as Colombia. These plants bear airy panicles of small flowers, sometimes with red buds; flowers open to a creamy white.

CULTIVATION: Tolerant of sun or part-shade, they need moist, fertile, humus-rich soil that does not dry out. Most are easily increased by layering, or heel cuttings of half-hardened wood in a peat-sand mixture; they may need mist propagation. They can be difficult to root.

Holodiscus discolor

CREAMBUSH, OCEAN SPRAY

☀/◐ ❄ ↔ 12 ft (3.5 m) ↑ 12 ft (3.5 m)

Native to western North America. Leaves broadly egg-shaped, with 4 to 8 lobes, scalloped margins, deep green above, white felty below. Flowers in plume-like creamy panicles in summer. Zones 4–10.

HOMALOCLADIUM

This genus in the knotweed (Polygonaceae) family consists of 1 curious evergreen shrub from the Solomon Islands, often grown as a container plant. Leafless at flowering time, it has flat, ribbon-like, jointed stems and tiny flowers in spring. The fruit is enclosed by a fleshy red to purple berry. Some botanists consider it to be no more than a bizarre species of *Muehlenbeckia*.

CULTIVATION: Easily grown and tolerant of light frosts, *Homalocladium* prefers a light, rich, moist, well-drained soil or a regular potting mix in a protected, partially shaded position. Propagation is either from fresh seed sown in spring or from cuttings taken in summer.

Holmskioldia sanguinea

Homalocladium platycladum

syn. *Muehlenbeckia platyclada*

CENTIPEDE PLANT, RIBBON BUSH, TAPEWORM PLANT

◐ ❄ ↔ 6 ft (1.8 m) ↑ 6–10 ft (1.8–3 m)

Unusual evergreen shrub. Distinctive, flat, green, ribbon-like, jointed stems. Whitish green flowers, in small clusters at joints of branches, in spring; narrow green leaves. Zones 10–12.

HYDRANGEA

There are about 100 species of deciduous and evergreen shrubs, trees, and climbers in this Hydrangeaceae family genus, native to eastern Asia, and North and South America. Leaves are usually large and oval with serrated edges. Flowerheads comprise very small fertile flowers surrounded by larger, 4-petalled, sterile florets, conical, flat-topped (lacecap), or rounded (mophead). Colors range from white through to red, purple, and blue.

CULTIVATION: Hydrangeas grow in a wide range of conditions. However, they will do better in good soil with compost and light feeding. Grow in sun or dappled shade, ensuring they have ample moisture. Grow *H. macrophylla* cultivars to suit the soil pH. Color can be changed by dressing with aluminium sulphate for blue and with lime for red. Prune in late winter, and remove old wood. Propagate species from seed in spring, tip cuttings in late spring, or hardwood cuttings in winter; propagate cultivars from cuttings only.

Hydrangea arborescens
SMOOTH HYDRANGEA

☼/◐ ❋ ↔ 8 ft (2.4 m) ↕ 3–12 ft (0.9–3.5 m)

Native to North America, from moist shady sites. Deciduous shrub, open habit, often spreading from suckers. Flat creamy white flowerheads, in summer, numerous tiny fertile flowers surrounded by a few sterile florets. *H. a.* subsp. *radiata,* deep green leaves. *H. a.* 'Annabelle' ★, large white mophead flowerheads; 'Grandiflora', slightly uneven mopheads of pure white sterile flowers. Zones 3–10.

Hydrangea aspera
syn. *Hydrangea villosa*

☼/◐ ❋ ↔ 10 ft (3 m) ↕ 10 ft (3 m)

Variable deciduous species native to eastern Asia. Lacecap flowers, held above foliage, to 10 in (25 cm) wide, pale mauve sterile florets, tiny bright purplish blue fertile flowers in center. *H. a.* f. *kawakamii*, pink-veined leaves. *H. a.* subsp. *sargentiana*, large leaves, velvety above, bristly beneath; flat-topped flowerheads, pinkish white sterile florets surrounding mauve fertile flowers. *H. a.* 'Mauvette', mauve dome-shaped flowerheads to 6 in (15 cm) across; 'Peter Chappell', large downy leaves, flat-topped flowerheads of white sterile florets surrounding creamy pink fertile flowers. Zones 7–10.

Hydrangea heteromalla

☼/◐ ❋ ↔ 10 ft (3 m) ↕ 10–15 ft (3–4.5 m)

Deciduous species from China and Himalayas. Leaves usually broadly lance-shaped, downy beneath in some forms. Lacecap flowers, white to pink sterile florets, greenish white fertile flowers, in summer. 'Jermyn's Lace', pink-tinged greenish white flowers. Zones 6–9.

Hydrangea macrophylla
syn. *Hydrangea hortensis*

BIGLEAF HYDRANGEA, FLORIST'S HYDRANGEA, GARDEN HYDRANGEA, HORTENSIA

☼/◐ ❋ ↔ 8 ft (2.4 m) ↕ 10 ft (3 m)

Long-cultivated species from coastal areas of Japan. Deciduous shrub, large shiny leaves, pinkish blue flat-topped flowers. Cultivars

usually grow 3–6 ft (0.9–1.8 m) high, divided into two groups: mophead (hortensias) and lacecap. More than 500 mophead cultivars, with globular heads of showy sterile florets; suitable for coastal gardens. About 20 lacecap cultivars, with flat-topped formation of outer sterile florets, central fertile flowers.

MOPHEAD CULTIVARS
'Alpenglühen' ★, medium-sized robust plant, maintaining rosy red color even in slightly acid soil; 'Ami Pasquier', rich crimson to purple flowers all summer, leaves turn red in autumn; 'Enziandom' (syn. 'Gentian Dome'), compact shrub to 5 ft (1.5 m) tall, needing acid soil to produce gentian blue flowers; 'Hamburg', large serrated petals of deep rose to purple or blue, depending on soil pH; 'Madame Emile Mouillère', grows to 6 ft (1.8 m), one of best white mopheads; 'Nigra', distinctive black stems, small flowerheads from pink to blue depending on soil pH; 'Nikko Blue' ★, growing to 5 ft (1.5 m), blue flowers; 'Pia', very dwarf form; 'President Doumer', rich cherry red flowers in small clusters on top of small, dark green, serrated leaves; and 'Soeur Thérèse', growing up to 6 ft (1.8 m) tall, pure white variety. Other cultivars include 'Altona', 'Amethyst', 'Générale Vicomtesse de Vibraye', 'Miss Belgium', 'Montgomery', and 'Parzifal'.

LACECAP CULTIVARS
'Fireworks Pink', double, star-shaped, pink florets around outer edge of each flowerhead; 'Hobella', soft pink flowers ageing to green, then to cherry red; 'Libelle', stunning heads of white sterile florets surrounding deep blue fertile flowers; 'Love You Kiss', large white flowerheads, each petal with red margin, red-tinted leaves; and 'Mariesii', pale pink to light blue flowers. Other cultivars include 'Geoffrey Chadbund', 'Lanarth White', 'Lilacina', and 'Sea Foam'. Zones 5–11.

Hydrangea macrophylla, Mophead, 'Enziandom'

Hydrangea arborescens 'Annabelle'

Hydrangea 'Preziosa'

Hydrangea paniculata
PANICLE HYDRANGEA

☼/☀ ❄ ↔ 10 ft (3 m) ↑ 6–20 ft (1.8–6 m)

Deciduous species from Japan and southeastern China. Conical flowerheads, densely packed, creamy white sterile and fertile flowers, often in arching shape, in late summer–autumn. 'Grandiflora', creamy white sterile flowers on panicles up to 18 in (45 cm) long; 'Kyushu', smaller bush, panicles of creamy white sterile and fertile flowers; 'Praecox', early flowering; 'Tardiva', late flowering; 'Unique', round-ended panicles larger than those of 'Grandiflora'. Zones 3–10.

Hydrangea 'Preziosa'

☼/☀ ❄ ↔ 5 ft (1.5 m) ↑ 5 ft (1.5 m)

Erect shrub with distinctive reddish stems, red-flushed leaves. Small globular flowerheads change from creamy white through shades of pink to reddish purple. Zones 6–10.

Hydrangea quercifolia
OAK-LEAFED HYDRANGEA

☼/☀ ❄ ↔ 8 ft (2.4 m) ↑ 3–8 ft (0.9–2.4 m)

Deciduous shrub from southeastern USA. Large, lobed, green leaves turn crimson in autumn. Creamy white flowers, on conical panicles to 10 in (25 cm) long, in summer, become pinkish in autumn. 'Snow Flake', double flowers; 'Snow Queen', exceptional autumn foliage colors. Zones 5–10.

Hydrangea serrata
syn. *Hydrangea macrophylla* subsp. *serrata*

☼/☀ ❄ ↔ 5 ft (1.5 m) ↑ 3–6 ft (0.9–1.8 m)

Deciduous species from Japan and Korea, closely related to *H. macrophylla*. Flat-topped flowerheads, sterile florets of white, pink, or blue surrounding white or blue fertile flowers, in summer, color changing with age. 'Bluebird', neat shrub, blue lacecap flowers, carried for long time, foliage turns red in autumn; 'Grayswood', flowerheads with bluish purple fertile flowers surrounded by sterile florets, changing color to white, pink, and crimson. Zones 6–10.

HYMENOSPORUM

Consisting of a single evergreen tree species, this genus in the pittosporum (Pittosporaceae) family is from subtropical areas of Australia's east coast where grows in rainforests. Cultivated for many years for its creamy white flowers, which turn yellow as they age, it is a slender, often open tree with mid-green shiny foliage.
CULTIVATION: Though it likes a spot in full sun, it can grow in part-shade but may not flower as profusely. Moist humus-enriched soil will suit this plant as it does not like to be deprived of moisture when conditions are dry. Propagate from seed or cuttings.

Hymenosporum flavum
NATIVE FRANGIPANI

☼ ❄ ↔ 12 ft (3.5 m) ↑ 30 ft (9 m)

Slender tree. Light foliage coverage, widely spaced horizontal branches bear shiny deep green leaves. Fragrant cream blossoms, ageing to yellow, in spring. Zones 9–11.

HYPERICUM

Belonging to the St John's-wort (Clusiaceae) family, this genus has more than 400 species of deciduous, semi-evergreen and evergreen annuals, herbaceous perennials, shrubs, and trees. They occur world-wide in various habitats, and have simple smooth-edged leaves in opposite pairs and usually yellow 5-petalled flowers with a central bunch of many stamens. Some are used locally as medicinal plants.
CULTIVATION: Most will thrive in sun or partial shade in good garden soil. *H. calycinum* takes root along its prostrate branches in dry shade, but also does well in partial shade. *H. olympicum* is a good rock-garden plant, and needs sharp drainage. Most North American species prefer damper conditions. Evergreen species are best sheltered from cold drying winds. Propagate from seed in autumn, though it may not come true. Take softwood cuttings in spring, half-hardened cuttings in summer.

Hymenosporum flavum

Hypericum balearicum

☼ ❄ ↔ 10 in (25 cm) ↑ 10 in (25 cm)

From Balearic Islands. Evergreen, densely branched shrub. Warty glandular stems and leaves. Leaves oblong to egg-shaped, wavy edges. Solitary, starry, golden yellow flowers in summer. Zones 7–9.

Hypericum beanii

☼ ❄ ↔ 6 ft (1.8 m) ↑ 2–6 ft (0.6–1.8 m)

Vigorous, evergreen, bushy shrub native to Yunnan and Guizhou Provinces in China. Mid-green leaves elliptic to lance-shaped, with pale underside. Golden yellow flowers, bowl- to star-shaped, in summer. Zones 7–10.

Hypericum calycinum
AARON'S BEARD, CREEPING ST JOHN'S WORT, ROSE OF SHARON

☀ ❄ ↔ 5 ft (1.5 m) ↑ 8–24 in (20–60 cm)

Native to parts of Bulgaria and Turkey. Evergreen or semi-evergreen shrub, rooting branches. Elliptic or oblong leaves, dark green above, paler below. Bright yellow flowers in mid-summer–autumn. Good ground-cover plant for dry shade. Zones 6–9.

Hypericum empetrifolium

☼ ❀ ↔ 3 ft (0.9 m)   ↑ 2 ft (0.6 m)

Native to southeastern Europe, Turkey, and Libya. Dwarf, cushion-forming, evergreen shrub. Narrow leaves mid-green in whorls of 3. Cylindrical cymes of up to 40 golden yellow star-shaped flowers in summer. **H. e. subsp. *oliganthum*** (syn. *H. e.* var. *prostratum* of gardens), 2 in (5 cm) tall. Zones 8–9.

Hypericum 'Hidcote'

☼ ❀ ↔ 4 ft (1.2 m)   ↑ 4 ft (1.2 m)

Likely cross between *H. × cyathiflorum* 'Gold Cup' and *H. calycinum*. Dense evergreen or semi-evergreen shrub. Leaves dark green, lance-shaped. Large, bowl-shaped, deep yellow flowers in summer–autumn. Zones 7–10.

Hypericum lancasteri

☼ ❀ ↔ 3 ft (0.9 m)   ↑ 3 ft (0.9 m)

Native to China. Deciduous shrub, purple-red young growth. Leaves oblong to triangular lance-shaped, mid-green. Cymes of yellow bowl- or star-shaped flowers in summer. Zones 7–10.

Hypericum × moserianum

Hypericum × moserianum

☼ ❀ ↔ 24–32 in (60–80 cm)   ↑ 12–16 in (30–40 cm)

Attractive, arching, semi-deciduous. Lance-shaped leaves to 2 in (5 cm) long. Flowers yellow, to 2½ in (6 cm) wide, in summer and autumn. '**Tricolor**', variegated form. Zones 7–10.

Hypericum olympicum

☼ ❀ ↔ 15 in (38 cm)   ↑ 10 in (25 cm)

Dwarf deciduous shrub native to Greece and southern Balkans. Oblong, elliptic, gray-green leaves, glaucous underside. Cymes of 5 golden yellow star-shaped flowers in summer. Zones 6–10.

Hypericum prolificum

☼ ❀ ↔ 5 ft (1.5 m)   ↑ 6 ft (1.8 m)

Loosely branched shrub from central and eastern USA and southern Canada. Leaves narrow, oblong, elliptical or lance-shaped, leaf

edges sometimes recurved, underside features pale waxy bloom. Golden yellow flowers borne in summer. Zones 4–9.

Hypericum 'Rowallane'

☼ ❀ ↔ 4 ft (1.2 m)   ↑ 6 ft (1.8 m)

Semi-evergreen shrub, chance hybrid between *H. leschenaultii* and *H. hookerianum* 'Charles Rogers'. Leaves egg-shaped or oblong to lance-shaped, dark green above, paler green and crinkly below. Rich golden flowers, in small cymes, in late summer–autumn. Zones 8–10.

HYPOESTES

An acanthus (Acanthaceae) family genus of 40 perennials, subshrubs, and shrubs from open woodland regions of Africa, Madagascar, Arabia, tropical Asia, and Australasia, some decoratively foliaged species are used as indoor plants or grown as annuals in cooler areas; others are valued for their autumn flowers. Evergreen leaves are held opposite on upright stems and in some species are velvety to touch. **CULTIVATION:** Grow in humus-rich well-drained soil. Water freely in summer but keep drier in the cold months. These plants do well in part-shade with protection from drying winds. Propagate in spring from seed, or from stem cuttings taken in spring to summer.

Hypoestes aristata

RIBBON BUSH

◑ ❅ ↔ 26 in (65 cm)   ↑ 3 ft (0.9 m)

From southern Africa. Evergreen shrubby plant, upright stems. Downy mid-green leaves. Masses of small purple flowers, in upper leaf axils, in autumn. Zones 9–11.

Hypoestes phyllostachya

POLKA-DOT PLANT

◑ ❅ ↔ 30 in (75 cm)   ↑ 3 ft (0.9 m)

Subshrub from Madagascar, widely used as indoor plant in cold areas. Pink-speckled green leaves. Soft tender stems, becoming woody near base. '**Splash**', larger pink markings. Zones 10–12.

Hypericum calycinum

Hypoestes aristata

IDESIA

WONDER TREE

The sole species in this genus in the governor's-plum (Flacourtiaceae) family is a medium-sized deciduous tree found naturally in Japan, Korea, Taiwan, and nearby parts of China. Its large foliage makes it an excellent shade tree. Bright red berries hang in large pendulous clusters long after the foliage has fallen. The flowers are unisexual but the plants are debatably dioecious: so-called female plants often bear fruit without the presence of male plants, though fruiting is better with a cross-pollinator.

CULTIVATION: Although reasonably frost hardy, *Idesia* can be severely damaged by late spring frosts that arrive after the foliage has expanded. It prefers a climate with a warm summer, a long autumn, and a short winter without late frosts. While the soil should be well drained, the tree will cope with most soil types. Prune foliage to shape when young, otherwise trim lightly after the fruit has fallen. Propagate from seed or from half-hardened cuttings.

Idesia polycarpa

☼ ✽ ↔ 35 ft (10 m) ↑ 50 ft (15 m)

Upright tree with rounded crown. Deep green leaves, heart-shaped, to 8 in (20 cm) long, red leaf stalks. Flowers tiny, in large sprays, yellow-green, fragrant. Red berries on bare branches. Zones 6–10.

ILEX

HOLLY

This widely distributed genus, belonging to the holly (Aquifoliaceae) family, contains more than 400 species of evergreen or deciduous trees, shrubs, and climbers. Used for its foliage and berries since Roman times, holly has long been associated with Northern Hemisphere festivals celebrating the winter solstice and Christmas. Wood of some species is used for veneers and musical instruments; leaves are used as tea substitutes or in tisanes. Male and female flowers usually grow on separate trees, thus plants of both sexes are required for the production of berries.

CULTIVATION: North American hollies prefer neutral to acid soils, while the Asian and European species will grow in most soils that are moderately fertile, well drained, and humus-rich. Green hollies will also grow in part- or full shade (but not deep shade). Variegated hollies require a position in full sun for best effect. Propagate from half-hardened cuttings in late summer or early autumn. Seed germination may take 2 or 3 years. Tender species need greenhouse protection in winter in colder climates.

Ilex × altaclerensis

HIGHCLERE HOLLY

☼ ✽ ↔ 20 ft (6 m) ↑ 70 ft (21 m)

Hybrid group of evergreen trees or shrubs of garden origin, cross between *I. aquifolium* and *I. perado*. More robust than *I. aquifolium*, with larger broader leaves. Berries mostly red. 'Camelliifolia', stems with purple hue, and red berries; 'Golden King', dark green leaves edged yellow; 'Hendersonii', vigorous tree, brown-red berries; 'Lawsoniana', compact female shrub with yellow-streaked stems, gold and green markings in center of leaves, brownish red berries; 'Platyphylla', broad, glossy, dark green, spine-toothed leaves; 'Purple Shaft', columnar, vigorous, fruits profusely. Zones 6–10.

Ilex aquifolium

COMMON HOLLY, ENGLISH HOLLY

☼ ✽ ↔ 25 ft (8 m) ↑ 40–80 ft (12–24 m)

Occurs over southern and western Europe, North Africa, and western Asia. Glossy dark green leaves, elliptic, spine-toothed edges. Male and female flowers usually borne on separate trees. Berries red, sometimes yellow or orange. 'Amber', female cultivar, to 20 ft (6 m) tall, bright green leaves, amber berries; 'Argentea Marginata', female cultivar, dark green leaves edged creamy white; 'Argentea Marginata Pendula' (syn. 'Argentea Pendula'), weeping female tree with spiny, cream-margined, elliptic leaves; 'Ferox Argentea', spiny leaves with cream margins; 'Handsworth New Silver', female, with elongated, spiny, cream-edged leaves, dark purple stems; 'J. C. van Tol', broad female tree, dark green leaves, scarlet berries; 'Madame Briot', vigorous female form, egg-shaped dark green leaves with gold margins, vivid red fruit; 'Pyramidalis', self-fertile cultivar, yellowish green stems, spiny bright green leaves; 'Pyramidalis Fructu Luteo', female conical shrub or small tree, yellow berries; 'Silver Milkmaid', female cultivar, pale green to yellow stems, spiny mid-green leaves with silver-white markings. Other popular cultivars include 'Aurifodina', 'Bacciflava', 'Gold Flash', 'Golden Milkboy', and 'Silver Queen'. Zones 6–10.

Ilex × aquipernyi

☼ ✽ ↔ 12 ft (3.5 m) ↑ 20 ft (6 m)

Evergreen tree or shrub of garden origin, hybrid between *I. aquifolium* and *I. pernyi*. Elongated glossy green leaves, strong spines. Red berries. 'San Jose' ★, female form, green leaves with up to 9 spines. Red fruit. Zones 6–10.

Idesia polycarpa

Ilex cassine

Ilex crenata

Ilex × *koehneana*

Ilex cassine

DAHOON HOLLY

☼ ❄ ↔ 15 ft (4.5 m) ↕ 40 ft (12 m)

Evergreen tree native to Cuba and southeastern USA. Pointed or rounded, glossy, dark green leaves with pronounced midrib, leaf edges either smooth or toothed near apex. Yellow or red berries. Zones 6–10.

Ilex cornuta

CHINESE HOLLY, HORNED HOLLY

☼ ❄ ↔ 6–12 ft (1.8–3.5 m) ↕ 6–12 ft (1.8–3.5 m)

Dense, evergreen, rounded shrub native to China and Korea. Oblong dark green leaves, variable spines. Large red berries, long-lasting. '**Burfordii**', free-fruiting female form, red berries, leaves with terminal spines; '**Dwarf Burford**', to 8 ft (2.4 m) high, dense habit, dark red berries. Zones 6–10.

Ilex crenata

JAPANESE HOLLY

☼ ❄ ↔ 12 ft (3.5 m) ↕ 15 ft (4.5 m)

Evergreen shrub or small tree from Korea, Japan, and Sakhalin Island. Small deep green leaves, minutely scalloped. Flowers white; fruit mainly glossy black, sometimes white or yellow. '**Convexa**' (syn. 'Bullata'), female, purple-green stems, abundant black fruit; '**Golden Gem**', compact female, to 3 ft (0.9 m) high, golden yellow leaves, prefers full sun; '**Helleri**', spreading female shrub, dark green leaves, black fruit; '**Ivory Tower**', female, late-ripening white fruit; '**Mariesii**' (syns *I. c.* var. *nummularioides*, *I. mariesii*), very slow-growing cultivar, dark green leaves, black fruit; '**Shiro Fukurin**' (syns 'Fukarin', 'Snow Flake'), upright female, rounded leaves with cream markings, black fruit; and '**Sky Pencil**', narrowly columnar female. Zones 6–10.

Ilex decidua

POSSUMHAW, WINTERBERRY

☼ ❄ ↔ 6–15 ft (1.8–4.5 m) ↕ 6–20 ft (1.8–6 m)

Native to southeastern and central USA. Upright deciduous shrub, rarely a tree. Mid-green leaves, sprout in late spring, oval or egg-shaped, scalloped, crowded on short lateral spurs. Berries orange or red, sometimes yellow, last well into winter. Zones 6–10.

Ilex glabra

GALLBERRY, INKBERRY

☼ ❄ ↔ 10 ft (3 m) ↕ 10 ft (3 m)

Erect evergreen shrub from eastern North America. Glossy dark green leaves, almost smooth-edged, slightly toothed near apex. Berries round, black. Shallow rooting. *I. g.* f. *leucocarpa*, white fruit; '**Ivory Queen**', popular form. *I. g.* '**Compacta**' ★, to 4 ft (1.2 m) high, denser foliage than species, black berries. Zones 3–10.

Ilex × *koehneana*

☼ ❄ ↔ 12 ft (3.5 m) ↕ 20 ft (6 m)

Evergreen shrub or tree, hybrid between *I. aquifolium* and *I. latifolia*. Strongly resembles *I. latifolia*, but more spiny; sometimes wrongly sold as that plant. Zones 7–10.

Ilex × *meserveae*

BLUE HOLLY, HYBRID BLUE HOLLY, MESERVE HOLLY

☼ ❄ ↔ 10 ft (3 m) ↕ 6–15 ft (1.8–4.5 m)

Of garden origin, hybrid of *I. aquifolium* and *I. rugosa*. Small, often blue-green leaves. Red berries on female plants. '**Blue Angel**', compact female shrub, slow growing, to 12 ft (3.5 m) high, royal purple stems, blue-green leaves, least hardy; '**Blue Boy**', male, grows to 10 ft (3 m) high; '**Blue Girl**', female, red berries; '**Blue Maid**', dense female shrub, red berries; '**Blue Prince**', male, lustrous bright green leaves; '**Blue Princess**', female shrub, prolific red berries. Zones 6–10.

Ilex mitis

CAPE HOLLY

☼ ❄ ↔ 20 ft (6 m) ↕ 30 ft (9 m)

Thick-trunked evergreen tree from wet regions of south and east Africa. Smooth-edged leaves, oblong to lance-shaped; juvenile leaves red. White flowers in spring–summer. Red berries. Zones 8–11.

Ilex opaca

AMERICAN HOLLY

☼ ❄ ↔ 35 ft (10 m) ↕ 50 ft (15 m)

From USA. Leaves oblong to elliptic, smooth-edged or spiny, matt green above, yellow-green beneath. White flowers. Red, orange, or yellow berries. '**Hedgeholly**', hardy, compact; '**Morgan Gold**', golden fruit; '**Old Faithful**', large berries, less hardy. Zones 5–9.

Ilex, Hybrid Cultivar, 'Nellie R. Stevens'

Ilex pedunculosa

☼ ❅ ↔ 20 ft (6 m) ↑ 30 ft (9 m)

Evergreen tree from China, Japan, and Taiwan. Leaves glossy, dark green, egg-shaped, pointed tips, smooth-edged, spineless. White flowers; red fruit. Zones 5–9.

Ilex pernyi

PERNY'S HOLLY

☼ ❅ ↔ 12 ft (3.5 m) ↑ 30 ft (9 m)

From Gansu and Hubei Provinces in China. Evergreen shrub, smaller in cultivation. Leaves almost stalkless, dark green, triangular to rectangular. Yellow flowers in late spring. Red berries. Zones 5–10.

Ilex serrata

FINETOOTH HOLLY, JAPANESE WINTERBERRY

☼ ❅ ↔ 10 ft (3 m) ↑ 15 ft (4.5 m)

Native to Japan and China. Bushy deciduous shrub, purple new twigs. Finely toothed, oval, dark green leaves, downy coating on both surfaces. Pink flowers, small red berries. Zones 5–10.

Ilex verticillata

BLACK ALDER, WINTERBERRY

☼ ❅ ↔ 15 ft (4.5 m) ↑ 15 ft (4.5 m)

Deciduous shrub from eastern North America. Bright green leaves, obovate or lance-shaped, toothed, fine downy below. White flowers; red, yellow, or orange berries. *I. v.* f. *aurantiaca*, orange berries. *I. v.* 'Winter Red' ★, female, dark green leaves, red berries. Zones 3–9.

Ilex vomitoria

CAROLINA TEA, YAUPON

☼/❉ ❅ ↔ 12 ft (3.5 m) ↑ 20 ft (6 m)

Evergreen shrub or small tree native to southeastern USA and Mexico. Glossy dark green leaves, elliptic to egg-shaped, scalloped

edges. White flowers, red berries. 'Nana', to 3 ft (0.9 m) high; 'Pendula', lax branches, clear red fruit. Zones 6–10.

Ilex Hybrid Cultivars

☼ ❅ ↔ 5–15 ft (1.5–4.5 m) ↑ 8–20 ft (2.4–6 m)

Hollies extensively hybridized. 'China Boy', very hardy, male, grows quickly to 8 ft (2.4 m); 'China Girl', very hardy, evergreen female, masses of bright red berries; 'Ebony Magic', evergreen female, leaves with wavy margin and up to 22 spines, leaf stems almost black, orange-red berries; 'John T. Morris', male, dark evergreen foliage, 'Nellie R. Stevens', evergreen female, orange-red berries; 'September Gem', evergreen female, narrow dark green leaves, red berries; 'Sparkleberry', deciduous female, bright red berries. Zones 6–10.

ILLICIUM

This genus of over 40 evergreen shrubs and trees in the star-anise (Illiciaceae) family is found in moist shaded areas of India, East Asia, and the Americas. Leaves and flowers are fragrant, and members of the genus supply aromatic oils used in some perfumes. *I. verum* is the source of the Chinese spice star-anise. These trees were originally included in the same genus as magnolias because of their resemblance to them. Flowers range in color from cream to reddish purple and are followed by star-shaped fruit. The genus name comes from the Latin for "allurement," in reference to the perfume of some species. **CULTIVATION:** *Illicium* species will survive in full sun but do best in a sheltered position out of direct sunlight, in a moist, well-drained, acid soil. Propagate from half-hardened cuttings taken in summer or by layering in autumn.

Illicium floridanum, fruit

Illicium anisatum

ANISE SHRUB, JAPANESE ANISE, JAPANESE STAR-ANISE

❉ ❅ ↔ 20 ft (6 m) ↑ 25 ft (8 m)

Conical evergreen shrub from China, Taiwan, and Japan. Aromatic wood, leaves, bark. Greenish yellow flowers in mid-spring. Fruit woody, poisonous. Variegated form available. Zones 7–11.

Illicium floridanum

FLORIDA ANISE TREE, POLECAT TREE, PURPLE ANISE

❉ ❅ ↔ 8 ft (2.4 m) ↑ 10 ft (3 m)

Aromatic, bushy, evergreen shrub from southeastern States of USA. Slightly furrowed, smooth, dark brown trunk. Slender, leathery, deep green leaves. Showy, star-shaped, reddish purple flowers in late spring–early summer. 'Album', white flowers; 'Variegatum', variegated leaves; 'Woodland Ruby' ★, red-pink flowers. Zones 8–11.

INDIGOFERA

The source of the purple-blue dye indigo, this genus in the pea-flower subfamily of the legume (Fabaceae) family includes some 700 species of perennials, shrubs, and trees that are widespread in the tropics and subtropics. Leaves vary, but they are typically pinnate, often made up of many small leaflets. The flowers are primarily in pink, mauve, and purple shades, carried in long racemes or spikes. They usually open in summer but may occur year-round in mild climates. Small seed pods follow.

CULTIVATION: The shrubby species are usually neat bushes, often deciduous, that vary in hardiness depending on their origins. They generally grow best in full sun with light well-drained soil and ample summer moisture. If necessary, prune after flowering or in late winter. Propagate from seed or half-hardened cuttings. Many species produce suckers that can be replanted.

Illicium anisatum

Indigofera australis
AUSTRALIAN INDIGO
☼ ❄ ↔6 ft (1.8 m) ↑6 ft (1.8 m)
Evergreen from Australia. Leaves pinnate, 9 to 21 blue-green leaflets, to 1 in (25 mm) long, hairy underside. Racemes of mauve-pink to magenta-red flowers in summer. Brown seed pods. Zones 9–11.

Indigofera decora ★
☼ ✳ ↔4 ft (1.2 m) ↑30 in (75 cm)
Widely cultivated, deciduous, spreading, suckering shrub from China and Japan. Leaves to 8 in (20 cm) long, 25 to 40 leaflets. Large racemes of light pink flowers in summer. Zones 6–10.

Indigofera heterantha
syn. *Indigofera gerardiana*
☼ ✳ ↔8 ft (2.4 m) ↑8 ft (2.4 m)
Deciduous shrub from northwestern Himalayas, smaller in cultivation. Densely twiggy plant, short pinnate leaves. Massed racemes of bright pink to light red flowers in summer. Zones 7–10.

Indigofera kirilowii
☼ ✳ ↔3–6 ft (0.9–1.8 m) ↑2–5 ft (0.6–1.5 m)
Deciduous shrub from Korea, nearby parts of China, and Kyushu, Japan. Leaves pinnate, bright green, 13 leaflets. Smothered in short racemes of rose pink flowers in spring–early summer. Zones 5–10.

Indigofera potaninii
☼ ✳ ↔4 ft (1.2 m) ↑3–5 ft (0.9–1.5 m)
Sometimes sold as *I. amblyantha*. True species is deciduous shrub from southwestern China. Differs from *I. amblyantha* in shorter leaves, fewer leaflets, densely hairy below. Larger flowers, usually mauve, in summer–autumn. Zones 5–9.

IOCHROMA
These large-leafed evergreen shrubs from Central America and Andean South America have a rather lax habit with long brittle branches. Although there are around 15 species within this genus, only 5 or 6 are generally used in horticulture. The soft foliage of most species is a downy mid-green. In common with other members of the nightshade (Solanaceae) family, the late summer flowers, usually held in clusters of drooping tubular blooms, are in shades of purple, orange, red, or white.

CULTIVATION: These plants need a sunny position with wind protection to ensure their quick-growing soft-stemmed branches are not

damaged. Plant in well-drained moisture-retentive soil and ensure they are given ample water during summer. Suitable for pot culture in cooler areas, they can be pruned to shape in early spring without undue loss of blossom. Propagate from cuttings or seed.

Iochroma coccineum
☼ ❄ ↔6 ft (1.8 m) ↑10 ft (3 m)
Soft-stemmed shrub from Central America. Soft, gray-green, felty leaves. Small clusters of tubular scarlet flowers with yellow throat in summer. Zones 9–11.

Iochroma cyaneum
syn. *Iochroma tubulosum*
☼ ✳ ↔5 ft (1.5 m) ↑10 ft (3 m)
Quick-growing shrub from northwestern South America. Large felty leaves, sometimes partly obscuring purple tubular flowers held in large pendent clusters in summer. Zones 8–11.

Iochroma grandiflorum
☼ ❄ ↔6 ft (1.8 m) ↑8 ft (2.4 m)
From Ecuador. Downy green leaves. Large purple flowers, in clusters of 5 or 6, in summer–autumn. Zones 9–11.

Indigofera decora

Iochroma grandiflorum

ISOPOGON

The majority of the 35 species in this southern Australian genus of the protea (Proteaceae) family are found in Western Australia. They are attractive evergreen shrubs with tough dissected foliage and showy flowers that form dense globular heads, generally in shades of yellow and pink. The rounded or egg-shaped cone-like fruiting heads are usually borne terminally and persist for a long time, giving some members of the genus the common names of cone bush or drumsticks.

CULTIVATION: These plants like full sun and light well-drained soil. Some species are best suited to winter rainfall areas, especially those from Western Australia. Pruning is not usually necessary, except when young to form the basis of a well-branched shrub. Most species will tolerate occasional light frosts. Propagate from cuttings or from seed, which may be slow to germinate.

Isopogon formosus   *Itea ilicifolia*

Isopogon anemonifolius
DRUMSTICKS
☼ ❀ ↔4 ft (1.2 m) ↑6 ft (1.8 m)

Erect bushy shrub found in eastern Australia. Flat dull green leaves divided into 3 segments, then again divided and lobed, with purplish tinge. Soft yellow flowers in terminal rounded heads, 1½ in (35 mm) across, in spring–early summer. Zones 9–11.

Isopogon dubius
☼ ❀ ↔5 ft (1.5 m) ↑5 ft (1.5 m)

Bushy upright shrub from Western Australia. Flat, grayish green, prickly leaves, divided into 3 segments. Rose pink flowers, in terminal heads, in late winter–spring. Zones 9–11.

Isopogon formosus ★
ROSE CONE FLOWER
☼ ❀ ↔6 ft (1.8 m) ↑6 ft (1.8 m)

Erect or spreading shrub from Western Australia. Narrow prickly leaves divided into short cylindrical segments. Mauve-pink flowers in cone-like heads, 2½ in (6 cm) wide, in winter–spring. Zones 9–11.

ITEA
SWEETSPIRE

Very attractive but not widely cultivated, the 10 evergreen and deciduous shrubs and small trees in this genus present an interesting

Isopogon dubius

combination of foliage and flowers. Although they are members of the gooseberry (Grossulariaceae) family, their foliage is often more reminiscent of members of the holly (Aquifoliaceae) family. Found naturally in Asia, with a sole eastern North American representative, the evergreens offer dark lustrous leaves throughout the year, while the deciduous species have brilliant autumn foliage color. The catkin-like racemes are not colorful and are really more of a novelty for their contrast with the foliage.

CULTIVATION: Frost hardiness varies, but the commonly grown species are reasonably tough and will thrive in most well-drained soils with a position in full sun or partial shade. They are, however, not drought tolerant and need ample summer moisture. Propagate from seed or from half-hardened cuttings.

Itea ilicifolia
HOLLYLEAF SWEETSPIRE
☼ ❀ ↔10 ft (3 m) ↑15 ft (4.5 m)

Widely cultivated evergreen shrub from western China. Narrow erect habit. Deep green holly-like leaves, 2–4 in (5–10 cm) long, edged with small spines. Cream to pale yellow flowers, on racemes to 15 in (38 cm) long, honey scented, in summer. Zones 7–10.

Itea virginica
SWEETSPIRE, VIRGINIA WILLOW
☼ ❀ ↔5 ft (1.5 m) ↑4–10 ft (1.2–3 m)

Deciduous clump-forming shrub from eastern North America. Arching stems, 2–4 in (5–10 cm) long, serrated-edged leaves, develop vivid red and orange tones in autumn. Racemes of tiny, honey-scented, cream flowers, 2–6 in (5–15 cm) long, erect rather than pendulous. 'Henry's Garnet', well-known cultivar. Zones 5–9.

IXORA
JUNGLE FLAME

Common throughout the wet tropics, this genus of about 400 evergreen shrubs and small trees belongs to the madder (Rubiaceae) family. The genus name is from the Portuguese name for the Hindu deity, Siva, to whom the blooms are dedicated. The flowers are usually produced in showy clusters, ranging from scarlet, pink, or yellow to white, and are sometimes fragrant. Attractive glossy leaves and a compact habit make them suitable for containers or massed plantings. The 1- or 2-seeded drupe, mostly red, ripens to black. CULTIVATION: Frost tender, many species will not tolerate a temperature much below 55°F (13°C), and prefer bright indirect sun. The soil should be friable, with added sharp sand and leaf mold. Pinch out the tips when young to encourage branching, and prune older plants after flowering. Propagate from seed in spring, or from half-hardened cuttings, taken from non-flowering shoots, in summer.

Ixora casei

☀ ✤ ↔ 8 ft (2.4 m) ↕ 12 ft (3.5 m)

Medium evergreen shrub from Caroline Islands in tropical Pacific. Large glossy leaves, to 12 in (30 cm) long. Very large compact flowerheads carry numerous, small, orange to red flowers in summer. 'Super King' bears large vivid red flowers. Zones 10–12.

Ixora chinensis

☀ ✤ ↔ 5 ft (1.5 m) ↕ 6 ft (1.8 m)

Small, rounded, evergreen shrub from tropical parts of East Asia, particularly China and Taiwan. Glossy deep green leaves. Flowers in very large, showy, terminal clusters, to 4 in (10 cm) across, bright orange, in late spring–autumn. 'Nora Grant', coral red flowers; 'Prince of Orange' ★, prolific orange-red flowers. Zones 10–12.

Ixora chinensis 'Prince of Orange'

Ixora coccinea

FLAME OF THE WOODS

☀ ✤ ↔ 8 ft (2.4 m) ↕ 8 ft (2.4 m)

Bushy rounded shrub from tropical Asia, mainly India and Sri Lanka. Leaves glossy, dark green. Small brilliant orange-red flowers, in large round clusters, most of year in tropics. Zones 11–12.

Ixora Hybrid Cultivars

☀ ✤ ↔ 1–3 ft (0.3–0.9 m) ↕ 1–6 ft (0.3–1.8 m)

Numerous *Ixora* hybrid cultivars, most derived from *I. coccinea*. 'Exotica', bright red flowers fade to orange, creating two-toned flowerhead; 'Frances Perry', deep yellow flowers; 'Fraseri', vivid salmon pink flowers; 'Herrera's White', white flowers; 'Orange Glow', bright orange flowers; 'Pink Delight', pink flowers; 'Rosea', rose pink flowers; 'Sunkist', dwarf shrub to 3 ft (0.9 m), small glossy leaves, flowers of apricot-yellow, age to brick red; 'Sunny Gold', orange-amber flowers; 'Thai King', orange-red flowers. Other cultivars include 'Aurora' and 'Florida Sunset'. Zones 11–12.

JACARANDA

The genus comprises about 50 species of deciduous and evergreen trees and shrubs belonging to the trumpet-vine (Bignoniaceae) family. They are native to the drier areas of tropical and subtropical Central and South America and have elegant, fern-like, bipinnate leaves, some pinnate or simple. Mauve-blue, rarely pink or white, funnel- or bell-shaped flowers in terminal or axillary panicles appear in spring–summer.
CULTIVATION: Jacarandas will grow quickly in fertile well-drained soil in full sun. Protect from the wind and frost when young.

They are relatively frost hardy once established. Pruning is not necessary for outdoor specimens. Water freely in the growing season and sparingly in winter. They are shallow-rooted heavy feeders, and shrubs planted nearby may suffer. Propagation is from seed in late winter or early spring, and from half-hardened cuttings taken in summer.

Jacaranda cuspidifolia

☀ ❋ ↔ 30 ft (9 m) ↕ 15–40 ft (4.5–12 m)

Native to Brazil, Argentina, Bolivia, and Paraguay. Large leaves with up to 20 pairs of leaflets on each pinna. Large bright blue-violet flowers in big clusters. Fruit nearly spherical, white to pale brown. Zones 10–11.

Jacaranda mimosifolia

BLUE HAZE TREE, BRAZILIAN ROSEWOOD, FERN TREE, JACARANDA

☀ ❋ ↔ 20–35 ft (6–10 m) ↕ 25–50 ft (8–15 m)

Fast-growing deciduous tree from drier areas of South America. Mid-green bipinnate leaves may turn rich yellow in late winter before falling. Terminal clusters of hanging, bell-shaped, mauve-blue flowers on mostly leafless branches in late spring–early summer. 'White Christmas', white flowers. Zones 10–11.

JASMINUM (see page 779)

Jasminum humile

ITALIAN JASMINE, ITALIAN YELLOW JASMINE

☀/❋ ❄ ↔ 12 ft (3.5 m) ↕ 12 ft (3.5 m)

Evergreen or semi-evergreen shrub from Middle East to China. Short pinnate leaves, up to 7 leaflets. Clusters of yellow flowers in summer. 'Revolutum', fragrant, with large leaves. Zones 8–10.

Jacaranda mimosifolia

Jasminum nudiflorum

Jatropha multifida

Jasminum mesnyi
PRIMROSE JASMINE, YELLOW JASMINE
☼/◐ ❄ ↔ 10 ft (3 m) ↑ 10 ft (3 m)
Evergreen sprawling shrub native to western China. Clump of arching cane-like stems. Leaves trifoliate, semi-glossy, bright green. Flowers unscented, bright yellow, semi-double, in summer. Zones 8–10.

Jasminum nudiflorum
WINTER JASMINE
☼/◐ ❄ ↔ 10 ft (3 m) ↑ 10 ft (3 m)
Sprawling deciduous shrub from northern China. Mass of slightly arched, whippy, green canes, dark green trifoliate leaves. Bright yellow blooms, in winter, when all else is bare. Zones 6–9.

JATROPHA
This variable genus of the euphorbia (Euphorbiaceae) family comprises some 170 species of succulent perennials and evergreen or deciduous shrubs, rarely trees. All species contain a milky latex that may irritate the skin. They are found in tropical to warm-temperate regions of the world, mainly Central and South America. Leaves are usually palmately lobed, though some are lobeless. Small clusters of purple, yellow, scarlet, or red flowers occur in summer. All plant parts are poisonous.
CULTIVATION: These plants appreciate a fertile, well-drained, sandy soil and full sun, but most will tolerate part-shade. Frost tender, in temperate zones they can be grown in a greenhouse. Place half-hardened cuttings in cool shade to allow the cutting ends to dry before rooting, or propagate from seed in spring or summer.

Jatropha integerrima
syns *Jatropha hastata, J. pandurifolia*
PEREGRINA, SPICY JATROPHA
☼ ❄ ↔ 4–8 ft (1.2–2.4 m) ↑ 10–20 ft (3–6 m)
Spreading evergreen tree native to Cuba, Hispaniola, and Puerto Rico. Leaves 3-lobed to fiddle-shaped, rich green, bronze underside. Small, funnel-shaped, 5-petalled, rose red flowers throughout year, but mostly in warm weather. Seeds and sap poisonous. Zones 10–12.

Jatropha multifida
CORAL PLANT, PHYSIC NUT
☼ ❄ ↔ 10 ft (3 m) ↑ 12 ft (3.5 m)
Large evergreen shrub or small tree from Mexico to Brazil. Rounded leaves, deeply divided into 7 to 11 blades, dark green above, whitish below. Small scarlet flowers on green or red stalks, above foliage, in summer. Egg-shaped fruit contains up to 3 seeds. Zones 10–12.

JUGLANS
The walnuts, a genus of the Juglandaceae family, comprise about 20 species of deciduous trees. They are distributed over the temperate zones of the Americas, southeastern Europe, and Southeast Asia. They have alternate compound leaves and monoecious flowers, borne in spring. The fruit is a hard-shelled nut enclosed in a fleshy green drupe, the kernels being prized as food.
CULTIVATION: They thrive on deep, alluvial, well-drained soil with a high organic content, and an assured water supply, in a cool humid climate. Severely prune after 1 year to force strong single-trunk growth, then stop at 12 ft (3.5 m) or so to induce lateral branches. Seed can be collected as soon as it is ripe in early autumn and stored in cool conditions until it is sown in early spring.

Juglans ailanthifolia
syn. *Juglans sieboldiana*
JAPANESE WALNUT
☼ ❄ ↔ 40 ft (12 m) ↑ 50 ft (15 m)
Upright tree from Japan. Leaves 11 to 17 leaflets, covered in dark red fine hairs. Bark striped pale and dark gray. Male catkins 6–12 in (15–30 cm) long, female flowers deep red. Fruits covered in adhesive down. Zones 4–9.

Juglans cinerea

Juglans californica
☼ ❄ ↔ 30 ft (9 m) ↑ 30 ft (9 m)
Native of southern California, USA. Large shrub or small tree, attractive leaves composed of 11 to 15 lance-shaped leaflets. Zones 7–10.

Juglans cinerea
BUTTERNUT, BUTTERNUT WALNUT, WHITE WALNUT
☼ ❄ ↔ 50 ft (15 m) ↑ 60 ft (18 m)
From New Brunswick, Canada, to Georgia, USA. Fast-growing species, usually smaller in cultivation.

Juglans ailanthifolia

Shoots sticky. Leaves oblong, notched edges, hairy, yellow-green. Fruit solitary or in clusters. Can be short lived. Zones 4–9.

JUNIPERUS

This genus consists of some 60 generally slow-growing evergreen trees and shrubs in the cypress (Cupressaceae) family, occurring in the Northern Hemisphere. All species are long lived, performing particularly well on alkaline soils. Juvenile leaves are awl-shaped (needle-like), and adult leaves are scale-like and stem-clasping. When crushed, the leaves of most species are aromatic. The small, fleshy, berry-like fruit are actually cones that ripen to blue-black or reddish. Usually separate male and female plants are found.
CULTIVATION: Although drought tolerant and tough, these plants are susceptible to fungal attack, needing an open airy situation. Well-drained soils are essential. Regular light pruning maintains shape, but do not cut bare wood. Propagation from fresh seed is best, although named cultivars should be either grafted or grown from a cutting in winter.

Juniperus chinensis

CHINESE JUNIPER
☼ ❄ ↔ 15 ft (4.5 m) ↑ 30 ft (9 m)
Native to China and Japan. Variable species in habit and size. Blunt-tipped adult leaves, prickly juvenile leaves, both on lower branches and within tree. Berries small, round, blue-green. *J. c.* var. *sargentii*, low growing. *J. c.* 'Aurea', golden adult leaves, yellowish green juvenile leaves, to 20 ft (6 m); 'Blaauw', vigorous shrub to 5 ft (1.5 m); 'Expansa Variegata', dwarf spreading shrub to 3 ft (0.9 m); 'Femina', good bonsai subject; 'Kaizuka', large upright shrub or small tree, spreading branches; 'Keteleeri' ★, distinctive spiralled habit of blunt-tipped closely held scales; 'Mountbatten', dense columnar habit, gray-green awl-shaped leaves; 'Oblonga', inner leaves dark green, awl-shaped, prickly, outer leaves scale-like; 'Olympia', small conical tree; 'Parsonii', dwarf shrub eventually mounding to 3 ft (0.9 m) in center; 'Shoosmith', conical tree, bright green foliage; 'Spartan', columnar form, dark green foliage; 'Variegata', mostly juvenile leaves on long branchlets when young, then progressively develops adult leaves, at all stages irregularly flecked with creamy yellow or white. Zones 4–9.

Juniperus communis 'Pendula'

Juniperus osteosperma, in the wild, Utah, USA

Juniperus communis

COMMON JUNIPER
☼ ❄ ↔ 3–15 ft (0.9–4.5 m) ↑ 20 ft (6 m)
Variable evergreen shrub or small tree widespread in Northern Hemisphere. Narrow-columnar in mild areas, tendency to spread in colder climates. Silver-backed leaves, needle-like, prickly; fruit green ripening to glossy black with whitish bloom. *J. c.* var. *montana* (syn. *J. c.* 'Nana'), slow-growing ground cover. *J. c.* 'Compressa', compact, narrow, slow-growing column to 3 ft (0.9 m); 'Depressa Aurea' ★, wide-spreading ground cover to 2 ft (0.6 m) high, foliage dense, brownish green, becoming more bronze in winter; 'Depressed Star', rounded spreading habit, light green foliage; 'Hibernica' (syn. 'Stricta'), slender column to 10 ft (3 m) high, dense foliage, prominent silvery reverse; 'Pendula', graceful weeping branches. Zones 2–8.

Juniperus conferta

SHORE JUNIPER
☼ ❄ ↔ 5–8 ft (1.5–2.4 m) ↑ 2 ft (0.6 m)
From Japan and Russian island of Sakhalin. Wide-spreading, fast-growing, prostrate, salt tolerant. Light green to blue-green foliage, very prickly and dense. Small berry-like fruit ripen to brown. 'Blue Lagoon' and 'Blue Pacific', bluer foliage; 'Emerald Sea', gray-green foliage; 'Sunsplash', green and gold variegated foliage. Zones 5–9.

Juniperus deppeana

ALLIGATOR JUNIPER, CHEQUERBOARD JUNIPER
☼ ❄ ↔ 7 ft (2 m) ↑ 20 ft (6 m)
Broad gray-barked tree from Arizona and New Mexico, USA, and northern Mexico. Blue-green leaves. *J. d.* var. *pachyphlaea*, sometimes sold as 'Conspicua', conical, coarse-textured, Mexican tree, silvery gray leaves, distinctive red-brown bark in square plates. Foliage of adult type. Performs best in cool dry conditions. Zones 7–9.

Juniperus horizontalis

CREEPING JUNIPER, HORIZONTAL JUNIPER
☼ ❄ ↔ 12 ft (3.5 m) ↑ 18 in (45 cm)
From northern North America, found on coastal cliffs and stony hillsides. Vigorous ground-hugging shrub with long trailing branches. Leaves gray-green or bluish, often with purplish tinge in winter. 'Bar Harbor', mat forming, blue-green foliage, tips turn mauve in winter; 'Blue Chip', blue-green leaves, variegated gold; 'Douglasii', prostrate to 2 ft (0.6 m) high, blue-green foliage turns purplish in autumn–winter; 'Prince of Wales', mat forming; 'Repens', blue-green leaves; 'Wiltonii', blue-foliaged, prostrate, trailing. Zones 4–10.

Juniperus osteosperma

UTAH JUNIPER
☼ ❄ ↔ 20 ft (6 m) ↑ 12–20 ft (3.5–6 m)
From eastern California to Montana, and New Mexico, USA. Short thick trunk, forking low, broad irregular crown. Dull olive-green foliage, small red-brown cones. Zones 4–9.

Juniperus sabina

Juniperus × *pfitzeriana*

syn. *Juniperus* × *media*

☼ ❋ ↔ 5–15 ft (1.5–4.5 m) ↕ 4–10 ft (1.2–3 m)

Collection of garden hybrids derived mainly from *J. chinensis*. Adult and juvenile leaves usually present simultaneously. Adult leaves stem-clasping scales; juvenile leaves triangular, sharp, protruding. Branches wide spreading, lifted just above horizontal. Dull green, adult, scale-like leaves release unpleasant scent when crushed. Many have white or blue-black fruit, globular or rounded. '**Golden Sunset**', low-growing shrub; '**Pfitzeriana Aurea**', greenish yellow foliage; '**Wilhelm Pfitzer**', vigorous, spreading, shade-tolerant shrub with sturdy ascending branches and pendulous tips, leaves mostly green and scale-like. Zones 4–10.

Juniperus procumbens

BONIN ISLAND JUNIPER, CREEPING JUNIPER, JAPANESE GARDEN JUNIPER

☼ ❋ ↔ 12 ft (3.5 m) ↕ 30 in (75 cm)

From western China. Stiff and wiry habit, prickly blue-green leaves. Small berry-like cones, brown-green, each contains 2 or 3 seeds. '**Nana**', smaller leaves, softer texture, more conical habit. Zones 4–9.

Juniperus recurva

COFFIN JUNIPER, DROOPING JUNIPER, HIMALAYAN JUNIPER

☼ ❋ ↔ 15 ft (4.5 m) ↕ 30 ft (9 m)

From southwestern China, Myanmar, and Himalayas. Weeping sprays of aromatic foliage, in whorls of 3 needle-like gray-green leaves. Bark peels off in reddish brown strips. Fruit small, round, fleshy, berry-like, ripens to glossy blue-black. *J. r.* var. *coxii*, slow growing, with smaller leaves. Zones 7–9.

Juniperus sabina

SAVIN JUNIPER

☼ ❋ ↔ 15 ft (4.5 m) ↕ 12 ft (3.5 m)

Variable, spreading, self-layering species from southern and central Europe. Dark green foliage with disagreeable odor when crushed.

Leaves awl-shaped on young plants, scale-like on adult. Fruit small, ovoid, blue-black berry with whitish bloom, with 1 to 3 seeds. '**Calgary Carpet**', low-growing form; '**Skandia**', mid-green foliage; '**Tamariscifolia**', spreading, green to blue-green foliage. Zones 4–9.

Juniperus scopulorum

ROCKY MOUNTAINS JUNIPER

☼ ❋ ↔ 15 ft (4.5 m) ↕ 30 ft (9 m)

From western North America and Texas, USA. Small tree or shrub with sturdy spreading branches; tightly held, scale-like leaves, light to blue-green. Small round fruit. '**Blue Arrow**', pencil-shaped, blue-green foliage, '**Blue Heaven**', blue-green foliage; '**Horizontalis**', spreading, blue-green foliage; '**Mountaineer**', bright green foliage; '**Repens**', prostrate, blue-green foliage; '**Skyrocket**', very narrow columnar form to 10 ft (3 m) tall, silvery blue foliage, arguably narrowest of all conifers; '**Tabletop**', spreading, blue-green foliage; '**Tolleson's Blue Weeping**', pendulous; '**Wichita Blue**', conical, blue-gray foliage. Zones 5–9.

Juniperus squamata

HOLLYWOOD JUNIPER, SINGLESEED JUNIPER, SQUAMATA JUNIPER

☼ ❋ ↔ 15 ft (4.5 m) ↕ 2–20 ft (0.6–6 m)

Extremely variable species from central Asia and China. May be mound-like shrub, small shrubby tree, or prostrate ground cover. Bark red-brown and flaky. Dense, juvenile-type, awl-shaped leaves, grayish green to silvery blue-green, upper surface marked pale green or white. '**Blue Carpet**', spreading form, blue-green foliage; '**Blue Star**', rounded shrub, very blue, small, dense; '**Chinese Silver**', medium to large, dense, multi-stemmed shrub, leaves strongly silvery blue; '**Meyeri**', open vase shape, leaves very blue when young, turning dark green with age. Zones 4–9.

Juniperus virginiana

EASTERN RED CEDAR, PENCIL CEDAR, RED CEDAR

☼ ❋ ↔ 12–20 ft (3.5–6 m) ↕ 40 ft (12 m)

From central and eastern North America. Upright tree, becoming more open with age. Bark reddish brown, peels in long strips. Small, adult, closely held scale leaves with pointed tip, glaucous green, purplish in winter. Fragrant timber traditionally used for casings of lead pencils. '**Burkii**' ★, narrowly pyramidal habit, blue-foliaged shrub becoming steel-blue in cold winters; '**Manhattan Blue**', popular pencil-shaped cultivar. Zones 2–8.

Juniperus × *pfitzeriana* '*Golden Sunset*'

JUSTICIA

syns *Adhatoda, Beloperone, Drejerella, Jacobinia, Libonia*

This largely tropical and subtropical American genus of the acanthus (Acanthaceae) family encompasses more than 400 species of perennials, subshrubs, and shrubs. The shrubby species are evergreen, their leaves usually simple pointed ovals in opposite pairs, sometimes hairy or with a velvety surface. The flowers are clustered, sometimes in upright panicles at the branch tips, or in looser, more open heads. The true flowers are often small, the flowerheads made colorful and showy by large bracts.

CULTIVATION: A feature of gardens in warm climates and popular house and greenhouse plants elsewhere, most justicias do not tolerate severe frosts. Some tolerate being frosted to the ground, reshooting in spring, but most need mild winter conditions. Justicias prefer moist well-drained soil in sun or partial shade with shelter from strong winds. Water regularly during the growth period. Keep compact by regular tip pinching or a light trimming after flowering. Propagate from seed or half-hardened cuttings.

Justicia adhatoda

syn. *Adhatoda vasica*

ADHATODA, MALABAR NUT, PHYSIC NUT

☀/◐ ❄ ↔ 3–5 ft (0.9–1.5 m) ↑ 6–8 ft (1.8–2.4 m)

Evergreen shrub, native to southern India and Sri Lanka. Erect growth habit; mid-green lance-shaped leaves. Flowers white, red to purple veining, in summer. Powder-coated leaves, flowers, roots, and seed pods used in Indian medicine. Zones 10–12.

Justicia aurea

☀ ❄ ↔ 3 ft (0.9 m) ↑ 3–5 ft (0.9–1.5 m)

From Mexico and Central America. Similar to better-known *J. carnea*, but foliage slightly lighter green; heads of yellow flowers rather than pink of *J. carnea*. Flowers in late summer–autumn. Often reshoots if foliage cut back by frost. Zones 9–12.

Justicia brandegeeana

syns *Beloperone guttata, Drejerella guttata*

SHRIMP PLANT

☀/◐ ❄ ↔ 26 in (65 cm) ↑ 36 in (90 cm)

Evergreen shrub from Mexico. Curved array of overlapping pink and yellow bracts enclose small white flowers with red markings. Elliptical downy leaves, to 3 in (8 cm) long. 'Fruit Cocktail', yellow-green bracts. Zones 9–11.

Justicia carnea

BRAZILIAN PLUME

☀/◐ ❄ ↔ 3 ft (0.9 m) ↑ 3–6 ft (0.9–1.8 m)

Evergreen shrub from northern South America. Leaves velvet-textured, conspicuously veined. Plume-like spikes of deep pink flowers, at branch tips, throughout year, especially late summer. Pinch back when young to keep compact. Zones 10–12.

Justicia rizzinii

syns *Jacobinia pauciflora, Libonia floribunda*

☀/◐ ❄ ↔ 10–22 in (25–55 cm) ↑ 10–22 in (25–55 cm)

Hardy, densely twiggy shrub from Brazil. Small, leathery, oval leaves, often with bronze tints in winter, also main flowering season. 'Firefly', heavier flowering, scarlet red flowers with glowing golden yellow tips, flared tubes, 1 in (25 mm) long. Zones 9–11.

Justicia spicigera

syn. *Justicia ghiesbreghtiana*

MEXICAN HONEYSUCKLE, MOHINTLI

☀/◐ ❄ ↔ 5 ft (1.5 m) ↑ 6 ft (1.8 m)

Found from Mexico to Colombia. Upright shrub, deeply veined oval leaves to 6 in (15 cm) long. Leaves with fine down on underside, smooth upper surface. Flowers to 1½ in (35 mm) long, in warmer months, in bright shades of orange to red. Zones 10–12.

KALMIA

A genus of 7 species of shrubs in the heath (Ericaceae) family, most are evergreen. They are native to northeastern USA; a single species occurs in Cuba. They are grown for their attractive foliage and their showy flowers, ranging in color from pale pink to deep red. Leaves are smooth, opposite or alternate, sometimes found in whorls, deep green above, paler beneath, occasionally stalkless. Flowers are generally carried in terminal corymbs. The fruit is a small capsule containing very small seeds.

CULTIVATION: Kalmias are at home in slightly acid, peaty soil but resent clay and lime in any form. Adequate water is needed on hot summer days. Dappled shade under tall deciduous trees in a cool moist climate is ideal. Little pruning is necessary apart from the removal of spent flowers. Propagate from seed. Firm tip cuttings taken in late summer through to winter may be struck; alternatively, simple layers can be set down in autumn and severed a year later.

Kalmia angustifolia

SHEEP LAUREL

☀ ❄ ↔ 5 ft (1.5 m) ↑ 3 ft (0.9 m)

From northeastern USA. Dwarf shrub, slowly spreading to dense bush. Leaves smooth, ovate-oblong, to ¾ in (18 mm) long. Pinkish red flowers in mid-summer. All plant parts poisonous. 'Rubra', flowers over long period; 'Rubra Nana', dwarf form. Zones 2–9.

Justicia carnea

Justicia rizzinii 'Firefly'

Kalmia angustifolia

Kalopanax septemlobus

Kerria japonica 'Pleniflora'

Koelreuteria bipinnata

Kalmia latifolia

CALICO BUSH, MOUNTAIN LAUREL

☼ ❄ ↔ 10 ft (3 m) ↑ 10 ft (3 m)

Dense shrub from eastern Canada to Gulf of Mexico. Leaves dark green, smooth above, paler beneath, to ½ in (12 mm) long. Flower buds crimped on edge; open to shell pink, purplish markings inside. 'Carousel', mid-pink flowers; 'Clementine Churchill', rosy pink flowers; 'Elf', dwarf with faded pink flowers; 'Minuet', pink flowers with purplish margins; 'Myrtifolia', pale pink blooms; 'Nipmuck', dark red buds open to almost white; 'Olympic Fire', rich crimson flowers; 'Ostbo Red' ★, vivid red buds open to faded pink; 'Pink Charm', crimson flowers; 'Silver Dollar', white flowers with red anthers; 'Snow Drift', white blooms. Zones 3–9.

Kalmia polifolia

EASTERN BOG LAUREL, SWAMP LAUREL

☼ ❄ ↔ 3 ft (0.9 m) ↑ 2 ft (0.6 m)

Dwarf shrub from northeastern America. Thin leaves, dark glossy green above, silvery gray beneath. Vivid pinkish purple flowers, in large terminal clusters, in early spring. Zones 3–9.

KALOPANAX

This genus of the ivy (Araliaceae) family contains a lone species of tree native to the cool deciduous forests of eastern Asia. It has scattered stout prickles on the trunk and branches, especially on the young new growth. The leaves are large and palmately lobed. The flowerheads of small white flowers are followed by ornamental clusters of bluish black berries.

CULTIVATION: Despite its tropical appearance, this hardy species should be grown in deep, moist, fertile soil. It will grow in sun or part-shade and makes an attractive specimen or shade tree. Propagation is from seed or half-hardened cuttings taken in summer.

Kalopanax septemlobus

syn. *Kalopanax pictus*

CASTOR ARALIA, HARA-GIRI, TREE ARALIA

☼ ❄ ↔ 10–30 ft (3–9 m) ↑ 20–60 ft (6–18 m)

Round-headed, sparingly branched tree. Leaves on long stalks, 5 to 7 pointed palmate lobes, finely toothed margins, dark green above, lighter below. Large rounded clusters of small flowers in late summer. *K. s.* var. *maximowiczii*, lance-shaped leaf lobes. Zones 5–10.

KERRIA

This genus with a single species in the rose (Rosaceae) family is native to China and Japan. Leaves are alternate, toothed, egg-shaped, and dark green. It is a low, suckering, deciduous shrub with bright yellow 5-petalled flowers, 2 in (5 cm) across, and graceful cane-like stems with rather sparse but attractive foliage.

CULTIVATION: It will grow in any moderately fertile soil with free drainage, preferring a sunny or lightly shaded position and a cool moist climate. Several of the older flowering shoots should be removed at the base after flowering each year to make room for new shoots; no further pruning is necessary. It is easily propagated; soft-tip or half-hardened cuttings taken in spring or summer strike readily, or stems can be layered and lifted a year later.

Kerria japonica

☼/☼ ❄ ↔ 5 ft (1.5 m) ↑ 6 ft (1.8 m)

Found in mountains of Japan and in southwestern China. Bright green leaves, simple and alternate, 2–4 in (5–10 cm) long, prominent veins, downy beneath, turn yellow in autumn. Deep yellow flowers, on short terminal and axillary spurs, in early–late spring. 'Pleniflora' (syn. 'Flore Pleno'), double flowers, taller, more vigorous; 'Simplex', single flowers, arching; 'Variegata', creamy white variegated foliage, low-spreading habit. Zones 5–10.

KIGELIA

This genus within the trumpet-vine (Bignoniaceae) family consists of a lone species. A tropical to subtropical evergreen tree, it is a native of central and southern Africa characterized by long pendent racemes of striking red to orange flowers, often reaching 6 ft (1.8 m) in length. The flowers are followed by large, brownish gray, woody fruit, up to 18 in (45 cm) in length, on very long stalks.

CULTIVATION: *Kigelia* will grow in any rich and well-drained soil, in a warm climate and in a protected sunny position. Water regularly during the growing season. Propagate from seed.

Kigelia africana

syn. *Kigelia pinnata*

SAUSAGE TREE

☼ ☽ ↔ 12 ft (3.5 m) ↑ 40 ft (12 m)

From central and southern Africa. Evergreen tree; pinnate leaves with 7 to 9 leaflets. Reddish orange bell-shaped flowers in summer, open at night with disagreeable odor that attracts pollinating bats. Fruit large, woody, resemble sausage, inedible. Zones 10–12.

KOELREUTERIA

There are only 3 species of deciduous small trees in this genus within the soapberry (Sapindaceae) family. Their natural habitat is dry woodland in open valleys in China, Korea, and Taiwan, 1 species also in Fiji. Best suited to warm climates with an extended growing season, they are moderately frost hardy and are widely grown as ornamentals for the beauty of their flowers and seed heads. Flowers are used medicinally and as a source of yellow dye in China.
CULTIVATION: Koelreuterias prefer a quite fertile, well-drained soil and thrive in full sun. Propagation is from root cuttings taken in late winter or from seed sown in autumn in sheltered conditions. Seed can also be stratified in the refrigerator and sown in spring. Plants grown from seed are very variable and root cuttings from a good tree are preferable.

Koelreuteria bipinnata
syn. *Koelreuteria integrifoliola*
CHINESE FLAME TREE, PRIDE OF CHINA
☼ ❉ ↔ 25 ft (8 m) ↑ 30 ft (9 m)
Native to Yunnan Province in southwestern China. Bipinnate leaves, elliptical to oblong leaflets, finely toothed, mid-green, turn gold in autumn. Yellow flowers, red spot at petal base, in large panicles, in summer–autumn. Red seed heads. Zones 8–11.

Koelreuteria paniculata ★
CHINA TREE, GOLDEN RAIN TREE, VARNISH TREE
☼ ❉ ↔ 30 ft (9 m) ↑ 30 ft (9 m)
Spreading tree from China and Korea. Leaves pinnate, sometimes bipinnate, leaflets elliptical-oblong, scalloped edges. Young foliage turns red to green with age, yellows in autumn. Panicles of small yellow flowers in summer. Fruit capsules rosy pink or red when ripe. *K. p.* var. *apiculata*, bipinnate leaves, light yellow flowers. *K. p.* 'Fastigiata', columnar habit. Zones 6–10.

KOLKWITZIA

There is just one species in this genus within the woodbine (Caprifoliaceae) family—a deciduous shrub occurring in the wild among rocky outcrops in the mountainous areas of Hubei Province, China. It is grown in gardens for its floriferous spring show.
CULTIVATION: *Kolkwitzia* grows in full sun in well-drained fertile soil. When planted in very cold areas it needs protection from cold spring winds, but in general it is frost hardy. Propagation is from cuttings taken from young wood in late spring or early summer or from suckers, which can be removed and grown on. Prune after flowering to retain a tidy shape.

Kolkwitzia amabilis
BEAUTY BUSH
☼ ❉ ↔ 12 ft (3.5 m) ↑ 12 ft (3.5 m)
Bushy deciduous shrub; long, upright or arching shoots. Leaves opposite, broadly egg-shaped, tapered, rounded tip. Corymbs of bell-shaped flowers, white to pink, yellow throat, in late spring–early summer. 'Pink Cloud' ★, slightly larger flowers. Zones 4–9.

KUNZEA

This genus of the myrtle (Myrtaceae) family, containing about 35 species of evergreen shrubs, is endemic to Australia, except for *K. ericoides*, which also occurs in New Zealand. Kunzeas have small, aromatic, heath-like leaves, and are cultivated mainly for their profuse honey-scented flowers with masses of protruding stamens that give them a fluffy appearance. The flowers appear mostly in spring, attracting honeyeaters and insectivorous birds.
CULTIVATION: They prefer a mild winter climate, full sun or part-shade, and a well-drained soil. Prune lightly from an early age and after flowering to encourage compact bushy growth. Propagate from seed or half-hardened tip cuttings taken in early summer.

Kunzea ambigua
TICK-BUSH
☼ ⬧ ↔ 12 ft (3.5 m) ↑ 12 ft (3.5 m)
Evergreen shrub from eastern Australia. Arching branches; small crowded leaves, dark green, narrow-linear. Masses of small creamy white flowers, in upper leaf axils, in spring–early summer. Zones 9–11.

Kunzea ambigua

Kunzea baxteri
SCARLET KUNZEA
☼ ⬧ ↔ 8 ft (2.4 m) ↑ 8 ft (2.4 m)
Many-stemmed spreading shrub from Western Australia. Crowded linear leaves. Crimson flowers, in dense spikes, in late winter–spring. May be grown in coastal gardens. Zones 9–11.

Kunzea parvifolia
VIOLET KUNZEA
☼ ❉ ↔ 5 ft (1.5 m) ↑ 5 ft (1.5 m)
Open twiggy shrub from southeastern Australia. Minute, heath-like, downy leaves. Masses of fluffy deep mauve flowers, in small terminal clusters, in late spring–early summer. Zones 8–10.

Kolkwitzia amabilis

Laburnum alpinum

Kunzea pulchella

☼ ⚘ ↔ 6 ft (1.8 m) ↕ 6 ft (1.8 m)

From semi-arid regions in southern Western Australia. Spreading or arching branches. Gray-green, silky hairy leaves. Bright red flowers in terminal spikes. Bird-attracting plant, suited to dry-summer climate. Pinch out tips lightly after flowering. Zones 9–11.

+ *LABURNOCYTISUS*

This is a hybrid between the genera *Laburnum* and *Cytisus,* the + sign indicating a graft hybrid. This particular hybrid arose in the French nursery of M. Jean-Louis Adam around 1825. Adam had been grafting the purple broom, *Cytisus purpureus,* onto stems of the common laburnum, *Laburnum anagyroides,* with the object of producing a long-stemmed broom. Most of the resulting plants turned out as expected, but one produced a branch with flowers of a curious brownish color and foliage intermediate between that of the broom and the laburnum. Adam propagated from this plant, producing plants with characteristics of both the parents, which were then named after him to acknowledge his work.

CULTIVATION: Cultivation requirements are the same as for *Laburnum.* The plants grow well in a cool-temperate climate, preferably with uniform annual rainfall. They require moderately fertile soil with good drainage. Seeds germinate readily if they are soaked in warm water for 24 hours before sowing.

+ *Laburnocytisus adamii*

☼ ❈ ↔ 15 ft (4.5 m) ↕ 25 ft (8 m)

Variable tree, some branches producing yellow flowers of laburnum, others with clusters of purple broom flowers, and yet others with muddy beige flowers, in short racemes. Leaves 3-palmate and dark green; leaflets about 2 in (5 cm) long. Pea-like flowers borne in late spring. Zones 5–9.

LABURNUM

This is a genus of only 2 species of small deciduous trees, allied to *Genista* in the pea-flower subfamily of the legume (Fabaceae) family, found natually in central and southern Europe. The leaves are trifoliate and alternate. The plants are widely grown for their long drooping racemes of yellow pea-flowers, which are produced in spring and early summer. All parts of the plant, especially the seeds, are poisonous.

CULTIVATION: Laburnums grow well in a cool-temperate climate, preferably with uniform annual rainfall; any moderately fertile soil with good drainage will suit them. It may be necessary to carry out some early shaping by way of removing competing leaders, but otherwise very little pruning is required. In larger gardens laburnums are popularly planted to form an arch of foliage. The seeds germinate readily if they are soaked in warm water for 24 hours before sowing. Position the plants where they will be sheltered from winter frosts.

Laburnum alpinum

SCOTCH LABURNUM

☼ ❈ ↔ 25 ft (8 m) ↕ 25 ft (8 m)

Small spreading tree from mountain regions of Europe. Leaflets deep shiny green on upper surface, paler and hairy on lower surface. Racemes of yellow flowers borne in mid-summer. Seed pods flattened, smooth, shiny. Popular cultivars include 'Pendulum', slow-growing form with pendulous branches; 'Pyramidale', upright branches. Zones 3–9.

Laburnum anagyroides

COMMON LABURNUM, GOLDEN CHAIN TREE

☼ ❈ ↔ 25 ft (8 m) ↕ 25 ft (8 m)

Small tree. Leaves dull green to gray-green, oval to elliptic, to 3 in (8 cm) long, hairy on undersurface. Drooping racemes of vivid yellow flowers, crowded along branches, in late spring–early summer. 'Pendulum', slender drooping branches. Zones 3–9.

Laburnum × watereri 'Vossii'

Laburnum × watereri

GOLDEN CHAIN TREE, LABURNUM

☼ ❈ ↔ 25 ft (8 m) ↕ 25 ft (8 m)

Hybrid between *L. alpinum* and *L. anagyroides,* which resembles *L. alpinum,* but has leaves and pods that are more densely hairy. Yellow flowers occur in packed racemes. Best-known clonal form, 'Vossii' ★, similar to parent but is more prolific, with longer flower racemes, to 2 ft (0.6 m). Zones 3–9.

LAGERSTROEMIA

CRAPE MYRTLE

A favorite genus in the loosestrife (Lythraceae) family, consisting of 53 species of evergreen or deciduous, small to large trees, it occurs from southern and eastern Asia to northern Australia. The plants have attractive, often peeling bark and simple, variable, usually opposite leaves that in many species provide brilliant autumn color. In summer they famously bear showy panicles of flowers with crinkled petals and a crape-like texture in differing shades of pink, mauve, and white. For all these reasons, these trees are a popular inclusion in many gardens. The fruit is a capsule. The timber of some species has been used to manufacture bridges, furniture, and railway sleepers.

CULTIVATION: These trees are generally easy to grow, as they adapt to a wide variety of soil types. They grow best in well-drained soil in a sunny position and some tolerate light frosts. Propagate from seed or half-hardened cuttings in summer, or from hardwood cuttings in early winter. Powdery mildew can be a problem in older plants, but newer cultivars are more disease resistant.

Lagunaria patersonia

Lagerstroemia floribunda
☼ ✣ ↔ 15 ft (4.5 m) ↑ 40 ft (12 m)
Native to Myanmar, southern Thailand, and Malay Peninsula. Trunk with gray bark; open crown. Leaves broad, somewhat glossy. Mauve-pink flowers, to 2 in (5 cm) across, occur in few-flowered sprays. Zones 11–12.

Lagerstroemia indica
CRAPE MYRTLE
☼ ❄ ↔ 20 ft (6 m) ↑ 20 ft (6 m)
From China and Japan. Often forms multi-stemmed deciduous tree, with wide-spreading, flat-topped, open habit when mature. Bark smooth, pinkish gray, mottled. Leaves small, dark green, turn orange-red in autumn. White, pink, mauve, purple, or carmine flowers with crimped petals, in panicles to 8 in (20 cm) long. For cultivars often included here, see *Lagerstroemia* Hybrid Cultivars entry. Zones 7–11.

Lagerstroemia indica

Lagerstroemia speciosa
syn. *Lagerstroemia flos-reginae*
PRIDE OF INDIA, QUEEN CRAPE MYRTLE
☼ ✣ ↔ 30 ft (9 m) ↑ 30–50 ft (9–15 m)
From India and China to Australia. Deciduous tree with mottled, smooth, gray-yellow, peeling bark. Leaves dark green, shiny, duller beneath, turn coppery red in autumn. Erect panicles of white, mauve, purple, or pink flowers in summer–autumn. Zones 10–12.

Lagerstroemia Hybrid Cultivars
CRAPE MYRTLE
☼ ❄ ↔ 8–25 ft (2.4–8 m) ↑ 15–25 ft (4.5–8 m)
In recent decades US National Arboretum, Maryland, has released series of hybrids between *L. indica* and Japanese species *L. faurei*, combining flower size of first with hardiness, mildew resistance, and bark color of second. 'Natchez', to about 25 ft (8 m) high, cinnamon bark often mottled with cream, white flowers; 'Tuscarora', fast growing, to 25 ft (8 m), dark coral pink flowers. An older group of hybrids originated in Australia, reportedly as backcrosses of *L. indica* × *L. speciosa* onto *L. indica*; these are upright and bear large panicles of deep heliotrope flowers. Zones 7–11.

LAGUNARIA
This genus comprising a single species in the mallow (Malvaceae) family, native to Norfolk and Lord Howe Islands, off eastern Australia, and a small stretch of coastal Queensland, Australia, was named after Andres de Laguna, a sixteenth-century Spanish physician and botanist. It is an evergreen tree growing to 50 ft (15 m) or more; there are, however, several distinct geographic forms, differing mainly in the quantity of soft downy hairs occurring on the simple alternate leaves. The flowers are hibiscus-like, with a conspicuous staminal column; the fruit is a leathery capsule. It is useful for park and street planting, especially in coastal areas, as it can withstand salt-laden winds.

CULTIVATION: This tree grows best in well-drained fertile soil in a warm-temperate or subtropical climate. It requires little or no pruning. Propagate from seed sown in spring; they germinate readily in warm humid areas.

Lagunaria patersonia
syn. *Hibiscus patersonius*
NORFOLK ISLAND HIBISCUS, WHITE OAK
☼ ✤ ↔ 15 ft (4.5 m) ↑ 25–50 ft (8–15 m)
Species named after William Paterson, who was second Lieutenant Governor of New South Wales, Australia. Solitary rosy to mauve-pink flowers with golden yellow anthers, borne in upper axils, in summer. Contact with kidney-shaped seeds, enclosed by fine sharp hairs, can cause skin irritation. 'Royal Purple', shiny green leaves and crimson flowers. Zones 10–11.

LANTANA

A small genus of about 150 species of evergreen shrubs within the vervain (Verbenaceae) family, these plants are mostly found in tropical America. They have scrambling, somewhat prickly stems, simple opposite leaves that are rough on both surfaces, and small flowers grouped in dense flattened or hemispherical heads, with the youngest flowers at the center.

CULTIVATION: Lantanas will tolerate quite harsh conditions but are at their best in light fertile soils with free drainage. They flower freely in a sunny open position in a frost-free climate, and although they are generally suitable for coastal areas, they should be given some protection from salt-laden winds. Regular tip pruning when the plants are young will help the formation of a compact shape, but in later years little or no pruning is necessary. Propagate from seed sown in spring or from half-hardened cuttings taken in summer. Soft-tip cuttings can be taken at any time of the year.

Lantana camara

Lantana camara

LANTANA

☼ ❄ ↔ 8–30 ft (2.4–9 m) ↑ 4–12 ft (1.2–3.5 m)

Evergreen shrub native to West Indies and Central America. Flowers in shades ranging from creamy white through yellow, orange, and pink to brick red, heads often appearing bicolored owing to florets ageing to another color. Wild forms are particularly invasive colonizers, and proclaimed as noxious weeds in some warm-climate countries, including some States of Australia. Sterile or near-sterile forms available. *L. c.* var. *crocea*, golden yellow to orange flowers. *L. c.* **'Chelsea Gem'**, mainly scarlet flowers, some orange; **'Orange Carpet'**, trailing habit, orange flowers; **'Patriot Dove Wings'**, cascading habit, pale yellow flowers soon turning white; **'Patriot Rainbow'**, compact, about 16 in (40 cm) wide and high, bicolored florets from deep pinkish red to creamy yellow; **'Schloss Ortenburg'**, multi-colored florets from yellow to orange or pink; **'Variegata'** (syn. 'Lemon Swirl'), pale green cream-edged leaves, yellow flowers. Zones 9–12.

Larix decidua

Larix laricina, in the wild, Ontario, Canada

Lantana montevidensis

syn. *Lantana sellowiana*

TRAILING LANTANA

☼ ❄ ↔ 10 ft (3 m) ↑ 3 ft (0.9 m)

Evergreen trailing shrub native to central eastern region of South America. Leaves dark green, oblong to lance-shaped, roughly toothed. Flowers rosy lilac, 1 in (25 mm) across, bright yellow flush in throat, slightly fragrant, in winter and throughout year. **'Alba'**, white-flowered cultivar popular in USA. Zones 9–11.

LARIX

The larches, members of the pine (Pinaceae) family, comprise the largest genus of deciduous conifers; they are found in north Europe, over much of Asia from Siberia to as far south as the mountains of northern Myanmar, and in northern North America. They are among the earliest trees to come into leaf in spring, the leaves being carried on both long and short shoots. The upright summer-ripening cones, borne on the shorter shoots, persist on the tree for some time. With age, branches tend to droop in a graceful manner. The leaves are needle-like and usually vivid green, sometimes blue-green in summer, turning butter yellow to old gold in autumn. Some species yield valuable timber that is strong and heavy.

CULTIVATION: Larches are adaptable to most soils, though wet soils are best avoided for all but 1 or 2 species. All larches need plenty of light. Species hybridize readily, both in the wild and in cultivation. Propagate from seed.

Larix decidua

syn. *Larix europaea*

EUROPEAN LARCH

☼ ✱ ↔ 12–20 ft (3.5–6 m) ↑ 165 ft (50 m)

Native to mountains of central and eastern Europe, introduced to Britain around 1600. Conical crown becoming broader with age, with some wide-spreading horizontal as well as erect branches. Bark smooth gray, fissured on old trees, coarsely ridged. Leaves tender light green; mature cones yellowish. **'Corley'**, dwarf spreading tree; **'Pendula'**, strongly weeping habit. Zones 2–8.

Larix kaempferi

syn. *Larix leptolepis*

JAPANESE LARCH

☼ ✱ ↔ 12–20 ft (3.5–6 m) ↑ 100 ft (30 m)

Common in Japan. Long low branches sweeping out and up, upper branches sweeping upward; scaly rusty brown bark. Leaves gray-green; female flowers pink or cream; cones brown. **'Pendula'** ★ and **'Stiff Weeping'** both have pendulous branches. Zones 4–9.

Larix laricina

AMERICAN LARCH, EASTERN LARCH, TAMARACK LARCH

☼ ✱ ↔ 12–20 ft (3.5–6 m) ↑ 60 ft (18 m)

Found across most of northern North America, growing in sphagnum bogs and swamps. Crown open, often with twisted hooped

branches. Bark pink to reddish brown, finely flaking, not fissured. Leaves short, soft, needle-like, turn yellow in autumn. Zones 2–8.

Larix × marschlinsii
syn. *Larix* × *eurolepis*
DUNKELD LARCH, HYBRID LARCH
☼ ✲ ↔ 20 ft (6 m) ↑ 90 ft (27 m)
Hybrid between *L. decidua* and *L. kaempferi*. Intermediate between parents, differing in having yellow, slightly waxy-bloomed shoots and conical cones. Leaves thin, gray-green, to 1½ in (35 mm) long. '**Varied Directions**', pendulous branches. Zones 2–9.

Larix occidentalis
WESTERN LARCH
☼ ✲ ↔ 15 ft (4.5 m) ↑ 180 ft (55 m)
Native to North America. Bark purplish gray, fissured; crown open, narrowly conical. Leaves bright green. Cones rich purple in summer; orange and yellow bracts ripen purple-brown. Zones 3–9.

LAVANDULA
LAVENDER
The 28 species of evergreen aromatic shrubs and subshrubs in this genus belong to the large mint (Lamiaceae) family. They occur mainly around the Mediterranean, with a few in western Asia and the Canary and Cape Verde Islands. Their natural habitat is dry and exposed rocky areas. The narrow leaves are usually grayish green, often toothed or in some species pinnately divided. The spikes of small purple flowers vary in their intensity of color and perfume. Cultivated species belong to 3 groups: the hardy **Spica** (English lavender) **Group**, with mostly basal smooth-edged leaves and long slender flower spikes; the slightly more tender **Stoechas Group**, with flower spikes terminating in a "top-knot" of colored bracts; and the tender **Ptero-stoechas Group**, with pinnately divided leaves. Some of the Spica Group lavenders are cultivated commercially for their aromatic foliage and flower-heads, distilled to produce the lavender oil widely used in perfumes, toiletries, and air fresheners.
CULTIVATION: Lavenders are excellent for hot dry sites, containers, hedging, and positions where they can be brushed against to release their aroma. They need well-drained soil that is not too fertile. Hardy species are pruned after flowering. All lavenders can be propagated from seed, or from tip cuttings in spring or half-hardened cuttings in autumn.

Lavandula dentata 'Ploughman's Blue'

Lavandula × allardii
HYBRID LAVENDER
☼ ✲ ↔ 3 ft (0.9 m) ↑ 3 ft (0.9 m)
Thought to be cross between *L. dentata* and *L. latifolia*. Vigorous grower. Leaves gray, relatively wide, roundly toothed. Long narrow spikes of dark purple flowers, carried well above foliage, in summer. Zones 8–11.

Lavandula angustifolia, Provence, France

Lavandula angustifolia ★
syns *Lavandula officinalis, L. spica, L. vera*
ENGLISH LAVENDER
☼ ✲ ↔ 4 ft (1.2 m) ↑ 2–3 ft (0.6–0.9 m)
Spica Group species native to Mediterranean region. Bushy shrub, with narrow, gray, slightly downy leaves. Fragrant deep purple flower spikes in early summer. '**Alba**', white flowers; '**Beechwood Blue**', low-growing; '**Folgate**', light gray-green foliage, bright blue flowers; '**Hidcote**', densely packed spikes of purple flowers; '**Imperial Gem**', narrow gray leaves, deep purple flowers; '**Loddon Blue**', to 20 in (50 cm) tall, bright silvery gray foliage; '**Martha Roderick**', compact mounding habit, bright lavender flowers; '**Munstead**' ★, dwarf, popular for edging; '**Princess Blue**', pale lavender flowers; '**Rosea**', pink flower spikes; '**Royal Purple**', deep purple flowers. Zones 5–10.

Lavandula dentata
TOOTHED LAVENDER
☼ ☽ ↔ 5 ft (1.5 m) ↑ 3–5 ft (0.9–1.5 m)
Stoechas Group species native to Mediterranean region, Madeira, and Cape Verde Islands. Leaves narrow, grayish green, bluntly toothed; stems slightly downy. Pale purple flower spikes on long stems above foliage. *L. d.* var. *candicans,* grayer in appearance, with flowers deeper purple. *L. d.* '**Ploughman's Blue**', lilac flower spikes on long stems to 12 in (30 cm), good for hedging and tubs. Zones 9–11.

Lavandula × intermedia
☼ ✲ ↔ 3 ft (0.9 m) ↑ 3 ft (0.9 m)
Various hybrids between *L. angustifolia* and *L. latifolia* known by this name. Characteristics intermediate between 2 species, flowers paler than *L. angustifolia*. Frequently grown for cut flowers and oil production. '**Gray Hedge**', attractive silvery gray foliage, purple flowers, popular as hedging plant; '**Grosso**' ★, most commonly grown for oil production, fine-leafed, long dark purple flowers; '**Provence**' ★, attractive cultivar popular in USA; '**Seal**', vigorous, very free flowering, with pale purple flower spikes. Zones 7–10.

Lavandula lanata

WOOLLY LAVENDER

☼ ❊ ↔ 3 ft (0.9 m) ↕ 3 ft (0.9 m)

Native to mountains of southern Spain. Leaves different from other species in Spica Group: wider, and covered in whitish gray down. Spikes of purple flowers, held well above foliage, in summer. Dislikes humidity. Zones 7–10.

Lavandula latifolia

SPIKE LAVENDER

☼ ❊ ↔ 4 ft (1.2 m) ↕ 3 ft (0.9 m)

Native to western Mediterranean region. Rather like *L. angustifolia*, but with broader grayish green leaves and purple flower spikes carried on long stalks, which are frequently in 3 branches. Flowers later in summer than *L. angustifolia*. Zones 7–10.

Lavandula pinnata

CANARY ISLAND LAVENDER

☼ ❊ ↔ 3 ft (0.9 m) ↕ 3 ft (0.9 m)

Native to Canary Islands. Pterostoechas Group species, lightly covered in fine short hairs. Leaves green to gray, pinnate, with broad lobes. Flowerheads of soft purple spikes, usually branched into 3, in summer. '**Sidonie**', hybrid thought to have *L. pinnata* as parent; free flowering in warm climates, bearing deep purple flower spikes on long branching stalks for most of year from late winter. Zones 9–11.

Lavandula stoechas

FRENCH LAVENDER, ITALIAN LAVENDER, SPANISH LAVENDER

☼ ❊ ↔ 24 in (60 cm) ↕ 24 in (60 cm)

Variable species from Mediterranean region. Leaves fine grayish green. Plump flower spikes of deep purple topped by prominent petal-like bracts in summer. Can become invasive. *L. s.* **subsp.** *pedunculata*, fatter and rounder spikes with longer bracts. *L. s.* '**Alba**', dull white flower spikes; '**Avonview**', fast growing,

Lavandula pinnata

24–32 in (60–80 cm) tall, sterile bracts long and pink, bracts of fertile heads purple with fine green mid-stripe; '**Helmsdale**', compact, with burgundy-purple flowers; '**Kew Red**', to 10 in (25 cm) tall, pink flowers; '**Major**', flowering profusely with spikes of deepest intense purple; '**Marshwood**', slightly bigger, to 3 ft (0.9 m), large plump spikes of purple flowers topped with very long mauve bracts; '**Otto Quast**', popular American cultivar; '**Regal Splendour**', deep purple flowers, lavender bracts; '**Willow Vale**', unusual wavy-edged and crinkled purple bracts. Zones 8–11.

Lavandula viridis

GREEN LAVENDER

☼ ❊ ↔ 30 in (75 cm) ↕ 36 in (90 cm)

Stoechas Group species from southern areas of Portugal and Spain and island of Madeira. Aromatic plant. Green foliage; stems covered in fine hairs. Unusual whitish green flower spikes in summer. Zones 8–11.

LAVATERA

TREE MALLOW

There are 25 species of evergreen or deciduous annuals, biennials, perennials, and softwooded shrubs in this genus within the mallow (Malvaceae) family found from the Mediterranean to the northwestern Himalayas, and in parts of Asia, Australia, California (USA), and Baja California (Mexico). The leaves are usually palmately lobed and slightly downy, and most species have attractive hibiscus-like flowers with prominent staminal columns, in colors ranging from white to a rosy purple. *Lavatera* is closely related to *Malva*, and following recent botanical studies several of its species have been reclassified as *Malva* species.

CULTIVATION: Shrubby mallows are suitable for planting in mixed borders, where they will bloom abundantly throughout summer. They should be grown in full sun in light well-drained soil. Too rich a soil will result in an excess of foliage at the expense of flowers. Prune after flowering to prevent legginess. Mallows tend to be short lived; softwood cuttings taken in spring or early summer strike readily and are the usual method of propagation for shrubby species.

Lavatera olbia

TREE LAVATERA, TREE MALLOW

☼ ❊ ↔ 5 ft (1.5 m) ↕ 6 ft (1.8 m)

From western Mediterranean region. True form of *L. olbia* is rarely cultivated; plant sold under that name is usually *L. × clementii*. Evergreen shrub. Bristly stems; downy lobed leaves; reddish purple flowers. Zones 8–10.

LEPTOSPERMUM

This genus in the myrtle (Myrtaceae) family is made up of about 80 species of evergreen shrubs or small trees with small narrow leaves that are often aromatic, occasionally lemon-scented, when crushed. Mostly Australian, 1 species is widespread in New Zealand and 2 are found in Southeast Asia. They are collectively known as tea-trees; the leaves of some species were used as a tea substitute by Captain James Cook's crew when they landed in Australia in

Lavatera olbia

Leptospermum rotundifolium

Leptospermum spectabile

Leptospermum squarrosum

1770 and later by early settlers in Australia. The flowers are small and open with a wide nectar cup and 5 petals that are mostly white or shades of pink and occasionally red. Small woody capsules often persist for a long period. They are sometimes used as cut flowers. CULTIVATION: Tolerating an occasional light frost, they are best suited to well-drained soil in full sun; some species will tolerate wet conditions and nearly full shade. Light feedings with slow-release fertilizers in spring are beneficial. Prune regularly after flowering to retain bushiness. Propagate from seed or half-hardened cuttings in summer; propagate cultivars from cuttings to retain characteristics.

Leptospermum laevigatum

COAST TEA-TREE

☼ ❄ ↔ 10–15 ft (3–4.5 m) ↑ 10–20 ft (3–6 m)

Widespread in eastern coastal areas of Australia. Tall dense shrub or small tree with deciduous flaky bark. Leaves small, gray-green, with rounded tip. Conspicuous white flowers in spring. Considered weed in South Africa. 'Reevesii', compact form. Zones 9–11.

Leptospermum nitidum

☼ ❄ ↔ 6 ft (1.8 m) ↑ 8 ft (2.4 m)

Rounded shrub endemic to wet heaths in Tasmania, Australia. Leaves small, crowded, glossy; new growth silky-hairy, often copper-colored. Masses of small white flowers in summer. Zones 8–10.

Leptospermum petersonii

LEMON-SCENTED TEA-TREE

☼ ❄ ↔ 10 ft (3 m) ↑ 20 ft (6 m)

From east coast of Australia. Shrub or small tree with slightly weeping habit. Leaves narrow-lanceolate, lemon-scented when crushed. Small white flowers in early summer. Popular street tree. Needs additional water during dry periods. Zones 9–11.

Leptospermum rotundifolium

syn. *Leptospermum scoparium* var. *rotundifolium*

ROUND-LEAFED TEA-TREE

☼ ❄ ↔ 10 ft (3 m) ↑ 6 ft (1.8 m)

From southeastern Australia. Leaves dark green, almost round. Attractive flowers, 1¼ in (30 mm) across, in shades of pink, mauve, or more rarely lavender, in spring. Persistent glossy capsules.

Prefers well-drained soil. 'Julie Ann', to about 12 in (30 cm) high, spreading habit, showy pale mauve flowers. Zones 8–10.

Leptospermum scoparium

MANUKA, TEA-TREE

☼ ❄ ↔ 6 ft (1.8 m) ↑ 6 ft (1.8 m)

Native of New Zealand, Tasmania (Australia), and southeastern corner of mainland Australia. Small prickly leaves. Showy white flowers, to 1¼ in (30 mm) across, in spring–summer. Fast growing; requires pruning to shape after flowering. 'Apple Blossom', pink-flushed white flowers; 'Autumn Glory', deep pink single flowers, bright green foliage; 'Big Red', covered in striking red flowers; 'Burgundy Queen', deep red double flowers, bronze-colored foliage; 'Gaiety Girl', dark-centered, pink, semi-double flowers, and reddish new growth; 'Helene Strybing', pink flowers, popular in USA; 'Kiwi', dwarf form with single light red flowers in late spring–early summer; 'Lambethii', large, dark-centered, single pink flowers; 'Nanum Kea', profuse pink flowers; 'Pink Cascade' ★, weeping branches, white flowers with pink flush; 'Pink Pearl', pink flowers, popular in USA; 'Ray Williams', white flowers streaked pink; 'Red Damask', dark green to bronze foliage, double crimson flowers; 'Ruby Glow', purple-red semi-double flowers. Zones 8–10.

Leptospermum spectabile

BLOOD-RED TEA-TREE

☼ ❄ ↔ 6 ft (1.8 m) ↑ 10 ft (3 m)

Rare shrub from small area near Sydney, New South Wales, Australia, growing along banks of Colo River. Narrow pointed leaves. Showy flowers, about 1 in (25 mm) across, with smallish deep red petals around very large receptacle glistening with nectar, in late spring. Zones 8–11.

Leptospermum squarrosum

syn. *Leptospermum persiciflorum*

PEACH-FLOWERED TEA-TREE

☼ ❄ ↔ 5 ft (1.5 m) ↑ 6 ft (1.8 m)

Erect open shrub from southeastern Australia, growing on poor sandstone soils around Sydney. Tiny, dark green, pointed leaves. Large white to bright pink flowers, on older thicker branches, in autumn. Requires good drainage. Zones 8–11.

Leschenaultia biloba

LESCHENAULTIA

syn. *Lechenaultia*

This Australian genus belonging to the Goodeniaceae family comprises about 26 species, the majority occurring in southwestern Western Australia, but with 3 in central Australia and 2 in far northern Australia, one of which also occurs in New Guinea. The genus includes perennials, subshrubs, and shrubs, with leaves that are usually small and very narrow. The flowers are the striking feature; although small and sometimes borne singly, they are profuse and in some species are very intensely colored. The flowers have 5 petals, which are fused at the base, each with a smooth central band and a broad crinkled margin; in some species they are spread in a hand-like form, in others they form more of a tube.

CULTIVATION: Perfect drainage and light gritty soils give the best results when growing these plants, and few species will survive, let alone thrive, where the soil stays cold and wet over winter. These plants tolerate light frosts and will withstand more cold if kept dry during winter. They prefer a position in full sun; water occasionally during the growing season. Other than a little tidying up after flowering, trimming is seldom needed. Propagate from seed or half-hardened tip cuttings of non-flowering stems.

Leschenaultia biloba

☼ ⁑ ↔ 24 in (60 cm) ↑ 24 in (60 cm)

Best-known leschenaultia, found in Perth region of Western Australia. Leaves sparse, rather dull gray-green. Magnificent sprays of gentian blue flowers in winter. Lighter colored and white-flowered forms available. Zones 10–11.

Leschenaultia formosa

☼ ⁑ ↔ 24 in (60 cm) ↑ 12 in (30 cm)

From southern Western Australia. Similar to *L. biloba*, but leaves slightly larger. Distinctive flowers, usually vivid red, sometimes tending toward orange; borne singly, they smother bush in late winter. Zones 9–11.

LEUCADENDRON

This genus is a member of the protea (Proteaceae) family, and comprises approximately 80 diverse evergreen shrubs and small trees. All species are naturally found in South Africa's Western Cape province and the far west of Eastern Cape, except for 3 species, which are isolated in eastern KwaZulu-Natal. Borne on separate male and female plants in winter to spring, the flowers are produced in dense heads, the females commonly concealed among rather woody scales, the males in rather looser cone-like structures. The longer bracts surrounding both male and female flowerheads are often colorful, giving each head the appearance of a single "flower." They are much-sought after as cut flowers because of their long vase life. The leaves are simple, often leathery in texture, and spirally arranged. Most species are insect pollinated but a few are wind pollinated. The cone-like fruits yield seed that ripens in summer.

CULTIVATION: The vast majority of species require perfect drainage, preferring humus-rich, acid, basaltic or sandy loams low in phosphorus. They generally prefer an open, sunny, frost-free position with good air circulation. Propagate from seed sown in autumn, from cuttings, or by grafting or budding.

Leucadendron argenteum

SILVER TREE

☼ ⁑ ↔ 6–20 ft (1.8–6 m) ↑ 20–30 ft (6–9 m)

Rare in wild, occurring on slopes of Table Mountain, South Africa. Beautiful tree; trunk with whorled branches, smooth gray bark with distinctive horizontal leaf scars. Leaves lance-shaped, to 6 in (15 cm) long, silvery, silky, with glistening sheen. Female flowers, in silvery cone-like heads with pinkish tinge, occur in summer. Produces silvery cone-like fruit. Zones 9–10.

Leucadendron eucalyptifolium

☼ ❄ ↔ 8 ft (2.4 m) ↑ 20 ft (6 m)

Shrub with somewhat eucalyptus-like leaves, long, narrow, bright green, each with distinctive twist. Flowerhead bracts turning bright yellow; fragrant flowers in winter–spring. Persistent cone-like fruit. Popular with florists. Responds to pruning. Zones 8–10.

Leucadendron salicifolium

☼ ❄ ↔ 6 ft (1.8 m) ↑ 10 ft (3 m)

Vigorous evergreen shrub, growing from sea level to high altitudes in moist acid soils along stream banks. Leaves green, smooth, narrow, sharply pointed, with twist. Light green-yellow bracts in winter–early spring. Very popular species with florists. Zones 8–10.

Leucadendron sessile

Leucadendron sessile

☼ ❄ ↔ 3 ft (0.9 m) ↑ 5 ft (1.5 m)

From mountains east of Cape Town, South Africa. Tolerates heavy clay; requires constant moisture, depends on sea mists in its native habitat. Leaves green, elliptical, smooth. Yellow flowerhead bracts, turning red with age, in winter. Zones 8–10.

Leucadendron, Hybrid Cultivar, 'Superstar'

Leucadendron tinctum

☼ ❋ ↔ 4 ft (1.2 m) ↕ 4 ft (1.2 m)

Low shrub from Western Cape, South Africa. Leaves oblong, gray-green, rounded tip, held close to stems. Distinctive pink-flushed flower bracts in winter. Fragrant cones. Zones 8–10.

Leucadendron Hybrid Cultivars

☼ ⧉ ↔ 4–8 ft (1.2–2.4 m) ↕ 4–8 ft (1.2–2.4 m)

Hybrids have large showy bracts, compact growth habit, interesting foliage. **'Cloudbank Jenny'** (syn. 'Cloudbank Ginny'), cream bracts, orange cones; **'Duet'**, red-edged yellow bracts, yellow cones; **'Pisa'**, yellow bracts, silvery green cones; **'Safari Sunset'** ★, vivid red bracts; **'Silvan Red'**, slim bracts; **'Sundance'**, bright yellow to gold bracts; **'Superstar'**, small red and yellow bracts. Zones 9–11.

LEUCAENA

Part of the mimosa subfamily of the legume (Fabaceae) family, the 20-odd species of evergreen trees and shrubs in this genus range from southern Texas, USA, and Mexico to South America. All have feathery foliage and fluffy globular heads of white flowers. The leaves are bipinnate, with many small leaflets or fewer larger ones. Dark brown pods hang in drooping clusters from the branches. CULTIVATION: These fast-growing plants thrive in a wide range of soils; routine care is minimal. They respond to pruning or coppicing, which quickly produces regrowth. Widely planted in tropical and subtropical areas as screen or shade trees, in cool-temperate climates they may be grown under glass. Propagate from seed, which needs soaking in warm water for 24 hours to soften it before planting, or from half-hardened cuttings.

Leucaena leucocephala

syn. *Leucaena glauca*

LEAD TREE, WHITE POPINAC

☼ ✦ ↔ 15 ft (4.5 m) ↕ 30 ft (9 m)

Vigorous, fast-growing, evergreen tree; abundantly naturalized in tropical areas. Gray-green bipinnate leaves; young stems deep copper color. Fluffy balls of creamy white flowers, on short stalks, borne in spring. Drooping clusters of dark brown, broad, flat pods borne during summer months. Zones 10–12.

LEUCOPHYTA

The sole species in this genus in the daisy (Asteraceae) family is an evergreen shrub native to the coasts of southern Australia. Rather reminiscent of lavender cotton (*Santolina chamaecyparissus*), it develops into a dense mound of wiry stems clothed in tiny, almost scale-like, silver-gray leaves. In summer and autumn small, knob-like, white to creamy yellow flowerheads lacking ray florets open from silvery buds. CULTIVATION: Very much a coastal plant and highly resistant to salt spray, it adapts well to cultivation and can be trimmed as a low border or hedge, good for accenting darker foliage. It dislikes hot humid conditions and appreciates full sun and good air movement. The soil should be light and well drained. While tough and drought resistant, it is short lived and will eventually die out from the center; hard pruning will not rejuvenate it. Light pinching back year round can keep it more compact and vigorous. Propagate from half-hardened tip cuttings.

Leucophyta brownii

Leucophyta brownii

syn. *Calocephalus brownii*

CUSHION BUSH

☼ ⧉ ↔ 3 ft (0.9 m) ↕ 3 ft (0.9 m)

Intricately branched dome of bright silvery foliage. Inconspicuous yellowish flowerheads, to ½ in (12 mm) across. Western Australian race has longer leaves, to ½ in (12 mm). Zones 9–11.

LEUCOSPERMUM

PINCUSHION

Unlike many plants in related genera of the protea (Proteaceae) family, leucospermums, often referred to as pincushion proteas, owe their beauty to their flowers, in roundish pincushion-like heads with long conspicuous styles. There are approximately 50 species, all evergreen shrubs, and all from a narrow coastal belt in South Africa's Western Cape province, except for a handful in eastern South Africa, one extending to Zimbabwe. The majority are compact shrubs, which flower abundantly in spring. The thick leaves are generally broadest near the tip, which usually has several rather blunt teeth. CULTIVATION: All require well-drained soil in an open sunny situation. Some species tolerate light frosts; all prefer a dry summer with low humidity. Winter watering is desirable. Pruning is usually unnecessary apart from cutting flowers. Propagate from seed or cuttings or by grafting, which is used for many of the hybrid cultivars.

Leucospermum bolusii

BOLUS PINCUSHION, GORDON'S BAY PINCUSHION

☼ ❋ ↔ 5–6 ft (1.5–1.8 m) ↕ 5–6 ft (1.5–1.8 m)

Evergreen shrub with stout, erect, branching stems. Leaves greenish gray, sword- to oval-shaped, notched at tip. Yellow to apricot pincushion-like flowers, 4 in (10 cm) in diameter, produced in spring. Zones 8–10.

Leucospermum cordifolium ★
syn. *Leucospermum nutans*
NODDING PINCUSHION
☼ ❋ ↔ 6 ft (1.8 m) ↑ 6 ft (1.8 m)

Shrub with open habit; some cultivars almost prostrate. Gray-green foliage. Apricot, pink, orange, or red flowers in spring. Tolerant of clay soils; frost tender when young. 'Aurora', apricot-yellow flowers; 'Fire Dance', scarlet flowerheads; 'African Red', florets with distinctive red striping and yellow styles. Zones 8–10.

Leucospermum tottum
FIREWHEEL PINCUSHION
☼ ❋ ↔ 5 ft (1.5 m) ↑ 5 ft (1.5 m)

Dense evergreen shrub. Leaves narrow-elliptical, gray-green, covered with fine hairs. Rounded scarlet flowers with creamy styles in spring–summer. Several hybrid cultivars available, some extending flowering season into mid-summer. 'Scarlet Ribbon', compact rounded habit, to 5 ft (1.5 m), frosted appearance, scarlet flowers in late spring. Zones 8–10.

Leucospermum 'Veldfire'
☼ ❋ ↔ 5 ft (1.5 m) ↑ 5 ft (1.5 m)

L. glabrum hybrid. Yellow-orange flowers, often age to crimson-red, with bright orange styles, in mid-spring–summer. Zones 8–10.

LEUCOTHOE
Found mainly in eastern Asia and the USA, this genus belonging to the heath (Ericaceae) family, as now understood, consists of only 6 species of evergreen and deciduous shrubs. Many more species formerly included in it are now separated as the genus *Agarista*. They usually have simple leathery leaves, dark green with toothed edges; some show a tendency to produce variegated foliage. The deciduous species often color well in autumn. The flowers are small, bell- or urn-shaped, and usually cream to pink. Opening in spring to early summer in racemes or panicles, they can be quite showy. CULTIVATION: Most species prefer shade from the hottest sun and should be grown in cool, moist, humus-rich soil that is open and

Leucospermum cordifolium

well drained. Other than light trimming to shape, pruning is seldom necessary. Propagation from seed is usually slow, so air-layering or half-hardened cuttings are more often used. Some species produce suckers that can be grown on.

Leucothoe fontanesiana
syns *Leucothoe catesbaei*, *L. walteri*
SWITCH IVY
☼ ❋ ↔ 7 ft (2 m) ↑ 6 ft (1.8 m)

From southeastern USA. Evergreen shrub with arching stems. Leaves long-pointed, to 4 in (10 cm) long, glossy upper surface, toothed edges; red-tinted new growth. White lily-of-the-valley-like flowers, in short racemes, in spring. 'Rainbow' ★ (syn. 'Girard's Rainbow'), foliage variegated green, cream, and pink. Zones 5–10.

Leucothoe racemosa
FETTER BUSH, SWEET BELLS
☼ ❋ ↔ 5 ft (1.5 m) ↑ 3–8 ft (0.9–2.4 m)

Deciduous shrub from eastern USA. Leaves to 2½ in (6 cm) long, finely toothed edges; autumn foliage develops intense yellow, orange, and cherry red tones. Short racemes of white to cream flowers in spring–summer. Zones 5–9.

LEYCESTERIA
This genus in the woodbine (Caprifoliaceae) family consists of 6 species of deciduous or semi-evergreen shrubs from western China and the Himalayas as far west as Pakistan. They have small tubular flowers, borne over a long period, with colored bracts. The soft berries mature so quickly that they are often carried at the same time as the flowers. In favorable climates these plants may become invasive weeds. CULTIVATION: Grow in moderately fertile soil in a sunny or part-shade location, though the flower bracts and fruit color better in full sun. Less hardy species can be overwintered in a greenhouse in colder climates. Propagate from seed in autumn or spring or by taking softwood cuttings in summer.

Leycesteria formosa
HIMALAYAN HONEYSUCKLE
☼ ❋ ↔ 6 ft (1.8 m) ↑ 6 ft (1.8 m)

Native to Himalayas and western China. Leaves long, dark green, slightly heart-shaped at base, smooth-edged or slightly toothed, undersurface paler and downy. Whitish flowers with purple bracts, on pendent spikes, in summer–autumn. Fruit ripening deep red-purple to black. Weed in Australia and New Zealand. Zones 7–10.

LIBOCEDRUS
This genus of 6 species of coniferous trees in the cypress (Cupressaceae) family is found in wet forest areas of New Caledonia, New Zealand, and southwestern South America, with 2 further species from New Guinea sometimes placed in the genus *Papuacedrus*. They are cypress-like trees with bright green foliage that has distinct adult and juvenile forms. Bark peels in stringy vertical strips, and male and female cones, borne on the same tree, are very small.

Leucothoe racemosa

Libocedrus plumosa, in the wild, New Zealand

CULTIVATION: The New Zealand and South American species can be grown outdoors in moderately frosty climates but the others may require greenhouse cultivation. Outdoors these conifers will grow in any reasonable deeply worked soil; some shade should be given when young. Water well in dry spells. Propagation is usually from seed, which is best sown fresh. Cuttings are difficult to strike.

Libocedrus plumosa ★

KAWAKA

☼ ❋ ↔ 10 ft (3 m) ↑ 40 ft (12 m)

From New Zealand. Pyramidal form, maintained for many years. Slow growing in cultivation, reaching only about 8 ft (2.4 m) after 10 years. Branchlets compressed, flattened, giving soft feathery appearance; leaves rich green, scale-like. Zones 8–11.

LIGUSTRUM

PRIVET

This genus of about 50 species of both deciduous and evergreen trees and shrubs is part of the olive (Oleaceae) family. Most are found in the Himalayas and eastern Asia, with one in Europe and North Africa. All have simple opposite leaves with smooth edges and bear panicles of scented white flowers at the branch or stem tips, followed by small blue-black drupes. In warmer climates the seed is produced in large quantities and is popular with birds, which has resulted in several species becoming weeds. *L. japonicum* and *L. ovalifolium* are weeds in the USA and New Zealand; *L. lucidum* and *L. sinense* have become pests in eastern Australia. Varieties with colored foliage can be grown with less risk but are apt to revert.
CULTIVATION: They are not particular about soil or exposure to the sun. Seed can be sown as soon as ripe; colored forms are best propagated from firm tip cuttings taken in late spring or summer.

Ligustrum japonicum

JAPANESE PRIVET

☼ ❋ ↔ 8 ft (2.4 m) ↑ 10 ft (3 m)

From Japan and Korea. Compact, very dense, evergreen shrub. Leaves camellia-like, shiny, olive green. Large panicles of white flowers in late summer–early autumn. Zones 5–10.

Ligustrum lucidum

BROAD-LEAFED PRIVET, GLOSSY PRIVET, WAXLEAF PRIVET

☼ ❋ ↔ 30 ft (9 m) ↑ 30 ft (9 m)

Large evergreen shrub or small tree from China. Leaves pointed, shiny, deep green, to 6 in (15 cm) long. Large panicles of white flowers in autumn. 'Excelsum Superbum', pale green leaves edged yellow; 'Tricolor', narrow deep green leaves, predominantly marked with gray-green, edged with pale creamy yellow. Zones 7–11.

Ligustrum ovalifolium

CALIFORNIA PRIVET, OVAL-LEAFED PRIVET

☼ ❋ ↔ 12 ft (3.5 m) ↑ 12 ft (3.5 m)

Cultivated for hedging. Leaves shiny, deep green, falling in very cold climates. White flowers in mid-summer. 'Argenteum', leaves with creamy white margins; 'Aureum', the golden privet, green-centered leaves with wide yellow margins, or all yellow. Zones 5–10.

LINDERA

This genus in the laurel (Lauraceae) family consists of about 80 species of deciduous and evergreen trees and shrubs, all from East Asia except for 3 from North America. They have an open habit and aromatic alternate leaves, smooth-edged or 3-lobed. The leaves color in autumn on deciduous species. Heads of star-shaped yellow flowers appear in the leaf axils during spring, followed by clustered berry-like fruit.
CULTIVATION: Suitable for a woodland or other informal garden, in a shady position when young, all species transplant well and will survive in ordinary, somewhat acidic, soil. Established trees require little or no care but may be pruned if they become ungainly. Propagate from seed sown when fresh; if the seed must be stored, do not allow it to dry. Otherwise propagate from cuttings taken in summer or by air-layering.

Lindera obtusiloba

☼ ❋ ↔ 25 ft (8 m) ↑ 30 ft (9 m)

From East Asia. Branches gray-yellow, sometimes flushed purple. Aromatic leaves turn pale gold in autumn. Tiny, yellow-green, star-shaped flowers, in umbels on previous year's growth, in early spring, before leaves. Fruit glossy dark red to black. Zones 6–9.

Ligustrum lucidum 'Excelsum Superbum'

Lindera obtusiloba

Liquidambar formosana

Liquidambar orientalis

Liquidambar styraciflua

LIQUIDAMBAR

SWEET GUM

In the witchhazel (Hamamelidaceae) family, this genus comprises 4 species of tall deciduous trees found in North and Central America, East Asia, and Turkey. The meaning of the name is much as it appears: it refers to the resin, known as storax, exuded by the winter buds. The trees have an attractive conical or rounded form, and the palmately lobed leaves are similar to those of maples but arranged spirally on the twig instead of in opposite pairs. In autumn the foliage changes color dramatically to shades of orange, red, and purple. Spring flowers are greenish and inconspicuous, in small spherical heads, but the brown fruiting heads that follow are spiky and decorative.

CULTIVATION: These are large trees requiring plenty of room to develop; their site should be chosen carefully, as they dislike being transplanted. They require a sunny site in deep rich soil with plenty of moisture. Propagate from seed in autumn or softwood cuttings in summer, or by air-layering.

Liquidambar formosana

CHINESE LIQUIDAMBAR, FORMOSAN GUM

☼ ❊ ↔ 30 ft (9 m) ↑ 60 ft (18 m)

From mountains of east, central, and southern China, Taiwan, northern Vietnam, Laos, and South Korea. Straight trunk, gray-white bark, fissures with age. Leaves broad, 3-lobed, serrated margins, downy below. Inconspicuous greenish yellow flowers; spiky fruit. Zones 8–11.

Liquidambar orientalis

ORIENTAL SWEET GUM, TURKISH LIQUIDAMBAR

☼ ❊ ↔ 15 ft (4.5 m) ↑ 25–50 ft (8–15 m)

From southwestern Turkey. Broad crown; bark thick, orangey brown, cracking into small plates. Leaves 5-lobed, smaller than other species, turn orange in autumn. Zones 8–11.

Liquidambar styraciflua

LIQUIDAMBAR, SWEET GUM

☼ ❊ ↔ 35 ft (10 m) ↑ 70 ft (21 m)

Native to eastern USA, highlands of southern Mexico, and Central America. Bark dark grayish brown, deeply furrowed. Leaves large, 5 to 7 tapering lobes, coloring brilliantly in shades of orange, red, and purple in autumn. Cultivars selected for their autumn colors include 'Burgundy', deep red; 'Festival', yellow, peach, pink; 'Lane Roberts', deep reddish purple; 'Palo Alto', orange and red; and 'Worplesdon', orangey yellow and purple. Other cultivars include 'Aurea', yellow-striped leaves; 'Golden Treasure', leaves with yellow margins; 'Gumball', dwarf form with rounded shape; 'Rotundiloba' ★, leaves with rounded lobes; and 'Variegata', leaves splashed with yellow. Zones 5–11.

LIRIODENDRON

This genus belonging to the magnolia (Magnoliaceae) family was

Liriodendron tulipifera

believed to consist of just a single species naturally found in North America, until a second similar species was found in central China in 1875. Both species form quite tall, fast-growing, deciduous trees with long straight trunks and unusually shaped 4-lobed leaves that turn a delightful translucent yellow in autumn. The greenish bell-shaped flowers have a tangerine tint at the petal bases. They somewhat resemble a tulip, hence the common name of tulip tree. Capsule-like fruit follow the flowers. Hybrids between the 2 species are now in cultivation.

CULTIVATION: Liriodendron species grow best in a fertile soil, in a cool climate in partial shade, with protection from drying winds. Some shaping of the plant in the early stages of growth to establish a single trunk may be necessary. Propagate from seed sown in a position protected from winter frosts. Cultivars may be apical-grafted in early spring onto 1- or 2-year-old seedling understocks.

Liriodendron tulipifera

NORTH AMERICAN TULIP TREE, TULIP TREE

☼ ❊ ↔ 40 ft (12 m) ↑ 100 ft (30 m)

Found east of Mississippi River, USA, from Gulf States up to St Lawrence River and Great Lakes. Leaves quite large. Solitary flowers, 6 petalled, yellow-green with orange-yellow blotch at base, in spring. 'Aureomarginatum', yellow-edged leaves; 'Fastigiatum' ★, upright columnar habit, growing to only about half height of species. Zones 4–10.

LITHOCARPUS

This genus of about 300 oak-like evergreen trees in the beech (Fagaceae) family is found on mountain slopes of East and Southeast Asia and New Guinea, with 1 species from western USA. Leathery smooth-edged or toothed leaves are spirally arranged but crowded toward the ends of seasonal growths. Tiny flowers are borne on stiff catkins near branch tips in spring, females close to catkin bases, males above. Seeds (acorns) mature in the second year. *Lithocarpus* differs from *Quercus* in that the male catkins are erect rather than pendulous and the acorns are crowded onto spikes.

CULTIVATION: Most enjoy cool moist winters and dry summers. Plant in moderately fertile acid to neutral soil in full sun or part-shade. Shelter from cold drying winds in cooler climates. Propagate from seed sown in autumn.

Lithocarpus densiflorus

TANBARK OAK

☀ ❀ ↔ 40 ft (12 m) ↑ 100 ft (30 m)

From northern California and southern Oregon, USA. Bark thick, furrowed, red-brown. Young shoots woolly white; leaves stiff, leathery, toothed, prominently veined, with rusty hairs on underside, turning leaden hue with age. Tiny whitish male flowers. Egg-shaped acorns. *L. d.* var. *echinoides*, to 10 ft (3 m) high, leaves smaller, less toothed, than species. Zones 7–9.

LITHODORA

A genus in the borage (Boraginaceae) family of 7 species of low hairy shrubs or subshrubs, it is native to western and southern Europe, North Africa, and Asia Minor. Plentiful, deep dark green, simple leaves are about 1 in (25 mm) long and evergreen when grown within the zone range, though they are susceptible to frost burn. Covered with many small vibrant blue or purple flowers in late spring or early summer, their low-growing habit makes them ideal for ground covers, rockeries, and borders.

CULTIVATION: Grow in well-drained acid soil in full sun to part-shade; they can become leggy in too much shade. Propagate from seed in spring or tip cuttings in mid- to late summer.

Lithodora diffusa

syn. *Lithospermum diffusum*

☀/◐ ❀ ↔ 24–36 in (60–90 cm) ↑ 6–12 in (15–30 cm)

From France, Spain, and Portugal. Green linear leaves; blue flowers in mid-spring–early summer. With age, it tends to cease producing foliage and flowers in center. 'Grace Ward', low-creeping form, bright azure flowers; 'Heavenly Blue' ★, petals edged with brilliant white; 'Star', petals edged with clear white, giving them starry appearance. Zones 7–9.

LOMATIA

There are 12 species in this genus of the protea (Proteaceae) family, 9 from eastern Australia and 3 from South America. All are shrubs or small trees, with a few reaching 60 ft (18 m) in rainforests. Leaves vary from smooth-edged to toothed to deeply divided. Small flowers, white, cream, yellow, or rarely pink, are borne on spikes in leaf axils or at branch tips. The fruit is leathery, with 2 rows of winged seeds.

CULTIVATION: Some require a sheltered, moist, frost-free position, others tolerate some dryness and some frosts. Generally, acid well-drained soils give best results. Propagate from fresh seed or cuttings taken in mid-summer from young growth that is not too soft.

Lomatia ferruginea

☀ ❋ ↔ 15 ft (4.5 m) ↑ 30 ft (9 m)

From rainforests of Argentina and Chile. Evergreen tree with divided, dark green, fern-like leaves on brown felty stems. Clusters of red and yellow flowers, in leaf axils, in summer. Cultivated in warmer parts of UK since mid-nineteenth century. Zones 9–10.

Lomatia ferruginea

Lomatia polymorpha

☀ ❀ ↔ 5 ft (1.5 m) ↑ 6–12 ft (1.8–3.5 m)

From Tasmania, Australia. Leaves narrow, deep green to yellow-green. Large cream flowers in late spring. Zones 8–10.

LONICERA (see page 781)

Lonicera fragrantissima

WINTER HONEYSUCKLE

☀ ❀ ↔ 8 ft (2.4 m) ↑ 6 ft (1.8 m)

From China. Leaves dull green. Small, strongly scented, cream flowers, in pairs in leaf axils, in winter–spring. Red fruit. Zones 5–9.

Lithodora diffusa 'Star'

Lonicera involucrata

TWINBERRY

☼ ❄ ↔ 3 ft (0.9 m) ↕ 3 ft (0.9 m)

Deciduous shrub from Mexico, western USA, and southern Canada. Leaves to 5 in (12 cm) long. Short-tubed yellow to red flowers in spring. Deep purple berries with large purple-red bracts. Zones 4–10.

Lonicera maackii

☼ ❄ ↔ 15 ft (4.5 m) ↕ 15 ft (4.5 m)

Deciduous shrub native to East Asia. Leaves 3 in (8 cm) long, purple-stemmed. Fragrant white flowers, ageing to yellow, in spring–summer. Tiny dark red to black berries. Zones 2–9.

Lonicera nitida

syn. *Lonicera ligustrina* subsp. *yunnanensis*

BOX HONEYSUCKLE

☼ ❄ ↔ 10 ft (3 m) ↕ 12 ft (3.5 m)

Shrubby evergreen from central and southwestern China. Leaves tiny, dark green, purple toned in winter. Small cream flowers in spring. Purple-black berries. Dense bushy habit. Zones 7–10.

Lonicera × purpusii

☼ ❄ ↔ 8 ft (2.4 m) ↕ 10 ft (3 m)

Semi-deciduous hybrid between winter-flowering *L. fragrantissima* and *L. standishii*. Fragrant creamy white flowers, in clusters of 2 to 4, in winter–early spring. 'Winter Beauty', red berries. Zones 6–9.

Lonicera syringantha

☼ ❄ ↔ 7 ft (2 m) ↕ 10 ft (3 m)

From China and Tibet. Deciduous shrub with upright stems, graceful arching habit. Leaves blue tinted. Small, paired, fragrant, soft lilac flowers in spring–summer. Red berries. Zones 4–9.

Lonicera tatarica

TATARIAN HONEYSUCKLE

☼ ❄ ↔ 7 ft (2 m) ↕ 10 ft (3 m)

From central Asia and southern Russia. Deciduous shrub; parent of many hybrids and available in wide range of cultivars. Leaves with blue-gray underside. Flowers in white and pink shades, in spring–summer. Pale orange to red fruit. Zones 3–9.

LOPHOMYRTUS

This genus native to New Zealand belongs to the myrtle (Myrtaceae) family and is closely allied to *Myrtus* itself. It consists of 2 species of small evergreen trees or shrubs, which are grown primarily for their interesting foliage, though with age they also develop attractive dappled or streaked smooth bark. The species hybridize freely. CULTIVATION: Grow in full sun for the best leaf coloration, in reasonably fertile well-drained soil. In cool-temperate climates they are best given a warm sheltered site and protection in winter. Prune for hedging or to maintain a dense shrubby form, or to a single trunk as a small tree. Species can be propagated from seed in spring but are usually propagated from half-hardened cuttings in autumn. *L. × ralphii* and its cultivars can only be propagated from cuttings.

Lophomyrtus bullata ★

RAMARAMA

☼ ❄ ↔ 8 ft (2.4 m) ↕ 8–12 ft (2.4–3.5 m)

Small tree. Leaves small, oval, puckered surface, greener in shade, develop bronzy purplish tones in sun. Small fluffy cream flowers in summer. Dark reddish purple berries. Zones 9–10.

Lophomyrtus × ralphii

☼ ❄ ↔ 5 ft (1.5 m) ↕ 6 ft (1.8 m)

Hybrid with characteristics intermediate between parent species, *L. bullata* and *L. obcordata*. Leaves more rounded than those of *L. bullata* and much less puckered; flowers for longer period over summer. 'Gloriosa' (syn. *L. × ralphii* 'Variegata'), leaves variegated cream and tinged pink; 'Indian Chief', dark reddish brown leaves; 'Kathryn', purplish red, glossy, oval leaves with puckered surface; 'Pixie', bronze-green leaves, chocolate-purple when young. Zones 9–11.

LOPHOSTEMON

This genus is a member of the myrtle (Myrtaceae) family, which includes important plants such as the eucalypts. Its 6 species of evergreen trees are native to Australia and New Guinea. The leaves are spirally arranged and crowded toward the end of the branchlets. The white flowers, with 5 petals and 5 showy feather-like groups of fused stamens, are grouped in short cymes in the upper leaf axils. The fruit is a woody capsule like that of some *Eucalyptus* species, though *Lophostemon* is not closely related to *Eucalyptus*.

Lonicera maackii

Lophomyrtus × ralphii

Lophostemon confertus

CULTIVATION: These trees should be planted in fertile free-draining soil. They will survive outdoors in regions with very light winter frosts in a warm sheltered site but in cool-temperate climates need greenhouse protection. Propagate from seed in spring or autumn. Variegated cultivars are propagated by budding or grafting.

Lophostemon confertus
syn. *Tristania conferta*
BRUSH BOX
🌣 ☀ ↔ 30 ft (9 m) ↑ 130 ft (40 m)
Found in east-coast Queensland and northeast New South Wales, Australia. Densely foliaged tree, pink-brown peeling bark. Leaves long-pointed, elliptical, dark green above, olive green below. White flowers, 1 in (25 mm) wide, fluffy stamens, in summer. Zones 10–12.

Luma apiculata

LOROPETALUM
Currently this genus is believed to comprise a single species of evergreen dome-shaped shrub or small tree from the woodland regions of the Himalayas, China, and Japan. One of the witch-hazel (Hamamelidaceae) family, it is grown for its distinctive flowers and its horizontal branching habit. Leaves are alternate, simple, and smooth-edged, and the small flowers, borne in tight heads of 3 to 6 flowers in the leaf axils, each have 4 twisted strap-like petals. The fruit is a small nut-like capsule containing 2 seeds.
CULTIVATION: This trouble-free plant grows best in fertile, humus-rich, well-drained soil in full sun. As it flowers on the last season's wood, prune after flowering, and only to enhance the shape. Propagate from cuttings taken in summer.

Luculia gratissima

Loropetalum chinense
FRINGE FLOWER
🌣 ❄ ↔ 8 ft (2.4 m) ↑ 6–15 ft (1.8–4.5 m)
Bushy shrub. Leaves small, dull green, oval. Slightly perfumed, creamy white, fringed flowerheads in spring. *L. c.* f. *rubrum,* bronze-foliaged form sometimes sold as 'Burgundy'. *L. c.* 'Plum Delight', purple-red foliage and flowers; 'Sizzling Pink', red spring foliage and bright pink flowers. Zones 8–11.

LUCULIA
This genus in the madder (Rubiaceae) family comprises 5 species of deciduous flowering shrubs and small trees found in elevated forest regions of the Himalayas, from northern India to western China. They are prized both for their attractive foliage and pro-lific clusters of pink, red, or white flowers in the form of a slender tube opening to a broad 5-lobed disc. The fruit is a capsule with 2 chambers containing flattened seeds. Although technically decid-uous, there is no long period of leaflessness, as the new foliage appears at about the same time as the old leaves are dropping.
CULTIVATION: Tolerating only mild frosts, they prefer a moderate summer temperature and grow well in moderately fertile, moist, well-drained soil with humus. They need protection from the wind and do not like competition from other roots. Plant in part-shade or sun; provide adequate water and fertilize regularly from spring to

autumn. Prune back old flowering shoots after flowering. In frost-prone areas, grow them in a greenhouse. Propagate from seed in spring or from half-hardened cuttings in summer.

Luculia grandifolia
🌣/◑ ☀ ↔ 7 ft (2 m) ↑ 12–20 ft (3.5–6 m)
From Bhutan. Leaves large, deep green, ellip-tic to ovate; reddish purple veins, stalks, mar-gins. Large clusters of 16 to 20 very fragrant, white, tubular flowers in summer. Zones 9–10.

Luculia gratissima
🌣/◑ ☀ ↔ 10–15 ft (3–4.5 m) ↑ 10–20 ft (3–6 m)
Large shrub or small tree native to Himalayas. Leaves ovate-oblong to lance-shaped, dark green. Large trusses of fragrant, slender, rosy pink flowers in autumn–mid-winter. Egg-shaped fruit. Zones 9–10.

LUMA
This genus, found in Argentina and Chile, includes just 4 species of densely foliaged, round-headed, evergreen shrubs and trees. In the myrtle (Myrtaceae) family and closely allied to *Myrtus,* they have small aromatic leaves and 4-petalled white flowers with a central mass of stamens. The flowers usually open in spring and early summer, and are followed by dark berries. The bark can also be an attractive feature, as in some species it peels and is a warm cinnamon tone on the outside and white to pink underneath.
CULTIVATION: Species are easily cultivated in any mild climate with adequate rainfall, preferring moist well-drained soil and a position in sun or light shade. Although usually neat growers, they benefit from being lightly trimmed to shape; if allowed to become over-grown, they can be rejuvenated with heavy pruning, best done over 2 or 3 seasons. Propagate from seed or half-hardened tip cuttings.

Luma apiculata ★
syns *Myrtus apiculata, M. luma*
PALO COLORADO, TEMU
🌣/◑ ☀ ↔ 20 ft (6 m) ↑ 20 ft (6 m)
Large shrub or small tree. Flaking warm brown bark. Leaves deep olive green, glossy. Small white flowers, each with over 150 stamens, in spring–summer. Small dark purple-red fruit. Zones 9–10.

LUPINUS *(see page 503)*

Lupinus arboreus
TREE LUPIN, YELLOW BUSH LUPINE

☼ ❋ ↔ 4–8 ft (1.2–2.4 m) ↕ 3–7 ft (0.9–2 m)

Bushy evergreen shrub native to central coastal California, USA, mostly on seashores. Leaves grayish green, smooth above, woolly hairs beneath. Loose racemes of flowers, usually bright yellow, occasionally blue or lavender, in spring–summer. *L. a.* var. *eximius*, hairier stems and leaves, yellow and blue flowers. Zones 8–10.

MACKAYA

This single-species genus is a member of the acanthus (Acanthaceae) family, which also includes the well-known perennial bear's breeches, *Acanthus mollis*. Native to southern Africa, it is an evergreen shrub that grows as an understory plant in forests, often along stream banks. Leaves are very deep green with soft wavy edges. Flowers are tubular with wide-open petals, usually mauve. They occur at the ends of branches from spring to autumn.
CULTIVATION: Grow in moist well-drained soil in full sun or part-shade in a sheltered position. Propagate from seed or from half-hardened cuttings in spring.

Mackaya bella ★

☼/◗ ◗ ↔ 4 ft (1.2 m) ↕ 8 ft (2.4 m)

Develops spreading habit over time. Glossy deep green leaves, wavy edges. Tubular flowers, 5 flaring petals, mauve with darker veining, in loose spikes at ends of branches, in spring–autumn. Zones 9–11.

MACLURA

Notable for their spiny branches, dye-bearing flowers, and interesting fruit, this genus from the mulberry (Moraceae) family contains 12 species of evergreen or deciduous shrubs, trees, and climbers. It occurs worldwide in warm-temperate to tropical regions. There are separate male and female trees. They usually have simple, pointed, ovate leaves, sometimes with a downy underside. Male and female flowers are similar in color (yellow to green shades); female flowers occur in larger clusters. The fruit is spherical, maturing to yellow or orange.
CULTIVATION: Frost hardiness and drought tolerance varies. Most are easily grown in any moist well-drained soil in full sun or part-shade. Brighter positions usually result in more fruit, while shade promotes foliage; thus male trees are best planted with a little shade, while females do better in sun. Prune in winter after the fruit falls, but if winter frost damage is likely, delay pruning until spring. Propagate from seed, from half-hardened cuttings in summer, or from hardwood cuttings in winter.

Maclura pomifera
OSAGE ORANGE

☼/◗ ❋ ↔ 30 ft (9 m) ↕ 50 ft (15 m)

Deciduous tree from Arkansas to Texas, USA. Lustrous leaves, 2–6 in (5–15 cm) long, bright yellow tones in autumn. Tiny green flowers in early summer. Fruit glossy, wrinkled surface. Zones 6–10.

Mackaya bella   *Maclura pomifera*

Maclura tricuspidata
syn. *Cudrania tricuspidata*

☼ ❋ ↔ 15 ft (4.5 m) ↕ 25 ft (8 m)

Thorny deciduous tree native to central China and Korea. Shiny green leaves. Green flowers with small spherical heads, tiny, tightly packed, in summer. Edible round red berries. Leaves are alternative food source for silkworms. Zones 7–10.

MAGNOLIA

Comprising around 100 evergreen and deciduous species and countless cultivars, this genus within the magnolia (Magnoliaceae) family occurs naturally throughout Asia and North America. The flowers are primitive, and many are fragrant. They are pollinated largely by beetles. The flowers are often seen to advantage on bare limbs before the foliage appears, and this simplicity contributes to their universal appeal. Fruit are often cone-like showy clusters, pink or red with colorful seeds, these sometimes suspended on fine threads.
CULTIVATION: Although some species will tolerate lime, most do better in well-drained acid soils rich in manure and humus. Generally fast growing, their fleshy surface roots are easily damaged by cultivation. For this reason they are best left undisturbed. Wind and late frosts can also damage the large flowers. Light shade is generally ideal. Propagate by taking cuttings in summer or sowing seed in autumn. Grafting should be carried out in winter.

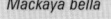

Lupinus arboreus

Magnolia acuminata
CUCUMBER TREE

☼ ❋ ↔ 30 ft (9 m) ↕ 100 ft (30 m)

Deciduous tree from eastern North America. Large oval leaves, blue-green below, hairy. Flowers metallic green to yellow-green, upright petals, in summer. Unripe fruit resemble cucumbers. Zones 4–9.

Magnolia campbellii
CAMPBELL'S MAGNOLIA, PINK TULIP TREE

☼ ❋ ↔ 30 ft (9 m) ↕ 100 ft (30 m)

Tree from Himalayan forests in southwest China to eastern Nepal. Large oval leaves, bronze when young, paler reverse. Huge slightly fragrant flowers, pale to deep pink, before leaves, in late winter–early spring. Seedlings take 30 years to flower, grafted varieties 5 years, using understock of *M.* × *soulangeana*. *M. c.* subsp. *mollicomata*, flowering younger, earlier in season, slightly larger flowers, more cold hardy; 'Lanarth', huge cyclamen-purple flowers. *M. c.* 'Charles Raffill', deep rose pink buds opening to rose-purple outside, white-flushed rose-purple inside; 'Darjeeling' dark rose-purple flowers. Zones 7–9.

Magnolia delavayi

☼/◐ ❄ ↔ 30 ft (9 m) ↑ 35 ft (10 m)

From southern Yunnan Province, China. Evergreen with large dark green leaves, gray-green underside. Large creamy white flowers, fragrant, short lived, opening at night, in late summer. Zones 8–10.

Magnolia denudata

JADE ORCHID, LILY TREE, YULAN

☼/◐ ❄ ↔ 30 ft (9 m) ↑ 30 ft (9 m)

Deciduous tree or shrub native to central China. Leaves alternate, green underside. Flowers white, fragrant, chalice-shaped, symbol of purity, emerge on bare wood before foliage appears, in summer. An exquisite magnolia, plant flowers within 3 years. Zones 6–9.

Magnolia grandiflora

Magnolia fraseri

EAR-LEAFED MAGNOLIA, FRASER'S MAGNOLIA

☼ ❄ ↔ 30 ft (9 m) ↑ 40 ft (12 m)

Broadly spreading, open-branched, deciduous tree from southeast USA. Young bronze foliage becomes pale green. Fragrant flowers, vase-shaped becoming saucer-shaped, creamy white, green flush to outer petals, in late spring–early summer. Zones 6–9.

Magnolia grandiflora

BULL BAY, GREAT LAUREL MAGNOLIA, SOUTHERN MAGNOLIA

☼ ❄ ↔ 35 ft (10 m) ↑ 35 ft (10 m)

Evergreen tree from central Florida to North Carolina and west to Texas, USA. Leaves stiff, leathery, deep glossy green, rusty-furry underside. Large, creamy white, saucer-shaped flowers, fragrant, in early summer. Woody fruit. 'Exmouth', glossy green leaves, rusty-felted beneath, huge fragrant flowers borne from early age;

'Ferruginea', erect form, dense habit, leaf underside richly red-felted; 'Goliath', many huge globular flowers in mid-summer; 'Little Gem', smaller leaves, slightly smaller flowers appear when young. Zones 6–9.

Magnolia kobus

KOBUS MAGNOLIA

☼ ❄ ↔ 30 ft (9 m) ↑ 40 ft (12 m)

From Japan and Korea. Oval leaves dark green, smooth, paler underside. Lightly fragrant, creamy white flowers, streaked pink at base, in early spring, before foliage. Species considered by some to be represented by forms now named *M.* × *loebneri* and *M. stellata. M. k.* var. *borealis*, more vigorous, larger leaves, sparser flowers. Zones 4–8.

Magnolia liliiflora

syn. *Magnolia quinquepeta*

LILY-FLOWERED MAGNOLIA

☼ ❄ ↔ 15 ft (4.5 m) ↑ 10 ft (3 m)

Small deciduous tree or large shrub from central China; smaller than other species. Fully hardy. Oval dark green leaves, paler and downy on reverse. Purplish pink, waxy, goblet-shaped, lily-like flowers, to 3 in (8 cm) wide, appear with foliage, in spring–summer. 'Nigra', wine purple flowers, paler purplish inside. Zones 6–11.

Magnolia × loebneri

LOEBNER MAGNOLIA

☼ ❄ ↔ 20 ft (6 m) ↑ 30 ft (9 m)

M. kobus and *M. stellata* hybrid. Deciduous tree or shrub. Leaves narrow, dark green, long oval-shaped. Flowers large, white, often pink beneath, in spring–summer. 'Leonard Messel', spreading tree; 'Merrill' ★, white flowers. Zones 4–8.

Magnolia macrophylla

BIGLEAF MAGNOLIA, UMBRELLA TREE

☼ ❄ ↔ 30 ft (9 m) ↑ 50 ft (15 m)

Deciduous tree from moist forests of southeast USA. Leaves large, oval, thin-textured, downy reverse. Cup-shaped creamy yellow flowers in early–mid-summer. Round pink fruit cluster. Zones 4–8.

Magnolia grandiflora

Magnolia kobus

Magnolia liliiflora 'Nigra'

Magnolia stellata 'Royal Star'

glossy. Flowers erect, white to rose pink, with deeper color beneath, in spring–summer, before foliage, even on young trees. '**Alexandrina**', large erect flowers, white inside, flushed rosy purple outside, darker veins; '**Brozzonii**', very large, elongated, white flowers, pink-purple veins at base; '**Burgundy**', purple-pink flowers; '**Lennei**', globular flowers, very concave, thick fleshy petals magenta-purple outside, creamy white inside; '**Lennei Alba**', ivory white; '**Picture**', deep maroon to burgundy, fading to white at petal tips; '**Rustica Rubra**', deep rosy pink petals outside, fading to pink-white inside. Zones 4–9.

Magnolia sprengeri
SPRENGER'S MAGNOLIA

☼ ❆ ↔ 25 ft (8 m) ↑ 40 ft (12 m)

Deciduous spreading tree from China. Leaves dark green, oval, felty underside when young. Flowers fragrant, pink, before foliage, in spring. *M. s.* var. *diva*, white flowers. Zones 7–9.

Magnolia salicifolia
WILLOW-LEAFED MAGNOLIA

☼ ❆ ↔ 20 ft (6 m) ↑ 40 ft (12 m)

Shrub or deciduous tree found along streams in Japan. Narrow pale green leaves, glaucous below; lemon-anise scent from leaves, bark, and wood when bruised. Flowers white, fragrant, before foliage, in spring. '**Wada's Memory**', popular cultivar. Zones 6–9.

Magnolia sargentiana

☼ ❆ ↔ 25 ft (8 m) ↑ 60 ft (18 m)

Deciduous tree from China. Leaves deep green, glossy, underside grayish. Flowers purplish pink to white, in spring. *M. s.* var. *robusta*, larger, more shrubby plant, earlier flowers. Sometimes regarded as form of *M. dawsoniana*. Zones 7–9.

Magnolia sieboldii
OYAMA MAGNOLIA, SIEBOLD'S MAGNOLIA

☼ ❆ ↔ 25 ft (8 m) ↑ 20 ft (6 m)

Large, spreading, deciduous shrub from Japan, Korea, and southern China. Leaves felty-white beneath. Spot-flowering, pure white, fragrant, nodding blooms, in late spring–late summer. Small pinkish fruit. *M. s.* subsp. *sinensis*, broadly oval leaves, felty underside; flowers white, cup-shaped, pendulous, strongly lemon-scented, in late spring, with leaves; large pink fruit. Zones 6–9.

Magnolia × soulangeana
SAUCER MAGNOLIA, TULIP MAGNOLIA

☼ ❆ ↔ 20 ft (6 m) ↑ 20 ft (6 m)

Deciduous low-branched tree or large shrub from cross between *M. denudata* and *M. liliiflora*. Leaves short, oval, dark green,

Magnolia stellata
STAR MAGNOLIA

☼ ❆ ↔ 10 ft (3 m) ↑ 15 ft (4.5 m)

Deciduous rounded shrub from highlands of Honshu Island, Japan. Leaves dark green, oval. Clusters of fragrant ivory white flowers, strap-like with curved reflexed petals, in late winter before foliage. Regarded by some as variety of *M. kobus* of garden origin. '**Chrysanthemiflora**', double flowers, white petals, reverse flushed pink; '**Pink Star**', pale pink almost white flowers; '**Rosea**', petals pale pink reverse; '**Royal Star**', abundant, double, snow white flowers; '**Waterlily**' ★, larger, more abundant, pale pink petals. Zones 5–9.

Magnolia, Hybrid Cultivar, 'Judy'

Magnolia × veitchii
VEITCH'S MAGNOLIA

☼ ❆ ↔ 15 ft (4.5 m) ↑ 100 ft (30 m)

Hybrid of *M. denudata* and *M. campbellii*. Leaves bronze-purple to dark green. Flowers upright, fragrant, pink at base, suffusing to white, in mid-spring before foliage. Zones 6–9.

Magnolia virginiana
SWAMP LAUREL, SWEET BAY

☼ ❆ ↔ 20 ft (6 m) ↑ 30 ft (9 m)

From coastal swamps in USA. Evergreen or deciduous. Glossy leaves, silvery below. Lemon-scented cream or white cup-shaped flowers in late summer. Zones 6–9.

Magnolia wilsonii
WILSON'S MAGNOLIA

☼ ❆ ↔ 20 ft (6 m) ↑ 20 ft (6 m)

Spreading deciduous shrub from western China. Narrow, elliptical, dark green leaves, paler felty reverse. White flowers, fragrant, saucer-shaped, pendent, in spring–early summer. Zones 6–9.

Magnolia Hybrid Cultivars

☼ ❄ ↔ 20–30 ft (6–9 m) ↑ 20–40 ft (6–12 m)

Since success of first *M. × soulangeana* hybrids, breeders have focused on producing bigger brighter magnolias. Notable are De Vos & Kosar's Eight Little Girls, Gresham hybrids from America, and those by Jury family of New Zealand. '**Ann**', deep pink base fades to pale pink on tips; '**Apollo**', rosy pink buds, rosy red flowers, in spring; '**Betty**', petals deep rose; '**Charles Coates**', scented, creamy white flowers in spring; '**Elizabeth**', primrose yellow fragrant flowers in late spring, dark green leaves; '**Freeman**', dark green, leathery, glossy leaves, fragrant white flowers in summer; '**Galaxy**', soft pink flowers with creamy white interior, upright, medium-sized to large, tulip-shaped, before foliage, in early spring; '**George Henry Kern**', small, strappy-petalled, white to pale pink flowers with mauve petal reverse; '**Gold Star**', yellow flowers; '**Heaven Scent**', one of Gresham hybrids, beautiful free-flowering, scented, narrow, deep pink, cup-shaped blooms in early spring; '**Iolanthe**', very large-flowered Jury hybrid; '**Jane**', deep pink flowers with deeper vein, in early spring; '**Judy**', small flowers, sometimes scented; '**Manchu Fan**', velvety cream flowers; '**No. 4**', pink flowers fade to white at tips, erect petals, turned back at tips; '**Pink Alba Superba**', deep pink cup-shaped flowers, in spring; '**Pinkie**', petals pink underneath, white on top; '**Randy**', very deep pink underside, triangular shrub or small tree; '**Ricki**', pale pink flowers, deeper underside, very erect petals; '**Rouged Alabaster**', creamy flowers, flushed with rose pink; '**Royal Crown**', flowers dark red to violet with white interior, outside tepals reflexed to resemble crown, in spring; '**Susan**', pale pink flowers deepening near center, faint ribbing; '**Vulcan**', cyclamen pink flowers; '**Yellow Lantern**', yellow flowers. Zones 6–9.

MAHONIA

This genus from the barberry (Berberidaceae) family of some 70 species of evergreen shrubs is found in Asia and North America, some species extending into Central America. Leaves are often very spiny and may be trifoliate or pinnate with relatively large leaflets; leaves may be carried alternately, or in whorls, with several changes of color during maturation. Sprays of small yellow flowers, often scented, appear between spring

Mahonia fremontii

and early winter. Fruit is usually blue-black edible berries with a grape-like powdery bloom. Botanists have long debated whether *Mahonia* should be maintained as a genus distinct from *Berberis*. Most British and Continental botanists have recognized both genera, while there is a strong school in North America, where the characteristics distinguishing the two groups tend to break down, that prefers to place all species in a broadly defined *Berberis*. Recent studies have given support to the latter classification, and *Mahonia* is recognized here only pending a more comprehensive survey.

CULTIVATION: Mahonias vary in hardiness. Most commonly grown species are temperate-zone plants tolerant of moderate to hard frosts, while some tropical Asian species withstand only light frosts. They prefer moist, well-drained, fertile soil rich in humus. Protect from the summer sun. Pruning is seldom necessary. Propagate from cuttings, or rooted suckers that grow at the base of established plants.

Mahonia aquifolium

OREGON HOLLY GRAPE

☼ ❄ ↔ 8 ft (2.4 m) ↑ 6 ft (1.8 m)

Suckering clump-forming shrub from western North America. Pinnate leaves composed of 5 to 13 spiny holly-like leaflets, dark green in summer, strong red tints in winter. Erect racemes of yellow to golden yellow flowers in late winter. Purple-black fruit. '**Compacta**', tiny, round, yellow flowers; '**Green Ripple**', green rippled leaves. Zones 5–10.

Mahonia fortunei

☼ ❄ ↔ 3 ft (0.9 m) ↑ 7 ft (2 m)

Chinese shrub, notable foliage. Leaves to 10 in (25 cm) long; dark green leaflets, 4 in (10 cm) long, pale underside. Leaflets bronze when young, toothed rather than spiny. Short racemes of bright yellow flowers in autumn. Zones 7–10.

Mahonia fremontii

DESERT MAHONIA

☼ ❄ ↔ 7 ft (2 m) ↑ 12 ft (3.5 m)

Drought-tolerant shrub from southwestern USA and Mexico. Open branching habit. Leaves pale green, strongly glaucous in best forms, 3 to 7 spiny toothed leaflets. Clusters of soft yellow flowers in summer. Deep yellow to red fruit. Zones 8–11.

Mahonia 'Golden Abundance'

☼ ❄ ↔ 3 ft (0.9 m) ↑ 6–8 ft (1.8–2.4 m)

Often listed as cultivar of *M. aquifolium*, but is probably hybrid. Densely foliaged, glossy, holly-like leaves. Golden yellow flowers, in large clusters, in summer. Purple-blue berries. Zones 6–9.

Mahonia japonica

☼ ❄ ↔ 10 ft (3 m) ↑ 6 ft (1.8 m)

Spreading shrub native to Japan; cultivated in China and Taiwan. Long leathery leaves, with 19 spiny dark green leaflets. Fragrant bright yellow flowers, in upright or arching racemes, in late winter. Small blue-black fruit. **Bealei Group**, upright shrubs, native to western China, deep olive green leaflets, scented pale yellow flowers in late winter. Zones 6–10.

Mahonia aquifolium

Mahonia lomariifolia

◗ ❄ ↔ 8 ft (2.4 m) ↑ 10 ft (3 m)

Upright shrub from Myanmar and western China. Leaves bronze ageing to dark green, 20 to 40 spiny leaflets. Erect spikes of fragrant yellow flowers in autumn–spring. Purple-blue fruit. Zones 7–10.

Mahonia × *media*

◗ ❄ ↔ 12 ft (3.5 m) ↑ 15 ft (4.5 m)

M. japonica and *M. lomariifolia* hybrid. Vigorous upright plant, foliage reddens in winter. Erect racemes of yellow flowers in summer. 'Arthur Menzies', bright yellow flower spikes; 'Buckland', fragrant flowers, long arching racemes; 'Charity', tall, flowers in winter; 'Winter Sun', horizontal racemes in autumn. Zones 7–10.

Mahonia repens

CREEPING MAHONIA

◗ ❄ ↔ 36 in (90 cm) ↑ 18 in (45 cm)

Suckering shrub from northwest North America. Blue-green leaves, reddening in winter, to 10 in (25 cm) long, 5 leaflets, very spiny. Flowers deep yellow, fragrant, in spring. Blue-black fruit. 'Denver Strain', dark green leaves. Zones 6–9.

Mahonia repens

MALPIGHIA

Found in tropical America and the islands of the Caribbean, this genus encompasses 45 species of evergreen shrubs and trees from the self-named Malpighiaceae family. They bear opposite pairs of sometimes hairy, rounded to lance-shaped leaves that may be smooth-edged or conspicuously toothed. Flowers are very distinctive because of the long-stemmed petals held clear of the central staminal cluster. The flowers may be borne singly or in small corymbs and are followed by small brightly colored drupes. CULTIVATION: These tropical plants will not tolerate frosts or prolonged cool conditions, but are otherwise easy to grow, provided they are given moderately fertile well-drained soil, occasional feeding, and water during dry periods. Most species can be trimmed back quite hard if necessary. Propagate from seed or cuttings.

Mahonia × *media*

Malpighia coccigera

BARBADOS HOLLY, MINIATURE HOLLY, SINGAPORE HOLLY

◗ ⊗ ↔ 30 in (75 cm) ↑ 30 in (75 cm)

Small shrub native to West Indies. Glossy deep green leaves, 1 in (25 mm) long, deeply toothed. Covered with pink to mauve flowers in summer. Red drupes. Zones 10–12.

Malpighia glabra

ACEROLA, BARBADOS CHERRY

◗ ⊗ ↔ 4 ft (1.2 m) ↑ 10 ft (3 m)

Shrub from southern Texas (USA), Caribbean, Central America, and northern areas of South America. Leaves glossy, smooth-edged, 4 in (10 cm) long. Pale to deep pink or red flowers in summer, followed by small, round, red, edible fruit. Zones 9–12.

MALUS

APPLE, CRABAPPLE

This well-known genus is found in temperate regions right around the Northern Hemisphere. The apples and crabapples comprise a large genus of around 30 species of ornamental and fruiting, small to medium-sized, deciduous trees belonging to the rose (Rosaceae) family. Nearly all have soft green leaves. The fruits are pomes; not all crabapples are edible, some being too bitter for the human palate. The cultivated apple is one of the most widely grown of all edible fruits, and the many species and cultivars of crabapple are valued as ornamental trees. CULTIVATION: *Malus* will grow in all cool-temperate regions. Apples and crabapples flower in spring and most cultivated varieties of apple require a cross-pollinator in order to produce fruit. While cultivated apples require careful winter pruning, crabapples, being largely ornamental, need less attention. Propagate by grafting onto an apple rootstock, some of which produce a dwarfed plant.

Malus baccata

SIBERIAN CRABAPPLE

☼ ❄ ↔ 40 ft (12 m) ↑ 40 ft (12 m)

Rounded erect tree from Siberia. Buds pinkish, open to single, white, fragrant flowers. Fruit red, sometimes yellow, on long thin stems. Resistant to most apple diseases. *M. b.* var. *mandshurica*, from Japan and northeast China, lightly serrated leaves, underside initially downy, single white flowers, red fruit; 'Midwest', larger creamy white flowers. *M. b.* 'Jackii', spreading habit, stouter branches; 'Spring Snow', drooping white flowers. Zones 2–9.

Malus coronaria

AMERICAN CRABAPPLE, AMERICAN SWEET CRABAPPLE

☼ ❄ ↔ 30 ft (9 m) ↑ 30 ft (9 m)

Large wide-limbed tree from eastern USA. Buds dark pink, single flowers, fragrant, pale pink to pink-white or salmon pink. Green fruit unpalatable. Susceptible to scab and rust diseases. *M. c.* var. *angustifolia*, short trunk, spreading branches, highly fragrant rose-colored flowers, susceptible to disease. *M. c.* var. *dasycalyx*, leaves paler beneath, woolly calyx; 'Charlottae', apricot to deep pink buds, light pink semi-double to double flowers. Zones 4–9.

Malus × *gloriosa*

Malus × *micromalus*

Malus × *purpurea*

Malus floribunda

JAPANESE FLOWERING CRABAPPLE

☼ ❄ ↔ 20 ft (6 m) ↕ 12 ft (3.5 m)

From Japan. Leaves green, serrated, tapered. Buds dark pink to red, opening to single light pink or nearly white flowers in late spring. Fruit yellow and red, ½ in (12 mm) in diameter. May be affected by powdery mildew. Long cultivated. Zones 4–9.

Malus × *gloriosa*

☼ ❄ ↔ 7–10 ft (2–3 m) ↕ 10 ft (3 m)

Hybrid shrub of *M. pumila* 'Niedzwetzkyana' and *M.* × *scheideckeri*. Heavily toothed leaves, red-tinted when young. Purple-red flowers, 1½ in (35 mm) wide. Yellow fruit, ½ in (12 mm) wide, in spring. 'Oekonomierat Echtermeyer', pendulous bronze foliage. Zones 4–9.

Malus halliana

☼ ❄ ↔ 10 ft (3 m) ↕ 15 ft (4.5 m)

Small tree with loose open habit, from China. Leaves oblong, dark green, often purple-tinted. Red stalks. Flowers bright rose, nodding, in late spring. Fruit purplish, ripening late. Disease resistant. *M. h.* var. *spontanea*, shorter, smaller whitish flowers, greenish yellow fruit. *M. h.* 'Parkmanii', bronze-green glossy leaves, flowers double or semi-double, flesh-pink; fruit red to red-purple. Zones 4–9.

Malus hupehensis

HUPEH CRABAPPLE, TEA CRABAPPLE

☼ ❄ ↔ 25 ft (8 m) ↕ 15 ft (4.5 m)

Open spreading tree from China and India. Leaves deep green, violet when young. Buds pink, open to single, white, fragrant flowers in spring. Fruit green-yellow, slight red cheek. Zones 4–10.

Malus ioensis

IOWA CRABAPPLE, PRAIRIE CRABAPPLE

☼ ❄ ↔ 20 ft (6 m) ↕ 20 ft (6 m)

Native to midwest USA. Leaves dark green, deeply serrated, yellowish green underside. Flowers white tinged with pink, fragrant, in spring. Fruit shiny green. Highly susceptible to disease, several resistant clones produced. 'Plena', fully double pink flowers; 'Prairifire' ★, dark pink buds and flowers. Zones 2–9.

Malus × *micromalus*

☼ ❄ ↔ 15 ft (4.5 m) ↕ 15 ft (4.5 m)

Small Japanese tree, hybrid between *M. baccata* and *M. spectabilis*. Dark brown stems, waxy serrated leaves taper to fine point. Pink blooms, in clusters of 3 to 5 flowers, in spring. Yellow somewhat pointed fruit, ½ in (12 mm) wide. Zones 4–9.

Malus × *purpurea*

☼ ❄ ↔ 25 ft (8 m) ↕ 20 ft (6 m)

Very early flowering, hybrid of *M.* × *atrosanguinea* and *M. pumila* 'Niedzwetzkyana'. Deep green leaves. Dark flowers fade to pale mauve, in late spring. 'Aldenhamensis', blooms up to 3 times per season, leaves red-green to bronze-green, single and semi-double pinkish red flowers; 'Eleyi', deep red-purple foliage, purple to red flowers, subject to leaf diseases; 'Lemoinei', red flowers. Zones 4–9.

Malus sargentii

SARGENT'S CRABAPPLE

☼ ❄ ↔ 15 ft (4.5 m) ↕ 6 ft (1.8 m)

Densely branched. Leaves broadly oval, sharp-tipped, heavy, bright green, lobed, serrated edges. Flowers white, single, fragrant, in spring. Fruit tiny, crimson to purple. Blooms in alternate years. 'Rosea', deep red-pink buds, white flowers, dark red fruit. Zones 4–9.

Malus × *scheideckeri*

☼ ❄ ↔ 8 ft (2.4 m) ↕ 15 ft (4.5 m)

Slow-growing, small, upright tree, hybrid of *M. floribunda* and *M. prunifolia*. Coarsely serrated leaves. Flowers faded rose pink, usually semi-double, in thick clusters on branches, in late spring. Fruit slightly ribbed, yellow-orange. Tolerates pruning. 'Exzellenz Thiel', pale pink to white flowers; 'Red Jade', drooping red fruit. Zones 4–9.

Malus sieboldii

Malus sieboldii

☼ ❄ ↔ 10 ft (3 m) ↕ 15 ft (4.5 m)

Slow-growing, small to medium-size, rounded tree from Japan. Lobed or simple leaves. Buds red to carmine, open to single white flowers in spring. Fruit very small, red. Disease resistant. *M. s.* var. *arborescens*, larger leaves, white flowers, reddish fruit. Zones 4–9.

Malus, Hybrid Cultivar, 'Red Sentinel'

Malus sylvestris
COMMON CRABAPPLE, WILD CRABAPPLE

☀ ❁ ↔ 10 ft (3 m) ↑ 30 ft (9 m)

From Europe. Small tree with dense rounded crown, dark bark. Some branches thorny. Flowers white or pink, followed by sour yellow-green or reddish fruit. Zones 3–9.

Malus tschonoskii

☀ ❁ ↔ 20 ft (6 m) ↑ 40 ft (12 m)

From Japan. Sturdy upright habit. Green leaves turn purple, orange, bronze, yellow, and crimson in autumn. Flowers white with pink hue, in spring. Fruit insignificant. Susceptible to most apple diseases. Zones 6–10.

Malus × *zumi*

☀ ❁ ↔ 10 ft (3 m) ↑ 15 ft (4.5 m)

Small downy-stemmed tree, pyramidal habit. Natural Japanese hybrid of *M. baccata* var. *mandshurica* and *M. sieboldii*. Leaves taper to fine point, scalloped to lobed edges. Pink buds, in spring, open to white flowers, 1¼ in (30 mm) wide. Small red fruit. *M.* × *z.* var. *calocarpa*, smaller flowers, leaves smooth-edged on fruiting spurs, lobed elsewhere. Zones 5–9.

Malus Hybrid Cultivars

☀ ❁ ↔ 5–25 ft (1.5–8 m) ↑ 10–40 ft (3–12 m)

Numerous crabapple cultivars raised, many in USA. Most grown for floral display, some for decorative fruit, and larger fruit of some eaten fresh or as preserves. Parent with most influence is *M. pumila* 'Niedzwetzkyana', originating from single tree with red flowers and purple-red new foliage, discovered in central Asia before 1900. 'Adirondack', 12 ft (3.5 m) high, white flowers with traces of pink, fruit red to orange-red; 'Almey', deep reddish pink flowers, small fruit; 'Beverly', 20 ft (6 m) high, white single flowers, red fruit; 'Brandywine', 20 ft (6 m) high, double fragrant flowers of rose pink, yellow-green fruit; 'Butterball', 25 ft (8 m) high, pinkish

white flowers, orange-yellow fruit; 'Chilko', single purple-pink flowers, red to crimson fruit; 'Christmas Holly' ★, 15 ft (4.5 m) high, single white flowers, fruit holly-like, bright red; 'Dolgo', white flowers; 'Fiesta', 15 ft (4.5 m) high, single white flowers, fruit coral to orange-gold; 'Golden Hornet', single white flowers, fruit lime-yellow; 'Gorgeous', single white flowers, fruit crimson to orange-red; 'Harvest Gold', single white flowers, golden fruit, disease resistant; 'John Downie', single white flowers, fruit orange with red cheeks, disease resistant; 'Madonna', 20 ft (6 m) high, flowers large, double, fragrant, white; 'Mary Potter', 20 ft (6 m) high, bright pink flowers, deep red to purple-red fruit; 'Naragansett', 12 ft (3.5 m) high, single white flowers, pink hue, shiny cherry red fruit, disease resistant; 'Pink Perfection', sterile, pink and white double flowers; 'Profusion', 20 ft (6 m) high, deep rose pink single flowers, fruit maroon to blood red; 'Red Sentinel', early white flowers, red fruit; 'Royalty', 15 ft (4.5 m) high, purple-red flowers and fruit; 'White Angel' (syn. 'Inglis'), white flowers, small red fruit; 'White Cascade', 15 ft (4.5 m) high, single white flowers, green-yellow fruit, disease resistant; 'Winter Gold', 20 ft (6 m) high, single white flowers, fruit bright lemon yellow. Zones 4–9.

MALVAVISCUS

This genus consists of 3 species of Central and South American evergreen shrubs from the mallow (Malvaceae) family. Their broad downy leaves are often lobed. They have unusually shaped flowers, borne singly in the leaf axils or in small clusters at the ends of branches. They are bright orange-red and usually held upright.

The long petals stay partly furled, never really opening fully, and from their center emerges a long hibiscus-like column. Small red berries follow the flowers.

CULTIVATION: Although able to withstand the very lightest frosts, these shrubs are best grown in warm subtropical to tropical areas. They thrive in moist, humus-rich, well-drained soil and can be grown in sun or part-shade. Their branches have a tendency to die back and are often attacked by boring grubs, so some pruning, thinning, and trimming is necessary. Propagate from seed or half-hardened cuttings.

Malvaviscus penduliflorus

Malvaviscus arboreus
TURK'S CAP, WAX MALLOW

☀ ❁ ↔ 10 ft (3 m) ↑ 12–15 ft (3.5–4.5 m)

Shrub from southern Texas and Florida, USA, to Peru and Brazil. Velvety ovate to heart-shaped leaves, may be 3-lobed. Long-stemmed rich red flowers, face upward or slightly bent, in summer. *M. a.* var. *drummondii*, brilliant reddish orange hibiscus-like flowers, swirled petals never fully open, in late summer–autumn. Zones 8–12.

Malvaviscus penduliflorus
syn. *Malvaviscus arboreus* var. *penduliflorus*
CARDINAL'S HAT, SLEEPING HIBISCUS

☀ ✿ ↔ 10 ft (3 m) ↑ 12–15 ft (3.5–4.5 m)

Mexican shrub, similar to *M. arboreus*. Less hairy leaves. Larger, pendulous rather than upright, red flowers in summer. Zones 11–12.

MAYTENUS

This genus of the spindle-tree (Celastraceae) family, with more than 200 species, occurs in southern Europe, Africa, tropical and eastern Asia, Central and South America, and Australia. Trees, shrubs, or scrambling shrubs, all are evergreen, some with rhizomes. Leaves are simple, smooth-edged or toothed. The small, usually whitish flowers can be bisexual; there may be separate males and females on the same plant or on different plants. The leathery or woody fruit are 2- to 5-celled capsules; in a few species they are fleshy, the seeds partly or wholly surrounded by a fleshy aril. Extracts from some species have been locally used for medicinal purposes.
CULTIVATION: Frost hardiness varies. All species should be grown in a sunny position in well-drained soil. Propagate from seed sown while as fresh as possible, or from cuttings.

Maytenus boaria ★

MAITEN, MAYTEN

☼ ❄ ↔ 30 ft (9 m) ↑ 70 ft (21 m)

Tree or large shrub from forests in Chile, Argentina, Bolivia, Paraguay, and southern Brazil. Glossy dark green leaves with finely toothed edges. Small, greenish, separate male and female flowers in spring. Fruit 3- to 5-celled, orange-red, aril red. Zones 8–11.

MEGASKEPASMA

The sole species in this genus from the acanthus (Acanthaceae) family is an evergreen shrub from Venezuela. It is a lushly foliaged plant with flowers that are striking in both color and shape. These appear throughout most of the year. This plant is a must for any warm-climate garden; it is also useful as a plant for large conservatories and greenhouses.
CULTIVATION: This shrub needs warmth, moisture, and humidity to do well. Given the right climate, a humus-rich soil, and regular feeding, it is the very epitome of a luxuriant tropical plant. Because its stems are soft and pliable it can be espaliered against a sheltered wall in cooler zones. Propagate from seed or half-hardened cuttings.

Megaskepasma erythrochlamys

BRAZILIAN RED CLOAK

☼ ▨ ↔ 4 ft (1.2 m) ↑ 10 ft (3 m)

Evergreen shrub from Venezuela. Heavily veined, semi-glossy, mid-green leaves. White or pale pink flowers, on upright red spikes, almost enclosed by red bracts; held above foliage. Zones 10–12.

MELALEUCA

There are approximately 220 species in this genus of evergreen shrubs and trees, mostly native to Australia, from the myrtle (Myrtaceae) family. Some species are known as paperbarks for their ornamental, papery-textured, creamy white or pale brown bark that peels off in layers, but the majority have non-papery bark. The nectar-rich flowers, with numerous stamens united into 5 bundles, are grouped into dense spikes or heads and range in color from white, yellow, and orange to pink, red, and purple. Small woody seed capsules often persist on the branches.
CULTIVATION: Most melaleucas are easily grown in full sun or part-shade in acidic well-drained soil. Fast-growing and adaptable plants, they can withstand pollution, some degree of coastal exposure, and moist poorly drained soil. Most species will withstand light frosts if given full sun; some species will tolerate heavy frosts. Shrubby species respond well to clipping after flowering and can be used for hedges and screens. Propagate from seed or cuttings.

Melaleuca armillaris

BRACELET HONEY MYRTLE

☼ ▨ ↔ 12 ft (3.5 m) ↑ 25 ft (8 m)

Tall shrub or small tree from southeastern coastal Australia. Spreading canopy of narrow dark green leaves. White flowers, in small cylindrical heads, in late spring–summer. Zones 9–11.

Melaleuca bracteata

BLACK TEA-TREE, RIVER TEA-TREE

☼ ▨ ↔ 20 ft (6 m) ↑ 30 ft (9 m)

Variable shrub or small tree from tropical and central Australian watercourses. Soft, linear, bright green leaves. Profuse creamy white flowers, in heads at branch ends or in short spikes, in spring. 'Golden Gem', to 6 ft (1.8 m) high, rich golden yellow leaves, colorful in early spring; 'Revolution Gold', reddish young stems, golden foliage, bushy upright habit, to 12 ft (3.5 m) high; 'Revolution Green', to 10 ft (3 m) high, fine bright green foliage. Zones 9–12.

Melaleuca fulgens

SCARLET HONEY MYRTLE

☼ ❄ ↔ 6 ft (1.8 m) ↑ 10 ft (3 m)

Erect shrub from semi-arid Western Australia. Narrow linear leaves. Spikes of red, orange, or pink flowers, on older stems, in spring–summer. *M. f.* subsp. *steedmanii*, leaves obovate, flat. Zones 8–11.

Maytenus boaria

Megaskepasma erythrochlamys

Melaleuca fulgens

Melaleuca quinquenervia, in the wild, New Caledonia

Melaleuca hypericifolia
HILLOCK BUSH

☼ ❄ ↔ 15 ft (4.5 m) ↑ 15 ft (4.5 m)

Tall, often spreading shrub from southeastern Australia. Slightly pendulous branches, oblong leaves in opposite pairs. Showy orange-red flowers, in cylindrical spikes, to 2 in (5 cm) long, in late spring–mid-summer. Tolerates exposure to salt-laden winds. Zones 9–11.

Melaleuca incana
GRAY HONEY MYRTLE

☼ ❄ ↔ 10 ft (3 m) ↑ 10 ft (3 m)

Dense weeping shrub from southwest Western Australia, grows naturally in wet situations. Gray-green linear leaves, often softly hairy, prominent oil glands. Creamy yellow flowers, in oval spikes, at branch ends, in early spring–mid-summer. Zones 8–11.

Melaleuca lateritia
ROBIN REDBREAST BUSH

☼ ❄ ↔ 3 ft (0.9 m) ↑ 6 ft (1.8 m)

Multi-stemmed shrub from Western Australia. Light green linear leaves, aromatic when crushed. Spikes to 3 in (8 cm) long of orange-red flowers, in spring–summer, other times sporadically. Zones 9–11.

Melaleuca leucadendra
CAJEPUT, WEEPING PAPERBARK

☼ ❄ ↔ 30 ft (9 m) ↑ 90 ft (27 m)

Spreading tree, pendulous branches and foliage, from tropical northern Australia. White to pale brown papery bark. Curved, thin-textured, lance-shaped leaves. Nectar-rich creamy white flowers, in spikes, in autumn–winter. Zones 10–12.

Melaleuca linariifolia
FLAX-LEAFED PAPERBARK, SNOW IN SUMMER

☼ ❄ ↔ 10 ft (3 m) ↑ 20 ft (6 m)

Bushy tree from eastern Australia. Creamy papery bark. Soft dark green foliage. Masses of creamy white flowers, in spikes, to 1½ in (35 mm) long, in early summer. 'Snowstorm' ★, prolific-flowering, to 5 ft (1.5 m) tall. Zones 8–11.

Melaleuca pulchella
☼ ❄ ↔ 6 ft (1.8 m) ↑ 6 ft (1.8 m)

Spreading shrub from southern coastal heathland of Western Australia. Small, crowded, oblong leaves. Mauve-pink flowers, large, curved claw-like stamens, in late spring–summer. Zones 8–11.

Melaleuca quinquenervia
BROAD-LEAFED PAPERBARK

☼ ❄ ↔ 20 ft (6 m) ↑ 30–50 ft (9–15 m)

Found in swampy areas in coastal eastern Australia, New Guinea, and New Caledonia. Thick, creamy, papery bark. Leathery lance-shaped leaves. Spikes of nectar-rich creamy white flowers, at ends of branches or in leaf axils, in late spring. Zones 10–12.

Melaleuca radula
GRACEFUL HONEY MYRTLE

☼ ❄ ↔ 6 ft (1.8 m) ↑ 6 ft (1.8 m)

Spreading, rather open shrub from Western Australia. Leaves narrow, linear, with raised oil glands. Pink to purple flowers, in long loose spikes, on older wood, in winter–spring. Zones 8–11.

Melaleuca thymifolia
THYME HONEY MYRTLE

☼ ❄ ↔ 3 ft (0.9 m) ↑ 3 ft (0.9 m)

Small, spreading, aromatic shrub from damp places in eastern Australia. Slender branches, small narrow-elliptic leaves. Fringed, claw-like, mauve-purple flowers, in irregular clusters, 1½ in (35 mm) long, on older wood, throughout year. 'Cotton Candy', mauve flowers; 'White Lace', white flowers. Zones 8–11.

MELASTOMA

This genus of around 70 species of tropical and subtropical shrubs from the melastoma (Melastomataceae) family is allied to the similar *Tibouchina*, and occurs primarily in tropical Asia. These plants have attractive heavily veined leaves that are often bristly above, with a downy underside. The leaves are oblong to lance-shaped with smooth edges, their size varying with the species. The flowers, borne in small heads at the ends of branches, are 5-petalled, usually in pink to soft purple shades, and are sometimes scented; they appear from 2 small bracts and have bristly calyces. Small, usually inconspicuous berries follow.
CULTIVATION: These tender warm-climate shrubs are best grown in reasonably fertile, moist, humus-rich, well-drained soil in sun or part-shade. They can be pruned after flowering, or in spring in cooler climates, to remove any winter damage. Propagation is usually from half-hardened cuttings taken in summer.

Melastoma malabathricum

Melastoma malabathricum
☼ ❄ ↔ 5 ft (1.5 m) ↑ 6–8 ft (1.8–2.4 m)

Shrub from India and Southeast Asia, where its red berries are used medicinally. Scaly branches; 3- to 5-veined, velvety, broad, lance-shaped leaves. Up to 5 mauve to purple flower-heads, almost year-round. Zones 10–12.

MELIA

This small genus of 3 species in the mahogany (Meliaceae) family is native to southern Asia, Australasia, and tropical Africa. All are deciduous trees with alternate bipinnate leaves and showy flowers in long panicles. They are valued for their rapid growth and adaptability to a range of soils and climates, including dry conditions. CULTIVATION: These trees need good drainage. Severe frost will defoliate them, but is unlikely to do permanent damage. Pruning is not normally necessary, apart from the removal of competing leaders in the early stages. Propagate from seed in spring.

Melia azedarach

PERSIAN LILAC, WHITE CEDAR

☼ ❄ ↔ 25 ft (8 m) ↑ 20–80 ft (6–24 m)

Melia azedarach

Metasequoia glyptostroboides

Fast-growing tree from southwest Asia to China and Japan and south to Australia. Variable species. Pointed mid-green leaflets. Fragrant lilac flowers, in loose panicles, in summer. Clusters of persistent, rounded, yellow, bead-like fruit, toxic to animals and young children, but not to birds. Zones 8–12.

MELIANTHUS

This genus of 6 species of often leggy shrubs native to South Africa is a member of the honey-flower (Melianthaceae) family. *M. major* is naturalized in India. Small flowers borne in erect bracted racemes produce a large quantity of nectar. Vigorous growers, they are often treated like perennials, being cut back severely to shoot again and inhibit their straggling tendencies. CULTIVATION: Not frost hardy, they grow well in full sun or part-shade in free-draining but moisture-retentive soil. Propagate from seed in spring, softwood cuttings in spring and summer, or rooted suckers in spring.

Melianthus major

Melianthus major

HONEY FLOWER

☼/◐ ❄ ↔ 3 ft (0.9 m) ↑ 6–10 ft (1.8–3 m)

Shrub native to hilly grasslands of South Africa. Large, decorative, pinnate leaves, 20 in (50 cm) long, up to 17 oval leaflets, toothed, gray-green. Racemes of brick red tubular flowers in spring–midsummer. Used in folk medicine. Can be invasive. Zones 8–11.

METASEQUOIA

A genus of a single species of conifer in the cypress (Cupressaceae) family, this plant was long thought to be extinct, known only from fossil remains found in China. In 1941 a Chinese botanist visited a village between Hubei and Sichuan and noticed a deciduous conifer known locally as *shuiskan*. It was found that the tree was identical to the fossil remains. Seed was collected in 1947 and sent to the Arnold Arboretum in the USA, from where it was distributed to botanic gardens throughout the world. Finally named and described in 1948, it has become a popular ornamental tree both in and outside China. The bark is reddish brown, darkening with age. The leaves are green and flattened and turn reddish brown in autumn.

CULTIVATION: *Metasequoia* species grow rapidly, particularly in a moist but well-drained soil, and have proved hardy and relatively resistant to atmospheric pollution. It is highly regarded as an ornamental for large gardens and parks in cool-temperate areas. Propagate from seed.

Metasequoia glyptostroboides ★

DAWN REDWOOD

☼ ❄ ↔ 20 ft (6 m) ↑ 70 ft (21 m)

Vigorous, quick-growing, deciduous conifer. Cinnamon brown bark. Flattened linear leaves, on short branchlets, turn tawny pink and old gold in autumn. Pendulous dark brown cones on long stalks. Zones 5–10.

METROSIDEROS

This genus is a member of the large myrtle (Myrtaceae) family, which includes *Eucalyptus* and *Psidium* (guava). It is found in South Africa, the Pacific Islands, Australia, and New Zealand. *Metrosideros* contains 50 species of evergreen shrubs, trees, and woody climbers with simple, opposite, often leathery leaves that can be aromatic. Flowers consist of numerous stamens and are crowded into rounded heads, usually in shades of red, pink, or white. CULTIVATION: *Metrosideros* species are best suited to warmer climates, but will grow in any reasonably fertile well-drained soil. *M. excelsa*, in particular, will grow in dry soils of lower fertility and in very exposed coastal conditions. It can be pruned for hedging and used as shelter. In cool climates, plants can be grown in pots, overwintered in a greenhouse and placed outdoors for summer. Propagate from seed sown in spring, or half-hardened cuttings taken in summer.

Metrosideros excelsa ★

NEW ZEALAND CHRISTMAS TREE, POHUTUKAWA

☼ ❄ ↔ 25 ft (8 m) ↑ 15–50 ft (4.5–15 m)

Shrubby coastal tree from New Zealand. Thick, leathery, oval leaves, dark green above, gray felted below. Red-crimson bottle-brush-like flowerheads in early summer. Young trees susceptible to frost. 'Fire Mountain', orangey scarlet flowers. Zones 9–11.

Metrosideros polymorpha

Michelia yunnanensis

Microbiota decussata

Metrosideros kermadecensis
KERMADEC POHUTUKAWA

☼ ❄ ↔ 15 ft (4.5 m) ↑ 20 ft (6 m)

Native to Kermadec Islands, New Zealand. Similar to *M. excelsa,* but smaller leaves and flowers. Blooms spasmodically year-round. 'Variegatus', wide creamy yellow margin on leaves. Zones 9–11.

Metrosideros polymorpha
OHI'A LEHUA

☼ ⚘ ↔ 20 ft (6 m) ↑ 20–50 ft (6–15 m)

Low prostrate shrub or tree from Hawaiian Islands. Bark rough, fissured. Oval to rounded leaves, felted beneath. Bottlebrush-like flowerheads, red to pink and yellow, in spring–summer. Zones 11–12.

MICHELIA

This genus of about 45 species of mostly evergreen trees and shrubs in the magnolia (Magnoliaceae) family is native to tropical and subtropical regions of Asia. All have simple leaves and solitary flowers in leaf axils that are strongly perfumed, especially after nightfall. Oils from some species are extracted for use in perfumes. CULTIVATION: *Michelia* species grow best in a reasonably fertile, well-drained, and lime-free soil in a sunny position with shelter from strong winds. They are not reliably frost hardy. Pruning is seldom necessary apart from the removal of competing leaders. Propagate from seed sown as soon as it is hardened in a warm and humid atmosphere.

Michelia champaca
CHAMPACA

☼ ❄ ↔ 10 ft (3 m) ↑ 100 ft (30 m)

Erect evergreen tree from eastern Himalayan foothills. Leaves bright green, shiny above, dull beneath. Cup-shaped flowers, deep yellowish cream, heavily perfumed, in mid-summer–mid-autumn. Fruit pale yellow-green, spotted brown. Zones 10–11.

Michelia doltsopa
☼ ❄ ↔ 20 ft (6 m) ↑ 30 ft (9 m)

Mostly evergreen tree native to western China and eastern Himalayas. Pendulous dark green leaves. Cup-shaped flowers, white to deep cream, greenish hue at base, heavily perfumed, in late winter–spring. 'Silver Cloud' ★, profuse white flowers. Zones 9–11.

Michelia figo
BANANA SHRUB, PORT-WINE MAGNOLIA

☼ ❄ ↔ 10 ft (3 m) ↑ 15 ft (4.5 m)

Medium to large shrub from southeastern China. Small, dark green, glossy leaves. Small purple-brown flowers in spring–summer. Fragrance resembles bananas and vintage port. Zones 9–11.

Michelia yunnanensis
☼ ❄ ↔ 7 ft (2 m) ↑ 15 ft (4.5 m)

Slow-growing shrub or small tree native to China. Brownish velvety covering on young leaves and buds. Leaves variably sized, shaped. Flowers yellow-white, little scent, in late winter–spring. Zones 10–11.

MICROBIOTA
RUSSIAN CYPRESS, SIBERIAN CARPET CYPRESS

This conifer genus in the cypress (Cupressaceae) family contains just one species, commonly found in the mountains of southeastern Siberia above the timber line. It is a small shrub with male and female cones borne on separate plants. CULTIVATION: This shrub is quite adaptable to cultivation in milder climates in moist soil. Propagate from seed or cuttings of half-hardened shoots taken in summer.

Microbiota decussata ★
RUSSIAN CYPRESS

☼ ❄ ↔ 5 ft (1.5 m) ↑ 2 ft (0.6 m)

Flattened short branches with tiny, scale-like, almost triangular, overlapping leaves. Cones at ends of short branches in summer; females egg-shaped. Foliage turns bronze in cold winters. Zones 3–9.

MILLETTIA

There are about 90 species in this tropical genus of trees, shrubs, and climbers from Africa and southern Asia. They are members of the pea-flower subfamily of the legume (Fabaceae) family. The leaves are alternate and compound, with a terminal leaflet and a pronounced swelling where the leaf stalk joins the stem. Flowers, in large spikes or panicles, are pink, mauve, red, or shades of these colors. Pods are often large, splitting in halves to release round seeds. CULTIVATION: These plants require rich moist soil and ample water in summer. Propagate from seed only, and the seed must be very fresh. Soak overnight in hot water prior to sowing.

Millettia grandis
SOUTH AFRICAN IRONWOOD

☼ ⚘ ↔ 30 ft (9 m) ↑ 20–40 ft (6–12 m)

Medium-sized tree from low-altitude coastal eastern South Africa, briefly deciduous in early summer. Leaves compound, 6 to 7 pairs of oblong leaflets, undersurface with silky hairs. Purple pea-flowers, upright spikes, in summer. Fruit large, woody, flat pods. Zones 9–11.

MIMOSA

Allied to *Acacia*, this genus in the mimosa subfamily of the legume (Fabaceae) family consists of some 480 species of herbs, vines, shrubs, and trees. Most are from South and Central America, southern USA, Asia, and Africa. They have bipinnate leaves and often spiny stems. The tiny flowers are white, pink, or lilac, and have long multiple stamens and 4 or 5 petals. They are borne singly or in stalked rounded heads, or in spikes or racemes. The prickly flat seeds split open when mature. Some species are invasive.
CULTIVATION: They are best suited to well-drained moderately fertile soil in a sunny frost-free site. Propagate from seed, usually pre-soaked in hot water, or cuttings taken from young growth.

Mimosa pudica
SENSITIVE PLANT

☼ ⚘ ↔ 3 ft (0.9 m) ↑ 3 ft (0.9 m)

Native to tropical America. Prickly branching stems. Leaves make "sleep-movements" at night. Leaflets fold together when touched, stalks droop. Light pink to lilac flowers in summer. Zones 10–12.

MONTANOA

In the daisy (Asteraceae) family, this genus from tropical America comprises about 20 species of vines and shrubs. They are erect species with short branches and square stems. The hand-shaped leaves are large and covered with fine hairs. The flowers resemble dahlias, are white with a yellow center, are borne in clusters, and appear throughout summer and into autumn. Reddish brown seeds are borne in the old flowerheads, which have a papery feel.
CULTIVATION: Grown for both foliage and flower display, these frost-tender plants need a warm full-sun position in fertile well-watered soil. Once the flowers have finished, the long canes can be hard pruned. Propagate from seed or from root cuttings.

Montanoa bipinnatifida
MEXICAN TREE DAISY

☼ ⚘ ↔ 7 ft (2 m) ↑ 10–20 ft (3–6 m)

Evergreen shrub, sometimes tree-like, from southern Mexico. Sparse deeply dissected leaves, on fast-growing brittle canes. Masses of single white daisy flowers in autumn. Zones 10–12.

MORELLA
WAXBERRY

This genus consists of deciduous and evergreen shrubs and trees in the family Myricaceae, all until recently treated as species of *Myrica*. The 40 or so *Morella* species are mostly tropical, mainly from Africa and the Americas, but there are several from cooler areas as well. All have dark gray or brown, slightly rough bark; leaves are simple, arranged spirally on the twigs, mostly narrow and tapering to the

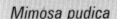

Mimosa pudica

Montanoa bipinnatifida

base, often toothed. Flowers are small and of different sexes, which may be on different plants. Fruit are small globular drupes, rough-surfaced and often wax-coated, in many small clusters.
CULTIVATION: Species vary in hardiness, but are not difficult to cultivate in suitable climates and will thrive in well-drained soil that is not strongly alkaline or prone to prolonged drought. Plant in sun to half-day shade, water well in sun, and trim to shape if necessary. Propagate from seed, layers, or half-hardened cuttings.

Morella cerifera
syn. *Myrica cerifera*
WAX MYRTLE

☼ ❋ ↔ 15 ft (4.5 m) ↑ 30 ft (9 m)

Large evergreen shrub or small tree native to most of Central America, West Indies, southern Mexico, and southeastern USA; thrives in shade of other trees. Broad-based lance-shaped leaves. Flowers small, pale yellow-brown, in summer. Tiny fruit. Zones 6–11.

Morella pensylvanica
syn. *Myrica pensylvanica*
BAYBERRY, CANDLEBERRY

☼ ❋ ↔ 4 ft (1.2 m) ↑ 6–10 ft (1.8–3 m)

Semi-evergreen to deciduous shrub, native to coastal eastern North America. Spreading suckering growth habit. Lance-shaped leaves, smooth or toothed edges. Tiny pale gray fruit in summer. Zones 2–8.

Millettia grandis

MURRAYA

This small genus in the rue (Rutaceae) family is related to *Citrus* and consists of 4 species from tropical Asia to Australia. They are shrubs or trees with pinnate dark green leaves, and white perfumed flowers in large panicles. Fruit are small globe- to egg-shaped berries. CULTIVATION: Most are adaptable, but grow best in well-drained mulched soil with added moisture and fertilizer during the growing season. They tolerate full sun to part-shade and perform best in a warm frost-free climate. Propagate from seed or cuttings.

Murraya paniculata
COSMETIC BARK, JASMINE ORANGE, ORANGE JESSAMINE
↔ 10 ft (3 m) ↑ 10 ft (3 m)

Globe-shaped shrub from Southeast Asia to Australia, many branches. Pinnate leaves pale green, maturing to dark glossy green. Orange blossom-like flowers, white, sweetly perfumed, in spring. Orange to red berries. Zones 10–12.

MUSSAENDA

This genus contains about 100 species of evergreen subshrubs, shrubs, and climbers native to tropical areas of Africa and Asia. It belongs to the madder (Rubiaceae) family. They have pointed elliptical leaves, opposite or in whorls. Small tubular flowers borne throughout the year are of secondary importance to the colorful enlarged sepals that accompany them. CULTIVATION: Plant in a tropical greenhouse in temperate climates. They require direct sunlight and should be watered well in the growing season. In warmer climates they can be grown outdoors in sun or part-shade, in rich well-drained soil. Propagate from seed sown in spring, or half-hardened cuttings taken in summer.

Mussaenda erythrophylla
ASHANTI BLOOD
↔ 5 ft (1.5 m) ↑ 10 ft (3 m)

Evergreen shrub native to tropical Africa. Erect or climbing, slightly downy, reddish stems. Flowers in dense, slightly drooping panicles,

Murraya paniculata

Mussaenda, Hybrid Cultivar, 'Queen Sirikit'

cream to pink and red, brilliant red sepals, in spring. 'Flamingo', bright pink sepals; 'Pink Dancer', salmon pink sepals. Zones 11–12.

Mussaenda Hybrid Cultivars
↔ 5–7 ft (1.5–2 m) ↑ 10 ft (3 m)

Hybrids often placed under *M. philippica* but may have originated from crosses between *M. erythrophylla* and *M. frondosa*. 'Aurorae', bushy shrub to 10 ft (3 m) high, yellow flowers, sepals large, white, pendulous; 'Queen Sirikit', salmon pink sepals. Zones 11–12.

MYOPORUM

This genus in the boobialla (Myoporaceae) family contains around 30 species, the majority from Australia, others from Mauritius,

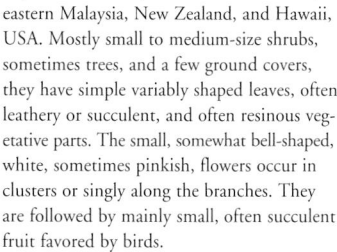

eastern Malaysia, New Zealand, and Hawaii, USA. Mostly small to medium-size shrubs, sometimes trees, and a few ground covers, they have simple variably shaped leaves, often leathery or succulent, and often resinous vegetative parts. The small, somewhat bell-shaped, white, sometimes pinkish, flowers occur in clusters or singly along the branches. They are followed by mainly small, often succulent fruit favored by birds. CULTIVATION: Most species are fairly adaptable, requiring good drainage and full sun or part-shade. Many will tolerate alkaline soils, medium to heavy frosts, and lengthy dry periods. Prune lightly to maintain shape. Propagate from fresh seed, cuttings, or by division of layered stems for ground covers.

Myoporum floribundum
WEEPING BOOBIALLA
↔ 8 ft (2.4 m) ↑ 10 ft (3 m)

Native of New South Wales and Victoria, Australia. Spreading habit, weeping branches. Leaves narrow, dark green, aromatic when crushed. White, rarely mauve, perfumed flowers, in massed clusters of false spikes, in winter–summer. Zones 9–11.

Myoporum laetum
NGAIO
↔ 10 ft (3 m) ↑ 15–30 ft (4.5–9 m)

Large shrub or small tree from New Zealand. Green fleshy leaves, lance-shaped to oblong or obovate, sticky shoot tips. White bell flowers, purple spots, in cymes, in summer. Maroon fruit. Zones 9–11.

MYRICA
syn. *Gale*

As now understood (following the removal of most species to *Morella*), this genus consists of only 2 species, one widespread in northern Europe, Asia, and North America, the other restricted to the lower slopes of California's Sierra Nevada. It gives its name to the Myricaceae family. The plants are deciduous low shrubs spreading by suckers, occurring in the wild in boggy ground and along stream banks. Leaves are small, toothed near their tip, aromatic when crushed, and arranged spirally on the reddish twigs. Flowers are small, in groups of catkins appearing before the leaves, and of

Myoporum floribundum

Myrtus communis

Nageia nagi

different sexes on different plants but the plants may switch sexes. Fruit are small, dry, flattened drupes with tiny resin dots. CULTIVATION: Occasionally planted in woodland gardens for their fragrant foliage, they tolerate wet ground but grow equally well in well-drained soil as long as moisture is adequate. Propagate from seed, which should be cold-stratified, or by division of clumps.

Myrica gale
syns *Gale belgica, G. palustris*
BOG MYRTLE, SWEET GALE
☼/◑ ❉ ↔4 ft (1.2 m) ↕3–6 ft (0.9–1.8 m)
Deciduous shrub found from Europe to Japan and North America. Leaves 1–2½ in (2.5–6 cm) wide, toothed. Buff-yellow fruit, in massed spikes, in summer. Grows well in damp soil. Zones 3–9.

MYRTUS
Although *Myrtus* was once a large genus in the myrtle (Myrtaceae) family, the Southern Hemisphere species have now been classified under other genera, leaving only 2 species, both native to the Mediterranean region. These are evergreen shrubs with simple, opposite, dark green leaves and small, fragrant, white flowers in summer. CULTIVATION: Grow these shrubs in a moderately fertile well-drained soil in a mild climate. Normally self-shaping into a rounded bush, they will respond to light tip-pruning in late winter, which produces denser foliage and a more compact habit. They prefer a position sheltered from cold drying winds. Propagate from half-hardened cuttings taken any time between spring and early winter.

Myrtus communis
COMMON MYRTLE, TRUE MYRTLE
☼ ❉ ↔10 ft (3 m) ↕10 ft (3 m)
Shrub from Mediterranean region. Leaves dark green above, paler beneath, aromatic when crushed. Flowers solitary, in upper axils, white, reddish pink shading on reverse; conspicuous stamens, in spring. Oval purplish berries. 'Citrifolium', cream flowers; 'Variegata', leaves with cream margin. Zones 8–11.

NAGEIA
This conifer genus in the plum-pine (Podocarpaceae) family consists of 6 species and occurs in

the south of India, China, and Japan, in Thailand, the Malay Peninsula, the Philippines, Indonesia, New Guinea, and New Caledonia. They are evergreen trees with broad, lance-shaped, multi-veined leaves, unusual in conifers. CULTIVATION: Only *N. nagi* is cultivated, requiring well-drained soil and water during dry periods. Propagate from seed or cuttings.

Nageia nagi
syn. *Podocarpus nagi*
NAGI
◑ ❉ ↔15 ft (4.5 m) ↕70 ft (21 m)
Native to Japan, China, and Taiwan. Smooth dark brown bark, ageing to gray; almost horizontal branches. Leaves oval or oblong, glossy deep green, paler underside, parallel veins. Seed cones occur singly, bluish green, globular, ripen in late autumn. Zones 8–10.

NANDINA
HEAVENLY BAMBOO, SACRED BAMBOO
Just a single species of small evergreen shrub is contained in this genus. Despite its common name, this plant is a member of the barberry (Berberidaceae) family. It is grown for its colorful foliage and the bright red berries it bears in autumn. Plants are either male or female; some hermaphroditic cultivars are now available. CULTIVATION: *Nandina* is easily grown in a rich soil that is moist but well drained. Leaf color is more intense when planted in full sun. For the best berry crops, make a group planting to ensure cross-pollination. Leggy older stems can be cut back to the base in summer. Propagate from cuttings taken in summer, as seed can be quite difficult to germinate.

Nandina domestica

Nandina domestica
HEAVENLY BAMBOO
☼ ❉ ↔4 ft (1.2 m) ↕7 ft (2 m)
Native from India to Japan. Leaves bipinnate or tripinnate, lance-shaped, soft, tinted pinkish red when young, dark green and glossy with age; yellow, red, and purplish hues in winter. Small creamy white flowers in summer. Popular cultivars include 'Filamentosa', 'Firepower', 'Gulf Stream', 'Harbor Dwarf', 'Nana' (syn. 'Pygmy'), 'Nana Purpurea', 'Richmond', and 'Woods Dwarf'. Zones 7–10.

NEILLIA

This genus in the rose (Rosaceae) family contains 10 deciduous species that are closely related to *Spiraea* and are found in Asia, from the eastern Himalayas to the western side of the Malay Peninsula. They are arching shrubs with prominently veined 3-lobed leaves that color to yellow in autumn. In winter their attractive form, with a zigzag pattern of twigs, is revealed. Slender panicles or racemes of small bell-shaped flowers are borne in spring or summer.

CULTIVATION: Although not widely grown, these shrubs are easily cultivated in all but the driest soils, in full sun or part-shade. After flowering, cut out old stems at ground level to encourage new growth and retain the arching habit. Propagate from seed, from cuttings in summer, or by the removal of suckers in autumn.

Neillia sinensis ★

☼ ❀ ↔ 7 ft (2 m) ↑ 10 ft (3 m)

Native to central China. Upright habit. Smooth brown branchlets, bark exfoliates. Lobed leaves, serrated edges, purplish bronze when young. Short terminal racemes of white to pale pink bell-shaped flowers in spring–summer. Zones 6–10.

Neillia thibetica

syn. *Neillia longiracemosa*

☼ ❀ ↔ 6 ft (1.8 m) ↑ 6 ft (1.8 m)

Native to western China. Deciduous shrub with upright habit. Branchlets covered in fine down. Serrated-edged leaves prominently veined, downy beneath. Slender racemes, to 6 in (15 cm) long, of pale pink bell-shaped flowers in summer. Zones 6–10.

NERIUM

OLEANDER

This genus of a single species from North Africa, the Middle East, northern India, and southern China belongs to the dogbane (Apocynaceae) family. It is a long-flowering evergreen shrub or small tree, with simple, smooth-edged, narrow leaves, and yellow, white, pink, and tangerine flowers. Petals are fused into a narrow tube but flaring from the end into a disc or a shallow cup, and the flowers are borne in terminal clusters.

CULTIVATION: Tolerant of salt-laden winds and dry sandy soils, it can be invasive. It will grow in almost any type of soil except wet, but likes full sun, and tolerates light frosts if given a sheltered position. For a dense shrubby habit, remove flowering shoots and prune well-established plants in winter every 3 years. As these plants are extremely poisonous, wear protective clothing when pruning and dispose of prunings carefully (do not burn). Propagate from half-hardened cuttings taken in autumn, or seed in spring.

Nerium oleander

☼ ❀ ↔ 8 ft (2.4 m) ↑ 10 ft (3 m)

Evergreen shrub. Many erect shoots from base. Leaves dark green above, paler below. Flowers in late spring–early autumn, and sporadically until early winter. Many single- and double-flowered cultivars in range of colors. Double cultivars have petals crimped,

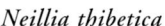

Neillia thibetica

waved on outer edge. 'Casablanca', faded pink flowers, almost white; 'Delphine', single dark purplish red flowers; 'Docteur Golfin', single, mauve tinged, cherry red flowers; 'Splendens', deep rose pink double flowers; 'Splendens Giganteum Variegatum', creamy yellow edge to leaves. Zones 8–11.

NEVIUSIA

Related to *Kerria*, this genus consists of a single species of deciduous shrub in the rose (Rosaceae) family. It is a threatened species in its native Alabama, USA. It increases in width by means of rooted branches. The white flowers are petal-less, with many prominent stamens.

CULTIVATION: This shrub is suitable for the border or woodland edge. It grows in moderately fertile soils and should be watered well in periods of drought. After flowering, the old and dead wood should be cut out at the base. Propagate from seed or cuttings, or by division.

Neviusia alabamensis

ALABAMA SNOW WREATH

☼/◐ ❀ ↔ 5 ft (1.5 m) ↑ 5 ft (1.5 m)

From State of Alabama in southern USA. Suckering plant, forms wide multi-stemmed shrub. Leaves have serrated edges, downy beneath. Small flowers, with fluffy mass of white stamens, in spring. Zones 5–9.

NOTHOFAGUS

SOUTHERN BEECH

There are approximately 35 species in this genus, native to temperate South America, New Zealand, New Guinea, New Caledonia, and southeastern Australia including Tasmania. Members of the beech (Fagaceae) family, all are evergreen or deciduous forest trees, with straight trunks and light lacy foliage. In native habitats, they are more stunted and more sparsely foliaged at higher altitudes. Leaves are dark green, or occasionally red, with mostly toothed edges, and commonly arranged in more or less a single plane. Tiny flowers are followed by nutlets. The timber is fine grained and valued for cabinetwork.

Neviusia alabamensis

CULTIVATION: A moderately rich and well-drained acid soil is preferred with shelter from salt-laden winds. They require regular watering until established. Propagate from fresh seed in autumn, from hardwood cuttings in summer, or by layering.

Nothofagus antarctica

ANTARCTIC BEECH, NIRRE

☼ ✳ ↔ 20 ft (6 m) ↑ 40 ft (12 m)

From Chile. Fast-growing deciduous tree, open habit, often with twisted trunk and main limbs. Leaves small, dark green, glossy, rounded to heart-shaped, irregularly toothed margins, turn yellow in autumn. Zones 8–9.

Nothofagus cunninghamii

MYRTLE BEECH, TASMANIAN BEECH

☼ ✳ ↔ 8–30 ft (2.4–9 m) ↑ 5–100 ft (1.5–30 m)

From cool-temperate forests in Tasmania and Victoria, Australia. Evergreen straight-trunked tree, variable habit. Dark green crown; small, shiny, toothed leaves in fan-like fronds. Young foliage reddish tinge. Best grown on basaltic soils. Zones 8–9.

Nothofagus fusca

NEW ZEALAND RED BEECH, RED BEECH

☼ ✳ ↔ 25 ft (8 m) ↑ 100 ft (30 m)

From New Zealand. Bark dark rusty brown to almost black, furrowed, flaking on old trees. Coarsely serrated oval leaves, turn bright red on young trees in winter, remain green on older trees before falling. Zones 8–9.

Nothofagus menziesii

NEW ZEALAND SILVER BEECH

☼ ✳ ↔ 30 ft (9 m) ↑ 60 ft (18 m)

Native to New Zealand. Evergreen tree, can develop massive trunk. Distinctive, horizontally banded and flaking, gray bark. Dense dark green leaves, tiny, oval to round, coarsely serrated. New spring foliage light green. Zones 8–9.

Nothofagus solanderi

BLACK BEECH, MOUNTAIN BEECH, NEW ZEALAND BEECH

☼ ✳ ↔ 25 ft (8 m) ↑ 60 ft (18 m)

From hilly and mountain habitats in New Zealand. Evergreen tree, distinctive black bark. Leaves shiny, bronze-green, small, oblong, paler on reverse, in fan-like sprays. Masses of small red-brown flowers in spring. Timber valued for construction. *N. s.* var. *cliffortioides*, oval leaves, more sharply pointed. Zones 8–9.

NYSSA

This is a small genus that includes about 5 species of deciduous trees from North America and eastern and southeastern Asia. It is a member of the dogwood (Cornaceae) family. They are all noted for their spectacular foliage in autumn, which ranges in color from soft green to pale yellow, gold, orange, and brown. Most species

Nothofagus solanderi var. *cliffortioides*, in the wild, New Zealand

inhabit moist land on the edges of streams, lakes, and swamps, and are rarely successful on dry soils. The leaves are simple, the flowers are inconspicuous, and the fruit are small and bluish.

CULTIVATION: These plants prefer well-drained, moist, fertile soil in full sun or part-shade. Little pruning is required, apart from the removal of competing leaders in the early stages. Propagate from seed collected as soon as it is ripe in autumn. Sow immediately, before it dries out. Alternatively, species can be propagated from half-hardened cuttings in mid-summer.

Nyssa aquatica

COTTON GUM, TUPELO GUM, WATER TUPELO

☼ ✳ ↔ 15 ft (4.5 m) ↑ 50 ft (15 m)

Native to southeastern USA, rare in wild. Erect stems, dome-shaped crown. Leaves ovate-oblong, downy underneath, serrated. Flowers greenish white, in axillary clusters, in summer. Fruit deep mauve. Zones 5–10.

Nyssa sinensis

CHINESE TUPELO

☼ ✳ ↔ 30 ft (9 m) ↑ 40 ft (12 m)

Rare species from China, beautiful small tree or large shrub, open habit. Leaves narrowly ovate, to 6 in (15 cm) long, juvenile foliage red. Leaves turn to almost every shade of red and yellow in autumn. Zones 7–10.

Nyssa sinensis

Nyssa sylvatica ★

BLACK GUM, BLACK TUPELO, SOUR GUM, TUPELO

☼ ✳ ↔ 30 ft (9 m) ↑ 50 ft (15 m)

Native to North America, from Canada to Gulf of Mexico. Deciduous tree with predominantly horizontal branches. Smooth-edged leaves, shiny dark green, paler beneath; turn shades of orange, scarlet, and purplish red in autumn. Small bluish black fruit. 'Sheffield Park', leaves start to color 2 to 3 weeks earlier than species; 'Wisley Bonfire', symmetrical form. Zones 3–10.

Ochna kirkii, fruitlet

Odontonema schomburgkianum

Olea capensis

OCHNA

There are around 80 species of deciduous and evergreen trees and shrubs included in this genus, a member of the family Ochnaceae, all occurring in Africa and Asia. The leaves of all species are simple, alternate, and have toothed margins. The flowers are borne singly or in clusters, with 5 to 10 petals that fall soon after the flower opens. In the fruit, the 5 sepals and the floral receptacle become swollen and brightly colored, with 3 or more fleshy 1-seeded fruitlets attached, usually contrasting in color when ripe.
CULTIVATION: These plants are marginally frost hardy, so they need shelter from frosts in their early years, but otherwise they can be grown in a range of well-drained soils in either full sun or part-shade in tropical and subtropical climates. Propagation is from seed or cuttings.

Ochna kirkii
☀ ❊ ↔ 7 ft (2 m) ↑ 10 ft (3 m)
From Mozambique, found along streamsides. Leaves thick, leathery, oblong to elliptic, heart-shaped base, with toothed margins. Yellow flowers, borne in terminal clusters, in spring. Bright red calyx. Zones 10–11.

Ochna serrulata
CARNIVAL BUSH, MICKEY MOUSE PLANT
☀ ❊ ↔ 7 ft (2 m) ↑ 12 ft (3.5 m)
Small tree from eastern South Africa. Bark smooth, brown. Leaves elliptic, glossy, dark green, paler undersurface, toothed margins. Fragrant yellow flowers in spring–early summer. Fleshy bright red calyx, fruitlets globular, black when ripe. Serious environmental weed in some areas. Zones 9–11.

ODONTONEMA

Native to the tropical regions of America, this genus in the acanthus (Acanthaceae) family consists of some 25 species of evergreen perennial herbs and shrubs with opposite pairs of simple, glossy green, smooth-edged leaves. They are grown for their delightful, waxy-textured, 2-lipped or 5-lobed, tubular flowers in colors of red, yellow, or white that are carried in upright terminal spikes or, in some species, drooping sprays.
CULTIVATION: Frost tender, these warm-climate plants need rich soil and regular watering. They like well-drained soil in full sun

or bright filtered light in a spot that is sheltered from the wind. Keep them neat and bushy by pinching out the growing tips. Propagate from cuttings in summer.

Odontonema callistachyum
syn. Odontonema strictum
FIRESPIKE
☀ ⚘ ↔ 3–6 ft (0.9–1.8 m) ↑ 6 ft (1.8 m)
Evergreen shrub native to Central America. Upright growth habit, with glossy, wavy-edged, oblong leaves tapering to fine point. Showy inflorescences of waxy-textured crimson flowers, borne at branch tips, through most of year. Excellent container plant for large conservatories. Zones 10–12.

Odontonema schomburgkianum
☀ ⚘ ↔ 2 ft (0.6 m) ↑ 6 ft (1.8 m)
Erect sparsely branched shrub from Colombia. Pale green leaves, lance-shaped to oblong, to 8 in (20 cm) long. Waxy crimson to scarlet flowers, in slender drooping racemes to 3 ft (0.9 m) long, in spring. Zones 10–12.

OLEA
OLIVE
This famous genus, which belongs to the olive (Oleaceae) family, includes some 20 species of evergreen shrubs and trees with a wide distribution throughout the warm-temperate areas of the world (excluding the Americas). With age, the branches become wonderfully gnarled and twisted, adding an interesting dimension to the garden. Each leaf is usually a simple narrow ellipse, deep green above and greenish white below. The flowers are massed in panicles. They are followed by the familiar fleshy drupes, each of which contains a hard pit or stone.
CULTIVATION: Olives vary in hardiness, though none are very frost tolerant, especially when the plants are young. If grown for their fruit, olives require a climate with distinct seasons. Flowering, cropping, and ripening are invariably best on trees grown in full sun with relatively mild winters and long hot summers that gradually decline into autumn. Olives are tolerant of most soil types and are very drought tolerant once they are established; fertile well-drained soil will yield a better crop. Propagate from seed, heel cuttings, or suckers.

Olea capensis

BLACK IRONWOOD

☼ ❊ ↔ 15 ft (4.5 m) ↑ 50 ft (15 m)

South African species. Glossy deep green leaves. White flowers in spring. Small black fruit, edible after appropriate treatment but seldom used. Heartwood is very hard, sometimes used for producing small items such as bowls, utensils, and handles. Zones 9–11.

OLEARIA

syn. *Pachystegia*

There are about 180 species of evergreen shrubs and small trees in this genus, of the daisy (Asteraceae) family. Most are native to Australia, with some from New Zealand, New Guinea, and Lord Howe Island. The leaves are sometimes aromatic and vary in size but are usually leathery with gray, white, or buff, tiny, soft hairs on the underside. Daisy flowers range in color from white to pink, blue, and purple and are often borne so profusely that they smother the foliage. CULTIVATION: Most species grow in well-drained moderately fertile soil in either full sun or part-shade. In cool-temperate climates the majority are not reliably hardy below about 23°F (–5°C) and need the protection of a warm wall. Prune after flowering to maintain the plant's bushy habit. Some are suitable for hedging and shelter planting, tolerating strong winds, including coastal conditions. Propagate from seed or from half-hardened cuttings taken in summer and autumn.

Olearia furfuracea

Olearia albida

DAISY BUSH, TANGURU

☼ ❊ ↔ 7 ft (2 m) ↑ 10 ft (3 m)

Vigorous species found in coastal forests of New Zealand's North Island. Erect shrub or small tree with oblong leaves, downy white underside. Large panicles of white daisy flowers in summer–autumn. Zones 8–10.

Olearia furfuracea

☼ ❊ ↔ 7 ft (2 m) ↑ 8–15 ft (2.4–4.5 m)

Native to New Zealand's North Island. Well-branched shrub or small tree. Dark green oblong leaves, buff hairy coating beneath, wavy margins. Large clusters of small white daisy flowers in summer. Zones 8–11.

Olearia insignis

syn. *Pachystegia insignis*

MARLBOROUGH ROCK DAISY

☼ ❊ ↔ 3–7 ft (0.9–2 m) ↑ 3–7 ft (0.9–2 m)

Spreading shrub from New Zealand. White or brown down on stems and underside of leathery oval leaves. Large, glistening, white daisy flowers with yellow center, open from felted drumstick-like heads, in summer. Zones 9–11.

Olearia macrodonta

☼ ❊ ↔ 7 ft (2 m) ↑ 7 ft (2 m)

New Zealand species similar to mountain holly (*O. ilicifolia*). Wider grayish green leaves, toothed, musky aroma when crushed. Large rounded clusters of white daisy flowers in summer. Zones 8–11.

Olearia phlogopappa

DUSTY DAISY BUSH

❊ ↔ 7 ft (2 m) ↑ 8 ft (2.4 m)

Extremely floriferous species, native to eastern Australia from New South Wales to Tasmania. Variable species with narrow oblong leaves, deep green to bluish green above, white or gray hairy coating beneath. Terminal clusters of showy daisy flowers, white, pink, mauve, or blue, in spring. *O. p.* var. *subrepanda*, lower growing shrub of subalpine vegetation, generally under 3 ft (0.9 m) in height, leaves only ½ in (12 mm) long. Many selections for flower color have been made, with cultivar names such as *O. p.* 'Blue Gem', 'Comber's Mauve' ★, and 'Rosea'. Zones 8–10.

Olearia × scilloniensis

☼ ❊ ↔ 8 ft (2.4 m) ↑ 10 ft (3 m)

Originated in an English garden; parents believed to be *O. phlogopappa* and *O. stellulata*. Well-branched shrub. Dark green wavy-edged leaves, paler underside. Crowded panicles of white daisy flowers in spring. Zones 8–10.

Olearia traversii

CHATHAM ISLAND AKEAKE

☼ ❊ ↔ 10 ft (3 m) ↑ 15 ft (4.5 m)

Shrub or small tree native to Chatham Islands of New Zealand. Attractive, pale, deeply furrowed bark. Broadly oval leaves, shiny dark green above, white hairy coating beneath. Insignificant summer flowers. Grown for attractive foliage; used as hedging, particularly in coastal areas. Zones 8–11.

Olearia phlogopappa

ONCOBA

The 39 species of shrubs and small trees in this genus are native to tropical and southern Africa. This genus is a member of the governor's-plum (Flacourtiaceae) family. Their evergreen leaves may be leathery or thin and are alternately arranged; some species are armed with spines. The fragrant flowers are borne for long periods and may be red, white, or orange. They have spreading petals with prominent stamens.

CULTIVATION: In cool-temperate climates these are greenhouse plants, but in warm frost-free areas they can be grown outside where the spiny species can make an effective barrier hedge. Grow in full sun in a fertile well-drained soil. Propagate from seed.

Oncoba spinosa
SNUFF BOX TREE

☼ ⁍ ↔ 6 ft (1.8 m) ↑ 6–10 ft (1.8–3 m)

Spiny shrub from eastern and central Africa and southern Arabia. Narrow serrated-edged leaves. Fragrant white flowers, mass of yellow stamens, which fall as flower ages, resemble camellia. Round fruit with hard, shiny, brown shell. Used to make snuff boxes and rattles in Africa. Zones 9–12.

OPLOPANAX

Related to ginseng, this genus of 2 species of prickly, deciduous, semi-prostrate or erect shrubs in the ivy (Araliaceae) family is native to temperate areas of the Northern Hemisphere. The tan bark is covered with slender stiff prickles. The green leaves are deeply lobed. The flower panicles, which appear in late spring to mid-summer, are white or greenish white and are followed by red flat berries, which are inedible.

CULTIVATION: Grow in a very moist shaded area in acidic soil. Propagate from seed (which can take as long as 18 months to germinate), or from suckers and root cuttings. Layering is also an effective method of propagation. Pruning with great care.

Oncoba spinosa

Oplopanax horridus
DEVIL'S CLUB

◐/◑ ❋ ↔ 5 ft (1.5 m) ↑ 3–10 ft (0.9–3 m)

Found from Michigan to Oregon and southeast Alaska, USA. Deciduous shrub with spiny branches. Leaves similar to maple. White flowers, in pyramidal clusters, in late spring–early summer. Shiny red berries. Zones 4–9.

ORPHIUM

Named after Orpheus, a character from Greek mythology, this genus contains a single species native to coastal regions of south-western South Africa, and is a member of the gentian (Gentianaceae) family. It is a small softwooded shrub that is grown for its glistening pink to mauve saucer-shaped flowers, up to 2 in (5 cm) across, that are carried at the tips of the branches in summer.

CULTIVATION: Marginally frost hardy, this plant will grow in a sunny position in any well-drained soil, provided it is watered regularly in dry periods. Tip prune in spring to encourage a compact habit. Propagation is from cuttings in late summer.

Orphium frutescens

Orphium frutescens
STICKY FLOWER

☼ ⁍ ↔ 18 in (45 cm) ↑ 24 in (60 cm)

Small evergreen shrub from South Africa's southwestern coast. Rather succulent, pale green, stem-clasping leaves, to 2 in (5 cm) long. Slightly sticky, 5-lobed, satiny flowers, in summer. Withstands moderate coastal exposure. Zones 9–11.

OSMANTHUS

This genus of about 15 species of slow-growing evergreen shrubs and small trees in the olive (Oleaceae) family is native to East Asia, except 1 or 2 species in the USA and 1 in the Caucasus. All have simple opposite leaves, some with spiny margins, and small, 4-petalled, white or yellow flowers, often strongly perfumed. The round fruit is dark blue.

CULTIVATION: The plants prefer moderately fertile well-drained soil in full sun, and a cool moist climate. Propagate from half-hardened cuttings.

Osmanthus × burkwoodii ★
syn. × Osmarea burkwoodii

☼ ❋ ↔ 10 ft (3 m) ↑ 10 ft (3 m)

Hybrid between O. delavayi and O. decorus; resilient thick-set shrub. Leaves dark glossy green, leathery, finely toothed. Flowers white, very fragrant, produced in profusion, in late spring. Zones 6–9.

Osmanthus delavayi

☼ ❋ ↔ 8 ft (2.4 m) ↑ 8 ft (2.4 m)

Slow-growing shrub from western China. Strong arching branches. Leaves smooth, dark green above, paler beneath. Flowers white, highly perfumed, in terminal, occasionally axillary, clusters of 5 or 6, in late winter–spring. Purplish black fruit. Zones 7–9.

Osmanthus × fortunei

☼ ❋ ↔ 10 ft (3 m) ↑ 10 ft (3 m)

Hybrid between O. fragrans and O. heterophyllus; compact robust shrub. Leaves large, prominently veined on upper surface, edged with sharp teeth, sometimes smooth-edged on mature plants. Small, fragrant, white flowers in autumn. '**San Jose**', cream to orange flowers. Zones 7–11.

Osmanthus fragrans
FRAGRANT OLIVE, SWEET OLIVE, SWEET OSMANTHUS
☼ ❋ ↔ 20 ft (6 m) ↑ 20 ft (6 m)
Evergreen species from China and Japan. Leaves smooth, dark green above, paler underneath. Flowers tubular, pure white, very fragrant, in late winter–mid-summer. *O. f.* f. *aurantiacus*, smooth-edged leaves, orange flowers. Zones 7–11.

Osmanthus heterophyllus
HOLLY OSMANTHUS
☼ ❋ ↔ 12 ft (3.5 m) ↑ 12 ft (3.5 m)
Evergreen shrub or small tree found in Taiwan and on main islands of Japan. Leaves oppositely arranged, smooth, dark glossy green. Small, fragrant, pure white flowers, carried in clusters, in autumn–early winter. '**Aureomarginatus**', leaves margined and splashed with broad patches of pale yellow; '**Aureus**', yellow-edged leaves; '**Goshiki**', cream and red-brown variegated leaves; '**Purpureus**', deep purple-green leaves; '**Variegatus**', leaves irregularly margined, marked with creamy white. Zones 7–11.

Osmanthus delavayi

OSTRYA
HOP HORNBEAM
This genus in the birch (Betulaceae) family contains about 10 species of deciduous trees related to *Betulus* and *Carpinus*. They grow throughout temperate Northern Hemisphere regions in open woodland. The alternate leaves have conspicuous veining and toothed edges, and are often hairy. The male catkins resemble the flowers of hornbeams *(Carpinus)*. The female flowers, on the same tree, develop into catkins that look like those of hops *(Humulus)*, with overlapping bracts.
CULTIVATION: These slow-growing trees are not commonly seen in cultivation, but they do make good specimen trees. They prefer well-drained fertile soil in either sun or shade. Propagate in spring from fresh seed, in pots protected from frosts. Seed which has dried out must be stratified to break its dormancy. Graft cultivars onto *Carpinus betulus* rootstocks in the colder months.

Ostrya carpinifolia
HOP HORNBEAM
☼ ❋ ↔ 70 ft (21 m) ↑ 70 ft (21 m)
Native to southern Europe and Turkey. Shoots with fine growth of hairs. Green leaves with pointed tip and doubly toothed edges, turning golden to pale yellow in autumn. Female flower clusters creamy white at first, turning brown in autumn. Zones 6–9.

Ostrya virginiana ★
EASTERN HOP HORNBEAM, IRONWOOD
☼ ❋ ↔ 35 ft (10 m) ↑ 50 ft (15 m)
From eastern North America. Dark brown bark. Leaves dark green above, paler underside, lance-shaped, double-serrated edges. Yellow male catkins in spring; female fruit clusters white at first, ripening to brown. Zones 4–9.

OXYDENDRUM
The single species of deciduous shrub or small tree in this genus is native to North America, and belongs to the heath (Ericaceae) family. It has a slender trunk, which is sometimes multi-stemmed, with rusty red fissured bark. Small white flowers appear in summer, and in autumn the leaves color vividly before they fall.
CULTIVATION: This plant is suitable for growing as a specimen or in open woodland. Grown in full sun, flowering is better and the autumn colors more intense. It needs an acid soil that is moist but well drained. Plants are slow growing and take time to become established. Propagate from seed in autumn or spring, or softwood cuttings in summer.

Oxydendrum arboreum ★
SORREL TREE, SOURWOOD
☼ ❋ ↔ 10 ft (3 m) ↑ 6–10 ft (1.8–3 m)
From eastern USA. Pointed glossy leaves, finely toothed; shades of red, purple, and yellow in autumn. Fragrant white flowers, on slender spreading racemes at branch tips, in summer. Zones 5–9.

Ostrya carpinifolia

Ostrya virginiana

Oxydendrum arboreum

Pachira aquatica

Pachystachys lutea

Paeonia delavayi var. lutea

PACHIRA

Native to regions throughout tropical America, this genus of about 20 species of evergreen or deciduous trees in the mallow (Malvaceae) family are cultivated as ornamentals for their handsome palmately lobed leaves and large flowers with a conspicuous tassel-like group of stamens fused into a tube at the base. Flowers last for a very short time and in some species are often hidden among thick foliage which is fully developed at the time of flowering. The woody fruiting capsules contain many kidney-shaped seeds embedded in a fleshy pulp.

CULTIVATION: Frost tender, these plants require a warm climate and a well-drained moist situation in full sun. Propagate from seed or cuttings taken in autumn.

Pachira aquatica

SHAVING BRUSH TREE

☼ ✲ ↔ 10 ft (3 m) ↑ 20 ft (6 m)

Evergreen tree native from Mexico to northern South America. Large compound leaves, 5 to 9 leaflets. Large creamy white or greenish flowers, red-tipped stamens, in summer. Brown fruiting capsules; edible seeds are roasted like chestnuts. Zones 10–12.

PACHYSTACHYS

The 12 species of evergreen perennials and shrubs in this genus, a member of the acanthus (Acanthaceae) family, are native to tropical America. They are closely related to *Justicia*, with similar showy terminal flower spikes. The tubular flowers are 2-lipped and have large overlapping bracts. The opposite leaves are quite large with a rather wrinkled surface due to their prominent veining.

CULTIVATION: In cool climates these are treated as indoor or greenhouse plants, but in warm humid areas they can be grown outside. They require a fertile, moist, but well-drained soil in a partially shaded situation. Propagation is best done from softwood cuttings taken in summer.

Pachystachys lutea

GOLDEN CANDLES

☀ ✲ ↔ 20 in (50 cm) ↑ 36 in (90 cm)

Native to Peru. Shorter narrower leaves than other species. Long flowering season, with terminal spikes of showy golden yellow bracts that hold white tubular flowers. Zones 10–12.

PAEONIA (see page 527)

Paeonia delavayi

MAROON TREE PEONY

☼/☀ ✲ ↔ 5 ft (1.5 m) ↑ 7 ft (2 m)

Deciduous suckering shrub from western China. Leaves large, deeply cut, dark green above, bluish green below. Flowers saucer-shaped, dark red, deep gold anthers, in spring. Pod-like fruit with colored sepals. *P. d.* var. *lutea* (syn. *P. lutea*), lemon yellow single flowers in mid-spring. *P. d.* var. *ludlowii* (syn. *P. lutea* var. *ludlowii*), larger than *P. d.* var. *lutea*, less divided leaves, more open flowers. Zones 6–9.

Paeonia × lemoinei

☼/☀ ✲ ↔ 6 ft (1.8 m) ↑ 6 ft (1.8 m)

Crosses between *P. delavayi* var. *lutea* and *P. suffruticosa*, inheriting strong yellow coloring of *P. delavayi* var. *lutea*, usually flushed red in center or colors blended giving shades of orange. 'Roman Child', dark red blotches at petal base; 'Souvenir de Maxime Cornu' (syns 'Kinshe', 'Souvenir de Professeur Maxime Cornu'), soft orange at flower center, red margins. Zones 6–9.

Paeonia rockii

syn. *Paeonia suffruticosa* 'Joseph Rock'

ROCK'S VARIETY

☼ ✲ ↔ 3 ft (0.9 m) ↑ 7 ft (2 m)

From northern Sichuan, southern Gansu, and Qinghai Provinces, China. Woody stems. Coarsely toothed, bipinnate, bright green leaves. Single white flowers, with notched petals, distinguished by deep purple central blotch. 'Fen He', pink flowers. Zones 7–10.

Paeonia suffruticosa

MOUTAN, TREE PEONY

☼/☀ ✲ ↔ 7 ft (2 m) ↑ 7 ft (2 m)

Upright shrub from northwestern China west to Bhutan. Smooth mid-green leaves variously cut and lobed, with bluish green below. Large, sometimes double, white, pink, yellow, or red flowers, solitary, petals fluted, frilled on edges, in mid-spring. 'Godaishu', white flowers, semi-double; 'Hiro-no-yuki', large, semi-double, white flowers; 'Louise Mouchelet', pale pink flowers; 'Mountain Treasure', white flowers, purplish blotches at petal bases; 'Shin-Shium-Ryo', yellow flowers; 'Zenobia', rich magenta blooms. Zones 4–9.

PANDANUS

The evergreen screw pines, with about 700 species in the family Pandanaceae, are found in east Africa, Madagascar, tropical Asia, the Pacific Islands, and northern Australia. Most are tree-like, often with trunks supported by stilt roots. Stems are commonly branched with terminal rosettes of long, leathery, strap-like, spiny-toothed, parallel-veined leaves arranged in distinct spirals. Male and female flowers are borne in dense spikes on separate plants. Resembling a pineapple, the woody or fleshy fruiting heads of compound drupes, many edible after cooking, can be red, pink, or yellow.
CULTIVATION: These plants need full sun and moist well-drained soil in warm humid environments. Propagate from seed, soaked for 24 hours before sowing, or from offsets or rooted suckers.

Pandanus tectorius
syns *Pandanus odoratissimus, P. pedunculatus*
BEACH SCREW PINE, PANDANG
☼ ⚘ ↔ 10–20 ft (3–6 m) ↑ 12–25 ft (3.5–8 m)
From coasts and islands of Pacific and Indian Oceans, as far as Hawaii (USA) to east, Sri Lanka to west, Okinawa (Japan) to north, and New South Wales (Australia) to south. Short trunk, supported by strong stilt roots and broadly spreading branches. Leaves spiny edges, midribs on underside. Male flowers cream, sweetly scented, in dense spikes among large white bracts, at various times of year. Fruiting heads up to 8 in (20 cm) long, segments usually with grooved sides, ripening deep red.
'**Baptistii**' (syn. *P. baptistii*), to 3 ft (0.9 m) tall, arching spineless leaves with yellow stripes; '**Sanderi**' (syn. *P. sanderi*), to 12 ft (3.5 m) tall, leaves small, fine striping of paler green and gold; '**Variegatus**', leaves with broad gold stripes, purple-brown spines; '**Veitchii**' (syn. *P. veitchii*), leaves striped cream, spines green to yellow. Zones 10–12.

PARASERIANTHES

A member of the mimosa subfamily of the legume (Fabaceae) family, this genus of 4 species occurs from Indonesia to tropical Australia and the

Paraserianthes lophantha

Solomon Islands. All species were previously included in the genus *Albizia. P. moluccana* holds the record for the world's fastest growing tree—just over 35 ft (10 m) in 13 months. These shrubs or trees are found in lowland rainforests and in moist areas.
CULTIVATION: Propagate from seed, which germinates readily without pre-treatment, unlike most members of this subfamily. They are fast-growing plants in well-drained acid soils in full sun.

Paraserianthes lophantha
syn. *Albizia lophantha*
CAPE LEEUWIN WATTLE
☼ ⚘ ↔ 10 ft (3 m) ↑ 25 ft (8 m)
From Indonesia, and naturalized in Australia. Fast-growing small tree, leaves bipinnate, many small leaflets. Small creamy flowers, inconspicuous petals, long prominent stamens, in spring. Long, flat, brownish pods; many black seeds. Can become invasive; considered a weed in South Africa and parts of Australia. Zones 9–10.

PARKINSONIA
syn. *Cercidium*
A member of the cassia subfamily of the legume (Fabaceae) family, this genus of 12 evergreen or deciduous trees and shrubs is found in warmer arid regions of North America. It has narrow leaves and racemes of yellow flowers. The fruit is a flattish pod.
CULTIVATION: *Parkinsonia* species prefer rich well-drained soils in a protected position. Propagate from seed, which should be scarified for successful germination.

Parkinsonia aculeata
JERUSALEM THORN, PALO VERDE
☼/◑ ⚘ ↔ 20 ft (6 m) ↑ 30 ft (9 m)
Found on ephemeral watercourses of southwest USA and Mexico, naturalized in many countries. Spiny shrub or tree, drooping branches, pinnate leaves in pairs, with 25 pairs of leaflets. Clusters of yellow flowers in spring. Long narrow seed pods. Zones 9–11.

PARMENTIERA
From Mexico and Central America, this small genus of less than 10 species of evergreen shrubs or trees, often with spines, belongs to the trumpet-vine (Bignoniaceae) family. Bell-shaped or funnel-like, white or greenish flowers are borne singly or in small clusters. The opposite compound leaves are made up of 3 leaflets. The linear or narrow cylindrical fleshy fruit bears a similarity to candles.
CULTIVATION: Frost tender, they can be cultivated in tropical and subtropical gardens where they prefer fertile, moist, but well-drained soil in sun. Propagate from seed or half-hardened cuttings in summer.

Parmentiera cereifera
CANDLE TREE
☼ ⚘ ↔ 10 ft (3 m) ↑ 20 ft (6 m)
Small tree native to Panama. Elliptic to almost diamond-shaped leaflets, 2 in (5 cm) long. Waxy, greenish white, tubular flowers, to 3 in (8 cm) long. Greenish yellow fruit. Zones 10–12.

Pandanus tectorius (tree at rear), Queensland, Australia

PARROTIA

This genus of a single species in the witchhazel (Hamamelidaceae) family is native to northern Iran and Azerbaijan, where it is found in the forests south and southwest of the Caspian Sea. It was named after Dr F. W. Parrot, a German plant collector who travelled through the Middle East in the early nineteenth century. It is grown mainly for its beautiful leaf color, especially in spring and autumn. It is a useful small tree for street planting and a very suitable species for parks and gardens in cool climates, where the foliage colors brilliantly.

CULTIVATION: Any moderately fertile soil with free drainage is suitable, including chalk soils; exposure to full sun is desirable. Propagation is usually from seed, which should be collected just before being expelled from the capsules, and sown immediately, taking up to 18 months to germinate. Softwood cuttings taken in summer are sometimes used.

Parrotia persica

Paulownia tomentosa

Parrotia persica

IRON TREE, PARROTIA, PERSIAN IRONWOOD, PERSIAN WITCH HAZEL

☼ ❄ ↔ 20 ft (6 m) ↕ 25–40 ft (8–12 m)

Small deciduous tree, short trunk with flaking bark. Leaves simple, alternate, leathery, shallowly toothed, pale lettuce-green; crimson, scarlet, orange, and yellow tones in autumn. Flowers small, bright red stamens, green calyx, enclosed in bract of dark brown hairy scales, in late winter–spring. 'Pendula' ★, drooping branches, slowly develops into dome-shaped mound. Zones 5–9.

PAULOWNIA

This is a genus of about 6 species in the foxglove (Scrophulariaceae) family, native to East Asia. All are deciduous trees with handsome leaves that in some species are very large in the juvenile stage, and bear large panicles of flowers in spring. Paulownias have been cultivated in China for more than 3,000 years, both for their strong light timber, and for their attractive flowers; the bark, wood, leaves, flowers, and fruit all have medicinal uses. They are characterized by their extremely rapid growth rate.

CULTIVATION: Paulownias do best in a moderately fertile and free-draining soil with adequate summer water. Protection from wind is important, especially in the early stages when the large leaves are easily damaged. Although quite hardy, dormant flower buds can be damaged by late frosts. The young trees are sometimes pruned back to 2 or 3 basal buds in order to encourage the vigorous growth of a single trunk. Propagation is from seed or root cuttings.

Pavonia hastata

Paulownia fortunei

POWTON, WHITE-FLOWERED PAULOWNIA

☼ ❄ ↔ 40 ft (12 m) ↕ 60 ft (18 m)

Found mainly in Yangtze delta area of China. Tall tree, straight-trunked, with rounded crown. Flowers open before leaves appear, in upright terminal panicles, 4 in (10 cm) long, white to cream, mauve or soft violet. Zones 6–10.

Paulownia tomentosa

EMPRESS TREE, HAIRY PAULOWNIA, PRINCESS TREE

☼ ❄ ↔ 30 ft (9 m) ↕ 50 ft (15 m)

Native to northern and central China, Korea, and Japan. Medium-sized tree, broad spreading crown. Pinkish lilac flowers in upright terminal panicles, 50 to 60 flowers in each panicle. Heart-shaped leaves downy, pale green maturing darker green, turning yellow-brown in autumn. 'Lilacina', lilac-purple flowers, hairy on outside, pale lemon yellow on inside; 'Sapphire Dragon', prominent clusters of creamy buff flowers. Zones 5–10.

PAVONIA

Found in the tropics and subtropics, especially in the Americas, this genus of the mallow (Malvaceae) family is composed of around 150 species of perennials, subshrubs, and shrubs. Easy-care plants, they are suitable for tropical gardens or can be grown as house or greenhouse plants elsewhere. The leaves may be simple or lobed, with serrated or toothed edges. The flowers vary in color and most often occur singly in the leaf axils but may be in terminal clusters or panicles. The petals fold back to reveal a hibiscus-like central column of stamens. Dry seed capsules follow.

CULTIVATION: All species are sensitive to frost and most cannot tolerate prolonged exposure to cool conditions. They respond well to container cultivation. Plant in moist well-drained soil in sun or partial shade and provide some protection from strong winds as the foliage is easily damaged. Propagate from seed or half-hardened tip cuttings.

Pavonia × gledhillii

☼ ✿ ↔ 3 ft (0.9 m) ↕ 5 ft (1.5 m)

Hybrid between Brazilian species *P. makoyana* and *P. multiflora*. Upright shrub. Deep green lance-shaped leaves, serrated edges. Flowers with bright red ring of narrow epicalyx bracts around dull purplish calyx, tubular purple corolla, in leaf axils, at branch tips, much of year. 'Rosea', dark pink flowers. Zones 10–12.

Pavonia hastata

☼ ⌘ ↔ 2 ft (0.6 m) ↕ 3 ft (0.9 m)

Native to southern Brazil, Uruguay, Paraguay, and Bolivia, naturalized in southeast USA and Australia. Subshrub or shrub reshoots if cut to ground by frost. Lance-shaped leaves, toothed edges. Flowers usually red, may be white with red basal spotting. Zones 9–12.

PELTOPHORUM

Consisting of 8 species of evergreen or deciduous trees from the cassia subfamily of the legume (Fabaceae) family, this genus occurs in the tropical savannah and coastal forests of Africa, Asia, the Americas, and northern Australia. Some species have been harvested for timber, others widely planted as ornamentals. The glossy green leaves are bipinnate, up to 18 in (45 cm) long, the ultimate leaflets being in 15 pairs, each about ½ in (12 mm) long. Prominent terminal panicles up to 24 in (60 cm) long bear many fragrant yellow flowers, with crinkly edges to the petals. Brown fruit pods contain several seeds.

CULTIVATION: These plants are only suitable for gardens in the tropics. Young plants require some shelter when first planted, but when established, full sun and well-drained moist soil are necessary. Like most legumes, propagation is from seed which requires pre-treatment such as soaking in boiling water or scarification of the seed coat.

Peltophorum pterocarpum

YELLOW FLAME TREE

☼ ✈ ↔ 30 ft (9 m) ↕ 50 ft (15 m)

Found in tropical India, Southeast Asia, Malay Archipelago, New Guinea, and Australia's "Top End." Medium-sized tree, with spreading branches. Leaves consist of bipinnate leaflets, 10 to 20 pairs. Terminal panicles of numerous fragrant yellow flowers in summer. Flat, brown, leathery pods. Zones 11–12.

PERSOONIA

This is an Australian genus of about 90 species of evergreen shrubs, or sometimes small trees, in the protea (Proteaceae) family, named for the eighteenth-century German botanist and mycologist Christian Hendrik Persoon. They have very attractive bright green leaves with smooth edges, and masses of almost stalkless, small, tubular, yellow flowers that have 4 rolled-back segments when they open. The flowers are followed by succulent yellow or green fruit, sometimes produced in large heavy clusters. These plants are commonly called geebungs, a version of the Dharuk Aboriginal word *jibbong*, referring to the edible fruit of some species.

CULTIVATION: They are best suited to full sun or part-shade, light acidic soil, and very good drainage. They respond well to pruning or regular clipping. Propagation is from heat-treated seed or from young tip cuttings (which are notoriously difficult to strike).

Persoonia pinifolia

PINELEAF GEEBUNG

☼ ⌘ ↔ 10 ft (3 m) ↕ 10–15 ft (3–4.5 m)

From eastern Australia. Erect shrub with slightly drooping branchlets and soft pine-like foliage. Profuse golden yellow flowers, in leaf axils at branch tips, in late summer–autumn. Small, pale green, succulent fruit. Zones 9–11.

PHELLODENDRON

This is a genus of 10 species of deciduous trees from temperate East Asia, which belongs to the rue (Rutaceae) family. Notable for their aromatic foliage and corky bark, these trees have large pinnate leaves composed of broad leaflets that are often glossy. The flowers are small and yellow-green in color and are carried in panicles, followed by small, black, fleshy fruit. The autumn foliage, however, is often bright yellow and can be quite spectacular in some years.

CULTIVATION: Most species in this genus need a climate with seasons that are well differentiated, and a cool winter is important to ensure proper dormancy. On the other hand, they handle hot summers and harsh sun with ease, though the foliage is easily damaged by strong winds. They seem to thrive in any well-drained soil with a position in full sun. Plants may be propagated from seed, from cuttings, by layering, or by grafting.

Phellodendron amurense ★

AMUR CORK TREE

☼ ✳ ↔ 40 ft (12 m) ↕ 50 ft (15 m)

Found in northern China. Corky pale gray bark. Strongly aromatic leaves composed of 9 to 13 broad leaflets, dark glossy green upper side, blue-green underside, turning yellow in autumn. Panicles of small yellow-green flowers in early summer. Clusters of fruit held erect above foliage. Zones 3–9.

Phellodendron amurense

PHILADELPHUS

MOCK ORANGE

Occurring within the hydrangea (Hydrangeaceae) family, this genus from temperate regions of Central and North America, southeast Europe, the Himalayas, and Asia includes 60 or so species of mainly deciduous shrubs. They usually have peeling bark. They are frequently grown for ornamental purposes, but are also cultivated for their scented double or single flowers, as specimen shrubs in woodland, or in a shrub border.
CULTIVATION: They grow well in full sun or partial shade, or in deciduous open woodland in moderately fer-
tile well-drained soil, but flower better in full sun. If grown in pots, a loam-based compost is best, and regular feeding and watering are necessary throughout the growing season. Propagate from softwood cuttings taken in summer or hardwood cuttings taken in autumn and winter.

Philadelphus coronarius

SWEET MOCK ORANGE, SYRINGA

☼ ❋ ↔ 8 ft (2.4 m) ↕ 10 ft (3 m)

Native to southern Europe and western Asia. Deciduous upright shrub, peeling bark. Egg-shaped leaves have irregular shallow toothing, with down on main veins. Very fragrant almost white flowers, on short terminal racemes, in early summer. 'Aureus' ★, compact growth, golden leaves turn lime green with age, fragrant flowers, best in part-shade; 'Bowles' Variety', leaves with white margins; 'Variegatus', leaves have wide white margins. Zones 5–9.

Philadelphus incanus

☼ ❋ ↔ 6 ft (1.8 m) ↕ 12 ft (3.5 m)

Erect shrub native to Hubei and Shaanxi Provinces in China. Branches hairy when young, peeling with age. Leaves oval to ellip-tical, larger on non-flowering shoots. White blooms, in racemes of up to 11 individual flowers, in late summer. Zones 5–9.

Philadelphus, Hybrid Cultivar, 'Manteau d'Hermine'

Philodendron bipinnatifidum

Philadelphus inodorus

☼ ❋ ↔ 4 ft (1.2 m) ↕ 10 ft (3 m)

Native to eastern USA. Arching shrub, bark peels in second year. Leaves variable in size, shape, and amount of hair on either side, faintly toothed or smooth-edged. Several white flowers, in cymes, in summer. Zones 5–9.

Philadelphus lewisii

INDIAN ARROWWOOD, LEWIS MOCK ORANGE, LEWIS SYRINGA

☼ ❋ ↔ 10 ft (3 m) ↕ 10 ft (3 m)

State flower of Idaho, USA. Arching shrub native to west of North America. Leaves bright green, egg-shaped, margins occasionally finely toothed. Racemes of 5 to 11 mildly scented flowers in early summer. Zones 5–9.

Philadelphus mexicanus

MEXICAN MOCK ORANGE

☼ ◐ ↔ 8 ft (2.4 m) ↕ 15 ft (4.5 m)

Evergreen climbing shrub native to Guatemala and Mexico. Pendulous branches, long bristles on current growth, oval leaves may have toothed margins. Rose-scented lemon-white flowers, often solitary, in summer. Zones 9–10.

Philadelphus Hybrid Cultivars

☼ ❋ ↔ 6–8 ft (1.8–2.4 m) ↕ 30 in–10 ft (75 cm–3 m)

Most early hybrid cultivars created by French plant breeder Pierre Lemoine; crosses of *P. coronarius* and *P. microphyllus*, often grouped as *P. × lemoinei*. Influence of *P. inodorus* and *P. insignis* prompted new hybrid names *P. × cymosus* and *P. × polyanthus*, respectively. Crosses between earlier hybrids and *P. coulteri* grouped under *P. × purpureomaculatus*. Finally, group emerged in which *P. pubescens* showed influence, under name *P. × virginalis*. 'Avalanche', early Lemoine hybrid, to 6 ft (1.8 m) tall, scented white flowers; 'Beau-clerk', later English hybrid, large, fragrant, single, cup-shaped, white flowers, pink-tinged center, in early–mid-summer; 'Belle Etoile', *P. × purpureomaculatus* hybrid, purple-red central splash on flowers, pineapple fragrance; 'Boule d'Argent', *P. × polyanthus* hybrid, com-pact slightly arching shrub to 5 ft (1.5 m) tall, double or semi-double flowers in summer; 'Bouquet Blanc', *P. × cymosus* hybrid, profuse semi-double flowers; 'Buckley's Quill', to 6 ft (1.8 m), fragrant double flowers in early–mid-summer, up to 30 quill-like petals per flower; 'Dame Blanche', Lemoine hybrid, cream colored semi-double flowers; 'Fimbriatus', Lemoine hybrid, compact fine-cut petal edges; 'Glacier', *P. × virginalis* hybrid, compact shrub to 5 ft (1.5 m) in height and spread, fragrant double white flowers in mid-summer; 'Innocence', Lemoine hybrid, to 10 ft (3 m), yel-low foliage, fragrant white flowers in summer; 'Manteau d'Hermine', Lemoine hybrid, to 30 in (75 cm) high, creamy double flowers in summer. Other *P. × virginalis* types include 'Minnesota Snowflake', double white flowers; 'Natchez', single flowers; 'Rosace', *P. × cymosus* hybrid, semi-double flowers; 'Schneesturm', *P. × virginalis* hybrid, pure white double flowers; 'Sybille', *P. × purpureomaculatus* hybrid, purple patches in center of single white flowers; 'Virginal', *P. × virginalis* hybrid, fragrant double white flowers. Zones 5–9.

PHILODENDRON *(see page 785)*

Philodendron bipinnatifidum
syn. *Philodendron selloum*

TREE PHILODENDRON

☼/◐ ⚜ ↔ 10 ft (3 m) ↑ 10 ft (3 m)

Native to southeastern Brazil. Large tree-like shrub with stout aerial roots. Spectacular, shiny, deep green leaves, to 3 ft (0.9 m) long, deeply divided, lobed, broadly ovate, somewhat arrow-shaped at base; leaf stalks as long as leaves. Spathes green to purplish red on outside, red-edged cream on inside. Zones 10–12.

PHLOMIS *(see page 538)*

Phlomis chrysophylla
☼ ⚜ ↔ 3 ft (0.9 m) ↑ 4 ft (1.2 m)

Small evergreen subshrub native to Lebanon. Erect branching stems. Broad oval leaves, covered in golden down when young and fade to yellowish gray when mature. Bright golden yellow flowers, in whorls in leaf axils, in summer. Zones 7–10.

Phlomis fruticosa
JERUSALEM SAGE

☼ ⚜ ↔ 30 in (75 cm) ↑ 30 in (75 cm)

Evergreen shrub from Mediterranean region. Leaves green and felty; bright yellow flowers in summer. Tolerates coastal conditions. Prune vigorously, to half its size, in autumn. Zones 7–10.

Phlomis italica
☼ ⚜ ↔ 12 in (30 cm) ↑ 12 in (30 cm)

Subshrub from Balearic Islands, Spain. Leaves narrow, oblong, with white hairs. Flowers pink or pale lilac, in well-spaced whorls of 6, with grayish white calyces, in summer–autumn. Zones 8–11.

PHOTINIA

This genus in the rose (Rosaceae) family consists of around 60 species of evergreen and deciduous shrubs and trees, most from the Himalayas to Japan and Sumatra, Indonesia. The leaves are often strikingly colored when young, especially in spring. The flowers are small, mostly white, with 5 petals, and grow in dense, flattish, clustering panicles along

Phlomis fruticosa

shoots or at their tips. The fruit are small pomes, usually red. Evergreen species are popular plants for hedging; deciduous species are more reliable than evergreens in flowering.
CULTIVATION: Most *Photinia* species are fairly adaptable, with good drainage being a key requirement. For best results, plant in a well-drained fertile soil in a sunny position. Prune to promote dense growth. Propagate from seed or cuttings.

Photinia davidiana
syn. *Stransvaesia davidiana*

☼ ⚜ ↔ 20 ft (6 m) ↑ 25 ft (8 m)

Large evergreen shrub or small tree from western China. Leaves leathery, elliptical to inversely lance-shaped, dark green; older

Photinia villosa

leaves may color red in autumn. Clustering panicles of small white flowers in summer. Small, red, hanging, persistent fruit. Zones 7–10.

Photinia × fraseri
FRASER PHOTINIA

☼ ⚜ ↔ 15 ft (4.5 m) ↑ 15 ft (4.5 m)

Hybrid between *P. glabra* and *P. serratifolia*, developed in USA. Large shrub, many stems, leathery dark green leaves, finely serrated margins, new leaves bronze to bright red. Small white flowers, in panicles, in spring. 'Red Robin' ★, compact cultivar from New Zealand with shiny red new growth; 'Robusta', widely grown for its flushes of brilliant red new growth, encouraged by repeated trimming. Zones 8–10.

Photinia glabra
JAPANESE PHOTINIA

☼ ⚜ ↔ 12 ft (3.5 m) ↑ 15 ft (4.5 m)

From Japan. Small tree with narrow-domed crown, bright red new leaves mature to green. Small white flowers, in clustering panicles, in summer. Small, fleshy, red drupes ripen to black. 'Rubens', popular for hedging in cool climates. Zones 7–10.

Photinia serratifolia
syn. *Photinia serrulata*

CHINESE HAWTHORN

☼ ⚜ ↔ 25 ft (8 m) ↑ 30 ft (9 m)

Native to China. Small tree, leathery oblong leaves, saw-toothed margins. Young copper-red foliage ages to dark green. Small white flowers, in clustering panicles, in spring. Red berries. Zones 7–10.

Photinia villosa
syn. *Pourthiaea villosa*

ORIENTAL PHOTINIA

☼ ❋ ↔ 15 ft (4.5 m) ↑ 15 ft (4.5 m)

Native to China, Korea, and Japan. Deciduous tree or large shrub, often vase-shaped. Downy young shoots. Elliptical to obovate dark green leaves, sharply serrated, bronze when young; yellow, orange, and red in autumn. Panicles of small white flowers in spring. Red fruit. Zones 4–9.

PHYGELIUS

This genus of evergreen subshrubs from South Africa is in the fox-glove (Scrophulariaceae) family. It consists of only 2 species, which have been crossed to produce hybrids. They are often grown as herbaceous perennials where winters fall below freezing. Soft green leaves grow on erect stems; pendent tubular flowers in warm tones appear in late summer. When grown as a perennial, the suckering or running rootstock can form attractive clumps 3 ft (0.9 m) wide. CULTIVATION: Given fertile, moist, humus-enriched soil, these plants will thrive in a morning sun position in warmer climates, but need the protection of a wall or a similar warm spot to minimize frost damage in cold climates. They are fleshy-leafed plants that dislike dry conditions, so they should be well watered throughout summer. Propagate from cuttings taken in summer.

Phygelius aequalis

☀ ❄ ↔ 3 ft (0.9 m) ↑ 3 ft (0.9 m)
South African suckering shrub. Upright stems, soft bright green foliage, dusky pink tubular flowers. Sensation/'Sani Pass', cerise to mauve flowers; 'Trewidden Pink', soft flesh pink flowers; 'Yellow Trumpet', larger leaves and flowers. Zones 8–10.

Phygelius capensis ★

CAPE FIGWORT, CAPE FUCHSIA
☀ ❄ ↔ 22 in (55 cm) ↑ 6 ft (1.8 m)
Well-clothed suckering shrub. Soft green leaves, lance-shaped. Masses of orange tubular flowers, distinctive recurved lobes. Zones 8–10.

Phygelius × rectus

☀ ❄ ↔ 4 ft (1.2 m) ↑ 4 ft (1.2 m)
Cross between P. aequalis and P. capensis. Compact suckering shrub. Dark green leaves, upright stems. Masses of pendent tubular flowers. 'African Queen', pale red flowers; 'Moonraker', creamy yellow flowers; 'Salmon Leap', deeply lobed orange blooms. Zones 8–10.

PHYLICA

Primarily native to South Africa, this genus in the buckthorn (Rhamnaceae) family has around 150 species of evergreen shrubs. A few are cultivated for their flowerheads, long lasting when cut. Leaves are dark green with a lighter underside, usually with a coating of silky silvery hairs. The true flowers are often petal-less or with fine filamentous petals, and are usually nearly enclosed by large feathery bracts or surrounded by white woolly hairs. CULTIVATION: Plant in light, gritty, well-drained, slightly acidic soil and full sun. They tolerate high humidity, but their foliage suffers in prolonged rain. Coastal conditions suit them. Added humus and water will give lusher foliage, but a looser habit and fewer flowers. Prune by removing spent flowers and general tidying. Propagate from seed or half-hardened cuttings from non-flowering stems.

Phygelius × rectus 'Moonraker'

Phylica plumosa

syn. Phylica pubescens
FLANNEL FLOWER
☀ ❄ ↔ 3 ft (0.9 m) ↑ 3–6 ft (0.9–1.8 m)
South African shrub densely covered with fine hairs. Tiny white flowers; hairy buff bracts. Deep green foliage. Flowerheads in early winter. Zones 9–11.

PHYLLOCLADUS

CELERY PINE
A genus of 5 or 6 coniferous trees or shrubs in the family Podocarpaceae, it comes from the Philippines and Malay Peninsula to New Zealand and Tasmania, Australia. Its "leaves" are flattened extended stems (phylloclades) resembling celery leaves. Male and female cones are on the same or different trees. CULTIVATION: Grow in moist well-drained soil in sun or part-shade, watering during dry spells. Propagate from seed or half-hardened cuttings taken in autumn; the cuttings can be difficult to strike.

Phyllocladus glaucus

TOA TOA
☀/◐ ❄ ↔ 10–15 ft (3–4.5 m) ↑ 35–50 ft (10–15 m)
From New Zealand. Whorls of large, gray-green, compound phylloclades. Thick branches radiate in whorls up trunk. Fruiting body looks like pine cone. Rare in wild. Zones 10–11.

Phyllocladus trichomanoides

NEW ZEALAND CELERY-TOP PINE, TANEKAHA
☀ ❄ ↔ 20 ft (6 m) ↑ 70 ft (21 m)
New Zealand native, faster growing than other species, smaller in cultivation. Conical in shape, symmetrical whorled branches;

Phylica plumosa

Phyllocladus glaucus

Physocarpus opulifolius

attractive, gray-brown, mottled bark. Bright green leathery phylloclades resemble small celery leaves. Zones 8–11.

PHYSOCARPUS

NINEBARK

From North America and temperate northeastern Asia, the 10 deciduous shrubs in this genus in the rose (Rosaceae) family have showy flowerheads, foliage that is attractive in spring, sometimes in autumn, and flaking bark. Most have conspicuously veined and lobed leaves. Flowers are white or pale pink, small, and massed in rounded corymbs. Inflated fruit with 3 to 5 lobes ripen in late summer. CULTIVATION: They are best grown in full sun in fertile well-drained soil that is moist in summer. They are not fussy, but dislike lime; foliage exposed to drought becomes desiccated and brown. Plants form thickets of stems; thin these and cut back the remaining growth after flowering. Propagate from seed or half-hardened cuttings.

Physocarpus monogynus

MOUNTAIN NINEBARK

☼ ✳ ↔ 4 ft (1.2 m) ↕ 4 ft (1.2 m)

From central USA. Thicket of arching stems. Toothed rounded leaves to 2 in (5 cm) long, 3 to 5 lobes. Flat heads of small white flowers, around 2 in (5 cm) wide, in spring–summer. Zones 5–9.

Physocarpus opulifolius

COMMON NINEBARK, NINEBARK

☼ ✳ ↔ 15 ft (4.5 m) ↕ 10 ft (3 m)

From central and eastern North America. Leaves usually 3-lobed, light green, toothed margins. Corymbs of flowers, mostly white, but may be pink-tinged or entirely pink, in late spring–early summer. *P. o.* var. *intermedius* (syn. *P. intermedius*), compact form, slightly smaller leaves, more densely packed flowerheads. *P. o.* 'Dart's Gold' ★, golden yellow foliage; 'Diabolo', burgundy foliage; 'Luteus', golden new growth, ageing to deep green, then bronze; 'Nanus', dense covering of small deep green leaves. Zones 2–9.

PHYTOLACCA

From temperate, warm-temperate, and subtropical regions, this genus in the pokeweed (Phytolaccaceae) family comprises 35 species of perennials, subshrubs, and deciduous or evergreen shrubs and trees, usually upright, with simple, often large leaves that can develop vivid colors in autumn. Their petal-less flowers are followed by conspicuous berries that in many species are poisonous. CULTIVATION: Apart from variable frost hardiness and an intolerance of drought, most species are easily grown in moist, moderately fertile, well-drained soil in sun or part-shade. Prune at any time, but winter is often best as it will not affect the flower and fruit production or the autumn color. Propagate from seed, from rooted basal shoots, or from cuttings taken during the growing season.

Phytolacca dioica

BELLA SOMBRA TREE, OMBU

☼ ◗ ↔ 30 ft (9 m) ↕ 50 ft (15 m)

Evergreen tree native to South America; buttressed multi-stemmed trunk. Leaves leathery, 4 in (10 cm) long, purple midrib. Racemes of tiny white flowers; golden berries ripen to black. Zones 10–11.

Picea engelmannii, in the wild, Colorado, USA

PICEA

SPRUCE

About 45 species make up this genus of resinous evergreen conifers in the pine (Pinaceae) family, from cool latitudes or high altitudes in the Northern Hemisphere. Most are large symmetrical trees, favoring deep, rich, acidic, well-drained soils in mountainous areas. The foliage is green, blue, silver, or gray, and consists of needle-like leaves on short, persistent, peg-like projections from the shoots. The cones are pendulous at maturity. CULTIVATION: Some are slow growing, but all are wind-firm, and taller species make good windbreaks in large gardens. They tolerate a range of soils and climates, but dislike mild areas or polluted atmospheres. Smaller cultivars are suitable bonsai subjects. Propagation is from seed or, for cultivars, firm cuttings or grafting.

Picea abies

COMMON SPRUCE, NORWAY SPRUCE

☼ ✳ ↔ 20 ft (6 m) ↕ 200 ft (60 m)

Native to southern Scandinavia and other parts of northern Europe. Columnar habit, slow growing, smaller in cultivation. Thick reddish brown bark, spreading branches, 4-sided dark green leaves. Light brown cones, erect at first, becoming pendulous, to 8 in (20 cm) long. 'Clanbrassiliana', dwarf to 5 ft (1.5 m) tall, spread of 8 ft (2.4 m); 'Cupressina', 60 ft (18 m) tall; 'Echiniformis', dwarf, long prickly foliage; 'Gregoryana', rounded dwarf to 30 in (75 cm) wide; 'Humilis', dwarf to less than 18 in (45 cm) tall; 'Nidiformis' (bird's nest spruce), branches form nest-shaped central depression; 'Pendula', drooping branches; 'Reflexa', mat-forming to 12 ft (3.5 m) wide; 'Tabuliformis', prostrate branches. Other cultivars include 'Cranstonii', 'Gracilis', 'Little Gem', 'Maxwellii', 'Procumbens', 'Pumila', 'Pyramidalis', and 'Repens'. Zones 2–9.

Picea engelmannii

ENGELMANN SPRUCE

☼ ✳ ↔ 15 ft (4.5 m) ↕ 150 ft (45 m)

North American evergreen; dense columnar-pyramidal habit. Leaves sharp-pointed, 4-angled, gray-blue. Cylindrical pendulous cones, green flushed with purple. Zones 1–8.

Picea glauca
DWARF ALBERTA SPRUCE, WHITE SPRUCE

☼ ❋ ↔ 12–20 ft (3.5–6 m) ↑ 80 ft (24 m)

Slow-growing evergreen conifer from Canada, grown commercially for paper making. Bright green shoots in spring; 4-angled, aromatic, needle-like leaves, on drooping branchlets. Small narrow cones. *P. g.* var. *albertiana* 'Alberta Globe', mound-forming conifer, to 12 ft (3.5 m) tall; 'Conica' ★, slow growing to a perfect conical form, fine blue-green foliage, deepening with age to gray-green, widely regarded as one of best dwarf conifers, reaching only 6 ft (1.8 m) in height. *P. g.* 'Alberta Blue', blue-green foliage; 'Densata', slow-growing form, blue-green needle-like leaves; 'Echiniformis' and 'Nana', dwarf forms; 'Rainbow's End', conical form, attractive yellow young growth. Zones 1–8.

Picea jezoensis
YEZO SPRUCE

☼ ❋ ↔ 25 ft (8 m) ↑ 120 ft (36 m)

From Japan and northeast Asia. Branches with upturned tips sweep to ground level. Gray bark fissured with age, shed in plates. Flat dark green leaves, glaucous beneath. Small cylindrical cones crimson when young, maturing to rich brown. Zones 8–10.

Picea mariana
AMERICAN BLACK SPRUCE

☼ ❋ ↔ 10 ft (3 m) ↑ 60 ft (18 m)

Pyramidal evergreen conifer from USA. Whorled branches, narrow, blue-green, blunt-tipped leaves. Many small persistent purple-brown cones. Distinctive densely hairy shoots. 'Doumetii', broader-leafed than species; 'Nana', more rounded dwarf form. Zones 1–8.

Picea omorika
SERBIAN SPRUCE

☼ ❋ ↔ 20 ft (6 m) ↑ 100 ft (30 m)

From Bosnia and Serbia. Elegant, evergreen, narrow pyramidal form. Fast-growing drooping branches upturned at ends. Flattened, blunt-tipped, needle-like, bright green leaves, grayish beneath. 'Nana', dwarf form, rounded to conical. Zones 4–9.

Picea omorika

Picea pungens

Picea orientalis
CAUCASIAN SPRUCE

☼ ❋ ↔ 20 ft (6 m) ↑ 100 ft (30 m)

From sheltered sites in Caucasus and Turkey. Upright, pyramidal, slow-growing, evergreen conifer. Pendulous branches to ground level. Short glossy green leaves. Short, pendulous, purplish cones. Brick red flower catkins in spring. 'Aureospicata', upward-curving branches; 'Connecticut Turnpike', shorter denser cultivar. Zones 3–9.

Picea pungens
COLORADO BLUE SPRUCE

☼ ❋ ↔ 20 ft (6 m) ↑ 100 ft (30 m)

Evergreen pyramidal conifer from western USA. Gray bark. Horizontal branches bear stiff, sharp, needle-like, blue-green leaves. Most cultivars fall into **Glauca Group** with paler blue-gray foliage, such as 'Compacta', silvery green foliage; 'Glauca Compacta', silvery blue foliage. Other Glauca Group cultivars include 'Globosa', 'Hoopsii', 'Koster', and 'Moerheimii'. Zones 2–10.

Picea sitchensis
ALASKA SPRUCE, SITKA SPRUCE

☼ ❋ ↔ 25 ft (8 m) ↑ 100 ft (30 m)

From west coast of North America. Broadly conical evergreen conifer, planted for timber. Narrow stiff leaves, green above, silvery beneath, tips sharply pointed. Favored Christmas tree. Zones 4–8.

Picea smithiana
syn. *Picea morinda*

WEST HIMALAYAN SPRUCE

☼ ❋ ↔ 20 ft (6 m) ↑ 75 ft (23 m)

Pyramidal evergreen conifer from north India. Horizontal branches, cascading foliage. Needle-like, finely pointed, dark green leaves surround branches. Pendulous, shiny, brown-purple cones. Zones 6–8.

PIERIS

This genus belonging to the heath (Ericaceae) family comes mainly from subtropical and temperate regions of the Himalayas. Widely cultivated, the best known of the 7 species are popular evergreen shrubs for gardens in temperate climates, but the genus also includes a vine and some shrubby species from the eastern regions of the USA and from the West Indies. Typically, the leaves are simple pointed ellipses, often with serrated edges, and the flowers are bell-shaped, downward-facing, and carried in panicles. They usually open in spring, and are sometimes scented.

CULTIVATION: Like most members of the erica family, *Pieris* species prefer cool, moist, well-drained soil with ample humus. A position in full sun yields more flowers; light shade results in lusher foliage. Heavy pruning is seldom required as the plants are naturally tidy; light trimming and pinching back is all that is necessary. Propagate from half-hardened cuttings or by layering.

Pieris floribunda
FETTER BUSH

☼ ❋ ↔ 7 ft (2 m) ↑ 6 ft (1.8 m)

From southeastern USA. Pointed serrated-edged leaves to 3 in (8 cm) long. Flowers white, ¼ in (6 mm) long, carried in showy

Pieris japonica

PIMELEA

This genus consists of about 100 species in the daphne (Thymelaeaceae) family. Evergreen shrubs or subshrubs of Australasian origin, they are valued for their spectacular spring flowering. Some species, known as rice flowers, are highly valued as cut flowers. Flower color is variable within a species, ranging from white to deep pink; some species produce yellow or purple flowers. Terminal starry flowers with open reflexed tubes appear in showy heads, sometimes surrounded by prominent colored bracts. Fruit are small, and dry or fleshy. CULTIVATION: They prefer well-drained acidic soils enriched with organic matter, and full sun or part-shade. They are tolerant of wind and salt-laden air, but dislike heavy frost. They respond to regular light pruning. Life expectancy is usually short. Propagate from tip cuttings in late spring to summer, or seed when it can be obtained. Germination may be slow.

panicles, in spring. Flowerheads differ from those of Asian species, being stiffer and held more erect. Zones 5–9.

Pieris 'Forest Flame'

☼ ❈ ↔ 6 ft (1.8 m) ↑ 12 ft (3.5 m)

Hybrid between *P. formosa* 'Wakehurst' and *P. japonica*. Strongly upright shrub, kept compact by pruning. Panicles of white flowers in spring. Young foliage bright red, changing to pink, then cream, then pale green, then dark green. Zones 6–9.

Pieris formosa

☼ ❈ ↔ 7 ft (2 m) ↑ 10–20 ft (3–6 m)

Native to Himalayan region. Leaves slightly glossy with finely serrated edges. Flower panicles mainly erect but with tendency to droop, flowers white or sometimes pink-tinted. *P. f.* var. *forrestii*, vivid red new growth, fragrant white flowers in drooping panicles; *P. f.* 'Wakehurst', leaves ageing from red to pink to green. Zones 6–10.

Pieris japonica
syn. *Pieris taiwanensis*
JAPANESE PIERIS, LILY-OF-THE-VALLEY BUSH

☼ ❈ ↔ 8 ft (2.4 m) ↑ 8–10 ft (2.4–3 m)

Species now includes *P. taiwanensis*, found in Japan, Taiwan, and eastern China. Leaves pink to bronze when young, ageing to dark green. Floral racemes erect or drooping, flowers usually white, in spring. 'Bert Chandler', light pink new growth turns yellow, then green; 'Christmas Cheer', early white and pink flowers; 'Karenoma', red-brown new growth; 'Little Heath', dwarf form, white-edged leaves; 'Mountain Fire' ★, reddish new leaves; 'Robinswood', green leaves, yellowish green edges, bright red new growth; 'Valley Valentine', purple-red flowers; 'Variegata', cream and green foliage, young leaves pink-tinted; 'Whitecaps', white flowers. Zones 6–10.

Pimelea ferruginea
ROSY RICE FLOWER

☼ ❈ ↔ 3 ft (0.9 m) ↑ 3 ft (0.9 m)

Commonly seen species from Western Australia. Tolerant of salt spray. Oval leaves, shiny green, pointed, arranged along stems. Clusters of pink, open, tubular flowers, on branch tips, in spring, and intermittently at other times. 'Bonne Petite', profuse clusters of pink flowers. Zones 8–10.

Pimelea physodes

Pimelea nivea
WHITE COTTON BUSH

☼ ❈ ↔ 3 ft (0.9 m) ↑ 6 ft (1.8 m)

Sometimes straggly evergreen shrub from Tasmania, Australia. White, or occasionally pink, star-shaped flowers, in large heads, in summer. White hairs cover plant, except upper surface of small, round to oval, glossy, dark green leaves. Zones 8–9.

Pimelea physodes
QUALUP BELLS

☼ ❈ ↔ 2 ft (0.6 m) ↑ 3 ft (0.9 m)

From Western Australia. Small hanging flowers surrounded by large red bracts. Popular cut flower. Thrives in harsh silica soil of Stirling Ranges. Can be difficult to cultivate outside its natural range. Zones 9–10.

Pimelea prostrata
NEW ZEALAND DAPHNE

☼ ❈ ↔ 36 in (90 cm) ↑ 6 in (15 cm)

From New Zealand. Evergreen prostrate shrub, dense foliage. Leaves tiny, blue-gray, along wiry stems, in 4 rows. Small white flowers in summer. Small white berries. Excellent embankment and spillover plant. Zones 8–10.

Pinus bungeana

Pinus densiflora

Pinus halepensis, in the wild, Spain

PINUS

PINE

This very variable genus of conifers in the pine (Pinaceae) family has around 110 species, found throughout Europe, Asia, north-western Africa, North and Central America, and the West Indies. They grow in a range of climates and conditions, from tropical equatorial forests to the extreme cold at the edge of the Arctic Circle. Predominantly large trees, only a couple of species are shrubs. The leaves are needle-like, and may be quite small to as long as 18 in (45 cm). They are generally found in bundles of 3 or 5, with never more than 8 in a group. The seed cones vary in shape, color, and dimension. The genus includes some of the world's most important timber species.

CULTIVATION: Most can easily withstand cold and extended dry periods, and also tolerate a range of soils, although they must have full sun. Some species are popular for bonsai. Propagation of the species is from seed; the cultivars are grafted.

Pinus banksiana

JACK PINE

☼ ❀ ↔ 20 ft (6 m) ↑ 60 ft (18 m)

Native to southern Canada and northeastern USA. Straight tree, irregular in outline, short twisted leaves growing in pairs. Light brown cones slightly curved. Grown and harvested for pulpwood, power poles, and railway ties, and planted for land rehabilitation and for trade in Christmas trees. Zones 2–8.

Pinus bungeana

LACEBARK PINE

☼ ❀ ↔ 20 ft (6 m) ↑ 60 ft (18 m)

Multi-trunked tree from northwestern China. Stiff leaves give off smell of turpentine when crushed. Cones small and egg-shaped. Gray-green peeling bark, splotched white and brown. Zones 5–9.

Pinus canariensis

CANARY ISLAND PINE

☼ ⚘ ↔ 25 ft (8 m) ↑ 130 ft (40 m)

From Canary Islands. Straight solid main trunk, dense oval crown of 6–12 in (15–30 cm) needles that tend to droop. Attractive dark reddish brown bark, shiny brown cones. Naturalized in Australia and South Africa. Zones 9–11.

Pinus cembra

AROLLA PINE, SWISS STONE PINE

☼ ❀ ↔ 15 ft (4.5 m) ↑ 30 ft (9 m)

From central Europe. Narrow-conical to almost columnar, branching from ground. Densely foliaged with stiff 3 in (8 cm) needles, dark green, twisted. Small cones on very old trees. Zones 4–8.

Pinus contorta

LODGEPOLE PINE, SHORE PINE

☼ ❀ ↔ 25 ft (8 m) ↑ 75 ft (23 m)

Tree native to western North America, from Alaska to Mexico. Variable in habit, generally tall, straight, conical. Dense, stiff, dark green needles; small, asymmetrical, orange-brown cones. Zones 5–9.

Pinus coulteri

BIG-CONE PINE, COULTER PINE

☼ ❀ ↔ 30 ft (9 m) ↑ 100 ft (30 m)

From dry mountain slopes of California, USA. Fast-growing conifer. Long, stiff, glaucous green needles in bundles of 3. Huge, spiny, brown cones. Tolerates wind and drought. Zones 8–10.

Pinus densiflora

JAPANESE RED PINE

☼ ❀ ↔ 20 ft (6 m) ↑ 70 ft (21 m)

Tree from Japan, Korea, and China. Open irregular crown. Green leaves 5 in (12 cm) long, in tufts at ends of branches. Bark reddish brown, cones dull brown. 'Pendula' ★, vigorous, semi-prostrate; 'Umbraculifera', slow growing, shaped like umbrella. Zones 4–9.

Pinus halepensis

ALEPPO PINE

☼ ⚘ ↔ 20 ft (6 m) ↑ 60 ft (18 m)

Mediterranean tree, low branches, flattened top. Leaves 4 in (10 cm) long, curved, twisted. Medium-sized cones persist for years. Naturalized in Australia, South Africa, and New Zealand. Zones 8–11.

Pinus heldreichii

BOSNIAN PINE

☼ ❀ ↔ 20 ft (6 m) ↑ 60 ft (18 m)

Found on western Balkan Peninsula southward to Greece. Sometimes shrubby tree. Irregular outline, open habit. Leaves stiff and sharp. Cones in clusters of 2, 3, or 4, opening when ripe. **P. h. var.** *leucodermis*, used as ornamental; '**Compact Gem**', dwarf. *P. h.* '**Smidtii**', compact dwarf, bright green needles. Zones 6–9.

Pinus lambertiana

SUGAR PINE

☼ ❄ ↔ 20 ft (6 m) ↑ 150 ft (45 m)

Occurs from central Oregon, USA, to northern Baja California, Mexico. Narrow irregular crown. Needles stiff, sharp, bluish. Pendulous cones, 20 in (50 cm) long, on long stalks. Zones 7–9.

Pinus longaeva

ANCIENT PINE, GREAT BASIN BRISTLECONE PINE

☼ ❄ ↔ 15 ft (4.5 m) ↑ 60 ft (18 m)

From dry subalpine peaks of western USA. Famous for its longevity with ages of over 5,000 years recorded. Small stiff leaves, medium-sized cones. Often crooked in form. Zones 5–8.

Pinus merkusii

SUMATRAN PINE

☼ ❄ ↔ 20 ft (6 m) ↑ 150 ft (45 m)

Only species found south of equator, in Sumatra, Indonesia, and also in Philippines. Conical to rounded crown, stiff needles 8 in (20 cm) long. Cones single or pairs. Zones 9–12.

Pinus monticola

WESTERN WHITE PINE

☼ ❄ ↔ 20 ft (6 m) ↑ 100 ft (30 m)

From northwestern North America. Large tree, narrow crown, solid straight main trunk. Foliage dense, leaves to 4 in (10 cm) long. Narrow cylindrical cones. Zones 4–9.

Pinus mugo

DWARF MOUNTAIN PINE, MUGO PINE, SWISS MOUNTAIN PINE

☼ ❄ ↔ 12 ft (3.5 m) ↑ 25 ft (8 m)

From mountains of central Europe. Small tree, often shrub-like, windswept habit. Long, bright green, needle leaves in pairs. Cones small, dark brown. '**Green Candles**', dense shrub; '**Honeycomb**', very compact rounded form, yellowish foliage; '**Paul's Dwarf**', tiny needle-like leaves; '**Slowmound**', tiny needle-like leaves; '**Tannenbaum**', very erect symmetrical form; '**Teeny**', dwarf. Zones 2–9.

Pinus nigra

AUSTRIAN PINE, BLACK PINE, CORSICAN PINE

☼ ❄ ↔ 25 ft (8 m) ↑ 120 ft (36 m)

Variable species, naturally occurring in southern Europe. Straight central trunk, silvery gray. Stiff needles 6 in (15 cm) long, cones light brown, glossy. Naturalized in New Zealand and parts of USA. '**Hornibrookiana**', dwarf forming compact mound. Zones 4–9.

Pinus palustris

LONG-LEAF PINE, PITCH PINE

☼ ❄ ↔ 15 ft (4.5 m) ↑ 100 ft (30 m)

Naturally found in southeastern USA. Open crown, straight trunk. Long leaves to 18 in (45 cm) in length, clustered at branch tips.

Pinus parviflora

Brown cones have short thorns. Seedlings look much like tuft of grass before traditional tree trunk develops. Zones 7–10.

Pinus parviflora

JAPANESE WHITE PINE

☼ ❄ ↔ 20 ft (6 m) ↑ 80 ft (24 m)

From Japan. Smaller in cultivation; slow growing. Dense rounded crown; stiff, curved, blue-green leaves. Oval to cylindrical red-brown cones. '**Adcock's Dwarf**', to 30 in (75 cm). Zones 4–9.

Pinus patula

MEXICAN PINE, PATULA PINE, WEEPING PINE

☼ ❄ ↔ 30 ft (9 m) ↑ 50 ft (15 m)

From mountains of Mexico. Broadly conical; horizontal branches; stout trunk; weeping foliage. Long pale green needles in groups of 3. Clusters of 2 to 5 brown, conical, curved cones. Zones 8–10.

Pinus pinaster

CLUSTER PINE, MARITIME PINE

☼ ❄ ↔ 30 ft (9 m) ↑ 100 ft (30 m)

From Mediterranean; world's main source of resin. Long, stiff, shiny, gray-green needles, in pairs. Bark with deep red-brown fissures between gray plates. Orange-brown cones. Zones 7–10.

Pinus pinea

ROMAN PINE, STONE PINE, UMBRELLA PINE

☼ ❄ ↔ 20 ft (6 m) ↑ 80 ft (24 m)

From southern Europe and Turkey. Flat-topped conifer; leaning trunk; fissured reddish gray bark. Needles bright green, in pairs. Rounded cones, shiny, brown, resinous. Large edible seeds known as "pine nuts." Drought tolerant once established. Zones 8–10.

Pinus ponderosa

PONDEROSA PINE, WESTERN YELLOW PINE

☼ ❄ ↔ 20 ft (6 m) ↑ 130 ft (40 m)

From western North America. Conical open crown; solid straight trunk; fissured pale yellow bark. Stiff pointed leaves to 10 in (25 cm) long. Prickly brown cones to 6 in (15 cm) long. Zones 3–9.

Pinus ponderosa, in the wild, California, USA

Pinus resinosa, in the wild, Minnesota, USA

Pinus sylvestris, in the wild, Scotland

Pinus wallichiana

Pinus radiata

syn. *Pinus insignis*

MONTEREY PINE, RADIATA PINE

☼ ❄ ↔ 25 ft (8 m) ↑ 100 ft (30 m)

From coastal central California, USA, and Guadalupe and Cedros Islands off Mexico. Tall tree; straight trunk, irregular open crown. Leaves 3–6 in (8–15 cm) long. Cones asymmetrically conical, 5 in (12 cm) long. Very important timber tree in Australia, New Zealand, and Chile. Zones 8–10.

Pinus resinosa

RED PINE

☼ ❄ ↔ 20 ft (6 m) ↑ 100 ft (30 m)

From northeastern USA and southeastern Canada. Trunk straight, crown narrow oval. Reddish brown bark. Sharp pointed leaves to 5 in (12 cm) long. Symmetrical oval to conical cones. Zones 2–8.

Pinus roxburghii

CHIR PINE, HIMALAYAN LONG-LEAF PINE

☼ ❄ ↔ 15 ft (4.5 m) ↑ 100 ft (30 m)

Broad-crowned tree from Himalayan foothills. Mottled gray and light brown bark. Sharp-pointed pendulous leaves. Cones 8 in (20 cm) long. Zones 6–11.

Pinus strobus

EASTERN WHITE PINE, WHITE PINE

☼ ❄ ↔ 20 ft (6 m) ↑ 165 ft (50 m)

From southeastern Canada and northeastern USA. Straight trunk, irregular crown of horizontal branches. Leaves blue-green; pendulous cones. 'Banzai Nana', bright green foliage; 'Fastigiata', upcurved branches; 'Horsford', compact foliage; 'Pendula', weeping branches; 'Prostrata', low spreading habit; 'Radiata', dwarf form. Zones 3–9.

Pinus sylvestris

SCOTCH PINE, SCOTS PINE

☼ ❄ ↔ 20 ft (6 m) ↑ 100 ft (30 m)

From Europe and northern Asia. Round-crowned tree, straight trunk, smaller in cultivation. Pairs of bluish green leaves. Gray-green symmetrical cones, 2½ in (6 cm) long. *P. s.* var. *lapponica*, smaller leaves and cones; *P. s.* var. *mongolica*, leaves up to 4 in (10 cm) long. *P. s.* 'Argentea' (syn. 'Edwin Hillier'), silver-blue foliage; 'Fastigiata', narrow erect habit, to 25 ft (8 m) tall; 'Moseri', dwarf form, yellowish needles; 'Saxatilis', low growing, dark green leaves; 'Troopsii', appealing foliage; 'Watereri', bluish leaves, slow growing, can be invasive in cool high-rainfall areas. Zones 2–9.

Pinus taeda

LOBLOLLY PINE

☼ ❄ ↔ 25 ft (8 m) ↑ 100 ft (30 m)

Leading timber tree, southeastern USA. Dense oval crown, straight trunk, lower half often free of branches. Twisted bright green leaves; oval to conical cones, 4 in (10 cm) long. Zones 7–11.

Pinus thunbergii

JAPANESE BLACK PINE

☼ ❄ ↔ 20 ft (6 m) ↑ 130 ft (40 m)

Tall tree from Japan and South Korea. Irregular outline, single main trunk often curved. Dense dark green leaves, small oval cones. 'Majestic Beauty' and 'Tsukasa', both compact and hardy. Zones 5–9.

Pinus wallichiana

BHUTAN PINE, BLUE PINE, HIMALAYAN PINE

☼ ❄ ↔ 20 ft (6 m) ↑ 150 ft (45 m)

Very tall tree with conical crown from Himalayas. Blue-green leaves to 8 in (20 cm) long, frequently arching or drooping. Cones very long, thin and cylindrical, hanging from branch tips. Zones 6–9.

PIPER

Belonging to the pepper (Piperaceae) family, this large genus of about 2,000 species of shrubs, trees, and woody-stemmed climbers is widely distributed in tropical regions. Smooth-edged, alternate, prominently veined leaves are often aromatic. Tiny flowers, borne in a dense axillary spike or raceme, are followed by small, single-seeded fruit. *P. nigrum* is the source of the black and white pepper used throughout the world as a seasoning.

CULTIVATION: All species are frost tender. In temperate climates, they make decorative indoor plants, climbing species needing some support structure. Indoors they are best suited to humid conditions and good light. Outdoor plants require a protected position in moist, fertile, well-drained soil in full sun or part-shade. Propagate from seed, half-hardened cuttings or by division.

Piper aduncum
COW'S FOOT, FALSE KAVA, FALSE MATICO, JOINTWOOD, SPIKED PEPPER
☀ ✦ ↔ 8–17 ft (2.4–5 m) ↑ 17–25 ft (5–8 m)

Multi-branched shrub or small tree native to Central America and northern South America. Trunk to 4 in (10 cm) or more in diameter. Erect branches; smooth gray bark. Cord-like flexible flower spikes grow from stems. Leaves opposite, alternate, elliptical, to 10 in (25 cm) long, tapered pointed tip. Berry with small black seeds. All plant parts have peppery taste and odor. Plant used medicinally as aromatic stimulant, to prevent gonorrhea and hemorrhoids, for relief of ulcers. Zones 10–12.

PISTACIA
This small genus in the cashew (Anacardiaceae) family consists of around 9 species from the Mediterranean region, eastern and southeastern Asia, Central America, and southern USA. They are mainly deciduous trees with compound, mostly pinnate leaves terminated by a pair of leaflets, and panicles of small-petalled flowers. The flowers are followed by peppercorn-like fruit produced on the female plants; male plants are separate. Some species are important for their oils and edible seeds.
CULTIVATION: Most species originate in dry, warm-temperate regions, and are fairly adaptable. They grow best in a well-drained moderately fertile soil in full sun. Propagate from seed, cuttings, budding, or grafting.

Pistacia chinensis
CHINESE PISTACHIO
☀ ❋ ↔ 15 ft (4.5 m) ↑ 25–50 ft (8–15 m)

Deciduous tree from China and Taiwan. Mostly pinnate leaves, 10 to 12 leathery dark green leaflets, turn shades of orange, red,

Pistacia chinensis

and yellow in autumn. Panicles of inconspicuous reddish flowers in summer. Small bluish fruit. Popular shade tree. Zones 7–10.

Pistacia lentiscus
LENTISCO, MASTIC TREE
☀ ❋ ↔ 12 ft (3.5 m) ↑ 12 ft (3.5 m)

Native of Mediterranean region. Aromatic evergreen tree or shrub. Pinnate leaves of 2 to 7 pairs of glossy, leathery, dark green leaflets, terminated by pair of leaflets. Panicles of small flowers in spring. Small black fruit. Zones 8–11.

PITTOSPORUM
This genus consists of about 200 species of evergreen trees and shrubs in the family Pittosporaceae. They are found in Africa, southern and eastern Asia, Australia, New Zealand, and the Hawaiian Islands, USA. The foliage is usually glossy with

Pittosporum eugenioides

leaves arranged alternately or in whorls. The small flowers, 5-petalled, may be cup-shaped or reflexed, single or in clusters, and some have a sweet fragrance. Capsules contain seeds with a sticky coating. Some species are useful for shelter, hedging, borders, or containers. They can be clipped for formal situations and to keep the foliage dense.
CULTIVATION: Most species will grow in sun or part-shade in any well-drained soil. In cool-temperate climates they may require the protection of a sunny wall, or they can be grown in the conservatory or greenhouse. Propagation is from seed, which germinates erratically, or from half-hardened cuttings taken in summer or autumn. Cultivars are propagated from cuttings only.

Pittosporum crassifolium
KARO
☀ ❂ ↔ 8 ft (2.4 m) ↑ 10–20 ft (3–6 m)

Robust New Zealand species, withstands coastal conditions. Dark green leaves, thick and leathery, white hairy coating beneath. Flowers small, dark red, noticeably fragrant in evening, in early summer. Down-covered fruit, shiny black seeds. Zones 9–11.

Pittosporum eugenioides
LEMONWOOD, TARATA
☀ ❋ ↔ 12 ft (3.5 m) ↑ 40 ft (12 m)

From New Zealand, smaller in cultivation. Glossy, light green, oval leaves, distinct pale midrib and wavy edges, release lemony aroma when crushed. Small creamy yellow flowers, honey-scented, in spring–summer. Popular for hedging and specimen planting. 'Variegatum', features irregularly marked creamy edges to its leaves. Zones 8–11.

Pittosporum 'Garnettii'
☀ ❋ ↔ 7 ft (2 m) ↑ 7–10 ft (2–3 m)

Hybrid between P. tenuifolium and P. ralphii. Attractive oval leaves, creamy white variegations flushed pink. Solitary dark purple flowers, along branches, in spring. Zones 8–11.

Pittosporum tenuifolium
KOHUHU

☼ ❄ ↔15 ft (4.5 m) ↑15–20 ft (4.5–6 m)

Variable species, native to New Zealand, usually large shrub. Dense foliage; thin, slightly leathery, oblong leaves with wavy edges. Small flowers, reflexed petals, dark red, almost black, in spring, strong honey fragrance. Capsules turn black on maturity. **'Deborah'**, grayish green leaves with creamy margins flushed with pink; **'Eila Keightley'** (syn. 'Sunburst'), rounded leaves with central yellow variegations; **'Irene Paterson'**, slower-growing form with almost white leaves speckled with pale green; **'James Stirling'**, blackish red branchlets, silvery green leaves; **'Marjory Channon'**, popular cultivar in USA; **'Tom Thumb'**, dwarf variety, foliage ages to dark purple; **'Variegatum'**, cream-edged green leaves; **'Warnham Gold'**, light green leaves change to creamy yellow and gold. Zones 8–11.

Pittosporum tobira
JAPANESE PITTOSPORUM, TOBIRA

☼ ❄ ↔7 ft (2 m) ↑20 ft (6 m)

Erect bushy shrub native to China and Japan. Leathery oblong leaves, dark glossy green, rolled edges. Orange-scented flowers, flaring petals creamy white, lemony yellow with age, in spring–early summer. **'Nanum'**, bright green leaves; **'Variegatum'**, leaves have irregularly marked white margin; **'Wheeler's Dwarf'**, compact miniature to 24 in (60 cm) high. Zones 9–11.

Pittosporum undulatum
SWEET PITTOSPORUM, VICTORIAN BOX

☼ ❄ ↔20 ft (6 m) ↑15–40 ft (4.5–12 m)

Native to eastern Australia. Vigorous species. Shiny, dark green, pointed, oval leaves, wavy edges. Creamy white flowers, sweetly

scented, in terminal clusters, in spring. Orangey brown capsules. Has become weed outside its natural forest habitat. Zones 9–11.

PLATANUS
PLANE TREE

This genus in the plane (Platanaceae) family consists of about 8 species from the northern temperate zone, including Eurasia, North America, and Mexico. These deciduous trees have inconspicuous spring flowers; globe-shaped fruit on hanging stalks; large, alternate, palmately lobed, simple leaves; and ornamental, flaking, mottled bark. They are useful large shade trees. Many species are highly tolerant of compacted soils and air pollution and will grow well in both temperate and cool climates.

Platycladus orientalis

CULTIVATION: Most species are adaptable, as can be seen by the many cases of street trees in less than optimal conditions, but they perform best on deep, productive, alluvial soils with a consistent water source, such as a permanent stream, in full sun. Pruning is not essential, though it is desirable in the early years if a single trunk is to be established. Propagate from seed, cuttings, or by layering.

Platanus × *hispanica*
syns *Platanus* × *acerifolia*, *P.* × *hybrida*
LONDON PLANE

☼ ❄ ↔60 ft (18 m) ↑100 ft (30 m)

Believed to be hybrid between *P. occidentalis* and *P. orientalis*. Rounded pyramidal form. Gray to light brown bark, variable bright green leaves, usually 5-lobed. Fruit small. Tolerates heat, drought and pollution. **'Pyramidalis'**, upright cultivar with coarse bark, leaves 3-lobed, often slightly toothed. Zones 4–9.

Platanus occidentalis
AMERICAN PLANE, BUTTON-BALL, BUTTONWOOD, SYCAMORE

☼ ❄ ↔70 ft (21 m) ↑150 ft (45 m)

Native to USA and Canada. Very tall deciduous tree, broad open crown, spreading branches. Attractive flaking bark, 3 to 5 bright green shallow-lobed leaves. Single hanging nutlets, sometimes in pairs. Timber used for furniture and pulp. Zones 4–9.

Platanus orientalis
ORIENTAL PLANE

☼ ❄ ↔70 ft (21 m) ↑100 ft (30 m)

Large, spreading, deciduous tree from southeastern Europe to western Asia. Huge trunk with mottled, brown, gray, and greenish white bark. Dark green leaves, palmately lobed. Inconspicuous flowers in early spring. Clusters of 2 to 6 globe-shaped fruit. *P. o.* var. *insularis*, bright green leaves, toothed lobes; hairy fruit. Zones 5–9.

Platanus racemosa
ALISO, CALIFORNIA PLANE, CALIFORNIA SYCAMORE, WESTERN SYCAMORE

☼ ❄ ↔75 ft (23 m) ↑100 ft (30 m)

Large, strong-growing, deciduous tree naturally found from southern California, USA, to Mexico. Dark green leaves, 3 to

Platanus × *hispanica*

5 deep lobes, downy underside. Clusters of 2 to 7 bristly hanging fruit turn brown when mature. Zones 7–10.

PLATYCLADUS

At times put in the genus *Thuja*, this genus, within the cypress (Cupressaceae) family, is now considered distinct. It contains only 1 species, an evergreen coniferous tree featuring flattened spray-like branchlets of lightly aromatic foliage. Native to Korea, China, and northeastern Iran, it is rarely seen outside eastern Asia in its typical form, but rather as one of its numerous cultivars. These generally have a more rounded low-branching habit and are highly ornamental and dependable. Many are suitable for hedging. Dwarf varieties are excellent in rock gardens or containers and as a low border.
CULTIVATION: Grow this fully hardy genus in a moist well-drained soil in a sunny position protected from strong winds. Prune lightly in spring. Propagate from seed or cuttings.

Plumeria obtusa

Platycladus orientalis
syn. *Thuja orientalis*
CHINESE ARBOR-VITAE
☀ ❋ ↔ 15 ft (4.5 m) ↑ 40 ft (12 m)
Small conical tree, upward-curving branches. Small, mid-green, scale-like leaves in flattened vertical sprays. Fleshy, ovoid, female cones, ripen to waxy silvery sheen. '**Aurea Nana**' ★, dense oval shape to 3 ft (0.9 m) high, creamy yellow foliage darkens to rich green in autumn–winter; '**Balaton**', soft light green foliage; '**Elegantissima**', compact conical bush to 15 ft (4.5 m) tall, golden yellow foliage develops bronze tones in winter; '**Meldensis**', dwarf rounded bush to 3 ft (0.9 m), with soft blue-green foliage, purplish toning in winter; '**Rosedalis**', to 5 ft (1.5 m) tall, fine soft foliage, changes from bright yellow in spring to sea green in summer, has purplish tones in winter. Zones 6–11.

PLUMBAGO
LEADWORT
There are about 15 species of annuals, perennials, and shrubs in this genus, which is a member of the leadwort (Plumbaginaceae) family. They are widely distributed throughout the tropical and subtropical regions of the world. They have simple light to mid-green leaves and can become rather sparsely foliaged and twiggy if they are not regularly trimmed. Their main attraction is their flowers, which appear throughout the warmer months. Carried on short racemes, they are very narrow tubes tipped with 5 relatively large lobes. The flowers come in white or various shades of pink and blue.
CULTIVATION: The taller shrubby species can be trained as climbers if they are grown against a wall. The shorter forms do well in containers. Plumbagos are not fussy about soil, as long as it is moist and well drained. Prune the plants in late winter to thin out the summer's congested growth and remove any wood that has been damaged by frost. Plant in full sun; propagate from seed, half-hardened cuttings, or layers.

Plumbago auriculata
syn. *Plumbago capensis*
CAPE LEADWORT, PLUMBAGO
☀ ❄ ↔ 7 ft (2 m) ↑ 15 ft (4.5 m)
Native to South Africa. Tough vigorous shrub with long arching stems. Profuse pale blue flowers in warmer months. '**Alba**', white flowers; '**Escapade Blue**', light blue flowers; '**Royal Cape**' ★, darker blue flowers. Zones 9–11.

Plumbago auriculata

Plumbago indica
☀ ✦ ↔ 3 ft (0.9 m) ↑ 5 ft (1.5 m)
Sprawling shrub or subshrub from Southeast Asia. Long spikes of deep pink, pale red, or purple-red flowers in warmer months, intermittently at other times. Zones 10–12.

PLUMERIA
This small genus in the dogbane (Apocynaceae) family contains about 8 species from tropical America. Mostly deciduous or semi-evergreen shrubs and small trees, they have simple smooth-edged leaves arranged alternately or spirally toward the ends of fleshy branches, which have a poisonous milky sap. They are grown for their fragrant flowers, which have 5 petals arranged in a propeller-like form and joined at the base into a narrow tube, produced in clusters on the ends of branches.
CULTIVATION: Easily cultivated in a warm humid climate in a sunny position protected from strong cold winds, in cooler climates they require a warm frost-free position in a well-drained moderately fertile soil. Propagate from stem cuttings; these are most successful if taken in late winter when the plant is dormant. Allow the cut end to seal before inserting it into the growing medium.

Plumeria obtusa
PAGODA TREE, WHITE FRANGIPANI
☀ ✦ ↔ 12 ft (3.5 m) ↑ 25 ft (8 m)
Native to Bahamas and Greater Antilles. Evergreen in tropical climates. Leaves rounded or blunt tip. Fragrant flowers, white with yellow center. '**Singapore White**' ★, popular cultivar. Zones 10–12.

Podocarpus latifolius

Plumeria rubra ★
FRANGIPANI

☼ ☀ ↔ 15 ft (4.5 m) ↑ 25 ft (8 m)

From Central America, Mexico, and Venezuela. Deciduous tree, spreading branches, broad rounded shape. Leaves large, dark green, shiny. Strongly fragrant funnel-shaped flowers, variable in color, in summer–autumn. *P. r.* **var.** *acutifolia*, panicles of yellow-centered white flowers with wide petals. *P. r.* 'Bridal White', 3 in (8 cm) wide, mildly scented, white to creamy white flowers with small yellow center and long deep green leaves with red edges; 'Celandine', golden yellow flowers; 'Dark Red', rich red flowers; 'Rosy Dawn', yellow flowers tinged pink; 'Starlight', flowers to 4 in (10 cm) wide, white with apricot to yellow center. Zones 10–12.

PODALYRIA

Containing some 25 species of evergreen shrubs and trees, this South African genus is in the pea-flower subfamily of the legume (Fabaceae) family. It is notable for its downy foliage and young growth, and for the attractive pea-flowers, which are usually in shades of pink and mauve. The leaves are simple smooth-edged ellipses with a covering of fine hairs, which gives them a silvery or pale golden sheen. The flowers, carried singly or in pairs in the leaf axils, open from similarly downy buds and are lightly scented.
CULTIVATION: These plants prefer light well-drained soil and a sunny position. They are drought tolerant once established and thrive in coastal conditions. Prune lightly after flowering to keep them compact. Propagate from seed, half-hardened cuttings, or layers.

Podalyria calyptrata
SWEET PEA BUSH

☼ ❆ ↔ 12 ft (3.5 m) ↑ 12 ft (3.5 m)

Large shrub or small tree. Dark green leaves, silvery sheen from coating of short fine hairs. Pale pink to lavender flowers, 1¼ in (30 mm) wide, in spring–early summer. Zones 9–10.

Podalyria calyptrata

PODOCARPUS

Widely distributed in warm-temperate areas of the Southern Hemisphere to tropical zones of eastern Asia and Japan, this genus in the plum-pine (Podocarpaceae) family consists of around 100 species of evergreen trees and shrubs. They have simple, usually spirally or alternately attached leaves that are mostly flat and narrow. The male and female plants are usually separate. Female flowers turn into round drupe-like fruit, often on a fleshy red or purple receptacle.
CULTIVATION: Most *Podocarpus* species prefer a well-drained soil in a sunny position protected from cold strong winds. Once established, they will tolerate extended dry periods. Propagate from seed, preferably fresh, or from cuttings.

Podocarpus elatus
BROWN PINE, PLUM PINE

☼ ❆ ↔ 20 ft (6 m) ↑ 50 ft (15 m)

Native to Queensland and New South Wales, Australia. Tall shrub or tree. Deep green leathery leaves, oblong to linear. Single greenish fruit. Especially suited for bonsai and hedging. Zones 9–12.

Podocarpus latifolius
YELLOWWOOD

☼ ☀ ↔ 15 ft (4.5 m) ↑ 90 ft (27 m)

Large evergreen shrub or tree native to Africa, from Sudan south to KwaZulu-Natal, South Africa. Smooth dark gray bark, peeling in long strips; leaves rigid, dark green, narrowly elliptical, 1¼–4 in (3–10 cm) long, tinged blue above. Male and female cones resemble small pine cones, female cone developing into small, fleshy, berry-like fruit, red tinged with purple. National tree of South Africa. Zones 10–11.

Podocarpus lawrencei
MOUNTAIN PLUM PINE

☼ ❆ ↔ 4 ft (1.2 m) ↑ 12 ft (3.5 m)

Very variable species, dwarf to tall shrub. Deep green linear leaves, bluish tinge above, paler below. Seed greenish on enlarged, pinkish red, fleshy stalk. Low-growing variants used as ground covers. Zones 7–10.

Podocarpus macrophyllus
KUSAMAKI, LOHAN PINE

☼ ❆ ↔ 20 ft (6 m) ↑ 60 ft (18 m)

Native to China and Japan. Outer branches droop. Dark green, leathery, linear to lance-shaped leaves, bluish green below. Fruit on succulent purplish red stalk. 'Maki', smaller leaves. Zones 7–11.

Podocarpus totara
TOTARA

☼ ❆ ↔ 25 ft (8 m) ↑ 80 ft (24 m)

Long-lived New Zealand tree. Dense rounded crown, giant trunk, timber highly prized, resistant to marine borers. Linear, leathery, dark green leaves. Single seeds on ends of reddish fleshy stalks. 'Aureus', grows to 10 ft (3 m) tall, with narrow conical form and yellow foliage. Zones 8–11.

POLYALTHIA

This genus of around 100 species of shrubs or trees belongs to the custard-apple (Annonaceae) family. It is widespread in tropical regions, particularly in Southeast Asia, with a few species occurring in Australia. They have large glossy leaves that have very fine oil dots and are aromatic when crushed. Borne singly or in clusters on older leafless wood, the open star-like flowers have 6 to 8 petals. Decorative clusters of succulent berry-like fruit follow.
CULTIVATION: All species demand warm frost-free conditions. They prefer moist, humus-rich, well-drained soil in full sun or part-shade. Water during dry periods. Propagate from fresh seed or cuttings.

Polyalthia longifolia
INDIAN WILLOW
☼ ✤ ↔ 3–10 ft (0.9–3 m) ↑ 50 ft (15 m)
From Sri Lanka. Columnar form, short side branches down to base. Pendulous, bright green, elliptic leaves. Small greenish yellow flowers, in axillary clusters, in summer. Zones 11–12.

POLYGALA

Covering over 500 species of almost every growth form, except tall trees, this genus, a member of the milkwort (Polygalaceae) family, is very widespread. The foliage ranges from small and linear to large and oval but is usually simple with smooth edges. The flowers have a pea-flower-like structure with distinct wings and a keel, which usually has a feathery tuft unique to polygalas. The flowers, carried in clusters or racemes, come in a range of colors, with purple and pink dominant, and are followed by small seed pods.
CULTIVATION: While frost hardiness varies, most prefer a light well-drained soil with a position in sun or part-shade. European and American alpine species are ideal subjects for pots or troughs. Shrubby species can be trimmed or pruned to shape in spring. Propagate from seed, layers, or cuttings.

Polygala × dalmaisiana
☼ ᛒ ↔ 3 ft (0.9 m) ↑ 3–10 ft (0.9–3 m)
Evergreen shrub, hybrid between *P. oppositifolia* and *P. myrtifolia*; compact if trimmed occasionally. Mid-green, 1 in (25 mm) long leaves. Magenta to pale purple flowers, most of year. Zones 9–11.

Polygala myrtifolia
☼ ᛒ ↔ 3–6 ft (0.9–1.8 m) ↑ 6 ft (1.8 m)
South African evergreen shrub. Elliptic to oblong, mid-green leaves, often develop purplish tints in winter. Small clusters of pale-tufted purple-pink flowers most of year. Trim to keep compact. Zones 9–11.

POLYSCIAS

This genus of around 150 species of evergreen shrubs to large trees is part of the ivy (Araliaceae) family. It is found in tropical and subtropical regions of Africa, Southeast Asia, Australia, and the Pacific Islands. They have alternate compound leaves that are pinnate to tripinnate and tend to be spirally arranged toward the ends of the branches. Very small greenish white or purplish flowers are produced in terminal racemes, which are often prominent and profuse. The fruit is a rounded or slightly compressed berry that turns purplish black when ripe.

Polyalthia longifolia

Polygala myrtifolia

CULTIVATION: Most species are only suited to warm-temperate to tropical climates and prefer well-drained acidic soils in sun to part-shade. Provide extra water during extended dry periods. Propagate from fresh seed, cuttings in summer, or by division of root suckers.

Polyscias elegans
CELERY WOOD
◑ ᛒ ↔ 15 ft (4.5 m) ↑ 100 ft (30 m)
Tree native to east Australia and New Guinea. Bipinnate leaves, glossy dark green leaflets, celery fragrance. Tiny purple flowers, in terminal panicles, in autumn–winter. Purple-black fruit. Zones 9–12.

Polyscias filicifolia
FERN-LEAF ARALIA
◑ ✤ ↔ 4 ft (1.2 m) ↑ 15 ft (4.5 m)
Shrub native to Pacific Islands. Deeply dissected leaves, many small, bright green, toothed leaflets, prominent purple veining. Tiny star-shaped flowers in summer. Zones 11–12.

Polyscias guilfoylei
GERANIUM ARALIA
◑ ✤ ↔ 8 ft (2.4 m) ↑ 20 ft (6 m)
Shrub native to eastern Malay Peninsula, northern Australia, and Polynesia. Pinnate leaves, leaflets toothed, white margins. Yellowish green flowers in summer. Tiny purplish black fruit. Zones 11–12.

Polyscias elegans, in center

POPULUS

ASPEN, POPLAR

There are about 35 species in this genus, comprising deciduous trees that range over much of the temperate Northern Hemisphere. They are in the willow (Salicaceae) family. Many poplars have deltoid-shaped leaves, but leaf shapes, sizes, and textures vary widely. Tiny flowers on pendulous catkins appear before the foliage. Small capsules follow the flowers, often filled with cotton-like down. Male and female catkins are usually on separate trees.
CULTIVATION: Poplars prefer a position in full sun in deep, moist, well-drained soil. Short-lived, they seldom exceed 60 years. They have vigorous invasive root systems and some can sucker heavily, which makes them a problem near drains and paving. Prune to shape; propagate from winter hardwood cuttings.

Populus alba

BOLLEANA POPLAR, SILVER POPLAR, WHITE POPLAR
☼ ❉ ↔ 40 ft (12 m) ↑ 80 ft (24 m)
Vigorous tree from Europe and North Africa to central Asia. Can become weed. Young stems and leaves have downy white hairs, upper surface ages to deep green. Leaves broad-based, egg-shaped, coarsely toothed edges. 'Nivea', chalky white; 'Pendula', weeping branches; 'Raket' (syn. 'Rocket'), upright form. Zones 3–10.

Populus balsamifera

BALSAM POPLAR, TACAMAHAC
☼ ❉ ↔ 25 ft (8 m) ↑ 80 ft (24 m)
Northern North American and Russian species. Fragrant resin coats young twigs, buds, and new foliage; gives bronze coloration. Leaves roughly egg-shaped. Zones 3–8.

Populus × canadensis

CANADIAN POPLAR, CAROLINA POPLAR, HYBRID POPLAR
☼ ❉ ↔ 35 ft (10 m) ↑ 80 ft (24 m)
Hybrid between *P. deltoides* and *P. nigra*. Leaves egg-shaped to triangular, sparsely toothed edges, leaf stalks red. 'Aurea', new growth golden; 'Eugenei', tall columnar habit, new growth bronze;

Populus fremontii, in the wild, Arizona, USA

'Robusta', dense foliage, strongly upright columnar habit; 'Serotina', male form, conical habit, comes into leaf late. Zones 4–9.

Populus × canescens

GRAY POPLAR, TOWER POPLAR
☼ ❉ ↔ 40 ft (12 m) ↑ 100 ft (30 m)
Natural hybrid between *P. alba* and *P. tremula*. Rounded crown of large triangular to oval leaves, toothed at edges, felted beneath. Yellow-gray bark, scarred and fissured. Zones 4–9.

Populus deltoides

COTTONWOOD, EASTERN COTTONWOOD
☼ ❉ ↔ 60 ft (18 m) ↑ 100 ft (30 m)
From eastern half of North America. Leaves deltoid, coarse-toothed edges. Buds, new shoots, and leaves covered in balsam-scented resin. Zones 2–10.

Populus fremontii

ALAMILLO, FREMONT COTTONWOOD, WESTERN COTTONWOOD
☼ ❉ ↔ 40 ft (12 m) ↑ 100 ft (30 m)
Western North American tree. Stocky trunk. Yellow-green, broad-based, deltoid leaves, tapering to point, toothed. Female trees shed masses of seed "cotton." Zones 7–10.

Populus grandidentata

BIGTOOTH ASPEN
☼ ❉ ↔ 30 ft (9 m) ↑ 60 ft (18 m)
From eastern North America. Leaves on shorter older twigs very sharply toothed, on younger longer shoots, more ovoid, with wavy rather than toothed edges. Short branches form narrow rounded crown. Zones 3–9.

Populus lasiocarpa

CHINESE NECKLACE POPLAR
☼ ❉ ↔ 35 ft (10 m) ↑ 50–80 ft (15–24 m)
From southwestern China. Rounded crown, young stems initially have woolly coating. Glossy gray-green leaves, very large, egg- to heart-shaped, downy underside. Zones 5–10.

Populus nigra

BLACK POPLAR, THEVES POPLAR
☼ ❉ ↔ 60 ft (18 m) ↑ 100 ft (30 m)
Native to Europe, North Africa, and western Asia. Round-headed, with thick trunk, deeply fissured, knotted and gnarled, gray bark. Triangular to diamond-shaped leaves, brilliant yellow tones in autumn. 'Italica', broadly columnar, orange young twigs, more intense autumn color; 'Lombardy Gold', bright golden yellow foliage in summer–autumn. Zones 2–10.

Populus nigra 'Italica'

Populus simonii

☼ ❉ ↔ 25 ft (8 m) ↑ 80–100 ft (24–30 m)
From northwestern China. Narrow crown, pendulous branch tips. Young twigs and leaf stalks red. Leaves fresh green, can exceed 4 in (10 cm) in length. 'Pendula', weeping branches. Zones 2–9.

Posoqueria latifolia

Potentilla fruticosa 'Ochraleuca'

Pouteria cainito

Populus tremula

ASPEN, EUROPEAN ASPEN, QUAKING ASPEN, SWEDISH ASPEN

↔35 ft (10 m) ↑50 ft (15 m)

From northwest Europe south to North Africa and east to Siberia. Dark fissured bark. Leaves gray-green, tremble in breeze, finely hairy, lighter below; yellow, orange, and red in autumn. Zones 2–9.

Populus tremuloides ★

AMERICAN ASPEN, QUAKING ASPEN, TREMBLING ASPEN

↔30 ft (9 m) ↑50 ft (15 m)

North American tree. Slender, upright; yellow-gray bark. Leaves broad, glossy, dark green, serrated edges, turn yellow in autumn. Zones 1–9.

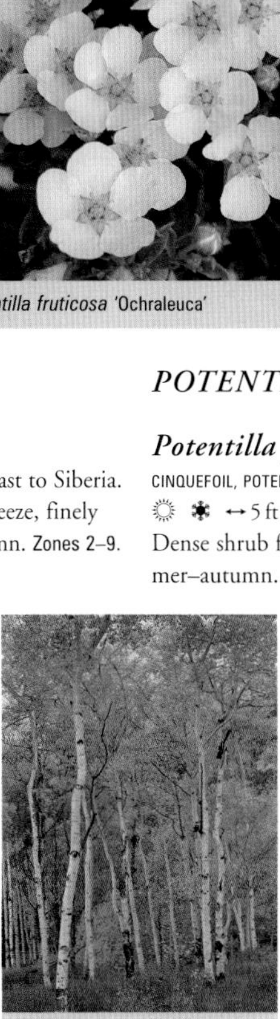

Populus tremuloides

Populus trichocarpa

BLACK COTTONWOOD

↔35 ft (10 m) ↑80–120 ft (24–36 m)

Native to western North America; furrowed dark gray bark, brittle branches. Leaves leathery, shallowly toothed, dark glossy green above, pale brown to nearly white beneath, turn yellow in autumn. **'Fritz Pauley'**, male cultivar. Zones 7–10.

POSOQUERIA

This genus of some 12 species of evergreen shrubs or trees in the madder (Rubiaceae) family comes from tropical America and the West Indies. The tubular flowers are very fragrant, white or red, and exceptionally long. The flowers each have 5 spreading petal lobes and are borne in large crowded clusters at branch tips in spring. Large glossy leaves are smooth-edged and arranged in opposite pairs. The fruit is a plum-sized, fleshy, yellow berry with several seeds. CULTIVATION: Frost tender, they require a humus-enriched well-drained soil in a warm sheltered position in full sun or part-shade. Propagate from half-hardened cuttings taken in late summer.

Posoqueria latifolia

BRAZILIAN OAK

↔15 ft (4.5 m) ↑6–20 ft (1.8–6 m)

From Mexico to South America and West Indies. Glossy green leaves, prominent veins. Pure white, perfumed, tubular flowers, in dense terminal clusters, in spring. Edible yellow fruit. Zones 10–12.

POTENTILLA *(see page 546)*

Potentilla fruticosa

CINQUEFOIL, POTENTILLA, SHRUBBY CINQUEFOIL

↔5 ft (1.5 m) ↑5 ft (1.5 m)

Dense shrub from Northern Hemisphere. Yellow flowers in summer–autumn. Small palmately arranged leaves with 5 to 7 narrow leaflets. ***P. f.* var. *dahurica,*** white, sometimes yellow, disc-shaped flowers. ***P. f.* 'Daydawn'**, yellow flowers tinged pink; **'Katherine Dykes'**, lemon yellow flowers; **'Ochraleuca'**, lemony white flowers; **'Tangerine'** ★, orange flowers. Zones 3–9.

POUTERIA

A genus of evergreen trees in the sapodilla (Sapotaceae) family, they are found in tropical and subtropical Asia, Australasia, and South America. Trees have a milky sap and alternately arranged, paper or leathery, ornamental leaves. The small tubular flowers are green or white to yellow, borne along branches, and followed by often edible fruit. CULTIVATION: Species with edible fruit require greenhouse cultivation outside warm subtropical areas. They grow in a range of soils but must have good drainage and light feeding. Propagate from fresh seed; graft fruit species.

Pouteria cainito

syns ***Lucuma caimito, Pouteria caimito***

ABIU

↔15 ft (4.5 m) ↑35 ft (10 m)

Native to northern South America. Oblong leaves 4–8 in (10–20 cm) long. Flowers greenish white. Oval, smooth, pale yellow, edible fruit, sweet pulp eaten fresh or used in ice creams. Zones 10–11.

Pouteria campechiana

syns ***Lucumis campechiana, L. nervosa***

CANISTEL, EGGFRUIT, SAPOTE BORRACHO

↔25 ft (8 m) ↑60 ft (18 m)

Found in Central America from Mexico to Panama. Papery leaves arranged in spirals. Small greenish white flowers. Yellow to greenish brown fruit. Orangey yellow pulp, edible, sweet. Zones 10–11.

PRINSEPIA

Native to northern China, Taiwan, and the Himalayas, and part of the rose (Rosaceae) family, this is a genus of about 4 species of deciduous thorny shrubs grown for their ornamental glossy leaves, attractive arching branches, and fragrant, yellow or white, blossom-like flowers. Crowded bright green leaves, smooth-edged or sparsely toothed, are arranged alternately along the stems. The pendent, cherry-like, edible fruit is at first yellow, ripening to red or purple. CULTIVATION: Frost hardy, *Prinsepia* species grow best in a well-drained moderately fertile and moist soil in full sun or part-shade. They must have room to spread, so position them where the thorny branches will not be a nuisance. Propagate from seed or cuttings.

Prostanthera lasianthos

Prinsepia sinensis ★
CHERRY PRINSEPIA

☼ ❄ ↔ 6 ft (1.8 m) ↑ 6 ft (1.8 m)
Spreading, rather open shrub from northeastern China. Bright green lance-shaped leaves to 3 in (8 cm) long. Fragrant flowers, bright yellow, 5-petalled, along entire stem length, in spring. Edible red cherry-like fruit. Zones 5–9.

Prinsepia uniflora
☼ ❄ ↔ 6 ft (1.8 m) ↑ 5 ft (1.5 m)
Arching shrub from northwest China. Sharp spines; narrow, dark green, oblong leaves to 2½ in (6 cm) long. Fragrant white flowers, along stems, in early spring–summer. Red to purplish black cherry-like fruit. Zones 5–9.

Prosopis glandulosa var. *torreyana*

PROSOPIS

Native mainly to tropical and warmer arid parts of North and South America, with a few in Africa and Asia, this genus of some 40 species of shrubs and trees is closely related to *Mimosa* and belongs to the mimosa subfamily of the legume (Fabaceae) family. They have spiny branches and bipinnate leaves with numerous pairs of tiny olive green leaflets. Fragrant, nectar-rich, greenish white to dull yellow flowers are borne in axillary spike-like catkins. The elongated, pale yellow, bean-like pods are a valuable source of food. The pods and young shoots are also valued as livestock feed in hot climates with very little rainfall. The aromatic timber gives off a slightly sweet smoke and is used for barbecues and smoking foods. CULTIVATION: These fast-growing, tough plants are easily grown in a warm dry climate. They prefer deep well-drained soil in full sun. Although most species tolerate only light frosts, they are extremely drought-resistant and provide welcome shade in arid regions. Propagate from seed or half-hardened cuttings.

Prosopis glandulosa
HONEY MESQUITE

☼ ❄ ↔ 25 ft (8 m) ↑ 30 ft (9 m)
Deciduous shrub or small tree from southern USA and northern Mexico. Spiny stems, bipinnate leaves. Fluffy yellow flowers, nectar-rich, in racemes, in spring–summer. Pale yellow linear pods. Prohibited plant in some countries. *P. g.* var. *torreyana* (syn. *P. juliflora* var. *torreyana*), smaller with shorter leaves. Zones 8–11.

Prosopis velutina
syn. *P. glandulosa* subsp. *velutina*
VELVET MESQUITE

☼ ❄ ↔ 15–40 ft (4.5–12 m) ↑ 15–40 ft (4.5–12 m)
Large shrub or medium-sized tree from southwest USA and northwest Mexico. Smooth dark brown bark; spine-covered velvety branches. Narrow, dull green, compound leaves with 2 to 3 leaflets, each with 15 to 20 pairs of minor leaflets with finely hairy surfaces. Clusters of small pale yellow to yellow-green flowers in late spring–early summer, sometimes again in autumn. Slender brown pods. Zones 8–11.

PROSTANTHERA

This Australian genus of around 100 species of evergreen shrubs belongs to the mint (Lamiaceae) family. Most have aromatic opposite leaves on squarish stems and produce masses of spring and summer flowers in shades of blue, mauve, or purple, sometimes white or red, rarely yellow. The tubular flowers are usually 2-lipped and 3-lobed, often in clusters around the upper part of the stem. CULTIVATION: Fast-growing but short-lived, they require a warm climate, excellent drainage, and a sheltered position. They can be planted beneath the light overhead cover of trees with open foliage. Tip prune from an early age and after flowering to ensure compact bushy growth. Propagate from half-hardened tip cuttings in summer.

Prostanthera cuneata
ALPINE MINT BUSH

☼/◑ ❄ ↔ 5 ft (1.5 m) ↑ 3 ft (0.9 m)
From southeastern Australia. Dense, very aromatic shrub. Thick oval leaves along stems, dotted with oil glands. Large white or pale mauve flowers, purple blotches in throat, in summer. Zones 8–9.

Prostanthera lasianthos ★
VICTORIAN CHRISTMAS BUSH

◑ ❄ ↔ 12 ft (3.5 m) ↑ 15 ft (4.5 m)
Tall shrub or small tree of southeastern Australia. Toothed lance-shaped leaves to 5 in (12 cm) long. Sprays of white to pale mauve flowers, purple and orange spots in throat, in summer. Zones 8–10.

Prostanthera nivea
SNOWY MINT BUSH

☼/◑ ✷ ↔ 7 ft (2 m) ↑ 12 ft (3.5 m)

Erect bushy shrub native to eastern Australia. Softly hairy branches, narrow-ovate leaves to 1½ in (35 mm) long. Abundant, white to pale mauve flowers, yellow-spotted throat, in spring. Zones 9–11.

Prostanthera ovalifolia
PURPLE MINT BUSH

◑ ✷ ↔ 6 ft (1.8 m) ↑ 6 ft (1.8 m)

Shrub from eastern Australia. Aromatic oval leaves, 1½ in (35 mm) long. Mass of purple or mauve flowers, darker spotted throat, in spring. 'Variegata', leaves with yellow edges. Zones 9–11.

PROTEA
Proteas belong to the family Proteaceae. The 100 or so evergreen trees and shrubs in *Protea* are all indigenous to Africa. They have bisexual flowers in cone-like heads with colored leaf-like bracts at the base, and are greatly valued for floristry because of their beauty and long vase life. Most flower between autumn and late spring. CULTIVATION: Undemanding once established, they are fairly specific in requirements—an open sunny situation and very free-draining, gravelly, sandy, or basaltic loam, generally acid, and a climate with most rainfall in winter. They will not tolerate fertilizers rich in phosphorus. Light frosts are tolerated once established. Summer mulching is desirable but cultivation of the soil surface is resented. Good air circulation discourages fungal diseases. Regular flower removal encourages less straggly growth. Propagate from seed, cuttings, or grafting. Hybrid cultivars are usually grown from cuttings.

Protea aurea
☼ ✸ ↔ 10 ft (3 m) ↑ 10 ft (3 m)

Evergreen sprawling shrub. Foliage soft silvery when young, becoming leathery with age, leaves oval-shaped. Flowers cream, pink, or red, in autumn–winter, spot flowering at other times. Zones 8–10.

Protea cynaroides ★
GIANT PROTEA, KING PROTEA

☼ ✸ ↔ 7 ft (2 m) ↑ 7 ft (2 m)

Floral emblem of South Africa. Evergreen shrub. Bluntly oval leathery leaves and numerous, wide, bowl-shaped flowers with silky white hairs and pointed pink bracts, in mid-winter–early summer. Sought-after by florists worldwide. Zones 8–10.

Protea eximia
syn. *Protea latifolia*
DUCHESS PROTEA, RAY-FLOWERED PROTEA

☼ ✸ ↔ 10 ft (3 m) ↑ 10 ft (3 m)

Evergreen upright shrub from South Africa's Cape region. Gray-green broadly oval to heart-shaped leaves. Large pink to dark crimson flowers, with dark crimson center, at any time, but with winter flush. Zones 8–10.

Protea grandiceps
PEACH PROTEA, PRINCESS PROTEA, RED SUGARBUSH

☼ ✸ ↔ 5 ft (1.5 m) ↑ 5 ft (1.5 m)

Evergreen protea native to South Africa's Cape region. Leathery, oval, gray-green leaves. Large light peach-pink bracts, fringed reddish purple, white stamens, in late winter–early summer. Zones 8–10.

Protea lacticolor
☼ ✸ ↔ 7 ft (2 m) ↑ 7–15 ft (2–4.5 m)

Evergreen shrub or slender tree native to Cape region of South Africa. Blue-green foliage stiff and thick. Narrow spring buds open to cream flowers, with shell pink bracts, in autumn–early winter. Zones 8–10.

Protea magnifica
BEARDED PROTEA, QUEEN PROTEA

☼ ✸ ↔ 5 ft (1.5 m) ↑ 5 ft (1.5 m)

Variable evergreen shrub from South Africa's Cape region. Flowers vary from cream to pink or red with fringe of white or black at center, bracts also fringed with white. Regular pruning establishes pleasing shape. Zones 8–10.

Protea neriifolia
BLUE SUGARBUSH, OLEANDER-LEAFED PROTEA, PINK MINK

☼ ✸ ↔ 7 ft (2 m) ↑ 7 ft (2 m)

Erect evergreen shrub from south coast of South Africa's Cape region. Foliage resembles oleander. Long fluffy flowerheads from cream and pink to crimson, black feathery "beards" to bracts, in autumn–spring. **White Brow**, light crimson flowers. Zones 8–10.

Protea aurea

Protea cynaroides

Protea neriifolia

Protea repens
HONEY PROTEA, SUGARBUSH

☼ ❋ ↔ 7 ft (2 m) ↑ 8 ft (2.4 m)

Open, erect shrub from slopes of coastal mountains in Western Cape, South Africa. Nectar-rich flowers, greenish white to pale pink or claret red, with white or yellowish pink-tipped bracts, waxy appearance, in early autumn–winter. Zones 8–10.

Protea scolymocephala
GREEN BUTTON PROTEA, GREEN PROTEA, MINI PROTEA

☼ ❋ ↔ 3 ft (0.9 m) ↑ 3 ft (0.9 m)

From western mountain ranges of South Africa's Cape region. Small evergreen shrub, irregular spiky growth. Tiny flowers, around 1½ in (35 mm) wide, yellowy green or red with pink-tipped bracts, in early winter–spring. Zones 8–10.

Protea speciosa
BROWN-BEARDED SUGARBUSH

☼ ❋ ↔ 3 ft (0.9 m) ↑ 3 ft (0.9 m)

Found in South Africa's Western Cape province. Multi-stemmed shrub from group commonly known as bearded sugarbushes. Leaves gray-green, usually oblong. Flowerheads pink, or sometimes cream, in summer–autumn. Now classed as endangered species. Zones 9–10.

Protea venusta

☼ ❋ ↔ 8 ft (2.4 m) ↑ 30 in (75 cm)

Low-growing hardy shrub, at elevations up to 6,000 ft (1,800 m), sometimes covered in snow. Oval blue-green leaves. Held face-upward, small white flowerheads surrounded by pink-tipped rounded bracts in summer–autumn. Zones 8–10.

Protea Hybrid Cultivars

☼ ❋ ↔ 10 ft (3 m) ↑ 5–8 ft (1.5–2.4 m)

Most widely used parent species is *P. neriifolia*. 'Clark's Red', to 7 ft (2 m) tall, glaucous oval leaves, bright red flowerheads in mid-summer; 'Frosted Fire', bright rosy red flowers, waxy white-fringed bracts, in late autumn–late winter; 'Pink Ice' ★, bright pink flowerheads with silvery white fringed bracts, giving frosted appearance; 'Pink Mink', deep pinkish red bracts, tipped black; 'Polar Blush', pink flowers, white frilled bracts, in autumn; 'Satin Mink', pink bracts, tipped black; 'Silvertips', deep reddish bracts with profuse silvery white wool toward their tips. Zones 8–10.

PRUNUS

This widely grown genus is naturally widespread throughout the northern temperate regions of the world and mountain parts of Africa and includes a range of shrubs and trees, mostly deciduous. A rose (Rosaceae) family member, it is best known for the edible stone fruits (cherries, plums, apricots, peaches, and nectarines) and their ornamental flowering cousins. The leaves are usually simple pointed ellipses, often with serrated edges, and sometimes have brilliant autumn colors. Flowers are 5-petalled, carried singly or in clusters, and range in color from white through to dark pink, followed by fleshy fruit with a single seed enclosed in a hard stone. CULTIVATION: Although hardiness varies with the species, most need some winter chilling to flower and fruit properly. Wind protection is important. Most species prefer cool, moist, well-drained soil that is both fertile and rich in humus. Correct pruning techniques are important for the fruiting varieties. Propagate the species from seed, the fruiting forms by grafting, and the ornamentals by grafts or, in some cases, from cuttings.

Prunus × *amygdalo-persica*
FLOWERING ALMOND

☼ ❋ ↔ 20 ft (6 m) ↑ 20 ft (6 m)

Hybrid of *P. dulcis* and *P. persica*. Ornamental flowers; inedible green fruit. 'Pollardii', typical form, large bright pink flowers in late winter before foliage expands. Zones 4–9.

Prunus × *blireana*
DOUBLE PINK FLOWERING PLUM

☼ ❋ ↔ 15 ft (4.5 m) ↑ 15 ft (4.5 m)

Cross between *P. cerasifera* cultivar and form of *P. mume*. Small deciduous tree, drooping branch tips, bronze new growth. Large, bright pink, double flowers. 'Moseri', small-flowered cultivar with red-tinted foliage. Zones 5–10.

Prunus campanulata
TAIWAN CHERRY

☼ ❋ ↔ 25 ft (8 m) ↑ 30 ft (9 m)

Deciduous tree from Taiwan and south Japan. Leaves large, doubly serrated, color in autumn. Flowers deep cerise, pendulous in clusters, open before foliage. Small purple-black fruit. Winter flowers in mild climates. Zones 7–10.

Protea repens

Prunus caroliniana

CAROLINA LAUREL-CHERRY, WILD ORANGE

☀ ❄ ↔ 20 ft (6 m) ↑ 40 ft (12 m)

Evergreen tree found in southern USA. Glossy, elliptical, smooth-edged leaves. Cream flowers, densely massed in racemes, in spring. Small, shiny, black fruit. Used for hedging. Zones 7–11.

Prunus cerasifera

CHERRY PLUM, FLOWERING PLUM, MYROBALAN

☀ ❄ ↔ 30 ft (9 m) ↑ 30 ft (9 m)

Eurasian species found in many cultivated varieties. Deciduous large shrub or small tree. Leaves bronze tinted, fairly small, veins on underside, hairy. White flowers; small yellow to red fruit. *P. c.* subsp. *divaricata*, lax habit, smaller yellow flowers. *P. c.* '**Hessei**', shrubby, light green foliage, snow white flowers; '**Lindsayae**', reddish young foliage maturing to green, pale pink flowers; '**Newport**', shrubby in habit, bronze foliage, small white to pale pink flowers; '**Nigra**', deep purple-black foliage; '**Pendula**', weeping growth habit; '**Pissardii**', red to purple leaves, white flowers opening from pink buds, plum-red fruit; '**Thundercloud**', tall cultivar, deep bronze foliage, pink flowers. Zones 4–10.

Prunus glandulosa

DWARF FLOWERING ALMOND

☀ ❄ ↔ 5 ft (1.5 m) ↑ 5 ft (1.5 m)

Lovely deciduous shrub from China and Japan. Densely branched, rather narrow leaves, finely serrated edges. Smothered in deep pink to red flowers in spring. Dark red fruit. Prune to near ground level after flowering to encourage strong growth, with heavy flowering next season. '**Alba Plena**', white double flowers; '**Sinensis**', large leaves, pink double flowers. Zones 4–9.

Prunus ilicifolia

HOLLY-LEAFED CHERRY, ISLAY

☀ ❄ ↔ 20 ft (6 m) ↑ 25 ft (8 m)

Densely branched evergreen shrub or small tree native to California, USA. Leathery, glossy, green, holly-like leaves, spiny edges. Small creamy white flowers in racemes. Red or yellow fruit. Zones 9–11.

Prunus cerasifera

Prunus maackii

Prunus padus

Prunus incisa

FUJI CHERRY

☀ ❄ ↔ 15 ft (4.5 m) ↑ 15–20 ft (4.5–6 m)

Deciduous tree from Japan. White to pale pink flowers, incised petals, in spring, on bare wood. Serrated-edge leaves yellow, orange, and red tones in autumn. Fruit small, purple-black. Zones 6–9.

Prunus laurocerasus

CHERRY LAUREL, LAUREL CHERRY

☀ ❄ ↔ 30 ft (9 m) ↑ 20 ft (6 m)

Evergreen Eurasian shrub or small tree. Lustrous deep green leaves. Racemes of tiny creamy white flowers in spring. Small black fruit. '**Etna**', finely toothed shiny leaves; '**Zabeliana**', low-growing to 3 ft (0.9 m) high, narrow pale green leaves. Zones 7–10.

Prunus lusitanica

PORTUGAL LAUREL

☀ ❄ ↔ 30 ft (9 m) ↑ 20 ft (6 m)

Native to Iberian Peninsula. Evergreen with large, glossy, deep green leaves. Racemes of cream flowers. Fruit deep purple to near-black. *P. l.* subsp. *azorica*, Azores cherry laurel, shrubby, rarely exceeding 12 ft (3.5 m) tall, smaller leaves, shorter racemes. Zones 7–10.

Prunus maackii ★

AMUR CHOKE CHERRY, MANCHURIAN CHERRY

☀ ❄ ↔ 25 ft (8 m) ↑ 50 ft (15 m)

From Korea and nearby parts of China, smaller in cultivation. Small cream flowers, in racemes, in spring. Purple-tinted leaves, peeling papery bark, light orange-red shade. Small black fruit. Zones 2–9.

Prunus padus

BIRD CHERRY, EUROPEAN BIRD CHERRY, MAYDAY TREE

☀ ❄ ↔ 25 ft (8 m) ↑ 30–50 ft (9–15 m)

Found from Europe to Japan. Deciduous tree, often shorter in cultivation. Drooping branch tips. Racemes of numerous white flowers in spring. Tiny black fruit. '**Aucubifolia**', yellow-speckled leaves; '**Colorata**', pink flowers, purple-tinted young branches; '**Pendula**', strongly drooping branches; '**Plena**', semi-double flowers; '**Stricta**', strongly erect racemes. Zones 3–9.

Prunus, Sato-zakura Group, 'Kiku-shidare'

Prunus pensylvanica

PIN CHERRY, RED CHERRY

☼ ❋ ↔ 30 ft (9 m) ↑ 30 ft (9 m)

Deciduous North American tree. Conspicuously toothed leaves to 4 in (10 cm) long. Tiny white flowers, in clusters of up to 8 blooms, in spring. Tiny red fruit. Zones 2–9.

Prunus sargentii

SARGENT CHERRY

☼ ❋ ↔ 35 ft (10 m) ↑ 50 ft (15 m)

Native to Japan, smaller in cultivation. Red-toothed leaves, 4 in (10 cm) long. Clusters of large, frilly, dusky pink flowers. Small red cherries. Zones 4–9.

Prunus, Sato-zakura Group

JAPANESE FLOWERING CHERRY

☼ ❋ ↔ 30 ft (9 m) ↑ 20–40 ft (6–12 m)

Large group, composed mainly of hybrids, probably derived from *P. serrulata*, ornamentals grown for early–mid-spring flower display. 'Alborosea', white to pink double flowers; 'Kanzan' (syn. 'Sekiyama'), strongly upright growth when young, clusters of bright pink double flowers, vivid autumn foliage; 'Kiku-shidare' (syn. 'Cheal's Weeping Cherry'), pendulous growth, pink double flowers; 'Okumiyako' (syn. 'Shimidsu-sakura'), flat-topped tree with large, white, double flowers from pink buds; 'Shirotae' (syn. 'Mt Fuji'), massed, large, single to semi-double, white flowers, golden autumn foliage; 'Ukon', pale green semi-double flowers. Zones 5–9.

Prunus serotina

BLACK CHERRY, CAPULIN, RUM CHERRY

☼ ❋ ↔ 30 ft (9 m) ↑ 100 ft (30 m)

Deciduous tree found in North America. Glossy, mid-green, finely serrated leaves, lighter undersurface, over 3 in (8 cm) long. White flowers, in short pendulous racemes, in spring. Small near-black fruit. Zones 3–9.

Prunus spinosa

BLACKTHORN, SLOE

☼ ❋ ↔ 15 ft (4.5 m) ↑ 20 ft (6 m)

Deciduous shrub or small tree found in Eurasia and North Africa, covered in sharp spines. Small white flowers, prune-like black fruit. Recorded in hedgerows from ancient times. Zones 4–10.

Prunus × *subhirtella*

SPRING CHERRY

☼ ❋ ↔ 25 ft (8 m) ↑ 50 ft (15 m)

Broad deciduous tree from Japan, smaller in cultivation. Serrated leaves to 3 in (8 cm) long. Flowers small, white or pink, before foliage. Tiny purple-black fruit. 'Autumnalis', early flowering, white flowers with hint of pink; 'Autumnalis Rosea', pink flowers; 'Fukubana', early flowering, double pink flowers; 'Pendula', long lived, weeping habit; 'Pendula Rosea', weeping habit, pink flowers; 'Stellata', clusters of starry, single, pink flowers. Zones 5–9.

Prunus tenella

DWARF RUSSIAN ALMOND

☼ ❋ ↔ 5 ft (1.5 m) ↑ 5 ft (1.5 m)

Deciduous Eurasian shrub, similar in habit to flowering quince (*Chaenomeles*). Leaves larger, dull yellow fruit smaller. Deep pinkish red flowers. Zones 2–9.

Prunus triloba

DWARF FLOWERING ALMOND, FLOWERING PLUM, ROSE TREE OF CHINA

☼ ❋ ↔ 12 ft (3.5 m) ↑ 12 ft (3.5 m)

From China. Pale pink flowers, semi or fully double, before or with leaf buds. Leaves 2½ in (6 cm) long, often 3-lobed. Red fruit with downy skin. 'Multiplex', soft pink flowers. Zones 5–9.

Prunus × *yedoensis*

TOKYO CHERRY, YOSHINO CHERRY

☼ ❋ ↔ 30 ft (9 m) ↑ 40 ft (12 m)

Hybrid between *P.* × *subhirtella* and *P. speciosa*. Upright tree with spreading crown. Deep green serrated leaves, turn vivid orange and red in autumn. Racemes of scented white flowers in spring. Tiny black fruit. 'Shidare-yoshino' ★, weeping branches, profuse snow white flowers. Zones 5–9.

PSEUDERANTHEMUM

From tropical regions, this genus of the acanthus (Acanthaceae) family contains about 60 species of small evergreen perennials, shrubs, or subshrubs. They are grown for their often prominently veined leaves and white flowers flecked or flushed red or mauve.

Prunus triloba 'Multiplex'

CULTIVATION: Suited to warm-climate gardens, the frost-tender members of this genus need well-drained soil enriched with organic matter in a protected, partially shaded position. Outside the tropics they are best grown as greenhouse or conservatory plants. They prefer bright filtered light and regular water and fertilizer during the growing season. Tip prune from an early age to encourage a bushy habit or, if the plants become leggy, cut back hard in spring. Propagate from half-hardened cuttings or by division.

Pseuderanthemum atropurpureum

☀ ❀ ↔ 3 ft (0.9 m) ↑ 4 ft (1.2 m)

Erect evergreen shrub from Polynesia. Showy, deep purple, ovate, pointed leaves, marked with pink or green along veins. Tubular white flowers with purple markings in center, in dense terminal spikes, in summer. Zones 11–12.

Pseuderanthemum reticulatum

☀ ❀ ↔ 3 ft (0.9 m) ↑ 3 ft (0.9 m)

Evergreen bushy shrub from Vanuatu. Golden stems, bright green ovate leaves, wavy margins, network of creamy yellow lines. White tubular flowers, cerise markings in throat, in terminal panicles, in summer. '**Andersonii**', yellow blotches on foliage. Zones 11–12.

PSEUDOLARIX

The sole species in this genus, part of the pine (Pinaceae) family, is a larch-like deciduous conifer from eastern China, with leaves larger and strappier than true larches. Young foliage is bright green but changes to fiery hues of yellow, orange, and red-brown before falling with the first hard frosts.

CULTIVATION: Although hardy to quite severe frosts, young plants may be damaged by very early or late freezes. This tree prefers deep, fertile, humus-rich, well-drained soil with a position in sun or morning shade. Trees that are too shaded will develop poor autumn color. Naturally upright and conical, this tree needs little pruning, other than to lightly shape or tidy the branches. Propagation is usually from seed.

Pseuderanthemum reticulatum 'Andersonii'

Pseudolarix amabilis

Pseudopanax ferox

Pseudolarix amabilis

GOLDEN LARCH

☀ ✱ ↔ 25 ft (8 m) ↑ 100 ft (30 m)

Upright conifer. Deeply fissured, warm red-brown bark. Leaves to 2 in (5 cm) long, in whorls on short sideshoots. Female cones purplish, to 3 in (8 cm) long, persist on tree after shedding their seed. '**Nana**' ★, 3 ft (0.9 m) tall, with spreading habit, one of several dwarf cultivars. Zones 6–9.

PSEUDOPANAX

syns *Neopanax, Nothopanax*

There are about 20 species of evergreen shrubs or small trees in this genus of the ivy (Araliaceae) family. Most are native to New Zealand and the rest are found in Chile and Tasmania, Australia. They have ornamental and interesting foliage, which in several species undergoes a distinct metamorphosis from juvenile to mature stages. The leaves are simple or palmate and may have toothed edges. Tiny, greenish, male or female flowers are borne in large clusters, sometimes on separate trees, and the small fruit that follow are often black.

CULTIVATION: Cultivated for their attractive foliage and, in species such as *P. crassifolius*, for their striking form, members of this genus will grow in any fertile well-drained soil in sun or part-shade. Most will tolerate at least light frost, but should be given a warm sheltered site in cool areas or grown in a greenhouse or conservatory. Propagate from seed or from half-hardened cuttings taken in autumn.

Pseudopanax arboreus

FIVE-FINGER

☀ ❦ ↔ 15 ft (4.5 m) ↑ 10–20 ft (3–6 m)

Rounded tree native to New Zealand. Leathery palmate leaves, 5 to 7 leaflets, deep shiny green with serrated edges. Tiny flowers in winter. Small purplish berries on female trees. Zones 9–11.

Pseudopanax ferox

TOOTHED LANCEWOOD

☀ ❦ ↔ 7 ft (2 m) ↑ 15 ft (4.5 m)

Native to New Zealand. Distinct juvenile and adult stages. Grown for its dramatic juvenile form. Narrow leathery leaves to 20 in (50 cm) long; large coarse-toothed edges. Dark green with bronze tones, orangey-red midrib. Zones 9–11.

Pseudopanax lessonii

HOUPARA

☀ ❦ ↔ 7 ft (2 m) ↑ 12 ft (3.5 m)

Attractive foliage shrub native to New Zealand's North Island. Thick, glossy, dark green leaves, 3 to 5 broadly oval leaflets, shallowly toothed near tips. '**Cyril Watson**', slow growing, very bushy, displays 2 leaf forms on same plant, 3 to 5 short broad lobes, coarsely toothed, or simple with shallowly toothed margins, very thick, leathery, glossy fresh green; '**Gold Splash**', dark green leaves with bright yellow splashed along veins and midribs. Zones 9–11.

PSEUDOTSUGA

DOUGLAS FIR

There are 6 to 8 species of coniferous trees within this genus in the pine (Pinaceae) family. All are evergreen forest trees from western North America, Mexico, Taiwan, Japan, and China. They are major timber trees used for power poles, railway sleepers, plywood, and wood pulp and are also a source of Oregon balsam. Some trees reach 300 ft (90 m) in height in their native habitat, but this is rare in cultivation. The foliage and cones are frequently used as Christmas decorations, as the foliage sheds its needles less readily than other species. The linear leaves grow radially on the shoots. The female cones have 3-pronged bract scales protruding from between the cone scales; the cylindrical male cones are smaller. CULTIVATION: These hardy trees prefer colder climates and will grow in any well-drained soil in full sun. Propagate the species from seed in spring, or graft cultivars in late winter.

Pseudotsuga menziesii

syns *Pseudotsuga douglasii, P. taxifolia*
DOUGLAS FIR
☀ ❄ ↔ 15–30 ft (4.5–9 m) ↑ 80–150 ft (24–45 m)
Native to North America, from British Columbia to California. Fast growing, long lived. Bark has corky plates, deep fissures developing with age. Narrow leaves, dark blue-green above, 2 white bands beneath, juvenile foliage apple-green in spring. Female cones produced on mature trees. *P. m.* var. *glauca*, glaucous blue leaves, smaller cones. *P. m.* 'Densa' and 'Fletcheri' are dwarf forms. Zones 4–9.

PSIDIUM

This tropical American genus, in the myrtle (Myrtaceae) family, contains about 100 species of evergreen shrubs or trees, several of which are grown for their edible fruit. They branch freely, almost to the ground, and have thick opposite leaves, some with prominent veins.

Pseudotsuga menziesii, in the wild, Utah, USA

The white 5-petalled flowers have numerous stamens. The fruit is a rounded or pear-shaped berry ripening to red or yellow. CULTIVATION: Members of this genus need a warm to hot climate, moist but well-drained soil with protection from strong winds, and regular watering during summer. They are pruned to tree form, and after fruiting to retain a compact shape. Propagate from seed or cuttings, or by layering or grafting.

Psidium cattleianum

CHERRY GUAVA, STRAWBERRY GUAVA
☀ ❄ ↔ 8 ft (2.4 m) ↑ 10–20 ft (3–6 m)
Red-barked, dense, evergreen shrub. Elliptic, shiny, green leaves. Flowers white, solitary, to 1 in (25 mm) wide. Small, round, dark red or yellow fruit, dark red flesh, rich in vitamin C. Zones 9–11.

PSORALEA

As now understood, this is a genus of around 20 species of evergreen shrubs and subshrubs from southern Africa in the pea-flower subfamily of the legume (Fabaceae) family. Many other species were formerley included in *Psoralea* but are now distributed among at least 4 other genera. Leaves are mostly small and crowded, simple or compound (trifoliate or pinnate), and dotted with tiny black glands. Flowers are borne prolifically, in short dense spikes, and are mostly blue, purplish, or white; small grayish pods follow. CULTIVATION: Cold-hardiness varies, though few will tolerate any but the lightest frosts. They prefer light but reasonably moist well-drained soil, and will flower best in full sun. Propagate from seed or half-hardened cuttings.

Psoralea pinnata

AFRICAN SCURF-PEA, BLUE PEA BUSH
☀ ❄ ↔ 7 ft (2 m) ↑ 6–10 ft (1.8–3 m)
South African shrub. Leaves with 5 to 11 narrow deep green leaflets, often with fine hairs. Clusters of violet to bright blue flowers, with white wings, in late spring–summer. Has become weed in parts of southern coastal Australia. Zones 9–11.

PTELEA

Despite looking rather more like lilacs than oranges, and bearing sycamore-like fruit, the 11 deciduous shrubs or small trees in this North and Central American genus are *Citrus* relatives, and belong to the rue (Rutaceae) family. This is only apparent in the aromatic oil glands of the leaf, which is usually trifoliate, with a dominant central leaflet flanked by a smaller one on each side. The leaves often become bright yellow in autumn. The small white to pale green flowers are scented and clustered together in conspicuous cymes. They appear first in spring or early summer, then sporadically later. Small, 2-seeded, winged fruit, a little like hop seeds, follow. CULTIVATION: Species from southern USA and northern Mexico are a little tender. Otherwise, most are adaptable and easily grown in any well-drained soil in sun or part-shade. In areas with hot summers, some shade from the afternoon sun is advisable. Propagate from seed, layers, or grafts.

Psoralea pinnata

Ptelea trifoliata

Pterocarpus indicus

Pterostyrax hispida

Ptelea angustifolia

WESTERN HOP TREE

☼ ❄ ↔ 12 ft (3.5 m) ↕ 12 ft (3.5 m)

Shrub from northern Mexico and southern USA. Fine hairs on young foliage and new stems. Mature leaves usually smooth, blue-green below. Flowers in early summer. Fruit rounded. Zones 8–10.

Ptelea trifoliata

COMMON HOP TREE

☼ ❄ ↔ 12 ft (3.5 m) ↕ 25 ft (8 m)

From eastern and central USA. Leaves mid-green, 3 leaflets, semi-glossy, paler below, slightly notched edges. Pale green flowers in early summer. Fruit to 1 in (25 mm) wide. 'Aurea', yellow-green foliage; 'Glauca', blue-green foliage. Zones 5–10.

PTEROCARPUS

This genus, in the pea-flower subfamily of the legume (Fabaceae) family, contains some 20 species of tropical trees or climbers highly regarded for their ornamental timber. They have wide graceful crowns and large pinnate leaves, and are usually deciduous in the dry season. Racemes of scented yellow to orange pea-flowers are borne just before, or with, new leaves. Flat rounded pods follow, their edges often extended into parchment-like wings.

CULTIVATION: These plants need a warm frost-free climate, moist well-drained soil, and full sun. Propagate from seed or cuttings.

Pterocarpus indicus

BURMESE ROSEWOOD

☼ ✦ ↔ 35 ft (10 m) ↕ 80 ft (24 m)

Broadly spreading tree widespread in tropical Asia, from India to Philippines. Pinnate leaves, leaflets to 4 in (10 cm) long. Sprays of yellow scented flowers in spring. Wood is rose-scented. Zones 11–12.

PTEROCARYA

There are 10 deciduous trees in this genus, which belongs to the walnut (Juglandaceae) family, and these are found from the Caucasus to the temperate areas of East Asia and Southeast Asia. The leaves are pinnate and can be quite large, sometimes with more than 20 leaflets up to 4 in (10 cm) long. The foliage seldom shows much autumn color. In spring, long bract-studded catkins of tiny green flowers open, developing into strings of winged nutlets with hard shells that become brown as they ripen.

CULTIVATION: Most species are tolerant of quite severe frosts and will thrive in any reasonably fertile, moist, well-drained soil with a position in full sun. Propagate from seed, suckers, or cuttings.

Pterocarya fraxinifolia

CAUCASIAN WINGNUT

☼ ❄ ↔ 60 ft (18 m) ↕ 80 ft (24 m)

Found from the Caucasus to northern Iraq. Dark deeply furrowed bark, leaves to 15 in (38 cm) long, with 11 to 21 leaflets. Catkins yellow-green shade. Zones 7–9.

Pterocarya stenoptera

☼ ❄ ↔ 40 ft (12 m) ↕ 70 ft (21 m)

Chinese species notable for leaves to 15 in (38 cm) long with up to 23 leaflets; new foliage downy. Fine tan down covers young twigs. Catkins often longer than leaves. Zones 7–9.

PTEROSTYRAX

The 3 species of deciduous shrubs or trees in this genus, belonging to the storax (Styracaceae) family, are native to eastern Asia. Leaves are alternately arranged, with serrated edges; numerous long open panicles of small flowers are borne in spring or summer.

CULTIVATION: These quick-growing plants prefer deep, rich, acid soil in a sheltered position in sun or part-shade. Prune after flowering to retain their shape. Propagate from seed or half-hardened cuttings.

Pterostyrax corymbosa

☼ ❄ ↔ 20 ft (6 m) ↕ 40 ft (12 m)

Spreading shrub or tree from Japan. Dark green leaves, bristly toothed margins. Small, fragrant, white, bell-shaped flowers, in panicles, in spring. Zones 6–10.

Pterostyrax hispida ★

EPAULETTE TREE

☼ ❄ ↔ 20 ft (6 m) ↕ 25 ft (8 m)

From Japan and China. Large leaves, finely serrated edges. Panicles of fragrant creamy white flowers, to 8 in (20 cm) long, in summer. Small, green, bristly fruit. Zones 6–10.

PYCNOSTACHYS

Native to tropical and southern Africa, these 40 or so species of perennials and softwooded shrubs are grown for their dense terminal spikes of 2-lipped deep blue flowers. Members of the mint (Lamiaceae) family, they have squarish stems and opposite or whorled leaves that are often aromatic when bruised.
CULTIVATION: These plants need a warm frost-free climate and are best suited to fertile, moist, but well-drained soil in full sun. In cool areas they are grown in the greenhouse or conservatory, with a plentiful supply of water during the growing season. Propagate from seed or cuttings.

Pycnostachys urticifolia

☼ ✤ ↔ 4 ft (1.2 m) ↕ 8 ft (2.4 m)

Shrub with erect branching stems. Oval leaves, 5 in (12 cm) long, toothed edges. Tubular deep blue to purple flowers, in dense terminal spikes to 4 in (10 cm) long, in summer–autumn. Zones 9–12.

PYRACANTHA

FIRETHORN

This small genus in the rose (Rosaceae) family consists of 9 species of mostly spiny shrubs, from eastern Asia and southeast Europe. They have simple leaves that are often toothed on the margins, and whitish flowers in corymbs are produced at the ends of branches. The flowers are followed by masses of red, orange, or yellow fruit, which persist into winter. Most species perform best in cool moist climates, where they are useful landscape subjects for the shrubbery or used as espalier specimens or for hedging. Pyracantha species can naturalize in favorable areas.
CULTIVATION: Most species are fairly adaptable shrubs tolerating exposed sites in full sun. They perform best in a fertile well-drained soil. Pruning is not essential but may be helpful to control size; hedges can be pruned from early to mid-summer. Watch for fireblight, scab, and wilt problems. Propagate from seed or cuttings.

Pyracantha angustifolia

NARROW-LEAFED FIRETHORN, ORANGE FIRETHORN

☼ ✤ ↔ 12 ft (3.5 m) ↕ 12 ft (3.5 m)

Native to southwest China. Spiny bushy shrub, horizontal branches. Dark green shiny leaves, gray and furry beneath. Dense corymbs of small white flowers in mid-summer. Yellow to deep orange berries. Zones 7–10.

Pyracantha coccinea

EUROPEAN FIRETHORN, SCARLET FIRETHORN

☼ ✤ ↔ 15 ft (4.5 m) ↕ 15 ft (4.5 m)

Dense shrub from southern Europe, Turkey, and Caucasus. Shiny, dark green, ovate to lance-shaped, toothed leaves, new growth finely downy. Small white flowers. Attractive scarlet berries on downy stalks. 'Lalandei' ★, strong growth habit, to 20 ft (6 m) tall, glossy bright orange-red fruit. Zones 5–9.

Pyracantha crenulata

HIMALAYAN FIRETHORN

☼ ✤ ↔ 12 ft (3.5 m) ↕ 15 ft (4.5 m)

Spiny shrub or small tree from southern slopes of Himalayas. Rusty downy new shoots. Glossy dark green leaves, notched margins. Corymbs of up to 30 small white flowers. Dark red berries. Zones 7–10.

Pyracantha koidzumii

TAIWAN FIRETHORN

☼ ✤ ↔ 12 ft (3.5 m) ↕ 12–15 ft (3.5–4.5 m)

Many-branched species native to Taiwan. Reddish downy young stems become smooth and purplish with age. Leaves dark green, glossy above, paler below. Small white flowers, in corymbs, in summer. Berry variable colors, sometimes orange-scarlet. Zones 7–10.

Pyracantha rogersiana

ROGERS FIRETHORN

☼ ✤ ↔ 12 ft (3.5 m) ↕ 12 ft (3.5 m)

Shrub from China; develops broad bun shape with age. Mid-green glossy leaves to 1½ in (35 mm) long. Small white flowers, in corymbs, mostly from 2-year-old branches, in spring. Yellow to orange-red berries. 'Flava', yellow berries. Zones 8–10.

Pyracantha Hybrid Cultivars

☼ ✤ ↔ 6–10 ft (1.8–3 m) ↕ 5–10 ft (1.5–3 m)

Spreading shrubs; good for hedges and shrub borders. 'Golden Charmer', vigorous arching shrub, rounded orange-yellow fruit; 'Harlequin', pink-flushed leaves, cream margins; 'Mohave', dark green leaves, masses of persistent bright orange-red fruit; 'Shawnee', spiny shrub, masses of white flowers, yellow to light orange fruit; 'Sparkler', leaves strikingly mottled; 'Watereri', compact yet vigorous shrub, bright red fruit. Other cultivars include 'Golden Dome', 'Orange Charmer', and 'Orange Glow'. Zones 5–9.

Pycnostachys urticifolia

Pyracantha angustifolia

Pyracantha crenulata

Pyrus calleryana

PYRUS

PEAR

Widely distributed through Europe and Asia, this genus of about 20 species is related to the apple *(Malus)* and belongs to the rose (Rosaceae) family. It comprises mostly deciduous trees of small to medium size, some thorny, with simple leaves that sometimes color to yellow and red in autumn. Flowers are mostly white, and are followed by fruit, edible in some species, that vary in size and shape. CULTIVATION: Pears will grow in most moderately fertile soils and prefer cool-temperate climates. Ornamental species are deep-rooted, drought tolerant, and reasonably tolerant of atmospheric pollution; pruning is seldom necessary. Fruiting forms require a cross-pollinator to set fruit. *Pyrus* species can be propagated from very fresh seed, but clonal forms are propagated by grafting to keep them true to type.

Pyrus calleryana

CALLERY PEAR

☼ ❊ ↔ 40 ft (12 m) ↑ 40 ft (12 m)

From southeastern China, Korea, Japan, and Taiwan. Ornamental tree, branches thorny. Glossy green leaves turn red in late autumn. Flowers white, unpleasant scent. Small pitted brown fruit on slender stalks. 'Bradford', non-thorny, flowers heavily in spring; Chanticleer/'Glen's Form' ★, scarlet autumn color, similar but narrower in form. Zones 5–10.

Pyrus nivalis

SNOW PEAR

☼ ❊ ↔ 20 ft (6 m) ↑ 30 ft (9 m)

Native to southern Europe. Small tree, thornless. Smooth-edged oval or egg-shaped leaves. White flowers, in racemes as young leaves open, in spring. Fruit small, round, yellowish green. Zones 5–9.

Pyrus salicifolia

SILVER PEAR, WILLOW-LEAFED PEAR

☼ ❊ ↔ 15 ft (4.5 m) ↑ 25 ft (8 m)

From Caucasus. Small graceful tree with slender drooping branches. Narrow willow-like leaves, silvery when young, age to grayish

green shiny upper surface. Flowers creamy white. Small, brown, pear-shaped fruit. 'Pendula', smaller, with fully pendulous branches; 'Silver Cascade', silvery gray foliage. Zones 4–9.

Pyrus ussuriensis

MONGOLIAN PEAR, USSURIAN PEAR

☼ ❊ ↔ 20 ft (6 m) ↑ 50 ft (15 m)

From northeastern China, Korea, and northern Japan. Yellowish green leaves ovate or rounded, bristle-toothed, crimson-bronze in autumn. Broad corymbs of white flowers in early spring. Fruit greenish brown, ripen in autumn–winter. Zones 4–9.

QUERCUS

OAK

This large genus of some 600 species, both evergreen and deciduous, is a member of the beech (Fagaceae) family. Most are trees, a few are shrubs, widely distributed throughout the Northern Hemisphere. Many are large trees that live to a great age. Fruit (acorns) are partly enclosed in a cup. All have simple leaves, often toothed or deeply lobed, in some turning to spectacular tones of red or yellow-brown in autumn. Male and female flowers are carried on separate catkins on the same tree, usually in early spring. CULTIVATION: Oaks grow well in deep alluvial valley soils; only some of the Mediterranean and western North American species are tolerant of poor dry soil. Most enjoy cool moist conditions. Some early pruning may be needed to help establish a single straight trunk. Seed, sown as soon as ripe in summer or autumn, will germinate readily; cultivars and sterile hybrids are usually grafted in late winter or early spring.

Quercus agrifolia

Quercus acutissima

JAPANESE CHESTNUT OAK, JAPANESE OAK

☼ ❊ ↔ 40 ft (12 m) ↑ 80 ft (24 m)

Deciduous tree native to Japan, Korea, China, and Himalayas. Dark gray bark, roughly ridged and fissured. Narrow, oblong, chestnut-like leaves, polished green, edged with bristle-tipped teeth, persist until winter. Oval acorns half-enclosed in cups. Zones 5–10.

Quercus agrifolia

CALIFORNIA LIVE OAK, COAST LIVE OAK

☼ ❊ ↔ 35 ft (10 m) ↑ 40 ft (12 m)

From California and Mexico. Evergreen tree or large shrub, branched almost to ground. Smooth black bark, roughens with age. Leaves oval or rounded, hard-textured, edged with spine-tipped teeth, smooth underside. Acorns half-enclosed in cups. Zones 8–10.

Quercus alba

AMERICAN WHITE OAK, STAVE OAK, WHITE OAK

☼ ❊ ↔ 100 ft (30 m) ↑ 100 ft (30 m)

Large deciduous tree from southeastern Canada and eastern USA. Straight, often massive trunk, spreading branches. Bark dark gray. Oval leaves deeply and irregularly lobed, green when young, purple-crimson in autumn. Acorns in shallow scaly cups. Zones 3–9.

Quercus bicolor

SWAMP WHITE OAK

☼ ❄ ↔ 40 ft (12 m) ↑ 80 ft (24 m)

Found growing naturally in southeastern Canada and eastern USA. Matures into well-developed trunk, with ascending branches. Bark pale gray with thick ridges that are blackish gray. Leaves egg-shaped, shallowly lobed, shiny green, grayish and felted on underside. Acorns in clusters. Zones 4–10.

Quercus canariensis

ALGERIAN OAK, CANARY OAK, MIRBECK'S OAK

☼ ❄ ↔ 40 ft (12 m) ↑ 80 ft (24 m)

Semi-deciduous fast-growing tree from North Africa, southern Portugal, and Spain. Leaves large, egg-shaped or oval, shallowly lobed, dark shiny green on upper surface, paler on underside. Hemispheric acorns. Succeeds in heavy clay or shallow chalky soil. Zones 7–10.

Quercus bicolor

Quercus castaneifolia

syn. *Quercus afares*

CHESTNUT-LEAFED OAK

☼ ❄ ↔ 60 ft (18 m) ↑ 100 ft (30 m)

Found in Caucasus, Iran, and Algeria. Deciduous tree, develops broadly domed crown. Leaves oblong or narrowly oval, tapered at both ends, with coarse teeth, shiny dark green on upper surface, grayish downy on underside. Acorns dark brown. 'Green Spire', broadly columnar form with compact habit. Zones 6–10.

Quercus cerris

TURKEY OAK

☼ ❄ ↔ 75 ft (23 m) ↑ 100 ft (30 m)

Large, fast-growing, deciduous tree from southern Europe and Middle East. Slender crown when young, becoming broad-domed. Bark dull gray, roughly fissured. Leaves oval or oblong, shallowly lobed, coarsely toothed. Stalkless acorns enclosed in mossy cups. 'Argenteovariegata' (syn. 'Variegata'), leaves with conspicuous creamy white margin; 'Laciniata', leaves with narrow spreading lobes. Zones 7–10.

Quercus chrysolepis

CANYON LIVE OAK, MAUL OAK

☼ ❄ ↔ 30 ft (9 m) ↑ 70 ft (21 m)

From southwestern USA and Mexico. Variable, slow-growing, evergreen tree or large shrub, with generous spreading crown. Bark rather thick, smooth, gray-brown tinged with red. Leaves oval or ovate, spine-toothed, downy. Acorns almost stalkless. Zones 7–10.

Quercus coccinea

SCARLET OAK

☼ ❄ ↔ 40 ft (12 m) ↑ 70 ft (21 m)

From eastern and central USA. Deciduous tree with wide-spreading branches. Leaves oblong or elliptic, shiny dark green above, paler beneath, few leaves turn bright deep red, later whole crown colors in autumn. Acorns in shallow cups. 'Splendens', larger leaves, more reliable autumn color. Zones 2–9.

Quercus dentata

DAIMYO OAK

☼ ❄ ↔ 30 ft (9 m) ↑ 50 ft (15 m)

Deciduous tree naturally found in Japan, Korea, and China. Horizontal branches arise from short sinuous bole. Leaves like those of giant form of *Q. robur*, up to 15 in (38 cm) long and 8 in (20 cm) wide; most leaves turn brown and remain on tree during winter. Scaly cups half-enclose egg-shaped acorns. Zones 7–9.

Quercus douglasii

BLUE OAK

☼ ❄ ↔ 20 ft (6 m) ↑ 70 ft (21 m)

Native to California. Deciduous large shrub to medium-sized tree, rounded crown. Bark thin, gray, scaly. Leaves bluish with lobed margins. Small cone-shaped acorns in shallow hairy cups. Zones 6–11.

Quercus falcata

SOUTHERN RED OAK, SPANISH OAK

☼ ❄ ↔ 35 ft (10 m) ↑ 80 ft (24 m)

Deciduous tree from southern USA. Bark thick, nearly black, deeply furrowed. Leaves egg-shaped to ovate, shallowly 3-lobed or deeply 5- to 7-lobed, dark green above; pale gray-green and woolly beneath. Acorns nearly stalkless. *Q. f.* var. *pagodifolia*, bark smoother, becoming scaly with age, larger leaves. Zones 8–10.

Quercus frainetto

FARNETTO, HUNGARIAN OAK

☼ ❄ ↔ 60 ft (18 m) ↑ 100 ft (30 m)

Native to southern Italy, Balkans, and Hungary. Large, fast-growing, deciduous tree, broad-domed and wide-spreading. Bark pale gray, closely fissured. Leaves egg-shaped and deeply lobed. Acorns egg-shaped, half-enclosed in cups. 'Hungarian Crown', with erect habit. Zones 7–10.

Quercus coccinea

Quercus ilex

Quercus gambelii
GAMBEL OAK, ROCKY MOUNTAIN WHITE OAK
☼ ❋ ↔ 25 ft (8 m) ↑ 30 ft (9 m)
Deciduous tree from central west USA. Shrubby in harsh winters; underground runners form clumps. Leaves with 3 to 6 deep lobes on each side, fine hairs beneath. Acorns ovoid. Zones 4–9.

Quercus garryana
OREGON OAK, OREGON WHITE OAK
☼ ❋ ↔ 15 ft (4.5 m) ↑ 15 ft (4.5 m)
Deciduous tree from western USA. Short stout trunk, spreading crown. Leaves oval, deeply cut, shiny dark green above, paler and slightly hairy beneath. Acorns stalkless or nearly so. Zones 5–10.

Quercus × hispanica
SPANISH OAK
☼ ❋ ↔ 25 ft (8 m) ↑ 100 ft (30 m)
Natural cross between Q. suber and Q. cerris. Variable tree, sometimes nearly evergreen. Bark has thick fissures. Dark green lobed leaves. Acorns oblong to egg-shaped. 'Lucombeana', tall, resembles Q. cerris, pale gray shallowly fissured bark, long leaves. Zones 6–10.

Quercus ilex
HOLLY OAK, HOLM OAK
☼ ❋ ↔ 60 ft (18 m) ↑ 70 ft (21 m)
Found naturally in southern Europe and North Africa. Large evergreen tree, broad-domed crown, branching close to ground. Bark brownish or black. Leaves leathery, glossy, smooth-edged or toothed, dark green above, grayish and downy below. Pointed acorns held in cups with many rows of small fluted scales. Zones 7–11.

Quercus kelloggii
CALIFORNIAN BLACK OAK
☼ ❋ ↔ 40 ft (12 m) ↑ 60–90 ft (18–27 m)
From California and Oregon, USA. Medium-sized to large deciduous tree with large, open, globe-like crown. Bark thick, divided

Quercus macrocarpa

by deep furrows into wide ridges. Leaves deeply lobed, bristle-toothed, shiny yellow-green above, paler, usually hairy beneath. Acorns carried on short stalks. Zones 7–10.

Quercus laurifolia
LAUREL OAK
☼ ❋ ↔ 60 ft (18 m) ↑ 60 ft (18 m)
Semi-evergreen tree from eastern USA. Bark thick, nearly black, furrowed. Leaves glossy green, oblong or egg-shaped, smooth-edged, can be shallowly lobed. Acorns stalkless or nearly so. Zones 6–11.

Quercus lyrata
OVERCUP OAK
☼ ❋ ↔ 30 ft (9 m) ↑ 60 ft (18 m)
Deciduous tree from southeastern USA with open crown and large crooked branches. Leaves oblong to egg-shaped, deeply and irregularly lobed, dark green above; paler, smooth or white-hairy beneath. Acorns stalkless or nearly so. Zones 8–10.

Quercus macrocarpa
BURR OAK, MOSSYCUP OAK
☼ ❋ ↔ 40 ft (12 m) ↑ 120 ft (36 m)
Found in northeastern and central North America. Large deciduous tree, massive trunk, spreading branches. Bark coarsely ridged, scaly, gray-brown. Leaves egg-shaped, conspicuously lobed. Young shoots and leaf undersurface covered in pale down. Acorns large, cups with long recurved scales. Zones 4–9.

Quercus mongolica
MONGOLIAN OAK
☼ ❋ ↔ 40 ft (12 m) ↑ 100 ft (30 m)
From Japan, Korea, northeastern China, Mongolia, and eastern Siberia. Deciduous tree with thick smooth branches. Leaves short, oval to oblong, strongly lobed, in clusters at branch ends. Egg-shaped acorns. Zones 4–9.

Quercus gambelii (golden foliage), in the wild, Colorado, USA

Quercus muehlenbergii

CHINQUAPIN OAK, YELLOW CHESTNUT OAK, YELLOW OAK

☼ ❋ ↔ 40 ft (12 m) ↕ 100 ft (30 m)

Deciduous tree found in central and southern USA. Grayish bark fissured vertically. Leaves oblong to lance-shaped, coarsely toothed, yellow-green above, pale and downy beneath; turn to rich reds and crimsons in autumn. Acorns half-enclosed in scaly cups. Zones 5–9.

Quercus nigra

WATER OAK

☼ ❋ ↔ 40 ft (12 m) ↕ 50 ft (15 m)

Broad-domed deciduous tree native to southern USA. Bark dark gray, develops scaly ridges. Leaves egg-shaped, variously lobed, glossy deep green, persist until winter, on slender stalks. Acorns enclosed in shallow cups. Zones 6–10.

Quercus palustris

PIN OAK, SWAMP OAK

☼ ❋ ↔ 60 ft (18 m) ↕ 100 ft (30 m)

Native to southeastern Canada and eastern USA. Large, dense, deciduous tree, slender branches droop at their extremities. Bark silver-gray becoming purplish gray with age. Leaves deeply lobed, shiny green; turn scarlet in autumn, persist until winter. Acorns in shallow hairy cups. Zones 3–10.

Quercus petraea

syn. *Quercus sessilis*

DURMAST OAK, SESSILE OAK

☼ ❋ ↔ 75 ft (23 m) ↕ 150 ft (45 m)

Found naturally in central and southeastern Europe. Spreading deciduous tree, similar to *Q. robur* but with stalkless acorns and more upright branches. Bark gray, deeply fissured. Leaves large, usually downy on underside. **'Columna'**, erect compact habit; **'Longifolia'**, exceptionally long leaves. Zones 5–9.

Quercus phellos

WILLOW OAK, WILLOW-LEAFED OAK

☼ ❋ ↔ 40 ft (12 m) ↕ 100 ft (30 m)

Large deciduous tree, slender branches, native to eastern USA. Bark smooth, gray, becomes fissured with age. Leaves narrow, willow-like, glossy green above, turn yellow and orange in autumn. Small acorns enclosed in shallow cups. Zones 5–10.

Quercus robur

COMMON OAK, ENGLISH OAK, PEDUNCULATE OAK

☼ ❋ ↔ 70 ft (21 m) ↕ 100 ft (30 m)

Large, long-lived, deciduous tree native to Europe, western Asia, and North Africa. Bark pale gray, closely fissured into short, narrow, vertical plates. Leaves shallowly lobed. Long-nosed acorns in shallow cups. May be invasive in cool climates. *Q. r.* subsp. *pedunculiflora,* leaves with fewer lobes, bluish underside. *Q. r.* f. *fastigiata,*

Quercus suber

Quercus robur

columnar habit. *Q. r.* **'Concordia'** (golden oak), leaves suffused with golden yellow; **'Pendula'**, drooping branches. Zones 3–10.

Quercus rubra

syn. *Quercus borealis*

NORTHERN RED OAK, RED OAK

☼ ❋ ↔ 70 ft (21 m) ↕ 100 ft (30 m)

Deciduous tree from eastern Canada to Texas, USA. Broad head, horizontal branches. Bark smooth, silvery gray, can become brown-gray with age. Leaves large, oval to egg-shaped, lobed, turn red then red-brown to yellow and brown on old trees before falling. Dark red-brown acorns, on short stalks, in shallow scaly cups. **'Schrefeldii'**, more deeply lobed leaves, lobes overlapping. Zones 3–9.

Quercus shumardii

SHUMARD OAK

☼ ❋ ↔ 40 ft (12 m) ↕ 100 ft (30 m)

Native of prairie States of central USA. Large deciduous tree, wide-spreading crown. Bark thick, furrowed. Leaves 5- to 7-lobed, toothed, dark green above, paler below; turn red or golden brown in autumn. Acorns in thick shallow cups. *Q. s.* var. *schneckii,* smoother bark, less deeply lobed leaves. Zones 5–9.

Quercus suber

CORK OAK

☼ ❋ ↔ 70 ft (21 m) ↕ 70 ft (21 m)

Native to southwestern Europe and North Africa. Short-stemmed, wide-spreading, evergreen tree. Thick rugged bark provides cork. Leaves leathery, broadly toothed, shiny green above, grayish green and felted below. Egg-shaped acorns in scaly cups. Zones 8–10.

Quercus texana
syn. *Quercus buckleyi*
SPANISH OAK
☀ ❄ ↔ 50–70 ft (15–21 m) ↕ 50–70 ft (15–21 m)
From Texas and Oklahoma, USA. Broad deciduous tree, often branching close to ground. Leaves with 2 or 3 pairs of lobes, up to 5 in (12 cm) long, mature to yellow-green. Acorns ripen in second year; only base held in cup. Zones 7–10.

Quercus velutina
BLACK OAK, YELLOW BARK OAK
☀ ❄ ↔ 75 ft (23 m) ↕ 100 ft (30 m)
Large deciduous tree found in central and southern USA. Bark dark gray, smooth, deeply fissured with age. Leaves large, deeply lobed, glossy dark green above, downy below. Acorns half-enclosed in scaly cups. Zones 3–9.

Quercus virginiana
LIVE OAK
☀ ❄ ↔ 35 ft (10 m) ↕ 70 ft (21 m)
From southeastern USA, Mexico, and Cuba. Wide-spreading evergreen. Bark charcoal gray, fissured. Twigs downy, leaves elliptic or oblong, leathery, smooth-edged, glossy dark green above, grayish to whitish hairs below. Acorns singly or in clusters. Zones 7–11.

Quercus wislizeni
INTERIOR LIVE OAK
☀ ❄ ↔ 35 ft (10 m) ↕ 80 ft (24 m)
Large evergreen shrub or rounded tree from Mexico and California, USA. Bark thick, nearly black, deeply furrowed with scaly ridges. Leaves holly-like, oblong to ovate, slender spiny teeth. Acorns mature in first autumn. Zones 8–10.

QUILLAJA
There are about 3 species in this genus of evergreen shrubs or trees from South America, which is the only member of the family Quillajaceae. They have shiny, bright green, thick, and leathery leaves and white hairy flowers that appear in clusters of 3 to 5 blooms in spring. The fruit comprises 5 leathery follicles that open out into a star shape. The bark of some species is used as soap and for medicinal purposes.
CULTIVATION: These plants need a warm climate and a moist fertile soil that is well drained. Grow in a protected part-shaded position. Propagate from seed or cuttings.

Quillaja saponaria
SOAPBARK TREE
☀ ❄ ↔ 15–25 ft (4.5–8 m) ↕ 50–60 ft (15–18 m)
Evergreen tree native to Peru and Chile. Shiny, short-stalked, oval leaves. Purple-centered white flowers in spring. Thick dark bark contains saponin, lathers in water, used as soap substitute. Zones 8–10.

RADERMACHERA
This genus in the trumpet-vine (Bignoniaceae) family is made up of around 15 species, mostly trees or shrubs, from tropical Southeast Asia. The compound leaves may be bipinnate or tripinnate. The tubular to trumpet-shaped flowers, often fragrant and in shades of orange, green-yellow to yellow, pink, and white, are borne in loose panicles, mostly at the ends of branches. The capsular fruit contain flat seeds that are winged at each end. Some species are used for timber in their native regions.
CULTIVATION: Most species are fairly adaptable, but give the best results in a well-drained fertile soil in full sun to part-shade. Protection from strong winds is necessary, as is moderate irrigation during the growing period. Prune after flowering to maintain a bushy habit. Propagate from seed or cuttings, or by aerial layering.

Radermachera sinica
ASIAN BELL
☀ ✈ ↔ 15 ft (4.5 m) ↕ 30 ft (9 m)
Shrub or small tree from Southeast Asia. Dark green, glossy, bipinnate leaves, 8 ovate to lance-shaped leaflets. Scented deep yellow or white flowers, open at night, in spring–summer. Popular indoor foliage plant in cooler climates. Zones 10–12.

REHDERODENDRON
This is a small genus of 9 species of deciduous shrubs and small trees in the storax (Styracaceae) family, native to the woods of China and northern parts of Vietnam. Only *R. macrocarpum* is in cultivation, being valued for its masses of delightfully fragrant, drooping, white, bell-shaped flowers in spring. The flowers are followed by large winged seeds and richly colored leaves in autumn.
CULTIVATION: These plants grow well in deep humus-rich soil that doesn't dry out, in a sheltered site among other trees or facing into the morning sun. Propagation is from seed, which can be quite slow to germinate, or from half-hardened cuttings taken in summer and given bottom heat.

Rehderodendron macrocarpum
☀ ❄ ↔ 15–17 ft (4.5–5 m) ↕ 25–35 ft (8–10 m)
From mountains of western China. Small tree with flat layers of branches. Leaves up to 6 in (15 cm) long, color well before they shed. White, scented, bell-shaped flowers, to 2½ in (6 cm) across, held in drooping clusters, in spring. Ridged seed pods. Zones 8–10.

Quillaja saponaria

Radermachera sinica

REINWARDTIA

This small genus of 1 or 2 species of subshrubs with softwooded stems in the flax (Linaceae) family is named after Professor Kaspar Reinwardt, one-time director of the Leiden Botanic Gardens in the Netherlands. They are evergreen only in warm climates, with simple alternate leaves and slender, yellow, tubular flowers with 5 spreading petals.

CULTIVATION: They are best grown in a light fibrous soil with free drainage, in a warm position sheltered from wind. Pruning should be severe, almost to half-height, in late winter in order to encourage suckering from the base; this should be followed by a good mulching and deep watering. Propagate from soft-tip cuttings, which may be taken from the young growths in early spring.

Reinwardtia indica

YELLOW FLAX BUSH

☼ � ↔ 2 ft (0.6 m) ↑ 3 ft (0.9 m)

From northern India, mostly in foothills of Himalayas. Soft erect stems sucker to form large clump. Smooth soft-textured leaves, elliptic to oval, bright green above, duller underneath. Bright butter yellow flowers in late autumn–spring. Zones 9–11.

Reinwardtia indica

RETAMA

Once included among other broom genera such as *Genista,* the 4 shrubby brooms that make up this genus, which is a member of the pea-flower subfamily of the legume (Fabaceae) family, are found in the Mediterranean region and the Canary Islands. While they are usually leafless when mature, as the chlorophyll-bearing green stems perform the functions of foliage, young plants often carry small linear leaves which sometimes also appear on adult plants in spring. Often rather untidy and wiry-stemmed, these shrubs are at their best in spring when smothered with flowers. These may be white or yellow, sometimes with purplish markings, and are often scented. The flowers are followed by conspicuous, somewhat inflated seed pods that are sometimes downy.

Retama monosperma

CULTIVATION: Best grown in full sun, and drought tolerant once established, these tough shrubs prefer a reasonably fertile, light, well-drained soil. They can be trimmed after flowering, but could never be called neat. Propagate from seed, which should be soaked before sowing, or from summer cuttings.

Retama monosperma

syn. *Genista monosperma*

SILVER BROOM

☼ � ↔ 10 ft (3 m) ↑ 10 ft (3 m)

Native to Spain and northern Africa. Upright near-leafless plant with slender arching branches, silvery and downy when young, becoming grayish green as plant matures. Short racemes of small, white, fragrant pea-flowers, backed by purplish calyces, in spring. Zones 9–11.

RHAMNUS

There are more than 125 species within this genus in the buckthorn (Rhamnaceae) family. Mostly prickly evergreen or deciduous shrubs or trees, they are found throughout the Northern Hemisphere, as well as Brazil, eastern Africa, and South Africa, in woodland and heathland areas. The simple dark green leaves can be smooth-edged or toothed. The flowers are insignificant; some are fragrant. Green, blue-green, and yellow dyes are made from some species, while others are used medicinally, or wood is used commercially for turning. They are also cultivated for their ornamental foliage and berries.

CULTIVATION: Depending on the species, these shrubs or trees prefer moist to very dry conditions in full sun or part-shade, in moderately fertile soil. Some species tolerate alkaline soil and coastal sites. Propagate by sowing seed in autumn, as soon as it is ripe, giving protection from winter frosts; or from softwood cuttings of deciduous species in early summer. Half-hardened cuttings can be taken from evergreen species in summer, and layering can be done in either autumn or spring.

Rhamnus alaternus

ITALIAN BUCKTHORN

☼ ❋ ↔ 12 ft (3.5 m) ↑ 15 ft (4.5 m)

Evergreen shrub native to Mediterranean and Caucasus regions. Leaves leathery, dark green, shiny. Small yellow-green flowers in late spring–early summer. Fruit ripens to black in late summer. Tolerates dry soil conditions, pollution, and salt-laden air. '**Argenteo-variegata**' (syn. 'Variegata'), slightly less hardy than species, leaves with marbled grayish green center and white edges. Zones 7–10.

Rhamnus californica

COFFEEBERRY

☼ ❋ ↔ 10 ft (3 m) ↑ 12 ft (3.5 m)

Evergreen to semi-evergreen upright shrub from western USA. Red new growth, shiny green leaves. Clusters of pale greenish yellow flowers in late spring–early summer. Round red berries ripen to black. Zones 7–10.

Rhamnus californica

Rhamnus imeretina

Rhaphiolepis indica

Rhamnus cathartica

BUCKTHORN, COMMON BUCKTHORN

☼ ❋ ↔ 15 ft (4.5 m) ↕ 20 ft (6 m)

Deciduous, thorny, thicket-forming shrub from temperate Asia, Europe, and Africa. Green leaves elliptic to oval, finely toothed edges, turn yellow in autumn. Yellow-green flowers in late spring to early summer. Red fruit ripens to black. Zones 3–9.

Rhamnus crocea

REDBERRY

☼ ❋ ↔ 7 ft (2 m) ↕ 6 ft (1.8 m)

Native to Baja California, Mexico, and north to southwest Oregon, USA. Evergreen spreading shrub with thorny twigs. Leaves glossy, egg-shaped to elliptic, slightly toothed edges. Small flower clusters followed by red fruit. Zones 7–11.

Rhamnus frangula

ALDER BUCKTHORN

☼ ❋ ↔ 15 ft (4.5 m) ↕ 15 ft (4.5 m)

Deciduous shrub from North Africa, Europe, and parts of Russia. Shiny, dark green, oval leaves, paler beneath, turn red in autumn. Axillary clusters of small, greenish, hermaphroditic flowers in spring to summer. Fruit ripens from red to black. Zones 3–9.

Rhamnus imeretina

☼ ❋ ↔ 15 ft (4.5 m) ↕ 10 ft (3 m)

Deciduous shrub native to Black Sea region. Oval to oblong leaves, prominent veins, dull green above, felty lighter underside, turn dark brownish purple in autumn. Axillary clusters of unisex greenish flowers in summer. Fruit ripens to black. Zones 6–9.

Rhamnus prinoides

SOUTH AFRICAN DOGWOOD

☼ ❊ ↔ 15 ft (4.5 m) ↕ 25 ft (8 m)

From mountains of eastern South Africa and tropical Africa. Ever-green leaves leathery, deep green above, paler olive below. Cream flowers in spring–early summer. Red berries ripen black. Zones 9–11.

RHAPHIOLEPIS

There are up to 10 species of evergreen shrubs in this genus of the rose (Rosaceae) family, allied to *Photinia*. Originating in East and Southeast Asia, these plants do not bear spines or thorns; they have leathery deep green leaves and clusters of white or pink flowers in spring, often blooming again in autumn. Flowers are followed by blue-black berries that are highly attractive to some birds, which distribute the seeds.

CULTIVATION: Considered tough low-maintenance plants that are suitable for seaside planting, these shrubs can withstand quite hard pruning, which makes them ideal for hedges. Plant them in full sun in reasonable soil topped up with an organic mulch into which branches can be layered to produce further plants. The soil should be forked over as little as possible as the plants resent root disturbance. In addition to layering, the plants can be propagated from either cuttings or seed.

Rhaphiolepis × delacourii

HYBRID INDIAN HAWTHORN

☼ ❋ ↔ 8 ft (2.4 m) ↕ 6 ft (1.8 m)

Name applied to plants intermediate in character between parents *R. indica* and *R. umbellata*. First were deliberate crosses made by M. Delacour at Cannes shortly before 1900. Cultivars from these crosses include 'Coates' Crimson', slow growing, glossy green leaves, dark pink flowers in spring–summer; 'Spring Song', light pink flowers held for long time; and 'White Enchantress', dwarf form with small white flowers. Zones 8–11.

Rhaphiolepis indica

INDIAN HAWTHORN

☼ ❋ ↔ 8 ft (2.4 m) ↕ 8 ft (2.4 m)

From southern China. Leaves leathery, serrated, narrow, pointed, dark green above, olive green beneath. Pinkish brown new growths. Pink-tinted white flowers in clusters, at ends of branches, in spring. Invasive in warm-temperate climates. 'Ballerina', pink flowers; Springtime/'Monme', small flowers, bronzy new growth. Zones 8–11.

Rhaphiolepis umbellata

☼ ❋ ↔ 7 ft (2 m) ↕ 6 ft (1.8 m)

Dense mound-like shrub from coastal areas of southern Japan and Korea. Broad, thick, grayish green leaves, rounded tip, recurved edges. Bunches of white perfumed flowers in spring–early sum-mer, spasmodically into winter in warmer areas. Blue-black berries. 'Minor' ★, dwarf form, smaller leaves and flowers. Zones 8–11.

Rhododendron albrechtii

Rhododendron alutaceum

Rhododendron arboreum

RHODODENDRON

syn. *Ledum*

AZALEA, RHODODENDRON

This very diverse genus of 800 or more species of mostly evergreen and some deciduous shrubs is widely distributed across the Northern Hemisphere, with the majority growing in temperate to cool regions. Particular concentrations occur in western China, the Himalayas, and northeastern Myanmar, while the Vireya rhododendrons grow mostly at higher altitudes throughout tropical southeastern Asia, as far south as the northern tip of Australia, with more than 200 species occurring on the island of New Guinea alone. Deciduous azalea species are scattered across cooler Northern Hemisphere climates, notably in Europe, China, Japan, and North America.

Rhododendrons vary in form from tiny, ground-hugging, prostrate and miniature plants adapted to exposed conditions, to small trees, often understory species in the forests of mountainous areas. Many species grow at altitudes of 3,000 ft (900 m) or more, and some can grow in the branches of trees or on rock faces. As members of the heath (Ericaceae) family, they are closely related to heathers (*Erica* and *Calluna* species) and have similar growing requirements. Some rhododendrons have solitary flowers but most bear terminal racemes, known as "trusses," of up to 24 or more blooms, in a wide palette of colors including white, pink, red, yellow, and mauve, excluding only shades of pure blue. Flowers may be a single color but are often multi-colored, with spots, stripes, edging, or a single blotch of a different color in the throat of the flower. With the exception of some Vireya species and hybrids, fragrant rhododendrons are always white or very pale pink. Blooms vary in size and shape but are generally bell-shaped, with a broad tube ending in flared lobes, and usually single. Flowers with double petals do occur, particularly among evergreen azaleas, which may also be "hose-in-hose," when the calyx is enlarged and the same color as the petals.

Most rhododendrons flower from early spring (early season) to early summer (late season), although some bear spot flowers briefly in autumn, and Vireya rhododendrons can flower at various times during the year, often in winter. Deciduous azaleas flower in spring on bare branches, usually before new leaf growth starts to emerge. The fruit is a many-seeded capsule, normally woody but sometimes soft, and sometimes bearing wings or tail-like appendages.

The genus is divided into 2 botanically distinct groups known as lepidotes and elepidotes, and these groups are subdivided further into the various rhododendron types. Plants from one group may not breed with plants from the other, thus limiting the options for hybridizers. The leaves, and sometimes the flowers and other parts, of lepidote rhododendrons are covered with scales, thought to aid transpiration. This group includes many cool-climate evergreen plants, such as the Vireya rhododendrons. The rest of the genus, the elepidote rhododendrons, with no scales on leaf or flower parts, includes the remaining cool-climate evergreen plants and the evergreen and deciduous azaleas. Azaleas were originally classified as a separate genus but are now regarded as botanically part of *Rhododendron*. Vireya rhododendrons can be grown in just about any climate as long as protection from frost is provided. Many are well suited to growing in hanging baskets and containers. The nectar of some species and some flower parts is poisonous.

CULTIVATION: Establishing an ideal growing environment before planting is the key to success with rhododendrons. Many of the problems likely to afflict them in the home garden can be minimized by maintaining soil quality and ensuring adequate ventilation. All prefer acidic soils between pH 4.5 and 6, high in organic matter and freely draining. A cool root run is essential; apply a deep mulch of organic material, which will also help to reduce moisture loss and control weed growth, while minimizing disturbance of the delicate roots. Many rhododendrons, particularly those with larger leaves, prefer a shaded or part-shaded aspect. They are ideally suited to planting under deciduous trees. While most prefer some protection from wind, sun, and frost, many others are tolerant of these conditions and some are well suited to exposed rock gardens.

Evergreen rhododendrons may be propagated by taking tip cuttings of new growth in spring, while deciduous azaleas are best grown from hardwood cuttings in winter. Plants may be grown from seed but germination and development is slow, and hybrids grown from seed are unlikely to be the same as the parent. Layering enables new plants to be created from low-hanging branches pinned to the ground and covered in a moist organic medium such as sphagnum moss. Plants which are difficult to propagate and establish by other means can be grafted onto the roots of stronger plants with more vigorous root systems. Regular pruning of rhododendrons is not necessary other than as required to control size, maintain shape, and to remove any damaged or diseased material; some species and hybrids actually resent pruning. Cultivated rhododendrons are compact and attain only about half the height of similar plants growing in the wild. The growing habit of all species and hybrids is related to the amount of shade the plant receives.

Rhododendron aberconwayi

☀ ❄ ↔ 4 ft (1.2 m) ↑ 6 ft (1.8 m)

Upright evergreen shrub from western China. Thick, smooth, glossy, dark green, elliptic leaves. Delicate, saucer-shaped, pale rose flowers, to 1½ in (35 mm) long, crimson or purple spots, in trusses of 5 to 12 blooms, in late spring–early summer. Zones 7–9.

Rhododendron albrechtii

☀ ❄ ↔ 4 ft (1.2 m) ↑ 7 ft (2 m)

Deciduous azalea native to central and northern Japan. Compact shrub. Whorls of 5 finely toothed leaves, gray hairy coating below. Openly bell-shaped, reddish purple flowers, in trusses of 3 to 5 blooms, in mid- to late spring. Zones 5–8.

Rhododendron alutaceum

☀/☀ ❄ ↔ 5–12 ft (1.5–3.5 m)
↑ 7–15 ft (2–4.5 m)

Large bushy shrub found in southwestern China. Broad, leathery, lance-shaped leaves, 2–6 in (5–15 cm) long, dense tan to red-brown hairs on underside. Trusses of up to 12 white to pale pink, funnel-shaped, red-spotted flowers, to 1½ in (35 mm) long, in early spring. Zones 7–10.

Rhododendron campylogynum

Rhododendron arborescens

☀ ❄ ↔ 8 ft (2.4 m) ↑ 10 ft (3 m)

Deciduous azalea native to woodlands of Appalachian region of eastern USA. Fragrant flowers white or pink, funnel-shaped, open with or after bright green obovate leaves. Zones 4–8.

Rhododendron arboreum

☀ ❄ ↔ 15 ft (4.5 m) ↑ 60 ft (18 m)

Slow-growing tree species common in Himalayan rhododendron forests, also in southern India, western China, and Thailand. Leaves tough, broad, green above; hairy brown coating below. Flowers fleshy, narrowly bell-shaped, 2 in (5 cm) wide, white or pink to blood red, in trusses of 15 to 20 blooms, in spring. *R. a.* subsp. *cinnamomeum*, leaves with reddish brown hairs beneath. *R. a.* subsp. *delavayi*, red-flowered form. Zones 7–9.

Rhododendron arizelum

☀ ❄ ↔ 6–25 ft (1.8–8 m) ↑ 6–25 ft (1.8–8 m)

Variable evergreen shrub or small tree from northeastern Myanmar, northeastern India, and western China. Bell-shaped flowers yellow, cream, or deep rose pink, in trusses of 12 to 25 blooms, mid- to late season. Oval-shaped leaves, velvety coating beneath. Zones 8–9.

Rhododendron augustinii

☀ ❄ ↔ 2–10 ft (0.6–3 m) ↑ 3–20 ft
(0.9–6 m)

Compact, freely flowering, variable, evergreen shrub from China. Elliptic leaves, hairy beneath. Flowers mauve-blue to purple, greenish spots; funnel-shaped, in trusses of 2 to 6 blooms, mid- to late season. Zones 6–9.

Rhododendron austrinum

FLORIDA AZALEA

☀ ❄ ↔ 10 ft (3 m) ↑ 10 ft (3 m)

Rarely grown, freely flowering, deciduous azalea from southeastern USA. Fragrant, funnel-shaped, creamy yellow to golden yellow, orange, or red flowers, with distinctive long protruding stamens, bloom before or as downy leaf shoots open. Zones 6–9.

Rhododendron calophytum

☀ ❄ ↔ 20 ft (6 m) ↑ 15 ft (4.5 m)

Native to China. Evergreen small tree, shorter in cultivation. Long, dark green, smooth leaves curl and droop in colder weather. White or pink bell-shaped flowers, with distinct purple basal blotch, early to mid-season. Zones 6–9.

Rhododendron campanulatum

☀ ❄ ↔ 15 ft (4.5 m) ↑ 15 ft (4.5 m)

From Himalayas. Shrub or small tree, varies widely in form and height. Smooth leaves, underside densely covered with brown woolly hairs. Bell-shaped flowers, lavender-blue or white to pale mauve, with purple spots, in trusses of 6 to 12 blooms, in spring. Zones 5–8.

Rhododendron campylogynum

☀ ❄ ↔ 30 in (75 cm) ↑ 18 in (45 cm)

Creeping evergreen shrub from eastern India and northeastern Myanmar. Dark green leaves, white or silvery hairy underside. Nodding creamy white or bright pink flowers, in delicate trusses of 1 to 3 blooms, in late spring–summer. Zones 7–9.

Rhododendron calophytum

Rhododendron concinnum

Rhododendron canescens

FLORIDA PINXTER AZALEA, PIEDMONT AZALEA, SWEET AZALEA

☀ ❋ ↔ 8 ft (2.4 m) ↑ 15 ft (4.5 m)

Deciduous azalea native to eastern USA, from North Carolina southward and west to Oklahoma. Oblong to lance-shaped leaves. Scented pink flowers, funnel-shaped, before or with leaves, in spring. White- or magenta-flowered forms occur. Zones 6–10.

Rhododendron catawbiense ★

CATAWBA RHODODENDRON, MOUNTAIN ROSEBAY

☀ ❋ ↔ 10 ft (3 m) ↑ 10 ft (3 m)

From eastern USA; robust evergreen similar in form to *R. ponticum*. Glossy dark green leaves, broadly elliptic to obovate. Funnel-shaped faintly spotted flowers, lilac-purple, in compact trusses of 15 to 20 blooms, in late spring–early summer. Important parent of many frost-hardy hybrids. Zones 4–9.

Rhododendron ciliatum

☀ ❋ ↔ 6 ft (1.8 m) ↑ 6 ft (1.8 m)

Evergreen species from Himalayas. Young shoots and upper surface of elliptic leaves distinctively bristly. Bell- to funnel-shaped flowers, white or white flushed with pink, in trusses of 2 to 4 blooms, in spring. Zones 7–9.

Rhododendron cinnabarinum

☀ ❋ ↔ 7 ft (2 m) ↑ 10 ft (3 m)

Evergreen species from Himalayas and north Myanmar. Roundish, glaucous, green leaves. Waxy, red to orange, narrowly bell-shaped flowers, in trusses of 3 to 9 blooms, mid- to late season. Zones 6–9.

Rhododendron concinnum

☀ ❋ ↔ 6–10 ft (1.8–3 m) ↑ 6–20 ft (1.8–6 m)

Vigorous evergreen shrub or small tree from western China. Smooth dark green leaves, scaly above, gray-brown scales underneath. Purple or red-purple funnel-shaped flowers, scaly on outside, in trusses of 2 to 8, in mid- to late spring. **Pseudoyanthinum Group**, ruby red flowers. Zones 7–9.

Rhododendron dauricum

☀ ❋ ↔ 8 ft (2.4 m) ↑ 8 ft (2.4 m)

From northern latitudes in East Asia, from eastern Siberia to Japan. Evergreen straggly shrub, scaly young shoots, densely scaly dark green leaves, hairy beneath. Widely funnel-shaped flowers, pink or violet-pink, singly or in pairs, early season. Zones 5–8.

Rhododendron decorum

☀ ❋ ↔ 8 ft (2.4 m) ↑ 20 ft (6 m)

Native to western China, northeastern Myanmar, and Laos. Evergreen shrub or small tree. Large smooth leaves to 8 in (20 cm) long. Scented, white to pale pink, funnel-shaped flowers, in trusses of 8 to 12 blooms, late in season. *R. d.* subsp. *diaprepes,* larger leaves and flowers. Zones 7–9.

Rhododendron degronianum

☀ ❋ ↔ 7 ft (2 m) ↑ 8 ft (2.4 m)

Evergreen species from central and southern Japan. Shiny, dark green, deeply veined leaves, fawn-colored felt-like hairs underneath. Pink, rose, reddish, or white bell-shaped flowers, in trusses of 6 to 15 blooms, mid- to late season. *R. d.* subsp. *yakushimanum* (syn. *R. yakushimanum*), slow- and low- growing spreading form, glossy dark green leaves, distinctive recurved margins, compact trusses of 8 to 12 rose-colored buds and pink flowers. Zones 7–9.

Rhododendron edgeworthii

☀ ❅ ↔ 6 ft (1.8 m) ↑ 6 ft (1.8 m)

Evergreen species from Himalayas, upper Myanmar, and southwestern China. Deeply textured, wrinkled leaves, brown hairy coating, scales beneath. Fragrant, white, funnel-shaped flowers, occasionally flushed with pink, in trusses of 2 to 3 flowers, midseason. Zones 9–10.

Rhododendron falconeri

☀ ❅ ↔ 30 ft (9 m) ↑ 40 ft (12 m)

Native to Himalayas. Evergreen with brown flaking bark. Large, wrinkled, dark mat green leaves, white with reddish hairy coating underneath. Fragrant, creamy white to pink or pale cream, bell-shaped flowers, in large trusses of 12 to 25 blooms, mid- to late

Rhododendron falconeri

Rhododendron fortunei

season. *R. f.* subsp. *eximium*, more persistent hairy coating under leaves, regarded by some as separate species, *R. eximium*. Zones 9–10.

Rhododendron flammeum

FLAME AZALEA

☀ ⚘ ↔ 3 ft (0.9 m) ↑ 6 ft (1.8 m)

Freely flowering deciduous azalea from eastern states of USA, from Georgia to South Carolina. Compact shrub, slender branches. Scarlet flowers open with leaves in late spring to early summer. Rare in cultivation. Zones 10–11.

Rhododendron forrestii

☀ ❄ ↔ 48 in (120 cm) ↑ 4 in (10 cm)

Creeping, prostrate, evergreen shrub native to western China and northeastern Myanmar. Leaves leathery, dark green, purple-red beneath. Bright scarlet tubular-campanulate flowers, singly or in pairs, mid- to late season. Used in breeding programs. *R. f.* subsp. *papillatum*, narrow leaves, light brown beneath; 'Scarlet Runner', scarlet flowers. *R. f.* Repens Group, dwarf forms with creeping habit, leaves extensively veined, red flowers; 'May Day', scarlet flowers. Zones 8–9.

Rhododendron fortunei

☀ ❄ ↔ 8 ft (2.4 m) ↑ 15 ft (4.5 m)

Widespread in its native eastern China. Evergreen, broadly upright, sometimes spreading shrub or tree. Rough grayish brown bark; reddish, bluish, or purplish leaf stalks. Fragrant, pale pink, rose, lilac to white, bell-shaped flowers, in trusses of 6 to 12 blooms, late in season. *R. f.* subsp. *discolor*, abundant pink flowers, late season; *R. f.* Houlstonii Group, soft pink to light purple flowers, mid-season. Zones 6–9.

Rhododendron griffithianum

☀ ❄ ↔ 10 ft (3 m) ↑ 60 ft (18 m)

Himalayan evergreen tree species with open habit. Flaking peeling bark; smooth oblong leaves. Fragrant flowers, white, shades of pale pink, or even yellowish, in trusses of 3 to 6 blooms, mid- to late season. Zones 8–9.

Rhododendron haematodes

☀ ❄ ↔ 5 ft (1.5 m) ↑ 5 ft (1.5 m)

Evergreen shrub naturally found in western China and northeastern Myanmar. Young shoots densely bristly; mature leaves matted with fawn to reddish brown hairs underneath. Fleshy, tubular to bell-shaped, scarlet to deep crimson flowers in late spring–early summer. *R. h.* subsp. *chaetomallum*, bristly young shoots and leaf stems. Zones 7–9.

Rhododendron impeditum

☀ ❄ ↔ 12 in (30 cm) ↑ 12 in (30 cm)

Compact ground-covering evergreen from western China. Dense, shiny, dark green, scaly foliage. Violet to purple funnel-shaped flowers, in small trusses of 1 to 3 blooms, mid-season. Zones 4–8.

Rhododendron impeditum

Rhododendron jasminiflorum

Rhododendron indicum

INDIAN AZALEA, JAPANESE EVERGREEN AZALEA

☀ ❄ ↔ 2 ft (0.6 m) ↑ 3 ft (0.9 m)

Variable evergreen species from southern Japan. Densely branched; low, sometimes prostrate habit. Mass of shiny dark green leaves. Red broadly funnel-shaped flowers, singly or in pairs, in spring. 'Balsaminiflorum', dwarf form, salmon red double flowers; 'Macranthum', compact shrub, orange-red flowers. Zones 6–9.

Rhododendron intricatum

☀ ❄ ↔ 5 ft (1.5 m) ↑ 5 ft (1.5 m)

Fast-growing, delicately branched, evergreen shrub from western China. Small, mat, smooth, grayish green leaves, densely scaly below. Tiny flowers, pale lavender to dark purple-blue, short stamens, in compact trusses of 2 to 10 blooms, mid- to late season. Zones 5–8.

Rhododendron jasminiflorum

☀ ⚘ ↔ 22 in (55 cm) ↑ 22 in (55 cm)

Vireya species found in Malay Peninsula, Philippines, and Sumatra. Leaves have scaly undersides. Trusses of 6 to 12 tubular flowers, white, sometimes flushed pink, in winter. Used in hybridizing. Spreading habit makes it ideal for hanging baskets. Zones 10–11.

Rhododendron kaempferi

KAEMPFER AZALEA

☀ ❄ ↔ 4 ft (1.2 m) ↑ 4 ft (1.2 m)

Densely branched shrub native to Japan; deciduous in cool climates. Red-brown bristles on young shoots. Salmon or brick red, funnel-shaped flowers, in trusses of 2 to 4 blooms, in late spring. Zones 5–8.

Rhododendron kiusianum

KYUSHU AZALEA

☀ ❄ ↔ 3 ft (0.9 m) ↑ 3 ft (0.9 m)

Parent of Kurume Group of azaleas. Evergreen species from Kyushu, Japan; deciduous at higher altitudes. Much-branched, often prostrate shrub with small hairy leaves. Funnel-shaped flowers, rose-purple, purple, red, pink, or white, in trusses of 2 to 3 blooms, in late spring. 'Mountain Gem', rose-purple flowers. Zones 6–9.

Rhododendron konori
☀ ✿ ↔ 6 ft (1.8 m) ↑ 12 ft (3.5 m)
Vireya species from New Guinea. Large leaves, mat green, bluish tinge, reddish brown hairy coating underneath. Fragrant white or pinkish flowers, in trusses of 5 to 8 blooms, in winter. Zones 10–11.

Rhododendron lacteum
☀ ❄ ↔ 12 ft (3.5 m) ↑ 12 ft (3.5 m)
Evergreen shrub or small tree found in western China. Leaves have hairy underside. Large, bell-shaped, cream flowers, sometimes flushed pink, to 2 in (5 cm) long, in large compact trusses of 15 to 30 blooms, in spring. Prefers well-sheltered position. Zones 7–9.

Rhododendron laetum
☀ ✿ ↔ 4 ft (1.2 m) ↑ 10 ft (3 m)
Vireya species native to northwestern New Guinea, more compact in cultivation. Broad elliptic leaves. Large funnel-shaped flowers of pure golden yellow, ageing to red, orange, or salmon, in open trusses of 6 to 8 blooms, in autumn–spring. Zones 10–11.

Rhododendron leucaspis
☀ ❄ ↔ 4 ft (1.2 m) ↑ 4 ft (1.2 m)
Compact, rounded, evergreen shrub from western China. Hairy elliptic leaves. Flowers bell-shaped, milky white, often tinged pink, singly, in 2s or 3s. Protect from late winter frosts. Zones 7–9.

Rhododendron lochiae
AUSTRALIAN RHODODENDRON
☀ ✿ ↔ 2 ft (0.6 m) ↑ 3 ft (0.9 m)
Slow-growing, compact, bushy Vireya species from northeastern tip of Australia. Scaly young shoots, dark green broadly obovate leaves, scaly underneath. Bright scarlet funnel-shaped flowers, in loose trusses of 2 to 7 blooms, in winter. Zones 10–11.

Rhododendron luteiflorum
syn. *Rhododendron glaucophyllum* var. *luteiflorum*
☀/☀ ❄ ↔ 18–32 in (45–80 cm) ↑ 12–36 in (30–90 cm)
Alpine species from northern Myanmar. Aromatic, pointed oval to lance-shaped, olive green leaves, around 1 in (25 mm) long. Nodding, yellow-green to yellow, 1 in (25 mm) long flowers, in trusses of 3 to 6 blooms, in mid-spring. Zones 6–9.

Rhododendron lutescens
☀ ❄ ↔ 15 ft (4.5 m) ↑ 20 ft (6 m)
From western China, straggly habit, gray or brown flaking bark. Bright bronze-red young foliage in spring, show of color in autumn. Small, delicate, pale yellow, funnel-shaped flowers, long stamens, in trusses of 1 to 3 blooms, in late winter–early spring. Zones 7–9.

Rhododendron luteum
PONTIC AZALEA
☀ ❄ ↔ 8 ft (2.4 m) ↑ 12 ft (3.5 m)
Widely grown deciduous azalea from eastern Europe, used extensively in breeding programs. Foliage colors red, orange, and purple in autumn. Tubular, funnel-shaped, clear yellow flowers, in trusses of 7 to 12 blooms, before leaves in spring. Zones 5–9.

Rhododendron macgregoriae
☀ ✿ ↔ 7 ft (2 m) ↑ 15 ft (4.5 m)
Shrub or small tree, most widespread of New Guinea's Vireya rhododendrons. Leaves with scaly underside. Flowers light yellow to dark orange or red, narrow corolla tube, in trusses of 8 to 15 flowers, in winter. Zones 10–11.

Rhododendron macrophyllum
☀ ❄ ↔ 12 ft (3.5 m) ↑ 12 ft (3.5 m)
Evergreen shrub from western North America. Dark green leaves, paler underside, smooth-edged. Bell-shaped flowers, white to pink, yellow spots, in trusses of 9 to 20 blooms, late in season. Zones 6–9.

Rhododendron maddenii
☀ ❄ ↔ 8 ft (2.4 m) ↑ 25 ft (8 m)
From Himalayas, southwestern China, Myanmar, and Vietnam. Leaves smooth, thick, brownish, hairy below, heavy scaling. Large funnel-shaped flowers, white, often flushed pink or purple, yellow basal blotch, in trusses of 1 to 11 blooms, in late spring. Zones 9–10.

Rhododendron mallotum
☀ ❄ ↔ 12 ft (3.5 m) ↑ 20 ft (6 m)
Evergreen shrub or small tree from western China and northeastern Myanmar. Young leaf shoots and thick, stiff, leathery leaves have gray or brown hairy coating. Trusses of up to 20 tubular bell-shaped, red or crimson flowers in early spring. Zones 7–9.

Rhododendron lacteum

Rhododendron lutescens

Rhododendron luteum

Rhododendron nuttallii

Rhododendron occidentale

Rhododendron orbiculatum

Rhododendron maximum

GREAT LAUREL RHODODENDRON, ROSEBAY RHODODENDRON

☀ ❄ ↔ 7 ft (2 m) ↕ 6 ft (1.8 m)

Compact, spreading, evergreen shrub from eastern North America. Smooth leaves, fine hairy coating underneath. Bell-shaped flowers, white to pinkish purple, with yellow-green spots, in late spring– early summer. 'Summertime', white flowers, tips of petals flushed reddish purple. Zones 3–8.

Rhododendron megeratum

☀ ✂ ↔ 15 in (38 cm) ↕ 15–30 in (38–75 cm)

Very early-flowering, evergreen, prostrate species found in north-eastern India, northeastern Myanmar, and western China. Leaves small, almost circular, whitish hairy coating below. Broad, bell-shaped, creamy white to yellow flowers. Zones 9–10.

Rhododendron minus

☀ ❄ ↔ 3–5 ft (0.9–1.5 m) ↕ 3–5 ft (0.9–1.5 m)

Small evergreen from North America. Pointed elliptic leaves, densely scaly below. Flowers usually scaly, white to pink or mauve, in trusses of 6 to 12 blooms, in mid-spring. **Carolinianum Group**, pink or pale rose-purple flowers in summer. Zones 4–9.

Rhododendron molle

DECIDUOUS AZALEA

☀ ❄ ↔ 4 ft (1.2 m) ↕ 4 ft (1.2 m)

Small deciduous azalea native to eastern China. Funnel-shaped flowers golden yellow or orange color, large greenish blotch, in trusses of 6 to 12 blooms, with or before mid-green leaves, in mid-spring. **R. m. subsp. japonicum** (syn. *R. japonicum*), from Japan, yellow or orange flowers, one parent of Mollis hybrids. Zones 7–9.

Rhododendron mucronulatum

KOREAN RHODODENDRON

☀ ❄ ↔ 3 ft (0.9 m) ↕ 6 ft (1.8 m)

Straggly deciduous shrub from eastern Russia, northern and central China, Mongolia, Korea, and Japan. Elliptic to lance-shaped leaves. Funnel-shaped bright mauve-pink flowers, protruding stamens, blue anthers, in spring, before foliage. 'Alba', white flowers; 'Cornell Pink' ★, large clear pink flowers; 'Crater's Edge', deep pink flowers; 'Mahogany Red', wine red flowers tinged bronze. Zones 4–8.

Rhododendron neriifolium

☀/❄ ❄ ↔ 6–12 ft (1.8–3.5 m) ↕ 10–20 ft (3–6 m)

Large shrub or small tree from western China to northern Myanmar. Long, pointed elliptic to lance-shaped, dark green leaves, waxy pale blue below. Tubular bell-shaped flowers, in trusses of up to 12 blooms, usually bright red to deep pink, rarely yellow. Zones 7–10.

Rhododendron nuttallii

☀ ✂ ↔ 20 ft (6 m) ↕ 35 ft (10 m)

Evergreen large shrub or small tree from Himalayas, western China, northern Myanmar, and northern India. Purplish brown bark, crimson-purple young growth. Creamy white bell-shaped flowers, yellow throat, in trusses of 7 blooms, in mid- to late spring. Zones 9–10.

Rhododendron × obtusum

KURUME AZALEA

☀ ❄ ↔ 3 ft (0.9 m) ↕ 3 ft (0.9 m)

Natural hybrid between *R. kiusianum* and *R. kaempferi*, from Japan. Twiggy, sometimes prostrate shrub. Densely bristly brown leaf shoots; bright green leaves. Bright red, scarlet, or crimson funnel-shaped flowers, in trusses of 1 to 3 blooms, in late spring. Zones 6–9.

Rhododendron occidentale

WESTERN AZALEA

☀ ❄ ↔ 5 ft (1.5 m) ↕ 5 ft (1.5 m)

Variable deciduous azalea from western USA. Bright green foliage turns bronze, then scarlet, crimson, or yellow in autumn. Fragrant, white or light pink, funnel-shaped flowers, deep yellow blotch, in mid-spring. Zones 6–9.

Rhododendron orbiculare

☀ ❄ ↔ 10 ft (3 m) ↕ 10 ft (3 m)

Evergreen from western China. Rounded bright green leaves, deeply notched bases. Rose to deep red bell-shaped flowers, up to 2½ in (6 cm) long, in trusses of 7 to 10 blooms, in spring. Zones 6–9.

Rhododendron orbiculatum

☀ ✈ ↔ 3 ft (0.9 m) ↕ 3 ft (0.9 m)

Compact Vireya rhododendron from Borneo. Thick rounded leaves. Large, orchid-like flowers, white or silvery pink, in loose trusses of up to 5 blooms. Good specimen for hanging baskets. Zones 10–11.

Rhododendron periclymenoides

coating on young shoots; dark green leaves. Large trusses of 20 to 30 bell-shaped creamy white flowers, flushed rose, in late winter–early spring. Protect in cooler areas. Zones 9–10.

Rhododendron quinquefolium
FIVE-LEAF AZALEA

◐ ❊ ↔ 4 ft (1.2–2.4 m) ↕ 8–25 ft (2.4–8 m)
Deciduous azalea from central Japan. Oval-shaped leaves, in whorls of 4 to 5, at ends of branches. Pure white flowers, with green spots, in late spring. '**Five Arrows**', white flowers spotted with olive green. Zones 6–8.

Rhododendron racemosum

◐ ❊ ↔ 5 ft (1.5 m) ↕ 5 ft (1.5 m)
Variable evergreen shrub from western China. Smooth leathery leaves. Funnel-shaped flowers, white to pale pink, in trusses of up to 6 blooms, in spring. '**Forrest**', dwarf form, pink flowers; '**Glendoick**', taller, deep pink flowers; '**Rock Rose**', bright purplish pink flowers. Zones 5–8.

Rhododendron pachysanthum

◐ ❊ ↔ 3 ft (0.9 m) ↕ 4 ft (1.2 m)
Compact, rounded, evergreen shrub from Taiwan. Dark green leaves, dense brownish hair on underside. New growth felted all over with pale brownish hairs. Trusses of 8 to 10, sometimes 20, bell-shaped white flowers, densely spotted with crimson, in spring. Zones 7–9.

Rhododendron periclymenoides
syn. *Rhododendron nudiflorum*
PINXTERBLOOM AZALEA

◐ ❊ ↔ 8 ft (2.4 m) ↕ 10 ft (3 m)
Deciduous azalea from eastern North America. Trusses of 6 to 12 fragrant funnel-shaped flowers, white, pale pink, or violet-red, with distinctive long stamens and long corolla tube, open just before or with bright green leaves, in late spring. Zones 3–9.

Rhododendron ponticum
PONTIC RHODODENDRON

◐ ❊ ↔ 20 ft (6 m) ↕ 25 ft (8 m)
Native to Mediterranean region. Vigorous evergreen shrub or small tree with smooth leaves. Compact trusses of 10 to 15 pale mauve or lilac-pink funnel-shaped flowers, to 2 in (5 cm) long, in mid- to late spring. Makes useful hedge or windbreak, but can become invasive weed. '**Silver Edge**', similar to '**Variegatum**', which has creamy white and green variegated leaves; less vigorous and invasive than species. Zones 6–9.

Rhododendron protistum

◐ ❊ ↔ 15 ft (4.5 m) ↕ 100 ft (30 m)
Evergreen species from western China and northern Myanmar; usually tall shrub in cultivation. Dense, yellowish gray, hairy

Rhododendron ponticum

Rhododendron reticulatum

◐ ❊ ↔ 4 ft (1.2 m) ↕ 4 ft (1.2 m)
Freely flowering, hardy, evergreen azalea from Japan. Leaves hairy initially, become smooth. Reddish purple to magenta bell-shaped flowers, to 2 in (5 cm) wide, carried singly or in pairs, in mid- to late spring. Zones 6–9.

Rhododendron rubiginosum

◐ ❊ ↔ 20 ft (6 m) ↕ 30 ft (9 m)
Evergreen species from west China and northeast Myanmar. Smooth aromatic leaves. Bell-shaped flowers, pink, rose, or lilac shades, in trusses of 4 to 8 blooms, in spring. Zones 7–9.

Rhododendron schlippenbachii
ROYAL AZALEA

◐ ❊ ↔ 15 ft (4.5 m) ↕ 15 ft (4.5 m)
Deciduous azalea from Korea and far eastern Russia. Light green leaves, in whorls at ends of branches, turn bronze in autumn. Funnel-shaped star-like flowers, pale pink or white, open with or shortly after leaves, in late spring. Zones 4–8.

Rhododendron scopulorum

◐ ❊ ↔ 8 ft (2.4 m) ↕ 15 ft (4.5 m)
Native to southwestern China. Dark green grooved leaves; pale green, scaly below. Fragrant, white or pink, widely funnel-shaped flowers, in trusses of 2 to 7 blooms, mid- to late season. Zones 9–10.

Rhododendron sinogrande

◐ ❊ ↔ 30 ft (9 m) ↕ 50 ft (15 m)
Evergreen understory tree from western China and northern Myanmar. Long, dark green, heavily wrinkled leaves; silvery white, pale

brown, or tan coating underneath. Creamy white or yellow flowers, in trusses of 15 to 30 blooms, in mid-spring. Zones 8–9.

Rhododendron spinuliferum
☀ ❄ ↔ 8 ft (2.4 m) ↑ 10 ft (3 m)

Evergreen shrub native to western China. Smooth, dark purple-brown bark. Juvenile leaves hairy, mature leaves smooth. Narrow tubular flowers, crimson, brick red, or orange, in trusses of 1 to 5 blooms, in mid-spring. Zones 8–9.

Rhododendron stamineum
☀ ❄ ↔ 10 ft (3 m) ↑ 10 ft (3 m)

Evergreen shrub or small tree from western China. Smooth leaves. Trusses of 1 to 3 funnel-shaped blooms, white with yellow blotch, stamens longer than corolla, in mid- to late spring. Zones 9–10.

Rhododendron thomsonii
☀ ❄ ↔ 2–20 ft (0.6–6 m) ↑ 2–20 ft (0.6–6 m)

Evergreen species from Himalayas. Red-brown, fawn, or pink bark. Thick, leathery, rounded leaves. Bell-shaped flowers, red or crimson, darker spots, in trusses of 6 to 13 blooms, in spring. Zones 6–9.

Rhododendron tomentosum
syn. *Ledum palustre*
CRYSTAL TEA, MARSH LEDUM, WILD ROSEMARY
☀/❂ ❄ ↔ 3 ft (0.9 m) ↑ 1–4 ft (0.3–1.2 m)

Evergreen shrub from northern and central Europe, northern Asia, and northern North America. Red-brown hairs on young shoots; dark green leaves with incurved edges. Clusters of white flowers, at branch tips, in late spring–early summer. Zones 2–8.

Rhododendron trichostomum
☀ ❄ ↔ 3 ft (0.9 m) ↑ 5 ft (1.5 m)

Variable evergreen shrub from western China; normally compact, tiny, twiggy, intricately branched, miniature bush. Aromatic, stiff, narrow, leathery, dark green leaves. Tiny flowers white, pink, or rose, in spherical trusses of 8 to 20 blooms, in late spring. Zones 7–9.

Rhododendron veitchianum
☀ ❄ ↔ 8 ft (2.4 m) ↑ 8 ft (2.4 m)

Spreading evergreen shrub from Laos, Myanmar, Thailand, and Vietnam, often grows epiphytically. Smooth, peeling, reddish

brown bark. Dark green leaves, paler below. Large, highly fragrant, pure white, funnel-shaped flowers, yellow blotch, in trusses of up to 5 blooms, in late spring–early summer. **Cubittii Group**, bristle-edged leaves, fragrant pink flowers. Zones 9–10.

Rhododendron viscosum
SWAMP AZALEA, SWAMP HONEYSUCKLE
☀ ❄ ↔ 8 ft (2.4 m) ↑ 8 ft (2.4 m)

Deciduous azalea native to eastern and central North America. New leaf growth yellowish or grayish brown. Dark green leaves, paler below. Funnel-shaped white flowers, spicy fragrance, in trusses of 4 to 9 blooms, in late spring–early summer. Zones 4–9.

Rhododendron wardii
☀ ❄ ↔ 15 ft (4.5 m) ↑ 25 ft (8 m)

Evergreen shrub from western China. Grayish brown bark. Leaves leathery, dark green, rounded; pale green, glaucous below. Saucer-shaped pale yellow or bright yellow flowers, in loose trusses of 5 to 14 blooms, in late spring. Zones 7–9.

Rhododendron schlippenbachii

Rhododendron williamsianum
☀ ❄ ↔ 4 ft (1.2 m) ↑ 5 ft (1.5 m)

Evergreen shrub native to western China. Bristly young shoots, rounded leaves, reddish glands beneath. Bell-shaped flowers, pale pink with darker spots, in 2s or 3s, in spring. Zones 7–9.

Rhododendron yedoense
KOREAN AZALEA, YODOGAWA AZALEA
☀ ❄ ↔ 3 ft (0.9 m) ↑ 3 ft (0.9 m)

Deciduous or semi-deciduous azalea from Korea. Compact densely branched shrub, foliage turns rich orange and crimson in autumn. Fragrant, double, funnel-shaped, lilac-purple flowers, in trusses of 2 to 4 blooms, in late spring. Originally named from this double-flowered cultivated form, wild plants subsequently named *R. y.* var. *poukhanense* ★, feature single pale to deep pink flowers. Zones 5–8.

Rhododendron zoelleri
☀ ↯ ↔ 3 ft (0.9 m) ↑ 6 ft (1.8 m)

Vireya rhododendron from New Guinea and Moluccas. Elliptic leaves. Large flowers of pinkish orange to yellow, in open trusses of up to 8 funnel-shaped blooms, in autumn–spring. Zones 10–11.

Rhododendron spinuliferum

Rhododendron williamsianum

Rhododendron, Hybrid Cultivar, Hardy Small,
'Chrysomanicum'

Rhododendron, Hybrid Cultivar, Hardy Medium,
'Purple Splendor'

Rhododendron, Hybrid Cultivar, Hardy Tall,
'Lem's Cameo'

Rhododendron Hybrid Cultivars

Rhododendron hybrids are cultivated as ornamental plants, valued
for their masses of colorful flowers and year-round foliage in a great
diversity of form; some are also sought-after for their attractive
textured bark and rich flower fragrance.

HARDY SMALL HYBRIDS

◑ ❋ ↔ 12–40 in (30–100 cm) ↕ 12–40 in (30–100 cm)
Variable group, ranging from those derived from tiny alpine species,
to dense mounding bushes with large leaves and upright flower
trusses. 'Blue Tit', small leaves, abundant grayish blue flowers;
'Bric-à-Brac', small, rounded, downy leaves, small white flowers
with faint pink markings on upper lobes, contrasting chocolate-
colored anthers; 'Carmen', dwarf form, less than 12 in (30 cm)
high, deep red bell-shaped flowers, in trusses of 2 to 5 blooms,
early to mid-season; 'Chevalier Félix de Sauvage', medium-sized
coral rose flowers with dark blotch in center, in trusses of 12
blooms, early to mid-season; 'Chikor', soft yellow flowers, delicate foliage turns red in winter; 'Chrysomanicum', bright buttercup yellow flowers, in trusses of 8 blooms, very early in season;
'Cilpenense', shiny deep forest green foliage, blush pink bell-shaped
flowers with deeper pink shading, early in season; 'Creeping Jenny'
(syn. 'Jenny'), bright red funnel-campanulate flowers, in large loose
trusses of 5 to 6 blooms, early to mid-season; 'Curlew', abundant
soft yellow flowers with green-brown markings; 'Dora Amateis',
pure white fragrant flowers, lightly spotted green, in trusses of
3 to 6 blooms, early to mid-season; 'Elizabeth', bright red funnel-
campanulate flowers, in loose trusses of 6 to 8 blooms, early to
mid-season; 'Ginny Gee', dark pink flowers shading to shell pink,
with white stripes, in trusses of 4 to 5 blooms, early to mid-season;
'Jingle Bells', orange flowers with red throat that fade to yellow,
mid-season; 'May Day', cerise or light scarlet funnel-shaped flowers,
in loose trusses of 8 blooms, early to mid-season; 'Ptarmigan',
delicate foliage, densely scaly underneath, broadly funnel-shaped
white flowers, in terminal clusters of several trusses of 2 to 3
blooms, early to mid-season; 'Ramapo', pinkish violet flowers,
early to mid-season, almost circular leaves with distinctive deep
metallic hue in winter; 'Scarlet Wonder', bright cardinal red bell-
shaped flowers with wavy edges, in trusses of 5 to 7 blooms, mid-
season; 'Snow Lady', dark green hairy leaves, white flowers with
dark anthers, early to mid-season. Zones 6–9.

HARDY MEDIUM HYBRIDS

◑ ❋ ↔ 2–6 ft (0.6–1.8 m) ↕ 3–6 ft (0.9–1.8 m)
Plants best suited to general cultivation; encompasses hundreds
of beautiful plants that bloom in full color range over entire flowering season. 'Blue Diamond', deep lilac-blue flowers, early to mid-
season; 'Bow Bells', cup-shaped light pink flowers, in loose trusses
of 4 to 7 blooms, early to mid-season; 'Creamy Chiffon', salmon-
orange buds, creamy yellow double flowers, mid- to late season;
'Fabia', scarlet flowers, shading to orange in tube, in drooping
trusses of bell-shaped blooms, mid-season; 'Furnivall's Daughter',
bright pink flowers with cherry blotch, in conical trusses of 15
blooms, mid-season; 'Goldflimmer', striking variegated foliage,
mauve flowers, late in season; 'Helene Schiffner', pure white flowers
with faint yellow to brown markings, in upright dome-shaped
trusses; 'Hotei', canary yellow bell-shaped flowers with darker
throat, in round trusses of 12 blooms, mid-season; 'Humming
Bird', deep pink to red bell-shaped flowers, in loose trusses of
4 to 5 blooms, early to mid-season; 'Lady Clementine Mitford'
(syn. 'Lady C. Mitford'), glossy green leaves covered with silver
hairs when young, soft peach pink flowers, darker at edges, slight
yellow eye, mid- to late season; 'Markeeta's Prize', leathery dark
green leaves, scarlet-red flowers, in trusses of 12 blooms, mid-season;
'Mrs A. T. de la Mare', large, white, upright flowers with faint green
blotch, in large dome-shaped trusses of 12 to 14 blooms, mid-
season; 'Mrs Furnivall', widely funnel-shaped light rose pink
flowers, paler at center, with conspicuous deep sienna blotch, in
large trusses, mid- to late season; 'President Roosevelt', strongly
variegated leaves, frilled flowers, white flushed red with bold red
edging, in medium-sized conical trusses, early to mid-season;
'Purple Splendor', very dark purple flowers, with blackish blotch,
in dome-shaped to spherical trusses, mid- to late season; 'Sappho',
medium-sized, white, widely funnel-shaped flowers with striking
deep maroon-black blotch, in large conical trusses, mid- to late
season; 'The Hon. Jean Marie de Montague' (syn. 'Jean Mary
Montague'), thick emerald green leaves, large bright scarlet flowers,
in dome-shaped trusses of 10 to 14 blooms, mid-season; 'Vanessa
Pastel', brick red flowers, changing to apricot then to deep cream,
with bronze-yellow throat, in trusses, mid- to late season; 'Winsome',
reddish winter buds open to rosy cerise flowers, mid-season; 'Yellow
Hammer', small, light green, scaly leaves, very deep yellow tubular
flowers, in trusses of 3 blooms, early to mid-season. Zones 6–9.

HARDY TALL HYBRIDS

☀ ❄ ↔ 5–17 ft (1.5–5 m) ↑ 6–35 ft (1.8–10 m)

After many years, taller hybrids eventually become tree-like and demand more space. 'Anna Rose Whitney', large mid-green leaves, upright trusses of deep pink flowers; 'Betty Wormald', pastel pink flowers, paler center and light purple spotting, in huge dome-shaped trusses, late season; 'Crest' (syn. 'Hawk Crest'), bright primrose yellow flowers, slightly dark around throat, in large dome-shaped trusses, mid-season; 'Cunningham's White', white flowers, yellowish green at center; 'David', deep red bell-shaped flowers, frilly margins, in loose trusses, early to mid-season; 'Fastuosum Flore Pleno', medium-sized, semi-double, mauve flowers, in loose trusses, mid- to late season; 'Gomer Waterer', white flowers open from slightly pink-tinged buds, mid- to late season; 'Lem's Cameo', widely bell-shaped, apricot-cream and pink flowers, with small scarlet blotch, in large dome-shaped trusses of about 20 blooms, mid-season; 'Loder's White', slightly fragrant flowers, white, edged pale lilac, yellow tinge in throat, in large conical trusses, mid-season; 'Mrs Charles E. Pearson', pale pinkish mauve flowers edged lavender, heavy chestnut spotting, in large conical trusses, mid- to late season; 'Mrs G. W. Leak', bright pink flowers, deep reddish carmine blotch, crimson markings, in large, compact, conical trusses, early to mid-season; 'Scintillation', pastel pink flowers, yellowish brown flare in throat, in large trusses of about 15 blooms, mid-season; 'Sir Charles Lemon', white flowers faintly spotted in throat, in large round trusses, early to mid-season; 'Souvenir de Doctor S. Endtz', rose pink buds open to pink funnel-shaped flowers, marked with crimson ray, in domed trusses of 15 to 17 blooms, mid-season; 'Susan', lavender flowers fade to nearly white, dark margins, purple spots, in rounded trusses of about 12 blooms, mid-season; 'Taurus', large trusses of bright red flowers, faint black spotting. Zones 6–9.

TENDER HYBRIDS

☀/☀ ❄ ↔ 3–10 ft (0.9–3 m) ↑ 3–17 ft (0.9–5 m)

Lowland southern Asian hybrids intolerant of heavy or repeated frosts; large colorful flowers, often also heavy fragrance and lush foliage. 'Countess of Haddington' (syn. 'Eureka Maid'), fragrant white flowers flushed rose, in loose trusses, mid- to late season; 'Fragrantissimum', large, perfumed, white, trumpet-shaped flowers, tinged pink, in loose trusses, early to mid-season; 'Princess Alice' (syn. 'Caerhays Princess Alice'), fragrant white flowers, flushed pink, in loose trusses, early to mid-season. Zones 9–10.

VIREYA HYBRIDS

☀/☀ ✛ ↔ 12–60 in (30–150 cm) ↑ 18–72 in (45–180 cm)

Hybrids of tropical Southeast Asian species, featuring vivid coloration, fragrant flowers, non-seasonal flowering. 'Bold Janus', very large, lightly perfumed, apricot flowers, edged pink; 'Coral Flare', large coral pink flowers, in trusses of 3 to 7 blooms, throughout year; 'Cristo Rey', orange flowers, yellow center; 'Dresden Doll', waxy, heavily veined, lime green leaves, deep salmon pink flowers with cream throat; 'Littlest Angel', petite, waxy, deep red flowers, in trusses of 4 blooms; 'Ne Plus Ultra', bright red, tubular, funnel-shaped flowers, in trusses of 8 to 14 blooms, waxy foliage; 'Popcorn', trusses of 10 to 14 pale cream flowers, with white lobes; 'Princess Alexandra', open trusses of tubular, medium-sized, slightly flared white flowers, sometimes with blush of pale pink. Zones 10–12.

YAK HYBRIDS

☀ ❄ ↔ 2–5 ft (0.6–1.5 m) ↑ 1–6 ft (0.3–1.8 m)

Hybrids in which dominant parent is *R. degronianum* subsp. *yakushimanum*. Low growing, very hardy, attractive foliage; abundant flowers, usually in combinations of pink and white. 'Bashful', camellia pink flowers, deeper shades of rose, reddish brown blotch, early in season; 'Doc', rose pink flowers with deeper rims and spots on upper lobes, in rounded trusses of 9 blooms, mid-season; 'Dopey', glossy, red, bell-shaped flowers, paler toward edges, dark brown spots on upper lobes, in spherical trusses of 16 blooms, mid-season; 'Golden Torch', soft yellow flowers, in compact trusses of 13 to 15 blooms, mid- to late season; 'Grumpy', orange buds open to creamy flowers tinged pink, in rounded trusses of 11 blooms, mid-season; 'Hoppy', white flowers with greenish speckling, in ball-shaped trusses of 18 blooms, mid-season; 'Hydon Dawn', flowers with pink frilled petals fading toward edges, with reddish brown spots, in large, compact, rounded trusses of 14 to 18 blooms, mid-season; 'Percy Wiseman', pink funnel-shaped flowers fade to white, with pale yellow center and orange spots, in trusses of 14 blooms, mid-season; 'Peste's Blue Ice', deep purplish pink flowers fade to very pale purple, lightly spotted green, in trusses of 21 blooms, mid-season; 'Polaris', abundant pinkish purple flowers, lighter shading at center; 'Renoir', deeply bell-shaped rose pink flowers with white throat and crimson spots, in rounded trusses of 11 blooms, mid-season; 'Surrey Heath', rose pink flowers with lighter center, mid-season; 'Titian Beauty', turkey red flowers, mid-season. Zones 7–9.

Rhododendron, Hybrid Cultivar, Tender, 'Countess of Haddington'

Rhododendron, Hybrid Cultivar, Vireya, 'Cristo Rey'

Rhododendron, Hybrid Cultivar, Yak, 'Grumpy'

DECIDUOUS AZALEA HYBRIDS

Deciduous azaleas are multi-stemmed from the ground, never forming a central trunk. The leaves are thin, and the large, often sticky, winter buds contain both the flowers and the spring foliage flush. Flowers are trumpet-shaped, flaring from a narrow tube, and are mostly in shades of cream to salmon, yellow, orange, and scarlet. Deciduous azaleas bloom in spring with or before the new leaves; if they are to flower well, they need a climate with fairly cold winters.

GHENT HYBRIDS

✳ ✺ ↔ 3–6 ft (0.9–1.8 m) ↑ 5–8 ft (1.5–2.4 m)
Very hardy hybrids; large bushes flower in late spring–early summer, with large trusses of small blooms, up to 2 in (5 cm) wide, often fragrant, with long tubes, mostly single, but occasionally double. 'Coccineum Speciosum', bright orange-red flowers; 'Daviesii', fragrant white flowers with yellow flare; 'Narcissiflorum', double yellow flowers, shaded darker at center and on petal reverse; 'Vulcan', deep red flowers with orange blotch. Zones 5–9.

ILAM AND MELFORD HYBRIDS

✳/✺ ✺ ↔ 4–7 ft (1.2–2 m) ↑ 4–10 ft (1.2–3 m)
Bred in New Zealand; Knap Hill and Exbury hybrids crossed with *R. calendulaceum*, *R. viscosum*, and *R. molle* to create larger fragrant flowers. 'Gallipoli', apricot flowers with orange markings; 'Ilam Ming', orange flowers with yellow flare; 'Yellow Beauty', golden yellow flowers with faintly spotted orange blotch. Zones 5–9.

KNAP HILL AND EXBURY HYBRIDS

✳/✺ ✺ ↔ 4–7 ft (1.2–2 m) ↑ 4–10 ft (1.2–3 m)
Large bushy shrubs; leaves of most turn bronze then red or yellow before falling in autumn. Large, open, sometimes fragrant, richly colored flowers, up to 4 in (10 cm) wide, in large trusses of up to 30 blooms. 'Berryrose', fragrant orange-red flowers with vivid yellow blotch; 'Cannon's Double', low-growing cultivar, creamy yellow flowers; 'Gibraltar', bright orange-red flowers; 'Homebush', semi-double crimson-pink flowers; 'Hotspur Red', deep orange flowers, almost red; 'Klondyke', deep golden orange flowers with orange-yellow blotch; 'Satan', brilliant red flowers; 'Silver Slipper', snow white flowers, flushed pink, with yellow flare. Zones 5–9.

Rhododendron, Hybrid Cultivar, Deciduous Azalea, Mollis, 'Christopher Wren'

MOLLIS HYBRIDS

✳/✺ ✺ ↔ 5–7 ft (1.5–2 m) ↑ 5–8 ft (1.5–2.4 m)
Ghent hybrids crossed with *R. molle* and *R. molle* subsp. *japonicum*; large hardy shrubs, with single sometimes fragrant flowers to 2 in (5 cm) wide, from mid-spring, in creams, yellows, oranges, and reds. Difficult to propagate from cuttings; buy seedlings when in flower. 'Christopher Wren', large yellow flowers with strong orange blotch; 'Doctor M. Oosthoek', vivid reddish orange flowers, lighter blotch; 'Spek's Orange', deep orange buds open to orange-red flowers; 'Winston Churchill', orange-red flowers. Zones 6–9.

OCCIDENTALE HYBRIDS

✳/✺ ✺ ↔ 6–10 ft (1.8–3 m) ↑ 6–10 ft (1.8–3 m)
Mollis hybrids crossed with *R. occidentale*; usually forming broad spreading shrub with white or pale pink fragrant flowers, to 3 in (8 cm) wide, open after leaves in mid-spring. Deep yellow blotch on flowers. Slow growing; most heat-, drought-, and humidity-tolerant of all deciduous azaleas. 'Delicatissimum', pink-flushed white to cream flowers, orange flare; 'Exquisitum', frilled, fragrant, pale pink flowers, orange flare, darker reddish buds; 'Magnificum', white to yellow flowers flushed pink, yellow flare. Zones 7–10.

EVERGREEN AZALEA HYBRIDS

Evergreen azalea hybrids are multi-stemmed plants. Leaves are of 2 types: spring leaves surround flowerheads and are crowded at the ends of the previous year's shoots; the summer growth flush produces longer leaves, more widely spaced on the branchlet. Flowers are widely funnel-shaped, in shades from white to pink, red, and purple, often bicolored. Most of these azaleas flower well in warmer temperate climates where winter frost is mild or even absent.

BELGIAN INDICA HYBRIDS

✳/✺ ✺ ↔ 3–6 ft (0.9–1.8 m) ↑ 2–5 ft (0.6–1.5 m)
Hybrids using *R. simsii*; damaged by repeated frosts. Compact heavy-flowering plants, among most widely grown azaleas. 'Advent Bells' (syns 'Adventglocke', 'Chimes'), strong purple-red, semi-double, cup-shaped flowers; 'Comtesse de Kerchove', soft pink, medium-sized, double flowers edged white; 'Eri Schaume', coral pink double flowers edged white; 'Helmut Vogel', long-flowering shrub, purplish red semi-double or double flowers; 'James Belton', white to pale pink flowers, darker pink stamens; 'Leopold Astrid', large, frilled, double, white flowers bordered rose red; 'Red Wings', ruffled hose-in-hose deep red blooms, long flowering, compact sun-tolerant shrub. Zones 8–11.

RUTHERFORD INDICA HYBRIDS

✳/✺ ❂ ↔ 4–8 ft (1.2–2.4 m) ↑ 3–8 ft (0.9–2.4 m)
Larger than Belgian hybrids, many have hose-in-hose flowers with ruffled or frilled petals, in reddish orange, pinks, purples, and white. 'Firelight', bright red flowers; 'Gloria USA', semi-double hose-in-hose flowers, salmon pink or white, red throat, white petal margins; 'Purity', white flowers; 'Rose Queen', deep purplish pink, semi-double, hose-in-hose flowers, white throat, darker blotch; 'White Gish', to 3 ft (0.9 m) high, white, semi-double, hose-in-hose flowers, greenish yellow markings; 'White Prince', white, semi-double, hose-in-hose flowers, red throat, sometimes flushed pink. Zones 9–11.

SOUTHERN INDICA HYBRIDS

☼/◐ ❄ ↔6–12 ft (1.8–3.5 m) ↕5–10 ft (1.5–3 m)

Vigorous sun-tolerant plants, hardier than Belgian hybrids. Early flowering, usually with single flowers, 2 in (5 cm) wide, in shades of pink, red, and dark purple; flowers sometimes striped. No hose-in-hose forms in this group. 'Alphonse Anderson', pale pink flowers, darker blotch; 'Brilliantina' (syn. 'Brilliant'), deep pink flowers, purple-red blotch; 'Duc de Rohan', salmon flowers, rose throat; 'Exquisite', fragrant lilac-pink flowers; 'Glory of Sunninghill', large, single, orange-red flowers; 'Pride of Dorking', carmine or deep pink flowers, bronze-red and orange forms available; 'Redwing', cerise flowers; 'Snow Prince', rounded bush, abundant flowers, mostly white; 'Splendens', salmon pink flowers. Zones 8–11.

KAEMPFERI OR MALVATICA HYBRIDS

☼/◐ ❄ ↔3–7 ft (0.9–2 m) ↕2–8 ft (0.6–2.4 m)

Late spring- or early summer-flowering hybrids from cross between hardy *R. kaempferi* and *R.* 'Malvaticum'. Large flowers mostly single, occasionally double or hose-in-hose, and tend to fade in full sunlight. 'Blue Danube', strong purplish pink flowers, deep purplish red midrib, deep red blotches; 'Cleopatra', upright shrub, deep pink flowers; 'Double Beauty', pink hose-in-hose flowers, mid-season; 'Fedora', deep purplish pink flowers; 'John Cairns', orange-red flowers; 'Othello', red flowers; 'Orange King', reddish orange flowers; 'Sunrise', reddish orange flowers. Zones 6–10.

Vuyk Hybrids

☼/◐ ❄ ↔3–7 ft (0.9–2 m) ↕2–8 ft (0.6–2.4 m)

Developed from original Kaempferi hybrids; very similar to them but more compact. Some Mollis azalea parentage initially suggested, now seems unlikely. 'Palestrina', snow white flowers, light green throat; 'Vuyk's Rosyred', deep pink-red flowers; 'Vuyk's Scarlet', vivid red flowers. Zones 6–10.

KURUME HYBRIDS

☼/◐ ❄ ↔2–4 ft (0.6–1.2 m) ↕2–4 ft (0.6–1.2 m)

Large, normally single flowers, in shades of pink or white, appear early to mid-season in wide range of strong colors, including pinks, reds, and purples; occasionally striped or "freckled," sometimes hose-in-hose, flowering abundantly. Hardy, slow growing; best planted in fully exposed positions. 'Fairy Queen' (syn. 'Aioi'), small, semi-double, hose-in-hose, almond-blossom pink flowers; 'Hatsugiri', vivid reddish purple flowers, pink spotting in throat; 'Hinomayo', strong purplish pink flowers; 'Irohayama', white flowers, pale lavender at edges; 'Kasane-kagaribi' (syn. 'Rositi'), shrub with low, dense, spreading growth, yellowish to salmon pink flowers; 'Kure-no-yuki', white hose-in-hose flowers; 'Mother's Day', dense low-growing bush, abundant cherry red colored flowers; 'Seikai' (syn. 'Madonna'), white, semi-double, hose-in-hose flowers; 'Taka-sago' (syn. 'Cherryblossom'), white hose-in-hose flowers, flushed with deep red or pale pink, dark spots; 'Vida Brown', pink-red hose-in-hose flowers; 'Ward's Ruby', blood red flowers, less hardy than other Kurume azaleas. Zones 7–10.

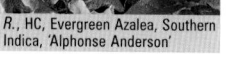

R., HC, Evergreen Azalea, Southern Indica, 'Alphonse Anderson'

R., HC, Evergreen Azalea, Kaempferi, Vuyk, 'Palestrina'

SATSUKI HYBRIDS

☼/◐ ❄ ↔24–48 in (60–120 cm) ↕12–36 in (30–90 cm)

Late-flowering, low-growing, spreading plants cultivated for centuries in Japan, most likely originate from crosses between *R. indicum* and *R. eriocarpum* or *R. simsii*. Valued in Japan for their landscaping qualities and were also traditionally used for bonsai and container cultivation. Gumpo series of dwarf plants useful in rockeries. 'Banzai', white flowers flushed with pink; 'Gumpo', large white flowers with petals wavy-edged; 'Gumpo Lavender', large, single, lavender flowers; 'Gumpo Pink', ruffled, single, pink flowers edged with white; 'Gumpo Salmon', ruffled salmon pink flowers; 'Gumpo Stripe', white flowers with mauve-red stripes and flecks; 'Gumpo White' pretty frilly white flowers; 'Gyoten', single flowers, up to 3 in (8 cm) across, pale pink with white edges, yellowish blotch and often with random red or white stripes; 'Hitoya-no-Haru', large lilac-pink flowers, olive green spotting in throat; 'Kunpu', pale pink, wavy-edged, single flowers, 2½ in (6 cm) in diameter; 'Man-saku', salmon pink flowers, rounded wavy petals; 'Nani-Wagata', abundant white flowers; 'Osakazuki', smallish, deep pink, single blooms, darker blotch in throat; 'Otome', white and pink flowers; 'Shin-Kyo', light salmon pink flowers, 'Shinnyo-no-Hikari', white flowers with green throat; 'White Shiko', white flowers with green blaze. Zones 7–11.

Rhododendron, HC, Evergreen Azalea, Belgian Indica, 'Eri Schaume'

AZALEODENDRON HYBRIDS

☼/◐ ❄ ↔2–7 ft (0.6–2 m) ↕2–8 ft (0.6–2.4 m)

Group of hybrids lies between deciduous azaleas and other (evergreen) rhododendrons; usually semi-evergreen, flowering in summer, sometimes have fragrant flowers. 'Broughtonii Aureum', yellow flowers; 'Dot', salmon pink flowers; 'Glory of Littleworth', cream flowers, flushed orange; 'Govenianum', deep mauve fragrant flowers; 'Hardijzer Beauty', purplish pink flowers; 'Martine', soft pink flowers; 'Ria Hardijzer', deep pink-red flowers. Zones 8–10.

RHODOLEIA

There is some doubt about the number of species in this genus, in the witchhazel (Hamamelidaceae) family. Some authorities consider that there is just a single variable species in several countries, from southern China to Indonesia, others have recognized up to 7 species. Most, if not all, of the plants in cultivation seem to have originated from material collected in Hong Kong. The range of variability within the species is not evident and the "other" species are not at all well known. All the forms are very similar: they are small evergreen trees with thick dark green leaves that are paler on the underside, and pendent bunches of reddish flowers surrounded by reddish bracts during spring.

CULTIVATION: These plants are somewhat frost tolerant and should be grown in a well-drained, acid, sandy soil to which plenty of organic matter has been added. Conditions should be the same as for azaleas and camellias. Propagate from seed or cuttings.

Rhus lancea

Rhodoleia championii

◐ ❄ ↔ 12 ft (3.5 m) ↕ 20 ft (6 m)

Variable species from southern China to Indonesia. Forms small tree. Thick oval leaves, whitish underside. Stems and leaf stalks yellowish red. Pendent bunches of pinkish red flowerheads in late winter–early spring. **Zones 8–11.**

RHUS

SUMAC

There are about 200 species of deciduous or evergreen trees, shrubs, and climbers in this genus within the cashew (Anacardiaceae) family. Widely distributed throughout the temperate and subtropical regions of the world, they are used to produce laquer, dyes, tannin, wax, and drinks. *Rhus* species are mainly grown in the garden for their good autumn color, interesting foliage, and fruit, which can persist on the tree into winter and often drop off only when the new leaves appear.

CULTIVATION: They grow in full sun in moderately fertile, moist, but free-draining soil with shelter from wind. Propagate from root cuttings in winter, half-hardened stem cuttings in late summer, or divided root suckers when the plant is dormant. Sow seed in autumn. Feed and water well in the growing season; do not feed in winter.

Rhus aromatica

FRAGRANT SUMAC, LEMON SUMACH, POLECAT BUSH

☼ ❄ ↔ 5 ft (1.5 m) ↕ 3–5 ft (0.9–1.5 m)

Suckering deciduous shrub native to eastern North America. Palmate leaves, oval toothed leaflets, aromatic. Small yellow flowers, in panicles, in spring. Round red fruit. 'Gro-Low' ★, to 2 ft (0.6 m) high, fragrant deep yellow flowers. **Zones 3–9.**

Rhodoleia championii

Rhus chinensis

CHINESE GALL, NUTGALL

☼ ❄ ↔ 15 ft (4.5 m) ↕ 20 ft (6 m)

Erect deciduous tree native to Japan and China. Leaves compound, mid-green, 3 to 7 oblong leaflets, scalloped edges, turn red in autumn. White conical clusters of flowers appear in late summer–early autumn. Rounded scarlet fruit. **Zones 8–11.**

Rhus copallina

DWARF SUMAC, MOUNTAIN SUMAC, SHINING SUMAC

☼ ❄ ↔ 5 ft (1.5 m) ↕ 5 ft (1.5 m)

Erect deciduous shrub from eastern North America. Dark green pinnate leaves, 15 lance-shaped leaflets, winged stalks. Yellowish green flowers, on upright panicles, in summer. Rounded red fruit. Foliage turns red in autumn. **Zones 5–9.**

Rhus glabra

SCARLET SUMAC, SMOOTH SUMAC, VINEGAR TREE

☼ ❄ ↔ 8 ft (2.4 m) ↕ 8 ft (2.4 m)

Bushy deciduous shrub from North America and Mexico. Bronze-colored stems, whitish bloom. Pinnate leaves, deep blue-green leaflets, turn rich red in autumn. Dense upright panicles of greenish red flowers in summer. Round, crimson, hairy fruit. **Zones 2–9.**

Rhus lancea

KAREE, WILLOW RHUS

☼ ◗ ↔ 25 ft (8 m) ↕ 25 ft (8 m)

Evergreen tree native to South Africa. Leaves dark green above, paler below, 3 lance-shaped leaflets. Tiny yellow-green flowers in late summer. Fruit glossy brown. **Zones 9–11.**

Rhus lucida

☼ ◗ ↔ 12 ft (3.5 m) ↕ 12 ft (3.5 m)

Evergreen tree or shrub from South Africa. Leaves 3 shiny dark green leaflets. Off-white flowers in spring. Small, glossy, brown fruit. **Zones 9–11.**

Rhus microphylla

CORREOSA, DESERT SUMAC, SCRUB SUMAC

☼ ❄ ↔ 4–6 ft (1.2–1.8 m) ↕ 6–10 ft (1.8–3 m)

Rounded deciduous shrub from southern USA and northern Mexico. Compound leaves with up to 9 leaflets; usually evergreen but can

Ribes sanguineum

shed leaves in cold or dry conditions. Tight spikes of tiny white flowers in spring. Tiny orange-red fruit. Zones 8–11.

Rhus pendulina
syn. *Rhus viminalis*
☼ ⁑ ↔ 15 ft (4.5 m) ↑ 15 ft (4.5 m)
Evergreen South African tree or shrub, willow-like in habit. Trifoliate leaves, lance-shaped leaflets. Light green flowers in summer. Small oblong fruit. Zones 9–11.

Rhus typhina
STAGHORN SUMAC, STAG'S HORN SUMAC
☼ ❋ ↔ 15 ft (4.5 m) ↑ 15 ft (4.5 m)
Deciduous tree or shrub from eastern North America. Can reach 30 ft (9 m) high in wild. Pinnate leaves, up to 31 dark green leaflets, turn flame red in autumn. Green-yellow flowers in summer. Felty red fruit. 'Dissecta', finely divided leaves. Zones 3–9.

RIBES
CURRANT
Mainly from the northern temperate regions, with some species native to South America, this genus of around 150 species of shrubs is in the gooseberry (Grossulariaceae) family. Some are ornamental; others are grown for their fruit. They are usually deciduous, with twiggy or wiry stems. Usually with 3 to 5 lobes, the leaves often have scalloped or toothed edges and bristly hairs. The flowers are small, sometimes in racemes, followed by often bristly, many-seeded, frequently edible berries. Some species are important commercial or home garden crops.
CULTIVATION: Some species are not self-fertile and must be planted in groups to ensure good fruiting. Apart from this, and the need for some winter chilling, most *Ribes* plants are quite easily grown, requiring little more than a well-drained soil, moisture in summer, and some shade from the very hottest summer sun. Both rust and mildew can cause problems with some species, but disease-resistant cultivars are often available. Propagation is from seed or cuttings, or by layering.

Ribes alpinum
ALPINE CURRANT, MOUNTAIN CURRANT
☼ ❋ ↔ 3 ft (0.9 m) ↑ 3–6 ft (0.9–1.8 m)
Deciduous shrub found in Europe and extending to North Africa. Smooth purple-red stems, leaves usually 3-lobed. Erect racemes of tiny yellow-green flowers in spring. Bitter red fruit. 'Aureum', yellow-green young growth; 'Green Mound', non-fruiting low-growing form; 'Pumilum', low and spreading with small leaves; 'Schmidt', slower growing, smaller than species. Zones 2–9.

Ribes aureum
GOLDEN CURRANT, GOLDEN FLOWERING CURRANT
☼ ❋ ↔ 6 ft (1.8 m) ↑ 6 ft (1.8 m)
Deciduous bush from western USA and northwestern Mexico. Leaves 3-lobed, coarsely toothed. Pendent racemes of strongly scented yellow flowers in spring. Fruit purple-black. *R. a.* var. *gracillimum*, unscented red flowers. Zones 2–9.

Ribes fasciculatum
CLUSTERED REDCURRANT
☼ ❋ ↔ 4 ft (1.2 m) ↑ 5 ft (1.5 m)
Deciduous shrub from temperate East Asia. Leaves rounded, downy, 3 to 5 lobes, toothed edges. Yellow flowers in spring; females scented. Smooth red fruit, yellow flesh. Plants of both sexes required for cropping. *R. f.* var. *chinense*, larger, leaves to 4 in (10 cm) long. Zones 5–9.

Ribes speciosum

Ribes magellanicum
☼ ❋ ↔ 6 ft (1.8 m) ↑ 6–8 ft (1.8–2.4 m)
Deciduous shrub from southern parts of Argentina and Chile. Leaves with 3 to 5 lobes. Drooping racemes of creamy yellow flowers, age to soft gold tone, in spring. Fruit red-black. Zones 8–10.

Ribes sanguineum
FLOWERING CURRANT, WINTER CURRANT
☼ ❋ ↔ 10 ft (3 m) ↑ 10 ft (3 m)
Deciduous shrub from western USA. Branches warm red-brown. Leaves dark green, 3 to 5 lobes, downy beneath. Pendent racemes of soft pink to red flowers in spring, before leaves. Fruit deep blue-black with white bloom. *R. s.* var. *glutinosum*, leaves less downy than species. *R. s.* 'Brocklebankii', clear pink scented flowers; 'Claremont', almost white flowers, ageing to deep pink; 'Elk River Red' ★, blooms bright rose red, very early in season, can become weedy; 'Inverness White', greenish white flowers in long sprays; 'King Edward VII', compact, with deep pink flowers; 'Plenum', red double flowers; 'Pulborough Scarlet', red flowers; 'Spring Showers', pink flowers; 'Tydeman's White', white flowers. Zones 6–10.

Ribes speciosum
FUCHSIA-FLOWERED CURRANT
☼ ❋ ↔ 10 ft (3 m) ↑ 12 ft (3.5 m)
Evergreen bushy upright shrub from California, USA. Thorny stems, small smooth leaves, 3 to 5 lobes, toothed edges. Flowers bright red, pendulous, with long red stamens; singly, pairs, or groups of 3, in summer. Fruit bristly and red. Zones 8–10.

Robinia × slavinii

Robinia viscosa

RICINOCARPOS

This genus, a member of the euphorbia (Euphorbiaceae) family, contains 16 species, 1 from New Caledonia, the others from eastern and southern Australia. All are woody shrubs that grow to 10 ft (3 m) tall, often less. Male and female flowers are separate, but appear in groups of a few males and 1 female. Male flowers have 5 white or pink petals with a bunch of united stamens in the center. Female flowers have smaller petals with a 3-celled ovary in the center. The fruit is relatively large, over ½ in (12 mm) wide. CULTIVATION: All species grow in acid sandy soils in various habitats. Frost hardiness varies, with western Australian species being the most tolerant. Propagation has been achieved using seed and cuttings. Treating seed with smoke or water may improve the rate of germination.

Ricinocarpos pinifolius
WEDDING BUSH

◗ ⦆ ↔ 3 ft (0.9 m) ↑ 3 ft (0.9 m)

Evergreen shrub occurring in all eastern States of Australia. Narrow leaves, margins rolled under. White flowers, to 1 in (25 mm) in diameter, in spring. Prefers soil that is extremely free-draining and acidic. Zones 9–11.

RICINUS

This single-species genus, a member of the euphorbia (Euphorbiaceae) family, comes from northeastern Africa, but has naturalized throughout the tropical regions of the world. Although it is technically a shrub, it is considered a prized annual in many cold-climate gardens (but a weed in warmer regions), and is grown for its deeply lobed and often colored leaves. CULTIVATION: R. communis requires fertile soil with ample organic matter added to ensure moisture retention and free drainage. This plant's brittle stems need to be protected from winds and frost. When grown from seed, care must be taken as the seed coats and other parts of the plant are extremely toxic.

Ricinus communis
CASTOR BEAN PLANT, CASTOR OIL PLANT

☼ ⦆ ↔ 3 ft (0.9 m) ↑ 5–15 ft (1.5–4.5 m)

Fast-growing evergreen shrub from northeastern Africa; can grow to 40 ft (12 m) high in wild. Somewhat brittle stems; distinctive, lobed, green leaves. Smaller-growing cultivars include 'Cambodgensis', purple-black stems, dark purple leaves; 'Red Spire', red stems, bronze-green foliage; and 'Zanzibarensis', taller, with large, white-veined, green leaves. Zones 9–12.

ROBINIA

The 20 or so species of deciduous trees and shrubs in this genus, in the pea-flower subfamily of the legume (Fabaceae) family, are found mainly in eastern USA. They bear pendulous racemes of white, cream, pink, or lavender pea-flowers, followed by flat seed pods. The leaves are pinnate, and are often quite large; some species have vivid yellow autumn colors. Stems may have fierce thorns. CULTIVATION: These tough adaptable plants grow quickly and tolerate most soil types provided they are well drained. They are, however, rather brittle, with branches that are prone to break or tear in strong winds. It is best to prune when young to establish a strongly branched structure. Some species sucker freely and the suckers can be used for propagation, otherwise they are propagated from stratified seed or cuttings. Special growth forms are usually grafted.

Ricinocarpos pinifolius

Robinia hispida
ROSE ACACIA

☼ ✳ ↔ 10 ft (3 m) ↑ 10 ft (3 m)

Large shrub from southeastern USA; dense and bushy, suckering. Branches covered in red bristles. Leaves with 7 to 15 leaflets, dark green above, gray-green below, bristles at tips. Flowers magenta to purple, in small racemes, in late spring. Zones 5–9.

Robinia pseudoacacia
BLACK LOCUST, FALSE ACACIA

☼ ✳ ↔ 35 ft (10 m) ↑ 50 ft (15 m)

Most widely grown robinia, parent of many cultivars, native to eastern and central USA. Thorny stems, red-tinted when young. Leaves with 19 bright green leaflets. White to cream flowers, in racemes, in summer. 'Appalachia', narrowly erect form; 'Aurea', greenish yellow spring foliage; 'Bessoniana', thornless rounded form; 'Coluteoides', very rounded, compact, with closely crowded leaflets; 'Frisia', bright golden foliage, thornless, few flowers; 'Inermis', thornless form, upright habit; 'Tortuosa', twisted branches; 'Umbraculifera', rounded form, dense foliage. Zones 3–10.

Robinia × slavinii

☼ ✳ ↔ 10 ft (3 m) ↑ 15 ft (4.5 m)

Shrubby hybrid between R. kelseyi and R. pseudoacacia. Leaves deep green and pinnate; rose pink racemes in spring. 'Hillieri', tree-like growth habit, pink flowers with distinct mauve tint. Zones 5–9.

Robinia viscosa

CLAMMY LOCUST

☼ ❋ ↔ 20 ft (6 m) ↑ 30 ft (9 m)

Deciduous tree native to southeastern USA. Sticky, dark brown, young stems with thorns. Leaves composed of 13 to 25 dark green leaflets, gray hairs beneath. Flowers pink with yellow markings, in tightly packed racemes, in late spring. Zones 3–10.

ROELLA

This genus, a member of the bellflower (Campanulaceae) family, consists of about 30 species, all from the Cape region of South Africa. They are perennials or small evergreen shrubs, mostly with slender branchlets clothed in small leaves, and attractive bell-shaped flowers borne singly or in short spikes at the branch tips.

CULTIVATION: At least 1 species was introduced to greenhouse cultivation in Europe by the late eighteenth century, part of the fad for Cape plants that continued to the mid-nineteenth century. Their requirements are similar to those of the Cape ericas, namely a gritty acid soil with perfect drainage, and a constant supply of moisture. Propagate from seed or tip cuttings.

Roella ciliata

☼ ❀ ↔ 2 ft (0.6 m) ↑ 3 ft (0.9 m)

Slender erect shrub native to South Africa's Western Cape. Small pointed leaves, bristle-haired edges. Large bell-shaped flowers, violet-blue petals, much darker blue zone in throat, at end of branches, in late spring–early summer. Zones 9–10.

ROLDANA

This genus of bushy daisies from Central America includes some 50-odd species and is a member of the daisy (Asteraceae) family. While many are annuals or perennials, the genus also includes a few shrubs. The leaves are usually large and rounded to hand-shaped with shallow lobes, dark green on top and often considerably lighter on the underside. The leaves and young stems are covered with fine hairs that can sometimes be dense enough to become felted. The flowers, which are most commonly bright yellow, are carried in corymbs and occur throughout the year if the climate is mild enough.

CULTIVATION: Many species are frost tender, though the hardiest of them will withstand light frosts and relatively cool winters. They prefer moist, well-drained, fertile soil and flower best if grown in sun. Foliage is often more luxuriant with a little shade. Propagate from seed or cuttings in general, but in some cases by division.

Roldana petasitis

syn. *Senecio petasitis*

☼ ❀ ↔ 6–10 ft (1.8–3 m) ↑ 6–10 ft (1.8–3 m)

Native to Central America. Leaves with 7 or more pointed lobes, densely felted beneath. Yellow daisy flowers in flat-topped corymbs or in spikes, in winter. Zones 9–11.

RONDELETIA

This small genus of evergreen shrubs and small trees in the madder (Rubiaceae) family, from Central America, is named for Professor Guillaume Rondelet, a sixteenth-century French naturalist. These

Roldana petasitis

shrubs and trees have opposite leaves and terminal or axillary inflorescences of red, yellow, pink, or white tubular flowers that are rich in nectar.

CULTIVATION: *Rondeletia* species need a warm position in full sun, and may be damaged by frost. A light friable soil that drains freely is ideal. Pruning should be moderately severe after flowering, with flowering shoots cut back to within several nodes of the previous season's growth. Propagation is from half-hardened leafy tip cuttings, 2–4 in (5–10 cm) long, which can be taken during spring.

Rondeletia amoena

☼ ❀ ↔ 8 ft (2.4 m) ↑ 10 ft (3 m)

Native to Mexico and Central America. Evergreen shrub, many erect stems rising from base. Dense foliage, leaves pale bronze-green, ageing to dark glossy green above, hairy below. Small salmon pink flowers, in terminal cymes, faint perfume, in spring. Zones 10–12.

Rondeletia odorata

FRAGRANT RONDELETIA

☼ ✿ ↔ 3 ft (0.9 m) ↑ 5 ft (1.5 m)

From Panama. Small evergreen shrub; upright, vase-shaped. Leaves elliptic-ovate, dark velvety green above, reddish green below. Flowers in terminal clusters, orange-scarlet to crimson, bright yellow throat, sweetly fragrant, in late summer–autumn. Zones 11–12.

Rondeletia odorata

ROSA

ROSE

Rosa is one of the most widely grown and best loved of all plant genera. It belongs to the large rose (Rosaceae) family, which includes favorite fruiting plants such as apples, plums, and strawberries as well as ornamentals. Since ancient times roses have been valued for their beauty and fragrance as well as for their medicinal, culinary, and cosmetic properties. There are 100 to 150 species of rose, ranging in habit from erect and arching shrubs to scramblers and climbers. Most species are deciduous and have prickles or bristles. They are found in temperate and subtropical zones of the Northern Hemisphere; none are native to the Southern Hemisphere.

The pinnate leaves are usually comprised of 5 to 9, sometimes more, serrated-edged leaflets. Flowers range from single, usually 5-petalled, blooms to those with many closely packed petals. They are borne singly or in clusters. Many are intensely fragrant. Most species and old garden roses flower only once, but many modern cultivars are repeat-blooming. Rose fruit (hips or heps) are rich in vitamin C. They are usually orangey red, but can be dark. They may be small and in clusters or single large fruits.

Roses have been bred for many centuries and are divided into recognized groups. Old garden roses were originally bred from a handful of species and include groups such as Gallica and Alba. In the late eighteenth century the repeat-flowering China rose *(R. chinensis)* arrived in Europe and subsequent cross-breeding extended the number of Old Rose groups further. The Tea Roses, also repeat-flowering, followed in the nineteenth century, and 50 years later a Frenchman bred the first Large-flowered Rose, heralding the start of modern rose breeding. Large-flowered, Polyantha, Cluster-flowered, and Shrub Roses proliferated in the twentieth century. While most of the species and Old Roses are in shades of pink, red, purple, or white, modern rose-breeding programs have seen the color range increase to include shades of yellow and orange. CULTIVATION: Roses can be grown in separate beds or mixed borders, as ground covers, climbing up arches and pergolas, scrambling up trees, as hedging, and in containers. Roses generally require a site that is sunny for most of the day, as shade inhibits flowering. They should not be overcrowded and there should be good air movement around the plants, factors that help reduce the risk of disease. Roses will grow in most well-drained medium-loamy soils in which compost or organic manure has been incorporated. When planting,

the point at which the plant is grafted should be about 1 in (25 mm) below the soil. Granular or liquid rose fertilizer can be applied once or twice a year from spring. Plants should be watered well in dry periods and a mulch will help to conserve moisture in summer.

Prune roses to maintain healthy growth, a good shape, and to let light into the plant. Various pruning regimes are promoted for different rose groups, but recent research has shown that a simple "tidying up" of dead wood may be just as effective. Most pruning is done when the plants are dormant in winter. Repeat-flowering roses should be deadheaded to encourage further blooms.

Fungal diseases such as rust, black spot, and mildew can be a problem, particularly in humid areas. Insect pests can also be troublesome, the most common being aphids. Others include spider mites, thrips, leafhoppers, froghoppers, and scale. Fungicidal and insecticidal sprays, both chemical and organic, are available to combat these problems. Roses planted in a position previously occupied by another rose can suffer rose sickness—to prevent this, replace a generous amount of the old soil with a fresh supply.

Most roses are very hardy and indeed benefit from a period of winter cold, but some of the old Tea Roses are a little tender and are better suited to warm-temperate climates. In warm areas roses often grow much larger than their cool-climate counterparts and can be more prone to problems caused by mild winters not killing off pests and diseases. Propagation in commercial quantities is usually from budding, but the gardener can take hardwood cuttings in autumn or softwood cuttings in summer. While hybrid plants will not come true from seed, the species can be propagated in this way. Seed will need to be stratified before planting.

Rosa acicularis

✳ ❊ ↔ 4 ft (1.2 m) ↕ 6 ft (1.8 m)

Widespread species, found throughout northern areas of Europe, Asia, and America. Lax shrub, densely packed bristles of varying lengths, grayish green foliage. Mildly fragrant, single, deep pink flowers in summer. Hips bright red, pear-shaped. Zones 2–9.

Rosa beggeriana

✳ ❊ ↔ 8 ft (2.4 m) ↕ 8 ft (2.4 m)

Deciduous shrub from central Asia. Grayish green leaves. Small white flowers, in clusters of 8 or more at end of new shoots, in mid-summer. Small, round, reddish hips. Zones 4–9.

Rosa canina

Rosa davurica

Rosa eglanteria

Rosa blanda

HUDSON BAY ROSE, MEADOW ROSE, SMOOTH ROSE

☼ ❄ ↔ 3 ft (0.9 m) ↑ 3–7 ft (0.9–2 m)

Brown-stemmed shrub from eastern and central North America, similar to *R. canina*. Few prickles near base; dull green leaves. Mildly fragrant, single, mid-pink flowers in summer. Ovoid to pear-shaped red hips. Zones 3–9.

Rosa californica

☼ ❄ ↔ 6 ft (1.8 m) ↑ 7 ft (2 m)

From west of Sierra Nevadas in USA south to Baja California, Mexico. Stout prickles on stems; leaves mid-green. Single, slightly fragrant, pink flowers, in clusters, in summer. Round orange-red hips. *R. c. plena,* flowers deeper pink than species. Zones 5–10.

Rosa canina

COMMON BRIAR, DOG ROSE

☼ ❄ ↔ 10 ft (3 m) ↑ 10 ft (3 m)

Vigorous suckering shrub native to UK and Europe. Prickly stems; leaves with 5 to 7 leaflets. Scented flowers, single, pale or blush pink, occasionally white, in summer. Orangey red hips. Zones 3–10.

Rosa chinensis

CHINA ROSE

☼ ❄ ↔ 8 ft (2.4 m) ↑ 20 ft (6 m)

Variable species from China. Lustrous leaves, 3 to 5 leaflets. Single red, pink, or white flowers in summer. Hips greenish brown to scarlet. Zones 7–10.

Rosa cinnamomea plena

syn. *Rosa majalis*

CINNAMON ROSE, MAY ROSE

☼ ❄ ↔ 5 ft (1.5 m) ↑ 6 ft (1.8 m)

Deciduous shrub from central northeastern Europe. Purplish stems, downy grayish green leaves. Single to double flowers, mid- to purplish pink, in early summer. Elongated hips, dark red. Zones 6–10.

Rosa davurica

☼ ❄ ↔ 4 ft (1.2 m) ↑ 3–5 ft (0.9–1.5 m)

Deciduous shrub found in northeastern Asia and northern China. Small leaves, straight prickles. Groups of 1 to 3 pink flowers in summer. Small, oval, red hips. Zones 5–9.

Rosa ecae

☼ ❄ ↔ 4 ft (1.2 m) ↑ 4 ft (1.2 m)

Much-branched suckering shrub native to Afghanistan and Pakistan. Very prickly stems. Small, fern-like, aromatic leaves. Buttercup-sized yellow flowers in spring. Shiny red-brown hips. Zones 7–10.

Rosa eglanteria

syn. *Rosa rubiginosa*

BRIAR ROSE, EGLANTINE, SWEET BRIAR

☼ ❄ ↔ 10 ft (3 m) ↑ 10 ft (3 m)

Deciduous shrub from Europe and western Asia. Arching prickly stems, apple-scented leaves. Small, single, pink, fragrant flowers

Rosa gallica

Rosa foetida persiana

in summer. Ovoid orangey red hips. Considered weed in Australia, New Zealand, and North America. Zones 4–10.

Rosa elegantula

syn. *Rosa farreri*

☼ ❄ ↔ 8 ft (2.4 m) ↑ 3–7 ft (0.9–2 m)

Dense suckering shrub from northwestern China. Fern-like foliage, grayish green, turns purple and crimson shades in autumn. Small single flowers, white to rose pink, in summer. 'Persetosa', stems thickly covered in red bristles. Zones 6–10.

Rosa foetida

AUSTRIAN BRIAR, AUSTRIAN YELLOW

☼ ❄ ↔ 6 ft (1.8 m) ↑ 3–10 ft (0.9–3 m)

Erect shrub native to Asia. Large blackish thorns, bright green leaves. Single flowers, deep yellow with prominent stamens, unpleasant aroma, in summer. Round red hips. *R. f. bicolor* (Austrian copper rose), coppery orange flowers; *R. f. persiana* (Persian yellow rose), double yellow flowers. Zones 4–10.

Rosa gallica

FRENCH ROSE, RED ROSE

☼ ❄ ↔ 4 ft (1.2 m) ↑ 4 ft (1.2 m)

Low suckering shrub native to southern, central, and eastern Europe. Lightly bristled, leathery, dark green leaves. Mildly fragrant flowers, usually single, soft to deep pink, prominent light yellow stamens. Small ovoid hips, brick red. *R. g. officinalis* ★ (apothecary's rose, Provins rose), slightly smaller, with quite large, semi-double, heavily perfumed, crimson flowers, can become weedy. *R. g. versicolor* (syn. 'Rosa Mundi'), sport of *R. g. officinalis*, identical except for its striped white, pink, and crimson flowers. Zones 5–10.

Rosa gigantea

☼ ❄ ↔ 20–40 ft (6–12 m) ↑ 30–60 ft (9–18 m)

Near-evergreen native to northeastern India, upper Myanmar, and western China. Thorny stems, glossy deep green leaves. Flowers cream, white, or pink, in early summer. Large red hips. Zones 8–11.

Rosa laxa

Rosa moyesii fargesii

Rosa pendulina

Rosa glauca
syn. *Rosa rubrifolia*

REDLEAF ROSE

☼ ❋ ↔ 6 ft (1.8 m) ↑ 6 ft (1.8 m)

Deciduous shrub native to Europe. Arching stems dark purplish red when young, leaves bluish gray. Flowers deep pink fading to white near center, in summer. Ovoid hips, purplish red. Zones 3–10.

Rosa hemisphaerica

SULFUR ROSE

☼ ❋ ↔ 7 ft (2 m) ↑ 7 ft (2 m)

Well-branched shrub from southwestern Asia. Stiffly upright stems with scattered thorns, leaves grayish green. Double flowers cupped, deep sulfur yellow, in summer. Round dark red hips. Zones 6–10.

Rosa hugonis
syn. *Rosa xanthina* f. *hugonis*

☼ ❋ ↔ 6 ft (1.8 m) ↑ 7 ft (2 m)

Chinese species; very similar to *R. xanthina*. Differs from *R. xanthina* in having broader leaflets and primrose yellow flowers to well over 2 in (5 cm) wide. Zones 5–10.

Rosa laxa

☼/☽ ❋ ↔ 5–10 ft (1.5–3 m) ↑ 7–8 ft (2–2.4 m)

Shrub from Siberia and northwestern China. Arching stems, bristly, some large recurved thorns. Leaves up to 9 leaflets, to nearly 2 in (5 cm) long, toothed, underside can be sparsely hairy. Clusters of 1 to 6 white to pale pink flowers in summer. Red fruit. Zones 5–9.

Rosa macrophylla

☼ ❋ ↔ 10 ft (3 m) ↑ 10 ft (3 m)

Native to Himalayas. Dark red stems almost thornless, leaves purplish green. Cerise-pink single flowers in summer. Orangey red bristly hips. Zones 7–10.

Rosa marginata
syn. *Rosa jundzillii*

☼ ❋ ↔ 8 ft (2.4 m) ↑ 3–8 ft (0.9–2.4 m)

Suckering shrub native to eastern Europe. Moderately thorny, with thorns few in number, slender and scattered. Dark green leaves, can be downy on underside. Slightly fragrant, single, pale to bright pink flowers in summer. Red hips, round or ovoid. Zones 5–10.

Rosa minutifolia

☼/☽ ✂ ↔ 4 ft (1.2 m) ↑ 4 ft (1.2 m)

Near-evergreen small bush from California, USA, and Baja California, Mexico. Hairy; dense covering of fine red-brown spines. Pinnate leaves, under 1 in (25 mm) long, leaflets under ¼ in (6 mm) long. Purple-pink or white single flowers in summer. Zones 9–11.

Rosa moyesii

☼ ❋ ↔ 10 ft (3 m) ↑ 10 ft (3 m)

Deciduous shrub from western China. Stout erect stems, scattered thorns, dark green leaves. Single deep red flowers in summer. Pendulous, flagon-shaped, orange-red hips. *R. m. fargesii*, reddish pink flowers. Zones 5–10.

Rosa multiflora

JAPANESE ROSE

☼ ❋ ↔ 10 ft (3 m) ↑ 10–15 ft (3–4.5 m)

Robust shrub from eastern Asia and Japan. Prickly stems, leaves with 7 to 9 leaflets. Clusters of small, single, creamy white flowers in summer. Small, rounded, red hips. *R. m. carnea*, white to pale pink flowers. *R. m. cathayensis*, single rosy pink flowers. Zones 5–10.

Rosa nitida

☼ ❋ ↔ 4 ft (1.2 m) ↑ 3 ft (0.9 m)

Suckering shrub native to eastern North America. Slender prickly stems, small fern-like leaves, turning crimson in autumn. Small, single, fragrant, deep pink flowers in summer. Dark scarlet hips. Suitable for ground cover. Zones 3–10.

Rosa nutkana

☼ ❋ ↔ 7 ft (2 m) ↑ 6–10 ft (1.8–3 m)

Vigorous rose native to western North America. Almost thornless purplish brown stems, dark grayish green leaves. Fragrant single flowers, medium pink, in summer. Small, round, red hips. *R. n. hispida*, fragrant pink flowers. Zones 4–10.

Rosa pendulina

☼ ❋ ↔ 5 ft (1.5 m) ↑ 2–7 ft (0.6–2 m)

Deciduous shrub from mountains of central and southern Europe. Arching reddish purple stems, almost thornless. Leaves dark green. Deep pink or purplish pink single flowers, prominent yellow stamens, in summer. Red elongated hips, often pendulous. Zones 5–10.

Rosa pisocarpa
CLUSTER ROSE

☼ ✳ ↔ 4 ft (1.2 m) ↑ 3–7 ft (0.9–2 m)

Deciduous shrub from western North America. Arching stems, small leaves, bristly at base. Small single flowers in clusters, rosy pink, in summer. Small, bright red, shiny hips. Zones 6–10.

Rosa primula
AFGHAN YELLOW ROSE, INCENSE ROSE

☼ ✳ ↔ 5 ft (1.5 m) ↑ 5–10 ft (1.5–3 m)

Species native to central Asia and China. Deciduous shrub, erect branching habit, thorny brown stems. Aromatic fern-like foliage. Perfumed single flowers, primrose yellow, prominent stamens, in spring. Smooth, rounded, reddish maroon hips. Has been confused with *R. ecae* in cultivation. Zones 5–10.

Rosa roxburghii
BURR ROSE, CHESTNUT ROSE

☼ ✳ ↔ 7 ft (2 m) ↑ 7 ft (2 m)

Deciduous shrub native to western China. Branches angular, bark peels with age. Leaves with 15 small light green leaflets. Double pink flowers, prickly calyx and receptacle, fragrant, in summer. Yellow-ish green hips covered in short prickles. *R. r. normalis*, single flowers. Zones 5–10.

Rosa rugosa
BEACH ROSE, JAPANESE ROSE, RAMANAS ROSE

☼ ✳ ↔ 5–8 ft (1.5–2.4 m) ↑ 5–8 ft (1.5–2.4 m)

Vigorous deciduous shrub native to Japan and eastern Asia. Stout prickly stems. Dark green leaves, wrinkled surface. Scented single flowers, light to deep pink, in summer–autumn. Round rich red hips. *R. r. alba*, pink buds, large white flowers, large tomato red hips; *R. r. rubra*, single deep pink-purple flowers. Zones 2–10.

Rosa sempervirens
EVERGREEN ROSE

☼ ✳ ↔ 20–35 ft (6–10 m) ↑ 1–6 ft (0.3–1.8 m)

Semi-evergreen shrub native to south Europe. Scrambling or trailing stems. Mid- to dark green foliage. Fragrant, white, single flowers, in clusters, in early summer. Small orange-red hips. Zones 7–10.

Rosa sericea
MALTESE CROSS ROSE

☼ ✳ ↔ 8 ft (2.4 m) ↑ 10 ft (3 m)

From western China and Himalayas. Vigorous. Stout erect branches, large hooked thorns, fern-like foliage. Single, white, 4-petalled flowers in spring. Pear-shaped bright red hips. *R. s. omeiensis* (syn. *R. omeiensis*), large wedge-shaped thorns. Zones 6–10.

Rosa setipoda

☼ ✳ ↔ 5 ft (1.5 m) ↑ 8 ft (2.4 m)

Deciduous shrub from western China. Shrubby branching habit, stout stems, thick well-spaced thorns. Foliage aromatic when crushed. Large clusters of single flowers, pale pink, prominent yellow stamens, in summer. Bristly, flagon-shaped, deep red hips. Zones 6–10.

Rosa roxburghii normalis

Rosa spinosissima
syn. *Rosa pimpinellifolia*
BURNET ROSE, SCOTCH BRIAR

☼ ✳ ↔ 4 ft (1.2 m) ↑ 3–7 ft (0.9–2 m)

Suckering rose from Europe and Asia. Prickly stems, coarse fern-like leaves. Single creamy white flowers in spring. Small, round, black, shiny hips. *R. s. altaica*, pure white flowers. Zones 4–10.

Rosa stellata
DESERT ROSE

☼ ✳ ↔ 3 ft (0.9 m) ↑ 3 ft (0.9 m)

Deciduous shrub from hot southwestern areas of USA. Forms dense spiny thicket. Light green wedge-shaped leaflets, small, slightly hairy. Single pink flowers in mid-summer. Soft spines on flower buds and red hips. *R. s. mirifica*, flowers pink to purplish red. Zones 6–10.

Rosa sweginzowii

☼ ✳ ↔ 15 ft (4.5 m) ↑ 12 ft (3.5 m)

Native to northern and western China. Large thorns, bristly reddish stems. Light to mid-green leaves, heavily toothed, rounded leaflets. Small clusters of deep pink flowers, in mid-summer. Bottle-shaped orange-red hips. Zones 6–10.

Rosa virginiana
VIRGINIA ROSE

☼ ✳ ↔ 5 ft (1.5 m) ↑ 5 ft (1.5 m)

Sometimes suckering shrub native to eastern North America. Leaves shiny green, color in autumn. Single deep pink flowers, yellow stamens, in mid-summer. Round red hips. Zones 3–10.

Rosa wichurana
syn. *Rosa luciae* var. *wichurana*
MEMORIAL ROSE

☼ ✳ ↔ 20 ft (6 m) ↑ 6 ft (1.8 m)

Dense spreading shrub or short climber from eastern Asia. Stout thorns on trailing stems; glossy green leaves almost evergreen. Clusters of single, fragrant, white flowers in summer. Small, dark red, oval hips. Regarded by some as not distinct from *R. luciae*. Zones 5–10.

Rosa spinosissima

Rosa willmottiae

MISS WILLMOTT'S ROSE

☼ ❀ ↔ 5 ft (1.5 m) ↑ 6 ft (1.8 m)

Deciduous shrub native to China. Arching habit, grayish green fern-like foliage. Single light purplish pink flowers, prominent yellow stamens, in summer. Small, ovoid, orangey red hips. Zones 6–10.

Rosa woodsii

WESTERN WILD ROSE

☼ ❀ ↔ 5 ft (1.5 m) ↑ 3–7 ft (0.9–2 m)

Stiffly branching shrub native to North America. Stems purplish brown when young, very prickly. Foliage colors in autumn. Mid-pink single flowers, in small clusters, in summer. Bright red hips. *R. w. ultramontana*, smaller flowers than species. Zones 4–10.

MODERN ROSES

The term "Modern Roses" is misleading, as a number of them were developed in the latter half of the 1800s, at the same time as some of the Old Rose groups. Modern Roses are famous for their repeat-flowering qualities, floriferousness, and availability of yellow and orange flower colors. Large-flowered (Hybrid Tea) Roses crossed with Polyanthas resulted in Cluster-flowered (Floribunda) Roses; others have followed. A breeding program initiated by the Canadian Department of Agriculture in the early 1900s produced some very hardy roses, some tolerant to Zone 1. Modern Roses are divided into Bush, Shrub, Climbing, Miniature, and Ground Cover Roses.

BUSH ROSES

Bush Roses usually grow no more than 5 ft (1.5 m) tall. They have a long flowering season and are suitable for flowerbeds and borders. Complex crossings of the various groups make classification difficult, with some Large-flowered Roses bearing flowers in large clusters, and taller-growing Cluster-flowered Roses being more shrub-like.

Rosa, Modern Rose, Cluster-flowered, 'Chinatown'

Cluster-flowered (Floribunda) Roses

☼ ❀ ↔ 3–6 ft (0.9–1.8 m) ↑ 4–7 ft (1.2–2 m)

Result of cross between small cluster-flowered Polyantha Roses and Large-flowered Roses. Individual blooms usually smaller than those of Large-flowered Roses, in large crowded clusters, flowers usually flatter when fully open, mostly double or semi-double. 'Amber Queen', large, cup-shaped, clear amber-yellow flowers; 'Apricot Nectar', cupped golden-apricot flowers, well-scented; 'Betty Boop' ★ (syn. 'Centenary of Federation'), highly fragrant single blooms, creamy white to yellow, shading to red toward petal edges; 'Brass Band' ★, lightly scented blooms, apricot shades; 'Chinatown', long-stemmed fragrant blooms, bright yellow with pink highlights at petal edges; 'City of Belfast', large clusters of scarlet-red blooms; 'City of London', very fragrant, cupped, double flowers, soft pink fading to blush; 'Dearest', very fragrant, large, salmon pink flowers, prominent yellow stamens; 'Dicky' (syn. 'Anisley Dickson'), lightly scented, orange-pink, double flowers; 'Elizabeth of Glamis' (syn. 'Irish Beauty'), named for UK's Queen Mother, very fragrant well-shaped flowers, clear salmon pink; 'Fragrant Delight', strong perfume, large flowers, soft salmon-orange shades; 'Frensham', deep red semi-double flowers; 'Gavno' (syn. 'Buck's Fizz'), soft orange blooms; 'Glad Tidings', velvety dark red blooms; 'Gold Badge' ★, large, rich yellow, double flowers; 'Hannah Gordon' (syn. 'Raspberry Ice'), creamy white petals suffused deep pink at edges; 'Iceberg' ★ (syns 'Fée des Neiges', 'Schneewittchen'), large clusters of pure white flowers; 'Lilac Charm', almost-single rose, large petals of pale lilac, red stamens; 'Lilli Marleen', large, velvety, deep red flowers; 'Livin' Easy' ★ (syn. 'Fellowship'), fiery orange-red blooms; 'Ma Perkins', large cupped flowers, pink and salmon; 'Margaret Merril', very fragrant, large, white flowers with hint of pink at center; 'Mariandel' ★, red semi-double flowers with mild fragrance; 'Matangi', so-called "hand-painted" rose, appears to be brushed with secondary colors, bright orangey vermilion with silvery white central eye and petal reverse; 'Matilda' (syn. 'Seduction'), large, white, double flowers, petals delicately edged with pink; 'Picasso', "hand-painted" rose, flowers brushed with deep pink, carmine, and silvery white; 'Prima' (syn. 'Many Happy Returns'), semi-double flowers of palest pink; 'Queen Elizabeth', long pointed buds open to large, high-centered, clear pink blooms; 'Radox Bouquet' (syn. 'Rosika'), very fragrant cupped blooms, soft rose pink; 'Rosemary Rose', camellia-like flowers, deep pinkish red, in large clusters with distinctive maroon foliage; 'Sexy Rexy' ★, large clusters of soft salmon pink camellia-like flowers; 'Sheila's Perfume' ★, very fragrant yellow flowers edged red; 'Southampton' (syn. 'Susan Ann'), apricot flowers flushed orange and red; 'Sunsprite' (syns 'Friesia', 'Korresia'), rounded buds open to very fragrant double flowers of bright yellow; 'Sweet Dream' ★, double blooms, soft apricot-orange; 'Trumpeter', brilliant scarlet-orange flowers. Zones 4–10.

Rosa, Modern Rose, Large-flowered, 'Fragrant Cloud'

Large-flowered (Hybrid Tea) Roses

☼ ❄ ↔ 3–6 ft (0.9–1.8 m) ↕ 5–8 ft (1.5–2.4 m)

Most popular of all roses; thousands have been bred. Generally sturdy plants, with upright bushy habit and mid- to dark green, often glossy leaves. Very large flowers usually double or semi-double, borne singly or in clusters. Elegant long-pointed buds; when open retain high center, to varying degrees, as outer petals reflex. Large-flowered Rose usually acknowledged as first is 'La France', bred in 1867. Only very small selection of vast numbers available included here. 'Abbeyfield Rose', rich deep pink double flowers; 'Alec's Red', plump black-red buds open to double well-perfumed flowers; 'Alexander', lightly scented, double, vermilion blooms; 'Brandy', large, sweetly perfumed, apricot flowers; 'Carina', fragrant double blooms of rosy pink; 'Congratulations', high-centered clear rose pink flowers on long stems; 'Dainty Bess', large single flowers of silvery rose pink, prominent golden-brown stamens; 'Deep Secret' (syn. 'Mildred Scheel'), very dark, deep crimson-red flowers, velvety-textured, very fragrant; 'Double Delight', very fragrant creamy pink flowers, darkening to cherry red at edges; 'Elina' ★ (syn. 'Peaudouce'), lemony yellow flowers fading to cream at edges; 'Fragrant Cloud' (syns 'Duftwolke', 'Nuage Parfumé'), highly perfumed coral red flowers; 'Indian Summer', fragrant double blooms in orange shades; 'Ingrid Bergman' ★, named for actress, deep red velvety blooms, long lasting, good for picking; 'Irish Gold' (syn. 'Grandpa Dickson'), very prickly plant, elegant lemony yellow flowers; 'Just Joey' ★, large coppery orange flowers that pale to soft pink at edge of petals; 'La France', high-centered, well-perfumed, silvery pink flowers; 'Lady Rose', high-centered bright salmon and orange flowers emerge from long pointed buds; 'Love', high-centered scarlet flowers, silvery white reverse on petals; 'Lovely Lady', fragrant, double, rosy pink flowers emerge from long buds; 'Loving Memory' (syns 'Burgund 81', 'Red Cedar'),

Rosa, Modern Rose, Patio, 'Queen Mother'

high-centered bright crimson blooms on long stems; 'Mme Butterfly', very fragrant soft pink flowers emerge from long buds; 'Mrs Oakley Fisher', single deep buff-yellow flowers, prominent amber stamens; 'Moonstone' ★, lightly scented, large, white flowers, highlighted with shades of soft pink; 'National Trust', large, high-centered, bright red flowers; 'New Zealand' ★ (syn. 'Aotearoa New Zealand'), soft pink fragrant flowers open from long pointed buds; 'Olympiad' ★, brilliant red, velvety, double flowers, delicately scented; 'Pascali', considered one of best whites, long, nearly thornless stems topped with ivory white flowers; 'Paul Shirville' (syn. 'Heart Throb'), perfumed, high-centered, pink flowers with hint of salmon; 'Peace', probably most famous and popular Large-flowered Rose of all, large pale yellow flowers suffused with creamy pink; 'Perfume Delight', cupped deep pink flowers, very fragrant; 'Pot o' Gold', bright yellow blooms touched with gold, very fragrant; 'Precious Platinum' (syns 'Opa Pötschke', 'Red Star'), bright red high-centered flowers with velvety sheen; 'Pristine', long pointed buds open to reveal large, shapely, white flowers flushed with pale pink; 'Remember Me', coppery orange flowers; 'Royal William', large, rich red, velvety blooms; 'Savoy Hotel', fully double soft pink flowers, deeper colored on petal reverse, lightly scented; 'Shot Silk', globular silky-petalled blooms of salmon pink with yellow base; 'Silver Jubilee', silvery pink and apricot flowers with deeper colored reverse; 'Sunblest' (syn. 'Landora'), rich yellow flowers emerge from slim buds; 'Sutter's Gold', deep yellow flowers flushed with orange and pink; 'Touch of Class' (syn. 'Maréchale LeClerc'), long-stemmed high-centered flowers in shades of cream, coral, and salmon pink; 'Valencia' ★, fragrant, apricot-yellow, double blooms; 'White Lightnin', vigorous plant, well-scented pure white flowers; 'White Wings', long pointed buds open to large, single, white flowers, prominent chocolate brown stamens. Zones 4–10.

Patio (Dwarf Cluster-flowered) Roses

☼ ❄ ↔ 18–36 in (45–90 cm) ↕ 18–30 in (45–75 cm)

More recent group, result of much cross-breeding between Polyantha Roses, Miniature Roses, and Cluster-flowered Roses; classification can be difficult because of this. Usually bushier and slightly taller than Miniatures; most resemble Cluster-flowered Roses with all parts proportionately smaller. Suitable for beds and borders as well as for patios and growing in containers. Some popularly grown examples of this group are 'Anna Ford', which bears long pointed buds opening to cup-shaped deep orange flowers with yellow eye; 'Boys' Brigade', single crimson flowers with paler eye; 'Brass Ring' (syn. 'Peek-a-Boo'), deep peachy orange buds opening to peach and pale apricot, fading to pink at edges; 'Dainty Dinah', soft coral red flowers on spreading plant; 'Festival', carrying clusters of striking deep red flowers, semi-double; 'Queen Mother' ★, delicate pink semi-double flowers; and 'Rexy's Baby', offspring of Cluster-flowered (Floribunda) Rose 'Sexy Rexy', which produces pale pink flowers deepening to salmon pink at center. Zones 4–11.

Rosa, Modern Rose, Polyantha, 'Gloire du Midi'

Polyantha Roses

☼ ❀ ↔ 2–3 ft (0.6–0.9 m) ↑ 2–4 ft (0.6–1.2 m)

Only a few of these small roses still available. Very hardy, withstanding winter cold of northern Europe, very free flowering, with small pompon-like flowers covering plants for months. '**Baby Faurax**', small, amethyst-violet, pompon flowers; '**Cameo**', semi-double blooms in shades of salmon and coral pink; '**Gloire du Midi**', orange-red blooms; '**Mlle Cécile Brünner**', profuse shell pink flowers open from long pointed buds; '**Mevrouw Nathalie Nypels**', pink semi-double flowers, sweet fragrance; '**Nypels Perfection**', semi-double blooms in shades of pink; '**Pinkie**', cupped, semi-double, very fragrant rosy pink flowers; '**The Fairy**', large crowded clusters of small, very double, clear pink flowers smother plant constantly throughout summer; '**White Cécile Brünner**', slightly fragrant, double, white flowers with yellow center; '**White Pet**' (syn. 'Little White Pet'), sometimes classed as Cluster-flowered Rose, small, pompon-like, white flowers, with pink tint in bud; '**Yesterday**', purple-pink double blooms emerge from dark buds. Zones 3–10.

SHRUB ROSES

Shrub Roses, usually bigger and more vigorous than Bush Roses, range from 4–10 ft (1.2–3 m) in height. Flower formation varies considerably and some cultivars flower only once in the season. Suitable for specimen or shrubberies and mixed borders, some can be trained as small climbers or pillar roses.

Hybrid Rugosa Roses

☼ ❀ ↔ 5–10 ft (1.5–3 m) ↑ 2–7 ft (0.6–2 m)

Distinctive group with stout bristly branches and coarse wrinkled leaves that often color to buttery yellow in autumn. Tough and healthy plants, many have very fragrant flowers; blooms range from single to double, in shades of pink and crimson, with a few white and yellow. As group they span eras of Old and Modern Roses, with plants being bred from late 1800s to present day. '**Agnes**', dense bush, bearing very fragrant, creamy yellow, double flowers; '**Blanc Double de Coubert**', vigorous plant with heavily perfumed semi-double flowers of purest white; '**Dr Eckener**', very

large, heavily perfumed, semi-double flowers in soft shades of pale yellow and coppery rose, fading to pale pink; '**Fimbriata**' (syns 'Dianthiflora', 'Phoebe's Frilled Pink'), small, white, double flowers, frilled petal edges resembling *Dianthus*; '**Frau Dagmar Hartopp**', large, single, silvery pink flowers, sometimes darker; '**Hansa**', fragrant, double, pink-purple flowers; '**Henry Hudson**' (one of Explorer Series), hardy to Zone 1, fragrant white flowers, tinged with pink; '**Martin Frobisher**' (Explorer Series), hardy to Zone 1, fragrant soft pink flowers; '**Roseraie de l'Haÿ**', dense and vigorous bush, with large, semi-double, extremely fragrant flowers of rich crimson-purple; '**Scabrosa**', modern introduction with large, single, cerise flowers; '**Souvenir de Philémon Cochet**', fully double flowers, white with pale pink center; '**Thérèse Bugnet**', large fragrant flowers, up to 4 in (10 cm) in diameter, opening reddish pink, maturing to light pink; '**Vanguard**', large, double, apricot-pink to salmon flowers, highly aromatic. Zones 3–10.

Rosa, Modern Rose, Hybrid Rugosa, 'Scabrosa'

Modern Shrub Roses

☼ ❀ ↔ 4–8 ft (1.2–2.4 m) ↑ 4–8 ft (1.2–2.4 m)

Plants bred from variety of different parents; various sizes and growth habits, flowers in all colors and from single to double. '**Adelaide Hoodless**', hardy to Zone 1, semi-double clear red flowers in clusters of up to 35 blooms; '**Anna Zinkeisen**', double flowers of ivory white, lemon tones at base; '**Berlin**', semi-double flowers of rich red, paling at center, prominent yellow stamens; '**Bonica**' ★ (syn. 'Bonica 82'), double light pink flowers, rather frilled petals; '**Canary Bird**' (syn. *R. xanthina* 'Canary Bird'), fragrant, single, canary yellow flowers, prominent stamens; '**Cantabrigiensis**' (syn. *R. × cantabrigiensis*), large pale primrose flowers; '**Cerise Bouquet**', semi-double deep pink-red flowers; '**Champlain**' (from Explorer Series), slightly fragrant, dark red, velvety flowers, hardy to Zone 2; '**Eddie's Jewel**', repeat-flowering form; '**Flower Carpet**' ★, semi-double rich pink flowers with light scent; '**Fred Loads**', large, almost-single, bright salmon pink flowers on large trusses; '**Fritz Nobis**', once-flowering shrub, large double flowers of light pink to soft salmon; '**Geranium**' ★, more compact habit, good display of larger hips; '**Golden Wings**', single

Rosa, Modern Rose, Modern Shrub, English, 'Golden Celebration'

pale primrose yellow flowers, prominent gold stamens; '**Goldstern**', large golden yellow blooms emerge from elegant, long, pointed buds; '**J. P. Connell**', hardy to Zone 2, clusters of 3 to 8 lemon yellow flowers fade to cream; '**Lavender Dream**', clusters of flattish lilac-pink flowers, may be slightly fragrant; '**Nevada**', almost-single white flowers, up to 4 in (10 cm) across, prominent yellow stamens; '**Phantom**', slightly fragrant saucer-shaped flowers, rich deep red petals, bright yellow stamens; '**St John's Rose**' (syns *R. × richardii, R. sancta*), dark green leaves, single flowers, mildly fragrant, clear delicate pink; an ancient hybrid, flowers have been found in Egyptian tombs; '**Sally Holmes**' ★, large, creamy white, single flowers open from soft apricot-pink buds; and '**Westerland**', fragrant, apricot, double blooms.

English Roses (also classed as Modern Shrub Roses). In early 1960s Englishman David Austin began breeding program that crossed Old and Modern Roses. Combines flower forms and fragrance of Old Roses with growth habits, repeat-flowering ability, and wider color range of Modern Roses. '**Abraham Darby**' ★, large, orange-pink, fully double flowers; '**Charles Rennie Mackintosh**', fragrant blooms open rose pink, age to lilac-pink; '**Constance Spry**', large, cupped, soft pink flowers, myrrh-like fragrance, in late spring–summer; '**Gertrude Jekyll**', very fragrant, rich pink, very double flowers; '**Golden Celebration**' ★, highly fragrant, deep yellow, double flowers in summer–autumn; '**Graham Thomas**', long-stemmed, rich yellow, double flowers, sweetly scented; '**Jude the Obscure**', strongly scented yellow blooms; '**Mary Rose**', rich rose pink flowers; '**Winchester Cathedral**', fragrant white blooms; '**Windrush**', large semi-double flowers, pure soft lemon, prominent yellow stamens, very sweetly perfumed.

Hybrid Musk Roses. Although placed in Modern Shrub Roses, group often thought of as "Old." First introduced in 1913 by Rev. Joseph Pemberton; most of group bred by him. Name relates to fragrance, inherited very indirectly from musk rose *(R. moschata)*. Shrubby habit, often with dark green leaves and purplish stems, long flowering season, clusters of single to double flowers. Good specimen or shrubbery plants. '**Belinda**' ★, mid-pink flowers,

Rosa, Modern Rose, Miniature, 'Rosmarin'

often highlighted with white at petal base; '**Buff Beauty**', double apricot blooms age to buff-yellow; '**Cornelia**', small, double, very pale pink flowers with orange base, musk-like fragrance; '**Danaë**', double blooms open yellow, age to white; '**Erfurt**', fragrant, semi-double, pink blooms, shaded yellow toward petal base; '**Moonlight**', one of first Hybrid Musk Roses, clusters of almost-single creamy white flowers, prominent yellow stamens; '**Mozart**', large white eye accents pink single flowers; '**Penelope**', semi-double blooms of palest pink, age to white; '**Prosperity**', large clusters of double white flowers on long arching stems. Zones 4–10.

Rosa, Modern Rose, Modern Shrub, Hybrid Musk, 'Cornelia'

MINIATURE ROSES

Among the more recent large groups to be developed, Miniature Roses of the style we know today first appeared in the late 1930s. Their tiny flowers are perfect replicas in miniature of those of the large rose bushes. What they lack in scent, they more than make up for in intricate beauty.

Miniature Roses

☼ ❀ ↔ 12–18 in (30–45 cm) ↕ 8–24 in (20–60 cm)

Perfect miniature replicas of Bush Roses, with tiny leaves and dainty buds and flowers. Useful for edging borders; make very good container plants. Some roses classed as Miniatures are somewhat taller, but bear small flowers and leaves. '**Air France**' (syns '**American Independence**', '**Rosy Meillandina**'), double flowers of clear rose pink; '**Autumn Splendour**' ★, light fruity fragrance, large, double, yellow-orange flowers, deeper coloring at petal edges intensifies with age; '**Baby Darling**', double apricot flowers; '**Baby Love**' ★, small, single, buttercup yellow flowers, prominent stamens; '**Cachet**' ★, large, unscented, white blooms; '**Cider Cup**', rich apricot double blooms, lightly scented; '**Cinderella**', pearly white flowers lightly flushed with pink; '**Fairy Tale**', small, delicately perfumed, pink flowers, mature to pale pink; '**Gentle Touch**', small, soft pink, double flowers, lightly scented; '**Gourmet Popcorn**' ★, lightly scented, semi-double, snow white flowers; '**Holy Toledo**', double flowers of apricot-orange; '**Hot Tamale**', striking pink-orange flowers, either singly or in clusters; '**Hula Girl**', long pointed buds open to deep salmon pink flowers; '**Irresistible**' ★, fragrant double blooms, almost pure white, becoming pink-tinged toward center; '**Little Red Devil**', well-perfumed, double, deep red flowers; '**Loving Touch**', long pointed buds open to fragrant high-centered flowers in apricot tones; '**Magic Carrousel**' ★, double flowers, creamy white, petals red-edged; '**My Valentine**', high-centered deep red flowers; '**Party Girl**' ★, fragrant, soft apricot-yellow, double blooms; '**Pride 'n' Joy**', profuse orange blooms, fruit-like perfume; '**Red Ace**' (syns '**Amanda**', '**Amruda**'), velvety deep red blooms; '**Rosina**' (syns '**Josephine Wheatcroft**', '**Yellow Sweetheart**'), semi-double blooms of clear yellow; '**Rosmarin**', slightly fragrant double flowers range in color from pale pink to pale red, depending on air temperature; '**Snow Carpet**', small, very double, white flowers; '**Sweet Magic**', orange semi-double blooms; '**Tapis Jaune**', profuse, double, yellow, small flowers. Zones 4–11.

OLD (HERITAGE) ROSES

Under the umbrella term "Old Roses" fall a number of groups containing roses that, through deliberate breeding, have similar characteristics to each other. Some of the oldest groups, such as Gallica, contain roses that have been cultivated for centuries, while other groups, like Bourbon, are the product of nineteenth-century breeding. The term "Old Rose" is a misnomer, as some Old groups contain plants bred more recently, and the term is often used in reference to shrubs such as the Hybrid Musks (included here under Modern Roses), which are of twentieth-century origin. Many people consider that it is a rose's attributes rather than its date of introduction that earn it the title of "Old." Some of the Old Rose groups, such as the Teas, include climbing plants, and there are also Old groups of climbers and ramblers, like the Noisettes.

OLD NON-CLIMBING ROSES

For as long as roses have been cultivated, gardeners have been improving on the wild species. Old Non-climbing Roses, which include groups such as the China Roses and Damask Roses, may be once-flowering and limited in color range, but they more than make up for those failings with delicate tones, unusually shaped flowers, and fragrance that combine to conjure up a bygone era.

Alba Roses

☼ ❋ ↔ 6–10 ft (1.8–3 m) ↕ 2–8 ft (0.6–2.4 m)
Very hardy group. Light bluish green foliage; very fragrant pale-colored flowers, usually double or semi-double, blooming once, in mid-summer. '**Alba Maxima**' (syns 'Bonnie Prince Charlie's Rose', 'Jacobite Rose', 'White Rose of York'), large, pure white, double flowers; '**Félicité Parmentier**', flat double flowers, salmon pink, fade to pale pink; '**Königin von Dänemark**' ★ (syn. 'Queen of Denmark'), smaller double flowers of deeper pink than other Albas; '**Mme Plantier**', rather flat, double, white flowers, buds often tinged reddish pink; '**Maiden's Blush**' fragrant, creamy white to very light pink, double flowers. Zones 4–10.

Bourbon Roses

☼ ❋ ↔ 5–8 ft (1.5–2.4 m) ↕ 4–7 ft (1.2–2 m)
First Bourbon Rose was hybrid between *R. chinensis* and a Damask Rose; occurred naturally on Ile de Bourbon. Highly perfumed, many with repeat-flowering characteristics. Flowers semi-double or double, often cupped or with quartered arrangement of petals. Susceptible to fungal diseases in humid areas. '**Boule de Neige**', globular, double, white blooms, sometimes with reddish purple tinge on petal edges; '**Honorine de Brabant**', light pink cupped flowers, faint rose spotting on inner surface; '**Louise Odier**', very double rose pink flowers; '**Mme Isaac Pereire**', heavily perfumed, large, double flowers, magenta-rose; '**Mme Pierre Oger**', cupped, double, translucent silvery pink flowers; '**Reine Victoria**', cupped double flowers, silky texture, lilac-pink; '**Souvenir de la Malmaison**', double flowers, flattened and quartered, flesh pink, quickly pulped by wet weather. Its sport, '**Souvenir de St Anne's**', semi-double form, yellow stamens, survives bad weather. '**Zéphirine Drouhin**', no thorns, rich pink, semi-double, fragrant flowers. Zones 6–10.

Centifolia Roses

☼ ❋ ↔ 4–8 ft (1.2–2.4 m) ↕ 2–8 ft (0.6–2.4 m)
Centifolia means "one hundred leaves," refers to crowded petals on large flowers. Flowers in shades of pink, white, and occasionally purplish magenta. Generally flower only once, in early summer. Bush often prickly, coarse, quite lax growth. '**Fantin-Latour**', fragrant, soft pink, double blooms; '**Petite de Hollande**', small, scented, double, rose pink blooms; '**Petite Lisette**', small, fragrant, pink pompon flowers; '**Reine des Centfeuilles**', fragrant pink flowers, to 2½ in (6 cm) across; '**Rose de Meaux**', small, pink, slightly frilly flowers, resemble *Dianthus*; '**The Bishop**', flowers slightly earlier than most, purplish magenta blooms; '**Tour de Malakoff**', tall lax bush, fragrant purplish magenta blooms fade to lilac. Zones 5–10.

China Roses

☼ ❋ ↔ 3–6 ft (0.9–1.8 m) ↕ 3–6 ft (0.9–1.8 m)
Low growing with airy, often spindly growth; sparsely foliaged. Repeat-blooming flowers, usually quite small and lightly fragrant, semi-double or double, in shades of pink, with some crimson and flame tints. '**Archduke Charles**', pink to crimson flowers mature to deeper shade, banana-scented; '**Comtesse du Caÿla**', loosely semi-double, scented flowers in flame shades; '**Gloire des Rosomanes**', hardy rose, large, cup-shaped, semi-double, pink to crimson flowers, in spring–autumn; '**Green Rose**' (syn. 'Viridiflora'), green leaf-like sepals with red-brown serrated edges, rather than colored petals; '**Le Vésuve**', large slightly fragrant flowers, pink or red, depending on whether grown in sun or shade; '**Louis XIV**', almost-double

Rosa, Old Rose, Alba, 'Alba Maxima'

Rosa, Old Rose, Bourbon, 'Souvenir de la Malmaison'

Rosa, Old Rose, Centifolia, 'Petite Lisette'

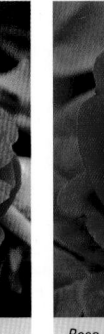

Rosa, Old Rose, Hybrid Perpetual, 'Baron Girod de l'Ain'

Rosa, Old Rose, Moss, 'William Lobb'

Rosa, Old Rose, Portland, 'Rose du Roi'

scented flowers, deep crimson, yellow stamens; '**Mutabilis**' ★, taller, single yellow flowers open from buff red-streaked buds, change in color through shades of pink and soft crimson; '**Old Blush**' (syns 'Common Monthly', 'Parsons' Pink'), semi-double silvery pink flowers; '**Sophie's Perpetual**', few thorns, scented mid-pink flowers, darker pink shading on some outer petals. Zones 7–10.

Damask Roses

☼ ❋ ↔ 5–8 ft (1.5–2.4 m) ↕ 3–7 ft (0.9–2 m)

Crusaders returning from Middle East took first Damask Roses to Europe. Often untidy bushes, prickly, downy grayish leaves; majority flower only once, in spring or summer. Flowers double or semi-double, pale shades of pink and white, most fragrant. '**Autumn Damask**' (syn. 'Quatre Saisons'), fragrant mid-pink blooms; '**Blush Damask**', profuse flowers in summer, mid-pink in center, lighter pink toward outer petals; '**Celsiana**', clusters of semi-double clear pink flowers; '**Gloire de Guilan**', double flowers, flattened and quartered when fully open; '**Ispahan**', longer flowering, intensely perfumed, clear pink, double flowers; '**Mme Hardy**', double white flowers, petals arranged around green "button" eye; '**Rose de Rescht**', deep pink double flowers; '**Summer Damask**', clusters of very fragrant, semi-double, pink flowers; '**York and Lancaster**', semi-double flowers white, blush pink, or 2-toned. Zones 5–10.

Gallica Roses

☼ ❋ ↔ 4–6 ft (1.2–1.8 m) ↕ 4–6 ft (1.2–1.8 m)

Mostly compact plants. Foliage usually dark green, not very prickly. Sweetly perfumed double or semi-double flowers in shades of pink or magenta-purple. Flower only once, in spring or summer. '**Belle de Crécy**', fragrant, rich pink and purple, double blooms; '**Belle Isis**', double flowers, flattened when fully open, flesh pink, fade to white near edges; '**Cardinal de Richelieu**', scented, dark red-purple, double flowers; '**Charles de Mills**' ★, fragrant, rich purple, double flowers; '**Complicata**', large single flowers, bright pink, paler at center, large stamens; '**Duc de Guiche**', fragrant, deep pink-purple, double blooms; '**Duchesse d'Angoulême**', semi-double to double, mid-pink flowers, fragrant, in summer; '**Duchesse de Montebello**', small, double, fragrant, pink flowers; '**Président de Sèze**', scented double flowers, magenta to cerise at center, shade to lilac-pink at outer petals; '**Tuscany**', purple-red double flowers, yellow stamens; '**Tuscany Superb**', fragrant purple-red flowers. Zones 5–10.

Hybrid Perpetual Roses

☼ ❋ ↔ 3–6 ft (0.9–1.8 m) ↕ 4–7 ft (1.2–2 m)

Complex parentage involving several rose groups, including Bourbons and Chinas. Repeat flowering. Large, double, usually fragrant blooms in shades of pink to red. '**Baron Girod de l'Ain**', crimson flowers, petals edged white; '**Baronne Prévost**', deep pink flowers, flattened when open; '**Comtesse Cécile de Chabrillant**', fragrant pink flowers; '**Frau Karl Druschki**' (syns 'Reine des Neiges', 'Snow Queen', 'White American Beauty'), globular white blooms; '**Général Jacqueminot**', fragrant, purple-red, double blooms on long stems; '**Henry Nevard**', red, highly fragrant, double flowers, up to 30 petals each; '**Marchesa Boccella**' ★, fragrant double flowers, pink, almost white on outer petals; '**Maurice Bernardin**', clusters of large, red, fragrant blooms; '**Paul Neyron**', mid-pink, cupped, fragrant flowers, up to 50 petals each; '**Reine des Violettes**', sweetly scented purple to violet flowers; '**Souvenir du Docteur Jamain**', deep ruby red semi-double flowers, full sun will scorch petals; '**Sydonie**', quartered mid-pink flowers; '**Ulrich Brunner Fils**', fragrant, cupped, pinkish red flowers open from rich red buds. Zones 5–10.

Moss Roses

☼ ❋ ↔ 5–8 ft (1.5–2.4 m) ↕ 3–7 ft (0.9–2 m)

First Moss Rose occurred as sport of a Centifolia. Named for mossy growth on stems and buds. Degree and type of mossing varies, some hard and prickly, others soft and downy. Large, double, fragrant blooms, flowering once, in spring or summer. '**Catherine de Würtemberg**', slightly scented, rich pink flowers; '**Comtesse de Murinais**', flattened double flowers opening soft pink, fading to white; '**Gloire des Mousseux**', large light pink flowers; '**Henri Martin**', deep pink-red semi-double blooms; '**Mme Louis Lévêque**', pink silky-petalled flowers, double, cupped; '**William Lobb**', semi-double purplish magenta flowers. Zones 5–10.

Portland Roses

☼ ❋ ↔ 3–5 ft (0.9–1.5 m) ↕ 2–4 ft (0.6–1.2 m)

Small group closely allied to Damasks and Gallicas, foliage usually resembles one or other. Most bear fragrant, double, repeat-blooming flowers in shades of pink to red. '**Duchess of Portland**' (syn. 'Portland Rose'), single or semi-double cerise-red flowers; '**Mme Knorr**', large, heavily perfumed, rich pink, double flowers; '**Rose du Roi**', heavily scented, rich red, double flowers. Zones 5–10.

Rosa, Old Rose, Tea, 'Monsieur Tillier'

Scots Roses

☼ ❈ ↔ 5–8 ft (1.5–2.4 m) ↕ 3–7 ft (0.9–2 m)

Group became prominent early in nineteenth century when breeding program began from seedlings of malformed *R. spino-sissima*. Quite tough plants, with fern-like foliage and prickly stems. Flowers range from single to double in white and cream shades to yellow, and from light to deepest pink and red. Most flower only once, in spring or summer. Hips all unusually dark in color, blackish maroon when fully ripe. 'Aïcha', large, semi-double, fragrant, yellow flowers, vigorous grower; 'Andrewsii' (syn. 'Andrew's Rose'), large, semi-double to double, mid-pink flowers, often cream toward petal base; 'Double White Burnet', highly fragrant white flowers, can be semi-double to double in form; 'Dunwich Rose', soft yellow single flowers, with prominent yellow stamens; 'Falkland', fragrant, semi-double, cupped blooms of lilac-pink fading to white; 'Karl Förster', lightly scented, creamy white, double flowers, prominent stamens when fully open, and repeat flowering; 'Single Cherry', thorny stems, deep red single flowers, bright yellow stamens; 'Stanwell Per-petual', arching bush, grayish green foliage, very fragrant double flowers of soft pink (paler with age), long flowering season; 'William III', fragrant semi-double flowers of rich maroon, becoming lighter with age. Zones 4–10.

Sweet Briar Roses

☼ ❈ ↔ 5–10 ft (1.5–3 m) ↕ 4–8 ft (1.2–2.4 m)

Apple-scented foliage of this group inherited from its *R. eglanteria* parent and is its main distinguishing feature. Majority are large, rather untidy bushes, which are best suited for planting in hedgerows or wild gardens. Flowers are usually single or semi-double, and occur in shades of pink to deep red and white. 'Amy Robsart', prolific flower bearer, almost-single, highly fragrant, deep pink blooms; 'Lady Penzance', most strongly scented foliage of group, single coppery pink flowers, prominent stamens; 'Magnifica', dense scented foliage that can be pruned to form hedge, with crimson semi-double flowers; 'Manning's Blush', densely foliaged, large, fully double, white flowers flushed

with pink; 'Meg Merrilies', extremely vigorous and prickly rose bush, deep pink to bright crimson, semi-double, scented flowers. Zones 4–10.

Tea Roses

☼ ❈ ↔ 3–6 ft (0.9–1.8 m) ↕ 3–7 ft (0.9–2 m)

Tea Roses arrived in Europe from Asia in early nineteenth century. Name thought to come from being shipped on boats that were also carrying tea rather than for any particular tea scent from leaves or flowers. With their repeat-flowering ability and yellow coloring of some blooms, they, together with Chinas, revolution-ized rose breeding. Foliage large and glossy. Double flowers often have long pointed buds. Flower color varies from creamy yellows and white through to pretty shades of pink and red. They grow better in warmer climates. 'Agnes Smith', free-flowering, flowers rose pink in cooler weather, turning paler pink in hotter months; 'Catherine Mermet', high-pointed buds opening to light salmon pink; 'Duchesse de Brabant' (syns 'Comtesse de Labarthe', 'Com-tesse Ouwaroff'), free-flowering, cupped, double, pink flowers; 'Francis Dubreuil', velvety, dark red, double flowers; 'Freiherr von Marschall', rich red, ageing to deep pink, fragrant, double flowers; 'Lady Hillingdon', long, pointed, deep yellow buds open to loose, semi-double, buff-yellow flowers; 'Mme de Tartas', lightly scented double blooms in delicate shade of blush pink; 'Mrs Reynolds Hole', fragrant, rich purple-pink, double flowers; 'Monsieur Tillier', rosy pink with salmon tonings, double flowers with darker shading; 'Niphetos', double white flowers opening from creamy buds; 'Perle des Jardins', very double, often quar-tered, sulfur yellow flowers; 'Rosette Delizy', light pink to pale yellow petals, darker pink veins; 'Souvenir d'un Ami', double flowers in varying shades of deep rose pink to salmon. Zones 7–11.

Rothmannia globosa

Miscellaneous Old Garden Roses

☼/◑ ❈ ↔ 20–48 in (50–120 cm) ↕ 2–6 ft (0.6–1.8 m)

In some instances parentage of Old Roses is hard to establish or plants simply do not seem to fit any particular category. This miscellan-eous group is mixed lot, though that in no way lessens their beauty. 'Duplex' (syn. 'Wolley Dodd's Rose'), repeat-flowering, semi-double blooms; 'Dupontii', plentiful grayish green leaves, sweetly perfumed single flowers, petals clear creamy white; 'Empress Josephine', grayish green leaves, fragrant double flowers, dark pink with darker vein-ing, flushed with lilac and purple; 'Fortuniana', of garden origin in China, dark green leaves, large, scented, double flowers creamy white; 'Harison's Yellow' (the yellow rose of Texas), of garden origin in USA, said to have been carried west by pioneers and planted wherever they stopped, small double flowers, deep clear yellow; 'Mermaid', fragrant, single, pale yellow blooms; 'Polliniana', white flowers, sometimes flushed palest of pink; 'The Garland', scented semi-double blooms in shades of pink, light yellow, and white. Zones 6–9.

ROTHMANNIA

This is a genus of about 20 evergreen shrubs or small trees in the madder (Rubiaceae) family that are cultivated largely for their glossy foliage, which is often strongly veined, and their bell-shaped or tubular flowers, which are often fragrant. They are native to Africa, Madagascar, and Asia. Fruit are brown pods containing seeds. CULTIVATION: Although adaptable to most soils, *Rothmannia* species prefer well-composted neutral or slightly acid soil in a protected and sunny position. They are frost and drought resistant. Propagate from seed in spring or half-hardened cuttings in early summer.

Rothmannia globosa
syn. *Gardenia globosa*
BELL GARDENIA, CAPE JASMINE, SEPTEMBER BELLS, TREE GARDENIA
☼ ❄ ↔ 6–10 ft (1.8–3 m) ↑ 12–20 ft (3.5–6 m)
Native of South Africa. Evergreen shrub, similar to gardenia. Textured, glossy green, veined, elliptic to narrow leaves. Fragrant, white, bell-shaped flowers, singly or in cymes, in spring. Zones 9–11.

RUBUS

There are more than 250 species of shrubs, often with prickles on stems and leaves, within this genus from the rose (Rosaceae) family. Found throughout the world, some are cultivated for their ornamental value and as a useful food source, others are regarded as weeds. Most species have biennial stems or canes, which means they produce fruit only on second-year wood; leaves on first and second year's growth are often a different shape. CULTIVATION: The wide distribution of this genus means it has a variety of habitats. Most species thrive in fertile, humus-rich, moist, free-draining soil. Many grow in full sun to light shade, and some grow in deeper shade under deciduous trees. Propagate by dividing suckering species in spring or take half-hardened cuttings from evergreen species, or softwood or hardwood cuttings from deciduous species, or layer. Grow from stratified seed in spring.

Rubus crataegifolius

Rubus biflorus
☼ ❄ ↔ 10 ft (3 m) ↑ 10 ft (3 m)
Deciduous shrub from China and Himalayas. Prickly erect stems, white bloom on bare young stems. Leaves pinnate, 3 to 5 leaflets, dark green, white downy underside. Flowers white, singly or in small clusters, in summer. Yellow edible fruit. Zones 7–9.

Rubus cockburnianus
☼ ❄ ↔ 8 ft (2.4 m) ↑ 8 ft (2.4 m)
Deciduous Chinese shrub. Prickly stems, white bloom in colder months. Dark green leaves, 9 egg-shaped leaflets, furry white underside. Saucer-shaped pale purple flowers, in racemes, in summer. Unappetizing black fruit. Zones 6–10.

Rubus crataegifolius
KOREAN RASPBERRY
☼ ❄ ↔ 5 ft (1.5 m) ↑ 8 ft (2.4 m)
Deciduous shrub from temperate East Asia. Leaves deeply lobed, good color in autumn. Small white flowers. Large, juicy, bright red fruit. Zones 5–9.

Rubus fruticosus
BLACKBERRY
☼ ❄ ↔ 10–25 ft (3–8 m) ↑ 3–6 ft (0.9–1.8 m)
Prickly scrambling shrub, variable in leaf shape and plant form, from temperate Northern Hemisphere. Arching entangling stems, up to 25 ft (8 m) long; savage backward-pointing thorns. Stout, branching, creeping underground roots. Compound leaves, 3 to 5 toothed oval leaflets, prickly stalks and midribs. Many-flowered clusters of white to pink, 5-petalled flowers in spring–summer. Red berries turn black when ripe. Can become invasive. Zones 4–7.

Rubus odoratus
PURPLE-FLOWERING RASPBERRY, THIMBLEBERRY
☼ ❄ ↔ 8 ft (2.4 m) ↑ 8 ft (2.4 m)
From eastern North America. Deciduous erect shrub, vigorous arching stems, peeling bark. Toothed leaves, 5 lobes, hairy underside. Fragrant lilac-pink flowers in summer–autumn. Flat reddish orange fruit. 'Albus', white flowers. Zones 3–9.

Rubus pentalobus
syns *Rubus calycinoides, R. fockeanus* of gardens
☼ ❄ ↔ 3–7 ft (0.9–2 m) ↑ 4 in (10 cm)
Taiwanese, evergreen, low-growing, spreading shrub. Dark green, 3- to 5-lobed leaves, wrinkled edges, heart-shaped base, paler and often woolly underside. Solitary white flowers in summer. Round red fruit. Zones 8–11.

Rubus biflorus

Rubus spectabilis
SALMONBERRY

☼ ✳ ↔ 6 ft (1.8 m) ↑ 6 ft (1.8 m)

Native to North America. Deciduous shrub, upright stems, tiny thorns. Leaves have 3 egg-shaped leaflets. Pink to purple solitary flowers in spring. Egg-shaped pale orange to yellow fruit. Can become invasive. Zones 5–9.

Rubus thibetanus

☼ ✳ ↔ 6–8 ft (1.8–2.4 m) ↑ 6–8 ft (1.8–2.4 m)

Native to western China. Thicket-forming deciduous shrub, prickly stems with white bloom in winter. Leaves fern-like, dark green above, felty white below. Red-purple flowers, solitary or in small terminal racemes, in summer. Round black fruit. Zones 6–10.

Rubus tricolor

☼ ✳ ↔ 8–15 ft (2.4–4.5 m) ↑ 2 ft (0.6 m)

Native to western China. Low-growing evergreen or semi-evergreen shrub, bristly stems. Shiny dark green leaves, 3-lobed, felty white beneath. White saucer-shaped flowers, singly or in sparse terminal racemes, in summer. Edible red fruit. Zones 7–9.

Rubus ursinus

☼ ✳ ↔ 3–10 ft (0.9–3 m) ↑ 20–36 in (50–90 cm)

Evergreen shrub native to California, USA. Upright or prostrate habit. Leaves with 3 to 5 leaflets, hairy above, felty white underneath. Male and female flowers on separate plants, white, in prickly corymbs, in spring–summer. Black hairy fruit. Zones 7–9.

RUELLIA (see page 558)

Ruellia macrantha
CHRISTMAS PRIDE

◑ ⅀ ↔ 20 in (50 cm) ↑ 6 ft (1.8 m)

Short-lived species native to Brazil. Erect stems, rounded crown of hairy, dark green, oval to lance-shaped leaves. Large, deep pink, trumpet-shaped flowers, darker veins, in winter. Zones 10–12.

RUSPOLIA

The 4 species of evergreen shrubs in this genus, which is a member of the acanthus (Acanthaceae) family, are native to Africa. They have oval opposite leaves and bear spikes or panicles of flowers in shades of red or yellow with flaring petal lobes.
CULTIVATION: In cool climates, species of *Ruspolia* make attractive flowering shrubs for the conservatory or greenhouse, where they should be shaded during the hottest part of the day. In very warm and tropical climates, grow outdoors in a humus-rich soil. Propagate from softwood cuttings taken in late spring.

Ruspolia hypocrateriformis

◑ ✛ ↔ 3 ft (0.9 m) ↑ 3 ft (0.9 m)

Small shrub from tropical and southern Africa; semi-trailing habit. Smooth leaves, to 3 in (8 cm) long. Flowers deep reddish pink,

tubular, with darker throat, in showy terminal panicles, appear over many months. Zones 10–12.

RUSSELIA

This genus of about 50 evergreen subshrubs and shrubs found from Mexico to Colombia is a member of the foxglove (Scrophulariaceae) family. The commonly grown species has arching stems, but *Russelia* species vary in habit and may be erect, arching, or spreading. They also vary in foliage, some species having much-reduced, scale-like leaves, others having heart-shaped leaves up to 4 in (10 cm) long. The flowers, however, are more distinctive, being flared pendulous tubes that appear through much of the year.
CULTIVATION: These plants are marginally frost tender and perform best in a mild climate. They flower most heavily when grown in full sun, and they prefer a gritty well-drained soil that can be kept moist in the warmer months. Trim lightly to encourage a neat bushy habit. Propagation is usually either from cuttings or by removing self-rooted layers.

Ruellia macrantha

Russelia equisetiformis
CORAL PLANT

☼ ⅀ ↔ 8 ft (2.4 m) ↑ 5 ft (1.5 m)

Native to Mexico. Arching weeping stems, leafless or nearly so, leaves reduced to small scales, closely held to wiry green stems. Small, bright red, tubular flowers, throughout year. Excellent spillover plant for wall or bank. Zones 9–12.

RUTTYA

This genus in the acanthus (Acanthaceae) family contains 3 species of evergreen shrubs that are native to tropical areas of eastern Africa. They have oval opposite leaves and bear colorful tubular flowers on short spikes.
CULTIVATION: In tropical and subtropical climates these plants are easily grown in a fertile well-drained soil, and are ideal for shrub borders. In cooler climates they make attractive flowering plants for the greenhouse or conservatory. Young plants should be pinched out to encourage bushiness. Propagation is from seed or from half-hardened cuttings.

Ruspolia hypocrateriformis

Russelia equisetiformis

Ruttya fruticosa
JAMMY-MOUTH

☼ ⬥ ↔ 5 ft (1.5 m) ↑ 12 ft (3.5 m)

Bushy shrub native to eastern Africa. Oval leaves. Flowers orangey red, petals fused into 2 lips, lower lip marked with dark brown blotch, in terminal spikes, appear over several months. 'Scholesii' ★, yellow flowers, lower lip marked with black blotch. Zones 10–12.

SALIX
OSIER, WILLOW

This large genus in the willow (Salicaceae) family consists of around 400 species, most from cold and temperate Northern Hemisphere regions. They range from trees to creeping shrublets, mostly decid-uous, with leaves often lance-shaped and toothed. The small flowers are usually insect-pollinated and are borne in a catkin; male and female flowers often appear on separate trees. The capsular fruit contain wind-dispersed hairy seeds. Many willows are widely grown for their timber, used for basketry and cricket bats. The bark is used medicinally, as it contains salicin, from which aspirin is derived. CULTIVATION: Most are fairly adaptable if they are adequately watered during the growing season and the soil is well drained, not swampy. Propagate from seed, by layering, or from cuttings, which root easily even up to branch size.

Salix alba, New Zealand

Salix alba
WHITE WILLOW

☼ ❋ ↔ 30 ft (9 m) ↑ 80 ft (24 m)

Broadly columnar tree native to western Asia and Europe. Droop-ing branch tips, dark gray deeply fissured bark. Narrow lance-shaped leaves, silky and white when young; dark green above, bluish green beneath with age. Thin catkins, with leaves, in spring. 'Vitellina', bright yellow young shoots prominent in winter. Zones 2–10.

Salix amygdaloides
PEACH-LEAFED WILLOW

☼ ❋ ↔ 25 ft (8 m) ↑ 70 ft (21 m)

Tree native to western North America. Young growth smooth and yellow or reddish brown. Oval to lance-shaped leaves, finely serrated mar-gins, bluish or grayish green beneath, downy when young. Female catkins to 4 in (10 cm). Zones 5–10.

Salix arctica
ARCTIC WILLOW

☼ ❋ ↔ 24–48 in (60–120 cm) ↑ 4 in (10 cm)

Creeping shrub, native to higher latitudes of Europe, Asia, and North America. Thick glossy twigs, leathery oval leaves networked with veins. Dark purple catkins. Zones 1–8.

Salix babylonica
PEKING WILLOW, WEEPING WILLOW

☼ ❋ ↔ 35 ft (10 m) ↑ 40 ft (12 m)

Native to northern China; brought to Middle East via trade routes, then to Europe in 1700s. Most planted trees belong to single female

Salix caprea

clone. Long vertically pendulous branches; leaves tapering to long fine point, finely toothed, smooth, bluish-gray beneath. Non-weeping ancestral Chinese trees named *S. b.* f. *pekinensis* (syn. *S. matsudana*); they include 'Crispa', slow-growing, leaves twisted or spirally curled; 'Navajo' (syn. *S. matsudana* 'Navajo'), broad, umbrella-shaped dense crown, very large; 'Tortuosa' (syn. *S. matsudana* 'Tortuosa'), contorted shape, upright in habit, twigs twisted and curled, used in floristry; 'Umbraculifera' (syn. *S. mat-sudana* 'Umbraculifera'), broad rounded habit. Zones 5–10.

Salix 'Boydii'

☼ ❋ ↔ 2 ft (0.6 m) ↑ 3 ft (0.9 m)

Natural hybrid found in 1870s in Scotland. Slow-growing dwarf shrub, twigs persistently downy, gnarled appearance. Round gray leaves also downy. Small dark gray catkins, rarely produced. Zones 5–9.

Salix caprea
FLORIST'S WILLOW, PUSSY WILLOW

☼ ❋ ↔ 10–20 ft (3–6 m) ↑ 15–35 ft (4.5–10 m)

Small tree or shrub from Europe to northeastern Asia. Elliptical to oblong leaves, slightly glossy, dark green above, gray and felted below, dull yellow in winter. Plump silky male catkins in spring. 'Pen-dula' (Kilmarnock willow), weeping branches, yellow-brown shoots, gray male catkins. Zones 5–10.

Salix cinerea
GRAY WILLOW

☼ ❋ ↔ 8 ft (2.4 m) ↑ 10 ft (3 m)

Shrubby species found from UK and continental Europe to west-ern Asia. Covered in fine gray down, remaining on twigs through second season. Narrow leaves dull green above, gray beneath. Silky catkins appear before leaves. Zones 2–9.

Salix fragilis

Salix daphnoides
VIOLET WILLOW

☼　❋　↔ 20 ft (6 m)　↑ 35 ft (10 m)

Vigorous erect tree or shrub, native to Europe and central Asia to Himalayas. Plum-colored bloom on young shoots. Long narrow leaves, glossy dark green above, bluish green below. Small, broad, silky male catkins in late winter–spring. Zones 5–10.

Salix discolor
AMERICAN PUSSY WILLOW

☼　❋　↔ 15 ft (4.5 m)　↑ 25 ft (8 m)

Shrub or small tree native to North America. Purplish brown shoots, downy at first. Oval leaves, bright green above, bluish gray beneath. Catkins appear before leaves, in late winter–spring. Zones 2–9.

Salix elaeagnos
HOARY WILLOW, ROSEMARY WILLOW

☼　❋　↔ 20 ft (6 m)　↑ 20 ft (6 m)

Shrub or small tree native to central Europe, Turkey, and southwestern Asia. Twigs gray and downy, becoming smooth, reddish yellow to brown. Dark green leaves, long, narrow, felted white beneath. Catkins appear before leaves, in spring. *S. e.* subsp. *angustifolia*, creeping stems, thin narrow leaves. Zones 4–9.

Salix fargesii

☼　❋　↔ 10 ft (3 m)　↑ 10 ft (3 m)

Chinese shrub. Large red winter buds. Leaves serrated edges, glossy dark green above, silky dull green below. Long slender catkins, with leaves, in spring. Zones 6–10.

Salix 'Flame'
FLAME WILLOW

☼　❋　↔ 20 ft (6 m)　↑ 20 ft (6 m)

Large shrub or round-headed small tree, most likely hybrid of *S. alba*. Young branches bright red. Leaves lance-shaped, downy when young, turn bright yellow, in autumn, contrasting with red twigs. Prune in spring to encourage bright new growth. Zones 5–9.

Salix fragilis
BRITTLE WILLOW, CRACK WILLOW

☼　❋　↔ 35 ft (10 m)　↑ 50 ft (15 m)

Broadly spreading tree native to Europe and northern Asia. Dark gray bark, deeply fissured, twigs break easily at joints. Long narrow leaves, silky, becoming dark green above, bluish green below. Slender catkins appear with leaves. Zones 6–10.

Salix gracilistyla
ROSEGOLD PUSSY WILLOW

☼　❋　↔ 10–15 ft (3–4.5 m)　↑ 10–15 ft (3–4.5 m)

Shrub native to eastern Asia. Oblong leaves. Catkins before leaves, in late winter; male catkins red, later orange, then yellow, female catkins silky gray. 'Melanostachys' ★ (syn. *S. melanostachys*), male form; black catkins with red-tipped yellow stamens. Zones 6–10.

Salix hastata
HALBERD WILLOW

☼　❋　↔ 7 ft (2 m)　↑ 5 ft (1.5 m)

Dense erect shrub native to mountainous areas of central Europe and northeastern Asia. Twigs become purple in second year. Leaves variable, oblong to slightly rounded, dull green above, glaucous beneath. Small plump catkins appear with leaves, in spring. 'Wehrhahnii', attractive silvery catkins. Zones 6–9.

Salix helvetica
SWISS WILLOW

☼　❋　↔ 3 ft (0.9 m)　↑ 2–5 ft (0.6–1.5 m)

Shrub from European alpine regions. Forms small spreading mound of densely interlaced twigs, larger in cultivation than species. Red-brown stems. Leaves glossy green, serrated edges, downy underside. Smothered in small silver-gray catkins in spring. Zones 5–9.

Salix integra
DAPPLED WILLOW, JAPANESE WILLOW

❋　↔ 12 ft (3.5 m)　↑ 10–15 ft (3–4.5 m)

Slender shrub from Japan and Korea; like *S. purpurea*, but leaves lighter shade of green. Drooping, purplish branches. Slender catkins before leaves. 'Hakura Nishiki', pink leaf buds and stems. Zones 6–10.

Salix lanata
ARCTIC WILLOW, WOOLLY WILLOW

☼　❋　↔ 6 ft (1.8 m)　↑ 2–4 ft (0.6–1.2 m)

Slow-growing shrub native to northern areas of Europe. Stout branchlets, densely woolly, gnarled with age. Oval to rounded leaves covered in silvery silky hairs, becoming dull green on upper surface. Bright golden catkins, after leaves, in spring. Zones 2–9.

Salix nigra

Salix lindleyana

☼　❋　↔ 30 in (75 cm)　↑ 2 in (5 cm)

Alpine species found in Himalayas. Forms dense mats of small, green, rosemary-like leaves on reddish stems. Leaves turn attractive yellow in autumn. Tiny catkins appear with leaves. Zones 5–10.

Salix repens | Salix reptans

Salix magnifica

☼ ❊ ↔ 10 ft (3 m) ↑ 20 ft (6 m)

Tree native to China. Magnolia-like foliage, smooth purplish shoots and buds. Blunt oval leaves, grayish green, yellowish green midrib and veining. Female catkins appear in spring with leaves. Zones 7–10.

Salix nakamurana

☼ ❊ ↔ 36 in (90 cm) ↑ 12 in (30 cm)

Slow-growing dwarf shrub native to Japan. Stout arching stems eventually form mound. Leaves large in relation to plant size, almost round, light green, silvery hairs. Catkins also silvery. Zones 6–10.

Salix nigra

BLACK WILLOW

☼ ❊ ↔ 15 ft (4.5 m) ↑ 10–30 ft (3–9 m)

North American large shrub or small tree. Rough bark, yellowish twigs. Narrow, pointed, pale green leaves with finely serrated margins. Catkins on short downy shoots, with leaves, in spring. Zones 4–10.

Salix purpurea

ALASKA BLUE WILLOW, ARCTIC WILLOW, PURPLE OSIER WILLOW

☼ ❊ ↔ 15 ft (4.5 m) ↑ 15 ft (4.5 m)

Shrub or small tree found from Europe to northern Africa, central Asia, and Japan. Arching purplish shoots, narrow oblong leaves, bluish green above, paler beneath. Red catkins, becoming purplish black, appear in spring before leaves. 'Nana' (syn. *S. purpurea* f. *gracilis*), gray-green leaves, thin shoots; 'Pendula', thin pendulous branches. Zones 5–10.

Salix repens

CREEPING WILLOW

☼ ❊ ↔ 5 ft (1.5 m) ↑ 8 in–5 ft (20 cm–1.5 m)

Creeping shrub from Europe, Turkey, south-western Asia, and Siberia. Downy shoots become smooth. Small tapering leaves, green above, silvery below. Small catkins in spring. Zones 5–10.

Salix reptans

ARCTIC CREEPING WILLOW

☼ ❊ ↔ 18–36 in (45–90 cm) ↑ 2 in (5 cm)

Dwarf from far northern Asia and Russia. Reddish brown branches. Leaves green, dense long hairs, wrinkled above, paler bluish beneath. Erect catkins, long-haired black-tipped scales. Zones 2–8.

Salix reticulata

NET-LEAFED WILLOW

☼ ❊ ↔ 15 in (38 cm) ↑ 6 in (15 cm)

Dwarf shrub from northern Europe, North America, and Asia. Oval to rounded leaves, dark green, wrinkled above, white beneath. Small, erect, mauve-tipped catkins, after leaves, in spring. Zones 1–8.

Salix × rubens

☼ ❊ ↔ 25 ft (8 m) ↑ 35 ft (10 m)

Natural hybrid of *S. alba* and *S. fragilis*, native to central Europe. Olive twigs tinged yellow or red. Lance-shaped leaves, bright green above, glaucous beneath. Cylindrical catkins. Zones 6–10.

Salix × sepulcralis

☼ ❊ ↔ 40 ft (12 m) ↑ 40 ft (12 m)

Hybrid between *S. alba* and *S. babylonica*, of garden origin. Habit and foliage similar to but slightly less weeping than *S. babylonica*. Fissured bark. Slender catkins similar to *S. alba*. Zones 6–10.

Salix taxifolia

☼ ❊ ↔ 7–10 ft (2–3 m) ↑ 10–15 ft (3–4.5 m)

Shrub from southern North America and Mexico. Narrow leaves, branches slightly furry. Tiny male and female catkins. Zones 8–10.

Salix viminalis

COMMON OSIER, HEMP WILLOW

☼ ❊ ↔ 15 ft (4.5 m) ↑ 8–20 ft (2.4–6 m)

Shrub from Europe to northeast Asia and Himalayas. Long flexible shoots, thick gray hair when young. Narrow leaves dull green above, silvery silky below. Catkins before leaves, in spring. Zones 4–10.

Salix × sepulcralis, UK

SALVIA

SAGE

The largest genus in the mint (Lamiaceae) family, *Salvia* contains annuals, perennials, and softwooded evergreen shrubs. They grow in habitats ranging from coastal to alpine; over half the 900 or so species are native to the Americas. The leaves are opposite and carried on squared hairy stems, and are aromatic when crushed. The flowers are tubular, with the petals split into 2 straight or flaring lips. Colors may be shades of blue to purple and pink to red, as well as white and some yellows.

CULTIVATION: The shrubby sages grow in a range of soil types, but dislike heavy wet soil. Most do best in full sun; all require a well-drained situation. Prune in spring to remove straggly, bare, and frost-damaged stems. Propagate most shrubby species from softwood cuttings taken throughout the growing season. Seed of all species can be sown in spring.

Salvia apiana

BEE SAGE, CALIFORNIA WHITE SAGE

☼ ↔ 3 ft (0.9 m) ↑ 4 ft (1.2 m)

Shrub from southwestern California, USA. Silvery covering of fine hairs. Leaves very aromatic. White or pale lavender flowers, in loose whorls above foliage, in spring. Zones 9–11.

Salvia aurea

syn. *Salvia africana-lutea*

BEACH SAGE, BROWN SALVIA, GOLDEN SAGE

☼ ↔ 3 ft (0.9 m) ↑ 3–5 ft (0.9–1.5 m)

Stiff well-branched shrub from coastal areas of South Africa. Small, aromatic, grayish green leaves. Whorls of large yellow flowers, fading to orangey brown, in summer–autumn. Prominent greenish brown calyces. **'Kirstenbosch'**, dwarf cultivar to 3 ft (0.9 m) high and wide, aromatic silvery leaves. Zones 9–11.

Salvia canariensis

CANARY ISLAND SAGE

☼ ↔ 3 ft (0.9 m) ↑ 4–7 ft (1.2–2 m)

Shrub native to Canary Islands. Stems covered in dense white hairs. Leaves soft, arrowhead-shaped, grayish green, hairy. Lilac-pink flowers, showy purplish red calyces, in spring–summer. **'Alba'**, pink calyces, white flowers. Zones 9–11.

Salvia clevelandii

CALIFORNIA BLUE SAGE, CLEVELAND SAGE

☼ ❄ ↔ 15–26 in (38–65 cm) ↑ 24–48 in (60–120 cm)

Shrub from California, USA. Aromatic, oval to lance-shaped, gray-green leaves, toothed edges, wrinkled upper surface. Whorls of fragrant, lavender-blue, rarely white, flowers, on erect flower spikes, in summer. **'Winifred Gilman'** ★, drought-tolerant. Zones 8–10.

Salvia fruticosa

GREEK SAGE, TRILOBA SAGE

☼ ❄ ↔ 2 ft (0.6 m) ↑ 3 ft (0.9 m)

Evergreen shrub from east Mediterranean region. Rough gray-green leaves. Spikes of small 2-lipped flowers, pink or mauve, at stem ends. May develop cherry-sized galls from insect sting. Zones 8–10.

Salvia × jamensis

☼ ↔ 27–40 in (70–100 cm) ↑ 27–40 in (70–100 cm)

Shrubby hybrid between *S. microphylla* and *S. greggii*. Glossy green oval leaves. Flowers in range of solid colors, including reds, pinks, oranges, apricots, and yellows, also some bicolored forms, in summer–autumn. **'Cinega de Oro'**, pale yellow flowers. Zones 9–11.

Salvia karwinskii

KARWINSKI'S SAGE

☼ ↔ 4 ft (1.2 m) ↑ 8 ft (2.4 m)

Shrubby species from Central America. Large felted leaves. Abundant, large, showy heads of red-pink flowers in winter. Zones 10–11.

Salvia leucophylla

CHAPARRAL SAGE, GRAY SAGE, PURPLE SAGE

☼ ❄ ↔ 3 ft (0.9 m) ↑ 5 ft (1.5 m)

Well-branched shrub native to hot, dry, stony hillsides of California, USA. Whitish gray, hairy leaves. Whorls of pinkish purple flowers, on pinkish stems, in autumn. **'Figuero'**, smaller, silvery foliage; **'Point Sal Spreader'** ★, prostrate form, grayer leaves. Zones 8–11.

Salvia mexicana

MEXICAN SAGE

☼ ↔ 7 ft (2 m) ↑ 10 ft (3 m)

Vigorous grower native to Mexico. Smooth to slightly hairy leaves, almost heart-shaped, mid-green to grayish green. Spikes of deep

Salvia clevelandii

Salvia fruticosa

Salvia leucophylla

purple flowers, from large green calyces, held well above foliage, in autumn. 'Limelight', chartreuse stems and calyces. Zones 9–11.

Salvia regla
MOUNTAIN SAGE

☼ ⬥ ↔ 3 ft (0.9 m) ↑ 4 ft (1.2 m)

Shrub found in Texas, USA, and Mexico. Erect woody habit, upper stems dark red-brown. Leaves triangular with wavy edges. Large bright scarlet-red flowers in autumn. 'Royal', tubular orange flowers; 'Huntington', orange-red flowers. Zones 9–10.

SAMBUCUS
ELDER, ELDERBERRY

This genus from the world's temperate areas encompasses around 25 species of perennials, shrubs, and small trees that are mostly deciduous, from the woodbine (Caprifoliaceae) family. Some are ornamental, others invasive weeds. Elders have pinnate leaves, and the umbel-like heads of small white to creamy yellow flowers develop into quick-ripening berries, usually red to black.
CULTIVATION: Elders are not difficult to grow, and some species are only too easily cultivated. They are not fussy about soil type as long as the ground remains fairly moist in summer, nor are they worried by brief periods of water-logging in winter. Most species are very frost hardy, and will reshoot even when cut to the ground by frost. Prune trees to shape as necessary, and propagate from seed or cuttings.

Sambucus canadensis

Sambucus canadensis
AMERICAN ELDER, AMERICAN ELDERBERRY, SWEET ELDER

☼ ❄ ↔ 12 ft (3.5 m) ↑ 8–12 ft (2.4–3.5 m)

Deciduous shrub from eastern North America, sometimes suckering. Leaves have 7 leaflets with serrated edges, smooth or woolly below. Cream flowers in summer, tiny purple-black berries. 'Goldfinch', reddish young leaves. Zones 3–9.

Sambucus ebulus
DANE'S ELDER, DANEWORT, DWARF ELDER

☼ ❄ ↔ 3–7 ft (0.9–2 m) ↑ 5–7 ft (1.5–2 m)

From southern Europe through northern Africa to Iran. Leaves divided, up to 9 leaflets to 6 in (15 cm) long. Tiny flowers in flattish heads to 4 in (10 cm) wide, followed by black berries, in summer. Zones 5–10.

Sambucus nigra
BLACK ELDER, EUROPEAN ELDER

☼ ❄ ↔ 10–20 ft (3–6 m) ↑ 8–30 ft (2.4–9 m)

Deciduous shrub or small tree from Europe, North Africa, and western Asia. Self-sows and suckers freely. Weed in many areas, but cultivated for edible flowers and fruit. Leaves have 3 to 9 dark green leaflets with serrated edges. Large heads of scented white flowers in spring–early summer. Purple-black berries. 'Aurea', golden yellow foliage; 'Aureomarginata', paler variegated foliage, berries grow on pink stems; 'Guincho Purple', deep green leaves turn very dark

Sanchezia speciosa

purple; 'Laciniata', deeply dissected leaflets; 'Marginata', gold- to cream-edged foliage; 'Pulverulenta', musk-scented flowers; 'Viridis', pale green flowers and fruit. Zones 5–10.

Sambucus racemosa
EUROPEAN RED ELDER, RED ELDERBERRY

☼ ❄ ↔ 12 ft (3.5 m) ↑ 12 ft (3.5 m)

Deciduous shrub found in most of temperate Eurasia. Leaves with 5 leaflets, coarsely serrated edges. Panicles of pale green to cream flowers in spring–early summer, followed by clusters of very small red berries. 'Plumosa Aurea', dissected yellow foliage; 'Tenuifolia', dwarf, deeply cut foliage, purple new growth. Zones 4–9.

SANCHEZIA
Named after Josef Sanchez, an early Spanish professor of botany, this genus of about 20 species of soft-stemmed shrubs, climbers, and perennials from the acanthus (Acanthaceae) family is native to tropical America. Sanchezia species are grown for their attractive leaves, which are carried in opposite pairs, and for their tubular flowers, each with 5 lobes, and often with conspicuous colorful bracts. Fruit are oblong capsules containing 6 to 8 seeds.
CULTIVATION: Frost tender, these are warm-climate plants that need good soil and regular watering. They prefer well-drained soil, in full sun or bright filtered light, in a position sheltered from wind. Water potted specimens adequately during the growing season, and keep just moist at other times. Plants can be kept neat and bushy by pinching out the growing tips. Propagate from cuttings taken in spring or summer.

Sanchezia speciosa
syn. Sanchezia nobilis

☼ ⬥ ↔ 5 ft (1.5 m) ↑ 5 ft (1.5 m)

Bushy evergreen shrub from South America. Large, leathery, dark green, oblong-ovate leaves, yellow or white veins. Tubular yellow flowers, bright red bracts, on ends of spikes, in summer. Zones 10–12.

Santolina rosmarinifolia

SANTALUM

This genus of around 25 species of evergreen shrubs and small trees of the sandalwood (Santalaceae) family comes from Southeast Asia, Australia, and some Pacific Islands. It includes a number of trees noted for their scented wood and oils. Some Australian species bear edible fruit, and have been researched as commercial food crops. They usually rely on the roots of other plants to supply their water and nutrients. The host may be another tree, a shrub, a dense ground-covering plant, or a well-established lawn with a vigorous root system. CULTIVATION: Grow in warm low-rainfall areas with full sun and light well-drained soil. Species will tolerate saline soils and periods of dryness, but they resent root disturbance and poor drainage. They may be propagated from seed, but early growth is often slow, and grafted plants are preferred for orchard crops.

Santalum acuminatum

QUANDONG, SWEET QUANDONG

☀ ❋ ↔ 12 ft (3.5 m) ↑ 20 ft (6 m)
Large shrub or small tree, widespread in inland Australia. Spindly erect trunk, open crown of pale olive green lance-shaped leaves. Panicles of small whitish cream flowers, at ends of stems, sporadically throughout year. Shiny, red, edible fruit. Zones 9–11.

Santalum lanceolatum

NORTHERN SANDALWOOD

☀ ❋ ↔ 15 ft (4.5 m) ↑ 20 ft (6 m)
Tall shrub or small tree from tropical Australia. Pendulous spreading branches, lance-shaped leaves. Cream or pale green flowers, in leaf axils or in panicles at ends of branches, in spring–summer. Dark blue or purplish edible fruit. Zones 10–12.

SANTOLINA

This Mediterranean genus from the daisy (Asteraceae) family is composed of some 18 species of largely similar evergreen shrubs

that form low hummocks. The slender stems are crowded with narrow leaves that have finely toothed or lobed margins. They are often clothed in silvery hairs, as are the leaf stalks. Clusters of button-like flowerheads, usually bright yellow, appear in summer. CULTIVATION: Fully to moderately frost hardy, these shrubs thrive in a warm sunny position and are ideal for dry banks and as border plants. They need perfect drainage and do not like overly wet winters, but are not fussy about soil type as long as it is reasonably loose and open. Species respond well to regular trimming to keep the bushes neat and compact. It is also advisable to remove the dead flowerheads, as they are not attractive once they have dried. Propagate from small cuttings or by removing self-rooted layers.

Santolina rosmarinifolia

GREEN SANTOLINA

☀ ❋ ↔ 36 in (90 cm) ↑ 12–24 in (30–60 cm)
Bushy shrub native to southwestern Europe. Sparsely downy linear leaves, fine narrow teeth, closely spaced. Clusters of ¾ in (18 mm) wide bright yellow flowerheads in mid-summer. 'Morning Mist ★', compact form; 'Primrose Gem', light lemon flowers. Zones 7–10.

SAPINDUS

There are about 13 species in this tropical and subtropical genus, most from the Americas and Asia. These evergreen and deciduous trees, shrubs, and climbers belong to the soapberry (Sapindaceae) family. They are grown mostly as ornamental and shade trees.

Santalum lanceolatum

They have alternate simple or pinnate leaves, which in some species color attractively to shades of yellow in autumn. They bear clusters of small 5-petalled flowers with prominent hairy stamens in summer, and these are followed by a crop of fleshy berry-like fruit. These berries are rich in saponins (glycosides that foam in water), and are used to yield a soap substitute in some countries. CULTIVATION: Most species are fairly adaptable, and will tolerate poor soil as long as it is well drained. They prefer a sheltered position that is in full sun. Propagation is either from seed or cuttings.

Sapindus drummondii

WESTERN SOAPBERRY, WILD CHINA TREE

☀ ❋ ↔ 30 ft (9 m) ↑ 50 ft (15 m)
Deciduous tree from southern USA and Mexico, occupying harsh dry habitats. Pinnate leaves, 18 mid-green leaflets, turning golden yellow in autumn. Small white flowers, in panicles at ends of branches, in summer. Rounded orange-yellow fruit. Zones 8–10.

Sapindus mukorossi

CHINESE SOAPBERRY

☀ ❋ ↔ 20 ft (6 m) ↑ 40–80 ft (12–24 m)
Deciduous tree found from India eastward through China to Japan. Large pinnate leaves. White flowers, in panicles at ends of branches, in summer. Yellow to orange-brown fruit used as soap substitute; black seeds used for beads. Zones 8–11.

Sapindus saponaria
FALSE DOGWOOD, SOAPBERRY, WING-LEAFED SOAPBERRY

☼ ⚘ ↔ 20 ft (6 m) ↑ 30 ft (9 m)

Evergreen tree from tropical America. Pinnate leaves to 12 in (30 cm) long. White flowers, in panicles to 6 in (15 cm) long, in summer. Glossy, orange-brown, saponin-rich fruit, used as soap. Zones 10–12.

SAPIUM
This is a genus of around 100 species of mainly evergreen trees and shrubs in the euphorbia (Euphorbiaceae) family, the majority from tropical America, Asia, and Africa, with a smaller number from warm-temperate regions such as South Africa. Leaves are simple and often toothed, while the flowers are small and petal-less, carried in catkin-like spikes at the ends of branchlets, with male and female flowers on different parts of the spike; the fruit is a capsule with 1 to 3 seeds. Some species are important for timber, and the latex of some has been put to various uses.
CULTIVATION: They can be grown in a frost-free climate with ample summer rainfall. Plant in full sun and in moderately fertile soil. Propagate from fresh seed, collected as the capsules shatter.

Sapium integerrimum
DUIKER-BERRY

☼ ⚘ ↔ 20 ft (6 m) ↑ 10–20 ft (3–6 m)

Native to eastern South Africa and adjacent Mozambique, often "pioneer" tree on forest margins, briefly deciduous in dry season. Branching low, irregular crown, drooping branches; oblong to elliptic leaves, shiny deep green above, pale blue-green beneath. Yellowish flowers in spring–summer. Fruit yellow-green, to 1 in (25 mm) wide, 3-seeded. Zones 10–12.

SARACA
A genus of about 70 species of small evergreen trees in the cassia subfamily of the legume (Fabaceae) family, it comes from the tropical forests of India, extending to China and Southeast Asia. The trees are grown for their dense upturned flower clusters in shades of yellow, orange, and red. Individual flowers have no petals; instead, they have 4 brightly colored sepals at the top of a tube with slender projecting stamens up to 8 in (20 cm) long. The leaves are pinnate with paired leaflets; they are soft, dangling, pinkish purple when young, maturing to a bright glossy green. These trees grow beneath taller trees in their natural habitat, and therefore like to be in shade, preferably that of taller trees.
CULTIVATION: Frost tender, they require a warm humid climate and a moist well-drained soil enriched with organic matter. In cooler areas, cultivate as greenhouse plants. Propagated from seed in autumn or winter.

Saraca cauliflora
syn. *Saraca thaipingensis*

☀ ⚘ ↔ 25 ft (8 m) ↑ 30 ft (9 m)

Tree from Thailand to Malay Peninsula. Compound leaves with 6 to 8 pairs of oblong leaflets, reddish when young. Night-fragrant yellow flowers, gradually deepening in color to red, at beginning and end of tropical dry season. Narrow, oblong, leguminous fruit. Zones 11–12.

SARCOBATUS
Native to western North America, this genus contains only 1 species and belongs to the rose (Rosaceae) family. It is a dense spiny shrub with arching branches and narrow fleshy leaves. Male and female flowers appear on the same plant, and both are usually small, with the male flowers forming catkin-like spikes. The enlarging calyx of the female flowers develops into a leathery fruit with a broad papery wing toward the middle.
CULTIVATION: Moderately frost hardy, this species grows best in a warm sheltered position in full sun and well-drained soil. Propagation is from seed.

Sarcobatus vermiculatus
GREASEWOOD

☼ ❄ ↔ 7 ft (2 m) ↑ 6 ft (1.8 m)

Rounded spreading shrub with arching branches. Narrow, fleshy, gray-green leaves to 1½ in (35 mm) long. Spikes of male flowers to 1¼ in (30 mm) long. Hard yellow wood used for fuel. Zones 5–10.

SARCOCOCCA
CHRISTMAS BOX, SWEET BOX

This genus in the box (Buxaceae) family consists of evergreen monoecious shrubs cultivated for their ornamental value. Their natural habitats are damp woods and dense forests in western China, the Himalayas, and the mountains of Southeast Asia. Male flowers have visible anthers; female flowers grow below the male flowers.
CULTIVATION: They grow best in neutral to alkaline soil, with plenty of humus added. Once established, they will tolerate drier conditions in shade. They can be grown in full sun, but will need more moisture. Most tolerate years of negligence and air pollution. Propagation is from seed, by division of suckering species, or by taking half-hardened cuttings in late summer. Hardwood cuttings can be taken in winter and propagated in an area protected from winter frosts.

Sarcococca confusa

☽ ❄ ↔ 7 ft (2 m) ↑ 7 ft (2 m)

Evergreen shrub. Leathery, dark green, elliptical to lance-shaped leaves, pale underside. Clusters of cream flowers, female form very fragrant, in mid-winter. Red berries ripen to black. Zones 6–10.

Sapindus mukorossi   *Saraca cauliflora*

Sarcococca hookeriana

☼ ❄ ↔ 6 ft (1.8 m) ↑ 5 ft (1.5 m)

Evergreen, thicket-forming, often suckering shrub native to China. Lance-shaped deep green leaves. Clusters of scented white flowers, males with deep pink anthers, in late autumn–winter. Black fruit. *S. h.* subsp. *humilis* ★, ground-cover plant, shiny bluish black fruit. *S. h.* var. *digyna*, slender leaves, white flowers with off-white anthers. *S. h.* 'Purple Stem', young magenta shoots, pink-tinted flowers. Zones 6–10.

Sarcococca ruscifolia

☼ ❄ ↔ 3 ft (0.9 m) ↑ 3 ft (0.9 m)

Thick bushy suckering shrub native to western China and Himalayas. Glossy, deep green, broadly lance-shaped leaves. Clusters of creamy white perfumed flowers throughout winter. Dark red fruit. Zones 8–10.

Sarcococca saligna

☼ ❄ ↔ 3 ft (0.9 m) ↑ 3 ft (0.9 m)

Suckering, evergreen, thicket-forming shrub native to Himalayas from Nepal to Afghanistan. Narrow, lance-shaped, pale green leaves. Male flowers green, female flowers greenish white, in winter–early spring. Egg-shaped dark purple fruit. Zones 7–10.

SASSAFRAS

This genus includes just 3 species in the laurel (Lauraceae) family. They are deciduous trees with a rather scattered distribution, occurring in temperate East Asia and eastern North America. They have been cultivated for their aromatic oils, which repel pests and so are valuable in the furniture industry. *Sassafras* leaves may be smooth-edged or lobed, are downy on their underside, and sometimes develop vivid autumn colors. Racemes of tiny, petal-less, yellow-green flowers appear in spring with the developing leaves, and are followed by blue-black drupes.
CULTIVATION: They are reasonably frost hardy. They prefer deep, fertile, well-drained soil, and will grow in either sun or part-shade. They tend to produce multiple trunks, and clever pruning can be directed to encourage this habit or to produce a single-trunked tree, as the situation dictates. Propagation is from seed, suckers, or root cuttings.

Sassafras albidum

Sassafras albidum

SASSAFRAS

☼ ❄ ↔ 30 ft (9 m) ↑ 50 ft (15 m)

North American tree, may be many-trunked. Oval leaves, up to 3 lobes, dark green, downy underside, turn gold and red in autumn. Underbark is source of sassafras oil. Zones 5–9.

SCHEFFLERA

syns *Brassaia, Dizygotheca, Heptapleurum*

This large genus in the ivy (Araliaceae) family consists of around 900 species, occurring in tropical and subtropical regions throughout the world, usually in moist environments, with the majority found from Southeast Asia to the Pacific Islands. Mostly shrubs, trees, scrambling climbers, or epiphytes, they have leaves composed of usually rounded leaflets of similar sizes and arranged in whorls held on a long stalk. Small flowers are produced in umbels, panicles, racemes, or spikes, and are followed by small black or purple fruit. Cultivated for their ornamental foliage, they are suitable for the garden in frost-free climates, or they can be used as pot plants, both indoors and outside.
CULTIVATION: Most are fairly adaptable, tolerating full sun to part-shade. They prefer well-drained moderately fertile soil with adequate moisture during growth periods. Propagate from seed, which is sown as soon as it is ripe, from cuttings, or by aerial layering.

Schefflera actinophylla

syn. *Brassaia actinophylla*

OCTOPUS TREE, QUEENSLAND UMBRELLA TREE

☼ ❅ ↔ 12 ft (3.5 m) ↑ 30 ft (9 m)

Rainforest shrub or tree from New Guinea and northern and northeastern Australia. Many trunks; glossy light green leaflets. Radiating spikes of small red flowers, on ends of branches, in late summer–early spring. Fruit reddish black. Zones 10–12.

Schefflera arboricola

DWARF UMBRELLA TREE, HAWAIIAN ELF SCHEFFLERA

☼ ❅ ↔ 3 ft (0.9 m) ↑ 3–5 ft (0.9–1.5 m)

From Taiwan. Rounded shrub with palmate leaves, 7 to 11 glossy bright green leaflets. Small yellowish flowers, on panicles near branch tips, in spring–summer. Golden berries. Popular house plant. 'Jacqueline', leaves irregularly splashed pale yellow. Zones 10–12.

Schefflera elegantissima

ARALIA, FALSE ARALIA

☼ ❅ ↔ 10 ft (3 m) ↑ 50 ft (15 m)

Tree native to New Caledonia, smaller in cultivation. Juvenile stage is unbranched and well-foliaged, leaves consisting of 7 to 11 long, narrow, deeply serrated leaflets. Lustrous dark green leaflets become wider and more broadly toothed with maturity. Black berries. Zones 10–12.

Schefflera umbellifera

BASTARD CABBAGE TREE, FOREST CABBAGE TREE

☼ ❅ ↔ 25 ft (8 m) ↑ 30 ft (9 m)

Tree native to southern and southeastern Africa. Older specimens have dense rounded crowns and fissured resinous bark. Leaves

Schefflera actinophylla

Schinus terebinthifolius

comprise 5 oblong leaflets crowded near branch tips on long stalks. Panicles of small yellowish green flowers. Black berries. Zones 10–12.

SCHIMA

There is just a single species of evergreen tree in this genus, which is a member of the camellia (Theaceae) family. Native to the area from India to Southeast Asia and Indonesia, it is a small tree with glossy leaves and single white flowers that are borne in late summer. CULTIVATION: This tree requires a sheltered frost-free environment and a humus-rich acid soil. In cool climates it can be grown in containers in the greenhouse or conservatory. Propagate from seed or half-hardened cuttings.

Schima wallichii

☼ ❄ ↔ 20 ft (6 m) ↑ 25 ft (8 m)
Tree with dense bushy head. Large, leathery, glossy, green leaves, bronze red when young, arranged in spirals. White flowers, mildly fragrant, prominent yellow stamens, in late summer. Zones 9–11.

SCHINUS

Found in Central and South America, this genus from the cashew (Anacardiaceae) family includes some 30 species of evergreen shrubs and trees. They are notable for their attractive pinnate leaves, sometimes weeping branches, and their sprays of brown-red drupes. The fruit develop from racemes of tiny flowers— usually white, yellow-green, or pale pink— that open in spring or summer. There are separate male and female flowers, and these may occur on the same plants or on different plants. CULTIVATION: Hardiness varies with the species, though no *Schinus* species is extremely frost tolerant and many are frost tender, preferring a warm climate. Most species are very drought tolerant once established, and are best grown in well-drained soil in full sun. Propagate from seed or cuttings.

Schinus molle

PEPPER TREE
☼ ❄ ↔ 50 ft (15 m) ↑ 50–60 ft (15–18 m)
Spreading evergreen tree, with drooping branches, naturally found in South America. Finely divided, pinnate leaves. Small yellow-white flowers in spring. Clusters of pea-sized red berries. Used as street tree in southern Europe; can become weedy in some conditions. *S. m.* var. *areira* (syn. *S. areira*), semi-weeping habit, dark green leaves have aromatic resin, pink to red-brown berries, drought and heat tolerant. Zones 9–11.

Schinus terebinthifolius

BRAZILIAN PEPPER TREE
☼ ❄ ↔ 15 ft (4.5 m) ↑ 20 ft (6 m)
Shrub or small tree from southern Brazil, Argentina, and Paraguay. Leathery pinnate leaves with light underside, covering of fine hairs when young. Small flowers open white from pale green buds. Bright red fruit. Zones 9–12.

SCHOTIA

This small genus in the cassia subfamily of the legume (Fabaceae) family consists of 4 or 5 species from southern Africa. They are deciduous or semi-evergreen shrubs or trees with alternate leaves that have an even number of leaflets. The red or pink flowers have 5 petals, and are borne in panicles that occur along or at the ends of branches or directly from older wood in spring. Fruit are pods, usually leathery, flat, and oblong; in some species the round flat seeds are high in protein and form part of the local diet. These plants come from hot, dry, tropical, and subtropical semi-desert regions, including deciduous woodland and scrub that may be rocky. They are grown for their handsome foliage and attractive flowers.
CULTIVATION: These plants perform best in warm frost-free areas in a well-drained soil and a sunny position that is protected from strong winds. Propagation is either from seed or cuttings.

Schotia latifolia

Schotia brachypetala

AFRICAN WALNUT, TREE FUCHSIA
☼ ❄ ↔ 15–25 ft (4.5–8 m) ↑ 50 ft (15 m)
Deciduous large shrub or small tree naturally found in Zimbabwe, Mozambique, and South Africa. Rough grayish brown bark. Shiny, green, pinnate leaves; leaflets reddish when young. Fragrant crimson flowers, in large, showy, dense panicles, on leafless stems, in summer. Oblong bean-like pods, edible seeds. Zones 9–12.

Schotia latifolia

BEAN TREE, ELEPHANT HEDGE
☼ ❄ ↔ 25 ft (8 m) ↑ 50 ft (15 m)
Variable-shaped tree from eastern South Africa. Leaflets in pairs, 3 to 5 per leaf, narrow rounded bases. Panicles of almost-stalkless pinkish flowers at ends of branches. Hard pods. Zones 9–12.

SCIADOPITYS

This remarkable conifer genus has its own family, Sciadopityaceae, and consists of a single species of evergreen tree endemic to the mountains of Japan. The most striking attribute of *Sciadopitys* is its foliage, as it features 2 kinds of leaves: brown scale-leaves arranged spirally on elongated intervals of stem, and long, green, leaf-like needles radiating in whorls of up to 30 at the end of each interval. Male and female cones are borne on the same tree. The seed cones are like small pine cones, and have broad thin scales at their tips.
CULTIVATION: Plants are easily grown in cool climates as long as rainfall is adequate and summers are warm and humid. They prefer a reasonably sheltered position and deep fertile soil. Growth is slow but steady. Propagate from seed, though germination is poor unless seeds are stratified and then chilled for 3 months before sowing.

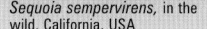

Sequoia sempervirens, in the wild, California, USA

Sequoiadendron giganteum

Sciadopitys verticillata

JAPANESE UMBRELLA PINE, UMBRELLA PINE

☼ ❄ ↔ 20 ft (6 m) ↑ 70 ft (21 m)

Conifer tree. Habit neat, conical, branches to ground level. Young plants grown in shade are more elongated. Rich brown bark peels in vertical strips. Whorls of deep glossy green leaves. Zones 6–9.

SENNA

This genus has about 350 species of tropical and warm-temperate trees, shrubs, and a few climbers, most from the Americas, Africa, Australia, and Asia. It is a member of the cassia subfamily of the legume (Fabaceae) family. All species have pinnate leaves, and almost all are evergreen. Most have yellow flowers, a few have pink flowers, but all are very showy when in flower. Many are the source of chemical compounds used medicinally. Fruit are long, flat, or rounded pods. Many species have become invasive weeds in countries where they have escaped cultivation.
CULTIVATION: Many species are frost tender. Grow in well-drained soil in open sunny positions. Species that originate from low-rainfall desert regions appear to be more frost hardy. Propagation is usually from seed, which germinates readily after pre-treatment, or from cuttings.

Senna didymobotrya

Senna alata

syn. *Cassia alata*

RINGWORM CASSIA

☼ ✈ ↔ 15 ft (4.5 m) ↑ 30 ft (9 m)

Shrub or tree from American tropics; naturalized elsewhere. Leaves large, 20 pairs of leaflets. Spikes of bright yellow flowers in late summer–early autumn. Winged pods age to brown. Zones 10–12.

Senna artemisioides

syn. *Cassia artemisioides*

FEATHERY CASSIA, SILVER CASSIA

☼ ❧ ↔ 7 ft (2 m) ↑ 7 ft (2 m)

Occurs throughout arid inland of mainland Australia. Has many varied forms. Typical plant is round shrub, with silvery gray leaves,

2 to 6 pairs of narrow leaflets. Yellow flowers appear in leaf axils in spring–autumn. Narrow flat pods. *S. a.* subsp. *filifolia* (syns *S. eremophila*, *S. nemophila*), pinnate leaves, 1 to 4 pairs of very narrow leaflets, leaf stalk flattened; less frost tolerant than other forms. *S. a.* subsp. *sturtii*, bright yellow flowers year-round. Zones 9–11.

Senna corymbosa

syn. *Cassia corymbosa*

☼ ❄ ↔ 8 ft (2.4 m) ↑ 10 ft (3 m)

Native to Uruguay and Argentina; naturalized in southern USA. Shrub or small tree with spreading habit. Long, light green, pinnately divided leaves with oval leaflets. Racemes of golden yellow flowers in spring–autumn. Zones 8–11.

Senna didymobotrya

syn. *Cassia didymobotrya*

☼ ❧ ↔ 10 ft (3 m) ↑ 10 ft (3 m)

Large evergreen shrub, originally from tropical Africa to Southeast Asia, now widely naturalized. Large leaves, leathery leaflets, downy when young. Erect flower spikes, golden yellow flowers emerging from blackish buds. Downy seed pods. Zones 10–12.

Senna multijuga

syn. *Cassia multijuga*

☼ ❧ ↔ 20 ft (6 m) ↑ 25 ft (8 m)

Small tree native to northern South America. Found in open grasslands and forests. Leaves 12 in (30 cm) long, with 40 or more pairs of leaflets. Terminal panicles of small yellow blooms in late summer–autumn. Fruit matures to black. Zones 9–12.

Senna polyphylla

syn. *Cassia polyphylla*

☼ ✈ ↔ 12 ft (3.5 m) ↑ 25 ft (8 m)

Shrub or small tree found in Caribbean region. Stiff branches clothed with small leaves composed of 13 pairs of olive green leaflets with slightly downy underside. Clusters of golden yellow flowers at various times throughout year, depending on climatic conditions. Pendulous flattened pods. Zones 10–12.

Senna siamea
syn. *Cassia siamea*
KASSOD TREE
☀ ✿ ↔ 35 ft (10 m) ↕ 40 ft (12 m)
Evergreen tree from Myanmar to Indonesia. Leaves pinnate, glossy dark green leaflets, young leaves often reddish. Yellow flowers, at ends of branched spikes, in spring–early summer. Long flat pods. Leaves and seeds reported to be poisonous. Zones 10–11.

Senna splendida
GOLDEN WONDER
☀ ✿ ↔ 8–12 ft (2.4–3.5 m) ↕ 10–15 ft (3–4.5 m)
Spreading shrub or small tree native to Brazil. Slender hanging branches. Glossy pinnately divided leaves with oblong leaflets. Racemes of yellow flowers in autumn. Long drooping cylindrical seed pods. Zones 10–12.

SEQUOIA
This famous genus from the cypress (Cupressaceae) family contains just a single species of coniferous tree native to the coastal areas of Oregon and California, USA. It is recognized as the tallest plant species in the world, with plants in the wild growing to over 360 ft (110 m) high.
CULTIVATION: This tree is suitable only for parks and large gardens, as it can reach 90 ft (27 m) in 20 years under ideal conditions. It does not grow well in cities as it dislikes pollution. Any good well-drained soil will suit it, but it does best in cool humid areas. It will coppice from the stump of a felled tree. Propagate from seed or from heeled cuttings.

Sequoia sempervirens
CALIFORNIA REDWOOD, COAST REDWOOD
☀ ❄ ↔ 15–25 ft (4.5–8 m) ↕ 150 ft (45 m)
Tree develops conical shape. Bark deeply ridged, reddish brown, very thick, spongy, exfoliating in strips. Dark green yew-like leaves arranged in ranks along stems. Small, reddish brown, barrel-shaped cones. 'Adpressa', slow-growing dwarf cultivar, grayish green leaves, will reach 90 ft (27 m) tall in about 100 years. Two cultivars have almost horizontal branches: 'Aptos Blue', teal foliage with drooping tips, site carefully as it sets abundant seed; 'Soquel', greener foliage with curling tips. Zones 8–10.

SEQUOIADENDRON
There is just a single species of coniferous tree in this genus from the cypress (Cupressaceae) family, which was formerly included in *Sequoia*. It is found in small groves in the Sierra Nevada foothills in California, USA. This species is the largest living organism (though *Sequoia* is taller), with trees acquiring massive bulk; the biggest existing specimen is named "General Sherman," and is estimated to weigh 2,460 tons (2,500 tonnes). It is also one of the longest living trees on the planet, with specimens in the range of 1,500 to 3,000 years old.

CULTIVATION: With its great bulk, this tree is suitable only for parks and very large gardens. For planting in lines or avenues, trees should be spaced at least 70 ft (21 m) apart. They will grow in a wide range of conditions but dislike pollution. Propagate from seed or cuttings.

Sequoiadendron giganteum
syn. *Wellingtonia gigantea*
BIG TREE, GIANT SEQUOIA, SIERRA REDWOOD
☀ ❄ ↔ 20–35 ft (6–10 m) ↕ 150–165 ft (45–50 m)
Often confused with *Sequoia sempervirens*. Similar conical shape, thick, reddish brown, spongy bark. Branches curve downward, then up at tip. Leaves compressed, scale-like, spirally arranged on stems. Larger cones than *Sequoia*. 'Pendulum', hanging branches. Zones 7–10.

SERRURIA
One of the many southern African genera in the protea (Proteaceae) family, *Serruria* encompasses some 55 species of evergreen shrubs, which are notable for their delicate inflorescences that often make excellent and very popular cut flowers. Most species have leaves that are very finely dissected, often so finely as to resemble needle-like foliage. A few species have simple undivided leaves. The flowerheads, which may be clustered or carried singly, are usually composed of several small hairy flowers that are largely concealed within showy bracts. Hard nut-like fruit follow.
CULTIVATION: Often tricky to cultivate outside their natural range, these species tend to be short lived. They have the typical protea requirements: low-phosphate, slightly acidic, gritty, very well-drained soil, a position in sun or part-shade, and good ventilation. If exposed to damp cool conditions in winter they tend to rot. They are also marginally frost hardy. Propagation is from seed or from cuttings, which are often slow to strike and prone to collapse.

Serruria 'Sugar 'n' Spice'
☀ ❀ ↔ 4 ft (1.2 m) ↕ 4 ft (1.2 m)
Originated as hybrid between *S. florida* and *S. rosea*. Combines large flowerheads and broad bracts of first species with richer pink coloring of second. Zones 9–10.

Serruria 'Sugar 'n' Spice'

Sesbania punicea

SESBANIA

Widespread in the tropics and subtropics, this genus in the pea-flower subfamily of the legume (Fabaceae) family includes some 50 species of evergreen and deciduous leguminous herbs, shrubs, and trees. They have pinnate leaves that can be quite large, but their main feature is their racemes of pea-flowers. These develop in the leaf axils and usually open in summer. Angular seed pods follow. CULTIVATION: Demanding a warm climate, most *Sesbania* species are quick growing and short lived. They can look rather untidy unless they are kept neatly trimmed, but usually make up for it with a colorful display of flowers. They thrive in a moderately fertile, deep, well-drained soil, and a position in full sun or part-shade. Water well during the flowering season, but keep dry during the cooler months. Propagate from seed or half-hardened cuttings.

Sesbania punicea
ORANGE WISTERIA SHRUB

☼ ᎒ ↔ 4 ft (1.2 m) ↑ 6 ft (1.8 m)

Shrub found in southern Brazil, Argentina, and Uruguay; naturalized in southeastern USA. Mid- to dark green leaves, 6 to 20 pairs of leaflets. Vivid orange flowers in racemes. Zones 9–11.

SHEPHERDIA

There are only 3 species of deciduous or evergreen shrubs in this genus from the oleaster (Elaeagnaceae) family. They are native to North America, where they grow on exposed slopes and dry rocky sites. They have simple opposite leaves and bear small petal-less flowers; male and female flowers are produced on separate plants. CULTIVATION: These shrubs will grow in a range of conditions, and can tolerate poor dry sites. They like full sun and free-draining soil. Propagation is from seed or cuttings.

Shepherdia argentea ★
BUFFALO BERRY, SILVER BUFFALO BERRY, SILVERBERRY

☼ ❋ ↔ 12 ft (3.5 m) ↑ 12 ft (3.5 m)

Well-branched shrub with spiny branches and silvery oblong leaves. Small yellowish white flowers in spring. Female plants produce glossy, red, pea-sized fruit. Zones 2–9.

Shepherdia canadensis
BUFFALO BERRY

☼ ❋ ↔ 8 ft (2.4 m) ↑ 8 ft (2.4 m)

Spreading shrub. Leaves dark yellowish green above, white below. Creamy yellow flowers. Yellow to red fruit. Zones 2–9.

SIMMONDSIA

This genus has only 1 species, a common shrub native to the desert regions of southwestern USA and northern Mexico. It is the sole genus of the jojoba (Simmondsiaceae) family, which is related to the box (Buxaceae) family. Sometimes cultivated in hot arid climates as an ornamental plant and for erosion control, it is more widely known and valued for its seeds, which are the source of jojoba oil, a clear waxy oil used in cosmetics and soaps. CULTIVATION: This species requires a warm to hot climate and a well-drained dry soil in full sun. It is very drought tolerant. Lightly prune regularly to shape. Propagate from seed.

Simmondsia chinensis
GOAT NUT, JOJOBA

☼ ᎒ ↔ 6 ft (1.8 m) ↑ 8 ft (2.4 m)

Evergreen shrub from USA and Mexico. Hairy young stems. Small, leathery, oblong, gray-green leaves. Male and female flowers on separate plants. Clusters of cup-shaped yellow male flowers, or bell-shaped greenish female flowers, in leaf axils, in summer. Fruit capsules contain single seed. Zones 9–12.

SKIMMIA

This genus of 4 slow-growing species belonging to the rue (Rutaceae) family is native to the Himalayas and eastern Asia. They are evergreen shrubs or small trees that tolerate shade and seaside conditions in cool-temperate regions. The leaves are simple, smooth-edged, and mostly broad and glossy; they are slightly aromatic when crushed due to minute oil cavities. The small flowers are white, yellow, or pink-tinged, and borne in short dense clusters at the branch tips. Some species produce male and female flowers on different plants, so both sexes need to be grown in close proximity to ensure the production of the colorful winter-borne berries. CULTIVATION: They are easily grown in cooler climates in soil that contains plenty of organic matter and has adequate drainage. Plants can be trimmed into compact shapes or as hedges. Propagate from tip cuttings; seed can be used but the plant's sex cannot be predicted.

Skimmia × confusa
☼/◑ ❋ ↔ 4 ft (1.2 m) ↑ 2–10 ft (0.6–3 m)

Mound-forming shrub, hybrid between *S. anquetilia* and *S. japonica*. Leaves pointed, aromatic. Perfumed off-white flowers, in large clusters, in late winter. 'Kew Green', popular cultivar. Zones 7–10.

Skimmia japonica
☼ ❋ ↔ 20 ft (6 m) ↑ 20 ft (6 m)

Dense, dome-shaped, medium-sized shrub from Japan. Leathery leaves. Flowers white, fragrant, in panicles, in spring. Clusters of red globular fruit. *S. j.* subsp. *reevesiana*, white flowers, dull pink berries; 'Chilan Choice', fragrant flowers, red berries. *S. j.* 'Cecilia Brown', bright green glossy leaves, white flowers open from red buds;

'**Fructo Alba**', cream flowers; '**Kew White**', narrow glossy leaves, fragrant cream flowers; '**Robert Fortune**', pale leaves, dark edge; '**Rubella**' ★, male cultivar, white flowers, yellow anthers. Zones 7–10.

Skimmia laureola

☼ ❋ ↔ 3–10 ft (0.9–3 m) ↑ 2–40 ft (0.6–12 m)

Spreading shrub or erect tree from Himalayas and western China. Dark green leaves. Unisexual or both male and female flowers on same plant. Flowers creamy white, fragrant, in spring. Zones 7–10.

SOLANUM

syns *Cyphomandra, Lycianthes*

Distinguished by potato *(S. tuberosum)* in its many forms, this genus in the nightshade (Solanaceae) family includes some 1,400 species of annuals, perennials, vines, shrubs, and trees with a cosmopolitan distribution, most from tropical America. The trees and shrubs may be deciduous or evergreen, and many are armed with thorns. While variable, their flowers are all remarkably similar, being simple, small, 5-petalled structures carried singly or in clusters with a central cone of yellow stamens. Fleshy berries follow the flowers. The berries are usually somewhat poisonous and, because of their conspicuous color, may be attractive to children.

CULTIVATION: Hardiness varies: although a few species are really frost tolerant, most are tender. They are generally easily grown in any well-aerated well-drained soil; some have become serious weeds in various parts of the world. Most species prefer sun or part-shade. Propagate from seed or cuttings, or in a few cases by division.

Solanum aviculare

KANGAROO APPLE, PORO PORO

☀ ❂ ↔ 3–12 ft (0.9–3.5 m) ↑ 3–12 ft (0.9–3.5 m)

Quick-growing evergreen shrub from Australia and New Zealand. Leaves dark green, tip end can be divided into 2 or 3 long lobes. Purple flowers. Fruit ripen green to purple to orange. Zones 9–11.

Solanum capsicastrum

FALSE JERUSALEM CHERRY

☼ ❂ ↔ 24 in (60 cm) ↑ 12–24 in (30–60 cm)

Brazilian native, evergreen shrub. Leaves 2–3 in (5–8 cm) long, often wavy-edged. White flowers. Small, orange to red, egg-shaped fruit. Often grown as house or greenhouse plant. Zones 10–12.

Solanum giganteum

AFRICAN HOLLY

☼ ❂ ↔ 10 ft (3 m) ↑ 12 ft (3.5 m)

Large shrub or small tree found from tropical Africa to Sri Lanka. Spiny trunks, prickle-covered silvery white branches. Leaves lance-shaped, dark green, silvery white felting beneath. Purple flowers in panicles. Small, glossy, red fruit. Zones 10–12.

Solanum mammosum

NIPPLE FRUIT

☼ ✦ ↔ 3 ft (0.9 m) ↑ 5 ft (1.5 m)

Native of tropical America, behaves as annual or shrubby perennial. Hair-covered stems whippy and spiny, with angularly lobed or toothed leaves. Inflorescences of purple flowers. Orange fruit. Zones 10–12.

Solanum pseudocapsicum

JERUSALEM CHERRY

☼ ❂ ↔ 4 ft (1.2 m) ↑ 3–6 ft (0.9–1.8 m)

Evergreen shrub from South America. Dark green leaves, wavy edges. Small white flowers, showy bright orange fruit. Many cultivars, variably colored fruit: cream, yellow, orange, and red. Fruit eaten by birds but poisonous to humans. Zones 9–11.

Solanum pyracanthum

☼ ✦ ↔ 2–3 ft (0.6–0.9 m) ↑ 3–6 ft (0.9–1.8 m)

Shrubby biennial or perennial from tropical Africa and Madagascar. Rust-colored felted stems. Lobed leaves; eye-catching long orange spines on midrib, which provide effective protection from herbivores. Bluish violet flowers, borne in dense clusters, in summer. Zones 10–12.

Solanum rantonnetii

syn. *Lycianthes rantonnetii*

BLUE POTATO BUSH, PARAGUAY NIGHTSHADE

☼ ❂ ↔ 7 ft (2 m) ↑ 6 ft (1.8 m)

Grown as scrambling shrub or semi-climber, long-flowering species from Argentina and Paraguay. Leaves have wavy edges. Fragrant purple to violet-blue flowers in summer. Red fruit. Trim to keep plants compact and shrubby. '**Royal Robe**', long-blooming, rich purple flowers. Zones 9–11.

Simmondsia chinensis

Skimmia × confusa

Solanum pseudocapsicum

Sophora davidii

Sophora japonica

Sophora tomentosa

SOPHORA

This widespread genus from the pea-flower subfamily of the legume (Fabaceae) family includes more than 50 species of evergreen, deciduous, or briefly deciduous shrubs and trees. They have pinnate leaves, often composed of many tiny leaflets. The flowers are pea-like, usually cream or yellow, and frequently have a prominent keel; they are carried in racemes or panicles. Spring is the principal flowering season, though the tropical species tend to be less seasonal in their flowering. Woody winged seed pods follow the flowers.
CULTIVATION: While hardiness varies with the species, most adapt well to cultivation and thrive in any well-drained soil with a position in sun or light shade. Propagate from seed, cuttings, or, in some cases, by grafting. The seed is particularly moisture resistant and must be soaked in warm water to soften it before sowing. Its moisture resistance allows the seed to survive prolonged exposure to seawater and this feature accounts for the rather unusual distribution patterns of some *Sophora* species.

Sophora arizonica
ARIZONA MOUNTAIN LAUREL, ARIZONA NECKLACE
☼ ❄ ↔ 8–10 ft (2.4–3 m) ↑ 10–15 ft (3–4.5 m)
Evergreen, slow-growing, spreading shrub or small tree from Arizona, USA. Silvery green pinnately divided leaves. Profuse wisteria-like bunches of fragrant violet flowers in spring, followed by bean-like seed pods, thought to be poisonous. Zones 8–10.

Sophora davidii
☼ ❄ ↔ 10 ft (3 m) ↑ 10 ft (3 m)
Deciduous shrub from China. Short leaves, up to 20 small leaflets. Flowers purple-blue with whitish tips to white, in short racemes at stem tips, in summer. Zones 6–9.

Sophora japonica
CHINESE SCHOLAR TREE, PAGODA TREE
☼ ❄ ↔ 35 ft (10 m) ↑ 50 ft (15 m)
Deciduous tree from China and Korea, long cultivated in Japan. Smaller in cultivation. Leaves light to mid-green, 16 leaflets, downy underside. Drooping panicles, 6–10 in (15–25 cm) long, fragrant creamy white flowers in mid-summer. 'Pendula', weeping habit in both flowers and foliage, usually grafted on upright standard trunk; 'Princeton Upright', to 60 ft (18 m) tall; 'Regent' ★, white flowers; 'Violacea', pale mauve-pink flowers. Zones 5–9.

Sophora microphylla
KOWHAI
☼ ❄ ↔ 20 ft (6 m) ↑ 20–30 ft (6–9 m)
Evergreen or briefly deciduous tree native to New Zealand. Fine twigs, sharp-angled nodes. Leaves small, tiny olive green leaflets. Pendulous clusters of golden yellow flowers in spring. Zones 8–10.

Sophora prostrata
DWARF KOWHAI
☼ ❄ ↔ 7 ft (2 m) ↑ 6 ft (1.8 m)
New Zealand evergreen shrub, prostrate in windswept locations. Densely interlaced branches. Small leaves, 8 tiny deep green leaflets. Flowers deep yellow to light orange, in late winter, often hidden among branches. 'Little Baby', bizarre branching habit. Zones 8–10.

Sophora secundiflora
FRIJOLITO, MESCAL BEAN, TEXAS MOUNTAIN LAUREL
☼ ❄ ↔ 15 ft (4.5 m) ↑ 30 ft (9 m)
Evergreen shrub or small tree native to Texas and New Mexico, USA, and nearby Mexico. Leaves with 3 to 5 pairs of leaflets. Racemes of fragrant violet-blue flowers in early spring. Zones 8–11.

Sophora tetraptera
KOWHAI, YELLOW KOWHAI
☼ ❄ ↔ 15 ft (4.5 m) ↑ 15–40 ft (4.5–12 m)
National flower of New Zealand, also found in Chile, evergreen. Leaves with 20 to 40 tiny leaflets. Young leaves, branches, and flower buds covered in fine brown down. Racemes of golden yellow flowers in spring. Zones 8–10.

Sophora tomentosa
SILVERBUSH
☼ ❅ ↔ 8 ft (2.4 m) ↑ 30 ft (9 m)
Large deciduous shrub or small tree from tropical Asia and Africa. Leaves with 18 leaflets. Silver-gray down on leaves and young branches. Flowers in racemes, unusual light yellow-green shade, in spring–summer. Zones 10–12.

SORBARIA

This genus, native to Asia, is a member of the rose (Rosaceae) family and is commonly called false spirea as the flowers are similar to *Spiraea*. There are 4 species of deciduous, usually suckering shrubs with pinnate leaves. They produce large panicles of small white flowers in summer followed by masses of small brownish seed capsules that often persist into winter.

CULTIVATION: They prefer a fertile moisture-retentive soil in sun or part-shade and should be planted in a position with protection from strong winds, which may damage the foliage. Cut back in early spring and remove any old weak branches at ground level. Propagate by removing suckers or from cuttings taken in summer.

Sorbaria kirilowii

syn. *Sobaria arborea*

TREE FALSE SPIREA, URAL FALSE SPIREA

☼ ❋ ↔ 20 ft (6 m) ↑ 17 ft (5 m)

Large, deciduous, spreading, Chinese shrub with slender pointed leaflets. White flowers, on panicles to 12 in (30 cm) long, in mid-summer. Spicy fragrance. Zones 5–7.

Sorbaria sorbifolia

FALSE SPIREA

☼ ❋ ↔ 10 ft (3 m) ↑ 10 ft (3 m)

Suckering shrub native to Asia, stiff erect stems. Pinnate leaves, finely serrated margins; colorful autumn foliage. White flowers, in large plumes, in summer. Zones 2–9.

Sorbaria tomentosa

☼ ❋ ↔ 15 ft (4.5 m) ↑ 20 ft (6 m)

Wide-spreading, branching, Himalayan shrub. Pinnate leaves, to 21 narrow finely serrated leaflets. Yellowish white flowers, in large panicles, in summer. Zones 6–10.

SORBUS

MOUNTAIN ASH

The 100-odd species of deciduous shrubs and trees in this genus from the northern temperate zones belong to the rose (Rosaceae) family. The foliage is usually pinnate with serrated-edged leaflets, but may be simple and oval to diamond-shaped. Clusters of white or cream, sometimes pink-tinted, spring flowers, somewhat unpleasantly scented, are followed by heads of berry-like pomes that ripen through summer and autumn. Some species develop russet- to red-toned foliage in autumn.

CULTIVATION: Most *Sorbus* species are very hardy and prefer a cool climate, suffering in high summer temperatures. They are best grown in moderately fertile, deep, humus-enriched soil with ample summer moisture, but adapt well to most conditions. Plant in sun or part-shade, prune to shape in autumn or winter, and propagate from stratified seed or by grafting. Fireblight can cause significant damage.

Sorbus alnifolia

KOREAN MOUNTAIN ASH

☼ ❋ ↔ 25 ft (8 m) ↑ 50 ft (15 m)

From Japan and Korea. Leaves with heavily serrated edges; orange and red in autumn. Young stems red-brown, bright green young foliage. Flowers white; fruit red or yellow. Zones 6–9.

Sorbus alnifolia

Sorbus americana ★

AMERICAN MOUNTAIN ASH

☼ ❋ ↔ 20 ft (6 m) ↑ 20–30 ft (6–9 m)

Shrubby tree from central and eastern USA. Leaves with 17 bright green leaflets, gray-green underside, turn yellow in autumn. Resinous buds, white flowers, in spring. Bright red fruit. Zones 2–9.

Sorbus aria

WHITEBEAM

☼ ❋ ↔ 25 ft (8 m) ↑ 20–40 ft (6–12 m)

Broad-crowned tree from Europe. Elliptical leaves, deep green, felty white when young. White flowers in spring. Orange-red fruit. 'Lutescens', conical growth habit, light green foliage. Zones 5–9.

Sorbus × arnoldiana

☼ ❋ ↔ 20 ft (6 m) ↑ 15–40 ft (4.5–12 m)

Garden hybrid of temperate Eurasian *S. aucuparia* and *S. discolor*. Small dark green leaflets, gray-green beneath. Small cream flower-heads. Pink berries. '**Carpet of Gold**', erect branches. Zones 5–9.

Sorbus aucuparia

EUROPEAN MOUNTAIN ASH, MOUNTAIN ASH, ROWAN

☼ ❋ ↔ 20 ft (6 m) ↑ 15–40 ft (4.5–12 m)

Hardy tree found over much of northern Eurasia. Dark green to bronze pinnate leaves, coarsely serrated leaflets, turn orange and red in autumn. Unpleasantly scented flowers. Orange berries. Zones 2–9.

Sorbus cashmiriana

☼ ❋ ↔ 20 ft (6 m) ↑ 30 ft (9 m)

Tree native to Kashmir region of Himalayas. Young branches red, dark green pinnate leaves, light green underside. Pink-tinted white flowers in spring. White to yellow-green fruit. Zones 5–9.

Sorbus chamaemespilus

DWARF WHITEBEAM

☼ ❋ ↔ 3–6 ft (0.9–1.8 m) ↑ 3–6 ft (0.9–1.8 m)

Shrub from central Europe. Simple dark green leaves, finely serrated edges, sometimes felted below. Flowers deep pink. Red fruit. Zones 6–9.

Sorbus cashmiriana

Sorbus commixta
JAPANESE ROWAN

☼ ❋ ↔ 20 ft (6 m) ↑ 20–30 ft (6–9 m)

Native to Korea and Japan. Pinnate leaves, 15 leaflets, open from sticky red buds, first bronze, then light green, glaucous underside; turn yellow to red in autumn. Flowers white, fruit red. '**Embley**', red autumn foliage lasts into winter; '**Jermyns**', vividly colored autumn foliage, large clusters of orange-red fruit. Zones 6–9.

Sorbus decora
SHOWY MOUNTAIN ASH

☼ ❋ ↔ 15 ft (4.5 m) ↑ 30 ft (9 m)

Often small and shrubby tree found in northeastern North America. Leaves with 17 leaflets. Loose white flowerheads in spring. Clusters of small red fruit. Zones 2–8.

Sorbus esserteauiana
☼ ❋ ↔ 35 ft (10 m) ↑ 50 ft (15 m)

Tree native to western China. Leaves open from red buds, 13 bright green leaflets, downy underside, turn red in autumn. Massed panicles of white flowers. Red fruit. Zones 6–9.

Sorbus forrestii
☼ ❋ ↔ 20 ft (6 m) ↑ 25 ft (8 m)

Similar species to commonly grown *S. hupehensis*, but with larger fruit, pure white when ripe, persisting well into winter after leaves have fallen. Zones 7–9.

Sorbus × hostii
☼ ❋ ↔ 10 ft (3 m) ↑ 12–15 ft (3.5–4.5 m)

Hybrid between *S. chamaemespilus* and *S. mougeotii*, very similar to *S. mougeotii* except leaves a little longer, somewhat sharper teeth. Flowers pink to pale red, like those of *S. chamaemespilus*. Red fruit follow. Zones 6–9.

Sorbus hupehensis
☼ ❋ ↔ 20 ft (6 m) ↑ 30 ft (9 m)

Tree from central and western China. Pinnate leaves, dull gray-green above, lighter below, turn strong pink tones, redden then

Sorbus hupehensis

fall in autumn. White flowers in spring. Small white berries, blush pink as they ripen. *S. h.* var. *obtusa* (syn. *S. h.* 'Rosea'), up to 25 ft (8 m) tall. *S. h.* '**Coral Fire**', red bark, red autumn foliage, pinkish red fruit. Zones 6–9.

Sorbus intermedia
SWEDISH MOUNTAIN ASH, SWEDISH WHITEBEAM

☼ ❋ ↔ 20 ft (6 m) ↑ 20–30 ft (6–9 m)

Usually small, sometimes shrubby, Scandinavian native. Felted young stems, simple oval leaves, small basal lobes. Densely branched heads of small flowers in spring. Orange-red berries. '**Brouwers**', compact upright habit, small clusters of dark red berries. Zones 5–9.

Sorbus latifolia
FONTAINEBLEAU SERVICE TREE

☼ ❋ ↔ 20 ft (6 m) ↑ 30–50 ft (9–15 m)

Strong-growing European tree, conical growth, bronze young branches. Oak-like lobed leaves, serrated edges, dark green above, yellowish felting on underside. Woolly heads of creamy white flowers. Green fruit speckled with brown. Zones 5–9.

Sorbus megalocarpa
LARGE-FRUITED WHITEBEAM

☼ ❋ ↔ 8 ft (25 m) ↑ 30 ft (9 m)

Shrub or tree native to China. Simple wavy- to shallowly toothed-edged leaves. Creamy white flowers in dense clusters. Rusty brown pomes. Zones 6–9.

Sorbus mougeotii
☼ ❋ ↔ 15 ft (4.5 m) ↑ 40 ft (12 m)

Large shrub or small tree found in mountains of northern Europe. Simple, broad, ovate leaves, shallow lobes, pale gray down beneath. Small heads of cream flowers. Green fruit become red as they ripen. Zones 6–9.

Sorbus pohuashanensis
☼ ❋ ↔ 20 ft (6 m) ↑ 70 ft (21 m)

Round-headed tree naturally found throughout mountains of northern China, smaller in cultivation. Pinnate leaves, felted underside. Woolly clusters of cream flowers. Orange-red to red fruit. Zones 5–9.

Sorbus reducta
DWARF CHINESE MOUNTAIN ASH

☼ ❋ ↔ 6 ft (1.8 m) ↑ 15 in (38 cm)

Low shrubby species from western China and Myanmar. Clump of suckering stems, bristly young stems. Pinnate leaves, reddish stalks. Flowers not abundant; fruit cherry red. '**Gnome**', smaller, compact form. Zones 6–10.

Sorbus sargentiana
SARGENT'S ROWAN

☼ ❋ ↔ 20 ft (6 m) ↑ 20–30 ft (6–9 m)

Western Chinese ornamental. Pinnate leaves, sticky buds, leaflets bright green, slightly serrated edges; lighter, downy beneath. Vivid autumn foliage. Flowers in clusters; small red berries. Zones 6–9.

Sorbus thibetica

☀ ❄ ↔ 30 ft (9 m) ↑ 50 ft (15 m)

Wild form of Chinese *S. thibetica* seldom seen cultivated. Most known as such are cultivar **'John Mitchell'** (syn. *S.* 'Mitchellii'), broad-headed tree. Simple, rounded, bright green leaves, white-felted underside. Flowers creamy white, fruit orange-red. Zones 8–10.

Sorbus × thuringiaca

OAK-LEAFED MOUNTAIN ASH

☀ ❄ ↔ 25 ft (8 m) ↑ 30–40 ft (9–12 m)

Hybrid between *S. aria* and *S. aucuparia*. Pinnate leaves, finely serrated leaflets. Small red fruit. **'Fastigiata'**, upright growth. Zones 6–9.

Sorbus torminalis

CHEQUER TREE, WILD SERVICE TREE

☀ ❄ ↔ 25 ft (8 m) ↑ 30–50 ft (9–15 m)

From Europe, western Asia, and North Africa. Green-brown bark. Leaves bright green, simple, lobed, serrated edges, redden in autumn. Lax spring flower clusters, brown-speckled olive fruit. Zones 6–10.

Sorbus vilmorinii

☀ ❄ ↔ 15 ft (4.5 m) ↑ 20 ft (6 m)

Spreading shrub or small tree native to western China. Buds and young branches warm red-brown shade. Leaves pinnate, serrated edges, gray-green underside. Loose open flower clusters, pink or pink-flushed white fruit. **'Pearly King'**, larger fruit. Zones 6–9.

Sorbus Hybrid Cultivars

☀/❂ ❄ ↔ 7–15 ft (2–4.5 m) ↑ 10–25 ft (3–8 m)

Range in size, from dwarf to tree-like forms. Foliage type and fruit color vary, all tend to be heavy cropping; often have bright foliage in autumn. **'Coral Beauty'**, strong *S. aucuparia* influence, brilliant orange-scarlet fruit; **'Joseph Rock'**, probable hybrid, 20–30 ft (6–9 m) tall, pinnate leaves, deeply serrated leaflets, turn orange or purple-red in autumn, flowers white, fruit ripen cream to golden yellow; **'Pearly King'**, pale pearl pink fruit; **'Sunshine'**, yellow fruit. Zones 6–9.

SPARMANNIA

AFRICAN HEMP, HOUSE LIME

This genus of 3 to 7 species of evergreen large shrubs or small trees comes from the linden (Tiliaceae) family, and occurs in woodland areas of southern Africa and Madagascar. Much cultivated as house plants, they will stand some neglect and continue to flower regularly in temperate climates. The simple or palmate leaves are toothed and covered in soft hairs, as are the stems. The flowers, which are produced on umbels, are usually white, or sometimes purple or pink, with prominent stamens. The seed capsule contains several seeds and is prickly on the outside. In warm climates, these are useful border plants.

Spartium junceum, France

Sparmannia africana

CULTIVATION: These plants require full sun and a rich well-drained soil, plus regular pruning to maintain their shape if grown in pots. Water very little during winter dormancy. Propagate by sowing seed or air layering in spring; half-hardened cuttings can be rooted in summer, but they require heat from beneath in cooler climates.

Sparmannia africana

AFRICAN LINDEN, CAPE STOCK ROSE

☀ ❂ ↔ 10 ft (3 m) ↑ 20 ft (6 m)

Large shrub or small tree native to South Africa. Hairy stems, light green hairy leaves, shallow lobes. White flowers, bright yellow or reddish purple stamens, in late spring–summer. **'Flore Pleno'** (syn. 'Plena'), double white flowers; **'Variegata'**, variegated leaves, large white flowers. Zones 9–11.

SPARTIUM

All but 1 species in this genus of brooms from the pea-flower subfamily of the legume (Fabaceae) family have now been transferred, most of them to *Genista*. The remaining species is a deciduous shrub native to the Mediterranean region and southwestern Europe. Leafless for much of the year, but green-stemmed, it produces a few small leaves in spring, usually as it comes into bloom.

CULTIVATION: It is easily grown in any well-drained soil with a position in full sun. It can be cut back hard after flowering to encourage bushiness. Pruning also helps to prevent excessive self-sowing, which can be a problem if too many seed pods are left to ripen. Propagation is from seed or cuttings.

Spartium junceum

SPANISH BROOM

☀ ❄ ↔ 10 ft (3 m) ↑ 10 ft (3 m)

Many-stemmed shrub. Strongly scented, bright yellow pea-flowers, in large racemes on new growth, in spring–early summer, later in cool climates. Flat dark brown seed pods. Zones 8–10.

SPATHODEA

The sole species in this genus from the trumpet-vine (Bignoniaceae) family is an evergreen tree found in the warmer areas of Africa. It has a domed crown, dark green compound leaves, and large bell-shaped flowers with a spathe-like calyx. Flowers are yellow at the base on the outside, becoming bright red near the mouth. They are a bright orange inside, merging to orangey red on the lobes.

CULTIVATION: It is best grown in fertile well-drained soil with plenty of organic matter, which helps keep the soil moist during hot summers. It is frost tender and needs shelter from wind, especially salt-laden wind. The strongest leading shoot should be kept free of competition until the trunk is 7 ft (2 m) or more tall, when the crown may be allowed to develop naturally. Seed can be sown in spring in a warm environment.

Spathodea campanulata
syn. Spathodea nilotica
AFRICAN TULIP TREE
↔ 25 ft (8 m) ↑ 25–35 ft (8–10 m)
Evergreen tree native to tropical central and western Africa. Broad-domed crown. Leaves compound on short stalks; leaflets shiny, dark green, paler and dull underneath. Bell-shaped flowers, in racemes, in late spring–mid-summer. Fruit slender capsule. Zones 11–12.

Spathodea campanulata

SPIRAEA

BRIDAL WREATH, SPIREA
This genus has about 70 species of mainly deciduous, sometimes semi-evergreen, flowering shrubs in the rose (Rosaceae) family. It is valued for its flowering and foliage qualities. Leaves are simple and alternate, variously toothed and lobed. The genus is found in many northern temperate areas, mainly in eastern and southeastern Asia and in North America.

CULTIVATION: They thrive in most soils, though some grow poorly on chalk, and prefer a sunny position and cool moist conditions. They fall into 2 groups for pruning: those that flower on the current year's growth, which can be hard pruned in spring, and those that flower on the previous year's growth, which should have the old flowering shoots removed just after flowering. Propagation is from soft-tip or half-hardened cuttings during the summer months.

Spiraea 'Arguta'
BRIDAL WREATH
↔ 4 ft (1.2 m) ↑ 5–7 ft (1.5–2 m)
Dense shrub. Thin hairless branches. Inversely lance-shaped to oval leaves, smooth edges or a few teeth. Clusters of white flowers along branches in spring. Zones 4–10.

Spiraea betulifolia
BIRCHLEAF SPIREA
↔ 3 ft (0.9 m) ↑ 3 ft (0.9 m)
Dwarf shrub found in Japan and northeastern Asia. Forms mound of brown hairless shoots. Round to egg-shaped leaves. Flowers white, in closely packed corymbs, in mid-summer. *S. b.* var. *aemiliana*, to 12 in (30 cm) high, broad rounded leaves. Zones 5–10.

Spiraea × billardii
↔ 7 ft (2 m) ↑ 7 ft (2 m)
Spreading shrub, hybrid between *S. douglasii* and *S. salicifolia*. Hairy upright stems. Oblong to lance-shaped leaves, sharp teeth, gray downy underside. Red flowers, in densely packed panicles, in summer. '**Triumphans**', small leaves, slightly downy underside, flowers deep pink, sometimes hint of purple. Zones 4–10.

Spiraea × brachybotrys
↔ 6 ft (1.8 m) ↑ 8 ft (2.4 m)
Vigorous shrub, hybrid between *S. canescens* and *S. douglasii*. Arching branches, egg-shaped to oblong leaves, teeth at tip, velvety gray underside. Light red flowers, in dense panicles, in summer. Zones 4–10.

Spiraea cantoniensis
REEVES' SPIREA
↔ 8 ft (2.4 m) ↑ 6 ft (1.8 m)
Deciduous or semi-evergreen shrub native to China. Arching hairless branches. Diamond-shaped leaves, glaucous underside, conspicuously toothed or 3-lobed. White flowers, in spherical clusters, in mid-summer. '**Flore Pleno**' (syn. 'Lanceata'), double flowers, most popular form of *S. cantoniensis* in cultivation. Zones 5–11.

Spiraea × cinerea
GREFSHEIM SPIREA
↔ 5 ft (1.5 m) ↑ 5 ft (1.5 m)
Garden hybrid between *S. hypericifolia* and *S. cana*. Small, rather pale green leaves. Branch tips covered with tiny white flowers, a few in leaf axils of lower branches, in spring. '**Compacta**', under 3 ft (0.9 m) tall, arching branches; '**Grefsheim**', early-flowering, slightly pendulous branches, narrower leaves. Zones 5–9.

Spiraea cantoniensis 'Flore Pleno'

Spiraea douglasii
WESTERN SPIREA

☼ ❋ ↔ 6 ft (1.8 m) ↑ 6 ft (1.8 m)

Suckering shrub from northwestern USA; naturalized in parts of Europe. Forms thicket of red shoots. Oblong leaves, downy gray below. Purplish pink flowers, in panicles, in mid-summer. Zones 4–10.

Spiraea fritschiana
KOREAN SPIREA

☼ ❋ ↔ 5 ft (1.5 m) ↑ 3 ft (0.9 m)

Mounding shrub native to Korea. Glaucous foliage, purplish tones in autumn. Large clusters of white flowers, sometimes tinged pink, in summer. Zones 4–9.

Spiraea japonica
JAPANESE SPIREA

☼ ❋ ↔ 4 ft (1.2 m) ↑ 6 ft (1.8 m)

Upright shrub from Japan, China, and Korea. Lance- to egg-shaped leaves. Pink flowers, in clusters, in summer. *S. j.* var. *albiflora*, pale green leaves, white flowers. *S. j.* 'Anthony Waterer', purplish red flowers; 'Bullata', dwarf slow-growing shrub, deep pinkish red flowers; 'Bumalda', dwarf form, leaves can be variegated pink and off-white; 'Crispa', purplish pink flowers; 'Dart's Red', bright pink flowers; 'Firelight', ovate leaves, purple-pink flowers; 'Gold Mound' ★, golden leaves turn chartreuse; Golden Princess/'Lisp', foliage ages bronze to yellow; 'Goldflame', orange autumn leaves, red flowers; 'Little Princess', pink flowers; Magic Carpet/'Walbuma', bronze-red leaves turn chartreuse, pink flowers; 'Nana', dwarf, dark pink flowers; 'Neon Flash', lance-shaped leaves, pink flowers; 'Shirobana', red buds open to deep pink and white flowers. Zones 3–10.

Spiraea nipponica
NIPPON SPIREA

☼ ❋ ↔ 6 ft (1.8 m) ↑ 6 ft (1.8 m)

Vigorous bushy shrub native to Japan. Leaves oval or inversely egg-shaped, teeth at tip. White flowers, in clusters at ends of branches, in mid-summer. *S. n.* var. *tosaensis*, smaller leaves; many sold under this name are cultivar 'Snowmound'. *S. n.* 'Halward's Silver',

Spiraea douglasii · *Spiraea japonica* var. *albiflora*

smaller than species, produces abundant white flowers; 'Rotundifolia', broader leaves, larger flowers than most other cultivars; 'Snowmound', green leaves, tinted blue. Zones 5–10.

Spiraea prunifolia
BRIDAL WREATH SPIREA, SHOE BUTTON SPIREA

☼ ❋ ↔ 7 ft (2 m) ↑ 7 ft (2 m)

Rounded bush native to China. Usually grown in form 'Plena', dense shrub with egg-shaped leaves, edged with very small teeth, which turn reddish orange in autumn. Double white flowers, in closely packed clusters, in spring. Zones 4–10.

Spiraea thunbergii
THUNBERG SPIREA

☼ ❋ ↔ 7 ft (2 m) ↑ 5 ft (1.5 m)

Shrub native to China, extensively naturalized in Japan. Thin hairy stems, narrow hairless leaves, toothed margins. White flowers, in small clusters, in spring. 'Okon', early flowering. Zones 4–10.

Spiraea tomentosa
HARD HACK, STEEPLEBUSH

☼ ❋ ↔ 7 ft (2 m) ↑ 7 ft (2 m)

Robust thicket-forming shrub from eastern USA. Brown velvety coating on young stems; tooth-edged leaves, downy yellow-gray underside. Crimson flowers in late summer. Zones 4–10.

Spiraea trichocarpa
KOREAN SPIREA

☼ ❋ ↔ 4 ft (1.2 m) ↑ 6 ft (1.8 m)

Shrub native to Korea. Stiff spreading branches, pointed leaves, few teeth toward tip, bluish underside. Rounded dense clusters of white flowers, crowded along outer branches, in summer. Zones 5–9.

Spiraea × *vanhouttei*
BRIDAL WREATH SPIREA, VAN HOUTTE SPIREA

☼ ❋ ↔ 4 ft (1.2 m) ↑ 6 ft (1.8 m)

Robust shrub, hybrid between *S. cantoniensis* and *S. trilobata*. Leaves inversely egg-shaped to diamond-shaped, lobed, toothed edges. White flowers, in dense umbels, in mid-summer. Zones 5–11.

Spiraea trichocarpa

Stachyurus chinensis

STACHYURUS

Subject to recent revisions, this genus in the family Stachyuraceae includes 6 to 10 species of deciduous shrubs and trees from the Himalayan and temperate East Asian region. While generally not spectacular plants, they have the attraction of blooming in late winter and early spring, before or just as the leaves are developing. They produce drooping racemes of small cream to pale yellow flowers at every leaf bud. The leaves are lance-shaped and are usually around 6 in (15 cm) long.
CULTIVATION: They prefer a humus-rich, well-drained, acidic soil in sun or light shade. They are not hardy in the coldest regions but thrive in areas with distinct yet relatively mild winters. Hard late spring frost may damage the flowers and young leaves. Propagate from seed or from half-hardened cuttings.

Stachyurus chinensis

☀ ❄ ↔ 8 ft (2.4 m) ↑ 8 ft (2.4 m)
Deciduous shrub native to China. Leaves 2–6 in (5–15 cm) long ovals, taper at tip. Pale yellow flowers, in racemes, in early spring. '**Magpie**', light green, cream, and pink variegated foliage. Zones 7–9.

Stachyurus praecox

☀ ❄ ↔ 6–12 ft (1.8–3.5 m) ↑ 6–12 ft (1.8–3.5 m)
Shrub native to Japan. Branches tiered. Leaves 6 in (15 cm) long, color slightly in autumn. Drooping racemes of small pale yellow flowers in late winter–early spring, before foliage. Zones 7–10.

STAPHYLEA

BLADDERNUT
This genus of around 11 species of deciduous shrubs and small trees, belonging to the bladdernut (Staphyleaceae) family, is found over much of the northern temperate zone. They have large trifoliate to pinnate leaves, and long leaflets with serrated edges tapering to

a point. Panicles of pale pink to white flowers are produced at the ends of branches, mainly in spring, followed by the 2- to 3-lobed inflated seed pods that give the genus its common name. The seed pods dry and brown as they ripen. The foliage may develop attractive autumn tones.
CULTIVATION: Mostly very hardy, bladdernuts thrive in nearly all well-drained moist soils in full sun or partial shade. The bushes tend to form a thicket, or if pruned after flowering they can be thinned to one or a few main stems and made tree-like. Propagate from seed or summer cuttings; rooted suckers can sometimes be removed and grown on.

Staphylea bumalda

JAPANESE BLADDERNUT
☀ ❄ ↔ 6 ft (1.8 m) ↑ 7 ft (2 m)
Deciduous shrub native to Japan. Leaves trifoliate, lance-shaped leaflets, sharply serrated edges, down on underside veins. Panicles of white flowers in spring. Pods about 1 in (25 mm) wide, 2-lobed. Zones 4–9.

Staphylea colchica

CAUCASIAN BLADDERNUT
☀ ❄ ↔ 10 ft (3 m) ↑ 10–15 ft (3–4.5 m)
Deciduous shrub from Caucasus region. Leaves with 3 to 5 glossy green, finely toothed leaflets. Flowers to ½ in (12 mm) wide, white, fragrant. Seed pods 3-lobed, 3 in (8 cm) across. '**Colombieri**', ovate, finely serrated. Zones 6–9.

Staphylea holocarpa

CHINESE BLADDERNUT
☀ ❄ ↔ 10 ft (3 m) ↑ 15 ft (4.5 m)
Chinese native, shrub or tree. Trifoliate leaves, leaflets with hairy underside. Flowers in drooping panicles, open white from pink buds. Pods around 2 in (5 cm) wide. Zones 6–9.

Staphylea pinnata

Staphylea pinnata

EUROPEAN BLADDERNUT
☀ ❄ ↔ 15 ft (4.5 m) ↑ 15 ft (4.5 m)
Temperate Eurasian shrub. Leaves with 3, 5, or 7 leaflets taper to fine point, serrated edges, glaucous underside. Flowers white, red-tipped sepals, in late spring. Seed pods 1 in (25 mm) wide. Zones 6–9.

Staphylea trifolia

BLADDERNUT, EASTERN BLADDERNUT
☀ ❄ ↔ 15 ft (4.5 m) ↑ 15 ft (4.5 m)
Shrub from eastern USA. Leaves trifoliate, 2–3 in (5–8 cm) long leaflets, finely pointed, sharply serrated edges, fine hairs beneath, change color in autumn. White flowers 1½ in (35 mm) wide, in short panicles; 3-lobed fruit. Zones 5–9.

STENOCARPUS

This genus of 25 species of evergreen trees or large shrubs, in the protea (Proteaceae) family, is from Southeast Asia, the Malay Peninsula to New Caledonia, and Australia. They feature simple

alternate leaves. Tubular flowers, usually red to orange, are borne in umbels, sometimes partly hidden by the foliage. The fruit is a narrow follicle containing winged seeds.
CULTIVATION: Species need a warm site, preferably near the coast but with shelter from salt-laden winds. They prefer a light, sandy, well-drained soil with plenty of organic matter, as well as plentiful summer water. Seed sown when ripe in winter germinate readily in a warm environment; clonal varieties may be grafted on seedling understocks. These species require little or no pruning.

Stenocarpus salignus
RED SILKY OAK, SCRUB BEEFWOOD
☼ ⬩ ↔ 10–15 ft (3–4.5 m) ↑ 100 ft (30 m)
Tree from northeastern Australia. Dark brown scaly bark. Leaves ovate to lance-shaped, leathery, paler beneath. Creamy white flowers, in umbels of 10 to 20 blooms, in spring–summer. Zones 9–12.

Stenocarpus sinuatus
FIREWHEEL TREE, QUEENSLAND FIREWHEEL TREE
☼ ⬩ ↔ 15 ft (4.5 m) ↑ 120 ft (36 m)
Tree from eastern Australia. Gray to brown bark. Leathery leaves, shiny green above, duller beneath. Orange-scarlet flowers, in umbels of 15 to 20 blooms, in upper axils. Zones 9–12.

STEPHANANDRA
This genus of 4 species of deciduous shrubs in the rose (Rosaceae) family is native to eastern Asia. They are valued for their foliage, which often has orange autumn tones. Panicles of white or pale green flowers, shaped like tiny stars, with a profusion of stamens, are borne in summer.
CULTIVATION: They will grow in most soils in sun or part-shade, but prefer moist loam. Maintain shape by hard pruning in spring. Propagate in autumn from cuttings or by division.

Stephanandra incisa
CUTLEAFED STEPHANANDRA, LACE SHRUB
☼ ✳ ↔ 10 ft (3 m) ↑ 6 ft (1.8 m)
Shrub from Japan and Korea. Egg-shaped, deeply toothed, lobed leaves, yellow-green in autumn. Dense panicles of pale green to white flowers in mid-summer. 'Crispa' ★, dwarf. Zones 4–10.

Stephanandra tanakae
☼ ✳ ↔ 8 ft (2.4 m) ↑ 10 ft (3 m)
Shrub native to Japan. Arching branches. Deeply toothed leaves, egg-shaped to triangular, 5 lobes, pink-brown when young. Small white flowers in summer, which are not a feature. Zones 4–10.

STERCULIA
This tropical genus of around 150 species of deciduous or evergreen trees or shrubs gives its name to the family Sterculiaceae. They have broad, dark green, smooth-edged or lobed leaves. Small flowers are borne in often-pendulous racemes or panicles. Individual flowers are petal-less, but the urn-shaped calyx is usually colorful. The fruit consists of up to 5 boat-shaped woody or leathery follicles, pink to red when ripe, that open to display shiny black seeds.

Stephanandra incisa

Stenocarpus sinuatus

CULTIVATION: These fast-growing plants need a warm climate and fertile, moist, well-drained soil. Grow in sun and protect from winds. Water regularly when young. Propagate from fresh seed.

Sterculia murex
LOWVELD CHESTNUT
☼ ⬩ ↔ 10–20 ft (3–6 m) ↑ 20–40 ft (6–12 m)
South African deciduous tree. Gray-brown, nearly black, cracked bark. Compound leaves, 5 to 10 oblong to lance-shaped leaflets. Waxy yellow flowers, brown or red-pink marks, in spring. Woody fruit. Zones 9–11.

Sterculia quadrifida
PEANUT TREE
☼ ⬩ ↔ 20 ft (6 m) ↑ 40 ft (12 m)
Bushy tree from northern Australia and New Guinea. Ovate to heart-shaped leaves. Scented, greenish yellow, bell-shaped flowers, in racemes, in late summer. Leathery scarlet follicles. Zones 10–12.

STEWARTIA
The 9 species of deciduous trees and shrubs from eastern North America and temperate East Asia in this genus are from the camellia (Theaceae) family. The leaves are simple and short-stemmed with serrated edges. The spring flowers, usually white, are borne singly or in clusters. The bark often flakes away to reveal a range of colors.
CULTIVATION: Generally preferring cool, moist, well-drained, humus-rich soil and a position in sun or partial shade, most species are adaptable and will grow well in any position that does not dry out in summer. If it becomes necessary, trim plants after flowering. Propagate from stratified seed or from summer cuttings.

Stewartia malacodendron
SILKY CAMELLIA, VIRGINIA STEWARTIA
☼ ✳ ↔ 10 ft (3 m) ↑ 15–30 ft (4.5–9 m)
From southeastern USA. Downy young shoots, new leaves. Leaves finely toothed edges, downy below, color in autumn. Flowers borne singly, blue-gray anthers, purplish filaments, in summer. Zones 7–9.

Stewartia monadelpha

TALL STEWARTIA

☼ ❋ ↔ 20 ft (6 m) ↑ 50 ft (15 m)

Tree from Japan and Korea. Red-brown bark sheds. Downy young shoots, leaves densely hairy on underside veins. Foliage turns pinkish red in autumn. Flowers 1½ in (35 mm) wide. Zones 6–9.

Stewartia ovata

MOUNTAIN STEWARTIA

☼ ❋ ↔ 15 ft (4.5 m) ↑ 15–20 ft (4.5–6 m)

Shrub from southeastern USA. Leaflets with sparsely toothed edges, downy underside, turn yellow in autumn. Flowers 2 in (5 cm) long. Zones 5–9.

Stewartia pseudocamellia ★

JAPANESE STEWARTIA

☼ ❋ ↔ 15 ft (4.5 m) ↑ 20–50 ft (6–15 m)

From Japan. Light reddish brown bark sheds. Leaves with serrated edges, downy underside, bright red in autumn. Flowers with frilly-edged petals, golden anthers, in spring. Zones 5–9.

Stewartia pseudocamellia

Stewartia pteropetiolata

☼ ❋ ↔ 12 ft (3.5 m) ↑ 20 ft (6 m)

Shrub or small tree native to southern China and Korea. Toothed-edged leaves, small wing-like bracts on stalks. Small flowers, jagged-edged white petals, gold anthers, in mid- to late summer. Zones 5–9.

Stewartia sinensis

CHINESE STEWARTIA

☼ ❋ ↔ 20 ft (6 m) ↑ 15–30 ft (4.5–9 m)

From China. Flaking red-brown bark. Stems and leaves downy when young, leaves taper to fine point, serrated edges, purple-red in autumn. Fragrant flowers have yellow anthers. Zones 6–9.

STRELITZIA

Native to South Africa, the 4 or 5 species in this genus are large evergreen perennials in the strelitzia (Strelitziaceae) family. Usually treated as shrubs or trees, they are clump-forming and have very long oblong to lance-shaped leaves that are borne on stout stalks. A large bud or spathe borne at the end of the stem is usually held clear of the foliage; from it opens a succession of strikingly colored flowers, each with a long projecting corolla and wing-like sepals.

CULTIVATION: They prefer full sun or part-shade, and are tender to all but the lightest frosts. Soil should be well-drained and moist, but most species will tolerate brief periods of drought once established and prefer to be kept on the dry side in winter. Roots are very strong, so take care when siting. Propagate from seed or by removing suckers. Division is possible.

Strelitzia nicolai

GIANT BIRD OF PARADISE, NATAL WILD BANANA

☼ ⸙ ↔ 15 ft (4.5 m) ↑ 30 ft (9 m)

Found in KwaZulu-Natal and Eastern Cape, South Africa. Leaves and leaf stalks often over 4 ft (1.2 m) long. Flowers light greenish to purple-blue, white projecting corolla, open from red-brown spathes, in late spring–early summer. Zones 10–12.

STREPTOSOLEN

This genus from the nightshade (Solanaceae) family is doubtfully distinct from *Browallia*. The single species is from tropical South America. It has a scrambling habit and simple alternate leaves, and is popular in warm climates for its spectacular red to orange flowers.

CULTIVATION: Plant in full sun with shelter from cold winds, in a light, fibrous, well-drained soil. It should be well watered during dry weather, and is intolerant of frost. Frequent tip pruning in the first few years will help develop a densely foliaged bush and, thereafter, regular light pruning after flowering will maintain its shape. Soft-tip cuttings can be taken in late spring or summer, half-hardened cuttings in autumn.

Streptosolen jamesonii

syn. *Browallia jamesonii*

MARMALADE BUSH, ORANGE BROWALLIA

☼ ⸙ ↔ 5 ft (1.5 m) ↑ 7 ft (2 m)

Evergreen shrub. Leaves simple, alternate, finely hairy, dark green, paler beneath. Inflorescence in 2 forms: one is mixture of yellows and reds to orange, other has pure yellow flowers, in early to late spring. Zones 9–11.

STRYCHNOS

This genus of around 150 species of woody climbers, shrubs, and small trees, from the logania (Loganiaceae) family, occurs mainly in tropical and subtropical regions of the world. Some species contain highly toxic

Strelitzia nicolai

Streptosolen jamesonii

Strychnos decussata

Styphelia tubiflora

alkaloids, most notably *Strychnos nux-vomica*, the chief source of the drug strychnine. The plants have fairly large, smooth-edged, oval leaves borne in opposite pairs at right angles to each other, with 3 to 5 major veins originating from the base of the leaf. Often spines are present in the leaf axils. The creamy white, funnel-shaped or bell-shaped flowers, borne in small clusters at the ends of branches, are often perfumed, sometimes unpleasantly. The rounded berry-like fruit has a smooth hard rind or shell and fleshy juicy pulp.
CULTIVATION: Most species are suited to only warm-temperate to tropical climates and prefer well-drained acidic soils in a sunny to part-shaded position. Provide supplementary watering during extended dry periods. Propagate from seed or cuttings.

Strychnos decussata
CAPE TEAK, CHAKA'S WOOD
☀ ☘ ↔ 15 ft (4.5 m) ↑ 30 ft (9 m)
Small tree from eastern South Africa and tropical East Africa. Small leaves glossy dark green. Small greenish white flowers in spring to early summer. Globular orange or red berries. Zones 10–12.

Strychnos spinosa
NATAL ORANGE
☀ ☘ ↔ 12 ft (3.5 m) ↑ 20 ft (6 m)
Spiny shrub or small tree native to Madagascar, and tropical and southern Africa. Leathery oval leaves. Greenish white star-shaped flowers, in clusters, in spring. Yellow edible fruit. Zones 10–12.

STYPHELIA
This genus is a member of the epacris (Epacridaceae) family, with all 14 species occurring in Australia. Other species have been placed in this genus in the past, but are now correctly placed in other genera. All species are woody shrubs, often sparsely branched; some are small, some almost prostrate. Their leaves are stiff with parallel veins and a sharp point. The green, pink, or red flowers are long and tubular with the 5 petals rolled back, exposing the hairy interior and leaving the stamens protruding.
CULTIVATION: These plants require acid soils that are free draining but do not dry out. Organic matter in the soil and mulching seem to improve the chances of success. Propagation is not easy, unfortunately; cuttings do not strike readily and seed germination is often slow and erratic.

Styphelia tubiflora
☀ ❋ ↔ 30 in (75 cm) ↑ 24 in (60 cm)
Straggly shrub, occurs only in New South Wales, Australia. Leaves narrow, sharp point. Flowers red, 1 in (25 mm) long, in winter. Small berry-like fruit containing 5 seeds. Zones 8–9.

STYRAX
Found over much of the northern temperate and subtropical zones, this genus gives its name to the storax (Styracaceae) family. It has some 100 species of deciduous and evergreen shrubs and trees. Foliage usually comprises simple rounded leaves with serrated edges, obvious veins, and a pointed tip. Leaves are usually small to medium-sized, but a few species have large felted leaves. Flowers, which are usually fragrant, hang in clusters beneath the foliage of the previous season's wood. They are white, occasionally with a flush of pink, and open in spring to be followed by 1- or 2-seeded drupes.
CULTIVATION: They prefer a cool moist climate with clearly defined seasons that is not too cold in winter. Hardiness varies with the species' native range. Propagate from seed, which often needs stratification to germinate well, or by taking cuttings in summer.

Styrax americanus ★
☀ ❋ ↔ 8 ft (2.4 m) ↑ 10 ft (3 m)
Deciduous shrub from southeastern USA. Branches coated with down when young. Dark green leaves elliptical, serrated edges, pale, downy below. Pendulous clusters of flowers in late spring. Zones 6–10.

Styrax benzoin
BENZOIN
☀ ☘ ↔ 10–20 ft (3–6 m) ↑ 20 ft (6 m)
Evergreen tree from highlands of Sumatra, Indonesia. Stout trunk and main branches, heavy covering of resinous gray-brown bark. Leaves 4–6 in (10–15 cm) long, finely toothed along edges. Flower panicles carry up to 20 small white blooms. Zones 10–11.

Styrax grandifolius
BIG-LEAFED SNOWBELL
☀ ❋ ↔ 15 ft (4.5 m) ↑ 15 ft (4.5 m)
Deciduous large shrub or small tree native to southeastern USA. Leaves large, downy coating, underside gray, yellowish elsewhere. Fragrant flowers, in racemes, in spring. Zones 8–10.

Sutherlandia frutescens

Styrax japonicus
JAPANESE SNOWBELL, JAPANESE SNOWDROP TREE,
SNOWBELL TREE

☀ ❈ ↔ 15 ft (4.5 m) ↕ 20–30 ft (6–9 m)
Deciduous tree from Japan. Lightly branched.
Downy young stems. Leaves glossy dark green,
shallowly toothed edges. Short pendulous
flower clusters in late spring–early summer.
'Fargesii', vigorous cultivar with larger leaves;
'Pink Chimes', pale pink flowers. Zones 5–9.

Styrax obassia
BIG-LEAFED STORAX, FRAGRANT SNOWBELL
☀ ❈ ↔ 20 ft (6 m) ↕ 35 ft (10 m)
Tree native to Japan. Rounded oval leaves to 8 in (20 cm) long,
dark green, very fine serrations, densely downy beneath. Flowers
on 4–8 in (10–20 cm) long racemes, in late spring. Zones 6–10.

SUTHERLANDIA
BALLOON PEA

The 5 species of evergreen shrubs in this genus from the pea-flower
subfamily of the legume (Fabaceae) family are natives of South
Africa. They have pinnate leaves made up of many small finely hairy
leaflets. The red to purple pea-flowers have a large keel, and are followed by inflated bladder-like seed pods, hence the common name.
CULTIVATION: Apart from being susceptible to frost damage, *Sutherlandia* species are easily grown in light well-drained soil in full sun.
Seedlings grow quickly and often flower in their first year; in cool
winter areas with long summers the plants can be treated as annuals.
Cut back older plants to keep them compact. Propagate from seed,
soaked before sowing, or from half-hardened summer cuttings.

Sutherlandia frutescens
BALLOON PEA, CAPE BLADDER PEA, DUCK PLANT
☀ ❇ ↔ 5 ft (1.5 m) ↕ 5 ft (1.5m)
Found in open areas and dry woodlands of southern Africa. Soft-
wooded shrub; drooping pinnate leaves with 13 to 21, small, finely
hairy leaflets. Pendulous clusters of orange-red flowers in late winter. Inflated pale green, sometimes red-tinged, seed pods. Zones 9–11.

Styrax japonicus

SWIETENIA
MAHOGANY

From tropical regions throughout Central America and the
West Indies, this is a small genus of about 3 species of evergreen
or semi-deciduous trees belonging to the mahogany (Meliaceae)
family. Grown as shade and street trees in the tropics, they are
highly prized for their reddish brown hardwood timber, commercially known as mahogany, that is used in cabinetwork,
paneling, and ship-building. Large pinnate leaves have smooth
shiny leaflets. Small, 5-petalled, greenish white flowers are borne
in panicles in the leaf axils or at the ends of branches. Woody
capsules contain winged seeds.
CULTIVATION: Frost tender, they need a sunny protected position in
a deep well-drained soil. Provide supplementary watering during
dry periods. Propagate from seed or cuttings.

Swietenia macrophylla
HONDURAS MAHOGANY
☀ ✶ ↔ 25 ft (8 m) ↕ 150 ft (45 m)
Tall, straight, evergreen tree native to lowland
tropical American forests, shorter in cultivation.
Pinnate leaves, 8 to 12 lance-shaped leaflets.
Large woody fruit, chestnut brown winged
seeds. Cultivated for timber. Zones 10–12.

Swietenia mahogani
WEST INDIES MAHOGANY
☀ ✶ ↔ 15 ft (4.5 m) ↕ 80 ft (24 m)
Dome-shaped West Indian tree. Pinnate leaves,
4–8 in (10–20 cm) long, 4 or 5 oval leaflets.
Small greenish yellow flowers, in clusters, in
spring. Large woody fruit, 4 in (10 cm) wide. Zones 11–12.

SYMPHORICARPOS
CORALBERRY, SNOWBERRY

Allied to the honeysuckles *(Lonicera),* the 17 deciduous shrubs in
this genus from the woodbine (Caprifoliaceae) family are mainly
found in North and Central America, with 1 species from China.
They have opposite pairs of usually simple leaves with blunt rounded
tips. Small white or pink flowers appear in spring and may be carried
singly or in clusters. The fruit is the dominating feature of most
species. The berry-like drupes are near-spherical, and last well into
winter when they stand out clearly on the then leafless stems.
CULTIVATION: Most species are very frost hardy and prefer to grow
in a distinctly seasonal temperate climate. They are not fussy about
soil type as long as it is well drained, but will crop more freely if
fed well and watered during dry spells. Plant in sun or part-shade
and prune or trim to shape in winter after the fruit is past its best.
Propagation is most often from winter hardwood cuttings.

Symphoricarpos albus ★
COMMON SNOWBERRY, SNOWBERRY
☀ ❈ ↔ 4–6 ft (1.2–1.8 m) ↕ 4–6 ft (1.2–1.8 m)
Shrub with slightly differing varieties over most of North America.
Wiry stems, suckering habit. Clusters of small pink flowers in
spring. Berries, pale green at first, ripen to strikingly pure white.

S. a. var. *laevigatus* (syn. *S. rivularis*), native to western North America, upright habit, forms dense thickets, fruits more heavily than eastern forms. Zones 3–9.

Symphoricarpos × chenaultii
CHENAULT CORALBERRY

☀ ❋ ↔ 5 ft (1.5 m) ↑ 6–8 ft (1.8–2.4 m)
Garden hybrid between *S. microphyllus* and *S. orbiculatus*. Deciduous shrub, downy young stems, dark green leaves, glaucous, slightly downy beneath. Small spikes of pink flowers, near branch tips, in summer. Red-and-white spotted or mottled fruit. '**Hancock**', low spreading habit, rarely exceeds 20 in (50 cm) high.
Zones 5–9.

Symphoricarpos mollis
☀ ❋ ↔ 3 ft (0.9 m) ↑ 3 ft (0.9 m)
From western USA. Compact shrub, velvety new stems and young leaves. Foliage downy on underside. Inconspicuous pinkish white flowers in spring. White berries, ¼ in (6 mm) in diameter. Zones 7–9.

Symphoricarpos orbiculatus
CORALBERRY, INDIAN CURRANT

☀ ❋ ↔ 6 ft (1.8 m) ↑ 6 ft (1.8 m)
From eastern USA and Mexico. Dark green leaves, gray underside, red tints in autumn. Flowers white, flushed pink, in summer. Small berries ripen from dull white to deep red. Zones 3–9.

SYMPLOCOS
This genus gives its name to the family Symplocaceae. It consists of 250 species of trees and shrubs, some evergreen and some deciduous, occurring in woodlands throughout Asia, Australasia, and North and South America, in tropical and warm-temperate regions. Their leaves are simple and alternate. Some of the species accumulate aluminum in their tissues and these plants have yellow-green leaves and blue fruit. Other species have egg-shaped fruit that are black, purple, or white. The flowers are yellow or white and are borne in a variety of inflorescences.
CULTIVATION: Well-drained, acid to neutral soils are required, in a full sun position. The species in cultivation respond well to regular feeding. Frost tolerance varies between species, depending on the climate of their original habitat. Propagation is from fresh seed or cuttings, and both methods are quite reliable.

Symplocos paniculata
SAPPHIRE BERRY

☀ ❋ ↔ 15 ft (4.5 m) ↑ 15 ft (4.5 m)
Deciduous, bushy, spreading shrub or small tree from eastern Asia and Himalayas. Oval, slightly

Syncarpha vestita, in the wild, South Africa

Swietenia macrophylla

hairy, dark green leaves, toothed margins. Small, white, sweet-smelling flowers, borne in clusters, in late spring–summer. Egg-shaped blue fruit. Zones 7–9.

SYNCARPHA
EVERLASTING

This genus of around 25 species of perennials and subshrubs endemic to the Cape region of South Africa belongs to the daisy (Asteraceae) family. They have a low shrubby habit, usually with several erect stems densely covered with thickly downy leaves that are narrowly elliptical and often semi-succulent. Showy, papery, "everlasting" flowerheads, usually white to cream with a small cluster of golden disc florets at the stem tips, can smother a small plant. Most species flower in spring or after rain.
CULTIVATION: These plants are tolerant of irregular light frosts and are also drought resistant once established. Plant in a sunny position with gritty soil that provides excellent drainage. A little added humus for moisture retention will help the plants through summer. Remove spent flowerheads but otherwise trim only very lightly to shape. Propagation is usually from seed, which, as with other plants often exposed to fires, has been found to germinate better if it is smoke treated.

Syncarpha vestita
syn. *Helichrysum vestitum*
CAPE EVERLASTING

☀ ❀ ↔ 12–20 in (30–50 cm) ↑ 12–20 in (30–50 cm)
Found in rocky habitats. Clump of upright stems with mid-green leaves to 2 in (5 cm) long, densely covered with silvery white down. Abundance of creamy white flowerheads give bush overall silvery appearance. Zones 9–10.

SYNCARPIA

This genus in the myrtle (Myrtaceae) family contains 2 species found in the coastal areas of eastern Australia. Both are tall straight trees that have simple opposite leaves with noticeable venation and thick fibrous bark. From the same family as the eucalypts, they have petal-less flowers with numerous stamens and capsular fruit containing many seeds. These are important hardwood timber trees and make very good ornamental subjects for parks and large gardens. Wood from *S. hillii* was used for sidings in the building of the Suez Canal and for wharves in other countries.
CULTIVATION: These trees perform best in a moist well-drained soil in areas free from frost and protected from strong winds. Propagate from seed sown in a humid environment.

Syncarpia glomulifera, in the wild, New South Wales, Australia

Syncarpia glomulifera

TURPENTINE

☀ ⧉ ↔ 25 ft (8 m) ↑ 100 ft (30 m)

Tall straight tree with dense crown, straight trunk, fibrous persistent bark. Ovate to narrow-ovate dull green leaves, whitish gray, hairy beneath, aromatic when crushed. Cream flowers, long stamens, in spring–summer. Multiple capsular fruit. Zones 9–12.

SYRINGA

LILAC

This genus, which a member of the olive (Oleaceae) family, is made up of 23 species of vigorous, deciduous, flowering shrubs, most of them native to northeast Asia, with 2 species only in Europe. Of the European species one, *S. vulgaris*, the common lilac, is known to have been grown in the gardens of western Europe since the sixteenth century; today, it is represented by more than 1,500 named cultivars. The plants have simple pointed elliptical to heart-shaped leaves in opposite pairs, and produce upright panicles of small 4-petalled flowers, usually in spring. The flowers may be single

Syringa × *prestoniae*

or double, and occur in conspicuous clusters. Almost all are strongly sweet smelling, although not every cultivar is noted for its fragrance. *Syringa* species are popular cool-climate shrubs.
CULTIVATION: Their main requirements are a well-drained soil and a position in sun or light shade; they thrive in a sandy gravelly soil, preferably one that is slightly alkaline, but do not do well in heavy clay. Propagate from seed, but the results may be variable. They can be grown from cuttings of the current year's growth, or by layering.

Syringa × chinensis

CHINESE LILAC

☀ ❋ ↔ 12 ft (3.5 m) ↑ 12 ft (3.5 m)

Group of hybrids between *S. laciniata* and *S. vulgaris*. Upright rounded bushes with slender branches, and oval medium to dark green leaves. Large panicles of flowers, white to pinkish lavender to reddish, highly fragrant, in late spring. 'Saugeana' ★, reddish mauve flowers. Zones 4–9.

Syringa emodi

HIMALAYAN LILAC

☀ ❋ ↔ 12 ft (3.5 m) ↑ 15 ft (4.5 m)

From western Himalayas. Upright branches, leaves oblong to elliptical, half main vein tinged purple. Flowers tinged pinkish mauve in bud, open to white, in early summer. Zones 4–9.

Syringa × hyacinthiflora

AMERICAN HYBRID LILAC, EARLY FLOWERING LILAC, HYACINTH LILAC

☀ ❋ ↔ 15 ft (4.5 m) ↑ 15 ft (4.5 m)

Hybrids of *S. oblata* and *S. vulgaris*. Ovate leaves, often red-bronze, purple-red tones in autumn. Single or double flowers in early spring. 'Blue Hyacinth', pale purple to light blue flowers; 'Charles Nordine', lilac-pink flowers; 'Laurentian', rose pink buds. Zones 4–9.

Syringa × josiflexa

☀ ❋ ↔ 7 ft (2 m) ↑ 8–10 ft (2.4–3 m)

Hybrid of *S. josikaea* and *S. reflexa*. Erect shrub, broadly lance-shaped leaves, magenta flowers in early summer. 'Anna Amhoff' and 'Elaine', both with single white flowers; 'Bellicent', perfumed pink flowers; 'Lynette', single purple flowers. Zones 5–9.

Syringa josikaea

HUNGARIAN LILAC

☀ ❋ ↔ 10 ft (3 m) ↑ 12 ft (3.5 m)

One of only 2 European lilacs, occurs in mountain regions of central to eastern Europe. Leaves leather-like, glossy green. Flowers dark blue-violet, in summer. Requires rich soil. Zones 5–9.

Syringa laciniata

CUT-LEAFED LILAC

☀ ❋ ↔ 10 ft (3 m) ↑ 12 ft (3.5 m)

From Chinese Province of Gansu, one of first oriental lilacs introduced to West. Tall shrub, smooth-edged and cut leaves. Pale lavender flowers, small clusters along branches, in spring. Zones 5–9.

Syringa meyeri
DWARF KOREAN LILAC, MEYER LILAC

☼ ❋ ↔4 ft (1.2 m) ↑5 ft (1.5 m)

Found in garden near Beijing, China, in 1909, unknown in wild. Low compact shrub, sturdy upright branches. Flowers in small clusters, pale lilac to lilac-purple, sometimes whitish lavender, in spring, repeat late summer–early autumn. 'Palibin', smallest of all lilacs, to 4 ft (1.2 m) high, pinkish lavender flowers; 'Superba', deep pink flowers, fade with age, long flowering season. Zones 4–9.

Syringa oblata
BROADLEAF LILAC

☼ ❋ ↔10 ft (3 m) ↑12 ft (3.5 m)

Native to China and Korea, like *S. vulgaris*, but flowers in mid-spring. Loose strongly fragrant panicles. *S. o.* subsp. *dilatata*, heart-shaped leaves, fragrant pale purple flowers. Zones 5–9.

Syringa pekinensis
syn. *Syringa reticulata* subsp. *pekinensis*

CHINESE TREE LILAC, PEKING LILAC

☼ ❋ ↔12 ft (3.5 m) ↑15 ft (4.5 m)

Tall shrub or tree collected in Beijing area, China, in 1742. Dark green leaves. Tiny flowerheads, creamy white, in mid-summer. Bark peels into papery curls with age. Zones 5–9.

Syringa potaninii
syn. *Syringa pubescens* subsp. *potaninii*

☼ ❋ ↔6 ft (1.8 m) ↑6–8 ft (1.8–2.4 m)

Discovered in southern Gansu Province of China in 1885. Upright vase-like habit. Variable leaves, broad-elliptic to oblong-elliptic, downy on both surfaces. Flowers light rose-purple to whitish purple, generally fading to near-white, in late spring. Zones 5–9.

Syringa × prestoniae
NODDING LILAC, PRESTON LILAC

☼ ❋ ↔12 ft (3.5 m) ↑12 ft (3.5 m)

Garden hybrid between *S. reflexa* and *S. villosa*. Dark green leaves, slightly glaucous, faintly downy underside. Slightly drooping panicles of scented soft pink to light purple flowers in early summer. 'Desdemona', rich purple-pink to blue flowers; 'Elinor', purple-tinged buds open to mauve flowers; 'James MacFarlane', soft pink flowers, spreading habit to over 8 ft (2.4 m) wide. Zones 4–9.

Syringa pubescens

☼ ❋ ↔12 ft (3.5 m) ↑12 ft (3.5 m)

From China. Numerous slender branches. Flowers fragrant, buds pale purple, mature to pale lilac with pinkish wash. *S. p.* subsp. *microphylla* (syn. *S. microphylla*), slightly shorter leaves, shorter panicles of more pinkish flowers in spring and earlier summer; 'Superba', heavy-flowering, slightly darker flowers over long season. *S. p.* subsp. *patula* (syn. *S. patula*), larger leaves, purplish new growths; 'Miss Kim', darker pink buds. *S. p.* 'Excellens', white flowers, pale flesh pink buds; 'Sarah Sands', very pale mauve-pink flowers, more compact clusters. Zones 5–9.

Syringa reflexa

☼ ❋ ↔12 ft (3.5 m) ↑12 ft (3.5 m)

Found in central China in 1901, used extensively in hybridizing. Erect stems, large ovate leaves. Flower buds deep bright red, opening to pale rose, in early summer. Flower clusters sometimes pendent like those of *Wisteria* species. Zones 5–9.

Syringa reticulata
JAPANESE TREE LILAC

☼ ❋ ↔15 ft (4.5 m) ↑30 ft (9 m)

Tree lilac native to Japan. Round top. Large plumes of feathery white blooms, with protruding yellow anthers, in summer, contrast well with dark green foliage. Flowers have strong fragrance. Bark reddish brown, peels on younger branches. 'Ivory Silk', abundant ivory flowers, blooms young. Zones 3–9.

Syringa × swegiflexa

☼/◗ ❋ ↔5 ft (1.5 m) ↑10 ft (3 m)

Garden hybrid between *S. reflexa* and *S. sweginzowii*. Upright shrub, pointed oval leaves, downy underside. Slender, pendent, many-flowered, red to dusky pink panicles to over 6 in (15 cm) long, in late spring. Zones 6–9.

Syringa reflexa

Syringa sweginzowii

☼ ❋ ↔6 ft (1.8 m) ↑10 ft (3 m)

Neat upright shrub found in northern Sichuan Province, China, around 1893. Small leaves. Brownish red stems covered with pink florets, in open clusters, in late spring–early summer. Spicy fragrance. Zones 3–9.

Syringa tigerstedtii

☼ ❋ ↔8 ft (2.4 m) ↑8 ft (2.4 m)

Slender shrub discovered in Sichuan Province, China, in 1934. Widely spaced flower clusters, purplish pink to white, on inflorescences to around 10 in (25 cm) in length, in summer. Zones 4–9.

Syringa tigerstedtii

Syringa tomentella

☼ ✳ ↔ 10 ft (3 m) ↕ 10 ft (3 m)

Neat compact shrub, found in Sichuan Province, China, in 1891. Smooth pale gray bark. Leaves elliptic to oblong, downy underside. Pink buds, paler pink flowers fade to white, in summer. Zones 4–9.

Syringa vulgaris

COMMON LILAC, FRENCH HYBRID LILAC

☼ ✳ ↔ 20 ft (6 m) ↕ 20 ft (6 m)

One of 2 species native to Europe, with 14 subspecies reflecting geographic variations. Typical form has blue flowers, but cultivars can have deep purple and white flowers. Blooms appear in late spring–early summer.

Single-flowered cultivars include '**Andenken an Ludwig Späth**', dark reddish flowers; '**Charles X**', crimson blooms in conical panicles; '**Congo**', purple-red flowers, lighter with age; '**Maréchal Foch**', large bright purplish red flowers; '**Maud Notcutt**', panicles of white blooms; '**President Lincoln**', flowers closest to true blue; '**Primrose**', pale yellow flowers in small panicles; '**Sensation**', purplish red blooms with white margins to petals; '**Vestale**', white flowers; and '**Volcan**', dark red to purple flowers.

Double-flowered cultivars include '**Ami Schott**', medium blue flowers with deeper tones; '**Ann Tighe**', crimson-purple buds, pink flowers; '**Belle de Nancy**', purplish red buds open to pale purple-pink flowers; '**Charles Joly**', dark purple-red blooms; '**Edith Cavell**', pale yellow buds open to white flowers; '**Madame Antoine Buchner**', reddish pink to mauve flowers; '**Madame Lemoine**', pale yellow buds open to snow white flowers; '**Monique Lemoine**', late-blooming white flowers; '**Mrs Edward Harding**', deep purplish red flowers, shaded pink; '**Olivier de Serres**', large panicles of lavender-blue flowers; '**Paul Thirion**', red-purple buds becoming lovely lilac-pink flowers; '**Victor Lemoine**', thin panicles of flowers ranging from lavender-pink to lilac-blue in color; and '**William Robinson**', abundant pale pink flowers. Zones 4–9.

Syringium francisii

Syringa vulgaris 'Ann Tighe'

Syringa wolfii

syn. *Syringa formosissima*

☼ ✳ ↔ 12 ft (3.5 m) ↕ 15 ft (4.5 m)

Tall shrub from northeastern China and Korea. Bright green elliptic leaves. Large pyramidal inflorescence, 12 in (30 cm) long, lilac-colored flowers, slightly fragrant, in late spring. Color may vary from pale lavender to darker purple. Zones 4–9.

SYZYGIUM

This large genus belonging to the myrtle (Myrtaceae) family consists of around 1,000 species, the majority occurring in Southeast Asia, Australia, and Africa. Mostly evergreen trees and shrubs, they have simple opposite leaves that are often smooth and hairless. The flowers, with numerous long stamens, usually occur in panicles along or at the ends of branches; petals and sepals are smaller than the stamens. The fruit is a succulent, mostly red, purple, blue, black, or white edible berry. Mostly tropical and subtropical species, they are cultivated for ornamental and medicinal uses, as well as for food and wood; many species are popular for hedging and topiary.

CULTIVATION: *Syzygium* species perform best in moist, well-drained, deep, fertile soil in sun or shade. Propagate from seed sown as soon as ripe in spring or from cuttings in summer. In Australia, galls can disfigure the foliage. Scale may also be a problem.

Syzygium australe

syn. *Eugenia paniculata* of gardens

BRUSH CHERRY, MAGENTA CHERRY

☼ ❅ ↔ 20 ft (6 m) ↕ 25 ft (8 m)

Shrub or small tree native to Australian rainforests. Upper stems brownish green. Opposite rounded leaves, mid-green when mature. White flowers, in small dense panicles, in summer. Large, red, fleshy, edible berries. Zones 9–12.

Syzygium francisii

GIANT WATER GUM

☼ ❅ ↔ 70 ft (21 m) ↕ 80 ft (24 m)

Medium to large tree native to Australia. Prominent buttressed trunk. Bark slightly flaky.

Tabebuia chrysantha

Tabernaemontana elegans

Glossy, dark green leaves, ovate to elliptical, wavy edges. Panicles of flowers with cream stamens in early–late summer, followed by violet-purple globe-shaped berries. Zones 10–12.

Syzygium jambos
syn. *Eugenia jambos*
ROSE APPLE

☼ ❄ ↔ 15 ft (4.5 m) ↑ 20 ft (6 m)

Large shrub or small tree from Malay Peninsula and Indonesia. Leathery, dark green, lance-shaped leaves, shiny pink when new. Large showy flowers, creamy white stamens, rich in nectar, in summer. Fragrant, pink to yellow, edible fruit. Zones 10–12.

Syzygium luehmannii
syn. *Eugenia luehmannii*
SMALL-LEAFED LILLYPILLY, RIBERRY

☼ ❄ ↔ 30 ft (9 m) ↑ 50 ft (15 m)

Tree from northeastern Australia. Leaves glossy dark green, ovate to lance-shaped, pale pink-red when young. Panicles of small creamy white flowers in summer. Pink pear-shaped fruit. Zones 9–12.

Syzygium paniculatum
syn. *Eugenia paniculata*
AUSTRALIAN BRUSH CHERRY, MAGENTA BRUSH CHERRY

☼ ❄ ↔ 20 ft (6 m) ↑ 25 ft (8 m)

Native to eastern Australia. Dense foliage, oblong to lance-shaped leaves, glossy dark green, copper-brown when young. Fluffy creamy white flowers in summer. Crimson-purple berries. Zones 9–12.

Syzygium wilsonii
POWDERPUFF LILLYPILLY

☼ ❄ ↔ 7 ft (2 m) ↑ 6 ft (1.8 m)

Scrambling shrub from Queensland, Australia. Smooth dark green leaves, narrowly oval, bronze or red new growth. Deep red flowers in spring–early summer. White berries.

TABEBUIA
GOLDEN TRUMPET TREE

This genus in the trumpet-vine (Bignoniaceae) family comprises 100 species of trees or shrubs native to tropical areas of the Americas

Syzygium luehmannii

and Caribbean. They may be briefly deciduous or evergreen and have simple or compound, 3- to 7-fingered leaves. They produce large crowded panicles of showy, frequently fragrant, trumpet-shaped flowers in a variety of colors, followed by bean-like pods. CULTIVATION: *Tabebuia* species are best grown in the greenhouse in cool-temperate climates. In tropical and subtropical areas they make attractive specimen trees and may produce flowers sporadically throughout the year. Propagate from seed, cuttings, or air layers.

Tabebuia chrysantha

☼ ❄ ↔ 20 ft (6 m) ↑ 20–50 ft (6–15 m)

Open-crowned tree from Mexico to Venezuela. Gray bark becomes fissured, scaly. Leaves 5-fingered, slightly hairy, in pointed oblong leaflets. Yellow trumpet flowers, in large clusters, in spring, followed by long seed pods. Zones 11–12.

Tabebuia rosea
PINK POUI

☼ ❄ ↔ 30 ft (9 m) ↑ 90 ft (27 m)

Variable species from Mexico to Colombia, and Venezuela. Leaves 3- to 7-fingered, in pointed oval leaflets. Flowers white to pale pink, with yellow throat, in loose clusters, in spring. Zones 11–12.

TABERNAEMONTANA

This genus of about 100 species of evergreen shrubs and small trees belongs to the dogbane (Apocynaceae) family. Found in tropical and subtropical regions of the world, they have large glossy green leaves and waxy, usually white, funnel-shaped flowers with 5 wide-spreading curved petals. Flowers are borne throughout the warmer months and are fragrant, particularly at night. These plants have a milky sap and are recognized by the paired boat- to egg-shaped fruit joined to a common stalk. CULTIVATION: These warm-climate frost-tender plants require regular watering. They need good soil that is well-drained but moisture-retentive, in full sun or bright filtered light, and shelter from wind. Plants can be kept neat and bushy by lightly trimming. Propagate from seed or cuttings.

Tabernaemontana divaricata
syns *Ervatamia coronaria, E. divaricata*
CRAPE GARDENIA, CRAPE JASMINE, PINWHEEL FLOWER

☼ ❄ ↔ 5 ft (1.5 m) ↑ 6 ft (1.8 m)

Evergreen shrub or small tree from India to Yunnan Province, China, and northern Thailand. Leathery elliptic leaves. Large, waxy, fragrant white flowers, in small clusters, in summer. Perfume more noticeable at night. 'Flore Pleno', double flowers. Zones 11–12.

Tabernaemontana elegans
TOAD TREE

☼ ❄ ↔ 10 ft (3 m) ↑ 10–20 ft (3–6 m)

Deciduous shrub or small tree from southern Africa. Opposite, glossy, dark green, oblong leaves. Sweetly scented trumpet-shaped flowers, in small panicles, in spring–summer. Zones 9–12.

Tamarix parviflora

TAIWANIA

The single conifer species in this genus, which belongs to the cypress (Cupressaceae) family, is related to *Cryptomeria*. It is native to Taiwan, with a variety being found in southwestern China and Myanmar. It is well known for the way the bark peels off in long strips. The foliage is bluish green, forming a rather cone-shaped crown on a very tall tree. The foliage becomes scaly with age and produces male and female cones in shades of brown. On some varieties, the cones can be in shades of gray and green.
CULTIVATION: This species prefers a sheltered sunny position in an acid soil that is moist but well drained. Propagate from seed.

Taiwania cryptomerioides

Taiwania cryptomerioides
☼ ❄ ↔ 35 ft (10 m) ↑ 180 ft (55 m)
Tall tree with conical or columnar crown, much smaller in cultivation. Bark exfoliates in strips. Variable bluish green leaves, narrow and pointed on juvenile plants, scale-like on adults. Small brown male and female cones in summer. *T. c.* **var.** *flousiana*, from China and Myanmar, cones grayish green stained with maroon. Zones 8–11.

TAMARINDUS

There is one species of evergreen tree in this genus, which is a member of the cassia subfamily of the legume (Fabaceae) family. Originally from tropical Africa, it is naturalized and cultivated in many other tropical areas. It has a wide crown, often spreading. The soft green leaves resemble fern fronds. The flowers are cream or yellowish, often with a red tinge. The seed pods are long and bean-like and are a dull brown when ripe. Apart from its ornamental value, the tree has many other uses. Its bean-like pods are used in a number of culinary ways: in curries, chutneys, drinks, and sweetmeats. Parts of the tree are also used medicinally.
CULTIVATION: This tree requires a sunny site in a tropical or subtropical climate. It will tolerate a range of soil types. In temperate climates it can be grown in the greenhouse but will not develop its full size. Propagate from seed or softwood cuttings.

Tamarindus indica
TAMARIND
☼ ✢ ↔ 35 ft (10 m) ↑ 90 ft (27 m)
Attractive tree originally from Africa but found in most tropical climates. Open spreading crown, fern-like bright green leaves. Racemes of small cream or orange-yellow flowers, flushed with red, in summer. Bean-like pods, to 6 in (15 cm) long, brittle and grayish brown when fully ripe. Zones 11–12.

TAMARIX
TAMARISK SALT CEDAR
This genus consists of 50 species of deciduous shrubs and small trees belonging to the tamarisk (Tamaricaceae) family, which are found in Europe, India, North Africa, and Asia. Most of the species occur on coastal flats, river estuaries, and on saline soil. They have brown, deep red, and sometimes purple bark; the main feature is the mass of attractive drooping branches covered in fine foliage. The flowers come in shades of pink and appear in drooping panicles. *Tamarix* are often used as windbreak hedging for exposed gardens near the sea; some species are also grown to stop the erosion of sand dunes. The galls of some species are used to tan leather.
CULTIVATION: In coastal areas, *Tamarix* species are happy to grow in well-drained soil in a sunny position, while in inland areas they prefer soil that is slightly moister, as well as shelter from cold drying winds. Shrubs should be pruned regularly to prevent root movement in severe winds. Propagate from just-hardened seed sown in an area that is protected from frost, or half-hardened cuttings in summer, or hardwood cuttings in winter.

Tamarix chinensis
CHINESE TAMARISK, SALT CEDAR
☼ ❄ ↔ 10 ft (3 m) ↑ 15 ft (4.5 m)
Small tree or shrub native to temperate zones of eastern Asia. Densely branched with fine drooping branchlets. Bark brown to blackish, leaves bluish green. Drooping panicles of pink flowers, on current year's wood, in summer. Zones 7–10.

Tamarix gallica
FRENCH TAMARISK, FRENCH TREE, MANNA PLANT
☼ ❄ ↔ 10 ft (3 m) ↑ 12 ft (3.5 m)
Small tree or shrub native to Mediterranean area. Bark reddish brown to purple; blue-green stalkless leaves, small and narrow. Pink flowers, in cylindrical racemes, on current year's wood, in summer. Larger in favorable conditions. Zones 5–10.

Tamarix parviflora
EARLY TAMARISK
☼ ❄ ↔ 20 ft (6 m) ↑ 15 ft (4.5 m)
Small tree or large shrub from Europe. Slender, arching, purple branches, pointed narrow leaves. Racemes of pale pink flowers, on older wood, in late spring. Zones 5–9.

Tamarix ramosissima
syn. *Tamarix pentandra*

☼ ❄ ↔15 ft (4.5 m) ↑15 ft (4.5 m)

Shrub or small tree from eastern Europe to central Asia. Upright arching branches. Leaves narrow, lance-shaped, pointed. Dense racemes of pink flowers in late summer–late autumn. '**Pink Cascade**', deep pink flowers; '**Rubra**', magenta flowers. Zones 2–10.

TAXODIUM

This group of 3 species from North America and Mexico belongs to the cypress (Cupressaceae) family. These deciduous or semi-deciduous trees are found growing in or near water. In these swampy conditions mature trees often produce aerial roots known as "knees" or pneumatophores, which allow the roots to breathe. These majestic conical trees bear foliage that resembles that of the yew (*Taxus*), with fissured peeling bark on buttressed trunks. Both male and female cones are held on the same tree, the small male cones in pendulous groups, the females scattered along the branches.
CULTIVATION: These plants will grow in either a clay or sandy soil as long as it remains relatively moist. They can withstand very low winter temperatures, where their foliage color turns to vivid rust tones before the leaves fall to reveal a fine tracery of branches. Propagate from seed, except for cultivars, which need to be grafted.

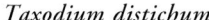
Taxodium mucronatum

Taxodium distichum
BALD CYPRESS, SWAMP CYPRESS

☼ ❄ ↔20 ft (6 m) ↑75 ft (23 m)

Fast-growing tree from North America. Deeply fissured fibrous bark exfoliates in long strips. Initially conical outline broadens, becomes irregular as tree matures. Fine leaves light green, in spring, age to deep green before turning rusty red in autumn. *T. d.* var. *imbricatum* (syn. *T. ascendens*), clasping bright green leaves; '**Nutans**', initially upright, pendulous tips with maturity. *T. d.* '**Shawnee Brave**', compact bright green leaves, ideal for hedges. Zones 6–10.

Taxodium mucronatum
MEXICAN SWAMP CYPRESS, MONTEZUMA CYPRESS

☼ ❄ ↔50 ft (15 m) ↑100 ft (30 m)

Tree from Mexico and southern Texas, USA. Evergreen in warmer climates, semi-deciduous in cooler areas. Pendulous foliage very similar to *T. distichum*. Clasping leaves, bright green turning rusty brown in autumn. Cones long, often warty. Zones 8–11.

TAXUS
YEW

This small evergreen conifer genus belonging to the yew (Taxaceae) family consists of around 7 species occurring in cool-temperate regions of the Northern Hemisphere and some more tropical mountain regions, including the Philippines and Mexico. Most are small to medium trees, with sharply pointed, linear or slightly sickle-shaped leaves, often with prominent olive green midribs.

Most species have separate male and female plants and flower in spring. The single seed found on the female plant is partly clothed in a red fleshy covering (or aril) that is sweet and edible; the rest of the plant, including the seed, is poisonous. They make useful specimen or hedge plants, and handsome topiary subjects.
CULTIVATION: Slow growing but long lived, most species are fairly adaptable in cool regions, tolerating sun or shade, frost, alkaline soils, exposure, and pollution. Propagate from seed sown as soon as hardened, from cuttings, or by grafting.

Taxus baccata
COMMON YEW, ENGLISH YEW

☼ ❄ ↔25 ft (8 m) ↑50 ft (15 m)

Slow-growing tree from Europe, North Africa, and western Asia. Very long lived, dense manybranched head. Reddish brown bark, dark green linear leaves, paler yellowish green below. Male cones yellow and scaly. Female flowers on separate plants, in summer. **Aurea Group** (golden yew), golden yellow young growth turning greener with age; '**Dovastonii Aurea**', male plant, low and spreading, dense foliage; '**Dwarf White**', low and spreading, moderately dense foliage, new growth whitish but soon turning green; '**Fastigiata**' (Irish yew), female plant, dark green leaves; **Fastigiata Aurea Group** (golden Irish yew), smaller than 'Fastigiata', golden yellow leaves; '**Nutans**', to less than 20 in (50 cm) high, dark green leaves; '**Repandens**', spreading female, to 3 ft (0.9 m) high, green leaves; '**Semperaurea**', male, to 10 ft (3 m) high, ascending branches of bright yellow young growth changing to russet-yellow in winter; '**Standishii**', female, golden leaves, columnar habit. Zones 5–10.

Taxus chinensis
CHINESE YEW

☼ ❄ ↔15 ft (4.5 m) ↑20 ft (6 m)

Shrub from China. Leaves stiff, sharp, taper abruptly, glossy green, curling outward on top, gray-green below, in 2 ranks. Pollen cones yellowish maturing to brown, in summer. Zones 6–10.

Taxus baccata

Taxus cuspidata

JAPANESE YEW

☼ ❀ ↔ 20 ft (6 m) ↑ 50 ft (15 m)

Erect tree from Japan, normally seen as shrub in gardens. Horizontal or ascending branches; spirally arranged, dark green, linear leaves. New shoots red-brown, fleshy aril red when ripe, in summer. Suitable for hedging and topiary, tolerant of pollution. *T. c.* var. *nana*, low-spreading shrub with dense growth. *T. c.* 'Capitata', strong upright foliage; 'Densa', female compact form with dark green leaves; 'Densiformis', dwarf, to 3 ft (0.9 m) tall. Zones 4–9.

Taxus × *media*

ANGLO-JAP YEW, HYBRID YEW

☼ ❀ ↔ 20 ft (6 m) ↑ 25 ft (8 m)

Hybrid between *T. baccata* and *T. cuspidata*. Tree or shrub suitable for hedging. Linear olive green leaves, prominent white midribs beneath. Seed partly covered by scarlet aril, in summer. 'Brownii', to 10 ft (3 m) high, dark green leaves, spherical shape; 'Dark Green Spreader', shrub with very dense deep green foliage; 'Everlow', low, rounded, up to 8 ft (2.4 m) high; 'Hatfieldii', male columnar form to 6 ft (1.8 m) high; 'Hicksii', columnar, dense growth, popular for hedges; 'Nigra', compact dark green foliage. Zones 5–9.

TECOMA

syns *Stenolobium, Tecomaria*

YELLOW BELLS

There are 13 species of mostly evergreen trees and scrambling shrubs in this genus belonging to the trumpet-vine (Bignoniaceae) family. They are found from southern Arizona, USA, to Mexico and the West Indies, and as far south as northern Argentina. One species (*T. capensis*), is native to southern and eastern Africa. Pinnate leaves are borne in opposite pairs; leaflets have toothed edges. Funnel-shaped or narrowly bell-shaped flowers are borne in showy terminal clusters in yellow, orange, or red, with 5 unequal petals. The fruit is a smallish pod splitting into 2 halves.

CULTIVATION: Fine ornamentals for the tropical and subtropical garden, in cool climates they can only be grown as potted shrubs in a greenhouse or conservatory. They like a sunny but sheltered position and reasonably fertile soil with good drainage. Propagate

from fresh seed, or from tip cuttings or larger cuttings from the previous year's growth. Suckering species can be divided or layered.

Tecoma capensis

syns *Bignonia capensis, Tecomaria capensis*

CAPE HONEYSUCKLE

☼ ❅ ↔ 7 ft (2 m) ↑ 10 ft (3 m)

Adaptable shrub, partly climbing habit, from eastern and southern Africa. Glossy green pinnate leaves. Orange-red to scarlet tubular flowers, in racemes at ends of branches, in spring–autumn. Tolerates salt spray, drought, wind. 'Aurea', golden yellow flowers. Zones 9–12.

Tecoma castaneifolia

☼ ❅ ↔ 8–12 ft (2.4–3.5 m) ↑ 15–25 ft (4.5–8 m)

Evergreen species from Ecuador. Upright tree, leathery elliptic leaves, very hairy underside. Yellow flowers, 2 in (5 cm) long, in spring–autumn. Beanpod-like capsules, 5 in (12 cm) long. Zones 10–12.

Tecoma stans

syns *Bignonia stans, Stenolobium stans*

SHRUBBY TRUMPET FLOWER, YELLOW BELLS, YELLOW ELDER

☼ ❅ ↔ 10 ft (3 m) ↑ 15–30 ft (4.5–9 m)

Small tree or large open shrub native to southern USA and Central and South America. Leaves oblong, lance-shaped, toothed, bright green leaflets. Yellow flowers, funnel-shaped, in terminal racemes or panicles, in late winter–summer. Capsules ripen brown. Zones 10–12.

TELANTHOPHORA

This genus, which is a member of the daisy (Asteraceae) family, was previously included in *Senecio* and contains 14 species of mostly evergreen trees and shrubs native to Central America. The stems are usually downy and have few branches. Large leaves have wavy or toothed edges. Yellow flowers are daisy-like and carried in terminal clusters. They flower profusely from late spring through summer.

CULTIVATION: These are easily grown plants that tolerate a range of soils in sun or part-shade. They are frost tender and in cool-temperate climates will require greenhouse protection. Propagate from seed.

Telanthophora grandifolia

syn. *Senecio grandifolius*

☼ ❅ ↔ 12 ft (3.5 m) ↑ 20 ft (6 m)

Evergreen shrub or small tree native to Mexico. Downy stems, large oval leaves, with wavy, lobed, or toothed edges. Yellow daisies, in large showy clusters, in late summer–early spring. Zones 9–11.

TELOPEA

WARATAH

Known for their spectacular flowerheads in shades of red, there are just 5 species in this southeastern Australian genus of evergreen shrubs and small trees belonging to the protea (Proteaceae) family. They have dark green, prominently veined leaves with toothed or lobed edges and leathery pods up to 5 in (12 cm) long that contain many seeds. The flowerheads are large and waxy and have a ring of bright red bracts. The Australian Aboriginal name for *T. speciosissima* is "waratah," now the accepted common name for the genus. All species are highly ornamental garden plants.

Tecoma capensis

Telanthophora grandifolia

Telopea speciosissima, in the wild, Australia

CULTIVATION: Waratahs require a deep, well-drained, acidic soil in full sun or part-shade. They have a low resistance to alkaline soils and excessive phosphorus, and prefer not to be overfed. Frost tolerance varies with the species. Tip prune from an early age to encourage branching, and after flowering cut old flowered stems back to halfway. Propagate from seed in spring, or from cuttings.

Telopea mongaensis

☀ ❄ ↔ 10 ft (3 m) ↑ 10 ft (3 m)

Multi-branched bushy shrub from southern New South Wales, Australia. Dark green, smooth, leathery leaves, smooth-edged or broadly lobed, yellowish green when young. Large, open, crimson flowerheads, at branch ends, in late spring–early summer. Zones 8–10.

Telopea oreades

GIPPSLAND WARATAH

☀ ❁ ↔ 10 ft (3 m) ↑ 10–30 ft (3–9 m)

Found in sheltered wet forests of southeastern Australia. Smooth lance-shaped leaves often have glaucous underside. Globular deep crimson flowerheads, up to 3 in (8 cm) across, in early summer. Zones 9–10.

Telopea speciosissima ★

WARATAH

☀ ❁ ↔ 5 ft (1.5 m) ↑ 10 ft (3 m)

Erect slender shrub, floral emblem of New South Wales, Australia. Toothed leathery leaves, prominent veins. Red dome-shaped flowerheads, surrounded by ring of bright red bracts, in spring. Grown commercially for high-quality cut flowers. 'Corroboree', vigorous growth, narrow leaves, large domed flowerheads with relatively

inconspicuous bracts; 'Flaming Beacon', large rich red bracts, red florets tipped white; 'Olympic Flame', released to mark 2000 Sydney Olympic Games, tall grower, exceptionally large high-domed flowerheads; 'Wirrimbirra White', creamy white flowers. Zones 9–10.

Telopea truncata

TASMANIAN WARATAH

☀ ❄ ↔ 10 ft (3 m) ↑ 10 ft (3 m)

From subalpine mountainous areas of Tasmania, Australia. Deep green smooth-edged leaves on new growth. Underside of new leaves and unopened flowers usually covered with soft brown hairs. Slightly flattened red flowerheads in late spring. Zones 8–10.

TEPHROSIA

Belonging to the pea-flower subfamily of the legume (Fabaceae) family, this genus contains about 400 species of usually evergreen perennials or shrubs native to tropical and subtropical areas of the world. They show considerable variation and may be erect or sprawling, with alternate leaves comprising 1 to 41 leaflets. The flowers are borne in pairs or clusters. They are typical of those in the pea-flower family and range in color from orange to purple. CULTIVATION: Most species are frost tender but if given a protective mulch in winter in cooler areas they should resprout from the base in spring. They prefer well-drained soil and can tolerate quite arid conditions. Propagate from seed, which requires hot water treatment.

Tephrosia grandiflora

☀ ❁ ↔ 3 ft (0.9 m) ↑ 2–5 ft (0.6–1.5 m)

Shrubby species native to South Africa. White or rusty down on stems. Pinnate leaves, 9 to 15 leaflets, white-hairy beneath. Clusters of purple-pink flowers in spring–early summer. Zones 9–11.

Tephrosia grandiflora

TERMINALIA

The name of this genus of about 200 species of evergreen or deciduous trees refers to the leaves, which are often clustered near the shoot tips. It is a member of the family Combretaceae. Found in tropical regions from Asia, India, Sri Lanka, and south to Polynesia and parts of Australia, these trees often grow near the coast and their trunks are frequently buttressed. They are grown for the ornamental qualities of their large, handsome, often leathery leaves and sprays of flowers as well as for dyes, oils, nuts, and some medicinal purposes. CULTIVATION: *Terminalia* species grow in any reasonably fertile soil that is well drained and in full sun. In cool areas they need to have greenhouse protection. Propagate from seed.

Terminalia arostrata

NUTWOOD

☀ ❁ ↔ 6–10 ft (1.8–3 m) ↑ 17–35 ft (5–10 m)

Semi-deciduous drought-resistant tree from northern and western Australia. Upright trunk, drooping branches, fissured bark, rounded crown. Leathery, broadly oval-shaped leaves. Spikes of tiny creamy flowers in summer. Berries dark purple or black, edible. Zones 9–11.

Tetradium ruticarpum

TERNSTROEMIA

This genus of 85 species of evergreen trees and shrubs is a member of the camellia (Theaceae) family. These plants are found in Asia, Africa, and the Americas. The large glossy leaves are leathery, sometimes with a serrated edge. The single white flowers are 5-petalled and appear in summer. The seed capsules are red.
CULTIVATION: These plants will grow well in a fertile, humus-rich, acid soil that is moisture retentive but well drained. Pinch out the shoot tips to encourage branching. Propagate from seed or from half-hardened cuttings in late summer.

Ternstroemia japonica ★
syn. *Ternstroemia gymnanthera*
☼ ❄ ↔ 10 ft (3 m) ↑ 12 ft (3.5 m)
Shrub or small tree native to Japan. Thick, leathery, glossy, oval leaves. Hanging clusters of small white flowers, lightly perfumed, in summer. Round red fruit split to reveal red seeds. 'Variegata', dark green leaves marbled gray, cream edges pink in autumn. Zones 8–11.

TETRACLINIS

This conifer genus in the cypress (Cupressaceae) family contains 1 species, native to northwestern Africa and southeastern Spain. It is a very dense tree with a strong thick trunk that is crowded with branches. Typical of conifers, it has branchlets that are flat and splayed with slightly brittle thin leaves. Tiny erect cones appear at the tips of the branches.
CULTIVATION: This is a frost-tender species that requires greenhouse cultivation in cool climates. In mild climates it is a good choice for dry areas, being very drought tolerant. It should be planted in well-drained soil. Propagate from seed or cuttings.

Tetraclinis articulata
ALERCE, ARAR, JUNIPER GUM PLANT
☼ ❄ ↔ 25 ft (8 m) ↑ 50 ft (15 m)
Conifer from northwestern Africa and southern Spain. Broad conical crown, thick trunk with closely packed branches. Cypress-like

foliage, branchlets in flat open sprays, scale-like leaves in whorls of 4. Small, erect, glaucous cones, at branch tips, in summer. Zones 9–11.

TETRADENIA

Found in southern Africa and Madagascar, this genus of 5 deciduous or semi-deciduous shrubs belongs to the mint (Lamiaceae) family. These shrubs are aromatic with semi-succulent stems that, along with the foliage, are often coated with a fine down. The light green to gray-green leaves are heart-shaped to rounded, usually with deeply lobed edges. The honey-scented flowers are minute but are massed in whorled panicles that can smother the plant.
CULTIVATION: Tolerating only the lightest frosts, they prefer a position in full sun or part-shade with light well-drained soil. Plants will flower more freely if watered well during the growing season but will tolerate short periods of drought. Cut back after flowering to encourage compact growth. Propagate from seed or cuttings.

Tetradenia riparia
syn. *Iboza riparia*
MOSCHOSMA, NUTMEG BUSH
☼ ❄ ↔ 8 ft (2.4 m) ↑ 8–10 ft (2.4–3 m)
Shrub from South Africa. Leaves rounded, light sage green, velvety hairs. Heads of scented pale pink to mauve flowers in winter–early spring. Leaves, young stems emit spicy aroma if crushed. Zones 10–11.

TETRADIUM

Native to the area from the Himalayas through to East and Southeast Asia, this small genus of about 9 species of deciduous and evergreen shrubs and trees belongs to the rue (Rutaceae) family. They are grown for their aromatic foliage, masses of small sweetly scented flowers, and the generous clusters of capsular fruit, which contain dark red to black seeds that are poisonous in some species.
CULTIVATION: Most species are very frost hardy. To thrive, they need a fertile, moist, but well-drained soil in full sun or part-shade. Prune to remove damaged foliage and spent flowerheads. Propagate from seed in autumn, or from cuttings in late winter.

Tetradium daniellii

Tetradium daniellii
syn. *Euodia daniellii*
KOREAN EUODIA
☼ ❄ ↔ 40 ft (12 m) ↑ 50 ft (15 m)
Large tree native to southwestern China and Korea. Large pinnate leaves, 11 ovate or lance-shaped, glossy, dark green leaflets, turn russet in autumn. Small, white, perfumed flowers, in terminal sprays, in late summer–early autumn. Small pear-shaped fruit. Zones 8–10.

Tetradium ruticarpum
syn. *Euodia ruticarpa*
☼ ❄ ↔ 15 ft (4.5 m) ↑ 30 ft (9 m)
Small tree naturally found in China and Taiwan. Leaves smooth, glossy and dark green above, greenish brown and densely hairy

below. Sprays of small white or yellowish green flowers in late summer. Round red to black fruit. Zones 9–11.

TETRATHECA

BLACK-EYED SUSAN

This Australian genus is a member of the family Tremandraceae and comprises about 40 species of low-growing evergreen shrubs with fine green leaves on slender stems. Nodding bell-like flowers are pink or purple with a black eye that is not readily seen. CULTIVATION: Give these shrubs a well-drained position in part-shade to ensure they are trouble-free in both garden and pot culture. Propagate from half-hardened cuttings.

Tetratheca thymifolia ★

◑ ⁍ ↔2 ft (0.6 m) ↑2 ft (0.6 m)

Mound-forming shrub from Australia. Small green leaves held on dainty stems. Profusion of deep pink bell-like blooms in spring. White-flowering forms also available. Zones 9–11.

TEUCRIUM (see page 589)

Teucrium fruticans

BUSH GERMANDER, SHRUBBY GERMANDER

☼ ❋ ↔6 ft (1.8 m) ↑4 ft (1.2 m)

Evergreen shrub native to southern Spain, Portugal, and Italy, as well as North Africa. Dense white hairs on stems and underside of grayish leaves. Flowers pale lilac-blue, in summer. Zones 8–10.

THEVETIA

This small genus belonging to the dogbane (Apocynaceae) family includes around 8 species native to tropical America. They are trees and shrubs with simple alternate leaves spirally arranged. Their plentiful summer flowers are showy, often yellow, and funnel-shaped, and are produced at the ends of shoots. The fruit is squat and berry-like. The genus is closely related to *Nerium,* which includes the poisonous plants commonly known as oleanders. All parts of *Thevetia* plants are highly poisonous, including the milky sap. CULTIVATION: Most members of this genus are fairly adaptable but will give the best results when planted in a mulched, well-drained, sandy soil with plenty of water during summer. They will tolerate full sun to part-shade. Propagate from seed or cuttings.

Thevetia peruviana

syn. *Thevetia neriifolia*

LUCKY NUT, YELLOW OLEANDER

☼ ⁍ ↔8 ft (2.4 m) ↑15 ft (4.5 m)

Upright shrub or small tree from Central America, Peru, and West Indies. Linear to narrowly lance-shaped leaves, shiny dark green. Fragrant funnel-shaped flowers, apricot-yellow, in cymes, in summer. Fleshy fruit. All parts of plant are poisonous. Zones 10–12.

THRYPTOMENE

This genus consists of around 40 species of evergreen shrubs from Australia. It is a member of the myrtle (Myrtaceae) family, and is allied to the genus *Baeckia*. These shrubs have wiry stems and small linear leaves that are usually aromatic when crushed. Their tiny starry flowers are white, pink-tinted, or pink and are abundant on every small side shoot, coloring the plant in late winter and spring. The flowers are rich in nectar, which gives them a honeyed scent. CULTIVATION: *Thryptomene* species prefer a light well-drained soil, in full sun, and will do best if kept free from frosts. These shrubs will not tolerate prolonged wet and cold conditions, but are otherwise easily grown. They make excellent cut flowers, and one of the best ways to keep the bush compact is to trim the flowering branches for use indoors. Propagation of *Thryptomene* species is from small tip cuttings of non-flowering stems.

Thryptomene calycina

GRAMPIANS THRYPTOMENE

☼ ⁍ ↔8 ft (2.4 m) ↑4–6 ft (1.2–1.8 m)

Evergreen shrub from Grampian Mountains of western Victoria, Australia. Branches carry somewhat flattened sprays of dark green foliage. Prolific display of star-shaped white flowers, open from pink buds, in winter to spring. Trim lightly during and after flowering. Zones 9–11.

Thryptomene saxicola

ROCK THRYPTOMENE

☼ ⁍ ↔5 ft (1.5 m) ↑3–5 ft (0.9–1.5 m)

Shrub found naturally on rocky hillside outcrops in most of southern Australia. Mass of wiry stems, sprays of small rounded leaves. White or pale pink flowers in late winter–spring. Give it a light annual trim after flowering. Prefers well-drained conditions. Zones 9–10.

Tetratheca thymifolia

Teucrium fruticans

Thryptomene saxicola

THUJA
syn. *Platycladus*
ARBORVITAE, RED CEDAR, WHITE CEDAR

This genus consists of 5 coniferous evergreen trees within the cypress (Cupressaceae) family. Their natural habitat is North America and East Asia, in high rainfall woodland or damp, cold, coastal and lowland plains. Bark is reddish brown and comes off in long vertical strips on mature trees. Leaflets are flattened and scale-like. Solitary male cones grow on the ends of branchlets, and the solitary female cones, with 6 to 12 overlapping scales, grow lower down. These are important timber trees as well as being used for hedging and in floristry. The aromatic foliage can cause skin allergies.
CULTIVATION: Young trees do well in full sun in deep, moist, well-drained soil, but need shelter from cold drying winds. They will survive boggy areas that are too wet for other conifers. Propagate by sowing seed in winter in an area protected from frosts, or by rooting half-hardened cuttings in late summer.

Thuja occidentalis
AMERICAN ARBORVITAE, EASTERN ARBORVITAE, WHITE CEDAR
☼ ❊ ↔ 15 ft (4.5 m) ↑ 30–70 ft (9–21 m)
Large conifer native to eastern North America. Conical form, rounded at top with dense foliage. Bark hangs in orange-brown strips. Crowded, flattened, dull green branchlets, grayish green underside. Female cones have 8 to 10 pairs of smooth scales, in summer. 'Caespitosa', slow-growing shrub, 12 in (30 cm) high; 'Filiformis', thin pendent branchlets, grows to 25 ft (8 m) high, golden yellow leaves; 'Golden Globe', height and width of 3 ft (0.9 m); 'Nigra', grows to about 30 ft (9 m) high, narrowly conical form, branches down to ground, very dark green foliage that retains color through winter; 'Ohlendorffii', retains juvenile foliage; 'Pyramidalis Compacta', column of fairly dense, compact, bright green foliage to about 12 ft (3.5 m) high but no more than 4 ft (1.2 m) wide, tapering to pointed leader, fast-growing, good for screens and hedges; 'Rheingold', pink tints when young, turns golden bronze in cold winters; 'Silver Queen', green-yellow foliage; 'Smaragd', conical shrub, bright green foliage; 'Tiny Tim', dwarf form, rust-colored winter foliage; 'Wintergreen', broadly conical; 'Woodwardii', compact shrub with light green foliage. Zones 2–10.

Thuja plicata
GIANT ARBOR, WESTERN RED CEDAR
☼ ❊ ↔ 15 ft (4.5 m) ↑ 70–120 ft (21–36 m)
Tall columnar tree native to western North America, often with buttressed bole. Flattened horizontal sprays of leaves, mid- to dark green, pale green to gray-white below. Female cones have 4 to 5 pairs of scales, each one with tiny hook, in summer. 'Atrovirens', makes compact hedge; 'Aurea', narrow conical habit, gold-tipped shoots soon revert to yellowish green; 'George Washington', broadly conical, long leading shoot; 'Hillieri', height and spread of 6–10 ft (1.8–3 m), bluish green foliage; 'Stoneham Gold', young leaves golden, age to green; 'Sunshine', yellow-green foliage; 'Zebrina', conical, green leaves with yellow stripes. Zones 5–10.

Thuja standishii
JAPANESE ARBORVITAE
☼ ❊ ↔ 20 ft (6 m) ↑ 100 ft (30 m)
Large tree native to Japan, split reddish brown bark. Open crown, broadly conical. Flattened branchlets green above, white below. Female cones have 4 pairs of scales, in summer. Zones 6–9.

THUJOPSIS
The single species of conifer tree in this genus is a member of the cypress (Cupressaceae) family and is native to Japan. It resembles the better known *Thuja* but has broader and flatter branchlets that are almost horizontal with tips lifting. The bark is brownish, often tending to red. The deep glossy green leaves are larger than those of *Thuja* species, and have a silvery underside.
CULTIVATION: Extremely slow growing, this tree should be planted in a sheltered position in moisture-retentive soil. It is very hardy but must have high humidity. Propagate from seed or cuttings.

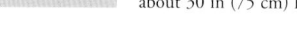
Thuja standishii

Thujopsis dolabrata
DEERHORN CEDAR, FALSE ARBORVITAE, HIBA, HIBA CEDAR
☼ ❊ ↔ 20 ft (6 m) ↑ 100 ft (30 m)
From Japan. Conical crown, almost horizontal branches, upswept at tips. Reddish brown bark exfoliates in strips. Leaves deep glossy green, silvery underside. Slow growing, just 8 ft (2.4 m) after 5 to 10 years in garden. 'Nana', grows to about 30 in (75 cm) high. Zones 6–10.

THUNBERGIA (see page 791)

Thunbergia erecta
BUSH CLOCK VINE, KING'S MANTLE
☼ ◐ ↔ 7 ft (2 m) ↑ 6–8 ft (1.8–2.4 m)
Erect free-standing or twining shrub from tropical western Africa to South Africa. Toothed ovate leaves. In summer, solitary, cream-centered, violet-blue flowers follow sun. Zones 10–12.

Tibouchina lepidota 'Alstonville'

TIBOUCHINA

syns *Lasiandra, Pleroma*

GLORY BUSH, LASIANDRA

This large genus belonging to the meadow-beauty (Melastomataceae) family consists of around 350 species, most naturally found in tropical South America. They are mostly shrubs or small trees, perennials, and scrambling climbers with large, hairy, prominently veined, simple leaves, which are oppositely arranged, often on square stems. The large, showy, 5-petalled flowers are violet, purple, pink, or white and may be borne singly or in panicles at the ends of branches. The flowers are followed by capsular fruit containing spirally curved seeds. *Tibouchina* species are generally only suitable for warm to hot areas that are frost free, although well-established plants that are properly acclimatized may tolerate light frosts. Tibouchinas make very attractive horticultural subjects, and some grow well in large pots or tubs.

CULTIVATION: Most tibouchinas are fairly adaptable to a variety of conditions, but they perform best in warm areas in a light well-drained soil with a high organic content. They prefer a situation in full sun with plentiful water during summer. Protect from strong winds and prune after flowering. Propagate from seed or cuttings taken in late spring or summer.

Tibouchina granulosa

GLORY BUSH

☼ ❄ ↔ 10 ft (3 m) ↑ 12–35 ft (3.5–10 m)

Large shrub or small tree native to southeastern Brazil. Thick branching stems, lance-shaped to oblong leaves, shiny dark green, hairy underneath. Variable-colored flowers, violet to rose-purple or pink, in panicles at ends of branches, in autumn. '**Rosea**', smaller purple to rosy magenta flowers. Zones 10–12.

Tibouchina heteromalla

☼ ❄ ↔ 4 ft (1.2 m) ↑ 3 ft (0.9 m)

Small spreading shrub from Brazil. Many erect stems, broadly ovate velvety leaves, bright green; whitish green and very hairy beneath. Violet flowers, in erect panicles at ends of branches, in summer–autumn. Zones 10–12.

Tibouchina lepidota

GLORY BUSH

☼ ❄ ↔ 10 ft (3 m) ↑ 12 ft (3.5 m)

Bushy shrub native to Ecuador and Colombia, taller and more tree-like in its natural environment. Ovate-oblong to oblong lance-shaped leaves, dark green, paler on underside. Panicles of violet-purple flowers, with violet-purple stamens, in late summer–early winter. '**Alstonville**', prolific display of vibrant purple flowers. Zones 10–12.

Tibouchina macrantha

LARGE-FLOWERED GLORY BUSH

☼ ❄ ↔ 8 ft (2.4 m) ↑ 10 ft (3 m)

Shrub or small tree from Brazil. Dark green leaves, bumpy surface, paler beneath. Large violet to purple flowers, around 4–6 in (10–15 cm) across, at ends of branches, in late summer–spring. Zones 10–12.

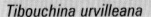
Tibouchina urvilleana

Tilia americana 'Redmond'

Tibouchina urvilleana

syns *Lasiandra semidecandra, Tibouchina semidecandra*

GLORY BUSH, PRINCESS FLOWER

☼ ❄ ↔ 10 ft (3 m) ↑ 15 ft (4.5 m)

Fast-growing shrub from Brazil. Dense rounded form, red hairy stems. Oblong-ovate leaves, dark green, serrated edges. Purple-violet flowers, purple stamens, singly or in panicles, in summer. '**Edwardsii**', similar to species, but larger flowers. Zones 9–12.

TILIA

BASSWOOD, LINDEN

Tilia has been revised down to just 45 species of deciduous trees belonging to the linden (Tiliaceae) family. They occur in eastern and central North America, Europe, as well as most of temperate Asia. They are upright single-trunked trees with a rounded or conical crown of foliage. The bark is silver-gray and smooth, and with great age it becomes fissured. The leaf shape is usually oval to heart-shaped with serrated edges, tapering to a fine point. The foliage is usually mid-green but develops vibrant yellow tones in autumn. Small, cream, scented, separate male and female flowers with large bracts are produced in small clusters from late spring. These trees produce conspicuous pale green fruit.

CULTIVATION: These very hardy trees prefer a temperate climate with 4 distinct seasons. They thrive in deep well-drained soil and should be given plenty of moisture in summer. Trim young trees to shape. Propagate from the copiously produced seed, which needs stratification; from cuttings or layers; or, for special forms, by grafting.

Tilia americana

AMERICAN LINDEN, BASSWOOD

☼ ✳ ↔ 40 ft (12 m) ↑ 100 ft (30 m)

Broad-crowned tree from central and eastern North America. Leaves up to 6 in (15 cm) long, almost as broad, serrated edges, paler green below, tapering abruptly to point. Clustered, pale yellow, fragrant flowers in mid-summer. *T. a.* var. *caroliniana* (syns *T. australis, T. caroliniana*), leaves generally smaller, more heavily serrated, blue-green on underside. *T. a.* var. *heterophylla* (syn. *T. heterophylla*), leaves white-felted on underside, sometimes sparsely. *T. a.* '**Ampelophylla**', large-lobed leaves; '**Fastigiata**', narrow conical habit; '**Macrophylla**', very large leaves; '**Redmond**', conical growth habit. Zones 3–9.

Tilia cordata

LITTLE-LEAF LINDEN, SMALL-LEAFED LIME

☼ ❋ ↔ 40 ft (12 m) ↑ 80–100 ft (24–30 m)

Wide-crowned tree found over most of temperate Europe from Wales, UK, to western Russia. Dark green rounded leaves, serrated, taper to narrow tip. Clusters of 5 to 7 fragrant cream flowers in summer. 'Greenspire' ★, strong-growing form with narrow crown; 'Rancho', conical habit, glossy leaves. Zones 3–9.

Tilia × *euchlora*

☼ ❋ ↔ 40 ft (12 m) ↑ 70 ft (21 m)

Hybrid most likely of *T. cordata* × *T. dasystyla* parentage. Arching branches, become increasingly more pendulous with age. Leaves deep glossy green, pale blue-green hairy beneath. Cream flower-heads, relatively large, attractive to bees, in summer. Zones 4–9.

Tilia × *europaea*

syn. *Tilia* × *vulgaris*

COMMON LIME, EUROPEAN BASSWOOD

☼ ❋ ↔ 40 ft (12 m) ↑ 100 ft (30 m)

T. cordata × *T. platyphyllos* hybrid. Tall, broad, conical crown, branches well down trunk. Leaves dark green, heart-shaped, hairy underside veins. Yellow autumn color. Cream flowers, in clusters, in summer, attractive to bees. 'Pallida', pale green leaves; 'Wratislaviensis', golden yellow leaves when young. Zones 5–9.

Tilia japonica

JAPANESE LIME

☼ ❋ ↔ 20 ft (6 m) ↑ 50 ft (15 m)

Tree found in Japan and nearby parts of China. Small pointed leaves, somewhat glaucous underside. Fragrant creamy yellow flowers in summer. Its relatively small size and upright growth habit make it attractive specimen for avenue planting. Zones 6–10.

Tilia oliveri

OLIVER'S LIME

☼ ❋ ↔ 30 ft (9 m) ↑ 100 ft (30 m)

Tall tree native to western China. Particularly large leaves, light to mid-green, silver-white underside, tend to be held horizontally.

Clusters of 7 to 10 flowers in summer. 'Chelsea Sentinel', densely foliaged, broad, upright column with weeping branches. Zones 6–9.

Tilia platyphyllos

BROAD-LEAFED LIME

☼ ❋ ↔ 50 ft (15 m) ↑ 100 ft (30 m)

Dome-shaped tree found in various forms from western Europe to southwest Asia. Stems very hairy when young. Small clusters of pale yellow flowers in early summer. Fruit persist after leaves fall. 'Laciniata', dome shape, yellow flowers from crown; 'Orebro', shorter and broader, slightly deeper green foliage. Zones 5–9.

Tilia tomentosa

EUROPEAN WHITE LIME, SILVER LIME, SILVER LINDEN

☼ ❋ ↔ 50 ft (15 m) ↑ 80–100 ft (24–30 m)

Dense conical to dome-shaped tree from areas around Black Sea. Rounded heart-shaped leaves, very dark green, coarsely serrated edges, fine gray down below. Dull white summer flowers. 'Brabant', broadly conical; 'Nijmegen', mottled gray bark. Zones 6–9.

TIPUANA

From northern South America, this genus, which is a member of the pea-flower subfamily of the legume (Fabaceae) family, consists of a single species. It is an evergreen tree widely grown for its outstanding floral display and overall attractive appearance. It has a wide flat crown covered in dark green foliage. In spring, the tree bursts into a profusion of deep yellow flowers at the tips of the branches. It has become a favorite shade and avenue tree in subtropical regions of the world. In cool or dry conditions it may be deciduous, but is bare for only a short period.

CULTIVATION: This tree needs a warm climate and a fertile, moist, but well-drained soil in sun. Pruning is rarely necessary, but young specimens may be shaped in late winter. It is sensitive to frost. Propagate from scarified seed in spring, which must be pre-treated by rubbing them briefly on sandpaper and soaking in cold water.

Tipuana tipu

syn. *Tipuana speciosa*

PRIDE OF BOLIVIA, TIPU TREE

☼ ⚘ ↔ 25 ft (8 m) ↑ 100 ft (30 m)

Fast-growing slender tree from northern South America. Spreading, slightly flattened crown. Dark green pinnate leaves, composed of 11 to 21 glaucous, green, oblong leaflets. Profuse racemes of orange-yellow flowers in spring. Woody winged seed pods. Zones 9–12.

TOONA

syn. *Cedrela*

This small genus in the mahogany (Meliaceae) family consists of 4 or 5 species occurring from southern and eastern Asia to eastern Australia that were once included in the genus *Cedrela*. All are evergreen or deciduous trees with pinnate leaves. They are valuable timber trees, particularly *T. ciliata* which is suitable for temperate to tropical regions. *T. sinensis* suits cooler areas.

CULTIVATION: They are best grown in deep, well-drained, fertile soil in sun with plentiful watering. Grow them in a moist climate and protect from strong winds. Propagate from seed or suckers.

Tilia japonica   *Tipuana tipu*

Toona ciliata

Toona ciliata

syns *Cedrela toona*, *Toona australis*
AUSTRALIAN RED CEDAR, RED CEDAR

☼ ⚘ ↔ 20 ft (6 m) ↑ 120 ft (36 m)

Beautiful deciduous tree from moist rainforests of northeastern Queensland to southeastern New South Wales, Australia. Spreading crown, glossy green pinnate leaves composed of ovate leaflets. New foliage bronzy red color, in late spring. Small, fragrant, white or pink flowers in spring. Zones 9–12.

Toona sinensis

syn. *Cedrela sinensis*
CHINESE TOON

☼ ❋ ↔ 30 ft (9 m) ↑ 40 ft (12 m)

Variable deciduous tree from China and Southeast Asia. Dark green pinnate leaves, with 8 to 12 pairs of leaflets, turn orange-yellow in autumn; rosy pink new growth. Hanging panicles of perfumed, small, white flowers in spring. '**Flamingo**', suckering growth to 20 ft (6 m) high, new leaves bright pink changing to creamy yellow then green. Zones 6–11.

TORREYA

This genus consists of 7 species of evergreen coniferous shrubs or trees belonging to the yew (Taxaceae) family. It is native to North America and Asia, and is found in sheltered woodland and moist riverside situations. The species vary from shrubs to trees with a wide-open crown. The leaves are glossy, fine, sharp needles, yew-like, with a paler underside. Some of the leaves will emit a scent when crushed. The fruit is a seed, smooth or furrowed, dull green to purplish in color. The kaya nut of Japan (*T. nucifera*) is edible and the oil is used for cooking in that country. The timber of

T. taxifolia is used for fencing; however, this is an endangered species surviving in the wild in only a few small areas in the States of Florida and Georgia, USA. CULTIVATION: These plants require shelter from cold or drying winds and grow in moist fertile soil with good drainage in full sun or part-shade. Propagate from half-hardened cuttings in late summer, or sow seed as soon as it is ripe in an area protected from frost. Label well as germination may take up to 2 years.

Torreya californica

CALIFORNIA NUTMEG, CALIFORNIA NUTMEG YEW

☼ ❋ ↔ 25 ft (8 m) ↑ 80 ft (24 m)

Tall tree native to California, USA, only species to adapt to cool seaside climates. Open crown, broadly conical. Somewhat pendulous shoots. Leaves yew-like, dark green needles, paler on underside, scented when crushed. Greenish purple female cones in summer. Zones 7–10.

Torreya nucifera

JAPANESE NUTMEG YEW, KAYA NUT

☼ ❋ ↔ 25 ft (8 m) ↑ 50–80 ft (15–24 m)

Tree or shrub native to Japan. Leaves glossy dark green above, blue-white stomatal bands beneath, scented when crushed. Olive green female cones have edible kernel. Zones 7–10.

Torreya californica

TOXICODENDRON

Widely distributed in temperate and subtropical regions of North America and East Asia, this is a genus of 6 to 9 species of trees, shrubs, and woody climbers belonging to the cashew (Anacardiaceae) family. It is closely related to *Rhus* and some highly noxious species that were previously included in *Rhus* have now been transferred to this genus, including the poison ivy of North America, *T. radicans*. The cultivation of a few species is prohibited in some places; however, when *Toxicodendron* species are cultivated they are grown mainly for their brilliantly colored autumn foliage and sometimes ornamental fruit. They all contain a milky or resinous sap that is highly caustic and capable of producing dermatitis or a severe allergic reaction in susceptible people. CULTIVATION: Frost hardy, these plants all require full sun and a well-drained soil. Locate as background plants away from lawns or walkways, where people are least likely to touch them. Propagate from seed in summer, or from cuttings.

Toxicodendron diversilobum

syn. *Rhus diversiloba*
CALIFORNIAN POISON OAK, WESTERN POISON OAK

☼ ❋ ↔ 7 ft (2 m) ↑ 8 ft (2.4 m)

Erect, occasionally climbing, shrub from western USA. Compound leaves, leaflets smooth-edged or lobed, hairy underside. Panicles of greenish white flowers in summer. Creamy white fruit. Contact can produce severe dermatitis. Zones 5–10.

Toxicodendron succedaneum

Trevesia palmata

Tristania neriifolia

Toxicodendron succedaneum

syn. *Rhus succedanea*

POISON SUMAC, RHUS TREE, WAX TREE

☼ ❈ ↔ 20 ft (6 m) ↑ 30 ft (9 m)

Large deciduous shrub or small spreading tree from eastern parts of Asia. Compound leaves of 9 to 15 oval pointed leaflets, shiny green, orange-red to scarlet in autumn. Tiny pale yellow flowers in early summer. Waxy yellowish brown drupes. Highly poisonous and not recommended for small home gardens. Zones 5–10.

Toxicodendron vernix

syn. *Rhus vernix*

POISON ELDER, POISON SUMAC

☼ ❈ ↔ 10 ft (3 m) ↑ 10 ft (3 m)

Deciduous shrub or small tree from temperate eastern North America. Pinnate leaves, 7 to 13 oblong leaflets, smooth edges, color brilliantly in autumn. Small yellow flowers in early summer. May produce dermatitis on contact. Zones 3–9.

TREVESIA

The 12 species of shrubs and trees in this genus, which is a member of the ivy (Araliaceae) family, are found from the Himalayas to southern China and Southeast Asia. Often forming dense clumps, they have thick stems that may be prickly. The large palmately lobed leaves are carried in clusters near the branch tips. Large terminal clusters of small creamy flowers are borne in summer.

CULTIVATION: They require greenhouse or conservatory protection in cold climates. In humid tropical areas they will need a sheltered and partly shaded site in moisture-retentive, deep, fertile soil. Propagate from seed or softwood cuttings.

Trevesia palmata

◑ ❅ ↔ 12 ft (3.5 m) ↑ 30 ft (9 m)

Native from India to southern China and Southeast Asia. Can grow unbranched or develop into wide-crowned shrub or tree. Stout thorny stems and unusual palmately lobed leaves. Large clusters of off-white flowers in spring. Zones 10–12.

TRIADICA

A genus of 3 species of small to medium deciduous trees in the euphorbia (Euphorbiaceae) family, from eastern and southern

Asia, they were formerly included in the larger genus *Sapium*. The sap is milky; leaves are elliptical to almost circular, dark green above but paler and bluish beneath. Flowers are small and petal-less, in catkin-like spikes at branchlet tips, and are followed in summer by distinctive capsules; these shed the fruit walls at maturity to reveal 3 conspicuous round seeds, each coated with a thick layer of chalky-white wax and persisting on the tree in autumn. The wax has had many uses, including candles and soap.

CULTIVATION: Only one species has been widely cultivated, originally for its seed wax in China, later as an ornamental tree. It prefers a subtropical to warm-temperate climate with hot summers, and a sunny position in any reasonably fertile, well-drained soil. Propagate from fresh seed, or half-hardened cuttings when in leaf.

Triadica sebifera

syn. *Sapium sebiferum*

CHINESE TALLOW TREE

☼ ❈ ↔ 15–20 ft (4.5–6 m) ↑ 20–30 ft (6–9 m)

From central and southern China and southern Japan, small tree with rounded crown. Leaves long-stalked, 2–4 in (5–10 cm) long, round to almost diamond-shaped, dull dark green, turning orange to deep red in autumn even in warm climates. Yellow-green flowers in late spring–early summer; ¼ in (6 mm) wide white seeds in autumn. Has become weed in parts of southern USA. Zones 8–11.

TRISTANIA

This is a single-species genus from Australia and is a member of the myrtle (Myrtaceae) family. Several closely related species were included in this genus in the past, but have now been placed in other genera. A shrub or small tree, it has smooth sometimes flaking bark. The leaves are opposite, lance-shaped, with obvious oil glands. It blooms in summer, producing small, yellow, rather insignificant flowers that appear in bunches, giving it a more heavily flowered appearance. It produces a 3-celled fruit capsule. *Tristania* is limited in its distribution, occurring from just north of Sydney to just south and west, along the banks and beds of streams.

CULTIVATION: *Tristania* adapts particularly well to garden situations. Well-drained sandy soils, acid to neutral pH, and water during dry periods are required for good growth. It is somewhat frost tender and grows best in full sun. Propagate from seed or cuttings.

Tristania neriifolia

DWARF WATER GUM, WATER GUM

☼ ⚡ ↔ 7 ft (2 m) ↕ 15 ft (4.5 m)

Shrub or small tree from mid-coast of New South Wales, Australia. Smooth or flaking bark. Leaves opposite, narrow, lance-shaped, with numerous prominent oil glands. Small yellow flowers, in bunches in upper axils, in summer. Zones 10–11.

TRISTANIOPSIS

This genus, a member of the myrtle (Myrtaceae) family, consists of 40 species, the majority of which are found in the moist forest areas of eastern Australia, in New Caledonia, Indonesia, and parts of Southeast Asia. Most are shrubs or trees with simple alternate leaves without any obvious venation. Small clusters of cymes occur along the branches, composed of 5-petalled flowers that are yellow to white, often with many stamens. The fruit is a capsule that contains mostly winged seeds. This group of plants was once included in the closely related genus *Tristania*. Many species make useful screen or hedge plants. CULTIVATION: Most species are fairly adaptable but perform best in warmer climates in a moist well-drained soil in full sun or part-shade. Prune to shape. Propagate from seed.

Tristaniopsis laurina

syn. *Tristania laurina*

KANUKA BOX, WATER GUM

☼ ⚡ ↔ 20 ft (6 m) ↕ 60 ft (18 m)

Tall tree native to eastern Australia. Dense canopy of oblong to lance-shaped leaves, glossy dark green above, paler below. Nectar-rich, small, yellow flowers, in cymes along branches, in summer. Round fruiting capsules. Smaller in cultivation. Tolerates medium frosts and compacted wet soils. Zones 10–12.

Tristaniopsis laurina

TROCHODENDRON

This genus, a member of the family Trochodendraceae, contains a single species of evergreen tree or shrub that has attractive tiered branches and is native to Japan, Korea, and Taiwan. The leaves are glossy and bright green and grow spirally near the tips of the stems. The green and petal-less flowers are produced in upright clusters from late spring. The genus name means "wheel tree," which refers to the spoke-like arrangement of the flower stamens. In the wild this plant will often start life as an epiphyte growing on *Cryptomeria japonica*. Its wood resembles that of coniferous trees and it is thought to be a quite primitive plant. CULTIVATION: Although interesting and attractive, this species is very slow growing in cultivation. It requires a fertile moisture-retentive soil in part-shade with protection from cold winds. Propagate from seed or half-hardened cuttings.

Trochodendron aralioides

WHEEL TREE

◑ ❄ ↔ 25 ft (8 m) ↕ 70 ft (21 m)

Tall tree from Japan, Korea, and Taiwan; in cultivation it will slowly grow to about 15 ft (4.5 m) high. Tiered branches bear simple glossy green leaves in spirals near stem tips. Upright clusters of 10 to 12 small, green, petal-less flowers in late spring. Zones 8–10.

TSUGA

HEMLOCK SPRUCE

These 10 or 11 evergreen, monoecious, coniferous trees from North America and Asia belong to the pine (Pinaceae) family. They grow in mountainous areas in their southern distribution, and in wet cool coastal areas and plains in the north. Most young trees are shade tolerant. They have flattened linear leaves with whitish silver bands on the underside. The female cones become pendent as they ripen and drop off in the second year. They are grown mainly for their timber and ornamental cultivars. CULTIVATION: *Tsuga* species grow in humus-rich, slightly acid, neutral to marginally alkaline soil in shade to sun. All need moist well-drained soil and shelter from cold winds. In poor dry soil these plants make weedy specimens. Propagate by sowing seed in pots in an area protected from winter frosts, or by rooting half-hardened cuttings in late summer to autumn.

Tsuga canadensis

CANADIAN HEMLOCK, EASTERN HEMLOCK

☼ ❄ ↔ 30 ft (9 m) ↕ 80–120 ft (24–36 m)

Evergreen tree native to eastern North America, in cultivation often smaller, multi-stemmed. Gray hairy young shoots; linear leaves arranged in 2 rows. Leaves toothed, mid-green above, silver underneath. Female cones brown, grow on end of branchlets. 'Aurea', grows to 25 ft (8 m) tall, young foliage golden, turns green as it matures; 'Bennett', dwarf cultivar with lighter green leaves; 'Cole's Prostrate', low-growing ground cover that reaches up to 12 in (30 cm) tall; 'Gracilis', slow-growing dwarf; 'Jacqueline Verkade', dwarf cultivar of globular form; 'Minuta', very compact form; 'Pendula ★', mound-forming slow-growing shrub with pendent branches, reaches 12 ft (3.5 m) in height. Zones 4–9.

Trochodendron aralioides

Tsuga heterophylla, in the wild, Washington, USA

The flowers, borne singly or in small clusters, are fragrant and range from pale yellow to gold. CULTIVATION: Gorses are tough and adaptable plants that thrive under a wide range of growing conditions. Generally they prefer a moist, light, well-drained soil, but they will tolerate winter damp and grow well on sandy soils near the coast. In New Zealand, where common gorse *(U. europaeus)* is a weed, farmers often tame it and use it for roadside hedging.

Ulex europaeus
COMMON GORSE, FURZE, GORSE, WHIN
☼ ❄ ↔ 7 ft (2 m) ↕ 8 ft (2.4 m)
Associated with Scotland but found over much of west Europe. Dense many-branched shrub covered with fine hairs and ½ in (12 mm) long spines. Flowers fragrant, golden yellow, in late winter–spring. '**Flore Pleno**', sterile form, preferable for cultivation. Zones 6–10.

Tsuga heterophylla
WESTERN HEMLOCK
☼ ❄ ↔ 20–30 ft (6–9 m) ↕ 60–120 ft (18–36 m)
Large tree native to western North America. Horizontal branches have pendent tips; glossy dark green leaves. Egg-shaped female cones. Shade tolerant, needs protection from wind. Timber and bark used commercially. '**Argenteovariegata**', white young shoots; '**Laursen's Column**', dwarf, narrow and columnar. Zones 6–10.

Tsuga mertensiana
MOUNTAIN HEMLOCK
☼ ❄ ↔ 20 ft (6 m) ↕ 50 ft (15 m)
Slow-growing tree, native to western North America. Blue-green leaves, blunt tips. Young cones purple, mature to dark brown, in summer. '**Glauca Nana**', to 10 ft (3 m) high, silver-gray foliage. Zones 4–9.

Tsuga sieboldii
SOUTHERN JAPANESE HEMLOCK
☼ ❄ ↔ 25 ft (8 m) ↕ 50–100 ft (15–30 m)
Multi-stemmed tree native to southern Japan. Shiny tan young shoots; leaves with notched tips. Leaves dark glossy green above, pale green to white underside. Shiny yellowish tan young cones ripen to brown in summer. Zones 6–10.

Ulex europaeus

ULEX
Cultivated as ornamentals in some areas, but among the worst of weeds in others, gorses can provoke quite extreme reactions when gardeners meet farmers. This genus from the pea-flower subfamily of the legume (Fabaceae) family is from North Africa and western Europe, and is made up of some 20 species of densely branched, fiercely spiny shrubs. Young plants have fuzzy trifoliate leaves but the foliage is reduced to a chlorophyll-bearing spine in adults.

ULMUS
ELM
There are 45 species of elms in the family Ulmaceae. Most are trees, some very large, but a few are shrubs. Although most are deciduous and very hardy, a few are semi-evergreen and not so tough. They occur in northern temperate zones and even extend into the subtropics. They are generally round-headed trees with bark often furrowed or fissured though seldom corky, except on young shoots. Leaves are usually elliptic with conspicuous veins and serrated edges. Flowers are inconspicuous, but the papery winged fruit (samaras) that follow can be showy.
CULTIVATION: In the main, elms are tough plants that adapt well to cultivation, growing successfully in a range of soils provided the drainage is good. However, in some areas populations have been decimated by Dutch elm disease, a fungal infection carried by small beetles with wood-boring larvae. Propagate from seed or by grafting.

Ulmus americana
AMERICAN ELM, WHITE ELM
☼ ❄ ↔ 100 ft (30 m) ↕ 100 ft (30 m)
Largest of North American elms. Impressive tree, deep gray furrowed bark. Large leaves turn bright yellow in autumn. '**Augustine**', vigorous grower, columnar habit; '**Columnaris**', columnar habit. Zones 3–9.

Ulmus carpinifolia
syn. *Ulmus minor*
FIELD ELM, SMOOTH-LEAFED ELM
☼ ❄ ↔ 70 ft (21 m) ↕ 50–70 ft (15–21 m)
Native to central and southern Europe, including UK. Leaves 2–4 in (5–10 cm) long, serrated edges, golden orange autumn tones. '**Variegata**', white-speckled leaves. Zones 5–10.

Ulmus crassifolia
CEDAR ELM

☼ ❉ ↔ 40 ft (12 m) ↑ 70–100 ft (21–30 m)

Found in southern USA. Young twigs edged with "wings" of bark. Rather stiff leaves, about 2 in (5 cm) long, toothed edges, downy underside. Zones 7–10.

Ulmus glabra
SCOTCH ELM, WYCH ELM

☼ ❉ ↔ 70 ft (21 m) ↑ 100 ft (30 m)

Large tree from northern Europe to western Asia. Deeply toothed, dark green, rounded, 2–6 in (5–15 cm) leaves sometimes lobed at base, turn yellow in autumn. Lime green fruit in spring. '**Camperdownii**' ★, low-growing, spreading crown of weeping branches; '**Exoniensis**', erect conical habit; '**Pendula**', (syn. 'Horizontalis'), horizontal spreading branches. Zones 5–9.

Ulmus × *hollandica*
DUTCH ELM

☼ ❉ ↔ 80 ft (24 m) ↑ 100 ft (30 m)

Naturally occurring hybrid between *U. glabra* and *U. carpinifolia*. Strong, heavily veined, serrated, deep green leaves turn yellow in autumn. '**Groenveldt**', disease-resistant; '**Jacqueline Hillier**', shrubby, to 8 ft (2.4 m) tall; '**Major**', wide-spreading crown, broad leaves; '**Modolina**', vase-shaped crown. Zones 5–9.

Ulmus japonica

☼ ❉ ↔ 60 ft (18 m) ↑ 100 ft (30 m)

Large broad-headed tree native to Japan and nearby parts of temperate northeastern Asia. Young stems have corky yellow-brown bark, roughly oval leaves taper abruptly to point, coarsely toothed edges. Small purplish flowers, pale green fruit. Zones 5–9.

Ulmus laevis
RUSSIAN ELM

☼ ❉ ↔ 30 ft (9 m) ↑ 70 ft (21 m)

From France to eastern Europe and Caucasus. Dark gray to brown bark, open spreading crown. Broad rough-textured leaves, 4 in (10 cm) long, gray hairs beneath. Zones 4–9.

Ulmus parvifolia
CHINESE ELM

☼ ❉ ↔ 30 ft (9 m) ↑ 70 ft (21 m)

Disease-resistant tree from Japan, Korea, and China, near-evergreen in mild climates. Round crown, smooth flaking bark, fine branches. Mature fruit in autumn. '**Frosty**', compact shrub, white-toothed leaves; '**True Green**', reliably evergreen in mild winters. Zones 5–10.

Ulmus procera
ENGLISH ELM

☼ ❉ ↔ 50 ft (15 m) ↑ 70–100 ft (21–30 m)

Stately English tree now rare due to Dutch elm disease. Leaves deep green, serrated-edged, bright yellow in autumn. Pale green fruit, most sterile, in spring. '**Argenteovariegata**', white-speckled leaves; '**Louis van Houtte**', very popular yellow-leafed cultivar, especially bright in autumn; '**Purpurea**', slight purplish tint to young foliage. Zones 4–9.

Ulmus pumila
CHINESE ELM, SIBERIAN ELM

☼ ❉ ↔ 20–30 ft (6–9 m) ↑ 20–35 ft (6–10 m)

Native to cool-temperate Asia. Coarsely textured, serrated leaves, color slightly in autumn. '**Den Haag**', disease-resistant tall form, with open crown. Zones 3–9.

Ulmus 'Sapporo Autumn Gold'

☼ ❉ ↔ 35 ft (10 m) ↑ 50 ft (15 m)

Hybrid notable for its resistance or tolerance of Dutch elm disease. Strongly upright habit when young, eventually develops broad crown. Soft yellow-green new spring foliage matures to lime green; golden yellow autumn foliage. Zones 4–9.

Ulmus 'Sarniensis'
JERSEY ELM, WHEATLEY ELM

☼ ❉ ↔ 23–25 ft (7–8 m) ↑ 75–80 ft (23–24 m)

Hybrid between *U. carpinifolia* and *U.* × *hollandica*. Very erect upright habit, with broad-based conical crown. Heavily serrated dark green leaves to 4 in (10 cm) long. Sets copious quantities of fruit, most sterile. Makes good lawn tree. Zones 7–10.

Ulmus laevis

Ulmus parvifolia

Ulmus 'Sarniensis'

Ulmus thomasii

CORK ELM, ROCK ELM

☀ ❄ ↔ 40 ft (12 m) ↑ 100 ft (30 m)

Native to eastern North America. Upright tree, narrow rounded crown. Young branches with distinctly corky bark. Leaves 2–4 in (5–10 cm) long, heavily serrated. Seldom color much in autumn. Zones 2–9.

UMBELLULARIA

Related to the laurels *(Laurus)*, the sole species in this genus from the family Ulmaceae is an aromatic evergreen tree found naturally only in Oregon and California, USA. It has tough leathery leaves and male and female flowers carried on separate flowerheads. The foliage is so strongly aromatic that crushing it in the hand and sniffing it can cause an instant though usually brief headache. It was widely used medicinally by native North Americans. Its timber is quite dense and used in woodturning for mainly ornamental objects or utensils.

CULTIVATION: Tolerant of light to moderate frosts and not particularly fussy about the soil type, California laurel grows best in deep, moist, humus-enriched, well-drained soil with a position in full sun or partial shade. Propagation is either from seed or half-hardened cuttings.

Umbellularia californica

CALIFORNIA LAUREL, HEADACHE TREE

☀ ❄ ↔ 35 ft (10 m) ↑ 50–70 ft (15–21 m)

Densely foliaged spreading crown, scaly red-brown bark. Strongly aromatic, glossy deep green, oval to lance-shaped leaves. Clusters of small yellow flowers, at branch tips, in spring. Purplish olive-like berries 1 in (25 mm) long. Zones 8–10.

VACCINIUM (see page 718)

Vaccinium crassifolium

CREEPING BLUEBERRY

◐ ❄ ↔ 3 ft (0.9 m) ↑ 15 in (38 cm)

From southeastern USA. Low evergreen shrub takes root as it spreads. Tiny leaves, thick and leathery, finely serrated edges. Flowers very small, white, white with pink markings, or pink, in small clusters, in late spring. Purple-black fruit. Zones 7–10.

Vaccinium nummularia

◐ ❄ ↔ 12–15 in (30–38 cm) ↑ 12–15 in (30–38 cm)

Small evergreen shrub found in Himalayas, Bhutan, and northeastern Indian province of Sikkim. Leaves rounded, finely serrated, ¾ in (18 mm) long. Small clusters of tiny pink flowers. Berries edible, deep blue-black. Zones 7–10.

Vaccinium stamineum

DEERBERRY

◐ ❄ ↔ 3 ft (0.9 m) ↑ 5 ft (1.5 m)

Deciduous shrub found in eastern and southern USA. Leaves smooth-edged, covered with minute hairs, develop good autumn color. Sprays of small white to cream flowers borne in spring. Greenish yellow to blue-green berries. Host for blueberry maggot fly. Zones 5–9.

Vaccinium vitis-idaea

COWBERRY

◐ ❄ ↔ 2–4 ft (0.6–1.2 m) ↑ 6 in (15 cm)

Creeping evergreen shrub found over much of cool-temperate Northern Hemisphere. Tiny oval leaves deep green, with black spotting on underside; develop bronze tones in winter. Clusters of white to pink flowers in late spring. Bright red berries in autumn. Zones 2–8.

VERTICORDIA

This genus from the myrtle (Myrtaceae) family is endemic in Australia; most of its 97 species occur in the southwest of the country. All are woody shrubs. The small leaves are opposite in alternating pairs, and have oil glands. The flowers are the attractive feature, with colors ranging from white to yellow, mauve, and red, and with the calyx of each flower deeply divided and appearing feathery. The petals of some species are also divided or lobed. Habitats are generally heaths and low scrubs, on sandy or gravelly soils that have an acid pH.

CULTIVATION: The majority of species do not do well in regions where summer rainfall is high or frequent. Propagate from seed or cuttings. Seeds are few and fertility is usually low. While cuttings are not always reliable, some species do strike readily. Grafting onto rootstocks of related genera that have proved reliable in a variety of garden situations has been successful with some species.

Vaccinium vitis-idaea

Verticordia grandis, in the wild, Western Australia

Verticordia plumosa

Verticordia chrysantha
☼ ❈ ↔ 2 ft (0.6 m) ↑ 2 ft (0.6 m)
Shrub from southern sandplains of Western Australia. Small linear leaves. Feathery flowers, in dense yellow heads, in spring. Grafting onto rootstocks of *Darwinia citriodora* has been successful. Zones 8–9.

Verticordia grandis
☼ ❈ ↔ 3 ft (0.9 m) ↑ 7 ft (2 m)
From sandheaths to north of Perth in Western Australia. Straggling shrub with opposite, almost circular, grayish green leaves. Few brilliant scarlet flowers, 1 in (25 mm) across, in upper leaf axils, in spring. Zones 8–9.

Verticordia plumosa
☼ ❈ ↔ 20 in (50 cm) ↑ 20 in (50 cm)
Variable species, with gray-green leaves about ¼ in (6 mm) long. Dense terminal heads of pinkish flowers in spring. Propagation successful from seed and cuttings. Most commonly cultivated *Verticordia*. Zones 8–9.

VESTIA
The single species in this genus within the nightshade (Solanaceae) family is an evergreen shrub growing in the Chilean woodland. It is grown for its flowers and foliage; the alternate, shiny, deep green leaves emit an unpleasant smell when crushed. The yellow-green flowers are pendent. CULTIVATION: It prefers well-drained soil in a site sheltered from full sun and frost. Water and feed moderately during the growing season, and reduce watering in the dormant period. Propagate from cuttings in summer, or seed in autumn or spring.

Vestia foetida
syn. *Vestia lycioides*
☼ ❅ ↔ 5 ft (1.5 m) ↑ 6 ft (1.8 m)
Erect evergreen shrub native to Chile. Thin, glossy, green leaves. Pale yellow, tubular, pendent flowers in spring–late summer. Green seed capsules turn pale brown. Zones 9–10.

Vestia foetida

VIBURNUM
This genus in the woodbine (Caprifoliaceae) family consists of easily grown, cool-climate, deciduous, semi-evergreen or evergreen, shrubby plants that are grown for their pretty flowers, autumnal leaf color, and berries. Most have erect branching stems, paired leaves, a spread about two-thirds their height, and display their small white flowers in dense clusters. (Those plants that resemble the lace-top *Hydrangea* species bear sterile florets at the outer edges of the cluster.) The buds and petals, particularly in cultivars, may be softly colored in tints of pink, yellow, and green. CULTIVATION: Light open positions and light well-drained soils are preferred. Many are drought tender. Prune the evergreens by clipping in late spring and the deciduous species by removing entire old stems after flowering. For a good berry display grow several plants in the same area. Propagate from cuttings taken in summer, or from seed in autumn.

Viburnum × *burkwoodii*

Viburnum betulifolium
☼ ❈ ↔ 10 ft (3 m) ↑ 10 ft (3 m)
Upright, arching, deciduous shrub native to western China. Bark smooth, purple-brown. Bright green roundly oval leaves, glossy underside. Tiny white flowers, in flat-topped clusters, in early summer. Persistent, round, glowing red berries. Zones 6–8.

Viburnum × bodnantense
☼ ❈ ↔ 7 ft (2 m) ↑ 10 ft (3 m)
Large, upright, deciduous shrub, hybrid of *V. farreri* and *V. grandiflorum*. Long, oval, mid-green leaves, paler beneath, noticeably veined, color in autumn. Persistent, pinkish white to red, fragrant flowers, in dense clusters on bare wood, in late autumn–early spring. 'Charles Lamont', large bright pink flowers; 'Dawn', distinctive, deep pink, fragrant flowers that fade with age. Zones 7–9.

Viburnum × burkwoodii
BURKWOOD'S VIBURNUM
☼ ❈ ↔ 8 ft (2.4 m) ↑ 8 ft (2.4 m)
Open bushy shrub, English hybrid of *V. carlesii* and *V. utile*. Evergreen dark leaves, shiny above, felted below, bronze when young, turn yellow. Flowers in rounded clusters, intense fragrance, in early spring, pink in bud, white on opening. 'Anne Russell', deciduous, valued for its small size, neat compact habit; 'Park Farm Hybrid', red autumnal foliage. Zones 6–9.

Viburnum × carlcephalum
FRAGRANT SNOWBALL VIBURNUM
☼ ❈ ↔ 8 ft (2.4 m) ↑ 8 ft (2.4 m)
Deciduous shrub, garden hybrid between *V. carlesii* and *V. macrocephalum* f. *keteleeri*. Lustrous leaves redden in autumn. Pink buds, mildly scented pink flowers, in spring, lighten with age. Zones 5–9.

Viburnum carlesii

Viburnum carlesii
KOREAN SPICE VIBURNUM
☼ ❆ ↔ 7 ft (2 m) ↕ 8 ft (2.4 m)
Dense, deciduous, rounded shrub from open scrub of Korea and Japan. Mid-green leaves, paler beneath, oval shape, bronze-tinted when young, purple-red in autumn. Clustered crimson-pink buds, pink flowers fade to white. 'Aurora' ★, light green young leaves, red buds, pink flowers; 'Diana', red flowers fade to purple. Zones 9–11.

Viburnum 'Cayuga'
☼ ❆ ↔ 6 ft (1.8 m) ↕ 6 ft (1.8 m)
Hybrid of *V. carlesii* and *V. × carlcephalum*. Leaves have soft orange tones in autumn. Pink buds; flowers scented, outer flowers pink, those in center white. Fruit deep purple-red to black. Zones 8–10.

Viburnum davidii
☼ ❆ ↔ 4 ft (1.2 m) ↕ 4 ft (1.2 m)
Low-growing, dense, evergreen, mound-forming shrub from woods of western China. Glossy green leather-like leaves, 3 distinctive main veins. Small off-white flowers, in stiff well-spaced clusters, in late spring. Bright, oblong, midnight blue berries. Zones 6–8.

Viburnum farreri

Viburnum macrocephalum

Viburnum dentatum
ARROWWOOD, SOUTHERN ARROWWOOD
☼ ❆ ↔ 10 ft (3 m) ↕ 10 ft (3 m)
Dense, deciduous, bushy shrub found naturally across North America. Stems erect and branching. Leaves broadly oval, coarsely toothed, redden in autumn. Flat clusters of tiny white flowers in late spring–early summer. Dark blue oblong fruit. 'Ralph Senior', vigorous bushy habit, large leaves. Zones 2–6.

Viburnum dilatatum
LINDEN VIBURNUM
☼ ❆ ↔ 8 ft (2.4 m) ↕ 10 ft (3 m)
Deciduous bushy shrub from China and Japan. Leaves large, oval, coarse, roundish, toothed, dark green, good autumn coloring. Tiny, creamy white, star-shaped flowers, in clusters, in late spring or summer. Oval scarlet fruit persist. 'Catskill', broad low-growing habit, smaller leaves than species, good autumn coloring; 'Erie', pink fruit, rich autumn colors; 'Iroquois', shorter than species, reddish yellow fruit. Zones 5–8.

Viburnum erubescens
☼ ❆ ↔ 10 ft (3 m) ↕ 20 ft (6 m)
Deciduous to near-evergreen shrub or small tree found from Himalayan region southward to Sri Lanka. Leaves elliptic, serrated edges, downy underside. Small pendulous clusters of pink-tinted white flowers in summer. Red fruit ripen to black. Zones 6–11.

Viburnum farreri
syn. *Viburnum fragrans*
☼ ❆ ↔ 8 ft (2.4 m) ↕ 10 ft (3 m)
Upright deciduous shrub native to northern China. Leaves oval, veined, tapering, bronze when young, red when mature. Sweetly scented persistent flowers pale pink or white, before leaves, in mid-autumn–spring. Edible scarlet berries, poisonous stones. Zones 6–9.

Viburnum × globosum
☼ ❆ ↔ 3–4 ft (0.9–1.2 m) ↕ 3–4 ft (0.9–1.2 m)
Evergreen *V. davidii × V. lobophyllum* hybrid, usually seen as selected form 'Jermyn's Globe', neat rounded shrub. Lustrous, leathery, heavily veined, red-stemmed leaves. Heads of massed small white flowers open from red-tinted buds. Small dark blue fruit. Zones 7–10.

Viburnum × hillieri
☼ ❆ ↔ 7 ft (2 m) ↕ 6–8 ft (1.8–2.4 m)
English-raised hybrid, cross between *V. erubescens* and *V. henryi*. Evergreen shrub with elliptic leaves, shallowly irregularly serrated edges. Small panicles of white flowers in summer. Red fruit ripen to black. Typical form usually sold as 'Winton'. Zones 6–10.

Viburnum japonicum
☼ ❆ ↔ 8 ft (2.4 m) ↕ 8 ft (2.4 m)
Robust evergreen shrub from Japan. Leaves long, leathery, lustrous, oval, dark green above, paler beneath. Tiny, white, strongly scented flowers, in clusters, in early summer. Berries red, persist through winter. Zones 7–9.

Viburnum × *juddii*

JUDD VIBURNUM

☼ ❋ ↔ 7 ft (2 m) ↕ 6 ft (1.8 m)

Deciduous *V. bitchiuense* and *V. carlesii* cross. Spreading habit. Leaves elongated, oval, dull dark green. Sweetly fragrant, pink budded, white starry flowers, in rounded clusters, in spring. Zones 5–9.

Viburnum lantana

WAYFARING TREE

☼ ❋ ↔ 12 ft (3.5 m) ↕ 15 ft (4.5 m)

Robust deciduous shrub or small tree native to Europe and northwest Asia. Oblong-oval dull green leaves, can turn rusty crimson in autumn. Creamy white flowers, in terminal clusters, in late spring–early summer. Red oblong fruit mature to black. 'Mohican' ★, darker leaves, reddish orange fruit mature to black; 'Versicolor', light yellow new leaves age to golden yellow. Zones 3–6.

Viburnum lantanoides

syn. *Viburnum alnifolium*

HOBBLE BUSH

☼/❂ ❋ ↔ 15 ft (4.5 m) ↕ 15 ft (4.5 m)

Deciduous shrub native to North America. Branches downy when young. Large leaves veined, broadly oval, turn yellow and red in autumn. Large white flowers, in lace-top clusters, in late spring–early summer. Oblong purple-black fruit. Zones 3–6.

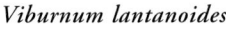
Viburnum nudum

Viburnum lentago

NANNYBERRY, SHEEPBERRY, WILD RAISIN

☼/❂ ❋ ↔ 10 ft (3 m) ↕ 20 ft (6 m)

Slender, branching, vigorous, deciduous shrub or small tree from North America. Broadly oval, lustrous, dark green leaves, attractive autumn hues. Creamy white fluffy flowers, in clusters, in spring–early summer. Oval bluish black berries. Zones 2–5.

Viburnum macrocephalum

CHINESE SNOWBALL BUSH/TREE

☼ ❋ ↔ 15 ft (4.5 m) ↕ 15 ft (4.5 m)

Chinese species with spreading branches. Showy pompon-like clusters of white flowers, opening from almost luminous green buds, in spring. May be semi-evergreen in mild winters. Dark green oval-oblong leaves, downy on underside. *V. m.* f. *keteleeri*, lacecap-like flowers. *V. m.* 'Sterile', sterile and berryless. Zones 6–9.

Viburnum nudum

POSSUM-HAW VIBURNUM, SMOOTH WITHE-ROD

☼ ❋ ↔ 6 ft (1.8 m) ↕ 10 ft (3 m)

Deciduous erect shrub native to eastern USA and Canada. Oval glossy leaves, prominent veins, minutely toothed edges, turn reddish purple in autumn. Flowers white or pale yellow, in summer. Blue-black fruit. Zones 6–9.

Viburnum opulus

COMMON SNOWBALL, EUROPEAN CRANBERRY, EUROPEAN SNOWBALL, GUELDER ROSE

☼ ❋ ↔ 15 ft (4.5 m) ↕ 15 ft (4.5 m)

Vigorous parent plant to many popular deciduous garden shrubs. Native hedgerow habitat from Siberia to Algeria. Deep green vine-like leaves, paler downy underside, redden in autumn. Lace-top clusters of white flowers in early summer. Lustrous, semi-translucent, red fruit. 'Aureum', bright yellow spring foliage, yellow-green in summer, easily scorched by sun; 'Nanum', dwarf cultivar of dense multi-stemmed habit, to 2 ft (0.6 m) tall, with small crowded leaves, rarely flowers; 'Notcutt's Variety', tall vigorous shrub to 12 ft (3.5 m) high, fine foliage color in autumn, large red fruit last into winter; 'Roseum' (syn. 'Sterile'), showy, snowball-like, greenish white flower clusters in mid-spring with leaves; 'Xanthocarpum', white flowers, mid-green leaves, berries glossy, partly translucent, yellow. Zones 3–9.

Viburnum plicatum

syn. *Viburnum plicatum* var. *tomentosum*

DOUBLEFILE VIBURNUM, JAPANESE SNOWBALL

☼ ❋ ↔ 10 ft (3 m) ↕ 8 ft (2.4 m)

From China and Japan. Vigorous, deciduous, spreading shrub with tiered branches. Leaves pleated surface, bright green in spring, mid-green in summer, burgundy-red in autumn. Profuse flat umbels of small, cream, fertile flowers in late spring–early summer, ringed by larger, white, sterile flowers. Small red fruit. 'Fireworks', reddish black fruit, purple-red autumn foliage; 'Grandiflorum', white flowers turn pink; 'Lanarth', spreads to 15 ft (4.5 m); 'Mariesii', large flat heads of mainly sterile flowers, rarely fruiting; 'Nanum Semperflorens' (syn. *V. watanabei*), slow-growing, small flowerheads in warmer months; 'Pink Beauty', white flowers age to pink; 'Roseum', white flowers age to deep pink; 'Shasta', 7 ft (2 m) tall, deep purple-red autumn foliage, large white flowers; 'Summer Snowflake', compact shrub, long-lasting white flowers, purple-red autumn foliage. Zones 4–9.

Viburnum lantana

Viburnum prunifolium
BLACK HAW

☀ ❋ ↔ 12 ft (3.5 m) ↑ 20 ft (6 m)

Spreading deciduous shrub or small tree from eastern North America. Leaves roundish oval, finely and sharply toothed. Reddish buds open to small, white, flat-topped clusters of flowers in spring–early summer. Yellow-green berries ripen blue-black. Zones 3–9.

Viburnum rhytidophyllum

☀ ❋ ↔ 8 ft (2.4 m) ↑ 10 ft (3 m)

Stout, upright, fast-growing, evergreen shrub. Leaves long, narrow, wrinkled, veined, leathery, dark green, gray or yellow woolly below. Terminal clusters of small, fluffy, yellowish to pinkish white flowers in early summer. Oval red fruit ripen black. '**Aldenhamense**', leaves with yellow tinge; '**Roseum**', deep pink flowers turn lighter with age. Zones 6–8.

Viburnum sieboldii

☀ ❋ ↔ 15 ft (4.5 m) ↑ 10 ft (3 m)

Spreading deciduous shrub from Japan. Young growth downy. Leaves large, veined, oblong-oval, glossy, dark green above, paler below. Panicles of tiny creamy white flowers in late spring–early summer. Red fruit ripen black. '**Seneca**', up to 30 ft (9 m) high, clusters of white flowers followed by persistent red fruit, ripening to almost black. Zones 4–8.

Viburnum tinus
LAURUSTINUS

☀ ❋ ↔ 8–10 ft (2.4–3 m) ↑ 8–10 ft (2.4–3 m)

Native to Mediterranean region. Dense evergreen shrub that has been popular for centuries as hedging plant. Leaves dark green, glossy, oblong-oval, pointed. Flattened heads of white, pink, or pinkish white flowers, strongly fragrant. Blue-black berries. Several named forms grow in sun or shade, tolerate coastal conditions, and are semi-tolerant of summer drought. '**Eve Price**', elongated leaves and light pink flowers; '**Lucidum**', particularly glossy leaves; '**Purpureum**', bronzed new growth; '**Robertson**', small whitish flowers; '**Variegatum**', leaves margined in yellow. Zones 7–9.

Viburnum tinus

Viburnum trilobum
syns *Viburnum americanum*, *V. opulus* var. *americanum*
AMERICAN HIGHBUSH CRANBERRY, CRANBERRY BUSH

☀ ❋ ↔ 10 ft (3 m) ↑ 10 ft (3 m)

Deciduous shrubby plant from North America. Dark leaves, broadly oval, deeply serrated, turn red shade in autumn. Showy, flat-topped, white flowerheads in early summer. Bright scarlet edible berries. '**Bailey Compact**' and '**Compactum**', attractive autumn foliage; '**Wentworth**', vigorous cultivar, tolerant of damp soils, very brightly colored long-lasting fruit. Zones 2–8.

Viburnum utile

☀ ❋ ↔ 5 ft (1.5 m) ↑ 6 ft (1.8 m)

From China. Evergreen, slender, open shrub with dark shiny leaves. Flowers white, in dense rounded clusters, in spring. Oval berries. Zones 7–9.

Viburnum veitchii
CHINESE WAYFARING TREE

☀ ❋ ↔ 5 ft (1.5 m) ↑ 5 ft (1.5 m)

Deciduous upright shrub from central China. Sharply toothed mid-green leaves. White flowers, in flat rayed clusters. Red berries ripen black. Zones 5–9.

VIRGILIA

This is a small South African genus of evergreen trees in the pea-flower subfamily of the legume (Fabaceae) family, named after Virgil, the classical Latin poet (70–19 BC). They are popular garden plants, chosen for their attractive fern-like foliage, showy flowers, and extremely rapid growth rate, although they have a rather short life span, especially in warm moist climates. The fruit are flat pods typical of legumes.
CULTIVATION: These trees thrive in well-drained light soil with adequate summer moisture, but are likely to fall over in heavy shallow soil. While they are adaptable to many different garden situations, they do require shelter from frost when young. Propagation is from seed, sown in spring in a position protected from winter frosts. Pre-soak the seed for a day before sowing.

Viburnum veitchii

Warszewiczia coccinea

Virgilia oroboides
syn. *Virgilia capensis*
CAPE LILAC, TREE-IN-A-HURRY
☼ ⟊ ↔ 15 ft (4.5 m) ↑ 30 ft (9 m)
Erect evergreen tree, broadly conical crown, native to South Africa. Fast-growing but often short-lived species. Leaves alternate, with 11 to 31 leaflets. Lightly perfumed pea-flowers, pink-purple with dark burgundy veins, in spring–summer. Zones 9–11.

VITEX
This unusual genus that encompasses several seemingly very different species is made up of some 250 species of evergreen and deciduous shrubs in the family Verbenaceae, and has a widespread distribution in the tropical, sub-tropical, and warm-temperate zones. The foliage is usually digitately divided with up to 7 leaflets, and may be smooth-edged or toothed. The flowers are clustered in panicles, racemes, or cymes, and come in a wide range of colors. CULTIVATION: As expected of a genus with tropical members, many species of *Vitex* are frost tender, but some are quite hardy and will tolerate moderate frosts. In general, *Vitex* species prefer to avoid the extremes of soil moisture, being tolerant of neither drought nor waterlogging. Plant them in moist, fertile, well-drained soil and water them well in summer. Most grow best with at least half-sun. Hard pruning is seldom required but trim to shape as necessary. Propagation is from seed or cuttings.

Vitex agnus-castus ★
CHASTE TREE
☼ ❋ ↔ 15 ft (4.5 m) ↑ 15 ft (4.5 m)
Aromatic shrub or small tree found from southern Europe to western Asia, naturalized in mild areas. Leaves gray-green, with 5 to 9

Vitex agnus-castus

narrow leaflets, downy underside. Dusty white buds open to scented lilac flowers in summer–autumn. Purple drupes. Zones 7–10.

Vitex lucens
PURIRI
☼ ⟊ ↔ 10–15 ft (3–4.5 m) ↑ 30–50 ft (9–15 m)
Evergreen tree from New Zealand. Lustrous deep green leaves, with 3 to 5 wavy-edged leaflets. Sprays of 1 in (25 mm) long pink to red flowers in autumn–winter. Pinkish red drupes. Zones 9–11.

WARSZEWICZIA
This genus in the madder (Rubiaceae) family contains 4 species of shrubs or trees native to tropical America. They are slightly hairy plants with opposite leaves and terminal panicles of small funnel-shaped flowers with showy bracts.
CULTIVATION: In cool climates grow these plants in a greenhouse. In warmer areas they can be grown outdoors in a moist well-drained soil in a sunny situation. Propagate from seed or from greenwood cuttings in spring.

Warszewiczia coccinea
☼ ⟊ ↔ 10 ft (3 m) ↑ 15 ft (4.5 m)
Leaves oblong, 6–24 in (15–60 cm) long. Terminal panicles, up to 20 in (50 cm) long, of small yellow flowers, 1 or 2 calyx lobes enlarged into showy, bright red, petal-like bracts, appear year round. Zones 10–12.

WEIGELA
CARDINAL BUSH, WEIGELA
The 10 or 12 species of this genus within the woodbine (Caprifoliaceae) family are deciduous long-lived shrubs native to eastern Asia, with opposite oblong to elliptic leaves. Cultivated for their bell- or funnel-shaped flowers, produced in late spring and early summer, they have pink, red, white, or sometimes yellow blooms, growing on the previous year's wood.
CULTIVATION: They do well in moist but well-drained fertile soil in sun or part-shade. Remove older branches after flowering to encourage vigorous growth. Propagate by sowing seed in autumn in an area protected from winter frosts, or from half-hardened cuttings in summer. Seed may not come true, as weigelas tend to hybridize freely.

Weigela decora
☼ ❋ ↔ 5–7 ft (1.5–2 m) ↑ 10–15 ft (3–4.5 m)
Species native to Japan, with leaves 4 in (10 cm) long. In spring–early summer bears white trumpet flowers to 1½ in (35 mm) long, ageing to cerise-red. Zones 6–10.

Weigela floribunda
☼ ❋ ↔ 8 ft (2.4 m) ↑ 10 ft (3 m)
Deciduous shrub native to Japan. Slender toothed leaves slightly hairy above, white and woolly beneath. Up to 3 dark red flowers in each leaf axil, in spring–summer. Zones 6–10.

Weigela florida

bell-shaped pink to red flowers; **'Bristol Ruby'**, carmine red flowers; **'Candida'**, vivid green leaves, bell-shaped white flowers; **'Chameleon'**, around 6 ft (1.8 m) tall, finely serrated mid-green leaves, pastel pink flowers, grows in sun or part-shade; **'Eva Rathke'**, dark green leaves, funnel-shaped dark purple flowers; **'Florida Variegata'** (syn. *W. florida* 'Variegata'), cream-edged leaves, rich pink trumpet flowers to 1¼ in (30 mm) long; **'Looymansii Aurea'**, yellowish leaves, rich pink flowers with paler pink center, foliage will scorch in hot sun, and lose its color in heavy shade; **'Madame Lemoine'**, pale pink flowers fading to white; **'Minuet'**, 30 in (75 cm) high with coppery oval leaves, bell-shaped magenta flowers; **'Newport Red'** ★ (syn. 'Vanicek'), tall, very hardy, with dark red flowers; **'Praecox Variegata'** (syn. *W. praecox* 'Variegata'), slightly scented pink trumpet flowers with soft yellow center, leaves have creamy yellow margins turning white as they age; **'Red Prince'**, lushly foliaged, long-lasting dark red flowers. Zones 5–10.

Weigela florida
OLD-FASHIONED WEIGELA, WEIGELA

☼ ❄ ↔ 8 ft (2.4 m) ↑ 8 ft (2.4 m)

From East Asia, larger in wild. Oblong leaves, pointed tips, toothed margins, felty underside. Funnel-shaped dark pink to nearly white flowers in spring–summer. **'Alexandra'** (syn. 'Wine & Roses'), recent cultivar with purple spring foliage becoming almost blackish and glossy in summer, flowers bright rose red, plant compact form, under 5 ft (1.5 m) in height; **'Foliis Purpureis'**, coppery foliage with dark pink flowers, compact habit to 3 ft (0.9 m); **'Java Red'**, purple-tinged foliage, dark pink flowers. Zones 5–10.

Weigela japonica

☼ ❄ ↔ 10 ft (3 m) ↑ 10 ft (3 m)

Native to Japan, larger in wild. Leaves dark green. Spring flowers solitary or in pairs, white, turning red later. *W. j.* var. *sinica*, taller than species, light pink flowers turn deeper pink. Zones 6–10.

Weigela middendorffiana

☀ ❄ ↔ 5 ft (1.5 m) ↑ 5 ft (1.5 m)

Erect shrub from eastern Asia. Vivid green leaves. Solitary or paired flowers, bell-shaped, pale yellow with orange or red throat markings, in summer. Protect from strong winds. Zones 4–10.

Weigela praecox

☼ ❄ ↔ 7 ft (2 m) ↑ 8 ft (2.4 m)

Erect densely branched shrub native to Korea, northeastern China, and Japan. Parent of numerous early-flowering cultivars. Leaves dark green, hairy underside. Fragrant, pink, funnel-shaped flowers, with yellow throat, in late spring–early summer. Zones 5–10.

Weigela Hybrid Cultivars

☼ ❄ ↔ 5–8 ft (1.5–2.4 m) ↑ 5–12 ft (1.5–3.5 m)

Great plants for placing in borders, hybrids between number of *Weigela* species. Range of cultivars to choose from very extensive, with many color possibilities. **'Abel Carrière'**, dark green leaves,

Weigela middendorffiana

WEINMANNIA

This genus of 150 to 190 species of evergreen shrubs and trees in the family Cunoniaceae is widespread, from Central and South America, to the Pacific region and tropical Asia. The cultivated species are grown mainly for their dense dark foliage and their wand- or bottlebrush-like racemes of flowers, which are usually white or cream. The foliage is usually pinnate and made up thick leathery leaflets that are often toothed and which may differ in size and shape between juvenile and adult plants.

CULTIVATION: While hardiness varies somewhat with the species, none are extremely frost tolerant. They prefer relatively mild winter conditions and a moist, humus-rich, well-drained soil that does not dry out in summer. Plant in full sun or part-shade and trim plants lightly to shape after flowering. Propagation is either from seed or from half-hardened cuttings.

Weinmannia racemosa
KAMAHI

☼ ⚘ ↔ 8–15 ft (2.4–4.5 m) ↑ 30 ft (9 m)

New Zealand shrub or tree, taller in wild. Leaves simple, dark green to bronze, serrated edges. Juvenile plants often have 3-part leaves. White bottlebrush-like flowers in summer. Very attractive to bees. Zones 9–10.

Weinmannia trichosperma
MADEN, TINEO

☼ ⚘ ↔ 5–12 ft (1.5–3.5 m) ↑ 70 ft (21 m)

Large shrub or tree native to Chile and Argentina. Remains bushy for many years. Pinnate leaves, composed of 11 to 13 toothed leaflets, each 1 in (25 mm) long. Flowers creamy white, on long spikes. Zones 9–10.

WESTRINGIA

This is an Australian genus in the mint (Lamiaceae) family consisting of 25 species. All are shrubs with angled stems and foliage usually arranged in whorls of 3 to 5 small leaves. Small tubular flowers are 2-lipped, the upper lip having 2 lobes and the lower lip 3 lobes, and are produced in the leaf axils over a long period. The fruit is divided into 4 tiny nutlets hidden in the persistent calyx. Most grow in coastal heathlands, scrublands, forests, and sandy or rocky areas. They are useful landscape subjects for regions with mild winters and are often seen as hedging or screening plants. CULTIVATION: Most are fairly adaptable in a well-drained soil with full sun, tolerating salty winds and exposed conditions. They require adequate water in summer. Prune after flowering to maintain a compact shape. Propagate from cuttings.

Westringia fruticosa
COASTAL ROSEMARY, NATIVE ROSEMARY
☼ ❄ ↔ 7 ft (2 m) ↑ 6 ft (1.8 m)
From east-coastal Australia. Leaves linear, gray above, felty white below, in whorls of 4 around stems. White flowers, lower lobe dotted brownish or purplish, for most of year. Tolerant of wind, drought, and salt. Zones 9–11.

Westringia 'Wynyabbie Gem'
☼ ❄ ↔ 5 ft (1.5 m) ↑ 4 ft (1.2 m)
Popular hybrid between *W. eremicola* and *W. fruticosa*. Bushy shrub with fine dark green foliage. Small bluish pink flowers in groups at branch tips, most of year. May not be long lived. Zones 9–11.

WIDDRINGTONIA
This is a genus in the cypress (Cupressaceae) family containing 3 species, 2 native to South Africa and 1 distributed more widely from tropical Africa south to Cape Town, South Africa. All are evergreen shrubs or trees with fragrant timber. Timber cutting and bushfires have decimated the populations of these trees. Juvenile leaves are needle-like and spirally arranged on the young twigs. The adult leaves are scale-like, arranged in an opposite or alternate pattern, and closely pressed against the stems. Male and female cones are borne on the same plant, the males are catkin-like, the females are woody. The seeds are egg-shaped with a thin wing. CULTIVATION: They do not adapt well to cultivation. Early growth is slow, and the plants sometimes languish and can fail to thrive.

Maintaining them as compact plants in a large pot may be a better option. They grow best in a humid mild climate. Propagation is from seed, which germinates readily, or from cuttings.

Widdringtonia nodiflora
MLANJE CEDAR, MOUNTAIN CEDAR, MOUNTAIN CYPRESS
☼ ❄ ↔ 6–12 ft (1.8–3.5 m) ↑ 40 ft (12 m)
Surviving in wild only in relatively inaccessible sites. Grayish bark peels in long strips. Tiny leaves. Cones ripen in early autumn, seeds black with red wing. Zones 9–11.

Widdringtonia schwarzii
WILLOWMORE CEDAR
☼ ❄ ↔ 15–30 ft (4.5–9 m) ↑ 120 ft (36 m)
Only known from small area just east of Cape Town, South Africa. Bark flaky, leaves arranged in opposite pairs. Male cones catkin-like, female cones globular, dark brown. Seeds flattish with prominent wing. Zones 8–9.

Widdringtonia schwarzii

WIGANDIA
The 5 members of this genus belonging to the waterleaf (Hydrophyllaceae) family are evergreen shrubs from Central and South America. Large, alternate, oval to oblong leaves can be up to 18 in (45 cm) long. The undersurface of the deep green leaves is covered in white hairs, often stinging. Violet-blue flowers are borne from spring to autumn in large, terminal, 1-sided panicles. CULTIVATION: These plants need moist but well-drained soil in full sun. They are frost tender, and make good container specimens. Propagation is from seed or from cuttings taken in spring.

Wigandia caracasana
syn. *Wigandia urens* var. *caracasana*
☼ ✦ ↔ 12 ft (3.5 m) ↑ 15 ft (4.5 m)
Found in jungles of Mexico, Colombia, and Venezuela. Variable species, often small spreading tree. Rough-textured deep green leaves, oval, with wavy edges and hairy white underside. Flowers violet to purple, with white throat, form in long terminal clusters. Zones 10–12.

Weinmannia trichosperma

Westringia 'Wynyabbie Gem'

Wigandia caracasana

WOLLEMIA

This genus belonging to the araucaria (Araucariaceae) family consists of a single species, endemic to the Wollemi National Park, 93 miles (150 km) northwest of Sydney, Australia. It comes from warm-temperate forests and emerges over coachwood and sassafras trees within sandstone canyons of the National Park. An extremely rare, endangered, and remarkable conifer, it has spongy nodular bark and an unusual branching pattern producing a double crown effect. The old leaves do not fall individually—instead, the tree sheds whole branches. *W. nobilis* was discovered in 1994. The chance discovery reinforces the importance of conservation areas in preserving both plant and animal species. The tree yields the anti-cancer drug taxol.
CULTIVATION: Because this genus is so new to horticulture, cultivation information is limited. It can be seen growing at the Royal Botanic Gardens in Sydney, and young plants can now be purchased from nurseries. Propagation from seed, cuttings, and tissue culture has been undertaken and research in these areas continues.

Wollemia nobilis
WOLLEMI PINE
☼ ⁑ ↔ 4–10 ft (1.2–3 m) ↑ 120 ft (36 m)
Very rare majestic conifer. Fern-like juvenile leaves dark green and waxy on underside; 4-ranked adult leaves yellow-green, stiff, long, and narrow. Cylindrical male cones on separate branches to globular female cones, which contain winged seeds. Zones 9–11.

XANTHOCERAS

The 1 species of deciduous shrub or small tree in this genus is native to northern China and is a member of the soapberry (Sapindaceae) family. It has pinnate leaves clustered near the branch tips and bears clusters of 5-petalled flowers. Fruit are thick-walled green capsules resembling the fruit of chestnut trees.

Wollemia nobilis

Xanthoceras sorbifolium

CULTIVATION: Although quite hardy, this species needs a long hot growing season to flower well, so in cooler areas should be given the shelter of a warm wall. Grow in a well-drained fertile soil and prune to maintain a compact shape. Propagate from seed, cuttings, or suckers.

Xanthoceras sorbifolium ★
☼ ❋ ↔ 10 ft (3 m) ↑ 25 ft (8 m)
Shrub or small tree with wide rounded habit, dark green pinnate leaves, and sharply toothed leaflets. Fragrant white flowers have crimson blotch at their base, and are borne in sprays, in spring–summer. Zones 6–9.

ZANTHOXYLUM

This is a widespread genus of around 250 species of deciduous or evergreen spiny shrubs and trees with pinnate leaves and aromatic bark from North and South America, Africa, Asia, and Australia. They are members of the rue (Rutaceae) family, and are grown for their attractive habit and handsome aromatic foliage, and sometimes for their fruit, which are dried and used for spices. Some species have medicinal uses and others provide a fine timber for woodworking.
CULTIVATION: Depending on the species, they are frost hardy to frost tender. They need a fertile, moist, but well-drained soil with a position in full sun or part-shade. Pruning is rarely necessary, but young specimens may be shaped in early spring. Propagate from seed, cuttings, or rooted suckers.

Zanthoxylum americanum
NORTHERN PRICKLY ASH, PRICKLY ASH, TOOTHACHE TREE
☼ ❋ ↔ 15 ft (4.5 m) ↑ 25 ft (8 m)
Deciduous large shrub or small tree naturally found in eastern North America. Spiny stems and aromatic pinnate leaves. Very small yellow-green flowers, in clusters, before leaves, in spring. Fruit is black berry. Zones 4–10.

Zanthoxylum piperitum
JAPANESE PEPPER
☼ ❋ ↔ 10 ft (3 m) ↑ 20 ft (6 m)
Deciduous, bushy, spiny shrub or small tree native to China, Korea, and Japan. Aromatic, glossy, dark green, pinnate leaves composed of many oval leaflets, which turn yellow in autumn. Small yellow-green flowers, in small clusters, in spring. Tiny orange-colored berries. Zones 7–10.

Zanthoxylum planispinum
☼ ❋ ↔ 8 ft (2.4 m) ↑ 12 ft (3.5 m)
Deciduous shrub native to Japan, Korea, and China. Spreading prickly stems. Pinnate leaves, stem-clasping leaflets to 4 in (10 cm) long. Pale yellow flowers, in small clusters, in spring. Tiny, warty, red berries. Zones 7–10.

Zanthoxylum simulans

FLAT-SPINE PRICKLY ASH, PRICKLY ASH

☼ ❄ ↔ 7–25 ft (2–8 m) ↕ 7–25 ft (2–8 m)

Rounded, spreading, deciduous shrub or small tree from China and Taiwan. Broad flattened spines on finely hairy branches. Compound leaves have 7 to 11 smooth, toothed, oval to oblong leaflets, to 2 in (5 cm) long, with prickly midrib. Slender cymes of reddish green flowers in midsummer, followed by red to black berries in autumn. Zones 5–8.

ZELKOVA

Allied to the elms *(Ulmus)* but not troubled by Dutch elm disease, the 5 deciduous trees in this genus are members of the family Ulmaceae, and are found in China, Taiwan, and Japan, as well as in the Caucasus and Crete, Greece. They have simple, pointed, elliptical leaves with conspicuous veins and heavily serrated edges. The foliage often develops attractive autumn colors. In some species the bark is an attractive feature, flaking to reveal interesting patterns and colors. The separate male and female flowers are largely inconspicuous, as are the small nut-like fruit.

CULTIVATION: Quite frost hardy, these spreading round-headed trees develop a better shape if sheltered from strong winds when they are young. They also benefit from pruning to encourage a strong single trunk. Plant in deep, fertile, well-drained soil in full sun. Propagation is from seed, from root cuttings of the young potted plants, or by grafting.

Zelkova carpinifolia

CAUCASIAN ZELKOVA

☼ ❄ ↔ 25 ft (8 m) ↕ 100 ft (30 m)

Native to Caucasus. May develop several trunks. Round-headed tree, upright gray-barked branches, weep at tips. Young stems very downy, veins on underside of serrated leaves. Flowers pleasantly scented. Zones 5–9.

Zelkova serrata

JAPANESE ZELKOVA

☼ ❄ ↔ 50 ft (15 m) ↕ 60–100 ft (18–30 m)

Widely cultivated; from Japan, Taiwan, and eastern China. Wide-spreading crown, bark flakes to reveal range of colors and textures. Heavily toothed, veined leaves, fine hairs on underside veins. Foliage turns gold and russet in autumn. 'Goblin', 3 ft (0.9 m) high dwarf cultivar; 'Green Vase' ★, vase-shaped form, brilliant green foliage; 'Village Green', fast-growing, rich green leaves. Zones 5–9.

ZENOBIA

The single species in this genus in the heath (Ericaceae) family is a deciduous or semi-evergreen shrub found in southeastern USA, on open heathland and in pine forest clearings. Notable for its beautiful flowers and their pleasant scent, this plant's foliage sometimes develops attractive red tints in autumn.

CULTIVATION: This plant prefers cool, moist, humus-rich, acidic soil conditions. It is very frost hardy, and prefers a situation in part-shade. If necessary, trim the plant to shape after flowering. Propagate from either seed or summer cuttings. Alternatively, try removing rooted layers or suckers.

Zanthoxylum planispinum

Zenobia pulverulenta ★

☼ ❄ ↔ 4 ft (1.2 m) ↕ 3–10 ft (0.9–3 m)

From southeast Virginia to South Carolina, USA. Retains much of its foliage in mild winters, deciduous elsewhere. Narrowly elliptical leaves, light green, covered with powdery bluish bloom. Heads of bell-shaped, nodding, scented white flowers in late spring. 'Quercifolia', retains shallowly lobed foliage often seen on juvenile plants. Zones 5–10.

ZIZIPHUS

This tropical and subtropical genus consists of 80 or so species of evergreen or deciduous trees and shrubs in the buckthorn (Rhamnaceae) family. Some have spiny branches with double armaments—1 hooked and 1 straight thorn at each node. They have alternate shiny green leaves, mostly with 3 prominent veins from the base. The insignificant flowers are greenish, white, or yellow, and arranged in axillary clusters; they are followed by small fleshy fruit that are sometimes edible. The genus is best known in horticulture for *Z. jujuba*, the jujube, which has been cultivated in China since antiquity.

CULTIVATION: They are ideally grown in a deep moisture-retentive soil that is well drained, and prefer a sunny position. Shelter from strong winds and water regularly during the growing season. Tip prune to maintain compact growth. Propagate from seed or root cuttings. Improved fruiting varieties may be obtained from grafting.

Ziziphus mucronata

BUFFALO THORN

☼ ❄ ↔ 10–20 ft (3–6 m) ↕ 17–35 ft (5–10 m)

Evergreen tree from South Africa. Crooked trunk and drooping branches, usually covered with pairs of spines, 1 curved and 1 straight. Glossy drooping leaves conspicuously 3-veined from base. Inconspicuous yellowish flower clusters. Roundish russet-colored fruit, dry meal-like pulp. Used in traditional medicine. Zones 7–9.

Zelkova serrata

Ziziphus mucronata, in the wild, South Africa

Annuals and Perennials

At the heart of many garden displays are annuals and perennials, which collectively offer an almost unrivaled choice of brilliantly colored blooms, across a wide range of garden situations. Annual plants have a frenetic life with only a short time to grow, flower, and set seed; they have no means of living through hard times, except as seed, so they must complete their life in a single season.

Perennials (more accurately known as herbaceous perennials to differentiate them from woody perennials such as trees) typically take more than a year to reach flowering size, but once they have, they bloom every year. Exceptions to this are monocarpic perennials such as the South American *Puya mirabilis*—they gradually build up the strength to flower, only then to die, having set thousands of seeds.

In the past, the traditional herbaceous border was a joy to behold, but its short season led many gardeners to abandon this type of garden. However, it is making a comeback, as today's range of herbaceous plants means that pretty perennials can enhance our gardens throughout much of the year, from hellebores flowering in late winter, and bergenias during spring, through to the last flowers of Japanese anemones in autumn.

As well as offering stunning deep red blooms that are excellent as cut flowers, *Gaillardia* × *grandiflora* 'Burgunder' is both drought and heat tolerant.

Annual and Perennial Finder

The following cultivation table features at-a-glance information for every species or hybrid with an individual entry in the Annuals and Perennials chapter of this book. Simply find the plant you wish to know more about, and run your eye along the row to discover its height and spread, whether it is frost tolerant or not, the aspect it prefers, and more.

The type of plant is abbreviated to **A**, **B**, or **P**:
A – the plant is an annual.
B – the plant is a biennial.
P – the plant is a perennial.

The climate(s) that each plant needs to thrive in the outdoors are given (some plants will grow in more than one climate), abbreviated to **C**, **W**, or **T**:
C – the plant prefers a cool climate.
W – the plant prefers a warm-temperate or subtropical climate.
T – the plant prefers a tropical climate.

The group that the plant belongs to is abbreviated to **B**, **C**, **G**, or **NA**:
B – the plant is a bromeliad.
C – the plant is carnivorous.
G – the plant is a gesneriad.
NA – the plant does not fit into one of the three groups given above.

The flowering and planting seasons are abbreviated to **A**, **W**, **Sp**, or **Su**:
A – the plant bears flowers or should be planted in autumn.
W – the plant bears flowers or should be planted in winter.
Sp – the plant bears flowers or should be planted in spring.
Su – the plant bears flowers or should be planted in summer.

Plant name	Height	Spread	Type	Climate	Group	Showy flowers	Showy foliage	Scented flowers	Planting season	Flowering season	Grow in pot/tub	Frost tolerant	Full Sun	Half Sun	Heavy shade
Abelmoschus manihot	3–6 ft (0.9–1.8 m)	3 ft (0.9 m)	P	W/T	NA	◆			W/Sp	Su	◆		◆		
Abelmoschus moschatus	4–6 ft (1.2–1.8 m)	30 in (75 cm)	A	W/T	NA	◆		◆	Sp	Su	◆		◆		
Acaena caesiiglauca	2 in (5 cm)	32 in (80 cm)	P	C/W	NA		◆		W/Sp	Su	◆	◆	◆	◆	
Acaena microphylla	2 in (5 cm)	20 in (50 cm)	P	C/W	NA	◆			W/Sp	Su	◆	◆	◆	◆	
Acanthus mollis	7 ft (2 m)	40–60 in (100–150 cm)	P	C/W	NA	◆	◆		W/Sp	Su		◆	◆	◆	◆
Acanthus spinosus	36 in (90 cm)	40–60 in (100–150 cm)	P	C/W	NA	◆	◆		W/Sp	Su		◆	◆	◆	◆
Achillea filipendulina	24–48 in (60–120 cm)	24–48 in (60–120 cm)	P	C/W	NA	◆			W/Sp	Su		◆	◆		
Achillea millefolium	12–30 in (30–75 cm)	18–30 in (45–75 cm)	P	C/W	NA	◆			W/Sp	Su/A		◆	◆		
Achillea ptarmica	30 in (75 cm)	30 in (75 cm)	P	C/W	NA	◆			W/Sp	Su		◆	◆		
Achillea Hybrid Cultivars	12–40 in (30–100 cm)	18–30 in (45–75 cm)	P	C/W	NA	◆			W/Sp	Su		◆	◆		
Achimenes longiflora	20–24 in (50–60 cm)	12–20 in (30–50 cm)	P	W/T	G	◆	◆		W/Sp	Su/A	◆			◆	
Achimenes Hybrid Cultivars	3–6 in (8–15 cm)	10–15 in (25–38 cm)	P	W/T	G	◆	◆		W/Sp	Su/A	◆			◆	
Aconitum carmichaelii	7 ft (2 m)	24–36 in (60–90 cm)	P	C	NA	◆			W/Sp	Su/A		◆	◆	◆	
Aconitum napellus	5–6 ft (1.5–1.8 m)	24–32 in (60–80 cm)	P	C	NA	◆			W/Sp	Su/A		◆	◆	◆	
Aconitum Hybrid Cultivars	4 ft (1.2 m)	24 in (60 cm)	P	C	NA	◆			W/Sp	Su/A		◆	◆	◆	
Acorus calamus	4 ft (1.2 m)	3–7 ft (0.9–2 m)	P	C	NA	◆	◆		W/Sp	Su		◆	◆	◆	
Acorus gramineus	16 in (40 cm)	18–36 in (45–90 cm)	P	C/W	NA		◆		W/Sp	Su		◆	◆	◆	
Aechmea caudata	36 in (90 cm)	24 in (60 cm)	P	W	B	◆	◆		Sp	Su	◆				◆

Plant name	Height	Spread	Type	Climate	Group	Showy flowers	Showy foliage	Scented flowers	Planting season	Flowering season	Grow in pot/tub	Frost tolerant	Full Sun	Half Sun	Heavy shade
Aechmea chantinii	40 in (100 cm)	20 in (50 cm)	P	W/T	B	◆	◆		Sp	Su	◆				◆
Aechmea fasciata	27 in (70 cm)	16 in (40 cm)	P	W/T	B	◆	◆		Sp	Su	◆				◆
Aechmea fulgens	20 in (50 cm)	20 in (50 cm)	P	W/T	B	◆			Sp	Su	◆				◆
Aechmea gamosepala	30 in (75 cm)	10 in (25 cm)	P	W	B	◆			Sp	Su	◆	◆	◆		
Aechmea nudicaulis	27–36 in (70–90 cm)	8 in (20 cm)	P	W/T	B	◆			Sp	Su	◆			◆	
Aechmea ornata	36 in (90 cm)	7 ft (2 m)	P	W	B	◆	◆		Sp	Su	◆				
Aechmea recurvata	8–16 in (20–40 cm)	8 in (20 cm)	P	W	B	◆			Sp	Su	◆			◆	
Aechmea Hybrid Cultivars	12–36 in (30–90 cm)	12–24 in (30–60 cm)	P	W/T	B	◆	◆		Sp	Su	◆			◆	
Aethionema grandiflorum	8–18 in (20–45 cm)	12–24 in (30–60 cm)	P	C	NA	◆			W	Sp/Su	◆	◆	◆		
Aethionema 'Warley Rose'	6 in (15 cm)	12 in (30 cm)	P	C	NA	◆			W	Sp/Su	◆	◆	◆		
Agapanthus inapertus	40–60 in (100–150 cm)	40–50 in (100–130 cm)	P	C/W	NA	◆			W/Sp	Su		◆	◆		
Agapanthus praecox	40 in (100 cm)	40–50 in (100–130 cm)	P	W	NA	◆			W/Sp	Su		◆	◆		
Agapanthus Hybrid Cultivars	15–60 in (38–150 cm)	12–30 in (30–75 cm)	P	C/W	NA	◆			W/Sp	Su	◆	◆	◆		
Agastache cana	20–24 in (50–60 cm)	12–18 in (30–45 cm)	P	W	NA	◆			W/Sp	Su			◆		
Agastache foeniculum	20–32 in (50–80 cm)	18–24 in (45–60 cm)	P	W	NA	◆			W/Sp	Su			◆		
Agastache rugosa	24–48 in (60–120 cm)	24 in (60 cm)	P	W	NA	◆			W/Sp	Su			◆		
Agastache rupestris	18–36 in (45–90 cm)	18 in (45 cm)	P	W	NA	◆			W/Sp	Su			◆		
Agastache Hybrid Cultivars	2–6 ft (0.6–1.8 m)	1–3 ft (0.3–0.9 m)	P	W	NA	◆			W/Sp	Su			◆		
Ageratum houstonianum	6–30 in (15–75 cm)	6–20 in (15–50 cm)	A	W/T	NA	◆			Sp	Su	◆		◆		
Aglaonema commutatum	24–36 in (60–90 cm)	24 in (60 cm)	P	W/T	NA		◆		any	Su	◆			◆	◆
Aglaonema costatum	12 in (30 cm)	24 in (60 cm)	P	W/T	NA		◆		any	Su	◆				◆
Aglaonema crispum	24–48 in (60–120 cm)	18–30 in (45–75 cm)	P	W/T	NA		◆		any	Su	◆			◆	◆
Ajuga pyramidalis	6–8 in (15–20 cm)	12–24 in (30–60 cm)	P	C/W	NA	◆	◆		W/Sp	Sp/Su	◆	◆	◆	◆	
Ajuga reptans	4–8 in (10–20 cm)	12–48 in (30–120 cm)	P	C/W	NA	◆	◆		W/Sp	Sp/Su	◆	◆	◆	◆	◆
Alcea rosea	2–8 ft (0.6–2.4 m)	2–3 ft (0.6–0.9 m)	B	C/W	NA	◆			Sp	Su		◆	◆		
Alchemilla mollis	12–20 in (30–50 cm)	12–32 in (30–80 cm)	P	C	NA	◆			W/Sp	Su		◆	◆	◆	
Alchemilla xanthochlora	12–20 in (30–50 cm)	16–24 in (40–60 cm)	P	C	NA	◆			W/Sp	Su		◆	◆		
Alkanna orientalis	8–12 in (20–30 cm)	8–12 in (20–30 cm)	A	C/W	NA	◆		◆	W/Sp	Sp/Su		◆	◆		
Alkanna tinctoria	12–36 in (30–90 cm)	12–36 in (30–90 cm)	P	C	NA				W/Sp	Sp/Su		◆	◆		
Alocasia × *amazonica*	40–60 in (100–150 cm)	20–40 in (50–100 cm)	P	W/T	NA		◆		W/Sp	Su	◆				◆
Alocasia cuprea	40 in (100 cm)	30 in (75 cm)	P	W/T	NA		◆		W/Sp	Su	◆			◆	

Plant name	Height	Spread	Type	Climate	Group	Showy flowers	Showy foliage	Scented flowers	Planting season	Flowering season	Grow in pot/tub	Frost tolerant	Full Sun	Half Sun	Heavy shade
Alocasia sanderiana	40–60 in (100–150 cm)	20–36 in (50–90 cm)	P	W/T	NA		◆		W/Sp	Su	◆			◆	◆
Alpinia purpurata	8–12 ft (2.4–3.5 m)	2–4 ft (0.6–1.2 m)	P	W/T	NA	◆			W/Sp	Any	◆		◆	◆	
Alpinia zerumbet	6–10 ft (1.8–3 m)	2–3 ft (0.6–0.9 m)	P	W/T	NA	◆			Sp	Sp/Su	◆		◆	◆	
Alstroemeria psittacina	28–36 in (70–90 cm)	16–20 in (40–50 cm)	P	W	NA	◆			W/Sp	Su	◆	◆	◆	◆	
Alstroemeria Hybrid Cultivars	18–48 in (45–120 cm)	12–24 in (30–60 cm)	P	W	NA	◆			W/Sp	Su/A	◆	◆	◆	◆	
Alternanthera bettzichiana	2–3 ft (0.6–0.9 m)	2–3 ft (0.6–0.9 m)	A	W/T	NA		◆		Sp	Su			◆	◆	
Amaranthus caudatus	36–48 in (90–120 cm)	24 in (60 cm)	A	W/T	NA	◆	◆		Sp	Su			◆		
Amaranthus tricolor	24–36 in (60–90 cm)	30 in (75 cm)	A	W	NA		◆		Sp	Su			◆		
Amsonia tabernaemontana	36 in (90 cm)	36–48 in (90–120 cm)	P	C/W	NA	◆			W/Sp	Sp/Su		◆	◆	◆	
Anagallis monelli	12–20 in (30–50 cm)	12–20 in (30–50 cm)	P	C/W	NA	◆			W/Sp	Sp/Su		◆	◆		
Anaphalis margaritacea	32–40 in (80–100 cm)	16–24 in (40–60 cm)	P	C	NA	◆			W/Sp			◆	◆	◆	
Anaphalis triplinervis	32–36 in (80–90 cm)	16–20 in (40–50 cm)	P	C	NA	◆	◆		W/Sp			◆	◆	◆	
Anchusa azurea	48 in (120 cm)	32 in (80 cm)	P	C/W	NA	◆			W/Sp	Sp/Su		◆	◆	◆	
Anchusa capensis	20 in (50 cm)	16 in (40 cm)	B	W	NA	◆			Sp	Su			◆		
Androsace lanuginosa	3 in (8 cm)	12–18 in (30–45 cm)	P	C	NA	◆			W/Sp	Su/A		◆	◆		
Androsace rotundifolia	4–6 in (10–15 cm)	8 in (20 cm)	P	C	NA	◆			W/Sp	Sp/Su		◆	◆		
Anemone blanda	4–8 in (10–20 cm)	6–12 in (15–30 cm)	P	C	NA	◆			A/W	W/Sp		◆		◆	◆
Anemone coronaria	16–24 in (40–60 cm)	8–16 in (20–40 cm)	P	C/W	NA	◆			A/W	Sp	◆	◆	◆	◆	
Anemone hupehensis	20–36 in (50–90 cm)	16–40 in (40–100 cm)	P	C	NA	◆			W/Sp	Su/A		◆	◆	◆	
Anemone × hybrida	32–60 in (80–150 cm)	20–48 in (50–120 cm)	P	C	NA	◆			W/Sp	Su/A		◆	◆	◆	
Anemone nemorosa	4–12 in (10–30 cm)	6–16 in (15–40 cm)	P	C	NA	◆			A/W	Sp		◆		◆	◆
Anemone pavonina	12 in (30 cm)	12–16 in (30–40 cm)	P	C	NA	◆			A/W	Sp		◆	◆	◆	
Anemone sylvestris	6–12 in (15–30 cm)	6–20 in (15–50 cm)	P	C	NA			◆	W	Sp/Su		◆		◆	
Angelonia angustifolia	18 in (45 cm)	12 in (30 cm)	A/P	W	NA	◆			Sp	Su	◆		◆		
Anigozanthos flavidus	10 ft (3 m)	3 ft (0.9 m)	P	W	NA	◆			W/Sp	Su			◆		
Anigozanthos manglesii	12–20 in (30–50 cm)	36 in (90 cm)	P	W	NA	◆			A/Sp	W/Sp			◆		
Anigozanthos Hybrid Cultivars	1–6 ft (0.3–1.8 m)	8–30 in (20–75 cm)	P	W	NA	◆			W/Sp	Sp/Su			◆	◆	
Antennaria dioica	8 in (20 cm)	24–36 in (60–90 cm)	P	C	NA	◆	◆		W/Sp	Su		◆	◆		
Anthemis punctata	16–24 in (40–60 cm)	12–20 in (30–50 cm)	P	C/W	NA	◆	◆		W/Sp	Su		◆	◆		
Anthemis tinctoria	24–36 in (60–90 cm)	20–40 in (50–100 cm)	P	C/W	NA	◆	◆		W/Sp	Sp–A		◆	◆		
Anthericum liliago	24–36 in (60–90 cm)	12 in (30 cm)	P	C/W	NA	◆			A/W	Sp		◆	◆		

Plant name	Height	Spread	Type	Climate	Group	Showy flowers	Showy foliage	Scented flowers	Planting season	Flowering season	Grow in pot/tub	Frost tolerant	Full Sun	Half Sun	Heavy shade
Anthurium andraeanum	20–48 in (50–120 cm)	12–24 in (30–60 cm)	P	W/T	NA	◆	◆		Any	Sp–A	◆			◆	◆
Anthurium scherzerianum	24–30 in (60–75 cm)	12–20 in (30–50 cm)	P	W/T	NA	◆	◆		Any	Sp–A	◆			◆	◆
Anthurium warocqueanum	24–60 in (60–150 cm)	3–10 ft (0.9–3 m)	P	T	NA		◆		Any	Sp–A				◆	◆
Antirrhinum majus	12–60 in (30–150 cm)	6–20 in (15–50 cm)	A	C/W	NA	◆			Sp/Su	Sp–A		◆	◆	◆	
Antirrhinum molle	8–16 in (20–40 cm)	6–8 in (15–20 cm)	P	C/W	NA	◆			Sp/Su	Sp–A			◆	◆	◆
Aponogeton distachyos	24–32 in (60–80 cm)	32–40 in (80–100 cm)	P	W	NA			◆	W/Sp	Su			◆	◆	
Aquilegia caerulea	8–24 in (20–60 cm)	8–16 in (20–40 cm)	P	C	NA	◆			W/Sp	Sp/Su		◆	◆	◆	
Aquilegia canadensis	12–30 in (30–75 cm)	12–20 in (30–50 cm)	P	C/W	NA	◆			W/Sp	Sp/Su			◆		
Aquilegia chrysantha	32–36 in (80–90 cm)	12–32 in (30–80 cm)	P	C/W	NA	◆			W/Sp	Sp/Su			◆	◆	
Aquilegia formosa	20–36 in (50–90 cm)	12–20 in (30–50 cm)	P	C	NA	◆			W/Sp	Sp/Su			◆	◆	
Aquilegia, McKana Group	32–48 in (80–120 cm)	12–20 in (30–50 cm)	P	C/W	NA	◆			W/Sp	Sp/Su			◆	◆	
Aquilegia vulgaris	12–36 in (30–90 cm)	8–18 in (20–45 cm)	P	C/W	NA	◆			W/Sp	Sp/Su			◆	◆	
Aquilegia Hybrid Cultivars	18–36 in (45–90 cm)	12–24 in (30–60 cm)	P	C/W	NA	◆			W/Sp	Sp/Su			◆	◆	
Arabis × *arendsii*	4–8 in (10–20 cm)	12–24 in (30–60 cm)	P	C	NA	◆			W/Sp	Sp/Su		◆	◆	◆	
Arabis blepharophylla	4–6 in (10–15 cm)	6–8 in (15–20 cm)	P	C	NA	◆			W/Sp	Sp/Su			◆	◆	
Arabis caucasica	6–12 in (15–30 cm)	8–20 in (20–50 cm)	P	C	NA	◆			W/Sp	Sp/Su			◆	◆	
Arctotis acaulis	6–12 in (15–30 cm)	12–40 in (30–100 cm)	P	W	NA	◆			A–Sp	Any		◆	◆	◆	
Arctotis × *hybrida*	8–16 in (20–40 cm)	8–20 in (20–50 cm)	A/P	W	NA	◆			A–Sp	Any			◆		
Arctotis venusta	16–24 in (40–60 cm)	8–16 in (20–40 cm)	A	W	NA	◆			Sp	Sp–A			◆		
Arenaria montana	4–6 in (10–15 cm)	9–24 in (23–60 cm)	P	C	NA	◆			W/Sp	Sp/Su		◆	◆	◆	
Arenaria purpurascens	4–6 in (10–15 cm)	9–24 in (23–60 cm)	P	C	NA	◆			W/Sp	Sp/Su		◆	◆	◆	
Argemone mexicana	36 in (90 cm)	12–16 in (30–40 cm)	A	W	NA	◆	◆		Sp	Su/A		◆	◆		
Aristea ecklonii	18–32 in (45–80 cm)	18–32 in (45–80 cm)	P	W	NA	◆			A/W	Sp/Su			◆	◆	
Aristea major	3–5 ft (0.9–1.5 m)	24–36 in (60–90 cm)	P	W	NA	◆			W/Sp	Su			◆	◆	
Aristolochia clematitis	12–30 in (30–75 cm)	24 in (60 cm)	P	C/W	NA			◆	W/Sp	Su			◆	◆	
Armeria alliacea	8–18 in (20–45 cm)	6–8 in (15–20 cm)	P	C/W	NA	◆			W/Sp	Su		◆	◆	◆	
Armeria juniperifolia	6 in (15 cm)	6–8 in (15–20 cm)	P	C/W	NA	◆			W/Sp	Su		◆	◆	◆	
Armeria maritima	8–12 in (20–30 cm)	8–16 in (20–40 cm)	P	C/W	NA	◆			W/Sp	Su		◆	◆	◆	
Armeria pseudarmeria	8–16 in (20–40 cm)	16–40 in (45–100 cm)	P	C/W	NA	◆			W/Sp	Su		◆	◆		
Artemisia lactiflora	5 ft (1.5 m)	24 in (60 cm)	P	C/W	NA	◆			W/Sp	Su			◆	◆	
Artemisia ludoviciana	36 in (90 cm)	36 in (90 cm)	P	C/W	NA		◆		W/Sp	Su			◆	◆	

Plant name	Height	Spread	Type	Climate	Group	Showy flowers	Showy foliage	Scented flowers	Planting season	Flowering season	Grow in pot/tub	Frost tolerant	Full Sun	Half Sun	Heavy shade
Artemisia pontica	32 in (80 cm)	24 in (60 cm)	P	C	NA		♦		W/Sp	Su		♦	♦		
Artemisia 'Powis Castle'	2 ft (0.6 m)	4 ft (1.2 m)	P	C/W	NA		♦		W/Sp	Su		♦	♦		
Artemisia stelleriana	18–24 in (45–60 cm)	18 in (45 cm)	P	C	NA		♦		W/Sp	Su		♦	♦		
Arthropodium cirratum	20–30 in (50–75 cm)	24 in (60 cm)	P	W	NA	♦	♦		A–Sp	Su	♦		♦	♦	
Aruncus dioicus	2–6 ft (0.6–1.2 m)	4 ft (1.2 m)	P	C	NA	♦	♦		W/Sp	Su				♦	
Asclepias linaria	24–36 in (60–90 cm)	24–36 in (60–90 cm)	P	W	NA	♦			W	Sp–A			♦		
Asclepias tuberosa	24–36 in (60–90 cm)	12 in (30 cm)	P	C/W	NA	♦			W/Sp	Sp–A		♦	♦		
Asparagus densiflorus	30–36 in (75–90 cm)	36 in (90 cm)	P	W	NA			♦	A/W	Sp/Su	♦	♦	♦		
Asparagus macowanii	6 ft (1.8 m)	8 ft (2.4 m)	P	W	NA	♦	♦		A/W	Su			♦	♦	
Asperula gussonei	4 in (10 cm)	6–12 in (15–30 cm)	P	C/W	NA	♦			A/W	Sp/Su			♦	♦	
Asperula orientalis	8–12 in (20–30 cm)	16–24 in (40–60 cm)	A	C/W	NA	♦			Sp	Su		♦	♦	♦	
Asphodeline lutea	36–48 in (90–120 cm)	12 in (30 cm)	P	C/W	NA	♦		♦	A/W	Sp/Su		♦	♦		
Asphodelus aestivus	40 in (100 cm)	24 in (60 cm)	P	C/W	NA	♦			A/W	Sp		♦	♦		
Asphodelus albus	36 in (90 cm)	24 in (60 cm)	P	C/W	NA	♦			A/W	Sp		♦	♦		
Aspidistra elatior	16–24 in (40–60 cm)	16–36 in (40–90 cm)	P	C/W	NA		♦		Any	Sp/Su					♦
Astelia chathamica	3–6 ft (0.9–1.8 m)	5 ft (1.5 m)	P	W	NA		♦		Any	Su		♦	♦	♦	
Astelia nervosa	3–7 ft (0.9–2 m)	5 ft (1.5 m)	P	W	NA		♦		Any	Su		♦	♦	♦	
Aster alpinus	4–10 in (10–25 cm)	8–32 in (20–80 cm)	P	C	NA	♦			A/W	Sp/Su	♦	♦	♦		
Aster amellus	24–27 in (60–70 cm)	12–20 in (30–50 cm)	P	C	NA	♦			W	A			♦		
Aster ericoides	32–40 in (80–100 cm)	20–32 in (50–80 cm)	P	C	NA	♦			W	Su/A		♦	♦	♦	
Aster × frikartii	20–30 in (50–75 cm)	16–24 in (40–60 cm)	P	C	NA	♦			W/Sp	A		♦	♦	♦	
Aster lateriflorus	3–4 ft (0.9–1.2 m)	2–4 ft (0.6–1.2 m)	P	C	NA	♦			W	A		♦	♦	♦	
Aster novae-angliae	4–5 ft (1.2–1.5 m)	2–4 ft (0.6–1.2 m)	P	C	NA	♦			W/Sp	A		♦	♦	♦	
Aster novi-belgii	36–48 in (90–120 cm)	24–32 in (60–80 cm)	P	C	NA	♦			W/Sp	A		♦	♦	♦	
Aster turbinellus	4 ft (1.2 m)	3 ft (0.9 m)	P	C	NA	♦			W/Sp	A		♦	♦	♦	
Astilbe × arendsii	2–6 ft (0.6–1.8 m)	12–32 in (30–80 cm)	P	C	NA	♦	♦		W/Sp	Sp/Su					♦
Astilbe chinensis	to 7 ft (2 m)	12–20 in (30–50 cm)	P	C	NA	♦			W/Sp	Sp/Su			♦	♦	
Astilbe japonica	2–3 ft (0.6–0.9 m)	3 ft (0.9 m)	P	C	NA	♦			W/Sp	Sp/Su				♦	
Astilbe simplicifolia	12–16 in (30–40 cm)	8–16 in (20–40 cm)	P	C	NA	♦			W/Sp	Sp/Su				♦	
Astilbe thunbergii	20–24 in (50–60 cm)	12–20 in (30–50 cm)	P	C	NA	♦			W/Sp	Sp/Su				♦	
Astilbe Hybrid Cultivars	2–3 ft (0.6–0.9 m)	3 ft (0.9 m)	P	C	NA	♦	♦		W/Sp	Sp/Su				♦	♦

Plant name	Height	Spread	Type	Climate	Group	Showy flowers	Showy foliage	Scented flowers	Planting season	Flowering season	Grow in pot/tub	Frost tolerant	Full Sun	Half Sun	Heavy shade
Astilboides tabularis	40–60 in (100–150 cm)	40–60 in (100–150 cm)	P	C/W	NA	◆	◆		W	Su		◆			◆
Astrantia major	24–32 in (60–80 cm)	16–24 in (40–60 cm)	P	C	NA	◆			W/Sp	Su		◆		◆	
Astrantia maxima	27–36 in (70–90 cm)	20–24 in (50–60 cm)	P	C	NA	◆			W/Sp	Su		◆		◆	
Atriplex hortensis	7–8 ft (2–2.4 m)	16–20 in (40–50 cm)	A	C/W	NA		◆		Sp	Su		◆	◆		
Aubrieta deltoidea	3 in (8 cm)	12 in (30 cm)	P	C/W	NA	◆			W/Sp	Sp/Su	◆	◆	◆	◆	
Aubrieta Hybrid Cultivars	3–6 in (8–15 cm)	8–24 in (20–60 cm)	P	C/W	NA	◆			W/Sp	SpSu	◆	◆	◆		
Aurinia saxatilis	8–12 in (20–30 cm)	16–24 in (40–60 cm)	P	C/W	NA	◆			W/Sp	Sp/Su	◆	◆	◆		
Baileya multiradiata	8–20 in (20–50 cm)	4–12 in (10–30 cm)	P	C/W	NA	◆			W/Sp	Sp–A		◆	◆		
Ballota acetabulosa	40 in (100 cm)	24–32 in (60–80 cm)	P	C/W	NA	◆	◆		W/Sp	Su		◆	◆	◆	
Ballota pseudodictamnus	12–20 in (30–50 cm)	24–48 in (60–120 cm)	P	C/W	NA		◆		W/Sp	Su		◆	◆		
Baptisia australis	2–4 ft (0.6–1.2 m)	4 ft (1.2 m)	P	C	NA	◆			W/Sp	Su		◆	◆		
Bassia scoparia	8–60 in (20–150 cm)	8–60 in (20–150 cm)	A	W	NA		◆		Sp	Su/A		◆	◆		
Begonia coccinea	48 in (120 cm)	24 in (60 cm)	P	W/T	NA	◆	◆		W/Sp	Sp	◆			◆	◆
Begonia × *erythrophylla*	8–16 in (20–40 cm)	16–24 in (40–60 cm)	P	W/T	NA		◆		Sp/Su	W/Sp	◆			◆	◆
Begonia fuchsioides	36 in (90 cm)	20 in (50 cm)	P	W/T	NA	◆	◆		Sp/Su	W	◆			◆	◆
Begonia grandis	24 in (60 cm)	12–18 in (30–45 cm)	P	W/T	NA	◆			Sp	Su/A	◆	◆	◆	◆	
Begonia masoniana	12 in (30 cm)	12–16 in (30–40 cm)	P	W/T	NA		◆		W/Sp	Sp/Su	◆			◆	◆
Begonia metallica	48 in (120 cm)	20–32 in (50–80 cm)	P	W/T	NA	◆	◆		Sp/Su	Su/A	◆			◆	◆
Begonia, Cane-like Group	2–6 ft (0.6–1.8 m)	20–32 in (50–80 cm)	P	W/T	NA	◆	◆		Sp/Su	Any	◆			◆	◆
Begonia, Rex Cultorum Group	12–24 in (30–60 cm)	16–24 in (40–60 cm)	P	W/T	NA		◆		Sp/Su	Sp/Su	◆			◆	◆
Begonia, Rhizomatous Group	6–8 in (15–20 cm)	12–30 in (30–75 cm)	P	W	NA		◆		Sp/Su	Any	◆			◆	◆
Begonia, Semperflorens Group	12 in (30 cm)	12 in (30 cm)	A/P	W	NA	◆	◆		Sp	Su/A	◆		◆	◆	
Begonia, Shrub-like Group	12–36 in (30–90 cm)	18–48 in (45–120 cm)	P	W/T	NA	◆	◆		Sp/Su	Any	◆			◆	◆
Begonia, Thick-stemmed Group	12–18 in (30–45 cm)	12–18 in (30–45 cm)	P	W/T	NA	◆	◆		Sp/Su	Any	◆			◆	◆
Begonia, Trailing or Scandent Group	6–12 in (15–30 cm)	18–36 in (45–90 cm)	P	W/T	NA			◆	Sp	Su/A	◆			◆	◆
Begonia, Tuberous Group	12–32 in (30–80 cm)	12–20 in (30–50 cm)	P	W	NA	◆			Sp	Su/A	◆	◆		◆	◆
Bellis perennis	2–4 in (5–10 cm)	4–8 in (10–20 cm)	P	C	NA		◆		W/Sp	Sp/Su	◆	◆		◆	
Bergenia cordifolia	16 in (40 cm)	48 in (120 cm)	P	C	NA	◆	◆		A/W	W/Sp		◆		◆	
Bergenia crassifolia	12 in (30 cm)	16–32 in (40–80 cm)	P	C	NA	◆	◆		A/W	Sp		◆		◆	
Bergenia × *schmidtii*	12 in (30 cm)	24–48 in (60–120 cm)	P	C	NA	◆	◆		A/W	W/Sp		◆		◆	

Plant name	Height	Spread	Type	Climate	Group	Showy flowers	Showy foliage	Scented flowers	Planting season	Flowering season	Grow in pot/tub	Frost tolerant	Full Sun	Half Sun	Heavy shade
Bergenia Hybrid Cultivars	8–16 in (20–40 cm)	16–32 in (40–80 cm)	P	C	NA	◆	◆		A/W	Sp		◆	◆	◆	
Bidens ferulifolia	24–36 in (60–90 cm)	12–18 in (30–45 cm)	A/P	W	NA	◆			Sp	Su/A		◆	◆		
Billbergia amoena	24 in (60 cm)	12 in (30 cm)	P	W	B	◆	◆		W/Sp	Sp/Su	◆				◆
Billbergia elegans	12 in (30 cm)	4 in (10 cm)	P	W	B	◆	◆		W/Sp	Sp/Su	◆				◆
Billbergia euphemiae	24 in (60 cm)	8 in (20 cm)	P	W	B	◆	◆		W/Sp	Sp/Su	◆				◆
Billbergia nutans	10 in (25 cm)	6 in (15 cm)	P	W	B	◆	◆		W/Sp	Sp/Su	◆				◆
Billbergia pyramidalis	20 in (50 cm)	6 in (15 cm)	P	W	B	◆	◆		W/Sp	Sp/Su	◆				◆
Billbergia zebrina	40 in (100 cm)	6 in (15 cm)	P	W	B	◆	◆	◆	W/Sp	Sp/Su	◆				◆
Billbergia Hybrid Cultivars	24 in (60 cm)	8 in (20 cm)	P	W	B	◆	◆		W/Sp	Sp/Su	◆				◆
Boltonia asteroides	3–5 ft (0.9–1.5 m)	5 ft (1.5 m)	P	C/W	NA	◆			W/Sp	Su/A		◆	◆	◆	
Boykinia jamesii	2–6 in (5–15 cm)	6–8 in (15–20 cm)	P	C	NA	◆			W/Sp	Su		◆	◆		◆
Brachyscome iberidifolia	2–16 in (5–40 cm)	8–12 in (20–30 cm)	A	W	NA	◆			W/Sp	Sp/Su			◆		
Brachyscome multifida	8–16 in (20–40 cm)	12–40 in (30–100 cm)	P	W	NA	◆			W/Sp	Sp–A			◆		
Brachyscome Hybrid Cultivars	18 in (45 cm)	18 in (45 cm)	P	W	NA	◆			W/Sp	Sp/Su	◆		◆	◆	
Bromelia pinguin	4 ft (1.2 m)	7 ft (2 m)	P	W/T	B	◆			W/Sp	Sp/Su			◆		
Bromelia serra	24 in (60 cm)	7 ft (2 m)	P	W/T	B	◆	◆		W/Sp	Sp/Su			◆		
Brunnera macrophylla	20 in (50 cm)	16–32 in (40–80 cm)	P	C	NA	◆	◆		A/W	Sp		◆		◆	
Calamintha grandiflora	2 ft (0.6 m)	3–4 ft (0.9–1.2 m)	P	C/W	NA	◆			W/Sp	Su		◆	◆	◆	
Calamintha nepeta	32 in (80 cm)	3–5 ft (0.9–1.5 m)	A/P	C/W	NA	◆			W/Sp	Su		◆	◆		
Calathea burle-marxii	5 ft (1.5 m)	3–5 ft (0.9–1.5 m)	P	W/T	NA	◆			W/Sp	Sp/Su	◆				◆
Calathea makoyana	24–32 in (60–80 cm)	16–32 in (40–80 cm)	P	W/T	NA		◆		W/Sp	Sp/Su	◆				◆
Calathea picturata	16–24 in (40–60 cm)	20–27 in (50–70 cm)	P	W/T	NA		◆		W/Sp	Sp/Su	◆				◆
Calathea zebrina	40 in (100 cm)	32–48 in (80–120 cm)	P	W/T	NA	◆	◆		W/Sp	Sp/Su	◆				◆
Calceolaria, Herbeohybrida Group	8–20 in (20–50 cm)	12–16 in (30–40 cm)	A/P	W	NA	◆			Su/A	W/Sp				◆	
Calceolaria integrifolia	4 ft (1.2 m)	8–12 in (20–30 cm)	P	W	NA	◆			W/Sp	Sp–A			◆	◆	
Calendula officinalis	12–24 in (30–60 cm)	12–18 in (30–45 cm)	A	C/W	NA	◆			A/W	Sp–A	◆	◆	◆		
Calibrachoa Hybrid Cultivars	3–8 in (8–20 cm)	12–24 in (30–60 cm)	P	W	NA	◆			Sp	Sp–A	◆	◆	◆		
Callistephus chinensis	12–36 in (30–90 cm)	8–12 in (20–30 cm)	A	W	NA	◆			Sp	Su/A	◆		◆		
Caltha palustris	12–24 in (30–60 cm)	16–24 in (40–60 cm)	P	C	NA	◆	◆		A/W	Sp/Su		◆	◆	◆	
Campanula carpatica	6–12 in (15–30 cm)	12–16 in (30–40 cm)	P	C	NA	◆			W/Sp	Su		◆	◆	◆	
Campanula cochlearifolia	3 in (8 cm)	10 in (25 cm)	P	C	NA	◆			W/Sp	Su		◆	◆	◆	

Plant name	Height	Spread	Type	Climate	Group	Showy flowers	Showy foliage	Scented flowers	Planting season	Flowering season	Grow in pot/tub	Frost tolerant	Full Sun	Half Sun	Heavy shade
Campanula garganica	6 in (15 cm)	6–12 in (15–30 cm)	P	C	NA	◆			W/Sp	Su	◆	◆	◆		
Campanula glomerata	12–36 in (30–90 cm)	12–24 in (30–60 cm)	P	C	NA	◆			W/Sp	Su		◆	◆		
Campanula isophylla	6 in (15 cm)	12–18 in (30–45 cm)	P	C	NA	◆			W/Sp	Su	◆	◆	◆		
Campanula lactiflora	3–5 ft (0.9–1.5 m)	2 ft (0.6 m)	P	C	NA	◆			W/Sp	Su		◆	◆		
Campanula medium	24–36 in (60–90 cm)	12 in (30 cm)	B	W	NA	◆			Sp	Su	◆	◆	◆		
Campanula persicifolia	24–36 in (60–90 cm)	18 in (45 cm)	P	C	NA	◆			W/Sp	Su		◆	◆		
Campanula portenschlagiana	6 in (15 cm)	18–24 in (45–60 cm)	P	C	NA	◆			W/Sp	Su	◆	◆	◆	◆	
Campanula poscharskyana	6–8 in (15–20 cm)	18–24 in (45–60 cm)	P	C	NA	◆			W/Sp	Su/A	◆	◆	◆		
Campanula punctata	12 in (30 cm)	18 in (45 cm)	P	C	NA	◆			W/Sp	Su		◆	◆		
Campanula pyramidalis	4–7 ft (1.2–2 m)	2 ft (0.6 m)	B	W	NA	◆			Sp	Su	◆		◆		
Campanula rapunculoides	36 in (90 cm)	24 in (60 cm)	P	C	NA	◆			W/Sp	Su		◆	◆	◆	
Campanula rotundifolia	6–12 in (15–30 cm)	10–18 in (25–45 cm)	P	C	NA	◆			W/Sp	Su		◆	◆		
Campanula takesimana	24 in (60 cm)	18 in (45 cm)	P	C/W	NA	◆			W/Sp	Su		◆	◆		
Canistrum fosterianum	24 in (60 cm)	8 in (20 cm)	P	W	B	◆	◆		Sp	Su	◆				◆
Canna glauca	4–6 ft (1.2–1.8 m)	1–3 ft (0.3–0.9 m)	P	W/T	NA	◆	◆		W/Sp	Su		◆	◆		
Canna indica	4–7 ft (1.2–2 m)	20–32 in (50–80 cm)	P	W/T	NA	◆	◆		W/Sp	Su/A		◆	◆		
Canna iridiflora	10 ft (3 m)	20–32 in (50–80 cm)	P	W/T	NA	◆	◆		W/Sp	Su/A		◆	◆		
Canna Hybrid Cultivars	2–7 ft (0.6–2 m)	3 ft (0.9 m)	P	W/T	NA	◆	◆		W/Sp	Su/A	◆	◆	◆		
Carthamus tinctorius	24–40 in (60–100 cm)	16–20 in (40–50 cm)	A	C/W	NA	◆			Sp	Su		◆	◆		
Catananche caerulea	24–30 in (60–75 cm)	12–18 in (30–45 cm)	P	C/W	NA	◆			Sp	Su		◆	◆		
Catharanthus roseus	24 in (60 cm)	16 in (40 cm)	P	W/T	NA	◆			Sp	Su/A	◆		◆	◆	
Celmisia sessiliflora	2–6 in (5–15 cm)	6–40 in (15–100 cm)	P	C	NA	◆	◆		W/Sp	Su		◆	◆		
Celmisia spectabilis	8–12 in (20–30 cm)	20–48 in (50–120 cm)	P	C	NA	◆	◆		W/Sp	Su		◆	◆		
Celosia argentea	3–7 ft (0.9–2 m)	16–24 in (40–60 cm)	A	W	NA	◆	◆		Sp/Su	Su/A			◆		◆
Centaurea cineraria	20–36 in (50–90 cm)	12–24 in (30–60 cm)	P	C/W	NA		◆		Sp	Su		◆	◆		
Centaurea cyanus	12–36 in (30–90 cm)	8–16 in (20–40 cm)	A/B/P	C/W	NA	◆			W/Sp	Sp/Su		◆	◆		
Centaurea dealbata	32–40 in (80–100 cm)	16–24 in (40–60 cm)	P	C	NA	◆	◆		Sp	Su		◆	◆		
Centaurea macrocephala	32–40 in (80–100 cm)	20–24 in (50–60 cm)	P	C	NA	◆	◆		Sp	Su		◆	◆		
Centaurea montana	24–32 in (60–80 cm)	12–40 in (30–100 cm)	P	C	NA	◆			W/Sp	Sp/Su		◆	◆		
Centranthus ruber	32–40 in (80–100 cm)	16–27 in (40–70 cm)	P	C/W	NA	◆		◆	W/Sp	Sp/Su		◆	◆	◆	
Cephalotus follicularis	15 in (38 cm)	8 in (20 cm)	P	W	C	◆			A/W	Sp	◆			◆	

Plant name	Height	Spread	Type	Climate	Group	Showy flowers	Showy foliage	Scented flowers	Planting season	Flowering season	Grow in pot/tub	Frost tolerant	Full Sun	Half Sun	Heavy shade
Cerastium boissieri	6–10 in (15–25 cm)	8–16 in (20–40 cm)	P	C/W	NA	♦	♦		W/Sp	Sp/Su	♦	♦	♦		
Cerastium tomentosum	4–6 in (10–15 cm)	40 in (100 cm)	P	C/W	NA	♦	♦		W/Sp	Sp/Su	♦	♦	♦		
Chelidonium majus	12–36 in (30–90 cm)	12–36 in (30–90 cm)	B/P	C	NA	♦			W/Sp	Su		♦		♦	♦
Chelone glabra	20–32 in (50–80 cm)	16–20 in (40–50 cm)	P	C	NA	♦			W/Sp	Su/A	♦	♦	♦	♦	
Chelone lyonii	40–48 in (100–120 cm)	24–36 in (60–90 cm)	P	C	NA	♦			W/Sp	Su/A	♦	♦	♦	♦	
Chlorophytum comosum	12–24 in (30–60 cm)	12–24 in (30–60 cm)	P	W	NA		♦		Sp	Su	♦			♦	
Chlorophytum laxum	8–12 in (20–30 cm)	8–12 in (20–30 cm)	P	W/T	NA		♦		Sp	Su	♦			♦	
Chrysanthemum × grandiflorum	1–5 ft (0.3–1.5 m)	18–36 in (45–90 cm)	P	C/W	NA	♦			W/Sp	A	♦	♦	♦	♦	
Chrysanthemum weyrichii	4 in (10 cm)	16–24 in (40–60 cm)	P	C/W	NA	♦			W/Sp	Su/A	♦	♦	♦	♦	
Chrysogonum virginianum	6–10 in (15–25 cm)	24 in (60 cm)	P	C	NA	♦			A/W	Sp/Su	♦			♦	♦
Clarkia amoena	24 in (60 cm)	12 in (30 cm)	A	C/W	NA	♦			Sp	Sp/Su	♦	♦	♦		
Clarkia pulchella	12–18 in (30–45 cm)	12 in (30 cm)	A	C/W	NA	♦			Sp	Sp/Su	♦	♦	♦		
Clarkia unguiculata	24–30 in (60–75 cm)	12 in (30 cm)	A	C/W	NA	♦			Sp	Sp/Su	♦	♦	♦		
Clematis integrifolia	3 ft (0.9 m)	3–5 ft (0.9–1.5 m)	P	C	NA	♦			W/Sp	Sp–A	♦	♦	♦	♦	
Clematis recta	3–5 ft (0.9–1.5 m)	3–4 ft (0.9–1.2 m)	P	C	NA	♦			W/Sp	Su	♦	♦	♦	♦	
Cleome sesquiorygalis	5 ft (1.5 m)	20 in (50 cm)	A	W/T	NA	♦			Sp	Su/A	♦		♦	♦	
Clivia caulescens	24 in (60 cm)	3–7 ft (0.9–2 m)	P	W	NA	♦			W	Sp	♦			♦	
Clivia miniata	16–24 in (40–60 cm)	24–40 in (60–100 cm)	P	W	NA	♦			W	Sp	♦			♦	
Clivia nobilis	16–24 in (40–60 cm)	20–36 in (50–90 cm)	P	W	NA	♦			W	Sp	♦			♦	
Codonopsis clematidea	32 in (80 cm)	20–60 in (50–150 cm)	P	C	NA	♦			W/Sp	Su/A		♦	♦		
Collinsia bicolor	12–24 in (30–60 cm)	6–12 in (15–30 cm)	A	C/W	NA	♦			Sp	Sp/Su	♦	♦	♦		
Columnea 'Early Bird'	48 in (120 cm)	18 in (45 cm)	P	W/T	G	♦	♦		Any	Sp–A	♦			♦	
Columnea gloriosa	12 in (30 cm)	18 in (45 cm)	P	W/T	G	♦	♦		Any	Sp/Su	♦			♦	♦
Columnea microphylla	6 ft (1.8 m)	2 ft (0.6 m)	P	W/T	G	♦	♦		Any	Sp/Su	♦			♦	♦
Columnea scandens	12 in (30 cm)	24 in (60 cm)	P	W/T	G	♦	♦		Any	Sp/Su	♦			♦	♦
Commelina tuberosa	12–36 in (30–90 cm)	18–30 in (45–75 cm)	P	W/T	NA	♦			W	Sp–A			♦	♦	
Consolida ajacis	32–40 in (80–100 cm)	6–12 in (15–30 cm)	A	W	NA	♦			Sp	Su			♦	♦	
Convolvulus cneorum	2 ft (0.6 m)	2 ft (0.6 m)	P	W	NA	♦	♦		W/Sp	Sp/Su	♦		♦		
Convolvulus sabatius	8–12 in (20–30 cm)	24–60 in (60–150 cm)	P	W	NA	♦			W/Sp	Sp/Su	♦	♦	♦		
Convolvulus tricolor	20–40 in (50–100 cm)	12–32 in (30–80 cm)	A/P	W	NA	♦	♦		Sp	Sp/Su	♦		♦	♦	
Coreopsis grandiflora	24 in (60 cm)	12–20 in (30–50 cm)	P	C/W	NA	♦			Sp	Sp/Su	♦	♦	♦	♦	

Plant name	Height	Spread	Type	Climate	Group	Showy flowers	Showy foliage	Scented flowers	Planting season	Flowering season	Grow in pot/tub	Frost tolerant	Full Sun	Half Sun	Heavy shade
Coreopsis lanceolata	24 in (60 cm)	12–16 in (30–40 cm)	P	C	NA	◆			W/Sp	Su	◆	◆	◆	◆	
Coreopsis 'Sunray'	20 in (50cm)	12–16 in (30–40 cm)	P	C/W	NA	◆			Sp	Sp/Su	◆	◆	◆	◆	
Coreopsis tinctoria	4 ft (1.2 m)	16–24 in (40–60 cm)	A	C/W	NA	◆			Sp	Su		◆	◆	◆	
Coreopsis verticillata	36 in (90 cm)	16 in (40 cm)	P	C/W	NA	◆			Sp	Su	◆	◆	◆	◆	
Cornus canadensis	4–6 in (10–15 cm)	36 in (90 cm)	P	C	NA	◆	◆		W	Su		◆		◆	
Corydalis cashmeriana	10 in (25 cm)	12–32 in (30–80 cm)	P	C/W	NA	◆			W/Sp	Sp/Su		◆		◆	
Corydalis flexuosa	12 in (30 cm)	12–32 in (30–80 cm)	P	C/W	NA	◆		◆	W/Sp	Sp/Su		◆		◆	
Corydalis ochroleuca	8–16 in (20–40 cm)	12–32 in (30–80 cm)	P	C/W	NA	◆			W/Sp	Sp/Su		◆		◆	
Corydalis wilsonii	12–16 in (30–40 cm)	12–32 in (30–80 cm)	P	C/W	NA	◆			A/W	Sp		◆		◆	
Cosmos bipinnatus	4–7 ft (1.2–2 m)	2–4 ft (0.6–1.2 m)	A	C/W	NA	◆			Sp	Su			◆	◆	
Cosmos sulphureus	5–7 ft (1.5–2 m)	32–48 in (80–120cm)	A	C/W	NA	◆			Sp	Su		◆	◆	◆	
Costus igneus	20 in (50 cm)	20–40 in (50–100 cm)	P	W/T	NA	◆			A	W	◆			◆	
Costus pulverulentus	5–10 ft (1.5–3 m)	2–5 ft (0.6–1.5 m)	P	W/T	NA	◆			W	Sp–A	◆			◆	
Cryptanthus acaulis	2 in (5 cm)	6 in (15 cm)	P	W	B		◆		Any	Sp/Su					◆
Cryptanthus bivittatus	2 in (5 cm)	10 in (25 cm)	P	W/T	B		◆		Any	Sp/Su	◆				◆
Cryptanthus fosterianus	2 in (5 cm)	16 in (40 cm)	P	W/T	B		◆		Any	Sp/Su					◆
Cryptanthus 'Rainbow Star'	16 in (40 cm)	16 in (40 cm)	P	W/T	B		◆		Any	Sp/Su	◆				◆
Cryptanthus zonatus	2 in (5 cm)	12 in (30 cm)	P	W/T	B		◆		Any	Sp/Su					◆
Ctenanthe burle-marxii	18 in (45 cm)	12–18 in (30–45 cm)	P	W/T	NA		◆		Any	Sp/Su	◆				◆
Ctenanthe lubbersiana	18–24 in (45–60 cm)	18–24 in (45–60 cm)	P	W/T	NA		◆		Any	Sp/Su	◆				◆
Ctenanthe oppenheimiana	36 in (90 cm)	24–36 in (60–90 cm)	P	W/T	NA		◆		Any	Sp/Su	◆				◆
Cynoglossum amabile	20–24 in (50–60 cm)	12 in (30 cm)	B	C/W	NA	◆			W/Sp	Sp/Su		◆	◆	◆	
Cynoglossum nervosum	24–30 in (60–75 cm)	24 in (60 cm)	P	C	NA	◆			W/Sp	Sp/Su		◆	◆	◆	
Dampiera diversifolia	4–20 in (10–50 cm)	40–60 in (100–150 cm)	P	W	NA	◆			W	Sp/Su			◆	◆	
Darlingtonia californica	24–40 in (60–100 cm)	8–10 in (20–25 cm)	P	C	C	◆	◆		A/W	Sp/Su	◆	◆	◆	◆	
Darmera peltata	5–7 ft (1.5–2 m)	3–10 ft (0.9–3 m)	P	C/W	NA	◆	◆		W	Sp		◆			◆
Delphinium × belladonna	12–40 in (30–100 cm)	6–20 in (15–50 cm)	P	C	NA	◆			W	Sp/Su		◆	◆	◆	
Delphinium cardinale	3–7 ft (0.9–2 m)	8–20 in (20–50 cm)	P	C/W	NA	◆			W	Su		◆	◆	◆	
Delphinium elatum	2–6 ft (0.6–1.8 m)	8–20 in (20–50 cm)	P	C	NA	◆			W	Su		◆	◆	◆	
Delphinium grandiflorum	12–40 in (30–100 cm)	12–24 in (30–60 cm)	P	C	NA	◆			W	Su		◆	◆	◆	
Delphinium nudicaule	12–24 in (30–60 cm)	8–16 in (20–40 cm)	P	C/W	NA	◆			W	Sp/Su		◆	◆	◆	

Plant name	Height	Spread	Type	Climate	Group	Showy flowers	Showy foliage	Scented flowers	Planting season	Flowering season	Grow in pot/tub	Frost tolerant	Full Sun	Half Sun	Heavy shade
Delphinium Hybrid Cultivars	4–7 ft (1.2–2 m)	1½–3 ft (0.5–0.9 m)	P	C/W	NA	◆			W	Sp/Su		◆	◆		
Derwentia perfoliata	12–26 in (30–65 cm)	20–60 in (50–150 cm)	P	C	NA	◆	◆		W/Sp	Sp/Su		◆	◆		
Deuterocohnia brevifolia	2–4 in (5–10 cm)	4–12 in (10–30 cm)	P	C/W	B	◆	◆	◆	W	Sp	◆	◆	◆	◆	
Deuterocohnia lorentziana	4 in (10 cm)	4 in (10 cm)	P	C/W	B	◆	◆	◆	W	Sp	◆				◆
Dianella tasmanica	40 in (100 cm)	12 in (30 cm)	P	W/T	NA	◆			A/W	Sp/Su		◆		◆	
Dianthus alpinus	4–6 in (10–15 cm)	6–12 in (15–30 cm)	P	C	NA	◆		◆		Sp/Su	◆	◆	◆		
Dianthus barbatus	12–24 in (30–60 cm)	6–12 in (15–30 cm)	A/P	C	NA	◆			W/Sp	Sp/Su	◆	◆	◆	◆	
Dianthus caryophyllus	20–32 in (50–80 cm)	8–16 in (20–40 cm)	P	C	NA	◆		◆	W	Sp/Su	◆	◆	◆	◆	
Dianthus deltoides	8–16 in (20–40 cm)	6–12 in (15–30 cm)	P	C	NA	◆				Sp/Su		◆	◆	◆	
Dianthus gratianopolitanus	6–8 in (15–20 cm)	8–16 in (20–40 cm)	P	C	NA	◆				Sp/Su		◆	◆	◆	
Dianthus plumarius	6–14 in (15–35 cm)	8–16 in (20–40 cm)	P	C	NA	◆				Sp/Su		◆	◆	◆	
Dianthus superbus	20–30 in (50–75 cm)	12–20 in (30–50 cm)	P	C	NA	◆				Sp/Su		◆	◆	◆	
Dianthus Hybrid Cultivars	8–15 in (20–38 cm)	6–12 in (15–30 cm)	A/P	C	NA	◆				Sp/Su		◆	◆	◆	
Diascia barberae	12 in (30 cm)	12–16 in (30–40 cm)	P	W	NA				W/Sp	Su	◆	◆	◆		
Diascia rigescens	16–20 in (40–50 cm)	24 in (60 cm)	P	W	NA				W/Sp	Su	◆	◆	◆	◆	
Diascia vigilis	20 in (50 cm)	48 in (120 cm)	P	W	NA				W/Sp	Su/A	◆	◆	◆		
Diascia Hybrid Cultivars	8–18 in (20–45 cm)	12–24 in (30–60 cm)	P	W	NA				W/Sp	Su	◆	◆	◆		
Dicentra cucullaria	12–16 in (30–40 cm)	20–40 in (50–100 cm)	P	C	NA	◆	◆		A/W	Sp		◆	◆	◆	
Dicentra eximia	12–26 in (30–65 cm)	20–40 in (50–100 cm)	P	C	NA	◆	◆		A/W	Sp		◆	◆	◆	
Dicentra formosa	12–26 in (30–65 cm)	20–40 in (50–100 cm)	P	C	NA	◆	◆		A/W	Sp		◆	◆	◆	
Dicentra spectabilis	40–56 in (100–140 cm)	20–40 in (50–100 cm)	P	C	NA	◆	◆		A/W	Sp		◆	◆	◆	
Dichorisandra thyrsiflora	3–10 ft (0.9–3 m)	3 ft (0.9 m)	P	W/T	NA	◆	◆		A/W	Su/A	◆				
Dicliptera suberecta	18–24 in (45–60 cm)	18–24 in (45–60 cm)	P	C/W	NA	◆			W	Su/A	◆	◆	◆		
Dieffenbachia seguine	3–6 ft (0.9–1.8)	18–24 in (45–60 cm)	P	W/T	NA		◆		Any	Sp/Su	◆			◆	
Dietes bicolor	32–36 in (80–90 cm)	24–36 in (60–90 cm)	P	W	NA	◆			W	Sp/Su			◆	◆	◆
Dietes grandiflora	20–27 in (50–70 cm)	20–27 in (50–70 cm)	P	W	NA	◆			W	Su					◆
Digitalis grandiflora	40 in (100 cm)	20–24 in (50–60 cm)	B/P	C	NA	◆			A/W	Sp/Su		◆		◆	
Digitalis lutea	24–40 in (60–100 cm)	16–24 in (40–60 cm)	P	C	NA	◆			A/W	Sp/Su		◆		◆	
Digitalis mertonensis	20–30 in (50–75 cm)	16–20 in (40–50 cm)	P	C	NA	◆			A/W	Sp/Su		◆		◆	
Digitalis purpurea	5–6 ft (1.5–1.8 m)	12–32 in (30–80 cm)	B	C	NA	◆			A/W	Su		◆	◆	◆	
Dimorphotheca sinuata	12–18 in (30–45 cm)	12 in (30 cm)	A	W	NA	◆			Sp	Sp/Su	◆		◆		

Plant name	Height	Spread	Type	Climate	Group	Showy flowers	Showy foliage	Scented flowers	Planting season	Flowering season	Grow in pot/tub	Frost tolerant	Full Sun	Half Sun	Heavy shade
Dionaea muscipula	4 in (10 cm)	8 in (20 cm)	P	C/W	C		◆		W	Sp	◆	◆	◆	◆	
Dodecatheon dentatum	4–16 in (10–40 cm)	6–12 in (15–30 cm)	P	C	NA	◆			A/W	Sp/Su	◆	◆	◆	◆	
Dodecatheon hendersonii	8–15 in (20–38 cm)	6–12 in (15–30 cm)	P	C	NA	◆			A/W	Sp/Su	◆	◆	◆	◆	
Dodecatheon meadia	8–18 in (20–45 cm)	12 in (30 cm)	P	C	NA	◆			A/W	Sp	◆	◆	◆	◆	
Dorotheanthus bellidiformis	2–6 in (5–15 cm)	8–16 in (20–40 cm)	A	W	NA	◆			Sp	Su			◆		
Doryanthes excelsa	8–20 ft (2.4–6 m)	10 ft (3 m)	P	W	NA	◆	◆		W	Sp/Su			◆		
Doryanthes palmeri	3–10 ft (0.9–3 m)	3–10 ft (0.9–3 m)	P	W/T	NA	◆	◆		W	Sp			◆		
Drosera binata	12 in (30 cm)	8 in (20 cm)	P	W	C		◆		W	Sp	◆	◆	◆		
Drosera capensis	6 in (15 cm)	6 in (15 cm)	P	W	C	◆			W	Sp	◆	◆	◆		
Drosera pulchella	½ in (12 mm)	1¼ in (30 mm)	P	W	C		◆		W	Sp	◆	◆	◆		
Drosera rotundifolia	2 in (5 cm)	4 in (10 cm)	P	W	C	◆			W	Sp	◆	◆	◆		
Drosera zonaria	1 in (2.5 cm)	3 in (8 cm)	P	W	C		◆		W	Sp	◆	◆	◆		
Drosophyllum lusitanicum	12 in (30 cm)	16 in (40 cm)	P	W	C	◆	◆		A/W	Sp			◆		
Dryas octopetala	3–4 in (8–10 cm)	40 in (100 cm)	P	C	NA	◆			A/W	Su			◆	◆	
Dyckia remotiflora	40 in (100 cm)	16 in (40 cm)	P	W	B	◆	◆	◆	A/W	Sp/Su	◆				◆
Echinops bannaticus	4 ft (1.2 m)	2 ft (0.6 m)	P	C	NA	◆			W	Su/A		◆	◆	◆	
Echinops ritro	12–24 in (30–60 cm)	16–24 in (40–60 cm)	P	C	NA	◆			W	Su/A		◆	◆	◆	
Echinops sphaerocephalus	3–7 ft (0.9–2 m)	16–32 in (40–80 cm)	P	C	NA	◆			W	Su/A		◆	◆	◆	
Echium candicans	6 ft (1.8 m)	6 ft (1.8 m)	P	W	NA	◆			Any	Sp/Su			◆		
Echium vulgare	18–24 in (45–60 cm)	18–24 in (45–60 cm)	A/B	C/W	NA	◆			Sp	Su		◆	◆		
Edmondia pinifolia	12 in (30 cm)	12 in (30 cm)	P	W	NA	◆			W/Sp	Sp	◆	◆	◆		
Eichhornia crassipes	12 in (30 cm)	18 in (45 cm)	P	W/T	NA	◆			W/Sp	Sp			◆		
Elodea canadensis	36 in (90 cm)	indefinite	P	C/W	NA		◆		Any	Su		◆	◆		
Emilia sonchifolia	6–20 in (15–50 cm)	6–10 in (15–25 cm)	A	W	NA	◆			Sp	Su	◆		◆		
Ensete ventricosum	30 ft (9 m)	15 ft (4.5 m)	P	W/T	NA	◆	◆		W/Sp	Su	◆		◆		
Epilobium angustifolium	3–8 ft (0.9–2.4 m)	3–8 ft (0.9–2.4 m)	P	C	NA	◆			Sp	Su/A			◆	◆	
Epilobium canum	1–3 ft (0.3–0.9 m)	3–7 ft (0.9–2 m)	P	W	NA	◆	◆		W/Sp	Su/A			◆	◆	
Epilobium septentrionale	6–12 in (15–30 cm)	24–36 in (60–90 cm)	P	W	NA	◆	◆		W/Sp	Su/A			◆	◆	
Epimedium × cantabrigiense	12–24 in (30–60 cm)	12–18 in (30–45 cm)	P	C	NA	◆	◆		W	Sp		◆		◆	
Epimedium grandiflorum	8–12 in (20–30 cm)	8–12 in (20–30 cm)	P	C	NA	◆	◆		W	Sp		◆			◆
Epimedium × perralchicum	14–16 in (35–40 cm)	20–24 in (50–60 cm)	P	C	NA	◆	◆		W	Sp		◆		◆	

Plant name	Height	Spread	Type	Climate	Group	Showy flowers	Showy foliage	Scented flowers	Planting season	Flowering season	Grow in pot/tub	Frost tolerant	Full Sun	Half Sun	Heavy shade
Epimedium perralderianum	14–16 in (35–40 cm)	20–24 in (50–60 cm)	P	C	NA	◆	◆		W	Sp		◆			◆
Epimedium × versicolor	10–12 in (25–30 cm)	10–12 in (25–30 cm)	P	C	NA	◆	◆		W	Sp		◆			◆
Episcia cupreata	8–12 in (20–30 cm)	12–24 in (30–60 cm)	P	W/T	G	◆	◆		W/Sp	Su	◆			◆	◆
Episcia dianthiflora	8 in (20 cm)	18–36 in (45–90 cm)	P	W/T	G	◆			W/Sp	Su	◆			◆	◆
Episcia Hybrid Cultivars	8–20 in (20–50 cm)	32–40 in (80–100 cm)	P	W/T	G	◆			W/Sp	Sp–A	◆			◆	◆
Eranthis hyemalis	3–4 in (8–10 cm)	3–4 in (8–10 cm)	P	C	NA	◆			Su/A	W/Sp		◆		◆	
Erigeron glaucus	6–12 in (15–30 cm)	12–24 in (30–60 cm)	P	C/W	NA	◆			W/Sp	Sp/Su		◆	◆		
Erigeron karvinskianus	1–2 ft (0.3–0.6 m)	2–5 ft (0.6–1.5 m)	P	W	NA	◆			W/Sp	Sp–A	◆	◆	◆		
Erigeron pulchellus	6–16 in (15–40 cm)	8–16 in (20–40 cm)	B/P	C	NA	◆			W/Sp	Su		◆	◆		
Erigeron 'Rosa Jewel'	18–30 in (45–75 cm)	16–24 in (40–60 cm)	P	C	NA	◆			W/Sp	Su		◆	◆		
Erigeron speciosus	18–30 in (45–75 cm)	16–24 in (40–60 cm)	P	C	NA	◆			W/Sp	Su		◆	◆		
Eriogonum arborescens	5 ft (1.5 m)	5 ft (1.5 m)	P	W	NA	◆			W/Sp	Su/A			◆	◆	
Eriogonum giganteum	8 ft (2.4 m)	10 ft (3 m)	P	W	NA	◆	◆		W/Sp	Su/A			◆	◆	
Eriogonum umbellatum	6–18 in (15–45 cm)	3–4 ft (0.9–1.2 m)	P	C/W	NA	◆			W/Sp	Su			◆	◆	
Erodium chrysanthum	4–6 in (10–15 cm)	12–16 in (30–40 cm)	P	C/W	NA	◆			W/Sp	Su		◆	◆		
Erodium corsicum	8 in (20 cm)	12 in (30 cm)	P	C/W	NA	◆			W/Sp	Sp/Su		◆	◆		
Erodium reichardii	1–2 in (2.5–5 cm)	10 in (25 cm)	P	C/W	NA	◆			W/Sp	Su		◆	◆		
Erodium × variabile	6–12 in (15–30 cm)	10 in (25 cm)	P	C/W	NA	◆			W/Sp	Su		◆	◆		
Eryngium alpinum	24 in (60 cm)	24 in (60 cm)	P	C	NA	◆			W/Sp	Su		◆	◆	◆	
Eryngium amethystinum	28 in (70 cm)	20 in (50 cm)	P	C/W	NA	◆			W/Sp	Su		◆	◆	◆	
Eryngium bourgatii	16 in (40 cm)	16 in (40 cm)	P	C/W	NA	◆			W/Sp	Su		◆	◆	◆	
Eryngium giganteum	5 ft (1.5 m)	32 in (80 cm)	P	C	NA	◆			W/Sp	Su		◆	◆	◆	
Eryngium × oliverianum	24–40 in (60–100 cm)	20–24 in (50–60 cm)	P	C	NA	◆			W/Sp	Su		◆	◆	◆	
Eryngium variifolium	20–30 in (50–75 cm)	16–20 in (40–50 cm)	P	C/W	NA	◆			W/Sp	Su		◆	◆	◆	
Erysimum bicolor	36 in (90 cm)	24 in (60 cm)	P	W	NA	◆		◆	W	Sp–A			◆	◆	
Erysimum cheiri	24 in (60 cm)	16 in (40 cm)	B/P	C/W	NA	◆		◆	W/Sp	Sp–A			◆	◆	
Erysimum Hybrid Cultivars	24–36 in (60–90 cm)	24 in (60 cm)	P	C/W	NA	◆			W	Sp–A			◆	◆	
Eschscholzia caespitosa	10 in (25 cm)	10 in (25 cm)	A	W	NA	◆			Sp	Sp–A	◆	◆	◆		
Eschscholzia californica	8–24 in (20–60 cm)	8–16 in (20–40 cm)	A/P	C/W	NA	◆			W/Sp	Sp–A	◆	◆	◆		
Etlingera elatior	10–20 ft (3–6 m)	5–8 ft (1.5–2.4 m)	P	W/T	NA	◆			Sp	Su/A			◆	◆	
Eupatorium perfoliatum	3–5 ft (0.9–1.5 m)	3–5 ft (0.9–1.5 m)	P	C	NA	◆	◆		W/Sp	Su/A		◆	◆		

Plant name	Height	Spread	Type	Climate	Group	Showy flowers	Showy foliage	Scented flowers	Planting season	Flowering season	Grow in pot/tub	Frost tolerant	Full Sun	Half Sun	Heavy shade
Eupatorium purpureum	6–10 ft (1.8–3 m)	6–10 ft (1.8–3 m)	P	C	NA	♦	♦	♦	W/Sp	Su/A		♦	♦	♦	
Eupatorium rugosum	3–6 ft (0.9–1.8 m)	3–6 ft (0.9–1.8 m)	P	C	NA	♦	♦		W/Sp	Su/A		♦		♦	
Euphorbia amygdaloides	20–32 in (50–80 cm)	24–40 in (60–100 cm)	P	C/W	NA	♦	♦		W/Sp	Sp/Su		♦	♦	♦	
Euphorbia characias	6 ft (1.8 m)	5 ft (1.5 m)	P	W	NA	♦	♦		A/W	W–Su		♦	♦		
Euphorbia cyparissias	16 in (40 cm)	24 in (60 cm)	P	C/W	NA	♦	♦		W/Sp	Sp/Su		♦	♦		
Euphorbia griffithii	36 in (90 cm)	36 in (90 cm)	P	C/W	NA	♦	♦		W/Sp	Su		♦		♦	
Euphorbia marginata	40 in (100 cm)	20 in (50 cm)	A	C/W	NA		♦		Sp	Su		♦	♦	♦	
Euphorbia myrsinites	10 in (25 cm)	20 in (50 cm)	P	C/W	NA	♦	♦		A/W	Sp		♦	♦		
Euphorbia nicaeensis	24 in (60 cm)	24 in (60 cm)	P	C/W	NA	♦			W/Sp	Sp/Su		♦	♦		
Euphorbia polychroma	24 in (60 cm)	24 in (60 cm)	P	C/W	NA	♦	♦		W/Sp	Sp/Su		♦	♦		
Euphorbia schillingii	4 ft (1.2 m)	5 ft (1.5 m)	P	C/W	NA	♦			W/Sp	Su		♦		♦	
Euphorbia seguieriana	20 in (50 cm)	32 in (80 cm)	P	C	NA	♦			W/Sp	Su		♦	♦		
Euphorbia sikkimensis	36 in (90 cm)	36 in (90 cm)	P	C/W	NA	♦	♦		W/Sp	Su		♦		♦	
Euryale ferox	3 ft (0.9 m)	5 ft (1.5 m)	A/P	W	NA	♦	♦		Sp	Su			♦	♦	
Eustoma grandiflorum	24–32 in (60–80 cm)	20 in (50 cm)	A/P	W	NA	♦			Sp	Su	♦	♦	♦	♦	
Evolvulus glomeratus	10–18 in (25–45 cm)	24–36 in (60–90 cm)	P	W/T	NA	♦			Sp	Sp–A	♦		♦		
Exacum affine	12–18 in (30–45 cm)	12 in (30 cm)	A/P	W/T	NA	♦		♦	Sp	Sp–A	♦		♦		
Farfugium japonicum	24–40 in (60–100 cm)	24–40 in (60–100 cm)	P	W	NA		♦		W/Sp	W		♦		♦	
Felicia amelloides	16–24 in (40–60 cm)	24 in (60 cm)	P	W	NA	♦			W/Sp	Su	♦		♦		
Felicia fruticosa	36 in (90 cm)	36 in (90 cm)	P	W	NA	♦			W/Sp	Sp/Su			♦		
Filipendula purpurea	36–48 in (90–120 cm)	18 in (45 cm)	P	C	NA	♦	♦		A/W	Su		♦		♦	
Filipendula rubra	3–7 ft (0.9–2 m)	2 ft (0.6 m)	P	C	NA	♦	♦		A/W	Su		♦		♦	
Filipendula ulmaria	24–48 in (60–120 cm)	12–18 in (30–45 cm)	P	C	NA	♦	♦	♦	A/W	Su		♦		♦	
Filipendula vulgaris	24–36 in (60–90 cm)	18 in (45 cm)	P	C	NA	♦			A/W	Su		♦		♦	
Fittonia albivenis	6 in (15 cm)	12–24 in (30–60 cm)	P	W/T	NA		♦		Any	Any	♦				♦
Gaillardia aristata	20 in (50 cm)	32 in (80 cm)	P	C/W	NA	♦			W/Sp	Su/A		♦	♦		
Gaillardia × grandiflora	24 in (60 cm)	40 in (100 cm)	P	C/W	NA	♦			W/Sp	Su/A		♦	♦		
Gaillardia pulchella	24 in (60 cm)	16 in (40 cm)	A	W	NA	♦			Sp	Su/A			♦		
Galium odoratum	18 in (45 cm)	36 in (90 cm)	P	C	NA	♦		♦	W/Sp	Sp/Su				♦	
Galium verum	3–4 ft (0.9–1.2 m)	3 ft (0.9 m)	P	C	NA	♦			W/Sp	Su/A				♦	
Gaura lindheimeri	48–60 in (120–150 cm)	40 in (100 cm)	P	C/W	NA	♦			A/Sp	Sp/Su		♦	♦	♦	

Plant name	Height	Spread	Type	Climate	Group	Showy flowers	Showy foliage	Scented flowers	Planting season	Flowering season	Grow in pot/tub	Frost tolerant	Full Sun	Half Sun	Heavy shade
Gazania rigens	8 in (20 cm)	40 in (100 cm)	P	W	NA	◆			W/Sp	Sp–A	◆		◆		
Gazania Hybrid Cultivars	4–6 in (10–15 cm)	20 in (50 cm)	P	W	NA	◆			W/Sp	Sp–A	◆		◆		
Genlisea violacea	1 in (2.5 cm)	2 in (5 cm)	P	W/T	C			◆	W/Sp	Sp/Su	◆				◆
Gentiana acaulis	4 in (10 cm)	12 in (30 cm)	P	C	NA	◆			W/Sp	Sp/Su	◆	◆		◆	
Gentiana asclepiadea	16 in (40 cm)	24–40 in (60–100 cm)	P	C	NA	◆			W/Sp	Su/A	◆	◆		◆	
Gentiana saxosa	8 in (20 cm)	12 in (30 cm)	P	C/W	NA	◆			W/Sp	Su	◆	◆	◆		
Gentiana septemfida	12 in (30 cm)	16 in (40 cm)	P	C	NA	◆			W/Sp	Su/A	◆	◆	◆		
Gentiana sino-ornata	6 in (15 cm)	12 in (30 cm)	P	C	NA	◆			W/Sp	A	◆	◆	◆		
Gentiana verna	2 in (5 cm)	8–12 in (20–30 cm)	P	C	NA	◆			W/Sp	Sp/Su	◆	◆		◆	
Geranium × *cantabrigiense*	8 in (20 cm)	24 in (60 cm)	P	C/W	NA	◆			W/Sp	Su	◆	◆	◆	◆	
Geranium cinereum	6 in (15 cm)	20 in (50 cm)	P	C/W	NA	◆			W/Sp	Su		◆	◆	◆	
Geranium dalmaticum	6 in (15 cm)	20 in (50 cm)	P	C/W	NA	◆			W/Sp	Su		◆	◆	◆	
Geranium endressii	18 in (45 cm)	24 in (60 cm)	P	C/W	NA	◆			W/Sp	Sp/Su		◆	◆	◆	
Geranium himalayense	18 in (45 cm)	40 in (100 cm)	P	C/W	NA	◆			W/Sp	Su		◆	◆	◆	
Geranium incanum	40 in (100 cm)	40 in (100 cm)	P	C/W	NA	◆			W/Sp	Su		◆	◆		
Geranium macrorrhizum	20 in (50 cm)	40 in (100 cm)	P	C/W	NA	◆			W/Sp	Su		◆	◆	◆	
Geranium maculatum	27 in (70 cm)	40 in (100 cm)	P	C/W	NA	◆			W/Sp	Sp/Su		◆	◆	◆	
Geranium maderense	60 in (150 cm)	60 in (150 cm)	P	C/W	NA	◆	◆		W/Sp	Sp/Su		◆	◆		
Geranium × *magnificum*	20 in (50 cm)	40 in (100 cm)	P	C/W	NA	◆			W/Sp	Su		◆	◆	◆	
Geranium × *oxonianum*	24 in (60 cm)	48 in (120 cm)	P	C/W	NA	◆			W/Sp	Su		◆	◆	◆	
Geranium phaeum	32 in (80 cm)	16 in (40 cm)	P	C/W	NA	◆			W/Sp	Su		◆	◆	◆	
Geranium pratense	48 in (120 cm)	40 in (100 cm)	P	C/W	NA	◆			W/Sp	Su		◆	◆		
Geranium psilostemon	24–40 in (60–100 cm)	16–24 in (40–60 cm)	P	C/W	NA	◆			W/Sp	Su		◆	◆	◆	
Geranium × *riversleaianum*	4 in (10 cm)	24 in (60 cm)	P	C/W	NA	◆			W/Sp	Su		◆	◆	◆	
Geranium sanguineum	8 in (20 cm)	16 in (40 cm)	P	C/W	NA	◆			W/Sp	Su		◆	◆	◆	
Geranium sylvaticum	27 in (70 cm)	40 in (100 cm)	P	C/W	NA	◆			W/Sp	Su			◆	◆	
Geranium wallichianum	6 in (15 cm)	24 in (60 cm)	P	C/W	NA	◆			W/Sp	Su		◆	◆	◆	
Geranium Hybrid Cultivars	8–36 in (20–90 cm)	24–48 in (60–120 cm)	P	C/W	NA	◆			W/Sp	Su		◆	◆	◆	
Gerbera jamesonii	27 in (70 cm)	30 in (75 cm)	P	W	NA	◆			Sp	A–Sp	◆	◆	◆		
Gerbera Hybrid Cultivars	8–18 in (20–45 cm)	12 in (30 cm)	P	W	NA	◆			Sp	A–Sp	◆			◆	
Geum chiloense	30 in (75 cm)	20 in (50 cm)	P	C/W	NA	◆			W/Sp	Su		◆	◆	◆	

Plant name	Height	Spread	Type	Climate	Group	Showy flowers	Showy foliage	Scented flowers	Planting season	Flowering season	Grow in pot/tub	Frost tolerant	Full Sun	Half Sun	Heavy shade
Geum montanum	12 in (30 cm)	20 in (50 cm)	P	C	NA	◆			W/Sp	Sp/Su	◆	◆	◆	◆	
Geum rivale	12 in (30 cm)	30 in (75 cm)	P	C/W	NA	◆			W/Sp	Sp/Su		◆	◆	◆	
Geum triflorum	16 in (40 cm)	16 in (40 cm)	P	C/W	NA	◆			W/Sp	Sp/Su			◆	◆	
Geum Hybrid Cultivars	36 in (90 cm)	36 in (90 cm)	P	C/W	NA	◆			W/Sp	Sp/Su	◆	◆	◆	◆	
Gillenia trifoliata	48 in (120 cm)	48 in (120 cm)	P	C	NA	◆			W	Sp/Su				◆	
Glaucium flavum	40 in (100 cm)	16 in (40 cm)	B/P	C/W	NA	◆	◆		Sp	Su		◆	◆		
Globba winitii	36 in (90 cm)	24 in (60 cm)	P	W	NA	◆			Sp	Su				◆	
Gloxinia perennis	24 in (60 cm)	15 in (38 cm)	P	W/T	G	◆			Sp	Su/A	◆			◆	
Gloxinia sylvatica	24 in (60 cm)	24 in (60 cm)	P	W/T	G	◆			Sp	Su/A				◆	
Gomphrena globosa	24 in (60 cm)	18 in (45 cm)	A	W	NA	◆			Sp	Su			◆	◆	
Gunnera manicata	6–10 ft (1.8–3 m)	10–15 ft (3–4.5 m)	P	C/W	NA		◆		W	Sp/Su			◆	◆	
Gunnera prorepens	2–4 in (5–10 cm)	12–18 in (30–45 cm)	P	C/W	NA		◆			Sp/Su			◆	◆	
Guzmania lingulata	12 in (30 cm)	8 in (20 cm)	P	W/T	B	◆	◆		W/Sp	Sp/Su	◆				◆
Guzmania musaica	20 in (50 cm)	16 in (40 cm)	P	W/T	B	◆	◆		W/Sp	Sp/Su					◆
Guzmania wittmackii	30 in (75 cm)	36 in (90 cm)	P	W/T	B	◆	◆		W/Sp	Sp/Su					◆
Guzmania Hybrid Cultivars	18–36 in (45–90 cm)	10–24 in (25–60 cm)	P	W/T	B	◆	◆		W/Sp	Sp/Su					◆
Gynura aurantiaca	7–8 ft (2–2.4 m)	4 ft (1.2 m)	P	W/T	NA		◆		Sp	W	◆				◆
Gypsophila cerastioides	3 in (8 cm)	8 in (20 cm)	P	C	NA	◆			W/Sp	Sp	◆	◆	◆	◆	
Gypsophila paniculata	48 in (120 cm)	48 in (120 cm)	P	C	NA	◆		◆	W/Sp	Su		◆	◆	◆	
Gypsophila repens	4 in (10 cm)	24 in (60 cm)	P	C	NA	◆			W/Sp	Sp/Su			◆	◆	
Gypsophila ‘Rosenschleier’	12 in (30 cm)	36 in (90 cm)	P	C	NA	◆			W/Sp	Sp/Su			◆	◆	
Hedychium coccineum	7–10 ft (2–3 m)	2–5 ft (0.6–1.5 m)	P	W/T	NA	◆		◆	W	A			◆	◆	
Hedychium coronarium	10 ft (3 m)	2–5 ft (0.6–1.5 m)	P	W/T	NA	◆		◆	W	Sp			◆	◆	
Hedychium gardnerianum	8 ft (2.4 m)	3–5 ft (0.9–1.5 m)	P	W	NA	◆		◆	W	Su/A			◆	◆	
Hedychium greenei	7 ft (2 m)	32–48 in (80–120 cm)	P	W/T	NA	◆		◆	W	Su		◆	◆	◆	
Helenium autumnale	5 ft (1.5 m)	3 ft (0.9 m)	P	C	NA	◆			W/Sp	Su/A			◆	◆	
Helenium Hybrid Cultivars	40 in (100 cm)	40 in (100 cm)	P	C	NA	◆			W/Sp	Su/A			◆	◆	
Heliamphora heterodoxa	18 in (45 cm)	12 in (30 cm)	P	W/T	C		◆		W/Sp	W	◆		◆	◆	
Heliamphora minor	3 in (8 cm)	6 in (15 cm)	P	W	C		◆		W/Sp	Sp	◆	◆	◆	◆	
Helianthus annuus	10–17 ft (3–5 m)	2–4 ft (0.6–1.2 m)	A	C/W	NA	◆			Sp	Su			◆	◆	
Helianthus maximilianii	7–10 ft (2–3 m)	2–3 ft (0.6–0.9 m)	P	C/W	NA	◆			Sp	A			◆	◆	

Plant name	Height	Spread	Type	Climate	Group	Showy flowers	Showy foliage	Scented flowers	Planting season	Flowering season	Grow in pot/tub	Frost tolerant	Full Sun	Half Sun	Heavy shade
Helianthus × *multiflorus*	7 ft (2 m)	2 ft (0.6 m)	P	C/W	NA	◆			Sp	Su/A		◆	◆		
Helianthus salicifolius	10 ft (3 m)	2–4 ft (0.6–1.2 m)	P	C/W	NA	◆			Sp	A		◆	◆		
Helianthus Hybrid Cultivars	4–7 ft (1.2–2 m)	3–4 ft (0.9–1.2 m)	P	C/W	NA	◆			Sp	Su			◆		
Helichrysum ecklonis	4–16 in (10–40 cm)	16–24 in (40–60 cm)	P	W	NA	◆			W/Sp	Su	◆		◆		
Helichrysum frigidum	4 in (10 cm)	12 in (30 cm)	P	W	NA	◆	◆		W/Sp	Sp/Su	◆		◆	◆	
Helichrysum milfordiae	6 in (15 cm)	12 in (30 cm)	P	W	NA	◆			A/W	Sp			◆		
Helichrysum petiolare	12–18 in (30–45 cm)	5 ft (1.5 m)	P	W	NA	◆			W/Sp	W			◆		
Helichrysum splendidum	5 ft (1.5 m)	3 ft (0.9 m)	P	W	NA			◆	W/Sp	A/W		◆	◆		
Heliconia bihai	7–17 ft (2–5 m)	2–7 ft (0.6–2 m)	P	W/T	NA	◆			W/Sp	Sp–A					◆
Heliconia caribaea	7–17 ft (2–5 m)	2–7 ft (0.6–2 m)	P	W/T	NA	◆			W/Sp	Sp–A					◆
Heliconia latispatha	10 ft (3 m)	3–4 ft (0.9–1.2 m)	P	W/T	NA	◆			W/Sp	Sp–A					◆
Heliconia psittacorum	2–7 ft (0.6–2 m)	20–32 in (50–80 cm)	P	W/T	NA	◆			W/Sp	Sp–A					◆
Heliconia wagneriana	12 ft (3.5 m)	4–7 ft (1.2–2 m)	P	W/T	NA	◆			W/Sp	Sp–A					◆
Heliopsis helianthoides	2–5 ft (0.6–1.5 m)	1–2 ft (0.3–0.6 m)	P	C	NA	◆			W/Sp	Su/A		◆	◆		
Heliopsis Hybrid Cultivars	4 ft (1.2 m)	1–2 ft (0.3–0.6 m)	P	C	NA	◆			W/Sp	Su/A		◆	◆		
Heliotropium arborescens	3 ft (0.9 m)	20 in (50 cm)	P	W/T	NA	◆	◆	◆	Sp	Sp/Su			◆		
Helleborus argutifolius	40 in (100 cm)	24–40 in (60–100 cm)	P	C/W	NA	◆	◆		A/W	W/Sp			◆	◆	◆
Helleborus foetidus	24–32 in (60–80 cm)	24–40 in (60–100 cm)	P	C	NA	◆	◆		A/W	W/Sp			◆	◆	◆
Helleborus × *hybridus*	16 in (40 cm)	16–24 in (40–60 cm)	P	C	NA	◆	◆		A/W	W/Sp				◆	◆
Helleborus lividus	16 in (40 cm)	24 in (60 cm)	P	C/W	NA	◆	◆		A/W	W/Sp				◆	◆
Helleborus niger	12 in (30 cm)	12–20 in (30–50 cm)	P	C	NA	◆			A/W	W/Sp				◆	◆
Helleborus × *nigercors*	24 in (60 cm)	24 in (60 cm)	P	C	NA	◆			A/W	W/Sp				◆	◆
Helleborus orientalis	16 in (40 cm)	16–24 in (40–60 cm)	P	C	NA	◆			A/W	W				◆	◆
Hemerocallis dumortieri	16 in (40 cm)	16–24 in (40–60 cm)	P	C/W	NA	◆		◆	W	Sp/Su		◆	◆	◆	
Hemerocallis fulva	3 ft (0.9 m)	4–5 ft (1.2–1.5 m)	P	C/W	NA	◆			W	Sp/Su		◆	◆	◆	
Hemerocallis lilio-asphodelus	24–40 in (60–100 cm)	40–48 in (100–120 cm)	P	C/W	NA	◆		◆	W	Sp/Su			◆	◆	
Hemerocallis middendorffii	18 in (45 cm)	20–24 in (50–60 cm)	P	C/W	NA	◆		◆	W	Sp/Su			◆	◆	
Hemerocallis minor	20 in (50 cm)	20–24 in (50–60 cm)	P	C/W	NA	◆			W	Sp/Su		◆	◆	◆	
Hemigraphis alternata	4 in (10 cm)	12–18 in (30–45 cm)	P	W/T	NA		◆		Sp	Any	◆			◆	
Hemigraphis repanda	4 in (10 cm)	12–18 in (30–45 cm)	P	W/T	NA		◆		Sp	Any	◆			◆	
Hepatica nobilis	3–4 in (8–10 cm)	4–6 in (10–15 cm)	P	C	NA	◆			W	Sp		◆			◆

Plant name	Height	Spread	Type	Climate	Group	Showy flowers	Showy foliage	Scented flowers	Planting season	Flowering season	Grow in pot/tub	Frost tolerant	Full Sun	Half Sun	Heavy shade
Hesperis matronalis	32–36 in (80–90 cm)	16–20 in (40–50 cm)	B/P	C/W	NA	◆		◆	Sp	Sp/Su		◆	◆	◆	
Heuchera americana	18 in (45 cm)	16 in (40 cm)	P	C/W	NA	◆	◆		A–Sp	Sp–A		◆	◆	◆	
Heuchera × brizoides	12–30 in (30–75 cm)	12–18 in (30–45 cm)	P	C/W	NA	◆	◆	◆	A–Sp	Sp–A		◆	◆	◆	
Heuchera maxima	24 in (60 cm)	16–20 in (40–50 cm)	P	C/W	NA	◆	◆		A–Sp	Sp–A		◆	◆	◆	
Heuchera micrantha	24 in (60 cm)	12–16 in (30–40 cm)	P	C/W	NA	◆	◆		A–Sp	Sp–A		◆	◆	◆	
Heuchera sanguinea	24 in (60 cm)	12–16 in (30–40 cm)	P	C/W	NA	◆	◆		A–Sp	Sp–A		◆	◆	◆	
Heuchera Hybrid Cultivars	12–36 in (30–90 cm)	12–18 in (30–45 cm)	P	C/W	NA	◆	◆		A–Sp	Sp–A		◆	◆	◆	
× Heucherella tiarelloides	18 in (45 cm)	18 in (45 cm)	P	C/W	NA	◆	◆		W/Sp	Sp/Su		◆	◆	◆	
× Heucherella Hybrid Cultivars	16–20 in (40–50 cm)	12–16 in (30–40 cm)	P	C/W	NA	◆	◆		W/Sp	Sp/Su		◆	◆	◆	
Hibiscus cannabinus	12 ft (3.5 m)	6 ft (1.8 m)	A/P	W/T	NA				Sp	Sp–A			◆		
Hibiscus Herbaceous Hybrids	18 in–5 ft (45 cm–1.5 m)	2–4 ft (0.6–1.2 m)	P	C/W	NA	◆			W/Sp	Sp–A		◆	◆		
Hosta crispula	36 in (90 cm)	24 in (60 cm)	P	C/W	NA		◆		W/Sp	Su		◆		◆	◆
Hosta fortunei	36 in (90 cm)	32–48 in (80–120 cm)	P	C/W	NA		◆		W/Sp	Su		◆		◆	◆
Hosta lancifolia	18 in (45 cm)	16–20 in (40–50 cm)	P	C/W	NA		◆		W/Sp	Su		◆		◆	◆
Hosta minor	24 in (60 cm)	16 in (40 cm)	P	C/W	NA	◆	◆		W/Sp	Su		◆		◆	◆
Hosta plantaginea	26 in (65 cm)	32 in (80 cm)	P	C/W	NA	◆		◆	W/Sp	Su		◆		◆	◆
Hosta sieboldii	20 in (50 cm)	32 in (80 cm)	P	C/W	NA	◆	◆		W/Sp	Su		◆		◆	◆
Hosta × tardiana	16 in (40 cm)	16–20 in (40–50 cm)	P	C/W	NA		◆		W/Sp	Su		◆		◆	◆
Hosta tardiflora	12 in (30 cm)	20 in (50 cm)	P	C/W	NA		◆		W/Sp	Su		◆		◆	◆
Hosta tokudama	18 in (45 cm)	32–48 in (80–120 cm)	P	C/W	NA		◆		W/Sp	Su		◆		◆	◆
Hosta undulata	12 in (30 cm)	16–20 in (40–50 cm)	P	C/W	NA		◆		W/Sp	Su		◆		◆	◆
Hosta ventricosa	40 in (100 cm)	24–32 in (60–80 cm)	P	C/W	NA	◆	◆		W/Sp	Su		◆		◆	◆
Hosta Hybrid Cultivars	6–36 in (15–90 cm)	12–60 in (30–150 cm)	P	C/W	NA	◆	◆		W/Sp	Su		◆		◆	◆
Houttuynia cordata	6–12 in (15–30 cm)	over 40 in (100 cm)	P	C/W	NA	◆	◆		W/Sp	Su		◆	◆	◆	◆
Hunnemannia fumariifolia	18–36 in (45–90 cm)	10 in (25 cm)	A/P	W	NA	◆	◆		Sp	Su		◆	◆		
Hydrastis canadensis	12 in (30 cm)	8 in (20 cm)	P	C	NA		◆		W/Sp	Sp		◆			
Iberis amara	12 in (30 cm)	12–20 in (30–50 cm)	A	C/W	NA	◆			Sp	Su	◆		◆	◆	
Iberis gibraltarica	12 in (30 cm)	20–24 in (50–60 cm)	P	C/W	NA	◆			Sp	Su		◆	◆	◆	
Iberis sempervirens	12 in (30 cm)	20–24 in (50–60 cm)	P	C/W	NA	◆			Sp	Sp/Su	◆	◆	◆	◆	
Iberis umbellata	12 in (30 cm)	16 in (40 cm)	A	C/W	NA	◆			Sp	Sp/Su			◆	◆	
Impatiens balsamina	27 in (70 cm)	12 in (30 cm)	A	W/T	NA	◆			Sp	Sp–A	◆			◆	◆

Plant name	Height	Spread	Type	Climate	Group	Showy flowers	Showy foliage	Scented flowers	Planting season	Flowering season	Grow in pot/tub	Frost tolerant	Full Sun	Half Sun	Heavy shade
Impatiens hawkeri	3–7 ft (0.9–2 m)	16–40 in (40–100 cm)	P	W/T	NA	◆			Sp	All	◆			◆	◆
Impatiens New Guinea Hybrids	10–48 in (25–120 cm)	16–40 in (40–100 cm)	P	W/T	NA	◆			Sp	All	◆			◆	◆
Impatiens niamniamensis	36 in (90 cm)	16 in (40 cm)	P	W/T	NA	◆			Sp	All	◆			◆	◆
Impatiens sodenii	3–7 ft (0.9–2 m)	3–7 ft (0.9–2 m)	P	W/T	NA	◆			Sp	Su	◆			◆	◆
Impatiens walleriana	8–24 in (20–60 cm)	8–20 in (20–50 cm)	A/P	W/T	NA	◆			Sp	Sp–A	◆			◆	◆
Incarvillea delavayi	20–24 in (50–60 cm)	12–16 in (30–40 cm)	P	C	NA	◆			W/Sp	Su		◆	◆		
Incarvillea emodi	16–20 cm (40–50 cm)	12–16 in (30–40 cm)	P	C	NA	◆			W/Sp	Sp			◆		
Inula grandiflora	20–24 in (50–60 cm)	36–40 in (90–100 cm)	P	C/W	NA	◆			W/Sp	Su/A		◆	◆		
Inula helenium	8–10 ft (2.4–3 m)	3–4 ft (0.9–1.2 m)	P	C/W	NA	◆			W/Sp	Su/A		◆	◆	◆	
Inula magnifica	5–6 ft (1.5–1.8 m)	3–5 ft (0.9–1.5 m)	P	C/W	NA	◆			W/Sp	Su/A		◆	◆		
Ipomopsis rubra	3–6 ft (0.9–1.8 m)	18 in (45 cm)	B/P	C/W	NA	◆			W/Sp	Su/A			◆		
Iresine herbstii	18–24 in (45–60 cm)	12–18 in (30–45 cm)	A/P	W/T	NA		◆		Sp	Su	◆		◆		
Iris chrysographes	12–20 in (30–50 cm)	12 in (30 cm)	P	C/W	NA	◆			A/W	Sp/Su		◆	◆		
Iris cristata	4–5 in (10–12 cm)	12–20 in (30–50 cm)	P	C/W	NA	◆		◆	A/W	Sp		◆		◆	
Iris douglasiana	20–32 in (50–80 cm)	18 in (45 cm)	P	C	NA	◆			A/W	Su		◆	◆		
Iris ensata	36 in (90 cm)	40 in (100 cm)	P	C	NA	◆			A/W	Su		◆	◆		
Iris foetidissima	18–30 in (45–75 cm)	18–30 in (45–75 cm)	P	C/W	NA	◆			A/W	Sp				◆	◆
Iris × fulvala	18–30 in (45–75 cm)	10 in (25 cm)	P	C	NA	◆			A/W	Sp		◆	◆		
Iris germanica	24–48 in (60–120 cm)	18–24 in (45–60 cm)	P	C	NA	◆			A/W	Sp		◆	◆		
Iris innominata	8–10 in (20–25 cm)	10 in (25 cm)	P	C/W	NA	◆			A/W	Sp		◆	◆	◆	
Iris japonica	24–32 in (60–80 cm)	18–24 in (45–60 cm)	P	C/W	NA	◆			A/W	Sp		◆		◆	
Iris laevigata	2–5 ft (0.6–1.5 m)	5 ft (1.5 m)	P	C	NA	◆			A/W	Su		◆	◆	◆	
Iris missouriensis	12–20 in (30–50 cm)	12 in (30 cm)	P	C	NA	◆			A/W	Sp/Su		◆	◆		
Iris pallida	36–48 in (90–120 cm)	12 in (30 cm)	P	C	NA	◆		◆	A/W	Su		◆	◆		
Iris pseudacorus	4–5 ft (1.2–1.5 m)	5–7 ft (1.5–2 m)	P	C	NA	◆			A/W	Sp/Su		◆	◆		
Iris pumila	4–6 in (10–15 cm)	4–6 in (10–15 cm)	P	C	NA	◆		◆	A/W	Sp		◆	◆		
Iris sibirica	18–48 in (45–120 cm)	8–24 in (20–60 cm)	P	C	NA	◆			A/W	Sp/Su		◆	◆		
Iris spuria	4–7 ft (1.2–2 m)	3–7 ft (0.9–2 m)	P	C	NA	◆			A/W	Sp		◆	◆		
Iris tectorum	12–16 in (30–40 cm)	12 in (30 cm)	P	C	NA	◆			A/W	Su		◆		◆	
Iris unguicularis	12–15 in (30–38 cm)	16–20 in (40–50 cm)	P	C/W	NA	◆			A/W	W/Sp		◆	◆	◆	
Iris versicolor	8–32 in (20–80 cm)	10 in (25 cm)	P	C	NA	◆			A/W	Su		◆	◆		

Plant name	Height	Spread	Type	Climate	Group	Showy flowers	Showy foliage	Scented flowers	Planting season	Flowering season	Grow in pot/tub	Frost tolerant	Full Sun	Half Sun	Heavy shade
Iris, Arilbred Hybrids	10–27 in (25–70 cm)	12 in (30 cm)	P	C/W	NA	●			Su/A	Sp			●	●	
Iris, Bearded Hybrids	8–40 in (20–100 cm)	12–36 in (30–90 cm)	P	C/W	NA	●			A/W	Sp/Su			●	●	
Iris, Californian Hybrids	12 in (30 cm)	10–20 in (25–50 cm)	P	C/W	NA	●			A/W	Sp			●	●	
Iris, Louisiana Hybrids	18–60 in (45–150 cm)	3–7 ft (0.9–2 m)	P	C/W	NA	●			A/W	Sp/Su			●	●	●
Iris, Oncocyclus Hybrids	4–24 in (10–60 cm)	40 in (100 cm)	P	C/W	NA	●			A/W	Sp			●	●	
Iris, Siberian Hybrids	18–48 in (45–120 cm)	8–24 in (20–60 cm)	P	C/W	NA	●			W	Sp/Su			●	●	
Iris, Spuria Hybrids	30–48 in (75–120 cm)	18–24 in (45–60 cm)	P	C/W	NA	●			A/W	Sp/Su			●	●	
Ismelia carinata	32–40 in (80–100 cm)	12–16 in (30–40 cm)	A	W/T	NA	●			Sp	S/A			●	●	
Jasione laevis	8–20 in (20–50 cm)	8–10 in (20–25 cm)	P	C	NA	●			W/Sp	Su			●	●	
Kirengeshoma palmata	48 in (120 cm)	30 in (75 cm)	P	C	NA	●	●		W/Sp	Su/A		●			●
Knautia arvensis	5 ft (1.5 m)	12 in (30 cm)	P	C/W	NA	●			W/Sp	Su/A			●	●	
Kniphofia caulescens	4 ft (1.2 m)	20 in (50 cm)	P	C/W	NA	●			W/Sp	Su/A			●	●	
Kniphofia northiae	5 ft (1.5 m)	40 in (100 cm)	P	W	NA	●			W/Sp	Sp–A			●	●	
Kniphofia × praecox	4–5 ft (1.2–1.5 m)	20–40 in (50–100 cm)	P	C/W	NA	●			W/Sp	Su–W			●	●	
Kniphofia rooperi	4 ft (1.2 m)	20–24 in (50–60 cm)	P	W	NA	●			W/Sp	Su/A	●		●	●	
Kniphofia thomsonii	4 ft (1.2 m)	16–24 in (40–60 cm)	P	W	NA	●			W/Sp	Su/A			●	●	
Kniphofia uvaria	4 ft (1.2 m)	24 in (60 cm)	P	C/W	NA	●			W/Sp	Su–W			●	●	
Kniphofia Hybrid Cultivars	2–5 ft (0.6–1.5 m)	12–20 in (30–50 cm)	P	W	NA	●			W/Sp	Su–W	●		●	●	
Kohleria digitaliflora	12–24 in (30–60 cm)	12–24 in (30–60 cm)	P	W/T	G	●			Sp	Su/A	●		●		
Kohleria eriantha	3–4 ft (0.9–1.2 m)	3–4 ft (0.9–1.2 m)	P	W/T	G	●		●	Sp	Sp/Su	●		●		
Lamium galeobdolon	8–16 in (20–40 cm)	48 in (120 cm)	P	C/W	NA		●		W/Sp	Su			●	●	●
Lamium garganicum	8–16 in (20–40 cm)	48 in (120 cm)	P	C/W	NA	●			W/Sp	Su			●	●	
Lamium maculatum	6–20 in (15–50 cm)	24–60 in (60–150 cm)	P	C/W	NA		●		W/Sp	Su			●	●	●
Lamium orvala	40 in (100 cm)	40 in (100 cm)	P	C/W	NA	●			W/Sp	Su			●	●	
Lathyrus aureus	24–36 in (60–90 cm)	40 in (100 cm)	P	C/W	NA	●			Sp	Sp/Su	●		●	●	
Lathyrus laxiflorus	12 in (30 cm)	16–24 in (40–60 cm)	P	C	NA	●			W/Sp	Su			●	●	
Lathyrus odoratus	8 ft (2.4 m)	40 in (100 cm)	A	C/W	NA	●			Sp	Su			●	●	
Lathyrus splendens	7–10 ft (2–3 m)	3–7 ft (0.9–2 m)	P	W	NA	●			Sp	Sp/Su			●	●	
Lathyrus vernus	12–24 in (30–60 cm)	24–40 in (60–100 cm)	P	C	NA	●			W/Sp	Sp		●	●	●	
Lavatera × clementii	6 ft (1.8 m)	6 ft (1.8 m)	P	C/W	NA	●			W/Sp	Su/A			●	●	
Lavatera thuringiaca	6 ft (1.8 m)	3–4 ft (0.9–1.2 m)	P	C/W	NA	●			W/Sp	Su/A			●	●	

Plant name	Height	Spread	Type	Climate	Group	Showy flowers	Showy foliage	Scented flowers	Planting season	Flowering season	Grow in pot/tub	Frost tolerant	Full Sun	Half Sun	Heavy shade
Lavatera trimestris	24–48 in (60–120 cm)	18–36 in (45–90 cm)	A	C/W	NA	◆			Sp	Su		◆	◆		
Leonotis nepetifolia	3–4 ft (0.9–1.2 m)	8–12 in (20–30 cm)	A	W	NA	◆			Sp	W		◆	◆		
Leonotis ocymifolia	8 ft (2.4 m)	3 ft (0.9 m)	P	W	NA	◆			Sp	Su–W			◆		
Leontopodium alpinum	6 in (15 cm)	4–9 in (10–22 cm)	P	C	NA	◆	◆		W/Sp	Su	◆	◆	◆		
Lespedeza thunbergii	3–8 ft (0.9–2.4 ft)	5–10 ft (1.5–3 m)	P	C	NA	◆			W/Sp	Su/A		◆	◆		
Leucanthemum × superbum	48 in (120 cm)	40 in (100 cm)	P	C/W	NA	◆			W/Sp	Sp–A	◆	◆	◆	◆	
Leucanthemum vulgare	40 in (100 cm)	24 in (60 cm)	P	C	NA	◆			W/Sp	Su		◆	◆	◆	
Lewisia columbiana	12 in (30 cm)	8 in (20 cm)	P	C	NA	◆			W/Sp	Sp/Su	◆	◆	◆	◆	
Lewisia cotyledon	6–12 in (15–30 cm)	8 in (20 cm)	P	C	NA	◆			W/Sp	Sp/Su	◆	◆	◆	◆	
Lewisia 'Pinkie'	6–8 in (15–20 cm)	8 in (20 cm)	P	C	NA	◆			W/Sp	Sp/Su	◆	◆	◆	◆	
Lewisia rediviva	4 in (10 cm)	8 in (20 cm)	P	C	NA	◆			W/Sp	Sp/Su	◆	◆	◆	◆	
Lewisia tweedyi	8 in (20 cm)	8 in (20 cm)	P	C	NA	◆			W/Sp	Sp/Su	◆	◆	◆	◆	
Liatris aspera	40 in (100 cm)	12–20 in (30–50 cm)	P	C/W	NA	◆			W/Sp	Su/A		◆	◆		
Liatris pycnostachya	60 in (150 cm)	10–18 in (25–45 cm)	P	C/W	NA	◆			W/Sp	Su/A		◆	◆		
Liatris spicata	60 in (150 cm)	10–18 in (25–45 cm)	P	C/W	NA	◆			W/Sp	Su/A		◆	◆		
Libertia formosa	18–36 in (45–90 cm)	24 in (60 cm)	P	W	NA	◆	◆		W/Sp	Sp		◆	◆		
Libertia grandiflora	30 in (75 cm)	24 in (60 cm)	P	W	NA	◆	◆		W/Sp	Sp		◆	◆		
Libertia ixioides	8–12 in (20–30 cm)	24 in (60 cm)	P	W	NA		◆		W/Sp	Sp		◆	◆		
Libertia peregrinans	15–27 in (38–70 cm)	20 in (50 cm)	P	W	NA		◆		W/Sp	Sp		◆	◆	◆	
Ligularia dentata	30–60 in (75–150 cm)	40–60 in (100–150 cm)	P	C/W	NA	◆	◆		W/Sp	Su/A		◆		◆	◆
Ligularia przewalskii	7 ft (2 m)	40–48 in (100–120 cm)	P	C	NA	◆	◆		W/Sp	Su/A		◆		◆	◆
Ligularia stenocephala	60 in (150 cm)	32–40 in (80–100 cm)	P	C/W	NA	◆	◆		W/Sp	Su/A		◆		◆	◆
Ligularia Hybrid Cultivars	3–7 ft (0.9–2 m)	32–60 in (80–150 cm)	P	C	NA	◆	◆		W/Sp	Su/A		◆		◆	◆
Limonium brassicifolium	16 in (40 cm)	12 in (30 cm)	P	W	NA	◆			Sp	Su			◆	◆	
Limonium perezii	27 in (70 cm)	20 in (50 cm)	P	W	NA	◆			Sp	Sp/Su			◆	◆	
Limonium sinuatum	16 in (40 cm)	16 in (40 cm)	A/P	W	NA	◆			Sp	Su			◆	◆	
Linaria maroccana	8–10 in (20–25 cm)	6–12 in (15–30 cm)	A	W	NA	◆			Sp	Su			◆	◆	
Linaria purpurea	20–36 in (50–90 cm)	6–12 in (15–30 cm)	P	C/W	NA	◆			Sp	Su/A			◆	◆	
Linum 'Gemmell's Hybrid'	6 in (15 cm)	8 in (20 cm)	P	C/W	NA	◆			A/Sp	Su			◆	◆	
Linum grandiflorum	15–18 in (38–45 cm)	12 in (30 cm)	A	W	NA	◆			Sp	Su			◆	◆	
Linum narbonense	12–24 in (30–60 cm)	12–18 in (30–45 cm)	P	C/W	NA	◆			Sp	Sp–A			◆	◆	

Plant name	Height	Spread	Type	Climate	Group	Showy flowers	Showy foliage	Scented flowers	Planting season	Flowering season	Grow in pot/tub	Frost tolerant	Full Sun	Half Sun	Heavy shade
Linum perenne	12–18 in (30–45 cm)	12 in (30 cm)	P	C/W	NA	◆			Sp	Su		◆	◆		
Liriope muscari	12 in (30 cm)	18 in (45 cm)	P	C/W	NA	◆	◆		W/Sp	A	◆	◆	◆	◆	
Liriope spicata	10 in (25 cm)	18 in (45 cm)	P	C/W	NA	◆	◆		W/Sp	Su	◆	◆	◆	◆	
Lobelia cardinalis	36 in (90 cm)	12–16 in (30–40 cm)	P	C/W	NA	◆	◆		W/Sp	Su/A		◆	◆	◆	
Lobelia erinus	8 in (20 cm)	12–16 in (30–40 cm)	A/P	C/W	NA	◆			Sp	Su/A	◆	◆	◆	◆	
Lobelia × gerardii	60 in (150 cm)	20–24 in (50–60 cm)	P	C/W	NA	◆			W/Sp	Su		◆	◆	◆	
Lobelia laxiflora	3 ft (0.9 m)	4 ft (1.2 m)	P	W	NA	◆			Sp	Su			◆	◆	
Lobelia siphilitica	24 in (60 cm)	16 in (40 cm)	P	C/W	NA	◆			W/Sp	Su/A		◆	◆	◆	
Lobelia tupa	6 ft (1.8 m)	3 ft (0.9 m)	P	W	NA	◆	◆		Sp	Su/A		◆	◆		
Lobularia maritima	10 in (25 cm)	8–16 in (20–40 cm)	A/P	C/W	NA	◆			Sp	Sp–A		◆	◆		
Lotus berthelotii	8 in (20 cm)	3–6 ft (0.9–1.8 m)	P	W	NA	◆	◆		A/Sp	Sp/Su	◆		◆		
Lotus maculatus	8 in (20 cm)	3–6 ft (0.9–1.8 m)	P	W	NA	◆	◆		A/Sp	Sp/Su	◆		◆		
Ludwigia peruviana	20 in–8 ft (50 cm–2.4 m)	20 in–8 ft (50 cm–2.4 m)	P	C/W	NA	◆			Sp	Sp–A		◆	◆		
Lunaria annua	30 in (75 cm)	12 in (30 cm)	B	C/W	NA	◆			A/Sp	Sp/Su		◆	◆	◆	
Lunaria rediviva	36–42 in (90–105 cm)	24 in (60 cm)	P	C/W	NA	◆		◆	A/Sp	Sp/Su		◆	◆	◆	
Lupinus chamissonis	2–7 ft (0.6–2 m)	4–10 ft (1.2–3 m)	P	W	NA	◆			Sp	Sp/Su			◆		
Lupinus polyphyllus	24–60 in (60–150 cm)	20–40 in (50–100 cm)	P	C	NA	◆			W/Sp	Su		◆		◆	
Lupinus texensis	12–24 in (30–60 cm)	12 in (30 cm)	A	C/W	NA	◆			A/W	Sp	◆	◆	◆		
Lupinus Hybrid Cultivars	2–4 ft (0.6–1.2 m)	2–5 ft (0.6–1.5 m)	P	C	NA	◆			W/Sp	Sp/Su	◆	◆	◆		
Lychnis × arkwrightii	12–30 in (30–75 cm)	16–24 in (40–60 cm)	P	C/W	NA	◆			W/Sp	Su			◆	◆	
Lychnis chalcedonica	20 in (50 cm)	12–16 in (30–40 cm)	P	C/W	NA	◆			W/Sp	Su		◆	◆	◆	
Lychnis coronaria	16–32 in (40–80 cm)	20–40 in (50–100 cm)	B/P	C/W	NA	◆	◆		W/Sp	Su			◆	◆	
Lychnis flos-cuculi	30 in (75 cm)	16 in (40 cm)	P	C	NA	◆			W/Sp	Su		◆	◆	◆	
Lychnis flos-jovis	32 in (80 cm)	16 in (40 cm)	P	C	NA	◆			W/Sp	Su		◆	◆	◆	
Lychnis viscaria	24 in (60 cm)	16 in (40 cm)	P	C/W	NA	◆			W/Sp	Su		◆	◆	◆	
Lysichiton americanus	3–4 ft (0.9–1.2 m)	4–5 ft (1.2–1.5 m)	P	C/W	NA	◆	◆		A/W	Sp		◆	◆	◆	
Lysimachia ciliata	40 in (100 cm)	20 in (50 cm)	P	C/W	NA	◆			W/Sp	Su		◆	◆	◆	
Lysimachia clethroides	40 in (100 cm)	24 in (60 cm)	P	C/W	NA				W/Sp	Su		◆		◆	
Lysimachia congestiflora	6 in (15 cm)	8–16 in (20–40 cm)	P	C/W	NA	◆			W/Sp	Sp		◆	◆		
Lysimachia ephemerum	40 in (100 cm)	16–24 in (40–60 cm)	P	C/W	NA	◆			W/Sp	Su		◆		◆	
Lysimachia nummularia	2–4 in (5–10 cm)	24–40 in (60–100 cm)	P	C/W	NA	◆	◆		W/Sp	Su		◆		◆	◆

Plant name	Height	Spread	Type	Climate	Group	Showy flowers	Showy foliage	Scented flowers	Planting season	Flowering season	Grow in pot/tub	Frost tolerant	Full Sun	Half Sun	Heavy shade
Lysimachia punctata	40 in (100 cm)	16–24 in (40–60 cm)	P	C/W	NA	◆			A/Sp	Su		◆		◆	
Lythrum salicaria	24–60 in (60–150 cm)	24 in (60 cm)	P	C/W	NA	◆			A/Sp	Su/A		◆	◆	◆	
Macleaya cordata	8 ft (2.4 m)	3 ft (0.9 m)	P	C/W	NA	◆	◆		A/Sp	Su		◆	◆		
Macleaya microcarpa	8 ft (2.4 m)	3 ft (0.9 m)	P	C/W	NA	◆	◆		A/Sp	A		◆	◆		
Maianthemum bifolium	5–6 in (12–15 cm)	40–48 in (100–120 cm)	P	C/W	NA	◆			W/Sp	Sp		◆			◆
Maianthemum canadense	7–8 in (18–20 cm)	36–40 in (90–100 cm)	P	C	NA	◆	◆	◆	W/Sp	Sp		◆		◆	
Maianthemum racemosum	2–3 ft (0.6–0.9 m)	2–4 ft (0.6–1.2 m)	P	C/W	NA	◆			W/Sp	Su		◆			◆
Malcolmia maritima	14 in (35 cm)	12 in (30 cm)	A	C/W	NA	◆		◆	Sp	Sp/Su	◆	◆	◆		
Malva alcea	40 in (100 cm)	24 in (60 cm)	P	C/W	NA	◆			Sp	Su/A		◆	◆		
Malva moschata	40 in (100 cm)	18 in (45 cm)	P	C/W	NA	◆			Sp	Su		◆	◆		
Malva sylvestris	3 ft (0.9 m)	7–25 ft (2–8 m)	B/P	C/W	NA	◆			Sp	Su/A		◆	◆		
Maranta leuconeura	10–12 in (25–30 cm)	10–12 in (25–30 cm)	P	W/T	NA		◆		Sp	Sp/Su	◆				◆
Marrubium incanum	20 in (50 cm)	24 in (60 cm)	P	C/W	NA	◆			Sp	Su		◆	◆		
Matthiola incana	32 in (80 cm)	12 in (30 cm)	B	C/W	NA	◆		◆	W/Sp		◆	◆	◆	◆	
Matthiola longipetala	20 in (50 cm)	10 in (25 cm)	A	C/W	NA	◆			Sp			◆	◆		
Mazus radicans	2 in (5 cm)	12 in (30 cm)	P	C	NA	◆	◆		Su/A	Sp/Su		◆			
Mazus reptans	2 in (5 cm)	20 in (50 cm)	P	C	NA	◆			Su/A	Sp/Su		◆			
Meconopsis betonicifolia	3–6 ft (0.9–1.8 m)	8–20 in (20–50 cm)	P	C	NA	◆			W/Sp	Sp/Su		◆		◆	◆
Meconopsis cambrica	12–24 in (30–60 cm)	8–16 in (20–40 cm)	P	C/W	NA	◆			W/Sp	Sp/Su		◆		◆	
Meconopsis grandis	4 ft (1.2 m)	16–24 in (40–60 cm)	P	C	NA	◆			W/Sp	Sp/Su		◆		◆	
Meconopsis horridula	32 in (80 cm)	16 in (40 cm)	P	C	NA	◆			W/Sp	Su		◆		◆	
Meconopsis napaulensis	6–8 ft (1.8–2.4 m)	20–32 in (50–80 cm)	P	C/W	NA	◆			W/Sp	Sp/Su		◆		◆	◆
Meconopsis × sheldonii	4 ft (1.2 m)	16–24 in (40–60 cm)	P	C	NA	◆			W/Sp	Sp/Su		◆		◆	
Melampodium leucanthum	24 in (60 cm)	24 in (60 cm)	P	C/W	NA	◆		◆	W/Sp	Sp–A		◆	◆		
Melampodium paludosum	24 in (60 cm)	36 in (90 cm)	A	W/T	NA	◆		◆	W/Sp	Sp–A	◆		◆		
Mentha × gracilis	12 in (30 cm)	36 in (90 cm)	P	C	NA		◆		W/Sp	Su/A		◆	◆		
Mentha pulegium	8–12 in (20–30 cm)	20 in (50 cm)	P	C/W	NA	◆			W/Sp	Su/A	◆	◆	◆	◆	
Mentha requienii	¾ in (1.8 cm)	27 in (70 cm)	P	C/W	NA	◆			W/Sp	Su	◆	◆	◆	◆	
Mentha × villosa	3 ft (0.9 m)	5 ft (1.5 m)	P	C	NA	◆			W/Sp			◆	◆		
Menyanthes trifoliata	10–16 in (25–40 cm)	8–12 in (20–30 cm)	P	C	NA	◆		◆	W/Sp			◆	◆		
Mertensia sibirica	12–18 in (30–45 cm)	12 in (30 cm)	P	C	NA	◆			W/Sp	Sp/Su		◆		◆	

Plant name	Height	Spread	Type	Climate	Group	Showy flowers	Showy foliage	Scented flowers	Planting season	Flowering season	Grow in pot/tub	Frost tolerant	Full Sun	Half Sun	Heavy shade
Mertensia simplicissima	6 in (15 cm)	18 in (45 cm)	P	C	NA	◆			W/Sp	Sp–A		◆	◆		
Mertensia virginica	12–24 in (30–60 cm)	12–24 in (30–60 cm)	P	C	NA	◆			W/Sp	Sp		◆		◆	
Meum athamanticum	18–24 in (45–60 cm)	12–18 in (30–45 cm)	P	C	NA		◆		Sp	Su		◆	◆		
Mimulus aurantiacus	4 ft (1.2 m)	3 ft (0.9 m)	P	C/W	NA	◆			W/Sp	Sp/Su		◆	◆		
Mimulus cardinalis	32–36 in (80–90 cm)	24–27 in (60–70 cm)	P	C/W	NA	◆			W/Sp	Su		◆	◆	◆	
Mimulus guttatus	36 in (90 cm)	36 in (90 cm)	A/B	C/W	NA	◆			W/Sp	Sp–A		◆	◆		
Mimulus luteus	12–16 in (30–40 cm)	24–32 in (60–80 cm)	P	C/W	NA	◆			W/Sp	Sp–A		◆	◆		
Mimulus ringens	3–4 ft (0.9–1.2 m)	4–5 ft (1.2–1.5 m)	P	C	NA	◆			W/Sp	Su		◆	◆		
Mimulus Hybrid Cultivars	8–36 in (20–90 cm)	12–32 in (30–80 cm)	P	C/W	NA	◆			W/Sp	Sp–A		◆	◆		
Minuartia stellata	2 in (5 cm)	18 in (45 cm)	P	C/W	NA	◆			Sp/Su	Su	◆		◆		
Mirabilis jalapa	20–24 in (50–60 cm)	20–24 in (50–60 cm)	P	W	NA			◆	W/Sp	Su		◆	◆		
Mitchella repens	3 in (8 cm)	24 in (60 cm)	P	C	NA			◆	W/Sp	Su					◆
Moltkia × intermedia	8–10 in (20–25 cm)	16–20 in (40–50 cm)	P	C	NA	◆			W/Sp	Su		◆	◆		
Monarda didyma	3–4 ft (0.9–1.2 m)	24–40 in (60–100 cm)	P	C	NA	◆		◆	W/Sp	Su		◆	◆	◆	
Monarda fistulosa	3–4 ft (0.9–1.2 m)	24–40 in (60–100 cm)	P	C	NA	◆		◆	W/Sp	Su		◆	◆	◆	
Monarda Hybrid Cultivars	20–60 in (50–150 cm)	20–32 in (50–80 cm)	P	C	NA	◆		◆	W/Sp	Su/A		◆	◆	◆	
Musa ornata	6–10 ft (1.8–3 m)	6 ft (1.8 m)	P	W/T	NA	◆	◆		W/Sp	Su			◆		
Musa velutina	5 ft (1.5 m)	3 ft (0.9 m)	P	W/T	NA	◆	◆		W/Sp	Sp			◆		
Myosotidium hortensia	12–16 in (30–40 cm)	24–40 in (60–100 cm)	P	C	NA	◆	◆		W/Sp	Su		◆	◆	◆	◆
Myosotis alpestris	12 in (30 cm)	16 in (40 cm)	P	C	NA	◆			A–Sp	Sp		◆	◆	◆	
Myosotis sylvatica	6–16 in (15–40 cm)	8–16 in (20–40 cm)	B/P	C	NA	◆			A–Sp	Su		◆	◆	◆	
Nelumbo lutea	7 ft (2 m)	7 ft (2 m)	P	C/W	NA	◆	◆	◆	W/Sp	Su		◆	◆		
Nelumbo nucifera	7 ft (2 m)	7 ft (2 m)	P	W/T	NA	◆	◆	◆	W/Sp	Su			◆		
Nemesia caerulea	16–24 in (40–60 cm)	16–24 in (40–60 cm)	P	W	NA	◆			A/Sp	Su	◆		◆	◆	
Nemesia strumosa	6–20 in (15–50 cm)	8–16 in (20–40 cm)	A	W	NA	◆			Sp–A	Su	◆		◆	◆	
Nemesia Hybrid Cultivars	6–16 in (15–40 cm)	8–16 in (20–40 cm)	A	W	NA	◆			Sp–A	Su	◆		◆	◆	
Nemophila maculata	8–12 in (20–30 cm)	12–20 in (30–50 cm)	A	C/W	NA	◆			Sp/Su	Su			◆	◆	
Nemophila menziesii	4–6 in (10–15 cm)	12–20 in (30–50 cm)	A	C/W	NA	◆			Sp/Su	Su			◆	◆	
Neomarica caerulea	24–36 in (60–90 cm)	12 in (30 cm)	P	W/T	NA	◆			A/W	Su			◆		
Neoregelia carolinae	12 in (30 cm)	24 in (60 cm)	P	W/T	B	◆	◆		W/Sp	Sp/Su	◆				◆
Neoregelia concentrica	12 in (30 cm)	32 in (80 cm)	P	W/T	B	◆	◆		W/Sp	Su	◆				◆

Plant name	Height	Spread	Type	Climate	Group	Showy flowers	Showy foliage	Scented flowers	Planting season	Flowering season	Grow in pot/tub	Frost tolerant	Full Sun	Half Sun	Heavy shade
Neoregelia marmorata	20 in (50 cm)	40 in (100 cm)	P	W/T	B	♦	♦		W/Sp	Su	♦				♦
Neoregelia Hybrid Cultivars	6–20 in (15–50 cm)	4–40 in (10–100 cm)	P	W/T	B		♦		W/Sp	Sp/Su	♦				♦
Nepenthes alata	15 ft (4.5 m)	20 in (50 cm)	P	W/T	C		♦		W/Sp	Su	♦	♦		♦	
Nepenthes ampullaria	20 ft (6 m)	20 in (50 cm)	P	W/T	C		♦		W/Sp	Su	♦		♦	♦	
Nepenthes burbidgeae	40 ft (12 m)	16 in (40 cm)	P	W/T	C		♦		W/Sp	Su	♦			♦	
Nepenthes fusca	35 ft (10 m)	14 in (35 cm)	P	W/T	C		♦		W/Sp	Su	♦			♦	
Nepenthes lowii	25 ft (8 m)	26 in (65 cm)	P	W/T	C		♦		W/Sp	Su	♦			♦	
Nepenthes maxima	10 ft (3 m)	30 in (75 cm)	P	W/T	C		♦		W/Sp	Su	♦			♦	
Nepenthes rajah	7 ft (2 m)	40 in (100 cm)	P	W/T	C		♦		W/Sp	Su	♦			♦	
Nepenthes spathulata	7 ft (2 m)	20 in (50 cm)	P	W/T	C		♦		W/Sp	Su	♦			♦	
Nepenthes tentaculata	7 ft (2 m)	20 in (50 cm)	P	W/T	C		♦		W/Sp	Su	♦			♦	
Nepenthes × ventrata	7 ft (2 m)	16 in (40 cm)	P	W/T	C		♦		W/Sp	Su	♦	♦		♦	
Nepenthes ventricosa	7 ft (2 m)	16 in (40 cm)	P	W/T	C		♦		W/Sp	Su	♦			♦	
Nepeta camphorata	18 in (45 cm)	24 in (60 cm)	P	C/W	NA	♦		♦	W/Sp	Su		♦	♦	♦	
Nepeta clarkei	24–36 in (60–90 cm)	24 in (60 cm)	P	C/W	NA	♦		♦	W/Sp	Su		♦	♦	♦	
Nepeta × faassenii	24 in (60 cm)	40 in (100 cm)	P	C/W	NA	♦		♦	W/Sp	Su		♦	♦	♦	
Nepeta grandiflora	24 in (60 cm)	24 in (60 cm)	P	C/W	NA	♦		♦	W/Sp	Su		♦	♦	♦	
Nepeta sibirica	40 in (100 cm)	40 in (100 cm)	P	C/W	NA	♦		♦	W/Sp	Sp/Su		♦	♦	♦	
Nicotiana alata	24–36 in (60–90 cm)	12 in (30 cm)	A/P	C/W	NA	♦		♦	Sp	Su	♦	♦	♦	♦	
Nicotiana langsdorffii	5 ft (1.5 m)	15 in (38 cm)	A	C/W	NA	♦			Sp	Su		♦	♦	♦	
Nicotiana × sanderae	15–24 in (38–60 cm)	10 in (25 cm)	A	C/W	NA	♦		♦	Sp	Sp/Su	♦	♦	♦	♦	
Nicotiana sylvestris	3–5 ft (0.9–1.5 m)	18–24 in (45–60 cm)	A	C/W	NA	♦		♦	Sp	Su			♦	♦	
Nidularium fulgens	12 in (30 cm)	32 in (80 cm)	P	W/T	B	♦	♦		W/Sp	Sp/Su	♦				♦
Nidularium innocentii	14 in (35 cm)	36 in (90 cm)	P	W/T	B	♦	♦		W/Sp	Sp/Su	♦				♦
Nidularium Hybrid Cultivars	12–20 in (30–50 cm)	20–40 in (50–100 cm)	P	W/T	B	♦	♦		W/Sp	Sp/Su					♦
Nierembergia caerulea	8–15 in (20–38 cm)	8 in (20 cm)	A/P	W	NA	♦			Sp	Su			♦		
Nierembergia repens	2 in (5 cm)	18 in (45 cm)	P	W	NA	♦			Sp	Su			♦		
Nigella damascena	20 in (50 cm)	10 in (25 cm)	A	C/W	NA	♦			Sp/Su	Su			♦	♦	
Nolana humifusa	4–6 in (10–15 cm)	12 in (30 cm)	A/P	W/T	NA	♦			Sp	Su			♦		
Nolana paradoxa	4–6 in (10–15 cm)	12 in (30 cm)	A/P	W/T	NA	♦			Sp	Su			♦	♦	
Nuphar lutea	3–15 in (8–38 cm)	3–8 ft (0.9–2.4 m)	P	C/W	NA	♦	♦	♦	W/Sp	Su		♦	♦	♦	

Plant name	Height	Spread	Type	Climate	Group	Showy flowers	Showy foliage	Scented flowers	Planting season	Flowering season	Grow in pot/tub	Frost tolerant	Full Sun	Half Sun	Heavy shade
Nymphaea alba	3–15 in (8–38 cm)	3–10 ft (0.9–3 m)	P	C/W	NA	◆	◆		W/Sp	Su		◆	◆		
Nymphaea caerulea	3–15 in (8–38 cm)	3–12 ft (0.9–3.5 m)	P	W/T	NA	◆	◆	◆	W/Sp	Sp/Su			◆		
Nymphaea × daubenyana	3–15 in (8–38 cm)	3–6 ft (0.9–1.8 m)	P	W/T	NA	◆	◆	◆	W/Sp	Sp/Su			◆		
Nymphaea lotus	3–15 in (8–38 cm)	3–12 ft (0.9–3.5 m)	P	W/T	NA	◆	◆	◆	W/Sp	Sp/Su			◆		
Nymphaea mexicana	3–15 in (8–38 cm)	3–12 ft (0.9–3.5 m)	P	W/T	NA	◆	◆		W/Sp	Sp/Su			◆		
Nymphaea odorata	3–15 in (8–38 cm)	3–8 ft (0.9–2.4 m)	P	C/W	NA	◆	◆	◆	W/Sp	Su		◆	◆		
Nymphaea tetragona	3–15 in (8–38 cm)	12–48 in (30–120 cm)	P	C/W	NA	◆	◆	◆	W/Sp	Su		◆	◆		
Nymphaea, Hardy Hybrids	3–15 in (8–38 cm)	3–8 ft (0.9–2.4 m)	P	C/W	NA	◆	◆	◆	W/Sp	Sp/Su		◆	◆		
Nymphaea, Tropical Day-Blooming Hybrids	3–15 in (8–38 cm)	3–12 ft (0.9–3.5 m)	P	W/T	NA	◆	◆	◆	W/Sp	Sp/Su			◆		
Nymphaea, Tropical Night-Blooming Hybrids	3–15 in (8–38 cm)	3–12 ft (0.9–3.5 m)	P	W/T	NA	◆	◆	◆	W/Sp	Sp/Su			◆		
Nymphoides crenata	2–5 ft (0.6–1.5 m)	6 ft (1.8 m)	P	W	NA	◆	◆		W/Sp	Sp–A			◆		
Nymphoides peltata	12 in (30 cm)	3–8 ft (0.9–2.4 m)	P	C/W	NA	◆	◆		W/Sp	Su		◆	◆		
Ochagavia carnea	20 in (50 cm)	32 in (80 cm)	P	W	B	◆	◆		Sp	W		◆	◆		
Oenothera acaulis	6 in (15 cm)	16–24 in (40–60 cm)	B/P	C/W	NA	◆			W/Sp	Su			◆		
Oenothera caespitosa	4–10 in (10–25 cm)	24 in (60 cm)	P	C	NA	◆		◆	W/Sp	Su			◆		
Oenothera 'Crown Imperial'	16–20 in (40–50 cm)	12 in (30 cm)	P	C/W	NA	◆			W/Sp	Su			◆		
Oenothera fruticosa	20–32 in (50–80 cm)	12–16 in (30–40 cm)	B/P	C/W	NA	◆			W/Sp	Su			◆		
Oenothera 'Lemon Sunset'	40 in (100 cm)	16–32 in (40–80 cm)	P	C/W	NA	◆		◆	W/Sp	Su			◆		
Oenothera macrocarpa	8–16 in (20–40 cm)	16–32 in (40–80 cm)	P	C/W	NA	◆			W/Sp	Su			◆		
Oenothera speciosa	12–24 in (30–60 cm)	12–24 in (30–60 cm)	P	C/W	NA	◆			W/Sp	Su/A		◆	◆		
Oenothera versicolor	24 in (60 cm)	16 in (40 cm)	P	C/W	NA	◆			W/Sp	Su			◆		
Omphalodes cappadocica	8 in (20 cm)	12–18 in (30–45 cm)	P	C	NA	◆			A/Sp	Sp/Su			◆		◆
Omphalodes linifolia	12–18 in (30–45 cm)	6–10 in (15–25 cm)	A	C	NA	◆		◆	A/Sp	Su		◆	◆		
Omphalodes verna	6 in (15 cm)	24 in (60 cm)	P	C	NA	◆			A/Sp	Sp			◆		◆
Onopordum acanthium	8–10 ft (2.4–3 m)	6–7 ft (1.8–2 m)	B	C/W	NA	◆	◆		W/Sp	Su			◆		
Onopordum acaulon	6 in (15 cm)	12–18 in (30–45 cm)	A/B	C/W	NA		◆		W/Sp	Su		◆	◆		
Ophiopogon japonicus	12 in (30 cm)	18 in (45 cm)	P	C/W	NA		◆		A/Sp	Su		◆	◆	◆	
Ophiopogon planiscapus	12–18 in (30–45 cm)	18 in (45 cm)	P	C/W	NA		◆		A/Sp	Su		◆	◆	◆	
Origanum amanum	2–4 in (5–10 cm)	6 in (15 cm)	P	W	NA	◆			W/Sp	Su/A		◆	◆		

Plant name	Height	Spread	Type	Climate	Group	Showy flowers	Showy foliage	Scented flowers	Planting season	Flowering season	Grow in pot/tub	Frost tolerant	Full Sun	Half Sun	Heavy shade
Origanum × hybridum	8 in (20 cm)	12 in (30 cm)	P	W	NA	◆	◆		W/Sp	Su/A	◆		◆		
Origanum Hybrid Cultivars	4–12 in (10–30 cm)	12–24 in (30–60 cm)	P	C/W	NA	◆	◆		W/Sp	Su/A	◆	◆	◆		
Orontium aquaticum	12–18 in (30–45 cm)	18–24 in (45–60 cm)	P	C/W	NA	◆			W/Sp	Su			◆	◆	
Orthophytum navioides	4 in (10 cm)	40 in (100 cm)	P	W	B		◆		W/Sp	Su	◆				◆
Orthophytum Hybrid Cultivars	10 in (25 cm)	4 in (10 cm)	P	W	B		◆		W/Sp	Su	◆				◆
Orthosiphon aristatus	36 in (90 cm)	36 in (90 cm)	P	W/T	NA	◆			W/Sp	Sp/Su					◆
Osteospermum ecklonis	20–40 in (50–100 cm)	20–40 in (50–100 cm)	P	W	NA	◆			W/Sp	Sp–A			◆	◆	
Osteospermum jucundum	12–20 in (30–50 cm)	20–32 in (50–80 cm)	P	W	NA	◆			W/Sp	Sp–A			◆	◆	
Osteospermum Hybrid Cultivars	8–12 in (20–30 cm)	16–24 in (40–60 cm)	P	W	NA	◆			W/Sp	Sp–A			◆		
Otacanthus caeruleus	36 in (90 cm)	20 in (50 cm)	P	W/T	NA	◆			Sp	Any	◆		◆	◆	
Oxalis acetosella	2–4 in (5–10 cm)	18–36 in (45–90 cm)	P	C/W	NA	◆			W/Sp	Su	◆		◆	◆	◆
Oxalis oregana	7–8 in (18–20 cm)	40 in (100 cm)	P	C/W	NA	◆	◆		W/Sp	Sp–A	◆				◆
Pachysandra procumbens	6–12 in (15–30 cm)	12–18 in (30–45 cm)	P	C	NA		◆	◆	W/Sp	Sp					◆
Pachysandra terminalis	8–12 in (20–30 cm)	18 in (45 cm)	P	C/W	NA		◆	◆	W/Sp	Sp					◆
Paeonia cambessedesii	24 in (60 cm)	24 in (60 cm)	P	W	NA	◆			W	Sp			◆	◆	
Paeonia × chamaeleon	20 in (50 cm)	20 in (50 cm)	P	C	NA	◆			W	Sp			◆		
Paeonia lactiflora	24 in (60 cm)	24 in (60 cm)	P	C	NA	◆		◆	W	Su			◆		
Paeonia mascula	24–36 in (60–90 cm)	24 in (60 cm)	P	C	NA	◆			W	Sp			◆		
Paeonia mlokosewitschii	40 in (100 cm)	40 in (100 cm)	P	C	NA	◆			W	Sp			◆		
Paeonia officinalis	15–24 in (38–60 cm)	24 in (60 cm)	P	C	NA	◆			W	Sp			◆		
Paeonia peregrina	20 in (50 cm)	20 in (50 cm)	P	C	NA	◆			W	Sp			◆	◆	
Paeonia tenuifolia	20–27 in (50–70 cm)	20–27 in (50–70 cm)	P	C/W	NA	◆			W	Sp			◆		
Paeonia veitchii	24 in (60 cm)	20 in (50 cm)	P	C/W	NA	◆			W	Su			◆		
Paeonia Hybrid Cultivars	30–36 in (75–90 cm)	30–36 in (75–90 cm)	P	C	NA	◆		◆	W	Sp			◆		
Papaver alpinum	10 in (25 cm)	8–16 in (20–40 cm)	P	C	NA	◆			W/Sp	Su	◆	◆	◆	◆	
Papaver atlanticum	18 in (45 cm)	8–12 in (20–30 cm)	P	C/W	NA	◆			W/Sp	Su			◆	◆	
Papaver commutatum	16 in (40 cm)	16 in (40 cm)	A	W	NA	◆			W/Sp	Su			◆	◆	
Papaver × hybridum	8–20 in (20–50 cm)	6–10 in (15–25 cm)	P	C/W	NA	◆			W/Sp	Sp/Su			◆	◆	
Papaver nudicaule	12–16 in (30–40 cm)	8–12 in (20–30 cm)	P	C/W	NA	◆			A–Sp	Sp/Su			◆	◆	
Papaver orientale	24–40 in (60–100 cm)	12–20 in (30–50 cm)	P	C/W	NA	◆	◆		W/Sp	Su			◆	◆	
Papaver rhoeas	36–48 in (90–120 cm)	12–16 in (30–40 cm)	A	C/W	NA	◆			W/Sp	Su			◆	◆	

Plant name	Height	Spread	Type	Climate	Group	Showy flowers	Showy foliage	Scented flowers	Planting season	Flowering season	Grow in pot/tub	Frost tolerant	Full Sun	Half Sun	Heavy shade
Papaver somniferum	36–48 in (90–120 cm)	12–24 in (30–60 cm)	A	C/W	NA	◆	◆		W/Sp	Su			◆	◆	
Paradisea liliastrum	16–24 in (40–60 cm)	10–12 in (25–30 cm)	P	C/W	NA	◆		◆	W/Sp	Su			◆	◆	◆
Parahebe × bidwillii	4 in (10 cm)	6 in (15 cm)	P	C/W	NA	◆			W/Sp	Su	◆	◆	◆		
Parahebe cataractae	12 in (30 cm)	24 in (60 cm)	P	C/W	NA	◆			W/Sp	Su			◆	◆	
Parahebe lyallii	8 in (20 cm)	18 in (45 cm)	P	C/W	NA	◆			W/Sp	Su	◆	◆	◆		
Paris polyphylla	36–40 in (90–100 cm)	8–12 in (20–30 cm)	P	C/W	NA	◆	◆		W/Sp	Su		◆		◆	◆
Paris quadrifolia	8–16 in (20–40 cm)	10–12 in (25–30 cm)	P	C	NA	◆			W/Sp	Su		◆		◆	◆
Pelargonium australe	12 in (30 cm)	20 in (50 cm)	P	W	NA	◆			W/Sp	Sp/Su			◆		
Pelargonium crispum	30 in (75 cm)	36 in (90 cm)	P	W	NA	◆	◆		W/Sp	Su	◆		◆		
Pelargonium graveolens	48 in (120 cm)	26 in (65 cm)	P	W	NA		◆	◆	W/Sp	Su			◆		
Pelargonium odoratissimum	12 in (30 cm)	24 in (60 cm)	P	W	NA		◆	◆	W/Sp	Sp/Su			◆		
Pelargonium quercifolium	3–5 ft (0.9–1.5 m)	24–32 in (60–80 cm)	P	W	NA	◆	◆		W/Sp	Sp/Su			◆		
Pelargonium rodneyanum	8–12 in (20–30 cm)	12–20 in (30–50 cm)	P	W	NA	◆	◆		Su/A	Sp			◆		
Pelargonium tomentosum	20 in (50 cm)	40 in (100 cm)	P	W	NA	◆	◆		W/Sp	Sp/Su	◆		◆		
Pelargonium Hybrid Cultivars	6–60 in (15–150 cm)	8–40 in (20–100 cm)	P	W	NA	◆	◆		W/Sp	Sp–A	◆		◆		
Peltandra virginica	12–36 in (30–90 cm)	12–36 in (30–90 cm)	P	C	NA	◆	◆		W/Sp	Sp			◆		
Penstemon barbatus	40 in (100 cm)	12–20 in (30–50 cm)	P	C/W	NA	◆			W/Sp	Su		◆	◆	◆	
Penstemon campanulatus	12–24 in (30–60 cm)	8–12 in (20–30 cm)	P	W	NA	◆			W/Sp	Sp/Su			◆	◆	
Penstemon davidsonii	4 in (10 cm)	20–24 in (50–60 cm)	P	C/W	NA	◆			W/Sp	Su			◆	◆	
Penstemon digitalis	5 ft (1.5 m)	12–24 in (30–60 cm)	P	C/W	NA	◆			W/Sp	Su			◆	◆	
Penstemon fruticosus	16 in (40 cm)	20 in (50 cm)	P	C/W	NA	◆			W/Sp	Sp/Su			◆	◆	
Penstemon grandiflorus	40 in (100 cm)	12–20 in (30–50 cm)	P	C/W	NA	◆			W/Sp	Su			◆	◆	
Penstemon heterophyllus	12–20 in (30–50 cm)	8–12 in (20–30 cm)	P	W	NA	◆			W/Sp	Su			◆	◆	
Penstemon hirsutus	16–32 in (40–80 cm)	8–12 in (20–30 cm)	P	C/W	NA	◆			W/Sp	Su		◆	◆	◆	
Penstemon isophyllus	27 in (70 cm)	40 in (100 cm)	P	W	NA	◆			W/Sp	Sp			◆	◆	
Penstemon pinifolius	16 in (40 cm)	16–24 in (40–60 cm)	P	W	NA	◆			W/Sp	Su			◆	◆	
Penstemon procerus	6–16 in (15–40 cm)	12–16 in (30–40 cm)	P	C/W	NA	◆			W/Sp	Su			◆	◆	
Penstemon strictus	32 in (80 cm)	12–16 in (30–40 cm)	P	C/W	NA	◆			W/Sp	Su		◆	◆	◆	
Penstemon superbus	5–6 ft (1.5–1.8 m)	20–32 in (50–80 cm)	P	W	NA	◆			W/Sp	Su			◆	◆	
Penstemon Hybrid Cultivars	24–48 in (60–120 cm)	8–16 in (20–40 cm)	P	C/W	NA	◆			W/Sp	Su		◆	◆	◆	
Pentas lanceolata	6 ft (1.8 m)	3 ft (0.9 m)	A/P	W/T	NA	◆			Sp	Su			◆		

Plant name	Height	Spread	Type	Climate	Group	Showy flowers	Showy foliage	Scented flowers	Planting season	Flowering season	Grow in pot/tub	Frost tolerant	Full Sun	Half Sun	Heavy shade
Peperomia argyreia	6–12 in (15–30 cm)	6–9 in (15–22 cm)	P	W/T	NA		◆		Any	Any	◆			◆	◆
Peperomia caperata	6–10 in (15–25 cm)	6–10 in (15–25 cm)	P	W/T	NA		◆		Any	Any	◆			◆	◆
Peperomia clusiifolia	6–10 in (15–25 cm)	6–10 in (15–25 cm)	P	W/T	NA		◆		Any	Any	◆				◆
Peperomia griseoargentea	6–8 in (15–20 cm)	6–8 in (15–20 cm)	P	W/T	NA		◆		Any	Any	◆				◆
Peperomia obtusifolia	6–8 in (15–20 cm)	6–8 in (15–20 cm)	P	W/T	NA		◆		Any	Any	◆				◆
Peperomia orba	4–6 in (10–15 cm)	4–6 in (10–15 cm)	P	W/T	NA		◆		Any	Any	◆				◆
Pericallis × hybrida	16–32 in (40–80 cm)	16–40 in (40–100 cm)	P	W	NA	◆			Any	Sp/Su	◆			◆	◆
Perilla frutescens	24–40 in (60–100 cm)	18–24 in (45–60 cm)	A	W	NA	◆	◆		Sp	Su/A		◆	◆	◆	
Perovskia atriplicifolia	30–60 in (75–150 cm)	18–36 in (45–90 cm)	P	C	NA	◆			W/Sp	Su/A		◆	◆		
Persicaria affinis	8–10 in (20–25 cm)	20–24 in (50–60 cm)	P	C/W	NA	◆			W/Sp	Su			◆	◆	
Persicaria amplexicaulis	3–4 ft (0.9–1.2 m)	3–4 ft (0.9–1.2 m)	P	C	NA	◆	◆		W/Sp	Su/A			◆	◆	
Persicaria bistorta	6–30 in (15–75 cm)	6–30 in (15–75 cm)	P	C	NA	◆			W/Sp	Su				◆	
Persicaria capitata	3–6 in (8–15 cm)	6–12 in (15–30 cm)	P	C/W	NA	◆	◆		W/Sp	Su/A			◆	◆	
Persicaria orientalis	36–60 in (90–150 cm)	15–18 in (38–45 cm)	A	C/W	NA	◆			W/Sp	Su/A			◆	◆	
Persicaria virginiana	24–48 in (60–120 cm)	32–60 in (80–150 cm)	P	C/W	NA		◆		W/Sp	Su			◆	◆	
Petunia axillaris	12–20 in (30–50 cm)	16–24 in (40–60 cm)	A	W	NA			◆	Sp	Su			◆	◆	
Petunia × hybrida	4–16 in (10–40 cm)	8–40 in (20–100 cm)	A	C/W	NA	◆			Sp	Sp–A			◆	◆	
Petunia integrifolia	12–20 in (30–50 cm)	16–24 in (40–60 cm)	A/P	W	NA	◆			Sp	Su	◆		◆	◆	
Phacelia campanularia	6–24 in (15–60 cm)	6–24 in (15–60 cm)	A	C/W	NA	◆			Sp	Sp			◆	◆	
Phacelia tanacetifolia	6–60 in (15–150 cm)	4–24 in (10–60 cm)	A	C/W	NA	◆			Sp	Sp			◆	◆	
Phlomis cashmeriana	36 in (90 cm)	36 in (90 cm)	P	W	NA	◆	◆		W/Sp	Su			◆	◆	
Phlomis 'Edward Bowles'	36 in (90 cm)	36 in (90 cm)	P	W	NA	◆	◆		W/Sp	Su			◆	◆	
Phlomis purpurea	24 in (60 cm)	24 in (60 cm)	P	W	NA	◆	◆		W/Sp	Su			◆		
Phlomis russeliana	36 in (90 cm)	24 in (60 cm)	P	W	NA	◆	◆		W/Sp	Su			◆	◆	
Phlomis tuberosa	36 in (90 cm)	36 in (90 cm)	P	W	NA	◆	◆		W/Sp	Su			◆	◆	
Phlox adsurgens	4–6 in (10–15 cm)	12–20 in (30–50 cm)	P	C/W	NA	◆			W/Sp	Sp/Su	◆		◆	◆	
Phlox bifida	4–8 in (10–20 cm)	12–16 in (30–40 cm)	P	C/W	NA			◆	W/Sp	Sp/Su			◆	◆	
Phlox divaricata	12–18 in (30–45 cm)	24–40 in (60–100 cm)	P	C	NA	◆			W/Sp	Sp			◆	◆	◆
Phlox douglasii	2–6 in (5–15 cm)	12–20 in (30–50 cm)	P	C/W	NA	◆			W/Sp	Sp/Su			◆	◆	
Phlox drummondii	6–16 in (15–40 cm)	8–16 in (20–40 cm)	A	C/W	NA	◆			Sp	Su			◆	◆	
Phlox maculata	27 in (70 cm)	16 in (40 cm)	P	C/W	NA	◆			W/Sp	Su			◆	◆	◆

Plant name	Height	Spread	Type	Climate	Group	Showy flowers	Showy foliage	Scented flowers	Planting season	Flowering season	Grow in pot/tub	Frost tolerant	Full Sun	Half Sun	Heavy shade
Phlox paniculata	24–48 in (60–120 cm)	16–40 in (40–100 cm)	P	C/W	NA	♦			W/Sp	Su		♦	♦	♦	
Phlox stolonifera	6–10 in (15–25 cm)	20–40 in (50–100 cm)	P	C/W	NA	♦			W/Sp	Sp	♦	♦	♦	♦	
Phlox subulata	2–4 in (5–10 cm)	12–20 in (30–50 cm)	P	C/W	NA	♦			W/Sp	Sp/Su	♦	♦	♦	♦	
Phormium cookianum	4–8 ft (1.2–2.4 m)	7–8 ft (2–2.4 m)	P	C/W	NA		♦		Any	Su		♦	♦		
Phormium tenax	10–15 ft (3–4.5m)	7–10 ft (2–3 m)	P	C/W	NA		♦		Any	Su		♦	♦		
Phormium Hybrid Cultivars	1–6 ft (0.3–1.8 m)	1–6 ft (0.3–1.8 m)	P	C/W	NA		♦		Any	Su	♦	♦	♦		
Physalis alkekengi	12–24 in (30–60 cm)	12–24 in (30–60 cm)	P	C	NA				W/Sp	Su		♦	♦		
Physostegia virginiana	32–48 in (80–120 cm)	12–20 in (30–50 cm)	P	C/W	NA	♦			W/Sp	Su/A		♦	♦	♦	
Phytolacca americana	12 ft (3.5 m)	3 ft (0.9 m)	P	C/W	NA	♦	♦		W/Sp	Su/A		♦	♦		
Pilea involucrata	4–18 in (10–45 cm)	6–12 in (15–30 cm)	P	W/T	NA		♦		Any	Su	♦			♦	
Pilea peperomioides	6–20 in (15–50 cm)	6–20 in (15–50 cm)	P	W/T	NA		♦		Any	Su	♦			♦	
Pinguicula emarginata	1½ in (35 mm)	4 in (10 cm)	P	W	C	♦			Sp	Su		♦	♦	♦	
Pinguicula moranensis	2 in (5 cm)	10 in (25 cm)	P	W	C	♦			Sp	Su		♦	♦	♦	
Pinguicula vulgaris	6 in (15 cm)	5 in (12 cm)	P	C	C	♦			Sp	Su	♦	♦	♦	♦	
Pistia stratiotes	4–6 in (10–15 cm)	4–6 in (10–15 cm)	P	W/T	NA		♦		Su	Su			♦		
Pitcairnia atrorubens	32 in (80 cm)	8 in (20 cm)	P	W/T	B	♦			Any	Su					♦
Pitcairnia heterophylla	20 in (50 cm)	20 in (50 cm)	P	W/T	B	♦			Any	Su	♦				♦
Platycodon grandiflorus	27 in (70 cm)	24 in (60 cm)	P	C	NA	♦			W/Sp	Su		♦	♦	♦	
Plectranthus ciliatus	2–4 in (5–10 cm)	4 in (10 cm)	P	W	NA	♦	♦		W/Sp	A/W	♦			♦	
Plectranthus ecklonii	5 ft (1.5 m)	3 ft (0.9 m)	P	W	NA	♦			W/Sp	A			♦		
Plectranthus forsteri	3–8 ft (0.9–2.4 m)	10 ft (3 m)	P	W	NA	♦			W/Sp	Su/A				♦	
Plectranthus neochilus	18 in (45 cm)	24 in (60 cm)	P	W	NA	♦	♦		W/Sp	Su			♦	♦	
Plectranthus oertendahlii	8–12 in (20–30 cm)	36 in (90 cm)	P	W	NA	♦	♦		W/Sp	Any	♦			♦	
Plectranthus verticillatus	12 in (30 cm)	40 in (100 cm)	P	W	NA	♦			W/Sp	Su				♦	
Podophyllum peltatum	24 in (60 cm)	24 in (60 cm)	P	C	NA	♦	♦	♦	W/Sp	Sp		♦	♦		
Polemonium caeruleum	12–36 in (30–90 cm)	12–20 in (30–50 cm)	P	C	NA	♦			A–Sp	Sp/Su		♦	♦		
Polemonium pulcherrimum	20–24 in (50–60 cm)	20–24 in (50–60 cm)	P	C	NA	♦			A–Sp	Sp/Su		♦	♦		
Polemonium reptans	8–27 in (20–70 cm)	12–27 in (30–70 cm)	P	C	NA	♦			A–Sp	Sp/Su		♦	♦		
Polygala chamaebuxus	2–6 in (5–15 cm)	15 in (38 cm)	P	C	NA	♦			W/Sp	Sp			♦		
Polygonatum × hybridum	36 in (90 cm)	12–24 in (30–60 cm)	P	C	NA	♦	♦	♦	W/Sp	Sp/Su		♦		♦	♦
Polygonatum odoratum	36 in (90 cm)	24 in (60 cm)	P	C	NA	♦	♦	♦	W/Sp	Sp/Su		♦			♦

Plant name	Height	Spread	Type	Climate	Group	Showy flowers	Showy foliage	Scented flowers	Planting season	Flowering season	Grow in pot/tub	Frost tolerant	Full Sun	Half Sun	Heavy shade
Pontederia cordata	48 in (120 cm)	27 in (70 cm)	P	C	NA	◆	◆		W/Sp	Su		◆	◆		
Portea petropolitana	7 ft (2 m)	3 ft (0.9 m)	P	W/T	B	◆	◆		W/Sp	Su	◆			◆	
Portulaca grandiflora	6–12 in (15–30 cm)	6–12 in (15–30 cm)	A	W	NA	◆			Sp	Su	◆	◆	◆		
Potamogeton perfoliatus	2 in (5 cm)	15 ft (4.5 m)	P	C/W	NA		◆		W/Sp			◆	◆		
Potentilla alba	10 in (25 cm)	10 in (25 cm)	P	C	NA	◆			W/Sp	Sp/Su	◆	◆	◆		
Potentilla atrosanguinea	36 in (90 cm)	36 in (90 cm)	P	C	NA	◆			W/Sp	Su/A		◆	◆		
Potentilla aurea	12 in (30 cm)	12 in (30 cm)	P	C	NA	◆			W/Sp	Sp/Su		◆	◆		
Potentilla megalantha	8–12 in (20–30 cm)	8–12 in (20–30 cm)	P	C	NA	◆			W/Sp	Su/A	◆	◆	◆		
Potentilla nepalensis	12–24 in (30–60 cm)	12–24 in (30–60 cm)	P	C	NA	◆			W/Sp	Su		◆	◆		
Potentilla neumanniana	3–4 in (8–10 cm)	6–12 in (15–30 cm)	P	C	NA	◆			W/Sp	Sp					
Potentilla nitida	2–4 in (5–10 cm)	5–16 in (12–40 cm)	P	C	NA	◆	◆		W/Sp	Su		◆	◆		
Potentilla × tonguei	6–10 in (15–25 cm)	12–20 in (30–50 cm)	P	C	NA	◆			W/Sp	Su		◆	◆		
Primula alpicola	16–36 in (40–90 cm)	10–16 in (25–40 cm)	P	C	NA	◆			A–Sp	Sp/Su		◆		◆	◆
Primula auricula	4–8 in (10–20 cm)	6–16 in (15–40 cm)	P	C	NA	◆			A–Sp	Sp	◆	◆		◆	◆
Primula beesiana	32 in (80 cm)	20 in (50 cm)	P	C	NA	◆			A–Sp			◆		◆	◆
Primula bulleyana	24 in (60 cm)	12–27 in (30–70 cm)	P	C	NA	◆			A–Sp	Sp/Su		◆		◆	◆
Primula capitata	10–15 in (25–38 cm)	12–18 in (30–45 cm)	P	C	NA	◆	◆		W/Sp	Sp/Su	◆	◆		◆	◆
Primula denticulata	8–12 in (20–30 cm)	10–18 in (25–45 cm)	P	C	NA	◆			A–Sp	Sp/Su		◆		◆	◆
Primula elatior	6–12 in (15–30 cm)	6–16 in (15–40 cm)	P	C	NA	◆			A–Sp	Sp/Su		◆		◆	◆
Primula farinosa	8 in (20 cm)	12 in (30 cm)	P	C	NA	◆			A–Sp	Sp	◆	◆		◆	◆
Primula florindae	36 in (90 cm)	8–16 in (20–40 cm)	P	C/W	NA	◆		◆	A–Sp	Sp/Su		◆		◆	◆
Primula japonica	18 in (45 cm)	12–24 in (30–60 cm)	P	C	NA	◆			A–Sp	Sp/Su		◆		◆	◆
Primula juliae	2 in (5 cm)	6–10 in (15–25 cm)	P	C	NA	◆			A–Sp	Sp		◆		◆	◆
Primula × kewensis	12 in (30 cm)	12–18 in (30–45 cm)	P	C/W	NA	◆		◆	A/W	Sp	◆				
Primula malacoides	12 in (30 cm)	16 in (40 cm)	A	C/W	NA	◆			A/W	W/Sp	◆		◆	◆	
Primula obconica	8 in (20 cm)	8–16 in (20–40 cm)	A	C/W	NA	◆			A/W	W/Sp		◆		◆	◆
Primula, Pruhonicensis Hybrids	4–12 in (10–30 cm)	6–16 in (15–40 cm)	P	C	NA	◆			A–Sp	W/Sp		◆		◆	◆
Primula × pubescens	6 in (15 cm)	10 in (25 cm)	P	C	NA	◆			A–Sp	Sp	◆	◆		◆	◆
Primula pulverulenta	36 in (90 cm)	20 in (50 cm)	P	C	NA	◆			A–Sp	Sp/Su		◆		◆	◆
Primula rosea	4–6 in (10–15 cm)	6–15 in (15–38 cm)	P	C	NA	◆			A–Sp	Sp	◆	◆		◆	◆
Primula sieboldii	12 in (30 cm)	12–24 in (30–60 cm)	P	C	NA	◆			A–Sp	Sp/Su		◆		◆	◆

Plant name	Height	Spread	Type	Climate	Group	Showy flowers	Showy foliage	Scented flowers	Planting season	Flowering season	Grow in pot/tub	Frost tolerant	Full Sun	Half Sun	Heavy shade
Primula sikkimensis	12–36 in (30–90 cm)	10–24 in (25–60 cm)	P	C	NA	◆			A–Sp	Sp/Su		◆		◆	◆
Primula veris	12 in (30 cm)	16 in (40 cm)	P	C	NA	◆		◆	A–Sp	Sp/Su		◆		◆	◆
Primula vulgaris	4–6 in (10–15 cm)	6–16 in (15–40 cm)	P	C	NA	◆		◆	A–Sp	Sp	◆	◆		◆	◆
Prunella grandiflora	12–24 in (30–60 cm)	12–24 in (30–60 cm)	P	C	NA	◆			Sp	Su		◆	◆		
Prunella laciniata	9–12 in (22–30 cm)	9–12 in (22–30 cm)	P	C	NA	◆			Sp	Sp/Su		◆	◆		
Psylliostachys suworowii	12–36 in (30–90 cm)	12–16 in (30–40 cm)	A	C/W	NA	◆			Sp	Su/A	◆	◆	◆		
Pulmonaria angustifolia	8–16 in (20–40 cm)	16–40 in (40–100 cm)	P	C	NA	◆	◆		A–Sp	Sp		◆		◆	◆
Pulmonaria mollis	16 in (40 cm)	40 in (100 cm)	P	C	NA	◆	◆		A–Sp	Sp/Su		◆		◆	
Pulmonaria rubra	12–18 in (30–45 cm)	20–40 in (50–100 cm)	P	C	NA	◆	◆		A–Sp	Sp/Su		◆		◆	
Pulmonaria saccharata	12–16 in (30–40 cm)	16–32 in (40–80 cm)	P	C	NA	◆	◆		A–Sp	Sp		◆		◆	
Pulmonaria vallarsae	12–18 in (30–45 cm)	20–40 in (50–100 cm)	P	C	NA	◆	◆		A–Sp	Sp/Su		◆		◆	
Pulmonaria Hybrid Cultivars	8–16 in (20–40 cm)	16–40 in (40–100 cm)	P	C	NA	◆	◆		A–Sp	Sp		◆		◆	
Pulsatilla albana	8 in (20 cm)	8 in (20 cm)	P	C	NA	◆	◆		A/W	Sp/Su		◆	◆	◆	
Pulsatilla halleri	10 in (25 cm)	12 in (30 cm)	P	C	NA	◆	◆		A/W	Sp		◆	◆	◆	
Pulsatilla patens	6–10 in (15–25 cm)	8–12 in (20–30 cm)	P	C	NA	◆	◆		A/W	Sp		◆	◆	◆	
Pulsatilla pratensis	12 in (30 cm)	16 in (40 cm)	P	C	NA	◆	◆		A/W	Sp		◆	◆	◆	
Pulsatilla vulgaris	8–15 in (20–38 cm)	8–16 in (20–40 cm)	P	C	NA	◆	◆		A/W	Sp		◆	◆	◆	
Puya berteroniana	15 ft (4.5 m)	7 ft (2 m)	P	C/W	B	◆	◆		A/W	Sp/Su		◆	◆		
Puya chilensis	15 ft (4.5 m)	7 ft (2 m)	P	C/W	B	◆	◆		A/W	Sp/Su		◆	◆		
Puya venusta	40 in (100 cm)	20 in (50 cm)	P	W	B	◆	◆		A/W	Sp/Su		◆	◆		
Quesnelia liboniana	32 in (80 cm)	4 in (10 cm)	P	W/T	B	◆			W	Sp					◆
Quesnelia marmorata	24 in (60 cm)	4 in (10 cm)	P	W/T	B	◆			W	Sp					◆
Ramonda myconi	4–5 in (10–12 cm)	7–8 in (18–20 cm)	P	C	G	◆			W/Sp	Sp/Su	◆	◆		◆	
Raoulia australis	½ in (12 mm)	12 in (30 cm)	P	C	NA		◆		W/Sp	Su	◆	◆	◆		
Raoulia eximia	12 in (30 cm)	20 in (50 cm)	P	C	NA		◆		W/Sp	Su	◆	◆	◆		
Ratibida columnifera	24 in (60 cm)	18 in (45 cm)	P	C	NA	◆			W/Sp	Su/A		◆	◆		
Ratibida pinnata	48 in (120 cm)	12–18 in (30–45 cm)	P	C	NA	◆			W/Sp	Su/A		◆	◆		
Rehmannia elata	40–60 in (100–150 cm)	20–32 in (50–80 cm)	P	W	NA	◆			W/Sp	Sp/Su		◆		◆	
Reineckea carnea	8 in (20 cm)	6–12 in (15–30 cm)	P	C/W	NA	◆		◆	W/Sp	Sp		◆		◆	
Reseda lutea	20–27 in (50–70 cm)	20–27 in (50–70 cm)	A	C/W	NA				Sp	Su		◆	◆		
Reseda luteola	36–48 in (90–120 cm)	8–12 in (20–30 cm)	A/P	C/W	NA	◆			W/Sp	Su		◆	◆		

Plant name	Height	Spread	Type	Climate	Group	Showy flowers	Showy foliage	Scented flowers	Planting season	Flowering season	Grow in pot/tub	Frost tolerant	Full Sun	Half Sun	Heavy shade
Reseda odorata	12–24 in (30–60 cm)	7–8 in (18–20 cm)	A	C/W	NA	◆		◆	Sp	Su		◆	◆		
Rheum australe	5 ft (1.5 m)	5 ft (1.5 m)	P	C	NA		◆		W/Sp	Su		◆	◆	◆	
Rheum palmatum	5–8 ft (1.5–2.4 m)	5 ft (1.5 m)	P	C	NA		◆		W/Sp	Su		◆	◆	◆	
Rhodanthe chlorocephala	12–24 in (30–60 cm)	8–12 in (20–30 cm)	A	W	NA	◆			A–Sp	W–Su			◆		
Rhodanthe manglesii	12–18 in (30–45 cm)	6–12 in (15–30 cm)	A	W	NA	◆			W/Sp	Sp		◆	◆		
Rhodanthemum gayanum	8–12 in (20–30 cm)	24–40 in (60–100 cm)	P	W	NA	◆			W/Sp	W/Sp	◆	◆	◆		
Rhodanthemum hosmariense	4–8 in (10–20 cm)	12–16 in (30–40 cm)	P	W	NA	◆	◆		W/Sp	Sp–A	◆		◆		
Rodgersia aesculifolia	5–7 ft (1.5–2 m)	3–7 ft (0.9–2 m)	P	C	NA	◆	◆		W/Sp	Su			◆		◆
Rodgersia pinnata	32–48 in (80–120 cm)	3–7 ft (0.9–2 m)	P	C	NA	◆	◆		W/Sp	Su			◆		◆
Rodgersia podophylla	32–48 in (80–120 cm)	3–7 ft (0.9–2 m)	P	C	NA		◆		W/Sp	Su			◆		◆
Rodgersia sambucifolia	24–36 in (60–90 cm)	24–48 in (60–120 cm)	P	C	NA	◆	◆		W/Sp	Su			◆		◆
Romneya coulteri	8 ft (2.4 m)	7 ft (2 m)	P	C/W	NA	◆		◆	W/Sp	Su/A		◆	◆		
Rudbeckia fulgida	40 in (100 cm)	24–48 in (60–120 cm)	P	C/W	NA	◆			W/Sp	Su/A		◆	◆		
Rudbeckia 'Herbstsonne'	6 ft (1.8 m)	3 ft (0.9 m)	P	C/W	NA	◆			W/Sp	Su/A		◆	◆		
Rudbeckia hirta	5–7 ft (1.5–2 m)	32–48 in (80–120 cm)	B/P	C/W	NA	◆			W/Sp	Su/A		◆	◆		
Rudbeckia laciniata	7–10 ft (2–3 m)	3–7 ft (0.9–2 m)	P	C/W	NA	◆			W/Sp	Su/A		◆	◆		
Rudbeckia nitida	5–7 ft (1.5–2 m)	32–48 in (80–120 cm)	P	C/W	NA	◆			W/Sp	Su/A		◆	◆		
Rudbeckia occidentalis	5–7 ft (1.5–2 m)	32–48 in (80–120 cm)	P	C/W	NA		◆		W/Sp	Su		◆	◆		
Ruellia brittoniana	24–36 in (60–90 cm)	18–24 in (45–60 cm)	P	W	NA	◆			W/Sp	Sp–A		◆	◆		
Ruellia makoyana	6–12 in (15–30 cm)	15–18 in (38–45 cm)	P	W/T	NA	◆	◆		W/Sp	All	◆		◆		
Rumex sanguineus	20–40 in (50–100 cm)	12–36 in (30–90 cm)	P	C/W	NA		◆		W/Sp	Su		◆	◆		
Rumex vesicarius	8–10 in (20–25 cm)	6–8 in (15–20 cm)	A	C/W	NA	◆			W/Sp	Sp		◆	◆		
Ruscus aculeatus	30–40 in (75–100 cm)	40 in (100 cm)	P	C/W	NA		◆		W/Sp	Sp		◆	◆		◆
Ruscus hypoglossum	18–26 in (45–65 cm)	40 in (100 cm)	P	C/W	NA		◆		W/Sp	Sp		◆	◆		◆
Sagina subulata	1 in (25 mm)	12 in (30 cm)	P	C	NA		◆		W/Sp	Su		◆	◆	◆	
Sagittaria graminea	20 in (50 cm)	12 in (30 cm)	P	All	NA	◆	◆		W/Sp	Su		◆	◆		
Saintpaulia ionantha	4–10 in (10–25 cm)	8–16 in (20–40 cm)	P	W/T	G	◆	◆		Sp	All	◆				◆
Saintpaulia shumensis	2–6 in (5–15 cm)	6–10 in (15–25 cm)	P	W/T	G	◆	◆		Sp	All	◆				
Saintpaulia Hybrid Cultivars	2–8 in (5–20 cm)	4–12 in (10–30 cm)	P	W/T	G	◆	◆		Sp	All	◆				
Salpiglossis sinuata	16–24 in (40–60 cm)	8–12 in (20–30 cm)	A	W	NA	◆			Sp	Su/A	◆	◆	◆	◆	
Salvia argentea	24–36 in (60–90 cm)	24–36 in (60–90 cm)	P	W	NA	◆	◆		W/Sp	Su			◆	◆	

Plant name	Height	Spread	Type	Climate	Group	Showy flowers	Showy foliage	Scented flowers	Planting season	Flowering season	Grow in pot/tub	Frost tolerant	Full Sun	Half Sun	Heavy shade
Salvia blepharophylla	8–12 in (20–30 cm)	20–27 in (50–70 cm)	P	W	NA	◆			W/Sp	Su/A				◆	
Salvia buchananii	12–20 in (30–50 cm)	12 in (30 cm)	P	W	NA	◆	◆		W/Sp	Su/A				◆	
Salvia cacaliifolia	36 in (90 cm)	12–20 in (30–50 cm)	P	W	NA	◆			W/Sp	Su/A			◆	◆	
Salvia chiapensis	16–24 in (40–60 cm)	16–24 in (40–60 cm)	P	W	NA	◆			W/Sp	Sp–A			◆	◆	
Salvia coccinea	40 in (100 cm)	20–32 in (50–80 cm)	A	W	NA	◆			Sp	Su/A			◆		
Salvia discolor	32–40 in (80–100 cm)	32–40 in (80–100 cm)	P	W	NA	◆	◆		W/Sp	Su/A			◆		
Salvia dorisiana	36–48 in (90–120 cm)	36 in (90 cm)	P	W	NA	◆		◆	Sp	W			◆		
Salvia elegans	6 ft (1.8 m)	3 ft (0.9 m)	P	C/W	NA	◆			W/Sp	Sp–A		◆	◆		
Salvia farinacea	36–48 in (90–120 cm)	24 in (60 cm)	A/P	W	NA	◆	◆		Sp	Su/A			◆		
Salvia fulgens	48 in (120 cm)	30 in (75 cm)	P	W	NA	◆			W/Sp	Su			◆		
Salvia gesneriiflora	26 in (65 cm)	10 in (25 cm)	P	W	NA	◆			W/Sp	Su			◆		
Salvia greggii	12–36 in (30–90 cm)	12–36 in (30–90 cm)	P	W	NA	◆			W/Sp	Su/A			◆		
Salvia guaranitica	4–5 ft (1.2–1.5 m)	16–27 in (40–70 cm)	P	C/W	NA	◆			W/Sp	Su/A			◆		
Salvia indica	24–36 in (60–90 cm)	24 in (60 cm)	P	W	NA	◆			A/W	Sp			◆		
Salvia involucrata	5 ft (1.5 m)	5 ft (1.5 m)	P	W	NA	◆	◆		W/Sp	Su/A			◆	◆	
Salvia leucantha	36 in (90 cm)	36 in (90 cm)	P	W	NA	◆			W/Sp	Su			◆		
Salvia microphylla	4 ft (1.2 m)	3 ft (0.9 m)	P	W	NA	◆			W/Sp	Su/A			◆	◆	
Salvia nemorosa	24–36 in (60–90 cm)	12–24 in (30–60 cm)	P	C/W	NA	◆			W/Sp	Sp			◆	◆	
Salvia patens	12–24 in (30–60 cm)	12–24 in (30–60 cm)	P	W	NA	◆			W/Sp	Su/A					◆
Salvia pratensis	36 in (90 cm)	12 in (30 cm)	P	C/W	NA	◆			W/Sp	Sp/Su			◆	◆	
Salvia przewalskii	12–24 in (30–60 cm)	12–24 in (30–60 cm)	P	W	NA	◆			W/Sp	Su		◆	◆		
Salvia roemeriana	12 in (30 cm)	12 in (30 cm)	P	C/W	NA	◆			W/Sp	Su		◆	◆	◆	
Salvia spathacea	12–36 in (30–90 cm)	12–36 in (30–90 cm)	P	C/W	NA	◆	◆		W/Sp	Sp/Su			◆	◆	
Salvia splendens	8–48 in (20–120 cm)	8–32 in (10–80 cm)	A/P	W	NA	◆			Sp	Su/A			◆		
Salvia × sylvestris	20–40 in (50–100 cm)	20–40 in (50–100 cm)	P	C/W	NA	◆			W/Sp	Su			◆		
Salvia uliginosa	3–6 ft (0.9–1.8 m)	3 ft (0.9 m)	P	W	NA	◆			W/Sp	Su/A			◆		
Salvia verticillata	40 in (100 cm)	32 in (80 cm)	P	C/W	NA	◆			W/Sp	Su		◆	◆		
Salvia viridis	12–24 in (30–60 cm)	12 in (30 cm)	A	C/W	NA	◆			Sp	Su/A			◆		
Salvia Hybrid Cultivars	20–60 in (50–150 cm)	16–48 in (40–120 cm)	A	C/W	NA	◆			Sp	Su/A		◆	◆	◆	
Sanguinaria canadensis	8 in (20 cm)	4 in (10 cm)	P	C	NA	◆			A/W	Sp		◆		◆	◆
Sanguisorba canadensis	48–60 in (120–150 cm)	24–36 in (60–90 cm)	P	C	NA	◆			W/Sp	Su		◆	◆		
Sanvitalia procumbens	6–8 in (15–20 cm)	12 in (30 cm)	A	C/W	NA	◆			Sp	Su		◆	◆		

Plant name	Height	Spread	Type	Climate	Group	Showy flowers	Showy foliage	Scented flowers	Planting season	Flowering season	Grow in pot/tub	Frost tolerant	Full Sun	Half Sun	Heavy shade
Saponaria ocymoides	6–12 in (15–30 cm)	12–20 in (30–50 cm)	P	C/W	NA	◆			W/Sp	Su	◆	◆	◆		
Saponaria officinalis	12–24 in (30–60 cm)	20–40 in (50–100 cm)	P	C/W	NA	◆			W/Sp	Su/A	◆	◆	◆		
Saponaria × olivana	2 in (5 cm)	8 in (20 cm)	P	C/W	NA	◆			W/Sp	Sp	◆	◆	◆		
Sarracenia alata	27 in (70 cm)	12 in (30 cm)	P	C/W	C		◆	◆	W/Sp	Sp		◆	◆		
Sarracenia × catesbaei	18 in (45 cm)	12 in (30 cm)	P	C/W	C		◆	◆	W/Sp	Sp		◆	◆		
Sarracenia × exornata	14 in (35 cm)	12 in (30 cm)	P	C/W	C		◆	◆	W/Sp	Sp		◆	◆		
Sarracenia flava	30 in (75 cm)	12 in (30 cm)	P	C/W	C		◆	◆	W/Sp	Sp		◆	◆		
Sarracenia 'Juthatip Soper'	18 in (45 cm)	12 in (30 cm)	P	C/W	C		◆	◆	W/Sp	Sp		◆	◆		
Sarracenia leucophylla	24 in (60 cm)	12 in (30 cm)	P	C/W	C		◆	◆	W/Sp	Sp		◆	◆		
Sarracenia minor	24 in (60 cm)	12 in (30 cm)	P	C/W	C		◆	◆	W/Sp	Sp		◆	◆		
Sarracenia × mitchelliana	18 in (45 cm)	12 in (30 cm)	P	C/W	C		◆	◆	W/Sp	Sp		◆	◆		
Sarracenia × moorei	40 in (100 cm)	12 in (30 cm)	P	C/W	C		◆	◆	W/Sp	Sp		◆	◆		
Sarracenia oreophila	24 in (60 cm)	12 in (30 cm)	P	C/W	C		◆	◆	W/Sp	Sp		◆	◆		
Sarracenia psittacina	10 in (25 cm)	20 in (50 cm)	P	C/W	C		◆	◆	W/Sp	Sp		◆	◆		
Sarracenia purpurea	12 in (30 cm)	24 in (60 cm)	P	C/W	C		◆	◆	W/Sp	Sp		◆	◆		
Sarracenia × readii	24 in (60 cm)	12 in (30 cm)	P	C/W	C		◆	◆	W/Sp	Sp		◆	◆		
Sarracenia × stevensii	24 in (60 cm)	12 in (30 cm)	P	C/W	C		◆	◆	W/Sp	Sp		◆	◆		
Saxifraga andersonii	4 in (10 cm)	12 in (30 cm)	P	C	NA	◆			W/Sp	Sp	◆	◆	◆		
Saxifraga callosa	10 in (25 cm)	8 in (20 cm)	P	C	NA	◆			W/Sp	Su		◆	◆		
Saxifraga cochlearis	8 in (20 cm)	6 in (15 cm)	P	C	NA	◆			W/Sp	Su		◆	◆		
Saxifraga oppositifolia	1 in (2.5 cm)	8 in (20 cm)	P	C	NA	◆			W/Sp	Su		◆	◆	◆	◆
Saxifraga paniculata	6 in (15 cm)	10 in (25 cm)	P	C	NA	◆			W/Sp	Su		◆	◆	◆	
Saxifraga spathularis	8–12 in (20–30 cm)	6–8 in (15–20 cm)	P	C/W	NA	◆			W/Sp	Su			◆	◆	◆
Saxifraga stolonifera	16 in (40 cm)	12 in (30 cm)	P	C/W	NA	◆	◆		W/Sp	Su		◆	◆	◆	
Saxifraga umbrosa	12 in (30 cm)	12 in (30 cm)	P	C/W	NA	◆			W/Sp	Sp/Su		◆		◆	
Saxifraga × urbium	12 in (30 cm)	18–36 in (45–90 cm)	P	C	NA	◆			W/Sp	Su			◆	◆	
Saxifraga Hybrid Cultivars	3–12 in (8–30 cm)	6–18 in (15–45 cm)	P	C	NA	◆			W/Sp	Sp/Su		◆	◆	◆	
Scabiosa atropurpurea	16–36 in (40–90 cm)	16–30 in (40–75 cm)	A/B/P	C/W	NA	◆		◆	Sp	Su/A			◆	◆	
Scabiosa caucasica	20–36 in (50–90 cm)	16–18 in (40–45 cm)	P	C/W	NA	◆			W/Sp	Su/A			◆	◆	
Scabiosa columbaria	24 in (60 cm)	16 in (40 cm)	B/P	C/W	NA	◆			W/Sp	Su			◆		
Scabiosa lucida	12 in (30 cm)	12–20 in (30–50 cm)	P	C/W	NA	◆			W/Sp	Su/A			◆	◆	
Scaevola aemula	6 in (15 cm)	20 in (50 cm)	P	W	NA	◆			W/Sp	Sp/Su	◆		◆		

Plant name	Height	Spread	Type	Climate	Group	Showy flowers	Showy foliage	Scented flowers	Planting season	Flowering season	Grow in pot/tub	Frost tolerant	Full Sun	Half Sun	Heavy shade
Schaueria flavicoma	36 in (90 cm)	24 in (60 cm)	P	W/T	NA	♦	♦		W/Sp	Sp/Su	♦		♦		
Schizanthus pinnatus	8–20 in (20–50 cm)	8–16 in (20–40 cm)	A	W	NA	♦			Sp	Su/A		♦	♦	♦	
Schizanthus × wisetonensis	12–20 in (30–50 cm)	12 in (30 cm)	A	W	NA	♦			Sp	Su		♦	♦	♦	
Scleranthus biflorus	2–4 in (5–10 cm)	12 in (30 cm)	P	C	NA		♦		Sp	Su		♦	♦	♦	
Scrophularia auriculata	36–48 in (90–120 cm)	36–48 in (90–120 cm)	P	C/W	NA		♦		W/Sp	Su		♦			♦
Scutellaria alpina	6–10 in (15–25 cm)	18 in (45 cm)	P	C	NA	♦			W/Sp	Sp/Su	♦	♦	♦		
Scutellaria baicalensis	16 in (40 cm)	8 in (20 cm)	P	C	NA	♦			W/Sp	Su	♦	♦	♦		
Scutellaria galericulata	12–24 in (30–60 cm)	8–12 in (20–30 cm)	P	C/W	NA	♦			W/Sp	Su		♦	♦		
Scutellaria incana	24–48 in (60–120 cm)	24 in (60 cm)	P	C/W	NA	♦			W/Sp	Su/A	♦	♦	♦		
Scutellaria indica	6 in (15 cm)	12 in (30 cm)	P	C/W	NA	♦			W/Sp	Su		♦	♦		
Scutellaria orientalis	12–18 in (30–45 cm)	6–10 in (15–25 cm)	P	C/W	NA	♦			W/Sp	Su		♦	♦		
Sedum spectabile	27 in (70 cm)	16–32 in (40–80 cm)	P	C/W	NA	♦	♦		W/Sp	Su/A		♦	♦		
Sedum telephium	24 in (60 cm)	24–32 in (60–80 cm)	P	C/W	NA	♦	♦		W/Sp	Su		♦	♦		
Sedum Hybrid Cultivars	12–24 in (30–60 cm)	12–24 in (30–60 cm)	P	C/W	NA	♦	♦		W/Sp	Su/A		♦	♦		
Semiaquilegia ecalcarata	12 in (30 cm)	8–10 in (20–25 cm)	P	C	NA	♦	♦		W/Sp	Su	♦	♦	♦	♦	♦
Senecio cineraria	20 in (50 cm)	16 in (40 cm)	P	C/W	NA		♦		A–Sp	Su		♦	♦		
Senecio vira-vira	16–24 in (40–60 cm)	12–24 in (30–60 cm)	P	W	NA		♦		A–Sp	Su		♦	♦		
Senna hebecarpa	4–6 ft (1.2–1.8 m)	24 in (60 cm)	P	C/W	NA	♦			W/Sp	Su		♦	♦		
Serissa japonica	18 in (45 cm)	18 in (45 cm)	P	W	NA	♦	♦		W/Sp	Sp–A	♦		♦		
Shortia galacifolia	6 in (15 cm)	10 in (25 cm)	P	C	NA	♦	♦		Su/A	Sp	♦	♦			♦
Shortia soldanelloides	6 in (15 cm)	10 in (25 cm)	P	C	NA	♦	♦		Su/A	Sp	♦	♦			♦
Sidalcea candida	24–36 in (60–90 cm)	20 in (50 cm)	P	C/W	NA	♦			W/Sp	Su		♦	♦		
Sidalcea malviflora	24–40 in (60–100 cm)	16–30 in (40–75 cm)	P	C/W	NA	♦			W/Sp	Sp–A		♦	♦	♦	
Sidalcea oregana	48 in (120 cm)	20 in (50 cm)	P	C/W	NA	♦			W/Sp	Su		♦	♦		
Sidalcea Hybrid Cultivars	24–32 in (60–80 cm)	16–24 in (40–60 cm)	P	C/W	NA	♦			W/Sp	Sp–A		♦	♦		
Silene acaulis	2 in (5 cm)	4 in (10 cm)	P	C	NA	♦			W/Sp	Sp/Su		♦	♦		
Silene alpestris	6–12 in (15–30 cm)	12 in (30 cm)	P	C	NA	♦			W/Sp	Su		♦	♦	♦	
Silene dioica	24 in (60 cm)	12 in (30 cm)	P	C	NA	♦			W/Sp	Su		♦	♦		
Silene fimbriata	40 in (100 cm)	24 in (60 cm)	P	C	NA	♦			W/Sp	Su		♦	♦	♦	
Silene laciniata	36 in (90 cm)	8 in (20 cm)	P	C/W	NA	♦			W/Sp	Su		♦	♦		
Silene schafta	4 in (10 cm)	8 in (20 cm)	P	C	NA	♦			W/Sp	Su/A	♦	♦	♦		
Silene uniflora	4–8 in (10–20 cm)	4 in (10 cm)	P	C	NA	♦			W/Sp	Su		♦	♦		

Plant name	Height	Spread	Type	Climate	Group	Showy flowers	Showy foliage	Scented flowers	Planting season	Flowering season	Grow in pot/tub	Frost tolerant	Full Sun	Half Sun	Heavy shade
Silphium laciniatum	5–10 ft (1.5–3 m)	3–4 ft (0.9–1.2 m)	P	C	NA	◆			W/Sp	Su		◆	◆	◆	
Silphium perfoliatum	5 ft (1.5 m)	3 ft (0.9 m)	P	C/W	NA	◆			W/Sp	Su		◆	◆	◆	
Silphium terebinthinaceum	7–10 ft (2–3 m)	3–6 ft (0.9–1.8 m)	P	C	NA	◆			W/Sp	Su		◆	◆	◆	
Silybum marianum	4 ft (1.2 m)	2 ft (0.6 m)	B	C/W	NA	◆	◆		W/Sp	Sp/Su			◆	◆	
Sinningia canescens	10 in (25 cm)	10 in (25 cm)	P	W/T	G	◆	◆		Sp	Su	◆			◆	◆
Sinningia cardinalis	8–12 in (20–30 cm)	12 in (30 cm)	P	W/T	G	◆			Sp	Su	◆			◆	◆
Sinningia × pumila	4–6 in (10–15 cm)	6–12 in (15–30 cm)	P	W/T	G	◆			Sp		◆			◆	◆
Sinningia speciosa	8–12 in (20–30 cm)	12–20 in (30–50 cm)	P	W/T	G	◆			Sp	Su	◆			◆	◆
Sisyrinchium 'Biscutella'	12 in (30 cm)	6 in (15 cm)	P	C/W	NA	◆			W/Sp				◆	◆	
Sisyrinchium 'Californian Skies'	12 in (30 cm)	8 in (20 cm)	P	C/W	NA	◆			W/Sp	Su/A			◆	◆	
Sisyrinchium californicum	24 in (60 cm)	6 in (15 cm)	P	C/W	NA	◆			W/Sp	Su			◆	◆	
Sisyrinchium graminoides	20 in (50 cm)	8 in (20 cm)	P	C/W	NA	◆			W/Sp	Su/A			◆	◆	
Sisyrinchium idahoense	5 in (12 cm)	6 in (15 cm)	P	C/W	NA	◆			W/Sp	Su			◆	◆	
Sisyrinchium striatum	32 in (80 cm)	14 in (35 cm)	P	W	NA	◆			W/Sp	Su			◆	◆	
Smithiantha zebrina	18–24 in (45–60 cm)	10–18 in (25–45 cm)	P	W/T	G	◆	◆		W/Sp	Su	◆			◆	
Solanum quitoense	7 ft (2 m)	7 ft (2 m)	P	W/T	NA		◆		Sp	Su					
Soldanella alpina	3–6 in (8–15 cm)	8 in (20 cm)	P	C	NA	◆			W/Sp	Sp/Su	◆	◆	◆	◆	
Soldanella carpatica	3–6 in (8–15 cm)	8 in (20 cm)	P	C	NA	◆			W/Sp	Sp			◆	◆	
Soldanella villosa	6–12 in (15–30 cm)	8–12 in (20–30 cm)	P	C	NA	◆			W/Sp	Sp		◆	◆	◆	
Soleirolia soleirolii	2–4 in (5–10 cm)	2–4 ft (0.6–1.2 m)	P	W/T	NA		◆		Any	Su	◆		◆	◆	
Solenostemon scutellarioides	12–24 in (30–60 cm)	12–24 in (30–60 cm)	P	W/T	NA		◆		Sp/Su	Su			◆	◆	
Solidago bicolor	40 in (100 cm)	24 in (60 cm)	P	C	NA	◆			W/Sp	Su/A		◆	◆	◆	
Solidago californica	40–48 in (100–120 cm)	24–32 in (60–80 cm)	P	C/W	NA	◆			W/Sp	A		◆	◆	◆	
Solidago canadensis	60 in (150 cm)	40 in (100 cm)	P	C	NA	◆			W/Sp	Su/A		◆	◆	◆	
Solidago rugosa	60 in (150 cm)	40 in (100 cm)	P	C	NA	◆			W/Sp	Su/A		◆	◆	◆	
Solidago virgaurea	40 in (100 cm)	24 in (60 cm)	P	C	NA	◆			W/Sp	Su/A		◆	◆	◆	
Solidago Hybrid Cultivars	24–60 in (60–150 cm)	12–48 in (30–120 cm)	P	C	NA	◆			W/Sp	Su/A		◆	◆	◆	
× Solidaster luteus	32–36 in (80–90 cm)	12–15 in (30–38 cm)	P	C/W	NA	◆			W/Sp	Su/A		◆	◆	◆	
Spathiphyllum cannifolium	40 in (100 cm)	40 in (100 cm)	P	W/T	NA	◆	◆		W/Sp	Sp/Su	◆				◆
Spathiphyllum wallisii	24–48 in (60–120 cm)	20–40 in (50–100 cm)	P	W/T	NA	◆	◆	◆	W/Sp	Sp/Su	◆				◆
Spathiphyllum Hybrid Cultivars	12–72 in (30–180 cm)	12–60 in (30–150 cm)	P	W/T	NA	◆	◆		W/Sp	Sp/Su	◆				◆
Sphaeralcea coccinea	6–18 in (15–45 cm)	6–12 in (15–30 cm)	P	C/W	NA	◆			W/Sp	Su			◆	◆	

Plant name	Height	Spread	Type	Climate	Group	Showy flowers	Showy foliage	Scented flowers	Planting season	Flowering season	Grow in pot/tub	Frost tolerant	Full Sun	Half Sun	Heavy shade
Sphaeralcea munroana	8–36 in (20–90 cm)	12–27 in (30–70 cm)	P	C/W	NA	◆			W/Sp	Su		◆	◆		
Stachys byzantina	18 in (45 cm)	24 in (60 cm)	P	C	NA		◆		A/Sp	Sp/Su		◆	◆		
Stachys citrina	8 in (20 cm)	12 in (30 cm)	P	C	NA	◆	◆		A/Sp	Su		◆	◆		
Stachys coccinea	24 in (60 cm)	18 in (45 cm)	P	C/W	NA	◆			A/Sp	Sp–A		◆	◆		
Stachys macrantha	18–24 in (45–60 cm)	12–18 in (30–45 cm)	P	C	NA	◆	◆		A/Sp	Su		◆	◆		
Stachys officinalis	12–36 in (30–90 cm)	18–36 in (45–90 cm)	P	C	NA	◆			A/Sp	Su/A		◆	◆		
Stellaria holostea	20–24 in (50–60 cm)	3–7 ft (0.9–2 m)	P	C/W	NA	◆			W/Sp	Sp/Su		◆			◆
Stokesia laevis	10–30 in (25–75 cm)	8–16 in (20–40 cm)	P	C/W	NA	◆			Sp	Su/A	◆	◆	◆	◆	
Strelitzia juncea	5 ft (1.5 m)	3–5 ft (0.9–1.5 m)	P	W/T	NA	◆	◆		W/Sp	Sp/Su	◆		◆		
Strelitzia reginae	6 ft (1.8 m)	3 ft (0.9 m)	P	W/T	NA	◆	◆		W/Sp	W/Sp	◆		◆		
Streptocarpus candidus	12 in (30 cm)	10–16 in (25–40 cm)	P	W/T	G	◆		◆	W/Sp	Su	◆			◆	◆
Streptocarpus caulescens	12–20 in (30–50 cm)	12–20 in (30–50 cm)	P	W/T	G	◆			W/Sp	Su–W	◆			◆	◆
Streptocarpus cyaneus	6–8 in (15–20 cm)	12–20 in (30–50 cm)	P	W/T	G	◆			W/Sp	Sp/Su	◆			◆	◆
Streptocarpus glandulosissimus	12–20 in (30–50 cm)	12–20 in (30–50 cm)	P	W/T	G	◆			W/Sp	All	◆			◆	◆
Streptocarpus kirkii	12–16 in (30–40 cm)	8–12 in (20–30 cm)	P	W/T	G	◆			W/Sp	W	◆			◆	◆
Streptocarpus saxorum	4–6 in (10–15 cm)	8–16 in (20–40 cm)	P	W/T	G	◆			W/Sp	All	◆			◆	◆
Streptocarpus wendlandii	12 in (30 cm)	30 in (75 cm)	P	W/T	G	◆			W/Sp	Su	◆			◆	
Streptocarpus Hybrid Cultivars	12–20 in (30–50 cm)	12–20 in (30–50 cm)	P	W/T	G	◆			W/Sp	Sp/Su	◆			◆	◆
Strobilanthes anisophyllus	5 ft (1.5 m)	5 ft (1.5 m)	P	W/T	NA		◆		W/Sp	Su/A				◆	
Strobilanthes dyerianus	36 in (90 cm)	36 in (90 cm)	P	W/T	NA		◆		W/Sp	Sp/Su				◆	
Strobilanthes gossypinus	3–5 ft (0.9–1.5 m)	20–30 in (50–75 cm)	P	W/T	NA		◆		W/Sp	Su				◆	
Stromanthe sanguinea	3–5 ft (0.9–1.5 m)	2–3 ft (0.6–0.9 m)	P	W/T	NA	◆	◆		W/Sp	Su				◆	◆
Stylidium graminifolium	10–20 in (25–50 cm)	10 in (25 cm)	P	W	NA	◆			W/Sp	Su	◆		◆		
Stylidium lineare	6–12 in (15–30 cm)	4 in (10 cm)	P	W	NA	◆			A/Sp	Su/A	◆		◆		
Stylophorum diphyllum	18 in (45 cm)	12 in (30 cm)	P	C	NA	◆	◆		A–Sp	Sp		◆			◆
Stylophorum lasiocarpum	12 in (30 cm)	12 in (30 cm)	P	C	NA	◆	◆		A–Sp	Sp		◆			◆
Sutera cordata	3 in (8 cm)	20 in (50 cm)	P	W	NA	◆			Sp	All	◆		◆		
Sutera grandiflora	40 in (100 cm)	24 in (60 cm)	P	W	NA	◆			Sp	Su/A	◆		◆		
Swainsona formosa	3–4 ft (0.9–1.2 m)	3–7 ft (0.9–2 m)	P	W	NA	◆			W/Sp	W–Su			◆		
Swainsona galegifolia	2 ft (0.6 m)	6 ft (1.8 m)	P	W	NA	◆			W/Sp	Sp/Su			◆		
Symphyandra hofmannii	12–24 in (30–60 cm)	6–12 in (15–30 cm)	P	C	NA	◆			W/Sp	Su		◆	◆	◆	
Symphytum asperum	4–5 ft (1.2–1.5 m)	5–7 ft (1.5–2 m)	P	C/W	NA	◆	◆		W/Sp	Su		◆	◆		

Plant name	Height	Spread	Type	Climate	Group	Showy flowers	Showy foliage	Scented flowers	Planting season	Flowering season	Grow in pot/tub	Frost tolerant	Full Sun	Half Sun	Heavy shade
Symphytum caucasicum	24–32 in (60–80 cm)	24–32 in (60–80 cm)	P	C/W	NA	♦	♦		W/Sp	Su		♦	♦		
Symphytum 'Goldsmith'	10–12 in (25–30 cm)	12–20 in (30–50 cm)	P	C/W	NA	♦	♦		W/Sp	Sp/Su		♦	♦	♦	
Symphytum grandiflorum	15–16 in (38–40 cm)	20–24 in (50–60 cm)	P	C/W	NA	♦	♦		W/Sp	Sp/Su		♦	♦		
Symphytum 'Hidcote Blue'	18–20 in (45–50 cm)	18–20 in (45–50 cm)	P	C/W	NA	♦	♦		W/Sp	Sp/Su		♦	♦		
Symphytum ibericum	16 in (40 cm)	12 in (30 cm)	P	C/W	NA	♦			W/Sp	Sp/Su		♦	♦	♦	
Synthyris missurica	16–24 in (40–60 cm)	12 in (30 cm)	P	C	NA	♦			W/Sp	Sp/Su			♦	♦	♦
Synthyris reniformis	2–6 in (5–15 cm)	4 in (10 cm)	P	C	NA	♦			W/Sp	Sp/Su			♦	♦	♦
Tacca integrifolia	24–48 in (60–120 cm)	24 in (60 cm)	P	W/T	NA	♦	♦		A/W	Sp/Su	♦		♦		
Tagetes lucida	16–40 in (40–100 cm)	16–32 in (40–80 cm)	P	W/T	NA	♦			Sp	Su		♦	♦	♦	
Tagetes patula	8–20 in (20–50 cm)	6–12 in (15–30 cm)	A	W	NA	♦			Sp	Su/A		♦	♦		
Tagetes tenuifolia	12–32 in (30–80 cm)	12–24 in (30–60 cm)	A	W	NA	♦			Sp	Su/A		♦	♦		
Tagetes Hybrid Cultivars	8–12 in (20–30 cm)	6–12 in (15–30 cm)	A	W	NA	♦			Sp	Sp–A		♦			
Talinum paniculatum	40 in (100 cm)	16–20 in (40–50 cm)	P	W	NA	♦			W/Sp	Sp/Su			♦	♦	
Tanacetum balsamita	36 in (90 cm)	18 in (45 cm)	P	C/W	NA	♦	♦		Sp	Su/A		♦	♦		
Tanacetum camphoratum	27 in (70 cm)	20 in (50 cm)	P	W	NA	♦	♦		Sp	Su/A		♦	♦		
Tanacetum coccineum	18–30 in (45–75 cm)	18 in (45 cm)	P	C/W	NA	♦			Sp	Su/A			♦		
Tanacetum corymbosum	36 in (90 cm)	18 in (45 cm)	P	C/W	NA	♦			Sp	Su/A			♦		
Tanacetum niveum	36 in (90 cm)	24 in (60 cm)	P	C/W	NA	♦	♦		Sp	Sp/Su		♦	♦		
Tapeinochilos ananassae	5–7 ft (1.5–2 m)	2–3 ft (0.6–0.9 m)	P	W/T	NA				W/Sp	Su					♦
Telekia speciosa	4–6 ft (1.2–1.8 m)	4–6 ft (1.2–1.8 m)	P	C	NA			♦	W/Sp	Su		♦	♦		
Tellima grandiflora	24 in (60 cm)	24 in (60 cm)	P	C/W	NA	♦	♦		A–Sp	Su		♦			♦
Teucrium chamaedrys	12–24 in (30–60 cm)	24–36 in (60–90 cm)	P	C/W	NA	♦	♦		W/Sp	Su		♦	♦		
Teucrium cossonii	8 in (20 cm)	24 in (60 cm)	P	W	NA	♦			W/Sp	Sp–A		♦	♦		
Teucrium hircanicum	24 in (60 cm)	24 in (60 cm)	P	C/W	NA	♦			W/Sp	Su/A			♦		
Teucrium polium	4–16 in (10–40 cm)	6–12 in (15–30 cm)	P	C/W	NA		♦		W/Sp	Su			♦		
Teucrium scorodonia	24 in (60 cm)	18 in (45 cm)	P	C/W	NA	♦	♦		W/Sp	Su/A		♦	♦	♦	
Thalia dealbata	3–6 ft (0.9–1.8 m)	20–30 in (50–75 cm)	P	W	NA	♦			W/Sp	Su			♦		
Thalictrum aquilegiifolium	60 in (150 cm)	20–40 in (50–100 cm)	P	C/W	NA	♦	♦		W/Sp	Su		♦	♦	♦	
Thalictrum delavayi	4–5 ft (1.2–1.5 m)	16–24 in (40–60 cm)	P	C/W	NA	♦			W/Sp	Su			♦	♦	
Thalictrum dioicum	12–30 in (30–75 cm)	12–16 in (30–40 cm)	P	C/W	NA	♦			W/Sp	Su			♦	♦	♦
Thalictrum flavum	40 in (100 cm)	16–20 in (40–50 cm)	P	C/W	NA	♦			W/Sp	Su			♦	♦	
Thalictrum kiusianum	6–12 in (15–30 cm)	12–20 in (30–50 cm)	P	C/W	NA	♦	♦		W/Sp	Su			♦		

Plant name	Height	Spread	Type	Climate	Group	Showy flowers	Showy foliage	Scented flowers	Planting season	Flowering season	Grow in pot/tub	Frost tolerant	Full Sun	Half Sun	Heavy shade
Thalictrum minus	3–5 ft (0.9–1.5 m)	20–32 in (50–80 cm)	P	C/W	NA	♦	♦		W/Sp	Su		♦	♦	♦	
Thalictrum rochebruneanum	40 in (100 cm)	16–20 in (40–50 cm)	P	C/W	NA	♦	♦		W/Sp	Su		♦	♦	♦	
Thermopsis rhombifolia	36 in (90cm)	24 in (60 cm)	P	C/W	NA	♦			W/Sp	Sp/Su		♦	♦		
Thermopsis villosa	3–5 ft (0.9–1.5 m)	2 ft (0.6 m)	P	C/W	NA	♦			W/Sp	Sp/Su		♦	♦		
Thymus caespititius	2 in (5 cm)	15 in (38 cm)	P	C/W	NA	♦			W/Sp	Sp		♦	♦		
Thymus × citriodorus	6–12 in (15–30 cm)	24 in (60 cm)	P	C/W	NA	♦	♦		W/Sp	Su		♦	♦		
Thymus Coccineus Group	3–4 in (8–10 cm)	14 in (35 cm)	P	C/W	NA	♦			W/Sp	Su		♦	♦		
Thymus herba-barona	4 in (10 cm)	24 in (60 cm)	P	C/W	NA	♦			W/Sp	Su		♦	♦		
Thymus mastichina	6–12 in (15–30 cm)	16 in (40 cm)	P	C/W	NA	♦			W/Sp	Su		♦	♦		
Thymus polytrichus	2 in (5 cm)	24 in (60 cm)	P	C/W	NA	♦			W/Sp	Su		♦	♦		
Thymus pseudolanuginosus	1–3 in (2.5–8 cm)	24 in (60 cm)	P	C/W	NA	♦	♦		W/Sp	Su		♦	♦		
Tiarella cordifolia	12 in (30 cm)	16–20 in (40–50 cm)	P	C	NA	♦			W/Sp	Su		♦		♦	♦
Tiarella polyphylla	12–18 in (30–45 cm)	16–20 in (40–50 cm)	P	C	NA				W/Sp	Sp/Su		♦		♦	♦
Tiarella wherryi	8–12 in (20–30 cm)	16–20 in (40–50 cm)	P	C	NA	♦			W/Sp	Su		♦		♦	♦
Tiarella Hybrid Cultivars	12–18 in (30–45 cm)	16–20 in (40–50 cm)	P	C	NA	♦			W/Sp	Su		♦		♦	♦
Tillandsia aeranthos	6 in (15 cm)	6 in (15 cm)	P	W/T	B	♦			W/Sp	Su					♦
Tillandsia bergeri	6 in (15 cm)	6 in (15 cm)	P	W/T	B	♦			W/Sp	Su					♦
Tillandsia butzii	12 in (30 cm)	4 in (10 cm)	P	W/T	B		♦		W/Sp	Su					♦
Tillandsia crocata	8 in (20 cm)	6 in (15 cm)	P	W/T	B	♦		♦	W/Sp	Su					♦
Tillandsia cyanea	10 in (25 cm)	10 in (25 cm)	P	W/T	B	♦		♦	W/Sp	Su					♦
Tillandsia dyeriana	6 in (15 cm)	6 in (15 cm)	P	W/T	B	♦			W/Sp	Su					♦
Tillandsia fasciculata	40 in (100 cm)	20 in (50 cm)	P	W/T	B	♦			W/Sp	Su					♦
Tillandsia fuchsii	8 in (20 cm)	4 in (10 cm)	P	W/T	B	♦			W/Sp	Su					♦
Tillandsia imperialis	20 in (50 cm)	16 in (40 cm)	P	W/T	B	♦	♦		W/Sp	Su					♦
Tillandsia ionantha	2 in (5 cm)	3 in (8 cm)	P	W/T	B		♦		W/Sp	Su					♦
Tillandsia leiboldiana	24 in (60 cm)	10 in (25 cm)	P	W/T	B	♦	♦		W/Sp	Su					♦
Tillandsia lindenii	27 in (70 cm)	16 in (40 cm)	P	W/T	B	♦	♦	♦	W/Sp	Su					♦
Tillandsia magnusiana	6 in (15 cm)	6 in (15 cm)	P	W/T	B		♦		W/Sp	Su					♦
Tillandsia recurvata	4 in (10 cm)	2½–8 in (6–20 cm)	P	W/T	B	♦			W/Sp	Su				♦	
Tillandsia streptophylla	18 in (45 cm)	8 in (20 cm)	P	W/T	B		♦		W/Sp	Su					♦
Tillandsia stricta	8 in (20 cm)	6 in (15 cm)	P	W/T	B	♦			W/Sp	Su					♦
Tillandsia tectorum	20 in (50 cm)	12 in (30 cm)	P	W/T	B	♦	♦		W/Sp	Su					♦

Plant name	Height	Spread	Type	Climate	Group	Showy flowers	Showy foliage	Scented flowers	Planting season	Flowering season	Grow in pot/tub	Frost tolerant	Full Sun	Half Sun	Heavy shade
Tillandsia tenuifolia	6 in (15 cm)	6 in (15 cm)	P	W/T	B	◆			W/Sp	Su					◆
Tillandsia usneoides	24 in (60 cm)	4 in (10 cm)	P	W/T	B		◆	◆	W/Sp	Su					◆
Tillandsia Hybrid Cultivars	4–36 in (10–90 cm)	4–24 in (10–60 cm)	P	W/T	B	◆	◆	◆	W/Sp	Su					◆
Tithonia rotundifolia	3–6 ft (0.9–1.8 m)	2 ft (0.6 m)	A	W	NA	◆			Sp	Su/A			◆		
Tolmiea menziesii	18–24 in (45–60 cm)	3–6 ft (0.9–1.8 m)	P	C/W	NA		◆		Any	Sp/Su	◆	◆			◆
Torenia fournieri	12 in (30 cm)	10 in (25 cm)	A	W/T	NA	◆			Sp	Sp/Su	◆			◆	◆
Torenia Hybrid Cultivars	12–15 in (30–38 cm)	10 in (25 cm)	A	W/T	NA	◆			Sp	Sp–A	◆			◆	◆
Townsendia formosa	12–16 in (30–40 cm)	10–12 in (25–30 cm)	P	C/W	NA	◆			W/Sp	Su		◆	◆		
Townsendia parryi	10–15 in (25–38 cm)	10–15 in (25–38 cm)	B/P	C	NA	◆			W/Sp	Su		◆	◆		
Trachelium caeruleum	24–36 in (60–90 cm)	18 in (45 cm)	P	W	NA	◆			Sp	Su			◆		
Trachystemon orientalis	2–3 ft (0.6–0.9 m)	3–7 ft (0.9–2 m)	P	C/W	NA	◆	◆		W/Sp	W/Sp		◆			◆
Tradescantia Andersoniana Group	8–20 in (20–50 cm)	12–48 in (30–120 cm)	P	C/W	NA	◆			W/Sp	Sp–A		◆	◆		
Tradescantia fluminensis	12–20 in (30–50 cm)	24–60 in (60–150 cm)	P	W	NA	◆	◆		W/Sp	Su			◆		◆
Tradescantia spathacea	15 in (38 cm)	12–16 in (30–40 cm)	P	W/T	NA		◆		W/Sp	Any	◆				◆
Tradescantia virginiana	12–20 in (30–50 cm)	20–48 in (50–120 cm)	P	C/W	NA	◆			W/Sp	Su		◆	◆		
Tradescantia zanonia	24–40 in (60–100 cm)	5 ft (1.5 m)	P	W/T	NA		◆		W/Sp	Su–W				◆	◆
Trichostema lanatum	2–5 ft (0.6–1.5 m)	2 ft (0.6 m)	P	W	NA	◆			A/Sp	Sp/Su		◆	◆		
Tricyrtis formosana	36 in (90 cm)	18 in (45 cm)	P	C	NA	◆			Sp	Su/A		◆			◆
Tricyrtis hirta	36 in (90 cm)	24 in (60 cm)	P	C	NA	◆			W/Sp	A		◆			◆
Tricyrtis macrantha	30 in (75 cm)	24 in (60 cm)	P	C	NA	◆			Sp	A		◆			◆
Tricyrtis macropoda	30 in (75 cm)	24 in (60 cm)	P	C	NA	◆			Sp	Su		◆			◆
Trifolium pannonicum	8 in (20 cm)	8 in (20 cm)	P	C	NA	◆			W/Sp	Su		◆	◆	◆	
Trifolium repens	2 in (5 cm)	8–16 in (20–40 cm)	P	C/W	NA	◆	◆		W/Sp	Su		◆	◆	◆	
Trifolium rubens	12–24 in (30–60 cm)	18–24 in (45–60 cm)	P	C/W	NA	◆			W/Sp	Su		◆	◆	◆	
Trifolium uniflorum	2–4 in (5–10 cm)	8–16 in (20–40 cm)	P	C/W	NA	◆			W/Sp	Sp/Su		◆	◆	◆	
Trillium chloropetalum	20 in (50 cm)	20 in (50 cm)	P	C	NA	◆	◆	◆	A/W	Sp		◆			◆
Trillium cuneatum	24 in (60 cm)	16 in (40 cm)	P	C	NA	◆	◆	◆	A/W	Sp		◆			◆
Trillium erectum	20 in (50 cm)	20 in (50 cm)	P	C	NA	◆			A/W	Sp		◆			◆
Trillium grandiflorum	18 in (45 cm)	20 in (50 cm)	P	C	NA	◆			A/W	Sp		◆			◆
Trillium luteum	18 in (45 cm)	18 in (45 cm)	P	C	NA	◆	◆	◆	A/W	Sp		◆		◆	◆
Trillium ovatum	20 in (50 cm)	20 in (50 cm)	P	C	NA	◆			A/W	Sp		◆			◆
Trillium sessile	12 in (30 cm)	12–16 in (30–40 cm)	P	C	NA	◆	◆		A/W	Sp		◆			◆

Plant name	Height	Spread	Type	Climate	Group	Showy flowers	Showy foliage	Scented flowers	Planting season	Flowering season	Grow in pot/tub	Frost tolerant	Full Sun	Half Sun	Heavy shade
Trollius chinensis	36 in (90 cm)	18 in (45 cm)	P	C	NA	◆			W/Sp	Su		◆	◆	◆	
Trollius × cultorum	24–36 in (60–90 cm)	18 in (45 cm)	P	C	NA	◆			W/Sp	Su		◆	◆	◆	
Trollius europaeus	24 in (60 cm)	18 in (45 cm)	P	C	NA	◆			W/Sp	Sp/Su		◆	◆	◆	
Tropaeolum ciliatum	20 ft (6 m)	20 ft (6 m)	P	W	NA	◆	◆		W/Sp	Su		◆		◆	◆
Tropaeolum majus	10 ft (3 m)	10 ft (3 m)	A	W	NA	◆	◆		W/Sp	Su			◆	◆	
Tropaeolum peregrinum	8 ft (2.4 m)	8 ft (2.4 m)	P	W	NA	◆		◆	W/Sp	Su/A			◆	◆	
Utricularia alpina	12 in (30 cm)	6 in (15 cm)	P	W	C	◆			W/Sp	Sp/Su	◆				
Utricularia bisquamata	2 in (5 cm)	3 in (8 cm)	P	W	C	◆			W/Sp	Sp/Su	◆				
Utricularia calycifida	6 in (15 cm)	4 in (10 cm)	P	W	C	◆			W/Sp	Sp/Su	◆				
Utricularia dichotoma	6–18 in (15–45 cm)	8 in (20 cm)	P	W	C	◆			W/Sp	Sp/Su	◆				
Utricularia inflata	12 in (30 cm)	12 in (30 cm)	P	W/T	C	◆			W/Sp	Sp/Su			◆		
Utricularia menziesii	3 in (8 cm)	2 in (5 cm)	P	W	C	◆			W/Sp	Sp/Su	◆				
Utricularia praelonga	18 in (45 cm)	12 in (30 cm)	P	W/T	C	◆			W/Sp	Sp/Su			◆		
Utricularia reniformis	18 in (45 cm)	18 in (45 cm)	P	W/T	C	◆	◆		W/Sp	Sp/Su			◆		
Utricularia uniflora	8 in (20 cm)	3 in (8 cm)	P	W	C	◆			W/Sp	Sp/Su			◆		
Uvularia grandiflora	12–24 in (30–60 cm)	12–24 in (30–60 cm)	P	C/W	NA	◆	◆		Sp–A	Sp/Su		◆			◆
Uvularia perfoliata	16 in (40 cm)	12–18 in (30–45 cm)	P	C/W	NA	◆			Sp–A	Sp/Su		◆			◆
Valeriana montana	10 in (25 cm)	10 in (25 cm)	P	C	NA	◆			A/Sp	Su		◆		◆	
Valeriana phu	36 in (90 cm)	18 in (45 cm)	P	C	NA			◆	A/Sp	Su		◆	◆		
Vancouveria chrysantha	12 in (30 cm)	12 in (30 cm)	P	C	NA	◆	◆		A–Sp	Sp/Su				◆	
Vancouveria hexandra	12 in (30 cm)	12 in (30 cm)	P	C	NA	◆	◆		A–Sp	Sp/Su				◆	◆
Veratrum album	24 in (60 cm)	24 in (60 cm)	P	C/W	NA	◆	◆		A/Sp	Su				◆	
Veratrum nigrum	24–48 in (60–120 cm)	24 in (60 cm)	P	C/W	NA	◆	◆		A/Sp	Su				◆	
Verbascum acaule	4 in (10 cm)	4 in (10 cm)	P	C/W	NA	◆			W/Sp	Sp–A		◆	◆	◆	
Verbascum blattaria	5–6 ft (1.5–1.8 m)	12–20 in (30–50 cm)	B	C/W	NA	◆			W/Sp	Su/A		◆	◆	◆	
Verbascum bombyciferum	6–8 ft (1.8–2.4 m)	24–40 in (60–100 cm)	B	C/W	NA	◆	◆		W/Sp	Su		◆	◆	◆	
Verbascum chaixii	36–48 in (90–120 cm)	12–24 in (30–60 cm)	P	C/W	NA	◆			W/Sp	Su		◆	◆	◆	
Verbascum dumulosum	8 in (20 cm)	12–16 in (30–40 cm)	P	W	NA	◆			W/Sp	Su			◆	◆	
Verbascum olympicum	5–6 ft (1.5–1.8 m)	20–40 in (50–100 cm)	B/P	C/W	NA	◆			W/Sp	Su			◆	◆	
Verbascum phoeniceum	8–16 in (20–40 cm)	12–16 in (30–40 cm)	B/P	C/W	NA	◆			W/Sp	Su			◆	◆	
Verbascum thapsus	6–7 ft (1.8–2 m)	20–32 in (50–80 cm)	B	C/W	NA	◆			W/Sp	Su		◆	◆	◆	
Verbascum Hybrid Cultivars	12–60 in (30–150 cm)	12–20 in (30–50 cm)	P	C/W	NA	◆	◆		W/Sp	Sp–A		◆	◆	◆	

Plant name	Height	Spread	Type	Climate	Group	Showy flowers	Showy foliage	Scented flowers	Planting season	Flowering season	Grow in pot/tub	Frost tolerant	Full Sun	Half Sun	Heavy shade
Verbena bonariensis	3–5 ft (0.9–1.5 m)	24 in (60 cm)	A/P	C/W	NA	◆			Sp	Sp–A		◆	◆		
Verbena canadensis	8 in (20 cm)	16 in (40 cm)	P	C	NA	◆			W/Sp	Sp–A		◆	◆		
Verbena rigida	24–36 in (60–90 cm)	12 in (30 cm)	P	W	NA	◆			W/Sp	Su		◆	◆		
Verbena tenera	12–20 in (30–50 cm)	12–20 in (30–50 cm)	P	W	NA	◆			W/Sp	Su			◆		
Verbena tenuisecta	12–20 in (30–50 cm)	12–20 in (30–50 cm)	A/P	W	NA	◆			W/Sp	Su			◆		
Verbena Hybrid Cultivars	12–24 in (30–60 cm)	24–40 in (60–100 cm)	P	C	NA	◆			W/Sp	Su/A	◆	◆	◆		
Veronica alpina	2–6 in (5–15 cm)	8–16 in (20–40 cm)	P	C	NA	◆			W/Sp	Sp/Su		◆	◆	◆	
Veronica austriaca	6–16 in (15–40 cm)	10–24 in (25–60 cm)	P	C/W	NA	◆			W/Sp	Sp/Su	◆	◆	◆		
Veronica beccabunga	4–6 in (10–15 cm)	8–20 in (20–50 cm)	P	C	NA	◆			W/Sp	Su		◆	◆	◆	
Veronica chamaedrys	6–10 in (15–25 cm)	12–20 in (30–50 cm)	P	C	NA	◆			W/Sp	Sp/Su		◆	◆	◆	
Veronica cinerea	2–4 in (5–10 cm)	6–10 in (15–25 cm)	P	C/W	NA	◆			W/Sp	Su		◆	◆	◆	
Veronica gentianoides	12–24 in (30–60 cm)	12–24 in (30–60 cm)	P	C	NA	◆			W/Sp	Sp/Su		◆	◆		
Veronica longifolia	20–48 in (50–120 cm)	16–30 in (40–75 cm)	P	C	NA	◆			W/Sp	Su/A		◆	◆		
Veronica pectinata	2–8 in (5–20 cm)	12–16 in (30–40 cm)	P	C	NA	◆			W/Sp	Sp/Su		◆	◆		
Veronica petraea	4–6 in (10–15 cm)	8–12 in (20–30 cm)	P	C	NA	◆			W/Sp	Su/A		◆	◆		
Veronica prostrata	2–4 in (5–10 cm)	8–16 in (20–40 cm)	P	C	NA	◆			W/Sp	Sp/Su		◆	◆		
Veronica spicata	12–24 in (30–60 cm)	12–32 in (30–80 cm)	P	C	NA	◆			W/Sp	Su	◆	◆	◆		
Veronica wormskjoldii	4–12 in (10–30 cm)	8–20 in (20–50 cm)	P	C	NA	◆			W/Sp	Su		◆	◆		
Veronicastrum virginicum	2–6 ft (0.6–1.8 m)	1–3 ft (0.3–0.9 m)	P	C	NA	◆			W/Sp	Su		◆	◆		
Victoria amazonica	10–12 in (25–30 cm)	15–20 ft (4.5–6 m)	P	W/T	NA	◆	◆	◆	W/Sp	Su/A			◆		
Victoria 'Longwood Hybrid'	10–12 in (25–30 cm)	12–40 ft (3.5–12 m)	P	W/T	NA	◆	◆	◆	W/Sp	Su/A			◆		
Viguiera multiflora	30–40 in (75–100 cm)	30–40 in (75–100 cm)	P	W/T	NA	◆			W/Sp	Su			◆		
Vinca difformis	12 in (30 cm)	5–10 ft (1.5–3 m)	P	C/W	NA	◆			W/Sp	Sp		◆	◆	◆	◆
Vinca major	18 in (45 cm)	5–10 ft (1.5–3 m)	P	C/W	NA	◆	◆		W/Sp	Sp–A		◆	◆	◆	◆
Vinca minor	8 in (20 cm)	5–10 ft (1.5–3 m)	P	C/W	NA	◆	◆		W/Sp	Sp–A	◆	◆	◆	◆	◆
Viola adunca	2–4 in (5–10 cm)	12–16 in (30–40 cm)	P	C	NA	◆	◆		W/Sp	Sp		◆		◆	◆
Viola blanda	3–6 in (8–15 cm)	12–20 in (30–50 cm)	P	C	NA	◆	◆		W/Sp	Sp		◆		◆	◆
Viola canina	4–12 in (10–30 cm)	12–20 in (30–50 cm)	P	C	NA	◆	◆		W/Sp	Su		◆		◆	◆
Viola cornuta	6–12 in (15–30 cm)	8–14 in (20–35 cm)	A/P	C/W	NA	◆			W/Sp	Sp/Su		◆	◆	◆	
Viola cucullata	4–6 in (10–15 cm)	8–16 in (20–40 cm)	P	C	NA	◆			W/Sp	Sp/Su		◆	◆	◆	
Viola hederacea	2–3 in (5–8 cm)	6–12 in (15–30 cm)	P	W	NA	◆	◆		W/Sp	Sp–A		◆		◆	
Viola jooi	2–4 in (5–10 cm)	8–14 in (20–35 cm)	P	C/W	NA	◆	◆		W/Sp	Sp/Su		◆	◆	◆	

Plant name	Height	Spread	Type	Climate	Group	Showy flowers	Showy foliage	Scented flowers	Planting season	Flowering season	Grow in pot/tub	Frost tolerant	Full Sun	Half Sun	Heavy shade
Viola odorata	4–6 in (10–15 cm)	12–24 in (30–60 cm)	P	C/W	NA	◆	◆	◆	W/Sp	Sp/Su	◆	◆		◆	◆
Viola pedata	4–6 in (10–15 cm)	8–16 in (20–40 cm)	P	C	NA	◆	◆		W/Sp	Sp		◆		◆	
Viola riviniana	4–6 in (10–15 cm)	8–24 in (20–60 cm)	P	C	NA	◆	◆		W/Sp	Sp/Su		◆		◆	◆
Viola septentrionalis	4–6 in (10–15 cm)	6–16 in (15–40 cm)	P	C	NA	◆	◆		W/Sp	Sp/Su		◆		◆	◆
Viola sororia	2–6 in (5–15 cm)	6–16 in (15–40 cm)	P	C	NA	◆	◆		W/Sp	Sp/Su	◆			◆	◆
Viola tricolor	4–14 in (10–35 cm)	6–16 in (15–40 cm)	A/B/P	C/W	NA	◆			W/Sp			◆	◆	◆	
Viola Hybrid Cultivars	6–12 in (15–30 cm)	8–16 in (20–40 cm)	A/P	C/W	NA	◆			W/Sp	W–Su	◆	◆	◆	◆	
Vriesea carinata	14 in (35 cm)	12 in (30 cm)	P	W/T	B	◆	◆		W/Sp	Sp/Su					◆
Vriesea erythrodactylon	16 in (40 cm)	16 in (40 cm)	P	W/T	B		◆		W/Sp						◆
Vriesea fenestralis	40 in (100 cm)	27 in (70 cm)	P	W/T	B	◆	◆		W/Sp	Sp					◆
Vriesea fosteriana	60 in (150 cm)	40 in (100 cm)	P	W/T	B		◆		W/Sp	Sp/Su					◆
Vriesea malzinei	32 in (80 cm)	16 in (40 cm)	P	W/T	B	◆	◆		W/Sp	Sp/Su	◆				◆
Vriesea saundersii	24 in (60 cm)	16 in (40 cm)	P	W/T	B	◆	◆		W/Sp						◆
Vriesea splendens	40 in (100 cm)	20 in (50 cm)	P	W/T	B	◆	◆		W/Sp	Sp/Su					◆
Vriesea Hybrid Cultivars	16–36 in (40–90 cm)	8–20 in (20–50 cm)	P	W/T	B	◆	◆		W/Sp	Sp/Su					◆
Wachendorfia thyrsiflora	4–7 ft (1.2–2 m)	2–4 ft (0.6–1.2 m)	P	W	NA	◆			W/Sp	Su			◆		
Waldsteinia fragarioides	2 in (5 cm)	12–20 in (30–50 cm)	P	C	NA	◆	◆		W/Sp	Sp			◆	◆	◆
Waldsteinia ternata	6 in (15 cm)	24 in (60 cm)	P	C	NA	◆	◆		W/Sp	Sp/Su			◆		◆
Wittrockia superba	16 in (40 cm)	55 in (140 cm)	P	W/T	B	◆	◆		W/Sp	Sp/Su	◆				◆
Xanthorrhoea australis	3 ft (0.9 m)	3 ft (0.9 m)	P	W	NA	◆	◆	◆	A/Sp	Sp			◆		
Xanthorrhoea glauca	20 ft (6 m)	3 ft (0.9 m)	P	W	NA	◆	◆	◆	A/Sp	Sp			◆		
Xanthorrhoea johnsonii	7 ft (2 m)	3 ft (0.9 m)	P	W	NA	◆	◆	◆	A/Sp	Sp			◆		
Xanthorrhoea quadrangulata	7–10 ft (2–3 m)	4–7 ft (1.2–2 m)	P	W	NA	◆	◆	◆	A/Sp	A			◆		
Xanthosoma undipes	7–10 ft (2–3 m)	7–10 ft (2–3 m)	P	W/T	NA	◆	◆		A/W/Sp	Sp/Su					◆
Xeranthemum annuum	10–36 in (25–90 cm)	10–36 in (25–90 cm)	A	C/W	NA	◆			Sp	Su/A			◆	◆	
Xerochrysum bracteatum	36 in (90 cm)	16 in (40 cm)	A/P	W	NA	◆			Sp	Su	◆		◆	◆	
Zaluzianskya ovata	8–10 in (20–25 cm)	20–24 in (50–60 cm)	P	W	NA	◆			W/Sp	Su/A			◆		
Zingiber spectabile	5–7 ft (1.5–2 m)	3 ft (0.9 m)	P	W/T	NA		◆		W/Sp						◆
Zingiber zerumbet	6–8 ft (1.8–2.4 m)	3 ft (0.9 m)	P	W/T	NA	◆	◆		W/Sp				◆	◆	
Zinnia angustifolia	8–16 in (20–40 cm)	12–20 in (30–50 cm)	A	W	NA	◆			Sp	Su	◆		◆		
Zinnia elegans	8–40 in (20–100 cm)	8–18 in (20–45 cm)	A	W	NA	◆			Sp	Su			◆		
Zinnia haageana	24 in (60 cm)	12–24 in (30–60 cm)	A	W	NA	◆			Sp	Su	◆		◆	◆	

ABELMOSCHUS

This genus belonging to the mallow (Malvaceae) family consists of about 15 species of annuals, perennials, and soft-wooded shrubs native to warmer parts of Asia and Africa. Allied to *Hibiscus*, its flowers have a single bract wrapping around the base of the sepals, splitting down one side as the flower expands. Leaves are usually maple-like or divided into finger-like lobes. Flowers are often showy, in shades of pink, red, or yellow, and are followed by elongated pods. *Abelmoschus esculentus* is grown as a vegetable (okra). The leafy young shoots of most species can be used as pot greens.

CULTIVATION: These plants do best in a sunny sheltered position and well-drained soil, fertilized in summer. Propagate from basal cuttings or seed sown in late spring.

Abelmoschus manihot
syn. *Hibiscus manihot*
AIBIKA
☼ ❄ ↔ 3 ft (0.9 m) ↕ 3–6 ft (0.9–1.8 m)
Shrubby Southeast Asian perennial. Large, deeply lobed leaves. Pale yellow flowers with a dark purplish eye appear at the branch tips, in summer. Zones 8–12.

Abelmoschus moschatus
syn. *Hibiscus abelmoschus*
MUSKMALLOW
☼ ❄ ↔ 30 in (75 cm) ↕ 4–6 ft (1.2–1.8 m)
Variable species from tropical Asia to northern Australia. Stems and leaves bear bristly hairs; leaf lobes triangular. Flowers white, pink, or yellow, with a dark eye, in summer. Ornamental strains grown as annuals. '**Mischief**' and '**Oriental Pink**', colorful cultivars. The **Pacific Series**, scarlet and pink flowers. Zones 10–12.

ACAENA
BIDDY BIDDY, NEW ZEALAND BURR, SHEEP'S BURRS

This genus of creeping perennials and evergreen subshrubs is a member of the rose (Rosaceae) family. It contains about 100 species native to California and Hawaii, USA, Central and South America, Australia, and New Zealand, often found growing in mountainous areas. The leaves are small and often fern-like, bright green to grayish blue and bronze-purple. Tiny spherical to spike-like flowerheads are held above the foliage, and the spiny burrs that follow are very ornamental in some species. They are ideal as ground cover plants and for growing over walls.

CULTIVATION: These grow readily in poor soil but must be well drained. They prefer full sun but tolerate light shade. Most are hardy but they may be deciduous in areas with prolonged frosts. Propagate from rooted stem pieces or seed in autumn and spring.

Acaena caesiiglauca
☼ ❄ ↔ 32 in (80 cm) ↕ 2 in (5 cm)
A New Zealand species with small pinnately divided leaves of bluish gray, silky beneath. Small white flowerheads are held well above the foliage, followed by brown spiny burrs. Zones 6–10.

Acaena microphylla
☼ ❄ ↔ 20 in (50 cm) ↕ 2 in (5 cm)
From New Zealand's North Island, this ground-hugging species has fine ferny foliage of green or bronze. The tiny cream flowers are followed by eye-catching, spiny, red burrs in late summer. '**Kupferteppich**' (syn. *A. m.* '**Copper Carpet**') has green to bronze leaves. Zones 6–10.

Abelmoschus moschatus 'Oriental Pink'

ACANTHUS
BEAR'S BREECHES

From the acanthus (Acanthaceae) family, this genus includes 30 species of perennials and shrubs from the temperate and tropical Old World regions. Cultivated species are valued for their bold, often near-evergreen foliage and upright flower spikes. The leaves, which form a basal clump, are usually large, glossy, and pinnately lobed, lobes toothed or spiny. The flowers are tubular, tend to be mauve and white, and partially enclosed within conspicuous bracts. Large seed pods follow.

CULTIVATION: Species are mostly cold tolerant but prefer mild winters. Plant in moist, well-drained, humus-rich soil. Many have heavy roots and divide easily, otherwise raise from spring-sown seed. May self-sow freely and can sucker.

Acanthus mollis
BEAR'S BREECHES
☼/◐ ❄ ↔ 40–60 in (100–150 cm) ↕ 7 ft (2 m)
From southern Europe and northwest Africa. Deep green, deeply toothed, soft-spined, pinnate or doubly pinnate leaves up to 36 in (90 cm) long. White flowers flushed pale purple in toothed mauve bracts on stems up to 2 m (7 ft) tall. '**Candelabrum**', large-lobed flowers on sometimes branching stems. Zones 6–10.

Acanthus spinosus
☼/◐ ❄ ↔ 40–60 in (100–150 cm) ↕ 36 in (90 cm)
Found around the Mediterranean. Similar to *Acanthus mollis* but with leaves more deeply divided, broader and spinier. White,

Acanthus spinosus 'Lady Moore'

sometimes mauve-tinted flowers in spiny bracts. '**Lady Moore**', variegated leaves and purple and white flowers. Zones 6–10.

ACHILLEA

MILFOIL, YARROW

This genus of about 100 species of clumping or mat-forming perennial plants is a member of the large daisy (Asteraceae) family. They are found throughout Europe and northern and western Asia in a range of habitats, including alpine. Some can be invasive. The foliage is usually finely divided with a fern-like appearance and is often aromatic. Usually grouped in flat corymbs, the small flowerheads are white and pale cream, lemon, and pink, with many cultivars in brighter colors.

CULTIVATION: Most yarrows can easily be grown in well-drained soil in full sun. They can tolerate quite poor conditions and are frost hardy to 5°F (–15°C). Alpine species require perfect drainage and protection from winter rain if downy-leafed. Propagation is by division or from seed.

Achillea filipendulina

☀ ❄ ↔ 24–48 in (60–120 cm) ↕ 24–48 in (60–120 cm)
Robust species from central and western Asia. Divided, hairy, aromatic leaves to 8 in (20 cm) long. Tiny gold flowers crowded in flattened flowerheads, to 4 in (10 cm) across, in summer. '**Cloth of Gold**', '**Gold Plate**', and '**Parker's Variety**' are improved cultivars 4–6 ft (1.2–1.8 m) high with bright golden flowerheads up to 6 in (15 cm) across. '**Schwellenburg**', about 18 in (45 cm) high with lemon yellow flowers. Zones 5–10.

Achillea millefolium

MILFOIL, YARROW

☀ ❄ ↔ 18–30 in (45–75 cm) ↕ 12–30 in (30–75 cm)
Weedy species from western Asia and Europe. Naturalized in temperate regions, too invasive for most gardens. Fern-like leaves. Flat sprays of small dull white flowerheads in summer–autumn. '**Cerise Queen**', cherry red, vigorous. Zones 3–10.

Achillea ptarmica

SNEEZEWORT

☀ ❄ ↔ 30 in (75 cm) ↕ 30 in (75 cm)
From Europe. Vigorous spreading mats of dark green, narrow, serrated leaves. Loose heads of small white flowers in summer. Tolerant of damp sites. '**The Pearl**', profuse double white flowers. Zones 6–10.

Achimenes, Hybrid Cultivar, 'Lachs Charm'

Achillea Hybrid Cultivars

☀ ❄ ↔ 18–30 in (45–75 cm) ↕ 12–40 in (30–100 cm)
Numerous cultivars in bright shades make excellent border plants. Anthea/'**Anblo**', pale yellow flowers, silvery foliage; '**Apfelblüte**' (syn. Apple Blossom), rose pink flowers; '**Coronation Gold**', bright yellow; '**Fanal**' (syn. 'The Beacon'), crimson-red, yellow centers; '**Heidi**', bright salmon, yellow centers; '**Lachsschönheit**', salmon fading to pale pink; '**Moonshine**', bright yellow flowers over silvery foliage; and '**Paprika**', bright red, yellow centers. Quick to flower from seed are '**Taygetea**', gray foliage, lemon yellow

Achillea, Hybrid Cultivar, 'Paprika'

flowers; '**Terracotta**', rusty orange; '**Walther Funcke**', red, yellow centers; '**Wesersandstein**', salmon fading to cream. Zones 3–10.

ACHIMENES

Found in tropical Americas, including the West Indies, this genus is a member of the African violet (Gesneriaceae) family and has some 25 species of winter-dormant fleshy-stemmed perennials ranging from ground covers, usually cultivated in hanging baskets, to shrubby species. Deep green, somewhat fleshy, simple elliptical to lance-shaped, tooth-edged leaves are covered with fine downy hair. The flowers are long-tubed with 5 lobes on 2 lips—2 lobes above, 3 below. Flowers appear in the leaf axils, either singly or in small groups.

CULTIVATION: Some are grown as house or greenhouse plants, others as annuals. All thrive outdoors in tropical and subtropical gardens. Plant rhizomes in spring in moist, humus-rich, well-drained soil in a bright but not too hot position. Feed and water well while in growth; dry off in autumn. Propagate by division.

Achimenes longiflora

◐ ❁ ↔ 12–20 in (30–50 cm)
↕ 20–24 in (50–60 cm)
Shrubby species found from Mexico to Panama. Deep green, lance-shaped leaves. White, mauve, purple to maroon flowers to 2½ in (6 cm) wide, borne singly. Zones 10–12.

Achimenes Hybrid Cultivars

◐ ❁ ↔ 10–15 in (25–38 cm) ↕ 3–6 in (8–15 cm)
Achimenes hybrids vary in size, growth habit, and flower color. '**Endeavor**', deep orchid pink flowers, leaves bronzy; '**Glacier**', 24 in (60 cm) tall, upright, white flowers tinted blue; '**Lachs Charm**', bright reddish pink flowers, small purple blotch; '**Peach Blossom**', trailer with salmon pink flowers; '**Pendant Purple**', vigorous trailer with bright purple-blue flowers; '**Ruby**', 12 in (30 cm) tall, bushy with masses of deep purple-red flowers; and '**Show-off**', to 16 in (40 cm), bushy, heavy crop of lavender-pink flowers. Zones 10–12.

Aconitum napellus

Aconitum carmichaelii

ACONITUM

BADGER'S BANE, MONKSHOOD, WOLFSBANE

This genus in the buttercup (Ranunculaceae) family has around 100 species of often tuberous biennials and perennials found in northern temperate zones. Completely dormant over winter, they quickly develop a clump of deeply lobed fan-shaped leaves from which emerge erect stems bearing racemes of hooded or helmet-shaped flowers, usually white, creamy yellow, or mauve-blue to purple in color. Flowers mainly from summer to autumn. Monkshood sap contains several toxic alkaloids, principally aconitine. CULTIVATION: *Aconitum* species are mostly very hardy and easily grown in full sun or half-sun in moist, humus-rich, well-drained soil. Propagation is by division when dormant or from seed.

Aconitum carmichaelii

☼/☀ ❄ ↔ 24–36 in (60–90 cm) ↕ 7 ft (2 m)

From China. Upright growth with dark green, 3- to 5-lobed, toothed, leathery leaves with pale undersides. Dense spikes of white to mauve helmet-shaped flowers, deep purple inside. Cultivars include 'Arendsii' and 'Kelmscott' (Wilsonii Group) ★. Zones 3–9.

Aconitum napellus

FRIAR'S CAP, HELMET FLOWER, MONKSHOOD

☼/☀ ❄ ↔ 24–32 in (60–80 cm)
↕ 5–6 ft (1.5–1.8 m)

Found in Europe and temperate Asia. Upright perennial with dark green slightly hairy leaves with 5 to 7 toothed lobes. Bright purple-blue helmet-shaped flowers in dense heads atop tall stems, late summer–autumn. Zones 5–9.

Aconitum Hybrid Cultivars

☼/☀ ❄ ↔ 24 in (60 cm) ↕ 4 ft (1.2 m)

Several hybrid monkshoods, varying in size, color, and flowering season, are sometimes listed under the name *A.* × *cammarum* (*A. variegatum* × *A. napellus),* but as they are not all of this parentage this grouping seems inappropriate. Popular hybrids include 'Bressingham Spire', strongly upright, with long spikes

of purple-blue flowers; *A.* × *cammarum* 'Grandiflorum Album', large heads of white flowers; 'Ivorine', with creamy white flowers; 'Spark's Variety', tall, non-twining, open plant, bright purple-blue flowers; and 'Stainless Steel', gray-green foliage and white-centered metallic blue flowers. Zones 4–9.

ACORUS

SWEET FLAG

Making up the family Acoraceae, this rather sedge-like genus of 2 evergreen perennial species occurs around pond margins in temperate East Asia and southeast USA. The narrow iris-like leaves in fans are often variegated in the cultivated forms. In summer they produce flowers in which the typically showy arum spathe is leaf-like and inconspicuous. The flowerhead (spadix) is pronounced but not a feature. CULTIVATION: *Acorus* species are tough and easily grown. Plant in damp or boggy soil, preferably by a pond, and cut back or divide occasionally to encourage fresh young leaves. Propagation is by division or from seed if available.

Acorus calamus

CALAMUS, FLAGROOT, MYRTLE FLAG, SWEET CALAMUS, SWEET FLAG

☼/☀ ❄ ↔ 3–7 ft (0.9–2 m) ↕ 4 ft (1.2 m)

Originally from temperate Eurasia and eastern North America but now widely naturalized in the Northern Hemisphere. Has iris-like leaves to 5 ft (1.5 m) long and a narrow yellow-green spadix to 4 in (10 cm) long. 'Variegatus' ★ has cream and yellow variegated leaves. Zones 3–10.

Acorus gramineus

☼/☀ ❄ ↔ 18–36 in (45–90 cm) ↕ 16 in (40 cm)

From Japan and possibly nearby mainland Asia, very similar to *A. calamus* but smaller grassy leaves, to 18 in (45 cm) long. Spadix broad and up to 3 in (8 cm) long. Several foliage cultivars, including 'Hakuro-nishiki', 'Ôgon' (syn. 'Wogon'), 'Pusillus', and 'Variegatus' (syn. 'Aureovariegatus'). Zones 5–10.

Acorus gramineus 'Hakuro-nishiki'

AECHMEA

This genus is a member of the pineapple (Bromeliaceae) family and has around 80 species, ranging in size from 4 in (10 cm) to 7 ft (2 m) in diameter, and more than 500 cultivars. They come from the humid regions of Central America, ranging from the upper reaches of the Amazon and the hot dry areas of Bahia in Brazil to cooler areas in the southern parts of Brazil and Argentina. Most grow on trees in their natural environment, though some grow on rocks. The edges of the leaves are toothed, with the teeth ranging from very fine to most vicious. The flowerheads vary from short to elongated cones. Many have bright red banner-like primary bracts under the flower branches, which attract hummingbirds. The small-petalled flowers come in various colors. The fruit can be brightly colored, from yellow to red to blue to purple.

CULTIVATION: Recommended for indoor culture if in flower; for greenhouse or conservatory in cool-temperate areas; or outdoors, with protection from direct continuous sunlight and extremes of rain, in warm-temperate, subtropical, and tropical areas. Water when potting mix is dry. No extra fertilizer needed if potting mix is of good quality. Propagate from seed or by offset.

Aechmea caudata
☀ ⚘ ↔ 24 in (60 cm) ↑ 36 in (90 cm)
Originates in the southern part of Brazil and is hardier than most other species. Leaves, to 40 in (100 cm) long, form an open funnel-shaped rosette. Flower stem to 36 in (90 cm) high; flowerhead erect, to 10 in (25 cm) long, with side spikes at the base, yellow petals. *A. c.* var. *variegata*, a more robust variegated form. Zones 9–11.

Aechmea chantinii
☀ ⚘ ↔ 20 in (50 cm) ↑ 40 in (100 cm)
Originates in the upper reaches of the Amazon and likes hot humid conditions. Leaves to 40 in (100 cm) long, with strong white cross-banding, forming a loose funnel-shaped rosette. Flower stem to 40 in (100 cm) high; flowerhead open, with mainly yellow side spikes on long stems; orange flowers. Lower side spikes have large bright red primary bracts that hang down. This species has numerous cultivars, usually describing the leaf color, for example, '**Ash Blond**', '**Black Goddess**', and '**Green Ice**'. Variegated cultivars include '**Samurai**' and '**Shogun**'. Zones 9–12.

Aechmea fasciata
☀ ⚘ ↔ 16 in (40 cm) ↑ 27 in (70 cm)
From southern parts of Brazil. Leaves to 3 ft (0.9 m) long, forming a slender funnel-shaped rosette. Leaves strongly cross-banded in white and in some forms almost totally covered with white scales. Flower stem to 27 in (70 cm) high. Flowerhead conical, bracts pink with a light covering of white scales. Flowers blue, ageing to red. There are variegated forms, and non-spined forms such as '**Morgana**' and '**Kiwi**'. Zones 9–12.

Aechmea fulgens
☀ ⚘ ↔ 20 in (50 cm) ↑ 20 in (50 cm)
From eastern Brazil. Leaves 16 in (40 cm) long, forming a dense funnel-shaped rosette. Flower stem to 20 in (50 cm) high. Flowerhead to 8 in (20 cm) high, narrowly pyramidal with a few red side branches at the base. Dark red flowers scattered along branches, blue petals soon changing to red. Zones 9–12.

Aechmea gamosepala
MATCHSTICK PLANT
☀ ❄ ↔ 10 in (25 cm) ↑ 30 in (75 cm)
From southern parts of Brazil. Leaves to 22 in (55 cm) long, forming a dense funnel-form rosette. Flower stem to 30 in (75 cm) high. Flowerhead a narrow cylinder to 10 in (25 cm) long, with flowers standing at right angles from the center stem like matches, red with blue petals. Zones 8–11.

Aechmea fasciata

Aechmea nudicaulis
☀ ⚘ ↔ 8 in (20 cm) ↑ 27–36 in (70–90 cm)
Found from southern Mexico to southern Brazil. Variable in size. Leaves 36 in (90 cm) long, green through to reddish, commonly with white bands, forming a tight tube. Flowerhead cylindrical with many flowers sticking out from the center stem. Bright red bracts under flowerhead. Flowers mainly yellow. Zones 9–12.

Aechmea ornata
☀ ⚘ ↔ 7 ft (2 m) ↑ 36 in (90 cm)
From southern Brazil. Leaves green, 36 in (90 cm) long, with small teeth, forming open rosette. Flowerhead a short cylinder with bristles and many flowers on all sides. Petals red or blue. Large red erect bracts under flowerhead. *A. o.* var. *hoehneana*, blue-petalled form. *A. o.* var. *nationalis*, variegated form. Zones 9–11.

Aechmea recurvata
☀ ❄ ↔ 8 in (20 cm) ↑ 8–16 in (20–40 cm)
From southern Brazil. Leaves green, to 16 in (40 cm) long, moderately spined, forming an open rosette from a bulbose base. Flowerhead almost globular, red bracts on the outside, reddish purple petals. '**Aztec Gold**' is variegated. Zones 8–11.

Aechmea Hybrid Cultivars
☀ ⚘ ↔ 12–24 in (30–60 cm) ↑ 12–36 in (30–90 cm)
Nearly all the more popular *Aechmea* species have been used in the breeding of hybrids. '**Bastantha**', leaves light yellowish green, red below; '**Burning Bush**', bright red flower stem and branches, cream flowers; '**Fascini**', large green rosette with branched long-lasting carmine flowers; '**Fia**', gray-green leaves, red bracts, flowers with yellow ovaries and red sepals; '**Foster's Favorite**', red-black leaves, pendent flowerhead, coral petals tipped blue; '**Friederike**', spineless; '**J C Superstar**', open funnel-shaped rosette, red bracts, pale petals; '**Royal Wine**', light green leaves, maroon undersides, orange and blue flowers; '**Shelldancer**', leaves apple green with red tips, side spikes, flowers white at base, petals blue. Zones 9–12.

Aechmea recurvata 'Aztec Gold'

AETHIONEMA

STONE CRESS

The 40-odd species in this genus of the cabbage (Brassicaceae) family are annuals and perennials distributed from Europe and the Mediterranean to southwest Asia. Most are low, spreading, or mounding plants that thrive in rockery conditions. They have simple, small, fleshy leaves on wiry stems that can become a tangled mass of branches and foliage tufts. In spring and summer flower-heads form at stem tips, bearing dense clusters of tiny 4-petalled flowers. Well-grown plants are smothered in blooms.

CULTIVATION: These plants are hardy to repeated frosts but per-haps a little tender for harsh continental winters. Plant in full sun in gritty well-drained soil with extra humus for moisture retention. Many appreciate a light dressing of dolomite. Water if necessary when flowering but otherwise keep dry. Propagate from seed or cuttings or by layering. May self-sow.

Aethionema grandiflorum

☼ ❄ ↔ 12–24 in (30–60 cm)
↑ 8–18 in (20–45 cm)
Found in the Caucasus and nearby parts of Iran and Iraq. Can mound up to form a moderately sized shrub. Blue-green foli-age and bright pink flowers, each slightly more than ½ in (12 mm) wide. Zones 7–9.

Aethionema 'Warley Rose'

☼ ❄ ↔ 12 in (30 cm) ↑ 6 in (15 cm)
Most widely grown *Aethionema*. Blue-green foliage. Flowers bright rosy red, borne profusely from late spring to sum-mer's end. May be short lived. Zones 6–9.

AGAPANTHUS

AFRICAN LILY, LILY-OF-THE-NILE

This southern African genus consists of 10 species of fleshy-rooted perennials of the onion (Alliaceae) family. Long, strappy, fleshy leaves form dense clumps of evergreen or deciduous foliage. Tall flower stems with heads of tubular to bell-shaped flowers, usually blue, are held above the foliage. Flowers of evergreens appear over a long season in frost-free climates, and in summer elsewhere. Their narrow, rather upright habit makes them ideal border plants. Dwarf forms are superb in large rockeries or containers.

CULTIVATION: Easily grown in any well-drained soil in sun or half-sun, they will withstand drought and poor soil but produce more flowers with good conditions. Slugs and snails often damage the young foliage. Propagate by division in winter or raise from seed.

Agapanthus inapertus

DRAKENSBERG AGAPANTHUS, DROOPING AGAPANTHUS

☼ ❄ ↔ 40–50 in (100–130 cm) ↑ 40–60 in (100–150 cm)
Deciduous, from southeastern South Africa. Dense clumps of blue-tinted leaves to 27 in (70 cm) long. Pendulous, purple-blue, sometimes white, tubular flowers on stems to 5 ft (1.5 m) tall.
A. i. subsp. *hollandii*, taller stems and flared flowers. Zones 7–10.

Agapanthus praecox

☼ ❄ ↔ 40–50 in (100–130 cm) ↑ 40 in (100 cm)
Evergreen, fleshy, bright green leaves to 27 in (70 cm) long. Wide-opening pale to mid-blue flowers on stems to 36 in (90 cm) tall. Most widely cultivated species in warm-temperate gardens.
A. p. subsp. *orientalis*, smaller, forms dense foliage clumps with tightly packed heads of small bright blue flowers. Zones 8–11.

Agapanthus Hybrid Cultivars

☼ ❄ ↔ 12–30 in (30–75 cm) ↑ 15–60 in (38–150 cm)
Variable group, ranging from plants for large gardens to those for rockeries or tubs. Mainly easily grown in areas with not too severe winters. Cultivars include '**Baby Blue**', dwarf, with bright blue flowers on 12–16 in (30–40 cm) stems; '**Elaine**', upright, vigorous, deep purple-blue flowers on 4 ft (1.2 m) high stems; '**Ellamae**', bright violet-blue flowers on stems to 5 ft (1.5 m); '**Henryi**', dwarf, narrow leaves, white flowers on 18 in (45 cm) stems; '**Lilliput**', dwarf, dark blue flowers on 18 in (45 cm) tall stems; '**Loch Hope**', large heads of dark blue flowers, 4 ft (1.2 m) stems, late-flowering; Midnight Blue/'**Monmid**', compact, deep purple-blue flowers on 16 in (40 cm) stems; '**Peter Pan**', dwarf, mid-blue flowers on 12 in (30 cm) stems; '**Queen Anne**', bright blue flowers on 24 in (60 cm) stems; '**Rancho White**', white flowers on stems to 18 in (45 cm); '**Storm Cloud**', intense purple-blue flowers on 4 ft (1.2 m) stems; and '**Tinkerbell**', leaves edged cream, pale blue flowers on 16 in (40 cm) stems. Zones 7–11.

Agapanthus inapertus

AGASTACHE

GIANT HYSSOP, MEXICAN HYSSOP

There are 20 species of very aromatic perennials in this genus, a member of the mint (Lamiaceae) family. They are native to North America, China, and Japan where they grow in dry scrub and fields. Leaf shape varies from pointed oval to almost triangular or lance shaped, the margins being shallowly to finely toothed. Flowers may be red, orange, rose, violet, blue, or white, typically tubular with two lips. They are borne in densely packed whorls on spikes or narrow panicles in summer and are very popular with bees.

CULTIVATION: Grow in well-drained soil in a sunny position. Most species tolerate some frost; give the more tender ones a warm shel-tered site in cooler climates or grow as annuals. They can be prone to fungal diseases in summer. Propagate from seed or cuttings.

Agastache cana

HUMMINGBIRD PLANT, MOSQUITO PLANT

☼ ❄ ↔ 12–18 in (30–45 cm) ↑ 20–24 in (50–60 cm)
Woody-based perennial from southern USA. Slightly downy triangular or pointed oval leaves. Flower spikes to 12 in (30 cm) long, whorls of rose-colored tubular flowers. '**Heather Queen**' ★ has bright pink flowers. Zones 7–11.

Agastache foeniculum

syns *Agastache anethiodora, A. anisata*
ANISE HYSSOP

☼ ❄ ↔ 18–24 in (45–60 cm)
↑ 20–32 in (50–80 cm)

Very aromatic plant from North America.
Leaves triangular to pointed oval with toothed
margins, downy beneath. Short, densely
packed flower spikes bear small violet-blue
flowers. Zones 8–10.

Agastache rugosa

HUO XIANG, KOREAN MINT, WRINKLED GIANT HYSSOP

☼ ❄ ↔ 24 in (60 cm) ↑ 24–48 in (60–120 cm)

Erect perennial from China and Japan.
Coarsely toothed ovate leaves, hairy undersides. In summer, short compact spikes bear
small tubular flowers of violet to rose.
'**Honeybee White**' and '**Honeybee Blue**'
('Licorice Blue' may be the prior name for
this) are compact plants. Zones 7–11.

Ageratum houstonianum 'Azure Pearl'

Agastache rupestris

LICORICE MINT, SUNSET HYSSOP, THREADLEAF GIANT HYSSOP

☼ ❄ ↔ 18 in (45 cm) ↑ 18–36 in (45–90 cm)

A very aromatic species found from southwest-
ern USA to northern Mexico. Grayish green thread-like leaves. Orange flowers with
lavender calyces in summer. '**Sunset**', slightly shorter. Zones 5–9.

Agastache Hybrid Cultivars

☼ ❄ ↔ 1–3 ft (0.3–0.9 m) ↑ 2–6 ft (0.6–1.8 m)

The crossing of several species has resulted in cultivars of varying
heights and colors. Cultivars include '**Apricot Sunrise**', grayish
green foliage, orange flowers; '**Blue Fortune**', bluish purple flowers;
'**Firebird**', coppery orange tones; '**Tangerine Dreams**', similar to
'Apricot Sunrise' but taller; '**Tutti Frutti**', grayish
green leaves, raspberry red flowers. Zones 7–10.

AGERATUM

FLOSS FLOWER

Found in the tropical Americas, including the
West Indies, this genus containing 43 species of
annuals, perennials, and shrubs is a member of
the daisy (Asteraceae) family. Best known for the
annual bedding species, *Ageratum houstonianum*,
the genus is characterized by flowerheads in which
the ray florets are tubular filaments rather than
petal-like, creating a fine feathery effect. The size
of the plants varies considerably with the species,
but most of the garden forms are compact and
have hairy or felted leaves, generally with toothed edges.
CULTIVATION: Plant in full sun in gritty well-drained soil that
remains moist during the flowering season. Most perennial and
shrubby species can tolerate only light frosts and may be grown
outdoors only in mild areas. Raise annuals from seed, usually
sown in spring; propagate perennials from half-hardened cuttings.

Agastache foeniculum

Ageratum houstonianum

☼ ❄ ↔ 6–20 in (15–50 cm) ↑ 6–30 in (15–75 cm)

Annuals from Central America and West Indies. Pointed oval to
poplar-shaped, downy, tooth-edged, dull green leaves to nearly
4 in (10 cm) long. Large dense or open heads of blue or lavender
flowers. Garden forms include pink and white flowers. Popular
cultivars include '**Azure Pearl**', 12 in (30 cm) tall, mid-blue
flowers; '**Blue Danube**', up to 6 in (15 cm) tall, mound forming,
blue flowers; '**Blue Horizon**', 24–30 in (60–75 cm) tall, purple-
blue flowers; '**Blue Lagoon**', 8 in (20 cm) tall, neat rounded blue
flowers; '**Blue Mink**' ★, 12 in (30 cm) tall, light dusky blue
flowers; '**Pacific**', 8 in (20 cm) tall, purple-blue flowers; and
'**Red Top**', 24–28 in (60–70 cm) tall, bushy purple-red flowers.
Among several seedling strains of uniform size
one of the best is the **Hawaii Series**—neat
rounded plants around 8 in (20 cm) tall—
including: '**Hawaii Blue**', '**Hawaii Pink Shell**',
'**Hawaii Royal**', and '**Hawaii White**'. Zones 10–12.

AGLAONEMA

This genus in the arum (Araceae) family has some
25 species of herbaceous evergreens, found from
eastern India to southern China and south to
Indonesia and the Philippines. Clustered fleshy
stems are short, or may grow slowly to over 3 ft
(0.9 m) long. Leaves crowded at stem tips are
mostly ovate or elliptical, somewhat leathery, and
often patterned in gray or cream. Flower spikes
project from among the leaf bases. Red or yellow fruits are berry-
like. Used indoors, or outdoors under trees in tropical gardens.
CULTIVATION: Require a humid, virtually frost-free environment
and grow best in filtered light; some tolerate deep shade. Pot in
a free-draining medium and feed regularly through summer; remove longer stems. Propagate from stem cuttings or by division.

Aglaonema costatum

Aglaonema commutatum

☀/◐ ❄ ↔ 24 in (60 cm) ↑ 24–36 in (60–90 cm)

Most widely cultivated species, from the Philippines and eastern Indonesia. Stems sprawl as they elongate. Leaves narrowly ovate, dull dark green with feathery gray markings. *A. c.* var. *maculatum*, leaves with light green markings. *A. c.* 'Pseudobracteatum', larger areas of white and pale green along veins; 'Treubii', narrower deep green leaves, pale gray pattern; 'White Rajah', erect thin leaves, much more white and cream than green. Zones 10–12.

Aglaonema costatum

☀/◐ ❄ ↔ 24 in (60 cm) ↑ 12 in (30 cm)

From the Malay Peninsula, low-growing plant with short trailing stems and short dark green leaves with paler midrib; flower spikes few, with white spathe, to 1½ in (35 mm) long, in summer. 'Foxii', scattered, small, white spots, white midrib. Zones 10–12.

Aglaonema crispum

syn. *Aglaonema robelinii*

PAINTED DROP-TONGUE

☀/◐ ❄ ↔ 18–30 in (45–75 cm)
↑ 24–48 in (60–120 cm)

Robust clumping plant with erect stems, from Philippines. Elliptical leaves to 12 in (30 cm) long, gray with dark green zone along midrib. Flower spikes clustered, spathe yellowish, to 3 in (8 cm) long. Zones 10–12.

AJUGA

BUGLE

Members of the mint (Lamiaceae) family, the 40-odd, low, spreading annuals and perennials in this genus occur throughout temperate Eurasia, Africa, and Australia, and are widely naturalized elsewhere. Many spread by fleshy stems, others self-layer as they grow. Leaves are in whorls on narrow angular stems. Conical, short-stemmed, upright flowerheads with small, often purple-blue flowers appearing from the axils of leaf bracts, bloom mainly from late spring into summer. Use as a quick ground cover around small shrubs or in containers, but take care to control their spread.

CULTIVATION: Most grow very freely in any well-drained soil. Some need to be cut back routinely. Propagation of perennials is by division or from self-rooted layers; annuals from seed.

Ajuga pyramidalis

PYRAMID BUGLE

☀/◐ ❄ ↔ 12–24 in (30–60 cm) ↑ 6–8 in (15–20 cm)

Mat-forming European perennial. Rosettes of dark green, finely toothed leaves to 4 in (10 cm) long. Leafy pyramidal flowerheads with mauve-blue flowers backed by purple-bronze bracts. 'Metallica Crispa', wavy-edged purple-bronze foliage. Zones 6–10.

Ajuga reptans

☀/◐ ❄ ↔ 12–48 in (30–120 cm) or more ↑ 4–8 in (10–20 cm)

A temperate Eurasian native. Sometimes invasive. Foliage often purple tinted. Flowers in blue to purple shades, sometimes pink. Cultivars include 'Atropurpurea', deep purple-bronze foliage, dark flowers; 'Braunherz', very dark, glossy, purple-bronze leaves; 'Burgundy Glow', gray-green leaves, reddish markings; 'Burgundy Lace', purple-bronze, cream, and green variegation; 'Catlin's Giant', bronze-green leaves, tall flower spikes; 'Jungle Beauty', large deep green leaves, bright purple-blue flowers; 'Jungle Bronze', vigorous and upright, large wavy-edged bronze leaves; 'Multicolor' (syns 'Rainbow', 'Tricolor'), cream, pink, and green foliage; 'Pink Elf', compact, deep pink flowers; 'Pink Surprise', bronze, gray, and green variegated foliage, bronze in winter, pink flowers; and 'Purple Torch', bronze foliage, pink flowers. Zones 5–10.

ALCEA

HOLLYHOCK

A member of the mallow (Malvaceae) family, this genus contains about 60 species of biennials and short-lived perennial herbs native to central and southwestern Asia. Some are naturalized around the Mediterranean. Flowers, to 4 in (10 cm) across and borne on stems to 7 ft (2 m) tall in summer, have 5 petals and may be pink, purple, yellow, or white. Stamens form a prominent central column, usually yellow. A quintessential English cottage garden style plant. CULTIVATION: Grow in a sunny position in rich soil, moist but well drained. Stake plants on exposed sites and water in dry spells. Rust is a problem, and it is best to renew plants each year. Propagate from seed sown in late summer or early spring.

Alcea rosea

Alcea rosea

syn. *Althaea rosea*

HOLLYHOCK

☀ ❄ ↔ 2–3 ft (0.6–0.9 m) ↑ 2–8 ft (0.6–2.4 m)

Cultivated and naturalized in many places but thought to originate from Turkey or Asia. Rounded leaves have 3 to 7 lobes. Flowers single or double, to 4 in (10 cm) across, shades of pink, purple, yellow, and white. Wide range of cultivars and seed lines. 'Nigra', dark maroon single flowers. Zones 3–10.

ALCHEMILLA

BEAR'S FOOT, LADY'S MANTLE, LION'S FOOT

This widespread genus of around 300 species of clump-forming soft-stemmed perennials from Eurasia, Africa, and Central and South America belongs to the rose (Rosaceae) family. Foliage, on fine stems that often self-layer, is hand-shaped with rounded lobes, covered in fine hairs. Sprays of tiny yellow-green flowers are borne from late spring.
CULTIVATION: Cultivated species are temperate-zone plants that prefer cool, moist, well-drained conditions with shade from the hottest sun. Propagation is usually by division when dormant, but can be raised from seed.

Alchemilla mollis ★

LADY'S MANTLE

☼/◐ ❋ ↔ 12–32 in (30–80 cm) ↑ 12–20 in (30–50 cm)
Mounding spreading species found from Romania to Greece and Iran. Toothed leaves, finely hairy above, densely hairy below. Sprays of yellow-green flowers in summer. Zones 4–9.

Alchemilla xanthochlora

◐ ❋ ↔ 16–24 in (40–60 cm) ↑ 12–20 in (30–50 cm)
Mounding and spreading European species. Yellow-green, kidney-shaped, toothed, 9- to 11-lobed leaves, hairless above, hairy below. Yellow-green flowers in summer. Zones 5–9.

ALKANNA

This is a genus of about 30 frost-hardy annual and perennial species found from southern Europe to Iran, and it is a member of the borage (Boraginaceae) family. The plants have branching terminal inflorescences with a long tubular corolla and a downy ring in the center. The leaves are smooth-edged and hairy. Fruits are elongated calyces.
CULTIVATION: These plants prefer rich warm soil in an open sunny position. Propagate from seed.

Alkanna orientalis

☼ ❋ ↔ 8–12 in (20–30 cm) ↑ 8–12 in (20–30 cm)
Annual found from southwest Europe to southwest Asia. White or yellow scented flowers to ½ in (12 mm) wide. Hairy green to whitish green leaves to 3 in (8 cm) long, lance-shaped or narrowly egg-shaped. Zones 6–9.

Alkanna tinctoria

ALKANET, DYER'S BUGLOSS

☼ ❋ ↔ 12–36 in (30–90 cm) ↑ 12–36 in (30–90 cm)
Perennial from central and southern Europe. Bright purplish blue flowers to ½ in (12 mm) wide with funnel-shaped corolla. Bristly, smooth-edged, linear to egg-shaped leaves to 3 in (8 cm) long. Extensive root system and a hairy angular stem. Zones 5–8.

ALOCASIA

Comprising 70 species, this genus of the arum (Araceae) family occurs in a variety of habitats, from lowland rainforests to roadsides, swamps, and mountain regions from tropical southern Asia, Indonesia, Malaysia, New Guinea, and Australia, to islands of the Pacific. The species are perennial, evergreen, very small to massive herbs, even tree-like, with corms, runners, or aboveground stems. Leaves are several with sheathing leaf stalk, simple, broadly or narrowly arrowhead-shaped, with entire or deeply lobed margins, but usually heart-shaped at the base. The major veins are often strikingly prominent in some species. Inflorescences are borne at or near the apex of the leafy plant, 2 or more together, the spathes constricted, the spadix in 4 parts, lowermost female, then sterile, then male, then a sterile appendage. The female flower has no petals or sepals, consisting only of the single-celled ovary and stigma. Male flowers consist of 3 to 8, stalkless, narrow anthers united into a pyramid shape. Fruit is a globular berry containing several seeds.
CULTIVATION: Propagate from seed and stem cuttings or by division of fleshy stem. All species require warm moist conditions in shady sheltered locations, and are grown in greenhouses and conservatories in all regions but the tropics.

Alocasia × *amazonica*

☀ ⚘ ↔ 20–40 in (50–100 cm) ↑ 40–60 in (100–150 cm)
A hybrid of *A. lowii* and *A. sanderiana*, its origins are unknown. Leaves to 24 in (60 cm) long and 12 in (30 cm) wide, arrowhead-shaped, upperside dark green, midrib yellow-greenish white, other veins silvery white. Underside dull purple, major veins green-white. Leaf stalk green, 18 in (45 cm) long. '**Magnifica**', more intensely silver coloration on upperside, all purple below; '**Randall**', larger in all parts. Zones 11–12.

Alocasia × *amazonica*

Alocasia cuprea

☀ ✤ ↔30 in (75 cm) ↑to 40 in (100 cm)

Occurs in forests of Malaysia and Borneo. Perennial herb, fleshy-stemmed, leaf stalks 24 in (60 cm) long, leaf blades oblong to oval, somewhat arrowhead-shaped, surface raised between the lateral veins giving a quilted appearance, upperside with dark green and copper-colored areas, underside reddish purple. Spathes purple, to 6 in (15 cm) long. Flowers in summer. Zones 11–12.

Alocasia sanderiana

syns *Alocasia sanderana, A. sanderi, Schizocasia sanderiana*

☀/☀ ✤ ↔20–36 in (50–90 cm) ↑40–60 in (100–150 cm)

Perennial herb. Common in cultivation but endangered in the wild; its only known habitat is the moist forests of Mindanao in the Philippines. Leaves broadly arrowhead-shaped, shiny, blackish green on the upperside, main veins and edges silvery white, underside green, 20 in (50 cm) long, leaf stalks 24 in (60 cm) long. Spathe is greenish, shorter than leaves, flowering intermittent. Attractive cultivars include '**Nobilis**' and '**Van Houtte**'. Zones 11–12.

ALPINIA

GINGER LILY

The 200 species of fleshy-stemmed perennials in this genus, which belongs to the ginger (Zingiberaceae) family, are native to tropical regions of Asia, Australia, and some Pacific islands. Lance-shaped leaves are arranged in 2 ranks along reed-like stems from 3–12 ft (0.9–3.5 m) tall depending on the species. The inflorescences are usually showy and long-lasting. The true flowers are often enclosed at first within colorful bracts.
CULTIVATION: In warm climates grow in sun or half-sun in fertile moist soil. Most species will withstand a little frost but need 4 to 5 months of growth to flower, so in cool climates start earlier indoors or grow under glass in bright filtered light, water plentifully and maintain high humidity. Propagate from seed or by division.

Alpinia zerumbet

Alpinia purpurata

RED GINGER

☀/☀ ✤ ↔2–4 ft (0.6–1.2 m) ↑8–12 ft (2.4–3.5 m)

From Melanesia. Large leaves, up to 32 in (80 cm) long, prominent midribs. The long-lasting rich red flowerheads are borne on upright inflorescences for much of the year. Zones 10–11.

Alpinia purpurata

Alpinia zerumbet

syns *Alpinia nutans, A. speciosa*

PINK PORCELAIN LILY, SHELL GINGER

☀/☀ ✤ ↔2–3 ft (0.6–0.9 m) ↑6–10 ft (1.8–3 m)

From eastern Asia and New Guinea. Most widely grown species. Glossy leathery leaves. Pendulous inflorescence to 16 in (40 cm) long. Pale pink or white bracts at first enclose yellow and red flowers, borne in spring and summer. '**Variegata**', pale yellow striped leaves. Zones 9–11.

ALSTROEMERIA

LILY OF THE INCAS, PERUVIAN LILY

This genus in the Alstroemeriaceae family has around 50 species of fleshy-rooted perennials. Found in South America, often at altitude, they are known for their long-lasting beautifully marked flowers but notorious for their vigorous roots and self-sowing. *A. psittacina* is considered a weed in some areas. Foliage is mid-green, usually lance-shaped, and slightly twisted. It is carried on tall stems that terminate in many flowered heads of 6-petalled lily-like blooms of many shades.
CULTIVATION: Though rather frost tender—the roots should be insulated with mulch—these species are easily grown in any sunny position with moderately fertile well-drained soil that can be kept moist during the flowering season. Propagate by division when dormant, or from seed.

Alstroemeria psittacina

syn. *Alstroemeria pulchella*

☀/☀ ❄ ↔16–20 in (40–50 cm) ↑28–36 in (70–90 cm)

This Brazilian species has leaves up to 3 in (8 cm) long, and heads of red-flushed green flowers with maroon flecks, borne in summer. '**Royal Star**' (syn. 'Variegata') is variegated. Zones 8–10.

Alstroemeria Hybrid Cultivars

☀ ❄ ↔12–24 in (30–60 cm) ↑18–48 in (45–120 cm)

Alstroemerias hybridize freely, and in recent years the range has increased enormously. Popular hybrids include '**Aimi**', 2 ft (0.6 m) tall, pink-blushed pale creamy yellow flowers with deep brown flecks; '**Amanda**', white-flushed pink flowers with green petal tips and dark flecks; '**Apollo**', 3 ft (0.9 m) tall, white flowers with deep yellow center and brown flecks; '**Belinda**', soft yellow flowers with darker center and brown flecks; '**Blue Heaven**', 3–4 ft (0.9–1.2 m) tall, lavender blue flowers with pale center and red-brown flecks; '**Blushing Bride**', 3 ft (0.9 m) tall, white flowers with faint pink blush; '**Evening Song**', 3 ft (0.9 m) tall, deep magenta flowers with yellow throat and dark flecks; '**Friendship**', 3 ft (0.9 m) tall, soft yellow flowers with deep brown markings and a darker center, and hint of purple at the petal tips; '**Fuego**' ★, 5–6 ft (1.5–1.8 m) tall, fiery red flowers with small yellow throat; Ilona/'**Stalona**', soft orange-red flowers with creamy yellow throat and dark flecks; Irena/'**Statiren**', white-flushed pink flowers with near-red mid-stripe and dark flecks; '**Marina**', 20–30 in (50–75 cm) tall, magenta-pink flowers with small yellow throat and dark flecks; '**Marissa**', 3 ft (0.9 m) tall, rose pink flowers lightening to cream mid-petal with yellow throat and dark flecks; '**Napoli**', magenta-purple flowers with faint yellow throat and dark flecks; '**Odessa**', 3–4 ft (1–1.2 m) tall, white flowers flushed and tipped deep red-pink, with yellow throat and red flecks; Olga/'**Stalog**', white flowers with yellow center and red flecks; '**Orange Gem**', 3 ft (0.9 m) tall, orange flowers with golden yellow throat and dark flecks; '**Orange Glory**', 3 ft (0.9 m) tall, deep orange flowers with dark markings and golden throat; Queen Elizabeth The Queen Mother/'**Stamoli**', brown-marked cream flowers flushed with pink; Rebecca/'**Stabec**', 3 ft (0.9 m) tall, cream flowers with deep pink blotches, yellow center and dark flecks; '**Red Beauty**', 3 ft (0.9 m) tall, with black-flecked, red-orange flowers with yellow-throats, '**Romy**', 4–5 ft (1.2–1.5 m) tall, white flowers with yellow center and red flecks; '**Tessa**', 30 in (75 cm) tall, brown-flecked red flowers with small yellow center; and '**Yellow Friendship**', black-flecked bright yellow flowers.

The **Little Miss Series** are dwarf plants, 6–12 in (15–30 cm) tall, with large flowers, strong stems and a long flowering period. They include '**Little Miss Olivia**', '**Little Miss Roselind**', '**Little Miss Sophie**', and '**Little Miss Tara**'.

The Dutch-raised **Princess Series** is a range of compact hybrids that grow 12–18 in (30–45 cm) tall and are long flowering because they are sterile. They are ideal as potted plants. This series includes Princess Daniela/'**Stapridani**', Princess Ivana/'**Staprivane**', Princess Monica/'**Staprimon**', Princess Morana/'**Staprirana**', Princess Oxana/'**Staprioxa**', Princess Pamela/'**Stapripame**', Princess Sissi/'**Staprisis**', and Princess Zavina/'**Staprivina**'. Zones 7–10.

ALTERNANTHERA

CHAFF FLOWER, COPPERLEAF, JOYWEED

A genus of about 200 low, compact, trailing or erect, aquatic, annual or perennial herbs from tropical to subtropical Americas belonging to the amaranth (Amaranthaceae) family. The spikes of small flowers have bracts but no petals. They are often grown for their brightly colored foliage, which is smooth-edged or densely toothed. **CULTIVATION:** Adaptable to most soils, they do best in a protected, warm, sunny position in rich soil with frequent watering. Regularly clip plants for border displays. In cooler climates plants should be lifted after first frosts. Propagate by division or from cuttings taken in late summer or spring.

Alstroemeria, Hybrid Cultivar, 'Apollo'

Alternanthera bettzichiana

CALICO PLANT

☼ ☀ ↔ 2–3 ft (0.6–0.9 m) ↕ 2–3 ft (0.6–0.9 m)

Annual or short-lived perennial native to Brazil. Erect habit; insignificant flowers; narrow spoon-shaped leaves of khaki to yellow, with red to purple markings. Usually grown for its foliage. '**Brilliantissima**' has vivid red leaves. Zones 10–12.

AMARANTHUS

There are about 60 species of weedy annuals and short-lived perennials in this genus, which is a member of the amaranth (Amaranthaceae) family. They have a worldwide distribution, often being found in wasteland areas. Species range from tall to prostrate, with long, often drooping, tassels of small red or green flowers. Individual flowers are either male or female and may be borne on separate plants. Some species are cultivated as leaf or grain crops in tropical areas, while those with dramatic flowers or colorful foliage are popular in the ornamental garden and for floristry. **CULTIVATION:** These are easily grown in well-drained fertile soil in full sun. Protect tall varieties from strong wind. In cooler climates sow seed under glass in early spring and plant out after danger of frosts has passed. In warmer areas seed can be sown outdoors later in the season.

Amaranthus caudatus 'Green Tails'

Amaranthus caudatus

LOVE-LIES-BLEEDING, TASSEL FLOWER, VELVET FLOWER

☼ ❄ ↔ 24 in (60 cm) ↕ 36–48 in (90–120 cm)

Native to Peru, Africa, and India, this annual or short-lived perennial has dull green leaves, as well as drooping crimson-purple tassels, up to 12 in (30 cm) long, in summer. Cultivars include '**Green Tails**' and '**Viridis**' (syn. '**Green Thumb**'). Zones 8–11.

Amaranthus tricolor
CHINESE SPINACH, JOSEPH'S COAT, TAMPALA

☼ ❄ ↔ 30 in (75 cm) ↑ 24–36 in (60–90 cm)

Bushy annual from Africa and Asia. Grown as a leaf vegetable or, in varieties which have colorful foliage, for its ornamental value. Appearing in summer, the flower spikes are green or red. 'Joseph's Coat' has red and gold upper leaves. Zones 8–11.

AMSONIA
BLUE STAR

Found from southern Europe, through temperate Asia including Japan, and in North America, this genus of the dogbane (Apocynaceae) family has some 20 species of perennials and subshrubs characterized by milky sap and simple narrow leaves. Flowers, though small, are an unusual shade of blue and mass in heads above the foliage. While not spectacular, most species are distinctive, adding something different to the perennial border. CULTIVATION: These plants prefer a climate with distinct seasons. Most are easily cultivated in a quite sunny position with well-drained soil kept moist in the growing season. Propagate perennials by division during dormancy or as growth starts. Those with firmer stems will also grow from summer cuttings.

Amsonia tabernaemontana
BLUE DOGBANE, BLUE STAR

☼/❂ ❄ ↔ 36–48 in (90–120 cm) ↑ 36 in (90 cm)

Clump-forming perennial of eastern USA. Upright green stems, simple lance-shaped leaves to 3 in (8 cm) long. Heads of pale blue flowers in mid-spring–late summer. Zones 4–9.

ANAGALLIS
PIMPERNEL

This primrose (Primulaceae) family genus includes 20 species, found over much of the globe, especially temperate zones. The soft-stemmed, low, spreading plants, mostly biennials or perennials, behave as annuals in cold climates. The leaves are small and simple. The small flowers are brightly colored, pink, red, or blue. Some may be weeds, but are not invasive.

Anaphalis triplinervis 'Sommerschnee'

CULTIVATION: Grow in a sunny spot with moist well-drained soil. Cultivated species are easily maintained by pinching to shape; not invasive. Propagate from seed, base cuttings, or layers.

Anagallis monelli
BLUE PIMPERNEL

☼/❂ ❄ ↔ 12–20 in (30–50 cm) ↑ 12–20 in (30–50 cm)

Mediterranean native, small perennial. Dark green leaves. Flowers single but abundant, bright blue, red-tinted undersides. Cultivars include 'Pacific Blue' ★ and 'Phillipii'. Zones 7–10.

ANAPHALIS
PEARLY EVERLASTING

This genus in the daisy (Asteraceae) family consists of around 100 species of perennials that may be upright, low and bushy, or trailing. Though found across northern temperate zones and on tropical mountains, a feature common to all is that the foliage and stems are covered with a fine white to gray hair. Leaves are simple, linear to lance-shaped, attached to stems without stalks. Flowerheads form dense downy heads, and while they lack ray florets, papery white bracts create a similar effect. Cut flowers last well but the plants are grown as much for their foliage. CULTIVATION: Mostly very hardy. Plant in full sun with gritty well-drained soil kept moist in summer. Dry winter conditions are preferable. Cut back hard in spring to encourage strong new growth. Propagate from seed, base cuttings, or by division.

Anaphalis margaritacea
PEARLY EVERLASTING

☼ ❄ ↔ 16–24 in (40–60 cm) ↑ 32–40 in (80–100 cm)

Widespread in northern temperate areas. Leaves gray-green above with white hair below. In summer, flowerheads are clustered in corymbs to 6 in (15 cm) wide with opalescent bracts. Zones 3–9.

Anaphalis triplinervis
☼ ❄ ↔ 16–20 in (40–50 cm) ↑ 32–36 in (80–90 cm)

Central Asian species, found from Afghanistan to southwest China. Clump-forming. Spatula-shaped gray-green leaves to 4 in (10 cm) long. Dome-shaped heads of white flowerheads in summer. 'Sommerschnee', larger, with silvery white flowers. Zones 5–9.

ANCHUSA
ALKANET, BUGLOSS

Classified in the borage (Boraginaceae) family, this genus includes some 35 species of biennials and perennials from Europe, western Asia, and Africa. They are strong growers, usually clump-forming, with upright stems and simple, pointed, elliptical leaves that can be quite large at the base of the clump. Heads of small 5-petalled flowers in shades from pale blue to purple open through late spring and summer. CULTIVATION: Species thrive in most conditions except very poor soil, deep shade, or drought. Ample feeding and mulching in winter and water in the growing season promotes flowering. Perennials may be divided in winter or very early spring; annuals or biennials must be raised from seed, preferably sown in autumn so young plants can start growth early in spring.

Anchusa azurea

syn. *Anchusa italica*

☼/◐ ❋ ↔ 32 in (80 cm) ↑ 48 in (120 cm)

Perennial, native to the Mediterranean region and western Asia. Bristly red-tinted stems with lower leaves to 12 in (30 cm) long. Flowers blue to purple, ½ in (12 mm) wide, 5-petalled, in late spring–summer. Cultivars include '**Dropmore**', compact and bushy, large deep blue flowers; and '**Opal**', compact, grayish foliage, light blue flowers. Zones 3–9.

Anchusa capensis

☼ ⚘ ↔ 16 in (40 cm) ↑ 20 in (50 cm)

Hairy biennial from South Africa with narrow lance-shaped leaves to 5 in (12 cm) long. White-centered bright blue flowers through summer. Treated as a spring-sown annual where summers are long. Zones 9–11.

ANDROSACE

ROCK JASMINE

This genus of 100 species of annual, biennial, and perennial herbs belongs to the primrose (Primulaceae) family. They are alpine plants from northern temperate regions, growing in scree at high altitudes and in turf at lower altitudes. The dainty flowers, usually less than ½ in (12 mm) across, have short tubular bases flaring to flat open-faced petals. They are white, pink, or red with a central eye that is often yellow or orange.

CULTIVATION: These plants need perfect drainage, good air circulation, and careful watering. Grow in a cool greenhouse or outdoors in troughs in a low-fertility gritty mix. Prevent collar rot with a gritty mulch on the soil surface and water from beneath. Cover outdoor troughs with glass in winter to protect from rain. Propagate from seed (germination may take 2 years), or cuttings or runners of some species.

Androsace lanuginosa ★

☼ ❋ ↔ 12–18 in (30–45 cm) ↑ 3 in (8 cm)

From the Himalayas. Prostrate perennial forming a mat of foliage covered in silvery hairs. Small dense heads of pale pink, darker-eyed flowers in summer–early autumn. '**Leichtlinii**' has deeper pink flowers. Zones 6–9.

Androsace rotundifolia

☼ ❋ ↔ 8 in (20 cm) ↑ 4–6 in (10–15 cm)

Hairy perennial from northern India. Rosettes of small, round, lobed leaves; densely packed, pale pink flowers, in spring–early summer. Zones 4–9.

ANEMONE

WINDFLOWER

Widespread in temperate regions of both hemispheres, this genus is a member of the buttercup (Ranunculaceae) family, and has some 120 species of perennials. Their roots may be tuberous, fleshy-

Anchusa azurea

stemmed or fibrous, and develop into clumps of finely divided foliage. Bowl-shaped flowers, single or in small clusters, sit on wiry stems well above the foliage. Most species flower in spring shortly after the foliage appears, but some continue into early summer and a few species bloom in autumn.

CULTIVATION: The wood anemones prefer woodland conditions with dappled shade, but most species thrive in a sunny border with moist well-drained soil. Propagation is by division in winter when dormant, or from seed in the case of strains grown as annuals.

Anemone blanda

◐/☼ ❋ ↔ 6–12 in (15–30 cm) ↑ 4–8 in (10–20 cm)

Found from southeastern Europe to the Caucasus region. Strong fleshy stems and ferny base leaves. Flowers 1–1¾ in (25–40 mm) wide, white, blue, mauve, or pink, from late winter. '**Atrocaerulea**' (syn. 'Ingramii'), deep blue flowers; '**Radar**', white-centered deep magenta-pink flowers; '**White Splendour**', tall grower, large white flowers, pink-tinted inside. Zones 5–9.

Anemone coronaria

FLORIST'S ANEMONE, WIND POPPY, WINDFLOWER

☼/◐ ❋ ↔ 8–16 in (20–40 cm) ↑ 16–24 in (40–60 cm)

Tuberous-rooted native of southeastern Europe and northern Mediterranean. Finely divided ferny base foliage and simple leaves on flower stems. Large spring flowers in most shades except yellow. Parent of many cultivars and a large range of garden hybrids, such as the **Mona Lisa Series**, which grow to 24 in (60 cm) tall with flowers to 4 in (10 cm) wide in all colors. Zones 8–10.

Anemone blanda

Anemone hupehensis var. japonica

Anemone pavonina

Anemone sylvestris

Anemone hupehensis

◑/◉ ❄ ↔ 16–40 in (40–100 cm) ↕ 20–36 in (50–90 cm)
Fibrous-rooted, late summer- to autumn-flowering species from China and Japan. Coarsely toothed, lightly downy, 3-part foliage. Upright branching flower stems with large flowers, usually white but often in pink shades. Fluffy seedheads follow. *A. h.* var. *japonica, A. h.* var. *japonica* 'Prinz Heinrich', and *A. h.* 'Hadspen Abundance' are attractive forms. Zones 6–9.

Anemone × hybrida

◑/◉ ❄ ↔ 20–48 in (50–120 cm) ↕ 32–60 in (80–150 cm)
Garden hybrids of uncertain origin. 'Géantes des Blanches', 4 ft (1.2 m) tall, large, white, semi-double flowers; 'Honorine Jobert' ★, 4 ft (1.2 m) tall, large, white, single flowers with pale pink reverse; 'Margarete', 3 ft (0.9 m) tall, pink double flowers; 'September Charm' (syn. *A. hupehensis* 'September Charm'), 30 in (75 cm) high, tall, pink flowers, often drooping. Zones 6–9.

Anemone nemorosa

WINDFLOWER, WOOD ANEMONE
◑/◉ ❄ ↔ 6–16 in (15–40 cm) ↕ 4–12 in (10–30 cm)
Fleshy-stemmed, spring-flowering, European native usually found in woodlands. Leaflets are in 3s, coarsely toothed, and/or finely divided. Flowers are around 1 in (25 mm) wide, usually white in the wild but garden forms come in a range of mauve and pink shades. Cultivars include 'Allenii', 'Pallida', 'Robinsoniana', and 'Vestal'. Zones 5–9.

Anemone pavonina

ANEMONE OF GREECE
◉/◑ ❄ ↔ 12–16 in (30–40 cm) ↕ 12 in (30 cm)
Clump-forming tuberous species native to the Mediterranean region. Three-part base foliage deeply divided and ferny, bright green. In spring, 2–4 in (5–10 cm) wide flowers in a range of colors. Allow to dry off after flowering. Zones 8–10.

Anemone sylvestris

SNOWDROP ANEMONE, SNOWDROP WINDFLOWER
◉ ❄ ↔ 6–20 in (15–50 cm) ↕ 6–12 in (15–30 cm)
A spreading fleshy-stemmed European species that is found to occur in a range of conditions from lowland woods to subalpine

regions. The species has deeply divided, deep green, hand-shaped leaves and, appearing from late spring, scented white flowers that are up to 3 in (8 cm) wide, often slightly drooping. These are followed by fluffy seedheads. Cultivars include 'Elise Fellman' (syn. 'Flore Pleno') and 'Grandiflora'. Zones 4–9.

ANGELONIA

There are some 30 species of subshrubs or perennials in this genus in the foxglove (Scrophulariaceae) family. Native to central and southern America, they grow in damp open spaces. Leaves are usually small and simple. The short, 5-lobed, tubular flowers are mauve, blue, or white and are produced for much of the year. In cool and temperate climates these are usually treated as annuals.
CULTIVATION: Grow in a sunny position in a moist but well-drained light soil. Indoors they require bright filtered light in a potting mix with added organic matter and should be kept moist. Propagate from seed or softwood cuttings, or by division.

Angelonia angustifolia

◉ ❖ ↔ 12 in (30 cm) ↕ 18 in (45 cm)
From Mexico and West Indies. Small pointed leaves with serrated edges, and racemes of mauve to violet flowers in summer. Colored strains are available in white (alba), purple, purple and white, and rose pink. Zones 9–11.

ANIGOZANTHOS

KANGAROO PAW
This genus contains 11 species of evergreen sword-leafed perennials of the bloodroot (Haemodoraceae) family, all of which are confined naturally to southwestern Australia. The foliage is dark green and varies from grassy to iris-like. Spikes or panicles of intriguingly furry tubular blooms are borne on stems 1–6 ft (0.3–1.8 m) tall, usually in warmer months. Flowers are around 1¼ in (30 mm) long and occur in green and warm shades of gold, pink, red, and russet brown, depending on the species. The flower stems last well when cut.
CULTIVATION: Plant in a sunny position with perfect drainage. Better if watered well in the growing season but will tolerate drought. Blackened foliage signals ink disease, which can be very damaging, as can slugs and snails. Propagation in gardens is mostly by careful division. Species may be raised from seed.

Anigozanthos flavidus

GREEN KANGAROO PAW, TALL KANGAROO PAW

☼ ⚘ ↔ 3 ft (0.9 m) ↑ 10 ft (3 m)

Found in moist positions in forested regions of southern and southwestern Australia on sandy and gravelly soils. Summer-flowering perennial with green leaves to 3 ft (0.9 m) long. Flowering stems smooth, green, to 10 ft (3 m) tall. Hairy, tubular flowers are green or yellow-green, sometimes red, orange, or pink. Zones 9–11.

Anigozanthos manglesii

MANGLES' KANGAROO PAW, RED AND GREEN KANGAROO PAW

☼ ⚘ ↔ 36 in (90 cm) ↑ 12–20 in (30–50 cm)

Usually a short-lived perennial, this species occurs on well-drained sandy soils along the western coast of Western Australia. Leaves flat, smooth, gray-green. Flower stems red, woolly, hairy, rarely branched. Tubular flowers green, red at base, in late winter–early summer. Zones 9–10.

Anigozanthos manglesii

Anigozanthos Hybrid Cultivars

☼/◐ ⚘ ↔ 8–30 in (20–75 cm) ↑ 1–6 ft (0.3–1.8 m)

There are now many attractive cultivars being offered to the gardening public. Cultivars include '**Autumn Sunrise**' ★, orange flowers in late spring–summer; '**Big Red**', many red flowers; '**Copper Charm**', tall scapes of orange flowers in spring; '**Dwarf Delight**', red hairs on yellow-green flowers; '**Hickman's Delight**', dark green leaves, dark red flowers; '**Little Jewel**', glossy green evergreen leaves, red flowers in spring; '**Mini Red**', compact plant, dense clusters of red flowers; '**Patricia**', red-brown flowers in spring; '**Pink Joey**', pale, purplish pink flowers; '**Red Cross**', large deep burgundy-colored flowers with a yellow spot at the base; '**Regal Claw**', red to orange flowers over most of the year; '**Ruby Jools**', leaves semi-deciduous, flowers red-green; '**Space Age**', red flowers; '**Spence's Spectacular**', red-brown flowers, deciduous leaves; '**Sue Dixon**', flowers red near base merging to yellow-green near lobes; and '**Velvet Harmony**', very dark, woolly, purplish flowers. The **Bush Gems Series** comes in a wide variety of colors. Zones 9–11.

ANTENNARIA

CAT'S EARS, EVERLASTING, LADIES' TOBACCO, PUSSY-TOES

Found in the northern temperate zone, especially in Asia and North America, this genus in the daisy (Asteraceae) family includes some 45 species of near-evergreen perennials characterized by a low, spreading habit and densely felted foliage. Flowerheads, on felted stems well above the foliage, are small, lack ray florets (petals), and are held within dry bracts. They are usually white, cream or pink, the foliage and growth habit perhaps being more important than the flowers.

CULTIVATION: These plants are used mainly as small-scale ground covers for rockeries and alpine troughs and to provide a foliage color contrast for showier plants. Grow in a sunny position with well-drained, somewhat gritty soil that can be kept moist in summer. Established plants can be divided or will self-layer, or fresh stocks can be raised from seed.

Antennaria dioica

CATSFOOT

☼ ❄ ↔ 24–36 in (60–90 cm) ↑ 8 in (20 cm)

Widespread in northern temperate zone. Mat-forming with felted, silver-gray, spatula-shaped leaves. White, cream, pink, or red flowerheads, on sturdy stems, in summer. Zones 5–9.

ANTHEMIS

DOG FENNEL

This genus in the daisy (Asteraceae) family contains around 100 species. These aromatic perennials and small shrubs are found mainly in the Mediterranean region and western Asia. Their leaves are usually very finely divided, sometimes gray-green or silvery, and form a base foliage clump with the yellow or white, rarely mauve, daisy flowers held above it.

CULTIVATION: Hardy, easily grown in moist, fertile, well-drained soil in full sun. Cut back after flowering for bushiness. May be short-lived. but easily propagated from cuttings and seed; some perennials may be divided.

Anthemis punctata

☼ ❄ ↔ 12–20 in (30–50 cm) ↑ 16–24 in (40–60 cm)

Found in Europe, the Mediterranean islands, and North Africa. Woody-based perennial with silky, white, pinnate leaves to around 4 in (10 cm) long. Abundant white flowerheads in summer. *A. p.* subsp. *cupaniana* ★ from Sicily has silver-gray foliage and is a vigorous grower. Zones 7–9.

Anthemis tinctoria

DYER'S CHAMOMILE, YELLOW CHAMOMILE

☼ ❄ ↔ 20–40 in (50–100 cm) ↑ 24–36 in (60–90 cm)

A shrubby perennial found from Europe to western Asia. Masses of golden flowerheads during the warmer months. Popular cultivars include 'E. C. Buxton' (syn. 'Mrs E. C. Buxton'), '**Golden Rays**', '**Sauce Hollandaise**', and '**Wargrave Variety**' (syn. 'Wargrave'). Zones 6–9.

Anthemis tinctoria 'Wargrave Variety'

Anthurium andraeanum

ANTHERICUM

There are over 50 species of perennial herbs in this genus which belongs to the agave (Agavaceae) family. They are found in southern Europe, Turkey, and Africa, growing in dry meadows and open scrub. They have short fleshy stems and fleshy roots and form clumps of narrow grass-like leaves. The flowering stems are tall and slender and bear airy sprays of white starry flowers in late spring and early summer.
CULTIVATION: Grow in full sun in fertile well-drained soil. Most species prefer alkaline conditions. Do not allow to dry out during the growth period. Propagate from seed or by division.

Anthericum liliago
ST BERNARD'S LILY
⚬ ❄ ↔ 12 in (30 cm) ↕ 24–36 in (60–90 cm)
Native to alpine meadows of southern Europe. Grass-like leaves to 16 in (40 cm) long. Starry white flowers, 1 in (2.5 cm) wide, borne on slender stems, in late spring. *A. l.* var. *major* has taller flowering stems and somewhat bigger flowers. Zones 7–9.

ANTHURIUM

This genus from the tropical Americas belongs to the arum (Araceae) family and encompasses around 900 species of evergreen perennials and climbers. They are widely grown as houseplants but also grown outdoors in the tropics. The large, elliptical, lance- or arrow-shaped leaves are usually held upright on stiff stems that emerge from a stout rootstock that may also produce aerial roots. The flowerheads consist of a shield-shaped spathe surrounding a protruding spadix. The spathe and spadix tend to be the same colour, often bright red. Anthuriums last well as cut flowers and are an important industry in Hawaii.
CULTIVATION: Mainly epiphytes in the wild, they adapt well to container and garden cultivation, thriving in bright humid conditions with moist humus-rich soil. Completely intolerant of frost, they cope with cool conditions quite well, though prolonged warmth is required for flowering.

Anthurium andraeanum
FLAMINGO FLOWER
◐/☀ ⚘ ↔ 12–24 in (30–60 cm) ↕ 20–48 in (50–120 cm)
From Colombia and Ecuador. Dark green arrowhead-shaped leaves up to 20 in (50 cm) long on equally long stalks. Bright, deep red, glossy, heavily veined, heart-shaped spathe with white to cream spadix and red fruit. Cultivars include '**Lady Ruth**', probably of hybrid origin, '**Rhodochlorum**', '**Rubrum**', and '**Small Talk Pink**'. Zones 11–12.

Anthurium scherzerianum ★
◐/☀ ⚘ ↔ 12–20 in (30–50 cm) ↕ 24–30 in (60–75 cm)
Compact terrestrial species from Costa Rica. Popular house plant. Narrow elliptical to lance-shaped leaves to 10 in (25 cm) long on slightly shorter stems. Stems extend beyond foliage, often red. Spathes bright red, broad. Spadix orange to red, twisted. Fruit red. Zones 11–12.

Anthurium warocqueanum
QUEEN ANTHURIUM
◐/☀ ⚘ ↔ 3–10 ft (0.9–3 m) ↕ 24–60 in (60–150 cm)
From Colombia. Spreading ground cover sometimes climbing to over 5 ft (1.5 m). Stunning pendent, elongated, heart-shaped leaves to 3 ft (0.9 m) long, dark green with velvety texture and large pale-green veins. Flowers on short stems among foliage. Spathe green and spadix yellow green. Zone 12.

ANTIRRHINUM
SNAPDRAGON
Found in temperate Northern Hemisphere areas, this genus of around 40 species of annuals, perennials, and subshrubs belongs to the figwort or foxglove (Scrophulariaceae) family. Most species are compact, forming a low mound of simple rounded to lance-shaped leaves, sometimes with a gray-green tint. Flowering stems develop from late spring and carry heads of the familiar lobed blooms.
CULTIVATION: These species grow best in a fertile, moist, humus-rich soil in full sun. The Mediterranean species are reasonably drought tolerant but need moisture to flower well. Rust diseases can cause problems in humid conditions. Propagation is from seed, though the perennial species will grow from cuttings of non-flowering stems.

Antirrhinum majus, Chimes Series, 'Chimes Red'

Antirrhinum majus
◐/◑ ❄ ↔ 6–20 in (15–50 cm)
↕ 12–60 in (30–150 cm)
Southwest European perennial, usually treated as an annual. Upright bushy habit, dark green, elliptical leaves. Flowers in upright racemes, usually pink in wild, but cultivated in most colors except blue. Popular seedling series include the dwarf **Candelabra Series** and **Chimes Series,** particularly '**Chimes Red**' ★, the mid-height **Sonnet Series**, and the slightly taller, often double-flowered **Liberty Series**. Zones 7–10.

Antirrhinum molle

☼/◐ ❄ ↔6–8 in (15–20 cm) ↑8–16 in (20–40 cm)

Native to Portugal and northeastern Spain. Downy elliptical leaves, flowers pale pink or white with yellow throat and downy exterior. 'Avalanche', white flowers with a small yellow patch on lower lip, blooms for most of the year. Zones 7–10.

APONOGETON

A member of the family Aponogetonaceae, this genus consists of some 44 species of aquatic herbaceous perennials from many tropical and subtropical areas, some of which have become weedy in areas where they are not native. The foliage can be submerged or floating, rather like that of a waterlily. The flowers are produced in a compound panicle that sits above the water. These can make attractive pond plants, and the more tropical species are often used in indoor heated aquariums. CULTIVATION: Plant *Aponogeton* species in mud in the bottom of a pond, either in full sun or half-shade. Propagation is from fresh seed, or by division.

Aponogeton distachyos

CAPE POND WEED, WATER HAWTHORN

☼/◐ ❄ ↔32–40 in (80–100 cm) ↑24–32 in (60–80 cm)

From South Africa, this species is naturalized in parts of Australia. It has oblong floating leaves. Its white and purple scented flowers are seen in a forked spike just above water level, during summer. The flowers are edible. Zones 9–11.

AQUILEGIA

COLUMBINE, GRANNY'S BONNET

This genus in the buttercup (Ranunculaceae) family has about 70 species, found over much of the temperate and subarctic Northern Hemisphere. Fine-stemmed, often blue-green foliage emerges from a woody rootstock. Flowering stems usually reach above the foliage and carry spurred, bell-shaped, often pendulous flowers. Some are short-flowering, others bloom through much of late spring and summer. CULTIVATION: An adaptable genus, with species suitable for woodland, rockeries, and perennial borders. Generally they prefer a cool-winter climate and a place in half-sun with cool, moist, humus-rich, well-drained soil. Often attracts aphids. Some species can be divided when dormant but propagation is usually from seed. May self-sow, can be invasive.

Aquilegia caerulea

BLUE COLUMBINE, ROCKY MOUNTAIN COLUMBINE

☼/◐ ❄ ↔8–16 in (20–40 cm) ↑8–24 in (20–60 cm)

From high woodlands and mountains of western USA. Large flowers. White to cream petals, blue or pink sepals, long spurs. Zones 3–9.

Aquilegia canadensis

CANADA COLUMBINE, MEETING HOUSES, ROCK BELLS, WILD COLUMBINE

◐ ❄ ↔12–20 in (30–50 cm) ↑12–30 in (30–75 cm)

Found over much of eastern North America. Soft yellow, red-spurred flowers are borne on many-branched, wiry stems. Prefers rockery or woodland conditions. Flowers popular with hummingbirds. Zones 2–10.

Aquilegia canadensis

Aquilegia chrysantha

GOLDEN COLUMBINE

◐ ❄ ↔12–32 in (30–80 cm) ↑32–36 in (80–90 cm)

Found in southern USA. Vigorous tall stems and large bright yellow flowers with long curved spurs, slightly paler in color. Several cultivars available, including double-flowered, white, and very tall types. 'Denver Gold', huge flowers to 3 in (8 cm) wide; 'Yellow Queen', larger, brighter yellow flowers than species. Zones 3–10.

Aquilegia formosa

WESTERN COLUMBINE

◐ ❄ ↔12–20 in (30–50 cm) ↑20–36 in (50–90 cm)

From western USA, this species has a graceful open habit with many small, orange-red, short-spurred flowers on each of its stems. An excellent source of nectar for hummingbirds, butterflies and bees. A number of cultivars are available, including dwarf types, and it is widely hybridized. Zones 3–9.

Aquilegia, McKana Group

☼/◐ ❄ ↔12–20 in (30–50 cm) ↑32–48 in (80–120 cm)

These hybrids between several North American species cover a wide color range. Most of the hybrids in the group are tall upright plants with long-spurred flowers and contrasting colors of corolla and sepals. Zones 3–10.

Aquilegia chrysantha

Aquilegia, Hybrid Cultivar, Songbird Series, 'Cardinal'

Aquilegia vulgaris

☼/◐ ❄ ↔ 8–18 in (20–45 cm) ↕ 12–36 in (30–90 cm)

Found over most of Europe. Ferny foliage; flowers with hooked spurs in white and shades of blue, mauve, and red, including double-flowered forms. The wild species is seldom seen in gardens but there are many cultivars. Single-flowered cultivars include 'Heidi', purple-red-stemmed, nodding, soft pink flowers; 'Hensol Harebell', short-spurred, mauve-blue flowers; and 'Nivea' (syn. 'Munstead White'), gray-green foliage; pure white flowers. Double-flowered cultivars can be divided into the following groups. **Flore Pleno Group,** elongated flowers, rounded petals, includes 'Graeme Iddon', tall, white flowers, has spawned a range of double-flowered forms; and 'Rougham Star', flowers with white inner petals, mauve-blue outer petals and sepals. **Stellata Group,** star-shaped double flowers, radiating pointed petals, includes 'Black Barlow', deep purple to near black flowers; 'Blue Barlow', double blue flowers; 'Nora Barlow' ★, green, white, and pink pompon-like flowers; and 'Rose Barlow', mid-pink and cream flowers. **Vervaeneana Group,** marbled green and gold foliage and variable flower color. Zones 3–10.

Aquilegia Hybrid Cultivars

☼/◐ ❄ ↔ 12–24 in (30–60 cm) ↕ 18–36 in (45–90 cm)

Aquilegias have been so widely hybridized, particularly among the American species, that there are now hybrids in almost any conceivable size and flower color. *A.* 'Crimson Star', 24 in (60 cm) tall, large, red-spurred cream flowers. The **Butterfly Series** includes 'Brimstone', cream and soft yellow; and 'Holly Blue', white to pale mauve petals, powder blue sepals. The **Songbird Series,** compact foliage clump, 24 in (60 cm) flower stems, large flowers in many shades, includes 'Bluebird', very large flowers,

white petals, soft blue sepals; 'Cardinal', white petals with pink markings, dark red sepals; 'Dove', pure white; 'Goldfinch', bright yellow; 'Redwing', white to cream petals, deep red sepals; and 'Robin', white to pale pink petals, dusky deep pink sepals. The **State Series** includes 'Alaska', pure white flowers; 'Colorado', semi-double flowers, mauve and white petals with purple sepals; 'Florida', yellow petals, creamy white sepals; 'Kansas', bright yellow petals, vivid red sepals; and 'Louisiana', creamy white petals, deep red sepals. Zones 4–10.

ARABIS

ROCK CRESS

This genus belongs to the cabbage (Brassicaceae) family and has around 120 species of annuals and perennials, mainly evergreen and sometimes woody-stemmed. Widespread in the northern temperate zones, especially Eurasia and western North America, they tend to be small plants that are often most at home in rock crevices. Their leaves are simple, sometimes downy or gray-green, and are often borne in tufted rosettes. In spring and early summer they carry upright sprays of small 4-petalled flowers, usually white or purple.

CULTIVATION: Most are hardy and easily grown in any temperate climate. Plant in a sunny position with well-drained soil that remains moist in summer. Ideal in rockeries or spilling over banks. Many species appreciate a light dressing of lime. Remove spent flowerheads to keep tidy and encourage continued blooming. Propagation is mainly from seed, though perennials will grow from base cuttings and a few species can be divided with care.

Arabis × arendsii

☼/◐ ❄ ↔ 12–24 in (30–60 cm) ↕ 4–8 in (10–20 cm)

Garden hybrid between *A. aubrietoides* and *A. caucasica.* Usually low and spreading, with tufted foliage clumps. Flower stems up to 6 in (15 cm) high, with deep pink flowers. 'Compinkie' (syn. *A. caucasica* 'Compinkie'), bright pink flowers; 'Monte Rosa', maroon flowers; 'Rubin', wine red flowers. Zones 5–9.

Arabis blepharophylla

☼/◐ ❄ ↔ 6–8 in (15–20 cm) ↕ 4–6 in (10–15 cm)

Californian perennial with small rosettes of deep to bright green leaves. Flowers deep pink to purple-red. 'Frühlingszauber' (syn. 'Spring Charm') is a compact cultivar with bright magenta flowers. Zones 7–9.

Arabis caucasica 'Schneehaube'

Arabis caucasica

☼/◐ ❄ ↔ 8–20 in (20–50 cm) ↕ 6–12 in (15–30 cm)

Perennial from southern European mountains. Gray-green leaves. White flowers, rarely pink, from spring to early summer. Sometimes confused with *A. alpina* in cultivation. 'Pinkie', bright pink flowers; 'Flore Pleno', more upright growth habit, white double flowers; 'Schneehaube' (syn. 'Snowcap'), low and spreading with white flowers; 'Variegata', white-edged leaves, masses of white flowers. Zones 4–9.

ARCTOTIS

AFRICAN DAISY

Found from the southern tip of Africa northward to Angola, this genus in the daisy (Asteraceae) family consists of around 50 species of low spreading annuals and perennials that often produce masses of large and brightly colored flowerheads. The leaves are simple, usually lance-shaped and frequently have felted undersides. For much of the year in mild climates the foliage is topped by 1–4 in (2.5–10 cm) wide flowers in a range of colors.
CULTIVATION: They thrive in light well-drained soil and full sun. They are drought tolerant but will flower more heavily if watered well in the growing season. Propagate from seed, though perennials grow readily from cuttings of non-flowering stems.

Arctotis acaulis

☀ ❊ ↔ 12–40 in (30–100 cm) ↕ 6–12 in (15–30 cm)
Clumping rosette-forming perennial. Wavy, lobed, or toothed leaves. Flowerheads to 4 in (10 cm) wide, ray florets mainly in yellow, orange, or red shades, disc florets deep purple. '**Magenta**', long-stemmed purple-red flowers. Zones 8–10.

Arctotis × hybrida 'Red Devil'

Arctotis × hybrida

☀ ❊ ↔ 8–20 in (20–50 cm) ↕ 8–16 in (20–40 cm)
Compact plants, usually with silvery foliage. Often treated as annuals in cool climates. Many popular named cultivars and seedling strains. '**Flame**' ★, bright orange flowers; '**Mahogany**', deep red-brown flowers; '**Red Devil**', bright red. Zones 9–11.

Arctotis venusta

BLUE-EYED AFRICAN DAISY

☀ ❊ ↔ 8–16 in (20–40 cm) ↕ 16–24 in (40–60 cm)
Annual with deeply lobed to almost pinnate, downy, gray-white leaves and heavily ribbed flower stems. Flowers in cultivation are variably colored but wild plants usually have deep magenta ray florets and purple-blue disc florets. Zones 9–11.

ARENARIA

SANDWORT

This genus of about 160 low-growing, largely perennial, woody herbs and some annuals from the pink (Caryophyllaceae) family is found across the temperate Northern Hemisphere. They are ideal rock-garden plants and compact ground covers. The branching stems bear masses of dense, often hairy foliage. Abundant, small, star-like flowers, normally white and 5-petaled, grow in cymes or solitary. The shallow root system can make them drought sensitive. Fruit is a cylindrical or ovoid capsule with 6 lobes.
CULTIVATION: Most species need partial shade and protection from hot afternoon sun, especially in hot climates. They will tolerate poor soils, but the soil should be moist, sandy, and well drained. Shallow roots will require mulching or frequent watering around, but not over, the plant. Propagate by division, from seed in autumn or spring, or from softwood cuttings in early summer.

Arenaria montana

☀/◑ ❊ ↔ 9–24 in (23–60 cm) ↕ 4–6 in (10–15 cm)
Vigorous perennial from southwestern Europe. Loose mats of narrow, gray-green, hairy leaves. Small white flowers, in spring–early summer. '**Avalanche**', more profuse, larger white flowers. Zones 4–8.

Arenaria purpurascens

☀/◑ ❊ ↔ 9–24 in (23–60 cm) ↕ 4–6 in (10–15 cm)
Evergreen, tufted, mat-forming perennial with small, sharply pointed, glossy leaves, from northern Spain. Many small clusters of 1 to 4 tiny, pale to deep purplish pink flowers, in early spring–summer. '**Elliot's Variety**', abundant pink flowers. Zones 4–8.

ARGEMONE

A genus of 23 species of annual or perennial herbs and a shrub, in the poppy (Papaveraceae) family. Occurs in North and South America, West Indies, and Hawaii, in drier plant communities, commonly colonizing. Erect stems are produced from fleshy roots, leaves entire or deeply lobed, prickly or smooth, bluish green. Flowers broad and shallow, white, yellow, or mauve, in clusters or singly, in summer–autumn. Fruits are prickly pods, containing many blackish seeds. Stems contain a yellowish latex.
CULTIVATION: Propagate from seed. Grow in full sun in well-draining gravelly soils. Self-seeding occurs with some species.

Argemone mexicana

MEXICAN POPPY, PRICKLY POPPY

☀ ❊ ↔ 12–16 in (30–40 cm) ↕ to 36 in (90 cm)
Erect, spreading annual. Leaves deeply lobed, with silvery spines. Yellow flowers, to 3 in (8 cm) across, in summer–autumn. A weed from southern USA to Central America. '**White Lustre**', white flowers; '**Yellow Lustre**', orange-yellow flowers. Zones 8–10.

ARISTEA

This genus belonging to the iris (Iridaceae) family has about 50 mainly evergreen species of fleshy-stemmed perennials found in Africa from the tropics to South Africa and Madagascar. They have upright sword-shaped leaves, in fans. The 6-petalled flowers, borne on branching stems with somewhat flattened segments, occur in shades of blue, lavender, and purple, and are short-lived. The flowering season ranges from late winter to summer.
CULTIVATION: Tolerant of only light frosts, most prefer to grow in sun or half-sun with a light but humus-rich, moist, well-drained soil. Plants can be divided but resent disturbance, so they are usually propagated from seed, which may be sown in autumn in frost-free areas, otherwise in spring.

Aristea ecklonii

☼/☽ ❄ ↔ 18–32 in (45–80 cm)
↑ 18–32 in (45–80 cm)
A South African species. Arching leaves to 24 in (60 cm) long. Loose panicles of 1 in (25 mm) wide bright blue to magenta flowers carried in late spring–summer. Zones 8–11.

Aristea major

☼/☽ ❄ ↔ 24–36 in (60–90 cm) ↑ 3–5 ft (0.9–1.5 m)
From the Cape region of South Africa. Blue-green leaves, 3–4 ft (0.9–1.2 m) long. Rootstock can form a trunk. Dense clusters of soft blue flowers, to 1½ in (35 mm) wide, in summer. Zones 9–10.

ARISTOLOCHIA (see page 768)

Aristolochia clematitis

☼/☽ ❄ ↔ 24 in (60 cm) ↑ 12–30 in (30–75 cm)
Native to Europe and naturalized in the UK and North America. Herbaceous species with heart-shaped leaves. Small dull greenish yellow flowers appear among the foliage in summer. Zones 6–10.

ARMERIA

SEA PINK, THRIFT
Armeria belongs to the leadwort (Plumbaginaceae) family. The genus comprises around 80 species of herbaceous and shrubby

Aristea major

perennials found in Eurasia, North Africa, and the American Pacific coast. They form clumps of simple linear leaves, with rounded heads of tiny flowers with colorful bracts held in spring and summer.
CULTIVATION: They occur in a wide range of environments and are easily cultivated, being especially at home in rockeries. Most are hardy and prefer moist well-drained soil and a position in full or half-sun. Propagate from seed or cuttings, or by the careful division of well-established clumps.

Armeria alliacea

☼/☽ ❄ ↔ 6–8 in (15–20 cm) ↑ 8–18 in (20–45 cm)
Cushion-forming species found from Portugal to southern Germany. Narrow strappy leaves to 6 in (15 cm) long. Flower stems to 18 in (45 cm) tall. White flowerheads, ¾ in (18 mm) wide. Zones 7–10.

Armeria juniperifolia

☼/☽ ❄ ↔ 6–8 in (15–20 cm) ↑ 6 in (15 cm)
Small shrubby perennial native to Spain. Very short, finely hairy, aromatic, grassy leaves. Flower stems less than 2 in (5 cm) long. Pink to magenta flowerheads, ½ in (12 mm) wide. 'Bevan's Variety' is a compact cultivar with dark foliage and short-stemmed pink flowerheads. Zones 8–10.

Armeria maritima

☼/☽ ❄ ↔ 8–16 in (20–40 cm) ↑ 8–12 in (20–30 cm)
This mounding perennial or subshrub is found across the northern temperate zone. It has grassy deep green leaves to 4 in (10 cm) long. Flower stems grow to 12 in (30 cm) tall with 1 in (25 mm) wide heads of white, pink, or red flowers. A. m. subsp. californica, from California, USA, mounds to 6 in (15 cm) high and has lavender-pink flowerheads on short stems. A. m. 'Bee's Ruby', 'Bloodstone' ★, 'Corsica', 'Isobel Burdett', 'Rubrifolia', and 'Vindictive' are attractive cultivars. Zones 4–10.

Armeria pseudarmeria

☼ ❄ ↔ 16–40 in (40–100 cm) ↑ 8–16 in (20–40 cm)
This dwarf subshrub or woody-based perennial is a native of coastal Portugal. Has fine grassy leaves around 1 in (25 mm) long. Flower stems are tall compared to the plant, with white to

Armeria maritima

deep pink flowerheads to 2 in (5 cm) wide. **'Rubra'**, is a red-flowered cultivar; **'Westacre Beauty'** has soft pink flowers. Zones 8–10.

ARTEMISIA

This genus of about 300 species of evergreen herbs and shrubs is spread throughout northern temperate regions with some also found in southern Africa and South America. It is a member of the daisy (Asteraceae) family but they bear small dull white or yellow flower-heads without ray florets. The attractive foliage is well dissected and of palest gray to silver. The plants are frequently aromatic. Tarragon, the popular culinary herb, is a member of this genus *(Artemisia dracunculus)*. CULTIVATION: These shrubs are ideal for hot dry areas as most can withstand considerable drought. They should be grown in full sun in well-drained soil. Their silvery leaves provide an attractive foliage contrast in borders, and when clipped some species can be used as a low hedge. Prune quite hard in spring and lightly clip at flowering time if the flowers are not wanted. Propagation is usually from softwood or half-hardened cuttings in summer.

Artemisia 'Powis Castle'

Artemisia lactiflora
WHITE MUGWORT
☼ ❄ ↔ 24 in (60 cm) ↕ 5 ft (1.5 m)
From China. A perennial species forming clumps of green divided leaves. Tall showy plumes of tiny cream flowers in midsummer. Requires more moisture than most species. Mahogany stems and purplish green foliage are a feature of the **Guizhou Group**. Zones 4–10.

Artemisia ludoviciana
syns *Artemisia gnaphalodes, A. purshiana*
CUDWEED, SILVER WORMWOOD, WESTERN MUGWORT, WHITE SAGE
☼ ❄ ↔ 36 in (90 cm) ↕ 36 in (90 cm)
Native to USA. Perennial herb with white downy stems and narrow, silvery gray, aromatic foliage. Sprays of tiny grayish white flowers in summer. *A. l.* subsp. *mexicana* var. *albula* has lance-shaped leaves, white and hairy. *A. l.* **'Silver Queen'** and **'Valerie Finnis'** are attractive cultivars. Zones 5–10.

Artemisia pontica
ROMAN WORMWOOD
☼ ❄ ↔ 24 in (60 cm) ↕ 32 in (80 cm)
This fleshy-stemmed perennial comes from central and eastern Europe. It has downy, grayish green, feathery foliage and is aromatic. Sprays of tiny yellow flowers in summer. Zones 4–9.

Artemisia 'Powis Castle' ★
☼ ❄ ↔ 4 ft (1.2 m) ↕ 2 ft (0.6 m)
Similar to *A. arborescens* but its habit is more sprawling, with woody stems usually lying on the ground. This is possibly a hybrid between *A. arborescens* and *A. pontica*. Zones 7–10.

Artemisia stelleriana
BEACH WORMWOOD, DUSTY MILLER, OLD WOMAN
☼ ❄ ↔ 18 in (45 cm) ↕ 18–24 in (45–60 cm)
Evergreen fleshy-stemmed perennial from northeastern Asia and eastern USA. Heavily felted gray-white leaves, deeply lobed. Sprays of tiny yellow flowers in summer. **'Boughton Silver'** and **'Mori'** are white-leafed prostrate forms. Zones 3–9.

ARTHROPODIUM

This genus in the family Laxmanniaceae has about 12 species of evergreen or deciduous fleshy-stemmed perennials found mostly in Australia and New Zealand. Plants form clumps of linear leaves. The white to pale mauve and violet flowers have 6 petals with yellow and purple stamens. They are borne in panicles. CULTIVATION: In warm areas, grow in well-drained soil in sun or half-sun. Where frosts are worse, choose a warm sheltered site or grow in a greenhouse. Propagate from seed or by division.

Arthropodium cirratum

Arthropodium cirratum
RENGARENGA, ROCK LILY
☼/◐ ⧖ ↔ 24 in (60 cm) ↕ 20–30 in (50–75 cm)
Variable evergreen species, native to New Zealand. Fleshy strap-shaped leaves, to 24 in (60 cm) long, may have bluish green overtones. Flowering stems bear airy panicles of starry white flowers, early to mid-summer. Zones 9–11.

ARUNCUS
GOAT'S BEARD
This genus is a member of the rose (Rosaceae) family and contains 2 or 3 species of deciduous perennials native to northern temperate and subarctic regions. They are grown for their large fern-like leaves and tiny flowers. CULTIVATION: Grow in moist soil in half-sun. Propagate by division in autumn or early spring, or from seed sown in autumn.

Aruncus dioicus
syns *Aruncus sylvester, A. vulgaris, Spiraea aruncus*
GOAT'S BEARD
◐ ❄ ↔ 4 ft (1.2 m) ↕ 2–6 ft (0.6–1.8 m)
From Europe and northern Asia. Imposing plant forming large clumps. Panicles of cream flowers, up to 20 in (50 cm) long, in summer. Weed in much of Australia. Zones 3–9.

ASCLEPIAS

MILKWEED

This American and African genus is a member of the dogbane (Apocynaceae) family and comprises over 100 species, including annuals, perennials, subshrubs, and shrubs. These plants have simple, narrow, elliptical to lance-shaped leaves. They produce heads of small 5-petalled flowers followed by seed pods, sometimes oddly shaped, tightly packed with small seeds, each with a small parachute of silky down. All parts of the plants exude a milky sap if they are cut, hence the common name. The sap is poisonous in some species.
CULTIVATION: Easily grown in light, well-drained soil in full sun, milkweeds will, however, have more luxuriant foliage and will flower more heavily if well-fed and watered. They grow readily and quickly from seed, and can be treated as annuals or short-lived perennials. Some species can be propagated from cuttings. Trim to shape, not into bare wood, as plants can be slow to recover from harsh pruning.

Asclepias linaria

PINE-NEEDLE MILKWEED, PINELEAF MILKWEED, THREADLEAF MILKWEED

☼ ❄ ↔ 24–36 in (60–90 cm) ↕ 24–36 in (60–90 cm)
From arid areas of California and Arizona, USA, and Mexico. Shrubby perennial with fine needle-like foliage. Flowers for long periods with small, white, 5-petalled flowers in clusters to 2 in (5 cm) wide. Zones 9–11.

Asclepias tuberosa ★

BUTTERFLY WEED, PLEURISY ROOT

☼ ❄ ↔ 12 in (30 cm) ↕ 24–36 in (60–90 cm)
Native to eastern and southern USA. Woody-based perennial herb. Narrow lance-shaped leaves on crowded stems. Heads of yellow, orange, or vermilion flowers. Pointed seed head to 6 in (15 cm) long. Zones 3–9.

Asclepias tuberosa

ASPARAGUS

syns *Myrsiphyllum, Protasparagus*
ASPARAGUS

A genus of about 300 perennial herbs, shrubs, or climbers that grow from a tuberous rhizome. Mostly from Africa and Asia, they belong to the asparagus (Asparagaceae) family. Leaves are small, scaly, and often spiny. Cladophylls (flattened stems that function as a leaf) are green and often needle-like. The green, yellow, or white flowers are small. Fruit is a round berry.
CULTIVATION: These plants prefer rich moist soils in a protected position with filtered sunlight. Propagate by division of crowded roots or from seed. Edible asparagus *(A. officinalis)* is grown from 1-year-old crowns planted in mid- to late winter, spaced 12 in (30 cm) apart, in heavily mulched rows 4–6 ft (1.2–1.8 m) apart. Harvest when spears are 6–10 in (15–25 cm) tall by breaking off at ground level. Full production in 2 to 3 years after planting; plants can produce for up to 25 years.

Asparagus densiflorus

syn. *Protasparagus densiflorus*
ASPARAGUS FERN, EMERALD FERN, FOXTAIL SHRUB, SPRENGER ASPARAGUS

☼ ❄ ↔ 36 in (90 cm) ↕ 30–36 in (75–90 cm)
Evergreen trailing plant, native to subtropical South Africa. Thick tuberous roots. No leaves but needle-like branchlets or cladophylls on green or brown, wiry, spiny stems. Small white flowers on axillary racemes in spring and summer. Small bright red berries in winter. Popular cultivars include '**Compactus**' (syn. 'Nanus'), '**Deflexus**', '**Myersii**', and '**Sprengeri**' *(syn. A. sprengeri)*. Zones 7–11.

Asparagus macowanii

syns *Asparagus zuluensis, Protasparagus macowanii*
☼/◑ ❄ ↔ 8 ft (2.4 m) ↕ 6 ft (1.8 m)
From the South African provinces of Eastern Cape, KwaZulu-Natal, and Mpumalanga. Robust plant with many stems about 1 in (25 mm) thick, springing like giant asparagus spears from a raised root-mass, each whitish stem living for many years, branched above into dense, fine, pale-green foliage. Profuse pure white flowers in mid-summer. Small blackish berries in winter. Zones 9–11.

ASPERULA

WOODRUFF

A genus of around 100 species of annuals, perennials, and small shrubs in the madder (Rubiaceae) family found from Europe through Asia to Australia. Most are mat-forming, with spreading sometimes bristly stems clothed with whorls of simple, narrow, sometimes faintly downy leaves. Some are more upright, often spreading by runners. Tiny, bell- or funnel-shaped, 4-petalled flowers appear in the leaf axils, or in clusters at the stem tips, from spring through summer. The heavy-flowering species smother themselves in bloom.

CULTIVATION: Plant in a bright position with moist, fertile, well-drained soil and trim after flowering. The smaller species are marvellous rockery plants. Propagate from seed, base cuttings, by division or layers, as appropriate.

Asperula gussonei

❀ ❄ ↔ 6–12 in (15–30 cm) ↑ 4 in (10 cm)

Sicilian perennial that forms a mat or tufts of silvery blue-gray whorled leaves around ½ in (12 mm) long. Densely packed heads of up to 15, minute, pale pink to red flowers. Zones 7–10.

Asperula orientalis

syn. *Asperula azurea*

BLUE WOODRUFF

❀/❀ ❄ ↔ 16–24 in (40–60 cm) ↑ 8–12 in (20–30 cm)

Annual from southern Europe, western Asia, and the Middle East. Rangy upright habit with widely spaced whorls of green leaves to 2 in (5 cm) long. Terminal heads of lavender-blue funnel-shaped flowers. Often self-sows. Zones 8–10.

ASPHODELINE

This genus is a member of the asphodel (Asphodelaceae) family. It has 18 to 20 species of fleshy-stemmed perennial or biennial herbs native to southern Europe where they grow on rocky slopes and in scrubby areas. They are clump-forming plants with grayish green linear leaves, sometimes with slightly serrated margins. The flowers are about 1¼ in (30 mm) across and are borne in spring and summer. They have 6 flaring petals, yellow or white tinged pink, and are scented in some species.

CULTIVATION: Useful plants for the border, rockery, or for naturalizing. Grow in moderately fertile soil in full sun. Propagate from seed or by division of clumps.

Asphodeline lutea ★

JACOB'S ROD, KING'S SPEAR, YELLOW ASPHODEL

❀ ❄ ↔ 12 in (30 cm) ↑ 36–48 in (90–120 cm)

From the Mediterranean. Narrow silvery leaves to 12 in (30 cm) long. Fragrant yellow flowers, borne on stiff spikes, in late spring–summer. Decorative seed pods. Zones 7–10.

ASPHODELUS

There are 12 species of clump-forming, swollen-rooted perennials in this genus in the asphodel (Asphodelaceae) family. They are found from the Mediterranean to the Himalayas, growing in scrub and on rocky slopes. The leaves are linear, up to 24 in (60 cm) long, and may be flat or cylindrical. The flowers have 6 whorled tepals and are white or pink with green or brown veining. Flowering stems vary in length, from 7 ft (2 m) tall in one species to non-existent in another, which flowers within the basal rosette.

CULTIVATION: *Asphodelus* is best grown in moderately fertile soil in a position that receives full sun. Some of the species, such as the low-growing *A. acaulis,* are better suited to the rockery as they require sharp drainage. Propagate from seed or by division.

Asperula orientalis

Asphodelus aestivus

❀ ❄ ↔ 24 in (60 cm) ↑ 40 in (100 cm)

Native to the Canary Islands and Mediterranean regions. Long, flat, basal leaves, flowering stems with short side branches. Its flowers are starry white, with a central brown stripe on each petal. Spring-flowering species. Zones 7–10.

Asphodelus albus

❀ ❄ ↔ 24 in (60 cm) ↑ 36 in (90 cm)

Native to southern and western Europe and northern Africa, this species has linear leaves that are up to 24 in (60 cm) long. Flowering stems, 12–36 in (30–90 cm) tall, bear white to pale pink flowers, with a pinkish brown stripe on each petal, in spring. Zones 6–10.

ASPIDISTRA

Found from the Himalayas to Japan, the 8 evergreen perennial species in this genus belong to the family Ruscaceae. Spreading from thick rhizomes, they form clumps of tough, deep green, elliptical to lance-shaped leaves that emerge directly from the ground on a strong leaf stalk, either singly or in small clusters. Small, stemless, purple-red to brown, bell- to urn-shaped flowers open from spring.

CULTIVATION: Easily grown outdoors in a mild temperate climate, preferring a shady spot with warm, moist, well-drained soil. They spread well, making an excellent large-scale ground cover.

Asphodeline lutea

Aspidistra elatior

BAR ROOM PLANT, CAST-IRON PLANT

☀ ❄ ↔ 16–36 in (40–90 cm) ↑ 16–24 in (40–60 cm)

A Chinese native. Veined, overarching, leathery leaves to 24 in (60 cm) long emerge singly. Flowers unobtrusive, bell-shaped, cream with purple spots to overall purple. Popular house plant, coping well with lack of light. Zones 7–10.

Aster × frikartii 'Mönch'

CULTIVATION: Mostly frost tolerant, they prefer well-drained soil that stays moist in the growing season. A sunny, airy, open position ensures maximum flowering and minimum mildew, a problem in humid conditions. Cut back hard after flowering. Propagate by winter division or from spring softwood cuttings.

Aster alpinus
ALPINE ASTER

☼ ❄ ↔ 8–32 in (20–80 cm)
↑ 4–10 in (10–25 cm)
Spreading, sometimes mounding perennial from mountains of southern Europe. Simple spatula- to lance-shaped base foliage. In spring and summer, masses of short-stemmed daisies, to slightly under 2 in (5 cm) wide, in white and all shades of pink, mauve, and purple. Zones 3–9.

Aster amellus

☼ ❄ ↔ 12–20 in (30–50 cm) ↑ 24–27 in (60–70 cm)
Upright Eurasian perennial. Faintly downy stems, green lance-shaped leaves around 2 in (5 cm) long. In autumn, terminal clusters of 2 in (5 cm) wide daisies, violet pink in the wild. Popular cultivars include 'Framfieldii', 'Jacqueline Genebrier', 'King George', 'Sonia', and 'Veilchenkönigin'. Zones 5–9.

Aster ericoides
HEATH ASTER

☼/◑ ❄ ↔ 20–32 in (50–80 cm) ↑ 32–40 in (80–100 cm)
Branching, bushy, North American perennial with narrow leaves to 2½ in (6 cm) long. Blooms in summer and autumn with masses of small daisies on leafy flower stems. Many cultivars, of which 'Pink Cloud' ★, to 3 ft (0.9 m) tall, with bronze new growth and billows of small pink flowers, is typical. Zones 3–9.

Aster × frikartii

☼/◑ ❄ ↔ 16–24 in (40–60 cm) ↑ 20–30 in (50–75 cm)
Garden hybrid between *A. amellus* and *A. thomsonii*. Upright perennial with dark green, elongated, lance-shaped base leaves. In autumn, branching sprays of 2 in (5 cm) wide daisies in shades of lavender and purple-blue. 'Mönch' and 'Wunder von Stäfa' are two cultivars with lavender-blue flowers. Zones 4–9.

Aster lateriflorus

☼/◑ ❄ ↔ 2–4 ft (0.6–1.2 m) ↑ 3–4 ft (0.9–1.2 m)
This upright to spreading North American perennial has base leaves to 6 in (15 cm) long, and is autumn-flowering, with sprays of pink-centered white to lavender-pink flowers on downy wiry stems. *A. l.* var. *horizontalis* is a spreading variety with brown-centered cream flowers. *A. l.* 'Prince' ★ is a typical cultivar and grows to 24 in (60 cm) tall, with bronze leaves and pink-centered white flowerheads. Zones 3–9.

ASTELIA

This genus is a member of the family Asteliaceae and contains 25 species of clump-forming evergreen perennials with attractive sword-like leaves. Most species are native to New Zealand with others scattered around Southern Hemisphere islands and Australia. Their natural habitat ranges from alpine areas to lowland forests, and many species are epiphytes. They are primarily grown for their foliage, which has a silvery sheen. The leaves can range in length from 3 in (8 cm) to 7 ft (2 m). The flowers are unisexual and insignificant but are followed by red berries.
CULTIVATION: Most are frost hardy and can be grown outdoors in a fertile moisture-retentive soil in full sun or half-sun. In very cold areas they need a warm sheltered position, or a greenhouse. Propagate by division in spring.

Astelia chathamica

☼/◑ ❄ ↔ 5 ft (1.5 m) ↑ 3–6 ft (0.9–1.8 m)
From New Zealand's Chatham Islands. Ornamental species forming clumps of broad, arching, sword-like leaves with a deep silvery sheen. Zones 8–10.

Astelia nervosa

☼ ❄ ↔ 5 ft (1.5 m) ↑ 3–7 ft (0.9–2 m)
A variable species from New Zealand. Foliage ranges from reddish tones through green to silver, leaves 2–7 ft (0.6–2 m) long. Named color forms are often available. Zones 8–10.

ASTER
MICHAELMAS DAISY

Found across the temperate Northern Hemisphere and into South America, this group of 250 species of mainly herbaceous perennials is the type genus for the daisy (Asteraceae) family. Upright plants that often sprawl under the weight of their foliage and flowers, they usually have simple linear to lance-shaped leaves, sometimes hairy and/or serrated. A few species flower in spring but most bloom in late summer and autumn, producing large heads of small to medium-sized daisies in a range of colors, all with a central eye of purple or yellow.

Aster novae-angliae
NEW ENGLAND ASTER

☼/☀ ❄ ↔ 2–4 ft (0.6–1.2 m) ↑ 4–5 ft (1.2–1.5 m)

A bushy autumn-flowering perennial that comes from eastern North America. It has lance-shaped base leaves up to 5 in (12 cm) long, and dense sprays of yellow-centered soft purple flowerheads up to 1¾ in (40 mm) wide. Cultivars include '**Andenken an Alma Pötschke**', cerise pink flowers; '**Barr's Pink**', small, deep pink, double flowers; '**Harrington's Pink**', small, soft pink, semi-double flowers; '**Hella Lacy**', violet-blue flowers; and '**Purple Dome**', dwarf, covered in purple flowers. Zones 2–9.

Aster novi-belgii
MICHAELMAS DAISY, NEW YORK ASTER

☼/☀ ❄ ↔ 24–32 in (60–80 cm)
↑ 36–48 in (90–120 cm)

This North American perennial is similar to *A. novae-angliae* except that it is slightly shorter and its leaves are more noticeably toothed. Over 400 cultivars have been raised and include '**Coombe Violet**', tall, deep purple flowers; '**Ernest Ballard**', 30 in (75 cm) tall, bright pink, named after the famous hybridizer; '**Little Red Boy**', masses of bright cerise-red flowers; '**Marie Ballard**', lavender blue, very fully double flowers; and '**Professor Anton Kippenberg**', lavender blue flowers. Zones 2–9.

Aster novae-angliae
'Andenken an Alma Pötschke'

Aster turbinellus

☼/☀ ❄ ↔ 3 ft (0.9 m) ↑ 4 ft (1.2 m)

Branching, multi-stemmed, autumn-flowering perennial from eastern USA. Lance-shaped 3 in (8 cm) long base leaves, fringed with fine hairs. Flowerheads 1 in (25 mm) wide, pink, borne singly on the stems but in large numbers. Zones 5–9.

ASTILBE
FALSE SPIRAEA

Found mainly in temperate East Asia, this perennial genus of the saxifrage (Saxifragaceae) family includes just 12 species that have been extensively selected and hybridized. Their toothed pinnate or bipinnate leaves sprout directly from rhizomes and soon form a large foliage clump. Long-stemmed plumes of tiny flowers appear in spring and summer, in white and all shades of pink, mauve, and red.
CULTIVATION: Astilbes are not drought tolerant nor do they thrive in the hot summer sun. Instead they prefer moist, humus-rich, woodland soil and dappled sunlight. They often thrive around pond margins but also tolerate being in well-drained soils.

Astilbe × *arendsii*

☀ ❄ ↔ 12–32 in (30–80 cm) ↑ 2–6 ft (0.6–1.8 m)

This group of garden hybrids involves several parent species. Both flowers and foliage are highly variable. Popular named forms include '**Anita Pfeifer**', 24 in (60 cm) tall, finely divided foliage and feathery sprays of pink flowers; '**Brautschleier**' (syn. '**Bridal Veil**'), 30 in (75 cm) tall, white flowers, early-flowering;

'**Bumalda**', 24 in (60 cm) high, white flowers with a faint pink blush, bronze foliage; '**Fanal**' ★, 24 in (60 cm) tall, dark, red-tinted foliage, deep red flowers; '**Federsee**', 24 in (60 cm) tall, sprays of deep pink flowers; '**Gertrud Brix**', 24 in (60 cm) tall, deep red flowers, bronze foliage; '**Gloria**', 27 in (70 cm) tall, deep pink flowers; '**Hyazinth**', 36 in (90 cm) tall, bright green foliage, lilac-pink flower sprays; '**Irrlicht**', 24 in (60 cm) tall, purple-tinted foliage and white flower sprays; '**Mainz**', 24 in (60 cm) tall, deep rose-pink flowers; '**Rosa Perle**' (syn. '**Pink Pearl**'), 30 in (75 cm) tall, silvery to pink flowers; **Showstar Group**, dwarf seedling strain in a mixed color range; '**Spinell**', 36 in (90 cm) tall, orange-red flowers; '**Venus**', 36 in (90 cm) tall, bright green foliage, sprays of pink flowers; '**Weisse Gloria**', 36 in (90 cm) tall, sprays of white flowers; and '**William Reeves**', 24 in (60 cm) tall, deep pinkish red flowers. Zones 6–9.

Astilbe chinensis

☀ ❄ ↔ 12–20 in (30–50 cm)
↑ to 7 ft (2 m)

Native to China and Japan. Foliage with large and coarsely toothed leaflets. Flowerheads short-stemmed with strongly upright plumes. Several natural varieties, including: *A. c.* var. *davidii*, bronze young leaves and purple-pink flower plumes to 7 ft (2 m) tall; *A. c.* var. *pumila*, just 10 in (25 cm) tall, with green foliage and dense plumes of deep pink flowers; and *A. c.* var. *taquetti* '**Superba**', with magenta flowers on brown stems to 4 ft (1.2 m) tall. *A. c.* '**Visions**', 18 in (45 cm) tall, honey-scented, deep pink to red flower sprays and bronze foliage. Zones 5–9.

Astilbe japonica

☀ ❄ ↔ 3 ft (0.9 m) ↑ 2–3 ft (0.6–0.9 m)

Endemic to Japan, known chiefly by its cultivars and hybrids. Leaves bi- or tripinnate, flowers white, in pyramidal panicles to 8 in (20 cm) long in late spring–early summer. Zones 5–9.

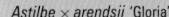

Astilbe × arendsii 'Gloria'

Astilbe chinensis 'Visions'

Astilbe simplicifolia

☀ ❊ ↔ 8–16 in (20–40 cm) ↑ 12–16 in (30–40 cm)

Compact Japanese species. Foliage often simple, glossy, ovate, and lobed but sometimes more deeply divided. Starry white flowers in narrow upright plumes. Several cultivars, including '**Bronze Elegance**' and '**Hennie Graefland**'. Zones 7–9.

Astilbe thunbergii

☀ ❊ ↔ 12–20 in (30–50 cm)
↑ 20–24 in (50–60 cm)

Early-flowering Japanese species with sharply toothed pinnate foliage, broad olive to bronze-green leaflets, sometimes downy. Flowers small but densely massed, opening white and ageing to pink. Zones 7–9.

Astilbe Hybrid Cultivars

☀ ❊ ↔ 3 ft (0.9 m) ↑ 2–3 ft (0.6–0.9 m)

These cultivars have *A. japonica* as a major part of their heritage. '**Betsy Cuperus**', 36 in (90 cm) tall, arching panicles of soft pink flowers; '**Deutschland**', 20 in (50 cm) tall, pure white flowers; '**Europa**', 24 in (60 cm) high, pale pink flowers; '**Montgomery**', 30 in (75 cm) tall, red flowers, red-tinted foliage; '**Red Sentinel**', 24–36 in (60–90 cm) high, bronze leaves, open sprays of red flowers on red stems; '**Straussenfeder**' (syn. 'Ostrich Feather'), 36 in (90 cm) high, salmon pink to soft red flowers in arching sprays. Zones 6–9.

ASTILBOIDES

A genus of the saxifrage (Saxifragaceae) family containing only one species, a herbaceous perennial once included in the genus *Rodgersia*. It comes from China and differs from its former relatives mainly in its leaf shape. It is grown for its huge leaves and racemes of tiny white flowers that occur in summer.
CULTIVATION: It grows best in moist soils in a cool sheltered spot and is usually seen at its best near water. Propagation is from seed or by division when dormant.

Astilbe, Hybrid Cultivar, 'Red Sentinel'

Astilboides tabularis

syn. *Rodgersia tabularis*

☀ ❊ ↔ 40–60 in (100–150 cm) ↑ 40–60 in (100–150 cm)

This impressive perennial has huge, bright green, circular leaves to 36 in (90 cm) across, with the stem attached to the center. Above the foliage are its large fluffy heads of tiny white flowers, produced in summer. Zones 7–10.

ASTRANTIA

MASTERWORT, PINCUSHION FLOWER

Primarily European, this genus of 10 species of perennials also occurs westward to Asia, often in alpine meadows or woodlands. Belonging to the carrot (Apiaceae) family, they bear their small pastel-toned flowers in small dome-shaped heads (umbels). The true flowers are often less showy than the surrounding papery bracts. The foliage, which forms a basal clump and spreads by runners, is hand-shaped, with 3 to 7 toothed lobes.
CULTIVATION: Apart from an intolerance of prolonged dry conditions, these grow freely in any cool-temperate garden with moderately fertile free-draining soil. Foliage may be lusher in shade, a consideration with variegated cultivars, but they usually flower best in at least half-sun. Propagate by division when dormant or from seed, which needs stratification.

Astrantia major

GREATER MASTERWORT

☀ ❊ ↔ 16–24 in (40–60 cm) ↑ 24–32 in (60–80 cm)

From central and eastern Europe. Leaves with 3 to 7, broad, toothed lobes. Floral bracts white through red, often green tinted or veined. *A. m.* subsp. *involucrata*, long narrow bracts creating a lacy flowerhead; '**Moira Reid**', pink-tinted early blooms; '**Shaggy**', green-tipped white flowers. *A. m.* var. *rosea*, green-tinted pale pink inflorescences. *A. m.* '**Rubra**' ★, deep purple-red inflorescence; '**Ruby Wedding**', dark wine red flowers; '**Sunningdale Variegated**', pink-flushed white flowerheads. Zones 6–9.

Astrantia maxima

☀ ❊ ↔ 20–24 in (50–60 cm) ↑ 27–36 in (70–90 cm)

Large leaves with 3 to 5 finely toothed lobes. Pink flowerheads, lighter center, bracts fused to create a ruff, in summer. Zones 6–9.

ATRIPLEX (see page 88)

Atriplex hortensis

FAT HEN, FRENCH SPINACH, MOUNTAIN SPINACH, ORACH, SALTBUSH, SEA PURSLANE

☀ ❊ ↔ 16–20 in (40–50 cm) ↑ 7–8 ft (2–2.4 m)

An erect annual from Asia, with grayish leaves, that has naturalized in most temperate parts of the world. Leaves heart-shaped to triangular, slightly serrated, 4–6 in (10–15 cm) long, green or purplish brown, and used in cooking. Terminal clusters of insignificant green or red flowers, without petals, in summer, followed by tiny brown plate-like seeds. *A. h.* var. *rubra*, purple leaves. *A. h.* '**Cuptorosea**' and '**Rosea**' are popular. Zones 6–11.

Astrantia major

AUBRIETA
AUBRETIA

Found from Europe to Central Asia, the 12 evergreen cushion or mat-forming perennials of this genus are members of the cabbage (Brassicaceae) family. They are smothered in tiny, 4-petalled, purple, mauve, or white blooms in spring and early summer. The foliage is small and simple, usually dull gray-green and finely downy, often with small lobes or teeth. They are excellent choices for rockeries, flower borders, or spilling over banks.
CULTIVATION: Hardy in most temperate zones, aubrietas prefer gritty well-drained soil in full or half-sun. Water during the flowering season and give an occasional light dressing of lime. Although perennial, at nurseries aubrietas are often sold with the bedding annuals and may be treated as such. However, if left to grow on they become far more impressive plants. Propagate from seed, layers, or small basal cuttings or by division.

Aubrieta, Hybrid Cultivar, 'Whitewell Gem'

Aubrieta deltoidea ★
☼/◐ ❁ ↔ 12 in (30 cm) ↕ 3 in (8 cm)
Found in southwest Europe, especially around the Aegean Sea. Leaves diamond-shaped, smooth edged or with 2 to 6 conspicuous teeth. Pale lavender through magenta to purple flowers up to 1 in (25 mm) in diameter. **Zones 7–10.**

Aubrieta Hybrid Cultivars
☼ ❁ ↔ 8–24 in (20–60 cm) ↕ 3–6 in (8–15 cm)
Garden hybrids are derived from several species. All are mat-forming, but otherwise highly variable. '**Argenteovariegata**', silver-edged leaves and purple flowers; '**Blue Cascade**', strongly trailing habit, may mound, purple-blue flowers; '**Blue King**', mauve-blue flowers in abundance; '**Bressingham Pink**', clusters of large, pink, double flowers; '**Campbellii**', mauve-blue double flowers; '**Doctor Mules**', neat, compact habit with attractive violet-blue flowers; '**Hendersonii**', low spreader with purple flowers, well suited to rock walls and banks; '**Novalis Blue**', bright mauve-blue flowers; '**Rokey's Purple**', deep purple flowers; '**Whitewell Gem**', purple-violet flowers. **Zones 7–10.**

AURINIA

A genus of 7 species of perennials and biennials of the cabbage (Brassicaceae) family, found in central and southern Europe and eastward to Turkey and the Black Sea region. They are small carpeting plants that form loose basal rosettes of leaves that emerge from a sometimes thickened rootstock. Leaves are often covered with fine hairs, giving them a silver-gray appearance. Heads of small bright yellow or white flowers open from spring, often almost hiding the foliage.
CULTIVATION: Best suited to a cool-temperate climate where frosts are not severe, these are superb plants for rockeries or alpine troughs. They prefer full sun and need perfectly drained gritty soil, kept moist in spring and early summer. All may be propagated from seed, and the perennials can also be grown from self-layered pieces or by taking small tip cuttings.

Aurinia saxatilis 'Compacta'

Aurinia saxatilis
syn. *Alyssum saxatile*
BASKET OF GOLD, YELLOW ALYSSUM
☼ ❁ ↔ 16–24 in (40–60 cm) ↕ 8–12 in (20–30 cm)
Central and southeastern Europe. Low, carpeting perennial with small silver-gray leaves. Sprays of pale to bright yellow flowers, from spring. Hardiest species by far. '**Citrina**' is heavy-blooming, bright yellow flowers; '**Compacta**' has golden flowers on 8 in (20 cm) high stems. **Zones 3–9.**

BAILEYA

This small genus from western North America is part of the daisy (Asteraceae) family. It comprises just 3 species of annuals and perennials; one, *B. multiradiata*, is sometimes grown for a bright splash of color in summer and autumn, especially in arid areas. *Baileya* species have opposite pairs of hairy, gray-green, pinnate leaves and have an open habit, rarely growing to more than 12–16 in (30–40 cm) tall. Their cosmos-like yellow flowerheads are held clear of the foliage on long stems, appearing from early summer and continuing until the first frosts.
CULTIVATION: *Baileya* plants thrive in semi-desert conditions and, although sometimes considered weeds, they are one of the most reliable and colorful summer annuals for arid gardens. Plant in full sun and water only to get plants established or if dry conditions persist. Remove spent flowerheads to prolong blooming. Propagation is from seed, which may be sown in situ or started under cover and then transplanted.

Baileya multiradiata
DESERT BAILEYA, DESERT MARIGOLD, PAPER DAISY, WILD MARIGOLD
☼ ❁ ↔ 4–12 in (10–30 cm) ↕ 8–20 in (20–50 cm)
Native to southern USA and Mexico. Short-lived perennial with grayish green foliage. Bright yellow flowers, 2 in (5 cm) across and resembling marigolds, are borne from spring to autumn. Needs perfect drainage to prevent rotting. **Zones 7–10.**

Baptisia australis

CULTIVATION: Grow in full sun in deep, well-drained, neutral or slightly acidic soil. Most species grow happily in poorly nourished soils. Stake tall plants in exposed positions. Propagate by division or from seed.

Baptisia australis

syn. *Baptisia caerulea*
BLUE FALSE INDIGO

☼ ❄ ↔ 4 ft (1.2 m) ↕ 2–4 ft (0.6–1.2 m)
Native to central and eastern USA, but threatened in some states. Upright or spreading bushy perennial with bluish green foliage. Spikes of purplish blue flowers in summer. Erect, inflated, dark gray seed pods can be dried for floral arrangements. Zones 5–9.

BALLOTA

Found from Europe through the Mediterranean region to western Asia, this mint (Lamiaceae) family genus is composed of 35 species of perennials and subshrubs. Bushy and spreading, they are grown primarily for their hairy gray-green stems and foliage, which in the best forms are heavily felted. The leaves may be evergreen or deciduous and are aromatic, oval to heart-shaped, with conspicuously toothed edges. In summer, small upright spikes of white, cream, or lilac-pink flowers appear.
CULTIVATION: Plants tolerate hardy to moderate frosts and are very easily grown in full or half-sun in a moist well-drained soil. Cut the evergreen types back hard in spring. Will naturalize and can become quite invasive. Propagate by division, or from basal cuttings or seed.

Ballota acetabulosa

☼/◐ ❄ ↔ 24–32 in (60–80 cm) ↕ 40 in (100 cm)
Shrubby semi-evergreen perennial. Native to Greece, Turkey, and eastern Mediterranean islands. Woolly stems and foliage. Leaves heart-shaped, pale green, to 2 in (5 cm) long, with toothed edges. Up to 12 purple-marked white flowers per head, ½ in (12 mm) wide, in summer. Zones 8–10.

Ballota pseudodictamnus

☼ ❄ ↔ 24–48 in (60–120 cm) ↕ 12–20 in (30–50 cm)
Evergreen subshrub found from Turkey through Crete to North Africa. Rounded, toothed, felted, gray-green leaves to 2 in (5 cm) long. White or mauve flowers with darker spotting, in large green calyces, in summer. Zones 8–10.

BAPTISIA

FALSE INDIGO, WILD INDIGO

Belonging to the pea-flower subfamily of the legume (Fabaceae) family, this genus contains about 17 species of perennial herbs native to the USA. They grow in sand, gravel, and other poor soils in dry woodlands and open areas. Plants have a shrubby habit, spreading or erect, to 7 ft (2 m) tall, with trifoliate leaves. Spikes of lupin-like flowers are white, yellow, or purplish blue. Once used in dye-making as a substitute for true indigo.

BASSIA

A genus of 26 densely branching, shrubby annuals or perennials belonging to the goosefoot (Chenopodaceae) family, *Bassia* plants are found in warm-temperate parts of the Northern Hemisphere. One species is grown for its foliage. Leaves are usually narrow and smooth-edged, and the flowers are normally inconspicuous spikes. Fruits are achenes (small, dry, single-seeded fruits).
CULTIVATION: Sow seed in spring where plants are to grow, in most soils, including saline. Propagate from seed or cuttings.

Bassia scoparia

syns *Kochia scoparia, K. trichophylla*
BELVEDERE, BURNING BUSH, FIREBUSH, FIREWEED, KOCHIA, SUMMER CYPRESS

☼ ❄ ↔ 8–60 in (20–150 cm) ↕ 8–60 in (20–150 cm)
Annual originally from temperate Asia, now naturalized through Europe and North America. Narrow flat leaves, normally mid-green, turning purple-red in late summer. Small inconspicuous flower clusters same color as leaves. With maturity, plant breaks off at base and rolls away, dispersing seed. Zones 8–11.

BEGONIA

Found through the tropics and subtropics but most diverse in the Americas, this group of around 900 species of perennials, shrubs, and climbers belongs to the family Begoniaceae. They may be fibrous- or rhizome-rooted or tuberous, with foliage emerging from the rootstock or held on cane-like stems. Leaves variable but are often lobed and finely hairy. Flowers are also variable.
CULTIVATION: Mostly frost tender, they are treated as annuals outdoors or grown indoors in cool climates. Plants prefer a bright but not sunny position with fertile, cool, moist, soil rich in humus. Water and feed well. Watch for fungal diseases. Propagate by division or from offsets, leaf cuttings, or seed, depending on type.

Begonia coccinea

ANGEL-WING BEGONIA

◐/● ✴ ↔ 24 in (60 cm) ↕ 48 in (120 cm)
Fibrous-rooted, from Brazil. Stems upright, succulent. Lush green, pointed, wing-shaped leaves, to 6 in (15 cm) long, red undersides. Large racemes of bright red flowers in spring. Zones 10–12.

Begonia × *erythrophylla*

BEEFSTEAK BEGONIA

☀/☀ ❋ ↔ 16–24 in (40–60 cm) ↑ 8–16 in (20–40 cm)

Rhizome-rooted. Rounded wavy leaves, deep green, red below, with hairs. Small pink flowers in winter–spring. Zones 10–12.

Begonia fuchsioides

FUCHSIA BEGONIA

☀/☀ ❋ ↔ 20 in (50 cm) ↑ 36 in (90 cm)

From Venezuela. Fibrous-rooted species. Succulent upright stems. Toothed, pointed, wing-shaped leaves, to 2 in (5 cm) long, bright green above, red-tinted below. Pendulous sprays of pink to red 1¼ in (30 mm) wide flowers in winter. Zones 10–12.

Begonia grandis

EVANS' BEGONIA, HARDY BEGONIA

☀/☀ ❋ ↔ 12–18 in (30–45 cm) ↑ 24 in (60 cm)

From China and Japan. Perennial with loose sprays of flower clusters over large clump of leaves. Green heart-shaped leaves, thick, succulent, ruby red veins on lower surfaces. Flowers pink, in drooping cymes, appear in late summer–autumn. 'Heron's Pirouette' blooms from early summer until autumn. Zones 6–9.

Begonia masoniana

IRON CROSS BEGONIA

☀/☀ ❋ ↔ 12–16 in (30–40 cm) ↑ 12 in (30 cm)

Rhizome-rooted, from New Guinea. Leaves asymmetrical, pointed, wing- to heart-shaped, to 8 in (20 cm) long, toothed, hairy, with puckered surface, light green with dark central markings. Upright sprays of small pale green flowers in spring–summer. Zones 10–12.

Begonia metallica

METALLIC-LEAF BEGONIA

☀/☀ ❋ ↔ 20–32 in (50–80 cm) ↑ 48 in (120 cm)

Fibrous-rooted, from Brazil. Leaves asymmetrical, pointed oval, to 6 in (15 cm) long, serrated edges, steely purple-blue upper surface veining. Many-flowered sprays of single 1¼ in (30 mm) wide, light to deep pink flowers in summer–autumn. Zones 10–12.

Begonia Hybrid Cultivars

Begonia is such a large genus and many of the species interbreed so freely that countless hybrids have been introduced over the years. These largely fall into eight quite clear-cut groups. While there are several subgroups, these are the main divisions.

CANE-LIKE GROUP

☀ ❋ ↔ 20–32 in (50–80 cm) ↑ 2–6 ft (0.6–1.8 m)

Tall upright stems. Leaves, usually wing-shaped, vary in size, texture, and color; may be deeply lobed, feathery; often silvery or red-tinted. Small red, pink, or salmon flowers in sprays. 'Flamingo Queen', pink flowers, spotted leaves; 'Honeysuckle', fragrant pink flowers; 'Irene Nuss' ★, coral pink flowers, bronze leaves; 'Looking Glass', pink flowers, leaves silvery; 'Orange Rubra', orange flowers, mid-green leaves. Zones 9–11.

REX CULTORUM GROUP

☀/☀ ❋ ↔ 16–24 in (40–60 cm) ↑ 12–24 in (30–60 cm)

Leaves large, exquisitely colored and marked, heavily veined and textured, velvety, often hairy at edges. Upper surfaces have combinations of bronze-green, bright green, silver, pink, and white; undersides usually purple-red. Clusters of small pink flowers. 'Merry Christmas', pink flowers, red leaves; 'Silver Queen', pink flowers, silvery leaves; 'Tinsel', purple-tinged leaves. Zones 10–12.

RHIZOMATOUS GROUP

☀/☀ ❋ ↔ 12–30 in (30–75 cm) ↑ 6–8 in (15–20 cm)

Grow from spreading or upright rhizomes. Often fleshy leaves, to 12 in (30 cm) wide. Leaf shape, texture, and color variable, often red-tinted undersides and wavy edges. Flowers few to many, mostly pink. Cultivars include 'Munchkin' and 'Tiger Paws'. Zones 9–11.

SEMPERFLORENS GROUP

☀/☀ ❋ ↔ 12 in (30 cm) ↑ 12 in (30 cm)

Small bushy perennials, usually treated as bedding annuals. Bright green or red, glossy, waxy leaves. Small, white, pink, or red flowers, usually single. Suit cool, fairly moist summers. **All Round Series**, bronze or green foliage; **Alfa Series**, vigorous plants, bronze foliage, including 'Alfa Pink'; **Ambassador Series**, compact with mid-green foliage; **Cocktail Series**, single flowers, bronze foliage; **Expresso Series**, bronze foliage, including 'Expresso Scarlet'; **Inferno Series**, vigorous and resilient, including 'Inferno Apple Blossom'; **Olympia Series**, green foliage, including 'Olympia White'; **Prelude Series**, early blooming, rich green foliage; **Senator Series**, early blooming, bronze foliage. Zones 9–11.

Begonia coccinea

Begonia, Cane-like Group, 'Flamingo Queen'

Begonia, Rex Cultorum Group, 'Tinsel'

SHRUB-LIKE GROUP

☀/◐ ❄ ↔ 18–48 in (45–120 cm) ↑ 12–36 in (30–90 cm)

Bushy plants with dense growth habit; leaves variably sized, colored, and textured, hairy or smooth, often red-veined. Flowers usually pink or cream, sometimes red or white, usually small and clustered. Popular cultivars include 'Cockatoo', 'Ginny', 'Red Amigo', 'Richmondensis' ★, and 'Thurstonii'. Zones 9–12.

THICK-STEMMED GROUP

☀/◐ ❄ ↔ 12–18 in (30–45 cm)
↑ 12–18 in (30–45 cm)

Strong fleshy stems. Variably colored leaves, more than 6 in (15 cm) long, deeply toothed, lobed, or smooth-edged. Small flowers, usually white or pink, sometimes scented. 'Boomer', bronze leaves, white flowers. Zones 9–12.

TRAILING OR SCANDENT GROUP

☀/◐ ❄ ↔ 18–36 in (45–90 cm)
↑ 6–12 in (15–30 cm)

Low spreading plants with lax stems. Usually grown in hanging baskets but sometimes climbing. Leaves usually small to medium-sized, smooth or hairy, often dark green. Sprays of small white, pink, or red flowers, often scented. Zones 9–12.

TUBEROUS GROUP

☀/◐ ❄ ↔ 12–20 in (30–50 cm) ↑ 12–32 in (30–80 cm)

These grow from large flat tubers, producing short, heavy, succulent stems carrying large, often hairy leaves. Huge range of flower types and colors, including many that resemble roses. They are suitable for indoor or outdoor cultivation, flowering mainly from mid-summer to frost. Popular cultivars include 'Coppelia', 'Fairlight', and 'Roy Hartley'. The Non-Stop Series and Pin-up Series ★ include a variety of attractive plants. Zones 8–10.

BELLIS

BELLIS DAISY, BRUISEWORT, LAWN DAISY

This European and Mediterranean genus of 7 species of annual and perennial daisies (family Asteraceae) includes the common

Begonia, Tuberous Group, 'Coppelia'

daisy *(B. perennis)*. Cultivated forms have much larger flowerheads with many more ray florets and a wider color range than wild plants. *Bellis* plants form flat rosettes of spoon- to kidney-shaped leaves and carry their flowerheads on individual stems.

CULTIVATION: Best in cool-temperate climates in a sunny or part-shaded open position with good air movement and soil that remains moist during the growing season. White rust and mildew can occur in humid conditions. The fancy cultivars are propagated by division, the others from seed.

Bellis perennis

Bellis perennis

BELLIS DAISY, ENGLISH DAISY

☀ ❄ ↔ 4–8 in (10–20 cm) ↑ 2–4 in (5–10 cm)

Originally from temperate Eurasia but now naturalized in most temperate zones. Leaves 1–2 in (25–50 mm) long, broad, spatula-shaped. White flowers, sometimes tinted pink, with yellow centers, from late winter. Popular cultivars include 'Dresden China', the Pomponette Series, and 'Rob Roy'. Zones 4–10.

BERGENIA

PIGSQUEAK

Found in Asia, from Afghanistan to Mongolia, this genus of the saxifrage (Saxifragaceae) family is made up of 8 species of perennials. Large leathery leaves sprout from tough, woody, fleshy stems. Leaves are broad, often light green, and usually at least 8 in (20 cm) long. They are complemented by long-stemmed heads of 5-petalled flowers in spring. Species most often have pink flowers but garden forms occur in white and shades of pink, red, and mauve.

CULTIVATION: For lush foliage, plant in cool moist conditions in part-shade in soil rich in humus. Plants in full sun often flower well but at the expense of their leaves, which burn. Excellent in large rockeries. Propagate by division after flowering.

Bergenia cordifolia

HEARTLEAF SAXIFRAGE, PIGSQUEAK

☀ ❄ ↔ 48 in (120 cm) ↑ 16 in (40 cm)

Found in the mountains of Siberia and Mongolia. Rounded toothed-edged leaves, to 8 in (20 cm) long, on strong stalks. Bright pink flowers on red stems from late winter.Popular cultivars include 'Perfecta', 'Purpurea', and 'Redstart'. Zones 3–10.

Bergenia crassifolia

☀ ❄ ↔ 16–32 in (40–80 cm) ↑ 12 in (30 cm)

From Siberia and Mongolia. Shallowly toothed, rounded leaves up to 8 in (20 cm) long, but can be considerably smaller. Magenta to cerise flowers on strong red stems. Zones 3–9.

Bergenia × *schmidtii*

☀ ❄ ↔ 24–48 in (60–120 cm) ↑ 12 in (30 cm)

Variable hybrid with large rounded leaves and deep pink to magenta flowers. Blooms very early, in winter and early spring; protect the flowers from frost. Zones 5–10.

Bergenia Hybrid Cultivars

☀/◐ ❋ ↔ 16–32 in (40–80 cm) ↑ 8–16 in (20–40 cm)

These plants need some sunlight for the best leaf color. Cultivars include 'Abendglut' (syn. 'Evening Glow'), compact, wavy-edged red-tinted foliage, purple-red semi-double flowers; 'Ballawley' (syn. 'Delbees'), glossy leaves, purple-tinted in winter, red flowers; 'Bressingham White', pure white flowers; 'Eroica', bronze- to purple-tinted foliage, purple-red flowers; 'Morgenröte' (syn. 'Morning Blush'), large bronze green leaves and deep purple-red flowers; 'Rosi Klose', dark green leaves, pink flowers; 'Silberlicht' (syn. 'Silver Light'), large leaves, white flowers ageing to pink; and 'Sunningdale', bronze-to red-tinted winter foliage, deep lavender-pink flowers. Zones 3–9.

BIDENS

BEGGAR'S TICK, BURR MARIGOLD, SPANISH NEEDLES, STICK TIGHT, TICKSEED

This genus of about 200 annual and perennial species belongs to the daisy (Asteraceae) family. It has a worldwide distribution, with its largest numbers in temperate and tropical Africa and America. The few ornamental forms are used as annual bedding plants. The sticking hooks on the seeds help them to become dispersed over wide areas.

CULTIVATION: These plants require little more than a sunny well-drained site with reasonable moisture-retentive soil. Plant after frosts in very cold climates. Propagate from seed or by division of the perennial forms.

Bidens ferulifolia

APACHE BEGGARTICKS

☀ ❋ ↔ 12–18 in (30–45 cm) ↑ 24–36 in (60–90 cm)

From Arizona (USA), Mexico, and Guatemala. Annual or perennial with ferny foliage. Golden wide-rayed daisies, about 1¼ in (30 mm) across, from late summer to autumn. 'Golden Goddess' and 'Goldmarie' are improved selections. 'Golden Eye', Goldie/ 'Innbid', and 'Peters Goldteppich' ★, trailing cultivars. Zones 8–11.

BILLBERGIA

This bromeliad (Bromeliaceae) family genus has 65 species and some 500 cultivars. It can be divided into 2 main groups: one from the warmer parts of South America and Mexico, the other from Brazil. Leaves form a tubular rosette, and come in all colors and markings; colors are more evident when plants are grown in good light. Flowerheads usually vary from spherical to cylindrical and can have a long stem, so the flowerhead hangs outside the leaf tube. Beneath the flowerhead are large, banner-like, red bracts. Flowers are long, thin, and tubular, topped with petals of many different colors in odd combinations.

Billbergia nutans

CULTIVATION: Indoor culture recommended if in flower; in greenhouse in cool-temperate areas; outdoors with protection from direct sunlight and rain in warm-temperate, subtropical, and tropical areas. Water when potting mix is dry. Adding fertilizer to good quality potting mix is not necessary. Propagate from seed or offsets.

Bergenia, Hybrid Cultivar, 'Sunningdale'

Billbergia amoena

☀ ❊ ↔ 12 in (30 cm) ↑ 24 in (60 cm)

Native to southern Brazil. Leaves green to red, sometimes with white spots. Flowerhead erect, mainly green, with up to 20 flowers; petals green, sometimes with blue tips. Beneath flowerhead are 7 or 8 red bracts, erect or drooping. Zones 9–10.

Billbergia elegans

☀ ❊ ↔ 4 in (10 cm) ↑ 12 in (30 cm)

Native to southern Brazil. Leaves green with white bands, becoming reddish in good light. Flowerhead erect but sometimes slightly bent, salmon pink, up to 8 flowers with blue-tipped green petals. Several salmon pink bracts below flowerhead. Zones 9–10.

Billbergia euphemiae

☀ ❊ ↔ 8 in (20 cm) ↑ 24 in (60 cm)

Native to eastern Brazil. Leaves green, sometimes purple. Flower stem erect to slightly bent. Flowerhead mainly yellow, to 6 in (15 cm) long, with up to 30 flowers, petals purple. This species is not as hardy as some of the other *Billbergia* species. Zones 9–10.

Billbergia nutans

FRIENDSHIP PLANT, QUEEN'S TEARS, TARTAN FLOWER

☀ ❋ ↔ 6 in (15 cm) ↑ 10 in (25 cm)

From southern Brazil to Uruguay. Leaves green, thin, to 24 in (60 cm) long. Flowerheads nodding, few green and pink flowers, blue-edged petals. Commonly grown bromeliad, but plants may really be the hybrid cultivar 'Albertii'. Zones 8–10.

Billbergia pyramidalis

☀ ⬍ ↔ 6 in (15 cm) ↑ 20 in (50 cm)

From eastern Brazil. Leaves light to dark green, sometimes with narrow white bands, teeth small. Flowerhead erect, mainly red with frosting, pyramidal shape, up to 40 flowers. Many large red bracts beneath flowerhead. Petals red with bluish tips. *B. p.* var. *concolor (syn. B. p.* var. *thyrsoidea)*, large, wide, pale green leaves and faint blue hue to petal ends. Zones 9–10.

Billbergia zebrina

☀ ⬍ ↔ 6 in (15 cm) ↑ 40 in (100 cm)

From southern Brazil and adjacent countries. Leaves to 3 in (8 cm) wide, pale green with white cross-bands. Flowerhead hanging, to 16 in (40 cm) long, felty, yellowish green. Up to 8 large pale pink to rose bracts above flowerhead. Zones 9–10.

Billbergia Hybrid Cultivars

☀ ⬍ ↔ to 8 in (20 cm) ↑ to 24 in (60 cm)

A range of hybrids with beautiful flowers. 'Afterglow', green-petalled flowers, large red bracts; 'Albertii', green-petalled flowers, blue petal edges; 'Breauteana', drooping flowerhead, mainly light pink with dark blue petals; 'Catherine Wilson', erect flowerhead, mainly green, with rose-colored bracts below; 'Domingos Martins', flowerhead to 6 in (15 cm) long, almost totally red, petals blue; 'Euphemie Waterman', compact flowerhead, leaves maroon with silvery bands; 'Fascinator', drooping flowerhead comprising about 15 blooms, petals green with blue edges, large red bracts; 'Hallelujah', flowerhead mainly light green, erect, up to 10 flowers with blue tips; 'Manda's Othello', flowerhead erect, mainly pale pink with blue-tipped petals, red bracts beneath; 'Muriel Waterman', flowerhead slightly bent, mainly green to pale pink with blue petals, flowers rarely; 'Platinum', flowerhead felty, erect, then curved, up to 14 flowers, pale green and pale red with dark blue-tipped petals; 'Poquito Blanco', flowerhead erect with few flowers, mainly pale pink, petals pale green with purple edges; 'Windii', large rose red bracts cover hanging flowerhead, mainly green and white, petals green with blue edges. Zones 9–10.

BOLTONIA

FALSE CHAMOMILE

A genus of about 8 species in the daisy (Asteraceae) family, these tall perennials are found in central and eastern USA and northeastern Asia, where they grow in moist soils. Their upright leafy stems bear masses of daisy-like flowers in late summer and autumn. The flowers have a yellow eye and are white, pink, mauve, or purple in color.
CULTIVATION: Showy and easily grown in borders or "wild" gardens, these plants can be cultivated in any moderately fertile soil in full sun or part-shade. Stake in exposed positions. Regular division will maintain vigor. Propagate by division or from seed.

Billbergia zebrina

Boltonia asteroides

☼ ✻ ↔ 5 ft (1.5 m) ↑ 3–5 ft (0.9–1.5 m)

Clump-forming perennial from eastern USA. Leaves narrow, to 4 in (10 cm) long. Erect leafy stems bear masses of starry white daisies in late summer–autumn. *B. a.* var. *latisquama*, taller plant bearing large mauve daisies. *B. a.* 'Snowbank', strong grower to 7 ft (2 m) tall, white daisies. Zones 4–10.

BOYKINIA

There are about 9 species of perennial herbs in this genus in the saxifrage (Saxifragaceae) family. They are native to moist woodlands of North America and Japan. They have creeping rhizomes and form clumps of rounded or kidney-shaped leaves. The tiny flowers are borne on crowded panicles. They are white, yellowish green, or purple. CULTIVATION: Best suited to "wild" or woodland gardens, or rockeries. Grow in moist well-drained soil in light shade. Propagate by division.

Boykinia jamesii

syn. *Telesonix jamesii*

◑ ✻ ↔ 6–8 in (15–20 cm) ↑ 2–6 in (5–15 cm)

Compact low-growing species from northwestern USA. Leaves small, toothed, kidney-shaped. Flowers small, purple-red, in early summer. Grow in cool greenhouse or trough. Zones 5–9.

BRACHYSCOME

syn. *Brachycome*

DAISY

A popular genus of annuals, perennials, and subshrubs in the daisy (Asteraceae) family. There are 90 to 100 species in the genus, with many cultivars. They occur throughout Australia from coastal to alpine habitats. Leaves are small, bright green, and generally multi-lobed, divided, and/or toothed. Plants can form mats or be suckering or rounded compact bushes. Flowers are a typical daisy type in shades of pink, mauve, blue, purple, lemon, and white, generally with yellow centers. These daisies are popular in rock gardens, pots, hanging baskets, on banks, and at the front of garden borders. Some cultivars have arisen by chance but others are the result of deliberate breeding programs to improve color selections and the size of the flowers.
CULTIVATION: Any well-drained soil in either full or half-sun will do; some plants are more drought/frost tolerant than others. Propagation is from seed, with named cultivars propagated from cuttings or by division.

Brachyscome iberidifolia

SWAN RIVER DAISY

☼ ⬍ ↔ 8–12 in (20–30 cm) ↑ 2–16 in (5–40 cm)

Erect annual daisy with pinnate leaves. Flowers 1 in (25 mm) in diameter in blue, purple, or white throughout spring–summer.

Can be frost tender. Cultivars include '**Blue Mist**', attractive blue flowers; '**Blue Star**' ★, purple-tinted flowers with quilled petals, lightly scented. Zones 9–11.

Brachyscome multifida
CUT-LEAF DAISY, HAWKESBURY RIVER DAISY

☼ ◗ ↔ 12–40 in (30–100 cm) ↑ 8–16 in (20–40 cm)

Soft, much-divided foliage on a mounding form. Flowers generally purple but can be pink or white. Likes well-drained soil and will tolerate frost. May layer but does not sucker. *B. m.* **var.** *dilatata*, rounded form, leaves more wedge-shaped than species; '**Break O' Day**', hardier and more compact than species, bears deep mauve flowers from spring to autumn. *B. m.* '**Evan**', cushion-like, deep mauve flowers from spring to autumn; '**White Surprise**', similar to species, except flowers are white. Zones 9–11.

Brachyscome Hybrid Cultivars
☼/◗ ◗ ↔ 18 in (45 cm) ↑ 18 in (45 cm)

These hybrids, mostly of *B. angustifolia* and *B. iberidifolia*, are compact heavy-flowering plants. '**Blue Haze**', compact, low growing, mauve-blue flowers; '**City Lights**', mounding form with large light lavender blue flowers; '**Just Jayne**', compact plant that does sucker, bearing white to pale pink flowers in autumn; '**New Amethyst**', fine foliage, small dark purple flowers in spring–autumn; '**Strawberry Mousse**', reddish mid-green foliage, spoon-shaped lobed leaves, bright pink flowers; '**Toucan Tango**' (syn. '**Ultra**'), lacy foliage, violet-blue flowers year round; '**Valencia**', mauve-pink flowers 1½ in (35 mm) in diameter, flowers year round in tropics. Zones 9–11.

BROMELIA
In 1753 Linnaeus named *Bromelia pinguin*, and this genus gave the bromeliad (Bromeliaceae) family its name. Found in Mexico, the Caribbean islands, and Central America south to Argentina. Leaves are long, narrow, and leathery with large curved spines along edges. When flowering the center turns bright red and a dense head or panicle of flowers emerges. There are about 50 species, but only 6 are popularly grown. Perhaps the most hardy is *B. serra*, with *B. pinguin* and its variegated form the most common.

CULTIVATION: Recommended for a greenhouse in cool-temperate areas, or outdoors in warm-temperate, subtropical, and tropical areas. Bromelias send out underground fleshy stems, so are best grown in large tubs. Water when potting mix is dry. No extra fertilizer. Propagate from seeds or offsets.

Bromelia pinguin
PINGUIN, PINUELA

◗ ◗ ↔ 7 ft (2 m) ↑ 4 ft (1.2 m)

Clumping species from tropical America. Many rosettes, each with up to 40 spiny leaves to 6 ft (1.8 m) long and 2 in (5 cm) wide, light gray-green flushed with red. Large panicles of white to pink flowers; small, fleshy, yellow fruits. Zones 10–12.

Brachyscome iberidifolia 'Blue Star'

Brunnera macrophylla

Bromelia serra
☼ ◗ ↔ 7 ft (2 m) ↑ 24 in (60 cm)

From Bolivia to northern Argentina. Leaves green, short spines on edges. Flower stem short. Flowerhead globular, 2½ in (6 cm) wide. Petals blue-purple. Bright red, stiff, spiny bracts up to 8 in (20 cm) long beneath the flowerhead. Zones 9–11.

BRUNNERA
This genus of 3 species of fleshy-stemmed herbaceous perennials of the borage (Boraginaceae) family comes from temperate Eurasia. The species are closely related to the forget-me-nots and resemble them in flower. Sprays of tiny blue or white flowers appear in spring. However, the rounded to heart-shaped leaves of *Brunnera* are far larger than those of the common forget-me-nots and, as the garden forms are often variegated, the foliage is as much a feature as the flowers.

CULTIVATION: These plants are most at home in a temperate climate with cool summers. Extremely hardy and easily grown in woodland conditions with dappled sunlight and moist, humus-rich, well-drained soil. Propagate from seed or division of established clumps near the end of the dormant period, *Brunnera* species often naturalize.

Brunnera macrophylla
◗ ❊ ↔ 16–32 in (40–80 cm) ↑ 20 in (50 cm)

A Eastern European perennial with finely hairy, broad, heart-shaped leaves to 6 in (15 cm) long on 8 in (20 cm) stalks. Soft blue flowers are held above the foliage on 20 in (50 cm) stems. '**Hadspen Cream**', one of several variegated cultivars, cream-spotted light green leaves, blue flowers. Zones 3–9.

Calamintha nepeta

CALAMINTHA

CALAMINT

This mint (Lamiaceae) family genus is made up of 7 species of
sometimes shrubby perennials found in the northern temperate
zones excluding East Asia. The foliage is evergreen in mild climates but in cool winters plants may die back to a basal clump.
Their aromatic pointed oval leaves are often slightly glossy and
have toothed edges. Flower stems develop in summer and carry
tubular pink to mauve flowers in the leaf axils near their tips.
CULTIVATION: Hardiness varies with the species, although the majority will tolerate quite severe frosts. Plant in a bright but not
baking position with moist, humus-rich, well-drained soil. Some
species have vigorous rhizomes and these can be slightly invasive.
Propagation is by division, or from basal cuttings or seed.

Calamintha grandiflora

LARGE-FLOWERED CALAMINT

☼◐/◑ ✳ ↔ 3–4 ft (0.9–1.2 m) ↑ 2 ft (0.6 m)
Native to southern Europe and North Africa.
Bushy plant with spreading rootstock. Dark
green, downy, toothed leaves to 3 in (8 cm) long.
Flowers 1½ in (35 mm) long, pink to mauve,
borne singly or up to 5 in a cluster. 'Variegata'
(syn. 'Fornsett Form'), compact. Zones 5–10.

Calamintha nepeta

LESSER CALAMINT

◑ ✳ ↔ 3–5 ft (0.9–1.5 m) ↑ 32 in (80 cm)
Spreading rhizome-rooted perennial found from
Britain to southern Europe. Downy gray-green
stems and leaves, to 1¼ in (30 mm) long. Aromatic. Flowers
mauve-pink, ½ in (12 mm) long, up to 15 in a cluster. Zones 6–10.

CALATHEA

Found from Mexico to northern Argentina, this large genus of
300 evergreen, tuberous, or rhizome-rooted perennials belongs
in the arrowroot (Marantaceae) family. They are upright in habit,
with bold and often strikingly marked elliptical foliage, and they
are commonly grown as house plants. There are 3 basic forms of
calatheas: dense clumps of short-stemmed leaves; more open

clumps of leaves with long leaf stalks; and those
with their foliage on cane-like stems. Leaves can
be as much as 5 ft (1.5 m) long, though 6–10 in
(15–25 cm) is more common. The flowers,
backed by colored bracts, are usually held in
a cone-like structure.
CULTIVATION: Calatheas require warm, humid,
frost-free conditions. A draft-free shaded position
with moist, humus-rich, well-drained soil is best.
Propagate by division.

Calathea burle-marxii

☀ ⚘ ↔ 3–5 ft (0.9–1.5 m) ↑ 5 ft (1.5 m)
Upright cane-stemmed Brazilian species with
leaves often over 24 in (60 cm) long, and bright
green with a yellow-green midrib and gray-green
undersides. Large heads of cream to yellow flowers, which are
sometimes tinted blue or purple. Zones 11–12.

Calathea makoyana

CATHEDRAL WINDOWS, PEACOCK PLANT

☀ ⚘ ↔ 16–32 in (40–80 cm) ↑ 24–32 in (60–80 cm)
From Brazil. Short-stemmed, 12 in (30 cm) long, translucent
leaves, midrib and main vein darker green bordered with cream,
green and maroon below. White flowers, green bracts. Zones 11–12.

Calathea picturata

☀ ⚘ ↔ 20–27 in (50–70 cm) ↑ 16–24 in (40–60 cm)
From Brazil. Short-stemmed leaves to 10 in (25 cm) long, dark
green with white along midrib and inside margin, maroon undersides. The white patches often join to form white-
centered leaves. White flowers. Zones 11–12.

Calathea makoyana

Calathea zebrina

ZEBRA PLANT

☀ ⚘ ↔ 32–48 in (80–120 cm) ↑ 40 in (100 cm)
From Brazil. Short canes with velvety, light and
dark green banded leaves to 27 in (70 cm) long,
pale midrib, maroon undersides. White to mauve
flowers with purple-brown bracts. Zones 11–12.

CALCEOLARIA

Found from Mexico to southern South America,
this genus of 300 species or so in the foxglove
(Scrophulariaceae) family includes perennials
and shrubs. Leaves tend to be light green and are
covered with fine hairs and small glands that make them sticky.
Flowers are very distinctive. They are 2-lipped with a small hooded
upper lip and a large lower lip that is inflated and pouch-like.
Yellow, orange, and red shades dominate the flower colors.
CULTIVATION: While calceolarias vary in their frost hardiness and
sun tolerance, they prefer cool moist soil conditions. Work high-
humus compost into soil before planting. Shrubby species become
untidy after a few years; pruning rejuvenates them, but replace-
ment with new plants is usually more successful. Seed germinates
well, but tip cuttings strike quickly and are the preferred method.

Calceolaria, Herbeohybrida Group

LADIES' PURSES, POCKETBOOK PLANT, SLIPPER FLOWER

☀️ ❄ ↔ 12–16 in (30–40 cm) ↑ 8–20 in (20–50 cm)

These perennials are treated as annuals. Large winter flowers in shades of reds, oranges, and yellows (some speckled or blotched), characteristic pouch-like lip and hairy leaves. **Sunset Series** produces bushy plants and short-stemmed flowers for a long period; flowers scarlet, yellow, rich red, and copper-orange. '**Sunset Red**', brilliant red to orange flowers. Zones 9–11.

Calceolaria integrifolia

☀️/◐ ❄ ↔ 2–6 ft (0.6–1.8 m) ↑ 4 ft (1.2 m)

Native to Chile. Most commonly cultivated species. Woody shrubby perennials. Leaves toothed, light green, sticky, slightly puckered, fine brown hairs beneath. Flowers yellow or rusty orange, sometimes with contrasting spots, borne all year, particularly abundant in warmer months. Trim in early spring. Popular cultivars include '**Goldbouquet**', '**Golden Nugget**', '**Kentish Hero**' ★, and '**Russet**'. Zones 8–10.

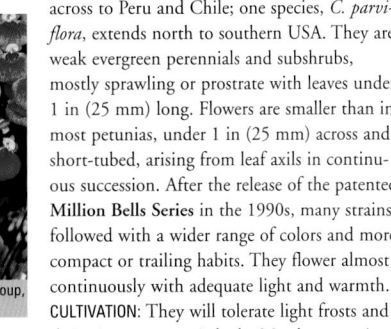

Calceolaria, Herbeohybrida Group, Sunset Series, 'Sunset Red'

CALENDULA

A genus of about 20 species of annual and perennial herbs in the daisy (Asteraceae) family. They are found around the Mediterranean area and Atlantic Islands where they are often found growing on disturbed ground, particularly *C. officinalis*, which is a widespread garden escapee. All have alternate simple leaves; some of these are aromatic. The cheerful yellow or orange daisies appear for long periods throughout the year. The common name marigold is today also associated with some *Tagetes* species. CULTIVATION: Very easily grown in any well-drained soil in full sun. Sow seed in situ or under glass in spring in cooler areas, or earlier in warmer areas. Successive sowings and deadheading will result in a display over many months, from spring to autumn in cooler areas and throughout the year in warm ones.

Calendula officinalis ★

COMMON MARIGOLD, POT MARIGOLD, SCOTCH MARIGOLD

☀️ ❄ ↔ 12–18 in (30–45 cm) ↑ 12–24 in (30–60 cm)

Originally from southern Europe but now widely naturalized. Bushy annual with slightly downy leaves. Orange or yellow daisies, to 3 in (8 cm) wide, in spring–autumn. **Bon Bon Series**, a mix of apricot, yellow, and orange flowers; '**Dwarf Gem**', double, large, apricot, yellow, and orange daisies; **Fiesta Gitana Group** ★, a mix of cream, yellow, orange, and bi-colored flowers; '**Greenheart Orange**', orange petals and a green center to flowers; '**Orange Salad**', petals are a saffron substitute; **Kablouna Series**, short ray florets and prominent quilled centers, mixed yellow, orange, and apricot flowers; **Pacific Beauty Series**, tall-stemmed, yellow, orange, and apricot flowers; '**Radio**', orange flowers, quilled petals resembling cactus-type dahlia. Zones 6–10.

CALIBRACHOA

syn. *Petunia* (in part)

A genus in the nightshade (Solanaceae) family, *Calibrachoa* is closely related to *Petunia* and its 25 species are found across much the same region of South America, from southern Brazil across to Peru and Chile; one species, *C. parviflora*, extends north to southern USA. They are weak evergreen perennials and subshrubs, mostly sprawling or prostrate with leaves under 1 in (25 mm) long. Flowers are smaller than in most petunias, under 1 in (25 mm) across and short-tubed, arising from leaf axils in continuous succession. After the release of the patented **Million Bells Series** in the 1990s, many strains followed with a wider range of colors and more compact or trailing habits. They flower almost continuously with adequate light and warmth. CULTIVATION: They will tolerate light frosts and thrive in sun or semi-shade. Mostly grown in pots or baskets; can be treated as annuals or short-lived perennials. Plant in a free-draining medium and apply weak fertilizer at intervals throughout the growing season, pinch back the longer shoots to increase the number of flowers. Water only when the soil is almost dry. Propagate from tip cuttings but be aware that propagation for sale may infringe plant patents.

Calibrachoa Hybrid Cultivars

☀️/◐ ❄ ↔ 12–24 in (30–60 cm) ↑ 3–8 in (8–20 cm)

Valued for their low mounding or trailing habit and profusion of small flowers, mid-spring–late autumn or virtually year-round in warm climates. **Million Bells Series** are yellow-throated flowers in shades from white to lemon, pink, red, and purple, mounding to 6 in (15 cm). Flowers in the **Trailing Million Bells Series** are only 3 in (7 cm) or so high, spilling over edges of baskets or planter boxes. Flowers in the **Colorburst Series** come in cherry, red, rose and violet. Flowers of the German-bred **Minifamous Series** (syn. Selecta Series) include some rich colors, especially oranges, reds, and yellows, and also bicolors. The **Liricashower Series** include strong reds and yellows as well as pastels, with flat open blooms. Zones 8–11.

Calibrachoa, Hybrid Cultivar, 'Colorburst Violet'

CALLISTEPHUS

CHINA ASTER

The sole species in this genus is an annual daisy in the family Asteraceae, from China. However, despite being just one species, it has been developed into an array of garden varieties, which have flowers in white and all shades of pink, mauve-blue, red, and purple in single- and double-flowered styles, all of which last well when cut. It is naturally a sturdy upright plant, though dwarf forms are available.

CULTIVATION: Plant in the full sun with moist well-drained soil and feed occasionally with liquid fertilizer. Err on the cautious side with feeding or you may produce foliage at the expense of flowers. Raise from seed. Spring-sown seed begins flowering by early summer; stagger sowing for a succession of blooms.

Callistephus chinensis

Callistephus chinensis

☼ ❄ ↔ 8–12 in (20–30 cm)
↑ 12–36 in (30–90 cm)
Dark green, pointed oval leaves to over 3 in (8 cm) long, with coarsely toothed edges. Flowerheads are 2–4 in (5–10 cm) across, borne singly on long stems. **Milady Series Mixed**, strong-growing and bushy yet compact series growing to around 10 in (25 cm) tall, available in a wide color range. Zones 8–11.

CALTHA

This buttercup (Ranunculaceae) family genus contains 10 species of herbaceous perennials, widespread in temperate regions of both hemispheres. Often very much like buttercups in general appearance, they have fleshy, bright to deep green, kidney- to heart-shaped leaves on sturdy leaf stalks and develop into mounding clumps of foliage. Flowers white to pale yellow or gold; although petalless, their 5 or more petal-like sepals give them a buttercup-like appearance. Double-flowered forms are common. Flowering season varies.

CULTIVATION: These plants are mostly very frost tolerant with a preference for damp soil and partly shaded conditions, though ordinary well-drained humus-rich garden soil in a woodland environment is perfectly acceptable. Their roots spread readily. Most are easily propagated by division.

Caltha palustris

syn. *Caltha polypetala*
KING CUP, MARSH MARIGOLD
☼/☀ ❄ ↔ 16–24 in (40–60 cm)
↑ 12–24 in (30–60 cm)
Widespread throughout the northern temp-erate zone. Upright or spreading habit, with kidney-shaped leaves, 4–8 in (10–20 cm) wide. Bright golden yellow flowerheads on upright stems, in late spring–early summer. Several double-flowered cultivars with round-ed heads available, including '**Flore Pleno**' and the dark-leafed '**Monstrosa**'. Zones 3–9.

Caltha palustris 'Flore Pleno'

CAMPANULA

This large genus of about 300 species of hardy annual, biennial, and perennial plants belongs to the bellflower (Campanulaceae) family. It contains a number of popular and beautiful garden plants. Many are native to Mediterranean areas, the Balkans, and Caucasus region. Some are from North America and temperate Asia. Their growth habit is ground-hugging and clump-forming, or erect and branching. A few species are invasive. Leaves are usually alternately arranged. Flowers are in shades of blue, mauve, pale pink, and white. They range from large drooping bells to delicate open stars, and are borne on panicles, spikes, or singly. The variety of species allows for choices for a range of garden types.

CULTIVATION: Most species grow easily in any reasonably fertile well-drained soil in sun or half-sun. Some alpine species require grittier soil and dislike winter wet. Propagate from seed, basal cuttings or by division.

Campanula carpatica

syn. *Campanula turbinata*
CARPATHIAN BELLFLOWER, TUSSOCK BELLFLOWER
☼/☀ ❄ ↔ 12–16 in (30–40 cm) ↑ 6–12 in (15–30 cm)
From the Carpathian Mountains. Low-growing spreading peren-nial forming a thick clump of small, bright green, egg-shaped leaves. In summer the plant is covered with pale blue or white, upward facing, open cup-shaped flowers, 1–2 in (2.5–5 cm) in diameter. Eccellent ground cover. *C. c. f. alba* has white flowers. *C. c.* cultivars include '**Blaue Clips**', blue flowers; '**Blue Moonlight**', very open flowers, light grayish-blue; '**Chewton Joy**', light blue petals edged with deeper blue. Zones 3–9.

Campanula cochlearifolia

syn. *Campanula pusilla*
FAIRIES' THIMBLES
☼ ❄ ↔ 10 in (25 cm) ↑ 3 in (8 cm)
Creeping fleshy-stemmed perennial from the European Alps. Forms tight clumps of small rounded leaves. Bell-shaped pale lavender-blue flowers hang from wiry stems for long periods over summer. *C. c.* var. *alba* has white flowers. The *C. c.* Baby Series includes '**Blue Baby**', prolific, pale blue flowers; '**Bavaria Blue**', a very compact plant with dark blue flowers; '**Elizabeth Oliver**', double pale blue flowers. Zones 6–9.

Campanula garganica

syn. *Campanula elatines* var. *garganica*
☼ ❄ ↔ 6–12 in (15–30 cm) ↑ 6 in (15 cm)
Native to Italy. Low-growing perennial forms tight clumps of small light green leaves. Masses of small, starry, light blue flowers on lax panicles, for long periods in summer. '**Dickson's Gold**' (syn. 'Aurea'), golden foliage. Zones 5–9.

Campanula glomerata
CLUSTERED BELLFLOWER

☼ ❊ ↔ 12–24 in (30–60 cm)
↑ 12–36 in (30–90 cm)

Perennial, native to Europe and Asia. Forms
clumps by suckering. Bristly stems, purplish
blue flowers. Long flowering period over
summer. *C. g.* var. *acaulis*, very dwarf plants.
C. g. 'Nana', 'Purple Pixie', and 'Superba' all
have deep purple flowers. Zones 4–9.

Campanula isophylla
FALLING STARS, ITALIAN BELLFLOWER, STAR OF BETHLEHEM

☼ ❊ ↔ 12–18 in (30–45 cm) ↑ 6 in (15 cm)

From northern Italy, trailing perennial with
small heart-shaped leaves. Smothered in 1 in
(25 mm) wide, starry, mid-blue flowers in
summer. Suitable for hanging baskets. Protect
from winter wet. Cultivars include 'Alba',
'Stella Blue', and 'Stella White'. Zones 7–9.

Campanula portenschlagiana

Campanula lactiflora
MILKY BELLFLOWER

☼ ❊ ↔ 2 ft (0.6 m) ↑ 3–5 ft (0.9–1.5 m)

From the Caucasus region. Upright perennial. Well-branched,
leafy, arching stems. Milky blue bell-shaped flowers in wide
showy panicles in summer. 'Alba', white flowers; 'Loddon Anna',
soft pinkish white flowers; 'Macrantha', large violet-purple flowers;
'Prichard's Variety', violet-blue flowers. Zones 5–9.

Campanula medium
CANTERBURY BELLS, CUP AND SAUCER

☼ ❊ ↔ 12 in (30 cm) ↑ 24–36 in (60–90 cm)

Native to southern Europe. Biennial. Soft,
hairy, lance- shaped leaves. Showy bell-shaped
white, pink, or blue flowers, in summer.
Popular as cut flowers. 'Calycanthema' has
petal-like calyx. Zones 8–10.

Campanula persicifolia
PEACH-LEAFED BELLFLOWER, WILLOW BELLFLOWER

☼ ❊ ↔ 18 in (45 cm)
↑ 24–36 in (60–90 cm)

Native to Europe, eastern Asia, and northern
Africa. Perennial. Narrow wavy-edged leaves.
Open, blue, bell-shaped flowers, on showy
stems in summer. Long-flowering. Many
single and double cultivars, including
'Bennett's Blue' (syn. 'Wortham Belle'), 'Boule de Neige', 'Chettle
Charm', 'Fleur de Neige', and 'Planiflora' (syn. 'Nitida'). Zones 4–9.

Campanula punctata

Campanula portenschlagiana
syn. *Campanula muralis*

☼/❊ ❊ ↔ 18–24 in (45–60 cm) ↑ 6 in (15 cm)

From southern Europe. A vigorous alpine perennial with small
heart-shaped leaves. It is smothered through the summer months

with erect starry flowers of lavender-blue. 'Resholdt's Variety'
produces deep vivid blue flowers. Zones 4–9.

Campanula poscharskyana
SERBIAN BELLFLOWER

☼ ❊ ↔ 18–24 in (45–60 cm) ↑ 6–8 in (15–20 cm)

Native to Croatia. Vigorous alpine perennial. Bears starry flowers,
lavender to violet, in summer–autumn. Spreads rapidly in rock
gardens. 'Blue Gown', large mid-blue flowers; 'Blue Waterfall',
vigorous and free-flowering, dark blue flowers with lighter centers;
'E. H. Frost' bears milky white starry flowers; 'Erich G. Arends'
has blue flowers; 'Lisduggan Variety', lavender-pink flowers;
'Multiplicity' ★, double lavender-blue flowers;
'Stella', bright blue flowers. Zones 6–9.

Campanula punctata
syn. *Campanula nobilis*

☼ ❊ ↔ 18 in (45 cm) ↑ 12 in (30 cm)

From Siberia and Japan. A somewhat invasive
perennial forming clumps of pointed heart-
shaped leaves. Tubular, pendulous, bell-
shaped flowers, cream, flushed with pink and
spotted inside with red. *C. p.* f. *rubriflora*,
narrow cream flowers tinged pink to purple,
heavily spotted with red inside. *C. p.* 'Cherry
Bells', cherry red with paler edging. Zones 6–9.

Campanula pyramidalis
CHIMNEY BELLFLOWER

☼ ❊ ↔ 2 ft (0.6 m) ↑ 4–7 ft (1.2–2 m)

From Europe. Short-lived clumping perennial usually grown as
biennial. Broad, pointed, serrated-edged leaves. Tall branching
stems of densely packed open bell-shaped flowers in pale blue
or white. Summer-flowering. Best grown in the conservatory
in cooler areas. Zones 8–10.

Campanula rapunculoides

☼/◑ ❉ ↔ 24 in (60 cm) ↕ 36 in (90 cm)

Native to Europe. Robust, invasive perennial forming large patches of serrated nettle-like leaves. Tall stems of nodding bell-shaped flowers in shades of blue to violet in summer. Zones 4–9.

Campanula rotundifolia

BLUEBELL, HAREBELL

◑ ❉ ↔ 10–18 in (25–45 cm) ↕ 6–12 in (15–30 cm)

Found throughout much of the Northern Hemisphere. Fleshy-stemmed perennial. Heart-shaped leaves forming rosettes. Dainty bell-shaped flowers, white to deep blue, on slender stems during summer. Buds upright but flowers hang when opened. Zones 3–9.

Campanula takesimana

◑ ❉ ↔ 18 in (45 cm) ↕ 24 in (60 cm)

From Korea, a rather invasive fleshy-stemmed perennial. Forms basal rosettes of large leaves. Bears tall stems of long, drooping, tubular bellflowers in summer. Flowers creamy white on outside, and spotted maroon inside. **'Beautiful Trust'** (syn. 'Beautiful Truth') has drooping spidery petals, pure white; **'Elizabeth'** ★, prolific and long flowering. Zones 4–9.

CANISTRUM

These bromeliads from eastern to southeastern Brazil belong to the pineapple (Bromeliaceae) family. There are only 7 species. They form erect spreading rosettes to 24 in (60 cm) high and 16 in (40 cm) wide. The leaves sometimes have black teeth, are generally narrow and green, and some have dark markings. The flower stem is long and the globular flowerhead is enclosed by mainly red (sometimes orange) bracts, which may spread outward. The petals are white to rose to yellow in color.
CULTIVATION: These plants are recommended for indoor culture if in flower, for greenhouse or similar in cool-temperate areas, or outdoors with protection from direct continuous sunlight and extremes of rain in warm-temperate, subtropical, and tropical areas.

Canna iridiflora

Canistrum fosterianum

❉ ✂ ↔ 8 in (20 cm) ↕ 24 in (60 cm)

A tubular rosette a little flared at the top, leaves green with variable black markings on the outside. The flowerhead, to 4 in (10 cm) in diameter, appears just above the leaf tube and has spreading red bracts. Petals are white. Zones 9–12.

CANNA

CANNA LILY, INDIAN SHOT

Found throughout the New World in tropical and subtropical areas and widely naturalized elsewhere, this Cannaceae family genus has 9 species. They are vigorous plants with strong, upright, reed-like pseudostems that sprout from rhizomes and which bear long lance-shaped leaves. Heads of striking lily-like flowers, usually in shades of yellow, tangerine, and red, are borne.

CULTIVATION: Although they are often tropical in origin most can withstand light frosts as dormant roots if well insulated with mulch. Plant in full sun in moist, humus-rich, well-drained soil and feed well. Propagate selected forms by division in early spring. Seeds will often self-sow but rarely result in superior plants.

Canna glauca

☼ ❉ ↔ 1–3 ft (0.3–0.9 m) ↕ 4–6 ft (1.2–1.8 m)

Native to wetlands of tropical America. Bluish green pointed leaves to 20 in (50 cm) long. Large pale yellow flowers in summer. Zones 8–12.

Canna indica

syn. *Canna edulis*

INDIAN SHOT, QUEENSLAND ARROWROOT

☼/◑ ❉ ↔ 20–32 in (50–80 cm) ↕ 4–7 ft (1.2–2 m)

Widespread in the tropics. Leaves to 20 in (50 cm) long, often purple-tinted. Flowerheads upright, usually simple but sometimes branched. Red to orange flowers, rarely pink, often with contrasting spots, to slightly over 2 in (5 cm) wide. Zones 8–12.

Canna iridiflora

☼/◑ ❉ ↔ 20–32 in (50–80 cm) ↕ 10 ft (3 m)

Found from Costa Rica to Peru. Banana-like blue-green leaves to 4 ft (1.2 m) long. They bear simple or few-branched heads of semi-pendent, long-tubed, deep pink to orange flowers from late summer to mid-autumn. Many plants cultivated under this name are now thought to be the hybrid *C. × ehemanii*. Zones 8–12.

Canna Hybrid Cultivars

☼/◑ ❉ ↔ 3 ft (0.9 m) ↕ 2–7 ft (0.6–2 m)

Large range of garden hybrids with complex and often uncertain parentage. The names *C. × generalis* and *C. × orchioides* have been used for these plants in the past. Ranging in size from 24 in (60 cm) dwarfs to over 7 ft (2 m) tall. Wide range of flower colors and forms. **'Durban'**, 4 ft (1.2 m) tall, with yellow-striped purple-red leaves, bright red flowers; **'Erebus'**, 6 ft (1.8 m) tall, silvery blue-green leaves, salmon pink flowers; **'Lucifer'** ★, 30 in (75 cm) high, dark foliage and yellow-edged red flowers; **'Minerva'**, 5 ft (1.5 m) tall, white and green striped foliage, yellow flowers opening from red buds over a long season; **'Pink Sunburst'**, 3 ft (0.9 m) high, pink-tinted yellow and green striped leave and salmon pink flowers; **'Red King Humbert'**, 7 ft (2 m) tall, bronze foliage and blood red flowers; **'Roi Humbert'**, 7–8 ft (2–2.4 m) tall, deep bronze foliage, orange-red flowers, sometimes yellow-marked; **'Striata'** (syn. 'Pretoria'), 6 ft (1.8 m) tall, leaves banded in light and dark shades of green, orange-pink flowers; Tropicanna/'Phasion', 7 ft (2 m) tall, vivid purple-red and yellow-orange striped foliage, bright orange flowers. Zones 8–12.

CARTHAMUS

A genus of 14 species of thistle-like annuals and perennials of the daisy (Asteraceae) family. Found mainly around the Mediterranean

and in western Asia, one species, the common *C. tinctorius*, now has a much wider distribution. Other species are seldom grown as they tend to become invasive. They are upright plants with stems that branch near the top to make a bushy clump of foliage. The leaves tend to be simple or pinnate with spine-tipped teeth. The whole plant is covered in fine downy hairs. Thistle-like heads with yellow, gold, pink, or violet ray florets appear in summer. Spiny bracts surround the base of the flowerheads.
CULTIVATION: They are easily grown in any sunny position with light, gritty, well-drained soil. Sometimes used as a quick filler in annual or perennial borders, they are more likely to be seen as a field-grown commercial crop or as a weed on waste ground.

Carthamus tinctorius
FALSE SAFFRON, SAFFLOWER
✺ ✽ ↔ 16–20 in (40–50 cm) ↑ 24–40 in (60–100 cm)
Native to the Mediterranean region. Lower leaves may be simple or pinnate, sometimes spiny; those on flower stem usually simple and spine-tipped. Flowerheads yellow, gold to orange or red, rarely white. Summer-flowering. 'Orange Gold' has intensely golden yellow flowerheads. Zones 4–10.

CATANANCHE
CUPID'S DART
This small genus, belonging to the daisy (Asteraceae) family, contains 5 species of annual or perennial herbs found in countries bordering the Mediterranean, inhabiting dry grassy areas. Leaves are usually long and narrow and arise at base of clump. Flowering stems are thin and wiry, bearing cornflower-like flowers of blue, white, or yellow. Bracts below the flowers are transparent and papery, often with a silver tinge.
CULTIVATION: *C. caerulea* is usually the only species seen in cultivation. Grow in full sun in any well-drained soil. It tends to be short-lived as a perennial, especially when grown in heavy clay, and can be treated as an annual. Plants propagated from seed will flower in the first year. Propagate by division in winter.

Catananche caerulea
BLUE CUPIDONE, BLUE SUCCORY, CUPID'S DART
✺ ✽ ↔ 12–18 in (30–45 cm)
↑ 24–30 in (60–75 cm)
Native to southwestern Europe and northern Africa. Low clumps of narrow, lance-shaped, grayish green leaves, sometimes with a few long teeth. Delicate stems of blue to mauve flowers, like cornflowers in color and appearance, in summer. 'Major' has flowers of deep blue. Zones 7–10.

Catharanthus roseus

CATHARANTHUS
Although related to the common periwinkle (*Vinca*), the 8 annuals and perennials of this genus, in the dogbane (Apocynaceae) family, are less hardy and tolerate little or no frost. All Madagascan natives, they are bushy plants with simple elliptical leaves on semi-succulent stems. Flat, 5-petalled flowers, mainly in pink and mauve shades, appear at the stem tip and leaf

Canna, Hybrid Cultivar, **Tropicanna**/'Phasion'

axils. Considered a weed in the tropics and subtropics, the commonly cultivated species *C. roseus* is a perennial often grown as a greenhouse plant or summer bedder in temperate gardens.
CULTIVATION: Very easily grown in sun or part-shade, periwinkles are drought tolerant but flower more heavily with summer moisture. Pinch back to encourage bushiness. In cool areas where winter frost would be fatal, bring plants indoors or discard and replace in spring. Propagate from seed or half-hardened summer cuttings.

Catharanthus roseus
syn. *Vinca rosea*
MADAGASCAR PERIWINKLE, ROSE PERIWINKLE
✺/❂ ✼ ↔ 16 in (40 cm) ↑ 24 in (60 cm)
Upright perennial from Madagascar. Glossy deep green leaves with pale midrib, to 2 in (5 cm) long. Mauve-throated, soft pink to red, 5-petalled flowers, with red "eye." 'Albus', white flowers; 'Blue Pearl', 18 in (45 cm) tall, white-centered lavender blue to mauve flowers; 'Blush Cooler', very pale pink flowers, light red center, one of the compact, 12 in (30 cm) tall, heavy-flowering **Cooler Series**; 'Pacifica Punch', deep pink flowers with slightly darker center, one of the 18 in (45 cm) tall **Pacifica Series**; 'Parasol', white flowers to 2 in (5 cm) wide, with red eye; the **Pretty Series**, very heat-tolerant; 'Stardust Orchid', cream-centered deep pink flowers, up to 16 in (40 cm) tall. Zones 11–12.

CELMISIA

MOUNTAIN DAISY, SNOW DAISY

Mainly from New Zealand, with a few species in southeastern Australia, this genus in the daisy (Asteraceae) family has some 60 species of perennials and subshrubs that frequently occur in subalpine and alpine regions where they often dominate the vegetation and may carpet large areas. They form basal rosettes or tufts of simple narrow leaves, sometimes ribbed, often with a covering of downy hair on the undersides. This hair can also cover the upper surfaces of young leaves. Woody stems can develop at the base, especially among the larger spreading species. The flowerheads are simple daisies with white ray florets around a central swelling of golden yellow disc florets. They are borne one head to a stem and appear mainly around mid-summer.
CULTIVATION: Only a few species adapt well to cultivation; many are difficult to grow outside their natural environment. They prefer a cool-summer temperate climate and should be planted in gritty, humus-rich, moist, well-drained soil in full or half-sun. Propagate from seed or by division.

Celmisia sessiliflora

WHITE CUSHION DAISY

☼/◐ ❄ ↔ 6–40 in (15–100 cm)
↑ 2–6 in (5–15 cm)
From South and Stewart Islands, New Zealand, common at altitude. Densely branched subshrub forming cushions of stiff, thick, silvery leaves less than 1 in (25 mm) long. Flowerheads abundant, usually at foliage level. Zones 7–9.

Celmisia spectabilis

COTTON DAISY, COTTON PLANT

☼/◐ ❄ ↔ 20–48 in (50–120 cm)
↑ 8–12 in (20–30 cm)
New Zealand species, found from the central North Island southward. The leaves are bright green, 4–6 in (10–15 cm) long with silver to buff-colored hairs, and grow in dense tufts. Plants can spread with age as a dense ground cover. Flowerheads to 2 in (5 cm) wide, on sturdy downy stems, in summer. Zones 7–9.

CELOSIA

COCKSCOMB, WOOLFLOWER

Found in the tropics of Asia, Africa, and the Americas, this genus of around 50 species of annuals and perennials belongs to the amaranth (Amaranthaceae) family. *C. argentea* var. *cristata*, an annual, is the only widely cultivated species and it has been developed into many variably flowered and colored seedling strains. Upright plants, some are up to 6 ft (1.8 m) tall, though most are far smaller. They have simple lance-shaped leaves up to 6 in (15 cm) long and tiny vivid yellow, orange, or red flowers massed in upright plumes or combs (cristate).
CULTIVATION: Although it can be grown far outside its natural range, *Celosia* needs ample warmth to perform well. Plant in fertile well-drained soil in full sun and water well. Raise from seed.

Celosia argentea

☼/◐ ✿ ↔ 16–24 in (40–60 cm) ↑ 3–7 ft (0.9–2 m)
Quick-growing annual, widespread in the tropics. Leaves lance-shaped to 6 in (15 cm) long. Tiny white flowers in upright spikes to 3 in (8 cm) long. Usually seen as *C. a.* var. *cristata;* cultivated forms have green, purple, or red foliage and many flower colors and styles: **Childsii Group**, rounded to globose flowerheads; **Cristata** or **Cockscomb Group**, flowerheads terminal, flattened and broad, resembling a rooster's comb; **Plumosa Group**, upright plumes of flowers, not always terminal, cultivars include 'Apricot Brandy', 'Forest Fire', 'Castle Mix', 'New Look', and 'Venezuela'; **Pyramidalis Group**, flowerheads broad-based, tapering evenly to a point, often included with Plumosa Group. Zones 11–12.

CENTAUREA

CORNFLOWER, KNAPWEED, STAR THISTLE

Widespread in temperate zones, this genus is a member of the daisy (Asteraceae) family and encompasses around 450 species of annuals, perennials, and subshrubs. A variable lot, most species are readily identifiable by their thistle-like flowerheads, which emerge from an egg-shaped receptacle known as an involucre. The flowerheads often have distinctly different inner and outer florets, with the outer having 5 longer petals. The range of flower colors includes white, yellow, pink, blue, and mauve. Plant size varies with the species; common features are pinnately lobed foliage, often silver-gray, and an upright habit.
CULTIVATION: Plant in full sun, in light well-drained soil. Good ventilation will lessen any mildew problems. Annuals can be raised from seed; perennials also propagated by division or from softwood cuttings of non-flowering stems.

Celosia argentea var. cristata, Plumosa Group, 'Venezuela'

Centaurea cineraria ★

syn. *Centaurea gymnocarpa*
DUSTY MILLER

☼ ❄ ↔ 12–24 in (30–60 cm) ↑ 20–36 in (50–90 cm)
From western and southern Italy. Perennial sometimes treated as an annual. Very decorative silver-gray pinnate leaves, Flowerheads purple-pink. Zones 7–10.

Centaurea cyanus

BACHELOR'S BUTTON, BLUEBOTTLE, CORNFLOWER

☼ ✿ ↔ 8–16 in (20–40 cm) ↑ 12–36 in (30–90 cm)
Annual or biennial from temperate Eurasia. Narrow green to blue-green leaves, sometimes silvery when young. Flowerheads are usually blue in the species but garden forms include white and a wide range of pink and blue shades. The flowering season is from late spring to summer; deadheading will prolong flowering. 'Blue Diadem', large, ruffled, double, deep blue heads; the **Florence Series**, a dwarf strain, to around 14 in (35 cm) high, wide color range. Zones 2–10.

Centaurea dealbata

Centaurea dealbata
PERSIAN CORNFLOWER

☼ ❋ ↔16–24 in (40–60 cm) ↕32–40 in (80–100 cm)

Caucasian and northern Iranian perennial. The pinnate leaves, to 8 in (20 cm) long, are green above with gray furry undersides. Pink to purple flowerheads are borne in summer. 'Steenbergii', large, vigorous, with attractive deep pink flowerheads. Zones 3–9.

Centaurea macrocephala
GLOBE CORNFLOWER

☼ ❋ ↔20–24 in (50–60 cm) ↕32–40 in (80–100 cm)

Erect perennial native to the Caucasus region. Green lance-shaped leaves covered with minute silvery hairs. Large yellow flowerheads. Zones 3–9.

Centaurea montana
MOUNTAIN BLUET, PERENNIAL CORNFLOWER

☼ ❋ ↔12–40 in (30–100 cm) ↕24–32 in (60–80 cm)

Perennial from mountains of Europe. Spreads by rhizomes and may form large clump of broad, green, lance-shaped leaves, sometimes pinnate at base. Flowerheads violet to purple-blue. 'Alba', low-growing, white-flowered cultivar. Zones 3–9.

CENTRANTHUS

This genus belongs to the valerian (Valerianaceae) family, and consists of 12 species of annual and perennial subshrubs from Europe and the Mediterranean, of which only one, *Centranthus ruber*, is widely cultivated. Forming clumps of upright stems with simple, lance-shaped, blue-green leaves and topped with inflorescences of tiny honey-scented flowers, the species can be 2–5 ft (0.6–1.5 m) tall. The flowers are most often a dusky crimson shade but may be white or pink.
CULTIVATION: These drought-tolerant and adaptable plants are very easily grown in any sunny well-drained position. Alkaline soil is preferred but not essential. To prevent seeding, cut back flower stems as soon as they fade. *C. ruber* is inclined to self-sow and is considered a weed in parts of New Zealand.

Centranthus ruber
JUPITER'S BEARD, RED VALERIAN

☼/◖ ❋ ↔16–27 in (40–70 cm) ↕32–40 in (80–100 cm)

Found in Europe, North Africa, and western Asia. Blue-green oval to lance-shaped leaves, are sometimes finely toothed, to 3 in (8 cm) long. Tiny, fragrant, deep rose pink to red flowers massed in upright heads. 'Albus' has white flowers. Zones 6–10.

CEPHALOTUS

A carnivorous pitcher plant and the only genus in the family Cephalotaceae, this is only found on the southwestern coast of Western Australia. Its small but very strong pitchers resemble little moccasins. Although a perennial, its growth slows and sometimes stops in the cool winters. In spring the plant produces non-carnivorous waxy leaves; as the weather warms, the carnivorous pitchers develop. Formed in a rosette, the outward-facing pitchers are covered in fine white hairs. The pitchers have a ribbed rim, a central rib, and 2 side ribs that slope toward the opening. In half-sun the pitchers are bright green but turn dark burgundy in full sun. Insects are attracted to the plant by the bright colors and the nectar just inside the pitcher's rim.
CULTIVATION: Grow in pots in a mixture of 3 parts peat, 1 part vermiculite and 2 parts sand or in a sunny bog garden. They do best in full sun (the pots can stand in water trays in summer); keep the soil just damp in the cooler months as plants are prone to root rot. Use a soil fungicide every few months. In its natural habitat, temperatures can reach up to 104°F (40°C) in summer but the winter nights are cool to cold. Propagate by division or from stem cuttings in late spring to early summer.

Cephalotus follicularis
ALBANY PITCHER PLANT, WESTERN AUSTRALIAN PITCHER PLANT

◖ ❁ ↔8 in (20 cm) ↕15 in (38 cm)

Robust rootstock that produces many short stems bearing 2 types of leaves: simple, spoon-shaped, green, fleshy, oval; and leaves modified to a pitcher-shaped container with a hinged lid, green, brown or red. Flowering stem can be 2 ft (0.6 m) high. Zone 9.

Cephalotus follicularis

CERASTIUM

A genus of about 100 species in the pink (Caryophyllaceae) family. Mostly annuals or perennials, the majority are vigorous carpeting ground covers or tufting plants; many are classed as weeds. Mainly found in Europe and North America, from temperate to arctic zones. Generally the leaves are small and are often hairy, giving a silvery appearance. The flowers are usually small and white. They are popular in rock gardens or massed in borders.
CULTIVATION: A well-drained soil in a position in full sun is a must for these plants. Some species can cope with poor or rocky soils. Propagation is from seed, cuttings, or by division.

Cerastium boissieri

syn. *Cerastium boissierianum*
✷ ✽ ↔ 8–16 in (20–40 cm)
↑ 6–10 in (15–25 cm)
European species, found particularly in Spain. Hairy white leaves. White flowers. Does well in sunny dry rock crevices. Zones 6–11.

Cerastium tomentosum

SNOW-IN-SUMMER
✷ ✽ ↔ 40 in (100 cm) ↑ 4–6 in (10–15 cm)
This species ranges widely through mountains of Europe and western Asia. A vigorous mat-former, this plant has whitish-woolly foliage. Profuse heads of starry white flowers, to 1 in (25 mm) wide, in spring–summer. Zones 6–11.

CHELIDONIUM

There is just one species of biennial or perennial herb in this genus of the poppy (Papaveraceae) family. It is native to Europe and western Asia and naturalized in the eastern USA. Variable species, branching from the base and with pinnate leaves, often with a 3-lobed terminal leaflet. Golden yellow flowers, to 1 in (25 mm) wide with 4 petals, are borne in loose terminal clusters.
CULTIVATION: This plant is suitable for the wild garden and shady corners in a range of soil types. It self-sows readily. Propagate from seed sown in situ.

Chelidonium majus

GREATER CELANDINE
✷/◑ ✽ ↔ 12–36 in (30–90 cm) ↑ 12–36 in (30–90 cm)
From Europe, western Asia, naturalized elsewhere. Brittle leafy stems. Summer-flowering. *C. m.* var. *laciniatum*, deeply cut leaves. *C. m.* 'Flore Pleno', more common double form. Zones 6–9.

CHELONE

SHELL FLOWER, TURTLE'S HEAD
This North American genus in the foxglove (Scrophulariaceae) family contains 6 species of herbaceous perennials. They have opposite leaves and bear tubular flowers with 2 lips. White to purple blooms are produced from mid-summer till cold weather arrives. They are long lasting if cut; seed heads can be dried.
CULTIVATION: These are happy in moisture-retentive soil in a half-sun to sunny position. Propagate by division, or from seed.

Chelone glabra

SNAKE HEAD, TURTLE'S HEAD
◑/◐ ✽ ↔ 16–20 in (40–50 cm) ↑ 20–32 in (50–80 cm)
From eastern and southern North America. White flowers, often stained pink or purple, to 1 in (25 mm) long, throughout summer and autumn. Zones 3–9.

Chelone lyonii ★

◑/◐ ✽ ↔ 24–36 in (60–90 cm) ↑ 40–48 in (100–120 cm)
Tall upright species, mainly found in Tennessee and North Carolina, USA. Deep pink flowers with a yellow beard on the inside lower lip, to 1 in (25 mm) long, throughout summer and into autumn. Zones 4–9.

CHLOROPHYTUM

This genus in the sisal (Agavaceae) family contains about 215 species of fleshy-stemmed perennials native to tropical and subtropical regions of Africa, Asia, and 1 species extending to northern Australia. They range in height from 4–24 in (10–60 cm), with linear to lance-shaped leaves arising from the rootstock. Small white flowers are borne in loose sparse panicles, and the flowering stems form new plantlets in some species.
CULTIVATION: A few species are cultivated for their foliage. The most commonly seen is the popular house plant *C. comosum*. In warmer

Chlorophytum comosum 'Variegatum'

areas where outdoor cultivation is possible, grow in light shade in well-drained soil. Can be grown as a ground cover. Indoor plants need bright indirect light and watering well when in full growth.

Chlorophytum comosum

SPIDER PLANT
◐ ❀ ↔ 12–24 in (30–60 cm) ↑ 12–24 in (30–60 cm)
From South Africa. Leaves to 16 in (40 cm) long, green or striped white. Loose panicles of small starry flowers. Can be invasive in mild moist climates. 'Variegatum', white or cream margins; 'Vittatum', recurved leaves with central white stripe. Zones 9–11.

Chlorophytum laxum

◐ ❀ ↔ 8–12 in (20–30 cm) ↑ 8–12 in (20–30 cm)
From tropical Africa to Southeast Asia and northern Australia. Fleshy-rooted perennial with linear leaves striped creamy white. Small white flowers are borne in loose panicles. Zones 10–12.

CHRYSANTHEMUM

syn. *Dendranthema*
Although once referred to as *Dendranthema*, the florists' chrysanthemum is now correctly known under its old name. There are about 40 species, mainly from East Asia.
CULTIVATION: Florists' chrysanthemums prefer a heavier richer soil and will tolerate some shade. Pinch back when young and disbud to ensure the best flower show. Annual species are raised from seed; the florists' forms by division when dormant or from half-hardened summer cuttings.

Chrysanthemum × *grandiflorum*

syn. *Dendranthema* × *grandiflorum*

FLORISTS' CHRYSANTHEMUM

☀️/❄️ ❄ ↔ 18–36 in (45–90 cm) ↑ 1–5 ft (0.3–1.5 m)

Encompassing a large group of hybrids, chrysanthemums are available from florists throughout the year; under garden conditions they are autumn-flowering. Although they tend to have similar lobed aromatic leaves, chrysanthemums occur in a wide range of plant sizes and flower types and are classified in groups based on flower characteristics. The United States National Chrysanthemum Society Standards recognizes these 13 classes.

1. **Irregular incurved:** Very large ball-shaped heads, with incurving florets, the lower ones often loose and irregular, creating a skirt. 'Gold Creamest', 'Palisade', and 'Shamrock' are examples.

2. **Reflexed:** Medium-sized to large heads, regular, downward curving florets, overlap neatly like scales or feathers. Included in this class are 'Euro', 'Fiji', and Robin/'Yorobi'.

3. **Regular incurved:** Heads 4–6 in (10–15 cm) wide, near-spherical heads, upward-curving florets. Includes 'Heather James'.

4. **Decorative:** Compact, rather flattened heads, distinct but short ray florets, no visible disc florets. Includes most of those known as spray chrysanthemums. Usually over 18 in (45 cm) tall. Popular examples include Barbara/'Yobarbara', 'Fortune', 'Margaret', 'Red Headliner', 'Salmon Margaret', 'Storm King', Sundoro/'Yosun', 'Wendy', and 'Wildfire'.

5. **Intermediate incurved:** Similar to irregular incurved but with smaller flowerheads, still around 6 in (15 cm) wide. Includes 'Primrose Allouise' and 'Royal Touch'.

6. **Pompon:** Small, densely petalled, spherical heads ranging from 1–4 in (2.5–10 cm) wide. Usually under 18 in (45 cm) tall. Popular hybrids include 'Carillon', 'Cheers', and 'Ping Pong'.

7. **Single and semi-double:** Simple heads, often very large, visible and clearly defined disc florets surrounded by one or more rows of ray florets. Singles sometimes known as 'daisies.' This group includes 'Amber Enbee Wedding', 'Buckeye', 'Golden Megatime', 'Megatime', 'Poser', 'Splendor', 'Tiger', and 'Tracy'.

8. **Anemone:** Basically semi-double in structure with a clearly defined halo of outer ray florets but smaller ray florets clustered and mounding at the center, and concealing the disc. Includes 'Day's End', 'Pennine Marie', 'Pennine Oriel', 'Powder Puff', 'Score', 'Sunny Le Mans', and 'Yellow Pennine Oriel'.

9. **Spoon:** Semi-double heads, clearly defined disc florets. Ray florets long, narrow, broaden to spoon shape at tips. Cultivars include 'Citrine', and 'Seminole'.

10. **Quill:** Large, regularly shaped heads, long, straight tubular florets open at tips. Includes 'Pennine Flute'.

11. **Spider:** Long, drooping, tubular florets, either narrow or broad, and often coiled or recurved at the tips. Popular hybrids include 'Dusky Queen', 'Mixed Spider', and 'Yellow Knight' ★.

12. **Brush or Thistle:** Very narrow, often twisted florets, lower of which stand out at right angles from stem.

13. **Unclassified:** Catch-all grouping covering blooms yet to be formally classified or not falling into any other categories. Includes 'Angora', 'Beacon', 'Bronze Cassandra', 'Cherry Nathalie', 'Eastleigh', 'George Griffiths', 'Harlekijn', 'Lemon Fiji', 'Mancetta Bride', 'Mavis', 'Myss Madi', 'Pennine Lace', 'Pink Gin', 'Roy Coopland', 'Rynoon', 'Southway Swan', and 'Weldon'. Zones 5–10.

Chrysanthemum weyrichii

syn. *Dendranthema weyrichii*

MIYABE DAISY

☀️/❄️ ❄ ↔ 16–24 in (40–60 cm) ↑ 4 in (10 cm)

Spreading perennial native to Japan. Leaves fleshy, glossy bright green, on purple-tinted stems. Short-stemmed flowerheads 1½ in (40 mm) wide with white or pink ray florets, in summer–autumn. 'Pink Bomb' and 'White Bomb', heavy-flowering. Zones 4–9.

CHRYSOGONUM

Part of the daisy (Asteraceae) family, this genus contains only one species—a low perennial herb native to eastern USA. It is a good ground cover for partly shaded borders and edges of woodlands. CULTIVATION: Plants prefer moist well-drained soil and part- to full shade. Propagate by division in early spring or early autumn; it also self-sows. Self-sown seedlings may be transplanted.

Chrysogonum virginianum

GOLDEN STAR, GREEN AND GOLD

☀️/❄️ ❄ ↔ 24 in (60 cm) ↑ 6–10 in (15–25 cm)

Coarse hairy leaves, serrated margin. Flowers yellow with 5 slightly notched petals, 1–1½ in (25–35 mm) wide, flowers from spring to early summer, and sporadically during summer. Will grow in colder areas provided it gets good snow cover. Zones 5–9.

Chrysanthemum × *grandiflorum*, 7. Single, 'Tiger'

Chrysanthemum × *grandiflorum*, 11. Spider, 'Mixed Spider'

Chrysanthemum weyrichii

CLARKIA
FAREWELL TO SPRING, GODETIA

This genus of 33 species of annual herbs belongs to the evening-primrose (Onagraceae) family. The majority are native to western North America. They are cultivated for their showy funnel-shaped flowers, which occur in shades of pink, red, purple, and sometimes yellow and white, from late spring to summer. The petals are often splashed with red or white. The flowers are long-lasting.
CULTIVATION: Grow in full sun in low to moderately fertile well-drained soil. They dislike hot humid conditions, so in warmer areas seed should be sown in autumn so that the plants will flower before the summer heat becomes intense. In cooler areas sow in early spring.

Clarkia amoena
syns *Clarkia grandiflora*, *Godetia amoena*
SATIN FLOWER
☼ ❀ ↔ 12 in (30 cm) ↑ 24 in (60 cm)
Showy species from northern California, USA. Densely packed spikes of cup-shaped flowers of pink to lavender, sometimes darkening at the base or shading to white, centers usually splashed with dark red. 'Grandiflora' (syn. 'Whitneyi'), flowers in shades of rose, pink, lavender, red, and white. Zones 7–10.

Clarkia pulchella
☼ ❀ ↔ 12 in (30 cm) ↑ 12–18 in (30–45 cm)
Found from the Rocky Mountains to the Pacific Coast, USA. Compact species. Frilly flowers of bright pink to lavender, sometimes with white or purple veining. Double forms of mixed colors are most commonly grown. Zones 7–10.

Clarkia unguiculata
syn. *Clarkia elegans*
☼ ❀ ↔ 12 in (30 cm) ↑ 24–30 in (60–75 cm)
From California. Commonly grown species with many cultivars. Flowers, 1 in (25 mm) across, ranging through pink, purple, and red shades, also yellow and white. Zones 7–10.

CLEMATIS (see page 772)

Clematis integrifolia
☼/◐ ❀ ↔ 3–5 ft (0.9–1.5 m) ↑ 3 ft (0.9 m)
Deciduous perennial or subshrub found from Europe to central Asia. Simple, lance-shaped leaves with downy undersides. Pendulous, flattened, bell-shaped flowers, to 4 in (10 cm) wide, deep violet-blue. Zones 3–9.

Clematis recta
☼/◐ ❀ ↔ 3–4 ft (0.9–1.2 m) ↑ 3–5 ft (0.9–1.5 m)
From southern and central Europe. Summer-flowering perennial with 5 to 7 blue-green leaflets. Small white flowers. Zones 3–9.

Clarkia pulchella, double mixed

CLEOME
SPIDER FLOWER

This largely tropical and subtropical genus of around 150 species of annuals and perennials belongs to the small caper (Capparidaceae) family. The commonly grown species are upright summer annuals. Their large palmate leaves have fine-toothed edges and stems that are sometimes spiny. Their 4-petalled flowers have long, protruding, filament-like stamens and are carried in apical heads with the filaments facing outward.
CULTIVATION: In areas with a warm summer the annuals are easily grown in any sheltered sunny position with moist, fertile, free-draining soil. Deadheading the flowers encourages longer blooming. With the exception of a few species, the perennials will not tolerate frost and need at least subtropical conditions. Propagate from spring-sown seed.

Cleome sesquiorygalis
syn. *Cleome spinosa*
SPIDER FLOWER
☼/◐ ◑ ↔ 20 in (50 cm) ↑ 5 ft (1.5 m)
Upright annual from southern Brazil, Paraguay, and northern Argentina. Palmate leaves with 5 to 7 finely toothed hairy leaflets to over 4 in (10 cm) long. Flowers clustered in terminal heads, petals to 1¼ in (30 mm) long with long filaments. In white and many shades of pink to purple. Several seedling strains and named forms, such as the Queen Series: 'Cherry Queen', 'Helen Campbell' (syn. 'White Queen'), 'Mauve Queen', 'Pink Queen', 'Purple Queen', 'Rose Queen', 'Ruby Queen'. Zones 10–12.

CLIVIA
FIRE LILY

This genus in the amaryllis (Amaryllidaceae) family consists of 4 species of perennials from southern Africa. Clump-forming with stocky rhizomes, they have long, bright green, strappy leaves and at various times, depending on the species, produce strong flower stems topped with heads of large funnel-shaped flowers in shades of yellow, orange, and red. Red berries follow flowering.
CULTIVATION: Tolerating only light frosts but otherwise quite easily grown, clivias are superb as greenhouse container plants. Outdoors they will be happiest when grown in dappled shade. Water well during the warmer months and allow to dry off for winter. Propagation is usually by division.

Cleome sesquiorygalis

Clivia caulescens
◐ ◑ ↔ 3–7 ft (0.9–2 m) ↑ 24 in (60 cm)
Spring-flowering species with leaves up to 6 ft (1.8 m) long, often drooping under their own weight. Flowers are pendulous,

green and yellow-tipped, salmon pink to soft red, tubular to narrow, funnel-shaped. Zones 10–11.

Clivia miniata

FIRE LILY

☀ ☒ ↔ 24–40 in (60–100 cm)
↕ 16–24 in (40–60 cm)

Leaves to 24 in (60 cm) long, sometimes quite broad. Wide open, funnel-shaped, yellow-throated, orange to nearly red flowers. Spring-flowering. *C. m.* f. *citrina*, primrose yellow flowers; cultivars include '**Kirstenbosch Yellow**' and '**Vico Yellow**', probably a hybrid. *C. m.* '**Aurea**', '**Flame** ★', '**Megen**', and '**Striata**' are attractive cultivars. Zones 9–11.

Clivia nobilis

GREENTIP FIRE LILY

☀ ☒ ↔ 20–36 in (50–90 cm)
↕ 16–24 in (40–60 cm)

Hardiest and most easily grown *Clivia*. Leaves to 18 in (45 cm) long, very finely toothed, producing a rough texture. Heads of green-tipped, yellow to red flowers. Spring-flowering. Zones 9–11.

CODONOPSIS

BONNET BELLFLOWER

This genus in the bellflower (Campanulaceae) family has around 30 species of herbaceous perennials that will climb on structures but prefer to scramble through surrounding vegetation. They have wiry, often twining stems and simple light-textured leaves of variable shape. The flowers are nodding, bell-shaped, with conspicuous calyces, and although fairly large they are often a pale blue-green color that merges well with the foliage. CULTIVATION: They are mostly very hardy and easily grown in any temperate climate with reasonable summer rainfall. They prefer woodland conditions with dappled light and cool, moist, humus-rich, well-drained soil. Try to remove the tangle of dry foliage and stems after it has died off, otherwise it may become very untidy. Propagate by division when dormant, or raise from seed.

Codonopsis clematidea

☀ ❀ ↔ 20–60 in (50–150 cm) ↕ 32 in (80 cm)

From central Asia. Slightly downy, 1 in (25 mm) long leaves tinted blue-green. In summer, very pale blue bell-shaped flowers, orange and black markings within. Zones 4–9.

COLLINSIA

This genus of 25 species of hardy annuals belongs to the foxglove (Scrophulariaceae) family. They are native to western North America and Mexico. They are grown for their attractive, tubular, 2-lipped flowers that are borne in whorls on slender stems. The flowers are in shades of white, lilac, rose, violet, and blue, and are often bicolored. Flowering is in spring and summer. CULTIVATION: Grow these plants in a rich, moist, but well-drained soil in sun or half-sun. They can also be grown as pot plants in a

Clivia miniata 'Vico Yellow'

conservatory, with shade from the hottest sun and a fortnightly dressing of weak liquid fertilizer. Propagate from seed.

Collinsia bicolor

syn. *Collinsia heterophylla*

CHINESE HOUSES, INNOCENCE

☀ ❀ ↔ 6–12 in (15–30 cm) ↕ 12–24 in (30–60 cm)

From California. Slender plants with lance-shaped leaves. Tubular 2-lipped flowers, borne on spikes in whorls of 2 to 7 blooms. Upper lip and tube are white, lower lip is rosy purple. Zones 7–10.

COLUMNEA

This mainly epiphytic genus of the African violet family (Gesneriaceae) contains around 160 species native to the New World tropics. They have arching to trailing or pendulous stems that form a crown of foliage. The small leaves are oval to lance-shaped and flowers are tubular. Red and orange are common flower colors; white, yellow, pink, and maroon also occur. CULTIVATION: Intolerant of frost, these are house or greenhouse plants outside the subtropics. They need a steady temperature, not necessarily hot, dappled light and shelter from cold drafts. Allow to dry in winter. Propagate from half-hardened tip cuttings.

Columnea 'Early Bird' ★

☀ ⟟ ↔ 18 in (45 cm) ↕ 48 in (120 cm)

Easily cultivated, consistent bloomer. Tolerates drought. Bright yellow flowers, red-orange edges, 2–3 in (5–8 cm) wide. Small, shiny, mid-green leaves, darker tips. Zones 11–12.

Columnea gloriosa ★

GOLDFISH PLANT

☀/☀ ⟟ ↔ 18 in (45 cm) ↕ 12 in (30 cm)

Central American species. Stems arch up before trailing. Hairy, pointed, oval leaves. Yellow-throated orange-red flowers borne singly, with hooded upper lip. Zones 11–12.

Columnea microphylla

❄/☀ ⚡ ↔ 2 ft (0.6 m) ↑ 6 ft (1.8 m)

Costa Rican species. Long, trailing stems. Red-haired rounded leaves less than ½ in (12 mm) long, with red undersides. Flowers borne singly, up to 3 in (8 cm) long, yellow markings, large hooded upper lip. Calyces often red-tinted, finely toothed. Zones 11–12.

Columnea scandens

❄/☀ ⚡ ↔ 24 in (60 cm) ↑ 12 in (30 cm)

From the West Indies and Central America. Cascading, sometimes arching stems. Deep green leaves, fine red hairs. Narrow flowers, singly or in pairs, fine-haired, nearly 3½ in (9 cm) long, red or yellow. Zones 11–12.

COMMELINA

DAY FLOWER, WIDOW'S TEARS

There are around 100 species of mainly perennial herbs in this genus, which gives its name to the spiderwort (Commelinaceae) family. They are native to mainly tropical and subtropical regions. The roots are often tuberous and the stems are usually slender and sprawling, rooting at the nodes. The flowers are held within spathe-like folded bracts. Commonly grown species have blue flowers, but white, yellow, rose, and lilac flowers occur. CULTIVATION: Grow in full sun in any well-drained soil. In cooler climates the tuberous species should be lifted in autumn. Propagate from seed or cuttings.

Commelina tuberosa

❄/☀ ⚡ ↔ 18–30 in (45–75 cm) ↑ 12–36 in (30–90 cm)

Variable perennial with tuberous roots, occurring from southern Mexico to Peru, in mountains. "Typical" form is low, spreading, and mounding. Brilliant blue flowers open continuously in spring–autumn. **Coelestis Group** (syn. *Commelina coelestis*) includes taller, more erect forms, larger flowers. Zones 9–12.

Columnea microphylla

CONSOLIDA

LARKSPUR

This Eurasian genus in the buttercup (Ranunculaceae) family has around 40 species. Larkspurs have fine feathery foliage, and about half their height is taken up with the upright, sometimes branching heads of their 5-petalled flowers. Pretty in the garden, they also make excellent cut flowers. Some parts of the plant, especially the seeds, are poisonous.
CULTIVATION: Plant these in fertile well-drained soil in full sun. They thrive in most conditions and will often self-sow, although the flowers of wild seedlings rarely amount to much. They may need staking. Raise from seed.

Consolida ajacis

syns *Consolida ambigua, Delphinium ajacis*
LARKSPUR

❄/☀ ⚡ ↔ 6–12 in (15–30 cm) ↑ 32–40 in (80–100 cm)

Mediterranean native with lacy finely cut foliage in basal clumps and wiry upright stems bearing heads of many spurred flowers in shades of blue, pink, or white. Garden forms occur in wide color range and include double flowers. **Giant Imperial Series**, including **'Giant Imperial Blue Spire'**, **'Giant Imperial Pink Perfection'**, and **'Giant Imperial White King'**, double flowers covering the entire color range with long spikes that last well and keep their color when dried. The **Dwarf Hyacinth Series** has short tightly packed spikes. Zones 9–11.

CONVOLVULUS

This genus of the family Convolvulaceae contains around 100 species of twining climbers, soft-stemmed shrubs, and herbaceous perennials from many temperate regions. The leaves are mostly narrow and thin textured. The widely flared funnel-shaped flowers bloom in succession over a long period.
CULTIVATION: Most *Convolvulus* species are hardy plants adaptable to a range of soils and situations, but all prefer a sunny position. Trim shrubby species regularly to encourage density of growth. They are easily propagated from cuttings.

Convolvulus cneorum

SILVERBUSH

❄ ❄ ↔ 2 ft (0.6 m) ↑ 2 ft (0.6 m)

From the Mediterranean. Bun-shaped plant, dense weak stems. Silvery, thin, narrow, silky leaves. White to pale pink flowers, darker pink stripes, flared, funnel-shaped, in spring–summer. Requires free drainage, good air circulation. Suited to coastal gardens, tolerates summer dryness. Zones 8–10.

Convolvulus sabatius ★

syn. *Convolvulus mauritanicus*

❄/☀ ❄ ↔ 24–60 in (60–150 cm) ↑ 8–12 in (20–30 cm)

Low spreading perennial species. Native to Italy and North Africa. Trailing stems. Fine-haired, gray-green, oval leaves to 1½ in (35 mm) long. Groups of 1 to 3 flowers in the leaf

Convolvulus tricolor

axils, pale mauve to purple, sometimes pink, to 1 in (25 mm) in diameter. Zones 8–10.

Convolvulus tricolor

☀/◐ ✽ ↔ 12–32 in (30–80 cm)
↕ 20–40 in (50–100 cm)

Found through southern Europe and in North Africa. Annual or short-lived shrubby or small climbing perennial. Small, pointed, oval leaves. Flowers to 2 in (5 cm) wide, borne singly in the leaf axils, in blue shades, often with a yellow throat. **Ensign Series**, brightly colored flowers with contrasting markings: **'Blue Ensign'**, white-edged, yellow-throated, deep blue flowers. Zones 8–10.

COREOPSIS

TICKSEED

Found in the Americas, especially in southwestern USA and Mexico, the 80-odd annuals and perennials (rarely shrubs) in this genus belong to the daisy (Asteraceae) family. They are compact plants that flower profusely, providing spectacular summer color. Most are shrubby plants, 2–4 ft (0.6–1.2 m) tall, with narrow, sometimes lobed leaves. The flowers are usually golden yellow, though garden forms occur in a variety of shades. The tips of the ray florets are often toothed as if cut with pinking shears.
CULTIVATION: Plant in a sunny position in light well-drained soil. These flower better with summer moisture but are quite drought tolerant. All can be raised from seed; the perennials will also grow from divisions or small basal cuttings from non-flowering stems.

Coreopsis grandiflora

☀/◐ ✽ ↔ 12–20 in (30–50 cm) ↕ 24 in (60 cm)

Bushy perennial from central and southern USA. Leaves to 4 in (10 cm) long; lower leaves often entire, upper tending towards pinnate. Long-stemmed flowerheads to slightly over 2 in wide, with around 8 ray florets. In the wild, colors range from pale yellow to gold. Flowers from late spring. **'Calypso'**, 14 in (35 cm) tall, cream variegated foliage, small red spots on ray florets; **'Early Sunrise'**, 18 in (45 cm) tall, gold double flowers; **'Kelvin Harbutt'**, up to 36 in (90 cm) tall, golden yellow flowerheads with red-brown disc florets. Zones 7–10.

Coreopsis lanceolata

☀/◐ ✽ ↔ 12–16 in (30–40 cm)
↕ 24 in (60 cm)

Tough perennial from central and southeastern USA. Leaves to 6 in (15 cm) long, lance-shaped to linear. Yellow flowerheads to 2½ in (6 cm) wide, usually with around 8 ray florets, in summer. A weed in Australia. **'Baby Gold'**, 16 in (40 cm) tall, golden flowers; **'Baby Sun'** (syn. 'Sonnenkind'), 12 in (30 cm) tall, gold flowers; **'Sterntaler'**, 16 in (40 cm) tall, gold flowers, ray florets with bronze-red basal blotch. Zones 3–9.

Coreopsis 'Sunray'

Coreopsis 'Sunray' ★

☀/◐ ✽ ↔ 12–16 in (30–40 cm) ↕ 20 in (50 cm)

Compact bushy plant with entire and pinnate foliage, bright green, leaflets often narrow. Glowing yellow double flowers from late spring. Often listed as a *C. grandiflora* cultivar. Zones 7–10.

Coreopsis tinctoria

☀/◐ ✽ ↔ 16–24 in (40–60 cm) ↕ 4 ft (1.2 m)

Summer-flowering annual found over much of North America. Leaves usually narrow and entire, sometimes pinnate, to 4 in (10 cm) long. Many small flowerheads, ray florets yellow, reddening at base, disc florets red-brown. **'Mahogany Midget'**, 12 in (30 cm) tall, all-over red-brown flowerheads. Zones 6–10.

Coreopsis verticillata

☀/◐ ✽ ↔ 16 in (40 cm) ↕ 36 in (90 cm)

Upright perennial from southeastern USA. Sticky doubly pinnate leaves, 3 leaflets per section, may be very narrow, to 2½ in (6 cm) long. Bright yellow flowerheads to 2 in (5 cm) wide, in summer. Attractive cultivars include **'Golden Gain'**, 20 in (50 cm) tall, narrow leaf segments, bright yellow flowers; **'Grandiflora'** (syn. 'Golden Shower'), 24 in (60 cm) tall, large bright yellow flowers; **'Moonbeam'**, 20 in (50 cm) tall, soft yellow flowers; and **'Zagreb'**, 12 in (30 cm) tall, pale gold flowers. Zones 6–10.

CORNUS (see page 126)

Cornus canadensis

BUNCHBERRY, CREEPING DOGWOOD

◐ ✽ ↔ 36 in (90 cm) ↕ 4–6 in (10–15 cm)

Cornus canadensis

Found from Greenland to Alaska. Hardy, low, deciduous perennial, spreading by rhizomes. Whorls of ovate to lance-shaped leaves, vivid red autumn color. Large white bracts around flowerheads. Summer-flowering. Red edible fruit. Likes cool moist conditions. Zones 2–8.

CORYDALIS

The 300-odd species of annuals and perennials in this genus belong to the poppy (Papaveraceae) family. Mainly confined to the northern temperate zones, the perennials spread by rhizomes or tubers to form clumps of ferny, often blue-green foliage. Their flowers are borne in racemes and are tubular, with 4 tiny petals and a long spur. The flowers are showy, combining well with the delicate foliage. The blue-flowered *C. flexuosa* and its cultivars are probably the most widely grown of the genus.
CULTIVATION: These plants are mostly very hardy, preferring temperate climates that have distinct seasons. Woodland or rockery conditions are best, with moist, cool, humus-rich, well-drained soil. If soil remains moist, they will grow in full sun, though part-shade is preferable. Propagate by division or from seed.

Corydalis flexuosa 'Père David'

Corydalis cashmeriana

☀ ❊ ↔ 12–32 in (30–80 cm) ↑ 10 in (25 cm)
Perennial from the Himalayas. Bright green ferny foliage with leaflets to 1 in (25 mm) long. Bright blue flowers, conspicuously spurred, ½–1 in (12–25 mm) long, in racemes of up to 8 blooms. Late spring- to summer-flowering. Zones 5–9.

Corydalis flexuosa

☀/☀ ❊ ↔ 12–32 in (30–80 cm) ↑ 12 in (30 cm)
Perennial from southwestern China. Blue-green leaves die after flowering. Bright blue flowers, mildly scented, spurred, to 1 in

(25 mm) long, in spring–early summer. Attractive cultivars include 'Bronze Leaf', leaves purplish, especially at tips, light blue flowers; 'China Blue', deep blue flowers; 'Père David', bright blue flowers to 2 in (5 cm) long; and 'Purple Leaf', deep blue flowers, purplish foliage. Zones 5–9.

Corydalis ochroleuca

☀ ❊ ↔ 12–32 in (30–80 cm) ↑ 8–16 in (20–40 cm)
Southern European perennial. Leaves strongly blue-green. Flowers very pale yellow to cream, ½ in (12 mm) long. Zones 5–9.

Corydalis wilsonii

☀ ❊ ↔ 12–32 in (30–80 cm)
↑ 12–16 in (30–40 cm)
Chinese perennial. Bright green to bronze-green, finely divided, ferny leaves to 4 in (10 cm) long. Small racemes of bright yellow flowers with yellow-green tips, in spring. Zones 7–9.

COSMOS

MEXICAN ASTER

This genus of the daisy (Asteraceae) family is found in the Americas from the tropics to the warm temperate zones. It contains 26 species, including both annuals and perennials, of which 3 are commonly grown. The common annual cosmos (*C. bipinnatus*) has fine feathery foliage and showy, large, wide-open flowers with 8 ray florets. It is available in many colors and varieties, from dwarf to 7 ft (2 m) tall. The common perennial species have broader leaves and smaller flowers than the annual *C. bipinnatus*, but are interesting for their colors and scents.
CULTIVATION: Annual species should be planted out only when all danger of frost has passed; perennials tolerate occasional moderate frosts. Plant in full sun with moist, well-drained soil. Do not overfeed or the plants may become top-heavy; they may need staking anyway. Propagate the annuals from seed and the perennials from basal cuttings.

Cosmos bipinnatus

☀/☀ ❊ ↔ 2–4 ft (0.6–1.2 m) ↑ 4–7 ft (1.2–2 m)
Annual native to Mexico and southern USA. Ferny pinnate leaves to over 4 in (10 cm) long, with very fine narrow leaflets. Flowerheads large and long-stemmed. Pink to lavender flowers in the wild, but many garden forms and seedling strains. 'Candystripe', 24 in (60 cm) tall, white flowers with red stripes; 'Dazzler', 4 ft (1.2 m) tall, bright crimson flowers; 'Picotee' 30 in (75 cm) tall, white to pale pink flowers flushed and edged deep pinkish red; Sensation Series, 3–4 ft (0.9–1.2 m) tall, wide color range; Sonata Series, 24–36 in (60–90 cm) tall, simple, daisy-like flowers in shades of pink and white; 'Sweet Dreams', 30–36 in (75–90 cm), soft pink flowers with darker center. Zones 7–11.

Cosmos sulphureus

☀/☀ ❊ ↔ 32 in–48 in (80 cm–120 cm) ↑ 5–7 ft (1.5–2 m)
Annual found from northern South America to Mexico. Pinnate, sometimes faintly hairy leaves to 14 in (35 cm) long.

Cosmos bipinnatus

Flowerheads deep yellow through orange to red. Several seedling strains. '**Bright Lights**', to 4 ft (1.2 m) tall, yellow, orange and red shades; '**Cosmic Yellow**', to 24 in (60 cm) tall, bright yellow single and semi-double flowers; **Ladybird Series**, 12–16 in (30–40 cm) tall, pale yellow to deep red flowers; '**Sunny Red**', 12–16 in (30–40 cm) tall, bright red flowers. Zones 7–11.

COSTUS
SPIRAL FLAG, SPIRAL GINGER

This genus in the ginger (Zingiberaceae) family has around 90 rhizome-rooted perennial species and is found throughout the tropics. They form clumps of strong cane-like stems with lance-shaped leaves, usually around 8–10 in (20–25 cm) long, spiralling around them. Their spikes of 3-petalled flowers, subtended by bracts and sometimes a ruff of leaves, are bright, flat, and crepe-textured. They usually bloom in the warmer months; then the spike develops into a cone-like fruit, best removed to encourage repeat flowering.

CULTIVATION: Many can survive in mild climates if the soil does not freeze and the summers are warm enough to encourage strong growth. Propagate from seed, from spring basal cuttings, or by dividing clumps in late winter or very early spring.

Costus igneus
FIERY COSTUS

◑ ⊰ ↔ 20–40 in (50–100 cm) ↕ 20 in (50 cm)

Brazilian species with purple-tinted stems and 4–8 in (10–20 cm) long, dark green leaves with reddish undersides. Bright orange flowers through winter. Little or no dormant period. Zones 10–12.

Costus pulverulentus

◑ ⊰ ↔ 2–5 ft (0.6–1.5 m) ↕ 5–10 ft (1.5–3 m)

Found from southern Mexico to Peru. Narrow, velvety, blue-green leaves to 12 in (30 cm) long, with red-tinted undersides and silvery veins. Upright inflorescences to 3 in (7.5 cm) long, with bright red flowers. Zones 10–12.

CRYPTANTHUS
EARTH STARS

The 50 species of this genus in the pineapple (Bromeliaceae) family are found from eastern to southern Brazil, growing in the ground or on rocks, under the protection of trees or bushes. They are generally small and flattened, with an irregular star shape. The triangular leaves are stiff and broad and of many colors, often with crossbands or longitudinal stripes. There are 2 main groups. One has no flower stem and the flowerhead nestles in the center of the plant; there is male dominance in the flowers in the center but female dominance in the outer flowers. The other group has similar flowers throughout the flowerhead, which is on a short stem. The petals are white for both groups.

CULTIVATION: These need more moisture than most bromeliads, and protection in the winter. They are best grown in shallow pots, and are recommended for indoor culture and greenhouse

Cryptanthus zonatus

Costus pulverulentus

conditions in cool-temperate areas, or outdoors with protection from direct continuous sunlight and extremes of rain in warm-temperate, subtropical, and tropical areas. Water when potting mix is dry. Fertilizer extra to that already incorporated in good quality potting mix is not necessary. Propagate from offsets.

Cryptanthus acaulis

◑ ⊰ ↔ 6 in (15 cm) ↕ 2 in (5 cm)

The most common and most hardy of the genus; can survive 32°F (0°C). Plant more circular in general shape than the more usual oval. Leaves triangular, to 4 in (10 cm), a scurfy green, sometimes reddish. Zones 9–10.

Cryptanthus bivittatus

◑ ⊰ ↔ 10 in (25 cm) ↕ 2 in (5 cm)

Plant resembles an open star. Leaves dark green with 2 broad, longitudinal, white or pinkish stripes. The center of '**Starlite**' (syn. '**Starlight**') is cream to light pink instead of dark green; '**Pink Starlite**', center stripe dark green, rest of leaf hot pink. Zones 10–12.

Cryptanthus fosterianus

◑ ⊰ ↔ 16 in (40 cm) ↕ 2 in (5 cm)

Narrow oval plant, irregular in shape. Leaves to 12 in (30 cm) long, thick and fleshy, wavy along the edges, coloring maroon with wavy gray crossbands. Zones 10–12.

Cryptanthus 'Rainbow Star'

◑ ⊰ ↔ 16 in (40 cm) ↕ 16 in (40 cm)

Variegated plant, leaves striped in green, white, and pink. Two forms, one stiffer leafed than other. Best allowed to offset freely; when settled into a large clump it will flower. Zones 10–12.

Cryptanthus zonatus

◑ ⊰ ↔ 12 in (30 cm) ↕ 2 in (5 cm)

Oval plant, irregular in shape. Leaves grow to 8 in (20 cm) long and are thick, fleshy, wavy along edges, mainly green, with wavy, shiny, gray crossbands. Zones 10–12.

Ctenanthe oppenheimiana 'Tricolor'

CTENANTHE

This genus in the arrowroot (Marantaceae) family contains about 15 species of evergreen perennials. They are native to Costa Rica and Brazil, where they grow on damp forest floors and in scrub. Arising from rhizomes, stems are single or branching, with leaves arising from sheaths at the nodes. The leaves are leathery, oblong, pointed, usually matt, often with colored markings.
CULTIVATION: In suitably warm climates grow in a shady sheltered position. In temperate climates they are cultivated as indoor plants. Grow in bright filtered light. During active growth, water moderately and apply liquid fertilizer fortnightly. Propagate by division or from cuttings.

Ctenanthe burle-marxii
☀ ❁ ↔ 12–18 in (30–45 cm) ↑ 18 in (45 cm)
From Brazil. Leaves to 6 in (15 cm) long, pale green, with sickle-shaped darker markings on upperside and dark purple beneath. Leaf sheaths also tinged purple. Zones 10–12.

Ctenanthe lubbersiana ★
☀ ❁ ↔ 18–24 in (45–60 cm) ↑ 18–24 in (45–60 cm)
From Brazil. Widely branching stems with narrow oblong leaves, deep green with yellow variegation on upperside, pale green beneath. Zones 10–12.

Ctenanthe oppenheimiana
syn. *Maranta lubbersiana*
NEVER NEVER PLANT
☀ ❁ ↔ 24–36 in (60–90 cm) ↑ 36 in (90 cm)
From eastern Brazil. Bushy plant with leathery oblong leaves to 16 in (40 cm) long, green, with silvery marking on upperside and deep red beneath. 'Tricolor', dark green leaves with irregular creamy yellow markings. Zones 10–12.

CYNOGLOSSUM

HOUND'S TONGUE
This genus in the borage (Boraginaceae) family has around 55 species of annuals, biennials, and perennials, found mainly in the temperate zones. They have simple, elongated, elliptical to lance-shaped leaves, often densely covered with fine hairs, that form a basal foliage clump. Upright flower stems emerge from the clump, branching into racemes of small 5-petalled flowers, usually in vivid blue shades. The flowers appear mainly in summer.
CULTIVATION: Most will tolerate quite severe short frosts, if not prolonged freezing. Perfect drainage is essential and summer moisture will improve flowering, so incorporate extra grit and humus. Deadhead the plants frequently to prolong flowering. Taller types may need to be staked or tied back. *Cynoglossum* are ideal for border planting. They can be raised from seed; the perennial species can also be propagated from basal cuttings.

Cynoglossum amabile
CHINESE FORGET-ME-NOT
☀/❁ ❋ ↔ 12 in (30 cm) ↑ 20–24 in (50–60 cm)
Biennial from temperate East Asia. Oval to lance-shaped basal leaves to 8 in (20 cm) long, often finely hairy. Sprays of white, pink, or blue flowers, ¼ in (6 mm) wide. 'Firmament', dwarf cultivar, gray-green leaves and slightly pendulous bright blue flowers. Zones 7–10.

Cynoglossum nervosum
HAIRY HOUND'S TOOTH
☀/❁ ❋ ↔ 24 in (60 cm) ↑ 24–30 in (60–75 cm)
Bushy upright perennial, native to the Himalayas. Oblong green leaves with short stiff hairs; intense blue flowers, in late spring, last for about 4 weeks. Soil must be well drained. Very suitable for a woodland setting, or for an informal garden. Zones 4–9.

DAMPIERA

Endemic to Australia, this large genus of 66 species is part of the Goodeniaceae family. Most of the species are perennial herbs with a few shrubby species occurring in a range of soil types from pure sand to clay, and in habitats from forests and woodlands to arid parts of the continent, and from sea level to montane. Most species occur in the southwest of Western Australia. Leaf shape ranges from simple and smooth-edged to lobed or toothed, basal or alternate on the stems, glabrous to densely woolly hairy. The flowers are an irregular shape, borne singly or in terminal or axillary clusters. Color is predominantly blue with some species' flowers being mauve to purple, only a couple of species being white, pink, or yellow. A few species produce suckers.
CULTIVATION: Propagation is from stem or leaf cuttings, or by division of the suckering species. Seeds are not easily obtained, but even when available, germination is not assured. Smoke treatment has been successful with germinating some of the western species, but cultivation of most of these has been rather difficult in non-Mediterranean climates of eastern Australia and elsewhere. Several other species now commonly cultivated. Tissue culture is a propagation method.

Dampiera diversifolia ★
☀ ❋ ↔ 40–60 in (100–150 cm) ↑ 4–20 in (10–50 cm)
A perennial prostrate herb from habitats in southwestern Australia, suckering readily in cultivated forms. Lance-shaped,

glabrous, slightly toothed basal leaves. Prostrate stems with smaller leaves, narrow and not toothed. Purple-blue flowers, borne in leaf axils during spring to summer, in great profusion, almost obscuring rest of plant. Zones 8–10.

DARLINGTONIA

CALIFORNIA PITCHER PLANT, COBRA LILY

This is a single species genus, belonging to the pitcher-plant (Sarraceniaceae) family, which also includes *Heliamphora* and *Sarracenia*. The plant grows in and around springs and streams, in sphagnum bogs, and wherever it has access to cool running water. Found at both high and low altitudes in northern California and southern Oregon, USA, this carnivorous herbaceous perennial is characterized by the cobra-like head of the pitcher, which resembles a snake poised to strike, fangs and all! Insects are attracted by the bright green or dark red pitchers and smell of nectar from around the rim. The nectar lures an insect to where it is trapped by downward pointing hairs and dissolved in liquid at base of pitcher. Unlike that of *Sarracenia*, this liquid does not contain digestive enzymes and the insect's body is broken down by bacteria.
CULTIVATION: These plants should be grown in sphagnum moss, in concrete or terracotta pots standing in a saucer of water, in full or half-sun. The most important key to growing *Darlingtonia* plants successfully is to keep their roots cool. In warm to hot weather, use chilled water. Propagate by removing the new plantlets that grow on the end of the fleshy stem.

Darlingtonia californica ★
☼/◐ ❄ ↔ 8–10 in (20–25 cm) ↑ 24–40 in (60–100 cm)
Perennial pitcher plant. Slender pitchers have bulbous hood with fishtail or fang-like tongues protruding from the hood's base. Red and green nodding flowers stand singly on a leafless stalk, in spring–late summer. Zones 6–9.

DARMERA

syn. *Peltiphyllum*
This genus of one species is native to western North America and is a member of the saxifrage (Saxifragaceae) family. It is a large herbaceous perennial, found along stream sides and in damp woods, grown for its dramatic foliage and early flowers. It is recommended for a bog garden or fernery.
CULTIVATION: Plant in moist to wet soils, rich in organic matter, in a cool sheltered site. Propagate by division of established clumps, although raising from seed is an option if sown fresh.

Darmera peltata
syn. *Peltiphyllum peltatum*
◐ ❄ ↔ 3–10 ft (0.9–3 m) ↑ 5–7 ft (1.5–2 m)
Herbaceous perennial with rounded heads of tiny pink flowers prior to foliage in very early spring. Huge leaves soon follow like bright green umbrellas. Dwarf form also grown. Zones 6–10.

DELPHINIUM

This genus is sometimes known as larkspur, although that name is best reserved for its relatives in the genus *Consolida*. A member of the buttercup (Ranunculaceae) family, *Delphinium* consists of around 250 species of annuals, biennials, and perennials. Most species form a basal clump of finely divided or lobed foliage, from which develops an upright spike bearing long-spurred, 4-petalled flowers backed by 5 sepals that sometimes become bract-like. Plant sizes vary markedly with the species: the smaller species may not exceed 12 in (30 cm) tall, while the fancy hybrids can grow to over 7 ft (2 m). Flower colors vary, but *Delphinium* is best known for the intense blue flowers it often produces.
CULTIVATION: They do best in an open airy position that lessens the risk of mildew. However, the more exposed the location, the more important it is that the plants are staked to prevent damage from wind. Plant in moist, humus-rich, fertile soil and water well while in flower. Propagate from seed or basal cuttings, or by division.

Delphinium × belladonna
☼/◐ ❄ ↔ 6–20 in (15–50 cm)
↑ 12–40 in (30–100 cm)
Perennial hybrid crosses between *D. elatum* and *D. grandiflorum*. Compact, sometimes dwarf, with finely divided dark green foliage. Flowers to 1¼ in (30 mm) wide. Many selected forms, including '**Bellamosum**', intensely dark blue flowers; '**Blue Sensation**', bright mid-blue flowers; and '**Cliveden Beauty**', light sky blue flowers. Zones 3–9.

Delphinium × belladonna

Delphinium cardinale
☼/◐ ❄ ↔ 8–20 in (20–50 cm) ↑ 3–7 ft (0.9–2 m)
A short-lived perennial, sometimes annual or biennial, from California, USA. Dark green, finely divided, basal foliage. Wiry upright flower stems; widely spaced red flowers, with yellow centers, in summer. Zones 8–10.

Darlingtonia californica

Delphinium grandiflorum 'Tom Pouce'

Delphinium elatum

☼/◑ ❄ ↔ 8–20 in (20–50 cm) ↕ 2–6 ft (0.6–1.8 m)
Summer-flowering Eurasian perennial. Downy or hairy leaves with 5 to 7 lobes toothed or further divided. Strong upright flower stems, dense racemes of blue flowers, in summer. Zones 3–9.

Delphinium grandiflorum

syn. *Delphinium chinense*

☼/◑ ❄ ↔ 12–24 in (30–60 cm) ↕ 12–40 in (30–100 cm)
Perennial from temperate East Asia. Low bushy foliage clump, very finely divided bright green leaves. Racemes of vivid blue flowers, sometimes quite tall and upright, usually short and lax. 'Blue Butterfly', masses of deep blue flowers on short stems; 'Tom Pouce', bright gentian blue flowers. Zones 3–9.

Delphinium nudicaule

☼/◑ ❄ ↔ 8–16 in (20–40 cm) ↕ 12–24 in (30–60 cm)
Perennial from California, USA. Short-lived, sometimes annual or biennial. Leaves coarsely lobed, secondary divisions fine, downy, dull green. Wiry flower stems with widely spaced, orange-red flowers marked yellow on upper lips, from late spring. Zones 8–10.

Delphinium Hybrid Cultivars

☼ ❄ ↔ 1½–3 ft (0.5–0.9 m) ↕ 4–7 ft (1.2–2 m)
Extensively selected and hybridized to produce the Elatum Group, which includes 'Albert Shepherd', medium height, light blue flowers with pink flush and buff center; 'Angela Harbutt', medium to tall, pinkish mauve; 'Blue Dawn', medium to tall, bright deep blue with white eye; 'Blue Lagoon', medium to tall, pure dark blue with light eye; 'Blue Nile', low-growing, clear mid-blue with contrasting white center; 'Bruce', tall, deep violet-purple with lavender to gray eye; 'Cassius', medium height, mid-blue often suffused with mauve, black center; 'Claire', low-growing, pale pink to nearly white at the center; 'Clifford Park', medium height, shades of pink; 'Conspicuous', medium height, mauve with large brown center; 'Constance Rivett', medium height, pure white; 'Cupid', short, blue with white eye; 'Emily

Hawkins', tall and strong-growing, lavender suffused with blue, buff center; 'Fanfare', tall, pale silvery mauve, early flowering; 'Faust', tall, intense almost metallic deep blue with hint of purple; 'Fenella', medium height, bright pure blue with black center; 'Gillian Dallas', medium height, gray-blue with white center, late flowering; 'Giotto', medium height, purple-blue with mustard center; 'Harlekijn', deep violet, semi-double with blackish center; 'Kathleen Cooke', medium height, mid-blue with white eye; 'Langdon's Royal Flush', medium height, dusky pink with white center; 'Loch Leven', low-growing, light blue with white eye; 'Lord Butler', low-growing, soft mid-blue with white eye, compact and heavy flowering; **Magic Fountain Series** ★, seedling strain, in wide color range; 'Michael Ayres', medium height, deep pinkish violet with dark center; 'Mighty Atom', short semi-double, deep mauve, late flowering; 'Min', medium height, lavender with dark veining; the **New Century** hybrids, to over 4 ft (1.2 m) tall, come in a wide range of colors; 'Our Deb', mid-sized, soft pink with dark eye; 'Rosemary Brock', medium height, soft mid-pink with a buff center; 'Sandpiper' ★, tall, white with black center; 'Spindrift', medium height, flower variable, usually turquoise shade but sometimes also with blue or pink flowers; 'Sungleam', medium height, creamy yellow with yellow eye; 'Thamesmead', short to medium, gentian blue with black eye; 'Tiddles', medium height, semi-double, dusky mauve; and 'Walton Gemstone', medium height, pale lavender blue flowers with white eye. Zones 3–9.

DERWENTIA

This small genus of 8 species is a member of the foxglove (Scrophulariaceae) family, and occurs in subalpine to lower mountain regions of southeastern Australia. They are evergreen perennials or subshrubs, with the ability to re-sprout from the rootstock. Leaves are opposite and variously shaped, some species being highly glaucous. White, blue, or mauve flowers are borne in dense spikes in spring and summer.

CULTIVATION: Propagation is usually from cuttings, with most success being from fresh new growth taken from sprouting rootstocks. Seeds are not readily obtained, but if available they should be sown when fresh.

Delphinium, Hybrid Cultivar, 'Albert Shepherd'

Delphinium, Hybrid Cultivar, 'Clifford Park'

Derwentia perfoliata

syns *Parahebe perfoliata*, *Veronica perfoliata*

DIGGER'S SPEEDWELL

☼ ❄ ↔ 20–60 in (50–150 cm) ↕ 12–26 in (30–65 cm)

Occurs in a range of habitats from central New South Wales, generally above 1,640 ft (500 m) altitude, south to eastern and central western Victoria, Australia. Small shrubby perennial with woody rootstock. Stems mostly held erect, glaucous, with finely toothed, oval-shaped, leathery leaves, in 2s or 3s at nodes. Bluish flowers in terminal and axillary spikes, in spring–summer. Propagate from seeds and cuttings. Zones 8–9.

DEUTEROCOHNIA

syn. *Abromeitiella*

Mainly found from northern Argentina, Peru, and Bolivia, this genus of 15 species is a member of the pineapple (Bromeliaceae) family. The rosette-forming plants are sun-loving and prickly, growing in the ground or on rocks, and they form large clumps. There are 2 groups of species: one consists of low-growing plants that look like cushions in the wild, generally with green tubular flowers; the other group is made up of larger plants that have mainly yellow flowers on long stems. The genus is unique among bromeliads because it has perennial flowering shoots that produce new branches each year.

CULTIVATION: Smaller species can be grown indoors, larger species are best in greenhouses or conservatories in cool-temperate areas, or outdoors in warm-temperate, subtropical, and tropical areas. Water when dry; do not over-fertilize. Propagate from seed or offsets.

Deuterocohnia lorentziana

Deuterocohnia brevifolia ★

syn. *Abromeitiella brevifolia*

☼/◑ ❄ ↔ 4–12 in (10 cm) ↕ 2–4 in (5–10 cm)

From northern Argentina. The plants eventually form broad mounds. Triangular green leaves, with a few spines along edge. Flowers green, tubular, solitary, and stalkless among leaves. *D. b.* subsp. *chlorantha*, more flexible spines on leaf. Zones 8–10.

Deuterocohnia lorentziana

syn. *Abromeitiella lorentziana*

◉ ❄ ↔ 4 in (10 cm) ↕ 4 in (10 cm)

From northern Argentina. Clump-forming plants. Triangular grayish leaves, few spines along edge. Petals tubular, green. Zones 8–10.

DIANELLA

A member of the daylily (Hemerocallidaceae) family, this genus of evergreen perennials has some 20 species from Australia, New Zealand, and Pacific Islands. One tropical species *(D. ensifolia)* extends to mainland Asia as far as China, Japan, and India, and to East Africa and Madagascar. *Dianella* are herbaceous plants with fibrous roots, often with underground rhizomes. The stems are creeping or erect, bearing a terminal fan of leaves. The leaves are grass-like, in 2 ranks, sheathing at the base and often with the lower edges folded and fused together. Inflorescence is a loose panicle with flowers on nodding stalks. The flowers have perianth segments, in 2 whorls of 3, blue to white, sometimes tinged green or purple. Fruit is a pale blue to dark purple-blue berry. Seeds are black and shiny.

CULTIVATION: In warmer regions they are grown in borders or wild plantings; elsewhere best under glass. Some will tolerate temperatures down to 20°F (–7°C) or even lower, others are frost tender. Tolerate light shade. These plants are easily propagated by division or from seed.

Dianella tasmanica

syns *Dianella archeri*, *D. densa*, *D. hookeri*

BLUE FLAX-LILY, TASMANIAN FLAX-LILY

◑ ❄ ↔ 12 in (30 cm) ↕ 40 in (100 cm)

Occurs in forests of southeastern Australia. Tufted perennial, rarely forms clumps. Leaves to 40 in (100 cm) long, green, inflorescences may exceed the leaves in length. Blue flowers in spring–summer. Large globular berries, bluish purple, containing many shiny black seeds. Zones 8–10.

DIANTHUS

CARNATION, PINK

The 300 or so species in this genus in the pink (Caryophyllaceae) family are tufting or spreading perennials largely from the Eurasian region. Most have narrow, somewhat grassy, blue-green leaves emerging directly from a dense basal clump or on wiry spreading stems. The flowers are simple 5-petalled structures, often with a powerful spicy scent. Flower stem length varies greatly. The common flower color is pink, and the petal edges ragged, which appear as if cut with pinking shears. Most species flower from late spring.

CULTIVATION: Plant in a bright, open position in moist, well-drained, humus-rich soil. Most appreciate a little lime and need regular feeding to prevent center of clump from dying out. Propagate from seed or small basal cuttings known as "slips," or by division.

Dianella tasmanica

Dianthus alpinus

☼/◑ ❄ ↔ 6–12 in (15–30 cm) ↕ 4–6 in (10–15 cm)

Short-lived perennial from European Alps. Leaves dark green and grassy. Flowers deep pinkish red with darker spots, white eye. 'Joan's Blood', maroon-centered with deep red flowers. Zones 3–9.

Dianthus gratianopolitanus 'Baker's Variety'

Dianthus, Hybrid Cultivar, Annual Bedding, Melody Series, 'Melody Pink Blush'

Dianthus, Hybrid Cultivar, Perennial, Perpetual-flowering, Self, 'Terra'

Dianthus barbatus ★

SWEET WILLIAM

☼/☽ ❄ ↔ 6–12 in (15–30 cm) ↑ 12–24 in (30–60 cm)

Short-lived, southern European perennial usually grown as annual. Clump of lance-shaped leaves. Pinked flowers clustered in heads. Seedling strains in many colors and patterned forms. **Auricula-eyed Group**, contrasting colored ring near center. Zones 4–9.

Dianthus caryophyllus

CARNATION

☼/☽ ❄ ↔ 8–16 in (20–40 cm) ↑ 20–32 in (50–80 cm)

Perennial from Mediterranean region. Leaves sheathed, gray-green to blue-green, on wiry spreading stems. Flowerheads on upright, sometimes spindly stems, strongly fragrant. Wild plants have pink flowers, garden forms many colors. **Knight Series** includes 'Crimson Knight', 'White Knight', and 'Yellow Knight'. Zones 8–10.

Dianthus deltoides

MAIDEN PINK

☼/☽ ❄ ↔ 6–12 in (15–30 cm) ↑ 8–16 in (20–40 cm)

Eurasian perennial, forming carpet, sometimes mounding, of small green to blue-green leaves with spreading narrow-leafed stems around the edge. Flowers usually borne singly, in pink shades, often with dark central spotting, pinked. 'Albus', white flowers; 'Brilliancy', deep crimson flowers. Zones 3–9.

Dianthus gratianopolitanus

syn. *Dianthus caesius*

CHEDDAR PINK

☼/☽ ❄ ↔ 8–16 in (20–40 cm) ↑ 6–8 in (15–20 cm)

Mat-forming perennial native to central and western Europe. Older leaves can be small and very densely packed. Fragrant pink to crimson flowers, usually borne singly, pinked. 'Baker's Variety' and 'Flore Pleno', semi-double flowers. Zones 3–9.

Dianthus plumarius

PINK

☼/☽ ❄ ↔ 8–16 in (20–40 cm) ↑ 6–14 in (15–35 cm)

Perennial from eastern and central Europe. Loose tuft of blue-green foliage. Flowers pink or white, often with darker markings or center. Zones 3–9.

Dianthus superbus

☼/☽ ❄ ↔ 12–20 in (30–50 cm) ↑ 20–30 in (50–75 cm)

Strong-growing Eurasian perennial with spreading stems. Flowers usually borne singly, with pink to purple-pink, highly scented, deeply cut petals. *D. s.* **var.** *longicalycinus,* mauve to light purple flowers with elongated calyx. Zones 4–9.

Dianthus Hybrid Cultivars

☼/☽ ❄ ↔ 6–12 in (15–30 cm) ↑ 8–15 in (20–38 cm)

The many carnations and pinks and their cultivars are divided into groups based on growth habit, flower color and style. Zones 8–10.

ANNUAL BEDDING DIANTHUS

Although sometimes really perennial, these small plants are grown as annuals. In many ways they resemble sweet William (*D. barbatus*), but they are available in a wider range of sizes and growth forms, including some suitable for hanging baskets. Popular annual dianthus include **Floral Lace Series**, masses of small flowers with pinked edges; and **Melody Series**, mainly single-colored in pink shades and white.

PERENNIAL DIANTHUS

Countless hybrids have been raised, either as garden plants or for the cut-flower trade. There are three main groups of dianthus hybrids that are further divided, primarily by flower type.

Border carnations

Tall growers that are derived from *D. caryophyllus*. Flowers are usually strongly scented, often fully double, with or without pinked edges. They bloom mainly in spring and early summer, and are divided as follows:

Fancies: Flowers basically one color but with flecks, spots, or small sectors of another color. 'Brookham Fancy', yellow flowers with pink flecks.

Selfs: Flowers all one color. 'Cathlene Hitchcock', soft pink flowers; 'Fiery Cross', vivid red; 'Golden Cross' soft yellow; 'Grey Dove', dusky mauve.

Clove-scented: Flowers strongly scented, color may be variable. 'Candy Clove', red-striped white flowers.

Picotees: One base color edged with another color. The edging width is variable. 'Eva Humphries', purple-edged white.

Perpetual-flowering Carnations

The tallest carnations, often with flower stems that need staking or tying. Not hardy to repeated severe frosts, and best grown in mild climates for their year-round flowering.

The rare Malmaison carnation has strong foliage and flower stems, and very intense clove perfume. 'Duchess of Westminster', with large cream flowers, is the most widely grown Malmaison.

Perpetuals are widely cultivated as greenhouse plants for florists. Popular forms, all doubles unless stated otherwise, follow:

Fancies: 'Bright Rendez-vous', creamy white flowers, with soft pink lacing; 'Cheerio', pinkish white and red; 'Crimson Tempo', rich red; 'Havana', red and yellow; 'Impulse', creamy white, deep pinkish red; 'New Tempo', pinkish white and red; 'Rendez-vous', white laced with deep pink; 'Tempo', white with fine red lacing, a few red sectors; 'Tundra', yellow laced with light red; 'Yellow Rendez-vous', soft yellow laced with deep pink.

Selfs: 'Delphi', white flowers; 'Mambo', bright yellow; 'Moutarde', yellow; 'Pink Dona', shades of pink ; 'Prado', creamy pale green; 'Raggio di Sole', orange; 'Terra', salmon to pink.

Spray carnations: Flowers usually smaller, 5 to 6 per stem. 'Fiorella', yellow and red; 'Ibiza', yellow; 'Kortina', purple-red.

Pinks

Developed from *D. plumarius* but often crossed with other species and hybrids. The most common cross is with the perpetual-flowering carnations, which gave rise to the Allwoodii Pinks. Flowers may or may not be fragrant, nearly always pinked edges.

Fancies: 'Dad's Favourite' (syn. 'Dad's Favorite'), white flowers, maroon lacing and center, double; 'Gran's Favourite', white, pinkish red lacing, double; 'Red Ensign', deep pink, white lacing.

Selfs: 'Becky Robinson', deep pink flowers; 'Bovey Belle', purple, double; 'Carmine Letitia Wyatt', deep pink, semi-double, scented; 'Devon Pride', bright pink; 'Dwarf Helen', pink, double; 'Inglestone', bright pink; 'Lemsii', small, pink; 'Letitia Wyatt' ★, bright pink, double, scented; 'Lionheart', red, sometimes lighter edges, single, scented; 'Neon Star', bright purple-pink, single, scented; 'Valda Wyatt', pink, double, scented; 'Whatfield Cancan', soft pink, frilled double, scented; 'White Joy', white, sometimes flushed pale pink, double.

Allwoodii Pinks: Usually *D. plumarius* × *D. alpinus* hybrids. 'Whatfield Ruby', vivid crimson flowers, gray foliage.

Bicolors: 'Cranmere Pool', white to pale pink flowers, deep red center, double; 'Doris' ★, light pink with purple-red center, double; 'Houndspool Ruby' (syn. 'Ruby Doris'), deep pink with crimson center, double, sport of 'Doris'; 'Monica Wyatt', pink with red center, double; 'Peach Mambo', cream with soft orange-pink center, double; 'Rose Monica Wyatt', deep pink with red center, double.

Old-Fashioned Pinks: Usually forms of *D. plumarius* but are sometimes hybrids or just varieties of indeterminate origin. 'Earl of Essex', deep pink, double flowers; well-known, very fragrant; 'Mrs Sinkins', white double flowers; 'Pike's Pink', pink semi-double flowers.

DIASCIA

TWINSPUR

This South African genus of around 50 species of annuals and perennials belongs to the foxglove (Scrophulariaceae) family. They are generally low mounding or spreading plants with upright or semi-trailing stems and small oval to elliptical leaves with toothed edges. The flowers, in shades of mauve, pink, and soft orange, are tiny but showy, because they are massed in racemes at the stem tip, mainly in the summer.

CULTIVATION: Plant these in a bright open position with good air movement, and well-drained humus-rich soil that is kept moist throughout the flowering season. Pinch back to keep the plants bushy, and deadhead regularly to encourage continued blooming. Propagate from seed or from cuttings.

Diascia barberae

☼/◗ ❄ ↔ 12–16 in (30–40 cm) ↕ 12 in (30 cm)

From the Drakensberg region of southern Africa. Upright or sprawling perennial. Flowers bright pink, with conspicuous spurs and small yellow patch, maroon edge and spots. 'Blackthorn Apricot', low growing, apricot-pink to soft orange flowers; 'Fisher's Flora', heart-shaped leaves, dark-centered flowers with two yellow spots; 'Ruby Field', pinkish red flowers. Zones 8–10.

Diascia rigescens

☼/◗ ❄ ↔ 24 in (60 cm) ↕ 16–20 in (40–50 cm)

From Drakensberg region of southern Africa. Sprawling perennial. Pointed oval leaves, sometimes with fine red edge. Upright flower spikes, closely spaced flowers, less open heads than other species. Deep pink flowers, distinct keel on the lower lobe. Zones 8–10.

Diascia vigilis

☼/◗ ❄ ↔ 48 in (120 cm) ↕ 20 in (50 cm)

From Drakensberg region of southern Africa. Strong-growing perennial with slightly glossy fleshy leaves. Soft pink flowers, small dark spots in the throat. Continues flowering later than other species. 'Jack Elliott', larger mid-pink flowers. Zones 8–10.

Diascia vigilis

Dicentra spectabilis

Diascia **Hybrid Cultivars**

☀ ❋ ↔ 12–24 in (30–60 cm) ↕ 8–18 in (20–45 cm)
The species tend to interbreed freely when cultivated and produce many intermediate hybrids. Attractive examples include
Coral Belle/'Hecbel', narrow, slightly glossy leaves, coral red
flowers, semi-trailing habit, good in baskets; 'Joyce's Choice',
heart-shaped leaves, apricot-pink flowers; 'Langthorn's Lavender,
pretty pink-mauve flowers; 'Lilac Belle', small leaves, light purple
flowers with a conspicuous lower lip; Little Dancer/'Pendan',
small heart-shaped leaves, vivid pink flowers, very good in
baskets; Redstart/'Hecstart', coral pink to red flowers; 'Rupert
Lambert' ★, deep pink flowers, to around 10 in (25 cm) tall and
twice as wide, blooms from summer through to autumn; 'Salmon
Supreme', light salmon pink flowers with darker spots; Sydney
Olympics/ 'Hecsyd', light salmon pink flowers, compact, heavy-
flowering; and 'Twinkle', dark foliage, purple-pink flowers, trailing habit, good in baskets. Zones 8–10.

DICENTRA

BLEEDING HEART
This genus of around 20 species of annuals and perennials from
North America and Asia belongs in the poppy (Papaveraceae)
family, though the resemblance may not be obvious. Most species
have roots adapted as storage organs, as tap roots, rhizomes, or
tubers. The foliage, ferny and often finely cut, disappears for
winter, but redevelops quickly with the arrival of spring, the
larger species often making noticeable daily growth. The flowers
have 4 petals, the outer pair creating a pouched structure that
largely envelops the inner pair. The pendulous flowers appear
in spring, and are borne in clusters on stems rising above the
foliage, mostly in white, pink, or cream shades.
CULTIVATION: These species prefer a cool moist soil that is humus-
rich, fertile, and well drained. They thrive in woodlands and perennial borders, and the smaller forms also do well in rockeries.
Best lightly shaded from hottest sun. Propagate from seed or
basal cuttings, or by division.

Dicentra cucullaria

DUTCHMAN'S BREECHES
☼/❂ ❋ ↔ 20–40 in (50–100 cm)
↕ 12–16 in (30–40 cm)
Perennial from eastern North America. Leaves
green, lacy, fern-like, with blue-green undersides,
finely divided. Small flowers, heart-shaped but
inner petals protruding, white or pink, tipped
yellow. Flowers look like upside-down bloomers.
May cause dermatitis in some people. Zones 5–9.

Dicentra eximia

STAGGERWEED, TURKEY CORN
☼/❂ ❋ ↔ 20–40 in (50–100 cm)
↕ 12–26 in (30–65 cm)
Perennial found over much of the USA. Blue-green
leaves are finely divided. Sprays of pink or white
heart-shaped flowers. The plant is somewhat toxic
to stock. Zones 5–9.

Dicentra formosa

syn. *Dicentra eximia* of gardens
WILD BLEEDING HEART
☼/❂ ❋ ↔ 20–40 in (50–100 cm) ↕ 12–26 in (30–65 cm)
Perennial, native to western North America. Ferny leaves with
blue-green undersides. Panicles up to 30 flowers, most commonly
deep pink, sometimes yellow, and rarely white. *D. formosa* and *D.
eximia* have been confused in cultivation and it now appears that
they may be one quite variable species. 'Aurora', gray-green
leaves, white flowers; 'Bacchanal', gray-green foliage, pinkish red
flowers; 'Bountiful', light blue-green leaves, deep pink flowers;
'Langtrees', very compact, blue-green leaves, pink-tinted cream
flowers; 'Luxuriant' ★, blue-green foliage, deep cherry pink to
red flowers; 'Stuart Boothman', blue-green leaves with narrow
leaflets, deep pink flowers on short stems; 'Zestful', light blue-
green foliage and deep purple-pink flowers. Zones 4–9.

Dicentra spectabilis

BLEEDING HEART
☼/❂ ❋ ↔ 20–40 in (50–100 cm) ↕ 40–56 in (100–140 cm)
Vigorous perennial from Japan, northeastern China, and Russia's
far east. Leaves coarsely divided. Upright often red-tinted flower
stems with up to 15 large, pink, heart-shaped flowers with slightly
protruding white inner petals. 'Alba', pure white flowers. Zones 6–9.

DICHORISANDRA

This genus of about 25 species from Central and South America
belongs to the spiderwort (Commelinaceae) family. All are perennials, sometimes becoming shrubby, with soft stems and glossy
green leaves, sometimes striped with cream or purple. The small
flowers are borne in dense terminal spikes and are blue or purple.
CULTIVATION: *Dichorisandra* species are best grown in shady or
only partly sunny, sheltered positions in moist soil. They are
somewhat frost tender but in cold climates plants can be overwintered in a greenhouse. Propagation is from division or from
cuttings taken in summer.

Dichorisandra thyrsiflora
BLUE GINGER

☀ ❄ ↔ 3 ft (0.9 m) ↑ 3–10 ft (0.9–3 m)

From northern South America. Dark green glossy leaves. Terminal clusters of purple-blue flowers, on stems to 10 ft (3 m) high, depending upon growing conditions. Zones 9–12.

DICLIPTERA

This genus of about 150 annual and perennial herbs and shrubs belongs to the acanthus (Acanthaceae) family, and is native to tropical and warm-temperate regions. Stems are usually 6-angled. Flowers are borne in terminal clusters with 2-lipped tubular corollas, expanding toward the throat.
CULTIVATION: These plants are easily grown in average well-drained soils in full sun and will tolerate some shade and drought. Suited to containers or hanging baskets. Propagate from seed or cuttings.

Dichorisandra thyrsiflora

Dicliptera suberecta
syns *Jacobina suberecta*, *Justicia suberecta*
HUMMINGBIRD PLANT, KING'S CROWN

☀ ❄ ↔ 18–24 in (45–60 cm) ↑ 18–24 in (45–60 cm)

Perennial subshrub from Uruguay. Slender, velvety, gray foliage on erect or arching stems. Simple smooth-edged leaves. Two-lipped, rusty reddish orange, tubular flowers. Summer- to autumn-flowering. Zones 7–11.

DIEFFENBACHIA
DUMB CANE, MOTHER-IN-LAW'S TONGUE, TUFTROOT

This genus of about 25 evergreen, erect, perennial herbs from tropical America belongs to the arum (Araceae) family and is grown for the patterned foliage. Large oval-shaped leaves, spotted or streaked with cream, spread out from a stout central stem. Flowers are borne on long spikes with a green boat-shaped spathe blade. These are very poisonous plants; contact with the sap will cause the tongue to swell.
CULTIVATION: *Dieffenbachia* are ideal as houseplants in bright light and rich moist soil, preferring full sun or partial shade and high humidity. Protect from frost or plant in frost-free areas. Propagate from stem or root cuttings or by division of established clumps.

Dieffenbachia seguine
SPOTTED DUMBCANE

☀/❄ ✿ ↔ 18–24 in (45–60 cm)
↑ 3–6 ft (0.9–1.8 m)

Variable perennial from tropical America. Cane-like stems; large, leathery, oval-shaped leaves, with pointed tips. 'Amoena', very robust, thick stems, large green leaves evenly marked in cream; 'Exotica', compact form, pointed oval-shaped leaves sprinkled

with ivory cream; 'Maculata', bright green leaves spotted with cream; 'Rudolph Roehrs', leaves mostly yellow, spotted with ivory, ribbed, deep green margin; 'Superba', fresh green leaves variegated with creamy white; 'Tropic Snow' (syns 'Snow Queen', 'Tropic Topaz', 'Hi-color'), dense tall plant, known by its heavy cream leaf markings. Zones 10–12.

DIETES

This genus belongs to the iris (Iridaceae) family and has 6 species of evergreen clumping plants, 5 from southern Africa and 1 from Lord Howe Island, Australia. The flat flowers are held above the leaves. They make strong bold feature plants. The flowers individually only last a day or two, but the flowering season can last a long time.
CULTIVATION: Able to endure only very light frosts, they will tolerate sun or deep shade, poor soils, and dry conditions. Propagate from seed; they can be divided, but tend to resent disturbance.

Dietes bicolor

☼/☀ ✿ ↔ 24–36 in (60–90 cm) ↑ 32–36 in (80–90 cm)

Well-known rhizomatous species from the East Cape, South Africa. Long, arching, deep green, strap-like leaves overtopped by flat lemon flowers with contrasting, brown, basal blotches. Spring- to summer-flowering. Zones 9–11.

Dietes grandiflora
syn. *Dietes iridioides* 'Johnsonii'
WILD IRIS

☀ ✿ ↔ 20–27 in (50–70 cm) ↑ 20–27 in (50–70 cm)

Perennial from forests of South Africa. Sword-shaped dark green leaves, broader than *D. bicolor*. Large white flowers marked with yellow and brown blotches. Summer-flowering. Zones 9–11.

Dieffenbachia seguine

Digitalis purpurea, Excelsior Group

DIGITALIS

FOXGLOVE

This genus, once confined to Eurasia and North Africa, now occurs in most temperate regions of the world. A member of the foxglove (Scrophulariaceae) family, it has around 20 species of biennials and perennials. They form a basal clump of coarse, often elliptical, heavily veined leaves. The upright flower stems carry smaller leaves and many downward-facing, 4-lobed, bell-shaped flowers that open progressively upwards along the spike in a long flowering period. Most flower from late spring into summer, in pink, lavender, purple, yellow, cream, or white. All parts of the plants are toxic if swallowed; the leaves may irritate the skin.
CULTIVATION: These are easily cultivated in most temperate areas. Plant in moist, humus-rich soil, water well in spring, and while in flower. Biennials must be raised from seed, but perennials will also grow from basal offshoots.

Digitalis grandiflora

syn. *Digitalis ambigua*
LARGE YELLOW FOXGLOVE
☼/◐ ✳ ↔ 20–24 in (50–60 cm) ↑ 40 in (100 cm)
European biennial or short-lived perennial. Lush dark green leaves, toothed; leafy flower stems. Flowers pale yellow, darker veining. 'Carillon', to 24 in (60 cm) tall, primrose yellow flowers. Zones 4–9.

Digitalis lutea

STRAW FOXGLOVE
☼/◐ ✳ ↔ 16–24 in (40–60 cm) ↑ 24–40 in (60–100 cm)
Native to Europe and North Africa. Leaves dark green, hairless, finely to heavily serrated. Soft yellow or white flowers. Zones 4–9.

Digitalis mertonensis

STRAWBERRY FOXGLOVE
☼/◐ ✳ ↔ 16–20 in (40–50 cm) ↑ 20–30 in (50–75 cm)
Widely grown perennial garden hybrid. Large, downy, pinkish red to purple-pink flowers. Compact plant with lush foliage and tightly packed flowers. Zones 4–9.

Digitalis purpurea

COMMON FOXGLOVE
☼/◐ ✳ ↔ 12–32 in (30–80 cm)
↑ 5–6 ft (1.5–1.8 m)
Biennial from western Europe and now widely naturalized, often considered a weed. Strongly upright flower stems. Many pink, purple, or white flowers, heavily spotted within, from early summer. *D. p.* subsp. *heywoodii*, silvery foliage, white and cream flowers. *D. p.* f. *albiflora*, flowers often free of throat markings. *D. p.*, Excelsior Group, flowers surrounding the stem, in a mix of colors; 'Sutton's Apricot', creamy salmon pink flowers. Zones 4–9.

DIMORPHOTHECA

This genus of 7 species of annuals, perennials, and subshrubs is a member of the daisy (Asteraceae) family. They are native to southern and tropical Africa. Stems may be upright or sprawling and the leaves simple or divided, sometimes scented. They flower prolifically from spring to late summer. The typical daisy flowers have white or yellow rays that are purplish blue or coppery beneath, creating an attractive contrast.
CULTIVATION: Grow in full sun in a well-drained soil. In cooler areas the protection of a hot sunny wall will promote flowering. Propagate annuals from seed; others from seed or cuttings.

Dimorphotheca sinuata

NAMAQUALAND DAISY
syn. *Dimorphotheca aurantiaca* of gardens
☼ ❀ ↔ 12 in (30 cm) ↑ 12–18 in (30–45 cm)
Native to South Africa. Annual with narrow coarsely toothed leaves. Dark-centered daisies in range of colors from white to orange, including some pastel shades. Zones 9–11.

DIONAEA

This single-species genus belongs to the sundew (Droseraceae) family. The Venus flytrap is found in coastal areas of North and South Carolina, USA, in damp acidic soil. It captures its prey in traps that snap shut when the trap's trigger hairs have been touched more than once in quick succession. Digestive enzymes enter the trap and the soft tissue of the insect is dissolved.
CULTIVATION: Grow in pots containing either just peat moss or 1 part sand to 3 parts peat, in full sun to half-sun. Water by tray; when winter dormancy approaches, remove pots from trays and only water once a week. Remove any black leaves or traps. Repot every couple of years. Propagate by division at the end of winter.

Dionaea muscipula ★

VENUS FLYTRAP
☼/◐ ✳ ↔ 8 in (20 cm) ↑ 4 in (10 cm)
Leaves green, each leaf blade having 2 eyelid-shaped fringed lobes. Each lobe has 3 fine trigger hairs. Small white flowers on a leafless stalk, at the end of spring. 'Akai Ryu', bright

burgundy traps in full sun; 'Fang' and 'Sawtooth', edges of the traps have jagged "teeth" rather than a fringe. Zones 8–11.

DODECATHEON

AMERICAN COWSLIP, SHOOTING STARS

This charming genus of some 14 species of small rosette-forming herbaceous perennials is a member of the primrose (Primulaceae) family, and is native to North America. These plants produce several flowers per stem, in spring, with fully reflexed petals like those of a cyclamen.
CULTIVATION: These frost-hardy plants grow naturally in moist meadows and mountain pastures, and usually perform best in a cool rock garden or pot. Propagate from freshly sown seed in autumn; division in late winter, just before the plants break dormancy, is also possible.

Dodecatheon dentatum

☼/◑ ❄ ↔ 6–12 in (15–30 cm)
↕ 4–16 in (10–40 cm)
North American species, found from Oregon and Washington through Idaho to Arizona, USA. Rosette-forming herbaceous perennial. Leaves oblong to lance-shaped, bright green, sometimes with finely toothed margins. White flowers, turned-back petals, yellow anthers. Spring- to early summer-flowering. Zones 5–9.

Dodecatheon hendersonii

MOSQUITO-BILLS, SAILOR'S CAP

☼/◑ ❄ ↔ 6–12 in (15–30 cm) ↕ 8–15 in (20–38 cm)
From California, USA. Deep green, fleshy, oval leaves. Flowers in heads of 2 to 3. Pinkish purple turned-back petals, yellow anthers. Zones 6–9.

Dodecatheon meadia

syn. *Dodecatheon pauciflorum*
AMERICAN COWSLIP, EASTERN SHOOTING STAR, SHOOTING STAR

☼/◑ ❄ ↔ 12 in (30 cm) ↕ 8–18 in (20–45 cm)
From eastern USA. Oblong leaves. Flowers in heads of 10 to 20, turned-back petals usually purple, cream to white base, sometimes pink or white. *D. m.* f. *album*, white flowers. Zones 3–9.

DOROTHEANTHUS

LIVINGSTONE DAISY

This genus of 6 species of succulent annuals, belonging to the iceplant (Aizoaceae) family, is confined to South Africa. They are spreading or mounding plants with thickened leaves that have a crystalline surface, creating a sugar-coated look. The flowers are daisy-like, often very abundant, in a range of colors, mainly shades of pink or white but also yellow, orange, red, and purple. Mostly ephemeral, these subdesert plants can race into growth with the arrival of rain. In frost-free climates they may grow at any time but in temperate areas they are mainly summer-flowering. CULTIVATION: Plant in spring in a bright sunny position to ensure maximum flowering time. Soil should be light, gritty, and well-drained, but the plants do need occasional watering when they are flowering. Deadhead frequently to encourage blooms over a longer period. In cooler climates, sow seed under glass in winter or spring. Propagation is from seed.

Dorotheanthus bellidiformis

☼ ▯ ↔ 8–16 in (20–40 cm) ↕ 2–6 in (5–15 cm)
From South Africa. Low spreading plant. Red-tinted stems, fleshy gray-green leaves, rough textured surface. Daisy-like flowers in mainly pink to purple shades but also white. Garden forms with yellow and multi-colored flowers may be hybrids. Zones 9–11.

DORYANTHES

This genus of 2 species of large perennial herbs has its own family, Doryanthaceae, and occurs in woodlands, open forests, and rocky hillsides on well-draining soils in eastern Australia. The leaves are lance-shaped and pointed. Flower stalks can exceed the leaves in length by 2 to 3 times. Flowers are in terminal heads, each large, red, and with 6 equal segments. Fruits are 3-celled capsules. Plants are long-lived in cultivation.
CULTIVATION: Propagation is usually from seeds, but flowering could be up to 10 years from germination. Division of clumps, or from suckers, will produce flowering plants more quickly.

Doryanthes excelsa

GIANT LILY, GYMEA LILY, ILLAWARRA LILY

☼ ▯ ↔ 10 ft (3 m) ↕ 8–20 ft (2.4–6 m)
Found in woodlands on sandy soils in the central coast region of New South Wales, Australia. Leaves bright or slightly yellowish green, generally stiff and erect. Flower stalk, to 20 ft (6 m) long, terminating in a dense head of many red flowers, in spring–summer. Each flower contains large quantities of nectar. Dark colored capsules. Zones 9–11.

Dionaea muscipula

Dodecatheon meadia

Doryanthes palmeri

SPEAR LILY

☼ ❋ ↔ 3–10 ft (0.9–3 m) ↕ 3–10 ft (0.9–3 m)

From northern New South Wales and southern Queensland, Australia. Leaves long, bright green, lance-shaped, cylindrical appendage at apex. Flower stalks to 17 ft (5 m) long, tending to arch. Brownish flowers in spring. Capsules greenish. **Zones 10–12.**

DROSERA

SUNDEW

A diverse genus of more than 130 carnivorous plants found on every continent except Antarctica, *Drosera* belongs to the sundew (Droseraceae) family. Almost half the species are native to Australia but are also found in South America, New Zealand, and Borneo. Their size and shape is varied. The tentacle-covered leaves can be erect, climbing, fan-leafed, or arranged in a rosette. All species trap prey by luring an insect to sticky, dew-like liquid sparkling on the red tentacles on the sundew's leaves.
CULTIVATION: Growing conditions for *Drosera* vary but they can be divided into the groups below. Some species grow in both tropical and temperate zones. Many grow easily from leaf cuttings.

Tropical species: Grow in sphagnum moss, in pots in tray of water in shade. Need high humidity. Best if temperature does not fall below 59°F (15°C).

Subtropical species: Use a soil mix of 3 parts peat and 2 parts sand; keep soil damp. Full sun to part-shade. Some species tolerate light frosts, but are best treated as an annual in colder areas. Grow in a greenhouse or on a sunny windowsill.

Temperate species: Use a soil mix of 3 parts peat to 2 parts sand. Stand containers in water. Full sun in temperate climates, part-shade in warmer areas. Plants usually dormant in winter.

Tuberous species: Use a soil mix of 3 parts peat to 2 parts sand. Pots should be kept dry and out of direct sunlight during summer dormancy. Start to water by tray as winter approaches and new growth appears. Protect from frosts.

Drosera binata

FORKED SUNDEW

☼ ❋ ↔ 8 in (20 cm) ↕ 12 in (30 cm)

From east coast of Australia and New Zealand. Leaf blades fork into "Y" shape. Slender green to yellow leaves, densely covered with tentacles. Temperate to subtropical (*see* Cultivation). **Zones 8–10.**

Drosera capensis

CAPE SUNDEW

☼ ❋ ↔ 6 in (15 cm) ↕ 6 in (15 cm)

From the Cape region of South Africa, found growing in bogs, marshes, and wet grasslands. Slender green leaves, covered in fine red tentacles; ends of leaves are rounded and curl around trapped prey. Older plants produce a woody trunk with green foliage at top. Pretty pink flowers on leafless stalk in spring. Does not experience dormancy in winter. Easy sundew to grow. Temperate to subtropical (*see* Cultivation). **Zones 8–11.**

Drosera pulchella

PRETTY SUNDEW

☼ ❋ ↔ 1¼ in (30 mm) ↕ ½ in (12 mm)

Found in swamps, wet peat, and damp sandy soil in Western Australia. Rosette sundew with round, tentacled, green leaves on broad stalks. Flowers in spring on 2 or 3 leafless stalks; can be white, pink, orange, or dark red with metallic sheen. Dormant in wild in hot dry summer, but not in cultivation if plant is kept moist. Subtropical (*see* Cultivation). **Zones 9–11.**

Drosera rotundifolia

ROUND-LEAFED SUNDEW

☼ ❋ ↔ 4 in (10 cm) ↕ 2 in (5 cm)

Most widely distributed of temperate sundews, found in Asia, Europe, and North America in sphagnum bogs. Cup-shaped leaves on fine stalk. Tiny flowers, white to pink, on leafless stalk, in spring–summer. Temperate (*see* Cultivation). **Zones 3–9.**

Drosera zonaria

PAINTED SUNDEW

☼ ❋ ↔ 3 in (8 cm) ↕ 1 in (2.5 cm)

Sundew from Western Australia. Rounded leaves with short stems in overlapping rosette. Green leaves, usually red around the edges. Flowers white, rare. Tuberous (*see* Cultivation). **Zones 8–10.**

DROSOPHYLLUM

DEWY PINE, PORTUGUESE SUNDEW

A carnivorous single species genus of the sundew (Droseraceae) family, the Portuguese sundew is found in Spain, Morocco, and Portugal. A small perennial shrub, it grows in dry sandy soil on coastal hills, often among short fir trees *(Pinus pinaster)*. The

Drosera binata

Drosera capensis

Drosera zonaria

plant has a dewy appearance, caused by the droplets of sticky mucus on the leaves. Small insects get trapped on the leaves by the very sticky liquid; the leaves then secrete a digestive enzyme which dissolves the prey's soft tissue.

CULTIVATION: Grow in mix of 3 parts sand to 1 part peat, add a teaspoon of limestone or dolomite to a 6 in (15 cm) clay pot. Place the clay pot in a plastic pot containing live sphagnum moss (ensure the plastic pot has a large drainage hole), in full sun. Water by tray, never from above. Allow the pot to dry out for one day each month. Small plantlets frequently appear among the branches, and these can be removed and planted once they have 10 or 12 leaves; dip stem in rooting hormone and plant in mix of 1 part sand to 2 parts peat.

Drosophyllum lusitanicum
☼ ❄ ↔ 16 in (40 cm) ↑ 12 in (30 cm)
Woody base. Up to 100 slender green leaves covered in sticky red liquid; leaves uncurl outwardly. Bright yellow flowers appear in spring. Zones 8–10.

DRYAS
MOUNTAIN AVENS
This small genus of 3 species, all evergreen mat-forming plants from arctic and Northern Hemisphere alpine regions, belongs to the rose (Rosaceae) family. The foliage resembles that of the oak *(Quercus),* although on a miniature scale. The flowers have 8 petals, unlike most Rosaceae members. They are comparatively large, white or lemon in color, and are produced in summer, held well clear of the foliage, and followed by large fluffy seed heads.
CULTIVATION: These prefer a sunny moist aspect in non-tropical climates in a rock garden or between pavers. They are ideal ground covers over small bulbs. Propagate by division, or from cuttings or freshly sown seed.

Dryas octopetala ★
MOUNTAIN AVENS
☼ ❄ ↔ over 40 in (100 cm) ↑ 3–4 in (8–10 cm)
Northern European species. Glossy, dark green, oak-shaped leaves, white reverse turns coppery in winter. White flowers, in summer. Fluffy seed heads. Zones 3–9.

DYCKIA
This genus in the pineapple (Bromeliaceae) family consists of more than 120 species, mostly from Brazil, Argentina, and neighboring countries, with only a few in cultivation. They are clump-forming plants. The leaves are triangular, usually green and very succulent, with mostly weak teeth on the edges. The generally long flower stems do not emerge from the plant's center, which means the plant does not die after flowering as with most other members of the Bromeliaceae. The flowerhead is sometimes single, sometimes open-branched, each branch having many well-spaced yellow to orange flowers.
CULTIVATION: Grow in well-drained sandy soil mix, in greenhouses or conservatories, in cool-temperate areas, or outdoors in warm-

Dryas octopetala

temperate, subtropical, and tropical areas. Water when potting mix is dry. Do not over-fertilize. Propagate from seed or offsets.

Dyckia remotiflora
☼ ❄ ↔ 16 in (40 cm) ↑ 40 in (100 cm)
Found from southern Brazil to Argentina. Terrestrial bromeliads. Slow clump-forming plants. Narrow, triangular, dark green leaves. Flowerhead a single stem with a few yellow flowers scattered on all sides. Mainly grown in open rockeries. Zones 9–11.

ECHINOPS
GLOBE THISTLE
This genus, containing about 120 species of thistle-like perennials found from Europe eastward to central Asia and southward to the mountains of Africa, is from the daisy (Asteraceae) family. The leaves are spine-tipped and usually deeply lobed, and may be simple or have up to 3 large leaflets. The flowers, appearing in summer–early autumn, are small, mostly white to mauve-blue, borne in spherical heads without ray florets, and backed by often spiny basal bracts, which are sometimes colored. The flowerheads are sometimes dried but tend to disintegrate rather quickly.
CULTIVATION: These are mostly very hardy plants and easily grown in any temperate climate garden with a moderately fertile, well-drained soil. They are best grown in a fairly open position to reduce the risk of mildew. Propagated mainly from seed but easily divided in late winter.

Echinops bannaticus
☼/◐ ❄ ↔ 2 ft (0.6 m) ↑ 4 ft (1.2 m)
Found from Greece to the Czech Republic. Upright stem; finely hairy leaves, angularly lobed almost to the midrib, a few narrow spines; downy stems. Gray-blue flowerheads, to 2 in (5 cm) across, lighter in bud. '**Blue Globe**', dark blue flowerheads, 2½ in (6 cm) across; '**Taplow Blue**', bright steel blue flowerheads. Zones 3–9.

Echinops bannaticus 'Taplow Blue'

Echinops ritro

☼/◐ ✽ ↔ 16–24 in (40–60 cm) ↕ 12–24 in (30–60 cm)
Eurasian species. Leaves finely hairy, narrow, triangular, deeply lobed, with small spines. Flowerheads deep steel blue to purple, rarely white, to nearly 2 in (5 cm) wide. *E. r.* **subsp.** *ruthenicus* (syn. *E. ruthenicus)*, leaves with small spines and white woolly hair on undersides, steel blue flowerheads; *E. r.* **'Blue Glow'**, large light blue flowerheads. Zones 3–9.

Echinops sphaerocephalus

☼/◐ ✽ ↔ 16–32 in (40–80 cm) ↕ 3–7 ft (0.9–2 m)
Native to southern and central Russia. Downy deeply lobed leaves, short spines, white hair on undersides. White to pale ash gray flowerheads, to over 2 in (5 cm) across. Zones 3–9.

ECHIUM

This genus contains about 60 species in the borage (Boraginaceae) family, a large proportion of which are endemic to the Canary Islands and Madeira. Some of these endemics are shrubs or giant biennials. The remaining species are found in parts of the Mediterranean region, through western Asia, and in parts of Africa. These are nearly all smaller annuals, biennials, or perennials, generally beginning as a rosette of narrow leaves clothed in stiff hairs. Bell-shaped flowers, usually blue, pink, purple, or reddish in color, are carried in branched, usually erect, spikes in spring and summer.
CULTIVATION: The shrubby species of *Echium* thrive best with only moderate amounts of fertilizer and water. The herbaceous species can be fertilized and watered more liberally. All do best in full sun. The species that are from the Canary Islands are less frost hardy than the European species. They are usually propagated from seed, but cuttings may be taken in spring or summer. These plants have a tendency to self-seed in mild climates, so they must be positioned carefully.

Echium candicans

Echium candicans ★

syn. *Echium fastuosum*
PRIDE OF MADEIRA

☼ ◁ ↔ 6 ft (1.8 m) ↕ 6 ft (1.8 m)
Native to the Canary Islands and Madeira. Thick-stemmed, soft-wooded, evergreen shrub, with large densely hairy leaves, to 10 in (25 cm) long. Clusters of about 8 blue flowers with protruding pink to lilac-purple stamens, borne in a spiky panicle, in early spring–early summer. May naturalize in cool climates. Zones 9–10.

Echium vulgare

BLUE WEED, VIPER'S BUGLOSS
☼ ✽ ↔ 18–24 in (45–60 cm)
↕ 18–24 in (45–60 cm)
From Europe and western Asia. Biennial usually grown as an annual. Often confused with *E. plantagineum* but bristlier, with smaller flowers. Branching spikes of intense violet-blue flowers, to ¾ in (18 mm), in summer. Zones 7–10.

EDMONDIA

This small genus, containing 3 species of perennials and small shrubs in the daisy (Asteraceae) family, is confined to the Cape region of South Africa. The flowerheads are composed of disc florets only, the daisy appearance is given by the papery bracts surrounding the flowerheads.
CULTIVATION: Best grown in relatively frost-free regions in well-drained soil in full sun. Propagate from seed in spring or from cuttings during summer or autumn.

Edmondia pinifolia

Edmondia pinifolia

☼ ✽ ↔ 12 in (30 cm) ↕ 12 in (30 cm)
Evergreen perennial. Small narrow leaves, white felting on undersurface. The flowerheads are surrounded by crimson bracts, borne at branch tips, in spring. Zones 8–9.

EICHHORNIA

This genus contains 7 species from tropical America, and belongs to the pickerelweed (Pontederiaceae) family. The plants are rhizomatous aquatics, usually perennial, with floating or submerged leaves. The stems are short and floating, and may be detaching or rooted in mud. The shiny hairless leaves form either floating or emergent rosettes; when free-floating they have tufts of thread-like roots below. Leaves have either narrow cylindrical stalks or, in floating species, elliptical stalks inflated with air-filled tissue. The inflorescence is a spike or panicle; flowers have 6 lobes, arising from a tube at the base, and are usually violet to blue with white or yellow markings. Fruit is a many-seeded capsule.
CULTIVATION: These plants do not tolerate frost and generally require water at least 6 in (15 cm) deep. They respond to dissolved nutrients with faster growth; in hotter climates growth is so rapid that planting is not recommended in any but small ponds. Some species are prohibited in some areas as a weed. Propagation is by division.

Eichhornia crassipes
WATER HYACINTH

☼ ❄ ↔ 18 in (45 cm) ↑ 12 in (30 cm)

Usually a free-floating plant. Swollen leaf stalks and leaf blades raised above the water act as sails. Violet-blue flowers in summer; some selections tinted pink or yellow. Introduced as an ornamental, but has spread to choke many tropical waterways and naturalize in many parts of the world. Regarded as a noxious weed in many countries, its use must be carefully planned. Zones 10–12.

ELODEA
syn. *Anacharis*

This genus in the frogbit (Hydrocharitaceae) family contains 12 species. These prolific freshwater plants, native to North and South America, are useful in aquariums, ponds, and water gardens. Because they are submersed, they protect spawning and young fish; they also counteract algae build-up. Some species are free floating, some rooted. Even in aquariums, rooted species can grow to 15 ft (4.5 m).
CULTIVATION: For best results, grow in full sun in slow-moving or still water. Under ideal conditions, *Elodea* can spread rapidly. Reproduce from cuttings.

Elodea canadensis
CANADIAN PONDWEED, WATERWEED

☼ ❄ ↔ indefinite ↑ 36 in (90 cm)

From North America. Excellent perennial oxygenator for water gardens, can become invasive. Densely branched stems, whorls of dark green pointed leaves, minute white flowers in summer. Dies back in winter. Zones 3–10.

EMILIA

There are about 24 species of rather sparse annual herbs in this genus in the daisy (Asteraceae) family. They are found throughout Polynesia, India, and tropical Africa. Their foliage is reminiscent of sow thistles, and the finely rayed flowers, which are borne singly or in small corymbs, are in bright shades of purple, scarlet, yellow, or orange.
CULTIVATION: These are easily grown in most soils in full sun; plant close together for the best effect. Propagate from seed.

Emilia sonchifolia
FLORA'S PAINTBRUSH, TASSEL FLOWER

☼ ❄ ↔ 6–10 in (15–25 cm) ↑ 6–20 in (15–50 cm)

Annual from tropical Asia and Africa. Rosettes of lyre-shaped leaves, sometimes bluish green. Tassel-like flowers in shades of scarlet, brilliant orange, or yellow in summer. Zones 9–11.

ENSETE

Members of the banana (Musaceae) family, to which this genus belongs, are really giant, tree-like, perennial herbs. *Ensete* is a

Emilia sonchifolia

genus of 7 species of ornamental bananas found in tropical Asia and Africa. The large solitary trunk or pseudostem is composed of the sheathing bases of the huge leaves, the blades of which are easily frayed by strong winds. Flowers are carried in large pendulous inflorescences at the end of arching stems, and develop into small, dry, inedible bananas containing hard seeds.
CULTIVATION: These are easy to grow, and do not require as much warmth as their edible relatives. The plants will survive all year in a mild frost-free climate; otherwise, treat them as annuals. Plant in moist, rich, well-drained soil in full sun or part-shade. They are usually propagated from seed, though it is sometimes possible to remove and strike basal suckers with roots.

Ensete ventricosum
ABYSSINIAN BANANA, ETHIOPIAN BANANA

☼ ❄ ↔ 15 ft (4.5 m) ↑ 30 ft (9 m)

African species. Huge crown of leaves, to 20 ft (6 m) long, tinted purple. '**Maurelii**', large, broad, red-tinged leaves. Zones 9–12.

EPILOBIUM
WILLOW HERB

This genus of about 200 species of annuals, perennials, and subshrubs in the evening primrose (Onagraceae) family is found in temperate climates around the world. Some are weedy. They are mostly rhizomatous plants. The leaves are opposite, and usually 4-ranked. Flowers are mostly pink or white, borne in succession in upper leaf axils, with long calyx tube and 4 petals, which are often notched. Fruit is a slender capsule. Some species from western North America have a more shrubby habit and scarlet flowers.
CULTIVATION: These plants are best suited to wild gardens or areas where they can spread freely. Grow in full sun in moisture-retentive soil. Alpine species need perfect drainage and protection from the hottest sun. Propagation is from seed or cuttings.

Eichhornia crassipes

Epilobium angustifolium, in the wild, Wyoming, USA

Epilobium angustifolium

syn. *Chamerion angustifolium*

FIREWEED, FRENCH WILLOW, GREAT WILLOW HERB, ROSEBAY WILLOW HERB

⚛ ✳ ↔ 3–8 ft (0.9–2.4 m) ↕ 3–8 ft (0.9–2.4 m)

Found throughout Northern Hemisphere. Invasive vigorous perennial. Willowy stems; narrow alternately arranged leaves. Racemes of pink to purplish flowers in summer–early autumn. Zones 3–9.

Epilobium canum

syns *Zauschneria californica, Z. cana*

CALIFORNIA FUCHSIA, ZAUSCHNERIA

⚛ ✳ ↔ 2–3 ft (0.6–0.9 m) ↕ 1–3 ft (0.3–0.9 m)

Ranging from Oregon and Wyoming to California and New Mexico, USA, and northwestern Mexico. Variable semi-deciduous plant; foliage gray-green; brilliant scarlet funnel-shaped flowers 1–2 in (2.5–5 cm) long, in summer–autumn. 'Solidarity Pink', reddish pink flowers. *E. c.* subsp. *latifolium* (syn. *Zauschneria californica* subsp. *latifolia*), leaves broader, less grayish. Zones 8–10.

Epilobium septentrionale

syns *Epilobium canum* subsp. *septentrionale, Zauschneria septentrionalis*

HUMBOLDT COUNTY FUCHSIA, WHITE LEAF FUCHSIA

⚛ ✳ ↔ 24–36 in (60–90 cm) ↕ 6–12 in (15–30 cm)

A mat-forming, semi-evergreen perennial from California, USA. Short, oval to lance-shaped, gray to gray-green leaves. Succession of tubular scarlet flowers in late summer-autumn. 'Select Mattole', silvery gray leaves. Zones 7–10.

EPIMEDIUM

BARRENWORT, BISHOP'S HAT, BISHOP'S MITER, HORNY GOAT WEED

This genus has about 44 species. Both evergreen and deciduous, they are clumping to slightly running perennials in the barberry (Berberidaceae) family that are found mainly in Asia but extend to the Mediterranean. They have attractive foliage, which is often

their biggest asset, and the dainty spring flowers occur in a range of colors, often with long curved spurs.

CULTIVATION: Most prefer a cool shaded aspect under deciduous trees in humus-rich soil; many are quite drought tolerant once established. Propagate by division in late winter.

Epimedium × cantabrigiense

⚛ ✳ ↔ 12–18 in (30–45 cm) ↕ 12–24 in (30–60 cm)

Heart-shaped evergreen leaves, downy beneath, with a few marginal spines. Stems of dainty red and pale yellow flowers in spring. Zones 5–9.

Epimedium grandiflorum

☀ ✳ ↔ 8–12 in (20–30 cm) ↕ 8–12 in (20–30 cm)

From Japan, China, and Northern Korea. Widespread more or less deciduous species. clumping habit. Heart-shaped leaves. Small spurred flowers in shades of white, yellow, pink or purple. More selected clones than any other species. 'Lilacinum', lilac flowers; 'Lilafee', magenta flowers; 'Rose Queen' ★, deep pink flowers with white-tipped spurs. Zones 5–9.

Epimedium × perralchicum

☀ ✳ ↔ 20–24 in (50–60 cm) ↕ 14–16 in (35–40 cm)

Forms large solid clumps of evergreen foliage, bronze when young. Sprays of bright yellow spurless flowers. 'Frohnleiten', spikier foliage and larger flowers. Zones 7–9.

Epimedium perralderianum

☀ ✳ ↔ 20–24 in (50–60 cm) ↕ 14–16 in (35–40 cm)

From northern Africa. Evergreen with a slowly spreading habit. Leaves with 3 toothed leaflets, bronze ageing to green. Yellow flowers with short brown spurs. Zones 7–9.

Epimedium × versicolor

☀ ✳ ↔ 10–12 in (25–30 cm) ↕ 10–12 in (25–30 cm)

Range of evergreen clump-forming garden hybrids. Spiny-edged leaves often richly colored with bronze when young. Pink and yellow flowers have short spurs that do not exceed the length of the calyx. 'Neosulphureum', soft lemon flowers; 'Sulphureum', bright yellow flowers with slightly longer spurs. Zones 5–9.

Epimedium × versicolor 'Sulphureum'

EPISCIA

This genus of 9 species from tropical America belongs to the African violet (Gesneriaceae) family. They are epiphytic or terrestrial herbs and are exceptional in the family in having runners. The leaves are opposite, often colored, and in equal or unequal pairs; when unequal the smaller one is often deciduous. The

flowers are borne in stalked racemes in the leaf axils, and may be clustered or solitary. The calyx has 5 green or colored sepals, which are sometimes joined at the base. The corolla is funnel-shaped with 5 spreading lobes. The fruit is a 2-valved capsule containing many elliptical seeds.
CULTIVATION: In temperate areas *Episcia* need greenhouse culture and are often grown in hanging baskets, but in the tropics they can be grown outside. These plants are difficult to overwinter in the poor light of temperate regions, but can be readily propagated from cuttings, which root easily, or from seed.

Episcia cupreata
CARPET PLANT, FLAME VIOLET
☼/☀ ✴ ↔12–24 in (30–60 cm)
↑8–12 in (20–30 cm)
Native to Central and South America. Ever-green creeping perennial. Leaves oval, brown to dark green, wrinkled, downy, flecked with copper and purple underneath. Clusters of scarlet flowers with a yellow ring, throat sometimes spotted with purple, in summer.
'Acajou', lighter-colored leaves, silvery mark-ings; 'Chocolate Soldier', large brown leaves with silvery gray center band; 'Country Cowgirl', silvery green pebble-textured leaves with copper-green margins; 'Metallica', copper leaves marked with silver, red flowers; 'Silver Sheen', bright copper-green margins on leaves, yellow, lilac, or red flowers; 'Tetra', large orange-red flowers with wavy lobes, orange-yellow inside; 'Tropical Topaz', bright yellow flowers. Zones 10–12.

Episcia dianthiflora
syn. *Alsobia dianthiflora*
LACE-FLOWER VINE
☼/☀ ✴ ↔18–36 in (60–90 cm) ↑8 in (20 cm)
Found from southern Mexico to Costa Rica. Low-growing ever-green perennial. Leaves dark green, toothed, elliptical to oval-shaped, to 1¾ in (40 mm) long, often veined with purple-red. Solitary, pearly white, tubular flowers, spotted with purple at base, conspicuously fringed rounded petals, in summer. Zones 10–12.

Episcia Hybrid Cultivars
☼/☀ ✴ ↔32–40 in (80–100 cm) ↑8–20 in (20–50 cm)
The best of the many hybrid cultivars tend to be compact plants that flower heavily, often with marked foliage. 'Chocolate 'n' Cherries', very dark bronze foliage, yellow-dotted bright red flowers; 'Star of Bethlehem', dark bronze leaves with red under-sides, distinctive bright pink flowers with a broad white margin; 'Toy Silver', very dwarf, with leaves of dark green heavily veined with silver-gray, bright red flowers. Zones 10–12.

ERANTHIS
WINTER ACONITE
The 7 species in this genus of small tuberous plants from the but-tercup (Ranunculaceae) family are found in the damp deciduous woodlands of Europe and Asia. In similar cool, damp, summer-shady situations they colonize and extend their territory. The

Episcia cupreata

cupped golden flowers, each held on a single stem, are encircled with pronounced green "ruffs," and appear in late winter.
CULTIVATION: Transplant in early spring while the plants are in leaf. Grow in moisture-retentive soil, with plenty of winter sun. Propagate by dividing the tubers or from seed.

Eranthis hyemalis
☼ ❀ ↔3–4 in (8–10 cm) ↑3–4 in (8–10 cm)
Originally found from southern France to Bulgaria; now natural-ized over a far wider range. Brilliant golden flowers, like butter-cups, often appearing before snow-melt, held on short curved stems. Stems elongate and straighten as the flower develops. Bright green, lobed, and circular basal leaves emerge after the flowers fade. Plant beneath decid-uous trees in alkaline soils. Zones 5–8.

ERIGERON
FLEABANE
The 200 or so species of annuals and peren-nials in this genus in the daisy (Asteraceae) family are found throughout temperate regions, particularly in North America, and grow in a variety of habitats. Their daisy flowers usually have numerous narrow rays in shades of white, pink, or lavender, occasionally yellow. Cultivars extend the color range. Plants vary from the low alpine species, suitable for a rock garden, to larger-flowered species growing to 30 in (75 cm) or more. They flower profusely over a long season.
CULTIVATION: Apart from the alpine species, which need protec-tion in winter and very good drainage, most are easily grown in full sun in any reasonable soil. Propagate from seed or by division.

Erigeron glaucus
BEACH ASTER, SEASIDE DAISY
☼ ❀ ↔12–24 in (30–60 cm) ↑6–12 in (15–30 cm)
From western USA. Somewhat succulent straggly perennial, with broadly oval leaves. Large gold-centered daisies with lilac to violet rays in late spring–early summer. 'Arthur Menzies', compact form, pink daisies; 'Rose Purple', pink-purple daisies. Zones 3–10.

Erigeron glaucus

Erigeron speciosus 'Quakeress'

Erigeron karvinskianus

syn. *Erigeron mucronatus*

MEXICAN DAISY, SANTA BARBARA DAISY

☼ ❄ ↔ 2–5 ft (0.6–1.5 m) ↑ 1–2 ft (0.3–0.6 m)

Perennial from highlands of southern Mexico, Central America, and Venezuela. Mounds of small toothed leaves on slender stems. Airy masses of small, white to pink, yellow-centered daisies all year round in frost-free areas, from spring to autumn in colder regions. Popular ground cover, but sometimes a weed. Zones 8–11.

Erigeron pulchellus

ROBIN'S PLANTAIN

☼ ❄ ↔ 8–16 in (20–40 cm) ↑ 6–16 in (15–40 cm)

Native to North America. Biennial or short-lived perennial with creeping rhizomes. Leaves spoon-shaped. Dainty pale pink or pale purple daisies with yellow centers in summer. Zones 4–9.

Erigeron 'Rosa Jewel'

☼ ❄ ↔ 16–24 in (40–60 cm) ↑ 18–30 in (45–75 cm)

An attractive hybrid with bright pink daisy-like flowers, similar to *E. speciosus* in other respects. Zones 3–9.

Erigeron speciosus

☼ ❄ ↔ 16–24 in (40–60 cm)

↑ 18–30 in (45–75 cm)

From northwestern USA. Popular perennial. Prolific blue daisies with yellow centers in summer. *E. s.* var. *macranthus*, slightly larger flowers. Many cultivars in shades of pink and blue. 'Rosa Jewel' ★ (syn. 'Pink Jewel'), bright pink flowers; 'Quakeress', light mauve-pink flowers. Zones 3–9.

ERIOGONUM

WILD BUCKWHEAT

This genus from western North America belongs to the knotweed (Polygonaceae) family, and includes about 150 annuals, perennials, and small evergreen shrubs of varied habit, most of which grow from a basal rosette of leaves. Small flowers appear in dense

Erodium chrysanthum

clusters or umbels, and the fruit is a 3-angled achene. *Eriogonum* species are good rockery or background plants for drier gardens. CULTIVATION: Adaptable to a wide range of climates, they will grow in sun or part-shade in a well-drained, preferably sandy, soil. They require plenty of water in warm conditions but need to be drier in winter. Remove spent flowerheads. Propagate from seed sown in spring or from cuttings. The root clumps of perennial species may be divided.

Eriogonum arborescens

SANTA CRUZ ISLAND BUCKWHEAT

☼/◗ ❄ ↔ 5 ft (1.5 m) ↑ 5 ft (1.5 m)

From California, USA. Peeling bark. Narrow near-linear leaves with slightly rolled edges and felted undersides. White to pale pink flowers, in downy inflorescences 2–6 in (5–15 cm) wide, in early summer–autumn. Good cut flower. Zones 9–10.

Eriogonum giganteum

SAINT CATHERINE'S LACE

☼ ❄ ↔ 10 ft (3 m) ↑ 8 ft (2.4 m)

From the Santa Barbara Islands off southern California, USA. Rounded evergreen shrub, with a central trunk, and leathery, oval, grayish white leaves. Flat clusters of woolly flowerheads, to 12 in (30 cm) across, white slowly fading to rusty red. Summer-flowering. Zones 9–11.

Eriogonum umbellatum

SULFUR FLOWER

☼ ❄ ↔ 3–4 ft (0.9–1.2 m) ↑ 6–18 in (15–45 cm)

From northwestern USA and southwestern Canada. Variable, low-spreading, perennial herb. Rosettes of spatula-shaped, purplish-tinged, stalked leaves, finely hairy underneath, in winter. Loose ball-like clusters of bright sulfur yellow or cream flowers in summer. Zones 6–10.

ERODIUM

HERONSBILL, STORKSBILL

This genus in the geranium (Geraniaceae) family includes 60 species of perennials and a few annuals and subshrubs. They are found in sunny rocky areas in mountainous regions of Europe, Asia, Australia, and South America. Some are mat-forming, others are erect, growing to 20 in (50 cm) tall. The leaves are lobed or pinnately divided, often finely and ornately, sometimes silvery gray. The charming 5-petalled flowers have 5 stamens. Some species carry male and female flowers on separate plants. The flowers are pink, red, purple, blue, yellow, or white, and often veined or stained with darker tones. CULTIVATION: Grow the smaller species in rockeries, pots, or a greenhouse; the taller plants are ideal in borders. Heronsbills need full sun and well-drained slightly alkaline soil. Propagate annuals from seed; perennials from seed or cuttings, or by division.

Erodium chrysanthum

☼ ❄ ↔ 12–16 in (30–40 cm) ↕ 4–6 in (10–15 cm)
From Greece. Low tufts of ferny silvery leaves. Saucer-shaped pale lemon flowers, to ¾ in (18 mm) across, in summer. Zones 7–10.

Erodium corsicum

☼ ❄ ↔ 12 in (30 cm) ↕ 8 in (20 cm)
From Corsica and Sardinia. Short-lived mat-forming perennial. Downy silvery gray foliage. Small, crumpled, oval leaves with wavy margins. Flowers rose pink, to ¾ in (18 mm) across, in late spring–summer. 'Rubrum', deeper pink flowers. Zones 8–10.

Erodium reichardii
ALPINE GERANIUM

☼ ❄ ↔ 10 in (25 cm) ↕ 1–2 in (2.5–5 cm)
From Majorca and Corsica. Mat-forming species. Small, crinkled, scallop-edged leaves. Delicate white flowers with pink veins, to ½ in (12 mm) across, in summer. Good choice for rock garden. 'Charm', white flowers. Zones 7–10.

Erodium reichardii 'Charm'

Erodium × variabile

☼ ❄ ↔ 10 in (25 cm) ↕ 6–12 in (15–30 cm)
These hybrids of *E. corsicum* and *E. reichardii* are intermediate between the parents. 'Bishop's Form', deep pink flowers with reddish veins; 'Derek' (syn. *E. reichardii* 'Derek'), very compact, with deep pink flowers; 'Flora Pleno', small, pale or deep pink, double flowers; 'Roseum', pink flowers veined with crimson. Zones 7–10.

ERYNGIUM

Belonging to the carrot (Apiaceae) family, this genus of more than 200 species of annuals, biennials, and perennials is found throughout most of the temperate world. Although the flower stems often carry rudimentary leaves, the foliage, which can be very spiny, is almost entirely basal, often forming a large clump. Unlike most umbellifers, with their open airy flowerheads, the flowerheads of *Eryngium* are thistle-like, with the flowers clustered in a central cone surrounded by spiny bracts, often in shades of metallic blue or silver gray. Flowerheads and foliage last well when cut and have a certain charm when dried. Summer is the main flowering season. CULTIVATION: Their hardiness varies with the species, though most will tolerate at least moderate frosts. Some are drought tolerant; most are comfortable in moist well-drained soil with regular watering during the growing season. Propagate by division or from seed.

Eryngium alpinum

☼/◐ ❄ ↔ 24 in (60 cm) ↕ 24 in (60 cm)
Perennial, found from western France to the Balkans. Long-stemmed leaves, deeply lobed, spiny, triangular to heart-shaped, to 6 in (15 cm) long. Purple-blue flowerheads surrounded by a large feathery ruff of spiny, 2½ in (6 cm) long, metallic purple-blue bracts. 'Blue Star', to 30 in (75 cm) tall, bracts more blue than purple. Zones 6–9.

Eryngium amethystinum
AMETHYST SEA HOLLY

☼/◐ ❄ ↔ 20 in (50 cm) ↕ 28 in (70 cm)
Found around the Adriatic to Sicily. Perennial. Leaves to 6 in (15 cm) long, palmately lobed and further divided into narrow spine-tipped segments. Many near-spherical purple-blue flowerheads surrounded by narrow, spiny, purple-tinted bracts, to 2 in (5 cm) long. Zones 7–9.

Eryngium bourgatii
MEDITERRANEAN SEA HOLLY

☼/◐ ❄ ↔ 16 in (40 cm) ↕ 16 in (40 cm)
Native to Spain and the Pyrenees. Perennial, forms low clump of foliage. Leaves much-divided, spiny, rounded, to 3 in (8 cm) across. Branching inflorescence of many flowerheads, to over ½ in (12 mm) wide, with up to 12 narrow light mauve-blue bracts that are not always spiny. 'Oxford Blue', attractive silver-blue bracts and darker flowerheads. Zones 5–10.

Eryngium giganteum
MISS WILLMOTT'S GHOST

☼/◐ ❄ ↔ 32 in (80 cm) ↕ 5 ft (1.5 m)
Perennial, native to Caucasus region. Long-stemmed triangular leaves, to 6 in (15 cm) long, deeply toothed, and spiny. Green to silvery mauve-blue flowerhead, surrounded by up to 10 large, spiny, silver-white bracts. Zones 6–9.

Eryngium bourgatii cultivar

Eryngium × *oliverianum*

☼/◐ ✽ ↔ 20–24 in (50–60 cm) ↕ 24–40 in (60–100 cm)
Perennial with long-stemmed, spiny, toothed leaves, rounded to heart-shaped, with 3 lobes on basal leaves. Bright metallic blue flowerheads, to 1¾ in (40 mm) across, with up to 15 narrow, spiny, purple bracts. Zones 5–9.

Eryngium variifolium

☼/◐ ✽ ↔ 16–20 in (40–50 cm)
↕ 20–30 in (50–75 cm)
Native to North Africa. An evergreen perennial forming a thistle-like basal rosette of white-marbled, dark green, toothed leaves. Flowerheads purple-blue, to 1 in (25 mm) across, with up to 7 narrow, spiny, white-centered bracts. Zones 7–9.

ERYSIMUM

syn. *Cheiranthus*
WALLFLOWER

This genus in the cabbage (Brassicaceae) family, containing some 80 species of sometimes shrubby annuals and perennials, now includes many species formerly classified under *Cheiranthus*. The narrow green to blue-green leaves with shallow lobes are unremarkable, but the 4-petalled flowers are brightly colored, often fragrant, and frequently appear over a long season. In mild climates the bushy forms flower all year round. The hybrids come in a wide variety of colors.
CULTIVATION: Although most species of *Erysimum* are very hardy, they prefer a temperate climate with distinct seasons. Plant in

Erysimum, Hybrid Cultivar, 'Bowles' Mauve'

moist humus-rich soil and water well during the flowering period. They are often quite drought tolerant, but these plants will flower more abundantly with regular watering, feeding, trimming, and deadheading. Propagation of annual species is by seed; perennials can be propagated from seed, from small cuttings of non-flowering stems, or sometimes by division.

Erysimum bicolor

syn. *Cheiranthus bicolor*
☼/◐ ✽ ↔ 24 in (60 cm) ↕ 36 in (90 cm)
Found in the Canary Islands and Madeira. Shrubby perennial with pointed, toothed, lance-shaped leaves. Scented flowers appear from spring onward, opening cream to orange-brown and ageing to mauve. Zones 9–10.

Erysimum cheiri

syn. *Cheiranthus cheiri*
WALLFLOWER
☼/◐ ✽ ↔ 16 in (40 cm) ↕ 24 in (60 cm)
A native of southern Europe. Shrubby perennial, usually cultivated as biennial. Narrow deep green foliage; the lower leaves to 8 in (20 cm) long, becoming smaller higher up. Large heads of yellow and/or orange flowers. The cultivated forms, which are most likely hybrids, include 'Cloth of Gold', deep golden yellow flowers; Fair Lady (quite often called My Fair Lady) Strain, to 18 in (45 cm) tall, blooms in range of pastel shades; 'Fire King Improved', 16 in (40 cm) tall, brilliant orange-red flowers; 'Harpur Crewe', yellow double flowers; and Prince Series, stocky, to 18 in (45 cm) tall, in wide color range. Zones 7–9.

Erysimum Hybrid Cultivars

☼/◐ ✽ ↔ 24 in (60 cm) ↕ 24–36 in (60–90 cm)
These bushy hybrids are of uncertain parentage. Though not long-lasting, they are easily propagated and flower virtually continuously. 'Bowles' Mauve' ★ (syn. 'E. A. Bowles'), best known, masses of small mauve-purple flowers; 'Gold Shot', 18 in (45 cm) tall, golden yellow flowers; 'Sunlight', yellow-flowered low spreader, about 4 in (10 cm) tall, ; 'Wenlock Beauty', magenta flowers ageing to mauve; 'Winter Cheer', two-tone orange and light purple flowers. Zones 7–10.

ESCHSCHOLZIA

CALIFORNIA POPPY

Native to western North America and now widely naturalized, this genus in the poppy (Papaveraceae) family is made up of about 8 annuals and short-lived perennials. They have fine feathery foliage, often a rather grayish green, and in summer produce masses of bright golden yellow 4- to 8-petalled poppies that only open on sunny days. Modern seed strains come in many flower colors; the flowers are followed by long seed capsules.
CULTIVATION: These are easily grown in any sunny position with light, gritty, very well-drained soil, and often self-sow and naturalize. Most are very frost hardy and tolerate poor soil. Propagate from seed, which is best sown where it is required to grow.

Erysimum cheiri, Fair Lady Strain

Eschscholzia caespitosa

TUFTED CALIFORNIA POPPY

☼ ❀ ↔ 10 in (25 cm) ↑ 10 in (25 cm)

From northern California and Oregon, USA. Fast-growing annual. Leaves very finely divided, feathery, green to blue-green. Bright yellow flowers, 2 in (5 cm) across. 'Sundew', to 6 in (15 cm) tall, lemon yellow flowers. Zones 7–10.

Eschscholzia californica

CALIFORNIA POPPY

☼ ❀ ↔ 8–16 in (20–40 cm) ↑ 8–24 in (20–60 cm)

From western USA and northern Baja California, Mexico. Now regarded as weed in parts of Australia. Annual or short-lived perennial. Leaves variable but usually finely divided, feathery, blue-green. Cup-shaped flowers to over 2 in (5 cm) across, usually bright orange but often yellow, rarely cream or pink. Seedling strains available in many colors and forms, including double flowers. 'Dali', interesting soft apricot-colored flowers with 2 rows of petals; 'Red Chief', striking red flowers. Zones 6–10.

ETLINGERA

About 60 species of rhizomatous perennials occur in this genus, which is a member of the ginger (Zingiberaceae) family, and is found from Sri Lanka to New Guinea. The stems are cane-like and the long leaves are borne in 2 ranks. Terminal flowerheads arise from the rhizomes on separate leafless stems; these are made up of small flowers and are surrounded by large, colorful, petal-like bracts. CULTIVATION: In suitably warm climates grow these plants in sun or part-shade in moist humus-rich soil. In cool climates grow indoors in bright filtered light and maintain high humidity. Water well and feed regularly during growth periods. Propagation is from seed or by division.

Etlingera elatior

syns *Nicolaia elatior*, *Phaeomeria magnifica*, *P. speciosa*

PHILIPPINE WAX FLOWER, TORCH GINGER

☼/◑ ✿ ↔ 5–8 ft (1.5–2.4 m) ↑ 10–20 ft (3–6 m)

From western Indonesia and the Malay Peninsula. Spectacular plant with large linear leaves. Cone-like heads of pink to bright red, densely packed, small flowers and waxy bracts of the same color, the outer bracts large and flaring, in summer–autumn. Zones 11–12.

EUPATORIUM

In the broadest sense, this is a genus of more than 450 species, but some botanists have preferred to split off several other genera, leaving only about 40 species in a more narrowly defined *Eupatorium*. As the genus is traditionally understood, *Eupatorium* includes annuals, perennials, subshrubs, and shrubs within the daisy (Asteraceae) family, and is native to eastern North America, Central America and South America, with a very few species in Europe and Asia. All the species of *Eupatorium* have whorled or opposite leaves on simple or branched stems, the stems terminating in corymbs or panicles of small flowerheads, which are the plants' most decorative feature. The fruit is plumed, like thistledown. The flowers are attractive to butterflies. CULTIVATION: These plants require a sunny position in well-drained but moist fertile soil. Growing tips can be pinched back to encourage compact growth. Propagate in spring from seed or cuttings of green wood, or by dividing root clumps when the plant is dormant; protect from frosts.

Eschscholzia californica

Eupatorium perfoliatum

BONESET, THOROUGHWORT

☼ ❀ ↔ 3–5 ft (0.9–1.5 m) ↑ 3–5 ft (0.9–1.5 m)

Native to southeastern USA. Aromatic herbaceous perennial. Erect, branching, hairy stems. Lance-shaped leaves, opposite, wrinkled, toothed, to 8 in (20 cm) long; downy underside. Pairs of leaves joined at base. Large, flat-topped, terminal, compound heads of 10 to 40 tubular white flowers, sometimes tinged with purple, from late summer to autumn. Flowering does not occur until the second year. Zones 3–4.

Eupatorium purpureum ★

JOE PYE WEED, TRUMPET WEED

☼/◑ ❀ ↔ 6–10 ft (1.8–3 m) ↑ 6–10 ft (1.8–3 m)

From eastern USA. Herbaceous perennial. Strong dark red stems. Large whorls of elliptical leaves that are finely toothed, with a purplish tinge. Inflorescence of a half-rounded panicle with 5 to 15 fragrant flowerheads, purple or pale pink to green-ish yellow or rose-purple, in late summer–autumn. *E. p.* subsp. *maculatum* (syn. *E. maculatum*), smaller, with a flat-topped panicle of 15 pale or rose purple flower-heads. Zones 3–9.

Etlingera elatior

Eupatorium rugosum

syn. *Ageratina altissima*

FALL POISON, SNOW THOROUGHWORT, WHITE SNAKEROOT

☼ ❀ ↔ 3–6 ft (0.9–1.8 m) ↑ 3–6 ft (0.9–1.8 m)

From northeastern North America. Perennial herb. Hairy stems. Leaves opposite, elliptical, grayish to purplish green, toothed. Flat-topped clusters of white flowers, at stem tips, in late summer. 'Braunlaub', young foliage and flowers tinted brown. Zones 4–6.

Euphorbia amygdaloides 'Purpurea'

Euphorbia charantias subsp. wulfenii 'Bosahan'

Euphorbia griffithii 'Fireglow'

EUPHORBIA

This large genus of about 2,000 species of annuals, perennials, shrubs, and trees, both evergreen and deciduous, is distributed throughout the world. It gives its name to the large and diverse family Euphorbiaceae. *Euphorbia* alone takes in a very diverse range of forms and natural habitats, from spiny and succulent cactus-like species occurring mainly in hot dry areas to leafy perennials from cool-temperate climates. All species contain a poisonous milky sap which can cause severe irritation if it contacts the skin and, if rubbed into the eyes, may bring on temporary blindness. The true flowers are tiny, with separate male and female forms attached to a smooth cup-like structure, or cyathium. Cyathia are generally accompanied by bracts, which may be larger and are often colored, such as the scarlet bracts of poinsettia *(E. pulcherrima)*. These cyathia and bracts may be arranged in repeatedly branched inflorescences and sometimes form large flowerheads. The flowering times of many species are rainfall dependent; in temperate climates with even rainfall, the likely flowering time is from late spring to mid-summer.
CULTIVATION: Provide similar growing conditions to the plant's natural habitat. In cool-temperate climates most succulent and subtropical species will require greenhouse protection; some will grow in dry rock gardens. Avoid the toxic sap when pruning and disposing of branches. Some species can only be propagated from seed, others can be grown from stem-tip cuttings or by division.

Euphorbia amygdaloides
WOOD SPURGE

☼/◐ ❄ ↔ 24–40 in (60–100 cm) ↑ 20–32 in (50–80 cm)
From temperate Eurasia. Sspreading, mounding, leafy perennial. Soft stems densely foliaged with spatula-shaped leaves, to over 3 in (8 cm) long; often purple-tinted with a slight sheen. Sprays of showy yellow-green flowerheads throughout spring and summer. *E. a.* var. *robbiae*, more robust dark foliage, spreading rosettes. *E. a.* 'Purpurea', stems and foliage strongly tinted with purple-red, new growth is red-wine colored. Zones 7–10.

Euphorbia characias

☼ ❄ ↔ 5 ft (1.5 m) ↑ 6 ft (1.8 m)
Various forms from the Mediterranean region and southern Europe. Perennial subshrub or shrub with soft stems. Narrow, elliptical, gray-green leaves. Heads of up to 20 small purple-green or yellow flowers, backed by conspicuous yellow-green whorled bracts, usually in late winter–early summer. The yellow-green-flowered *E. c.* subsp. *wulfenii* ★, with its various cultivars, is more widely cultivated than the species; 'Bosahan', variegated leaves, pale yellow flowers; 'John Tomlinson', 16 in (40 cm) long heads of bright yellow-green flowers. Zones 8–10.

Euphorbia cyparissias
CYPRESS SPURGE

☼/◐ ❄ ↔ 24 in (60 cm) ↑ 16 in (40 cm)
Widespread in Europe. Perennial, spreads by rhizomes, forms a clump of narrow stems with narrow green leaves, 1¾ in (40 mm) long, which may redden in sun or drought. Yellow-green inflorescence surrounded by mauve- to red-tinted feathery bracts in late spring to mid-summer. 'Fens Ruby', bright red bracts, near-yellow flowerheads, very compact. Zones 4–9.

Euphorbia griffithii

☼ ❄ ↔ 36 in (90 cm) ↑ 36 in (90 cm)
From the Himalayas. Widely grown and usually a perennial, can become shrubby in mild climates. Narrow leaves are, to 5 in (12 cm) long, dark green, tinted pink to orange. Flowerheads, with vivid orange-red bracts in summer, develop coppery tones with age. 'Fireglow', vivid red bracts. Zones 5–10.

Euphorbia marginata
GHOST WEED, SNOW ON THE MOUNTAIN

☼/◐ ❄ ↔ 20 in (50 cm) ↑ 40 in (100 cm)
Native to North America. Annual. Dense mound of light green, soft, downy leaves, to 3 in (8 cm) long, edged in white, sometimes entirely white at the top of the plant. White bracts in summer. Contact with sap can cause severe skin problems. Zones 4–10.

Euphorbia myrsinites ★
CREEPING SPURGE, DONKEY TAIL

◐ ❄ ↔ 20 in (50 cm) ↑ 10 in (25 cm)
From Eurasia. Clump-forming perennial with sprawling stems. Leaves spiralled, finely toothed, pointed, fleshy, blue-green, to 1¾ in (40 mm) long. Bright green cyathia with chrome yellow bracts in spring. Zones 6–10.

Euphorbia nicaeensis

☼ ❋ ↔ 24 in (60 cm) ↑ 24 in (60 cm)

From Europe. Attractive bushy perennial. Stems often tinged red and well covered with narrow bluish gray leaves. Floral bracts are a contrasting yellow-green. Zones 6–10.

Euphorbia polychroma

CUSHION SPURGE

☼ ❋ ↔ 24 in (60 cm) ↑ 24 in (60 cm)

From Eurasia. Clump-forming perennial. Bright green, elliptical, velvety leaves, to about 2 in (5 cm) long. Bright yellow-green, sometimes red-tinted, flowerheads in spring–summer. 'Major', compact, chrome yellow flowerheads. Zones 6–9.

Euphorbia schillingii

☼/◐ ❋ ↔ 5 ft (1.5 m) ↑ 4 ft (1.2 m)

From Nepal. Shrubby perennial. Bright green leaves, narrow, elliptical, to 3 in (8 cm) long. Showy yellow-green flowerheads with rounded green bracts, in summer. Zones 7–9.

Euphorbia seguieriana

☼/◐ ❋ ↔ 32 in (80 cm) ↑ 20 in (50 cm)

Found from central Europe to Pakistan and Siberia. Woody-based perennial. Forms clump of blue-green stems; similarly colored, pointed, linear leaves, to 1½ in (35 mm) long. Large heads of yellow-green cyathia and yellow bracts, in summer. *E. s.* subsp. *niciciana,* less crowded flowerheads. Zones 5–9.

Euphorbia schillingii

Euphorbia sikkimensis ★

☼/◐ ❋ ↔ 36 in (90 cm) ↑ 36 in (90 cm)

From the eastern Himalayas. Rhizome-rooted perennial with upright stems and narrow elliptical leaves, up to 4 in (10 cm) long, and often red-tinted. Attractive pink new growth. Showy orange-red flowerheads in summer. Zones 6–9.

EURYALE

This genus has just one species and belongs to the waterlily (Nymphaeaceae) family. It is found from northern India to China and Japan. It is a very large, perennial, aquatic plant with a massive rhizome. The leaves are round, ribbed, and very prickly. Flowers consist of 4 sepals and numerous petals, which are shorter than the sepals. The fruit is a prickly berry with many seeds.
CULTIVATION: This is often grown as an annual in tropical greenhouses, where it is raised from seed sown immersed in water at 70–73°F (21–23°C).

Euryale ferox

☼ ❋ ↔ 5 ft (1.5 m) ↑ 3 ft (0.9 m)

Leaves 2–5 ft (0.6–1.5 m) across; upperside dull green, with sparse prickles; undersurface reddish, densely armed with prickles. Summer flowers often do not open, remaining more or less submerged. Sepals green; petals red to purple or lilac. Zones 8–11.

EUSTOMA

LISIANTHUS, PRAIRIE GENTIAN, TEXAS BLUEBELL

This genus of family Gentianaceae has 3 species of annuals or short-lived perennials found from southern USA to northern South America. They form clumps of fleshy oval to narrowly elliptical leaves, producing showy 5- to 6-petalled, funnel- to bell-shaped flowers, up to 2 in (5 cm) wide, in summer. Some species carry flowers singly, but the cultivated plants have many-flowered stems up to 24 in (60 cm) long, with blooms in a wide range of colors and in double-flowered forms.
CULTIVATION: These are usually grown as annuals. Slow-growing, they need prolonged warm conditions to flower well. Plant in full or half-sun with fertile, moist, well-drained soil. The heavy flower stems are best staked. May be propagated by cuttings but better if raised fresh from seed.

Eustoma grandiflorum ★

syns *Eustoma russellianum, Lisianthus grandiflorus*

☼/◐ ❋ ↔ 20 in (50 cm) ↑ 24–32 in (60–80 cm)

Annual or short-lived perennial from southern USA and Mexico. Upright blue-green stems; fleshy, blue-green, pointed oval leaves, to 3 in (8 cm) long. Heads of bell-shaped flowers, to 2½ in (6 cm) across. **Echo** mixed color strain, to 24 in (60 cm) tall, in lilac-, blue-, pink-, yellow-, and white-flowered forms as well as picotee-edged; '**Forever Blue**', to 12 in (30 cm) tall, large purple-blue flowers; **Heidi Series**, to 18 in (45 cm) tall, in many colors; **Mermaid Series**, including early-flowering dwarf '**Lilac Rose**', light purple-pink single flowers. Zones 9–11.

Eustoma grandiflorum 'Forever Blue'

EVOLVULUS

This genus of about 100 species comes mostly from tropical and warm-temperate parts of the Americas. It belongs to the bindweed (Convolvulaceae) family. These plants are annuals, perennials, or subshrubs, often creeping but never climbing. The leaves are small, simple, and often narrow. The inflorescences are borne in the leaf axils or at the ends of the stems, each with one to several flowers with 5 small sepals. The corolla is funnel-shaped to flat, blue or pink to white, and has a lobed to smooth margin. The dry seed capsule is spherical to ovate in shape and contains 1 to 4 small seeds.

CULTIVATION: These plants thrive in well-drained soil in full sun. Propagate by root division or from cuttings; the shorter-lived species are readily raised from seed.

Evolvulus glomeratus

syn. *Evolvulus pilosus* of gardens

☼ ❄ ↔ 24–36 in (60–90 cm)
↑ 10–18 in (25–45 cm)
American species, found from South Dakota and Montana to Texas and Arizona, USA. Evergreen perennial. Dense mound of foliage emerging from mass of rhizomes; leaves gray-green with soft silky hairs. Long succession of brilliant blue flowers with a small white eye, 1 in (25 mm) across, in spring–autumn, wilting after noon in hot weather. Sold under the names 'Blue Daze', 'Hawaiian Blue Eyes', and 'Sapphire', but these are doubtfully distinct as cultivars. Often grown in hanging baskets. Zones 9–11.

Evolvulus glomeratus

EXACUM

There are about 25 species of tender annuals, biennials, and perennials in this genus, which is a member of the gentian (Gentianaceae) family and is native to the Old World tropics. The leaves are opposite, oval or elliptic, and often stalkless. Clusters of flowers, sometimes fragrant, are borne on leafy stems. The flowers consist of a narrow tube flaring to 5 flattened petal lobes with protruding yellow stamens.

CULTIVATION: These are popular in temperate regions as pot plants for the house or conservatory. Grow in well-drained but moist potting mix in a well-lit position. These plants can also be grown outdoors as a bedding annual but they are suitable for permanent outdoor cultivation only in humid tropical and subtropical areas. Propagation is from seed.

Exacum affine

GERMAN VIOLET, PERSIAN VIOLET

☼ ⚘ ↔ 12 in (30 cm) ↑ 12–18 in (30–45 cm)
A native of the island of Socotra at the mouth of the Red Sea. Annual or short-lived perennial with pointed oval leaves. Small fragrant flowers, ranging in color from sky blue to pale and deep violet, in spring–autumn. Zones 10–12.

FARFUGIUM

This genus of only 2 species belongs to the daisy (Asteraceae) family, and is native to East Asia. The handsome plants are evergreen perennials with large, deep green, kidney-shaped leaves and clusters of yellow daisies from autumn to winter.

CULTIVATION: Members of this genus are hardy, and easily grown in temperate zones in cool, moist, humus-rich soil. They will grow in damp areas but prefer woodland conditions with good drainage. Full sun is tolerated, but foliage will become lusher in partial shade. Good indoor pot plants in colder climates. Propagation is by division in late winter and spring.

Farfugium japonicum

syn. *Ligularia tussilaginea*

☀ ❄ ↔ 24–40 in (60–100 cm) ↑ 24–40 in (60–100 cm)
Native to Japan, evergreen herbaceous perennial. The only species usually cultivated. Large, kidney-shaped, rich green leaves. Yellow flowers, widely spaced rays, in winter. 'Argenteum', leaves edged with white; 'Aureomaculatum' ★ (leopard plant), irregular yellow spots on leaf; 'Crispatum' (syn. 'Cristata'), green leaves, crumpled crested edges. Zones 8–11.

FELICIA

This is a genus of about 80 species of annuals, perennials, subshrubs, and shrubs belonging to the daisy (Asteraceae) family, mostly evergreen. Most species are from South Africa, with a few species from eastern Africa and Arabia. Preferring open, sunny, low-humidity areas, most species need frost-free conditions. These plants are grown for their mainly blue flowerheads with yellow disc florets. Mauve, pink, and white forms are also available, as are some new cultivars. The shrubby forms are popular as annual container and patio plants, and will overwinter in a greenhouse in colder areas.

CULTIVATION: Members of this genus grow outdoors in moderately fertile soil, but prolonged damp conditions can kill them. When grown in containers they need a loam-based compost with added grit for drainage. The flowering season can be prolonged by removing dead flowers. Propagation is from seed sown in spring, or by taking stem-tip cuttings in summer and overwintering them in frost-free conditions.

Felicia fruticosa

Felicia amelloides

syns *Agathaea coelestis, Felicia aethiopica*
BLUE DAISY, BLUE MARGUERITE

☼ ❄ ↔ 24 in (60 cm) ↑ 16–24 in (40–60 cm)

South African perennial, trailing and/or upright stems. Fine-haired leaves light green.
Solitary flowers, vivid yellow disc florets, light
to dark blue ray florets. Summer-flowering.
'**Blue Eyes**', deep blue flowers; '**Santa Anita**',
heavy flowering, hardier. Zones 9–10.

Felicia fruticosa

☼ ❄ ↔ 36 in (90 cm) ↑ 36 in (90 cm)

Evergreen species, native to South Africa.
Linear leaves densely packed. Ray florets pink,
purple, or white, with yellow disc. Fruits are
hairy. Lengthy flowering season through
spring–summer; can be extended by deadheading. Zones 9–11.

Fittonia albivenis 'Nana'

FILIPENDULA

DROPWORT, MEADOWSWEET

This genus in the rose (Rosaceae) family has about 10 species of
tuberous clump-forming perennials. They are native to northern
temperate regions, where they are usually found growing in damp
habitats. These tall attractive plants have large divided leaves, and
bear plumes of tiny white or pink flowers.
CULTIVATION: Grow in part-shade in moist humus-rich soil that
does not dry out in summer. Propagate from seed or by division.

Filipendula purpurea

◑ ❄ ↔ 18 in (45 cm) ↑ 36–48 in (90–120 cm)

Native to Japan. Stems and leaf stalks often
purple. Stiff, palmate, dark green leaves.
Plumes of small deep pink to purplish
red flowers, in summer. Zones 6–9.

Filipendula rubra

QUEEN OF THE PRAIRIE

◑ ❄ ↔ 2 ft (0.6 m) ↑ 3–7 ft (0.9–2 m)

From eastern USA. Vigorous perennial, forming large clumps of deeply divided foliage.
Tall stems of peachy pink flowers are borne
in plumes in summer. '**Venusta**' ★ (syn.
'Magnifica'), deep rose flowers. Zones 2–9.

Filipendula vulgaris

Filipendula ulmaria

MEADOWSWEET, QUEEN OF THE MEADOWS

◑ ❄ ↔ 12–18 in (45–60 cm) ↑ 24–48 in (60–120 cm)

From Europe and Western Asia. Clump-forming perennial.
Stems tinged red to purple. Large divided leaves, dark green
uppersurface, paler-colored and hairy underside. Showy plumes
of creamy white fragrant flowers in summer. '**Aurea**', golden
yellow foliage; '**Flore Pleno**', double white flowers; '**Rosea**', soft
pink flowers; '**Variegata**', dark green leaves with bright yellow
central marking. Zones 3–9.

Filipendula vulgaris

syn. *Filipendula hexapetala*
DROPWORT

◑ ❄ ↔ 18 in (45 cm) ↑ 24–36 in (60–90 cm)

From Europe and northern and central Asia. Tuberous with
deeply cut fern-like leaves. Small white flowers, often tinged reddish purple, borne in feathery heads in summer. Zones 3–9.

FITTONIA

Usually seen as house plants, the 2 species of low, spreading,
evergreen perennial in this tropical South American genus belong
to the acanthus (Acanthaceae) family. The plants form a mat of
stems that root as they creep across the ground.
The stems and undersides of the oval leaves
are downy. The foliage is the main attraction,
not the rather inconspicuous spikes of tiny
creamy white flowers. The leaves are deep
green to olive, sometimes red-tinted, with
pink to red, or silvery white veins.
CULTIVATION: These do not tolerate prolonged
cool conditions, let alone frost; they need a
warm, humid, draft-free environment with
moist, well-drained, humus-rich soil. They
thrive in terrariums and are easily propagated
by removing small rooted pieces.

Fittonia albivenis

MOSAIC PLANT

☀ ⚘ ↔ 12–24 in (30–60 cm) ↑ 6 in (15 cm)

From Ecuador, Peru, and the western edge of Brazil. Mat-forming,
with stems rooting at nodes. Leaves broadly rounded at tip, dark
green with network of contrasting veins. Flowers small, cream,
for much of the year. '**Nana**', smaller leaves. **Argyroneura Group**
(syns *F. argyroneura, F. verschaffeltii* var. *argyroneura*), leaves deep
green, veined white or faintly pink. **Verschaffeltii Group** (syn.
F. verschaffeltii), leaves dark bronzy green, veins pink. Zones 11–12.

GAILLARDIA
BLANKET FLOWER, FIREWHEEL

This genus of around 30 species of annual, biennial, and perennial daisies (family Asteraceae) occurs mainly in southern Canada, USA, and Mexico. In summer and autumn the small plants are covered with 2–4 in (5–10 cm) wide flowerheads. The ray florets are typically red at the center with a yellow outer half. Garden forms occur in a range of warm tones.
CULTIVATION: Hardiness varies with the species. Plant in a sunny open position with gritty well-drained soil that remains moist during the growing season. Deadhead on a regular basis. Propagate from seed or basal cuttings, or by division.

Gaillardia aristata
☼ ❄ ↔ 32 in (80 cm) ↑ 20 in (50 cm)

Perennial, widespread in western North America. Very hairy stems and leaves, with basal leaves to 8 in (20 cm) long. Narrow lance-shaped leaves may have small basal lobes and/or toothed edges. Flowerheads to 4 in (10 cm) wide with ray florets to more than 1 in (25 mm) long, yellow or yellow with red base; disc florets usually same color as base of ray florets. Zones 6–10.

Gaillardia × grandiflora
☼ ❄ ↔ 40 in (100 cm) ↑ 24 in (60 cm)

Garden hybrid between G. aristata and G. pulchella. 'Burgunder' (syn. 'Burgundy'), deep red flowers; 'Dazzler', 12 in (30 cm) tall, red ray florets tipped golden yellow; 'Indian Yellow', bright golden yellow flowers; Goblin/'Kobold' ★, 16 in (40 cm) tall, red ray florets with yellow border; 'Gaiety' and 'Monarch', hybrids and double-flowered forms in mixed red and gold shades. Zones 5–10.

Gaillardia pulchella
☼ ❄ ↔ 16 in (40 cm) ↑ 24 in (60 cm)

Fast-growing hairy annual from northeastern Mexico and neighboring parts of eastern and central USA. Leaves to over 3 in (8 cm) long, sometimes lobed and/or toothed. Flowerheads around 2½ in (6 cm) wide, ray florets yellow, red, or red with yellow tips. 'Lollipop', to 18 in (45 cm) tall, yellow, red, and orange; 'Red Plume',

Gaillardia × grandiflora Goblin/'Kobold'

12–18 in (30–45 cm) tall, red double flowers; 'Yellow Plume', 12–18 in (30–45 cm) tall, yellow double flowers. Zones 8–10.

GALIUM
BEDSTRAW, CLEAVERS, WOODRUFF

A widespread genus in the madder (Rubiaceae) family with around 400 species of often sprawling annuals and perennials, this includes a few useful species and some rather persistent weeds. Plants are characterized by weak angular stems that spread through surrounding growth and may adhere to it by sticky coatings and/or fine hooked hairs. The small bright green leaves are sometimes in opposite pairs but more often in distinct whorls at intervals. Tiny white or yellow flowers, either solitary or in small clusters, appear in the leaf axils and at the stem tips.
CULTIVATION: Hardiness varies; most thrive in temperate climates. Easily grown in any well-drained soil in full sun or half-sun. Mostly propagated from seed; perennials also by division.

Galium odoratum
syn. Asperula odorata
SWEET WOODRUFF, WOODRUFF
❄ ❄ ↔ 36 in (90 cm) ↑ 18 in (45 cm)

The most attractive species. Aromatic carpet-forming perennial from Europe and North Africa. Stiff, narrow, prickly, elliptic leaves, to 2 in (5 cm) long, and with rough margins, in 6 to 8 neat whorls. Fragrant white flowers, 1½ in (35 mm) across, in terminal clusters, in spring–summer. Zones 3–9.

Galium verum
OUR LADY'S BEDSTRAW, YELLOW BEDSTRAW
❄ ❄ ↔ 3 ft (0.9 m) ↑ 3–4 ft (0.9–1.2 m)

Clump-forming perennial from North America, Europe, and Asia. Small narrow leaves, to 1¼ in (30 mm) long, in whorls of 6 or 8, rough margins rolled under and tipped with bristles. Dense spikes of small, star-shaped, bright yellow flowers in summer–autumn. Can be invasive and weedy. Zones 2–10.

GAURA

The 21 annual and perennial species in this North American genus are well worth growing. Members of the evening primrose (Onagraceae) family, they generally form a clump of irregularly shaped basal leaves from which emerge wiry stems bearing graceful, airy, 4-petalled, white to soft pink flowers. The stems may be more than 36 in (90 cm) tall and appear throughout the warmer months. Various pink-flowered and dwarf cultivars are available.
CULTIVATION: Gaura species prefer full sun with light, gritty, well-drained soil. While drought-tolerant, they flower better with summer moisture. Deadhead routinely and cut back hard after flowering. Propagate from seed in autumn and spring, or from basal cuttings in summer.

Gaura lindheimeri
☼/❄ ❄ ↔ 40 in (100 cm) ↑ 48–60 in (120–150 cm)

Vigorous heavy-flowering perennial from Texas and Louisiana, USA. Forms a clump of upright stems with narrow, elliptical, toothed leaves to 4 in (10 cm) long. Sprays of pink-tinted white

Gaura lindheimeri 'Whirling Butterflies'

flowers to over 1 in (25 mm) wide, upper petals large and wing-like, in spring–summer. '**Corrie's Gold**', foliage edged in golden yellow; '**Karalee Petite**', 24 in (60 cm) tall, deep pink flowers; '**Siskiyou Pink**', bright pink flowers; '**Whirling Butterflies**', 24 in (60 cm) tall, heavy-blooming, large flowers. Zones 5–9.

GAZANIA

TREASURE FLOWER

The 16 species of annuals and perennials belonging to this genus in the daisy (Asteraceae) family are found mainly in South Africa, with 1 species extending the range to the tropics. They are low, near-evergreen, clump-forming plants with simple, narrow, lance-shaped, sometimes downy leaves with paler undersides. Their flowers, which appear throughout the warmer months, are large, brightly colored, often interestingly marked, and always showy. While the species usually have yellow or orange flowers, garden forms are available in a large color range.

CULTIVATION: Apart from being somewhat frost tender and resenting wet winters, they are easily grown in any open sunny position with gritty very free-draining soil. They appreciate additional humus but will grow in poor dry soils. Propagation is by division, or from basal cuttings or seed.

Gazania rigens

TREASURE FLOWER

☼ ✤ ↔40 in (100 cm) ↕8 in (20 cm)
Perennial with fleshy stems that strike root as they spread, forming large leafy clump. Leaves to over 4 in (10 cm) long, smooth-edged or near-pinnately lobed, deep green to bronze above, white hair below. Long-stemmed flowerheads to 3 in (8 cm) wide, ray florets orange with black base, disc florets yellow or reddish orange. *G. r.* var. *uniflora*, small flowerheads, yellow ray florets, and silvery foliage. *G. r.* '**Variegata**', foliage variegated with gold or cream, orange flowers. Zones 9–11.

Gazania Hybrid Cultivars

☼ ✤ ↔20 in (50 cm) ↕4–6 in (10–15 cm)
There is a wide variety of garden forms, sizes, and flower colors. '**Aztec**', soft silvery gray foliage, white ray florets shading to purple-brown at the center; '**Aztec Queen**', yellow ray florets with red-brown base; '**Blackberry Ripple**', buff ray florets with purple midstripe; '**Bronze Gnome**', compact, bronze double flowers; '**Christopher Lloyd**', ray florets light red, darkening near center, green base; '**Cookei**', silvery gray foliage, burnt orange petals shading to taupe toward center; '**Copper King**', large copper-red flowers; '**Cream Dream**', silver-gray foliage, cream ray florets with green base; '**Fiesta Red**', rusty red ray florets with orange base; '**Michael**', dark foliage, yellow ray florets with black base; '**Moonglow**', golden double flowers. Also available as mixed color seedling strains: **Chansonette Series**, early-flowering; **Daybreak** and **Mini-star Series**, compact; **Talent Series**, gray-leafed. Zones 9–11.

GENLISEA

CORKSCREW PLANT

This genus of carnivorous plants belonging to the bladderwort (Lentibulariaceae) family has about 15 species. They come from Africa, Madagascar, and South America, growing in very wet soils along watercourses and in swampy savannahs. These small perennial plants produce 2 types of leaves: green spoon-shaped or lance-shaped leaves above the ground and carnivorous corkscrew-like leaves below ground. These carnivorous leaves fork into 2 prongs, at the base of which is a mouth in which very small prey are captured. Once inside the mouth, the prey cannot escape because inward-pointing hairs block their way, forcing them up through the trap into the digestive chamber.

CULTIVATION: These plants do best in tropical conditions; grow them in a greenhouse in cooler climates. They should be planted in sphagnum moss or a mix of 1 part sand to 1 part peat. Keep the soil waterlogged and provide filtered light. Propagation is from leaf cuttings.

Gazania, Hybrid Cultivar, 'Christopher Lloyd'

Genlisea violacea

◑ ✤ ↔2 in (5 cm) ↕1 in (2.5 cm)
Native of Brazil. Dense rosettes of green, 1 in (2.5 cm) long, spoon-shaped leaves. Violet-like flowers on 4 in (10 cm) leafless stalks. Zones 9–12.

GENTIANA

GENTIAN

This genus has around 400 widely distributed species of annuals, biennials, and perennials and is the type genus for its family, the Gentianaceae. Most form a compact clump of simple pointed leaves, sometimes in rosettes. The trumpet- or bell-shaped flowers may be blue, white, cream, yellow, or purple.

CULTIVATION: Gentians prefer a climate with distinct seasons and grow best in full sun/half-sun with moist, well-drained, humus-rich soil, perhaps with a little dolomite lime. The small species thrive in rockeries. Propagate by division or from seed.

Gentiana acaulis

◐ ✼ ↔ 12 in (30 cm) ↑ 4 in (10 cm)
Found from Spain to the Balkans. Perennial. Clump of short-stemmed, 1 in (25 mm) long, elliptical leaves in basal rosettes. Solitary, deep blue, green-spotted, flared bell-shaped flowers to 2 in (5 cm) long. Spring- to early summer-flowering. 'Rannoch', 2 in (5 cm) tall, dark-centered, deep blue flowers with fine green and/or white stripes. Zones 3–9.

Gentiana asclepiadea

WILLOW GENTIAN
◐ ✼ ↔ 24–40 in (60–100 cm) ↑ 16 in (40 cm)
Eurasian herbaceous perennial with arching stems to 24 in (60 cm) long. Finely tapering, 2–3 in (5–8 cm) long, oval to lance-shaped leaves. Narrow bell-shaped flowers to 1¼ in (30 mm) long, in clusters of 2 to 3 in leaf axils, mauve to purple-blue with darker spotting. Summer- to autumn-flowering. Zones 6–9.

Gentiana saxosa

◐ ✼ ↔ 12 in (30 cm) ↑ 8 in (20 cm)
Near-prostrate herbaceous perennial from New Zealand. Rosettes of purple-tinted, spatula-shaped, basal leaves, to more than 1¼ in (30 mm) long. Short upright flower stems with purple-veined, white, open bell-shaped flowers, solitary or in small heads. Summer-flowering. Zones 8–9.

Gentiana septemfida ★

◐ ✼ ↔ 16 in (40 cm) ↑ 12 in (30 cm)
Native to western and central Asia. Perennial with spreading, sometimes upright stems. Paired pointed oval leaves to nearly 1¾ in (40 mm) long and clusters of light-spotted, bright blue, bell-shaped flowers, to 1¾ in (40 mm) long. Summer- to autumn-flowering. *G. s.* var. *lagodechiana*, branching stems, solitary flowers. Zones 3–9.

Gentiana sino-ornata

◐ ✼ ↔ 12 in (30 cm) ↑ 6 in (15 cm)
Spreading perennial from western China and Tibet. Stems root as they spread. Loose rosettes of narrow lance-shaped leaves to more than 1¼ in (30 mm) long. Solitary, vivid blue, funnel-shaped flowers, to more than 2 in (5 cm) long, lighter inside, with purple and white bands. Autumn-flowering. Zones 6–9.

Gentiana verna

◐ ✼ ↔ 8–12 in (20–30 cm) ↑ 2 in (5 cm)
Prostrate European perennial. Leaves bright green, oval, to 1 in (25 mm) long. Starry vivid blue flowers, pale-centered, usually solitary, to 1 in (25 mm) wide, in spring–summer. Zones 5–9.

GERANIUM

CRANESBILL
The plants often called geraniums in fact belong in the genus *Pelargonium*. While both genera are members of the geranium (Geraniaceae) family, true geraniums are a very different group of some 300 species of perennials and subshrubs, sometimes evergreen, that are widespread in temperate zones. Their leaves, usually palmately lobed, with toothed lobes, are often finely hairy. They bloom in summer and have simple, flat, 5-petalled flowers in pink or purple-blue shades, less commonly white or purple-black. The flowers develop into long narrow fruits.
CULTIVATION: Most species are hardy and will grow in a range of conditions, preferring full sun or half-sun and moist humus-rich soil. The rhizomes can be invasive. Propagate from seed, cuttings, or by division. May self-sow.

Geranium × cantabrigiense

◐/◐ ✼ ↔ 24 in (60 cm) ↑ 8 in (20 cm)
A low spreading *G. macrorrhizum* × *G. dalmaticum* hybrid. Aromatic, bright green, rounded leaves, to 3 in (8 cm) wide, divided into 7 toothed lobes. Flowers to 1 in (25 mm) wide, pink or white with pink center. 'Biokovo', pink-flushed white flowers; 'Cambridge', deep pink to magenta flowers. Zones 5–9.

Geranium cinereum

◐/◐ ✼ ↔ 20 in (50 cm) ↑ 6 in (15 cm)
Found in southern Europe and Turkey. Spreading perennial, rosettes of 5- to 7-lobed gray-green leaves, to 2 in (5 cm) wide. Small heads of often dark-veined white to deep pink flowers, to 1 in (25 mm) wide. 'Purple Pillow', very compact habit, striking funnel-shaped purple-red flowers. Zones 5–9.

Geranium dalmaticum

◐/◐ ✼ ↔ 20 in (50 cm) ↑ 6 in (15 cm)
Small slow-spreading native of Albania and southwest Balkans. Glossy 5- to 7-lobed leaves, to 1¾ in (40 mm) wide. Airy sprays

Gentiana acaulis

Geranium × cantabrigiense

Geranium dalmaticum

of bright pink 5-petalled flowers to more than 1¼ in (30 mm) wide, in summer. Zones 5–9.

Geranium endressii

☼/❋ ❄ ↔ 24 in (60 cm) ↕ 18 in (45 cm)

Long-flowering evergreen perennial from the Pyrenees. Basal leaves 5-lobed, to 6 in (15 cm) wide, upper leaves 3- to 5-lobed and smaller. Foliage reddens in winter. Heads of dark-veined bright pink flowers to 1¾ in (40 mm) wide. **'Beholder's Eye'**, good for use as ground cover, dark pink flowers; **'Castle Drogo'**, pink flowers with large petals that overlap each other. Zones 5–9.

Geranium himalayense

☼/❋ ❄ ↔ 40 in (100 cm) ↕ 18 in (45 cm)

Found from northern Afghanistan to Nepal. Spreading habit with hairy stems and leaves. Basal leaves to 8 in (20 cm) wide, 7-lobed and toothed, upper leaves considerably smaller. Airy sprays of deep purple-blue flowers, to more than 2 in (5 cm) wide, often pink- or white-centered. **'Baby Blue'**, compact habit, vivid bright blue flowers; **'Gravetye'** (syn. 'Alpinum'), intense blue flowers, red-tinted autumn foliage; **'Plenum'** (syn. 'Birch Double'), compact habit, small leaves, purple-blue double flowers. Zones 4–9.

Geranium incanum

☼/❋ ❄ ↔ 40 in (100 cm) ↕ 40 in (100 cm)

Evergreen South African species, with branching main stems; long-stemmed, aromatic, bright green leaves, sometimes paired, finely cut into 5 narrow toothed lobes, downy white undersides. Airy sprays of long-stemmed, light-centered, magenta flowers to more than 1¼ in (30 mm) wide. Zones 8–11.

Geranium macrorrhizum

☼/❋ ❄ ↔ 40 in (100 cm) ↕ 20 in (50 cm)

Spreading clump-forming perennial native to southern Europe. The leaves are 4–8 in (10–20 cm) wide, with 5 to 7 lobes, toothed and further divided. Flower stems to 12 in (30 cm) tall. Densely clustered heads of pink to purple-red flowers in summer. **'Album'**, white flowers with red-tinted sepals; **'Bevan's Variety'**, small leaves, bright magenta flowers; **'Czakor'**, low-growing, magenta flowers with dark sepals; **'Ingwersen's Variety'**, light glossy green leaves, pale pink flowers. Zones 4–9.

Geranium maculatum

☼/❋ ❄ ↔ 40 in (100 cm) ↕ 27 in (70 cm)

Bushy North American perennial found from Manitoba, Canada, to Kansas, USA. Basal leaves to 8 in (20 cm) wide, upper leaves to 4 in (10 cm) wide, 5- to 7-lobed, further divided and toothed. Heads of upward-facing deep pink flowers, to 1¾ in (40 mm) wide, in late spring–summer. Zones 4–9.

Geranium maderense

Geranium maderense

☼/❋ ❅ ↔ 60 in (150 cm) ↕ 60 in (150 cm)

This native of Madeira is regarded as the largest geranium. Shrubby habit with rosettes of deeply lobed and divided leathery leaves, to 12 in (30 cm) wide, long purple-tinted stalks. Large, hairy, purple-stemmed flowerheads with many dark-veined deep pink to magenta flowers, to 1¾ in (40 mm) wide. Zones 9–11.

Geranium × magnificum

☼/❋ ❄ ↔ 40 in (100 cm) ↕ 20 in (50 cm)

Garden hybrid. Leaves to 4 in (10 cm) wide, 9- to 11-lobed, toothed; hairy stems. Heads of dark-veined purple flowers to more than 1¾ in (40 mm) wide, in mid-summer. Zones 5–9.

Geranium × oxonianum

☼/❋ ❄ ↔ 48 in (120 cm) ↕ 24 in (60 cm)

Hybrid between *G. endressii* and *G. versicolor*. Spreads to cover large area. Leaves with 5 fairly shallow lobes, 2–4 in (5–10 cm) wide, sometimes larger. Masses of dark-veined light pink flowers to 1 in (25 mm) wide. *G. × o.* f. *thurstonianum,* deep purple-pink flowers, thin petals. *G. × o.* **'A. T. Johnson'**, pale silvery pink flowers; **'Claridge Druce'**, vigorous, hairy stems, dark leaves, deep pink flowers; **'Rose Clair'**, small with purple to pink flowers; **'Sherwood'**, starry flowers with very narrow pale pink petals; **'Wargrave Pink'**, many soft orange-pink flowers. Zones 5–9.

Geranium phaeum

Geranium phaeum

BLACK WIDOW

☼/❋ ❄ ↔ 16 in (40 cm) ↕ 32 in (80 cm)

Upright, bushy, European perennial with 9-lobed leaves, larger at the base. Heads of 1 in (25 mm) wide flowers, mauve, maroon, to dark purple-red, sometimes near-black. **'Album'** ★, large white flowers; **'Lily Lovell'**, large purple flowers. Zones 5–9.

Geranium pratense 'Mrs Kendall Clark'   Geranium sylvaticum   Geranium, Hybrid Cultivar, 'Patricia'

Geranium pratense
MEADOW CRANESBILL

❁/❂ ❋ ↔ 40 in (100 cm) ↕ 48 in (120 cm)
Sturdy spreading perennial found from central Europe to western Himalayas. Upright stems, leaves 4–8 in (10–20 cm) wide, 7 to 9 deep pinnate lobes, toothed. Flowerheads crowded to rather open; blue flowers to 2 in (50 mm) wide. 'Mrs Kendall Clark', pale flowers with translucent veins; 'Splish-splash', pale flowers randomly sectored and flecked with light purple-blue. Zones 5–9.

Geranium psilostemon

❁/❂ ❋ ↔ 16–24 in (40–60 cm) ↕ 24–40 in (60–100 cm)
Upright slightly spreading perennial from northeastern Turkey. Leaves 2–8 in (5–20 cm) wide, deeply lobed, and further divided. Erect heads of black-centered magenta flowers, to over 1¼ in (30 mm) wide. Zones 6–9.

Geranium × riversleaianum

❁/❂ ❋ ↔ 24 in (60 cm) ↕ 4 in (10 cm)
Garden hybrid. Low spreading habit with small, 7-lobed, bronze green leaves. Open heads of dark-veined, funnel-shaped, pink flowers, to more than 1¼ in (30 mm) wide. 'Mavis Simpson', light-centered flowers; 'Russell Prichard', deep pink flowers, sharply toothed leaves. Zones 7–10.

Geranium sanguineum
BLOODY CRANESBILL

❁/❂ ❋ ↔ 16 in (40 cm) ↕ 8 in (20 cm)
Low, slowly spreading, bushy Eurasian perennial. Leaves 2–4 in (5–10 cm) wide, 5- to 7-lobed, further divided. Many flowers, borne singly, magenta to purple-red, to over 1¼ in (30 mm) wide. *G. s.* var. *striatum* is small plant with dark-veined soft pink flowers, of which 'Splendens' is taller form. *G. s.* Alan Bloom/ 'Bloger', small leaves, compact habit, deep magenta flowers; 'Album', white flowers; 'Max Frei', similar to Alan Bloom/'Bloger' but darker foliage, longer flower stems. Zones 5–9.

Geranium sylvaticum

❂ ❋ ↔ 40 in (100 cm) ↕ 27 in (70 cm)
Native to Europe and northern Turkey, usually growing in moist places. Leaves finely hairy, 2–8 in (5–20 cm) wide, 7 to 9 deep lobes, further divided and toothed. Dense heads of usually mauve-blue but sometimes white to magenta flowers, to 1¼ in (30 mm) wide. 'Album', pure white flowers; 'Mayflower', purplish blue flowers with pale centers. Zones 4–9.

Geranium wallichianum

❁/❂ ❋ ↔ 24 in (60 cm) ↕ 6 in (15 cm)
Spreading mountain perennial found from northeastern Afghanistan to Kashmir. Paired, 3- to 5-lobed, deeply divided and toothed leaves, about 3 in (8 cm) wide, often long-stemmed. Bowl-shaped, light-centered, magenta or light purple flowers, to over 1¼ in (30 mm) wide. 'Buxton's Variety' ★ (syn. 'Buxton's Blue'), prostrate habit and light-centered bright mauve-blue flowers. Zones 7–10.

Geranium Hybrid Cultivars

❁/❂ ❋ ↔ 24–48 in (60–120 cm) ↕ 8–36 in (20–90 cm)
Geraniums tend to sport readily and interbreed freely, so there are many garden forms in assorted sizes and flower colors. 'Ann Folkard', trailing habit, yellow-green foliage, magenta flowers with dark-center; 'Ballerina', red-veined purple-pink flowers, notched petal tips; 'Frances Grate', silvery foliage, reddish purple flowers; 'Johnson's Blue' ★, 18 in (45 cm) tall, bushy to semi-trailing habit, bright blue to purple-blue flowers; 'Nimbus', 16 in (40 cm) tall, glossy foliage, starry purple flowers; 'Patricia', spreading, rather open habit with black-centered magenta-pink flowers; 'Philippe Vapelle', 16 in (40 cm) tall, large leaves, densely foliaged, dark-veined lavender blue flowers; 'Pink Spice', trailing, dark bronze foliage, small pink flowers; 'Rambling Robin', mounding, spreading habit, lavender-blue flowers; Rozanne/'Gerwat', to 20 in (50 cm) tall, variegated foliage, large violet-blue flowers; 'Sue Crûg', bushy habit, mauve-pink flowers, with darker centers and veins. Zones 6–9.

GERBERA
BARBERTON DAISY, TRANSVAAL DAISY

Some 40 species of daisy (Asteraceae) family perennials make up this genus, best known for its winter-flowering South African representatives; other species occur in western and southern Asia. Resembling highly sophisticated dandelions, they have a basal rosette of deeply lobed and softly toothed spatula- to lance-shaped leaves, and from the center of the rosette emerge strong flower stems, each bearing one large daisy head. Available in a wide color range and double flowers.

CULTIVATION: Gerberas are tender but can tolerate light frosts if kept barely moist in winter. Plant in full sun with deep, light, humus-rich soil with added grit for drainage. Popular as a house plant and cut flower. Propagation is from seed or by careful division after flowering.

Gerbera jamesonii ★
BARBERTON DAISY
☼ ❄ ↔ 30 in (75 cm) ↑ 27 in (70 cm)
Native to South Africa and Swaziland. Long-stemmed, deep green, dandelion-like leaves with coarse lobes and finely hairy undersides. Leaves can be more than 24 in (60 cm) long but usually considerably smaller. Flowerheads long-stemmed, to 4 in (10 cm) wide, usually in yellow, orange, or red shades. Zones 8–11.

Gerbera Hybrid Cultivars
❂ ❄ ↔ 12 in (30 cm) ↑ 8–18 in (20–45 cm)
These plants produce a long succession of large flowerheads throughout much of the year, in both pastel and strong colors. **Dwarf Pandora Series**, large single blooms on short stems, in a mix of reds, oranges, yellows, pinks, and whites, usually 3 to 6 open at any one time. **Fantasia Double Series**, very large double blooms with quilled central florets, in a range of soft colors. **Happipot Series**, large blooms in vivid shades, deep green leaves. Zones 9–11.

GEUM
AVENS
This genus in the rose (Rosaceae) family, consisting of around 40 species and perennials, is widely distributed in the temperate regions. The plants are either rosette-forming or spread by rhizomes or runners, with their finely hairy pinnate or lobed leaves arising directly from the roots. From late winter to late summer, depending on the species, they produce flower stems bearing showy flowers that resemble tiny single roses, usually in bright shades of yellow, orange, pink, or red. Bristly dry fruits follow the flowers.

CULTIVATION: The small species are popular for rockeries, while larger forms suit perennial borders. Plant in a sunny position with moist well-drained soil that does not become compacted. Propagate by division when dormant, or raise from seed.

Geum chiloense
☼/❂ ❄ ↔ 20 in (50 cm) ↑ 30 in (75 cm)
Heavy-flowering Chilean perennial that has been extensively developed in cultivation. Basal rosette of long leaves divided into many toothed 1 in (25 mm) lobes. Erect flower stems with terminal panicles of bright red flowers. Summer-flowering. 'Farncombe', orange-yellow, semi-double, upward facing flowers; 'Werner Arends' (syn. 'Borisii'), many light orange-red semi-double flowers. Zones 5–9.

Geum chiloense
'Werner Arends'

Geum montanum
ALPINE AVENS
☼/❂ ❄ ↔ 20 in (50 cm) ↑ 12 in (30 cm)
Native to the mountains of central and southern Europe. Creeping rhizome-rooted perennial. Rosettes of bright green pinnate leaves, to 6 in (15 cm) long, large terminal leaflet making up half that length. Small heads of bright yellow flowers, to more than 1 in (25 mm) wide, in spring–early summer. Zones 6–9.

Geum rivale
INDIAN CHOCOLATE, WATER AVENS
☼/❂ ❄ ↔ 30 in (75 cm) ↑ 12 in (30 cm)
Eurasian and North American native forming a small clump and spreading by rhizomes. Slightly pendulous heads of creamy yellow flowers within downy purple-red calyces. Leaves to 12 in (30 cm) long, pinnate, with 7 to 13 toothed leaflets. 'Leonardii' (syn. 'Leonard's Variety'), soft orange-red flowers. Zones 3–9.

Geum triflorum
LION'S BEARD, OLD MAN'S WHISKERS, PRAIRIE SMOKE, PURPLE AVENS
☼/❂ ❄ ↔ 16 in (40 cm) ↑ 16 in (40 cm)
North American species. Ferny leaves, to 6 in (15 cm) long, gray-green, sometimes very downy. Flower stems to 16 in (40 cm) tall, with clusters of small, maroon-tinted, yellow flowers. Zones 6–9.

Geum Hybrid Cultivars
☼/❂ ❄ ↔ to 36 in (90 cm) ↑ 36 in (90 cm)
Geums hybridize freely. 'Beech House Apricot', flower stems to 8 in (20 cm), light yellow to apricot flowers; 'Coppertone', pale-apricot flowers; 'Fire Opal', 30 in (75 cm) tall, semi-double orange-red flowers; 'Lady Stratheden', 24 in (60 cm) tall, bright yellow double flowers; 'Mrs J. Bradshaw' ★, 24 in (60 cm) tall, bright red semi-double flowers; 'Starker's Magnificum', flower stems to 16 in (40 cm), flowers soft orange-pink; 'Tangerine', 5 in (12 cm) flower stems, bright orange flowers. Zones 6–9.

Gerbera Hybrid Cultivar

GILLENIA

This North American genus of 2 species of rhizome-rooted perennials belongs to the rose (Rosaceae) family. They form shrubby
clumps of upright, arching, branching stems bearing stemless
trifoliate leaves with toothed leaflets that turn orange in autumn.
Loose sprays of 5-petalled flowers appear from spring to summer,
with calyces that last long after the flowers have fallen, enlarging
and reddening as the small seed heads develop.
CULTIVATION: These are very hardy but do best when protected
from hot sun. They are easily grown in dappled light and moist,
humus-rich, well-drained soil. Propagate from stratified seed,
or by dividing established clumps as they
enter or leave dormancy in autumn or spring.

Gillenia trifoliata
BOWMAN'S ROOT, INDIAN PHYSIC

☀ ❄ ↔ 48 in (120 cm) ↑ 48 in (120 cm)
Found in eastern North America, from
Ontario to Georgia. Leaves with serrated
pointed oval leaflets to nearly 3 in (8 cm)
long. Flowers to 1 in (25 mm) wide, white,
sometimes pink- or purple-tinted. Zones 4–9.

GLAUCIUM
HORNED POPPY, SEA POPPY

This genus in the poppy (Papaveraceae) family has around
25 species of annuals, biennials, and perennials and is found from
Europe to North Africa, central and western Asia, often in coastal
areas. They are similar in general appearance to poppies but are
clearly differentiated by the long horn-shaped seed capsules that
follow the flowers. Most species have blue-green leaves, toothed
and often pinnately lobed, in a basal rosette. Upright, sometimes
branching flower stems with small leaves emerge from the rosette
in summer, and carry 4-petalled flowers, usually 2–4 in (5–10 cm)
wide, in warm shades of yellow, orange, or red.
CULTIVATION: These plants are hardy to moderate frosts and are
very easily grown in any temperate climate with reasonably warm
summers. Plant in full sun with light, rather gritty, free-draining

Gloxinia sylvatica

soil. Most species, even the perennial ones, are propagated
from seed and may self-sow, though rarely invasively.

Glaucium flavum
YELLOW-HORNED POPPY

☀ ❄ ↔ 16 in (40 cm) ↑ 40 in (100 cm)
Biennial or short-lived perennial from Europe, North Africa,
and the Middle East. Hairy, pinnately lobed, toothed, blue-green
leaves. Branching stems with bright yellow or orange flowers, to
2 in (5 cm) wide. Narrow curved seed pods, to 12 in (30 cm) long.
G. f. f. *fulvum*, grayish foliage, orange-yellow flowers. Zones 7–10.

Glaucium flavum

GLOBBA

There are about 70 species of tender, fleshy-
stemmed, rhizomatous perennials in this
genus, which is a member of the ginger
(Zingiberaceae) family. They are native to
forested areas of southeastern Asia and northeastern India. The lance-shaped to oblong
leaves are carried on reed-like pseudostems to
3 ft (0.9 m) tall. Pendulous terminal racemes
bear oddly shaped flowers, often spurred,
with protruding stamens and colorful bracts.
CULTIVATION: In warm areas grow these plants outdoors in a shady
well-drained situation. In cooler climates start plants indoors in
spring and place outside after danger of frost has passed, or grow
indoors in bright indirect light with high humidity. Propagate
from the bulbils produced on the flowering stems.

Globba winitii

☀ ❄ ↔ 24 in (60 cm) ↑ 36 in (90 cm)
From Thailand. The most commonly grown species. Long leaves,
heart-shaped bases, hairy beneath. Flowers have magenta bracts
with yellow floral parts. Zones 9–11.

GLOXINIA

Not to be confused with *Sinningia*, which includes the florist's
gloxinia, this genus of some 8 species of perennials and subshrubs
in the African violet (Gesneriaceae) family occurs in Central
America and tropical South America. They are mostly small plants
that form bushy clumps of stems bearing opposite pairs of simple
pointed oval leaves, often finely toothed. The stems and foliage
are usually covered with fine velvety hairs. Single or paired
funnel- or bell-shaped flowers appear in the leaf axils.
CULTIVATION: These adapt well to pot cultivation and are usually
grown as house or greenhouse plants outside the tropics. They
prefer even warm temperatures, absence of cool drafts, and ample
humidity. Plant in half-sun or full shade in moist, humus-rich,
free-draining soil. Propagate from seeds or stem or leaf cuttings.

Gloxinia perennis

☀ ❄ ↔ 15 in (38 cm) ↑ 24 in (60 cm)
Perennial from Colombia to Peru. Heart-shaped, hairy, toothed
leaves, to 8 in (20 cm) long, pale red underneath. Solitary lower
flowers, upper flowers in racemes with bell-shaped pale purple
corollas, purple-blotched throat, late summer–autumn. Zones 10–12.

Gloxinia sylvatica

☀ ⚘ ↔ 24 in (60 cm) ↑ 24 in (60 cm)

Native to Bolivia and Peru. Mounds, then spreads by runners, to become slightly trailing. Lustrous, narrow, lance-shaped leaves. Orange-red to red bell-shaped flowers, to 1 in (25 mm) long, held clear of the foliage in terminal clusters, in cooler months. 'Bolivian Sunset', red flowers with orange interior. Zones 10–12.

GOMPHRENA

Native to tropical parts of the Americas and Australia, the 90-odd annuals and perennials in this genus are members of the amaranth (Amaranthaceae) family. The flowers are borne in small, usually upright, heads. The cultivated species form bushy mounds with leaves that are simple narrow oblongs in opposite pairs. The stems are finely hairy, the leaves less so. The flower-heads are borne on wiry stems and held just above the foliage. Each head is a short plume of many tiny flowers, usually creamy yellow, mauve, or pink in the species.
CULTIVATION: Out of the tropics these plants are treated as annuals; they need long warm summers to flower. Plant in moist humus-rich soil and water well; do not overfeed. Propagate from seed.

Gomphrena globosa

BACHELOR'S BUTTON, GLOBE AMARANTH

☼ ❁ ↔ 18 in (45 cm) ↑ 24 in (60 cm)

From Panama and Guatemala. Bushy annual with slightly hairy pointed leaves. Flowers papery and round, white through to red, purple, and yellow, in summer. 'Lavender Lady', lavender-colored flowers; 'Strawberry Fields', flowers scarlet to crimson. Zones 7–11.

GUNNERA

There are 40 to 50 species of fleshy stemmed perennials in this genus in the family Gunneraceae. They are native to Australasia, South Africa, South America, and the Pacific. Species range from tiny ground huggers to spectacular giants of 7 ft (2 m) or more. Grown for their foliage, which may be round to oval, heart-shaped or deeply lobed, with or without toothed margins. Tiny greenish yellow or red flowers are borne on spikes in summer, and followed by red, orange, yellow, or white berries.
CULTIVATION: These are excellent plants for waterside planting. Grow in moisture-retentive soils in full sun. Cover the crowns of large species with a protective mulch in winter. Propagate from seed or by division.

Gunnera manicata

syn. *Gunnera brasiliensis*

GIANT RHUBARB

☼ ❁ ↔ 10–15 ft (3–4.5 m) ↑ 6–10 ft (1.8–3 m)

Spectacular species from South America. Rhubarb-like leaves, 7 ft (2 m) or more across, sharply toothed, spiny beneath. Tiny greenish red flowers on erect spikes 3–6 ft (0.9–1.8 m) tall. Zones 7–9.

Gunnera prorepens

☼ ❁ ↔ 12–18 in (30–45 cm) ↑ 2–4 in (5–10 cm)

Mat-forming stoloniferous perennial from New Zealand. Small, round-toothed, ovate leaves, bronze to purplish green. Male and

Gunnera manicata

female flowers on separate plants; the female plants bear short spikes of dense red berries after flowering. Zones 8–10.

GUZMANIA

This genus of about 200 usually epiphytic species and more than 200 hybrids belongs to the bromeliad (Bromeliaceae) family. The plants are found mainly in Ecuador and Colombia and also in Central America and the West Indies. They grow up to 40 in (100 cm) high and wide but are mostly smaller, with green, spine-less, strap-like leaves, sometimes finely lined or cross-banded on the undersides, forming an open rosette. The flower stem is usually conspicuous and the flowerhead is globular to cylindrical, with side branches and flowers on all sides. Beneath each branch or flower there are generally brilliantly colored bracts in yellow to orange to red shades. Petals are white or yellow.
CULTIVATION: Recommended for indoor culture if in flower, for greenhouse in cool-temperate areas, or outdoors with protection from continuous sunlight and excessive heat in warm-temperate, subtropical, and tropical areas. Prefers a damp atmosphere and a constant warm temperature. Water when potting mix is dry. Do not over-fertilize. Propagate from seed or offsets.

Guzmania lingulata

☀ ⚘ ↔ 8 in (20 cm) ↑ 12 in (30 cm)

Widespread from the West Indies and Central America to Bolivia and Brazil. Leaves 18 in (45 cm) long, forming a dense spreading rosette. Flower stem usually shorter than leaves. Flowerhead globular with up to 50 flowers, petals white, nestling in a bed of large red to pink bracts. *G. l.* var. *cardinalis* has bright red hooded bracts, foliage often striped. *G. l.* 'Estrella', orange-red flower-head; 'Empire', smaller form with orange-red star-shaped flower-head; 'Fortuna', white-tipped brilliant red bracts; 'Rondo', similar to 'Empire' but with red-striped leaves. Zones 10–12.

Guzmania musaica

☀ ✈ ↔ 16 in (40 cm) ↕ 20 in (50 cm)

From Panama and Colombia. Strap-like leaves, to 27 in (70 cm) long, can be totally green on both sides, or green on top and purple beneath, or with fine, dark, irregular, transverse lines, forming an open rosette. Flower stem shorter than leaves. Spherical flowerhead, with up to 25 white flowers mainly pointing upward. Below each flower is a small red bract. Zones 10–12.

Guzmania wittmackii

☀ ✈ ↔ 36 in (90 cm) ↕ 30 in (75 cm)

From Colombia and Ecuador. Green strap-like leaves, 32 in (80 cm) long, forming an open funnel-shaped rosette. Flower stem equal in length to leaves. Flowerhead long and slender with very small branches. Below each branch is a long thin bract, to 3 in (8 cm) long, which can be red, orange, white, or even green. Flowers have long white petal tube, about 3 in (8 cm) long. Zones 10–12.

Guzmania Hybrid Cultivars

☀ ✄ ↔ 10–24 in (25–60 cm)
↕ 18–36 in (45–90 cm)

Most of these have brilliantly colored and large inflorescence bracts. '**Amaranth**', green leaves with brownish lines on undersides, intense raspberry-purple flower bracts, petals white; '**Attila**', dark green rosette, red bracts, yellow flowers; '**Caroline**', bright green rosette, pinkish red bracts; '**Cherry**', leaves reddish green with faint striping at the base, vibrant cherry red bracts, yellow flowers. '**Cherry Smash**', '**Grand Prix**' ★, '**Grapeade**', '**Orangeade**', and '**Samba**', similar but have different-colored bracts. Some forms also have variegated leaves. Zones 9–12.

GYNURA

VELVET PLANT

This genus of some 50 species of perennials and subshrubs belongs in the daisy (Asteraceae) family and comes from the tropics, ranging from Java through Thailand to China all the way to East Africa. Often brightly colored, the flowers are small. These plants are grown for their handsome velvet-covered foliage.
CULTIVATION: Except in the tropics, where they can be grown outside in part-shade, these plants are usually grown indoors. Propagate from cuttings; fresh young stock grown each year is best.

Gynura aurantiaca

PURPLE VELVET PLANT, ROYAL VELVET PLANT, VELVET PLANT

☀ ✈ ↔ 4 ft (1.2 m) ↕ 7–8 ft (2–2.4 m)

Trailing, soft-wooded, evergreen plant from Java. Rich purple bristles cover the 8 in (20 cm) long, spearhead-shaped, scalloped

Guzmania, Hybrid Cultivar, 'Grand Prix'

leaves and stems. Small orange flowers, to 1 in (25 mm) wide, in open clusters, in winter. '**Purple Passion**' (syn. *G. sarmentosa* of gardens), more trailing, stems and leaves covered with purple bristles. Zones 10–12.

GYPSOPHILA

BABY'S BREATH

Related to the pink (Caryophyllaceae) family, the 100-odd annuals and perennials in this genus occur naturally in temperate Eurasia. They can be spreading mat-forming plants studded with pink or white blooms, or upright shrubby species with billowing heads of tiny flowers. Leaves are simple linear to lance-shaped, sometimes rather fleshy, and often blue-green. *G. paniculata* and its cultivars are very popular cut flowers.
CULTIVATION: *Gypsophila* means lime-loving, but most species are happy in any neutral to slightly alkaline soil that is fertile, moist, and well-drained. Mat-forming species are superb rockery plants. Plant in full sun. Larger types will often rebloom if cut back after their first flush. Propagate from basal cuttings or seed.

Gypsophila cerastioides

☼/☀ ❄ ↔ 8 in (20 cm) ↕ 3 in (8 cm)

Mat-forming perennial from the Himalayas. Small, downy, gray-green leaves with small sprays of pink-veined white or mauve flowers to over ½ in (12 mm) wide. Zones 5–9.

Gypsophila repens

Gypsophila paniculata

BABY'S BREATH

❋/❋ ❋ ↔ 48 in (120 cm) ↑ 48 in (120 cm)

Rhizome-rooted perennial found from central Europe to central Asia. Forms a bushy clump of narrow blue-gray leaves to 3 in (8 cm) long, often hidden below billowing panicles massed with tiny white or pink flowers. '**Bristol Fairy**' ★, the most widely grown form, has relatively large white double flowers. Zones 4–9.

Gypsophila repens

❋/❋ ❋ ↔ 24 in (60 cm) ↑ 4 in (10 cm)

Mat-forming perennial from the mountains of central and southern Europe. Narrow, pointed oval, blue-green leaves to more than ½ in (12 mm) long. Sprays of up to 25 tiny, white, pink, or mauve flowers. '**Rosa Schönheit**' (syn. 'Rose Beauty'), rose pink flowers. Zones 4–9.

Gypsophila 'Rosenschleier'

syn. *Gypsophila* 'Rosy Veil'

❋ ❋ ↔ 36 in (90 cm) ↑ 12 in (30 cm)

Pale pink-flowered hybrid. Blue-green leaves. Zones 4–9.

HEDYCHIUM

GARLAND LILY, GINGER LILY

This genus is a member of the ginger (Zingiberaceae) family and includes some 40 species of perennials with heavy rhizomes from which emerge strong cane-like pseudostems with large leaves like those of canna lilies. Native to tropical Asia, the Himalayan region, and Madagascar, they have naturalized elsewhere and have become troublesome at times, one species being a serious pest in northern New Zealand. Ginger lilies are grown mainly for their colorful and fragrant flowerheads, in which are clustered many slender-tubed flowers with protruding anthers. The flowers appear in summer and are mainly in yellow or pink shades. CULTIVATION: They are mostly tolerant of very light frosts and capable of reshooting from the rootstock. Plant in sun or shade with fertile, moist, humus-rich, well-drained soil. Cut back the spent flower stems and any old, unproductive canes to encourage fresh growth. Propagate by division or from seed.

Hedychium coccineum

RED GINGER LILY, SCARLET GINGER LILY

❋/❋ ❋ ↔ 2–5 ft (0.6–1.5 m) ↑ 7–10 ft (2–3 m)

Himalayan native with very narrow leaves to 20 in (50 cm) long. Heads of pink, orange, or red flowers with similarly colored lower lip and filaments. Autumn-flowering. '**Tara**', large spikes of orange flowers. Zones 7–12.

Hedychium coronarium

BUTTERFLY LILY, GARLAND FLOWER, WHITE GINGER

❋/❋ ❋ ↔ 2–5 ft (0.6–1.5 m) ↑ 10 ft (3 m)

Indian species with lance-shaped leaves to 24 in (60 cm) long and a little more than 4 in (10 cm) wide. Heads of very fragrant white butterfly-like flowers with yellow-green markings. Spring-flowering. '**F. W. Moore**', soft yellow-brown flowers with orange markings. Zones 8–12.

Hedychium greenei

Hedychium gardnerianum

GINGER LILY, KAHILI GINGER

❋/❋ ❋ ↔ 3–5 ft (0.9–1.5 m) ↑ 8 ft (2.4 m)

Northern Indian and Himalayan native. Leaves to 16 in (40 cm) long. Dense spikes of many cream and yellow flowers with conspicuous red filaments. Summer- to autumn-flowering. Very vigorous species. Zones 8–11.

Hedychium greenei

❋/❋ ❋ ↔ 32–48 in (80–120 cm) ↑ 7 ft (2 m)

Summer-flowering native of Bhutan. Very narrow leaves to 10 in (25 cm) long and bright red flowers in 5 in (12 cm) long spikes. May form bulbils in the leaf axil near flowerheads. Zones 8–12.

HELENIUM

SNEEZEWEED

This mainly North American genus in the daisy (Asteraceae) family contains about 40 species of annuals, biennials, and perennials. Most form an upright foliage clump and have simple lance-shaped leaves, usually covered with fine hairs. From mid-summer into autumn they produce large flowerheads with a central cone of disc florets and large often slightly drooping ray florets. Yellow and orange to red shades are common. CULTIVATION: Hardiness of these plants varies but most species are very frost tolerant. Plant in a sunny, open position in moist, well-drained soil. Regular removal of dead flowers prolongs flowering; alternatively pick the flowers for use as a cut flower to encourage repeat flowering. Propagation is by division, or from basal cuttings or seed.

Helenium autumnale

SNEEZEWEED

❋ ❋ ↔ 3 ft (0.9 m) ↑ 5 ft (1.5 m)

North American perennial making a dense clump of stems with narrow, usually serrated, leaves to 6 in (15 cm) long topped with many 2 in (5 cm) wide, bright yellow to golden flowerheads each with up to 20 reflexed ray florets. '**Sunshine Hybrid**' is a seedling strain with yellow, orange, red-brown, and red flowers in a range of color patterns. Zones 3–9.

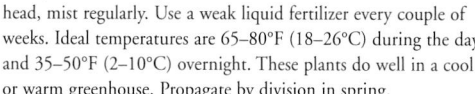
Helenium, Hybrid Cultivar, 'Waldtraut'

Helenium Hybrid Cultivars

☀ ❀ ↔ 40 in (100 cm) ↑ 40 in (100 cm)

These are heavy-flowering plants usually more compact than the species. 'Moerheim Beauty', red-brown to red flowers, strongly downward-angled ray florets; Pipsqueak/'Blopip', 18 in (45 cm) tall, yellow ray florets and red-brown disc florets; 'Waldtraut' ★, burnt orange and gold flowers; 'Wyndley', gold to tawny brown ray florets, brown disc florets. Zones 5–9.

HELIAMPHORA

MARSH PITCHER, SUN PITCHER

A carnivorous genus of 9 known species in the pitcher plant (Sarraceniaceae) family, native to Brazil, Guyana, and Venezuela. They have tubular green to red pitchers that range from 1¾ in (40 mm) to 20 in (50 cm) in height, and most have a small overhanging cap. The pitchers are arranged in a rosette attached to a stem at the base. Insects are attracted to the plant by the bright colors and nectar under the lid of the pitcher. The upper interior of the pitcher is covered in downward-pointing hairs, and then it becomes smooth and slippery. Insects slide into the well of water and are digested by the plant. CULTIVATION: Grow in full sun in sphagnum or a mix of 4 parts peat to 1 part perlite. In very hot weather pots should be placed in shade or in trays of water. Keep soil moist, water overhead, mist regularly. Use a weak liquid fertilizer every couple of weeks. Ideal temperatures are 65–80°F (18–26°C) during the day and 35–50°F (2–10°C) overnight. These plants do well in a cool or warm greenhouse. Propagate by division in spring.

Heliamphora heterodoxa

☀/◑ ❅ ↔ 12 in (30 cm) ↑ 18 in (45 cm)

From Venezuela. Lime green pitchers, usually red toward the top. Pitcher lid green on young plants, red on older ones. Pink and white flowers in early to mid-winter. Easy to grow. Zones 10–12.

Heliamphora minor

☀/◑ ❅ ↔ 6 in (15 cm) ↑ 3 in (8 cm)

From Auyan Tepuis and Chimanta Tepuis in Venezuela. The smallest species. Cone-shaped, green to red, 3 in (8 cm) high pitchers. Emerging pitchers are covered in fine white hairs; older pitchers have hairs along central seam and near rim. Pink flowers in spring. *H. m.* × *heterodoxa*, pale pink flowers. Zones 8–10.

HELIANTHUS

SUNFLOWER

This genus of 70 annuals and perennials in the daisy (Asteraceae) family is from the Americas and is best known for the common or giant sunflower *(H. annuus)*, which is both popular as an ornamental and widely grown commercially for its seeds and the oil extracted from them. Other species are smaller and tend to have lance-shaped rather than heart-shaped leaves. Most have bristly stems. The flowers are held above the foliage and are nearly always yellow. Double-flowered forms are common. Flowerheads turn to follow the sun. CULTIVATION: Plant in a sunny, open position with fertile, moist, well-drained soil. Mildew can be a problem but usually only when the plants are past their best. Propagate annuals from seed and perennials also by division and from basal cuttings.

Helianthus annuus

COMMON SUNFLOWER

☀ ❀ ↔ 2–4 ft (0.6–1.2 m) ↑ 10–17 ft (3–5 m)

Quick-growing annual native to USA. Broad, bristly, toothed, pointed heart-shaped leaves to 16 in (40 cm) long. Flowerheads to 12 in (30 cm) wide from mid-summer, ray florets yellow around a purple-brown disc. 'Music Box', mixed color seedling strain with 2-tone ray florets, 30 in (75 cm) tall; 'Ring of Fire', 5 ft (1.5 m) tall, flower 5 in (12 cm) wide, yellow and red ray florets; 'Ruby Eclipse', 6 ft (1.8 m) tall, red-tinted primrose ray florets, red at base, no pollen; 'Sunrich Orange', 5 ft (1.5 m) tall, bright orange ray florets, no pollen; 'Teddy Bear', 3 ft (0.9 m) tall, fully double, golden yellow flowers 5 in (12 cm) wide. Zones 4–11.

Helianthus annuus 'Ruby Eclipse'

Helianthus maximilianii

☀ ❀ ↔ 2–3 ft (0.6–0.9 m) ↑ 7–10 ft (2–3 m)

Erect perennial found from Texas, USA, to southern Canada. Forms a bushy base of 8 in (20 cm) long, often shallowly toothed, blue-green, lance-shaped, rough-textured leaves. Deep golden yellow flowerheads to 4 in (10 cm) wide in autumn. Zones 4–9.

Helianthus × *multiflorus*

☀ ❀ ↔ 2 ft (0.6 m) ↑ 7 ft (2 m)

Garden hybrid. Perennial. Coarsely hairy, lance-shaped lower leaves to 8 in (20 cm) long. Flowerheads to nearly 5 in (12 cm) wide, often double, from late summer until first frost. 'Capenoch Star', 5 ft (1.5 m) tall, soft yellow flowerheads; 'Loddon Gold', 5 ft (1.5 m) tall, golden yellow, double flowerheads. Zones 5–9.

Helianthus salicifolius

☀ ✹ ↔ 2–4 ft (0.6–1.2 m) ↑ 10 ft (3 m)

Perennial, native to south-central USA. Drooping, slightly hairy, narrowly lance-shaped leaves to 8 in (20 cm) long. Flowerheads to 3 in (8 cm) wide, yellow ray florets around a dark disc, in autumn. 'Golden Pyramid', 5 ft (1.5 m) tall, has a double row of yellow ray florets. Zones 4–9.

Helianthus Hybrid Cultivars

☀ ✹ ↔ 3–4 ft (0.9–1.2 m)
↑ 4–7 ft (1.2–2 m)

These hybrid cultivars are robust hardy plants popular with gardeners. 'Italian White', 5 ft (1.5 m) tall, very pale yellow flowers; 'Monarch', 6 in (15 cm) wide flowerheads, double row of golden ray florets; 'Moonshadow', 4 ft (1.2 m) tall, near-white ray florets; 'Newcutt Gold', rich yellow flowers; 'Sunbeam', 5 ft (1.5 m) tall, golden ray florets, outer disc florets yellow around a green center; 'Sunny', double row of bright yellow blooms; 'Vanilla Ice', 5 ft (1.5 m) tall, starry, flowerheads, creamy yellow ray florets around a dark disc. Zones 5–10.

HELICHRYSUM

A member of the daisy (Asteraceae) family, this genus was formerly estimated to have over 600 mainly perennial species, but many of these are now considered better placed in other genera; some are yet to be formally renamed. The plants have simple, often heavily felted leaves, usually in pale green to gray-green shades. Tiny flowers, usually quite heavily clustered and conspicuous, lack ray florets or petals but have white to yellow, pink, or purple papery bracts around each flowerhead.
CULTIVATION: Most species tolerate drought once established. Plant in full sun with light, gritty, very well-drained soil. Their frost hardiness varies, but few will tolerate prolonged cold; if wet at the same time, they tend to rot before they are killed by frost. Any trimming or shaping should be done in spring. Propagation is from seed (some species self-sow freely), or layers can be pegged down at any time, or half-hardened tip cuttings, which strike well in both summer and autumn.

Helichrysum ecklonis

☀ ✹ ↔ 16–24 in (40–60 cm) ↑ 4–16 in (10–40 cm)

Carpeting South African perennial, sometimes upright habit. Rosettes of oblong leaves to 8 in (20 cm) long with patchy covering of down, sometimes cobweb-like. Flowerheads solitary, to 1¼ in (30 mm) wide, white to purple. Summer-flowering. Zones 9–11.

Helichrysum frigidum

☀ ✹ ↔ 12 in (30 cm) ↑ 4 in (10 cm)

Mat-forming plant from Sardinia and Corsica. Forms a dense carpet with many narrow, ¼ in (6 mm) long, white to gray downy leaves. Numerous white flowerheads to ½ in (12 mm) wide, solitary. Excellent for rock gardens. Spring- to summer-flowering. Zones 8–10.

Helichrysum milfordiae

☀ ✹ ↔ 12 in (30 cm) ↑ 6 in (15 cm)

Cushion-forming plant from South Africa. Densely downy, spatula-shaped, leaves to ½ in (12 mm) long. Deep pink to red buds open to white flowerheads, to 1½ in (35 mm) wide. Spring-flowering. Zones 8–10.

Helichrysum milfordiae

Helichrysum petiolare

LICORICE PLANT, LIQUORICE PLANT

☀ ✹ ↔ 5 ft (1.5 m) ↑ 12–18 in (30–45 cm)

South African native. Forms a mounding ground cover. Long soft stem; rounded leaves to over 1¼ in (30 mm) long. Leaves and stems covered in pale gray down. Small, dull white flowerheads loosely clustered. Winter-flowering. 'Limelight', distinctive pale yellow-green foliage; 'Variegatum', gray and cream variegated leaves. Zones 9–11.

Helichrysum splendidum

☀ ✹ ↔ 3 ft (0.9 m) ↑ 5 ft (1.5 m)

From eastern and southern Africa. Narrowly lance-shaped leaves to over 2 in (5 cm) long with a thin covering of down. Tiny yellow to orange flowerheads clustered together. Autumn- to winter-flowering. Zones 8–11.

HELICONIA

FALSE BIRD OF PARADISE, LOBSTER CLAW, WILD PLANTAIN

Widespread in the American tropics, southern Asia, and the Pacific Islands, this group of around 100 species of evergreen perennials is from the banana (Musaceae) family. Ranging from small clumps to tree-like species and with large leaves resembling those of canna lilies or bananas, they are impressive foliage plants but their main feature is the floral inflorescence in which small flowers are each backed by a colorful bract that overlaps with the next flower to form a long spiral. Most members of this genus bloom continuously.
CULTIVATION: All but a very few species will not do well in prolonged cool conditions. Plant in a part-shaded, warm, sheltered place with moist, humus-rich, well-drained soil. Water and feed well. Remove spent inflorescences to encourage flowering. Propagate by division, or from offsets or seed if available.

Helichrysum frigidum

Heliconia bihai

MACAW FLOWER, WILD PLANTAIN

☀ ❄ ↔ 2–7 ft (0.6–2 m) ↕ 7–17 ft (2–5 m)

From Central America and tropical South America. Forms clump of banana-like stems with leaves often red-veined, to 6 ft (1.8 m) long, though usually much shorter. Long upright inflorescence with up to 20 green-edged red bracts around green-tipped white flowers. '**Aurea**', bracts with a broad gold edge; '**Chocolate Dancer**', deep red-brown bracts edged gold; '**Emerald Forest**', narrow bright green bracts; '**Schaefer**', brilliant red bracts edged orange; '**Yellow Dancer**', yellow bracts tipped green. Zones 10–12.

Heliconia caribaea

BALISIER, WILD PLANTAIN

☀ ❄ ↔ 2–7 ft (0.6–2 m) ↕ 7–17 ft (2–5 m)

From West Indies. Banana-like stems; pointed elliptical leaves to 4 ft (1.2 m) long. Short upright inflorescence, up to 15 golden yellow to red bracts, often green-tipped. Flowers white, green-tipped. '**Barbados Flat**', flat inflorescence, red-brown bracts edged yellow; '**Gold**', golden yellow bracts; '**Flash**', bracts with yellow base, red center, green edges. Zones 10–12.

Heliconia latispatha

☀ ❄ ↔ 3–4 ft (0.9–1.2 m) ↕ 10 ft (3 m)

Found from southern Mexico to Colombia and Venezuela. Broad, sometimes red-edged leaves to over 5 ft (1.5 m) long. Upright inflorescence, long narrow bracts, yellow with a broad red edge. Zones 10–12.

Heliconia psittacorum

PARAKEET FLOWER, PARROT FLOWER

☀ ❄ ↔ 20–32 in (50–80 cm)
↕ 2–7 ft (0.6–2 m)

From eastern Brazil and the southern West Indies. Banana-like growth habit; slender stems; narrow leaves to 20 in (50 cm) long, edges and stalks often red. Tall, upright inflorescence. Few large bracts, pink, orange, or red. Cultivars in range of colors. '**Strawberries and Cream**', creamy yellow bracts tinged pink. Zones 10–12.

Heliconia wagneriana

☀ ❄ ↔ 4–7 ft (1.2–2 m) ↕ 12 ft (3.5 m)

Banana-like species found from Central America to northern Colombia. Wavy-edged leaves to over 6 ft (1.8 m) long. Inflorescence upright, to 18 in (45 cm) long. Bracts deep pink, orange, or red with creamy yellow keel and green edges. Zones 10–12.

HELIOPSIS

FALSE SUNFLOWER, OX-EYE

From North America, this genus of 13 species of loosely branched, erect, perennial herbs is a member of the daisy (Asteraceae) family. Flowerheads of bright yellow daisy-like flowers are produced from mid-summer to autumn, over a long period.

Heliconia caribaea

CULTIVATION: Fully frost hardy, these plants prefer full sun and average soil kept moist during summer. Staking may be needed. Propagate from seed or divide clumps in spring or autumn.

Heliopsis helianthoides

EVERLASTING SUNFLOWER, FALSE SUNFLOWER, SMOOTH OX-EYE

☀ ❄ ↔ 1–2 ft (0.3–0.6 m) ↕ 2–5 ft (0.6–1.5 m)

Perennial found from Ontario, Canada, to Florida and Mississippi, USA. Smooth, oval- to sword-shaped, coarse-toothed, leaves, to 6 in (15 cm) long. Many terminal flowerheads of yellow daisy-like flowers, to 3 in (8 cm) across. *H. h.* var. *scabra*, double orange-yellow flowers, very rough stems and leaves; '**Incomparabilis**', single orange-yellow flowers; '**Light of Loddon**', double bright golden orange flowers. Zones 3–9.

Heliopsis Hybrid Cultivars

☀ ❄ ↔ 1–2 ft (0.3–0.6 cm) ↕ 4 ft (1.2 m)

Perennials with mid-green leaves. '**Goldgefieder**' (ox-eye), late-flowering, 4–5 ft (1.2–1.5 m) tall, double golden flowers; Loraine Sunshine/'**Helhan**', dwarf, white leaves with green veins, large golden yellow flowers. Zones 3–9.

HELIOTROPIUM

This is a genus in the borage family (Boraginaceae) with about 250 species of annuals, perennials, subshrubs, and evergreen shrubs from tropical and warmer temperate climates around the world. The fragrant flowers can be white, yellow, blue, or purple.

CULTIVATION: Most of the species prefer fertile free-draining soils, summer moisture and shelter from cold. Full sun to filtered light is their favored habitat. Shelter from frosts. Prune moderately after flowering to encourage new shoots. Propagate from soft-tip cuttings or half-hardened cuttings in a warm and moist situation.

Heliotropium arborescens

CHERRY PIE, COMMON HELIOTROPE

☀ ❄ ↔ 20 in (50 cm) ↕ 3 ft (0.9 m)

From Peru, Ecuador, and Bolivia. Spreading, evergreen plant. Narrow oval leaves dark and shiny above, paler reverse. Abundant fragrant mauve to purple flowers, from early spring to late summer. '**Black Beauty**' ★, very dark purple-black flowers; '**Chatsworth**', purple flowers; '**Fragrant Delight**', dark purple flowers; '**Iowa**', purple-tinted foliage, dark purple flowers; '**Lord Roberts**', compact growth, violet flowers; '**Marine**', compact growth, purple-blue flowers; '**Princess Marina**', dark violet-blue flowers. Zones 9–12.

HELLEBORUS

LENTEN ROSE, WINTER ROSE

This genus of 15 species of buttercup (Ranunculaceae) family perennials is found in the temperate zone from Europe to

western China. They are mainly low-growing plants with short-stemmed, often toothed, palmate foliage emerging direct from a rhizome. The simple, 5-petalled, bowl-shaped flowers appear from mid-winter into spring and occur in unusual shades of green, dusky pink, and maroon as well as white. At the center of the flower are prominent greenish nectaries and yellow stamens.
CULTIVATION: Most prefer woodland conditions with deep, fertile, humus-rich, well-drained soil and dappled shade. Some of the smaller types are well suited to rock gardens. Many are near-evergreen but benefit from having old foliage removed when dormant. Propagate by division or from seed, which may require 2 periods of stratification. Naturalizes in suitable climates.

Heliotropium arborescens

Helleborus argutifolius
syns *Helleborus corsicus,*
H. lividus subsp. *corsicus*
☀/◐ ❄ ↔ 24–40 in (60–100 cm) ↑ 40 in (100 cm)
Native to islands of Corsica, France, and Sardinia, Italy. Evergreen, leathery leaves with soft-spined toothed leaflets to 8 in (20 cm) long, sometimes gray-green. Large heads of green flowers to 2 in (5 cm) wide. Winter- to spring-flowering. 'Janet Starnes', mottled cream foliage; 'Pacific Frost', mottled cream and pink foliage, narrow leaflets, pale flowers, sometimes maroon-tinted. Zones 7–10.

Helleborus foetidus
BEAR'S FOOT, STINKING HELLEBORE, STINKWORT
☀/◐ ❄ ↔ 24–40 in (60–100 cm) ↑ 24–32 in (60–80 cm)
Evergreen found from Britain to Hungary. Foliage is pungent if crushed. Dark green leaves with 5 to 13 narrow leaflets, longest to 8 in (20 cm) long, toothed. Green flowers, often red-tinted, bell-shaped, 1 in (25 mm) wide, on upright stems. 'Green Giant', bright green flowers; 'Miss Jekyll', fragrant flowers; Sierra Nevada Group, 12 in (30 cm) high; Wester Flisk Group, red-tinted stems and leaves, gray-green flowers. Zones 6–9.

Helleborus × hybridus
☀/◐ ❄ ↔ 16–24 in (40–60 cm)
↑ 16 in (40 cm)
Hybrids of *H. orientalis* and other species. 'Alberich', purple-black flowers; 'Banana Split', large creamy yellow flowers; 'Blue Spray', bell-shaped smoky purple flowers; 'Fred Whitsey', white flowers with purple spots and streaks; 'Hades', dark-speckled gray-blue flowers; 'Mardi Gras', red-blotched white flowers; 'Pleiades', dwarf, red-flecked white flowers; 'Southern Belle', lavender flowers on tall stems; 'Trotter's Spotted', large purple-spotted white flowers. Zones 5–9.

Helleborus niger

Helleborus lividus
☀/◐ ❄ ↔ 24 in (60 cm) ↑ 16 in (40 cm)
Evergreen from Mallorca, Spain. Simple 3-part, deep green, purple-tinted leaves. Flowers bright green flushed purple to all purple, from mid-winter. May rot in cold wet winters. Zones 8–10.

Helleborus niger
CHRISTMAS ROSE
☀/◐ ❄ ↔ 12–20 in (30–50 cm) ↑ 12 in (30 cm)
Evergreen from Alps of northern Italy to southern Germany. Deep green, leathery, serrated leaves, with 5 to 9 broad leaflets, to 8 in (20 cm) long. White flowers on strong stems, sometimes flushed pink. Winter- to spring-flowering. *H. n.* subsp. *macranthus,* large flowers, blue-green leaves. *H. n.* 'Potter's Wheel', white flowers to 4 in (10 cm) wide; 'White Magic', dark-stemmed white flowers, pink-tinted with age. Zones 3–9.

Helleborus × nigercors
☀/◐ ❄ ↔ 24 in (60 cm) ↑ 24 in (60 cm)
Leaves evergreen, large, gray-green, 3 to 7 leaflets coarsely toothed and often soft-spined. Heads of large blue-green-tinted white flowers from mid-winter. Zones 7–10.

Helleborus orientalis ★
LENTEN ROSE
☀/◐ ❄ ↔ 16–24 in (40–60 cm)
↑ 16 in (40 cm)
Semi-evergreen from northern Turkey and Greece. Leaves with 7 to 9 leaflets. Flowers pure white to red-black, often dark-spotted. Winter-flowering. *H. o.* subsp. *abchasicus,* red to purplish flowers; *H. o.* subsp. *a.,* Early Purple Group (syn. *Helleborus atrorubens*), flowers greenish purple. *H. o.* subsp. *guttatus,* white flowers, dark-spotted. *H. o.* subsp. *orientalis,* white flowers. Zones 5–9.

Hemerocallis minor

HEMEROCALLIS

DAYLILY

Daylilies are so named because each of their funnel- to bell-shaped flowers lasts just one day, though they carry a succession of blooms from late spring until autumn. Once classified with the true lilies, this group of 15 species of rhizome-rooted perennials from temperate East Asia is now the type genus for its own family, the Hemerocallidaceae. They form clumps of grassy or iris-like leaves with sometimes branching racemes of 6-petalled flowers in a range of warm yellow, apricot, and red shades. All parts of the plant, especially the buds and flowers, are edible. CULTIVATION: They are hardy and easily grown in a sunny or part-shaded position with fertile, moist, well-drained soil. Slugs and snails often badly disfigure the foliage. Take care when siting as the flowers turn to face the sun. Rust disease is a problem in some areas. Propagation is usually by division.

Hemerocallis dumortieri

LEMON LILY
☼/◑ ❊ ↔ 16–24 in (40–60 cm)
↑ 16 in (40 cm)
Compact, early-flowering species from Korea and eastern Russia. Very narrow leaves to 14 in (35 cm) long. Flower stems, red-tinted, unbranched and only slightly exceeding foliage height, bearing just 2 to 4 fragrant golden flowers to a little over 2 in (5 cm) wide, backed by broad bracts. Zones 4–9.

Hemerocallis fulva

☼/◑ ❊ ↔ 4–5 ft (1.2–1.5 m) ↑ 3 ft (0.9 m)
Wild origin uncertain, may be a hybrid. Leaves to over 24 in (60 cm) long, strappy. Flower stems usually 2-branched with up to 20, dark-striped, light orange-brown, 3–4 in (8–10 cm) wide flowers. **Kwanzo** (syn. 'Kwanzo Flore Pleno'), dark-centered

double flowers; **'Kwanzo Variegata'**, same flowers, creamy white-edged foliage. Zones 4–9.

Hemerocallis lilio-asphodelus

CUSTARD LILY
☼/◑ ❊ ↔ 40–48 in (100–120 cm)
↑ 24–40 in (60–100 cm)
An early-flowering Chinese species. Very narrow sickle-shaped leaves to over 24 in (60 cm) long. Wiry, branching flower stems carry up to 12 night-scented pale yellow flowers to 3 in (8 cm) wide. Zones 4–9.

Hemerocallis middendorffii

☼/◑ ❊ ↔ 20–24 in (50–60 cm)
↑ 18 in (45 cm)
Native to Japan and nearby mainland north-eastern Asia. Leaves strappy, to 12 in (30 cm) long. Flower stems unbranched, with scented yellow flowers clustered together. Zones 5–9.

Hemerocallis minor

☼/◑ ❊ ↔ 20–24 in (50–60 cm) ↑ 20 in (50 cm)
From Japan and nearby parts of China. Very narrow leaves to 18 in (45 cm) long. Flower stems with 2 or sometimes more branches bearing up to 5 soft yellow flowers to over 2 in (5 cm) wide. Zones 4–9.

HEMIGRAPHIS

This genus, which is a member of the acanthus (Acanthaceae) family, contains about 90 species of annuals, perennials, and subshrubs that are native to tropical Asia. They have low-growing slender stems with opposite leaves that usually have toothed or scalloped margins. The foliage is the most attractive feature of most species. The small flowers are tubular with 5 petal lobes and have conspicuous bracts. They are carried on terminal spikes, which appear intermittently through the year.
CULTIVATION: In tropical and subtropical regions these plants can be grown as ground cover outdoors in positions in partial shade. In other areas they are suitable for indoor plants and as ground cover in the tropical greenhouse. In these situations they require filtered light and plentiful watering during the growing period. Propagation is from cuttings.

Hemigraphis alternata

Hemigraphis alternata

syn. Hemigraphis colorata
METAL LEAF, RED IVY
❊ ✦ ↔ 12–18 in (30–45 cm) ↑ 4 in (10 cm)
From India and Java. Prostrate perennial rooting at the nodes. It is grown for its attractive, scallop-edged, oval leaves, which are purple beneath and dark bluish green above with a metallic sheen. Flowers are small and white. **'Exotica'** has puckered leaves with rolled margins. Zones 11–12.

Hemigraphis repanda

☀ ✦ ↔ 12–18 in (30–45 cm) ↑ 4 in (10 cm)

Native to Malaysia. Prostrate perennial rooting at the nodes. Slender stems flushed with maroon. Lance-shaped leaves with scalloped edges are satiny gray flushed with maroon or purple. Zones 11–12.

HEPATICA

This is a small genus of 10 species belonging to the buttercup (Ranunculaceae) family, closely related to *Anemone*. They are native to northern temperate zones in woodland settings. The leaves are basal, usually 3- to 5-lobed, leathery in texture, and often persist throughout winter. The flowers, produced in very early spring, are bowl-shaped and borne one per stem and are white, pink, and blue to purple.
CULTIVATION: As they are woodlanders by nature, a cool aspect in humus-rich soil is best, and as the plants are small in stature, the intimacy of a small pocket in a shaded rock garden makes a good setting. Propagate from freshly sown seed or by division of selected clones, which will take time to re-establish.

Hepatica nobilis

☀ ❋ ↔ 4–6 in (10–15 cm) ↑ 3–4 in (8–10 cm)

European native. Mid-green leaves with 3 rounded lobes, underside sometimes purplish. Open bowl-shaped flowers, to 1 in (25 mm) across, in shades of white through pink to blue and almost purple. Many selections in a range of colors and with double flowers. Zones 5–9.

HESPERIS

This genus belongs to the cabbage (Brassicaceae) family and consists of 60 biennials and short-lived perennials of upright habit from central and southwest Asia and the Mediterranean region. Erect stems are clothed with oblong leaves and topped with open clusters of 4-petalled flowers in shades of yellow, white, or purple, often sweetly scented, particularly in the evenings.
CULTIVATION: These plants are suitable for the border or wild garden. They will do best in full sun or light shade and prefer a neutral to alkaline soil. Although they tolerate poor soils, they will perform better if the ground is enriched. Inspect periodically for mildew. Propagation is from seed, which will usually self-sow, or from cuttings of the sterile double forms.

Hesperis matronalis

DAMASK VIOLET, DAME'S VIOLET, SWEET ROCKET

◐/☀ ❋ ↔ 16–20 in (40–50 cm) ↑ 32–36 in (80–90 cm)

Well-known biennial or short-lived perennial from southern Europe through to central Asia. Dark green leaves to 8 in (20 cm) long. Clusters of scented flowers, 1¾ in (40 mm) across, in late spring–summer. Forms with both white and lilac, single and double flowers are grown. Zones 3–10.

Heuchera americana

HEUCHERA

ALUM ROOT, CORAL BELLS

This genus, a member of the saxifrage (Saxifragaceae) family, consists of around 55 near-evergreen perennials native to North America. The species form a dense clump of basal foliage with rounded to kidney-shaped, toothed leaves on thin wiry leaf stalks. The branching flower stems are also very fine and from late spring to autumn carry sprays of tiny flowers, usually 5-petalled but sometimes petal-less.
CULTIVATION: They are mostly very hardy and adaptable and are suitable for perennial borders or rock gardens, depending on size. Plant in full or half-sun with fertile, moist, humus-rich, well-drained soil. Remove flower stems as they fade. Propagate by division or from seed sown fresh in early autumn.

Heuchera americana

ROCK GERANIUM

◑/◐☀ ❋ ↔ 16 in (40 cm) ↑ 18 in (45 cm)

Evergreen North American native with downy, broad, lobed, heart-shaped leaves about 3 in (8 cm) long, sometimes white mottled. Upright flower stems with narrow heads of faintly pink-tinted cream flowers. 'Garnet', leaves which are red when young, turning bronze-veined green, developing a red center in winter; 'Lace Ruffles', ruffled, silver-mottled leaves, white flowers; 'Ring of Fire', red-veined green foliage turning pink in winter with pale edges; 'Velvet Night', darkest purple-black leaves overlaid with metallic purple. Zones 4–10.

Heuchera × brizoides

◑/◐☀ ❋ ↔ 12–18 in (30–45 cm) ↑ 12–30 in (30–75 cm)

These are a mixed group, sharing simple green, lobed, heart-shaped leaves and differing mainly in flower color. **Bressingham hybrids**, with graceful, airy flowerheads, many shades of pink, red, and white; Firefly/'Leuchtkäfer', coral pink, faintly scented; 'Freedom', dwarf form, flowers bright pink; 'June Bride', white flowers. Zones 4–10.

Heuchera × brizoides

Heuchera maxima

Heuchera, Hybrid Cultivar, 'Strawberry Candy'

Heuchera maxima

☼/◐ ❄ ↔16–20 in (40–50 cm) ↕24 in (60 cm)
Evergreen species from western USA. Rounded, toothed leaves to more than 6 in (15 cm) wide, underside veins downy. Pinkish white flowers in warmer months. Zones 6–10.

Heuchera micrantha

☼/◐ ❄ ↔12–16 in (30–40 cm) ↕24 in (60 cm)
Western North American species with broad, shallowly lobed, heart-shaped leaves to more than 3 in (8 cm) long. Open sprays of small white to cream flowers in warmer months. *H. m.* var. *diversifolia* 'Palace Purple', deep purple-red leaves and stems, small white flowers. Zones 5–9.

Heuchera sanguinea

☼/◐ ❄ ↔12–16 in (30–40 cm)
↕24 in (60 cm)
Evergreen, from New Mexico and Arizona, USA. Roughly kidney-shaped leaves to 2 in (5 cm) wide, with irregular lobes and downy undersides. Bright red flowers. 'Brandon Pink', bright coral-pink flowers, green and white leaves; 'Monet', white-variegated green foliage, red flowers; 'Northern Fire', pinkish red flowers, green leaves, vigorous; 'Singham', bright green leaves, hot pink flowers; 'Snow Storm', white-mottled foliage, red flowers; 'Splendens', deep red flowers; 'Virginalis', white flowers. Zones 3–9.

Heuchera Hybrid Cultivars

☼/◐ ❄ ↔12–18 in (30–45 cm) ↕12–36 in (30–90 cm)
In recent years many *Heuchera* hybrids have been introduced, with interesting foliage. 'Amber Waves', light golden bronze foliage and deep pink flowers; 'Autumn Haze', purple leaves overlaid silver, pink flowers; 'Chocolate Ruffles' ★, deep bronze-green foliage with purple-brown overtones, white flowers; 'Fireglow', red blooms; 'Mint Frost', green leaves overlaid silver, cream flowers; 'Persian Carpet', silver-marked red to purple-red leaves,

buff flowers; 'Petite Marble Burgundy', compact, silver-marked, purple-red leaves, pinkish flowers; 'Pewter Moon', silver-veined deep purple-red foliage; 'Pewter Veil', purple-red foliage overlaid silver-gray; 'Plum Pudding', purple-brown leaves with red undersides, cream flowers; 'Red Spangles', plain green leaves, bright red flowers; 'Ruby Veil', deep maroon and silver-gray upper leaves, purple-red undersides; 'Santa Ana Cardinal' *(H. maxima × H. sanguinea)*, tall, rounded bright green leaves, deep pink to red flowers; 'Snow Angel', red flowers, white-flecked green foliage; 'Strawberry Candy', green leaves overlaid silver, pink flowers; 'Wendy' ★ *(H. maxima × H. sanguinea)*, large light green leaves, soft pink flowers. **Canyon Series**, compact evergreen hybrids with small, lobed, rounded to heart-shaped leaves, usually deep green, sometimes with hint of purple; many tiny flowers in upright, airy sprays. Original varieties include 'Canyon Delight', tall, deep pink to red; 'Canyon Pink', bright pink. **Canyon Quartet Series** includes 'Canyon Bell', short stems, bright red flowers; 'Canyon Chimes', tall stems, red flowers; 'Canyon Duet', bicolor red and white flowers; and 'Canyon Melody', smaller plant, pink and white flowers. Zones 5–10.

× HEUCHERELLA

This group of garden hybrids in the saxifrage (Saxifragaceae) family are crosses between the genera *Heuchera* and *Tiarella*. They are sterile hybrids with evergreen maple-shaped leaves that often color well in winter and sprays of tiny dainty pale pink to white flowers on upright stems in late spring.
CULTIVATION: These hybrids are best grown in humus-rich moist soils in cool woodland-type aspects where they make attractive slow-moving ground covers. Propagation is by division.

× Heucherella, Hybrid Cultivar, 'Viking Ship'

× Heucherella tiarelloides

☼/◐ ❄ ↔18 in (45 cm) ↕18 in (45 cm)
Smooth, light green, divided leaves heart-shaped at the base. Stems of pink flowers above foliage in spring–summer. Zones 5–9.

× Heucherella Hybrid Cultivars

☼/◐ ❄ ↔12–16 in (30–40 cm)
↕16–20 in (40–50 cm)
Evergreen perennials with striking foliage. 'Bridget Bloom', heart-shaped mid-green leaves, heavy brown markings, white flower spikes in spring–autumn; 'Dayglo Pink', mid-green leaves, chocolate-colored inlay, purple foliage tones in winter, brilliant pink flowers; 'Kimono', tawny flowers, in summer–autumn; 'Viking Ship', silver leaves in spring, coral-pink flowers. Zones 5–9.

HIBISCUS (see page 178)

Hibiscus cannabinus

BIMLI, DECCAN HEMP, INDIAN HEMP, KENAF
☼ ⚘ ↔6 ft (1.8 m) ↕12 ft (3.5 m)
Fast-growing annual or short-lived, shrubby perennial, thought to be from East Indies. Long stems used for fiber. Pale yellow,

sometimes pale purple flowers in racemes, reddish purple column and center. Leaves prickly, deeply lobed, serrated. Zones 10–12.

Hibiscus Herbaceous Hybrids
☼ ❋ ↔ 2–4 ft (0.6–1.2 m)
↑ 18 in–5 ft (45 cm–1.5 m)
Perennials derived mainly from *H. moscheutos*. Leaves vary from toothed to deeply lobed. Succession of large, flat to funnel-shaped flowers from upper leaf axils in shades from white or pale pink to dark red, sometimes with dark eye. 'Davis Creek', deep pink to red flowers; 'Lady Baltimore', pink flowers; 'Miss Kitty', yellow flowers. Zones 5–10.

HOSTA
syn. *Funkia*
PLANTAIN LILY

This genus from the agave (Agavaceae) family contains about 40 perennial species. Hostas are clump-forming, and grown primarily for their large, bold, heart-shaped leaves. In addition to green, blue, and grayish tones, some cultivars have variegated or yellow-green foliage. The flowers are funnel-shaped and borne in racemes atop erect stems. They are usually white, mauve, or purple, appear from mid-summer, and are sometimes scented. CULTIVATION: Although sun-tolerant cultivars have been raised, hostas prefer shaded conditions with moist, cool, humus-rich, well-drained soil. Water and feed well during the growing season. Propagate by dividing as the first buds show. The young shoots are very vulnerable to slug and snail damage.

Hosta crispula
SAZANAMI GIBOSHI
◐/◉ ❋ ↔ 24 in (60 cm) ↑ 36 in (90 cm)
From Japan, though not known in the wild. Deeply veined, pointed oval to lance-shaped leaves to 10 in (25 cm) long, deep green with white edges, usually twisted with wavy edges rolled around leaf stalk. Pale mauve flowers on tall stem. Zones 6–10.

Hosta fortunei
◐/◉ ❋ ↔ 32–48 in (80–120 cm) ↑ 36 in (90 cm)
Wild status uncertain—it is perhaps Japanese but may be a garden hybrid from Europe. Wavy, deep green, heart- to lance-shaped leaves tapering to a fine point, often variegated. Mauve flowers on leafy stems. 'Albomarginata', large white-edged leaves; 'Albopicta', large, thin leaves, maturing to green with hint of cream; 'Antioch', dark green leaves, yellow edge turning cream; 'Aurea', leaves yellow, turning light green; 'Aureomarginata', clearly defined gold-edged leaves; 'Elizabeth Campbell', leaves with broad green edge and light green central zone; 'Francee', white-edged deep green leaves, slightly puckered; 'Gold Haze', like 'Aurea' but slower to turn green; 'Gold Standard', green-gold leaves, clearly defined dark green edge; 'Goldbrook Gold', yellow-gold leaves; 'Joker', gray-green to blue-green leaves; 'Mary Marie Ann', bright green edges around a broad yellow-green center; 'Minuteman', bright green leaves, with irregular broad white

edge; 'North Hills', mid-green leaves with irregular narrow white edge; 'Striptease', heart-shaped blue-green leaves with narrow cream and green central zone; 'Whirlwind', mid-green, broad yellow-gold center. Zones 6–10.

Hosta lancifolia
◐/◉ ❋ ↔ 16–20 in (40–50 cm)
↑ 18 in (45 cm)
Not known in the wild. Narrow, deep green, lance-shaped leaves to around 6 in (15 cm) long, tapering to a fine point. Flower stems leafy, flowers purple. Zones 6–10.

Hosta minor
KIRIN GIBOSHI
◐/◉ ❋ ↔ 16 in (40 cm) ↑ 24 in (60 cm)
Korean species long cultivated in Japan. Clump of small, dark green, pointed oval to heart-shaped leaves to 3 in (8 cm) long. Comparatively tall flower stem with deep mauve flowers. Zones 6–10.

Hosta plantaginea
AUGUST LILY, MARUBA
◐/◉ ❋ ↔ 32 in (80 cm) ↑ 26 in (65 cm)
Native to China and Japan. Grown as much for flowers as foliage. Leaves bright green, wavy, deeply veined, lance-shaped tapering to fine point, to 10 in (25 cm) long. Flowers white, may be mauve-tinted, large, scented. *H. p.* var. *japonica* (syn. *H. p.* var. *grandiflora*), taller flower stems, larger flowers. *H. p.* 'Honey Bells', mauve-tinted flowers; 'Venus', double flowers. Zones 8–10.

Hosta sieboldii
KOBA GIBOSHI
◐/◉ ❋ ↔ 32 in (80 cm) ↑ 20 in (50 cm)
Native to Japan and Sakhalin Island. Finely pointed, often undulating and puckered, lance-shaped leaves to 6 in (15 cm) long, deep green with white edges. Mauve flowers. *H. s.* f. *kabitan*, small, green-edged golden leaves; *H. s.* 'Krossa Cream Edge', narrow, cream-edged leaves; 'Wogon', lime green leaves. Zones 5–10.

Hibiscus, Herbaceous Hybrid, 'Davis Creek'

Hosta fortunei 'Whirlwind'

Hosta × *tardiana*

◐/☀ ❄ ↔16–20 in (40–50 cm) ↕16 in (40 cm)

Hybrids between *H. sieboldiana* var. *elegans* and *H. tardiflora*. Mainly forming mounding clumps of heavily veined blue-green leaves, sometimes variegated. Flower stems fairly short, flowers cream to pale mauve. 'Brother Ronald', dark blue-green leaves to over 6 in (15 cm) long; 'Camelot', wide spreading, broad, heart-shaped, intensely blue-green leaves to 8 in (20 cm) long, lavender flowers; 'Devon Blue', pointed, gray-marked, blue-green leaves to over 6 in (15 cm) long; 'Halcyon', heart-shaped blue-green leaves to 8 in (20 cm) long, many lavender-gray flowers; 'Moody Blues', broad, intensely blue-green leaves, pale lavender flowers. Zones 6–10.

Hosta tardiflora

◐/☀ ❄ ↔20 in (50 cm) ↕12 in (30 cm)

Unknown in the wild. Prominently veined, glossy, olive green, sometimes undulating, lance-shaped leaves to 6 in (15 cm) long. Flower stem to 14 in (35 cm) long but held at around a 45° angle, flowers mauve in cream to purple bracts. Zones 6–10.

Hosta tokudama

TOKUDAMA GIBOSHI

◐/☀ ❄ ↔32–48 in (80–120 cm) ↕18 in (45 cm)

Unknown in the wild, long cultivated in Japan. Broad oval to heart-shaped leaves, puckered surface, bright blue-green, to 10 in (25 cm) long and wide. Flowers lavender-gray to white. *H. t.* f. *aureonebulosa*, leaves irregular, large central yellow-green area. *H. t.* 'Love Pat', possibly of hybrid origin, heavily textured, deep blue-green leaves, mauvish white flowers. Zones 6–10.

Hosta undulata

SUJI GIBOSHI

◐/☀ ❄ ↔16–20 in (40–50 cm) ↕12 in (30 cm)

Unknown in the wild, long cultivated in Japan. Dark green leaves, narrow central band of creamy white, pointed elliptical, wavy edged, to nearly 6 in (15 cm) long. Flowers pale purple within greenish white bracts. 'Albomarginata', leaves with white edges, wavy but not twisted; 'Variegata' *(syn. H. u. var. undulata)*, leaves with central area cream and 2-tone green; 'Univittata', large leaves with narrow central creamy white zone; 'White Christmas', white leaves with narrow irregular green edge. Zones 6–10.

Hosta ventricosa

MURASAKI GIBOSHI

◐/☀ ❄ ↔24–32 in (60–80 cm) ↕40 in (100 cm)

Chinese species long cultivated in Japan. Deep green, broad, often wavy, heart-shaped leaves to 10 in (25 cm) long. Tall flower stems, light purple flowers. *H. v.* var. *aureomaculata*, young leaves with bright yellow center. *H. v.* 'Peedee Elfin Bells', pendulous flowers. Zones 6–10.

Hosta Hybrid Cultivars

◐/☀ ❄ ↔12–60 in (30–150 cm) ↕6–36 in (15–90 cm)

In recent decades hostas have been among plant breeders' favorites, and extensive hybridizing has produced a myriad of foliage forms. 'Allan P. McConnell', medium height, dark green with white edge, purple flowers; 'August Moon', tall, wavy yellow-gold leaves, lavender flowers; 'Blue Moon', low-growing, small blue-green leaves, white flowers; 'Brim Cup', tall, puckered, light yellow-green leaves with irregular green center, mauve flowers; 'Candy Hearts', tall blue-green leaves, pale mauve flowers; 'County Park', tall, broad, flat, mid-green leaves, white flowers; 'Devon Gold', medium height, small yellow-green leaves, purple flowers; 'Floradora', medium height, neat heart-shaped mid-green leaves, pale mauve flowers; 'Gold Edger', low-growing, golden green leaves, white flowers; 'Green Piecrust', tall, large mid-green wavy-edged leaves, lavender flowers; 'Ground Sulphur', medium height, low spreader, bright yellow-green leaves; 'Island Charm', medium height, small pink-stemmed bright green leaves with yellow center, lavender flowers; 'Julie Morss', medium height, yellow-gold leaves with green edges, lavender-pink flowers; 'June', medium height, small yellow-centered blue-green leaves, violet flowers; 'King Michael', tall, large lustrous mid-green leaves, white flowers; 'Krossa Regal', tall, long-stemmed blue-green leaves, white to pale mauve flowers; 'Lady Isobel Barnett', tall, very large mid-green leaves with creamy yellow margin, white to pale lavender flowers; 'Medusa', medium height, narrow green-edged cream leaves, purple flowers; 'Midwest Magic', tall, yellow-green leaves with darker edges, lavender flowers; 'Patriot', tall, dark green leaves with broad white edge, violet flowers; 'Paul's Glory', medium height, heavily puckered yellow-centered blue-green leaves, lavender flowers; 'Pearl Lake', tall, small mid-green leaves, many lavender flowers; 'Pizzazz', medium height, broad

Hosta tardiflora

Hosta undulata 'White Christmas'

Hosta, Hybrid Cultivar, 'August Moon'

blue-green leaves with thin irregular yellow edges, pale mauve flowers; '**Radiant Edger**', tall, small mid-green leaves with yellow-green edges, mauve flowers; '**Royal Standard**', tall, glossy mid-green leaves, fragrant white flowers; '**Ryan's Big One**', tall, very large puckered blue-green leaves, pale lavender flowers; '**September Sun**', tall, leaves initially yellow-green becoming green-edged, white flowers; '**Shade Fanfare**', medium height, puckered white-edged blue-green leaves, pale mauve flowers; '**Summer Music**', medium height, slightly twisted dark green leaves with white to cream center, pale mauve flowers; '**Tall Boy**', tall, long-stemmed mid-green leaves, purple flowers on tall stems; '**Torchlight**', medium height, dark green leaves with broad white edge, lavender flowers; '**Veronica Lake**', medium height, blue-green leaves with white to light green edges, pale mauve flowers; '**Wide Brim**', tall, blue-green leaves with creamy yellow edge, mauve flowers; '**Yellow Waves**', low-growing, small yellow-gold leaves, mauve flowers. Zones 6–10.

HOUTTUYNIA

This genus of a only single species from East Asia belongs to the lizard's-tail (Saururaceae) family. It is a widely spreading herbaceous perennial with heart-shaped leaves and cones of tiny yellow flowers surrounded by 4 white petal-like bracts. The leaves can be eaten raw or cooked and have a peppery taste.
CULTIVATION: This grows well in moist to wet soil, even slightly submerged in water, and is happy in full sun or half-shade. It can become invasive and hard to remove; grow in pots kept off the ground to restrict spread. Propagate by division.

Houttuynia cordata

☼/◑ ❋ ↔ over 40 in (100 cm)
↕ 6–12 in (15–30 cm)
Herbaceous plant China and Japan. Aromatic heart-shaped leaves to 3½ in (9 cm) long, deep green often stained burgundy. White-bracted flower clusters atop red stems from mid-summer onward. '**Chameleon**' (syns *H. c.* 'Court Jester', *H. c.* 'Tricolor', *H. c.* 'Variegata'), slightly less vigorous, leaves broadly edged in yellow and stained red; '**Flore Pleno**', masses of white bracts arranged like little cones. Zones 5–10.

HUNNEMANNIA

GOLDEN CUP, MEXICAN TULIP POPPY

This genus belongs to the poppy (Papaveraceae) family and contains one fast-growing species of perennial that is often grown as an annual. It is native to highland areas of Mexico. Although rather woody at the base, it is of delicate appearance with finely divided bluish gray foliage. The clear yellow flowers may be single or semi-double, and are up to 3 in (8 cm) in diameter, appearing in summer.
CULTIVATION: Grow in full sun in a well-drained soil. It will not tolerate wet conditions in the cooler months. Deadhead regularly to encourage a longer flowering season. Care should be taken not to disturb the roots on transplanting. Propagate from seed.

Houttuynia cordata 'Chameleon'

Hunnemannia fumariifolia

☼ ❋ ↔ 10 in (25 cm) ↕ 18–36 in (45–90 cm)
Perennial or annual. Attractive bluish gray filigree leaves. Satiny flowers clearest yellow, held above foliage in summer. Zones 8–10.

HYDRASTIS

This genus, a member of the buttercup (Ranunculaceae) family, contains only 2 species of low-growing perennial herbs, one native to Japan and the other to eastern North America.
CULTIVATION: These grow best in conditions similar to its natural habitat—the forest floor. Plant in a shady position with rich moist soil that has been enriched with leafmold. Add more leafmold or similar organic matter every year. Propagate from seed or by division.

Hunnemannia fumariifolia

Hydrastis canadensis

EYE ROOT, GOLDENSEAL, GROUND RASPBERRY, INDIAN DYE,
JAUNDICE ROOT, ORANGEROOT, TURMERIC, YELLOW PUCCOON
☼ ❋ ↔ 8 in (20 cm) ↕ 12 in (30 cm)
Perennial woodland herb from eastern North America. Each stem has 2 large, serrated, 5-lobed, wrinkled leaves; small white flowers in spring. Raspberry-like fruit, in cluster of red berries, follows in summer. Endangered species. All parts poisonous. Zones 6–8.

IBERIS

CANDYTUFT

Popular for the bold effect of their massed heads of white, pink, mauve, or purple flowers, the 30-odd annuals, perennials, and subshrubs in this genus in the cabbage (Brassicaceae) family are found from western and southern Europe to western Asia. They usually have simple, small, narrow leaves; when not flowering they form a rounded bush. Their flowerheads open in summer, on short stems holding them clear of the foliage.
CULTIVATION: Plant in a sunny position with light yet moist, well-drained soil. A light dressing of dolomite lime is appreciated. Deadhead regularly. Propagate the annuals from seed and the perennials and subshrubs from seed or small cuttings.

Iberis gibraltarica

Iberis amara

ANNUAL CANDYTUFT

☼/◐ ❄ ↔ 12–20 in (30–50 cm) ↑ 12 in (30 cm)

Western European annual. Small, lance-shaped, sometimes toothed leaves often hidden under massed heads of white, pink, or purple flowers in summer. Zones 7–11.

Iberis gibraltarica

GIBRALTAR CANDYTUFT

☼/◐ ❄ ↔ 20–24 in (50–60 cm) ↑ 12 in (30 cm)

Evergreen species from Gibraltar. Forms neat mound of narrow stems with rosettes of small leaves at tips. Heads of white, lavender, or pink-tinted flowers in summer. Zones 7–10.

Iberis sempervirens

☼/◐ ❄ ↔ 20–24 in (50–60 cm) ↑ 12 in (30 cm)

Spreading evergreen plant from southern Europe with small oblong leaves, mainly clustered at stem tips. Flowerheads to 2 in (5 cm) wide, usually white, in spring–summer. **'Flore-Plena'**, compact habit, double flowers; **'Purity'**, to 8 in (20 cm) high; Snowflake/**'Schneeflocke'** ★, low-growing, silvery white flowers; **'Weisser Zwerg'** (syn. 'Little Gem'), 6 in (15 cm) high, early flowers. Zones 7–10.

Iberis umbellata

☼/◐ ❄ ↔ 16 in (40 cm) ↑ 12 in (30 cm)

Annual from southern Europe. Very narrow lance-shaped leaves may be toothed. Purple flowers in spring–summer. **Flash Series**, white, shades of pink, mauve, purple, and red flowers. Grow from autumn-sown seed in mild areas; summer annual elsewhere. Zones 7–10.

IMPATIENS

BALSAM, BUSY LIZZIE, WATER FUCHSIA

The type genus giving its name to the balsam (Balsaminaceae) family is home to around 850 species of annuals, perennials, and subshrubs found worldwide except in Australasia, South America,

and the polar regions. These are generally soft-stemmed plants with simple, pointed, lance-shaped leaves, often with toothed edges. Flowers in many colors appear throughout the year in mild areas and have 5 petals, an upper standard and the lower 4 fused into 2 pairs, the sepals also partly fused to form a spur. Ripe seed pods explosively eject their contents at a touch.
CULTIVATION: Grow the annuals as summer plants in cooler climates outside the recommended zones; perennials need mild winter conditions. Provide shade from the hottest sun and plant in deep, cool, moist, humus-rich soil. Feed well. Propagate annuals from seed, the perennials also by cuttings. Some species self-sow and are slightly invasive.

Impatiens balsamina

BALSAM

◐/● ❖ ↔ 12 in (30 cm) ↑ 27 in (70 cm)

Vigorous upright annual from East Asia. Toothed lance-shaped leaves. Flowers to nearly 2 in (5 cm) wide, clustered, in many colors, mainly plain, mauve to red shades. Conspicuous seed pods burst when ripe. Garden seedling strains include **Camellia-flowered Series**, large double flowers; and **Tom Thumb Series**, low-growing double-flowered. Zones 10–12.

Impatiens hawkeri

syn. *Impatiens schlechteri*

◐/● ❖ ↔ 16–40 in (40–100 cm) ↑ 3–7 ft (0.9–2 m)

Shrubby, continuous-flowering, evergreen perennial from New Guinea and Solomon Islands. Heavy fleshy stems; pointed oval to lance-shaped leaves, toothed, usually red or red-tinted. Long-spurred flowers to over 3 in (8 cm) wide, white, or pink, red, and purple shades. Zones 10–12.

Impatiens New Guinea Hybrids

◐/● ❖ ↔ 16–40 in (40–100 cm) ↑ 10–48 in (25–120 cm)

These are usually cultivars of *I. hawkeri* or hybrids with *I. lineari-folia*. They are available in many striking combinations of flower and foliage. **Bonita Series** includes Improved Quepos/**'Kimpque'**, bright reddish flowers, dark red-tinted green leaves, and Sarchi/**'Kisar'**, deep magenta flowers, dark green leaves; **Celebration Series**, **'Light Lavender II'**, mauve flowers, mid-green leaves; Celebrette Hot Pink/**'Balcebhopi'**, vivid magenta flowers and mid-green leaves; **Paradise Series**, includes Pascua/**'Kipas'**, deep pink flowers, mid-green leaves, Tagula/**'Kigula'**, pale pink flowers with red upper petal, dark green leaves, and Timor/**'Kitim'**, deep orange-red flowers, red-tinted bright green leaves; **'Tango'** ★, bright orange flowers, bronze-green leaves. Zones 10–12.

Impatiens niamniamensis

Impatiens niamniamensis

◐/● ❖ ↔ 16 in (40 cm) ↑ 36 in (90 cm)

Continuous-flowering evergreen perennial from tropical east Africa. Deeply toothed leaves. Large, heavy-textured, long-spurred, deep red flowers with yellow upper petal. Zones 10–12.

Impatiens sodenii

☼/☀ ☘ ↔ 3–7 ft (0.9–2 m) ↕ 3–7 ft (0.9–2 m)

Shrubby evergreen perennial from tropical east Africa. Whorls of toothed lance-shaped leaves. Long-stemmed flowers to over 2 in (5 cm) wide, in lavender and pink shades or white, in summer. Zones 10–12.

Impatiens walleriana

syns *Impatiens holstii, I. sultani*

☼/☀ ☘ ↔ 8–20 in (20–50 cm)
↕ 8–24 in (20–60 cm)

Continuous-flowering, shrubby, evergreen, tropical east African perennial; often treated as annual. Fleshy, succulent stems; toothed lance-shaped leaves, often red-tinted. Spurred flat-faced flowers, evenly sized petals; most colors except yellow and blue. '**Blackberry Ice**', double purple-red flowers; **Carousel Mix**, rosebud doubles in wide range of colors; **Dazzler Series**, many single flowers in warm pastel shades; **Deco Series**, spreading, single flowers in all shades; **Fiesta Series**, rosebud double flowers in many shades including bicolors; **Garden Leader Series** comes in a wide range of colors; **Ice Series**, white-marked foliage, rosebud double flowers in all shades; **Merlot Series**, bright green foliage, single flowers in all colors; **Super Elfin Series**, very compact, single flowers in all shades; **Tempo Series**, compact plants, large flowers; '**Victorian Rose**', spreading habit, semi-double deep pink flowers. Double and variegated cultivars are propagated from cuttings, the rest from seed. Zones 10–12.

Impatiens sodenii

INCARVILLEA

This group of 14 species from central and eastern Asia includes annuals and perennials, some of which are slightly woody, and belongs in the trumpet-vine (Bignoniaceae) family. Depending on which species you plant, they can make exotic-looking rock-garden or border plants. The flowers are trumpet-shaped with flared and often undulated edges, and are usually a bright pink to magenta, although yellow forms have been discovered. Most species have a long flowering period; besides the decorative value of the flowers, the foliage is usually also attractive.

CULTIVATION: Grow in moisture-retentive but not wet soil, sheltered from the hottest afternoon sun. Propagate from fresh seed or by division, although established plants resent disturbance.

Incarvillea delavayi

☀ ☘ ↔ 12–16 in (30–40 cm) ↕ 20–24 in (50–60 cm)

Rosette-forming species from western China. Long compound leaves. Up to 10 large rich pink trumpets per stem, to 3 in (8 cm) across, with yellow throat, held above the foliage, in early to mid-summer. '**Snowtop**', white with yellow throat. Zones 6–9.

Incarvillea emodi

☀ ☘ ↔ 12–16 in (30–40 cm) ↕ 16–20 in (40–50 cm)

Rosette-forming perennial from Afghanistan, Pakistan, and northern India. Large leaves; stems of deep pink trumpets with yellow throat, each bloom 2½ in (6 cm) long, in spring. Zones 7–9.

INULA

Members of this large genus in the daisy (Asteraceae) family are found in a wide range of habitats, from Europe through to sub-tropical Africa and Asia. Most are herbaceous perennials, with some biennials and annuals, the perennial species being those most commonly grown. Some can be invasive. The basal leaves tend to be largest, the leaves reducing in size toward the top of the stems. All have yellow daisy flowers produced mainly in summer.

CULTIVATION: Despite the range of habitats from which they originate, most species like a sunny aspect and rich moist soil. The dwarf species are suited to the larger rock garden, while the taller species can be planted in the wilder parts of the garden or among other perennials in the border. Propagation is from seed or by division.

Inula grandiflora

syns *Inula glandulosa, I. orientalis*

☼ ☀ ↔ 36–40 in (90–100 cm) ↕ 20–24 in (50–60 cm)

From the Caucasus region. Smooth-edged hairy leaves, to 5 in (12 cm) long. Yellow flowers, to 3 in (8 cm) across. Zones 6–10.

Inula helenium

ELECAMPANE

☼/☀ ☀ ↔ 3–4 ft (0.9–1.2 m) ↕ 8–10 ft (2.4–3 m)

Tall, robust, somewhat invasive species from temperate Eurasia. Large hairy lower leaves, to 27 in (70 cm) long, serrated and undulating edges. Spikes of yellow daisy flowers. Zones 5–10.

Inula magnifica

syn. *Inula afghanica*

☼ ☀ ↔ 3–5 ft (0.9–1.5 m) ↕ 5–6 ft (1.5–1.8 m)

Robust, impressive, herbaceous perennial from Caucasus region. Large, deep green, basal leaves, to 10 in (25 cm) long, hairy beneath. Large open clusters of yellow daisies. Zones 6–10.

Inula helenium

IPOMOPSIS

This genus in the phlox (Polemoniaceae) family has 24 species of annuals and perennials that are native to western North America, with outlying species found in Florida, USA, and temperate South America. Leaves often form a basal rosette and may be either smooth or pinnately divided. The tubular flowers, in shades of red, yellow, pink, white, or violet, are borne in loose racemes in spring and summer.

CULTIVATION: In cooler climates they can be grown as temporary summer bedding or in the conservatory or greenhouse. Elsewhere, grow in full sun in fertile well-drained soil. Propagate from seed.

Ipomopsis rubra
syn. *Gilia rubra*
STANDING CYPRESS

☼ ❄ ↔ 18 in (45 cm) ↕ 3–6 ft (0.9–1.8 m)

From South Carolina, Florida, and Texas, USA. Erect unbranched perennial or biennial. Basal rosettes of thread-like leaves. Stems of tubular flowers, scarlet with speckled yellow throats, from summer to autumn. Zones 7–10.

IRESINE
BLOODLEAF

There are about 80 species of annuals, perennials, and subshrubs in this genus, which belongs to the amaranth (Amaranthaceae) family. They are native to the Americas and Australia. The simple leaves are often brilliantly colored with contrasting veins, and it is for this feature that these plants are cultivated. The spikes of small white or green flowers are of little ornamental significance.

CULTIVATION: Grow outdoors all year round in tropical and subtropical areas. In cooler regions, grow outside in summer. Plant in well-drained moisture-retentive soil in full sun for best leaf coloring. Can be used in summer bedding schemes and in pots, both indoors and outdoors. Pinch growing tips to maintain bushiness. Propagate from cuttings, seed, or by division.

Iresine herbstii
BEEF PLANT, BEEF STEAK PLANT, BLOOD-LEAF

☼ ❂ ↔ 12–18 in (30–45 cm) ↕ 18–24 in (45–60 cm)

Native to Brazil. Perennial, often renewed annually in cultivation. Green, purple, or red stems. Pointed oval leaves, deep purple with pink veins to green with yellow veins. '**Aureo-reticulata**', green, gold, and red leaves; '**Brilliantissima**', crimson leaves. Zones 9–12.

IRIS

Iris is the type genus for the family Iridaceae. The 300-odd species, which are divided into various sections, and scattered over the northern temperate zones, occur in bulbous, rhizomatous, and fibrous-rooted forms. The sword-shaped foliage, often arranged in fans, is sometimes variegated. The flowers have 6 petals, usually in the fleur-de-lis pattern of 3 upright standards and 3 downward-curving falls, which may be bearded, beardless, or crested, and occurring in all colors.

Iresine herbstii 'Brilliantissima'

CULTIVATION: Bog irises need a sunny position in damp soil. Woodland irises thrive in dappled sunlight with moist well-drained soil. Bearded irises need sun, and dry soil after flowering. Rockery irises need a sunny spot in moist, well-drained, gritty soil. Propagate by division when dormant, less commonly by seed.

Iris chrysographes
GOLD NET IRIS, GOLD PATTERN IRIS

☼ ❄ ↔ 12 in (30 cm) ↕ 12–20 in (30–50 cm)

Fleshy-stemmed beardless iris from China, Myanmar, and Tibet. Strappy grayish green leaves. Flowers purple-black, gold streaks on falls. '**Black Knight**', purple-black flowers. Zones 7–10.

Iris cristata
CRESTED IRIS

❂ ❄ ↔ 12–20 in (30–50 cm) ↕ 4–5 in (10–12 cm)

Dainty herbaceous woodlander from eastern USA, with exposed, creeping, fleshy stems, and fans of bright green strappy leaves. Produces lightly scented light blue to purple flowers, on stems to height of leaves, with white markings on falls and yellow crests. Spring-flowering. A white-flowered form also grown. Zones 6–10.

Iris douglasiana

☼ ❄ ↔ 18 in (45 cm) ↕ 20–32 in (50–80 cm)

Fleshy-stemmed beardless iris from California and Oregon, USA. Loose clumps of dark green ribbed leaves. Branching flower stems. Blooms, in summer, vary in color from cream to deep reddish purple, veining usually in darker tones. Zones 7–9.

Iris ensata ★
syn. *Iris kaempferi*
JAPANESE WATER IRIS, WOODLAND IRIS

☼ ❄ ↔ 40 in (100 cm) ↕ 36 in (90 cm)

Native to Europe, Asia, and North America. Tall, dark green, strappy, grass-like foliage. Single, occasionally branched stems of

Iris chrysographes 'Black Knight'

flowers vary in color from red, purple, or blue, held well above foliage, in early summer. Will grow in shallow water. Not tolerant of dry hot conditions. '**Flying Tiger**', white flowers, heavily veined in violet; '**Hekito**', deep blue flowers, blue-tipped; '**Hue and Cry**', red-veined plum-red flowers; '**Rose Queen**', soft pink flowers, darker veined falls; '**Variegata**', purple-red flowers, variegated foliage; '**Yaemo-miji**', cerise-purple flowers streaked with white. Zones 5–8.

Iris foetidissima
GLADDON, GLADWYN, ROAST BEEF PLANT,
STINKING GLADWYN
☀/◐ ❋ ↔ 18–30 in (45–75 cm)
↕ 18–30 in (45–75 cm)
Vigorous, fleshy-stemmed, beardless iris, native to Europe and north Africa. Glossy, deep green, sword-shaped leaves, odorous when crushed. Spring flowers unspectacular, buff-yellow and dusty dull purple. '**Variegata**', boldly white-striped leaves. Zones 6–10.

Iris × fulvala
☀ ❋ ↔ 10 in (25 cm) ↕ 18–30 in (45–75 cm)
Hybrid beardless irises. Purplish red flowers, in summer. Needs very moist soil. Zones 7–10.

Iris germanica
☀ ❋ ↔ 18–24 in (45–60 cm)
↕ 24–48 in (60–120 cm)
Rhizomatous bearded iris. Origin uncertain, widely naturalized. Blue, white, and yellow flowers, to 4 in (10 cm) wide, yellow beards. Zones 5–9.

Iris innominata
☀/◑ ❋ ↔ 10 in (25 cm) ↕ 8–10 in (20–25 cm)
Fleshy-stemmed beardless iris, native to Oregon and California, USA, with narrow dark green leaves. Slender-petalled flowers, cream to purple, with darker veining, in summer. Zones 8–10.

Iris japonica
syns *Iris chinensis*, *I. fimbriata*
◑ ❋ ↔ 18–24 in (45–60 cm) ↕ 24–32 in (60–80 cm)
Fleshy-stemmed crested iris from central China and Japan. Shiny dark green leaves in fans. Pale lavender flowers with orange markings, ruffled and fringed at margins, borne on branching airy stems, in spring. Zones 8–10.

Iris laevigata
JAPANESE WATER IRIS, RABBIT EAR IRIS
☀/◑ ❋ ↔ 5 ft (1.5 m) ↕ 2–5 ft (0.6–1.5 m)
From Japan. Robust upright irises, grow in water and boggy areas. Will naturalize on edges of swamps and ponds. Tall spikes

Iris ensata 'Flying Tiger'

Iris pseudacorus 'Variegata'

of purple, mauve, and white flowers, above foliage, in summer. Large floppy petals hang gracefully toward the ground. '**Variegata**', to 16 in (40 cm) tall, green leaves striped with large white veins, purple-blue flowers, on short stems. Zones 3–9.

Iris missouriensis
☀ ❋ ↔ 12 in (30 cm) ↕ 12–20 in (30–50 cm)
Fleshy-stemmed beardless iris from western North America. Narrow grayish green leaves. White, blue, or purple flowers, long narrow falls, in late spring–summer. Zones 3–8.

Iris pallida
syns *Iris glauca*, *I. odoratissima*
DALMATIAN IRIS
☀ ❋ ↔ 12 in (30 cm) ↕ 36–48 in (90–120 cm)
Fleshy-stemmed bearded iris from the European Alps. Stiff, sword-like, bluish green foliage. Large fragrant flowers, blue with yellow beards, in early summer. *I. p.* **subsp.** *cengialti* ★ (syn. *I. cengialti*), greener leaves than species, dark purple flowers. *I. p.* '**Argentea Variegata**', white stripes on leaf edges; '**Variegata**', creamy yellow leaf markings. Zones 5–9.

Iris pseudacorus
YELLOW FLAG
☀ ❋ ↔ 5–7 ft (1.5–2 m) ↕ 4–5 ft (1.2–1.5 m)
Robust, potentially weedy water iris from Europe, Middle East, and northern Africa. Long, upright, rich green leaves die down in winter. Bright yellow flowers with brown markings on falls, 4 in (10 cm) across, just below the tallest leaves. '**Variegata**', boldly cream-variegated leaves fade to green after flowering. Zones 6–10.

Iris tectorum

Iris unguicularis

Iris versicolor

Iris pumila
DWARF BEARDED IRIS

☼ ❋ ↔ 4–6 in (10–15 cm) ↕ 4–6 in (10–15 cm)

Dainty rock-garden iris, found from eastern Europe to the Ural Mountains of Russia. Solitary flowers, perfumed, blue, purple, or yellow, in mid-spring. Zones 5–10.

Iris sibirica

☼ ❋ ↔ 8–24 in (20–60 cm) ↕ 18–48 in (45–120 cm)

From Europe and northern Asia. Rhizomatous beardless iris. Thin, grassy, bright green leaves. Purple-blue flowers, dark veins on falls, to 3 in (8 cm) wide, in late spring–summer. Zones 4–9.

Iris spuria

☼ ❋ ↔ 3–7 ft (0.9–2 m) ↕ 4–7 ft (1.2–2 m)

From northern and northwestern Iran. Colonizing iris. Flowers from pale and dark blues through to whites, creams, and mauves. Plants need rich warm soils. *I. s.* subsp. *halophila*, pale to deep yellow flowers, dark green strappy foliage. Zones 6–9.

Iris tectorum
ROOF IRIS

☼ ❋ ↔ 12 in (30 cm) ↕ 12–16 in (30–40 cm)

Native to China. Fleshy-stemmed crested iris. Light green leaves. Bluish purple flowers, darker veining, in early summer. Zones 6–9.

Iris unguicularis
syn. *Iris stylosa*
ALGERIAN IRIS, WINTER IRIS

☼/❁ ❋ ↔ 16–20 in (40–50 cm) ↕ 12–15 in (30–38 cm)

Evergreen species from Mediterranean region. Grows well in hot dry aspects. Tough grassy leaves and pale lavender to blue flowers, hidden among leaves, in winter–early spring. 'Mary Barnard', deep violet-blue flowers. Zones 7–10.

Iris versicolor

☼ ❋ ↔ 10 in (25 cm) ↕ 8–32 in (20–80 cm)

From eastern USA. Vigorous, water-loving, fleshy-stemmed, beardless iris. Broad, ribbed, green foliage. Many small flowers in bluish purple shades, with darker veining, carried on branching flower spikes. Summer-flowering species. Zones 4–9.

Iris Hybrid Cultivars
ARILBRED HYBRIDS

☼ ❋ ↔ 12 in (30 cm) ↕ 10–27 in (25–70 cm)

Large flowers in a range of purple shades and yellow, with colored markings, in early spring. Require a dry dormant summer season. 'Oyez', 24 in (60 cm) high, white flowers, dark purple veins on standards and falls. Zones 3–9.

BEARDED HYBRIDS

☼ ❋ ↔ 12–36 in (30–90 cm) ↕ 8–40 in (20–100 cm)

Hardy perennials. Grown from rhizomes. Will produce more flowers in cooler climates. Upright pale blue-green foliage. Large heads of flowers, in blues, purples, and browns through to oranges, whites, and yellows, in late spring. Flowers have standards and falls, with a distinctive beard on each fall. Do not cover rhizomes with soil, as they will rot and die. Need well-drained and fertile soil in full sun. Divide every 5 to 7 years.

Miniature Dwarf Bearded Hybrids: Less than 8 in (20 cm) high. Small flowers, 1½–3 in (35–80 mm) wide, in spring.

Standard Dwarf Bearded Hybrids: Flower well in cool maritime climates. Height of 8–15 in (20–38 cm). Form good clumps. Flowers in late spring. Need good cold period through winter to perform well. 'Bromyard', early season, blue-gray standards, blue-purple and ocher falls, blue-gray beards; 'Eyebright', yellow flowers with deep brown lines, creamy yellow beards; 'Flower Shower', ruffled flowers in violet and white; 'Honington', cream-yellow flowers; 'Rain Dance', early season, violet-blue flowers, matching violet-blue beards; 'Tirra Lirra', mauve flowers.

Intermediate Bearded Hybrids: These hybrids reach 16–27 in (40–70 cm) high. Medium-sized plants bear blooms that are also medium-sized. Will flower well in most areas, flowers well able to support themselves on their stems. Do well in wind-prone areas, but need full sun. 'Arctic Fancy', pure white flowers with purple markings; 'Eye Magic', yellow flowers, with red thumbprint on falls; 'Happy Mood' ★, creamy flowers edged in lavender; 'Maui Moonlight', mid-season, rich lemon flowers. Other popular Intermediate Bearded Hybrids include 'Katie-Koo', 'Miss Carla', 'Sherbet Lemon', and 'Templecloud'.

Miniature Tall Bearded Hybrids: Sharing a similar flowering season to the Tall Bearded Hybrids, and reaching similar height to Border Bearded Hybrids, these hybrids produce smaller flowers on wiry stems. **'Bumblebee Deelite'**, yellow standards, maroon falls edged with yellow; **'Frosted Velvet'**, two-tone flowers with white centers, rich velvet purple falls edged in white.

Border Bearded Hybrids: Flowering at same time as Tall Bearded Hybrids, but with somewhat smaller flowers held on stalks 16–27 in (40–70 cm) high. **'Apricot Frosty'**, white flowers, deep apricot falls, apricot beards; **'Brown Lasso'**, deep butterscotch and yellow flowers, petals edged in pale lavender.

Tall Bearded Hybrids: Well-branched spikes of robust large flowers, may be ruffled or smooth-edged. Can reach height of 27–40 in (70–100 cm). Good for cutting. **'Apricorange'**, orange flowers; **'Berry Sherbet'**, early flowering, pink and violet flowers; **'Blue-Eyed Brunette'**, ruffled bronze flowers, blue beards; **'Breakers'**, mid-blue ruffled flowers; **'Celebration Song'**, late season, pinkish standards, lavender-blue falls; **'Champagne Elegance'** ★, apricot flowers, yellow standards, white falls edged in apricot, yellow-red beards, large number of blooms; **'Cinderella's Coach'**, pumpkin orange flowers, bright red to tangerine beards, ruffled flowers; **'Cupid's Arrow'**, pink to maroon flowers; **'Dazzling Gold'**, mid-season, yellow and red flowers; **'Designing Woman'**, rosy lilac standards and falls, coral beards, very wavy and ruffled blooms; **'Dusky Challenger'**, large, ruffled, black-purple flowers; **'Early Light'**, creamy yellow ruffled flowers; **'Good Morning America'**, mid-season, pale blue flowers; **'Hello Darkness'**, mid-season, rich velvet black flowers; **'Honky Tonk Blues'**, mid-season, blue-violet, heavily washed over a white base, giving a soft blue effect, wide ruffled blooms; **'Incantation'**, mid-season, bluish standards, pure white falls; **'In Town'**, mid-season, lilac blue standards, with slightly ruffled purple falls; **'Jesse's Song'**, white center bleeding into violet, lemon beard, violet edging; **'Stepping Out'**, similar to 'Jesse's Song'; **'Thornbird'**, yellowish standards, greenish brown falls; **'Vanity'**, pink flowers, salmon pink beards. Other attractive Tall Bearded Hybrids include **'Bewick Swan'**, **'Meg's Mantle'**, **'Paradise'**, **'Paradise Bird'**, **'Phil Keen'**, **'Precious Heather'**, and **'Sun Miracle'**. Zones 3–9.

CALIFORNIAN HYBRIDS

☼/☀ ❄ ↔ 12 in (30 cm)
↑ 10–20 in (25–50 cm)
Hybrids of about 6 iris species from California and Oregon, sometimes known as Pacific Coast Hybrids, wide color range, from yellow to pink and purple. Long bloom period from spring. **'Broadleigh Carolyn'**, compact white flowers, mauve-purple veining and yellow blotches in eye; **'Broadleigh Rose'**, rich rose pink flowers, yellow and cream blotches in eye; **'Broadleigh Sybil'**, creamy apricot standards, deep rose pink falls. Zones 5–9.

LOUISIANA HYBRIDS

☼/☀ ❄ ↔ 3–7 ft (0.9–2 m) ↑ 18–60 in (45–150 cm)
Adaptable to growing in water and also on edges of ponds and rivers. Will grow in ordinary garden soil if given plenty of water. Need well-prepared soil, with good amount of humus. Will grow in full sun or part-shade. Flowers from pinks, yellows, and blues to oranges, purples, and browns. **'Marie Caillet'**, ruffled violet-blue flowers, yellow signals. Zones 6–9.

ONCOCYCLUS HYBRIDS

☼ ❄ ↔ 40 in (100 cm) ↑ 4–24 in (10–60 cm)
Similar to bearded iris, but smaller. One flower on each stem. Characteristic large blotch and dark veining on flowers. Adaptable to hot dry climates. Large seed heads in autumn. Zones 7–9.

SIBERIAN HYBRIDS

☼ ❄ ↔ 8–24 in (20–60 cm) ↑ 18–48 in (45–120 cm)
Adaptable irises, happy in heavy clay soils. Flower spikes taller than foliage, up to 5 flowers on each stem; flowers blue-violet or white. Flowers of **'Annemarie Troeger'** in 2 shades of blue, white signals; **'Harpswell Happiness'**, ruffled white flowers; **'Pink Haze'**, lavender-pink flowers, red-violet veins on falls; **'White Swirl'**, pure white flowers, yellow blotches, flared outer petals. Zones 4–9.

Iris, Hybrid Cultivar, Bearded, Tall, 'Cinderella's Coach'

SPURIA HYBRIDS

☼ ❄ ↔ 18–24 in (45–60 cm)
↑ 30–48 in (75–120 cm)
Tall plants with large flowers in white and yellow to red and purple shades, in spring–summer. **'Shelford Giant'**, mid-season, large lemon and white flowers. Zones 4–9.

Iris, Hybrid Cultivar, Louisiana, 'Marie Caillet'

Ismelia carinata

ISMELIA

This genus of around 5 species of annuals and short-lived perennials in the daisy (Asteraceae) family, which was established with
the break-up of the genus *Chrysanthemum*, may prove to be
indistinguishable from *Xanthopthalmum*. Found around the
Mediterranean region and on Madeira and the Canary Islands,
they are bushy plants with upright stems that sometimes become
woody at the base. The foliage is pinnately lobed, sometimes
with very narrow lobes, and may be toothed. The daisy-like
flowerheads are often brightly colored and appear in abundance.
CULTIVATION: These plants are intolerant of repeated frosts but are
otherwise very adaptable in mild climates. Plant in a bright position with light well-drained soil. Water well when in bud and
flower, but otherwise keep rather dry. Usually raised from seed,
although perennial species may also be propagated from half-
hardened stem cuttings.

Ismelia carinata
syns *Chrysanthemum carinatum, Ismelia versicolor*
☼☼/◐ ⚘ ↔ 12–16 in (30–40 cm) ↕ 32–40 in (80–100 cm)
Annual of obscure origin, probably from Morocco. Upright stems;
bright green, fleshy, pinnately lobed leaves. Flowerheads to 4 in
(10 cm) diameter, disc florets dark, ray florets multicolored in
yellow, orange, and red tones with light base, in summer–early
autumn. 'Court Jesters', popular mixed color strain. Summer
annual in cool areas. Zones 10–12.

JASIONE
SHEEP'S BIT
There are about 20 species of annuals, perennials, and biennials
in this genus, which belongs to the bellflower (Campanulaceae)
family. These plants are native to Europe and regions of the
Mediterranean, where they grow in grassland. Plants form tufts

of narrow grassy foliage. Their small blue flowers are borne in
compact terminal heads reminiscent of scabious, and are surrounded by 1 or more rows of bracts. Flowers occur in summer.
CULTIVATION: The small *Jasione* species are best grown in the rock
garden while the taller ones are suitable for the front of the border. Grow in full sun in a well-drained sandy soil. Propagation
is by division or from seed.

Jasione laevis
syn. *Jasione perennis*
SHEEP'S BIT, SHEPHERD'S SCABIOUS
☼ ⚘ ↔ 8–10 in (20–25 cm) ↕ 8–20 in (20–50 cm)
From southern and western Europe. Perennial forming dense
tufts of narrow leaves. The blue flowerheads are a little over 1 in
(25 mm) wide and have numerous bracts. 'Blaulicht' (syn. 'Blue
Light') has globose flowerheads of vivid blue. Zones 5–9.

KIRENGESHOMA
This genus of a single species, a woodland perennial from Japan
and Korea, is a member of the hydrangea (Hydrangeaceae)
family. These plants have large, maple-like, soft green leaves, and
drooping thick-petalled flowers, shaped like a shuttlecock, are
produced in late summer.
CULTIVATION: Give *Kirengeshoma* a cool shaded aspect, sheltered
from the wind, in moist humus-rich soil. Propagation is from
seed freshly sown or by careful division of established clumps.

Kirengeshoma palmata
☀ ⚘ ↔ 30 in (75 cm) ↕ 48 in (120 cm)
Elegant, arching, herbaceous perennial from Japan and Korea.
Leaves to 8 in (20 cm) long on black stems. Pale lemon flowers
to 1½ in (35 mm) long, in late summer. Zones 5–9.

KNAUTIA
This genus of some 60 species of annuals and herbaceous perennials is a member of the teasel (Dipsacaceae) family. They can be
found in Europe, the Caucasus region, Siberia, and the Mediterranean region in a wide range of habitats, from woods to meadows
and rocky hillsides. They have flowers very like those of *Scabiosa*
species, consisting of a cluster of small flowers that look like a
single bloom. Their open airy habit makes them useful in the
border or the wild garden.
CULTIVATION: Grow these plants in any well-drained fertile soil
in full sun. Propagation is usually from seed and they will usually
self-seed, sometimes to the extent of weediness.

Knautia arvensis
syn. *Scabiosa arvensis*
BLUE BUTTONS, FIELD SCABIOUS
☼ ⚘ ↔ 12 in (30 cm) ↕ 5 ft (1.5 m)
Upright clumping perennial from Europe through to Siberia
via the Caucasus, Iran, and central Asia. Hairy dull green leaves,
smooth-edged through to indented, and up to 10 in (25 cm)
long. Erect branched flower stems. Soft lilac-blue flowerheads,
1½ in (35 mm) across, from mid-summer through to cooler
months. Zones 6–10.

KNIPHOFIA

RED-HOT POKER, TORCH LILY

Most of the nearly 70 species in this genus in the asphodel (Asphodelaceae) family are South African clump-forming perennials with grassy to sword-shaped, often evergreen, foliage that emerges from vigorous rhizomes. They are grown for their spikes of intensely colored, usually orange and/or yellow flowers, borne mainly from autumn to spring in bottlebrush heads at the top of strong, tall, upright stems. Many hybrids and cultivars are available in a variety of sizes and flower colors.
CULTIVATION: Hardiness varies, though none will tolerate repeated heavy frosts. Plant in an open sunny position in moist, humus-rich, well-drained soil. Water and feed well during active growth. Most will tolerate salt winds and thrive near the coast. Propagation is usually by division after flowering or from seed.

Kniphofia caulescens

☼/◐ ❄ ↔ 20 in (50 cm) ↕ 4 ft (1.2 m)

Tough evergreen alpine species. Narrow but thick blue-green leaves on "trunk" to 12 in (30 cm) high. Coppery flower stems and densely packed heads of pink-tinted cream flowers opening from red buds, in late summer–autumn. Zones 7–10.

Kniphofia northiae

☼/◐ ❄ ↔ 40 in (100 cm) ↕ 5 ft (1.5 m)

Evergreen perennial. Thick, broader, slightly blue-green leaves with deep central keel. Dense cylindrical heads of yellow flowers opening from red buds, in late spring–autumn. Zones 8–10.

Kniphofia × *praecox*

RED-HOT POKER

☼/◐ ❄ ↔ 20–40 in (50–100 cm) ↕ 4–5 ft (1.2–1.5 m)

Wild hybrids from South Africa, also garden hybrids. Evergreen perennial. Dense basal clumps of narrow deeply channeled leaves. Strong upright flower stems. Cylindrical to rounded heads of bright orange, yellow, or cream flowers, mainly in late summer–winter. Zones 7–10.

Kniphofia rooperi

☼/◐ ❄ ↔ 20–24 in (50–60 cm) ↕ 4 ft (1.2 m)

Evergreen perennial. Thick leaves with conspicuous keels. From late summer, large spherical heads of bright red flowers appear; lower flowers often yellow-green. Zones 8–10.

Kniphofia thomsonii

☼/◐ ◔ ↔ 16–24 in (40–60 cm) ↕ 4 ft (1.2 m)

From Kenya. Usually evergreen. Narrow leaves. Strong flower stems, large cylindrical heads of deep dusky red flowers, yellow-gold at base of head, in mid-summer to autumn. *K. t.* var. *snowdenii* is deciduous. Zones 9–11.

Kniphofia uvaria

☼/◐ ❄ ↔ 24 in (60 cm) ↕ 4 ft (1.2 m)

Evergreen perennial. Thick, deeply channeled leaves. Strong flower stems with ovoid heads of yellow-tipped, bright orange-red, tubular flowers, in late summer–autumn. Parent of many garden hybrids. Zones 5–10.

Kniphofia Hybrid Cultivars

☼/◐ ❄ ↔ 12–20 in (30–50 cm) ↕ 2–5 ft (0.6–1.5 m)

Many hybrids. 'Bees' Sunset', deciduous, leaves with serrated edges, yellow-orange flowers on dark stems to 3 ft (0.9 m) tall; 'Green Jade', evergreen, flowers initially pale cream ageing through cream to white, 5 ft (1.5 m) stems; 'Ice Queen', deciduous, green buds open pale yellow and age to off-white, 5 ft (1.5 m) stems; 'Little Maid', deciduous, fine grassy leaves, green buds open soft yellow and age to cream, 24 in (60 cm) stems; 'Painted Lady', dusky red flowers age to orange-pink, 3 ft (0.9 m) stems; 'Primrose Beauty', fine grassy foliage, bright yellow flowers, 24 in (60 cm) stems; 'Royal Standard', deciduous, bright yellow flowers open from red buds, stocky 3 ft (0.9 m) stems; 'Sunset', orange to red flowers; 'Tetbury Torch', broad, slightly blue-green leaves, golden yellow flowers open from orange buds, 3 ft (0.9 m) stems; 'Yellowhammer', spring-flowering, bright yellow flowers, 4 ft (1.2 m) stems. Zones 8–10.

Kniphofia caulescens

Kniphofia northiae

Kniphofia, Hybrid Cultivar, 'Little Maid'

Kniphofia, Hybrid Cultivar, 'Primrose Beauty'

Lamium maculatum 'Pink Pewter'

KOHLERIA

These 50 hairy herbs and shrubs, native to tropical Central and South America, are part of the African violet (Gesneriaceae) family, and are often cultivated as house plants. Large rhizomes grow across the soil surface and the thick, serrated, hairy or velvety leaves are often mottled with red. Trumpet-shaped flowers with erect, thick, hairy sepals and tubular corollas, usually in colors ranging from yellow through red to purple, are covered with red hairs and spotted on the inside with a contrasting color.
CULTIVATION: These plants prefer moist well-drained soil, kept drier in winter, in full sun or part-shade. Propagate in spring by division of rhizomes or from seed sown in spring.

Kohleria digitaliflora
syn. *Kohleria warscewiczii*
☀ ❄ ↔ 12–24 in (30–60 cm)
↕ 12–24 in (30–60 cm)
Erect perennial from Colombia. Hairy white stems and dark green narrowly oval to sword-shaped leaves to 8 in (20 cm) long. Stalked clusters of very hairy flowers with white corolla tubes to 1¼ in (3 cm) long, flushed with deep rose, and green lobes spotted with purple, in summer–autumn. Zones 8–10.

Kohleria eriantha
☀ ❄ ↔ 3–4 ft (0.9–1.2 m) ↕ 3–4 ft (0.9–1.2 m)
Shrubby perennial from tropical Colombia. Reddish, densely hairy stems and oval to spear-shaped, deep green, velvety leaves, to 5 in (12 cm) long, with hairy red margins. Clusters of up to 4 drooping flowers, fuzzy, with corolla tubes to 2 in (5 cm) long, of scarlet-orange, with lobes ¼ in (6 mm) across, spotted with yellow, in late spring–summer. Zones 8–10.

LAMIUM
DEAD-NETTLE
This is the type genus for the mint (Lamiaceae) family. This group of about 50 species of low-growing annuals and perennials, which often spreads by rhizomes or runners, occurs naturally in Europe, North Africa, and temperate Asia, but some are also

widely naturalized elsewhere and have become weeds. The opposite pairs of toothed, pointed, heart-shaped leaves resemble those of stinging nettles but lack the sting. They can be eaten as a salad vegetable. The small flowers, usually yellow, pink, or white, emerge in spring near the stem tips in leafy heads (verticillasters).
CULTIVATION: These are very hardy and easily grown in any partly shaded or shaded position in moist, humus-rich, well-drained soil. Variegated forms often need more light to maintain their color. Propagate at any time from cuttings or by division.

Lamium galeobdolon
syns *Galeobdolon luteum, Lamiastrum galeobdolon*
YELLOW ARCHANGEL
☀/◐ ❄ ↔ 48 in (120 cm) ↕ 8–16 in (20–40 cm)
Vigorous, creeping or scrambling, near-evergreen perennial from temperate Eurasia. Leaves narrow, dark green, to over 2 in (5 cm) long, deeply toothed edges. Heads of up to 10 yellow flowers, to ¾ in (18 mm) long, in summer. 'Hermann's Pride' ★, narrow leaves, silver streaks and spots; 'Silver Angel', low spreader, stems initially upright, silver-marked leaves. Zones 6–10.

Lamium garganicum
☀/◐ ❄ ↔ 48 in (120 cm) ↕ 8–16 in (20–40 cm)
From Europe, western Asia, and North Africa. Mat-forming, spreading, scrambling, near-evergreen perennial. Leaves broad, dull mid-green, toothed, triangular, to 3 in (8 cm) long. Heads of up to 8 widely spaced purple-pink to red flowers, to over 1 in (25 mm) long, in summer. Zones 6–10.

Kohleria eriantha

Lamium maculatum
☀/◐ ❄ ↔ 24–60 in (60–150 cm)
↕ 6–20 in (15–50 cm)
From Europe, western Asia, and North Africa. Spreading, sometimes mounding or scrambling, near-evergreen perennial. Stems long, rooting as they spread, with downy, toothed, pointed oval to triangular, often white-marked leaves, to over 3 in (8 cm) long. Heads of up to 8 widely spaced pinkish red to purple, rarely white, flowers, to ¾ in (18 mm) long, in summer. 'Album', silver blotched leaves, white flowers; 'Anne Greenaway', tricolor foliage, silver center outlined in dark green on yellow-green base, light purple flowers; 'Aureum', yellow-green leaves with white centers, pink flowers; 'Beacon Silver', silver leaves with thin green margin, pink to purplish flowers; 'Pink Nancy', silver leaves with thin green margin, pale pink flowers; 'Pink Pewter', green leaves overlaid with silver-gray, deep pink flowers; 'White Nancy', silver leaves with thin green margin, white flowers. Zones 4–10.

Lamium orvala
☀/◐ ❄ ↔ 40 in (100 cm) ↕ 40 in (100 cm)
Vigorous bushy perennial found from southern to central Europe. Dark green leaves, toothed, pointed oval, to 6 in (15 cm) long. Flowerheads consist of a few pinkish red to purple flowers,

¾ in (18 mm) long, appearing in summer. Trim occasionally to retain its compact shape. Does not spread. Zones 6–10.

LATHYRUS
SWEET PEA, VETCHLING, WILD PEA

This genus in the pea-flower subfamily of the legume (Fabaceae) family has 110 species of annuals and perennials from Eurasia, North America, temperate South America, and the mountains of east Africa. Many are climbers, others are low-spreading plants, and some are shrubby. The climbers support themselves with tendrils growing at the tips of the pinnate leaves, where the terminal leaflets would normally be. The typical pea-flowers occur in many colors, and may be borne singly or in racemes.
CULTIVATION: The non-climbing perennials will tolerate partial shade, but otherwise grow these species in sunny well-ventilated conditions. Plant in moist well-drained soil; provide stakes or wires for climbers. Propagate the annuals from seed sown in early spring, or in autumn–winter in mild climates, and the perennials by division when dormant.

Lathyrus odoratus 'Brian Clough'

Lathyrus aureus
☼/◗ ❄ ↔ 40 in (100 cm) ↕ 24–36 in (60–90 cm)
From the Balkans. Bushy herbaceous perennial. Leaves with up to 12 leaflets. Racemes of golden yellow flowers, often tinted orange, ¾ in (18 mm) across, in late spring–summer. Zones 6–10.

Lathyrus laxiflorus
☼/◗ ❄ ↔ 16–24 in (40–60 cm) ↕ 12 in (30 cm)
From southeastern Europe. Low, somewhat spreading perennial. Paired lance-shaped leaflets, to 1¾ in (40 mm) long. Sprays of up to 6 white-centered violet flowers, ¾ in (18 mm) across, in summer. Zones 7–9.

Lathyrus odoratus
SWEET PEA
☼ ❄ ↔ 40 in (100 cm) ↕ 8 ft (2.4 m)
From Italy and the Mediterranean islands. Highly scented annual climber. Paired blue-green leaflets. Racemes of up to 3 violet and purple-red flowers in summer. Garden forms are heavier flowering, very wide range of colors. 'Alan Williams', buff-pink and white flowers; 'Annie Good', pink tonings; 'Anniversary' ★, white with pink edge; 'Bijou Mix', only 12 in (30 cm) tall, many colors; 'Brian Clough', orange and white; 'Charlie's Angel', blue and lavender; 'Cream Southbourne', pale cream; 'Eclipse', deep lavender; 'Evening Glow', mid-pink and orange; 'Firebird', orange-red; 'Jill Walton', cream and pale pink, darker edge; 'Lilac Ripple', white and mauve; 'Midnight', deep purple-red; 'Noel Sutton',

deep blue; 'Sea Wolf', lavender; 'Spencer Mixed', large-flowered mixed color strains; 'Teresa Maureen', lavender and cerise, purplish edge; 'Wiltshire Ripple', brown-red and white; 'Winner', red flowers suffused with orange. Cultivars with small, fragrant, single flowers, often known as **Heirloom** style, include 'Blanche Ferry', pink and white bicolor; 'Cupani', compact, very fragrant, purple and red flowers; 'Old Spice Mix', very fragrant flowers in wide color range, including bicolor and striped; and 'Painted Lady', very pale pink and deep cherry red flowers. Zones 8–11.

Lathyrus splendens
PRIDE OF CALIFORNIA
☼ ❄ ↔ 3–7 ft (0.9–2 m) ↕ 7–10 ft (2–3 m)
From northern Baja California, Mexico. Shrubby, sometimes scrambling, evergreen perennial. Leaves tendril-tipped, with up to 10 leaflets to nearly 3 in (8 cm) long. Racemes of up to 12 violet to purple-red flowers, 1¾ in (40 mm) across. Zones 8–10.

Lathyrus vernus
SPRING VETCH
☼ ❄ ↔ 24–40 in (60–100 cm) ↕ 12–24 in (30–60 cm)
From Europe. Semi-evergreen perennial. Leaves with 1 to 2 pairs of leaflets. Racemes of up to 15 flowers, ¾ in (18 mm) across, purple-red ageing to blue-green, in early spring. 'Alboroseus', pink and white flowers; 'Rosenelfe', pale pink flowers. Zones 4–9.

LAVATERA (see page 200)

Lavatera × clementii
☼ ❄ ↔ 6 ft (1.8 m) ↕ 6 ft (1.8 m)
Vigorous upright plants. Sometimes short lived. 'Barnsley' ★, masses of pale pink flowers; 'Bredon Springs' ★, deep pink flowers; 'Rosea', tall, gray-tinted foliage, dusky pink flowers. Zones 8–10.

Lavatera × clementii 'Barnsley'

Lavatera thuringiaca
TREE MALLOW
☼ ❋ ↔ 3–4 ft (0.9–1.2 m) ↑ 6 ft (1.8 m)
Shrubby evergreen perennial from central Europe. Rose pink
flowers for several months in summer–autumn. Zones 8–11.

Lavatera trimestris
ANNUAL MALLOW, REGAL MALLOW, ROSE MALLOW,
ROYAL MALLOW
☼ ❋ ↔ 18–36 in (45–90 cm)
↑ 24–48 in (60–120 cm)
Bushy easy-to-grow annual native to Mediterranean region. No need to stake. Silky cup-
shaped flowers. '**Ruby Regis**', to 24 in
(60 cm) tall, cerise pink flowers; '**Silver Cup**',
24 in (60 cm) tall, pink flowers. Zones 8–10.

LEONOTIS
Comprising 15 species, this genus of soft-
wooded annuals, perennials, and evergreen
to semi-deciduous subshrubs in the mint (Lamiaceae) family,
with the exception of one widely distributed tropical species,
occurs wild in tropical and southern Africa. Opposite pairs of
mid-green leaves are borne on upright squarish stems, and in late
summer to winter whorls of narrow 2-lipped flowers are arranged
densely around the stems.
CULTIVATION: These are warm-climate plants that can be grown
under cover in frost-prone areas. They need moderately fertile
soil in full sun and ample water in the growing season. The
somewhat brittle stems can be cut back in spring. Propagate
from seed or from softwood cuttings in summer.

Leonotis nepetifolia
☼ ❋ ↔ 8–12 in (20–30 cm) ↑ 3–4 ft (0.9–1.2 m)
From India and Africa; now naturalized
in parts of North America. Upright annual.
Serrated leaves, to 5 in (12 cm) long. Curved
orange trumpet-flowers in winter. Zones 8–11.

Leonotis ocymifolia
syn. *Leonotis leonurus*
LION'S TAIL, WILD DAGGA
☼ ❂ ↔ 3 ft (0.9 m) ↑ 8 ft (2.4 m)
Clump-forming plant, semi-deciduous or
evergreen depending on climate. Upright
stems. Bright orange woolly flowers in late
summer–winter. '**Alba**' and '**Harrismith
White**', white-flowered plants. Zones 9–11.

LEONTOPODIUM
A rock garden favorite, *Leontopodium* is a member of the daisy
(Asteraceae) family. The approximately 60 species are hardy,
herbaceous, alpine perennials. Most are native to the mountain
regions of east and central Asia, with only one species occurring
in Europe. The gray-green leaves are basal or alternate, and
coated with white hairs. The flowerheads are small and white.

In the wild, these tufted herbs grow in alpine meadows,
on scree slopes, and among rocks, in cool to cold climates.
CULTIVATION: These plants require a well-drained gritty or sandy
soil and a sunny position. They will not tolerate damp conditions,
and generally prefer cooler temperatures. Propagate from seed.

Leontopodium alpinum

Leontopodium alpinum
EDELWEISS
☼ ❋ ↔ 4–9 in (10–22 cm) ↑ 6 in (15 cm)
The only European species, from the Alps,
Carpathians, and Pyrenees. Creeping short-
lived perennial. Leaves silvery gray, 2–3 in
(5–8 cm) long. Star-shaped white flowers
with central yellow floret surrounded by long
floral bracts in early summer. Zones 4–8.

LESPEDEZA
This genus is a member of the large pea-
flower subfamily of the legume (Fabaceae)
family. It contains about 40 species of usually
prostrate annuals and perennials and deciduous shrubs, which are
found in eastern and tropical Asia, Australia, and eastern USA.
The leaves are trifoliate, and the flowers are small but are usually
borne in long racemes.
CULTIVATION: Grow these in a sunny position in deep, well-drained,
fertile soil. In cooler areas they need a warm wall for protection.
In spring prune out dead growth and cut back hard to rejuvenate
the plant. Propagate from seed or from half-hardened cuttings.

Lespedeza thunbergii
MIYAGINO-HAGI, THUNBERG BUSH CLOVER
☼ ❋ ↔ 5–10 ft (1.5–3 m) ↑ 3–8 ft (0.9–2.4 m)
From Japan and China. An erect semi-evergreen or deciduous
shrubby perennial. Long, wiry, widely spreading, interlacing
branches; arching fountain-like habit. Bluish
green compound leaves with 3 sharp-tipped
leaflets, smooth above, finely hairy beneath.
Dense drooping racemes of numerous pea-
flowers with rose-purple corollas in late
summer–autumn. '**Alba**', white flowers;
'**Albiflora**', smaller leaflets, small white flowers
with violet markings; '**Edo Shindori**', pink
and white flowers; '**Gibraltar**', profuse lavender pink flowers. Zones 4–9.

LEUCANTHEMUM
This genus from Europe and northern Asia
contains 33 species of annual and perennial
daisies (family Asteraceae), most of which
have flowerheads with white ray florets, usually around a central
boss of golden disc florets. They form often large clumps of deep
green, usually toothed, linear to spatula-shaped leaves. The flowers
appear from spring to autumn, depending on the species. Garden
forms include pompon-centered flowers and various colors.
CULTIVATION: Grow in a sunny position in moist well-drained soil.
Feeding and watering will result in more luxuriant plants but not

Leonotis nepetifolia

necessarily more flowers. Tall types may need staking. Propagate the species from seed, cultivars and hybrids by division or from basal cuttings.

Leucanthemum × *superbum*

syns *Chrysanthemum maximum* of gardens, *C. superbum*

SHASTA DAISY

☼/◐ ❈ ↔ 40 in (100 cm) ↑ to 48 in (120 cm)

Garden hybrid. Many upright flower stems emerging from dense basal clump of dark green, toothed, spatula-shaped leaves, to 8 in (20 cm) long. Flowerheads solitary, to 4 in (10 cm) across, ray florets white, disc florets golden yellow. 'Aglaia' ★, white semi-double flowers; 'Becky', large, single, white flowers in spring–summer; 'Cobham Gold', creamy yellow double flowers; 'Esther Read', feathery semi-double flowers; 'Horace Read', feathery double flowers; 'Marconi', very large, double, white flowers; 'Silberprinzesschen', single white flowers in spring–autumn; 'Snow Lady', single white flowers in spring–autumn; 'Snowcap', large, white, single flowers; 'T. E. Killin', yellow-centered, white, semi-double flowers; 'Wirral Supreme', anemone-centered white flowers. Zones 5–10.

Leucanthemum × *superbum*

Leucanthemum vulgare

syn. *Chrysanthemum leucanthemum*

OX-EYE DAISY

☼/◐ ❈ ↔ 24 in (60 cm) ↑ 40 in (100 cm)

From Europe and northern Asia. Perennial, forming basal clump of toothed leaves, to 4 in (10 cm) long. Flower stems sometimes branched, with small leaves, flowerheads 1–3 in (2.5–8 cm) across, ray florets white, disc florets yellow, in summer. Zones 3–9.

LEWISIA

BITTER ROOT

This is a genus of 19 species of exquisite, semi-succulent, evergreen and deciduous, alpine and subalpine perennials in the purslane (Portulacaceae) family. They are found in western North America from New Mexico to southern Canada and usually form basal rosettes of fleshy, linear, lance- or spatula-shaped leaves. Their starry many-petaled flowers may be solitary or clustered and are borne in shades of yellow, apricot, and pink at the ends of short wiry stems from mid-spring through to early summer. CULTIVATION: Most have deep tap roots and prefer gritty free-draining soil; keep moist in the growing season but otherwise dry. Plant in full or half-sun and use gravel mulch around the crown to prevent rotting. Deciduous species generally only reproduce from seed, but evergreens can also be propagated from offsets.

Lewisia columbiana

☼/◐ ❈ ↔ 8 in (20 cm) ↑ 12 in (30 cm)

Found over much of North America west of the Rockies. Evergreen. Crowded, fleshy, narrow, basal leaves, 1–4 in (2.5–10 cm)

long. Many-flowered heads of pink-veined white to magenta flowers, to 1 in (25 mm) across, with up to 11 petals, in spring–summer. Zones 5–9.

Lewisia cotyledon

☼/◐ ❈ ↔ 8 in (20 cm) ↑ 6–12 in (15–30 cm)

From California and Oregon, USA. Evergreen. Loose rosette of spatula-shaped leaves, to over 4 in (10 cm) long, often blue-green and/or pink-tinted, edges often wavy, rarely toothed. Panicles of 7- to 10-petaled flowers, to 1¾ in (40 mm) across, in spring–summer. Flowers usually purple-pink. *L. c.* f. *alba*, white flowers. **Sunset Group**, shades of yellow, orange, pink, and red; 'White Splendour', dark green foliage, pure white flowers. Zones 5–9.

Lewisia 'Pinkie'

☼/◐ ❈ ↔ 8 in (20 cm) ↑ 6–8 in (15–20 cm)

Evergreen hybrid. Resembles a compact *L. cotyledon* with slightly narrower leaves. Many broad-petaled apricot pink flowers with dark pink centers. Zones 5–9.

Lewisia rediviva

BITTERROOT

☼/◐ ❈ ↔ 8 in (20 cm) ↑ 4 in (10 cm)

Found over much of subalpine and alpine western North America. Deciduous. Dense basal tuft of many narrow leaves, to 2 in (5 cm) long. Flowers solitary, to over 2 in (5 cm) across, with up to 6 petals in pink to purple shades or white. Zones 4–9.

Lewisia tweedyi

☼/◐ ❈ ↔ 8 in (20 cm) ↑ 8 in (20 cm)

From Washington State, USA, and British Columbia, Canada. Evergreen. Small clump of often purple-tinted, broad, lance-shaped leaves, to 3 in (8 cm) long. Up to 8 soft pink or yellow, 7- to 12-petaled flowers, to over 2 in (5 cm) across, in spring–summer. Zones 5–9.

LIATRIS

BLAZING STAR, GAYFEATHER, SNAKE ROOT

Native to eastern North America and growing from corms or modified flattened roots, the 35 species of perennials in this genus of the daisy (Asteraceae) family make a bold splash of color in summer; very easy to grow. They form clumps of simple linear to lance-shaped leaves, sometimes finely hairy, bearing 24–60 in (60–150 cm) tall stems, topped with long, quite un-daisy-like, bottlebrush spikes of filamentous purple-pink flowers.
CULTIVATION: While hardiness varies, most species are frost resistant. They can be grown in any sunny position in moist, humus-rich, well-drained soil. Place at back of borders to disguise the foliage clump and make use of flower stem's height. Propagate by division or from seed.

Liatris aspera

ROUGH BLAZING STAR

☼/◑ ❄ ↔ 12–20 in (30–50 cm) ↕ 40 in (100 cm)

Found across most of eastern North America. Leaves narrow, to 6 in (15 cm) long. Spikes of up to 20 purple flowerheads in mid-summer to autumn. Zones 5–10.

Liatris pycnostachya

BUTTON SNAKE ROOT

☼/◑ ❄ ↔ 10–18 in (25–45 cm) ↕ 60 in (150 cm)

Native to southeastern USA. Strongly upright habit. Leaves narrow, sometimes downy, to 4 in (10 cm) long. Densely crowded purple-red flowerheads, in spikes to 12 in (30 cm) long, in mid-summer–autumn. 'Alexander', dark green foliage, purple flowerheads. Zones 3–10.

Liatris spicata ★

BLAZING STAR, BUTTON SNAKE ROOT, GAYFEATHER

☼/◑ ❄ ↔ 10–18 in (25–45 cm) ↕ 60 in (150 cm)

Found across most of eastern USA. Upright habit. Leaves narrow, sometimes linear, to 8 in (20 cm) long. Dense spikes, to 24 in (60 cm) long, with purple-red flowerheads in mid-summer to autumn. 'Callilepsis Purple', 24 in (60 cm) high, dark purple flowerheads; 'Floristan', 32 in (80 cm) high, deep violet flowerheads; 'Floristan White', 32 in (80 cm) high, white flowerheads; 'Kobold' (syn. 'Goblin'), 20 in (50 cm) high, dense heads of purple-pink flowers. Zones 3–10.

LIBERTIA

The 9 species of perennial rhizomatous plants in this genus, a Southern Hemisphere member of the iris (Iridaceae) family, have a creeping or tufted growth habit and a prolonged flowering season. They occur in eastern Australia, New Zealand, New Guinea, and the Andes of South America. The strap-like leaves are produced in sparse to dense tufts. The flowers, usually white and recognizably iris-like in form, are borne in clusters at the top of straight stems. Often the leaves partially obscure the flowers.
CULTIVATION: Most species are quite tolerant of both drought and poor soils; however, they will respond visibly to softer conditions and light feeding. Some species may be used for roadside plantings. Propagate in spring by division or from seed.

Liatris pycnostachya

Ligularia przewalskii

Libertia formosa

SHOWY LIBERTIA, SNOWY MERMAID

☼ ◈ ↔ 24 in (60 cm) ↕ 18–36 in (45–90 cm)

Chilean species. Clumping perennial. Dark green leaves, narrow, strap-shaped, and leathery. Tall spikes of white or pale yellow flowers in late spring. Zones 9–10.

Libertia grandiflora

MIKOIKOI, NEW ZEALAND IRIS, TUKAUKI

☼ ❄ ↔ 24 in (60 cm) ↕ 30 in (75 cm)

From New Zealand. Clumping perennial. Leaves green to yellowy green, narrow, leathery. Tall spike of white flowers, in dense clusters, in spring, followed by attractive, yellow, pear-shaped seed capsules. Zones 8–11.

Libertia ixioides

MIKOIKOI, NEW ZEALAND IRIS, TUKAUKI

☼ ❄ ↔ 24 in (60 cm) ↕ 8–12 in (20–30 cm)

From New Zealand. Clumping perennial. Leaves green to orange-brown, narrow, leathery. Spike of white flowers in late spring. Zones 8–11.

Libertia peregrinans

☼/◑ ❄ ↔ 20 in (50 cm) ↕ 15–27 in (38–70 cm)

From New Zealand. Long-running rhizomes. Leaves obviously veined, turning orange-brown in cold weather. White flowers with yellow anthers in spring. Needs well-drained soil. Zones 8–10.

LIGULARIA

This temperate Eurasian genus of the daisy (Asteraceae) family has some 125 species of perennials. In spring these vigorous

plants soon develop into clumps of long-stalked, broad, basal leaves, usually kidney- to heart-shaped, with toothed edges. In summer and autumn flowering stems develop, ranging from broadly forking panicles of large yellow to orange daisies to tall spike-like racemes of numerous smaller heads.
CULTIVATION: Most species are very hardy. Grow in full to half-sun, in deep, fertile, humus-rich soil kept moist through the year. Cut back when flowers and foliage fade. Propagate by division when dormant or from seed.

Ligularia dentata
☼/◐ ❄ ↔ 40–60 in (100–150 cm) ↕ 30–60 in (75–150 cm)
From China and Japan. Vigorous clump-forming perennial. Impressive foliage. Leaves rounded to kidney-shaped, deeply toothed, with downy undersides, often red-tinted, to 16 in (40 cm) wide. Strong upright flower stems branching broadly with many gold to orange flowerheads to 4 in (10 cm) across. 'Desdemona', purple-red leaves, orange flowers on stems to 48 in (120 cm). Zones 4–10.

Ligularia przewalskii
SHAVALSKI'S LIGULARIA
☼/◐ ❄ ↔ 40–48 in (100–120 cm) ↕ 7 ft (2 m)
Northern Chinese vigorous perennial. Leaves deeply palmately lobed and toothed, basal leaves to 12 in (30 cm) long and wide. Stems dark purple-red. Narrow spikes of many spidery golden yellow flowerheads. Zones 4–9.

Ligularia stenocephala
☼/◐ ❄ ↔ 32–40 in (80–100 cm) ↕ 60 in (150 cm)
Native to Japan, China, and Taiwan. Leaves heart-shaped to tri-angular, toothed, basal leaves to 12 in (30 cm) long and wide. Stems deep purple-red. Deep yellow flowerheads, to over 2 in (5 cm) across. Zones 5–10.

Ligularia Hybrid Cultivars
☼/◐ ❄ ↔ 32–60 in (80–150 cm)
↕ 3–7 ft (0.9–2 m)
Bred with both foliage and flowers in mind, hy-brid ligularias are bold architectural plants ideally suited to moist partly shaded corners, especially near ponds and streams. 'Gregynog Gold', coarsely toothed green leaves, and pyramidal spikes of orange flowers; 'The Rocket', dark black-green stems contrasting with numerous bright yellow flowerheads; 'Weihenstephan', large deep golden yellow flowerheads; 'Zepter', slightly shorter than the species but with more densely crowded golden yellow flowerheads. Zones 5–9.

LIMONIUM
SEA LAVENDER, STATICE
Genus of about 150 species of mainly summer-flowering annuals, perennials, and small shrubs in the leadwort (Plumbaginaceae) family, widely distributed around the world, but with the main

concentration in southern Europe and North Africa. Most are low-growing, forming mounds of basal leaf rosettes. The leaves vary in size and tend to be lance- or spatula-shaped. Flowers are minute but showy, borne in billowing sprays held well clear of the foliage on branching wiry stems, in white, cream, and mauve to purple shades. The flowers are still widely sold as "statice."
CULTIVATION: Many species are somewhat frost tender, thriving in coastal conditions, with a preference for sheltered sunny locations and light, well-drained, yet moist soil. If the flowers are not cut for indoor use, they should be removed, as allowing the plants to set seed can shorten their life. Propagate from seed or root cuttings, or by division, depending on the plant type.

Limonium brassicifolium
☼/◐ ✤ ↔ 12 in (30 cm) ↕ 16 in (40 cm)
From Canary Islands. Perennial with a woody rhizome producing winged stems and 4–12 in (10–30 cm) long, broad, pointed oval leaves. Panicles of many single-flowered spikes with purple calyces and a white corolla. Zones 9–11.

Limonium perezii
☼/◐ ✤ ↔ 20 in (50 cm) ↕ 27 in (70 cm)
From Canary Islands. Broad oval leaves, to 6 in (15 cm) long. Flower stems downy. Large heads of flowers with deep purple calyces and creamy yellow to white corolla. Zones 9–11.

Limonium sinuatum
syn. *Statice sinuata*
☼/◐ ✤ ↔ 16 in (40 cm) ↕ 16 in (40 cm)
Native to Mediterranean region. Perennial, often short-lived and treated as annual. All parts downy. Leaves lance-shaped, 1–4 in (2.5–10 cm) long. Flower stems winged, with many short compact spikes of papery flowers in summer. White, lavender, or pink flowers; cultivars in many colors. Can be invasive. 'Art Shades', pastel tones, most colors; **California Series**, bright tones, most colors; 'Forever Gold', deep golden yellow flowers. Zones 9–11.

Limonium brassicifolium

Linum grandiflorum 'Rubrum'

LINARIA

SPURRED SNAPDRAGON, TOADFLAX

From the foxglove (Scrophulariaceae) family, this genus encompasses about 150 species of annuals and perennials found in Europe (mainly around the Mediterranean) and temperate Asia. Toadflaxes are closely related to snapdragons, with similar but smaller flowers. They are easy to cultivate but stop flowering in hot weather. For best effect, plant in masses, as the individual plants are wispy.
CULTIVATION: Grow in full or half-sun in well-drained soil. Cut perennials down to ground level in autumn. Propagate annuals and perennials from seed; perennials also by division and from cuttings. Sow seed outdoors in late autumn or early spring (even when snow is still on ground) or indoors. Annuals also self-seed.

Linaria maroccana

ANNUAL TOADFLAX, BUNNY RABBITS, MOROCCO TOADFLAX

☼ ⚘ ↔ 6–12 in (15–30 cm) ↕ 8–10 in (20–25 cm)
From Morocco; naturalized in northeastern USA. Annual. Leaves narrow, grass-like, alternate. Profuse tiny snapdragon-like flowers in white, yellow, pink, red, and dark blue to purple shades in early summer. 'Fairy Bouquet', flowers ranging from lavender, purple, and pink to crimson; 'Fantasy Blue', dwarf form, compact habit, will grow year-round in mild climates; 'Northern Lights', faintly violet-scented, jewel-like, bicolored flowers in pink, red, yellow, and purple; Soda Pop Series, magenta-rose, blue, or pink flowers. Zones 9–11.

Linaria purpurea

PURPLE TOADFLAX

☼ ❀ ↔ 6–12 in (15–30 cm) ↕ 20–36 in (50–90 cm)
From southern Europe. Narrow bushy perennial. Slender gray-green leaves. Bright blue-purple flowers with white stripes in mid-summer–early autumn. 'Canon Went', tall, with grayish foliage and soft pink flowers. Zones 5–10.

LINUM

FLAX

This genus, which gives its name to the family Linaceae, comprises about 180 species of tender and hardy annuals, biennials, perennials, and subshrubs, with flax, *L. usitatissimum*, the important fiber and oilseed plant included among them. Native to temperate or subtropical regions of the world though mainly from the Northern Hemisphere. They are delicate but easy-to-grow plants. The stems are erect and branching, and the gray-green leaves are simple and narrow. The cup- to funnel-shaped 5-petalled flowers are carried in branched clusters at the stem tips, lasting only one day. Colors vary with the variety but are mostly shades of blue or yellow, less commonly red, pink, or white. However, they are produced in great numbers throughout summer.
CULTIVATION: For the best flowering effect, grow in well-drained humus-rich soil in full sun. Provide shelter in cool climates. Annuals and perennials are easily raised from seed or from cuttings of named varieties. Plant out perennials in autumn or early spring; sow annual species in early autumn or spring. Thin seedlings as needed.

Linum 'Gemmell's Hybrid'

☼ ❀ ↔ 8 in (20 cm) ↕ 6 in (15 cm)
Short golden yellow form best grown at the front of a border or in the rock garden. Zones 6–9.

Linum grandiflorum

FLOWERING FLAX

☼ ❀ ↔ 12 in (30 cm) ↕ 15–18 in (38–45 cm)
From Algeria. Annual. Slender stems; narrow, pointed, pale green leaves. Single, clear rose to purple, saucer-shaped flowers, 1½ in (35 mm) across, in early–late summer. 'Bright Eyes', to 15 in (38 cm) tall, white flowers, 2 in (5 cm) across, with carmine eye; 'Rubrum' (scarlet flax), to 12 in (30 cm) tall, brilliant crimson flowers. Zones 7–10.

Linum narbonense

☼ ❀ ↔ 12–18 in (30–45 cm) ↕ 12–24 in (30–60 cm)
From southern Europe. Perennial. Leaves gray-green, narrow. Rich blue cup-shaped flowers, 1–1¼ in (25–30 mm) across, with white eye, in late spring–autumn. Usually dies back in winter but may be evergreen in mild climates. 'Heavenly Blue', more compact, with ultramarine flowers. Zones 5–9.

Linum perenne

PERENNIAL BLUE FLAX

☼ ❀ ↔ 12 in (30 cm) ↕ 12–18 in (30–45 cm)
From Europe. Vigorous but short-lived perennial. Many sky blue flowers, 1 in (25 mm) across, in early–late summer. Easy to raise from seed; self-seeds freely. Zones 4–9.

LIRIOPE

LILY TURF

This small genus in the family Ruscaceae has 5 or 6 species of evergreen or semi-evergreen frost-hardy perennials. From acid-soil woodland habitats in East Asia. Tough, mat-forming, trouble-free plants, which soon establish a dense fibrous root system and in some species develop nutrient-storing fleshy tubers. The grass-like leaves are arching, linear, and dense. Flowers are clustered and grape-like on blunt stems, usually showy for extended late summer period, followed by black, berry-like seeds. CULTIVATION: Grow in shade in mild climates; allow more sun in cold climates. Propagate by division or by fresh ripe seed sown in a sandy medium.

Liriope muscari 'Monroe White'

Liriope muscari

☼/☀ ❋ ↔ 18 in (45 cm) ↕ 12 in (30 cm)

Native to China, Taiwan, and Japan. Woodland plant; drought-tolerant, tough, sturdy, evergreen, spreading ground cover. Leaves narrow, glossy deep green. Dense, bead-like, steely deep lavender flowers, held on blunt spikes, in late autumn. 'Christmas Tree', large form, resplendent flowers; 'John Burch', large flowers on tall spikes, wide leaves with yellow-green central stripe; 'Majestic', violet flowers; 'Monroe White', numerous white flowers, requires full shade; 'Variegata', leaves boldly edged in yellow. Zones 4–10.

Liriope spicata

☼/☀ ❋ ↔ 18 in (45 cm) ↕ 10 in (25 cm)

From China and Vietnam. Drought-tolerant evergreen ground cover. Leaves glossy, dark, dense. Pale lavender flowers in late summer. 'Silver Dragon', compact, to about 8 in (20 cm) tall, narrow dark leaves silver striped, pale purple flowers. Zones 5–10.

LOBELIA

Lobelia is a large, enormously variable, and widespread genus of the bellflower (Campanulaceae) family, including over 350 species of annuals, perennials, and shrubs. Other than the annuals, with their massed summer display of blue, white, or pink flowers, cultivated lobelias are mainly perennials from the Americas, most of which form a basal clump of simple leaves, from which emerge upright flower stems bearing spikes of tubular 5-lobed flowers, the lower 3 lobes enlarged. CULTIVATION: Requirements vary but most *Lobelia* species prefer a sunny position with moist well-drained soil. Tall types may need staking. Propagate the annuals from seed sown in spring and the perennials by division or from basal cuttings.

Lobelia cardinalis

CARDINAL FLOWER

☼/☀ ❋ ↔ 12–16 in (30–40 cm) ↕ 36 in (90 cm)

North American short-lived perennial forming clump of upright stems with often red-tinted, narrow, pointed oval to lance-shaped leaves, to 4 in (10 cm) long. Long spikes of bright red flowers, to over 1 in (25 mm) wide, from summer to autumn. Zones 6–9.

Lobelia erinus

BEDDING LOBELIA, EDGING LOBELIA

☼/☀ ❋ ↔ 12–16 in (30–40 cm) ↕ 8 in (20 cm)

South African, small, long-flowering perennial usually treated as an annual. Dense mounding habit; fine stems; small, often purple-tinted, deep green leaves, roughly oval, toothed. Masses of small pale-centered flowers, blue, mauve, purple. Seedling strains differ mainly in size and growth habit. **Cascade Series**, for hanging baskets; 'Kathleen Mallard', mounding, with deep blue double flowers; '**Mrs. Clibran**', mounding, with dark blue flowers; **Palace Series**, dwarf and heavy flowering, for borders and pots; '**Periwinkle Blue**', trailer, bright blue flowers; **Regatta Series**, trailer, mixed colors; **Royal Jewels** seed mix, flowers in blue, mauve, and purple-red shades. Zones 8–11.

Lobelia × gerardii

☼/☀ ❋ ↔ 20–24 in (50–60 cm) ↕ 60 in (150 cm)

Garden hybrid. Vigorous perennial forming a clump of upright stems with pointed oval to elliptical leaves, to 6 in (15 cm) long, mainly crowded at base. Large heads of white-marked pink or violet to purple flowers. 'Bee's Flame', bronze foliage, red flowers; 'Cherry Ripe', dark green leaves, red flowers; **Compliment Series**, seedling strain, blue or red flowers; 'Fan Scarlet', green foliage, purple-red flowers; 'Queen Victoria' ★, deep red foliage and stems, bright red flowers; 'Russian Princess', green foliage, green flowers. 'Tania', red-tinted foliage, deep magenta flowers; 'Vedrariensis', red-tinted foliage, purple flowers. Zones 7–10.

Lobelia laxiflora

TORCH LOBELIA

☼/☀ ❋ ↔ 4 ft (1.2 m) ↕ 3 ft (0.9 m)

From southern Arizona, USA, through the Mexican highlands to Colombia, occurring in oak and pine forests. Variable species with shrubby habit. Leaves pointed, lance-shaped. Long-stalked tubular flowers, scarlet with yellow tips, in summer. Zones 8–11.

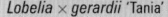
Lobelia × *gerardii* 'Tania'

Lobelia laxiflora

Lobelia tupa

Lobelia siphilitica

BLUE CARDINAL FLOWER

☼/◐ ❈ ↔ 16 in (40 cm) ↑ 24 in (60 cm)

From eastern USA. Bushy perennial with mainly basal foliage. Leaves pointed oval to lance-shaped, toothed, to 4 in (10 cm) long. Flower stems upright, with long spikes of deep blue flowers, to 1 in (25 mm) across, in summer–autumn. Zones 5–9.

Lobelia tupa

☼ ❈ ↔ 3 ft (0.9 m) ↑ 6 ft (1.8 m)

From Chile, growing in sandy hills near the sea. Attractive leaves lightly felted, grayish green. Terminal spikes of scarlet or brick-red flowers in summer–autumn. Zones 8–10.

LOBULARIA

ALYSSUM, BEDDING ALYSSUM

This genus of 5 species of annuals and perennials belongs to the cabbage (Brassicaceae) family and is from the northern temperate zones. They are small mounding plants with simple linear to lance-shaped leaves, sometimes with fine silvery hairs. Tiny, often sweet-scented flowers appear in the warmer months, in rounded heads. Garden forms are available in white and shades of primrose, apricot, mauve, and purple.

CULTIVATION: These plants are hardy, and easily grown in sun in light free-draining soil. Water to encourage flowering, but plants often remain more compact if kept dry. Propagate from seed, or the seed may be broadcast; often self-sows.

Lobularia maritima

BEDDING ALYSSUM

☼ ❈ ↔ 8–16 in (20–40 cm) ↑ 10 in (25 cm)

Widespread in northern temperate zones. Annual or short-lived perennial. Narrow dull green leaves, about 1 in (25 mm) long. Tiny flowers in massed rounded heads. Usually white to cream

flowers. Cultivars vary in size and color. **'Carpet of Snow'**, to 4 in (10 cm) tall, pure white flowers; **Easter Bonnet Series**, to 6 in (15 cm) tall, flowers white and pink to purple; **'Snow Crystals'**, to 8–10 in (20–25 cm) tall, large white flowers. Zones 7–10.

LOTUS

This genus in the pea-flower subfamily of the legume (Fabaceae) family has around 150 species of annuals, perennials, and deciduous and evergreen subshrubs. They are found almost worldwide in open grasslands and rocky places. The leaves are small and pinnate, often with only 4 or 5 leaflets and sometimes closely hairy, giving them a silvery appearance. The pea-flowers are white to yellow, pink, or red, and are borne singly or in clusters in the leaf axils. The most colorful are species from the Canary Islands and Madeira, with yellow or red flowers. The trailing types are suited to hanging baskets or pots.

CULTIVATION: Most prefer well-drained soil in full sun. Propagate from seed in spring or autumn, from cuttings in early summer.

Lotus berthelotii

CORAL GEM, PARROT'S BEAK, PELICAN'S BEAK

☼ ⚘ ↔ 3–6 ft (0.9–1.8 m) ↑ 8 in (20 cm)

From the Canary Islands. Popular, trailing, evergreen plant. Leaves silvery gray, with needle-like leaflets. Yellow-orange to red flowers, 1½ in (35 mm) long, in spring–summer. Zones 10–11.

Lotus maculatus

syn. *Heinekenia maculata*

FIRE VINE

☼ ⚘ ↔ 3–6 ft (0.9–1.8 m) ↑ 8 in (20 cm)

From the Canary Islands. Trailing perennial well suited to hanging baskets and pots. Mid-green needle-like leaflets.

Lotus maculatus 'Gold Flash'

Yellow-tipped red-orange flowers in spring–summer. 'Amazon Sunset', long-flowering, with silvery leaves and deep red flowers; 'Gold Flash', red-orange flowers; 'New Gold Flash', improved form of 'Gold Flash', abundant red-orange flowers. Zones 10–11.

LUDWIGIA
syn. *Jussiaea*

This genus of about 75 herbaceous or woody, aquatic or marginal perennials belongs to the evening-primrose (Onagraceae) family and is widely distributed in bogs and marshes in warmer climates in both the Northern and Southern Hemispheres. The leaves are simple. The inconspicuous flowers may be solitary, arising from the leaf axils, or in clusters at the branch tips. They may be white or yellow, and have a long calyx tube with 4 or 5 sepals and 4 spreading petals (or sometimes no petals).
CULTIVATION: Grow near to, or in, shallow water in acid soil in a protected sunny position. Propagate from cuttings or by division.

Ludwigia peruviana
COMMON PRIMROSE WILLOW, EVENING PRIMROSE, PERUVIAN PRIMROSE WILLOW
☼ ❈ ↔ 20 in–8 ft (50 cm–2.4 m) ↕ 20 in–8 ft (50 cm–2.4 m)
Occurring from southeastern USA to South America. Woody shrubby perennial growing out from air-filled roots at water's edge to form floating mat, sometimes free-floating. Leaves finely hairy, oval, with impressed veins, deciduous in cooler climates. Solitary bright yellow flowers, clawed, with rounded petals, in late spring–autumn. Rusty red sepals remaining attached to brown seed capsule in star shape. Zones 7–10.

LUNARIA
This genus of 3 species of biennials and herbaceous perennials belongs to the cabbage (Brassicaceae) family. They are best raised in containers, as they can be somewhat weedy and invasive. They are primarily grown for their silvery flat seed pods, which are used in dried flower arrangements.
CULTIVATION: Grow these species in full sun or partial shade in light, fertile, moist, well-drained soil. Propagate the perennials from seed or by division in autumn or spring. Propagate biennials and annuals from seed in spring. These plants will readily self-seed.

Lunaria annua
HONESTY, MONEY PLANT, MONEYWORT, SILVER DOLLAR
☼/❂ ❈ ↔ 12 in (30 cm) ↕ 30 in (75 cm)
Fast-growing biennial from southern Europe. Has naturalized in parts of Europe and North America. Leaves bright green, alternate, heart-shaped, coarsely serrated. Rosy magenta, white, or violet-purple flowers, with 4 petals, in spring or early summer,

followed by circular seed pods covered with silvery translucent membrane. *L. a.* var. *albiflora*, white flowers. *L. a.* 'Variegata', variegated crimson flowers. Zones 8–10.

Lunaria rediviva
☼/❂ ❈ ↔ 24 in (60 cm)
↕ 36–42 in (90–105 cm)
Native to Europe. Hairy-stemmed perennial with somewhat smaller flowers and seed pods than the annual species. Pale mauve flowers, sweetly scented. Spring- to summer-flowering. Zones 8–10.

Lunaria rediviva

LUPINUS
LUPIN, LUPINE

There are about 200 species of annuals, perennials, and evergreen shrubs in this genus in the pea-flower subfamily of the legume (Fabaceae) family. They are native to North and South America, southern Europe, and northern Africa, usually found in dry habitats. Many have ornamental flowers, borne in showy terminal panicles or racemes. The leaves are palmate, with 5 to 15 leaflets, and the stems are often covered in fine soft down.
CULTIVATION: Although these generally tolerate poor dry conditions, they are best grown in full sun in moderately fertile well-drained soil. Propagate from seed or cuttings. The seedlings should be planted out when small, as these plants dislike root disturbance.

Lupinus chamissonis
☼ ❂ ↔ 4–10 ft (1.2–3 m) ↕ 2–7 ft (0.6–2 m)
From seashores of California, USA. Often mound-forming shrub. Leaves gray to blue-green from dense hairs. Blue flowers, on 4 in (10 cm) long spikes, from mid-spring to mid-summer. Tolerates drought and salt spray. Zones 9–10.

Lupinus polyphyllus
BLUE-POD LUPINE
❂ ❈ ↔ 20–40 in (50–100 cm)
↕ 24–60 in (60–150 cm)
From mountains of western North America, from British Columbia to California, growing in moist ground. Perennial with thick rootstock, chief ancestor of Russell lupins. Leaves large, basal, long-stalked, up to 17 leaflets, to 6 in (15 cm) long. Dense tapering spikes of very showy flowers, usually blue, often in shades of red, purple, or pink, in early–mid-summer. Zones 5–9.

Lupinus texensis
TEXAS BLUEBONNET
☼ ❈ ↔ 12 in (30 cm) ↕ 12–24 in (30–60 cm)
From Texas, USA. Drought-tolerant annual blooming in early–late spring with dark blue and white flowers. Must be planted in well-drained soil. Zones 7–10.

Ludwigia peruviana

Lupinus, Hybrid Cultivar, 'Candy Floss'

Lupinus Hybrid Cultivars

☀ ❁ ↔ 2–5 ft (0.6–1.5 m) ↑ 2–4 ft (0.6–1.2 m)
Many of the later perennial hybrids are infor-
mally referred to as Russell lupins, and can be
invasive. **Band of Nobles Series**: rich colors of
blue, purple, intense reds ('The Page'); deep
pinks, creamy whites ('Noble Maiden'); and
many bicolors ('The Governor', blue and
white, 'The Chatelaine', soft pink and white).
'**Bishop's Tipple**', to 48 in (120 cm) tall,
mauve and lilac flowers with ivory flecks;
'**Blue Moon**', to 18 in (45 cm) tall, late-
blooming, tall narrow spikes of mauve-blue and white flowers;
'**Candy Floss**', to 24 in (60 cm) tall, delicate blush pink and
white flowers, becoming deep pink with age; '**Chandelier**',
36–40 in (90–100 cm) tall, yellow flowers in early summer;
Gallery Series, compact plants, to 20 in (50 cm) tall, 10 to
12 spikes of red, blue, or pink sweet-pea-like flowers in late
spring or early summer; '**My Castle**', 30–36 in (75–90 cm) tall,
bright brick-red blooms; '**Pagoda Prince**', 36–48 in (90–120 cm)
tall, early-blooming, soft lilac to purple and white bicolor flowers;
'**Red Arrow**', to 36 in (90 cm) tall, pure red flowers flecked with
yellow, ageing to mulberry; '**Terracotta**', 36–48 in (90–120 cm)
tall, early-blooming, large rusty-colored bells. Zones 3–9.

LYCHNIS

CAMPION, CATCHFLY

This genus of 20 species of biennials and perennials in the pink
(Caryophyllaceae) family is found in the northern temperate
zone. *Lychnis* species are quite variable, often forming large
clumps of foliage, sometimes with silver-gray leaves. While their
flowers are simple 5-petalled structures, they are brightly colored
and showy, occurring in heads usually held well clear of the foliage, maximizing the summer color effect.

CULTIVATION: They are mostly very hardy and easily grown in sun
or part-shade in moist well-drained soil. The silvery *L. coronaria*
prefers fairly dry conditions, but most others can be given routine

watering. Deadhead frequently to encourage
continuous flowering. Propagate from seed or
from basal cuttings or by division, depending
on the growth form.

Lychnis × *arkwrightii*

☀/❁ ❁ ↔ 16–24 in (40–60 cm)
↑ 12–30 in (30–75 cm)
Garden hybrids. Sometimes short-lived perennials. Bristly bright to dark green foliage.
Small heads of vivid flowers, held above foliage, in summer. '**Vesuvius**', to 18 in (45 cm)
tall, dark green to purplish foliage, large,
striking, orange-red flowers. Zones 6–10.

Lychnis chalcedonica

MALTESE CROSS

☀/❁ ❁ ↔ 12–16 in (30–40 cm)
↑ 20 in (50 cm)
Upright, bristly, Eurasian perennial forming
clump of large, pointed, oval, basal leaves
with smaller leaves up the flower stems.
Heads of up to 50 small bright red flowers
in summer. Zones 4–10.

Lychnis coronaria

DUSTY MILLER, ROSE CAMPION

☀/❁ ❁ ↔ 20–40 in (50–100 cm)
↑ 16–32 in (40–80 cm)
From southeastern Europe. Spreading
mounding biennial or short-lived perennial.

Lychnis × *arkwrightii* 'Vesuvius'

Stems and foliage with dense silver-gray hairs. Leaves lance-
shaped, to about 3 in (8 cm) long, often smaller. Small heads
of flowers, usually in vivid shades of pink or purple-red. '**Alba**',
white flowers; '**Atrosanguinea**', very light foliage and deep magenta
flowers; '**Oculata**' ★, red-centered white flowers. Zones 4–10.

Lychnis flos-cuculi

RAGGED ROBIN

☀/❁ ❁ ↔ 16 in (40 cm) ↑ 30 in (75 cm)
Bristly Eurasian perennial. Basal leaves broad, lance- to spatula-
shaped; upper leaves almost linear. Open flowerheads, with few
pale purple flowers with fine petals divided in two. Zones 6–9.

Lychnis flos-jovis

☀/❁ ❁ ↔ 16 in (40 cm) ↑ 32 in (80 cm)
From Europe. Upright alpine perennial. Downy white stems and
foliage. Leaves lance- to spatula-shaped, broader at base. Small
heads of bright red flowers with petals divided in two, sometimes
almost completely, in summer. Zones 5–9.

Lychnis viscaria

GERMAN CATCHFLY, VISCARIA

☀/❁ ❁ ↔ 16 in (40 cm) ↑ 24 in (60 cm)
Found from Europe to Siberia. Upright perennial, with stems
and leaves bristly, and sticky leaf bases. The leaves are elliptical to

lance-shaped. The flower spikes are narrow, carrying small mauve to purple-red flowers, in summer. *L. v.* subsp. *atropurpurea*, deep purple flowers. *L. v.* 'Flore Pleno' (syn. 'Splendens Plena'), bright magenta double flowers; 'Splendens', pale to deep pink single flowers. Zones 4–10.

LYSICHITON

SKUNK CABBAGE

The 2 species in this genus in the arum (Araceae) family grow in bogs in northeast Asia and western North America. They are herbaceous rhizomatous perennials with large paddle-shaped leaves, preceded in spring by almost stemless arum-type flowers of yellow or white. Spikes of green-skinned fruit follow in summer. CULTIVATION: Plant in damp to wet humus-rich mud in sun or semi-shade in cool climates. They usually take several years to settle down and flower. Propagate from seed sown as soon as it is ripe. Division is possible, but given the habitat and the deeply buried rhizomes, this would be a very messy and difficult job.

Lysichiton americanus

YELLOW SKUNK CABBAGE

↔ 4–5 ft (1.2–1.5 m)

↑ 3–4 ft (0.9–1.2 m)

From western North America. Flowers with bright yellow spathe, rising to 16 in (40 cm), in early spring, followed by tall, bright green, paddle-shaped leaves. Zones 6–10.

LYSIMACHIA

LOOSESTRIFE

This genus of about 150 species of perennials and subshrubs belonging to the primrose (Primulaceae) family is found over much of Europe and Asia, as well as in North America and South Africa. A few species are low-spreading plants, but most are clump-forming perennials with narrow lance-shaped leaves and upright spikes of small 5-petalled flowers, often in shades of yellow, rarely white or purple-pink. The flowers appear from early summer to autumn. CULTIVATION: Some species prefer the damp soil of pond edges or stream banks, others thrive in rockeries, but most are perfectly happy in full sun or half-sun in moist well-drained garden soil. Propagate by division or from basal cuttings or layers, depending on the growth type.

Lysimachia ciliata

↔ 20 in (50 cm) ↑ 40 in (100 cm)

From North America. Perennial with upright stems and whorls of lance-shaped leaves, to nearly 6 in (15 cm) long. The yellow flowers, solitary or paired, appear in the upper leaf axils, in summer. 'Purpurea', deep purple-red foliage. Zones 4–10.

Lysimachia clethroides

GOOSENECK LOOSESTRIFE

↔ 24 in (60 cm) ↑ 40 in (100 cm)

Native to China and Japan. Upright perennial with narrow, finely downy, lance-shaped leaves, to 5 in (12 cm) long. Produces densely packed spikes of small white flowers, at the stem tips, during summer. The initially nodding flower spikes later become erect. Can become invasive. Zones 4–9.

Lysimachia congestiflora

↔ 8–16 in (20–40 cm) ↑ 6 in (15 cm)

From temperate East Asia. Perennial, forming densely foliaged mound of dark green, often red-tinted, pointed oval leaves, topped with clusters of golden yellow flowers in late spring. Prefers damp soil. 'Outback Sunset', yellow-green leaves with darker central zone. Zones 7–10.

Lysimachia ephemerum

↔ 16–24 in (40–60 cm) ↑ 40 in (100 cm)

From southwestern Europe. Upright perennial. Opposite pairs of narrow, lance-shaped, gray-green to blue-green leaves, to 6 in (15 cm) long. Terminal spikes of small white flowers, initially curved, later becoming erect. Summer-flowering. Zones 7–10.

Lysimachia congestiflora 'Outback Sunset'

Lysimachia nummularia

CREEPING JENNY, MONEYWORT

↔ 24–40 in (60–100 cm)

↑ 2–4 in (5–10 cm)

Found in Europe, Turkey, and the Caucasus region. Low-spreading, sometimes mounding perennial. Leaves light-textured, wavy-edged, rounded, to 1 in (25 mm) wide. Bright yellow flowers, usually solitary, sometimes paired, in leaf axils, in summer. Can become invasive. 'Aurea', bright yellow-green to golden foliage. Zones 4–10.

Lysimachia punctata

↔ 16–24 in (40–60 cm) ↑ 40 in (100 cm)

Upright Eurasian perennial. Opposite pairs and/or whorls of downy, finely pointed, lance-shaped leaves, to 3 in (8 cm) long. Terminal heads or spikes of bright yellow flowers, to over ½ in (12 mm) across, in summer. 'Alexander', striking cream-edged foliage. Zones 5–10.

Lysichiton americanus

LYTHRUM

This genus of about 35 species is a member of the loosestrife (Lythraceae) family. It comprises mainly herbaceous perennials but includes some annuals and small herbs. Two of the hardy herbaceous perennials have been used to produce very adaptable varieties that grow in a wide range of conditions, thriving just about anywhere except in full shade. *(See note of caution for L. salicaria.)* The flowers are small, rather star-shaped, and carried in racemes. They are attractive cut and in borders.
CULTIVATION: Grow in ordinary garden soil in full or half-sun. Ideal conditions would be a damp or wet spot in part-shade, where some species can become invasive. Cut back in autumn. Propagate by dividing the roots in autumn or spring. Named varieties will not come true from seed.

Lythrum salicaria
PURPLE LOOSESTRIFE, STRIPED LOOSESTRIFE
☼/◐ ❋ ↔ 24 in (60 cm) ↑ 24–60 in (60–150 cm)
From temperate Eurasia, Africa, and Australia, but widely naturalized in North America. Invasive, declared illegal in some areas; both it and *L. virgatum* should be used with caution. Mid-green leaves. Spikes, 9–12 in (22–30 cm) long, of small red-purple flowers in early summer–early autumn. '**Blush**', large-petalled blushed pale pink flowers; '**Feuerkerze**' (syn. 'Firecandle'), tall plant for back of border, intensely rosy red flowers; '**Robert**', bright cerise pink flowers. Zones 3–10.

MACLEAYA
PLUME POPPY
This genus is a member of the poppy (Papaveraceae) family and includes 2 species of hardy herbaceous perennials, sometimes sold under the name *Bocconia*. These bold attractive plants can be invasive, forming dense thickets, and spread by means of underground suckers. They have scalloped, deeply lobed, heart-shaped, gray to olive green leaves, 6–8 in (15–20 cm) long. Tiny flowers are borne in large plume-like panicles, 12 in (30 cm) long.

Lythrum salicaria

CULTIVATION: Plant in autumn or early spring in a sheltered sunny position in deep loamy soil. Remove spent flowerheads and cut down stems in autumn. Soils with high fertility will encourage their invasive nature. Propagate from seed or by division of roots in autumn or early spring. Plants will self-seed.

Macleaya cordata
syn. *Bocconia cordata*
PLUME POPPY, TREE CELANDINE
☼ ❋ ↔ 3 ft (0.9 m) ↑ 8 ft (2.4 m)
Plume poppy from China and Japan. Lower stem has large deeply lobed leaves, gray-green above, gray-white beneath. Feathery plumes, to 36 in (90 cm) tall, of small, pearly white or pink flowers in summer. Zones 3–10.

Macleaya microcarpa
syn. *Bocconia microcarpa*
☼ ❋ ↔ 3 ft (0.9 m) ↑ 8 ft (2.4 m)
Plume poppy from central China. Leaves grayish green to olive with white undersides, downy. Flowers pink outside, bronze inside. Autumn-flowering. Can be very invasive. '**Coral Plume**', pinker flowers; '**Kelway's Coral Plume**', showy deep buff to coral flowers. Zones 3–10.

MAIANTHEMUM
syn. *Smilacina*
FALSE SOLOMON'S SEAL
This genus consists of about 35 species of herbaceous perennials in the family Ruscaceae, most from eastern Asia and North America but with a few in the highlands of Central America and one extending across northern Asia and into Europe. They have creeping underground rhizomes and erect or arching, unbranched stems, each bearing 2 to 15 ovate leaves, usually in 2 rows. Plants will grow into clumps or, in some species, into substantial colonies. Small white flowers are borne in spring and summer in terminal panicles or spikes, followed by small red berries.
CULTIVATION: All species grow best in moist humus-rich soils in full sun or partial shade under deciduous shrubs and trees. Plants should not be allowed to dry out when in leaf. Propagate by division while dormant, or by sowing seed as soon as it is ripe.

Maianthemum bifolium
FALSE LILY-OF-THE-VALLEY, MAY LILY
◐ ❋ ↔ 40–48 in (100–120 cm) ↑ 5–6 in (12–15 cm)
Spreading perennial found from western Europe to Japan. Upright unbranched stems bearing 2 heart-shaped leaves to 3 in (8 cm) long. Narrow spike of tiny flowers in spring. *M. b.* subsp. *kamtschaticum* (syn. *M. dilatatum*), stems to 14 in (35 cm) high, leaves to 8 in (20 cm) long. Zones 3–10.

Maianthemum canadense
syn. *Unifolium canadense*
TWO-LEAFED SOLOMON'S SEAL
◐ ❋ ↔ 36–40 in (90–100 cm) ↑ 7–8 in (18–20 cm)
Woodland plant, native to Canada and northern parts of USA. Good ground cover. Leaves oval, 1 to 3 per stem, to 4 in (10 cm)

long. Tiny, fragrant, white flowers, on spikes
2 in (5 cm) long, in spring. Zones 1–7.

Maianthemum racemosum
syn. *Smilacina racemosa*
FALSE SOLOMON'S SEAL, FALSE SPIKENARD
☀/◐ ❄ ↔ 2–4 ft (0.6–1.2 m)
↑ 2–3 ft (0.6–0.9 m)
Occurs right across USA and in parts of
northern Mexico. Arching cane-like stems,
each with up to 12 pointed oval leaves to 6 in
(15 cm) long. Panicles to 6 in (15 cm) long of
tiny creamy white flowers in summer. Red-
tinted green berries. Zones 4–10.

MALCOLMIA
MAHON STOCK, MALCOLM STOCK, VIRGINIA STOCK
This genus of the cabbage (Brassicaceae) fam-
ily includes some 35 species of annuals and perennials, found
from southwest Europe to Afghanistan. They are mainly small
mounding plants, with variably shaped foliage that is often finely
hairy with toothed edges. The purplish red, often fragrant flowers
are 4-petalled, carried in open racemes, and appear from spring
to autumn, varying with the species.
CULTIVATION: Hardiness of these species varies, though most do
best in fairly mild climates. Plant in full sun with free-draining
soil that can be kept moist. Avoid over-watering or over-feeding,
which can result in very few flowers. Propagate common annuals
from seed; perennials from basal cuttings.

Malcolmia maritima
VIRGINIA STOCK
☀ ❄ ↔ 12 in (30 cm) ↑ 14 in (35 cm)
Native of Greece and Albania. Fast-growing
annual with upright branching stems. Leaves
hairy, 2 in (5 cm) long, elliptical, smooth-
edged or toothed. Racemes of fragrant pinkish
purple flowers, to 1 in (25 mm) wide, in
spring–summer. Zones 8–11.

MALVA
MALLOW, MUSK MALLOW
Like the hollyhock, to which it is related,
Malva is a member of the mallow (Malvaceae)
family. These easily cultivated plants are native
to Europe, North Africa, and Asia, but have
naturalized in other areas. This genus contains at least 30 species
of annuals, biennials, and short-lived herbaceous perennials that
are similar to hollyhocks, but bushier and with smaller leaves.
The single flowers are 5-petalled, appearing in shades of white,
pink, blue, or purple.
CULTIVATION: Grow in herbaceous or annual borders. They do
best in a sunny position but will tolerate partial shade in well-
drained soil. Remove spent flowers to encourage a second flowering; cut down to the ground in autumn. Propagate from cuttings
or seed in spring. Plants will self-seed.

Maianthemum racemosum

Malva moschata 'Alba'

Malva alcea
☀ ❄ ↔ 24 in (60 cm) ↑ 40 in (100 cm)
Southern European herbaceous perennial, naturalized in USA.
Deeply lobed light green leaves with toothed edges. Mauve-pink
flowers, in mid-summer to mid-autumn. Zone 3–10.

Malva moschata
MUSK MALLOW
☀ ❄ ↔ 18 in (45 cm) ↑ 40 in (100 cm)
European perennial. Narrow, finely cut, mid-green leaves; musky
smell when brushed or crushed. Abundant, saucer-shaped, rose-
pink flowers, in summer. 'Alba', white flowers;
'Rosea', pink flowers. Zones 3–10.

Malva sylvestris
CHEESES, COMMON MALLOW, HIGH MALLOW
☀ ❄ ↔ 7–25 ft (2–8 m) ↑ 3 ft (0.9 m)
Biennial or perennial from Europe. Leaves
green, alternate, to 4 in (10 cm) long. Flowers
rose-purple with dark veins, in early summer–
early autumn. 'Primley Blue', bluish purple
flowers, dark blue veins. Zones 3–9.

MARANTA
PRAYER PLANT
This genus of the arrowroot (Marantaceae)
family includes around 32 species of evergreen tropical perennials from the forests of
Central and South America and the West Indies. The elliptical
leaves are spread flat by day and closed "in prayer" at night;
they are usually attractively blotched and veined. The tiny, white,
2-lipped flowers are insignificant. These plants can be grown as
attractive indoor foliage plants in cooler climates.
CULTIVATION: Grow these as house plants in a light, warm, humid
site or in a greenhouse out of direct sun. Potting mix should be
well-drained but never wet. In tropical climates they make good
ground covers under the shade of trees. Propagate by division or
from basal cuttings in spring with bottom heat.

Maranta leuconeura

PRAYER PLANT, RABBIT TRACKS, TEN COMMANDMENTS

☀ ✣ ↔ 10–12 in (25–30 cm) ↑ 10–12 in (25–30 cm)

Perennial herb from Brazil. Almost prostrate, spreading rhizome. Leaves broad, dark green, oval, zoned gray or maroon, veined silver, red, or purple above, grayish green or maroon below, fold upward at night. Solitary spike of white or violet flowers, spotted purple, in spring–summer. *M. l.* var. *kerchoveana* (rabbit's foot), grayish green leaves, purplish brown to dark olive blotches on both sides of midrib. *M. l.* 'Erythroneura' (syn. 'Erythrophylla') (herringbone plant), velvety blackish green leaves, red veins, lime green central zone; 'Tricolor', large oval leaves, strong red veining, dark green blotches on each midrib. Zones 10–11.

Maranta leuconeura

MARRUBIUM

HOREHOUND

This is a genus of some 40 species of woolly gray-leafed perennials from Asia, the Mediterranean region, and North Africa. They are members of the mint (Lamiaceae) family, and as such usually feature rounded leaves that have quite a strong smell. They have square stems and 2-lipped pink to mauve flowers. Some species can become invasive.

CULTIVATION: These sun-loving perennials are drought-tolerant and enjoy a dry summer climate. Prune hard each winter to clean up the plant and encourage bushiness. Propagate by division or from spring-sown seed, which is inclined to germinate in an erratic fashion.

Marrubium incanum

syn. *Marrubium candidissimum*

☼ ❄ ↔ 24 in (60 cm) ↑ 20 in (50 cm)

Perennial from Italy and the Balkans. Densely woolly white shoots; gray-green, scalloped, rounded leaves. Dense clusters of pale mauve to nearly white flowers, in summer. Zones 6–10.

Marrubium incanum

Matthiola incana, Vintage Series, 'Vintage Lavender'

MATTHIOLA

GILLYFLOWER, STOCK

This genus, a member of the cabbage (Brassicaceae) family, contains 55 mainly temperate Eurasian species of annuals, perennials, and subshrubs. They usually have simple leaves, often gray-green and sometimes toothed. Their flowers, which are 4-petalled and often evening-scented, are borne on upright, often branching stems. There are many garden strains available in a wide range of flower forms and colors.

CULTIVATION: Plant in full sun with moist well-drained soil. A light dressing of lime is beneficial. Taller types need shelter from strong wind or can be supported by staking. Propagate mostly from seed, which can be sown in succession for continuous spring and summer flowering.

Matthiola incana

BROMPTON STOCK

☼/❂ ❄ ↔ 12 in (30 cm) ↑ 32 in (80 cm)

Woody-based biennial from southern and western Europe. Leaves elliptical, gray-green, downy, 2 in (5 cm) long. Upright spikes of scented purple, pink, or white flowers, in summer. Long seed pods. 'Annua' (ten weeks stock), matures and flowers in one season; Cinderella Series, single-stemmed, most colors; Lady Series, biennial, branching, dense spikes, most colors, many double flowers; Vintage Series, compact plants, branching, most colors, many doubles. Zones 8–11.

Matthiola longipetala

NIGHT-SCENTED STOCK

☼/❂ ❄ ↔ 10 in (25 cm) ↑ 20 in (50 cm)

Summer-flowering annual found from Greece and the Middle East to the Crimean region. Narrow leaves, to 3 in (8 cm) long, toothed or pinnately lobed. Creamy yellow or pink 4-petalled flowers, 1 in (25 mm) across, with evening fragrance, borne in summer. Horned seed pods. *M. l.* subsp. *bicornis*, usually double flowers. Zones 8–11.

MAZUS

The 30 species of ground-covering and mat-forming perennials in this genus belonging to the foxglove (Scrophulariaceae) family are found in Asia, Australia, and New Zealand. The foliage color varies from mid- to bright greens through to brown and bronze shades. The prostrate stems hug the ground and new roots form as the plant creeps along. Often found in damp sheltered areas, they creep through and over rocks. The narrow tubular flowers sit up on the mats of foliage in spring and summer. The flowers vary in color from purples and blues through to pale lavender, white, and yellow. Depending on the species, flowers may have a splash of lilac-mauve in the throat, or be marked with white and yellow. They are excellent ground cover plants.

CULTIVATION: These plants prefer full sun, good drainage, and open porous soils. Propagate from half-hardened stem cuttings in summer and autumn.

Mazus radicans

syn. *Mimulus radicans*

☼ ❄ ↔ 12 in (30 cm) ↑ 2 in (5 cm)

New Zealand perennial species. Round bronze-brown leaves, 1¼–2 in (3–5 cm) long, with very tight, nearly impenetrable, foliage mats. Flowers are white, lilac streaked, and 1½–2 in (3.5–5 cm) across, in spring–summer. Zones 7–9.

Mazus reptans

☼ ❄ ↔ 20 in (50 cm) ↑ 2 in (5 cm)

Himalayan species. Mid-green, almost glossy leaves cover its stems. Flowers purple-blue, ¾ in (18 mm) wide, with dark center fleck, in spring–summer. Zones 7–9.

MECONOPSIS

The 40 or more species in this genus are mainly native to the Himalayan region, with one notable exception. The genus belongs to the poppy (Papaveraceae) family, and includes annuals, biennials, and perennials, some of which die after flowering. The genus is known for its blue-flowered species, but the other more traditional poppies of yellow, pink, or red are often more easily grown. They form compact mounds of coarsely hairy lower leaves that may be round, pinnately lobed, or deeply toothed. The flowers, carried singly on short stems or in heads on taller stems, open in spring or summer.

CULTIVATION: Most species grow best in woodland conditions in a cool-temperate climate with reliable rainfall. Plant in a sheltered part-shaded position with moist, deep, humus-rich, well-drained soil. Water well in spring and early summer. Propagate from seed.

Meconopsis betonicifolia

BLUE POPPY

☼/◑ ❄ ↔ 8–20 in (20–50 cm) ↑ 3–6 ft (0.9 m–1.8 m)

Perennial, often short-lived, from Himalayan China. Stems and foliage bristly, golden brown hairs. Oblong, often shallowly serrated leaves, to 12 in (30 cm) long. Open heads of up to 6 bright blue flowers, to 2 in (5 cm) long, in late spring–early summer. *M. b.* var. *alba*, white flowers. Zones 7–9.

Meconopsis cambrica

WELSH POPPY

☼ ❄ ↔ 8–16 in (20–40 cm) ↑ 12–24 in (30–60 cm)

Perennial, native to western Europe. Small clumps of ferny mid-green leaves, to 8 in (20 cm) long. Flowers solitary, on hairy stems, bright yellow, to 2 in (5 cm) wide, in late spring–summer. Often self-sows freely. *M. c.* var. *aurantiaca*, orange flowers. Zones 6–10.

Meconopsis grandis

☼ ❄ ↔ 16–24 in (40–60 cm) ↑ 4 ft (1.2 m)

Himalayan perennial. Foliage and stems have rusty brown hairs. Lower leaves to 12 in (30 cm) long, elliptical, serrated to coarsely toothed. Long-stemmed flowers, in groups of 3 or more, deep blue to purple-blue, in late spring–early summer. Zones 5–9.

Mazus reptans

Meconopsis horridula

☼ ❄ ↔ 16 in (40 cm) ↑ 32 in (80 cm)

Often short-lived Himalayan perennial. Very bristly foliage and stems. Leaves elliptical, gray-green, to 10 in (25 cm) long. Long-stemmed flowers in upper leaf axils, solitary or paired, blue to light purple or white, in summer. Zones 6–9.

Meconopsis napaulensis

syn. *Meconopsis wallichii*

SATIN POPPY

☼/◑ ❄ ↔ 20–32 in (50–80 cm) ↑ 6–8 ft (1.8–2.4 m)

Vigorous upright perennial. Found from central Nepal to southwestern China. Stems and foliage covered with fine hairs. Leaves deeply lobed. Red or purple flowers, rarely blue or white, on drooping heads, in spring–summer. Zones 8–10.

Meconopsis × sheldonii

☼ ❄ ↔ 16–24 in (40–60 cm) ↑ 4 ft (1.2 m)

Colorful, easy-to-grow garden hybrid. Bristly oblong leaves, 6–10 in (15–25 cm) long. Leafy flower stems. Blue flowers, 1¼ in (30 mm) wide, in upper axils, in spring–summer. Zones 6–9.

MELAMPODIUM

The 37 annual or perennial herbs and subshrubs in this genus from the daisy (Asteraceae) family are native to the warmer parts of North America and Mexico. They have narrow to oval toothed or simple leaves, and carry heads of daisy-like flowers with white to yellow ray florets and yellow disc florets.

CULTIVATION: These plants are best suited to a sunny position in moist well-drained soil, although they will tolerate dry conditions. During winter reduce the amount of water given. They can be propagated from seed.

Meconopsis grandis

Melampodium paludosum 'Showstar'

Melampodium leucanthum

BLACKFOOT DAISY

☼ ❋ ↔ 24 in (60 cm) ↑ 24 in (60 cm)

Short-lived, mound-forming, shrubby perennial found from Mexico to Colorado, USA. Leaves smooth or divided into 6 lobes. Honey-scented flowerheads, white to cream ray florets, in spring–autumn. Zones 4–11.

Melampodium paludosum

BUTTER DAISY, GOLD MEDALLION FLOWER

☼ ✣ ↔ 36 in (90 cm) ↑ 24 in (60 cm)

Annual herb, from Mexico. Light green oblong leaves on purplish green stems. Solitary, yellow, daisy-like flowers, darker centers, in late spring–early autumn. May self-seed in suitable conditions. '**Showstar**', golden yellow daisy-like flowers. Zones 11–12.

MENTHA (see page 746)

Mentha × gracilis

☼ ❋ ↔ 36 in (90 cm) ↑ 12 in (30 cm)

Low-growing, ground-hugging perennial from temperate Eurasia. Crinkly, dark green, rounded leaves with minty, slightly ginger taste. Tubular lilac flowers, in summer–autumn. '**Variegata**' (variegated ginger mint), leaves with yellow streaks. Zones 7–9.

Mentha pulegium

PENNYROYAL

☼/◑ ❋ ↔ 20 in (50 cm) ↑ 8–12 in (20–30 cm)

Carpeting, spreading, aromatic herb from southwest and central Europe, and the Mediterranean to Iran. Small, dark green,

sometimes gray, leaves, flat on stems. Balls of tubular lilac flowers, on top of foliage, in summer–autumn. Oils deter houseflies. Zones 7–10.

Mentha requienii

syn. *Mentha corsica*

CORSICAN MINT

☼/◑ ❋ ↔ 27 in (70 cm) ↑ ¾ in (1.8 cm)

Carpeting herb from France and Italy. Tight mats of tiny leaves spread on creeping stems. Dark green foliage, pales in hot sun, very aromatic when rubbed. Tiny heads of lavender flowers, in summer. Zones 7–10.

Mentha × villosa

BOWLES MINT

☼ ❋ ↔ 5 ft (1.5 m) ↑ 3 ft (0.9 m)

Spreading mound-forming mint. Delicate hairs on round bright green leaves. Large spikes of pink tubular flowers. Summer-flowering. Zones 5–8.

MENYANTHES

This genus of a single species of perennial aquatic or marginal herbs is native to the cooler regions of Europe, Asia, and North America and gives its name to the Menyanthaceae family. Grown for both its attractive foliage and fragrant flowers, it has smooth, dark green, compound leaves with elliptic to oval leaflets, with slightly serrated edges. These are carried on sheathed stalks arising from a thick, rooting, creeping, then rising rhizome. It carries erect racemes of 10 to 20 short-lived flowers. These heavily fringed and bearded blooms each feature 5 petals that are white, flushed with pink.

CULTIVATION: This plant prefers an open, sunny position in shallow water. Keep tidy by removing fading flowerheads and foliage. Propagate from seed or by division of overcrowded clumps in spring.

Menyanthes trifoliata

Menyanthes trifoliata

BOG BEAN, BUCK BEAN, MARSH TREFOIL

☼ ❋ ↔ 8–12 in (20–30 cm)
↑ 10–16 in (25–40 cm)

Smooth, dark green, compound leaves; elliptic to oval leaflets, slightly serrated edges, on sheathed stalks. Erect racemes of short-lived, fringed, white flowers, flushed pink, in summer. Zones 3–9.

MERTENSIA

This genus, found in Europe, temperate Asia, and North America, is a member of the borage (Boraginaceae) family. It contains about 40 species of hardy herbaceous perennials, although only 4 or 5 are cultivated. Their leaves are usually lance-shaped and hairy. Most species are relatively small and

produce terminal panicles of usually blue tubular or bell-shaped flowers in spring. Some species are used in wild or rock gardens.
CULTIVATION: Plant these in full sun or half-sun in early spring. The plants prefer soil that is moist, well-drained, and rich in humus. Propagate from seed or by division after flowering.

Mertensia sibirica
SIBERIAN BLUEBELLS
☼ ✳ ↔ 12 in (30 cm) ↑ 12–18 in (30–45 cm)
Perennial from East Asia, northern China, and Siberia. Light green leaves on long stems. Deep blue-purple funnel-shaped flowers, in spring–early summer. Zones 3–7.

Mertensia simplicissima
syn. *Mertensia asiatica*
OYSTER PLANT
☼ ✳ ↔ 18 in (45 cm) ↑ 6 in (15 cm)
Perennial, native to Japan and Korea. Long trailing stems of fleshy silver-gray leaves. Sky blue flowers, in spring–early autumn. Needs well-drained soil. Zones 5–9.

Mertensia virginica
syn. *Mertensia pulmonaroides*
BLUEBELLS, COWSLIP, ROANOKE BELLS,
VIRGINIA BLUEBELLS
☀ ✳ ↔ 12–24 in (30–60 cm)
↑ 12–24 in (30–60 cm)
Perennial from North America. Oval gray-green leaves, 8 in (20 cm) long. Very attractive blue-purple flowers, in nodding clusters, in spring. Foliage dies after blooming, so plant among other perennials. Zones 3–9.

MEUM
BALDMONEY, BEARWORT, SPIGNEL
This monotypic genus is a member of the carrot (Apiaceae) family. Its single species is a herbaceous perennial native to temperate Europe where it grows in grassland and rough rocky areas, usually on limestone. It forms a clump of finely divided, feathery, aromatic, rich green foliage. In summer small white to pinkish flowers are borne in the umbels that are typical of the carrot family. Both the roots and leaflets are edible, having a warm spicy taste.
CULTIVATION: Grow these plants in a sunny position in well-drained but moisture-retentive fertile soil at the front of the border. Suitable for naturalizing in sunny wild gardens. Propagate from seed or by division.

Meum athamanticum
☼ ✳ ↔ 12–18 in (30–45 cm) ↑ 18–24 in (45–60 cm)
Perennial herb, native to Europe. Forms clumps of attractive, fresh green, feathery foliage. Umbels of small white flowers, sometimes flushed purple, in summer. Zones 6–9.

MIMULUS
MONKEY FLOWER, MUSK
While it is best known for its annuals and perennials, this mostly American genus in the foxglove (Scrophulariaceae) family has some 180 species and includes a few shrubs. *Mimulus* are vigorous plants with stems covered in fine hairs and sticky glands, which may also be present on the leaves. The flowers form in the leaf axils and are short tubes with widely flared throats. The annuals and perennials often have flowers with vividly contrasting color patterns; this is less common among the shrubs.
CULTIVATION: In suitably mild climates, *Mimulus* are easy to grow, provided they are given full sun and a well-drained soil that remains moist through summer. They are quick growing, and may be inclined to become untidy unless routinely pinched back. They tend to be short lived. Propagate from seed or half-hardened cuttings.

Mimulus aurantiacus
BUSH MONKEY FLOWER
☼ ✳ ↔ 3 ft (0.9 m) ↑ 4 ft (1.2 m)
Upright plant found in western USA from southern Oregon to California. Narrow, bright to dark green leaves, serrated edges. Stems and foliage have sticky coating. Flowers funnel-shaped, yellow, gold, and orange, in spring–summer. Zones 8–10.

Mimulus cardinalis
SCARLET MONKEY FLOWER
☼/☼ ✳ ↔ 24–27 in (60–70 cm)
↑ 32–36 in (80–90 cm)
Vigorous clumping herbaceous perennial from southern North America. Roots down when a stem touches ground. Stems are sticky. Leaves to 5 in (12 cm) long. Scarlet tubular flowers, in leaf axils, in summer. Zones 6–10.

Mimulus cardinalis

Mimulus guttatus
syn. *Mimulus langsdorfii*
COMMON LARGE MONKEY FLOWER, GAP MOUTH
☼ ✳ ↔ 36 in (90 cm) ↑ 36 in (90 cm)
Mat-forming, branching, annual or biennial herb, occurring from Alaska, USA, to Mexico. Rounded, toothed or slightly divided, mid-green leaves. Hairy heads of bright yellow tubular flowers, with red to brown spots, in spring–early autumn. Zones 4–8.

Mimulus luteus
MONKEY MUSK, YELLOW MONKEY FLOWER
☼ ✳ ↔ 24–32 in (60–80 cm) ↑ 12–16 in (30–40 cm)
Vigorous spreading perennial found from Chile, naturalized in other moist habitats. Leaves to 1¼ in (30 mm) long. Yellow tubular flowers, to 2 in (5 cm) long, in leaf axils, in spring–autumn. 'Variegatus', variegated foliage, less vigorous. Zones 7–10.

Mimulus, Hybrid Cultivar, 'Puck'

Mimulus ringens
ALLEGHENY MONKEY FLOWER

☼ ❋ ↔ 4–5 ft (1.2–1.5 m) ↕ 3–4 ft (0.9–1.2 m)

Perennial herb from North America and Europe. Smooth, 4-cornered, narrowly winged stems. Narrow green leaves. Violet-blue tubular flowers, occasionally white or pink, thin throat, on erect stalks, in summer. Zones 3–9.

Mimulus Hybrid Cultivars

☼ ❋ ↔ 12–32 in (30–80 cm) ↕ 8–36 in (20–90 cm)

Mimulus hybrids are strong and vigorous with a wide range of striking colors to choose from. 'Highland Park', varying shades from apricot to tomato red; 'Highland Pink', strong red velvet colors with paler undersides; 'Malibu Red', larger blooms in rich red; 'Puck', clear yellow; 'Roter Kaiser', larger trumpet-shaped blooms in rich red. Zones 3–9.

MINUARTIA
SANDWORT

This genus belonging to the pink (Caryophyllaceae) family contains about 100 annuals and perennials that are widely distributed through the temperate and arctic regions of the Northern Hemisphere. Many of the perennials have a mat-forming habit, and are often very compact. The plants have narrow leaves and clusters of 5-petalled open flowers; some of the neater ones are suited to rock gardens.
CULTIVATION: *Minuartia* species require a moist, rich, well-drained soil in an open sunny position. Propagate from seed in spring or cuttings in late summer.

Minuartia stellata
syns *Alsine parnassica, A. stellata*

☼ ❋ ↔ 18 in (45 cm) ↕ 2 in (50 mm)

Cushion-forming plant from eastern Mediterranean grasslands. Smooth, short, pointed leaves. White flowers, about 2½ in (6 cm) wide, elongated, 5 partially opening petals, in summer. Zones 4–9.

MIRABILIS

A genus of about 50 species of annuals and tuberous-rooted perennials in the four-o'clock (Nyctaginaceae) family, native to

southern North America, Central America, and South America. The leaves are in opposite pairs and are simple and smooth-edged, modified into small bracts below the flower clusters. The flowers are short lived and fragrant, and are available in a wide range of bright colors.
CULTIVATION: Grow these plants in a sunny moist aspect in rich soil. In frost-prone areas, lift the tubers of perennials and store as you would dahlias. Propagate annual species from seed sown where it is to grow, or by division of tuberous perennial species.

Mirabilis jalapa
FOUR O'CLOCK FLOWER, MARVEL OF PERU, VIERUURTJIE

☼ ❋ ↔ 20–24 in (50–60 cm) ↕ 20–24 in (50–60 cm)

Widespread in tropical and subtropical regions of the Americas, so widely cultivated and naturalized that its exact origin is uncertain. Bushy herbaceous perennial. Tuberous roots and leaves to 4 in (10 cm) long. Short-lived, flared, trumpet-flowers, 2 in (5 cm) wide, mainly magenta, or yellow, red, or white, striped, in summer. Zones 8–11.

MITCHELLA
PARTRIDGE BERRY

There are 2 species of trailing, mat-forming, evergreen herbs in this genus belonging to the madder (Rubiaceae) family. One is native to North America and the other to Japan and Korea. They grow naturally in rather sandy soils on wooded hillsides. Dark green leaves are glossy and broadly oval. Small white or pinkish flowers are borne in pairs in summer. They are tubular with flaring lobes and velvety interiors. Although fairly inconspicuous they have a pleasant fragrance. The pea-sized scarlet berries have a noticeable dimple and are edible but have little flavor. They persist on the plant for long periods.
CULTIVATION: Grow these plants as ground cover in shady areas or in the rock garden in a rich soil, neutral to acid. Propagate from pieces of stem from which roots have emerged, or from seed.

Mitchella repens

☼ ❋ ↔ 24 in (60 cm) ↕ 3 in (8 cm)

Trailing prostrate perennial from North America. Roots along the stems. Small rounded leaves, whitish veins. Small pinkish white flowers, in summer. Scarlet berries. Zones 3–9.

MOLTKIA

This genus, belonging to the borage (Boraginaceae) family, is composed of 6 species of perennials, some of which become shrubby, especially in mild climates. Found from Italy through to Greece and into western Asia, they are small plants with hairy dark green foliage. Related to *Lithospermum*, they usually have a more upright, less spreading growth habit and considerably larger leaves than their relatives. In summer they bear cymes of small, tubular, 5-petalled flowers in shades of mauve, blue, and sometimes yellow.
CULTIVATION: Sun-loving plants, these are hardy to moderate frosts and reasonably drought tolerant once established. They thrive in well-drained gritty soil, of most soil types, to which some humus has been added to aid moisture retention, and are lime tolerant.

Light trimming after winter or after flowering will keep them tidy, though often they are not long lived. Propagate from seed, layers, or small cuttings.

Moltkia × *intermedia*

☼ ❄ ↔ 16–20 in (40–50 cm) ↑ 8–10 in (20–25 cm)
Spreading herbaceous perennial, native to Europe and Asia. Narrow bristly leaves, up to 6 in (15 cm) long. Indigo blue tubular flowers, up to ¾ in (18 mm) wide, in summer. Zones 5–8.

MONARDA

BEE BALM, BERGAMOT, HORSEMINT
This genus, a member of the mint (Lamiaceae) family, contains 16 species of annuals and perennials from North and Central America. They form large clumps, dying away completely in winter but recovering quickly in spring to form thickets of angled stems, densely clothed in lance-shaped leaves, often red-tinted and hairy, with serrated edges. In summer the top of each stem carries several whorls of tubular flowers backed by leafy bracts.
CULTIVATION: Very hardy, these plants are easily grown in any open sunny position with moist well-drained soil. Mildew is often a problem in late summer and good ventilation is important. Propagate by division when dormant, or from basal cuttings.

Monarda didyma ★

BEE BALM, OSWEGO TEA
☼/◑ ❄ ↔ 24–40 in (60–100 cm) ↑ 3–4 ft (0.9–1.2 m)
Perennial species from Canada and USA. Finely downy, often purple-red-tinted, serrated leaves, to 6 in (15 cm) long. Flowerheads 2 in (5 cm) wide, usually red shades. Summer-flowering. 'Cambridge Scarlet', heavy-flowering, bright light red; 'Mahogany', purple-red flowers, persistent red-brown bracts. Zones 4–9.

Monarda fistulosa ★

☼/◑ ❄ ↔ 24–40 in (60–100 cm)
↑ 3–4 ft (0.9–1.2 m)
Perennial found from Canada to Mexico. Very similar to *M. didyma*. Leaves seldom over 4 in (10 cm) long, may be smooth-edged. Flowers lavender to pink, in summer. Zones 4–9.

Monarda Hybrid Cultivars

☼/◑ ❄ ↔ 20–32 in (50–80 cm)
↑ 20–60 in (50–150 cm)
The 2 most commonly grown species, *M. didyma* and *M. fistulosa*, hybridize freely resulting in excellent garden varieties. 'Beauty of Cobham', 50 in (130 cm) high, lavender-pink flowers; 'Cambridge Scarlet' ★, large ruby red flowers; 'Croftway Pink' ★, 40 in (100 cm) tall, bright mid-pink flowers; 'Ruby Glow', 24 in (60 cm) tall, bright red flowers, red-tinted foliage; 'Scorpion', 40 in (100 cm) tall, purple-pink flowerheads, purple-red-tinted foliage; 'Vintage Wine', 27 in (70 cm) high, deep purple-red flowers. Zones 4–9.

Monarda fistulosa

MUSA

BANANA
There are about 40 species in this genus of evergreen suckering perennials found from Asia to Australia. They belong to the banana (Musaceae) family. Leaves are large, paddle-shaped, and smooth-edged. The flowers appear on a spike that can be pendent or erect. The female or hermaphrodite flowers are near the base and the male flowers are near the tip. The fruit can be long, slim, and curved, or stubby, nearly round, sausage-shaped, or cylindrical. Although they are usually grown commercially for the fruit, some species are cultivated for their foliage or flowers.
CULTIVATION: *Musa* species are found in light woodland and forest margins and will do best in humus-rich fertile soil in full sun, with shelter from wind. In temperate areas where frosts occur, grow in a greenhouse in loam-based compost with added leafmold. Water and feed regularly during the growing months. Propagate by division of suckers, or by seed in spring.

Musa ornata

FLOWERING BANANA
☼ ⚘ ↔ 6 ft (1.8 m) ↑ 6–10 ft (1.8–3 m)
Ornamental suckering perennial, native to Myanmar and Bangladesh. Waxy green leaves, 6 ft (1.8 m) long. Inflorescences of flowers, orange to yellow, light purple bracts, in summer. Yellow or pink fruit. Zones 11–12.

Musa velutina

VELVET BANANA
☼ ◗ ↔ 3 ft (0.9 m) ↑ 5 ft (1.5 m)
Rhizomatous plant from northeastern India. Dark green leaves, paler undersides, red midrib. Red bracts, white or yellowish flowers. Spring-flowering. Pink velvety fruit, will split when ripe. Zones 9–12.

Musa ornata

MYOSOTIDIUM

The sole species in this genus in the borage (Boraginaceae) family is endemic to the wet, windswept Chatham Islands off the east coast of New Zealand. It has very large, leathery, glossy leaves on stalks like small rhubarb stalks. In spring and early summer, rounded heads of tiny, 5-petalled, bright blue to purple-blue flowers appear among the leaves.

CULTIVATION: This prefers cool-temperate conditions with no extremes of cold or heat. Plant in part- or full shade with moist, humus-rich, well-drained soil. Water and feed well for best results. Watch for aphids. Propagate from seed rather than by division, as established clumps are best left to naturalize.

Myosotidium hortensia

CHATHAM ISLANDS FORGET-ME-NOT

☀/☀ ❄ ↔ 24–40 in (60–100 cm)
↕ 12–16 in (30–40 cm)
Evergreen perennial. Forms clump of long-stemmed, deeply veined, dark green, heart- to kidney-shaped leaves to 12 in (30 cm) long. Upright flower stems, large heads crowded with white-centered blue flowers, in early summer. Zones 8–10.

MYOSOTIS

FORGET-ME-NOT

Around 100 species of annuals, biennials, and perennials belong to this genus of the borage (Boraginaceae) family. They are found in Europe, Asia, Africa, North and South America, Australia, and New Zealand. Most are small tufted plants with simple, usually lance-shaped leaves that are sometimes grayish and often finely hairy. Their 5-petalled flowers are tiny but quite showy and are usually borne in sprays on short branching stems. Most bloom in spring and early summer and are commonly white, cream, pink, or various shades of blue and mauve.

CULTIVATION: Easily grown in any position, sunny or shady, that remains moist during summer. Alpine species benefit from a gritty free-draining soil. Propagate perennials by careful division in late winter, otherwise raise from seed, which often self-sows.

Nelumbo nucifera

Myosotis alpestris

☀ ❄ ↔ 16 in (40 cm) ↕ 12 in (30 cm)

Long-flowering temperate Eurasian and North American perennial. Simple, bright green, pointed oval to lance-shaped leaves, to 3 in (8 cm) long. Small sprays of bright to dark blue tiny flowers, in spring. 'Alba', white flowers. Zones 3–9.

Myosotis sylvatica

BEDDING FORGET-ME-NOT

☀ ❄ ↔ 8–16 in (20–40 cm)
↕ 6–16 in (15–40 cm)

Biennial to short-lived perennial, often treated as an annual, from Europe and Asia. Bright green leaves, to 4 in (10 cm) long. Spikes of pale-centered, tiny flowers, blue or pink, in summer. 'Blue Ball', deep blue flowers; 'Music', large deep blue flowers; 'Royal Blue Improved', many deep blue flowers; 'Spring Symphony Blue', bright blue; Victoria Series, blue, pink, and white flowers. Zones 5–10.

Myosotis sylvatica

NELUMBO

This genus of 2 species of aquatic perennials belongs to the lotus (Nelumbonaceae) family. One species is native to eastern North America, and the other is found throughout Asia and in Australia. The round leaves are borne umbrella-like on long stalks, usually above the water. The showy fragrant flowers are also borne on long stalks, often over 36 in (90 cm) tall, in shades of pink, yellow, and white. They are followed by decorative seed heads. Stalks, rootstock, and seeds are all edible.

CULTIVATION: In warm subtropical climates, they can be grown in outdoor ponds. In cool-temperate climates, plant in shallow water or in tubs. Plant rhizomes in baskets or beds of heavy rich soil mix. Grow in calm water in full sun. Propagate by division of rhizomes or from seed.

Nelumbo lutea

syn. *Nelumbium luteum*

AMERICAN LOTUS, WATER CHINQUAPIN, YANQUAPIN

☀ ❄ ↔ 7 ft (2 m) ↕ 7 ft (2 m)

From eastern North America. Round bluish green leaves, to 24 in (60 cm) across. Pale yellow flowers, to 10 in (25 cm) wide, in summer. Flat-topped seed heads studded with small holes resemble showerheads. Zones 4–9.

Nelumbo nucifera

syn. *Nelumbium nelumbo*

SACRED LOTUS

☀ ❄ ↔ 7 ft (2 m) ↕ 7 ft (2 m)

Found from Iran to Japan and in Australia. Bluish green wavy-edged leaves on prickly stems. Very fragrant pink or white flowers, to 12 in (30 cm) wide, in summer. 'Carolina Queen', large pink flowers, creamy at base; 'Momo Botan', smaller with dark pink to rosy red flowers; 'Mrs Perry D. Slocum', deep pink flowers, ageing to creamy yellow; 'Sharon', large double flowers, pink to red; 'Speciosum' with light pink flowers. Zones 9–12.

Nemesia caerulea

Nemesia, Hybrid Cultivar, 'Fragrant Cloud'

Nemophila menziesii 'Pennie Black'

NEMESIA

Confined to South Africa, this genus belonging to the foxglove (Scrophulariaceae) family includes around 65 species of annuals, perennials, and subshrubs. They form small mounds of toothed linear to lance-shaped foliage. Their flowers, borne in clusters on short stems, have a conspicuous lower lobe, often with a blotch of contrasting color. The annuals are popular short-lived bedding plants in a range of bright colors. The less colorful perennials are sometimes mildly scented and ideal for borders, rockeries, or pots. CULTIVATION: Grow in a sunny position in light free-draining soil that is kept moist. Pinch back to keep compact. Sow annuals in succession for continuous bloom. Perennials will tolerate light frosts and grow from cuttings of non-flowering stems. Propagate from seed in late autumn or early spring.

Nemesia caerulea

☼/◐ ❄ ↔16–24 in (40–60 cm) ↕16–24 in (40–60 cm)
Woody-based perennial from South Africa. Bright green, narrow, lance-shaped leaves, often finely toothed. Heads of small pink to light purple-blue flowers with yellow eye, in summer. Bluebird/ 'Hubbird', violet flowers with yellow eye. Zones 8–10.

Nemesia strumosa

☼/◐ ❋ ↔8–16 in (20–40 cm) ↕6–20 in (15–50 cm)
Fast-growing mounding annual native to South Africa. Lower leaves to 3 in (8 cm) long, bright green, toothed, upper leaves much smaller. Small flowers in crowded heads, often in warm shades of yellow-orange and apricot, sometimes purple or white, in summer. 'Blue Gem', bright blue flowers; 'KLM', two-tone flowers, dark blue upper petals, white lower petals. Zones 9–11.

Nemesia Hybrid Cultivars

☼/◐ ✿ ↔8–16 in (20–40 cm) ↕6–16 in (15–40 cm)
Many hybrids have been bred to produce early-flowering compact plants in a wide range of colors. 'Fleurie Blue', low spreader, bright blue flowers; 'Fragrant Cloud', fragrant pale pink and white flowers; 'Innocence', pure white flowers, each with a small yellow throat; Maritana Series, low-spreading, heavy-flowering plants, wide color range including bicolors; Sachet Series, compact, heavy-flowering, often fragrant plants in single colors, such as 'Blueberry Sachet', blue to purple, and 'Vanilla Sachet', white; 'Sundrops', compact rounded plants in warm tones. Zones 11–12.

NEMOPHILA

There are 11 species of annuals in this genus, a member of the waterleaf (Hydrophyllaceae) family. Native to western North America, they have small pinnate leaves on wiry stems, and form spreading mounds of ferny foliage that are smothered in small 5-petalled flowers, usually borne singly in the leaf axils, in late spring and summer. The plants are graceful and often intriguingly colored, with flowers in various shades and patterns of blue and white. They are most at home in full to half-sun. CULTIVATION: These are superb plants for narrow borders, banks, hanging baskets, and window boxes. They require moist well-drained soil. Propagation is from seed, which is best sown in situ, as once it has germinated, the young plants resent disturbance.

Nemophila maculata

FIVE SPOT
☼ ❋ ↔12–20 in (30–50 cm) ↕8–12 in (20–30 cm)
Annual species from central California, USA. Initially upright, later spreading. Soft green pinnate leaves, up to 7 lobes. White flowers, purple blotch near petal tip, in summer. Zones 7–11.

Nemophila menziesii

☼ ❋ ↔12–20 in (30–50 cm) ↕4–6 in (10–15 cm)
Low spreading annual from California, USA. Ferny light green leaves, up to 11 lobes. Many white-centered mid-blue flowers, sometimes entirely white, in summer. N. m. subsp. atromaria, white flowers spotted with purple-black. N. m. 'Oculata', pale blue flowers with purple-black center; 'Pennie Black', very dark purple-black flowers, edged with white. Zones 7–11.

NEOMARICA

This genus of 15 species of tender rhizomatous perennials is a member of the iris (Iridaceae) family. They are native to tropical America and western Africa. The thick leaves are erect and sword-shaped, with strong veins or ribs, and are arranged in fans. Tall stems bear short-lived, flattened, iris-like flowers, in summer. The outer petals are larger and spreading; the inner 3 petals are upright and reflexed. Some species have fragrant flowers. CULTIVATION: In suitably warm climates, grow outdoors in a sunny position in well-drained soil. In temperate areas, grow in the greenhouse in a fertile well-drained mix, in bright filtered light or full sun. Propagate by division or from seed.

Neomarica caerulea

syn. *Marica caerulea*

☼ ⚘ ↔ 12 in (30 cm) ↑ 24–36 in (60–90 cm)

Rhizomatous perennial, native to Brazil. Leaves mid-green, sword-shaped, erect. Flowers on tall stems, 3–4 in (8–10 cm) wide, pale blue to lilac outer petals, deep blue inner petals, marked with yellow, white, and brown, in summer. Flowers rarely last more than one day but are quickly replaced. Zones 11–12.

NEOREGELIA

These variable members of the bromeliad (Bromeliaceae) family range from small tubular plants to large, flat, circular plants. Their leaves are generally strap-like, forming a rosette, and they can be green, silvery green, purplish, banded, spotted, striped in white, cream, or red, or marbled in a number of colors, or even tipped red. In some species the center leaves turn red or reddish blue, sometimes white. The flower stem is short, and the globular flowerhead, with up to 100 flowers, generally nestles in the center of the leaf rosette. This genus contains over 70 species, mainly from South America. One group from southeastern Brazil are common and easy to grow, especially in tropical to warm-temperate areas. This group provides almost all of the nearly 3,000 hybrids listed for this genus.

CULTIVATION: Grow *Neoregelia* indoors or in a conservatory or greenhouse in cool-temperate areas, or outdoors with protection from direct sunlight and extremes of rain in warmer areas. Water when the potting mix is dry. Try to keep the water in the leaf rosette clean. Do not add extra fertilizer. Propagate from offsets.

Neoregelia carolinae

☼ ⚘ ↔ 24 in (60 cm) ↑ 12 in (30 cm)

From Rio de Janeiro, Brazil. About 20 green leaves, with a few small spines on edges. Flower stem short. Flowerhead globular, with up to 50 flowers opening over a long period. Center leaves turn red before flowering. Petals blue. *N. c. f. tricolor,* variegated form. Zones 11–12.

Neoregelia, Hybrid Cultivar, 'Empress'

Neomarica caerulea

Neoregelia concentrica

☼ ⚘ ↔ 32 in (80 cm) ↑ 12 in (30 cm)

Brazilian species. Leaves strap-like, green with varying purple blotches and broken stripes, with large black teeth on edges, forming a spreading rosette. Center leaves turn purple just before flowering, lasting for many weeks. Flower stem short. Flowerhead globular, with up to 100 flowers, in summer. Petals bluish. Zones 11–12.

Neoregelia marmorata

☼ ⚘ ↔ 40 in (100 cm) ↑ 20 in (50 cm)

Brazilian species. Leaves strap-like, green with many purplish spots and splashes, underside has reverse colors, medium-sized teeth on edges, forming an open funnel-shaped rosette. Flower stem short. Flowerhead globular, with up to 40 flowers, in summer. Petals white. Zones 11–12.

Neoregelia Hybrid Cultivars

☼ ⚘ ↔ 4–40 in (10–100 cm) ↑ 6–20 in (15–50 cm)

Mostly from Australia, Brazil, and USA, these are all easy to grow in warm areas. 'Amazing Grace', upright rosette in pale lime green, the whole plant blushes red in good light at flowering; 'Barbie Doll', light green leaves, red tips; 'Beef Steak', magnificent, symmetrically layered, wide-leafed rosette; 'Blushing Bride', center turns bright red on flowering; 'Bobby Dazzler', broad rich red leaves, heavy apple green spotting; 'Charm', bright wine red leaves, tiny lime green spots—impostors grown from seed have large spotting; 'Chili Verde', rich red in center at flowering; 'Chirripo', glazed centrally in rich reddish purple; 'Debbie', shy bloomer, inner leaves at first almost vertical; 'Empress', strap-like green and pink leaves; 'Fireball', shy flowering, petals blue; 'George's Prince', pale lilac leaves; 'Gespacho', wide red leaves with yellow-green markings; 'Green Apple', leaves apple green; 'Lambert's Pride', leaves with red to orange-red barring; 'Manoa Beauty', leaves with unique speckling in yellow-green; 'Medallion', inner leaves form dense crested rosette of brilliant red; 'Meyendorffii', center turns red at flowering; 'Midnight', deep burgundy central leaves, almost black; 'Ounce of Purple', dull green leaves covered in tiny purple spots; 'Painted Desert', symmetrical rosette of yellow-green leaves, developing more color in strong light; 'Passion', chartreuse-green leaves with hot lilac-pink intense areas; 'Perfection', yellow-cream central variegation; 'Red of Rio', mahogany red with small random green markings; 'Rosella', at flowering, green part of leaves turns red; 'Spots and Dots', dark red spots, blotches, and wavy lines; 'Takemura Grande', greenish plum-colored; 'Vulkan', varying darker purple blotches and broken stripes. Zones 11–12.

NEPENTHES

MONKEY CUPS, TROPICAL PITCHER PLANT

A remarkable genus of carnivorous plants, *Nepenthes* are found through tropical Southeast Asia, with outlying species in Australia and Madagascar. They belong to their own pitcher-plant

Nepenthes alata

Nepenthes ampullaria

Nepenthes rajah

(Nepenthaceae) family. In all, there are over 70 species, divided into 2 main groups: highland species and lowland species. Tropical pitcher plants are climbers that reach up high into the jungle canopy. They have 2 types of pitchers: rounded lower ones, and upper pitchers that are longer and narrower. The flowers are small, with dozens carried along an upright stem. Attracted by bright colors and sweet nectar around the pitcher rim, the prey—usually insects, but sometimes small birds and even rats—once inside, slips down the waxy sides into the digestive liquid and drowns. CULTIVATION: Lowland species can be grown outside in tropical and subtropical regions. In the tropics, use an open soil like bark chips, while in subtropical and temperate areas, use a mix of equal parts peat and scoria. In cooler areas, they are best grown in a warm greenhouse or conservatory. Water overhead, never by tray. Most species prefer part-shade and high humidity. Fertilize with a light foliar feed once a month in spring and summer. Highland species prefer a cooler night temperature. Propagate from stem cuttings; plant in sphagnum moss. Mist regularly.

Nepenthes alata
WINGED NEPENTHES
☼/◑ ✦ ↔ 20 in (50 cm) ↑ 15 ft (4.5 m)
Native to the Philippines, Malaysia, and Sumatra, in highlands and lowlands. Stem prostrate or climbing. Elongated green leaves, to 10 in (25 cm) long. Pitchers cylindrical, bulbous at base, green in shade, pinkish in full sun. Lower pitchers 4 in (10 cm) long, with 2 fringed wings; upper pitchers to 10 in (25 cm) long, with 2 wings. Also a spotted form. Zones 11–12.

Nepenthes ampullaria
☼/◑ ✦ ↔ 20 in (50 cm) ↑ 20 ft (6 m)
From Borneo, Malaysia, New Guinea, Singapore, and Sumatra. Lowland climbing species, woody vine, leaves to 10 in (25 cm) long. Lower pitchers squat, about 3 in (8 cm) high, with 2 fringed wings, large spur behind lid. Upper pitchers rare. Zones 11–12.

Nepenthes burbidgeae
PAINTED PITCHER PLANT
☼ ✦ ↔ 16 in (40 cm) ↑ 40 ft (12 m)
Beautiful climbing highland species native to Borneo. Lower pitchers ivory or cream with burgundy blotches, rim with burgundy stripes. Upper pitchers funnel-shaped, pale green with purple to burgundy blotches. Zones 11–12.

Nepenthes fusca
☼ ✦ ↔ 14 in (35 cm) ↑ 35 ft (10 m)
From the highlands of Borneo. Tubular lower pitchers to 6 in (15 cm) long, with 2 fringed wings, usually purple with green blotches. Upper pitchers are similar size but funnel-shaped, green with purple blotches. Zones 11–12.

Nepenthes lowii
☼ ✦ ↔ 26 in (65 cm) ↑ 25 ft (8 m)
Unusual highland species from Borneo. Lower pitchers cylindrical, with 2 prominent ribs. Upper pitchers hourglass-shaped, deep red inside, green to red outside. Lid is upright, the interior covered with bristly hairs. Zones 11–12.

Nepenthes maxima
☼ ❄ ↔ 30 in (75 cm) ↑ 10 ft (3 m)
Beautiful varied highland species found in Borneo, New Guinea, and Malaku and Sulawesi Islands, Indonesia. Three-angled climbing stem. Lower pitchers to 8 in (20 cm) high with 2 prominent wings. Upper pitchers usually tubular but can be slightly funnel-shaped. Color varies from yellow-green to white with burgundy blotches, to purple with white blotches. *N. m.* × *mixta*, 6–8 in (15–20 cm) pitchers, very easy to grow. Zones 8–12.

Nepenthes rajah
☼ ✦ ↔ 40 in (100 cm) ↑ 7 ft (2 m)
Magnificent highland species from Borneo. *N. rajah* is the "king" of *Nepenthes*. Usually a scrambling vine rather than a climber. Lower pitchers are oval-shaped, to 14 in (35 cm) high, burgundy to purple, with large mouth and even larger lid. Upper pitchers are similar except they are funnel-shaped. Zones 11–12.

Nepenthes spathulata
☼ ✦ ↔ 20 in (50 cm) ↑ 7 ft (2 m)
Beautiful highland species native to southern Sumatra. Lower pitchers are green, with large bright red rim and 2 lightly fringed wings. Upper pitchers are more slender and totally green. *N. s.* × *maxima*, pitchers spotted with red. Zones 11–12.

Nepenthes tentaculata

☀ ⚘ ↔ 20 in (50 cm) ↕ 7 ft (2 m)

Small, scrambling, highland species from Borneo and Sulawesi. Lower pitchers are cream to green, burgundy blotches, narrowing toward mouth, with 2 heavily fringed wings. Upper pitchers burgundy to purple, with prominent ribs. Lid covered with thick bristles. Zones 11–12.

Nepenthes × *ventrata*

☀ ❉ ↔ 16 in (40 cm) ↕ 7 ft (2 m)

Naturally occurring hybrid; varies considerably in size and color. Pitchers usually cylindrical, bulging a little in lower third, totally green or almost bronze to red, with many variations in between. Robust easily grown plant. Zones 8–12.

Nepenthes ventricosa ★

☀ ❉ ↔ 16 in (40 cm) ↕ 7 ft (2 m)

Lovely highland species from the Philippines. Pitchers hourglass-shaped, without wings or ribs, yellow to green, often red in upper half, with red rim. *N. v.* × *mikei*, green pitchers spotted with red. Zones 8–12.

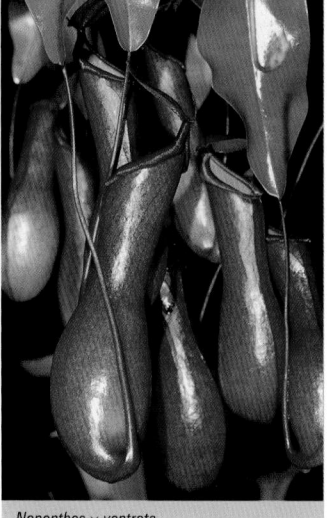

Nepenthes × *ventrata*

NEPETA

CATMINT, CATNIP

A member of the mint (Lamiaceae) family, this genus of around 250 mainly temperate Eurasian and North African aromatic perennials is represented in cultivation by just a few species, and one widely grown hybrid group. Commonly grown in herbaceous borders or for edging large beds, they are valued for the hazy effect created by their gray-green foliage and mauve-blue to purple flowerheads. They are mainly low-growing sprawling plants, with small toothed leaves. In summer, the foliage disappears under upright spikes of tiny flowers.
CULTIVATION: Grow in full sun with light free-draining soil. Pinch back in spring to encourage compact growth, and water well. Propagate from seed or cuttings of non-flowering stems.

Nepeta camphorata

☼/☀ ❉ ↔ 24 in (60 cm) ↕ 18 in (45 cm)

Very aromatic species from Greece. Somewhat sticky, toothed, pointed, oval leaves, to 1 in (25 mm) long. Foliage and stems camphor-scented when crushed. Heads of fairly widely spaced, purple-spotted, white flowers, in summer. Zones 8–10.

Nepeta clarkei

HIMALAYAN CATMINT

☼/☀ ❉ ↔ 24 in (60 cm) ↕ 24–36 in (60–90 cm)

Himalayan native. Leaves light green to silvery, broad-based, toothed, lance-shaped, in whorls at base, in opposite pairs on flower stems. Long upright spikes of purple-blue flowers, white lower lobes, in summer. Zones 6–10.

Nepeta × *faassenii* ★

☼/☀ ❉ ↔ 40 in (100 cm) ↕ 24 in (60 cm)

Often sprawling hybrid. Leaves toothed, lance-shaped to pointed oval. Spikes of lavender to purple-blue flowers, in summer. 'Walker's Low', mounding habit, lavender-blue flowers. Zones 3–10.

Nepeta grandiflora

☼/☀ ❉ ↔ 24 in (60 cm) ↕ 24 in (60 cm)

Bushy eastern European species. Leaves toothed, downy, broad-based, pointed oval. Spikes of lavender-blue flowers in summer. 'Bramdean', compact flowerheads; 'Dawn to Dusk', gray-green foliage, mauve flowers. Zones 3–10.

Nepeta sibirica

SIBERIAN CATMINT

☼/☀ ❉ ↔ 40 in (100 cm) ↕ 40 in (100 cm)

Quick-growing native of Siberia. Leaves sparsely hairy, toothed, dark green. Flowerheads crowded but individual whorls widely spaced, blue to soft purple, in spring–summer. Zones 3–9.

NICOTIANA

TOBACCO

Famous as the source of tobacco leaf, this genus, which is a member of the nightshade (Solanaceae) family, encompasses over 65 species, the bulk of which are annuals and perennials, most native to tropical and subtropical America, with a smaller number in Australia and the South Pacific. A few species are shrubby in habit, though they tend to be softwooded and short-lived. The leaves are usually very large and covered with fine hairs, sticky to the touch, and may exude a fragrance when crushed. The flowers are tubular or bell-shaped, usually white or in pastel shades of green, pale yellow, pink, or soft red, and if fragrant their scent is generally released at night. Some species, notably *N. alata,* are grown especially for their fragrant blooms
CULTIVATION: Most tobacco species are marginally frost tolerant. They grow best in warm humid climates with ample summer rainfall, in full sun or partial shade. The soil should be well drained and reasonably fertile. Cut back old flower stems to encourage reblooming. Propagate from seed sown in spring, though some will grow from cuttings. Some species may self sow.

Nicotiana alata

syn. *Nicotiana affinis*

FLOWERING TOBACCO, JASMINE TOBACCO

☼/☀ ❉ ↔ 12 in (30 cm) ↕ 24–36 in (60–90 cm)

Native to South America. Sticky-stemmed perennial often grown as an annual. Rosette-forming. Large oval leaves. Tall flower stems. Clusters of narrow, tubular, greenish white flowers with flaring starry ends, in summer. They are very fragrant and open at night. Zones 4–11.

Nicotiana langsdorffii

☼ ❋ ↔ 15 in (38 cm) ↑ 5 ft (1.5 m)

Native to Brazil. Upright tall annual with dark green, deeply veined, ovate leaves. Masses of twiggy flower spikes, lime green tubular flowers. Summer-flowering. Zones 8–11.

Nicotiana × sanderae

☼/◑ ❋ ↔ 10 in (25 cm)
↑ 15–24 in (38–60 cm)

Garden hybrid between *N. alata* and *N. forgetiana*. Bushy hairy-leafed annual. Slightly crinkled, wavy, dark green, ovate leaves. Fragrant, flaring, tubular flowers, red, purple, and white, open all day. **Domino Series**, compact, upward-facing flowers in antique shades such as salmon pink; 'Lime Green', bright yellow-green flowers; **Nikki Series**, prolonged flowering, red, pink, yellow, and white flowers; **Saratoga Series**, uniform in size, flowers in mixed color range of reds, pinks, white, and lime. Zones 7–10.

Nicotiana sylvestris

☼/◑ ❋ ↔ 18–24 in (45–60 cm) ↑ 3–5 ft (0.9–1.5 m)

Native to Argentina. Vigorous annual with very large sticky leaves. Tall stems bear terminal panicles of long, white, pendulous flowers, very fragrant, in summer. Zones 8–11.

Nicotiana × sanderae, Nikki Series

Nicotiana sylvestris

NIDULARIUM

From southern and eastern Brazil, this genus contains 45 species and belongs to the bromeliad (Bromeliaceae) family. Closely related to *Neoregelia*, these medium-sized plants prefer shadier conditions. They have small-toothed strap-like leaves, mainly green, often with darker green spots, and sometimes purplish on either side, forming an open rosette with some water-holding capacity. The flower stem varies from short to just emerging above the water level in the leaf tank. The flowerhead is globular, with flat flower clusters, and large, stiff, flattened bracts, mostly red but sometimes greenish. Each flowerhead contains many flowers, with petals that are white, red, or blue, but which never open wide. CULTIVATION: Grow indoors if in flower, or in a greenhouse or conservatory in cool-temperate areas, or outdoors with shade protection in warm-temperate, subtropical, and tropical areas. Water when potting mix is dry. Extra fertilizer is not necessary. Propagate from offsets.

Nidularium fulgens

Nidularium fulgens

☼ ⚘ ↔ 32 in (80 cm) ↑ 12 in (30 cm)

From Rio de Janeiro, Brazil. Leaves strap-like, green, with scattered dark green spots, teeth up to almost ¼ in (6 mm) long on edges, forming broad funnelform rosette. Flowerhead globular, with up to 10 flat flower clusters and large bright red to orange bract with strong teeth and spreading widely, in spring–summer. Petals blue with white edges. Zones 11–12.

Nidularium innocentii

☼ ⚘ ↔ 36 in (90 cm) ↑ 14 in (35 cm)

Native to southeast Brazil. Leaves green, or with purplish wine underneath, small teeth on edges forming a dense funnelform rosette. Flowerhead globular, with up to 9 flat flower clusters, and a large broad bract, green with a red tip to totally red, in spring–summer. Petals greenish. Several variegated forms available. Zones 11–12.

Nidularium Hybrid Cultivars

☼ ⚘ ↔ 20–40 in (50–100 cm)
↑ 12–20 in (30–50 cm)

Diverse color range and ease of care. Most prefer a subtropical garden. 'Madonna', white bracts becoming bright red at flowering, petals white; 'Miranda', variegated form of 'Madonna'; 'RaRu', apple green rosette, whitish pink flowers; 'Ruby Lee', leaves with longitudinal lines throughout on a background of green, or green and red, or totally red. Zones 10–12.

Nigella damascena 'Miss Jekyll'

Nierembergia caerulea 'Purple Robe'

Nolana paradoxa

NIEREMBERGIA

CUPFLOWER

There are about 23 species of annuals, perennials, and subshrubs in this genus, which is a member of the nightshade (Solanaceae) family. They are native to South America where they grow in moist sunny situations. They are slender-stemmed plants, creeping, spreading, or erect, with small narrow leaves. The showy flowers are open and upward-facing, in shades of blue, purple, or white, often with yellow throats. They are borne for long periods from summer to autumn.

CULTIVATION: Grow these in a sunny sheltered position in gritty moisture-retentive soil. In cold climates grow in pots or as annuals. Plants flower in the first year from seed. Propagate all species from seed, and perennials also by division or from cuttings.

Nierembergia caerulea

syn. *Nierembergia hippomanica*

☼ ❄ ↔ 8 in (20 cm) ↕ 8–15 in (20–38 cm)

From Argentina. Small, upright, densely branching perennial often grown as an annual. Narrow pointed leaves. Numerous lavender flowers with yellow throats, in summer. 'Purple Robe', darker purple flowers with yellow throats. Zones 9–11.

Nierembergia repens

syn. *Nierembergia rivularis*

☼ ❄ ↔ 18 in (45 cm) ↕ 2 in (5 cm)

Native to South America. Low spreading rhizomatous perennial with spoon-shaped leaves. Flaring white flowers, about 1 in (25 mm) wide, tinged with yellow or pink at base, in summer. May be invasive. Zones 9–11.

NIGELLA

FENNEL FLOWER, LOVE-IN-A-MIST, WILD FENNEL

This genus of about 15 species of annuals, from the Mediterranean region and western Asia, is a member of the buttercup (Ranunculaceae) family. All the species are easy to grow and feature finely divided green foliage with bushy growth. Flower colors are sky blue and mixes of white, blue, pink, purple, mauve, and rosy red. Nigellas bloom profusely and make good cut flowers. Their decorative seed pods and foliage are also used in dried floral arrangements.

CULTIVATION: Grow in full sun to half-sun in any well-drained soil and fertilize once a month with a relatively high phosphorus fertilizer. Deadhead to prolong flowering. Propagate from seed sown directly where it is to grow, since *Nigella* seedlings resent being transplanted. Plants will reseed.

Nigella damascena

LOVE-IN-A-MIST

☼ ❄ ↔ 10 in (25 cm) ↕ 20 in (50 cm)

European species. Bright green finely cut foliage, somewhat like fennel. Fluffy flowers, in blue, pink, or white. Make successive plantings for blooms all summer. 'Miss Jekyll', semi-double, sky blue flowers. Zones 8–10.

NOLANA

CHILEAN BELLFLOWER

This genus of around 18 perennials from South America belongs to the nightshade (Solanaceae) family. They are grown as annuals in the Northern Hemisphere. These are heat-tolerant sprawling plants, frequently found in maritime areas in their native habitat. Their leaves are spoon-shaped. The showy, tubular, blue or purple flowers have white throats and 5 lobes. The flowers open in the sun but stay closed on cloudy days. They are attractive edging plants and a good choice in a hanging basket.

CULTIVATION: Drought tolerant, these plants will grow in any sandy garden soil in full sun. Propagate from seed, sown directly where it is to grow, in spring.

Nolana humifusa

SNOWBIRD

☼ ✦ ↔ 12 in (30 cm) ↕ 4–6 in (10–15 cm)

Quite rare species from Peru. Leaves mid-green, oval. Long trailing stems with small, bell-shaped, pale blue flowers, in summer. Zones 11–12.

Nolana paradoxa

☼ ✦ ↔ 12 in (30 cm) ↕ 4–6 in (10–15 cm)

From Chile. Trailing plant, suitable for rock gardens or hanging baskets. Mid-green oval leaves, pointed. Large blue-purple flowers, pale yellow or white throats, in summer. 'Blue Bird', blue flowers, white throat. Zones 11–12.

NUPHAR

This genus belongs to the waterlily (Nymphaeaceae) family. It contains about 25 species of aquatic perennial herbs, native to temperate regions of the Northern Hemisphere, growing in still or slow-moving water. The large oval to round leaves may be floating, submerged, or held above the water. Floating and emergent leaves are leathery. The small flowers are held above the water and have prominent yellow sepals, with smaller yellow petals.
CULTIVATION: Plant rhizomes in baskets containing a rich soil mix. Baskets can be lowered gradually to acclimatize plants to the water depth. Grow in full sun in still water. They can be invasive where conditions suit. Propagate from seed or by division.

Nuphar lutea
YELLOW WATERLILY
☼/◖ ❋ ↔ 3–8 ft (0.9–2.4 m) ↕ 3–15 in (8–38 cm)
Widespread in northern temperate regions. Invasive plant with broadly oval or rounded, floating or emergent, leathery and shiny leaves. Produces small, globular, bright yellow flowers, in summer. Blooms emit a distinct odor. Zones 4–9.

NYMPHAEA

This genus of aquatic perennials, in the waterlily (Nymphaeaceae) family, is of varied distribution in ponds over most of the world. There are about 50 species, split into hardy and tropical groups. The leaves are broadly oval or round, with the base cleft in 2 lobes. Flowers with pointed or rounded petals cover the color spectrum. They may be on stalks above the foliage, or sit at water level. Some are fragrant or night-opening.
CULTIVATION: Hardy water lilies are suitable for permanent pond positions in temperate climates. Tropical plants need a summer water temperature of 65–70°F (18–21°C), and a winter temperature of 50°F (10°C). Plant rhizomes in baskets in a rich soil mix, the water depth varying with plant size. Grow in full sun in still water. Propagate by dividing rhizomes.

Nymphaea alba
EUROPEAN WHITE LILY
☼ ❋ ↔ 3–10 ft (0.9–3 m) ↕ 3–15 in (8–38 cm)
From temperate Eurasia and northern Africa. Round leaves, 12 in (30 cm) across, red then green. Floating white flowers, 8 in (20 cm) wide, open during day, in summer. Zones 5–9.

Nymphaea caerulea
syn. *Nymphaea capensis*
CAPE BLUE WATERLILY
☼ ✚ ↔ 3–12 ft (0.9–3.5 m)
↕ 3–15 in (8–38 cm)
From southern and eastern Africa. Round wavy-edged leaves, to 16 in (40 cm) wide. Fragrant blue flowers, held above foliage, open during day, in spring–summer.
'Colorata' *(syn. N. colorata)*, smaller leaves with overlapping lobes, and smaller, mauve to blue flowers. Zones 10–12.

Nymphaea × *daubenyana*
☼ ✚ ↔ 3–6 ft (0.9–1.8 m) ↕ 3–15 in (8–38 cm)
Hybrid of garden origin. Small, fragrant, light blue flowers held well above the water. New plants arise within axils of leaves and stalks. Day-opening, in spring–summer. Zones 11–12.

Nymphaea lotus
EGYPTIAN WATERLILY, LOTUS, WHITE LILY
☼ ✚ ↔ 3–12 ft (0.9–3.5 m) ↕ 3–15 in (8–38 cm)
From Egypt and tropical southeastern Africa. Large, rounded, wavy-edged leaves to 20 in (50 cm) wide. Flowers, to 10 in (25 cm) wide, white, fragrant, usually night-opening, closing the following noon, in spring–summer. Zones 11–12.

Nymphaea mexicana
YELLOW WATERLILY
☼ ✚ ↔ 3–12 ft (0.9–3.5 m) ↕ 3–15 in (8–38 cm)
From southern USA and Mexico. Vigorous plant with round to oval leaves, green blotched with purplish brown. Lightly fragrant flowers, pale to bright yellow, in spring–summer. Zones 10–12.

Nymphaea odorata
FRAGRANT WATERLILY, POND LILY
☼ ❋ ↔ 3–8 ft (0.9–2.4 m) ↕ 3–15 in (8–38 cm)
From eastern USA. Round dull green leaves to 10 in (25 cm) wide. Fragrant white flowers open during day, in summer. Zones 3–10.

Nymphaea tetragona
syn. *Nymphaea pygmaea*
PYGMY WATERLILY
☼ ❋ ↔ 12–48 in (30–120 cm) ↕ 3–15 in (8–38 cm)
Found throughout Europe, Asia, and Japan. Small, oval, dark green leaves, dull red beneath. Slightly fragrant flowers, about 2 in (5 cm) wide, white with yellow stamens, in summer. 'Alba', small leaves, purple beneath, white flowers. Zones 3–9.

Nymphaea tetragona 'Alba'

Nymphaea Hybrid Cultivars

Nymphaea hybrids are divided into hardy and tropical hybrids, with the tropical hybrids further divided into day- and night-blooming hybrids.

HARDY HYBRIDS

☼ ❄ ↔ 3–8 ft (0.9–2.4 m) ↕ 3–15 in (8–38 cm)

Suitable for cooler climates. Day-blooming flowers, usually held close to water level, all colors except blue shades. Some "changeables," altering their coloring dramatically as they age. 'Charlene Strawn', scented yellow flowers held above water; 'Ellisiana', scented deep pink to red flowers; 'Fire Crest', scented clear pink flowers with red stamens; 'Gladstoneana', large white flowers with gold stamens; 'Gonnère', large pure white flowers; 'James Brydon', large-cupped, bright red, scented flowers; 'Odorata Sulphurea Grandiflora', mottled leaves and large, starry, bright yellow flowers; 'Pink Sensation', rich pink flowers held above water; 'Pygmaea Helvola', mottled leaves, bright yellow flowers, orange stamens; 'Texas Dawn', large yellow flowers; 'William B. Shaw', large creamy pink flowers; 'William Falconer', blood red flowers with yellow stamens.

Marliacean hybrids, from mid-nineteenth century, still popular. 'Marliacea Albida', white; 'Marliacea Carnea', soft pink with yellow stamens; 'Marliacea Chromatella', soft yellow. Zones 3–10.

TROPICAL DAY-BLOOMING HYBRIDS

☼ ⚘ ↔ 3–12 ft (0.9–3.5 m) ↕ 3–15 in (8–38 cm)

These hybrids need a water temperature of 70°F (21°C). Some produce flowers to 15 in (38 cm) wide. All colors, including blue shades, are covered. Flowers are usually held above the foliage. 'Evelyn Randig', hot pink flowers; 'General Pershing', deep pink fragrant flowers, to 12 in (30 cm) across; 'Margaret Randig', deep blue-purple scented flowers; 'Mrs George H. Pring', scented, white, star-shaped flowers, to 10 in (25 cm) across; 'Pamela', starry sky blue flowers; 'Panama Pacific', deep plum flowers with yellow stamens; 'Pink Platter', open soft pink flowers. Zones 11–12.

TROPICAL NIGHT-BLOOMING HYBRIDS

☼ ⚘ ↔ 3–12 ft (0.9–3.5 m) ↕ 3–15 in (8–38 cm)

These need a water temperature of 70°F (21°C). Flowers open about dusk and close by the following noon. They are mostly in shades of red, pink, and white. 'Emily Grant Hutchings', rich pinkish red cupped flowers, to 12 in (30 cm) wide; 'Mrs George C. Hitchcock', large clear pink flowers with orange stamens; 'Red Flare', starry, vivid red, scented flowers; 'Sir Galahad', flowers of starry white with yellow stamens; 'Sturtevantii', pearly pink scented flowers; 'Trudy Slocum', large, flat, white flowers with yellow stamens. Zones 11–12.

NYMPHOIDES

This genus of about 20 species of aquatic perennial herbs belongs to the bogbean (Menyanthaceae) family. They are of cosmopolitan distribution. The floating leaves are oval to round with heart-shaped bases. Starry 5-petalled flowers of yellow or white are borne on stems above the water.

CULTIVATION: Most species are invasive and not suitable for small ponds. Grow in full sun, in still water, planting the rhizomes in a rich soil mix. Propagate from seed or by division.

Nymphoides crenata

WAVY MARSHWORT

☼ ⚘ ↔ 6 ft (1.8 m) ↕ 2–5 ft (0.6–1.5 m)

From Australia, growing in water up to 5 ft (1.5 m) deep, can persist on drying mud. Leaves to 5 in (12 cm) wide with shallow wavy teeth. Flowers yellow, to 1¼ in (35 mm) across, with fringed petals, in many-flowered umbels, in spring–autumn. Zones 9–11.

Nymphoides peltata

YELLOW FLOATING HEART

☼ ❄ ↔ 3–8 ft (0.9–2.4 m) ↕ 12 in (30 cm)

Native to temperate Eurasia and naturalized in North America. Small, mottled, heart-shaped, floating leaves. Bright yellow, starry, fringed flowers, in summer. Zones 6–10.

OCHAGAVIA

The 4 members of this genus in the bromeliad (Bromeliaceae) family are native to Chile. They form clumps of dense non-water-retaining rosettes. The leaves are very numerous, narrow and stiff, with many teeth on the edges. The stemless globular flowerhead, with up to 50 flowers, is sunk in the middle of the leaf rosette and surrounded with bright red bracts. The flower petals are mainly in shades of red. The innermost leaves are sometimes reddish at the base. These plants require winter temperatures down to around 32°F (0°C) to promote flowering.

Nymphaea, Hybrid Cultivar, Hardy, 'Ellisiana'

Nymphaea, Hybrid Cultivar, Tropical Day-blooming, 'Margaret Randig'

Nymphaea, Hybrid Cultivar, Tropical Night-blooming, 'Trudy Slocum'

CULTIVATION: These are recommended for pot culture in a green-house or conservatory in cold-temperate areas, or for outdoor culture in cool- to warm-temperate areas. Water when potting mix is dry. Do not overfertilize. Propagation is mainly from offsets.

Ochagavia carnea

☼ ❊ ↔ 32 in (80 cm) ↕ 20 in (50 cm)

From Chile. Clumping plant of dense rosettes, to 20 in (50 cm) across. Leaves green, stiff, with strongly toothed edges. Flower-head bears up to 50 pink-petalled flowers, surrounded by large fluffy pink bracts, in winter. Zones 8–10.

OENOTHERA

EVENING PRIMROSE

This genus of more than 120 species of annuals, biennials, and perennials in the evening-primrose (Onagraceae) family is found in temperate zones of the Americas. Some have tap roots and tend to be upright, others have fibrous roots and a more sprawling habit. These plants' most attractive feature is their short-lived but pretty summer flowers, which are cup-shaped, 4-petalled, and mainly yellow, sometimes pink, in color. Many species open from evening or night, sometimes not lasting beyond the following morning. Elongated seed capsules follow.

CULTIVATION: Mostly very hardy, these tough adaptable plants prefer full sun and light, gritty, free-draining soil. Summer watering produces stronger growth, but they will tolerate drought. Fibrous-rooted species can be divided when dormant, otherwise propagate from seed or basal cuttings. May self-sow and naturalize.

Oenothera acaulis

☼ ❊ ↔ 16–24 in (40–60 cm) ↕ 6 in (15 cm)

Biennial or perennial from Chile. Spreading clump of often red-tinted stems. Irregularly lobed pinnate leaves. White flowers, ageing to pale pink, to 3 in (8 cm) wide, in summer. Zones 5–10.

Oenothera caespitosa

FRAGRANT EVENING PRIMROSE, WHITE EVENING PRIMROSE

☼ ❊ ↔ 24 in (60 cm) ↕ 4–10 in (10–25 cm)

Low, bushy, mounding perennial, native to western USA. Loose rosettes of variably sized leaves, narrow lance- to spatula-shaped, shallowly toothed, wavy edges. Fragrant white flowers ageing to pink, to 2½ in (6 cm) wide, open in evening, in summer. Zones 4–9.

Oenothera 'Crown Imperial'

☼ ❊ ↕ 12 in (30 cm) ↕ 16–20 in (40–50 cm)

Hybrid. Forms clump of bright green, lance-shaped, basal leaves. Upright flower stems, fritillary-like heads of bright yellow flowers, to over 1¼ in (30 mm) wide, in summer. Zones 7–10.

Oenothera fruticosa

☼ ❊ ↔ 12–16 in (30–40 cm) ↕ 20–32 in (50–80 cm)

Sometimes short-lived biennial or perennial from eastern North America. Leaves to over 4 in (10 cm) long, lance-shaped, midrib

Ochagavia carnea

and stems usually red-tinted. Heads of golden yellow flowers, in summer. *O. f.* subsp. *glauca*, broad blue-green leaves, red-tinted when young. *O. f.* 'Fyrverkeri' (syns 'Feuerwerkeri', 'Fireworks'), foliage tinted purple-red, bright yellow flowers. Zones 4–9.

Oenothera 'Lemon Sunset'

☼ ❊ ↔ 16–32 in (40–80 cm) ↕ 40 in (100 cm)

Erect hybrid perennial of uncertain parentage. Forms mounding clump of small deep green leaves. Red stems. Fragrant flowers, to 4 in (10 cm) in diameter, light yellow, ageing to deep pink or red, in summer. Zones 5–9.

Oenothera macrocarpa

MISSOURI PRIMROSE, OZARK SUNDROPS

☼ ❊ ↔ 16–32 in (40–80 cm)

↕ 8–16 in (20–40 cm)

Spreading, sometimes mounding perennial from south-central USA. Stems initially erect then sprawling. Downy leaves, to 3 in (8 cm) long. Bright yellow flowers, to 4 in (10 cm) wide, in summer. Zones 5–9.

Oenothera speciosa

WHITE EVENING PRIMROSE

☼ ❊ ↔ 12–24 in (30–60 cm)

↕ 12–24 in (30–60 cm)

Oenothera 'Lemon Sunset'

Perennial from southwestern USA and Mexico. Upright mounding habit. Rosettes of broad lance-shaped leaves, usually irregularly toothed, sometimes lobed. Flowers open white, ageing to deep pink, in summer–early autumn. 'Alba', white flowers; 'Rosea', pale pink flowers; 'Siskiyou', pale pink to mauve flowers. Zones 5–10.

Oenothera versicolor

☼ ❊ ↔ 16 in (40 cm) ↕ 24 in (60 cm)

Native range unclear, possibly of garden origin. Upright perennial; red-tinted stems; narrow elliptic leaves taper to fine point, toothed. Terminal heads of bright orange flowers ageing to red, in summer. Zones 6–10.

OMPHALODES

NAVELSEED, NAVELWORT

There are about 28 species of annuals, biennials, and perennials in this genus, which belongs to the borage (Boraginaceae) family. They are native to Europe, northern Africa, Asia, and Mexico, where they grow in habitats such as shady rocks and cliffs, damp woodland, or streamsides. The leaves vary from heart-shaped to lance-shaped and may be slightly hairy. The small blue or white flowers are borne in terminal clusters, in spring or early summer, and resemble forget-me-nots.

CULTIVATION: Most species prefer a cool, somewhat shaded situation in any moist but well-drained soil high in organic matter. Low-growing species are suitable for rockeries or make excellent ground covers, while taller plants can be grown in the border. Propagate all species from seed in spring. Perennials can also be propagated by division in autumn, but care should be taken as they resent root disturbance.

Onopordum acaulon

Omphalodes cappadocica

NAVELWORT

◐ ✽ ↔ 12–18 in (30–45 cm) ↕ 8 in (20 cm)

Native to Turkey. Perennial, forming low clumps of heart-shaped leaves. Small, blue, forget-me-not flowers, in early–mid-summer. 'Cherry Ingram', taller vigorous form, deeper blue flowers; 'Starry Eyes', darker blue central stripe on each pale petal, creating a starry effect. Zones 6–9.

Omphalodes linifolia

VENUS' NAVELWORT

☼ ✽ ↔ 6–10 in (15–25 cm)
↕ 12–18 in (30–45 cm)

From western Europe. Annual with narrow grayish green leaves. Sprays of slightly scented white flowers, borne profusely in summer. Unlike other members of the genus, should be grown in a sunny situation. Zones 6–9.

Omphalodes verna

BLUE-EYED MARY, CREEPING FORGET-ME-NOT

◐ ✽ ↔ 24 in (60 cm) ↕ 6 in (15 cm)

Native to Europe. Low-growing perennial, suitable for ground cover. Long, creeping, rooting stems; pointed oval to heart-shaped leaves. White-centered, blue, forget-me-not flowers, in spring. Zones 6–9.

Omphalodes cappadocica

ONOPORDUM

This genus of about 40 thistles in the daisy (Asteraceae) family is from the Mediterranean region and western central Asia. They are gray-leafed plants, in some cases of impressive dimensions, with white cobwebbed foliage well armed with vicious spines. They are biennials and in their second year produce purple thistle-flowers on candelabra-like thorny and webbed stems, followed by the classic feathery seeds that are caught by the wind to be spread far and wide.

CULTIVATION: Grow in any sunny well-drained site. Propagation is from seed, best sown where it is to grow. Care must be taken in

choice of site as these plants can become invasive out of their native environment. On reaching seeding stage the plants will look shabby and should be removed.

Onopordum acanthium

COTTON THISTLE, SCOTCH THISTLE

☼ ✽ ↔ 6–7 ft (1.8–2 m) ↕ 8–10 ft (2.4–3 m)

Found from southern Europe to central Asia. Impressive biennial starting as rosette of large, spiny, woolly leaves; in second year sends up branched, prickly, gray stem topped by purple thistle-flowers surrounded by fierce spines, in summer. White-flowered form sometimes grown. Zones 6–10.

Onopordum acaulon

STEMLESS THISTLE

☼ ✽ ↔ 12–18 in (30–45 cm) ↕ 6 in (15 cm)

Annual from Spain and northwestern Africa. Considered a weed in many places. Low stemless rosette with white, woolly, spiny leaves. White or purple flowerheads open from yellow buds, sitting within center of rosette, in summer. Zones 7–10.

OPHIOPOGON

MONDO GRASS

This is a small genus of 4 species of evergreen perennials from Japan belonging to the family Ruscaceae. They form clumps of grassy leaves arising from underground rhizomes, and in summer bear small lily-like flowers of white to purple that are followed by blue-black berries. These grass-like plants are related to lilies, not grasses. They are cultivated for their attractive foliage and have become popular both as ground covers and for edging. Cultivars with dwarf, giant, and variously colored leaves are available.

CULTIVATION: Grow in full sun or part-shade in moist but well-drained soil. All species will withstand at least short periods of frost but in cooler areas they can be treated as bedding or container plants. Propagation is from seed sown in autumn or by division in spring.

Ophiopogon japonicus

☀/◐ ✲ ↔ 18 in (45 cm) ↕ 12 in (30 cm)

Native to Japan; popular species for ground cover. Very narrow, dark green, curving leaves form dense mats. White to pale lilac flowers, on short stems, in summer. 'Kyoto Dwarf', tightly clumped, grows 2–4 in (5–10 cm) high; 'Nana', slightly taller, to 5–6 in (12–15 cm) high. Zones 7–10.

Ophiopogon planiscapus 'Nigrescens'

Ophiopogon planiscapus

☀/◐ ✲ ↔ 18 in (45 cm)
↕ 12–18 in (30–45 cm)

From Japan. Similar to *O. japonicus*. Form most usually seen is the cultivar 'Nigrescens' (syns 'Arabicus', 'Black Dragon', 'Ebony Knight'), commonly known as black mondo grass. Lower growing plant, purple-black foliage. Zones 6–10.

ORIGANUM (see page 748)

Origanum amanum

☀ ✲ ↔ 6 in (15 cm) ↕ 2–4 in (5–10 cm)

Native to eastern Mediterranean and Turkey. Slow-growing mat-forming plant. Light green heart-shaped leaves. Tubular rosy pink flowers, on whorled spikes, in late summer–autumn. Zones 8–10.

Origanum × hybridum

☀ ◐ ↔ 12 in (30 cm) ↕ 8 in (20 cm)

Hybrid between *O. dictamnus* and *O. sipyleum*. Downy, grayish green, oval leaves. Pink flowers, in drooping clusters of bracts, from late summer to autumn. 'Santa Cruz', pink to purple flowers held above foliage. Zones 9–11.

Origanum Hybrid Cultivars

☀ ✲ ↔ 12–24 in (30–60 cm)
↕ 4–12 in (10–30 cm)

Some hybrids are grown for their globular flowerheads with shell-like pink to red bracts, while others have less showy flowers but attractive aromatic foliage. 'Barbara Tingey', small, rounded, bluish leaves, flowers green at first, ageing to rosy pink; 'Betty Rollins', crowded dark green leaves, small pink flowers, in summer; 'Kent Beauty', small rounded leaves, small pink flowers enclosed within drooping, overlapping, pink and green bracts; 'Norton Gold', aromatic bright golden foliage in spring, later becoming greenish gold, with pinkish purple flowers. Zones 6–9.

ORONTIUM

GOLDEN CLUB

This genus in the arum (Araceae) family contains only a single species of aquatic perennial. It is native to streams and shallow lakes and ponds of North America. The oblong leaves may be floating or upright. The narrow yellow spadix is borne on a long white stalk above a small green spathe, which withers and drops at flowering.

CULTIVATION: Grow these in large tubs or as a marginal plant in water 4–18 in (10–45 cm) deep. Grow in full sun in a fertile soil mix. Propagation is by division or from seed.

Orontium aquaticum

GOLDEN CLUB

☀ ✲ ↔ 18–24 in (45–60 cm) ↕ 12–18 in (30–45 cm)

Native to eastern USA. Aquatic perennial with leathery oblong leaves, to 12 in (30 cm) long, dark metallic green. Erect white flowering stems, to 24 in (60 cm) long, in summer. Zones 7–10.

Origanum, Hybrid Cultivar, 'Kent Beauty'

Origanum, Hybrid Cultivar, 'Betty Rollins'

ORTHOPHYTUM

Mainly from restricted locations in the dry areas of eastern Brazil, the 30 species in this genus belong to the bromeliad (Bromeliaceae) family. These clump-forming plants grow in the ground or on rocks, with or without elongating stems. The furry or smooth leaves, edged with strong teeth, form an open non-water-retaining rosette. Non-stemmed species have stalkless flowerheads that nestle in the center of the rosette, or long-stalked flowerheads. CULTIVATION: These plants are recommended for indoor culture in cool-temperate areas, or for outdoor culture with protection from continuous direct sunlight and extremes of rain in warm-temperate to tropical areas. Water when potting mix is dry. Do not over-fertilize. Propagation is usually by offsets.

Orthophytum navioides
☀ ❄ ↔ 40 in (100 cm) ↕ 4 in (10 cm)
From eastern Brazil. Dense flattened rosettes; leaves small-toothed, very narrow. Globular flowerhead, up to 10 white-petalled flowers. Most of plant turns red at flowering. Zones 9–10.

Orthophytum Hybrid Cultivars
☀ ❄ ↔ 4 in (10 cm) ↕ 10 in (25 cm)
These hybrids are bred for color and texture of foliage and inflorescence bracts. Cultivars include 'Blaze', 'Copper Penny', 'Iron Ore', and 'Star Lights'. Zones 9–10.

ORTHOSIPHON

Genus of about 40 species found in tropical regions of Africa, Asia, and Australasia, belonging to the mint (Lamiaceae) family. They are mainly softwooded shrubs with simple leaves in opposite pairs that may be smooth-edged or toothed. The elongated tubular flowers, with long prominent stamens, are borne in spiked whorls for long periods in spring and summer. CULTIVATION: Frost tender, these plants prefer a protected sunny or shaded spot and a moist, moderately fertile, well-drained soil. Trim excess growth regularly, especially after flowering, to maintain density. Propagation is usually from seed or from cuttings.

Orthosiphon aristatus
CAT'S MOUSTACHE, CAT'S WHISKERS
☀ ✿ ↔ 36 in (90 cm) ↕ 36 in (90 cm)
Found from Southeast Asia to northern Australia, often growing near streams. Dark green ovate leaves, coarsely toothed edges. White or pale mauve flowers, in terminal racemes, in spring–summer. Zones 10–12.

OSTEOSPERMUM

Mainly from southern Africa, this genus in the daisy (Asteraceae) family comprises some 70 species of annuals, perennials, and sub-shrubs. They are valued for their carpeting of flowers during the warmer months, and year-round in mild areas. They are mainly low, mounding or spreading plants with simple, broadly toothed, elliptic to spatula-shaped leaves. The flowerheads are large, with

Orthosiphon aristatus

showy ray florets, mainly in pinks and purples, or white. Disc florets are purple-blue, contrasting with the golden anthers. CULTIVATION: Most tolerate only light frosts and do better in mild climates. They prefer a sunny position with light well-drained soil. Pinch back and deadhead to keep compact. Propagate annuals from seed and perennials from tip cuttings.

Osteospermum ecklonis
☀ ❄ ↔ 20–40 in (50–100 cm) ↕ 20–40 in (50–100 cm)
Native to South Africa. Narrow, downy, lance-shaped leaves, edges often irregularly toothed. Ray florets white, deep purple-blue undersides; disc florets blue, flowers produced throughout most of year. Zones 8–11.

Osteospermum jucundum
syn. Osteospermum barberae of gardens
☀ ❄ ↔ 20–32 in (50–80 cm)
↕ 12–20 in (30–50 cm)
South African perennial. Narrow lance-shaped leaves, irregularly toothed. Flowerheads over 4 in (10 cm) wide, ray florets mauve-pink to purple, disc florets purple-black, in late spring–autumn. O. j. subsp. compactum, high-altitude form, many small flowers; 'Purple Mountain' ★, purple-pink ray florets. O. j. 'Blackthorn Seedling', purple-pink ray florets. Zones 8–10.

Osteospermum Hybrid Cultivars
☀ ❄ ↔ 16–24 in (40–60 cm)
↕ 8–12 in (20–30 cm)
Osteospermum species hybridize freely, especially in cultivation. New forms are constantly being introduced. Most are low spreading. 'Buttermilk', warm buff-yellow petals, dark reverse; 'Hopleys', pink flowers; 'Pink Whirls' ★, pink ray florets, crimped, dark reverse; 'Pixie', soft pink flowers; 'Silver Sparkler', variegated leaves, white flowers; 'Stardust', deep pink flowers; 'Sunny Dark Gustaf', pink and white flowers; 'Weetwood', white flowers with blue eye; 'Whirligig', gray-green foliage, dusky gray-green flowers, crimped ray florets. Seedling strains include the Nasinga Series, various colors, some have crimped ray florets, and the Symphony Series, mainly bright warm colors. Zones 9–11.

OTACANTHUS

Native to Brazil, this genus of 4 species of soft-wooded evergreen shrubs is a member of the foxglove (Scrophulariaceae) family. These plants have simple smooth-edged leaves borne in opposite pairs and attractive spikes of snapdragon-like flowers. CULTIVATION: These frost-tender plants require a humus-enriched well-drained soil in a warm sheltered position in full sun or partial shade. Pinch out tips in spring to promote bushy growth. Propagate from half-hardened cuttings.

Otacanthus caeruleus
☀/❄ ✿ ↔ 20 in (50 cm) ↕ 36 in (90 cm)
Upright plant; woody stems; bright green leaves, lance-shaped, rough-textured. Violet-blue tubular flowers, 2 flat lobes, about

1 in (25 mm) across, most of year. 'Little Boy Blue', attractive cultivar. Zones 10–12.

OXALIS (see page 658)

Oxalis acetosella
CUCKOO BREAD, WOOD SORREL
☼/☀ ❋ ↔ 18–36 in (45–90 cm)
↕ 2–4 in (5–10 cm)
Creeping perennial ground cover from North America, Asia, and Europe. Clover-shaped leaves. White flowers, veined with purple, in summer. *O. a.* **var.** *subpurpurascens*, rose pink flowers with purple veins. Zones 3–10.

Oxalis oregana
RED WOOD SORREL
☀ ❋ ↔ 40 in (100 cm) ↕ 7–8 in (18–20 cm)
Creeping perennial. Native to the woods of western North America. Leaves with 3 mid-green leaflets. Flowers pink to lilac, sometimes white, to 1 in (25 mm) across, from spring to autumn. Zones 7–10.

PACHYSANDRA
SPURGE
Pachysandra belongs to the box (Buxaceae) family and contains 5 species of low-growing shrubby or creeping perennials native to North America and East Asia. Some are deciduous, some are semi-evergreen or evergreen, depending on the climate. They are used for ground cover in shady places and although slow to get started they are reliable once established. They spread by underground runners and have the advantage of being able to grow over tree roots. They have a compact growth and attractive tidy foliage, growing in whorls at the tip of the stem. The flowers are insignificant but scented and appear in spring.
CULTIVATION: Ideal conditions for these plants include a shady position, in moist slightly acidic soil, with organic matter incorporated. If too much light is admitted to their growing area,

Osteospermum, Hybrid Cultivar, 'Sunny Dark Gustaf'

the foliage will turn yellow and the plants will not grow well. Propagation is by division or from cuttings taken in summer.

Pachysandra procumbens
ALLEGHENY PACHYSANDRA, ALLEGHENY SPURGE
☀ ❋ ↔ 12–18 in (30–45 cm) ↕ 6–12 in (15–30 cm)
Found from eastern Kentucky to Florida and Louisiana, USA. Deciduous in colder areas, semi-evergreen or evergreen elsewhere. Leaves dull green, tinged gray; may be mottled with brown or gray colorings. Small white or pinkish flowers in spring. Zones 5–9.

Pachysandra terminalis
JAPANESE PACHYSANDRA, JAPANESE SPURGE
☀ ❋ ↔ 18 in (45 cm) ↕ 8–12 in (20–30 cm)
Native to Japan. Shiny dark green leaves, slightly toothed edges. Small white flowers in spring. Withstands heavy shade and tree roots. 'Green Spike', popular cultivar; '**Variegata**', green and gray-green leaves variegated with creamy white. Zones 5–10.

PAEONIA
PEONY
There are 30 or so species in this genus belonging to the peony (Paeoniaceae) family. While most of the species are herbaceous perennials native to temperate parts of the Northern Hemisphere, the genus also contains shrubs and subshrubs known as tree peonies, which have persistent woody stems, brilliantly colored flowers, and highly decorative foliage.
CULTIVATION: *Paeonia* species are best suited to deep fertile soils of basaltic origin, heavily fed annually with organic matter; soils should not be allowed to dry out in summer. Protection from strong winds and scorching sun is essential, and they require some protection from early spring frost. The only pruning that is necessary is the removal of spent flowerheads and dead or misplaced shoots. Propagation is from seed, which can be slow and difficult, or by division of herbaceous peonies, or by apical grafting of tree peonies, with the graft union being buried 3 in (8 cm) below soil level.

Oxalis oregana

Paeonia cambessedesii
MAJORCAN PEONY

☼ ❄ ↔ 24 in (60 cm) ↕ 24 in (60 cm)

From the Balearic Islands. Leathery ovate leaves, purple-suffused veining, wavy edges; reddish stems. Single flowers, deep rose to magenta, darker veins, in spring. Zones 8–9.

Paeonia × chamaeleon

☼ ❄ ↔ 20 in (50 cm) ↕ 20 in (50 cm)

Naturally occurring hybrid between *P. mlokosewitschii* and *P. caucasica*, from mountains of Georgia. Oval bluish green leaflets. Flower color variable, from pink to creamy yellow, in late spring. Zones 6–9.

Paeonia lactiflora
syn. *Paeonia albiflora*
CHINESE PEONY

☼ ❄ ↔ 24 in (60 cm) ↕ 24 in (60 cm)

Perennial, native to steppes and scrub of Siberia, Tibet, and China. Erect stems; lobed, pointed leaves; good autumn color. Two or more scented white flowers per stem, to 4 in (10 cm) diameter, in early–mid-summer. Parent of thousands of cultivars and hybrids. Easy to grow in well-drained soil; tolerates winter temperatures to −22°F (−30°C). Cultivars mostly taller, to 40 in (100 cm) high, including: 'A La Mode', scented white flowers, petals shiny, serrated, mid-spring; 'Angel Cheeks', double pink flowers; 'Barrington Belle', deep red outer petals, gold-edged pink or deep red, petal-like staminodes (narrow inner petals); 'Bowl of Beauty', large, rose pink, rounded outer petals, mass of creamy staminodes; 'Carrara', tall, white outer petals, mass of white staminodes; 'Cora Stubbs', tall, pale lilac outer petals, cream and pale pink petaloids; 'Dawn Pink', large, single, pink flowers, late spring; 'Duchesse de Nemours', scented, double cream flowers flushed pale yellow toward center; 'Globe of Light', petals almost white-edged, becoming bright pink toward center, free flowering, early summer; 'Haku-Gah', white flowers; 'Heirloom' ★, fully double pale pink flowers; 'Helen', old cultivar, single pink flowers; 'Kelway's Supreme', scented, single or semi-double, blush pink flowers, free flowering, late spring to mid-summer; 'Miss America', beautiful, large, semi-double, scented, pure white flowers flushed creamy yellow at center, spring; 'Moonstone', large flowers, blush pink fading to white; 'Nellie Shaylor', red flowers; 'Peppermint', double flowers, opening blush pink, fading to white, cream flush at center, outer petals with crimson streak, early summer; 'Pillow Talk', fully double, outer petals rose pink, pale yellow staminodes surround pink center, late spring; 'Pink Lemonade', anemone- or double-flowered, pink and yellow petals; 'Pink Princess' (syn. 'Pink Dawn'), rather crinkled petals, pale pink outer edge, fading to white at center; 'Reine Wilhelmine', fully double, scented, rose pink flowers, fine carmine markings in center, very free flowering, early summer; 'Requiem', spicy-scented, single blush cream flowers, free flowering, late spring; 'Sarah Bernhardt', fully double, scented, large, rose pink flowers fading to blush on outer edges; 'Sorbet', fully double, rose pink outer petals surrounding ring of finely fringed cream petals enclosing pink center; 'White Wings', scented, purple-streaked buds opening to pure white single flowers, mid-summer. Zones 6–9.

Paeonia mascula
MALE PEONY

☼ ❄ ↔ 24 in (60 cm) ↕ 24–36 in (60–90 cm)

Variable species from forests of southern Europe. Large, spreading clumps; dark green ovate leaves, bluish green below. Single flowers, 5 in (12 cm) wide, usually deep rose red or pink, sometimes magenta or white, in mid- to late spring. Good autumn color. *P. m.* subsp. *arietina*, from Turkey and eastern Europe, leaves biternate, narrowly elliptic, light or dark green, bluish green below, red or pink single flowers; 'Mother of Pearl', single, large, pale pink flowers; 'Northern Glory', single, carmine flowers; 'Purple Emperor', single magenta flowers; 'Rosy Gem', rosy pink, single flowers. *P. m.* subsp. *russoi,* shorter, from Mediterranean islands and central Greece; mid-green oval leaflets, purple below, purplish stems; flowers single, deep pink, in mid-spring. Zones 8–9.

Paeonia mlokosewitschii ★
CAUCASIAN PEONY, MOLLY THE WITCH

☼ ❄ ↔ 40 in (100 cm) ↕ 40 in (100 cm)

One of the most famous peonies, from sunny hillsides and oak forests of the Caucasus. Oval leaves, blue-green above, lighter below, good autumn color. Bowl-shaped flowers, clear glowing yellow, in late spring. Zones 6–9.

Paeonia cambessedesii

Paeonia lactiflora 'Heirloom'

Paeonia officinalis 'Rosea Plena'

Paeonia officinalis
FEMALE PEONY

☼ ❄ ↔ 24 in (60 cm) ↑ 15–24 in (38–60 cm)

Native to Europe. Lower leaves dark green, biternate, deeply cut into narrow segments. Single flowers, 5 in (12 cm) across, magenta to deep red. 'Rosea Plena', double flowers, bright pink; 'Rubra', single, deep red flowers; 'Rubra Plena' (syn. 'Memorial Day'), double flowers, deep red, very vigorous. Zones 8–9.

Paeonia peregrina
RED PEONY OF CONSTANTINOPLE

☼/◑ ❄ ↔ 20 in (50 cm) ↑ 20 in (50 cm)

From the Balkans and Turkey. Shiny, dark green, biternate leaves, up to 18 segments, turning yellow in autumn. Deep red, cup-shaped, single flowers up to 5 in (12 cm) across, in mid- to late spring. 'Fire King', shiny petals, scarlet; 'Otto Froebel', red; 'Sunbeam', orange-red. Zones 8–9.

Paeonia tenuifolia
☼ ❄ ↔ 20–27 in (50–70 cm) ↑ 20–27 in (50–70 cm)

Herbaceous species, found from southeastern Europe to the Caucasus. Finely dissected feathery leaves; single, blood red, bowl-shaped flowers to 3 in (8 cm) across, yellow stamens, in spring. 'Plena', full double red selection. Zones 8–9.

Paeonia veitchii
☼ ❄ ↔ 20 in (50 cm) ↑ 24 in (60 cm)

From central China, found in subalpine meadows and scrub. Bronze-green deeply divided leaves; good autumn color. Slightly nodding, single flowers, deep rosy pink, 2 or more per stem, in early summer. Ideal for rock gardens. Zones 8–9.

Paeonia Hybrid Cultivars
☼ ❄ ↔ 30–36 in (75–90 cm) ↑ 30–36 in (75–90 cm)

Breeding of herbaceous peonies has resulted in countless cultivars including: 'America', large, single, scented, scarlet flowers; 'Avant Garde', single flowers, pale pink petals with darker veins; 'Blaze', single red flowers, golden yellow centers; 'Buckeye Belle', unusual semi-double flowers, very dark red, crinkled petals; 'Burma Ruby', single red flowers; 'Claire de Lune', large single flowers, palest yellow; 'Coral Charm', large, semi-double, coral peach flowers; 'Defender', single blooms, rich crimson, lightly scented; 'Early Windflower', small, single, white flowers; 'Fairy Princess', single red flowers; 'Flame', single, orange-tinted, bright red flowers; 'Gauguin', large, single, yellow flowers with red center; 'Hakuo-jisi' (syns 'King of White Lion', 'White Tailed Lion'), Japanese tree peony, double white flowers flushed purple toward center; 'Honor', single deep pink flowers; 'Moonrise', single flowers, pale yellow, ageing to rich cream; 'Nymph', single flowers, delicate pink, yellow at center; 'Paula Fay', semi-double, bright pink, scented flowers, flushed white in center; 'Pink Hawaiian Coral', scented, semi-double, coral pink flowers, white stripe on outer

Paeonia, Hybrid Cultivar, 'Sanctus'

petals; 'Prairie Moon', single to semi-double flowers, pale yellow; 'Red Charm', fully double, deep red, ruffled petals; 'Salmon Surprise', single salmon pink flowers; 'Sanctus', single white flowers; 'Scarlett O'Hara', single bright red flowers; 'Vesuvian', deep, dark red flushed purple, almost black flowers; and 'Yellow Dream', large, scented, double flowers, rich yellow. Zones 6–9.

PAPAVER
POPPY

This widespread group of around 50 species of annuals and perennials gives its name to the poppy (Papaveraceae) family. Bristly upright flower stems emerge from basal rosettes of usually finely lobed, often hairy, leaves, each with one nodding bud, rarely 2 or 3. The flowers most often have 4 crape-like petals around a central ovary topped with a prominent stigmatic disc.
CULTIVATION: Most poppies are very hardy and prefer a sunny position with light, moist, and well-drained soil. Propagate perennial poppy cultivars by root cuttings, otherwise raise from seed.

Papaver alpinum
ALPINE POPPY

☼/◑ ❄ ↔ 8–16 in (20–40 cm) ↑ 10 in (25 cm)

Variable perennial from mountains of southern Europe, possibly conglomerate of closely related species. Basal clump of finely divided, downy, gray-green to blue-green leaves. Orange, yellow, or white flowers borne singly in summer. Zones 5–9.

Papaver atlanticum
☼/◑ ❄ ↔ 8–12 in (20–30 cm) ↑ 18 in (45 cm)

Moroccan perennial. Broad, hairy, lance-shaped leaves, coarsely toothed or lobed. Flowers usually solitary, stems sometimes forked, light orange to red, in summer. 'Flore Pleno', orange double flowers on stocky stems. Zones 6–10.

Papaver commutatum

Flower stems usually leafy on lower half. Solitary flowers, to 4 in (10 cm) wide, red, orange, or pink, often darker blotched. Cultivars include '**Black and White**', large white flowers with black center; '**Cedric Morris**' ★, very hairy leaves, dark-blotched soft pink flowers; the **Goliath Group**, sturdy plants, very large flowers in bright colors with dark centers, such as '**Beauty of Livermere**', deep red with small black blotches; '**Mrs Perry**', large salmon pink flowers with dark blotches; and '**Princess Victoria Louise**', ruffled apricot pink flowers with dark blotches. Zones 3–9.

Papaver commutatum

☀/❂ ❄ ↔ 16 in (40 cm) ↕ 16 in (40 cm)

Annual from western Asia. Leaves to 6 in (15 cm) long, sometimes shallowly lobed. Red flowers with black basal blotches, 2 in (5 cm) wide, in summer. '**Lady Bird**', slightly taller, bright red flowers liberally splashed with black. Zones 8–10.

Papaver × hybridum

ROUGH POPPY

☀/❂ ❄ ↔ 6–10 in (15–25 cm) ↕ 8–20 in (20–50 cm)

Naturally occurring hybrid. Eurasian annual. Finely divided pinnate leaves to 4 in (10 cm) long. Bright red flowers with purple blotch at base of petals. Zones 6–9.

Papaver nudicaule

syns *Papaver croceum*, *P. miyabeanum*
ARCTIC POPPY, ICELAND POPPY

☀/❂ ❄ ↔ 8–12 in (20–30 cm)
↕ 12–16 in (30–40 cm)

Perennial, native to subarctic regions. Pinnate leaves, often light blue-green, hairy. Solitary long-stemmed flowers to 3 in (8 cm) wide, in many colors, in spring–summer. *P. n.* var. *croceum*, orange to orange-red flowers. *P. n.* '**Pacino**', yellow flowers on stocky stems; mixed-color seedling strains include **Meadhome's Strain**, and **Artist Mixed**. Zones 2–10.

Paradisea liliastrum

Papaver orientale

ORIENTAL POPPY

☀/❂ ❄ ↔ 12–20 in (30–50 cm) ↕ 24–40 in (60–100 cm)

Summer-flowering western Asian perennial. Forms sturdy clump of bristly, pinnate, often blue-green leaves to 10 in (25 cm) long.

Papaver rhoeas

CORN POPPY, FIELD POPPY, FLANDERS POPPY

☀/❂ ❄ ↔ 12–16 in (30–40 cm)
↕ 36–48 in (90–120 cm)

Vigorous hardy annual from Old World temperate zones. Pinnate leaves to 6 in (15 cm) long. Bristly flower stems, solitary bright red flowers to 3 in (8 cm) wide, sometimes with black basal blotch, in summer. Mixed color strains include '**Mother of Pearl**', in pastel shades, and **Shirley Mixed**, single or double flowers, range of colors. Zones 5–9.

Papaver somniferum

OPIUM POPPY

☀ ❄ ↔ 12–24 in (30–60 cm) ↕ 36–48 in (90–120 cm)

From southeastern Europe and western Asia. Vigorous annual. Leaves light blue-green, heavy textured, deeply cut with jagged teeth. Strong leafy flower stems. Flowers 4 in (10 cm) wide, white, mauve, or purple, sometimes with a dark basal blotch, in summer. *P. s.* var. *paeoniflorum*, deep blue-green leaves, maroon-black, double, peony-like flowers. *P. s.* '**Hen and Chickens**', lavender flowers; '**White Cloud**', tall, white, double flowers. Zones 7–10.

PARADISEA

PARADISE LILY, ST BRUNO'S LILY

A genus of 2 species in the asphodel (Asphodelaceae) family, native to the woods and alpine pastures of Europe. Perennials with a short underground rhizome, strappy basal leaves, and stems of fragrant white trumpet flowers in summer. Excellent cut flowers. CULTIVATION: These species prefer moist but well-drained humus-rich soil in full sun or partial shade. Propagate from seed sown fresh or divide when dormant.

Paradisea liliastrum

☀/❂ ❄ ↔ 10–12 in (25–30 cm) ↕ 16–24 in (40–60 cm)

Clump-forming perennial. Narrow, gray-green, grass-like foliage to 10 in (25 cm) long. Upright spikes of slightly drooping, fragrant, white trumpets to 2½ in (6 cm) long, in summer. '**Major**' has larger trumpets. Zones 7–9.

PARAHEBE

Revised in recent years, this genus of some 30 species belonging to the foxglove (Scrophulariaceae) family grows largely in New Zealand with a few species in Australia and New Guinea. Low, spreading plants best regarded as subshrubs, sometimes developing a few woody branches with age. The leaves, on pliable wiry stems, are small, dark green, and elliptical, often with toothed edges. Racemes of small, rounded flowers, usually white, pink, or mauve with contrasting veining, appear in late spring and summer.
CULTIVATION: Parahebes are easily cultivated in moist well-drained soil and a reasonably sunny aspect. They tolerate moderate frosts but will not withstand drought without becoming sparsely foliaged and untidy. If necessary, trim back after flowering. Propagate from seed, layers (which often form naturally), or by small tip cuttings taken in summer–autumn.

Parahebe × bidwillii

☀ ❄ ↔ 6 in (15 cm) ↕ 4 in (10 cm)
Native to New Zealand. Mat-forming sub-shrub; cross between *P. decora* and *P. lyallii*. Tiny, round, leathery, dark green leaves. Small, saucer-shaped, white flowers stained crimson. Summer-flowering. Zones 6–11.

Parahebe catarractae

☀ ❄ ↔ 24 in (60 cm) ↕ 12 in (30 cm)
New Zealand native. Serrated lance-shaped leaves; purple-red-tinted stems. Flowers white, purple veining. Pale blue, pink, and mauve-flowered forms, such as 'Falling Skies'. Zones 8–10.

Parahebe lyallii

☀ ❄ ↔ 18 in (45 cm) ↕ 8 in (20 cm)
Native to New Zealand. Dense mound of fine stems; leaves less than ½ in (12 mm) long, with toothed edges. White to pale pink flowers, held in sprays above the foliage, in summer. Zones 8–10.

PARIS

A genus of over 20 species of perennials in the honey-flower (Melanthiaceae) family, found in woodlands from Europe across to eastern Asia. Extremely slow-growing rhizomes produce erect stems, with a whorl of leaves at the top surrounding the flowers. The summer flowers have spidery or lance-shaped petals.
CULTIVATION: Grow in a cool aspect with moist not wet humus-rich soil. Propagate from seed, which can take 2 years or more to germinate, or by division of old clumps when dormant.

Paris polyphylla

syn. *Daiswa polyphylla*
☀/◐ ❄ ↔ 8–12 in (20–30 cm) ↕ 36–40 in (90–100 cm)
Perennial, found from the Himalayas to Myanmar and Thailand. Upright stems; lance-shaped leaves to 7 in (18 cm) long. Flowers

with narrow green sepals, thread-like yellow petals, purple ovary. *P. p.* var. *yunnanensis* f. *alba*, white filament-like petals. Zones 6–9.

Paris quadrifolia

HERB PARIS
☀/◐ ❄ ↔ 10–12 in (25–30 cm) ↕ 8–16 in (20–40 cm)
Perennial from Europe and East Asia. Upright stems; leaves to 6 in (15 cm) long. Flowers with 4 mid-green sepals and narrow white petals. Blue-black seed capsules. Zones 6–9.

PELARGONIUM

STORKSBILL
Most of the 250 species of annuals, perennials, and subshrubs in this genus of the geranium (Geraniaceae) family come from South Africa, a few from the rest of Africa, the Middle East, and Australia. The rounded or hand-shaped leaves have conspicuous lobes, fine hairs, and darker blotches. The simple 5-petalled flowers are often massed and/or brightly colored.
CULTIVATION: Tolerant of light frosts only, many pelargoniums are treated as annuals in areas with cold winters. Plant most species in a position in full sun in light well-drained soil. Propagate annuals and species from seed; perennials and shrubs from cuttings.

Pelargonium australe

☀ ⚘ ↔ 20 in (50 cm) ↕ 12 in (30 cm)
Perennial from southeastern Australia including Tasmania. Rather straggling habit; downy, rounded, 5- to 7-lobed leaves to 4 in (10 cm) across. Clusters of 5 to 10 dark-veined pale pink or white flowers to slightly over ½ in (12 mm) wide, from spring to summer. Zones 9–10.

Pelargonium crispum

LEMON-SCENTED GERANIUM
☀ ⚘ ↔ 36 in (90 cm) ↕ 30 in (75 cm)
South African aromatic shrub. Small, 3-lobed leaves, crinkled edges. Pink flowers, dark markings, ¾ in (18 mm) wide. Foliage has strong lemon scent when crushed. Cultivars with small fragrant leaves include 'Major', larger leaves; 'Minor', upright habit with tiny leaves; 'Peach Cream', pink flowers, subtle peach scent; 'Variegatum', cream-edged leaves. Zones 9–11.

Pelargonium graveolens

ROSE-SCENTED GERANIUM
☀ ⚘ ↔ 26 in (65 cm) ↕ 48 in (120 cm)
South African summer-flowering species, possibly a hybrid. Erect stems; rounded, deeply divided leaves release strong scent of rosewater when crushed. Foliage and young stems covered with fine hairs. Clusters of small, purple-veined, pink flowers. 'Lady Plymouth', compact growth, cream-edged strongly scented leaves, often used in floral decorations. Zones 9–11.

Parahebe catarractae

Paris polyphylla

Pelargonium odoratissimum

APPLE GERANIUM

☼/◐ ✳ ↔ 24 in (60 cm) ↑ 12 in (30 cm)

Low-spreading perennial from South Africa. Apple-scented leaves, rounded, pale green, and toothed, to around 1½ in (35 mm) wide. Branching flower stems with heads of up to 10, ½ in (12 mm) wide, red-marked, white flowers, in spring–summer. Zones 9–11.

Pelargonium quercifolium

ALMOND GERANIUM, OAK-LEAF GERANIUM

☼ ✳ ↔ 24–32 in (60–80 cm) ↑ 3–5 ft (0.9–1.5 m)

South African native. Upright growth habit; hairy, aromatic, deeply lobed leaves, often with toothed edges, olive green, dark central zone. Small heads of ½ in (12 mm) wide purple-pink flowers in spring–summer. Zones 9–11.

Pelargonium rodneyanum

MAGENTA STORKSBILL

☼ ✳ ↔ 12–20 in (30–50 cm) ↑ 8–12 in (20–30 cm)

Spreading, tuberous perennial. Native to Australia. Dark green, elongated, heart-shaped leaves to 4 in (10 cm) long, notched edges. Short wiry stems, heads of small bright pink flowers, in spring. Zones 9–11.

Pelargonium tomentosum

☼ ✳ ↔ 40 in (100 cm) ↑ 20 in (50 cm)

South African perennial. Peppermint-scented, 3- to 5-lobed, velvety, rounded leaves, around 3 in (8 cm) wide. Erect stems; heads of white flowers, to over ½ in (12 mm) wide. Upper petals purple-marked. Spring- to summer-flowering. Zones 9–11.

Pelargonium Hybrid Cultivars

☼ ✳ ↔ 8–40 in (20–100 cm) ↑ 6–60 in (15–150 cm)

Pelargonium species interbreed freely; there is a range of hybrid groups of mostly compact plants with large showy flowers.

Pelargonium, Hybrid Cultivar, Angel, 'Suffolk Garnet'

Ivy-Leafed Hybrids: Derived mainly from *P. peltatum*. Large range of growth forms. Very hardy for outdoor planting; tolerant of humidity and damp soil. 'Barbe Bleu', deep purple double flowers ageing to deep red; 'Crocketta', light veined leaves, white flowers with red markings; 'Evka', white-edged leaves, bright red flowers; and 'Mutzel', gray-green and white variegated leaves, bright red flowers.

Angel Hybrids: Similar to Regal Hybrids, but usually only 12 in (30 cm) tall or less. They do not produce double flowers. 'Captain Starlight', upper petals purple-red, lower petals pink-flushed white; 'Oldbury Duet', white-edged bright green leaves, upper petals burgundy with mauve markings, lower petals shades of mauve; 'Quantock Marjorie', upper petals purple-red, lower petals very pale pink; 'Quantock Matty', upper petals deep purple, lower petals pink-flushed white; 'Quantock Rita', upper petals maroon, lower petals pink-flushed white; 'Quantock Star', upper and lower petals dark red with broad pale pink edge; 'Spanish Angel', upper petals purple-red edged with mauve, lower petals mauve with maroon blotch and veins; 'Suffolk Garnet', large red flowers; 'The Culm', royal purple upper petals with delicate mauve edging, lower petals lavender pink with deeper pink markings; 'Tip Top Duet', upper petals maroon, lower petals lavender.

Dwarf Hybrids: Resembling Zonal Hybrids in foliage and stature; differing from Angel Hybrids often with fully double blooms. 'Beryl Read', pink flowers, darker blotch; 'Brackenwood', salmon pink double flowers; 'Brenda', mid-pink flowers, red blotch; 'Brookside Flamenco', vivid pink double flowers; 'Hope Valley', golden yellow leaves, pink double flowers; 'Little Alice', deep green leaves, dark salmon pink flowers; 'Orion', orange-red double flowers; 'Redondo', large, red, double flowers.

Regal Hybrids: Also known as Martha Washington Hybrids. Around 20 in (50 cm) tall, though plant size ranges from dwarfs under 12 in (30 cm) tall through to shrubs of 4 ft (1.2 m) or more. Flowers large, reminiscent of evergreen azaleas; may be single or double; huge range of colors and patterns. 'Askham Fringed Aztec', frilly white flowers with red veining; 'Australian Mystery', cut-edged upper petals, magenta with lighter veining, lower petals white with magenta veining and blotch; 'Bert Pearce', large, frilly, pink flowers with red veining; 'Bosham', pink with dark purple-red upper blotch and magenta veining; 'Cherry Orchard', bright red with lighter center and dark red upper veining; 'Delhi', white flowers tinted dark pink at petal edge; 'Eileen Postle', bright mid-pink with purple-red upper blotch; 'Harbour Lights', bright pink with pink-edged, dark-blotched, light red upper petals; 'Joan Morf', white flushed mid-pink with red upper blotch; 'Kimono', lavender-pink with white throat, deep magenta veining; 'Lara Susan', single, pale pink-edged purple-red upper petals, near white lower petals with small purple-red blotch; 'Lavender Sensation', lavender-pink with purple-red upper blotch; 'Lord Bute', simple single flowers, dark maroon with narrow bright pink edge; **'Rembrandt'** ★, purple edged with mauve-pink; **'Rimfire'**, black-red with red to pink edge; **'Rosmaroy'**, bright pink, pale red upper blotch, lower spotting; **'Springfield Black'**, dark purple-red, lighter center; **'Super Spot-on-bonanza'**, white flecked and sectored bright orange-red; **'Virginia Louise'**, pale pink, blotched deeper pink.

Scented-leafed Hybrids: Grown mainly for aroma of foliage; flowers can be very showy. **'Camphor Rose'**, minty camphor scent, small lavender flowers; **'Lara Ballerina'**, sharp citrus scent, white to pale pink flowers flushed with purple-red; **'Lara Starshine'**, mild citrus scent, many small, deep pinkish red flowers; **'Pink Champagne'**, dwarf habit, green and gold foliage, bright pink double flowers.

Unique Hybrids: Woody-based perennials; most have *P. fulgidum* parentage. Aromatic foliage; large flowers. **'Bolero'**, single, vivid pink flowers, darker center; **'Mystery'**, red flowers with darker blotch; **'Scarlet Unique'**, rich red flowers, velvety leaves; **'Shrubland Pet'** (syn. 'Shrubland Rose'), dwarf form, rose-red petals, deeper colored toward edges.

Zonal Hybrids: Mainly of *P. inquinans × P. zonale* parentage, many now classified as *P. × hortorum*. Low bushy habit; succulent stems; light green, kidney-shaped to rounded, shallowly lobed leaves with dark zonal markings. Heads of brightly colored flowers, held above foliage on upright stems in warmer months, year-round in frost-free areas. Many cultivars and seedling strains, including: **'Dolly Vardon'**, tricolored leaves, red and green with creamy white edges, red single flowers; and **'Retah's Crystal'**, variegated leaves, large soft pink flowers. Stellar forms have narrow, pointed petals and more sharply lobed leaves. These include: **'Annsbrook Gemini'**, bright pink double flowers with red flecks; **'Bird Dancer'**, very dark foliage, spidery, salmon pink, single flowers; **'Grandad Mac'**, dark foliage, orange-pink double flowers; **'Laura Parmer'**, dark foliage, mid-pink single flowers; **'Mrs Pat'**, golden brown leaves, salmon pink single flowers; **'Pagoda'**, pale pink double flowers; **'Red Cactus'**, starry bright red flowers with long petals; **'Vancouver Centennial'**, red leaves with light green edges, small, bright magenta, single flowers. Zones 9–11.

Pelargonium, Hybrid Cultivar, Regal, 'Delhi'

Pelargonium, Hybrid Cultivar, Regal, 'Rembrandt'

PELTANDRA

ARROW ARUM

The 3 aquatic, rhizomatous, perennial herbs in this genus of the arum (Araceae) family inhabit the bogs and marshes of eastern North America. They have simple arrowhead-shaped leaves on long sheathed stalks, and spikes of tiny unisexual flowers, carried on stalks as long or longer than the leaf stalks, and enclosed by wavy spathes with overlapping edges. The fruit is a berry.

CULTIVATION: Arrow arums thrive in full sun or half-sun in damp, acidic soil adjacent to water, or in water up to 12 in (30 cm) deep. Propagate by division in spring or from seed, which should be stratified prior to sowing.

Peltandra virginica

GREEN ARROW ARUM, TUCKAHOE

☼ ❄ ↔ 12–36 in (30–90 cm) ↕ 12–36 in (30–90 cm)

From eastern and southeastern USA. Large, glossy, dark green leaves, 12–36 in (30–90 cm) long, in spring, on long succulent stalks. Yellowish green spathe, up to 8 in (20 cm) long, edged with white or yellow; erect whitish green flower spike; green berries in late summer–autumn. Zones 5–9.

PENSTEMON

This genus of around 250 species of perennials and subshrubs in the foxglove (Scrophulariaceae) family is found from Alaska to Guatemala, with one straggler in cool-temperate Asia. Some are shrubby, some mat-forming, but most form clumps of simple linear to lance-shaped leaves in opposite pairs. Their flowers, borne mainly in summer on upright terminal spikes reminiscent of foxgloves *(Digitalis)*, are tubular to bell-shaped, with 2 upper lobes and 3 larger lower lobes.

CULTIVATION: Some species and garden forms are frost tender, and considerable work has recently been put into producing hardy hybrids. Plant in full or half-sun with moist well-drained soil. Propagate by division or from cuttings of non-flowering stems. The species may be raised from seed.

Penstemon barbatus

BEARDLIP, CORAL PENSTEMON

☼/❄ ❄ ↔ 12–20 in (30–50 cm) ↕ 40 in (100 cm)

Perennial from Colorado, Arizona, and New Mexico, USA. Narrow lance-shaped leaves to 3 in (8 cm) long. Heads of pink to red flowers, extended upper lobes, in summer. **'Coccineus'**, bright red flowers; **'Elfin Pink'**, bright pink flowers; **'Rose Elf'**, deep pink flowers; **'Schooley's Yellow'**, bright yellow flowers. Zones 3–9.

Penstemon digitalis 'Husker Red'

Penstemon procerus var. tolmiei

Penstemon campanulatus

☀/◐ ❄ ↔ 8–12 in (20–30 cm) ↑12–24 in (30–60 cm)
Perennial from mountains of Mexico and Guatemala. Narrow,
toothed, lance-shaped leaves, to 3 in (8 cm) long. Deep pink
to purple flowers, in late spring–early summer. Zones 9–10.

Penstemon davidsonii

☀/◐ ❄ ↔ 20–24 in (50–60 cm) ↑4 in (10 cm)
Low spreading perennial from western USA. Forms mat of fine
stems; ½ in (12 mm) long elliptical leaves. Short inflorescences
of bright pink flowers in summer. Zones 6–9.

Penstemon digitalis

FOXGLOVE BEARDTONGUE
☀/◐ ❄ ↔ 12–24 in (30–60 cm) ↑5 ft (1.5 m)
Perennial from central USA. Leaves glossy, purple-tinted, blue-
green, 4–6 in (10–15 cm) long. Purple-pink flushed white flowers
in summer. 'Husker Red', deep purple-red foliage. Zones 3–9.

Penstemon fruticosus

SHRUBBY PENSTEMON
☀/◐ ❄ ↔ 20 in (50 cm) ↑16 in (40 cm)
Perennial from western USA. Bushy clump of mostly erect stems;
lance-shaped leaves to 2 in (5 cm) long, sometimes toothed. Lavender to purple flowers in spring–summer. Zones 4–9.

Penstemon grandiflorus

LARGE BEARDTONGUE
☀/◐ ❄ ↔ 12–20 in (30–50 cm) ↑40 in (100 cm)
Perennial found in central USA from North Dakota to Texas.
Leathery, rounded, blue-green leaves, 1–4 in (2.5–10 cm) long.
lavender to pale blue flowers in summer. 'Prairie Snow', heavy-
blooming, white flowers. Zones 3–9.

Penstemon heterophyllus

FOOTHILLS PENSTEMON
☀/◐ ❄ ↔ 8–12 in (20–30 cm) ↑12–20 in (30–50 cm)
Shrubby Californian perennial. Narrow, dark green to blue-green
leaves to 2 in (5 cm) long. Fairly short heads of lavender-pink

to bright blue flowers, in summer. 'Blue Bedder' ★, compact,
bright blue flowers; 'Heavenly Blue', dark mauve-blue to blue
flowers. Zones 8–10.

Penstemon hirsutus

☀/◐ ❄ ↔ 8–12 in (20–30 cm) ↑16–32 in (40–80 cm)
Clump-forming perennial from eastern North America. Erect
stems; toothed lance-shaped leaves, 2–4 in (5–10 cm) long,
downy uppersurfaces. Slightly pendulous flowers, purple with
white-edged lobes, in late summer. 'Pygmaeus', 6 in (15 cm)
tall, purple flowers. Zones 3–9.

Penstemon isophyllus

☀/◐ ❄ ↔ 40 in (100 cm) ↑27 in (70 cm)
Mexican perennial. Purple-tinted stems initially spreading, then
upright. Leaves leathery, lance-shaped, to 1½ in (35 mm) long,
with slightly rolled edges. Inflorescence to 12 in (30 cm) long;
5-lobed, white-haired, red flowers. Spring-flowering. Zones 9–11.

Penstemon pinifolius

☀/◐ ❄ ↔ 16–24 in (40–60 cm) ↑16 in (40 cm)
Perennial from Arizona and New Mexico, USA, and nearby parts
of Mexico. Very narrow filament-like leaves. Bright red flowers in
summer. 'Mersea Yellow', bright yellow flowers. Zones 8–10.

Penstemon procerus

SMALL-FLOWERED PENSTEMON
☀/◐ ❄ ↔ 12–16 in (30–40 cm) ↑6–16 in (15–40 cm)
Perennial from northwestern North America. Slender stems; broad,
dark green, lance-shaped leaves, 2 in (5 cm) long. White-centered
lavender-blue and purple-pink flowers in summer. *P. p.* var. *tolmiei*, 4 in (10 cm) tall, bright lavender-blue flowers. Zones 3–9.

Penstemon strictus

STIFF BEARDTONGUE
☀/◐ ❄ ↔ 12–16 in (30–40 cm) ↑32 in (80 cm)
Clumping perennial from mountains of southwestern USA.
Long-stemmed spatula-shaped basal leaves to over 3 in (8 cm)

Penstemon heterophyllus

long, upper leaves linear to lance-shaped. Narrow heads of large-lobed violet to purple-blue flowers in summer. Zones 3–9.

Penstemon superbus

☼/◐ ❄ ↔ 20–32 in (50–80 cm) ↑ 5–6 ft (1.5–1.8 m)

Vigorous, erect, Mexican perennial. Blue-green, leathery, pointed oval leaves to 6 in (15 cm) long, sometimes partly or entirely encircling stems. Bright red flowers in summer. Zones 9–11.

Penstemon Hybrid Cultivars

☼/◐ ✹ ↔ 8–16 in (20–40 cm) ↑ 24–48 in (60–120 cm)

Modern hybrids bred with large flowers, compact habit, bright colors, and frost tolerance. 'Alice Hindley', mauve flowers, white center; 'Andenken an Friedrich Hahn' (syn. 'Garnet'), flowers paler at first, becoming purple-red; 'Apple Blossom', pink-tipped, white flowers; 'Burgundy', deep purple-red flowers; 'Chester Scarlet' ★, bright red flowers, darker throat stripes; 'Countess of Dalkeith', deep purple flowers, white throat; 'Hewell Pink Bedder', gray-green foliage, reddish pink flowers; 'Hidcote Pink', gray-green foliage, deep pink flowers, darker throat markings; 'Maurice Gibbs', purple-red flowers, white throat; 'Myddleton Gem', vivid pinkish red flowers, white throat; 'Osprey', pink flowers, white throat; 'Peace', pink and white flowers; 'Pennington Gem', deep pink flowers, red-marked white throat; 'Raven', purple-red flowers, white throat; 'Rich Ruby', purple-red flowers, darker throat; 'Schoenholzeri' (syn. 'Firebird'), deep red flowers; 'Stapleford Gem', violet and light purple tones; 'White Bedder', white flowers, sometimes pink in bud, compact habit. Zones 6–10.

PENTAS

Mainly biennials and perennials, the 30 to 40-odd species in this genus of the madder (Rubiaceae) family from tropical parts of Arabia, Africa, and Madagascar also include a few shrubs. They have ovate to lance-shaped leaves and small flowers in showy terminal heads. Flowers in all shades of pink, white, purple, mauve, and red. Dry seed heads follow the flowers.

CULTIVATION: These tender plants will not tolerate frosts or prolonged cold conditions. Cultivated outdoors in the tropics and subtropics, they are treated as house or greenhouse plants elsewhere. They are not drought tolerant and need plenty of moisture while actively growing and flowering. Plant in a moist, fertile, humus-rich, well-drained soil. Keep stem tips pinched back to ensure a compact habit. Propagate from seed or half-hardened cuttings, which strike quickly.

Pentas lanceolata

STAR CLUSTER

☼ ✚ ↔ 3 ft (0.9 m) ↑ 6 ft (1.8 m)

Found from Yemen to tropical east Africa, smaller in cultivation. Dark green velvety leaves. Large heads of flowers, white through

shades of pink to magenta to lavender-blue, in summer. 'New Look Red' ★, scarlet flowers; 'New Look Rose', deep pink flowers. The Butterfly Series includes 'Butterfly Blush', 'Butterfly Cherry Red', and 'Butterfly Light Lavender'. Zones 10–12.

PEPEROMIA

Genus of around 1,000 evergreen herbs from the pepper (Piperaceae) family, mainly originating from South America, with 17 species from Africa, and valued for their ornamental foliage. They feature fleshy leaves, usually on long stalks, and dense, erect, slender spikes of minute bisexual flowers, normally whitish cream, which are mostly produced in late summer.

CULTIVATION: In warm climates *Peperomia* species can be grown as ground covers or as epiphytes on tree trunks. Otherwise, they can be grown in pots or hanging baskets in light, well-drained compost; a soil-less mixture is best for epiphytic species. Avoid over-watering; protect from slugs and snails. Propagation is by division or from stem, tip, or leaf cuttings.

Peperomia caperata

Peperomia argyreia

syn. *Peperomia sandersii*

WATERMELON BEGONIA, WATERMELON PEPPER

◐/☀ ❄ ↔ 6–9 in (15–22 cm) ↑ 6–12 in (15–30 cm)

Evergreen succulent perennial from northern South America to Brazil. Broadly heart-shaped, thick, wrinkled, dark green, concave leaves, pointed at tip, rounded at base, silvery gray above, with dark green stripes resembling watermelon rind, on erect red stalks. White flower spikes covered with tiny yellowish white flowers. 'Emerald Ripple', corrugated, deep green leaves, greenish white flower spikes on pinkish stalks; 'Little Fantasy', dwarf form; 'Silver Ripple', tight clusters of showy, deeply corrugated or ribbed heart-shaped leaves, with variable colors from green to red and even variegated, often highlighted with frosted ridges; 'Tricolor' (syn. 'Variegata'), small leaves with broad white borders. Zones 9–12.

Peperomia caperata

◐/☀ ❄ ↔ 6–10 in (15–25 cm) ↑ 6–10 in (15–25 cm)

Bushy perennial from Brazil. Heart-shaped, dark green, deeply veined leaves; pinkish stems. White flowers. Zones 10–12.

Peperomia clusiifolia

◐/☀ ❄ ↔ 6–10 in (15–25 cm) ↑ 6–10 in (15–25 cm)

Erect semi-succulent perennial, native to the West Indies and parts of northern South America. Oval to elliptical, glandular leaves, 3 in (8 cm) long, pointed or rounded tips, taper toward base; mid-green or tinged with purple, with edges flushed with maroon, and a reddish main vein, on dark red stalks. 'Variegata', light green leaves, variegated with cream toward the edges and red margins. Zones 9–11.

Peperomia griseoargentea
IVY-LEAF PEPPER, PLATINUM PEPPER, SILVER-LEAF PEPPER
☀ ⟂ ↔ 6–8 in (15–20 cm) ↑ 6–8 in (15–20 cm)
Erect perennial herb from Brazil. Heart-shaped, leathery leaves, 1½ in (35 mm) long, pointed tips, rounded base, grayish green above, paler beneath, with deeply impressed veins, on pale green to pink stalks. Zones 9–11.

Peperomia obtusifolia
AMERICAN RUBBER PLANT, BABY RUBBER PLANT, PEPPER-FACE
☀ ⚼ ↔ 6–8 in (15–20 cm) ↑ 6–8 in (15–20 cm)
Erect or sprawling perennial found from Mexico to northern South America and the West Indies. Stems to 6 in (15 cm) long. Alternate, thick, elliptical to oval leaves, to 4 in (10 cm) long, rounded tips, wedge-shaped at base, winged stalks. '**Golden Gate**', yellow-blotched leaves; '**Variegata**', more pointed variegated pale green leaves, marked with cream or yellow toward edges; '**White Cloud**', bluish green leaves, yellow markings. Zones 10–12.

Peperomia orba
☀ ⟂ ↔ 4–6 in (10–15 cm) ↑ 4–6 in (10–15 cm)
Bushy erect perennial. Leathery and hairy, oval or elliptical, dull green leaves, lighter central stripe, pointed tips, rounded at base. Spikes of tiny green flowers. Zones 9–11.

PERICALLIS
CINERARIA
This genus of 14 species of perennials and shrubs in the daisy (Asteraceae) family, are mostly Canary Island natives. With soft, bristly or hairy leaves, some of the species carry their flowers singly but cultivated plants produce large heads of daisies. Pink to purple is the predominant flower color in the wild, but the hybrids occur in a wide range of shades.
CULTIVATION: Cinerarias prefer temperate climates; in cool areas treat as summer annuals or winter-flowering indoor plants. They like shade in summer but require more light in winter. Plant in humus-rich, cool, moist, well-drained soil. Usually propagated by seed, but the shrubby types will grow from cuttings.

Pericallis × *hybrida*
CINERARIA
❁/☀ ⟂ ↔ 16–40 in (40–100 cm)
↑ 16–32 in (40–80 cm)
Perennial hybrids ranging from small mounding plants to taller, more open, shrubby forms. Compact types have downy, angular, heart-shaped leaves, toothed edges, sometimes purplish undersides; flowerheads clustered, often densely, in a wide range of colors, from early spring to summer. Zones 9–11.

PERILLA
A genus of 6 annual herbs in the mint (Lamiaceae) family, found naturally in Asia from India to Japan. They feature tight dense spikes of tiny flowers with a 5-toothed bell-shaped calyx, and a

Pericallis × *hybrida*

shorter 5-lobed corolla tube. Opposite pairs of leaves are often variegated or colored. Fruit consists of 4 joined nutlets.
CULTIVATION: Space plants about 12 in (30 cm) apart, in rich but well-drained soil and full sun to light shade. Sow seeds outdoors in warm soil; the seeds require light to sprout. Deadhead to prevent invasive self-sowing.

Perilla frutescens var. *crispa*

Perilla frutescens
BEEFSTEAK PLANT, CHINESE BASIL, WILD SESAME
❁/❁ ❊ ↔ 18–24 in (45–60 cm)
↑ 24–40 in (60–100 cm)
Erect, finely hairy, annual herb; resembles basil. Native to the Himalayas and eastern Asia. Leaves purple or green, sometimes speckled with purple, often wrinkled, broadly oval, heavily serrated, pointed, 1½–5 in (3.5–12 cm) long, cinnamon-like scent. Spikes of small, white, pink, or reddish flowers, corolla to 4 mm across, in late summer to autumn. *P. f.* var. *crispa* (syn. *P. f.* var. *nankinensis*), with extra-crinkled bronze or dark purplish brown leaves. Zones 8–11.

PEROVSKIA
A genus of 7 deciduous subshrubs or perennials in the mint (Lamiaceae) family, and native to central Asia and the Himalayas. They are grown for their grayish foliage and large sprays of small blue flowers produced in late summer and autumn.
CULTIVATION: Plant in a sunny well-drained position. Prune heavily each winter. Propagate from softwood or half-hardened cuttings.

Perovskia atriplicifolia

RUSSIAN SAGE

☼ ❄ ↔ 18–36 in (45–90 cm) ↕ 30–60 in (75–150 cm)

Deciduous perennial from Iran, Afghanistan, and western Pakistan. Upright stems; grayish green leaves, 2–2½ in (5–6 cm) long, coarsely toothed to lobed, pungent when crushed. Narrow spikes of tiny, tubular, blue to lavender flowers in late summer–autumn. Zones 5–9.

PERSICARIA

KNOTWEED

A large and somewhat confused genus of between 50 and 80 species in the knotweed (Polygonaceae) family, found around the world. Many are alternatively listed in the genera *Bistorta, Polygonum, Tovara, Antenoron,* or *Aconogonon*. Most cultivated species are creeping perennials or occasionally subshrubs, grown for their attractive foliage or for their upright or drooping spikes of small flowers, which are usually pink turning to red as they age. Some can be quite weedy. CULTIVATION: Most knotweeds like a moist to very moist soil, in full sun to partial shade. Propagate by division or from softwood cuttings in spring.

Persicaria affinis

syns *Bistorta affinis, Polygonum affine*

☼ ❄ ↔ 20–24 in (50–60 cm) ↕ 8–10 in (20–25 cm)

Evergreen creeping perennial from the Himalayas. Upright stems; leaves to 6 in (15 cm) long. Upright spikes of tiny pink flowers in late summer. 'Darjeeling Red', larger leaves, flowers pink then red; 'Superba', tiny pink flowers turn red then brown. Zones 3–10.

Persicaria amplexicaulis

syns *Bistorta amplexicaulis, Polygonum amplexicaule*

KNOTWEED, MOUNTAIN FLEECE

☼ ❄ ↔ 3–4 ft (0.9–1.2 m) ↕ 3–4 ft (0.9–1.2 m)

Upright perennial, native to the Himalayas. Large, dense, bushy, slowly spreading clumps. Stem-clasping, dark green, sword-shaped to oval, pointed leaves, 3–10 in (8–25 cm) long, heart-shaped at base, downy underneath, on long stalks. Dense, bottlebrush-like, erect flower spikes, 3–6 in (8–15 cm) long; tiny rose red to purple or white flowers from early summer to early autumn. 'Firetail', low-growing, bright crimson flowers. Zones 4–9.

Persicaria bistorta

syn. *Polygonum bistorta*

BISTORT, EASTER LEDGES, SNAKEWEED

☼ ❄ ↔ 6–30 in (15–75 cm) ↕ 6–30 in (15–75 cm)

Perennial from northern Europe and northern and western Asia. Wavy, triangular, oval, or oblong leaves, 4–8 in (10–20 cm) long, rounded tips, flattened bases, winged stalks. Dense cylindrical spikes of white or rose pink flowers in summer. 'Superba' ★ (syn. 'Superbum'), dense spikes of soft pinkish red flowers. Zones 3–9.

Persicaria capitata

syn. *Polygonum capitatum*

KNOTWEED

☼ ❄ ↔ 6–12 in (15–30 cm) ↕ 3–6 in (8–15 cm)

Spreading perennial from the Himalayas. Silvery grayish green heart-shaped or oval leaves, 1–2 in (25–50 mm) long, with purplish maroon bands. Dense trailing heads of pink to red flowers from summer–autumn. Can become invasive in warmer regions. 'Magic Carpet', creeping form, to 4 in (10 cm) high. Zones 5–10.

Persicaria orientalis

syn. *Polygonum orientale*

KISS-ME-OVER-THE-GARDEN-GATE, ORIENTAL PERSICARY, PRINCE'S FEATHER

☼ ❄ ↔ 15–18 in (38–45 cm) ↕ 36–60 in (90–150 cm)

Annual, native to eastern and southeastern Asia and northern Australia, naturalized in North America. Oval leaves, 4–8 in (10–20 cm) long, bronze-green, soft fine hairs, branching stems. Drooping many-branched spikes of bead-like, pink, rose-purple, or white flowers, in late summer–early autumn. Zones 8–10.

Persicaria virginiana

syn. *Polygonum virginianum*

☼/❂ ❄ ↔ 32–60 in (80–150 cm) ↕ 24–48 in (60–120 cm)

Large perennial found from the Himalayas to Japan, and in northeastern USA. Pointed oval leaves, up to 6 in (15 cm) long, downy to bristly, dark markings. Tiny, pink-tinted, greenish white flowers, in late summer. 'Painter's Palette', variegated leaves, cream with yellow, green, and red-brown patches. Zones 5–9.

PETUNIA

This tropical South American genus in the nightshade (Solanaceae) family includes some 35 species of annuals, perennials, and shrubs. Most are low spreading plants with soft, downy, rounded leaves and large funnel-shaped flowers with 5 fused lobes. CULTIVATION: Plant in full sun in moist, humus-rich, well-drained soil. Flowers are vulnerable to water spray and wet weather, although modern types are sturdier. Most are raised from seed; the more reliably perennial forms all grow well from cuttings.

Persicaria bistorta

Petunia × *hybrida*, Surfinia Series, Surfinia Blue Vein/'Sunsolos'

Petunia axillaris

LARGE WHITE PETUNIA

☼/◑ ☀ ↔16–24 in (40–60 cm) ↕12–20 in (30–50 cm)
Annual from Argentina, Uruguay, and southern Brazil. Sticky, short-haired, thin leaves, rounded tips. Conical white or creamy yellow flowers, night-scented, in summer. Zones 10–12.

Petunia × *hybrida*

☼/◑ ❄ ↔8–40 in (20–100 cm) ↕4–16 in (10–40 cm)
Garden hybrids, generally low, spreading, short-lived perennials treated as annuals. 'Colorwave', a distinct cultivar propagated vegetatively. Forms are sometimes grouped in classes such as Grandiflora (large flowers), Milliflora (small flowers, compact habit), and Multiflora (many flowers, spreading habit). Popular forms include: **Carpet Series**, mounding bushes in many colors; **Celebrity Series**, compact, heavy-flowering, several color mixes; **Daddy Series**, shades of pink and purple, large flowers, veins in contrasting colors; **Fantasy Series**, very compact, many small flowers, good container plant; **Giant Victorious Series**, all-double flowers, huge color range including bicolors and picotées; **Marco Polo Series**, double-flowered, mainly pinks, mauves, and purples; **Mirage Series**, large single flowers, often light colors, striking contrasting dark veins; **Super-cascade Series**, compact but with trailing habit, wide color range; **Surfinia Series**, mainly purples, pinks, and blues; **Wave Series**, mounding bushes, large flowers. Zones 9–10.

Petunia integrifolia

☼/◑ ❄ ↔16–24 in (40–60 cm) ↕12–20 in (30–50 cm)
Annual or short-lived perennial from Argentina. Sticky, downy, elliptical leaves. Long-tubed violet flowers, purple-pink interior, to nearly 2 in (5 cm) wide, in summer. Zones 8–10.

PHACELIA

SCORPION WEED

This genus of about 150 glandular, hairy, annual, biennial, or perennial herbs belongs to the waterleaf (Hydrophyllaceae) family, and originates from North and South America. The plants have alternate leaves, divided or smooth-edged, and they bear dense terminal heads of white to purple flowers, which have a narrow 5-lobed calyx and an open to spreading bell-shaped corolla with lobed petals. The capsular fruits contain one to many brownish seeds with a pitted or furrowed appearance. The bristly hairs of this plant may cause severe dermatitis, and some species can become invasive and weedy.
CULTIVATION: Sow seed for both annuals and biennials in spring where plants are to grow, in full sun in fertile well-drained soil. Perennial species can be propagated by division.

Phacelia campanularia

syn. *Phacelia minor* var. *campanularia*

CALIFORNIA BLUEBELL, DESERT BLUEBELL, WILD CANTERBURY BELL

☼ ❄ ↔6–24 in (15–60 cm) ↕6–24 in (15–60 cm)
Annual herb from southern California, USA. Erect stems; elliptical to oval, hairy, toothed leaves. Dark blue bell-shaped flowers in early spring. Oval fruits, 40 to 80 pitted seeds. Zones 7–10.

Phacelia tanacetifolia

FIDDLENECK

☼ ❄ ↔4–24 in (10–60 cm) ↕6–60 in (15–150 cm)
Moderately fast-growing annual from California, USA, to Mexico. Covered with bristly hairs; erect, sparsely branched stem; compound, oval to oblong, toothed or lobed leaves. Blue, lilac, or mauve flowers in spring. Fruits have 1 or 2 wrinkled pitted seeds. Zones 7–10.

Phacelia tanacetifolia

PHLOMIS

This genus of about 100 low-growing shrubs, subshrubs, and herbs in the mint (Lamiaceae) family is found through Europe and Asia, from the Mediterranean regions to China. Most have felted leaves and tubular flowers in whorls along the stems. The yellow, cream, pink, mauve, or purple flowers have 2 lips at the tips.
CULTIVATION: Most are quite frost hardy, and best planted in exposed sunny positions. Drought tolerant, they generally resent receiving too much water in summer. Propagate from seed or tip cuttings from non-flowering shoots.

Phlomis cashmeriana

☼ ❄ ↔36 in (90 cm) ↕36 in (90 cm)
Native to Kashmir and the western Himalayas. Very woolly stems; narrow oval leaves, downy, white undersides. Pale lilac flowers, in crowded whorls, in summer. Zones 8–11.

Phlomis 'Edward Bowles'

☼ ❄ ↔ 36 in (90 cm) ↕ 36 in (90 cm)

Robust hybrid of uncertain parentage. Pointed oval, bright green, felted leaves, up to 6 in (15 cm) in length, wrinkled surfaces. Whorls of sulfur yellow flowers. Summer-flowering. Zones 7–11.

Phlomis purpurea

☼ ❄ ↔ 24 in (60 cm) ↕ 24 in (60 cm)

From Spain and Portugal. Woolly-stemmed; narrow, wrinkled, leathery, grayish green leaves, very hairy undersides. Whorls of downy purple to pink flowers in summer. Zones 8–11.

Phlomis russeliana

☼ ❄ ↔ 24 in (60 cm) ↕ 36 in (90 cm)

Native to just a small area of western Syria; common in cultivation. Long-stemmed heart-shaped leaves, fine hairs, especially on under-sides. Spikes of pale yellow hooded flowers in summer. Does not thrive in prolonged wet conditions. Zones 7–9.

Phlomis russeliana

Phlomis tuberosa

☼ ❄ ↔ 36 in (90 cm) ↕ 36 in (90 cm)

Tuberous-rooted deciduous perennial found from central Europe to central Asia. Lightly hairy, pointed oval leaves to 10 in (25 cm) long. Whorls of purple to pink flowers, more crowded near stem ends, in summer. Zones 6–10.

PHLOX

This North American genus of 67 annuals and perennials belongs in the phlox (Polemoniaceae) family. All types have similar terminal heads of small bell-shaped flowers with long widely flaring tubes, but growth habits differ markedly. Annual species tend to be small mounding bushes; the ground-hugging rock phlox has tiny leaves; trailing forms have long stems; and border phlox species are upright and bushy, often with plenty of foliage.
CULTIVATION: All *Phlox* species prefer well-drained soil that can be kept moist; annual and rock phlox need full sun; border and trailing forms will take part shade. Border phlox need good ventilation to prevent late-season mildew. Propagate by seed, by division, or from cuttings.

Phlox adsurgens

WOODLAND PHLOX

☼/☀ ❄ ↔ 12–20 in (30–50 cm) ↕ 4–6 in (10–15 cm)

Spreading perennial from western USA. Stem tips sometimes partly erect; oval leaves, ½–1 in (12–25 mm) long. Open flower-heads of pink to purple blooms in late spring–summer. Zones 6–10.

Phlox bifida

SAND PHLOX

☼/☀ ❄ ↔ 12–16 in (30–40 cm) ↕ 4–8 in (10–20 cm)

Tufted perennial from central USA. Sparse hairy leaves, elliptical to near-linear. Honey-scented, starry, white to lavender flowers, with notched petals, in spring–summer. Zones 6–10.

Phlox divaricata

BLUE PHLOX, WILD SWEET WILLIAM

☼/☀ ❄ ↔ 24–40 in (60–100 cm) ↕ 12–18 in (30–45 cm)

Spreading low-clump-forming perennial from central North America. Wiry stems; pointed oval to narrow lance-shaped leaves. Small heads of lavender-pink, mauve, or white flowers in spring. *P. d.* subsp. *laphamii* is best known for cultivar 'Chattahoochee' ★, 6 in (15 cm) tall, lavender flowers with red eye. Zones 4–9.

Phlox douglasii

☼/☀ ❄ ↔ 12–20 in (30–50 cm) ↕ 2–6 in (5–15 cm)

Perennial from northwestern USA. Usually mat-forming, sometimes stem tips ascend slightly. Fine downy stems; very narrow hair-fringed leaves. Flowers in showy, tightly clustered heads, mainly in deep pink, red, mauve, and purple, in spring–early summer. 'Boothman's Variety', dark-centered lavender flowers; 'Crackerjack', compact habit, magenta flowers; 'Kelly's Eye', pale pink flowers, purple-red center; 'Red Admiral', mounding to 4 in (10 cm) high, crimson flowers; 'Rosea', silvery pink flowers. Zones 5–10.

Phlox drummondii

☼/☀ ❄ ↔ 8–16 in (20–40 cm) ↕ 6–16 in (15–40 cm)

Annual from Texas, USA; now widely established as a wild-flower. Upright, sometimes sprawling stems; pointed oval to narrow lance-shaped leaves. Showy heads of small flowers, often with notched petals, bright lavender to purple-red. Summer-flowering. Mixed color seedling strains include **Beauty Series**, many colors, including yellow; **Brilliancy Series**, wide color range; **Buttons and Bows Series**, mainly bright colors, often with contrasting eye; **Phlox of Sheep Series**, primrose-centered, pastel shades including yellow, orange-red, and apricot; **Tapestry Series**, wide range of pastel shades with contrasting eye color, fragrant. Zones 6–10.

Phlox divaricata subsp. *laphamii* 'Chattahoochee'

Phlox maculata

MEADOW PHLOX, WILD SWEET WILLIAM

☼/◑ ❄ ↔ 16 in (40 cm) ↑ 27 in (70 cm)

Erect rhizome-rooted perennial from eastern USA. Thick, lustrous, dark green leaves, usually pointed oval, sometimes linear. Densely packed heads of pink, violet, or white flowers, often with purplish centers, in summer. 'Alpha', fragrant lavender pink flowers; 'Omega', fragrant white flowers, deep violet centers. Zones 5–10.

Phlox paniculata

BORDER PHLOX, SUMMER PHLOX

☼/◑ ❄ ↔ 16–40 in (40–100 cm) ↑ 24–48 in (60–120 cm)

Eastern USA perennial. Upright stems; pointed oval to lance-shaped leaves, often toothed, sometimes downy. Large rounded flowerheads, usually pink, lavender, and purple, in summer. Cultivars include 'Brigadier', apricot pink; 'Europa', white, scarlet eye, honey-scented; 'Eva Cullum', dark pink, deep pink center; 'Eventide', mauve-blue; 'Fujiyama' ★, white; 'Le Mahdi', purple-blue; 'Mother of Pearl', pale silvery pink; 'Prospero', lavender to light purple; 'Starfire', deep red; 'Tenor', scarlet; 'White Admiral', pure white; 'Windsor', white, suffused lavender blue. Zones 4–10.

Phlox stolonifera

☼/◑ ❄ ↔ 20–40 in (50–100 cm) ↑ 6–10 in (15–25 cm)

Mounding perennial from southeastern USA. Spreads by underground runners. Broad, pointed, oval leaves. Lax heads of about 6 violet to purple flowers in spring. 'Blue Ridge', glossy foliage, bright mid-blue flowers. Zones 4–9.

Phlox subulata

MOSS PHLOX, MOUNTAIN PHLOX

☼/◑ ❄ ↔ 12–20 in (30–50 cm) ↑ 2–4 in (5–10 cm)

Prostrate mat-forming perennial from eastern USA. Small, narrow, pointed leaves. Few blooms per head, but densely clustered; usually pink to lavender or white, often with notched petals, in spring–early summer. Cultivars include 'Bonita', bright pink; 'Emerald Blue', mid-blue; 'Emerald Pink', vivid pink; 'Late Red', purple-red; 'McDaniel's Cushion', bright pink; 'Scarlet Flame', deep purple-red. Zones 3–9.

PHORMIUM

FLAX LILY, NEW ZEALAND FLAX

Phormium is a genus of only 2 species of large evergreen perennials in the daylily (Hemerocallidaceae) family, and is restricted

Phlox paniculata

to New Zealand and Norfolk Island. The leaves are long and fibrous, and in summer the plants produce large candelabras of upright curved flowers, dripping nectar that is highly attractive to birds. Glossy decorative seed pods follow.

CULTIVATION: Give these plants a sunny spot in moisture-retentive soil; in frosty climates, cover them in winter. Propagate from seed, or by division of the colored leaf or dwarf clones in early spring.

Phormium cookianum

syn. *Phormium colensoi*

NEW ZEALAND MOUNTAIN FLAX

☼ ❄ ↔ 7–8 ft (2–2.4 m) ↑ 4–8 ft (1.2–2.4 m)

Arching leaves to 5 ft (1.5 m) long. Yellow-green flowers, thick petals. Glossy brown seed pods, curled and pendulous. *P. c.* subsp. *hookeri* 'Cream Delight', narrow creamy yellow bands toward edges of leaves, broader bands further in; 'Tricolor', leaves with irregular bands of creamy yellow and fine red edges. Zones 8–11.

Phormium tenax

NEW ZEALAND FLAX, NEW ZEALAND HEMP

☼ ❄ ↔ 7–10 ft (2–3 m) ↑ 10–15 ft (3–4.5 m)

Large species with upright leaves to 10 ft (3 m) long, usually gray-green in the wild forms of the species. Upright flowers, waxy, red-brown trumpets. Upright black seed heads. Purpureum Group, darker leaves. Zones 8–10.

Phormium Hybrid Cultivars

☼ ❄ ↔ 1–6 ft (0.3–1.8 m) ↑ 1–6 ft (0.3–1.8 m)

In the wild and in cultivation, the 2 *Phormium* species hybridize readily. Large number of cultivars available, in dwarf to tall sizes, with weeping or erect foliage, and range of colors and variegations. Cream and green striped cultivars include: 'Duet', to 3 ft (0.9 m); 'Tricolor', to 4 ft (1.2 m); and 'Yellow Wave', to 3 ft (0.9 m). Variegated cultivars in tones of pink, red, and bronze include: 'Rainbow Maiden' (syn. 'Maori Maiden') and 'Sundowner', both erect forms, and 'Evening Glow' and 'Pink Panther', both weeping forms. Cultivars with dark purple to black foliage include: 'Bronze Baby' and 'Tom Thumb', dwarf forms, and 'Black Prince' and 'Dark Delight', taller weeping forms. Zones 8–11.

PHYSALIS

GROUND CHERRY, HUSK TOMATO

This genus in the nightshade (Solanaceae) family consists of about 80 erect, bushy, or sprawling annual and rhizomatous perennial herbs. It is widely distributed, especially in the Americas, but also in temperate Eurasia and Australia. Alternate simple or divided leaves, sometimes roughly opposite and often in groups of 2 or 3, grow from erect or straggling stems, sometimes woody at the base. Nodding, mostly solitary flowers, on short stalks or none, grow from the leaf axils, with widely bell-shaped to open, blue, yellowish, or white corollas. The bell-shaped calyx features 5 lobes and enlarges into a papery husk enclosing the spherical, 2-celled, greenish, yellowish, orange, or purple fruits, which contain many seeds. The husks split open as fruits ripen in late summer to autumn. Unripe berries may be toxic to humans and livestock, although those of some species are edible.

CULTIVATION: Sow seed in autumn or early spring and plant out seedlings of annual species in a warm, sunny, exposed or part-shaded position, in fertile well-drained soil. Perennials can be propagated by division of rhizomes or from tip cuttings in spring.

Physalis alkekengi

ALKEKENGI, BLADDER CHERRY, CHINESE LANTERN, WINTER CHERRY
☼ ✳ ↔ 12–24 in (30–60 cm)
↑ 12–24 in (30–60 cm)
Perennial from central and southern Europe, and from western Asia to Japan. Long, creeping, underground rhizomes. Erect, leafy, finely glandular, hairy stems. Mid-green triangular to oval leaves, to 5 in (12 cm) long. Inconspicuous drooping flowers, calyx expands to 2 in (5 cm) enclosing the fruit, yellow to cream corolla, red to scarlet berries, in late summer. '**Gigantea**' (syn. 'Monstrosa'), larger growing, larger fruits. Zones 4–9.

PHYSOSTEGIA

FALSE DRAGON HEAD, OBEDIENT PLANT
A member of the mint (Lamiaceae) family, this North American genus has 2 species of upright perennials, one widely cultivated. They normally form a clump of unbranched stems, with simple, dark green, toothed, narrow, elliptical to lance-shaped leaves. In summer to autumn flowerheads of many 5-lobed tubular to bell-shaped blooms, mainly pink and purple, develop at most stem tips. CULTIVATION: These plants are hardy, and are easily grown in full or half-sun in moist well-drained soil. They spread by rhizomes that can become invasive, but provided the clumps are broken up occasionally this causes few problems. Propagate by division.

Physostegia virginiana

OBEDIENT PLANT
☼/☀ ✳ ↔ 12–20 in (30–50 cm)
↑ 32–48 in (80–120 cm)
Summer- to autumn-flowering perennial from eastern USA. Upright stems; narrow, toothed, lance-shaped leaves. Narrow conical flower spikes to 8 in (20 cm) long, downy, tubular, purple-pink flowers. Cultivars include '**Alba**', '**Rose Queen**', '**Rosea**', '**Summer Snow**', '**Variegata**', and '**Vivid**'. Zones 5–10.

PHYTOLACCA (see page 237)

Phytolacca americana

POKE, POKEBERRY, POKEWEED
☼ ✳ ↔ 3 ft (0.9 m) ↑ 12 ft (3.5 m)
Perennial from North and Central America. Can be herbaceous in severe winters. Young stems purple-red; leaves take on purple-red and pink tones in autumn. Racemes of tiny cream to pink flowers in summer–autumn. Clusters of berries follow, turning red and purple-black as they ripen. Zones 4–10.

Phytolacca americana

Phormium cookianum, in the wild, New Zealand

PILEA

This genus of about 600 creeping, sprawling, or erect annual or perennial herbs, sometimes with a woody base, is a member of the nettle (Urticaceae) family, and is native to tropical regions worldwide except for Australia. The leaves are usually opposite, often unequal, smooth-edged or serrated, covered with calcium deposits that give the appearance of opalescent spots. Minute whitish green flowers that become pinkish brown are produced on solitary flowerheads or loose panicles. The fruits are achenes. CULTIVATION: These plants require abundant moisture during active growth, in any moist well-drained soil, out of direct sunlight and drafts. Pinch out terminal buds to encourage compact bushy growth. Propagate perennial species from stem cuttings or by division in spring or summer, and annual species from seed in spring or autumn.

Pilea involucrata

FRIENDSHIP PLANT, PANAMICA
☀ ⚘ ↔ 6–12 in (15–30 cm) ↑ 4–18 in (10–45 cm)
Evergreen, bushy, hairy, trailing to erect herb. From tropical regions of Central and South America. Branches 8–12 in (20–30 cm) long; hairy, oval, toothed leaves, to 2½ in (6 cm) long, marked with bronze, red, or silver. Tiny pink or red flowers in summer. Cultivars include '**Moon Valley**', and '**Norfolk**'. Zones 10–12.

Pilea peperomioides

☀ ⚘ ↔ 6–20 in (15–50 cm) ↑ 6–20 in (15–50 cm)
Erect herb from the West Indies. Smooth elongated stems; succulent, elliptical to nearly circular, pale green, prominently veined leaves, to 3½ in (9 cm) long, on stalks to 2½ in (6 cm) long. Insignificant flowers in summer. Zones 10–12.

Pinguicula emarginata × P. vulgaris

Pinguicula moranensis

Pistia stratiotes

PINGUICULA

BUTTERWORTS, PINGS

A varied genus of more than 75 carnivorous plants belonging to the bladderwort (Lentibulariaceae) family, found in a variety of damp tropical and temperate habitats in North America, Asia, and Europe. In South America they favor drier conditions, sometimes as epiphytes. Most are perennials, with fibrous roots, very pale to bright green leaves forming a rosette, and beautiful flowers held singly on leafless stems. Some species form a tight winter resting-bud (hibernacula). Tiny glandular hairs covering the leaves produce a greasy mucilage.

CULTIVATION: Tropical species prefer an equal mix of sand, peat, and perlite, and filtered sun; keep moist in spring and summer, and just damp in winter, when succulent non-carnivorous leaves form. Feed each week in spring and summer with a weak foliar fertilizer. In temperate areas, grow in a warm greenhouse or on a sunny windowsill. Propagate from leaf cuttings of winter leaves. Temperate species prefer an equal mix of peat and sand or vermiculite, and filtered light. If grown in pots, water by tray in spring and summer; keep plants with hibernacula fairly dry in winter. Propagate from leaf cuttings. Re-pot in winter.

Pinguicula emarginata

/ ❋ ↔ 4 in (10 cm) ↕ 1½ in (35 mm)

From Mexico, found in damp sandy soil. Oval leaves, 2 in (5 cm) long. White to violet flowers, with violet to purple veins. *P. e.* × *P. vulgaris*, purple or violet flowers spotted with white. Zones 8–11.

Pinguicula moranensis ★

syn. *Pinguicula caudata*

❋ ↔ 10 in (25 cm) ↕ 2 in (5 cm)

From Mexico. Oval leaves, to 5 in (12 cm) long, slightly curved edges, sometimes tinged pink. Lavender or pink flowers, sometimes pink and white or all white. Zones 8–11.

Pinguicula vulgaris ★

COMMON BUTTERWORT

/ ❋ ↔ 5 in (12 cm) ↕ 6 in (15 cm)

From rocky mountainous areas of Europe and North America, in open grass or bogs. Leaves yellow to green, curved inward at edge. Single violet-like flowers on 6 in (15 cm) tall stems. Zones 2–7.

PISTIA

SHELL FLOWER, WATER LETTUCE

This genus, with just 1 aquatic evergreen herb, belongs to the arum (Araceae) family. Found on Lake Victoria, on Africa's Nile River, it is now widely distributed through the tropics. It has spreading feathery roots and floating rosettes of broadly wedge-shaped, ribbed, bluish green leaves in lettuce-like arrangements.

CULTIVATION: Water lettuce is best grown in aquariums and ponds in warmer climates, in a protected sunny position, out of direct sunlight in the middle of the day. Propagation is by division of plantlets in summer.

Pistia stratiotes

❋ ↔ 4–6 in (10–15 cm) ↕ 4–6 in (10–15 cm)

Aquatic herb. Rosettes of oval to hairy, round, bright green leaves, to 8 in (20 cm) long; fine, water-repellent hairs. Small flowers without petals, enclosed by a leaf-like spathe. Zones 9–11.

PITCAIRNIA

There are more than 350 species in this genus, one of the more primitive genera in the bromeliad (Bromeliaceae) family, found throughout more humid areas in the American tropics, with a single species native to Guinea, in West Africa. The few species in cultivation are very popular. Species vary greatly in size, most growing in the ground but sometimes on rocks, rarely on trees. Leaves are generally narrow and grass-like, sometimes wider, the edges sometimes toothed, forming an open erect rosette. Some species have both grass-like and short, very prickly leaves. Conspicuous red, sometimes yellow, white, or violet flowerheads are held on long slender stems above leaves. The fruit is a dry capsule.

CULTIVATION: Recommended for greenhouse or conservatory cultivation in cool temperate areas, and outdoors with protection from direct continuous sunlight in warmer areas. Water when potting mix is almost dry. Extra feeding is not necessary. Propagation is by seed or offsets.

Pitcairnia atrorubens

❋ ↔ 8 in (20 cm) ↕ 32 in (80 cm)

Found from Mexico to Colombia. Erect, open, rosettes; strap-like leaves, few small teeth. Flower stem erect; cylindrical flowerhead, erect bright red bracts spiraling to top, whitish petals. Zones 10–12.

Pitcairnia heterophylla

☀ ⚘ ↔ 20 in (50 cm) ↑ 20 in (50 cm)

From Mexico to Venezuela and Peru. Large bulb; forms clumps; leaves very thin, brown, very spiny. Short flower stem or second set of leaves emerges from center of leaf rosette. Leaves narrow, smooth-edged, to 27 in (70 cm) long. Globular flowerhead, up to 10 flowers, reddish, petals of red, orange, or white. Zones 10–12.

PLATYCODON

BALLOON FLOWER, CHINESE BELLFLOWER

The sole species in this genus in the bellflower (Campanulaceae) family is a vigorous herbaceous perennial found in Japan and nearby parts of China. It forms a clump of bold, lance-shaped leaves with toothed edges. The flowers open from enlarged, balloon-like buds and are cup- to bell-shaped, white, pink, or blue, with 5 broad lobes.

CULTIVATION: Suitable for a distinctly seasonal temperate climate. Plant in sun or part-shade in moist, humus-rich, well-drained soil. May be raised from seed; cultivars by division.

Platycodon grandiflorus

Platycodon grandiflorus

BALLOON FLOWER, CHINESE BELLFLOWER

☀/☀ ❀ ↔ 24 in (60 cm) ↑ 27 in (70 cm)

Broad lance-shaped, toothed leaves; sturdy, usually upright, sometimes sprawling stems. Bell-shaped blue, purple, white, or pink flowers open from inflated buds in summer. 'Apoyama', low growing, large deep lavender flowers; 'Fuji Blue' ★, erect habit, flowers large, blue; 'Fuji White', white flowers; 'Perlmutterschale' (syn. 'Mother of Pearl'), large pale pink flowers; 'Sentimental Blue', dwarf habit, large mauve-blue flowers. Zones 4–9.

PLECTRANTHUS

Over 200 species of annuals, perennials, and shrubs make up this large genus of herbaceous, semi-succulent or succulent plants in the mint (Lamiaceae) family. They come from Africa, Asia, Australia, and the Pacific Islands. Most are grown for their attractive evergreen foliage and ease of growing, either in the garden, in pots, or as hanging basket specimens in greenhouses where necessary. Although individual tubular flowers are usually insignificant, the massed flower display provided by the spikes is impressive.

CULTIVATION: Many of these undemanding plants can be grown as ground covers in lightly shaded areas in warmer climates or as easy-care specimens for pot or basket. Others of shrub-like proportions can be grown in a warm sheltered position. Any fertile soil or potting mix will suit; provide ample water during growing season. They are quite rapid growers; the succulent stems are easily pruned and can be used for propagating.

Plectranthus ciliatus

☀ ⚘ ↔ 4 in (10 cm) ↑ 2–4 in (5–10 cm)

Straggling evergreen herb or shrub. Native to eastern South Africa; spreads by runners. Hairy trailing stems; opposite pairs of shining hairy leaves, to 5 in (12 cm) long, purple beneath, dotted with glands. Tiny flowers, white corolla tube, 2-lobed upper lip, purple dots in lower lip, in winter–autumn. Dark brown nutlets follow the flowers. Zones 9–11.

Plectranthus ecklonii

☀ ⚘ ↔ 3 ft (0.9 m) ↑ 5 ft (1.5 m)

Bushy South African plant. Mid-green tapering leaves, prominent veining. Upright clusters of pale lilac flowers in autumn. Zones 9–11.

Plectranthus forsteri

☀ ⚘ ↔ 10 ft (3 m) ↑ 3–8 ft (0.9–2.4 m)

Sprawling herb from eastern Australia and nearby Pacific Islands. Oval, serrated, hairy leaves. Pale to mid-blue or mauve flowers. 'Marginatus' (syn. 'Variegatus'), white flowers, leaves variegated with cream. Zones 8–10.

Plectranthus neochilus

FLY BUSH, LOBSTER FLOWER, SKUNK LEAF

☀/☀ ⚘ ↔ 24 in (60 cm) ↑ 18 in (45 cm)

Sprawling succulent perennial from southern Africa. Mat-forming branches; succulent fragrant leaves, prominent veins, strong garlic-like smell when crushed. Flowerheads distinctly 4-sided, to 4 in (10 cm) long. Blue 2-lipped flowers emerge from large overlapping bracts throughout most of summer. Zones 8–11.

Plectranthus oertendahlii

☀ ⚘ ↔ 36 in (90 cm) ↑ 8–12 in (20–30 cm)

Semi-succulent, freely branching, perennial herb. Native to South Africa. Oval to nearly round, purple, hairy, scalloped leaves, to 1½ in (35 mm) long, white veins above, reddish green beneath. White or pale mauve flowers, irregularly during the year. Zones 10–11.

Plectranthus ciliatus

Plectranthus verticillatus

SWEDISH IVY

↔ 40 in (100 cm) ↑ 12 in (30 cm)

Succulent, sprawling, perennial herb from Southeast Asia, Swaziland, and Mozambique. Smooth or slightly hairy stems, to over 40 in (100 cm) long; leaves oval to rounded, toothed, to 1½ in (35 mm) long; Single or pairs of cymes; 1 to 3 white to pale mauve flowers, speckled with purple, without stalks. Zones 9–11.

PODOPHYLLUM

MAY APPLE

This genus of 7 perennial herbs from the barberry (Berberidaceae) family, found from eastern North America to eastern Asia and the Himalayas, grows from stout rhizomes. Large, palm-shaped, lobed leaves, on long stalks, and groups of single or several, overlapping, ruff- or parasol-like flowers with 6 to 9 petals, rise on erect stems, to 16 in (40 cm) tall. Large, fleshy, egg-shaped berries follow the flowers. CULTIVATION: Most may apples prefer a shady position, often in wet or marshy ground. Propagate by division or from seed.

Podophyllum peltatum

AMERICAN MANDRAKE, DEVIL'S APPLE, HOG-APPLE, INDIAN APPLE, MAY APPLE

↔ 24 in (60 cm) ↑ 24 in (60 cm)

From woodlands of eastern USA south to Texas. Single, round, simple, forked stem; 2 leaves, to 12 in (30 cm) across, with 3 to 9 lobes, finely hairy beneath. Flowering stem with 2 to 3 leaves or leafless; solitary, nodding, fragrant flowers, white or rose pink petals, with toothed points, in spring. Fruit is single berry, greenish yellow, occasionally red, flesh pulpy; ripens in late summer, only part of plant not poisonous. Zones 4–6.

POLEMONIUM

JACOB'S LADDER, SKY PILOT

A genus of 25 erect or spreading or rhizomatous annual or sometimes short-lived perennial herbs from the phlox (Polemoniaceae) family, native from temperate to Arctic regions of the Americas, Europe, and Asia. Plants have pinnate leaves with simple or divided leaflets, with or without stalks. Heads of 5-lobed, tubular,

Polemonium reptans

bell- or funnel-shaped flowers, in blue, purplish, white, or yellow, grow from the leaf axils or at the ends of sprawling or erect stems. Fruit contain 3 to 10 brown or black seeds per compartment. CULTIVATION: These plants grow well in sun or part-shade in rich, well-drained, moist, loamy soil. Propagate by division in autumn or early spring, or from seed sown in autumn or winter.

Polemonium caeruleum

CHARITY, GREEK VALERIAN, JACOB'S LADDER

↔ 12–20 in (30–50 cm) ↑ 12–36 in (30–90 cm)

Hairy and glandular perennial, found from northern and central Europe and northern Asia. Leaves to 16 in (40 cm) long, 11 to 27 sword-shaped to oblong leaflets, growing from a central base.

Blue flowers, occasionally white, widely bell-shaped corollas, oval lobes, in late spring–summer. *P. c.* subsp. *caeruleum*, many blue flowers, stamens protruding beyond corolla. *P. c.* Brise d'Anjou/'Blanjou' ★, variegated form. Zones 2–4.

Polemonium caeruleum, Brise d'Anjou/'Blanjou'

Polemonium pulcherrimum

SHOWY POLEMONIUM, WESTERN SKY PILOT

↔ 20–24 in (50–60 cm) ↑ 20–24 in (50–60 cm)

Erect, clumping, deciduous perennial. From moist to dry, often rocky slopes in northwestern North America. Slender branching rhizomes; sprawling or erect stems, 4 to 10, soft hairs; leaves grow from central base, 9 to 37 bright green, oval leaflets, fine hairs. Dense glandular clusters of flowers, bell-shaped, blue, violet, or white corolla, 2 leaf-like bracts, yellow inside, on stalks to 1 in (25 mm) long, in late spring–summer. Zones 4–7.

Polemonium reptans

ABSCESS ROOT, CREEPING JACOB'S LADDER, GREEK VALERIAN

↔ 12–27 in (30–70 cm) ↑ 8–27 in (20–70 cm)

Erect or spreading perennial, native to eastern USA. Fleshy roots; many erect, smooth, hollow, branching, herbaceous stems, sometimes tinged red, growing from small crown. Leaves 8 in (20 cm) long; 7 to 19 elliptical to oval, dull green leaflets, silvery green beneath. Drooping flowers; densely glandular, bell-shaped calyx; lilac to light blue, funnel-shaped corolla, in spring–early summer. 'Blue Pearl', to 10 in (25 cm) high, blue flowers. Zones 4–7.

POLYGALA (see page 247)

Polygala chamaebuxus

↔ 15 in (38 cm) ↑ 2–6 in (5–15 cm)

Tiny spreading shrublet from mountains of central Europe. Long, elliptical, leathery, glossy leaves. White-winged, yellow-keeled, pea-flowers. *P. c.* var. *grandiflora*, purple-winged flowers. Zones 6–9.

POLYGONATUM

SOLOMON'S SEAL

There are approximately 50 species in this genus, which is a member of the family Ruscaceae. They are found in the temperate zones of the Northern Hemisphere. Spreading by slow-growing underground rhizomes, most of these easy-to-grow herbaceous perennials are fully hardy. The taller species have graceful arching stems, attractive leaves, and carry the delicate flowers in small pendulous clusters from the upper leaf axils. Small blue-black berries often follow the flowers.

CULTIVATION: Plant in a shady or partly shady position in a rich, moist, peaty soil. Cut the stems down to soil level in late autumn. Mulch annually with leaf mold. Propagate from seed or divide the rhizomes in spring or autumn.

Polygonatum × *hybridum*
syn. *Polygonatum multiflorum* of gardens

◐/☀ ✿ ↔ 12–24 in (30–60 cm) ↕ 36 in (90 cm)

Oval green leaves turn a buttery yellow color in autumn. White, green-tipped, bell-shaped flowers hang from arching stems in late spring–early summer. Protect roots from sun. Zones 3–9.

Polygonatum odoratum
syn. *Polygonatum officinale*

ANGULAR SOLOMON'S SEAL

☀ ✿ ↔ 24 in (60 cm) ↕ 36 in (90 cm)

From Europe, northern Iran, Siberia, and Japan. Grows in woods, in limestone. Flowers mid-spring to early summer. 'Flore Pleno' ★, double flowers; 'Variegatum', white leaf edges and tips. Zones 3–9.

PONTEDERIA

A genus of 5 perennial aquatic or marginal herbs, members of the pickerel-weed (Pontederiaceae) family, from the east of North and South America and the Caribbean. Erect or prostrate stems grow from a branching, often submerged rhizome, with smooth-edged, sword-shaped, dark green leaves on long stalks. Spikes of small tubular flowers are produced, usually blue with 3 lobes, the largest lobe spotted with yellow.

CULTIVATION: Plant these perennials in full sun in ponds and bog gardens, in water 8–12 in (20–30 cm) deep. Propagate in spring by division or from seed.

Pontederia cordata
PICKEREL RUSH, PICKEREL WEED, WAMPEE

☼ ✿ ↔ 27 in (70 cm) ↕ 48 in (120 cm)

Deciduous marginal water plant found mostly in eastern North America and the Caribbean. Dense cylindrical spikes, 1–6 in (2.5–15 cm) long; blue to white flowers, to ¾ in (18 mm) wide; erect stalks, to 14 in (35 cm) tall, in late summer. Zones 2–5.

PORTEA

There are 8 species, all from the eastern states of Brazil, in this genus belonging to the bromeliad (Bromeliaceae) family. They are medium to large plants, with green strap-like leaves, toothed on the edges, forming an open rosette. The flowerhead is branched, sometimes reaching 5 ft (1.5 m) tall, each flower borne on a slender stem. The petals are generally blue-violet but sometimes red.

CULTIVATION: These plants are recommended for greenhouse or conservatory cultivation in cool temperate areas, or outdoors with protection from direct continuous sunlight and extremes

Pontederia cordata

of rain in warm temperate, subtropical, and tropical areas. Water when potting mix is dry. Extra feeding is not necessary. Propagation is mainly from offsets.

Portea petropolitana

◐ ✈ ↔ 3 ft (0.9 m) ↕ 7 ft (2 m)

From central eastern Brazil. Open rosette of long, toothed-edged, strap-like, green leaves. Flower stem to 32 in (80 cm) tall, many-branched, pyramidal flowerheads to 4 ft (1.2 m) high, each branch with open cluster of red-stemmed violet flowers, long red bract below each branch. *P. p.* var. *extensa*, longer branches, stunning in flower. Zones 10–12.

PORTULACA

PURSLANE

This genus of some 40 species occurring in the warmer parts of the world is a member of the purslane (Portulacaceae) family. They are mostly succulent herbs, usually with tuberous roots. The leaves are flat or cylindrical, opposite or spirally arranged, usually with hairs in their axils, though these are absent in the Australian species (subgenus *Portulacella*). Flowers are solitary or in heads, surrounded by a whorl of bracts formed by the upper leaves, the Australian species with distinct stalks. There are 2 sepals and usually 5 pink, purple, or yellow petals, which open in direct sun and close in shade. There are 8 to many stamens. The fruit is a small conical capsule, opening when the top falls off to release the many small seeds. The various species are often very difficult to distinguish. Some are grown as ornamentals, some for eating.

CULTIVATION: *Portulaca* species are easily grown from seed in well-drained soils in sunny but sheltered positions.

Portulaca grandiflora, Sundial Series, 'Sundial Fuchsia'

Portulaca grandiflora

syn. *Portulaca pilosa* subsp. *grandiflora*
ELEVEN-O'CLOCK, GARDEN PORTULACA, MOSS ROSE, ROSE MOSS, SUN PLANT

☀ ❋ ↔ 6–12 in (15–30 cm) ↕ 6–12 in (15–30 cm)

Slow-growing annual. Native to Brazil, Argentina, and Uruguay. Partially prostrate or climbing stem, to 12 in (30 cm) long, reddish twigs; alternate, thick, fleshy, lance-shaped, cylindrical, pale green leaves. Single or double flowers of rose, red, purple, lavender, yellow, or white, often striped, open only in sunlight. '**Sundance**', semi-double flowers remain open most of the day. Other popular cultivars include: '**Double Mix**', '**Margarita Rosita**', the **Sundial Series**, and '**Tutti Frutti Mix**'. Zones 8–10.

POTAMOGETON

PONDWEED

A genus of about 90 aquatic perennials from the pondweed (Potamogetonaceae) family, widely distributed, mostly in temperate regions of the Northern Hemisphere. They have submerged or floating, simple, elliptical, flat, green, leathery, alternate leaves growing from cylindrical or flattened upright stems, rooting at the lower nodes and usually growing from a bottom-rooting, simple or branched rhizome. Fleshy cylindrical spikes of inconspicuous flowers grow on stalks above or below the water. Plants also produce small, bulb-like, winter buds and stalkless, egg-shaped, floating fruit.
CULTIVATION: They suit aquariums and pond cultivation, in full sun. Propagate from stem cuttings in spring and summer, by division, or by planting out bulb-like winter buds.

Potamogeton perfoliatus

CLASPING LEAF PONDWEED, PERFOLIATE PONDWEED, REDHEAD GRASS

☀ ❋ ↔ 15 ft (4.5 m) ↕ 2 in (5 cm)

Freshwater pondweed. Native to eastern North America, temperate Eurasia, and eastern Australia. Branching, densely crowded stem. Stalkless, deep green, glossy, oval to heart-shaped, submerged leaves, up to 4 in (10 cm) long, heart-shaped base. Spikes of small green flowers in summer. Zones 3–10.

POTENTILLA

This is a large genus of some 500 species in the rose (Rosaceae) family from the Northern Hemisphere. While most are herbaceous perennials, the shrubby species are very hardy, thriving in most soils, in sun and in partial shade. The flowers are like small single roses, and are produced over a long period, from spring throughout summer and, in some species, well into autumn.
CULTIVATION: These plants prefer a fertile well-drained soil. Cultivars with orange, red, or pink flowers tend to fade in very strong sunshine and should be given a position where they receive some shade in the hottest part of the day. Propagation is usually from seed in autumn or cuttings in summer.

Potentilla alba

WHITE CINQUEFOIL

☀ ❋ ↔ 10 in (25 cm) ↕ 10 in (25 cm)

Low-growing, spreading, mat-forming, perennial herb from central, southern, and eastern Europe. Lower leaves dark green, palm-shaped, 5 oblong leaflets, to 2½ in (6 cm) long; stem leaves smaller, simple or divided into leaflets, silvery silky at first. Sprays of 5 white single flowers in spring–summer. Zones 3–9.

Potentilla atrosanguinea

syns *Potentilla argyrophylla* var. *atrosanguinea*, *P. leucochroa*
RED CINQUEFOIL

☀ ❋ ↔ 36 in (90 cm) ↕ 36 in (90 cm)

Clump-forming perennial herb from grassland and thickets of the Himalayas and western China. Branching stems; few branches. Semi-evergreen leaves, 3 elliptical to oval, toothed, silky leaflets, up to 3 in (8 cm) long, white hairs beneath, on long stems. Clusters of deep red to reddish purple, orange, or yellow flowers, usually with dark eyes, in late summer–early autumn. Zones 3–9.

Potentilla aurea

syns *Potentilla chrysocraspeda*, *P. halleri*, *P. ternata*

☀ ❋ ↔ 12 in (30 cm) ↕ 12 in (30 cm)

Rounded, mat-forming, perennial herb with woody base. Native to grassland and thickets of the European Alps and the Pyrenees. Hand-shaped leaves grow from a central base;
5 oblong leaflets, silver hairs along the edges and veins, toothed at tips; smaller leaves on stems. Loose clusters of few golden yellow flowers, with deeper orange centers. Spring- to summer-flowering. Zones 3–9.

Potentilla nepalensis 'Miss Willmott'

Potentilla megalantha

syn. *Potentilla fragiformis*

☀ ❋ ↔ 8–12 in (20–30 cm)
↕ 8–12 in (20–30 cm)

Clump-forming, softly hairy, tufted perennial herb. Native to Japan and the Siberian and North American tundra. Soft, palm-shaped, thick basal leaves to 3 in (8 cm) wide, 3 broad oval leaflets, scalloped edges; leaves finely hairy underneath. Solitary, rich bright yellow, 5-petalled, saucer-shaped flowers. Summer- to autumn-flowering. Zones 5–9.

Potentilla nitida 'Rubra'

Potentilla nepalensis

CINQUEFOIL

☀ ❀ ↔ 12–24 in (30–60 cm) ↕ 12–24 in (30–60 cm)

Clump-forming perennial herb. Found in thickets and grassland of the western Himalayas. Slender, erect, leafy, branching, purple stems. Palmate strawberry-like leaves, 1¼–3 in (3–8 cm) long, on tall stalks, 5 oval coarsely toothed leaflets, grow from a central base. Pink, purplish red, or crimson 5-petalled flowers in summer. 'Miss Willmott' ★ (syn. 'Willmottiae'), dwarf form, salmon pink flowers, darker pink center and veining. Zones 5–8.

Potentilla neumanniana

syns *Potentilla crantzii, P. tabernaemontani, P. verna*

SPRING CINQUEFOIL

☀ ❀ ↔ 6–12 in (15–30 cm) ↕ 3–4 in (8–10 cm)

From temperate northern, western, and central Europe. Prostrate, mat-forming, evergreen, perennial herb. Sprawling woody stem, spreads by runners. Spicily scented, strawberry-like, shiny, hand-shaped, deep green leaves, usually 5 leaflets, occasionally 3, up to 1½ in (35 mm) long, with toothed tips. Up to 12 buttery yellow 5-petalled flowers in spring. 'Nana' (syn. *P. verna* 'Nana'), vivid green leaves, gold flowers. Zones 5–8.

Potentilla nitida

☀ ❀ ↔ 5–16 in (12–40 cm) ↕ 2–4 in (5–10 cm)

From rocky areas of European Alps. Dense, tufted, downy, carpet-forming, perennial herb. Compound leaves; 3 silvery, silky leaflets, oval to nearly sword-shaped, to ½ in (12 mm) long, with 3-toothed tips. White or deep pink flowers in summer. 'Rubra', pink to rose-pink flowers. Zones 3–8.

Potentilla × tonguei

☀ ❀ ↔ 12–20 in (30–50 cm) ↕ 6–10 in (15–25 cm)

Perennial herb of garden origin. Sprawling, non-rooting stems; compound leaves, 3 to 5 narrowly oval, coarsely toothed leaflets. Apricot corolla and carmine red eye, in summer. Zones 3–5.

PRIMULA

COWSLIP, POLYANTHUS, PRIMROSE

This widespread, mainly Northern Hemisphere, perennial genus gives its name to the family Primulaceae. Most primulas form basal rosettes of heavily veined leaves from which emerge the flower stems, sometimes with just a single bloom, but often with a large terminal head or several well-shaped whorls of flowers. CULTIVATION: The majority of *Primula* species prefer dappled shade in woodland gardens and moist, humus-rich, well-drained soil. So-called bog primroses like damper conditions and often naturalize along streams. Propagate from seed or by dividing thriving clumps when dormant.

Primula alpicola

◐/☀ ❀ ↔ 10–16 in (25–40 cm) ↕ 16–36 in (40–90 cm)

Native to the Himalayas. Prefers wet peaty soil. Toothed elliptical leaves. Flowers white, yellow, mauve, purple, on stems with powdery white coating, in late spring–early summer. Zones 6–9.

Primula auricula

◐/☀ ❀ ↔ 6–16 in (15–40 cm) ↕ 4–8 in (10–20 cm)

From mountains of southern Europe. Clump-forming; foliage and stems with dusty coating. Leaves fleshy, light green, rounded to broad lance-shaped, usually toothed; heads of few to many flat, ½–1 in (12–25 mm) wide spring flowers on 6 in (15 cm) stems, in the wild mostly yellow or purple-red with yellow center, some with white band. Cultivars include 'Alicia', dark purple-red, edges lighter; 'Beatrice', purple, mauve border, cream center; 'Butterwick', red-brown, golden yellow center; 'C. W. Needham', dark purple-blue, yellow-green center; 'Dales Red', red, heavy powdery white coating and white band, yellow center; 'Hawkwood', red, white edge and band, yellow center; 'Jeannie Telford', purple-red, mauve edge, cream center; 'Lavender Lady', light purple,

Primula alpicola

white center; 'Lucy Locket', buff yellow, cream center; 'Rowena', maroon, lavender edges, yellow center, white band; 'Sirius', coffee-colored, purplish red markings, yellow center; 'Spring Meadows', cream, yellow-green center, light green edges; and 'Trouble', pinkish beige double flowers. Zones 3–9.

Primula beesiana

◐/☀ ❀ ↔ 20 in (50 cm) ↕ 32 in (80 cm)

Native to Himalayan area of western China. Narrow, toothed leaves lengthen as seed heads ripen. Candelabra-style flowerheads with up to 8 whorls; flowers deep pink, yellow-centered, in summer. Zones 5–9.

Primula bulleyana

◐/☀ ❀ ↔ 12–27 in (30–70 cm) ↕ 24 in (60 cm)

Native to southwestern China. Basal rosette; leaves toothed and tapering to narrow base. Candelabra-style flowerheads with up to 7 whorls of golden yellow to orange flowers in late spring–early summer. Zones 6–9.

Primula denticulata

Primula juliae

Primula, Pruhonicensis Hybrid, 'Iris Mainwaring'

Primula capitata

☽/☀ ❋ ↔ 12–18 in (30–45 cm) ↑ 10–15 in (25–38 cm)
From the Himalayas. Stems and undersides of foliage powdery
white; leaves coarsely toothed. Sturdy erect flower stems, somewhat flattened heads of many small, violet to purple flowers, in
late spring–early summer. Zones 5–9.

Primula denticulata

DRUMSTICK PRIMULA

☽/☀ ❋ ↔ 10–18 in (25–45 cm) ↑ 8–12 in (20–30 cm)
Found from mountains of Afghanistan to Myanmar. Flower stems
and undersides of toothed leaves are downy white. Overwinters
as conical bud; rounded heads of mauve to purple-red, rarely
white, flowers in spring, with or before new leaves. Zones 5–9.

Primula elatior

OXLIP

☽/☀ ❋ ↔ 6–16 in (15–40 cm) ↑ 6–12 in (15–30 cm)
Eurasian perennial. Forms clump of long-stemmed, toothed,
rounded to elliptical leaves, undersides sometimes downy. Rather
wiry flower stems; heads of pale yellow flowers, in spring–early
summer. Zones 5–9.

Primula farinosa

☽/☀ ❋ ↔ 12 in (30 cm) ↑ 8 in (20 cm)
Found from Scotland to northwestern Pacific. Bright green leaves,
spatula-shaped, wavy edges can be toothed or smooth. Short
flower stems; heads of usually a few, sometimes many, bright
pink, starry flowers, notched petals. Spring-flowering. Zones 4–9.

Primula florindae

☽/☀ ❋ ↔ 8–16 in (20–40 cm) ↑ 36 in (90 cm)
Native to Tibet. Long-stemmed, broad pointed oval, toothed
leaves. Tall sturdy flower stems; heads of up to 40 scented yellow
flowers in late spring–early summer. **Keillour Group** (hybrids with
P. × *waltonii*), flowers in oranges, reds, and yellow tones. Zones 6–9.

Primula japonica

☽/☀ ❋ ↔ 12–24 in (30–60 cm) ↑ 18 in (45 cm)
Native to Japan. Clump-forming; broad, coarsely toothed, spatula-
shaped leaves to 10 in (25 cm) long. Stems bear up to 6 whorls

of white, pink, magenta to red flowers, to ¾ in (18 mm) wide,
in late spring–early summer. '**Postford White**', white flowers, pink
eye; '**Valley Red**', bright pinkish red flowers. Zones 5–9.

Primula juliae

☽/☀ ❋ ↔ 6–10 in (15–25 cm) ↑ 2 in (5 cm)
Native to the Caucasus. Rounded, toothed leaves, red-tinted
leaf stems. Flowers among foliage, solitary, mauve to purple-red,
conspicuous yellow eye, in spring. Flowers can appear before
foliage. Zones 5–9.

Primula × kewensis

☽/☀ ❄ ↔ 12–18 in (30–45 cm) ↑ 12 in (30 cm)
Hybrid, probably between *P. floribunda* and *P. verticillata*. Faintly
powdery, toothed, spatula-shaped leaves. Closely spaced whorls of
fragrant yellow flowers in spring. Zones 9–10.

Primula malacoides

☼/☀ ❋ ↔ 16 in (40 cm) ↑ 12 in (30 cm)
From China. Winter-flowering, usually short lived; treated as annual. Long-stemmed, downy, rounded leaves, lobed and coarsely
toothed. Numerous flower stems; heads of up to 20 lavender
flowers. Cultivars in pink, lavender, purple, and white. Zones 8–10.

Primula obconica

GERMAN PRIMROSE, POISON PRIMROSE

☽/☀ ❄ ↔ 8–16 in (20–40 cm) ↑ 8 in (20 cm)
Perennial from southern China. Broad elliptical leaves; fine
downy hairs, frequently causing contact dermatitis. Open heads
of up to 15 lavender to purple flowers, notched petals, in winter.
Mixed-color seed strains include '**Libre Mixed**', large flowers in
apricots, pinks, mauves, purples, and white. Zones 9–10.

Primula, Pruhonicensis Hybrids

POLYANTHUS

☽/☀ ❋ ↔ 6–16 in (15–40 cm) ↑ 4–12 in (10–30 cm)
Complex group of garden and natural hybrids, ranging from very
small, long-lived, rock-garden types, such as '**Wanda**' (purple-red
flowers) to large showy hybrid polyanthus (usually mixed color
seedling selections, such as the **Crescendo**, **Kaleidoscope**, **Pacific
Giants**, and **Rainbow Series**), which are often treated as annuals.

Also single-flowered hybrids; rosebud-double-flowered types ("double primroses"); hose-in-hose, appearing to have two blooms sleeved one within the other, and "gold-" or "silver-laced" forms with light-edged brownish black flowers. Popular single-flowered forms include: **'Dorothy'**, pale yellow flowers; **'Guinevere'** (syn. 'Garryard Guinevere'), bronze-green leaves, white flowers, red stems and sepals; **'Iris Mainwaring'**, mauve-blue suffused with pink; **'Old Port'**, deep purple-red; **'Schneekissen'**, dark green foliage, pure white flowers; and **'Velvet Moon'**, very dark foliage, deep velvet red flowers. Double primroses include: **'April Rose'**, deep red flowers; **Bon Accord Series**, series of doubles mainly named by color, such as **'Bon Accord Purple'**; **'Ken Dearman'**, apricot-pink suffused with yellow, deep pink buds; and **'Sunshine Susie'**, bright yellow to gold flowers. Zones 7–9.

Primula × pubescens
☼/◐ ❄ ↔ 10 in (25 cm) ↕ 6 in (15 cm)
Hybrid between *P. auricula* and *P. hirsuta*. Leaves often powdery, toothed, usually quite rounded, to 4 in (10 cm) long. Small flowerheads, short stems, most shades, except darker blue. **'Boothman's Variety'** (syn. 'Carmen'), deep crimson, white center; **'Harlow Car'**, cream; **'Wharfedale Buttercup'**, sulfur yellow. Zones 5–9.

Primula pulverulenta
☼/◐ ❄ ↔ 20 in (50 cm) ↕ 36 in (90 cm)
Native to China. Coarsely toothed leaves to 12 in (30 cm) long. Tall flower stems, candelabra-like; several whorls of purple-red flowers, dark red centers, in late spring–summer. **Bartley hybrids**, typically dark-centered pink-red flowers. Zones 6–9.

Primula rosea
☼/◐ ❄ ↔ 6–15 in (15–38 cm) ↕ 4–6 in (10–15 cm)
From northwest Himalayas. Toothed leaves develop slowly, often flushed bronze when young. Glowing deep pink flowers appear before foliage, or before it is fully expanded. Heads of up to 12 flowers, notched petal tips, in spring. **'Grandiflora'**, large flowers on tall stems. Zones 6–9.

Primula sieboldii
☼/◐ ❄ ↔ 12–24 in (30–60 cm) ↕ 12 in (30 cm)
Native to Japan and nearby parts of temperate mainland Asia. Leaves very coarsely toothed, indented heart-shaped base. White, pink, or purple flowers, in small heads, in late spring–summer. **'Blush Pink'** ★, bright pink flowers, hint of apricot; **'Cloth of Mist'**, pale lavender flowers; **'Mikado'**, dark purple-pink flowers. Zones 5–9.

Primula sikkimensis
☼/◐ ❄ ↔ 10–24 in (25–60 cm)
↕ 12–36 in (30–90 cm)
Native to Nepal and the Chinese western Himalayas. Dark green, serrated to toothed leaves.

Primula rosea

Heads of partly pendulous flowers, white to yellow and funnel-shaped, sturdy erect stems, in late spring–early summer. Zones 6–9.

Primula veris
COWSLIP
☼/◐ ❄ ↔ 16 in (40 cm) ↕ 12 in (30 cm)
Eurasian species. Leaves smooth-edged to coarsely toothed, 2–8 in (5–20 cm) long, undersides sometimes downy. Downy flower stems, heads of up to 16 fragrant yellow flowers, in late spring–early summer. *P. v.* subsp. *columnae,* pointed oval leaves, downy white undersides; *P. v.* subsp. *macrocalyx,* large hairy calyces, larger flowers, rounded leaves. Zones 5–9.

Primula vulgaris
ENGLISH PRIMROSE, PRIMROSE
☼/◐ ❄ ↔ 6–16 in (15–40 cm)
↕ 4–6 in (10–15 cm)
European species. Leaves toothed, sometimes coarsely, undersides often faintly downy. Fragrant pale yellow flowers emerge at ground level on thin stems in spring. Extensively hybridized. *P. v.* subsp. *sibthorpii*, very compact, light mauve-pink flowers. *P. v.* **'Blaue Auslese'** (syn. 'Blue Selection'), lavender blue flowers; **'Quaker's Bonnet'**, lavender pink flowers. Zones 6–9.

PRUNELLA
syn. *Brunella*
HEAL ALL, SELF-HEAL
These 7 semi-evergreen, spreading, sprawling perennial herbs in the mint (Lamiaceae) family are from temperate Eurasia, North Africa, and North America. Leaves are opposite with generally smooth-edged blades, on stalks from the base of the plant or from the stems. Bluish violet or purplish red, tubular to bell-shaped flowers, with an erect, hooded, 2-lipped corolla with 3 lobes, are surrounded by leaf-like bracts. Fruit is an egg-shaped nutlet.
CULTIVATION: They grow well in sun or shade in dry to moist well-drained soil. Propagate from seed or by division in spring.

Primula sieboldii 'Mikado'

Prunella grandiflora 'Loveliness'

Prunella grandiflora

BIGFLOWER, LARGE SELF-HEAL, SELF-HEAL

☀ ❊ ↔ 12–24 in (30–60 cm) ↕ 12–24 in (30–60 cm)

European mat-forming herb. Woody branching stems; tiny, oval to sword-shaped leaves, scalloped edges. Off-white, pale blue, or purple flowers, deep violet lips, in summer. 'Loveliness' ★, pale lilac flowers; 'Pink Loveliness', pink flowers. Zones 4–9.

Prunella laciniata

☀ ❊ ↔ 9–12 in (22–30 cm) ↕ 9–12 in (22–30 cm)

From southwestern and central Europe. Lobed or divided leaves, to 3 in (8 cm) long, densely covered with fine hairs. Spikes of yellowish white flowers, sometimes rose pink or purple, in spring–summer. Zones 6–9.

PSYLLIOSTACHYS

A genus of around 10 species of annuals in the leadwort (Plumbaginaceae) family, ranging in the wild from the eastern Mediterranean and Black Sea region to central Asia. Often treated in the past as species of the larger genus *Limonium* (statice). The leaves are mostly in a basal rosette and may be deeply lobed. Flowers are tiny, usually pink, in small clusters that are densely crowded onto branched cylindrical spikes.

CULTIVATION: *Psylliostachys* species are readily grown in full sun in any reasonably fertile soil. Water freely in warmer months, do not over-fertilize. Sow seed in spring, covering seed trays as germination requires darkness and even then may be erratic.

Psylliostachys suworowii

syns *Limonium suworowii, Statice suworowii*

☀ ❊ ↔ 12–16 in (20–40 cm)
↕ 12–36 in (30–90 cm)

Erect branching annual. Native to central Asia and Iran. Glossy green leaves, 6 in (15 cm) or more long, wavy-edged to deeply lobed. Flowers pale pink to deep rose pink, in summer–early autumn. Zones 7–10.

PULMONARIA

LUNGWORT

This genus of 14 temperate Eurasian perennials of the borage (Boraginaceae) family overcomes its rather unappealing name by being indispensable for woodland, perennial border, and rock-garden cultivation. Their simple, long-stemmed, lance-shaped leaves are sometimes white spotted and can grow to a considerable size. The first flowers, while welcome, are sparse but, as spring warms further, the plants carry larger heads of small 5-petalled blooms. Flowers are usually blue, though white and pink forms are common.

CULTIVATION: Lungworts are very hardy and need a temperate climate with distinct seasons. They can be grown in full sun, but are best cultivated in moist, humus-rich, well-drained soil, in a partly shaded position. Propagate by division, or from basal cuttings or seed.

Pulmonaria angustifolia

BLUE COWSLIP, BLUE LUNGWORT

◑/☀ ❊ ↔ 16–40 in (40–100 cm) ↕ 8–16 in (20–40 cm)

Native to Europe. Spreading mat of unspotted, pointed oval leaves to 12 in (30 cm) long. Heads of bright blue flowers in spring. Often blooms before foliage is fully expanded. *P. a.* subsp. *azurea*, intense gentian blue flowers, no purple tones. Zones 3–9.

Pulmonaria mollis

◑/☀ ❊ ↔ 40 in (100 cm) ↕ 16 in (40 cm)

European species. Leaves downy, usually unspotted, to 20 in (50 cm) long. Flowers violet to purple-blue; in early spring–summer. Several pink- or white-flowered cultivars. Zones 6–9.

Pulmonaria rubra

◑/☀ ❊ ↔ 20–40 in (50–100 cm) ↕ 12–18 in (30–45 cm)

Native to Europe. Leaves often spotted white or silver-gray. Small heads of light red flowers, sometimes mauve tinted; flower stems tend to be erect. Spring- to early summer-flowering. 'Bowles' Red', white-spotted leaves, red-pink flowers; and 'David Ward', creamy white-edged leaves, red-pink flowers. Zones 6–9.

Pulmonaria saccharata

JERUSALEM SAGE

◑/☀ ❊ ↔ 16–32 in (40–80 cm)
↕ 12–16 in (30–40 cm)

Native to northern Italy, flowers after foliage is well developed. Spring leaves are small, lance-shaped, spotted, summer leaves larger. Flowers white, or shades of mauve to purple or purple-red. Argentea Group, silver-mottled leaves, mauve-blue flowers; 'Dora Bielefeld', white- or lighter green-spotted leaves, mauve-pink flowers;

Pulmonaria saccharata

'Janet Fisk', silver-spotted and marbled leaves, purple flowers opening from red buds; 'Leopard', white-spotted leaves, purplish pink flowers; and 'Mrs Moon', white-spotted leaves, red-tinted mauve flowers. Zones 3–9.

Pulmonaria vallarsae

◑/☀ ✳ ↔ 20–40 in (50–100 cm)
↑ 12–18 in (30–45 cm)

Northern Italian species. Forms clump of
finely hairy, often white-spotted or variegated
leaves. First flowers appear with new growth,
red-tinted buds open to purple flowers, in
early spring–early summer. Zones 6–9.

Pulmonaria Hybrid Cultivars

◑/☀ ✳ ↔ 16–40 in (40–100 cm)
↑ 8–16 in (20–40 cm)

Lungworts hybridize freely, in the wild and
in cultivation; many widely grown hybrids.
Modern forms tend to have showy variegated
foliage and short flower stems. '**Benediction**',
silver-flecked leaves, mauve-blue flowers;
'**Beth's Pink**', broad spotted leaves, mauve-
pink flowers; '**Blue Pearl**', small rounded
leaves, light blue flowers; '**High Contrast**',
silver-gray leaves, with irregular green edges,
flowers deep pink ageing to purple-blue; '**Lewis Palmer**', white-
spotted leaves, purple-blue flowers; '**Margery Fish**' ★, silver-
mottled foliage, pink flowers ageing to blue; '**Purple Haze**',
white-spotted leaves, purple flowers; '**Roy Davidson**', long silver-
spotted leaves, light blue flowers; '**Silver Mist**', leaves spotted silvery white, red-pink flowers; '**Silver Streamers**', large silver-gray
leaves with ruffled edges, pink flowers darkening with age;
'**Sissinghurst White**', large white-spotted leaves, white flowers,
produced early in season; '**Smoky Blue**', dark green white-spotted
leaves, purplish blue flowers; and '**Trevi Fountain**', silver-spotted
leaves, open sprays of deep blue flowers. Zones 6–9.

Pulmonaria, Hybrid Cultivar, 'Silver Mist'

PULSATILLA

PASQUE FLOWER

These beautiful Eurasian and North American
relatives of the anemones race into growth in
early spring. They are members of the buttercup (Ranunculaceae) family. They form
clumps of ferny leaves, which are silvery in
most species from a dense covering of fine
hairs. Long-stemmed, very graceful, cup- or
bell-shaped flowers in a wide color range.
Carried singly, the blooms have 5 to 8 petals
and a prominent boss of golden stamens.
CULTIVATION: Pasque flowers need a seasonal
temperate climate. They grow well in wood-
land conditions but are at their best in rock gardens with sun or
part-shade, in gritty, humus-rich, well-drained yet moist soil.
Propagate by division when dormant, or raise from seed.

Pulsatilla vulgaris

Pulsatilla albana

☼/◑ ✳ ↔ 8 in (20 cm) ↑ 8 in (20 cm)

From alpine meadows of the Caucasus and northeastern Turkey.
Finely cut pinnate foliage. Hairy stems and buds; nodding, bell-
shaped, yellow flowers, in late spring–early summer. Zones 5–9.

Pulsatilla halleri

☼/◑ ✳ ↔ 12 in (30 cm) ↑ 10 in (25 cm)

From mountains of central and southeastern Europe. Densely
covered with silky silvery hairs. Blooms often well advanced
before finely divided feathery foliage appears. Flowers erect,
usually upward-facing, violet to lavender blue. Zones 5–9.

Pulsatilla patens

EASTERN PASQUE FLOWER

☼/◑ ✳ ↔ 8–12 in (20–30 cm) ↑ 6–10 in (15–25 cm)

Found from northern Europe to Siberia and Alaska, USA. Leaves
lightly hairy, heavy textured, less finely divided than most silvery
species. Flowers quite late in season, purple
shades, sometimes with yellow tint, rarely
white, stems silky. Zones 4–9.

Pulsatilla pratensis

☼/◑ ✳ ↔ 16 in (40 cm) ↑ 12 in (30 cm)

Found throughout most of Europe. Entire
plant covered with dense, silky, silvery hairs.
Foliage very finely divided. Pendent, narrow
bell-shaped flowers, to 1½ in (40 mm) wide,
mauve to deep purple. Spring-flowering.
P. p. subsp. *bohemica,* small flowers, very
dark purple. Zones 5–9.

Pulsatilla vulgaris

syn. *Anemone pulsatilla*

PASQUE FLOWER

☼/◑ ✳ ↔ 8–16 in (20–40 cm) ↑ 8–15 in (20–38 cm)

From Britain through Europe to Ukraine. Covered in fine, silky,
silvery hairs. Very finely divided feathery foliage. Mauve to purple
flowers usually upward-facing, open bell-shaped, in spring. '**Alba**',
white flowers; '**Papageno**' (syn. *P. v.* subsp. *grandis* 'Papageno'),
mixed color strain; '**Rubra**', red flowers. Zones 5–9.

Puya berteroniana

Puya venusta

PUYA

More than 200 species, mainly from the South American Andes, make up this ground-dwelling genus in the bromeliad (Bromeliaceae) family, most of which prefer colder conditions than other bromeliads. Many are large plants forming trunks, and are not often seen in private gardens; they are popular in botanic gardens in subtropical areas. One species reaches a height of 35 ft (10 m) in flower; the smallest species reaches only 3 in (8 cm) high. They form rosettes of narrow-triangular leaves, usually with large spines along the edges. Flowerheads may be cylindrical or pyramidal and branched, and the flowers are generally large and showy. CULTIVATION: Recommended for greenhouse, conservatory, or outdoor cultivation in cool temperate areas; some species will adapt to warmer areas if kept on the dry side. Water when potting mix is dry. Extra feeding may speed up their slow-growing habit. Propagation is by seed or from offsets of most species.

Puya berteroniana
☼ ❊ ↔ 7 ft (2 m) ↕ 15 ft (4.5 m)
From central Chile. Forms trunk with age. Leaves green, narrow-triangular, strongly toothed edges; form dense rosette. Flower stem stout, to 10 ft (3 m) high. Flowerhead to 40 in (100 cm) long and 20 in (50 cm) wide, up to 100 side branches, each with about 15 large blue-green flowers. Upper part of branches without flowers. Zones 7–9.

Puya chilensis
☼ ❊ ↔ 7 ft (2 m) ↕ 15 ft (4.5 m)
From central Chile. Forms trunk with age. Leaves green, narrow-triangular, strongly toothed edges; form dense rosette. Stout erect flower stem to 12 ft (3.5 m) tall. Flowerhead over 40 in (100 cm) long, up to 100 side branches, each with up to 12 large yellow flowers. Upper part of branches without flowers. Zones 7–9.

Puya venusta
☼ ❊ ↔ 20 in (50 cm) ↕ 40 in (100 cm)
From coastal Chile. Clump-forming, branching plant. Leaves gray-green, narrow-triangular, toothed-edged; form dense rosette.

Flower stem stout, bright red. Flowerheads reddish, like pine cones, at end of some branches, flowers deep violet. Zones 8–9.

QUESNELIA

The 16 species in this genus in the bromeliad (Bromeliaceae) family are indigenous to southeastern Brazil and fall into two main groups: one containing plants that form large clumps and have a flowerhead in the form of an elongated cone with startlingly bright, red, erect bracts; the other made up of plants that are not clump-forming and mostly having an open flowerhead reminiscent of *Billbergia* but with the petals uniform rather than opening at an angle. The leaves are green and strap-like, with some teeth on the edges, forming an open rosette. Petals may be red, blue, or yellow. CULTIVATION: Recommended for indoor culture in the greenhouse or conservatory in cool-temperate areas, or outdoors with protection from direct continuous sunlight and extremes of rain in warmer areas. Water when soil is dry. Extra feeding is generally not necessary. Propagation is mainly by offsets.

Quesnelia liboniana
☀ ❄ ↔ 4 in (10 cm) ↕ 32 in (80 cm)
From Brazil's Rio de Janeiro area. Forms offsets on small rhizomes; leaves few, strap-like, few teeth on edges, forming a tube that soon flares out. Slender flower stem; short cylindrical flowerhead, with about 8 well-separated red flowers emerging at all angles. Petals are blue. Zones 9–12.

Quesnelia marmorata
☀ ❄ ↔ 4 in (10 cm) ↕ 24 in (60 cm)
From central eastern Brazil. Few stiff, strap-like leaves, dark green or brown irregular cross-bands and toothed edges, forming tight tube that flares at top. Flowerhead just emerging from leaf tube, pyramidal, spreading branches on all sides becoming smaller toward top. Large red bracts below branches tend to droop. Flowers mainly violet, petals blue. Zones 10–12.

RAMONDA

The 3 species in this small genus in the African violet (Gesneriaceae) family are evergreen, rosette-forming, alpine plants, found from the mountains of northeastern Spain to the Balkans. The flowers, held well above the rich green heavily veined leaves in late spring and early summer, are 4- or 5-petalled, somewhat flat-faced, and come in white to pink and lavender to violet-blue. CULTIVATION: These plants are for cool to cold climates only, and due to their dislike of winter wet they are usually grown in a cool greenhouse or on their sides in a drystone wall. Propagation is quite difficult from seed. They are usually propagated by division or, better still, from leaf cuttings taken in late summer.

Ramonda myconi
syn. *Ramonda pyrenaica*
◑ ❊ ↔ 7–8 in (18–20 cm) ↕ 4–5 in (10–12 cm)
Rosette-forming perennial. Native to northeastern Spain. Ovate, hairy, crinkled, rich green leaves. Violet-blue 5-petalled flowers, to 1 in (25 mm) across, yellow anthers, in clusters held above leaves, in

late spring–early summer. 'Rosea', pink-flowered form; a white form is also grown. Zones 6–9.

RAOULIA
SCABWEED

Found in screes or open rocky places from sea level to alpine areas throughout New Zealand, the 20 to 30 species of tiny-leafed, cushion- or mat-forming, evergreen perennials or subshrubs that make up this genus are members of the daisy (Asteraceae) family. The leaves are green or silvery in appearance, caused by minute silky hairs. The flowers are tiny, disc-like, and pale white, cream, or yellow. Many botanists now regard *Raoulia* as an unnatural group and propose that some of the species should go into a distinct genus, *Psychrophyton*.
CULTIVATION: Grow *Raoulia* species in full sun in moist well-drained soil. They will do well in pots, troughs, or rock gardens. Propagate from seed or from sections of the mat (rooted stems).

Raoulia australis
syn. *Raoulia lutescens*
COMMON MAT DAISY, GOLDEN SCABWEED
☼ ❊ ↔ 12 in (30 cm) ↑ ½ in (12 mm)
From New Zealand's South Island. Mat-forming perennial; layers itself as it creeps. Tiny leaves, gray or silver. Yellow flowers, 5 mm wide, in summer. Zones 7–9.

Raoulia eximia
TUTAHUNA, VEGETABLE SHEEP
☼ ❊ ↔ 20 in (50 cm) ↑ 12 in (30 cm)
From New Zealand's South Island. Dense cushion-like perennial, eventually forming large mounds. Tiny flowers, yellowish white. Summer-flowering. These plants resemble sheep sitting down, giving rise to one of the common names. Zones 7–9.

RATIBIDA
CONEFLOWER

This genus in the daisy (Asteraceae) family contains 5 biennial or perennial species that are found throughout North America, from Ontario, Canada, through to New York, Minnesota, South Dakota, Nebraska, south to Georgia and Texas, USA, and into northern Mexico. These plants are stiff and erect, with deeply cut leaves that are covered with rigid hairs. The flowerheads are similar to those of *Rudbeckia* species but have fewer ray florets and a round or cylindrical central disc, unlike the flat disc of the *Rudbeckia* flowerheads. The crushed seed heads have an aromatic anise scent.

Ramonda myconi 'Rosea'

CULTIVATION: Ideal for casual settings, in native flower gardens, or cottage gardens. Plant in full sun in a very well-drained soil. Propagation is from seed, which will self-sow.

Ratibida columnifera
MEXICAN HAT, PRAIRIE CONEFLOWER
☼ ❊ ↔ 18 in (45 cm) ↑ 24 in (60 cm)
Perennial, from North America and Mexico. Hairy gray-green leaves. Flowers bright yellow or brown-purple, in drooping rays; cylindrical or columnar brown floral disc. Summer- to autumn-flowering. Zones 4–9.

Ratibida pinnata
GRAY-HEAD CONEFLOWER, PRAIRIE CONEFLOWER, YELLOW CONEFLOWER
☼ ❊ ↔ 12–18 in (30–45 cm) ↑ 48 in (120 cm)
Perennial from eastern North America. Leaves lance-shaped, blue-green, toothed. Yellow ray flowers, rounded brown disc, from mid-summer to early autumn. Zones 3–8.

Ratibida columnifera, in the wild, Mexico

REHMANNIA
CHINESE FOXGLOVE

This genus of up to 9 species of herbaceous perennials in the fox-glove (Scrophulariaceae) family is native to the woods and hills of China. The foliage is heavily serrated and hairy to sticky. The blooms, produced over a long period, are usually a magenta-pink with patterns of brown and yellow in the throat.
CULTIVATION: Grow these perennials in moisture-retentive but not wet, humus-rich soil in a spot that receives lots of light but not the very hottest sun. Propagate from seed, or from stem cuttings early in the growth cycle, or more usually by division.

Rehmannia elata
syn. *Rehmannia angulata* of gardens
CHINESE FOXGLOVE

☀ ❄ ↔ 20–32 in (50–80 cm) ↑ 40–60 in (100–150 cm)
Vigorous suckering perennial from China. Lobed hairy leaves, to 10 in (25 cm) long, in basal foliage. Slightly drooping trumpet flowers, to 4 in (10 cm) long, heavily spotted in throat, in late spring–summer. Zones 8–10.

REINECKEA

This genus, a member of the family Ruscaceae, contains 1 species of grassy-leafed, rhizomatous, evergreen perennial, and is native to China and Japan. Its prostrate stems form clumps of narrow glossy foliage. Flowering stems, to 6 in (15 cm) in height, bear small fragrant flowers in varying shades of pink.
CULTIVATION: This perennial will do well in half-sun in a rich, moisture-retentive, but well-drained soil. Where summers are cool, flowering may be limited. Propagate from seed or by division.

Reineckea carnea
☀ ❄ ↔ 6–12 in (15–30 cm) ↑ 8 in (20 cm)
Native to China and Japan. Clump-forming perennial. Narrow arching leaves. Pink buds open to near-white flowers, spreading starry petals, in late spring. Small scarlet berries. Zones 7–10.

RESEDA
MIGNONETTE

This genus of some 50 to 60 species of annuals and perennials gives its name to the mignonette (Resedaceae) family. Although mainly from the Mediterranean area, some species come from India, Asia, and East Africa. They have small leaves that can be smooth-edged or lobed to toothed, and bear tiny flowers in up-right spikes that are rarely showy, usually green or white, and in some species sweetly fragrant. All are good bee-attractant plants.
CULTIVATION: These plants will all grow well in a sunny site in fer-tile, well-drained, and preferably alkaline soil. Propagate from seed planted in position and thin out as seedlings get larger.

Reseda lutea
YELLOW MIGNONETTE
☀ ❄ ↔ 20–27 in (50–70 cm) ↑ 20–27 in (50–70 cm)
From the Mediterranean to Iran. Annual herb; deep roots; many erect, very fast-growing stems; leaves with simple blades or 1 to 3 deep lobes, with or without stalks. Flowers with 4 to 8 white-edged sepals, 4 to 8 yellow petals, each with 2 to 3 lobes, in sum-mer. Erect 3-part capsule contains smooth seed. Zones 7–9.

Reseda luteola
☀ ❄ ↔ 8–12 in (20–30 cm) ↑ 36–48 in (90–120 cm)
From Europe and central Asia. Upright annual or short-lived per-ennial. Leaves smooth-edged, to 1 in (25 mm) long. Sometimes branched, upright, 24 in (60 cm) tall flower spikes; tiny, yellow-green, unscented flowers, in summer. Zones 6–10.

Reseda odorata
BASTARD ROCKET, MIGNONETTE, SWEET RESEDA
☀ ❄ ↔ 7–8 in (18–20 cm) ↑ 12–24 in (30–60 cm)
Annual from the Mediterranean region. Smooth-edged leaves, oc-casionally 3-lobed. Loose clusters of highly scented, tiny, greenish white flowers, soft orange stamens, in early summer. Zones 6–10.

RHEUM
RHUBARB

This genus of 50 robust perennials, native to a wide area of tem-perate Asia, includes several ornamental foliage plants as well as the popular edible rhubarb, and belongs to the knotweed (Poly-gonaceae) family. The large leaves, which are often wavy-edged or palmately lobed, are borne on stout stalks and form basal clumps. The small greenish white or red tinged flowers are wind-pollinated and borne in large panicles on strong upright stems.

Rehmannia elata

Reineckea carnea

Reseda lutea

Rhodanthe chlorocephala

CULTIVATION: Ornamental *Rheum* species make excellent feature plants. They do best when grown in sun or part-shade in a rich, deep, moisture-retentive but well-drained soil. Edible rhubarb should be planted at a 30–36 in (75–90 cm) spacing in a deeply cultivated soil with plenty of compost added. Plants require plenty of moisture but should be well-drained. Propagate from seed or by division; cultivars are propagated by division of the crown.

Rheum australe
syn. *Rheum emodi*
HIMALAYAN RHUBARB, RED-VEINED PIE PLANT
❀/❀ ❄ ↔ 5 ft (1.5 m) ↕ 5 ft (1.5 m)
From the Himalayas. Leaves rounded or broadly oblong, prominently veined, wavy edges. Stout red-tinged flowering stalks; dense clusters of small white to red flowers in summer. Zones 6–9.

Rheum palmatum
❀/❀ ❄ ↔ 5 ft (1.5 m) ↕ 5–8 ft (1.5–2.4 m)
Native to northwestern China. Deeply lobed and toothed leaves, to 40 in (100 cm) wide, purplish red when young. Fluffy panicles of small pink flowers, on tall stems, in summer. *R. p.* var. *tanguticum*, more robust, very deeply lobed leaves. *R. p.* 'Atrosanguineum', cerise flowers, leaves open vivid red; and '**Bowles' Crimson'**, leaves crimson beneath. Zones 6–9.

RHODANTHE
STRAWFLOWER
This genus in the daisy (Asteraceae) family, one of several in the complex *Helichrysum* group, was extensively revised in the early 1990s and is now considered to be exclusively Australian. The 40 species in the genus are annuals, perennials, and small shrubs with simple, narrow, light green to silver-gray leaves. They are rather sprawling plants, grown for their long-lasting flowers, which are made colorful by dry papery bracts enclosing the yellowish flowerheads. Some species have long-stemmed flowerheads that last well when cut. Some are ephemeral plants native to desert regions, remaining in the ground as seeds for many years ready to burst into a carpet of bloom with the arrival of rain. CULTIVATION: Hardiness varies but most are surprisingly tough and are ideal for dry banks or rockeries. Plant in full sun with

light, gritty, very free-draining soil. These plants will tolerate poor soil. Propagate from seed or cuttings. Some will self-layer.

Rhodanthe chlorocephala
syn. *Helipterum roseum*
❀ ❄ ↔ 8–12 in (20–30 cm) ↕ 12–24 in (30–60 cm)
Annual from southwestern Australia; usually erect or rounded. Narrow gray-green leaves, around 1 in (25 mm) long. Flowerheads 1–2 in (25–50 mm) wide, white to pink papery bracts around a conspicuous soft yellow disc, from late spring to early summer; winter-flowering in mild areas. *R. c.* subsp. *rosea*, flowerheads with bright pink ray florets; *R. c.* subsp. *splendida*, white flowerheads with many ray florets. Zones 9–11.

Rhodanthe manglesii
syn. *Helipterum manglesii*
SWAN RIVER EVERLASTING
❀ ❄ ↔ 6–12 in (15–30 cm) ↕ 12–18 in (30–45 cm)
Western Australian annual. Erect stems; pointed oval to narrow heart-shaped, gray-green to blue-green leaves, to 2 in (5 cm) long. Many white to pink flowerheads, 1¼ in (30 mm) wide, in spring or after rain. 'Sutton's Rose', attractive cultivar. Zones 8–11.

RHODANTHEMUM
A mainly alpine Eurasian and North African genus of some 15 to 20 species that was established with the revision of *Chrysanthemum* in the 1960s to 1990s, and belongs to the daisy (Asteraceae) family. These shrubby perennials have ferny, usually silver-gray foliage, sometimes in whorls or loose rosettes, and develop into dense mounds. In spring and early summer they are covered in wiry-stemmed flowerheads with white ray florets, often pink-tinted, around a yellow disc. In mild areas flowers occur less heavily throughout the year.
CULTIVATION: Although generally frost tolerant, few *Rhodanthemum* species will withstand prolonged cold damp winter conditions. They are best grown in an alpine house or dry winter climate. Plant in full sun or half-sun in gritty free-draining soil with a little added humus. Water in summer and feed very lightly. Propagation is from seed or from small basal cuttings of non-flowering shoots.

Rodgersia podophylla

Rhodanthemum gayanum

syns *Chrysanthemum gayanum, C. mawii, Pyrethropsis gayana*
☼ ❊ ↔ 24–40 in (60–100 cm) ↕ 8–12 in (20–30 cm)
Low-growing perennial subshrub. Native to Morocco and Algeria. Forms dense spreading cushion; lacy, finely divided, dark
green, glossy foliage. Abundant, bright pink, daisy-like flowers,
yellow to burgundy centers, from winter to spring. Zones 8–10.

Rhodanthemum hosmariense

syns *Chrysanthemum hosmariense,*
Pyrethropsis hosmariensis
MOROCCAN DAISY
☼ ❊ ↔ 12–16 in (30–40 cm)
↕ 4–8 in (10–20 cm)
Spreading, drought-resistant, bushy perennial
herb. Native to Morocco's Atlas Mountains.
Forms compact cushion; finely cut silvery
gray leaves. Scaly decorative floral buttons
in winter open to white daisy-like flowers
with yellow centers, from spring to autumn,
scattered blooms throughout year. Zones 8–10.

RODGERSIA

The 6 large perennial species of this genus are members of the
saxifrage (Saxifragaceae) family. Found naturally among the woodlands and streamsides of temperate Asia, these plants have a preference for damp conditions. They have large pinnate leaves with
toothed edges and are grown primarily as foliage plants. Their
astilbe-like plumes of tiny flowers are also attractive, although
they are quite short lived. The foliage develops quickly in spring,
and the flowers, which are white, cream, or pink in color, open
at about the time the leaves reach their maximum size.
CULTIVATION: Plant *Rodgersia* species in a position in part-shade
or full shade in cool, moist, humus-rich soil. Although these
plants prefer constant moisture, they are not happy in stagnant
boggy conditions and often do better when planted alongside
moving water rather than ponds. Propagation is from seed or
by division when dormant.

Rodgersia aesculifolia

☀ ❊ ↔ 3–7 ft (0.9–2 m) ↕ 5–7 ft (1.5–2 m)
From China. Large palmate leaves, to over 16 in (40 cm) long,
reminiscent of horse chestnut *(Aesculus)* foliage. White flowers,
in dense panicles, to 24 in (60 cm) long, in summer. Zones 5–9.

Rodgersia pinnata

☀ ❊ ↔ 3–7 ft (0.9–2 m) ↕ 32–48 in (80–120 cm)
Native to southwestern China. Leaves partly pinnate, with 5 to
9 dark green, deeply veined leaflets, to 8 in (20 cm) long. Deep
pink to red, rarely white, flowers, in long-stemmed panicles held
well clear of foliage, in summer. 'Rosea', deep pink flowers;
'Superba' ★, bronze- to purple-tinted foliage, large panicles of
pink flowers. Zones 6–9.

Rodgersia podophylla

☀ ❊ ↔ 3–7 ft (0.9–2 m) ↕ 32–48 in (80–120 cm)
Native to Japan and Korea. Broad palmate leaves, usually 5-lobed,
to over 12 in (30 cm) long and wide, with lobes at tips. Foliage
reddens in autumn, sometimes brilliantly. White flowers, in
heads to 12 in (30 cm) long, in summer. Zones 6–9.

Rodgersia sambucifolia

☀ ❊ ↔ 24–48 in (60–120 cm) ↕ 24–36 in (60–90 cm)
Perennial from China. Pinnate leaves, to over 12 in (30 cm)
in length; up to 11 deeply veined, finely hairy, dark green leaflets. Flat-topped, often rather open panicles
of white to light pink flowers. Summer-
flowering. Zones 6–9.

Rodgersia pinnata 'Rosea'

ROMNEYA

This is a genus of only 2 species in the
poppy (Papaveraceae) family, native to western North America and Mexico, both with
glaucous stems and deeply cut leaves. The
flowers are large, 6-petalled, white and
poppy-like, with a central mass of golden
yellow stamens. *Romneya* species are sometimes difficult to establish but once settled
they spread quickly by underground stems,
so should be allowed plenty of space.
CULTIVATION: These attractive plants thrive in a warm sunny
position and are quite frost hardy. They prefer a fertile and well-
drained soil and resent being transplanted. Propagation is from
seed or from cuttings.

Romneya coulteri

CALIFORNIA TREE POPPY
☼ ❊ ↔ 7 ft (2 m) ↕ 8 ft (2.4 m)
Small to medium-sized shrubby perennial from southern
California, USA. Persistent stems; leaves silvery gray, finely
cut. Flowers solitary, buds smooth, slightly conical, opening to
large white flowers, crumpled crape-like petals, in late summer
to mid-autumn. Cultivars include 'Butterfly', smaller flowers,
pure white ruffled petals; 'White Cloud', large white flowers,
silvery gray leaves. Zones 7–10.

RUDBECKIA

BLACK-EYED SUSAN, CONEFLOWER

This North American genus contains 15 species of perennials in the daisy (Asteraceae) family. They are popular in gardens for their great hardiness, ease of cultivation, and late-season flower display. Most are fairly bulky plants, over 4 ft (1.2 m) tall, and carry masses of large golden yellow daisies, usually with dark brown to black disc florets. Available in dwarf, double-flowered, and variously colored forms, they bloom from late summer until cut back by frost.

CULTIVATION: Plant in a sunny open position in moist well-drained soil. Deadhead to encourage continued blooming. Mildew can occur but usually only late in the season. Propagate by division, from basal cuttings or seed.

Romneya coulteri

Rudbeckia fulgida

BLACK-EYED SUSAN, ORANGE CONEFLOWER

☼/❂ ❈ ↔ 24–48 in (60–120 cm) ↑ 40 in (100 cm)

Perennial from southeastern USA. Lance-shaped leaves, to over 4 in (10 cm) long, often bristly. Flowerheads to almost 3 in (8 cm) wide, ray florets yellow to orange, disc florets dark purple-brown, in summer–autumn. Several natural varieties, including: *R. f.* **var.** *deamii*, 24 in (60 cm) tall, hairy pointed oval leaves; *R. f.* **var.** *speciosa*, 36 in (90 cm) tall, hairy elongated lance-shaped leaves; and *R. f.* **var.** *sullivantii*, 36 in (90 cm) tall, pointed oval leaves often downy, flowerheads to 4 in (10 cm) wide; **'Goldsturm'**, to 24 in (60 cm) tall, slightly larger flower-heads. Zones 4–9.

Rudbeckia 'Herbstsonne'

syn. *Rudbeckia* 'Autumn Sun'

☼ ❈ ↔ 3 ft (0.9 m) ↑ 6 ft (1.8 m)

Vigorous *R. nitida* hybrid; perennial with strongly erect habit. Flowerheads to well over 4 in (10 cm) wide, yellow ray florets, tall yellow-green cone. Summer- to autumn-flowering. Zones 3–10.

Rudbeckia hirta

BLACK-EYED SUSAN

☼/❂ ❈ ↔ 32–48 in (80–120 cm)
↑ 5–7 ft (1.5–2 m)

Biennial or short-lived perennial, native to central USA. Dwarf forms often treated as annuals. Narrow, 4 in (10 cm) long, lance-shaped leaves, toothed. Flowerheads to nearly 4 in (10 cm) wide, ray florets yellow, disc florets purple-brown, in summer–autumn. Cultivars and seedling strains include **'Becky Mix'**, 10 in (25 cm) tall, mixed color dwarf seedling strain with yellow-, orange-, and red-flowered forms; **'Irish Eyes'** ★, olive green disc florets; **'Marmalade'**, 18 in (45 cm) tall,

golden orange ray florets; **'Rustic Dwarfs'**, 24 in (60 cm) tall, flowers in warm shades of gold, orange, terracotta, and red-brown; **'Toto'**, 10 in (25 cm) tall, golden yellow ray florets, large deep purple-brown disc florets. Zones 4–9.

Rudbeckia laciniata

CUT-LEAF CONEFLOWER

☼/❂ ❈ ↔ 3–7 ft (0.9–2 m) ↑ 7–10 ft (2–3 m)

Vigorous North American perennial. Leaves deeply lobed to pinnate, bluish-green, often with hairy undersides. Flowerheads over 5 in (12 cm) wide, ray floret yellow, disc florets yellow-green, in late summer–autumn. **'Goldquelle'** (syn. 'Gold Drop'), 30 in (75 cm) tall, large, yellow, fully double flowerheads; **'Hortensia'** (syn. 'Golden Glow'), 6 ft (1.8 m) tall, yellow double flowerheads. Zones 3–9.

Rudbeckia nitida

SHINY CONEFLOWER

☼/❂ ❈ ↔ 32–48 in (80–120 cm) ↑ 5–7 ft (1.5–2 m)

Perennial, native to North America. Leaves to 6 in (15 cm) long, deeply lobed, almost to midrib. Flowerheads to 4 in (10 cm) wide, ray florets yellow, disc florets yellow-green, in late summer–autumn. Zones 3–9.

Rudbeckia occidentalis

☼/❂ ❈ ↔ 32–48 in (80–120 cm) ↑ 5–7 ft (1.5–2 m)

Perennial, native to western USA. Pointed oval leaves, to over 4 in (10 cm) long, sometimes toothed. Flowerheads to over 3 in (8 cm) wide, yellow ray florets, central cone brown-black, to over 2 in (5 cm) high. Summer-flowering. **'Green Wizard'**, no ray florets but elongated bright green sepals around a large near-black disc. Zones 7–10.

Rudbeckia hirta

RUELLIA

Mostly from tropical and subtropical regions, with a few species in temperate North America, this is a genus containing some 150 species of evergreen perennials and soft-stemmed shrubs, belonging to the acanthus (Acanthaceae) family. They are grown for their showy funnelform flowers, usually red, pink, or mauve, that may occur singly, or in dense terminal panicles or axillary clusters. The attractive, smooth-edged, oblong to lance-shaped leaves have prominent veins.
CULTIVATION: Although some species from temperate America are quite frost hardy, most need a warm climate and a fertile, moist, well-drained soil in partial shade. In cooler areas they are grown indoors or in a greenhouse. Water potted specimens adequately during the growing season and keep just moist during winter. Trim excess growth regularly and especially after flowering to maintain density of foliage. Propagation is from seed or soft-wood cuttings in spring.

Ruellia brittoniana
COMMON RUELLIA
☼ ❄ ↔ 18–24 in (45–60 cm) ↕ 24–36 in (60–90 cm)
Upright evergreen perennial shrub from Mexico and southwestern USA. Purple fleshy stems; lower branches drooping over with age and taking root. Narrow, sword-shaped, serrated, dark green leaves, prominent purple veins. Funnel-shaped, purple or blue, petunia-like flowers, 2 in (5 cm) long, in leaf axils, from mid-spring until first autumn frosts. Dies back in winter and self-seeds aggressively. 'Alba' (syn. 'Clean White Katie'), low-growing form, up to 8 in (20 cm) high, white flowers throughout summer; 'Chi Chi', 24–36 in (60–90 cm) tall, pale pink flowers throughout summer; 'Katie' (dwarf blue bells), low-growing form, 6–8 in (15–20 cm) high, purple flowers all summer; 'Texas Blue', up to 10 in (25 cm) tall, purple summer flowers. Zones 8–11.

Ruellia makoyana
MONKEY PLANT, TRAILING VELVET PLANT
☀ ✿ ↔ 15–18 in (38–45 cm) ↕ 6–12 in (15–30 cm)
Perennial from Brazil. Spreading habit; trailing branching stems. Variegated leaves, 2–3 in (5–8 cm) long, velvet-textured, veined

Ruscus aculeatus

white above and purple beneath. Brilliant reddish purple trumpet-shaped flowers, to 2 in (5 cm) wide, growing from leaf axils, all year round, mostly autumn–spring. Zones 10–12.

RUMEX
DOCK, SORREL
This genus, comprising some 200 species of annuals, biennials, and often tap-rooted perennials, belongs to the knotweed (Polygonaceae) family. Its members are distributed worldwide, and are found in most countries with temperate climates. The leaves are usually basal and the typically small flowers are produced in terminal racemes or spikes. The seeds are enclosed in a papery membrane that allows them to float. Although some species are ornamental and some are edible, this genus also includes some dreadfully weedy species that have hitchhiked around the world with human travelers.
CULTIVATION: Most *Rumex* species do best in a deep, fertile, and moist to even damp soil in full sun. Propagation is usually from seed, which will often self-sow; root cuttings are another option.

Rumex sanguineus
BLOODY DOCK, RED-VEINED DOCK
☼ ❄ ↔ 12–36 in (30–90 cm) ↕ 20–40 in (50–100 cm)
Clumping species. Native to Europe, southwestern Asia, and northern Africa. Dark stems; lance-shaped bright green leaves, to 6 in (15 cm) long, beetroot red veins. Panicles of tiny green flowers, from early to mid-summer. Brown seeds. Zones 6–10.

Rumex vesicarius
syn. *Acetosa vesicaria*
ROSY DOCK
☼ ❄ ↔ 6–8 in (15–20 cm) ↕ 8–10 in (20–25 cm)
Annual from northern Africa and southwest Asia. Fleshy leaves, spearhead-shaped, to ¾ in (18 mm) long. Tiny flowers, deep pink, in panicles, in late spring. Conspicuous fruits, rose pink, bladder-like. A weed in arid southern Australia. Zones 6–10.

RUSCUS

This genus, containing about 6 species of evergreen subshrubs from the Mediterranean region, belongs to the family Ruscaceae. The plants form clumps, spreading slowly by underground rhizomes. Their leaves are more correctly called "cladodes," which are flattened stems that function as a leaf. The real leaf is a small protuberance on the surface of the cladode, from whence emerge the tiny greenish or white starry flowers. These are followed by red pea-sized fruits if both male and female plants are present. Some forms appear to be hermaphroditic.
CULTIVATION: These hardy plants perform well in dry shade. Grow in well-drained soil in a position in full sun to half-sun. Propagate from seed or by division.

Ruscus aculeatus
BUTCHER'S BROOM
☼/☀ ❄ ↔ 40 in (100 cm) ↕ 30–40 in (75–100 cm)
From southern Europe and the Mediterranean region. Clump-forming; spreads by rhizomes. Small, oval-shaped, leathery, dark

green cladodes, ¾–1¼ in (18–
30 mm) long, prickly tips. Bright
red berries in summer–winter.
Zones 6–10.

Ruscus hypoglossum
☀/◐ ❄ ↔ 40 in (100 cm)
↑ 18–26 in (45–65 cm)
Native to southern Europe and
elsewhere in the Mediterranean
region. Clumping subshrub;
spreads by rhizomes. Oval mid-
green cladodes, to 4 in (10 cm)
long. Arching stems; green flowers;
red fruit. Flowers and fruit borne
on a cladode under a tongue-like
leaf. Zones 7–11.

SAGINA
PEARLWORT

This Northern Hemisphere genus
contains approximately 20 species
of annual and perennial, ground-

Sagina subulata

covering, mat-forming plants, which are found growing on rocky
outcrops in the wild. Members of the pink (Caryophyllaceae)
family, a great number of the species in this genus are garden
weeds, and can prove extremely difficult to eradicate because
of their highly developed reproductive system. Their fine linear
leaves are arranged in pairs, and they quickly form dense mats
of growth that cover both soil and rocky areas. Tiny white 4-
or 5- petalled flowers are typically borne in spring and summer.
CULTIVATION: Pearlworts do not like prolonged periods of hot dry
weather; they prefer low temperatures and cool free-draining
soils, with full sun or part-shade. Some of the golden forms of
pearlwort will die if temperatures exceed 86°F (30°C). These
plants can be propagated very easily, either from seed in spring
or by division at any time of year.

Sagina subulata
GOLDEN PEARLWORT
☀/◐ ❄ ↔ 12 in (30 cm) ↑ 1 in (25 mm)
Mat-forming perennial. Native to central Europe. Soft foliage;
forms dense ground-covering mounds; leaves bright green, tiny.
Solitary white flowers in summer. 'Aurea', lime green to canary
yellow foliage. Zones 4–7.

SAGITTARIA
ARROWHEAD

This genus of some 30 mostly perennial species is distributed
throughout the world, but is particularly well represented in
the Americas. It belongs to the family Alismataceae. *Sagittaria*
species are aquatic plants, usually with flowers of a single sex
on the same plant. Some have rhizomes or runners; many have
tubers, which are sometimes edible. The leaves are smooth-
edged, and are borne below, on, or above the water. The flowerheads are erect, floating, or submerged, in racemes or panicles,

rarely umbel-like. The 3-petalled flowers are white, sometimes
with a pink spot. Fruits are compressed achenes, with a conspicuous dorsal wing and sometimes lateral wings.
CULTIVATION: *Sagittaria* species are grown as marshy garden or
pond-edge plants. They can also be grown in deep fast-flowing
water and will tolerate light shade. Weighted tubers thrown
into water to 24 in (60 cm) deep will grow well. Propagation
is by division in spring.

Sagittaria graminea
☀ ❄ ↔ 12 in (30 cm) ↑ 20 in (50 cm)
Cormous aquatic perennial. Native to eastern USA. Narrow,
strap-like, submerged leaves, emergent leaves being wider and
pointed. Upright flowering stems; whorls of white 3-petalled
male flowers above small, green, petal-less female flowers.
Summer-flowering. *S. g.* var. *platyphylla*, flowers with longer
beaks. Zones 6–12.

SAINTPAULIA
AFRICAN VIOLET

This genus of 20 perennials from tropical East Africa is a member of the African violet (Gesneriaceae) family. Only a few species
are cultivated, with the majority of those grown being hybrids or
cultivars. They are soft-stemmed rosette-forming plants, generally
low-growing, with finely hairy, rounded leaves that have toothed
edges and long stalks. The velvety 5-petalled flowers are produced
in clusters at the center of the rosettes throughout the year.
CULTIVATION: Rarely grown outdoors, even in the tropics, African
violets are popular pot plants that prefer constant temperatures,
moderate to high humidity, and fertile, moist, humus-rich soil.
They need bright but not sunny conditions. Propagate from
leaf-stalk cuttings. The seed is very fine, and is cultured rather
like orchid seed.

Saintpaulia, Hybrid Cultivar, 'Patty'

Saintpaulia ionantha

AFRICAN VIOLET, USAMBARA VIOLET

☀ ✦ ↔ 8–16 in (20–40 cm) ↕ 4–10 in (10–25 cm)

Perennial, native to Tanzania. Rounded to heart-shaped, downy, wavy-edged or softly toothed leaves. Sprays of flowers held above the foliage, 8 to 10 blooms per head. Flowers pale lavender to purple or white, with violet throat. Zones 11–12.

Saintpaulia shumensis

☀ ✦ ↔ 6–10 in (15–25 cm)
↕ 2–6 in (5–15 cm)

Perennial, native to Tanzania. Slightly glossy, rounded, hairy, serrated to toothed leaves, undersides often red-tinted. Heads of up to 5 flowers, to over 2 in (5 cm) wide, white to pale mauve, sometimes with darker markings. Zones 11–12.

Saintpaulia Hybrid Cultivars

☀ ✦ ↔ 4–12 in (10–30 cm)
↕ 2–8 in (5–20 cm)

All the plants in this group are commonly known as hybrids, but most of the widely grown and popular African violets are in fact cultivars of *S. ion-antha* (although some are true hybrids between *S. ionantha* and other species, such as *S. shumensis*). Compact, lavishly foliaged, long-flowering plants; attractive flowers range in color from mainly pink to purple, but may also come in white, in near-red shades, and in yellow. Hybrids and cultivars include 'Akira', lush dark foliage, deep crimson flowers; 'Chantiana', dwarf form, bright pink double flowers; 'Chimera Monique', dwarf form, white flowers, dark purple edges; 'Concord', deep maroon flowers, white edges; 'Diana', very dark foliage, deep red velvety flowers; 'Dorothy', pink flowers, fine white edges; 'Emi', very profuse pale mauve flowers, light edges; 'Hisako', deep purple-blue flowers, fine white edges; 'Irish Flirt', white flowers suffused with green, double; 'Jolita', dwarf form, lavender double flowers; 'Melodie Kimi', purple upper petal, white lower petals with broad purple edges; 'Milky Way Trail', pure white flowers; 'Optimara Colo-rado', bright purplish red flowers; 'Patty', purple-red and white

flowers; 'Rococo Pink', semi-double, dusky dark pink flowers; 'Shades of Autumn', cream variegated foliage, ruffled pink and mauve flowers, semi-double; 'Zoja', purple-blue flowers, white edges, semi-double. Zones 11–12.

SALPIGLOSSIS

This genus containing 2 species of annuals or short-lived perennials is a member of the nightshade (Solanaceae) family. Natives of the southern and central Andes, they are small upright plants with alternate, simple linear to elliptical, dark green leaves with finely toothed edges. The stems and foliage are rather sticky to the touch. The petunia-like flowers are funnel-shaped and 5-lobed; they are borne singly in the leaf axils near the stem tips, and are strikingly colored and patterned, often velvety-textured. Seedling strains in a range of sizes and colors are widely available.

CULTIVATION: Treated as annuals, *Salpiglossis* species are best grown in an area with cool moist summer conditions. Plant in a sunny position with fertile, moist, well-drained soil, and water well. They make excellent cut flowers and are useful for border plant-

Salpiglossis sinuata, Festival Strain

ing. Taller plants may need staking. In mild almost frost-free regions these species can be overwintered. They are usually propagated by seed sown in situ.

Salpiglossis sinuata

PAINTED TONGUE

☀/◐ ❋ ↔ 8–12 in (20–30 cm)
↕ 16–24 in (40–60 cm)

Annual, biennial, or short-lived perennial, usually treated as an annual. Native of Chile. Narrow, dark green, sticky leaves to 4 in (10 cm) long, often toothed, sometimes lobed. Heads of funnel-shaped flowers, to 2 in (5 cm) wide, yellow to reddish purple, darker veins and markings, in summer–autumn. Mixed color seedling strains include **Bolero Hybrids**, 12 in (30 cm) tall, wide color range; **Casino Mixed**, 12 in (30 cm) tall, wide color range with contrasting veining; **Emperor Royal Series**, 24 in (60 cm) tall, large petunia-like flowers, conspicuously veined; and **Festival Strain**, dark red-maroon flowers. Zones 8–11.

SALVIA (see page 298)

Salvia argentea

SILVER SAGE

☀ ❋ ↔ 24–36 in (60–90 cm) ↕ 24–36 in (60–90 cm)

Perennial, native to southern Europe. Large, woolly, silvery-looking leaves form flat rosette up to 36 in (90 cm) wide on young plants. Tall candelabra-like stems; white flowers produced in second year. Pinch out developing flower stem to promote foliage growth. Zones 8–11.

Salvia blepharophylla

EYELASH-LEAFED SAGE

☼ ❄ ↔ 20–27 in (50–70 cm) ↑ 8–12 in (20–30 cm)

Native to Mexico. Mat-forming perennial, spreads by runners. Glossy green oval leaves, edged with tiny hairs; tubular flowers, vibrant orange-red, in early summer–late autumn. Zones 9–11.

Salvia buchananii

syn. *Salvia bacheriana* of gardens

BUCHANAN'S SAGE

☼ ❄ ↔ 12 in (30 cm) ↑ 12–20 in (30–50 cm)

Perennial, probably originating from Mexico. Clump-forming; rich, glossy, oval leaves ¾–2 in (18 mm–5 cm) long. Velvety flowers, hot magenta, mainly from summer to autumn. Zones 10–11.

Salvia cacaliifolia

CACALIA SAGE

☼ ❄ ↔ 12–20 in (30–50 cm) ↑ 36 in (90 cm)

Suckering perennial from Central America. Bright green arrowhead-like leaves. Royal blue flowers; green calyces. Blooms year round in mild climates, from mid-summer to autumn in cooler climates. Zones 10–11.

Salvia coccinea

Salvia chiapensis

CHIAPAS SAGE

☼/❄ ❄ ↔ 16–24 in (40–60 cm) ↑ 16–24 in (40–60 cm)

Perennial, native to Mexico. Glossy olive green leaves to 3 in (8 cm) in length. Cerise-pink flowers, velvety green calyces. Long-flowering in mild climates. Zones 9–11.

Salvia coccinea

syn. *Salvia coccinea* var. *pseudococcinea*

TEXAS SAGE, TROPICAL SAGE

☼ ❄ ↔ 20–32 in (50–80 cm) ↑ 40 in (100 cm)

Annual or short-lived shrub from tropical South America; in mild climates may be perennial, elsewhere treated as annual. Mostly triangular, hairy leaves, scalloped edges. Flowers usually scarlet, may be red, pink, or white. '**Lady in Red**', red flowers. Zones 9–12.

Salvia discolor

ANDEAN SILVER SAGE

☼/❄ ❄ ↔ 32–40 in (80–100 cm) ↑ 32–40 in (80–100 cm)

Perennial from Peru. White, wiry, sprawling stems; leaves green above, silver below. Dark purple to navy blue flowers, green calyces and silver bracts, in late summer–early autumn. Zones 9–11.

Salvia dorisiana

FRUIT-SCENTED SAGE, PEACH SAGE

☼ ❄ ↔ 36 in (90 cm)

↑ 36–48 in (90–120 cm)

From Honduras; hairy heavily branched plant; long velvety leaves. Spikes of bright pink loosely tubular flowers, 2 in (5 cm) long, in winter. Flowers and leaves scented; flowers attract hummingbirds. Zones 10–12.

Salvia elegans

PINEAPPLE SAGE

☼ ❄ ↔ 3 ft (0.9 m) ↑ 6 ft (1.8 m)

From high mountain regions of Central Mexico and Guatemala. Perennial or sub-shrub; shorter growth habit in cold areas. Light green leaves, soft and downy, finely serrated edges. Crushed leaves have distinctive pineapple aroma. Small, narrow, scarlet-red flowers in well-spaced whorls, from spring to autumn. Flowers attract hummingbirds. '**Scarlet Pineapple**' (syn. *S. rutilans*), stronger pineapple scent than the species, larger flowers. Zones 8–11.

Salvia farinacea

MEALY SAGE

☼ ❄ ↔ 24 in (60 cm) ↑ 36–48 in (90–120 cm)

Popular perennial, often treated as an annual, from Texas and New Mexico, USA. Leaves oval, green, glossy. Flowers at ends of stems in shades of blue, purple, or white; dusted with flour-like substance. Cultivars include '**Strata**', shorter habit, blue flowers, mealy white stem and calyces; '**Victoria**', blue flowers, blue stems and calyces; '**Victoria Blue**', shorter habit, flowers deeper blue, larger. Zones 9–11.

Salvia dorisiana

Salvia elegans

Salvia farinacea (purple flowers)

Salvia fulgens

CARDINAL SAGE

☼ ⚘ ↔ 30 in (75 cm) ↑ 48 in (120 cm)

Perennial subshrub. Native of Mexico. Woody-stemmed and shrubby in mild climates. Ovate to poplar-shaped leaves, cleft at base, toothed edges, downy undersides. Spikes of 2 to 6 bright red flowers, densely coated with soft hairs, in summer. Zones 9–10.

Salvia gesneriiflora

☼ ⚘ ↔ 10 in (25 cm) ↑ 26 in (65 cm)

Perennial shrub or subshrub occurring from Mexico to Colombia. Dense mound of hairy, somewhat wrinkled, ovate leaves with toothed edges. Flower spikes to 8 in (20 cm) long; orange-red flowers, 2 in (5 cm) long, resembling those of *Columnea* species, in summer–autumn. 'Tequila', large shrub, scarlet flowers, black calyx. Zones 9–11.

Salvia greggii

AUTUMN SAGE

☼ ⚘ ↔ 12–36 in (30–90 cm)
↑ 12–36 in (30–90 cm)

Variable species from Texas, USA, and Mexico. Hybridizes freely with related *S. microphylla*. Small leathery leaves, usually smooth. Flowers usually red or shades of pink, purple, and white, in summer–late autumn. Cultivars named for flower color include 'Alba', 'Iced Lemon', 'Peach', and 'Raspberry Royale'. Zones 9–11.

Salvia guaranitica ★

syns *Salvia ambigens, S. concolor*

ANISE-SCENTED SAGE

☼ ❅ ↔ 16–27 in (40–70 cm) ↑ 4–5 ft (1.2–1.5 m)

South American perennial, suckering lightly to form large clumps. Flowers on 10 in (25 cm) long spike, true blue with green calyces, in early summer–autumn. 'Black and Blue', shorter cultivar, less

spreading, blue flowers, almost black calyces; 'Blue Enigma', shorter cultivar, earlier flowering, deep blue flowers, green calyces; 'Costa Rica Blue', tall cultivar, violet-blue flowers, yellow-green calyces. Zones 8–11.

Salvia indica

☼ ⚘ ↔ 24 in (60 cm) ↑ 24–36 in (60–90 cm)

Perennial, native to the Middle East. Hairy gray leaves, edges scalloped; forms mound of basal foliage. Tall spikes of purple flowers, white markings on bottom lip. Spring-flowering. May die down during warmer months. Zones 9–11.

Salvia involucrata

ROSELEAF SAGE

☼/◐ ⚘ ↔ 5 ft (1.5 m) ↑ 5 ft (1.5 m)

Perennial from Mexico. Some wood at base. Purplish green leaves. Beetroot red flowers and calyces. Summer- to autumn-flowering. 'Bethellii', more compact, sometimes suckering, large heart-shaped leaves, flowers sugar pink. Zones 9–11.

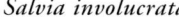

Salvia involucrata

Salvia leucantha

MEXICAN BUSH SAGE, VELVET SAGE

☼ ⚘ ↔ 36 in (90 cm) ↑ 36 in (90 cm)

Native to Mexico and tropical America. Woolly stems; soft, narrow, wrinkled leaves, dull green, thickly felted beneath. White or purple flowers; purple velvety calyces, in late summer. 'Midnight' (syn. 'Purple Velvet'), purple flowers. Zones 9–11.

Salvia microphylla

LITTLE-LEAFED SAGE

☼ ❅ ↔ 3 ft (0.9 m) ↑ 4 ft (1.2 m)

Variable species, widespread in its native southern USA and Mexico. Slightly hairy serrated-edged leaves; blackcurrant-like aroma when crushed. Flower color variable, shades of pink, red, and deep purple, in summer–autumn. *S. m.* var. *microphylla*, crimson flowers, heavily blooming; 'La Foux', shrubby, glossy green oval leaves, flowers hot pink to red with purple stems and calyces. *S. m.* 'Coral', deep salmon pink flowers; 'Huntington Red', bright scarlet flowers; 'Kew Red', deep red flowers; 'La Trinidad Pink', bright pink to magenta flowers; 'Newby Hall', vivid deep scarlet flowers; 'Pink Blush', magenta-pink flowers; 'San Carlos Festival', continual display of crimson flowers. Zones 8–11.

Salvia nemorosa

BALKAN CLARY, STEPPE SAGE

☼ ❆ ↔ 12–24 in (30–60 cm)
↑ 24–36 in (60–90 cm)

Perennial found from Europe to central Asia. Simple, oval to oblong, wrinkled, green

Salvia leucantha

Salvia patens

Salvia roemeriana

Salvia × sylvestris 'Mainacht'

leaves. Racemes of mauve to purple flowers, sometimes white to pink, in summer–autumn. **'Lubecca'** (syn. *S.* × *superba* 'Lubecca'), dwarf cultivar, gray-green leaves, tall spikes of mauve flowers with rich burgundy bracts, in spring; **'Ostfriesland'** (syn. 'East Friesland'), vivid violet-blue flowers, slightly taller than 'Lubecca', in late spring. Zones 5–10.

Salvia patens
GENTIAN SAGE

☀ ❦ ↔ 12–24 in (30–60 cm) ↑ 12–24 in (30–60 cm)
Perennial from Mexico. Dies back to tubers in winter. Oval green leaves to 8 in (20 cm) long. Spikes of gentian blue flowers, in pairs, 12 in (30 cm) long, green calyces, in summer–autumn. **'Cambridge Blue'**, sky blue flowers. Zones 9–11.

Salvia pratensis
MEADOW CLARY, MEADOW SAGE

☀ ❋ ↔ 12 in (30 cm) ↑ 36 in (90 cm)
Perennial of meadows across Europe. Basal clump of rich green wrinkled leaves with irregular edges. Violet flowers (also blue, pink, and white forms), brown calyces, green bracts, in spring. **Haematodes Group** (syn. *S. haematodes*), large erect sprays of pale lilac-blue flowers, reddish brown stems, in summer; **'Indigo'**, superb indigo blue flowers in early summer. Zones 4–10.

Salvia przewalskii
☀ ❋ ↔ 12–24 in (30–60 cm)
↑ 12–24 in (30–60 cm)
Chinese species; forms basal clump of yellow-green foliage. Some leaves grow to 12 in (30 cm) long. Much-branched stems; flowers purplish red, reddish brown calyces, in summer. Zones 8–11.

Salvia roemeriana
CEDAR SAGE

☀/☀ ❋ ↔ 12 in (30 cm) ↑ 12 in (30 cm)
Small perennial. Native to Arizona and Texas, USA, and Mexico. Rounded geranium-like leaves. Bright red flowers on 8 in (20 cm) long stalks, in summer. Zones 8–11.

Salvia spathacea
CRIMSON SAGE, HUMMINGBIRD SAGE, PITCHER SAGE

☀/☀ ❋ ↔ 12–36 in (30–90 cm) ↑ 12–36 in (30–90 cm)
From California, USA. Suckering perennial; forms large mats. Large spear-shaped leaves. Tall stems; crimson-pink flowers, prominent reddish black calyces and bracts, in early spring–summer. **'Powerline Pink'**, taller stems, pink flowers. Zones 8–11.

Salvia splendens
SCARLET SAGE

☀ ❦ ↔ 8–32 in (20–80 cm) ↑ 8–48 in (20–120 cm)
Native of Brazil. Variable perennial, often treated as an annual. Upright growth habit; many-branched. Oval bright green to dark green leaves, serrated edges. Spikes of flowers, usually red, from summer to autumn; many cultivars in other colors. Popular cultivars include **'Blaze of Fire'**, brillian orange-red flowers; **'Empire Purple'**, deep reddish purple flowers; **'Red Arrows'**, bright red flowers; **'Red Riches'** (syn. 'Ryco'), early-blooming, vivid scarlet flowers, dark green leaves; **'Scarlet King'**, traditional bedding variety, big dense spikes of scarlet flowers, dark green foliage; **Sizzler Series**, compact foliage, early-flowering, long-lasting, flowers burgundy, lavender, pink, red, salmon, white, and bicolored; **'Vanguard'**, compact, early flowering, dark leaves, red flowers; **'Vista Salmon'**, compact, well-branched, dark green leaves, well-packed spikes of salmon flowers, pink inner petals. Zones 9–11.

Salvia spathacea

Salvia × sylvestris
☀ ❋ ↔ 20–40 in (50–100 cm)
↑ 20–40 in (50–100 cm)
Very hardy and widespread European perennial. Small narrow leaves; scalloped edges. Flowers usually purple. Summer-flowering. **'Blauhügel'** (syns 'Blue Hills', 'Blue Mount'), deep blue flower spikes on low plants to 15 in (38 cm) high; **'Mainacht'** (syn. 'May Night'), midnight violet flowers, in early spring; **'Tänzerin'**, erect, deep violet flower spikes to 32 in (80 cm) long. Zones 5–10.

Salvia uliginosa

BOG SAGE

☼ ❄ ↔ 3 ft (0.9 m) ↑ 3–6 ft (0.9–1.8 m)

From Brazil, Uruguay, and Argentina. Clump-forming perennial; spreads by underground runners. Yellowish green lance-shaped leaves on erect stems. Whorls of small sky blue and white flowers in late summer–autumn. Needs moist soil. Zones 9–11.

Salvia verticillata

LILAC SAGE

☼ ❄ ↔ 32 in (80 cm) ↑ 40 in (100 cm)

Perennial, widespread throughout Europe and western Asia, naturalized in North America. Leafy clump of hairy, pale green leaves. Branched inflorescences; whorls of lavender-violet flowers, green calyces, in summer. '**Alba**', white flowers, lime green calyces; '**Purple Rain**', slightly smaller than species, dusky purple flowers, violet calyces. Zones 6–10.

Salvia viridis

syn. *Salvia horminum*

ANNUAL SAGE, PAINTED SAGE, PURPLE-TOP

☼ ❄ ↔ 12 in (30 cm) ↑ 12–24 in (30–60 cm)

Slender annual found from the Mediterranean across to Crimea, Ukraine. Tiny flowers bloom in leaf axils; petal-like top bracts are purple, pink, or white with darker veining. '**Tricolor Mixed**', improved form with blue, pink, or cream bracts. Zones 8–10.

Salvia Hybrid Cultivars

☼/☽ ❄/❄ ↔ 16–48 in (40–120 cm) ↑ 20–60 in (50–150 cm)

Hybrids have been developed from a wide range of species—some are known crosses, others chance seedlings—and are a diverse group. Grown mainly for their flowers, but many cultivars also have attractive or unusual foliage. Many are probably perennial, but are often treated as annuals, especially in cold climates. '**Costa Rica Blue**', vibrant green heart-shaped leaves, bright blue flowers; '**Hot Lips**', white, red, and red/white flowers on same plant; '**Indigo Spires**' ★, deep violet flowers, double white bee-line, lower lip, dark purple calyces; '**Maraschino**', sprawling plant, long-flowering, cherry red flowers; '**Phyllis's Fancy**', long-flowering, white flowers, bluish tinge, calyces

Salvia verticillata 'Purple Rain'

Salvia uliginosa

Salvia, Hybrid Cultivar, 'Plum'

purple; '**Plum**', flowers bright magenta, calyces deep reddish purple; '**Purple Majesty**', flowers and calyces rich dark purple, growing in spikes 10 in (25 cm) long. Zones 6–10.

SANGUINARIA

BLOODROOT, RED PUCCOON

This genus, belonging to the poppy (Papaveraceae) family, consists of a single species that is found only in eastern North America. The plant is a hairless perennial that grows in woodlands. It has a branching rhizome, usually with a single palmately incised leaf. The small, white, starry flowers appear early, unfurling to reveal their rounded scalloped shape. The fruit capsules open from the middle to both the base and the apex. The many seeds have a juicy aril that is attractive to ants, which then help to disperse the seeds. This plant is an ephemeral and will die down by mid-summer—so mark its location. It will eventually spread to make a good woodland ground cover.

CULTIVATION: Grow this plant in half-sun or shade in rich moist soil, and keep well watered. It prefers a damp shaded area, where it can be left to spread. Sow seed when ripe, or divide rhizomes when the plant is dormant.

Sanguinaria canadensis

☽/● ❄ ↔ 4 in (10 cm) ↑ 8 in (20 cm)

Native to eastern North America. Perennial woodland plant. Branching rhizome; large leaves, up to 12 in (30 cm) wide, green-gray, deep indentations. Starry white or pinkish flowers, 1 per stalk. Spring-flowering. Many-seeded fruit capsules follow the flowers. Ephemeral, dies back in mid- to late summer. '**Flore Pleno**' and '**Multiplex**' (syn. 'Plena') have showy double white flowers. Zones 2–8.

SANGUISORBA *(see page 753)*

Sanguisorba canadensis

CANADIAN BURNET, GREAT BURNET

☼ ❄ ↔ 24–36 in (60–90 cm) ↑ 48–60 in (120–150 cm)

Clump-forming perennial found from Newfoundland, Canada, through Michigan, and south to Georgia, USA. Bright green compound leaves, small regular indentations on edges. White bottlebrush-like flowers, in late summer. Zones 4–8.

SANVITALIA

This genus of 7 species extends from southwestern USA through Central America to northwestern South America, and belongs to the daisy (Asteraceae) family. They are small ornamental shrubs or low-growing perennials or annuals. The leaves are opposite, with sheathing bases, and may be smooth-edged or lobed. The flowers resemble daisies. Outer florets have orange to yellow to white rays; disc florets are usually a deep purple.
CULTIVATION: Garden species are usually annuals, and are best suited to an open sunny position in well-drained good soil. Propagate from seed sown in situ in spring or autumn.

Saponaria ocymoides

Sanvitalia procumbens
CREEPING ZINNIA
☼ ❋ ↔ 12 in (30 cm) ↕ 6–8 in (15–20 cm)
Native to southwestern USA and Mexico. Low spreading annual; forms mats of hairy, mid-green, ovate leaves. Heads of many bright yellow to orange daisies, purple-black centers, in summer. 'Aztec Gold', bright yellow daisies, green centers; 'Gold Braid', double golden daisies; 'Mandarin Orange', bright orange flowers, black centers. Zones 6–11.

SAPONARIA
SOAPWORT
This genus, belonging to the pink (Caryophyllaceae) family, contains some 20 species of temperate Eurasian annuals and perennials that contain saponin, a glycoside that forms a soapy colloidal solution when mixed with water, and the extract is sometimes used in detergents and foaming agents. They are mainly low-growing, ranging from tufted mounds to fairly wide-spreading ground covers. They have blue-green linear to spatulate leaves, sometimes toothed, and in summer they are smothered in heads of small, starry, 5-petalled, pink flowers.
CULTIVATION: *Saponaria* species are mainly very hardy and easily grown, and do best spilling over banks or in perennial borders or rockeries. They prefer gritty, moist, free-draining, humus-rich soil, however, they will tolerate slightly alkaline soil. Propagate from cuttings or seed, or by layering.

Saponaria officinalis

Saponaria ocymoides
ROCK SOAPWORT
☼ ❋ ↔ 12–20 in (30–50 cm) ↕ 6–12 in (15–30 cm)
Found from Spain to the Balkans. Mound-forming, alpine perennial; small, downy, lance-shaped leaves. Clusters of tiny deep pink flowers, sometimes red or white, in summer. 'Rubra Compacta' ★, dense mounding habit, deep crimson flowers. Zones 3–10.

Saponaria officinalis
BOUNCING BET, SOAPWORT
☼ ❋ ↔ 20–40 in (50–100 cm) ↕ 12–24 in (30–60 cm)
Perennial found over much of Europe. Billowing mound of wiry stems, green to gray-green; pointed oval leaves to ½ in (12 mm) long. Heads of 5 or more small flowers, pale to bright pink, sometimes red or white, in late summer–autumn. Cultivars include 'Rosea Plena' and 'Rubra Plena'. Zones 4–10.

Saponaria × olivana
☼ ❋ ↔ 8 in (20 cm) ↕ 2 in (5 cm)
Dwarf cushion-forming hybrid. Dense mound; tiny green to gray-green leaves. Abundant pink flowers in late spring. Zones 3–10.

SARRACENIA
AMERICAN PITCHER PLANT, TRUMPET PITCHER
The 8 species in this genus are carnivorous pitcher plants in the family Sarraceniaceae. They hybridize easily, both in the wild and in cultivation. They are found in swamps, wetlands, and pine forest edges, mainly in southeastern USA. They are perennial, growing from a rhizome, and the leaves or pitchers form a basal rosette. Most have long tubular pitchers. The nodding scented flowers grow singly on tall leafless stalks. Inside, downward-pointing hairs prevent their prey—usually small insects—from escaping out of a well of digestive liquid.
CULTIVATION: Grow in full sun in peat moss or a mix of peat and sand. Water by tray, keeping level constant. Suits warmish temperate climate, with cold winters for dormancy. Most will withstand light frosts. Propagate by division during winter dormancy. Divide and repot potted plants every 2 to 3 years.

Sarracenia × exornata

Sarracenia alata ★

FLYCATCHER, PALE PITCHER PLANT

☼ ❄ ↔ 12 in (30 cm) ↑ 27 in (70 cm)

Pitcher plant from Texas, Louisiana, Mississippi, and Alabama, USA. Light green pitchers to 26 in (65 cm) high, sometimes red veined, red pitcher lid. Yellow to white flowers, 2 in (5 cm) wide, on long stalks, in spring. *S. a.* × *S. flava* 'Maxima', vigorous, pitchers to 24 in (60 cm), flowers yellow to green. Zones 7–9.

Sarracenia × catesbaei

☼ ❄ ↔ 12 in (30 cm) ↑ 18 in (45 cm)

Hybrid of *S. purpurea* × *S. flava*. Tall pitchers, large frilled lid, red veined to fully red. Flowers in late spring–summer. Zones 7–9.

Sarracenia × exornata

☼ ❄ ↔ 12 in (30 cm) ↑ 14 in (35 cm)

Naturally occurring hybrid of *S. purpurea* × *S. alata*. Pitchers red veined to totally burgundy, frilled lid. Zones 7–9.

Sarracenia flava ★

YELLOW TRUMPET

☼ ❄ ↔ 12 in (30 cm) ↑ 30 in (75 cm)

Varied pitcher plant found along the Atlantic coastal plain of USA. Tall pitchers, widening toward the mouth, large green lid. Yellow to greenish yellow flowers in spring. 'Red Veined', red veined, red around throat. Zones 7–9.

Sarracenia 'Juthatip Soper'

☼ ❄ ↔ 12 in (30 cm) ↑ 18 in (45 cm)

Stunning award-winning cultivar of *S. mitchelliana* crossed with very pink form of *S. leucophylla*. Rich reddish purple pitchers. Zones 7–9.

Sarracenia leucophylla

WHITE TRUMPET

☼ ❄ ↔ 12 in (30 cm) ↑ 24 in (60 cm)

Pitcher plant found along Atlantic coastal plain of USA. Showy species, beautiful pitchers, green at base, top white, red veined.

Deep burgundy flowers, fragrant, in spring. *S. l.* × *S. oreophila*, robust, narrow, bright green pitchers, crimson veining. Zones 7–9.

Sarracenia minor

HOODED PITCHER PLANT

☼ ❄ ↔ 12 in (30 cm) ↑ 24 in (60 cm)

Found on floating sphagnum islands in North and South Carolina, Georgia, and Florida, USA. Pale green to red pitchers, hood curls over pitcher mouth. Upper pitcher covered with fenestrations. Yellow flowers in spring. Zones 7–9.

Sarracenia × mitchelliana

☼ ❄ ↔ 12 in (30 cm) ↑ 18 in (45 cm)

Hybrid of *S. purpurea* and *S. leucophylla*. Curved pitchers, hood usually ruffled, lower parts green, red and white around top and hood. Zones 7–9.

Sarracenia × moorei

☼ ❄ ↔ 12 in (30 cm) ↑ 40 in (100 cm)

Cross between *S. flava* and *S. leucophylla*. Very tall pitchers, 40 in (100 cm) or more. 'Brook's Hybrid', red around throat, pink to red flowers. Zones 7–9.

Sarracenia oreophila

BUGLE GRASS, FROG BONNETS, GREEN PITCHER PLANT

☼ ❄ ↔ 12 in (30 cm) ↑ 24 in (60 cm)

Rare pitcher plant from Alabama, Georgia, and North and South Carolina, USA. Green pitchers, red veined to almost totally red, wide mouth, heart-shaped lid. Pale yellow fragrant flowers. Endangered species since 1979. Zones 7–9.

Sarracenia psittacina

LOBSTER POT, PARROT PITCHER PLANT

☼ ❄ ↔ 20 in (50 cm) ↑ 10 in (25 cm)

Unusual species, native to southeastern coastal plain of USA. Pitchers grow upward, then fall back horizontally, forming a rosette with pitcher openings facing center of plant. Pitchers

Sarracenia 'Juthatip Soper'

Sarracenia × moorei 'Brook's Hybrid'

green to red, puffed up hood. Red flowers. Prefers very wet soil; can survive flooding, during which it preys on small swimming creatures. Zones 7–9.

Sarracenia purpurea ★
HUNTSMAN'S CAP, NORTHERN PITCHER PLANT, SIDESADDLE PLANT

☼ ❄ ↔ 24 in (60 cm) ↑ 12 in (30 cm)

Found east of Canadian Rockies and southward along coastal USA to Gulf of Mexico. Green to purple bulging pitchers 12 in (30 cm) high, prominent rib, hood ruffled or unruffled. Green, pink, or burgundy flowers. *S. p.* subsp. *venosa*, fat green to red pitchers. *S. p.* f. *heterophylla*, narrow, green, wide mouth pitchers. Zones 2–9.

Sarracenia × readii
☼ ❄ ↔ 12 in (30 cm) ↑ 24 in (60 cm)

Naturally occurring cross between *S. leucophylla* and *S. rubra*. Bright green slender pitchers, ruffled lids white and veined with red. Zones 7–9.

Sarracenia × stevensii
☼ ❄ ↔ 12 in (30 cm) ↑ 24 in (60 cm)

Origins of this Dutch hybrid are disputed; believed to be a cross between *S. rubra* and *S. leucophylla*. Green pitchers, heavily veined with red. Zones 7–9.

SAXIFRAGA

This genus in the saxifrage (Saxifragaceae) family is very extensive, comprising a wide range of perennial, annual, or biennial ground-hugging plants, many of which are alpines. They are found throughout much of the temperate and subarctic zones of the Northern Hemisphere, with outposts in places such as Ethiopia, Mexico, and the Arctic. There are some 480 known species, as well as numerous garden hybrids. The 3 main sections that are of garden interest are the "mossies," the "silvers," and the Kabschia and Engleria subsections. These plants are not only diverse in themselves but come from a variety of habitats, such as exposed mountains and moist woodlands.
CULTIVATION: Being shallow-rooted plants, *Saxifraga* species require free-draining relatively fertile soil and a position in either sun or part-shade. Propagate by division at any time, or from seed in autumn.

Saxifraga andersonii
☼ ❄ ↔ 12 in (30 cm) ↑ 4 in (10 cm)

Cushion-forming perennial. Native to Nepal and Tibet. Loose rosettes of gray-green leaves. Tall flower stalks, to 4 in (10 cm) high; clear white or pink flowers. Spring-flowering. Zones 6–8.

Saxifraga callosa
syn. *Saxifraga lingulata*

☼ ❄ ↔ 8 in (20 cm) ↑ 10 in (25 cm)

Evergreen perennial from western and eastern Spain, the southwestern alpine areas of Europe, Sardinia, Sicily, and southern Italy. Rosettes of broad, round, silver-gray foliage growing in dense clumps. White flowers, star-shaped, ½ in (12 mm) wide, in early summer. Grows on limestone formations. Zones 7–9.

Saxifraga cochlearis
SNAIL SAXIFRAGE

☼ ❄ ↔ 6 in (15 cm) ↑ 8 in (20 cm)

Very tight, dense, mat-forming cushion plant from the maritime Alps of France. Rosettes of mid-green spoon-shaped leaves. Tall hairy stems, 4 in (10 cm) high; clusters of red-spotted white flowers in summer. 'Probynii', pure white flowers. Zones 7–8.

Saxifraga oppositifolia

Saxifraga oppositifolia
PURPLE MOUNTAIN SAXIFRAGE

☼/◐ ❄ ↔ 8 in (20 cm) ↑ 1 in (2.5 cm)

Very small, clumping and dense mat-forming perennial herb from arctic-latitude mountains of Europe, western Asia, and North America. Rosettes of stiff, elliptical, dark green leaves. Single, almost stemless, dark red to purple to pale pink flowers in summer. Zones 1–7.

Saxifraga callosa

Saxifraga, Hybrid Cultivar, 'Purple Robe'

Saxifraga paniculata
syn. *Saxifraga aizoon*
☼ ❉ ↔ 10 in (25 cm) ↑6 in (15 cm)
Mat-forming perennial from Canada, Norway, Greenland, and Iceland. Rosettes of narrow gray-green leaves, 2½ in (6 cm) long, lime-encrusted edges. Creamy white to pink flowers, in early summer. Zones 1–6.

Saxifraga spathularis
ST PATRICK'S CABBAGE
☼/◐ ❉ ↔ 6–8 in (15–20 cm) ↑8–12 in (20–30 cm)
Summer-flowering species. Native to Ireland, Spain, and Portugal. Forms clumped rosettes; rounded, 1–2 in (25–50 mm) long, leathery, bright green leaves, coarsely toothed edges. Wiry stems; sprays of tiny pinkish purple flowers. Zones 5–9.

Saxifraga stolonifera
syn. *Saxifraga sarmentosa*
MOTHER OF THOUSANDS, STRAWBERRY BEGONIA
☼/◐ ❉ ↔ 12 in (30 cm) ↑16 in (40 cm)
Perennial from East Asia. Rounded, kidney-shaped, mid- to dark green, serrated leaves form dense mounds of foliage. Tall loose stems, 16 in (40 cm) long; white flowers, spotted with red or yellow, in summer. 'Eco Butterfly', golden yellow leaves, green centers; 'Harvest Moon', moon-shaped golden green to reddish leaves; 'Tricolor', leaves edged in tones of red, white, and/or pink. Zones 5–10.

Saxifraga umbrosa
☼ ❉ ↔ 12 in (30 cm) ↑12 in (30 cm)
From the Pyrenees. Clump-forming perennial; stiff rosettes of green leaves. Flowers on 10 in (25 cm) long stems, rose pink, irregular red blotches, in late spring–early summer. Zones 1–5.

Saxifraga × urbium
syn. *Saxifraga umbrosa* 'London Pride'
LONDON PRIDE
☼ ❉ ↔ 18–36 in (45–90 cm) ↑12 in (30 cm)
Of garden origin; quick-growing ground-covering perennial. Large rosettes of spoon-shaped, leathery, dark green leaves. Arching stems; small pale pink flowers in summer. 'Aureovariegata', variegated leaves, gray-green and gold. Zones 6–7.

Saxifraga Hybrid Cultivars
☼/◐ ❉/❉ ↔ 6–18 in (15–45 cm)
↑3–12 in (8–30 cm)
Saxifraga species hybridize freely in the wild, and many garden plants are of indeterminate parentage. Suited to rock and alpine gardens. Cultivars include 'James Bremner', 6 in (15 cm) tall, creamy white flowers; 'Purple Robe', dense foliage cushion, many tall sprays of purple-pink flowers; 'Southside Seedling' dark green spoon-shaped leaves in rosettes, arching panicles of white saucer-like flowers; 'Tumbling Waters' (syn. *S. longifolia* 'Tumbling Waters'), dark green rosettes, arching racemes of star-shaped white flowers; 'Whitehill', gray-green foliage with crusty white edges, white flowers on stems to 12 in (30 cm) tall. Zones 6–9.

SCABIOSA
SCABIOUS
Belonging to the teasel (Dipsacaceae) family, the genus comprises around 80 species of annuals and perennials found throughout Europe, parts of Africa, and Japan. Most species form a spreading basal clump of light green to gray-green, rounded to lance-shaped leaves with deeply incised notches or lobes. A few species have an erect or branching habit. The flowers are individually tiny, but occur in rounded to flattened composite heads on stems held clear of the foliage. White and pale yellow to soft pink or powder blue and mauve are the usual colors.

CULTIVATION: *Scabiosa* species are hardy and easily grown in any sunny position in fertile, moist, free-draining, slightly alkaline soil. Propagate annuals from seed and perennials from seed and basal cuttings, or by division.

Scabiosa atropurpurea 'Chile Black'

Scabiosa atropurpurea
EGYPTIAN ROSE, MOURNFUL WIDOW, SWEET SCABIOUS
☼/◐ ❉ ↔ 16–30 in (40–75 cm)
↑16–36 in (40–90 cm)
Annual, biennial, or short-lived perennial herb from southern Europe. Basal cluster of light green to gray-green, lobed or toothed leaves, to 6 in (15 cm) long, upper leaves shorter and more deeply lobed, almost pinnate. Flowerheads crimson to deep purple-black, fragrant, to 2 in (5 cm) wide, in summer–early autumn. 'Blue Cockade', 36 in (90 cm) tall,

rounded, deep blue, double flowerheads; **'Chile Black'**, 24 in (60 cm) tall, deep black-red flowers with minute flecks of lavender; **'Peter Ray'**, 24 in (60 cm) tall, large purple-black flowerheads; **'Salmon Queen'**, 36 in (90 cm) tall, deep salmon pink to light red double flowers. Zones 8–10.

Scabiosa caucasica

☼/❁ ❄ ↔ 16–18 in (40–45 cm) ↕ 20–36 in (50–90 cm)
Perennial, native to the Caucasus region. Gray-green to blue-green leaves, basal foliage lance-shaped, large, smooth-edged; upper leaves lobed almost to midrib. Powder blue flowers bloom in heads to 3 in (8 cm) wide. Summer- to autumn-flowering. Cultivars include **'Alba'**, white flowers; **'Bressingham White'**, white flowers; **'Clive Greaves'** ★, pale lavender blue flowers; **'Fama'**, bright blue flowers; **'Floral Queen'**, tall, vigorous, flowers light blue; **'Miss Willmott'**, tall, flowers cream; **'Nachtfalter'**, dark purple flowers; **'Pink Lace'**, bright pink flowers. Zones 4–10.

Scabiosa columbaria

☼/❁ ❄ ↔ 16 in (40 cm) ↕ 24 in (60 cm)
Biennial or short-lived perennial from temperate Eurasia and North Africa. Stems and foliage gray-green, woolly; basal leaves smooth-edged to deeply lobed, upper leaves pinnate, often further divided. Lavender to purple-blue flowerheads to 1¾ in (40 mm) wide, in summer. *S. c.* **var.** *ochroleuca*, 36 in (90 cm) tall, primrose flowerheads. *S.c.* **'Butterfly Blue'**, 28 in (70 cm) tall, lavender blue; **'Pink Mist'**, 24 in (60 cm) tall, light pink. Zones 6–10.

Scabiosa lucida

☼ ❄ ↔ 12–20 in (30–50 cm) ↕ 12 in (30 cm)
Low spreading perennial from central Europe. Deeply divided, hairy, dark green to silvery leaves. Lavender-pink to purple-red flowerheads to 1¾ in (40 mm) wide. Summer- to autumn-flowering. **'Rosea'**, pale pink flowers. Zones 5–10.

SCAEVOLA

This genus from the family Goodeniaceae contains nearly 100 plants from Australia and islands in the Indian and Pacific Oceans, and includes shrubs, subshrubs, and perennials. Many have a ground-hugging habit, and provide reliable ground cover in temperate areas. The leaves of most species are small, somewhat succulent, often hairy, and usually carried on short, often brittle stems. The foliage is covered in fan-shaped flowers in varying shades of blue, sometimes white, over a long period from mid-winter onward.
CULTIVATION: Full sun and freely draining soil are the main requirements. Many species are resistant to salt spray, making them ideal plants for coastal sites, but they do need a frost-free position. Propagate from cuttings taken in the warmer months.

Scaevola aemula

☼ ❂ ↔ 20 in (50 cm) ↕ 6 in (15 cm)
Perennial from southern and eastern Australia. Variable, usually prostrate habit; oblong, wedge-shaped, toothed leaves. Pale mauve-blue fan-shaped flowers, 1¼ in (30 mm) wide, along stems. Spring- to summer-flowering. Cultivars include **'Blue Fan'**, **'Blue Wonder'**, and **'New Wonder'**, more vigorous and upright growth habit; **'Mauve Clusters'** ★, mauve-pink flowers; **'Purple Fanfare'**, large flowers produced throughout most of year. Zones 9–11.

Scaevola aemula

SCHAUERIA

This genus, a member of the acanthus (Acanthaceae) family, contains 8 species of evergreen shrubs and subshrubs, native to Brazil. They are grown for their spikes of narrow tubular flowers; the bristly calyces give a brush-like appearance.
CULTIVATION: In tropical climates, plant *Schaueria* species outdoors in a rich moist soil. In cool climates they are suitable for the conservatory or greenhouse, but will require shading during the hottest part of the day. Propagate by softwood cuttings.

Schaueria flavicoma

☼ ✈ ↔ 24 in (60 cm) ↕ 36 in (90 cm)
Erect perennial subshrub from Brazil. Glossy green leaves, prominent pale veins and midribs. Dense spikes of narrow, soft yellow, tubular flowers; downy to bristly yellow-green calyces. Zones 10–12.

Schaueria flavicoma

SCHIZANTHUS
POOR MAN'S ORCHID

This Chilean genus of 12 species of annuals and biennials belongs to the nightshade (Solanaceae) family, although the relationship is not an obvious one. The species are small upright plants around 12 in (30 cm) tall, with soft, green, ferny foliage, often covered with fine hairs. Flowers are borne in branching panicles that are held above the foliage. They are beautifully marked and shaped, with a prominent lower lip, hence the common name. Modern strains are available in a wide range of colors and sizes.
CULTIVATION: These plants are easily grown as annuals where summer temperatures are warm and consistent. Elsewhere they are best treated as greenhouse plants, as they are intolerant of cold. Grow in a bright position in fertile, moist, well-drained soil. Raise from seed, with several sowings to ensure continued flowering.

Schizanthus pinnatus
↔ 8–16 in (20–40 cm) ↕ 8–20 in (20–50 cm)
Annual; bushy habit; lance-shaped, usually lobed, light green leaves. Tightly clustered heads of flat flowers, lobes almost evenly sized, in summer–autumn. White-throated deep pink flowers, yellow and black central markings. Garden forms in many colors. Zones 9–11.

Schizanthus × wisetonensis
↔ 12 in (30 cm) ↕ 12–20 in (30–50 cm)
Garden hybrid annual; *S. pinnatus* × *S. grahamii* parentage. Several cultivars resembling *S. pinnatus* in foliage and habit. Flowers in various colors. Zones 9–11.

Schizanthus × wisetonensis

SCLERANTHUS

This genus, a member of the pink (Caryophyllaceae) family, contains up to 10 species that occur naturally in Europe, Asia, Africa, South America, Australia, New Guinea, and New Zealand. Perennials or annuals, they have a densely tufted ground-covering habit. The small, linear, usually green leaves are joined at the base of the stems. The pale creamy green flowers are small, often less than ¼ in (6 mm) wide, and are hard to see on some species. The plants are shallow-rooted, and generally all species creep along the ground, forming dense cushions.

Scleranthus biflorus

CULTIVATION: These plants like sun or shade, but not long periods of dry or heavy wet weather. Propagate from stem cuttings in autumn or from fresh seed.

Scleranthus biflorus
↔ 12 in (30 cm) ↕ 2–4 in (5–10 cm)
From New Zealand; dense, perennial, mat-forming plant. Tiny, needle-like, bright green, sometimes lime green, foliage. Conspicuous pale creamy green flowers, in summer. Zones 5–9.

SCROPHULARIA
FIGWORT

The members of this genus of some 200 species in the foxglove (Scrophulariaceae) family are mainly perennials. Often marsh-dwellers, they come mostly from temperate parts of the Northern Hemisphere, although some species are found as far south as Central America. The stems are 4-angled; their leaves may be compound or simple, and alternate or opposite. The flowers are usually small, like tiny, fat, inflated foxgloves *(Digitalis)* with a lower lip, in bronze, copper, or dull red. Some species are garden weeds.
CULTIVATION: Most species grow well in moist humus-rich soil in dappled shade; some are aquatic. Propagation is by seed sown in situ, or from basal cuttings taken in spring.

Scrophularia auriculata
syn. *Scrophularia aquatica*
WATER BETONY, WATER FIGWORT
↔ 36–48 in (90–120 cm) ↕ 36–48 in (90–120 cm)
Vigorous marginal aquatic species from western Europe. Opposite leaves, to 10 in (25 cm) long, slightly toothed. Open sprays of tiny, rounded, reddish brown flowers, drooping lip, yellowish green interior, in summer. 'Variegata', leaves with bold white edges. Zones 5–10.

SCUTELLARIA
HELMET FLOWER, SKULLCAP

This genus of about 300 species of annuals and perennials is a member of the mint (Lamiaceae) family. They are found mostly in temperate Northern Hemisphere regions, where they grow in scrub, open woodland, and grassland. The roots are often rhizomatous, and the plants are erect or sprawling, ranging from 6 in (15 cm) to 4 ft (1.2 m) high. The leaves are opposite and simple, sometimes pinnate or toothed. The 2-lipped tubular flowers emerge from hooded calyces, which give the genus its common names. The blue, white, or yellow flowers appear in summer singly, in pairs, or on the ends of spikes. A number of species are grown ornamentally, and some are used in herbal medicine for their anti-spasmodic properties.
CULTIVATION: Plant taller species in borders and smaller species at the edges of borders or in rock gardens. Grow in full sun in any reasonable soil. Water well in dry summers. Propagate from seed or by division.

Scutellaria alpina

☼ ❄ ↔ 18 in (45 cm) ↑ 6–10 in (15–25 cm)

Found in mountains from southern Europe to Siberia. Sprawling perennial; often roots at nodes; mats of small oval leaves. Small flowers in crowded racemes, purple to pale pink, often with yellow on lower lip, in late spring–early summer. *S. a.* subsp. *supina*, soft lemon flowers. *S. a.* 'Arcobaleno', bluish purple to white, rose, and pale yellow flowers, contrasting colors on lower lip. Zones 5–9.

Scutellaria baicalensis

☼ ❄ ↔ 8 in (20 cm) ↑ 16 in (40 cm)

Found from Siberia to Japan. Sprawling plant; stems often suffused with purple; small, narrow, slightly hairy leaves. Dense heads of velvety, purple, tubular flowers, white lower lip, in summer. Zones 5–9.

Scutellaria galericulata

☼ ❄ ↔ 8–12 in (20–30 cm) ↑ 12–24 in (30–60 cm)

Erect or spreading perennial from temperate Eurasia and North America. Pointed leaves to 2 in (5 cm) long. Flowers lavender-blue, white marks within; lower lip sometimes paler with dark blue speckling. Summer-flowering. Zones 5–9.

Scutellaria incana

DOWNY SKULLCAP

☼ ❄ ↔ 24 in (60 cm) ↑ 24–48 in (60–120 cm)

Bushy perennial from eastern North America. Oval leaves, to 3 in (8 cm) long, grayish green, with minute hairs. Dense panicles of velvety purplish blue flowers in summer–autumn. Zones 4–9.

Scutellaria indica

☼ ❄ ↔ 12 in (30 cm) ↑ 6 in (15 cm)

Low-growing mat-forming perennial; native to Japan, Korea, and China. Small, rounded, grayish green leaves, toothed edges. Pale purplish blue flowers in summer. *S. i.* var. *parvifolia* ★, dark green leaves, relatively large lavender-blue flowers. Zones 5–9.

Scutellaria orientalis

☼ ❄ ↔ 6–10 in (15–25 cm) ↑ 12–18 in (30–45 cm)

Low mounding subshrub; native to southeastern Europe. Small oval leaves, dark green above, woolly gray beneath. Dense racemes of lemon yellow flowers, sometimes tinged or spotted with red. Summer-flowering. Zones 7–10.

SEDUM *(see page 843)*

Sedum spectabile ★

syn. *Hylotelephium spectabile*

ICE PLANT

☼ ❄ ↔ 16–32 in (40–80 cm)
↑ 27 in (70 cm)

Perennial from Korea and nearby parts of China. Erect thickened stems; fleshy, toothed, elliptical leaves, 2–4 in (5–10 cm) long. Large 3-branched heads of small pink to red flowers

Scutellaria orientalis

in late summer–autumn. 'Brilliant' ★, pink flowers; 'Iceberg', white flowers, sometimes tinted with pink; 'Indian Chief', deep pink to purple-red flowers. Zones 6–10.

Sedum telephium

syn. *Hylotelephium telephium*

LIVE-FOREVER, ORPINE

☼ ❄ ↔ 24–32 in (60–80 cm) ↑ 24 in (60 cm)

Found from eastern Europe to Japan. Perennial; erect thickened stems; fleshy, toothed, pointed oval leaves, to 3 in (8 cm) long. Heads of many purple-red flowers in late summer. *S. t.* subsp. *maximum* 'Atropurpureum', deep purple-red foliage, red flowers. *S. t.* 'Matrona', stems tinted red, very pale pink flowers; 'Mohrchen', deep red flowers, purple-red foliage. Zones 6–10.

Sedum Hybrid Cultivars

☼ ❄ ↔ 12–24 in (30–60 cm) ↑ 12–24 in (30–60 cm)

Several popular interspecies garden hybrids are placed in the subgenus *Hylotelephium*; these are mainly autumn-flowering, though foliage is also attractive. 'Herbstfreude' (syn. 'Autumn Joy') (*S. telephium* × *S. spectabile*), blue-green foliage, salmon pink flowers ageing to bronze; 'Ruby Glow' (*S. cauticolum* × *S. telephium*), purple-green foliage, often pink-edged, deep red flowers; 'Vera Jameson' ('Ruby Glow' × *S. telephium* subsp. *maximum* 'Atropurpureum'), purple foliage, light pink flowers. Zones 6–10.

Sedum, Hybrid Cultivar, 'Ruby Glow'

Semiaquilegia ecalcarata

Senecio cineraria 'Silver Dust'

Serissa japonica 'Flore Pleno'

SEMIAQUILEGIA

This genus, belonging to the buttercup (Ranunculaceae) family, contains 7 species of low perennial plants closely related to *Aquilegia*. Native to Asia, they grow in high mountain grassland and scrub in damp conditions. The lacy foliage resembles maidenhair fern *(Adiantum)*, with leaves comprised of 3 leaflets. The nodding flowers are in shades of pink, red, and purple, often plump with many petals, but lacking the spurs typical of *Aquilegia* species.
CULTIVATION: Suitable for the rock garden, these plants should be grown in full sun to half-sun. They require a moist but well-drained soil. Propagate from seed or by division.

Semiaquilegia ecalcarata
☼/◑ ❀ ↔ 8–10 in (20–25 cm) ↑ 12 in (30 cm)
Perennial species, native to western China. Clumps of deeply divided ferny foliage, often with purplish tinge. Nodding cup-like flowers, pink to purple, in loose panicles, in summer. Zones 6–9.

SENECIO *(see page 846)*

Senecio cineraria
syn. *Cineraria maritima*
DUSTY MILLER, SEA RAGWORT
☼ ❀ ↔ 16 in (40 cm) ↑ 20 in (50 cm)
From southern Europe; naturalized in southern England. Mounding subshrub; leaves deeply dissected and lobed, intensely silver-white. Small heads of yellow daisies in summer. 'Cirrus', grayish blue rounded-lobed leaves; 'Silver Dust' ★, broad, deeply cut, pewter leaves; 'Silver Lace', rounded leaves deeply lobed but less dissected; 'White Diamond', finely dissected white leaves, compact habit. Zones 7–10.

Senecio vira-vira
syn. *Senecio leucostachys*
DUSTY MILLER
☼ ❀ ↔ 12–24 in (30–60 cm) ↑ 16–24 in (40–60 cm)
Shrubby perennial; native to Argentina. Covered in dense white hairs. Lacy effect of finely divided, soft, silvery gray leaves. Small, creamy, button-like flowers in summer. Zones 8–11.

SENNA *(see page 304)*

Senna hebecarpa
WILD SENNA
☼ ❀ ↔ 24 in (60 cm) ↑ 4–6 ft (1.2–1.8 m)
Native to eastern USA; endangered in some states. Well-foliaged perennial; pinnately divided leaves. Yellow flowers in large racemes in summer. Long black seed pods. Zones 4–9.

SERISSA

The sole species in this genus from the madder (Rubiaceae) family is a small, densely branched, evergreen shrub from warm-temperate Southeast Asia. It is a neat little bush with tiny leaves that emit an unpleasant smell when crushed. It produces small white flowers followed by berries, but it is often grown as a foliage plant; there are several variegated cultivars.
CULTIVATION: Somewhat frost tender, *Serissa* likes a warm, moist, humid climate and a rich soil with plenty of humus. For cooler climates, it makes an excellent greenhouse or conservatory plant. Propagate from cuttings or from self-layered pieces.

Serissa japonica
syn. *Serissa foetida*
☼ ❊ ↔ 18 in (45 cm) ↑ 18 in (45 cm)
Attractive plant; popular bonsai subject. White flowers in spring–autumn. 'Flore Pleno', very compact bush with double flowers; 'Mount Fuji', very compact, leaves edged and striped with white; 'Variegata Pink', pink flowers, white-edged leaves. Zones 9–11.

SHORTIA
syn. *Schizocodon*
This genus in the family Diapensiaceae comprises 6 dainty, rhizomatous, clumping, evergreen perennials. Five are native to East Asia, the other to the woodlands of southeastern USA. The leaves are heart-shaped, rounded, or elliptical, toothed and leathery, and are usually glossy dark green, often turning red in winter. In early spring they bear bell-, trumpet-, or funnel-shaped, white to deep pink flowers with toothed or fringed petals.
CULTIVATION: All appreciate humus-rich, acidic, moist but well-drained soil and part- to full shade. They are a challenge to grow in dry regions, even with adequate water; regions with cool damp summers are preferred. Sow seed when ripe in autumn, or propagate by basal cuttings in early summer or runners in mid-summer.

Shortia galacifolia
OCONEE BELLS

❀ ❈ ↔ 10 in (25 cm) ↑ 6 in (15 cm)

Perennial species; native of southeastern USA. Large clump of roundish glossy green leaves, scalloped edges, bronze-red in winter. Nodding, rose-flushed white, bell-shaped flowers, toothed edges. Spring-flowering. Zones 6–9.

Shortia soldanelloides
FRINGE BELLS, FRINGED GALAX

❀ ❈ ↔ 10 in (25 cm) ↑ 6 in (15 cm)

Evergreen perennial from Japan. Round coarsely toothed leaves. Pinkish rose flowers, deeply fringed, whitish edges, in spring. *S. s.* var. *ilicifolia,* smaller, with smaller sparsely and coarsely toothed leaves, white or occasionally pink flowers. Zones 6–9.

SIDALCEA
FALSE MALLOW

This genus, containing about 22 annual and perennial species, is a member of the mallow (Malvaceae) family. Native to western parts of North America, these plants can be found growing on lime-free sandy grasslands along stream beds, and in damp mountain meadows. Resembling a small hollyhock (*Alcea rosea*), to which they are related, they have glossy, round, palmately lobed basal leaves and stiffly upright flower spikes that bear stalkless or short-stemmed, white, pink, or purple, open, cup-shaped flowers at the ends. These are popular plants for perennial borders, and many improved varieties are bred for their color and length of flowering.

CULTIVATION: *Sidalcea* species require a humus-rich free-draining soil in a sunny position. They will flower freely throughout summer if spent flower spikes are removed. Propagation is by division or from seed.

Sidalcea candida
❀ ❈ ↔ 20 in (50 cm) ↑ 24–36 in (60–90 cm)

From Utah, New Mexico, Wyoming, and Colorado, USA. Roundish, 7-lobed, glossy leaves on long stalks. White flowers with bluish anthers, on branching stems, in early summer. Parent, with *S. malviflora,* of many modern cultivars. Zones 5–9.

Sidalcea malviflora
CHECKERBLOOM

❀/❀ ❈ ↔ 16–30 in (40–75 cm) ↑ 24–40 in (60–100 cm)

Clump-forming perennial found from Oregon, USA, to Baja California, Mexico. Erect stems; 7- to 9-lobed leaves, 1–2 in (25–50 mm) long, shallow-toothed. Racemes of many pink to lavender flowers, 1–2 in (25–50 mm) wide, from spring to autumn. Zones 6–10.

Sidalcea oregana
❀ ❈ ↔ 20 in (50 cm) ↑ 48 in (120 cm)

Found from Washington to California and Nevada, USA. Round basal leaves, shallow-lobed, up to 6 in (15 cm) across, stem leaves shiny green and segmented. Small deep pink flowers in dense racemes in summer. Zones 5–9.

Sidalcea Hybrid Cultivars
❀/❀ ❈ ↔ 16–24 in (40–60 cm) ↑ 24–32 in (60–80 cm)

Compact heavy-blooming plants, flowers usually held well above foliage. 'Elsie Heugh', dainty shell pink flowers; 'Little Princess', miniature, compact, soft pink flowers; 'Rose Queen' ★, deep rose pink flowers; 'Sussex Beauty', large pale pink flowers; 'Monarch', taller cultivar, pink flowers. Zones 6–10.

SILENE
CAMPION, CATCHFLY, CUSHION PINK

This large and varied genus in the pink (Caryophyllaceae) family contains about 500 annuals and perennials widely distributed throughout the Northern Hemisphere and southern Africa. The flowers are 5-petalled, generally white or shades of pink, and may be solitary or borne in one-sided spikes. The leaves and stems of many species are downy and sticky to the touch.

CULTIVATION: Good drainage is essential for cultivation of these plants, as is a light loamy soil in a sunny position. Propagation is from seed or cuttings, or by division.

Silene acaulis
CUSHION PINK, MOSS CAMPION

❀ ❈ ↔ 4 in (10 cm) ↑ 2 in (5 cm)

Perennial from Eurasia and North America extending into higher mountain regions further south. Low, dense, tufted cushion; bright green linear leaves. Solitary deep pink to purple flowers sit just above foliage. Numerous cultivars. Zones 2–8.

Silene alpestris
syns *Heliosperma alpestre, Silene quadrifida*

❀/❀ ❈ ↔ 12 in (30 cm) ↑ 6–12 in (15–30 cm)

Found from the southern European Alps to Caucasus region. Low loose cushion of linear-lanceolate leaves. Starry flowers, white, rarely pink, with cleft or fringed petals, in summer. Zones 5–9.

Sidalcea, Hybrid Cultivar, 'Elsie Heugh'

Silene dioica

RED CAMPION

☼/◑ ❄ ↔ 12 in (30 cm) ↑ 24 in (60 cm)

From woods, rocky hillsides, and cliffs of Europe. Perennial; rosettes of downy leaves. Tall, stiff, branching stems; bright pink flowers, rarely white, in summer. Zones 6–10.

Silene fimbriata

☼/◑ ❄ ↔ 24 in (60 cm) ↑ 40 in (100 cm)

Perennial, native to damp woodlands of the Caucasus region. Rosettes of dark green, hairy, oval leaves. Open panicles of fringed white flowers, swollen globular calyces. Early summer-flowering. Zones 5–8.

Silene laciniata

FRINGED INDIAN PINK, MEXICAN CAMPION

☼ ❄ ↔ 8 in (20 cm) ↑ 36 in (90 cm)

From California and New Mexico, USA, and Mexico. Narrow oval leaves. Upright stems; large, starry, crimson flowers. Zones 7–10.

Silene schafta

☼ ❄ ↔ 8 in (20 cm) ↑ 4 in (10 cm)

Perennial from Caucasus region. Upright stems; small, bright green, linear leaves form loose mat. Star-shaped, rosy magenta flowers, cleft petals, in late summer–autumn. Zones 5–9.

Silene uniflora

syn. *Silene vulgaris* subsp. *maritima*

BLADDER CAMPION, SEA CAMPION

☼ ❄ ↔ 4 in (10 cm) ↑ 4–8 in (10–20 cm)

Perennial, native to coasts of western Europe and North Africa. gray-tinged oval to spathulate leaves. Upright flower stems; profuse, solitary, white blooms, pronounced inflated calyx like a small bladder. Summer-flowering. **'Robin Whitebreast'** (syn. 'Flore Pleno'), gray leaves, abundant double white flowers. Zones 5–9.

Silphium perfoliatum

SILPHIUM

This genus of 23 species of coarse-leafed perennials native to central and eastern North America is in the daisy (Asteraceae) family. The simple to deeply divided leaves are opposite to whorled, the basal ones forming a rosette, those on the inflorescence stalks spirally arranged. The daisy-like flowerheads are large and have numerous outer rayed white or yellow florets growing in 2 or 3 rows, with small yellow disc florets.

CULTIVATION: Mostly suited to the wild garden, *Silphium* species grow in a position in full sun or very light shade in any soil that is not too nitrogen-rich. Seed is the best method of propagation, because the deep root system of larger species makes them difficult to propagate vegetatively.

Silphium laciniatum

COMPASS PLANT

☼/◑ ❄ ↔ 3–4 ft (0.9–1.2 m) ↑ 5–10 ft (1.5–3 m)

From central USA. Strongly erect, hairy, fern-like leaves, 4–16 in (10–40 cm) long, aligned north–south. Clusters of bright yellow flowerheads in summer. Zones 4–9.

Silphium perfoliatum

CUP PLANT

☼/◑ ❄ ↔ 3 ft (0.9 m) ↑ 5 ft (1.5 m)

From damp woodlands and prairies of eastern North America. Forms large clump of rough, irregularly toothed, ovate leaves, upper leaves stem-clasping. Stiffly upright stems branching toward top; single yellow daisy flowers. Zones 5–10.

Silphium terebinthinaceum

PRAIRIE DOCK

☼/◑ ❄ ↔ 3–6 ft (0.9–1.8 m) ↑ 7–10 ft (2–3 m)

From southern Canada to southeastern USA. Dense clump of large, long-stemmed basal leaves, to over 12 in (30 cm) long, heart-shaped at base, toothed or lobed near tip. Erect red-brown flower stems; sprays of 1–2 in (25–50 mm) wide golden flowerheads with many ray florets, in summer. Zones 4–9.

SILYBUM

This genus, belonging to the daisy (Asteraceae) family, contains just 2 species of annual or biennial plants grown for their ornamental foliage. They are native to the Mediterranean region and eastern Africa, where they grow in sunny free-draining areas. They are robust upright plants forming basal rosettes from which the stout flowering stems arise. The long leaves are lobed or pinnate with extremely spiny edges. They have prominent white veins or variegations. The purple thistle flowers are borne on tall stems in spring or summer.

CULTIVATION: Ideal candidates for border planting, grow *Silybum* species in full sun and in free-draining soil. To prolong the display of attractive foliage, the flowering stem can be removed. When allowed to flower, seed will self-sow freely. Young plants need protection from slugs and snails.

Silene fimbriata

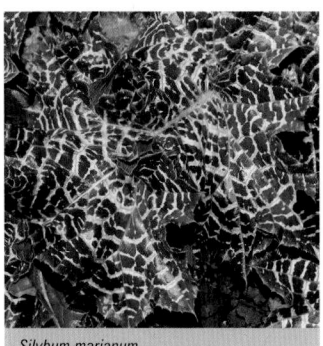
Silybum marianum

Sinningia cardinalis

Sinningia speciosa, Lawn Hybrid

Silybum marianum

BLESSED THISTLE, OUR LADY'S MILK THISTLE

☼ ❀ ↔ 2 ft (0.6 m) ↑ 4 ft (1.2 m)

Biennial, native to Europe; naturalized in the Americas. Basal rosette of long, deeply lobed, dark green leaves, with prominent white veins and spiny edges. Purplish thistle flowers. Spring- to summer-flowering. Zones 6–10.

SINNINGIA

GLOXINIA

This genus, a member of the African violet (Gesneriaceae) family, is made up of about 40 species of tuberous perennials and small shrubs found from Mexico to Argentina. The commonly cultivated species are perennials with large lance- to heart-shaped leaves made velvety by a dense covering of fine hairs. The well-known florist's gloxinia (S. speciosa) has large, upward-facing, bell-shaped flowers; other species have tubular flowers, which are sometimes scented.
CULTIVATION: These plants prefer warm humid conditions with a bright but not sunny exposure and moist, well-drained, humus-rich soil. They are widely grown as indoor or greenhouse plants in pots, and are also raised outdoors as a summer annual, or year-round in warm areas. The flower trumpets collapse if filled with water. Propagate by lifting and dividing plants after the foliage has died back, or by seed or leaf-stalk cuttings. Tubers may be stored dry.

Sinningia canescens

☼/☀ ⚘ ↔ 10 in (25 cm) ↑ 10 in (25 cm)

Perennial, native to Brazil. Heavy thickened tubers; upright stems; heart-shaped, velvety, deep green leaves, finely toothed. Small heads of up to 5 long-stemmed, tubular, bright orange flowers. Zones 11–12.

Sinningia cardinalis

☼/☀ ⚘ ↔ 12 in (30 cm) ↑ 8–12 in (20–30 cm)

Tuberous perennial from Brazil. Paired, long-stemmed, rounded to heart-shaped, velvety deep green, finely toothed leaves. Red tubular flowers, overarching upper lip, in heads of many blooms, not all open at same time. 'Innocent', low-growing cultivar, tubular white flowers. Zones 11–12.

Sinningia × pumila

☼/☀ ⚘ ↔ 6–12 in (15–30 cm) ↑ 4–6 in (10–15 cm)

Low mounding garden hybrid between S. pusilla and S. eumorpha. Short-stemmed, rounded, velvety leaves. Slightly flared, mauve, tubular flowers, to 1¼ in (30 mm) long. Zones 11–12.

Sinningia speciosa

FLORIST'S GLOXINIA, GLOXINIA

☼/☀ ⚘ ↔ 12–20 in (30–50 cm) ↑ 8–12 in (20–30 cm)

Brazilian species, popular house plant. Lush, deep green, velvety, soft-toothed, rounded to heart-shaped leaves. Upright flower stems; large bell-shaped flowers, mauve to purple with light center and contrasting spots. Cultivars have larger flowers and wider color range, including 'Boonwood Yellow Bird', yellow flowers; 'Buell's Queen Bee', white flowers, 2 conspicuous pink blotches; and 'Kiss of Fire', many small bright red flowers. Seedling strains such as Lawn Hybrids ★ available as individual colors or mixed. Zones 10–12.

SISYRINCHIUM

This genus contains about 90 species of annuals and perennials, and is a member of the iris (Iridaceae) family. These plants are native to North and South America, but have also been known to naturalize in other temperate countries. They produce clumps of stiff, upright, linear or sword-shaped leaves, which arch out into a fan shape. During spring and summer, clusters of trumpet-shaped flowers appear on spikes that hold the flowers just above the top of the foliage.
CULTIVATION: While frost tolerance varies with the species, these are otherwise undemanding plants that will do well when grown in poor to moderately fertile, well-drained soil. Though they will tolerate some shade, they do best in a position in full sun. Both species and cultivars propagate readily from seed and the rhizomatous clumps divide easily in autumn and spring.

Sisyrinchium 'Biscutella'

☼ ❀ ↔ 6 in (15 cm) ↑ 12 in (30 cm)

Clumping evergreen perennial; mid-green linear leaves. Upright flower stems; spikes of pale yellow flowers, dark brown to purple veining, to 1 in (25 mm) across; short-lived. Summer-flowering. Zones 7–9.

Sisyrinchium 'Californian Skies'

Sisyrinchium 'Californian Skies'

☼ ❋ ↔ 8 in (20 cm) ↑ 12 in (30 cm)

Hybrid with dark green lance-shaped foliage. Sturdy flower stems; mid-blue flowers in summer–late autumn. Zones 8–9.

Sisyrinchium californicum

syns *Sisyrinchium boreale*, *S. brachypus*
GOLDEN EYE GRASS

☼ ❋ ↔ 6 in (15 cm) ↑ 24 in (60 cm)

Found from California, USA, to British Columbia, Canada. Semi-evergreen perennial; often short-lived. Linear to sword-shaped gray-green leaves, 4–6 in (10–15 cm) long. Sturdy stems; star-shaped yellow flowers, 1 in (25 mm) wide, in summer. Zones 8–10.

Sisyrinchium graminoides

syns *Sisyrinchium angustifolium*, *S. bermudiana*
BLUE-EYED GRASS

☼ ❋ ↔ 8 in (20 cm) ↑ 20 in (50 cm)

Tight clump-forming perennial from North America. Rush-like dark green foliage year round. Star-shaped flowers, dark blue with distinctive yellow center dot, in summer–autumn. Zones 5–10.

Sisyrinchium idahoense

syns *Sisyrinchium bellum*, *S. birameum*
CALIFORNIAN BLUE-EYED GRASS

☼ ❋ ↔ 6 in (15 cm) ↑ 5 in (12 cm)

Found from Washington and Idaho to California, USA. Semi-evergreen clump-forming perennial; narrow, sword-shaped, dark green foliage. Stiff upright stems; star-shaped violet-blue flowers, yellow throats, in summer. Zones 4–9.

Sisyrinchium striatum

syn. *Phaiophleps nigricans*

☼ ❋ ↔ 14 in (35 cm) ↑ 32 in (80 cm)

From Chile and Argentina. Clump-forming upright perennial; gray-green linear foliage. Sturdy spikes of pale yellow star-shaped flowers push up on stems through foliage, in summer. 'Aunt May', creamy yellow variegated foliage. Zones 8–10.

SMITHIANTHA

This genus of 4 species of rhizomatous perennials belongs to the African-violet (Gesneriaceae) family, and grows in high-rainfall mountain areas of tropical Mexico. They are compact plants with one to several short fleshy stems and broadly heart-shaped leaves with a coating of velvety hairs. Borne in erect racemes, the long-stalked flowers are trumpet-shaped with upward-turned mouths, spotted on the inside. Many attractive hybrid cultivars exist.
CULTIVATION: Grown as conservatory or indoor plants except in the humid tropics and subtropics, these plants prefer high light levels but not direct sun and should not be allowed to dry out except during their winter dormancy period, when they should be kept dry. Resume watering in late spring. Propagate by division of rhizomes before growth begins in spring.

Smithiantha zebrina

☼ ✳ ↔ 10–18 in (25–45 cm) ↑ 18–24 in (45–60 cm)

Known in Europe since 1840 and cultivated around the world, now rare in the wild in Mexico. Leaves 6 in (15 cm) long, irregularly banded along veins with brownish purple. Racemes of few flowers in summer, stalks erect, but flowers pointing down, orange to red on outside, inside yellow with red spots. Zones 10–12.

SOLANUM (see page 307)

Solanum quitoense

NARANJILLA

☼ ✳ ↔ 7 ft (2 m) ↑ 7 ft (2 m)

Shrubby perennial, native to South America; straggly growth habit; densely covered with fine hairs. Stems and leaves light green, purple toned; leaves angularly lobed. Clusters of white flowers. Tomato-like edible orange fruit. Zones 10–12.

SOLDANELLA

This genus, belonging to the primrose (Primulaceae) family, contains 10 species of tiny alpine perennials native to the European Alps, the Carpathians, and the Balkans. They grow naturally in short damp turf and rocky places in the mountains. Plants form basal rosettes of leathery round or kidney-shaped leaves. The flowering stems often penetrate the snow cover in early spring. They bear heads of 1 to 6 hanging flowers in shades of blue to violet and white. The small funnel-shaped or bell-shaped flowers have fringed petals and are very dainty in appearance.
CULTIVATION: Grow in well-drained rich soil that in most cases should be neutral to slightly acid. Plant in an open cool position with protection from the hot midday sun. Protect from winter wet and also from slugs at flowering time. Alternatively, grow in a cool greenhouse in a gritty soil mix in bright filtered light with good ventilation. Propagation is from seed or by division.

Soldanella alpina

ALPINE SNOWBELL

☼ ❋ ↔ 8 in (20 cm) ↑ 3–6 in (8–15 cm)

From the Pyrenees and Alps, Europe. Leathery, kidney-shaped to round, dark green leaves. Violet flowers, crimson markings inside, 2 to 4, on 6 in (15 cm) stems, in spring–early summer. Zones 5–9.

Soldanella carpatica

☼ ❋ ↔ 8 in (20 cm) ↕ 3–6 in (8–15 cm)

From the Carpathian Mountains, Europe. Broad dark green leaves, to 2 in (5 cm) wide. Flowers small, fringed, violet, 2 to 5 blooms on 6 in (15 cm) stems, in spring. Zones 5–9.

Soldanella villosa

☼ ❋ ↔ 8–12 in (20–30 cm) ↕ 6–12 in (15–30 cm)

Perennial from the Pyrenees, Europe. Round or kidney-shaped leaves to 2½ in (6 cm) wide, pale green beneath. Hairy flowering stalks, to 12 in (30 cm) high; 3 to 4 violet fringed flowers per stalk in early spring. Zones 5–9.

Soldanella alpina

SOLEIROLIA

BABY'S TEARS, MIND-YOUR-OWN-BUSINESS

The sole species in this genus is an evergreen mat-forming perennial native to the islands of the western Mediterranean, notably Corsica, and widely naturalized in warm countries. It is a member of the nettle (Urticaceae) family. The branches are fine and root at the nodes. The tiny leaves are almost circular and spirally arranged but appear alternate. The white flowers are pink-tinged, minute, solitary, 4-petalled, and held in the leaf axils.

CULTIVATION: Makes a neat ground cover in greenhouses, and in terraria, for temperate regions. Its invasive habit makes it less welcome in warmer climates. Plant in humus-rich well-drained soil; it is intolerant of scorching midday sun. Propagate by division.

Soleirolia soleirolii

syn. *Helxine soleirolii*

ANGEL'S TEARS, BABY'S TEARS, MIND-YOUR-OWN-BUSINESS

☼/◑ ☀ ↔ 2–4 ft (0.6–1.2 m) ↕ 2–4 in (5–10 cm)

From Corsica and nearby islands, widely naturalized in Europe; creeping mat-forming perennial. Can be invasive. Tightly packed, small, rounded, bright green leaves. Tiny, 4-petalled, solitary flowers, white tinged with pink, in summer. 'Aurea', yellowish green leaves. Zones 9–12.

SOLENOSTEMON

This genus, belonging to the mint (Lamiaceae) family, contains 60 species of shrubby plants native to tropical Africa and Asia. They may be erect, prostrate, or sprawling and are sometimes downy or succulent. Some of the species were previously included in the closely related genera *Plectranthus* and *Coleus*. Species of *Solenostemon* are grown for their colorful foliage that is often strikingly blotched or variegated, the leaves being pointed oval with toothed or scalloped edges. The flowers have little importance for their appearance, and are the typical tubular 2-lipped flowers of the mint family.

CULTIVATION: In cool temperate climates, grow *Solenostemon* species in the conservatory, as house plants, or outdoors as annual bedding plants. In frost-free areas the plants can remain outdoors. Grow in any reasonable soil or potting mix in direct sunlight. Pinch back the growing tips regularly to maintain the plant's bushy shape and to prevent flowering. Propagation is easy from seed or from cuttings of desired plants.

Solenostemon scutellarioides

syns *Coleus blumei*, *C. scutellarioides*, *Plectranthus scutellarioides*

COLEUS, PAINTED NETTLE

☼/◑ ☀ ↔ 12–24 in (30–60 cm) ↕ 12–24 in (30–60 cm)

From southeastern Asia. Shrubby plant; square, semi-succulent, lightly downy stems. Pointed oval, scallop-edged leaves, extremely variable, with green, red, purple, white, and yellow combinations. Insignificant flowers. 'Cantigny Royale', reddish purple leaves; 'Crimson Ruffles', crimson leaves, lighter veins, ruffled edges; 'Crinkly Bottom', deep blue-purple leaves, bright green edges; 'Display', burnt orange leaves, bright green edges; **Dragon Series**, large leaves, serrated-edged, scarlet to purple and black, gold edging; 'Frogs-foot Purple', magenta leaves with deep purple edges; 'Jupiter', beet red crinkly leaves, edged pale green; 'Kiwi Fern', deeply serrated crimson leaves, edged lemon; 'Lemon Dash', brilliant green leaves, yellow center; 'Muriel Pedley', blood red leaves, splashed yellow, bright green edges; 'Pineapple Beauty', deep maroon splashed, golden green leaves; **Rainbow Series**, variegated in greens, creams, and purples, irregularly marked leaves of yellow, red, copper, purple, and green, including 'Rainbow Fringed Mix', cut frilly edged leaves; 'Solar Eclipse', serrated edges; 'Walter Turner', red to dark red leaves, bright green edges; 'White Pheasant', serrated-edged rich green leaves, pale lemon center; 'Winsley Tapestry', highly serrated bright green leaves, beet red center; 'Winsome', vivid green leaves, vivid red to black centers. Zones 10–12.

Solenostemon scutellarioides, Dragon Series, 'Black Dragon'

SOLIDAGO

GOLDENROD

Although a few species are found in other temperate regions, this genus of around 100 species of perennials is primarily North American, and belongs to the daisy (Asteraceae) family. They form clumps of upright, sometimes branching stems, the upper half of which develops panicles of tiny golden yellow flowers. The leaves may be linear, lance-shaped, or pointed oval, and usually have toothed edges. Often, by the time flowering starts in late summer, many of the lower leaves have withered somewhat.
CULTIVATION: Very hardy plants, easily grown in full sun or half-sun in any position, in reasonably fertile, moist, and well-drained soil. They will grow in poor soil and withstand drought but will not flower well or reach maximum size in such conditions. Propagate from seed, basal cuttings, or by division. May self-sow.

Solidago bicolor

SILVERROD

☼/◗ ❋ ↔ 24 in (60 cm) ↑ 40 in (100 cm)
Perennial, native to eastern and central North America. Broad lance-shaped leaves, smooth-edged or toothed, to 8 in (20 cm) long. White to pale yellow flowerheads, in upright spikes, sometimes widely spaced, in late summer–autumn. Zones 4–9.

Solidago californica

CALIFORNIA GOLDENROD

☼/◗ ❋ ↔ 24–32 in (60–80 cm) ↑ 40–48 in (100–120 cm)
From southwestern USA east to New Mexico and south to Mexico. Narrow, pointed oval leaves, to more than 4 in (10 cm) long. Deep yellow flowerheads, in slightly overarching spikes, in autumn. Zones 8–10.

Solidago canadensis

☼/◗ ❋ ↔ 40 in (100 cm) ↑ 60 in (150 cm)
Erect species widespread throughout North America. Narrow lance-shaped leaves, to 4 in (10 cm) long, serrated edges. Short

Solidago canadensis

panicles of golden yellow flowers in late summer–autumn. *S. c.* subsp. *elongata*, minutely bristly stems and leaves. Zones 3–9.

Solidago rugosa

ROUGH-STEMMED GOLDENROD

☼/◗ ❋ ↔ 40 in (100 cm) ↑ 60 in (150 cm)
From eastern North America. Densely foliaged basal clump; broad lance-shaped leaves to over 5 in (12 cm) long, bristly, toothed. Small bright yellow flowerheads in late summer. 'Fireworks', heavy flowering, starburst-like array of panicles. Zones 3–9.

Solidago virgaurea

☼/◗ ❋ ↔ 24 in (60 cm) ↑ 40 in (100 cm)
Herbaceous perennial, native to Europe. Downy, finely toothed, broad lance-shaped leaves, to 4 in (10 cm) long near plant base, becoming smaller higher up. Elongated branching sprays of yellow flowers. Summer- to autumn-flowering. Zones 5–9.

Solidago Hybrid Cultivars

☼/◗ ❋ ↔ 12–48 in (30–120 cm)
↑ 24–60 in (60–150 cm)
Goldenrods, especially the hardier species from northern North America, interbreed freely, often producing vigorous heavy-flowering hybrids that generally make better garden plants. Examples include: 'Cloth of Gold', 24 in (60 cm) high, flowers deep yellow; 'Golden Wings', 60 in (150 cm) tall, toothed lance-shaped leaves, feathery panicles of bright yellow flowers; 'Goldenmosa' ★, 40 in (100 cm) tall, with strongly erect cane-like stems and small, overarched, bright yellow plumes; and 'Summershine', panicles of golden yellow flowers. Zones 4–9.

Solidago californica

× *SOLIDASTER*

This is a hybrid genus, arising in cultivation, of a single clump-forming perennial. It is most probably a cross between *Solidago canadensis* and *Aster ptarmicoides*, both members of the daisy (Asteraceae) family, and was found in 1910 in a nursery in Lyons, France. It bears tiny daisy flowers from late summer through to autumn. This plant is an ideal candidate for border plantings, and the blooms make good cut flowers for fresh or dried floral arrangements.

CULTIVATION: This attractive plant will grow well in a sunny well-drained border with moist but not wet soils. It will do best in a non-humid Mediterranean climate: it is fully frost hardy. Propagation is by dividing dormant plants in winter or from basal cuttings taken in spring.

× *Solidaster luteus*
syn. × *Solidaster hybridus*

☼ ❋ ↔ 12–15 in (30–38 cm)
↕ 32–36 in (80–90 cm)

Erect clump-forming perennial; leaves to 6 in (15 cm) long. Sprays of tiny daisy flowers, soft yellow, darker disc florets, from late summer to autumn. 'Lemore', profuse flowers, paler yellow. Zones 6–10.

SPATHIPHYLLUM

PEACE LILY

This genus of 36 species of evergreen perennials originates mainly in the American tropics, and is a member of the arum (Araceae) family. Peace lilies are large clump-forming plants with strong rhizomes, from which emerge lush, dark green, long-stemmed leaves that taper to a fine point and have a prominent midrib and veining. The tiny flowers, which are usually cream, are borne on an upright spike backed and partially enclosed by a large leafy spathe, which is often pure white but may be cream or pale green. In recent years, peace lilies have gained a reputation for their ability to remove vaporized solvents from the atmosphere. This characteristic, along with their ability to flower with fairly low light levels, has resulted in peace liles being widely used as pot plants in shopping malls and offices.

CULTIVATION: *Spathiphyllum* species will perform best in a warm humid environment with fertile, deep, moist, humus-rich, well-drained soil. Water and feed well. Propagate by division.

Spathiphyllum cannifolium

☀ ✛ ↔ 40 in (100 cm) ↕ 40 in (100 cm)

Evergreen perennial, native to tropical South America and Trinidad. Long-stemmed leaves, lighter colored, less heavily veined than most species, on long stalk. Spathe usually folded back, white inside, green-tinted exterior. White to pale gray-green spadix. Zones 11–12.

Spathiphyllum wallisii

☀ ✛ ↔ 20–40 in (50–100 cm) ↕ 24–48 in (60–120 cm)

From Panama and Costa Rica. Dark green, heavily veined, lustrous, lance-shaped leaves, to 14 in (35 cm) long. Spathes white, ageing to green. White spadix, fragrant flowers. 'Clevelandii', large spathes, drooping leaves, deeply veined, glossy, to 16 in (40 cm) long, flowers indoors. Zones 11–12.

Spathiphyllum Hybrid Cultivars

☀ ✛ ↔ 12–60 in (30–150 cm) ↕ 12–72 in (30–180 cm)

A number of hybrid peace lilies have been raised, ranging from the fairly compact, heavy-flowering '**Tasson**', to the largest hybrid cultivar in general cultivation, '**Sensation**', which reaches over 6 ft (1.8 m) in height. Zones 11–12.

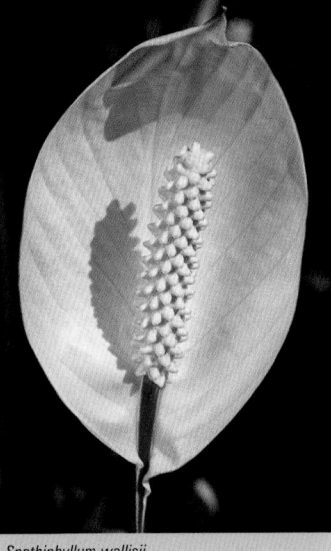

Spathiphyllum wallisii

SPHAERALCEA
syn. *Iliamna*

FALSE MALLOW, GLOBE MALLOW

This genus consists of 60 species belonging to the mallow (Malvaceae) family. Deciduous or evergreen perennials, sub-shrubs, and shrubs, they are native to the dry, even volcanic, mountain slopes of the warmer areas of North America, South America, and South Africa. The leaves are arranged in spirals, come in a variety of shapes, and are usually downy and toothed. The saucer-shaped flowers are red, pale purple, pink, white, orange, or yellow, and are produced singly in clusters or inflorescences.

CULTIVATION: Grow outdoors in full sun in well-drained moderately fertile soil and provide protection from winter moisture. If grown in pots, provide added grit to loam-based compost and feed and water moderately. Propagate by sowing seed in spring and dividing perennials at the same time. In areas with heavy winter rain, they are best protected in a cool greenhouse as excess wet, rather than cold, often kills the hardier species.

Sphaeralcea coccinea
syn. *Malvastrum coccineum*

GLOBE MALLOW, PRAIRIE MALLOW, RED FALSE MALLOW

☼ ❋ ↔ 6–12 in (15–30 cm) ↕ 6–18 in (15–45 cm)

Found from southern Canada to Arizona, USA. Well-branched perennial; white or gray felted stems. Pinnately parted leaves, rough-textured, grayish green. Short racemes of orange to red flowers in summer. Zones 4–9.

Sphaeralcea munroana

☼ ❋ ↔ 12–27 in (30–70 cm) ↕ 8–36 in (20–90 cm)

Short-lived perennial; native to western North America. Felted gray stems; small, deeply toothed, 5-lobed, hairy leaves. Apricot-pink to red or orange saucer-shaped flowers in summer. Zones 4–9.

STACHYS

BETONY, HEDGE NETTLE, WOUNDWORT

There are about 300 species in this genus in the mint (Lamiaceae) family, and they range from stoloniferous and rhizomatous perennials through to a few evergreen shrubs. In the wild these plants can be found in a range of situations, from dry mountain areas through to scrub areas, wastelands, meadows, and streamsides, particularly in northern temperate zones. The hairy, soft to touch, lance-shaped, sometimes round leaves vary in color from pale silvery grays to greens. Flowers are tubular, sometimes hooded, and vary from red, pink, and purple through to white and yellow. The foliage is often aromatic, lending itself to many uses in the ornamental garden.

CULTIVATION: *Stachys* species require well-drained open soil in full sun. They do not cope well in shade or humid areas. Propagate from seed in spring and autumn or from softwood cuttings when material is available.

Stachys byzantina

syns *Stachys lanata, S. olympica*

LAMBS' EARS, WOOLLY BETONY

☼ ❄ ↔ 24 in (60 cm) ↕ 18 in (45 cm)

Ground-hugging perennial found from the Caucasus region to Iran. Oblong to elliptical gray-green leaves with silvery white down. Upright stems of pink to purple flowers in late spring–early summer. 'Cotton Boll' ★ (syn. 'Sheila McQueen'), longer leaves, modified cottonball-like flowers. Zones 4–8.

Stachys citrina

☼ ❄ ↔ 12 in (30 cm) ↕ 8 in (20 cm)

Spreading, low-growing, woody perennial. Native to Turkey. Ovate, minutely serrated, delicately downy, soft green leaves. Spikes of yellow flowers in summer. Zones 5–7.

Stachys coccinea

SCARLET HEDGE NETTLE

☼ ❄ ↔ 18 in (45 cm) ↕ 24 in (60 cm)

Mounding perennial species found from Arizona and Texas, USA, to Mexico. Ovate to lance-shaped, slightly downy, crinkly, mid-green leaves. Upright stems of scarlet-pink flowers from mid-spring to late autumn. Zones 7–9.

Stachys byzantina

Stachys coccinea

Stachys macrantha

syns *Stachys grandiflora, S. spicata*

BIG BETONY

☼ ❄ ↔ 12–18 in (30–45 cm) ↕ 18–24 in (45–60 cm)

Upright hairy perennial from northeastern Turkey and northwestern Iran. Rosettes of wide, ovate, crinkly, veined, dark green leaves, to 3 in (8 cm) long. Spikes of hooded dark cerise-purple flowers, 1¼ in (3 cm) wide, on erect stems, in summer. 'Superba', bright cerise-purple flowers. Zones 5–7.

Stachys officinalis

syn. *Stachys betonica*

BISHOP'S WORT, WOOD BETONY

☼ ❄ ↔ 18–36 in (45–90 cm) ↕ 12–36 in (30–90 cm)

Perennial from Europe. Upright, almost completely hairless, oblong, wrinkled, mid-green leaves, to 5 in (12 cm) long. Erect stems of oblong flower spikes; purple, reddish pink, or white flowers in early summer–early autumn. 'Alba', white flowers; 'Rosea Superba', rose pink flowers. Zones 5–8.

STELLARIA

CHICKWEED, STITCHWORT

This large genus of plants belongs to the pink (Caryophyllaceae) family. About 120 species are distributed worldwide; they are annuals and perennials with brittle stems and generally tiny white flowers. Some species, such as *S. media*, commonly known as chickweed, are weeds.

CULTIVATION: *Stellaria* species with some ornamental value are only suitable in wild gardens, as fillers under large shrubs, or as light airy plants among bolder woodland perennials. Grow these plants in humus-rich soil in half-sun and propagate by division or from seed.

Stellaria holostea

GREATER STITCHWORT

☼ ❄ ↔ 3–7 ft (0.9–2 m) ↕ 20–24 in (50–60 cm)

Suckering perennial from Europe, North Africa, and western Asia. Narrow leaves to 3 in (8 cm) long. Open airy sprays of dainty white flowers in spring–early summer. Zones 5–10.

Stellaria holostea

STOKESIA

STOKES ASTER

The sole species in this genus in the daisy (Asteraceae) family has been extensively developed in cultivation. This late summer- to autumn-flowering perennial from southeastern USA is an upright plant with 6–8 in (15–20 cm) long lance-shaped leaves and large cornflower-like heads of white, yellow, or mauve to deep purple-blue flowers.
CULTIVATION: Plant in full sun or half-sun in light free-draining soil. Water and feed well. Watch for mildew in late summer. Propagate by division near end of dormant period or from seed.

Stokesia laevis

STOKES ASTER

☼/◐ ❋ ↔ 8–16 in (20–40 cm)
↑ 10–30 in (25–75 cm)
Found from South Carolina to Louisiana and northern Florida, USA. Narrow, deep green, lance-shaped leaves, smooth-edged, sometimes spiny-toothed at base. Flowerheads to 4 in (10 cm) wide, solitary or in small clusters, usually mauve to purple. '**Blue Danube**' ★, 16 in (40 cm) tall, deep blue with white center; '**Bluestone**', 10 in (25 cm) tall, bright blue; '**Mary Gregory**', pale yellow with darker center; '**Purple Parasols**', 20 in (50 cm) tall, deep violet-blue; '**Silver Moon**', 18 in (45 cm) tall, pure white; '**Wyoming**', 20 in (50 cm) tall, very dark blue flowers. Zones 6–10.

Stokesia laevis 'Purple Parasols'

STRELITZIA

Originating in South Africa, the 4 or 5 species in this genus are large evergreen perennials in the strelitzia (Strelitziaceae) family. Usually treated as shrubs or trees, they are clump-forming and have very long oblong to lance-shaped leaves that are borne on stout stalks. A large bud or spathe, borne at the end of the stem, is usually held clear of the foliage; from it opens a succession of flowers, each with a long projecting corolla and wing-like sepals, often in a striking range of contrasting colors.
CULTIVATION: They prefer full sun or partial shade, and are tender to all but the lightest frosts. Plant in moist well-drained soil; most species will tolerate brief periods of drought once established and prefer to be kept on the dry side in winter. Roots are very strong, so take care when siting. Propagate from seed, by removing suckers, or by division.

Strelitzia juncea

syns *Strelitzia* × *kewensis* var. *juncea*,
S. reginae var. *juncea*
☼ ⅋ ↔ 3–5 ft (0.9–1.5 m) ↑ 5 ft (1.5 m)
Native to South Africa's Cape region; ever-green perennial. Thick, rush-like, grayish green leaves lack blades, tapering to point. Orange flowers emerge from beaked bract, like those of *S. reginae*. Zones 10–12.

Strelitzia reginae

BIRD OF PARADISE

☼ ⅋ ↔ 3 ft (0.9 m) ↑ 6 ft (1.8 m)
Leaves 12–30 in (30–75 cm) long; stems to 6 ft (1.8 m) tall. Deep purple-blue corolla, orange calyces, in winter–spring. Cultivars include '**Kirstenbosch Gold**' and '**Mandela's Gold**' ★. Zones 10–12.

STREPTOCARPUS

CAPE PRIMROSE

Although widespread in the African and Asian tropics and sub-tropics, most of the cultivated plants in this genus of around 130 species of annuals and perennials are natives of southern Africa, and belong to the African violet (Gesneriaceae) family. Despite the di-versity of form among species in the genus, they share some features. The leaves are vel-vety and heavily veined. The flowers are long-tubed, primrose-like, usually with 5 petals; they occur in heads on short upright stems.
CULTIVATION: Cold tolerance varies, though none withstand more than the lightest frost. Plant in a bright but not sunny, warm, draft-free position, in fertile, moist, humus-rich, well-drained soil. Propagate by division, from leaf-stalk cuttings or from seed.

Streptocarpus candidus

◐/☀ ⅃ ↔ 10–16 in (25–40 cm) ↑ 12 in (30 cm)
From South Africa. Vertical rhizome; rosettes of deep green, heavily veined, irregularly toothed leaves. Heads of up to 25 pale mauve to white flowers, usually fragrant, in summer. Zones 10–11.

Streptocarpus caulescens

◐/☀ ⅃ ↔ 12–20 in (30–50 cm) ↑ 12–20 in (30–50 cm)
From Tanzania and Kenya; erect to sprawling perennial. Woody-based stems; broad, pointed oval leaves. Airy sprays of up to 12 white-centered purple flowers, in autumn–winter. Zones 11–12.

Strelitzia reginae

Streptocarpus, Hybrid Cultivar, 'Party Doll'

Streptocarpus cyaneus

◐/☀ ✦ ↔ 12–20 in (30–50 cm)
↑ 6–8 in (15–20 cm)
From South Africa. Rosettes of toothed leaves
up to 16 in (40 cm) long. Dark-veined light
pink to violet flowers, usually paired, on stems
to 6 in (15 cm) long, in spring–summer. *S. c.*
subsp. *polackii*, mauve-pink flowers, leaves
and stalks red-tinted. Zones 10–11.

Streptocarpus glandulosissimus

◐/☀ ✦ ↔ 12–20 in (30–50 cm)
↑ 12–20 in (30–50 cm)
Kenyan species; upright to sprawling habit.
Downy pointed oval leaves to over 4 in
(10 cm) long, often smaller. Airy sprays of
violet flowers, most of year. Zones 11–12.

Streptocarpus kirkii

◐/☀ ✦ ↔ 8–12 in (20–30 cm) ↑ 12–16 in (30–40 cm)
Native to Kenya and Tanzania. Erect stems become woody and
trailing as they mature. Opposite pairs of sparsely hairy, pointed
oval, serrated or smooth-edged leaves. Airy sprays of up to 10
small violet-pink flowers, deep purple spots in throat. Winter-
flowering. Zones 11–12.

Streptocarpus saxorum

syn. *Streptocarpella saxorum*
◐/☀ ✦ ↔ 8–16 in (20–40 cm) ↑ 4–6 in (10–15 cm)
Compact, long-flowering species, native to Kenya and Tanzania.
Low spreading clump of velvety pointed oval leaves to 1¼ in
(30 mm) long. Relatively large, solitary or paired, white to pale
mauve flowers, small upper lobes. Blooms throughout most of
year. Zones 10–12.

Streptocarpus wendlandii

◐/☀ ✦ ↔ 30 in (75 cm) ↑ 12 in (30 cm)
South African native. Single, very large, heart-
shaped, finely toothed, deep green leaf, to
30 in (75 cm) long, covered with fine hairs,
red underside. Small, white to mauve, purple-
marked flowers, in summer. Zones 10–12.

Streptocarpus Hybrid Cultivars

◐/☀ ✦ ↔ 12–20 in (30–50 cm)
↑ 12–20 in (30–50 cm)
Wide-ranging group of fancy-flowered, compact, rosette-forming hybrids developed by
interbreeding mainly South African species.
Flower most heavily from spring into summer, sometimes blooming sporadically year-
round. Cultivated as house plants. 'Albatross',
white flowers, yellow throat; 'Amanda', blue,
dark-veined, white throat; 'Bethan', mauve,
yellow throat; 'Blue Heaven', pale lavender,
semi-double, white throat; 'Blushing Bride',
white flushed pink, semi-double, long-tubed;
'Bristol's Very Best', magenta, double; 'Carys',
mauve-blue, purple-blue throat and veining;
'Chorus Line', white with mauve-blue veining, double; 'Concord Blue', continual pale
violet-blue mid-pink, purple-red center;
'Falling Stars', pale lavender, white throat;
'Flexii White', white, dark purple veins;
'Happy Snappy', red, yellowish throat;
'Heidi', mauve-blue; 'Jennifer', dark blue,
white throat; 'Kim', purple, white throat;
'Lisa', pink, white throat; 'Lynette', soft
deep burgundy; 'Megan', deep purple, yellow throat; 'Melanie', mauve-blue, purple-
pink veining; 'Midnight Flame', intense
bright red; 'Nymph', bright purple, yellow
throat; 'Party Doll', purple-edged, pale lavender, yellow throat; 'Passion Pink', deep
pink with dark lines; 'Pink Souffle', frilly
pink double; 'Rosebud', deep pink, double; 'Rosemary', light
pink, double; 'Ruby' ★, pure deep crimson; 'Sian', bright blue,
white and yellow throat; 'Sophie', purple-red, dark throat;
'Tina', pale pink, dark pink center and veining. Zones 10–11.

Streptocarpus wendlandii

STROBILANTHES

This genus of more than 250 species of evergreen or deciduous
perennials and soft-stemmed shrubs is native to tropical Asia
and Madagascar, and belongs to the acanthus (Acanthaceae)
family. A few species are grown both indoors and out for their
attractive tubular or funnel-shaped flowers, in varying shades of
blue and purple. *Strobilanthes* species have colorful purplish foliage; the opposite paired leaves are frequently of unequal size.
CULTIVATION: Frost tender, these plants require a warm climate
and prefer a position in full sun or part-shade in well-drained
humus-enriched soil. They can be pruned lightly to shape, or

clipped to form a hedge. The new growth has the most attractive coloring. Propagation is from seed, cuttings, or by division.

Strobilanthes anisophyllus

GOLDFUSSIA

↔5 ft (1.5 m) ↑5 ft (1.5 m)

Shrubby plant, native to Assam in northern India. Narrow silvery purple leaves in unequal-sized pairs. Tubular flowers, lavender-blue, 1 in (25 mm) long, at ends of branches, in late summer–autumn. Zones 10–11.

Strobilanthes dyerianus

syn. *Perilepta dyeriana*

↔36 in (90 cm) ↑36 in (90 cm)

Originally a native of Myanmar. Evergreen species grown mostly as an indoor plant for its attractive foliage. Lance-shaped iridescent purple leaves, to 6 in (15 cm) long, toothed edges. Short spikes of funnel-shaped pale blue flowers, held above leaves, in spring–summer. Zones 10–12.

Strobilanthes gossypinus

↔20–30 in (50–75 cm) ↑3–5 ft (0.9–1.5 m)

Shrubby species native to southern India and Sri Lanka. Green leaves, 2–4 in (5–10 cm) long, lance-shaped, tapering to fine point, densely coated with cream hairs. Small heads of soft blue to lavender flowers clustered at stem tip and in upper leaf axils, in summer. Zones 10–12.

STROMANTHE

This genus of 15 species of leafy perennials growing 3–10 ft (0.9–3 m) high belongs to the arrowroot (Marantaceae) family. In their native Central and South America they grow on the forest floor, where they are rampant and often weedy. Their appearance is similar to related plants such as *Ctenanthe* and *Maranta* with long oblong ornamental leaves, which emerge from sheathed stems. The leaves are often marked or veined with white or lighter or darker shades of green. Although they are grown as house plants for their foliage, the flowers often have showy colorful bracts, which add interest to their ornamental appeal.

CULTIVATION: In suitably warm climates grow these plants in a shady and sheltered position. In temperate climates they are widely cultivated as indoor plants. Grow in bright filtered light in a rich soil mix. During active growth, water moderately and apply liquid fertilizer fortnightly. Propagation is by division or from cuttings.

Stromanthe sanguinea

↔2–3 ft (0.6–0.9 m) ↑3–5 ft (0.9–1.5 m)

Handsome foliage plant, native to Brazil. Large, thick, glossy, oblong leaves, emerge from pinkish red sheaths, dark green above, purple beneath. White flowers, showy red floral bracts. **'Stripestar'**, leaves with distinctive white stripes. Zones 10–12.

Stylidium lineare

Strobilanthes gossypinus

STYLIDIUM

TRIGGERPLANT

This genus, belonging to the self-named triggerplant (Stylidiaceae) family, contains around 110 species of perennials. Most are native to Australia, where they often grow in sandy coastal areas. The foliage is usually grass-like, sometimes with short leaves on narrow stems. The dainty flowers, in white, pink, or yellow, are borne on upright spikes in summer. Stamens and stigma are fused in a column; when an insect alights on the flower, they react like a trigger, hitting the insect's back and thereby transferring pollen. It is this unusual trigger mechanism, which is only activated on warm sunny days, that gives the genus its common name.

CULTIVATION: In very warm dry areas, plant *Stylidium* species in well-drained sandy soil, but these plants are better suited to pot culture. In cool temperate climates they can be grown in the greenhouse in full light in a sandy potting mix. They should be watered moderately when in growth, but plants should be kept almost dry in winter. Propagate from seed or cuttings or by division.

Stylidium graminifolium

TRIGGERPLANT

↔10 in (25 cm) ↑10–20 in (25–50 cm)

Native to eastern and southern Australia; found from coastal to mountain regions. Variable perennial; stiff grass-like leaves. Spikes of pale pink to magenta flowers, on hairy stems, in summer. Zones 9–11.

Stylidium lineare

↔4 in (10 cm) ↑6–12 in (15–30 cm)

Native to New South Wales, Australia. Small plant forming rosettes of short, narrow, grass-like leaves. Upright central stems; spikes of dainty pink flowers. Summer- to autumn-flowering. Zones 9–11.

Sutera cordata

SUTERA

This genus of about 130 perennials and annuals from the foxglove (Scrophulariaceae) family originates from South Africa. They have become well known in recent years as hanging basket plants. Small, rounded, toothed, green leaves sit on thin stems that hug the ground. Starry white, mauve, lilac, pink, or blue flowers sit face-up on the foliage. These plants can produce flowers for up to 10 months of the year.
CULTIVATION: *Sutera* species are adaptable to sun and shade and require free-draining fertile soil. During warmer months they need extra water to keep blooming. Propagate from stem cuttings in autumn or by sowing seed in spring.

Sutera cordata
syn. *Bacopa cordata*
☼ ❄ ↔ 20 in (50 cm) ↑ 3 in (8 cm)
Low-growing, ground covering, South African perennial, pale green leaves all year. Pure white flowers, delicate yellow eye, almost year round in warm climates. 'Blue Showers', lilac to pale blue flowers; 'Lavender Showers', pale lavender star-shaped flowers; 'Snowflake', tiny white flowers in leaf axils; 'Snowstorm' ★, large white flowers, more compact growth habit. Zones 9–10.

Sutera grandiflora
PURPLE MORNING GLORY PLANT
☼ ❄ ↔ 24 in (60 cm) ↑ 40 in (100 cm)
Bushy perennial, native to South Africa. Small, elliptical, green leaves. Lavender-blue flowers with white throat. Summer- to autumn-flowering. Zones 9–11.

STYLOPHORUM

This genus in the poppy (Papaveraceae) family contains 3 species of hairy perennials, and is native to eastern North America and eastern Asia, where they grow in woodlands. They form basal rosettes of long divided, irregularly lobed and toothed leaves. The stem leaves are much smaller and usually stalkless. Clear yellow or orange, 4-petalled, saucer-shaped flowers are borne in small clusters in spring. The blooms are followed by narrow cylindrical seed pods that are covered in fine silvery hairs.
CULTIVATION: *Stylophorum* species are woodland plants suitable for shady positions in the garden. Unlike most plants in the poppy family, which resent disturbance, these plants can be readily transplanted, and will perform best in any reasonably fertile moist but well-drained soil. Propagate from seed or by division.

Stylophorum diphyllum

Stylophorum diphyllum
CELANDINE POPPY, WOOD POPPY
☼ ❄ ↔ 12 in (30 cm) ↑ 18 in (45 cm)
Downy perennial, native to eastern USA. Deeply and irregularly lobed leaves, scalloped or toothed edges. Simple, yellow, saucer-shaped, 4-petalled flowers, to 2 in (5 cm) wide, on delicate stems, in spring. Zones 5–9.

Stylophorum lasiocarpum
CHINESE CELANDINE POPPY
☼ ❄ ↔ 12 in (30 cm) ↑ 12 in (30 cm)
Perennial from central and eastern China. Long irregularly lobed and toothed leaves, rather like those of the dandelion (*Taraxacum* species). Clear yellow, 4-petalled, saucer-shaped flowers, in clusters, 4–5 in (10–12 cm) wide, in spring. Zones 5–9.

SWAINSONA

Around 50 species of perennials and subshrubs from the pea-flower subfamily of the legume (Fabaceae) family, all but one of the species in this genus are Australian natives. They are leguminous plants and have small racemes of ridged pea-flowers, often red or pink, but also occur in mauve- or white-flowered forms. The foliage is pinnate, usually with many small leaflets, often gray-green and covered in fine downy hairs. The flowering season varies—some species bloom in winter, others in spring to summer, and those from very arid areas burst into bloom after rain.
CULTIVATION: Although some *Swainsona* species will tolerate very light frosts, most perform best in a mild frost-free climate in a position in full sun. They vary in their soil requirements; those species from hot arid areas prefer to be dry over winter, while those from cooler zones require constant moisture. Good drainage is also most important. Propagation is from seed, which needs to be soaked before sowing, or from half-hardened summer cuttings.

Swainsona formosa

syn. *Clianthus formosus*

GLORY PEA, STURT'S DESERT PEA

☼ ✤ ↔ 3–7 ft (0.9–2 m) ↑ 3–4 ft (0.9–1.2 m)

Sprawling subshrub. Silky, grayish green, pinnate leaves. Showy pea-flowers to 3 in (8 cm) long, in clusters of 5 to 6; brilliant red, black spot, from winter–summer. Zones 9–11.

Swainsona galegifolia

☼ ✤ ↔ 6 ft (1.8 m) ↑ 2 ft (0.6 m)

Upright or trailing perennial or softwooded shrub from eastern Australia. Gray- to dark green pinnate leaves, 25 tiny leaflets edged with fine hairs. Pink, mauve, purple, white, or reddish purple pea-flowers, in spring–summer. Zones 9–11.

SYMPHYANDRA

RING BELLFLOWER

This genus of some 12 rather short-lived perennial species, occurs from the eastern Mediterranean region to central Asia, and belongs to the bellflower (Campanulaceae) family. They differ from *Campanula* merely in the anthers being united to form a collar around the style. The basal leaves are often heart-shaped and toothed, with long stalks. The flowers are held in racemes or panicles. The calyx has 5 long lobes; the corolla is bell-shaped with 5 lobes. There are 5 stamens with free filaments and united anthers. The fruit is a capsule. CULTIVATION: These plants suit the herbaceous border or rock garden in temperate areas. They grow best in good well-drained soils. Some die after flowering, though setting seed freely. They can be propagated by careful division of the fleshy rootstocks or from seed sown in autumn.

Symphyandra hofmannii

☼/◐ ✤ ↔ 6–12 in (15–30 cm) ↑ 12–24 in (30–60 cm)

From Bosnia and Herzegovina. Can be monocarpic in cultivation. Rosette-forming; leaves oval to lance-shaped. Pendulous cream or pale yellow bell-flowers, in racemes, in summer. Zones 4–9.

SYMPHYTUM

COMFREY, KNITBONE

This genus contains 35 species of hardy perennials belonging to the borage (Boraginaceae) family. Of temperate Eurasian origin, they favor damp woodlands, streamsides, and wasteland. Plants are characterized by vigorous growth and prolific flowering. A basal rosette of coarse tapering leaves emerges from a fleshy tap root. Clusters of small bell-shaped flowers, red-tipped in bud, reddish to blue in bloom, are arranged in 1-sided coils at the tips of branching stems. Hummingbirds are attracted to the flowers. Comfrey has a long history of use in herbal medicine. If taken internally in quantity, comfrey could be carcinogenic. CULTIVATION: *Symphytum* species favor damp soil and will grow in full sun or partial shade. They are adaptable to dry conditions where their growth is restrained. They can be grown in full sun

Swainsona formosa

in cold climates if the soil is heavy and moisture-retentive. Control and propagate these plants by chopping out extra growth; they should be cut back after blooming.

Symphytum asperum

PRICKLY COMFREY

☼ ✤ ↔ 5–7 ft (1.5–2 m) ↑ 4–5 ft (1.2–1.5 m)

From Europe, the Caucasus region, and Iran. Oval bristly leaves to 10 in (25 cm) long. Small tubular flowers, initially pink, ageing to blue or lilac, in summer. Zones 5–10.

Symphytum caucasicum

☼ ✤ ↔ 24–32 in (60–80 cm) ↑ 24–32 in (60–80 cm)

Native to the Caucasus region. Basal leaves mid-green, 10 in (25 cm) long. Flared trumpets of rich blue flowers, to ½ in (12 mm) long, in summer. 'Eminence', smaller than the species, leaves gray tinged, blue flowers in early summer. Zones 5–10.

Symphytum 'Goldsmith' ★

syns *Symphytum ibericum* 'Jubilee', *S. i.* 'Variegatum'

☼/◐ ✤ ↔ 12–20 in (30–50 cm) ↑ 10–12 in (25–30 cm)

Spreading bristly perennial. Leaves to 10 in (25 cm) long, irregularly and broadly edged with yellow. Drooping blue and white flowers, to ¾ in (18 mm) long, open from pink buds, in late spring–early summer. Zones 5–10.

Symphytum grandiflorum

☼ ✤ ↔ 20–24 in (50–60 cm) ↑ 15–16 in (38–40 cm)

Native to Europe and the Caucasus region. Deciduous species; rosette-forming; bristly leaves, to 10 in (25 cm) long. Clusters of trumpet-shaped flowers open to pale yellow from red-tipped buds, at the end of branching stems, in late spring–early summer. Zones 5–10.

Symphytum 'Goldsmith'

Symphytum 'Hidcote Blue'

☀ ✳ ↔ 18–20 in (45–50 cm) ↕ 18–20 in (45–50 cm)
Leaves to 10 in (25 cm) long. Red buds, pale blue trumpets, to ¾ in (18 mm) long, in late spring–early summer. Zones 5–10.

Symphytum ibericum

syn. *Symphytum grandiflorum* of gardens
☀/☀ ✳ ↔ 12 in (30 cm) ↕ 16 in (40 cm)
Creeping rhizomatous perennial, native to Turkey and eastern Europe. Hairy oval leaves. Clusters of pendulous tubular cream flowers in spring–summer. Can be invasive. Zones 5–10.

SYNTHYRIS

KITTENTAILS
This genus, belonging to the foxglove (Scrophulariaceae) family, contains 14 species of perennials from northern and western North America where they are found growing in woodland and alpine areas. Closely related to *Veronica*, they are low-growing, rhizomatous, tufted plants. The leathery leaves, which are heart-shaped, kidney-shaped, or deeply cut, become smaller and bract-like on the flowering stems. The flowers are blue or violet-blue with a short tube and 4 erect or spreading lobes.
CULTIVATION: The woodland species will tolerate quite poor soils such as those occurring under deciduous trees, but will do best in a fertile well-drained soil with added organic matter in light shade. Alpine species will perform best in a sunny open site with protection from the hottest summer sun. Propagation is from seed or by division.

Tacca integrifolia

Synthyris missurica

☀/☀ ✳ ↔ 12 in (30 cm) ↕ 16–24 in (40–60 cm)
Tufted perennial native to northern and western North America. Dark green, leathery, heart-shaped to kidney-shaped, toothed leaves. Bright bluish purple tubular flowers, in loose spikes, in spring–summer. 'Alba', white flowers. Zones 3–9.

Synthyris reniformis

SNOW QUEEN, SPRING QUEEN
☀/☀ ✳ ↔ 4 in (10 cm) ↕ 2–6 in (5–15 cm)
From moist shady forests of Washington and Oregon, USA. Round to heart-shaped leaves, shallowly lobed, paler beneath. Short racemes of bluish purple flowers in early spring. Zones 6–9.

TACCA

This genus, comprising 10 species native to the African and Asian tropics with 9 from the Malay Archipelago alone, is now a member of the yam (Dioscoreaceae) family, though it was formerly placed in Taccaceae. The plants are herbaceous perennials that arise from tubers. The long-stalked leaves have blades that are smooth and elliptical, or deeply dissected. The hermaphrodite flowers are regular, in cymes surrounded by a whorl of bracts and are pollinated by flies. The 6 tepals are petal-like, greenish to brown-purple. The fruit is a berry or more rarely a capsule with 10 to many seeds. These plants are found in semi-evergreen monsoon forests and are useful foliage plants in tropical gardens. They are used as flowering pot plants for indoor decoration in more temperate countries.
CULTIVATION: In the tropics these perennials are grown in shaded sites with humus-rich soils; in temperate regions they need a humid greenhouse. To maintain vigor, such plants should be re-rooted and repotted every 2 years. They are propagated by division or from cuttings from old tubers. Seeds sown on the soil surface will yield flowering plants in 3 years.

Tacca integrifolia

BAT FLOWER, BAT PLANT, WHITE BAT FLOWER
☀ ◗ ↔ 24 in (60 cm) ↕ 24–48 in (60–120 cm)
Perennial from eastern India, southern China, and Indonesia. Vertical rhizome; large, broad, oblong or sword-shaped leaves. Long-stalked heads of nodding bat-like flowers, green to dark purplish black bracts (white in one popular form), green to dark purple bracteoles, in spring–summer. Zones 10–12.

TAGETES

MARIGOLD
All but one of the 50 or so species of this genus in the daisy (Asteraceae) family comes from the American tropics and sub-tropics. They are mainly upright annuals or perennials with dark green, sometimes aromatic, pinnate leaves with toothed edges. The flowers are usually yellow or orange, and often daisy-like.
CULTIVATION: Marigolds prefer a warm sunny position in light well-drained soil. Water well and feed if the foliage begins to yellow. Deadhead frequently to ensure continuous blooming is maintained. Propagate from seed, which is usually started indoors in early spring.

Tagetes, Hybrid Cultivar, Safari Series, 'Safari Red'

Tagetes, Hybrid Cultivar, Atlantis Series, 'Atlantis Primrose'

Tagetes, Hybrid Cultivar, 'Jolly Jester'

Tagetes lucida

MEXICAN MINT, SPANISH TARRAGON, SWEET MACE

☼/◑ ⦂ ↔ 16–32 in (40–80 cm) ↕ 16–40 in (40–100 cm)

Perennial from Mexico and Guatemala. Woody-based, branching a little way up stem. Lance-shaped leaves, toothed, pleasantly aromatic. Small bright golden yellow flowerheads in late summer. Can be used as tarragon substitute. Zones 9–11.

Tagetes patula

FRENCH MARIGOLD

☼ ✛ ↔ 6–12 in (15–30 cm) ↕ 8–20 in (20–50 cm)

Compact bushy annual from Mexico and Guatemala. Pinnate leaves, narrow, toothed, lance-shaped segments. Flowers solitary or in small clusters, usually yellow to orange, in early summer–autumn. Garden forms available in many colors. Zones 11–12.

Tagetes tenuifolia

SIGNET MARIGOLD, STRIPED MARIGOLD

☼ ✛ ↔ 12–24 in (30–60 cm) ↕ 12–32 in (30–80 cm)

Annual, found naturally from Mexico to Colombia. Sometimes narrowly upright, usually bushy, with fine branches. Pinnate, many-toothed leaves, narrow lance-shaped segments. Abundant bright yellow flowerheads, short ray florets, in early summer–autumn. 'Starfire', seedling mix in various shades of yellow, orange, and red. Zones 11–12.

Tagetes Hybrid Cultivars

☼ ✛ ↔ 6–12 in (15–30 cm) ↕ 8–12 in (20–30 cm)

Mainly derived from *T. patula*. Border marigolds make ideal summer bedding plants. Usually marketed as seedling series, in mixed or single colors; mostly double flowers with few visible ray florets, chiefly in yellow, orange, and red. **Antigua Series**, flowerheads up to 3 in (8 cm) wide; **Atlantis Series**, pompon-like flowerheads up to 4 in (10 cm) wide; **Bonanza Series**, crested flowerheads up to 2 in (5 cm) wide; **Boy Series**, crested flowerheads up to 1½ in (35 mm) wide; **Crush Series**, flowerheads to 4 in (10 cm) wide; **Disco Series**, many single flowers up to 2 in (5 cm) wide; **Gate Series**, double flowerheads up to 3 in (8 cm) wide; **Girl Series**, dwarf, double flowerheads; **Inca Series**, flowerheads up to 5 in (12 cm) wide; **'Jolly Jester'**, red petals with yellow striping; **Little Hero Series**, double flowerheads up to 2 in (5 cm) wide;

'Naughty Marietta' ★, single yellow flowers, red mid-band; **Safari Series**, double flowers to 3 in (8 cm) wide; **Zenith Series**, heavy foliage, double flowers to 3 in (8 cm) wide. Zones 11–12.

TALINUM

This genus of over 40 species of succulent shrubs or herbs from Africa and the Americas, belongs to the purslane (Portulacaceae) family. They usually have deciduous leaves and branches arising from a perennial tuber or caudex. Leaves are alternate, often irregularly spaced, flat to cylindrical, more or less succulent and often soft and limp. Flowerheads are often solitary and usually held at the stem tips. The flowers open once, often for only a few hours, some setting seed without opening. The seed pod is a 3-chambered, spherical or oval capsule. Some are regarded as weeds. CULTIVATION: These plants are extremely easy to grow in any well-drained soil. Most mature plants will readily set seed. Underground roots may be raised for display. Propagate from seed.

Talinum paniculatum

JEWELS OF OPAR

☼/◑ ⦂ ↔ 16–20 in (40–50 cm) ↕ 40 in (100 cm)

Found from southern USA to central Argentina, naturalized in tropics and subtropics. Leaves elliptical to oblong. Small flowers, 5-petalled, pink, yellow, or white, in spring–summer. Seed pods yellow. Often a weed. Zones 9–10.

Tagetes tenuifolia 'Starfire'

Tanacetum corymbosum subsp. *clusii*

Tanacetum camphoratum

TANACETUM

This genus of about 70 annuals and perennials belonging to the daisy (Asteraceae) family originates in northern temperate regions. Foliage is diverse, often strongly aromatic, sometimes silvery, and can be fringed, ferny, scalloped, or toothed. Flowers are daisy-like or rayless buttons, mainly yellow, white, and red, produced in a mass on vigorous plants of mounding, upright, or shrubby habit. **CULTIVATION:** These plants require poor to moderately fertile well-drained soil, full sun, and dry growing conditions. There are forms that are suitable for a variety of situations, from rock gardens and borders to natural- izing. Cut back plants after blooming to encourage new growth and to prevent pro- lific self-seeding of some types. Propagate by division or from seed in spring.

Tanacetum balsamita
syns *Balsamita major,*
Chrysanthemum balsamita
ALECOST, COSTMARY
☼ ❄ ↔ 18 in (45 cm)
↑ 36 in (90 cm)
Hardy mat-forming perennial found growing naturally from central Asia to Europe. Silvery gray leaves, scalloped, slightly hairy, aromatic. Small, white, button-like flowers with yellow eye, in late summer–autumn. Zones 6–10.

Tanacetum camphoratum
DUNE DAISY
☼ ❄ ↔ 20 in (50 cm)
↑ 27 in (70 cm)
Rare perennial from temperate zones of North America. Bright green serrated foliage all year round. Bright yellow button-like flowers, 1 in (25 mm) wide. Summer- to autumn-flowering. In some areas, can die back over winter months. Zones 8–10.

Tanacetum coccineum
syns *Chrysanthemum coccineum, Pyrethrum coccineum*
PAINTED DAISY, PYRETHRUM
☼ ❄ ↔ 18 in (45 cm) ↑ 18–30 in (45–75 cm)
Compact low-growing perennial found from southwest Asia and the Caucasus. Fern-like, elliptical to oblong, silver-gray, aromatic foliage. White, pink, or red daisy flowers, yellow eye, in early summer–late autumn. Oils of leaves used to deter pests. Cultivars include '**Brenda**', bright cerise-pink flowers with yellow eye; '**Eileen May Robinson**', larger pale pink flowers with soft yellow eye; '**James Kelway**' ★, vibrant crimson-pink flowers. Zones 5–9.

Tanacetum corymbosum
☼ ❄ ↔ 18 in (45 cm) ↑ 36 in (90 cm)
Woody perennial, native to southern and central Europe. Clump- forming plant; leaves mid-green, elliptical to oblong, aromatic. Clusters of white daisy-like flowers, from early summer to late autumn. *T. c.* **subsp.** *clusii*, white daisy-like flowers, drooping petals. Zones 6–9.

Tanacetum coccineum

Tanacetum niveum
SILVER TANSY
☼ ❄ ↔ 24 in (60 cm) ↑ 36 in (90 cm)
Superb species, native to southern and cen- tral Europe. Mound-forming; striking silver-gray, deeply cut, fragrant leaves. Hundreds of *Chrysanthemum*-like flowers, white with yellow centers, in late spring– summer. Zones 6–9.

TAPEINOCHILUS

This genus is a member of the ginger (Zingiberaceae) family and contains about 15 species of perennial herbs that are found in Southeast Asia, Indonesia, New Guinea, and Australia. Like the related *Costus*, they are plants of the forest floor and have spirally arranged leaves. As is typical of the ginger family, the flowers are of less significance than the colorful showy bracts that surround them, which are usually red. The flowerheads may be on leafy shoots or a separate flowering stem.
CULTIVATION: In tropical areas, *Tapeinochilus* species can be grown in a shady border in rich, moist but well-drained soil. In cool-temperate climates, grow these plants in the greenhouse in a rich soil-based mix, providing high humidity, plenty of water, and fortnightly feeding in summer. They should be watered sparingly in winter and humidity should be reduced. Propagation is from seed or bulbils or by division.

Tapeinochilus ananassae

Tapeinochilus ananassae
☀ ⚘ ↔ 2–3 ft (0.6–0.9 m) ↕ 5–7 ft (1.5–2 m)
Rhizomatous perennial found from Malaysia to Australia. Cane-like stems; spirally arranged, bright green, oblong leaves. Yellow flowers held within a cone-like structure of densely packed overlapping red bracts, in summer. Zones 11–12.

TELEKIA

This genus, comprising a single species found from central Europe eastward to the Caucasus region, is a member of the daisy (Asteraceae) family. The plant is a coarse perennial herb. Leaves are large and heart-shaped, deeply toothed, and hairy, with long stalks. The large flowerheads have ray florets and form loose terminal corymbs. The receptacle has scales, which persist after flowering. The whorl of bracts is cup-shaped and the bracts are heart-shaped and herbaceous. Ray florets are female, each with a very long, narrow, yellow petal. The dry fruits are linear and flattened.
CULTIVATION: This plant grows wild by streamsides and in wet woodlands up to the subalpine zone. It is easily grown in open or lightly shaded moist places in a garden but can readily become invasive. Propagate by division or from seed.

Telekia speciosa
syn. *Buphthalmum speciosum*
OXEYE DAISY, TELEKIA SUNFLOWER
☀ ✳ ↔ 4–6 ft (1.2–1.8 m) ↕ 4–6 ft (1.2–1.8 m)
Strongly scented perennial. Coarsely serrated leaves, finely hairy underneath. Clusters of 2 to 8 flowerheads, up to 35 tiny yellow ray florets, in summer. Zones 3–9.

TELLIMA

This genus in the saxifrage (Saxifragaceae) family contains just a single species of perennial herb. Native to western North America, it is found in cool moist woodland and rocky areas. The hairy, heart-shaped or round, lobed or toothed leaves form spreading clumps. In summer, tall wiry stems bear spikes of small creamy flowers, tinged with green and red. The blooms deepen in color as they age.
CULTIVATION: Fringecups are ideal plants for cool woodland gardens, shady borders, and rockeries. They prefer moist humus-rich soil. Propagate by division in autumn or from seed sown in spring.

Tellima grandiflora
FRINGECUPS
☀ ✳ ↔ 24 in (60 cm) ↕ 24 in (60 cm)
Perennial herb. Almost round, lobed, hairy, basal leaves, 2–4 in (5–10 cm) wide. Creamy flowers with deeply fringed petals, in summer. **Rubra Group** (syn. 'Purpurea'), rounder leaves, scallop-edged, tinted bronze, green, flowers fringed with pink. Zones 6–9.

TEUCRIUM

GERMANDER
This genus of about 100 species of herbs, shrubs, and subshrubs is a member of the mint (Lamiaceae) family. They are found growing in warm-temperate regions, but are particularly concentrated around the Mediterranean region. The shrubs are attractive and often colorful flowering plants. All have characteristic squarish stems with opposite leaves that are usually downy or hairy, oval to lance-shaped, and have notched or slightly toothed edges. The summer flowers are borne in whorls on loose stems and are cream, purple, or pink.
CULTIVATION: These reliable plants are mostly frost hardy, and will perform best in a sunny position with well-drained soil. While they will tolerate the dry heat of the inland, they prefer coastal conditions. Lightly prune the ends of the branchlets to remove spent inflorescences and stimulate lateral growth immediately after the summer-flowering period. Propagation is best from firm tip cuttings taken in summer.

Tellima grandiflora

Teucrium chamaedrys
GROUND OAK, WALL GERMANDER
✻ ❀ ↔ 24–36 in (60–90 cm) ↕ 12–24 in (30–60 cm)
Woody-based perennial, native to central and southern Europe; naturalized further north. Small oval leaves, toothed edges, shiny green above, downy below. Whorls of pink to purple flowers, on terminal spikes, in summer. Zones 5–10.

Teucrium cossonii
syns *Teucrium gussonei, T. majorcum*
✻ ❀ ↔ 24 in (60 cm) ↕ 8 in (20 cm)
Low-growing shrubby perennial from the Mediterranean island of Majorca, Spain. Small, narrow, gray leaves. Whorls of lavender flowers, on short leafy spikes, almost year-round in warm climates. Zones 8–11.

Teucrium hircanicum
✻ ❀ ↔ 24 in (60 cm) ↕ 24 in (60 cm)
Woody-based perennial, native to western Asia and the Caucasus region. Soft, green, downy leaves, somewhat wrinkled on upper-surface. Terminal spikes of closely packed whorls of small purple to reddish purple flowers from summer to autumn. Zones 6–9.

Teucrium cossonii

Teucrium polium
GOLDEN GERMANDER
✻ ❀ ↔ 6–12 in (15–30 cm) ↕ 4–16 in (10–40 cm)
Low mound-forming subshrub from the Mediterranean and western Asia. Woody-based, with downy stems; small gray leaves, wrinkled surface. Small heads of white, yellow, pink, or purple velvety flowers in summer. Zones 7–10.

Teucrium scorodonia
MOUNTAIN SAGE, WOOD GERMANDER, WOOD SAGE
✻/❁ ❀ ❀ ↔ 18 in (45 cm) ↕ 24 in (60 cm)
From southern and western Europe. Downy rhizomatous perennial. Wrinkled, toothed, grayish green leaves. Small yellowish green flowers, in terminal spikes, in summer–autumn. 'Crispum Marginatum', crimped, frilly-edged, green leaves. Zones 6–10.

THALIA
ALLIGATOR FLAG
This genus of 12 aquatic perennial herbs belongs to the arrowroot (Marantaceae) family, and is native to the tropical and subtropical Americas and tropical Africa. Growing from thick rhizomes, the overlapping blue-green leaves have large sword-shaped to oval blades that fold upward at night, and long stalks with sheaths at the base. Two ranks of tubular, often waxy flowers are produced in curving tassel-like branches on long-stalked panicles that extend beyond the leaves.
CULTIVATION: These plants grow in water 12–18 in (30–45 cm) deep, or in moist to wet loamy soil in an open sunny position. Propagate by division in spring.

Thalia dealbata
POWDERY ALLIGATOR FLAG, WATER CANNA
✻ ❁ ↔ 20–30 in (50–75 cm)
↕ 3–6 ft (0.9–1.8 m)
Native to southeastern North America. Erect perennial; unbranching stems. Large, textured, grayish green leaves; fine red edges, powdery white underneath. Branching heads of 6-petalled, violet, waxy flowers, from late summer to early autumn. Zones 9–11.

THALICTRUM
MEADOW RUE
This genus of around 130 species of tuberous or rhizome-rooted perennials, belonging to the buttercup (Ranunculaceae) family, is found mainly in the northern temperate zone, with a few species straying south of the equator into the tropics. They are upright plants with lacy, pinnate, blue-green leaves that are reminiscent of *Aquilegia* or *Adiantum* (maidenhair fern) foliage. Tall elegant flower stems extend well above the foliage and from late spring to autumn, depending on the species, produce inflorescences of small fluffy flowers, which are mainly pink or mauve, but can be white and yellow.
CULTIVATION: *Thalictrum* species are useful plants in woodland gardens, borders, or rock gardens. The ferny foliage is an effective backdrop in floral arrangements. Usually very hardy, these plants are easily grown in temperate climates in full sun or half-sun in fertile, humus-rich, well-drained soil. Propagate these perennials by division, as the cultivated plants are mainly selected forms.

Thalictrum aquilegiifolium
FEATHERED COLUMBINE, FRENCH MEADOW RUE
✻/❁ ❀ ↔ 20–40 in (50–100 cm)
↕ 60 in (150 cm)
Multi-stemmed perennial found from Europe to Japan. Blue-green fern-like foliage, leaves to 12 in (30 cm) wide. Panicles of greenish white through pink to purple flowers, inconspicuous sepals, in early summer. Zones 6–9.

Thalictrum aquilegiifolium

Thalictrum delavayi

☀/◐ ❄ ↔ 16–24 in (40–60 cm)
↑ 4–5 ft (1.2–1.5 m)

Perennial, native to the Himalayas. Dark-stemmed; blue-green foliage. Erect showy heads of large, long-lasting, purple-pink, rarely white flowers, sepals similarly colored, yellow stamens. Summer-flowering. '**Hewitt's Double**' ★, double flowers, slightly shorter than the species. Zones 7–9.

Thalictrum dioicum

EARLY MEADOW RUE

◐/☀ ❄ ↔ 12–16 in (30–40 cm)
↑ 12–30 in (30–75 cm)

Found from Ontario, Canada, to Tennessee, USA. Aquilegia-like blue-green foliage; tiny leaflets, deeply scalloped edges. Flowers with pendulous pink filaments below conspicuous pale green, sometimes purple-tinted sepals, in summer. Zones 4–9.

Thalictrum flavum

FALSE RHUBARB, YELLOW MEADOW RUE

☀/◐ ❄ ↔ 16–20 in (40–50 cm)
↑ 40 in (100 cm)

Perennial, native to in southwestern Europe and North Africa. Finely divided, blue-green, aquilegia-like, pinnate foliage. Small heads of fluffy cream to yellow flowers, inconspicuous sepals. Flowers held above foliage on tall stems. Summer-flowering. *T. f.* subsp. *glaucum*, intensely blue-green foliage. Zones 6–10.

Thalictrum kiusianum

◐ ❄ ↔ 12–20 in (30–50 cm)
↑ 6–12 in (15–30 cm)

Small species, native to Japan. Dense clump of short-stemmed, small, doubly trifoliate, blue-green leaves, 3- to 5-lobed segments. Abundant small flowerheads, held above foliage, white to purple-pink blooms, inconspicuous sepals. Summer-flowering. Zones 8–10.

Thalictrum minus

☀/◐ ❄ ↔ 20–32 in (50–80 cm) ↑ 3–5 ft (0.9–1.5 m)

Erect perennial, found throughout Europe and Asia. Finely divided, blue-green, pinnate leaves. Panicles of yellow, sometimes purple-tinted flowers, inconspicuous sepals, in summer. Zones 6–9.

Thalictrum rochebruneanum

☀/◐ ❄ ↔ 16–20 in (40–50 cm) ↑ 40 in (100 cm)

Japanese perennial. Finely divided foliage, smooth-edged or lobed leaflets, to over 1 in (25 mm) long. Airy sprays of small pendulous flowers, many yellow filaments, showy purple-pink sepals, in summer. '**Lavender Mist**', large heads of tiny, bell-shaped, violet flowers. Zones 8–10.

Thalictrum rochebruneanum

Thalictrum delavayi

THERMOPSIS

FALSE LUPIN

This genus, which is a member of the pea-flower subfamily of the legume (Fabaceae) family, contains 23 species of rhizome-rooted perennial herbs. They are native to North America, Siberia, and parts of Asia, and are found growing in habitats such as riverbanks and open woods. The attractive 3-part leaves are often silvery. Their nectar-rich yellow or purple flowers are typical of the pea-flower family. The blooms are borne in spring or summer in dense or loose terminal racemes, often resembling lupins (*Lupinus*), a fact that is recognized in the common name applied to a number of the species.

CULTIVATION: *Thermopsis* species make ideal subjects for border planting and are suitable for naturalizing in larger areas. They are fully frost hardy plants, and will do well if planted in a position in full sun in any reasonably fertile soil that is moist but well drained. Some of the species can spread rapidly by their rhizomes. Propagate from seed or by division, which must be undertaken carefully as these deep-rooted plants resent disturbance.

Thermopsis rhombifolia

FALSE LUPIN, GOLDEN BANNER

☀ ❄ ↔ 24 in (60 cm) ↑ 36 in (90 cm)

Found from the Rocky Mountains to New Mexico, USA. Leaflets broadly oval, undersides coated with silvery hairs. Yellow, softly hairy flowers, densely or loosely packed in racemes to 12 in (30 cm) long. Spring- to summer-flowering. Upright downy seed pods. Zones 4–9.

Thermopsis villosa

syn. *Thermopsis caroliniana*

CAROLINA LUPIN

☀ ❄ ↔ 2 ft (0.6 m) ↕ 3–5 ft (0.9–1.5 m)

Stout perennial, native to southeastern USA. Bluish green leaves, downy undersides. Yellow flowers in terminal, downy, lupin-like racemes, in spring–summer. Silky-hairy seed pods. Zones 6–9.

THYMUS

THYME

Well known as the source of one of the most widely used culinary herbs, this genus in the mint (Lamiaceae) family is composed of around 350 species of mainly evergreen aromatic perennials and sub-shrubs, many of which become quite shrubby. The distribution range of the genus extends to most parts of Europe, temperate Asia, and northwest Africa, but the highest concentration is found around the Mediterranean and in the Middle East. Small wiry-stemmed plants, they have tiny, often downy leaves and heads of equally small, mauve, pink, or sometimes white flowers that are very attractive to bees. Late spring to mid-summer is the main flowering season. CULTIVATION: Frost hardiness varies with the species, though most *Thymus* species will withstand moderate frosts. Thyme grows best in light, rather gritty soil that has been enriched with humus for moisture retention. Plant in full sun and trim lightly after flowering to keep the plants compact and well-foliaged. When growing thyme indoors, place plant in a well-lit position. Propagate from seed, by removing naturally formed layers, or by taking half-hardened cuttings.

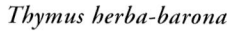

Thymus Coccineus Group

Thymus caespititius

☀ ❄ ↔ 15 in (38 cm) ↕ 2 in (5 cm)

Dwarf mat-forming shrub, found in Portugal and nearby parts of Spain, also Madeira and the Azores. Narrow, tiny, paddle-shaped leaves, edged with fine hairs. Flowers deep pink, lavender, or white, in late spring. Zones 7–10.

Thymus × *citriodorus*

LEMON-SCENTED THYME, LEMON THYME

☀ ❄ ↔ 24 in (60 cm) ↕ 6–12 in (15–30 cm)

Erect subshrub; of garden origin; *T. pulegioides* × *T. vulgaris* hybrid. Branching stems; glossy dark green leaves. Dense lavender-pink flowerheads in summer. Strong lemon scent. 'Aureus', upright spreading plant, gold-splashed leaves; 'Bertram Anderson' (golden lemon thyme), gray-green leaves suffused with gold, new growth tinged red; 'Lime', low, creeping, lime green foliage, white flowers; 'Silver Queen', silver-green to cream marbled foliage. Zones 5–10.

Thymus Coccineus Group

☀ ❄ ↔ 14 in (35 cm) ↕ 3–4 in (8–10 cm)

Mat-forming creeper, garden origin, possibly forms of *T. serpyllum*. Tiny dark green leaves. Magenta flowers, in terminal clusters, in summer. 'Coccineus Minor', dwarf form, tiny leaves, pink flowers. Zones 4–9.

Thymus herba-barona

CARAWAY THYME

☀ ❄ ↔ 24 in (60 cm) ↕ 4 in (10 cm)

Wide-spreading species from Corsica and Sardinia. Carpet of glossy dark green leaves, spicy scent. Loose clusters of pink-mauve flowers in mid-summer. Zones 7–9.

Thymus mastichina

☀ ❄ ↔ 16 in (40 cm)

↕ 6–12 in (15–30 cm)

Native of Spain and Portugal. Upright perennial; hairy shoots and leaves. Elliptical green leaves, aromatic. Clusters of white flowers. Summer-flowering. Zones 7–10.

Thymus polytrichus

☀ ❄ ↔ 24 in (60 cm) ↕ 2 in (5 cm)

Perennial, native to southern Europe. Tight mat-forming species; dark green oval leaves. Pale to deep purple flowers, splashed with white, in summer. *T. p.* subsp. *britannicus*, slightly downy foliage, dark pink flowers; 'Minor', dwarf habit, tiny pink and white flowers; 'Thomas's White' (syn. *T. praecox* subsp. *arcticus* 'Albus'), compact, crisp clear white flowers. Zones 5–9.

Thymus polytrichus subsp. *britannicus*

Thymus pseudolanuginosus

syn. *Thymus lanuginosus*

WOOLLY MOTHER-OF-THYME, WOOLLY THYME

☼ ❋ ↔ 24 in (60 cm) ↑ 1–3 in (2.5–8 cm)

Of unknown origin. Forms low-spreading mat of woolly leaves. Scentless pink flowers in early summer. Sparse flowering. Must have sharp drainage. Plant between rocks. Zones 5–9.

TIARELLA

This genus in the saxifrage (Saxifragaceae) family is made up of 5 perennials—4 from North America and 1 found from the Himalayas to Japan. They spread by rhizomes or an underground network of thin fleshy stems, forming clumps of lobed heart-shaped leaves with long stalks. The flower stems carry airy open racemes of tiny white and/or pink to red, 5-petalled flowers, in late spring and summer. Foliage and flower stems are covered in fine hairs. *Tiarella* has been crossed with *Heuchera* to produce the inter-generic hybrid × *Heucherella*.

CULTIVATION: *Tiarella* species are very hardy, especially the American species. They are easily grown in woodlands or perennial borders; spreading but seldom invasive. Plant in a position in half-sun or full shade in humus-rich, moist, well-drained soil. Propagation is by division in late winter to early spring or from seed.

Tiarella cordifolia

FOAMFLOWER

☼/◐ ❋ ↔ 16–20 in (40–50 cm) ↑ 12 in (30 cm)

Perennial, occurring naturally in eastern North America; spreads by underground stems. Stems and leaves finely hairy; leaves lobed, toothed, heart-shaped, up to 4 in (10 cm) in length, on long stalks.

Tiarella, Hybrid Cultivar, 'Tiger Stripe'

Airy sprays of tiny, often pink-tinted flowers, 5-petalled, on fine stems, in early summer. 'Major', salmon pink flowers that darken with age. Zones 3–9.

Tiarella polyphylla

☼/◐ ❋ ↔ 16–20 in (40–50 cm) ↑ 12–18 in (30–45 cm)

Found from the Himalayas to Japan. Toothed, 5-lobed, heart-shaped leaves, to nearly 3 in (8 cm) long and wide. Sturdy purple-red-tinted flower stems; branching sprays of small, pink-tinted, cream flowers, from late spring to early summer. 'Rosea', deep pink flowers. Zones 7–9.

Tiarella wherryi

☼/◐ ❋ ↔ 16–20 in (40–50 cm) ↑ 8–12 in (20–30 cm)

Perennial from North America, closely allied to *T. cordifolia*. Leaves usually have 5 pronounced lobes, reddening in autumn.

Racemes of narrow, cream, 5-petalled flowers open from base upward from pink to maroon buds. Summer-flowering. 'Bronze Beauty', red-brown leaves, pink flowers; 'Oakleaf' ★, leaves with dark center and more pronounced lobes, flowers strongly pink-tinted. Zones 5–9.

Tiarella Hybrid Cultivars

☼/◐ ❋ ↔ 16–20 in (40–50 cm) ↑ 12–18 in (30–45 cm)

North American species interbreed freely and intermediate forms are common. Range of attractive garden forms available. Culti-vars include 'Crow Feather', foliage with dark central feather marking intensifying in winter, cream to pink flowers on spikes; 'Dark Star', bright green leaves with dark center, pink-tinted white flowers; 'Elizabeth Oliver', deep maroon-veined foliage, maroon-tinted flowers; 'Spring Symphony', long-lobed dark-centered leaves, pale pink flowers from dark buds; and 'Tiger Stripe', dark-veined bronze foli-age, reddening in autumn, pink-tinted cream flowers. Zones 6–9.

TILLANDSIA

AIR PLANT

This large genus of over 500 mostly epiphytic species in the bromeliad (Bromeliaceae) family has a distri-bution range that extends from southern USA to southern Argent-ina. Plants vary in size from minute to 15 ft (4.5 m) tall in flower. Some species have leaves that are covered with moisture-absorbing gray-white hairs, while others have green strap-like leaves. The flowerheads are typically globular or pyramidal, with side-branches and prominent bracts that are showy and colorful. Flowers are mostly tubular, some-times scented, and are bluish, pink, white, or yellow. The seed has a feathery parachute.

CULTIVATION: Gray-leafed forms are usually grown attached to a substrate. Mist-spray weekly in cooler months, as often as daily (in the early morning) in warmer periods. They like some air movement. Green-leafed forms are generally grown in pots. Grow them indoors in light and airy situations, in a greenhouse or con-servatory in cool-temperate areas, outdoors with protection from direct sunlight and extremes of rain in warm areas. Propagation is mainly by offsets.

Tillandsia aeranthos

☀ ✣ ↔ 6 in (15 cm) ↑ 6 in (15 cm)

Clump-forming species, found from northeastern Argentina to southern Brazil. Narrow triangular leaves form elongated rosette. Flower stem red, a little taller than leaf rosette. Flower-head egg-shaped, mainly red, large dark blue petals. Summer-flowering. Zones 11–12.

Tillandsia butzii

Tillandsia crocata

Tillandsia cyanea

Tillandsia bergeri

☀ ✛ ↔ 6 in (15 cm) ↑ 6 in (15 cm)

From southeastern Argentina. Clump-forming; narrow triangular leaves, gray-green, form elongated rosette. Flower stem a little taller than leaf rosette, pale red. Egg-shaped flowerhead, mainly pale red; large, wavy, pale blue petals, in summer. Zones 11–12.

Tillandsia butzii

☀ ✛ ↔ 4 in (10 cm) ↑ 12 in (30 cm)

Found from southern Mexico to Panama. Tall, clump-forming; base of leaves forms dense globular bulb, gray-green with darker spots and broken lines, upper parts almost tubular, contorted, spreading. Flower stem red, slender. Flowerhead with few sword-shaped spikes, petals blue-violet, rolled into tight tube. Summer-flowering. Zones 11–12.

Tillandsia crocata

☀ ✛ ↔ 6 in (15 cm) ↑ 8 in (20 cm)

Tiny clump-forming species, found from Bolivia to southern Brazil. Leaves narrow, almost cylindrical, furry gray, in opposite rows on single plane. Short flowerhead, furry, gray, sword-shaped; on slender stem; wide-spreading petals bright yellow. Summer-flowering. Zones 11–12.

Tillandsia cyanea

☀ ✛ ↔ 10 in (25 cm) ↑ 10 in (25 cm)

Small plant from Ecuador. Closely linked with *Tillandsia lindenii,* often hybridizing. Leaves narrow triangular, green, often with red lines underneath, forming an open rosette. Flowerhead sword-shaped, fragrant, petals deep violet, sometimes white eye in center, in summer. Zones 11–12.

Tillandsia dyeriana

☀ ✛ ↔ 6 in (15 cm) ↑ 6 in (15 cm)

From Ecuador. Leaves strap-like, green and purple spotted, forming funnel-shaped rosette. Flower stem slender, soon hanging. Sword-shaped flowerhead, single or cluster of several branches, bright reddish orange, petals white, spreading wide, just emerging from bracts, in summer. Zones 11–12.

Tillandsia fasciculata

☀ ✛ ↔ 20 in (50 cm) ↑ 40 in (100 cm)

Large varied species, native to Mexico, Central America, and the West Indies. Narrow triangular leaves, gray-green, rigid; form open rosette. Simple sword-shaped spike or cluster of up to 10 spikes, wholly red or yellow, or yellow and red, petals purple, rolled into tube. Summer-flowering. Eight varieties are recognized. Zones 11–12.

Tillandsia fuchsii

☀ ✛ ↔ 4 in (10 cm) ↑ 8 in (20 cm)

Small species, found naturally in Mexico. Leaves almost tubular, very thin, and grayish, bottom part forms tight bulb, upper part spreading, forming globular rosette. Dark wine red flower stem. Cylindrical flowerhead, wine red, petals violet, rolled into tight tube, in summer. Zones 11–12.

Tillandsia imperialis

☀ ✛ ↔ 16 in (40 cm) ↑ 20 in (50 cm)

Large species from Mexico. Green, narrow triangular leaves, form spreading rosette. Cone-shaped flowerhead, many red overlapping bracts, tip bending outward and sometimes green; emerging petals violet, rolled tightly into a tube; in summer. Zones 11–12.

Tillandsia ionantha

Tillandsia ionantha

BLUSHING BRIDE

☀ ✛ ↔ 3 in (8 cm) ↑ 2 in (5 cm)

Variable clump-forming species native to Mexico and Central America. Narrow triangular leaves, gray-green, erect, tips bent outward, almost forming a ball. Hidden flowerhead, globular, with up to 5 flowers, petals violet, forming a tight tube. Summer-flowering. Center leaves turn bright red at flowering. 'Druid', albino form. Zones 11–12.

Tillandsia leiboldiana

☀ ✛ ↔ 10 in (25 cm) ↑ 24 in (60 cm)

Tall evergreen perennial, native to Mexico and Central America. Funnel-shaped rosette; strap-like green leaves. Erect to curved flower stem. Bright red, narrow pyramidal flowerhead, up to 12 side branches, large red bract below each, petals violet, rolled into tight tube. Summer-flowering. Variegated form also occurs. Zones 11–12.

Tillandsia lindenii

☀ ⚘ ↔ 16 in (40 cm) ↕ 27 in (70 cm)

Tall species, native to Ecuador and northern Peru. Open rosette; narrow triangular green leaves, striped red underneath. Tall flower stem; sword-shaped flowerhead, petals opening wide, deep blue, white eye in center, fragrant. Summer-flowering. Zones 11–12.

Tillandsia magnusiana

☀ ⚘ ↔ 6 in (15 cm) ↕ 6 in (15 cm)

Tiny species, found from southern Mexico to El Salvador. Globular rosette; leaves very thin, almost tubular, gray-green, furred. Flowerhead almost globular, violet petals rolled into tight tubes emerging above leaves, in summer. Zones 11–12.

Tillandsia recurvata

BALL MOSS

☀ ⚘ ↔ 2½–8 in (6–20 cm) ↕ 4 in (10 cm)

Minute clump-forming species, found from southern USA to Argentina. Stemmed leaves almost tubular, gray-green, furred, in opposite rows on single plane. Flowerhead with 1 or 2 flowers; petals pale violet or white, in summer. Zones 11–12.

Tillandsia streptophylla

☀ ⚘ ↔ 8 in (20 cm) ↕ 18 in (45 cm)

Tall species, found from southern Mexico to Honduras. Leaves narrow triangular, gray-green, bottom part forms erect bulb, top part bends downward, contorted, spiralling. Flowerhead pyramidal, up to 10 narrow sword-shaped side branches, gray-green; center axis and large bracts below branches bright red, petals purple, rolled into a tube. Summer-flowering. Zones 11–12.

Tillandsia stricta

☀ ⚘ ↔ 6 in (15 cm) ↕ 8 in (20 cm)

Widespread species, especially in eastern South America. Epiphytic; open rosette, sometimes with leaves pointing in the same direction; leaves narrow triangular, green-gray, covered with hairs. Flower stem curving downward. Flowerhead egg-shaped, many overlapping red bracts, petals blue, in summer. Zones 11–12.

Tillandsia tectorum

☀ ⚘ ↔ 12 in (30 cm) ↕ 20 in (50 cm)

Larger species, native to Ecuador and northern Peru. Open rosette; sometimes stemmed leaves, narrow triangular, gray with long gray wool. Flowerhead with up to 5 sword-shaped spikes, reddish gray, petals blue with white band, in summer. Dislikes wet conditions. Zones 11–12.

Tillandsia streptophylla

Tillandsia tenuifolia

☀ ⚘ ↔ 6 in (15 cm) ↕ 6 in (15 cm)

Tiny epiphytic species, native to eastern South America. Stems can reach up to 10 in (25 cm) in length. Leaves sometimes stemmed, narrow triangular, gray-green, usually forming open rosette, but sometimes pointing in one direction. Egg-shaped flowerhead, red overlapping bracts, petals white or blue. Summer-flowering. Zones 11–12.

Tillandsia usneoides

OLD MAN'S BEARD, SPANISH MOSS

☀ ⚘ ↔ 4 in (10 cm)
↕ 24 in (50 cm)

Tall narrow species; perennial herb; found from southern USA to Argentina. Forms large clumps; leaves clothed in woolly hairs, gray, opposite and on same plane, forming long strands that twist and twine. Single flowerhead, green petals, fragrant. Summer-flowering. Zones 11–12.

Tillandsia leiboldiana

Tillandsia Hybrid Cultivars

☀ ✦ ↔ 4–24 in (10–60 cm) ↑ 4–36 in (10–90 cm)

Cultivars are extremely varied in size, however, all produce showy and colorful flowers. Popular cultivars include '**Anita**', which has links with *Tillandsia cyanea* and *T. lindenii*, striking lavender instead of more usual light pink, with large, cinnamon-scented flowers; '**Creation**', hybrid between *T. platyrhachis* and *T. cyanea*, flowerhead erect, many spreading branches, sword-shaped spikes in pink to dark rose, spreading violet-blue flowers; '**Curly Slim**', leaves narrow triangular, gray-green, flowerhead pyramidal, gray-green with pinkish tinge, central axis dull red, petals purple; '**Curra**', numerous inner leaves turn red at flowering, conical flowerhead, many overlapping bright red bracts, emergent violet petals; '**Eric Knobloch**', gray-green leaves, forming a bulbose base, flowers pointing upward, petals violet; at time of flowering, upper half of plant blushes yellow-orange, orange-scarlet, then deep rosy red; and '**Wildfire**', flower stem appears to be an extension of plant, with up to 25 green bracts taking the place of leaves; brilliant red sword-shaped spike emerges from each bract, petals purplish. Zones 11–12.

TITHONIA

MEXICAN SUNFLOWER

This genus is made up of 10 species of annuals, perennials, and shrubs that are native to Mexico and Central America. It is a member of the daisy (Asteraceae) family. Quite shrubby species, they are robust plants, sometimes with hairy stems, and have alternate leaves that are often lobed. They bear large daisy flowers in shades of yellow and orangey scarlet.

CULTIVATION: These plants are useful for providing a bright spot in the garden in late summer and autumn. Grow in a well-drained, moderately fertile soil in full sun. Propagation is from seed or from cuttings.

Tithonia rotundifolia

syn. *Tithonia speciosa*

MEXICAN SUNFLOWER

☀ ✿ ↔ 2 ft (0.6 m) ↑ 3–6 ft (0.9–1.8 m)

Annual, native to Mexico and Central America; rapidly forming, large, many-branched plant. Velvety-hairy leaves, to 12 in (30 cm) long. Orange ray flowers, tufted yellow centers, from summer to autumn, or first frost. Cultivars include '**Aztec Sun**', 4 ft (1.2 m) tall, golden flowers; '**Fiesta del Sol**', earlier-blooming dwarf; '**Goldfinger**', bushy selection, deep orange flowers; and '**Torch**', orange-red flowers. Zones 9–10.

Tithonia rotundifolia 'Torch'

TOLMIEA

Native to the coastal mountains of western North America, from northern California and north to Alaska, USA, this genus in the saxifrage (Saxifragaceae) family contains a single mat-forming herbaceous perennial. It has shallowly lobed pale green leaves that are sometimes evergreen. Young plants are borne on the leaves where the leaf stalk and leaf blade meet.

CULTIVATION: This plant prefers neutral to acidic, cool, moist, humus-rich soil in partial to deep shade. Sun can scorch the leaves, particularly the variegated form. It is sometimes grown as a house plant, requiring cool temperatures and filtered light. Propagation is by division in spring, or from seed in autumn. Plantlets may also be removed from leaves in mid- to late summer and potted up.

Tolmiea menziesii

PICKABACK PLANT, PIGGYBACK PLANT, THOUSAND MOTHERS

☀ ❄ ↔ 3–6 ft (0.9–1.8 m) ↑ 18–24 in (45–60 cm)

Shade-loving perennial from the west coast of North America. Shallowly lobed leaves, slightly hairy, mid-green. Small, inconspicuous, reddish brown flowers, borne on top of 12–24 in (30–60 cm) stems, from late spring to summer. '**Taff's Gold**' (syns '**Maculata**', '**Variegata**'), leaves splashed with gold in spring; foliage fades somewhat in summer. Zones 6–9.

TORENIA

WISHBONE FLOWER

This is a genus of up to 50 species of low-growing, spreading, bushy annual and perennial plants from tropical parts of Africa and Asia. They are members of the foxglove (Scrophulariaceae) family. These plants are noted for their ability to bloom well in both shady and sunny conditions. The toothed oval leaves, up to 4 in (10 cm) long, cover the pale creamy green stems. The flowers are pale violet with dark blue-purple lower lips and a yellow throat blotch. A pair of stamens unites at the anthers in a shape resembling the wishbone of a chicken, hence the common name. The flowers generally appear from late spring and finish once the first frosts start.

CULTIVATION: These plants make excellent edging plants for beds, borders, and shade or woodland gardens, as well as for containers or window boxes. They need a warm spot in order to flourish and will not cope with frost, cold persistent winds, or cold windchill factors. They are best grown in consistently moist, organically rich, well-drained soils in part-shade to full sun. Propagate from seed in spring, or once the last of the frosts has finished.

Torenia fournieri

BLUEWINGS, WISHBONE FLOWER

☀ ◐ ✦ ↔ 10 in (25 cm) ↑ 12 in (30 cm)

Small bushy species, native to tropical Asia. Pale green lightly serrated leaves, 2 in (5 cm) long, form mounds on stems. Trumpet-shaped, pale purple flowers. Summer- to autumn-flowering. Ideal hanging basket plant. '**Blue Panda**', compact

Torenia fournieri 'Blue Panda'

habit, lilac-blue flowers; **Clown Series**, mix containing several colors, some with a contrasting rim to each flower. Zones 11–12.

Torenia Hybrid Cultivars

☼/◐ ⚘ ↔ 10 in (25 cm) ↑ 12–15 in (30–38 cm)

Cultivars expand the range of flower colors to include shades of burgundy, pink, rose, lavender, as well as white. '**Duchess Deep-blue**', deep purplish blue flowers with orange spotting; '**Duchess White and Blue**' ★, white flowers with very deep blue blotches; '**Duchess White and Pink**', white flowers with deep magenta markings. Zones 11–12.

TOWNSENDIA

This genus of about 21 annual or perennial herbs is a member of the daisy (Asteraceae) family, and is native to western North America. It features soft gray-green spatula-shaped leaves that are covered in very fine hairs. The flowers are very daisy-like with wide discs surrounded by pointed ribbed petals in grayish pink, pinkish white, and mauve. The disc florets are yellow.
CULTIVATION: These plants prefer a position in full sun with deep well-drained soil. Propagate from cuttings in spring or from seed when ripe.

Townsendia formosa

☼ ❊ ↔ 10–12 in (25–30 cm)
↑ 12–16 in (30–40 cm)
Tufting rhizomatous perennial from dry stony grasslands of southwestern USA. Spatula-shaped leaves, midribs and edges finely hairy. Purple or white ray florets and yellow disc florets, in summer. Zones 8–10.

Townsendia parryi

PARRY'S TOWNSENDIA
☼ ❊ ↔ 10–15 in (25–38 cm) ↑ 10–15 in (25–38 cm)
Biennial or short-lived hairy perennial from northwestern North America. Spatula-shaped leaves. Large solitary flowerheads, ray florets bluish purple or violet, disc florets yellow, in early summer. Prefers subalpine to alpine habitats. Zones 5–8.

TRACHELIUM

A small genus of 7 species of perennial herbs belonging to the bellflower (Campanulaceae) family. They are native to Mediterranean regions, and are usually found growing in rocky crevices. They range from tiny cushion-forming species to more robust, erect, woody-based plants. Their simple leaves are alternately arranged. The flowers, in shades of purple and white, usually appear in clusters in summer. They are tubular with prominently protruding styles. *T. caeruleum,* which is suitable for border planting, is most commonly seen, flowering from seed in its first year or grown as an annual.
CULTIVATION: Grow *Trachelium* species in a sunny position in reasonably fertile, well-drained soil. The smaller species, requiring perfectly drained alkaline soil, are better suited to the rock garden, pots, or alpine house. Provide protection from the hottest sun and from winter wet. Propagate from seed or cuttings.

Trachelium caeruleum ★

☼ ❊ ↔ 18 in (45 cm) ↑ 24–36 in (60–90 cm)
Upright perennial from the Mediterranean region. Serrated-edged, pointed, oval leaves. Rounded clusters of tiny, starry, pleasantly perfumed, purple flowers, in summer. Very long protruding styles give flowerheads a soft fluffy appearance. Zones 9–11.

Townsendia parryi, in the wild, Colorado, USA

Trachystemon orientalis

Tradescantia, Andersoniana Group, 'Bilberry Ice'

Tradescantia zanonia 'Mexican Flag'

TRACHYSTEMON

RUSSIAN BORAGE

This small genus of only 2 species of herbaceous perennials is a member of the borage (Boraginaceae) family and is native to eastern Europe. They have large bristly leaves, very similar to those of comfrey *(Symphytum),* and bright blue starry flowers in very early spring as the leaves come up. Only *T. orientalis* is in general cultivation.

CULTIVATION: These exceptionally hardy plants do best in light to heavy shade in moist humus-rich soil where they will make large weed-smothering clumps. Propagate by division when dormant. Plants will self-seed.

Trachystemon orientalis

syn. *Borago orientalis*

RUSSIAN BORAGE

☀ ❊ ↔ 3–7 ft (0.9–2 m) ↑ 2–3 ft (0.6–0.9 m)

Coarse herbaceous perennial from Europe. Paddle-shaped, bristly, green leaves, to 12 in (30 cm) long. Open sprays of bright blue starry flowers, white at center, to ¾ in (18 mm) across, in late winter–early spring. Zones 5–10.

TRADESCANTIA

SPIDER LILY, SPIDERWORT

This genus is made up of around 70 species of annuals and perennials from the Americas, and is a member of the spiderwort (Commelinaceae) family. It includes a few species that, while attractive as garden plants, have become serious pests in some areas. Tuberous or fibrous-rooted and often evergreen, they have rather succulent stems and fleshy, pointed elliptical, lance-shaped, or narrow leaves. The clusters of small 3-petalled flowers, subtended by bracts, appear throughout the warmer months. They are sometimes very bright magenta, though white, soft pink, and blue to mauve predominate. Variegated and colored foliage forms are common.

CULTIVATION: Most of these plants are tolerant of light to moderate frosts. Some prefer a sunny aspect and are drought tolerant, but most prefer part-shade and moist well-drained soil. Propagation is by division, or from self-struck layers, tip cuttings, or seed, depending on the growth form.

Tradescantia virginiana

Tradescantia Andersoniana Group

☀ ❊ ↔ 12–48 in (30–120 cm) ↑ 8–20 in (20–50 cm)

Often wrongly called *T. × andersoniana.* Hybrids of several species, mostly derived from *T. virginiana.* Mainly clumping hybrids with narrow foliage and flowering habits of *T. virginiana.* Hybrids include 'Bilberry Ice', blue-green foliage, pale silver-mauve flowers; 'Blue and Gold' (syn. 'Sweet Kate'), long, narrow, bright yellow leaves, vivid blue flowers; 'Concord Grape', blue-green foliage, deep magenta flowers; 'Innocence', bright green foliage, white flowers; 'Isis', green foliage, bright blue flowers; 'J. C. Weguelin', green foliage, striking sky blue flowers; 'Little Doll', very compact, bright green foliage, soft mauve-blue flowers; 'Osprey', green foliage, flowers white to palest mauve with mauve-blue center; 'Purple Dome', green foliage, deep purple flowers; and 'Zwanenburg Blue', green foliage, blue to violet flowers. Zones 7–10.

Tradescantia fluminensis

syn. *Tradescantia albiflora*

WANDERING JEW

☀/☀ ❊ ↔ 24–60 in (60–150 cm) ↑ 12–20 in (30–50 cm)

Somewhat invasive perennial from South America; naturalized in southern USA. Thick succulent stems, closely spaced. Broadly lance-shaped fleshy leaves, lighter central area, to over 3 in (8 cm) long; large white flowers. Cultivated forms occur in wide range of foliage colors and patterns. Zones 9–11.

Tradescantia spathacea

syn. *Rhoeo discolor*

BOAT LILY, CRADLE LILY, MOSES-IN-HIS-CRADLE

☀/☀ ❊ ↔ 12–16 in (30–40 cm)
↑ 15 in (38 cm)

From southern Mexico, Guatemala, and Belize. Short-stemmed clumping perennial; erect leaves, to 14 in (35 cm) long, broadly spear-shaped, dark green above, purple-red below. Small white flowers in boat-shaped bract near leaf base, all year. 'Vittata' ★ (syn. 'Variegata'), cream-and-pink striped foliage. Zones 10–12.

Tradescantia virginiana

☼ ❈ ↔ 20–48 in (50–120 cm) ↕ 12–20 in (30–50 cm)

Mounding spreading perennial, native to eastern USA. Narrow, rather grass-like leaves. Small heads of white, pink, mauve-blue, or purple flowers, similarly colored bracts, in summer. Widely hybridized to produce a range of garden forms. Zones 7–10.

Tradescantia zanonia

syn. *Campelia zanonia*

☼/☼ ❈ ↔ 5 ft (1.5 m) ↕ 24–40 in (60–100 cm)

Erect to spreading perennial from Central and South America. Leaves simple lance-shaped, silvery beneath. Inflorescence to 8 in (20 cm) long, tiny magenta-tinted white flowers, large purple-tinted green bracts, in summer–winter. 'Mexican Flag', leaves with broad cream stripes. Zones 10–12.

TRICHOSTEMA

This genus of 16 species of aromatic annuals and small shrubs is a member of the mint (Lamiaceae) family and is found throughout most parts of North America. They have simple lance-shaped leaves that have a woolly underside. They produce blue, or occasionally pink or white, tubular flowers, which resemble those of the related *Salvia* genus, during most of spring and summer.
CULTIVATION: The shrubby species should be grown in a well-drained soil of medium fertility. In cool climates they are best overwintered in the greenhouse. Propagate from seed sown in spring, or from half-hardened cuttings in autumn.

Trichostema lanatum

Trichostema lanatum

BLUE CURLS, WOOLLY BLUE CURLS

☼ ❈ ↔ 2 ft (0.6 m) ↕ 2–5 ft (0.6–1.5 m)

Shrubby species from California, USA. Dark green lance-shaped leaves, woolly beneath, rolled edges. Woolly, tubular, purple-blue flowers on 15 in (38 cm) spikes, in spring–summer. Zones 8–10.

TRICYRTIS

TOAD LILY

A genus of 16 graceful, rhizomatous, woodland perennials belonging to the lily-of-the-valley (Convallariaceae) family, and found growing in moist woodlands and on mountains and cliffs from the eastern Himalayas to the Philippines, and in Japan and Taiwan. Their oblong to lance-shaped, pointed, often glossy and sometimes spotted leaves clasp upright on arching stems. The star-, bell-, or funnel-shaped flowers are terminal or in upper leaf axils and can be pure white, golden yellow, lavender, or purple, usually spotted, with a somewhat waxen or iridescent quality. They usually bloom in late summer and autumn.
CULTIVATION: These perennials need moist, well-drained, humus-rich soil, and a position in part-shade to full sun. In warmer areas, they will do best in part-shade to full shade. Some species may be propagated from seed in autumn. All may be divided in spring when dormant.

Tricyrtis formosana

syn. *Tricyrtus stolonifera*

FORMOSA TOAD LILY

☼ ❈ ↔ 18 in (45 cm) ↕ 36 in (90 cm)

Erect species, native to Taiwan. Spreads by runners. Green leaves mottled deeper green. Brown or maroon buds open to white or pale lilac, purple-spotted flowers tinged yellow, in mid-summer to autumn. Zones 5–9.

Tricyrtis hirta

HAIRY TOAD LILY

☼ ❈ ↔ 24 in (60 cm) ↕ 36 in (90 cm)

From Japan. Arching stems; slightly hairy, soft green foliage. White flowers speckled with dark purple, along stems in leaf axils, in early to mid-autumn. Cultivars include 'Myazaki' and 'Myazaki Gold'. Zones 4–9.

Tricyrtis macrantha

☀ ❈ ↔ 24 in (60 cm) ↕ 30 in (75 cm)

Upright plant from Japan. Arching stems; glossy green, ovate-oblong, bamboo-like leaves. Brownish slightly fuzzy stems; pendulous bell-shaped flowers, lemon yellow with chocolate spots inside, in early autumn. Zones 7–9.

Tricyrtis macropoda

syn. *Tricyrtis dilatata*

☼ ❈ ↔ 24 in (60 cm) ↕ 30 in (75 cm)

Handsome species, native to China. Rhizomatous perennial; oblong-ovate leaves on erect stems. Branched inflorescences of lavender flowers, spotted with darker purple, in mid- to late summer. Zones 5–9.

Tricyrtis hirta

Trifolium pannonicum

Trifolium rubens

☼/◐ ❄ ↔ 18–24 in (45–60 cm)
↕ 12–24 in (30–60 cm)
Bushy perennial, native to southern Europe.
Silver-haired, deep green, trifoliate leaves,
elliptical leaflets. Large conical heads of
crimson flowers. Summer-flowering.
Zones 7–10.

Trifolium uniflorum ★

ONE-FLOWERED CLOVER

☼/◐ ❄ ↔ 8–16 in (20–40 cm)
↕ 2–4 in (5–10 cm)
Trailing rhizome-rooted perennial found
from Sicily to the eastern Mediterranean.
Trifoliate leaves, leaflets rounded, often
downy undersides. White flowers, sometimes
flushed with pink, solitary or in heads of up
to 3, in spring–summer. Zones 7–10.

TRIFOLIUM

CLOVER

A vitally important component of the world's pastures, at the
same time clover is far less welcome in lawns. A member of the
pea-flower subfamily of the legume (Fabaceae) family, it is found
naturally throughout the temperate and subtropical zones except
Australasia and consists of around 230 species of annuals, biennials, and perennials. Typically trifoliate and bright green, the
leaves may have up to 9 leaflets, sometimes darkly marked. The
individual flowers, which are carried in rounded heads, are very
much like pea-flowers.

CULTIVATION: Generally hardy and easily grown, clover is rarely
deliberately cultivated in gardens. Plant in full sun or half-sun in
moist well-drained soil. Propagate by division but usually self-sows.

Trifolium pannonicum

HUNGARIAN CLOVER

☼/◐ ❄ ↔ 8 in (20 cm) ↕ 8 in (20 cm)
Perennial from eastern Europe; upright bushy
habit. Fine silky hairs on stems and leaves.
Red-tinted stems; narrow elliptical leaflets.
Inflorescence erect, to 4 in (10 cm) long; soft
creamy yellow flowers, in summer. Zones 5–9.

Trifolium repens

WHITE CLOVER

☼/◐ ❄ ↔ 8–16 in (20–40 cm) ↕ 2 in (5 cm)
Low-growing widely naturalized perennial
from Europe. Creeping rhizomes; leaves usu-
ally trifoliate, leaflets rounded, finely serrated, deep green with
darker chevron markings. Tiny flowers, fragrant, white or soft
pink. Summer-flowering. Cultivars include '**Atropurpureum**',
red-bronze leaves, variable green edge; '**Green Ice**', 2-tone gray-
green foliage; '**Purpurascens**', vigorous, leaflets with central
purple-red zone; and '**Purpurascens Quadrifolium**', purplish
brown leaves with 4 leaflets. Zones 4–10.

TRILLIUM

WAKE ROBIN, WOOD LILY

This group of 30 rhizome-rooted, spring-flowering, woodland
perennials from North America and temperate Asia is the type
genus for the wake-robin (Trilliaceae) family. Ranging from the
tiny *T. rivale*, to 2 in (5 cm) high, to species 24 in (60 cm) tall
in flower, the genus is remarkably consistent in form. The leaflets are bright green, often mottled and usually broadly oval,
tapering to a point. At the center of the 3-leafed cluster is a
simple 3-petaled flower that may be white, cream, pink, or
deep maroon-red. The common name comes from their early
flowering habit—the plant that wakes the robin in spring.

CULTIVATION: Plant in part-shade or full shade in a cool, moist,
humus-rich, well-drained soil. All species die back completely in
autumn but race into growth in early spring.
Propagate by division or from seed.

Trillium chloropetalum

Trillium chloropetalum

◐/☼ ❄ ↔ 20 in (50 cm) ↕ 20 in (50 cm)
Perennial from California, USA. Thick
stems; rounded, often maroon-mottled leaves
developing rapidly from early spring to form
full ruff behind flowers. Fragrant, white to
greenish white, soft yellow, or maroon flowers
with slightly reflexed petals, in early spring.
T. c. var. *giganteum*, robust, usually dark
red-flowered form, with maroon-mottled
foliage. Zones 6–9.

Trillium cuneatum

SWEET BETSY, TOAD SHADE

◐/☼ ❄ ↔ 16 in (40 cm) ↕ 24 in (60 cm)
Variegated species from southeastern USA. Mottled gray-green
and olive foliage, said to resemble pattern of a toad's skin. Leaves
pointed oval, not quite making a full circle. Flowers burgundy to
yellowish green, musk-scented, in early spring. Zones 6–9.

Trillium erectum ★
BETHROOT, BIRTHROOT

◐/◉ ❋ ↔ 20 in (50 cm) ↑ 20 in (50 cm)

From eastern North America. Large, light textured, bright green leaves, sometimes making complete ruff. Flowers at or slightly above foliage level, dark velvety red, rarely white, narrow petals, unpleasantly scented, in early spring. Zones 4–9.

Trillium grandiflorum
GRAND TRILLIUM, SHOWY TRILLIUM

◐/◉ ❋ ↔ 20 in (50 cm) ↑ 18 in (45 cm)

Late-flowering species from eastern North America. Rounded to pointed oval leaves, sometimes overlapping to form full circle. Flowers opening white, ageing to pink, in early summer. *T. g.* f. *roseum* (syn. 'Roseum'), flowers pink, ageing to deep dusky shade. *T. g.* **'Flore Pleno'**, double flowers. Zones 5–9.

Trillium luteum
WOOD TRILLIUM, YELLOW WAKE ROBIN

◐/◉ ❋ ↔ 18 in (45 cm) ↑ 18 in (45 cm)

Native to southeastern USA. Broad pointed oval, mottled leaves, not overlapping. Yellow to yellow-green, very fragrant flowers, erect petals to over 3 in (8 cm) long, in early spring. Zones 5–9.

Trillium ovatum
WAKE ROBIN, WESTERN TRILLIUM

◐/◉ ❋ ↔ 20 in (50 cm) ↑ 20 in (50 cm)

Erect species, native to Oregon, USA. Conspicuously veined, deep green, pointed oval to rhomboidal leaves. Flowers held above foliage level on erect stems; white petals held almost horizontally, ageing to pink, musk-scented, in early spring. Zones 5–9.

Trillium sessile
TOAD SHADE

◐/◉ ❋ ↔ 12–16 in (30–40 cm) ↑ 12 in (30 cm)

Native to northeastern USA. Elliptical to rounded leaves with dark mottling, often slightly drooping, leaves encircle flower but seldom overlap. Flowers musk-scented, petals deep purple-red, sepals green tinted purple-red, in early spring. Zones 4–9.

TROLLIUS
GLOBE FLOWER

There are approximately 31 species of perennial herbs in this genus, which belongs to the buttercup (Ranunculaceae) family. They are found in almost all northern temperate regions from the Himalayas to Turkey, China, Europe, and North America. The roots are thick and fibrous and the plants form basal tufts or rosettes of palmately lobed and divided leaves with toothed edges. The flowers,

Trollius chinensis 'Golden Queen'

often cupped, are up to 3 in (8 cm) wide, with spirally arranged sepals and petals of white, yellow, or orange, sometimes tinged with red or lilac. They grow in damp sunny meadows and on stream banks, often in heavy soils.

Trillium cuneatum

CULTIVATION: These plants will grow best in full sun or part-shade in permanently moist soil or in boggy areas beside water. Propagate from seed or by division.

Trollius chinensis
syn. *Trollius ledebourii*

◐/◑ ❋ ↔ 18 in (45 cm) ↑ 36 in (90 cm)

Clumping species, found growing naturally in northern China. Deeply lobed, finely toothed leaves. Tall stems; bowl-shaped flowers, golden yellow, prominent stamens, in summer. **'Golden Queen' ★**, deep orange-yellow flowers. Zones 5–9.

Trollius × cultorum

◐/◑ ❋ ↔ 18 in (45 cm) ↑ 24–36 in (60–90 cm)

Garden hybrids; finely divided foliage; lemon to orange flowers, in summer. **'Cheddar'**, pale lemon to almost white flowers; **'Feuertroll'**, rich orangey yellow flowers; **'Orange Princess'**, orange flowers tinted with yellow. Zones 5–9.

Trollius europaeus
COMMON GLOBE FLOWER

◐/◑ ❋ ↔ 18 in (45 cm) ↑ 24 in (60 cm)

Variable species found in Europe, northern Asia, and far northern North America. Muchdivided, toothed leaves, 3- to 5-lobed. Globular lemon yellow flowers, to 2 in (5 cm) wide, in spring–summer. Zones 5–9.

TROPAEOLUM (see page 792)

Tropaeolum ciliatum

◐/◉ ❋ ↔ 20 ft (6 m) ↑ 20 ft (6 m)

Vigorous, climbing, herbaceous perennial, native to Chile. Leaves mid-green, 5 to 7 lobes. Bright golden yellow trumpet-shaped flowers, deep red center and veining. Summer-flowering. Capable of spreading over a large area in one season. Zones 8–10.

Tropaeolum majus

Tropaeolum majus

NASTURTIUM

☼/◐ ⚅ ↔ 10 ft (3 m) ↑ 10 ft (3 m)

Annual climber or scrambler found from Colombia to Bolivia. Near round, dull green leaves, sometimes shallowly lobed. Yellow, orange, and red, long-spurred flowers, to over 2 in (5 cm) wide, in summer. Now grown mainly in the form of seed-raised cultivars including **Alaska Series ★**, white-variegated foliage, most colors; '**Empress of India**', green to bluish green leaves, vivid red flowers; **Gleam Hybrids**, mixed or individual colors; '**Hermine Grashoff**', shallowly lobed leaves, orange-red double flowers; **Jewel Series ★**, white foliage variegation, most colors; '**Margaret Long**', shallowly lobed leaves, golden yellow shading to pink double flowers; '**Peach Melba**', pale yellow flowers, orange blotch on each petal; '**Peach Schnapps**', pinkish orange flowers, orange veining on each petal; '**Red Wonder**', low, slightly spreading, purple-blue leaves, deep red flowers; **Whirlibird Series**, low and spreading, most colors. **Zones 9–11.**

Tropaeolum peregrinum

CANARY CREEPER

☼/◐ ⚅ ↔ 8 ft (2.4 m) ↑ 8 ft (2.4 m)

Quick-growing perennial climber from Peru and Ecuador, often treated as an annual. Light green, 5-lobed leaves. Clusters of long-stemmed, 1 in (25 mm) wide, sulfur yellow to gold flowers, cut-edged petals. Summer- to autumn-flowering. **Zones 9–11.**

UTRICULARIA

BLADDERWORT

This genus in the bladderwort (Lentibulariaceae) family has around 200 species of small carnivorous plants. Highly adaptable, these plants grow in areas of perennial or seasonal wetness in a wide range of environments. Having no real root system, they form rhizomes or stolons with green leaves of varying size and shape and/or tiny stalked bladders, spreading rapidly in the growing season. Traps found on the stems or runners have tiny trigger hairs that "vacuum" insects into the bladder. Most have attractive 2-lipped flowers on slender scapes from spring to early summer. **CULTIVATION:** Growing conditions can be divided into 4 main groups. All can be grown in a peat/sand mix (4:1). Grow terrestrial species in part-shade in permanently wet peat soil occasionally flooded with shallow water. Allow seasonal species to dry out, then put in a shallow tray of water in the growing season. Tropical/epiphytic species prefer warm, wet, humid conditions in part-shade. Grow aquatic species in full sun in a small tank of water with a peat base, taking care to prevent algae from forming. Propagate by division in the growing season or from seed.

Utricularia alpina

ALPINE BLADDERWORT

◐ ⚅ ↔ 6 in (15 cm) ↑ 12 in (30 cm)

Perennial tropical epiphyte or ground species from highland rainforests of Central and South America and the West Indies. Oval leaves, 6 in (15 cm) long, arise from tuberous root stock. Up to 4 white and yellow flowers, to 2 in (5 cm) wide. **Zones 9–11.**

Utricularia bisquamata

syn. *Utricularia capensis*

◐ ⚅ ↔ 3 in (8 cm) ↑ 2 in (5 cm)

Terrestrial species from South Africa. Profuse small flowers on scapes to 1 in (25 mm) long, in a color combination of violet, orange, white, and yellow. Spreads by seed. **Zones 9–11.**

Utricularia calycifida

◐ ⚅ ↔ 4 in (10 cm) ↑ 6 in (15 cm)

Tropical species, native to Guyana, Venezuela, and Surinam. Teardrop-shaped leaves with purple streaks, sometimes tinged red. Several purple flowers with yellow center, on scapes to 6 in (15 cm) tall. **Zones 10–11.**

Utricularia bisquamata

Utricularia inflata

Utricularia reniformis

Utricularia dichotoma ★

FAIRY APRONS

☀ ❄ ↔ 8 in (20 cm) ↑ 6–18 in (15–45 cm)

Tropical and temperate terrestrial species from New Zealand and temperate Australia. Leaves to 1 in (25 mm) long. Pale pink to purple flowers, white to yellow centers, 1 to 2 pairs per scape. Zones 9–11.

Utricularia inflata

syn. *Utricularia ceratophylla*

FLOATING BLADDERWORT

☀ ❄ ↔ 12 in (30 cm) ↑ 12 in (30 cm)

North American tropical and subtropical perennial aquatic. Leaves to 7 in (18 cm) long. Star-shaped whorl of 5 to 7 hollow tubes make it float. To 17 yellow flowers per scape. Zones 9–11.

Utricularia menziesii

REDCOAT

☀ ❄ ↔ 2 in (5 cm) ↑ 3 in (8 cm)

From southwestern Western Australia. Leaves to 2 in (5 cm) long. Single orange to burgundy flower, yellow center. Forms a tuber during hot dry summer months. Zones 9–11.

Utricularia praelonga

☀ ❄ ↔ 12 in (30 cm) ↑ 18 in (45 cm)

Tropical and subtropical Brazilian species. Forms 2 types of leaves: long, thin; circular, flat on ground. Large yellow flowers on long stems. Zones 10–11.

Utricularia reniformis ★

☀ ❄ ↔ 18 in (45 cm) ↑ 18 in (45 cm)

Tropical terrestrial species from Venezuela and Guyana. Thick fleshy rhizomes bearing traps. Large kidney-shaped leaves. Tall spikes of long-lasting, large, pinkish violet flowers. Zones 10–11.

Utricularia uniflora

☀ ❄ ↔ 3 in (8 cm) ↑ 8 in (20 cm)

Perennial terrestrial found in the wet sandy soil of streams and on waterfall rockfaces of the Australian east coast. Small egg-shaped leaves; 1 to 2 mauve flowers on each slim stalk. Zones 9–11.

UVULARIA

BELLWORT, MERRYBELLS

This genus contains 5 species of easy-to-grow herbaceous perennials in the lily-of-the-valley (Convallariaceae) family. From eastern North America, they are found in moist, well-drained, deciduous woodlands. Stems are erect or arching; the lance-shaped leaves are a bright green. Leaves are perfoliate (wrapping around the stem at the base) on all species except *U. sessilifolia*. Yellow bell-shaped flowers dangle from the stem and have long, slender, pointed, slightly twisted

Utricularia praelonga

petals. Blooms last for 2 to 3 weeks in early spring to mid-summer, depending on species, but foliage remains visible all summer.

CULTIVATION: Grow these plants in shade in deep, moist, slightly acid soil. Propagate by dividing clumps in spring or autumn, from ripened seed in late summer, or by transplanting underground stems, which spread easily.

Uvularia grandiflora

BIG MERRYBELLS, GREAT MERRYBELLS

☀ ❄ ↔ 12–24 in (30–60 cm)
↑ 12–24 in (30–60 cm)

Found from Quebec to Ontario, Canada, south to Minnesota, Georgia, Tennessee, and Kansas, USA. Light green foliage, arching stems. Bright yellow flowers, from mid-spring to early summer. Fruit a small triangular capsule. *U. g.* var. *pallida*, pale sulfur yellow flowers. Zones 3–9.

Uvularia perfoliata

PERFOLIATE BELLWORT, STRAW BELL, WOOD MERRYBELLS

☀ ❄ ↔ 12–18 in (30–45 cm) ↑ 16 in (40 cm)

From Quebec to Ontario, Canada, south to Mississippi and Florida, USA. Flowers pale yellow from mid-spring to early summer. Zones 3–9.

VALERIANA

VALERIAN

This is a widely distributed (excluding Australasia) genus of vigorous annuals, hardy perennials, and small shrubs in the family Valerianaceae that favor moist habitats in woodlands, meadows, and mountainous regions. They are creeping or tap-rooted, and leaves vary from simple to lobed, pointed or deeply divided, sometimes arranged along the stems like the rungs of a ladder, disappearing near the top of the plant. Small flowers are produced, often in clusters, in pink, lavender-pink, white or yellow shades.

CULTIVATION: Grow in moist soil and full sun or part-shade. Propagate from seed in autumn or early spring, or from cuttings.

Uvularia grandiflora

Valeriana montana

☀ ❄ ↔ 10 in (25 cm) ↑ 10 in (25 cm)

From the Alps and the Caucasus region. Clumps of oval to round leaves. Small rounded clusters of lilac, pink, or white flowers in early summer. Zones 4–9.

Valeriana phu

☀ ❄ ↔ 18 in (45 cm) ↑ 36 in (90 cm)

Native to Europe and the Caucasus. Tall perennial; basal leaves mostly undivided. Tiny white flowers, in clusters, in summer. 'Aurea' leaves yellow when young. Zones 3–9.

VANCOUVERIA

This genus is made up of 3 species of herbaceous creeping perennials that are native to the woodlands of northwestern North America. Like *Epimedium*, they are members of the barberry (Berberidaceae) family and are useful ground covers in shady areas, but they will not do well in dry soil. Their leathery divided leaves grow on wiry stems from crowns arising from branched underground rhizomes. The small and pendulous flowers are held on tall stems above the foliage.

CULTIVATION: Grow *Vancouveria* species in partial shade in cool, moist, organic, acid soil. Additions of leaf mold or humus will ensure success. They will not perform well in areas with hot dry summers. Given ideal conditions they will spread quickly. Propagate by dividing the rhizomes in spring or autumn.

Vancouveria chrysantha

☀ ❄ ↔ 12 in (30 cm) ↑ 12 in (30 cm)

Creeping evergreen perennial from Oregon, USA. Stiff green leaves, bronze-tinged. Small golden yellow flowers in early summer. Zones 7–9.

Vancouveria hexandra ★

AMERICAN BARRENWORT

☀/☀ ❄ ↔ 12 in (30 cm) ↑ 12 in (30 cm)

Creeping perennial, found from Washington to California, USA. Deciduous; pale green foliage, similar to maidenhair fern (*Adiantum*). Drooping white flowers from late spring to early summer. Zones 7–9.

VERATRUM

FALSE HELLEBORE

This genus of rhizomatous herbaceous perennials, belonging to the bunchflower (Melanthiaceae) family, includes 20 species distributed throughout temperate Europe, North Africa, Asia, and North America that are usually found in damp meadows and open woodlands. Typically grown for their foliage, these plants feature alternate, pleated, prominently veined, mid- to dark green leaves, which form mounds. The numerous tiny flowers, typically bell-shaped, occur in white, green, brownish, or purple-black, and are held in terminal panicles. All parts of the plants are extremely toxic.

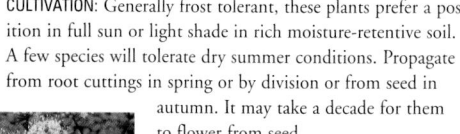

Valeriana montana

CULTIVATION: Generally frost tolerant, these plants prefer a position in full sun or light shade in rich moisture-retentive soil. A few species will tolerate dry summer conditions. Propagate from root cuttings in spring or by division or from seed in autumn. It may take a decade for them to flower from seed.

Veratrum album

WHITE FALSE HELLEBORE

☀ ❄ ↔ 24 in (60 cm) ↑ 24 in (60 cm)

Rhizomatous herb, native to Europe, North Africa, and northern Asia. Large, oblong or elliptic, pleated leaves. Dense racemes of green and white flowers. Summer-flowering. Zones 5–9.

Veratrum nigrum

BLACK HELLEBORE

☀ ❄ ↔ 24 in (60 cm) ↑ 24–48 in (60–120 cm)

Found from southern Europe to Siberia and Asia. Pleated, broadly elliptic to linear or lance-shaped leaves. Numerous purple-black flowers in dense racemes. Summer-flowering. Zones 6–9.

VERBASCUM

MOTH MULLEIN, MULLEIN

This genus of some 300 species of annuals, biennials, perennials, and subshrubs in the foxglove (Scrophulariaceae) family includes cultivated plants and many that have become weeds outside their natural temperate Eurasian and North African range. The commonly cultivated species usually form basal rosettes of large elliptic leaves, which are often heavily veined and sometimes felted. Tall upright flower spikes emerge from the rosettes, carrying massed, small, 5-petalled flowers, usually in white, yellow, or pink to lavender shades.

CULTIVATION: Hardiness varies with the species, but the majority of *Verbascum* species and cultivars prefer a sunny position with light, gritty, free-draining soil. They can tolerate summer drought but need moisture until after flowering. Propagate by division or from seed, depending on the growth form.

Verbascum acaule

☀/☀ ❄ ↔ 4 in (10 cm) ↑ 4 in (10 cm)

Tiny species, native to the Peloponnesian region of Greece. Tight rosette of dark green, toothed, elliptic leaves. Glowing yellow 5-petalled flowers throughout warmer months. Ideal for alpine troughs. Zones 7–10.

Verbascum blattaria

MOTH MULLEIN

☀/☀ ❄ ↔ 12–20 in (30–50 cm) ↑ 5–6 ft (1.5–1.8 m)

Widely naturalized temperate Eurasian biennial. Basal rosettes of downy, toothed, lance-shaped, green leaves, up to 10 in (25 cm) long. Strong, erect, leafy flower stems; many ¾ in (18 mm) wide, white, sometimes pale yellow or pink flowers. Cultivated forms may have considerably larger flowers. Zones 6–10.

Verbascum bombyciferum

☼/◐ ❄ ↔ 24–40 in (60–100 cm) ↑ 6–8 ft (1.8–2.4 m)

Western Asian biennial. Forms large rosettes of broadly oval, wavy-edged, white-felted leaves, to 20 in (50 cm) long. Flower stems to over 6 ft (1.8 m) tall, leafy at base but leafless from point where flowers commence. Stems and buds woolly, sometimes branching, flowers deep yellow, to over 1¼ in (30 mm) wide, in summer. 'Polarsommer' (syn. 'Arctic Summer'), yellow flowered cultivar, named for especially heavy silver felting on leaves. Zones 6–10.

Verbascum chaixii

NETTLE-LEAFED MOTH MULLEIN

☼/◐ ❄ ↔ 12–24 in (30–60 cm) ↑ 36–48 in (90–120 cm)

Perennial, occurring from central Europe to Spain and east to Russia. Forms clump of rosettes of deeply veined, toothed, gray-green to dark green, downy leaves, to 12 in (30 cm) long. Narrow erect flower stems; flowers less than 1 in (25 mm) wide, bright yellow with purple-red stamens, in summer. 'Album' ★, to 33 in (85 cm) tall, white flowers, mauve stamens. Zones 5–9.

Verbascum dumulosum

☼/◐ ❄ ↔ 12–16 in (30–40 cm) ↑ 8 in (20 cm)

Turkish perennial. Dense clump of velvety, toothed, soft green, basal leaves to 2 in (5 cm) long. Many 10- to 35-flowered heads of bright yellow blooms in summer. Zones 8–10.

Verbascum olympicum

☼/◐ ❄ ↔ 20–40 in (50–100 cm) ↑ 5–6 ft (1.5–1.8 m)

Turkish summer-flowering biennial or short-lived perennial. Forms dense basal clump of smooth-edged, lance-shaped, white, woolly leaves, around 12 in (30 cm) long, sometimes more than 24 in (60 cm) long. Branching leafy-based stems; dozens of 1 in (25 mm) wide, bright yellow flowers. Zones 6–10.

Verbascum phoeniceum

PURPLE MULLEIN

☼/◐ ❄ ↔ 12–16 in (30–40 cm) ↑ 8–16 in (20–40 cm)

Southern Eurasian biennial or short-lived perennial. Usually one large rosette of sparsely hairy, dark green, wavy-edged or finely toothed, pointed oval leaves, to 6 in (15 cm) long. Simple or few-branched stems with mauve to purple, rarely white, pink, or yellow flowers, around 1 in (25 mm) wide, in summer. Zones 6–10.

Verbascum thapsus

AARON'S ROD

☼/◐ ❄ ↔ 20–32 in (50–80 cm) ↑ 6–7 ft (1.8–2 m)

Extremely vigorous, widely naturalized, summer-flowering, temperate Eurasian biennial. Forms large rosettes of woolly white to gray leaves, up to 20 in (50 cm) long. Strong erect flower stem, usually leafy at base, many ½–1¼ in (12–30 mm) wide, deep yellow flowers. Zones 3–9.

Verbascum Hybrid Cultivars

☼/◐ ❄ ↔ 12–20 in (30–50 cm) ↑ 12–60 in (30–150 cm)

Moth mulleins hybridize freely, and British breeders in particular have produced a range of hybrids that combine lush velvety foliage with beautifully shaded flowers. Some of the best include members of the **Cotswold Group** such as 'Cotswold Beauty', to 48 in (120 cm) tall, with buff to apricot-pink flowers, purple-pink anthers; 'Gainsborough', to 48 in (120 cm) tall, bright yellow flowers, gray felted foliage; 'Mont Blanc', to 36 in (90 cm) high, pure white flowers, gray felted foliage; and 'Pink Domino', to 48 in (120 cm) tall, bright pink with a dark center. Other excellent cultivars include 'Helen Johnson', 24–32 in (60–80 cm) tall, variable dusky apricot-pink shades, gray-felted foliage; 'Jackie', to 24 in (60 cm) high, dusky pink with deep magenta center; 'Letitia', to 12 in (30 cm) tall, shrubby habit, many bright yellow flowers. Zones 6–10.

Verbascum chaixii 'Album'

Verbascum dumulosum

Verbascum olympicum

Verbascum, Hybrid Cultivar, 'Cotswold Beauty'

VERBENA

VERVAIN

This member of the self-named vervain (Verbenaceae) family contains 250 species of annuals, perennials, and subshrubs native to tropical and subtropical America. Plants are sprawling to erect; leaves are opposite and variously divided. Terminal flowerheads range from narrow and overlapping to broader, rounder clusters. Individual flowers are tubular with flaring, sometimes notched, lobes and blooms come in shades of purple, pink, red, and white. Some botanists, particularly in North America, recognize the genus *Glandularia* as distinct from *Verbena*. As such, *Glandularia* includes most lower-growing verbenas with more colorful flowers in short broad heads, in contrast to the erect slender spikes of flowers that characterize *Verbena* in the narrower sense.
CULTIVATION: Grow these plants in the border in full sun in moderately fertile, moist but well-drained soil. A number of cultivars are suitable for hanging baskets. Propagate annuals from seed and perennials from seed, cuttings, or by division.

Verbena bonariensis

PURPLE TOP, SOUTH AMERICAN VERVAIN, TALL VERBENA

☼ ❋ ↔ 24 in (60 cm) ↑ 3–5 ft (0.9–1.5 m)

South American perennial; also grown as annual. Erect, square, rough stems. Sparsely foliaged; lance-shaped serrated leaves. Tiny purple flowers in flat-topped clusters. Self-sows. Zones 7–10.

Verbena canadensis

syn. *Glandularia canadensis*

CREEPING VERVAIN, ROSE VERVAIN

☼ ❋ ↔ 16 in (40 cm) ↑ 8 in (20 cm)

From North America. Semi-prostrate perennial, rooting at nodes. Leaves toothed, deeply divided. Small showy heads of fragrant rosy pink to purple flowers, in spring–autumn. Zones 4–9.

Verbena rigida

syn. *Verbena venosa*

VEINED VERBENA

☼ ❋ ↔ 12 in (30 cm) ↑ 24–36 in (60–90 cm)

Creeping perennial, native to South America. Stiff upright stems; stalkless oblong leaves, rough, irregularly toothed. Vivid purple to magenta flowers, in clusters, in summer. 'Polaris', silver-blue flowers. Zones 8–10.

Verbena tenera

syn. *Glandularia tenera*

☼ ❀ ↔ 12–20 in (30–50 cm) ↑ 12–20 in (30–50 cm)

Shrubby, clumping perennial, found from Brazil to Argentina. Sprawling stems rooting at nodes; small, finely hairy, divided leaves. Elongated spikes of purplish or rose violet flowers. *V. t.* var. **maonetti**, reddish violet flowers edged with white; *V. t.* var. **pulchella**, spikes of rose-violet flowers. *V. t.* 'Kleopatra', crimson-pink flowers. Zones 9–11.

Verbena tenuisecta

syns *Glandularia tenuisecta*, *Verbena pulchella gracilior*

MOSS VERBENA

☼ ❀ ↔ 12–20 in (30–50 cm) ↑ 12–20 in (30–50 cm)

Annual or perennial from South America. Prostrate, sprawling, aromatic stems, square in cross-section. Leaves with 3 narrow, toothed leaflets. Spikes of broad-lobed lilac, mauve, purple, blue, or white flowers. Zones 9–11.

Verbena Hybrid Cultivars

syn. *Glandularia* Hybrid Cultivars

☼ ❋ ↔ 24–40 in (60–100 cm) ↑ 12–24 in (30–60 cm)

Fragrant perennials flowering from summer to autumn. 'Homestead Purple', vigorous, trailing dark green foliage, purple flowers; 'Imagination', violet-blue flowers; 'Peaches and Cream', peach and cream flowers; 'Quartz Burgundy', dwarf form, deep wine red flowers with tiny white eyes; 'Quartz Scarlet', vigorous, scarlet flowers; 'Silver Ann', vigorous, pale and deep pink flowers; 'Sissinghurst', mat-forming, magenta pink flowers, can be invasive; Tapien Series, low-growing, long-blooming, heat-resistant forms, in blue, violet-blue, lavender, and pink; Temari Series, low-growing, trailing, long-flowering, dense mats of ferny foliage, large flowerheads in pink, burgundy, blue, and scarlet. Zones 7–10.

VERONICA

BIRDSEYE, SPEEDWELL

This genus in the foxglove (Scrophulariaceae) family, containing 250 species of annuals and perennials, is widespread in northern temperate zones. Most are creeping mat-forming plants that sometimes strike root as they spread. The leaves tend to be small, oval to lance-shaped, often shallowly toothed, and rarely pinnately lobed. A few of the species have solitary flowers, but more often

Verbena bonariensis

Verbena tenera 'Kleopatra'

Verbena, Hybrid Cultivar, 'Homestead Purple'

many-flowered upright spikes develop in spring and summer. The color range is mainly white and pink to purple-blue shades, including some striking deep blue flowers.

CULTIVATION: Speedwells are mostly very hardy and easily grown in full sun to half-sun, with moist well-drained soil. Some are superb rock garden plants, others are suited to borders. Propagate from cuttings or seed, or by self-rooted layers or division.

Veronica alpina

☼/◐ ❄ ↔ 8–16 in (20–40 cm) ↑ 2–6 in (5–15 cm)

Creeping Arctic and temperate Eurasian perennial. Forms clump of wiry stems; pointed oval leaves, 1 in (25 mm) long, faintly toothed, sparsely hairy. Short erect spikes, few light-centered, purple flowers, ¼ in (6 mm) wide, in spring–summer. 'Alba', white-flowered form, but the name *Veronica alpina* 'Alba' is sometimes used in the nursery trade to refer to *Veronicastrum virginicum* 'Album', which is a completely different plant. Zones 2–9.

Veronica austriaca

☼/◐ ❄ ↔ 10–24 in (25–60 cm) ↑ 6–16 in (15–40 cm)

Spreading European perennial. Wiry stems; sparsely hairy, narrow lance-shaped, ½ in (12 mm) long leaves. Upright spikes of many bright purple-blue flowers, in late spring–summer. *V. a.* subsp. *teucrium*, broader, more deeply toothed leaves, parent of best garden forms, such as 'Crater Lake Blue' ★, 10 in (25 cm) tall, intense blue flowers; and 'Shirley Blue', 10 in (25 cm) tall, bright mid-blue flowers. Zones 6–10.

Veronica beccabunga

BROOKLIME

☼/◐ ❄ ↔ 8–20 in (20–50 cm)
↑ 4–6 in (10–15 cm)

Eurasian perennial. Fleshy, often red-tinted stems, upturned at tips. Oval leaves, 1¾ in (40 mm) long, usually finely toothed, Tiny lilac to purple flowers, in small clusters at stem tips and nearby axils, in summer. Zones 5–9.

Veronica chamaedrys

ANGELS' EYES, BIRD'S EYE, GERMANDER SPEEDWELL

☼/◐ ❄ ↔ 12–20 in (30–50 cm)
↑ 6–10 in (15–25 cm)

Temperate Eurasian perennial, widely naturalized in North America. Forms small mounding clump of bright green, sparsely hairy, and toothed, ½–1¾ in (12–40 mm) long, oval leaves. Flowers tiny, bright blue, white center, in sprays of up to 30 blooms, in late spring–summer. Zones 3–9.

Veronica cinerea

☼/◐ ❄ ↔ 6–10 in (15–25 cm) ↑ 2–4 in (5–10 cm)

Summer-flowering perennial from the Middle East and western Asia. Forms dense cushion; ½ in (12 mm) long, sometimes toothed leaves, covered with silver-gray hairs. Foliage color contrasts well with short spikes of light-centered deep blue to purple-blue flowers. Zones 5–9.

Veronica chamaedrys

Veronica gentianoides

☼/◐ ❄ ↔ 12–24 in (30–60 cm) ↑ 12–24 in (30–60 cm)

Spreading perennial from the Caucasus region and western Asia. Forms dense clump; upright stems, narrow, toothed, pointed oval leaves, to nearly 3 in (8 cm) long, at base of clump. Erect spikes, to 12 in (30 cm) long; abundant flowers, usually pale blue, sometimes white, in late spring–summer. Cultivars include 'Tissington White', white flowers; and 'Variegata', attractive cream-variegated foliage, pale blue flowers. Zones 4–9.

Veronica longifolia

☼/◐ ❄ ↔ 16–30 in (40–75 cm)
↑ 20–48 in (50–120 cm)

Found over much of continental Europe, widely naturalized in northeastern North America. Erect perennial; whorls of narrow, lance-shaped leaves, toothed, sometimes sparsely hairy. Basal leaves to over 4 in (10 cm) long, upper leaves much smaller. Terminal flower spikes to 10 in (25 cm) long, numerous tiny blue to lavender flowers. Summer- to autumn-flowering. Cultivars include 'Alba', to 36 in (90 cm) tall, flowers pure white; 'Blauriesin' (syn. 'Blue Giantess'), reaches up to 32 in (80 cm) tall, bright blue flowers; 'Lilac Fantasy', compact, flowers lilac; 'Pink Damask', to 36 in (90 cm) tall, soft pastel pink flowers; 'Rose Tone', to around 36 in (90 cm) high, rose pink flowers; and 'Schneeriesin', to 36 in (90 cm) tall, profuse white flowers. Zones 4–9.

Veronica longifolia

Veronica pectinata

☼/◐ ❄ ↔ 12–16 in (30–40 cm) ↑ 2–8 in (5–20 cm)

Evergreen southern Eurasian subshrub. Forms mat of hairy, deeply toothed or cut leaves, each around 1 in (25 mm) long. Racemes, up to 8 in (20 cm) long, form in leaf axils; numerous light-centered deep blue flowers, from late spring. Zones 3–9.

Veronica petraea

☼/◑ ✱ ↔ 8–12 in (20–30 cm) ↕ 4–6 in (10–15 cm)
Caucasian perennial. Forms small tuft; wiry, often purple-tinted
stems; downy, sometimes toothed leaves, to ¾ in (18 mm) long.
Stem tips usually erect; heads of up to 20 tiny flowers, blue or
pink, at tips and in nearby leaf axils, in summer–autumn.
'Madame Mercier', lilac-blue flowers. Zones 6–9.

Veronica prostrata

☼/◑ ✱ ↔ 8–16 in (20–40 cm) ↕ 2–4 in (5–10 cm)
European perennial. Forms small mat; wiry stems; toothed, nar-
row pointed oval leaves, to 1 in (25 mm) long. Spikes of many
small pale to deep blue flowers in late spring–summer. 'Heavenly
Blue', bright blue flowers; 'Spode Blue', deepest blue flowers;
'Trehane', golden leaves and violet-blue flowers. Zones 5–9.

Veronica spicata

☼/◑ ✱ ↔ 12–32 in (30–80 cm) ↕ 12–24 in (30–60 cm)
European perennial. Forms clump; erect stems; narrow lance-
shaped, 1–3 in (25–80 mm) long leaves, downy, finely toothed.
Terminal spikes of many ¼ in (6 mm) wide deep blue flowers in
summer. *V. s.* subsp. *incana,* velvety silver-gray to white flowers,
sometimes classified as distinct species, with cultivars including
'Rotfuchs' (syn. 'Red Fox'), 'Silbersee', and 'Wendy'. *V. s.*
'Barcarolle', bright pink flowers; 'Heidekind', purple-red flowers;
'Icicle', white flowers; 'Rosea', deep pink flowers; 'Sunny Border
Blue', dark violet-blue flowers over long season. Zones 3–9.

Veronica wormskjoldii

AMERICAN ALPINE SPEEDWELL
☼/◑ ✱ ↔ 8–20 in (20–50 cm) ↕ 4–12 in (10–30 cm)
Clump-forming perennial from North America and southern tip
of Greenland. Spreads by rhizomes; erect sparsely hairy stems;
pointed elliptic leaves to 2 in (5 cm) long sometimes toothed. Terminal heads of few tiny violet-blue blooms in summer. Zones 4–9.

VERONICASTRUM

Belonging to the foxglove (Scrophulariaceae) family, this genus of
2 upright perennials is from northeastern Asia and northeastern

Veronicastrum virginicum var. *sibiricum*

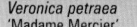

Veronica petraea
'Madame Mercier'

Veronica spicata 'Heidekind'

North America. The plants have whorls of simple leaves and a
terminal raceme or spikes of flowers. Blooms feature a calyx with
4 to 5 lobes, and a saucer-shaped corolla with 2 stamens.
CULTIVATION: These perennials like moist, humus-rich soil and will
grow in full sun or half-sun. Propagate from seed or by division.

Veronicastrum virginicum

syns *Leptandra virginica, Veronica virginica*
BLACKROOT, BOWMAN'S ROOT, CULVER'S ROOT
☼ ✱ ↔ 1–3 ft (0.3–0.9 m) ↕ 2–6 ft (0.6–1.8 m)
From northeastern America. Whorls of 4 to 7 simple, sword-
shaped, serrated leaves. Slender spikes, to 12 in (30 cm) tall, tiny
pale blue or white flowers in summer. *V. v.* var. *sibiricum,* narrow
spikes of lilac flowers. *V. v.* 'Album', white flowers; 'Pointed
Finger', lilac flowers; 'Roseum', soft pink flowers. Zones 3–6.

VICTORIA

GIANT WATER LILY
The 2 species of aquatic perennials in this genus, members of
the waterlily (Nymphaeaceae) family, are native to tropical South
America, where they are found growing in slow-moving or still
water. These giant plants are grown for their large flat leaves,
reputed to be able to bear the weight of a small child, and for
their beautiful perfumed flowers. Arising from stout rhizomes,
they produce floating round leaves, which can reach up to 7 ft
(2 m) wide, with upturned rims. Opening at night, the many-
petalled flowers are white at first, deepening to pink on the
second day, and purple on the third day before dying.
CULTIVATION: Ideal for large warm pools in tropical greenhouses,
these plants are usually grown as annuals because of their rapid
growth rate. Grow in full sun. Propagate from seed and gradually
increase pot size and water depth as plants grow.

Victoria amazonica

syn. *Victoria regia*
AMAZON WATER LILY, ROYAL WATER LILY
☼ ✲ ↔ 15–20 ft (4.5–6 m) ↕ 10–12 in (25–30 cm)
From the Amazon region. Leaves to 7 ft (2 m) wide, upturned
rim to about 6 in (15 cm) high. Leaf underside is reddish purple
and spiny. Perfumed flowers in summer and autumn. Zones 10–12.

Victoria 'Longwood Hybrid'

☀ ✦ ↔ 12–40 ft (3.5–12 m)
↑ 10–12 in (25–30 cm)
Vigorous hybrid of *V. amazonica* and *V. cruziana* raised at Longwood Gardens, Philadelphia, USA. Large leaves, to 8 ft (2.4 m) wide. Flowers open earlier in evening. Zones 10–12.

VIGUIERA

Native to North and South America, this genus, containing about 150 annual or perennial herbs and shrubs, is a member of the daisy (Asteraceae) family. They feature several stems that grow from a central base, and simple, alternate or opposite leaves. The solitary flowerheads, about 2 in (5 cm) across, are borne on long stalks, usually with yellow daisy-like flowers.
CULTIVATION: *Viguiera* species prefer a position in full sun, and will perform well in most well-drained soils. Propagate from seed.

Viguiera multiflora

☀ ✦ ↔ 30–40 in (75–100 cm) ↑ 30–40 in (75–100 cm)
Resinous perennial herb, native to southern, central, and western USA, and south to Mexico. Smooth-edged or sparsely toothed leaves, narrowly oval to sword-shaped. Yellow daisy-like flowers in summer. Zones 10–12.

VINCA
PERIWINKLE

This genus of 7 species of evergreen groundcovering perennials found in woodland areas of Europe, North Africa, and central Asia, belongs to the dogbane (Apocynaceae) family. These plants are distinctive for their opposite, simple, lance-shaped leaves that cover the slender, often cream or pale green, ground-hugging stems. The foliage varies in color from pale to dark green and many variations occur with attractive variegations. The star-shaped flowers are produced from spring through to late autumn, and vary in color from dark purple to blue and white.
CULTIVATION: These plants prefer a light free-draining soil with a reasonable level of organic matter, in sun or shade. The plant sends out long trailing and rooting shoots, which make new plants. They will spread indefinitely and can become invasive if neglected. Propagation is easy any time of year by separating the new offshoots or by layering new shoots.

Vinca difformis

☀/◐ ❄ ↔ 5–10 ft (1.5–3 m) ↑ 12 in (30 cm)
Low-growing evergreen perennial, native to North Africa, and southern and western Europe. Narrowly lance-shaped, glossy, dark green leaves, up to 3 in (8 cm) long. Flowers 5-petalled, soft blue, fading to white as the season develops. Early spring-flowering. Zones 8–9.

Victoria amazonica

Vinca major
BLUE BUTTONS, GREATER PERIWINKLE

☀/◐ ❄ ↔ 5–10 ft (1.5–3 m) ↑ 18 in (45 cm)
Mounding plant from western parts of Mediterranean. Arching stems; dark green leaves, 3½ in (9 cm) long. Rich violet-blue flowers from early spring to late autumn. 'Variegata' (syn. 'Elegantissima'), creamy white-streaked green leaves. Zones 7–11.

Vinca minor
CREEPING MYRTLE

☀/◐ ❄ ↔ 5–10 ft (1.5–3 m) ↑ 8 in (20 cm)
From Europe, southern Russia, and northern Caucasus. Mat-forming; dark green leaves, to 2 in (5 cm) long. Violet-blue star-shaped flowers from early spring to mid-autumn. 'Alba', white flowers; 'Argenteovariegata' (syn. 'Variegata'), variegated leaves pale lavender flowers; 'Atropurpurea', dark plum flowers; 'Azurea Flore Pleno', pale blue, frilly, double flowers; 'Bowles' Variety', pale lavender-blue flowers; 'Gertrude Jekyll', white flowers; 'Illumination', variegated leaves, mainly yellow, some green marking; 'Multiplex', double, red wine colored flowers; 'Ralph Shugert', deep green leaves, white variegations. Zones 4–9.

VIOLA
HEARTSEASE, PANSY, VIOLET

The type genus for the family Violaceae, *Viola* includes some 500 species of annuals, perennials, and subshrubs, found in all the world's temperate zones from the mountains of New Zealand to the subarctic. Most species are small clump-forming plants with lobed, elliptic, kidney- or heart-shaped leaves. All have 5-petalled flowers, with the lower petal often carrying dark markings. White, yellow, and purple predominate but flowers occur in every color, at least among the garden forms.
CULTIVATION: Pansies are mostly very hardy and easily grown in sun or shade. Woodland species prefer a humus-rich soil, while the rock-garden types like something grittier, but most do well in any moist well-drained soil. Propagation is from seed or basal cuttings or by division, depending on the growth form.

Vinca minor

Viola cornuta 'Magnifico'

Viola cornuta 'Pat Kavanagh'

Viola jooi

Viola adunca
HOOKED-SPUR VIOLET, PURPLE VIOLET, WESTERN DOG VIOLET

☼/◐ ❉ ↔ 12–16 in (30–40 cm) ↕ 2–4 in (5–10 cm)

Spreading perennial from northern USA. Heart-shaped to rounded leaves, up to 1¾ in (40 mm) long. Spurred lavender to violet flowers in spring, deepen in color with age. Zones 4–9.

Viola blanda
SWEET WHITE VIOLET, WILLDENOW VIOLET, WOODLAND WHITE VIOLET

☼/◐ ❉ ↔ 12–20 in (30–50 cm) ↕ 3–6 in (8–15 cm)

Stemless North American perennial. Shallowly toothed, sparsely downy, deep green, heart-shaped leaves, to over 2 in (5 cm) long. White flowers, dark central veining, in spring. Zones 2–9.

Viola canina
HEATH DOG VIOLET, HEATH VIOLET

◐ ❉ ↔ 12–20 in (30–50 cm) ↕ 4–12 in (10–30 cm)

Perennial found over much of northern temperate Eurasia. Deep green, shallowly toothed, pointed oval to heart-shaped leaves, to 1 in (25 mm) long. Erect stems; mauve, purple, or white flowers, pale yellow spur, in summer. Zones 6–9.

Viola cornuta
BEDDING PANSY, HORNED VIOLET

☼/◐ ❉ ↔ 8–14 in (20–35 cm) ↕ 6–12 in (15–30 cm)

Rhizome-rooted perennial from the Pyrenees and northern Spain; initially prostrate then more mounding. Oval, 1 in (25 mm) long, shallowly toothed leaves. Spurred, broad-petaled, violet flowers, darker veining, yellow center, in late spring–summer. **Alba Group**, white-flowered forms, '**Belmont Blue**' (syn. '**Boughton Blue**'), lilac flowers; '**Jewel White**', compact habit, white flowers; '**Magnifico**', white flowers, mauve-edged; '**Pat Kavanagh**', pale lemon yellow flowers; '**Victoria's Blush**', mid-pink flowers, narrow petals. Mixed color seedling strains include **Penny Series** and **Princess Series**. **Sorbet Series** includes '**Sorbet Black Delight**', almost black flowers; and '**Sorbet Coconut**', pure white flowers. Zones 7–10.

Viola cucullata
syn. *Viola obliqua*
MARSH BLUE VIOLET

☼/◐ ❉ ↔ 8–16 in (20–40 cm) ↕ 4–6 in (10–15 cm)

Perennial from North America. Low spreading habit; broad, pointed oval to kidney-shaped leaves, to more than 3 in (8 cm) wide, shallowly toothed. Short-spurred, 5-petalled, white flowers, washed with mauve to purple, in spring–early summer. Zones 4–9.

Viola hederacea
AUSTRALIAN VIOLET, TRAILING VIOLET

◐ ❉ ↔ 6–12 in (15–30 cm) ↕ 2–3 in (5–8 cm)

Small creeping perennial native to southeastern Australia. Broad, oval to kidney-shaped, sometimes shallowly toothed leaves, to over 1¼ in (30 mm) wide. Dark-centered pale lavender or white flowers throughout warmer months. Zones 8–10.

Viola jooi
☼/◐ ❉ ↔ 8–14 in (20–35 cm) ↕ 2–4 in (5–10 cm)

Perennial from southeastern Europe. Stemless habit; spreads by runners. Shallowly toothed heart-shaped leaves, to 3 in (8 cm) long. Short-spurred, dark-streaked, mauve flowers, in spring–summer. Zones 5–10.

Viola odorata
SWEET VIOLET

☼/◐ ❉ ↔ 12–24 in (30–60 cm) ↕ 4–6 in (10–15 cm)

Southern and western European perennial. Spreads by runners; heart-shaped dark green leaves, to over 2 in (5 cm) long. Highly fragrant, spurred, lavender, purple, yellow, or white flowers, in spring–early summer. Can be weedy. Numerous cultivars available, with single or double flowers in range of colors. '**Purple Robe**' ★, low spreading habit, masses of deep purple flowers. Zones 7–10.

Viola pedata
BIRD'S FOOT VIOLET, PANSY VIOLET

◐ ❉ ↔ 8–16 in (20–40 cm) ↕ 4–6 in (10–15 cm)

Stemless eastern North American perennial. Spreads by runners; foliage differs from most violets: palmate, with up to 5 narrow lobes. Spurred flowers, faintly downy petals, lavender with darker upper petals and veining, in spring. Zones 4–9.

Viola riviniana
DOG VIOLET, WOOD VIOLET

☼/◐ ❉ ↔ 8–24 in (20–60 cm) ↕ 4–6 in (10–15 cm)

European and North African perennial. Broad, pointed oval to rounded, toothed, often purple-tinted leaves, about 2 in (5 cm) long. Short-spurred lavender-blue flowers in spring–early summer. '**Purpurea**', purplish-tinted foliage. Zones 5–9.

Viola septentrionalis
NORTHERN BLUE VIOLET

☀️/◐ ❄️ ↔6–16 in (15–40 cm) ↕4–6 in (10–15 cm)

North American perennial; spreads by rhizomes. Pointed oval to rounded heart-shaped leaves, to 2 in (5 cm) long, edged with fine hairs. Downy dark-veined flowers, lavender, less commonly white or purple, in spring–early summer. Zones 4–9.

Viola sororia

☀️/◐ ❄️ ↔6–16 in (15–40 cm) ↕2–6 in (5–15 cm)

Eastern North American perennial. Leaves broad, rounded, light-textured, toothed, downy, up to 4 in (10 cm) long. Light-centered violet flowers, less commonly white with purple veining, in spring–early summer. 'Freckles', white flowers heavily purple-spotted; 'Priceana', flowers white, deep blue center. Zones 4–9.

Viola tricolor
HEARTSEASE, JOHNNY JUMP-UP, LOVE-IN-IDLENESS

☀️/◐ ❄️ ↔6–16 in (15–40 cm)
↕4–14 in (10–35 cm)

Annual, biennial, or perennial from temperate Eurasia; usually treated as an annual; often self-sows and naturalizes. Pointed oval to lance-like, shallowly lobed or toothed leaves. Small bicolored or multi-colored pansy flowers, often with face-like pattern, in spring–early summer. Many cultivars and seedling strains, such as 'Bowles' Black' (syn. 'E. A. Bowles'), intense velvety black flowers with small yellow center; 'Czar Bleu', pink to purple; and Tinkerbelle Series, small flowers in various pure shades and combinations. Zones 4–10.

Viola sororia 'Freckles'

Viola Hybrid Cultivars
PANSY, VIOLA

☀️/◐ ❄️ ↔8–16 in (20–40 cm) ↕6–12 in (15–30 cm)

Annual or short-lived perennial garden hybrids developed from *V. cornuta*, *V. tricolor*, *V. corsica*, and other mainly European species. Mostly neat, slowly spreading clumps of fleshy, dark green, shallowly lobed, ½–2 in (12–50 mm) long, pointed oval to lance-shaped leaves. Flowers variably sized from small to giant styles nearly 3 in (8 cm) wide. Virtually all colors and many beautiful combinations and patterns. Baby Face Series, bicolored to multi-colored flowers with central "face" markings; Banner Series, vigorous plants with massed display of mainly bright clear colors; Crystal Bowl Series, large flowers, bright pure colors; Delta Series, large flowers, wide color range in pure and bicolor; Dynamite Series, large flowers, pure colors and several multi-tone forms; Fama Series, semi-trailing habit, abundant mid-sized flowers, usually selfs but some pastel blends; Imperial Series, similar colors to 'Antique Shades' but larger flowers, such as 'Imperial Antique Shades', large heat-tolerant flowers in delicate pale creams, mauves, peachy apricots, blues, rosy pinks;

Joker Series, boldly patterned mid-sized flowers usually combining blue and another color; Panola Series, narrow leaves and abundant small flowers with dark faces; Penny Series, including 'Penny Primrose', creamy white upper petals, pale yellow lower petals, and 'Penny Violet Flare', deep violet petals; Turbo Series, hardy plants, bright colors; Ultima Series, fast-growing, large flowers, wide color range, including selfs, blotched and pastel types in lavender, scarlet, yellow, bronze-apricot, pale salmon orange, including Ultima Supreme, compact form bred to withstand very cold temperatures, with mid-sized early-flowering blooms; Universal Series, tolerant of hot and cold weather, 18 prolific bloomers, masses of early-flowering blooms with 13 clear colors, including blue, white, burgundy, orange, purple and yellow, or the typical pansy face; Velour Series, medium to large, velvet-textured flowers in intense shades, often with dark markings. Other cultivars include 'Antique Shades', mid-sized, dusky pink and apricot pastel tones; 'Black Moon', rich black petals; and 'Elaine Quin', deep velvety rosy mauve with cream stripes, giving a marbled effect.

Viola Group, more compact pansies, usually fragrant, flowers often patterned. 'Baby Lucia', clear blue blooms, 6 in (15 cm) high mounding plant, heavy bloomer, cold tolerant; 'Etain', cream-yellow petals edged with lavender, refreshing scent; 'Fiona', sweet scent, creamy white flowers, suffused with lavender-blue; 'Irish Molly' ★, gold-bronze yellow petals, dark maroon eye; 'Jackanapes', lower sections bright yellow, upper chocolate brown; 'Maggie Mott', a silvery mauve with creamy center and golden eye; 'Martin', violet flowers with a creamy center; 'Masterpiece', large ruffled flowers, purple-blue with bronze; 'Molly Sanderson', long-lasting, nearly black, velvety flowers with purple veins and golden eye, green heart-shaped leaves; 'Nellie Britton', originally called 'Haslemere', rosy pink; 'Vita', small dainty flowers, with delicate lavender-pink petals and a creamy eye.

Violetta Group, similar to Viola Group but smaller, more compact fragrant flowers. 'Dawn', pale cream flowers deepening to gold; 'Little David' ivory flowers; 'Melinda', white with mauve-blue edges and gold centers; 'Zoe', flowers soft lilac-purple and yellow. Zones 7–10.

Viola, Hybrid Cultivar, Viola Group, 'Irish Molly'

VRIESEA

From Mexico, Central and South America, and the West Indies, this genus of over 250 species and 650 listed hybrids in the bromeliad (Bromeliaceae) family is closely related to *Tillandsia*. They mainly have green leaves, only a few have gray-green leaves, and they have 2 small appendages at the base of each petal. The spineless leaves form a dense rosette capable of storing water. The flowerhead is usually colorful, and some can reach 7 ft (2 m) high. CULTIVATION: Grow indoors or in the greenhouse in cool-temperate areas, or outdoors with protection from prolonged sunlight and heavy rain in warm-temperate, subtropical, and tropical areas. Water when potting mix is dry. A foliar feed high in potash and low in nitrogen (other than in the form of urea) will increase flower size. Propagate from offsets.

Vriesea carinata
☀ ⚘ ↔ 12 in (30 cm) ↑ 14 in (35 cm)
From Rio de Janeiro, Brazil. Leaves strap-like, green, forming a funnel-shaped rosette. Flower stem erect, longer than the rosette. Flowerhead sword-shaped, made up of mainly red bracts with green edges. Petals tubular, yellow, green tipped. Zones 11–12.

Vriesea erythrodactylon
☀ ⚘ ↔ 16 in (40 cm) ↑ 16 in (40 cm)
From Brazil. Leaves strap-like, green, forming funnel-shaped rosette. Erect flower stem, shorter than rosette. Broadly sword-shaped flowerhead, center portion solid and green, outer edges deeply notched and red, with yellow tubular petals. Zones 11–12.

Vriesea fenestralis
☀ ⚘ ↔ 27 in (70 cm) ↑ 40 in (100 cm)
From Brazil. Broad rosette; strap-like green leaves, dark green, narrow, longitudinal lines and irregular, broken, thick crossbands. Sturdy flower stem, longer than rosette. Sword-shaped flowerhead, green bracts with red spots. Petals greenish white. Zones 11–12.

Vriesea fosteriana
☀ ⚘ ↔ 40 in (100 cm) ↑ 60 in (150 cm)
From Brazil. Spreading rosette; leaves strap-like, rigid, green or purplish, wavy broken crossbands in dark green, purple, or white. Flower stem erect, longer than rosette. Flowerhead sword-shaped, yellowish bracts with red spots. Petals creamish purple. Zones 11–12.

Vriesea malzinei
☀ ⚘ ↔ 16 in (40 cm) ↑ 32 in (80 cm)
Native to Mexico. Funnel-shaped rosette; leaves strap-like, green above, red below. Flower stem erect, longer than rosette.

Vriesea, Hybrid Cultivar, 'Mariae'

Cylindrical red flowerhead; pale green or yellow overlapping bracts; long, white, tubular petals with flared tips. Zones 11–12.

Vriesea saundersii
☀ ⚘ ↔ 16 in (40 cm) ↑ 24 in (60 cm)
Native to Brazil. Broad funnel-shaped rosette; leaves strap-like, leathery, dull green or gray-green above; undersides with small brown or purplish speckles. Erect flower stem, taller than rosette. Pyramidal flowerhead, 3 to 4 side-branches, bracts mainly yellow; bright yellow tubular petals. Zones 11–12.

Vriesea splendens
FLAMING SWORD
☀ ⚘ ↔ 20 in (50 cm) ↑ 40 in (100 cm)
From Venezuela and the Caribbean Islands. Broad funnel-shaped rosette; strap-like green leaves, often with broad dark irregular crossbands. Erect flower stem, about equal in length to rosette. Long, sword-shaped, bright red flowerhead, yellow tubular petals. Zones 10–12.

Vriesea Hybrid Cultivars
☀ ⚘ ↔ 8–20 in (20–50 cm)
↑ 16–36 in (40–90 cm)
Hybrids feature larger flower spike and strongly patterned foliage. 'Bananas', upright rosette, reddish flower stem, flowerhead sword-shaped at top, with up to 8 sword-shaped side-branches, mostly bright yellow but sometimes with reddish edges; 'Carlsbad', leaves pointed, green with red mottling, flushed red near base, flower stem red; 'Charlotte', broad sword-shaped flowerhead, with up to 7 side-branches, all red toward base, bright yellow above; 'Christiane', flowerhead bright red, yellow tubular petals; 'Eva', open rosette of strap-like leaves, green tinged maroon; 'Grafton Sunset', mainly golden orange flowerhead suffused with red, petals yellow; 'Gunther', flowerhead bright red; 'Komet', overlapping, mainly red, yellow-tipped bracts, pale yellow petals; 'Likely Lad', flowerhead pyramidal, red side-branches, each with up to 5 flowers and large red bract below each branch; 'Little Chief', flowerhead glossy orange tinted red; 'Mariae', petals tubular, yellow with green tips; 'Poelmanii', sword-shaped flowerhead, up to 7 bright red branches, yellow petals; 'Purple Cockatoo', flowerheads purple, deep serrations around edge resembling a cockatoo's crest; 'Red Chestnut', yellowish bracts with small reddish spots, creamish purple petals; 'Splendide', sword-shaped flowerhead, up to 4 bright red side-branches, pinkish yellow tubular petals. Zones 11–12.

WACHENDORFIA

This genus of some 25 species of mostly deciduous strappy-leafed perennials from South Africa is a member of the bloodroot

(Haemodoraceae) family. The deciduous species have bright red tubers, and both deciduous and the sole evergreen species have orange-red roots. The leaves are usually bright green and heavily pleated, with each leaf sheathing the next one in a flat fan arrangement. The yellow star-shaped flowers are produced in tall narrow spikes or, in the case of smaller species, in open clusters. Regarded as weeds in southern Australia.

CULTIVATION: In more or less frost-free climates, grow in a sunny moist position; in other areas, protect from frost by growing these plants in large pots which can be overwintered in a greenhouse. Raise from fresh seed or by division in late winter.

Wachendorfia thyrsiflora (at front), South Africa

Wachendorfia thyrsiflora

☼ ⧊ ↔ 2–4 ft (0.6–1.2 m)
↑ 4–7 ft (1.2–2 m)

Only evergreen species. Strongly pleated, rich green leaves to 40 in (100 cm) long. Star-shaped rich yellow flowers, to 1¼ in (30 mm) wide, on tall upright spikes, in early summer. Zones 10–11.

WALDSTEINIA

This genus of 6 species of creeping fleshy-stemmed perennials belongs to the rose (Rosaceae) family. They are native to northern temperate regions, where they are found in woodland areas. Plants form low mats of lobed and toothed leaves that are similar to those of the related strawberry and cinquefoil *(Potentilla)*. The leaves sometimes take on bronze tones in winter. The saucer-shaped, 5-petalled, yellow flowers are carried for long periods in spring and early summer.

CULTIVATION: *Waldsteinia* species are suited to the rock garden, the front of a border, or a woodland edge, and make useful ground covers. Grow in partial shade in moist but well-drained soils. Where soils remain moist in summer, they can be grown in full sun. Propagate by division of rooted runners or from seed.

Waldsteinia fragarioides

BARREN STRAWBERRY

☼/◑ ✽ ↔ 12–20 in (30–50 cm) ↑ 2 in (5 cm)

Mat-forming species, native to eastern USA. Trifoliate bronze-green leaves with toothed, pointed oval leaflets to nearly 3 in (8 cm) long. Clusters of up to 8 yellow flowers, ¾ in (18 mm) wide, in spring. Zones 3–9.

Waldsteinia ternata ★

◑ ✽ ↔ 24 in (60 cm) ↑ 6 in (15 cm)

Found from Europe to China and Japan. Dark green, 3-lobed, toothed, somewhat hairy leaves. Flowers borne in groups of 3 to 7 in spring–summer. Can become invasive. Zones 3–9.

Waldsteinia ternata

WITTROCKIA

This small genus of 6 species, related to *Canistrum,* is a member of the bromeliad (Bromeliaceae) family. They are medium to large plants from southeastern Brazil, with strap-like toothed leaves forming a broad cup-shaped rosette. The flowerhead bears many flowers, usually with bright red bracts around the bottom edge.

CULTIVATION: In cool-temperate areas. grow in a greenhouse or conservatory. In warm-temperate, subtropical, and tropical areas, grow outdoors with protection from prolonged sunlight and heavy rain. Propagate from offsets.

Wittrockia superba

☼ ✦ ↔ 55 in (140 cm) ↑ 16 in (40 cm)

Large plant from Rio de Janeiro, Brazil. Strap-like large-toothed leaves, dark green with bright red tip, forming broad cup-shaped rosette. Flower stem very short. Flowerhead globular, with many flowers, surrounded by bright red bracts. Petals white. Zones 10–12.

XANTHORRHOEA

Now classified in their own family—Xanthorrhoeaceae—there are around 30 species of grass trees found across Australia. They are slow-growing long-lived woody perennials with long narrow leaves that emerge in tufts from the extremities of the branches; there are also species that have substantial subterranean stems. The white or cream flowers are clustered on long-stalked spikes, and are usually produced in spring or as a reaction to fire. Leathery capsular fruits are clustered along the spikes.

CULTIVATION: The young plants may take 20 years to develop stems and more than 100 years to flower. Plant in an open sunny spot with well-drained soil. Propagation is from seed sown in spring or autumn in a coarse free-draining mix.

Xanthorrhoea quadrangulata, in the wild, South Australia

Xanthorrhoea australis

SOUTHERN GRASS TREE

☼ ⊗ ↔ 3 ft (0.9 m) ↑ 3 ft (0.9 m)

From southeastern Australia. May develop short trunk. Dense rosette; narrow arching leaves, finely hairy. Spring flowers, white or cream, fragrant, on long "spears," after many years. Zones 9–11.

Xanthorrhoea glauca

NARROW-LEAFED GRASS TREE

☼ ✽ ↔ 3 ft (0.9 m) ↑ 20 ft (6 ft)

From Great Dividing Range country of New South Wales and southeastern Queensland, Australia. Branched blackish trunks; Leaves bluish green. Flower spike to 7 ft (2 m) tall. Zones 8–11.

Xanthorrhoea johnsonii

QUEENSLAND GRASS TREE

☼ ⊗ ↔ 3 ft (0.9 m) ↑ 7 ft (2 m)

Fire-blackened trunk; bright green grass-like leaves. Huge cylindrical spikes, hundreds of nectar-rich cream flowers. Zones 9–10.

Xanthorrhoea quadrangulata

SQUARE-LEAF GRASS TREE

☼ ⊗ ↔ 4–7 ft (1.2–2 m) ↑ 7–10 ft (2–3 m)

From southern Australia. Trunk to 10 ft (3 m) tall; very narrow, tough, dark green leaves, quadrangular in section, to 24–36 in (60–90 cm) long. Narrow whitish flower spikes, 3–4 ft (0.9–1.2 m) tall, in autumn. Drought tolerant. Zones 9–11.

XANTHOSOMA

TANNIA, YAUTIA

This genus of around 50 species of tuberous-rooted perennials from tropical America belongs to the arum (Araceae) family. The leaves are variable, often long and arrowhead-shaped but sometimes pointed, oval, or divided into large segments. The flowerheads are usually short-stemmed, with a bulbous base and a green, white, or creamy yellow spathe that partly encloses a short spadix. CULTIVATION: These plants demand warm humid conditions with moist humus-rich soil. They will not tolerate frosts or prolonged

cold. Outside the tropics they are mainly cultivated as house or greenhouse plants. Propagate from seed or by division of clumps.

Xanthosoma undipes

☼ ⊗ ↔ 7–10 ft (2–3 m) ↑ 7–10 ft (2–3 m)

Found from Mexico to Peru; widely cultivated in the Caribbean. Stem to 7 ft (2 m) long. Broadly heart-shaped leaves, 20 in–7 ft (0.5–2 m) long, on stalks to 40 in (100 cm) long. Egg-shaped spathe tube, to 3 in (8 cm) long, yellowish green inside, limb to 10 in (25 cm) long. Zones 10–11.

XERANTHEMUM

This genus of 6 upright annual herbs in the daisy (Asteraceae) family is found from the Mediterranean region to southwestern Asia. They have alternate smooth leaves and solitary, terminal, disc-like flowerheads resembling daisy flowers, in white, mauve, rose, or lilac shades, with papery petal-like bracts. CULTIVATION: These plants prefer an open sunny position in most well-drained fertile soils. Propagation is from seed.

Xeranthemum annuum

COMMON IMMORTELLE

☼ ✽ ↔ 10–36 in (25–90 cm) ↑ 10–36 in (25–90 cm)

Found from southeastern Europe to the Caucasus and Iran, naturalized elsewhere. Upright branching stems; alternate, smooth, narrow, oblong leaves, with fine white hairs, denser underneath. Flowerheads have spreading, oblong, bright pink or white inner bracts and many florets, in summer–autumn. Zones 6–10.

XEROCHRYSUM

ALPINE EVERLASTING, ORANGE EVERLASTING

A small genus of 6 Australian species in the daisy (Asteraceae) family, formerly classified in the genus *Bracteantha*. They feature dry papery bracts, which are golden yellow in many species. CULTIVATION: These attractive daisies will do best in a position in full sun, in light well-drained soil. Propagate from seed.

Xerochrysum bracteatum

syns *Bracteantha bracteatum*, *Helichrysum bracteatum*
GOLDEN EVERLASTING, STRAWFLOWER

☼ ✽ ↔ 16 in (40 cm) ↑ 36 in (90 cm)

Australian annual or short-lived perennial. Narrow, pointed lance-shaped, often sticky, leaves to over 4 in (10 cm) long. Flowerheads to nearly 3 in (8 cm) wide, deep golden yellow. 'Bright Bikini' strain in all shades except blue and mauve; 'Coco', pale yellow flowers; 'Dargan Hill Monarch' (syn. *Bracteantha bracteata* 'Dargan Hill Monarch'), buttery yellow flowers; 'Golden Beauty', all-over deep golden yellow; 'Pink Sunrise', orange and cream flowerheads opening from pink buds; 'Princess of Wales', compact habit, golden yellow flowerheads. Zones 8–10.

ZALUZIANSKYA

A genus of about 35 species of sticky-leafed annuals, perennials, and subshrubs from southern and eastern Africa belonging to the foxglove (Scrophulariaceae) family. Their leaves are smooth or toothed and the flowers have 5 spreading notched petals at

the end of a long tube. The outside color of the flowers is quite different from the inside, and the majority are night scented.
CULTIVATION: These plants like full sun and a well-drained soil in almost frost-free climates. Where frost is usual, they can be grown in a cool greenhouse. Keep almost dry in winter. Take tip cuttings in the summer or sow seed in spring with bottom heat.

Zaluzianskya ovata
☼ ❄ ↔ 20–24 in (50–60 cm) ↑ 8–10 in (20–25 cm)
Brittle-stemmed evergreen perennial, native to South Africa. Toothed leaves to 1¾ in (40 mm) long. Flowers white inside, rich crimson on petal backs, in summer–autumn. Zones 10–11.

ZINGIBER
GINGER
This genus, containing about 60 herbaceous and evergreen rhizomatous, clumping, perennial herbs from Asia and northern Australia, gives its name to the ginger (Zingiberaceae) family. The leaves are usually narrow, and are arranged in 2 ranks on upright stems. The inflorescences, which are often intensely colored and cone-like with overlapping waxy-looking bracts, arise from the base of the plant in summer.
CULTIVATION: Most species are frost tender, although some prove surprisingly hardy in temperate gardens. The majority prefer nutrient-rich, well-drained, moist soil and full sun to part shade in warm humid conditions. Propagate by division in early spring.

Zingiber spectabile
BEEHIVE GINGER
☼ ❄ ↔ 3 ft (0.9 m) ↑ 5–7 ft (1.5–2 m)
From Malaysia. Deep green leaves; paler, downy beneath. Long inflorescences, yellow bracts turning scarlet. Small creamy flowers, 2-lobed purple lip with yellow spots, in late summer. Zones 9–12.

Zingiber zerumbet
syn. *Zingiber amaricans*
AWAPUHI, PINE-CONE GINGER, SHAMPOO GINGER
☼ ❄ ↔ 3 ft (0.9 m) ↑ 6–8 ft (1.8–2.4 m)
Upright species from India. Arching stems; shiny dark green leaves. Large cone-shaped inflorescences, pale green turning bright red. Flowers white with pale yellow lip in late summer. 'Variegatum' (syns *Z. darceyi*, *Z.* 'Darceyi'), smaller, more frost tender, leaves striped with cream. Zones 8–12.

ZINNIA
This genus of around 20 species of annuals, perennials, and small shrubs in the daisy (Asteraceae) family is found from south-central USA to Argentina, with its center in Mexico. Zinnias have soft light green leaves that range from linear to broadly spatula-shaped. The flowers of the wild species are typically daisy-like with conspicuous ray and disc florets. Modern seed strains are mainly doubles with the disc florets largely hidden or absent. The color range is very wide, though mostly warm tones.

CULTIVATION: Cultivated plants are mostly frost-tender summer annuals that should be grown in a sunny warm position sheltered from drafts, in moist and well-drained soil. Propagate from seed.

Zinnia angustifolia
☼ ❄ ↔ 12–20 in (30–50 cm) ↑ 8–16 in (20–40 cm)
Annual from southeastern USA and Mexico. Needle-like to narrow lance-shaped leaves. Bright orange ray florets, orange disc florets. 'Classic', white ray florets; 'Coral Beauty', orange-pink; 'Crystal White', white ray florets; 'Golden Eye', white ray florets, creamy yellow at center; 'Star White', white ray florets, orange disc. Zones 9–11.

Zinnia elegans
syn. *Zinnia violacea*
☼ ❄ ↔ 8–18 in (20–45 cm)
↑ 8–40 in (20–100 cm)
Popular garden flowers; some newer varieties are disease resistant. Cultivars include 'Aztek', white flowers; 'Canary Yellow', bright yellow flowers; Dreamland Series, double flowers, many colors; 'Envy', light green fully double flowers; 'Giant Purity', fully double white flowers; 'Halo', red flowers; Mammoth Exhibition Series, double flowers, large color range; Oklahoma Series, semi-double and fully double flowers, wide color range; 'Polar Bear', white double flowers; Profusion Series, single flowers, red, orange, or white; 'Pulcino', semi-double and fully double flowers, wide color range; Ruffles Series, double flowers in most colors; Splendor Series, fully double flowers, red, pink, orange, or yellow; Sun Series, double flowers, in a variety of bright warm colors. Zones 9–11.

Zinnia elegans, Ruffles Series, 'Cherry Ruffles'

Zinnia haageana
syn. *Zinnia angustifolia* of gardens
☼/◐ ❄ ↔ 12–24 in (30–60 cm) ↑ 24 in (60 cm)
From Mexico. Narrow lance-shaped leaves. Golden to red-brown ray florets, orange disc. Fully double-flowered forms include 'Old Mexico' and 'Stargold'. Zones 9–11.

Zingiber spectabile

Bulbs, Corms, and Tubers

Plants that produce underground organs such as bulbs, corms, or tubers are known as geophytes. This varied and large group includes many of the world's favorite ornamental garden plants and cut flowers, as well as being a source of food in many parts of the world. Bulbs, corms, and tubers are adaptations that enable the plant to survive times of the year unfavorable to aerial growth, such as cold winters and the dry season.

A bulb is a modified bud borne on a short thickened stem. Naked bulbs are made up solely of scaly but fleshy modified leaves surrounding the central developing flower stem, as with *Lilium;* on tunicated bulbs, the fleshy inner scales are covered with thin membranous scales, seen on daffodils and tulips. Corms are similar to bulbs, but instead of the scales of the underground bud forming the bulk of the organ, the thickened stem is the biggest part. Corms include *Freesia* and *Watsonia* plants. Tubers can be formed from both underground stems and swollen roots, and include potatoes and dahlias.

As well as beautiful flowers, scent is an important feature of some plants in this group. Hyacinths and some lilies have excellent fragrance and make ideal pot plants.

A woodland meadow of spring-flowering Spanish bluebells *(Hyacinthoides hispanica)* can be achieved on a smaller scale in most cool-climate gardens.

Bulb, Corm, and Tuber Finder

The following cultivation table features at-a-glance information for every species or hybrid with an individual entry in the Bulbs, Corms, and Tubers chapter of this book. Simply find the plant you wish to know more about, and run your eye along the row to discover its height and spread, whether it is frost tolerant or not, the aspect it prefers, and more.

The type of plant is abbreviated to **B**, **C**, or **T**:
B – the plant is a bulb.
C – the plant is a corm.
T – the plant is a tuber.

The climate(s) that each plant needs to thrive in the outdoors are given (some plants will grow in more than one climate), abbreviated to **C**, **W**, or **T**:
C – the plant prefers a cool climate.
W– the plant prefers a warm-temperate or subtropical climate.
T – the plant prefers a tropical climate.

The flowering, dormant, and planting seasons are abbreviated to **A**, **W**, **Sp**, or **Su**:
A – the plant flowers, is dormant, or should be planted in autumn.
W– the plant flowers, is dormant, or should be planted in winter.
Sp – the plant flowers, is dormant, or should be planted in spring.
Su – the plant flowers, is dormant, or should be planted in summer.

Plant name	Height	Spread	Type	Climate	Flowering season	Dormant season	Planting season	Bedding	Rock garden	Pots	Frost tolerant	Full sun	Half sun	Heavy shade
Allium aflatunense	3–5 ft (0.9–1.5 m)	12–24 in (30–60 cm)	B	C	Sp	W	Sp	◆			◆	◆		
Allium carinatum	12–24 in (30–60 cm)	6–12 in (15–30 cm)	B	C	Su	W	Sp	◆	◆		◆	◆		
Allium cernuum	12–27 in (30–70 cm)	6–12 in (15–30 cm)	B	C	Su	W	Sp	◆	◆		◆	◆		
Allium cristophii	8–20 in (20–50 cm)	8–12 in (20–30 cm)	B	C	Su	W	Sp	◆			◆	◆		
Allium cyaneum	5–10 in (12–25 cm)	5–10 in (12–25 cm)	B	C	Sp	W	Sp	◆	◆	◆	◆	◆		
Allium flavum	8–12 in (20–30 cm)	4–6 in (10–15 cm)	B	C	Su	W	Sp	◆	◆		◆	◆		
Allium giganteum	3–6 ft (0.9–1.8 m)	12–20 in (30–50 cm)	B	C	Su	W	Sp	◆			◆	◆	◆	
Allium howellii	12–20 in (30–50 cm)	6–8 in (15–20 cm)	B	C	Su	W	Sp		◆		◆	◆		
Allium karataviense	4–12 in (10–30 cm)	8–20 in (20–50 cm)	B	C	Sp	W	Sp	◆	◆	◆	◆	◆	◆	
Allium moly	8–12 in (20–30 cm)	8–12 in (20–30 cm)	B	C	Su	W	Sp	◆		◆	◆	◆	◆	
Allium oreophilum	4–8 in (10–20 cm)	6–8 in (15–20 cm)	B	C	Su	W	Sp		◆	◆	◆	◆		
Allium platycaule	4–6 in (10–15 cm)	8–12 in (20–30 cm)	B	C	Sp	W	Sp		◆		◆	◆		
Allium regelii	32–40 in (80–100 cm)	12–20 in (30–50 cm)	B	C	Su	W	Sp	◆			◆	◆	◆	
Allium stellatum	18 in (45 cm)	1–2 in (5–10 cm)	B	C	A	W	Sp	◆			◆	◆		◆
Amaryllis belladonna	24 in (60 cm)	12–20 in (30–50 cm)	B	W	Su/A	Su	Su	◆			◆	◆		
Amorphophallus bulbifer	3 ft (90 cm)	5 ft (1.2 m)	T	T	Su	W	Sp			◆				◆
Amorphophallus titanum	17–20 ft (5–6 m)	25 ft (8 m)	T	T	Su	W	Sp	◆						◆
Anemonella thalictroides	4–10 in (10–25 cm)	3–6 in (7–15 cm)	T	C	Sp	A	Sp		◆	◆	◆		◆	◆
Arisaema consanguineum	36 in (90 cm)	12 in (30 cm)	T	C/W	Su	W	Sp		◆	◆	◆			◆
Arisaema ringens	12 in (30 cm)	12 in (30 cm)	T	C	Sp	W	A	◆	◆	◆	◆			◆
Arisaema sikokianum	18 in (45 cm)	18 in (45 cm)	T	C	Su	W	Sp		◆	◆	◆			◆
Arisaema speciosum	24–36 in (60–90 cm)	18 in (45 cm)	T	W	Su	W	Sp			◆			◆	
Arisaema triphyllum	12–24 in (30–60 cm)	18 in (45 cm)	T	C	Su	W	Sp				◆			◆

Plant name	Height	Spread	Type	Climate	Flowering season	Dormant season	Planting season	Bedding	Rock garden	Pots	Frost tolerant	Full sun	Half sun	Heavy shade
Arum italicum	10–12 in (25–30 cm)	12–16 in (30–40 cm)	T	C/W	Sp	A/W	Sp			♦	♦		♦	♦
Arum maculatum	10 in (25 cm)	8–16 in (20–40 cm)	T	C	Sp	W	Sp			♦	♦		♦	♦
Babiana ringens	6–10 in (15–25 cm)	4 in (10 cm)	C	W	W/Sp	Su	A		♦	♦		♦		
Babiana rubrocyanea	6–12 in (15–30 cm)	4 in (10 cm)	C	W	W/Sp	Su	A		♦	♦		♦		
Babiana stricta	6–12 in (15–30 cm)	4 in (10 cm)	C	W	Sp	Su	A	♦	♦	♦		♦		
Belamcanda chinesis	36 in (90 cm)	12 in (30 cm)	B	W	Su	W	Sp/A	♦	♦			♦	♦	
Blandfordia grandiflora	32 in (80 cm)	10 in (25 cm)	T	C/W	Su	A	W							
Brodiaea coronaria	12 in (30 cm)	4 in (10 cm)	B	C/W	Sp	A/W	Sp		♦	♦	♦	♦		
Brunsvigia orientalis	20 in (50 cm)	18 in (45 cm)	B	W	Sp	Su	Sp			♦	♦	♦		
Bulbinella hookeri	36 in (90 cm)	24 in (60 cm)	T	C	Su	A	Sp		♦	♦		♦		
Bulbinella latifolia	36 in (90 cm)	24 in (60 cm)	T	W	W/Sp	Su	A			♦		♦		
Caladium bicolor	24 in (60 cm)	12 in (30 cm)	T	T	Su/A	W/Sp	Sp	♦		♦				♦
Calochortus amoenus	18 in (45 cm)	6 in (15 cm)	B	C	Sp	Su	Sp			♦	♦	♦		
Calochortus luteus	8–20 in (20–50 cm)	6 in (15 cm)	B	C	Sp	Su	Sp			♦	♦	♦	♦	
Calochortus superbus	16–24 in (40–60 cm)	6 in (15 cm)	B	C	Sp	Su	Sp		♦	♦	♦	♦	♦	
Camassia leichtlinii	24–48 in (60–120 cm)	20–60 in (50–150 cm)	B	C	Sp	A	Sp	♦			♦	♦	♦	
Camassia quamash	12–32 in (30–80 cm)	16–40 in (40–100 cm)	B	C	Sp	A	W				♦	♦	♦	
Cardiocrinum giganteum	7–15 ft (2–4.5 m)	3–5 ft (0.9–1.5 m)	B	C	Sp	A/W	Sp	♦			♦	♦		♦
Chasmanthe aethiopica	16–27 in (40–70 cm)	5–7 in (12–17 cm)	C	W	W/Sp	A	A	♦				♦	♦	
Chasmanthe floribunda	2–4 ft (60–120 cm)	12 in (30 cm)	C	W	W/Sp	A	A	♦				♦		
Chionodoxa forbesii	3–8 in (7–20 cm)	4–8 in (10–20 cm)	B	C	Su	A/W	Sp	♦	♦	♦	♦	♦		
Chionodoxa luciliae	4–6 in (10–15 cm)	3–6 in (7–15 cm)	B	C	Su	A/W	Sp	♦	♦	♦	♦	♦		
Colchicum autumnale	6–10 in (15–25 cm)	6–16 in (15–40 cm)	B	C	A	Su	Sp	♦	♦	♦	♦	♦	♦	
Colchicum byzantinum	6–12 in (15–30 cm)	6–16 in (15–40 cm)	B	C	A	Su	Sp	♦	♦	♦	♦	♦	♦	
Colchicum cilicicum	6–12 in (15–30 cm)	6–16 in (15–40 cm)	B	C	A	Su	Sp	♦	♦	♦	♦	♦	♦	
Colchicum speciosum	4–8 in (10–20 cm)	6–16 in (15–40 cm)	B	C	A	Su	Sp	♦	♦	♦	♦	♦	♦	
Colchicum 'The Giant'	10 in (25 cm)	8 in (20 cm)	C	C	A	Su	Su		♦	♦	♦	♦	♦	
Colchicum 'Waterlily'	8 in (20 cm)	8 in (20 cm)	C	C	A	Su	Su		♦	♦	♦	♦	♦	
Convallaria majalis	4–8 in (10–20 cm)	12–40 in (30–100 cm)	T	C	Sp	W	A	♦			♦		♦	♦
Crinum asiaticum	3–5 ft (0.9–1.5 m)	3 ft (0.9 m)	B	W/T	Sp/Su	A	W					♦		
Crinum bulbispermum	3 ft (90 cm)	3 ft (0.9 m)	B	W	Sp	Su	A			♦	♦	♦		
Crinum 'Ellen Bosanquet'	2–3 ft (60–90 cm)	2–3 ft (60–90 cm)	B	W/T	Su	A	Sp			♦	♦	♦		
Crinum moorei	4–5 ft (1.2–1.5 m)	4–5 ft (1.2–1.5 m)	B	W	Su	A	Sp				♦		♦	
Crinum × powellii	4 ft (1.20 m)	4 ft (1.2 m)	B	W	Su	A/W	Sp	♦		♦	♦		♦	

Plant name	Height	Spread	Type	Climate	Flowering season	Dormant season	Planting season	Bedding	Rock garden	Pots	Frost tolerant	Full sun	Half sun	Heavy shade
Crocosmia aurea	32–40 in (80–100 cm)	24–32 in (60–80 cm)	C	C/W	Su/A	W	W	♦		♦	♦	♦		
Crocosmia × crocosmiiflora	20–24 in (50–60 cm)	20–24 in (50–60 cm)	C	C/W	Su/A	W	W	♦		♦	♦	♦		
Crocosmia masoniorum	3–4 ft (0.9–1.2 m)	32–40 in (80–100 cm)	C	C/W	Su	W	W	♦		♦	♦	♦		
Crocosmia Hybrid Cultivars	18–36 in (45–90 cm)	12–24 in (30–60 cm)	C	C/W	Su/A	W	W	♦		♦	♦	♦		
Crocus chrysanthus	2 in (5 cm)	4 in (10 cm)	C	C	Sp	A/W	A	♦	♦	♦	♦	♦		
Crocus kotschyanus	3 in (8 cm)	4 in (10 cm)	C	C	A	Su	Su	♦	♦	♦	♦	♦		
Crocus speciosus	4–6 in (10–15 cm)	3 in (8 cm)	C	C	A	Su	Su	♦	♦	♦	♦	♦		
Crocus tommasinianus	3–4 in (8–10 cm)	3 in (8 cm)	C	C	Sp	A/W	A	♦	♦	♦	♦	♦		
Crocus vernus	4–5 in (10–12 cm)	4 in (10 cm)	C	C	Sp	A/W	A	♦	♦	♦	♦	♦		
Cyclamen cilicium	3–4 in (8–10 cm)	6–8 in (15–20 cm)	T	C	A	Su	A		♦	♦	♦		♦	♦
Cyclamen coum	4 in (10 cm)	6–12 in (15–30 cm)	T	C	W/Sp	Su	Su		♦	♦	♦		♦	♦
Cyclamen hederifolium	4 in (10 cm)	6–12 in (15–30 cm)	T	C	Su	Su	Su		♦	♦	♦		♦	♦
Cyclamen persicum	6–8 in (15–20 cm)	6–12 in (15–30 cm)	T	W	W/Sp	Su	Sp		♦	♦			♦	♦
Cyclamen purpurascens	4–6 in (10–15 cm)	6–12 in (15–30 cm)	T	C/W	Su	W	W		♦	♦	♦		♦	♦
Cyclamen repandum	4–6 in (10–15 cm)	6–12 in (15–30 cm)	T	C/W	Sp	A/W	A		♦	♦	♦		♦	♦
Cyrtanthus elatus	18 in (45 cm)	12 in (30 cm)	B	W	Su/A	W	W	♦	♦	♦		♦	♦	
Cyrtanthus mackenii	12 in (30 cm)	12 in (30 cm)	B	W	Sp	W	W	♦	♦	♦			♦	
Dahlia coccinea	7–10 ft (2–3 m)	2–4 ft (60–120 cm)	T	W	Su/A	W	Sp	♦			♦	♦	♦	
Dahlia imperialis	17–25 ft (2–4.5 m)	7–15 ft (2–4.5 m)	T	W	A	W/Sp	Sp	♦			♦	♦	♦	
Dahlia merckii	7 ft (2 m)	3 ft (0.9 m)	T	W	Su/A	W	Sp	♦	♦	♦	♦	♦	♦	
Dahlia scapigera	20 in (50 cm)	12–20 in (30–50 cm)	T	W	Su/A	W	Sp	♦		♦		♦		
Dahlia tenuicaulis	10–15 ft (3–4.5 m)	3–7 ft (0.9–2 m)	T	W	Su/A	W	Sp	♦			♦	♦	♦	
Dahlia Hybrid Cultivars	1½– 3 ft (0.5–0.9 m)	1–3 ft (30–90 cm)	T	W	Su/A	W	Sp	♦		♦		♦		
Dierama pulcherrimum	5 ft (1.5 m)	12 in (30 cm)	C	C/W	Su	A/W	W	♦	♦		♦	♦		
Eranthis × tuberinii 'Guinea Gold'	4–8 in (10–20 cm)	3–4 in (8–10 cm)	T	C	W		A	♦			♦		♦	
Eremurus himalaicus	36–48 in (90–120 cm)	30 in (75 cm)	T	C	Sp	Su/A	A	♦			♦	♦		
Eremurus robustus	7–10 ft (2–3 m)	36–48 in (90–120 cm)	T	C	Su	Su/A	A	♦			♦	♦		
Eremurus Hybrid Cultivars	4–7 ft (1.2–2 m)	24–40 in (60–100 cm)	T	C	Sp/Su	Su/A	A	♦			♦	♦		
Erythronium californicum	10 in (25 cm)	6 in (15 cm)	B	C	Sp	Su/A		♦	♦	♦	♦		♦	
Erythronium dens-canis	6–8 in (15–20 cm)	6 in (15 cm)	B	C	Sp	Su/A		♦	♦	♦	♦		♦	
Erythronium 'Pagoda'	6–12 in (15–30 cm)	8 in (20 cm)	B	C	Sp	Su/A		♦	♦	♦	♦		♦	
Erythronium revolutum	6–8 in (15–20 cm)	6 in (15 cm)	B	C	Sp	Su/A			♦	♦	♦		♦	
Erythronium tuolumnense	8–15 in (20–37 cm)	8 in (20 cm)	B	C	Sp	Su/A		♦	♦	♦	♦		♦	
Eucomis autumnalis	10–18 in (25–45 cm)	24 in (60 cm)	B	W	Su/A	W/Sp	W	♦		♦	♦	♦	♦	

Plant name	Height	Spread	Type	Climate	Flowering season	Dormant season	Planting season	Bedding	Rock garden	Pots	Frost tolerant	Full sun	Half sun	Heavy shade
Eucomis bicolor	12–24 in (30–60 cm)	12–24 in (30–60 cm)	B	C/W	Su	W/Sp	W	◆		◆	◆	◆		
Eucomis comosa	12–24 in (30–60 cm)	16 in (40 cm)	B	W	Su/A	W/Sp	W	◆		◆	◆	◆		
Freesia alba	4–6 in (10–15 cm)	3 in (7 cm)	C	W	W/Sp	Su	A	◆		◆		◆		
Freesia laxa	12–16 in (30–40 cm)	8–12 in (20–30 cm)	C	W	Sp/Su	Su/A	A	◆	◆	◆		◆		
Freesia Hybrid Cultivars	12–20 in (30–50 cm)	6–12 in (15–30 cm)	C	W	W/Sp	Su	A	◆		◆	◆	◆	◆	
Fritillaria acmopetala	16–18 in (40–45 cm)	1¾–2 in (4–5 cm)	B	C	Sp	Su/A	A		◆	◆	◆		◆	
Fritillaria camschatcensis	8–16 in (20–40 cm)	1¾–2 in (4–5 cm)	B	C	Sp/Su	Su/A	A		◆	◆	◆		◆	
Fritillaria graeca	2½–8 in (6–20 cm)	1¾–2 in (4–5 cm)	B	C	Sp/Su	Su/A	A		◆	◆	◆	◆		
Fritillaria imperialis	36–48 in (90–120 cm)	16 in (40 cm)	B	C	Sp	Su/A	A	◆		◆	◆	◆		
Fritillaria meleagris	7–8 in (18–20 cm)	1¾–2 in (4–5 cm)	B	C	Sp	Su/A	A	◆	◆	◆	◆	◆		
Fritillaria persica	4–36 in (10–90 cm)	3 in (8 cm)	B	C	Sp	Su/A	A	◆		◆	◆	◆		
Galanthus elwesii	4–6 in (10–15 cm)	4 in (10 cm)	B	C	W	Su/A	Sp	◆	◆	◆	◆		◆	
Galanthus ikariae	4–6 in (10–15 cm)	4 in (10 cm)	B	C	W/Sp	Su/A	Sp	◆	◆	◆	◆		◆	
Galanthus nivalis	6–8 in (15–20 cm)	4 in (10 cm)	B	C	W/Sp	Su/A	Sp	◆	◆	◆	◆		◆	
Galtonia candicans	4 ft (120 cm)	12 in (60 cm)	B	C	Su	A/W	Sp			◆	◆	◆		
Galtonia viridiflora	36 in (90 cm)	12 in (30 cm)	B	C/W	Su	A/W	Sp			◆		◆		
Gladiolus communis	40 in (80 cm)	12 in (30 cm)	C	C/W	Sp	A/W	A			◆		◆		
Gladiolus murielae	40 in (100 cm)	20 in (50 cm)	C	C/W	Su/A	W/Sp	Sp	◆		◆	◆	◆		
Gladiolus tristis	24 in (60 cm)	12 in (30 cm)	C	C	Sp	Su/A	A	◆		◆		◆		
Gladiolus Hybrid Cultivars	2–5 ft (60–150 cm)	12 in (30 cm)	C	W	Sp/Su	A/W	A/W	◆		◆		◆		
Gloriosa superba	6–8 ft (1.8–2.4 m)	12–20 in (30–50 cm)	T	W/T	Su/A	W/Sp	Sp			◆			◆	◆
Habranthus robustus	8–12 in (20–30 cm)	4 in (10 cm)	B	W	Su	Sp	Sp	◆	◆	◆		◆		
Habranthus tubispathus	6–10 in (15–25 cm)	3 in (7 cm)	B	W	Su	Sp	Sp	◆	◆	◆		◆		
Haemanthus albiflos	12 in (30 cm)	15 in (38 cm)	B	W	A/W	Su	A		◆	◆		◆		
Haemanthus sanguineus	12 in (30 cm)	6 in (15 cm)	B	C/W	Su/A	Sp	Sp		◆	◆	◆	◆		
Hippeastrum papilio	24 in (60 cm)	12–16 in (30–40 cm)	B	W	Sp	W			◆	◆		◆	◆	
Hippeastrum reticulatum	10–14 in (25–35 cm)	14–18 in (35–45 cm)	B	W	Su	W/Sp		◆		◆		◆	◆	
Hippeastrum vittatum	36 in (90 cm)	12 in (30 cm)	B	W	Su	W		◆	◆	◆		◆		
Hippeastrum Hybrid Cultivars	20–36 in (50–90 cm)	12–16 in (30–40 cm)	B	W/T	Sp/Su	W		◆	◆	◆		◆	◆	
Hyacinthoides hispanica	16–18 in (40–45 cm)	4–6 in (10–15 cm)	B	C	Sp	A	A	◆		◆	◆		◆	◆
Hyacinthoides non-scripta	8–16 in (20–40 cm)	2–6 in (5–15 cm)	B	C	Sp	A	A	◆		◆	◆		◆	◆
Hyacinthus orientalis	8–12 in (20–30 cm)	3 in (7 cm)	B	C	Sp	A/W	A	◆		◆	◆	◆		
Hymenocallis × festalis	24–32 in (60–80 cm)	12–24 in (30–60 cm)	B	W	Sp/Su	W	Sp			◆		◆		
Hymenocallis narcissiflora	20–24 in (50–60 cm)	12–24 in (30–60 cm)	B	W	Su	W	Sp	◆		◆		◆		

Plant name	Height	Spread	Type	Climate	Flowering season	Dormant season	Planting season	Bedding	Rock garden	Pots	Frost tolerant	Full sun	Half sun	Heavy shade
Hymenocallis 'Sulphur Queen'	20–24 in (50–60 cm)	12–20 in (30–50 cm)	B	W	Su	W	Sp	◆		◆	◆	◆		
Hypoxis capensis	8–24 in (20–60 cm)	8–24 in (20–60 cm)	C	W	Sp/Su	W	Sp	◆	◆	◆		◆		
Hypoxis hirsuta	4–8 in (10–20 cm)	2 in (5 cm)	C	C/W	Sp/Su		Sp		◆	◆	◆	◆		
Ipheion 'Alberto Castillo'	7–8 in (18–20 cm)	2 in (5 cm)	B	C/W	W/Sp	A	A	◆	◆	◆		◆	◆	
Ipheion uniflorum	4–8 in (10–20 cm)	2 in (5 cm)	B	C/W	W/Sp	A	A	◆	◆	◆	◆	◆		
Iris bucharica	18 in (45 cm)	6 in (15 cm)	B	C	Sp	A	A	◆	◆	◆		◆		
Iris reticulata	6 in (15 cm)	2 in (5 cm)	B	C	W/Sp	Su/A	A	◆	◆	◆		◆		
Iris, Dutch Hybrids	24–36 in (60–90 cm)	12–18 in (30–45 cm)	B	C	Sp	A	A	◆	◆	◆		◆		
Ixia maculata	8–20 in (20–50 cm)	6 in (15 cm)	C	W	Sp	Su/A	A	◆				◆		
Ixia paniculata	18–30 in (45–75 cm)	6 in (15 cm)	C	W	Sp/Su	A	W	◆					◆	◆
Ixia viridiflora	12–24 in (30–60 cm)	8 in (20 cm)	C	W	Sp	Su/A	A	◆				◆		
Ixiolirion tataricum	10–16 in (25–40 cm)	12–16 in (30–40 cm)	B	C	Sp/Su	A/W	A	◆	◆	◆	◆	◆		
Lachenalia aloides	12 in (30 cm)	8 in (20 cm)	B	W	W/Sp	Su/A	A	◆	◆	◆		◆	◆	
Lachenalia contaminata	6–10 in (15–25 cm)	8–10 in (20–25 cm)	B	W	Su	A/W	Sp		◆	◆		◆		
Ledebouria cooperi	2–4 in (5–10 cm)	2–3 in (5–7 cm)	B	W	Su	W	Sp		◆	◆				
Ledebouria socialis	2–4 in (5–10 cm)	2–3 in (5–8 cm)	B	W/T	Sp/Su	W	Sp		◆	◆	◆	◆		
Leucocoryne ixioides	16–18 in (40–45 cm)	3–4 in (8–10 cm)	B	W	Sp	Su/A	A	◆	◆	◆		◆		
Leucojum aestivum	18–22 in (45–55 cm)	12 in (30 cm)	B	C	W/Sp	A/W	A	◆			◆	◆		◆
Leucojum autumnale	6–10 in (15–25 cm)	2 in (5 cm)	B	C	Su/A	W/Sp	Sp	◆	◆	◆	◆	◆		
Leucojum vernum	12–30 in (30–75 cm)	12 in (30 cm)	B	C	Sp	A/W	A	◆	◆	◆		◆		◆
Lilium candidum	3–7 ft (1–2 m)	12–18 in (30–45 cm)	B	C	Su	W	A	◆		◆		◆		
Lilium columbianum	7–8 ft (2–2.4 m)	12–18 in (30–45 cm)	B	C	Su	W	A	◆		◆		◆		
Lilium davidii	3–5 ft (0.9–1.5 m)	12–18 in (30–45 cm)	B	C	Su	W	A	◆				◆		
Lilium formosanum	3–7 ft (1–2 m)	12–18 in (30–45 cm)	B	C/W	Su/A	W	A	◆				◆		
Lilium henryi	7–10 ft (2–3 m)	12–18 in (30–45 cm)	B	C	Su	W	A	◆				◆		
Lilium lancifolium	3–4 ft (90–120 cm)	12–18 in (30–45 cm)	B	C/W	Su	W	A	◆			◆	◆		
Lilium longiflorum	36–40 in (90–100 cm)	12–18 in (30–45 cm)	B	C/W	Sp	W	A	◆		◆		◆		
Lilium martagon	3–8 ft (0.9–2.4 m)	12–18 in (30–45 cm)	B	C	Su	W	A	◆		◆	◆	◆		
Lilium nepalense	27–40 in (40–100 cm)	12–18 in (30–45 cm)	B	C	Su/A	W	A	◆	◆	◆	◆	◆		
Lilium regale	5–7 ft (1.5–2 m)	12–18 in (30–45 cm)	B	C	Su	W	A				◆	◆		
Lilium speciosum	3–5 ft (0.9–1.5 m)	12–18 in (30–45 cm)	B	C	Su/A	W	A	◆				◆		
Lilium Hybrid Cultivars	30 in–7 ft (0.75–2 m)	12–24 in (30–60 cm)	B	C	Su	W	A	◆		◆	◆	◆	◆	
Lycoris aurea	18–24 in (45–60 cm)	18 in (45 cm)	B	C/W	Su/A	Sp	Sp	◆	◆	◆	◆	◆		
Moraea aristata	15–16 in (38–40 cm)	3 in (7 cm)	C	W	Sp	Su	A	◆	◆	◆		◆		

Plant name	Height	Spread	Type	Climate	Flowering season	Dormant season	Planting season	Bedding	Rock garden	Pots	Frost tolerant	Full sun	Half shade	Heavy shade
Moraea collina	6–14 in (15–35 cm)	3 in (8 cm)	C	W/T	W/Sp	Su	A	◆	◆	◆	◆	◆		
Moraea polystachya	32 in (80 cm)	3 in (8 cm)	C	W	A/W	Su	A	◆	◆	◆		◆	◆	
Moraea ramosissima	24–48 in (60–120 cm)	4 in (10 cm)	C	W	Sp/Su	A	A		◆			◆		
Moraea spathulata	20–40 in (50–100 cm)	4 in (10 cm)	C	W	W/Su	A	A	◆	◆	◆		◆		
Moraea villosa	12–16 in (30–40 cm)	5 in (12 cm)	C	W	W/Sp	A	A		◆	◆		◆		
Muscari armeniacum	8 in (20 cm)	2 in (5 cm)	B	C	Sp	Su	A	◆	◆	◆	◆	◆	◆	
Muscari azureum	4–6 in (10–15 cm)	2 in (5 cm)	B	C	Sp/Su	Su	A	◆	◆	◆	◆	◆	◆	
Muscari botryoides	4–6 in (10–15 cm)	2 in (5 cm)	B	C	Su	Su	A	◆	◆	◆	◆	◆	◆	
Muscari latifolium	8 in (20 cm)	2–4 in (5–10 cm)	B	C	Sp	Su	A	◆	◆	◆	◆	◆	◆	
Narcissus bulbocodium	4–6 in (10–15 cm)	12 in (30 cm)	B	C	Sp	Su/A	Su/A		◆	◆	◆	◆	◆	
Narcissus cyclamineus	6–8 in (15–20 cm)	12 in (30 cm)	B	C	Sp	Su/A	Su/A		◆	◆	◆	◆	◆	
Narcissus jonquilla	18 in (45 cm)	8 in (20 cm)	B	C	Sp	Su/A	Su/A	◆	◆	◆	◆	◆	◆	
Narcissus minor	8 in (20 cm)	4 in (10 cm)	B	C	Sp	Su/A	Su/A	◆	◆	◆	◆	◆	◆	
Narcissus obesus	7–8 in (18–20 cm)	12 in (30 cm)	B	C	Sp	Su/A	Su/A		◆	◆	◆	◆	◆	
Narcissus × odorus	14–16 in (35–40 cm)	12 in (30 cm)	B	C	Sp	Su/A	Su/A	◆	◆	◆	◆	◆	◆	
Narcissus poeticus	12–20 in (30–50 cm)	12 in (30 cm)	B	C	Sp	Su/A	Su/A	◆	◆	◆	◆	◆	◆	
Narcissus pseudonarcissus	8–14 in (20–35 cm)	12 in (30 cm)	B	C/W	Sp	Su/A	Su/A	◆	◆	◆	◆	◆	◆	
Narcissus tazetta	6–20 in (15–50 cm)	12 in (30 cm)	B	C/W	W/Sp	Su/A	Su/A	◆		◆	◆	◆		
Narcissus triandrus	5–10 in (12–25 cm)	12 in (30 cm)	B	C	Sp	Su/A	Su/A		◆	◆	◆	◆	◆	
Narcissus Hybrid Cultivars	6–18 in (15–45 cm)	10–20 in (25–50 cm)	B	C/W	Sp	Su/A	Su/A	◆		◆	◆	◆	◆	
Nerine bowdenii	16–18 in (40–45 cm)	12 in (30 cm)	B	W	A	Su	Su	◆	◆	◆	◆	◆		
Nerine flexuosa	16–18 in (40–45 cm)	6 in (15 cm)	B	W	A	Su	Su	◆		◆		◆		
Nerine sarniensis	16–18 in (40–45 cm)	6 in (15 cm)	B	W	A	Su	Su			◆		◆		
Nomocharis aperta	14–32 in (35–80 cm)	10 in (25 cm)	B	C	Su	W	A		◆	◆			◆	◆
Ornithogalum arabicum	16–30 in (40–75 cm)	24–48 in (60–120 cm)	B	W	Sp/Su	Su/A		◆		◆		◆		
Ornithogalum dubium	8–12 in (20–30 cm)	12–20 in (30–50 cm)	B	C/W	Sp	Su/A		◆		◆		◆		
Ornithogalum longibracteatum	2–4 ft (60–120 cm)	4 ft (1.2 m)	B	W	Sp/Su	Su	A			◆		◆		
Ornithogalum narbonense	24–36 in (60–90 cm)	24–48 in (60–120 cm)	B	C/W	Su	Su	A	◆	◆	◆	◆	◆		
Ornithogalum nutans	16–24 in (40–60 cm)	16–30 in (40–75 cm)	B	C	Sp	Su	A	◆		◆	◆	◆	◆	
Ornithogalum umbellatum	20 in (50 cm)	20–32 in (50–80 cm)	B	C	Sp	Su	A	◆	◆	◆	◆	◆	◆	
Oxalis adenophylla	3–4 in (7–10 cm)	5–6 in (12–15 cm)	B	C	Sp	W	Sp		◆	◆		◆		
Oxalis bowiei	8–10 in (20–25 cm)	6–8 in (15–20 cm)	B	W	A/W	Su	A		◆	◆		◆		
Oxalis enneaphylla	2½–3 in (6–8 cm)	4–6 in (10–15 cm)	T	W	Sp/Su	W	A		◆	◆	◆	◆	◆	
Oxalis hirta	10–12 in (25–30 cm)	4–6 in (10–15 cm)	B	C/W	A	Su	Su	◆	◆			◆		

Plant name	Height	Spread	Type	Climate	Flowering season	Dormant season	Planting season	Bedding	Rock garden	Pots	Frost tolerant	Full sun	Half sun	Heavy shade
Oxalis 'Ione Hecker'	2½–3 in (6–8 cm)	3–4 in (8–10 cm)	B	C	Su	W	Sp	♦	♦	♦	♦	♦	♦	
Oxalis purpurea	3–4 in (7–10 cm)	18 in (45 cm)	B	C/W	W	Su	Su	♦	♦	♦		♦		
Oxalis rubra	16 in (40 cm)	12 in (30 cm)	T	W	Su/A	W	Sp	♦				♦	♦	
Oxalis triangularis	8–10 in (20–25 cm)	16 in (40 cm)	T	W	Su	W	Sp	♦		♦		♦		♦
Oxalis versicolor	3–4 in (7–10 cm)	8 in (20 cm)	B	W	W	Su	A		♦	♦		♦		
Pinellia cordata	4–6 in (10–15 cm)	4–6 in (10–15 cm)	T	C	Su	W	Sp		♦	♦	♦		♦	
Polianthes tuberosa	48 in (120 cm)	20 in (50 cm)	T	W	Su/A	W	Sp	♦		♦		♦		
Ranunculus aconitifolius	24 in (60 cm)	40 in (100 cm)	T	C/W	Sp	A	A	♦		♦	♦		♦	♦
Ranunculus acris	24–40 in (60–100 cm)	24–48 in (60–120 cm)	T	C/W	Sp	A	A	♦		♦	♦	♦		
Ranunculus anemoneus	8–14 in (20–35 cm)	12–16 in (30–40 cm)	T	C/W	Sp	A	A		♦	♦	♦		♦	
Ranunculus asiaticus	18 in (45 cm)	10 in (25 cm)	T	C/W	Sp/Su	A	A	♦		♦		♦		
Ranunculus constantinopolitanus	16–30 in (40–75 cm)	12–32 in (30–80 cm)	T	C/W	Sp/Su	A	A	♦		♦	♦	♦		
Ranunculus ficaria	6 in (15 cm)	8–24 in (20–60 cm)	T	C/W	Sp	A	A		♦	♦	♦		♦	♦
Ranunculus flammula	4–12 in (10–30 cm)	32–60 in (80–150 cm)	T	C/W	Su	A	A			♦	♦	♦		
Ranunculus gramineus	8–20 in (20–50 cm)	6–12 in (15–30 cm)	T	C/W	Sp/Su	A	A	♦	♦	♦	♦	♦		
Ranunculus lingua	8–12 in (20–30 cm)	3–7 ft (0.9–2 m)	T	C/W	Su	A	A	♦		♦	♦	♦		
Ranunculus lyallii	24–48 in (60–120 cm)	24–48 in (60–120 cm)	T	C/W	Sp/Su	A	A			♦	♦		♦	♦
Ranunculus parnassifolius	2–4 in (5–10 cm)	8–12 in (20–30 cm)	T	C/W	Sp/Su	A	A		♦	♦	♦		♦	
Rhodohypoxis baurii	2½–4 in (6–8 cm)	2½–4 in (6–10 cm)	C	C	Su	A	Sp	♦	♦	♦		♦	♦	
Rhodohypoxis Hybrid Cultivars	2½–4 in (6–8 cm)	3–6 in (7–15 cm)	C	C	Su	A	A	♦	♦	♦		♦		
Romulea ramiflora	10–12 in (25–30 cm)	6–10 in (15–25 cm)	C	W	Sp	A	A		♦	♦		♦		
Roscoea alpina	10–12 in (25–30 cm)	5 in (12 cm)	T	C	Su	W	Sp	♦	♦	♦			♦	
Roscoea auriculata	12–20 in (30–50 cm)	5 in (12 cm)	T	C	Su	W	Sp	♦	♦	♦	♦		♦	
Roscoea 'Beesiana'	10–12 in (25–30 cm)	4–5 in (10–12 cm)	T	C	Su	W	Sp	♦	♦	♦			♦	
Roscoea cautleyoides	20–24 in (50–60 cm)	4–6 in (10–15 cm)	T	C	Su	W	Sp	♦	♦	♦			♦	
Roscoea humeana	8–10 in (20–25 cm)	5–6 in (12–15 cm)	T	C	Su	W	Sp	♦	♦	♦			♦	
Roscoea purpurea	12–16 in (30–40 cm)	5–6 in (12–15 cm)	T	C	Su	W	Sp	♦	♦	♦			♦	
Sandersonia aurantiaca	40 in (100 cm)	8 in (20 cm)	T	W	Su		Sp			♦		♦		
Saururus cernuus	12–18 in (30–45 cm)	36 in (90 cm)	T	C/W	Sp	W	A			♦	♦		♦	
Scadoxus multiflorus	20 in (50 cm)	24 in (60 cm)	B	W/T	Su	W/Sp	Sp	♦		♦		♦		
Scilla bifolia	3–6 in (7–15 cm)	3 in (7 cm)	B	C	Sp	W	A		♦	♦	♦	♦	♦	
Scilla hyacinthoides	36 in (90 cm)	12 in (30 cm)	B	W	Sp	W	A			♦	♦	♦		
Scilla liliohyacinthus	4 in (10 cm)	4 in (10 cm)	B	C	Sp	W	A		♦	♦	♦	♦	♦	
Scilla natalensis	36 in (90 cm)	20 in (50 cm)	B	W	Sp/Su	W	A	♦				♦	♦	♦

Plant name	Height	Spread	Type	Climate	Flowering season	Dormant season	Planting season	Bedding	Rock garden	Pots	Frost tolerant	Full sun	Half sun	Heavy shade
Scilla peruviana	12 in (30 cm)	18 in (45 cm)	B	W	Sp/Su	W	A	♦	♦	♦	♦	♦		
Scilla ramburei	6 in (15 cm)	4 in (10 cm)	B	C	Sp	W	A	♦	♦	♦	♦	♦		
Scilla siberica	6 in (15 cm)	3 in (8 cm)	B	C	Sp	W	A	♦	♦	♦	♦	♦	♦	
Scilla tubergeniana	5 in (12 cm)	4 in (10 cm)	B	C	Sp	W	A	♦	♦	♦	♦	♦		
Sparaxis fragrans	8–18 in (20–75 cm)	6–12 in (15–30 cm)	C	W	W/Sp	Su/A	A		♦	♦		♦	♦	
Sparaxis tricolor	8–16 in (20–40 cm)	8 in (20 cm)	C	W	Sp	Su/A	A	♦	♦	♦	♦	♦		
Sprekelia formosissima	12 in (30 cm)	8 in (20 cm)	B	W	Su/W	W	Sp			♦		♦		
Stenomesson miniatum	12–16 in (30–40 cm)	6 in (15 cm)	B	W	Sp/Su	W	Sp	♦	♦	♦		♦		
Sternbergia lutea	6 in (15 cm)	3 in (8 cm)	B	C	A	Su	Su	♦	♦	♦	♦	♦	♦	
Sternbergia sicula	3–4 in (8–10 cm)	3 in (8 cm)	B	C	A	Su	Su	♦	♦	♦	♦	♦	♦	
Tecophilaea cyanocrocus	4–5 in (10–12 cm)	2 in (5 cm)	C	C/W	Sp	W	A	♦	♦	♦	♦	♦		
Tigridia pavonia	24–48 in (60–120 cm)	12–20 in (30–50 cm)	C	W	Sp/Su	W	A		♦		♦	♦		
Triteleia grandiflora	12–24 in (30–60 cm)	8–12 in (20–30 cm)	C	C	Su	A	A	♦	♦	♦	♦	♦	♦	
Triteleia hyacinthina	18–24 in (45–60 cm)	8–12 in (20–30 cm)	C	C	Su	A	A	♦	♦	♦	♦	♦		
Triteleia ixioides	18–24 in (45–60 cm)	8–12 in (20–30 cm)	C	C/W	Su	A	A	♦	♦	♦	♦	♦		
Triteleia laxa	24–30 in (60–75 cm)	8–12 in (20–30 cm)	C	C	Su	A	A		♦	♦	♦	♦	♦	
Triteleia lilacina	12–20 in (30–50 cm)	6–10 in (15–25 cm)	C	C/W	Su	A	A	♦	♦	♦	♦	♦		
Tritonia crocata	10–18 in (25–45 cm)	4 in (10 cm)	C	C/W	Sp	Su	A	♦	♦	♦	♦	♦		
Tulbaghia alliacea	18–20 in (45–50 cm)	16–20 in (40–50 cm)	B	C/W	A	Sp	Sp	♦	♦	♦				
Tulbaghia cominsii	6–10 in (15–25 cm)	6 in (15 cm)	B	C/W	Sp/Su	W	Sp		♦	♦	♦	♦		
Tulbaghia natalensis	8–12 in (20–30 cm)	6 in (15 cm)	B	C/W	Su	W	Sp		♦	♦	♦	♦		
Tulbaghia simmleri	20–24 in (50–60 cm)	10–12 in (25–30 cm)	B	C/W	Sp/Su	W	Sp	♦	♦	♦	♦	♦		
Tulbaghia violacea	12–16 in (30–40 cm)	12 in (30 cm)	B	W	Sp/A	W	W		♦	♦	♦	♦		
Tulipa acuminata	18 in (45 cm)	2–4 in (5–10 cm)	B	C	Sp	Su/A	A		♦	♦	♦	♦		
Tulipa aucheriana	2–4 in (5–10 cm)	2–4 in (5–10 cm)	B	C	Sp	Su/A	A		♦	♦	♦	♦		
Tulipa clusiana	8–12 in (20–30 cm)	4 in (10 cm)	B	C	Sp	Su/A	A		♦	♦	♦	♦		
Tulipa fosteriana	12–16 in (30–40 cm)	4–6 in (10–15 cm)	B	C	Sp	Su/A	A	♦	♦	♦	♦	♦		
Tulipa greigii	6–10 in (15–25 cm)	6 in (15 cm)	B	C	Sp	Su/A	A		♦	♦	♦	♦		
Tulipa hageri	6–10 in (15–25 cm)	8 in (20 cm)	B	C	Sp	Su/A	A		♦	♦	♦	♦		
Tulipa humilis	4–6 in (10–15 cm)	2–4 in (5–10 cm)	B	C	Sp	Su/A	A	♦	♦	♦	♦	♦	♦	
Tulipa iliensis	8 in (20 cm)	2–4 in (5–10 cm)	B	C	Sp	Su/A	A		♦	♦	♦	♦		
Tulipa kaufmanniana	6–10 in (15–25 cm)	6 in (15 cm)	B	C	Sp	Su/A	A	♦	♦	♦	♦	♦		
Tulipa linifolia	4–6 in (10–15 cm)	4 in (10 cm)	B	C	Sp	Su/A	A			♦	♦	♦	♦	
Tulipa orphanidea	6–15 in (15–38 cm)	6 in (15 cm)	B	C	Sp	Su/A	A	♦	♦	♦	♦	♦	♦	

Plant name	Height	Spread	Type	Climate	Flowering season	Dormant season	Planting season	Bedding	Rock garden	Pots	Frost tolerant	Full sun	Half sun	Heavy shade
Tulipa praestans	6–20 in (15–50 cm)	6–8 in (15–20 cm)	B	C	Sp	Su/A	A	◆	◆	◆	◆	◆	◆	
Tulipa primulina	8 in (20 cm)	2–4 in (5–10 cm)	B	C	Sp	Su/A	A		◆	◆	◆	◆		
Tulipa sylvestris	10–18 in (25–45 cm)	4–6 in (10–15 cm)	B	C	Sp	Su/A	A		◆	◆	◆	◆	◆	
Tulipa tarda	4–6 in (10–15 cm)	6–8 in (15–20 cm)	B	C	Sp	Su/A	A		◆	◆	◆	◆	◆	
Tulipa turkestanica	8–10 in (20–25 cm)	6–10 in (15–25 cm)	B	C	Sp	Su/A	A		◆	◆	◆	◆		
Tulipa undulatifolia	12–20 in (30–50 cm)	6–10 in (15–25 cm)	B	C	Sp	Su/A	A				◆	◆	◆	◆
Tulipa urumiensis	4–6 in (10–15 cm)	4–6 in (10–15 cm)	B	C	Sp	Su/A	A				◆	◆		
Tulipa vvedenskyi	6–8 in (15–20 cm)	6–16 in (15–40 cm)	B	C	Sp	Su/A	A				◆	◆	◆	
Tulipa, Single Early Group (Group 1)	12–18 in (30–45 cm)	8–12 in (20–30 cm)	B	C	Sp	Su/A	A	◆		◆	◆	◆		
Tulipa, Double Early Group (Group 2)	12–16 in (30–40 cm)	8–12 in (20–30 cm)	B	C	Sp	Su/A	A	◆		◆	◆	◆		
Tulipa, Triumph Group (Group 3)	15–20 in (38–50 cm)	8–12 in (20–30 cm)	B	C	Sp	Su/A	A	◆		◆	◆	◆		
Tulipa, Darwin Hybrid Group (Group 4)	20–27 in (50–70 cm)	8–12 in (20–30 cm)	B	C	Sp	Su/A	A	◆		◆	◆	◆		
Tulipa, Single Late Group (Group 5)	18–30 in (45–75 cm)	8–12 in (20–30 cm)	B	C	Sp	Su/A	A	◆		◆	◆	◆		
Tulipa, Lily-flowered Group (Group 6)	15–24 in (38–60 cm)	8–12 in (20–30 cm)	B	C	Sp	Su/A	A	◆		◆	◆	◆		
Tulipa, Fringed Group (Group 7)	18–26 in (20–65 cm)	8–12 in (20–30 cm)	B	C	Sp	Su/A	A	◆		◆	◆	◆		
Tulipa, Viridiflora Group (Group 8)	12–20 in (30–50 cm)	8–12 in (20–30 cm)	B	C	Sp	Su/A	A	◆		◆	◆	◆		
Tulipa, Rembrandt Group (Group 9)	16–24 in (40–60 cm)	8–12 in (20–30 cm)	B	C	Sp	Su/A	A	◆		◆	◆	◆		
Tulipa, Parrot Group (Group 10)	18–22 in (45–55 cm)	8–12 in (20–30 cm)	B	C	Sp	Su/A	A	◆		◆	◆	◆		
Tulipa, Double Late or Peony-flowered Group (Group 11)	15–24 in (38–60 cm)	8–12 in (20–30 cm)	B	C	Sp	Su/A	A	◆		◆	◆	◆		
Tulipa, Kaufmanniana Group (Group 12)	10 in (25 cm)	6–10 in (15–25 cm)	B	C	Sp	Su/A	A	◆		◆	◆	◆		
Tulipa, Fosteriana Group (Group 13)	8–24 in (20–60 cm)	6–12 in (15–30 cm)	B	C	Sp	Su/A	A	◆		◆	◆	◆		
Tulipa, Greigii Group (Group 14)	8–12 in (20–30 cm)	6–12 in (15–30 cm)	B	C	Sp	Su/A	A	◆		◆	◆	◆		
Veltheimia bracteata	16–18 in (40–45 cm)	12 in (30 cm)	B	W	W/Sp	Su	A	◆	◆	◆			◆	
Watsonia borbonica	3–7 ft (1–2 m)	4 in (10 cm)	C	W	Su	A	A					◆		
Watsonia meriana	20–60 in (50–150 cm)	6 in (15 cm)	C	W	Sp/Su	A	A	◆	◆					
Watsonia pillansii	20–48 in (50–120 cm)	4 in (10 cm)	C	W	Su/A	A	A	◆			◆	◆		
Weldenia candida	5–6 in (12–15 cm)	6 in (15 cm)	T	C/W	Sp/Su	W	Sp		◆	◆		◆	◆	
Zantedeschia aethiopica	4–6 ft (1.2–1.8 m)	20–60 in (50–150 cm)	T	W	W/Sp	A	A			◆		◆		◆
Zantedeschia albomaculata	24–40 in (60–80 cm)	16–24 in (40–60 cm)	T	W	Su	W	Sp	◆		◆		◆		
Zantedeschia elliottiana	15 in (38 cm)	12–18 in (30–45 cm)	T	W	Su	W	Sp					◆		
Zantedeschia rehmannii	18 in (45 cm)	12–20 in (30–50 cm)	T	W	Su	W	Sp					◆		
Zantedeschia Hybrid Cultivars	1–6 ft (0.3–1.8 m)	1–5 ft (0.3–1.5 m)	T	W	Su	W	Sp	◆		◆		◆		
Zigadenus fremontii	20–36 in (50–90 cm)	2–5 in (5–12 cm)	B	C	Sp	A	A	◆	◆	◆	◆	◆		

ALLIUM

CHIVE, GARLIC, LEEK, ONION, ORNAMENTAL ONION

Genus of around 700 species of bulbous perennials and biennials, and the type genus for the onion (Alliaceae) family. Famous for their taste and pungency, many are essential ingredients in the world's cuisine. Foliage may be fine and grassy, strappy or hollow and tubular. Flowers are usually borne in rounded heads.
CULTIVATION: Plant in light well-drained soil. Propagate using offsets and bulbils, or from seed.

Allium aflatunense

☼ ❄ ↔ 12–24 in (30–60 cm) ↑ 3–5 ft (0.9–1.5 m)
Chinese species with 6 to 8, short, aromatic, blue-green, tubular leaves per bulb. Foliage dies before the flower stems develop in late summer. Dark-veined, lilac flowers. Zones 8–10.

Allium carinatum

KEELED GARLIC

☼ ❄ ↔ 6–12 in (15–30 cm) ↑ 12–24 in (30–60 cm)
From central and southern Europe to Russia and Turkey. Grassy leaves, 2 to 4 per bulb. Up to 30 purple-pink flowers. *A. c.* subsp. *pulchellum,* purplish flower stems. Zones 7–10.

Allium cernuum

LADY'S LEEK, NODDING ONION, WILD ONION

☼ ❄ ↔ 6–12 in (15–30 cm) ↑ 12–27 in (30–70 cm)
From southern Canada to northern Mexico. Flattened, bright green leaves to 8 in (20 cm) long, 4 to 6 per bulb. White, pink, or purplish flowers. 'Hidcote', purple-pink flowers. Zones 6–10.

Allium cristophii ★

STAR OF PERSIA

☼ ❄ ↔ 8–12 in (20–30 cm) ↑ 8–20 in (20–50 cm)
Found in central Asia and parts of Iran and Turkey. Narrow to broad blue-green leaves, downy undersides, 2 to 7 per bulb. Rounded head of small, starry, purple flowers. Zones 7–10.

Allium cyaneum

☼ ❄ ↔ 5–10 in (12–25 cm) ↑ 5–10 in (12–25 cm)
Perennial clump-forming bulb from China. Grassy foliage with very narrow leaves. Small blue or purplish flowers. Zones 5–9.

Allium flavum

SMALL YELLOW ONION

☼ ❄ ↔ 4–6 in (10–15 cm) ↑ 8–12 in (20–30 cm)
Found in southern Europe from France to Greece. Fine, cylindrical, blue-green leaves to 8 in (20 cm) long. Zones 7–10.

Allium giganteum

GIANT ALLIUM

☼/❋ ❄ ↔ 12–20 in (30–50 cm) ↑ 3–6 ft (0.9–1.8 m)
From central Asia. Strappy gray-green leaves. Large near-spherical heads of many tiny purple-pink flowers. Zones 7–9.

Allium howellii

☼ ❄ ↔ 6–8 in (15–20 cm) ↑ 12–20 in (30–50 cm)
Species from California, USA, with few grassy blue-green leaves that wither before the wiry flower stems develop fully. White to cream flowers edged with pink. Zones 8–10.

Allium karataviense

☼/❋ ❄ ↔ 8–20 in (20–50 cm) ↑ 4–12 in (10–30 cm)
Asian species with broad, gray-green leaves, often with a metallic purple sheen. Tiny, starry, white to pale mauve flowers. '**Ivory Queen**', pale green to cream flowers. Zones 7–9.

Allium moly

GOLDEN GARLIC

☼/❋ ❄ ↔ 8–12 in (20–30 cm) ↑ 8–12 in (20–30 cm)
European species with strappy blue-green leaves, 1 to 3 per bulb. Golden yellow flowers from late spring. '**Jeannine**', slightly larger heads of especially bright flowers. Zones 7–9.

Allium oreophilum

☼ ❄ ↔ 6–8 in (15–20 cm) ↑ 4–8 in (10–20 cm)
Found in the Caucasus region and Central Asia. Narrow blue-green leaves that extend beyond the height of the flower stem. Bright pink to purple bell-shaped flowers. Zones 7–9.

Allium platycaule

☼ ❄ ↔ 8–12 in (20–30 cm) ↑ 4–6 in (10–15 cm)
Native to mountains of western USA. Leaves are blue-green, usually flat to the ground, growing to 8 in (20 cm) long, 2 per bulb. Showy heads of tiny, starry, deep pink flowers. Zones 6–9.

Allium howellii

Allium carinatum subsp. *pulchellum*

Allium regelii

☼/◐ ❄ ↔ 12–20 in (30–50 cm) ↑ 32–40 in (80–100 cm)

Found in semi-desert areas of central Asia. Broad, strappy, coarse-edged, green leaves to 20 in (50 cm) long, 2 to 4 per bulb. Stems with up to 6 whorls of pale pink or purple flowers. Zones 7–10.

Allium stellatum

GLADE ONION, PRAIRIE ONION

☼/◐ ❄ ↔ 1–2 in (2.5–5 cm) ↑ 18 in (45 cm)

Perennial from central North America. Its 2 to 6 green flat leaves die back at flowering time. Blooms summer–autumn; flowers pinkish rose. *Stellatum* means starry and describes the flowers. Naturalizes easily. Zones 5–9.

AMARYLLIS

BELLADONNA LILY, JERSEY LILY, MARCH LILY, NAKED LADIES

This once large genus has now been reduced to just one species, an autumn-flowering bulb native to South Africa. It is the type genus for the ama-ryllis (Amaryllidaceae) family. Belladonna means "beautiful lady." Dormant for most of the warmer months, sturdy red-tinted flower stems appear from late summer and grow quickly to as much as 24 in (60 cm) tall. They are topped with heads of flowers in shades from very pale pink to deep magenta. Long strappy leaves soon follow.

CULTIVATION: Plant the bulbs with their tops exposed in a warm sunny location and water well from late summer to encourage flower production. They can withstand considerable drought when foliage is absent. Propagation is usually by division of established clumps once the foliage dies back.

Amaryllis belladonna

☼ ❄ ↔ 12–20 in (30–50 cm) ↑ 24 in (60 cm)

From South Africa's Cape region, this species forms clumps of glossy mid-green leaves to 20 in (50 cm) long. Foliage dies back from spring. Mildly scented, funnel-shaped flowers. 'Capetown', deep pink; 'Johannesburg', pale pink, white center; 'Major', deep pink, fragrant; and 'Purpurea', purple-pink. Zones 8–10.

Allium regelii

AMORPHOPHALLUS

This fascinating genus of the arum (Araceae) family of some 170 species occurs in tropical regions from West Africa eastwards to Polynesia. Most species are found in disturbed vegetation, in open savannahs, and limestone outcrops, very few in dense forests. Altitude ranges from sea level to 9,840 ft (3,000 m), and they flower with the onset of the wet season. All are terrestrial herbaceous perennials with underground tubers or fleshy stems. Plants may be small to massive, with a single leaf, rarely 2, produced from the stem and usually lasting only one season. The leaf stalk is generally cylindrical, ranging from green to purple, or blotchy. Inflorescences vary in shape, size, and color, but are composed of a spadix encircled by a spathe. Being pollinated by various bees or flies, the inflorescences emit odors that can be pleasant or disgusting to the human nose.

CULTIVATION: Propagate from seed or by division of fleshy stems or branching tubers. Some succeed in temperate climates but most require warmth and regulated wet and dry periods to flower. Too much moisture in the leafless stage can cause rotting.

Amaryllis belladonna

Amorphophallus bulbifer ★

☼ ☂ ↔ 5 ft (1.5 m) ↑ 3 ft (0.9 m)

Occurs in India, Bangladesh, Bhutan, and Nepal. Has a tuber up to 6 in (15 cm) in diameter, producing 1 to 2 leaves, leaf stalk smooth, fleshy, dark green, mottled with whitish pink spots. The inflorescence stalk is 4–27 in (10–70 cm) long, spathe oval to boat-shaped, 12 in (30 cm) long, outside grayish green with blackish green spots, inside at base dark pink, paler towards the top. The spadix is roughly the same length as the spathe. Zone 12.

Amorphophallus titanum

syn. *Amorphophallus selebicus*

TITAN ARUM

☼ ☂ ↔ 25 ft (8 m) ↑ 17–20 ft (5–6 m)

Huge species, tuber weighing up to 165 lb (75 kg), occurring in secondary forests in open situations and other aspects, up to 3,940 ft (1,200 m) altitude, on Sumatra. Leaf stalk up to 17 ft (5 m) tall, leaf blade up to 25 ft (8 m) across, divided, glossy green, leathery. Inflorescence short-stalked. Spathe vase-shaped to 6 ft (1.8 m) long, margin serrated and pleated, pale green outside, purplish brown inside. Spadix 3–10 ft (0.9–3 m) long. Large berries. Zones 9–12.

ANEMONELLA

Native to eastern North America, the single species in this genus, of the buttercup (Ranunculaceae) family, is a perennial herb with smooth tuberous roots. In spring, 2 to 5 flowers appear on thin stalks, with 5 to 10 sepals and numerous spreading, petal-like, white stamens but no corolla.

CULTIVATION: Heat tolerant but hardy to cold temperatures, preferring shade. Soil should be humus-rich and moist. Plant from containers in early spring, and water until established. Requires little maintenance thereafter and can be cut to ground level in winter. Propagate from seed when fresh or by division every 3 to 5 years during autumn.

Anemonella thalictroides
CROWFOOT, RUE ANENOME

☀ ❄ ↔ 3–6 in (8–15 cm) ↕ 4–10 in (10–25 cm)

This tuberous-rooted perennial comes from eastern North America. It has delicate 3-lobed leaflets and single white to pale pink flowers. *A. t. f. rosea* has pale pink flowers; **'Oscar Schoaf'** (syns 'Rosea Plena', 'Schoaf's Double Pink') also with pale pink flowers. *A. t.* **'Betty Blake'**, has cream flowers. Zones 4–8.

ARISAEMA

This genus of about 150 tuberous perennials in the arum (Araceae) family is found in Africa, North America, and Asia, usually in shade or woodland. Ornamental leaves and stems and bizarre flowers. Leaves may be compound or divided and stems are often mottled in pink to purplish shades. Large hooded flower spathes may be yellow, green, brown, red, or pink; striped or mottled. They surround the spadix, a central column of small true flowers. Orange-red berries form on the spadix.

CULTIVATION: Grow frost-tolerant species in shelter, part-shade, or woodland in cool peaty soil. Mulch in winter. Greenhouse-grown tropical species need a deep pot in a mix of leaf mold, grit, and slightly acid loam. Propagate from seed or by division of tubers.

Amorphophallus titanum

Arisaema consanguineum

☀ ❄ ↔ 12 in (30 cm) ↕ 36 in (90 cm)

From Himalayas and central China. A single leaf of 11 to 20 radiating leaflets to 16 in (40 cm) long. Spathe has long slightly drooping point, green and purple with narrow stripes. Flowers in early summer. Zones 7–10.

Arisaema ringens
syn. *Arisaema praecox*

☀ ❄ ↔ 12 in (30 cm) ↕ 12 in (30 cm)

From Japan, China, and Korea. Has two leaves each with 3 broad leaflets. The spathe is small, green and purple with white stripes, and remains in a curled position enclosing the spadix. Flowers are seen in early spring. Zones 7–10.

Arisaema sikokianum

☀ ❄ ↔ 18 in (45 cm) ↕ 18 in (45 cm)

From Japan. Two leaves with 3 to 5 leaflets with toothed margins. Upright spathe has a purple exterior, paler and striped inside. The spadix is prominent, white, club-shaped. Flowers appear in early summer. Zones 5–9.

Arisaema ringens

Arisaema speciosum
COBRA LILY

☀ ❄ ↔ 18 in (45 cm) ↕ 24–36 in (60–90 cm)

Native to Nepal and southwestern China. A single leaf with large leaflets flushed red at the margins. Mottled purple stems. Large hooded spathe, dark purple with white stripes. Spadix has a long thread-like appendage. Flowers in early summer. Zones 8–10.

Arisaema triphyllum
INDIAN TURNIP, JACK-IN-THE-PULPIT

☀ ❄ ↔ 18 in (45 cm) ↕ 12–24 in (30–60 cm)

From eastern North America. Has two leaves with 3 pointed leaflets. Spathe hooded, green to purple, striped green or white. Summer-flowering. Zones 4–9.

ARUM

Found from western Europe to the Himalayas and centered around the Mediterranean, this genus contains about 26 species of tuberous-rooted perennials, commonly known as lilies but actually of the arum (Araceae) family, of which it is the type genus. Lustrous dark green leaves, sometimes with lighter marbling, tend to be arrowhead-shaped and usually die away in summer or autumn. Inflorescence consists of a spathe ranging from green to yellow, dull purple or almost black with a cream to purplish spadix. Clustered berries, usually bright orange-red, follow flowers. The unpleasant scent and dark purple-red color of many arums mimics rotting flesh, attracts pollinating flies—unpleasant but effective.

CULTIVATION: Arums are best grown in half-sun in a temperate climate with cool humus-rich soil that remains moist over the summer. Propagation is by division when plants are dormant; new stocks can be raised from seed.

Arum italicum

☼/◐ ✳ ↔ 12–16 in (30–40 cm) ↑ 10–12 in (25–30 cm)

From southern and western Europe and North Africa. Leaves arrowhead-shaped, glossy deep green, often lighter marbled, dying back in late spring. Large pale green spathe, deep cream spadix. 'Marmoratum' ★, gray-green mottling. Zones 6–10.

Arum maculatum

CUCKOO PINT, JACK-IN-THE-PULPIT, LORDS AND LADIES

☼/◐ ✳ ↔ 8–16 in (20–40 cm) ↑ 10 in (25 cm)

European species with long-stemmed arrow-head-shaped leaves up to 8 in (20 cm) long. Purple-pink spadix, long pale green spathe. Orange-red fruit. Zones 6–9.

BABIANA

BABOON FLOWER

Genus of about 60 species of spring-flowering, cormous plants from the iris (Iridaceae) family. Most are native to southern Africa where they grow in coastal habitats. Leaves are lance-shaped, ribbed and hairy in some species. Funnel-shaped flowers, some scented, are borne on short spikes and range from white, cream, and yellow to rich pink, red, purple, and blue. Baboons eat the corms of some species.
CULTIVATION: Plant corms about 6 in (15 cm) deep in a warm position in well-drained soil. Plant deeper in cooler areas; mulch in winter or lift corms in autumn. Propagate from seed or offsets.

Babiana ringens

syn. *Antholyza ringens*

☼ ❀ ↔ 4 in (10 cm) ↑ 6–10 in (15–25 cm)

From Cape Peninsula in South Africa. Narrow lance-shaped leaves. Flowering spikes branched, densely packed with red funnel-shaped flowers with yellow lower lobes appear from late winter into spring. Zones 9–11.

Babiana rubrocyanea ★

RED-EYED BABOON FLOWER, WINE CUPS

☼ ❀ ↔ 4 in (10 cm) ↑ 6–12 in (15–30 cm)

From South Africa. Leaves ribbed, slightly hairy. Spirally arranged, funnel-shaped, blue flowers, dark red throats. Zones 9–11.

Babiana stricta

BABOON FLOWER

☼ ✳ ↔ 4 in (10 cm) ↑ 6–12 in (15–30 cm)

Babiana rubrocyanea

From southwestern South Africa, this is the most commonly grown species in the genus. Fan of ribbed hairy leaves. Spikes of pink to purplish blue to red cup-shaped flowers, in spirals, sometimes scented, in late spring. Cultivars include: 'Purple Star', dark reddish purple flowers with white stripes; 'White King', white blooms flushed pale blue; 'Zwanenburg Glory', violet flowers with pale blotches and darker throat. Zones 8–11.

BELAMCANDA

There are 2 species of short-lived rhizomatous perennials in this genus in the iris (Iridaceae) family, found across a wide area of Asia. Leaves are sword-like and arranged in fans. Flowers have 6 equal-sized flaring petals. Fruiting capsules split to reveal large black seeds. Some botanists suggest that they are better classified in the genus *Iris*.
CULTIVATION: Grow in sun or light shade in well-drained soil. Water well during the growing period. In cooler climates provide a protective mulch in winter. Propagate from seed or by division.

Belamcanda chinensis ★

syn. *Iris pampaninii*

BLACKBERRY LILY, LEOPARD LILY

☼ ✳ ↔ 12 in (30 cm) ↑ 36 in (90 cm)

Short-lived perennial found from far eastern Russia to Japan. Deciduous sword-like leaves. Borne on loose spikes, the flowers have 6 narrow flaring petals from yellow to orange, usually speckled crimson. Zones 8–10.

BLANDFORDIA

CHRISTMAS BELLS

Blandfordia is a genus of 4 species of erect, perennial, lily-like herbs from eastern Australia in many habitats, often swampy, and usually acid and sandy. Originally part of lily (Liliaceae) family, but now in the Blandfordiaceae family. Narrow, tough, grass-like leaves. Flowers 6-lobed, tubular, waxy, pendent and bell-like, hence the common name. Fruits are cylindrical and 3-celled, with each containing numerous, small, brown seeds.
CULTIVATION: Grow Christmas bells in constantly moist to wet, well-draining, sandy or acid, organic soil. Propagate from seed; often slow to germinate.

Belamcanda chinensis

Blandfordia grandiflora

CHRISTMAS BELLS

☀ ❄ ↔ 10 in (25 cm) ↑ 32 in (80 cm)

Found in heathy coastal habitats in eastern Australia. The leaves are grass-like, 32 in (80 cm) long, minutely toothed. The flowers to 2½ in (6 cm) long, are waxy, red or orange with yellow lobes, and appear in summer. Zones 8–10.

BRODIAEA

This genus of about 15 species of cormous plants is a member of the onion (Alliaceae) family. Most are native to western North America, where they grow in grass, scrub, and open forest. Over the years the genus has been extensively revised and several former members are now described under *Triteleia* and *Dichelostemma*. *Brodiaea* species have grass-like foliage, which usually dies back at flowering time. The pink, blue, or purple flowers are borne in loose umbels on stems ranging from 2–30 in (5–75 cm) tall and are bell-shaped or-flaring.

CULTIVATION: Grow in a light fertile soil in full sun. Plant closely for best flowering display. Keep moist during growth period but allow to dry out when dormant as corms are susceptible to rot. Provide a protective layer of mulch in winter in frosty areas, or-grow in pots in the greenhouse. Propagate by division of corms, removal of offsets, or from seed.

Brodiaea coronaria

syns *Brodiaea grandiflora*, *Hookera coronaria*

HARVEST BRODIAEA

☀ ❄ ↔ 4 in (10 cm) ↑ 12 in (30 cm)

From California and northwestern USA. Loose umbels of up to 12 purplish blue starry flowers are borne in late spring and into summer. Zones 8–10.

BRUNSVIGIA

There are about 20 species of bulbous plants in this genus, which is a member of the amaryllis (Amaryllidaceae) family. They are native to South Africa, where they grow in a variety of soils but all have a dormant period during the summer. They resemble amaryllis plants, to which they are closely related. The leaves are long and strap-like, and from late summer to autumn showy heads of pink to red, funnel-shaped, lily-like flowers are borne on tall stems. The bulbs can grow very large and usually take several years to flower.

CULTIVATION: In frost-free climates grow in well-drained soil in full sun in a position that is dry during the period of their summer dormancy. In colder areas grow in pots under glass. Bulbs should be planted almost on the soil surface. Water in autumn to bring bulbs into growth. Propagate from offsets in late summer or from seed in-autumn.

Brunsvigia orientalis ★

CANDELABRA FLOWER

☀ ❄ ↔ 18 in (45 cm) ↑ 20 in (50 cm)

From South Africa. Subterranean bulb producing strap-shaped leaves. Sturdy stems bear large umbels of pink to crimson narrow-petalled flowers. Zones 9–11.

Brunsvigia orientalis, in the wild, South Africa

BULBINELLA

This genus of 20 species of fleshy-rooted deciduous perennials is a member of the asphodel (Asphodelaceae) family. The majority are native to South Africa, but 6 are from New Zealand. They form clumps of long somewhat fleshy leaves. Yellow flowers are borne on tall stems in spikes.

CULTIVATION: Grow in sun or part-shade in free-draining but moisture-retentive soil that is neutral or slightly acidic. They are also suitable for growing in pots in the greenhouse. They dislike humidity. Propagate from seed or by root division.

Bulbinella hookeri

☀ ❄ ↔ 24 in (60 cm) ↑ 36 in (90 cm)

From alpine areas of New Zealand. Strap-like leaves. Spikes of starry yellow flowers in summer. Winter dormant. Zones 8–10.

Bulbinella latifolia ★

☀ ❄ ↔ 24 in (60 cm) ↑ 36 in (90 cm)

From South Africa. Narrow strappy leaves. Spikes of yellow to deep orange flowers from winter to late spring. Summer dormant. Propagate by root division. Zones 8–10.

CALADIUM

ANGEL WINGS, ELEPHANT EARS

This genus of 7 species of deciduous tuberous perennials from tropical America belongs to the arum (Araceae) family. The leaves, attractively splashed or veined with white or brilliant shades of pink and red, and up to 18 in (45 cm) long, are arrow-or heart-shaped and held above the stalks. The arum-like flowers are not considered to be of ornamental significance.

CULTIVATION: They thrive in tropical and warm climates. Grow outdoors in a moist but well-drained fertile soil, in a shady position. In colder climates grow in pots indoors. Use a moist, free-draining, coarse potting mix, and place in bright but not direct sunlight. Maintain high humidity. Water and feed regularly until leaves fade in autumn, then dry out for dormancy. The first leaves to appear each year may not show the colorful markings.

Caladium bicolor 'Scarlet Pimpernel'

Caladium bicolor

syns *Caladium × hortulanum, C. marmoratum, C. picturatum*
ANGEL WINGS, ELEPHANT EARS

☀ ⬩ ↔ 12 in (30 cm) ↑ 24 in (60 cm)

From the Amazon region of Brazil. Large green arrow-shaped leaves are irregularly splashed with varying amounts of white, pink, and red. Extensively bred to produce an extremely wide range of color forms, including: **'Carolyn Whorton'**, bright pink blotches, red veining, dark green at edges; **'Festiva'**, transparent red with green veining; **'Fire Chief'**, crimson heart, red veining, green margins; **'Kathleen'**, bright salmon heart, green margins; **'Lord Derby'**, transparent rose, dark veins, green margins; **'Mrs F. M. Joyner'**, white flushed with pink, dark red veins, and light green margins; **'Red Flash'**, bright red heart, red veining, dull green margins; **'Red Frill'** ★, deep red center becoming darker red toward the green margins; **'Rosebud'**, pink heart fading to white, pink veining, green margins; **'Scarlet Pimpernel'**, red heart, red veining, cream to light green margins; and **'White Christmas'**, white with green veining. Zones 10–12.

CALOCHORTUS

CAT'S EAR, FAIRY LANTERNS, MARIPOSA

This genus of about 60 species of hardy bulbous perennials belongs to the lily (Liliaceae) family. Natives of North America, they grow in perfectly drained areas in grassland, scrub, and forest, and from low to high altitudes. The leaf base is sword-shaped. Flowers vary greatly—some are dainty, others flamboyant; they may be pendulous and globe-shaped or upright and open. All have 2 distinct whorls of 3 colorful outer sepals and 3 inner petals. At the base of each petal is a nectar gland, often prominently displayed. Flowers are colored white, yellow, orange, red, or purple, and are often marked with red or chocolate brown.
CULTIVATION: Cultivation requirements vary. Difficult to grow. In general, they require a sheltered position in full sunlight or half sun and a gritty soil with excellent drainage. They are averse to humidity, preferring wet-winter dry-summer climates.

Calochortus amoenus

ROSE FAIRY LANTERN, SIERRA GLOBE TULIP

☀ ✳ ↔ 6 in (15 cm) ↑ 18 in (45 cm)

From central and southern California. Nodding flowers of deep rose pink or purple form on slender stems from spring–summer. Flowers narrowly bell-shaped or more globose. Zones 5–9.

Calochortus luteus

GOLD NUGGETS, YELLOW MARIPOSA TULIP

☀ ✳ ↔ 6 in (15 cm) ↑ 8–20 in (20–50 cm)

From central California. Slender stems carry bell-shaped yellow flowers, up to 3 in (8 cm) wide, usually with a brown spot at the base of each petal. Nectar gland is crescent-shaped. Zones 5–9.

Calochortus superbus

PROUD MARIPOSA

☀/☀ ✳ ↔ 6 in (15 cm) ↑ 16–24 in (40–60 cm)

Native to California. Bears bell-shaped white or cream flowers, streaked with purple, each petal with a maroon spot at the base surrounded by yellow. Outer petals lance-shaped, inner petals rounded and slightly hairy. Nectar gland is V-shaped. Zones 5–9.

CAMASSIA

CAMAS, QUAMASH

This genus consists of 5 species of bulbs in the sisal (Agavaceae) family, native primarily to western North America. The name comes from the Native American name, which is usually transliterated as quamash. They are tough and adaptable and one species, *C. leichtlinii*, has been extensively developed into garden forms. They have long narrow leaves and in late spring and early summer produce heads of 6-petalled flowers atop strong stems, reminiscent of some of the *Agapanthus*.
CULTIVATION: Mostly frost hardy and easily grown in any fertile, well-drained soil that does not dry out. Plant in full or half-sun. May be raised from seed but then take up to 5 years to bloom, and as most garden plants are cultivars, division when dormant during winter is preferred.

Calochortus luteus

Camassia leichtlinii

☀/☀ ✳ ↔ 20–60 in (50–150 cm) ↑ 24–48 in (60–120 cm)

Found from British Columbia in Canada to California, USA. Rather stiff green leaves to 24 in (60 cm) long. Short racemes on tall stems. Flowers creamy white to lavender-blue. **'Semiplena'**, semi-double cream to yellow flowers. *C. l.* subsp. *suksdorfii* is a widespread blue-flowered subspecies, of which **'Alba'** is a white-flowered cultivar and **'Blauwe Donau'** ('Blue Danube') has dark blue flowers. Zones 3–9.

Camassia quamash

CAMASH, CAMOSH, SWAMP SEGO

☀/☀ ✳ ↔ 16–40 in (40–100 cm) ↑ 12–32 in (30–80 cm)

Found over much of western USA. Slightly blue-green leaves to 20 in (50 cm) long. Flower racemes about one-third of the flower stem length. The pale blue to deep violet, rarely white, flowers grow to a width of over 2 in (5 cm). Zones 5–9.

CARDIOCRINUM

GIANT LILY

Found from the Himalayas to Japan. This lily (Liliaceae) family genus has just 3 species of bulbs that develop rapidly after winter dormancy, producing a clump of large, fleshy, heart-shaped leaves from which emerge tall flower stems that are usually in bloom before the summer solstice. Flowers are funnel-shaped, sometimes fragrant, and usually clustered near stem tips. Large seed pods follow. Giant lilies are equally impressive as foliage plants.
CULTIVATION: Best suited to woodland conditions in temperate climates where winters are not severe. Plant in fertile, moist, humus-rich, well-drained soil in bright shade or dappled sunlight. The bulb dies after flowering but produces several offsets. These bloom within 3 to 4 years and are a quicker way of securing flowers than raising seedlings, which can take 5 to 7 years to reach flowering age.

Cardiocrinum giganteum ★

HIMALAYAN GIANT LILY

☀/☀ ❄ ↔ 3–5 ft (0.9–1.5 m) ↕ 7–15 ft (2–4.5 m)
From Himalayan region to Myanmar and China. Leaves to 18 in (45 cm) long and nearly as wide. Leafy flower stems, very sturdy at the base, with fragrant, purple-red striped or flecked cream flowers, up to 8 in (20 cm) long. *C. g.* var. *yunnanense* from western and central China has green-tinted flowers. Zones 7–9.

CHASMANTHE

There are 3 species of cormous plants in this genus, which belongs to the iris (Iridaceae) family. Native to South Africa, they are closely related to *Crocosmia* and *Tritonia*. Sword-shaped leaves are arranged in fans. They flower in late winter to spring, bearing spikes of yellow, orange, or red tubular flowers. May, in sunny well-drained situations, prove moderately frost tolerant.
CULTIVATION: Easily grown in warm climates where they clump quickly and can become weedy. Grow in a warm sunny position in a well-drained soil. Propagate from seed or from offsets.

Chasmanthe aethiopica

syn. *Chasmanthe vittigera*
AFRICAN CORN FLAG

☀/☀ ❧ ↔ 5–7 in (12–18 cm) ↕ 16–27 in (40–70 cm)
From coastal South Africa, this plant grows from large corms that are renewed annually. The bright green lance-like leaves are arranged in fans, forming dense clumps. Bright vermilion-red flowers, held in single file on straight thrusting stems, in winter–early spring. Nectar enjoyed by honey-eating birds. Zones 9–11.

Chasmanthe floribunda

☀ ❧ ↔ 12 in (30 cm) ↕ 2–4 ft (0.6–1.2 m)
From Western Cape, South Africa. A fan of sword-shaped leaves often with a silky sheen. Orangey red flowers with yellow striping, arranged in 2 rows on stems to 4 ft (1.2 m) tall, during winter and spring. Zones 9–11.

CHIONODOXA

GLORY OF THE SNOW

These small, bulbous, summer-dormant plants are members of the hyacinth (Hyacinthaceae) family. In their native mountainous habitats of Crete, Cyprus, and western Turkey they bloom in early summer as the last snows melt. In milder climates the display is likely to be in early spring. Either way their clear colors, perky star-shaped flowers, and glossy emerald green leaves have great appeal. The bulbs are small and dressed in brown tunics.
CULTIVATION: Easily grown in half-sun and at lower altitudes and higher temperatures than those found in their native range. They require good drainage, an open situation, and some degree of frost. Divide the established clumps and gather the offsets in autumn and plant into gritty soil in a sunny position. Sow the seed during autumn into trays or beds containing a sandy mix. Germination takes place during the winter months.

Chionodoxa forbesii

syn. *Scilla forbesii*
☀ ❄ ↔ 4–8 in (10–20 cm) ↕ 3–8 in (8–20 cm)
From the mountains of western Turkey. Bears a few sparse leaves that reach 3–10 in (8–25 cm). Erect stems carry up to 12 downturned flowers. Slightly recurved petals, about ¾ in (18 mm) wide, are intensely blue with white central markings. Bulging white tubes. Cultivars include the well-known large but pale 'Pink Giant' ★. Zones 4–9.

Chionodoxa luciliae

syns *Chionodoxa gigantea, Scilla luciliae*
☀ ❄ ↔ 3–6 in (8–15 cm) ↕ 4–6 in (10–15 cm)
From mountains of western Turkey. Produces soft violet-blue flowers with small white central zone. Production, when climate and season suits, is prolific. Leaves, often slightly recurved, reach 3–8 in (8–20 cm) long. 'Alba', white petals; 'Gigantea', grows to 8 in (20 cm) high; 'Rosea', pinkish petals. Zones 4–9.

Chasmanthe aethiopica

Colchicum cilicicum

COLCHICUM

AUTUMN CROCUS, MEADOW SAFFRON, NAKED LADIES

A genus of around 45 species of corms that is the type genus for the family Colchicaceae. They are found from eastern Europe to North Africa and eastwards to China. They are not related to the true crocuses, but the name autumn crocus is an apt description of the habit and appearance of many of the species. The plants are dormant and leafless in summer. The flowers have 6 petals, in 2 whorls, and start to appear from early autumn before the foliage develops, or in spring. Double-flowered forms are available. *Colchicum* species are famous as the source of the cancer treatment drug colchicine, a mutagen that affects cell division. Colchicine is sometimes used to produce new plant cultivars.
CULTIVATION: Hardy, adaptable, and great favorites of rock garden enthusiasts, autumn crocuses thrive in zones with distinct seasons. Some need a hot dry summer to flower well but most like any fertile well-drained soil in full or half-sun. They do well in containers.

Colchicum autumnale
☼/◑ ❋ ↔6–16 in (15–40 cm) ↑6–10 in
(15–25 cm)
Late summer- to autumn-flowering species from western and central Europe. Long, white-tubed, purple-pink flowers, yellow anthers. Later, narrow to broad lance-shaped leaves. 'Alboplenum', white double flowers; 'Album', small white flowers; 'Plenum', lavender-pink double flowers. Zones 5–9.

Colchicum byzantinum
☼/◑ ❋ ↔6–16 in (15–40 cm) ↑6–12 in (15–30 cm)
From Turkey, Syria, and Lebanon. Lush, bright green, pleated leaves, in spring, to 12 in (30 cm) long. In autumn, soft lavender-pink flowers with long white tubes, pale brown anthers, purple-red stigma. Possibly a natural hybrid. Zones 6–9.

Colchicum cilicicum
☼/◑ ❋ ↔6–16 in (15–40 cm) ↑6–12 in (15–30 cm)
Native to Turkey, Syria, and Lebanon. Large lavender-pink to purple flowers on strong white stems. Yellow anthers. Bright green leaves to 16 in (40 cm) long emerge in spring. Zones 6–9.

Colchicum speciosum
☼/◑ ❋ ↔6–16 in (15–40 cm) ↑4–8 in (10–20 cm)
Found from northern Turkey westward to Iran and northward to Russia. In autumn, pale-centered bright mauve-pink flowers with sturdy stems. Golden-yellow anthers. In spring, broad, bright green, slightly arched leaves to 10 in (25 cm) long. 'Album', large, green-throated, white flowers. Zones 6–9.

Colchicum 'The Giant'
☼ ❋ ↔8 in (20 cm) ↑10 in (25 cm)
Large white-mottled lilac-pink flowers on strong stems, in autumn. Probably a hybrid with *C. bivonae*. Zones 6–9.

Colchicum 'Waterlily' ★
☼ ❋ ↔8 in (20 cm) ↑8 in (20 cm)
Large and very fully double flowers on fairly short stems. Probably a hybrid with a *C. autumnale* cultivar. Zones 6–9.

CONVALLARIA

LILY-OF-THE-VALLEY

Lily-of-the-valley has been cultivated since at least 1000 BCE. Belonging to the family Ruscaceae, the sole species in the genus is a low spreading perennial found over much of the northern temperate zone. Its vigorous rhizomes can colonize a large area and in spring produce bright green lance-shaped leaves and short-stemmed white flowerheads of bell-shaped blooms (there is a form with pale pink flowers), followed by red berries. It contains glycoside compounds used in heart medications.
CULTIVATION: Plant in dappled shade in moist, well-drained soil. A cool winter is needed for proper dormancy. Propagate by division.

Convallaria majalis

Convallaria majalis
◑/☼ ❋ ↔12–40 in (30–100 cm) ↑4–8 in (10–20 cm)
Fragrant waxy flowers in spring–early summer. *C. m.* var. *rosea*, small pale pink flowers, not as vigorous as white-flowered species. *C. m.* cultivars with variegated foliage include 'Albostriata', dark leaves with white to cream longitudinal stripes; 'Aureovariegata' (syn. 'Striata'), gold stripes; 'Aureomarginata', cream-to yellow-edged leaves; 'Hardwick Hall', broad leaves with pale margins; and 'Prolificans', unusually shaped flowers. Zones 3–9.

CRINUM

There are about 130 species of evergreen and deciduous bulbous plants in this genus, which belongs to the amaryllis

(Amaryllidaceae) family. They are found in tropical and subtropical zones, usually in coastal areas. The bulbs are large and the leaves broad and long, to 3 ft (0.9 m) or more. Thick flowering stems support large trumpet-shaped flowers with flaring lobes, narrow and spidery in some species. The flowers may be white or in shades of pink or rose, and are often fragrant.
CULTIVATION: In cool areas grow in pots in the conservatory or greenhouse. Elsewhere grow in a sheltered sunny or semi-shaded position in well-drained soil. Bulbs dislike being transplanted and take time to become established. Propagate from seed and offsets. Seed-grown plants take 3 years to flower.

Crinum asiaticum

POISON BULB

☀ ❄ ↔ 3 ft (0.9 m) ↕ 3–5 ft (0.9–1.5 m)

From tropical Asia. Large long-necked bulbs. Very leafy plant with broad bluish green leaves to 4 ft (1.2 m) long. Thick flowering stems bear heads of 20 to 30 fragrant white flowers with narrow spidery petals and long red stamens. *C. a.* var. *sinicum* (syn. *C. pedunculatum),* from Australia and some Pacific Islands, has larger leaves and taller flowering stems. Zones 10–12.

Crinum bulbispermum

syn. *Crinum longifolium*

☀ ❄ ↔ 3 ft (0.9 m) ↕ 3 ft (0.9 m)

A popular South African species. Large long-necked bulb. Tidy, channeled, arching leaves. Large, funnel-shaped, vibrant, fragrant flowers come in white, or in various shades of pink, with a dramatic red streak on each of the petals. Zones 7–10.

Crinum 'Ellen Bosanquet'

☀ ❄ ↔ 2–3 ft (0.6–0.9 m) ↕ 2–3 ft (0.6–0.9 m)

A hybrid of *C. moorei* and *C. zeylanicum*. Tidy foliage with soft slightly arching leaves. Heads of large, trumpet-shaped, rose red flowers in summer. Zones 7–12.

Crinum moorei

☀ ❄ ↔ 4–5 ft (1.2–1.5 m) ↕ 4–5 ft (1.2–1.5 m)

From South Africa. Extremely large long-necked bulb. Long, broad, rather untidy deciduous leaves. Tall flowering stems bear 6 to 12 fragrant, pale pink, trumpet-shaped flowers in summer. Zones 8–11.

Crinum × powellii

☀ ❄ ↔ 4 ft (1.2 m) ↕ 4 ft (1.2 m)

A hybrid of *C. moorei* and *C. bulbispermum*, thought to be of garden origin. Large long-necked bulb. Broad, upright, channeled leaves. Trumpet-shaped flowers of pink or white are borne on tall stems in clusters of 8 to 10. The popular cultivar **'Album'** has pure white flowers. Zones 7–10.

CROCOSMIA

FALLING STARS, MONTBRETIA

The iris (Iridaceae) family species in this genus come from the grasslands of tropical and South Africa. Their very handsome appearance, trouble-free lifestyles, vivid flowers, and erect lance-like leaves make them popular in cultivation. The leaves reach heights of 24–40 in (60–100 cm) and form dense clumps. They can be pleated and/or ribbed, and vary from pale green to mid-green to a brownish shade. The funnel-shaped flowers are held on long, wiry, often branching stems and appear in mid- to late summer. The plants are fully dormant in winter. The corms are disc-like, ivory white, and about 2½ in (6 cm) in diameter.
CULTIVATION: Sun, water, reasonably good drainage, and the regular division of overcrowded corms are the principal requirements of these tough but very attractive plants.

Crocosmia aurea

☀ ❄ ↔ 24–32 in (60–80 cm) ↕ 32–40 in (80–100 cm)

From streambeds, wet woodlands, and shady gorges. Tolerates shade. Flowers, held in double rows on erect sometimes branched spikes, range between burnt orange and chrome yellow. Leaves are papery and pale green. Zones 7–9.

Crinum bulbispermum

Crocosmia × crocosmiiflora

☀ ❄ ↔ 20–24 in (50–60 cm) ↕ 20–24 in (50–60 cm)

Robust hybrid between *C. aurea* and *C. pottsii*. Pale green leaves, arching branching flower stems. Sunny protected situations suit it best. Invasive in mild wet climates. **'Emily McKenzie'** (syn. 'Lady McKenzie'), grows to 24 in (60 cm), generous branched spikes of nodding dark orange flowers splashed with red; **'Solfatare'** (syn. 'Solphatare'), hybrid dating from the 1890s, yellow petals, smoky bronze papery leaves. Zones 5–10.

Crocosmia × crocosmiiflora

Crocosmia masoniorum

☀ ❄ ↔ 32–40 in (80–100 cm) ↑ 3–4 ft (0.9–1.2 m)

Robust plant from a mountainous habitat. Pleated mid-green leaves and single, arching stems of red-orange flowers. Likes moist sandy soils. 'Rowallane Yellow', yellow flowers. Zones 7–10.

Crocosmia Hybrid Cultivars

☀ ❄ ↔ 12–24 in (30–60 cm) ↑ 18–36 in (45–90 cm)

Many colorful, carefully selected, new and old named cultivars of much mixed parentage. Most bred for cool wet climates. All produce dense leaf-clumps and a generous supply of summer flowers. 'Citronella' (syn. 'Golden Fleece'), grows to 24 in (60 cm) high, mid-green leaves, yellow flowers with red-brown markings; 'Lucifer', large rich red flowers; 'Norwich Canary', orange buds open to bright yellow flowers with orange petal reverse; 'Star of the East' ★, large, light-centered, apricot pink to light orange flowers. Zones 7–10.

CROCUS

Genus of around 80 species of small, herbaceous, lily-like perennials in the iris (Iridaceae) family, found in a range of habitats from sea level to sub-alpine regions of central and southern Europe, northern Africa, central Asia, and western China. All have subterranean corms, from which inflorescences arise. Leaves are similar in shape but produced at different times: autumn-flowering species are leafless at flowering, growth returning in spring; spring-flowering species have leaves at flowering, and fruit is produced before winter. Flowers have a long tube originating from the top

Crocosmia masoniorum

of the corm and terminating in a colorful, tall, 6-segmented "flower." The ovary that forms the fruit is at the base of the floral tube. Seeds develop in the 3-celled capsular fruits.

CULTIVATION: Most grow over some years into compact clumps around 4–6 in (10–15 cm) in diameter. Plant bulbs 4 in (10 cm) apart or in widely spaced groups of more crowded bulbs. Propagate from seed, which germinates readily. Young seedlings should be kept in containers for 2 years before planting out.

Crocus chrysanthus

syns *Crocus annulatus*, *C. croceus*, *C. skorpilii*

☀ ❄ ↔ 4 in (10 cm) ↑ 2 in (5 cm)

Found in a range of habitats from Albania, Bulgaria, Greece, Macedonia, Serbia, Romania, and Turkey. Variable spring-flowering species, flowers fragrant, pale yellow to orange-yellow, sometimes striped bronze or purple on outer segments. Leaves 3 to 7, various lengths, gray-green. Many selections and hybrids. 'Blue Pearl' ★, flowers white, yellow throat, pale lilac-blue outer segments; 'E. A. Bowles', flowers deep lemon yellow, outer segments with bronze-green bases; 'Ladykiller', flowers white, deep purple markings on outer segments. Zones 6–8.

Crocus kotschyanus

syn. *Crocus zonatus*

☀ ❄ ↔ 4 in (10 cm) ↑ 3 in (8 cm)

Variable species from Russia, Turkey, Syria, and Lebanon. Flowers 1 to 2, white or bluish lilac, parallel veins darker, throat white or yellowish, sometimes hairy, in autumn. Leaves 4 to 6, not present at flowering, green. Corms upright or lying on side. Zones 6–8.

Crocus speciosus

☀ ❄ ↔ 3 in (8 cm) ↑ 4–6 in (10–15 cm)

From Russia, northern Iran, and Turkey. Widespread variable species. Flowers 1 to 2, fragrant, lilac-blue, darker veins present, exterior of segments often with silvery flush, throat whitish, in autumn. Leaves 3 to 5, emerging long after flowering, dark green. Zones 6–8.

Crocus tommasinianus ★

☀ ❄ ↔ 3 in (8 cm) ↑ 3–4 in (8–10 cm)

From Yugoslavia, Hungary, and Bulgaria. Flowers 1 to 2, in early spring, pale lilac to purple, often silvery or buff-colored on exterior segments, sometimes with darker purple on ends of segments, throat white. Leaves 3 to 4, equal in length to flowers, green with prominent longitudinal stripe. Zones 6–8.

Crocus vernus

DUTCH CROCUS

☀ ❄ ↔ 4 in (10 cm) ↑ 4–5 in (10–12 cm)

Most common *Crocus* species, found over much of Europe from Iberian Peninsula to western Russia. Flowers 1 to 2, in early spring, purple, lilac, white, striped darker in some populations. Leaves 2 to 4, mostly shorter than flowers. Zones 6–8.

Crocus speciosus

CYCLAMEN

ALPINE VIOLET, PERSIAN VIOLET, SOWBREAD

Distinctive in leaf and flower, the 19 species in this genus in the primrose (Primulaceae) family are tuberous perennials found in Europe in hills and mountains around the Mediterranean Sea and in western Asia. From flattened tubers, heart-shaped gray-green to blue-green leaves emerge, often patterned silver-gray. They bear one downward-facing flower per stem, in white or pink through purple to red, with reflexed petals. CULTIVATION: They need perfect drainage. Add some fibrous com-

Cyclamen hederifolium

post; plant tuber with its top at or just above soil level. Propagate from seed, as clumps flower better if left undivided.

Cyclamen cilicium

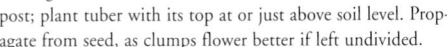 ❁ ↔ 6–8 in (15–20 cm) ↕ 3–4 in (8–10 cm)

From southwestern Turkey. Forms a neat clump of rounded heart-shaped leaves with toothed edges, green with silver-gray markings above, purple-red below. White to pale pink flowers, flushed deep pink, in autumn. Slightly twisted petals. Zones 7–9.

Cyclamen coum

syn. *Cyclamen atkinsii*

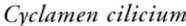 ❊ ↔ 6–12 in (15–30 cm) ↕ 4 in (10 cm)

From southeast Europe, the Caucasus, and the Middle East. Silver-gray and dark green-patterned, rounded, heart-shaped leaves with purple-red undersides. White, pink, or purple-pink flowers, darker at base. The leaves of the **Pewter Group** are strongly marked with silver-gray, including: '**Maurice Dryden**', green-edged silver leaves, white flowers; '**Tilebarn Elizabeth**', silver leaves with narrow green edges, pink flowers. Zones 6–9.

Cyclamen hederifolium

syn. *Cyclamen neapolitanum*

❊ ↔ 6–12 in (15–30 cm) ↕ 4 in (10 cm)

Found from southern Europe in to Turkey. Leaves from small to large, 2–6 in (5–15 cm) long, smooth-edged or serrated, overall dark green, or patterned silver-gray, green, or purple-red on undersides. Pale pink flowers. Often flowers with no foliage. Zones 6–9.

Cyclamen persicum

❊ ↔ 6–12 in (15–30 cm) ↕ 6–8 in (15–20 cm)

Native to the eastern Mediterranean, including Crete, Cyprus, and other islands, and also Libya. Variably colored and marked, heart-shaped leaves, serrated edges. White, mauve, or pink flowers, darker centers, in winter–spring. The florists' cyclamen was developed from this. Zones 9–10.

Cyclamen purpurascens

syn. *Cyclamen europaeum*

❊ ↔ 6–12 in (15–30 cm) ↕ 4–6 in (10–15 cm)

Central and eastern European species. Round leaves, bright to deep green, with variable silver-gray markings, red-tinted below. Strong-scented flowers in pink shades, rarely white, in late summer. **Silver Leafed Group** has strongly marked foliage. Zones 6–9.

Cyclamen repandum

❊ ↔ 6–12 in (15–30 cm) ↕ 4–6 in (10–15 cm)

Found around and on islands of the central and eastern Mediterranean. Broad, heart-shaped, dark green leaves, conspicuously scalloped and toothed, variable silver-gray markings above, purple-red below. Fragrant white to magenta flowers. Zones 7–10.

CYRTANTHUS

FIRE LILY

There are 47 evergreen or deciduous bulbous plants in this genus in the amaryllis (Amaryllidaceae) family. They are found in tropical and southern Africa, where they grow in a range of habitats.

Leaves form at the base of a loose rosette and are linear or strap-shaped. Funnel-shaped flowers, upright or pendulous, are usually borne in umbels on strong stems. Colors range from red and yellow to white. CULTIVATION: In warm areas can be grown in a sheltered situation with dappled shade, in well-drained sandy soil, but are best suited to pot culture. In cool areas grow under glass in indirect bright light. Water thoroughly and feed weekly when in growth. Propagate from seed or offsets.

Cyrtanthus elatus

Cyrtanthus elatus ★

syns *Cyrtanthus purpureus*, *Vallota speciosa*

GEORGE LILY, SCARBOROUGH LILY

❊ ↔ 12 in (30 cm) ↕ 18 in (45 cm)

Evergreen species from South Africa. Tall stems bear heads of 6 to 9 upright trumpet-shaped flowers of brilliant red. Zones 9–11.

Dahlia imperialis

Cyrtanthus mackenii

IFAFA LILY

❋ ✦ ↔ 12 in (30 cm) ↑ 12 in (30 cm)

From eastern Cape Province. A dainty plant with grass-like foliage, bearing fragrant, tubular, white or yellow flowers, narrow and curving, to 2 in (5 cm) long. *C. mackenii* blooms for long periods in spring–summer. Zones 9–11.

DAHLIA

There are around 30 species of tuberous-rooted perennials in this genus of the daisy (Asteraceae) family. From Mexico south to Colombia; in dwarf forms to tree-sized species that can grow to over 20 ft (6 m) high in one season. Most are immediately recognizable, with similar pinnate to tripinnate foliage, hollow cane-like stems and bright flowerheads. Wild species usually have single blooms; garden forms show many styles and colors. CULTIVATION: Full sun or partial shade with moist, fertile, humus-rich, well-drained soil. Tops die with first frosts, but provided the soil does not freeze or become waterlogged, tubers can be left in the ground for winter. Elsewhere, lift tubers, store in dry sand or sawdust in a frost-free place. Propagate small bedding strains from seed; divide tubers or take basal cuttings.

Dahlia coccinea

❂/❋ ❋ ↔ 2–4 ft (0.6–1.2 m) ↑ 7–10 ft (2–3 m)

From Mexico to Guatemala. This is one of main parents of the garden dahlias. Dark green, often purple-tinted, tripinnate leaves, toothed, pointed oval leaflets. Clusters of 2 to 3 flowerheads, with ray florets yellow through red to purple-red appear in summer–autumn. Zones 8–11.

Dahlia imperialis

TREE DAHLIA

❂/❋ ❋ ↔ 7–15 ft (2–4.5 m) ↑ 17–25 ft (5–8 m)

Found from Guatemala to Colombia. Huge bamboo-like stems. Many-flowered clusters of pink to lavender flowerheads. Blooms autumn–winter. Zones 8–11.

Dahlia merckii

❂/❋ ❋ ↔ 3 ft (0.9 m) ↑ 7 ft (2 m)

Mexican species. Leaves often finely divided and red-tinted. Clusters of delicate, upright or semi-pendulous, white to purple flowerheads from late summer. Zones 8–10.

Dahlia scapigera

❂/❋ ❋ ↔ 12–20 in (30–50 cm) ↑ 20 in (50 cm)

From Mexico. Very compact with foliage mostly in basal rosettes. Leaves with 3 to 7 pointed oval leaflets. Flowers usually borne singly, drooping, white to deep mauve. Zones 9–11.

Dahlia tenuicaulis

❂/❋ ❋ ↔ 3–7 ft (0.9–2 m) ↑ 10–15 ft (3–4.5 m)

Found in Mexico. Tree-like species. Leaves often bipinnate, with toothed, pointed, oval leaflets. Flowers, lilac pink to near magenta, in large clusters, with short rounded ray florets. Zones 9–11.

Dahlia Hybrid Cultivars

❂ ❋ ↔ 1–3 ft (30–90 cm) ↑ 1½–3 ft (0.5–0.9 m)

Although breeders are now trying to introduce other species into the mix, virtually all of our modern garden dahlias are *D. coccinea* × *D. pinnata* hybrids. This cross first appeared in Madrid, Spain, in 1789, not long after dahlias arrived in Europe from Mexico. Since that time, hybridizers have been able to produce a huge and remarkably dazzling range of garden plants.

Dahlias are divided into groups, based on the flower type; plant size and weather resistance also need to be considered. Large cultivars with huge intricate flowers are spectacular but rarely do well in open gardens exposed to the wind. Most dahlias reach their peak of bloom after the longest day and continue to flower until frost or winter cold intervenes. Zones 9–11.

The dahlia groups are as follows.

1. SINGLE-FLOWERED

This group comprises cultivars with simple wide-open single flowerheads. Usually small, they are often treated as summer bedding annuals. Larger forms may have 2 rows of ray florets but the disc florets are always present and clearly visible. 'Coltness Gem', dwarf bedding strain in several colors; and 'Yellow Hammer', bedding form, yellow flowers and contrasting bronze-green foliage.

2. ANEMONE-FLOWERED

Flowerheads have 1 or 2 rows of outer ray florets, sometimes slightly packed, similarly colored, tubular disc florets that often give the flowerhead a mounded center. 'Brio', orange scarlet with large group of disc florets, short reflexed rays; and 'Miss Saigon', dull orange to pink disc florets, reflexed pale pink rays.

3. COLLERETTE

Collerette flowerheads have 1 or 2 outer rows of flat ray florets, an inner row of short ray-like disc florets called the "collar," and a clear center or anther-bearing disc florets. 'Clair de Lune', yellow with a pale collar, is typical of the form.

4. WATERLILY

Fully double flowerheads with relatively few broad ray florets. They may be flat to slightly involute or revolute. (Involute florets are rolled along their length from underside to upperside; revolute florets are rolled the opposite way: upperside to underside.) This produces rather flat blooms lacking the high center that is characteristic of most double dahlias. Popular waterlily cultivars include 'Fascination', deep pink, semi-double flowers, dark foliage; 'Fürst Pückler', deep pinkish red, yellow flushed; 'Glorie van Heemstede', bright yellow double flowers; 'Nepos', white and lavender; and 'Vanessa', pale to deeper pink.

5. DECORATIVE

Double style, with no central disc, and broad, flat or slightly involute florets making a rounded head. In some classifications this group is subdivided into formal (very even petals that are neatly arranged) and informal (more open and less regular). The flowers are classified as giant, large, medium, small, or miniature depending upon their size. Giant flowers do not, however, necessarily mean giant plants: some of the largest flowers are borne on relatively small plants. 'Akita', dark red flushed with yellow; 'Arabian Night', a deep black-red turning red, and lightening with age; 'Audacity', an unusual combination of maroon with a light golden yellow center; 'Doris Duke', apricot-pink shade deepening at the center; 'Fiaker', light purple flowers; 'Formby Perfection', with magenta to lavender flowers; 'Orange Sun', bright orange flowers, flushed with red. 'Hamari Gold', giant flowers of deep golden amber; 'Hamilton Lillian', yellow- to apricot-pink; 'Hulin's Carnival', red, splashed white; 'Jennie', white to cream with a yellow center, flushed and edged with deep pink, fringed edges; 'Kelvin Floodlight', enormous bright yellow, fully double flowers; 'Pearl of Heensteded', pale pink, double flowers on thin stems; 'Peter', deep rose pink; 'Purple Joy', deep purple-red, darkening at the center; 'Santa Claus', fire engine red, edged in white; 'Stefan Bergerhof', bright orange; 'Suffolk Punch', deep purple; 'Tartan', white with deep purple markings; 'Ted's Choice', a deep purple-pink; 'Zingaro', cream with a yellow center, edged and flushed with a deep red-pink; and 'Zorro', with huge deep red flowers.

6. BALL

Ball-shaped flowerheads are globular but may be slightly flattened on top. Ray florets are broad, rounded at the tips and involute for half their length. They are divided by flower size into miniature, up to 4 in (10 cm) in diameter; small, 4–6 in (10–15 cm) in diameter; medium, 6–8 in (15–20 cm) in diameter; and large, over 8 in (20 cm) across. Popular ball cultivars include 'Black Pearl', deep maroon, almost black at center; 'Boy Scout', deep pink with a darker center; 'Charles Dickens', small pink flowers; 'Kathryn's Cupid', soft orange-pink double flowers; and 'Wootton Cupid', with dark pink flowers.

7. POMPON

Flowerheads nearly spherical. Similar to the ball style but with smaller flowers that give the impression of more tightly packed florets. Florets are involute for their entire length. Typical pompon cultivars include 'Aurwen's Violet', bright purple; 'Linos', bright yellow almost orange center; 'Lollipop', pinkish to mauve, outer ray florets ageing to pale pink; 'Mini Pompon Orange', orange, turning reddish in center; 'Night Queen', deepest black-red; and 'White Aster', evenly shaped, white flowers.

8. CACTUS

Fully double flowerheads with long quilled ray florets and no central disc. Quilling extends for at least half the length of the floret. Both cactus and semi-cactus forms are further subdivided into large- and small-flowered types and are available in a wide range of colors. Popular cultivars include 'Alfred Grille', yellow-centered turning deep pink to light red at the tips; 'Border Princess', with small orange and yellow flowers; 'Feuerwerk', a bright red with very narrow ray florets like a starburst firework in keeping with its name; 'Friquolett', fiery red with white tips; 'Hillcrest Royal', intense deep purple-red fully double flowers, with a strong quilted effect; 'Park Princess', bright pink with a yellow center, super reliable and often mass planted for effect; 'Wagschal's Goldkrone', golden yellow to light orange blooms.

Dahlia, Hybrid Cultivar, 6. Ball, 'Charles Dickens'

Dahlia, Hybrid Cultivar, 7. Pompon, 'White Aster'

Dahlia, Hybrid Cultivar, 8. Cactus, 'Border Princess'

9. SEMI-CACTUS

Not semi-double-flowered cactus forms, but fully double flowers with broad-based ray florets that are quilled for less than half their length. They may be straight or incurving. 'Aspen', white, somewhat twisted ray florets, yellowing toward the center; 'Color Magic', creamy yellow with irregular sectors, flakes and flecks of deep pink; 'Engelhardt's Jubiläum', deep golden yellow to light orange; 'Explosion', white to cream blooms with purple-red markings and center; 'Fürsten Elizabeth von Bismarck', cerise flowerheads; 'Golden Charmer', a golden yellow to pale orange; 'Goldener Reiner', golden yellow to light orange; 'Hamari Accord', a soft but bright yellow; 'Herzdame', orange, reddening at the tips, edges and center; 'Magic Moment', white, very full flowerheads; 'So Dainty', broad apricot-pink ray florets, with dark edges; 'Vulcan', orange-red with lighter tips; 'Wittemann's Best', bright red; and 'Wootton Impact', classic bronze in color.

10. MISCELLANEOUS

This is a catch-all group for the leftover species of dahlia that do not fit in the other groups. They are subdivided into several small groups. This group includes the very dwarf miniature cultivars. 'Bishop of Llandaff' is typical, with vivid red *Cosmos*-like flowerheads and deep red-tinted foliage; 'Jescot Julie', is a burnt orange, plum purple, orchid-flowering miniature.

DIERAMA

AFRICAN HAREBELL, ANGEL'S FISHING ROD, WAND FLOWER

From the high grasslands of southern Africa and Ethiopia, these perennial plants in the iris (Iridaceae) family form almost evergreen clumps of grassy gray-green foliage. Of the 40-plus species only a few are common in cultivation. Pendulous funnel-shaped flowers, in shades of wine red, pink, mauve, purple, and white, are held on long, graceful, arching, wiry stems and appear in summer. The corms, which are replaced annually, reproduce themselves one on top of another. Although these multitudinous corms often seem overcrowded, they are best left to sort themselves out as disturbance can be resented.

CULTIVATION: Open sunny sites and deep, rich, moist but well-drained soils suit them best, but keep well watered during early growth. Propagate from seed or by division. Some forms of *Dierama* can become weedy.

Dierama pulcherrimum

Dierama pulcherrimum

☼ ❋ ↔ 12 in (30 cm) ↕ 5 ft (1.5 m)

Graceful species from South Africa. Flowers bell-shaped, colors variable, commonly magenta pink, madder pink, rich sugary pinks, and deep purples. 'Album', pure white form. Zones 7–10.

ERANTHIS

WINTER ACONITE

In the wild these small tuberous plants from the buttercup (Ranunculaceae) family are found in the damp deciduous woodlands of Europe and Asia. In similar cool, damp, situations they colonize readily. The cupped golden flowers, each held on a single stem, are encircled with pronounced green "ruffs."

CULTIVATION: Transplant in early spring while the plants are in leaf; they can be temperamental if transplanted when dry during the summer months. Grow in moisture-retentive soil, with plenty of winter sun. Propagate by dividing the tubers or from seed.

Eranthis × tubergenii 'Guinea Gold'

☀ ❋ ↔ 3–4 in (8–10 cm) ↕ 4–8 in (10–20 cm)

A tough, vigorous, but sterile hybrid, product of *E. hyemalis* and *E. cilicica*. Given the right conditions, it quickly expands into decent-sized clumps. The flamboyant flowers are yellow, large, and held above bronzed "ruffs." Zones 5–8.

EREMURUS

DESERT CANDLE, FOXTAIL LILY

This genus of 40 to 50 species of fleshy-stemmed perennials belongs to the asphodel (Asphodelaceae) family. They are native to western and central Asia, where they grow in dry areas among rocks and in grassland. The statuesque plants form basal clumps of strap-shaped leaves and send up flower spikes to 10 ft (3 m) tall. The white, pink, or yellow flowers are borne in tapering spikes and resemble small starry lilies. Their prominently protruding stamens give the spike a soft fluffy appearance.

CULTIVATION: Grow in a rich, well-drained, sandy soil in sheltered position in full sun. Stake taller species. Protect from winter wet with mulch; remove before new growth emerges. Protect new growth from slugs and snails. Propagate from seed or divide carefully, avoiding damage to the fragile roots.

Eremurus himalaicus

☀ ❋ ↔ 30 in (75 cm) ↕ 36–48 in (90–120 cm)

From Afghanistan and northwestern Himalayas. One of the first species to flower in early summer. Narrow strap-shaped leaves. Bears dense heads of white, starry, lily-like flowers with protruding stamens in the late spring–summer. Zones 3–9.

Eremurus robustus

☀ ❋ ↔ 36–48 in (90–120 cm) ↕ 7–10 ft (2–3 m)

Native to Tajikistan, Kyrgyzstan, and Afghanistan. Vigorous species with leaves to 4 ft (1.2 m) long, often deciduous before flowering. Very showy densely packed spikes of pink flowers marked with brown and green in summer. Zones 6–9.

Eremurus Hybrid Cultivars

☼ ❋ ↔ 24–40 in (60–100 cm) ↑ 4–7 ft
(1.2–2 m)

Most *Eremurus* hybrids are free-flowering
and come in white and various shades of
pink, amber, orange, and yellow. '**Cleopatra**' ★, has deep orange flowers; **Erfo
Hybrids**, to 5–6 ft (1.5–1.8 m) tall, pastel
flowers; **Highdown Hybrids**, richly colored,
flowering in summer: '**Himrob**', pink flowers, late-flowering; **Ruiter Hybrids**, to 7 ft
(2 m), brightly colored: '**Moneymaker**',
pretty yellow flowers ageing to orange;
Shelford Hybrids, to 4 ft (1.2 m), richly
colored flowers in early summer. Zones 5–9.

ERYTHRONIUM

DOGTOOTH VIOLET, TROUT LILY

A member of the lily (Liliaceae) family,
this genus of bulbs is found in the wild in
North America, Asia, and across Europe;
some grow in a wide variety of habitats.
Flowers, held well above the leaves, hang
down, with distinctive, recurved, pointed
petals. The shiny leaves fan outward and, in many varieties,
are mottled, flecked, or spotted with silver, brown, maroon,
or bronze. This feature begins to fade as the season progresses.
CULTIVATION: Most thrive in cool damp climates and dappled
shade, but those from western North America can, if shaded, tolerate hot dry summers. None like humid heat; majority dislike
disturbance. Plant in autumn, keeping bulbs moist, about 2 in
(5 cm) below surface. To propagate, divide as leaves wilt, replanting immediately, or sow fresh seed in moisture-retentive soil.

Erythronium californicum

FAWN LILY

☼ ❋ ↔ 6 in (15 cm) ↑ 10 in (25 cm)

From California, USA. Vigorous clump-forming plant found on
the north-facing slopes of coastal pine forests. Mid-green leaves,
lightly patterned in purplish green. Flowers, sometimes 3 per
stem, appear in spring. The petals are creamy white with brownish to yellow staining on the petal reverse and at the base. Will
tolerate some heat. '**White Beauty**' (syn. *E. revolutum* 'White
Beauty') is easily grown, with glossy lettuce-green leaves marbled
with dark green. It puts on a glamorous show during the spring.
The flowers have white petals suffused with a clear cream at their
center, and the basal ring is flecked with maroon. Zones 4–9.

Erythronium dens-canis

DOG'S TOOTH VIOLET

☼ ❋ ↔ 6 in (15 cm) ↑ 6–8 in (15–20 cm)

From cool-temperate Europe and Asia. A variable plant, with
white, pale pink, rose pink, or lilac flowers, to 1½ in (35 mm)
across, held individually on straight stems, in spring–early
summer. These have protruding purple or blue anthers. The
leaves are long and mid-green, sometimes mottled or splotched

Eremurus, Hybrid Cultivar, 'Moneymaker'

with chocolate brown, purple-green, lettuce green, or silver, and sometimes plain.
The common name is derived from the
elongated fang-like shape of the bulb.
E. dens-canis can be grown through
thin grass. Zones 3–9.

Erythronium 'Pagoda'

☼ ❋ ↔ 8 in (20 cm) ↑ 6–12 in
(15–30 cm)

This is a vigorous decorative hybrid, with
glossy, deep green, mottled leaves. The
sulfur yellow flowers have deep yellow
anthers emerging from a highly visible
dark central ring. Each stem bears 3 to
4 blooms, during the spring. Zones 4–9.

Erythronium revolutum

TROUT LILY

☼ ❋ ↔ 6 in (15 cm) ↑ 6–8 in (15–20 cm)

From North America. A dainty variable
species. The flowers, 3 to 4 per stem,
appear in spring. The petals are cyclamen
pink, the stamens protruding, cream,
spreading, and recurved. The leaves are deep green, marbled, and
slightly wavy. There are many named selections. '**Pink Beauty**'
produces deep lavender-pink petals. Zones 4–9.

Erythronium tuolumnense

☼ ❋ ↔ 8 in (20 cm) ↑ 8–15 in (20–38 cm)

Native to the open evergreen forests of central California, USA.
The flower production of *E. tuolumnense* is sometimes sparse,
with 3 or 4 small flowers per stem in spring. The bright yellow
petals are sometimes veined in green, the anthers are yellow. The
leaves are plain, pale to mid-green, and are modestly waved at the
margins. This species will tolerate hot dry conditions, but it must
have shade throughout the summer months. Zones 4–9.

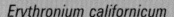

Erythronium californicum

Erythronium tuolumnense

EUCOMIS

PINEAPPLE LILY

These plants, which grow from large, ovate, shiny, greenish purple bulbs, gain their common name from the flowering stem's pineapple-like topknot. Mainly from the summer-rainfall eastern parts of southern Africa, they are members of the hyacinth (Hyacinthaceae) family. Leaves are broad, glossy, and can be plain or flecked; they appear with the flowers and form a basal rosette. Many tiny star-shaped flowers cluster around a single semi-erect stem in cylindrical formation. These striking plants lend themselves to greenhouse culture and are popular in cut-flower arrangements. In consequence, they are seen at many times of the year, but when left to themselves, they bloom in late summer to early autumn. There are numerous strains and cultivars.

CULTIVATION: They like rich, well-drained soil, a dry dormancy, and a moist growth period. Propagate from seed sown in spring or from offsets taken during the winter dormancy.

Eucomis bicolor

Eucomis autumnalis

WHITE PINEAPPLE LILY

☼/◐ ❋ ↔ 24 in (60 cm) ↑ 10–18 in (25–45 cm)

From eastern South Africa, widespread. Leaves broad, wavy-edged, green, to 18 in (45 cm) long. Flower stems upright, not lax, with 6 in (15 cm) long racemes of white flowers ageing to yellow-green in mid-summer–early autumn. There are several subspecies with widely varying foliage and flowers. Zones 8–11.

Eucomis bicolor

☼ ❋ ↔ 12–24 in (30–60 cm) ↑ 12–24 in (30–60 cm)

From eastern-central South Africa. Grows wild in wet meadows and on stream banks. It bears slightly ragged pendent flowers with green-white petals, that are sometimes marked with purple, and maroon-flecked stems in late summer. The leaves are undulating and oblong. Zones 7–9.

Eucomis comosa

☼ ❋ ↔ 16 in (40 cm) ↑ 12–24 in (30–60 cm)

Highly variable species from Eastern Cape and KwaZulu-Natal, South Africa. The leaves are wavy-edged. The flowers with green or whitish, pink or reddish, brown-purple or deep purple petals appear in late summer–early autumn. Some selections have purple leaves, but mid-green is more common, often with spotted undersides. Zones 8–10.

FREESIA

syn. *Anomatheca*

This genus is a member of the iris (Iridaceae) family and consists of 6 species of corms found in southern and central Africa. They are mainly small plants, forming clumps of simple narrow leaves, usually with a prominent midrib. In the warmer months they produce sprays of small, 6-petalled, sometimes fragrant flowers on wiry, often branching stems, held above the foliage.

CULTIVATION: Freesias, which are undemanding plants, are easily grown in any sunny position with moderately fertile well-drained soil. Provided the soil does not freeze to the depth of the corm, they can be left in the ground to overwinter; otherwise store dry in a frost-free place. Propagation is usually by breaking up established clumps while the plants are dormant. Freesias are easily raised from seed, and sometimes they will self-sow.

Freesia alba

syns *Freesia lactea*, *F. refracta* var. *alba*

☼ ◑ ↔ 3 in (8 cm) ↑ 4–6 in (10–15 cm)

Vigorous old garden inhabitant of confused nomenclature and possibly muddled ancestry. Strongly perfumed, prolific, small flowers. Petals variable; common coloration is cream splashed in onion-skin colors of gold, brown, purple, bronze, and rose. Stems short. Prefers dry summers, sharp drainage, poor soils. Zones 9–11.

Freesia laxa

syn. *Anomatheca laxa*

SCARLET FREESIA

☼ ❋ ↔ 8–12 in (20–30 cm) ↑ 12–16 in (30–40 cm)

From South Africa and Mozambique. Forms clumps of grassy leaves. Bears flowers in shades of pink to purple-red, sometimes white or pale blue. Self-sows. 'Joan Evans', only 6 in (15 cm) tall, with pale-centered pink flowers. Zones 8–11.

Freesia, Hybrid Cultivar, Royal Crown Series

Freesia Hybrid Cultivars

FLORIST'S FREESIAS

☀/◐ ✳ ↔6–12 in (15–30 cm) ↑12–20 in (30–50 cm)

This group of cultivars and hybrids has a complex parentage involving several known parents, such as *F. alba, F. corymbosa, F. leichtlinii, F. refracta*, and possibly a few others. They cover a wide range of plant sizes and flower colors, and vary greatly in the intensity of their fragrance. Popular hybrid cultivars in the pink double-flowered range include: '**Aphrodite**'; mixed-color seedling strains such as '**Parego's Blue**', blue tones; '**Parego's Red**', pink to red; **Royal Crown Series**, pink, yellow throats; '**Super Emerald**', shades of green. Zones 8–11.

FRITILLARIA

FRITILLARY

This genus of natives from the Mediterranean, Asia, and America contains about 100 species of perennial, herbaceous, bulbous plants that are members of the lily (Liliaceae) family. They are increasingly popular with domestic gardeners, who value them for their unusual coloring, delicate appearance, interesting formations, and odd, almost mechanical markings. The majority bloom in spring. The flowers are usually bell-shaped and somewhat pendent. Their scent is sometimes less than pleasing. The botanical name comes from the Latin *fritillus* (dice box), referring to the neat checked markings that some species bear on their petals and to the shape of the capsules.

CULTIVATION: The origin of each individual species is an important pointer. Many are seriously fussy about their needs, and the moisture levels, soil types, climate, and altitude of the original habitat should be taken into account in cultivation. Propagate from purchased bulbs (avoid if dried out), from bulb scales, from basal "rice-grain" bulbets, or from seed.

Fritillaria acmopetala

◐ ✳ ↔1¾–2 in (4–5 cm) ↑16–18 in (40–45 cm)

Found in vineyards and grain fields across western Asia and the eastern Mediterranean. Flowers are usually solitary, petals pale, shiny, green-yellow with chocolate-purple blotches. Leaves alternate, linear, gray-green. Prefers fertile well-drained soil. Less demanding than many. Zones 7–10.

Fritillaria camschatcensis

BLACK SARANA, ESKIMO POTATOES

☀/◐ ✳ ↔1¾–2 in (4–5 cm) ↑8–16 in (20–40 cm)

Widespread through northwestern America and northern Japan, in moist open woods and subalpine meadows. Leaves glossy, light green, lance-like, and held in whorls. Stems bear 2 to 3 flowers, grape-like, rich dark purple-brown petals with interior sheen, in late spring–early summer. Prefers humus-rich moisture-retentive soil and cool damp summers. Zones 4–9.

Fritillaria graeca

☀ ✳ ↔1¾–2 in (4–5 cm) ↑2½–8 in (6–20 cm)

Found on exposed rocky habitats in southern Greece, Albania, and Yugoslavia. The leaves are broad at the base, mid-green, and clustered around the stem. The flowers are solitary or paired, in

Fritillaria imperialis

broad, heavy, pendent bells, appearing in late spring–early summer; petals slightly incurving, green and red, often with central stripe. The plant prefers fertile soil, good drainage, and a dry dormancy. The robust *F. g.* subsp. *thessala* is the most common form in cultivation. Zones 7–9.

Fritillaria imperialis

CROWN IMPERIAL, TEARS OF MARY

☀ ✳ ↔16 in (40 cm) ↑36–48 in (90–120 cm)

Widespread from southern Turkey to Kashmir. Leaves mid-green, glossy, in whorls. Flowers large, bright, clustered at top of upright stems, appearing in late spring. Scent unpleasant, fox-like. Petals yellow, lemon yellow, orange, or red, commonly orange. Prefers a fertile well-drained soil. '**Aureomarginata**', margins of leaves lemon yellow; '**Lutea**', yellow petals. Zones 4–7.

Fritillaria meleagris

GUINEA HEN FLOWER, LEPER LILY, SNAKES HEAD FRITILLARY/LILY

☀ ✳ ↔1¾–2 in (4–5 cm) ↑7–8 in (18–20 cm)

Variable protected species, rare in the wild, found in grassy flood plains from southern England to western Russia. Leaves alternate, long, sharply pointed, gray-green. Flowers square-shouldered bells, sometimes paired, appearing in mid-spring; petal color is variable, distinctly checked maroon, dark purple, and/or murky pink. Prefers fertile well-drained soils and damp summers. *F. m.* var. *unicolor* subvar. *alba*, white petals; *F. m.* '**Aphrodite**', white petals with green veining. Zones 4–9.

Fritillaria persica

☀ ✳ ↔3 in (8 cm) ↑4–36 in (10–90 cm)

Robust variable species with changeable nomenclature. Found in the eastern Mediterranean region and inland, on rocky slopes and along the edges of cornfields. Leaves numerous, gray, alternate, lance-like. Flowers appear in conical racemes of 7 to 20 heads, lasting several weeks, in spring; petals are narrow, bell-shaped, plum-purple with gray bloom. It prefers deep, damp, fertile soil, protected from both late frosts and sun. The cultivar '**Adiyaman**' has darker petals than the species. Zones 5–9.

GALANTHUS

SNOWDROP

Probably the most welcome harbinger of spring, this normally late winter-flowering Eurasian genus of 15 bulbs in the amaryllis (Amaryllidaceae) family also includes a few species that bloom in autumn. Narrow grassy leaves usually break through shortly after mid-winter and are soon joined by short flower stems, each carrying one mildly scented, pendulous, white, 6-petalled flower. The name *Galanthus* comes from the Greek *gala* (milk) and *anthos* (a flower) and refers to the flower color. Inner 3 petals are short and green-tipped, and double-flowered forms are available. Flowering is often brief but occurs when most welcome.

CULTIVATION: They like cool-temperate climates and thrive in woodland or rockery conditions and humus-rich soil. Propagate from seed, but they usually multiply quickly enough so that division after the foliage dies back is more practical. Do not let the bulbs dry out.

Galanthus elwesii

GIANT SNOWDROP

🔆 ❄ ↔ 4 in (10 cm) ↕ 4–6 in (10–15 cm)

Robust plant with honey-scented winter flowers, to 1¼ in (3 cm) long, with 2 green markings on each inner petal, flaring in sunshine. Broadly oblong gray-green leaves, sometimes twisted. Zones 6–9.

Galanthus ikariae ★

🔆 ❄ ↔ 4 in (10 cm) ↕ 4–6 in (10–15 cm)

Highly variable species found from the Aegean to the Caucasus region. Broad, glossy, bright green leaves, up to 6 in (15 cm) long. Flowers to 1¼ in (30 mm) long, with large green marking at petal tips, from late winter–early spring. Zones 6–9.

Galanthus nivalis

COMMON SNOWDROP, ENGLISH SNOWDROP

🔆 ❄ ↔ 4 in (10 cm) ↕ 6–8 in (15–20 cm)

Small European species with flat, narrow, blue-green leaves to slightly under 4 in (10 cm) long. Flowers small, slightly scented, with green petal tips and central markings. **'Flore Pleno'**, small, beautiful white double flowers detailed in lime green. Zones 4–9.

Galanthus nivalis

Gladiolus communis subsp. *byzantinus*

GALTONIA

This southern African genus, belonging to the hyacinth (Hyacinthaceae) family, contains 3 species of bulbous perennials. Tall spires of white bell-shaped flowers bloom in late summer. Leaves are rather fleshy and strap-shaped, form a basal clump.

CULTIVATION: Grow in a sunny sheltered spot in a light, fertile, well-drained soil. Propagate from seed or division of offsets.

Galtonia candicans ★

SUMMER HYACINTH

🔆 ❄ ↔ 1 ft (0.3 m) ↕ 4 ft (1.2 m)

From Free State and KwaZulu-Natal, South Africa, and Lesotho. Strap-shaped leaves to 30 in (75 cm) long. Fragrant, drooping, bell-shaped, white flowers, base tinged green. Bulbs will rot in wet ground. Zones 5–9.

Galtonia viridiflora

🔆 ❄ ↔ 12 in (30 cm) ↕ 36 in (90 cm)

From Free State and KwaZulu-Natal, South Africa, and Lesotho. Bluish green leaves to 24 in (60 cm) long. Pale green bell-shaped flowers, flushed white at the petal edges. Zones 8–10.

GLADIOLUS

SWORD LILY

Think of the genus *Gladiolus,* and large-flowered hybrids, derived mainly from South African species, come to mind. But this genus in the iris (Iridaceae) family includes around 180 species of corms found from Europe to western Asia and South Africa, many quite different from the showy hybrids. Many are scented.

CULTIVATION: Plant the corms at 4 times their own depth. Plant in full sun with light well-drained soil. In cold areas corms will survive outdoors if planted below freezing depth, otherwise lift and store dry for winter. Propagation is by growing the cormlets on.

Gladiolus communis

🔆/🔆 ❄ ↔ 12 in (30 cm) ↕ 40 in (100 cm)

Southern European native. Narrow leaves to around half of the flower stem length. Flowerheads usually with 2 to 3 branches, up to 20 red- or white-marked pink flowers. *G. c.* **subsp.** *byzantinus* ★, pink-marked, purple-red flowers. Zones 6–10.

Gladiolus murielae

syns *Acidanthera bicolor, Gladiolus callianthus*

🔆/🔆 ❄ ↔ 20 in (50 cm) ↕ 40 in (100 cm)

From mountains of tropical east Africa. Compact clump of upright, broad, spear-shaped leaves to 20 in (50 cm). Many erect flower stems with solitary or paired, fragrant, white flowers with maroon blotch, in late summer–autumn. Zones 8–10.

Gladiolus tristis

MARSH AFRIKAANER

🔆/🔆 ❄ ↔ 12 in (30 cm) ↕ 24 in (60 cm)

South African species. Narrow leaves, thickened midrib, often twisting at tips. Up to 20 often widely spaced cream to yellow

Gladiolus, Hybrid Cultivar,
Grandiflorus Group, 'Her Majesty'

Gladiolus, Hybrid Cultivar,
Grandiflorus Group, 'Saxony'

flowers, sometimes marked purple or maroon, on wiry stems, appear from spring. Scented in evening. Zones 7–10.

Gladiolus Hybrid Cultivars

☼ ‡ ↔ 12 in (30 cm) ↑ 2–5 ft (0.6–1.5 m)

Some 10,000 *Gladiolus* hybrids have been raised, divided into groups with similar characteristics. Classifications vary in different parts of world but most recognize just 3 main groups: Grandiflorus, Nanus, and Primulinus. Common garden gladioli belong to Grandiflorus Group, and include 'Goldfinch', small, yellow, ruffled flowers; 'Her Majesty', large, white-throated, mauve to lavender flowers; and 'Saxony', large, yellow-throated, apricot flowers. Zones 9–11.

GLORIOSA

CAT'S CLAW, CLIMBING LILY, FLAME LILY, GLORY LILY

This genus from the autumn crocus (Colchicaceae) family presently consists of a single, highly variable, tuberous, perennial species from tropical Africa and Asia. The climbing scrambling plant ascends by means of glossy emerald leaves that taper into coiling clinging tendrils. The showy single flowers, borne in late summer and autumn, are held on short stems that emerge from the leaf axils. The petals are recurved, widely separated, and are bright yellow, red, or purple. Bicolors are common. All parts of the plant are toxic.

CULTIVATION: Glory lilies require good drainage and full sun to half-sun in order to thrive. Plant the large, red-brown, fang-shaped tubers in a horizontal position, taking great care as they are dangerously brittle. Water plentifully when in growth and liquid feed with weak solution every 2 weeks.

Gloriosa superba

CLIMBING LILY, CREEPING LILY, GLORY LILY

☀ ‡ ↔ 12–20 in (30–50 cm) ↑ 6–8 ft (1.8–2.4 m)

Tuberous perennial vine with 1 to 4 slender, scrambling, bright green stems, native to tropical Africa and Asia. Soft, oval- to spear-shaped, glossy, bright green leaves, 2–3 in (5–8 cm) long, with tendrils, 1¼–2 in (3–5 cm) long, at leaf tips. Flowers are solitary, yellow, red, purple, or bi-colored, 1¾–4 in (4–10 cm) long, on long stalks, from summer–autumn. Many cultivars including: 'Citrina', with yellow flowers striped with maroon;

'Grandiflora', with striking, large golden yellow flowers; 'Rothschildiana' ★, with bright red or scarlet petals fading to garnet and purple, yellow near the base and at margins, completely recurved, undulating; and 'Simplex', with deep orange and yellow flowers. Zones 9–12.

HABRANTHUS

This genus of about 10 bulbous perennials from Central and South America belongs to the amaryllis (Amaryllidaceae) family. The solitary, trumpet-shaped flowers, which appear after rain in summer and autumn, are held at an angle from their straight stems. The leaves are semi-erect, narrow, and linear. Some of the species are evergreen and some deciduous. The name comes from the Greek *habros*, meaning graceful—which they are.

CULTIVATION: Give these plants sharp drainage and a sandy loam. Apply a weak liquid feed while in growth and keep slightly moist while dormant. Propagation is best done from offsets or from fresh ripe seeds kept at 61°F (16°C).

Habranthus robustus

syn. *Zephyranthes robusta*

☼ ❄ ↔ 4 in (10 cm) ↑ 8–12 in (20–30 cm)

Robust plant, can become invasive in appropriate conditions. Flowers open funnel-shaped, solitary or paired, 2½ in (6 cm) across, in summer. Petals rose pink fading to almost white. The leaves are deep green, finely linear with a visible midrib, appearing after flowers and persisting until late spring. Zones 8–10.

Habranthus tubispathus

☼ ❄ ↔ 3 in (8 cm) ↑ 6–10 in (15–25 cm)

Robust, invasive in appropriate conditions. Flowers small, funnel-shaped, produced in succession throughout summer. Petals coppery red, orange, or yellow. Leaves appear after flowers and persist until late spring. 'Rosea', dark pink petals. Zones 8–10.

Gloriosa superba

HAEMANTHUS

From southern Africa, this bulbous genus of 21 species from the amaryllis (Amaryllidaceae) family divides into those whose growth and dormancy coincide with wet winter/dry summer climates and the evergreens that come from areas where rainfall is more evenly distributed. Typically numerous small flowers form a dense head with a surrounding decorative whorl of brightly colored, waxy spathes. Often, the large bulbs produce only 2 huge leaves. Some of the larger-growing species formerly included in this genus are now placed in the genus *Scadoxus*.
CULTIVATION: Plant with the neck protruding from the soil, keep wet and use weak liquid fertilizer while in growth; cut back moisture when leaves turn yellow. Propagate from offsets removed when growth resumes, or from ripe seed.

Haemanthus albiflos

☼ ✣ ↔ 15 in (38 cm) ↕ 12 in (30 cm)
Evergreen species from South Africa. Large oblong leaves. Thick green stems support greenish white flowers crowded with yellow-tipped stamens, creating a shaving-brush effect. Zones 9–11.

Haemanthus sanguineus

☼ ❋ ↔ 6 in (15 cm) ↕ 12 in (30 cm)
From South Africa's Western Cape. In summer and autumn, produces dense umbels of 100 small flowers in red, salmon-pink, or sugar pink. Stems dark red. Leaves paired, prostrate, dark green, appear after flowers. Deciduous. Zones 8–10.

HIPPEASTRUM

AMARYLLIS, KNIGHT'S STAR LILY
From the subtropics of Central and South America these bulbous, deciduous, spring- to summer-flowering perennials of the amaryllis (Amaryllidaceae) family are grown as pot plants in cooler climates. In the past, 1 to 3 single trumpet-shaped heads per stem and petals in red, white, or pink shades were common. Today the range of cultivars includes pale translucent yellows, doubles, and stems carrying up to 5 large, outward-facing heads. Leaves are strap-like. Stems are straight, stout, and hollow.
CULTIVATION: Grow outdoors in frost-free areas or as greenhouse plants elsewhere. Heavy feeders and drinkers while in growth; reduce water prior to a period of dry winter dormancy. Bulbs should be planted with the necks protruding from the soil. Provide total shelter from frost and rain in winter. Propagate from offsets or from fresh ripe seeds kept at 61°F (16°C).

Hippeastrum papilio

Hippeastrum papilio

BUTTERFLY AMARYLLIS
☼/☀ ✣ ↔ 12–16 in (30–40 cm) ↕ 24 in (60 cm)
From southern Brazil. Star-like flowers 2 to 3 per stem winter–spring. Petals striped pale green-cream, stained reddish chocolate. Leaves are dark green, purple at base, strap-like. Zones 9–10.

Hippeastrum, Hybrid Cultivar, 'Pamela'

Hippeastrum reticulatum

☼/☀ ✣ ↔ 14–18 in (35–45 cm) ↕ 10–14 in (25–35 cm)
From southern Brazil. Flowers long-tubed, downward-facing, crimson-pink, 3 to 4 per stem, in late summer. Leaves deep green, 2 in (5 cm) wide, with pale central marking. Zones 9–10.

Hippeastrum vittatum

ST JOSEPH'S LILY
☼ ✣ ↔ 12 in (30 cm) ↕ 36 in (90 cm)
Large, robust plant from the Peruvian Andes. Flowers are wide open stars, 5 to 6 per tall stout stem. Petals in variable arrangement of white with red stripes. Bright green leaves appear after flowers. Zones 9–10.

Hippeastrum Hybrid Cultivars

☼/☀ ✣ ↔ 12–16 in (30–40 cm) ↕ 20–36 in (50–90 cm)
Hippeastrum hybrid cultivars are available in a wealth of flower colors, and are ideal for container planting. '**Christmas Star**', stems with up to 8 brilliant red and white flowers; '**Pamela**' ★, 20 in (50 cm) high, robust miniature, free-flowering, small and fine blue-green stems, narrow leaves, flowers up to 5 per stem, perfect shape, petals clear bright red; '**Picotee**', 20 in (50 cm) high, up to 5 large flowerheads per stem, petals white, finely margined in red, flushed green at the base; '**Royal Velvet**', deep velvety blackcurrant red petals. Zones 9–12.

HYACINTHOIDES

syn. *Endymion*
BLUEBELL
With 3–4 species from western Europe and northern Africa, these vigorous bulbous plants, members of the hyacinth (Hyacinthaceae) family, bear azure, pendant, spring flowers. Some are fragrant. Leaves are linear to strap-shaped and fleshy. Hybrids between *H. hispanica* and *H. non-scripta* are common.

CULTIVATION: Best grown in the ground in damp-summer climates or in irrigated beds, beneath deciduous trees in humus-rich, moisture-retentive. Provide winter sun and summer shade. Keep moist. Sap can cause skin irritations. Propagate by division (the bulbs lie deep), or from ripe fresh seed.

Hyacinthoides hispanica ★

syns *Endymion hispanicus, Scilla campanulata, S. hispanica*
SPANISH BLUEBELL
☼◐/☀ ❄ ↔ 4–6 in (10–15 cm) ↑16–18 in (40–45 cm)
Flowers without fragrance, arranged loosely around a single erect stem, in spring. Petals commonly blue, also lilac-pink and white; anthers blue. Leaves broad, strap-shaped, glossy emerald green, copious, erect but usually prostrate after rain. Clump-forming. '**Excelsior**', large-flowered, with violet-blue petals adorned with a stripe; '**La Grandesse**', widely spaced, pure white bells. Zones 6–7.

Hyacinthoides non-scripta

syns *Endymion non-scriptus, Scilla non-scripta*
BLUEBELL, ENGLISH BLUEBELL, WILD HYACINTH
☼◐/☀ ❄ ↔ 2–6 in (5–15 cm) ↑8–16 in (20–40 cm)
A clump-forming colonizer of damp oak, beech, and chestnut woodlands. Flowers 6 to 10 per stem, narrow bells, are scented, arranged in drooping racemes on 1 side of stalk, in spring. Petals commonly azure blue; anthers creamy white. Stem bent like a shepherd's crook. Leaves narrow, glossy dark green. '**Alba**', common white form; '**Rosea**', lilac-pink flowers. Zones 5–10.

HYACINTHUS

HYACINTH
There are only 3 species in this bulbous perennial genus in the lily (Liliaceae) family. They come from western and central Asia. Many more have been developed for the cut-flower market and for container culture; the most common are the showy cultivars of *H. orientalis*. There are 3 basic forms: Dutch hyacinths, numerous flowerheads tightly packed around a central stem forming a dense cylinder; Roman hyacinths, less numerous flowerheads and a looser arrangement; and the Multiflora Group, which produces several stems of loosely set flowerheads. All are fragrant and lend themselves to container culture and forcing.

CULTIVATION: Plant in autumn under a light deciduous canopy, in well-drained moderately fertile soil. In containers, use a moisture-retentive mix, and keep in a cool dark place until roots are well developed, or suspend over water and keep in a cool dark place until the roots are well developed. Bulbs grown over water should be discarded after flowering. Give them sun in winter and shade in summer. Propagate from offsets or fresh ripe seed.

Hyacinthus orientalis

COMMON HYACINTH
☼◐/☀ ❄ ↔ 3 in (8 cm) ↑8–12 in (20–30 cm)
Flowers in 6 or 7 heads sparsely arranged at angles around a central stem, smallish, dainty, narrowly bell-shaped, waxy, fragrant. Petals blue, blue-mauve, pink, white, and cream. '**Amethyst**', mauve-violet petals; '**Bismarck**', lilac with pale margins; '**Blue Jacket**', navy with purple veins; '**Carnegie**', compact, pure white, late; '**City of Haarlem**', primrose yellow, late; '**Delft Blue**', soft blue flushed with mauve; '**Gipsy Queen**', salmon orange; '**Hollyhock**', compact, crimson, double; '**King of the Blues**', rich dark blue; '**Violet Pearl**', carmine-pink with pale margins. Zones 5–9.

HYMENOCALLIS

syn. *Ismene*
SACRED LILY OF THE INCAS, SPIDER LILY
Some of the 30 or so species of this bulbous, perennial, tropical and subtropical genus from Central and South America, in the amaryllis (Amaryllidaceae) family, were once classified as *Ismene*. Distinctive flowers have a central narcissus-like staminal cup and long, narrow, recurved, or streamer-like petals.

CULTIVATION: Deciduous species need a dry dormancy and a sunlit or semi-shaded position. Evergreen species thrive in damp, fertile, shaded soil. Plant with the bulb's neck protruding. Propagation is from offsets or fresh ripe seed. Clumps can be divided in winter.

Hymenocallis × festalis ★

☼ ✶ ↔ 12–24 in (30–60 cm) ↑24–32 in (60–80 cm)
Up to 4 flowers at right angles to the stout stem, pure white, fragrant, cup with spidery swept-back outer segments, usually in late spring. Stamens golden. Leaves clump-forming, deciduous, dark green, long and broad. Zones 9–11.

Hyacinthoides hispanica

Hymenocallis narcissiflora

SACRED LILY OF THE INCAS

◑ ⬗ ↔ 12–24 in (30–60 cm) ↑20–24 in (50–60 cm)

From the Peruvian Andes, growing in stony fields to 9,840 ft (3,000 m) above sea level. Flower a long daffodil-like cup, filaments stand out like aeroplane propellers, fragrant, white with touches of green, held above foliage. Flower stem emerges from 12 in (30 cm) false stem. Leaves deciduous, strap-like. '**Advance**', slightly elongated cup lobes, pure white version. Zones 9–11.

Hymenocallis '**Sulphur Queen**'

◑ ❄ ↔ 12–20 in (30–50 cm) ↑20–24 in (50–60 cm)

Scented hybrid cultivar. Cross between yellow-flowering Peruvian *H. amancaes* and *H. narcissiflora*. Narrow leaves to 20 in (50 cm) long. Large primrose yellow cup and white filaments. Zones 8–10.

HYPOXIS

STAR GRASS, STARFLOWER

With a wide habitat—through North America, Africa, Australia, and tropical Asia—only a few of this large (about 150 species) genus of low-growing, cormous, perennial plants in the starflower (Hypoxidaceae) family have been cultivated. Upturned star-like flowers open in sunlight, and have 6 radiating petals, outer 3 are wider than inner ones. Fibrous roots emerge from an annual corm. Leaves are linear, grass-like, and often hairy. **CULTIVATION:** Grow in light, well-drained soil and in sunlight. Dry off after flowering. Root disturbance is resented, as is frost. Propagate from offsets or fresh ripe seed.

Hypoxis capensis

WHITE STAR GRASS

☀ ⬗ ↔ 8–24 in (20–60 cm) ↑8–24 in (20–60 cm)

Perennial from South Africa. Leaves 4–12 in (10–30 cm) long. Solitary white or yellow flowers, spotted purple at center, in spring–summer. Zones 9–11.

Hypoxis hirsuta

☀ ❄ ↔ 2 in (5 cm) ↑4–8 in (10–20 cm)

From eastern North America. Flowers up to 7 per stem, yellow with greenish backs, from spring to summer. Leaves basal, hairy, ribbed, semi-erect. Zones 5–9.

IPHEION

In the past this genus, a member of the onion (Alliaceae) family, was incorporated in *Brodiaea*, *Triteleia*, and *Milla*, and some confusion remains in common horticulture. Some botanists have proposed *Ipheion* be merged with *Tristagma*. Native to South America, these bulbous perennials give off a strong smell of stale garlic when the leaves are bruised. The starry flowers are upward-facing and prolific. **CULTIVATION:** These easy-going plants thrive in well-drained sunny situations in warm climates, but need protection against frost in cold climates. Keep just moist during dormancy. Propagate from seed in spring or from offsets taken as the foliage dies down.

Ipheion uniflorum '**Wisley Blue**'

Ipheion '**Alberto Castillo**'

☀ ❄ ↔ 2 in (5 cm) ↑7–8 in (18–20 cm)

Narrow, gray-green leaves. Fragrant, large, white blooms held on strong flower stems from late winter to late spring. Zones 7–11.

Ipheion uniflorum

syns *Brodiaea uniflora*, *Tristagma uniflorum*, *Triteleia uniflora*

SPRING STAR FLOWER

☀ ❄ ↔ 2 in (5 cm) ↑4–8 in (10–20 cm)

From Argentina and Uruguay. Robust plant with weedy potential. Leaves mat-forming, linear, grassy, gray-green. Flowers starry, soap-scented, produced in succession over 6–8 weeks, from midwinter to mid-spring, opening only during sunlit hours. Petals silvery mauve, palest blue, white, with a pronounced midrib. '**Froyle Mill**', large deep purple petals; '**Wisley Blue**', a popular pale blue form, bluish petals, darker midrib. Zones 7–11.

IRIS *(see page 488)*

Iris bucharica

syn. *Iris orhioides*

☀ ❄ ↔ 6 in (15 cm) ↑18 in (45 cm)

Native of Russia and Afghanistan. Bulbous iris, distinctive, shiny green, channeled leaves that resemble dwarf maize. Creamy flowers, yellow-centered falls, small white standards, in upper leaf axils, in spring. Zones 5–9.

Iris bucharica

Iris reticulata

☀ ❄ ↔ 2 in (5 cm) ↑6 in (15 cm)

From the Caucasus region. Variable bulbous iris with very narrow channeled leaves. Solitary stemless flowers, narrow petals, in violet shades with gold markings on falls. '**Blue Veil**' and '**Cantab**' are popular cultivars. Zones 3–9.

DUTCH HYBRIDS

☀ ❄ ↔ 12–18 in (30–45 cm) ↑24–36 in (60–90 cm)

Bulbous irises with large spring blooms in shades of blue and purple, yellow and white. Grown for cut flower trade. '**Blue Diamond**', dark blue buds open to mid-blue flowers, yellow thumbprints at base of petals; '**Blue Magic**', deep blue flowers, yellow thumbprints; '**Cream Beauty**', ivory flowers, gold thumbprints; '**Madonna**', crisp white, yellow thumbprints; '**Telstar**', rich purple-blue flowers, golden yellow thumbprints. Zones 5–9.

IXIA

CORN LILY, WAND FLOWER

This South African genus in the iris (Iridaceae) family contains some 50 species of corms with fine grassy foliage, usually quite short in comparison to the wiry, often arching flower stems. Flowers are simple 5- or 6-petalled structures massed in spikes at the stem tips. Often brightly colored, they may also be pale with brighter markings, and occur in some unusual shades including pale blue-green.
CULTIVATION: Plant in a sunny position in light well-drained soil. Water well in spring but allow to dry off after flowering. Propagation is usually from offsets, less commonly from seed.

Ixia maculata

☼ ⁑ ↔ 6 in (15 cm) ↑ 8–20 in (20–50 cm)
Variable robust plant with weedy potential. Erect, wiry stems. Leaves are grassy and untidy, withering quickly after the flowers fade. Numerous large cupped flowers, petals in cream, purple-pink, cherry red, pink, yellow, orange shades, often with a dark eye, as well as stripes and bicolors, spring-flowering. Zones 9–10.

Ixia paniculata

syn. *Morphixia paniculata*
☼/☀ ⁑ ↔ 6 in (15 cm) ↑ 18–30 in (45–75 cm)
Robust species with weedy potential. Leaves a little broader than most species, to 24 in (60 cm) long. Flower stems long, heads of white to creamy yellow flowers, often pink- to red-tinted, petals sometimes darker at base, in spring–summer. Zones 9–10.

Ixia viridiflora

☼ ⁑ ↔ 8 in (20 cm) ↑ 12–24 in (30–60 cm)
This robust species is from the southwest Cape region, South Africa. Fine grassy leaves to 20 in (50 cm) long. Variable short-lived flowers in open stars, petals sea-green, turquoise, teal, aqua-blue, duck-egg blue, often with a dark central marking, appear from mid-spring. Zones 9–10.

IXIOLIRION

A genus of 4 bulbous perennial herbs from the family Tecophilaeaceae, originating from southwest and central Asia. The narrow grassy leaves grow from a central point, forming rosettes. In spring and summer tall slender stems carry umbels or loose racemes of funnel-shaped flowers in blue to violet shades.
CULTIVATION: Plant these bulbs in a sheltered sunny position in light, well-drained, sandy soil, allowed to become hot and dry in summer. Propagate from seed or by dividing the bulbs and removing the offsets in autumn.

Iris, Hybrid Cultivar, Dutch, 'Telstar'

Ixiolirion tataricum

SIBERIAN LILY, TARTAR LILY

☼ ❋ ↔ 12–16 in (30–40 cm) ↑ 10–16 in (25–40 cm)
Bulbous perennial from southwest and central Asia. Narrow, semi-erect, grass-like leaves. Abundant clusters of up to 4 flowers, on 16 in (40 cm) tall stems, blue or purple-blue tepals, darker stripe at center, in spring–early summer. Zones 5–9.

LACHENALIA

CAPE COWSLIP

Most of the 110 species of bulbs in this southern African genus, belonging to the hyacinth (Hyacinthaceae) family, occur in a small region of Western Cape, with a smaller number in Namibia. Interestingly colored, mainly winter- to spring-blooming flowers; highly variable foliage. Leaves are always basal, emerging directly from the bulb, but may be small or large; lance-shaped, heart-shaped, strappy or grassy; matt green, glossy green, plain, or mottled. Flowers come in many colors and are tubular or bell-shaped with 6 petals, the outer 3 forming a fleshy cup, from which the inner 3, often differently colored, protrude.
CULTIVATION: Frost tender but otherwise easily grown. Plant in full sun in humus-rich soil. Water and feed during active growth. Propagate by offset or by dividing established clumps.

Lachenalia aloides ★

☼/☀ ⁑ ↔ 8 in (20 cm) ↑ 12 in (30 cm)
Leaves 2 per bulb, broad, green to blue-green, often darker or maroon-spotted. Flowers tubular to funnel-shaped, greenish yellow to apricot. Consists of many forms; used extensively in hybridization. *L. a.* var. *aurea,* golden yellow flowers, greenish markings; '**Nelsonii**', densely purple-spotted leaves. *L. a.* '**Pearsonii**', leaves with red-brown spotting. Zones 9–10.

Lachenalia aloides var. *aurea*

Lachenalia contaminata

WILD HYACINTH

☼/◐ ☽ ↔ 8–10 in (20–25 cm) ↕ 6–10 in (15–25 cm)

Forms clump of up to 10 fine grassy leaves per bulb. Dense heads of small, cream, bell-shaped flowers with contrasting dark maroon tips; flower buds with emerald green tips. **Zones 9–10.**

LEDEBOURIA

AFRICAN SQUILL

Genus of about 30 species of bulbous perennials from sub-Saharan Africa, Madagascar, and India belonging to the hyacinth (Hyacinthaceae) family. Leaves are basal, sometimes grayish, often striped or spotted red or green. Inflorescence is a simple raceme with inconspicuous bracts, borne at branch tips. Flowers are small, the 6 outer segments purple or greenish and recurved. CULTIVATION: They grow well with cacti and succulents. In temperate climates they prefer a cool greenhouse in moderately rich compost.

Ledebouria cooperi

Ledebouria cooperi

syns *Scilla adlamii, S. cooperi*

☼ ❄ ↔ 2–3 in (5–8 cm) ↕ 2–4 in (5–10 cm)

Semi-evergreen bulb from South Africa. Leaves fleshy, to 10 in (25 cm) long, green with parallel purple stripes, setting off spikes of tiny deep purple-pink flowers in summer. **Zones 8–11.**

Ledebouria socialis ★

syns *Scilla socialis, S. violacea*

☼ ❄ ↔ 2–3 in (5–8 cm) ↕ 2–4 in (5–10 cm)

From South Africa. Evergreen with exposed bulb. Leaves broad, to 4 in (10 cm) long, gray with deep green blotches, purple beneath. Spikes of tiny, nodding, green bellflowers, on pink stalks, are held above the leaves. **Zones 8–12.**

LEUCOCORYNE

Some 12 or so species of bulbs from Chile comprise this small genus in the onion (Alliaceae) family. Bulbs have a dark brown tunic; leaves are narrow and usually lax, appearing in winter. Showy flowers, usually white, blue, or purple and often scented. CULTIVATION: In mild climates plant the bulbs 4 in (10 cm) deep in a sunny well-drained site in sandy fertile soil. In colder areas, grow in a greenhouse. Propagate by seed (plant will take some years to flower) or by small offset bulbs.

Leucocoryne ixioides

GLORY OF THE SUN

☼ ☽ ↔ 3–4 in (8–10 cm) ↕ 16–18 in (40–45 cm)

Found in Chile. *L. ixioides* has narrow grassy leaves. Heads of up to 12 open, starry, bright blue flowers with a white center, ¾ in (18 mm) across, in spring, as the leaves die down. **Zones 9–10.**

LEUCOJUM

SNOWFLAKES

A genus of 20 species of bulbs in the amaryllis (Amaryllidaceae) family, native to Europe, the Middle East, and North Africa. Better suited than the related snowdrops *(Galanthus)* to mild, warm climates. Their overall appearance is similar, the 6 white petals of the nodding flowers at the tops of the slender stems are of equal length; snowdrops have 3 long and 3 short petals. The linear leaves, said to be poisonous to stock, appear either with or before the flowers. CULTIVATION: Trouble-free, needing almost no maintenance. Propagate by division of offsets after flowering, or by sowing ripe fresh seed.

Leucojum aestivum

syn. *Leucojum aestivale*

SUMMER SNOWFLAKE

☼/◐ ❄ ↔ 12 in (30 cm) ↕ 18–22 in (45–55 cm)

Native to the damp woods of central and southern Europe. Robust, with strap-like leaves. Flowers delicate-looking, 1 to 5 per stem, white with green markings, sometimes scented; in wet-winter dry-summer climates the flowers appear in winter, in cooler wet-summer climates in summer. Needs moist conditions. **'Gravetye Giant'** ★, to 30 in (75 cm). **Zones 6–9.**

Leucojum autumnale

AUTUMN SNOWFLAKE

☼ ❄ ↔ 2 in (5 cm) ↕ 6–10 in (15–25 cm)

From western Europe and northwestern Africa. Thread-like leaves. Flowers are tiny, delicate-looking, scented, white bells, several per stem, sometimes lightly tinged with pink, with yellow anthers, in late summer–early autumn. **Zones 6–9.**

Leucojum vernum

SPRING SNOWFLAKE

◐ ❄ ↔ 12 in (30 cm) ↕ 12–30 in (30–75 cm)

From shady hillsides and woodlands of higher parts of central Europe; widely naturalized elsewhere. Flowers are large flared bells, 1¼ in (30 mm) across, held singly on straight stems, white marked with green or yellow, in spring. **Zones 5–8.**

Leucojum aestivum

LILIUM

LILY

There are about 100 species of these lilies spread across the northern temperate zone. Type genus for their family, Liliaceae, they are strongly upright plants with leafy aerial stems that die back to the bulb after flowering; bulbs are composed of many narrow, overlapping, fleshy scales with no outer covering (tunic). Leaves are short, usually linear to lanceolate. Flowers are borne at stem tips and may be solitary or in umbels or panicles; they may be bell-, trumpet-, or cup-shaped, or have strongly recurved sepals, producing the "turk's-cap" flower shape. They come in all colors, except for blue, and are often spotted or streaked. The genus *Lilium* is split into 9 main divisions, to each of which both species and hybrids may be assigned.

CULTIVATION: Lilies like sun for at least half the day, and moist, humus-rich, fertile, well-drained soil. Do not store bulbs dry; use moist sawdust or shredded paper. Propagate from offsets, from detached bulb scales, or from leaf axil bulbils or seed.

Lilium candidum

MADONNA LILY, WHITE LILY

☀ ❄ ↔ 12–18 in (30–45 cm) ↑ 3–7 ft (0.9–2 m)

Native to the Mediterranean region (Lebanon, Israel, Turkey, Greece). Up to 20 flowers per stem, pure white trumpets with reflexed tips and strong fragrance, in summer–autumn. Unlike most lilies, likes alkaline soil and a sunny aspect. Zones 6–9.

Lilium columbianum

COLUMBIA LILY, COLUMBIA TIGER LILY, OREGON LILY

◑ ❄ ↔ 12–18 in (30–45 cm) ↑ 7–8 ft (2–2.4 m)

From western North America. Lance-shaped leaves in whorls up the stems. Flowers strongly reflexed in turk's-cap fashion, yellow to orange-red spotted with maroon. Zones 5–9.

Lilium davidii

◑ ❄ ↔ 12–18 in (30–45 cm) ↑ 3–5 ft (0.9–1.5 m)

Native to western China. Slightly stoloniferous. Scattered leaves, to 4 in (10 cm) long. Up to 20 unscented, nodding, turk's-cap flowers, to 3 in (8 cm) across, bright vermilion-red spotted with black, in summer–early autumn. Zones 5–9.

Lilium formosanum

◑ ❄ ↔ 12–18 in (30–45 cm) ↑ 3–7 ft (0.9–2 m)

From Taiwan. Tall, elegant, with scattered leaves. Up to 10 blooms on each stem, but usually fewer, in summer–autumn. Flowers are trumpet-shaped, horizontal, 8 in (20 cm) long, scented, white stained purple. *L. f.* var. *pricei*, dwarf form, 1 or 2 flowers per stem. Zones 5–11.

Lilium henryi

◑ ❄ ↔ 12–18 in (30–45 cm) ↑ 7–10 ft (2–3 m)

From China. Stems, each holding up to 20 flowers, inclined to lean from the weight. Leaves relatively broad, scattered up the stems. Reflexed turk's-cap flowers, orange spotted with black. Zones 5–9.

Lilium nepalense

Lilium lancifolium

syn. *Lilium tigrinum*

DEVIL LILY, KENTAN, TIGER LILY

☀ ❄ ↔ 12–18 in (30–45 cm) ↑ 3–4 ft (0.9–1.2 m)

From eastern China, Japan, and Korea. Hardy well-known lily, probably an ancient hybrid. Scattered leaves, to 8 in (20 cm) long; black bulbils produced in leaf axils. Turk's-cap flowers, to

Lilium lancifolium

8 in (20 cm) across, orange with bold dark purple spots, are borne from summer to early autumn. Zones 4–10.

Lilium longiflorum

EASTER LILY

◑ ❄ ↔ 12–18 in (30–45 cm) ↑ 36–40 in (90–100 cm)

From Japan and Taiwan. Vigorous species. Scattered shiny leaves, to 7 in (18 cm) long. Horizontally held, strongly scented, trumpet-shaped flowers, to 7 in (18 cm) long, white with green central stripes, in summer–early autumn. Zones 5–11.

Lilium martagon

MARTAGON, TURK'S CAP

◑ ❄ ↔ 12–18 in (30–45 cm) ↑ 3–8 ft (0.9–2.4 m)

Native from northwestern Europe to Mongolia. The classic lily in turk's-cap form. Leaves broad, in whorls. Up to 50 flowers per stem, usually far fewer, to 2 in (5 cm) across, dull pink with darker spots, unpleasantly scented, in summer–early autumn. *L. m.* var. *album*, pure white flowers; *L. m.* var. *cattaniae*, deep wine-red flowers without spots. Zones 4–9.

Lilium nepalense ★

◑ ❄ ↔ 12–18 in (30–45 cm) ↑ 27–40 in (70–100 cm)

Himalayan. Rare and desirable species. Scattered leaves, to 6 in (15 cm) long. Drooping, flared, trumpet-shaped flowers, 6 in (15 cm) long, usually green-white with a large purple throat, in summer–early autumn. Zones 5–9.

Lilium regale

Lilium, Hybrid Cultivar, 4. American Species, Bellingham Hybrid

Lilium, Hybrid Cultivar, 7. Oriental, 'Cartouche'

Lilium regale

REGAL LILY

☼ ❁ ↔ 12–18 in (30–45 cm) ↑ 5–7 ft (1.5–2 m)

From China. Scattered leaves, to 5 in (12 cm) long. Up to 20 flowers per stem, flared trumpets, to 6 in (15 cm) long, held horizontally, white inside with purple flushes on the outside, in summer–early autumn. Zones 5–9.

Lilium speciosum

☼ ❁ ↔ 12–18 in (30–45 cm) ↑ 3–5 ft (0.9–1.5 m)

From China, Japan, and Taiwan. Scattered leaves, to 7 in (18 cm) long. Up to 12 pendent, fragrant, turk's-cap flowers per stem, to 7 in (18 cm) across, usually pale pink, deeper pink toward center, with deep pink spots, in summer–early autumn. *L. s.* var. *album*, purple stems, white flowers; *L. s.* var. *rubrum*, purple stems, dark carmine flowers, white edges. Zones 6–9.

Lilium Hybrid Cultivars

☼/☼ ❁ ↔ 12–24 in (30–60 cm) ↑ 30 in–7 ft (75 cm–2 m)

Most garden or florists' lilies are hybrid cultivars, nearly all from generations of breeding from many wild species. The classification of *Lilium* cultivars below is that used by the *International Lily Register*, kept by the Royal Horticultural Society. Zones 5–9.

1. ASIATIC HYBRIDS

These hybrids, derived from *L. amabile, L. bulbiferum, L. cernuum, L. concolor, L. davidii, L. lancifolium, L. leichtlinii, L. maculatum, L. × hollandicum,* and *L. pumilum,* typically have one or a few large trumpet-shaped flowers and occur in a huge range of colors and patterns. Although known as Asiatic, the geographic origins of these often overlap with the Oriental hybrids.

They are subdivided by their flower form into 3 categories: 1a, upward-facing flowers; 1b, outward-facing; 1c, pendent.

Asiatic hybrids include: 'Alaska', to 48 in (120 cm) tall, white flowers; 'Avignon', to 36 in (90 cm) tall, red and orange flowers; 'Chianti', to 32 in (80 cm) tall, pink flowers; 'Connecticut King', to 36 in (90 cm) tall, yellow flowers; 'Côte d'Azur', to 27 in (70 cm) tall, pink flowers; 'Montreaux', to 48 in (120 cm) tall, pink flowers; 'Navona', to 36 in (90 cm) tall, white flowers with yellow-green center; 'Polyanna', over 48 in (120 cm) tall, yellow flowers; 'Vivaldi', to 42 in (105 cm) tall, pink flowers.

2. TURK'S-CAP OR MARTAGON HYBRIDS

Hybrids between *L. martagon* and *L. hansonii,* or hybrids with one of those species as a parent. They have large heads of many small to medium-sized pendulous flowers. The mixed color selection known as the **Backhouse Hybrids** are the most widely grown lilies of this style.

3. *L. CANDIDUM* HYBRIDS

Hybrids of *L. candidum, L. chalcedonicum,* and some other related species, but not *L. martagon.* Typically tall and dark-stemmed. Fragrant, often white to cream, funnel-shaped flowers.

4. AMERICAN SPECIES HYBRIDS

Hybrids between American species, such as *L. canadense, L. maritimum, L. columbianum,* and *L. grayi.* They should be variable and interesting, but as yet this group is represented by just a few plants, of which the **Bellingham Hybrids**, with brown-spotted red and orange or red and yellow flowers, are the most common.

5. *L. LONGIFLORUM* AND *L. FORMOSANUM* HYBRIDS

Hybrids between or of these 2 species usually have large, green-tinted, white, trumpet-shaped flowers.

6. TRUMPET-SHAPED AND AURELIAN LILIES

Hybrids of *L. henryi* and related species, but not including those species that make up Division 7. This group is subdivided into 4 categories based on flower shape: 6a, trumpet-shaped flowers; 6b, bowl-shaped flowers; 6c, flat flowers with recurved tips; and 6d, strongly recurved flowers.

Popular Division 6 lilies include: 'Black Dragon', to 60 in (150 cm) tall, deep purple-red flowers with white interior; 'Pink Perfection', to 60 in (150 cm) tall, large, deep magenta flowers.

7. ORIENTAL HYBRIDS

Hybrids of *L. auratum, L. speciosum, L. japonicum,* and *L. rubellum.* Includes hybrids between these species and *L. henryi* but not with Trumpet or Aurelian hybrids. Subdivided into 4 categories based on flower shape: 7a, trumpet-shaped flowers; 7b, bowl-shaped flowers; 7c, flat flowers; and 7d, strongly recurved flowers.

Oriental hybrids include: 'Acapulco', to 36 in (90 cm) tall, mauve flowers; 'Cartouche', to 48 in (120 cm) tall, reddish pink flowers with dark mid-stripe and pale edges; 'Casa Blanca', to 54 in (135 cm) tall, white flowers; 'Expression' ★, to 36 in (90 cm) tall, white flowers; 'Muscadet', to 27 in (70 cm) tall, white, flushed pale pink flowers with red spots; 'Pesaro', to 36 in (90 cm) tall, deep pink flowers with pale center; 'Siberia', to 48 in (120 cm) tall, pure white flowers; 'Sissi', to 36 in (90 cm) tall, pink flowers; 'Sorbonne', to 48 in (120 cm) tall, deep pink flowers with pale edges; 'Star Gazer', to 36 in (90 cm) tall, pink flowers with red flecks and pale edges; 'Woodriff's Memory', to 36 in (90 cm), purplish-pink flowers with a yellow mid-stripe.

8. OTHER HYBRIDS

Miscellaneous hybrids not classified elsewhere. 'Virginia', 24–36 in (60–90 cm), white flowers greenish yellow at center. LA Hybrids appeared in the 1990s, named because they combined *L. longiflorum* with Asiatic Hybrids; 'Glossy Wings', to 36 in (90 cm) tall, strong salmon-pink flowers; 'Royal Fantasy', to 36 in (90 cm) tall, creamy yellow scented flowers; 'Royal Sunset', to 30 in (75 cm) tall, orange petals tipped scarlet, finely spotted; 'Wiener Blut' ★, to 30 in (75 cm) tall, tomato red flowers, major commercial cut flower.

Lycoris aurea

9. SPECIES

The species as they occur in the wild, include the many natural subspecies and varieties of *Lilium*. In this book the species all have their own entries.

LYCORIS

SPIDER LILY

These cousins of the South African genus *Nerine*, often found at the edges of fields in Japan and China, resemble nerines. A member of the amaryllis (Amaryllidaceae) family, *Lycoris* contains about 18 bulbous perennials, dormant in summer prior to flowering in late summer to early autumn. The spidery flowers have strongly reflexed petals and are borne in an umbel at the top of a straight stem. Linear leaves emerge from the base of the bulb after flowers and persist during winter.

CULTIVATION: They grow best in well-drained fertile soil, in areas with dry summers. If growing in a pot, do not transplant for several years. Withhold water from late spring to mid-summer.

Lycoris aurea

GOLDEN SPIDER LILY, HURRICANE LILY

☼ ❄ ↔ 18 in (45 cm) ↕ 18–24 in (45–60 cm)

From limestone areas of China and Japan. Leaves fleshy, gray-green. Flowers in golden shades, recurved at tips, petal margins slightly wavy, rather crowded at top of stem. Zones 7–10.

MORAEA

Belonging to the iris (Iridaceae) family, this genus consists of about 120 species of which only a few are commonly cultivated.

They are cormous perennials, which may be deciduous or semi-deciduous, originating in sub-Saharan Africa from Ethiopia to South Africa. Short-lived, iris-like, clustered flowers, often in brilliant colors, appear during spring and early summer.

CULTIVATION: A dry dormancy period in summer is essential, as is very sharp drainage. Propagate from seed, sowing summer-flowering species in spring and winter-growing species in autumn.

Moraea aristata

PEACOCK IRIS

☼ ∤ ↔ 3 in (8 cm) ↕ 15–16 in (38–40 cm)

Perennial species from Cape Town, South Africa, almost extinct in the wild. Leaves hairy. Flowers solitary, white, hint of smoky blue, central eye with concentric crescents of blue, green, violet, and black. Zones 9–11.

Moraea collina

syns *Homeria breyniana, H. collina*

☼ ❄ ↔ 3 in (8 cm) ↕ 6–14 in (15–35 cm)

From Southwest Cape region of South Africa. Flowers scented, upturned. Petals pale yellow, peach-pink, bronze-pink, or sugar pink, darker at base. Leaves linear, grayish green. Stems solitary or sparsely branched. Toxic to stock. Zones 8–12.

Moraea polystachya

☼/❂ ∤ ↔ 3 in (8 cm) ↕ 32 in (80 cm)

Perennial from Namibia and Botswana. Leaves are linear, almost flat, stems branched. Short-lived flowers, violet, marked yellow, with white edges, are produced in a long display in early autumn–winter. Tough; in stressful conditions may lie dormant for years. Zones 9–11.

Moraea ramosissima

☼ ∤ ↔ 4 in (10 cm) ↕ 24–48 in (60–120 cm)

Perennial from South Africa. Narrowly linear leaves, borne on much-branched stems. Yellow flowers, darker centers, appear in spring–early summer. Zones 9–11.

Moraea polystachya

Moraea villosa

Moraea spathulata
☼ ❋ ↔ 4 in (10 cm) ↑ 20–40 in (50–100 cm)
Evergreen perennial from Swaziland, Zimbabwe, Mozambique, and Mpumalanga,
South Africa. Yellow flowers, darker nectar
guides, appear on branching stems, opening
in morning, closing late afternoon, season variable but in summer is common. Zones 9–11.

Moraea villosa
PEACOCK IRIS
☼ ❋ ↔ 5 in (12 cm) ↑ 12–16 in (30–40 cm)
Perennial species from Western Cape, South
Africa. Basal leaves are channeled. Flowers
flat, to 3 in (8 cm) wide, white to orange or blue, with large,
deep blue, circular blotches at base of each of 3 petals, in late
winter–early spring. Rare in the wild. Zones 8–10.

MUSCARI
GRAPE HYACINTH
This genus, a member of the hyacinth (Hyacinthaceae) family,
contains some 30 species of spring-blooming bulbous perennials.
Originally from the Mediterranean basin and southwest Asia.
Popular in woodland gardens and bedding displays. Flowers, like
tiny upside-down bowls, hang in dense clusters from stems, in
spring. Lower florets open first. Voluminous foliage often untidy.
CULTIVATION: Feed with bone meal in spring. Divide overcrowded
clumps while dormant. Propagate from offsets, or sow fresh seed.

Muscari armeniacum
syn. *Muscari szovitsianum*
☼ ❋ ↔ 2 in (5 cm) ↑ 8 in (20 cm)
Bulbous perennial. Leaves mid-green, may collapse in rough
weather. Flowers in dense racemes, bright blue, pinched white
mouths. Needs winter sun. 'Blue Spike', large, double, soft blue
flowers; 'Cantab', vigorous, pale blue flowers, short stalks;
'Valerie Finnis' ★, pale lavender flowers, in dense showy spirals,
dark semi-erect leaves, may be related to *M. neglectum*. Zones 6–9.

Muscari azureum
syn. *Hyacinthella azurea*
☼ ❋ ↔ 2 in (5 cm) ↑ 4–6 in (10–15 cm)
Bulbous perennial from eastern Turkey. Leaves gray-green.
Flowers bright blue with darker stripe, bell-shaped. Zones 6–9.

Muscari botryoides
☼ ❋ ↔ 2 in (5 cm) ↑ 4–6 in (10–15 cm)
Bulbous perennial from central and southeastern Europe. Leaves
mid-green, narrowly spoon-shaped, semi-erect. Flowers spherical,
bright blue, pinched white mouths, in early summer. 'Album',
slender racemes of fragrant white flowers. Zones 6–9.

Muscari latifolium
☼ ❋ ↔ 2 in (5 cm) ↑ 8 in (20 cm)
Bulbous perennial from southwest Asia. Leaves mid-green, lance-
shaped. Blooms, extended urn shape, violet-black, with pinched
mouths, racemes are topped with paler sterile
flowers, in early summer. Requires plenty of
winter sun. Zones 6–9.

Muscari armeniacum 'Valerie Finnis'

NARCISSUS
DAFFODIL, JONQUIL
Part of the amaryllis (Amaryllidaceae) family,
this genus includes around 50 species of
mainly spring-flowering bulbs found from
Europe and North Africa to Japan and Australasia. They have grassy to strap-like leaves,
and the flowers almost always have the typical cup- or trumpet-shaped corona backed
by 6 petals. Garden forms abound in a range
of colors and flower types and are classed
according to flower shape and form. There are 12 divisions, listed
here under *Narcissus* Hybrid Cultivars. Wild species belonging to
Division 10 are listed first as individual entries.
CULTIVATION: Daffodils are mainly very hardy and adaptable, and
will thrive in borders, pots, or naturalized in lawns. They prefer
full sun/half-sun when in growth, and do well under deciduous
trees. Good drainage is important. Water well until the foliage
dies off. Propagate by breaking up established clumps.

Narcissus bulbocodium
HOOP-PETTICOAT DAFFODIL
☼ ❋ ↔ 12 in (30 cm) ↑ 4–6 in (10–15 cm)
From France, Portugal, and Spain. Fine dark green leaves, more
rounded than other *Narcissus*. Bright yellow to soft lemon flowers
with flared trumpet, narrow much-reduced petals in same color,
in early spring. *N. b.* var. *conspicuus* is a large-flowered rich
yellow form. Division 10. Zones 6–10.

Narcissus cyclamineus
☼/❋ ❋ ↔ 12 in (30 cm) ↑ 6–8 in (15–20 cm)
From northwestern Portugal and Spain. Dainty little species
much used in hybridizing; threatened in the wild. Dark green
strappy leaves. Bright yellow flowers with long narrow trumpet,
petals reflex right back, in early spring. Division 10. Zones 6–9.

Narcissus jonquilla
JONQUIL

❂/❂ ❋ ↔ 8 in (20 cm) ↑ 18 in (45 cm)

From Portugal and Spain. Narrow leaves, 2 to 4 per bulb. Thin flower stems, heads of small bright yellow flowers, seldom more than 1¼ in (30 mm) wide, with tiny cup-shaped corona, often strongly scented, in early spring. Division 10. Zones 4–9.

Narcissus minor
❂/❂ ❋ ↔ 4 in (10 cm) ↑ 8 in (20 cm)

Native to France and northern Spain. Short, upright, gray- to blue-green leaves, often channeled, 3 to 4 per bulb. Solitary, large-cupped, yellow flower to 1¾ in (40 mm) wide, in early spring. Corona usually has frilled edge. Division 10. Zones 4–9.

Narcissus obesus
syn. *Narcissus bulbocodium* subsp. *obesus*

❂ ❋ ↔ 12 in (30 cm) ↑ 7–8 in (18–20 cm)

A hoop-petticoat daffodil from Portugal. The foliage sits almost flat to the ground. Large yellow trumpets to 1 in (25 mm) long, in early spring. Division 10. Zones 6–10.

Narcissus × odorus
❂ ❋ ↔ 12 in (30 cm) ↑ 14–16 in (35–40 cm)

From southern Europe. Fragrant natural hybrid between *N. jonquilla* and *N. pseudonarcissus* with bright green curved leaves. Bright yellow flowers, 1 to 2 per stem, short trumpet, spreading petals, in early spring. 'Rugulosus', more robust form, up to 4 flowers per stem. Division 10. Zones 6–9.

Narcissus poeticus
PHEASANT'S EYE NARCISSUS, POET'S NARCISSUS

❂ ❋ ↔ 12 in (30 cm) ↑ 12–20 in (30–50 cm)

From Italy, France, and Switzerland. Erect green leaves, somewhat glaucous. Flowers 2¾ in (7 cm) across, 1 per stem, pure white flat petals, tiny cup-shaped trumpet, yellow with red rim, green center. Division 10. Zones 4–9.

Narcissus pseudonarcissus
LENT LILY, WILD DAFFODIL

❂ ❋ ↔ 12 in (30 cm) ↑ 8–14 in (20–35 cm)

This widespread European species is the classic Wordsworth daffodil. Thin, mid-green, erect leaves. Nodding yellow flowers to 2¾ in (7 cm) across, narrow trumpet and twisted petals, in early spring. Division 10. Zones 4–10.

Narcissus tazetta
BUNCH-FLOWERED NARCISSUS, JONQUIL, POLYANTHUS NARCISSUS

❂ ❋ ↔ 12 in (30 cm) ↑ 6–20 in (15–50 cm)

Variable species from the Mediterranean, naturalized in many places. Mid-green erect

Narcissus tazetta

leaves, twisted. Sweetly scented flowers, up to 1¾ in (4 cm) across, in clusters of up to 20, white petals, shallow yellow cup, in late winter. *N. t.* subsp. *lacticolor* (syn. *N. canaliculatus*), dwarf form of unknown origin, white petals, orange cups. The parent of many cultivars. Division 10. Zones 7–10.

Narcissus triandrus
ANGEL'S TEARS

❂/❂ ❋ ↔ 12 in (30 cm) ↑ 5–10 in (12–25 cm)

From Spain and Portugal. Leaves, strappy, tips often curled. The flowers 2½ in (6 cm) across, are cream with open cup-shaped trumpets, and reflexed petals, in spring. Division 10. Zones 4–9.

Narcissus Hybrid Cultivars
Daffodils hybridize freely and are favorites with plant breeders. The widely used Royal Horticultural Society classification system divides the many cultivars and hybrids into 12 groups or divisions based on the flower type and parentage.

DIVISION 1: TRUMPET
❂/❂ ❋ ↔ 12 in (30 cm) ↑ 12–16 in (30–40 cm)

Large-cupped flowers, with one bloom per stem. The corona (cup) must be at least as long as the perianth segment, that is, the length of the petals. Division 1 hybrids include: 'Attraction', creamy white perianth, bright yellow corona; 'Dutch Master', overall bright yellow; 'Gold Medal', bright yellow flowers, late flowering; 'Honeybird', green-tinged yellow perianth, white to cream corona; 'King Alfred', typical of group, bright golden yellow blooms; 'Las Vegas', pale cream perianth, bright yellow corona; 'Mount Hood', white to cream flowers, tall; 'Spellbinder' ★, soft to brighter yellow blooms with pale center; 'Standard Value', soft golden yellow flowers, held aloft on short stems; 'Unsurpassable', deep golden yellow blooms, tall, very early flowering; 'W. P. Milner', elegant form, flowers open lemon yellow, paling to white with age. Zones 5–10.

Narcissus, Hybrid Cultivar, 1. Trumpet, 'Standard Value'

DIVISION 2: LARGE-CUPPED

☼/☀ ❋ ↔ 12 in (30 cm) ↕ 12–16 in (30–35 cm)

The Division 2 plants are similar to the trumpet-flowered style with one flower per stem but with a smaller cup (corona) that should be shorter than the length of the perianth and at least one-third as long. Division 2 members include: 'Ambergate', deep yellow perianth, with orange corona; 'Berlin', yellow perianth, yellow corona with frilled bright orange edge; 'Blimey', primrose yellow perianth, corona of palest yellow; 'Camelot' ★, all-over yellow; 'Ceylon', yellow perianth, with orange corona; 'Chilli Belle', white perianth, with deep pink corona; 'Coquille', ivory perianth, orangey pink corona, deeper colored at rim; 'Fortune's Bowl', yellow perianth, with rich golden corona; 'Fragrant Breeze', cream perianth, with yellow corona, fragrant blooms; 'Golden Aura', brilliant yellow perianth, with yellow corona; 'Ice Follies', white perianth, with pale yellow corona; 'Modern Art', bright yellow perianth, with heavily ruffled orangey corona; 'Quasar', crisp white perianth, with deep orange-red and pink corona; 'Redhill', white perianth, orange-red corona; 'Saint Patrick's Day', all-over yellow; 'Salomé' ★, white perianth, with yellow corona; 'Woodland', ivory perianth, rich cream corona, with a hint of green; 'Zampatti', cream perianth, yellow and orange-gold corona. Zones 5–10.

DIVISION 3: SMALL-CUPPED

☼/☀ ❋ ↔ 12 in (30 cm) ↕ 12–14 in (30–35 cm)

Small-cupped flowers, with one bloom per stem and a cup length of less than one-third of the perianth length. Division 3 hybrids include 'Amor' ★, white perianth, with soft yellow corona; 'Barrett Browning', white perianth, with orange corona; 'Lough Areema', white perianth, with dark-edged greenish yellow corona; 'Red Ember', deep yellow perianth, with orange-red corona; 'Verger', white perianth, with red-edged golden corona. Zones 5–10.

DIVISION 4: DOUBLE

☼/☀ ❋ ↔ 12 in (30 cm) ↕ 10–14 in (25–35 cm)

These hybrids can have one or more flowers per stem. The corona or the perianth, or both, may be doubled. Popular doubles include: 'Bridal Crown', fully double, white and pale yellow; 'Candida', fully double, cream and pale yellow; 'Cheerfulness', fully double, creamy white, yellow center; 'Flower Drift', cream perianth, orange-red and yellow double corona; 'Madison', white double perianth, golden corona; 'Manly', fully double, white and bright yellow; 'Pink Paradise', white perianth, pink double corona; 'Tahiti', double perianth, yellow split orange corona; 'White Lion', fully double, pale yellow; 'Yellow Cheerfulness', yellow with some orange on central doubled petals. Zones 5–10.

DIVISION 5: TRIANDRUS

☼/☀ ❋ ↔ 8 in (20 cm) ↕ 6–10 in (15–25 cm)

These plants show clear evidence of *N. triandrus* parentage and usually have two or more pendent flowers per stem with reflexed perianth segments. 'Hawera', up to 5 pendulous soft-yellow flowers; 'Lapwing', white perianth, yellow corona; 'Thalia' ★, overall white to cream. Zones 5–10.

DIVISION 6: CYCLAMINEUS

☼/☀ ❋ ↔ 8 in (20 cm) ↕ 8–12 in (20–30 cm)

Hybrids of *N. cyclamineus* parentage with usually one flower per stem and perianth segments strongly reflexed, often almost to the stem. 'Dove Wings', soft yellow perianth, deep yellow corona; 'Jack Snipe', cream perianth, yellow corona; 'Jetfire', golden yellow perianth, orange corona. Zones 5–10.

DIVISION 7: JONQUILLA

☼/☀ ❋ ↔ 12 in (30 cm) ↕ 12–18 in (30–45 cm)

Plants with *N. jonquilla* parentage evident in their small fragrant flowers, in heads of 1 to 3, sometimes more, with a starry array of perianth segments. Some popular jonquils include: 'Bell Song', cream to pale yellow perianth, pink corona; 'Quail', overall deep golden yellow; 'Suzy', yellow perianth, orange corona; 'Trevithian', deep yellow perianth, darker corona. Zones 5–10.

DIVISION 8: TAZETTA

☼/☀ ❋ ↔ 18 in (45 cm) ↕ 12–18 in (30–45 cm)

Hybrids of *N. tazetta* with heads of 3 to 20 clustered, small, often highly scented flowers on sturdy stems. Popular for posies and corsages. The Tazetta hybrids include: 'Avalanche', white perianth, yellow corona; 'Geranium', white perianth, golden orange corona; 'Golden Dawn', yellow perianth, gold corona; 'Minnow', soft yellow perianth, darker corona; 'Ziva', white perianth, cream to pale yellow corona. Zones 5–10.

Narcissus, Hybrid Cultivar, 4. Double, 'Flower Drift'

Narcissus, Hybrid Cultivar, 5. Triandrus, 'Thalia'

Narcissus, Hybrid Cultivar, 6. Cyclamineus, 'Jack Snipe'

DIVISION 9: POETICUS

⚘/❀ ❄ ↔ 10 in (25 cm) ↑ 12–16 in (30–45 cm)

Hybrids of species belonging to the *N. poeticus* group. Distinctive, usually one flower per stem, with small disc-shaped corona edged in red. 'Actaea' ★, flat white petals, tiny cup-shaped trumpet, bright yellow, edged with red. 'Cantabile' and 'Felindre', popular cultivars. Zones 5–10.

DIVISION 10: WILD SPECIES

See the individual species entries.

DIVISION 11: SPLIT-CORONA

⚘/❀ ❄ ↔ 12 in (30 cm) ↑ 12–14 in (30–35 cm)

Unlike most daffodils with fused corona segments, split-corona forms have separate lobes, usually for more than half their length. 'Articol', white perianth with a pale dusky pink double corona; 'Egard', a white perianth with soft yellow corona; 'Sovereign', a white perianth with deep gold to orange corona. Zones 5–10.

Nerine sarniensis

DIVISION 12: MISCELLANEOUS

⚘/❀ ❄ ↔ 6–12 in (15–30 cm) ↑ 6–16 in (15–40 cm)

Division 12 includes daffodil garden forms that do not fall into any other division—for example, 'Jumblie', up to 3 flowers per stem, bright yellow. Zones 5–10.

NERINE

GUERNSEY LILY, SPIDER LILY

This genus in the amaryllis (Amaryllidaceae) family is from southern Africa and contains 23 species of autumn-flowering bulbs. Grassy to strappy leaves are evergreen or summer-deciduous. The flower stems carry many-flowered heads of long-tubed funnel-shaped flowers, each with 6 widely flared, reflexed, narrow petals. Bright pink and orange-red are the main colors; white forms are common.

CULTIVATION: They tolerate moderate frosts, but where the soil freezes, grow in pots that can be moved under cover. Plant in full sun/half-sun with the bulb neck exposed in a light, gritty, well-drained soil, with extra humus. Keep dry when dormant. Propagate by division, from offsets or seed. May self-sow.

Nerine bowdenii

⚘ ❄ ↔ 12 in (30 cm) ↑ 16–18 in (40–45 cm)

Well-known South African species. Leaves pale to dark green, glossy. Bright pink flowers with wavy edges, in clusters of up to 7, in autumn. Foliage comes up in early winter when flowering is over. 'Pink Triumph', deep pink flowers. Zones 8–11.

Nerine flexuosa

⚘/❀ ❄ ↔ 6 in (15 cm) ↑ 16–18 in (40–45 cm)

Almost evergreen species from South Africa. Leaves glossy green, to 12 in (30 cm) long. Pink flowers with wavy-edged petals, in clusters of up to 20, in autumn. 'Alba', commonly grown white form, ruffled edges. Zones 8–11.

Nerine sarniensis

GUERNSEY LILY

⚘ ✂ ↔ 6 in (15 cm) ↑ 16–18 in (40–45 cm)

South African species. Erect leaves, bright green. Heads of up to 20 brilliant orange-red flowers with wavy-edged petals and prominent stamens, in autumn. *N. s.* var. *curvifolia* f. *fothergillii* 'Major', larger and darker orange-red flowers. Zones 9–11.

NOMOCHARIS

A genus of 7 species closely related to *Lilium* and a member of the lily (Liliaceae) family, found from western China, through Tibet and northern Myanmar, into northern India. Bulbs consist of loose scales and leaves scattered up stems. Flowers are flat to open bowl-shaped, usually 1 to 9 per stem.

CULTIVATION: Provide a constantly moist, but not wet, humus-rich soil in a sheltered, humid environment. Propagate from seed.

Nomocharis aperta

❀/❀ ❄ ↔ 10 in (25 cm) ↑ 14–32 in (35–80 cm)

From western China. Oval leaves, pale green. Up to 6 nodding pale pink flowers, spotted deep purple, in summer. Zones 6–9.

ORNITHOGALUM

CHINCHERINCHEE, STAR OF BETHLEHEM

This genus of around 200 species of bulbs, in the hyacinth (Hyacinthaceae) family, is native to Europe, Western Asia, and Africa. Some form large clumps of grassy to strappy leaves, sometimes with a prominent midrib. In spring or summer, upright conical spikes of white to cream flowers appear, sometimes mildly scented, in whorls of 3, usually starry or cup-shaped.

CULTIVATION: Most European species tolerate mild frosts; lift South African species in winter. Plant in a sunny open position in any light well-drained soil. Water well when flowering.

Ornithogalum arabicum ★

☼/☀ ✤ ↔ 24–48 in (60–120 cm) ↑16–30 in (40–75 cm)
Native to the Mediterranean region. Heavily-textured leaves to
24 in (60 cm) long. Up to 20 large fragrant white or cream flowers,
conspicuous black ovaries, spring–early summer. Zones 9–10.

Ornithogalum dubium ★

☼/☀ ✤ ↔ 12–20 in (30–50 cm) ↑8–12 in
(20–30 cm)
Native to South Africa. Hair-fringed lance-
shaped leaves, to 4 in (10 cm). Crowded
heads of orange, red, yellow, or white
flowers, from winter to spring. Zones 8–10.

Ornithogalum longibracteatum

syn. *Ornithogalum caudatum*
FALSE SEA ONION, SEA ONION
☼/☀ ✤ ↔ 4 ft (1.2m) ↑2–4 ft (0.6–1.2 m)
Native to Cape region of South Africa. Green
bulb to 4 in (10 cm) diameter, sitting on surface of soil. Strappy, light green leaves, to
24 in (60 cm) long. Flower stems over 40 in
(100 cm) high, flowers small, green-striped, white,
largely enclosed within bracts, for most of year. Zones 9–10.

Ornithogalum narbonense

☼/☀ ✤ ↔ 24–48 in (60–120 cm) ↑24–36 in (60–90 cm)
Found from the Mediterranean to northern Iran. Very narrow
leaves, to 32 in (80 cm) long. Flower stems to 36 in (90 cm) tall;
heads of many small flowers, white with fine green center stripe,
in spring. Zones 7–10.

Ornithogalum nutans

☼/☀ ✤ ↔ 16–30 in (40–75 cm) ↑16–24 in (40–60 cm)
From Europe and Turkey. The plant has lax strappy leaves, to
16 in (40 cm) long. Nodding, translucent, attractive, green-
striped, white flowers, are borne on stems reaching up to 24 in
(60 cm) tall, during spring. Zones 6–9.

Ornithogalum dubium

Ornithogalum umbellatum

STAR OF BETHLEHEM
☼/☀ ✤ ↔ 20–32 in (50–80 cm) ↑20 in (50 cm)
Perennial from Europe and around the Mediterranean. Very
narrow leaves, to 12 in (30 cm) long, with pale midvein. Broad
heads of small, green-striped, white flowers, in spring. Zones 5–10.

OXALIS

A huge genus occurring worldwide of about
500 species belonging to the wood-sorrel
(Oxalidaceae) family. These mainly bulbous
plants also inlude evergreen ground-covering
perennials, succulents, and shrubs. Many
have clover-shaped leaves that close at night.
Flower buds are rolled like an umbrella and
open to bowl- or cup-shaped 5-petaled
blooms, some species opening only in full
sunlight. Some are troublesome weeds.
CULTIVATION: The bulbous winter-growers like
almost frost-free sunny sites, dry in summer.
Evergreen and woodland summer-growing
species prefer shade and moist soil. Some of
the succulent and shrubby forms, in all but frost-free climates,
should be grown as greenhouse plants. Propagation is from seed,
by division, or from cuttings of shrubby species.

Oxalis adenophylla

☼/☀ ✤ ↔ 5–6 in (12–15 cm) ↑3–4 in (8–10 cm)
A lovely clump-forming species from the Andes in Chile and
Argentina with fibrous bulbs. Suitable for rock gardens. The
gray-green leaves have up to 22 leaflets. Attractive pink, occasionally mauve, flowers, veined with purple, are produced in the late
spring. Zones 5–9.

Oxalis bowiei

syn. *Oxalis purpurata* var. *bowiei*
☼ ✤ ↔ 6–8 in (15–20 cm) ↑8–10 in (20–25 cm)
Summer-growing species from South Africa. Leaves with 3 leaflets, each to 1 in (25 mm) across. Flowers are bright pink, over
1½ in (35 mm) wide, held well above leaves. Zones 8–11.

Oxalis enneaphylla

SCURVY GRASS
☼/☀ ✤ ↔ 4–6 in (10–15 cm) ↑2½–3 in (6–8 cm)
Native to the Falkland Islands and Patagonia. Branched, slowly
spreading, scaly rhizomatous plant. The leaves have up to 20
gray-green pleated leaflets, giving them a crinkled appearance.
White to pink flowers, to 1 in (25 mm) across, borne from
spring to summer. 'Rosea' has deep pink flowers. Zones 6–9.

Oxalis hirta

☼ ✤ ↔ 4–6 in (10–15 cm) ↑10–12 in (25–30 cm)
Bushy bulbous species from South Africa. Upright leafy stems;
leaflets long and narrow; arranged in 3s but do not have classic
clover appearance. Flowers may be mauve through salmon to
bright pink, in autumn. Zones 8–10.

Oxalis hirta

Oxalis 'Ione Hecker' ★

☼/☽ ❋ ↔ 3–4 in (8–10 cm) ↑ 2½–3 in (6–8 cm)
Small rhizomatous hybrid between *O. enneaphylla* and *O. laciniata*. Finely divided foliage, tiny, semi-folded, gray-green leaflets. Produces large, violet-blue, purple-veined flowers. Zones 6–9.

Oxalis purpurea

☼ ❋ ↔ 18 in (45 cm) ↑ 3–4 in (8–10 cm)
Variable, strongly spreading bulbous perennial from South Africa. Leaves green, grayish, even purple, divided into 3 leaflets. Flowers white, yellow, pink, mauve, or purple. Zones 8–10.

Oxalis rubra

☼/☽ ❧ ↔ 12 in (30 cm) ↑ 16 in (40 cm)
Tuberous summer-growing perennial from Brazil and Argentina. Leaves with 3 leaflets are green marked with brown. Flowers white, lilac, pink, or red, in summer. Zones 9–11.

Oxalis 'Ione Hecker'

Oxalis triangularis

☀ ❋ ↔ 16 in (40 cm) ↑ 8–10 in (20–25 cm)
Summer-growing South American species; branching scaly rhizome. Leaves with 3 triangular leaflets, close at night; foliage deep purple suffused with violet. Slightly nodding pink flowers, in warmer months. *O. t.* subsp. *papilionacea* (syn. *O. regnellii*), bright green triangular leaves, pure white flowers. Zones 8–11.

Oxalis versicolor

BARBER'S POLE OXALIS, CANDY-CANE OXALIS
☼ ❧ ↔ 8 in (20 cm) ↑ 3–4 in (8–10 cm)
Winter-growing bulbous species from southern Africa. Neat clumps of fine foliage with 3 narrow leaflets. Flowers pure white, deep pink edges on outsides of petals. Zones 9–10.

PINELLIA

Genus of 6 species in the arum (Araceae) family from wooded regions of China, Korea, and Japan. Summer-growing tuberous perennials that have handsome leaves and strange usually green flowers consisting of a slightly hooded spathe with a long curving spadix. CULTIVATION: Grow *Pinellia* species in a semi-shaded aspect in moisture-retentive soil. Propagate from seed sown as soon as it is ripe, or by division of tubers when the plant is dormant. Some species produce tiny bulbils where the stem and leaf meet.

Pinellia cordata

❀ ❋ ↔ 4–6 in (10–15 cm) ↑ 4–6 in (10–15 cm)
Chinese species. Deep green spearhead-shaped leaves marked with white, and with purple undersides. It produces a single bulbil where the stem joins the leaf. Flowers are held at same level as the leaf and are green throughout. Zones 6–10.

POLIANTHES

This Mexican genus in the agave (Agavaceae) family comprises 13 species of strongly rhizomatous perennials forming clumps of linear to lance-shaped, sometimes strappy basal leaves, from which emerge upright flower stems bearing several pairs of very fragrant, waxy flowers backed by leafy bracts. The flowers of *P. tuberosa*, are cultivated for the perfume and florist trades. CULTIVATION: Plant in a sunny, sheltered position in fertile, moist, humus-rich, well-drained soil. Although perennial, they flower only once. Propagate by removing the strongest side-shoots before discarding spent crowns, or from seed.

Polianthes tuberosa

TUBEROSE
☼/☽ ❧ ↔ 20 in (50 cm) ↑ 48 in (120 cm)
Mexican perennial. Forms basal clump of narrow, strap-like, green to gray-green leaves. Racemes of fragrant, funnel-shaped, waxy, white flowers to 2 in (5 cm) long, with 6 widely flared lobes, on erect stems, are borne in summer–autumn. The popular cultivar 'The Pearl' is strongly scented, with attractive white, double flowers. Zones 9–10.

RANUNCULUS

BUTTERCUP
The type genus for the buttercup (Ranunculaceae) family, this widespread group encompasses some 400 species of annuals, biennials, and perennials, many of which are cultivated, others are admired in the wild, and some are despised as invasive weeds. The foliage varies markedly, though pinnate, glossy, leathery, kidney-shaped leaves predominate. The flowers too are often glossy and commonly have 5 petals. Most species produce yellow flowers but cultivated forms occur in many different colors. *Ranunculus* is Latin for little frog, a name given by the Roman Pliny due to the wet conditions in which they are often found growing. CULTIVATION: Buttercups are very hardy and will grow in a wide range of conditions, but generally prefer to have their roots kept cool and moist. Many have strong rhizomes that can be invasive. Bedding ranunculus "corms" can be lifted and stored dry. Propagate by division or from seed. Mildew can be a problem in autumn.

Polianthes tuberosa

Ranunculus aconitifolius

☼/☀ ❋ ↔ 40 in (100 cm) ↑ 24 in (60 cm)
Found in damp subalpine meadows of western and central European mountains. Forms a large clump of dark green, 3- to 5-lobed palmate leaves. White flowers, backed by purple-red-tinted sepals, in spring. 'Flore Pleno', a fully double-flowered form also known as fair maids of France or fair maids of Kent. Zones 6–9.

Ranunculus acris 'Flore Pleno'

Ranunculus acris

MEADOW BUTTERCUP

☀/◐ ❅ ↔ 24–48 in (60–120 cm) ↑ 24–40 in (60–100 cm)
Widely naturalized perennial from temperate Eurasia. Toothed leaves are 3- to 7-lobed. Small clusters of bright golden yellow flowers, in spring. Can be invasive. **'Flore Pleno'**, a double-flowered form that is also known as bachelor's buttons. Zones 5–10.

Ranunculus anemoneus

ANEMONE BUTTERCUP

☀/◐ ❅ ↔ 12–16 in (30–40 cm) ↑ 8–14 in (20–35 cm)
Alpine perennial from Mt Kosciuszko, New South Wales, Australia, with a low spreading habit. Basal leaves are 3- to 5-lobed and toothed. White flowers are solitary or paired, around 2 in (5 cm) wide, with up to 30 petals, in late spring. Zones 7–9.

Ranunculus asiaticus

◐/☀ ❅ ↔ 10 in (25 cm) ↑ 18 in (45 cm)
Rhizome-rooted southern Eurasian perennial. Finely divided, ferny, basal leaves; hairy upright flower stems. Large, often double flowers, in late spring–summer, mainly in yellow to red shades in the wild, but cultivated forms are available in many colors. Often sold as mixed color strains, such as **Bloomingdale Series**, 8 in (20 cm) tall, fully double flowers and compact habit, wide color range excluding mauve to purple shades; and **Tecolote Hybrids**, 18 in (45 cm) tall, very large double flowers, all colors except blue. Zones 8–10.

Ranunculus constantinopolitanus

☀/◐ ❅ ↔ 12–32 in (30–80 cm) ↑ 16–30 in (40–75 cm)
Perennial from southeastern Europe to the Middle East. Heart-shaped leaves are divided into 3 lobed, toothed segments. Glowing golden yellow flowers are clustered on erect stems, in spring to early summer. **'Flore Pleno'** (syns 'Plenus', 'Speciosus Plenus'), fully double flowers. Zones 6–9.

Ranunculus ficaria

COMMON BUTTERCUP, LESSER CELANDINE, PILEWORT

◐/☀ ❅ ↔ 8–24 in (20–60 cm) ↑ 6 in (15 cm)
Widely naturalized perennial from temperate Eurasia and North Africa. Forms a carpet of long-stemmed, lustrous dark green, heart-shaped leaves. Solitary, golden yellow, spring flowers. Mildly invasive. *R. f.* **'Brazen Hussy'** ★, dark bronze-green foliage and deep golden flowers. Zones 5–9.

Ranunculus flammula

LESSER SPEARWORT

◐/☀ ❅ ↔ 32–60 in (80–150 cm) ↑ 4–12 in (10–30 cm)
Semi-aquatic perennial indigenous to temperate Eurasia. Creeping stems strike root as they spread, and have narrow to broad, lance-shaped leaves. The pretty, bright yellow summer flowers are carried either singly or in small clusters. Zones 5–9.

Ranunculus gramineus

◐/☀ ❅ ↔ 6–12 in (15–30 cm) ↑ 8–20 in (20–50 cm)
Perennial from southern Europe and North Africa. Forms clumps. Gray-green to blue-green leaves, to 12 in (30 cm) long. Lemon yellow flowers, ¾ in (18 mm) wide, solitary or in groups of up to 3, in spring–summer. Zones 7–10.

Ranunculus lingua

GREATER SPEARWORT

◐/☀ ❅ ↔ 3–7 ft (0.9–2 m) ↑ 8–12 in (20–30 cm)
Semi-aquatic perennial found in shallow streams or continually damp areas from Europe to Siberia. Long spreading stems, striking roots as they grow; long-stemmed pointed oval leaves, to 8 in (20 cm) long. Clusters of bright yellow flowers, 2 in (5 cm) wide, in summer. Zones 4–9.

Ranunculus lyallii

Ranunculus lyallii

MOUNT COOK BUTTERCUP, MOUNT COOK LILY

☀/◐ ❅ ↔ 24–48 in (60–120 cm) ↑ 24–48 in (60–120 cm)
An attractive perennial from damp subalpine regions of New Zealand's South Island. Leathery, dark green, kidney-shaped leaves, to 16 in (40 cm) wide. Tall branching stems with panicles of pure white flowers, to 3 in (8 cm) wide, appear from late spring through to early summer. Zones 7–9.

Ranunculus parnassifolius

☀/◐ ❅ ↔ 8–12 in (20–30 cm) ↑ 2–4 in (5–10 cm)
Perennial native to southern Europe. Leathery, dark green, pointed oval, sometimes downy leaves, to 2 in (5 cm) long. Solitary white or light pink flowers, to 1 in (25 mm) wide, are borne in spring–summer. Zones 5–9.

RHODOHYPOXIS

Genus of about 6 low-growing, clump-forming, free-flowering, cormous perennials in the star-flower (Hypoxidaceae) family. Coming from the damp-summer climates of southern Africa, they rarely thrive in wet-winter dry-summer climates without some assistance. Leaves are generally grassy in character. Starry flowers, borne on slender stems about the height of the leaves, have 6 petals of equal length, arranged alternately in 2 ranks. CULTIVATION: In suitable conditions and lime-free soils, they can bloom from late spring until early autumn. Suitable for planting in peaty areas where dry winter dormancy period can be assured.

Rhodohypoxis baurii

RED STAR, ROSY POSY

☼ ❈ ↔ 2½–4 in (6–10 cm) ↑ 2½–4 in (6–10 cm)
Perennial from South Africa. Leaves are dull gray-green, grass-like, tuft-forming, lance-shaped, very hairy. Flowers held on short stems, upturned 6-petalled stars, almost flat, white through pink and red, throughout summer. *R. b.* var. *confecta*, white flowers reddening with age, a parent of many cultivars and hybrids. *R. b.* 'Tetra Red' ★, large dark pink-red flowers. Zones 8–9.

Rhodohypoxis Hybrid Cultivars

☼ ❈ ↔ 3–6 in (8–15 cm) ↑ 2½–4 in (6–10 cm)
There is often confusion between the numerous named hybrid cultivars, but they include the fairly distinctive '**Albrighton**', deep cherry-pink flowers; '**Appleblossom**', pale pink flowers; '**E. A. Bowles**', light candy pink petals; '**Fred Broome**', sugar pink petals, cream at base; '**Great Scott**', magenta petals; '**Harlequin**', pink flowers, flushed white; '**Monty**', bright cerise-pink flowers; '**Pinkeen**', narrow rich pink petals. Zones 8–9.

ROMULEA

Genus of some 80 or so species of small, crocus-like, cormous plants in the iris (Iridaceae) family, found from Europe through to South Africa. They have narrow to thread-like basal leaves from among which arise open funnel-shaped flowers on fine stems, singly or, in some species several to a stem, opening in succession. In most species the flowers open about midday, closing again at dark, and do not open at all on dull or wet days. CULTIVATION: The hardiest species can be grown in a sunny well-drained rock garden in areas that get little to no frosts; otherwise they must be container-grown in an alpine house and kept dry in summer. Propagation is by seed sown in autumn and by dividing the clumps of corms when dormant.

Romulea ramiflora

☼ ❈ ↔ 6–10 in (15–25 cm) ↑ 10–12 in (25–30 cm)
Dainty species from Mediterranean region. Erect or curved leaves. Pale lilac flowers, yellow or white throat, to 1 in (25 mm) across, in spring; produces 1 to 4 flowers per corm. Zones 8–10.

ROSCOEA

This genus of about 18 species of tuberous herbaceous perennials is a member of the ginger (Zingiberaceae) family. Summer growing, they are native to the Himalayas and China. They have often broad, heavily veined leaves sheathing the flower stems that support flowers almost orchid-like in their appearance. CULTIVATION: Grow in well-drained but humus-rich soil in a cool but not heavily shaded site. Plant the tubers about 6 in (15 cm) below the soil surface in late winter. Do not store dry. Propagate by division or from seed.

Roscoea alpina

◐ ❈ ↔ 5 in (12 cm) ↑ 10–12 in (25–30 cm)
Native to Nepal and Kashmir. Up to 4 leaves, to 4 in (10 cm) long, per tuber. Summer-produced flowers, pink or mauve, tend to be somewhat hidden among upper leaves. Zones 6–9.

Roscoea auriculata

◐ ❈ ↔ 5 in (12 cm) ↑ 12–20 in (30–50 cm)

Roscoea auriculata

From Nepal and Sikkim, India. It has up to 10 broad lance-shaped leaves, to 10 in (25 cm) long. The purple flowers, which are borne in late summer, measure 1½ in (35 mm) wide. Zones 6–9.

Roscoea 'Beesiana'

◐ ❈ ↔ 4–5 in (10–12 cm) ↑ 10–12 in (25–30 cm)
This hybrid is often thought to be the result of a cross between *R. purpurea* and *R. humeana,* but this is doubtful. The flowers can be yellow, red, pink, blue, or purple. Zones 6–9.

Roscoea cautleyoides

◐ ❈ ↔ 4–6 in (10–15 cm) ↑ 20–24 in (50–60 cm)
From China. The plant has up to 4 narrow leaves, to 16 in (40 cm) long. Flowers, held well above the leaves, usually yellow, but can also be purple or white, in early summer. Zones 6–9.

Roscoea humeana

◐ ❈ ↔ 5–6 in (12–15 cm) ↑ 8–10 in (20–25 cm)
Stocky Chinese species. Up to 3 leaves, not fully developed at flowering. Rich purple blooms, about 1½ in (4 cm) across, in early summer. Zones 7–9.

Rhodohypoxis baurii

Roscoea purpurea ★

syn. *Roscoea procera*

↔5–6 in (12–15 cm) ↑12–16 in (30–40 cm)

From the Himalayas. Up to 8 leaves. Rich purple flowers, sometimes white or marked white, to 2½ in (6 cm) wide. Zones 6–9.

SANDERSONIA

A genus consisting of a single species of scrambling to climbing tuberous perennial, which is a member of the autumn-crocus (Colchiacaceae) family. Now rare in its native South African habitat of KwaZulu-Natal, the species is widely cultivated in gardens and for the cut-flower trade.

CULTIVATION: Grow in full sun in a free-draining mix to which some well-rotted garden humus has been added. Poor soils are tolerated, and may even be preferable. Water well, and apply weak liquid feed every 10 days during the growth phase. Provide support for the climbing stems. Propagate from offsets in autumn, or by sowing ripe seed in a sandy mix in late winter.

Sandersonia aurantiaca ★

syn. *Sandersonia koetjape*

CHINESE LANTERN LILY, CHRISTMAS BELLS

↔8 in (20 cm) ↑40 in (100 cm)

Deciduous perennial, tuberous and scrambling to climbing. Leaves are a soft green, growing alternately along the stems; tips often develop into tendrils by which the plant scrambles. Flowers are lantern-shaped, glowing golden orange, pendent, on downturned stalks, in summer. Zones 9–11.

Sandersonia aurantiaca

SAURURUS

LIZARD'S TAIL

This genus of just 2 species—one from eastern Asia, and one from eastern North America—gives its name to the lizard's-tail (Saururaceae) family. They are tall, erect, rhizomatous, perennials that grow in bogs. They are often classed as tubers because of their fairly stout rootstock. Leaves are undivided and spirally arranged. The leaf-base is kidney- to heart-shaped; stipules are joined to the stalk. Flowerhead is a dense raceme on the ends of branches. Small ivory to white fragrant flowers, without sepals or petals, with 6, rarely 8, stamens. They produce no nectar, but have a faint scent. Round fruit is warty with just a single seed.

CULTIVATION: These are plants for bog gardens or damp woodlands. They are propagated by division, or from seed sown in pots that are always kept moist.

Saururus cernuus

LIZARD'S TAIL

↔36 in (90 cm) ↑12–18 in (30–45 cm)

Water plant from eastern USA. Forms small colonies by underground runners. Leaves are arrow- or heart-shaped. Bottlebrush-like flower spikes arch above foliage. Bead-like seeds resemble lizard's tail. Zones 5–10.

SCADOXUS

BLOOD LILY

A member of the amaryllis (Amaryllidaceae) family, this genus of 9 perennial species comes from the tropical regions of Africa and the Arabian Peninsula. They are closely related to species belonging to the genus *Haemanthus,* to which they bear a resemblance, and they also share the common name, blood lily. However, *Scadoxus* species are distinguished by the form and arrangement of their leaves, which do not have obvious midveins and are arranged in a rosette. *Scadoxus* also has fleshy-stemmed bulbs.

CULTIVATION: Plant bulbs in full sun or part-shade in fertile well-drained soil, with top of bulb above ground. When grown in pots, keep slightly damp while dormant; water well during the summer growth phase. In frost-prone areas, grow in the greenhouse. Propagate from seed or offsets.

Scadoxus multiflorus

syn. *Haemanthus multiflorus*

BLOOD LILY

↔24 in (60 cm) ↑20 in (50 cm)

Perennial from southern Africa. Large bulb. Almost evergreen, large fresh-green leaves, lance-shaped to oval, growing in an upright arching rosette. Flowers glowing salmon-red, large rounded heads of star-shaped florets, narrow petals, whiskery stamens, in summer. ***S. m.* subsp. *katherinae*** ★ (syn. *Haemanthus katherinae*), wavy undulating leaves. ***S. m.* 'Koning Albert'** (syn. *Haemanthus* 'King Albert'), coral-red flowers. Zones 9–11.

SCILLA

BLUEBELL, SQUILL

This genus of 90 species of bulbs of the hyacinth (Hyacinthaceae) family, is found from western Europe to Japan and in parts of Africa. They form clumps of grassy or strappy bright green leaves, and some, for example *S. peruviana*, can cover a large area in a relatively short time. Long flower stems carry conical heads of small, star-shaped, sometimes fragrant flowers. Although the flowering time varies with the species, it is usually spring. While species often have mauve to purple flowers, the cultivars occur in a wide color range. Extracts of squill bulbs have a long history of medicinal use, mainly as diuretics and expectorants.

CULTIVATION: Bluebells are mostly quite hardy and are easily cultivated in full or half-sun with moist, humus-rich, well-drained soil. When the clumps become large, lift and divide them, as the foliage dies back in autumn. They can be raised from seed, but take longer to flower.

Scilla bifolia

TWO-LEAFED SQUILL

↔3 in (8 cm) ↑3–6 in (8–15 cm)

From Europe. Each bulb produces 2, occasionally 3, green elongated leaves. Pretty, small deep blue-violet flowers, appear along with the leaves, in early spring. Zones 4–8.

Scilla hyacinthoides
HYACINTH SCILLA

☼ ❄ ↔12 in (30 cm) ↑36 in (90 cm)
Rare bulb from the Mediterranean. Strap-shaped green leaves. Strong stems each carry up to 100 small, violet-blue, star-shaped flowers, in mid-spring. Zones 8–11.

Scilla liliohyacinthus
PYRENEAN SQUILL

☼/◐ ❄ ↔4 in (10 cm) ↑4 in (10 cm)
From France and Spain. The leaves are broad, strap-like, mid-green, lustrous. Flowers are pale violet, with deep purple anthers, and appear in mid- to late spring. Zones 6–8.

Scilla natalensis ★
BLUE SQUILL

☼/◐ ❄ ↔20 in (50 cm) ↑36 in (90 cm)
From South Africa. Short dark green leaves. Long-lasting, graceful, starry, blue plumes of flowers, 50 to 100 per stalk, in spring–summer. Zones 7–10.

Scilla peruviana
CUBAN LILY, HYACINTH-OF-PERU

☼ ❄ ↔18 in (45 cm) ↑12 in (30 cm)
From the Mediterranean. The shiny green leaves are broad-pointed, and have fleshy stems. A rounded cushion of indigo-blue star-shaped flowers is produced from mid-spring–early summer. *S. p.* var. *venusta*, from Tunisia, mauve-blue flowers, leaves lie flat. Zones 8–11.

Scilla ramburei

☼ ❄ ↔4 in (10 cm) ↑6 in (15 cm)
From Spain and Portugal. Has 3 to 6, narrow, bright green curled, grasslike, leaves, and flattish nodding inflorescences of violet-blue flowers, ½–¾ in (12–18 mm) wide, spring. Robust, salt tolerant. Zones 7–10.

Scilla siberica
BLUE SQUILL, SIBERIAN SQUILL

☼/◐ ❄ ↔3 in (8 cm) ↑6 in (15 cm)
From Russia and southwest Asia. Strap-like, glossy, bright green leaves. Bright blue star-shaped flowers in groups of 3 to 5 per stem, in early spring. 'Spring Beauty', large blue flowers, taller. Zones 2–8.

Scilla tubergeniana ★
syn. *Scilla mischtschenkoana* 'Tubergeniana'

☼/◐ ❄ ↔4 in (10 cm) ↑5 in (12 cm)
From Iran and Russia. Cup-shaped white or pale blue flowers with deep blue veins in early spring. Shiny strap-like leaves follow flowers. Good in shady rock gardens. Zones 5–7.

Scilla peruviana

Scilla siberica 'Spring Beauty'

Sparaxis tricolor

SPARAXIS
HARLEQUIN FLOWER

Under suitable conditions, this South African genus of 6 species of corms in the iris (Iridaceae) family will naturalize and form large drifts. Leaves are grassy to sword-shaped, with prominent ribbing, developing quickly from late winter, followed by wiry spikes carrying just a few blooms or fan-like sprays of ¾ in (18 mm) wide, 6-petalled, funnel-shaped flowers that may be white, yellow, or shades of pink to orange and red, usually with a yellow center and contrasting colors in the throat. CULTIVATION: They are not hardy where the soil freezes but otherwise are easily grown in full sun in fertile, moist, well-drained soil. In cold areas, lift in autumn and replant in early spring for a late flower show. Propagation is from seed or by division.

Sparaxis fragrans

☼/◐ ⚘ ↔6–12 in (15–30 cm) ↑8–18 in (20–45 cm)
Grassy leaves to ½ in (12 mm) long. Un-branched flower stems, spikes of variably colored, fragrant flowers to over 2 in (5 cm) wide. Flowers yellow, often purple-red or black sectors and dark streaks. *S. f.* subsp. *acutifolia*, pointed golden yellow flowers. *S. f.* subsp. *grandiflora*, fragrant yellow-centered white flowers. Zones 9–10.

Sparaxis tricolor ★
VELVET FLOWER

☼/◐ ⚘ ↔8 in (20 cm) ↑8–16 in (20–40 cm)
Narrow sword-shaped leaves and 1 to 5 flower stems per corm, each with up to 5 darkly marked, yellow-centered, orange to red flowers to over 1 in (25 mm) wide. Readily naturalizes in suitable climates. Zones 9–10.

SPREKELIA

This single-species genus in the amaryllis (Amaryllidaceae) family is native to the dry winter/wet spring and summer climates of Central and South America. In cultivation, however, these bulbous perennials seem quite happy to sit in damp but well-drained situations during the winter months. They produce large red flowers in almost frost-free climates.
CULTIVATION: They flower best in well-established clumps and resent root disturbance. In frost-prone climates, grow in pots, moving into protected conditions during the colder months. When in growth, give a weak liquid feed every 10 days. Propagate from offsets taken in autumn, and by sowing ripe seeds.

Sprekelia formosissima ★
AZTEC LILY, JACOBEAN LILY, ST JAMES LILY
☼/◐ ❄ ↔ 8 in (20 cm) ↑ 12 in (30 cm)
Winter dormant or almost evergreen depending on conditions. Leaves strap-like, forming dense clumps. Flowers showy, solitary, 6-petalled, 3 upright and 3 pointing downward, dark red to orange-red. Flowering varies between late winter and summer. Zones 7–10.

Sprekelia formosissima

STENOMESSON

There are about 30 species of bulbous perennials in this genus, which belongs to the amaryllis (Amaryllidaceae) family. Most are uncommon in cultivation. They are found on high rocky slopes and in the meadows of the Andes in Peru, Bolivia, and Ecuador, where snow sometimes provides the protection from frost that these plants require.
CULTIVATION: Easily grown outside in frost-free climates, these plants can be cultivated under glass in colder climates provided temperatures do not fall below 44–50°F (7–10°C). Bulbs should be kept slightly moist when dormant in winter. Propagate from offsets or fresh seed sown ripe in sand.

Stenomesson miniatum ★
☼ ❄ ↔ 6 in (15 cm) ↑ 12–16 in (30–40 cm)
Almost evergreen in some conditions or winter dormant. The leaves are dark green, narrow, strap-like. The flowers orange to red, umbels of drooping tubular bells, on straight stalks, in spring–summer. Anthers creamy yellow, protruding. Zones 8–10.

Stenomesson miniatum

STERNBERGIA
AUTUMN CROCUS, AUTUMN DAFFODIL
There are 7 to 8 species in this genus of bulbous perennials, which belong to the amaryllis (Amaryllidaceae) family. They come from the sparse woodlands and winter-rainfall climates of southern Europe and central Asia. Often confused with *Crocus*, they can be distinguished by their leaves, which do not bear the pale midrib of the true crocus. The goblet-like flowers, however, are recognizably crocus-like. The majority bloom in autumn.
CULTIVATION: They do best when provided with sharp drainage, in summer heat, and a limy soil. They are intolerant of wet soggy root conditions in frost-prone climates. In containers, use equal parts of loam, leaf mold, and sand. Water sparingly and only during the growing season.

Sternbergia lutea ★
☼/◐ ❄ ↔ 3 in (8 cm) ↑ 6 in (15 cm)
Found from southern Europe to central Asia. Leaves black-green, linear, appear with flowers, persist until spring. Flowers large, bright yellow, goblet-like, in autumn. Zones 7–9.

Sternbergia sicula
☼/◐ ❄ ↔ 3 in (8 cm) ↑ 3–4 in (8–10 cm)
Vigorous species from Italy to southeastern Europe. Regarded by some as a subspecies of *S. lutea*, to which it has a marked resemblance, although a smaller size and more open star-like flowers. Zones 7–9.

TECOPHILAEA
BLUE CROCUS, CHILEAN CROCUS
Native to mountainous areas in Chile, this genus of just 2 species of cormous perennials has its own family (Tecophilaeaceae). It is rare to the point of extinction in the wild. However, collectors cherish them for their glamorous coloring, which varies between royal blue, gentian blue, and a pale true-blue. New growth occurs as the snows melt, and it is this protective blanket of snow that is thought to assist in the production of the spring-borne flowers.
CULTIVATION: Grow these plants in full sun in a fertile, well-drained soil. Watch for snails, which are major predators. When grown under glass, be sure to use a sandy fertile potting mix and water only when in growth. Propagation is from offsets or by sowing fresh ripe seed.

Tecophilaea cyanocrocus ★
CHILEAN CROCUS
☼ ❄ ↔ 2 in (5 cm) ↑ 4–5 in (10–12 cm)
Perennial from Chile. The leaves are narrow, lance-shaped, and emerge with the flowers. Flowers are a heavenly blue, with 6 petals variously marked in white, in early spring. It dislikes soggy wet winters; likes dryish sunny summers. Zones 8–10.

TIGRIDIA
JOCKEY'S CAP, TIGER FLOWER
This bulbous genus in the iris (Iridaceae) family comprises 23 species found in Mexico and Guatemala. They have sword- to lance-shaped leaves with pronounced longitudinal ribbing. Upright, sometimes-branched flower stems appear from late

spring through summer, carrying interestingly shaped and colored blooms with a bold tiger-stripe patterned central cup surrounded by 3 large lobes with 3 small lobes in between. Individual flowers last one day and occur in a range of shades.

CULTIVATION: Considering their origins, these are surprisingly hardy bulbs that will thrive anywhere the soil does not freeze to bulb depth. Elsewhere they can be lifted for winter and replanted in spring. Propagate from offsets or from seed.

Tigridia pavonia ★

☀ ⚘ ↔12–20 in (30–50 cm) ↑24–48 in (60–120 cm)

Long-flowering species native to Mexico. The basal leaves grow 12–20 in (30–50 cm) long. Flower stems are usually about 24 in (60 cm) long, sometimes longer. Flowers yellow to red with heavily red-marked yellow cup, from spring to summer. Zones 9–10.

TRITELEIA

The name of this genus of 15 species of corms from western North America was bestowed because the flowers are arranged in threes. Members of the onion (Alliaceae) family, they form clumps of long, narrow, rather grass-like leaves that are often starting to fade or may have died away before the upright flower stems appear. Usually 12–24 in (30–60 cm) tall and borne in late spring, they carry heads of funnel-shaped white, blue, or purple, rarely yellow, flowers. The corms of at least one species, *T. hyacinthina*, have been used as vegetables by Native Americans, eaten boiled and mashed.

CULTIVATION: These plants require full sun and fertile well-drained soil. Water them well during the growing season but allow them to dry off after flowering. Most species are very hardy provided the soil does not become waterlogged in winter. Propagate by breaking up established clumps after flowering, or from seed.

Triteleia grandiflora

DOUGLAS'S TRITELEIA, HOWELL'S TRITELEIA

☀/☽ ❄ ↔8–12 in (20–30 cm) ↑12–24 in (30–60 cm)

Clumping species found from British Columbia, Canada, to Utah, USA. Fine grass-like foliage. Each wiry flower stem bears

Triteleia ixioides

Tigridia pavonia

a head of mauve to blue, rarely white, funnel-shaped flowers with widely flared lobes, in summer. Zones 5–9.

Triteleia hyacinthina

☀/☽ ❄ ↔8–12 in (20–30 cm) ↑18–24 in (45–60 cm)

Found from British Columbia, Canada, to California, USA. Foliage grass-like. Usually several wiry flower stems with heads of around 10 white to lavender, bowl-shaped flowers, to 1 in (25 mm) wide, in summer. Zones 4–9.

Triteleia ixioides

GOLDEN BRODIAEA, PRETTY FACE

☀/☽ ❄ ↔8–12 in (20–30 cm) ↑18–24 in (45–60 cm)

Widespread in western USA. Grass-like foliage. Usually just 1 or 2 wiry flower stems with heads of about 10 golden yellow, widely flared, funnel-shaped flowers. 'Starlight', pale yellow flowers, may be a form of *T. i.* subsp. *scabra*. Zones 7–10.

Triteleia laxa

GRASSNUT, TRIPLET LILY

☀/☽ ❄ ↔8–12 in (20–30 cm) ↑24–30 in (60–75 cm)

Widespread in western USA. Flower stems are sturdy, with heads to 6 in (15 cm) wide. Flowers are funnel-shaped, lavender blue to white, around 2 in (5 cm) long, and are produced in summer. 'Koningin Fabiola' (syn. Queen Fabiola), vigorous, with stronger, more numerous flower stems; 'Sierra Giant', large cobalt blue flowers with shiny petals. Zones 6–9.

Triteleia lilacina

GLASSY HYACINTH

☀/☽ ❄ ↔6–10 in (15–25 cm) ↑12–20 in (30–50 cm)

Very grassy species from California, USA, with very fine foliage and wiry flower stems. Small lilac flowers with glassy, finely textured interior, in summer. Zones 7–10.

TRITONIA

This genus of 28 species of cormous deciduous perennials is a member of the iris (Iridaceae) family and comes from the grassy and stony hillsides of southern Africa. They are closely related to *Chasmanthe, Crocosmia, Ixia,* and *Montbretia,* with which they are often confused. To add to the confusion, many now nameless cultivars and hybrids survive in old gardens. These clump-forming plants have reed-like leaves and their flared trumpet stems are usually arranged in rows along single or branching stems. CULTIVATION: They need sharp drainage, dry summers and wet winters coupled with nutrition during growth. Some may become weedy. Propagate from offsets or by sowing fresh seed.

Tritonia crocata
syn. *Tritonia hyalina*
BLAZING STAR

☼ ❊ ↔ 4 in (10 cm) ↑ 10–18 in (25–45 cm)
Variable summer-dormant species from Africa is widespread in cultivation, rare in the wild. Leaves are erect and grass-like, stems are wiry. Open-cupped flowers, up to 10 per spike, are produced in bright orange, tawny red, or salmon red shades, in spring. 'Princess Beatrix' has brilliant red-orange flowers. Zones 8–10.

TULBAGHIA
SOCIETY GARLIC, WILD GARLIC

This genus, which is a member of the onion (Alliaceae) family, is known for its flowering habit. These bulbous perennials come from summer-rainfall areas in southern Africa, and those in cultivation adapt well to irrigated beds in dry-summer climates. They also pick well, pot well and, generally speaking, lead clumping trouble-free lives. The umbels of starry flowers are held well above the leaves. Many species carry a persistent stale garlic scent when crushed. The flowers of these garden-grown members perform well over extended periods, and some will even put on two flowery displays in a single year, depending on conditions. CULTIVATION: Grow in full sun in well-drained soils and water well while in growth. Provide a sheltered spot in cool climates. Propagate from offsets or by sowing fresh ripe seed.

Tulbaghia simmleri

Tulbaghia alliacea

☼ ❊ ↔ 16–20 in (40–50 cm) ↑ 18–20 in (45–50 cm)
Semi-evergreen perennial from Zimbabwe and South Africa. Green strappy leaves. Clusters of ½ in (12 mm) wide, green, slightly scented flowers with an orange center. Zones 8–10.

Tulbaghia cominsii

☼/◗ ❊ ↔ 6 in (15 cm) ↑ 6–10 in (15–25 cm)
A sweetly scented perennial from South Africa. Foliage narrow, linear, grooved, with stale garlic scent when crushed. Flowers pale lilac to white to cream, purplish throat, from spring to summer. Recent introduction to cultivation. Zones 8–10.

Tulbaghia natalensis ★

☼/◗ ❊ ↔ 6 in (15 cm) ↑ 8–12 in (20–30 cm)
Small perennial from Zimbabwe and South Africa. Leaves linear, light green, stale garlic scent when crushed. Flowers dark purple or white, slightly fragrant, in early to late summer. Zones 8–10.

Tulbaghia simmleri
syns *Tulbaghia fragrans, T. pulchella*
PINK AGAPANTHUS, SWEET GARLIC

☼ ❊ ↔ 10–12 in (25–30 cm) ↑ 20–24 in (50–60 cm)
Bulbous semi-evergreen perennial from South Africa. Comparatively broad gray-green leaves. Clusters of up to 40 scented mauve flowers, from spring to summer. 'Alba' (syn. *T. fragrans* 'Alba') is a pure white form. Zones 8–10.

Tulbaghia violacea ★

☼/◗ ❊ ↔ 12 in (30 cm) ↑ 12–16 in (30–40 cm)
Vigorous clump-forming plant from South Africa, with gray-green foliage. Clusters of up to 20 pink-mauve flowers produced almost year-round where frost is minimal. The whole plant has a strong garlic smell when crushed. Can become a weed if neglected. 'Silver Lace' (syn. 'Variegata'), slightly smaller variegated form with cream stripes. Zones 8–10.

TULIPA
TULIP

This genus, a member of the lily (Liliaceae) family, contains approximately 100 species of bulbs occurring naturally in northern temperate regions, especially in central Asia. Cultivated for at least 3,000 years, they reached Europe from Turkey in 1554. The Dutch "tulipomania" of the 1630s established tulips in folklore as well as gardens. The foliage is gray-green to blue-green and may be grass-like or quite broad, with contrasting markings. The flowers vary widely. The numerous hybrids and cultivars are divided into 15 groups based mainly on parentage and flower type. *Tulipa* species generally fall into the Miscellaneous Group (Group 15); any exceptions to this general rule are indicated in their individual entry. CULTIVATION: Tulips require a temperate climate and winter chilling, preferring a sunny position that does not bake in summer. Plant at around 6 in (15 cm) depth in autumn, watering well once foliage appears. Propagate hybrids and cultivars from offsets; species also from seed.

Tulipa acuminata
HORNED TULIP

☼ ❋ ↔ 2–4 in (5–10 cm) ↑ 18 in (45 cm)
Narrow species from Turkey. Gray-green foliage has undulating edges. Narrow, 3–5 in (8–12 cm) long flowers, scarlet and yellowish with curious, narrow, twisted tips. Zones 3–8.

Tulipa aucheriana
☼ ❋ ↔ 2–4 in (5–10 cm) ↑ 2–4 in (5–10 cm)
Tiny species from Iran and Syria. Dwarf plant with strap-like, deep green, almost prostrate leaves with wavy edges. The flowers are star-shaped, 1 to 3 per stem, deep rose pink with a yellow basal blotch, in mid-spring. Zones 5–8.

Tulipa clusiana
CANDY-STICK TULIP, LADY TULIP

☼ ❋ ↔ 4 in (10 cm) ↑ 8–12 in (20–30 cm)
From Iran, Iraq, and Afghanistan. Linear gray-green leaves with a soft bloom. Flowers open flat and star-shaped. They have a white interior, a dark blue base; outer petals are red edged white, in spring. *T. c.* var. *chrysantha* (syn. *T. chrysantha*), bright golden tepals with a red or purple-brown exterior. Zones 3–8.

Tulipa fosteriana
☼ ❋ ↔ 4–6 in (10–15 cm) ↑ 12–16 in (30–40 cm)
Outstanding species from eastern Uzbekistan. Oblong to broadly ovate, glossy green leaves. Faintly scented, vivid scarlet flowers with black basal blotch edged yellow. Mostly used in hybridizing. Group 13. Zones 5–8.

Tulipa greigii
☼ ❋ ↔ 6 in (15 cm) ↑ 6–10 in (15–25 cm)
Small species from central Asia. Lance-shaped to oblong leaves with a soft bloom, mottled and striped purple-brown. The solitary, cup-shaped, scarlet, yellow, or multicolored flowers with black or red blotch on a yellow base, appear in mid-spring. Group 14. Zones 5–8.

Tulipa hageri
☼/◑ ❋ ↔ 8 in (20 cm) ↑ 6–10 in (15–25 cm)
From the eastern Mediterranean. Each bulb has 2 to 7 grass-like leaves and 3 to 5 wide open, red flowers, contrasting buff exterior, about 2 in (5 cm) wide. Excellent rockery or alpine-garden plant. Zones 5–9.

Tulipa humilis
syns *Tulipa pulchella*, *T. violacea*

☼ ❋ ↔ 2–4 in (5–10 cm) ↑ 4–6 in (10–15 cm)
Variable species from southeastern Turkey, Iraq, and Azerbaijan. Linear gray-green leaves. Flowers bright rose pink to violet, basal blotches pink, purple to black, yellow, or blue, in early spring. Violacea Group, deep violet, yellow center. Zones 3–8.

Tulipa linifolia, Batalinii Group, 'Bronze Charm'

Tulipa orphanidea, Whittallii Group Cultivar

Tulipa iliensis
☼ ❋ ↔ 2–4 in (5–10 cm) ↑ 8 in (20 cm)
An attractive, erect species originating from central Asia, with channeled undulate leaves with a soft bloom. Clusters of 1 to 5 striking yellow flowers with red and dull green reverse, are borne in early spring. Zones 6–8.

Tulipa kaufmanniana
WATERLILY TULIP

☼ ❋ ↔ 6 in (15 cm) ↑ 6–10 in (15–25 cm)
Broad-flowered species from central Asia. Slightly narrow, wavy-edged, gray-green foliage. Spring flowers open flat, star-shaped, creamy white with yellow base, outer segments streaked with red; also pink, orange, and red forms. Group 12. Zones 3–8.

Tulipa linifolia
☼ ❋ ↔ 4 in (10 cm) ↑ 4–6 in (10–15 cm)
Variable species from central Asia, northern Iran, and Afghanistan. Lance-shaped, undulating, red-edged, gray-green leaves. Shiny red flowers with a cream-edged jet black blotch, in spring. Batalinii Group (syn. *T. batalinii*), formerly listed as a separate species, single soft yellow to apricot flowers; 'Bronze Charm', yellow with bronze markings. Zones 5–9.

Tulipa orphanidea
☼/◑ ❋ ↔ 6 in (15 cm) ↑ 6–15 in (15–38 cm)
Variable species from Turkey. Grass-like leaves, 2 to 7 per bulb. Orange-red flowers with a contrasting buff exterior, often green- or purple-tinted, 1 to 4 per bulb. Whittallii Group (syn. *T. whittallii*), star-shaped flowers, orange to red-brown. Zones 5–9.

Tulipa tarda

Tulipa turkestanica

Tulipa vvedenskyi

Tulipa praestans

☼/◐ ❋ ↔ 6–8 in (15–20 cm) ↑ 6–20 in (15–50 cm)
From central Asia. Leaves blue-green, 4 to 6 per bulb. Goblet-shaped, bright red flowers to 3 in (8 cm) wide, 1 to 5 per stem. **'Fusilier'**, up to 4 orange-red flowers per stem; **'Unicum'**, similar flowers but distinctive cream-edged foliage. Zones 5–9.

Tulipa primulina

☼ ❋ ↔ 2–4 in (5–10 cm) ↑ 8 in (20 cm)
Very rare species from northwestern Algeria. Gray-green leaves. Nodding flowers are held singly or in pairs, ivory to pale yellow tepals with rose pink or light green exterior, in spring. Zones 5–8.

Tulipa sylvestris

☼ ❋ ↔ 4–6 in (10–15 cm) ↑ 10–18 in (25–45 cm)
A tall species, naturalized in Europe, Iran, and North Africa. Network of thin fleshy stems. Narrow dark green leaves with a soft bloom. Fragrant flowers, clear yellow, exterior occasionally tinged green or red, petal tips reflexed, in spring. Zones 3–8.

Tulipa tarda

☼/◐ ❋ ↔ 6–8 in (15–20 cm) ↑ 4–6 in (10–15 cm)
Small species from central Asia. Leaves are narrow, deep green to blue-green. Flowers are small, starry, cream to yellow with a maroon- to green-tinted exterior, in spring. Zones 5–9.

Tulipa turkestanica

☼/◐ ❋ ↔ 6–10 in (15–25 cm) ↑ 8–10 in (20–25 cm)
Slightly clumping species from central Asia. Narrow blue-green foliage, 2 to 4 leaves per bulb. The small, starry, yellow-centered white to cream flowers, up to 12 per stem, are borne in spring. The flower stem is shorter than the foliage. Zones 5–9.

Tulipa undulatifolia

syn. *Tulipa eichleri*
☼/◐ ❋ ↔ 6–10 in (15–25 cm) ↑ 12–20 in (30–50 cm)
This narrow species from the Balkans, Turkey, Greece, Iran, and central Asia has wavy-edged blue-green leaves, fringed with very short hairs. Flower stems are wiry, with 1 flower per stem. The bright red flowers, with a dark central zone, are an open goblet shape, and appear in late spring. Zones 5–9.

Tulipa urumiensis

☼ ❋ ↔ 4–6 in (10–15 cm) ↑ 4–6 in (10–15 cm)
From northwestern Iran and eastern Turkey. Mostly subterranean stem; rosettes of linear leaves. Flowers cup-shaped, opening to bright golden yellow star, bronze-streaked reverse. Zones 3–8.

Tulipa vvedenskyi

☼/◐ ❋ ↔ 6–16 in (15–40 cm) ↑ 6–8 in (15–20 cm)
A small species from central Asia. Undulating, downy, blue-green, sometimes purple-tinted leaves, held near horizontally at ground level. Flowers vivid orange-red, single, with broad buff to pale green exterior mid-stripes, in mid-spring. Zones 3–9.

Tulipa Hybrid Cultivars

☼/◐ ❋ ↔ 4–12 in (10–30 cm) ↑ 4–30 in (10–75 cm)
Tulip hybrids are divided into 15 groups according to flower type. The flowers come in a bewildering array of forms and colors and include the Parrot Group with deeply cut petals, Viridifloras with green markings and those with broad splashes or "flames" of a contrasting color. Zones 6–9.

SINGLE EARLY GROUP (GROUP 1)

Single-flowered, single or multi-colored forms about 12–18 in (30–45 cm) tall, generally blooming within a month after spring equinox. **'Apricot Beauty'**, apricot-pink suffused soft orange; **'Christmas Dream'**, bright pink; **'Diana'**, pure white; **'Kiezer-kroon'**, Rembrandt Group look-alike, golden yellow with broad red flame; **'Van der Neer'**, bright purple, in cultivation since 1860.

DOUBLE EARLY GROUP (GROUP 2)

Fully double-flowered forms 12–16 in (30–40 cm) tall, generally blooming within a month after spring equinox. **'Baby Doll'**, golden yellow; **'Double Price'**, lavender-pink; **'Murillo'**, deep pink; **'Orange Nassau'**, deep red with lighter zones; **'Peach Blossom'**, deep pink flamed and flecked with white.

TRIUMPH GROUP (GROUP 3)

Single-flowered hybrids between single early and Darwin tulips, from 15–20 in (38–50 cm) tall, often with contrastingly colored petal edges or flecks. Generally bloom after the spring equinox. **'Abu Hassan'**, deep red with a yellow edge; **'Attila'**, pinkish purple; '**Couleur Cardinal**', bright red with purple-tinted base; '**Don Quichotte**', mauve-pink; '**Ice Follies**', Rembrandt Group look-alike, white with red flaming; '**Leen van der Mark**', cherry red with yellow edges ageing to white; '**Negrita**' ★, deep purple; '**New Design**', white with pink edge and white-edged foliage.

DARWIN HYBRID GROUP (GROUP 4)

Single-flowered hybrids between single late (Group 5) tulips and *T. fosteriana* and/or similar closely related species. They are 20–27 in (50–70 cm) tall, and in cool areas flower more than a month after spring equinox; also called Cottage tulips. '**Ad Rem**', orange-red blooms with a gold edge; '**Apeldoorn**', deep red with a yellow center; '**Apeldoorn's Elite**', red, edged with yellow; '**Daydream**', irregular mix of yellow, orange, and apricot; '**Elizabeth Arden**', orange-pink to red, yellow base; '**Golden Apeldoorn**', deep yellow; '**Ollioules**', dark pink with paler edges; '**Olympic Flame**', yellow with red flame.

SINGLE LATE GROUP (GROUP 5)

Single-flowered forms, 18–30 in (45–75 cm) tall, usually flower more than a month after spring equinox. '**Bleu Aimable**', purple suffused with lavender; '**Candy Club**', pale pink with dark central "kiss;" '**Dordogne**', soft orange edges, deepening to center; '**Douglas Bader**', soft pink; '**Dreamland**', deep pink, light edges, white base; '**Halcro**', deep red; '**Perestroyka**', white with purplish red markings; '**Queen of Night**', deep black-purple; '**Sorbet**', white flowers flamed cherry red; '**Union Jack**', a Rembrandt Group look-alike, white flowers, edged deep red.

LILY-FLOWERED GROUP (GROUP 6)

Long 2-toned flowers tapering at the center to distinct waist. Lily-flowered tulips, 15–24 in (38–60 cm) tall. Variable flowering time. '**Aladdin**', bright red with yellow edge and center; '**Ballade**', violet edged with white; '**China Pink**', deep pink with light tips and center; '**Elegant Lady**', soft gold turning to pink near tips; '**Queen of Sheba**', red with golden orange edge; '**West Point**', bright golden yellow; '**White Triumphator**', pure white.

FRINGED GROUP (GROUP 7)

Flowers with fringed edges, the fringe itself often in a contrasting color to the rest of the flower, usually with a crystalline texture, 18–26 in (45–65 cm) tall. '**Arma**', deep red with a crystalline fringe; '**Blue Heron**', dusky purple and mauve with white fringe; '**Burgundy Lace**' ★, wine red with crystalline edge.

VIRIDIFLORA GROUP (GROUP 8)

These tulips are around 12–20 in (30–50 cm) tall, with either strong green coloration in the base or an external flare up the center of each petal. '**Artist**', salmon suffused with orange and purple, and a green flame; '**China Town**', dusky light pink, with

Tulipa, Hybrid Cultivar, Single Early, 'Van der Neer'

darker edges and green flame; '**Golden Artist**', deep golden yellow, with a green flame that is edged with red; '**Groenland**', mid-pink, a narrow green flame with a broad pale pink edge.

REMBRANDT GROUP (GROUP 9)

Fancy-flowered, often multi-colored tulips with contrasting flares, flecks, and veining, usually on a base color of yellow, red, or white, patterns originating from a viral disease that led to the plants' slow decline; cultivars with such viral patterning are now banned from sale. Members of other groups can show similar color patterns. Modern Rembrandt look-alikes that fall into other groups include: '**Olympic Flame**' (Darwin Group); '**Kiezerkroon**' (Single Early Group); and '**Union Jack**', (Single Late Group).

PARROT GROUP (GROUP 10)

These hybrids, 18–22 in (45–55 cm) tall, largely result from sports within other groups and have deeply cut petals, often bicolored. '**Bird of Paradise**' has deep red flowers edged with gold; '**Blue Parrot**' is a deep mauve; '**Fantasy**', deep pink with purple-green flame near tips; '**Karel Doorman**', bright red edged with gold; '**Professor Röntgen**', orange-red flowers with a green-gold flame; '**Weber's Parrot**', twisted pale pink petals with a green flame and deep pink edges and tips.

DOUBLE LATE OR PEONY-FLOWERED GROUP (GROUP 11)

Very large, fully double flowers on stems 15–24 in (38–60 cm) tall. Bloom well after the spring equinox. '**Allegretto**', red flowers, golden edge; '**Angélique**', pink flowers, pale exterior; '**Carnaval de Nice**', white flowers, narrow red striping; '**Orange Princess**', deep orange center, lightening at edges, tipped with green.

Tulipa, Hybrid Cultivar, Double Early, 'Peach Blossom'

KAUFMANNIANA GROUP (GROUP 12)

Early-flowering cultivars and hybrids of *T. kaufmanniana,* around 10 in (25 cm) tall. Flowers open flat; sometimes called waterlily tulips; leaves plain or mottled; flowers usually bicolored or multi-colored in a variety of patterns. 'Ancilla', white, with orange-red-edged yellow center; 'Shakespeare', dusky salmon pink.

FOSTERIANA GROUP (GROUP 13)

Variably sized cultivars and hybrids of *T. fosteriana,* 8–24 in (20–60 cm) tall; foliage may be plain, mottled, or variegated; boldly colored flowers. 'Madame Lefeber' (syn. 'Red Emperor'), bright red; 'Orange Emperor', bright orange blending to a yellow base; 'Princeps' bears large bright red flowers; 'Purissima' (syn. 'White Emperor'), white with a creamy yellow center.

GREIGII GROUP (GROUP 14)

Sometimes known as rock or rockery tulips, these cultivars and hybrids of *T. greigii* rarely exceed 12 in (30 cm) tall. Purple-red marbled gray-green foliage, and commonly simple single flowers in one or two colors. 'Cape Cod', orange with gold edge; 'Oriental Splendour', deep yellow with red flame; 'Plaisir', cream with red flame; 'Red Riding Hood', bright red; 'Toronto' ★, bright salmon to orange.

MISCELLANEOUS GROUP (GROUP 15)

This is a catch-all group for species and their cultivars which are otherwise ungrouped (*see* individual species).

VELTHEIMIA

This genus of the hyacinth (Hyacinthaceae) family consists of 2 species from southern Africa. Huge papery bulbs protrude from the soil's surface. Decorative, glossy, undulating leaves. The well-held flowers, are followed by shimmering papery seed pods.
CULTIVATION: They like temperate climates and do well in wet-summer areas and in summer-irrigated beds. They resent root disturbance. Propagate by removing and replanting offsets while plant is dormant, or by sowing fresh ripe seed. Alternatively, mature leaves can be taken from the base of the bulb, set in sand and grown on in a mild even temperature.

Veltheimia bracteata ★
syn. *Veltheimia capensis*
FOREST LILY, TORCH LILY
☼ ⬧ ↔ 12 in (30 cm) ↑ 16–18 in (40–45 cm)
Robust, variable, summer-dormant perennial with long-lasting flowers in warm coral-red, pinkish purple, or murky white shades. Flowers are held in terminal racemes on straight mottled stems in spring. Decorative seed pods follow. Dark green, very glossy leaves form a rosette. As a container plant, place the bulb with top two-thirds protruding, water sparingly, and feed with a

low-strength, low-nitrogen liquid feed when in growth. 'Yellow Flame', pale yellow flowers. *V. capensis* is sometimes listed as a separate species, but is now considered by many to be a form of *V. bracteata.* It bears muted yellow, flesh pink, or murky white blooms, and is smaller than the common forms. Zones 9–11.

WATSONIA
BUGLE LILY

Genus of 52 species of sun-loving bulbous perennials from South Africa. Members of the iris (Iridaceae) family, they are cormous and clump forming; common garden-grown species hold their flowers well above the reed-like foliage. Spring-flowering species are dormant in summer and need wet-winter to dry-summer climates. Summer- and autumn-flowering species are either evergreen or winter dormant, and need damp summer climates. Those with narrow tubular flowers are thought to be pollinated by honey-eating birds; those with open cupped flowers by bees.
CULTIVATION: Protect from frost in cold climates. They require sharp drainage, an open sunny position and light liquid feed when in poor soils. Propagate from seed in spring or from off-sets just as the plants move into dormancy.

Watsonia meriania

Watsonia borbonica
syn. *Watsonia pyramidata*
☼ ⬧ ↔ 4 in (10 cm) ↑ 3–7 ft (0.9–2 m)
Leaves narrowly sword-shaped. Flowers are lightly scented, pale or deep pink, appearing in spring–early summer. Corms ¾–1¾ in (18–40 mm) wide. *W. b.* subsp. *ardernei* (syn. *W. ardernei*) is white, occasionally light pink, with flared trumpets. Can become invasive. Zones 9–10.

Watsonia meriania
☼ ⬧ ↔ 6 in (15 cm) ↑ 20–60 in (50–150 cm)
From southern Africa. Sword-shaped leaves. Flowers are small, dull pink to bright rose-red, rarely red or white, on branched spikes, long tube with flared trumpet, in summer. Potentially invasive, particularly *W. m.* subsp. *bulbillifera*, which has dull apricot flowers and ruby stems. Zones 9–10.

Watsonia pillansii
☼ ❄ ↔ 4 in (10 cm) ↑ 20–48 in (50–120 cm)
Leaves dense, evergreen. The orange and red-orange flowers are held in dense racemes, from summer to autumn. Requires well-drained damp conditions in summer. Zones 7–10.

WELDENIA

Single-species genus consisting of a very variable tuberous peren-nial found in the wilds of South America and in the summer-wet mountainous terrains of Mexico and Guatemala. A member of the spiderwort (Commelinaceae) family, it has long tuberous roots and tufts or rosettes of leathery lance-shaped leaves. Its cupped flowers are white with yellow anthers.

CULTIVATION: Grow in gritty soil in full sun or in a greenhouse. Protect from frost. Keep damp while in growth. Propagate from fresh ripe seed, from root cuttings, or by division in spring.

Weldenia candida
☼ ❄ ↔ 6 in (15 cm) ↑ 5–6 in (12–15 cm)
Large, leathery, lance-shaped leaves with wavy margins, rosette-forming. Flowers white, cupped, held among the leaves, in late spring–early summer. Tubers elongated. Zones 8–9.

ZANTEDESCHIA
ARUM LILY, CALLA LILY
This genus in the arum (Araceae) family comprises 6 species of rhizome-rooted perennials from southern Africa, with large, upward-facing, elongated heart-shaped leaves that taper to a long tip and can be speckled with translucent spots. The flower spathe is funnel-shaped and also tapers to a tip. The spadix may be enclosed within the spathe or protrude slightly. Although the white form is the best known, modern hybrids cover a wide color range. Both leaves and the flowers are supported by strong stalks. CULTIVATION: Some prefer damp conditions, but most will grow in full or half-sun in any garden soil that does not dry out. Propagate by division, or from basal offsets or seed.

Zantedeschia aethiopica
ARUM LILY, CALLA LILY
☼/☀ ❄ ↔ 20–60 in (50–150 cm) ↑ 4–6 ft (1.2–1.8 m)
From South Africa, this evergreen or semi-evergreen species develops large rhizomes and can form clumps of long-stemmed, 12–24 in (30–60 cm) long, arrowhead-shaped leaves. Tall flower stems topped with a white spathe, to 10 in (25 cm) long, around a yellow spadix. 'Childsiana' ★, compact, small leaves, pink-tinted flowers; 'Crowborough', 36 in (90 cm) tall; 'Green Goddess', 36 in (90 cm) tall, small greenish spathe; 'Hercules', 6 ft (1.8 m), giant-sized, white to very pale pink spathes. Zones 8–11.

Zantedeschia albomaculata
☼ ❀ ↔ 16–24 in (40–60 cm) ↑ 24–40 in (60–100 cm)
Perennial found from South Africa to tropical eastern Africa. Long-stemmed, white-spotted, arrowhead-shaped leaves. Sturdy flower stems with cup-shaped spathe, are usually white to cream, sometimes yellow or pink. Spadix pale to deep yellow. Zones 9–11.

Zantedeschia elliottiana ★
GOLDEN CALLA
☼ ❀ ↔ 12–18 in (30–45 cm) ↑ 15 in (38 cm)
Unknown in the wild and possibly of hybrid origin. Heavily white-spotted leaves, deep yellow 4–5 in (10–12 cm) long spathes. Zones 9–11.

Zantedeschia rehmannii
☼ ❀ ↔ 12–20 in (30–50 cm) ↑ 18 in (45 cm)
Native of South Africa and Swaziland. Narrow, unspotted, lance-shaped leaves, to 16 in (40 cm) long. Flowerheads often held below foliage level.

Zantedeschia, Hybrid Cultivar, 'Flame'

Spathes white, pink, or purple-red, to over 4 in (10 cm) long. 'Superba', deep pink spathes held above foliage level. Zones 9–11.

Zantedeschia Hybrid Cultivars
☼ ❀ ↔ 1–5 ft (0.3–1.5 m) ↑ 1–6 ft (0.3–1.8 m)
Developed through crossing smaller species. Generally compact. 'Flame', red-flecked yellow spathes deepening with age; 'Scarlet Pimpernel' ★, bright red spathes. Zones 9–11.

ZIGADENUS
DEATH CAMAS, ZYGADENE
Genus of 18 bulbous or rhizomatous perennial herbs, members of the lily (Liliaceae) family, native to temperate North America and northern Asia. Narrow, folded, and curved leaves grow from a central base. Terminal panicles or racemes of greenish white to yellowish white, bisexual flowers, in summer. Fruit is a capsule. Highly poisonous. CULTIVATION: They like full sun and well-drained soil. Propagate by division, or from seed.

Zigadenus fremontii
STAR LILY, STAR ZYGADENE
☼ ❄ ↔ 2–5 in (5–12 cm) ↑ 20–36 in (50–90 cm)
Perennial herb from southern Oregon, USA, to northern Baja California, Mexico. Grows from spherical bulbs. Narrow, slightly rough, curved leaves. Off-white or ivory flowers, in summer, on smooth stems. Zones 5–10.

Zigadenus fremontii

Grasses, Sedges, and Bamboos

The grass family features around 635 genera and more than 9,000 different species. They are some of the most adaptable plants on earth, occurring in almost all regions and on all continents, from the Arctic to the Antarctic peninsula. There are also a number of grass-like plants commonly and broadly referred to as grasses, including rushes, sedges, and cat tails (bulrushes).

True grasses are members of the Poaceae or Gramineae family, and are mainly annual or perennial herbs with hollow or solid stems. Their root systems may be tufted so that they form single clumps, sometimes quite densely bunched to form tussocks, or they may form quite extensive patches or colonies due to their rhizomatous stems, which either creep along the surface of the ground and root-in, or grow below the surface. Distinctive in their form, bamboos are actually giant grasses with over 500 ornamental forms in cultivation.

Grasses are some of the most important plants on Earth, as all of our grains and cereals such as wheat, oats, barley, maize, rice, and rye have been derived from wild grasses. For the gardener, grasses are important because of their ornamental uses, and for their suitability for lawns and sports fields.

Bambusa vulgaris 'Striata' adds a unique linear dimension to the tropical garden, as its erect golden yellow culms (stems) have green stripes of various widths.

Grass, Sedge, and Bamboo Finder

The following cultivation table features at-a-glance information for every species or hybrid with an individual entry in the Grasses, Sedges, and Bamboos chapter of this book. Simply find the plant you wish to know more about, and run your eye along the row to discover its height and spread, whether it is frost tolerant or not, the aspect it prefers, and more.

The type of plant is abbreviated to **G**, **S**, **B**, or **O**:
G – the plant is a grass.
S – the plant is a sedge.
B – the plant is a bamboo.
O – the plant is similar to, but not a part of, the grass, sedge, or bamboo groups.

The climate(s) that each plant needs to thrive in the outdoors are given (some plants will grow in more than one climate), abbreviated to **C**, **W**, or **T**:
C – the plant prefers a cool climate.
W– the plant prefers a warm-temperate or subtropical climate.
T – the plant prefers a tropical climate.

Plant name	Height	Spread	Type	Climate	Showy inflorescence	Showy foliage	Lawn/ground cover	Hedge/screen	Border/bedding	Pot plant	Frost tolerant	Full sun	Half sun	Heavy shade
Agrostis stolonifera	8–16 in (20–40 cm)	12–24 in (30–60 cm)	G	C/W			•				•	•		
Alopecurus pratensis	40–48 in (100–120 cm)	12–16 in (30–40 cm)	G	C/W	•	•			•		•	•	•	
Arrhenatherum elatius	18–60 in (45–150 cm)	6–8 in (15–20 cm)	G	C	•	•			•	•	•	•	•	
Arundo donax	10–20 ft (3–6 m)	7–15 ft (2–4.5 m)	G	C/W	•	•		•	•		•	•	•	
Bambusa multiplex	35 ft (10 m)	10 ft (3 m)	B	W/T	•	•		•	•		•	•		
Bambusa oldhamii	60 ft (18 m)	20–40 ft (6–12 m)	B	W/T		•		•			•	•		
Bambusa vulgaris	50 ft (15 m)	15–30 ft (4.5–9 m)	B	W/T		•		•				•		
Bouteloua curtipendula	24–32 in (60–80 cm)	12–18 in (30–45 cm)	G	C	•				•		•	•	•	
Bouteloua gracilis	24 in (60 cm)	12 in (30 cm)	G	C/W	•				•		•	•	•	
Butomus umbellatus	60 in (150 cm)	30 in (75 cm)	O	C	•	•					•	•		
Calamagrostis × acutiflora	5–7 ft (1.5–2 m)	36–40 in (90–100 cm)	G	C	•	•			•		•	•		
Carex comans	16 in (40 cm)	24–30 in (60–75 cm)	S	C/W		•			•		•	•	•	
Carex elata	3 ft (0.9 m)	3 ft (0.9 m)	S	C/W		•			•		•	•	•	
Carex grayi	30 in (75 cm)	30 in (75 cm)	S	C/W	•				•		•	•	•	
Carex morrowii	30 in (75 cm)	30 in (75 cm)	S	C/W		•			•		•	•	•	
Carex oshimensis	12 in (30 cm)	18 in (45 cm)	S	C/W		•						•	•	•
Chimonobambusa marmorea	7–10 ft (2–3 m)	10–17 ft (3–5 m)	B	C/W						•		•	•	•
Chimonobambusa tumidissinoda	10–20 ft (3–6 m)	20–40 ft (6–12 m)	B	C/W						•		•		•
Chusquea culeou	10–20 ft (3–6 m)	10–20 ft (3–6 m)	B	C/W		•		•			•	•		
Coix lacryma-jobi	40–48 in (100–120 cm)	36–40 in (90–100 cm)	G	W	•				•	•		•		
Cortaderia richardii	4–10 ft (1.2–3 m)	2–3 ft (60–90 cm)	G	C/W	•				•	•	•	•		
Cortaderia selloana	5–25 ft (1–8 m)	4–6 ft (1.2–1.8 m)	G	C/W	•				•	•	•	•		

Plant name	Height	Spread	Type	Climate	Showy inflorescence	Showy foliage	Lawn/ground cover	Hedge/screen	Border/bedding	Pot plant	Frost tolerant	Full sun	Half sun	Heavy shade
Cynodon dactylon	2–6 in (5–15 cm)	unlimited	G	W/T		◆					◆	◆	◆	
Cyperus albostriatus	24 in (60 cm)	12 in (30 cm)	S	W/T	◆				◆	◆		◆	◆	
Cyperus involucratus	3–5 ft (0.9–1.5 m)	24–40 in (60–100 cm)	S	W/T	◆					◆		◆	◆	
Cyperus papyrus	7–17 ft (2–5 m)	5–10 ft (1.5–3 m)	S	W/T	◆	◆				◆		◆	◆	
Dendrocalamus asper	60–100 ft (18–30 m)	40–80 ft (12–24 m)	B	W/T				◆				◆		
Deschampsia cespitosa	5–7 ft (1.5–2 m)	5 ft (1.5 m)	G	C/W	◆				◆	◆	◆	◆	◆	
Deschampsia flexuosa	36 in (90 cm)	8 in (20 cm)	G	C	◆	◆			◆	◆	◆	◆	◆	◆
Equisetum hyemale	3–5 ft (0.9–1.5 m)	12–24 in (30–60 cm)	O	C						◆	◆	◆		
Equisetum telmateia	20 in–6 ft (0.5–1.8 m)	12–24 in (30–60 cm)	O	C						◆	◆	◆		
Eriophorum vaginatum	12–32 in (30–80 cm)	6–12 in (15–30 cm)	S	C	◆					◆	◆	◆		
Fargesia murielae	12 ft (3.5 m)	2–4 ft (0.6–1.2 m)	B	C				◆	◆		◆	◆	◆	
Fargesia nitida	12 ft (3.5 m)	2–4 ft (0.6–1.2 m)	B	C				◆	◆	◆	◆	◆	◆	
Festuca californica	24–36 in (60–90 cm)	24 in (60 cm)	G	C		◆			◆		◆	◆	◆	
Festuca glauca	12 in (30 cm)	10 in (25 cm)	G	C/W		◆			◆	◆	◆	◆	◆	
Festuca valesiaca	6 in (15 cm)	6 in (15 cm)	G	C		◆			◆	◆	◆	◆		
Hakonechloa macra	To 24 in (60 cm)	Over 24 in (60 cm)	G	C/W		◆			◆	◆	◆			◆
Imperata cylindrica	24–72 in (60–180 cm)	8–12 in (20–30 cm)	G	W		◆			◆	◆		◆	◆	
Juncus effusus	5 ft (1.5 m)	30 in (75 cm)	O	C					◆	◆	◆	◆	◆	
Juncus patens	27 in (70 cm)	24 in (60 cm)	O	C/W		◆			◆		◆	◆	◆	◆
Lolium perenne	6–24 in (15–60 cm)	10–18 in (25–45 cm)	G	C/W			◆							
Lomandra longifolia	20–40 in (50–100 cm)	30–36 in (75–90 cm)	O	W	◆				◆	◆		◆		
Melica altissima	60 in (150 cm)	32 in (80 cm)	G	C/W	◆				◆	◆	◆	◆	◆	
Miscanthus floridulus	8 ft (2.4 m)	5 ft (1.5 m)	G	C	◆	◆			◆		◆	◆		
Miscanthus sacchariflorus	5 ft (1.5 m)	5 ft (1.5 m)	G	C	◆	◆			◆		◆	◆		
Miscanthus sinensis	15 ft (4.5 m)	4 ft (1.2 m)	G	C	◆	◆			◆		◆	◆	◆	
Molinia caerulea	16 in (40 cm)	16 in (40 cm)	G	C	◆	◆			◆	◆	◆	◆	◆	
Muhlenbergia rigens	36–60 in (90–150 cm)	24–48 in (60–120 cm)	G	C/W	◆				◆			◆	◆	
Otatea acuminata	25 ft (8 m)	20 ft (6 m)	B	W/T		◆		◆		◆		◆		
Pennisetum alopecuroides	4–5 ft (1.2–1.5 m)	18–24 in (45–60 cm)	G	C	◆	◆			◆	◆	◆	◆	◆	
Pennisetum setaceum	3–5 ft (0.9–1.5 m)	24–36 in (60–90 cm)	G	W	◆				◆	◆		◆		
Pennisetum villosum	2–4 ft (0.6–1.2 m)	18–24 in (45–60 cm)	G	C/W	◆	◆			◆	◆	◆	◆	◆	
Phalaris arundinacea	4–5 ft (1.2–1.5 m)	7–10 ft (2–3 m)	G	C/W	◆	◆			◆	◆	◆	◆	◆	
Phragmites australis	6–10 ft (1.8–3 m)	27–40 in (70–100 cm)	G	C	◆	◆			◆			◆	◆	

Plant name	Height	Spread	Type	Climate	Showy inflorescence	Showy foliage	Lawn/ground cover	Hedge/screen	Border/bedding	Pot plant	Frost tolerant	Full sun	Half sun	Heavy shade
Phyllostachys aurea	25 ft (8 m)	20–40 ft (6–12 m)	B	C/W		◆		◆			◆	◆	◆	
Phyllostachys bambusoides	40–70 ft (12–21 m)	20–60 ft (6–18 m)	B	C/W		◆		◆			◆	◆		
Phyllostachys edulis	40–75 ft (12–22 m)	30–100 ft (9–30 m)	B	C/W		◆		◆			◆	◆		
Phyllostachys nigra	25–50 ft (8–15 m)	20–50 ft (6–15 m)	B	C/W				◆			◆	◆		
Pleioblastus variegatus	28–40 in (70–100 cm)	40–60 in (100–150 cm)	B	C		◆			◆	◆	◆	◆	◆	
Poa cita	12–40 in (30–100 cm)	9–12 in (22–30 cm)	G	C					◆	◆	◆	◆		
Poa pratensis	24–36 in (60–90 cm)	12–24 in (30–60 cm)	G	C	◆	◆					◆	◆		
Pseudosasa japonica	17–20 ft (5–6 m)	15 ft (4.5 m)	B	C/W		◆		◆			◆	◆	◆	
Saccharum ravennae	10–15 ft (3–4.5 m)	40 in (100 cm)	G	C	◆	◆					◆	◆		
Sasa palmata	7 ft (2 m)	10–20 ft (3–6 m)	B	C/W		◆		◆			◆			◆
Sasa veitchii	5 ft (1.5 m)	10–20 ft (3–6 m)	B	C/W		◆		◆			◆			◆
Schoenoplectus lacustris	3–10 ft (0.9–3 m)	3–4 ft (0.9–1.2 m)	S	C	◆	◆					◆	◆		
Semiarundinaria fastuosa	20–30 ft (6–9 m)	7–10 ft (2–3 m)	B	C/W		◆		◆			◆	◆		
Sesleria tatrae	6–10 in (15–25 cm)	6–8 in (15–20 cm)	G	C	◆	◆	◆		◆	◆	◆	◆	◆	
Sorghastrum nutans	5–7 ft (1.5–2 m)	16–32 in (40–80 cm)	G	C/W	◆						◆	◆		◆
Spartina pectinata	3–10 ft (0.9–3 m)	18–24 in (45–60 cm)	G	C	◆	◆			◆		◆	◆	◆	
Sporobolus heterolepis	24–36 in (60–90 cm)	12–16 in (30–40 cm)	G	C	◆	◆					◆	◆		
Stenotaphrum secundatum	2–16 in (5–40 cm)	2–16 in (5–40 cm)	G	W/T			◆					◆	◆	
Stipa arundinacea	3 ft (0.9 m)	4 ft (1.2 m)	G	C/W	◆				◆	◆	◆	◆		
Stipa calamagrostis	3 ft (0.9 m)	4 ft (1.2 m)	G	C/W	◆				◆		◆	◆		
Stipa gigantea	8 ft (2.4 m)	4 ft (1.2 m)	G	C/W	◆	◆			◆		◆	◆		
Stipa splendens	8 ft (2.4 m)	4 ft (1.2 m)	G	C/W	◆	◆			◆		◆	◆		
Typha minima	2½–3 in (6–8 cm)	1¼–2 in (3–5 cm)	O	C/W	◆				◆	◆	◆	◆		
Typha orientalis	3–8 ft (0.9–2.4 m)	12–20 in (30–50 cm)	O	W	◆							◆		
Yushania anceps	15 ft (4.5 m)	15–30 ft (4.5–9 m)	B	C/W		◆		◆			◆	◆		
Zoysia 'Emerald'	1–2 in (25–50 mm)	1–2 in (25–50 mm)	G	C			◆				◆	◆		
Zoysia tenuifolia	1–2 in (25–50 mm)	1–2 in (25–50 mm)	G	C/W			◆				◆	◆		

AGROSTIS

BENT GRASS, BROWN TOP

Cosmopolitan genus of some 120 species of evergreen annuals and perennials of the grass (Poaceae) family, many spread by runners (stolons). Hardiness varies, but cultivated species are mostly frost hardy. Untrimmed, they develop into dense mounds of fine leaves and from late summer produce numerous inflorescences. CULTIVATION: When grown as lawn, keep growing steadily with frequent watering and feeding. Prone to fungal diseases. Avoid alkaline soil. Annual aeration and dethatching is recommended.

Agrostis stolonifera

CREEPING BENT GRASS

☼ ❄ ↔ 12–24 in (30–60 cm) ↕ 8–16 in (20–40 cm)

Gray-green foliage, short feathery inflorescence. Good for golf courses; too high-maintenance for domestic lawns. Considered a weed in many areas. Zones 3–10.

ALOPECURUS

FOXTAIL GRASS

Found throughout northern temperate zones, this genus of 25 species of annual and perennial grasses (family Poaceae) has long, soft, plume-like flower panicles. Leaves range from linear and hair-like to flat and quite broad. In summer, flowering stems bear cylindrical plumes of tiny bristled spikelets. Dying flowers are replaced by conspicuous seed heads. Cultivated forms often have larger flowerheads or variegated foliage.

CULTIVATION: Mostly very hardy and easily grown in temperate areas. Plant in moist well-drained soil in full or half-sun. Some species are invasive but are rarely serious weeds. Occasionally used as a meadow grass but too coarse for lawns. Propagate the annuals from seed and perennials or cultivars by division.

Alopecurus pratensis

MEADOW FOXTAIL

☼/◐ ❄ ↔ 12–16 in (30–40 cm) ↕ 40–48 in (100–120 cm)

A species that is widespread throughout Eurasia and also found in northeastern Africa. Long, relatively broad, smooth-surfaced leaves. Pale green flower panicles, to 4 in (10 cm) long, are often purple-tinted. 'Aureomarginatus' (syn. 'Aureovariegatus'), has leaves edged gold with longitudinal stripes; 'Aureus' ★, has golden yellow leaves. Zones 5–10.

ARRHENATHERUM

OAT GRASS

This genus, a member of the grass (Poaceae) family, consists of 6 perennials that are native to Europe, northern Africa, and northern and western Asia. The panicles are narrow, with flat 2-flowered spikelets. The stalk bases are sometimes swollen into bulbous or pear-shaped structures. The leaves are flat and strap-like, with usually hairless sheaths.

CULTIVATION: These species grow well in both partial shade and full sun. Soil should be dry to moist. Propagate from seed.

Alopecurus pratensis 'Aureomarginatus'

Arrhenatherum elatius

BULBOUS OAT GRASS, FALSE OAT, FRENCH RYE, OAT GRASS, ONION COUCH, STRIPED TUBER OAT GRASS, TUBER OAT GRASS

☼/◐ ❄ ↔ 6–8 in (15–20 cm) ↕ 18–60 in (45–150 cm)

Tussock-forming grass from Europe. Raceme is lance-shaped to oblong, lustrous, tinged with purple, containing spikelets of whitish flowers, in summer. Finely hairy pale green leaves, up to 16 in (40 cm) long × ½ in (12 mm) wide, turn light tan to brown in winter. *A. e.* subsp. *bulbosum*, chains of bulb-like swellings at stem bases; 'Variegatum', tuft-forming, herbaceous, perennial grass with swollen basal stem and hairless gray-green leaves with ivory white margins. Zones 4–9.

ARUNDO

GIANT REED

Genus of 3 species of giant, perennial grasses (family Poaceae) with cane-like stems, which comes from the Old World tropics and subtropics. Only one species, *A. donax* from the Mediterranean region, is widely cultivated and it has become a weed in some areas. Very strongly upright plants reminiscent of bamboo, they form a large clump of heavy, somewhat flattened stems with long narrow leaves. Large feathery flower panicles appear in autumn; often with a dusky pink tint. The foliage dies back over winter but does not usually disappear entirely.

CULTIVATION: These reeds do not require boggy conditions. Any well-drained moderately fertile soil kept moist through summer will do. As the plants most often cultivated are variegated forms, propagation is usually by division during the dormant period.

Arundo donax

☼/◐ ❄ ↔ 7–15 ft (2–4.5 m) ↕ 10–20 ft (3–6 m)

Dense clump of strong stems with 24 in (60 cm) long, gray-green leaves. Flower panicles to 24 in (60 cm) long, pink-tinted when young, maturing to silver-gray. 'Versicolor' ★ (syn. 'Variegata'), white-striped variegated foliage. There are several other variegated forms of varying patterns. Zones 7–11.

Arundo donax

Bambusa vulgaris 'Striata'

BAMBUSA

BAMBOO

Genus in the family Poaceae with about 120 species of giant grasses from low elevations of tropical and subtropical Asia, tropical America, Africa, and northern Australia. From 15 ft (4.5 m) to 80 ft (24 m) in height, they have smooth cylindrical stems grown from rhizomes, in loose to dense compact clumps. Stems (called culms) are mostly hollow, except at nodes (rings). From the higher nodes wiry lateral branches emerge bearing leaves. Large pale scale-leaves sheath young stems. Flowering is rare. CULTIVATION: Vigorous growers requiring a tropical or subtropical climate. Several are frost hardy. Plant in deep, fertile, loamy soil with ample water in summer in a sheltered, sunny site. Propagate from offsets buried in soil; flood, mulch, and feed well when new growth shows.

Bambusa multiplex

syn. *Bambusa glaucescens*

HEDGE BAMBOO

☼ ❄ ↔ 10 ft (3 m) ↑ 35 ft (10 m)

From southern China. Crowded deep green culms up to 1½ in (35 mm) in diameter, erect then arching at the top. Leaves small, bluish green undersurface. Mature plants produce arching flowering branches every few years. 'Alphonse Karr' ★, green-striped gold culms forming broad-headed clump; 'Fernleaf', to 20 ft (6 m) tall; 'Riviereorum', to 6 ft (1.8-m) tall; 'Silverstripe', pale stripes on new leaves and stems. Zones 8–12.

Bambusa oldhamii

OLDHAM BAMBOO

☼ ❄ ↔ 20–40 ft (6–12 m) ↑ 60 ft (18 m)

Native to southern China and Taiwan. Open clump of straight upright culms 24 in (60 cm) thick, bright green with white

bloom, ageing to yellow. Grown for edible shoots, hedging, paper pulp. Zones 9–12.

Bambusa vulgaris

COMMON OR YELLOW-STEMMED BAMBOO

☼ ❄ ↔ 15–30 ft (4.5–9 m) ↑ 50 ft (15 m)

Grown widely in tropical regions. Open clump of dark green culms 6 in (15 cm) thick, used for structural purposes, but their high starch content encourages insect and fungal attack. 'Maculata', culms become blotchy, eventually completely black; 'Striata' (syn. 'Vittata'), golden yellow culms with green stripes of various thicknesses; 'Wamin', short wide lower internodes (parts of culm between nodes), to 17 ft (5 m) tall. Zones 9–12.

BOUTELOUA

GRAMA GRASS

Found from southern USA and the West Indies to Central and South America, this genus of 39 annual or perennial grasses belongs to the family Poaceae. It features clusters or clumps of stiff slender flower stems. Panicles of flowers have one or many branches of delicate, stalkless, "mosquito-like" spikelets on wiry stems, in summer. The leaves with flat-or folded blades arise from a central base. CULTIVATION: These grasses like an open sunny position and will tolerate any type of garden soil. Propagate from seed.

Bouteloua curtipendula

SIDEOATS GRASS

☼ ❄ ↔ 12–18 in (30–45 cm) ↑ 24–32 in (60–80 cm)

Native to temperate areas from Canada to Argentina. Panicles of flowers with 30 to 80 branches; there are between 1 and 12 spikelets, each to ½ in (12 mm) long, per branch. Bluish green, rough or slightly hairy leaf blades, to ¼ in (6 mm) wide. Zones 4–9.

Bouteloua gracilis

Bouteloua gracilis ★

syns *Bouteloua oligostachya, Chondrosum gracile, C. oligostachyum*

BLUE GRAMA, MOSQUITO GRASS, NAVAJITA AZUL, NAVAJITA COMUN

☼ ❄ ↔ 12 in (30 cm) ↑ 24 in (60 cm)

A grass from the plains of southern Canada, USA, and Mexico. Dense arching panicles of flowers with 1 to 4 branches; 1 to 12 spikelets, each to ¼ in (6 mm) long, per branch. Narrow, wispy, sometimes hairy leaf blades, rough to touch. 'Lovington', flowers purple fading to yellow. Zones 8–10.

BUTOMUS

FLOWERING RUSH, GRASSY RUSH, WATER GLADIOLUS

A genus containing a single species of aquatic perennial herb from the family Butomaceae, native to Eurasia. The sword-like leaves, to 5 ft (1.5 m) tall, arise from the fleshy stems. The flower

stalk is to 3 ft (0.9 m) high, with terminal umbels of many flowers, often fragrant, with rose-pink tepals, ¼–¾ in (6–18 mm) wide, with 6 to 9 stamens and dark red anthers, in summer.
CULTIVATION: Plant in a warm sunny position in water that does not freeze, up to 6 in (15 cm) deep. Propagate by root division.

Butomus umbellatus

FLOWERING RUSH

☼ ❄ ↔ 30 in (75 cm) ↑ 60 in (150 cm)

Aquatic grass-like plant from Europe and Asia. Terminal umbels of rose-pink summer flowers borne on smooth, leafless, erect stem. Sword-like leaves, bronze-purple, maturing to green, arranged in rosette. Zones 5–9.

CALAMAGROSTIS

REED GRASS

A genus of around 250 species in the grass (Poaceae) family that is fairly widespread throughout temperate zones of the Northern Hemisphere. Only a few species are of orna-mental value and those in cultivation are mainly hybrids or selected forms. Some can be invasive. Their upright form and fluffy flowerheads that can be dried make them rather dramatic feature plants in the garden.
CULTIVATION: They prefer moist to damp soils in a sunny position. Propagate from seed; divide cultivars at the end of winter.

Calamagrostis × acutiflora

FEATHER REED GRASS

☼ ❄ ↔ 36–40 in (90–100 cm) ↑ 5–7 ft (1.5–2 m)

Clump-forming herbaceous hybrid between *C. arundinacea* and *C. epigejos* that arose naturally. Sterile. '**Overdam**' ★, variegated silver foliage; '**Stricta**', vertical form, feathery flowers. Zones 4–10.

CAREX

SEDGE

Genus of some 1,000 species of deciduous or evergreen grass-like perennials in the sedge (Cyperaceae) family, found throughout the world in damp and boggy ground. Many are native to north-ern temperate regions. Plants range from low-growing and tufted

Calamagrostis × acutiflora 'Stricta'

to tall and tussock-forming. Grass-like leaves may be flat, folded, or rolled and in various shades of green, red, or brown. They often have sharp cutting edges. Tiny insignificant flowers.
CULTIVATION: Easy-care plants, they are best in moisture-retentive soils. Propagate by division or from seed.

Carex comans

☼ ❄ ↔ 24–30 in (60–75 cm) ↑ 16 in (40 cm)

Native to New Zealand. Drooping sprawling plant. Fine narrow leaves curl at tips. Foliage varies from reddish brown to shades of gray and green. The tips are often blond. '**Frosted Curls**' ★, swirling mound of palest green or straw-colored foliage. Zones 7–10.

Carex elata

TUFTED SEDGE

☼ ❄ ↔ 3 ft (0.9 m) ↑ 3 ft (0.9 m)

Native to Europe, as far east as the Caucasus, and northern Africa. Dense tussock plant, spreads rapidly in wet situations. The bluish green leaves are folded with a flat tip. '**Aurea**' (known as Bowles golden sedge), golden leaves with green margins. Zones 7–10.

Carex grayi

MACE SEDGE, MORNING STAR SEDGE

☼ ❄ ↔ 30 in (75 cm) ↑ 30 in (75 cm)

From eastern North America. Upright clump-forming plant. Flat pale green leaves. Spiky seed heads resemble a mace. Zones 7–10.

Carex morrowii

◐ ❄ ↔ 30 in (75 cm) ↑ 30 in (75 cm)

Native to Japan. Tufted plant forming an upright clump. Thick, glossy leaves with rough margins. Usually seen in one of its culti-vated forms such as '**Expallida**' (syn. '**Variegata**'), leaves striped with white. Zones 8–10.

Carex oshimensis

☼/◐ ❄ ↔ 18 in (45 cm) ↑ 12 in (30 cm)

Tufted evergreen sedge. Dark green leaves. '**Evergold**' (syn. *C. sidericsticha* 'Variegata'), leaves striped gold and white. Zones 5–10.

Carex comans 'Frosted Curls'

Carex elata 'Aurea'

Carex grayi

CHIMONOBAMBUSA

Genus of about 40 species of bamboo from southern and eastern Asia in the grass (Poaceae) family. Small to medium-sized plants, often quite dense and bushy, with a strongly running habit, making them good for screens and hedges. Although they can be very invasive, they resent and will often fail in dry soils. CULTIVATION: Plant in moist soil in full sun or shade. Prune out old spent canes as needed and put down root barriers or trench around them once a year to control their spread. Propagate by division—just lift a section or use wayward runners.

Chimonobambusa marmorea
KAN-CHIKU, MARBLE SHEATH BAMBOO

☼/◐ ❄ ↔ 10–17 ft (3–5 m) ↑ 7–10 ft (2–3 m)

Introduced from Japan to Europe in 1889. Bushy species, slender black marbled stems that in strong light can completely blacken. Makes fine arching interior plant or ground cover in shady woodland. Zones 7–10.

Chimonobambusa tumidissinoda
syn. Qiongzhuea tumidinoda
CHINESE WALKING STICK

◐ ❄ ↔ 20–40 ft (6–12 m) ↑ 10–20 ft (3–6 m)

Endemic to small region in Yunnan, China. Shoots in late summer, and has rapidly unfurling willow-like foliage; aggressively spreading by rhizomes. Commercially grown for sweet shoots and for walking sticks and tobacco pipes. Zones 8–10.

CHUSQUEA

From Central and South America, the genus *Chusquea*, in the grass (Poaceae) family, has an estimated 200 species of clump-forming bamboos, including a number of species large enough to be treated as shrubs or trees. Though externally similar to other bamboos, except perhaps being longer, with more plumed foliage, they differ internally in having solid pithy-centered stems rather than the hollow stems. Bristly leaf sheaths do not drop. The leaf-like outgrowths are known as auricles. CULTIVATION: They prefer relatively cool, moist, humid conditions and will not tolerate prolonged dry conditions. Although they are not huge and do not produce runners, they can be vigorous in suitable climates, so choose a site that allows room for development. Frost hardiness varies, species from southern South America being the hardiest. Propagate by division.

Chusquea culeou

☼ ❄ ↔ 10–20 ft (3–6 m) ↑ 10–20 ft (3–6 m)

Chilean species. Develops into a large clump with tightly packed, solid, erect culms with bottlebrush-like branching. Most widely cultivated of the species. The stems and leaves are yellowish olive green, the papery leaf sheaths creamy white. The young stems are waxy coated, giving them a bluish appearance. Zones 7–9.

COIX

A small genus consisting of 6 species of annual and perennial plants in the grass (Poaceae) family that come from tropical Asia and are now naturalized in many other parts of the world. They have soft, green, arching leaves, like dwarf sweet corn, and hard black seeds that have been used as rosary beads. CULTIVATION: Grow in moist to damp soil in a sheltered sunny spot and plant out after frosts have finished in areas where these occur. Propagate from seed sown indoors in late winter in frosty areas or from self-sown seedlings elsewhere.

Coix lacryma-jobi
CHRIST'S TEARS, JOB'S TEARS

☼ ◑ ↔ 36–40 in (90–100 cm) ↑ 40–48 in (100–120 cm)

An annual or short-lived perennial species grown for its drooping stems of hard, glossy, gray to black seeds, to ½ in (12 mm) in diameter, and lush bright green leaves, to 20 in (50 cm) long. Zones 9–11.

Coix lacryma-jobi

CORTADERIA
PAMPAS GRASS

This genus of about 25 species of grasses belongs to the Poaceae family. With the exception of one New Guinea species, *Cortaderia* are native to South America and New Zealand, where they grow in a range of habitats from grassy plains to mountains. They are dense tussock-forming grasses growing to 10 ft (3 m) or more. Their long, stiff, flat leaves are crowded at the base, and the leaf margins range from rough to very sharp. Flowers are tall, showy, erect or arching plumes, in white, pale pink, or pale gold. CULTIVATION: Most are at least frost hardy, and can be grown as lawn specimens, in the garden border, by water, and for hedging. Grow in a sunny situation in any well-drained reasonably fertile soil. Cut or burn out dead material annually. Propagate from seed or by division.

Cortaderia richardii
TOETOE GRASS, TOITOI

☼ ❄ ↔ 2–3 ft (0.6–0.9 m) ↑ 4–10 ft (1.2–3 m)

Clump-forming tussock-like grass from New Zealand. Long, narrow, arching, strap-like, soft green leaves, with sharply serrated edges and shiny undersides. Tall arching plumes of pale yellow-gold, usually drooping flowers, carried on stalks up to 10 ft (3 m) long, extending beyond leaves, in summer–autumn. Zones 7–9.

Cortaderia selloana
syns Arundo selloana, Cortaderia argentea
PAMPAS GRASS

☼ ❄ ↔ 4–6 ft (1.2–1.8 m) ↑ 5–25 ft (1.5–8 m)

Large durable grass from southern South America. Narrow, arching, rough-surfaced leaves, forming dense fountain-like clumps. Silvery white oblong flower panicles, to 4 ft (1.2 m) long, tinged red or purple, in autumn. Regarded as a weed in Australia, New Zealand, and California, USA. '**Albolineata**' (syn. 'Silver Stripe'), compact, slow-growing, with white-edged leaves; '**Aureolineata**' (syn. 'Gold Band'), hardy, compact, with leaves broadly edged with rich yellow, later deep gold; '**Bertinii**', dwarf form, to 3 ft (0.9 m); '**Pumila**' (dwarf pampas grass), hardy dwarf form, up to 3–4 ft (0.9–1.2 m), narrow bluish green foliage; '**Rosea**', long plumes tinged pink; '**Sunningdale Silver**', sturdy, large, wind resistant, with dense white plumes to 12 ft (3.5 m). Zones 7–11.

CYNODON

Genus of 8 species of tropical and subtropical grasses, well represented in southern Africa, in the family Poaceae. Strong creeping stems root at the nodes as they spread and can also grow upward. The stems interweave and form a dense mat, made more impenetrable by their flat-bladed leaves. Small clusters of flower spikes form at the stem tips, but they are not showy and are unlikely to be seen when the grasses are used for lawns or routinely grazed pastures. The vigor of these grasses is both their appeal and their curse, as when they escape from cultivation they can be very invasive. An oft-quoted statistic claims that if the maximum logarithmic growth rates were sustained for a year, a patch measuring 10 feet square (3 meters square) would spread to cover 50 percent of the land surface of the world.
CULTIVATION: Most are tolerant of moderate frosts but will suffer in prolonged periods of frost. Plant in full sun to ensure dense growth, and water well in summer. Feed, aerate, and dethatch in spring. The plants are sometimes raised from seed, but more commonly planted as ready-to-lay rolls, or "plugs," of stolons.

Cortaderia richardii, in the wild, New Zealand

Cynodon dactylon
BAHAMA GRASS, BERMUDA GRASS
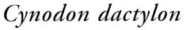 ↔ unlimited ↕ 2–6 in (5–15 cm)
Widespread species, found in warm temperate to tropical zones. Vigorous spreading grass forming dense turf. Tough stems up to 12 in (30 cm) long, broad-bladed leaves to 6 in (15 cm) long, often gray-tinted. Dense 2 in (5 cm) long flower spikes from late summer. '**U-3**', tough, coarse-bladed, suitable only for high-traffic lawns, not for fine turf. Zones 8–12.

CYPERUS

Around 600 species of annual and perennial sedges from all but the coldest parts of the world make up the type genus for the family Cyperaceae. Perhaps best known as the source of our earliest form of paper, papyrus, *Cyperus* includes other locally useful species that provide thatch and fuel, as well as ornamental species and several invasive weeds. From a clump of grassy basal foliage, *Cyperus* sedges produce strongly upright flower stems topped with flowerheads, usually

Cyperus involucratus

on umbels with leafy bracts. Their interesting appearance, and airy foliage and bracts, give the ornamental species their appeal.
CULTIVATION: Hardiness varies widely, subtropical and tropical species often being intolerant of frost. Otherwise, cultivation is straightforward. Plant *Cyperus* species in a bright position with moist, humus-rich soil and water well in summer. Many species will grow in damp to boggy conditions or even in shallow to quite deep water, though most are equally at home in well-drained soil. Propagate from seed or by division.

Cyperus albostriatus
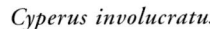 ↔ 12 in (30 cm) ↕ 24 in (60 cm)
South African species with many narrow leaves that are up to 20 in (50 cm) long, with 3 conspicuous pale veins. Flower stems, with broad, leafy, white-lined bracts, do not extend much above the height of the foliage. Will grow in wet soil. Zones 9–12.

Cyperus involucratus
syn. *Cyperus alternifolius* of gardens
↔ 24–40 in (60–100 cm) ↕ 3–5 ft (0.9–1.5 m)
Widespread in Africa. Short basal foliage clump and numerous 3-sided flower stems topped with many bracts to 16 in (40 cm) long, with rays to a little over 4 in (10 cm) long. Considered invasive in some areas. '**Variegatus**' ★, foliage with longitudinal cream striping. Zones 9–12.

Cyperus papyrus
EGYPTIAN REED, PAPYRUS
↔ 5–10 ft (1.5–3 m) ↕ 7–17 ft (2–5 m)
Vigorous, clump-forming, African species, with few or no basal leaves but many strong, deep green, 3-sided stems topped with dense umbels each of 100 or more drooping spikelet stalks. Will grow in water. *C. papyrus* is the "bulrush" of the Old Testament story of Moses. Zones 9–12.

DENDROCALAMUS

Genus of about 30 giant, clump-forming, perennial bamboos from India, Southeast Asia, China, and Indonesia, members of the grass (Poaceae) family. Mostly restricted to higher rainfall or mountain areas; they grow from short rhizomes. Members form loose to dense clumps with hollow to solid culms. There are numerous branches at a node, one or two larger than the rest. Long, narrow, strap-like, green leaves. CULTIVATION: Plant in spring in slightly acidic, loamy or sandy soil kept moist. Propagate by division or stem cuttings.

Dendrocalamus asper

PAI TONG, PRING BETUNG, SWEET BAMBOO

☼ ⁑ ↔ 40–80 ft (12–24 m) ↑ 60–100 ft (18–30 m)

From Southeast Asia. Stems reach 8–12 in (20–30 cm) in diameter, new shoots furry silver-brown, velvety. An important, large, structural bamboo, with edible shoots. Used for building, furniture making, and as livestock fodder. 'Hitam', from Indonesia, culms turn black with occasional green stripes; dark color is retained after harvest, green stripes becoming tan. Zones 9–12.

DESCHAMPSIA

HAIR GRASS

Genus of about 50 species of grasses in the grass (Poaceae) family. Clump-forming, can be herbaceous or evergreen. Found in temperate to cold regions, and many clones have been selected by growers, mainly in Germany. Graceful foliage. Airy flowerheads. CULTIVATION: Will grow in any good garden soil in sun or light shade. Clean out old spent flower stems in early spring. Propagate from seed; divide named clones in early spring.

Eriophorum vaginatum

Deschampsia cespitosa

syn. *Aira cespitosa*

TUFTED HAIR GRASS, TUSSOCK GRASS

☼/◐ ❋ ↔ 5 ft (1.5 m) ↑ 5–7 ft (1.5–2 m)

Native to North America, Asia, and Europe. Fine, rich, evergreen foliage. Masses of tiny summer flowers. *D. c. subsp. holciformis,* darker green foliage. *D. c. var. vivipara,* drooping plants that take root. Numerous clones include: *D. c.* Bronze Veil/'Bronzeschleier', bronze flowers; Golden Pendant/'Goldgehänge', slightly pendulous yellow flowers. Zones 5–10.

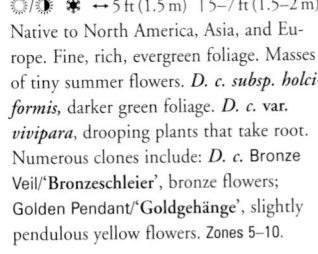

Deschampsia cespitosa

Deschampsia flexuosa

COMMON HAIR GRASS, CRINKLED HAIR GRASS, WAVY HAIR GRASS

☼/◐ ❋ ↔ 8 in (20 cm) ↑ 36 in (90 cm)

Found in Eurasia and the Americas. Fine, wavy, thread-like, green to olive leaves. Wiry flower stems with branching, spray-like, pink-tinted inflorescence. Zones 5–9.

EQUISETUM

HORSETAIL, SCOURING-RUSH

Genus of about 25 rush-like, flowerless, perennial herbs from the scouring-rush (Equisetaceae) family, found worldwide, except in Australia and New Zealand. Lumps of erect, cylindrical, jointed, bamboo-like stems. Leaves usually reduced to a ring of black or brown teeth at stem nodes; sometimes longer, straggly, and wiry. Spore-bearing cones at stem tips. CULTIVATION: Plant around water features, using garden soil or potting mix kept moist and well drained; stand pots in water. Propagate from spores or by division.

Equisetum hyemale

DUTCH RUSH, HORSETAIL RUSH, ROUGH HORSETAIL, SCOURING-RUSH,

☼ ❋ ↔ 12–24 in (30–60 cm) ↑ 3–5 ft (0.9–1.5 m)

Found in Eurasia and North America. An evergreen rush-like perennial that forms large colonies. Unbranched stems are rough, broad, rounded, ridged, to 5 ft (1.5 m) tall, with gray and black bands. 'Robustum', larger form, to 10 ft (3 m) tall. Zones 3–10.

Equisetum telmateia

GIANT HORSETAIL

☼ ❋ ↔ 12–24 in (30–60 cm) ↑ 20 in–6 ft (0.5–1.8 m)

Native to Eurasia, north Africa, and northern North America. Perennial. Erect, grooved, ivory white or pale green, sterile stems; smoothly ridged nodes and whorls of simple, feathery branches. Zones 5–10.

ERIOPHORUM

COTTON GRASS

Genus of about 22 grass-like perennial herbs, native to cooler regions of Eurasia, North America, and South Africa (1 species only), in the sedge (Cyperaceae) family. Common in bogs and other wet areas. Plants spread by rhizomes and have slender flat leaves on tufted, leafy, 3-angled stems. In spring stem tips bear dense spikelets of flowers with numerous perianth parts reduced to pale, cotton-like hairs that elongate with age to aid dispersal. CULTIVATION: Plant in full sun in damp garden soil or on the shallow margins of ponds. Propagate from seed or by division.

Eriophorum vaginatum ★

syns *Eriophorum callitrix, E. spissum, Scirpus faurieri*
COTTON GRASS, COTTONSEDGE, TUSSOCK COTTON GRASS, HARE'S TAIL

☼ ❀ ↔ 6–12 in (15–30 cm) ↕ 12–32 in (30–80 cm)

From the Northern Hemisphere's temperate regions. Tussock-forming sedge that dies back to rootstock annually, the basal portions of leaves and stems remaining green. Simple multi-flowered spikelet covered with white hairs, borne at stem tips. Zones 5–9.

FARGESIA

Himalayan bamboo genus, member of the grass (Poaceae) family. It contains 4 species, but there are also several cultivated varieties. Most are fairly compact, clumping, and non-invasive. Stems are fine and well foliaged, forming a dense impenetrable clump, useful as a screen. Flowers seldom appear on garden specimens. CULTIVATION: Easily grown in mild temperate areas in moist, humus-rich, well-drained soil in full sun or shade. Thin out old canes. Propagate by division, or from seed.

Fargesia murielae ★

syns *Sinarundinaria murielae, Thamnocalamus spathaceus*
UMBRELLA BAMBOO

☼ ❀ ↔ 2–4 ft (0.6–1.2 m) ↕ 12 ft (3.5 m)

From west and central China; important food of giant panda. Narrow apple green leaves, long drawn-out apex. Jointed culms, ½ in (12 mm) diameter, yellowish green. 'Simba', to 6 ft (1.8 m) high. Zones 5–10.

Fargesia nitida

syn. *Sinarundinaria nitida*
FOUNTAIN BAMBOO

☼ ❀ ↔ 2–4 ft (0.6–1.2 m) ↕ 12 ft (3.5 m)

From central China. Purplish culms to ½ in (12 mm) wide, branching in 2nd year, persistent purplish green sheaths.

Cascades of narrow, rough, tapered leaves. 'Anceps', narrower foliage, more open habit than species; 'De Belder', shorter, purple culms; 'McClure', reaches 18 ft (5.5 m) high; 'Nymphenburg', narrow foliage. Zones 5–10.

FESTUCA

FESCUE

Genus of some 300 species in the grass (Poaceae) family, widespread throughout the world. Small unassuming plants, they sometimes have distinctively colored foliage and showy flower plumes. Some of the finest lawn grasses available. Leaves are usually folded around the midrib, in some species making foliage very fine and hair-like. Flowerheads, which usually exceed foliage in height, are feathery and open. CULTIVATION: Most prefer temperate zones and tolerate most soils. Plant in full sun or partial shade. De-thatch and aerate annually. Green year-round, but in hot areas water well and do not mow too closely. Propagate by division, or from seed.

Festuca california

Festuca californica

CALIFORNIA FESCUE

☼ ❀ ↔ 24 in (60 cm) ↕ 24–36 in (60–90-cm)

From California, USA. Foliage green to bright blue; blue forms take on purplish tones once frosts commence. Pale creamy green flower spikes, in summer. 'Serpentine Blue' ★ (blue California fescue), rich silvery foliage, red-purple autumn tones. Zones 5–9.

Festuca glauca

BLUE FESCUE, GRAY FESCUE

☼ ❀ ↔ 10 in (25 cm) ↕ 12 in (30 cm)

Found throughout Europe. Densely tufted evergreen grass. Smooth blue-green leaves surround crown of plant. Creamy flower spikes appear from mid-summer, sitting well above the foliage. 'Blaufuchs' ★ (syn. Blue Fox), intense powder blue leaves, fade to cream at tips; 'Blauglut' (syn. Blue Glow), clump-forming, intense silver-blue foliage; 'Elijah Blue', soft powdery blue foliage, very compact; and 'Seeigel' (syn. Sea Urchin), very fine, upright, spiky, blue-green leaves, very compact. Zones 4–10.

Festuca glauca

Festuca valesiaca

WALLIS FESCUE

☼ ❀ ↔ 6 in (15 cm) ↕ 6 in (15 cm)

Tight, clump-forming, dwarf grass species from central Europe has soft powdery blue foliage. The bluish white flower spikes are held above foliage, in mid-summer. This plant needs well-drained soils, and is ideal in rockeries but not in very hot situations. Zones 5–9.

Imperata cylindrica 'Rubra'

HAKONECHLOA

A grass (Poaceae) family genus, it comprises one ornamental species and numerous cultivars. Slow-spreading, rhizomatous, perennial grass found in the mountains of the Tokaido district of southeast Honshu, Japan. Linear to lance-shaped blades grow to 12–36 in (30–90 cm) tall, and in mid- to late summer small airy inflorescences appear between the leaves, which turn orange to bronze in autumn. Variegated forms exist whose variegation is affected by siting and climatic conditions: in deep shade, yellow variegation is lime green; in partial shade in warm regions, the yellow parts turn a strong gold-yellow; grown in full sun in cool summer climates, yellow variegation bleaches to creamy white. CULTIVATION: Frost hardy. Prefers moist, humus-rich, well-drained soil in full or half-sun. Provide shade in hot dry areas. Generally disease free, it can be propagated by division in spring.

Hakonechloa macra
HAKONE GRASS, JAPANESE FOREST GRASS, URAHAGUSA
☼ ❀ ↔ over 24 in (60 cm) ↑ to 24 in (60 cm)
Slender, arching, green leaves with wiry stems form loose cascading mounds. Orange- to red-flushed autumn foliage persists into winter. Green-leafed form is more cold hardy (Zone 4), sun and drought tolerant, and faster grow-ing than cultivars, which both reach 12 in (30 cm) high. 'Alboaurea', mostly off-white and yellow variegated leaves with green, and red- to pink-flushed autumn foliage; 'Aureola', golden yellow leaves and thin green stripes, pinkish red tints in autumn. Zones 6–11.

IMPERATA

This genus in the grass (Poaceae) family, from warmer regions around the world, consists of about 8 species of perennial grasses with deep long-running rhizomes and erect tufts of long flat leaves. Tiny flowers are crowded into a plume-like spike topping a slender stalk; seeds are like thistledown, dispersed by the wind. They can form dense stands after removal of forest cover; in some areas they are regarded as weeds, though at the same time they may stabilize denuded soils on slopes. Some colored-leafed forms of *I. cylin-drica* are grown only for ornamental value. CULTIVATION: Ornamental forms may be grown in containers. Plant in fertile, moist, well-drained soil in full sun. Propagate from seed or by division of rhizomes.

Imperata cylindrica
BLADY GRASS, COGON GRASS, KUNAI GRASS
☼ ❅ ↔ 8–12 in (20–30 cm) ↑ 24–72 in (60–180 cm)
Perennial grass from most warmer parts of the Old World, naturalized in North America. Flat, semi-erect, narrow leaves to at least 20 in (50 cm) long. Silvery white panicles to 8 in (20 cm) long, sword-shaped spikelets. 'Rubra' ★ (syn. 'Red Baron'), leaves tinted wine red, scarlet in autumn. Zones 8–12.

JUNCUS
Genus of some 225 species of grass-like plants in the self-named Juncaceae or rush family, of cosmopolitan distribution. Found growing in wet soils such as bogs and water margins. The leaves may be flat, channeled, cylindrical, or reduced to sheaths at stem bases. Small green or brown flowers are borne in round heads or more open clusters at the stem ends. CULTIVATION: Many are invasive and few are grown ornamentally. They have some use around ponds or in wild gardening in wet areas. Grow in full sun or part-shade in heavy wet soil or shallow water. Propagate from seed or by division.

Juncus effusus
COMMON RUSH
☼ ❅ ↔ 30 in (75 cm) ↑ 5 ft (1.5 m)
Stiff, upright, twisted evergreen with rush-like leaves. Stems are rigid but smooth and look like a corkscrew. Tiny brown flowers appear in clusters in autumn, sitting above the foliage. Needs a moist soil. The cultivar 'Spiralis' (corkscrew rush) has mounding, curly, sometimes upright stems. Zones 6–9.

Juncus effusus

Juncus patens
CALIFORNIAN GRAY RUSH
☼/◗ ❅ ↔ 24 in (60 cm) ↑ 27 in (70 cm)
Steel blue-gray foliage, upright habit. Inconspicuous flowers appear in summer. Very tolerant of dry soils but will grow in shallow water. 'Carman's Gray', silvery gray, stiff, upright foliage, needs little room for roots; 'Elk Blue', intense steely blue foliage, wider leaves than the species. Zones 7–10.

LOLIUM

RYEGRASS

This genus comprises about 8 species of annual and perennial grasses (family Poaceae), native to temperate areas of Eurasia and northern Africa. They have smooth, erect, or shortly creeping rhizomes and narrow, flat or folded, strap-like leaves with cylindrical sheaths. They bear thin unbranched flowering spikes with 2 rows of flattened spikelets usually pressed tightly against the main axis, each spikelet bearing 5 to 9 green florets with yellow anthers. Ryegrasses are valued for pasture and fodder; some are used as lawn grasses, while some can be troublesome weeds. They shed large quantities of very fine pollen; close mowing of a lawn may prevent this problem. CULTIVATION: Adaptable to most well-drained soils in an open sunny position, though when used for lawns they can tolerate a certain amount of shade. In regions of light winter frost they are useful for lawns that remain green through winter. Propagate from seed.

Lolium perenne

ENGLISH RYEGRASS, PERENNIAL RYEGRASS

☼ ❋ ↔ 10–18 in (25–45 cm) ↕ 6–24 in (15–60 cm)

From temperate Eurasia and North Africa. Perennial grass distributed throughout the world as a lawn and pasture grass. 'Derby', early-flowering turf grass; 'Loretta', permanent and hard-wearing, light green turf grass; 'Manhattan', dark green fine-textured lawn and playing field turf; 'Pennfine', dense fine-textured lawn turf; 'Yorktown', low-growing, dark green, dense, fine-textured turf grass. Zones 5–10.

LOMANDRA

MAT-RUSHES

The 50 species in this genus in the family Laxmanniaceae are, with a few exceptions, confined to Australia. Evergreen, clump-forming, rush-like perennials or subshrubs with tiny flowers produced in spikes or panicles usually held low down among the leaves. Flowers are usually creamy white to lemon yellow, and the panicles are not particularly showy. Mat-rushes are used for soil stabilization, providing a habitat for small animals such as lizards. CULTIVATION: Once cultivated only by native plant enthusiasts, mat-rushes (mainly *L. longifolia*) are often used in Australia as roadside plantings owing to their drought tolerance. Because dead foliage builds up in the clumps, prune to the ground every so often, or set fire to in areas where this is feasible. Propagate from fresh seed or by dividing established clumps.

Lomandra longifolia

BASKET GRASS, SPINY-HEADED MAT-RUSH

☼ ❋ ↔ 30–36 in (75–90 cm) ↕ 20–40 in (50–100 cm)

From Eastern Australia. Sedge-like perennial forming large tussocks. Leaves stiff, flat, with several points at each tip. Narrow

panicle of dense clusters of small, fragrant, creamy yellow flowers with straw-colored spiny bracts, held in foliage, in the spring to early summer. These plants are widely grown for both ornament and for soil stabilization. Zones 8–12.

MELICA

MELIC

This genus of about 70 species, belongs to the grass (Poaceae) family. It is native to temperate regions of the world, excluding Australia. These cool-season growers usually become semi-dormant in summer. The foliage is quite unremarkable and they are grown for the creamy white flowerheads that mature in spring, which is quite early in the year for an ornamental grass. CULTIVATION: These hardy grasses need little more than a well-drained but moisture-retentive soil in full sun/half-sun. Prune down in the early winter before new growth starts. Propagate from seed in summer, or by dividing the large clumps.

Melica altissima

SIBERIAN MELIC, SIBERIAN MELICK

☼ ❋ ↔ 32 in (80 cm) ↕ 60 in (150 cm)

Tall grass species, native to eastern Europe and Siberia. Tall spikes of soft green strappy leaves. Fluffy, one-sided flowerheads, to 10 in (25-cm) long, in early summer. Can be dried for floral work. 'Atropurpurea' has mauve-pink flowerheads. Zones 5–10.

Melica altissima

MISCANTHUS

This genus, part of the grass (Poaceae) family, contains about 20 species found from Africa to East Asia. These tufted spreading plants have showy, green, silver, white, and mottled foliage, deciduous or evergreen. They are found in moist areas with free drainage. Commonly referred to as reeds, they have upright clumps of leaves that cascade from rounded upright stems. Masses of tall flowerheads usually appear in late summer through autumn, often remaining on plants through winter. They dry well, holding their form for months, so are ideal for floral work. Autumn tonings, orange, red, yellow, or purple. CULTIVATION: *Miscanthus* species prefer full sun and moist open soils. Used widely in ornamental gardens as features and for screening. To propagate, divide into small clumps in autumn, or sow seed in containers in spring after frosts. Division is best, as seed is often slow to germinate.

Miscanthus floridulus

AMUR SILVERGRASS

☼ ❋ ↔ 5 ft (1.5 m) ↕ 8 ft (2.4 m)

A tall grass plant from Southeast Asia, it can be deciduous or evergreen. It has arching mid-green leaves with silver midribs. Silver flower spikes appear in autumn. Zones 6–9.

Miscanthus sacchariflorus

SILVER BANNER GRASS

☼ ❊ ↔ 5 ft (1.5 m) ↑ 5 ft (1.5 m)

Deciduous creeping grass from Korea, Japan, and China. Forms dense clumps. The long green leaves hang from upright stems; orange-brown tonings in autumn. Wispy silver flowers appear in autumn–winter. Zones 5–9.

Miscanthus sinensis

EULALIA, JAPANESE SILVER GRASS

☼ ❊ ↔ 4 ft (1.2 m) ↑ 15 ft (4.5 m)

Tall clump-forming grass from Japan and China. Blue-green leaves turn vivid orange-reds and yellows in autumn. Flower spikes from silver-pink to reddish purple, in autumn. *M. s.* var. *condensatus*, taller form, wide leaves with cream central stripe; 'Cabaret' (Japanese silver grass), wide ribbon-like foliage, creamy white stripes, blush pink flowers; 'Cosmopolitan', improved form of *M. s.* 'Variegatus', wide, more upright, non-floppy stems and leaves, flowers sit above foliage. *M. s.* 'Gracillimus' ★ (maiden grass), upright clumps, narrow silver leaves, bright orange foliage; 'Kleine Silberspinne' (silver tower Japanese spider grass), delicate silvery foliage, spider-like flowers; 'Morning Light' ★ (morning light Japanese silver grass), narrow, green leaves, reddish bronze flowers fade to dusty cream; 'Strictus' (porcupine grass, banded miscanthus), clump-forming, stiff, upright, gold-banded leaves and stems, copper flowers, fade to cream; 'Variegatus' (variegated Japanese silver grass), loose, pendulous, green and white-striped foliage; 'Yaku jima' (Yaku jima Japanese silver grass), delicate fine-textured foliage, compact plant, reddish bronze flowers; 'Zebrinus' (zebra grass, banded miscanthus), long arching leaves, pale yellow, pinkish bronze flowers above foliage. Zones 5–9.

MOLINIA

MOOR GRASS

Genus of only 2 species of these deciduous, tuft-forming perennial grasses from temperate Eurasia. Members of the grass (Poaceae) family, they grow in wetland tussock areas. The stiff upright foliage changes color in autumn. Tall flower spikes sit high above the foliage from late spring to autumn. When the plants die down in winter, the foliage detaches itself from the plant, unlike most deciduous grasses that hold onto the old foli-

age through to the next season. Crown is thus free of any material over winter, giving a clean look for new growth in spring. CULTIVATION: These plants prefer moist open soils and will grow in sun or shade. Propagate from seed or by division in spring. The seed may not be true to type and is very slow to germinate.

Molinia caerulea

MOOR GRASS, PURPLE MOOR GRASS

☼/❉ ❊ ↔ 16 in (40 cm) ↑ 16 in (40 cm)

Perennial grass, native to Eurasia. Clumping form with slender sword-shaped leaves, slightly arching. Purple flowers on spikes above the foliage, in summer. *M. c.* subsp. *arundinacea*, long, pale gray-green, arching foliage, graceful purple to brown flower spikes, fade to vivid yellow, in late summer, prefers damp, boggy areas. *M. c.* 'Moorhexe' (witch moor grass), pale green foliage, neat clumps, purplish flowers on fine spikes; 'Variegata' ★ (variegated moor grass), mid-green leaves, creamy yellow to white variegations, upright brown flowers, slow to establish. Zones 5–9.

MUHLENBERGIA

MUHLY GRASS

A genus of around 160 species of mainly perennial grasses (in the family Poaceae), most native to warmer parts of North America, with a few in Asia as well. They are tussock-forming grasses, often making large clumps of fine foliage. They produce numerous long plume-like flowerheads in summer; the small crowded spikelets may be finely awned. They are generally evergreen but foliage may be killed by winter frost or wither in hot summers. CULTIVATION: Mostly easily grown in any sunny position with moist well-drained soil. The more tender species may be grown as annuals in colder areas, or potted and moved under cover over the winter months. Propagation is from seed but the best forms must be increased by division.

Muhlenbergia rigens

DEERGRASS

☼ ❊ ↔ 24–48 in (60–120 cm) ↑ 36–60 in (90–150 cm)

Found across southwestern USA from northern California to western Texas, also northern Mexico; large dense tussocks of fine, spreading, pale green foliage; many slender erect seed heads in summer with crowded small grayish spikelets. Zones 7–10.

Miscanthus sinensis 'Gracillimus'

Miscanthus sinensis 'Variegatus'

Molinia caerulea 'Variegata'

OTATEA

This Central American genus, a member of the grass (Poaceae) family, is composed of 2 species of shrubby bamboos. They have narrow arching stems, with a dense covering of long, thin, soft green leaves crowded near the end of the stems, creating a plume-like or pompon effect. The exposed parts of the stems turn dark brown to black in their second year. Although they spread by runners, they are not invasive and are easily controlled.
CULTIVATION: Unusually for bamboos, *Otatea* species can be hard to grow and can develop into rather sparse clumps. While hardy to light frosts and reasonably drought tolerant once established, they prefer warm conditions with summer moisture and fertile humus-rich soil in sun or part-shade. Propagate by division.

Otatea acuminata

☀ ⬍ ↔ 20 ft (6 m) ↕ 25 ft (8 m)
Bamboo found from Mexico to Nicaragua. Forms large clump of very narrow stems. Stems curve gracefully, moving in the breeze. Narrow leaves, to 6 in (15 cm) long, sheaths fall, revealing distinctive white powder below leaf nodes. *O. a.* subsp. *aztecorum* (Mexican weeping bamboo) has culms 1½ in (35 mm) in diameter, mostly obscured by prolific, long, narrow leaves. Zones 10–12.

Otatea acuminata subsp. *aztecorum*

PENNISETUM

Genus of about 80 clump- or mat-forming, rhizomatous or stoloniferous, annual or perennial grasses from the family Poaceae, native to tropical, subtropical, and warm temperate regions of Eurasia, Africa, Arabia, and Australasia. Round, hollow, prostrate to erect and tufted stems with solid swollen nodes. Alternate, narrow, strap-like, flat leaves rising from a central base and stems. Cylindrical or rounded, feathery, spike-like flowerheads grow at the stem ends or from leaf axils, and contain clusters of up to 4 sword-shaped to oblong spikelets, minute bisexual flowers with 3 stamens and 2 stigmas, in late summer and autumn. Fruit is an achene-like grain. Some species are cultivated for ornamental and foodcrop value.
CULTIVATION: They prefer moist, well-drained soil with either full sun or light shade. Propagate species from seed and hybrids by division in spring.

Pennisetum alopecuroides ★

syn. *Pennisetum japonicum*
CHINESE PENNISETUM, FOUNTAIN GRASS, SWAMP FOX-TAIL GRASS

☀/☀ ❄ ↔ 18–24 in (45–60 cm) ↕ 4–5 ft (1.2–1.5 m)
Clump-forming, upright, perennial grass, found from eastern Asia to northwestern Australia. Solitary, terminal, yellowish green to dark purple, cylindrical to narrowly oblong flowerheads, to 8 in (20 cm), with spikelets with purplish anthers and long bristles. Leaves to 24 in (60 cm) long. 'Cassian', to 4 ft (1.2 m) tall, foxtail-shaped flowerheads contrast with foliage, which turns gold with reddish tints in autumn; 'Hameln', clump-forming to 20 in (50 cm) high, with buff-colored flowerheads, golden leaves in autumn; 'Little Bunny', compact form, to 18 in (45 cm) tall, heads of whitish green flowers; 'Moudry', dark purple to black flowerheads, shiny dark green leaves, turning golden yellow then beige, in autumn. Zones 5–9.

Pennisetum setaceum

Pennisetum setaceum

FOUNTAIN GRASS
☀ ⬍ ↔ 24–36 in (60–90 cm) ↕ 3–5 ft (0.9–1.5 m)
Clumping, perennial grass native to tropical Africa, southwestern Asia, and Arabia, annual in cooler climates. Erect slender stem and very narrow, rough, rigid leaves, 8–26 in (20–65 cm) long. Feathery, erect or inclined flowerheads, to 12 in (30 cm) long, are tinged with pink to purple, and contain 1 to 3 purplish spikelets in summer. 'Atrosanguineum' has burgundy foliage, and soft reddish purple, nodding flower plumes borne in summer; 'Burgundy Giant', broad burgundy leaves, to 1 in (25 mm) wide, and whitish pink flowers on stalks up to 4 ft (1.2 m) long, bright green in summer, and turning golden brown in autumn. Zones 9–10.

Pennisetum villosum ★

syn. *Pennisetum longistylum*
FEATHERTOP
☀ ❄ ↔ 18–24 in (45–60 cm) ↕ 2–4 ft (0.6–1.2 m)
Spreading perennial grass, sometimes grown as an annual. Native to northeastern Africa. Forms loosely clumped, spreading mats. Sheathed leaves, bluish green blades. Solitary, plumed, cylindrical to almost spherical flower spikes, with feathery bristles, tinged with tawny brown to purple spikelets. Self-seeds. Zones 8–10.

Phragmites australis

PHALARIS

CANARY GRASS, GARDENER'S GARTERS, RIBBON GRASS

Genus of around 15 species of both clumping annual and running perennial plants in the grass (Poaceae) family come from a
wide range of habitats in North America, Asia, southern Africa,
and Europe. Only the perennial species (only in their variegated
forms) are usually grown in gardens. *P. canariensis,* an annual species long cultivated for birdseed, is now considered a major weed.
CULTIVATION: Easily grown in any well-drained to moist soil in a
sunny to part-shaded site. Can become weedy. Propagate annual
species from seed, and perennial species by division.

Phalaris arundinacea

GARDENER'S GARTERS, REED CANARY GRASS, RIBBON GRASS

☼/◐ ❄ ↔ 7–10 ft (2–3 m) ↑ 4–5 ft (1.2–1.5 m)

Hardy perennial from Europe, temperate Asia, and North
America. Soft arching leaves to 14 in (35 cm) long grow on
upright stems topped with soft fluffy flowerheads that are pale
green at first and turn buff with maturity. Usually grown in only
one of its variegated forms, such as 'Picta', which has leaves
boldly striped with white. Zones 4–11.

PHRAGMITES

REED

The 3 or 4 members of this genus in the family Poaceae are
widely distributed in swamps and wet areas in tropical and temperate climates. They are perennial grasses with thick rhizomes or
runners, and grow in dense stands. They have broad or narrow,
flat or folded, generally deciduous leaves with open sheaths, and
bear large, soft, hairy or feathery terminal panicles of spikelets
of 1 to 10 florets, on tall, erect, robust stems.
CULTIVATION: These reeds prefer a position in full sun in damp
soil, preferably near ponds or slowly moving water. Propagation
is from seed or by division.

Phragmites australis

syn. *Phragmites communis*

CARRIZO, COMMON REED, FEATHER GRASS

☼ ❄ ↔ 27–40 in (70–100 cm) ↑ 6–10 ft (1.8–3 m)

Widely distributed perennial grass. Stiff erect stems; narrow,
arching, flat, strap-like leaves with blades tapering to a long tip,
with rough margins and smooth sheaths. Flowerheads feathery,
erect or drooping, oblong to egg-shaped, tinged brown to purple
in summer–autumn. 'Rubra', reddish flowerheads; 'Variegatus',
leaves striped with bright yellow fading to white. Zones 4–11.

PHYLLOSTACHYS

This is the largest and best known genus of running bamboos
(family Poaceae), consisting of 50 or more species ranging from
the eastern Himalayas to Japan, most native to China. Medium
to tall, with widely spaced culms arising from deep long-running
rhizomes, they spread rapidly when conditions suit. Culm internodes are flattened or shallowly grooved on one side; each lower
node bears just 2 lateral branches, though there may be a third
smaller branch. Foliage is not distinctive. Flowers are rare and
inconspicuous. Genus includes species for edible shoots, as well
as many used in Asia for building, furniture, and similar items.
CULTIVATION: Some are frost hardy, and when grown near their
cold limit they remain fairly compact, though vigorous spreaders
in warmer areas. Spread can be contained by inserting concrete,
steel, or plastic barriers in the soil to about 24 in (60 cm). Grow
smaller species in tubs or planter boxes; water generously. Any
soil is fine. Provide ample moisture in summer. Propagate from
excavated lengths of rhizome, each with several culm bases.

Phyllostachys aurea

FISHPOLE BAMBOO, GOLDEN BAMBOO

☼/◐ ❄ ↔ 20–40 ft (6–12 m) ↑ 25 ft (8 m)

From southeastern China. Culms smooth olive-green to quite
yellowish, depending on exposure to sun, stronger ones 1–1½ in
(25–40 mm) thick but usually mixed with many smaller ones,
making dense bushy stands; bases of culms with crowded, often
crooked nodes. Versatile species, tolerating dry air. 'Holochrysa'
(syn. 'Kansai'), whole culm bright yellow, turning a transient red
in first season (in full sun); 'Flavescens Inversa', dark green
culms, contrasting bright yellow groove; 'Koi', golden culms,
prominent green groove. Zones 7–11.

Phyllostachys bambusoides

JAPANESE TIMBER BAMBOO

☼ ❄ ↔ 30–60 ft (6–18 m) ↑ 40–70 ft (12–21 m)

One of the largest timber bamboos, valued for construction
due to its thick, straight, strong culms, up to 6 in (15 cm) wide.
Native to China, long cultivated in Japan. The ornamental cultivars, mostly 25 ft (8 m) or smaller, include: 'Castilloni', which is
like 'Holochrysa' but with green groove and stronger apricot variegated foliage; 'Castilloni Inversa', reverse of 'Castilloni' with
randomly variegated foliage; 'Holochrysa' (syn. 'Allgold'), rich
golden culms; 'Kawadana', green culm subtly striped white and
finely white-striped foliage; 'Marliacea', corrugated internodes;
'Richard Haubrich', apricot-striped foliage. Zones 7–11.

Phyllostachys edulis

syns *Phyllostachys heterocycla, P. pubescens*

MAO ZHU, MOSO, MOUSOU CHIKU

☀ ❄ ↔ 30–100 ft (9–30 m) ↑ 40–75 ft (12–22 m)

Believed native to Japan, long cultivated in China. Most
important bamboo for edible shoots; also valued
as a timber bamboo. Culms up to 7 in (18 cm)
wide though 3–4 in (8–10 cm) is more usual,
densely hairy when young, pale matt green ageing
to deep yellowish; long branches and fine leaves
give a plume-like appearance. '**Aureovariegata**'
(syn. 'Gold Stripe'), 20 ft (6 m) tall, culms and
foliage striped golden; '**Spring Beauty**', fine white-
striped variegation in spring. Zones 6–10.

Phyllostachys nigra ★

BLACK BAMBOO

☀ ❄ ↔ 20–50 ft (6–15 m) ↑ 25–50 ft (8–15 m)

From China, long cultivated in Japan. Original
wild plants are not as black as commonly grown
form. New culms green, soon develop brown stip-
pling that transforms them to black. Probably the
most popular bamboo species. *P. n.* f. *henonis*,
larger culms, blue-gray in shade or golden green
in sun; *P. n.* '**Boryana**', like *P. n.* f. *henonis* but
developing brown cloud-like markings. Zones 7–10.

PLEIOBLASTUS

Genus in the grass (Poaceae) family, of about 20
species of mainly small-growing running bamboos from Japan
and China. Leaves lance-shaped. Over the years many attractive
variegated clones have been selected, many of which are still
grown as species because they haven't been properly classified.
CULTIVATION: Prefers well-drained but moist rich soil in full or
half-sun. Variegated clones need sun to keep their color. Most are
best pruned to ground level each spring. Propagate by division

Pleioblastus variegatus

syns *Arundinaria fortunei, A. variegata*

CHIGO-ZASA, DWARF WHITE-STRIPED-BAMBOO

☀ ❄ ↔ 40–60 in (100–150 cm) ↑ 28–40 in (70–100 cm)

Upright form from Japan with upright leaves to 6 in (15 cm)
long, boldly striped with white. Obviously a selection of an as
yet unidentified green-leafed species. Zones 5–10.

POA

BLUE GRASS, MEADOWGRASS, SPEAR GRASS

Genus of about 500 mostly perennial and some annual species
with slender to robust stems, members of the grass (Poaceae)
family. Native to cool temperate regions. Sheathed, narrow, strap-
like leaves with flat, folded, or curled blades, and raised, rough
veins. Flowerheads, on erect stems, 1–4 ft (0.3–1.2 m) tall, are
open or compact panicles of 2 to 6 spikelets, often tufted; long,
cobweb-like hairs with branches drooping or held close to stem.
CULTIVATION: They are adaptable to most soils in an open sunny
position. Propagation is from seed or by division.

Phyllostachys nigra

Poa cita ★

SILVER TUSSOCK

☀ ❄ ↔ 9–12 in (22–30 cm) ↑ 12–40 in (30–100 cm)

Perennial grass from New Zealand. It forms dense clumps of
tightly folded, leathery, sharply tipped, brownish or silvery green
leaves smooth above and fringed with hairs along
the margins, with a creamy brown, shiny sheath
with rough margins. Feathery pale green flowerheads consist of an open, slender, rough panicle
with twisted branches. Zones 7–9.

Poa pratensis

JUNE GRASS, KENTUCKY BLUEGRASS, MEADOW GRASS

☀ ❄ ↔ 12–24 in (30–60 cm) ↑ 24–36 in
(60–90 cm)

Loosely tufted perennial grass native to North
Africa and central Europe. Grows from long,
stout rhizomes, and is widely planted as a lawn
or pasture grass. Loose, spreading, pyramid-
shaped panicles have spreading branchlets of
cream-colored flower spikelets, to 8 in (20 cm)
long, in spring–early summer. The spikelets
often fall to one side. The leaves are flattened
or folded, smooth or rough, to 6 in (15 cm)
long, with open sheaths. Zones 3–6.

PSEUDOSASA

A genus of 6 species of bamboo in the grass
(Poaceae) family, from China, Japan, and Korea.
They can be clump-forming or running and vary from dwarf to
quite tall species. Some can be invasive. The stems are woody
and erect. Foliage usually lance-shaped and without hairs.
CULTIVATION: They will grow well in any moist fertile soil in full
sun or half-sun. Propagate by division in early spring.

Pseudosasa japonica

ARROW BAMBOO, METAKE

☀/◐ ❄ ↔ 15 ft (4.5 m) ↑ 17–20 ft (5–6 m)

Strong running species with upright stems that start green and
turn beige, forming branchlets in the second year. Leaves to 14 in
(35 cm) long, yellowish midrib and grayish reverse. Zones 6–10.

Poa cita

SACCHARUM

syn. *Erianthus*

This genus contains around 40 species of clumping or rhizomatous perennial grasses in the family Poaceae. Native to tropical and warm temperate regions worldwide, they grow by riversides and in rich soils in valleys. Their strong, cane-like, jointed stems are green to violet, with exposed roots near the base. Their long flat leaves are arranged in 2 ranks, and the tiny flowers are borne in attractive fluffy panicles. One species, *S. officinarum*, is a major crop from which several products are made, including sugar cane, rum, molasses, and wax. The genus is also host to a parasite, *Aeginetia indica*, which has purple flowers.

CULTIVATION: In cool temperate climates grow in the greenhouse in beds or large containers of rich damp loam. In warm regions grow outdoors in rich moist soil in full sun. These plants can be invasive in appropriate conditions. Propagate from seed, or, more usually, from stem cuttings.

Saccharum ravennae

syn. *Erianthus ravennae*
PLUME GRASS, RAVENNA GRASS

☼ ❄ ↔ 40 in (100 cm) ↑ 10–15 ft (3–4.5 m)

An upright, decorative, dominant grass from southern Europe. The green leaf blades have a white stripe. Silver plumes appear in late summer, turning gray with maturity. Do not plant in heavy clay soils. Zones 5–9.

Schoenoplectus lacustris

SASA

Sasa is the Japanese word for bamboo, and this genus has 60 species of small to medium-sized bamboos native to southeastern Russia, southern China, northern Japan, and Korea. Members of the grass (Poaceae) family, they have running rhizomes and arching culms, and the stems have a waxy white bloom at the nodes. The broad finely toothed leaves wither in winter; those of *S. veitchii* create ornamental white margins of "false parchment," which lowers leaf maintenance yet still suppresses competition from weeds and protects buds from severe cold. The tropical appearance of these plants is illusory: when weighed down with snow, the thin flexible culms protect against severe cold winds.

CULTIVATION: Grow these plants in a damp rich soil in part-shade. *Sasa* species spread rapidly, so careful siting is necessary; alternatively the plants can be confined in a large container. Propagate in spring by coiling the mature rhizomes into pots and covering them with potting compost. Tidy plants by clearing away the disheveled culms at the end of winter.

Sasa palmata

☼ ❄ ↔ 10–20 ft (3–6 m) ↑ 7 ft (2 m)

Native to Japan. Vigorous spreading species forms thick hedge. Stems may be streaked with purple. Palm-like foliage, long tapering leaves, bright shiny green all year, yellow midrib. '**Nebulosa**', brown cloud-like markings on mature culms. Zones 7–11.

Sasa veitchii

KUMA ZASA

☼ ❄ ↔ 10–20 ft (3–6 m) ↑ 5 ft (1.5 m)

From Japan. Ground-covering foliage tolerates dark dry locations. Stems purple-lined, glaucous. Short tapering leaves wither in winter to broad, papery, white margins. Zones 6–11.

SCHOENOPLECTUS

Genus of some 50 tufted or creeping annuals or perennials found throughout the world belongs in the sedge (Cyperaceae) family. Perennial species are found in deep to shallow water, annuals in seasonal wet depressions. Leaves are usually represented merely by a sheath, less often by a strap-like blade. The reddish brown summer flowerheads are generally held on long slender stems, and usually comprise a few to many spikelets, each containing numerous flowers. The fruits are achenes. Many species are used for basketry and mat-making in various parts of the world.

CULTIVATION: These plants are easily grown in full sun or shade in any moist soil. Some may become invasive, so care should be taken if growing them in non-native areas. Easily propagated by division or raised from seed.

Schoenoplectus lacustris

syn. *Scirpus lacustris*
BULRUSH, CLUBRUSH, TULE

☼ ❄ ↔ 3–4 ft (0.9–1.2 m) ↑ 3–10 ft (0.9–3 m)

Grass-like annual or perennial, found throughout Europe, Asia, Africa, and northern South America. Slow-spreading, clump of circular rush-like stems. Dense rust-colored flowerheads made up of over 100 spikelets, in summer–autumn. Leaves are used for

making mats and baskets. *S. l.* subsp. *tabernaemontani*, shorter
stems; its cultivar 'Zebrinus', less vigorous, usually less than 5 ft
(1.5 m) tall, bands of yellow to ivory on stems. Zones 4–11.

SEMIARUNDINARIA

This genus of bamboos is from Japan and contains 6 species,
which are also found wild in China. This leptomorph bamboo
is considered a natural bigeneric cross between *Phyllostachys* and
Pleioblastus. Members of the grass (Poaceae) family, they are usually running plants but tend to be more clumping in cooler climates. The stems are comparatively short-lived, and should be
regularly removed as they age to keep the plant tidy. The stems
usually have 3-short principal branches and up to 7 branches at
each node. Although they are regarded as shrubs, *Semiarun-
dinaria* species can reach up to 40 ft (12 m) tall.
CULTIVATION: Plant in moist but not wet soils in partly shaded
woodland situations. Not fussy about soil type, but prefer
humus-rich acid soil. Propagate by division of rhizomes.

Semiarundinaria fastuosa

syn. *Arundinaria fastuosa*

NARIHARA BAMBOO

☼/☀ ❄ ↔ 7–10 ft (2–3 m) ↑ 20–30 ft (6–9 m)

Erect clumping to running bamboo from Japan. Slender green
stems, with purple-brown stripes in direct sun. Leaves to 6 in
(15 cm) long, most numerous toward tops of stems. *S. f.* var.
viridis, bushier growth habit, with narrower, non-fading, dark
green leaves, easily propagated. Zones 7–10.

SESLERIA

MOOR GRASS

This genus of about 35 low-growing, mounding, perennial
grasses from the family Poaceae is native to Europe and
western Asia. These attractive grasses have
narrow leaf blades and dense rounded to
cylindrical panicles of flower spikes.
CULTIVATION: Moor grasses prefer rocky well-
drained soils in an open sunny position.
Propagation is by division.

Sesleria tatrae

☼/☀ ❄ ↔ 6–8 in (15–20 cm) ↑ 6–10 in
(15–25 cm)

A tufted or clump-forming perennial grass
from around the snowline in the Tatra
Mountains of Poland. It forms a dense clump
of very fine deep green leaves. The flowerheads are short
and appear on stocky stems, in summer. Zones 3–8.

Sesleria tatrae

SORGHASTRUM

Genus of around 16 species of annual and perennial grasses in
the family Poaceae from the American and African tropics. They
can form open, rather airy sprays or strong, densely foliaged
clumps of long, very narrow leaves, often rolled along the midrib.
Large feathery panicles, usually from late summer, are borne on
long stems that hold them well clear of the foliage.

Spartina pectinata

CULTIVATION: They are easily grown in any reasonably sunny position with moist, well-drained soil. Drought tolerant once established. Hardiness varies with the species. Propagate by seed;
perennials will also grow from division.

Sorghastrum nutans

INDIAN GRASS, WOOD GRASS

☼/☀ ❄ ↔ 16–32 in (40–80 cm) ↑ 5–7 ft (1.5–2 m)

Perennial grass from central and eastern USA. Narrow leaves to
24 in (60 cm) long. Pale to golden brown panicles, to over 12 in
(30 cm) long atop erect, wiry stems, in autumn. Zones 5–10.

SPARTINA

CORD GRASS, MARSH GRASS

This genus of 15 perennial species, members of the grass
(Poaceae) family, is native to western and southern Europe, the
Americas, northwestern and southern Africa,
and the South Atlantic islands. These plants
grow from rhizomes, with rigid upright stems
and tough flat or folded leaves with finely
hairy ligules. Flowerheads are stalkless spikelets, held close or spreading out. The name
comes from the Greek word *spartine*, a cord,
referring to the plant's tough flowering stems.
CULTIVATION: They prefer a position in full
sun and thrive in salty coastal marshes and
sand flats, but can adapt to any moist soil.
Propagate by division or from seed.

Spartina pectinata

FRESHWATER CORD GRASS, MARSH GRASS, SALT GRASS

☼ ❄ ↔ 18–24 in (45–60 cm) ↑ 3–10 ft (0.9–3 m)

Aggressively spreading perennial grass native to the wet prairies
of North America. Narrow, arching, leathery, flat leaves, to 4 ft
(1.2 m) long; they change from green to yellow to fawn. The
feathery columnar flowerheads, masses of tiny purple flowers,
are borne in autumn–winter. 'Aureomarginata' (syn. 'Variegata')
has arching olive green leaves, edged with golden yellow, and
purplish, hanging stamens. Zones 4–5.

SPOROBOLUS

DROPSEED, RUSHGRASS

Genus of about 100 perennial or annual species, widely distributed and naturalized, in the grass (Poaceae) family. Finely textured, hair-like, medium green leaves, 8–24 in (20–60 cm) long, typically form a dense arching mound, to 15 in (38 cm) tall. Leaves turn golden in autumn, fading to light bronze in winter. Open branching panicles, 12–27 in (30–70 cm) long, of small stalked spikelets, carry a single fragrant flower with pink and brown tints, on slender stems that rise well above the foliage, from late summer to autumn. Tiny spherical seeds drop from their hulls in autumn. Cultivated as ornamentals and for livestock feed.
CULTIVATION: Easily grown in a range of dry to medium-wet, well-drained soils in full sun. Drought tolerant. Propagate from seed.

Sporobolus heterolepis

PRAIRIE DROPSEED

☼ ❋ ↔ 12–16 in (30–40 cm) ↕ 24–36 in (60–90 cm)
North American prairie grass. Very fine bright green leaves, vivid orange in autumn. Airy, open, buff flower plumes on wiry stems, in summer. Drought tolerant once established. Zones 3–9.

STENOTAPHRUM

Genus of 7 annual or perennial mat-forming species native to tropical or subtropical regions. Members of the grass (Poaceae) family, they have creeping or rising stems, rooting at nodes. Short flattened racemes at stem ends, growing from the leaf axils, bear spikelets of 2 stalkless flowers on upright or sprawling, solid, flattened stems. Leaves can be thick, flat, or folded, and narrow to sword-shaped. They grow from the stems with a sheath at the base, with leaf blade held at right angles to stem. One species, *S. secundatum*, is used widely for lawns in the southern USA.
CULTIVATION: These plants prefer partial shade and moist soil. Propagation is usually from cuttings.

Stenotaphrum secundatum

BUFFALO GRASS, GRAMA, ST AUGUSTINE GRASS

☼/◕ ❅ ↔ 2–16 in (5–40 cm) ↕ 2–16 in (5–40 cm)
Hardy perennial grass, native to tropical regions. Popular warm-season lawn grass. Forms fans of smooth, flat, or folded, narrow, oblong leaves, to 6 in (15 cm) long. Stiff one-sided spikes, to 6 in (15 cm) long, green stalkless spikelets. 'Variegatum', leaves striped pale green and ivory, suited to indoor culture. Zones 9–11.

STIPA

FEATHER GRASS, NEEDLE GRASS, SPEAR GRASS

This is a wide and varied genus in the grass (Poaceae) family, containing about 200 species of tufted evergreen and deciduous grasses. Occurring as native plants on slopes in the world's temperate and warm-temperate regions, some of these pretty grasses are now widely grown in ornamental gardens. Many species formerly included in the genus *Stipa* are now reclassified under other genera such as *Austrostipa* and *Nassella*. *Stipa* species have fine-textured, linear, flat leaves that bear long panicles of feathery, often fluffy flowerheads. Some are grown for floral work, and they are often used in perennial borders and roadside plantings.
CULTIVATION: They need a fertile, medium to light soil in full sun. Trim back deciduous species in winter to ensure good growth. Propagate by division in summer or sow seed in pots in spring.

Stipa arundinacea

NEW ZEALAND WIND GRASS

☼ ❋ ↔ 4 ft (1.2 m) ↕ 3 ft (0.9 m)
Mid-sized New Zealand grass. Light green arching foliage, turns light orange with bronzy tones in sunlight. Spikelets of fluffy green flowers, tinted purple, in summer–autumn. Zones 8–10.

Stipa calamagrostis ★

syn. *Stipa lasiogrostis*

☼ ❋ ↔ 4 ft (1.2 m) ↕ 3 ft (0.9 m)
Deciduous perennial grass, native to southern Europe. Forms tufted clump. Linear blue-green leaves arch slightly during the season. Bears creamy silver plumes of nodding feathery flowers, in summer. Zones 7–10.

Stipa gigantea ★

GIANT FEATHER GRASS, GOLDEN OATS

☼ ❋ ↔ 4 ft (1.2 m) ↕ 8 ft (2.4 m)
Striking perennial grass from Spain and Portugal. Clumps of green to gray-green foliage. Loose panicles of flowers and seeds, in spring, become golden, persist through summer. Zones 6–10.

Stipa splendens

☼ ❋ ↔ 4 ft (1.2 m) ↕ 8 ft (2.4 m)
Deciduous perennial grass from central Asia and Russia. Tufted mounded plant. Dark green leaves, slightly arching habit. Purple-tinted white flower spikes, in summer. Zones 7–10.

Stipa arundinacea

Stipa gigantea

Stipa splendens

TYPHA

BULRUSH, CAT-TAIL, REED MACE

This genus, comprising some 10 to 12 species found almost throughout the world, makes up the family Typhaceae. These often very large perennials are from marshlands, where they can form extensive stands. The leaves arise from rhizomes and have sheathing bases; the leaf blade is very elongated and linear, flat or concave, with spongy internal tissue. The flowering stems are erect and spear-like, bearing dense cylindrical spikes of tightly packed wind-pollinated flowers. The male and female flowers are separate but on the same plant, the males borne in an upper distinct part, often differently colored. The fruits are tiny and plumed, like thistledown. They are released by disintegration of the female spike and float away on the breeze in vast numbers. The starch-rich rhizomes, and even the pollen, provide emergency food. The leaves are used in matting and chair-seating ("rush") and have been tried for paper-making. The plush formed by the female flowers has been used as a substitute for kapok.

CULTIVATION: Cultivation is easy in any moist soil. These rushes grow in water to 24 in (60 cm) or so deep, although seed germination takes place on damp mudbanks. Except for some of the smallest species, they are too invasive for use as aquatics in any but the largest ponds or artificial lakes. Propagate from seed or by rhizome division.

Typha orientalis, New Zealand

Typha minima

☼ ❊ ↔ 1¼–2 in (3–5 cm) ↑ 2½–3 in (6–8 cm)

Perennial from Europe, the Caucasus region, and Asia with narrow, sword-shaped, green leaves. Flower stalks shorter than leaves, bearing oblong, dark brown, terminal heads of scaly, finely hairy, upright, catkin-like flowers, in summer. Zones 3–11.

Typha orientalis

BROAD-LEAF CUMBUNGI, BULRUSH

☼ ❖ ↔ 12–20 in (30–50 cm) ↑ 3–8 ft (0.9–2.4 m)

Vigorous reed-like perennial found from northern Australia to the Philippines. Branching rhizomes; stout upright stems. Long narrow leaves. Cylindrical spikes of chestnut brown flowers produce masses of fluffy seed, summer. Can be invasive. Zones 9–11.

YUSHANIA

Yushania (Chinese for "jade mountain") is a large genus of over 80 species in the grass (Poaceae) family. Technically, *Yushania* species are cold hardy pachymorph bamboos, but the rhizome neck is so long that the culms arise at considerable distances, so they should be treated as spreaders. Found from China, Taiwan, and Southeast Asia to Madagascar and the mountains of East Africa. Typically shrubs, they are highly regarded as screens.

CULTIVATION: Propagation is by division, taken in winter with the culm and rhizome buds present.

Yushania anceps

☼ ❊ ↔ 15–30 ft (4.5–9 m) ↑ 15 ft (4.5 m)

Native to the Himalayan mountains of India. Erect culms, ¾ in (18 mm) in diameter, completely pendulous, bowed down by the weight of the foliage. Makes fine screens. 'Pitt White', smaller foliage, more vigorous, double the height of species. Zones 7–10.

ZOYSIA

ZOYSIA GRASS

This genus of 5 creeping, warm season, perennial grasses in the grass (Poaceae) family comes from Southeast Asia. These plants grow from both runners and rhizomes. Leaves are rounded to slightly flattened, stiff, and sharply pointed, with occasional hairs near the base, smooth margins and fine to coarsely textured surfaces. Short, slender, and sheathed terminal spikes or spikelets, each with 1 flower, on short stalks.

CULTIVATION: Plant in late spring to early summer for lawn turf. Adaptable to most soils in full sun; they are also shade-tolerant.

Zoysia 'Emerald'

☼ ❊ ↔ 1–2 in (25–50 mm) ↑ 1–2 in (25–50 mm)

Developed for lawn turf use. A hybrid between *Z. japonica* and *Z. tenuifolia*. Creeping, fast-growing, dark emerald green, perennial grass growing from underground runners. Fine dense texture; cold- and drought-tolerant. Zones 1–9.

Zoysia tenuifolia ★

KOREAN VELVET GRASS, MASCARENE GRASS

☼ ❊ ↔ 1–2 in (25–50 mm) ↑ 1–2 in (25–50 mm)

A slow-growing, creeping, ornamental, perennial grass from Southeast Asia that spreads by underground rhizomes. Low-growing ground cover, forms clumps or mounds. The fine, short, wiry, dark green leaves are up to 2 in (5 cm) long. The narrow, oblong spikelets of green flowers, to 2 in (5 cm) long, appear in late summer. Zones 6–10.

Fruit Trees, Nut Trees, and Other Fruits

Botanically, a fruit is a mature ovary, a home for the seed inside. It is also a delicious form of food. As we or other animals enjoy and are nourished by succulent fruits, we incidentally help disperse their seeds.

Not all botanical fruits function in the same way. Nuts are fruits whose mature ovaries are hard shells that provide protection. Other fruits ripen without any seeds at all. The seeds might be absent because they abort, as with seedless grapes, or because the ovary is able to swell and develop without the stimulus of seed development, as with seedless persimmons. These examples have been bred to be seedless.

For best-quality yields, most fruit plants need a helping hand. Fruiting demands considerable energy, so plants need to be positioned in full sunlight for maximum yields (even those plants that naturally inhabit shaded sites). Annual pruning is essential, which helps expose branches to sun and air, and fruit thinning—pinching off excess fruit—ensures good annual crops, as heavy fruiting one year leads to a reduced yield the next year.

Fruit and nut plants generally enjoy moist but well-drained fertile soils that are slightly acidic. Blueberries, cranberries, and lingonberries are notable exceptions, preferring infertile and very acidic soils.

The persimmon *(Diospyros kaki)* has been long cultivated in Japan for its edible fruit. More than 2,000 cultivars have been developed from this species.

Fruit and Nut Finder

The following cultivation table features at-a-glance information for every species or hybrid with an individual entry in the Fruit Trees, Nut Trees, and Other Fruits chapter of this book. Simply find the plant you wish to know more about, and run your eye along the row to discover its height and spread, whether it is frost tolerant or not, the aspect it prefers, and more.

The type of plant is abbreviated to **T**, **S**, **C**, or **P**:
T – the plant is a tree.   **C** – the plant is a climber.
S – the plant is a shrub.   **P** – the plant is a perennial.

The climate(s) that each plant needs to thrive in the outdoors are given, abbreviated to **C**, **W**, or **T**:
C – the plant prefers a cool climate.
W – the plant prefers a warm-temperate or subtropical climate.
T – the plant prefers a tropical climate.

The season in which the plant produces flowers or fruit is abbreviated to **A**, **W**, **Sp**, **Su**, or **T**:
A – the plant flowers or fruits in autumn.
W – the plant flowers or fruits in winter.
Sp – the plant flowers or fruits in spring.
Su – the plant flowers or fruits in summer.
T – tropical plants with flowers and/or fruit that appear at any time of year in tropical/monsoonal areas.

Edible parts of the plant are abbreviated to **F**, **N**, **D**, or **B**:
F – the fruit is eaten.   **D** – the drupe is eaten.
N – the nut is eaten.   **B** – the berry is eaten.

Plant name	Height	Spread	Type	Climate	Deciduous	Evergreen	Flowering season	Fruiting season	Part eaten	Frost tolerant	Full sun	Half sun	Heavy shade
Actinidia arguta	20–30 ft (6–9 m)	20–30 ft (6–9 m)	C	C	♦		Su	A	F	♦	♦		
Actinidia deliciosa	35 ft (10 m)	35 ft (10 m)	C	C/W	♦		Sp/Su	A/W	F	♦	♦		
Actinidia kolomikta	20–35 ft (6–10 m)	17–20 ft (5–6 m)	C	C	♦		Sp	A	F	♦	♦		
Anacardium occidentale	40 ft (12 m)	25 ft (8 m)	T	T		♦	T	T	N		♦		
Ananas comosus	30 in (75 cm)	30 in (75 cm)	P	W/T		♦	T	T	F				♦
Annona, Atemoya Group	10–15 ft (3–4.5 m)	6–9 ft (1.8–2.7 m)	S/T	W/T		♦	T	T	F		♦		
Annona cherimola	20 ft (6 m)	10 ft (3 m)	T	W/T	♦		T	T	F		♦		
Annona muricata	20 ft (6 m)	10 ft (3 m)	T	W/T		♦	T	T	F		♦		
Annona squamosa	25 ft (8 m)	10 ft (3 m)	T	W/T		♦	T	T	F		♦		
Artocarpus altilis	50 ft (15 m)	20 ft (6 m)	T	T		♦	T	T	F		♦		
Artocarpus heterophyllus	30–50 ft (9–15 m)	20 ft (6 m)	T	T		♦	T	T	F		♦		
Asimina triloba	30 ft (9 m)	20 ft (6 m)	T	C/W	♦		Sp	A	F	♦	♦		
Averrhoa bilimbi	50 ft (15 m)	15 ft (4.5 m)	T	T		♦	T	T	F		♦		
Averrhoa carambola	20 ft (6 m)	10 ft (3 m)	T	T		♦	T	T	F		♦		
Capparis spinosa	3 ft (0.9 m)	10 ft (3 m)	S	W/T		♦	Su/A	W	Buds		♦		
Carica papaya	30 ft (9 m)	12 ft (3.5 m)	T	W/T		♦	Sp/Su	A/W	F		♦		
Carya illinoinensis	100 ft (30 m)	70 ft (21 m)	T	C/W	♦		Sp	A	N	♦	♦		
Carya laciniosa	100 ft (30 m)	35 ft (10 m)	T	C	♦		Sp	A	N	♦	♦		
Carya ovata	80 ft (24 m)	70 ft (21 m)	T	C	♦		Sp	A	N	♦	♦		
Castanea mollissima	40 ft (12 m)	35 ft (10 m)	T	C	♦		Sp	A	N	♦	♦		
Castanea pumila	15 ft (4.5 m)	20 ft (6 m)	T	C	♦		Sp	A	N	♦	♦		

Plant name	Height	Spread	Type	Climate	Deciduous	Evergreen	Flowering season	Fruiting season	Part eaten	Frost tolerant	Full sun	Half sun	Heavy shade
Castanea sativa	60 ft (18 m)	40 ft (12 m)	T	C	◆		Sp	A	N	◆	◆		
Citrullus lanatus	3–6 ft (0.9–1.8 m)	10–20 ft (3–6 m)	C	W/T	◆		Sp/Su	Su/A	F		◆	◆	
Citrus × aurantiifolia	8–15 ft (2.4–4.5 m)	10 ft (3 m)	S	W/T		◆	Sp/Su	A/W	F		◆		
Citrus × aurantium	15 ft (4.5 m)	10 ft (3 m)	S	W/T		◆	Sp/Su	A/W	F		◆		
Citrus hystrix	10 ft (3 m)	6 ft (1.8 m)	S	W/T		◆	Sp/Su	A/W	F		◆		
Citrus japonica	6 ft (1.8m)	3 ft (0.9 m)	S	W/T		◆	Sp/Su	A/W	F		◆		
Citrus × limon	10–15 ft (3–4.5 m)	10 ft (3 m)	S	W/T		◆	Sp/Su	A/W	F		◆		
Citrus × limonia	20 ft (6 m)	12 ft (3.5 m)	T	W/T		◆	Sp/Su	A/W	F		◆		
Citrus maxima	20–40 ft (6–12 m)	10 ft (3 m)	T	W/T		◆	Sp/Su	A/W	F		◆		
Citrus medica	6–15 m (1.8–4.5 m)	8 ft (2.4 m)	S	W/T		◆	Sp/Su	A/W	F		◆		
Citrus reticulata	10–17 ft (3–5 m)	6–10 ft (1.8–3 m)	T	W/T		◆	Sp/Su	A/W	F		◆	◆	
Corylus avellana	15 ft (4.5 m)	15 ft (4.5 m)	S	C	◆		W/Sp	Su/A	N	◆	◆	◆	
Corylus colurna	80 ft (24 m)	25 ft (8 m)	T	C	◆		W/Sp	Su/A	N	◆	◆		
Corylus cornuta	10 ft (3 m)	10 ft (3 m)	S	C	◆		Sp	Su/A	N	◆	◆	◆	
Corylus maxima	30 ft (9 m)	15 ft (4.5 m)	T	C	◆		Sp	Su/A	N	◆	◆	◆	
Cucumis melo	16–28 in (40–70 cm)	7–10 ft (2–3 m)	C	W/T	◆		Sp/Su	Su/A	F		◆		
Cydonia oblonga	10–15 ft (3–4.5 m)	15 ft (4.5 m)	T	C	◆		Sp	A	F		◆		
Cydonia sinensis	20 ft (6 m)	10 ft (3 m)	T	C/W	◆		Sp	A	F		◆		
Diospyros kaki	50 ft (15 m)	25 ft (8 m)	T	C/W	◆		Sp	A/W	F	◆	◆		
Diospyros virginiana	50 ft (15 m)	10 ft (3 m)	T	C	◆		Sp	A/W	F	◆	◆		
Durio zibethinus	80 ft (24 m)	20 ft (6 m)	T	T		◆	T	T	F		◆		
Eriobotrya japonica	20 ft (6 m)	15 ft (4.5)	T	W		◆	A	Sp	F	◆	◆		
Ficus carica	35 ft (10 m)	15–30 ft (4.5–9 m)	T	W/T	◆		Sp	A	F		◆		
Fragaria × ananassa	6 in (15 cm)	40 in (100 cm)	P	C/W		◆	Sp/A	Sp/A	B	◆	◆		
Fragaria chiloensis	6 in (15 cm)	20 in (50 cm)	P	C/W		◆	Sp/Su	Su	B	◆	◆	◆	
Fragaria vesca	2 in (5 cm)	12 in (30 cm)	P	C		◆	Sp	Su	B	◆	◆	◆	
Fragaria Hybrid Cultivars	2–6 in (5–15 cm)	8–60 in (20–150 cm)	P	C/W		◆	Sp/Su	Su	B	◆	◆	◆	
Hylocereus undatus	17–30 ft (5–9 m)	15–25 ft (4.5–8 m)	C	W		◆	Sp/Su	A	F		◆		
Juglans major	50 ft (15 m)	30 ft (9 m)	T	C/W	◆		Sp	A	N		◆		
Juglans nigra	100 ft (30 m)	70 ft (21 m)	T	C/W	◆		Sp	A	N	◆	◆		
Juglans regia	40–60 ft (12–18 m)	35 ft (10 m)	T	C/W	◆		Sp	A	N	◆	◆		
Litchi chinensis	20–40 ft (6–12 m)	15 ft (4.5 m)	T	W		◆	W/Sp	Su/A	D		◆		
Macadamia integrifolia	50 ft (15 m)	20 ft (6 m)	T	W		◆	W/Sp	Su/A	N		◆	◆	

Plant name	Height	Spread	Type	Climate	Deciduous	Evergreen	Flowering season	Fruiting season	Part eaten	Frost tolerant	Full sun	Half sun	Heavy shade
Macadamia tetraphylla	40 ft (12 m)	20 ft (6 m)	T	W		◆	W/Sp	Su/A	N		◆	◆	
Malus pumila	50 ft (15 m)	20 ft (6 m)	T	C	◆		Sp	Su/A	F	◆	◆		
Mangifera indica	80 ft (24 m)	25 ft (8 m)	T	W/T		◆	T	T	D		◆		
Manilkara zapota	100 ft (30 m)	20 ft (6 m)	T	W/T		◆	Sp	A	B			◆	
Mespilus germanica	20 ft (6 m)	25 ft (8 m)	T	C	◆		Sp	A/W	F	◆	◆		
Morus alba	30–50 ft (9–15 m)	30 ft (9 m)	T	C/W	◆		Sp/Su	Su/A	F	◆	◆		
Morus nigra	50 ft (15 m)	40 ft (12 m)	T	C/W	◆		Sp	Su/A	F	◆	◆		
Morus rubra	50 ft (15 m)	40 ft (12 m)	T	C/W	◆		Sp	Su	F	◆	◆		
Musa acuminata	12–20 ft (3.5–6 m)	8 ft (2.4 m)	T (P)	W/T		◆	Su	A/W	F		◆		
Musa × paradisiaca	10–20 ft (3–6 m)	8 ft (2.4 m)	T (P)	W/T		◆	Su	A/W	F		◆		
Olea europaea	20–30 ft (6–9 m)	20 ft (6 m)	T	W		◆	Su	A/W	D	◆	◆		
Opuntia ficus-indica	15 ft (4.5 m)	15 ft (4.5 m)	S	W		◆	Sp/Su	A/W	F		◆		
Passiflora alata	20 ft (6 m)	8–20 ft (2.4–6 m)	C	W/T		◆	Su	A/W	F		◆	◆	
Passiflora edulis	15 ft (4.5 m)	8–15 ft (2.4–4.5 m)	C	W/T		◆	Su	A/W	F		◆	◆	
Passiflora mollissima	15 ft (4.5 m)	8–15 ft (2.4–4.5 m)	C	W		◆	Su	A/W	F		◆	◆	
Passiflora quadrangularis	50 ft (15 m)	10–20 ft (3–6 m)	C	W/T		◆	Su	A/W	F		◆	◆	
Persea americana	60 ft (18 m)	30 ft (9 m)	T	W		◆	Su	A/W	D		◆		
Phoenix dactylifera	70 ft (21 m)	30 ft (9 m)	T	W/T			Su	Su	F		◆		
Physalis peruviana	2–6 ft (0.6–1.8 m)	2–3 ft (0.6–0.9 m)	P	W		◆	Su	Su/A	B	◆	◆		
Pistacia vera	30 ft (9 m)	15 ft (4.5 m)	T	C/W	◆		Su	A	N		◆	◆	
Pouteria sapota	40 ft (12 m)	20 ft (6 m)	T	W		◆	T	T	F		◆		
Prunus americana	25 ft (8 m)	12 ft (3.5 m)	T	C	◆		Sp	Su	D	◆	◆		
Prunus armeniaca	25 ft (8 m)	15 ft (4.5 m)	T	C	◆		Sp	Su/A	D	◆	◆		
Prunus avium	50 ft (15 m)	20 ft (6 m)	T	C	◆		Sp	Su	D	◆	◆		
Prunus cerasus	20 ft (6 m)	15 ft (4.5 m)	T	C	◆		Sp	Su	D	◆	◆		
Prunus × domestica	30 ft (9 m)	15 ft (4.5 m)	T	C	◆		Sp	Su	D	◆	◆		
Prunus dulcis	20–30 ft (6–9 m)	15 ft (4.5 m)	T	C	◆		Sp	Su/A	N	◆	◆		
Prunus mume	20–30 ft (6–9 m)	25 ft (8 m)	T	C	◆		Sp	Su	D	◆	◆		
Prunus persica	8–20 ft (2.4–6 m)	6–20 ft (1.8–6 m)	S/T	C	◆		Sp	Su/A	D	◆	◆		
Prunus salicina	30 ft (9 m)	25 ft (8 m)	T	C	◆		Sp	Su	D	◆	◆		
Psidium guajava	30 ft (9 m)	15 ft (4.5 m)	T	W/T	◆		Sp	Su	B		◆		
Punica granatum	25 ft (8 m)	15 ft (4.5 m)	S/T	C/W	◆		Sp/Su	Su/A	F	◆	◆		
Pyrus communis	50 ft (15 m)	20 ft (6 m)	T	C	◆		Sp	Su/A	F	◆	◆		

Plant name	Height	Spread	Type	Climate	Deciduous	Evergreen	Flowering season	Fruiting season	Part eaten	Frost tolerant	Full sun	Half sun	Heavy shade
Pyrus pyrifolia	50 ft (15 m)	30 ft (9 m)	T	C	◆		Sp	Su/A	F	◆	◆		
Ribes gayanum	5 ft (1.5 m)	3 ft (0.9 m)	S	C/W		◆	Sp	Su	B		◆	◆	
Ribes nigrum	7 ft (2 m)	6 ft (1.8 m)	S	C	◆		Sp	Su	B		◆	◆	
Ribes odoratum	6 ft (1.8 m)	6 ft (1.8 m)	S	C	◆		Sp	Su	B		◆	◆	
Ribes rubrum	5–7 ft (1.5–2 m)	32–60 in (80–150 cm)	S	C	◆		Sp	Su	B		◆	◆	◆
Ribes uva-crispa	36 in (90 cm)	36 in (90 cm)	S	C	◆		Sp	Su	B		◆	◆	
Rubus arcticus	6–12 in (15–30 cm)	18–24 in (45–60 cm)	P	C	◆		Su	Su	B		◆	◆	
Rubus idaeus	5 ft (1.5 m)	4 ft (1.2 m)	S	C	◆		Sp/Su	Su	B		◆	◆	
Rubus loganobaccus	4–6 ft (1.2–1.8 m)	2–3 ft (0.6–0.9 m)	S	C	◆		Sp	Su	B		◆	◆	
Rubus occidentalis	10 ft (3 m)	10 ft (3 m)	S	C	◆		Sp	Su	B		◆	◆	
Rubus phoenicolasius	10 ft (3 m)	10 ft (3 m)	S	C	◆		Sp	Su	B		◆	◆	
Rubus Hybrid Cultivars	2–8 ft (0.6–2.4 m)	6–12 ft (1.8–3.5 m)	S	C	◆		Sp	Su	B		◆	◆	
Solanum betaceum	10 ft (3 m)	7 ft (2 m)	S	W		◆	Sp/Su	Su/A	F		◆		
Solanum melanocerasum	24 in (60 cm)	18 in (45 cm)	S	W/T	◆		Sp/Su	Su/A	F		◆		
Solanum muricatum	36 in (90 cm)	36 in (90 cm)	S	W/T		◆	Sp/Su	Su/A	F		◆		
Solanum sessiliflorum	7 ft (2 m)	4 ft (1.2 m)	S	W/T		◆	Sp	Sp/Su	F		◆		
Sorbus domestica	30–50 ft (9–15 m)	30 ft (9 m)	T	C	◆		Sp	Sp/Su	B		◆	◆	
Syzygium aqueum	35 ft (10 m)	20 ft (6 m)	T	W/T		◆	Sp	Su	B		◆		
Syzygium malaccense	40–80 ft (12–24 m)	15 ft (4.5 m)	T	W/T		◆	Su	Su/A	F		◆		
Terminalia catappa	90 ft (27 m)	35 ft (10 m)	T	T		◆	Su	Su/A	F		◆		
Theobroma cacao	25 ft (8 m)	10 ft (3 m)	T	T		◆	Sp	Su	F				◆
Ugni molinae	6 ft (1.8 m)	3 ft (0.9 m)	S	C/W		◆	Sp	Su/A	F		◆	◆	
Vaccinium ashei	3–15 ft (0.9–4.5 m)	7 ft (2 m)	S	C/W	◆		Sp	Su/A	B		◆		
Vaccinium corymbosum	3–6 ft (0.9–1.8 m)	5 ft (1.5 m)	S	C	◆		Sp	Su/A	B		◆		◆
Vaccinium macrocarpon	3 ft (0.9 m)	5–10 ft (1.5–3 m)	S	C		◆	Sp	Su/A	B		◆		
Vaccinium myrtillus	18 in (45 cm)	36 in (90 cm)	S	C	◆		Sp	Su/A	B		◆		◆
Vaccinium ovatum	3–5 ft (0.9–1.5 m)	4 ft (1.2 m)	S	C/W		◆	Sp	Su/A	B		◆		◆
Vaccinium parvifolium	6 ft (1.8 m)	6 ft (1.8 m)	S	C/W		◆	Sp	Su/A	B		◆		◆
Vaccinium Hybrid Cultivars	2–5 ft (0.6–1.5 m)	3–6 ft (0.9–1.8 m)	S	C	◆		Sp	Su/A	B		◆		
Vitis rotundifolia	100 ft (30 m)	10–20 ft (3–6 m)	C	C	◆		Sp	Su/A	F		◆	◆	
Vitis vinifera	35 ft (10 m)	15–30 ft (4.5–9 m)	C	C	◆		Su	Su/A	F		◆	◆	
Vitis 'Waltham Cross'	35 ft (10 m)	15–30 ft (4.5–9 m)	C	C	◆		Sp	Su/A	F		◆	◆	
Ziziphus jujuba	30 ft (9 m)	12 ft (3.5m)	T	C/W	◆		Sp	Su	F		◆	◆	

Actinidia deliciosa 'Hayward'

ACTINIDIA

This genus of about 60 species of evergreen and deciduous twining climbers from East Asia belongs to the family Actinidiaceae. They are grown for their handsome foliage and often scented creamy white flowers in spring. The fruit of some is edible, but both male and female plants are needed to produce these. They can be used to cover walls, pergolas, and dead or unattractive trees.
CULTIVATION: Plant in full sun to partial shade in any well-drained loamy soil that should not dry out. Prune in winter as necessary. Vines become heavy so provide support. There is little need for fertilizer. Propagate from seed sown in spring or autumn, from half-hardened cuttings, or by layering in late autumn or winter. Vines of both sexes are required for fruiting of most varieties.

Actinidia arguta

BOWER ACTINIDIA, BOWER VINE, COCKTAIL KIWI, DESSERT KIWI, HARDY KIWI, KOKUWA, SIBERIAN GOOSEBERRY, TARA VINE, YANG-TAO
☼ ❊ ↔ 20–30 ft (6–9 m) ↕ 20–30 ft (6–9 m)
Vigorous twining vine of variable habit from Japan, Korea, and northeastern China. Fragrant white flowers tinged green, purple anthers, in mid- to late summer. Leaves to 6 in (15 cm) long, oval, smooth, serrated. Fruit abundant, yellow-green, hairless, slightly acid flavor. '**Ananasnaya**' (syn. 'Anna'), vigorous female cultivar, large clusters of small sweet-smelling flowers; '**Issai**', self-pollinating form. Zones 4–9.

Actinidia deliciosa ★

syn. *Actinidia chinensis* of gardens
CHINESE GOOSEBERRY, KIWI FRUIT, YANTAO
☼ ❊ ↔ 35 ft (10 m) ↕ 35 ft (10 m)
Vigorous climber from China. Large, furry, green leaves to 8 in (20 cm) long. Scented cream flowers in spring, followed by tasty, brown, fuzzy fruit with green flesh and black seeds that ripen in early winter. '**Hayward**', large-fruited commercial form. Zones 7–10.

Actinidia kolomikta

syn. *Trochostigma kolomikta*
❊ ❊ ↔ 17–20 ft (5–6 m) ↕ 20–35 ft (6–10 m)
Climber from East Asia, grown for its handsome leaves, green or tipped with white or pink. Variegation develops as plant grows,

rarely evident in very young plants. Not produced commercially but, if both male and female plants present, fruit edible. '**September Sun**', richer variegated foliage. Zones 4–9.

ANACARDIUM

This tropical American genus of the cashew (Anarcardiaceae) family is made up of 11 species of evergreen or semi-deciduous small to medium trees with simple, smooth-edged, leathery leaves. Small flowers are borne in large panicles. Fruit, on fleshy (and edible) stems, is small, and curved like the enclosed seed, which is covered by a thin flesh containing a dangerously caustic juice.
CULTIVATION: These plants are successfully grown in a tropical monsoonal climate with a long dry season; they are prone to pests and diseases in wetter tropics. Intolerant of frost, they prefer well-drained, sandy, moderately fertile soils, and are tolerant of fierce sun or coastal salt spray. Propagate from seed. The best cultivars can be increased by grafting, cuttings, or air-layering.

Anacardium occidentale

ACAJOU, CASHEW
☼ ✦ ↔ 25 ft (8 m) ↕ 40 ft (12 m)
Origin uncertain, though southern India is largest supplier of nuts. Stalk—"cashew apple"—commonly used in refreshing drink. Zones 11–12.

ANANAS

PINEAPPLE
Currently there are 7 species in this genus of the pineapple (Bromeliaceae) family, but research by the pineapple industry has shown that there is very little difference between them. In nature they are prickly plants with many seeds in the fruit. Indigenous populations in Central America and northern South America selected the better plants over hundreds of years, resulting in the seedless fruit we enjoy today. Even the leaves are without teeth on the edges in some cultivars. Known as *Ananas* in its native region for thousands of years, how it came to be called "pineapple" is not recorded.
CULTIVATION: It is good for the greenhouse or conservatory in cool-temperate areas, or outdoors in warm-temperate, subtropical, and tropical areas. Water before the potting mix is totally dry. If good-quality potting mix is to be used, extra fertilizer is not necessary. Propagate mainly by basal offset.

Ananas comosus

PINEAPPLE
❊ ✦ ↔ 30 in (75 cm) ↕ 30 in (75 cm)
Leaves narrow, triangular, gray-green, to 30 in (75 cm) long, strong teeth on edges (some forms are spineless), forming open rosette. Flower stem short and stout. Flowerhead globular to cylindrical with many small flowers. Petals blue-lavender. Cultivars include '**Abacaxi**', '**Queen**', '**Red Spanish**', and '**Smooth Cayenne**'. Zones 9–10.

ANNONA

Widespread in the tropics of Africa and America, this genus of the custard-apple (Annonaceae) family includes some 100 species of evergreen or semi-deciduous shrubs and trees. Several are important either commercially or locally, particularly the

cherimoya and the custard apple. Most of the common species have aromatic, simple, oblong leaves with pronounced veins. Flowers are unusual, having 6 thick fleshy petals and a central mass of densely packed stamens and pistils. These develop into a fruit with a pulpy center and a sometimes spiny exterior.
CULTIVATION: Species need warm subtropical or tropical conditions, and shelter from strong winds. They are best in a sunny position with moist, well-drained, humus-rich soil. Flowering and fruiting can occur any time, and the plants should not dry out too much or fruit quality will suffer. Propagate from seed or by grafting.

Annona, Atemoya Group
ATEMOYA, CUSTARD APPLE
☀ ☘ ↔ 6–9 ft (1.8–2.7 m) ↑ 10–15 ft (3–4.5 m)
Hybrids between *A. cherimola* and *A. squamosa*. Spreading trees, large drooping leaves, many trumpet-shaped yellow flowers. Fruits with few seeds, flesh free from grainy texture. 'African Pride', dwarf, yields fruit 1–1½ lb (454–680 g) twice annually; 'Pink's Mammoth', large sweet fruit weighing up to 6½ lb (3 kg). Zones 10–12.

Annona muricata

Annona cherimola
CHERIMOYA, CUSTARD APPLE
☀ ☘ ↔ 10 ft (3 m) ↑ 20 ft (6 m)
Evergreen tree native to Peru and Ecuador. Leaves deep green, oval to lance-shaped, velvety beneath. Flowers fragrant, yellowish, purple spotting inside, covered in fine brown hairs. Fruit rounded, delicious fleshy pulp. 'El Bumpo', soft-skinned, sweet; 'Honeyhart', mid-sized, yellow-green; 'McPherson', mid-sized, dark green; 'Pierce', mid-sized, smooth-skinned; 'Spain', pineapple flavor. Zones 10–12.

Annona muricata
GUANABANA, SOURSOP
☀ ☘ ↔ 10 ft (3 m) ↑ 20 ft (6 m)
Evergreen tree from Central America and West Indies. Leaves glossy with age. Flowers yellow-green. Surface of ovoid dark green fruit has soft curved spines with white flesh. Zones 10–12.

Annona squamosa
CUSTARD APPLE, SWEETSOP
☀ ☘ ↔ 10 ft (3 m) ↑ 25 ft (8 m)
Evergreen tree native to tropical America. Scented leaves narrow, lance-shaped. Yellowish flowers with purple-spotted interiors. Fruit spherical, custard-like creamy white pulp inside. Zones 10–12.

ARTOCARPUS
This genus of around 50 species of evergreen and deciduous trees of the mulberry (Moraceae) family occurs wild in tropical Asia and the Malay Archipelago. It includes several commercially important fruits, notably breadfruit and jackfruit. The leaves may be large and simple or lobed, with large stipules at the stalk base. Separate male and female flowers are produced; males are borne in small catkins, females in large heads. Flowers are tiny, but the starchy, white-fleshed, compound fruit that follows is conspicuous and may be very large.

CULTIVATION: *Artocarpus* species require constantly warm moist conditions and prefer well-drained humus-rich soil. They will fruit more reliably and heavily if fed well. Plant in full sun or partial shade with shelter from strong winds. Propagate the species from seed and the cultivars from cuttings or aerial layers.

Artocarpus altilis
syns *Artocarpus communis*, *A. incisus*
BREADFRUIT
☀ ☘ ↔ 20 ft (6 m) ↑ 50 ft (15 m)
From East Asia. Broad crown of deeply lobed leaves to 30 in (75 cm) long. Spherical, 8 in (20 cm) wide, yellow-green fruit, eaten boiled or baked. Zones 11–12.

Artocarpus heterophyllus
JACKFRUIT
☀ ☘ ↔ 20 ft (6 m) ↑ 30–50 ft (9–15 m)
From India to Malay Peninsula. Simple, dark green leaves. Ripe fruit mustard shade. Yellow to pink flesh smells unpleasant but is edible. Zones 10–12.

ASIMINA
This genus of 7 or 8 evergreen or deciduous shrubs or trees from eastern North America is in the custard-apple (Annonaceae) family. White or purple, nodding, bell-shaped flowers appear in clusters.
CULTIVATION: Generally frost hardy, most species tolerate temperatures of 5°F (–15°C) or lower. They will grow in moist well-drained soil in sun or part-shade, though they are affected by long dry periods. They respond well to pruning and shaping and can be used for hedging, though this reduces flowers and fruit.

Artocarpus heterophyllus

Asimina triloba
PAWPAW

☼ ❋ ↔ 20 ft (6 m) ↑ 30 ft (9 m)

From eastern and central North America. Leaves oval, pointed, and narrow, up to 10 in (25 cm) long. Reddish brown pendulous flowers, around 2 in (5 cm) wide, in spring. Edible fruits ripen to yellowish brown in autumn. 'Prolific', early ripening; 'Rebecca's Gold', late ripening; 'Sunflower', large, late ripening; 'Taylor', small fruit, late ripening; and 'Wells', with golden orange flesh. Zones 5–10.

AVERRHOA

East Asian genus of 2 species of evergreen trees, of the wood-sorrel (Oxalidaceae) family. Foliage is pinnate, composed of quite large leaflets. The flowers, white to red or purple with white markings, are carried in short inflorescences, followed by 5-angled edible fruit, to 5 in (12 cm) long. CULTIVATION: Easily cultivated, other than requiring tropical or subtropical conditions. Thrive in warm sheltered positions with moist well-drained soil and high humidity. Propagate from seed, or grow fruiting cultivars from grafts or aerial layers.

Averrhoa bilimbi

Averrhoa bilimbi
BILIMBI, PICKLE FRUIT

☼ ✦ ↔ 15 ft (4.5 m) ↑ 50 ft (15 m)

Leaves composed of up to 40 leaflets, 5 in (12 cm) long. Inflorescences sprout directly from the branches. Flowers are purple to orange-red. The yellow-green fruit, shallowly angled, lacks the sweetness of *A. carambola*. Zones 11–12.

Averrhoa carambola ★
CARAMBOLA, FIVE-CORNER, STAR FRUIT

☼ ✦ ↔ 10 ft (3 m) ↑ 20 ft (6 m)

Leaflets blue-green on undersides, to 4 in (10 cm) long. They are sensitive to touch and light, folding at night or if handled. Dull red flowers appear for much of the year. The edible fruit is yellow-green to orange. Zones 11–12.

Carica papaya

CAPPARIS

This genus of around 250 species of shrubs, scrambling climbers, and small trees is from the caper (Capparidaceae) family. It contains both evergreen and deciduous plants, which grow in warm climates around the world. *C. spinosa* is the source of the edible capers used as a condiment and the only species occurring naturally in Europe. The simple leaves have paired and often hooked spines at the base. Flowers have early-shedding petals and long showy stamens, and fruit is berry-like. The species grow in a range of habitats, from dry open woodland, vine thickets, and rainforest, to rocky seashores. In some regions the foliage is eaten by the larvae of the caper white butterfly.
CULTIVATION: Needs vary, but most are sun-loving and prefer a reasonably fertile soil. Few tolerate more than very light frosts. *C. spinosa* requires hot dry summers and well-drained open soil. Propagate from freshly extracted seed or from half-hardened cuttings in summer.

Capparis spinosa
CAPER BUSH

☼ ⚘ ↔ 10 ft (3 m) ↑ 3 ft (0.9 m)

From southern Europe, Africa, Asia, and northern Australia. Scrambling shrub, semi-prostrate branches. Leaves very broad, rounded, arranged in 2 rows. Flowers white, pale purple stamens, on slender stalks, in summer–autumn. Unopened buds pickled in brine as capers. Fruits elongated, strongly ribbed. Zones 9–12.

CARICA (see page 107)

Carica papaya
PAPAYA, PAWPAW

☼ ✦ ↔ 12 ft (3.5 m) ↑ 30 ft (9 m)

Native to lowlands of tropical South America. Single trunk, ringed with leaf scars. Leaves to 24 in (60 cm) wide, stalk to 36 in (90 cm) long. Fruits mature to yellow or orange, contain yellow or pinkish flesh, black seeds. Zones 11–12.

CARYA
syn. *Hicoria*

This genus, belonging to the walnut (Juglandaceae) family, consists of about 25 species, most of which come from eastern North America, with some from Vietnam and China. These large deciduous trees have both functional male and female organs on the one plant. The gray-brown bark becomes scaly with age. The pinnate leaves are alternate with serrated-edged leaflets. Male inflorescence is a pendent branched catkin; female inflorescence is a terminal spike with up to 20 individual flowers. The fruit is a drupe. Commercially valuable for pecan nuts, and hard wood. Transplanting is difficult as they resent disturbance.
CULTIVATION: Seedlings develop a long tap root very early, so plant when young into deep, fertile, humus-rich but well-drained soil. Sow seed into a seed bed as soon as it is ripe. If growing in a pot, use one that is extra deep. Use good loam with added leafmold; cultivars require winter grafting.

Carya illinoinensis

Carya ovata

Castanea mollissima

Carya illinoinensis

syns *Carya olivaeformis, Juglans illinoinensis*

PECAN

☼ ❋ ↔ 70 ft (21 m) ↑ 100 ft (30 m)

Native to the southern and central USA and northern Mexico. Grows best in deep alluvial soil. Scaly gray bark, mid-green leaves, with up to 17 lance-shaped leaflets. Pecan nuts are an important crop exported worldwide. Some 500 cultivars are available: 'Pawnee' and 'Lucas' are early ripeners. Zones 6–11.

Carya laciniosa

BIG SHELLBARK HICKORY

☼ ❋ ↔ 35 ft (10 m) ↑ 100 ft (30 m)

From eastern USA. Bark peels in 3 ft (0.9 m) long curving plates. Leaves reach 18 in (45 cm) long with 5 to 7 leaflets. Fruit oval, 2 in (5 cm) long. Good timber tree. Zones 4–9.

Carya ovata

syns *Hicoria ovata, Juglans ovata*

LITTLE SHELLBARK HICKORY, SHAGBARK HICKORY

☼ ❋ ↔ 70 ft (21 m) ↑ 80 ft (24 m)

From eastern USA. Gray-brown peeling bark. The leaves are mid-green, with 5 leaflets, turning golden yellow in autumn. Fruit edible, splitting when ripe. Cultivars often hybrids with *C. cathayensis* or *C. laciniosa*. Zones 4–9.

CASTANEA

Belonging to the beech (Fagaceae) family, this is a small genus of about 12 species of sweet chestnuts native to temperate regions of the Northern Hemisphere, from North America across Europe and into eastern Asia. In habit they range from low suckering shrubs to tall trees. Several species are of economic importance, being grown for their sweet-tasting edible nuts, enclosed in a spiny whorl of bracts. The taller species are also valued for their use as ornamental trees, especially for their spectacular yellowish green drooping male catkins.

CULTIVATION: Sweet chestnuts prefer a well-drained and slightly acid soil; adequate rainfall is essential. Most are frost hardy down to Zones 4 or 5. Propagation is usually from seed which should be sown as soon as it is ripe; selected clones can be reproduced by grafts onto 1- or 2-year-old understocks, in early spring.

Castanea mollissima

CHINESE CHESTNUT

☼ ❋ ↔ 35 ft (10 m) ↑ 40 ft (12 m)

Native to central and eastern China and Korea. Ovate or oblong, coarsely serrated, short-stalked leaves, coarse white hair beneath. Edible nuts. Resistant to chestnut blight. Highly valued as an ornamental. 'Pendula', a popular cultivar. Zones 5–9.

Castanea pumila

ALLEGHENY CHINKAPIN, CHINQUAPIN

☼ ❋ ↔ 20 ft (6 m) ↑ 15 ft (4.5 m)

Large suckering shrub from eastern and southern areas of USA. Downy young shoots, young leaves white and furry on the undersides. 'Ashei' has less densely spiny bracts. Zones 6–9.

Castanea sativa

syn. *Castanea vesca*

CHESTNUT, SPANISH CHESTNUT, SWEET CHESTNUT

☼ ❋ ↔ 40 ft (12 m) ↑ 60 ft (18 m)

Native of the high forest areas of southern Europe and western Asia. Fast-growing deciduous tree. Glossy, dark green, coarsely serrated leaves, lighter and slightly furry beneath. Yellow-green catkins, in mid-summer. Edible nuts are a delicacy, "marrons glacés." Cultivars include 'Albomarginata' and 'Glabra'. Zones 5–9.

CITRULLUS

An African and Asian pumpkin (Cucurbitaceae) family genus of just 3 species of annual and perennial trailers and climbers, best known as the home of the watermelon (*C. lanatus*). Stems are covered with short coarse hairs and bear simple or branched tendrils in the leaf axils. Leaves are oval to palmate but often so deeply lobed that they appear pinnate. Foliage color ranges from blue-gray to deep green, sometimes with small translucent patches. Large, 5-lobed, bell-shaped, yellow flowers appear in the leaf axils and develop into rounded to elongated fruit, usually pale green with dark striping and mottling, and ranging from golf ball to larger than soccer ball size, weighing up 60 lb (27.25 kg).

CULTIVATION: Melons need a long warm growing season and good drainage to ripen. Water well and allow to dry off as the fruit nears ripeness. Usually propagated from seed, though *C. colocynthis* will grow from cuttings or layers.

Citrullus lanatus, in the wild, South Africa

Citrullus lanatus

syn. *Citrullus vulgaris*

WATERMELON

☼/❋ ❀ ↔ 10–20 ft (3–6 m) ↑36 in–6 ft (90 cm–1.8 m)

Annual climber or trailer from Namibia, naturalized elsewhere. Of indeterminate size, spreading or climbing throughout growing season. Oval, lobed, pinnate, green leaves with toothed edges and small translucent patches. Branched tendrils and pink- to red-fleshed, mottled, green fruit to over 20 in (50 cm) long. '**Candy Red**', oblong fruit weighing up to 40 lb (18 kg), ripens 85 days after petal fall; '**Dixie Queen**', bright red flesh, even round fruit to 50 lb (22.5 kg), 80-day ripening period; '**Fordhook Hybrid**', deep pink flesh, small fruit to 10 lb (4.5 kg), 74-day ripening period; '**Klondike RS57**', medium-sized fruit, pinkish red flesh, 85-day ripening period; '**New Queen**', round fruit; '**Sweet Favorite**', oblong, red-fleshed fruit to 20 lb (9 kg), 82-day ripening period; '**Triplesweet Seedless**' ★, round fruit, deep pink seedless flesh, to 20 lb (9 kg), 85-day ripening period. Zones 10–12.

CITRUS

syns *Eremocitrus, Fortunella, Microcitrus, Poncirus*

Ranging in the wild from China to India, Southeast Asia, New Guinea, and Australia, this genus comprises about 20 species of mostly evergreen shrubs and small trees and belongs to the family Rutaceae. Grown in warmer countries for their edible fruits—the oranges, lemons, limes, grapefruit, and mandarins, among others. Most cultivated citrus are ancient hybrids, derived from 3 wild species. Ornamental plants with dark glossy foliage; fragrant, starry, white flowers appear singly or in clusters at different times of the year. Twigs are often thorny; the spirally arranged leaves are jointed at the junction with the stalks, a relic of ancestral compound leaves (still compound in *C. trifoliata*). Their unique fruit structure identifies the genus: the tough skin, dotted with aromatic oil glands, encloses a white pith of varying thickness, inside which are the segments (carpels) with seeds embedded among juice-filled vesicles, or giant cells.

CULTIVATION: In frost-free conditions most species flourish in fertile well-drained soil in a sunny position protected from wind. During the growing season they need plenty of water and regular small applications of nitrogenous fertilizer to promote growth

and fruit size. They need very little pruning. Propagation is by budding, or by grafting the desired cultivar onto a suitable rootstock.

Citrus × *aurantiifolia*

syn. *Limonia aurantiifolia*

LIME

☼ ✿ ↔ 10 ft (3 m) ↑8–15 ft (2.4–4.5 m)

This popular plant is widely cultivated in Mexico, the West Indies, and Florida, USA. It has spreading prickly branches. Small, thin-skinned, oval to round, seeded fruit, greenish yellow, acid, juicy, green pulp. Limes thrive in tropical and subtropical regions. Zones 11–12.

Citrus × *aurantium*

syns *Citrus* × *paradisi, C. sinensis, C.* × *tangelo, C.* × *tangor*

☼ ❀ ↔ 10 ft (3 m) ↑15 ft (4.5 m)

This name has expanded to include oranges, grapefruits, tangelos, and tangors, all of which are believed to be hybrids between the mandarin *(C. reticulata)* and the shaddock *(C. maxima)*. These major citrus types are now treated as cultivar groups.

Grapefruit Group (syn. *C.* × *paradisi*): Rounded bushy tree to 30 ft (9 m). Large oval leaves, some spines. Large, thin-skinned, yellow fruits ripen late autumn–early spring. Some varieties withstand light frosts. Frost tolerant varieties '**Duncan**' and '**Marsh**' ★ have pale straw-colored flesh. '**Red Blush**' and '**Ruby**' have pink flesh and require a hot frost-free climate to develop good color.

Sour Orange Group: The Seville orange is the only widely grown member of this group. Tough spiny tree to 30 ft (9 m), highly perfumed flowers, aromatic thick peel, bitter-tasting fruit, ripens in autumn, used for marmalade. Withstands light frosts.

Sweet Orange Group (syn. *C. sinensis*): This group comprises the common eating oranges. Attractive, medium-sized, rounded tree to 25 ft (8 m) high. Glossy dark green leaves, beautiful, fragrant, white blossoms. Fruit is deep orange in color, and has sweet juicy flesh. These plants do best in a Mediterranean cli-

Citrus × *aurantium* 'Valencia'

mate. Some varieties tolerate light frosts. '**Ruby**', a popular "blood orange," has reddish skin, flesh, and juice; '**Valencia**' produces abundant fruit, relatively seedless. The navel subgroup of sweet oranges is normally seedless; well known '**Washington Navel**' is possibly one of the best eating oranges.

Tangelo Group (syn. *C.* × *tangelo*): Grows up to 30 ft (9 m), bears reddish orange fruit, pleasant acid-sweet flavor, good for juicing. Frost sensitive, needs a long hot growing season. Most ripen in spring. Best varieties are '**Minneola**', '**Orlando**', and '**Samson**'.

Tangor Group (syn. *C.* × *tangor*): to 12 ft (3.5 m) high. Fruit is intermediate in flavor and size between orange and mandarin, but more rounded than the latter. The cultivar '**Honey Murcott**', the original cross, has 3 in (8 cm) wide, thin-skinned, yellow-orange fruit, juicy, sweet, orange flesh.

'**Temple**', a deep orange-red easy-to-peel variety with a sweet rich flavor, ripens in spring. Zones 9–11.

Citrus hystrix
CAFFRE LIME, LEECH LIME, MAURITIUS PAPEDA
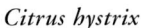 ↔ 6 ft (1.8 m) ↑ 10 ft (3 m)
Aromatic leaves flavor Thai and Malay dishes. Unusual leaves, leaf stalk swells to almost same width as blade. Small, rough, wrinkled fruit, little juice, rind used as flavoring. Zones 10–12.

Citrus japonica
syns *Fortunella japonica, F. margarita*
CUMQUAT
↔ 3 ft (0.9 m) ↑ 6 ft (1.8 m)
From southern China. Dense branches, oval leaves, small, round to oval, golden fruit. **Marumi Group**, round or flattened fruit; '**Sunstripe**', variegated foliage and fruit. **Nagami Group** (syn. *Fortunella margarita*), elongated thin-skinned fruit. Zones 9–10.

Citrus × limon
LEMON
↔ 10 ft (3 m) ↑ 10–15 ft (3–4.5 m)
An ancient hybrid; one parent is *C. medica,* the other uncertain. Smooth-skinned, acidic, yellow fruit, several flushes throughout the year. Best in a Mediterranean climate. '**Garey's Eureka**', thornless, fruits year round, mostly in summer; '**Lisbon**', vigorous, winter-bearing variety, suited to hot areas. Zones 9–11.

Citrus × limonia
RANGPUR LIME
↔ 12 ft (3.5 m) ↑ 20 ft (6 m)
Lemon/mandarin hybrid, originating in China. Thorny, many branches. Fragrant white flowers, pinkish tinge. Rounded fruit, deep yellow-orange, ripen in winter. Zones 10–12.

Citrus maxima
POMELO, SHADDOCK
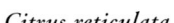 ↔ 10 ft (3 m) ↑ 20–40 ft (6–12 m)
Presumed native to Southeast Asia. it produces dense, large, glossy, oval to oblong leaves. Pale yellow fruit with yellowish to pink flesh. Zones 10–12.

Citrus medica
CITRON
↔ 8 ft (2.4 m) ↑ 6–15 ft (1.8–4.5 m)
From northern India. Shrub or small tree. Short stiff spines, large, oval, serrated leaves, purplish new growth. Large flowers, purplish outside, white within. Large wrinkled fruit, little juice, thick fragrant rind. The cultivar '**Etrog**' has a long-pointed apex. Zones 9–11.

Citrus reticulata
MANDARIN, SATSUMA, TANGERINE
↔ 6–10 ft (1.8–3 m) ↑ 10–17 ft (3–5 m)
From warm-temperate to subtropical East Asia. Small thorny tree. Lance-shaped leaves 2–4 in (5–10 cm) long, leaf stalks with small wings. Small, fragrant, white flowers, followed by oval to flattened, sweet-fleshed, golden fruit. '**Clementine**', large, rather acidic, spherical, orange-red fruit with few seeds; '**Dancy**', flattened orange-red fruit, good flavor, few to many seeds; '**Encore**', upright tree, few thorns, rounded orange-yellow fruit with darker spots, good flavor but many seeds; '**Fairchild**', round deep orange fruit, many seeds, bush near thornless, needs cross-pollination; '**Fremont**', early fruiting, good flavor, few seeds; '**Kinnow**', very hardy, thin leaves, flattened, orange-yellow, seedy fruit; '**Page**', round orange fruit, often very seedy, sometimes sold as an orange; '**Pixie**', small, very sweet, seedless. Some varieties that are marketed as mandarins or tangerines are in fact tangors, which are mandarin/orange hybrids (see *C.* × *aurantium*). Zones 9–11.

CORYLUS
Known as filberts, hazelnuts, cobnuts, and cobs, there are about 15 species of deciduous suckering shrubs and trees in this genus in the birch (Betulaceae) family, some garden grown. The flowers, both the long flouncing male catkins ("lambs' tails") and the inconspicuous female flowers, appear on last year's bare wood, the same plant carrying both sexes. Catkins are usually visible by late winter and fluff out in spring, when the female flowers appear. The husked edible nuts ripen in autumn.
CULTIVATION: They are easily grown in rich moist soils in full sun or part-shade. Propagate from detached suckers, mounding up soil beforehand to promote root growth. Early summer softwood cuttings are also used, treated with hormone powder. Seeds require cold stratification for about 3 months for germination. Nut production may require a different cultivar for pollination.

Citrus maxima

Citrus × *aurantium* 'Washington Navel'

Corylus avellana

COBNUT, EUROPEAN HAZELNUT

☼/◑ ❄ ↔ 15 ft (4.5 m) ↑ 15 ft (4.5 m)

Native of Europe, western Asia, North Africa. Thicket-like shrub. Coarse mid-green leaves turn yellow in autumn. Long pale yellow catkins in winter on bare branches; red female flowers in early spring. Nuts half covered in ragged husks. '**Aurea**', greenish yellow leaves; '**Contorta**', dense slow-growing shrub of twisted branches. Zones 4–8.

Corylus colurna

syn. *Corylus byzantina*

TURKISH HAZEL

☼ ❄ ↔ 25 ft (8 m) ↑ 80 ft (24 m)

Native of western Asia. Leaves veined, bluntly pointed, lightly lobed, turn yellow in autumn. Yellow catkins in late winter. Distinctive deeply fringed husks, cork-like corrugations on bark. Thrives in continental climates—hot summers, cold winters. Zones 4–8.

Corylus cornuta

syn. *Corylus rostrata*

BEAKED FILBERT

☼/◑ ❄ ↔ 10 ft (3 m) ↑ 10 ft (3 m)

Deciduous shrub from North America. Erect stems. Oval, lobed, serrated leaves. Catkins reach 1¼ in (30 mm) in length. Nuts with long tubular husks. *C. c.* **var.** *californica* grows to about 25 ft (8 m) high, bears shorter husks, longer catkins. Zones 4–8.

Corylus maxima

FILBERT

☼/◑ ❄ ↔ 15 ft (4.5 m) ↑ 30 ft (9 m)

Native of southern and eastern Europe and western Asia. Vigorous bushy shrub or small tree. Leaves large, heart-shaped, mid-green, new growth covered in sticky hairs. Large brown nuts, elongated lobed husks. '**Purpurea**', young leaves coppery purple tint, fade to leathery greenish purple. Zones 5–9.

CUCUMIS (see page 738)

Cucumis melo

CANTALOUPE, HONEYDEW, MELON, MUSKMELON

☼ ⸙ ↔ 7–10 ft (2–3 m) ↑ 16–28 in (40–70 cm)

Annual vines found in arid regions of Africa, Arabia, southwest Asia, and Australia. Wild types may be bitter, but cultivars produce a range of generally round sweet fruit with either smooth or rough skins. **Cantalupensis Group:** Sweet fragrant melons; the skin can be smooth, scaly, grooved or rough, but not netted. Usually round. **Inodorus Group:** Round or oval sweet melons with green, white, orange, pinkish, or yellowish green flesh. **Reticulatus Group:** Netted melons or cantaloupes, assorted shapes and sizes. Skins can be ribbed, warty, smooth, or netted. Seed cavity large in old varieties, smaller in newer varieties. Some varieties (muskmelons)

Corylus avellana 'Contorta'

have musky aroma. '**Ambrosia**', firm, luscious, extra sweet, juicy, peach-colored flesh. Zones 9–12.

CYDONIA

syn. *Pseudocydonia*

Genus of 2 species of long-lived, small, deciduous tree in the rose (Rosaceae) family, one from the Caucasus region and one from China. Allied to apples *(Malus)* and pears *(Pyrus)*, they bear large pome fruits with a waxy aromatic skin and hard flesh. Simple oval leaves; densely downy on new growth. White to pink flowers, almost stalkless and borne singly among leaves at ends of spring growths. Fruits ripen slowly to yellow through summer and persist well into autumn; woody seeds embedded in the flesh, which contains stone cells.

CULTIVATION: They prefer a temperate climate with well marked seasons and tolerate a range of soils. Plant in full sun; protect from wind. Can be propagated from seed or cuttings, but cultivated forms are normally grafted onto quince rootstocks. Quinces are self-fertile, so even a single tree is capable of producing fruit.

Cydonia oblonga

QUINCE

☼ ❄ ↔ 15 ft (4.5 m) ↑ 10–15 ft (3–4.5 m)

Originally from northern Iran, Turkey, and Armenia, later spread around Mediterranean, then northward through Europe. Rather crooked tree, umbrella-like rounded crown. Leaves very pale green, hairy beneath. Large, upright, white or pink flowers. Fruits round or pear-shaped, to 4 in (10 cm) long. '**Champion**', '**Lusitanica**' (syn. '**Portugal**'), and the Turkish '**Smyrna**' are 3 of the best cultivars. Zones 4–9.

Cydonia sinensis

syns *Chaenomeles sinensis*, *Pseudocydonia sinensis*

CHINESE QUINCE

☼ ❄ ↔ 10 ft (3 m) ↑ 20 ft (6 m)

From eastern China. Dappled bark, leaves and flowers slightly smaller than those of *C. oblonga*. Leaves brownish woolly beneath; vivid autumn coloring. Reddish pink flowers in spring. Fruit ovoid, to 7 in (18 cm) long, aromatic. Zones 5–10.

DIOSPYROS

EBONY, PERSIMMON

This genus in the ebony (Ebenaceae) family of some 475 species of evergreen and deciduous, tender and hardy, tropical and temperate shrubs and trees is a diverse group of plants. Some have economic importance, either for their timber or their fruit, while others are attractive ornamentals. Their foliage is usually quite simple and the leaves of the deciduous species can be very colorful in autumn. The flowers are unisexual, and to ensure better fruit production it helps to have several trees for cross-pollination. The fruits range from small fleshy berries to the pear-like persimmons.

Cydonia oblonga

CULTIVATION: With such a diverse genus it is difficult to generalize about cultivation needs. Only a few species will tolerate prolonged drought and most prefer moist well-drained soil that is reasonably fertile. Propagation is from seed or by root cuttings or grafting.

Diospyros kaki
JAPANESE DATE PLUM, PERSIMMON

☼ ❉ ↔ 25 ft (8 m) ↑ 50 ft (15 m)

Long cultivated in Japan, this species is not known in the wild. Deciduous tree, edible fruit. Choose named cultivars for fruit production where warmth is needed. 'Fuyu' ★, a low tannin variety, needs ample warmth; 'Hachiya', produces a large, tender-skinned, conical-shaped, pinkish orange fruit, not sweet, unpalatable until fully ripe and soft; 'Izu', a compact low tannin variety. Zones 8–10.

Diospyros virginiana
AMERICAN PERSIMMON, PERSIMMON

☼ ❉ ↔ 10 ft (3 m) ↑ 50 ft (15 m)

Native to eastern USA, deciduous tree, simple oval leaves color well in autumn. Small, edible, yellow fruit. Timber used for making golf woods. 'John Rick' ★, old-established fruiting cultivar grown for superior eating qualities. Zones 5–9.

DURIO
Night-flying bats pollinate flowers of the 28 species of tall evergreen trees in this genus, placed in the mallow (Malvaceae) family, and found from Myanmar to Malaysia and Indonesia in lowland rainforest. All have simple lance-shaped leaves, shiny on upper surface, lower surface grayish and covered with small scales. Creamy white flowers in clusters on stems and trunks. CULTIVATION: Like most tropical tree species, propagation is best from fresh seed, since viability is lost quickly. Grow in full sun or dappled shade, in moist humus-rich soil with good drainage. Apart from the durian, members of this genus are seldom grown.

Diospyros kaki, with ripe fruit

Durio zibethinus
DURIAN

☼ ⚘ ↔ 20 ft (6 m) ↑ 80 ft (24 m)

From Malaysia and Indonesia. Leaves lance-shaped, shining green, grayish beneath. Flowers on older wood, creamy white or pink. Fruits large, green to brown, covered in sharp spines. Zone 12.

ERIOBOTRYA
This genus from the rose (Rosaceae) family consists of about 10 species of evergreen trees and shrubs found from the eastern Himalayas to Southeast Asia and China. They are all tough plants with dull green, leathery, strongly veined leaves, felted underneath. The felted buds held at the branch tips develop into scented creamy flower clusters in the autumn. The showy, fragrant, fleshy, edible fruits are sweet, soft, and juicy at full ripeness. The best known species is the loquat, *E. japonica,* which is both edible and decorative, but attracts birds and fruit fly. CULTIVATION: They prefer subtropical conditions; although generally drought-tolerant, they need abundant moisture in winter to produce good fruit. All except strongly alkaline soils are suitable. Seedlings are easily propagated but variable, often producing fruit with large seeds and minimal flesh, but grafted selected varieties are available. Self-sown seedlings are common.

Eriobotrya japonica
LOQUAT

☼ ❉ ↔ 15 ft (4.5 m) ↑ 20 ft (6 m)

Long cultivated in Japan but native to central China. The common name derives from the Cantonese name, *lo kwat.* An evergreen tree valued for its luscious fragrant fruit in early spring. The leaves are large, dull green, and lance-shaped, with prominent veins and woolly undersides, occurring mostly at the branch tips. The flowers, which are usually self-fertile, develop from woolly buds in autumn. Zones 8–11.

Eriobotrya japonica

FICUS *(see page 159)*

Ficus carica
EDIBLE FIG

☼ ❄ ↔ 15–30 ft (4.5–9 m) ↑ 35 ft (10 m)

Cultivated over 5,000 years ago in western Asia, origins obscure. Deciduous tree, spreading rounded canopy. Smooth silvery-gray bark. Leaves 3- to 5-lobed, toothed edges. Tiny flowers. Purple-brown fruit. Used for dried figs. Prefers climates with long warm summers, dry atmosphere, on soils of low to medium fertility. '**Black Genoa**' ★, large tree, dull purple fruits, sweet dark red flesh; '**Brown Turkey**', pink-fleshed, brown-skinned figs, flavor sweet but slightly insipid; '**White Adriatic**', tall grower, pale greenish brown figs, tasty deep pink flesh. **Zones 10–12.**

FRAGARIA
STRAWBERRY

This genus of 12 perennials, a member of the rose (Rosaceae) family, is found in northern temperate zones and in Chile. Many botanists now believe that the distinction between *Fragaria* and the large, diverse genus *Potentilla* is artificial, and that strawberries should be included in *Potentilla*. It is likely that this reclassification will be generally accepted in the future. Among the most widely grown of the small fruits, strawberries are tough adaptable plants that spread by runners. Leaves grow in groups of 3, and are heart-shaped to rounded, with toothed edges. Clusters of pretty, white, 5-petalled flowers precede the fruits, which may be red, white, yellow, pink, or orange. The fruits are unusual in that they carry their seeds on the outside. **CULTIVATION:** Hardy in temperate zones in all but the coldest winters, strawberries need moist, fertile, well-drained soil, water to swell the fruit, and sun to ripen it. Planting atop mounds ensures good drainage. Cover with netting to keep the birds away from the fruit. Propagation is usually by layering, using either natural layers or runners, pegged down until the roots establish.

Fragaria × *ananassa*
GARDEN STRAWBERRY

☼ ❄ ↔ 40 in (100 cm) ↑ 6 in (15 cm)

From Holland. Low-growing ground cover; parent of many of the most successful strawberries around the world. Palmate, toothed, green leaves. White flowers with yellow centers in late spring–autumn. Medium-sized dark red fruits, in summer–autumn. '**Cambridge Rival**', large, firm, sweet fruit; '**Earlisweet**', popular early fruiting variety, rich flavor, medium-sized fruit; '**Eros**', mid-season, large, firm, glossy, red fruit, resistant to red stele; '**Symphony**', shiny, medium-sized fruit; '**Tioga**', large sweet fruit, heavy cropper, disease resistant; '**Redgauntlet**', vigorous growth habit, medium-sized fruit, mid-season; '**Tribute**', with medium to large, flavorful, firm fruit. **Zones 3–10.**

Fragaria chiloensis
BEACH STRAWBERRY

☼/◐ ❄ ↔ 20 in (50 cm) ↑ 6 in (15 cm)

From North and South America. Short thick leaves, hairy undersides. White flowers, rose-colored edible fruit with white flesh. Grows naturally in coastal areas. **Zones 4–10.**

Fragaria vesca
WILD STRAWBERRY

☼/◐ ❄ ↔ 12 in (30 cm) ↑ 2 in (5 cm)

From European woodland regions. Compact rosettes of dark green leaves on ground-hugging plant. Flowers white; dark red, sweet, edible fruits in summer. '**Alexandra**', smaller red berries, very sweet, plant habit slightly smaller than species; '**Fructo Albo**' (white wild strawberry), creamy white edible fruits. **Zones 5–9.**

Fragaria Hybrid Cultivars

☼/◐ ❄ ↔ 8–60 in (20–150 cm) ↑ 2–6 in (5–15 cm)

These are popular mainly for their ground-covering abilities, although some do produce edible fruits. The most popular hybrid cultivars include: '**Darselect**', large, firm, bright red berries; '**Lipstick**', ornamental variety, dark green leaves, deep pink flowers, small fruit; Pink Panda/'**Frel**', dark green, heavily veined, palmate foliage, sterile pink flowers, no fruit; '**Rosie**', ground-covering habit, sterile variety, rosy red flowers. **Zones 5–9.**

HYLOCEREUS
A genus of 18 species of climbing night-flowering cacti, in the Cactaceae family, from southern Mexico, the Caribbean, Central America, and northern South America. These clambering, climbing, or epiphytic plants produce aerial roots and may reach 35 ft

Fragaria × *ananassa* 'Symphony'

Fragaria chiloensis

Fragaria, Hybrid Cultivar, 'Rosie'

(10 m) wide and 7–10 ft (2–3 m) long. Usually stems have only 3 ribs, are segmented, green to bluish green, with a horny margin. Spines are absent or few, and always small. Flowers are large, nocturnal, white, rarely red. Floral tubes are strong with large naked scales. Seedpods are spherical to oval, usually red.
CULTIVATION: Easily grown in a compost-rich well-drained soil. May be raised from seed but are usually propagated from cuttings dried out for a week or two. Rest in winter.

Hylocereus undatus ★
DRAGON FRUIT, QUEEN OF THE NIGHT
☼ ⚘ ↔ 15–25 ft (4.5–8 m) ↑ 17–30 ft (5–9 m)
Of uncertain origin, long cultivated as an ornamental for its spectacular flowers and delicious fruits. Sprawling, climbing, producing many stout, 3-angled, jointed stems, with a wavy horny margin. Has 1 to 3 spines, short, conical, brown to gray, 3 mm long. Flowers from sides of stems, white, 10–12 in (25–30 cm) long. Fruit spherical to oval, bright red, with large often green scales, edible. Zones 10–11.

JUGLANS
The walnuts, a genus of the Juglandaceae family, comprise about 20 species of deciduous trees. They are distributed over the temperate zones of the Americas, southeastern Europe, and Southeast Asia. They have alternate compound leaves and monoecious flowers, borne in spring. The fruit is a hard-shelled nut enclosed in a fleshy green drupe, the kernels being prized as food. Some species produce hard, beautifully grained wood, valued for furniture making; some produce juglose, which can poison apple trees.
CULTIVATION: Walnuts thrive on deep, alluvial, well-drained soil with a high organic content, and an assured water supply, in a cool humid climate. Plantation trees are often severely pruned after one year to force strong single trunk growth, then stopped at 12 ft (3.5 m) or so to induce lateral branches; ornamental trees can be treated the same way. Seeds can be collected as soon as ripe in early autumn and stored in cool conditions until sown in early spring.

Juglans major
syn. *Juglans elaeopyren*
ARIZONA WALNUT, NOGAL
☼ ⚘ ↔ 30 ft (9 m) ↑ 50 ft (15 m)
New Mexico to Arizona, USA. Single upright trunk, slender crown. Leaves oblong to lance-shaped, 9 to 13 leaflets. Nuts with dark brown shells. Autumn foliage pale yellow. Zones 9–11.

Juglans nigra
AMERICAN WALNUT, BLACK WALNUT
☼ ❋ ↔ 70 ft (21 m) ↑ 100 ft (30 m)
Native of eastern and central USA and southeastern Canada. Dome-shaped crown, large leaves, 11 to 23 leaflets. Edible nuts dark brown. Grows quickly in warm areas on rich soils, usually slow elsewhere. 'Laciniata' has finely cut leaves. Zones 4–10.

Juglans major

Juglans regia
ENGLISH WALNUT, PERSIAN WALNUT, WALNUT
☼ ❋ ↔ 35 ft (10 m) ↑ 40–60 ft (12–18 m)
Native to southeastern Europe, the Himalayas, and China. Edible nuts. Bark pale gray. Smooth aromatic leaves, 7 leaflets; young leaves coppery purple turning green as they mature. Cultivars of the **Carpathian Group** are cold hardy, and popular in the USA, especially selected commercial clones **'Broadview'** and **'Buccaneer'**. **'Laciniata'** has deeply cut leaflets. Zones 4–10.

LITCHI
Genus in the soapberry (Sapindaceae) family of just one species, from southern China and Southeast Asia. Evergreen tree. Leaves are pinnate, with up to 8 oblong leaflets. Insignificant greenish white flowers are borne in large panicles in the upper leaf axils. Globular fruit contains a large seed enclosed in an edible juicy translucent white aril inside a thin hard skin.
CULTIVATION: Needs warm humid weather and high rainfall for vegetative growth but a cool dry spell to induce flowering, followed by warmth and humidity to ensure pollination. Hot dry winds are harmful at any time. Deep moist soil, regular watering, and protection from wind and cold provide ideal growing conditions. Remove non-fruiting flower panicles at harvest. Fruit turns bright red when ripe and is harvested immediately. Propagate by air-layering or grafting.

Litchi chinensis

Litchi chinensis
LYCHEE
☼ ⚘ ↔ 15 ft (4.5 m) ↑ 20–40 ft (6–12 m)
Spreading tree, with a thick canopy of dark green leaves reaching to the ground. Flowers in long panicles at branch tips, male and female flowers in the same panicle. Fruits round, about 1½ in (35 mm) in diameter, turning red when ripe. Zones 10–11.

Macadamia integrifolia

MACADAMIA

This genus from the protea (Proteaceae) family contains 8 species of evergreen rainforest trees, 7 from coastal eastern Australia; one from Sulawesi, Indonesia. In warm frost-free climates they grow into compact trees with large glossy leaves and long pendulous sprays of creamy white or pale pink blossoms. Self-pollinating, the round hard-shelled nuts ripen in late summer to autumn. Two species are cultivated commercially in Australia, Hawaii and California, USA.
CULTIVATION: Grow in a humus-rich well-drained soil in full sun or partial shade. They require an ample supply of water in dry periods. Propagate from seed, but trees will not bear fruit until at least 6 years old. Selected clones are commonly grafted or budded.

Macadamia integrifolia
SMOOTH-SHELLED MACADAMIA NUT
☼/◗ ❋ ↔ 20 ft (6 m) ↑ 50 ft (15 m)
From southeastern Queensland, Australia. Glossy oblong leaves, in whorls of 3, smooth, slightly wavy edges. Creamy white to pinkish flowers. Creamy white nut. Zones 9–11.

Macadamia tetraphylla
BOPPLE NUT, MACADAMIA NUT, QUEENSLAND NUT
☼/◗ ❋ ↔ 20 ft (6 m) ↑ 40 ft (12 m)
From subtropical rainforests of coastal eastern Australia. Whorls of dark green oblong leaves, prickly teeth. Long pendulous racemes of white or pinkish flowers, in winter–spring. Zones 9–11.

MALUS (see page 214)

Malus pumila
syns Malus × domestica, Pyrus malus
APPLE, CRABAPPLE, ORCHARD APPLE
☼ ❋ ↔ 20 ft (6 m) ↑ 50 ft (15 m)
The origins of eating apples were uncertain, but recent intensive botanical studies have virtually solved this puzzle and helped to establish correct botanical names. It was believed that apples were of ancient hybrid origin, so the name M. × domestica was used to distinguish them from wild species. But now DNA and other evidence has shown that only one wild species is involved, M. pumila, and fieldwork has revealed a large range of variation in wild populations. The wild range of M. pumila is from western China through mountain regions of Central Asia to Europe. Young leaves, flower stalks, and calyces vary in downiness. Pink buds open to white flowers suffused with pink. Fruits over 2 in (5 cm) in diameter. M. p. 'Niedzwetzkyana', the most significant parent of hybrid crabapples, has young leaves, buds, blossoms, fruit, bark, branches all purple-red.

Orchard apples run to many thousands of cultivars, some still popular after 200 years. Some can be eaten raw, some are better cooked, and a number are suitable only for cider. Apples often need a pollinator of a different cultivar to set good crops. 'Bramley's Seedling', late red fruit, best cooked; 'Cox's Orange Pippin', small, strong-flavored, orange to red fruit; 'Fuji' ★, white-fleshed red fruit with yellowish markings; 'Gala', good flavor, long-keeping, yellow-marked red fruit; 'Golden Delicious', white-fleshed, red-marked, golden yellow fruit; 'Honey Crisp', very juicy, yellow-marked red fruit, cold tolerant; 'James Grieve', yellow-fleshed red fruit, quite acidic; 'Red Delicious', deep red to black-red, strong-flavored; 'Scarlet Gala', red fruit. Recent varieties, such as 'Pacific Rose', are patent-protected. Zones 3–9.

Malus pumila 'Scarlet Gala'

MANGIFERA

Best known for the mango, M. indica, This genus is from the cashew (Anacardiaceae) family and consists of around 40 to 60 species originally from the tropical rainforests of India, Southeast Asia, and the Solomon Islands. Simple, leathery, smooth-edged leaves are reddish when young. Panicles of small bisexual and male flowers are produced on the same plant. The fruit is a large, fleshy, hanging drupe with a flat fibrous seed. Grown in tropical and warm-temperate countries for their handsome foliage and fruit. The timber of some species is used for floorboards and tea chests. The sap and plant parts may cause dermatitis.
CULTIVATION: They need deep well-drained soil with regular fertilizing, a warm frost-free climate, and warm dry weather to set fruit; regions with low rainfall during flowering must be selected for fruit production. Propagate from seed or by grafting.

Mangifera indica
MANGO
☼ ✥ ↔ 25 ft (8 m) ↑ 80 ft (24 m)
From Southeast Asia, especially Myanmar and eastern India. Young leaves red, ageing to shiny dark green. Yellowish or reddish flowers, in dense panicles. Fruit irregularly egg-shaped fleshy drupe. May be "alternate-bearing," fruiting heavily every 2 to 4 years. 'Campeche', deep yellow fruit with reddish pink tinge; 'Edward', medium to large fruit; 'Kensington Pride' (syn. 'Pride of Bowen'), Australian cultivar, propagated as seedling. Zones 11–12.

MANILKARA

This genus of around 70 species of evergreen trees belonging to the sapodilla (Sapotaceae) family has a wide distribution throughout the tropics. Leaves are usually simple and large with a thin, papery texture. Flowers form in the leaf axils and may be carried singly or in clusters. They are followed by fleshy berries containing only a few seeds. Some species yield a latex.
CULTIVATION: They are variable in their climatic preferences. Some come from the seasonally dry tropics but most prefer year-round warmth, moisture, and high humidity. They like well-drained humus-rich soil in part shade or full shade and can be trimmed lightly to maintain a pleasing shape. Propagate from seed or cuttings, but allow the latex that is exuded from the cut to dry before inserting the cutting into the potting mix.

Manilkara zapota
SAPODILLA
☼ ◐ ↔ 20 ft (6 m) ↑ 100 ft (30 m)
Commercially grown tree from Mexico to Costa Rica. Simple leaves, 6 in (15 cm) long. Small white flowers. Rough-skinned, egg-shaped, golden brown fruits, to 3 in (8 cm) long. Timber known as chicozapote. Zones 10–12.

Mangifera indica

MESPILUS

This genus within the rose (Rosaceae) family has one species, a deciduous tree that grows in mountain woodland and scrubland throughout southeast Europe and southwest Asia. It is a good ornamental shrub or tree with large single flowers that are usually white, sometimes with a pink flush, and good autumn foliage. It is now grown less for its fruit, which is only edible after frost, when it is described as "bletted" (slightly rotted); the high malic acid content is reduced and the sugar increased in this way.
CULTIVATION: Grows well in any good moisture-retentive soil with shelter from strong winds. Propagate from seed in autumn, or by bud-grafting in late summer. Can also be grafted onto hawthorn to form graft hybrids.

Mespilus germanica
MEDLAR
☼ ❋ ↔ 25 ft (8 m) ↑ 20 ft (6 m)
A large shrub or small tree from Europe. Thorny branchlets in the wild, but cultivated forms are usually thornless. Leaves alternate, oblong to lance-shaped, toothed, dull green above, felty underneath, red and yellow, in autumn. Profuse apple-blossom-like flowers, in spring. Round, fleshy, brown fruit, too astringent to eat until bletted. **'Breda Giant'**, apple-cinnamon flavored fruit; **'Dutch'**, ornamental tree; **'Large Russian'**, pink tinged flowers, spreading crown; **'Nottingham'**, good-flavored fruit; **'Royal'**, medium-sized fruit; **'Stoneless'**, seedless, small fruit. Zones 4–9.

MORUS
MULBERRY
There are about 12 species of deciduous trees and shrubs in this genus belonging to the mulberry (Moraceae) family. Most species are from Asia, a few are from North America and central Africa. Heart-shaped leaves with serrated edges are arranged alternately. Inconspicuous male and female flowers are borne on separate catkins, followed by fruits resembling raspberries. The black mulberry *(M. nigra)* has edible fruits; leaves of the white mulberry *(M. alba)* provide food for silkworms.
CULTIVATION: They grow in any reasonably fertile well-drained soil. Prune only in winter and keep to a minimum as the sap bleeds freely. Propagate from cuttings in spring or autumn; large pieces of branch (truncheons) up to 5 ft (1.5 m) long can be planted 20 in (50 cm) into the ground.

Morus alba
WHITE MULBERRY
☼ ❋ ↔ 30 ft (9 m) ↑ 30–50 ft (9–15 m)
Native to China. Leaves broadly oval, heart-shaped base, 2- to 3-lobed, coarsely toothed; silkworm food. Greenish male and female flowers, in separate clusters, in early summer. Fruit white, becoming pale pink then red. **'Bungeana'**, dense bright green foliage; **'Pendula'**, weeping form; **'Venosa'**, heavily veined mid-green leaves. Zones 4–10.

Morus nigra
BLACK MULBERRY
☼ ❋ ↔ 40 ft (12 m) ↑ 50 ft (15 m)
Deciduous tree from central or southwestern Asia. Wide dense crown, relatively short trunk, gnarled with age. Broadly oval to heart-shaped leaves, roughened uppersurface. Greenish flowers, in spring. Edible berries ripen to purplish black. Zones 5–10.

Morus rubra
RED MULBERRY
☼ ❋ ↔ 40 ft (12 m) ↑ 50 ft (15 m)
From eastern USA and southeastern Canada, rarely cultivated. Slightly heart-shaped leaves, sometimes lobed, roughened uppersurface, serrated edges. Ripe purple fruit in summer. Zones 5–10.

Mespilus germanica

Passiflora alata

MUSA *(see page 513)*

Musa acuminata

syn. *Musa cavendishii*

BANANA

☼ ❄ ↔ 8 ft (2.4 m) ↑ 12–20 ft (3.5–6 m)

From Southeast Asia and north Queensland, Australia. Paddle-shaped leaves, mid- to gray-green. Pendent flowers, yellow, white, or cream, in summer. Edible yellow fruit. **'Dwarf Cavendish'** (syn. 'Basrai'), smaller, yellow flowers and purple bracts. Zones 10–12.

Musa × paradisiaca

syn. *Musa sapientum*

BANANA, PLANTAIN

☼ ❄ ↔ 8 ft (2.4 m) ↑ 10–20 ft (3–6 m)

An *M. acuminata* and *M. balbisiana* cross, that includes cooking and eating bananas. Leaves large, green, oblong. Fruit yellow, pale pulp, seedless, in summer. Zones 10–12.

OLEA *(see page 226)*

Olea europaea

COMMON OLIVE

☼ ❄ ↔ 20 ft (6 m) ↑ 20–30 ft (6–9 m)

In cultivation since ancient times, evergreen tree from the Mediterranean region. Gnarled branches, fissured bark with age. Leaves leathery, silver undersides. Very long lived. Fruit is not edible off the tree, must be processed. *O. e.* subsp. *cuspidata* (syns *O. africana*, *O. cuspidata* and *O. e.* subsp. *africana*), to 25 ft (8 m) high, makes a good shade tree, self-seeds quite freely, can become invasive; leaves not silvery, pea-sized globular fruit. *O. e.* **'Manzanillo'** ★, leathery leaves, edible black fruit; **'Mission'**, a vigorous cold-hardy cultivar. Zones 8–10.

OPUNTIA *(see page 836)*

Opuntia ficus-indica

syns *Opuntia engelmannii*, *O. vulgaris*

INDIAN FIG, INDIAN FIG PEAR

☼ ❄ ↔ 15 ft (4.5 m) ↑ 15 ft (4.5 m)

Native to Mexico, naturalized elsewhere. Green or bluish green, flattened, oblong or rounded segments, areoles with 1 or 2 spines. Yellow flowers, in late spring to early summer. Purple edible fruits. Zones 9–11.

PASSIFLORA *(see page 784)*

Passiflora alata

☼/◐ ✛ ↔ 8–20 ft (2.4–6 m) ↑ 20 ft (6 m)

Vigorous climber from Amazonian Brazil and Peru. Winged stems, simple pointed oval leaves to 6 in (15 cm) long, edges may be finely toothed. Scented flowers up to 5 in (12 cm) wide, deep red petals, purple and white banded filaments, in summer. Ovoid to pear-shaped, edible, yellow fruit to 4 in (10 cm) long. Zones 10–12.

Passiflora edulis

GRANADILLA, PASSIONFRUIT, PURPLE GRANADILLA

☼/◐ ✛ ↔ 8–15 ft (2.4–4.5 m) ↑ 15 ft (4.5 m)

Summer-flowering climber from Brazil. Glossy, 3-lobed leaves to 4 in (10 cm) long. White flowers with white and purple banded filament. Ovoid edible fruit to around 3 in (8 cm) long, becom-

Opuntia ficus-indica

ing purple-black and wrinkled when ripe. *P. e. f. flavicarpa*, golden yellow fruit, hybrids between these 2 forms include: **'Lacey'** and **'Purple Gold'** ★, light purple fruit; **'Fredrick'** and **'Red Rover'**, red fruit. *P. e.* **'Edgehill'**, large purple-black fruit; **'Kahuna'**, pale purple fruit. Zones 10–12.

Passiflora mollissima

BANANA PASSIONFRUIT, CURUBA

☼/◐ ❄ ↔ 8–15 ft (2.4–4.5 m) ↑ 15 ft (4.5 m)

Vigorous summer- to autumn-flowering climber from northern South America. Leaves to 4 in (10 cm) long, 3-lobed, downy. Long-tubed bright mid-pink flowers. Edible, yellow, ovoid fruit to 3 in (8 cm) long. Zones 9–11.

Passiflora quadrangularis

GIANT GRANADILLA

☼/◐ ✛ ↔ 10–20 ft (3–6 m) ↑ 50 ft (15 m)

Climber from tropical South America. Pointed oval, leathery leaves. Flowers dusky gray-pink, with twisted blue, white, purple-red banded filaments. Bright yellow, ovoid fruit. Zones 10–12.

PERSEA

Belonging to the laurel (Lauraceae) family, this genus of around 200 species of evergreen shrubs or trees comes chiefly from subtropical and tropical America and Southeast Asia. *Persea* species have prominently veined alternate leaves, and bear panicles of small greenish flowers in the leaf axils. The fruits contain a single large stone, and may be large or small, pear-shaped or rounded; the yellowish green flesh is smooth and rich. The best-known species is the avocado (*P. americana*), long cultivated for its fruit. CULTIVATION: Best suited to a sheltered but sunny position in a well-drained soil rich in humus. Water moderately during the growing season. Little pruning is necessary once the plants are established. Propagation is from seed or from cuttings. Plants may take up to 7 years to bear fruit; grafted plants are recommended for varieties grown for their fruits.

Persea americana

ALLIGATOR PEAR, AVOCADO

☼ ⚘ ↔ 30 ft (9 m) ↑ 60 ft (18 m)

Native to Central America and the West Indies. Fast-growing; grafted trees are smaller. Leathery elliptical leaves, panicles of yellowish green flowers. Large dark green fruits, pear-shaped or rounded. '**Haas**', thick-skinned cultivar. Zones 9–11.

PHOENIX

This genus in the palm (Arecaceae) family consists of around 17 species, mostly from tropical and subtropical Africa, Madagascar, Canary Islands, Crete, and southern and western Asia. Solitary or clustered feather-leafed palms, with separate male and female plants, they have long pinnate leaves; lower leaflets on each frond reduced to stiff sharp spines. Panicles of small, 3-petalled, often yellow flowers are followed by yellow, orange, green, brown, or red to black fruits with 1 grooved seed. CULTIVATION: Most do best when well-watered in productive soils, but are fairly adaptable and tolerant of poorer drier soils in full sun as long as drainage is good. Propagate from seed, or from suckers from suckering varieties. Remove old fronds carefully.

Phoenix dactylifera

DATE PALM, EDIBLE DATE

☼ ⚘ ↔ 30 ft (9 m) ↑ 70 ft (21 m)

Commercially cultivated for at least 5,000 years. Graceful spreading crown, gray-green fronds, lower leaflets reduced to spines. Sweet edible fruits are produced only in hot dry climates. Commercially developed varieties have superior fruits. Zones 9–12.

PHYSALIS (*see page 540*)

Physalis peruviana

syn. *Physalis edulis*

CAPE GOOSEBERRY, GOLDEN BERRY, TEPAREE

☼ ❋ ↔ 2–3 ft (0.6–0.9 m) ↑ 2–6 ft (0.6–1.8 m)

Herbaceous spreading perennial, from Peru and Chile. Widely introduced elsewhere. Branches ribbed, spreading, often purplish; leaves nearly opposite, randomly toothed, velvety, pointed, mid-green, heart-shaped to oval, 2½– 6 in (6–15 cm) long; flowers

Persea americana 'Haas'

inconspicuous, bell-shaped, yellow, with 5 dark purple-brown markings, in summer. Purple-green hairy calyx becomes a straw-colored husk enclosing glossy, smooth-skinned, orange-yellow fruit; juicy pulp contains many tiny yellowish seeds. Fruits eaten fresh or stewed, canned, used in jams and sauces; worn as jewelry in Peru; used as a diuretic and anti-asthmatic in Colombia, and as a poultice or enema in South Africa. Zones 8–10.

PISTACIA (*see page 243*)

Pistacia vera

PISTACHIO

☼ ❋ ↔ 15 ft (4.5 m) ↑ 30 ft (9 m)

Native to western China; cultivated in the Mediterranean region and USA for its nut crop. Pinnate leaves; oval, shiny, paired leaflets, duller beneath. Panicles of flowers; small reddish fruit with bony shell contains the edible green or yellow seed. Zones 8–10.

POUTERIA (*see page 249*)

Pouteria sapota

syns *Calocarpum mammosum, C. sapota, Pouteria mammosa*

MAMEY SAPOTE, MARMALADE PLUM, SAPOTE

☼ ⚘ ↔ 20 ft (6 m) ↑ 40 ft (12 m)

Native of Central America and northern South America. Broad oblong leaves and small flowers clustered near branch tips. Large ovoid fruits, edible pulp in shades of orangey pink, that take 1 to 2 years to ripen. '**Magana**', fruit weighs up to 6 lb (2.75 kg). Zones 10–11.

PRUNUS (*see page 252*)

Prunus americana

AMERICAN PLUM, AMERICAN RED PLUM, GOOSE PLUM, HOG PLUM, WILD PLUM

☼ ❋ ↔ 12 ft (3.5 m) ↑ 25 ft (8 m)

Eastern and central North American tree with spiny branches, peeling dark brown bark. Leaves to 4 in (10 cm) long, white flowers. Small, yellow-fleshed, red to plum-blue fruit. Zones 3–9.

Pouteria sapota

Prunus armeniaca
APRICOT

☼ ❄ ↔ 15 ft (4.5 m) ↕ 25 ft (8 m)

Flat-topped tree, red-brown bark, leaves large, heavily serrated. Needs winter chilling, summer heat to produce fruit. Flowers white or pale pink, on bare wood, prone to damage from late frosts. Golden orange fruit. *P. a.* var. *ansu*, cultivated race, broader leaves, fruit's stone is rougher. Zones 5–10.

Prunus avium
GEAN, MAZZARD, SWEET CHERRY, WILD CHERRY

☼ ❄ ↔ 20 ft (6 m) ↕ 50 ft (15 m)

The main parent of edible cherries. Deciduous Eurasian tree with serrated-edged leaves. Flowers white, massed in small clusters, open before the new leaves. Purple-red fruit. 'Asplenifolia', deeply cut leaves; 'Cavalier', medium-sized to large fruit, black, produced early to mid-season; 'Plena' (syn. 'Multiplex'), peeling bark, orange-red autumn foliage, white double flowers. Zones 3–9.

Prunus cerasus
SOUR CHERRY

☼ ❄ ↔ 15 ft (4.5 m) ↕ 20 ft (6 m)

Found from southeastern Europe to India. Small, deep green, glossy leaves, finely serrated edges. Long-stemmed umbels of small white flowers. Fruit resembles sweet cherries. Zones 3–9.

Prunus × *domestica*
EUROPEAN PLUM, PLUM

☼ ❄ ↔ 15 ft (4.5 m) ↕ 30 ft (9 m)

The common plum has been grown since ancient times, a hybrid, probably between *P. spinosa* and *P. cerasifera* subsp. *divaricata*. Leaves to 4 in (10 cm) long, flowers white, soft-fleshed yellow or red-skinned fruit. 'Angelina Burdett' (syn. 'Angelina'), early fruiting, light red skin, yellow flesh; 'Bühlerfrühwetsch', purple-skinned; 'Coe's Golden Drop', mid-season, yellow skin, yellow flesh; 'Hauszwetsch' and 'Mount Royal', purple-skinned; 'President', mid- to late season, large, purplish blue skin, yellow flesh; **Reine Claude Group** (syn. Greengage Group), mid-season, greenish yellow skin, yellow flesh, largely self-fertile. Zones 5–9.

Prunus dulcis
ALMOND

☼ ❄ ↔ 15 ft (4.5 m) ↕ 20–30 ft (6–9 m)

Species native to eastern Mediterranean and North Africa. Narrow leaves with finely serrated edges, 5 in (12 cm) long. Large white or deep pink flowers, followed by edible kernels. 'Alba Plena' has white double flowers; 'Macrocarpa' has large pale pink flowers; 'Roseoplena' has pink double flowers. Zones 7–10.

Prunus mume
JAPANESE APRICOT, MEI

☼ ❄ ↔ 25 ft (8 m) ↕ 20–30 ft (6–9 m)

Early flowering deciduous tree from China. Rounded crown of leaves to 4 in (10 cm) long. Flowers, more than 1 in (25 mm) wide, soft fragrance, dusky rose pink. Yellow fruit. 'Beni-chidori', small, deep pink, double flowers; 'Dawn', large, light pink, double flowers; 'Geisha', dusky pink, semi-double flowers; 'Pendula', single pale pink flowers. Zones 6–10.

Prunus persica
syn. *Amygdalus persica*
NECTARINE, PEACH

☼ ❄ ↔ 6–20 ft (1.8–6 m) ↕ 8–20 ft (2.4–6 m)

Believed native to China. Leaves 4–6 in (10–15 cm) long; white or pink flowers. Fruiting cultivars can be subdivided as freestone or clingstone; white or yellow fleshed; early-, mid-, or late season. **Peach Group:** Fuzzy-skinned fruit. 'Cresthaven' and 'Jerseyglo', late-season, yellow, freestone; 'Texstar' early to mid-season, semi-freestone, yellow. **Nectarine Group:** Smooth-skinned fruit. 'Anderhone', large late-season fruit; 'Gold Mine' and 'Lord Napier' white flesh, freestone, mid-season. **Ornamental Group:** Flowers, mostly double, white or pink to red, some flecked. 'Klara Meyer', compact, deep pink double flowers. Zones 5–10.

Prunus salicina
JAPANESE PLUM

☼ ❄ ↔ 25 ft (8 m) ↕ 30 ft (9 m)

Deciduous tree from Japan and China. New shoots red, lush dark green foliage. White flowers in pairs or small clusters. Yellow to red fruit. 'Methley', purple-skinned, yellow-fleshed fruit; 'Red Heart', large red fruit. Zones 6–10.

PSIDIUM

This tropical American genus, in the myrtle (Myrtaceae) family, contains about 100 species of evergreen shrubs or trees; several are grown for their edible fruits. They branch freely, and have thick opposite leaves. The white 5-petalled flowers have numerous stamens. Fruit is a rounded or pear-shaped berry.

Prunus persica

Psidium guajava

Pyrus communis 'Doyenné du Comice'

Ribes nigrum 'Ben Connan'

CULTIVATION: They need a warm to hot climate, moist but well-drained soil, protection from strong winds. Water regularly during summer. Prune after fruiting to retain a compact shape. Propagate from seed or cuttings, or by layering or grafting.

Psidium guajava
GUAVA

☀ ✦ ↔15 ft (4.5 m) ↑30 ft (9 m)

Dark brown scaly bark; light to mid-green oval leaves, prominent veins, downy undersides. Large white flowers, in spring. Edible fruit, pink strongly aromatic flesh. Zones 10–12.

PUNICA

This genus in the loosestrife (Lythraceae) family contains only 2 species, both small, deciduous, fruiting trees native to the Mediterranean region, North Africa, Iran, and Afghanistan. They have simple lance-shaped leaves, scarlet flowers, and reddish yellow apple-shaped fruits.
CULTIVATION: Plant in well-aerated coarsely textured soil, enriched with organic matter. Lightly prune current year's growth in late winter. Propagate from seed sown in spring, or from soft-tip or half-hardened cuttings between spring and autumn.

Punica granatum
COMMON POMEGRANATE

☀ ❄ ↔15 ft (4.5 m) ↑25 ft (8 m)

Small tree, broad domed crown, lateral shoots thorny. Leaves opposite, broadly lance-shaped, reddish in spring, then bright green; turn yellow in autumn. Flowers with 5 to 8 bright scarlet petals, many stamens, late spring–late summer. Orange-red fruit, jelly-like crimson pulp. Cultivars include 'Nana', 'Nochi Shibari', and 'Wonderful', a double-flowered form. Zones 8–11.

PYRUS (see page 259)

Pyrus communis
CALLERY PEAR, COMMON PEAR, GARDEN-PEAR

☀ ❄ ↔20 ft (6 m) ↑50 ft (15 m)

Medium-sized tree with rounded or oval, glossy, green leaves. Thorny branches covered in white blossoms, in spring. Large, edible fruit. Cultivated for centuries. Over 1,000 named cultivars

raised. 'Beurré d'Anjou', very old French cultivar, smooth green fruit, slight red cheek or all red; 'Cascade', heavy bearer, almost globular fruit, bright red, some yellow showing through, white juicy flesh; 'Clapp's Favourite Liebling', small fruit, juicy flavor; 'Conference', large pear, with a long neck, brown skin, yellow-green showing through, sweet juicy flesh faintly pink-tinged; 'Doyenné du Comice' ★ (syn. 'Comice'), old French pear, with many variants, fruit smooth-skinned, ripening to pale green, sweet creamy flesh; 'Gellerts Butterbine', greenish yellow fruit, bronze-orange cheek; 'Red Bartlett', bright red fruit; 'Williams' Bon Chrétien' (syn. 'Bartlett'), bright green with a slight red cheek, ripening yellowish. Zones 2–9.

Pyrus pyrifolia
CHINA PEAR, NASHI PEAR, SAND PEAR

☀ ❄ ↔30 ft (9 m) ↑50 ft (15 m)

Native to China and Japan. Leaves oblong, serrated, in shades of orange and bronze, in autumn. Small white flowers appear just before or with emerging leaves. Small, hard, brown fruit. 'Chojuro', squat, russet brown, densely dotted fruit; 'Hosui', yellow-brown fruit; 'Nijisseiki' ★, green-yellow fruit; 'Shinko', medium-sized fruit of regular globular form. Zones 4–9.

RIBES (see page 279)

Ribes gayanum
CHILEAN BLACKCURRANT

☀ ❄ ↔3 ft (0.9 m) ↑5 ft (1.5 m)

Evergreen shrub from the Chilean Andes. Leaves covered in woolly down, 3 to 5 coarsely toothed lobes. Short upright racemes of yellow flowers, pleasant honey scent, in early summer. Edible black fruit has a downy coating. Zones 8–10.

Ribes nigrum
BLACKCURRANT

☀ ❄ ↔6 ft (1.8 m) ↑7 ft (2 m)

Deciduous shrub from Eurasia. Upright multi-stemmed habit. Downy pendent racemes of red-centered yellow-green flowers, in spring. 'Ben Connan', award-winning cultivar; 'Ben Lomond', late large fruit; 'Black Beauty', American cultivar; 'Boskoop Giant', large fruit; 'Jet', large dark fruit. Zones 5–9.

Ribes rubrum

Rubus, Hybrid Cultivar, 'Navajo'

Rubus idaeus 'Heritage'

Ribes odoratum

BUFFALO CURRANT, CLOVE CURRANT, GOLDEN CURRANT

☼ ❋ ↔ 6 ft (1.8 m) ↕ 6 ft (1.8 m)

From central USA. Spice-scented leaves, 3 to 5 lobes, toothed edges. Pendent racemes of sweetly scented yellow flowers. Edible black fruit. 'Xanthocarpum', orange-yellow berries. Zones 5–9.

Ribes rubrum

syns *Ribes sativum, R. silvestre, R. spicatum*

NORDIC CURRANT, REDCURRANT

☼/❋ ❋ ↔ 32–60 in (80–150 cm) ↕ 5–7 ft (1.5–2 m)

Smooth-stemmed shrub found from Scandinavia to eastern China. Leaves are 3- to 5-lobed, to 4 in (10 cm) in diameter. Upright to pendulous racemes of small red-flushed green flowers in early summer. Shiny red fruit. Cultivars include 'Red Lake', 'Macrocarpum', and 'White Grape'. Zones 3–9.

Ribes uva-crispa

GOOSEBERRY

☼ ❋ ↔ 36 in (90 cm) ↕ 36 in (90 cm)

Found through Europe to North Africa and the Caucasus region. Thorny many-branched bush. Leaves heart-shaped, green flowers. Bristly green fruit. Fruit of some ripen to yellow or red. Cultivars include: 'Crown Bob', 'Leveller' ★, and 'Roaring Lion'. Zones 5–9.

RUBUS (see page 293)

Rubus arcticus

ARCTIC BRAMBLE, CRIMSON BRAMBLE

☼ ❋ ↔ 18–24 in (45–60 cm) ↕ 6–12 in (15–30 cm)

Herbaceous rhizomatous perennial, native to boggy woods of the higher latitudes of Europe, Asia, and North America. Compound leaves with 3 to 5 oval, smooth, toothed leaflets. Clusters of 1 to 3 pink or red flowers, purple stamens, in summer. Red globular fruit. 'Kenai Carpet' (nagoonberry), pink flowers. Zones 1–7.

Rubus idaeus

RASPBERRY

☼ ❋ ↔ 4 ft (1.2 m) ↕ 5 ft (1.5 m)

Native to Europe, northern Asia, and North America. Deciduous erect shrub, prickly or bristly arching stems. Leaves pinnate, 7 oblong to egg-shaped leaflets. White spring–summer flowers on axillary or terminal racemes. Red fruit. *R. i.* subsp. *strigosus* has more bristly stems. *R. i.* 'Amity', large dark red fruit; 'Aureus', yellow fruit; 'Autumn Bliss' and 'Chilcotin', large red fruit; 'Fallgold', large, yellow fruit; 'Glen Moy', red summer fruit; 'Heritage', late-bearing cultivar; 'Taylor', red fruit. Zones 3–9.

Rubus loganobaccus

LOGANBERRY

☼ ❋ ↔ 2–3 ft (0.6–0.9 m) ↕ 4–6 ft (1.2–1.8 m)

Strongly growing herbaceous shrub developed in California in 1916 by Judge James Harvey Logan by crossing a blackberry, 'Aughinburgh', and a raspberry, 'Red Antwerp'. Vigorous prickly canes; leaves with 3 to 5 leaflets. Ruby red blackberry-shaped berries turn purplish red in early autumn when ripe. Zones 4–7.

Rubus occidentalis

BLACKCAP

☼ ❋ ↔ 10 ft (3 m) ↕ 10 ft (3 m)

Native to eastern and central North America. Deciduous shrub, prickly curved stems. Dark green leaves, 5 leaflets on non-flowering stems, 3 leaflets on flowering stems, white felty undersides. White flowers, in summer. Dark purple fruit. 'Brandywine', large purple-red fruit; 'Cumberland', 'Jewel', 'Morrison', and 'Munger', glossy black fruit; 'Sodus', purple fruit. Zones 3–9.

Rubus phoenicolasius

☼ ❋ ↔ 10 ft (3 m) ↕ 10 ft (3 m)

Native to China, Korea, and Japan. Deciduous shrub, spreading stems with red bristles. Leaves have 3 leaflets, are broadly egg-shaped, coarsely toothed and lobed, with white felty undersides. Light pink flowers in summer. Red cone-shaped fruit. Zones 5–9.

Rubus Hybrid Cultivars

☼ ❋ ↔ 6–12 ft (1.8–3.5 m) ↕ 2–8 ft (0.6–2.4 m)

Most *Rubus* hybrids have been bred for fruit production, with an emphasis on flavor and vigor. 'Benenden' ★ (syn. *R.* × *tridel*), white flowers, in late spring–early summer; 'Navajo', North American eating blackberry, thornless canes, smallish black fruit; 'Silvan', purple fruit; 'Tayberry', heavy yielding hybrid, sweet, fairly large, highly perfumed fruit, dark red when ripe. Zones 6–9.

SOLANUM *(see page 307)*

Solanum betaceum
syn. *Cyphomandra betacea*
TAMARILLO, TREE TOMATO
☼ ☽ ↔ 7 ft (2 m) ↑ 10 ft (3 m)
Bushy evergreen shrub from the Andes in Peru. Large heart-shaped leaves, with an unpleasant smell. Pale pink bell-shaped flowers, in spring–summer. Fruits early autumn. Zones 9–11.

Solanum melanocerasum
GARDEN HUCKLEBERRY
☼ ☽ ↔ 18 in (45 cm) ↑ 24 in (60 cm)
Bushy annual probably originating from western tropical Africa. Broadly oval leaves. Small white flowers. Black berries, ¾ in (18 mm) wide, through summer; edible if cooked. Zones 9–12.

Solanum muricatum
PEPINO, MELON PEAR, MELON SHRUB
☼ ☽ ↔ 36 in (90 cm) ↑ 36 in (90 cm)
Variable plant from the Andes. Flowers purple, or white, purple markings. Juicy, melon flavored, white, green, purple, or striped, oblong to pear-shaped, edible fruit. '**Ecuadorian Gold**', golden fruit, long fruiting season. Zones 9–12.

Solanum sessiliflorum
COCONA
☼ ✿ ↔ 4 ft (1.2 m) ↑ 7 ft (2 m)
From South America. Downy stems and large, oval, scallop-edged leaves. Yellowish green flowers. Pear-shaped orangey red edible fruit, mild tomato flavor, in spring–summer. Zones 10–12.

SORBUS *(see page 309)*

Sorbus domestica
SERVICE TREE
☼ ❋ ↔ 30 ft (9 m) ↑ 30–50 ft (9–15 m)
From southern Europe, North Africa, and western Asia, pinnate leaves, serrated edges, downy undersides. White flowers. Edible large berries yellow-green, ripening to red; sometimes used in jams and jellies. Zones 6–10.

SYZYGIUM *(see page 322)*

Syzygium aqueum
WATER APPLE, WATER ROSE APPLE
☼ ✿ ↔ 20 ft (6 m) ↑ 35 ft (10 m)
Tree from Malay Peninsula, Borneo, and New Guinea. Leathery leaves, dull light green. White, red, or dull purple flowers, in loose clusters, in summer. Glossy, pear-shaped, edible fruit, red or white. Zones 10–12.

Syzygium malaccense
syn. *Eugenia malaccense*
MALAY APPLE
☼ ✿ ↔ 15 ft (4.5 m) ↑ 40–80 ft (12–24 m)
Native to the Malay Peninsula. Soft leathery, dark green leaves, paler undersurface, new growth wine red, then pinkish. Clusters of cream or reddish purple flowers occur on branches or trunk, in summer. Edible red, pink, or white fruit. Zones 10–12.

TERMINALIA *(see page 327)*

Terminalia catappa
INDIAN ALMOND, KOTAMBA
☼ ✿ ↔ 35 ft (10 m) ↑ 90 ft (27 m)
Tree found in tropical Asia, parts of Polynesia, and northern Australia. Broad spreading crown, tiered horizontal branches. Semi-deciduous; large oblong leaves turn red before falling. Small white flowers in summer. Large greenish yellow and red edible fruits. Zones 11–12.

THEOBROMA
This genus from tropical America is a member of the cacao (Sterculiaceae) family and contains 20 species of evergreen trees; the best known is *T. cacao*, from which cocoa is obtained. They have alternately arranged simple leaves. Flowers arise directly from the leaf axils after the leaves have fallen and are followed by large fleshy fruits that contain many seeds.
CULTIVATION: Frost tender, they need a greenhouse in cool areas. In warm areas grow in a sheltered spot in fertile, moisture-retentive, yet well drained soil. Water and feed regularly in the growing season. Propagate from seed, sown fresh, or by air layering.

Solanum sessiliflorum

Syzygium aqueum

Terminalia catappa

Theobroma cacao
COCOA

☀ ✦ ↔ 10 ft (3 m) ↑ 25 ft (8 m)

Tree from Central and South America. Pointed oblong leaves, red when young. Clusters of small, creamy pink, slightly fragrant flowers borne directly on the trunk and thick branches, in spring. Ribbed seed pods ripen to purplish brown. Zones 11–12.

UGNI

Once included in the genus of the true myrtles (Myrtus), this variable group of approximately 10 species of evergreen shrubs from the temperate Americas is now in a genus of its own within the myrtle (Myrtaceae) family. They have simple oval leaves that are usually tough, leathery, and small. Their flowers are carried singly, in the leaf axils; they have 5 petals and tend to hang downwards. Fleshy berries, sometimes edible, follow the flowers and can become very aromatic as they near ripeness. CULTIVATION: A little frost tender when young, these plants dislike lime. Grow in cool, moist, humus-rich, well-drained soil in sun or part-shade. An annual trim, after either flowering or fruiting, will keep the growth compact. Propagate from seed, cuttings or by removing naturally formed layers.

Ugni molinae ★
CHILEAN CRANBERRY, CHILEAN GUAVA

☼ ❋ ↔ 3 ft (0.9 m) ↑ 6 ft (1.8 m)

Native to Chile and western Argentina. Wiry-stemmed shrub with glossy deep green leaves on red stems. Flowers are cream flushed with pink, with a cluster of 40 to 60 tiny stamens at the center, in spring to early summer. Red berries follow. Zones 8–10.

VACCINIUM
BLUEBERRY

This genus of around 450 species of evergreen and deciduous shrubs, small trees and vines includes the blueberries, cranberries, and huckleberries. Members of the heath (Ericaceae) family, they occur over much of the Northern Hemisphere, with a few species

found in South Africa. Their main feature is the small but colorful edible fruits. Flowers are urn-shaped, carried singly or in clusters. Leaves are simple, oval to lance-shaped, often pointed at the tip and sometimes serrated around the edges.
CULTIVATION: Vaccinium species prefer cool, moist, humus-rich soil that is acidic and well drained, with shelter from the hottest summer sun. The conditions preferred by Camellia and Rhododendron give the best results. Prune shrubby species to shape: after flowering if the fruit is not required, or at harvest. Propagate from seed, cuttings, layers, or in some cases, by division.

Vaccinium ashei
RABBIT-EYE BLUEBERRY

☀ ❋ ↔ 7 ft (2 m) ↑ 3–15 ft (0.9–4.5 m)

Shrub from southeastern USA. Usually deciduous, sometimes near-evergreen in mild winters. Broad, serrated-edged leaves. White to light red flowers, in spring. Edible, ½ in (12 mm) wide, purple-black fruit. Zones 8–10.

Vaccinium corymbosum
BLUEBERRY, HIGHBUSH BLUEBERRY

☀ ❋ ↔ 5 ft (1.5 m) ↑ 3–6 ft (0.9–1.8 m)

Deciduous shrub from eastern USA. Lance-shaped leaves develop orange tones, in autumn. White flowers, sometimes with a red tint, in clusters, in spring. Edible, blue-black berries. 'Earliblue' is a tall vigorous cultivar with large fruit. Zones 2–9.

Vaccinium corymbosum

Vaccinium macrocarpon
CRANBERRY

☀ ❋ ↔ 5–10 ft (1.5–3 m) ↑ 3 ft (0.9 m)

Native of eastern North America and northern Asia. Low-growing evergreen shrub, takes root as it spreads. Leaves dark green, lighter undersides. Flowers mauve with stamens extending beyond the petals. Fruit is red. Zones 2–9.

Vaccinium myrtillus
BILBERRY, BLAEBERRY, WHORTLEBERRY

☀ ❋ ↔ 36 in (90 cm) ↑ 18 in (45 cm)

Semi-deciduous shrub found from Europe to the cold near-Arctic of northern Asia. The 1 in (25 mm) long leaves have finely serrated edges, and hairs on the underside veins. Flowers are borne in small clusters, opening green and turning red with age. Edible blue-black berries. Zones 3–9.

Vaccinium ovatum
BOX BLUEBERRY, EVERGREEN HUCKLEBERRY

☀ ❋ ↔ 4 ft (1.2 m) ↑ 3–5 ft (0.9–1.5 m)

Found naturally in western North America, this evergreen shrub has 1 in (25 mm) long oval leaves with finely serrated edges. Small white to pale pink flowers, tinted with red, are produced in clusters in spring. The fruit is blue-black. Zones 7–10.

Ugni molinae

Vaccinium parvifolium
RED HUCKLEBERRY, RED WHORTLEBERRY

☀ ❄ ↔ 6 ft (1.8 m) ↑ 6 ft (1.8 m)

Found from Alaska to California, USA. A deciduous shrub with small leaves, 1 in (25 mm) long. Flowers ¼ in (6 mm) wide, green with red tints, in spring. Edible, pinkish red berries. Zones 6–10.

Vaccinium Hybrid Cultivars

☀ ❄ ↔ 3–6 ft (0.9–1.8 m) ↑ 2–5 ft (0.6–1.5 m)

There are many popular hybrids and cultivars, some of indeterminate origin. '**Beckyblue**', with medium-sized blue fruit; '**Elliott**', to 8 ft (2.4 m) tall, with a long-lasting display of orange-red autumn color; '**Lingonberry**', reddish pink tints; '**Ornablue**', bright red leaves during autumn; '**Sharpeblue**' ★, smallish sweet fruit. Zones 2–9.

Vitis vinifera 'Pinot Noir'

VITIS
GRAPE

This is a genus of 65 species of woody deciduous vines indigenous to the Northern Hemisphere, particularly North America, giving its name to the grape (Vitaceae) family. The vines climb by tendrils; leaves are mostly simple, toothed or lobed. Flowers are small, sometimes fragrant. Berries can be small and unpalatable or large and sweet and are often produced in bunches. There are many hundreds of cultivars, particularly of *Vitis vinifera,* the European wine grape.

CULTIVATION: These vines prefer deep, moderately fertile, well-drained, often chalky, alkaline soil. Full sun and warmth are necessary for best fruit ripening. Most commercial *V. vinifera* grapes are grafted onto *Phylloxera*-resistant American species rootstock. Propagate from hardwood cuttings in late winter; propagate *V. coignetiae* by layering or from seed.

Vitis rotundifolia
BULLACE, FOX GRAPE, MUSCADINE

☀ ❄ ↔ 10–20 ft (3–6 m) ↑ 100 ft (30 m)

From moist swampy areas in southeastern USA, this vigorous plant has tight, non-shredding bark. Its glossy, coarsely toothed, occasionally lobed, rounded leaves turn a soft yellow during the autumn months. The large, round, greenish to purplish fruit has a musky flavor. Zones 5–9.

Vitis vinifera
COMMON GRAPE VINE

☀ ❄ ↔ 15–30 ft (4.5–9 m) ↑ 35 ft (10 m)

From southern and central Europe. High-climbing. Variably sized leaves, rounded or palm-shaped, 3- to 7-lobed, toothed, heart-shaped at base. Late summer fruit. Source of most of the world's wine and table grape cultivars, including: '**Black Corinth**' (syn. 'Zante Currant'), tiny seedless black fruit, tiny yields; '**Cabernet Sauvignon**', small, black, and very seedy fruit; '**Chardonnay**', small round fruit, used for white wines; '**Chenin Blanc**', medium-sized yellow-green fruit; '**Flame Seedless**' ★,

Ziziphus jujuba

firm, crisp, red fruit; '**Gelber Muskateller**', small green fruit; '**Golden Chasselas**', firm, sweet, juicy, greenish yellow fruit; '**Merlot**', medium-sized blue-black fruit yielding soft wines; '**Muller-Thurgau**', medium-sized fruit with green to grayish skin; '**Muscat Hamburg**', large, sweet, black, seeded fruit; '**Muscat of Alexandria**', large, seeded, green to amber fruit with musky flavor and aroma; '**Pinot Gris**', distinctive gray-blue to brown-pink seeded fruit; '**Pinot Noir**', small to medium black fruit; '**Purpurea**' (syns 'Claret Vine', 'Tenturier'), ornamental, leaves dark purple in spring, purplish green in summer, red-purple in autumn; '**Schiava Grossa**' (syn. 'Black Hamburg'), medium to large fruit, dark purplish red to black; '**Silvaner**', medium sized blue to yellow-green fruit; '**Sultana**' (syns 'Sultanina', 'Thompson Seedless'), small, seedless, greenish table fruit; '**Trebbiano**' (syns 'Saint-Emilion', 'Trebbiano Toscano', 'Ugni Blanc'), medium-sized, golden yellow fruit, one of most widely planted grapes in the world; '**Zinfandel**', reddish black to black fruit. Zones 6–9.

Vitis 'Waltham Cross'
syns *Vitis* 'Dattier', *V.* 'Lady Finger'

☀ ❄ ↔ 15–30 ft (4.5–9 m) ↑ 35 ft (10 m)

This popular, older Middle Eastern variety may be a pure *V. vinifera* cultivar. Large, oval, sweet, juicy, gold-tinted white fruit. Zones 6–9.

ZIZIPHUS (see page 347)

Ziziphus jujuba
CHINESE DATE, CHINESE JUJUBE, COMMON JUJUBE

☀ ❄ ↔ 12 ft (3.5 m) ↑ 30 ft (9 m)

Widely distributed from southern Europe to China. Fast-growing, deciduous tree. Oval to lance-shaped serrated leaves. Axillary clusters of tiny creamy flowers, in late spring. Dark red plum-like fruits, eaten fresh, dried, preserved, or candied. Zones 7–10.

Vegetables and Herbs

Comprising a diverse range of plants, with a wide range of uses in the kitchen, vegetables can be defined as any of various herbaceous plants that have edible parts. Most vegetables are annuals, or are biennials and perennials grown as annuals, cropping in the same year as they are sown or planted. A few, such as asparagus, are perennials remaining in the ground for years. Vegetables roughly fall into five categories: root crops, brassicas and leafy crops, legumes, salad crops, and vegetables with edible fruit.

For millennia, herbs have been valued for their useful properties in flavoring foods and beverages, for imparting aromas, for dyeing yarns and fabrics, and for curing or alleviating the various ills of humankind. The epithet *officinalis,* which appears in many Latin herb names, means "from the apothecary," or drugstore, and indicates that the herb was approved for use. One of the most important herb families is Lamiaceae, which includes mint, lavender, thyme, and rosemary.

Growing your own vegetables and herbs is hugely satisfying and brings with it the opportunity to grow plants organically so that they are free from artificial chemicals. Most importantly, vegetables and herbs used straight from the garden have a much better taste.

Growing vegetables like this *Brassica oleracea* cultivar in your garden is rewarding—you have fresh produce at your fingertips, and save money too!

Vegetable and Herb Finder

The following cultivation table features at-a-glance information for every species or hybrid with an individual entry in the Vegetables and Herbs chapter of this book. Simply find the plant you wish to know more about, and run your eye along the row to discover its height and spread, whether it is frost tolerant or not, the aspect it prefers, and more.

The type of plant is abbreviated to **A, P, C,** or **S:**
A – the plant is an annual.
P – the plant is a perennial.
C – the plant is a climber.
S – the plant is a shrub.

The climate(s) that each plant needs to thrive in the outdoors are given (some plants will grow in more than one climate), abbreviated to **C, W,** or **T:**
C – the plant prefers a cool climate.
W – the plant prefers a warm-temperate or subtropical climate.
T – the plant prefers a tropical climate.

The planting and harvesting season is abbreviated to **A, W, Sp, Su,** or **Any:**
A – plant or harvest in autumn.
W – plant or harvest in winter.
Sp – plant or harvest in spring.
Su – plant or harvest in summer.
Any – plant or harvest in any season.

The part of the plant that is edible is abbreviated to **L, S, R, Fl, Fr,** or **M:**
L – the leaves are eaten.
S – the shoots are eaten.
R – the roots are eaten.
Fl – the flowerheads are eaten.
Fr – the fruit are eaten.
M – the plant is used medicinally (not taken internally).

The best soil type for the plant is abbreviated to **S, C, M,** or **A:**
S – the plant prefers sandy soil.
C – the plant prefers clay soil.
M – the plant grows in most soils.
A – the plant grows in water.

Plant name	Height	Spread	Type	Climate	Vegetable	Herb	Planting season	Harvest season	Part eaten	Soil type	Frost tolerant	Full sun	Half sun	Heavy shade
Abelmoschus esculentus	30–48 in (75–120 cm)	18–24 in (45–60 cm)	A	C/W	♦		Sp	Su/A	Fr	M	♦	♦		
Agrimonia eupatoria	24–48 in (60–120 cm)	20–40 (50–100 cm)	P	C/W		♦	Sp	Su/A	M	M	♦	♦	♦	
Allium ampeloprasum	2–6 ft (0.6–1.8 m)	12–24 in (30–60 cm)	P	C	♦		Sp/Su	A/W	R	M	♦	♦		
Allium cepa	12–24 in (30–60 cm)	4–8 in (10–20 cm)	P	C/W	♦		Sp/Su	A/W	R	M	♦	♦		
Allium fistulosum	20–24 in (50–60 cm)	8–12 in (20–30 cm)	P	C	♦		Sp/Su	A	R	M	♦	♦		
Allium sativum	12–32 in (30–80 cm)	12–16 in (30–40 cm)	P	C/W	♦		W	Su	R	M	♦	♦		
Allium schoenoprasum	6–20 in (15–50 cm)	4–12 in (10–30 cm)	P	C/W	♦		Sp	Sp/A	L	M	♦	♦	♦	
Allium tuberosum	20 in (50 cm)	8–12 in (20–30 cm)	P	C/W	♦		Sp	Sp/A	L	M	♦	♦	♦	
Aloe vera	32 in (80 cm)	24–48 in (60–120 cm)	P	W/T		♦	Any	Any	M	S		♦	♦	
Aloysia citriodora	10 ft (3 m)	10 ft (3 m)	S	W/T		♦	Any	Any	L	M		♦	♦	
Alpinia galanga	4–6 ft (1.2–1.8 m)	2–3 ft (0.6–0.9 m)	P	W	♦	♦	Sp	A	R	M		♦		
Althaea officinalis	4–7 ft (1.2–2 m)	4 ft (1.2 m)	P	C/W		♦	W/Sp	Su/A	M	M	♦	♦		
Amaranthus cruentus	36–60 in (90–150 cm)	30 in (75 cm)	A	W	♦		Sp	Su/A	L	M		♦	♦	
Amorphophallus konjac	36–50 in (90–130 cm)	7 ft (2 m)	P	W/T	♦		Sp	A	R	M				♦
Anethum graveolens	24–32 in (60–80 cm)	12–20 in (30–50 cm)	A	C/W		♦	Sp	Su/A	Fr	M	♦	♦	♦	
Angelica archangelica	6 ft (1.8 m)	5 ft (1.5 m)	P	C		♦	Sp	Su/A	Fr/S	M	♦	♦	♦	
Anthriscus cerefolium	20–24 in (50–60 cm)	10–12 in (25–30 cm)	A	C/W		♦	Sp/Su	Su/A	L	M			♦	♦

Plant name	Height	Spread	Type	Climate	Vegetable	Herb	Planting season	Harvest season	Part eaten	Soil type	Frost tolerant	Full sun	Half sun	Heavy shade
Apium graveolens	24–36 in (60–90 cm)	12–18 in (30–45 cm)	P	C	◆		Sp	Su/A	S	M	◆	◆		
Arachis hypogaea	8–12 in (20–30 cm)	24–36 in (60–90 cm)	A	W/T	◆		Sp	Su/A	Fr	S	◆	◆		
Aralia cordata	8 ft (2.4 m)	8 ft (2.4 m)	P	C/W	◆		W/Sp	Sp	S	M	◆	◆	◆	
Arctium lappa	5–7 ft (1.5–2 m)	4 ft (1.2 m)	A	C/W	◆	◆	Sp	Su/A	S/L	M	◆	◆		
Armoracia rusticana	3 ft (0.9 m)	3–5 ft (0.9–1.5)	P	C		◆	W/Sp	Sp/A	R	M	◆		◆	
Artemisia absinthium	36 in (90 cm)	36 in (90 cm)	S	C/W		◆	W/Sp	Sp/A	M	M	◆	◆		
Artemisia dracunculus	2–5 ft (0.6–1.5 m)	3 ft (0.9 m)	P	C		◆	W/Sp	Sp/A	L	M	◆	◆		
Artemisia vulgaris	5–8 ft (1.5–2.4 m)	4 ft (1.2 m)	P	C/W		◆	W/Sp	Sp/A	M	M	◆	◆		
Asparagus officinalis	3–5 ft (0.9–1.5)	3–5 ft (0.9–1.5)	P	C	◆		W	Sp	S	M	◆	◆		
Ballota nigra	16–40 in (40–100 cm)	24–60 in (60–150 cm)	P	C/W		◆	W/Sp	Sp/A	M	M	◆			◆
Bergera koenigii	15 ft (4.5 m)	12 ft (3.5 m)	S	W/T		◆	Any	Any	L/Fl	M		◆		
Beta vulgaris	27 in (70 cm)	27 in (70 cm)	A	C/W	◆		Sp/A	Su/W	L	M	◆	◆		
Borago officinalis	20–24 in (50–60 cm)	12–36 in (30–90 cm)	A	C/W		◆	Sp/Su	Su/A	L	M	◆	◆		
Brassica juncea	8–40 in (20–100 cm)	8–40 in (20–100 cm)	A	C/W	◆		Sp/Su	Su/A	L/Fr	M	◆			
Brassica napus	8–16 in (20–40 cm)	8–16 in (20–40 cm)	A	C/W	◆		Su/A	A/W	R	M	◆	◆		
Brassica oleracea	16 in (40 cm)	12 in (30 cm)	A	C/W	◆		Any	Any	L/Fl	M	◆	◆		
Brassica rapa	12–20 in (30–50 cm)	12–20 in (30–50 cm)	A	C/W	◆		Sp/Su	Su/A	L/R	M	◆	◆		
Campanula rapunculus	24–36 in (60–90 cm)	24 in (60 cm)	A	C	◆		Sp/Su	Su/W	L/R	M	◆	◆		
Capsicum annuum	8 in–5 ft (20 cm–1.5 m)	8–20 in (20–50 cm)	A	C/W	◆		Sp/Su	Su/A	Fr	M		◆		
Capsicum chinense	8 in–5 ft (20 cm–1.5 m)	8–20 in (20–50 cm)	A	W/T	◆		Sp/Su	Su/A	Fr	M		◆		
Capsicum frutescens	8 in–5 ft (20 cm–1.5 m)	8–20 in (20–50 cm)	A	W/T	◆		Sp/Su	Su/A	Fr	M		◆		
Carum carvi	24 in (60 cm)	12–18 in (30–45 cm)	P	C/W		◆	Sp/Su	Su/A	Fr	M	◆	◆		
Centella asiatica	2–12 in (5–30 cm)	12–36 in (30–90 cm)	P	W/T	◆	◆	Sp/Su	Su/A	L	M		◆		◆
Chamaemelum nobile	4–12 in (10–30 cm)	12 in (30 cm)	P	C/W		◆	Sp/Su	Su/A	L/Fl	M	◆	◆		
Chenopodium bonus-henricus	24 in (60 cm)	24 in (60 cm)	P	C/W	◆		Sp/Su	Su/A	L	M	◆			
Chenopodium quinoa	6 ft (1.8 m)	2 ft (0.6 m)	A	C/W	◆		Sp/Su	Su/A	S/Fr	M	◆	◆		
Cicer arietinum	8 in–3 ft (20 cm–0.9 m)	10–20 in (25–50 cm)	A	C/W	◆		Sp/Su	Su/A	Fr	M	◆	◆		
Cichorium endivia	8–20 in (20–50 cm)	8–20 in (20–50 cm)	A	C/W	◆		Sp/Su	Su/A	L	M		◆		
Cichorium intybus	20–48 in (50–120 cm)	24 in (60 cm)	P	C/W	◆		Sp/Su	Su/A	R/S/L	M		◆		
Colocasia esculenta	3–6 ft (0.9–1.8)	3–6 ft (0.9–1.8)	P	W/T	◆		Any	Any	R	M	◆	◆		
Coriandrum sativum	18–24 in (45–60 cm)	18–24 in (45–60 cm)	A	C		◆	Sp/Su	Su/A	L/S	M	◆	◆		
Crocus sativus	2 in (5 cm)	4 in (10 cm)	P	C		◆	W/Sp	A	Fl	M	◆	◆		
Cryptotaenia canadensis	3 ft (0.9 m)	20–27 in (50–70 cm)	A	C	◆	◆	Sp/Su	Su/A	L/S/R	M	◆			◆

Plant name	Height	Spread	Type	Climate	Vegetable	Herb	Planting season	Harvest season	Part eaten	Soil type	Frost tolerant	Full sun	Half sun	Heavy shade
Cucumis anguria	20 in (50 cm)	7–10 ft (2–3 m)	A	W/T	◆		Sp/Su	Su/A	Fr	M		◆		
Cucumis sativus	8–20 in (20–50 cm)	3–10 ft (0.9–3 m)	A	W/T	◆		Sp/Su	Su/A	Fr	M		◆		
Cucurbita maxima	12–20 (30–50 cm)	3–10 ft (0.9–3 m)	A	C/T	◆		Sp/Su	Su/A	Fr	M	◆	◆		
Cucurbita moschata	12–20 in (30–50 cm)	3–10 ft (0.9–3 m)	A	C/T	◆		Sp/Su	Su/A	Fr	M	◆	◆		
Cucurbita pepo	12–20 in (30–50 cm)	3–10 ft (0.9–3 m)	A	C/T	◆		Sp/Su	Su/A	Fr/Fl/L	M	◆	◆		
Cuminum cyminum	12 in (30 cm)	12 in (30 cm)	A	C/T		◆	Sp/Su	Su/A	Fr	M		◆		
Curcuma longa	3 ft (0.9 m)	30 in (75 cm)	P	W/T		◆	W/Sp	Su/A	R	M		◆	◆	
Cymbopogon citratus	3–5 ft (0.9–1.5 m)	1 ft (0.3 m)	P	W		◆	Sp/Su	Su/A	L	M		◆		
Cynara cardunculus	4–8 ft (1.2–2.4 m)	4–8 ft (1.2–2.4 m)	P	C/W	◆		W/Sp	Su/A	S/Fl	M	◆	◆		
Daucus carota	40 in (100 cm)	20 in (50 cm)	A	C	◆		Su	A/W	R	M	◆	◆		
Dioscorea alata	10 ft (3 m)	6 ft (1.8 m)	C	W/T	◆		Sp/Su	A/W	R	M		◆	◆	
Dioscorea batatas	10 ft (3 m)	6 ft (1.8 m)	C	C/T	◆		Sp/Su	A/W	R	M		◆	◆	
Dioscorea bulbifera	6–12 ft (1.8–3.5 m)	10 ft (3 m)	C	W/T	◆		Sp/Su	A/W	R	M		◆	◆	
Dioscorea esculenta	4–8 ft (1.2–2.4 m)	6 ft (1.8 m)	C	W/T	◆		Sp/Su	A/W	R	M		◆	◆	
Echinacea purpurea	60 in (150 cm)	40 in (100 cm)	P	C/W		◆	W/Sp	Su/A	M	M	◆	◆		
Elettaria cardamomum	5–8 ft (1.5–2.4 m)	5–8 ft (1.5–2.4 m)	P	W/T		◆	W/Sp	Su/A	R	M			◆	◆
Eruca vesicaria	16–40 in (40–100 cm)	12–24 in (30–60 cm)	A	C/W	◆		Sp/Su	Sp/A	L		◆	◆		
Foeniculum vulgare	3–7 ft (0.9–2 m)	18–36 in (45–90 cm)	P	C/W	◆	◆	W/Sp	Sp/A	R/L	M	◆	◆		
Glycine max	4–7 ft (1.2–2 m)	3 ft (0.9 m)	A	C/W	◆		Sp/Su	Su/A	Fr	M	◆	◆		
Glycyrrhiza glabra	36 in (90 cm)	36 in (90 cm)	P	C/W		◆	Sp/Su	Su/A	R	M	◆	◆		
Helianthus tuberosus	10 ft (3 m)	5 ft (1.5 m)	P	C	◆		Sp/Su	Su/A	R	M	◆	◆		
Helichrysum italicum	16 in (40 cm)	20 in (50 cm)	P	C/W		◆	W/Sp	Sp/A	M	S		◆		
Hyssopus officinalis	18–24 in (45–60 cm)	12 in (30 cm)	P	C/W		◆	W/Sp	Sp/A	M	M		◆		
Illicium verum	60 ft (18 m)	20 ft (6 m)	S	W		◆	Any	Su/A	Fr	M		◆		◆
Ipomoea batatas	10 ft (3 m)	10 ft (3 m)	A	W/T	◆		Sp	Su/A	R	M		◆		
Lablab purpureus	12–20 ft (3.5–6 m)	5–10 ft (1.5–3 m)	C	W/T	◆		Sp	Su/A	Fr	M		◆		
Lactuca sativa	4–12 in (10–30 cm)	4–12 in (10–30 cm)	A	C/W	◆		Sp	Su/A	L	M	◆	◆		
Lagenaria siceraria	10–30 ft (3–9 m)	10–20 ft (3–6 m)	C	W/T	◆		Sp	Su/A	Fr	M		◆		
Laurus nobilis	10–50 ft (3–15 m)	6–15 ft (1.8–4.5 m)	S	C/W		◆	Any	Any	L	M	◆	◆		
Lens culinaris	12–18 in (30–45 cm)	24 in (60 cm)	A	C/W	◆		Sp	Su/A	Fr	S		◆		
Leonurus cardiaca	24–36 in (60–90 cm)	12 in (30 cm)	P	C/W		◆	Sp	Su/A	L/S	M	◆	◆		
Levisticum officinale	7 ft (2 m)	40 in (100 cm)	P	C/W		◆	W/Sp	Sp/A	L/Fr	M	◆	◆	◆	
Lycium barbarum	10 ft (3 m)	15 ft (4.5 m)	S	C/W	◆		Any	Su/A	Fr	M	◆	◆		

Plant name	Height	Spread	Type	Climate	Vegetable	Herb	Planting season	Harvest season	Part eaten	Soil type	Frost tolerant	Full sun	Half sun	Heavy shade
Lycopersicon esculentum	2–8 ft (0.6–2.4 m)	12–24 in (30–60 cm)	A	W/T	◆		Sp/Su	Su/A	Fr	M		◆		
Lycopersicon Hybrid Cultivars	2–8 ft (0.6–2.4 m)	12–24 in (30–60 cm)	A	W/T	◆		Sp/Su	Su/A	Fr	M		◆		
Manihot esculenta	12 ft (3.5 m)	3 ft (0.9 m)	S	W/T	◆		Sp/Su	Su/A	R	M		◆		
Maranta arundinacea	4–6 ft (1.2–1.8 m)	24–40 in (60–100 cm)	P	T		◆	Sp/Su	Su/A	R	M		◆		
Marrubium vulgare	20 in (50 cm)	20 in (50 cm)	P	C/W		◆	W/Sp	Sp/A	M	M	◆	◆		
Matricaria recutita	6–20 in (15–50 cm)	6–20 in (15–50 cm)	A	C/W		◆	Sp	Sp/A	M	M	◆	◆		
Medicago sativa	32–40 in (80–100 cm)	32–40 in (80–100 cm)	A	C	◆		Sp/A	Sp/A	Fr	M	◆	◆		
Melissa officinalis	24–36 in (60–90 cm)	18 in (45 cm)	P	C		◆	Any	Sp/A	L	M	◆	◆	◆	
Mentha aquatica	3 ft (0.9 m)	3–7 ft (0.9–2 m)	P	C		◆	Any	Sp/A	L	A	◆	◆		
Mentha longifolia	4 ft (1.2 m)	3–6 ft (0.9–1.8 m)	P	C/W		◆	Any	Sp/A	L	M	◆	◆		
Mentha × piperita	24–36 in (60–90 cm)	36 in (90 cm)	P	C		◆	Any	Sp/A	L	M	◆	◆		
Mentha spicata	4 ft (1.2 m)	3–6 ft (0.9–1.8 m)	P	C/W		◆	Any	Sp/A	L	M	◆	◆		
Mentha suaveolens	36 in (90 cm)	36 in (90 cm)	P	C/W		◆	Any	Sp/A	L	M	◆	◆		
Myrrhis odorata	5–7 ft (1.5–2 m)	4–5 ft (1.2–1.5 m)	P	C/W		◆	Any	Sp/A	L	M	◆	◆		◆
Nepeta cataria	40 in (100 cm)	40 in (100 cm)	P	C/W		◆	Any	Sp/A	M	M	◆	◆	◆	
Nicotiana tabacum	3–5 ft (0.9–1.5 m)	18–24 in (45–60 cm)	A	W		◆	Sp/Su	Su/A	L	M		◆	◆	
Ocimum basilicum	12–24 in (30–60 cm)	12 in (30 cm)	A	W/T		◆	Sp/Su	Sp/A	L	M		◆		
Ocimum tenuiflorum	36 in (90 cm)	24 in (60 cm)	S	W/T		◆	Sp/Su	Sp/A	L	M		◆		
Oenanthe javanica	12–16 in (30–40 cm)	12–16 in (30–40 cm)	P	W/T	◆		Sp/Su	Sp/A	L/	C		◆	◆	
Origanum dictamnus	8–12 in (20–30 cm)	8–12 in (20–30 cm)	S	C/W		◆	Sp/Su	Sp/A	L	S	◆	◆		
Origanum majorana	24 in (60 cm)	18 in (45 cm)	P	C/W		◆	W/Sp	Sp/A	L	M	◆	◆		
Origanum onites	24 in (60 cm)	24 in (60 cm)	P	W		◆	Sp/Su	Sp/A	L	M	◆	◆		
Origanum vulgare	12–18 in (30–45 cm)	12 in (30 cm)	P	C		◆	W/Sp	Sp/A	L	M	◆	◆		
Oryza sativa	2–4 ft (0.6–1.2 m)	12–24 in (30–60 cm)	A	W/T	◆		Sp/Su	Sp/A	Fr	A		◆		
Oxalis tuberosa	10–12 in (25–30 cm)	6–8 in (15–20 cm)	A	C/W	◆		Sp/Su	Sp/A	R	M		◆		
Pachyrhizus erosus	10–20 ft (3–6 m)	3–6 ft (0.9–1.8 m)	C	W	◆		Sp/Su	Sp/A	R	S		◆		
Panax ginseng	6–8 in (15–20 cm)	8–12 in (20–30 cm)	P	C/W		◆	Sp	Su/A	M	M	◆			◆
Pastinaca sativa	3–5 ft (0.9–1.5 m)	18–24 in (45–60 cm)	A	C		◆	Sp/Su	A/W	R	M	◆	◆		
Persicaria odorata	6–18 in (15–45 cm)	6–18 in (15–45 cm)	A	W/T		◆	Sp/Su	Sp/A	L	C		◆		
Petroselinum crispum	12–36 in (30–90 cm)	9–36 in (22–90 cm)	A	C		◆	Sp/Su	Sp/A	L	M	◆	◆		
Phaseolus acutifolius	18–40 in (45–100 cm)	12–24 in (30–60 cm)	A	W	◆		Sp/Su	Su/A	Fr	M		◆	◆	
Phaseolus coccineus	4–6 ft (1.2–1.8 m)	24 in (60 cm)	A	C/W	◆		Sp/Su	Su/A	Fr	M		◆		
Phaseolus lunatus	24–36 in (60–90 cm)	9–12 in (22–30 cm)	A	W	◆		Su	A/W	Fr	M		◆	◆	

Plant name	Height	Spread	Type	Climate	Vegetable	Herb	Planting season	Harvest season	Part eaten	Soil type	Frost tolerant	Full sun	Half sun	Heavy shade
Phaseolus vulgaris	3–10 ft (0.9–3 m)	6–9 in (15–22 cm)	A	C/W	◆		Sp/Su	Su/A	Fr	M		◆		
Pimpinella anisum	20–24 in (50–60 cm)	16–20 (40–50 cm)	A	C		◆	Sp/Su	Su/A	Fr	M	◆	◆		
Pisum sativum	5–6 ft (1.5–1.8 m)	2 ft (0.6 m)	A	C	◆		Sp/Su	Su/A	Fr	M		◆		
Portulaca oleracea	40 in (100 cm)	20 in (50 cm)	A	C/W	◆		Sp/Su	Su/A	L	M	◆	◆		
Raphanus sativus	2–5 ft (0.6–1.5 m)	12–24 (30–60 cm)	A	C	◆		Sp/Su	Su/A	R	M	◆	◆		
Rheum × hybridum	3 ft (0.9 m)	3–6 ft (0.9–1.8 m)	P	C/W	◆		W	Sp/A	S	M	◆	◆		
Rorippa nasturtium-aquaticum	6–12 in (15–30 cm)	2–7 ft (0.6–2 m)	P	C/W	◆		Any	Sp/A	L	A		◆	◆	
Rosmarinus officinalis	7 ft (2 m)	6 ft (1.8 m)	S	C/W		◆	Any	Any	L	M	◆	◆		
Rumex acetosa	20–40 in (50–100 cm)	12–16 in (30–40 cm)	P	C/W	◆		W/Sp	Sp/A	L	M	◆	◆		
Rumex scutatus	16–18 in (40–45 cm)	12–16 in (30–40 cm)	P	C/W		◆	W/Sp	Sp/A	Fr	M	◆	◆		
Ruta graveolens	20 in (50 cm)	15 in (38 cm)	S	C		◆	Any		M	M	◆	◆		
Saccharum officinarum	12–20 ft (3.5–6 m)	3–6 ft (0.9–1.8 m)	P	W/T	◆		W/Sp	Su/A	S	M		◆		
Sagittaria sagittifolia	24–36 in (60–90 cm)	12 in (30 cm)	P	C/W/T	◆		W/Sp	Su/A	R	A		◆	◆	
Salvia officinalis	30 in (75 cm)	36 in (90 cm)	P	C/W		◆	Sp	Sp/A	L	M	◆	◆		
Salvia sclarea	36–48 in (90–120 cm)	36 in (90 cm)	P	C		◆	W/Sp	Sp/A	M	M	◆	◆		
Sanguisorba minor	30 in (75 cm)	12–16 in (30–40 cm)	P	C	◆	◆	W/Sp	Sp/A	L/M	M	◆	◆	◆	◆
Sanguisorba officinalis	30–36 in (75–90 cm)	24–36 in (60–90 cm)	P	C	◆		W/Sp	Sp/A	M	M	◆	◆		
Satureja hortensis	8 in (20 cm)	8 in (20 cm)	A	C		◆	Sp	Sp/A	L	M	◆	◆		
Satureja montana	20–36 in (50–90 cm)	12 in (30 cm)	S	C		◆	W/Sp	Sp/A	L	M	◆	◆		
Sechium edule	10 ft (3 m)	10–20 ft (3–6 m)	C	W/T	◆		Sp	Su/A	Fr	M		◆	◆	
Sesamum orientale	2–6 ft (0.6–1.8 m)	1–2 ft (0.3–0.6 m)	A	W/T		◆	Sp	Su/A	Fr	M		◆		
Smyrnium olusatrum	3–5 ft (0.9–1.5 m)	18–36 in (45–90 cm)	A	C/W	◆			Su/A	L/R/S	M		◆		
Solanum melongena	36 in (90 cm)	24 in (60 cm)	A	W/T	◆		Sp	Su/A	Fr	M		◆		
Solanum tuberosum	18–24 in (45–60 cm)	18 in (45 cm)	A	C/W	◆		Sp	Su/A	R	M		◆		
Sorghum bicolor	10–20 ft (3–6 m)	2–3 ft (0.6–0.9 m)	A	W/T	◆		Sp	Su/A	Fr	M		◆		
Spinacia oleracea	24–36 in (60–90 cm)	12–18 in (30–45 cm)	A	C	◆		W/Sp	Sp/A	L	M	◆	◆	◆	
Stachys affinis	20 in (50 cm)	36 cm (90 cm)	P	C	◆		Sp	Su/A	R	M		◆		
Symphytum officinale	5 ft (1.5 m)	6 ft (1.8 m)	P	C/W		◆	W/Sp	Sp/A	M	M		◆	◆	
Symphytum × uplandicum	6 ft (1.8 m)	4 ft (1.2 m)	P	C/W		◆	W/Sp	Sp/A	M	M		◆	◆	
Syzygium aromaticum	50 ft (15 m)	15 ft (4.5 m)	S	W/T		◆	W/Sp	Su/A	Fl	M		◆		
Tanacetum cinerariifolium	12–24 in (30–60 cm)	12 in (30 cm)	P	C/W		◆	W/Sp	Sp/A	M	S	◆	◆		
Tanacetum parthenium	24 in (60 cm)	12 in (30 cm)	P	C		◆	W/Sp	Sp/A	M	S	◆	◆	◆	
Tanacetum vulgare	36–48 in (90–120 cm)	36–48 in (90–120 cm)	P	C		◆	W/Sp	Sp/A	M	S	◆	◆	◆	

Plant name	Height	Spread	Type	Climate	Vegetable	Herb	Planting season	Harvest season	Part eaten	Soil type	Frost tolerant	Full sun	Half sun	Heavy shade
Taraxacum officinale	10–12 in (25–30 cm)	8 in (20 cm)	A	C/W	◆		Sp	Sp/A	L	M	◆	◆		
Tetragonia tetragonioides	8–12 in (20–30 cm)	24–40 in (60–100 cm)	A	C/W	◆		Sp	Sp/A	L	M	◆		◆	
Thymus serpyllum	1–4 in (2.5–10 cm)	36 in (90 cm)	S	C/W		◆	W/Sp	Sp/A	L	M	◆	◆		
Thymus vulgaris	12 in (30 cm)	10 in (25 cm)	S	C/W		◆	W/Sp	Sp/A	L	M	◆	◆		
Tragopogon porrifolius	24–36 in (60–90 cm)	6–12 in (15–30 cm)	A	C	◆		Sp	A	R	M	◆	◆		
Trapa natans	3–5 ft (0.9–1.5 m)	2–4 ft (0.6–1.2 m)	P	C	◆		Sp	Su/A	Fr	A	◆	◆		
Trichosanthes cucumerina	8–20 ft (2.4–6 m)	5–10 ft (1.5–3 m)	A	W/T	◆		Sp	Su/A	Fr/R	M		◆		
Trigonella foenum-graecum	12–24 in (30–60 cm)	8–12 in (20–30 cm)	A	W		◆	Sp	Su/A	Fr/M	M		◆		
Triticum aestivum	3–5 ft (0.9–1.5 m)	12–20 in (30–50 cm)	A	W	◆		W/Sp	Su/A	Fr	M		◆		
Triticum durum	3–5 ft (0.9–1.5 m)	12–20 in (30–50 cm)	A	W	◆		W/Sp	Su/A	Fr	M		◆		
Tropaeolum majus	10 ft (3 m)	10 ft (3 m)	C	W	◆		Sp	Su/W	R	M	◆	◆	◆	
Tropaeolum tuberosum	10 ft (3 m)	10 ft (3 m)	C	W	◆		Sp	Su/W	R	M	◆	◆	◆	
Urtica dioica	2–8 ft (0.6–2.4 m)	3–6 ft (0.9–1.8 m)	P	C	◆		W/Sp	Sp/A	L	M	◆	◆		
Valeriana officinalis	4–6 ft (1.2–1.8 m)	16–32 in (40–80 cm)	P	C/W		◆	W/Sp	Su/A	M	M	◆	◆		
Valerianella locusta	4–12 in (10–30 cm)	6–8 in (15–20 cm)	A	C/W	◆		Sp	Su/A	L	M	◆	◆		
Vicia faba	3–6 ft (0.9–1.8 m)	12 in (30 cm)	A	C/W	◆		A/W	Sp/Su	Fr	M	◆	◆		
Vigna mungo	12–24 in (30–60 cm)	24–36 in (60–90 cm)	A	W/T	◆		Sp	Su/A	Fr	M		◆		
Vigna radiata	5–6 ft (1.5–1.8 m)	8–12 in (20–30 cm)	A	W/T	◆		Sp	Su/A	Fr	M		◆		
Xanthophthalmum coronarium	18–30 in (45–75 cm)	12–24 in (30–60 cm)	A	W	◆		Sp	Su/A	L	M	◆	◆		
Zea mays	7–15 ft (2–4.5 m)	24–40 in (60–100 cm)	A	C/W	◆		Sp	Su/A	Fr	M	◆	◆		
Zingiber officinale	3–5 ft (0.9–1.5 m)	3 ft (0.9 m)	P	W/T		◆	W/Sp	A/W	R	M				◆

Allium cepa

ABELMOSCHUS *(see page 394)*

Abelmoschus esculentus

GUMBO, LADY'S FINGER, OKRA

☼ ❋ ↔ 18–24 in (45–60 cm) ↕ 30–48 in (75–120 cm)

Widely naturalized tropical annual, grown extensively as vegetable. Serrated leaves, 5 to 7 lobes. Solitary flowers, white or yellow marked with red or purple toward base. Fleshy pod-like fruit, green or red skin. Needs long frost-free season to produce fruit. 'Cajun Delight', heavy-cropping early-fruiting variety. Zones 7–9.

AGRIMONIA

AGRIMONY, COCKLEBUR, STICKLEWORT

Found throughout northern temperate zones, this rose (Rosaceae) family genus has 15 species of summer-flowering herbaceous perennials. They form clumps of strongly upright stems bearing irregularly pinnate, faintly aromatic leaves with coarsely toothed leaflets. Minute yet showy yellow flowers are massed in plume-like racemes. Burr-bearing seed heads follow. Agrimony has astringent and diuretic properties, and has long been used in herbal medicines, mainly as an infusion. It is also the source of a yellow dye. CULTIVATION: Easily grown in any temperate climate, they are not fussy about soil type if it's well-drained and doesn't dry out in summer. They may self-sow in situ but the seed does not germinate well in cultivation and is prone to damping off. Propagate by division.

Agrimonia eupatoria

Agrimonia eupatoria

HEMP AGRIMONY

☼/◑ ❋ ↔ 20–40 in (50–100 cm) ↕ 24–48 in (60–120 cm)

Found from Britain to Iran and North Africa. Leaves to 8 in (20 cm) long, with up to 14 pairs of leaflets with bristly undersides. Open flowerheads to 15 in (38 cm) long. Zones 6–10.

ALLIUM *(see page 627)*

Allium ampeloprasum

KURRANT, LEVANT GARLIC, WILD LEEK

☼ ❋ ↔ 12–24 in (30–60 cm) ↕ 2–6 ft (0.6–1.8 m)

Occurs in various forms from Ireland and southern England to Iran and North Africa. Flat, rough-edged, gray-green leaves to 20 in (50 cm) long, 4 to 10 per bulb. Spherical heads of hundreds of pink to red flowers, initially enclosed by papery bracts. **Porrum Group** (syn. *A. porrum*) comprises leeks. 'Colossal' and 'Unique', long-stemmed, quick-maturing cultivars. Zones 6–9.

Allium cepa

ONION, SCALLION, SPRING ONION

☼ ❋ ↔ 4–8 in (10–20 cm) ↕ 12–24 in (30–60 cm)

Biennial bulb, appears to be true species but is not known in wild. Cultivated widely as vegetable. Blue-green, flattened, cylindrical leaves to 16 in (40 cm) long, up to 10 per bulb. In summer, strong, tall, sometimes bulbil-bearing flower stems with heads of green-veined white flowers. Many cultivars in 3 groups. **Aggregatum Group** (scallions, spring onions) produces clustered bulbs, with no bulbil on flowerhead. **Cepa Group** (brown, white, and red onions) has single bulbs, with no bulbils on flower stem: 'Aristocrat', relatively large bulbs; 'Kelsae', large, soft onions; 'Kelsae Giant', very large bulbs; 'Red Baron', large, red-skinned, near-spherical onions; 'Tough Ball', round medium-sized bulbs that keep well; 'Paris Silver Skin', small onion often used for pickling; and 'Superstar', especially heavy-cropping. **Proliferum Group** produces single bulbs and clusters of bulbils around flowerhead. Zones 5–10.

Allium fistulosum

JAPANESE BUNCHING ONION, JAPANESE LEEK, WELSH ONION

☼ ❋ ↔ 8–12 in (20–30 cm) ↕ 20–24 in (50–60 cm)

Unknown in wild. Hollow leaves to 12 in (30 cm) long, 2 to 6 per bulb. In summer, small heads of green flowers on tall stems, sometimes forming bulbils. Zones 5–9.

Allium sativum

GARLIC

☼ ❋ ↔ 12–16 in (30–40 cm) ↕ 12–32 in (30–80 cm)

Strongly aromatic bulbs widely cultivated for culinary use; unknown in wild. Narrow blue-green leaves to 24 in (60 cm) long, often shorter. Flowers sporadically with few white to pale pink flowers. Zones 8–10.

Allium schoenoprasum

CHIVES

☼/◑ ❋ ↔ 4–12 in (10–30 cm) ↕ 6–20 in (15–50 cm)

Widespread in northern temperate zones. Fine, grassy, hollow, aromatic foliage. Rounded heads of small, pink, bell-shaped flowers in summer. 'Black Isle Blush', up to 12 in (30 cm) tall, mauve flowers; 'Forescate', to 20 in (50 cm) tall, gray-green leaves, deep purple-pink flowers; 'Pink Perfection', up to 12 in (30 cm) tall, many heads of bright pink flowers; and 'Silver Chimes', gray-green foliage and white flowers. Zones 5–10.

Allium tuberosum ★

CHINESE CHIVES, GARLIC CHIVES

☼/◐ ❄ ↔8–12 in (20–30 cm) ↑20 in (50 cm)

Southeast Asian species cultivated for garlic-flavored, narrow, grassy, angled stems, used as vegetable and in salads. Blue-green leaves to 12 in (30 cm) long, 4 to 9 per bulb. In late summer, scented white flowers in small heads on long stems. Zones 7–10.

ALOE (see page 808)

Aloe vera ★

syn. *Aloe barbadensis*

☼/◐ ❁ ↔24–48 in (60–120 cm) ↑32 in (80 cm)

Believed to be originally native to southern Arabia or nearby parts of Africa; naturalized in Mediterranean and tropical Africa. Forms clumps of stemless or suckering rosettes of light-spotted, narrow, fleshy, dark green leaves to 12 in (30 cm) long. Yellow 1¼ in (30 mm) long flowers on few-branched inflorescences in summer. Valued for its sap's medicinal properties. Zones 10–12.

ALOYSIA

Mostly from South America in subtropical and temperate climates, this genus of tender shrubs and perennials belongs in the vervain (Verbenaceae) family. All species contain volatile oils in their foliage, with fragrances resembling citrus, lavender, camphor, and mint, used in perfumery and traditional medicine. Small flowers cluster at branch ends (on current season's wood).
CULTIVATION: They prefer well-drained loam and summer rainfall or irrigation. They tolerate only light frosts so need a sheltered spot. Trim straggly growth to encourage new wood and maintain foliage density. Propagate from cuttings which strike in summer.

Aloysia citriodora

syn. *Aloysia triphylla*

LEMON-SCENTED VERBENA

☼ ❄ ↔10 ft (3 m) ↑10 ft (3 m)

From Argentina, Uruguay, and Chile. Semi-deciduous shrub. Lemon-scented foliage, rough-textured leaves in whorls of 3, used for flavorings, herbal teas, and potpourri. Flowers very pale lavender to white, in summer–autumn. Zones 8–12.

ALPINIA (see page 402)

Alpinia galanga

GALANGAL, SIAMESE GINGER

☼/◐ ❁ ↔2–3 ft (0.6–0.9 m) ↑4–6 ft (1.2–1.8 m)

From southeastern Asia. Large leaves to 20 in (50 cm) long. In summer branching inflorescence bears flowers of pale green and white with pink markings. Fleshy rhizome used in cooking and eastern herbal remedies. Zones 9–11.

ALTHAEA

This genus is a member of the mallow (Malvaceae) family and contains 12 species of annual and perennial herbs native to western

Aloysia citriodora

Europe and central Asia. They grow in moist or marshy ground at low altitudes. Rounded leaves are lobed to varying degrees. The 5-petalled flowers are only 1½ in (35 mm) across and have prominent tubes of fused stamens. They are borne in racemes or panicles in summer.
CULTIVATION: Suited to "wild" gardens, grow them in rich moist soil in a sunny spot. Propagate by division or from seed in spring.

Althaea officinalis

MARSH MALLOW, WHITE MALLOW

☼ ❋ ↔4 ft (1.2 m) ↑4–7 ft (1.2–2 m)

From Europe, naturalized in eastern USA. Lax plant with hairy, grayish, 3- to 5-lobed leaves. Small flowers, pale pink or white with purplish red tubes of fused stamens. Zones 3–10.

AMARANTHUS

There are about 60 species of weedy annuals and short-lived perennials in this genus, which is a member of the amaranth (Amaranthaceae) family, with a worldwide distribution. Species range from tall to prostrate, with long, often drooping, tassels of small red or green flowers. Individual flowers, either male or female, may be borne on separate plants.
CULTIVATION: They prefer well-drained fertile soil and protection from wind. In cool areas sow seed under glass in spring, planting after frost has passed. In warm areas, sow seed outdoors in late spring.

Amaranthus cruentus

syn. *Amaranthus paniculatus*

PRINCE'S FEATHER, PURPLE AMARANTH, RED AMARANTH

☼ ❋ ↔30 in (75 cm) ↑36–60 in (90–150 cm)

Native to Americas. Oval to lance-shaped leaves. Greenish to red tassels, erect or drooping. Reddish brown to black seeds. '**Golden Giant**', golden seed heads. Zones 8–11.

Amaranthus cruentus

Angelica archangelica

AMORPHOPHALLUS *(see page 628)*

Amorphophallus konjac

syns *Amorphophallus rivieri, Hydrosme rivieri*

DEVIL'S TONGUE, SNAKE PALM, UMBRELLA ARUM

☀ ❄ ↔ 7 ft (2 m) ↕ 36–50 in (90–130 cm)

Occurs in southern and southeastern China and Vietnam in forest margins and open areas, to 10,000 ft (3,050 m) altitude. Produces tuber to 12 in (30 cm) wide. Leaf up to 3 ft (0.9 m) tall, dirty whitish pink, with dark green and whitish spots, dull green on upper surface. Inflorescence long-stalked. Spathe broadly triangular, to 24 in (60 cm) long, whitish purple to blackish purple with blackish green spots. Spadix 6–44 in (15–110 cm) long. Zones 10–12.

ANETHUM

DILL

A genus of 2 species of annual or biennial herbs of the carrot (Apiaceae) family, only *A. graveolens* is commonly cultivated and is used (foliage and seeds) as a garnish or flavoring. It is similar in appearance to its relative, fennel. Dill flowers attract butterflies and can be used in wildflower gardens. Dill is used medicinally for indigestion, flatulence, and colic.
CULTIVATION: They are easily grown in a sunny well-drained position that is not too dry in summer. Though plants can be raised from seed and then transplanted, it may be easier to prepare a patch of soil and cast seed over it, lightly raking it in afterward.

Anethum graveolens

☀/☀ ❄ ↔ 12–20 in (30–50 cm) ↕ 24–32 in (60–80 cm)

Strongly aromatic southwest Asian annual with long, finely divided, ferny leaves; individual leaflets almost hair-like. Summer-borne heads of tiny yellow flowers followed by well-known seeds. Zones 8–10.

ANGELICA

A genus of about 50 biennials and perennials (including monocarpic species) belonging to the carrot (Apiaceae) family, it occurs over much of the temperate Northern Hemisphere. Most are grown as ornamentals for their bold foliage, but others are cultivated for herbal uses. Large, often pinnate leaves, deeply divided, are sometimes glossy, and usually have toothed edges. Foliage grows from a stout rootstock. In summer, compound flowerheads (umbels) of tiny white, cream, green, pink, or red flowers appear.
CULTIVATION: Plant in deep humus-rich soil with ample moisture. They will grow well in full sun but foliage is usually lusher with some shade. True perennial species may be divided, but annual and monocarpic species are raised from seed, best very fresh.

Angelica archangelica

☀/☀ ❄ ↔ 5 ft (1.5 m) ↕ 6 ft (1.8 m)

Monocarpic perennial found from Greenland through Europe to central Asia. Bipinnate leaves to 24 in (60 cm) long. Greenish white to cream flowers. Young stems often candied. Zones 4–9.

ANTHRISCUS

This is a genus of about 12 species consisting of annuals, biennials, and herbaceous perennials from Europe, North Africa, and Asia, some of which have become weedy in other countries. They have soft feathery foliage and the flat heads of tiny white flowers typical of the carrot (Apiaceae) family. Some species have marginal ornamental value in the wild-type garden, but because of their self-sowing tendencies they need to be planted with discretion.
CULTIVATION: Any well-drained, moisture-retentive soil in sun or half-sun will suit. Propagate from fresh seed, usually self-sown.

Anthriscus cerefolium

CHERVIL

☀ ❄ ↔ 10–12 in (25–30 cm) ↕ 20–24 in (50–60 cm)

Annual plant from Europe and western Asia; grown as food flavoring, tends to bolt in hot dry weather. Sow seed every few weeks to ensure continuous crops; germinates in 2 to 3 weeks, ready to harvest in about 6 weeks. Zones 7–10.

APIUM

CELERIAC, CELERY

A member of the carrot (Apiaceae) family, this genus of 20 biennial plants with fleshy bulbous roots comes from Europe and temperate Asia. Leaves are pinnate, and white flowers appear in compound short-stalked or stalkless umbels.
CULTIVATION: These plants are frost tolerant and drought tender. Plant seedlings 10–12 in (25–30 cm) apart in light, moist, well-drained soil enriched with organic matter, in a protected sunny position. Propagate from seed.

Apium graveolens

Apium graveolens

CELERY, WILD CELERY

☀ ❄ ↔ 12–18 in (30–45 cm) ↕ 24–36 in (60–90 cm)

Strongly aromatic perennial from southern Europe. Whitish flowers, in compound umbels arranged in panicles, in summer–autumn. Fruits small, ribbed, elliptical to oval seeds. Leaf segments, ½–2 in (12–50 mm) long, lance-shaped, toothed or lobed, on thick, long, grooved stalks. *A. g.* var. *dulce* (celery), erect leaves with closely overlapping enlarged leaf stalks, popular garden vegetable; *A. g.* var. *rapaceum* (celeriac), grossly swollen taproot, shortened edible leaves; '**Brilliant**', early maturing; *A. g.* var. *secalinum* (leaf celery), strong-flavored fragrant leaves on thin rounded stalks, used in soups and stews. *A. g.* '**Tricolor**', glossy green leaves tinted bronze at first, edged with cream and a silver central stripe; Zones 5–10.

ARACHIS

The peanut or groundnut, valued as an oilseed as well as for its high-protein "nuts," is one member of this genus of the pea-flower subfamily of the legumes (Fabaceae), which includes about 75 species of annuals and perennials. All are native to South America, the largest number occurring in Peru, Bolivia, and adjacent parts of Brazil and Argentina. Low growing and many stemmed, they have pinnate leaves with few leaflets, and flowers arising from lower leaf axils. The seed pod is remarkable for the way it develops below the soil surface, thrust under by its elongating stalk. Peanuts have been cultivated since ancient times.
CULTIVATION: Peanuts can be grown in the tropics wherever plentiful moisture is available in the summer growing season, but adapt to cooler climates as long as summers are hot and sufficiently long. Sow seeds in rows into well-tilled soil (limed if acid) when soil temperature is 59°F (15°C) or above. Raw peanuts from health-food shops are a source of seed. Feed regularly and water as for green beans; lift plants and harvest nuts when foliage yellows.

Arachis hypogaea

GOOBER, GROUNDNUT, PEANUT
☼ ❄ ↔ 24–36 in (60–90 cm) ↕ 8–12 in (20–30 cm)
Possibly of ancient hybrid origin, peanut is annual with mass of soft spreading stems. Leaves each with 4 rounded leaflets. Small yellowish flowers in spring–summer are self-pollinating, soon developing into pods pushed deep into soil. Zones 8–12.

ARALIA *(see page 83)*

Aralia cordata

JAPANESE SPIKENARD, UDO
☼/◐ ❄ ↔ 8 ft (2.4 m) ↕ 8 ft (2.4 m)
Herbaceous perennial from Japan, Korea, and nearby parts of China. Huge compound leaves with rounded, finely toothed, 6 in (15 cm) long leaflets. Blanched young stems used as vegetable in Japan. Large panicles of cream flowers in summer; black fruit. Zones 8–10.

ARCTIUM

A small genus of 10 species in the daisy (Asteraceae) family, they are erect biennials with large leaves and flowerheads with hooks on them that cling to clothing or fur. Native to parts of Europe and Asia, these bold-looking plants are grown not as ornamentals, but as a vegetable or for medicinal purposes. The leaves are large at the base and reduce in size farther

up the stems, and at the top its mauve flowers hide in the green spiked heads. The stalks can be peeled and cooked and very young leaves can be used in salads.
CULTIVATION: Grow in a moist well-enriched soil in half-sun. Propagate from seed sown where it is to grow. They will self-sow.

Arctium lappa

GREAT BURDOCK
☼ ❄ ↔ 4 ft (1.2 m) ↕ 5–7 ft (1.5–2 m)
Native to most of Europe and garden escapee in many other places. Large basal leaves to 20 in (50 cm) long, gray-green with whitish reverse. Burred flowerheads green with mauve stamens just protruding. Zones 3–10.

ARMORACIA

HORSERADISH
A genus of 3 species of perennials of the cabbage (Brassicaceae) family, they have strong deep tap roots from which emerge variably sized leaves, the largest of which can be up to 3 ft (0.9 m) long. The panicles of small white flowers are not a feature, and rather than allowing them to go to seed they are usually removed to encourage stronger foliage growth. Roots are used to make horseradish sauce, while the foliage and roots have diuretic properties.
CULTIVATION: They will grow in any temperate climate. For best root production plant in moist humus-rich soil, but take care as roots can be invasive in loose soil. Propagate by division.

Armoracia rusticana

HORSERADISH, RED COLE
☼ ❄ ↔ 3–5 ft (0.9–1.5 m) ↕ 3 ft (0.9 m)
Vigorous southern European native. Toothed, somewhat puckered leaves to 20 in (50 cm) long, pronounced midrib. Strong, rather invasive rootstock. '**Variegata**', slightly smaller leaves variegated with bold white or cream splashes. Zones 5–9.

Armoracia rusticana

ARTEMISIA *(see page 413)*

Artemisia absinthium
ABSINTHE, COMMON WORMWOOD, OLD MAN

☼ ✳ ↔ 36 in (90 cm) ↕ 36 in (90 cm)

From temperate areas of Europe, Asia, and North America. Shrubby species with finely divided, silky, gray leaves. Aromatic. Insignificant tiny flowers in summer. 'Lambrook Mist', very finely divided silky leaves; 'Lambrook Silver' ★, more compact shrub. Zones 4–10.

Artemisia dracunculus
syns *Artemisia dracunculina, A. dracunculoides, A. glauca*
DRAGON SAGEWORT, TARRAGON

☼ ✳ ↔ 3 ft (0.9 m) ↕ 2–5 ft (0.6–1.5 m)

Wild forms of tarragon range from European Russia through Central Asia and across Pacific to western North America, extending down Rockies as far as northern Mexico. Erect herbaceous perennial spreading by rhizomes. Leaves narrow, pointed, dull green to somewhat bluish. Flowers in tiny brownish heads in summer. *A. d.* var. *inodora*, Russian tarragon, representative of wild forms, more vigorous grower but has little flavor. *A. d.* 'Sativa', French tarragon, clone selected for its intense aromatic flavor, renowned for uses as culinary herb; it must be propagated from cuttings or division. Zones 5–9.

Artemisia vulgaris
MUGWORT

☼ ✳ ↔ 4 ft (1.2 m) ↕ 5–8 ft (1.5–2.4 m)

Tufted perennial from Europe and northern Africa. Reddish stems, divided green leaves, downy beneath. Small reddish brown flowers in summer–autumn. Oriental Limelight/'Janlim', to 18 in (45 cm) high and wide, finely cut leaves variegated yellow and green. Zones 3–10.

ASPARAGUS *(see page 414)*

Asparagus officinalis
ASPARAGUS

☼ ✳ ↔ 3–5 ft (0.9–1.5 m) ↕ 3–5 ft (0.9–1.5 m)

Herbaceous perennial from Europe, Asia, and North Africa grown extensively as foodcrop. Erect multi-branched stems. Rich green, feathery, almost plume-like cladophylls. Small, drooping, greenish white axillary flowers. Bright red berries. 'Larac', French seed-raised variety noted for adaptability, white spears. Zones 4–10.

BALLOTA *(see page 420)*

Ballota nigra
BLACK HOREHOUND

☽ ✳ ↔ 24–60 in (60–150 cm) ↕ 16–40 in (40–100 cm)

Perennial found from southern Europe to North Africa and Iran. Unpleasantly aromatic. Green nettle-like leaves to 3 in (8 cm) long, hairy rather than felted. Mauve flowers in leaf axils. Used in herbal remedies to treat worms. Zones 7–10.

Artemisia absinthium

BERGERA

Belonging to the rue (Rutaceae family), this genus consists of a single species of evergreen shrub or small tree from tropical Asia, until recently accepted as part of the genus *Murraya*. It differs in its longer pinnate leaves, smaller flowers in larger corymbs, and dark bluish fruit. The leaves and flowers contain essential oils.
CULTIVATION: It is easily grown in frost-free, warm-temperate to tropical climates, in any moderately fertile, well-drained soil, in a protected position. Propagate from seed or half-hardened cuttings.

Bergera koenigii
syn. *Murraya koenigii*
CURRY LEAF, CURRY TREE

☼ ⚘ ↔ 12 ft (3.5 m) ↕ 15 ft (4.5 m)

Evergreen tree from Asia. Aromatic leaves; leaflets long pointed tips, finely serrated edges. Small, white or yellow-tinted, fragrant flowers, at branch tips, in spring. Berries blue-black. Zones 10–12.

BETA
BEET

A member of the goosefoot (Chenopodiaceae) family, this genus contains one biennial species with 2 main forms. One is grown for its roots (beets), the other for its leaves (chards). Wild forms are often found on the Mediterranean coastline, western Europe, and parts of Asia growing at the high-tide mark. The leaves are small and glossy to large and crinkly or puckered. The insignificant flowers are followed by knobbly seeds in profusion. The leaves of both forms are edible. The roots have been used as a food source for centuries.
CULTIVATION: Beets favor light well-drained soil, that is not too rich. Chards prefer rich moist soil. Grow from seed.

Beta vulgaris, Cicla Group, 'Rhubarb Chard'

Beta vulgaris
BEET

☼ ✳ ↔ 27 in (70 cm) ↕ 27 in (70 cm)

Original wild or sea beet (also classified as *B. v.* subsp. *maritima*) grows on seashores of Europe, North Africa, and western Asia.

All cultivated beets are believed to be derived from it, including beetroot, sugar beet, fodder beets such as mangel-wurzel, chard, and spinach beet. Once treated as falling within *B. v.* subsp. *vulgaris*, this is now regarded as inaccurate. They should be divided among the following cultivar groups:

Cicla Group (syn. *B. v.* var. *cicla, B. v.* var. *flavescens*): Includes spinach beets, but also chards or silver beets with larger leaves puckered to varying degrees, stalk and midrib broad, white or colored, root not swollen. **'Bright Lights'** ★ (syns 'Five Colour Mix', 'Rainbow'), stems in shades of red, orange, yellow, pink, and white, or bicolored; **'Bright Yellow'**, yellow stems, green crinkly leaves; **'Lucullus'**, huge, crinkly or puckered, glossy, green leaves, wide white midrib and veins; **'Mostruosa'**, broad, bright green, puckered leaves; **'Rhubarb Chard'** ★, crimson stalks and dark green crinkly leaves.

Conditiva Group (syn. *B. v.* var. *conditiva*): Includes the root vegetables as well as beetroot, sugar beet, fodder beet, mangel-wurzel, and mangold. Root (actually stem) is swollen, leaf stalk slender, blade flat. Most have red or yellow roots and leaf stalks. **'Bull's Blood'** (syn. *B. v.* var. *crassa*), dark red leaves, red midrib and veins; **'Forono'** ★, cylindrical purple beet. Zones 8–11.

BORAGO

BORAGE, TAILWORT

Part of the borage (Boraginaceae) family, this genus is made up of just 3 species of annuals or short-lived perennials from Europe that are usually used in the herb garden or wilder spots where their self-seeding tendencies won't be a problem. The leaves are rough to touch, and the summer flowers are usually a rich blue. The flowers and aromatic young leaves are edible.

CULTIVATION: Any moisture-retentive soil in sun or half-sun will suit. Propagate from self-sown seed that will need to be thinned out.

Borago officinalis

BORAGE

☼ ❄ ↔ 12–36 in (30–90 cm) ↕ 20–24 in (50–60 cm)

Vigorous, self-seeding, upright annual. Rough leaves to 10 in (25 cm) long. Large open heads of rich blue flowers in summer

Borago officinalis

to 1 in (25 mm) across. *B. o.* f. *alba*, white-flowered form, comes true from seed as long as it is not near blue forms. Zones 5–10.

BRASSICA

The cabbage and its relatives are in the family Brassicaceae. The genus contains around 30 species, and a large number of cultivars have been derived from a few of these. Wild species occur mainly in Europe and temperate Asia. They are annuals, biennials, and perennials, depending on climate and treatment. Brassicas are known for their leaves (cabbages, kale, Asian greens), flowering parts (broccoli, cauliflower, brussels sprouts), seeds (rape/canola), stems (kohlrabi), or roots (turnip, swede). Leaves are generally large and waxy with a whitish bloom; flowers are usually yellow, sometimes white.

CULTIVATION: Brassicas like well-drained moist soil that has been enriched with well-rotted manure. Those grown for their leaves like added nitrogen. Propagate from seed.

Brassica juncea

BROWN MUSTARD, CHINESE MUSTARD, KAI-TSOI

☼ ❀ ↔ 8–40 in (20–100 cm) ↕ 8–40 in (20–100 cm)

Annual species, native to southern and eastern Asia, grown as leaf vegetable and for mustard seed. Leaves green, red, or purple, smooth or puckered, smooth-edged or toothed. Racemes of light yellow flowers. **'Red Giant'** (syn. *B. j.* var. *rugosa*), cool-season annual, crinkled leaves in shades of green, purple, and maroon.

Japonica Group (syn. *B. j.* var. *multiceps*): Very hardy, usually growing throughout winter. Leaves used raw or cooked, salted, and pickled; **'Mizuna'** ★, with a peppery taste. Zones 9–11.

Brassica napus

OIL-SEED RAPE, RUTABAGA, SWEDE, SWEDISH TURNIP

☼ ❄ ↔ 8–16 in (20–40 cm) ↕ 8–16 in (20–40 cm)

First grown in Sweden. Grown for its storage roots. Other forms, such as rape and canola, grown for their oil-bearing seed.

Napobrassica Group: Swedes and rutabaga—hardier and less watery than turnips; yellowish roots and blue-gray leaves.

Pabularia Group: Siberian kale, rosetting brassica with smooth purple or white leaves. Zones 8–11.

Brassica napus, canola crop

Brassica oleracea

WILD CABBAGE

☼ ❄ ↔ 12 in (30 cm) ↕ 16 in (40 cm)

Western European annual or perennial. Woody stem with dense head of overlapping blue-green leaves. Differs from cultivated types in its coarsely lyrate or pinnate leaf shape.

Acephala Group: Non-heading brassicas, both ornamental and edible; '**Blue Ridge**' and '**Redbor**', edible kales; '**Red Peacock**' and '**White Peacock**', dwarf ornamental kales; '**Winterbor**' ★, vigorous edible kale, curled, thick, blue-green leaves.

Alboglabra Group (syn. *B. o.* var. *alboglabra*): Close relative of European (Calabrese) broccoli, this group produces several small succulent heads instead of one large head.

Botrytis Group (syn. *B. o.* var. *botrytis*): Cauliflower and broccoli, the heads range in color from white and cream to pink, lime green, and purple. '**Early Emerald**', blue-green with large, domed, tight head; '**Perfection**' ★, mini cauliflower.

Capitata Group (syn. *B. o.* var. *capitata*): Cabbage, many forms developed. **Alba Subgroup:** Several hundred cultivars; large cabbages with flat heavy head and white interior: '**Dynamo**', '**Primax**', '**Red Express**', and '**Ruby Ball**' ★. **Savoy Subgroup:** Features crinkled leaves and greenish hearts, including '**Early Curly**', '**Primavoy**' ★, '**Savoy Express**', and '**Savoy King**' ★.

Gemmifera Group (syn. *B. o.* var. *gemmifera*): Brussels sprouts, first recorded in Belgium about 1750, sprouts are compact leaf buds produced directly from the main stem.

Gongylodes Group (syn. *B. o.* var. *gongylodes*): Kohlrabi, fast-growing cabbage grown for its swollen stem. Available in white or purple; '**Kolibri**' ★, purple skin with sweet, crunchy white flesh.

Italica Group (syn. *B. o.*, Cymosa Group): Sprouting or Italian broccoli, it has many long-stalked heads of green to purplish buds, which mature in succession. Calabrese types exhibit a single head: '**Emperor**', '**Eureka**', and '**Shogun**'. Zones 8–11.

Brassica rapa

syn. *Brassica campestris*

TURNIP

☼ ❄ ↔ 12–20 in (30–50 cm) ↕ 12–20 in (30–50 cm)

Species from which modern turnip, oil-seed turnip-rape, and Chinese cabbage have developed. Leaves green, lobed, jagged edges. Roots yellow or white flesh; yellow, white, green, or purple skin.

Chinensis Group (syn. *B. chinensis*): Pak-choy or bok choy, prominent white or green stems, with bright green, glossy leaves.

Pekinensis Group (syn. *B. pekinensis*): Pe-tsai or won-bok, crisp dark or light green leaves often have creamy center, thick white midribs. Commonly used as salad vegetable.

Rapifera Group: Turnips, long and thin (purplish red and white) or small and round (white). '**Atlantic**' ★, early cropper with purple top, harvest when size of golf ball. Zones 9–11.

CAMPANULA (see page 428)

Campanula rapunculus

RAMPION

☼ ❄ ↔ 24 in (60 cm) ↕ 24–36 in (60–90 cm)

Biennial from Europe, northern Africa, and Siberia. Oval pointed leaves. Small pale blue or white bell-flowers, on leafy stems, in summer. Taproots and leaves used as salad vegetables. Zones 4–9.

CAPSICUM

PEPPER

This genus of 10 species of which 5, mainly *C. annuum*, are used by people, belongs to the nightshade (Solanaceae) family. Natives of Mexico and Central and South America, most capsicums are perennials but are treated as annuals and are grown for their fruit. There are two main types of capsicums—hot or chilli peppers, hot to taste, and sweet or bell peppers, which are not so hot. Some are grown as ornamentals. Small white, cream, or purple flowers are followed by their hollow fruits, which are full of seeds. They need a long hot summer to fruit well.

CULTIVATION: A well-drained moist soil in full sun is best, with fertilizer applied early in the growing season to bulk up plants. Ease this off as they begin to set fruit. Propagate from seed.

Capsicum annuum

BELL PEPPER, CHILLI PEPPER, PAPRIKA

☼ ❄ ↔ 8–20 in (20–50 cm) ↕ 8 in–5 ft (20 cm–1.5 m)

Annual or short-lived perennial. Lance-shaped to ovate leaves to 5 in (12 cm) long. Fruits in many shapes. Color usually green, matures to red. Cultivar groups based on size and shape of fruit.

Cerasiforme Group: Small, spherical, aromatic fruit. '**Cherry Bomb**', hot fruit; '**Guantanamo**', lime green, smooth skin.

Brassica oleracea, Acephala Group cultivar

Brassica oleracea, Botrytis Group, 'Perfection'

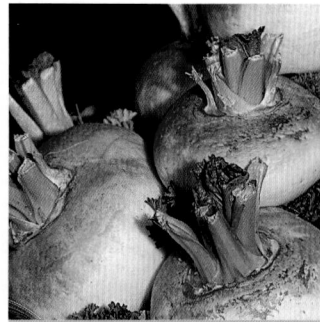

Brassica oleracea, Acephala Group, 'Blue Ridge'

Capsicum annuum, Cerasiforme Group, 'Guantanamo'

Capsicum annuum, Conoides Group, 'Shishito'

Capsicum annuum, Longum Group, 'Cayenne'

Conoides Group: Small hot chillies, more or less conical in shape. '**Apache**' ★, to 18 in (45 cm) tall; '**Jalapeño**' ★, Mexican variety, very hot; '**Mitla**', early 'Jalapeño' type; '**Shishito**', hot pepper, bright red when mature; '**Tam Vera Cruz**', developed by the Texas A & M University, grows to 3 ft (0.9 m) tall; '**Thai Miniature**' (syn. 'Thai Hot Small'), mounded with showy fruit.

Grossum Group: Sweet bell peppers, ripen to yellow, orange, red, brown, or purple-black, about 4–8 in (10–12 cm) long. Popular cultivars include '**Blue Jay**', '**Blushing Beauty**', '**Giant Marconi**', '**Jumbo Stuff**', '**Merlin**', '**Minibell Yellow**', '**Mohawk**', and '**Super Shepherd**'.

Longum Group: Quite hot fruits, including '**Cayenne**', slightly curved fruit, dried and powdered to make cayenne pepper; '**Sweet Banana**', pale yellowish fruit matures to red sweet flesh.

Ornamental Forms: Bred as ornamentals. Fruits often held upright, range of colors. Usually edible. '**Nosegay Pepper**', 6–8 in (15–20 cm) tall, mix of fruits in red, orange, and green.

Pimento Group: Original source of Spanish paprika. Heart-shaped fruit to 4 in (10 cm) long. Zones 6–12.

Capsicum chinense

☼ ⚘ ↔ 8–20 in (20–50 cm) ↕ 8 in–5 ft (20 cm–1.5 m)

From Western Amazon Basin. Extra hot species, some golden yellow in color. Best known is '**Habanero**', said to be 1,000 times hotter than 'Jalapeño'. Zones 10–12.

Capsicum frutescens

CHILLI, GOAT OR SPUR PEPPER

☼ ⚘ ↔ 8–20 in (20–50 cm) ↕ 8 in–5 ft (20 cm–1.5 m)

Originally from tropical areas of South America, widely grown in India and Asia. Best known cultivar is '**Tabasco**', from which tabasco sauce is made; upward pointing fruits. Zones 10–12.

CARUM

There are about 30 species of biennials and perennials in this genus, which belongs to the carrot (Apiaceae) family. They are found in temperate to subtropical regions. Their finely divided leaves are often aromatic and bear umbels of small white to pink flowers. The most commonly grown species is *C. carvi* (caraway), which is usually grown as a flavoring herb but its tap root is sometimes cooked in the manner of parsnips.

CULTIVATION: Grow in full sun in deep, fertile, well-drained soil. Propagate from seed sown in situ as plants dislike transplanting.

Carum carvi

CARAWAY

☼ ✳ ↔ 12–18 in (30–45 cm) ↕ 24 in (60 cm)

From Europe and western Asia, naturalized in USA. Pretty biennial with fine feathery foliage. Umbels of small white to pinkish flowers in summer. Licorice-flavored seeds. Zones 3–10.

CENTELLA

This genus of some 50 species, largely from southern Africa with one widespread in warmer parts of the world, belongs to the ivy (Araliaceae) family. Creeping or scrambling to erect perennials, they are sometimes woody at the base. Leaves are simple, linear to broadly kidney-shaped, solitary or grouped. The reddish or dirty white flowers are small, usually hermaphrodite and in simple umbels.

CULTIVATION: Only *C. asiatica* is in cultivation, as a medicinal plant. Grow outdoors in moist fertile soil in any warm climate, or as a summer annual in areas with severe winter frost and snow. It can become invasive. Propagate from rooted runners or seed.

Centella asiatica

syn. *Hydrocotyle asiatica*

ASIATIC PENNYWORT, GOTU KOLA, INDIAN PENNYWORT

☼/◐ ⚘ ↔ 12–36 in (30–90 cm) ↕ 2–12 in (5–30 cm)

Pantropical and Southern Hemisphere plant. Creeping perennial with prostrate stems rooting at nodes. Leaves of variable size, stalks kidney-shaped to rounded blades notched at base. Flowers tiny, reddish, in summer–autumn. Zones 9–12.

CHAMAEMELUM

CHAMOMILE

There are 4 species of annual and perennial herbs in this genus, which belongs to the daisy (Asteraceae) family. Native to Europe and to the Mediterranean, the fern-like foliage is aromatic, having a sharp apple scent when crushed. Typical daisy flowers are white with yellow centers. Leaves and flowers are used for tea.

CULTIVATION: Grow in full sun in well-drained soil. For lawns, place plants about 6 in (15 cm) apart and water well until established. Cut regularly. Propagate from seed or by rooted divisions.

Chamaemelum nobile

syn. *Anthemis nobile*

CHAMOMILE

☼ ❋ ↔ 12 in (30 cm) ↑ 4–12 in (10–30 cm)

Sprawling perennial from western Europe. Very aromatic fern-like foliage. Small white daisies with yellow center in summer. '**Treneague**', non-flowering cultivar suitable for lawns. Zones 4–10.

CHENOPODIUM

Part of the goosefoot (Chenopodiaceae) family, this genus consists of about 100 species of annuals and evergreen or deciduous perennials and shrubs, found in temperate climates around the world including arid regions and saline areas. Leaves are alternate, often toothed or lobed, and their surfaces may be covered with minute bladder-like whitish cells that often burst at an early stage; some species also have minute glands that secrete a sticky, pungent-smelling substance. Flowers are tiny and crowded in clusters in the leaf axils or on terminal branches; grain-like fruit are profuse, developing within the persistent perianth.

Chamaemelum nobile

CULTIVATION: Easily grown in any good garden soil in full sun, they are tough drought-tolerant plants, but if grown as vegetables should be kept well-watered and fertilized to promote leaf growth and delay seeding. Propagate from seed (or division for perennials) in spring.

Chenopodium bonus-henricus

GOOD KING HENRY

☼ ❋ ↔ 24 in (60 cm) ↑ 24 in (60 cm)

Herbaceous perennial from temperate Eurasia, naturalized in North America and British Isles. Leaves deep green, like spinach leaves, to 4 in (10 cm) long; flowers greenish, in long terminal spikes, in late spring–summer. Grown as leaf vegetable. Zones 5–10.

Chenopodium quinoa

INCA WHEAT, QUINOA

☼ ❋ ↔ 2 ft (0.6 m) ↑ 6 ft (1.8 m)

Once an important grain crop in highlands of Ecuador, Bolivia, and Peru; wild origin uncertain. Broad mid-green leaves. Erect stems carry plumes of red to yellow, black, or white seed heads. Dehulled grains high in protein, source of edible oil. Zones 8–11.

Chenopodium bonus-henricus

CICER

This genus of 40 species from central and western Asia to Ethiopia, Greece, Morocco, and the Canary Islands belongs to the pea-flower subfamily of the legume (Fabaceae) family. They are erect to creeping annuals or perennials. Leaves are pinnate or have 3 leaflets, sometimes with tendrils. Leaflets are toothed and the stipules are leafy. Flowers are small, white or violet, in few-flowered racemes arising in the leaf axils. The pods are oblong to elliptical and burst open at maturity to release 1 to 4 large seeds.

CULTIVATION: The only species that is widely cultivated is *C. arietinum* (chickpea). Grown in fields in light, well-drained, fertile soil, they need 4 to 6 months of warm dry conditions to crop satisfactorily. In India seeds are mostly planted in autumn and the peas harvested before the onset of the summer monsoon; in other areas sow in late spring for autumn harvest.

Cicer arietinum

CHICKPEA, EGYPTIAN PEA, GARBANZO BEAN

☼ ❋ ↔ 10–20 in (25–50 cm) ↑ 8 in–3 ft (20 cm–0.9 m)

Annual probably derived from *C. reticulatum* in southeastern Turkey. Sprawling to erect downy stems, leaves with up to 17 pairs of small leaflets. Flowers white to violet, in spring–early summer, followed by hairy pods to 1½ in (35 mm) long containing globular white, brown, or blackish seeds. Eaten fresh or dried. Seedlings, especially of '**Green Seeded**', eaten as bean sprouts; '**Kabuli Black**', drought tolerant and vigorous. Zones 8–11.

CICHORIUM

CHICORY, ENDIVE

A genus of 8 species in the daisy (Asteraceae) family and the tribe Lactuceae, *Cichorium* are annuals or perennials that originate from Europe, especially around western Asia and the Mediterranean, but are now naturalized in parts of North America and Australia. Grown for their edible roots (chicory) and leaves (endive, witloof, escarole), they come in a range of green or red leaves, either hairy or smooth. Flowers are most often a bright blue but sometimes pink or white, and resemble a dandelion or thistle. Their milky sap may irritate the skin.

CULTIVATION: These plants are generally seed-sown in spring and grown on through summer for a late autumn harvest. A deep, friable, well-fertilized soil with even moisture throughout the growing season is desirable. Some varieties can overwinter in the ground, but the resultant crop is not as good as the initial crop.

Cichorium endivia

ENDIVE, ESCAROLE

☼ ❀ ↔ 8–20 in (20–50 cm) ↑ 8–20 in (20–50 cm)

Grown for their large slightly bitter leaves for salads, also for cooking. Hearting varieties have outer leaves tied up (or covered with pot) to blanch hearts and reduce bitterness. '**Batavian Green**' ★, mild-flavored heart; '**Green Curled**', leaves divided and curled; '**Green Curled Ruffec**', finely cut frilled or ruffled leaves. Zones 9–11.

Cichorium intybus

CHICORY, RADICCHIO, WITLOOF

☼ ◗ ↔ 24 in (60 cm) ↑ 20–48 in (50–120 cm)

Roots used for coffee substitute; also grown for blanched forced shoots harvested in autumn–winter. Leaves green or red, blue flowers very ornamental. '**Alouette**', radicchio type, good flavor; '**Di Magdeburgo**', grown for white tapered root that is dried and powdered as coffee substitute; '**Early Treviso**', non-heading, slender, green leaves change to red as weather cools; '**Giulio**', compact radicchio; '**Greenlof**', tall upright heads with green outer leaves, white inside when blanched; '**Long Green**', green upright leaves, use like lettuce; '**Palla Rossa**' ★, compact radicchio type; '**Red-Rib**', bright red stems and veins; Red Treviso/'**Rossa di Treviso**', upright type, red leaves turn dark purple in winter; '**Rossa di Verona**' ★, hardy radicchio type, red leaves, large, tight, round heart; '**Rossana**', heat resistant; **Witloof Group**, fat white chicons (forced shoot) when roots are cut and blanched. Zones 9–11.

COLOCASIA

A genus of 6 species of tuberous perennials belonging to the arum (Araceae) family, they are native to tropical Asia and grow in naturally moist areas. Some are widely naturalized in other tropical and warm-temperate regions. Leaves, which can be very large, are arrow- or heart-shaped with prominent veins. The typical arum flower spike consists of a fleshy spike of minute flowers surrounded by a white to yellow spathe. In tropical areas the roots of *C. esculenta* are a staple food. Elsewhere they are grown for the ornamental quality of their leaves.

CULTIVATION: In warm climates grow in a fertile moisture-retentive soil, watering well in dry spells. If grown as a crop, plant at 24 in (60 cm) spacings, and top-dress monthly with a high-potash fertilizer. Tubers are ready for harvesting after about 8 months. In mild climates grow under glass with high humidity; water well.

Colocasia esculenta

syn. *Colocasia antiquorum*

COCOYAM, DASHEEN, TARO

☼ ❄ ↔ 3–6 ft (0.9–1.8 m) ↑ 3–6 ft (0.9–1.8 m)

From tropical eastern Asia; grown as a food crop. Prominently veined dark green leaves to 24 in (60 cm) long, arrow- or heart-shaped, with sturdy stems supporting them from below. '**Black Magic**', purplish black leaves; '**Fontanesii**', dark purple stems, dark green leaves with purple veins. Zones 8–12.

CORIANDRUM

CILANTRO, CORIANDER

Consisting of only 2 species, native to southwestern Asia and parts of North Africa, these slender, erect, annual herbs belong to the carrot (Apiaceae) family. Leaves are finely divided to lobed. Flowers appear in umbels, in shades of white to pink, with larger outer petals. Aromatic globular seeds follow the summer flowers.

Coriandrum sativum

CULTIVATION: Plant in sunny well-drained situations when frost risk has passed. Harvest leaves as required. Propagate from seed, harvested when it has ripened to a gray-brown color.

Coriandrum sativum

CHINESE PARSLEY, CILANTRO, CORIANDER

☼ ❄ ↔ 18–24 in (45–60 cm) ↑ 18–24 in (45–60 cm)

Native to eastern Mediterranean and western Asia. Annual herb, strongly aromatic. Foliage and seeds are popular food flavorings. Umbels of small flowers are white or pale purple. Zones 6–9.

CROCUS (see page 636)

Crocus sativus

SAFFRON CROCUS

☼ ❄ ↔ 4 in (10 cm) ↑ 2 in (5 cm)

Ancient source of dye and herbal medicine. A pound (450 g) of dried saffron takes 70,000 flowers! Sterile; reproduces by vegetative means. Large floral segments and styles. Flowers 1 to 5, fragrant, pale to deep lilac-purple or white, veins darker, in autumn. Zones 6–8.

CRYPTOTAENIA

This genus of 6 species from the north temperate zone and the mountains of tropical Africa belongs to the carrot (Apiaceae) family. The plants are perennials with strong taproots or rhizomes. Leaves are pinnate, sometimes reduced to 3 broad leaflets. Erect inflorescences are irregularly branched into loose umbels of tiny flowers, which soon give way to small flattened fruits.

CULTIVATION: Easily grown in any good soil in full sun, they self-seed freely. For tender leaves, water well and fertilize regularly.

Cryptotaenia canadensis

HONEWORT, WHITE CHERVIL

◖ ❄ ↔ 20–27 in (50–70 cm) ↑ 3 ft (0.9 m)

Perennial from North America, Asia, and Europe. Toothed leaves, lance-shaped leaflets. Tiny white flowers in summer. Zones 3–9.

CUCUMIS
CUCUMBER, MELON

A genus of about 25 species of trailing or climbing annuals in the pumpkin (Cucurbitaceae) family. Originating from warm to tropical areas of Africa and Asia, they are now grown worldwide. Their large, often hairy or prickly leaves can be smooth or may be lobed like a grape leaf. Separate male and female flowers are produced on the one plant and are usually yellow or orange. Fruits are generally green and either long and narrow or round, and are best eaten when young, as bitterness often develops as they mature. Skin can be smooth, bumpy, spiny, or ridged. **CULTIVATION:** Cucumbers are grown from seed and like a rich soil with lots of organic matter and a constant supply of moisture during the growing period. Melons are not as demanding.

Cucumis anguria
BURR CUCUMBER, JERUSALEM CUCUMBER, WEST INDIAN GHERKIN

☼ ⚛ ↔ 7–10 ft (2–3 m) ↑ 20 in (50 cm)

This species has 5-lobed leaves on a trailing vine. Light green spiny fruits, to 1¼–3 in (3–8 cm) long, picked when young for pickling. Grows from seed to harvest in 60 to 75 days. **Zones 9–12.**

Cucumis sativus
CUCUMBER, GHERKIN

☼ ⚛ ↔ 3–10 ft (0.9–3 m) ↑ 8–20 in (20–50 cm)

There are many different forms in this species, including field, greenhouse, gherkin, Sikkim, apple, and snake cucumbers. Some are more tolerant of cold or more "burpless" than others. **'Bush Champion'** ★, compact bush-type, bright green straight fruit; **Beit Alpha Group** (Lebanese cucumbers), thin-skinned, best picked and eaten at 8 in (20 cm) in length; **'Muncher'**, thin smooth skin, easily digestible; **'Spacemaster'**, disease resistant, compact, slender, dark green fruit, good for pickling when small and for slicing when mature; **'Sunsweet'**, lemon-shaped fruit, cream-colored when young and sweet (eat raw), yellowy orange when mature, with a sharper taste (eat cooked). **Zones 9–11.**

CUCURBITA
COURGETTE, GOURD, MARROW, PUMPKIN, SQUASH, ZUCCHINI

A trailing or climbing genus of about 27 species of annuals and perennials from North, Central and South America in the pump-kin (Cucurbitaceae) family. *Cucurbita* species are grown for both their edible and their ornamental fruit. Generally classified according to when they are harvested (summer or winter) or by their shape. Their leaves are often quite large, sometimes spotted or lobed, and usually rough or prickly, as are their stems. Flowers are yellow or orange, and are usually separate male and female. Fruit ranges in size from tiny to the largest fruit in the world, and can be eaten raw or cooked; it is also a nutritious stock feed. **CULTIVATION:** A very rich well-drained soil in full sun and a long warm growing season are essential for producing a good crop. Propagate from seed sown in spring.

Cucurbita maxima
AUTUMN SQUASH, GOURD, SQUASH, WINTER PUMPKIN, WINTER SQUASH

☼ ❄ ↔ 3–10 ft (0.9–3 m) ↑ 12–20 in (30–50 cm)

South American species with large round leaves. Divided into two main groups, the pumpkins and the gourds. There is a wide range of cultivars of both groups. Cultivars include: **'Atlantic Giant'** ★, the largest of the pumpkins and the largest fruit in the world—specimens weighing over 1,000 lb (450 kg) are not uncommon; **'Autumn Cup'**, butternut-type F1 hybrid. **Zones 8–11.**

Cucurbita moschata
BUTTERNUT, CANADA PUMPKIN, CROOKNECK SQUASH, PUMPKIN, WINTER SQUASH

☼ ❄ ↔ 3–10 ft (0.9–3 m) ↑ 12–20 in (30–50 cm)

Trailing, climbing, or bush species. Large leaves. Fruit usually has orange flesh and smooth skin. Stem flares out where it joins the fruit. **'Butternut'** ★, bottle-shaped, a buttery color. **Zones 8–11.**

Cucurbita pepo
COURGETTE, SUMMER SQUASH, VEGETABLE MARROW, ZUCCHINI

☼ ❄ ↔ 3–10 ft (0.9–3 m) ↑ 12–20 in (30–50 cm)

Trailing or bushy species. Many cultivars. Leaves are lobed, triangular, and prickly. Young leaves and flowers can also be eaten. Most are best eaten straight after harvest. **'Black Beauty'**, best eaten when 6–8 in (15–20 cm) long; **'Clarimore'**, hybrid Lebanese-type squash with light green, speckled, tapered fruit; **'Delicata'**, sweet potato squash; **'Early White'**, creamy white flesh; **'Eightball'**, dark green, speckled, zucchini-type squash; **'Gold Rush'** ★, golden yellow zucchini-type fruit; **'Table King'**, dark gray-green fruit, yellow-orange flesh. **Zones 8–11.**

Cucumis sativus 'Spacemaster'

Cucurbita maxima 'Atlantic Giant'

Cucurbita pepo 'Gold Rush'

CUMINUM

This genus of 4 species of annuals comes from the Mediterranean south to the Sudan and east to central Asia. It belongs to the carrot (Apiaceae) family. The leaves are finely divided and the flowers are in umbels, each umbel with a whorl of unequal bracts. The small notched petals are pink or white. The fruits ("seeds") are elliptical to oblong and flattened.
CULTIVATION: Only one species is known in cultivation: *C. cyminum* (cumin), the source of a major dried herb or spice. Grown in full sun in fertile well-drained soils, cumin needs 3 to 4 warm months to ripen its fruits. In cool countries it is raised under glass and planted out after frosts cease. Propagation is from seed.

Cuminum cyminum
CUMIN
☼ ❊ ↔ 12 in (30 cm) ↑ 12 in (30 cm)
From the Mediterranean. Much-branched annual with leaves to 4 in (10 cm) long, divided into threadlike segments. Numerous, tiny, white flowers in short-stalked umbels about 1 in (25 mm) wide, in early summer. Fruits about ¼ in (6 mm) long. Fruits used to flavor cheese, curry powder, and liqueurs. Zones 8–12.

CURCUMA

A genus of some 40 species of usually deciduous perennials with fleshy rhizomes and tuberous roots, upright to spreading reed- or cane-like pseudostems bearing lance-shaped leaves. Native to tropical and subtropical Asia, including northern Australia, it belongs to the ginger (Zingiberaceae) family. Flowers are borne on separate, usually leafy stems, in a cone-like head that soon develops brightly colored bracts largely enclosing the 3-petalled flowers. The flowerheads, which may reach 8 in (20 cm) long, are popular in floristry. Most species have local uses, either medicinally or for the mild ginger flavor of their rhizomes.
CULTIVATION: Grow in warm frost-free climates in moist, humus-rich, well-drained soil. Feed and water well during the growing season. Rhizomes may be stored dry for short periods. Most dormant during cooler months. Propagate from seed or by division.

Curcuma longa
syn. *Curcuma domestica*
TURMERIC
☼/❋ ◗ ↔ 30 in (75 cm) ↑ 3 ft (0.9 m)
Well-known culinary herb from India. Large aromatic rhizomes with orange flesh; leaves to 20-in (50 cm) long. Inflorescences to 8 in (20 cm) long, lower bracts white to pale green, upper bracts deep pink or white, yellow flowers. Zones 10–12.

CYMBOPOGON

This genus of 56 species of perennial grasses belongs to the Poaceae family. They are found in tropical and subtropical Asia, Africa, and Australia. The plants form into clumps, and have rather coarse leaves. Many species have aromatic foliage. The tiny flowers are borne in airy panicles.
CULTIVATION: Grow in moisture-retentive well-drained soil in full sun. In cooler areas grow indoors in pots, maintaining moderate humidity. Propagate from seed or by division.

Cymbopogon citratus

Cymbopogon citratus
LEMON GRASS
☼ ◗ ↔ 1 ft (0.3 m) ↑ 3–5 ft (0.9–1.5 m)
Native to southern India and Ceylon. Clumps of green to bluish green leaves with roughened margins. The strongly lemon-scented foliage is used as a flavoring in Asian cooking. Zones 9–11.

CYNARA

There are 10 species of perennial herbs in this genus, which belongs to the thistle tribe of the daisy (Asteraceae) family. Native to the Mediterranean, northwestern Africa, and the Canary Islands. They resemble giant thistles—large leaves with pointed lobes, sometimes spiny, tall heads of thistle-like flowers.
CULTIVATION: Grow in full sun in a-well-drained soil, sheltered from strong winds. Allow plenty of space for the large heavy leaves to develop. Propagate by seed or division.

Cynara cardunculus
CARDOON
☼ ❊ ↔ 4–8 ft (1.2–2.4 m) ↑ 4–8 ft (1.2–2.4 m)
Native to Mediterranean regions. Statuesque plant with thick, pointed-lobed, grayish green leaves to 5 ft (1.5-m) long. Large, purple, thistle-like flowers stand above the foliage in summer. Grown ornamentally, young stems can be cooked as a vegetable. **Scolymus Group** (globe artichoke), more compact plants, fatter head, florets less showy; popularly grown as a vegetable. Zones 7–11.

DAUCUS

This genus of about 22 species from the Mediterranean and Europe to central Asia, tropical Africa, Australasia, and the Americas, belongs to the carrot (Apiaceae) family; the carrot *(D. carota)* is its best known and only widely cultivated species. They are annuals or biennials that begin as a rosette of finely divided leaves arising from a taproot, elongating in the first or second year into a flowering stem bearing small white, often purple-flushed, or pale yellow flowers in compound umbels, the flowers are soon followed by small, dry, ribbed fruits, or "seeds."
CULTIVATION: Best in well rotted compost. Can stay in ground for some weeks. Water regularly; drying out causes splitting. Propagate from seed a few weeks before end of frost when soil is dry.

Daucus carota

CARROT

⚘ ✷ ↔ 20 in (50 cm) ↑ 40 in (100 cm)

From Europe, temperate Asia, and North Africa. Biennial, usually grown as annual, green fern-like foliage. Roots vary from cream to orange and red. Bracted umbels of creamy white flowers in second year, in late summer. ***D. c.* subsp. *sativus***, orange root, includes main carrot varieties: '**Canada**', disease, heat, and drought tolerant; '**Red Intermediate Stump Rooted 2**' ★, dark orange-red, sow in summer as can bolt if sown in spring; and '**Topweight**', a vigorous sweet-tasting variety, bolt resistant, a good all-purpose carrot. Zones 3–9.

DIOSCOREA

syns *Rajania, Tamus, Testudinaria*

YAM

Principal genus, comprising 850 species in all tropical and subtropical regions, especially in seasonal climates, in the yam (Dioscoreaceae) family of monocots. Rhizomes and annual shoots twine to the left or right. Attached to the rhizomes are one or more tubers, sometimes large, and starch-filled. Stems are erect or creeping, round in cross-section or angled, often armed with prickles especially near the base. Leaves are opposite or spirally arranged, smooth-edged to lobed or compound. Inflorescences are racemes or panicles from leaf axils; flowers are small. Fruit is a 1- or 3-winged capsule, or a berry. These are the true yams (as opposed to the sweet potato that is sometimes called yam). They are the source of diosgenin, a precursor in the synthesis of the steroidal hormones used in female contraceptive pills.

CULTIVATION: They are grown in rich soils in full sun or light shade and in temperate regions may occasionally be grown as ornamentals for their attractively colored foliage, though *D. elephantipes* is to be seen in collections of succulents. They are propagated by division of the dormant tuber or from the seed.

Dioscorea alata

Dioscorea alata

GUYANA ARROWROOT, WATER YAM, WHITE YAM

⚘/⚘ ⚓ ↔ 6 ft (1.8 m) ↑ 10 ft (3 m)

Native of tropical Asia. The most widely cultivated species, tubers can reach 8 ft (2.4 m) in length and 110 lb (50 kg) in weight. Stem is 4-angled, often with axillary tubers. Leaves are ovate to oblong, with a heart-shaped base. Zones 10–12.

Dioscorea batatas

CHINESE POTATO, CHINESE YAM, CINNAMON VINE

⚘/⚘ ✷ ↔ 6 ft (1.8 m) ↑ 10 ft (3 m)

From East Asia, and naturalized in USA. Tubers grow up to 36 in (90 cm) long. Stem is angled, twining to the right, with axillary tubers. White flowers are scented like cinnamon. Zones 8–11.

Dioscorea bulbifera

AERIAL YAM, AIR POTATO, OTAHEITE POTATO, OTAHEITE YAM

⚘/⚘ ⚘ ↔ 10 ft (3 m) ↑ 6–12 ft (1.8–3.5 m)

From tropical Asia. Tubers are small or absent, spherical in shape. The stem grows to 20 ft (6 m) with hard, corky-surfaced tubers in leaf axils. Leaves are ovate with a heart-shaped base. A troublesome weed in some areas. Zones 9–12.

Dioscorea esculenta

CHINESE YAM, IGNAME, LESSER YAM, POTATO YAM

⚘/⚘ ⚘ ↔ 6 ft (1.8 m) ↑ 4–8 ft (1.2–2.4 m)

From subtropical eastern Asia. The tubers are egg-shaped, developing near the surface of the soil, with sweet white flesh. The leaves are almost circular, there are 2 spines at the base of the stalk. Flowering is rare in cultivated plants. Zones 9–12.

ECHINACEA

CONEFLOWER

This genus, comprising 9 species of summer-flowering perennials, some of which grow as tall as 7 ft (2 m), belongs to the daisy (Asteraceae) family. Found in eastern USA and closely allied to *Rudbeckia* and *Helianthus*, they spread by rhizomes and after a few years can colonize large areas, though they are not difficult to control. The foliage is simple, usually lance-shaped, and sometimes toothed. The flowerheads are large and have relatively few ray florets, often deep purple-pink and downward facing, around a prominent, often dark, central cone of disc florets. The dried rhizomes and roots of coneflowers are widely used as an ingredient in herbal medicines; they are thought to fortify the immune system's power to ward off infection.

CULTIVATION: They grow very freely in temperate gardens, thriving in an open sunny position with well-drained humus-rich soil that is kept moist in summer. Staking is sometimes required, as they can grow quite tall. Propagate from seed or basal cuttings, or by division; they may self-sow.

Echinacea purpurea

Echinacea purpurea
syn. *Rudbeckia purpurea*
PURPLE CONEFLOWER
☼/◐ ❈ ↔ 40 in (100 cm) ↑ 60 in (150 cm)
Forms a clump of quick-growing strongly upright stems. Leaves are broad, toothed, pointed oval to lance-shaped, to 6 in (15 cm) long. Reflexed magenta-purple ray florets, to 3 in (8 cm) long, form around orange-brown disc florets opening from dark buds. *E. purpurea* is widely used in herbal medicines. 'Magnus' ★, intensely colored flowerheads; 'White Lustre', white ray florets, dark centers; 'White Swan' ★, white flowerheads. Zones 3–10.

ELETTARIA
A genus of 7 species found from India to the western Malay Archipelago, belonging to the ginger (Zingiberaceae) family. All are perennial herbs with creeping rhizomes. Leaves are in 2 ranks. Inflorescences are borne on prostrate shoots, with scale leaves arising directly from the rhizomes. Bracts surround several flowers; bracteoles and calyx are tube-shaped. The 3-petalled corolla sometimes forms a hood. The fruit is a spherical to elliptical capsule.
CULTIVATION: *E. cardamomum* (cardamom) grows in southern Indian hills under a forest canopy; few needs once established.

Elettaria cardamomum
CARDAMOM
◑/◕ ✦ ↔ 5–8 ft (1.5–2.4 m) ↑ 5–8 ft (1.5–2.4 m)
From India. Thick rhizome. Leaves to 24 in (60 cm) long, narrowly lanceolate, hairy beneath. Flower spike to 24 in (60 cm). The flowers have a white corolla with violet or pink stripes on the lip and a yellow margin. In Asia it is grown for its spicy seeds, used in cooking. Zones 10–12.

ERUCA
This genus has 3 species of annuals and perennials native to the Mediterranean region, and belongs to the cabbage (Brassicaceae) family. Leaves are pinnately lobed. Violet, yellow, or white 4-petalled flowers veined in contrasting colors are borne in racemes. The narrow seed pod splits into 2 halves, releasing several seeds.
CULTIVATION: Only *E. vesicaria* subsp. *sativa* is grown, as a salad green or as an oilseed. Raise from seed in open ground or, for early harvest in temperate regions, in trays under glass. For a succession of tender young shoots, sow seed fortnightly throughout the season. It likes added nitrogenous fertilizer and plenty of water. After leaves have been harvested, plants can regenerate up to 4 more flushes. Shade young plants in summer to stop bolting.

Eruca vesicaria
ARUGULA, ROCKET, ROQUETTE
☼/◐ ❈ ↔ 12–24 in (30–60 cm) ↑ 16–40 in (40–100 cm)
From the Mediterranean region. Short-lived perennial forming a clump of deeply lobed dark green leaves with an erect raceme of pale yellow flowers. *E. v.* subsp. *sativa* (syn. *E. sativa*) (garden or salad rocket) is an annual, with deeply divided leaves and 1 in (25 mm) wide pale yellow flowers with violet-veined petals in summer, pods to 1 in (25 mm) long, held erect. Zones 7–10.

FOENICULUM
FENNEL
A culinary herb, and in many areas a weed of waste ground, fennel belongs to the carrot (Apiaceae) family. It is an aromatic biennial or perennial from Europe and the Mediterranean region. It forms a clump of erect hollow stems with feathery foliage made up of many hair-like deep green to bronze leaflets. Heads of small yellow flowers appear through summer, then dry to become similarly shaped pale brown seed heads. It is invasive.
CULTIVATION: It will grow in most soils and climates, from cool-temperate to subtropical, in moderately fertile soil and a little summer moisture. Propagate from seed; perennial forms will also grow from divisions.

Eruca vesicaria subsp. *sativa*

Foeniculum vulgare
FENNEL
☼ ❈ ↔ 18–36 in (45–90 cm) ↑ 3–7 ft (0.9–2 m)
From Europe and the Mediterranean region, naturalized elsewhere. Hollow-stemmed aromatic perennial, soft, fine, green, fern-like foliage smelling of aniseed. Umbels of small yellow flowers in summer. *F. v.* var. *azoricum* (Florence fennel, finocchio), smaller annual grown as a vegetable; 'Perfection' and 'Zefo Fino'; *F. v.* 'Purpureum' (syns 'Bronze', 'Purpurascens'), all popular. Zones 5–10.

GLYCINE
SOYA BEAN, SOYBEAN
From Asia and Australia, this genus belongs to the pea-flower subfamily of the legume (Fabaceae) family. Although it includes some 9 to 18 species of perennials, some of them twining semi-climbers, it is known in cultivation for just one, *G. max*, the soya bean. All have trifoliate leaves but can produce foliage with up to 7 leaflets. Flowers, clustered in small inflorescences, are typically pea-flower-like, usually mauve or pink, followed by pods with 2 to 4 seeds: beans are used to produce a huge range of products.
CULTIVATION: To thrive, these tender plants must be kept growing steadily and without check. They need hot humid conditions and moist humus-rich soil. Water and feed well. Propagate from seed or cuttings of non-flowering basal shoots.

Glycine max
syn. *Glycine soja*
MANCHURIAN BEAN, SOJA BEAN, SOYA BEAN, SOYBEAN
☼ ❈ ↔ 3 ft (0.9 m) ↑ 4–7 ft (1.2–2 m)
Annual from northeast China. Compound leaves with oval leaflets up to 6 in (15 cm) long. Heads of 8 white to violet or pink pea-flowers. Hanging pods contain 2-to 4 rounded or flattened seeds. All parts covered with fine reddish brown hairs. Zones 7–8.

Hyssopus officinalis 'Sissinghurst'

the 2-lipped tubular flowers. *H. officinalis* has in the past been used in asthma and bronchitis remedies.
CULTIVATION: Grow in well-drained soil in a sunny situation. *H. officinalis* can be used as a low hedge. Pinch growing tips to encourage bushiness. Propagate from seed or cuttings.

Hyssopus officinalis
HYSSOP
☼ ❋   ↔ 12 in (30 cm)   ↑ 18–24 in (45–60 cm)
From southern and eastern Europe. Naturalized in USA. Variable shrubby perennial with aromatic foliage. Violet to blue flowers carried on thin spikes in late summer. 'Sissinghurst' has a dwarf, compact habit. Zones 3–10.

ILLICIUM *(see page 186)*

Illicium verum
CHINESE ANISE, STAR ANISE
◑ ❋   ↔ 20 ft (6 m)   ↑ 60 ft (18 m)
Native of China and North Vietnam. Star-shaped fruits used for spice and medicine. Leaves are lance-shaped, with a prominent mid-vein. Flowers whitish yellow, turning deep pink or purple-red, in early summer. Glossy brown fruits. Zones 8–11.

IPOMOEA *(see page 778)*

Ipomoea batatas
KUMARA, SWEET POTATO
☼ ⚎   ↔ 10 ft (3 m)   ↑ 10 ft (3 m)
Native to tropical regions. Important food crop with edible tubers, usually grown as a prostrate annual. Leaves oval to heart-shaped, lobed or toothed. Tubers have purple, red, or yellow skins, orange or white flesh. 'Blackie', ornamental variety, purple-black foliage; 'Vardaman', orange-fleshed tubers. Zones 9–12.

LABLAB
A genus of a single species in the pea-flower subfamily of the legume (Fabaceae) family, native to Africa but long grown in India, Southeast Asia, Egypt, and Sudan as a vegetable. Most parts of the plant are poisonous; the pods and seeds are edible only after they have been boiled thoroughly. It is a short-lived herbaceous perennial climber, often treated as a half-hardy annual in colder climates. The leaves consist of 3 triangular leaflets; the pea-flowers occur in various colors and are produced throughout summer, followed by edible pods.
CULTIVATION: Grow in a sunny well-drained site when danger of frost is past. Propagate by seed sown in spring.

Lablab purpureus
syns *Dolichos lablab, Lablab niger*
BANNER BEAN, BLACK BEAN, EGYPTIAN BEAN, HYACINTH BEAN, INDIAN BEAN
☼ ⚎   ↔ 5–10 ft (1.5–3 m)   ↑ 12–20 ft (3.5–6 m)
Perennial vine from tropical Africa. Purplish stems; alternate divided leaves, 3 broad oval leaflets. Elongated flowerheads of fragrant white, pink, or purple pea-flowers. Flat, often curved, maroon or purplish seed pods. Most plant parts poisonous; pods

GLYCYRRHIZA
There are 20 species of perennial herbs in this genus, which belongs to the pea-flower subfamily of the legume (Fabaceae) family. They have pinnate leaves and small pea-like flowers of white, violet, or yellow. One species, *G. glabra*, is grown for its sweet root, licorice, used in confectionery and medicines.
CULTIVATION: Grow these plants in full sun in rich, deeply cultivated, well-drained soil. Propagate from seed or division.

Glycyrrhiza glabra
LICORICE, LIQUORICE, SWEETWOOD
☼ ❋   ↔ 36 in (90 cm)   ↑ 36 in (90 cm)
Found from Mediterranean areas to southwestern Asia. Coarse deep-rooting plant with pinnately divided sticky leaves and loose spikes of pale blue to violet pea-flowers in summer. The thick dark reddish brown roots are harvested in autumn. Zones 7–9.

HELIANTHUS *(see page 476)*

Helianthus tuberosus ★
JERUSALEM ARTICHOKE
☼ ❋   ↔ 5 ft (1.5 m)   ↑ 10 ft (3 m)
Tuberous perennial found from Canada to southeastern USA. Coarsely hairy, toothed, lance-shaped or pointed oval leaves. Yellow flowerheads in autumn. Tubers edible. Zones 4–9.

HELICHRYSUM *(see page 477)*

Helichrysum italicum
syn. *Helichrysum angustifolium*
☼ ❋   ↔ 20 in (50 cm)   ↑ 16 in (40 cm)
Summer-flowering, bushy, aromatic perennial native to south-western Europe. Narrow, sparsely downy leaves. Tiny dull white to yellow flowerheads in small clusters. *H. i.* subsp. *serotinum* (curry plant) has foliage with a strong curry aroma. Zones 8–10.

HYSSOPUS
This genus in the mint (Lamiaceae) family contains about 10 species of perennials or small shrubs. The opposite leaves are lance-shaped and aromatic. Rather sparse flower spikes bear

and seeds edible if well boiled. '**Darkness**', violet-purple flowers, black seeds; '**Daylight**', white flowers, white seeds; '**Giganteus**', larger form, white flowers. Zones 9–12.

LACTUCA
LETTUCE

Genus of about 75 species of Northern Hemisphere annuals and perennials in the daisy (Asteraceae) family, which produce a rosette of entire, lobed, deeply divided, or blistered leaves. Leaf margins are smooth, undulating, serrated, or frilly; leaf color varies from green to brown or red. Masses of tiny flowers, usually white, yellow, or blue, are produced in a tall spike. The seeds are tiny and are white, gray, or black. Only one species, *L. sativa*, is widely cultivated for its edible leaves; the stems of some cultivars are also eaten. The milky sap or juice of lettuces is soporific.
CULTIVATION: Grow in rich well-drained soil in full sun. Do not dry out during the growing period or they will go to seed. Cool conditions needed for germination; seed can be sown almost year round.

Lablab purpureus

Lactuca sativa
COMMON LETTUCE

☼ ❄ ↔ 4–12 in (10–30 cm) ↑ 4–12 in (10–30 cm)

As usually understood, this species is known only in cultivation, but it is thought that it may be an ancient derivative of the wild Mediterranean prickly lettuce, *L. serriola*, now known as a common weed. There are many varieties of lettuce. Leaf shape, size, and color vary. Most are eaten raw, although they can be cooked. All need to be grown quickly to avoid bitterness. *L. s.* **var.** *augustana* (syn. *L. s.* var. *asparagina),* known as asparagus lettuce, celtuce, or Chinese lettuce, from Asia, is larger than the species and grown for its thickened stem, to 3 in (8 cm) wide, eaten raw or cooked; leaves are usually green, but there is a red form. *L. s.* '**Attico**', a mini, cos-type lettuce, resistant to bolting, tip burn, and downy mildew; '**Australiana Gialla**' (syn. 'Australian Yellow Leaf'), yellow-green color, slow to bolt; '**Bubbles**' ★, compact lettuce, notably blistered leaves; '**Cocarde**' ★ (arrowhead lettuce), a red oak-leaf type, large arrow-shaped leaves tinged red,

tender; '**Cos Verdi**', a crisp, cos-type lettuce, open upright heads and smooth-edged green leaves; '**Cosmic**', a cos-type lettuce; '**Crisp Mint**', with compact tall heads; '**Fortune**', a butterhead with a medium compact head; '**Grandpa Admires**', loose heads of pale green blushing bronze and red; '**Green Coral**', fast-growing loose-leaf type, frilly margins; '**Green Mignonette**', soft-leafed, hearting lettuce, blistered leaves; '**Green Oak Leaf**' (syn. 'A Couper Feuille de Chêne à Graine Noire'), deeply divided leaves; '**Iceberg**' ★, bred in the USA in the 1930s, a large, heavy, hearting lettuce, crisp outer green leaves, white heart; '**Italian Oak Leaf**', medium-sized, Italian-style lettuce, resistant to disease; '**Kendo**', a cos cross, green leaves overlaid with red; '**Little Gem**' ★ (syns 'Sucrine', 'Sugar Cos'), a semi-cos with dark green crumpled leaves; '**Musketeer**', resistant to downy mildew; '**Oak Leaf**', first listed in France in the 1770s, 3 main colors: green, dark green, and brown, a loose-leaf variety with deeply divided leaves; '**Red Mignonette**', a butterhead with small red and green heads; '**Red Oak Leaf**', a red-tinged form of the green 'Oak Leaf'; '**Red Salad Bowl**' ★, a red loose-leaf variety developed from 'Oak Leaf', serrated leaves; '**Romany**', a semi-cos, resistant to tip burn and downy mildew; '**Sunset**', a large red butterhead, good in cool areas; '**Valdor**' ★, a winter lettuce. Zones 6–11.

LAGENARIA
GOURD

This genus comprises 6 species of annual or perennial vines in the pumpkin (Cucurbitaceae) family, native to tropical regions, that use tendrils to climb. Leaves are heart-shaped or 3- to 5-lobed. Scented, white, male and female, bell-shaped flowers may be solitary or in racemes. Fruit may be up to 3 ft (0.9 m) long and comes in a variety of shapes but is often in the form of a club. The young fruit of some species is edible, but bitter.
CULTIVATION: These vines will adapt to most soils in an open sunny position. A trellis or similar support should be provided to keep gourds off the ground. Propagate from seed in late spring in temperate climates or at the beginning of the tropical wet season.

Lactuca sativa 'Cocarde'

Lactuca sativa 'Little Gem'

Lactuca sativa 'Red Salad Bowl'

Lagenaria siceraria

syns *Lagenaria leucantha, L. vulgaris*

BOTTLE GOURD, CROOKNECK GOURD, TRUMPET GOURD, WHITE-FLOWERED GOURD

☼ ⚘ ↔ 10–20 ft (3–6 m) ↑ 10–30 ft (3–9 m)

Tendril-climbing annual. Leaves hairy, oval to heart-shaped, toothed. Solitary, white, trumpet-shaped flowers in summer. Fruit is variably shaped, greenish yellow, edible. Zones 10–12.

LAURUS

LAUREL

There are just 2 species of evergreen trees and shrubs in this genus, which gives its name to the large and mainly tropical laurel (Lauraceae) family, one found around the Mediterranean region and the other native to the Canary Islands and the Azores. Botanists regard them as relics of the warmer evergreen "laurel forest" believed to have covered Europe before the last Ice Age. Foliage is leathery, deep green, and aromatic; small yellowish flowers arise along the branches in spring.
CULTIVATION: *L. nobilis* is the species commonly seen in cultivation. An adaptable plant, suitable for hedging, topiary, specimen planting, or containers, it tolerates coastal conditions. In cool-temperate climates grow against a warm wall. It needs a sunny site in fertile well-drained soil. Hedging should be trimmed in the summer. Propagate from seed sown in autumn or from half-hardened cuttings taken in summer.

Laurus nobilis

BAY LAUREL, BAY TREE, SWEET BAY, TRUE LAUREL

☼ ❊ ↔ 6–15 ft (1.8–4.5 m) ↑ 10–50 ft (3–15 m)

Native to the Mediterranean region. Densely branched small tree or shrub. Leaves glossy, dark green, slightly wavy margins. Small yellowish flowers; black egg-shaped fruit. Leaves are used as a herb. 'Aurea', yellow leaves. Zones 8–11.

LENS

LENTIL

This genus comprises 4 species of annuals closely related to peas and vetches, in the pea-flower subfamily of the legume (Fabaceae) family, native to the Mediterranean region, western Asia, and Africa. Leaves are pinnate, with the terminal leaflet modified into a tendril or short bristle. Small whitish pea-flowers are borne in the leaf axils. The fruit is a small flattened pod.
CULTIVATION: Best adapted to regions with hot dry summers and good winter or spring rainfall, or tropical plateau areas with a long dry season. They tolerate most open well-drained soils. Sow seed in spring; harvest in summer as the plants wither.

Lens culinaris

syns *Ervum lens, Lens ervoides, L. esculenta, L. nigricans*

☼ ❊ ↔ 24 in (60 cm) ↑ 12–18 in (30–45 cm)

The various cultivated races of lentils have been grouped under the names *L. ervoides* and *L. nigricans* but are now all treated as this one species. Erect to sprawling annual. Leaves pinnate, with

usually 6 pairs of narrow leaflets. Stalked clusters of 1 to 3 flowers; pods under ¾ in (18 mm) long, 1- or 2-seeded. Zones 7–11.

LEONURUS

There are 3 species of perennials in this genus, which belongs to the mint (Lamiaceae) family. They are found over a wide area of Europe and temperate Asia, growing on woodland margins, in gravelly or alkaline soil. Opposite leaves are lobed or toothed. The 2-lipped tubular flowers are pink or white, and borne on spikes in well-spaced whorls, emerging from bell-shaped calyces.
CULTIVATION: Grows in any soil. Propagate by seed or by division.

Leonurus cardiaca

MOTHERWORT

☼ ❊ ↔ 12 in (30 cm) ↑ 24–36 in (60–90 cm)

Native to continental Europe; naturalized in parts of Britain and the USA. Basal leaves palmately lobed, with 5 to 7 toothed lobes; stem leaves 3-lobed, narrower. Whorls of pinkish white flowers with spiny-tipped calyces, leafy flowering stems, in summer. Zones 3–10.

LEVISTICUM

Genus in the carrot (Apiaceae) family consisting of a single species of tall upright perennial with compound triangular leaves with a strong celery taste. Its leaves are used in salads; seeds for flavoring. In summer it produces flowerheads typical of the carrot family, with tiny green-yellow blooms. The true garden celery (*Apium graveolens* var. *dulce*) is more tender.
CULTIVATION: Plant in full sun in fertile, moist but well-drained soil. Propagate by freshly sown seed or division in spring.

Laurus nobilis

Levisticum officinale

LOVAGE, LOVE PARSLEY

☼/◐ ❊ ↔ 40 in (100 cm) ↑ 7 ft (2 m)

Native to the Mediterranean region. Umbelliferous perennial. Dark green, leathery, shiny leaves, similar to a carrot's but wider. Flower stalks thick and hollow, yellow flowers. Zones 3–10.

LYCIUM

This genus, belonging to the nightshade (Solanaceae) family, comprises some 100 species of deciduous and evergreen, often thorny shrubs that inhabit temperate, subtropical, and tropical regions worldwide. Branches are often thorn-tipped. Leaves are alternate or in clusters. Small funnel-shaped or tubular flowers, white, green, or purplish, are borne in the leaf axils. They bear showy, succulent, generally bright red berries. Some species have become troublesome weeds.
CULTIVATION: Ranging from frost hardy to frost tender, they like moderately fertile well-drained soil in a sunny spot. Some species tolerate sea spray. *Lycium* may be grown as a hedge or espaliered against walls. Prune in winter or early spring. All species propagate easily from seed in autumn. Hardwood cuttings may be taken in the winter, and softwood cuttings in the summer.

Lycopersicon, Hybrid Cultivar, 'Black Plum'

Lycopersicon, Hybrid Cultivar, 'Green Zebra'

Lycopersicon, Hybrid Cultivar, 'Sungold'

Lycium barbarum

syn. *Lycium chinense*

GOJI, GOU-QI, MATRIMONY VINE, WOLFBERRY

☼ ✻ ↔ 15 ft (4.5 m) ↑ 10 ft (3 m)

Deciduous shrub from southeastern Europe through Himalayas to China. Tubular, lilac-purple flowers in late spring–summer, followed by small orange or red berries, edible when ripe. Zones 6–10.

LYCOPERSICON

A genus in the nightshade (Solanaceae) family containing 7 species of aromatic herbs, some annuals, others short-lived perennials, occurring wild in western South America and the Galapagos Islands. They have erect or sprawling stems clothed in sticky hairs and deeply divided toothed leaves. Short racemes of yellow, star-shaped flowers with a 5-lobed calyx are borne in the leaf axils. The fruit is a fleshy berry with 2 or more chambers containing many seeds; the best-known species is *L. esculentum*.
CULTIVATION: In areas with a long warm growing season plant in fertile well-drained soil in an open sunny position. In cooler areas protect seedlings from late frosts. Propagate from seed; many varieties are grafted onto stronger root-stock for improved vigor.

Lycopersicon esculentum

syns *Lycopersicon lycopersicum*, *Solanum lycopersicum*

LOVE APPLE, POMODORO, TOMATO

☼ ⌖ ↔ 12–24 in (30–60 cm) ↑ 2–8 ft (0.6–2.4 m)

Native to western South America. Perennial, grown as an annual food crop. Stem erect or scrambling, hairy; leaves deeply cut, with up to 9 lobes. Up to 12 yellow, open, star-shaped flowers per raceme. *L. e.* var. *cerasiforme*, the original wild Peruvian cherry tomato from which cultivars have been bred, has small red fruit, ½–¾ in (12–18 mm) in diameter. Modern cultivars may have fleshy, rounded, cylindrical or oval-shaped fruit, to 6 in (15 cm) in diameter, usually red, but often yellow, orange, or blackish. '**Abraham Lincoln**', medium-sized fruit; '**Black Russian**', dark mahogany brown fruit; '**Costoluto di Marmande**', ribbed red fruit; '**Freude**' (syn. 'Gardener's Delight') ★, clusters of cherry tomatoes; '**Gold Nugget**', small, yellow or gold fruit; '**Goliath**', medium-sized, red fruit; '**Juliette**', clusters of grape-type fruit; '**Mexico Midget**', prolific, cherry-sized tomatoes; '**Moneymaker**' ★, medium-sized fruit; '**Mortgage Lifter**', large red beefsteak variety; '**Plum Dandy**', egg-shaped fruit; '**Sherry's**

Sweet Italian', pointed fruit, suited to sauces and tomato paste; '**Stupice**', suits cooler climates; '**Yellow Boy**' ★, bright yellow fruit; '**Yellow Pear-shaped**', small, yellow, sweet fruit. Zones 9–12.

Lycopersicon Hybrid Cultivars

☼ ⌖ ↔ 12–24 in (30–60 cm) ↑ 2–8 ft (0.6–2.4 m)

Several species, most notably *L. peruvianum*, hybridize with *L. esculentum*, resulting in a range of fruit. Popular cultivars include '**Black Plum**', '**Carmello**', '**Caspian Pink**', '**Early Girl**', '**Green Zebra**', '**Jolly**', '**Northern Exposure**', and '**Sungold**' ★. Zones 9–12.

MANIHOT

There are some 100 species of trees, shrubs, and herbs within this genus from the euphorbia (Euphorbiaceae) family native to tropical and warm-temperate regions of Central and South America. Leaves are palmate, lobed, with lance-shaped leaflets. *M. esculenta* has a cyanogen in its roots that must be extracted before eating.
CULTIVATION: Best in warm, wet conditions followed by a dry season. Propagate from mature cuttings planted in gritty loam.

Manihot esculenta

BITTER CASSAVA, MANIOC

☼ ⌖ ↔ 3 ft (0.9 m) ↑ 12 ft (3.5 m)

Shrubby tree from Central and South America. Tuberous roots. Fruit is 6-angled. '**Variegata**', yellow variegation. Zones 9–11.

Manihot esculenta 'Variegata'

MARANTA *(see page 507)*

Maranta arundinacea
ARROWROOT
☼ ✤ ↔ 24–40 in (60–100 cm) ↑ 4–6 ft (1.2–1.8 m)
Perennial herb from the West Indies and Central
America. Erect, fleshy, brittle, branching stems.
Smooth, oblong to sword-shaped, pointed leaves,
to 10 in (25 cm) long. Slender, open, branched
heads of small white flowers, in spring. This plant
is the source of arrowroot. Zones 11–12.

MARRUBIUM *(see page 508)*

Marrubium vulgare
COMMON HOREHOUND, WHITE HOREHOUND
☼ ❀ ↔ 20 in (50 cm) ↑ 20 in (50 cm)
Native to southern Europe, northern Africa, the
Canary Islands, and Asia. Leaves rounded, woolly,
gray. Small, 2-lipped flowers, in summer. Poor as a
garden plant, weedy outside native areas. Marginally
ornamental variegated form exists. Zones 3–10.

MATRICARIA
This genus of 5 species of usually annual herbs
belongs to the daisy (Asteraceae) family. Found
throughout temperate areas of Europe and Asia,
they have upright, branching, leafy stems with alternate, finely divided, light to bright green leaves. The foliage
is often aromatic. The freely borne flowers may be single or in
clusters and are either yellow and button-like or white daisies
with yellow centers. *M. recutita* is used in herbal medicine.
CULTIVATION: These herbs are easily grown in a sunny position in
well-drained soil. Propagate from seed, *in-situ,* in late summer.

Matricaria recutita
syn. *Matricaria chamomilla*
GERMAN CHAMOMILE, SWEET FALSE CHAMOMILE, WILD CHAMOMILE
☼ ❀ ↔ 6–20 in (15–50 cm) ↑ 6–20 in (15–50 cm)
Bushy annual, from Europe and western Asia, with fine, pinnately divided, aromatic foliage, and daisy-like flowers, with white
ray petals that flex downward, in summer–autumn. Zones 4–10.

Marrubium vulgare

Melissa officinalis

MEDICAGO
This genus of about 56 species of annuals, perennials, and shrubs is a member of the pea-flower subfamily of the legume (Fabaceae) family and
includes the important fodder crop *M. sativa*
(lucerne or alfalfa). Species are found over a range
of habitats in Europe, Africa, and Asia. Growth
habits vary but all have clover-like leaves and some
species have slightly downy foliage and stems. The
flowers are usually yellow and the seed pods that
follow are curved or twisted and often spiny.
CULTIVATION: Shrubby species grow in any fertile
well-drained soil. Plant in full sun; in cooler areas
they need the protection of a warm wall. Their
deep rooting systems make them useful for soil
stabilization. Propagate from seed, or from softwood or half-hardened cuttings taken in summer.

Medicago sativa
ALFALFA, LUCERNE, PURPLE MEDICK
☼ ❀ ↔ 32–40 in (80–100 cm) ↑ 32–40 in
(80–100 cm)
Perennial forage herb from Eurasia, naturalized
worldwide. Leaves with 3 oval to narrow leaflets,
toothed at tip, on short stalks. Blue to purple pea-
flowers, in dense racemes, in summer–autumn.
Sprouted seeds edible. Zones 4–8.

MELISSA
BALM
This hardy genus, which belongs to the mint (Lamiaceae) family,
contains 3 species of perennial herbs native to Europe and western and central Asia. When the small heart-shaped leaves are
crushed, a lemony scent is released. The flower spikes bear white
or yellow insignificant flowers. The leaves can be infused to make
a herbal tea or can be chopped and used in salads and soups.
CULTIVATION: Grow in borders, along path edges, in herb gardens
or containers, in full sun or half-sun in moist, well-drained soil.
They may die in soils that are wet in winter. Plants may self-seed.
Propagate from seed or cuttings, or by division of roots in spring.

Melissa officinalis
BEE BALM, LEMON BALM
☼/◐ ❀ ↔ 18 in (45 cm) ↑ 24–36 in (60–90 cm)
Herb from Europe. Green, oval, tooth-edged leaves in opposite
pairs. Insignificant white tubular flowers, in summer–early
autumn. 'Aurea', green leaves, gold splotches. Zones 5–9.

MENTHA
A genus of 25 species of aromatic rhizomatous perennials in
the mint (Lamiaceae) family. From Europe, Africa, Asia, and
Australia, they naturalize in damp moist areas. Shallow-rooted
plants, they spread easily. They have an upright branching habit
and form dense bushy plants from a few inches to 5 ft (1.5 m)
high. The tiny flowers are borne at the ends of the stems in clusters or spikes from ¼ in (6 mm) to 4 in (10 cm) long. Foliage is

aromatic. Many are used in teas and as food flavoring or for medicinal purposes; some are grown commercially for their essential oils. Species can be evergreen or deciduous.
CULTIVATION: Mints grow in any open, fertile, moist soil, in part-shade or full sun. Propagate by dividing the rhizomes throughout the year; roots will appear in a few weeks. Sow seed in spring.

Mentha aquatica
WATER MINT
☼ ❋ ↔ 3–7 ft (0.9–2 m) ↕ 3 ft (0.9 m)
Marginal water herb from temperate Eurasia. Strongly scented foliage, serrated dark green leaves on purple upright stems. Small purple flowers, in summer. Zones 7–9.

Mentha longifolia
syns *Mentha incana, M. sylvestris*
HORSE MINT
☼ ❋ ↔ 3–6 ft (0.9–1.8 m) ↕ 4 ft (1.2 m)
Tall, creeping herb from Europe and western Asia. Hairy, gray-green leaves, musty fragrance. Lilac to white flowers. Zones 6–9.

Mentha × piperita
PEPPERMINT
☼ ❋ ↔ 36 in (90 cm) ↕ 24–36 in (60–90 cm)
Fast-growing herb from Europe. Purplish stems. Long lance-shaped leaves, serrated edges, minty flavor and aroma. Mauve-pink flowers in summer. Sterile seeds. *M. × p.* f. *citrata* (bergamot mint), strong flavor, use in fruit salads, can be invasive; 'Chocolate' ★ (chocolate mint), chocolate fragrance and taste. *M. × p.* 'Logee's' (variegated peppermint), some leaves with pink and white markings. Zones 3–9.

Mentha spicata
SPEARMINT
☼ ❋ ↔ 3–6 ft (0.9–1.8 m) ↕ 4 ft (1.2 m)
Herb from Europe. Mid-green, narrow, pointed leaves, serrated edge. Creeping rhizomes; flowers pale mauve, pink, or white, in summer. *M. s.* var. *crispa* (curly spearmint), lance-shaped dark green leaves, may be red edge, pale mauve-pink flowers. Zones 3–10.

Mentha suaveolens
syn. *Mentha rotundifolia*
APPLE MINT, WOOLLY MINT
☼ ❋ ↔ 36 in (90 cm) ↕ 36 in (90 cm)
Herb from southwest Europe. Round pale green leaves, fine hairs and apple-like aroma. Flowers white to pink, in summer. 'Variegata' (syn. *M. rotundifolia* var. *variegata*) (pineapple mint), leaves gray-green. Zones 6–10.

MYRRHIS
SWEET CICELY
Containing a single species, an aromatic herbaceous perennial from Europe, this genus is a member of the carrot (Apiaceae) family. It has delicate, ferny, bright green leaves from spring until autumn and flat heads of tiny pure white flowers in summer.

Myrrhis odorata cultivar

CULTIVATION: Grow *Myrrhis* plants in an open sunny position. Propagate from seed; they can self-sow and become weedy.

Myrrhis odorata
GARDEN MYRRH, SWEET CICELY
☼ ❋ ↔ 4–5 ft (1.2–1.5 m) ↕ 5–7 ft (1.5–2 m)
Clumping herbaceous perennial. Hairy stems. Fine, ferny, aniseed-flavored leaves, to 18 in (45 cm) long. Tiny white flowers. Ridged dark brown seeds. Zones 5–10.

NEPETA (see page 518)

Nepeta cataria
CATMINT, CATNIP
☼/◑ ❋ ↔ 40 in (100 cm) ↕ 40 in (100 cm)
Bushy upright species, naturalized in Europe. Downy gray-green leaves. Spikes of mauve-spotted, white flowers. When crushed, 'Citriodora', has a lemon scent. Zones 3–10.

Nepeta cataria 'Citriodora'

NICOTIANA (see page 518)

Nicotiana tabacum
TOBACCO
☼/◑ ❋ ↔ 18–24 in (45–60 cm) ↕ 3–5 ft (0.9–1.5 m)
Native to South America. Annual or biennial, grown commercially for tobacco. Fragrant, greenish white to pinkish red flowers. 'Variegata', leaves variegated cream, flowers tinged pink. Zones 8–11.

OCIMUM

BASIL

This genus encompasses 35 species of annuals and perennials from tropical and subtropical Africa and Asia known for their aromatic foliage. These herbs belong to the mint (Lamiaceae) family and are generally erect bushy plants, with a distinctive branching habit and narrow oval to elliptic leaves. Foliage varies from pale to dark green through to dark red and purple. Whorls of tiny tubular flowers appear on short spikes in summer and vary from white to creamy green.

CULTIVATION: Grow in moist well-drained soil in a warm sunny site; they do not tolerate frost or cold temperatures. Propagate from seed in summer for annuals; from stem cuttings for perennials.

Ocimum basilicum

BASIL, SWEET BASIL

☼ ✛ ↔ 12 in (30 cm) ↑ 12–24 in (30–60 cm)

From tropical and subtropical Asia. Erect, upright, erect, bushy annual. Oval mid-green leaves, sometimes slightly serrated around edges, often hairy on topside of leaf. Whorls of creamy white flowers, in summer. *O. b.* var. *minimum* ★, (Greek bush basil) small compact leaves on compact plant, good flavor. *O. b.* 'Dark Opal' (purple leaf basil), dark red-purple, sometimes curly leaves, pale creamy green stems, pale pink flowers; 'Fino Verde Compatto' (Italian basil), compact plant, small mid-green leaves; 'Mini Purple', dwarf compact plant, dark purple foliage, hint of green through leaves; 'Red Rubin' ★, a selection from 'Dark Opal', more uniform and compact, foliage stays rich red-purple for longer; 'Ruffles' ★, green foliage, curly and frilly leaf edges; 'Siam Queen', rosy purple flowers, licorice flavor. Zones 10–12.

Ocimum basilicum

Ocimum tenuiflorum

syn. *Ocimum sanctum*

HOLY BASIL

☼ ⍓ ↔ 24 in (60 cm) ↑ 36 in (90 cm)

Deciduous shrub from India and Malaysia. Lightly hairy mid-green leaves, on purplish stems with visible hairs. Very spicy and pungent fragrance. Pale pink to purple flowers. Zones 9–10.

Origanum majorana

OENANTHE

This genus in the carrot (Apiaceae) family contains 30 species of perennial herbs, native to damp habitats of the Northern Hemisphere and southern Africa. Foliage is usually pinnately divided into small leaflets. Tiny white flowers borne on umbels are typical of the family. Some species are poisonous while, conversely, *O. javanica* is cultivated as a vegetable in Asia.

CULTIVATION: Suitable for naturalizing in wild gardens. Grow in damp fertile soil in full sun/shade. Propagate from cuttings or seed or by division.

Oenanthe javanica

syn. *Oenanthe japonica*

WATER CELERY, WATER DROPWORT

☼/☽ ⍓ ↔ 12–16 in (30–40 cm) ↑ 12–16 in (30–40 cm)

Found from India to Japan and into southeastern Asia. Likes boggy ground. Divided foliage resembles celery leaves. Umbels of small white flowers. Grown as a leafy vegetable crop in Asia. 'Flamingo', has green, cream, and pink leaves. Zones 9–12.

ORIGANUM

Found from the Mediterranean to east Asia and known mainly as a genus of perennials, including some of the best known culinary herbs, *Origanum* belongs to the mint (Lamiaceae) family. It has aromatic foliage on short stems. Flowers are borne in spikes with conspicuous bracts that enclose the flowers.

CULTIVATION: Grow in light well-drained soil in a sunny position. Hardiness varies, but most tolerate moderate frosts. Propagate from seed, small half-hardened cuttings, or by layering.

Origanum dictamnus

DITTANY OF CRETE

☼ ❈ ↔ 8–12 in (20–30 cm) ↑ 8–12 in (20–30 cm)

Small, Cretan evergreen shrub. Woolly white leaves, in opposite pairs. Drooping heads of pink flowers, enclosed within large pink bracts, in summer. Suitable for a cool greenhouse. Zones 7–10.

Origanum majorana

syn. *Majorana hortensis*

KNOTTED MARJORAM, SWEET MARJORAM

☼ ❈ ↔ 18 in (45 cm) ↑ 24 in (60 cm)

Native to the Mediterranean region, naturalized through Europe. Grayish green leaves used for flavoring. Stems root readily where they touch the soil. Small white to pink flowers. Zones 7–10.

Origanum onites

POT MARJORAM

☼ ❈ ↔ 24 in (60 cm) ↑ 24 in (60 cm)

Shrubby, mounding culinary herb, native of the Mediterranean region. Flexible wiry stems, aromatic bright green to sage green leaves, with a covering of very fine hairs. Small, soft pink, thyme-like flowers, in mid-summer. 'Aureum', bright yellow foliage, more popular than the species as an ornamental. Zones 8–10.

Origanum vulgare
COMMON MARJORAM, OREGANO, WILD MARJORAM

☼ ❋ ↔ 12 in (30 cm) ↕ 12–18 in (30–45 cm)

Variable species found from Europe to Asia. Popular culinary herb, more pungent flavor than marjoram. Dark green oval to round leaves. Small pink, purple, or white flowers, from summer to autumn. *O. v.* var. *humile,* compact creeping variety with deep green leaves. *O. v.* 'Aureum', small golden leaves; 'Dr Ietswaart', low growing with golden leaves; 'Gold Tip', yellow-tipped leaves; 'Polyphant' (syn. 'White Anniversary'), leaves edged with creamy white; 'Thumble's Variety', large yellowish green leaves. Zones 5–9.

ORYZA

A genus in the grass (Poaceae) family containing 19 species of annual and perennial grasses, including rice, native to damp and swampy areas of tropical Asia, Africa, and Australia. Flowering stems bear panicles of compressed flower spikelets. The ripened seed of *O. sativa,* rice, is an important staple food.

CULTIVATION: *O. sativa* has many cultivars that suit a range of climates and soil types; usually grown as an annual. It needs moist soil and, when grown as a food crop, is usually grown in a flooded system, the water being drained away at harvest.

Oryza sativa
RICE

☼ ⚘ ↔ 12–24 in (30–60 cm) ↕ 2–4 ft (0.6–1.2 m)

Native to southeastern Asia. Annual swamp grass with tapering leaves and a drooping flowering panicle. Most of the many cultivars belong to the Indica Group, more tropical, with longer lighter green leaves, longer kernels, or the Japonica Group, generally grown in more northern climates, with shorter darker green leaves, shorter kernels. 'Cigalon', cultivar from Japan. Zones 9–12.

OXALIS (see page 658)

Oxalis tuberosa
NEW ZEALAND YAM, OCA

☼ ❋ ↔ 6–8 in (15–20 cm) ↕ 10–12 in (25–30 cm)

Tuberous summer-growing perennial from Colombia. Knobbed red, yellow, or white tubers, edible. Stems upright, often red, with 3 leaflets per leaf. Wild form has small yellow flowers, in summer; many cultivated forms are non-flowering. Zones 7–11.

PACHYRHIZUS
YAM BEAN

This genus of about 6 twining, climbing herbs with massive, tuberous roots, within the pea-flower subfamily of the legume (Fabaceae) family, originates from tropical South America to Mexico; has naturalized in Florida, USA. Large compound leaves with 3 toothed leaflets. Green, blue, purple, white, or mauve pea-flowers in dense racemes, up to 8 in (20 cm) long, in spring, followed by clusters of flattened pods. Some species are grown for their edible roots, the only part of the plant not poisonous.

CULTIVATION: Sow seed in sandy soil in a warm, dry, sunny area, spacing about 12 in (30 cm) apart. Remove flowers to enhance root growth and harvest before first frost. Propagate from seed.

Oryza sativa

Pachyrhizus erosus
JICAMA, MEXICAN POTATO, MEXICAN TURNIP, YAM BEAN

☼ ⚘ ↔ 3–6 ft (0.9–1.8 m) ↕ 10–20 ft (3–6 m)

Central American herbaceous twining climber. Edible, starchy, tuberous root to 8 ft (2.4 m). Compound leaves, toothed leaflets. Flowers purple-violet to white. Bean-shaped pods. Zones 10–11.

PANAX
GINSENG

In the ivy (Araliaceae) family, this once large genus of Asian and eastern North American tuberous-rooted perennials has been reduced to just 5 species, with many former members now classified under *Polyscias.* Most species produce upright stems with whorls of palmate leaves made up of 3 to 7 leaflets. Small white flowers are followed by yellow, red, or near-black drupes.

CULTIVATION: Mostly cold hardy, it needs warm summers to do well. Plant in humus-rich, moist, well-drained soil away from the hottest sun and cold drafts. Water and feed well during the growing season. Propagate by division or from seed.

Panax ginseng
syn. *Panax schinseng*

GINSENG, NIN-SIN

☀ ❋ ↔ 8–12 in (20–30 cm) ↕ 6–8 in (15–20 cm)

Perennial herb from Korea and northeastern China. Carrot-shaped, branching, aromatic rootstock, valued in traditional medicine. Compound leaves, 5 elliptical to oval-shaped, finely serrated leaflets. Red berry-like fruit. Zones 4–8.

PASTINACA

Genus of 14 biennial or perennial herbs from Eurasia, from the carrot (Apiaceae) family, one of which, *P. sativa,* has edible roots. Simple or divided leaves, with segments sometimes deeply lobed. Compound umbels of small yellow flowers with no sepals but yellow oval petals curving inward. Fruit is flattened and elliptical with ridged edges.
CULTIVATION: Plant in full sun in rich soil. Sow seeds in spring in rows 16–18 in (40–45 cm) apart. Dig roots in autumn and store, or leave in ground until spring. Propagate from seed.

Pastinaca sativa

PARSNIP
☼ ❄ ↔ 18–24 in (45–60 cm) ↑ 3–5 ft
(0.9–1.5 m)
Strong-smelling, finely hairy biennial from Europe and western Asia. Angled or cylindrical, hollow or solid, grooved stems. Thick, white, edible rootstock. Base leaves divided, with 5 to 11 oval, curling, serrated lobes. Zones 4–8.

PERSICARIA *(see page 537)*

Persicaria odorata

syn. *Polygonum odoratum*
VIETNAMESE CORIANDER, VIETNAMESE MINT
☼ ➤ ↔ 6–18 in (15–45 cm) ↑ 6–18 in (15–45 cm)
Spreading, colony-forming, tropical perennial, grown as an annual in cooler climates, with erect jointed stems that fall and take root. Pink flowers in summer–autumn. Used fresh as both a medicinal herb and aromatic culinary herb. Zones 8–12.

PETROSELINUM

PARSLEY, ROCK PARSLEY, ROCK SELINEN
Genus of 3 annual or biennial tap-rooted herbs, members of the carrot (Apiaceae) family, native to temperate Eurasia. Erect or spreading, branching stems and divided foliage. Compound leaf blades are broadly oblong, triangular, or oval, with toothed or lobed leaflets, often ornately curled. In late summer to autumn compound umbels of small greenish yellow or reddish flowers appear, followed by flat, ribbed, oval seeds.
CULTIVATION: Sow seeds in moist well-drained soil in a sunny spot, about 6–8 in (15–20 cm) apart. Cut back frequently to maintain vigor. Propagate from seeds soaked in warm water before planting.

Persicaria odorata

Petroselinum crispum

syns *Petroselinum hortense, P. sativum*
CURLY PARSLEY, PARSLEY
☼ ❄ ↔ 9–36 in (22–90 cm) ↑ 12–36 in (30–90 cm)
Biennial herb, native to Europe and western Asia. Erect or spreading stems. Culinary and medicinal uses. Dark to bright

Petroselinum crispum

green, aromatic, edible leaves are mostly triangular, deeply divided, with toothed or deeply cut oval segments, sometimes flat, often curling. Terminal umbels of many small greenish yellow flowers. Many cultivars and varieties. '**Champion Moss Curled**', curled, finely cut, deep green leaves; '**Clivi**', neat dwarf form; '**Darki**', cold-tolerant, tightly curled dark green leaves; '**Italian Plain Leaf**', plain, flat, deeply cut leaves; '**Krausa**', triple-curled leaves; '**New Dark Green**', compact hardy form, emerald green leaves; '**Paramount**', closely curled leaves; *P. c.* **var.** *neapolitanum* (Italian parsley), flat uncurled leaves; *P. c.* **var.** *tuberosum* (Hamburg parsley, turnip-rooted parsley), fleshy, edible root. Zones 7–9.

PHASEOLUS

BEAN
Genus of about 20 annual or perennial, usually climbing herbs belonging to the pea-flower subfamily of the legume (Fabaceae) family, native to the Americas; several species grown widely as food crops. Compound leaves, with 3 smooth-edged or lobed leaflets. Sickle-shaped flower buds grow from the leaf axils and open as loose racemes of pea-flowers. Fruits are narrow oblong pods, often flattened, and contain several oval or flattened seeds.
CULTIVATION: Perennial species are often grown as annuals, sown and harvested during frost-free months. Grow in humus-rich well-drained soil in full sun. Water freely during growth and propagate from seed in autumn or spring.

Phaseolus acutifolius

DESERT BEAN, PAVI, TEXAS BEAN, WILD TEPARY BEAN
☼ ❄ ↔ 12–24 in (30–60 cm) ↑ 18–40 in (45–100 cm)
Drought-tolerant twining or sprawling annual herb, native to southwestern USA and Mexico. Compound leaves with 3 to 5 narrow, pointed, oval or sword-shaped leaflets, and few white, yellow, or pale purple flowers on short stalks. Slightly hairy oblong seed pods. Seeds, usually 2 to 10 per pod, are normally flat and buff colored, and resemble a small butterbean. The cultivated varieties are bush types, best suited for use as dried rather than fresh beans. *P. a.* **var.** *latifolius* (Tepary bean), bushy or-twining plant, larger leaflets and narrower fruits than the species; '**Golden**', prolific form, yellow seeds; '**Mitla Black**', black seeds, ideal for soups, crops twice a year; '**Sonoran Brown**', early-maturing form, tolerates drought and heat, brown seeds. Zones 8–11.

Phaseolus coccineus

DUTCH CASE-KNIFE BEAN, SCARLET RUNNER BEAN
☼ ❄ ↔ 24 in (60 cm) ↑ 4–6 ft (1.2–1.8 m)
Tall, twining, perennial vine, native to tropical Americas. Grown as an annual. Compound leaves with broad oval to heart-shaped

leaflets, to 5 in (12 cm) long. Long racemes of bright scarlet flowers in spring. Pods, to 12 in (30 cm) long, contain black seeds mottled red. *P. c.* var. *albonanus*, white seeds. *P. c.* var. *rubronanus*, erect form, red flowers. *P. c.* 'Albus', white seeds and flowers; 'Painted Lady' ★, red and white flowers. Zones 8–10.

Phaseolus lunatus

syn. *Phaseolus limensis*
LIMA BEAN
☼ ❄ ↔ 9–12 in (22–30 cm) ↑ 24–36 in (60–90 cm)
Twining or erect perennial, native to tropical South America. Grown widely as an annual. Long stalks bear leaves with oval to triangular leaflets, to 4 in (10 cm) long, and yellowish green, white, or lilac flowerheads. Pods, to 4 in (10 cm) long, containing 2 to 4 small, reddish brown, kidney-shaped seeds, appear from winter–spring. *P. l.* var. *lunonanus,* non-climbing bushy form; *P. l.* var. *salicis,* narrow spear-shaped leaves; *P. l.* 'Kate May Giant' and 'King of the Garden', good cropping forms. Zones 8–11.

Phaseolus vulgaris

FRENCH BEAN, HARICOT, KIDNEY BEAN, STRING BEAN
☼ ⚘ ↔ 6–9 in (15–22 cm) ↑ 3–10 ft (0.9–3 m)
Erect or twining annual from tropical Americas. Widely grown in cooler areas, but needs some protection. Compound leaves with rounded or oval leaflets. Racemes of up to 6 white, purple, or pink flowers in spring. Fruits are flat or nearly cylindrical pods, to 20 in (50 cm) long, containing elongated or spherical red, brown, black, white, or mottled seeds, harvested in summer. *P. v.* var. *humilis*, low-growing, non-climbing. *P. v.* 'Ferrari', 'Goldmarie' ★, 'Purple Speckled', popular cultivars. Zones 8–11.

PIMPINELLA

This genus of about 150 annual or perennial herbs with branching stems, members of the carrot (Apiaceae) family, is native to

Phaseolus coccineus 'Painted Lady'

temperate Eurasia and North Africa. Leaves may be simple, or divided with up to 3 leaflets. Umbels of small white or yellow flowers in summer, followed by oval fruits.
CULTIVATION: Grow in dry to marshy, wet, alkaline soils, in the sun. Propagate from seed.

Pimpinella anisum

ANISE, ANISEED
☼ ❄ ↔ 16–20 in (40–50 cm) ↑ 20–24 in (50–60 cm)
Annual, aromatic, finely hairy herb, native to eastern, central, and southern Europe, to the eastern Mediterranean, Syria and Egypt. Seeds have distinctive flavor. On its stems it bears rounded or oval leaves, finely cut into 3 narrow leaflets, and simple, broader, oval, toothed or slightly lobed leaves grow closer to the ground. In summer, umbrella-shaped clusters of yellow or white flowers. Zones 4–10.

PISUM

Genus of 2 bushy or climbing annual herbs from the pea-flower subfamily of the legume (Fabaceae) family, native to the Mediterranean area. Divided leaves have 4 to 6 opposite leaflets with leafy, rounded stipules and main axis ending as a tendril. Single, or groups of 2 or 3, butterfly-like flowers grow from leaf axils. Fruit is a flattened, oblong pod, containing few to several seeds.
CULTIVATION: A cool-season plant, in warmer climates plant from autumn into winter, and from summer to autumn in cooler climates, avoiding flowering and fruiting when frosts are likely. Peas prefer full sun in a rich, fertile, well-drained soil. Sow seed where plants are to grow. Pods are ready to harvest within 3 to 5 months of planting. Climbing plants require support.

Pisum sativum ★

FIELD PEA, GARDEN PEA, SUGAR PEA
☼ ❄ ↔ 2 ft (0.6 m) ↑ 5–6 ft (1.5–1.8 m)
Annual, native to southern Europe. Compound leaves with 3 nearly circular to oblong leaflets, with smooth-edged or toothed margins. Flowers are white with dark reddish purple markings. Elongated pods, to 6 in (15 cm) long, contain 3 to 10 seeds. *P. s.* var. *arvense*, stipules spotted with red, with angled and blotched seeds; *P. s.* var. *macrocarpa*, broad, flat, edible pod. Zones 7–9.

PORTULACA (see page 545)

Portulaca oleracea

syn. *Portulaca retusa*
COMMON PURSLANE, PUSSLEY
☼ ❄ ↔ 20 in (50 cm) ↑ 40 in (100 cm)
Soft, prostrate, fleshy annual, probably from India, now widely naturalized. Several or many, spreading to erect reddish brown stems forming mats of simple, flat, alternate or opposite, succulent, spatula- to egg-shaped leaves. Yellow flowers. Capsules contain dark brown to black, kidney-shaped seeds. Zones 7–10.

Phaseolus lunatus 'Kate May Giant'

Phaseolus vulgaris 'Purple Speckled'

RAPHANUS

RADISH

These 8 annual, biennial, or perennial herbs are members of the cabbage family (Brassicaceae), native to Europe and temperate Asia. Tall, branching habit, often with stems and leaves covered with hairs, and often with swollen, sometimes edible, tap roots. Leaves are divided or lobed; lower leaves appear on stalks, upper and stem leaves are nearly or completely stalkless. White or yellow flowers. Fruit is a jointed, narrow, grooved, long-beaked pod. Roots, seeds, and some flowers are edible.
CULTIVATION: Sow spring radish seed in spring and early autumn. Sow winter radishes in late summer. Adaptable to most soils in an open sunny position. Harvest seed pods when half-grown.

Raphanus sativus

RADISH

☼ ❋ ↔ 12–24 in (30–60 cm) ↑ 2–5 ft (0.6–1.5 m)

Annual or biennial herb, from southern Asia. Red, white, or yellow edible tap root. Rough, alternate, divided leaves. White to pale purple flowers strongly veined, in summer. **Caudatus Group** (syn. *R. caudatus*) (potting radish, rat-tail radish), non-tuberous root, thick seed pods used in pickles; **Longipinnatus Group** (daikon, Japanese radish, Chinese radish), deeply divided leaves, long white durable root; **Sativus Group**, common short-root radishes, root mostly pink or red but brown and "black" cultivars are also known. 'Cherriette', uniform, bright red, crisp, spherical roots; 'Cherry Belle' ★, cherry red spherical roots; 'Icicle' ★, heat-tolerant variety, roots pure white, crisp, carrot-shaped; 'Scarlet White-tipped', scarlet red spherical roots, white flesh. Zones 6–9.

RHEUM (see page 554)

Rheum × hybridum

syns *Rheum × cultorum*, *R. rhabarbarum* of gardens

RHUBARB

☼ ❋ ↔ 3–6 ft (0.9–1.8 m) ↑ 3 ft (0.9 m)

Hybrid of unclear origin. Stout edible stalks, large, wavy-edged, triangular leaves. Cultivars differ in flavor, degree of stalk color,

and harvest time. 'Cherry', thick red stalks; 'MacDonald', red stalks; and 'Victoria', thick green stalks shaded red. Zones 6–10.

RORIPPA

syn. *Nasturtium*

Genus of about 80 species of annuals and perennials in the cabbage (Brassicaceae) family, found around the world in temperate climates. Most are weak-stemmed plants, with smooth, lobed or toothed leaves and small 4-petalled yellow or white flowers.
CULTIVATION: Grow in well-aerated freshwater, preferably running and slightly alkaline; or grow in the bottom of a shallow trench in moist garden soil. Propagate from stem cuttings; or from seed.

Rorippa nasturtium-aquaticum

syn. *Nasturtium officinale*

WATERCRESS

☼ ❋ ↔ 2–7 ft (0.6–2 m) ↑ 6–12 in (15–30 cm)

Originating from temperate Eurasia but grown throughout the world. Hollow, crisp stems float in water, producing adventitious roots; they spread indefinitely. Variably lobed tender dark green leaves; small white flowers from spring to autumn. Zones 6–11.

ROSMARINUS

ROSEMARY

This genus is part of the large mint (Lamiaceae) family, and contains just 2 species of evergreen shrubs with short linear leaves. Small 2-lipped flowers are usually pale blue and borne along the branches.
CULTIVATION: Grow these plants in well-drained soil in a hot dry position; they will not tolerate wet winter conditions. Prune them after flowering has finished. Propagation is either from softwood or from half-hardened cuttings.

Rosmarinus officinalis ★

ROSEMARY

☼ ❋ ↔ 6 ft (1.8 m) ↑ 7 ft (2 m)

Native to the Mediterranean region. Variable habit. Aromatic, linear leaves, leathery with rolled edges, silvery beneath. Small light blue flowers, in spring–summer. *R. o.* var. *angustissimus* 'Benenden Blue', striking blue flowers, narrow leaves; *R. o.* 'Blue Lagoon', narrow leaves, blue flowers; 'Joyce DeBaggio' (syn. 'Golden Rain'), lower and more compact. Other cultivars include 'Majorca Pink', 'Roseus', 'Severn Sea', Silver Spires/'Wolres', 'Tuscan Blue' ★. The **Prostratus Group**, which are low spreading forms, includes 'Lockwood de Forest'. Zones 6–11.

RUMEX (see page 558)

Rumex acetosa

GARDEN SORREL, SOUR DOCK

☼ ❋ ↔ 12–16 in (30–40 cm) ↑ 20–40 in (50–100 cm)

Clumping Northern Hemisphere perennial, can be weedy. Slightly succulent, spearhead-shaped leaves. Red-brown flowers. Zones 3–10.

Rosmarinus officinalis 'Blue Lagoon'

Rumex scutatus
BUCKLER-LEAFED SORREL, FRENCH SORREL, GARDEN SORREL
☼ ❊ ↔ 12–16 in (30–40 cm) ↑ 16–18 in (40–45 cm)
Hardy clump-forming perennial native to Europe, western Asia, and northern Africa. Bright green spearhead-shaped leaves. Tiny green flowers. Brown seeds. Edible; used in sorrel soup. Zones 6–10.

RUTA
This genus of 8 species belongs to the rue (Rutaceae) family. Mostly subshrubs, some can become shrubby in mild climates. Found throughout temperate Eurasia. Grayish blue-green foliage. Small yellow flowers in summer, followed by insignificant greenish seed heads. CULTIVATION: Grow in well-drained soil, in full sun. Propagate from seed or cuttings.

Ruta graveolens ★
COMMON RUE, HERB OF GRACE, RUE
☼ ❊ ↔ 15 in (38 cm) ↑ 20 in (50 cm)
Subshrub from southern Europe. Glaucous stems and leaves, finely divided foliage. Tiny greenish yellow flowers. Toxic. '**Jackman's Blue**' ★, glaucous form; '**Variegata**', creamy foliage. Zones 5–9.

SACCHARUM (*see page 690*)

Saccharum officinarum
SUGAR CANE
☼ ⬥ ↔ 3–6 ft (0.9–1.8 m) ↑ 12–20 ft (3.5–6 m)
Believed to have originated from New Guinea. Stout upright juicy canes. Rich green leaves with roughened edges. Zones 9–12.

SAGITTARIA (*see page 559*)

Sagittaria sagittifolia
ARROWHEAD
☼ ❊ ↔ 12 in (30 cm) ↑ 24–36 in (60–90 cm)
Aquatic perennial found in temperate Eurasia. Large arrowhead-shaped leaves, very long pointed lobes. White flowers, often purple basal spots. Edible tuber. Zones 7–12.

SALVIA (*see page 298*)

Salvia officinalis ★
COMMON SAGE, GARDEN SAGE
☼ ❊ ↔ 36 in (90 cm) ↑ 30 in (75 cm)
Perennial native to Spain, the Balkans, and northern Africa. Oblong grayish green leaves. Flowers white to pink and purple. '**Berggarten**' ★, rounded leaves, flowers less often; '**Extrakta**', high-yielding medicinal oil; '**Icterina**', variegated leaves; '**Purpurascens**', reddish purple leaves; '**Purpurascens Variegata**', purple leaves, splashed white to cream; '**Tricolor**', leaves edged yellow and salmon pink. Zones 5–10.

Saccharum officinarum

Salvia sclarea
CLARY SAGE, CLEAR EYE
☼ ❊ ↔ 36 in (90 cm) ↑ 36–48 in (90–120 cm)
Perennial or biennial from southern Europe. Leaves heart-shaped and puckered. Small white-lilac or pale blue flowers in prominent rosy pink or mauve bracts. Musky aroma. '**Turkestanica**' ★, larger bluish or pinkish white flowers. Zones 4–9.

SANGUISORBA
syn. *Poterium*
BURNET
Genus comprising about 10 species of shrubs and rhizomatous perennials found in temperate parts of Eurasia, North America, and the Canary Islands, is a member of the rose (Rosaceae) family. Spirally arranged leaves. Flowers are small, either unisexual or hermaphroditic, green, white, or pink, stalkless, and arranged in dense heads. The calyx tube has 4 petal-like lobes, and there are no petals. Fruits are leathery achenes. CULTIVATION: Grow in moist rich soils that do not dry out in summer. Propagate by division, or from seed.

Sanguisorba minor
GARDEN BURNET, SALAD BURNET
☼/◖ ❊ ↔ 12–16 in (30–40 cm) ↑ 30 in (75 cm)
Perennial from Europe and western Asia. Basal green leaves. Flowerheads pink and rounded, in early to mid-summer. Young leaves give salads a cucumber flavor. Zones 3–8.

Sanguisorba officinalis
BURNET BLOODWORT, GREAT BURNET
☼ ❊ ↔ 24–36 in (60–90 cm) ↑ 30–36 in (75–90 cm)
Clump-forming perennial from temperate Eurasia. Medium green leaves. Deep red or dark purple flowers in summer. Zones 4–8.

SATUREJA
SAVORY
Genus of highly aromatic, small shrubs belonging to the mint (Lamiaceae) family, native to dry hillsides in the Mediterranean, the woods of North America, and the Himalayas. Four-angled, woody stems bear small, hairy, round to oval leaves. Pale lilac to white flowers in spring and summer. CULTIVATION: Grow in any fertile well-drained soil. Propagate from cuttings or by removal of rooted shoots.

Salvia sclarea

Satureja hortensis
SUMMER SAVORY
☼ ❊ ↔ 8 in (20 cm) ↑ 8 in (20 cm)
Annual from southern Europe. Erect hairy stems, long pointed leaves. Dense spikes of mauve to white flowers. Zones 5–9.

Satureja montana
WINTER SAVORY
☼ ❄ ↔ 12 in (30 cm) ↕ 20–36 in (50–90 cm)
Semi-evergreen shrublet from southern Europe and northern Africa. Small, highly fragrant, oblong leaves. Whorls of pale lilac summer flowers. Leaves similar in flavor and scent to thyme (*Thymus vulgaris*) used for seasoning. Zones 4–8.

SECHIUM
CHACO, CHAYOTE, CHOCHO
This genus, which belongs to the pumpkin (Cucurbitaceae) family, contains 6 to 8 species of climbing plants from the cooler mountain regions of tropical America. Bright green leaves, long-stalked and palmately lobed, heart-shaped bases. Star-shaped 5-lobed flowers are either male or female. Male flowers arise in long racemes, females are borne singly or in pairs. Large, green, ridged, oval fruits are fleshy and have hairy, spiny, or smooth skin. They contain a single seed that germinates within the fruit.
CULTIVATION: In temperate areas grow in a greenhouse with medium humidity in a well-drained, gritty soil. Water and feed regularly. In warm areas, grow outdoors in a free-draining soil. Propagate from cuttings or seed. Plant whole fruit if seed has germinated.

Sechium edule
CHAYOTE, CHOKO, CHRISTOPHINE
☼/◐ ❋ ↔ 10–20 ft (3–6 m) ↕ 10 ft (3 m)
Tuberous-rooted climber from Central America. Leaves have 3 to 5 lobes. Pale yellow male flowers in racemes to 12-in (30 cm) long; greenish female flowers. Edible greenish yellow fruits. Zones 9–12.

SESAMUM
There are about 15 species of annuals and perennials in this genus in the sesame (Pedaliaceae) family, native to Africa, India, and Sri Lanka. Leaves are simple or divided, opposite or alternate. Flowers are white, pink, or purple, bell-shaped, and 2-lipped, similar to foxgloves (*Digitalis*). Seed pods are oblong to cylindrical and are split longitudinally. The nutritious seeds of *S. orientale* have a variety of uses, including being used whole in cooking, ground to a paste for tahini, pressed for oil, and incorporated in stock feed.
CULTIVATION: Grow in tropical and subtropical areas in full sun in a rich, moist, but well-drained soil. Seed pods explode and disperse their seed, so they should be harvested before they dry out. Propagate from seed.

Sesamum orientale
syn. *Sesamum indicum*
BENNE, GINGELLY, SESAME
☼ ✦ ↔ 1–2 ft (0.3–0.6) ↕ 2–6 ft (0.6–1.8 m)
Annual species, originally from Africa. Hairy lance-shaped to oval leaves. Attractive white to pink tubular flowers, borne in leaf axils. When left on plant, dry seed pods explode, releasing numerous small seeds. Zones 10–12.

SMYRNIUM
This genus contains 7 species of biennial or monocarpic plants from western Europe and the Mediterranean region. They are tall rather coarse plants with leaves comprised of 3 broad leaflets. Small greenish yellow or yellow flowers in umbels typical of the carrot (Apiaceae) family, followed by shiny black or brown seeds, which readily self-sow. Leaves, roots, and stems of *S. olastrum* taste like celery. Foliage is aromatic.
CULTIVATION: Grow in moisture-retentive, well-drained fertile soil. When growing *S. olusatrum*, earth up in spring to blanch the stems as for celery. Propagate from seed.

Smyrnium olusatrum
ALEXANDERS, BLACK LOVAGE, HORSE PARSLEY
☼ ❋ ↔ 18–36 in (45–90 cm) ↕ 3–5 ft (0.9–1.5 m)
Biennial with stout ridged stems, native to Europe, widely naturalized elsewhere. Large, divided, shiny, dark green leaves, serrated margins. Small yellowish flowers. Shiny black seeds. Zones 6–10.

SOLANUM (see page 307)

Satureja montana

Solanum melongena
AUBERGINE, EGGPLANT, JEW'S APPLE
☼ ❂ ↔ 24 in (60 cm) ↕ 36 in (90 cm)
Bushy annual from southeastern Asia. Egg-shaped fruit. Stems sometimes spiny. Downy, oval, shallowly lobed leaves. Violet to light blue flowers. White to purple-black fruit, to 8 in (20 cm) wide. 'Black Beauty' ★, nearly black oval fruit; 'Bonica', early maturing; 'Ping Tung', clusters of long slender rich rosy mauve to purple fruit; and 'Turkish Orange', tiny squat orange-red fruits, which resemble tomatoes. Zones 9–12.

Solanum tuberosum
POTATO
☼ ❄ ↔ 18 in (45 cm) ↕ 18–24 in (45–60 cm)
From South America. Dark green leaves, white to pale violet flowers. Big range of cultivars. 'All Blue' and 'Salad Blue' have blue skin and lavender-blue flesh; 'Mimi', red skinned, cherry size; 'Red Duke of York' ★, red skin and yellow flesh. Zones 7–11.

SORGHUM
MILLET, SORGHUM
Genus of about 20 quick-growing, broad-leafed, annual or perennial grasses, members of the family Poaceae, originating from tropical and subtropical Africa, Asia, and Australia, except for 1 species from Mexico. Robust, usually upright stems form clumps. Leaves have flat or wavy margins in 2 ranks that overlap the waxy sheaths encircling the stem. Branching, usually upright, conical to oval-shaped panicles of flower spikelets, which yield round bluntly pointed seed. Grown for grain and forage and for the syrup extracted from the stalks of *S. vulgare* var. *saccharatum*.
CULTIVATION: Sorghum tolerates a wide range of fertile well-drained soils in an open sunny position. Propagate from seed.

Solanum melongena 'Bonica'

Solanum tuberosum 'Mimi'

Spinacia oleracea 'Viking'

Sorghum bicolor

GREAT MILLET, SORGHUM

✷ ⚘ ↔ 2–3 ft (0.6–0.9 m) ↑ 10–20 ft (3–6 m)

Believed to be of African origin. Narrow strap-like leaves, white midrib. Large dense panicles, to 24 in (60 cm) long, fertile spikelets, in summer. Large variously colored grains, which provide the staple diet for the people of many countries. Zones 9–12.

SPINACIA

SPINACH

Native to central Asia, this genus of 3 species of annuals or biennials lies within the goosefoot (Chenopodiaceae) family. Leaves are large and flat. Small flowers are either male or female, males borne on densely packed spikes, females in the leaf axils. *S. oleracea* is the commonly cultivated species grown for its edible leaves. CULTIVATION: Grow *S. oleracea* in deep rich soil to accommodate the taproot and top-dress with nitrogen. Water well in the growing period. Best suited to cool season growing in spring and autumn. Susceptible to downy mildew and leaf spot. Propagate from seed.

Spinacia oleracea

SPINACH

✷/◐ ❋ ↔ 12–18 in (30–45 cm) ↑ 24–36 in (60–90 cm)

Annual of uncertain origin, possibly from southwestern Asia. Large, bright green, oval to triangular, smooth or wrinkled leaves. Young leaves eaten raw in salads, older leaves cooked. '**Space**', smooth-leafed, good mildew resistance; '**Triathlon**' ★, vigorous, fast-growing; '**Viking**', large leaves, slow to bolt. Zones 6–9.

STACHYS (see page 580)

Stachys affinis

CHINESE ARTICHOKE

✷ ❋ ↔ 36 in (90 cm) ↑ 20 in (50 cm)

Tuberous perennial from China. Upright stems, crinkly leaves. Small white or pink flowers, in summer. Small, edible root tubers. Widely cultivated in Japan. Zones 4–8.

SYMPHYTUM (see page 585)

Symphytum officinale

COMFREY, COMMON COMFREY, ENGLISH COMFREY

✷/◐ ❋ ↔ 6 ft (1.8 m) ↑ 5 ft (1.5 m)

Vigorous plant with rangy habit from temperate Eurasia. Bell-shaped flowers, rose-purple crimson, mauve crimson, white, in spring–summer. '**Variegatum**', leaf margins are white. Zones 3–9.

Symphytum × uplandicum

syn. *Symphytum peregrinum*

RUSSIAN COMFREY

✷/◐ ❋ ↔ 4 ft (1.2 m) ↑ 6 ft (1.8 m)

Bristly plant of garden origin, may be a natural hybrid of *S. officinale* and *S. asperum*. Heavy clusters of rose-purple flowers, late spring–late summer. Useful background plant. '**Variegatum**', lilac flowers, yellow edged mid-green leaves. Zones 3–9.

SYZYGIUM (see page 322)

Syzygium aromaticum

syn. *Eugenia aromaticum*

CLOVE

✷ ⚘ ↔ 15 ft (4.5 m) ↑ 50 ft (15 m)

Conical to columnar small tree from the Moluccas, Indonesia. Aromatic, elliptical-shaped leaves. Summer flowers have pinkish yellow stamens. Purple berries. Flower buds exported as cloves. Zones 11–12.

Symphytum officinale

TANACETUM (see page 588)

Tanacetum cinerariifolium ★

syns *Chrysanthemum cinerariifolium*, *Pyrethrum cinerariifolium*

DALMATIA PYRETHRUM, INSECT FLOWER, PYRETHRUM

✷ ❋ ↔ 12 in (30 cm) ↑ 12–24 in (30–60 cm)

Perennial from the Balkans. Finely cut, silvery gray foliage on slender stems. The daisy-like flowers with white rays and a yellow center appear from late summer to autumn. Mulch where winters are severe. Needs hot dry conditions. It is the source of insecticidal pyrethrum. Zones 6–10.

Thymus serpyllum 'Snow Drift'

Tanacetum parthenium
syn. *Chrysanthemum parthenium*
FEVERFEW

☼/◐ ❋ ↔ 12 in (30 cm) ↑ 24 in (60 cm)

Short-lived perennial from southern Europe to the Caucasus. Ferny foliage. Summer flowers have flat yellow center surrounded by short, stubby, white petals. '**Aureum**', bright golden foliage, single yellow-tinted white flowers; '**Santana Lemon**', yellow button flowers, thinly rayed; '**Snowball**', tight ivory buttons; '**White Stars**', white flowers. Zones 4–9.

Tanacetum vulgare
GOLDEN BUTTONS, TANSY

☼/◐ ❋ ↔ 36–48 in (90–120 cm) ↑ 36–48 in (90–120 cm)

Perennial from Europe. Creeping roots and finely divided ferny foliage all along stem. Bright yellow flower clusters, spring to summer. Camphor scent. *T. v.* var. *crispum*, attractive arching foliage. *T. v.* '**Goldsticks**', longer stems, larger flowers. Zones 4–9.

TARAXACUM
DANDELION

Dandelions form a worldwide group of about 60 perennial or biennial weeds belonging to the daisy family (Asteraceae). They grow almost all over the Northern Hemisphere and different species are common in most parts of the world. They share a sturdy tap root, hollow stems with milky sap, toothed green leaves, and bright yellow flowers. All parts of the plant are edible. CULTIVATION: Grow as an annual, in rich friable soil in a sunny position. Propagation is usually from seed.

Taraxacum officinale
BLOWBALL, DANDELION, WET-A-BED

☼ ❋ ↔ 8 in (20 cm) ↑ 10–12 in (25–30 cm)

Common weed from the Northern Hemisphere. Leaves vary from broad to narrow, and from deeply cut edges, even fringed, to nearly smooth. Yellow ray flowers produce a ball of tufted

seeds dispersed by wind, from spring to summer. '**Thick-leaved Improved**', tender fleshy leaves. Zones 3–10.

TETRAGONIA
This small genus has its own family, Tetragoniaceae, and is found in New Zealand and Australia, naturalized elsewhere. The few species are short-lived perennials with dark green fleshy leaves of variable shapes, from triangular to oblong with shiny undersides. Stems are succulent with small daisy-like flowers in shades of pale green, cream to yellow, in spring. Fruits are square-shaped. CULTIVATION: Adaptable to most soils, in a sunny or partly shaded spot. Propagate from seed soaked in warm water, or from cuttings.

Tetragonia tetragonioides
NEW ZEALAND SPINACH, WARRIGAL GREENS

◐ ❋ ↔ 24–40 in (60–100 cm) ↑ 8–12 in (20–30 cm)

Short-lived prostrate perennial from New Zealand and Australia. Oblong to triangular, pointed, fleshy leaves, shiny underneath, edible. Succulent stems. Greenish yellow flowers. Zones 7–9.

THYMUS (see page 592)

Thymus serpyllum
CREEPING THYME, MOTHER-OF-THYME, WILD THYME

☼ ❋ ↔ 36 in (90 cm) ↑ 1–4 in (2.5–8 cm)

Variable, wide, mat-forming perennial found naturally from northern Europe to northwestern Spain. Tiny lavender-purple flowers. '**Annie Hall**', old reliable cultivar, early-blooming, fragrant, pink flowers; '**Pink Chintz**', gray-green leaves, pale pink flowers; '**Rainbow Falls**', gold-splashed deep green foliage, pink summer flowers; '**Russetings**', bronze-tinted foliage, bright pink flowers; '**Snow Drift**', with pure white flowers over a spreading mat; and '**Vey**', a neat, compact form, pale salmon pink flowerheads, darker in bud. Zones 4–9.

Thymus vulgaris
COMMON THYME

☼ ❋ ↔ 10 in (25 cm) ↑ 12 in (30 cm)

Woody-based perennial or subshrub found naturally around the western Mediterranean. Tiny lance-shaped leaves, downy undersides. White to pinkish purple flowers. '**Argenteus**', silver-edged foliage, best in pots; '**Aureus**', golden yellow foliage, reddish purple flowers; '**Compactus**', a dwarf, dense mound of gray-green leaves; '**Erectus**', upright growth, aromatic, conifer-like, gray-green needle leaves, white flowers; '**Silver Posie**', white-edged foliage, pale pink-mauve flowers. Zones 7–10.

TRAGOPOGON
GOAT'S BEARD

This genus is a member of the daisy (Asteraceae) family and contains about 50 species of tap-rooted annual, biennial, or perennial

herbs native to temperate Eurasia and the Mediterranean. Alternate linear leaves. Daisy flowers are yellow or purple, open in the morning, turning to face the sun before closing in the afternoon or in cloudy weather. Seed heads resemble thistledown.
CULTIVATION: Grow in any soil in full sun. Propagate from seed.

Tragopogon porrifolius
OYSTER PLANT, SALSIFY, VEGETABLE OYSTER
☼ ✳ ↔ 6–12 in (15–30 cm) ↑ 24–36 in (60–90 cm)
Biennial from the Mediterranean. Long, strap-like, bluish green leaves. Dusky purple daisy flowers. Grown for its edible root. Zones 5–9.

TRAPA
WATER CHESTNUT
The members of this genus, part of the water-chestnut (Trapaceae) family, consist of about 15 floating, aquatic, perennial herbs found from central Europe to eastern Asia and Africa. Their submerged stems have feathery roots usually rooted in mud. Leaves clustered toward the tips of the stems form rosettes; the leaves are toothed, floating, oval-shaped, held on swollen spongy stalks. Heads of 4 small white flowers emerge from the leaf axils. Hardened, horned, nut-like fruits are edible once they have been treated to remove toxins.
CULTIVATION: They prefer shallow water or wet muddy soil in a protected, sunny position. Propagate from seed.

Trapa natans
BULL NUT, JESUITS' NUT, WATER CHESTNUT
☼ ✳ ↔ 2–4 ft (0.6–1.2 m) ↑ 3–5 ft (0.9–1.5 m)
Aquatic perennial found from central Europe to eastern Asia and tropical Africa. Floating or prostrate stems; submerged leaves are narrow, linear; floating leaves triangular, leathery, forming rosettes. Insignificant flowers. Large, fleshy, nut-like fruit. Very invasive. Zones 5–8.

TRICHOSANTHES
Genus of some 15 species found from tropical Asia through to northern Australia and the Pacific Islands belonging to the pumpkin (Cucurbitaceae) family. Climbing or sprawling annuals or perennials. Tendrils are unbranched or with up to 5 branches. Leaves are simple or with 3 or 5 lobes, their edges smooth or toothed. Flowers are unisexual, males and females on the same plant or on different plants, with 5 white petals conspicuously fringed. Fruit is spherical to egg-shaped or very elongated, fleshy, with a smooth surface.
CULTIVATION: In temperate zones grow as greenhouse annuals, raised from seed sown in spring. In the tropics grow up buildings or hedges in sunny fertile sites. Propagate from seed.

Tragopogon porrifolius

Trichosanthes cucumerina
syn. *Trichosanthes anguina*
CLUB GOURD, SERPENT CUCUMBER, SNAKE GOURD
☼ ⚘ ↔ 5–10 ft (1.5–3 m) ↑ 8–20 ft (2.4–6 m)
Annual found from southern Asia to northern Australia. Compound leaves. White flowers. Cylindrical fruit. Zones 10–12.

TRIGONELLA
Genus of about 50 species from the Mediterranean region, the islands of the subtropical North Atlantic, and South Africa, with one species in Australia, in the pea-flower subfamily of the legume (Fabaceae) family. Perennial or annual herbs. Leaves have 3 toothed leaflets. Flowers in axillary racemes, umbels, or heads, small bracts. Calyx tube is short, bell-shaped with 5 lobes. Beaked fruit obovate, flattened or round in cross-section.
CULTIVATION: Best grown in well-drained soil in full sun. Propagate from seed sown in situ.

Trigonella foenum-graecum
FENUGREEK, GREEK CLOVER, GREEK HAY
☼ ⚘ ↔ 8–12 in (20–30 cm) ↑ 12–24 in (30–60 cm)
Annual herb from southern Europe and the Mediterranean. Compound leaves, 3 toothed oval-shaped leaflets. Ivory to yellow pea-flowers. Foliage and flowers bitter. Seeds edible. Zones 9–11.

TRITICUM
WHEAT
Genus of about 30 annual clumping grasses, from temperate regions of the Middle East and North Africa, a member of the grass (Poaceae) family, and belongs to the cereals group. Flat, strap-like leaves. Upright or sprawling, solid or hollow, cylindrical stems bear cylindrical or flattened spikelets of 3 to 7 florets with 3 stamens and yellow anthers, in summer. Ripe seed heads of *T. aestivum*, the world's most important cereal crop, are used for making bread flour. *T. durum* is also important as source of flour or pasta. There are more than 40,000 varieties of wheat.
CULTIVATION: Attractive but not often grown as a garden plant, wheat adapts to most soils in a sunny spot. Propagate from seed.

Triticum aestivum
BREAD WHEAT
☼ ⚘ ↔ 12–20 in (30–50 cm) ↑ 3–5 ft (0.9–1.5 m)
Found across the plains of the world wherever cereal crops are grown. Flat, rough, narrow, strap-like leaves. Smooth hollow flower stem. Bearded seed heads of oval kernels, usually yellowish brown, also red, white, blue, or purple. Flour ground from seeds used to make cereals and bread. Zones 9–11.

Trichosanthes cucumerina

Triticum durum
DURUM WHEAT, EMMER WHEAT
☼ ✤ ↔ 12–20 in (30–50 cm) ↕ 3–5 ft (0.9–1.5 m)
Grown across the flat plains of the world. Flat, rough, narrow, strap-like leaves. Smooth hollow flower stem. Flowers in dense, somewhat flattened, stalkless spikelets. Seed heads usually bearded; hard, oval-shaped, white, red, yellowish brown, or purple kernels ground to produce flour used to make pasta. Zones 9–11.

TROPAEOLUM (see page 792)

Tropaeolum majus
NASTURTIUM
☼/✤ ✤ ↔ 10 ft (3 m) ↕ 10 ft (3 m)
Annual climber or scrambler found from Colombia to Bolivia. Near round, dull green leaves, sometimes shallowly lobed. Flowers to over 2 in (5 cm) wide, in shades of yellow, orange, and red. Now grown mainly in the form of seed-raised cultivars in various colors, some double-flowered; some may be of hybrid origin, with other annual species such as *T. minus* and *T. peltophorum* in their parentage. **Alaska Series** ★, white-variegated foliage, most flower colors; '**Empress of India**', green to bluish green leaves, red flowers; **Gleam Hybrids**, mixed or individual colors; '**Hermine Grashoff**', orange-red double flowers; **Jewel Series** ★, white foliage variegation, in most flower colors; '**Margaret Long**', shallowly lobed leaves and golden yellow shading to pink double flowers; '**Peach Melba**', pale yellow flowers with orange blotch on each petal; '**Peach Schnapps**', pinkish orange with orange veining on each petal; '**Red Wonder**', spreading, purple-blue leaves, red flowers; **Whirlibird Series**, low and spreading. Zones 9–11.

Tropaeolum tuberosum
☼/✤ ✤ ↔ 10 ft (3 m) ↕ 10 ft (3 m)
Tuberous-rooted perennial climber from central Andes. Gray-green leaves. Solitary long-stemmed flowers, spur red, petals golden yellow to red, in summer. The large purple-marked yellow tubers are used as a vegetable in its native range. *T. t.* var. *lineamaculatum* 'Ken Aslet', orange flowers. Zones 8–10.

Valeriana officinalis

URTICA
STINGING NETTLE
This genus of 100 annual or perennial herbs, giving its name to the nettle (Urticaceae) family, is widely spread in temperate regions of the Northern Hemisphere. Leaves and stems of many species are covered with stinging hairs. The opposite, coarsely toothed, sword- to heart-shaped leaves have 3 to 5 prominent veins. Panicles or racemes of 4 small, inconspicuous flowers with no petals but 4 green sepals grow from the leaf axils in summer.
CULTIVATION: These plants are adaptable to most soils and positions in sun or shade. Propagate from seed or cuttings.

Urtica dioica
syn. **Urtica urens**
BIG STRING NETTLE, COMMON NETTLE, STINGING NETTLE
☼ ✤ ↔ 3–6 ft (0.9–1.8 m) ↕ 2–8 ft (0.6–2.4 m)
Perennial herb, widely naturalized. Square, bristly stems and leaves to 6 in (15 cm) long, covered with stinging hairs. Leaves used as food; stem fibre in rope, cloth, and paper. Zones 3–9.

VALERIANA (see page 603)

Valeriana officinalis
GARDEN HELIOTROPE, TRUE VALERIAN, VALERIAN
☼/✤ ✤ ↔ 16–32 in (40–80 cm) ↕ 4–6 ft (1.2–1.8 m)
From western Europe. Musk-scented flowers borne in 2–4 in (5–10 cm) wide pinkish white heads atop stems with paired deeply cut leaves in early summer. A famous sedative. Zones 3–10.

VALERIANELLA
CORN SALAD
This genus in the valerian (Valerianaceae) family contains 50 annual and biennial herbs occurring in North America, Europe, North Africa, and Asia. Upright, branching stems with simple, smooth-edged or toothed, succulent leaves. Dense, paired, terminal heads of flowers with bracts with a minute or non-existent calyx, and a small, 5-lobed, saucer-shaped to tubular corolla.
CULTIVATION: Adaptable plants, they grow well in most soils and positions. Propagate from seed.

Valerianella locusta
COMMON CORN SALAD, FETTICUS, LAMB'S LETTUCE
☼ ✤ ↔ 6–8 in (15–20 cm) ↕ 4–12 in (10–30 cm)
Annual native to Europe, northern Africa, and western Asia. Forms large rosette of slightly succulent, smooth-edged or slightly toothed, spoon-shaped to round leaves. Branched flower stalk with smaller stem leaves topped with rounded clusters of bluish mauve or white flowers. *V. l.* var. *olitoria*, bright green leaves. *V. l.* '**Blonde Shell**', gold leaves; '**Broad Leaved**', heat tolerant; '**Coquille de Louviers**', spoon-shaped leaves. Zones 5–9.

VICIA
VETCH
The members of this genus within the pea-flower subfamily of the legume (Fabaceae) family include around 140 mostly sprawling, annual or perennial herbaceous vines that often climb by

tendrils at the leaf tips. Widely distributed across temperate regions of the Northern Hemisphere. Divided leaves and butterfly-like flowers of lavender, white, or purple, occasionally yellow, followed by seeds carried in long pods.
CULTIVATION: Adaptable to most soils. Propagate from seed. Some self-seed readily.

Vicia faba
BROAD BEAN, HORSE BEAN

☼ ❄ ↔ 12 in (30 cm) ↕ 3–6 ft (0.9–1.8 m)
Upright annual, native to northern Africa and southwest Asia. Divided leaves without tendrils. White flowers with a dark purple blotch in leaf axils. Edible oblong seed pods. '**Red Epicure**', red flowers. Zones 8–10.

VIGNA
This genus, comprising some 150 species native throughout the tropics, but particularly in the Americas, is a member of the pea-flower subfamily of the legume (Fabaceae) family. The plants are erect or twining herbs with woody or tuberous rootstocks. Leaves have 1 to 3 elliptic to ovate leaflets. Flowers are in racemes or clustered together. Calyx is 2-lipped. The yellow, blue, or purple corolla has an upper petal generally with 2 to 4 appendages; the inner petals forming the keel are often beaked. The pod is cylindrical or flattened, straight or curved. The seeds are often kidney-shaped and sometimes have an aril.
CULTIVATION: Frost tender. In tropical areas grow in well-drained soil; in cooler areas grow in a greenhouse. Propagate from seed.

Vicia faba 'Red Epicure'

Vigna mungo
syn. *Phaseolus mungo*
BLACK GRAM

☼ ✦ ↔ 24–36 in (60–90 cm) ↕ 12–24 in (30–60 cm)
Spreading annual from Asia. Pointed, oval-shaped leaflets and yellow, pea-like flowers. Seed pods up to 2 in (5 cm) long. *V. m.* var. *radiata,* stems and seed pods covered with fine, short reddish hairs. Zones 10–12.

Vigna radiata
syns *Phaseolus aureus, P. radiatus*
GOLDEN GRAM, GREEN GRAM, MUNG BEAN

☼ ✦ ↔ 8–12 in (20–30 cm) ↕ 5–6 ft (1.5–1.8 m)
Annual vine native to India, Indonesia, and Southeast Asia. Finely hairy, with slender, twining stems and divided leaves. Yellowish purple, pea-shaped flowers. Finely hairy seed pods. Sprouted edible seeds. Zones 10–11.

XANTHOPHTHALMUM
Genus of 2 species of annuals from Europe, temperate Asia, and North Africa in the daisy (Asteraceae) family. They are branched

near the ground into several to many erect stems bearing toothed or lobed hairless leaves. Few daisy-like cream to yellow flower-heads at each branch tip. Free-seeding.
CULTIVATION: Easily grown in most soils in full sun. Apply nitrogenous fertilizer and keep soil moist. Sow seed in spring.

Xanthophthalmum coronarium
syn. *Chrysanthemum coronarium*
CROWN DAISY

☼ ❄ ↔ 12–24 in (30–60 cm) ↕ 18–30 in (45–75 cm)
Occurs across the Mediterranean region. Vigorous annual. Lower leaves often narrowly lobed. Profuse flowerheads with broad cream ray florets and yellow disc. Zones 8–11.

ZEA
Genus of 4 annual grasses, members of the grass (Poaceae) family, native to Central America. Strong upright stems with broad, smooth, strap-like leaves. Male flowers are at tops of stems, female flowers grow from leaf axils, with solid spathe-like core enclosed within the leaves, in summer. Fruit forms as massed grains (cobs or ears) around the core in late summer–autumn.
CULTIVATION: Adaptable to most soil types, they prefer an open sunny position. They can be propagated from seed.

Zea mays
CORN, MAIZE, MEALIE, INDIAN CORN, SWEET CORN

☼ ❄ ↔ 20–40 in (50–100 cm) ↕ 7–15 ft (2–4.5 m)
Upright, stout, robust stems. Smooth strap-like leaves in 2 ranks, with pointed tips and sheathed bases. Feathery male flowers in terminal panicles; female flowers in heads to 8 in (20 cm) long, growing from leaf axils, maturing to shining, yellow, white, or black grains, to 10 mm across, enclosed within the leaves. '**Black Aztec**', white ears that turn black when dried; '**Blue Jade**', dwarf bushy habit, deep bluish black kernels; '**Cuties Pops**', ornamental variety; '**Earlivee**', compact, early-maturing, yellow form, to 4 ft (1.2 m) high; '**Indian Summer**' ★, dense ears, 8 in (20 cm) long, with mixed kernels of white, yellow, red, and purple; '**New Excellence**', sweet yellow kernels. Zones 8–10.

ZINGIBER (see page 615)

Zingiber officinale
CANTON GINGER, COMMON GINGER, STEM GINGER

☼ ❄ ↔ 3 ft (0.9 m) ↕ 3–5 ft (0.9–1.5 m)
From tropical Asia, exact origin obscure. Narrow, glossy green leaves. Small green inflorescences with white and maroon flowers. Various forms, most are sterile. Grown for its aromatic root used in cooking and medicine. Zones 9–12.

Zea mays 'Indian Summer'

Climbers and Creepers

Plants that need a supporting structure to grow upon, such as a wall, trellis, or another plant, are known as climbers or creepers. Some plants have active mechanisms to help them cling, and there are different types of these mechanisms: some plants, such as clematis, have tendrils that attach themselves to something, while others, like *Pandorea pandorana*, attach themselves by twining up and around the support device. Clinging vines like ivy attach themselves to surfaces with adventitious roots.

Plants with a passive climbing system can have spines or stiff emergences (hook-shaped spikelets), which they use to attach themselves to other plants. Many roses are climbers and are armed with strong backward-pointing stem emergences.

For the gardener, climbers and creepers have many uses. They cover a fence or trellis, hide walls and bare ground, provide color and softness, release fragrance, provide shade, and reduce wind and noise. The care and cultivation of climbers and creepers depends greatly on the species. Some prefer shade while others, such as many bougainvillea species, prefer sun. Some like cool soils and root zones; the warmer the soil gets, the slower the roots are to develop. Provide adequate moisture, depending on the species, and fertilize as required.

Pendulous racemes of *Wisteria floribunda* blooms gracefully drape over an arbor. The flowers are fragrant, and will attract bees and butterflies to the garden.

Climber and Creeper Finder

The following cultivation table features at-a-glance information for every species or hybrid with an individual entry in the Climbers and Creepers chapter of this book. Simply find the plant you wish to know more about, and run your eye along the row to discover its height and spread, whether it is frost tolerant or not, the aspect it prefers, and more.

The type of plant is abbreviated to **A, P, W,** or **T:**
A – the plant is an annual.
P – the plant is a perennial.
W– the plant is woody.
T – the plant is a trailer.

The climate(s) that each plant needs to thrive in the outdoors are given (some plants will grow in more than one climate), abbreviated to **C, W,** or **T:**
C – the plant prefers a cool climate.

W– the plant prefers a warm-temperate or subtropical climate.
T – the plant prefers a tropical climate.

The season during which the plant produces flowers is abbreviated to **A, W, Sp, Su,** or **Any:**
A – the plant flowers in autumn.
W – the plant flowers in winter.
Sp – the plant flowers in spring.
Su – the plant flowers in summer.
Any – the plant flowers in any season.

The climbing mechanism that the plant uses is abbreviated to **C, Te, Tw,** or **S:**
C – the plant clings.
Te – the plant uses tendrils.
Tw – the plant twines.
S – the plant scrambles.

Plant name	Height	Spread	Type	Climate	Deciduous	Evergreen	Showy flowers	Flowering season	Climbing mechanism	Indoor use	Frost tolerant	Full sun	Half sun	Heavy shade
Aeschynanthus longicaulis	18–24 in (45–60 cm)	36 in (90 cm)	T	T		◆	◆	Su	—	◆				◆
Aeschynanthus radicans	5–6 ft (1.5–1.8 m)	18–36 in (45–90 cm)	T	T		◆	◆	Su	—	◆				◆
Akebia quinata	10 ft (3 m)	20 ft (6 m)	W	C/W	◆			Sp/Su	Tw			◆		◆
Allamanda cathartica	17 ft (5 m)	10 ft (3 m)	W	W/T		◆	◆	Su	C			◆		
Ampelopsis glandulosa	17 ft (5 m)	17 ft (5 m)	W	C/W	◆			Sp	Te		◆	◆	◆	
Antigonon leptopus	15 ft (4.5 m)	20 ft (6 m)	P	W/T		◆	◆	Su/A	Te			◆		
Aristolochia grandiflora	10 ft (3 m)	6 ft (1.8 m)	P	W/T		◆	◆	Su	Tw			◆	◆	
Aristolochia littoralis	20 ft (6 m)	15 ft (4.5 m)	W	W/T		◆		Su	Tw			◆	◆	
Asparagus asparagoides	5–6 ft (1.5–1.8 m)	3 ft (0.9 m)	P	C/W		◆		Su	Tw	◆	◆	◆		
Asparagus setaceus	12–48 in (30–120 cm)	24 in (60 cm)	P	W		◆		Su	Tw	◆			◆	
Beaumontia grandiflora	25 ft (8 m)	15 ft (4.5 m)	W	W/T		◆	◆	Su	Tw			◆		
Berberidopsis corallina	15 ft (4.5 m)	5–8 ft (1.5–2.4 m)	W	T		◆	◆	Su/A	Tw		◆		◆	
Bignonia capreolata	10–30 (3–9 m)	10 ft (3 m)	W	C/W		◆	◆	Su	Te		◆	◆	◆	
Bougainvillea × buttiana	17 ft (5 m)	10–20 ft (3–6 m)	W	W/T		◆	◆	Su	S			◆		
Bougainvillea glabra	10–12 ft (3–3.5 m)	15 ft (4.5 m)	W	W/T		◆	◆	Su	S			◆		
Bougainvillea spectabilis	12 ft (3.5 m)	15 ft (4.5 m)	W	W/T		◆	◆	Sp/Su	S			◆		
Bougainvillea Hybrid Cultivars	2–20 ft (0.6–6 m)	5–20 ft (1.5–6 m)	W	W/T		◆	◆	Su	S	◆		◆	◆	
Campsis grandiflora	25 ft (8 m)	8–15 ft (2.4–4.5 m)	W	C/W	◆		◆	Su/A	C		◆	◆		
Campsis radicans	35 ft (10 m)	8–15 ft (2.4–4.5 m)	W	C/W	◆		◆	Su/A	C		◆	◆		
Campsis × tagliabuana	17 ft (5 m)	8–15 ft (2.4–4.5 m)	W	C/W	◆		◆	Su/A	C		◆	◆		
Celastrus orbiculatus	30 ft (9 m)	10–20 ft (3–6 m)	W	C	◆			Su	Tw		◆	◆		
Celastrus scandens	20 ft (6 m)	20 ft (6 m)	T	C/W	◆			Su	Tw		◆	◆		
Cissus antarctica	17–25 ft (5–8 m)	3–10 ft (0.9–3 m)	W	W/T		◆		Sp/Su	Te	◆		◆	◆	

Plant name	Height	Spread	Type	Climate	Deciduous	Evergreen	Showy flowers	Flowering season	Climbing mechanism	Indoor use	Frost tolerant	Full sun	Half sun	Heavy shade
Cissus hypoglauca	17–60 ft (5–18 m)	20 ft (6 m)	W	W/T		◆		Sp/Su	Tw	◆			◆	
Cissus quadrangularis	60 in (150 cm)	32 in (80 cm)	P	W/T		◆		Sp/Su	Te	◆			◆	
Cissus rhombifolia	10 ft (3 m)	6 ft (1.8 m)	W	W/T		◆		Sp/Su	Te	◆		◆	◆	
Clematis alpina	8–10 ft (2.4–3 m)	5 ft (1.5 m)	W	C	◆		◆	Sp	Tw		◆	◆	◆	
Clematis armandii	20–30 ft (6–9 m)	7–10 ft (2–3 m)	W	C/W		◆	◆	Sp	Tw		◆	◆	◆	
Clematis chrysocoma	7–15 ft (2–4.5 m)	4–6 ft (1.2–1.8 m)	W	C/W	◆		◆	Su/A	Tw		◆	◆	◆	
Clematis cirrhosa	10–15 ft (3–4.5 m)	6 ft (1.8 m)	W	C/W		◆	◆	W/Sp	Tw		◆	◆	◆	
Clematis florida	15 ft (4.5 m)	5 ft (1.5 m)	W	C/W	◆		◆	Su	Tw		◆	◆	◆	
Clematis lanuginosa	7–10 ft (2–3 m)	4–8 ft (1.2–2.4 m)	W	C	◆		◆	Sp/Su/A	Tw		◆	◆	◆	
Clematis montana	15–25 ft (4.5–8 m)	10–20 ft (3–6 m)	W	C	◆		◆	Sp	Tw		◆	◆	◆	
Clematis paniculata	17–30 ft (5–9 m)	10–30 ft (3–9 m)	W	C/W		◆	◆	Sp/Su	Tw		◆	◆	◆	
Clematis patens	10–15 ft (3–4.5 m)	5–10 ft (1.5–3 m)	W	C	◆		◆	Sp/Su	Tw		◆	◆	◆	
Clematis tangutica	7–10 ft (2–3 m)	8–12 ft (2.4–3.5 m)	W	C	◆		◆	Su/A	Tw		◆	◆	◆	
Clematis × triternata	10–15 ft (3–4.5 m)	10–15 ft (3–4.5 m)	W	C			◆	Su	Tw		◆	◆	◆	
Clematis Hybrid Cultivars	4–20 ft (1.2–6 m)	5–15 ft (1.5–4.5 m)	W	C	◆		◆	Sp/Su/A	Tw		◆	◆	◆	
Clerodendrum splendens	7 ft (2 m)	7 ft (2 m)	W	W/T		◆	◆	Su	S	◆		◆		
Clerodendrum thomsoniae	15 ft (4.5 m)	15 ft (4.5 m)	W	W/T		◆	◆	Su	Tw			◆	◆	◆
Clytostoma callistegioides	10 ft (3 m)	20 ft (6 m)	W	W		◆	◆	Su	Te			◆		
Cobaea scandens	20–25 ft (6–8 m)	5–10 ft (1.5–3 m)	P	W	◆		◆	Su/A	Te	◆		◆		
Combretum bracteosum	12 ft (3.5 m)	7 ft (2 m)	W	W		◆	◆	Su	S			◆		
Congea tomentosa	10–30 ft (3–9 m)	20–40 ft (6–12 m)	W	T		◆	◆	Sp/Su/A	S			◆		
Distictis buccinatoria	6–15 ft (1.8–4.5 m)	10–20 ft (3–6 m)	P	W		◆	◆	Sp/Su	Te			◆		
Eccremocarpus scaber	10–15 ft (3–4.5 m)	7–10 ft (2–3 m)	P	W		◆	◆	Sp/Su	Te			◆		
Epipremnum pinnatum	12–20 ft (3.5–6 m)	6 ft (1.8 m)	W	W/T		◆		Sp/Su	C	◆		◆		
Fallopia baldschuanica	20–40 ft (6–12 m)	20–40 ft (6–12 m)	W	C	◆		◆	Su/A	Tw		◆	◆		
Fallopia japonica	3–7 ft (0.9–2 m)	3–7 (0.9–2 m)	P	C	◆		◆	Su/A	Tw		◆	◆		
Ficus pumila	10–30 ft (3–9 m)	unlimited	W	C/W		◆		Su	C	◆	◆	◆		◆
Gelsemium sempervirens	20 ft (6 m)	20 ft (6 m)	W	C/W		◆	◆	Su/A	Tw			◆	◆	
Hardenbergia comptoniana	10–15 ft (3–4.5 m)	3–10 ft (0.9–3 m)	W	W		◆	◆	W/Sp	Tw			◆	◆	
Hardenbergia violacea	3–10 ft (0.9–3 m)	3–7 ft (0.9–2 m)	W	W		◆	◆	W/Sp	Tw			◆	◆	
Hedera canariensis	15–20 ft (4.5–6 m)	20–60 ft (6–18 m)	W	C/W		◆		Sp/Su	C		◆			◆
Hedera colchica	20–35 ft (6–10 m)	20–60 ft (6–18 m)	W	C/W		◆		Sp/Su	C		◆		◆	◆
Hedera helix	35–50 ft (10–15 m)	20–60 ft (6–18 m)	W	C/W		◆		Sp/Su	C		◆			◆
Hedera hibernica	25–35 ft (8–10 m)	unlimited	W	C/W		◆		Sp/Su	C		◆			◆
Hibbertia scandens	8 ft (2.4 m)	unlimited	W	W		◆	◆	Sp/Su/A	Tw			◆	◆	
Hoya australis	2–6 ft (0.6–1.8 m)	2–6 ft (0.6–1.8 m)	W	W/T		◆	◆	Su	Tw	◆			◆	
Hoya carnosa	2–6 ft (0.6–1.8 m)	2–6 ft (0.6–1.8 m)	W	W/T		◆	◆	Su	Tw	◆			◆	

Plant name	Height	Spread	Type	Climate	Deciduous	Evergreen	Showy flowers	Flowering season	Climbing mechanism	Indoor use	Frost tolerant	Full sun	Half sun	Heavy shade
Humulus lupulus	17–20 ft (5–6 m)	10–30 ft (3–9 m)	P	W/T	◆		◆	Su	Tw		◆	◆		
Hydrangea petiolaris	50 ft (15 m)	17–35 ft (5–10 m)	W	C	◆		◆	Su	C		◆		◆	
Ipomoea alba	10–20 ft (3–6 m)	20–30 ft (6–9 m)	P	W/T		◆	◆	Su	Tw			◆		
Ipomoea horsfalliae	15–25 ft (4.5–8 m)	5–10 ft (1.5–3 m)	P	W/T		◆	◆	Su	Tw			◆		
Ipomoea lobata	10–15 ft (3–4.5 m)	3–6 ft (0.9–1.8 m)	P	W/T		◆	◆	Su	Tw			◆		
Ipomoea × multifida	3–10 ft (0.9–3 m)	3–6 ft (0.9–1.8 m)	P	W/T		◆	◆	Su/A	Tw	◆		◆		
Ipomoea nil	10–15 ft (3–4.5 m)	2–5 ft (0.6–1.5 m)	A	W/T	◆			Su	Tw			◆		
Ipomoea purpurea	5–10 ft (1.5–3 m)	5–10 ft (1.5–3 m)	A	C/W	◆			Sp/Su	Tw			◆		
Ipomoea tricolor	10 ft (3 m)	3 ft (0.9 m)	A	W/T	◆			Su	Tw			◆		
Jasminum azoricum	20 ft (6 m)	20 ft (6 m)	W	W/T		◆	◆	Su	Tw			◆	◆	
Jasminum beesianum	15 ft (4.5 m)	15 ft (4.5 m)	W	C/W		◆	◆	Sp/Su/A	S/Tw		◆	◆	◆	
Jasminum officinale	30 ft (9 m)	15 ft (4.5 m)	W	C/W		◆	◆	Su/A	S/Tw		◆	◆	◆	
Jasminum polyanthum	10–17 ft (3–5 m)	25 ft (8 m)	W	C/W		◆	◆	W/Sp/A	Tw			◆	◆	
Jasminum sambac	5–12 ft (1.5–3.5 m)	6 ft (1.8 m)	W	W		◆	◆	Any	Tw			◆		
Jasminum × stephanense	17 ft (5 m)	5–10 ft (1.5–3 m)	W	C/W	◆		◆	Su/A	Tw			◆		
Kennedia coccinea	7–10 ft (2–3 m)	10 ft (3 m)	W	W		◆	◆	Sp/Su	Tw			◆		
Kennedia nigricans	17–20 ft (5–6 m)	10–15 ft (3–4.5 m)	W	W		◆	◆	Sp/Su	Tw			◆		
Kennedia rubicunda	10–15 ft (3–4.5 m)	15 ft (4.5 m)	W	W		◆	◆	Sp/Su	Tw			◆		
Lapageria rosea	17 ft (5 m)	3–10 ft (0.9–3 m)	W	C/W		◆	◆	Su/A	Tw				◆	
Lathyrus grandiflorus	7 ft (2 m)	7 ft (2 m)	P	C/W	◆		◆	Su	Te		◆	◆		
Lathyrus latifolius	10 ft (3 m)	7 ft (2 m)	P	C	◆		◆	Su	Te		◆	◆		
Lonicera × brownii	10 ft (3 m)	8 ft (2.4 m)	W	C	◆		◆	Sp/Su	Tw			◆	◆	
Lonicera caprifolium	20 ft (6 m)	10 ft (3 m)	W	C	◆		◆	Sp/Su	Tw			◆	◆	
Lonicera etrusca	12 ft (3.5 m)	10 ft (3 m)	W	C/W		◆	◆	Sp/Su	Tw			◆	◆	
Lonicera × heckrottii	15 ft (4.5 m)	6 ft (1.8 m)	W	C	◆		◆	Sp/Su	Tw			◆	◆	
Lonicera × italica	10 ft (3 m)	5–10 ft (1.5–3 m)	W	C		◆	◆	Sp/Su	Tw			◆	◆	◆
Lonicera japonica	25–30 ft (8–9 m)	25 ft (8 m)	W	C/W		◆	◆	Sp/Su	Tw			◆	◆	
Lonicera periclymenum	12 ft (3.5 m)	8 ft (2.4 m)	W	C/W	◆		◆	Su	Tw			◆	◆	
Lonicera sempervirens	10–20 ft (3–6 m)	10 ft (3 m)	W	C/W		◆	◆	Sp/Su	Tw			◆	◆	
Lonicera × tellmanniana	7–20 ft (2–6 m)	5 ft (1.5 m)	W	C	◆		◆	Sp/Su	Tw			◆	◆	
Mandevilla × amabilis	15 ft (4.5 m)	15 ft (4.5 m)	W	W/T		◆	◆	Sp	Tw	◆			◆	
Mandevilla laxa	15 ft (4.5 m)	17 ft (5 m)	W	W/T		◆	◆	Sp/Su	Tw			◆	◆	
Mandevilla sanderi	17 ft (5 m)	17 ft (5 m)	W	W/T		◆	◆	Sp	Tw	◆		◆	◆	
Metrosideros carminea	40 ft (12 m)	3–10 ft (0.9–3 m)	W	W		◆	◆	Sp	C				◆	
Monstera deliciosa	35–50 ft (10–15 m)	8–20 ft (2.4–6 m)	W	W/T		◆		Su	C					◆
Muehlenbeckia complexa	5–15 ft (1.5–4.5 m)	10 ft (3 m)	W	C/W		◆		Sp	Tw		◆	◆		
Pandorea jasminoides	17 ft (5 m)	8–15 ft (2.4–4.5 m)	W	W		◆	◆	Su/A	Tw	◆		◆		

Plant name	Height	Spread	Type	Climate	Deciduous	Evergreen	Showy flowers	Flowering season	Climbing mechanism	Indoor use	Frost tolerant	Full sun	Half sun	Heavy shade
Pandorea pandorana	20 ft (6 m)	10–20 ft (3–6 m)	W	W		◆	◆	Sp/Su	Tw			◆		
Parthenocissus quinquefolia	40–50 ft (12–15 m)	30 ft (9 m)	W	C/W	◆			Su/A	C/Te		◆	◆	◆	
Parthenocissus tricuspidata	50–70 ft (15–21 m)	20 ft (6 m)	W	C/W	◆			Su/A	C/Te			◆	◆	
Passiflora amethystina	10 ft (3 m)	3–6 ft (0.9–1.8 m)	W	W		◆	◆	A	Te			◆	◆	
Passiflora caerulea	30 ft (9 m)	6–15 ft (1.8–4.5 m)	W	C/W		◆	◆	Su/A	Te			◆	◆	
Passiflora coccinea	12 ft (3.5 m)	12–30 ft (3.5–9 m)	W	W/T		◆	◆	Su/A	Te			◆	◆	
Passiflora incarnata	6 ft (1.8 m)	6–15 ft (1.8–4.5 m)	W	C/W		◆	◆	Su	Te			◆		
Passiflora racemosa	15 ft (4.5 m)	6–15 ft (1.8–4.5 m)	W	W		◆	◆	Su/A	Te			◆	◆	
Passiflora × violacea	20 ft (6 m)	6–15 ft (1.8–4.5 m)	W	W		◆	◆	Su	Te			◆	◆	
Passiflora Hybrid Cultivars	6–12 ft (1.8–3.5 m)	6–15 ft (1.8–4.5 m)	W	W		◆	◆	Su/A	Te			◆	◆	
Pelargonium peltatum	8 ft (2.4 m)	8 ft (2.4 m)	P	W		◆	◆	Any	S	◆		◆		
Petrea volubilis	20–60 ft (6–18 m)	10–20 ft (3–6 m)	W	W/T		◆	◆	Su	S			◆		
Philodendron domesticum	6–10 ft (1.8–3 m)	2–3 ft (0.6–0.9 m)	W	W/T		◆		Su	C	◆			◆	
Philodendron erubescens	6–10 ft (1.8–3 m)	3–8 ft (0.9–2.4 m)	W	W/T		◆		Su	C				◆	◆
Philodendron hederaceum	10–15 ft (3–4.5 m)	2–6 ft (0.6–1.8 m)	W	W/T		◆		Su	C	◆			◆	
Piper nigrum	10–25 ft (3–8 m)	12 ft (3.5 m)	P	T		◆		Su	Tw			◆		
Podranea ricasoliana	12–20 ft (3.5–6 m)	20 ft (6 m)	W	W		◆	◆	Su/A	S			◆		
Pueraria lobata	30–60 ft (9–18 m)	30–100 ft (9–30 m)	P	C/W	◆			Su	Tw		◆	◆		
Pyrostegia venusta	20–30 ft (6–9 m)	20 ft (6 m)	W	W		◆	◆	A/W/Sp	Tw			◆		
Quisqualis indica	35 ft (10 m)	25 ft (8 m)	W	T		◆	◆	Su/A	Tw			◆	◆	
Rosa banksiae	30 ft (9 m)	30 ft (9 m)	W	C/W		◆	◆	Sp	Tw/S		◆	◆		
Rosa bracteata	8 ft (2.4 m)	8 ft (2.4 m)	W	C/W		◆	◆	Su/A	S		◆	◆		
Rosa helenae	20 ft (6 m)	15 ft (4.5 m)	W	C/W	◆		◆	Su	S		◆	◆		
Rosa laevigata	30 ft (9 m)	20 ft (6 m)	W	C/W		◆	◆	Su	S		◆	◆		
Rosa moschata	10–35 ft (3–10 m)	10 ft (3 m)	W	C/W	◆		◆	Su	S		◆	◆		
Rosa, Cluster-flowered Climbing Roses	10–20 ft (3–6 m)	8–15 ft (2.4–4.5 m)	W	C/W	◆		◆	Su/A	S		◆	◆		
Rosa, Large-flowered Climbing Roses	7–17 ft (2–5 m)	7–17 ft (2–5 m)	W	C/W	◆		◆	Su/A	S		◆	◆	◆	
Rosa, Rambler Roses	10–25 ft (3–8 m)	10–25 ft (3–8 m)	W	C/W	◆		◆	Su	S		◆	◆		
Rosa, Modern Ground Cover Roses	12–24 in (30–60 cm)	5–12 ft (1.5–3.5 m)	T	C/W	◆		◆	Su/A	S		◆	◆		
Rosa, Ayrshire Roses	5–10 ft (1.5–3 m)	10–20 ft (3–6 m)	W	C	◆		◆	Su	S		◆	◆		
Rosa, Boursault Roses	8–12 ft (2.4–3.5 m)	8–12 ft (2.4–3.5 m)	W	C/W	◆		◆	Su	S		◆	◆		
Rosa, Climbing Tea Roses	10–20 ft (3–6 m)	10–25 ft (3–8 m)	W	C/W		◆	◆	Su/A	S		◆	◆		
Rosa, Laevigata Roses	10–25 ft (3–8 m)	10–20 ft (3–6 m)	W	C/W		◆	◆	Su	S		◆	◆		
Rosa, Noisette Roses	8–12 ft (2.4–3.5 m)	5–10 ft (1.5–3 m)	W	C/W	◆		◆	Su/A	S		◆	◆		
Rosa, Sempervirens Roses	8–15 ft (2.4–4.5 m)	10–20 ft (3–6 m)	W	C/W		◆	◆	Su	S		◆	◆		
Saritaea magnifica	25 ft (8 m)	8–15 ft 2.4–4.5 m)	W	W/T		◆	◆	Sp/Su	Tw			◆	◆	
Schisandra chinensis	25–35 ft (8–10 m)	20 ft (6 m)	W	C/W	◆		◆	Sp/Su	Tw		◆	◆	◆	

Plant name	Height	Spread	Type	Climate	Deciduous	Evergreen	Showy flowers	Flowering season	Climbing mechanism	Indoor use	Frost tolerant	Full sun	Half sun	Heavy shade
Schizophragma hydrangeoides	30 ft (9 m)	10 ft (3 m)	W	C/W	◆		◆	Su	C		◆		◆	
Senecio macroglossus	3–7 ft (0.9–2 m)	40 in (100 cm)	P	W/T		◆	◆	Sp/Su	Tw			◆		
Smilax aspera	10 ft (3 m)	24 in (60 cm)	P	W		◆		Sp	Te			◆		
Smilax glyciphylla	5–10 ft (1.5–3 m)	5–10 ft (1.5–3 m)	W	W		◆		Su	Te/Tw			◆	◆	
Solandra longiflora	10–20 ft (3–6 m)	8–15 ft (2.4–4.5 m)	W	W/T		◆	◆	W/Sp	S			◆		
Solandra maxima	20–50 ft (6–15 m)	10–30 ft (3–9 m)	W	W/T		◆	◆	Sp/Su	S			◆		
Solanum crispum	10–20 ft (3–6 m)	8–15 ft (2.4–4.5 m)	W	C/W			◆	Su	S/Tw		◆	◆		
Solanum jasminoides	10–20 ft (3–6 m)	8–15 ft (2.4–4.5 m)	W	W			◆	Su	S/Tw			◆		
Solanum seaforthianum	10–20 ft (3–6 m)	8–15 ft (2.4–4.5 m)	W	W/T			◆	Su	S			◆		
Solanum wendlandii	15 ft (4.5 m)	5–10 ft (1.5–3 m)	W	W/T			◆	Su	S			◆		
Sollya heterophylla	5–7 ft (1.5–2 m)	3–5 ft (0.9–1.5 m)	W	W		◆	◆	Su	Tw			◆		
Stauntonia hexaphylla	35 ft (10 m)	10–17 ft (3–5 m)	W	W		◆	◆	Sp/Su	Tw			◆	◆	
Strongylodon macrobotrys	20–40 ft (6–12 m)	5–10 (1.5–3 m)	W	W/T		◆	◆	Sp	Tw			◆	◆	
Strophanthus gratus	10–15 ft (3–4.5 m)	10 ft (3 m)	W	W/T		◆	◆	Sp/Su	S			◆		
Strophanthus speciosus	10 ft (3 m)	10 ft (3 m)	W	W/T		◆	◆	Su/A	S			◆		
Tecomanthe speciosa	20–30 ft (6–9 m)	5–10 ft (1.5–3 m)	W	W		◆	◆	A/W	S/Tw					◆
Thunbergia alata	10 ft (3 m)	10 ft (3 m)	A	W/T	◆		◆	Su	Tw	◆		◆	◆	
Thunbergia grandiflora	15 ft (4.5 m)	15 ft (4.5 m)	W	W/T		◆	◆	Su	Tw			◆	◆	
Thunbergia gregorii	6 ft (1.8 m)	6 ft (1.8 m)	P	W/T	◆		◆	Su	Tw			◆	◆	
Thunbergia mysorensis	20 ft (6 m)	20 ft (6 m)	W	W/T		◆	◆	Sp/Su	Tw			◆	◆	
Trachelospermum asiaticum	20 ft (6 m)	10–17 ft (3–5 m)	W	W		◆	◆	Su	Tw		◆	◆	◆	◆
Trachelospermum jasminoides	30 ft (0.9 m)	17–25 ft (5–8 m)	W	W		◆	◆	Su/A	Tw/S		◆	◆	◆	
Tropaeolum pentaphyllum	20 ft (6 m)	20 ft (6 m)	P	W	◆		◆	Su	Tw			◆	◆	
Tropaeolum polyphyllum	10 ft (3 m)	10 ft (3 m)	P	W	◆		◆	Su	Tw			◆	◆	
Tropaeolum speciosum	10 ft (3 m)	10 ft (3 m)	P	C/W	◆		◆	Su/A	Tw			◆	◆	◆
Tropaeolum tricolor	7 ft (2 m)	7 ft (2 m)	P	C/W	◆		◆	Sp/Su	Tw			◆	◆	
Tweedia caerulea	36 in (90 cm)	36 in (90 cm)	W/T	W		◆	◆	Su/A	S			◆		
Vigna caracalla	12–20 ft (3.5–6 m)	10 ft (3 m)	P	W	◆		◆	Su/A	Tw			◆		
Vitis amurensis	50 ft (15 m)	10–20 ft (3–6 m)	W	C/W	◆			Su	Te		◆	◆		
Vitis coignetiae	50 ft (15 m)	10–20 ft (3–6 m)	W	C/W	◆			Su	Te		◆	◆		
Vitis riparia	40 ft (12 m)	10–20 ft (3–6 m)	W	C/W	◆			Su	Te		◆	◆		
Wisteria brachybotrys	30 ft (9 m)	30 ft (9 m)	W	C	◆		◆	Sp	Tw		◆	◆	◆	
Wisteria floribunda	25 ft (8 m)	25 ft (8 m)	W	C	◆		◆	Sp	Tw		◆	◆	◆	
Wisteria × formosa	30 ft (9 m)	30 ft (9 m)	W	C	◆		◆	Sp	Tw		◆	◆	◆	
Wisteria frutescens	40 ft (12 m)	40 ft (12 m)	W	C	◆		◆	Sp	Tw		◆	◆	◆	◆
Wisteria macrostachya	25 ft (8 m)	25 ft (8 m)	W	C	◆		◆	Sp	Tw		◆	◆	◆	
Wisteria sinensis	35 ft (10 m)	35 ft (10 m)	W	C	◆		◆	Sp	Tw		◆	◆	◆	

AESCHYNANTHUS

BASKET PLANT, BLUSH WORT

Found in the tropics from India to New Guinea, mainly in the Malaysian Archipelago, this genus of around 100 species of often epiphytic perennials and subshrubs belongs in the African violet (Gesneriaceae) family. Often climbing or sprawling, with overarching stems, species tend to have simple, fleshy, pointed, elliptical leaves in opposite pairs. Flowers are curved tubes clustered at the stem tips, and can be brightly colored, often in red and orange shades, with an upper and lower lip, the lower with 3 small lobes.
CULTIVATION: Prefer even warmth and ample moisture. Often grown as house or greenhouse plants; mainly cultivated in hanging baskets and prefer a free-draining, humus-rich soil. The creeping species can be good ground cover in tropical gardens. Water and feed well in growing season. Propagate from cuttings or seed.

Aeschynanthus longicaulis

syn. *Aeschynanthus marmoratus*
☀ ✂ ↔ 36 in (90 cm) ↑ 18–24 in (45–60 cm)
From the Malay Peninsula and Indonesia. Evergreen trailing perennial; tubular yellowish green to greenish flowers, marked dark brown, in terminal clusters, in summer. Leaves oval and waxy, mottled light and dark green above, purplish red below. Zones 11–12.

Aeschynanthus radicans

LIPSTICK PLANT

☀ ✂ ↔ 18–36 in (45–90 cm) ↑ 5–6 ft (1.5–1.8 m)
Epiphytic evergreen vine from Malaysia. Slender trailing and arching stems originating in tree branches. Long, red, tubular flowers in dense terminal clusters. Leaves dark green, elliptical, fleshy and smooth-edged. Fruit to 1½ in (35 mm) long. Zones 11–12.

AKEBIA

CHOCOLATE VINE

Found in the small chocolate-vine (Lardizabalaceae) family, which includes some unusual plants, this genus from temperate East Asia

Akebia quinata

is made up of just 4 species of evergreen and deciduous twining vines. The extent of foliage loss depends on the degree of winter cold. Leaves are composed of several oval leaflets, the number varying with species. Flowers open in spring, are unisexual, and, while not showy, are distinctive as they occur in panicles and for their color, which ranges from bright maroon to purple-brown. If cross-pollinated, pulpy, sausage-like, blue to purple fruits follow the flowers and are edible, though insipid.
CULTIVATION: Preferring cool shaded conditions with moist humus-rich soil, they are undemanding and in suitable conditions can be vigorous growers that need frequent trimming. Propagate from seed that has been stratified for about 4 weeks or from softwood to half-hardened summer cuttings.

Akebia quinata

☀ ✳ ↔ 20 ft (6 m) ↑ 10 ft (3 m)
From Korea, Japan, and nearby parts of China. Leaves have 5 leaflets up to 2 in (5 cm) long. Vanilla-scented, maroon flowers; males very small, females about 1 in (25 mm) wide. Plants that fruit well will need support. Zones 5–10.

ALLAMANDA (see page 80)

Allamanda cathartica

CLIMBING ALLAMANDA, COMMON ALLAMANDA, GOLDEN TRUMPET
☼ ⚮ ↔ 10 ft (3 m) ↑ 17 ft (5 m)
From South America. A vigorous climber with whorls of glossy leathery leaves. Bears bright yellow trumpet-shaped flowers, to 5 in (12 cm) across, in summer. The seed capsules are prickly. 'Grandiflora', very large flowers in profusion; 'Hendersonii', smaller flowers with orange markings in throat; and 'Nobilis', larger, more flaring flowers. Zones 10–12.

AMPELOPSIS

A genus of 25 species of deciduous shrubs and tendril-bearing vines of the grape (Vitaceae) family. Native to North America and temperate Asia. Main features are the attractive grape-like fruit and colorful autumn foliage. Leaves are usually large, often toothed, and may be simple or deeply lobed. Sprays of tiny yellow-green flowers open in spring, followed by berries, often dark blue when ripe.
CULTIVATION: Prefer humid climate, cool winters, and no clear dry period. Plant in deep, humus-rich, well-drained soil. Water well when growing. Can be invasive, so trim often. Propagate from half-hardened summer cuttings, winter hardwood cuttings, or layers.

Ampelopsis glandulosa

☼/☀ ✳ ↔ 17 ft (5 m) or more ↑ 17 ft (5 m) or more
Strong-growing climber from Japan, Korea, and nearby China. Stems hairy when young. Leaves 3- to 5-lobed, toothed, up to 6 in (15 cm) long. Foliage reddens in autumn. Clusters of ¼ in (6 mm) wide purple to blue fruit. In gardens mainly as *A. g.* var. *brevipedunculata* (syn. *A. brevipedunculata*). 'Elegans' (syn. 'Tricolor'), deeply lobed leaves mottled with white, pink patches in autumn; rather frost tender and easily sun- or wind-burnt. Seldom fruits. Zones 4–10.

Aeschynanthus radicans

ANTIGONON

A Mexican and Central American genus comprising 3 species of quick-growing perennial vines of the knotweed (Polygonaceae) family. Evergreen in mild climates if the roots can be insulated with mulch. Can be grown in areas with light frosts that do not freeze the soil to any depth. Forming a dense canopy, the vines are smothered throughout the warmer months in floral racemes that derive most of their color, usually bright pink, from the sepals that surround the tiny flowers. Racemes terminate in a tendril that aids climbing. Three-angled fruits follow the flowers.
CULTIVATION: Plant in a sunny well-drained position; water well in summer. Frequent feeding encourages strong growth and heavy flowering. Pinch back to keep compact and remove spent flowers to prolong blooming. Propagate from seed or summer base cuttings, or by division of tubers in early spring.

Antigonon leptopus
CHAIN OF LOVE, CONFEDERATE VINE, CORAL VINE, MEXICAN CREEPER
☀ ❄ ↔ 20 ft (6 m) ↑ 15 ft (4.5 m)
A strong-growing tuberous-rooted climber found growing in Mexico. Pointed, heavily veined, elongated, heart-shaped leaves to around 4 in (10 cm) long, with strongly frilled margins. Minute flowers are enclosed by coral pink to red heart-shaped sepals. Zones 10–12.

ARISTOLOCHIA
BIRTHWORT, DUTCHMAN'S PIPE
This genus of about 300 species ranging from vigorous climbers to perennials, both deciduous and evergreen, found throughout tropical and temperate regions, is a member of the birthwort (Aristolochiaceae) family. Stems are usually thick and fissured; leaves vary from entire to lobed, often being heart-shaped. The flowers, which trap pollinating insects, have bladder-like bases and contorted, tubular shapes. They range from less than 3 in (8 cm) to giants of 20 in (50 cm) and many have an offensive smell. Flowers are mottled in shades of brown, pink, purple, and ivory. The common name, birthwort, comes from the herbal use of some species as an aid to childbirth.
CULTIVATION: Many of the vigorous climbers are hardy only to 23°F (−5°C) and better suit the greenhouse in cooler areas. Where suitable, grow outdoors in sun or half-sun in rich well-drained

soil. Climbers require support and can be pruned in late winter. Propagate from softwood cuttings or seed, or by division.

Aristolochia grandiflora
PELICAN FLOWER
☀/◐ ❄ ↔ 6 ft (1.8 m) ↑ 10 ft (3 m)
From Central America and West Indies. Deep green heart-shaped leaves. Very large contorted flowers with bladder-like base and lip with long narrow appendage; mottled purple, green, and cream. Summer-flowering. Zones 10–11.

Aristolochia littoralis
syn. Aristolochia elegans
CALICO FLOWER
☀/◐ ❄ ↔ 15 ft (4.5 m) ↑ 20 ft (6 m)
Native to Brazil. Naturalized in Central America and southern USA. Can be weedy in warm climates. Vigorous climber, heart-shaped leaves, grayish green beneath. Flowers have bladder-like bases with almost round lips; mottled chocolate purple and ivory. Summer-flowering. Zones 9–11.

Aristolochia littoralis

ASPARAGUS (see page 414)

Asparagus asparagoides
syns Myrsiphyllum asparagoides, Protasparagus aethiopicus
FLORIST'S SMILAX
☀ ❄ ↔ 3 ft (0.9 m) ↑ 5–6 ft (1.5–1.8 m)
Evergreen vine, native to South Africa. Vigorous, wiry stem. Solitary or paired, small, white flowers in leaf axils. Glossy green, alternate, leathery, oval branchlets or cladophylls. Fruits are red berries. 'Myrtifolius' is a small elegant variety. Zones 7–10.

Asparagus setaceus
syns Asparagus plumosus, Protasparagus plumosus
ASPARAGUS FERN, PLUMOSA FERN LILY
☀/◐ ❄ ↔ 24 in (60 cm) ↑ 12–48 in (30–120 cm)
Twining climber from southern and eastern Africa. Smooth, woody or wiry, green stems; strong thorns. Small white flowers. Red to black berries. Bright or dark green tiny cladophylls, in clusters of 8–20, in single plane. 'Cupressoides', compact, pyramid-shaped; 'Nanus', compact, shorter crowded cladophylls; 'Pyramidalis', pyramidal in shape; 'Robustus', strongly growing form. Zones 9–11.

BEAUMONTIA

This genus of 9 species of often rampant climbers from tropical Asia belongs to the oleander or dogbane (Apocynaceae) family. They are evergreen, though in subtropical gardens B. grandiflora loses many leaves in winter. Leaves are smooth and opposite. The large fragrant flowers are borne in corymbs, terminal and in the leaf axils. The calyx is 5-lobed and the corolla is funnel- or bell-shaped with 5 lobes. Stamens are attached near the base of the corolla tube and have slender filaments with arrow-shaped anthers. The fruit comprises a pair of thick woody follicles.
CULTIVATION: In temperate regions, grow these plants along walls of greenhouses or conservatories. They need hot moist conditions

Antigonon leptopus

Beaumontia grandiflora

Berberidopsis corallina

in the growing season. Propagate from seed or from half-hardened cuttings taken with a heel, rooted in sandy soil under mist.

Beaumontia grandiflora

EASTER LILY VINE, HERALD'S TRUMPET

☼ ❄ ↔ 15 ft (4.5 m) ↑ 25 ft (8 m)

Vigorous, woody, evergreen twiner, occurring in moist forests of Southeast Asia from India to Vietnam. Leaves large, oval-shaped, opposite, prominent veins, covered with brown-red hairs when young, glossy green when older. Flowers white, fragrant, trumpet-shaped, to 6 in (15 cm) long, in summer. Zones 10–12.

BERBERIDOPSIS

A genus of evergreen climbing shrubs in the Berberidopsidaceae family, it consists of one species from eastern Australia and one from South America, mainly from Chile, that is now rare in the wild and may even be extinct. Shrubs can be trained to 15 ft (4.5 m) in height, with a similar spread, and are grown for their ornamental foliage and pretty sprays of pendent pink to scarlet flowers, which appear from summer to early autumn. CULTIVATION: Plants grow best in moist woodland, in acid to neutral soil. They dislike hot summers, and prefer shelter in part-shade with root protection in winter. While moisture is essential, good free drainage is also needed. Propagate from seed in spring, half-hardened cuttings in late summer, or layered trailing branches in autumn. In areas prone to hard frost, grow in a greenhouse.

Berberidopsis corallina

CORAL PLANT

❄ ❄ ↔ 5–8 ft (1.5–2.4 m) ↑ 15 ft (4.5 m)

Evergreen climber from Chile. Heart-shaped to oval dark green leaves sometimes end in tiny spines. Flowers rounded, dark red, ½ in (12 mm) wide, on 2 in (5 cm) long scarlet stalks. Zones 8–9.

BIGNONIA

This genus belongs to the trumpet-vine (Bignoniaceae) family. It formerly contained a large number of species but reclassification has reduced it to just one climbing evergreen vine. Its natural habitat is rich moist woodland areas of southeastern USA. CULTIVATION: Grow in well-drained fertile soil in full sun or part-shade. In cooler climates grow in the greenhouse, with protection

from the hottest summer sun. Cut back previous season's growth by two-thirds in early spring. Mealybugs can be serious pests. Propagate from seed or by layering.

Bignonia capreolata

CROSS-VINE, QUARTER VINE, TRUMPET-FLOWER

☼/☼ ❄ ↔ 10 ft (3 m) ↑ 10–30 ft (3–9 m)

From southeastern USA. A vigorous summer-flowering vine, climbs by tendrils. Leaves opposite, deep green. Showy heads of flaring trumpet flowers 2 in (5 cm) long, deep orange to scarlet with darker throat. Flowers most prolifically in full sun. 'Tangerine Beauty', orange flowers with yellow throats. Zones 7–9.

BOUGAINVILLEA

The 14 species of this South American genus in the four-o-clock (Nyctaginaceae) family, seen in warm-temperate to tropical regions as spectacular climbers, are really scrambling shrubs and usually remain fairly compact or behave as ground covers if left free-standing. Leaves are thin, sometimes downy, and broadly elliptical with pointed tips; stems are protected by long narrow thorns, found at the leaf axils. Foliage is evergreen or deciduous, depending on the species and climate. True flowers, in groups of 1 to 3, are tubular, creamy white to yellow, around 1 in (25 mm) wide, largely hidden by brightly colored petal-like bracts. CULTIVATION: Bougainvilleas will not tolerate heavy or repeated frosts. They prefer light well-drained soil, a sunny position, and will perform better if watered well in summer but not overfed. They can withstand the heavy pruning necessary to keep the plants shrub-like. Propagate by taking firm cuttings in summer.

Bougainvillea × buttiana

☼ ❄ ↔ 10–20 ft (3–6 m) ↑ 17 ft (5 m)

A hybrid between *B. glabra* and *B. peruviana*. Broad leaves to over 4 in (10 cm) long with a downy midrib. Bracts small but densely packed. Popular hybrid cultivars include 'Afterglow', pink suffused orange, sparse foliage; 'Barbara Karst', red in full sun, deep carmine-pink in part-shade; 'Brilliant Variegated', mounding shrub, gray-green and silver variegated foliage, red-brown bracts; 'Coconut Ice', irregularly marked pink and white bracts; 'Enid Lancaster' (syns *B.* 'California Gold', 'Hawaiian Glow', 'Sunset', *B.* × *b.* 'Golden Glow'), soft yellow bracts age to gold; 'Killie Campbell' (syns *B.* 'Green Light', 'Rose Amber'), trailing habit, large bracts open orange-red and age to magenta; 'Lady Mary Baring',

Bougainvillea × buttiana
'Enid Lancaster'

quick-growing, yellow bracts; 'Louise Wathen' (syn. *B.* 'Orange King'), copper-orange bracts, tender; 'Mahara' (syns *B.* 'Manila Red', 'Princess Mahara'), dark green foliage, purple double bracts; 'Mrs Butt' (syn. *B.* 'Crimson Lake'), crimson red, needs heat to flower well; 'Purple Queen', bushy, deep purple bracts; 'Rainbow', pinkish red bracts develop various pink tones with age; 'Raspberry Ice' (syn. *B.* 'Raspberry Ice'), high, bushy, red new growth ages green with cream to golden edges, vivid magenta bracts, good ground cover; 'Rosenka', golden yellow ageing to soft pink, large papery bracts; and Texas Dawn/'Monas' (syns *B.* 'Purple King', 'Robyn's Glory'), large clusters of purple-pink bracts. Zones 9–12.

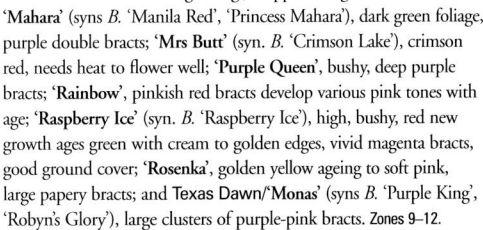

Bougainvillea glabra

Bougainvillea, Hybrid Cultivar, 'Elizabeth Doxey'

Campsis radicans

Bougainvillea glabra

PAPER FLOWER

☼ ❄ ↔ 15 ft (4.5 m) ↑ 10–12 ft (3–5 m)

Native to Brazil, a summer-flowering species, dark green foliage with few hairs. Leaves to 5 in (12 cm) long. When trained as a climber can grow to a height or spread of 30 ft (9 m). Flower bracts white to magenta. 'Alba', pure white bracts; 'Cypheri', deep pink bracts; 'Magnifica', masses of short-lived purple bracts; 'Sanderiana Variegated', mauve bracts, gray-green and cream variegated foliage. Zones 10–12.

Bougainvillea spectabilis

syn. *Bougainvillea brasiliensis*

☼ ❄ ↔ 15 ft (4.5 m) ↑ 12 ft (3.5 m)

Vigorous species from Brazil. Velvety leaves to 4 in (10 cm) long. Panicles of pink to purple bracts, in spring. Stems have vicious curved thorns. 'Thomasii' (syn. 'Rosea'), 15–20 ft (4.5–6 m) high, vigorous climber, deep reddish pink bracts. Zones 10–12.

Bougainvillea Hybrid Cultivars

☼/❄ ❄ ↔ 5–20 ft (1.5–6 m) ↑ 2–20 ft (0.6–6 m)

There are many hybrid bougainvilleas with obscure parentage. They are a variable group covering most sizes and colors. Popular hybrids include: 'Alexandra', 15–20 ft (4.5–6 m) high, vigorous, deep magenta-purple; 'Betty Hendry' (syn. 'Indian Maid'), 8–15 ft (2.4–4.5 m), long-flowering, red with occasional purple and yellow flecks; Camarillo Fiesta/'Monle', 15–20 ft (4.5–6 m), small leaves, magenta and copper bracts; 'Cherry Blossoms' (syns *B.* 'Bridal Bouquet', 'Limberlost Beauty'), 7 ft (2 m), compact, slow-growing, white bracts tinted pink, double; 'Closeburn' (syns 'Helen Johnson', 'Temple Fire', 'Tom Thumb'), 3–5 ft (0.9–1.5 m), spreading shrub, good in containers, coppery red bracts; 'Crimson Jewel', 2–4 ft (0.6–1.2 m), spreading trailing shrub, deep pinkish red bracts; Don Mario/'Monio', 12–15 ft (3.5–4.5 m), purple-red bracts; 'Elizabeth Doxey' (syns 'Apple Blossom', 'Jamaica White', 'Madonna'), 12–15 ft (3.5–4.5 m), white bracts; 'Elsbet', 8–12 ft (2.4–3.5 m), shrubby with dark leaves, small deep purple bracts; 'Hawaiian White', 15–20 ft (4.5–6 m), vigorous, white bracts with green veining; 'Isabel Greensmith', 12–15 ft (3.5–4.5 m), orange to coppery red bracts; 'Jamburi', 15–20 ft (4.5–6 m), vigorous, purple-red to red bracts; 'James Walker', 15–20 ft (4.5–6 m), vigorous, deep magenta, large bracts; 'Juanita Hatten', 8–15 ft (2.4–4.5 m), deep purple-pink

bracts; 'La Jolla', 3–6 ft (0.9–2 m), compact shrub, bright red bracts; 'Lavender Queen', 12–15 ft (3.5–4.5 m), soft purple bracts; 'Miss Manila' (syn. 'Tango'), 12–15 ft (3.5–4.5 m), pinkish red bracts; 'Oo-La-La', 4–8 ft (1.2–2.4 m), shrubby growth with deep magenta bracts; 'Pink Tiara', 8–15 ft (2.4–4.5 m), long-flowering, pale pink bracts; 'Purple Robe', 12–15 ft (3.5–4.5 m), large, bright purple-pink bracts; 'Rubyana', 15–20 ft (4.5–6 m), vigorous, dark foliage, purple-pink bracts; 'San Diego Red' (syn. 'Scarlett O'Hara'), 12–15 ft (3.5–4.5 m), massed bright scarlet bracts ageing to magenta, bronze young growth; 'Southern Rose', 12–15 ft (3.5–4.5 m), bright pink bracts; 'Sundance', 8–12 ft (2.4–3.5 m), orange-pink bracts; Tahitian Dawn/'Monari', 15–20 ft (4.5–6 m), vigorous, gold bracts ageing to pink; Torch Glow/'Pixie', (syns 'Pink Pixie', 'Smartipants'), shrubby, 3–6 ft (0.9–2 m), vivid magenta-pink bracts at stem tips. **Spectoperuviana Group** includes 'Mary Palmer', 12–15 ft (3.5–4.5 m), with both pink and white bracts; 'Mary Palmer's Enchantment', 15–20 ft (4.5–6 m), very vigorous, pure white bracts. Zones 9–12.

CAMPSIS

TRUMPET CREEPER, TRUMPET VINE

A genus of 2 species of flamboyant climbing plants, in the trumpet-vine (Bignoniaceae) family. One is native to China and Japan; the other is native to North America where it can be a weed. These vigorous deciduous vines have aerial roots to help them climb and long leaves with 7–11 broadly lance-shaped leaflets that are serrated along the margins. The large orange or red trumpet-shaped flowers have widely flaring lobes and are borne in clusters.

CULTIVATION: Grow over walls or fences in a well-drained soil in full sun. In cool climates grow in a warm sheltered position to encourage flowering. Tie *C. grandiflora* to a sturdy support as it produces relatively few aerial roots; *C. radicans* will also benefit from additional support. Prune hard in late winter–early spring to contain plants within their allotted space. Propagate from cuttings, layering, or seed.

Campsis grandiflora

syns *Bignonia chinensis*, *B. grandiflora*, *Campsis chinensis*, *Tecoma chinensis*, *T. grandiflora*

CHINESE TRUMPET CREEPER, CHINESE TRUMPET VINE

☼ ❄ ↔ 8–15 ft (2.4–4.5 m) ↑ 25 ft (8 m)

From Japan and China. Climber with few aerial roots. Orange to red trumpet-shaped flowers, 3–4 in (8–10 cm) long, are borne from summer through to autumn on large loose panicles up to 20 in (50 cm) long. '**Morning Calm**' produces deep peach flowers with a yellow interior. Zones 7–11.

Campsis radicans
syns *Bignonia radicans*, *Tecoma radicans*
COW-ITCH, TRUMPET CREEPER
☀ ❋ ↔ 8–15 ft (2.4–4.5 m) ↑ 35 ft (10 m)
From southeastern USA. Invasive in some States. Becomes rampant in rich soil. Climbs with aerial roots. Orange or red trumpet-shaped flowers, borne in terminal clusters during summer, are a little smaller than those of *C. grandiflora*. *C. r.* f. *flava* has deep bright yellow flowers. Zones 4–10.

Campsis × *tagliabuana*
syns *Bignonia tagliabuana*, *Tecoma hybrida*, *T. intermedia*
☀ ❋ ↔ 8–15 ft (2.4–4.5 m) ↑ 17 ft (5 m)
A hybrid of *C. grandiflora* and *C. radicans*. Robust vine, climbs with its aerial roots. In summer bears loose panicles of orange-scarlet trumpet-shaped flowers. '**Madame Galen**', large flaring flowers in rich salmon shades. Zones 6–10.

CELASTRUS
Although often twining and usually considered to be climbers, many of the 30-odd species in this genus in the spindle-tree (Celastraceae) family are shrubs that can be grown as free-standing plants or trained against a wall as espaliers. Widespread except in Europe, some are deciduous, with rather thin leaves that often have serrated edges. Most species have separate male and female plants; flowers of both sexes are small, 5-petalled, and cream to green in color occurring in small panicles. Both sexes are required to produce the showy fruit, which is a dry capsule containing a brightly colored fleshy aril, revealed as the capsule splits open. CULTIVATION: Easily grown in any well-drained soil in full sun or half-sun, *Celastrus* species vary in hardiness but they are generally tolerant of moderate frosts. They should be cut back immediately after fruiting, in spring, and can be pruned back quite severely if necessary. Propagation is from seed, layers, or half-hardened summer cuttings.

Celastrus orbiculatus
ORIENTAL BITTERSWEET
☀ ❋ ↔ 10–20 ft (3–6 m) ↑ 30 ft (9 m)
From temperate northeastern Asia. Deciduous species that needs regular trimming to keep it compact. Wiry stems tangled, interwoven, light green leaves. Flowers form in the leaf axils. Colorful fruit, splits open in autumn revealing an orange-yellow interior and usually pink arils. Zones 4–9.

Celastrus scandens
AMERICAN BITTERSWEET
☀ ❋ ↔ 20 ft (6 m) ↑ 20 ft (6 m)
Native to North America. Climbing or spreading as a large-scale ground cover. Leaves 4 in (10 cm) long, serrated, oblong, tapering quickly to a point. Yellow-green summer flowers. Clusters of fruits open to reveal yellow interior and pinkish red arils. Zones 3–10.

CISSUS
GRAPE IVY
This genus of around 200 species, mostly vines, found throughout tropical and subtropical parts of the world, belongs to the grape (Vitaceae) family. Some are shrublets and some have succulent or herbaceous stems. Leaves are usually simple, sometimes palmate, rarely with 3 distinct leaflets. They usually have simple or forked tendrils opposite the leaves, sometimes with adhesive discs. Flowers are stalked candelabra-like cymes opposite the leaves, usually on or at the end of lateral tendril-less shoots. They are hermaphroditic, with a cup-shaped calyx, 4 free petals, and 4 stamens. The disc is cup-shaped with a thick margin. The ovary has 2 compartments, each with 2 ovules. The style is round in cross-section, the stigma minute. Berries are spherical to egg-shaped, usually inedible, with 1 seed. CULTIVATION: Grow outdoors in warmer areas, or as house plants for their glossy foliage or succulent stems in cooler regions. Propagate from stem cuttings, or from seed for the succulent species.

Cissus antarctica
KANGAROO VINE
☀/◐ ▨ ↔ 3–10 ft (0.9–3 m) ↑ 17–25 ft (5–8 m)
From Australia. A vigorous vine. Branches downy when young. Shiny, dark green, pointed leaves, shallow-toothed margins, to 4 in (10 cm) long. Small green flowers. Edible, black, pea-sized fruit. Popular as a house plant. Zones 9–12.

Cissus hypoglauca
GIANT WATER VINE, JUNGLE VINE, NATIVE GRAPE
☀ ▨ ↔ 20 ft (6 m) ↑ 17–60 ft (5–18 m)
Vigorous climber from eastern rainforests of Australia. Compound leaves of 3–5 glossy oval leaflets, bluish on undersides. Clusters of small yellow flowers in early summer. Grape-like fruits from late summer to autumn. Zones 9–11.

Cissus quadrangularis
☀ ✚ ↔ 32 in (80 cm) ↑ 60 in (150 cm)
Succulent climber from Africa, southern Asia, and Malaysia. Four-angled stems, constricted at nodes. Heart-shaped or 3-lobed leaves to 2 in (5 cm), soon falling. Small greenish flowers. Although poisonous to stock, extracts of *C. quadrangularis* used medicinally. Zones 10–12.

Cissus hypoglauca

Cissus rhombifolia

VENEZUELA TREE VINE

☼/◗ ❄ ↔ 6 ft (1.8 m) ↑ 10 ft (3 m)

Climber native to tropical America, popular as a house plant. Stems and leaves have brownish or silvery down when young. Trifoliate leaves, rhomboid leaflets with serrated margins. 'Ellen Danica', larger glossy leaves with deep pointed lobes; 'Mandana', erect stems when young, larger more leathery leaves. Zones 10–11.

CLEMATIS

LEATHER VINE, TRAVELLER'S JOY, VIRGIN'S BOWER

This genus of over 200 species, in the buttercup (Ranunculaceae) family, encompasses a huge range of forms. *Clematis* species are mainly climbing or scrambling but sometimes shrubby or perennial, deciduous or evergreen, flowering at any time in any color, occurring in both northern and southern temperate zones and at higher altitudes in the tropics. Leaves may be simple or pinnate. Flowers are nearly always showy, with 4 to 8 petal-like sepals. Fluffy seed heads follow. CULTIVATION: Foliage should be in the sun while the roots are kept cool and moist.

Clematis armandii 'Snowdrift'

Incorporate plenty of humus-rich compost before planting, and water well. Clematis wilt disease is a problem in many areas. Propagate from cuttings or layers. Species may be raised from seed, but sex will be undetermined before flowering.

Clematis alpina ★

☼/◗ ❄ ↔ 5 ft (1.5 m) ↑ 8–10 ft (2.4–3 m)

Deciduous climber from Europe and northern Asia. Paired trifoliate leaves; serrated lance-shaped leaflets. Blue to mauve flowers, white stamens, spring–early summer. 'Frances Rivis' (syn. 'Blue Giant'), blue flowers; 'White Columbine', white flowers. Zones 5–9.

Clematis armandii

☼/◗ ❄ ↔ 7–10 ft (2–3 m) ↑ 20–30 ft (6–9 m)

A vigorous evergreen climber from central and western China. Leaves with 3 glossy, dark green, leathery leaflets to 6 in (15 cm) long, bronze-green when young. Clusters of white flowers, sometimes faintly pink-tinted, early spring. Flowers may smell slightly of urine. 'Apple Blossom', pink buds opening white; 'Snowdrift' ★, white, waxy, fragrant flowers in cascading panicles. Zones 8–10.

Clematis chrysocoma

☼/◗ ❄ ↔ 4–6 ft (1.2–1.8 m) ↑ 7–15 ft (2–4.5 m)

Deciduous climber from southwestern China. Trifoliate leaves; pointed oval leaflets, sometimes serrated, 1–2 in (2.5–5 cm) long. From summer to autumn 2 in (5 cm) wide, pink-tinted, white flowers are borne on long, downy, brown stems. Zones 7–10.

Clematis cirrhosa ★

syn. *Clematis calycina*

☼/◗ ❄ ↔ 6 ft (1.8 m) ↑ 10–15 ft (3–4.5 m)

From southern Europe and Mediterranean region. Evergreen climber; paired trifoliate leaves, small lobed leaflets. From winter–early spring,

small clusters of pendulous cream flowers, sometimes spotted purple-red. *C. c.* var. *balearica*, fragrant flowers, always spotted. *C. c.* var. *purpurascens* 'Freckles' ★, large-flowered, long-stemmed. Zones 7–10.

Clematis florida

☼/◗ ❄ ↔ 5 ft (1.5 m) ↑ 15 ft (4.5 m)

A deciduous or part evergreen climber from Japan and China. Paired trifoliate leaves, up to 2 in (5 cm) long leaflets, sometimes toothed. Flowers are 3 in (8 cm) in diameter, often green-tinted, white stamens, violet anthers, in summer. *C. f.* var. *flore-pleno* bears double flowers, white, striped green; *C. f.* var. *sieboldiana* (syn. 'Bicolor'), white flowers, purple-red stamens. *C. f.* Pistachio/ 'Evirida' produces large white flowers sometimes flushed pale green, with red stamens. Zones 7–10.

Clematis lanuginosa

☼/◗ ❄ ↔ 4–8 ft (1.2–2.4 m) ↑ 7–10 ft (2–3 m)

Chinese deciduous climber. Leaves are simple or trifoliate, leaflets up to 4 in (10 cm) long. Large flowers, from white to pale lavender, in groups of up to 3, produced during the warmer months. Zones 6–9.

Clematis montana

☼/◗ ❄ ↔ 10–20 ft (3–6 m) ↑ 15–25 ft (4.5–8 m)

Vigorous, spring-flowering, deciduous climber found growing from the Himalayas to central China. Deep green trifoliate leaves with toothed leaflets up to 4 in (10 cm) long. In spring, massed large sprays of white to pale pink flowers. *C. m.* var. *glabrescens*, very vigorous variety with mauve-pink flowers; *C. m.* var. *grandiflora*, very vigorous variety, to 40 ft (12 m) tall, white flowers. *C. m.* var. *rubens* ★, bronze new growth, with large pink flowers: 'Elizabeth', very pale pink flowers, vanilla scented; 'Marjorie' ★, semi-double with petal-like stamens, cream overlaid with orange-pink and copper; 'Tetrarose' ★, has very large deep pink flowers, strong growing with lush foliage; *C. m.* var. *sericea* (syns *C. chrysocoma* var. *sericea*, *C. spooneri*), downy young stems and reverse of sepals, white flowers in profusion; *C. m.* var. *wilsonii*, large sprays of tiny white flowers, fragrant; *C. m.* 'Snowflake', produces pure white flowers. Zones 6–9.

Clematis paniculata

☼/◗ ❄ ↔ 10–30 ft (3–9 m) ↑ 17–30 ft (5–9 m)

A native of New Zealand. Tough climber, dioecious, evergreen, flowering from spring through to early summer; large panicles of scented white flowers. Zones 7–10.

Clematis patens

☼/◗ ❄ ↔ 5–10 ft (1.5–3 m) ↑ 10–15 ft (3–4.5-m)

Vigorous climber naturally found in Japan and nearby parts of China. Pinnate leaves with 3 to 5 leaflets up to 4 in (10 cm) long. Flowering occurs from spring to early summer; white through mauve to blue flowers borne singly at tips of stems, purple-brown stamens. Zones 6–9.

Clematis tangutica

☀️/◐◗ ❄️ ↔ 8–12 ft (2.4–3.5 m) ↕ 7–10 ft (2–3 m)

Climber; Mongolia and northwestern China. Bright green pinnate leaves, toothed and/or lobed leaflets. Deep yellow bell-shaped flowers from late summer, lantern-shaped if sepals remain unfurled. Zones 5–9.

Clematis × *triternata*

☀️/◐◗ ❄️ ↔ 10–15 ft (3–4.5 m) ↕ 10–15 ft (3–4.5 m)

Garden hybrid between *C. flammula* and *C. viticella*. Simple or pinnate foliage, with smooth-edged, lance-shaped leaflets up to 3 in (8 cm) long. Masses of small, starry, pale lavender flowers, in summer. 'Rubromarginata', a heavy crop of white flowers edged and tipped with soft purple to wine red. Zones 6–9.

Clematis Hybrid Cultivars

☀️/◐◗ ❄️ ↔ 5–15 ft (1.5–4.5 m) ↕ 4–20 ft (1.2–6 m)

The many large-flowered hybrid clematis are broadly classified into 9 groups that vary in growth habit and flowering style depending on parentage. There is also a large range of ungrouped hybrids of indeterminate parentage. *Clematis* hybrids are now often grouped by flower size and pruning requirements (this varies because some flower on new growth, others on old wood) rather than on parentage, which is often obscure. Zones 5–9.

DIVERSIFOLIA GROUP

Hybrids mainly of *C. integrifolia*, *C. viticella*, *C. alpina*, and *C. macropetala*, sometimes listed under *C. integrifolia* or in the Viticella Group but meriting a classification of their own. Long-flowering climbers, usually grow 8–12 ft (2.4–3.5 m) tall, but can be low and compact; very hardy, bloom from late spring on new growth, typically with bell-shaped mauve to purple flowers, sometimes with petaloid centers. 'Arabella', large flowers, deep mauve-blue, variable number of sepals; 'Blue Bird', long mauve-blue sepals, creamy white double center; 'Blue Boy', mauve-blue flowers; 'Juuli', mauve-blue flowers, 5 sepals, low-growing, often less than 4 ft (1.2 m) tall.

FLORIDA GROUP

Climbers, from 8–12 ft (2.4–3.5 m) tall, flower spring–summer on previous year's wood. Early flowers are often double or semi-double; later blooms tend to be single, often very large. The group includes Arctic Queen/'Evitwo' with attractive double white blooms.

FORSTERI GROUP

Evergreen hybrids between several New Zealand species, notably *C. paniculata*, *C. marmoraria*, and *C. forsteri*. Most are low-spreading, but some are more vigorous climbers. Flowers usually white with hints of green; hardiness varies with parentage, though most survive well in zone 8. 'Avalanche', over 10 ft (3 m) tall; 'Early Sensation', around 5 ft (1.5 m); 'Lunar Lass', low spreader, lobed toothed leaves.

JACKMANII GROUP

These climbers grow up to 6–20 ft (1.8–6 m) tall and produce large flowers with a wide color range and usually with 4 sepals, in summer–autumn on new growth. 'Comtesse de Bouchaud', large pink flowers, cream stamens, very popular; 'Jackmanii', semi-pendulous deep purple flowers, 4 widely spaced sepals, cream stamens; 'Niobe', deep red flowers, yellow stamens.

LANUGINOSA GROUP

A group of climbers formerly known as *C.* × *lawsoniana*. Plants flower in summer–autumn on side shoots of current season's growth. Can reach 15 ft (4.5 m) tall, and bear large to very large single or double flowers. 'Marie Boisselot' (syn. 'Madame le Coultre'), vigorous, pale pink flowers ageing to white, cream to pale brown stamens; 'Nelly Moser', large lilac-pink flowers with wine red stripes, brown stamens; 'Silver Moon', silvery lilac flowers, yellow stamens.

PATENS GROUP

Compact climbers seldom growing to more than 12 ft (3.5 m) tall; flower in spring on previous season's wood. Flowers usually single and medium to large; sepals often have a darker mid-stripe and may have wavy edges. 'Blue Ravine', large mauve-blue flowers with faint purple-red markings, purple-red stamens; 'Gillian Blades', white flowers, may have blue blush, wavy edges; 'Henryi', very large white to cream flowers, up to 8 sepals, brown stamens.

TEXENSIS GROUP

A group of sprawling semi-climbing shrubs that can be trained to climb or left to form bushy mounds. They may also be cut back each year as herbaceous perennials. Flowers, usually bell-shaped, bloom in summer on new growth. 'Duchess of Albany', wide-open bell-shaped to starry flowers, deep pink, lighter at edges; 'Etoile Rose', nodding, bell-shaped, rose pink flowers.

Clematis florida var. *sieboldiana*

Clematis, Hybrid Cultivar, Jackmanii, 'Niobe'

Clematis, Hybrid Cultivar, Lanuginosa, 'Silver Moon'

VITICELLA GROUP

Vigorous climbers that grow 8–20 ft (2.4–6 m) tall. Flower on new growth, but in short intense bursts rather than over a longer season. Flowers may be single or double, seldom over 5 in (12 cm) wide, often smaller. '**Lady Betty Balfour**', strong-growing with deep violet-blue flowers, creamy yellow stamens; '**Minuet**', creamy white flowers, edged and tipped with lavender-pink, cream stamens; '**Ville de Lyon**' ★, deep pink flowers with yellow stamens.

UNGROUPED HYBRIDS

Ungrouped *Clematis* hybrids usually result from chance seedlings and display a range of sizes, flower types, and hardiness. All may grow 8–15 ft (2.4–4.5 m) tall, sometimes taller with suitable support. '**Helsingborg**', purple-blue flowers and stamens; '**Pastel Princess**', pastel pink flowers, mauve center.

CLERODENDRUM *(see page 121)*

Clerodendrum splendens

☼/◑ � ↔ 7 ft (2 m) ↑ 7 ft (2 m)

Scrambling or climbing tropical African shrub with lush, dark green, smooth-edged, broad, pointed, oval leaves to over 6 in (15 cm) long and sprays of many bright red flowers. Zones 10–12.

Clerodendrum thomsoniae

BLEEDING HEART VINE

☼/◐/● � ↔ 15 ft (4.5 m) ↑ 15 ft (4.5 m)

Vigorous, twining, evergreen climber from tropical West Africa. Smooth-edged, pointed, oval leaves to over 6 in (15 cm) long. Many-bloomed clusters of flowers with white calyces and dark red corolla, a striking contrast. Red to black fruit follow. Zones 10–12.

CLYTOSTOMA

The 9 species of evergreen vines in this genus, part of the trumpet-vine (Bignoniaceae) family, are native to tropical America. Leaves are compound with 2 leaflets. Clusters of flaring trumpet-shaped flowers, usually pink, are borne terminally or along the branches from spring to summer. The large seed pods are bristly or spiny.
CULTIVATION: In warm climates grow over walls and fences in full sun in well-drained soil and protect from strong winds. In cool climates grow in pots in the glasshouse and protect from direct sun when at its hottest. Propagate from cuttings or seed.

Clerodendrum splendens

Clytostoma callistegioides

Clytostoma callistegioides

syns *Bignonia callistegioides*, *B. speciosa*, *B. violacea*

ARGENTINE TRUMPET VINE, VIOLET TRUMPET

☼ � ↔ 20 ft (6 m) ↑ 10 ft (3 m)

Climber native to Argentina and southern Brazil. Dark green glossy leaves, bronzed when young. Flaring trumpet-shaped flowers, lilac-pink with purple veining, soft creamy center. Zones 10–11.

COBAEA

About 20 species of perennial climbers belong to this genus of the phlox (Polemoniaceae) family. They are native to Mexico and tropical South America. Plants have alternate lobed leaves and climb with tendrils. Cup-shaped flowers are bright green, violet, or purple, borne singly along the stems. The commonly grown species *C. scandens* has become naturalized in many warm areas.
CULTIVATION: Grow in a moisture-retentive but well-drained soil in a sunny position protected from strong winds. *C. scandens* grows rapidly and can be treated as an annual in cool climates or grown in the conservatory. Propagate from seed or cuttings.

Cobaea scandens

CATHEDRAL BELLS, CUP AND SAUCER VINE, MEXICAN IVY

☼ � ↔ 5–10 ft (1.5–3 m) ↑ 20–25 ft (6–8 m)

From Mexico. A vigorous vine with wide cup-shaped flowers to 2 in (5 cm) long. Color varies from white to deep purple. *C. s.* f. *alba* has white or creamy green flowers. Zones 9–11.

COMBRETUM *(see page 125)*

Combretum bracteosum

HICCUP NUT

☼ � ↔ 7 ft (2 m) ↑ 12 ft (3.5 m)

An evergreen from South Africa. Can be grown as a shrub, as a climber, or espaliered. Oval, dull green, sometimes red-tinted leaves, with pale undersides. Mass of orange-red flowerheads in summer. Smooth rounded fruit, local hiccup remedy. Zones 9–11.

CONGEA

This genus, consisting of about 7 species from Southeast Asia, belongs to the vervain (Verbenaceae) family. They are scrambling shrubs, often forming tangled masses of stems over other shrubs and small trees, with entire, simple, opposite leaves. Flowers are usually borne in a terminal panicle of small condensed cymes, each cyme surrounded by 3 conspicuous colored bracts that can be highly ornamental. The leathery fruit contains a single seed.
CULTIVATION: Grow in full sun and give support and plenty of space. In temperate regions they need to be planted in large pots and kept under glass, or they can be grown in the greenhouse border, requiring a rich loam with additional leafmold. Propagation is best done from seed, or from softwood or half-hardened cuttings.

Congea tomentosa

SHOWER ORCHID

☼ ✿ ↔ 20–40 ft (6–12 m) ↑ 10–30 ft (3–9 m)

From Thailand and Burma. A large shrub with long scrambling branches, densely mounding over fences or trees. Leaves to 8 in

(20 cm) long, usually with hairy undersides. Heads of small white flowers, surrounded by woolly-surfaced white to pink or mauve bracts to 1 in (25 mm) long. Zones 11–12.

DISTICTIS

This genus of 9 evergreen woody-stemmed climbers from Mexico and the West Indies belongs to the trumpet-vine (Bignoniaceae) family. The terminal racemes or panicles of colorful, tubular to trumpet-shaped, occasionally scented flowers appear from spring to summer. Branches are hexagonal with tendrils that cling to surfaces. Fruit is a 2-valved capsule containing winged seeds.
CULTIVATION: Grow in full sun in fertile, moist, well-drained soil. Not suited to hot humid conditions or cold or dry inland areas, but withstands light frost. Propagate from half-hardened cuttings in the growing season, or by layering in early spring.

Distictis buccinatoria

Distictis buccinatoria
syns *Bignonia cherere, Phaedranthus buccinatorius*
MEXICAN BLOOD TRUMPET
☀ ⚑ ↔ 10–20 ft (3–6 m) ↕ 6–15 ft (1.8–4.5 m)
Vigorous, evergreen, perennial climber or creeper from Mexico. Fast growing. Purple-red, large, tubular to funnel-shaped flowers, corolla about 3 in (8 cm) long, yellow in the throat and covered with minute yellow hairs. '**Mrs Rivers**', late-flowering, with dark mauve-pink flowers with a golden yellow throat. Zones 9–11.

ECCREMOCARPUS
CHILEAN GLORY FLOWER
A genus of 5 species of evergreen or herbaceous tendril climbers from South America, in the trumpet-vine (Bignoniaceae) family. Grown for their brightly colored lopsided trumpets, produced in abundance throughout the warmer months, and often used as quick cover plants, as they will hide almost anything in one growing season.
CULTIVATION: These plants prefer moist but well-drained soil in a sunny site sheltered from strong winds. Grow on wire-up fences, over arches, or through large shrubs and small trees. Can be treated as annuals in frost-prone areas. Propagate from seed; in frost-prone areas plant out young plants as soon as possible after frosts. In warmer climates they can self-sow and become invasive.

Eccremocarpus scaber
CHILEAN GLORY FLOWER
☀ ⚑ ↔ 7–10 ft (2–3 m) ↕ 10–15 ft (3–4.5 m)
From Chile and Peru. A fast-growing climber, and virtually the only species grown. Soft green compound leaves. Clusters of yellow, orange, or red tubular flowers, 1½ in (35 mm) long, in late spring–summer. Orange is the color of the wild form and the color most commonly cultivated. Zones 9–10.

EPIPREMNUM

This genus of some 15 species found from Southeast Asia to the western Pacific belongs to the arum (Araceae) family. They are

Epipremnum pinnatum 'Aureum'

evergreen climbers with distinct juvenile and mature phases. Adhesive roots emerge from aerial stems. The leaves are ovate to oblong or lanceolate, often pinnately divided or lobed, but entire on young plants. The leaf stalks have a "knee" and sheathe the stem at the base. In mature leaves veins are parallel. The inflorescence stalk is solitary. The spathe does not form a tube, and is purple to yellow or green and deciduous; the spadix is short and included within the spathe, and is covered with hermaphrodite flowers. The seeds are kidney-shaped and have tough coats. These climbers closely resemble species of *Monstera*.
CULTIVATION: In tropical regions species of *Epipremnum* are grown as scramblers up trees; however, in temperate regions they are usually seen as house plants or trained up sphagnum poles in greenhouses. A number of variegated forms are grown around villages in the western Pacific. The plants need filtered light and high humidity, but often they do not flower in cultivation, as flowering occurs only in the mature phase. They are easily propagated from stem cuttings or cuttings made from shoot tips, by air-layering, or, less usually, from fresh seed if available.

Epipremnum pinnatum
syn. *Rhaphidophora pinnata*
FALSE MONSTERA
☀ ✦ ↔ 6 ft (1.8 m) ↕ 12–20 ft (3.5–6 m)
A species found from Southeast Asia to New Guinea as well as in northern Queensland, Australia. An evergreen climber with a slender twining and branching stem. Downy, oval- to heart-shaped, pinnate leaves grow up to 3 ft (0.9 m) long, with holes along the midrib. The cream tubular flowers are marked with purple. '**Aureum**' (syns *Pothos aureus, Rhaphidophora aurea, Scindapsus aureus*) (commonly known as devil's ivy, golden pothos, and hunter's robe) has bright green heart-shaped leaves variegated with yellow or cream; '**Marble Queen**', the stems and moss green leaves are streaked with white; '**Tricolor**', off-white stems and leaves are variegated with white. Zones 10–12.

Ficus pumila 'Sonny'

FALLOPIA

syn. *Polygonum* in part, *Reynoutria*
FLEECE VINE, KNOTWEED, SILVER LACE VINE

This is a genus of about 25 woody-stemmed
annual or perennial herbs from the knotweed
(Polygonaceae) family, found across Northern
Hemisphere temperate regions though mostly
from East Asia. Panicles or spikes of small
funnel-shaped flowers appear from axils or ends
of branches. Fruit is 2- to 3-angled and nut-like.
CULTIVATION: They grow in sun or shade in any well-drained
garden soil, but will thrive in damper conditions. Propagate from
seed or by division from autumn to spring; propagate climbers
from semi-hardened cuttings in summer. Can become invasive.

Fallopia baldschuanica

syns *Bilderdykia baldschuanica, Polygonum baldschuanica*
MILE-A-MINUTE VINE, RUSSIAN VINE

☼ ❄ ↔ 20–40 ft (6–12 m) ↑ 20–40 ft (6–12 m)

Vigorous, woody, deciduous climber from Iran. Pale green heart-
shaped leaves, on long stalks. Broad drooping panicles of white
flowers, tinged pink, borne in summer–autumn. Zones 3–8.

Fallopia japonica

syns *Polygonum japonicum, Reynoutria japonica*
JAPANESE KNOTWEED, MEXICAN BAMBOO

☼ ❄ ↔ 3–7 ft (0.9–2 m) ↑ 3–7 ft (0.9–2 m)

A very vigorous, suckering, rhizomatous perennial from Japan.
Very invasive. Oval leaves with short stalks. Showy panicles of
tiny creamy white flowers, from late summer through to autumn.
F. j. var. *compacta* (syn. *Polygonum reynoutria*), compact form,
almost circular leaves, pink to reddish flowers; *F. j.* 'Spectabilis'
features red leaves marbled with yellow. Zones 3–8.

FICUS *(see page 159)*

Ficus pumila

CREEPING FIG

☼ ❄ ↔ unlimited ↑ 10–30 ft (3–9 m)

From China and Japan, self-clinging evergreen
climber. Small, flat, heart-shaped leaves. Thick,
vigorous, non-clinging branches with age, with
large fleshy leaves. Large, purplish green, barrel-
like figs develop on old plants. 'Dorthe', green
leaves, cream centers; 'Minima', smaller leaves;
'Sonny', cream leaves, green centers. Zones 8–11.

GELSEMIUM

CAROLINA JASMINE, YELLOW JESSAMINE

Gelsomino is the Italian name for jasmine, and
the 3 twining evergreen vines in this genus
resemble yellow-flowered jasmines, but they
are not even in the same family. *Gelsemium* is
in the logania (Loganiaceae) family, while
Jasminum is related to the olives (Oleaceae).
Found in North and Central America and
Southeast Asia, they have simple, pointed, oval
leaves, around 2 in (5 cm) long, and grow
slowly but steadily to cover a large area. The
flowers are mildly scented, small, yellow trumpets borne in clusters. As might be expected of
a genus related to the strychnine and curare
trees, *Gelsemium* is highly poisonous.
CULTIVATION: Suitable as a ground cover and for
container cultivation, as well as for training over
trellises and walls. While tolerant of moderate
frosts, they grow and flower better in a mild cli-
mate. Plant in a sunny spot with fertile, moist, well-drained soil. Trim
back if necessary. Propagate from half-hardened cuttings or seed.

Gelsemium sempervirens

Gelsemium sempervirens ★

☼/◐ ❄ ↔ 20 ft (6 m) ↑ 20 ft (6 m)

Found from southern USA to Guatemala. Jasmine-like, glossy
green, 2 in (5 cm) long, pointed elliptical leaves. Sprays of 1 in
(25 mm) long, scented, yellow flowers followed by dark fruits.
'Pride of Augusta' has double flowers. Zones 8–11.

HARDENBERGIA

This genus, a member of the pea-flower subfamily of the legumes, consists of just 3 species of evergreen climbing shrubs or
trailers. These highly adaptable plants are all native to Australia
where they often make quite an impact in late winter and early
spring when they flower. The spearhead-shaped leaves are glossy
and set off the cluster of small usually purple pea-flowers.
CULTIVATION: In the almost frost-free climates in which these
species grow best, they are used to cover banks, are trained over
fences and arbors, or are used to hide any eyesore in the garden.
They can be grown in full sun or light shade in well-drained to
dry soils. Propagation is best done from seed soaked in hot water
before sowing; selected cultivars are grown from cuttings.

Hardenbergia comptoniana

NATIVE LILAC, WILD WISTERIA VINE

 ↔ 3–10 ft (0.9–3 m) ↑ 10–15 ft (3–4.5 m)

Native to the southwestern part of Western Australia, from Perth to Albany, this is a vigorous evergreen climbing vine with 3 dark green leaflets per leaf, to 2½ in (6 cm) long. Masses of usually purple-blue flowers, to ½ in (12 mm) across, with green spots at their base, are produced in late winter. Zones 10–11.

Hardenbergia violacea

FALSE SARSAPARILLA

☼ ↔ 3–7 ft (0.9–2 m) ↑ 3–10 ft (0.9–3 m)

From Eastern Australia. A climbing or sprawling plant. Wiry stems with dark green, leathery, lance-shaped leaves. Racemes of deep purple pea-flowers smother the entire plant in late winter. 'Happy Wanderer' ★, a vigorous, free-flowing, climbing form; 'Minihaha', compact dwarf shrub to 6 in (15 cm) tall, with small leaves and deep mauve flowers during spring. Zones 9–11.

Hardenbergia violacea

HEDERA

IVY

This is a well-known genus of 11 species of evergreen climbers from Europe, Asia, and northern Africa that will cling by aerial roots to almost any surface. These plants, members of the ivy (Araliaceae) family, are used to clothe walls and grow up trees, as well as being efficient ground covers. They will grow in a wide range of soils and climates, and can become quite weedy outside their native habitats. The foliage usually changes shape to an adult form when it can no longer grow any taller, and cuttings taken from this wood will produce a shrubby form of the plant. The flowers are small, borne in clusters, and of little interest to anyone other than their fly pollinators. The berries that follow are usually black.

CULTIVATION: All species of ivy will grow in almost any soil that is not waterlogged, in aspects ranging from heavy shade to full sun, or in pots or other containers as indoor plants. Propagation of these climbing plants is from cuttings, which strike easily at almost any time of the year.

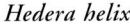

Hedera colchica 'Dentata'

Hedera canariensis

CANARY ISLAND IVY, NORTH AFRICAN IVY

☼ ❄ ↔ 20–60 ft (6–18 m) ↑ 15–20 ft (4.5–6 m)

From northern Africa and the Canary Islands. Large, leathery, slightly glossy, unlobed to shallowly lobed leaves, to 5 in (12 cm) long. 'Gloire de Marengo' (syn. *H. c.* 'Variegata'), leaves go from green through silvery-gray to white at the edges; 'Ravensholst', shallowly lobed bright green leaves to 6 in (15 cm). Zones 8–10.

Hedera colchica

BULLOCK'S HEART IVY, COLCHIC IVY, PERSIAN IVY

☼/☀ ❄ ↔ 20–60 ft (6–18 m) ↑ 20–35 ft (6–10 m)

Large-leafed species found from northern Iran to the Caucasus. Strong self-clinging climber. Foliage is rich deep green, leathery and generally unlobed, to 5 in (12 cm) long. 'Dentata', very large unlobed leaves to 9 in (22 cm) long, bright green on purple-flushed stems; 'Dentata Variegata', one of the boldest ivies grown, mottled gray-green leaves with wide, irregular, yellow edges; 'Sulphur Heart' (syn. 'Paddy's Pride'), rich green leaves, irregular yellow and light green central splashes. Zones 6–10.

Hedera helix

COMMON IVY, ENGLISH IVY

☼ ❄ ↔ 20–60 ft (6–18 m) ↑ 35–50 ft (10–15 m)

Well-known species, distributed over most of Europe. The most genetically unstable, there are hundreds of named clones. Typical form has 3- to 5-lobed, dark green, juvenile leaves, 1¾–2½ in (4–6 cm) long. When a plant has grown as tall as it can on its given support, it produces adult non-climbing branches that flower and fruit, and produce unlobed adult leaves. 'Amberwaves', squarish, 5-lobed, overlapping, yellow-green leaves; 'Atropurpurea', classic ivy leaves, green in summer, turning rich dark purple if exposed to light and enough cold; 'Buttercup', strongly climbing, 5-lobed, rounded, bright yellow leaves turn green in shade; 'Ceridwen', well-branched, ideal for pots, 3-lobed yellow variegated leaves, some of which are completely yellow; 'Cockle Shell', 3- to 5-lobed, round, cupped leaves; 'Glacier', widely grown, will climb or trail, with 3-lobed, mid gray-green leaves, irregularly edged with creamy white; 'Goldchild', dense form, good in pots, with 3-lobed leaves to 1¾ in (4 cm) long, boldly edged with yellow; 'Green Ripple' ★, shiny green rippled leaves with creamy yellow veins, can be vigorous to invasive; 'Harrison', 3-lobed leaves to 2½ in (6 cm) long, dark green veined white, turning purple with enough winter cold; 'Lalla Rookh', bright green form with 5-lobed leaves, irregularly and deeply toothed, good in pots or as ground cover; 'Manda's Crested', good ground cover, bright green leaves that turn bronze in cold weather, with 5 lobes that curl and twist; 'Misty', miniature, 5-lobed variegated leaves; 'Needlepoint', dense mat-forming selection with 3 to 5 deep green narrow lobes on leaves to 1 in (25 mm) long; 'Schafer Three' (syn. *H. h.* 'Calico'), a form with 3-lobed leaves splashed with creamy white, to 1¾ in (4 cm) by 1¾ in (4 cm); 'Treetop', adult non-climbing shrubby plant of the type often known as a tree ivy, with unlobed rich green leaves, selected off a plant of *H. h.* 'Pittsburgh'. Zones 5–10.

Hibbertia scandens

Hedera hibernica
syn. *Hedera helix* subsp. *hibernica*
ATLANTIC IVY, IRISH IVY

☀ ❄ ↔ unlimited ↑ 25–35 ft (8–10 m)

Not restricted to Ireland but native to much of western Europe. A species widely grown as a vigorous ground cover or climber. Differs from *H. helix* in its larger leaves, up to 3½ in (9 cm) long, with 5 lobes. Zones 6–10.

HIBBERTIA (see page 178)

Hibbertia scandens

☀ ❄ ↔ unlimited ↑ 8 ft (2.4 m)

Found growing in Queensland and New South Wales, Australia. A twining climber that can be grown as a ground cover. Slightly glossy narrow leaves, developing bronze tints. Flowers are bright yellow, with a slightly unpleasant scent. Zones 10–12.

HOYA
WAX FLOWER

This genus, in the milkweed (Asclepiadaceae) family, is native to Polynesia, Asia, and Australia. It contains 200 species of mainly climbing, sometimes shrubby or succulent, evergreen plants. They are woody-stemmed and some contain milky sap. In the wild, climbers will reach 20 ft (6 m) or more. Foliage is usually dark green and glossy. Their exquisite waxy flowers, often fragrant, look like fine porcelain. The thick petals are usually white or in shades of pink. The center of the flower has a corona that is starry in many species and often brightly colored.

CULTIVATION: In warm climates grow outdoors in semi-shade in a moist, rich, free-draining soil. Elsewhere hoyas are popular house plants, often grown in hanging baskets. Grow in bright filtered light in a well-drained potting mix. Water and feed regularly and maintain a high level of humidity. Propagate from cuttings.

Hoya australis ★

☀ ❄ ↔ 2–6 ft (0.6–1.8 m) ↑ 2–6 ft (0.6–1.8 m)

Twining and rooting Australia climber. Thick, shiny, succulent, dark green leaves. Umbels of small, starry, scented, white to pale pink flowers, with reddish purple coronas, in summer. Zones 10–12.

Hoya carnosa
WAX PLANT

☀ ❄ ↔ 2–6 ft (0.6–1.8 m) ↑ 2–6 ft (0.6–1.8 m)

Found from India to southeastern China. Climber widely grown as a house plant. Thick dark green leaves. Umbels of fragrant white to palest pink flowers have starry, white, red-centered coronas: 'Exotica', leaves variegated yellow and pink with green margins; 'Krinkle Kurl', twisted curly leaves; 'Variegata', leaves with a yellow central zone and pinker flowers. Zones 10–12.

HUMULUS

A genus of 2 species of herbaceous, climbing, and twining perennials from northern temperate regions; from the hemp (Cannabaceae) family. The plants naturalize in trees and woodland areas and can grow to 70 ft (21 m) in a season. Grown primarily for their attractive foliage, many cultivars have been selected for ornamental purposes. *H. lupulus* is grown for its fruits (hops), used to flavor beer. Spreading via underground suckers, they cover large areas quickly.
CULTIVATION: These plants need well-drained, moist, fertile soil. They die back to the ground over winter, and are prone to mildew in the damp. Propagate from semi-hardwood stem cuttings in late summer or by division when plants are dormant.

Humulus lupulus
BINE, COMMON HOP, EUROPEAN HOP

☀ ❄ ↔ 10–30 ft (3–9 m) ↑ 17–20 ft (5–6 m)

Well-known vigorous herbaceous twiner with rough stems. Source of hops. Suckers far and wide from its questing rhizomes. Leaves 3- to 5-lobed, to 6 in (15 cm) long. Female plants festooned with bracted hops in summer. Usually grown in gardens in its golden-leafed form, 'Aureus', which varies in color depending on how much light it gets. Zones 5–10.

HYDRANGEA (see page 180)

Hydrangea petiolaris ★
syn. *Hydrangea anomala* subsp. *petiolaris*

☀ ❄ ↔ 17–35 ft (5–10 m) ↑ 50 ft (15 m)

A climbing hydrangea from Russia, Korea, Taiwan, and Japan. Attractive dark green leaves; flowers with large lacecap blooms at the start of the season. May take several years to bear flowers. Do not prune. Often treated as a subspecies of *H. anomala*. Zones 4–9.

Hoya carnosa

IPOMOEA

This large and variable genus in the bindweed (Convolvulaceae) family is made up of twining climbers, annual or perennial herbs, shrubs, and small trees. Widely cultivated in tropical to warm-temperate areas for their showy flowers and vigorous growth, some species, including the sweet potato *(I. batatas)*, have tuberous roots used as food. Bell-shaped to tubular flowers usually open for just a day and appear in the leaf axils.

CULTIVATION: They prefer full sun and plenty of water in the growing season but will make the best of almost any conditions. Species other than annuals may be propagated from softwood or half-hardened cuttings in summer. Seeds are better started under glass. Give plants plenty of room and cut back after flowering. They may need support.

Ipomoea alba
syns *Calonyction aculeatum, Ipomoea bona-nox*
BELLE DE NUIT, MOONFLOWER
☼ ✱ ↔ 20–30 ft (6–9 m) ↑ 10–20 ft (3–6 m)
Found throughout tropical regions. Perennial climber with long-stalked heart-shaped leaves. White saucer-shaped flowers, to 6 in (15 cm) wide, open at night, fragrant. Summer-flowering species. Zones 10–12.

Ipomoea horsfalliae
CARDINAL CREEPER
☼ ⬧ ↔ 5–10 ft (1.5–3 m) ↑ 15–25 ft (4.5–8 m)
Perennial twining climber from the West Indies. Long palmate leaves, 3 to 5 lobes. Large clusters of flared deep pink to purple flowers. Zones 9–12.

Ipomoea lobata
syns *Mina lobata, Quamoclit lobata*
SPANISH FLAG
☼ ⬧ ↔ 3–6 ft (0.9–1.8 m) ↑ 10–15 ft (3–4.5 m)
Mexican perennial often grown as an annual. Variable smooth or deeply lobed leaves. Racemes of small, tubular, scarlet flowers, fade to yellow, giving a two-toned effect. Summer-flowering. Zones 9–12.

Ipomoea × multifida
syn. *Ipomoea × sloteri*
CARDINAL FLOWER
☼ ✱ ↔ 3–6 ft (0.9–1.8 m) ↑ 3–10 ft (0.9–3 m)
Of garden origin; hybrid of *I. coccinea* and *I. quamoclit*. Leaves deeply divided, several linear lobes. Funnelform flowers, 1–2 in (25–50 mm) wide, red with white centers, from summer to autumn. Zones 8–12.

Ipomoea nil
☼ ⬧ ↔ 2–5 ft (0.6–1.5 m) ↑ 10–15 ft (3–4.5 m)
Found throughout tropical regions. Annual climber with hairy stems. Broadly oval or 3-lobed leaves. Blue funnelform flowers, around 4 in (10 cm) wide, in clusters of 1 to 5, in summer. '**Chocolate**', pale chocolate brown flowers; '**Scarlett O'Hara**', red flowers. Zones 9–12.

Ipomoea purpurea
COMMON MORNING GLORY
☼ ✱ ↔ 5–10 ft (1.5–3 m) ↑ 5–10 ft (1.5–3 m)
Vigorous annual climber originally from Mexico, but now naturalized in many countries and often declared as a weed. Stems hairy, leaves whole to lobed, heart-shaped, 4 in (10 cm) wide. Flowers large, trumpet-shaped, in shades ranging from red through to pink, blue, white, and purple, opening in the morning and lasting only a day,

Ipomoea × multifida

Ipomoea horsfalliae

from spring–summer. *I. p.* var. *diversifolia*, leaves more often 3- to 5-lobed than smooth. Zones 7–11.

Ipomoea tricolor
MORNING GLORY
☼ ✱ ↔ 3 ft (0.9 m) ↑ 10 ft (3 m)
From Mexico and Central America. Annual climber with heart-shaped leaves. Bears wide funnel-shaped flowers that fade as the day progresses, sky blue, yellow interior base, in summer. '**Heavenly Blue**', blue flowers, white and yellow throat; '**Tie Dye**', leaves green, purple, and white. Zones 8–12.

JASMINUM
JASMINE
Famed for the fragrance of its flowers, this genus, which belongs to the olive (Oleaceae) family, is native to Africa, Europe, and Asia (with a single American species). The genus includes some 200 species of deciduous, semi-deciduous, and evergreen shrubs and woody-stemmed climbers. The foliage is usually pinnate or less commonly trifoliate and varies greatly in color and texture. The flowers, in clusters at the branch tips and leaf axils, are tubular with 5 widely flared lobes. Most commonly white, white flushed with pink, or yellow, and can be scentless to overpoweringly fragrant.
CULTIVATION: Jasmines vary greatly in their hardiness, depending on their origins, though few will tolerate repeated severe frosts. They are averse to drought, preferring moist, humus-rich, well-drained soil and a position in full sun or partial shade. In suitable climates most species grow rapidly and some can become rather invasive. They are readily propagated from seed, cuttings, or layers, which with some low-growing species may form naturally, making them difficult to contain.

Jasminum azoricum ★
AZORES JASMINE
☼/⬧ ⬧ ↔ 20 ft (6 m) ↑ 20 ft (6 m)
Evergreen climbing shrub from the Azores. Glossy, deep green, leathery leaves, 3 or sometimes 5 lance-shaped leaflets, up to 2 in (5 cm) long. Flowers are pure white, very scented, in loose panicles, produced in late summer. Zones 10–11.

Jasminum beesianum

☼/◐ ❋ ↔15 ft (4.5 m) ↑15 ft (4.5 m)

Scrambling or twining, Chinese, deciduous shrub. Simple, 2 in (5 cm) long, lance-shaped leaves in pairs. Small fragrant blooms in 3-flowered clusters, shades of pink from pale to deep rose, in late spring–autumn. Glossy black fruits. Zones 7–10.

Jasminum officinale

COMMON JASMINE, COMMON WHITE JASMINE, POETS' JASMINE, TRUE JASMINE

☼/◐ ❋ ↔15 ft (4.5 m) ↑30 ft (9 m)

Found from the Middle East to China. Sprawling, somewhat twining, deciduous shrub. Slightly downy pinnate leaves, 5 to 9 leaflets. White or very pale pink flowers, fragrant, early summer–autumn. Several variegated foliage cultivars, such as cream-edged 'Argenteovariegatum' and gold-blotched 'Aureum'. Zones 7–10.

Jasminum polyanthum

☼/◐ ❋ ↔25 ft (8 m) ↑10–17 ft (3–5 m)

Vigorous evergreen climber from southwestern China that twines and tangles through trees, trellises, and other structures. Dark green foliage, 5 to 7 leaflets, can have bronze tones in winter. Delicate pink buds from late winter open to white fragrant flowers, ¾ in (18 mm) wide, in spring. Flowers through to mid-autumn. Zones 7–9.

Jasminum sambac

ARABIAN JASMINE, ZAMBAC

☼ ⧉ ↔6 ft (1.8 m) ↑5–12 ft (1.5–3.5 m)

Woody-stemmed evergreen climber, can be treated as a lax shrub. Large simple, not pinnate, leaves, glossy deep green with a heavy texture. Clusters of up to 12 fragrant, waxy, white flowers that age to pale pink, are borne throughout the year. 'Grand Duke of-Tuscany', double-flowered cultivar. Zones 10–11.

Jasminum × stephanense

☼ ❋ ↔5–10 ft (1.5–3 m) ↑17 ft (5 m)

A *J. beesianum × J. officinale* hybrid from south-western China. Rampant, woody, twining, decid-uous climber, soft gray-green foliage that has a dull appearance. Bunches of fragrant pale pink flowers, ¾ in (18 mm) long, summer–autumn. Zones 8–10.

KENNEDIA

CORAL PEA

A genus of 16 species of evergreen climbers and trailers in the pea-flower subfamily of the legume (Fabaceae) family; all except one are endemic to Australia. Flowers are usually brightly colored and borne in spring and summer; they usually have a contrasting color at the base of the stand-ard. Flowers are followed by round to flattened pea-style pods. Leaves are composed of 3 leaflets. CULTIVATION: In nature these plants tolerate drought and poor soils and in near frost-free conditions will do so in gardens as well. They make attractive ground covers or can be grown on fences and arches in full to half-sun. They are usually raised from seed that must be soaked in hot water prior to sowing in spring.

Jasminum sambac

Kennedia nigricans

Kennedia coccinea

CORAL VINE

☼/◐ ⧉ ↔10 ft (3 m) ↑7–10 ft (2–3 m)

From southwestern Western Australia. Fast-growing twiner or ground cover with leathery, green, wedge-shaped leaflets to 3 in (8 cm) long. Bright red pea-flowers with yellow blotches, borne from spring through to summer. Zones 9–11.

Kennedia nigricans

BLACK BEAN, BLACK CORAL PEA

☼/◐ ⧉ ↔10–15 ft (3–4.5 m) ↑17–20 ft (5–6 m)

Very vigorous climber from Western Australia. Leaflets 5 in (12 cm) long. Black pea-flowers, yellow patches, spring–summer. Zones 9–11.

Kennedia rubicunda

DUSKY CORAL PEA

☼/◐ ⧉ ↔15 ft (4.5 m) ↑10–15 ft (3–4.5 m)

A strong-growing climber from coastal eastern Australia. Leaflets up to 6 in (15 cm) long. Deep red flowers with paler blotches, borne from spring to summer. Zones 9–11.

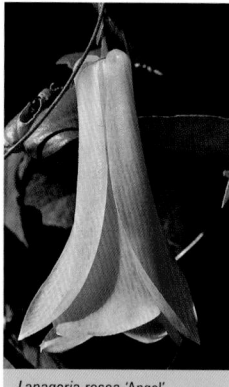
Lapageria rosea 'Angol'

LAPAGERIA

This genus consists of a single species of ever-green, climbing, woody plants from Chile that twine up trees, trellises, and fences. They are members of the small family Philesiaceae, allied to the sarsaparilla (Smilacaceae) family. Their upright stems need support to climb up and through structures. Without support the plant will scramble over the ground. Large, oval, dark green leaves are thick and leathery and have dis-tinctive ribbing along the length of the leaf. The large, pendent, bell-shaped flowers have 3 broad waxy outer segments overlapping the 3 narrower inner ones; predominantly a rosy red in wild populations, but cultivars can vary in color from deep crimson red to a range of pinks and creams. There have also been some reports of yellow forms of *Lapageria*. CULTIVATION: Sensitive to frost, they need a sheltered spot, away from all-day sun in summer. They like a cool area for their roots, and their branches head toward the light, which helps initiate flower bud development. They need free-draining, open, fertile soil, not waterlogged, with a neutral pH. Propagate from seed in spring; it may take up to 7 years for plants to flower from seed, and flower color may vary in seedlings. They can be grown in a greenhouse.

Lapageria rosea

CHILEAN BELLFLOWER, COPIHUE

☼/◐ ❁ ↔ 3–10 ft (0.9–3 m) ↑ 17 ft (5 m)

Chile's national flower. Leaves, to 5 in (12 cm) long, held on thin, smooth, rope-like stems. Large rosy red flowers, 4–6 in (10–15 cm) long, in summer–autumn. **'Angol'** (perhaps more correctly 'Ongol', though usually sold as 'Angol') has especially large salmon pink flowers; **'Nash Court'** produces soft shell pink flowers, the petals marked with dark red stripy mottling. Zones 8–9.

LATHYRUS *(see page 495)*

Lathyrus grandiflorus

EVERLASTING PEA, TWO-FLOWERED PEA

☼ ❁ ↔ 7 ft (2 m) ↑ 7 ft (2 m)

Found from Sicily to the southern Balkans. A climbing perennial. Angled stems; leaves tendril-tipped, paired leaflets. Sprays of up to 4 violet and pink flowers, 1¼ in (30 mm) wide, summer. Zones 6–10.

Lathyrus latifolius

PERENNIAL PEA

☼ ❁ ↔ 7 ft (2 m) ↑ 10 ft (3 m)

Found in central and southern Europe. A climbing perennial. Faintly angled stems; the leaves tendril-tipped, with paired leaflets. Racemes of up to 15 purple, pink, or white flowers, 1¼ in (30 mm) across, in summer. **'Albus'** (syn. 'Snow White'), pure white flowers; **'Pink Beauty'**, pink and red flowers; **'White Pearl'**, long-lasting white flowers. Zones 5–9.

LONICERA

HONEYSUCKLE

Honeysuckles, belonging to the woodbine (Caprifoliaceae) family, are often regarded as somewhat untidy second-class climbers, but in the right place they are among the easiest and most rewarding plants. Occurring widely throughout the Northern Hemisphere though chiefly in temperate Eurasia, the 180-odd species in the genus encompass climbers, ground covers, and shrubs, both evergreen and decid-uous, most of them very hardy. The foliage usually consists of opposite pairs of smooth-edged leaves, often somewhat leathery. The flowers, sometimes highly fragrant, vary in size; most are tubular at the base but divided at the mouth into 5 petals that are frequently arranged in 2 lips, an upper lip of 4 fused petals and a lower lip of a single petal. The fruit is an ornamental berry relished by birds, usually backed or partially enclosed by bract-like calyces that may color slightly.

CULTIVATION: Although honeysuckles are tough adaptable plants that will thrive in most conditions, they are generally best grown in rich, moist, humus-enriched, well-drained soil in full sun to partial shade. They can be raised from seed, though most are easily grown from layers or half-hardened cuttings. Cultivars and hybrids must be propagated from cuttings.

Lonicera × brownii

SCARLET TRUMPET HONEYSUCKLE

☼ ❁ ↔ 8 ft (2.4 m) ↑ 10 ft (3 m)

Garden-raised deciduous or semi-deciduous *L. sempervirens* × *L. hir-suta* hybrid, resembling *L. sempervirens,* with paired blue-green leaves. Whorls of pale orange to red unscented flowers in late spring to early summer. **'Dropmore Scarlet'**, strong growing, with larger leaves, long-tubed bright red flowers, mid-summer to autumn. Zones 5–9.

Lonicera caprifolium

ITALIAN HONEYSUCKLE

☼ ❁ ↔ 10 ft (3 m) ↑ 20 ft (6 m)

From Europe and western Asia. A species usually seen as a climber, but it can be grown as ground cover. Oval leaves in pairs. Whorls of very fragrant, pink-tinted creamy yellow flowers, to 2 in (5 cm) long, from spring to summer. Orange-red fruit. Zones 5–9.

Lonicera etrusca

☼ ❁ ↔ 10 ft (3 m) ↑ 12 ft (3.5 m)

From the Mediterranean. Scrambling semi-evergreen shrub or climber. Fused pairs of bright green or blue-green leaves with downy undersides. Whorls of fragrant flowers, cream with red tints, ageing to yellow, at branch tips, in summer–early autumn. **'Superba'**, red young growth, many-flowered panicles opening cream, ageing to yellow-orange. Zones 7–10.

Lathyrus grandiflorus

Lonicera × heckrottii

☼ ❁ ↔ 6 ft (1.8 m) ↑ 15 ft (4.5 m)

Hybrid, possibly between *L. sempervirens* and *L. × americana.* Sprawling deciduous climber with paired oblong to elliptical leaves, purplish when young, maturing to blue-green. Whorls of yellow-throated deep pink flowers, late spring–summer. Red fruit. **'Gold Flame'**, purple-red flowers, bright yellow inside. Zones 5–9.

Lonicera × *heckrottii* 'Gold Flame'

Lonicera × *italica*

☼/◐ ❋ ↔ 5–10 ft (1.5–3 m) ↑ 10 ft (3 m)

Evergreen vine with variegated leaves of pink, lime green, and cream. The spicy-scented, rose-purple, tubular flowers appear from mid-spring to mid-summer. Zones 5–9.

Lonicera japonica

HALL'S HONEYSUCKLE, JAPANESE HONEYSUCKLE

☼/◐ ❋ ↔ 25 ft (8 m) ↑ 25–30 ft (8–9 m)

From Japan, Korea, and China. Vigorous, evergreen (semi-evergreen in cold climates), twining vine. Leaves oblong, dark green, slightly downy on both sides. Produces fragrant white to pale yellow flowers in early summer–late autumn, followed by black berries. A weed in southeastern USA, Australia, and New Zealand. Zones 4–11.

Lonicera periclymenum

WOODBINE

☼ ❋ ↔ 8 ft (2.4 m) ↑ 12 ft (3.5 m)

From Eurasia. Twining, scrambling, deciduous or semi-evergreen shrub. Finely downy young leaves becoming smooth and blue-gray when mature. Very fragrant pinkish red flowers with creamy yellow interiors, in whorls of 3 to 5 blooms, in summer. Red fruit. Can become invasive. Zones 4–10.

Lonicera sempervirens

TRUMPET HONEYSUCKLE

☼/◐ ❋ ↔ 10 ft (3 m) ↑ 10–20 ft (3–6 m)

From eastern and southern USA. Deciduous twining vine with blue-green leaves; scarlet-orange trumpet-shaped blooms with yellow centers, borne on previous year's stems. Zones 4–10.

Lonicera × *tellmanniana*

REDGOLD HONEYSUCKLE, TELLMANN HONEYSUCKLE

☼/◐ ❋ ↔ 5 ft (1.5 m) ↑ 7–20 ft (2–6 m)

A deciduous, vigorous, twining climber with showy coppery gold flowers from late spring through to summer. Zones 6–9.

MANDEVILLA

Central and South American genus in the dogbane (Apocynaceae) family; contains some 120 species of mainly tuberous perennials, subshrubs, and twining vines. Leaves large, deep green, elliptical to lance-shaped with prominent elongated tips. Trumpet flowers, singly or in racemes, often large and sometimes fragrant, throughout the warmer months. They come in white to cream and various shades of pink. More commonly cultivated are the beautiful vigorous vines. CULTIVATION: Only a few species will tolerate any frost and all prefer a mild to warm climate, dappled sunlight, and moist, humus-rich, well-drained soil. Trim if necessary. All parts exude an irritant milky latex when cut. Feeding produces lush foliage but also rampant growth. Propagate from half-hardened stems in summer, or cuttings.

Mandevilla × *amabilis*

☼/◐ ⚘ ↔ 15 ft (4.5 m) ↑ 15 ft (4.5 m)

Vigorous climber, uncertain origins (probably *M. splendens* hybrid). Deeply veined, leathery leaves, 4–8 in (10–20 cm) long. Yellow-throated, dark-centered, pink flowers, in spring. Zones 11–12.

Mandevilla laxa

CHILEAN JASMINE

☼ ⚘ ↔ 17 ft (5 m) ↑ 15 ft (4.5 m)

Vigorous semi-evergreen to deciduous climber, native to Argentina. Elliptical leaves taper to fine point, dark green to bronze, downy, sometimes purplish undersides, to 3 in (8 cm) long. White flowers, 2 in (5 cm) wide, strongly scented, especially evenings, from late spring through to summer. Zones 9–11.

Mandevilla sanderi

☼/◐ ⚘ ↔ 17 ft (5 m) ↑ 17 ft (5 m)

Strong-growing Brazilian climber. Glossy, smooth-surfaced, leathery leaves, 3 in (8 cm) long. Deep pink yellow-throated flowers, to 2 in (5 cm) wide, up to 5 blooms per raceme, in spring. 'Scarlet Pimpernel', very deep pink to red flowers. Zones 11–12.

METROSIDEROS *(see page 219)*

Metrosideros carminea ★

AKAKURA

◐ ⚘ ↔ 3–10 ft (0.9–3 m) ↑ 40 ft (12 m)

Rare climber from New Zealand, climbs by clinging aerial roots. Small, deep green, rounded leaves. Bright crimson flowers, in spring. Cuttings from adult plants grow into small spreading shrubs. 'Carousel' ★, yellow leaf margins. Zones 9–11.

Mandevilla sanderi 'Scarlet Pimpernel'

Mandevilla laxa

Metrosideros carminea

MONSTERA
FRUIT SALAD PLANT, SWISS CHEESE PLANT, WINDOWLEAF

A genus of 22 species of epiphytic and climbing evergreen tropical plants from Central and South America; in the arum (Araceae) family. They are grown as handsome foliage plants indoors or in a greenhouse in all but tropical climates where they are often used to grow up tree trunks. Leaves often have large holes in them.
CULTIVATION: Grow in a humid warm spot, frost-free, in part-shade. Soil must be well drained and humus-rich. Stake or support climbing species. Propagate from freshly sown seed with bottom heat.

Monstera deliciosa
FRUIT SALAD PLANT, MEXICAN BREADFRUIT, SWISS CHEESE PLANT

☀ ⚘ ↔ 8–20 ft (2.4–6 m) ↑ 35–50 ft (10–15 m)

Impressive climber from southern Mexico to Panama. Extensive aerial root system. Leaves to 36 in (90 cm) long, irregular holes, often break edges. White arum-type flowers in suitable conditions, in summer. Edible cone-shaped fruit, to 10 in (25 cm) long. Zones 11–12.

MUEHLENBECKIA
WIRE VINE

This genus contains 15 species of evergreen or semi-deciduous sub-shrubs and shrubs in the knotweed (Polygonaceae) family. Plants are often twining, scrambling, or forming dense mounds of tangled stems. Found in South America, Australia, New Zealand, and New Guinea, often in hilly country, with some extending into the alpine zone. They are well adapted to harsh windswept conditions, with reduced foliage hidden within the mass of stems. Flowers are small and clustered in the leaf axils or at the branch tips. Small, 3-sided, nut-like fruit in a fleshy cup follow the flowers.
CULTIVATION: These plants tolerate light to moderate frosts but are not suited to continental climates. Their best features are their ground-hugging habit and resistance to wind. Plant in full sun with light, well-drained soil that can be kept moist in summer. Propagate from seed in autumn, or by layers, which often form naturally, or from hardwood cuttings in winter.

Muehlenbeckia complexa
MAIDENHAIR VINE, MATTRESS VINE, NECKLACE-VINE, WIRE VINE

☼ ❋ ↔ 10 ft (3 m) ↑ 5–15 ft (1.5–4.5 m)

Dense twining climber from New Zealand. Fine dark purple stems. Tiny bronze-green leaves. Tiny white flowers, in spring. White receptacle, one black nut. Zones 8–10.

PANDOREA

A small genus consisting of 6 species and several cultivars in the trumpet-vine (Bignoniaceae) family. This genus has been classified as *Bignonia* and *Tecoma* in the past. These woody evergreen climbers, which are grown for their flowers and foliage, are native to Australia, New Caledonia, Malaysia, and New Guinea, where they grow from sea level up to 9,840 ft (3,000 m). Leaflets are usually green and glossy, and the plant climbs by using tendrils. Flowers are 5-petalled, tubular, fragrant, and usually white, cream, buff, or pink.
CULTIVATION: They grow best in moist well-drained soil in full sun. Prune after flowering. Propagate from seed, cuttings or layers.

Pandorea pandorana

Pandorea jasminoides
syns *Bignonia jasminoides*, *Tecoma jasminoides*
BOWER-OF-BEAUTY, BOWER PLANT

☼ ⚘ ↔ 8–15 ft (2.4–4.5 m) ↑ 17 ft (5 m)

Vigorous twining climber with glossy bright green leaflets. White flowers with hot-pink throats, in abundance on large panicles, in spring–summer. Prefers rich moist soil. Zones 9–11.

Pandorea pandorana
syns *Bignonia pandorana*, *Pandorea doratoxylon*, *P. oxleyii*, *Tecoma australis*
WONGA WONGA VINE

☼ ⚘ ↔ 10–20 ft (3–6 m) ↑ 20 ft (6 m)

Vigorous twining climber, long whippy stems. Leaflets bright green and glossy. Flowers in abundance in late winter, small, usually white, cream, buff, pinkish, or maroon, often spotted purple. Zones 9–11.

PARTHENOCISSUS

A genus of 10 species of deciduous tendril-producing climbers in the grape (Vitaceae) family from East Asia and North America. Grown for their attractive foliage and, in most species, self-clinging habit. Leaves are either maple-shaped or divided into leaflets, and usually develop brilliant colors before they shed. Flowers are tiny and green, and, like the small black berries, have no ornamental value.
CULTIVATION: They will grow in any moderately fertile soil in sun or part-shade. Propagate from cuttings at almost any time or by removing rooted layers. Can also be raised from seed.

Parthenocissus quinquefolia
syn. *Vitis quinquefolia*
VIRGINIA CREEPER

☼/❋ ❋ ↔ 30 ft (9 m) ↑ 40–50 ft (12–15 m)

Fast-growing self-clinging climber from North America, Mexico, and Cuba. Suction cups on tendrils, 5 leaflets to 5 in (12 cm) long, turn brilliant scarlet before shedding. Zones 3–10.

Parthenocissus tricuspidata
BOSTON IVY, JAPANESE CREEPER

☼ ❋ ↔ 20 ft (6 m) ↑ 50–70 ft (15–21 m)

Strongly self-clinging species from China, Japan, and Korea; maple-shaped leaves to 8 in (20 cm) long, usually with 3 lobes, juvenile plants usually have leaves divided into 3 leaflets. Leaves overlap each other, turning brilliant colors before shedding. Zones 4–10.

Passiflora caerulea

PASSIFLORA

PASSIONFLOWER

Type genus for its family, Passifloraceae, the 500 or so species of passionflowers are mainly evergreen tendril-climbing vines from tropical America, though there are a few shrubby species and the range does extend to Asia and the Pacific Islands. Grown mainly for their flowers and fruit, the vigor of passionflowers makes them superb plants for covering unsightly objects. Flowers have an unusual structure, with a tubular calyx of 5 conspicuous sepals, usually 5 petals of the same size and color as the sepals, a corona of anthers, and 3 styles on an extended central tube. Fruits of many species are mildly to quite poisonous, though others are edible and delicious. CULTIVATION: Most species are frost tender and prefer a warm climate in full or half-sun with deep, moist, humus-rich, well-drained soil. Feed and water well. Trim to shape and remove any frosted foliage in spring. Propagate from seed or cuttings, or by layering.

Passiflora amethystina
syn. *Passiflora violacea* of gardens
☼/◐ ⚘ ↔ 3–6 ft (0.9–1.8 m) ↑10 ft (3 m)
From central Bolivia to northern Argentina. Autumn-flowering, with 3-lobed leaves to 5 in (12 cm) long. Flowers to 4 in (10 cm) wide, deep violet-pink, radiating white filaments. Zones 9–11.

Passiflora caerulea
BLUE PASSIONFLOWER
☼/◐ ❊ ↔ 6–15 ft (1.8–4.5 m) ↑30 ft (9 m)
From Brazil and Argentina. Tolerates repeated frosts, though partly deciduous in cold. Broadly palmate leaves, 3 to 9 lobes, often with toothed edges. Flowers to over 4 in (10 cm) wide, petals mostly creamy white, many radial purple and white banded filaments around a greenish center, in summer–autumn. Zones 7–10.

Passiflora coccinea
RED GRANADILLA, RED PASSIONFLOWER
☼/◐ ✢ ↔ 12–30 ft (3.5–9 m) ↑12 ft (3.5 m)
Vigorous summer-flowering climber from tropical South America. Deep green, heavily textured, toothed elliptical leaves to 6 in (15 cm)

long. Long-tubed flowers to 5 in (12 cm) wide, bright red with dark filaments around a pale pink to white center. Fruit yellow to orange, sometimes mottled, to 2 in (5 cm) long. Zones 10–12.

Passiflora incarnata
MAY APPLE, MAY POPS, WILD PASSIONFLOWER
☼/◐ ❊ ↔ 6–15 ft (1.8–4.5 m) ↑6 ft (1.8 m)
Vigorous climber from eastern USA. Evergreen in mild areas, dies back to ground in cold conditions but regrows up to 15 ft (4.5 m) in summer. Leaves 3-lobed, to 6 in (15 cm) long and wide, toothed edges and blue-green undersides. Lavender and white flowers to 3 in (8 cm) wide followed by ovoid, 2 in (5 cm) long fruit. Zones 6–10.

Passiflora racemosa
RED PASSIONFLOWER
☼/◐ ✢ ↔ 6–15 ft (1.8–4.5 m) ↑15 ft (4.5 m)
Brazilian species with pointed oval to 3-lobed leaves to 4 in (10 cm) long and wide. Large pendulous racemes of bright red, rarely white, flowers to 4 in (10 cm) wide, short white filaments. Zones 10–12.

Passiflora × *violacea*
syn. *Passiflora* × *caeruleoracemosa*
☼/◐ ◔ ↔ 6–15 ft (1.8–4.5 m) ↑20 ft (6 m)
A summer-flowering hybrid of *P. caerulea* and *P. racemosa*. Dark green palmate leaves, 5 deep lobes. Deep purple-pink flowers with darker filaments. Best known form is mauve-pink 'Eynsford Gem' with white filaments. Zones 9–11.

Passiflora Hybrid Cultivars
☼/◐ ❊ ↔ 6–15 ft (1.8–4.5 m) ↑6–12 ft (1.8–3.5 m)
There are many hybrid passionflowers, often based on *P. caerulea* to increase their hardiness, though some frost-tender hybrids have been raised specifically for tropical gardens. They include 'Amethyst'; 'Debby'; 'New Incense'; and 'Sunburst'. Zones 8–12.

PELARGONIUM *(see page 531)*

Pelargonium peltatum
IVY-LEAFED GERANIUM
☼ ◔ ↔ 8 ft (2.4 m) ↑8 ft (2.4 m)
Sprawling, scrambling, climbing South African perennial. Flowers continuously. Succulent rounded leaves, 5 triangular lobes, are often zonally marked. Short-stemmed heads of up to 9 flowers. Zones 9–11.

PETREA

BLUE BIRD VINE

A genus of 30 evergreen, woody-stemmed, twining climbers, shrubs, or small trees, in the vervain (Verbenaceae) family, native to tropical America and the West Indies. Plants have simple, opposite, leathery leaves and long racemes of blue, purple, violet, or white flowers, growing from leaf axils or at branch ends. Narrow, bell-shaped corolla tubes have 5 flared and rounded lobes, 4 stamens. Fruit is a drupe. CULTIVATION: Plant in full sun in fertile well-drained soil, and water regularly—less when not in growth. Plants may require support. Thin out crowded spring growth and protect against sucking insects. Propagate in summer from semi-ripe tip cuttings, or from seed.

Petrea volubilis
PURPLE WREATH, QUEEN'S WREATH, SANDPAPER VINE

☼ ✣ ↔ 10–20 ft (3–6 m) ↑ 20–60 ft (6–18 m)

Evergreen woody vine or subshrub with intertwining pale brown to ash gray branches covered with pores. From Central America and the West Indies. Rough-textured leaves, about 8 in (20 cm) long, are dark green, oblong or elliptical, lighter green underneath. Erect or drooping cylindrical flowerheads, 3–12 in (8–30 cm) long. Flowers have a lilac calyx with lobes longer than the tube, and an indigo to amethyst corolla with a densely hairy tube. Dead flowers fall to the ground, rotating like helicopter blades. 'Albiflora', white flowers. Zones 10–12.

PHILODENDRON
A genus in to the arum (Araceae) family and made up of around 500 species from tropical America and the West Indies. They are mainly epiphytic clinging vines with aerial roots, but the genus also includes some shrub-like and almost tree-like species. The large glossy leaves may be smooth-edged, variously lobed, or deeply divided in a feather-like pattern. Flowers are insignificant and without petals; held on a flower spike. Plant parts are poisonous, and contact with the sap may cause skin irritation. Suitable species can make attractive landscape plants in warm climates. Many are used as indoor plants.
CULTIVATION: Best in the tropics and subtropics, in a moist, well-drained, humus-rich soil with generous watering in growth phase. Many species tolerate low light, grow them in dappled shade. Propagate from seed, from cuttings, or by layering.

Philodendron domesticum
syn. *Philodendron hastatum*
ELEPHANT EAR PHILODENDRON, EMERALD DUKE PHILODENDRON

◑ ⚬ ↔ 2–3 ft (0.6–0.9 m) ↑ 6–10 ft (1.8–3 m)

Slow-growing, evergreen, woody-based climber native to northern South America. Has lustrous, coarse-textured, bright green leaves, arrowhead- to heart-shaped, 12–24 in (30–60 cm) long, waxy coating, prominent lobes at base, on thick stalks. Bears spathes of white or green flowers. Zones 10–12.

Philodendron erubescens
BLUSHING PHILODENDRON, RED-LEAF PHILODENDRON

◑/◐ ⚬ ↔ 3–8 ft (0.9–2.4 m) ↑ 6–10 ft (1.8–3 m)

Erect scrambling climber from Colombia. Large, lustrous dark green leaves with a coppery finish, oval to triangular, on long red stalks. Spadix of dark purple flowers, to 6 in (15 cm) long. Zones 10–12.

Philodendron hederaceum
syn. *Philodendron scandens*

◑ ⚬ ↔ 2–6 ft (0.6–1.8 m) ↑ 10–15 ft (3–4.5 m)

Evergreen tree-climbing vine from the West Indies, and much of northern South and Central America. Large, reddish green young leaves and oval to heart-shaped, leathery, dark green mature leaves, often purplish or violet below, long thick stalks, 5 to 6 pairs of prominent raised veins. Solitary flower spikes, with green spathes, white on the inside, and white spadix. Greenish white berries. Zones 10–12.

PIPER (see page 242)

Piper nigrum
BLACK OR WHITE PEPPER, COMMON PEPPER, MADAGASCAR PEPPER, PEPPER PLANT

☼ ⚬ ↔ 12 ft (3.5 m) ↑ 10–25 ft (3–8 m)

Climbing perennial vine from India and Myanmar. Round, woody, smooth, branching stems. Smooth, broadly tapered, oval to heart-shaped leaves, rounded at base, with pointed tips. Spikes of small, creamish green flowers, followed by fruit, a drupe, dark red when mature, the source of commercial black or white pepper. Zones 10–12.

PODRANEA
This genus is made up of 2 evergreen, twining, climbing shrubs, members of the trumpet-vine (Bignoniaceae) family and natives of South Africa, grown for their foxglove-like flowers. They have divided leaves and terminal, pyramid-shaped flowerheads. Fruit is a long capsule or pod containing winged seed.
CULTIVATION: These plants are best grown in full sun in any fertile, well-drained soil. They may require some support. Propagate by striking half-hardened cuttings in summer or from seed sown in spring.

Podranea ricasoliana

Podranea ricasoliana
syns *Pandorea brycei, P. ricasoliana,*
Tecoma ricasoliana
PINK TRUMPET VINE

☼ ✣ ↔ 20 ft (6 m) ↑ 12–20 ft (3.5–6 m)

Fast-growing, climber; slender, twining stems and compound leaves, 5 to 11 smooth-edged, green leaflets. Loose clusters of pale pink, fragrant, funnelform flowers, striped red, spring to autumn. Zones 10–11.

Philodendron hederaceum, in the wild, Costa Rica

Pueraria lobata

PUERARIA

A genus of about 20 herbaceous or woody, twining climbers in the pea-flower subfamily of the legume (Fabaceae) family, native to Southeast Asia and Japan. The compound leaves have 2 or 3 leaflets, and long flowerheads with butterfly-like flowers grow from the leaf axils or cluster in racemes at the ends of branches. These are followed by narrow flattened pods.
CULTIVATION: These plants prefer full sun in moist well-drained soil. Propagate from seed or cuttings, or by division of roots. They can be invasive.

Pueraria lobata
syn. *Pueraria montana* var. *lobata*
JAPANESE ARROWROOT, KUDZU VINE, THE VINE THAT ATE THE SOUTH
☼ ❄ ↔ 30–100 ft (9–30 m) ↕ 30–60 ft (9–18 m)
Fast-growing, semi-woody vine from China and Japan. Fleshy tuberous roots, very hairy stems. Alternate, finely hairy leaves with 2 to 3 oval to diamond-shaped leaflets. Erect racemes of large flowers grow from leaf axils in autumn. Many purple flowers, to ¾ in (18 mm) wide, with a distinct yellow patch on the largest petal. Fruit is a several-seeded, brown, finely hairy, flat legume. Zones 5–11.

PYROSTEGIA

These 4 evergreen, woody-stemmed, tendril climbers belong to the trumpet-vine (Bignoniaceae) family. Native to the tropical Americas, they are grown for their showy flowers. They have angled branches and compound leaves with 2, sometimes 3, oval leaflets, with or without a terminal tendril, and clusters, at the ends of branches, of flowers with curved, tubular corollas with protruding stamens.
CULTIVATION: They grow best in full sun in a fertile well-drained soil, and need support. Propagate from half-hardened cuttings in summer.

Pyrostegia venusta
syn. *Pyrostegia ignea*
FLAME VINE, GOLDEN SHOWER, ORANGE TRUMPET CREEPER, TANGO POI
☼ ✦ ↔ 20 ft (6 m) ↕ 20–30 ft (6–9 m)
Fast-growing, vigorously branching climber from Brazil, Paraguay, Bolivia, and northeastern Argentina. Smooth, papery or leathery leaflets, blunt tips. Orange flowers, in autumn–spring. Zones 8–10.

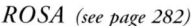
Pyrostegia venusta

QUISQUALIS

This genus in the family Combretaceae contains 16 species from tropical Africa and Southeast Asia. They are evergreen woody climbers or trailing plants grown in their steamy homelands for their tubular flowers that flare into 5 lobes and are used to cover walls or grow over arches. Leaves are simple and are usually in opposite pairs.
CULTIVATION: In tropical climates provide a well-drained but moist soil, not too fertile, to encourage growth at the expense of flowers. In temperate to cold climates they need a warm greenhouse, minimum temperature 56°F (13°C). They prefer full light, but shelter from the midday sun. Propagate from softwood cuttings or by layering.

Quisqualis indica
syn. *Combretum indicum*
RANGOON CREEPER
☼/❂ ✦ ↔ 25 ft (8 m) ↕ 35 ft (10 m)
From mainland Southeast Asia to New Guinea. Rampant evergreen climber, usually shrubby to begin with. Leaves up to 7 in (18 cm) long, smooth-edged with prominent veins. Perfumed, very narrow, tubular flowers initially white, ageing from pink to bright red, in summer–autumn. Zones 10–12.

ROSA *(see page 282)*

Rosa banksiae
BANKSIAN ROSE
☼ ❄ ↔ 30 ft (9 m) ↕ 30 ft (9 m)
Near-evergreen in mild climates, once-flowering climbing rose from western and central China. Leaves with 3 to 5 leaflets. Massed sprays of small white flowers, spring–early summer. *R. b. banksiae*, double, white, scented flowers; *R. b. lutea* ★, yellow double flowers. Zones 7–10.

Rosa bracteata
MACARTNEY ROSE
☼ ❄ ↔ 8 ft (2.4 m) ↕ 8 ft (2.4 m)
Evergreen species native to China but naturalized in southern USA. Forms a shrub or small climber in colder areas. Stems with hooked thorns; leaves dark green. Single white flowers with prominent yellow stamens, summer to autumn. Hips round, orangey red. Zones 7–10.

Rosa helenae
☼ ❄ ↔ 15 ft (4.5 m) ↕ 20 ft (6 m)
Rambling rose from central China. Young branches with purplish hue, stems well armed with strong curved prickles. Light green leaves, long narrow leaflets, pale undersides. Small, white, single, fragrant flowers, in corymbs, in summer. Large orange to red hips. Zones 5–10.

Rosa laevigata
CHEROKEE ROSE
☼ ❄ ↔ 20 ft (6 m) ↕ 30 ft (9 m)
From warm-temperate and subtropical East Asia, also naturalized in southeastern USA; shrubby if cut back hard. Evergreen foliage, deep green, leathery, glossy leaflets, toothed edges. Flowers large, single, white to cream, fragrant, summer. Bristly orange-red hips. Zones 7–10.

Rosa moschata

MUSK ROSE

☼ ❄ ↔ 10 ft (3 m) ↑ 10–35 ft (3–10 m)

Ancient species from southern Europe and Middle East. Arching or semi-climbing habit. Few thorns, shiny grayish green leaves. Single creamy flowers, fading to white, in loose clusters, in summer. Small, downy, ovoid, orange-red hips. The Himalayan musk rose, *R. m. nepalensis* (syn. *R. brunonii*) has fragrant white flowers. Zones 6–10.

MODERN CLIMBING ROSES

Modern climbing roses are usually long-flowering and not quite as rampant as the early introductions. They encompass a huge range of colors and frequently have double flowers. Non-rambling climbers are most often produced from Bush Rose sports, and some popular Bush Roses, such as 'Iceberg', also occur in climbing forms.

Cluster-flowered Climbing Roses

☼/❂ ❄ ↔ 8–15 ft (2.4–4.5 m) ↑ 10–20 ft (3–6 m)

Often the most satisfying of the climbers because their smaller flowers are more weather resistant while being just as showy as the larger-flowered forms. Their whippy stems are less inclined to break under the weight of blooms and are more easily trained. Cultivars include 'Climbing Iceberg', 'John Cabot', and 'Santa Catalina'. Zones 5–9.

Large-flowered Climbing Roses

☼/❂ ❄ ↔ 7–17 ft (2–5 m) ↑ 7–17 ft (2–5 m)

Large-flowered climbers have the same fancy double and large single flowers as their bushy cousins. They tend to have heavier, less pliable stems than other climbers and need support to prevent weather damage and to ensure long-lasting displays. Cultivars include 'Dublin Bay' ★, 'New Dawn' ★, and 'Pierre de Ronsard' ★. Zones 5–9.

Rambler Roses

☼/❂ ❄ ↔ 10–25 ft (3–8 m) ↑ 10–25 ft (3–8 m)

Often very thorny plants, Rambler Roses, principally of *R. wichurana* or *R. multiflora* parentage, differ from other Climbing Roses in not only elongating their stems, but also producing many vigorous new basal shoots each year. This results in a clump of cane-like stems. Pruning is mainly cutting out the older and less productive stems. Ramblers are usually once-flowering. Cultivars include 'Albéric Barbier', 'Excelsa', 'Rambling Rector', and 'Trier'. Zones 5–9.

Rosa, Modern Climbing Rose, Rambler, 'Trier'

MODERN GROUND COVER ROSES

☼ ❄ ↔ 5–12 ft (1.5–3.5 m) ↑ 12–24 in (30–60 cm)

Some of the modern sprawling Shrub Roses are classed as Ground Cover Roses. With their lax spreading habit they are useful for growing on banks and cascading over low walls, as well as for covering large areas of ground. More recent breeding has led to the introduction of a number of plants that are very long flowering and have a densely foliaged habit. Cultivars include 'Bassino', 'Diamant', and 'Pretty in Pink'. Zones 4–10.

OLD CLIMBING ROSES

Old Climbing Roses have a wide variety of growth habits. Most are hardy. Flowers may be single or double and are usually in shades of white, pink, and red. Some varieties are thornless, or nearly so. Flowering may occur in spring, summer, or recurrently. They are classified into a number of groups depending on parentage.

Ayrshire Roses

☼ ❄ ↔ 10–20 ft (3–6 m) ↑ 5–10 ft (1.5–3 m)

Medium-sized climbing or scrambling roses with *R. arvensis* parentage. Flowers borne in clusters or singly; may be single or double and vary in degree of fragrance. Flowers are white or in shades of pink. Cultivars include 'Ayrshire Queen' and 'Ruga'. Zones 6–9.

Boursault Roses

☼ ❄ ↔ 8–12 ft (2.4–3.5 m) ↑ 8–12 ft (2.4–3.5 m)

A small group of nearly thornless climbing roses. Dark green foliage. Double flowers, light pink to deep red, mildly fragrant. Cultivars include 'Amadis', 'Blush Boursault', and 'Gracilis'. Zones 6–10.

Climbing Tea Roses

☼ ❄ ↔ 10–25 ft (3–8 m) ↑ 10–20 ft (3–6 m)

Most are sports of the bush varietes. Best suited to warmer climates. Most flower for long periods. May be single or double, varying in fragrance. They come in all shades of white, pink, red, and yellow. Cultivars include 'Gloire de Dijon' and 'Sombreuil' ★. Zones 7–10.

Laevigata Roses

☼ ❄ ↔ 10–20 ft (3–6 m) ↑ 10–25 ft (3–8 m)

Vigorous sprawling or climbing roses; large, almost evergreen leaves. Large single (occasionally semi-double) flowers, white or pink. 'Cooper's Burmese', single flowers, ivory white, scented. Zones 7–10.

Noisette Roses

☼ ❄ ↔ 5–10 ft (1.5–3 m) ↑ 8–12 ft (2.4–3.5 m)

Vigorous climbing roses originally from cross of China and Musk Roses. Double flowers usually fragrant and recurring throughout season. Flowers in shades of white, cream, yellow, pink. Cultivars include 'Mme Alfred Carrière' ★ and 'Rêve d'Or'. Zones 7–11.

Sempervirens Roses

☼ ❄ ↔ 10–20 ft (3–6 m) ↑ 8–15 ft (2.4–4.5 m)

Usually evergreen, moderately vigorous climbers with lush foliage. Produce small double flowers, in shades of white and pink, borne in showy clusters. Cultivars include 'Adélaide d'Orléans', 'Félicité et Perpétué', and 'Spectabile'. Zones 7–10.

SARITAEA

The single species in this genus in the trumpet-vine (Bignoniaceae) family, is found in Ecuador and Colombia. The plant is a liane. The stems are almost round in cross-section, and are marked with longitudinal stripes. The leaves have 2 leaflets and a further 2 leaflet-like appendages at the base of the leaf stalk, plus a tendril at the tip. The large often showy flowers in shades of purple to red and rose pink are borne in panicles along or at the ends of the branches. The calyx is tubular, with an unlobed margin. The corolla is a tubular bell shape, and is hairy inside around the bases of the stamens. The fruit is a long flattened capsule containing 2 winged seeds.

CULTIVATION: These plants prefer bright filtered light and a well-drained moisture-retaining soil with plenty of humus; keep them moist. Propagate from cuttings or seed.

Saritaea magnifica
syns *Arrabidaea magnifica, Bignonia magnifica*
☼/❈ ✚ ↔ 8–15 ft (2.4–4.5 m) ↕ 25 ft (8 m)

Evergreen climber with leathery leaves and oblong leaflets to 4 in (10 cm) long. Narrow, tubular, rosy purple flowers, flaring petals, showy heads, in summer. Zones 10–12.

SCHISANDRA

This genus of some 25 species native to eastern Asia and eastern North America (where a single species is found) gives its name to the family Schisandraceae. They are aromatic woody lianes largely found in broad-leafed evergreen forests. The leaves are undivided and spirally arranged, with minutely toothed or scalloped edges. Small cup-shaped flowers are borne in clusters or as solitary blooms on the ends of branches. Male and female flowers can occur on the same plant or on separate plants. The brightly colored fruits are berry-like, each with 1 or 2 seeds. Grown for their short-lived fragrant flowers and their conspicuous red or black fruits.

CULTIVATION: Provide good soil, well-drained but moisture-retentive, and protection from midday sun. Grow in subtropical gardens or greenhouses in temperate regions. They can tolerate some lime. Propagate from seed or long half-hardened cuttings, from suckers, from root-cuttings taken in summer, or by layering in autumn.

Saritaea magnifica

Schisandra chinensis
☼/◑ ❈ ↔ 20 ft (6 m) ↕ 25–35 ft (8–10 m)

Vigorous woody twiner from China. Reddish young stems and rounded leaves. Cream to pale pink flowers, ¾ in (18 mm) wide. If both sexes are present, female flowers produce 6 in (15 cm) long drooping spikes of red or pink berries. Zones 4–10.

SCHIZOPHRAGMA

This genus of 2 deciduous ornamental woody climbers in the hydrangea (Hydrangeaceae) family is native to woodlands and cliffs of China, Korea, and Japan. Both species climb by means of short, adhesive, aerial roots. Leaves are attractive, pointed, few- to many-toothed, sometimes turning yellow in autumn. Bark flakes off older branches. Flowerheads consist of flat clusters of tiny fertile flowers and a ring of sterile, showy, outer florets, typically creamy white. Fruits are capsules. The vines can eventually grow very large, but can be slow to establish. They can be grown up trees, but need support until they develop their rootlets.

CULTIVATION: Rich well-drained soil is ideal, but they will grow in nearly any soil. They tolerate a wide range of light conditions, including shade, but flower best in full sun if the roots are shaded. Propagate from softwood cuttings in early to mid-summer, or from half-hardened cuttings in late summer. Few pest or disease problems.

Schizophragma hydrangeoides
JAPANESE HYDRANGEA VINE
◑ ❈ ↔ 10 ft (3 m) ↕ 30 ft (9 m)

Deciduous, woody, self-clinging climber from Korea and Japan. Pointed, toothed, dark green leaves. Flat clusters of creamy white flowers to 10 in (25 cm) wide, tiny fertile inner flowers, tear-drop-shaped outer ones, in summer. 'Moonlight', blue-green foliage, pewter markings and deep green veins; 'Roseum', pale pink flowers intensifying to rose. Zones 5–9.

SENECIO

There are 1,250 species in this genus of trees, shrubs, lianes, annuals, biennials, perennials, and some succulents in the daisy (Asteraceae) family; one of the largest genera of flowering plants. Leaves are lobed or smooth-edged. The daisy-like flowers are usually arranged in clusters, with or without florets. Flowers are usually yellow, but can be purple, white, red, or blue. Many species are toxic to livestock.

CULTIVATION: With such a large genus, cultivation requirements are diverse, so general guidelines only can be given. They grow in either moderately fertile well-drained soil in full sun, or in moderately fertile soil that retains moisture; a few will grow in bogs. Plants grown in pots in colder climates need fertile well-drained soil with added grit and leaf mold. They should be fed and watered moderately during the growing season. Propagation is from seed or cuttings.

Senecio macroglossus
☼ ⬧ ↔ 40 in (100 cm) ↕ 3–7 ft (0.9–2 m)

Slender twining climber from eastern South Africa, Zimbabwe, and Mozambique. Ivy-shaped, slightly succulent, shiny green leaves. The long-lasting cream to pale yellow daisies appear in spring–summer. 'Variegatus', dark green leaves marked with cream. Zones 9–12.

SMILAX

This genus of over 200 species of climbing plants gives its name to the sarsaparilla (Smilacaceae) family and is found throughout the world in temperate and tropical zones, but few species are cultivated. Stems are generally scrambling, wiry, often bearing spines; the plants support themselves with tendrils. They have glossy green, heart-shaped or triangular leaves. Insignificant small flowers are yellowish or greenish.
CULTIVATION: These plants do best with their roots in shade while the upper part of the plant climbs to reach the sun.

Smilax aspera

☼ ❄ ↔ 24 in (60 cm) ↑ 10 ft (3 m)
Evergreen climber from southern Europe, North Africa, and the Canary Islands. Angular, zigzag, prickly stems form dense tangle; leaves are ovate to heart-shaped, glossy and leathery. Fragrant, greenish flowers followed by red fruits, in late summer. Zones 8–10.

Smilax glyciphylla

Smilax glyciphylla

SWEET SARSAPARILLA
☼/◐ ❄ ↔ 5–10 ft (1.5–3 m) ↑ 5–10 ft (1.5–3 m)
Twining coastal eastern Australian species, also bears tendrils. Elongated lance- to heart-shaped leaves to 6 in (15 cm) long, strongly pink-tinted when young. Sprays of tiny greenish white flowers in summer. Black berries. Zones 9–11.

SOLANDRA

CHALICE VINE
A genus of 8 species of showy vigorous climbers in the nightshade (Solanaceae) family. They are native to tropical America where they grow in forests, often up buttressed trees near waterways. The alternately arranged simple leaves are usually leathery and shiny. The open trumpet-shaped flowers may be fragrant at night and are usually yellow or white, sometimes with purplish red stripes or markings. Some species were used by the Aztecs and other indigenous groups for their hallucinogenic properties, which are very dangerous and capable of causing death.
CULTIVATION: In warm climates, grow against walls and fences or over pergolas in full sun in a rich moist but well-drained soil. Grow in the greenhouse in cool-temperate climates. Excessive watering will promote foliage growth at the expense of flowers. Prune to contain size. Propagate from seed or from cuttings.

Solandra longiflora

Solandra longiflora

☼ ✦ ↔ 8–15 ft (2.4–4.5 m) ↑ 10–20 ft (3–6 m)
Vigorous climber native to the West Indies. Oval leaves to 4 in (10 cm) long. Fragrant white flowers, tinged purple, long corolla tube ending with flaring frilly-edged lobes. Zones 10–12.

Solandra maxima

syn. *Solandra hartwegii*
CUP OF GOLD
☼ ✦ ↔ 10–30 ft (3–9 m) ↑ 20–50 ft (6–15 m)
A rampant climber from Mexico and Central America. Glossy green oval leaves to 7 in (18 cm) long. The large, golden yellow,

funnel-shaped flowers are widely flared, with purple stripes along the center of each lobe. Zones 10–12.

SOLANUM *(see page 307)*

Solanum crispum

CHILEAN POTATO VINE
☼ ❄ ↔ 8–15 ft (2.4–4.5 m) ↑ 10–20 ft (3–6 m)
An evergreen climbing plant native to Chile. Pointed oval to lance-shaped leaves, often with wavy margins. Showy, crowded clusters, open, 5-lobed, purplish blue flowers with yellow stamens, borne in summer. 'Glasnevin', hardier, very free flowering. Zones 8–11.

Solanum jasminoides

POTATO VINE
☼ ❄ ↔ 8–15 ft (2.4–4.5 m) ↑ 10–20 ft (3–6 m)
An evergreen Brazilian climber. Vigorous, twiggy-stemmed, well-foliaged. Oval, lance-shaped or lobed leaves. Produces clusters of long-lasting, starry, white flowers, tinged blue, during summer. 'Album', pure white flowers. Zones 9–12.

Solanum seaforthianum

ST VINCENT LILAC
☼ ✦ ↔ 8–15 ft (2.4–4.5 m) ↑ 10–20 ft (3–6 m)
Attractive climber from Trinidad and South America. Entire or pinnate leaves. Starry pale violet flowers, narrow widely spreading petals, in dense clusters, appear in summer. Small, shiny, bright red berries. Seeds dispersed by birds. Zones 10–12.

Solanum wendlandii

GIANT POTATO CREEPER, PARADISE FLOWER, POTATO VINE
☼ ✦ ↔ 5–10 ft (1.5–3 m) ↑ 15 ft (4.5 m)
Evergreen climber native to Costa Rica. Prickly scrambling branches. Glossy pinnate leaves. Large lilac-blue flowers, in large showy clusters, in summer. Oval yellowish fruits to 4 in (10 cm) long. Zones 10–12.

Stauntonia hexaphylla

Strongylodon macrobotrys

SOLLYA

A genus of 3 species of evergreen, climbing, or twining shrubs from the pittosporum (Pittosporaceae) family, closely related to *Billardiera*. The plants are mainly found in southern Western Australia, and are established as a weed in parts of South Australia, Tasmania, and Victoria, Australia. Usually elliptical, the pale to dark green leaves in this genus can vary in shape; the stems twine around supporting structures such as other plants, trellises, or fences. These plants are cultivated for their attractive, star-shaped, bell-like flowers, which can range from blue to pale pink and white, and appear in summer.
CULTIVATION: They need full sunlight to provide the best show of flowers and prefer a well-drained fertile soil to thrive. Propagate from fresh seed in the spring or from softwood cuttings in late summer.

Sollya heterophylla
syn. *Sollya fusiformis*
BLUEBELL CREEPER
🔆 ⚘ ↔ 3–5 ft (0.9–1.5 m) ↕ 5–7 ft (1.5–2 m)
A twining climber from Western Australia. Mid- to dark green leaves. Can take time to fill out; often looks sparse. Intense blue flowers hang in groups, in summer. Can be invasive. *S. h.* **subsp.** *parviflora*, smaller, deeper blue flowers, vine habit. Zones 9–11.

STAUNTONIA

A genus of up to 16 species of evergreen and deciduous twining and climbing plants, in the chocolate-vine (Lardizabalaceae) family. From East Asia, they are now naturalized in many other countries. Quick-growing and ornamental plants, they are often chosen for their handsome palmate foliage and fragrant bell-like flowers. They are only hardy outdoors in milder areas, tolerating temperatures down to about 15°F (–10°C) when fully dormant. The young spring growth, however, can be damaged by late frosts. They are cultivated for their edible fruits in some countries, such as Japan.
CULTIVATION: Well-drained, moisture-retentive soil in a sheltered spot; grow best if roots are in shade and top is grown into sun. Propagate from seed in early spring; seed can take 18 months to germinate.

Stauntonia hexaphylla ★
🔆/◐ ✦ ↔ 10–17 ft (3–5 m) ↕ 35 ft (10 m)
Quick-growing climber from South Korea and Japan. Dark green leathery leaves. Fragrant white flowers tinged with violet, appear throughout spring and summer months. Zones 10–11.

STRONGYLODON

This genus of 12 species of vigorous evergreen or deciduous shrubs or twining climbers is native to tropical areas from the island of Madagascar eastward to Polynesia, but is especially numerous in the Philippines. It belongs to the pea-flower subfamily of the legume (Fabaceae) family. Leaves consist of 3 leaflets. Pea-flowers are borne in long, spectacular racemes; the seed pods are large and do not split open at maturity.
CULTIVATION: Grow outside in the tropics, in a heated greenhouse in temperate areas. Plants raised from seed are slow to reach flowering size; air-layering or propagation by cuttings gives quicker results.

Strongylodon macrobotrys
EMERALD CREEPER, JADE VINE
🔆/◐ ✦ ↔ 5–10 ft (1.5–3 m) ↕ 20–40 ft (6–12 m)
A tall woody climber from the Philippines. Dark green leaves, open pinkish bronze. Large, waxy, claw-like flowers, luminous bluish green or jade, in pendulous racemes, in spring. Zones 11–12.

STROPHANTHUS

This genus belongs to the dogbane (Apocynaceae) family and contains 38 species of evergreen shrubs and small trees found in tropical regions of Africa and Asia. Plants often have a semi-climbing habit and stems contain a milky latex. Leaves may be opposite or whorled. The showy flowers are funnel-shaped, and in some species the petal lobes are long and narrow. Strophanthin, a drug that acts in a similar way to digitalis (a heart muscle stimulant), is extracted from the seeds of some *Strophanthus* species.
CULTIVATION: In subtropical and tropical climates they can be grown outdoors in fertile soil that is moist but well drained. In cooler climates they can be grown in the greenhouse. Propagate from seed or from hardwood cuttings taken in the spring.

Strophanthus speciosus

Strophanthus gratus
CLIMBING OLEANDER, INDIA RUBBER VINE
🔆 ⚘ ↔ 10 ft (3 m) ↕ 10–15 ft (3–4.5 m)
Spreading semi-climbing shrub native to tropical western Africa. Leathery olive green leaves. Bears showy clusters of funnel-shaped white flowers, flushed pink or purple; rounded petal lobes have crimped edges. Zones 10–12.

Strophanthus speciosus
CORKSCREW FLOWER
🔆 ⚘ ↔ 10 ft (3 m) ↕ 10 ft (3 m)
Bushy spreading shrub from South Africa. Leaves in whorls of 3 to 4, leathery texture. Creamy yellow flowers marked with red, narrow petal lobes long and twisted, in summer and autumn. Ground seeds have been used for arrow-tip poison. Zones 10–12.

TECOMANTHE

A genus of 5 species of vigorous climbing plants in the trumpet-vine (Bignoniaceae) family. Its botanical name is derived from *Tecoma*, a genus to which it is closely related. Species are found in tropical and subtropical forests from Malaysia to New Zealand. Rich green leaves have 1 to 7 pairs of oblong leaflets with smooth or toothed edges.

Plants are grown for their showy clusters of large funnel-shaped flowers, resembling foxgloves, in shades of cream, red, and purple. CULTIVATION: In tropical and subtropical areas grow these plants in rich, moist but well-drained soil in partial shade. Provide a strong support such as an archway or trellis. In cool-temperate climates grow in the greenhouse in a free-draining soil mix enriched with organic material. Give them light shade in summer and water well when in growth. Propagate from seed or cuttings.

Tecomanthe speciosa ★
☀ ⧉ ↔ 5–10 ft (1.5–3 m) ↑ 20–30 ft (6–9 m)
A climber from Three Kings Islands, New Zealand, with large, glossy, dark green leaves. Clusters of large, creamy, tubular flowers on old wood, from autumn to winter. Only one plant known in the wild. Zones 9–11.

THUNBERGIA
From tropical Asia and Africa, and also found in South Africa and Madagscar, containing around 100 species of annuals, perennials, and shrubs that are members of the acanthus (Acanthaceae) family. They form an enormously varied group with many being vigorous twining climbers, others are shrubby in habit. Their leaves are usually pointed oval to heart-shaped, sometimes lobed or toothed. Flowers occur in a wide color range, but most often yellow, orange, and purple-blue shades, borne singly or in racemes and are generally long-tubed trumpets with 5 large lobes. CULTIVATION: These plants are mostly frost tender or tolerant only of very light frosts. Plant in a warm sheltered position in moist, humus-rich, well-drained soil. Many species are quite drought tolerant but generally perform best with frequent watering and feeding. Propagate from cuttings or seed, rarely by division.

Thunbergia alata
BLACK-EYED SUSAN VINE
☼/☀ ⧉ ↔ 10 ft (3 m) ↑ 10 ft (3 m)
Twining annual or perennial from tropical Africa. Quick-growing, many long stems. Leaves heart-shaped, toothed. Flowers numerous, usually orange with near-black throat, sometimes cream to yellow and/or evenly colored, in early summer. Zones 10–12.

Thunbergia grandiflora
BENGAL CLOCK VINE, BLUE TRUMPET VINE, SKY VINE, SKYFLOWER
☼/☀ ⧉ ↔ 15 ft (4.5 m) ↑ 15 ft (4.5 m)
Vigorous twining perennial from northern India. Downy pointed oval leaves, sometimes lobed or toothed. In summer, large, sky blue to violet flowers, occasionally solitary, usually in racemes. Zones 10–12.

Thunbergia gregorii
ORANGE CLOCK VINE
☼/☀ ⧉ ↔ 6 ft (1.8 m) ↑ 6 ft (1.8 m)
Perennial twiner from tropical Africa, often cultivated as an annual. Toothed, coarsely hairy, triangular leaves. The flowers are solitary but abundant, bright orange, throughout summer. Zones 10–12.

Thunbergia alata

Thunbergia mysorensis
☼/☀ ⧉ ↔ 20 ft (6 m) ↑ 20 ft (6 m)
Strong-growing, twining, perennial or shrub from India. Simple, often toothed, narrowly elliptic leaves. Spectacularly long pendulous racemes of yellow and red-brown flowers, late spring. Zones 10–12.

TRACHELOSPERMUM
CONFEDERATE JASMINE, STAR JASMINE
A genus of about 20 species of evergreen climbing and twining plants found in woodland areas from Japan to India, and part of the dogbane (Apocynaceae) family. The attractive, glossy, oval leaves are pointed at both ends. Stems will climb over supports and cling to walls and hard surfaces with great ease and abandon. Plants are popular for covering fences and pergolas or to clamber up tree trunks; also used to soften concrete and brick walls and absorb heat in urban landscapes. They work well as ground cover for larger areas and in containers and urns, making great indoor or greenhouse specimens. Indoors, they will reward with fragrant blossoms if supplied with at least a few hours of sun in winter. CULTIVATION: They are not particular as to soil but prefer well-drained spots with some organic matter. They grow well in sun or shade and need average amounts of water, but are somewhat drought tolerant once established. Propagate from half-hardened cuttings in summer.

Trachelospermum asiaticum
☼/☀ ❄ ↔ 10–17 ft (3–5 m) ↑ 20 ft (6 m)
A twining climber from Japan and Korea. Oval, dark green, glossy, leathery-looking leaves to 2 in (5 cm) long. Very fragrant, star-shaped, white flowers hang in clusters, in summer. Zones 8–10.

Trachelospermum jasminoides ★
syn. *Rhynchospermum jasminoides*
CONFEDERATE JASMINE, STAR JASMINE
☼/☀ ⧉ ↔ 17–25 ft (5–8 m) ↑ 30 ft (9 m)
A twining climber from Korea, Japan, and China. Oval to elliptical, dark green, glossy leaves, to 4 in (10 cm) long. Masses of highly fragrant white flowers in clusters, from summer to mid-autumn. This species can be grown as a ground-cover plant. 'Tricolor' ★, red, yellow, and green foliage; 'Variegatum' ★, with white-marked dark green foliage that can burn in hot sun. Zones 9–10.

Trachelospermum jasminoides 'Tricolor'

Trachelospermum jasminoides 'Variegatum'

Tropaeolum tricolor

TROPAEOLUM

CANARY BIRD VINE, FLAME CREEPER, NASTURTIUM

The type genus for the nasturtium (Tropaeolaceae) family, this group of over 80 species of sometimes tuberous annuals and perennials is found from southern Mexico to the southern tip of South America. Many climb using their twining leaf stalks. Though variable, the leaves are often shield-shaped and tinted blue-green. All have long-spurred 5-petalled flowers in a wide range of mainly warm shades.

CULTIVATION: Hardiness varies considerably in these species. Plant in full sun or half-sun in moist well-drained soil. May need trimming back occasionally. Propagate by division, from basal cuttings or seed.

Tropaeolum pentaphyllum

↔ 20 ft (6 m) ↑ 20 ft (6 m)

Extremely vigorous tuberous-rooted climber widespread in South America. Small 5-lobed leaves with purple leaf stalks. Leaves often obscured by pendent masses of dusky coral red to scarlet tubular flowers, in summer. Zones 8–11.

Tropaeolum polyphyllum

WREATH NASTURTIUM

↔ 10 ft (3 m) ↑ 10 ft (3 m)

An annual or perennial trailer or climber found growing in Chile and Argentina. Gray-green to blue-green leaves are 5- to 7-lobed; some forms have near-circular leaves. Clusters of bright yellow funnel-shaped flowers, partly contained in large calyces, produced throughout summer months. Zones 8–11.

Vigna caracalla

Tropaeolum speciosum

FLAME CREEPER, FLAME FLOWER, FLAME NASTURTIUM

↔ 10 ft (3 m) ↑ 10 ft (3 m)

Perennial climber from Chile. Mid-green to blue-green, palmate, 5- to 7-lobed leaves, often downy. Clusters of brilliant red, 1 in (25 mm) wide flowers, during summer and autumn. This species blooms well in shade. Zones 8–10.

Tropaeolum tricolor

↔ 7 ft (2 m) ↑ 7 ft (2 m)

Tuberous trailing or climbing perennial from Bolivia and Chile. Small, mid-green to blue-green, palmate leaves. Clusters of pendulous conical flowers, black-tipped red spurs, short cream to yellow petals, from spring to summer. Zones 8–11.

TWEEDIA

This genus in the milkweed (Asclepiadaceae) family contains a single species of twining or scrambling shrub from subtropical South America. It is sparsely branched with softly hairy stems and foliage. Oblong to heart-shaped leaves are up to 10 in (25 cm) long. Starry pale blue flowers are borne in summer and autumn.

CULTIVATION: These plants flower from seed in the first year so can be grown as an annual in cool-temperate zones or, alternatively, they can be grown under glass. In frost-free areas grow in full sun in well-drained, moderately fertile soil. Pinch back when young to encourage bushier growth. Propagate from seed or cuttings.

Tweedia caerulea

syn. *Oxypetalum caeruleum*

↔ 36 in (90 cm) ↑ 36 in (90 cm)

Twining or scrambling shrub from southern Brazil and Uruguay with lightly hairy grayish green leaves. Flowers starry pale blue, darken to lilac as they age, for long periods from summer. 'Heaven Bow', pretty pale blue to lilac flowers, look almost painted. Zones 10–12.

VIGNA (see page 759)

Vigna caracalla

syn. *Phaseolus caracalla*

CORKSCREW FLOWER, SNAIL BEAN, SNAIL FLOWER

↔ 10 ft (3 m) ↑ 12–20 ft (3.5–6 m)

Twining perennial from tropical South America. Finely hairy leaves with 3 oval-shaped leaflets. Fragrant white or yellow flowers, to 2 in (5 cm) across, pinkish purple wings. Coiled keel resembles a snail shell. Zones 10–11.

VITIS (see page 719)

Vitis amurensis ★

AMUR GRAPE

↔ 10–20 ft (3–6 m) ↑ 50 ft (15 m)

Vine or strong-growing shrub from northeast Asia. Reddish young shoots. Large, 3- to 5-lobed leaves turning rich red, orange, yellow, and purple in autumn. Fruit is oval, black, usually bitter, in late summer. Zones 4–9.

Vitis coignetiae

CRIMSON GLORY VINE

↔ 10–20 ft (3–6 m) ↑ 50 ft (15 m)

A native of Japan and Korea. A fast-growing, vigorous vine with large, rounded, toothed, 3- or 5-lobed, thickly textured, somewhat puckered leaves, becoming bronze, fiery red, and scarlet in the autumn months. The purple-black fruit is inedible. Zones 5–9.

Vitis riparia

FROST GRAPE, RIVERBANK GRAPE

☼ ❋ ↔ 10–20 ft (3–6 m) ↑ 40 ft (12 m)

Climbing or scrambling central North American native. Leaves typically 3-lobed, serrated, shiny green. Sweetly fragrant flowers. Round, somewhat tart but edible blackish purple fruit. 'Brant' has leaves turning purple and red with yellow-green edged veins in autumn. Fruit sweet, purple-black. Zones 2–8.

WISTERIA

Often seen covering verandahs and porches and capable of spreading a great distance, the 10 species of twining deciduous vines in this genus belong to the pea-flower subfamily of the legume (Fabaceae) family. They are native to China, Japan, and eastern USA. When young, the pinnate leaves are a soft bronze green but turn light green when mature. The flowers, primarily mauve in the species, occur in long racemes that start to open as the leaves expand. Cultivated forms range from white to various pink and purple tones.

CULTIVATION: Wisterias like their tops in sun and their roots in cool, moist, humus-rich, well-drained soil. These hardy, heavy-wooded, vigorous climbers need sturdy support and routine trimming. Propagate from cuttings or seed, by layering or grafting.

Wisteria brachybotrys

syn. *Wisteria venusta*

SILKY WISTERIA

☼/◑ ❋ ↔ 30 ft (9 m) ↑ 30 ft (9 m)

Vigorous Japanese climber with stems twining anticlockwise, densely downy when young. Leaves to 14 in (35 cm) long with 9 to 13, downy, pointed oval leaflets to 4 in (10 cm) long. Bears pendulous racemes to 6 in (15 cm) long of white, very fragrant, 1 in (25 mm) wide flowers. 'Murasaki Kapitan' (syn. *W. venusta* 'Violacea'), clockwise-twining with purple-keeled mauve flowers; and 'Shiro-kapitan' (syn. *W. sinensis* 'Prematura Alba'), similar to the species but produces shorter, sometimes pink-tinted racemes. Zones 6–9.

Wisteria floribunda ★

JAPANESE WISTERIA

☼/◑ ❋ ↔ 25 ft (8 m) ↑ 25 ft (8 m)

A clockwise-twining Japanese climber with leaves up to 14 in (35 cm) long, downy when young, 11 to 19 pointed oval leaflets to 3 in (8 cm) long. Pendulous racemes 16–40 in (40–100 cm) long, fragrant violet, purple, pink, white, or magenta-red flowers to ¾ in (18 mm) wide. 'Alba' (syn. 'Shîro-nôda'), long racemes with more than 100 faintly scented white flowers; 'Kuchi-beni', dark-keeled pale pink flowers in racemes up to 18 in (45 cm) long; 'Multijuga' (syn. 'Macrobotrys'), produces extremely long racemes of light purple flowers; 'Violacea Plena', clustered racemes to 16 in (40 cm) long with many lavender and purple double flowers. Zones 5–10.

Wisteria × formosa

☼/◑ ❋ ↔ 30 ft (9 m) ↑ 30 ft (9 m)

Garden hybrid between *W. floribunda* and *W. sinensis*. Clockwise-twining stems and leaves up to 14 in (35 cm) long, with 9 to 15 pointed oval leaflets to over 3 in (8 cm) long, silky when young. Dark-keeled violet flowers to ¾ in (18 mm) wide, very fragrant, all opening together on the raceme rather than in succession. 'Yae-kokuryû' (syn. 'Black Dragon'), lilac blooms. Zones 5–9.

Wisteria frutescens

AMERICAN WISTERIA

☼/◑ ❋ ↔ 40 ft (12 m) ↑ 40 ft (12 m)

Very vigorous clockwise-twining climber from eastern USA. Leaves to 12 in (30 cm) long, with 9 to 15 pointed oval leaflets around 2 in (5 cm) long. Racemes to 4 in (10 cm) long, often held horizontally or semi-erect; flowers bright purple, mildly scented. Zones 5–9.

Wisteria macrostachya

KENTUCKY WISTERIA

☼/◑ ❋ ↔ 25 ft (8 m) ↑ 25 ft (8 m)

Anticlockwise-twining climber found from Louisiana to Illinois, USA. Leaves up to 12 in (30 cm) long, with 7 to 11 leaflets, 2 in (5 cm) long, tapering to a fine point. Bears pendulous, 6–12 in (15–30 cm) long racemes of small pale pink and lavender flowers opening from deep pink buds. Zones 5–9.

Wisteria sinensis ★

CHINESE WISTERIA

☼/◑ ❋ ↔ 35 ft (10 m) ↑ 35 ft (10 m)

Rapid-growing anticlockwise-twining climber native to China. Leaves to 35 cm (14 in) long, 7 to 13 pointed elliptical leaflets up to 3 in (8 cm) long. The flowers are lavender and purple-blue, strongly scented, to 1 in (25 mm) wide, in pendulous racemes, 6–12 in (15–30 cm) long. 'Alba' bears white flowers; 'Sierra Madre' has fragrant, lavender-keeled, white flowers. Zones 5–10.

Wisteria floribunda

Cacti and Succulents

These beautiful and fascinating plants are wonderful examples of the adaptability of nature. In many parts of the world there is either too little rainfall or long periods of drought, conditions that most perennial plants would not be able to survive. Slow-growing cacti and other succulent plants have adapted in order to be able to grow in these areas, taking advantage of the minimal competition from faster-growing plants.

Succulent plants store moisture, which they then slowly use in order to survive until the next rain comes. Water may be stored in thick fleshy leaves, such as those seen on the jade tree *(Crassula ovata)*. Other plants, like *Stapelia* species, have thick swollen stems, and a third group has swollen roots or tubers, such as some species of *Ipomoea*.

One particular group of stem succulents is cacti. In order to be classified as a cactus, a plant must have several botanical characteristics, one of which is peculiar to the cactus family: the areole. It is a modified axillary bud from which the spines, branches, and flowers arise.

Cacti and succulents generally prefer a bright site. During the summer months, allow plants to dry between waterings; in winter, keep the plants more or less dry.

Many cacti and succulents have flowers that are striking in size, form, or color. The star-shaped red-and-yellow blooms of *Stapelia gigantea* appear in summer.

Cactus and Succulent Finder

The following cultivation table features at-a-glance information for every species or hybrid with an individual entry in the Cacti and Succulents chapter of this book. Simply find the plant you wish to know more about, and run your eye along the row to discover its height and spread, whether it is frost tolerant or not, the aspect it prefers, and more.

The type of plant is abbreviated to **C**, **S**, or **O**:
C – the plant is a cactus.
S – the plant is a sword-leaf.
O – the plant is another type of succulent.

The climate(s) that each plant needs to thrive in the outdoors are given (some plants will grow in more than one climate), abbreviated to **C**, **W**, or **T**:
C – the plant prefers a cool climate.
W – the plant prefers a warm-temperate or subtropical climate.
T – the plant prefers a tropical climate.

The type of spines or prickles the plant has is abbreviated to **F**, **M**, or **A**:
F – the plant has fierce spines or prickles.
M – the plant has moderate spines or prickles.
A – the spines or prickles are absent.

Plant name	Height	Spread	Type	Climate	Spines/prickles	Showy flowers	Tolerates wet soil	Tolerates moist soil	Needs perfect drainage	Frost tolerant	Full sun	Half sun	Heavy shade
Aeonium arboreum	6 ft (1.8 m)	4 ft (1.2 m)	O	W	A	◆		◆			◆		
Aeonium haworthii	24 in (60 cm)	32 in (80 cm)	O	W	A	◆		◆			◆		
Aeonium tabuliforme	12 in (30 cm)	24 in (60 cm)	O	W	A	◆		◆			◆		
Aeonium Hybrid Cultivars	12–24 in (30–60 cm)	8–24 in (20–60 cm)	O	W	A	◆		◆			◆	◆	
Agave americana	17–30 ft (5–9 m)	7–15 ft (2–4.5 m)	O	W	F	◆		◆		◆	◆		
Agave attenuata	3–7 ft (0.9–2 m)	24–60 in (60–150 cm)	O	W	A	◆		◆			◆		
Agave deserti	8–15 ft (2.4–4.5 m)	16–24 in (40–60 cm)	O	W	M	◆			◆		◆		
Agave lechuguilla	8–17 ft (2.4–5 m)	8–12 in (20–30 cm)	O	W	F	◆		◆		◆	◆		
Agave parryi	12–20 ft (3.5–6 m)	20–28 in (50–70 cm)	O	W	M	◆		◆		◆	◆		
Agave potatorum	15 ft (4.5 m)	3–8 ft (0.9–2.4 m)	O	W	F	◆			◆		◆		
Agave schidigera	7–12 ft (2–3.5 m)	40–60 in (100–150 cm)	O	W	A	◆		◆			◆		
Agave victoria-reginae	10–15 ft (3–4.5 m)	20–28 in (50–70 cm)	O	W	M	◆		◆			◆		
Alluaudia humbertii	17–20 ft (5–6 m)	20–25 ft (6–8 m)	C	W	F	◆		◆			◆		
Alluaudia procera	35–50 ft (10–15 m)	7–10 ft (2–3 m)	C	W	F	◆		◆			◆		
Aloe arborescens	10 ft (3 m)	6 ft (1.8 m)	O	W	F	◆		◆			◆		
Aloe aristata	20 in (50 cm)	24 in (60 cm)	O	W	M	◆		◆			◆		
Aloe brevifolia	20 in (50 cm)	20–32 in (50–80 cm)	O	W	M	◆		◆			◆		
Aloe descoingsii	12 in (30 cm)	16–24 in (40–60 cm)	O	W	M	◆			◆		◆	◆	
Aloe ferox	7–17 ft (2–5 m)	5–10 ft (1.5–3 m)	O	W	F	◆		◆			◆		
Aloe haworthioides	20 in (50 cm)	24–40 in (60–100 cm)	O	W	M	◆				◆	◆		
Aloe maculata	40 in (100 cm)	24–60 in (60–150 cm)	O	W	M	◆		◆			◆	◆	

Plant name	Height	Spread	Type	Climate	Spines/prickles	Showy flowers	Tolerates wet soil	Tolerates moist soil	Needs perfect drainage	Frost tolerant	Full sun	Half sun	Heavy shade
Aloe marlothii	12–15 ft (3.5–4.5 m)	7–10 ft (2–3 m)	O	W	F	♦		♦			♦		
Aloe mitriformis	30 in (75 cm)	3–7 ft (0.9–2 m)	O	W	M	♦		♦			♦	♦	
Aloe peglerae	24 in (60 cm)	15 in (40 cm)	O	W	F	♦		♦			♦		
Aloe plicatilis	15 ft (4.5 m)	7 ft (2 m)	O	W	M	♦		♦			♦		
Aloe polyphylla	30 in (75 cm)	16–32 in (40–80 cm)	O	W	F	♦		♦		♦	♦		
Aloe striatula	6 ft (1.8 m)	3 ft (0.9 m)	O	W	M	♦			♦	♦	♦		
Aloe variegata	20 in (50 cm)	20–32 in (50–80 cm)	O	W	M	♦		♦		♦	♦	♦	
Aporocactus flagelliformis	3–7 ft (0.9–2 m)	20 in (50 cm)	C	W	M	♦		♦			♦		
Aptenia cordifolia	2 in (5 cm)	16–40 in (40–100 cm)	O	W	A	♦			♦		♦	♦	
Ariocarpus retusus	10 in (25 cm)	15 in (38 cm)	O	W	A	♦			♦		♦		
Astrophytum asterias	2 in (5 cm)	4 in (10 cm)	C	W	A	♦			♦		♦		
Astrophytum capricorne	4–10 in (10–25 cm)	4–6 in (10–15 cm)	C	W	M	♦			♦		♦		
Astrophytum myriostigma	4–10 in (10–25 cm)	4–6 in (10–15 cm)	C	W	A	♦			♦		♦		
Astrophytum ornatum	12–40 in (30–100 cm)	12–40 in (30–100 cm)	C	W	F	♦	♦				♦		
Beaucarnea recurvata	25 ft (8 m)	6–8 ft (1.8–2.4 m)	O	W	A	♦		♦			♦		
Beschorneria yuccoides	4–6 ft (1.2–1.8 m)	7 ft (2 m)	S	W	A								
Bowiea volubilis	8–15 ft (2.4–4.5 m)	8 in (20 cm)	O	W	A				♦		♦		
Carnegiea gigantea	50 ft (15 m)	10 ft (3 m)	C	W	F	♦		♦					♦
Carpobrotus edulis	4–6 in (10–15 cm)	40–60 in (100–150 cm)	O	W	A	♦			♦		♦	♦	
Cephalocereus senilis	50 ft (15 m)	12–16 in (30–40 cm)	C	W	M	♦		♦			♦		
Cereus hildmannianus	10–17 ft (3–5 m)	4–7 ft (1.2–2 m)	C	W/T	M	♦		♦			♦	♦	
Cereus jamacaru	17–35 ft (5–10 m)	7–15 ft (2–4.5 m)	C	C	F	♦		♦			♦	♦	
Ceropegia linearis	4 in (10 cm)	unlimited	O	W/T	A			♦			♦		
Ceropegia sandersonii	6 ft (1.8 m)	5 ft (1.5 m)	O	W/T	A			♦			♦		
Cheiridopsis cigarettifera	4 in (10 cm)	6–12 in (15–30 cm)	O	W	A	♦			♦		♦		
Cheiridopsis pillansii	4 in (10 cm)	8–12 in (20–30 cm)	O	W	A	♦			♦	♦	♦		
Cleistocactus hyalacanthus	36 in (90 cm)	24–48 in (60–120 cm)	C	W	F	♦			♦	♦			
Cleistocactus strausii	3–10 ft (0.9–3 m)	3 ft (0.9 m)	C	W/T	F	♦		♦		♦	♦		
Conophytum pillansii	2–4 in (5–10 cm)	4–8 in (10–20 cm)	O	W	A	♦			♦		♦		
Conophytum quaesitum	2–4 in (5–10 cm)	6–8 in (15–20 cm)	O	W	A	♦			♦		♦		
Copiapoa cinerascens	4–8 in (10–20 cm)	6–24 in (15–60 cm)	C	W	F	♦			♦		♦	♦	
Copiapoa cinerea	8 in–4 ft (20 cm–1.2 m)	6–16 in (15–40 cm)	C	W	F	♦			♦		♦	♦	

Plant name	Height	Spread	Type	Climate	Spines/prickles	Showy flowers	Tolerates wet soil	Tolerates moist soil	Needs perfect drainage	Frost tolerant	Full sun	Half sun	Heavy shade
Copiapoa humilis	8 in (20 cm)	4–16 in (10–40 cm)	C	W	F	◆			◆		◆	◆	
Cotyledon orbiculata	1–5 ft (0.9–1.5 m)	20 in–4 ft (50 cm–1.2 m)	O	W	A	◆		◆			◆	◆	
Cotyledon tomentosa	12–20 in (30–50 cm)	12–27 in (30–70 cm)	O	W	A	◆		◆			◆	◆	
Cotyledon undulata	32 in–5 ft (80 cm–1.5 m)	20 in–4 ft (50 cm–1.2 m)	O	W	A	◆		◆			◆	◆	
Crassula atropurpurea	6–18 in (15–45 cm)	12 in (30 cm)	O	W	A	◆		◆			◆	◆	
Crassula hemisphaerica	8 in (20 cm)	12–20 in (30–50 cm)	O	W	A			◆			◆	◆	
Crassula lactea	16–24 in (40–60 cm)	12–20 in (30–50 cm)	O	W	A	◆		◆			◆	◆	
Crassula multicava	12–16 in (30–40 cm)	3–10 ft (0.9–3 m)	O	W	A	◆		◆			◆	◆	
Crassula muscosa	8–32 in (20–80 cm)	20–40 in (50–100 cm)	O	W	A			◆			◆	◆	
Crassula ovata	3–6 ft (0.9–1.8 m)	2–4 ft (0.6–1.2 m)	O	W	A	◆		◆			◆	◆	
Crassula perfoliata	2–4 ft (0.6–1.2 m)	18–36 in (45–90 cm)	O	W	A	◆		◆			◆	◆	
Crassula pyramidalis	4–10 in (10–25 cm)	4–8 in (10–20 cm)	O	W	A			◆			◆	◆	
Crassula rupestris	8–20 in (20–50 cm)	6–12 in (15–30 cm)	O	W	A	◆		◆			◆	◆	
Crassula Hybrid Cultivars	2–8 in (5–20 cm)	2–10 in (5–25 cm)	O	W	A	◆		◆			◆	◆	
Cylindropuntia bigelovii	3–8 ft (0.9–2.4 m)	2–3 ft (0.6–0.9 m)	C	W	F	◆					◆		
Cylindropuntia imbricata	10 ft (3 m)	4–7 ft (1.2–2 m)	C	C/T	F	◆			◆	◆	◆		
Cylindropuntia spinosior	7 ft (2 m)	3–5 ft (0.9–1.5 m)	C	C/W	F	◆			◆		◆	◆	
Cylindropuntia tunicata	2 ft (0.6 m)	4 ft (1.2 m)	C	C/W	F	◆				◆	◆	◆	
Cyphostemma juttae	6 ft (1.8 m)	6 ft (1.8 m)	O	W	A						◆		
Dasylirion acrotriche	10–20 ft (3–6 m)	5 ft (1.5 m)	S	W	F	◆		◆			◆	◆	
Dasylirion wheeleri	12–25 ft (3.5–8 m)	3 ft (0.9 m)	S	C/W	F	◆		◆		◆	◆		
Delosperma cooperi	6–20 in (15–50 cm)	24–32 in (60–80 cm)	O	C/W	A	◆		◆		◆	◆	◆	◆
Delosperma nubigenum	2–4 in (5–10 cm)	20 in (50 cm)	O	C/W	A	◆		◆		◆	◆	◆	
Dioscorea elephantipes	36 in (90 cm)	12 in (30 cm)	O	W	A					◆		◆	◆
Drosanthemum speciosum	24 in (60 cm)	40 in (100 cm)	O	W	A	◆		◆			◆		
Dudleya attenuata	12–16 in (30–40 cm)	16–24 in (40–60 cm)	O	W	A	◆		◆			◆	◆	
Dudleya candelabrum	14 in (35 cm)	14 in (35 cm)	O	W	A	◆		◆			◆	◆	
Dudleya farinosa	8–12 in (20–30 cm)	16–20 in (40–50 cm)	O	W	A	◆		◆		◆	◆		
Dudleya pulverulenta	40 in (100 cm)	20 in (50 cm)	O	W	A	◆		◆			◆		
Echeveria agavoides	6–8 in (15–20 cm)	8–12 in (20–30 cm)	O	W	A	◆		◆			◆	◆	
Echeveria elegans	6–8 in (15–20 cm)	12–16 in (30–40 cm)	O	W	A			◆			◆	◆	
Echeveria gibbiflora	48 in (120 cm)	20 in (50 cm)	O	W	A	◆		◆			◆		

Plant name	Height	Spread	Type	Climate	Spines/prickles	Showy flowers	Tolerates wet soil	Tolerates moist soil	Needs perfect drainage	Frost tolerant	Full sun	Half sun	Heavy shade
Echeveria gigantea	5–7 ft (1.5–2 m)	20 in (50 cm)	O	W/T		A			♦		♦		
Echeveria × imbricata	12–16 in (30–40 cm)	12–16 in (30–40 cm)	O	W/T		A			♦		♦		
Echeveria pulvinata	12–16 in (30–40 cm)	12–20 in (30–50 cm)	O	W		A			♦		♦		
Echeveria setosa	8–12 in (20–30 cm)	12–16 in (30–40 cm)	O	W		A			♦		♦		
Echeveria Hybrid Cultivars	6–24 in (15–60 cm)	4–18 in (10–45 cm)	O	W		A			♦		♦		
Echinocactus grusonii	50 in (130 cm)	32 in (80 cm)	C	W/T	♦	F			♦		♦		
Echinocactus polycephalus	12–24 in (30–60 cm)	12–24 in (30–60 cm)	C	W	♦	F			♦		♦		
Echinocereus engelmannii	12–20 in (30–50 cm)	12–20 in (30–50 cm)	C	C/W	♦	F			♦	♦	♦		
Echinocereus pectinatus	14 in (35 cm)	6–16 in (15–40 cm)	C	C/W	♦	M					♦		
Echinocereus pentalophus	8–12 in (20–30 cm)	20 in–7 ft (50 cm–2 m)	C	W	♦	F					♦		
Echinocereus rigidissimus	8 in (20 cm)	4 in (10 cm)	C	W	♦	M					♦		
Echinocereus triglochidiatus	12–16 in (30–40 cm)	8–20 in (20–50 cm)	C	C/W	♦	F			♦	♦	♦		
Echinocereus viridiflorus	2–5 in (5–12 cm)	4–12 in (10–30 cm)	C	C/W	♦	F					♦		
Echinopsis backebergii	6 in (15 cm)	4–8 in (10–20 cm)	C	W	♦	M			♦		♦		
Echinopsis chamaecereus	4 in (10 cm)	12 in (30 cm)	C	W	♦	M			♦		♦		
Echinopsis hertrichiana	6–16 in (15–40 cm)	6–12 in (15–30 cm)	C	W/T	♦	M					♦		
Echinopsis huascha	24 in (60 cm)	24 in (60 cm)	C	W	♦	F		♦			♦		
Echinopsis oxygona	12 in (30 cm)	12–24 in (30–60 cm)	C	W	♦	F					♦		
Echinopsis spachiana	5–7 ft (1.5–2 m)	40 in (100 cm)	C	W/T	♦	F					♦		
Echinopsis Hybrid Cultivars	6–18 in (15–45 cm)	6–12 in (15–30 cm)	C	W/T	♦	F					♦		
Epiphyllum oxypetalum	5–10 ft (1.5–3 m)	5–10 ft (1.5–3 m)	C	W/T		A			♦				♦
Espostoa lanata	7–25 ft (2–8 m)	3–10 ft (0.9–3 m)	C	W		M			♦		♦		
Espostoa senilis	7–15 ft (2–4.5 m)	3–7 ft (0.9–2 m)	C	W	♦	M			♦		♦		
Euphorbia caput-medusae	12 in (30 cm)	48 in (120 cm)	O	W		A		♦			♦	♦	
Euphorbia cooperi	15 ft (4.5 m)	6 ft (1.8 m)	O	W		M		♦			♦		
Euphorbia grandicornis	6 ft (1.8 m)	3 ft (0.9 m)	O	W		F		♦	♦	♦	♦		
Euphorbia × lomii	40 in (100 cm)	40 in (100 cm)	O	W/T	♦	M		♦			♦	♦	
Euphorbia milii	1–3 ft (0.3–0.9 m)	2–8 ft (0.6–2.4 m)	O	W		F		♦			♦		
Euphorbia neriifolia	20 ft (6 m)	4 ft (1.2 m)	O	W/T	♦	A		♦			♦		
Euphorbia obesa	8 in (20 cm)	6 in (15 cm)	O	W		A			♦		♦	♦	
Euphorbia tirucalli	15–30 ft (4.5–9 m)	7–12 ft (2–3.5 m)	O	W/T		A		♦			♦		
Euphorbia trigona	3–8 ft (0.9–2.4 m)	12–24 in (30–60 cm)	O	W		F		♦			♦		

Plant name	Height	Spread	Type	Climate	Spines/prickles	Showy flowers	Tolerates wet soil	Tolerates moist soil	Needs perfect drainage	Frost tolerant	Full sun	Half sun	Heavy shade
Ferocactus cylindraceus	10 ft (3 m)	20 in (50 cm)	C	W	F	♦		♦			♦		
Ferocactus emoryi	8 ft (2.4 m)	3 ft (0.9 m)	C	W	F	♦			♦		♦		
Ferocactus glaucescens	18 in (45 cm)	20 in (50 cm)	C	W	F	♦			♦		♦		
Ferocactus latispinus	12 in (30 cm)	16 in (40 cm)	C	W	F	♦			♦		♦		
Ferocactus wislizeni	10 ft (3 m)	32 in (80 cm)	C	W	F	♦	♦				♦		
Fouquieria splendens	30 ft (9 m)	6 ft (1.8 m)	O	C/W	F	♦		♦		♦	♦		
Furcraea bedinghausii	4–7 ft (1.2–2 m)	4–7 ft (1.2–2 m)	O	C/W	A	♦		♦			♦		
Furcraea selloa	4–7 ft (1.2–2 m)	4–7 ft (1.2–2 m)	O	C/W	M	♦		♦			♦	♦	
Gasteria bicolor	16 in (40 cm)	16 in (40 cm)	O	W	A	♦			♦		♦		♦
Gasteria glomerata	1½ in (4 cm)	3 in (8 cm)	O	W	A	♦			♦			♦	
Gibbaeum dispar	4–6 in (10–15 cm)	4–6 in (10–15 cm)	O	W	A	♦			♦		♦		
Gibbaeum pilosulum	3–5 in (8–12 cm)	8 in (20 cm)	O	W/T	A	♦			♦		♦	♦	
Glottiphyllum linguiforme	3–5 in (8–12 cm)	8 in (20 cm)	O	W	A	♦			♦		♦		
Glottiphyllum nelii	1–6 in (2.5–15 cm)	12 in (30 cm)	O	W	A	♦			♦		♦		
Graptopetalum amethystinum	4–6 in (10–15 cm)	3–5 in (8–12 cm)	O	W	A	♦			♦				♦
Graptopetalum paraguayense	4–12 in (10–30 cm)	5–12 in (12–30 cm)	O	W	A	♦			♦		♦		
Gymnocalycium bruchii	1½ in (35 mm)	20 in (50 cm)	C	W	M	♦			♦	♦	♦		
Gymnocalycium castellanosii	6 in (15 cm)	4 in (10 cm)	C	W	F	♦			♦	♦	♦		
Gymnocalycium ochoterenae	2–2½ in (5–6 cm)	4–5 in (10–12 cm)	C	W	F	♦			♦	♦	♦		
Gymnocalycium saglionis	6 in (15 cm)	12 in (30 cm)	C	W	F	♦			♦	♦	♦		
Hatiora gaertneri	12–20 in (30–50 cm)	12–20 in (30–50 cm)	C	W/T	M	♦		♦			♦	♦	
Hatiora rosea	12–16 in (30–40 cm)	8–12 in (20–30 cm)	C	W/T	M	♦					♦	♦	
Haworthia coarctata	8 in (20 cm)	6 in (15 cm)	O	W	A					♦		♦	
Haworthia cymbiformis	2 in (5 cm)	4 in (10 cm)	O	W	A					♦		♦	
Haworthia fasciata	6 in (15 cm)	6 in (15 cm)	O	W	M					♦		♦	
Haworthia reinwardtii	6 in (15 cm)	3 in (8 cm)	O	W	A					♦		♦	
Huernia zebrina	4 in (10 cm)	6 in (15 cm)	O	W/T	M	♦		♦					♦
Jatropha podagrica	20–36 in (50–90 cm)	10–12 in (25–30 cm)	O	W/T	A	♦		♦			♦		
Jovibarba hirta	4–6 in (10–15 cm)	10–12 in (25–30 cm)	S	C/W	A					♦	♦		
Kalanchoe beharensis	10 ft (3 m)	3 ft (0.9 m)	O	W/T	A			♦			♦		
Kalanchoe blossfeldiana	16 in (40 cm)	16 in (40 cm)	O	W/T	A	♦		♦			♦		
Kalanchoe daigremontiana	40 in (100 cm)	12 in (30 cm)	O	W/T	A	♦		♦			♦		

Plant name	Height	Spread	Type	Climate	Spines/prickles	Showy flowers	Tolerates wet soil	Tolerates moist soil	Needs perfect drainage	Frost tolerant	Full sun	Half sun	Heavy shade
Kalanchoe delagoensis	40 in (100 cm)	12 in (30 cm)	O	W/T	A	◆			◆		◆		
Kalanchoe fedtschenkoi	20 in (50 cm)	12 in (30 cm)	O	W/T	A	◆			◆		◆		
Kalanchoe manginii	12 in (30 cm)	12 in (30 cm)	O	W/T	A	◆		◆			◆		
Kalanchoe marmorata	50 in (130 cm)	36 in (90 cm)	O	W/T	A				◆		◆		
Kalanchoe pumila	8 in (20 cm)	18 in (45 cm)	O	W/T	A	◆			◆		◆		
Kalanchoe thyrsiflora	24 in (60 cm)	12 in (30 cm)	O	W/T	A	◆				◆	◆		
Kalanchoe tomentosa	15 in (38 cm)	7 in (18 cm)	O	W/T	A				◆		◆		
Lampranthus aurantiacus	6–12 in (15–30 cm)	8–18 in (20–45 cm)	O	W/T	A	◆		◆			◆		
Lampranthus glaucus	12–24 in (30–60 cm)	12–24 in (30–60 cm)	O	W/T	A	◆		◆			◆		
Lampranthus roseus	12–20 in (30–50 cm)	12–20 in (30–50 cm)	O	W/T	A	◆		◆			◆		
Leuchtenbergia principis	8–24 in (20–60 cm)	8–12 in (20–30 cm)	C	W	M	◆			◆		◆		
Lithops karasmontana	¾–1¼ in (2–3 cm)	4–8 in (10–20 cm)	O	W	A				◆		◆		
Lithops lesliei	1¼–2 in (3–5 cm)	4–8 in (10–20 cm)	O	W	A				◆		◆		
Lithops marmorata	¾–1¼ in (18–30 mm)	4–6 in (10–15 cm)	O	W	A				◆		◆		
Lithops meyeri	¾–1¼ in (18–30 mm)	3–6 in (8–15 cm)	O	W	A				◆		◆		
Lithops olivacea	¾–3 in (18 mm–8 cm)	4–8 in (10–20 cm)	O	W	A				◆		◆		
Lithops schwantesii	¾–1¼ in (18–30 mm)	3–6 in (8–15 cm)	O	W	A				◆		◆		
Lophophora williamsii	¾–2½ in (18–60 mm)	32–40 in (80–100 cm)	C	W	A				◆		◆		
Mammillaria albicoma	2–2½ in (5–6 cm)	1¼–5 in (3–12 cm)	C	W	M				◆		◆		
Mammillaria blossfeldiana	3–4 in (8–10 cm)	1¼–2 in (3–5 cm)	C	W	M	◆			◆		◆		
Mammillaria bocasana	4–8 in (10–20 cm)	12–24 in (30–60 cm)	C	W	M	◆			◆		◆		
Mammillaria carmenae	2–3 in (5–8 cm)	2–3 in (5–8 cm)	C	W	M	◆			◆		◆		
Mammillaria compressa	1½–2½ in (4–6 cm)	6 in (15 cm)	C	W	M	◆			◆		◆		
Mammillaria elongata	4–6 in (10–15 cm)	8–12 in (20–30 cm)	C	W	M				◆		◆		
Mammillaria hahniana	6–10 in (15–25 cm)	8–12 in (20–30 cm)	C	W	M				◆		◆		
Mammillaria klissingiana	4–6 in (10–15 cm)	2½–4 in (6–10 cm)	C	W	M	◆			◆		◆		
Mammillaria longimamma	3–5 in (8–12 cm)	3–5 in (8–12 cm)	C	W	F				◆		◆		
Mammillaria mazatlanensis	4–6 in (10–15 cm)	¾–1¾ in (18–40 mm)	C	W	M	◆			◆		◆		
Mammillaria melanocentra	3–5 in (8–12 cm)	4–6 in (10–15 cm)	C	W	F	◆			◆		◆		
Mammillaria moelleriana	6–12 in (15–30 cm)	3–4 in (8–10 cm)	C	W	M	◆			◆		◆		
Mammillaria mystax	4–6 in (10–15 cm)	3–4 in (8–10 cm)	C	W	M	◆			◆		◆		
Mammillaria plumosa	4–6 in (10–15 cm)	2½–16 in (6–40 cm)	C	W	M				◆		◆		

Plant name	Height	Spread	Type	Climate	Spines/prickles	Showy flowers	Tolerates wet soil	Tolerates moist soil	Needs perfect drainage	Frost tolerant	Full sun	Half sun	Heavy shade
Mammillaria prolifera	2½–4 in (6–10 cm)	8–12 in (20–30 cm)	C	W	M				◆		◆		
Mammillaria spinosissima	4–6 in (10–15 cm)	2½–3 in (6–8 cm)	C	W	M	◆				◆	◆		
Mammillaria supertexta	4–6 in (10–15 cm)	2–3 in (5–8 cm)	C	W	M	◆				◆	◆		
Melocactus azureus	5–18 in (12–45 cm)	6–8 in (15–20 cm)	C	W/T	F	◆				◆	◆		
Melocactus bahiensis	4–8 in (10–20 cm)	4–5 in (10–12 cm)	C	W/T	F	◆				◆	◆		
Melocactus curvispinus	2–12 in (5–30 cm)	3–12 in (8–30 cm)	C	W/T	F	◆				◆	◆		
Mesembryanthemum crystallinum	4–8 in (10–20 cm)	12–24 in (30–60 cm)	O	W	A	◆				◆	◆		
Mesembryanthemum guerichianum	2–4 in (5–10 cm)	8–18 in (20–45 cm)	O	W	A	◆				◆	◆		
Mesembryanthemum nodiflorum	6–8 in (15–20 cm)	36 in (90 cm)	O	W	A	◆				◆	◆		
Myrtillocactus cochal	15–17 ft (4.5–5 m)	10–15 ft (3–4.5 m)	C	W/T	F	◆				◆	◆		
Myrtillocactus geometrizans	15 ft (4.5 m)	10–15 ft (3–4.5 m)	C	W/T	F	◆				◆	◆		
Nolina parryi	5 ft (1.5 m)	5 ft (1.5 m)	S	W	A						◆	◆	◆	
Opuntia aciculata	36–60 in (90–150 cm)	36–60 in (90–150 cm)	C	W	F	◆			◆			◆		
Opuntia basilaris	2–3 ft (0.6–0.9 m)	4 ft (1.2 m)	C	W	M	◆				◆		◆		
Opuntia cochenillifera	12 ft (3.5 m)	8 ft (2.4 m)	C	W	M	◆			◆			◆		
Opuntia humifusa	8–12 in (20–30 cm)	36 in (90 cm)	C	C/W	M	◆			◆			◆		
Opuntia littoralis	12–24 in (30–60 cm)	12–48 in (30–120 cm)	C	W	F	◆			◆			◆		
Opuntia microdasys	18–24 in (45–60 cm)	18–24 in (45–60 cm)	C	W	M	◆				◆	◆	◆		
Opuntia polyacantha	12 in (30 cm)	48 in (120 cm)	C	C/W	F	◆				◆	◆	◆		
Oreocereus celsianus	7 ft (2 m)	40 in (100 cm)	C	W	F	◆				◆	◆	◆		
Oreocereus trollii	20 in (50 cm)	32 in (80 cm)	C	W	F	◆				◆	◆	◆		
Pachycereus marginatus	10–17 ft (3–5 m)	3–8 in (8–20 cm)	C	W/T	F	◆			◆			◆		
Pachycereus pringlei	35 ft (10 m)	24 in (60 cm)	C	W/T	F	◆				◆		◆		
Pachyphytum compactum	12 in (30 cm)	16 in (40 cm)	O	W	A	◆					◆	◆		
Pachypodium geayi	25 ft (8 m)	5 ft (1.5 m)	O	W/T	F	◆				◆		◆		
Pachypodium lamerei	20 ft (6 m)	6 ft (1.8 m)	O	W	F	◆				◆		◆		
Pachypodium rosulatum	5 ft (1.5 m)	3 ft (0.9 m)	O	W	F	◆				◆		◆		
Parodia alacriportana	3–5 in (8–12 cm)	2½–3 in (6–8 cm)	C	W	F	◆			◆			◆		
Parodia concinna	1¼–4 in (3–10 cm)	3–4 in (8–10 cm)	C	W	F	◆			◆			◆		
Parodia leninghausii	3–24 in (8–60 cm)	3–4 in (8–10 cm)	C	W	F	◆			◆			◆		
Parodia magnifica	3–12 in (8–30 cm)	3–6 in (8–15 cm)	C	W	F	◆			◆			◆		
Parodia ottonis	1¼–6 in (3–15 cm)	1¼–6 in (3–15 cm)	C	W	F	◆			◆			◆		

Plant name	Height	Spread	Type	Climate	Spines/prickles	Showy flowers	Tolerates wet soil	Tolerates moist soil	Needs perfect drainage	Frost tolerant	Full sun	Half sun	Heavy shade
Parodia scopa	2–20 in (5–50 cm)	2½–4 in (6–10 cm)	C	W	F	◆		◆			◆		
Pedilanthus tithymaloides	6 ft (1.8 m)	2 ft (0.6 m)	O	W/T	A			◆				◆	
Pelargonium crithmifolium	20 in (50 cm)	12–20 in (30–50 cm)	O	W	A	◆		◆			◆		
Pelargonium fulgidum	27 in (70 cm)	20–32 in (50–80 cm)	O	W	A			◆			◆		
Pelargonium incrassatum	12 in (30 cm)	12 in (30 cm)	O	W	A			◆			◆		
Pereskia aculeata	25–30 ft (8–9 m)	6–15 ft (1.8–4.5 m)	C	W/T	M			◆			◆		
Pereskia grandifolia	7–15 ft (2–4.5 m)	3 ft (0.9 m)	C	W	F			◆			◆		
Pleiospilos bolusii	2½ in (6 cm)	6 in (15 cm)	O	W	A			◆	◆	◆	◆		
Pleiospilos nelii	2–2½ in (5–6 cm)	1¾–2½ in (4–6 cm)	O	W	A			◆	◆	◆	◆		
Portulacaria afra	10 ft (3 m)	5 ft (1.5 m)	O	W	A			◆			◆	◆	
Rebutia aureiflora	2 in (5 cm)	3–8 in (8–20 cm)	C	W/T	M			◆			◆		
Rebutia fiebrigii	1¼–2 in (3–5 cm)	¾–3 in (18–80 mm)	C	W/T	M			◆			◆		
Rebutia marsoneri	1¼–4 in (3–10 cm)	1¼–8 in (3–20 cm)	C	W/T	M			◆			◆		
Rebutia perplexa	½–1 in (12–25 mm)	1–3 in (25–80 mm)	C	W/T	M			◆			◆		
Rebutia spinosissima	1¼–2½ in (3–6 cm)	1¾–8 in (4–20 cm)	C	W/T	M			◆			◆		
Rhipsalis cereuscula	24 in (60 cm)	12 in (30 cm)	C	W/T	A			◆			◆	◆	
Rhipsalis paradoxa	5–15 ft (1.5–4.5 m)	3 ft (0.9 m)	C	W/T	A			◆			◆	◆	
Rhodiola rosea	2–30 in (5–75 cm)	2–30 in (5–75 cm)	O	C	A	◆				◆	◆		
Ruschia caroli	8–12 in (20–30 cm)	12–18 in (30–45 cm)	O	W	A	◆			◆		◆		
Ruschia dichroa	8–12 in (20–30 cm)	12–16 in (30–40 cm)	O	W	A	◆			◆		◆		
Sansevieria cylindrica	16 in (40 cm)	5 ft (1.5 m)	O	W	A	◆		◆				◆	
Sansevieria trifasciata	5 ft (1.5 m)	3 ft (0.9 m)	O	W	A			◆				◆	
Schlumbergera × buckleyi	12 in (30 cm)	12–24 in (30–60 cm)	C	W/T	A	◆		◆					◆
Schlumbergera truncata	12 in (30 cm)	12–24 in (30–60 cm)	C	W/T	A	◆		◆					
Schlumbergera Hybrid Cultivars	12 in (30 cm)	12–24 in (30–60 cm)	C	W/T	A			◆				◆	◆
Sedum acre	2–4 in (5–10 cm)	12–24 in (30–60 cm)	O	C/W	A	◆		◆		◆	◆		
Sedum aizoon	16 in (40 cm)	20 in (50 cm)	O	C/W	A	◆		◆		◆	◆		
Sedum album	2–4 in (5–10 cm)	8–20 in (20–50 cm)	O	C/W	A	◆		◆		◆	◆		
Sedum cauticolum	4–6 in (10–15 cm)	8–20 in (20–50 cm)	O	C/W	A	◆				◆	◆		
Sedum dasyphyllum	2–4 in (5–10 cm)	8–16 in (20–40 cm)	O	C/W	A			◆		◆	◆		
Sedum dendroideum	6–12 in (15–30 cm)	12–16 in (30–40 cm)	O	C/W	A	◆		◆		◆	◆		
Sedum kamtschaticum	4–12 in (10–30 cm)	16–24 in (40–60 cm)	O	C/W	A	◆		◆		◆	◆		

Plant name	Height	Spread	Type	Climate	Spines/prickles	Showy flowers	Tolerates wet soil	Tolerates moist soil	Needs perfect drainage	Frost tolerant	Full sun	Half sun	Heavy shade
Sedum lydium	2–4 in (5–10 cm)	6–12 in (15–30 cm)	O	W	A	◆		◆			◆		
Sedum morganianum	20 in (50 cm)	4 ft (1.2 m)	O	W	A				◆		◆		
Sedum oreganum	6 in (15 cm)	12–16 in (30–40 cm)	O	C/W	A	◆				◆	◆		
Sedum rubrotinctum	10 in (25 cm)	12–24 in (30–60 cm)	O	W	A	◆					◆		
Sedum sieboldii	4 in (10 cm)	12–20 in (30–50 cm)	O	C/W	A	◆				◆	◆		
Sedum spathulifolium	6 in (15 cm)	24 in (60 cm)	O	C/W	A	◆		◆		◆	◆		
Sedum spurium	6 in (15 cm)	12–20 in (30–50 cm)	O	C/W	A	◆		◆			◆		
Selenicereus anthonyanus	10 ft (3 m)	7 ft (2 m)	C	W/T	M	◆		◆			◆	◆	
Selenicereus grandiflorus	17 ft (5 m)	7–10 ft (2–3 m)	C	W/T	M	◆		◆			◆	◆	
Sempervivum arachnoideum	5 in (12 cm)	5–10 in (12–25 cm)	O	C/W	A	◆				◆	◆		
Sempervivum calcareum	2–3 in (5–8 cm)	5–8 in (12–20 cm)	O	C/W	A					◆	◆		
Sempervivum marmoreum	1–2 in 2–5 cm)	4 in (10 cm)	O	C/W	A	◆				◆	◆		
Sempervivum montanum	¾ in (18 mm)	1¼–1¾ in (30–40 mm)	O	C/W	A	◆				◆	◆		
Sempervivum pumilum	¾ in (18 mm)	1–1¼ in (25–30 mm)	O	C/W	A					◆	◆		
Sempervivum tectorum	3–4 in (8–10 cm)	8 in (20 cm)	O	C/W	A	◆				◆	◆		
Sempervivum Hybrid Cultivars	4–8 in (10–20 cm)	4–16 in (10–40 cm)	O	C/W	A	◆				◆	◆	◆	
Senecio articulatus	12 in (30 cm)	16–20 in (40–50 cm)	O	W	A					◆	◆	◆	
Senecio rowleyanus	20–32 in (50–80 cm)	8–12 in (20–30 cm)	O	W	A						◆	◆	
Senecio serpens	12 in (30 cm)	24 in (60 cm)	O	W	A						◆		
Stapelia gigantea	8–10 in (20–25 cm)	8 in (20 cm)	O	W/T	A	◆		◆			◆		
Stapelia leendertiziae	8 in (20 cm)	6–8 in (15–20 cm)	O	W/T	A	◆		◆			◆		
Stenocactus coptonogonus	2–4 in (5–10 cm)	3–5 in (8–12 cm)	C	W	F	◆			◆		◆		
Stenocactus crispatus	3–5 in (8–12 cm)	3–5 in (8–12 cm)	C	W	F	◆			◆		◆		
Stenocactus multicostatus	3–5 in (8–12 cm)	4 in (10 cm)	C	W	F	◆			◆		◆		
Stenocereus beneckei	7–10 ft (2–3 m)	20–40 in (50–100 cm)	C	W	F	◆		◆			◆		
Stenocereus eruca	3–10 ft (0.9–3 m)	17–20 ft (5–6 m)	C	W	F	◆		◆			◆		
Synadenium compactum	10–20 ft (3–6 m)	6 ft (1.8 m)	O	W/T	A			◆			◆		
Synadenium grantii	12 ft (3.5 m)	4 ft (1.2 m)	O	W/T	A			◆			◆		
Thelocactus hexaedrophorus	1¼–3 in (3–8 cm)	3–6 in (8–15 cm)	C	W	M	◆			◆	◆	◆		
Thelocactus macdowellii	2–4 in (5–10 cm)	2–5 in (5–12 cm)	C	W	F	◆			◆		◆		
Thelocactus setispinus	3–5 in (8–12 cm)	2–4 in (5–10 cm)	C	W	F	◆			◆		◆		
Titanopsis calcarea	¾–1¾ in (18–40 mm)	20 in (50 cm)	O	W	A	◆			◆	◆	◆	◆	

Plant name	Height	Spread	Type	Climate		Spines/prickles	Showy flowers	Tolerates wet soil	Tolerates moist soil	Needs perfect drainage	Frost tolerant	Full sun	Half sun	Heavy shade
Tradescantia sillamontana	6–32 in (15–80 cm)	40 in (100 cm)	O	W	A				◆				◆	◆
Trichodiadema bulbosum	6 in (15 cm)	16–20 in (40–50 cm)	O	W	A	◆				◆	◆	◆		
Trichodiadema densum	6 in (15 cm)	16–20 in (40–50 cm)	O	W	A	◆				◆	◆	◆		
Turbinicarpus pseudomacrochele	¾–1¾ in (18–40 mm)	1–1½ in (25–35 mm)	C	W	M					◆		◆		
Turbinicarpus valdezianus	½–1 in (12–25 mm)	½–1 in (12–25 mm)	C	W	M	◆				◆		◆		
Welwitschia mirabilis	4 ft (1.2 m)	10 ft (3 m)	O	W	A					◆		◆		
Yucca aloifolia	25 ft (8 m)	10 ft (3 m)	S	W	F	◆			◆		◆	◆		
Yucca baccata	5 ft (1.5 m)	4 ft (1.2 m)	S	W	M	◆			◆			◆		
Yucca brevifolia	30–40 ft (9–12 m)	5 ft (1.5 m)	S	C/W	M	◆			◆		◆	◆		
Yucca elata	10 ft (3 m)	5 ft (1.5 m)	S	W	M	◆			◆			◆		
Yucca elephantipes	30 ft (9 m)	10 ft (3 m)	S	W	M	◆			◆			◆		
Yucca filamentosa	3 ft (0.9 m)	5 ft (1.5 m)	S	C/W	A	◆			◆		◆	◆		
Yucca flaccida	17–35 ft (5–10 m)	17–35 ft (5–10 m)	S	C/W	M	◆			◆		◆	◆		
Yucca gloriosa	6–8 ft (1.8–2.4 m)	6 ft (1.8 m)	S	C/W	M	◆			◆		◆	◆		
Yucca recurvifolia	4–8 ft (1.2–2.4 m)	4 ft (1.2 m)	S	W	A	◆			◆		◆	◆		
Yucca whipplei	3 ft (0.9 m)	4 ft (1.2 m)	S	C/W	F	◆			◆		◆	◆		

AEONIUM

This genus, a member of the stonecrop (Crassulaceae) family, contains around 30 species of often shrubby and woody-stemmed succulents with terminal rosettes of fleshy leaves. Mainly from the Canary Islands and Madeira, they can also be found in eastern and northern Africa, parts of the Mediterranean, and the Middle East. Their brittle branches, often arranged rather like a multi-headed candlestick, are covered with a papery bark. Pyramidal inflorescences of small flowers, which are usually yellow but sometimes red, pink, or white, develop in the centers of the rosettes, usually in spring, followed by brown seed heads. CULTIVATION: As with most succulents, once established aeoniums are very drought tolerant. They need full sun and perfect drainage, and in the wild can often be found on steep slopes with their roots anchored in crevices between rocks. They are easily propagated by removing rooted basal suckers, by treating the rosettes as cuttings, or by raising from seed.

Aeonium arboreum

☼ ☙ ↔ 4 ft (1.2 m) ↑ 6 ft (1.8 m)

From the west coast of Morocco, this heavily branching species has bright green sometimes red-tinted leaves in rosettes 6–8 in (15–20 cm) wide. Large conical heads of yellow flowers in spring. *A. a.* var. *holochrysum*, 7 ft (2 m) tall, showy sprays of yellow flowers in summer; *A. a.* 'Atropurpureum' ★, deep purple-bronze leaves; and the cream-variegated 'Variegatum'. Zones 9–11.

Aeonium haworthii

PINWHEEL

☼ ☙ ↔ 32 in (80 cm) ↑ 24 in (60 cm)

Mounding subshrub, occasionally branching stems with aerial roots, from the Canary Islands. Small rosettes with red-edged blue-green leaves to slightly over 2 in (5 cm) long. Pink-flushed

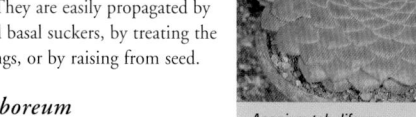

Aeonium tabuliforme

pale yellow flowers from spring. Drops much of its foliage while flowering. 'Variegatum' ★ has cream-variegated foliage that develops pink tints. Zones 9–11.

Aeonium tabuliforme ★

☼ ☙ ↔ 24 in (60 cm) ↑ 12 in (30 cm)

Low spreading biennial or perennial from the Canary Islands. Flat rosettes to 16 in (40 cm) wide, densely packed with spirals of pale green. Leaves often red-tinted and hair-fringed, to 8 in (20 cm) long. Flower stems tall and branching, yellow flowers. Usually dies after flowering. Zones 9–11.

Aeonium Hybrid Cultivars

☼/☀/❄ ☙ ↔ 8–24 in (20–60 cm) ↑ 12–24 in (30–60 cm)

A number of cultivars have arisen from either deliberate or accidental crosses between *Aeonium* species. They feature either more colorful foliage (bronze or variegated) or larger, more brightly colored flowers. Cultivars include 'Plum Purdy', 'Sunburst' ★, and 'Zwartkop' ★. Zones 9–11.

AGAVE

CENTURY PLANT

A genus of about 225 species, 50 subspecies, and varieties of rosette-shaped, succulent plants in the sisal (Agavaceae) family. They are found from southwest USA to Mexico, Central America and the Caribbean, into Colombia and Venezuela. The genus name comes from the Greek *agavos* (stately). Most species take decades to bloom, though many flower within 8–25 years in ideal conditions. After blooming they usually set seeds and some produce offsets or bulbils on the inflorescence. The leaves usually terminate in a strong sharp spike, and mostly have spiny teeth on the margins. Most species produce basal offsets to ensure survival when the mother plant dies after flowering. CULTIVATION: Grow in rich well-drained soil. Propagate from seed, offsets, or bulbils. Most species benefit from a rest in winter; many need protection from frost.

Agave americana

☼ ❄ ↔ 7–15 ft (2–4.5 m) ↑ 17–30 ft (5–9 m)

From northeastern Mexico. Variable, medium to large, hardy species with curving blue-gray leaves. Have 10–20 leaves, 5–8 ft (1.5–2.4 m) long, lance-shaped, toothed, flat to guttered, hard, often turned down with age. The inflorescence 17–50 ft (5–15 m) long with 15 to 35 branches. Many yellow, funnel-shaped flowers. *A. a.* var. *marginata*, yellow or white variegated stripes on leaf margins. *A. a.* 'Cornelius', compact with broad, yellow leaf margins; 'Mediopicta' ★, yellow-variegated mid-stripe on leaves; 'Mediopicta Alba' ★, white-variegated mid-stripe. Zones 8–11.

Aeonium, Hybrid Cultivar, 'Zwartkop'

Agave attenuata

Agave schidigera

Agave victoria-reginae 'Variegata'

Agave attenuata ★

☼ ⧗ ↔ 24–60 in (60–150 cm) ↑ 3–7 ft (0.9–2 m)
From just a few habitats in Mexico. Brittle, almost flat, rounded, lime-green to bluish green leaves, 10–28 in (25–70 cm) long, lacking teeth and terminal spine. Inflorescence an arching spike, 7–15 ft (2–4.5 m) long. Displays pale yellow flowers and offsets. 'Boutin Blue' ★ is a distinctly blue-gray cultivar. Zones 9–11.

Agave deserti

☼ ⧗ ↔ 16–24 in (40–60 cm) ↑ 8–15 ft (2.4–4.5 m)
From southern California and southwestern Arizona, USA, and northern Sonoran Desert areas of Mexico. Simple to clumping, with narrow bluish green to gray leaves, 6–16 in (15–40 cm) long. Small, sharp, marginal teeth. Inflorescence 8–15 ft (2.4–4.5 m) tall, branched. Flowers bright yellow. Zones 9–11.

Agave lechuguilla

SHIN DAGGER

☼ ❋ ↔ 8–12 in (20–30 cm) ↑ 8–17 ft (2.4–5 m)
Widespread, low-growing, densely clumping species from southern New Mexico and Texas, USA, and Chihuahua Desert areas of Mexico south to Hidalgo State. Leaves light to yellowish green with darker striations, upright, concaved, 10–20 in (25–50 cm) long, forming a narrow rosette. Thin, gray, horny leaf margins bear downward-pointing teeth. Inflorescence a spike, 8–17 ft (2.4–5 m) tall. Flowers yellow with tinges of purple. Zones 8–11.

Agave parryi ★

syn. *Agave patonii*

☼ ❋ ↔ 20–28 in (50–70 cm) ↑ 12–20 ft (3.5–6 m)
Compact solitary to suckering species from southeastern Arizona and southwestern New Mexico, USA, and Durango and Chihuahua, Mexico. Tight rosette of 100 to 150 leaves, 10–16 in (25–40 cm) long, straight to slightly rounded, ending in a sharp tip. Leaves smooth, rigid, flat to slightly concave, overlapping, light gray to blue-green, toothed margins. Inflorescence 12–20 ft (3.5–6 m) tall, 20 to 30 branches. Flowers yellow, tinged red. *A. p.* var. *huachucensis* ★, to 5 ft (1.5 m) wide. *A. p.* var. *truncata* ★, most attractive form with short, rounded leaves. Zones 7–11.

Agave potatorum

☼ ⧗ ↔ 3–8 ft (0.9–2.4 m) ↑ 15 ft (4.5 m)
From Puebla and Oaxaca, Mexico. Symmetrical plant with whitish gray-green leaves, deeply indented along margins, bearing large tubercles from which widely spaced, hooked, red-brown teeth arise. *A. p.* var. *verschaffeltii* ★ is distinguished by its whiter color and bigger tubercles on the leaf margins. Zones 9–11.

Agave schidigera

☼ ⧗ ↔ 40–60 in (100–150 cm) ↑ 7–12 ft (2–3.5 m)
From Chihuahua, Durango, Hidalgo, Zacatecas, San Luis Potosi, and smaller adjacent Mexican States. A solitary to non-suckering species. Leaves 12–20 in (30–50 cm) long, lacking teeth, straight to slightly incurving. Inflorescence is a spike, 7–12 ft (2–3.5 m) tall. Flowers greenish yellow with a tinge of purple. Zones 9–11.

Agave victoria-reginae ★

☼ ⧗ ↔ 20–28 in (50–70 cm) ↑ 10–15 ft (3–4.5 m)
Easily recognized, small to medium-sized, solitary species from Coahuila, Durango, and Nuevo Leon, Mexico. Has a dense, symmetrical, tightly packed rosette of hard, dark green, triangular leaves, 6–8 in (15–20 cm) long, marked with thick white lines or leaf bud imprints. 'Variegata', with distinctive yellow leaf margins, has recently been renamed as 'Golden Princess'. Zones 9–11.

ALLUAUDIA

All 8 species of *Alluaudia* are endemic to the arid southern and southwestern tip of Madagascar. They are members of the Didiereaceae family. All the species are sought-after collector plants and are still rare in cultivation. In habitat they start life as small xerophytic shrubs but most species eventually become tree-like, forming dense forests. Because of their heavily spined bodies, alluaudias resemble cacti and are in fact distant relatives. Unlike most cacti, however, alluaudias are covered in small fleshy deciduous leaves during their growing period. Both male and female flowers appear on the same plant and are often borne in huge numbers from the ends of mature branches.

CULTIVATION: *Alluaudia* species are easily grown from seeds but are more usually raised from cuttings that have been dried out for a week or two. They thrive in a rich well-drained soil and may grow rapidly when planted in the ground.

Alluaudia humbertii

☼ ⧗ ↔ 20–25 ft (6–8 m) ↑ 17–20 ft (5–6 m)
Untidy shrub to small tree consisting of many gray-brown, thin, flexible, intertwining branches covered in spines and pairs of small, round, green leaves. Red stamens of the flowers on male plants contrast with the all-white flowers on female plants. Zones 9–11.

Alluaudia procera ★

☼ ⚘ ↔ 7–10 ft (2–3 m) ↑ 35–50 ft (10–15 m)
The most common species of *Alluaudia* in cultivation. Wood from this tree-like species is used
for housing, fencing, boxes, and firewood. The
greenish yellow flowers are produced on massive
racemes bearing hundreds of blooms. Zones 9–11.

ALOE

Part of the asphodel (Asphodelaceae) family, this
genus comprises about 330 species of evergreen
succulent plants found through southern and
tropical Africa to Madagascar and the Arabian
Peninsula. They range from low-growing grass-
like perennials to trees, shrubs, and climbers.
Succulent leaves grow in rosettes or spirals at the
stem or branch tips, usually lance-shaped and
toothed or spiny. Red or yellow tubular flowers
are borne in racemes, often umbel-like, in late winter or spring.
With striking form and brilliant flowers, aloes are popular landscaping plants in warm dry areas; many grow well in containers.
CULTIVATION: Aloes need warm, dry, and well-drained conditions.
They can tolerate soils of low fertility. Most prefer full sun but
some smaller species do well in part-shade. In cool-temperate
climates they are suitable for greenhouse culture, and potted plants
can be moved outdoors during the summer months. Propagation
is by seed or, more easily, from stem cuttings or offsets.

Alluaudia procera

Aloe arborescens ★

KRANTZ ALOE

☼ ⚘ ↔ 6 ft (1.8 m) ↑ 10 ft (3 m)
From the bush and open forest in southern Africa. Leaves
toothed, blue-green, curved and tapering, up to 2 ft (0.6 m)
long, in rosettes at branch ends. Spikes of orange to red flowers
in winter. Suitable for growing in coastal areas. Zones 9–11.

Aloe aristata ★

LACE ALOE, TORCH PLANT

☼ ⚘ ↔ 24 in (60 cm) ↑ 20 in (50 cm)
From southern Africa. Dense clusters of stemless rosettes with
incurved, 4 in (10 cm) long, white-spotted green leaves tapering
to a filament-like tip. Leaves have white spines and soft white
teeth. Inflorescences to 20 in (50 cm) tall, often branched. Red
1½ in (35 mm) long flowers from late spring. Zones 9–11.

Aloe brevifolia ★

☼ ⚘ ↔ 20–32 in (50–80 cm) ↑ 20 in (50 cm)
Native to South Africa. Dense clusters of 4 in (10 cm) wide
rosettes of short, tightly packed, blue-green, soft-spined leaves.
Unbranched, 16 in (40 cm) tall, inflorescences of short, green-
tipped, red flowers are borne in summer. Zones 9–11.

Aloe descoingsii

☼/⚘ ⚘ ↔ 16–24 in (40–60 cm) ↑ 12 in (30 cm)
From Madagascar. Regarded as the smallest *Aloe*, with clustered
rosettes around 2 in (5 cm) wide, made up of 1¼ in (30 mm)

long, soft brown to olive green, white-spotted
leaves edged with very fine white teeth.
Inflorescences 6 in (15 cm) tall, unbranched,
with ½ in (12 mm) long, red-tipped, orange
flowers in winter. Zones 10–12.

Aloe ferox ★

BITTER ALOE, CAPE ALOE

☼ ⚘ ↔ 5–10 ft (1.5–3 m) ↑ 7–17 ft (2–5 m)
From South Africa's Cape region. Tree-like, with
heads of broad, fleshy, red-tinted, sometimes
spiny leaves to 40 in (100 cm) long, edged with
strong red-brown teeth. Branched inflorescences
with spikes of orange-red and golden yellow
flowers, 1½ in (35 mm) long, from late winter.
A. f. var. *candelabrum* (syn. *A. candelabrum*) has
neatly branched stems, inflorescences heavily
branched, and leaf tips slightly rolled. Zones 9–11.

Aloe haworthioides

☼ ⚘ ↔ 24–40 in (60–100 cm) ↑ 20 in (50 cm)
From Madagascar, this species has clusters of stemless, sometimes
suckering rosettes tightly packed with small, narrow, fleshy leaves
up to 2 in (5 cm) long, edged with white teeth. Unbranched
inflorescences to 12 in (30 cm) tall with ½ in (12 mm) long,
white to pale pink flowers. Zones 9–11.

Aloe maculata ★

syn. *Aloe saponaria*

SOAP ALOE, ZEBRA ALOE

☼/⚘ ⚘ ↔ 24–60 in (60–150 cm) ↑ 40 in (100 cm)
From southern Africa. Clumps of short-stemmed rosettes with
fleshy green leaves, light-spotted in bands. Teeth green to brown.

Aloe arborescens

Orange flowers on branching inflorescences in spring and summer. Zones 9–11.

Aloe marlothii ★
BERGAALWYN
☼ ✤ ↔ 7–10 ft (2–3 m) ↕ 12–15 ft (3.5–4.5 m)
South African. Tree-like, stem clothed with old leaves. Spine-studded and toothed green to gray-green leaves, 24–60 in (60–150 cm) long. Branching inflorescences to 32 in (80 cm) tall, orange to golden flowers in winter. Zones 9–11.

Aloe mitriformis ★
GOLD-TOOTH ALOE, KRANS AALWYN
☼/☀ ✤ ↔ 3–7 ft (0.9–2 m) ↕ 30 in (75 cm)
South African. Sprawling branching stems, ends ascending, rosettes of yellow-toothed green to blue-green leaves to 8 in (20 cm) long, sometimes white-spotted. Branched inflorescences to 24 in (60 cm) tall, with tubular scarlet flowers in summer. Zones 9–11.

Aloe marlothii, in the wild, Zimbabwe

Aloe peglerae
☼ ✤ ↔ 15 in (40 cm) ↕ 24 in (60 cm)
From near Pretoria in northern South Africa; rare in the wild. Often solitary rosette with overlapping bluish gray leaves, reddish in winter. Flowers dull red in dense cylindrical erect spikes, borne from mid-winter to early spring. Zones 9–10.

Aloe plicatilis ★
FAN ALOE
☼ ✤ ↔ 7 ft (2 m) ↕ 15 ft (4.5 m)
Well-branched shrub from Cape region in South Africa. Terminal leaves, arranged in 2 ranks of 12 to 16, dull green, flat, with rounded tips and minute teeth. Red flowers in winter. Zones 9–11.

Aloe polyphylla ★
☼ ❉ ↔ 16–32 in (40–80 cm) ↕ 30 in (75 cm)
Native of Lesotho. Short-stemmed rosettes with spirals of light-toothed, purple-edged, gray-green leaves to 12 in (30 cm) long. Branched inflorescences to 24 in (60 cm) high, with 2 in (5 cm) long, red to orange-pink flowers in spring. Very hardy. Zones 8–10.

Aloe striatula ★
BASUTO KRAAL ALOE
☼ ❉ ↔ 3 ft (0.9 m) ↕ 6 ft (1.8 m)
Species found in rocky places in Eastern Cape and Lesotho in southern Africa. Well-branched, terminal rosettes, downward curving, bright green, glossy leaves with white toothed edges. Conical flowerheads red to yellow in summer. Zones 8–11.

Aloe variegata ★
PARTRIDGE BREAST ALOE, TIGER ALOE
☼/☀ ❉ ↔ 20–32 in (50–80 cm) ↕ 20 in (50 cm)
This native of western southern Africa has clumps of stemless or short-stemmed rosettes of 4–6 in (10–15 cm) long, broad-based, triangular leaves, with white spots in bands, white edges, and white-striped undersides. Pink to dull red flowers, 1½ in (35 mm) long, in winter on few-branched inflorescences. Zones 8–11.

APOROCACTUS
RAT'S TAIL CACTUS
Pencil-thin, long, graceful, cascading branches covered with short golden brown spines and many flowers have long made this cactus a popular subject for hanging baskets. A member of the cactus (Cactaceae) family, it comes from the Mexican States of Oaxaca and Hidalgo. The name comes from the Greek *aporos,* meaning tangled, and refers to the plant's habit of branching profusely from the base. *Aporocactus* has been hybridized with several related epiphytic cactus genera to produce a variety of flower sizes and shapes in shades of pink, red, purple, orange, and yellow. The spherical seed pods may be spiny and are green to red and ½ in (12 mm) in diameter.
CULTIVATION: The plants are usually grown in hanging baskets. They need a well-drained humus-rich soil, a moderate level of watering, a position with some shade, and protection from frost. Plants may be grown from seed, but they are more usually raised from cuttings dried out for a week or more before planting. Give the plants a short rest after flowering, and then cuttings, 4–8 in (10–20 cm) long, can be taken.

Aporocactus flagelliformis ★
syn. *Disocactus flagelliformis*
RAT'S TAIL CACTUS
☼ ✦ ↔ 20 in (50 cm) ↕ 3–7 ft (0.9–2 m)
This old favorite has many, 3- to 8-ribbed, pendulous branches to 7 ft (2 m) long, arising profusely from the base. Spines ¾ in (18 mm), yellow to brown, in dense clusters along stems. Many flowers, pink to red, 2½–3 in (6–8 cm) long. Zones 11–12.

Aptenia cordifolia 'Red Apple'

APTENIA
HEARTLEAF ICEPLANT, HEARTS AND FLOWERS

A South African genus in the iceplant (Aizoaceae) family with 2 species—small, spreading, branching shrubs with fleshy succulent leaves covered in minute protuberances that make the leaves look as if covered with fine sugar crystals. The bright light green leaves, rounded to heart-shaped, taper to a broad point. Established plants may have a wide spread but are easily controlled. Small, purple-pink, daisy-like flowers, solitary or in 3s, appear at the stem tips in summer. The small, green, fleshy fruits redden as they mature.
CULTIVATION: Surprisingly hardy if kept dry in winter, they make a bold splash of color and thrive in a sunny well-drained position. Ideal for rockeries, as small-scale ground covers, or in hanging baskets. Will withstand prolonged drought but will not flower until watered. Propagate from seed or cuttings; may self-layer.

Aptenia cordifolia ★
☼/◐ ❄ ↔ 16–40 in (40–100 cm) ↕ 2 in (5 cm)
Native to the Eastern Cape region of South Africa. Heart-shaped leaves to 1 in (25 mm) long and wide. Intense magenta flowers. 'Red Apple' is an especially vigorous form, possibly a hybrid, that can be invasive; 'Variegata' has small cream-edged leaves. Zones 9–11.

ARIOCARPUS

Rare, small, slow-growing plants from arid to extreme desert areas of Texas, USA, and Mexico, the 6 species of this genus are part of the cactus (Cactaceae) family. They normally grow as solitary, spineless rosettes with short to long tubercles with tufts of wool between them, and in some species a woolly furrow along the upperside of each tubercle. They generally have thick skin and stout turnip-like roots, and may cluster with age. Species are usually wider than they are tall; some even grow flush with the soil. Most mimic their stony habitat, which renders them hard to locate, except when they flower, usually in autumn. Flowers come in shades of white, purple, pink, or yellow, and are mostly self-fertile. Seed pods are hidden in the woolly growing point. All Ariocarpus are listed in Appendix I of CITES, but illegal collecting has almost eliminated some species in certain habitats.

CULTIVATION: While habitat collected Ariocarpus are difficult to grow, seed-raised plants present few difficulties if grown in a pre-dominantly mineralized soil with a little humus and some gypsum. Keep completely dry in summer and winter and water thoroughly, but not frequently, in spring and autumn. Very slow growing.

Ariocarpus retusus
☼ ❄ ↔ 15 in (38 cm) ↕ 10 in (25 cm)
Occurs in several central Mexican States. Neat rosette of smooth, gray-green, unfurrowed tubercles pointing upward and outward, covered with thick wool at growing point. Flowers pale pink, to 2 in (50 mm) wide. A. r. var. furfuraceus, appears rock-like. Zones 9–11.

ASTROPHYTUM
BISHOP'S CAP, BISHOP'S MITER, GOAT HORN CACTUS, SEA URCHIN CACTUS

Astrophytum is an easily recognised and popular genus of small- to medium-sized members of the cactus (Cactaceae) family from Texas, USA, and Mexico. Usually solitary, with 5 to 8 ribs, they appear star-shaped when viewed from above. The genus name comes from the Greek astron, meaning star. Taxonomists have recently reduced the genus to just 4 species, but collectors recognize dozens of subspecies as well as hundreds of varieties and inter-species hybrids. Flowers are 1¼–2½ in (3–6 cm) wide, yellow or yellow with a red center. Astrophytums readily cross-pollinate to produce ¾–1¼ in (18–30 mm), spherical, scaly, dry seed pods that ripen quickly. These split open to reveal hundreds of cowry-shell-shaped, brown to black seeds.
CULTIVATION: Almost invariably grown from seed, astrophytums are easy to grow in a well-drained, moderately rich, preferably mineralized soil and given a distinct winter rest. They can be susceptible to over-watering, especially if the medium is not well drained.

Astrophytum asterias
SEA URCHIN CACTUS
☼ ❄ ↔ 4 in (10 cm) ↕ 2 in (5 cm)
From southern Texas, USA, and the Mexican States of Nuevo Leon and Tamaulipas. Smallest species, 8 low ribs, spineless, fine horizontal bands of hairs. Flowers 2–2½ in (5–6 cm) wide, yellow with a red center. Brown seed pods. Zones 9–11.

Astrophytum capricorne
GOAT HORN CACTUS
☼ ❄ ↔ 4–6 in (10–15 cm) ↕ 4–10 in (10–25 cm)
From the Chihuahua Desert of northern Mexico. Spherical to cylindrical, may grow to 40 in (100 cm) tall, has 7 or 8 well-defined ribs. Clusters of 5 to 10 twisted, flexible, black, brown, yellow, or gray spines along the ribs. Plant body may be very smooth, have many horizontal bands of whitish scurf, or be covered in scurf. Flowers yellow with a red center. Brown seed pods. A. c. var. senile, gray spines. A. c. f. aureum, golden spines when young. Zones 9–11.

Astrophytum myriostigma ★
BISHOP'S CAP, BISHOP'S MITER
☼ ❄ ↔ 4–6 in (10–15 cm) ↕ 4–10 in (10–25 cm)
From Central Mexico. The archetypical astrophytum, with 5 well-defined spineless ribs and an even spread of whitish scurf. A. m. var.

coahuilense, lower ribs than the type species, more cylindrical in shape, more densely covered in scurf. Some authorities regard this variety as a separate species. *A. m.* var. *strongylogonum*, rounded ribs and almost spherical shape; *A. m.* f. *nudum*, bright green plant body devoid of scurf, flowers yellow; seed pods brown. Zones 9–11.

Astrophytum ornatum ★

☼ ❈ ↔12–40 in (30–100 cm) ↕12–40 in (30–100 cm)

From Queretaro and Hidalgo, Mexico. Largest species, named for the ornate clusters of 5 to 11 sharp, 1¼–2 in (30–50 mm) long, needle-like spines. Spine clusters occur along the 7 to 8 ribs. Whitish scurf may be absent, dense, or in horizontal bands, giving rise to many named varieties. Flowers about 2 in (50 mm) wide, yellow. Seed pods, brown. *A. o.* var. *niveum* is covered in trichomes, *A. o.* f. *mirbelii* has bands of scurf, and *A. o.* f. *nudum* has none. Zones 9–11.

BEAUCARNEA

The 20 species of evergreen trees and shrubs in this genus in the dragon-tree (Dracaenaceae) family grow in arid regions ranging from northeastern Mexico to Nicaragua. The trunks become bulbous and swollen and have thick corky bark. Leaves are long, linear, and often grass-like. Plants take several years before they flower, when large panicles of tiny white flowers are carried.
CULTIVATION: Outdoor cultivation is only possible in warm, dry, and frost-free areas. In cooler areas plants can be grown in greenhouses or as indoor pot plants. Too much water in winter can cause the stem to rot. Propagate from seed or offsets in spring.

Beaucarnea recurvata ★

syn. *Nolina recurvata*
PONYTAIL PALM
☼ ❈ ↔6–8 ft (1.8–2.4 m) ↕25 ft (8 m)

Native of east-central Mexico. Popular indoor plant and dramatic landscaping feature. Narrow strap-like leaves, up to 3 ft (0.9 m) long, from a single bulbous trunk. Slow growing, branching occurs as it ages. Panicles of tiny white flowers are followed by pinkish fruit. Zones 9–11.

BESCHORNERIA

Native to Mexico, the 7 perennial rosette-forming species in this genus belong to the agave (Agavaceae) family. They resemble *Agave* but differ in that the stamens are shorter than the perianth segments. Leaves are up to 5 ft (1.5 m) long, lance- to sword-shaped, fleshy and bluish green, with rough margins. Surrounded by colorful bracts, flowers are clustered in racemes or panicles to 7 ft (2 m) or more tall. The 6 erect perianth segments are broadest toward the tips and are green tinged red; 6 stamens have delicate filaments and versatile anthers. The ovary is inferior, thin, with 3 compartments. The fruit is a capsule with many seeds.
CULTIVATION: Most *Beschorneria* species are frost tender, requiring full sun; provide greenhouse protection in cool regions. Propagate from seed, from suckers, or by division.

Beaucarnea recurvata

Beschorneria yuccoides

☼ ❈ ↔7 ft (2 m) ↕4–6 ft (1.2–1.8 m)

Dense clump of gray-green to blue-green sword-shaped leaves to more than 24 in (60 cm) long. Arching deep pink- to red-stemmed inflorescence with green flowers within large pinkish red bracts. Zones 9–11.

BOWIEA

This genus of 2 very similar species of perennial, South African succulent plants belongs to the hyacinth (Hyacinthaceae) family. The plants consist of many overlapping scales, which form a tight, pale green, spherical bulb that grows to 8 in (20 cm) above the soil. Dormant in winter, when the outer scales and many of the scale tips dry to a paper-like state, the plants burst into growth in late spring or summer, producing one or more very fast-growing stems that need to be supported by a trellis or stake. The stems are covered with many leafless side branches that may fall off.
CULTIVATION: *Bowiea* species prefer gritty well-drained soil and a position in full sun. Water rarely, except during the growing season. Propagate from seed.

Bowiea volubilis

Bowiea volubilis

☼ ❈ ↔8 in (20 cm) ↕8–15 ft (2.4–4.5 m)

Outer surface of bulb more or less covered in paper-like remnants of dead or dying scales, especially when dormant. Long vigorous stems bear many inconspicuous greenish white flowers. Zones 9–11.

CARNEGIEA

This genus of a single species belongs to the cactus (Cactaceae) family. Native to northern Mexico and southwestern USA. Slow growing, plants around 50 ft (15 m) in the wild are rare and over 100 years old. It may only flower when it reaches a height of 12 ft (3.5 m); it does not do well in cultivation. Heavy fines and strict regulations have stopped the practice of taking it from the wild for "desert gardens." Used in ceremonies by Native Americans.
CULTIVATION: Not hardy; in frost areas grow in a warm greenhouse. Grow in full light, but shade from full sun. After winter rest, during which it must not be watered, mist a few times, then start watering moderately; when in growth, water freely. Feed with a low nitrogen fertilizer monthly, reduce water and stop feeding in early autumn. Outdoors in frost-free areas grow in low humus, alkaline, well-drained soil.

Carnegiea gigantea, in the wild, Arizona, USA

Carnegiea gigantea
SAGUARO CACTUS
☀ ✤ ↔ 10 ft (3 m) ↑ 50 ft (15 m)
Produces between 12 and 24 ribs, sometimes more; areoles grow from the tops of ribs, non-flowering areoles, with up to 30 spines gray or brown, to 3 in (8 cm) long. White funnel-shaped flowers, followed by egg-shaped fruit in autumn. Zones 9–11.

CARPOBROTUS

An iceplant (Aizoaceae) family genus of around 25 species from southern Africa and Australia. Related to Lampranthus, Carpobrotus is distinctive in having fleshy berries. Plants form large spreading mats with yellow to red stems and long markedly 3-angled leaves. The flowers have purple to white or yellow petals and are borne singly or in groups of 3 on side branches. The fruits (known as "Hottentot figs" in South Africa) are fleshy and succulent and sometimes edible. All are rampant growers; some species have become naturalized in maritime habitats in North America and Europe, where they are aggressive weeds.
CULTIVATION: These iceplants are remarkably tough drought-tolerant plants for vegetating bare areas on poor soils, including coastal dunes. They thrive best in milder temperate climates, some species tolerating moderate frosts. Propagate from cuttings or seed; can be rapidly increased by pulling up the stems of any length and laying them flat under a light covering of sand.

Cephalocereus senilis

Carpobrotus edulis ★
HOTTENTOT FIG
☀/☀ ✤ ↔ 40–60 in (100–150 cm) ↑ 4–6 in (10–15 cm)
A South African native widely naturalized in temperate regions, especially on coastal dunes. Saber-shaped light green leaves to 3 in (8 cm) long, may be red-tinted in sun. Flowers yellow ageing to pink, to over 3 in (8 cm) wide. Fleshy red-tinted edible fruit. Zones 9–12.

CEPHALOCEREUS

This genus contains 5 species belonging to the cactus (Cactaceae) family. Many attempts have been made to classify the columnar cacti of Mexico. No doubt further reclassification will occur as research, including DNA testing, throws more light on the true relationship between Cephalocereus and related genera, Carnegia, Lemaireo-cereus, Mitrocereus, Neobuxbaumia, Neodawsonia, Pachycereus, and Piloso-cereus. The genus was established in 1838, its name is derived from the Greek, cephale, meaning head, with reference to the pseudocephalium—the area of thick wool and bristles normally found on the northern side of mature stems, through which flowers are produced in summer.
CULTIVATION: Easy to cultivate in a mineral-rich well-drained soil. They may be raised from seed or from cuttings that have been dried out for a week or two. Rest them in winter.

Cephalocereus senilis
OLD MAN CACTUS, OLD MAN OF MEXICO
☀ ✤ ↔ 12–16 in (30–40 cm) ↑ 50 ft (15 m)
From Hidalgo, Guanajuato, and the Metztitlan Valley of Mexico. A very popular and easily recognized cactus because of the distinctive long, twisted, gray or white spines that cover the stem of the plant and give it its species name, senilis, meaning aged, because it looks like a bearded old man. Plants are solitary or branched from the base, slow growing, and can eventually reach over 40 ft (12 m) in the wild. Ribs 20 to 30. Spines strong, 1 to 5 grayish white centrals, 20 to 30 white hair-like radials, thin, twisted. Pseudocephalium on side of mature branches, later covering growing point. Apricot, bell-shaped flowers, 3–4 in (8–10 cm) wide. Seed pods oval. Zones 9–11.

CEREUS

This genus in the Cactaceae family consists of about 40 species of columnar or tree-like cacti native to South America and the West Indies. Stems are strongly ribbed along their full length, spines short and unyielding. Most nocturnal flowering species are now in the genera *Selenicereus* and *Hylocereus*. The flowers emerge from the ribs and are usually white, followed by fruit that is oblong to round or egg-shaped, ripening to yellow and red; the fruits split to reveal black shiny seeds in white, pink, or even red pulp.
CULTIVATION: Grow in well-drained reasonably fertile soil in full sun; water well in the growing season. Reduce watering in autumn. Water in winter only if plant starts to shrivel. Propagate from seed during spring or cuttings from large specimens in summer.

Cereus hildmannianus ★

☼/☀ ❧ ↔ 4–7 ft (1.2–2 m) ↑ 10–17 ft (3–5 m)
Shrub or small tree from eastern Brazil. Strongly upright, with multi-branched green stems with 5 to 6 ribs. May be spineless or have small white areoles with a ¾ in (18 mm) long central spine and up to 12 radial brown spines. White flowers to 4 in (10 cm) in diameter. *C. h.* subsp. *uruguayensis* (syns *C. peruvianus* of gardens, *C. uruguayanus*), funnel-shaped flowers, green sepals, tipped red, inner tepals white. *C. h.* 'Monstrosus' (syn. *C. h.* var. *monstrosus*) has twisted and contorted blue-green stems. Zones 10–12.

Cereus jamacaru

☼/☀ ❧ ↔ 7–15 ft (2–4.5 m) ↑ 17–35 ft (5–10 m)
Impressive tree-sized cactus from northeastern Brazil. Short trunk to 24 in (60 cm) diameter topped with multi-branched 4- to 6-ribbed stems, blue-green ageing to gray. Clusters of 9 to 11 spines, short and pale on young growth, dark and long on mature stems. White and pale green flowers to 12 in (30 cm) long. Zones 10–12.

CEROPEGIA

A genus of 200-odd often succulent climbers, trailers, or shrubs in the dogbane (Apocynaceae) family. They come mainly from southern Africa but also from elsewhere in Africa, the Canary Islands, Southeast Asia, and northeast Australia. Allied to *Hoya* and *Stapelia*, they have succulent hoya-like foliage and/or stems and unusual 5-lobed lantern-shaped flowers that, as with *Stapelia*, are often rather unpleasantly scented as they are fly-pollinated and may trap visiting insects until pollination is effected.
CULTIVATION: All species dislike frost. They prefer a light gritty soil and can be allowed to dry out between waterings. The trailing species are widely cultivated as indoor hanging basket plants. Outdoors they suit the tropics and subtropics. Propagate from seed or cuttings, or by division. Some species develop small tubers, underground or on the stems, that can be removed and grown on.

Ceropegia linearis

☀ ❧ ↔ unlimited ↑ 4 in (10 cm)
Southern African trailer. Fine twining stems; small fleshy leaves, triangular to lance-shaped, rounded at the base, sometimes linear. Flowers short, broad-based, cream tubes with narrow red-brown lobes fused at tip. *C. l.* subsp. *woodii* ★, "string of hearts," "sweetheart" vine, trailing with heart-shaped leaves. Zones 10–12.

Ceropegia sandersonii ★
PARACHUTE PLANT, UMBRELLA FLOWER

☀ ❧ ↔ 5 ft (1.5 m) ↑ 6 ft (1.8 m)
From Mozambique and South Africa. Vigorous twining climber, tuberous roots. Heart-shaped leaves to 2 in (5 cm) long. Flowers distinctive, upward-facing with cream and green vase-shaped tube with lobes united, forming a canopy over the tube. Zones 10–12.

CHEIRIDOPSIS

A genus of 23 species of succulents from southern Africa, part of the iceplant (Aizoaceae) family. Most are clump-forming but a few are shrubby. Leaves are opposite and triangular in section, rarely flattened, the surface more or less velvety, distinguishing them from species of the allied genus *Argyroderma*. Each succeeding pair differs from the previous one in form, size, and relative unity of the leaves. Those most united wither in the resting period and form a sheath covering the succeeding pair of leaves. Flowers open during the day, are borne singly, and usually have yellow, rarely purple or red, petals.
CULTIVATION: In warm regions plants need full sun, low humidity, and protection from rain in summer when they are resting. Grow in a cool greenhouse in temperate regions; do not water in winter. They need rapid-draining soil as the leaves will split open if kept wet too long. Propagate from seed or from hardened cuttings.

Cheiridopsis cigarettifera

☼/☀ ❧ ↔ 6–12 in (15–30 cm) ↑ 4 in (10 cm)
From Western Cape, South Africa. Forms dense circular mats. Narrow, tapering, keeled leaves to slightly over 2 in (5 cm) long. Inner pairs are fused for about a third of their length, and gray-green with a waxy bloom and tiny translucent spots. Flowers in shades of yellow to golden yellow. Zones 9–11.

Cheiridopsis pillansii

☼/☀ ❊ ↔ 8–12 in (20–30 cm) ↑ 4 in (10 cm)
From Western Cape, South Africa. Leaves largely fused, forming a small, rounded, pale gray-green to blue-green succulent body, often with darker spotting. Where separate, lower leaves protrude. Flowers to 3 in (8 cm) wide, cream to straw yellow. Zones 8–11.

Cheiridopsis pillansii

CLEISTOCACTUS

A popular genus of 48 species of upright, sprawling, and even decumbent cacti (family Cactaceae) from southern Ecuador, Peru, Bolivia, western Brazil, Uruguay, Paraguay, and northern Argentina. The genus was named because the long tubular flowers, which are usually pollinated by hummingbirds, appear to be closed even when mature. (The Greek word *kleistos* means closed.) *Cleistocactus* species are popular because they are easy to grow and offer a wide variety of spine and flower colors. Flowers are produced along the upper portion of the stems, and may be red, maroon, pink, orange, yellow, white, or even a combination of up to 3 colors. There continues to be confusion as to what species should be included in the genus *Cleistocactus*. Currently it includes some or all of the species previously described as *Akersia, Binghamia, Bolivicereus, Borzicactella, Borzicactus, Clistanthocereus, Hildewinteria, Loxanthocereus, Maritimocereus, Seticereus, Seticleistocactus, Winteria,* and *Winterocereus*.

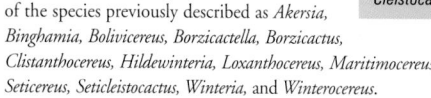

Cleistocactus strausii

CULTIVATION: They are easy to grow in a rich well-drained soil. Propagate from seed, or from cuttings that have been dried out for a week or two. Rest the plants in winter.

Cleistocactus hyalacanthus
syn. *Cleistocactus jujuyensis*

☼ ❄ ↔ 24–48 in (60–120 cm) ↕ 36 in (90 cm)

From northwestern Argentina and southeastern Bolivia; 18 to 22 ribs. Three central spines, yellow to brown, 20 to 30 radials, white to gray, needle-like, bristly. Flowers 1½ in (35 mm) long, purplish pink, outer petals slightly recurved. Seed pods red. Zones 8–12.

Cleistocactus strausii ★
SILVER TORCH CACTUS

☼ ❄ ↔ 3 ft (0.9 m) ↕ 3–10 ft (0.9–3 m)

Stunning cactus from Bolivia and northern Argentina. Plants dark green, with 25 to 30 ribs. Silvery white spines 4 centrals, creamy white, 30 to 40 radials, hair-like, white, completely obscuring the plant body. Flowers 3–4 in (8–10 cm) long, deep maroon, slightly curved. Seed pods red, spherical to club-shaped. Zones 8–12.

CONOPHYTUM

An iceplant (Aizoaceae) family genus of around 86 species of small, tufted, stemless succulents from southern Africa. Each shoot is reduced to 2 leaves fused into a cylindrical body that is flattened, notched or 2-lobed at the apex, with a small mouth-like opening between the lobes. Some species mimic the related *Lithops*, having a green "window" or translucent dots that allow light to penetrate to the green photosynthetic tissue within. New leaf pairs develop inside those of the previous season, older ones drying as shells that protect new ones in the dry season. Some species bloom during the day, others are nocturnal, flowers bursting through the central fissure, with petals white, yellow, purple, or bicolored.

CULTIVATION: Give these succulents full sun and low humidity all year. They are best grown in pots in sandy or gritty compost,

even in warm countries, to control soil moisture. Withhold water from late spring to mid-summer, when new growths are forming inside old sheaths. Propagate from seed or cuttings of leaf pairs with a small amount of stem; allow to dry before rooting.

Conophytum pillansii

☼ ❄ ↔ 4–8 in (10–20 cm) ↕ 2–4 in (5–10-cm)

From Western Cape. Flat-topped globose body, entirely fused or conspicuously divided. Velvety texture, light green to near red, mottled brown markings. Purple-red flowers. Zones 9–11.

Conophytum quaesitum

☼ ❄ ↔ 6–8 in (15–20 cm) ↕ 2–4 in (5–10 cm)

From Namibia and Namaqualand. Round to cylindrical, usually 2-lobed plant body, often keeled; gray-green to yellow-green, sometimes red-tinted and/or with brownish spots. White, cream or pink flowers, fragrant. Zones 10–11.

COPIAPOA
syn. *Pilocopiapoa*

A northern Chilean genus of around 20 species of low, often mounding cacti (family Cactaceae). The stems, which may be short and rounded or longer, tending towards cylindrical, are ribbed, but seldom heavily, and are often woolly at the top. Plants develop from a taproot that may emerge slightly from the soil, making the stem appear pinched at the base. Spines are often large in relation to plant size and tend to be curved. Flowers are short and funnel- to bell-shaped, usually clustered near the apex of the stems, and are most commonly yellow, rarely red.

CULTIVATION: Tolerant of only very light frosts; likely to rot in wet winter conditions. Otherwise these cacti are easily grown in full or half-sun with gritty free-draining soil. Water and feed occasionally in summer, keep dry at other times. New plants may be raised from seed, but offsets and divisions will establish more quickly.

Copiapoa cinerascens

☼/☀ ❄ ↔ 6–24 in (15–60 cm) ↕ 4–8 in (10–20 cm)

Slow to cluster, may for many years be a single stem. Stems gray-green and slightly downy, with 10–17 ribs, the neck of taproot

Copiapoa cinerea

often exposed. Curved gray-brown spines on woolly areoles. Creamy yellow flowers to 2 in (5 cm) wide in summer. Zones 10–11.

Copiapoa cinerea

☼/◐ ✦ ↔ 6–16 in (15–40 cm) ↑ 8 in–4 ft (20 cm–1.2 m)
Clustering or mounding, woolly-topped, globose or short cylindrical stems that may reach 10 in (25 cm) across. Up to 45 ribs, studded with areoles bearing short, often dark spines. Yellow flowers in summer, to 2 in (5 cm) wide. *C. c.* var. *columna-alba*, fewer ribs, flowers often smaller. *C. c.* var. *gigantea*, generally spinier than other species, orange-brown wool, ribs with rounded apices. Zones 10–11.

Copiapoa humilis

☼/◐ ✦ ↔ 4–16 in (10–40 cm) ↑ 8 in (20–cm)
Green to olive brown, simple or clustered stems, 9–17 ribs, partially exposed taproot. Slightly scented yellow-green to yellow flowers, to 1¾ in (40 mm) wide, from late-spring. Zones 10–11.

COTYLEDON

This formerly large stonecrop (Crassulaceae) family genus of succulents has been extensively revised, and now contains around a dozen species of evergreen, often rather woody-stemmed shrubs from South Africa. The leaves vary widely in shape, from flat and rounded to elongated and cylindrical, but are always fleshy and succulent, sometimes with a powdery white surface bloom of wax. The flowers, usually yellow, orange, or red, have 5 recurved petal-like sepals, are bell-shaped, and are borne in heads on strong stems that hold them well clear of the foliage. Flowers appear throughout the year, most abundantly in late spring. CULTIVATION: Tolerant of light frosts, they do best in mild climates with relatively dry winters. Plant in full sun or half-sun with gritty very free-draining soil. Routine deadheading and removal of old branches and dried leaves will keep plants tidy and flowering profusely. Propagation is from seed, cuttings, or offsets.

Cotyledon orbiculata ★

☼/◐ ✦ ↔ 20 in–4 ft (50 cm–1.2 m) ↑ 1–5 ft (0.9–1.5 m)
Bushy often densely branched shrub. Leaves variable, rounded to elongated, to over 4 in (10 cm) long, seldom hairy, pale green to silver-gray, with a powdery coating. Small, orange to red flowers, often densely clustered. Can be invasive in favorable climates. *C. o.* f. *variegata*, mid-green leaves with large pale sectors. Zones 9–11.

Cotyledon tomentosa ★

BEAR'S PAW
☼/◐ ✦ ↔ 12–27 in (30–70 cm) ↑ 12–20 in (30–50 cm)
Shrub branching near ground. Thick fleshy leaves, 1 in (25 mm) long with dense silver-gray to gray-green hairs and vestigial brown teeth. Short flower stems. Small, orange-red to yellow flowers, often downy. *C. t.* f. *variegata*, cream patches on foliage. Zones 10–11.

Cotyledon orbiculata

Cotyledon undulata ★

syn. *Cotyledon orbiculata* var. *undulata*
SILVER CROWN, SILVER RUFFLES
☼/◐ ✦ ↔ 20 in–4 ft (50 cm–1.2 m) ↑ 32 in–5 ft (80 cm–1.5 m)
Very similar to *C. orbiculata*, except that leaves are always silver-gray with wavy edges. Zones 9–11.

CRASSULA

This stonecrop (Crassulaceae) family genus has some 300 species of succulent annual, biennial, and perennial herbs and small shrubs. A few are found in Asia, Europe, Madagascar, Australia, and North America, but most are from southern Africa. Leaves usually opposite, fleshy, and vary in size, texture, color, and shape. Red, pink, green, or white, funnel- or star-shaped flowers, occasionally tubular, are sometimes carried singly but are more often in cyme-like branches. CULTIVATION: They prefer full sun or half-sun. Grow in well-drained average soil with added humus, or in pots in cactus compost. In areas with frost, grow under glass. Water sparingly in winter. Propagate from stem cuttings or set single leaves in soil from spring to mid-summer. Sow seeds in cactus compost with added sharp sand.

Crassula atropurpurea

☼/◐ ✦ ↔ 12 in (30 cm) ↑ 6–18 in (15–45 cm)
Erect or domed subshrub from Namibia and South Africa's Western Cape. Variable; leaves red-tinted in sun. Cream to pinkish flowers tiny. *C. a.* var. *anomala* (syn. *C. anomala*) ★ is compact. Zones 9–11.

Crassula hemisphaerica

ARAB'S TURBAN
☼/◐ ✦ ↔ 12–20 in (30–50 cm) ↑ 8 in (20 cm)
Low spreading perennial from South Africa. Rosettes or short stems of small, tightly spiralled, bristle-edged, gray-green to deep green leaves. Spikes of tiny, cream, tubular flowers in spring. Zones 9–11.

Crassula lactea

TAILOR'S PATCH

☼/◐ ✤ ↔ 12–20 in (30–50 cm) ↕ 16–24 in (40–60 cm)

From Eastern Cape, South Africa. Shrubby perennial, spreading or scrambling stems, green, pointed, hard-edged leaves to nearly 3 in (8 cm) long. White flowers, undersides sometimes pink, in autumn. Zones 9–11.

Crassula multicava ★

☼/◐ ✤ ↔ 3–10 ft (0.9–3 m) ↕ 12–16 in (30–40 cm)

From South Africa. Small, thin, rounded, gray-green leaves, on short, upright or spreading, sometimes branching stems. Rounded inflorescence of tiny, red-tipped, white to cream autumn flowers. Zones 9–11.

Crassula muscosa

MOSS CYPRESS, WATCH-CHAIN CYPRESS

☼/◐ ✤ ↔ 20–40 in (50–100 cm) ↕ 8–32 in (20–80 cm)

From South Africa, Namibia, and Lesotho. Tiny, overlapping, gray-green leaves on short scrambling stems, resembling thickened clubmoss. Inconspicuous inflorescences of up to 8 yellow-green flowers in summer. Zones 9–11.

Crassula ovata ★

syns Crassula arborescens of gardens, C. argentea of gardens, C. portulacea

DOLLAR PLANT, JADE TREE

☼/◐ ✤ ↔ 2–4 ft (0.6–1.2 m) ↕ 3–6 ft (0.9–1.8 m)

Native to most of South Africa. Upright branching shrub, thick stems and peeling bark. Fleshy rounded leaves, usually shiny dark green with red or pale green edges. Heads of pink-tinted white flowers in winter–early spring. 'Crosby's Compact' (syn. 'Crosby's Dwarf'), low compact habit, rarely exceeding 12 in (30 cm) high, red-tinted foliage; 'Hobbit', compact with thickened almost cylindrical, to thin slightly curled leaves, often with red tints; 'Hummel's Sunset' ★ (syn. 'Sunset'), vivid red leaves suffused with yellow and orange; 'Tricolor', bold cream-variegated foliage suffused with bright pink. Zones 10–11.

Crassula perfoliata

☼/◐ ✤ ↔ 18–36 in (45–90 cm) ↕ 2–4 ft (0.6–1.2 m)

Variable species of wide distribution in southern Africa. Subshrub, branching from base. Typical form has 4-ranked, channeled, long-tapering, gray-green leaves to 6 in (15 cm) long. White, pink, or red summer flowers in large, dense, terminal corymb. C. p. var. minor (syn. C. falcata), from Eastern Cape, flatter, sickle-shaped, mealy-whitish leaves turned on edge and flattened into one plane, brilliant red flowers. Zones 9–11.

Crassula pyramidalis

☼/◐ ✤ ↔ 4–8 in (10–20 cm) ↕ 4–10 in (10–25 cm)

From Northern Cape, South Africa. Short, sometimes branching stems with tiny, pointed, oval leaves in groups of 4, stacked to make a square-sectioned column. Few-flowered terminal heads of small white to cream blooms, in spring. Zones 9–11.

Crassula rupestris ★

BEAD VINE, BUTTONS ON A STRING

☼/◐ ✤ ↔ 6–12 in (15–30 cm) ↕ 8–20 in (20–50 cm)

Shrubby perennial from South Africa and Namibia. Short stems with slightly overlapping, thick, red-tinted, olive green, pointed, tiny, oval leaves. Tiny, red-tinted, white flowers in rounded heads. C. r. subsp. commutata, dense, upright, bushy; C. r. subsp. marnieriana, low, spreading, larger flowerheads. Zones 9–11.

Crassula Hybrid Cultivars

☼/◐ ✤ ↔ 2–10 in (5–25 cm) ↕ 2–8 in (5–20 cm)

Grown for their brightly colored, variably textured and shaped foliage, and wide range of shapes and sizes. 'Baby's Necklace' ★, small, bead-like, purplish red-edged leaves; 'Buddha's Temple' ★, hybrid of C. pyramidalis, rosettes of upward-curved, gray-green leaves tiered like a pagoda roof; 'Campfire', narrow bright green leaves, flushed vivid red; 'Coralita', rosettes of curly, gray-green leaves; 'Fernwood', tight rosettes of small bright green leaves; 'Frosty', tiny cream flowers; 'Moonglow' ★, soft-orange flowers; 'Morgan's Beauty' ★ (syn. 'Morgan's Pink'), showy, soft pink flowers open from glowing pink buds, age to red; 'Pagoda Village', purplish red-edged bronze-green leaves, tiered; 'Pastel', tiny, white to pink-tinted, cream flowers; 'Pink Pagoda', reddish seed heads; 'Springtime', tiny, pink-tinted, cream flowers in summer. Zones 9–11.

Crassula, Hybrid Cultivar, 'Pink Pagoda'

CYLINDROPUNTIA

A genus of 33 species of shrubby to tree-like opuntias from North America south to Mexico, with one species in South America and one in the West Indies. Part of the cactus (Cactaceae) family, Cylindropuntia are common in American deserts, and are usually known by their common name, cholla. Cylindropuntia species are distinguished from Austrocylindropuntia, their similar looking South American counterparts, in that their spines are always enclosed in a fine papery sheath. Stem joints vary from being tightly attached to easily detached, but most feature very distinct tubercles. Flowers are red, magenta, chartreuse, yellow, or bronze. Seed pods are fleshy or dry, spherical to club-shaped, red, brown, green, or yellow, with or without spines. CULTIVATION: Cultivation is easy in any well-drained soil, from seed or from entire seed pods that may be planted as if they were a cutting, and also from stems that have been dried out for a few days. Careful handling is recommended, as they are likely to irritate the skin. A brief rest from watering in winter is beneficial.

Cylindropuntia bigelovii

syn. Opuntia bigelovii

JUMPING CHOLLA, TEDDY-BEAR CHOLLA

☼ ✤ ↔ 2–3 ft (0.6–0.9 m) ↕ 3–8 ft (0.9–2.4 m)

From southwestern USA and northern Mexico. Variable in size, can exceed 8 ft (2.4 m) tall. Spiny cylindrical stem segments; spines pinkish straw to red-brown, and held in golden yellow sheaths that sprout from prominent tubercles. Yellow-green to green flowers, sometimes striped pale mauve; spineless, warty yellow fruits. Zones 9–11.

Cylindropuntia bigelovii, in the wild, California, USA

Cylindropuntia imbricata

syn. *Opuntia imbricata*

☼ ❋ ↔4–7 ft (1.2–2 m) ↑10 ft (3 m)

From Mexico and southwest USA. Shrubby, becoming tree-like. Long stem segments, somewhat flattened, many spines, tiny leaves. Purplish to red or yellowish flowers. Yellow fruits. Zones 7–12.

Cylindropuntia spinosior

syn. *Opuntia spinosior*

CANE CHOLLA

☼/❋ ❋ ↔3–5 ft (0.9–1.5 m) ↑7 ft (2 m)

From southwest USA and northwest Mexico. Shrubby to tree-like. Densely warty cylindrical segments. Pinkish ephemeral leaves, many small pale yellow to white spines. Red or magenta flowers, rarely yellow or white, spineless yellow fruits. Zones 7–11.

Cylindropuntia tunicata

syn. *Opuntia tunicata*

PRICKLY PEAR, TUNA

☼ ❋ ↔4 ft (1.2 m) ↑2 ft (0.6 m)

Native to Mexico and southwestern USA but naturalized in areas of South America. Forms a much-branched shrub. Whorls of blue-green stem segments, white areoles with white-sheathed cream or yellowish spines. Yellow flowers, spring to summer, followed by blue-green spineless fruit that persists for a long time. Zones 8–11.

CYPHOSTEMMA

Part of the grape (Vitaceae) family and related to *Cissus*, this genus includes many climbers and vines and a few shrubs among its 250 or so species. They occur in many tropical and subtropical regions of the world, mainly in seasonally dry climates, and include both evergreen and deciduous species. Many of the African species have a thickened base, swollen succulent stems, and fleshy, usually compound leaves; all adaptations to the drought conditions they must frequently endure. Tiny greenish flowers in flat-topped heads are followed by fleshy grape-like berries that may be edible.

CULTIVATION: Plant in full sun in a light, well-drained soil. Most prefer a warm frost-free climate, but some will tolerate light frosts. They will withstand more cold if kept dry over winter, and may rot if kept cold and damp for prolonged periods. Propagate from seed.

Cyphostemma juttae ★

syn. *Cissus juttae*

TREE GRAPE

☼ ❋ ↔6 ft (1.8 m) ↑6 ft (1.8 m)

From Namaqualand in Namibia. Deciduous shrub, thickened succulent stem. Leaves toothed, 3-part, glossy green, oval leaflet, downy undersides. Stems covered with peeling yellowish bark. Small yellow-green flowers in summer. Yellow to red-brown berries. Zones 9–11.

DASYLIRION

From southern USA and Mexico, this genus consists of 18 evergreen perennial species. *Dasylirion* (family Ruscaceae) is closely related to *Beaucarnea*. Single trunk topped with a head of linear leaves that in some species are over 3 ft (0.9 m) long and with edges often spiny-toothed. From among the foliage emerges a tall spike, bearing a vast number of creamy white flowers. Male and female flowers occur on separate plants, usually in the summer.

CULTIVATION: As with most dry-country plants, they demand good drainage and full sun. They will tolerate light to moderate frosts but suffer if kept wet and cold for prolonged periods. Soil should be light and gritty, though a little extra humus is appreciated. Propagate from seed.

Cyphostemma juttae

Dasylirion acrotriche

Dioscorea elephantipes

Dasylirion acrotriche

☼ ❋ ↔ 5 ft (1.5 m) ↕ 10–20 ft (3–6 m)
A Mexican species. The leaves are light green, and have very narrow, edges with teeth and hooked spines. Inflorescence usually upright to 12 ft (3.5 m) tall. Zones 8–11.

Dasylirion wheeleri ★

DESERT SPOON, SOTOL
☼ ❋ ↔ 3 ft (0.9 m) ↕ 12–25 ft (3.5–8 m)
A species found growing in arid parts of southeastern Arizona and Texas, USA. Leaves are blue-green and viciously spiny. The flower spike is very tall. Zones 7–11.

DELOSPERMA

Found mainly in southern Africa but also spread through eastern Africa to Saudi Arabia, this genus, a member of the iceplant (Aizoaceae) family, is composed of over 150 species of annuals, biennials, and perennials that often have a low spreading habit and can become shrubby. Most have a thickened, somewhat tuberous, central stem known as a "caudex," from which emerge fine stems clothed in succulent cylindrical leaves. The daisy-like

Delosperma cooperi

flowers are usually small, but are exceptionally bright and abundant. Most species flower in late spring.
CULTIVATION: Intolerant of repeated hard frosts, these plants are otherwise undemanding and easily grown in any gritty free-draining soil that can be kept moist during the flowering season. Ideal for covering dry banks and rock walls, they often naturalize in crevices. Propagate from seed, cuttings, or by layering, either natural or deliberately encouraged.

Delosperma cooperi

☼/◐ ❋ ↔ 24–32 in (60–80 cm) ↕ 6–20 in (15–50 cm)
From South Africa. Densely branched perennial that spreads quickly and may become shrubby. Narrow glandular leaves, sometimes gray-green. Pink to magenta flowers. Zones 7–10.

Delosperma nubigenum

☼/◐ ❋ ↔ 20 in (50 cm) ↕ 2–4 in (5–10 cm)
A native of South Africa, this is the hardiest of the *Delosperma*. It has a prostrate spreading stem with rosettes of short fleshy leaves, which are often red-tinted in sun, and bears flowers that are bright golden yellow to orange-red. Zones 7–10.

DIOSCOREA *(see page 740)*

Dioscorea elephantipes

syn. *Testudinaria elephantipes*
ELEPHANT'S FOOT
☼/◐ ❀ ↔ 12 in (30 cm) ↕ 36 in (90 cm)
Found growing on dry rocky slopes in southern Africa. A perennial with an exposed tuber covered in tough armor-like plates and stems twining to the left. Heart-shaped leaves. It bears yellowish green flowers, the males are in the erect inflorescences, the females in the nodding to spreading spiny ones. Zones 9–11.

DROSANTHEMUM

Found in South Africa and Namibia, this genus of succulents in the iceplant (Aizoaceae) family is made up of about 90 species of perennials, many trailing, the others mounding or shrubby. The leaves are succulent, cylindrical in section, covered in tiny protuberances and often small. The attraction lies largely in its dense carpeting habit and weight of bloom. Flowers are seldom very large but are incredibly abundant, frequently making a solid mass of color, in white or any shade of pink, purple, yellow, orange, or red, usually from late spring.
CULTIVATION: Hardiness varies; most species are intolerant of repeated frosts. Plant in an open sunny position in gritty, very free-draining soil with a little extra humus. Water when in flower, otherwise allow to survive on natural rainfall. Propagate from seed or cuttings or by layering.

Drosanthemum speciosum ★

☼ ❀ ↔ 40 in (100 cm) ↕ 24 in (60 cm)
From South Africa's Cape region. A shrub with upright branching stems. Leaves have a crystalline surface. Flowers are deep orange-red, occasionally purplish, green center, large, with many petals, giving a plumed effect. Zones 9–11.

DUDLEYA

This genus comprises some 40 species of rosette-forming perennials from southwestern USA and western Mexico. Members of the stonecrop (Crassulaceae) family, they are closely allied to *Echeveria*, in which genus they were once included. Many have gray or gray-green foliage, often with a powdery white bloom. The foliage withers with age but may remain attached to the plant. The flower stems tend to be upright, sometimes branching, and carry many small 5-petalled flowers, usually in spring. Old plants often have rosettes that have developed thickened stems or short trunks.
CULTIVATION: Although many species tolerate moderate frost, they need mild winters as they tend to grow during the cooler months. They usually do best when placed in full sun but may need a little shade inland. Water in autumn and spring but keep dry at other times. Rotting is the most common cause of failure, so be sure to plant in gritty free-draining soil. Propagate from seed, from offsets, or by division.

Dudleya farinosa

Dudleya attenuata

☼ ❊ ↔ 16–24 in (40–60 cm) ↕ 12–16 in (30–40 cm)
Native to California, USA, and Baja California, Mexico. A low-growing plant with narrow, cylindrical, powdery, gray- to blue-green leaves in open rosettes. Yellow flowers on branching stems. *D. a.* subsp. *orcuttii*, white flowers, tinted with pink. Zones 8–11.

Dudleya candelabrum

☼ ❊ ↔ 14 in (35 cm) ↕ 14 in (35 cm)
A native of California, USA, including some of the islands. This plant usually forms a single short-stemmed rosette of powdery gray-green leaves. Many small, soft yellow flowers are borne on stocky flower stems. Zones 8–11.

Dudleya farinosa

☼ ❊ ↔ 16–20 in (40–50 cm) ↕ 8–12 in (20–30 cm)
From the coast of California north to Oregon, USA. Branching at the base to form a clump of small, powder-coated, blue-green rosettes that develop strong red tints in the sun. Flower stems are usually short, with bright yellow flowers. Zones 8–10.

Dudleya pulverulenta

CHALK LETTUCE
☼ ❊ ↔ 20 in (50 cm) ↕ 40 in (100 cm)
Native to California, USA, and Baja California, Mexico. Usually forms a solitary rosette. Leaves broad, yellow-green with powdery white bloom. Sturdy flower stems with branching heads of red flowers. Zones 9–11.

ECHEVERIA

This genus of about 150 species of rosette-forming succulents in the stonecrop (Crassulaceae) family is found mainly in Mexico, with a few from Central America. It was named after Atanasio Echeverria Codoy, an eighteenth-century Spanish botanical artist.

Echeveria agavoides

Though superficially similar to, and sometimes confused with *Sempervivum*, *Echeveria* are generally far less frost hardy but more drought tolerant than their European cousins. Apart from a few species that are shrubby or more leafy and perennial-like, all form spiraling rosettes of flattened but fleshy, pointed, spoon-shaped leaves. The flowers, usually appearing in spring and early summer, are borne on short stems, either along the stem or in branching heads, and are simple, bell-shaped, 5-petalled, structures, often in shades of pink, red, yellow, or orange.
CULTIVATION: Most *Echeveria* species prefer full sun and mild winters with only light frosts. They may require some shade in very hot inland areas. Plant in light, gritty, very free-draining soil. Water in spring and when they are flowering, but otherwise keep dry, especially in winter. Propagate from seed or offsets, or by division.

Echeveria agavoides ★

☼ ❊ ↔ 8–12 in (20–30 cm) ↕ 6–8 in (15–20 cm)
This species forms clumps of small short-stemmed rosettes with red-edged light gray-green to blue-green leaves, to 3 in (8 cm) long. The forked inflorescence bears ½ in (12 mm) long orange-pink flowers, yellow inside. *E. a.* f. *cristata* has rosettes with many small leaves in rows across the center; *E. a.* var. *corderoyi* (syn. *E. a.* 'Red Edge') produces rosettes with numerous small leaves, inflorescence has 3 branches and smaller flowers. Zones 9–11.

Echeveria elegans ★

MEXICAN SNOWBALL, WHITE MEXICAN ROSE
☼ ❊ ↔ 12–16 in (30–40 cm) ↕ 6–8 in (15–20 cm)
Clusters of short-stemmed densely foliaged rosettes, 4 in (10 cm) wide, with pale gray-green leaves, to 2¾ in (65 mm) long, coated with a white powder. Simple 4–6 in (10–15 cm) long inflorescence with as many as 10 golden-centered deep pink flowers. 'Kesselringii' has globular rosettes of blue-gray leaves. Zones 9–11.

Echeveria gigantea 'Dee'

Echeveria pulvinata

Echeveria, Hybrid Cultivar, 'Morning Light'

Echeveria gibbiflora

☀ ❄ ↔ 20 in (50 cm) ↕ 48 in (120 cm)

Open rosettes, to 20 in (50 cm) in diameter, on unbranched stems, to 12 in (30 cm) tall. Leaves are broad, purple-tinted, wavy-edged, powdery, pale blue-green, to 14 in (35 cm) long. The branching inflorescence, to 36 in (100 cm) tall, has soft, brown-centered, red flowers that are backed by lavender calyces through the autumn–winter. *E. g.* var. *carunculata,* pale leaves, heavily distorted and covered with protuberances; *E. g.* var. *metallica,* silvery gray foliage with a metallic sheen. Zones 9–11.

Echeveria gigantea ★

☀ ❄ ↔ 20 in (50 cm) ↕ 5–7 ft (1.5–2 m)

Winter-flowering species with loose open rosettes, up to 16 in (40 cm) across, on unbranched stems, to 20 in (50 cm) tall. Leaves purple-edged, pale green, spatula-shaped, to 8 in (20 cm) long. Branching inflorescence, to 7 ft (2 m) tall, with deep pink-red flowers, over ½ in (12 mm) long. 'Dee', rosettes with broad blue-green leaves ageing red in the sun. Zones 10–12.

Echeveria × *imbricata* ★

☀ ❄ ↔ 12–16 in (30–40 cm) ↕ 12–16 in (30–40 cm)

Short-stemmed cup-shaped rosettes, to 10 in (20 cm) wide, with broad but thin gray-green to silver-gray leaves. Features branching inflorescences with yellow-centered deep pink flowers, up to ½ in (12 mm) long. Zones 9–12.

Echeveria pulvinata

CHENILLE PLANT, PLUSH PLANT

☀ ❄ ↔ 12–20 in (30–50 cm) ↕ 12–16 in (30–40 cm)

Branching stems forming dense mounding clusters of small rosettes with many finely downy, red-tinted, green to blue-green leaves, about 2 in (5 cm) long. Inflorescence, 8–12 in (20–30 cm) long, with up to 15 red-edged golden yellow to orange flowers from mid-winter. 'Ruby', velvety-textured red leaves. Zones 9–11.

Echeveria setosa

MEXICAN FIRECRACKER

☀ ❄ ↔ 12–16 in (30–40 cm) ↕ 8–12 in (20–30 cm)

Small clumping species, which forms 4–6 in (10–15 cm) wide rosettes of 2 in (5 cm) long green leaves covered with fine white hairs, becoming bristly with age. Inflorescence is 12 in (30 cm) long, with up to 10 red-tipped yellow flowers. Zones 9–11.

Echeveria Hybrid Cultivars

☀ ❄ ↔ 4–18 in (10–45 cm) ↕ 6–24 in (15–60 cm)

Many species hybridize freely, and garden hybrids are available in a wide range of sizes, flower colors, and growth forms. 'Arlie Wright', large gray leaves flushed with pink, heavily crimped edges, and a single rosette, to 16 in (40 cm) across; 'Dondo', an *E. dehrenbergii* × *E. setosa* hybrid, rosettes of gray-blue leaves with scalloped and pointed tips, golden yellow flowers; 'Fire Light' ★, rosette of broad leaves, blue-green rapidly ageing to deep glossy red, with frilled edges; 'Kirchneriana', massed 4 in (10 cm) wide pale powdery blue-gray rosettes, narrow leafy stems with small heads of orange-tipped yellow flowers in spring; 'Lace', similar but with more complexly frilled leaves; 'Morning Light' ★, clusters of small blue-green rosettes edged with pink; 'Powder Blue' ★, light blue-green rosettes, to 6 in (15 cm) across, light orange flowers; 'Princess Lace', pale green rosettes, to 12 in (30 cm) across, with the edges red and heavily crimped; 'Pulv-oliver', a shrubby *E. pulvinata* × *E. harmsii* hybrid, to 20 in (50 cm) tall, with small open rosettes of red-tinted, downy, light green leaves and soft orange flowers; 'Set-oliver' ★, an *E. harmsii* × *E. setosa* hybrid with rosettes of downy, thickened, red-tinted, light green leaves and orange-red flowers on 16 in (40 cm) tall inflorescences; 'Violet Queen' ★, clusters of 6 in (15 cm) wide, pink-edged, pale blue-green rosettes. The **Galaxy Series** are similar to 'Pulv-oliver' and 'Set-oliver', and bear flowers in a range of brilliant orange-reds with varying amounts of yellow on the petal tips. Zones 9–11.

ECHINOCACTUS

This genus in the cactus (Cactaceae) family, as now understood, comprises just 5 species native to Mexico and southwestern USA. Globular in growth habit for many years, with prominent spiny ribs and a woolly crown, most eventually become columnar, though none grow to any great height. In cultivation they are favored for their slow growth and symmetry. Flowers are usually in shades of yellow or pink, and tend to be short and not very spectacular, though they bloom for a long time in summer.
CULTIVATION: Tolerant of occasional light frosts but inclined to rot in damp conditions, especially in winter. Plant in light, very gritty,

free-draining soil. Water in summer but otherwise keep dry. Most grow best in full sun but some may need light shade in hot inland areas. Offsets are few but can be propagated; or raise from seed.

Echinocactus grusonii
GOLDEN BARREL CACTUS, MOTHER-IN-LAW'S CHAIR

☼ ⚥ ↔ 32 in (80 cm) ↑ 50 in (130 cm)

From central Mexico. Stems usually solitary, globular for many years. Crown very woolly; offsets rare. Up to 40 ribs with closely spaced areoles bearing many yellow spines, to 2 in (5 cm) long. Flowers yellow, brown at the tip, clustered around the crown. **Zones 9–12.**

Echinocactus polycephalus
☼ ⚥ ↔ 12–24 in (30–60 cm) ↑ 12–24 in (30–60 cm)

From northwestern Mexico and southwestern USA. Clumps of spherical to short cylindrical stems, each to 8 in (20 cm) wide, numerous 2–3 in (5–8 cm) long curved spines interwoven to form a dense matrix. Flowers yellow with faint pink stripes. **Zones 9–11.**

ECHINOCEREUS
HEDGEHOG CACTUS

This genus comprises about 60 species of cacti (family Cactaceae) found in Mexico and southern USA. The name comes from the Greek *echinos*, a hedgehog, and Latin/Greek *cereus*, a candle or taper, referring to the commonly occurring combination of densely packed spines and showy flowers. Most form clumps of cylindrical stems, which are sometimes elongated and may spread across the ground or clamber over low objects. The flowers form near the top of the stem, often developing from woolly areoles. Most open in spring or summer, and are usually large in comparison to the plant and often brightly colored or strikingly marked. CULTIVATION: Hardiness varies, but none will tolerate repeated hard freezes. Plant in light, gritty, very free-draining soil; keep dry in winter. Best grown in full sun, though in inland continental areas they may need shade from the hottest summer sun. Propagate from seed, offsets, or from stem cuttings.

Echinocereus engelmannii ★
STRAWBERRY HEDGEHOG CACTUS

☼ ✱ ↔ 12–20 in (30–50 cm) ↑ 12–20 in (30–50 cm)

From the western USA–Mexico border region. Clustering, upright, narrow, cylindrical stems with ribs densely covered with fine spines, to over 2 in (5 cm) long. Flowers are magenta to lavender, to 3½ in (9 cm) across, in summer. **Zones 7–11.**

Echinocereus pectinatus ★
☼ ⚥ ↔ 6–16 in (15–40 cm) ↑ 14 in (35 cm)

From southwestern USA and northern Mexico. Clusters of spherical to short cylindrical stems, rarely branched, to 5 in (12 cm) wide, 12 or more ribs carrying many light brown interlacing spines, to 1 in (25 mm) long. Flowers are green-centered white or pink to red-brown, to about 4 in (10 cm) wide, in summer. *E. p.* **var.** *dasyacanthus* (syn. *E. dasyacanthus*), yellow or white flowers. **Zones 9–11.**

Echinocereus pentalophus ★
LADY FINGER CACTUS

☼ ⚥ ↔ 20 in–7 ft (50 cm–2 m) ↑ 8–12 in (20–30 cm)

Found from eastern Mexico to Texas, USA. Clustering, narrow, sometimes sprawling, cylindrical stems with few ribs and a mix of spines ranging from very short to 2½ in (6 cm) long. Stems often red-tinted in sun. Deep pink flowers with a white to yellow-green throat, to 6 in (15 cm) across, in summer. **Zones 9–11.**

Echinocereus rigidissimus ★
☼ ⚥ ↔ 4 in (10 cm) ↑ 8 in (20 cm)

From northwestern Mexico to Arizona, USA. Solitary cylindrical stem, rarely branched, with 15 or more ribs bearing woolly tubercles, often pink-tinted, with many small spines held flat to the stem. White-centered pink to crimson flowers, to 3 in (8 cm) across, in early summer. **Zones 9–11.**

Echinocereus triglochidiatus ★
CLARET CUP

☼ ✱ ↔ 8–20 in (20–50 cm) ↑ 12–16 in (30–40 cm)

From the western USA–Mexico border region. Stems solitary or clumping, ovate to cylindrical, with about 10 ribs bearing woolly areoles with short radial spines around a central spine to nearly 2¾ in (7 cm) long. Long-tubed bright red flowers, to over 2 in (5 cm) across, in summer. *E. t.* **var.** *gurneyi*, compact form from the Chihuahuan desert grasslands; *E. t.* **var.** *melanacanthus* (syn. *E. coccineus*), found among mountain pines, forming mounds of up to several hundred small stems. **Zones 6–11.**

Echinocereus viridiflorus
☼ ✱ ↔ 4–12 in (10–30 cm) ↑ 2–5 in (5–12 cm)

From southwestern USA. Clusters of short, ovate to cylindrical stems with up to 12 ribs largely hidden beneath many fine needle-like spines. Flowers many-petalled, yellow-green, citrus-scented, to 1¼ in (30 mm) across, in summer. *E. v.* **subsp.** *davisii*, dwarf variety, only 1 in (25 mm) tall, often has solitary stems. **Zones 4–11.**

Echinocereus rigidissimus

Echinopsis backebergii

ECHINOPSIS

syns *Chamaecereus, Helianthocereus, Lobivia, Trichocereus*
EASTER LILY CACTUS, SEA URCHIN CACTUS

Species in this South American cactus genus (family Cactaceae) encompass a wide range of forms, from small, cylindrical, and clustering to tree-like with strong branching trunks. The genus has been expanded to include the species formerly placed in *Lobivia* and *Trichocereus*; it now comprises up to 120 species. Most have cylindrical stems with clearly defined ribs, and some also have tubercles bearing areoles with conspicuous and often fierce spines. Some species have spectacular, long-tubed, funnel-shaped flowers that are large in comparison to the plant. These are known as Easter lily cacti because they may bloom as early as Easter in the Northern Hemisphere, though their main flowering season is early to mid-summer. Some species are night-blooming, with attractive, fragrant, white flowers; others are day-blooming, with unscented flowers that occur in various shades of red, pink, yellow, or orange. CULTIVATION: As with most cacti, plant in full sun/half-sun in very free-draining, light, gritty soil and water well in summer but keep dry during winter. Most species will tolerate only occasional light frosts. Propagate from offsets where it is appropriate, from stem cuttings of the branching types, or from seed.

Echinopsis backebergii

syns *Echinopsis wrightiana, Lobivia wrightiana*
☼ ⚘ ↔ 4–8 in (10–20 cm) ↑ 6 in (15 cm)
Found in Peru and Bolivia. Forms clusters of dark gray-green, spherical stems with up to 15 ribs bearing short curved spines. Produces pink to violet flowers, to 4 in (10 cm) in diameter, often exceeding the stem width, in summer. Zones 10–12.

Echinopsis chamaecereus

syns *Chamaecereus silvestris, Lobivia silvestrii*
PEANUT CACTUS
☼ ⚘ ↔ 12 in (30 cm) ↑ 4 in (10 cm)
From Argentina. Mat-forming, with freely branching cylindrical stems, to 12 in (30 cm), and numerous lateral stems, 1–4 in (20–100 mm) long. Low ribs and tiny spines on stems. Orange-red flowers, to 2 in (5 cm) across, in early summer. Zones 9–11.

Echinopsis hertrichiana

syns *Lobivia incaiaca, L. hertrichiana*
☼ ⚘ ↔ 6–12 in (15–30 cm) ↑ 6–16 in (15–40 cm)
From Peru. Stems often solitary, spherical, becoming columnar and clustered with great age. Up to 22 deep ribs with small woolly areoles and few spines to 1¼ in (30 mm) long. Bright red flowers, about 2 in (5 cm) long and across. Zones 10–12.

Echinopsis huascha ★

syns *Lobivia huascha, Trichocereus andalgalensis*
☼ ⚘ ↔ 24 in (60 cm) ↑ 24 in (60 cm)
From Argentina. The stems are clustering, cylindrical, upright, sprawling, branching, to 2 in (5 cm) in diameter. Up to 17 ribs and many fine needle-like spines, to 3 in (8 cm) long. The floral areoles are densely hairy, opening to bright orange-red or yellow flowers, to 4 in (10 cm) long and 3 in (8 cm) across. Zones 9–11.

Echinopsis oxygona ★

syn. *Echinopsis multiplex*
☼ ⚘ ↔ 12–24 in (30–60 cm) ↑ 12 in (30 cm)
From southern Brazil and northern Argentina. Clusters of spherical to short cylindrical stems, to 6 in (15 cm) in diameter, with up to 15 ribs bearing spines to 1 in (25 mm) long. Green-tubed red flowers, to 10 in (25 cm) long and 4 in (10 cm) across, appear in summer. Cristate forms are common. Zones 9–11.

Echinopsis spachiana ★

syn. *Trichocereus spachianus*
GOLDEN TORCH CEREUS
☼ ⚘ ↔ 40 in (100 cm) ↑ 5–7 ft (1.5–2 m)
A native of Argentina. Shrubby species with tall cylindrical stems, each to 4 in (10 cm) in diameter, branching at the base, and 10 to 15 ribs with sturdy spines, to 2 in (5 cm) long. White flowers, to 10 in (25 cm) long and 6 in (15 cm) across. Zones 9–12.

Echinopsis Hybrid Cultivars

syns × *Chamaelobivia* Hybrid Cultivars, × *Lobivopsis* Hybrid Cultivars
☼ ⚘ ↔ 6–12 in (15–30 cm) ↑ 6–18 in (15–45 cm)
Most *Echinopsis* hybrid cultivars have been bred for their large flowers and glowing colors; they are derived from the large-flowered day-blooming species, including some formerly classified under *Lobivia*. Some such hybrids were thus treated as bigeneric hybrids. 'Arizona' produces crowded, large, funnel-shaped flowers, with apricot shading to yellow centers, and ageing dull pinkish; 'Chico Mendes' forms a compact mounding plant, with flowers to 5 in (13 cm) across, opening almost flat; petals are broad, and pinkish orange with deeper pink at the edges; 'Samantha Smith' has clustering short stems, and bears large flowers of apricot shading to a deeper color in the center. Zones 9–12.

EPIPHYLLUM

This genus consists of 19 species of epiphytic and lithophytic cacti (family Cactaceae) from Mexico, Central America, northern South America, and the Caribbean. Named from the Greek *epi*, upon, and *phyllon*, leaf, referring to the very large, white, night-blooming

flowers, borne on leaf-like stems. While many plants in collections and nurseries are labeled orchid cacti or *Epiphyllum* hybrids, the term orchid cactus is more correctly applied to hybrids of the genera *Selenicereus, Schlumbergera, Disocactus,* and *Pseudorhipsalis;* their flowers are neither night-blooming nor white. Many so-called *Epiphyllum* hybrids have no *Epiphyllum* ancestry. Stems of true *Epiphyllum* species are usually long and bear aerial roots; they are round in cross-section in the lower part but usually flattened and leaf-like toward the tips, with scalloped or toothed margins. Flowers often have very long floral tubes; outer perianth segments whitish, yellowish, or pinkish, inner petal-like ones pale yellow or white. Seed pods are oval to ovate, ridged, and spineless.
CULTIVATION: Easily grown in well-drained, rich, organic soil. Fertilize when flower buds forming; may also be lightly fertilized during growing period. Withhold water for 1 to 2 weeks after flowering. Propagate from seed or, more usually, from cuttings dried out for a week or two.

Epiphyllum oxypetalum

Epiphyllum oxypetalum ★
☼ ✿ ↔ 5–10 ft (1.5–3 m) ↑ 5–10 ft (1.5–3 m)
From Mexico and Central America. Profuse arching to pendent branches. Main stems flattened at tips, thin, with scalloped wavy margins. White funnel-shaped flowers, 5–7 in (12–17 cm) across, borne on long curved tubes with maroon-colored outer segments, summer. Crimson-red seed pods, fragrant when ripe. Zones 10–12.

ESPOSTOA
A genus of 16 beautiful columnar cacti from Bolivia, Ecuador, and Peru in the family Cactaceae. The genus was named in honor of the early twentieth century Peruvian botanist, Nicholas Esposto. Plants are shrubby to columnar and bear a long lateral cephalium on mature branches. Young plants are often clothed in a dense web of white wool, which protects them from their very harsh desert environment. The cylindrical branches bear many ribs. The night-blooming flowers are usually creamy white to reddish. Seed pods are spherical, juicy, and red to green, and may be naked or covered in tufts of hair. The genus now includes all former species of *Thrixanthocereus* and *Pseudoespostoa* and some species of *Facheiroa.*
CULTIVATION: These cacti are easily grown in a rich well-drained soil; withhold water in winter to avoid root rot. Grows faster in open ground than in pots. Propagate either from seed or from cuttings dried out for a week or two.

Espostoa lanata ★
COTTON BALL CACTUS, OLD MAN OF THE ANDES
☼ ❧ ↔ 3–10 ft (0.9–3 m) ↑ 7–25 ft (2–8 m)
Popular cactus from southern Ecuador to northern Peru. Columnar to shrubby, erect stems clothed in white wool, especially noticeable on seedlings. Ribs 20 to 25; central spines sparse, to 2 in (50 mm) long, often absent, radials numerous, short. Cephalium light gray to brown wool, to 15 ft (4.5 m) long. Purple funnelform flowers 1¼ in (30 mm) across; pear-shaped seed pods plum-colored. Zones 9–11.

Espostoa senilis ★
☼ ❧ ↔ 3–7 ft (0.9–2 m) ↑ 7–15 ft (2–4.5 m)
A native of Ancash in Peru. Shrubby to tree-like plants. Branches are gray-green and covered with brownish white hairs. Ribs 16 to 18. The 1 to 3 central spines are brown, up to 1¼ in (30 mm) long; the 60 or more radial spines are white, to ½ in (12 mm) long. Purple flowers, to 2½ in (6 cm) long and 1¾ in (40 mm) in diameter. Spherical green seed pods, up to ¾ in (18 mm) in diameter. Zones 9–11.

EUPHORBIA (see page 462)

Euphorbia caput-medusae ★
MEDUSA'S HEAD
☼/◐ ❧ ↔ 48 in (120 cm) ↑ 12 in (30 cm)
Species from South Africa. A succulent shrub with many spreading, tubercle-studded, cylindrical stems radiating from a central caudex, like the snakes on Medusa's head. Stems broaden at the tip, bearing tiny, often short-lived, linear leaves. Unusual cream flowerheads featuring fimbriated snowflake-shaped cyathia. Zones 9–10.

Euphorbia cooperi ★
TRANSVAAL CANDELABRA TREE
☼ ❧ ↔ 6 ft (1.8 m) ↑ 15 ft (4.5 m)
From southern and eastern Africa. Succulent tree with upwardly arching segmented branches, usually pentagonal in shape. Pairs of buff-colored spines accentuate margins. The small yellowish flowers arise between them usually in autumn–spring. Zones 9–11.

Euphorbia grandicornis ★
BIG-HORN EUPHORBIA, COW'S HORN EUPHORBIA
☼ ❄ ↔ 3 ft (0.9 m) ↑ 6 ft (1.8 m)
From southern Africa. A succulent species that is well armed with spines, up to 3 in (8 cm) long, which arise in pairs along the uneven margins of the upright, bright green, triangular branches. Flowers with very small yellowish green floral bracts appear between the spines. Zones 8–11.

Euphorbia cooperi, in the wild, South Africa

Euphorbia × lomii

GIANT CROWN OF THORNS

☼/◑ ⚘ ↔ 40 in (100 cm) ↑ 40 in (100 cm)

A garden hybrid between two Madagascan species, *E. lophogona* and *E. milii*. Very like the common crown of thorns, *E. milii*, but generally shorter, with broader stems. Densely prickly; light green leaves, to 6 in (15 cm) long, red-tinted in the sun. Salmon to red flowerheads and bracts occur at any time except during periods of severe drought. The **Somona Range** includes various flower colors, such as pale pink '**Merle**' and cerise '**Rosemarie**'. Zones 10–12.

Euphorbia milii ★

CROWN OF THORNS

☼ ◗ ↔ 2–8 ft (0.6–2.4 m) ↑ 1–3 ft (0.3–0.9 m)

From Madagascar. Erect or scrambling shrub, sparsely foliaged, bright green leaves near branch tips. Stems prickly. Tiny yellow flowers with bright red floral bracts appearing intermittently for long periods. *E. m.* var. *splendens* (syn. *E. splendens*), commonly cultivated, mound of tangled branches to 2 ft (0.6 m), pinkish red bracts; *E. m.* f. *lutea* ★, cream bracts. Zones 9–11.

Euphorbia neriifolia

HEDGE EUPHORBIA, OLEANDER SPURGE

☼ ⚘ ↔ 4 ft (1.2 m) ↑ 20 ft (6 m)

From India and Southeast Asia. Semi-succulent shrub or small tree. The whorled fresh green branches carry leathery spoon-like leaves near the tips. Flowerheads, with yellowish green bracts, in spring. The sap from this species has been used as a fish poison in India. Zones 10–12.

Euphorbia obesa ★

BASEBALL PLANT, GINGHAM GOLF BALL, KLIPNOORS

☼/◑ ◗ ↔ 6 in (15 cm) ↑ 8 in (20 cm)

From South Africa. Small succulent. Flat-topped cylindrical stem, near-spherical when young, green with faint purple banding, and tubercle-studded ribbing reminiscent of baseball stitching. Green flowerheads, mainly near stem tips, usually in spring to early summer. Zones 9–11.

Euphorbia obesa

Euphorbia × lomii

Euphorbia tirucalli

FINGER TREE, MILK BUSH, PENCIL BUSH, PENCIL TREE, RUBBER HEDGE

☼ ⚘ ↔ 7–12 ft (2–3.5 m) ↑ 15–30 ft (4.5–9 m)

Species from tropical and southern Africa, and India east to Indonesia. Large shrub or small tree with a dense crown of succulent, pale green, cylindrical branches. Small, short-lived, lance-shaped leaves. Insignificant flowers. Can be invasive. Zones 10–12.

Euphorbia trigona

☼ ◗ ↔ 12–24 in (30–60 cm) ↑ 3–8 ft (0.9–2.4 m)

From Namibia. Succulent cactus-like shrub. Branches all erect, 3-cornered, dark green mottled with white, with vertical ranks of spoon-shaped leaves and short reddish brown spines. Often seen as a house plant. '**Green Angel**' ★, stems and leaves always plain green; '**Red Devil**' ★, attractive cultivar with red leaves. Zones 9–11.

FEROCACTUS

BARREL CACTUS

A genus of 29 species of barrel-shaped cacti (family Cactaceae) from semi-arid areas of southwestern USA and Mexico, especially Baja California. The name refers to the strong stout spines, which are often savagely hooked. *Ferocactus* is distinguished from the closely related genus *Echinocactus* by the absence of wool at the growing tip. Most are solitary, a few branch, and some form mats and grow to massive proportions. Stems are spherical to columnar to barrel-shaped. Ribs range from few to many, often very deep and prominent. The large areoles usually have glands that secrete nectar that is attractive to ants and other insects. Flowers form near the growing tip and are short, funnelform or bell-shaped, with prominent scales. Seed pods are oval to spherical, dry or juicy at maturity. **CULTIVATION:** *Ferocactus* species are relatively easy to grow in rich, very well-drained, predominantly mineral soil, with moderate watering in warmer months but a distinct rest in winter. Full sun and low humidity are essential for good spination. Being mainly solitary, theses cacti are almost invariably raised from seed.

Ferocactus cylindraceus

syns *Ferocactus acanthodes*, *F. lecontei*, *F. tortulispinus*

CALIFORNIA BARREL CACTUS, COMPASS-CACTUS

☼ ◗ ↔ 20 in (50 cm) ↑ 10 ft (3 m)

From southern California, Nevada, Utah, and Arizona, USA, and Baja California and Sonora, Mexico. Solitary, spherical to cylindrical, 20 to 30 ribs with tubercles, slightly wavy ribs with transverse creases. Spines white, yellow, red, or gray; 10 centrals, 4 to 12 radials. Flowers bell-shaped, red, yellow, or orange. Seed pods yellow. Zones 9–11.

Ferocactus emoryi

syn. *Ferocactus covillei*

☼ ◗ ↔ 3 ft (0.9 m) ↑ 8 ft (2.4 m)

From central Arizona, USA, and Sonora, Sinaloa, and Baja California Sur, Mexico. Solitary, spherical to cylindrical, light to bluish green with 15 to 30 ribs, distinctly tuberculed when young. Spines whitish to reddish; 1 central, 7 to 9 radials. Flowers funnelform, mahogany red to red, tinged with yellow. Seed pods oval. *F. e.* **subsp. *rectispinus*,** smaller stems, 21 ribs. Zones 9–11.

Ferocactus glaucescens ★

☼ ❊ ↔ 20 in (50 cm) ↑ 18 in (45 cm)

From Hidalgo, Mexico. Solitary to many-stemmed, with slightly depressed tops, distinctly powdery pale bluish gray-green, 12 to 17 ribs, no tubercles, long merging areoles. Spines awl-shaped, yellow, 1 central, 6 to 7 radials. Flowers bell-shaped, yellow. Seed pods spherical, whitish or yellowish. Zones 9–11.

Ferocactus latispinus ★

☼ ❊ ↔ 16 in (40 cm) ↑ 12 in (30 cm)

From much of central Mexico. Solitary, light green, spherical to flattened, 20 or more deep tuberculed ribs. Spines reddish to yellowish to white; 4 centrals, 5 to 15 radials. Flowers funnelform, purplish pink or yellow, densely overlapping, fringed bracts. Seed pods oval, covered with scales. Zones 9–11.

Ferocactus wislizeni ★

ARIZONA BARREL CACTUS, CANDY BARREL-CACTUS

☼ ❊ ↔ 32 in (80 cm) ↑ 10 ft (3 m)

A cactus from central and southern Arizona, southern New Mexico, southwest Texas, USA, and northwest Mexico. Solitary giant, 20 to 30 ribs, barely tuberculed, widely spaced areoles when young, merging with age. Spines variable, white to red to gray, 4 centrals; 12 or so radials. Flowers funnelform, yellow to yellowish orange. Seed pods oval, green, turning yellow when ripe. The native Seri peoples of Mexico have used the spines as fishhooks, the flesh to make candies, and the dried floral remains as a dye for face paint. Zones 9–11.

FOUQUIERIA

This genus of 11 species of woody or succulent, spiny, deciduous shrubs and small trees occurs in arid regions in the southwest of North America, such as Baja California, Mexico. It is a member of the ocotillo (Fouquieriaceae) family. Small bright green leaves emerge after the irregular rains of those regions. All species have spines along the stems and branches. Some grow as columnar unbranched stems up to 50 ft (15 m) tall. Red, purple, cream, or yellow tubular flowers are produced at the tips of branches or stems after rain, usually in spring; they are followed by capsules that contain winged seeds.

CULTIVATION: They require full sun, in climates similar to those where they occur naturally. Too much rain, or over-watering, can be fatal. Since all species are frost tender when young, propagate from seed or cuttings in late spring to summer.

Fouquieria splendens ★

OCOTILLO

☼ ❄ ↔ 6 ft (1.8 m) ↑ 30 ft (9 m)

Occurs in the arid regions of northern Mexico, and southern California, New Mexico, and Texas, USA. Many-branched shrub; long, cylindrical, gray-green, spiny stems. Small green leaves

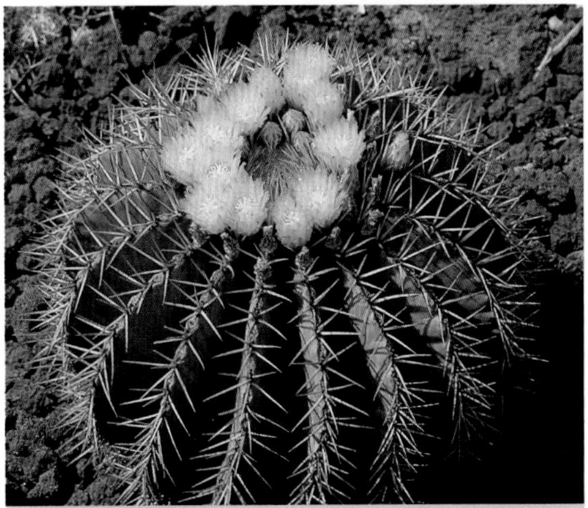

Ferocactus glaucescens

appear after rain, falling during long dry periods. Panicles of bell-shaped bright red flowers, in early spring–summer. Zones 7–11.

FURCRAEA

syn. *Fourcroya*

Up to 20 species have been credited to this genus of evergreen succulents in the agave (Agavaceae) family from Central and South America and the West Indies, but there may be far fewer. Like agaves, they have rosettes of sword-like leaves, ending in a spine and usually with prickly edges. The flowers have a shorter tube and more spreading petals. A trunk may develop below the rosette, and lateral shoots sprout from the plant base or the trunk. An inflorescence ends the life of a rosette, but may take several decades to appear; some are extremely tall. Once flowering finishes, the inflorescence usually develops aerial plantlets that eventually fall and take root.

CULTIVATION: *Furcraea* species are among the toughest of plants, and in warm climates they will grow and multiply with no attention paid to them at all. They have become invasive in some tropical countries. In cold climates they can be grown under glass, but they require a lot of space at maturity. Propagation is from offsets, aerial plantlets, or seed.

Furcraea bedinghausii

syn. *Furcraea roezlii*

☼ ❄ ↔ 4–7 ft (1.2–2 m) ↑ 4–7 ft (1.2–2 m)

A succulent perennial from Mexico. Features rosettes of bluish sword-shaped leaves with soft tips, forming a ball that eventually develops a trunk. Inflorescences of green flowers appear on tall stems. Zones 8–10.

Furcraea selloa

☼ ❄ ↔ 4–7 ft (1.2–2 m) ↑ 4–7 ft (1.2–2 m)

Succulent perennial from Mexico and Guatemala. Forms dense rosettes of 30 to 40 bright green leaves, with horny spines along the edges. Faintly scented white flowers flushed with green. *F. s.* f. ***marginata*** has white or yellow leaf edges. Zones 8–10.

Gasteria glomerata

Gibbaeum pilosulum

Glottiphyllym linguiforme

GASTERIA

These 15 or so compact, short-stemmed, succulent perennials, native to South Africa, belong to the asphodel (Asphodelaceae) family; the genus is closely allied to *Aloe*. The thick, fleshy, dark green leaves are spirally arranged in tight compact rosettes, and the pendulous, pink to vermilion, tubular flowers appear in simple or branched racemes. Fruit is a capsule; seeds are winged to aid dispersal. The genus name comes from the Greek word for stomach.
CULTIVATION: Easily grown in light, sandy, well-drained soil in a protected spot with sun or part-shade. Provide moderate water in summer, keep drier in winter. Propagate from leaf cuttings, or by dividing offsets and plantlets at stem tops.

Gasteria bicolor
DWARF GASTERIA
☼/◐ ✤ ↔ 16 in (40 cm) ↑ 16 in (40 cm)
From Eastern Cape. Smooth, strap-shaped, dark green leaves, 1¼–9 in (3–22 cm) long, rounded or pointed ends, arise from base, forming dense groups of up to 10 or more plants. Simple elongated raceme, 6–16 in (15–40 cm) in height, with reddish pink flowers, in spring–summer. Seed capsule contains small black seeds. *G. b.* var. *liliputana* (syn. *G. liliputana*), dwarf form, leaves spotted with white, to 2½ in (6 cm) long. Zones 9–11.

Gasteria glomerata
◐ ✤ ↔ 3 in (8 cm) ↑ 1½ in (4 cm)
A clump-forming perennial. Forms rosettes of dark green leaves. Orange-red flowers on spikes. Zones 9–10.

GIBBAEUM
syns *Imitaria, Muiria*
A genus of 17 species of succulent plants from the Karoo and Western Cape regions in South Africa in the iceplant (Aizoaceae) family. They are compact, rarely cushion-forming, plants with often thickened but rarely fleshy rhizomes and roots. The 3-angled leaves have green to grayish white surfaces; the long and weakly united leaves found on some species resemble a shark's head. Stalked single flowers come in different shades of purple, pink, or white; calyx is a 6-lobed tube, in some species united with the 6 petals. Up to 200 to 300 stamens, along with many staminodes, form a central cone in the flower. The capsule usually has 6 compartments.

CULTIVATION: These succulents require full sun and low humidity with no water during the resting period. Best grown under cover even in warm regions. They require very sharply drained compost to minimize the risk of splitting of leaves or root rot. Propagate from seed or from cuttings allowed to dry before rooting.

Gibbaeum dispar
☼/◐ ✤ ↔ 4–6 in (10–15 cm) ↑ 4–6 in (10–15 cm)
Erect, sturdy, clump-forming stem. Unequal pairs of leaves form a velvety, slightly glossy, egg-shaped body, gray-green tinged with red, with a deep fissure. The open, daisy-like, mauve-red to pink flowers are about ¼ in (6 mm) across. Zones 9–11.

Gibbaeum pilosulum
syns *Conophytum pilosulum, Mesembryanthemum pilosulum*
☼/◐ ✤ ↔ 8 in (20 cm) ↑ 3–5 in (8–12 cm)
Mat-forming; fused leaves form slightly glossy, light green, egg-shaped bodies, covered with fine white hairs, with a small notch in the top of each. Small mauve-red flowers in winter. Zones 9–12.

GLOTTIPHYLLUM
This genus of around 60 species from the Karoo and Cape regions of South Africa belongs to the iceplant (Aizoaceae) family. They are compact succulent plants with semi-prostrate forking stems. The leaves are very fleshy, tongue-shaped or cylindrical, sometimes of different lengths, in 2 or 4 ranks, bright glossy green or whitish, sometimes tinged purple. The single yellow flowers, sometimes stalked, are borne in summer.
CULTIVATION: Easily grown in low-fertility compost as long as it is well drained; little watering is required. Too much water or too many nutrients lead to lush watery leaves that are prone to damage from handling, rots, and winter cold. Plant in full sun and keep completely dry from late summer until spring. Propagate from seed or cuttings, allowing them to dry out well before rooting.

Glottiphyllym linguiforme
syns *Mesembryanthemum linguiforme, M. lucidum, M. scalpratum*
☼ ✤ ↔ 8 in (20 cm) ↑ 3–5 in (8–12 cm)
Mat-forming perennial with pairs of curved, glossy, fleshy, apple green, unequal leaves, 2–2½ in (5–6 cm) long, with rounded tip. Golden yellow flowers, 3 in (8 cm) wide, in autumn. Zones 9–11.

Glottiphyllym nelii
syn. *Gibbaeum pygmaeum*

✲ ✧ ↔ 12 in (30 cm) ↕ 1–6 in (2.5–15 cm)

A rambling perennial that forms rounded clumps. Unequal, semi-cylindrical, fleshy, light green, erect leaves, to 1½–2 in (3.5–5 cm) long, with rounded tips. Daisy-like golden yellow flowers, 1½ in (3.5 cm) across, produced from spring to summer. Zones 9–11.

GRAPTOPETALUM

These 12 species of succulent perennials native to Paraguay and Mexico to Arizona, USA, belong to the stonecrop (Crassulaceae) family. They form rosettes of fleshy leaves. The flowerheads are cymes bearing flowers with 5 spreading petals that are fused toward the base. **CULTIVATION:** Easily grown in light to medium very well-drained soil in an open sunny position. Propagation is from seed, from stem or leaf cuttings, or by division of the offsets.

Graptopetalum amethystinum
LAVENDER PEBBLES

☀ ✧ ↔ 3–5 in (8–12 cm) ↕ 4–6 in (10–15 cm)

Graptopetalum amethystinum

Clumping succulent perennial from Mexico. Forms rosettes of thick, blunt, rounded, blue-gray leaves, to 3 in (8 cm) long, with an amethyst tinge. Stout erect stems become prostrate with age. The terminal clusters of creamy white, bell-shaped flowers have red markings and are ½–1 in (12–25 mm) across, appearing from spring through to summer. Zones 9–11.

Graptopetalum paraguayense ★
GHOST PLANT, MOTHER OF PEARL PLANT

✲ ✧ ↔ 5–12 in (12–30 cm) ↕ 4–12 in (10–30 cm)

A small succulent perennial from Mexico. Stout stem forms rosettes, to 6 in (15 cm) across, at stalk ends. Thick, stiff, oval to wedge-shaped, whitish gray leaves, with a pinkish cast, 1½–2 in (3.5–5 cm) long, ridged undersurface. Young leaves pale purple. Terminal flowerhead, to 6 in (15 cm) tall, with up to 6 white star-shaped flowers, red-spotted, to ¾ in (18 mm) across, from late winter to early spring. *G. p.* **subsp.** *superbum* has succulent leaves with an eye-catching purplish gray bloom. Zones 9–11.

GYMNOCALYCIUM

A genus of 71 species of small cacti in the Cactaceae family from the Andes in Bolivia, southern Brazil, Paraguay, Uruguay, and Argentina. The genus name is derived from the Greek *gymnos* (naked) and *calyx* (bud), referring to the smooth flower buds. Many species are solitary, but several offset freely. They feature a depressed spherical to short cylindrical stem with 4 to 15 fairly rounded ribs. Many species have distinct "chins" below the usually large areoles. Spines are variable, from thin and weak to strong and stout. Flowers are diurnal, borne at or near the top of the plant, funnelform to bell-shaped, in shades of white, pink, yellow, or red, with large, broad, naked scales on the calyx. Seed pods are spherical to cylindrical. **CULTIVATION:** Easily grown in a rich well-drained soil. Propagate from seed, offsets, or cuttings that have been dried out for a week or two.

May also be grown by dividing clumps of older plants. Rest in winter, when plants often pull into the soil and appear rather shrivelled.

Gymnocalycium bruchii
syns *Gymnocalycium albispinum, G. lafaldense*

✲ ❄ ↔ 20 in (50 cm) ↕ 1½ in (35 mm)

From Cordoba province, Argentina. Depressed spherical trunk, freely offsets with age, gray-green stems, 12 low, rounded, warty, chinless ribs. Spines 1 to 3, dark white or brown, erect centrals, 12 to 14 backward-curving radials. Flowers pale mauve-pink to white. Seed pods spherical, bluish to whitish. Zones 8–11.

Gymnocalycium castellanosii
✲ ❄ ↔ 4 in (10 cm) ↕ 6 in (15 cm)

From La Rioja and Cordoba provinces, Argentina. Solitary, spherical to elongated-spherical trunk, 10 to 12 low wide ribs with distinct tubercles. Spines 1 central, 5 to 7 radials, whitish with dark tips. Flowers funnel-form to bell-shaped, white tinged pink. Seed pods spherical, green. Zones 8–11.

Gymnocalycium ochoterenae ★
✲ ❄ ↔ 4–5 in (10–12 cm) ↕ 2–2½ in (5–6 cm)

From Cordoba, La Rioja, and San Luis, Argentina. Solitary, spherical to flattened-spherical, olive green to brownish trunk, 14 to 16 ribs. Spines 1 to 7 radials only, bending backward, sometimes comb-like, brownish yellow to whitish yellow with dark tips. Flowers white with pink throats. Seed pods barrel-shaped, green to dull red. *G. o.* **subsp.** *vatteri*, 1 to 3 recurved spines; *G. o.* **subsp.** *herbertshofferianum*, 6 to 7 comb-like radial spines. Zones 8–11.

Gymnocalycium saglionis ★
✲ ❄ ↔ 12 in (30 cm) ↕ 6 in (15 cm)

From northern Argentina. Solitary, spherical, dull green trunk, 10 to 30 deep ribs, prominent rounded tubercles. Spines yellow-brown to red-black, 1 to 3 straight centrals, 10 to 15 radials. Flowers white or pink, red throat. Seed pods spherical, reddish. Zones 8–11.

Gymnocalycium castellanosii

HATIORA

syn. *Rhipsalidopsis*

A genus of 5 species of epiphytic or lithophytic cacti from Brazil belonging to the Cactaceae family. Several species resemble some members of the genus *Rhipsalis* but are distinguished by the fact that each stem segment grows to a predetermined size and shape before producing another segment. Stem shapes are variable, from flattened to cylindrical. The name *Hatiora* is an anagram of the family name of Thomas Hariot, a sixteenth-century Jamaican botanist. Plants are erect at first, then spreading, in time becoming pendulous. Flowers are diurnal, bell-shaped, yellow, pink or red, arising from the terminal stem segments.
CULTIVATION: Easily grown in rich well-drained soil. Propagate from seed or cuttings that have been dried out for a week or two. Rest in winter.

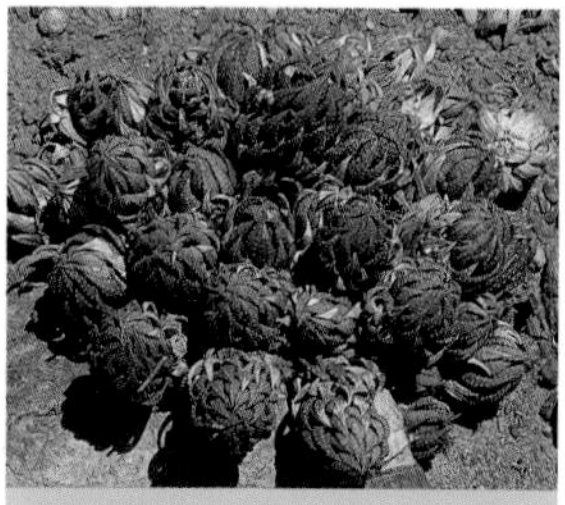
Haworthia coarctata

Hatiora gaertneri ★

syns *Schlumbergera gaertneri, Rhipsalidopsis gaertneri*

EASTER CACTUS

↔ 12–20 in (30–50 cm) ↑ 12–20 in (30–50 cm)

From Parana and Santa Catarina, Brazil. Pendent multi-branched shrub consisting of numerous dull green segments, brown bristles at the tips, from which 1 to 3 funnel-form red flowers arise. An important parent in many hybrids with other species of *Hatiora*. Zones 9–12.

Hatiora rosea ★

syn. *Rhipsalidopsis rosea*

EASTER CACTUS

↔ 8–12 in (20–30 cm) ↑ 12–16 in (30–40 cm)

From Parana to Rio Grande do Sol, Brazil. Erect to sprawling plant. Stem segments are flat to 3-sided, reddish becoming green, margins with 2 to 3 notches. Areoles from segment tips. Flowers terminal, diurnal, pink, funnelform. Zones 9–12.

HAWORTHIA

This genus in the lily (Liliaceae) family contains 70–160 species of dwarf succulent perennials native to southern Africa, grown for their interesting foliage. Plants form low spirally arranged rosettes and often resemble in miniature the related *Aloe*. Leaf form varies widely; shapes range from triangular to lance-shaped, margins toothed or even, and leaf tips blunt or sharp. Some have transparent "windows" to allow light into the middle of the plant. Leaf surfaces may be plain or patterned, smooth or roughened with tiny growths called tubercles. Some have a firm consistency, others are soft and juicy. Small 2-lipped flowers, borne on relatively tall stems, are usually white with 6 flaring petals.
CULTIVATION: Grow in a well-drained soil in semi-shade. Water well in summer but keep dry and protect from frosts in winter. Indoor plants will tolerate quite low light levels. Propagate from offsets or seed.

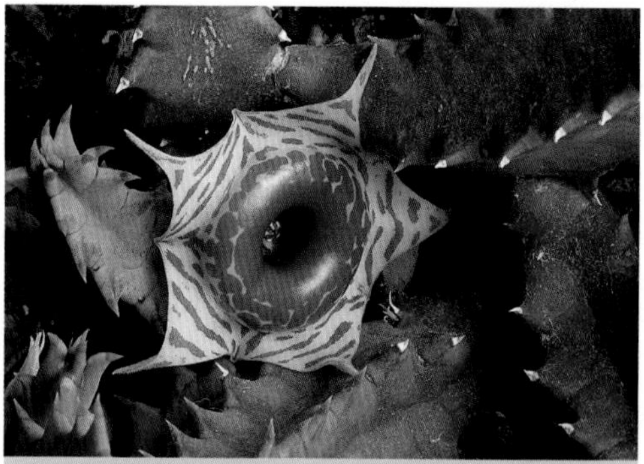
Huernia zebrina

Haworthia coarctata

↔ 6 in (15 cm) ↑ 8 in (20 cm)

South African. Dense columnar rosettes of overlapping, incurving, yellowish green, triangular leaves. Leaf surface covered with white or pale green tubercles. Zones 9–11.

Haworthia cymbiformis

↔ 4 in (10 cm) ↑ 2 in (5 cm)

South African. Stemless rosettes that offset freely. Soft, incurving, thick, triangular leaves translucent pale green with darker lines. *H. c.* var. *variegata,* cream leaves with splashes of green. Zones 9–11.

Haworthia fasciata ★

ZEBRA HAWORTHIA

↔ 6 in (15 cm) ↑ 6 in (15 cm)

From South Africa. Stemless rosettes of narrow, pointed, upright leaves, dark green, white striping on underside. Like *H. attenuata* but leaves are shorter and have a smoother surface. Zones 9–11.

Haworthia reinwardtii

↔ 3 in (8 cm) ↑ 6 in (15 cm)

From South Africa. Forms a tight columnar rosette of incurving triangular leaves. Closely resembles *C. coarctata* but leaves are slightly bigger and tubercles larger but less prominent. Zones 9–11.

HUERNIA

LIFE BUOY PLANT

There are about 70 species of small succulent perennials in this dogbane (Apocynaceae) family genus, native to dry areas of Africa and southern Arabia. They are leafless plants with fleshy angular stems often with small tubercles, and fleshy spines or bristles. The waxy flowers may be clustered or solitary and emerge from the plant base or stem tips. They are star- or bell-shaped and some species have a prominent fleshy central ring, hence "life buoy plant." They are usually strongly colored and marked in shades of red, maroon, yellow, and green, and have an unpleasant odor of varying intensity.
CULTIVATION: In suitably warm climates grow them outdoors in shade in free-draining soil or in a pot. Keep dry in winter. In the greenhouse they need bright shade. Water with care as plants rot easily. They are susceptible to root and stem mealy bugs.

Huernia zebrina ★

LITTLE OWL, OWL-EYES

☀ ⦂ ↔ 6 in (15 cm) ↑ 4 in (10 cm)

From South Africa, Botswana, and Namibia. Stems 5-angled with toothed edges. Basal flowers have a prominent raised central ring of maroon, sometimes marked yellow. Surrounding triangular lobes are pale yellow with reddish brown bands. Zones 10–12.

JATROPHA (see page 190)

Jatropha podagrica ★

GOUT PLANT, GUATEMALA RHUBARB, TARTOGO

☀ ⦂ ↔ 10–12 in (25–30 cm) ↑ 20–36 in (50–90 cm)

Small succulent shrub from Central America. Trunk is grotesquely swollen, becoming knobbly with age, gray. Round to oval 3- to 5-lobed leaves, dark green uppersurface, glaucous beneath. Terminal clusters of small brilliant orange-red to scarlet flowers held above the foliage on red or green stalks. Long flowering season, usually from winter to summer. Zones 10–12.

JOVIBARBA

A small genus of 6 species from the mountains of Europe and in the stonecrop (Crassulaceae) family. These rosetting succulents are often confused with the better known houseleeks *(Sempervivum)*, which in foliage they resemble. The insignificant flowers are 6-petalled and bell-shaped, whereas those of the houseleeks are star-shaped. CULTIVATION: Hardy succulents ideal in well-drained poor soil in the rock garden, dry stone walls, pots, or troughs. Remove old rosettes after flowering. Propagate by division; some species detach their own rosettes that then roll away to take root elsewhere.

Jovibarba hirta

☀ ❄ ↔ 10–12 in (25–30 cm) ↑ 4–6 in (10–15 cm)

A native of the mountains of central and southeastern Europe. Rosettes to 2 in (5 cm) across. Small flat leaves narrow or broadly lance-shaped, convex below, green with darker colored tips. Branching heads of small pale yellow flowers in summer. *J. h.* **var.** *neilreichii*, from lower Carpathian Mountains, narrow leaves arranged in open rosettes. Zones 6–10.

KALANCHOE

This genus in the stonecrop (Crassulaceae) family contains about 125 species of succulent shrubs, herbs, and climbers distributed throughout tropical regions of Africa, Madagascar, and parts of Asia. Usually grown for their interesting foliage forms, although the vibrantly colored flowers of *K. blossfeldiana* make it a popular house plant. Growth habits range from low sprawling subshrubs to tall tree-like plants, with a similar wide variation in leaves, from small to large and glossy to felted. CULTIVATION: Plants require indoor or greenhouse cultivation in all climates where frost is experienced; grow in a moderately fertile gritty potting mix. Can be grown outdoors in suitable climates in

Jovibarba hirta var. neilreichii | Kalanchoe beharensis

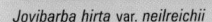

a sunny sheltered position in well-drained soil; keep fairly dry in winter. Propagate from stem or leaf cuttings, or seed sown in spring.

Kalanchoe beharensis

FELT PLANT, GIANT KALANCHOE

☀ ⦂ ↔ 3 ft (0.9 m) ↑ 10 ft (3 m)

Tree-like species from Madagascar, smaller in cultivation. Foliage stunning; large, thick, triangular leaves, heavily felted, silvery gray, light bronze overtones on uppersurface; wavy, uneven, toothed edges. Small, tubular, yellowish flowers seen rarely on mature specimens. 'Oak Leaf' ★, greenish yellow flowers. Zones 10–11.

Kalanchoe blossfeldiana

FLAMING KATIE

☀ ⦂ ↔ 16 in (40 cm) ↑ 16 in (40 cm)

Bushy perennial from Madagascar. Large, round, dark green, fleshy leaves. Heads of tubular scarlet flowers in clusters from early spring. Numerous cultivars, flowers in white, cream, yellow, orange, and red. Zones 10–12.

Kalanchoe daigremontiana

syn. *Bryophyllum daigremontianum*

MEXICAN HAT PLANT

☀ ✿ ↔ 12 in (30 cm) ↑ 40 in (100 cm)

Jatropha podagrica

From Madagascar. Upright perennial succulent with long with lance-shaped, silver-gray leaves, changing to green as temperatures fall. On leaf edges, plantlets appear that look like "Mexican hats"; these can be separated to produce new plants. Pendulous pale pink flowers in spring. Zones 10–12.

Kalanchoe delagoensis

syns *Bryophyllum tubiflorum*, *Kalanchoe tubiflora*

CHANDELIER PLANT

☀ ⦂ ↔ 12 in (30 cm) ↑ 40 in (100 cm)

Upright, unbranched succulent from Madagascar and South Africa. Cylindrical, long, pale green leaves with irregular red spots and small plantlets on the edge. In winter terminal clusters of pink, orange, or yellow pendent flowers will appear. Zones 9–12.

Lampranthus aurantiacus

LAMPRANTHUS

This genus of some 155 species belonging to the iceplant (Aizoaceae) family is found from southern Namibia to South Africa's Eastern Cape; there is also one species possibly native to Australia. They are creeping, sometimes erect subshrubs. The succulent leaves are linear to club-shaped, often triangular in section. The flowers are commonly large and brightly colored and produced profusely over long periods in spring–summer, making them useful for summer bedding and containers in temperate regions. A few are frost hardy, and can be grown all year round in sheltered sites. Some species formerly placed here have now been reclassified as *Oscularia*.
CULTIVATION: *Lampranthus* species need full sun and will thrive in poor well-drained soils. They are very easily propagated from stem cuttings, which can be rooted at almost any time of the year.

Kalanchoe fedtschenkoi
☼ ⚘ ↔12 in (30 cm) ↑20 in (50 cm)
Spreading succulent; Madagascar. Thick, fleshy, blue-green, round leaves, serrated edges. Tubular orange to red flowers, spring. *K. f.* 'Variegata' ★, blue-gray white-edged foliage. Zones 9–12.

Kalanchoe manginii
☼ ⚘ ↔12 in (30 cm) ↑12 in (30 cm)
From Madagascar. A sprawling succulent with notched, furry, green leaves. Groups of bright red flowers cover the plant in spring. Zones 10–12.

Kalanchoe marmorata
syn. *Kalanchoe somaliensis*
☼ ⚘ ↔36 in (90 cm) ↑50 in (130 cm)
From northeastern Africa. Sprawling succulent; branches from base of plant. Dusty gray leaves have distinctive brown markings. Panicles of white flowers in summer. Zones 10–12.

Kalanchoe pumila
☼ ⚘ ↔18 in (45 cm) ↑8 in (20 cm)
From Madagascar. Low-growing ground cover, cream-green leaves frosted white; serrated edges. Erect pink flowers, spring. Zones 11–12.

Kalanchoe thyrsiflora ★
☼ ⚘ ↔12 in (30 cm) ↑24 in (60 cm)
Southern African. Bushy succulent, white frosted green leaves with red margins. Tubular, fragrant, yellow flowers, spring. Zones 11–12.

Kalanchoe tomentosa ★
PANDA PLANT
☼ ⚘ ↔7 in (18 cm) ↑15 in (38 cm)
A small erect shrub that is native to Madagascar. Dense rosettes of oblong gray leaves, heavily felted, brown markings near tips. Small yellowish green flowers. Zones 10–12.

Kalanchoe tomentosa

Lampranthus aurantiacus ★
syn. *Mesembryanthemum aurantiacum*
ICE PLANT
☼ ⚘ ↔8–18 in (20–45 cm) ↑6–12 in (15–30 cm)
A succulent perennial with upright stems becoming prostrate with age. Leaves bluish green, tapering, minutely rough and spotted. Bears profuse daisy-like bright yellow or orange flowers in late spring. 'Sunman' bears golden yellow flowers. Zones 9–11.

Lampranthus glaucus
NOON FLOWER
☼ ⚘ ↔12–24 in (30–60 cm) ↑12–24 in (30–60 cm)
Bushy, low-spreading, succulent perennial with roughly dotted, flattened, 3-angled, gray-green leaves. Soft, sulfur yellow, daisy-like flowers in late spring. Fruit is a dry capsule. Zones 9–11.

Lampranthus roseus
syn. *Mesembryanthemum roseum*
☼ ⚘ ↔12–20 in (30–50 cm) ↑12–20 in (30–50 cm)
Short-lived, erect, shrubby, succulent perennial, sometimes grown as an annual, with slender branches and narrow curved leaves. Clusters of rose pink to reddish violet daisy-like flowers, with a slightly peppery smell, mid-spring to early summer. Zones 9–11.

LEUCHTENBERGIA

This genus of a single cactus species (family Cactaceae) is from the Chihuahuan Desert of Mexico and was named for the Duke of Leuchtenberg, the stepson of Napoleon Bonaparte. Agave-like, it has long leaf-like tubercles and long papery spines. Its large flowers open during the day and close at night, and often persist for several days. It lacks the ribs usually found in this family.

Rare in its natural habitat, it is often disguised by growing in or near clumps of *Agave lechuguilla* or near yuccas. Illegal collecting of wild plants continues to reduce numbers.
CULTIVATION: A solitary plant usually raised from seed. It needs very well-drained, purely mineral soil with a winter rest and judicious watering in spring and autumn, even in the growing seasons.

Leuchtenbergia principis
AGAVE CACTUS, PRISM CACTUS
☼ ✽ ↔ 8–12 in (20–30 cm) ↕ 8–24 in (20–60 cm)
Spherical to short cylindrical form, with long tap root. Covered in thin 3-sided tubercles. Thin, flat, yellow to gray, papery, 6 in (15 cm) spines at the ends of tubercles, often twisted, among the longest of all cactus spines. Large, fragrant, glossy yellow, funnel-shaped flowers. Green to yellow egg-shaped seed pods. Zones 9–11.

LITHOPS
LIVING STONES
This genus of 36 species of extreme succulents from the drier parts of southern Africa belongs to the iceplant (Aizoaceae) family. Compact plants sunk into the soil, comprising a solitary or repeatedly branched shoot. Each shoot consists for most of the year of only 2 leaves, fused into a cone with a flat or domed top marked with lines, dots, or translucent "windows," which camouflages the plants in their pebbly surroundings, reducing predation by animals. In areas of high light intensity, the plants of some species also have protective layers of calcium oxalate. The appearance of a single (rarely 2 or more) yellow or white flower through a fissure on top of the plant ends the season's growth; a new shoot develops in the axil of one or both leaves. The new shoots draw water from the old leaves, which remain around them as tough withered sheaths. Many species are highly variable in leaf coloration and markings; almost all species and varieties, as well as some hybrids, are in cultivation.
CULTIVATION: Plants can be grown in any well-drained compost of low fertility, but generally thrive best in sandy or gritty loam. Keep dry through winter; water sparingly in growing season from summer to early autumn (when they flower), starting only when the old pair of leaves has almost completely shriveled. Best grown under cover even in warm regions, in a large pot for their large root system. They can be grown with much of the plant above

the soil, as opposed to their natural habitat, where only the upper-surface is exposed. Best raised from seed; can also be divided.

Lithops karasmontana
☼ ✽ ↔ 4–8 in (10–20 cm) ↕ ¾–1¼ in (2–3 cm)
From Namibia. Highly variable species. Pairs of brown to brownish yellow leaves, uppersurface convex with darker marks and brownish pits and wrinkles, elliptical to kidney-shaped face, dark brown panel with fine lines on surface, forming body 1¼–1½ in (25–35 mm) across. White flowers in late summer–early autumn. *L. k.* subsp. *bella*, gray to buff body, convex face, dull olive panel; *L. k.* var. *lericheana*, smaller buff body, rounded pinkish face, olive green markings; *L. k.* var. *tischeri*, somewhat smaller body, kidney-shaped face, dark olive to chocolate panel. Zones 9–11.

Lithops lesliei
☼ ✽ ↔ 4–8 in (10–20 cm) ↕ 1¼–2 in (3–5 cm)
From South Africa. Egg-shaped, forming clumps 4 in (10 cm) or more wide. Pairs of thick, gray-green to buff or light velvet brown leaves forming body ¾–1¾ in (20–45 mm) across, top light reddish brown, dark brown mottling. Yellow flowers, summer–early autumn. Variable species; many subspecies and varieties have been distinguished. *L. l.* 'Albiflora', uppersurface of lobes buff marked with olive, white flowers; 'Albinica', pale gold face, panel dull olive, finely marked, white flowers; 'Storm's Albinigold', similar to *L. l.* 'Albinica', yellow flowers. Zones 9–11.

Lithops marmorata
☼ ✽ ↔ 4–6 in (10–15 cm) ↕ ¾–1¼ in (18–30 mm)
From South Africa. Clump-forming. Unequal pairs of swollen, fleshy, pale gray-green leaves, uppersurface convex with dark gray marks; body 1–1¼ in (25–30 mm) wide, narrowly kidney-shaped face, translucent dark gray or gray-green panel marked with jagged edges. White flowers, summer–early autumn. *L. m.* var. *elisae*, buff or beige body, panel markings vein-like. Zones 9–11.

Lithops meyeri
☼ ✽ ↔ 3–6 in (8–15 cm) ↕ ¾–1¼ in (18–30 mm)
A native of South Africa. Wrinkled pale gray body, ¾–1¼ in (18–30 mm) across, narrowly kidney-shaped face, darker translucent panel. Yellow flowers with a white center. Zones 9–11.

Leuchtenbergia principis

Lithops lesliei

Lithops marmorata

Lithops olivacea

☼ ❄ ↔ 4–8 in (10–20 cm) ↑ ¾–3 in (18 mm–8 cm)

Native to South Africa. Egg-shaped species forming clumps 6 in (15 cm) or more in diameter. Pairs of pale gray or beige to dark olive green leaves, uppersurface convex, kidney-shaped, with translucent olive window. The solitary yellow flowers with a white center appear in late summer–autumn. Zones 9–11.

Lithops schwantesii

☼ ❄ ↔ 3–6 in (8–15 cm) ↑ ¾–1¼ in (18–30 mm)

From Namibia. A very variable egg-shaped species forming clumps to 4 in (10 cm) across. Pairs of dark gray or dull buff leaves, uppersurface flat or convex, with sunken dark red or blue lines or dots, forming oblong to kidney-shaped body with olive gray panel marked with cinnamon lines. Yellow flowers in late summer–early autumn. *L. s.* **subsp.** *gebseri,* gray to tan body with a network of reddish brown lines; *L. s.* **subsp.** *steineckeana,* grayish white body, with semi-circular face, with grayish green dots; *L. s.* **subsp.** *terricolor,* buff to tan body, an

Lithops schwantesii

oblong to kidney-shaped face spotted with olive or mid-green, yellow flowers, sometimes with a white center. *L. s.* **var.** *marthae,* a fawn to gray body, gray panel etched with ocher; *L. s.* **var.** *rugosa,* gray-buff to pale lilac body, network of brown lines; *L. s.* **var.** *urikosensis,* fawn body with a deep fissure and covered with fine burnt sienna lines. Zones 9–11.

LOPHOPHORA

PEYOTE

Native to Mexico and southern Texas, USA, the just 2 species of small, spineless, low-growing, flattened spherical cacti with thickened tap roots that comprise this genus (family Cactaceae) are well known because of their long association with Native American religious and medicinal ceremonies. They contain the mind-altering drug mescaline, with the result that a considerable

amount of pharmacological, botanic, and horticultural research has been carried out on them. The name derives from the Greek *lophos,* meaning crest, and *phoreus,* meaning bearer, referring to the tufts of white hair borne at the growing point and sometimes evident on the areoles of the plant.

CULTIVATION: These cacti are quite easy to grow in any rich well-drained soil. They may be raised from seed, by division of mature clumps, or from cuttings that have been allowed to dry out for a week or two. Withhold water during the winter months.

Lophophora williamsii

DEVIL'S ROOT, DUMPLING CACTUS, MESCAL BUTTON, PEYOTE, WHITE MULE

☼ ❄ ↔ 32–40 in (80–100 cm) ↑ ¾–2½ in (18–60 mm)

From the Chihuahuan desert regions of Texas, USA, and northern Mexican States. A widespread variable species; its many common names reflect its narcotic effects. Often solitary but may form mats. Stems firm, gray-green; 5 to 15 well-defined ribs. Pink, pale pink, or occasionally red flowers in summer. Zones 9–11.

MAMMILLARIA

PINCUSHION CACTUS

This genus in the cactus (Cactaceae) family is made up of more than 150 low-growing, solitary or clustering, hemispherical, spherical, or columnar cacti from southwestern USA, Mexico, Central America, and northern South America. Rings of funnel-shaped flowers, in colors ranging from white through cream to pinks and reds, sometimes yellow, sometimes purplish or green, develop near the crown. The spiny green stems are spherical to cylindrical, and feature stiff spines. These clumping plants spread by growing offsets. The fruits are slender to spherical berry-like seed pods that grow between the tubercles.

CULTIVATION: These plants prefer well-drained soils in an open sunny position. Keep drier in winter. Propagate most species by division of offsets, or from seed in spring and summer.

Mammillaria albicoma

☼ ❄ ↔ 1¼–5 in (3–12 cm) ↑ 2–2½ in (5–6 cm)

A clustering cactus from northeastern central Mexico. The stem features hair-like bristles in the axils. Up to 4 straight, darkly tipped, white central spines, white radial spines. Creamy flowers bloom throughout spring. Zones 9–11.

Mammillaria blossfeldiana

☼ ❄ ↔ 1¼–2 in (3–5 cm) ↑ 3–4 in (8–10 cm)

A simple or clustering cactus indigenous to central Baja California, Mexico. Dark green stems are spherical to shortly cylindrical. Sparsely woolly axils do not have bristles. Central spines are dark, radial spines are pale yellow and dark-tipped. Pinkish white flowers, with rose stripes, produced during the summer months. Zones 9–11.

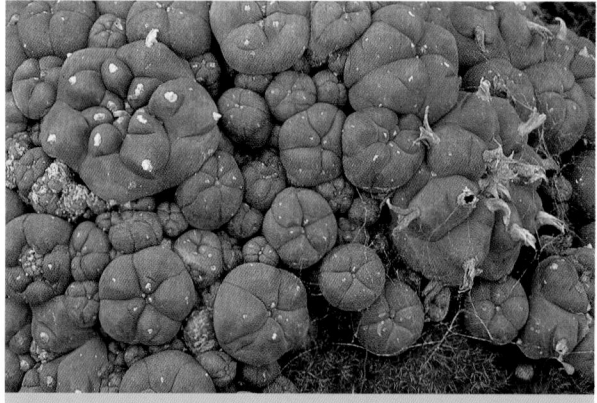

Lophophora williamsii

Mammillaria bocasana

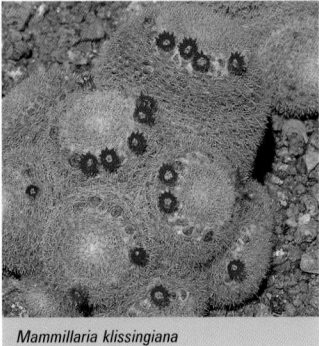
Mammillaria klissingiana

Mammillaria mystax

Mammillaria bocasana ★
POWDER-PUFF CACTUS
☼ ⟩ ↔ 12–24 in (30–60 cm) ↕ 4–8 in (10–20 cm)
A clump-forming perennial cactus native to central Mexico. The spherical stem is densely covered in spines. Axils are naked or with fine hairs or bristles; central spines red or brown, radial spines white. Flowers are creamy white or rose pink, borne in spring–summer. Red seed pods. Zones 9–11.

Mammillaria carmenae
☼ ⟩ ↔ 2–3 in (5–8 cm) ↕ 2–3 in (5–8 cm)
A clustering cactus from eastern central Mexico. Stem is spherical to egg-shaped, with no central spines but more than 100 pale radial spines. White flowers tinged pink or cream, with yellow stigmas, are produced in spring. 'Jewel' is available in two colors, intense pink or white. Zones 9–11.

Mammillaria compressa ★
☼ ⟩ ↔ 6 in (15 cm) ↕ 1½–2½ in (4–6 cm)
A clustering cactus from central Mexico. Flattened spherical stems; swollen angled tubercles. Woolly bristly axils. White to pale red spines, darker tips, 4 to 6 unequal. Dark purplish pink flowers, borne in spring. Zones 9–11.

Mammillaria elongata ★
LACE CACTUS
☼ ⟩ ↔ 8–12 in (20–30 cm) ↕ 4–6 in (10–15 cm)
Clump-forming perennial cactus from central Mexico. Features a columnar elongated stem, with up to 3 pale yellow to brown central spines and 14 to 25 yellow radial spines. Pale yellow flowers, sometimes tinged with pink, produced from spring to summer. Offsets freely. Zones 9–11.

Mammillaria hahniana ★
OLD LADY CACTUS, OLD WOMAN CACTUS
☼ ⟩ ↔ 8–12 in (20–30 cm) ↕ 6–10 in (15–25 cm)
Simple or clustering cactus native to Mexico. Spherical to columnar, with copious triangular to conical tubercles and long white bristles. White central spines are brown-tipped; radial spines are white and hair-like. Deep purplish pink flowers appear in spring. Fruits are spherical and red. Zones 9–11.

Mammillaria klissingiana
☼ ⟩ ↔ 2½–4 in (6–10 cm) ↕ 4–6 in (10–15 cm)
Simple then clustering cactus from central Mexico. Spherical to club-shaped stems. White bristles on axils; central spines nearly white, tips darker, radial spines nearly white. Pink summer flowers. Zones 9–11.

Mammillaria longimamma
syn. *Dolichothele longimamma*
☼ ✦ ↔ 3–5 in (8–12 cm) ↕ 3–5 in (8–12 cm)
Slow-growing, simple or clustering, perennial cactus from central Mexico. Very large tubercles, oblong to cylindrical in section. Spines pale brown, yellow, or white. Big, bright yellow flowers emerge from axils around the stems, in summer. Zones 11–12.

Mammillaria mazatlanensis
☼ ⟩ ↔ ¾–1¾ in (18–40 mm) ↕ 4–6 in (10–15 cm)
Clustering cactus from northwestern Mexico. Slender cylindrical stems, short conical tubercles, axils bare or a few small bristles. Central spines reddish brown, sometimes hooked; radial spines white. Carmine red flowers, green stigmas, in summer. Zones 9–11.

Mammillaria melanocentra
☼ ⟩ ↔ 4–6 in (10–15 cm) ↕ 3–5 in (8–12 cm)
Simple perennial cactus from northern Mexico. Flattened spherical stems, bluish green; large pyramid-shaped tubercles and axils woolly at first. Stout black central spine, unequal radial spines, black when young. Deep-pink flowers, in spring. Zones 9–11.

Mammillaria moelleriana
☼ ⟩ ↔ 3–4 in (8–10 cm) ↕ 6–12 in (15–30 cm)
A simple cactus from western to central Mexico. Spherical to slightly cylindrical stem, egg-shaped tubercles, bare axils. Central spines browny yellow to deep reddish brown; radial spines yellow to white. Pale pink flowers, dark stripe, in spring. Zones 9–11.

Mammillaria mystax
☼ ⟩ ↔ 3–4 in (8–10 cm) ↕ 4–6 in (10–15 cm)
Simple cactus, dividing later, from southern Mexico. Spherical to cylindrical stems; pyramid-shaped tubercles, bristly axils. Central spines purplish brown, later gray, distorted; white radial spines, brown-tipped. Dark purplish pink flowers, in spring. Zones 9–11.

Mammillaria plumosa ★

☼ ❄ ↔ 2½–16 in (6–40 cm) ↑ 4–6 in (10–15 cm)

A clustering, perennial cactus from northeastern Mexico that forms mounds. The spherical green stems are hidden by white feathery spines. There are cylindrical tubercles, and woolly axils. Tiny flowers, creamy white, with a hint of brownish pink, are produced in winter. Zones 9–11.

Mammillaria prolifera

STRAWBERRY CACTUS

☼ ❄ ↔ 8–12 in (20–30 cm) ↑ 2½–4 in (6–10 cm)

A perennial cactus from northeastern Mexico, southwestern USA, and the West Indies. It forms dense clumps; with axils almost bare. The straight central spines are white to reddish brown; the fine radial spines are white. Creamy yellow tubular flowers, may be pink-tinged, or brown-striped, emerge from spring to summer. Red berries taste like strawberries. Zones 9–11.

Mammillaria spinosissima ★

☼ ❄ ↔ 2½–3 in (6–8 cm) ↑ 4–6 in (10–15 cm)

Cactus from central Mexico. Simple, later clustering; cylindrical stems; oval to conical tubercles, slightly woolly axils. Central spines reddish brown or pale yellow; radial spines bristly, nearly white. Purplish pink flowers, in spring. Zones 9–11.

Mammillaria supertexta

☼ ❄ ↔ 2–3 in (5–8 cm) ↑ 4–6 in (10–15 cm)

A cactus native to southern Mexico. Simple, nearly spherical to cylindrical stems; crowded, small, conical tubercles, woolly axils; central spines white, sometimes tipped black, radial spines white. Small deep red or pink flowers, in spring. Zones 9–11.

MELOCACTUS

MELON CACTUS

This cactus (Cactaceae) family genus contains 33 species from tropical America, especially eastern Brazil and the Amazon Basin, Peru, Venezuela, the Caribbean, and Central America. These cacti are unbranched (unless they are damaged), the stems being spherical to columnar and strongly ribbed. The flower-bearing structure, or cephalium, is permanently distinct, bearing wool and usually bristles. Flowers are red to pink, small and tubular, usually covered by the wool. The fruit is a red, pink, or white, juicy berry, and is usually club-shaped.

CULTIVATION: Grow in a cactus compost that is both acidic and high in inorganic materials. *Melocactus* plants prefer a sunny position, low humidity, and just a little water in winter. In cool regions they need a heated greenhouse. The Brazilian species and *M. matanzanus*, a widely grown species from Cuba, are those in general cultivation; other species need higher winter temperatures. All species can be propagated from seed.

Melocactus azureus ★

☼ ✦ ↔ 6–8 in (15–20 cm) ↑ 5–18 in (12–45 cm)

A cactus from the limestone areas of eastern Brazil. Spherical to cylindrical, dark green to gray-green, sometimes with a fine bloom, 9 or 10 triangular ribs. Spines black to reddish, becoming gray, 7 to 11 radials. Flowers pink, on thick stems with reddish bristles, brown or white wool, in summer. Seed pods are white through to pale pink. Zones 11–12.

Melocactus bahiensis

☼ ✦ ↔ 4–5 in (10–12 cm) ↑ 4–8 in (10–20 cm)

Cactus found growing in eastern Brazil. Spherical to depressed spherical, pale to dark green, 8 to 14 low ribs, variable in shape. Spines are brown, reddish, or yellowish, overlaid with gray. Flowers are pink, on short, thick, woolly stems, produced during the summer months. Zones 11–12.

Melocactus curvispinus

syns *Melocactus guitartii*, *M. maxonii*, *M. ruestii*

☼ ✦ ↔ 3–12 in (8–30 cm) ↑ 2–12 in (5–30 cm)

Variable cactus found in Mexico, Central America, the Caribbean, Peru, Colombia, and Venezuela. Stems are depressed, spherical to short cylindrical, light to dark green, with a soft bloom. Erect central spines, 1 to 4, occasionally absent, 6 to 11 radials. Flowers pink to carmine to magenta, on small, thick, woolly stems with prominent reddish brown bristles, in summer. Seed pods are club-shaped. Zones 11–12.

Mammillaria prolifera

Melocactus bahiensis

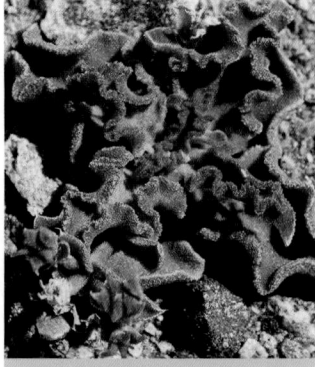

Mesembryanthemum guerichianum

MESEMBRYANTHEMUM

This genus, once interpreted in a far broader sense, contains 15 species of prostrate or creeping succulent annuals or biennials in the iceplant (Aizoaceae) family, and is native to South Africa and Namibia; several species are naturalized elsewhere. All parts of the plants are covered with tiny, glistening, watery, bubble-like cells. Rosettes of cylindrical or flattish, fleshy branches bearing succulent leaves of varying form grow from a central taproot. The glossy, daisy-like flowers are solitary or numerous, and come in a variety of shades from white to yellow or pink.
CULTIVATION: They require full sun and well-drained, very light, sandy soil. Propagate from seed in spring, or from cuttings.

Mesembryanthemum crystallinum
syn. *Cryophytum crystallinum*
☼ ❄ ↔12–24 in (30–60 cm) ↕4–8 in (10–20 cm)
A creeping annual or biennial from South Africa and Namibia. Spreading branches; leaves thick, sometimes fleshy, oval to spatula-shaped with wavy edges. Creamy white daisy-like flowers that open only in sunlight, in summer. Can be invasive. Zones 9–11.

Mesembryanthemum guerichianum
☼ ❄ ↔8–18 in (20–45 cm) ↕2–4 in (5–10 cm)
Highly succulent annual from South Africa and Namibia. Thick, fleshy, cylindrical stems. Opposite pairs of oval basal leaves, lower leaves larger than upper leaves. White or green to yellowish white and pink flowers, in summer. Zones 9–11.

Mesembryanthemum nodiflorum
☼ ❄ ↔36 in (90 cm) ↕6–8 in (15–20 cm)
Annual or biennial from South Africa, introduced widely elsewhere. Extremely succulent. Long, narrow, thick, grayish green leaves, a little hairy underneath, covered with large glandular hairs. Reddish buds then white flowers, summer. Zones 9–11.

MYRTILLOCACTUS

Four species of tree-like cacti from Guatemala and Mexico comprise this genus in the family Cactaceae. These densely branched cacti stand out in their natural habitat, often emerging from low scrub. The genus name comes from the Greek word *myrtus*, myrtle, and refers to the tiny fruits that resemble the fruits of the true myrtle. The bell-shaped flowers are small, and highly unusual for a cactus in that up to 9 flowers may be borne at any one time from a single areole. Fruits are small, spherical, and edible, and are widely utilized as a food, fresh or dried, throughout the range of the plants.
CULTIVATION: Easily cultivated in a rich, well-drained soil. Propagate from seed or from cuttings that have been dried out for a week or two before planting. Rest in winter.

Myrtillocactus cochal

Myrtillocactus cochal
☼ ❄ ↔10–15 ft (3–4.5 m) ↕15–17 ft (4.5–5 m)
Cactus from northern Baja California, Mexico. Densely branched, tree-like, usually short trunk, many blue-green stems with 5 to 6 ribs;

Nolina parryi, in the wild, Mexico

with or without a central spine, black to gray, 5 to 6 black radials. Flowers pale green to white, spring. Fruits red, spherical. Zones 10–12.

Myrtillocactus geometrizans ★
BILBERRY CACTUS, GARAMBULLA CACTUS, PADRE NUESTRO
☼ ✤ ↔10–15 ft (3–4.5 m) ↕15 ft (4.5 m)
Candelabra-shaped cactus from central Mexico. Usually with a distinct trunk or few main lower branches; many shorter, azure blue, upper branches, club-shaped, jointed, 5 or 6 smooth to rounded ribs. A single, dagger-like, black central spine, 5 to 9 radials, brown to black. Flowers are small, greenish white, in spring. The purplish fruits resemble grapes. Zones 11–12.

NOLINA

This genus in the family Ruscaceae consists of around 24 species of evergreen perennials related to *Yucca*, native to southern USA, Mexico, and Guatemala. Adapted to very dry climates, most have swollen bases that are conical, spherical, or bottle-shaped, with thick corky bark. The long narrow leaves are fibrous and tough. Flowers, usually blooming on mature plants, are very small, creamy white, and are borne densely on tall panicles. Some species are often split off into the genus *Beaucarnea*.
CULTIVATION: Most will withstand some frost. Grow outdoors in warm dry climates. In cooler regions grow in the greenhouse, in a well-drained mix. Propagate from seed or offsets.

Nolina parryi
PARRY'S BEARGRASS
☼ ❄ ↔5 ft (1.5 m) ↕5 ft (1.5 m)
From southwestern USA and Mexico. Slow-growing species, eventually forms thick stems, terminal rosettes of narrow leaves. Very like *N. bigelovii* but leaf edges minutely toothed and do not shred into fibers. Tiny white flowers on ends of long flower stalks, summer. Zones 8–11.

Opuntia littoralis, in the wild, Mexico

OPUNTIA

PRICKLY PEAR, TUNA

This genus in the cactus (Cactaceae) family contains more than 180 species that grow throughout the Americas, from southern Canada to the most southerly part of South America, and also in the West Indies and Galapagos Islands. They range widely from high-altitude to temperate-region and tropical lowland species. Stem segments are highly variable. The spring and summer, cup- or funnel-shaped flowers are followed by prickly egg-shaped fruits. Some species have become invasive. Most species have bristles that break off; these can cause irritation when they penetrate and stick in the skin. CULTIVATION: Opuntias dislike having their roots confined. Those grown outdoors do best in sandy, humus-enriched, moderately fertile, well-drained soil. Frost-hardy species need protection from too much winter wet; grow them in full sun under glass, with filtered light in hot summers. Feed regularly from spring to summer, and reduce or stop watering during winter months. Propagate in spring by sowing pre-soaked seed or by rooting stem segments.

Opuntia aciculata

syn. *Opuntia lindheimeri*

CHENILLE PRICKLY PEAR

☼ ⌘ ↔ 36–60 in (90–150 cm) ↑ 36–60 in (90–150 cm)

A shrubby species native to southwestern USA and northwestern Mexico. Flattened oblong to round stem segments are dotted with tufts of yellowish brown spines and bristles. Flowers yellow or red, borne in spring–summer. Zones 9–11.

Opuntia basilaris ★

BEAVER TAIL CACTUS

☼ ⌘ ↔ 4 ft (1.2 m) ↑ 2–3 ft (0.6–0.9 m)

Perennial from southwestern USA and northwestern Mexico. Oblong to rounded fleshy stems bluish gray, often tinged red, dotted with tufts of reddish bristles. Purplish red flowers, summer. Zones 9–11.

Opuntia cochenillifera

syn. *Nopalea cochenillifera*

COCHINEAL CACTUS

☼ ⌘ ↔ 8 ft (2.4 m) ↑ 12 ft (3.5 m)

Tree-like species, native to Mexico. Trunk up to 8 in (20 cm) in diameter. Flat oval stem segments, often spineless, to 10 in (25 cm) long. Bright red flowers, prominent stamens, in spring–summer. Zones 9–11.

Opuntia humifusa

PRICKLY PEAR CACTUS

☼ ❄ ↔ 36 in (90 cm) ↑ 8–12 in (20–30 cm)

A native of eastern North America. Forms spreading clumps of fleshy dull green leaves made up of sections that are lightly spiny. Yellow frilly flowers in early summer. Dark red fruit is inedible. Zones 5–10.

Opuntia littoralis

☼ ⌘ ↔ 12–48 in (30–120 cm) ↑ 12–24 in (30–60 cm)

From southwestern USA and northwestern Mexico. Sprawling shrub. Flattened oblong to nearly round stem segments, dotted with tufts of yellowish bristles and brown spines. Flowers yellow with red centers, spring–summer; red fruit. *O. l.* var. *vaseyi*, salmon flowers. Zones 9–11.

Opuntia microdasys ★

☼ ❄ ↔ 18–24 in (45–60 cm) ↑ 18–24 in (45–60 cm)

Central and northern Mexico. Thicket-forming shrub. Long, oblong, flattened, green stem segments, yellow bristles. Yellow flowers, often tinged red, spring–summer. 'Albispina', white bristles. Zones 8–11.

Oreocereus celsianus

Opuntia polyacantha

PLAINS PRICKLY PEAR, STARVATION PRICKLY PEAR

☼ ❄ ↔ 48 in (120 cm) ↑ 12 in (30 cm)

Mat-forming cactus found from northern Mexico to Canada, with flattened round stem segments. Clusters of 5 to 10 blue-green spines, 2 in (5 cm) long. Flowers yellow to yellow-green, in spring–summer. Dry, rather spiny fruits. Zones 3–10.

OREOCEREUS

A genus of 9 attractive columnar cacti (family Cactaceae) from the Andes at elevations above 9,840 ft (3,000 m) in southern Peru, northern Chile, southern Bolivia, and northern Argentina. They are all low shrubby cacti with cylindrical stems, sparsely branching from the base, 7–10 ft (2–3 m) tall, rarely developing a trunk. The ribs are tubercled or deeply indented between the areoles, which often bear long white hairs and stout dense spines. Flowers are diurnal, asymmetrical, tubular to funnelform, in red to purple or orange tones. Floral tubes are straight or somewhat curved, with scales and some hairs. Seed pods are fleshy or dry, usually bursting open from the base. All species of *Morawetzia* and some species of *Borzicactus* are now classified as *Oreocereus*.

CULTIVATION: These cacti are easily grown in a rich well-drained soil. Propagate from seed, or from cuttings that have been allowed to dry out for a week or two. Rest them in winter.

Oreocereus celsianus ★

syns *Borzicactus celsianus, B. fossulatus, Oreocereus maximus, O. neocelsianus*

OLD MAN OF THE ANDES

☼ ❅ ↔ 40 in (100 cm) ↕ 7 ft (2 m)

From southern Bolivia, southern Peru, and northern Argentina. Stems columnar, erect, 3–5 in (8–12 cm) in diameter, with 10 to 25 rounded warty ribs. Stems branch from base, covered in white hairs and heavy spines. Areoles large, white with wool and hairs. Spines yellow to reddish brown, 1 to 4 centrals, 7 to 9 radials. Purplish pink flowers, near stem tips, in summer. Seed pods spherical, scaly, green, ripening to yellow. Zones 8–10.

Oreocereus trollii

☼ ❅ ↔ 32 in (80 cm) ↕ 20 in (50 cm)

From southern Bolivia to northern Argentina. Stems short cylindrical, 2½–3 in (6–8 cm) wide, branching from base, pale green, stout, totally covered in dense white hairs almost covering the 15 to 25 strongly warty ribs. Red, yellow, or brown spines, 3 to 5 centrals, 10 to 15 radials. Flowers violet to red, in summer. Seed pods spherical. *O. t.* var. *crassineus*, slightly longer stems. Zones 8–10.

PACHYCEREUS

Genus of 9 species of large, tree-like cacti (family Cactaceae), all found in Mexico, with some straying into southern USA. They are upright plants, branching either at the base or further up the main stem. Shrubbier species may form clumps of unbranched stems. Stem ribbing is sharply angled, with clearly defined spine-bearing areoles along the ridges. The nocturnal flowers, usually white or in shades of pink, are tubular, around 2–3 in (5–8 cm) long, with protruding anthers.

CULTIVATION: As for all cacti, the soil should be very gritty and free draining, and the plants should receive sun for at least half the day. Some species will tolerate the occasional light frost, but in general they are warm-climate plants. Moisture is appreciated in summer, but wet conditions in winter can lead to rotting. Propagate from seed or, with the unusual cultivars, by grafting.

Pachycereus marginatus ★

MEXICAN FENCE POST CACTUS

☼ ✂ ↔ 3–8 in (8–20 cm) ↕ 10–17 ft (3–5 m)

From Mexico. Stout, vertical, columnar branches are used as living fences. Recognized by its 4 to 7 almost triangular ribs that bear elongated white to gray areoles. Spines yellow to gray, 1 to 3 centrals, 5 to 9 radials. Flowers funnelform, red to pink. Fruit spherical, with detachable spines and wool. Zones 10–12.

Pachycereus pringlei

CARDON

☼ ✂ ↔ 24 in (60 cm) ↕ 35 ft (10 m)

A species from northwestern Mexico. Tree-like with thick trunk, to 24 in (60 cm) in diameter. Branches are blue-green becoming yellow-green, bearing 10 to 15 deep ribs. Spines 1 to 3 centrals, gray with black tips, 7 to 10 radials, whitish to gray. Flowering ribs develop large felted areoles that bear white funnelform to bell-shaped flowers. Calyx is scaly with masses of brown hair. Fruit is spherical, with a dense covering of yellowish brown felt and bristles. Zones 10–12.

PACHYPHYTUM

This genus consisting of 12 small succulents from Mexico is a member of the stonecrop (Crassulaceae) family. The name comes from the Greek *pachys* (meaning thick) and *phyton* (meaning plant), referring to the thick smooth leaves of these profusely off-setting plants. Most species grow in a distinct rosette shape, with tightly packed leaves, often with a pruinose finish to them (that is, they are covered with a powdery bloom). *Pachyphytum* is closely related to the genus *Echeveria*, and numerous inter-generic hybrids are currently in cultivation.

CULTIVATION: Grow these succulents in a rich well-drained soil. Propagate by division of older plants, or from stem cuttings dried out for a few days, or from leaves placed on a bed of seed-raising mix. Cuttings and leaves will produce roots and new shoots within a few weeks in warmer months. May also be raised from seed. A brief rest from watering in winter is beneficial.

Pachycereus pringlei, in the wild, Mexico

Pachyphytum compactum ★

☼/◐ ❄ ↔ 16 in (40 cm) ↑ 12 in (30 cm)

From Mexico. Stems branch from base, bearing rosettes of tightly packed, short, cylindrical, dark green to gray-white leaves, tapering to point with keel below tip. Inflorescence, 16 in (40 cm) tall, of many green-tipped bell-shaped flowers, ⅓ in (8 mm) long. Zones 8–11.

PACHYPODIUM

The 17 species of this genus, in the dogbane (Apocynaceae) family, come from Madagascar and southern Africa. They are cactus-like deciduous succulents with very spiny main stems and usually few branches. Variable in size, the largest reaching 25 ft (8 m). Leaves are smooth-edged and sprout from the upper parts of stems and branches. The 4 South African species can stand cooler temperatures, but a minimum winter temperature of 50°F (10°C) is needed for most species. CULTIVATION: They need full sun and a fertile soil with maximum drainage. If growing in containers, do not water through the dormant (winter) period. Apply a low-nitrogen fertilizer once a month during the growing

Pachypodium lamerei

season. In warm climates they grow outdoors in sharply drained, moderately fertile soil. Propagate by sowing seed in pots in a propagator, or take stem tip cuttings in late spring.

Pachypodium geayi

☼ ✦ ↔ 5 ft (1.5 m) ↑ 25 ft (8 m)

Candelabra-shaped succulent tree from southern Madagascar with cigar- or bottle-shaped trunk up to 32 in (80 cm) across, branching after first flowering; branchlets carry spines in 3s, to ¾ in (18 mm). Leaves to 18 in (45 cm) long, narrow, usually hairy. Flowers yellow to white inside, fragrant. Zones 11–12.

Pachypodium lamerei ★

☼ ⋇ ↔ 6 ft (1.8 m) ↑ 20 ft (6 m)

From southern and southwestern areas of Madagascar. Tree-like species with a succulent, thick, thorny stem, branching at the top with age. Terminal clusters of glossy dark green leaves. Fragrant frangipani-like flowers, produced during summer. Fruit is shaped like a double banana. Zones 9–11.

Pachypodium rosulatum

☼ ⋇ ↔ 3 ft (0.9 m) ↑ 5 ft (1.5 m)

Native to Madagascar. Variable succulent, thorny stem with thick forked branches. New leaves hairy at first, becoming smooth, shiny, elliptic and frosted green in color. Slightly tubular yellow flowers, produced during summer months. Zones 9–11.

PARODIA

syns *Eriocactus, Notocactus, Wigginsia*

This genus of about 50 succulent perennials in the cactus (Cactaceae) family is native to South America, from southern Brazil to northwestern Argentina. They may be simple or clustering, and range in form from small and spherical to columnar cacti up to 3 ft (0.9 m) tall. The stems are usually small, green, spherical, or cylindrical, with tubercles arranged in ribs that often spiral around the stem. The yellow to red many-petalled flowers are short and funnel-shaped with hairy bristly tubes and narrow scales, borne on areoles, from spring to autumn. CULTIVATION: Prefer full sun or part-shade in very well-drained soil, with regular watering in summer, but less in winter. Propagation is from seed in spring or summer, from cuttings in summer or by division of the offsets.

Parodia alacriportana

syn. *Notocactus alacriportanus*

☼ ⋇ ↔ 2½–3 in (6–8 cm) ↑ 3–5 in (8–12 cm)

From southern Brazil. A simple or clustering species. Spherical to elongated stem, 1 to 31 vertical ribs with tubercles. Bristly, white, brown, or orange spines, ageing to gray, in a tuft at the top of the stem. Central spines 4 to 6, 1 often hooked, 14 to 20 radial spines. Golden yellow flowers in spring. *P. a.* subsp. *buenekeri* (syn. *P. buenekeri*), fewer central spines. Zones 9–11.

Parodia concinna

syn. *Notocactus tabularis*

☼ ⋇ ↔ 3–4 in (8–10 cm) ↑ 1¼–4 in (3–10 cm)

A usually simple species from southern Brazil and Uruguay. Flattened spherical stem elongates with maturity; 15 to 32 low ribs. Brown, reddish brown, or partly white to pale yellow spines,

Parodia alacriportana subsp. *buenekeri*

Parodia magnifica

Pedilanthus tithymaloides 'Variegatus'

bristly, curved or twisted; 4 to 6 central spines, sometimes more, 9 to 25 shorter radial spines held close to stem. Yellow flowers produced during spring. Zones 9–11.

Parodia leninghausii ★
syns *Eriocactus leninghausii, Notocactus leninghausii*
GOLDEN BALL CACTUS
☼ ❄ ↔ 3–4 in (8–10 cm) ↑ 3–24 in (8–60 cm)
From southern Brazil. Simple or clustering. Branching and becoming columnar with age. Cylindrical stem with slanted top, 30 to 35 straight ribs; 3 or 4 straight or curved, yellow or pale brown central spines, 15 to 20 or more radial spines. Lemon yellow flowers in summer, only at maturity. Zones 9–11.

Parodia magnifica ★
syns *Eriocactus magnificus, Notocactus magnificus*
☼ ❄ ↔ 3–6 in (8–15 cm) ↑ 3–12 in (8–30 cm)
From southern Brazil. Simple, occasionally clustering. Blue-green spherical to elongated stem, 11 to 15 straight pointed ribs; golden yellow spines. Sulfur yellow flowers, produced from late spring through to summer. Zones 9–11.

Parodia ottonis
syns *Notocactus acutus, N. ottonis*
☼ ❄ ↔ 1¼–6 in (3–15 cm) ↑ 1¼–6 in (3–15 cm)
Species from southern Brazil, Uruguay, northeastern Argentina, and southern Paraguay. Ball-shaped, solitary, later clustering. More or less spherical, variably colored stem, tapered at base; 6 to 15 rounded or pointed ribs. Hair-like, straight, curved, or twisted spines, 1 to 6 brown or yellow central spines, 4 to 15 off-white, yellow, or brown radial spines. Yellow, sometimes reddish orange, summer flowers. Zones 9–11.

Parodia scopa ★
syns *Notocactus scopa, N. soldtianus*
SILVER BALL CACTUS
☼ ❄ ↔ 2½–4 in (6–10 cm) ↑ 2–20 in (5–50 cm)
From southern Brazil, Uruguay, and northern Argentina. Simple or clumping, columnar. Dark green spherical to cylindrical stem, mostly obscured by spines; 25 to 40 low ribs with fine tubercles, 3 to 4 brown, red, or white central spines, 35 to 40 or more fine white or pale yellow radial spines. Bright yellow flowers during summer, in a ring around the top of the stem. Zones 9–11.

PEDILANTHUS
A member of the euphorbia (Euphorbiaceae) family, this genus contains around 14 species of clump-forming succulent shrubs or small trees native to drier regions of Central and South America, the West Indies, and southern USA. The fleshy leaves are light green or variegated with a thickened mid-rib. The greenish white flowers are enclosed by colorful bracts that are shaped like a bird's head. All *Pedilanthus* species contain a milky sap that could be poisonous if ingested.
CULTIVATION: These plants prefer a warm climate and partial shade in a very well-drained soil. Most species will withstand extended dry periods. Propagate from cuttings or from seed.

Pelargonium crithmifolium

Pedilanthus tithymaloides ★
DEVIL'S BACKBONE
◑ ❄ ↔ 2 ft (0.6 m) ↑ 6 ft (1.8 m)
From the West Indies and southern USA. Evergreen or deciduous succulent shrub. Has fleshy erect stems zigzagging at each node, mid-green boat-shaped leaves, and small, reddish green, tubular flowers with red bracts, in summer. 'Variegatus', commonly grown form, green leaves variegated white and red. Zones 9–12.

PELARGONIUM (see page 531)

Pelargonium crithmifolium
SAMPHIRE-LEAFED GERANIUM
☼ ✿ ↔ 12–20 in (30–50 cm) ↑ 20 in (50 cm)
A summer- to autumn-flowering South African and Namibian species with thick succulent stems and fleshy, gray-green, pinnate leaves to 6 in (15 cm) long. Heads of up to 8 starry white to pale pink flowers with reddish basal blotch. Zones 10–11.

Pelargonium fulgidum
☼ ❄ ↔ 20–32 in (50–80 cm) ↑ 27 in (70 cm)
Woody based spring- to early summer-flowering scrambling subshrub from South Africa. Succulent stems and pinnate silver-haired leaves to around 4 in (10 cm) long. Heads of bright red flowers. Zones 9–11.

Pelargonium incrassatum
☼ ❄ ↔ 12 in (30 cm) ↑ 12 in (30 cm)
Summer-dormant, tuberous, spring-flowering perennial from South Africa's Western Cape region. It forms basal rosettes of long-stemmed, silver-haired, pinnate leaves to around 2 in (5 cm) long. Sturdy stems carry heads of 10 to 20, rarely up to 40, deep mauve-pink flowers with much-reduced lower petals. Zones 9–11.

Pereskia grandifolia

PERESKIA

This genus is an unusual member of the cactus (Cactaceae) family, as its 16 species of trees, shrubs, and woody climbers have leaves. From southern Mexico and areas of Central and South America. The stems and leaves are not noticeably succulent but spines are numerous. Some species have tuberous roots. The clustered or solitary flowers are red, pink, or white. CULTIVATION: These rather tender plants need greenhouse cultivation in cool climates. In warm climates they can be grown outdoors in a light well-drained soil. They dislike humidity; keep dry in winter. Propagate from seed or cuttings.

Pereskia aculeata ★
BARBADOS GOOSEBERRY, LEMON VINE

☼ ¦ ↔ 6–15 ft (1.8–4.5 m) ↕ 25–30 ft (8–9 m)
Woody climber from tropical America with a thick, cane-like main stem. Sword-shaped, elliptical or oval leaves, 3–5 in (8–12 cm) long, with 2 or 3 spines emerging from the leaf tips. Panicles of numerous scented, white, yellow, or pinkish flowers, in autumn. *P. a.* var. *rubescens* (syn. *P. rubescens*), leaves variegated with red. Zones 9–12.

Pereskia grandifolia

☼ ¦ ↔ 3 ft (0.9 m) ↕ 7–15 ft (2–4.5 m)
A shrub or small tree from Brazil. Thin broadly lance-shaped leaves, brownish black spines. Flowers pink to purplish pink in clusters, from spring to autumn. Zones 9–11.

PLEIOSPILOS

A genus of 4 succulent species, often referred to as "split rock plants," in the iceplant (Aizoaceae) family, from the Little Karoo region of southern Africa. The genus name comes from the Greek *pleio* (full) and *spilos* (dots), referring to the dark green spots on the skin of these plants. They are small, compact and occasionally solitary, but usually clustering with 1 to 4 pairs of leaves per branch. Leaves are often purplish brown, thick, rock-like, fused at their bases and somewhat rounded. Flowers are large, yellow to reddish orange, occasionally white, borne on short stems. The seed pods have 9 to 15 compartments that open when wet. CULTIVATION: Grow these succulents in rich well-drained soil. Propagate from seed or stem cuttings dried out for a week or two, or by division of older clumps. Rest them in winter.

Pleiospilos bolusii

☼ ❄ ↔ 6 in (15 cm) ↕ 2½ in (6 cm)
From South Africa's eastern and western Cape region. Solitary to 3-branched, with hood-shaped leaves, flat on uppersurface, deeply keeled below. Flowers flat funnelform, yellow, about 2 in (5 cm) long. Seed pods flattened, spherical, 12 compartments. Zones 8–11.

Pleiospilos nelii ★

☼ ❄ ↔ 1¾–2½ in (4–6 cm) ↕ 2–2½ in (5–6 cm)
From South Africa's eastern and western Cape region. Easily distinguished by its hemispherical leaves, ¾–1¼ in (18–30 mm) long, flat on upper surface, without a keel on lower side. Flowers flat funnelform, salmon pink to yellow, rarely white. Seed pods flattened, spherical, 11 compartments. Zones 8–11.

PORTULACARIA

In a single-species genus of its own, this ornamental, evergreen, multi-branched, succulent belongs to the purslane (Portulacaceae) family and is native to South Africa. The branches are often held horizontally and develop twists to create a plant that has great character even when young. The leaves are less than 1 in (25 mm) long and rounded, with a smooth, glossy green surface. Clusters of pale pink flowers open from late spring and are followed by 3-lobed pink fruit (rarely seen in cultivation). CULTIVATION: Suitable for mild almost frost-free gardens, especially near the coast, it is an ideal plant for arid areas, well-drained raised beds or for growing in large containers. Prefers a light gritty soil and full sun or light partial shade. Thinning the branches to emphasize the plant's tree-like character can be most effective, otherwise light trimming is all that is required to keep it tidy. Propagate from seed or cuttings in summer.

Portulacaria afra

Portulacaria afra
CHINESE JADE PLANT, ELEPHANT BUSH, ELEPHANT'S FOOD, SPEKBOOM

☼/◗ ¦ ↔ 5 ft (1.5 m) ↕ 10 ft (3 m)
Bright green glossy foliage that contrasts well with the dark purple-brown of the branches. Abundance of small flowers. Zones 9–11.

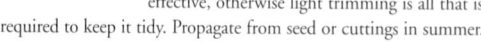

REBUTIA

syns *Aylostera, Weingartia*

These 40 evergreen, low-growing, simple or clustering cacti from the family Cactaceae are native to the mountains of Bolivia and northwestern Argentina. The small stems, 4 in (10 cm) wide or less, are lightly ribbed or with a warty surface, and have weak spines, with the radial and central spines often similar. Funnel-shaped flowers, which emerge from the lower part of the stem, are mostly yellow to red or white, with a sometimes bristly or scaly, slender, curved corolla, opening in daylight. The genus is named after P. Rebut, a nineteenth-century French cactus dealer.
CULTIVATION: *Rebutia* species prefer a gritty, well-drained, slightly acidic soil in an open sunny position. Propagate from seed that is less than 12 months old or by dividing offsets.

Rebutia aureiflora
syn. *Mediolobivia aureiflora*
☼ ⚘ ↔ 3–8 in (8–20 cm) ↥ 2 in (5 cm)
Clustering globular cactus from northwestern Argentina. Warty stems, often tinged red, 3 to 4 central spines, smaller radial spines. Broadly funnel-shaped yellow flowers, usually with a white throat and a paler tube, in summer. *R. a.* var. *rubelliflora*, over 10 radial spines, 1 darker central spine, deep orange flowers. Zones 9–12.

Rebutia fiebrigii ★
syns *Aylostera fiebrigii, Rebutia muscula*
☼ ⚘ ↔ ¾–3 in (18–80 cm) ↥ 1¼–2 in (3–5 cm)
A variable clumping cactus, native to Bolivia and northwestern Argentina. Stems to 2 in (5 cm) tall, depressed at the top, with a warty surface; brown-tipped central spines, white bristly radial spines. Funnel-shaped orange to red flowers, with a slender upcurved tube, are produced in summer months. Zones 9–12.

Rebutia marsoneri
syn. *Rebutia krainziana*
☼ ⚘ ↔ 1¾–8 in (4–20 cm) ↥ 1¼–4 in (3–10 cm)
A clumping cactus from northern Argentina. Pale green stem has a warty surface and nest-shaped clusters of reddish brown spines. Funnel-shaped yellow to orange-yellow or red flowers, borne in summer. Zones 9–12.

Rebutia perplexa
☼ ⚘ ↔ 1–3 in (25–80 mm) ↥ ½–1 in (12–25 mm)
A normally clumping cactus indigenous to Bolivia. Stems with flattened spherical heads. Tall, funnel-shaped, lilac-pink flowers, up to 1½ in (35 mm) in diameter. Zones 9–12.

Rebutia spinosissima
syns *Aylostera spinosissima, Rebutia hoffmannii*
☼ ⚘ ↔ 1¼–8 in (3–20 cm) ↥ 1¼–2½ in (3–6 cm)
Clustering cactus from northern Argentina. Forms flat clumps of light green stems, a little depressed at top; many bristly white spines, brown-tipped central spines. Funnel-shaped

apricot to orange flowers open from pink buds at the base of the stem, during spring. Fruit is small and spherical. Zones 9–12.

RHIPSALIS

A genus of 35 species of epiphytic cacti (family Cactaceae) from tropical America, especially the Caribbean and Brazil. They usually grow as pendulous shrubs with hundreds of intertwining branches, hence the genus name, from the Greek *rhips*, basketwork. Stems of most species are rounded in cross-section; others are angled, ribbed, winged, even flat. Most species are spineless, new stems usually arising singly or in clusters at the ends of older stems. Flowers are small, saucer-shaped, mostly white; fleshy fruits are small and spherical.
CULTIVATION: Easily grown in a humus-rich well-drained soil with regular liquid feeding; very sensitive to alkaline soil. Propagate from stem cuttings dried out for a week or two; also grown from seed. Need more water than most terrestrial cacti, but keep dry for 6 to 8 weeks in autumn to induce winter flowering.

Rhipsalis cereuscula
☼/◑ ⚘ ↔ 12 in (30 cm) ↥ 24 in (60 cm)
From northeastern and eastern South America. Shrubby, much-branched, pendent cactus; cylindrical stems, 4–12 in (10–30 cm) long, from which shorter stems, 4- or 5-angled, arise in clusters; areoles with 2 to 4 short bristles. Small white flowers at ends of stems, in spring. Zones 9–12.

Rhipsalis paradoxa ★
☼/◑ ⚘ ↔ 3 ft (0.9 m) ↥ 5–15 ft (1.5–4.5 m)
From southern Brazil. Large, freely branching, pendent, producing large clusters of new stems at tips of old ones. Stems short, pale green, 3- or 4-angled; angles discontinuous, in zigzag links, pairs or whorls of 3 to 8; areoles spineless, woolly. Single white flowers near stem tips, in summer. Fruits white tinged pink. Zones 9–12.

Rebutia fiebrigii

Rhodiola rosea

RHODIOLA

A genus of about 50 perennial herbs in the stonecrop (Crassulaceae) family, native to the Himalayas, northwestern China, central Asia, North America, and Europe. They feature a single rosette of stems with stalkless, smooth-edged to toothed, alternate, fleshy leaves growing from thick, fleshy, branching, woody rhizomes with brown, scaly, radical leaves. Stems bear dense spreading terminal heads of solitary to numerous 4- or 5-petalled flowers with 4 or 5 fleshy sepals, fused at the base, with 8 or 10 stamens and dark purple anthers. The erect fruit contains many brown seeds. The genus was named from the Greek, *rhodon*, a rose, referring to the rose-scented roots. Tibetans consider the root of *Rhodiola* to be a life-prolonging, wisdom-enhancing, sacred herb.
CULTIVATION: Plants prefer a position in full sun, and can adapt to most well-drained soils. Propagate from seed in spring or from softwood cuttings taken from non-flowering branches.

Rhodiola rosea
syn. *Sedum rosea*
GOLDEN ROOT, ROSE-ROOT
☼ ❄ ↔ 2–30 in (5–75 cm) ↕ 2–30 in (5–75 cm)
A perennial herb of extremely variable habit, native to dry sandy ground at higher altitudes and subarctic areas of Europe and Asia. Thick branching rhizome, fragrant when cut. Smooth, oblong, sometimes red-tinged leaves, to 1¾ in (40 mm) long, with rounded base and pointed tip, smooth-edged or irregularly toothed. Rarely more than 1 to 3 flowering stems with heads of 25 to 70 small greenish yellow flowers, in early summer. Zones 1–8.

RUSCHIA

A large genus of about 400 perennial species, from the drier parts of southern Africa, belonging to the iceplant (Aizoaceae) family. The plants are succulent shrubs or ground covers, with dark reddish brown internodes, some branches bearing spines derived from sterile parts of the flowerheads. Leaves in a pair are free to united, the free parts 3-angled

to round in cross-section. Flowers may be solitary or in branched flowerheads; they have pink, purple, or sometimes white petals.
CULTIVATION: Plants need full sun and thrive in poor well-drained soils. Propagate them from stem cuttings, which can be rooted at almost any time of the year.

Ruschia caroli
PURPLE DEW PLANT
☼ ❄ ↔ 12–18 in (30–45 cm) ↕ 8–12 in (20–30 cm)
Succulent ground-covering perennial from coastal western South Africa. Leaves to 4 in (10 cm) long. Purple flowers, up to 1 in (25 mm) across, in early spring–summer. Zones 10–11.

Ruschia dichroa
ICE PLANT
☼ ❄ ↔ 12–16 in (30–40 cm) ↕ 8–12 in (20–30 cm)
Succulent perennial from coastal western South Africa. Leaves to 2½ in (6 cm) long. Purple, white, or pink flowers, up to 1¾ in (4 cm) across, in summer. Zones 10–11.

SANSEVIERIA
BOWSTRING HEMP, MOTHER-IN-LAW'S TONGUE
A genus of over 50 species of perennial plants in the dragon-tree (Dracaenaceae) family, all native to tropical and southern Africa and the East Indies. Thick fibrous leaves generally form a rosette, either lying nearly flat on the ground or stiffly upright to 5 ft (1.5 m) tall. Flowers are held in a cluster or panicle on simple stems. Fiber from the leaves of *Sansevieria* species is traditionally used for making mats, rope, and bowstrings. Plants are generally cultivated for their decorative leaves, which may be variegated or mottled. They are important indoor plants in temperate climates.
CULTIVATION: They do not tolerate frost, and need shade from the afternoon sun, and only moderate water in summer. Keep dry in winter. Propagation is by division of offsets or from leaf cuttings.

Sansevieria cylindrica
CYLINDER SNAKE PLANT
☼ ❄ ↔ 5 ft (1.5 m) ↕ 16 in (40 cm)
Native to southern tropical Africa. Long, arching, leathery leaves, cylindrical in section, forming a low mound. Flowers are white, flushed with pink, in racemes up to 24 in (60 cm) long, held on a stiff stem, produced during summer months. Zones 10–11.

Sansevieria trifasciata
☼ ❄ ↔ 3 ft (0.9 m) ↕ 5 ft (1.5 m)
Native to tropical west Africa. Forms a dense clump of stiffly upright straight leaves, pale to dark green transverse bands. White flowers in late spring. 'Bantel's Sensation', ivory to ocher, dark green variegated leaves; 'Golden Hahnii', yellow linear striations; 'Hahnii', dark green leaves with pale green transverse bands; 'Laurentii', dark green leaves with paler transverse bands, golden stripes along the margins; 'Moonglow', compact, silver green leaves, edged dark green. Zones 10–11.

Ruschia dichroa

SCHLUMBERGERA

syn. *Zygocactus*

A genus of 6 popular species in the family Cactaceae that grow on rocks or in trees in Brazil, where hummingbirds pollinate the red, purple, pink, or white flowers. Stems are segmented, flattened to round in cross-section, with weak or no spines. Fruits are berry-like, sometimes ribbed. There are many cultivars, some with yellow flowers, which turn pink at low temperatures.

CULTIVATION: These plants are easily grown in heated greenhouses, on windowsills in small pots or hanging baskets in temperate regions, outdoors as epiphytes, or in rock gardens in warmer climates. They prefer slightly acidic humus-rich soils, with shade and high humidity throughout the summer and reduced water in winter. Rest winter-flowering plants in late summer. Most species will grow from cuttings that have been allowed to dry out for a week or so and then planted in humus-rich well-drained soil.

Schlumbergera truncata

Schlumbergera × *buckleyi*

CHRISTMAS CACTUS

☀ ⚘ ↔ 12–24 in (30–60 cm) ↑ 12 in (30 cm)

Garden hybrid between *S. truncata* and *S. russelliana*, long cultivated in northern Europe. Profuse cylindrical flowers with purple stigmas at stem tips, during winter months. Zones 10–12.

Schlumbergera truncata

syn. *Zygocactus truncatus*

CRAB CACTUS

☀ ⚘ ↔ 12–24 in (30–60 cm) ↑ 12 in (30 cm)

Stems scarcely woody at base. Stem segments to 3 in (8 cm) long, with 2 to 4 forward-pointing teeth on each side. Flowers up to 3 in (8 cm) long, variable colors, in autumn. Zones 10–12.

Schlumbergera Hybrid Cultivars

CHRISTMAS CACTUS, HOLIDAY CACTUS, ZYGO

☀/◐ ⚘ ↔ 12–24 in (30–60 cm) ↑ 12 in (30 cm)

Many vigorous hybrids have appeared over the last several decades, adding to the range of colors found in the species and early hybrids such as *S.* × *buckleyi*. Most have broad, thin segments with long teeth and large flowers in soft pastel shades of pink, cream and orange-yellow, often with white petal bases, as well as some deeper magenta shades. The name "holiday cactus" was coined because they bloom through November and December, which is the time of Thanksgiving and Christmas in the Northern Hemisphere. '**Christmas Cheer**', soft orange-red; '**Gold Charm**', strong bronzy-yellow; '**White Christmas**', silky white petals flushed pink at the base with a ring of deeper pink. Zones 10–12.

SEDUM

STONECROP

This very diverse group of succulent species in the stonecrop (Crassulaceae) family has many hybrids. Of Northern Hemisphere origins, with over 300 species they vary enormously in foliage and form. Some are shrubby, with flattened, oval, gray-green leaves;

others are trailing, with succulent jellybean-like leaves; and some form very compact mats. Most species produce small heads of tiny, bright yellow, 5-petalled flowers in summer and autumn. The autumn-flowering types have been reclassified, mainly to the genera *Hylotelephium* and *Rhodiola*. Their name is derived from the Latin *sedo* (to sit), referring to their low spreading habit. Some species have been used medicinally and as salad vegetables. Some, such as *S. spectabile*, are grown for their flowers; others, such as *S. rubrotinctum*, for their colorful plant bodies.

CULTIVATION: Plant in full sun in gritty well-drained soil. Most appreciate water at flowering time, but are otherwise drought tolerant. Propagate by division, from cuttings, or from seed, depending on the growth type.

Sedum acre

STONECROP, WALL PEPPER

☀ ❋ ↔ 12–24 in (30–60 cm) ↑ 2–4 in (5–10 cm)

Perennial native to Europe and North Africa. Spreading, slightly mounding mats of fine stems clothed with tiny, light green, overlapping, triangular leaves, often red-tinted in sun. Heads of small bright yellow flowers at the ends of stems in summer. '**Aureum**' features creamy yellow foliage variegations. Zones 5–10.

Sedum aizoon

☀ ❋ ↔ 20 in (50 cm) ↑ 16 in (40 cm)

Summer-flowering succulent native to temperate northern Asia. Upright stems, fleshy, toothed, 2–3 in (5–8 cm) long, lance-shaped leaves. Flat heads of golden yellow flowers. Zones 7–10.

Sedum album ★

☀ ❋ ↔ 8–20 in (20–50 cm) ↑ 2–4 in (5–10 cm)

Spreading mat-forming perennial from temperate regions of Eurasia and North Africa. Leaves ¼–¾ in (6–18 mm) long, often red-tinted, narrow and cylindrical. Heads of tiny white flowers appear during summer. '**Coral Carpet**', 2 in (5 cm) high cultivar, pink-tinted leaves, light pink flowers. Zones 6–10.

Sedum aizoon

Sedum rubrotinctum

Sedum sieboldii 'Mediovariegatum'

Sedum spathulifolium

Sedum cauticolum
syn. *Hylotelephium cauticolum*

☼ ❄ ↔ 8–20 in (20–50 cm) ↕ 4–6 in (10–15 cm)

Spreading ground cover, native to Japan. Wiry stems. Rounded, sometimes sparsely toothed, gray powder-coated, red-tinted leaves to 1 in (25 mm) long. Dense heads of small pink to near-red flowers from summer to early autumn. Zones 4–10.

Sedum dasyphyllum

☼ ❄ ↔ 8–16 in (20–40 cm) ↕ 2–4 in (5–10 cm)

A cushion-forming perennial species found growing around the Mediterranean region, with some apparently natural forms found growing in southwestern parts of the USA. Spreading pink-tinted stems. Tiny overlapping leaves are grayish to bluish green. Few-flowered heads of tiny, pink-tinted, white flowers are produced during summer months. Zones 8–11.

Sedum dendroideum

☼ ❄ ↔ 12–16 in (30–40 cm) ↕ 6–12 in (15–30 cm)

Spring-flowering Mexican subshrub. Usually one main stem and many side branches that are tipped with rosettes of bright green spatula-shaped leaves up to 1½ in (35 mm) long. Airy panicles of tiny yellow flowers appear in spring. Zones 8–11.

Sedum kamtschaticum
KAMCHATKA STONECROP

☼ ❄ ↔ 16–24 in (40–60 cm) ↕ 4–12 in (10–30 cm)

A succulent species found growing in Japan. Plants spread by rhizomes, produce low branching stems. Fleshy, coarsely toothed, deep green, lance-shaped leaves, under 2 in (5 cm) long. Flattish flowerheads of golden yellow blooms, borne in summer. *S. k.* var. *ellacombeanum* produces pale yellow flowers; *S. k.* 'Variegatum' features creamy white- and pink-variegated mid-green leaves, has golden yellow flowers. Zones 7–10.

Sedum lydium ★

☼ ❄ ↔ 6–12 in (15–30 cm) ↕ 2–4 in (5–10 cm)

Small tufted to cushion-forming Turkish perennial species. Stems root as they spread, and produce ¼ in (6 mm) long, fleshy, red-tipped leaves. Heads of numerous tiny, pink-tinted, white flowers borne during summer months. Zones 9–11.

Sedum morganianum ★
BURRO'S TAIL, DONKEY'S TAIL

☼ ❄ ↔ 4 ft (1.2 m) ↕ 20 in (50 cm)

Evergreen perennial of obscure origin, probably Mexican. Widely cultivated as hanging basket plant. Long trailing stems, and densely crowded, spirally arranged, pointed cylindrical, blue-green leaves. Small long-stemmed flowerheads of pink blooms produced from spring to summer. Zones 9–11.

Sedum oreganum

☼ ❄ ↔ 12–16 in (30–40 cm) ↕ 6 in (15 cm)

Spreading North American perennial. Succulent, green, club-shaped leaves to ¾ in (18 mm) long, red-tinted in autumn. Small yellow flowers, singly or in flat heads, in summer. Zones 6–10.

Sedum rubrotinctum

☼ ❄ ↔ 12–24 in (30–60 cm) ↕ 10 in (25 cm)

A mounding evergreen subshrub of obscure origin, probably Mexican. The arching stems root where they touch the ground. Leaves are thick and cylindrical, blunt-tipped, mid-green in color, red-tinted in sunlight. Loose heads of pale yellow flowers appear during spring months. 'Aurora' ★ features pale yellow-green leaves with a strong red tint. Zones 9–11.

Sedum sieboldii
syn. *Hylotelephium sieboldii*

☼ ❄ ↔ 12–20 in (30–50 cm) ↕ 4 in (10 cm)

Low spreading perennial species from Japan. Leaves up to ¾ in (18 mm), rounded, fleshy, long, gray- to blue-green, often tinted purple or red. Dense heads of tiny pale pink flowers in autumn. 'Mediovariegatum' ★, broad cream-centered leaves; 'Variegatum', cream-mottled blue-green leaves. Zones 7–10.

Sedum spathulifolium ★

☼ ❄ ↔ 24 in (60 cm) ↕ 6 in (15 cm)

Clump-forming perennial species from western North America. Spreads by long runners. Spatula-shaped fleshy leaves, often coloring to bronzy red, mainly clustered in rosettes at stem tips. Tiny flowers, bright yellow, from late spring to early summer. 'Cape Blanco' features silver-gray leaves; 'Purpureum' has foliage that is tinged purple-red. Zones 7–10.

Sedum spurium

☼ ❄ ↔ 12–20 in (30–50 cm) ↑ 6 in (15 cm)

Evergreen mat-forming perennial or subshrub, found from the Caucasus region to northern Iran. Spreading branches; opposite pairs of rounded, fleshy, toothed leaves, red-tinted in sunlight. Heads of small purple-red flowers, rarely white or pink, on erect stems, produced in summer. '**Dragon's Blood**', bears reddish pink flowers, sometimes red-tinged leaves; '**Variegatum**' features leaves that are edged pink and cream. Zones 7–10.

SELENICEREUS

MOON CACTUS, QUEEN OF THE NIGHT

This genus consisting of 28 species of thin-stemmed climbing plants in the family Cactaceae is from seasonal or tropical rainforests in the Americas. Named for Selene, the Greek moon goddess, in reference to its nocturnal flowers, this genus produces some of the largest of all cactus flowers. The floral tubes bear scales, bristles, and spines. Flowers are mainly white and perfumed, 5–16 in (12–40 cm) long, usually borne toward the end of the long, clambering, pencil-thick branches, which grow up to 17 ft (5 m) long. Branches have 3 to 12 ribs, covered in short or bristly spines. To see a fully opened flower, one must wait until after midnight on the one day of the year when the plant blooms.

CULTIVATION: These cacti are easily grown in a humus-rich well-drained soil, and are often grown on a frame or trellis, or in a hanging basket. Propagation is usually from cuttings that have been allowed to dry out for a few days. They may also be raised from seed. Give these plants a rest in winter.

Selenicereus anthonyanus

syn. *Cryptocereus anthonyanus*

☼/❄ ❄ ↔ 7 ft (2 m) ↑ 10 ft (3 m)

A distinctive clambering cactus from Mexico. Unusual stems and branches clustering from the base; branches bright green, flat, zigzag-shaped, with deep lobes. Areoles small, 3 short spines. Fragrant flowers, cream with magenta pericarpals, in summer. Zones 9–12.

Selenicereus grandiflorus ★

☼/❄ ❄ ↔ 7–10 ft (2–3 m) ↑ 17 ft (5 m)

Widely cultivated cactus found in eastern Mexico and the Caribbean. Stems deep green, ½–1 in (12–25 mm) in diameter, with 5 to 8 low ribs. Spines 6 to 18, bristle-like, whitish to brownish. Flowers white, fragrant, with pale yellow to brown pericarpals, borne in summer. Seed pods oval, red. Zones 9–12.

SEMPERVIVUM

HENS AND CHICKENS, HOUSELEEK

This member of the stonecrop (Crassulaceae) family, is a genus containing about 40 species of perennials from the mountains of central and southern Europe and eastward to Turkey and Iran, where the plants grow in rocks and crevices. The thick fleshy leaves may be dull or glossy, and are sometimes covered in a soft down of hairs. They form a flat crowded rosette and spread by offsets, in time becoming a dense tight mat. White, yellow, red, or purplish flowers are held in a cluster on stout fleshy stems during the summer months. Mainly grown for their colorful decorative leaves, these plants make excellent specimens for rock gardens and pots.

CULTIVATION: These perennials require a sandy well-drained soil and dry conditions. The smaller species prefer to nest tightly in narrow crevices, while the larger species need a soil that is richer in humus. *Sempervivum* species are easily propagated from offsets, and they hybridize readily.

Sempervivum arachnoideum ★

COBWEB HOUSELEEK

☼ ❄ ↔ 5–10 in (12–25 cm) ↑ 5 in (12 cm)

A species from the Pyrenees and the Carpathian mountains that forms dense rosettes of green or reddish leaves, their pointed tips connected by fine, cobweb-like, white hairs. The bright rose red flowers are produced in summer. *S. a.* subsp. *tomentosum* has particularly dense leaves with silvery cobwebbing and showy red flowers; *S. a.* 'Cebanse' has larger rosettes. Zones 5–9.

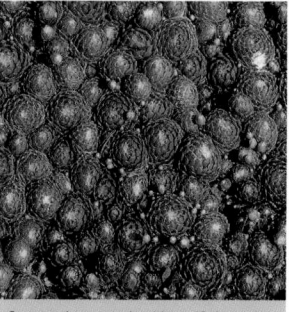

Sempervivum arachnoideum 'Cebanse'

Sempervivum calcareum

☼ ❄ ↔ 5–8 in (12–20 cm) ↑ 2–3 in (5–8 cm)

Indigenous to the Pyrenees, a species that is closely related to *S. tectorum*. Rosettes of brown-tipped gray-green leaves. '**Mrs Giuseppi**' produces gray-green rosettes, the red-tipped leaves darken in winter; '**Sir William Lawrence**' ★ produces larger more globose rosettes, its leaves feature prominent reddish tips. Zones 5–9.

Sempervivum calcareum 'Mrs Giuseppi'

Sempervivum marmoreum

☼ ❄ ↔ 4 in (10 cm) ↕ 1–2 in (2–5 cm)

A species from the Balkans and eastern Europe. Forms flat open rosettes of reddish to purplish tinged leaves, softly hairy when young, becoming smooth and glossy. Star-shaped mauve flowers with white edges. Many cultivars produce more red leaves, 'Brunneifolium', pink-brown leaves; 'Rubicundrum', red-tipped leaves; 'Rubrifolium', bright red-tipped leaves. Zones 5–9.

Sempervivum montanum

☼ ❄ ↔ 1¼–1¾ in (30–40 mm) ↕ ¾ in (18 mm)

Native to mountains of Europe. Very variable; forms clustered mats of dense open rosettes, fleshy, softly furry green leaves, many offsets on fine stems. Violet-purple flowers, during summer. *S. m.* subsp. *stiriacum*, larger, leaves with prominent brown-red tips. Zones 5–9.

Sempervivum pumilum

☼ ❄ ↔ 1–1¼ in (25–30 mm) ↕ ¾ in (18 mm)

A miniature species from the Caucasus region. It forms small rosettes of finely hairy, green leaves. Mauve flowers with white margins, are borne in summer. Zones 5–9.

Senecio serpens

Sempervivum tectorum ★

HEN AND CHICKENS, ST PATRICK'S CABBAGE

☼ ❄ ↔ 8 in (20 cm) ↕ 3–4 in (8–10 cm)

Found growing on mountains in Europe from the Pyrenees to the Balkans; naturalized in the UK. Vigorous and variable. Wide flat rosettes of very fleshy green leaves with reddish tips, many offsets on stout reddish stems. Mauve-red flowers produced in summer. Parent of many cultivars. Zones 5–9.

Sempervivum Hybrid Cultivars

☼/◐ ❄ ↔ 4–16 in (10–40 cm) ↕ 4–8 in (10–20 cm)

Sempervivum species hybridize freely and garden forms vary. Mostly grown for their foliage, a few have showy flowers. 'Booth's Red', dense, neat, purplish red rosettes, symmetrically arranged, to over 3 in (8 cm) wide; 'Commander Hay', a large mound of heavily red-tinted rosettes, each to over 6 in (15 cm) wide;

'Corona', many 1 in (25 mm) wide red-tinted rosettes, turning bright red in winter; 'Engle's Rubrum', 3 in (8 cm) wide gray-green rosettes heavily tinged with red; 'Hall's Hybrid', flat to 3 in (8 cm) wide rosettes, flushed with red at the base; 'Raspberry Ice', tight symmetrical rosettes, red-tinted, fringed with white hairs; 'Reginald Malby', large flat rosettes of deep red-brown tinged leaves; 'Reinhard', many small rosettes with deep purple-red leaf tips, showy pink flowers; 'Virgil', 3 in (8 cm) wide gray-green rosettes, flushed purple-blue with darker tips; 'White Eyes', central part of rosette yellowish green. Zones 6–10.

SENECIO

There are 1,250 species in this cosmopolitan genus of trees, shrubs, annuals, biennials, lianes, perennials, and some succulent species in the daisy (Asteraceae) family; this is one of the largest genera of flowering plants. The leaves are lobed or smooth-edged, and the daisy-like flowers are usually arranged in clusters, with or without florets. The flowers are usually yellow, but can be purple, white, red, or blue. Many species are toxic to livestock. CULTIVATION: With such a large genus, the cultivation requirements are diverse; therefore general guidelines only can be given. These species grow in either moderately fertile well-drained soil in full sun, or in moderately fertile soil that retains moisture; a few will grow in bogs. Plants that are grown in pots in colder climates need fertile well-drained soil with added grit and leaf mold. They should be fed and watered moderately during the growing season. Propagation is from seed or cuttings.

Senecio articulatus

CANDLE PLANT

☼/◐ ✦ ↔ 16–20 in (40–50 cm) ↕ 12 in (30 cm)

Shrubby succulent plant native to the Cape region of South Africa. Fleshy, jointed stems are grayish green, with inverted V-shaped markings below each leaf node. Bluish green leaves flat and broadly triangular, soft and fleshy, and often purple on the undersides. The inflorescences grow at the ends of branches; yellowish white florets with an unpleasant odor appear in winter. Zones 9–11.

Sempervivum, Hybrid Cultivar, 'Corona'

Sempervivum, Hybrid Cultivar, 'Virgil'

Sempervivum, Hybrid Cultivar, 'White Eyes'

Senecio rowleyanus ★

STRING OF BEADS

☼/◐ ❄ ↔ 8–12 in (20–30 cm) ↕ 20–32 in (50–80 cm)

Succulent perennial from Eastern Cape, South Africa. Creeping or pendent habit; thick mat of near-spherical leaves on thin bluish green stems, narrow "window" on uppersurface from tip to base. Single flowerheads at ends of branches. Lacks ray florets; white disc florets, mauve anthers, violet style, cinnamon perfume. Zones 9–10.

Senecio serpens ★

syn. *Kleinia repens*

BLUE CHALKSTICKS

☼ ❄ ↔ 24 in (60 cm) ↕ 12 in (30 cm)

Spreading South African shrub. Narrow, succulent, glaucous leaves with powdery white coating. White flowers in small heads in late spring; best removed to keep plant more lushly foliaged. Zones 9–11.

STAPELIA

CARRION FLOWER, STARFISH FLOWER

This genus belonging to the milkweed (Asclepiadaceae) family contains 99 species of succulent perennials. They are known as carrion flowers because of their putrid smell, which attracts flies for pollination. Most species are native to Africa where they grow in arid areas, often in the shade of scrub, grass, or rocks. Leaves are absent or short-lived on angular, thick, fleshy, toothed stems. The fleshy flowers, usually borne at the base of the plant, are flat and circular with 5 often pointed lobes, hence the common name of starfish flower. They are somewhat muted in shades of yellow, brown, purple, and red, and are often marked transversely with ridges or stripes of different colors.

CULTIVATION: In hot dry regions grow these perennials outdoors in full sun or part-shade. Elsewhere grow them in the greenhouse in a well-drained gritty potting mix with low humidity and bright filtered light. Withhold water in winter. Propagation is from seed or from stem cuttings.

Stapelia gigantea ★

GIANT STAPELIA

☼ ☀ ↔ 8 in (20 cm) ↕ 8–10 in (20–25 cm)

A species found growing from South Africa to Tanzania. Upright, 4-ridged, pale green, fleshy stems, small teeth along angles. Flowers up to 14 in (35 cm) wide, cream to yellow, with transverse crimson lines. Zones 10–12.

Stapelia leendertziae

☼ ☀ ↔ 6–8 in (15–20 cm) ↕ 8 in (20 cm)

From northern South Africa. Narrow, branching, hairy stems with small teeth. Dark purple cup-shaped flowers, downy on the outside, wrinkled interior surface. Zones 10–12.

STENOCACTUS

syn. *Echinofossulocactus*

A genus of 10 to 13 species of small low-growing cacti (Cactaceae family) from the Chihuahua Desert region of northern and central

Stapelia gigantea

Mexico. The name comes from the Greek *stenos*, narrow, referring to the thin wavy ribs that characterize most species. Usually solitary and spherical to cylindrical with age, most species have many narrow, often wavy ribs. The spines are well spaced along the ribs, straight, or upright and incurving, never hooked; the centrals are always uppermost in the spine cluster, the large and often dagger-like radials are always smaller and lower. The flowers are numerous, small, bell-shaped to funnelform, white to yellow, pink, or purple, with a red, purple, or brown mid-stripe. Seed pods are spherical and uniformly small in all species.

CULTIVATION: Grow in rich well-drained soil. Propagate from seed. Rest in winter. An ideal plant for inexperienced cactus growers.

Stenocactus coptonogonus ★

☼ ❄ ↔ 3–5 in (8–12 cm) ↕ 2–4 in (5–10 cm)

Solitary spherical cactus native to Mexico. Dark green, 10 to 15 stout ribs, depressed at the spine cluster. Distinctive spines, 3 to 7, upper 3 to 5 broad flattened centrals, pointed upward, remainder all downward-pointing radials. White flowers with purple mid-stripe. Zones 8–10.

Stenocactus crispatus

syns *Echinofossulocactus flexispinus*, *E. multiareolatus*

☼ ❄ ↔ 3–5 in (8–12 cm) ↕ 3–5 in (8–12 cm)

Solitary, flattened spherical, yellow green to dark green cactus from Mexico with 25 to 60 wavy ribs. Spines variable; straight, yellow or brown, 1 to 4 upward-pointing centrals, 2 to 10 downward-pointing radials. Bright pink-red flowers are borne in spring. Zones 8–10.

Stenocactus crispatus

Stenocactus multicostatus

syns *Stenocactus lloydii*, *S. zacatecasensis*

BRAIN CACTUS

☼ ❄ ↔ 4 in (10 cm) ↕ 3–5 in (8–12 cm)

A flattened spherical cactus indigenous to Mexico. Produces up to 120 very thin, sharp-edged, wavy ribs. Long, flexible, sword-like central spines; glassy, straight to curved radials. Flowers are white, with a purple mid-stripe. Zones 8–10.

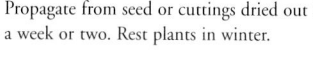
Stenocereus eruca

STENOCEREUS

A genus of 23 disparate species of columnar to tree-like cactus (Cactaceae) family members from southwestern USA, Central America, the Caribbean, Venezuela, and Colombia. The name comes from the Greek *stenos*, narrow, and refers to the numerous thin ribs of many of the species. The genus now includes all species previously classified as *Rathbunia* and *Machaerocereus*, and most of *Lemaireocereus*. Plants have stout, cylindrical, mostly green stems with numerous ribs. They may or may not have tubercles and the areoles may be woolly, but a common feature is very strong spines. Flowers are bell-shaped to funnelform, opening at night and lasting into the next day. Pericarpels are short, with many areoles, often spiny. Seed pods are spherical, fleshy, with deciduous spines. CULTIVATION: Grow in a rich well-drained soil. Propagate from seed or cuttings dried out for a week or two. Rest plants in winter.

Stenocereus beneckei

syns *Lemaireocereus beneckei*, *Rathbunia beneckei*
☼ ❄ ↔ 20–40 in (50–100 cm) ↕ 7–10 ft (2–3 m)
An upright to arching, thin, columnar cactus native to Mexico. Occasionally branching from the base, and with white powdery stems. Ribs 7 to 9, widely separated, straight black central spine, 2 to 5 grayish radials. White nocturnal flowers, brown, naked, and with scaly pericarpels. Zones 9–10.

Stenocereus eruca

syns *Lemaireocereus eruca*, *Rathbunia eruca*
CATERPILLAR CACTUS, CREEPING DEVIL
☼ ❄ ↔ 17–20 ft (5–6 m) ↕ 3–10 ft (0.9–3 m)
Prostrate plant from Mexico. It forms tangled mats of heavily spined dark green stems, 10 to 12 ribs. Spines have 1 to 3 stout, flattened, dagger-shaped, gray centrals, 10 to 15 rounded and whitish radials. Flowers are few, nocturnal, salverform, pinkish white to cream. Seed pods are spherical. Zones 9–10.

SYNADENIUM

This genus is made up of about 20 species of succulent shrubs and small trees native to central and east Africa and the Mascarene Islands. Being members of the euphorbia (Euphorbiaceae) family, species are closely related to *Euphorbia* and similarly have smooth fleshy stems that contain a milky sap. A few species are grown for their ornamental leaves, which are alternate, lance-shaped or oval and rather fleshy. All parts of the plant are highly poisonous, and contact with the sap can irritate the eyes, mouth, and skin. CULTIVATION: Most species prefer a warm dry climate. Grow in full sun in a moderately fertile well-drained soil. Water sparingly in winter and lightly prune in late winter to shape. Propagate from seed or from cuttings.

Synadenium compactum

☼ ❄ ↔ 6 ft (1.8 m) ↕ 10–20 ft (3–6 m)
A small tree indigenous to Kenya. Glossy green oval leaves, with a pronounced central rib. Very small greenish yellow flowers, near the ends of the stems, during autumn. 'Rubrum' (syn. *S. grantii* 'Rubrum') has lance-shaped to oval leaves, purple to rich bronze-red; 'Variegatum', features interesting foliage with patches of bright green and dark olive to grayish green. Zones 9–12.

Synadenium grantii ★

AFRICAN MILKBUSH, GRANT'S MILKBUSH
☼ ❄ ↔ 4 ft (1.2 m) ↕ 12 ft (3.5 m)
An erect succulent shrub native to tropical Africa, often smaller in cultivation. Fleshy light green leaves, finely toothed margins, spirally arranged near the ends of the stems. Small, bowl-shaped, deep red flowers borne in the autumn months. Zones 9–12.

Synadenium compactum 'Variegatum'

THELOCACTUS

This is a genus of 12 small solitary to clustering members of the cactus (Cactaceae) family from the Chihuahua Desert, Mexico through to Texas, USA. The stems are spherical to columnar, to 10 in (25 cm) tall and 8 in (20 cm) in diameter. The ribs are vertical or spiralling, with tubercles usually prominent, rounded to conical, often with extra floral nectaries that attract ants. The spines are variable but persistent, usually straight, up to 2½ in (6 cm) long. Funnel-shaped flowers appear from the growing tip, and come in various colors. Seed pods are spherical to oval, green to bright red, and can be dry to the touch. These plants are very popular with cacti collectors because of their easy culture, showy spines, and large flowers. CULTIVATION: These attractive cacti are easily grown in a rich well-drained soil. Propagate from seed, or by division of older plants, or from cuttings that have been allowed to dry out for a week or two. Give the plants a rest during the winter months.

Thelocactus hexaedrophorus

syns *Thelocactus fossulatus, T. lloydii*

☼ ❄ ↔ 3–6 in (8–15 cm) ↕ 1¼–3 in (3–8 cm)

Usually solitary species from Texas, USA. Spherical to flattened-spherical stems. Ribs indistinct; tubercles compressed, rounded; areoles with grooves. Spines reddish, brownish, or grayish white. Flowers white, sometimes with a reddish mid-stripe, produced in summer months. Seed pods green to magenta. Zones 9–11.

Thelocactus macdowellii

syns *Echinomastus macdowellii, Neolloydia macdowellii*

☼ ❄ ↔ 2–5 in (5–12 cm) ↕ 2–4 in (5–10 cm)

A solitary or clustering species from Texas, USA. Spherical stems, green to pale green, densely covered in spines. Ribs are indistinct; tubercles conical. Spines are white to grayish white. The magenta flowers are borne during summer. Seed pods are dry. Zones 9–11.

Thelocactus setispinus

syn. *Hamatocactus setispinus*

☼ ❄ ↔ 2–4 in (5–10 cm) ↕ 3–5 in (8–12 cm)

A solitary species from Mexico, rarely offsetting. Spherical to elongated spherical stems, yellow-green. Ribs are conspicuous, thin, wavy; tubercles are absent; areoles with extra floral nectaries. Spines are yellowish white to red, whitish, or reddish white. Flowers are yellow with a deep red throat, borne in summer. Seed pods are spherical, red, fleshy. Zones 9–11.

TITANOPSIS

This genus of 5 species is a member of the iceplant (Aizoaceae) family, from Namibia and South Africa. They are small succulents making rosettes of 6 to 8 tightly packed, very warty leaves. Leaves are broad, spoon-shaped, with a triangular widening at the tip, in shades of white, gray, pink, red, and brown. The daisy-like, yellow to orange flowers are honey-scented, opening in the afternoon, closing by dusk, and are stemless or with a short stem. Seed pods have from 5 to 10 chambers, but usually 6 chambers.

Titanopsis calcarea

The name, from the Greek *titanos,* chalk, *opsis,* appearance, refers to the calcium-filled warts on the ends of the leaves.

CULTIVATION: Quite easy to grow in a mineralized well-drained soil. Do not overwater; give a distinct winter rest. Usually propagated from seed, but may also be grown by careful division of older clumps.

Titanopsis calcarea

☼/❉ ❄ ↔ 20 in (50 cm) ↕ ¾–1¾ in (18–40 mm)

This tiny succulent is found among limestone rocks throughout Northern, Western, and Eastern Cape in South Africa. Rosettes of spoon-shaped leaves with truncated ends densely covered in reddish or gray-white tubercles, giving a greenish to bluish hue that mimicks its habitat. Flowers golden yellow to orange, in summer. Zones 8–10.

TRADESCANTIA (see page 598)

Tradescantia sillamontana

WHITE VELVET

◖❉◗/◉ ❄ ↔ 40 in (100 cm) ↕ 6–32 in (15–80 cm)

A perennial species from northern Mexico. Sometimes erect, or spreading and trailing. Fleshy lance-shaped leaves, to nearly 3 in (8 cm) long, purple-red tinted under a dense covering of silky silvery hairs. Small purple-magenta flowers, produced in summer months. Zones 9–11.

Tradescantia sillamontana

TRICHODIADEMA

The 34 shrubby species in this genus are members of the iceplant (Aizoaceae) family, and are found growing in Namibia and South Africa. Plants range from shrubby with long, slender, arched branches to short-stemmed subshrubs. Most species have woody to tuberous roots. Leaves are small, semi-cylindrical, uniquely tipped with a cluster of bristles, and usually glisten with tiny specialized water-storing cells. Small, solitary, daisy-like flowers are white, cream, yellow, or pink to purple, borne from winter into early summer. Seed pods usually have 5 or 6 compartments.

CULTIVATION: These shrubby plants are easy to grow in a mineral-rich, well-drained soil. Protect them from excessive rain during summer if planted outside; give them a short rest from watering in mid-winter. Propagate from seed, or more usually from cuttings allowed to dry out for a few days.

Trichodiadema bulbosum

☼ ❄ ↔ 16–20 in (40–50 cm) ↕ 6 in (15 cm)

A tiny shrub from South Africa. Tuberous roots, often partially raised for display. Leaves are short, cylindrical, appearing gray-green due to the covering of short white hairs. Flowers are deep purple, borne in early spring. Zones 8–10.

Trichodiadema densum

☼ ❄ ↔ 16–20 in (40–50 cm) ↕ 6 in (15 cm)

Shrub from South Africa. Thick fleshy roots; stems short. Leaves in tufts, densely crowded, green, covered with numerous, short, downy hairs and tipped with a tuft of white bristles. The dark red flowers are produced in early spring. Zones 8–10.

Welwitschia mirabilis

TURBINICARPUS

A genus of 24 species of tiny cactus in the family Cactaceae, most from limited habitats in northern Mexico. The plants are usually unbranched, spherical to slightly depressed spherical. Ribs are replaced by tubercles, sometimes indistinct. Areoles are at the tubercle tips and are often woolly and white. There are generally few spines but those that exist are flexible and not usually sharp. Growing from the stem tips, flowers are funnel-shaped, diurnal, in white, rose, or magenta. The seed pods are spherical. Many species have had several name changes; some botanists argue that *Turbinicarpus* species originated as stabilized juvenile forms of *Neolloydia* and should be included in that genus.
CULTIVATION: These cacti are easily grown in well-drained, purely mineral soil or soil with very little organic material. Rest them in winter, again in the heat of summer. Give them less than average water throughout spring and autumn. Propagate from seed.

Turbinicarpus pseudomacrochele
syn. *Strombocactus pseudomacrochele*
⚘ ⚘ ↔ 1–1½ in (25–35 mm) ↕ ¾–1¾ in (18–40 mm)
A solitary, occasionally clustering species from Mexico with spherical to short cylindrical stems, pale green to dark blue-green with woolly tips; tubercles low, tapering. Spines yellowish brown turning gray. Flowers are white, reddish purple, yellowish green, or magenta, in late spring. Seed pods green, spherical. *T. p.* subsp. *krainzianus* (syn. *Neolloydia krainziana*), dark green stems, smaller magenta to cream flowers. Zones 9–11.

Turbinicarpus valdezianus
syn. *Pelecyphora valdeziana*
⚘ ⚘ ↔ ½–1 in (12–25 mm) ↕ ½–1 in (12–25 mm)
Solitary species from Mexico with depressed spherical to hemispherical stems, the green color obscured by the dense feathery spines; tubercles are flattened. Flowers are white with a magenta mid-stripe, produced throughout the summer months. Seed pods dark greenish brown and spherical. Zones 9–11.

WELWITSCHIA

This genus, which makes up the family Welwitschiaceae, is made up of just one species found in the deserts and nearby woodland of southwest Africa. It is a long-lived perennial (up to 1,500 years) with a short exposed stem that can reach 40 in (100 cm) wide, and a long tap root. There are just 2 parallel-veined leaves growing from the base. With time these become shredded and look like multiple leaves. Male and female flowers, on separate plants, are in red cones at the apex of the plant. *Welwitschia* is rarely grown except in botanic gardens for its curiosity value.
CULTIVATION: It is cultivated from fresh seed under conditions suitable for cacti, with seedlings requiring careful watering in order to prevent rotting off. Often plants are grown in clay drainpipes to accommodate the tap root, which is easily damaged.

Welwitschia mirabilis
syn. *Welwitschia bainesii*
⚘ ⚘ ↔ 10 ft (3 m) ↕ 4 ft (1.2 m)
Tree with more of its trunk below than above ground. Two straplike olive green leaves arise from the top of the truncated stem, growing from the base. Male cones are brightly colored, possess stamens; female cones are greenish yellow and reddish brown with a style-like structure present. Zones 9–10.

YUCCA

Native to dry regions of North and Central America and the West Indies, the 40-odd species in this agave (Agavaceae) family genus include evergreen herbaceous perennials, as well as trees and shrubs. They have a strong bold form and rosettes of strap- to lance-shaped leaves. Bell- to cup-shaped flowers are held on usually erect panicles.
CULTIVATION: They grow best in loamy soil with good drainage, but will tolerate poor sandy soil. In colder regions it is best to grow tender species in large pots in loam-based potting compost and overwinter them indoors. Grown outdoors they need good light in summer, a monthly feed and careful watering. *Yucca* species range from frost hardy to frost tender. Propagate by sowing seed in spring, or by taking root cuttings in winter, or by removing suckers in spring.

Turbinicarpus valdezianus

Yucca aloifolia
DAGGER PLANT, SPANISH BAYONET
⚘ ❊ ↔ 10 ft (3 m) ↕ 25 ft (8 m)
From the West Indies, Mexico, and southeastern USA. A slow-growing shrub or small tree. Erect stem simple or branched, stiff, lance-shaped, toothed, gray-green leaves to 20 in (50 cm) long, sharply pointed. Bell-shaped, pendent, white flowers, on erect spikes, summer–autumn. Fleshy fruit. 'Marginata' ★, yellow leaf edges; 'Tricolor', leaves striped white or yellow in center. Zones 8–11.

Yucca baccata
BANANA YUCCA, BLUE YUCCA, SPANISH BAYONET
⚘ ⚘ ↔ 4 ft (1.2 m) ↕ 5 ft (1.5 m)
A native of northern Mexico and southwestern USA. Single-stemmed or branched, spent leaves persist on stem. Leaves green

with yellow or blue tinges, fine hairs on leaf edges. Bell-shaped flowers, in panicles, cream sometimes tinged purple. **Zones 9–11.**

'Ivory' is a freely flowering cultivar with spikes of ivory flowers that may have a green tinge. **Zones 6–9.**

Yucca brevifolia
JOSHUA TREE

☼ ❄ ↔ 5 ft (1.5 m) ↕ 30–40 ft (9–12 m)

Found from California to southwestern Utah, USA. Has branching habit, bark gray or orange-brown forming plates. Leaves straight and narrow, finely toothed edges. Flower spikes bear unpleasant smelling greenish flowers, tinged yellow or cream, in late spring. **Zones 7–10.**

Yucca elata
PALMELLA, SOAP WEED

☼ ⚜ ↔ 5 ft (1.5 m) ↕ 10 ft (3 m)

Found from Arizona to Texas, USA, and Mexico. Suckering shoots, multiple stems covered with dead leaves. New leaves light green, edged with fine hairs. Flower stalk is up to 6 ft (1.8 m) tall, flowers are creamy white, tinted pink or green. **Zones 9–11.**

Yucca elephantipes
syn. *Yucca guatemalensis*
GIANT YUCCA, SPINELESS YUCCA

☼ ⚜ ↔ 10 ft (3 m) ↕ 30 ft (9 m)

Native to Central America and Mexico. Large erect shrub or small tree. Narrow, leathery, mid-green leaves, to 3 ft (0.9 m) long, finely toothed edges. White or cream flowers borne on 3 ft (0.9 m) tall stalks, from summer through to autumn. **Zones 10–12.**

Yucca filamentosa ★
ADAM'S NEEDLE

☼ ❄ ↔ 5 ft (1.5 m) ↕ 3 ft (0.9 m)

From eastern USA. Usually trunkless, multiple suckering heads of 30 in (75 cm) long, filamentous, blue-green leaves. Flower stems to 10 ft (3 m) tall bear masses of pendulous cream flowers in summer. **'Bright Edge' ★**, dwarf cultivar with yellow-edged foliage, creamy flowers tinged green; **'Golden Sword' ★**, similar but larger; **'Ivory Tower'**, flowers creamy white tinged green. **Zones 6–10.**

Yucca flaccida
syn. *Yucca filifera*

☼ ❄ ↔ 17–35 ft (5–10 m) ↕ 17–35 ft (5–10 m)

A branching, evergreen, perennial shrub from North America. Dark bluish green, flexible, narrowly sword-shaped leaves, up to 22 in (55 cm) long, with sharp tips and yellow serrated margins ending in straight threads. Cylindrical heads of creamy white bell-shaped flowers, up to 2 in (5 cm) long, in panicles to around 5 ft (1.5 m) long, borne from summer to autumn. **'Golden Sword'** has green leaves with yellow margins;

Yucca brevifolia, in the wild, California, USA

Yucca gloriosa
CANDLE YUCCA, PALM LILY, ROMAN CANDLE

☼ ❄ ↔ 6 ft (1.8 m) ↕ 6–8 ft (1.8–2.4 m)

A species found growing from North Carolina to Florida, USA. Usually unbranched and tree-like. Stiff, thin, lance-shaped, blue-green leaves, ageing to dark green. White, pendent bell-shaped flowers, sometimes tinged with green, pink or purplish red on tall panicles, produced from summer to autumn. **'Variegata' ★** has leaves with yellow-cream stripes and edges. **Zones 7–10.**

Yucca recurvifolia
WEEPING YUCCA

☼ ❄ ↔ 4 ft (1.2 m) ↕ 4–8 ft (1.2–2.4 m)

Native to southeastern USA. Robust shrub, may have multiple stems. Leathery, bluish to deep green, tapered leaves, recurved and drooping in some forms, mostly straight in others. Large, creamy white, bell-shaped flowers, tall panicles, late summer to late autumn. **Zones 8–11.**

Yucca whipplei
OUR LORD'S CANDLE

☼ ❄ ↔ 4 ft (1.2 m) ↕ 3 ft (0.9 m)

Stiff-leafed stemless yucca ranges from southwestern USA into Baja California, Mexico. Rosettes of narrow, rigid, blue-green leaves, spiny tips, fine-toothed edges. The flowering panicle grows rapidly to 10–15 ft (3–4.5 m) high, with pendulous, small, white flowers, often green- or purple-tipped, from late summer into early autumn. *Y. w.* **subsp.** *parishii* is an unbranched race. **Zones 8–11.**

Yucca whipplei

Orchids

Orchids form one of the largest of all plant families, with 25,000 to 35,000 species in over 800 genera, and they can be found on all continents except Antarctica. They are diverse in size, growth habit, and flower color and shape, but all share a particular flower formation. They have three sepals and three petals; one petal differs from the other two and is called the labellum or lip. Located at the bottom of the flower, the labellum is often larger and different in color to the other petals, with various markings, and sometimes with a nectar-bearing spur at the base.

The most distinctive feature of an orchid flower is the reproductive organs. The stamens, style, and stigmas—separate in most plants—are joined in orchid flowers to form a structure called the column. As well, the pollen, instead of being loose, is in masses called pollinia. Pollination mechanisms are often complex, not to say bizarre.

Orchids may be either terrestrial (growing in soil), epiphytic (growing on the trunks or branches of trees), or lithophytic (growing on rocks). Over half of all orchids are epiphytes, such as *Vanda coerulea,* but the most widely cultivated orchids are hybrids; well over 100,000 hybrids have been registered.

Although associated with tropical regions, some orchids—such as *Cymbidium tracyanum*—are cool-growing plants that need protection from summer heat.

Orchid Finder

The following cultivation table features at-a-glance information for every species or hybrid with an individual entry in the Orchids chapter of this book. Simply find the plant you wish to know more about, and run your eye along the row to discover its height and spread, whether it has showy and/or scented flowers, whether it is drought and/or frost tolerant, the aspect it prefers, and more. The last column is marked for the plant if that plant is protected by Appendix I of CITES.

The type of plant is abbreviated to **E**, **L**, or **T**:
E – the plant is an epiphyte.
L – the plant is a lithophyte.
T – the plant is a terrestrial.

The temperature requirements that each plant needs to thrive are given (some plants will grow well in more than one temperature range), abbreviated to **W**, **I**, or **C**:
W – warm-growing plants that prefer a winter nighttime minimum of 60°F (16°C); these plants are very unforgiving if temperatures drop below 50°F (10°C), but can take high temperatures as long as the humidity is high.
I – intermediate-growing plants that prefer a winter nighttime minimum of 50°F (10°C); these plants can take cooler temperatures for short lengths of time.
C – cool-growing plants that prefer a winter nighttime minimum of 39°F (4°C); keep these plants cooler in summer.

Plant name	Height	Spread	Type	Temperature	Showy flowers	Scented flowers	Grow in pot	Grow on mount	Keep moist	Dry winter	Drought tolerant	Frost tolerant	Full sun	Half sun	Shade	CITES listed
Anguloa uniflora	16–24 in (40–60 cm)	12–24 in (30–60 cm)	T	I/C	♦		♦		♦					♦		
Ascocenda Hybrids	16–48 in (40–120 cm)	12–24 in (30–60 cm)	E	W	♦		♦						♦			
Ascocentrum garayi	5–12 in (12–30 cm)	5–10 in (12–25 cm)	E	W	♦		♦						♦			
Bletilla striata	12–24 in (30–60 cm)	12–48 in (30–120 cm)	T	C	♦		♦					♦	♦	♦		
Brassia arcuigera	12–24 in (30–60 cm)	8–16 in (20–40 cm)	E	W/I	♦	♦	♦	♦	♦					♦		
Brassia verrucosa	8–12 in (20–30 cm)	8–24 in (20–60 cm)	E	I	♦	♦	♦	♦	♦					♦		
Brassia Hybrids	12 in (30 cm)	24 in (60 cm)	E	W/I	♦	♦	♦	♦						♦		
Brassocattleya Hybrids	10 in (25 cm)	12 in (30 cm)	E	W/I/C	♦	♦	♦		♦		♦		♦	♦		
Brassolaeliocattleya Hybrids	8–24 in (20–60 cm)	8–24 in (20–60 cm)	E	W/I/C	♦	♦	♦				♦			♦		
Bulbophyllum Daisy Chain	5 in (12 cm)	12 in (30 cm)	E	W	♦		♦	♦						♦		
Bulbophyllum pectenveneris	3–6 in (8–15 cm)	16 in (40 cm)	E	W				♦	♦					♦		
Bulbophyllum rothschildianum	10 in (25 cm)	24 in (60 cm)	E	W/I/C	♦	♦	♦	♦	♦					♦		
Bulbophyllum wendlandianum	8–12 in (20–30 cm)	4–12 in (10–30 cm)	E	W/I/C	♦			♦	♦	♦				♦	♦	
Cattleya aurantiaca	5–24 in (12–60 cm)	6–24 in (15–60 cm)	E	W/I			♦						♦	♦		
Cattleya bicolor	8–48 in (20–120 cm)	8–24 in (20–60 cm)	E/L	W/I	♦								♦	♦		
Cattleya bowringiana	6–36 in (15–90 cm)	4–24 in (10–60 cm)	L	W/I	♦								♦	♦		
Cattleya intermedia	6–16 in (15–40 cm)	4–12 in (10–30 cm)	E	W/I	♦									♦		
Cattleya loddigesii	6–24 in (15–60 cm)	4–12 in (10–30 cm)	E	W/I	♦									♦		
Cattleya walkeriana	3–6 in (8–15 cm)	4–10 in (10–25 cm)	E	I	♦		♦							♦		
Cattleya Hybrids	8–32 in (20–80 cm)	8–24 in (20–60 cm)	E	I	♦		♦							♦		
Coelogyne Burfordiense	10–36 in (25–90 cm)	8–32 in (20–80 cm)	E	W	♦	♦	♦							♦		
Coelogyne flaccida	5–15 in (12–38 cm)	4–27 in (10–70 cm)	E	I/C	♦	♦	♦							♦		
Coelogyne pandurata	8–24 in (20–60 cm)	8–48 in (20–120 cm)	E	W	♦	♦	♦							♦		
Cymbidium erythrostylum	12–27 in (30–70 cm)	8–24 in (20–60 cm)	E	C	♦		♦		♦				♦	♦		
Cymbidium lowianum	12–48 in (30–120 cm)	8–36 in (20–90 cm)	T	I/C	♦		♦		♦				♦	♦		
Cymbidium tracyanum	12–48 in (30–120 cm)	8–36 in (20–90 cm)	E	C	♦	♦	♦		♦				♦	♦	♦	

Plant name	Height	Spread	Type	Temperature	Showy flowers	Scented flowers	Grow in pot	Grow on mount	Keep moist	Dry winter	Drought tolerant	Frost tolerant	Full sun	Half sun	Shade	CITES listed
Cymbidium Hybrids	12–48 in (30–120 cm)	8–36 in (20–90 cm)	T	I/C	◆		◆						◆	◆		
Cypripedium formosanum	4–10 in (10–25 cm)	4–12 in (10–30 cm)	T	C	◆		◆							◆		
Dactylorhiza elata	24 in (60 cm)	6 in (15 cm)	T	C	◆		◆					◆	◆	◆		
Dactylorhiza fuchsii	8–24 in (20–60 cm)	4–10 in (10–25 cm)	T	C	◆		◆					◆	◆	◆	◆	
Dendrobium bigibbum	4–24 in (10–60 cm)	8–24 in (20–60 cm)	E	W	◆		◆	◆			◆		◆			
Dendrobium chrysotoxum	8–16 in (20–40 cm)	8–24 in (20–60 cm)	E	W/I	◆		◆				◆		◆	◆		
Dendrobium crumenatum	8–24 in (20–60 cm)	8–24 in (20–60 cm)	E	W	◆	◆	◆	◆					◆	◆		
Dendrobium cuthbertsonii	1–3 in (2.5–8 cm)	2–8 in (5–20 cm)	E	I/C	◆		◆	◆	◆					◆		
Dendrobium discolor	1–6 ft (0.3–1.8 m)	1–4 ft (0.3–1.2 m)	E/L	W	◆		◆			◆			◆			
Dendrobium fimbriatum	1–7 ft (0.3–2 m)	1–4 ft (0.3–1.2 m)	E	I/C	◆	◆	◆				◆		◆	◆		
Dendrobium gibsonii	12–48 in (30–120 cm)	12–24 in (30–60 cm)	E	I	◆		◆						◆	◆		
Dendrobium gracilicaule	8–24 in (20–60 cm)	8–36 in (20–90 cm)	E/L	I/C		◆	◆	◆						◆		
Dendrobium johnsoniae	8–20 in (20–50 cm)	8–20 in (20–50 cm)	E	W	◆		◆						◆	◆		
Dendrobium kingianum	2–36 in (5–90 cm)	4–48 in (10–120 cm)	E/L	I/C	◆	◆	◆							◆		
Dendrobium lindleyi	8–16 in (20–40 cm)	8–16 in (20–40 cm)	E	W/I	◆		◆						◆	◆		
Dendrobium nobile	8–24 in (20–60 cm)	8–24 in (20–60 cm)	E	W/I/C	◆		◆			◆			◆	◆		
Dendrobium pulchellum	1–7 ft (0.3–2 m)	1–3 ft (0.3–0.9 m)	E	W	◆	◆	◆						◆	◆		
Dendrobium speciosum	4–48 in (10–120 cm)	1–10 ft (0.3–3 m)	E/L	I/C	◆	◆	◆	◆			◆		◆	◆		
Dendrobium spectabile	8–32 in (20–80 cm)	8–24 in (20–60 cm)	E	W	◆		◆						◆	◆		
Dendrobium tetragonum	4–27 in (10–70 cm)	4–20 in (10–50 cm)	E	I/C	◆	◆	◆	◆						◆		
Dendrobium thrysiflorum	8–24 in (20–60 cm)	8–36 in (20–90 cm)	E	W/I	◆		◆							◆		
Dendrobium victoriae-reginae	8–24 in (20–60 cm)	8–20 in (20–50 cm)	E	I/C	◆		◆			◆				◆		
Dendrobium, Australian Hybrids	4–24 in (10–60 cm)	8–30 in (20–75 cm)	E	I/C	◆	◆	◆							◆		
Dendrobium, "Hardcane" Hybrids	8–40 in (20–100 cm)	8–32 in (20–80 cm)	E	W	◆		◆							◆		
Dendrobium, "Nigrohirsute" Hybrids	8–16 in (20–40 cm)	8–16 in (20–40 cm)	E	W/I	◆		◆							◆		
Dendrobium, "Softcane" Hybrids	8–24 in (20–60 cm)	6–16 in (15–40 cm)	E	I/C	◆		◆						◆	◆		
Dendrochilum saccolabium	8–16 in (20–40 cm)	8–24 in (20–60 cm)	E	I	◆		◆		◆					◆		
Dendrochilum tenellum	8–16 in (20–40 cm)	8–32 in (20–80 cm)	E	I	◆	◆	◆							◆		
Disa Hybrids	8–32 in (20–80 cm)	4–10 in (10–25 cm)	T	C	◆		◆		◆				◆	◆		
Encyclia hanburyi	8–27 in (20–70 cm)	8–20 in (20–50 cm)	E	W/I	◆		◆	◆		◆			◆	◆		
Epidendrum ciliare	8–24 in (20–60 cm)	8–36 in (20–90 cm)	E	W/I	◆		◆	◆		◆			◆	◆		
Epidendrum ibaguense	8–48 in (20–120 cm)	8–48 in (20–120 cm)	E/T	W/I/C	◆		◆						◆	◆		
Epidendrum parkinsonianum	1–7 ft (0.3–2 m)	8–24 in (20–60 cm)	E	W/I	◆			◆					◆	◆		
Epidendrum secundum	8–36 in (20–90 cm)	8–48 in (20–120 cm)	T	W/I	◆		◆						◆	◆		
Epidendrum Hybrids	8–48 in (20–120 cm)	8–48 in (20–120 cm)	E	W/I/C	◆		◆						◆	◆		
Laelia anceps	8–48 in (20–120 cm)	8–36 in (20–90 cm)	E	W/I/C	◆	◆	◆	◆			◆		◆	◆		
Laelia Canariensis	8–40 in (20–100 cm)	8–24 in (20–60 cm)	E/L	W/I	◆		◆						◆	◆		
Laelia crispa	8–24 in (20–60 cm)	8–36 in (20–90 cm)	E/L	W/I	◆		◆						◆	◆		
Laelia purpurata	8–36 in (20–90 cm)	8–36 in (20–90 cm)	E	W/I	◆	◆	◆						◆	◆		

Plant name	Height	Spread	Type	Temperature	Showy flowers	Scented flowers	Grow in pot	Grow on mount	Keep moist	Dry winter	Drought tolerant	Frost tolerant	Full sun	Half sun	Shade	CITES listed
Laelia tenebrosa	8–32 in (20–80 cm)	8–36 in (20–90 cm)	E	W/I	◆	◆	◆						◆	◆		
Laeliocattleya Hybrids	4–36 in (10–90 cm)	4–30 in (10–75 cm)	E	W/I	◆		◆				◆		◆	◆		
Lycaste skinneri	4–24 in (10–60 cm)	8–24 in (20–60 cm)	E	I/C	◆	◆	◆							◆		
Lycaste Hybrids	4–24 in (10–60 cm)	8–24 in (20–60 cm)	E/T	W/I	◆		◆							◆		
Masdevallia tridens	4–12 in (10–30 cm)	4–8 in (10–20 cm)	T	I/C	◆		◆		◆					◆		
Masdevallia veitchiana	24 in (60 cm)	12 in (30 cm)	T	I/C	◆		◆		◆					◆		
Masdevallia Hybrids	4–24 in (10–60 cm)	4–12 in (10–30 cm)	T	I/C	◆		◆		◆					◆		
Maxillaria fractiflexa	4–24 in (10–60 cm)	8 in (20 cm)	E	I/C	◆									◆		
Maxillaria porphyrostele	4–24 in (10–60 cm)	4–8 in (10–20 cm)	E/L	W/I/C	◆		◆						◆	◆		
Maxillaria variabilis	4–24 in (10–60 cm)	4–8 in (10–20 cm)	E	W/I/C	◆		◆						◆	◆		
Miltonia clowesii	8–27 in (20–70 cm)	8–24 in (20–60 cm)	E	W/I	◆		◆	◆		◆				◆		
Miltonia Sandy's Cove	8–24 in (20–60 cm)	8–24 in (20–60 cm)	E	W/I	◆		◆	◆						◆		
Miltonia spectabilis	8–16 in (20–40 cm)	8–24 in (20–60 cm)	E	W/I	◆		◆							◆		
Miltoniopsis phalaenopsis	12 in (30 cm)	15 in (38 cm)	E	W/I	◆		◆			◆				◆		
Miltoniopsis vexillaria	8–16 in (20–40 cm)	8–24 in (20–60 cm)	E	W/I	◆		◆			◆				◆		
Miltoniopsis Hybrids	20 in (50 cm)	32 in (80 cm)	E	W/I	◆	◆	◆			◆				◆		
Odontioda Hybrids	8–36 in (20–90 cm)	8–24 in (20–60 cm)	E	C	◆		◆							◆		
Odontoglossum crispum	5–32 in (12–80 cm)	4–16 in (10–40 cm)	E	C	◆		◆			◆				◆		
Odontoglossum wyattianum	5–24 in (12–60 cm)	4–12 in (10–30 cm)	E	C	◆		◆			◆				◆		
Odontoglossum Hybrids	8–36 in (20–90 cm)	8–24 in (20–60 cm)	E	C	◆		◆			◆				◆		
Oncidium crispum	8–27 in (20–70 cm)	4–16 in (10–40 cm)	E	W/I	◆								◆	◆		
Oncidium flexuosum	8–60 in (20–150 cm)	8–36 in (20–90 cm)	E	W/I	◆			◆					◆	◆		
Oncidium sphacelatum	8–60 in (20–150 cm)	8–36 in (20–90 cm)	E	W/I	◆	◆	◆	◆					◆	◆		
Oncidium varicosum	5–32 in (12–80 cm)	4–16 in (10–40 cm)	E	W/I	◆		◆	◆					◆	◆		
Paphiopedilum bellatulum	2½–6 in (6–15 cm)	8–12 in (20–30 cm)	T	W/I	◆		◆							◆		◆
Paphiopedilum haynaldianum	4–32 in (10–80 cm)	12–24 in (30–60 cm)	E/L/T	W/I	◆		◆							◆		◆
Paphiopedilum henryanum	4–16 in (10–40 cm)	8–12 in (20–30 cm)	L	W/I	◆		◆							◆		◆
Paphiopedilum hirsutissimum	4–16 in (10–40 cm)	8–16 in (20–40 cm)	T	I/C	◆		◆							◆		◆
Paphiopedilum insigne	4–16 in (10–40 cm)	8–12 in (20–30 cm)	T	I/C	◆		◆							◆		◆
Paphiopedilum lowii	8–40 in (20–100 cm)	12–24 in (30–60 cm)	L/T	W/I	◆		◆							◆		◆
Paphiopedilum primulinum	4–24 in (10–60 cm)	8–16 in (20–40 cm)	T	W/I	◆		◆							◆		◆
Paphiopedilum rothschildianum	8–36 in (20–90 cm)	8–32 in (20–80 cm)	L/T	W/I	◆		◆							◆		◆
Paphiopedilum victoria-regina	4–27 in (10–70 cm)	8–24 in (20–60 cm)	L/T	W/I	◆		◆							◆		◆
Paphiopedilum villosum	4–16 in (10–40 cm)	8–12 in (20–30 cm)	T	I/C	◆		◆							◆		◆
Paphiopedilum Hybrids	4–24 in (10–60 cm)	4–8 in (10–20 cm)	T	I/C	◆		◆							◆	◆	
Phalaenopsis amabilis	12–36 in (30–90 cm)	8–20 in (20–50 cm)	E	W	◆		◆	◆	◆					◆		
Phalaenopsis equestris	4–12 in (10–30 cm)	5–12 in (12–30 cm)	E	W	◆		◆	◆	◆					◆		
Phalaenopsis lueddemanniana	4–16 in (10–40 cm)	6–16 in (15–40 cm)	E	W	◆		◆		◆					◆		
Phalaenopsis schilleriana	12–36 in (30–90 cm)	8–20 in (20–50 cm)	E	W	◆		◆		◆					◆		

Plant name	Height	Spread	Type	Temperature	Showy flowers	Scented flowers	Grow in pot	Grow on mount	Keep moist	Dry winter	Drought tolerant	Frost tolerant	Full sun	Half sun	Shade	CITES listed
Phalaenopsis Hybrids	8–36 in (20–90 cm)	5–24 in (12–60 cm)	E	W	♦		♦	♦	♦						♦	
Phragmipedium longifolium	8–36 in (20–90 cm)	12–24 in (30–60 cm)	T	W	♦		♦		♦					♦		♦
Pleione formosana	16 in (40 cm)	16 in (40 cm)	L/T	C	♦		♦			♦	♦		♦	♦		
Pleione Hybrids	8–16 in (20–40 cm)	8–16 in (20–40 cm)	T	C	♦		♦			♦			♦	♦		
Pleurothallis tuerckheimii	8–20 in (20–50 cm)	4–20 in (10–50 cm)	E	I			♦		♦					♦		
Pleurothallis villosa	1½–6 in (3.5–15 cm)	1½–6 in (3.5–15 cm)	E	I/C			♦							♦		
Potinara Hybrids	8–24 in (20–60 cm)	8–24 in (20–60 cm)	E	W/I	♦		♦				♦		♦			
Prosthechea michuacana	8–48 in (20–120 cm)	8–16 in (20–40 cm)	E	I			♦							♦		
Prosthechea vitellina	8–24 in (20–60 cm)	8–16 in (20–40 cm)	E	W	♦		♦	♦						♦		
Pterostylis curta	4–12 in (10–30 cm)	1½–3 in (3.5–8 cm)	T	I/C	♦		♦					♦		♦		
Renantanda Tuanku Bainun	8–48 in (20–120 cm)	8–32 in (20–80 cm)	E	W	♦		♦		♦				♦			
Renanthera coccinea	8–48 in (20–120 cm)	8–32 in (20–80 cm)	E	W	♦		♦						♦			
Renanthera Hybrids	1–8 ft (0.3–2.4 m)	8–36 in (20–90 cm)	E	W	♦		♦						♦			
Rhynchostele bictoniensis	8–24 in (20–60 cm)	8–16 in (20–40 cm)	E	I	♦		♦							♦		
Rhynchostele cordata	8–16 in (20–40 cm)	8–16 in (20–40 cm)	E	I	♦		♦							♦		
Rhynchostylis gigantea	8–24 in (20–60 cm)	8–20 in (20–50 cm)	E	W	♦		♦						♦	♦		
Rossioglossum grande	8–20 in (20–50 cm)	8–20 in (20–50 cm)	E	I/C	♦		♦			♦				♦		
Rossioglossum Rawdon Jester	8–20 in (20–50 cm)	8–20 in (20–50 cm)	E	I/C	♦		♦			♦				♦		
Sarcochilus fitzgeraldii	4–16 in (10–40 cm)	4–16 in (10–40 cm)	L	I/C	♦		♦							♦	♦	
Sarcochilus Hybrids	4–16 in (10–40 cm)	4–16 in (10–40 cm)	E/L	I/C	♦	♦	♦							♦	♦	
Sobralia macrantha	1–7 ft (0.3–2 m)	1–4 ft (0.3–1.2 m)	T	W/I	♦		♦		♦					♦		
Sobralia Mirabilis	36 in (90 cm)	36 in (90 cm)	T	W/I	♦		♦							♦		
Sophrocattleya Lana Coryell	4–16 in (10–40 cm)	4–16 in (10–40 cm)	E	W/I	♦		♦							♦		
Sophrolaeliocattleya Hybrids	4–16 in (10–40 cm)	4–16 in (10–40 cm)	E	W/I	♦		♦							♦		
Sophronitis coccinea	1½–5 in (3.5–12 cm)	2½–8 in (6–20 cm)	E	I/C	♦		♦	♦						♦		
Spathoglottis plicata	12–40 in (30–100 cm)	8–48 in (20–120 cm)	T	W/I	♦		♦		♦					♦		
Stanhopea nigroviolacea	8–20 in (20–50 cm)	8–24 in (20–60 cm)	E	W/I/C	♦	♦	♦		♦					♦		
Stanhopea oculata	8–20 in (20–50 cm)	8–20 in (20–50 cm)	E	W/I	♦	♦	♦		♦					♦		
Stanhopea wardii	8–20 in (20–50 cm)	8–20 in (20–50 cm)	E	W/I	♦	♦	♦		♦					♦		
Vanda coerulea	6–36 in (15–90 cm)	4–10 in (10–25 cm)	E	I/C	♦		♦						♦	♦		
Vanda sanderiana	8–48 in (20–120 cm)	8–20 in (20–50 cm)	E	W	♦		♦							♦		
Vanda tricolor	8–48 in (20–120 cm)	8–20 in (20–50 cm)	E	W/I	♦		♦						♦	♦		
Vanda Hybrids	8–48 in (20–120 cm)	8–20 in (20–50 cm)	E	W/I	♦		♦						♦	♦		
Vanilla planifolia	1–10 ft (0.3–3 m)	1–10 ft (0.3–3 m)	E	W/I		♦	♦	♦						♦		
Vuylstekeara Hybrids	4–24 in (10–60 cm)	4–20 in (10–50 cm)	E	I/C	♦		♦							♦		
Zygopetalum intermedium	4–16 in (10–40 cm)	4–16 in (10–40 cm)	E	I/C	♦	♦	♦		♦					♦		
Zygopetalum mackayi	4–16 in (10–40 cm)	4–16 in (10–40 cm)	E	I/C	♦	♦	♦		♦					♦		
Zygopetalum Hybrids	4–16 in (10–40 cm)	4–16 in (10–40 cm)	E/T	I/C	♦	♦	♦		♦					♦		

ANGULOA

TULIP ORCHID

The 10 species in this genus are epiphytes or terrestrials from mountainous regions of Colombia, Ecuador, Peru, Bolivia, and Venezuela, and are closely related to *Lycaste*, with fat pseudobulbs and large, thin, pleated leaves. The waxy tulip-shaped flowers do not open fully and are borne singly on erect stalks from the base of the pseudobulb in spring and summer, coinciding with new growth.

CULTIVATION: These plants require a cool to intermediate growing environment. Because their roots must not dry out during the growing season, they are best suited to containers. Water them well when in active growth. Propagation is by division.

Anguloa uniflora

✂ ☀ ↔ 12–24 in (30–60 cm) ↕ 16–24 in (40–60 cm)

From Venezuela, Colombia, Ecuador, Peru, and Bolivia. Flowers variable in color, with white to creamy base, finely to coarsely spotted pink, in summer–autumn. Some clones appear dark pink. Often confused with the closely related *A. virginalis*. Zones 10–11.

ASCOCENDA

Arguably one of the most popular of the orchid genera. Plants are artificial hybrids between the natural genera *Ascocentrum* and *Vanda*. Erect-growing to about 48 in (120 cm) high, these epiphytes have thick cord-like roots, strap-like channeled leaves, and long-lasting flowers. In tropical climates they bloom year round; elsewhere mainly in spring and summer. Colorful showy blooms are long lived. The influence of *Ascocentrum* has greatly reduced the plant size, injected a range of vibrant colors, and given the blooms a rounder shape.

CULTIVATION: Ideal plants for bark-filled wooden baskets, enjoying warm conditions and high light levels. The thick roots will often venture outside the pot or basket, and this culture should be encouraged, as the roots need unimpeded air circulation and must dry out quickly after watering. Propagation is by division of rooted basal shoots.

Ascocenda Hybrids

✂ ☀ ↔ 12–24 in (30–60 cm)
↕ 16–48 in (40–120 cm)

Ascocenda hybrids include **Carolaine 'Kathleen'**, pink flowers, heavily spotted darker pink to red, 5 *Vanda* species and *Ascocentrum curvifolium* in its parentage; **Fuchs Gold**, a fine hybrid developed by Robert Fuchs of R. F. Orchids, Florida, USA; **Fuchs Serval**, unusual hybrid with bold spotting and mustard-colored background; **Guo Chia Long**, yellow-orange blooms with maroon spotting; **Kwa Geok Choo**, hybrid made using the albino (green and white) form of *Vanda sanderiana;* **Pramote**, orange blooms (an influence from *Ascocentrum curvifolium*) that last well on the plant or as a cut flower, and mature plants will bloom a number of times during the warmer months; **'Pranam'**, clusters of apricot flowers; **Princess Mikasa**, with flower shape and color a legacy from *Vanda coerulea;* **Udomchai Beauty**, 4 different *Vanda* species and *Ascocentrum curvifolium* in its makeup; **Wichot**, primary hybrid between *Vanda bensonii* and *Ascocentrum ampullaceum*. Zones 11–12.

Ascocenda, Hybrid, Carolaine 'Kathleen'

ASCOCENTRUM

A monopodial genus of about 8 small compact epiphytic species from Southeast Asia. Plants erect growing, with short, strap-like, channeled leaves in 2 ranks. Larger plants may branch at the base, and have numerous, very thick, cord-like roots. Inflorescences appear from the stem at the leaf base. Mostly spring- and summer-flowering, but in the tropics larger plants can bloom year-round. *Ascocentrum* has been bred with members of *Vanda* to create the hybrid genus *Ascocenda*.

CULTIVATION: Best suited to container or basket culture, these species require warm conditions and high light levels. Water and feed well during active growth and throughout the flowering season. Roots need to dry out quickly after watering and do best if allowed to grow beyond the confines of the container. Propagate by division of mature basal shoots.

Ascocentrum garayi

✂ ☀ ↔ 5–10 in (12–25 cm)
↕ 5–12 in (12–30 cm)

From Thailand. Strap-like leaves. Bright orange spring flowers ensured its popularity in cultivation. Nurseries have selected horticulturally superior forms and propagated these from seed. Often confused with *A. miniatum*. Zones 10–12.

BLETILLA

CHINESE GROUND ORCHID

Genus of about 10 species of deciduous sympodial terrestrial orchids from temperate regions of China, Taiwan, and Japan, with corm-like pseudobulbs, from which 3 to 4 lance-shaped pleated leaves arise. Inflorescence is a terminal raceme and carries up to 12 flowers. They are dormant in autumn–winter, blooming with flush of new growth in early spring.

CULTIVATION: They need a well-drained but rich potting mixture that retains moisture, or grow them in the garden. Grow in semi-shade to full sun, with regular watering in spring and summer. Caterpillars can often disfigure the leaves, particularly young shoots after their dormancy. Will withstand cold winters, but new growth must be protected from any late heavy frosts. Propagate by division.

Ascocentrum garayi

Bletilla striata

🌿 ☼/◐ ❄ ↔ 12–48 in (30–120 cm) ↕ 12–24 in (30–60 cm)

Hardy species, frequently grown as a garden plant, often without the owner knowing it is an orchid! Leaves lance-shaped, to 18 in (45 cm) long. Up to 8 blooms, each 2 in (5 cm) wide, pale pink to rose-purple (rarely white), resembling a small *Cattleya* flower. Also a form with variegated leaf. Blooms in early spring–summer. Zones 6–11.

BRASSIA

SPIDER ORCHID

This genus of about 20 epiphytic sympodial orchids from tropical America is popular in cultivation due to their large, often strongly perfumed, spidery blooms. The arching inflorescences carry up to 12 blooms, which can reach over 12 in (30 cm) wide. These plants are very amenable to cultivation over a wide range of climatic conditions. **CULTIVATION:** Many of these species are from the lowlands and like warm, moist, and bright conditions. They grow well in pots in a bark-based medium. Larger plants look especially good in hanging baskets. In frost-free climates *Brassia* species can also be attached to garden trees that do not shed their bark. Propagation is by striking back-bulbs or by division.

Brassia arcuigera

syn. *Brassia longissima*

♀ ☼ ↔ 8–16 in (20–40 cm) ↕ 12–24 in (30–60 cm)

Costa Rica to Ecuador. Flowers among largest in genus, up to 10 in (25 cm) tall, with narrow yellow petals and sepals, heavily marked rustic brown, giving overall bronze cast; spring–summer. Zones 11–12.

Brassia verrucosa

syn. *Brassia brachiata*

♀ ☼ ↔ 8–24 in (20–60 cm) ↕ 8–12 in (20–30 cm)

Found from Mexico to Venezuela; very popular species; reliable late-spring bloomer. Narrow ovoid pseudobulbs; leaves to 18 in (45 cm) long, lance-shaped. Large fragrant flowers, 8 in (20 cm) wide, spidery, pale green to yellowish, with fine dark spotting at base. Performs well in shadehouse conditions in frost-free climates. Zones 10–12.

Brassia Hybrids

♀ ☼ ↔ 24 in (60 cm) ↕ 12 in (30 cm)

These hybrids are particularly vigorous and worth cultivating. Bloom best when grown as large, somewhat crowded specimens. Most have large, highly fragrant, spider-like blooms during spring and summer. **Chieftain**, maroon and yellow petals and sepals with maroon-spotted lemon yellow lip; **Chieftain × B. Rex**, lemon yellow flowers with red-brown spotting; **Edvah Loo**, primary hybrid between *B. arcuigera* and *B. gireoudiana*, both large-flowered species; **Memoria Fritz Boedeker**, yellow-green petals and sepals, creamy lip, all with red-brown markings; **Rex 'Christine' ★**, arguably most popular *Brassia* hybrid in cultivation, primary hybrid between *B. gireoudiana* and *B. verrucosa*, blooms at full potential when grown into a large plant; **Rising Star**, yellow-green petals and sepals, creamy lip, all with very dark spotting; **Spider's Feast**, impressive hybrid between *B.* Chieftain and *B. verrucosa*, which has all its blooms out at once and well presented on the flower spike; **Spider's Gold**, hybrid between *B.* Arania Verde and the large-flowered *B. arcuigera*. Zones 10–12.

BRASSOCATTLEYA

Artificial bigeneric sympodial genus, a hybrid between *Brassavola* and *Cattleya*. In most cases such hybrids have *Rhyncholaelia digbyana* (previously known as *Brassavola digbyana*) as one of the parents. Hybrids created using this species, which has predominantly green and white blooms, result in the other parent of the hybrid having a strong influence on the resulting flower shape. The showy blooms are often produced in large numbers and can be fragrant. **CULTIVATION:** Compact habit; grows well in small terracotta or plastic pots, baskets, or on slabs; must be allowed to dry out fully between waterings. Enjoy high light, intermediate to warm temperatures; can take cool temperatures in winter if kept dry. Propagate by division.

Brassocattleya Hybrids

♀ ☼/◐ ↔ 12 in (30 cm) ↕ 10 in (25 cm)

Large numbers of showy blooms, often pleasantly fragrant, in spring or autumn. **Binosa ★**, hybrid between *Brassavola nodosa* and *Cattleya bicolor*, long-lasting flowers; **Maikai**, large plant, splendid in bloom, a floriferous primary hybrid between *Brassavola nodosa* and *Cattleya bowringiana*; **November Bride 'Santa Clara'**, large flowers, pink to white; and **Sunny Delight**, primary hybrid between *Brassavola perrinii* and *Cattleya aurantiaca*, yellow to orange flowers. Zones 10–12.

BRASSOLAELIOCATTLEYA

Most of the "cattleya orchids" with large single or twin flowers seen at florists and orchid shows are actually members of the hybrid genus *Brassolaeliocattleya*, which is an artificial combination between the sympodial epiphytic orchid genera *Brassavola*, *Laelia*, and *Cattleya*. But many of the registered intergeneric hybrids listed as involving *Brassavola* have *Rhyncholaelia digbyana*, previously known as *Brassavola digbyana*, as one parent. This species imparts fragrance as well as a large fringed lip, a distinctive feature of many hybrids. **CULTIVATION:** They need semi-shade to strong light, but will burn if exposed to direct sunlight. Grow best in pots incorporating a coarse bark-based medium to ensure unimpeded drainage. Healthy plants will develop an extensive system of thick white roots, which are long-lived and branch freely. Plants require additional warmth on winter evenings, but will tolerate cooler winter temperatures for short periods if kept dry while dormant. Flowers are long lasting, so bring the plant indoors to be enjoyed when in bloom. Propagate by division.

Brassia verrucosa

Brassolaeliocattleya Hybrids

♀ ☀ ↔ 8–24 in (20–60 cm) ↑ 8–24 in (20–60 cm)

Durable plants with long-lasting blooms. **Alma Kee 'Tipmalee'**, bright yellow petals and sepals, red lip; **Dundas 'Olga'**, cerise flowers, ruffled lip, orange at throat; **Golden Tang**, deep yellow petals and sepals, orange lip peppered with reddish spots; **Hawaiian Satisfaction 'Romantic'**, unusual color combinations; **Lucky 'Golden Ring'**, huge, highly fragrant, long-lasting flowers with a large flared lip; **Rosemary Hayden 'Paradise'**, fine example of a traditional colored "cattleya," autumn-flowering; **Samba Splendor**, cerise flowers, ruffled lip golden orange and red at throat; **(Shades of Jade×Waikiki Gold)**, "splash-petalled" hybrid—flower gives impression of having 3 lips; actually lip color has been generically transposed onto the petals; **Toshi Aoki 'Pokai'** ★, popular and highly awarded yellow hybrid, bred in Hawaii; **Waianae Leopard**, cluster-type hybrid, heavily influenced by the spotted *Cattleya guttata*. Zones 10–12.

BULBOPHYLLUM

This huge and cosmopolitan genus contains more than 1,500 named species, and many more still being discovered. There are plants with flowers in all shapes, sizes, and colors. These sympodial orchids grow as epiphytes and lithophytes. Most species produce a cylindrical pseudobulb with a single leaf, which develops along a creeping rhizome. However, numerous species, particularly from Africa and Madagascar, are 2-leafed. This genus includes some of the world's smallest orchids, plus others that form massive plants. The flowers are unlike most orchids, and are highly specialized to attract specific pollinators. Most species have very mobile lips.

CULTIVATION: Most bulbophyllums are creeping plants that have only a short root system, which rarely branches. They grow well on tree-fern slabs and rafts, while the larger species may be grown in pots, baskets, or shallow saucers. In general, they prefer shaded conditions and constant moisture around the roots. Some species of *Bulbophyllum* only flower in response to wet and dry seasons, while others flower throughout the year. Propagate by division.

Bulbophyllum Daisy Chain

syn. *Cirrhopetalum* Daisy Chain

♀ ☀ ↔ 12 in (30 cm) ↑ 5 in (12 cm)

Primary hybrid between *B. makoyanum* and *B. amesianum*. Flowers presented like spokes of wheel. Blooms autumn–winter. Zones 11–12.

Bulbophyllum wendlandianum

Bulbophyllum pectenveneris

syn. *Bulbophyllum flaviflorum*

♀ ☀ ↔ 16 in (40 cm) ↑ 3–6 in (8–15 cm)

From China, Vietnam, Laos, and Thailand. Up to 10 short sprays of blooms, each 1¼ in (30 mm) long, most of flower made up of bright yellow fused lateral sepals; tiny purplish petals and lip. Zones 11–12.

Bulbophyllum rothschildianum ★

syn. *Bulbophyllum ornatissimum*

♀ ☀ ↔ 24 in (60 cm) ↑ 10 in (25 cm)

From India. Member of the *Cirrhopetalum* section of *Bulbophyllum*, generally characterized by having flowers in an umbel, lower sepals fused, and filaments and appendages on upper sepal and petals. These "flags" move in slightest breeze and help attract potential pollinators. Single leaf to 6 in (15 cm) long. Inflorescence to 6 in (15 cm) long, arises from base of mature pseudobulbs, bears around 3 unpleasantly scented flowers in autumn. Green and crimson flowers up to 4 in (10 cm) long, mostly made up of fused lower sepals. Zones 10–12.

Bulbophyllum wendlandianum ★

syn. *Bulbophyllum collettii*

♀ ☀/☀ ↔ 4–12 in (10–30 cm) ↑ 8–12 in (20–30 cm)

From Thailand and Myanmar. Spreading clump of rhizomes; short leathery leaves. Inflorescences emerge from new growths in late spring–early summer. Heads of up to 6 flowers, closely clustered to look like a single large bloom. Flowers yellow-green to orange, heavily suffused and striped red to brown to purple. Zones 10–12.

CATTLEYA

This tropical American genus is one of the most popular groups of orchids in cultivation, with over 50 species and literally thousands of hybrids. Sympodial rock- and tree-dwellers, they have showy, colorful, long-lasting, and often highly fragrant flowers on stout plants with club-shaped to cylindrical pseudobulbs. They are topped with 1 (unifoliate) or 2 (bifoliate) dull green leathery leaves. Thousands of hybrids have been made within the genus and related members of the *Cattleya* alliance or family, especially *Laelia*, *Rhyncholaelia* (often credited in hybrid lists under *Brassavola*), and *Sophronitis*.

CULTIVATION: All *Cattleya* species enjoy high light and intermediate to warm temperatures; some species will take cooler conditions in winter. Most need warmth in winter, but the Brazilian bifoliate autumn-flowering types will stand cooler winter temperatures for short periods, if kept dry while dormant. They must all have unimpeded drainage and a coarse bark-based medium. Most species will grow best in plastic or terracotta pots; must dry out between waterings. Healthy plants will develop an extensive system of thick white roots, which are long-lived and branch freely. Propagate by division.

Cattleya aurantiaca

♀ ☀/☀ ↔ 6–24 in (15–60 cm)

↑ 5–24 in (12–60 cm)

From Central America; smallest flowers of genus, with up to 12 glossy flowers, 2 in (5 cm) wide, ranging from yellow through shades of orange (most common color)

Cattleya aurantiaca 'Golden Dew'

Cattleya bicolor 'Golden Gate'

Cattleya walkeriana

♀ ☀ ↔ 4–10 in (10–25 cm)

↕ 3–6 in (8–15 cm)

Brazilian species. Unique flowering style—short specialized spike emerges from rhizome near base of previous growth, bearing 1 or 2 flat 4 in (10 cm) blooms that are generally lilac-pink to purple. *C. w.* var. *alba*, one of numerous albino forms, flowers of the purest white, many of which have allegedly been "line bred", may be hybrids. Zones 10–12.

to deep red, occasionally white, in summer. In some clones flowers do not open fully, while inferior forms are self-pollinating. 'Golden Dew', golden flowers, splash of red at throat, early blooming; 'Red', bright vermilion flowers. Zones 10–12.

Cattleya bicolor

♀/∧ ☼/☀ ↔ 8–24 in (20–60 cm) ↕ 8–48 in (20–120 cm)

A bifoliate species from Brazil. Cylindrical pseudobulbs; leathery leaves up to 4 in (10 cm) long. Up to 8 flowers, to 3 in (8 cm) in diameter, apple or olive green, sometimes with a coppery cast, and a contrasting purple lip. Blooms in autumn. *C. b.* var. *braziliensis*, larger but fewer blooms. *C. b.* 'Golden Gate', crimson-cupped blooms. Zones 10–12.

Cattleya bowringiana

∧ ☼/☀ ↔ 4–24 in (10–60 cm) ↕ 6–36 in (15–90 cm)

Strong, easily grown, species from Guatemala and Belize, found on rocky cliffs, in bright humid conditions. Forms large clusters of up to 20 rose-purple blooms, each 3 in (8 cm) wide, autumn. Zones 10–12.

Cattleya intermedia

♀ ☀ ↔ 4–12 in (10–30 cm)

↕ 6–16 in (15–40 cm)

Variable species, Brazil; range of shapes, sizes, and colors—pure white through shades of pink to deep purple. Up to 5 blooms, 3½ in (9 cm) wide, in spring. *C. i.* var. *alba*, fragrant white flowers; 'Breckinridge Snow', pure white and long-lasting. *C. i.* var. *amethystina*, white flowers, pink or lavender at lip; *C. i.* var. *aquinii*, splash-petalled form; and *C. i.* 'Do Hector', pinkish sepals and petals, lip deepening in color at tip. Zones 10–12.

Cattleya loddigesii

♀ ☀ ↔ 4–12 in (10–30 cm) ↕ 6–24 in (15–60 cm)

From Brazil and Argentina. Pseudobulbs cylindrical; leaves leathery. Up to 8 flowers, 4 in (10 cm) wide, in autumn. Pale pink to purple (rarely white) petals and sepals, sometimes finely speckled with darker purple, lip white, yellow, and purple. Color intensity of blooms can be improved if they are given strong light when in bud. Very similar to, and often confused with, *C. harrisoniana*. 'Blue Sky', with pale lavender-blue flowers, with white and yellow lip; and ('Pink Spots' × 'Monty'), pink flowers, yellow and pink lip. Zones 10–12.

Cattleya Hybrids

♀ ☀ ↔ 8–24 in (20–60 cm) ↕ 8–32 in (20–80 cm)

A selection of some popular cultivars and recent seedlings shows the variety of color available. Most bloom in spring or autumn. *C.* Bow Bells 'July', white flowers, golden yellow at throat; (Browniae × *loddigesii*) can be grown over a range of climates; protect from frosts; Earl 'Imperialis', bred from albino forms of *C. trianaei*, *C. gaskelliana*, and *C. mossiae*, large white blooms; Frasquita, tall-growing primary hybrid between *C. bicolor* and *C. velutina*, clusters of glossy brown flowers with bright purple lip; Hawaiian Comfort, compact grower, crisp pure white to cream blooms, excellent as cut flowers and in corsages; Humming Bird Hybrids, sprays of up to 8 flowers, often called "cluster cattleyas;" Luteous Forb, a primary hybrid between *C. luteola* and *C. forbesii*, clusters of apple green and yellow flowers. Zones 10–12.

COELOGYNE

A large diverse group of about 100 species of sympodial orchids from Asia. Plants form distinct pseudobulbs, linked by woody rhizomes. Depending on the species, from 1 to 3 leaves are produced from the top of each pseudobulb. Most members of this showy genus of epiphytes and lithophytes have white or green flowers, with contrasting lips displaying profuse brown markings.

Coelogyne Burfordiense

Flowering often occurs from the developing new growths, or from specialized points at the base of the previous year's pseudobulb. Some species have fragrant blooms. CULTIVATION: Generally from mountainous regions, about 80 percent of these species are suitable for growing in cool to intermediate conditions. However, there are species from the monsoonal tropical lowlands; generally easy to grow, will rapidly build into specimen plants if conditions are favorable. Most are grown in pots in a bark-based growing medium, but those species with pendulous flower spikes, or with long rhizomes, do best when grown in baskets. They enjoy humid conditions and regular watering year-round. Propagate by division.

Coelogyne Burfordiense

♀ ☀ ↔ 8–32 in (20–80 cm) ↕ 10–36 in (25–90 cm)

A large-growing hybrid between the tropical species *C. asperata* and *C. pandurata*; often confused with the latter. Large, 4 in (10 cm) wide, green flowers, lip almost black in color, on long arching inflorescences of about 12 blooms, in spring or summer. Zones 11–12.

Coelogyne flaccida

♀ ☀ ↔ 4–27 in (10–70 cm) ↕ 5–15 in (12–38 cm)

Variable, fragrant, spring-blooming species found growing from Nepal to China. Most clones have pendulous spikes of up to 14 cream to light bronze flowers. Reliable bloomer, very fast-growing. 'Caramel', sepals and petals caramel colored, with a contrasting lip; 'Dark', popular cultivar with ocher flowers. Zones 9–11.

Coelogyne pandurata

♀ ☀ ↔ 8–48 in (20–120 cm) ↕ 8–24 in (20–60 cm)

A robust species from Borneo, the Philippines, and Indonesia. Oblong to spherical pseudobulbs. Long arching inflorescences of up to 12 blooms, in spring or summer. Large flowers, 4 in (10 cm) wide, fragrant, green, with an almost black lip. Zones 11–12.

CYMBIDIUM

A genus of 50 or so species, distributed throughout southern and eastern Asia and into Australia. Most of the sympodial species from the mountains are terrestrial, with upright to arching flower spikes and blooms in many colors. They produce a fleshy pseudobulb with many long, durable, strap-like leaves. In lowlands, most cymbidiums grow epiphytically, in high light. Many species have long pendent inflorescences and thick leathery leaves. Over the past century tens of thousands of hybrids have been created, which are often loosely categorized by flower size: miniature, under 2½ in (6 cm); intermediate, 2½–3½ in (6–9 cm); and standard, over 3½ in (9 cm). These hybrids form the basis of an important pot-plant and cut-flower industry in temperate climates. Traditionally, the main flowering season has been winter to spring, but selective breeding is continually extending this. These orchids have been cultivated for centuries in China and Japan, where they are also valued for spiritual and medicinal purposes. Variegated-leafed and unusual flower forms are also highly prized. CULTIVATION: Most hybrid species are grown in commercially available "orchid composts," which are usually free-draining but retain some moisture. *Cymbidium* species are remarkably hardy. Epiphytic species prefer a mix incorporating a high percentage of coarse bark. They should be kept moist year-round, increasing watering and fertilizing from spring to autumn while they are actively growing. Most cool-growing species and complex hybrids need a nighttime drop in temperature of at least 18°F (10°C) during summer evenings, to help initiate flowering for the following season. This can be manipulated by giving the plants a regular light misting of water at sunset during the warmer months. Propagation is by division.

Cymbidium erythrostylum ★

♀ ☀/☀ ↔ 8–24 in (20–60 cm) ↕ 12–27 in (30–70 cm)

Species from Vietnam. Ovoid pseudobulbs. Erect inflorescences carry up to 10 blooms in autumn. Flowers white, 2½ in (6 cm); yellow and white lip netted with thick red-orange veins. Petals usually do not open fully, and tend to embrace the column and lip. Zones 9–10.

Cymbidium lowianum

🌱 ☀/☀ ↔ 8–36 in (20–90 cm) ↕ 12–48 in (30–120 cm)

Hardy species, found from Thailand to China. Up to 30 very long arching spikes, bearing olive green flowers, 3 in (8 cm) long, with contrasting cream and red lip, in spring. *C. l.* var. *concolor*, bright green sepals and petals, yellow and gold lip. Zones 9–11.

Cymbidium tracyanum

♀ ☀/☀ ❄ ↔ 8–36 in (20–90 cm) ↕ 12–48 in (30–120 cm)

A large species, found from Thailand to China. Flowers are strongly fragrant, 6 in (15 cm) long, light green, heavily marked, and striped with red-brown, giving blooms an overall deep bronze appearance. Flowers produced in autumn. Zones 8–11.

Cymbidium Hybrids

🌱 ☀/☀ ↔ 8–36 in (20–90 cm) ↕ 12–48 in (30–120 cm)

Thousands of *Cymbidium* hybrids have been registered, varying widely in shape and color. Many have been mericloned or tissue cultured to increase numbers to satisfy demand. **African Adventure 'Sahara Gold'**, sunset tones, some new colors are being developed; **Anita 'Pymble'**, green flowers on tall arching spikes; **Astronaut 'Raja'**, buttery yellow flowers flushed with red, lip spotted deep maroon; **Bulbarrow 'Friar Tuck'** ★, intermediate-style, distinctive color combination from *C. devonianum*; **Castle of Mey 'Pinkie'**, miniature, with up to 25 pinkish white cascading blooms on each stem; **Dilly 'Del Mar'**, yellow flowers, late-blooming; **Ice Ranch**, dusky pink and cream flowers, yellow and maroon lip; **John Woden**, large salmon pink blooms, with deep maroon spotted lip, on tall spikes; **Lady McAlpine 'Jersey'**, white flowers, lip white, maroon, and lemon; **Little Bighorn 'Prairie'** ★, intermediate hybrid, many upright inflorescences of mainly green blooms with white lips with maroon spots; **Mavourneen 'Jester'** ★, an unusual standard hybrid with lip colors transposed onto petals; **Pontac 'Trinity'**, bears purplish red flowers; **Sumatra 'Astrid'**, sprays of dark pink flowers, yellow lip with purple markings; **Sunshine Falls 'Green Fantasy'**, miniature-flowered, highly fragrant and floriferous, from *C. madidum* heritage; **Sylvia Miller 'Gold Cup'**, miniature, golden flowers, rosy tones on lip; **Tinsel 'Harriet'**, pink flowers on slender spike; **Valley Legend 'Gee Wizz'**, chartreuse flowers, lip yellow and deep red. Zones 9–11.

CYPRIPEDIUM

LADY'S SLIPPER

This deciduous genus consists of about 50 sympodial species found in North and Central America, Europe, and Asia. These plants are

Cymbidium erythrostylum

Cymbidium, Hybrid, Sunshine Falls 'Green Fantasy'

Cypripedium formosanum

characterized by a short rhizome, with up to 4 basal leaves, which are often pleated. The slender inflorescences carry up to 12 showy flowers, which appear from late spring and into summer, come in a range of colors, and feature an impressive, often contrasting, slipper-like lip. One of the rarest of terrestrial genera, they are protected, and should not be removed from the wild under any circumstances. **CULTIVATION:** In cool to temperate climates, these plants can be grown in pots or in the garden, in soils rich in decayed leaf matter. Will not grow in subtropical or tropical climates. Propagate by division.

Cypripedium formosanum

✹ ❋ ↔ 4–12 in (10–30 cm) ↑ 4–10 in (10–25 cm)
Mountain-dwelling species from Taiwan. Pair of attractive, fan-like, wavy leaves. Single pale pink flower, up to 3 in (8 cm) wide, with darker markings and large inflated lip. Dislikes warm temperatures; easy to grow in cool climates. Zones 6–9.

DACTYLORHIZA

MARSH ORCHID

A deciduous terrestrial genus of about 35 sympodial species native to Europe, the Mediterranean region, northern and western Asia, and North America. Orchids of the grasslands, often found growing in moist situations in bogs and drainage patterns. Most of the variable species have green leaves heavily spotted maroon, and long 2-pronged tubers from which the plant grows. Flower color is mostly confined to a range of pink tones, with finer and darker spotting. **CULTIVATION:** In cool to temperate climates they can be grown in pots or in the garden in soils rich in decayed leaf matter. Though members of this genus are quite frost hardy, they do appreciate protection from the most severe frosts. Constant moisture is needed throughout the warmer months, but plants must be kept drier in winter. Will not grow in subtropical or tropical climates. Propagation is by division.

Dactylorhiza elata

syn. *Orchis elata*
ROBUST MARSH ORCHID

✹ ❂/❂ ❋ ↔ 6 in (15 cm) ↑ 24 in (60 cm)
A European native. Plain, unspotted, green leaves. Spikes crowded with large deep violet flowers during summer. Zones 6–9.

Dactylorhiza fuchsii

syn. *Orchis fuchsii*
COMMON SPOTTED ORCHID

✹ ❂/❂ ❋ ↔ 4–10 in (10–25 cm) ↑ 8–24 in (20–60 cm)
European species; likes slightly alkaline limestone soils. Spotted leaves. Flowers pale pink to white. Summer-flowering species, often confused with closely related *D. maculata*. 'Rachel', white flowers. Zones 6–9.

DENDROBIUM

This genus has always been popular with orchid growers. It enjoys a wide distribution, from India and Sri Lanka, through Southeast Asia to southern China, New Guinea, Australia, and the Pacific Islands. They are almost exclusively epiphytes or lithophytes, with a sympodial growth habit. There is an amazing diversity of plant habit, flower form, and color in this genus of around 900 species. Almost all colors and combinations are represented in the flowers. Some species' individual blooms last for a few hours; others can persist for up to 9 months in pristine condition. Many hybrids have been developed for both orchid enthusiasts and the cut-flower industry in tropical countries. Most flowers marketed as "Singapore orchids" are actually *Dendrobium* hybrids, which last well as cut flowers. *D. nobile* and related species have been used to create thousands of colorful and long-lasting "softcane" *Dendrobium* hybrids. Over the past couple of decades, there have been many new Australian native *Dendrobium* hybrids. Very popular and relatively fast growing, they incorporate species such as *D. kingianum*, *D. speciosum*, and *D. tetragonum*.

Dactylorhiza fuchsii

CULTIVATION: Dendrobiums have a range of diverse cultural requirements. Quite a number of species and hybrids produce new plants off the older pseudobulbs. Once these aerials or "keikis" have hardened off and produced roots, remove them and grow as a new plant. In the dry season, the "softcane" types shed their leaves and are dormant. Once the rains come, the plants burst into flower and produce next season's growth. This deciduous feature is common with many of the *Dendrobium* species, which have evolved to adapt to distinct wet and dry seasons. Most dendrobiums can be grown in a bark-based medium with some types performing well on tree-fern or cork slabs. Some of the smaller-growing species from mountainous regions grow well in sphagnum moss that is kept damp. Propagate by division.

Dendrobium bigibbum

COOKTOWN ORCHID

♀ ❂ ↔ 8–24 in (20–60 cm) ↑ 4–24 in (10–60 cm)
From Australia, common in Cape York Peninsula. Spectacular purple blooms, on sprays of up to 20 flowers, in autumn. Must be kept dry in winter when dormant. *D. b.* var. *compactum* ★, small-growing form to 5 in (12 cm) tall, with chunky pseudobulbs. Zones 11–12.

Dendrobium chrysotoxum

♀ ❂/❂ ↔ 8–24 in (20–60 cm) ↑ 8–16 in (20–40 cm)
Robust plant; India to southern China. Swollen pseudobulbs produce sprays of to 25 golden yellow to orange waxy flowers late spring. *D. c.* var. *suavissimum* has a dark reddish orange blotch on lip. Zones 10–12.

Dendrobium crumenatum

DOVE ORCHID, PIGEON ORCHID

♀ ☼/☀ ↔ 8–24 in (20–60 cm)

↑ 8–24 in (20–60 cm)

From India, Southeast Asia. Needs a sudden drop in temperature, of about 18°F (10°C), to induce flowering; this takes place during tropical storms. Exactly 9 days later the plant, plus any others in the district, will profusely burst into bloom; flowers last only one day. Short inflorescence, several fragrant white flowers just over 1½ in (35 mm) wide. Zones 11–12.

Dendrobium gibsonii

Dendrobium nobile

Dendrobium cuthbertsonii ★

♀ ☀ ↔ 2–8 in (5–20 cm) ↑ 1–3 in (2.5–8 cm)

From New Guinea; a miniature plant with disproportionately large blooms. Flowers year-round, individual blooms can last up to 9 months under favorable conditions. Comes in range of bright colors, including red, orange, yellow, pink, white, plus bicolor forms. Keep plants moist; sphagnum moss is often used for potted plants. Zones 10–11.

Dendrobium discolor

♀/↑ ☼ ↔ 1–4 ft (0.3–1.2 m) ↑ 1–6 ft (0.3–1.8 m)

Tall-growing, variable, coastal species; Australia and New Guinea. Large spikes of undulating brown and yellow flowers, most of year. Enjoys strong light, does best when given a lot of room. Zones 11–12.

Dendrobium fimbriatum

♀ ☼/☀ ↔ 1–4 ft (0.3–1.2 m) ↑ 1–7 ft (0.3–2 m)

From Southeast Asia. Pure yellow to orange flowers, on small spikes, late spring. *D. f.* var. *oculatum*, more often cultivated, orange flowers, deep maroon blotch on lip. Zones 10–12.

Dendrobium gibsonii

♀ ☼/☀ ↔ 12–24 in (30–60 cm) ↑ 12–48 in (30–120 cm)

Uncommon species, from Nepal to China. Glossy golden blooms, with 2 deep maroon blotches on lip, summer to autumn. Zones 10–12.

Dendrobium gracilicaule

♀/↑ ☼/☀ ↔ 8–36 in (20–90 cm) ↑ 8–24 in (20–60 cm)

Australian species. Slender pseudobulbs. Small arching spikes of fragrant flowers, yellowish green, heavily blotched with red-brown on the back of the segments. Flowers in early spring. Zones 10–11.

Dendrobium johnsoniae

♀ ☀ ↔ 8–20 in (20–50 cm) ↑ 8–20 in (20–50 cm)

New Guinean; grows at elevations of 1,640–3,940 ft (500–1,200 m). Pseudobulbs spindle-shaped, with 4 to 5 leaves. Clusters of attractive, long-lasting, fragrant blooms, on short upright spikes, throughout warmer months. Flowers to 5 in (12 cm) wide, pure white, lip striped with purple, disproportionately large for size of the plant. Zones 11–12.

Dendrobium kingianum ★

♀/↑ ☀ ↔ 4–48 in (10–120 cm) ↑ 2–36 in (5–90 cm)

Popular and highly variable species found in Australia. Cone-shaped pseudobulbs. Up to 12 fragrant flowers off compact plants. Colors vary from pure white through most shades of pink to deep beetroot purple. White lip, sometimes blotched and splashed with lilac, through to solid deep purple, in spring. *D. k.* 'Steve', pale pink with darker tinges, dark lip. Many superior cultivars have been developed through selective line breeding of desirable forms. Zones 9–11.

Dendrobium lindleyi

syn. *Dendrobium aggregatum*

♀ ☼/☀ ↔ 8–16 in (20–40 cm) ↑ 8–16 in (20–40 cm)

Found from India to China. Pendent sprays of up to 20 lemon yellow to golden flowers, quite large considering its compact growth habit. Blooms from spring to summer. Zones 10–12.

Dendrobium nobile

♀ ☼/☀ ↔ 8–24 in (20–60 cm) ↑ 8–24 in (20–60 cm)

Found from India to China. Highly variable, one of the "softcanes;" great beginner's orchid. Deep purple to pure white flowers, many shades and bicolored combinations, spring. *D. n.* var. *cooksonianum*, unusual, with lip coloring in petals; *D. n.* var. *nobilius*, large, deep purple flowers; *D. n.* var. *virginale*, pure white flowers. Zones 9–12.

Dendrobium pulchellum

♀ ☼/☀ ↔ 1–3 ft (0.3–0.9 m) ↑ 1–7 ft (0.3–2 m)

Species found from Nepal to China. Can produce very long cane-like pseudobulbs. Up to 12, cream to apricot, fragrant flowers, with dark maroon blotches on lip, on pendent spikes off older leafless stems, borne in summer. Zones 11–12.

Dendrobium speciosum

KING ORCHID, ROCK LILY

♀/↑ ☼/☀ ↔ 1–10 ft (0.3–3 m) ↑ 4–48 in (10–120 cm)

Variable orchid from New South Wales, Australia; sister species recognized at specific level as *D. curvicaule, D. pedunculatum, D. rex,* and *D. tarberi.* Popular garden plant, thrives in frost-free climates, where it blooms from late winter to spring. Particularly large inflorescences crowded with white to yellow, highly fragrant flowers. A most robust plant. Zones 9–11.

Dendrobium spectabile

♀ ☼/☀ ↔ 8–24 in (20–60 cm) ↑ 8–32 in (20–80 cm)

Found growing naturally in New Guinea. A unique species with twisted and somewhat distorted floral segments, on inflorescences of up to 20 blooms, produced from spring through to summer. Blooms can last for some weeks. Zones 11–12.

Dendrobium tetragonum

♀ ☼ ↔ 4–20 in (10–50 cm) ↕ 4–27 in (10–70 cm)

Australian species; highly variable; 3 distinct geographical populations have been recognized at species level: *D. cacatua*, *D. capitisyork*, and *D. melaleucaphilum*. Semi-pendulous pseudobulbs, distinctly 4-angled in cross-section. Spidery blooms, cream to yellow-green, often with dark purple to brown blotches and borders on floral segments. Lip can be white or marked with brown to purple spots or striations. Blooms in spring–summer. 'Black Boy', attractive cultivar. Zones 9–12.

Dendrobium thyrsiflorum

♀ ☼ ↔ 8–36 in (20–90 cm) ↕ 8–24 in (20–60 cm)

Found from India to China; easily grown species. Clustered upright pseudobulbs. Short-lived pendent clusters of flowers in late spring. Floral segments white, sometimes with faint pink flush, lip bright yellow, resemble a bunch of grapes. Zones 10–12.

Dendrobium victoriae-reginae ★

♀ ☼ ↔ 8–20 in (20–50 cm) ↕ 8–24 in (20–60 cm)

From the Philippines; one of the few "blue" orchids. Up to 4 flowers, lilac to dark bluish purple and white, on short sprays, from nodes along branching pseudobulbs, throughout the year. It prefers cool moist conditions. Zones 9–11.

Dendrobium Hybrids

The numbers of *Dendrobium* hybrids have greatly increased in recent decades, particularly "hardcane" hybrids for the cut-flower market.

AUSTRALIAN HYBRIDS

♀ ☼ ↔ 8–30 in (20–75 cm) ↕ 4–24 in (10–60 cm)

This is a selection of some Australian hybrids, bred from indigenous species, such as *D. kingianum*, *D. speciosum*, and *D. tetragonum*. Most bloom in winter and spring, off the same pseudobulbs for a number of seasons. These compact plants will often produce masses of highly fragrant blooms. **Bardo Rose**, popular early primary hybrid; **Barry Simpson**, mauve and white flowers; **Brinawa Sunset**, hybrid between *D. Peewee* and *D. falcorostrum*; **Elegant Heart**, hybrid between *D. Peewee* and *D. speciosum*, developed in the 1980s by Walter Upton; **Hilda Poxon** ★, very popular primary hybrid between *D. speciosum* and *D. tetragonum*, blooms a number of times during year; **Jonathan's Glory**, a newer hybrid, similar to an improved *D. kingianum*; **Kim**, white flowers, faintly edged with mauve; **Lorikeet**, white flowers with magenta markings, especially on lip; **Maroon Star**, bright yellow

spider-like flowers, edged maroon; **Memoria Kevin Conroy**, deep pink flowers; **Our Reg**, deep crimson and cream flowers; **Ronnie Gee**, white flowers edged with deep crimson, especially on lip; **Warrior**, yellow-green petals and sepals, crimson and white lip; **Wonga**, creamy yellow flowers with deep red markings on lip; **Yondi Brolga**, superb hybrid made by the late Sid Batchelor; **Zeus**, starry purple flowers produced numerous times throughout year. Zones 9–11.

"HARDCANE" HYBRIDS

♀ ☼/☀ ↔ 8–32 in (20–80 cm) ↕ 8–40 in (20–100 cm)

Hybrids derived from many of the lowland tropical *Dendrobium* species such as *D. bigibbum*, *D. discolor*, and *D. phalaenopsis*. Blooms produced all year. **Chao Praya Rose**, magenta blooms, long-lived both on plant and as a cut flower; **Floralia**, white sepals and petals, rich yellow lip; **Nora Tokunaga**, white flowers with purple speckling, heavy purple stripes on lip; **Pua'ala**, triploid hybrid of *D. bigibbum*, *D. macrophyllum*, and *D. spectabile*, deep red flowers with white edges; **Sedona**, white sepals and petals, magenta lip; **Suzanne Neil**, deep pink-purple flowers; **Thai Pinky**, important horticultural plant for florist trade; **Thanaid Stripes**, heavily veined magenta blooms; and **White Fairy**, white flowers tinged with yellow. Zones 11–12.

"NIGROHIRSUTE" OR BLACK-HAIRED STYLE HYBRIDS

♀ ☼/☀ ↔ 8–16 in (20–40 cm) ↕ 8–16 in (20–40 cm)

These dendrobiums have short black hairs on the pseudobulbs and usually have white to cream blooms with contrasting colors on the lip. **Frosty Dawn**, a hybrid between *D.* Dawn Maree and *D.* Lime Frost, flowers spring–summer, blooms last about 8 weeks. Zones 10–12.

"SOFTCANE" HYBRIDS

♀ ☼/☀ ↔ 6–16 in (15–40 cm) ↕ 8–24 in (20–60 cm)

Hybrids derived from *D. nobile*, or closely related species. Short-lived leaves are shed from pseudobulbs before flowers appear in spring–early summer. Up to 5 flowers from each node along a naked pseudobulb, with potential for many long-lived blooms along the length of swollen stems. **Akatuki Queen**, bright mauve flowers, lip with dark blotch surrounded by white ring; **Bohemian Rhapsody**, primary hybrid between *D. cucullatum* and *D. loddigesii*; **Christmas Chime** 'Azuka', white flowers, petals with white tips, lip with dark blotch, white ring; **Colorado Springs**, white flowers, tinged mauve at tips, lip with yellow blotch; **Gatton Monarch**, mauve and white flowers, lip with dark blotch; **Golden Blossom 'Kogane'**, yellow flowers, crimson blotched lip; **Golden Blossom 'Venus'**, pale yellow flowers; **Hanafubuki**, white flowers, yellow-blotched lip; **Lilac Frost**, magenta flowers, lip marked with dark blotch; **Lovely Virgin 'Angel'**, magenta and white flowers, large yellow blotch on lip; **Maihime 'Beauty'**, deep pink and white flowers, lip with yellow throat; **Sagamusmi**, white flowers, lip faintly yellow; **Sailor Boy 'Pinkie'**, white flowers, tipped with mauve, lip with yellow blotch; **Stardust**, yellow flowers, lip darker markings; and **Yukidaruma 'King'** ★, arguably the most popular softcane hybrid. Zones 9–11.

Dendrobium victoriae-reginae

Dendrobium, Australian Hybrid, Hilda Poxon

Dendrochilum tenellum

DENDROCHILUM

CHAIN ORCHID

Members of this large genus of over 200 sympodial botanicals produce a single leaf per pseudobulb and are related to *Coelogyne*. Most are epiphytes that grow in mossy cloud forests in mountainous regions, where there are rarely significant temperature extremes. Only a few make their homes in the tropical lowlands. Main distribution center for the genus is the Philippines, with many species in Borneo and Sumatra, Indonesia. They bloom once a year, with the developing new growth; their small but often colorful flowers arranged in 2 rows and alternately along an inflorescence, spiralled in some species.

CULTIVATION: Easy to grow, with most being clump-forming and well suited to pot culture. Sphagnum moss may be used solely as a medium for the miniature growers and plants up to 4 in (10 cm) pot size. Larger plants grow well in a bark-based mix, with a small proportion of gravel, perlite, and chopped moss added. Fresh air and constant high humidity is important and these plants happily bloom in shaded conditions. Keep theses plants constantly moist and as cool as possible during hot summer months, and protect them from the chill in winter. Propagation is by division.

Dendrochilum saccolabium

♀ ☀ ↔ 8–24 in (20–60 cm) ↕ 8–16 in (20–40 cm)

Spectacular and horticulturally attractive species from the Philippines. Arching inflorescences with up to 40 glossy, round, dull to bright red flowers, during winter months. Zones 10–11.

Dendrochilum tenellum

♀ ☀ ↔ 8–32 in (20–80 cm) ↕ 8–16 in (20–40 cm)

From the Philippines; forms large clumps on moss-covered rainforest trees. "Unorchid-like" species in foliage; fine, cylindrical, grassy leaves. Tiny white–cream flowers in late winter–early spring. Zones 10–11.

DISA

Primarily a South African terrestrial orchid genus of over 100 species. While the famous *D. uniflora*, known colloquially as "The Pride of

Table Mountain," is well known to orchid growers, most species are only of botanical interest and few of these are in cultivation. In the wild, they are often seen growing on the fringes of marshlands or on the banks of flowing streams, in substrates that generally are low in nitrogen content, and they often grow in association with sphagnum moss. Numerous attractive hybrids have been bred. Many have a high percentage of *D. uniflora* in their pedigree, and generally exhibit hybrid vigor. The color range is also expanding, with whites, lemons, and pinks now supplementing the reds and oranges.

CULTIVATION: Live sphagnum moss has proved the best medium for cultivated plants. They are very particular about water quality, and rainwater is best. Keep plants moist all year. Do not sit them in trays of water for extended periods. Some growers have had success with "waterwell" containers. Mature specimens may produce daughter plants at edge of pot (or at times through the drainage holes!). These can be potted separately when large enough to handle. Repot the plants annually into fresh moss a few months after main summer flowering period. They enjoy cool to intermediate conditions. Propagate by division.

Disa Hybrids

✿ ☀/◑ ↔ 4–10 in (10–25 cm) ↕ 8–32 in (20–80 cm)

The following hybrids have been primarily bred from the popular and award-winning *D. uniflora*, developed to improve flower count and quality, as well as to expand color range. Summer-flowering. **Diores**, hybrid between *D. uniflora* and *D. Veitchii*, long-lasting flowers, popular for cutting; **Kewbett**, a hybrid between *D.* Betty's Bay and *D.* Kewensis; and **Watsonii**, a hybrid between *D. uniflora* and *D.* Kewensis. Zones 9–11.

Disa, Hybrid, Watsonii

ENCYCLIA

This complex genus contains more than 200 sympodial orchids from Mexico, and Central and South America, most of which are intermediate- to warm-growing species. This genus was once included within the related *Epidendrum*. Often clumping plants with a distinct pseudobulb, they are usually topped with 2 or 3 leaves. Recently, sections of *Encyclia* have been transferred to separate genera. In 1998 a large group of the "cockleshell" *Encyclia* species was moved into the genus *Prosthechea*. This met with some resistance, even though they are easily recognized by their "up-side down" flowers and lip that displays varying degrees of dark purple striation. Most of these species flower in summer and are also highly fragrant.

CULTIVATION: *Encyclia* species are readily grown, on cork slabs or potted in a well-drained bark-based medium. Most species have a dormant period from late autumn to early spring. The majority enjoy bright light conditions. Propagate by division.

Encyclia hanburyi

♀ ☀/◑ ↔ 8–20 in (20–50 cm) ↕ 8–27 in (20–70 cm)

From Mexico. Clusters of conical pseudobulbs; leaves up to 10 in (25 cm) long. Upright spikes of brown flowers, 1½ in (35 mm) wide, contrasting rosy purple lip, in spring–summer. Zones 10–12.

EPIDENDRUM

A large sympodial orchid genus from southern USA, Mexico, and Central and South America, with over 1,000 recognized species. Many gardeners are familiar with "crucifix" orchids, which are in fact "reed-stem" *Epidendrum* species and their hybrids. While most species have thin reed-like stems, some have thickened stems that form functional pseudobulbs. Many of these grow as terrestrials among grasses in bright spots, frequently in full sun. Most species, however, occur as lithophytes or epiphytes. *Epidendrum* belongs to the same group of genera as *Brassavola, Cattleya, Encyclia, Laelia, Rhyncholaelia,* and *Sophronitis.* CULTIVATION: As the various species come from a range of altitudes, some will suit most frost-free climates, but most enjoy bright and warm conditions. The "reed-stem" or "crucifix" types may be grown in the ground in frost-free climates. Some species have a dormancy period; many are in continual growth. Many species may be grown in a free-draining bark-based medium or tied onto slabs of cork or tree fern. Propagate by division.

Encyclia hanburyi

Epidendrum ciliare

♀ ☼/☀ ↔ 8–36 in (20–90 cm) ↕ 8–24 in (20–60 cm)
Variable Central American species. Like a cattleya in growth habit but without the telltale floral sheath. Can bear inflorescences of up to 8 flowers, summer–autumn. Blooms spidery, green, 4 in (10 cm); white lip. Needs strong light and a dry winter rest to bloom. Zones 10–12.

Epidendrum ibaguense

♀/❦ ☼/☀ ↔ 8–48 in (20–120 cm) ↕ 8–48 in (20–120 cm)
From Central and South America. A common and widespread species; the classic "reed-stem" or "crucifix" orchid that is popular in horticulture. Spherical heads of red to orange blooms, 1¼ in (30 mm) across; with a modified yellowish lip. Requires strong light; will continue to bloom throughout the year if grown under favorable conditions. Zones 9–12.

Epidendrum parkinsonianum ★

♀ ☼/☀ ↔ 8–24 in (20–60 cm) ↕ 1–7 ft (0.3–2 m)
Central American species. Pendulous growth habit; succulent purple-stained foliage. Up to 4 large greenish flowers, 5 in (12 cm) across, white lip, throughout spring. Grow on large slabs of cork or tree fern, or in small wooden baskets. Zones 10–12.

Epidendrum secundum

syn. *Epidendrum elongatum*
❦ ☼/☀ ↔ 8–48 in (20–120 cm) ↕ 8–36 in (20–90 cm)
"Reed-stem" epidendrum from Central America. Comes in a range of colors. Spherical heads of blooms, ¾ in (18 mm), borne throughout year. 'Clark', rich pink flowers, lip pink, white, and gold. Zones 10–12.

Epidendrum Hybrids

♀ ☼/☀ ↔ 8–48 in (20–120 cm) ↕ 8–48 in (20–120 cm)
Most common types in cultivation are the "reed-stem" or "crucifix" orchids, which come in a range of colors, deep reds predominating. The globular heads of blooms can re-bloom off the same flowering stem many times, and at any time of the year. While many older hybrids can grow up to 48 in (120 cm) tall, there are also more recent hybrids that are more compact growing, reaching only to 24 in (60 cm) tall, with larger and more brightly colored flowers. Cosmo Dream Color 'Momo 1', bright pink flowers, fringed lip, with a splash of golden yellow at throat; Hokulea, orange-red blooms, lip is golden yellow and bright orange; Hokulea 'Santa Barbara' ★, has compact growth habit, boldly colored blooms; Joseph Glow 'Seto Raspberry', orange-red flowers, lip orange and golden yellow with red spotting; Pacific Girl, bright orange blooms, lip bright yellow at center. White-flowering forms also available. Zones 9–12.

LAELIA

A genus from Mexico, Central America, and tropical South America of about 60 colorful, easily grown, showy sympodial orchids. These *Cattleya* relatives are generally lithophytic, though there are some epiphytic species. They also differ from that genus by having 8 pollen bundles or pollinia (*Cattleya* have 4). Generally smaller plants than most cattleyas, and mostly have 1 leaf per pseudobulb, though a few species have 2 or more leaves. Have been used in many artificial hybrids involving a range of related genera, including *Brassavola, Broughtonia, Cattleya, Epidendrum,* and *Sophronitis.* CULTIVATION: Most species require bright, warm, and moist conditions during summer while the plants are in active growth, and a cooler dry winter, when most species are dormant. Cultivated plants must have unimpeded drainage, and can be mounted or grown in pots using a coarse bark-based medium. Flowering plants may be enjoyed indoors while in bloom. Propagate by division.

Laelia anceps ★

♀ ☼/☀ ↔ 8–36 in (20–90 cm) ↕ 8–48 in (20–120 cm)
Extremely variable Mexican species. Long flattened inflorescences to over 40 in (100 cm) long, up to 5 large blooms in autumn–winter. Flowers to 5 in (12 cm) across, somewhat starry, colors range from white through shades of pink to deep lavender; lip color various combinations of white, yellow, orange, purple, and lilac. Albino (white), bicolored, and splash-petalled forms also in cultivation. Zones 10–12.

Epidendrum parkinsonianum   *Laelia anceps*

Laelia Canariensis

♀/∧ ☼/❂ ↔ 8–24 in (20–60 cm) ↕ 8–40 in (20–100 cm)
Popular primary hybrid of *L. anceps* and *L. harpophylla*. Blooms
in colors ranging from light purples to orange and yellow tones,
during winter and spring. Zones 10–12.

Laelia crispa

syn. *Sophronitis crispa*
♀/∧ ☼/❂ ↔ 8–36 in (20–90 cm) ↕ 8–24 in (20–60 cm)
From Brazil. Upright spike with up to 7 blooms, in late summer.
Flowers 5 in (12 cm) wide, white; lip predominantly purple with
yellow markings, floral segments with wavy edges. Zones 10–12.

Laelia purpurata

syn. *Sophronitis purpurata*
♀ ☼/❂ ↔ 8–36 in (20–90 cm) ↕ 8–36 in (20–90 cm)
The national flower of Brazil; has been called the
"Queen of the Laelias." Up to 5 blooms, to 8 in
(20 cm) across, produced off mature pseudobulbs
in summer. Tall-growing species come in a wide
range and combination of colors, from pure white
through all shades of pink, purple, and lilac.
Flared and trumpet-like lip in a similar color
range, with a network of stripes and solid color.
Also availble are albino (pure white), semi-alba,
splash-petalled, and bicolored forms. Numerous
varieties have been named, all defining a different
color form. Two of the most popular varieties are
L. p. var. *carnea* ★, crisp white blooms with a soft pink lip; and
L. p. var. *werkhauseri*, white blooms with a dark bluish purple lip
and a pleasant fragrance. Zones 10–12.

Laelia tenebrosa

syn. *Sophronitis tenebrosa*
♀ ☼/❂ ↔ 8–36 in (20–90 cm) ↕ 8–32 in (20–80 cm)
Large summer-flowering species from Brazil. Up to 3 blooms, 6 in
(15 cm) across. Petals and sepals are bronze with coppery hue; lip
is white with very heavy purple veining. Zones 10–12.

LAELIOCATTLEYA

This is an artificial bigeneric group of colorful orchid hybrids
between 2 epiphytic New World genera—*Laelia* and *Cattleya*.
They are generally robust plants with 1 or 2 leaves per pseudobulb, and come in a wide range of sizes, shapes, and colors—the
result of the combination of 2 genera that are themselves highly
variable. Almost all colors may be encountered, with the exception of black and sky blue. The flower size varies between around
2 in (5 cm) and 10 in (25 cm). Many of the larger-flowering
types are grown commercially for the cut-flower trade.
CULTIVATION: These attractive hybrids require warmth in winter
but will cope with cooler winter temperatures for short periods
provided that they are kept dry while dormant. They will enjoy
bright light conditions and must have unimpeded drainage and
a coarse bark-based medium. Healthy plants will develop an
extensive system of thick white roots that are both long-lived
and freely branching. Propagation is by division.

Laeliocattleya, Hybrid, Pink Favourite 'Jolly'

Lycaste, Hybrid, Albanensis

Laeliocattleya Hybrids

♀ ☼/❂ ↔ 4–30 in (10–75 cm)
↕ 4–36 in (10–90 cm)
Popular and easily grown examples include **C. G.
Roebling**, primary hybrid made over a century ago
between "blue-lipped" forms of *Cattleya gaskelliana*
and *Laelia purpurata*; **Chit Chat 'Tangerine'**, free-
flowering hybrid of *Cattleya aurantiaca* and *Laelia
Coronet*, vivid orange blooms; **Jim Burkhalter**,
between *Laeliocattleya* Jalapa and *Cattleya* Chocolate
Drop, apricot and pink flowers, deep pinkish red
lip; **Mini Purple 'Bette'** ★, popular primary hybrid
of compact-growing *Laelia pumila* and *Cattleya walkeriana*, pinkish
purple flowers; **Myrtle Johnson**, fine "splash-petalled" style, lip colors
also appearing on petals; **Pink Favourite 'Jolly'**, primary hybrid of
Laelia milleri and *Cattleya walkeriana*; **Tropical Pointer 'Cheetah'**,
Cattleya intermedia hybrid—gets its spots from one of its ancestors,
C. aclandiae. Depending on parentage, blooms can be produced for
most of year. Zones 10–12.

LYCASTE

These deciduous sympodial orchids are native to coastal and mountainous regions from Mexico to Bolivia. There are 45 distinct recognized species. They are cool- to warm-growing epiphytes or terrestrials
with fat pseudobulbs and large, thin, pleated leaves. Many of the
Central American species (particularly the yellow-flowered group,
which also have highly fragrant blooms) often leave sharp spines after
the previous season's leaves have fallen. The long-lasting flowers are
produced singly, on upright stalks from the base of the pseudobulb,
usually in spring and summer, coinciding with new growth. The
sepals open fully in most species, with the petals pushed forward,
often adjacent to the lip. There are numerous hybrids, mostly based
on the magnificent *L. skinneri*, which prefers cooler temperatures.
CULTIVATION: Best grown in pots, as their roots must not dry out in
growing season. Use a well-drained bark-based mix that incorporates
a moisture-retaining medium such as peat moss. Heavy feeders when
in active growth, and require copious watering. Leaves can burn in
summer if plants are exposed to direct light. Reduce watering when
plants are dormant in winter, allowing potting medium to dry for a
few days before re-wetting. Protect from frost. Propagate by division.

Lycaste skinneri

syn. *Lycaste guatemalensis*

♀ ☼ ↔ 8–24 in (20–60 cm) ↕ 4–24 in (10–60 cm)

Highly desirable and variable species from Guatemala, Honduras, and El Salvador. Large light to deep pink blooms, 5 in (12 cm) across, in groups of up to 6, in winter–early spring. Zones 9–11.

Lycaste Hybrids

♀/✿ ☼ ↔ 8–24 in (20–60 cm) ↕ 4–24 in (10–60 cm)

Many have hybrid vigor, are easier to grow, and bloom more readily than some of the species. *Lycaste* hybrids mostly flower winter–spring. **Albanensis**, primary hybrid between *L. lasioglossa* and *L. macrophylla*; **Imschootiana**, primary hybrid made over a century ago between *L. cruenta* and *L. skinneri*; **Koolena** ★, popular hybrid, as a showbench flower and for breeding, high percentage of *L. skinneri*; **Macama 'Aline'** and **Macama 'Atlantis'**, both hybrids between *L.* Sunrise and *L.* Koolena; **(Rowland × Shoalhaven)**, unregistered hybrid; **Shonan Harmony**, hybrid of *L.* Koolena and *L.* Headington; **Wyuna 'Pale Beauty'**, hybrid between *L.* Macama and *L. mathiasiae*. Zones 10–12.

MASDEVALLIA

FLAG ORCHID

There are almost 500 species in this genus, distributed in Central and South America. They are generally found in cloud forests in mountainous regions with fairly uniform conditions throughout the year. They have no pseudobulbs, produce clumps of single fleshy leaves, and store moisture in the roots and foliage. Species bloom at different times; peak seasons are winter and spring. They come in an amazing range of shapes, sizes, and bright colors, and most are single-flowered; larger-flowered species produce fewer blooms. The sepals often terminate with short or long tails, while the petals and lip are generally tiny. The many hybrids are more vigorous in cultivation.
CULTIVATION: Prefer small pots; sphagnum moss is the best medium. Will grow in pots with a bark and perlite mix if it does not dry out. Keep plants slightly potbound, moist, shaded, and in a cool humid environment all year, out of direct sunlight. Propagate by division.

Masdevallia tridens

syn. *Masdevallia ova-avis*

✿ ☼ ↔ 4–8 in (10–20 cm) ↕ 4–12 in (10–30 cm)

Multi-flowered orchid from Ecuador. Up to 8 nodding flowers, 1½ in (35 mm) wide, open simultaneously in spring. Blooms are pinkish cream, with dark maroon spots; sepal tails bright yellow. Zones 9–11.

Masdevallia veitchiana ★

✿ ☼ ↔ 12 in (30 cm) ↕ 24 in (60 cm)

From Peru, known from the Aztec city of Machu Picchu. Spikes of orange flowers, 5 in (12 cm) wide, with tiny bright purple tubercles, incandescent sheen in sunlight, in spring–summer. Zones 9–11.

Masdevallia Hybrids

✿ ☼ ↔ 4–12 in (10–30 cm) ↕ 4–24 in (10–60 cm)

Many hybrids have been developed. They exhibit hybrid vigor and many bloom several times a year. Popular hybrids include: **Adelina**, between *M. velifera* and *M. deformis*, gold and red flowers; **Carousel 'Parade'**, pink blooms, darker veining; **Charisma**, between *M. coccinea*

and the striped *M. yungasensis*, pale pink blooms, magenta striped; **Cinnamon Twist**, orange flowers, heavily spotted red-brown; **Copper Angel 'Highland'**, orange flowers; **Copperwing**, between *M. veitchiana* and *M. decumana*, deep yellow blooms, copper spotting; **Dean Haas**, orange blooms; **Delma Hart 'Paddy'**, creamy white flowers, gold throat; **Elegance**, yellow flowers, flushed pink; **Falcata 'North Degree'**, orange blooms, highlighted with red; **Machu Picchu**, between *M. ayabacana* and *M. coccinea*, superb magenta flowers; **(Magdalene × Marguerite)**, between 2 hybrids, deep red flowers, center fading slightly; **Marguerite**, between *M. infracta* and *M. veitchiana*, flowers with copper-red spotting; **Pixie Shadow**, between *M. infracta* and *M. schroederiana*, rich red flowers; **Prince Charming**, between *M. angulata* and *M. veitchiana*, flowers with ruby red banding deepening at center; **Redwing**, magenta blooms; **Rose-Mary**, between *M. coccinea* and pink-spotted *M. glandulosa*, rose pink flowers, orange at center; **Urubamba**, between *M. ayabacana* and *M. veitchiana*, orange blooms; and **Winter Blush**, between *M.* Angel Frost *(M. veitchiana × M. strobelii)* and *M. chaparensis*, golden orange blooms. Zones 9–11.

MAXILLARIA

A complex genus of some 600 epiphytic and lithophytic sympodial orchids from Mexico, and Central and South America. They exhibit an enormous range in plant habit and floral shape, size, and color. In most species, solitary blooms emerge from base of pseudobulbs; petals are smaller than sepals. They produce 1 to 3 leaves at top of pseudobulb. For such a large genus, there have been surprisingly few artificial hybrids, despite their obvious potential. They are related to *Lycaste*.
CULTIVATION: These orchids have varying growing requirements, but most cultivated species are cool- to intermediate-growers, enjoy bright light in a humid environment, and are easily grown in pots of a coarse bark-based mix. Many species, particularly the miniatures, also grow well on slabs of tree fern or cork. Propagate by division.

Maxillaria fractiflexa

♀ ☼ ↔ 8 in (20 cm) ↕ 4–24 in (10–60 cm)

Colombian; large-flowered. Tall mid-green leaves, strappy. Summer flowers up to 6 in (15 cm) wide, narrow sepals, mustard yellow to brown; twisted petals, cream; relatively small white lip. Zones 9–11.

Masdevallia, Hybrid, Cinnamon Twist

Maxillaria fractiflexa

Maxillaria porphyrostele
♀/⋀ ☼/☽ ↔ 4–8 in (10–20 cm) ↑ 4–24 in (10–60 cm)
From Brazil; hardy orchid. Round pseudobulbs; 2 strap-like leaves.
Bright yellow flowers, 2 in (5 cm) wide, long-lasting. Yellow lip,
red-brown markings near base. Blooms in early spring. Zones 9–12.

Maxillaria variabilis ★
♀ ☼/☽ ↔ 4–8 in (10–20 cm) ↑ 4–24 in (10–60 cm)
Variable species found from Mexico to Panama. Upright habit,
somewhat branching in older specimens.
Leaves green, long, strap-like. Flowers vary
from yellow, orange, brown, and red to a dark
claret-black, in spring–summer. Zones 9–12.

MILTONIA
Genus of sympodial orchids, about 10 epiphytic
species, mostly from Brazil. Showy blooms in a
large variety of colors. Vigorous plants that
quickly grow into specimen size. *Miltonia* species
have been hybridized with many of the related
genera, including *Brassia*, to produce *Miltassia*,
and with *Oncidium* to create the genus *Miltoni-
dium*. But many hybrids labeled as *Miltonia* species in collections
often refer to the closely related genus of pansy orchids, *Miltoniopsis*.
CULTIVATION: Can be grown on large slabs or plaques of cork or tree
fern, or potted in squat-style pots, as they have a shallow root system.
They will take bright light and high temperatures in summer, as long
as the humidity remains high. Need a cooler dry rest period in winter.
Reliable bloomers and, for best results, they should be fed regularly
throughout the growing season. However, the plants will still perform
well even with a level of neglect. Propagation is by division.

Miltoniopsis, Hybrid,
Zorro 'Yellow Delight'

Miltonia clowesii
♀ ☀ ↔ 8–24 in (20–60 cm) ↑ 8–27 in (20–70 cm)
Striking Brazilian orchid. Tall spikes of up to 8 yellow-brown, starry,
3 in (8 cm) wide flowers, with chestnut-brown bars and blotches, in
summer–autumn. Lip white, purple markings at base. Zones 10–12.

Miltonia Sandy's Cove
♀ ☀ ↔ 8–24 in (20–60 cm) ↑ 8–24 in (20–60 cm)
Hybrid orchid, of unusual color combination, with 5 species in its
ancestry. Golden brown tepals, with a contrasting plum-colored lip.
Flowers produced in spring. Zones 10–12.

Miltonia spectabilis
♀ ☀ ↔ 8–24 in (20–60 cm) ↑ 8–16 in (20–40 cm)
Variable Brazilian species. Flowers 3 in (8 cm) wide, singly or in pairs,
spring. Common form has white petals and sepals, broad lip, 2-tone
purple; also pink and purple forms and rare albino forms. Zones 10–12.

MILTONIOPSIS
PANSY ORCHID
A genus of 6 different sympodial orchids, mainly from Colombia and
Ecuador. They were once included within *Miltonia*, but botanically,
Miltoniopsis is closer to *Odontoglossum* than *Miltonia*. Many artificial
hybrids have been created within this showy genus, known as "pansy

orchids" because of their floral shape and color markings. Plants are
fragile with thin foliage. The leaves are usually bluish green and
narrow. The large flat blooms come in a range of colors. Care should
be taken with handling, as all parts scorch and bruise easily.
CULTIVATION: They prefer a narrow temperature range; they do not
want to go below 50°F (10°C) in winter or go over 79°F (26°C) in
summer. Foliage prefers a shaded humid position. Blooms will readily
mark if not provided with ample air movement. Best in small pots,
with sphagnum moss as the exclusive growing medium. Hybrids are
generally easier to grow than the species, due to
hybrid vigor. Propagate by division.

Miltoniopsis phalaenopsis
♀ ☀ ↔ 15 in (38 cm) ↑ 12 in (30 cm)
Colombian species, occurring at altitudes of
3,940–4,920 ft (1,200–1,500 m). Clumping;
grass-like foliage. Up to 5 shapely white flowers,
2½ in (6 cm) wide, in spring. Outstanding
broad white lip, yellow at base, distinguished by
a waterfall pattern of bright purple markings
often passed on to hybrids. Zones 11–12.

Miltoniopsis vexillaria
♀ ☀ ↔ 8–24 in (20–60 cm) ↑ 8–16 in (20–40 cm)
A species found growing naturally in Colombia and Peru; a
major parent among *Miltoniopsis* hybrids. Upright to arching
spikes of up to 8 flowers, up to 4 in (10 cm) in diameter, palest
pink to deep rose, borne in spring. Zones 11–12.

Miltoniopsis Hybrids
♀ ☀ ↔ 32 in (80 cm) ↑ 20 in (50 cm)
These hybrids offer a range of colors and patterns in white, pinks,
purples, reds, and yellows. Many are fragrant. **Beall's Strawberry Joy**,
rose pink blooms, deep strawberry red markings; **Cute 'Rodeo'**,

Miltonia Sandy's Cove

white-edged blooms, deep ruby red centers;
First Love 'Pink Lady', yellow-throated pink
blooms; **Hudson Bay**, white blooms brushed
rose pink; **Jean Carlson**, striking hot pink
blooms; **Red Knight**, pink and purple blooms;
Robert Strauss, creamy white blooms, red to
orange marking at centers; **Rouge 'California
Plum'** ★, 2-tone plum blooms, white-edged;
and **Zorro 'Yellow Delight'**, pale yellow
blooms with orange-red marking. Zones 11–12.

ODONTIODA

This is a cool-growing bigeneric hybrid
between the sympodial genera *Odontoglossum* and *Cochlioda*, with *C. noezliana*
giving bright red color to many of its hybrids. Sometimes the
Cochlioda influence is barely noticeable as the hybrids have been
repeatedly backcrossed onto other odontoglossums.
CULTIVATION: These plants prefer cool, moist, humid conditions in
part-shade, and thrive in pots. Use sphagnum moss or a fine-grade
bark mixture with perlite. Keep well-watered. Propagate by division.

Odontioda, Hybrid, Avranches

Odontoglossum wyattianum

Odontioda Hybrids

♀ ☀ ↔ 8–24 in (20–60 cm) ↕ 8–36 in (20–90 cm)

Most of these hybrids are winter and spring flowerers, with the
bloom size from 2–5 in (5–12 cm). **Avranches** ★, an albino hybrid
developed from white-flowered forms of the species; **Bugle Boy**,
red-orange blooms; **Durham River**, full shape from *Odontoglossum*
parent, with intense color coming from *Cochlioda*; (**Erik Jaeger ×
Helen Stead 'Geyserland'**), pink and white blooms with darker
markings; **Heatonensis × *Odontoglossum* Starlight**, unregistered
hybrid, spidery shape inherited from *Odontoglossum cirrhosum*;
La Fosse, most unusual color combination of maroon, white,
and yellow. (**Nichirei Sunrise × Ingmar**), vermilion and hot pink
blooms; **Ruby Eyes**, pink flowers with maroon patterning; **Sheila
Hands**, white blooms overlaid with brown and edged with pink;
and **Wearside Gate**, bright red blooms. Zones 9–10.

ODONTOGLOSSUM

This genus of about 60 cool-growing orchids from mountainous
regions of South America is related to *Oncidium* and *Miltoniopsis*.
Most have short to long spikes of large, showy, yellow and brown
blooms, often spidery. The popular ornamentals have been the
species with white and pink flowers and wider segments, giving the
effect of a round bloom. There are many hybrids in *Odontoglossum*
and its combinations with related genera. Some of the more popular combinations include *Colmanara* (× *Miltonia* × *Oncidium*),
Odontioda (× *Cochlioda*), and *Odontocidium* (× *Oncidium*).
CULTIVATION: They thrive in cool growing conditions in a part-shaded
spot. Grow in pots in a fine-grade bark mixture with perlite in a 5:1
ratio or in sphagnum moss. Keep well-watered. Propagate by division.

Odontoglossum crispum

♀ ☀ ↔ 4–16 in (10–40 cm) ↕ 5–32 in (12–80 cm)

From Colombia. Compressed pseudobulbs, each with 2 strap-like
leaves. Up to 12 or more large, widely opening blooms, 3 in (8 cm)
wide, with broad segments. Flowers white to pale rose, spotted or
blotched with red or purple. Blooms in autumn–winter. Zones 9–10.

Odontoglossum wyattianum

♀ ☀ ↔ 4–12 in (10–30 cm) ↕ 5–24 in (12–60 cm)

From Peru and Ecuador; found in mossy cloud forests at altitudes of
around 6,560 ft (2,000 m). Up to 8 tan-brown, 3 in (8 cm) wide
blooms, with a contrasting, broad, 2-toned purple lip, borne from
late winter to spring. Closely related to *O. harryanum*. Zones 9–11.

Odontoglossum Hybrids

♀ ☀ ↔ 8–24 in (20–60 cm) ↕ 8–36 in (20–90 cm)

Mostly winter- and spring-flowering hybrids. Blooms are 1½–5 in
(3.5–12 cm) wide. (**Augres × *nobile***), unregistered hybrid, white
blooms, contrasting yellow lip, deep pink border; (**Holiday Gold
× Geyser Gold**), golden yellow hybrid; **Illustre**, red-brown blooms
with white markings; **La Hougue Bie**, blooms with well-defined
yellow, white, and tan blotches; **Margarete Holm**, blooms with
white, yellow, and maroon markings; and **Mimosa 'Oda Marcet'**,
vivid plum-purple blooms with a velvety texture. Zones 9–10.

ONCIDIUM

DANCING LADY ORCHID

This large genus of sympodial orchids from tropical America contains
over 650 different species. Usually they produce yellow and brown
flowers on long branching inflorescences. Most have a distinct pseudobulb with up to 4 leaves at the apex. Inflorescences generally appear
from the leaf axil of recently matured growth. In many species, the lip
is most prominent feature. Bloom only once from the pseudobulb.
CULTIVATION: Most species are frequently grown mounted, which per-
mits unimpeded development of the root system and allows for quick
drying after watering. Some smaller species may be grown in pots.
Cultural requirements are varied, and depend largely on the habitat
and altitude of particular species. Most prefer intermediate growing
conditions. Propagation is by division.

Oncidium crispum

♀ ☀/☀ ↔ 4–16 in (10–40 cm) ↕ 8–27 in (20–70 cm)

From Brazil. Ovoid pseudobulbs; 2-leafed. Leathery leaves to 8 in
(20 cm) long. Branching inflorescence has 3 in (8 cm) wide blooms,
predominantly brown, some yellow patches, in summer. Zones 10–12.

Oncidium flexuosum

♀ ☼/☀ ↔ 8–36 in (20–90 cm)
↕ 8–60 in (20–150 cm)

A common and widespread species from South America. Climbing habit; long rhizomes between pseudobulbs. Tall branching spikes bear masses of long-lasting, bright yellow, ¾ in (18 mm) wide flowers, in mid-summer. Zones 10–12.

Oncidium sphacelatum

♀ ☼/☀ ↔ 8–36 in (20–90 cm)
↕ 8–60 in (20–150 cm)

Vigorous species native to Central America; adaptable throughout a range of climates in cultivation. Long, branched, and upright to arching inflorescences of typical brown and yellow blooms, each 1¼ in (30 mm) wide, in spring. Very hardy and reliable species. Zones 10–12.

Paphiopedilum haynaldianum

Oncidium varicosum

DANCING LADY ORCHID

♀ ☼/☀ ↔ 4–16 in (10–40 cm) ↕ 5–32 in (12–80 cm)

From Brazil; this species has been dominant in the production of "varicosum-type" *Oncidium* hybrids. Clustered pseudobulbs, each with up to 3 leaves. Upright branching inflorescences carry up to 70 long-lasting blooms throughout summer. The flowers are up to 2 in (5 cm) across; petals and sepals are small, yellow with brown markings; the lip is large, flat, round, bright yellow, and dominates the flower. Zones 10–12.

PAPHIOPEDILUM

SLIPPER ORCHID

The slipper orchids, with their distinctive modified lip or "pouch," have long been highly prized in horticulture. They are cultivated throughout the world, and countless hybrids have been produced from the 80 or so species. The range extends from India eastward across southern China to the Philippines and throughout Southeast Asia and Malaysia to New Guinea and the Solomon Islands. New species continue to be discovered, particularly in remote rainforest areas of Borneo and China. There is a huge amount of diversity within the genus: some are terrestrial, growing through the leaf litter on the forest floor; others are lithophytes that show a preference for limestone cliffs; others are epiphytes, happy to live in the major forks of rainforest trees. Most species produce a single flower, but some may have up to a dozen or more open at one time, and then there are others that flower sequentially. They are generally found in quite bright situations, but not receiving direct sunlight. These flowers, which come in a wide range of colors and forms, often last for well over a month in pristine condition. Most species have plain green strap leaves; others distinctive mottled foliage, which makes them attractive plants even when they are not in flower. Slipper orchids generally grow in quite moist and humid environments. They do not have pseudobulbs but store water in their fleshy leaves and thick hairy root system. The genus name comes from the temple to Aphrodite (Venus) at Paphos, and the Greek *pedilon*, meaning a slipper.

CULTIVATION: Slipper orchids are best grown in pots, in a well-drained bark-based medium. Select a pot size that fits the roots snugly, as they will not tolerate stagnant conditions around the root system. Pot the plant so that it is slightly buried, as often the roots will push it out of the mix, and any exposed new roots can become dry and not develop further. Keep plants shaded and moist during the warmer months, and mist foliage frequently. Many of the multi-flowered species need a drier rest in winter, along with a significant drop in day and night-time temperature. There are cool-, intermediate-, and warm-growing species. Propagation is by division.

Paphiopedilum bellatulum

☀ ↔ 8–12 in (20–30 cm) ↕ 2½–6 in (6–15 cm)

Native to Thailand and Myanmar. Waxy tessellated leaves; very short flower stem with a single 3 in (8 cm) wide bloom that rests on the leaves, in summer. Flowers are large, white, with sizeable dark maroon spots. Zones 10–12.

Paphiopedilum haynaldianum

♀/∧/☀ ↔ 12–24 in (30–60 cm) ↕ 4–32 in (10–80 cm)

From the Philippines. Plain green leathery leaves. Up to 5 flowers produced at the same time, 5 in (12 cm) wide, yellow to green, white, and mauve, marked with dark red blotches. Spring- and summer-blooming species. Zones 10–12.

Paphiopedilum henryanum

∧ ☀ ↔ 8–12 in (20–30 cm) ↕ 4–16 in (10–40 cm)

Stunning and distinctive species from China and Vietnam. Plain green leaves; single, 2½ in (6 cm) wide, colorful bloom. Dorsal sepal green with bold maroon spots, petals brownish purple, lip bright dark pink. Spring-flowering species. Zones 10–12.

Paphiopedilum hirsutissimum

☀ ↔ 8–16 in (20–40 cm) ↕ 4–16 in (10–40 cm)

Found from India to Indochina. Hairy flower stems; flowers yellow to green, with brown, and purple markings, 6 in (15 cm) wide, also covered in hairs. Winter- to spring-flowering. Zones 9–11.

Paphiopedilum insigne ★

♥ ☀ ↔ 8–12 in (20–30 cm) ↕ 4–16 in (10–40 cm)

From Nepal and northern India; commonly grown variable species, readily grows into a specimen. Leaves up to 12 in (30 cm) long. Glossy, brownish yellow, 5 in (12 cm) wide flowers, heavily spotted in red-brown, in winter. Zones 9–11.

Paphiopedilum lowii

∧/♥ ☀ ↔ 12–24 in (30–60 cm) ↕ 8–40 in (20–100 cm)

Variable multi-flowered species from Peninsular Malaysia, Borneo, and Indonesia. Similar to *P. haynaldianum*, but lacks spotting on dorsal sepal. Tall inflorescences, to 20 in (50 cm), bear up to 6 blooms in spring–summer. Flowers green, white, and deep purple, 6 in (15 cm) wide. 'Select', attractive cultivar. Zones 10–12.

Paphiopedilum primulinum

♥ ☀ ↔ 8–16 in (20–40 cm)
↕ 4–24 in (10–60 cm)

From Sumatra, Indonesia. Long spikes of many sequentially opening flowers, each 3 in (8 cm) wide, bright canary yellow, dorsal sepal tinged green. Blooms throughout year. *P. p.* var. *purpurescens*, purple-tinged flowers. Zones 10–12.

Paphiopedilum rothschildianum

∧/♥ ☀ ↔ 8–32 in (20–80 cm)
↕ 8–36 in (20–90 cm)

From Sabah in north Borneo; endemic to Mt Kinabalu, where it often occurs in large clumps; impressive and majestic species. Up to 5 dark-striped flowers on an upright spike; each flower up to 12 in (30 cm) across extended petals, in spring–summer. Zones 10–12.

Paphiopedilum victoria-regina

syn. *Paphiopedilum chamberlainianum*

∧/♥ ☀ ↔ 8–24 in (20–60 cm) ↕ 4–27 in (10–70 cm)

Species from central Sumatra in Indonesia; grows on forest floor or on mossy rocks. Leaves green with wavy edges. Arching to erect spikes, with up to 20 sequentially produced blooms. Large persistent bracts behind each flower. Blooms to 3 in (8 cm) wide; white-edged green dorsal sepal with dark lines or reddish spotting

Paphiopedilum rothschildianum

overlay, white to yellow-green and reddish undulated petals, with a pink lip. Can bloom throughout the year. Zones 10–12.

Paphiopedilum villosum

♥ ☀ ↔ 8–12 in (20–30 cm) ↕ 4–16 in (10–40 cm)

Found from India to Indochina. Commonly grown. Flowers, 5 in (12 cm) wide, glossy, bronze overlay. Dorsal sepal yellow to green with dark brown markings at base. Petals 2-tone; top half reddish brown, bottom half yellowish green. Winter–spring. Zones 10–11.

Paphiopedilum Hybrids

♥ ☀/☀ ↔ 4–8 in (10–20 cm)
↕ 4–24 in (10–60 cm)

While there are hundreds of possible combinations, there have been 3 basic styles of hybrids popular for over a century. "Maudiae"-type hybrids (*P. Maudiae*, an antique hybrid between *P. callosum* and *P. lawrenceanum*) have tessellated 2-tone foliage and single blooms with prominent stripes on the broad, white, dorsal sepal. Of these, the "albino" hybrids have green stripes on the dorsal sepal, with green petals and pouch; the "coloratum" hybrids are the same, but with purple stripes, while the "vinicolors" have deep beetroot-colored flowers and almost black stripes. Multifloral hybrids have become more popular, and often feature larger-flowered spectacular species, such as *P. stonei, P. rothschildianum, P. philippinense*, and, since its rediscovery, *P. sanderianum*. The third group are the "complex hybrids;" the large, round, single-flowered plants often seen at orchid shows. Ironically, despite being developed for over a century, there is only a handful of species in their pedigree. They are mostly multiple generation hybrids, with high ratios of *P. insigne, P. spicerianum*, and *P. villosum*, with minor influences of *P. bellatulum, P. charlesworthii, P. druryi, P. exul*, and *P. niveum*. Obviously, many of today's desirable species were unknown when most of this breeding was undertaken. Here is a selection of slipper orchid hybrids. **Darling**, hybrid of *P. Madame Martinet* and *P. lawrenceanum*; **Delophyllum**, hybrid of *P. delenatii* and *P. glaucophyllum*; **Gael**, albino "Maudiae-type"; **Gold Dollar**, hybrid of the yellow-flowered species *P. armeniacum* and *P. primulinum*; **Lebaudyanum**, hybrid of the multi-flowered species *P. haynaldianum* and *P. philippinense*; **Madame Martinet**, hybrid of *P. delenatii* and *P. callosum*; **Mitylene** and **Onyx**, albino "Maudiae-type" hybrids; **Oriental Enchantment**, albino "Maudiae-type" with white blooms striped bright green; **Pathfinder Norm**, "complex" or "exhibition" style; **Pinocchio**, hybrid between *P. primulinum* and *P. glaucophyllum*; **Rolfei**, hybrid between *P. bellatulum* and *P. rothschildianum*; **Saint Swithin**, hybrid of *P. philippinense* and *P. rothschildianum* with large flowers; and **Yospur**, hybrid between *P. delenatii* and *P. conco-bellatulum*, with round white blooms overlaid with some fine pepper spotting of purple. Zones 9–11.

Paphiopedilum hirsutissimum

Paphiopedilum, Hybrid, Gold Dollar

PHALAENOPSIS

MOTH ORCHID

These orchids are popular with florists and are often used for weddings. The 60 or so species in the genus are found throughout the tropical rainforests of Asia, and south to New Guinea and northern Australia. Most of the species exist in the wild as epiphytes, and the monopodial plants consist of only a few leathery, often deep green, leaves. There are also some species with attractive tessellated foliage.
CULTIVATION: *Phalaenopsis* species and hybrids require warm, humid, damp conditions, and will grow and bloom in quite deep shade. These orchids are mostly grown in pots in a bark-based medium, but a number of species perform well on long slabs of tree fern or cork when grown in the greenhouse. They are marketed as flowering pot plants, and are one of the most majestic flowers in horticulture; even better, they are the best orchids to grow indoors as they are compact in habit, will grow in a range of light conditions, and prefer a temperature range that is also pleasant for humans. Cut off the flower spike only after it has died and turned brown. As long as the stem remains green, there is the potential for more flowers to be produced along dormant eyes of the peduncle—the part of the flowering stem between the plant and the first flower. Most species and their hybrids can bloom all year, but peak flowering occurs in spring and summer.

Phalaenopsis amabilis ★

♀ ☀ ↔ 8–20 in (20–50 cm) ↕ 12–36 in (30–90 cm)
Species from Indonesia, Borneo, and the Philippines. Leaves broadly oval, to 20 in (50 cm) long. Long arching sprays of large, flat, pure white flowers, 3 in (8 cm) across. *P. rosenstromii* is a closely related species from northeastern Australia and New Guinea. Zones 11–12.

Phalaenopsis equestris

♀ ☀ ↔ 5–12 in (12–30 cm) ↕ 4–12 in (10–30 cm)
Popular miniature-flowered species from the Philippines and Taiwan. Branched sprays of numerous pink to rose-purple blooms, to 1¼ in (30 mm) wide. Flowers in autumn–spring. Zones 11–12.

Phalaenopsis lueddemanniana

♀ ☀ ↔ 6–16 in (15–40 cm) ↕ 4–16 in (10–40 cm)
Highly variable species from the Philippines. Greenish white flowers, 1½ in (35 mm) wide, with concentric purple barring that may give blooms an overall pink appearance. Old inflorescences often produce plantlets; remove these when roots have formed. Zones 11–12.

Phalaenopsis schilleriana

♀ ☀ ↔ 8–20 in (20–50 cm) ↕ 12–36 in (30–90 cm)
From the Philippines. Showy foliage mottled in green and silver. Branched inflorescence with numerous large flowers, pale pink to lilac to deep rose, 4 in (10 cm) wide, in winter–spring. Zones 11–12.

Phalaenopsis Hybrids

♀ ☀ ↔ 5–24 in (12–60 cm) ↕ 8–36 in (20–90 cm)
Many *Phalaenopsis* hybrids have been produced, and this is probably the most important commercial genus of orchids grown. Tens of thousands of plants are sold in flower annually throughout the world to cater for the flowering pot-plant trade. White *Phalaenopsis* hybrids, mostly derived from *P. amabilis*, are still one of the most popular flowers; these include **Cottonwood, Oregon Delight, Snow City,** and **Taisuco Adian.** Previously there were similar hybrids known under the generic name of *Doritaenopsis,* but these are all now classified as *Phalaenopsis.* There is some variation in color, apart from the classic white and pink standard hybrids. Bicolored hybrids include **Brother Pico Sweetheart, City Girl, Luchia Lip,** and **Quevedo.** Hybrids in pink and purple include **Brother Juno, Ho's Amaglad, Hwafeng Redqueen, Little Kiss, Night Shine, Sogo Firework, Sonoma Spots, Taisuco Pixie,** and (**Timothy Christopher** × *pulcherrima*). Candy stripe hybrids include **Brother Pico Pink, Formosa Mini, Hsinying Facia, Minho Stripes, Quilted Beauty,** and **Striped Eagle.** Hybrids in yellow-bronze shades include **Antique Gold, Brother Cefiro, Brother Golden Wish, Coral Harbor, Hakugin, Pumpkin Patch,** and **Taida Sunset.** More recently, new hybrids have been bred from some of the smaller, often rather unusual or brightly colored species, which have provided new shapes, sizes, and color combinations. Zones 11–12.

PHRAGMIPEDIUM

SOUTH AMERICAN SLIPPER ORCHID

A genus from Central and South America of about 20 species. The sympodial plants have multiple flowers, generally blooming sequentially; some robust species have branching spikes of blooms. Well known to orchid growers, their popularity rose dramatically in the early 1980s with the discovery of the bright red species *P. besseae,* which has been used to create many lovely orange and red hybrids. Most flower during warmer months, but some can bloom all year.
CULTIVATION: They have similar needs to those of *Paphiopedilum,* but require stronger light levels and frequent watering. They grow well in a bark-based medium with the addition of washed pea-sized river gravel and perlite. Some growers use pure sphagnum moss. Plants prefer deep plastic pots, and much success has been achieved by placing them in shallow saucers of water, 2 in (5 cm) deep. Propagate by division.

Phragmipedium longifolium

♀ ☀ ↔ 12–24 in (30–60 cm)
↕ 8–36 in (20–90 cm)
Variable species found growing naturally from Costa Rica to Ecuador. Predominantly green blooms, 6 in (15 cm) wide, red-brown markings on the narrow outstretched petals. Autumn-flowering species. Zones 11–12.

Phalaenopsis schilleriana

Phalaenopsis, Hybrid, Taida Sunset

PLEIONE

This small genus of about 20 mostly semi-alpine bulbous orchids is related to Coelogyne. Pleiones are found in a wide variety of mountain habitats, at high altitudes, from Nepal to China. They grow as terrestrials or epiphytes on mossy limbs or fallen rotting logs and produce Cattleya-like blooms, singly or in pairs, in early spring.
CULTIVATION: Pleiones are easy to cultivate in cool climates and do best if repotted annually in a rich, well-drained, terrestrial mix. Healthy plants will produce 2 new growths, which develop into new plants, as older pseudobulbs will shrivel and die. Keep the potting mix moist from spring to early autumn while plants are actively growing. They must be kept cool and dry during the winter months. Propagate by division of the dormant pseudobulbs in late winter.

Pleione formosana

/\/❦ ☀ ❄ ↔16 in (40 cm) ↑16 in (40 cm)
From China and Taiwan; hardiest species. Flowers to 4 in (10 cm), wide, in shades of pink; many named cultivars, also pure white forms, such as 'Clare'. Fringed lip with white and yellow base and small red-brown blotches. Some botanists consider *P. bulbocodioides* to be the same species. Zones 8–10.

Pleione Hybrids

❦ ☀ ❄ ↔8–16 in (20–40 cm) ↑8–16 in (20–40 cm)
There have been numerous hybrids created, using *P. formosana* as a foundation with other pink- and purple-flowered species, as well as incorporating some of the more difficult-to-grow, yellow-flowered species from China. **Alishan**, creamy-colored hybrid of *P.* Versailles and *P. formosana*; **Soufrière**, pale pink flowers, white-fringed lip with brownish red and yellow markings, hybrid of *P.* Versailles and *P. confusa*; **Tolima**, purple-flowered hybrid of *P. formosana* and *P. speciosa*; **Versailles**, vigorous pink- to purple-flowered hybrid of *P. formosana* and *P. limprichtii*, and **Zeus Weinstein**, hybrid of *P. formosana* and *P. forrestii*, flowers lilac-pink, lip yellowish with red markings. Zones 8–10.

PLEUROTHALLIS

A large genus of over 1,000 species of sympodial orchids from the American tropics. They are generally epiphytes of the mountainous rainforests, but many species grow in open situations, on rocks, or as terrestrials, generally in thick mosses. A single leaf is produced, often on a thin flattened "stem," called a ramicaul, as plants lack a pseudobulb. Flowers are produced from a spathe or sheath at the base of the leaf, either singly or on an inflorescence. There is an amazing range of color, shape, and size within the blooms of the various species. Plants range from miniatures to species that can grow over 3 ft (0.9 m) tall. Most are cool-growing, but there are also examples from lowland regions that require warm conditions in cultivation. They are mainly of interest to species orchid enthusiasts, who enjoy the challenge of growing these more unusual botanical subjects in their collections.
CULTIVATION: They have similar cultural needs to *Masdevallia*, but will generally tolerate a wider range of temperatures and stronger light intensities. They like to be somewhat potbound and prefer small pots. Keep them moist, shaded, and generally in a humid environment throughout the year, but avoid direct sunlight. Most species may be grown in sphagnum moss or in a fine bark mix, with some creeping species suitable for mounting on tree fern. Propagate by root division.

Pleione, Hybrid, Soufrière

Pleurothallis tuerckheimii

♀ ☀ ↔4–20 in (10–50 cm) ↑8–20 in (20–50 cm)
Robust Central American species. Long inflorescences of up to 20 reddish brown blooms, about 1 in (25 mm) tall, summer. Zones 10–11.

Pleurothallis villosa

syn. *Pleurothallis schiedei*
♀ ☀ ↔1½–6 in (3.5–15 cm) ↑1½–6 in (3.5–15 cm)
Somewhat bizarre miniature species found in Mexico and Guatemala. Short fine spikes of up to 5 tiny flowers, ranging from greenish yellow through orange-brown to deep maroon, darker spotting over sepals. White filaments dangle from the edges of the sepals, and move in the slightest breeze. Flowers from spring to autumn. Zones 9–11.

POTINARA

Potinara has 4 genera in its genetic make-up, being a blend of the sympodial genera *Brassavola*, *Cattleya*, *Laelia*, and *Sophronitis*. They are like sophrolaeliocattleyas, but differ in having an extra infusion of *Brassavola*. Flowers usually slightly larger than those of the parents.
CULTIVATION: They need part-shade to strong light, but will burn in direct sunlight. Grow best in pots using a coarse bark-based medium to ensure unimpeded drainage. Healthy plants develop an extensive system of thick white roots, which are long lived and branch freely. Plants will withstand cooler winter temperatures for short periods if kept dry while dormant. Flowers are long lasting; enjoy the plant indoors when in bloom. Propagate by division after flowering.

Potinara Hybrids

♀ ☀ ↔8–24 in (20–60 cm) ↑8–24 in (20–60 cm)
There is a huge color range in these attractive hybrids; bright yellow and reds predominate. Many can bloom more than once a year, but most flower in spring. **Afternoon Delight 'Magnificent'**, rich orange blooms; **Atomic Fireball**, large solid red blooms; (*Brassolaeliocattleya* **Regal Pokai** × *Potinara* **Pastushin's Gold**), reddish pink blooms, with ruffled deep red lip with yellow markings; **Burana Beauty ★**, 2-tone yellow and red splash-petalled hybrid; **Dal's Moon**, creamy flowers, ruffled edges and dark markings; **Little Toshie 'Gold Country'**, pure yellow, 3 in (8 cm) blooms, deep red lip. Zones 10–12.

PROSTHECHEA

COCKLESHELL ORCHID

This is a genus of around 100 species found growing naturally from Florida, USA, to Brazil. They were previously included within the vast genus *Encyclia*. Many species of these sympodial epiphytes and lithophytes are known as cockleshell orchids on account of the lip shape, which is often striped and always the uppermost part of the flower. In general, the individual blooms are long lived, with many having a strong and pleasant fragrance. The pseudobulbs are spindle-shaped, generally flattened with 2 distinctive edges along their length. Flowering inflorescences are produced from the apex of the 1 to 5 leaves, after the pseudo-bulbs have fully developed.

CULTIVATION: *Prosthechea* species are readily grown, either on cork or tree-fern slabs, in wooden slatted baskets, or potted in a well-drained bark-based medium. Most species have a dormant period from late autumn to early spring, when growth recommences. The majority of the species are summer flowering and enjoy bright light conditions. They are reliable bloomers in cultivation, with most species also tolerating a wide variation in temperature. Propagate by division of large specimens in spring.

Prosthechea michuacana | Pterostylis curta

Prosthechea michuacana

syn. *Encyclia michuacana*

♀ ☀ ↔ 8–16 in (20–40 cm) ↕ 8–48 in (20–120 cm)

A species from Central America. Tall, upright, branched inflorescences bear numerous reddish brown to olive green flowers, up to 1 in (25 mm) in diameter, with a predominantly white lip. Blooms during summer months. Zones 10–11.

Prosthechea vitellina

syn. *Encyclia vitellina*

♀ ☀ ↔ 8–16 in (20–40 cm) ↕ 8–24 in (20–60 cm)

Found growing from Mexico and Guatemala. Probably one of the showiest and most striking members of this genus, unique in having large orange-red blooms with broad segments. The erect inflorescences with up to 12 blooms, 1½ in (35 mm) across, are produced from summer to autumn. Zones 10–11.

PTEROSTYLIS

GREENHOOD ORCHID

This is a genus of approximately 120 species of temperate, deciduous, terrestrial orchids, known as "greenhoods"; the majority of the species occur in Australia. There are also representatives from New Zealand, New Caledonia, and New Guinea. Most species develop a rosette of leaves, with the single bloom produced on a slender stem, originating from the crown of the foliage. Blooms are usually green with reddish brown suffusions and transparent "light windows" to deceive pollinators that would normally avoid a darker area. The dorsal sepals and petals overlap to form a hood, giving these orchids their common name. The lip is sensitive, mobile, and capable of rapid movement; it is an important attractant for potential pollinators.

CULTIVATION: The colony-forming species in this genus are relatively easy to cultivate, flower, and multiply. They require moist, humid, and cool conditions when in growth from autumn to

spring. They are best grown in a well-drained terrestrial mix, containing a high proportion of peat moss and coarse sand. They go dormant in summer, at which time they should be kept dry, and revert to round white tubers about ½ in (12 mm) across. Repot greenhood orchids annually, repositioning the dormant tubers 2 in (5 cm) below the soil surface. Propagate from extra tubers that may form, or from seed.

Pterostylis curta

✿ ☀ ❉ ↔ 1½–3 in (3.5–8 cm) ↕ 4–12 in (10–30 cm)

An Australian species. Dark green and yellowish green flowers, 1½ in (35 mm) in diameter, with a light brown lip that has a distinctive slight twist. Blooms in early spring. Zones 8–11.

RENANTANDA

This is an artificial monopodial genus between *Renanthera* and *Vanda*. These epiphytic orchids are erect-growing, with strap-like channeled leaves in 2 ranks. Larger plants may branch at the base and have numerous, very thick, cord-like roots. Inflorescences appear from the stem at the base of the leaf. The hybrids are not as tall as many of the *Renanthera* species, as the *Vanda* influence has reduced the plant size while increasing the floral size and imparting wider petals to the bloom. In the tropics they bloom throughout the year, with a peak during the summer months.

CULTIVATION: These vandaceous epiphytes require warm to hot conditions with bright light, and are very well-suited to tropical gardens and greenhouses in climates away from the tropics. They are best grown in pots using a coarse grade of pine bark as the potting medium. The thick roots will often venture outside the confines of the pot or basket, and this culture should be encouraged, as the roots require unimpeded air circulation and must dry out quickly after watering. Propagate from cuttings with at least 3 roots attached.

Renantanda Tuanku Bainun

♀ ☀ ↔ 8–32 in (20–80 cm) ↕ 8–48 in (20–120 cm)

This is a hybrid between *Vanda* Keeree's Delight and *Renanthera storiei*. Produces shapely blooms, up to 3 in (8 cm) tall, red, with darker tessellation throughout the flower. Zones 11–12.

RENANTHERA

FIRE ORCHID

This robust monopodial genus, with some 15 species, is found throughout Malaysia, Indonesia, the Philippines, and New Guinea, where they grow in hot, humid, lowland conditions. Most species bear very bright long-lasting flowers on branched inflorescences. There have been a number of hybrids made both within the genus and with related genera, particularly to exploit the bright red colors and to improve the overall shape of the bloom.

CULTIVATION: These tall-growing vandaceous epiphytes require warm to hot conditions with strong light, and are best suited to tropical gardens and large greenhouses in climates away from the tropics. Because of their rambling habit they can prove difficult to confine to pots, and are best grown in wooden baskets or on large slabs of cork. In the tropics they bloom throughout the year, with a peak during summer. In this habitat they can be tied to the trunks of trees and grown in full sun. They will not withstand temperatures below 54°F (12°C). Propagation is from cuttings with at least 3 roots attached.

Renanthera, Hybrid, Monaseng

Renanthera coccinea

♀ ☼ ↔ 8–32 in (20–80 cm) ↕ 8–48 in (20–120 cm)
Widespread and variable species from Southeast Asia. Numerous blooms, 2 in (5 cm) wide, dark orange to deep red, with darker spotting peppered over flower, in spring–autumn. Zones 11–12.

Renanthera Hybrids

♀ ☼ ↔ 8–36 in (20–90 cm) ↕ 1–8 ft (0.3–2.4 m)
Vandaceous hybrids; blooming occurs in warmer months of year, or all year in the tropics; generally hardier than the species. Some of the attractive hybrids are **Monaseng**, bright orange bloom, heavily overlaid with red, has *R. imschootiana*, *R. monachica*, and *R. storiei* in its pedigree; **Tan Keong Choon**, striking red hybrid bred from *R. storiei*, *R. matutina*, and *R. philippinensis*; **Tom Thumb**, a red-flowered primary hybrid of *R. monachica* and *R. imschootiana*. Zones 11–12.

RHYNCHOSTELE

This is a genus consisting of some 16 species of sympodial orchids found from Mexico to the northern part of South America. They are related to *Odontoglossum*, and were previously included within that genus. They have egg-shaped, somewhat flattened pseudobulbs topped with up to 3 thin textured leaves. Most of the species in this genus have showy colorful flowers on short or long stems.

CULTIVATION: They will grow well potted in a fine-grade bark mixture with 20 percent perlite added. Sphagnum moss is also a popular potting medium. These orchids are most suitable for humid intermediate growing conditions, and require abundant water throughout the year. They prefer a position in part-shade, and are more tolerant of warm conditions than *Odontoglossum* species. Propagate by division.

Rhynchostele bictoniensis

syn. *Odontoglossum bictoniense*
♀ ☼ ↔ 8–16 in (20–40 cm) ↕ 8–24 in (20–60 cm)
Found from Mexico to Panama. Upright inflorescences of up to 14 blooms from winter to spring. Flowers 2 in (5 cm) across; petals and sepals vary from yellowish green to brown, with darker spotting and barring over segments; a broad white lip. Zones 10–11.

Rhynchostele cordata

syn. *Odontoglossum cordatum*
♀ ☼ ↔ 8–16 in (20–40 cm) ↕ 8–16 in (20–40 cm)
A species found growing naturally from Mexico to Venezuela. Starry blooms, 3 in (8 cm) wide, mustard-colored with dark brown blotches, from summer to autumn. Zones 11–12.

RHYNCHOSTYLIS

FOXTAIL ORCHIDS

This genus of monopodial plants contains only 4 or 5 species. These tropical, lowland, vandaceous species are erect-growing epiphytes, with thick, strap-like, channeled leaves in 2 ranks. Larger plants may branch at the base, and have numerous, cord-like, very thick roots. The inflorescences appear from the stem at the base of the leaf.

CULTIVATION: These plants grow in brightly lit situations, and require year-round warm conditions. They are best grown in wooden baskets, with the thick fleshy roots attaching to the timber and being allowed to ramble, as the roots require unimpeded air circulation and must dry out quickly after watering. Propagate from seed.

Rhynchostylis gigantea

♀ ☼/☼ ↔ 8–20 in (20–50 cm) ↕ 8–24 in (20–60 cm)
From Thailand and Indochina; the most popular cultivated species. Blooms 1¼ in (30 mm) across, range from white with pink spotting and blotching to various shades of purple to red. Also bicolored and pure white strains. Flowers late winter to spring. Zones 11–12.

Rhynchostele bictoniensis

Rhynchostylis gigantea

ROSSIOGLOSSUM

CLOWN ORCHIDS, TIGER ORCHIDS

This is a small group of 6 different but similar Central American species, which at one time were included under *Odontoglossum*. They have distinct somewhat flattened pseudobulbs with up to 3 broad leathery leaves at the apex. Flower spikes, which generally appear from the leaf axil of the semi-matured new growth, develop from late summer to autumn and bloom in late autumn and winter. They bloom only once from the pseudobulb.
CULTIVATION: They like warm moist conditions and bright light during main growing period, from late spring to autumn. Keep on

Rossioglossum grande

Sarcochilus fitzgeraldii

the dry side in winter and only water enough to keep pseudobulbs from shriveling. Best grown potted, in a bark-based mix, in cool to intermediate conditions. Propagate by division of large clumps.

Rossioglossum grande ★

syn. *Odontoglossum grande*
♀ ☼/☀ ↔ 8–20 in (20–50 cm) ↕ 8–20 in (20–50 cm)
Mexico and Guatemala. Stiff spikes of up to 8 blooms in winter. Flowers 6 in (15 cm) wide; chestnut brown bars across sepals, yellow and brown petals, lip creamy with red-brown markings. Zones 10–12.

Rossioglossum Rawdon Jester

♀ ☼/☀ ↔ 8–20 in (20–50 cm) ↕ 8–20 in (20–50 cm)
This is a cross between *R. grande* and *R.* Williamsianum (*R. grande* × *R. schlieperianum*); resembles robust forms of *R. grande*. Flowers from winter through to spring. Zones 10–12.

SARCOCHILUS

FAIRY ORCHID

This genus contains about 20 diminutive monopodial species. They are native to eastern Australia and New Caledonia, and may be epiphytic or lithophytic. Short inflorescences bear showy blooms in many shapes and colors, and mostly flower in spring and summer. Mainly cultivated are the lithophytic species; tree-dwelling species often grow as twig epiphytes. The lithophytes are clump-forming, whereas the epiphytes generally only have one growth.
CULTIVATION: Lithophytic species are easily cultivated in pots, in a coarse mixture such as 2 parts medium-grade pine bark, 1 part pea-sized gravel, and a handful of perlite. Epiphytic species should be grown on long narrow slabs of weathered timber or cork. They can easily succumb to crown rot. Most species will take cool to cold conditions, but need at least 70 percent shade in a humid environment. Protect from frost and avoid excessive heat. Keep moist, with high humidity and good air circulation. The clumping species may be propagated by division; epiphytes from seed.

Sarcochilus fitzgeraldii

∧ ☼/☀ ↔ 4–16 in (10–40 cm) ↕ 4–16 in (10–40 cm)
From Australia; grows in cool heavily shaded situations. Produces up to 12 white blooms, 1¼ in (30 mm) wide, light pink to dark crimson spots or bands in the center, throughout spring. Zones 9–11.

Sarcochilus Hybrids

♀/∧ ☼/☀ ↔ 4–16 in (10–40 cm) ↕ 4–16 in (10–40 cm)
Sarcochilus has been extensively line-bred and hybridized. Popular blends link the hardy lithophytic types such as *S. fitzgeraldii*, *S. ceciliae*, and *S. hartmannii* with some of the smaller-flowered but colorful epiphytic species. Use of *S. hirticalcar* expanded both color range and flowering times, so some hybrids bloom year-round. Individual blooms range from ¾ in (18 mm) to 1½ in (35 mm) wide. **Bobby-Dazzler**, pink and purple flowers, all year; **Burgundy on Ice 'Arctic Circle'**, white flowers, red marking at center and on lip; **First Light** ★, blooms with brown and tan tones and spotting; **Kate**, pink blooms, cross between *S. roseus* and *S.* Heidi; **Melba**, between *S. falcatus* and *S. hartmannii*; **Velvet**, pale to deep purple and pink flowers, year-round. Zones 9–11.

SOBRALIA

A genus of about 100 species, mostly terrestrials, found growing naturally from Mexico to tropical South America. Few are cultivated but availability is increasing. Popular species have huge *Cattleya*-like blooms, which are often short-lived, and are produced from the top of the leafy cane-like growths in summer.
CULTIVATION: To accommodate extensive roots, pot these plants into large deep containers in well-drained terrestrial mix with bark added. Intermediate to warm conditions suit most species. They enjoy strong light, and frequent watering and feeding during warmer months. Sit plants in saucers of water in summer. Keep dry in winter. Hardy species can be planted in gardens in frost-free climates in soil with a high percentage of organic matter. Propagate by division in spring.

Sobralia macrantha

✹ ☼/☀ ↔ 1–4 ft (0.3–1.2 m) ↕ 1–7 ft (0.3–2 m)
Found from Mexico to Costa Rica. Stems up to 7 ft (2 m) tall, often less in cultivation. Large flowers, to 10 in (25 cm) wide, rose-purple, in summer. *S. m.* var. *alba* bears white flowers. Zones 10–12.

Sobralia Mirabilis

✹ ☼/☀ ↔ 36 in (90 cm) ↕ 36 in (90 cm)
Registered in 1903; a cross between *S. macrantha* and *S.* Veitchii. Original cross had white petals with faintest pink blush around mid-pink wavy-edged lip much elongated at base. Later forms vary, mainly in lip color. Summer-flowering. Zones 11–12.

SOPHROCATTLEYA

Sophrocattleya is a bigeneric hybrid between the sympodial genera *Sophronitis* and *Cattleya*. Most of these hybrids have the cool-growing *Sophronitis coccinea* in their background, which gives smaller-growing plants, flowers that have a more filled-in shape, and many of the red tones. Yellow-flowered hybrids often have *Cattleya luteola* in their lineage. Mostly bloom in spring–summer; some flowering in autumn.

CULTIVATION: They enjoy bright light and cool to warm temperatures. They need a cooler and drier rest in winter when plants are dormant. They must all have unimpeded drainage and a coarse bark-based medium. They grow best in plastic or terracotta pots and must dry out between waterings. Healthy plants will develop an extensive system of thick white roots, which are long lived and freely branch. Propagate by division.

Sobralia Mirabilis

Sophrocattleya Lana Coryell ★

♀ ☀/◐ ↔ 4–16 in (10–40 cm)
↕ 4–16 in (10–40 cm)
Compact-growing hybrid of *Sophrocattleya* Beaufort and *Cattleya walkeriana*. Disproportionally large flowers, salmon pink to purple, throughout year. Zones 10–12.

SOPHROLAELIOCATTLEYA

A 3-way orchid hybrid from 3 sympodial genera: *Sophronitis, Laelia,* and *Cattleya*. Most hybrids have the cool-growing *Sophronitis coccinea* somewhere in their background, using its influence for shapely red blooms as well as its compact to miniature growth habit. The yellow-flowered hybrids often have *Cattleya luteola* in their lineage.

CULTIVATION: They do well in bright light and cool to warm temperatures. Give them a cooler and drier rest in winter when dormant. Best grown in plastic or terracotta pots, they need excellent drainage and a coarse bark-based medium. Allow to dry out between waterings. Healthy plants develop an extensive system of thick white roots, which are long lived and freely branch. Propagate by division.

Sophrolaeliocattleya Hybrids

♀ ☀/◐ ↔ 4–16 in (10–40 cm) ↕ 4–16 in (10–40 cm)
Depending on hybrid, flower size varies from 1½ in (35 mm) to 6 in (15 cm) across petals. Mostly spring- and summer-blooming, some flower in autumn. **Fire Lighter**, blooms readily off young plants, purplish red blooms; **Hazel Boyd 'Apricot Glow'** ★ popular clone of this successful American-bred hybrid between S. California Apricot and S. Jewel Box; **Jeweler's Art**, 5 in (12 cm) wide blooms, unusual orange-pink shades; **Mahalo Jack**, deep pink blooms; **Mine Gold 'Orchid Centre'**, yellow blooms, deep red lip; **Sunset Nugget**, burnt orange blooms, overlaid with fine red veining, deep red lip. Zones 10–12.

SOPHRONITIS

A small genus of about 8 brightly colored, sympodial, epiphytic and lithophytic orchids from Brazil and Bolivia. Closely related to the genus *Laelia*, in particular the Section Hadrolaelia, which includes species such as *L. dayana* and *L. pumila*. These laelias and *Sophronitis* share similarities in having single colorful blooms, and inflorescences without a sheath; however, the young leaves fold around the buds.

CULTIVATION: Most *Sophronitis* species are best grown in cool to intermediate conditions, in pots, using a bark-based mix for larger plants, and sphagnum moss for smaller ones. Repot every other year as they lose their roots in stale mix. They need medium light levels, a humid and part-shaded environment, and fresh air, and will not tolerate stagnant conditions. Reduce watering in winter. *Sophronitis* have been extensively used within the *Cattleya* alliance, creating compact plants and brightly colored full blooms. Propagation is by division.

Sophronitis coccinea

syn. *Sophronitis grandiflora*
♀ ☀ ↔ 2½–8 in (6–20 cm)
↕ 1½–5 in (3.5–12 cm)
Brazilian orchid. Large, round, flat blooms, to 3 in (8 cm) across, bright orange to red, in autumn–winter; very narrow lip, often yellow and orange markings. Zones 9–11.

SPATHOGLOTTIS

This group of 40 semi-deciduous to evergreen, tropical, terrestrial orchids is found from Southeast Asia, New Guinea, and northern Australia to nearby islands of the Pacific. They grow in grasslands and open forests in moist places. Small, conical, somewhat flattened pseudobulbs on or just below the soil surface. A few large pleated leaves and tall inflorescences of mainly pink and purple, occasionally yellow or white, showy flowers. Bloom all year in the tropics; warmer months in greenhouses in temperate climates.

CULTIVATION: Best in bright light. Warm conditions throughout the year are needed; they dislike temperatures below 50°F (10°C). Grow in deep pots in well-drained medium incorporating pine bark, sand, and peat moss. Keep moist; place pots in a saucer of water, about 2 in (5 cm) deep, during time of active growth in summer. Reduce watering in winter when plants are semi-dormant. Propagate by division.

Spathoglottis plicata

syn. *Spathoglottis vieillardii*
❦ ☀ ↔ 8–48 in (20–120 cm) ↕ 12–40 in (30–100 cm)
From Southeast Asia, Australia, and nearby Pacific Islands, naturalized in Hawaii, USA, where marketed as native. Erect spikes of up to 20 pink to purple, 1½ in (35 mm) wide blooms all year. Zones 11–12.

Sophrolaeliocattleya, Hybrid, Hazel Boyd 'Apricot Glow'

STANHOPEA

UPSIDE-DOWN ORCHID

A large popular genus of around 70 epiphytic orchids, found from Mexico to Brazil. Feature egg-shaped pseudobulbs, each with a single leaf. Plants are grown for their large, bizarre, and colorful blooms and amazing lip structure. Waxy blooms are fragrant; last for a few days. CULTIVATION: Grow these orchids in baskets to allow their pendent spikes to spear through the medium and burst into bloom. Use *Cymbidium* compost, sphagnum moss, fine-grade pine bark, or a combination of these materials. Mounted plants rarely stay moist enough, resulting in a bunch of yellowish shriveled back-bulbs. They appreciate constant moisture throughout the year and grow best in a part-shaded position. Leaves will burn in very strong light and low humidity. There are species suitable for cool to tropical climates, which flower over several months. Propagate by division.

Stanhopea nigroviolacea ★

syn. *Stanhopea tigrina* var. *nigroviolacea*

♀ ☀ ↔ 8–24 in (20–60 cm) ↕ 8–20 in (20–50 cm)

From Mexico; the most commonly seen species in cultivation. Pairs of yellowish green, 7 in (18 cm) wide blooms, heavily blotched with dark reddish brown. The pleasant powerful vanilla fragrance is often detected before sighting the blooms. Summer-flowering. Zones 9–12.

Stanhopea oculata

♀ ☀ ↔ 8–20 in (20–50 cm) ↕ 8–20 in (20–50 cm)

Elegant variable orchid found from Mexico to Brazil. Up to 8 flowers in late summer–autumn. Blooms ½ in (12 mm) wide, pale yellow overlaid with red-purple circular spots; cream lip marked with fine reddish pepper spotting, bright orange base. Zones 10–12.

Stanhopea wardii

♀ ☀ ↔ 8–20 in (20–50 cm) ↕ 8–20 in (20–50 cm)

Variable orchid found in Nicaragua, Costa Rica, Panama, Colombia, and Venezuela. Up to 10, bright yellow to orange, 5 in (12 cm) wide blooms, fine maroon spotting, in summer or autumn. Distinguished by very dark purple patch at lip base. Zones 10–12.

VANDA

syn. *Trudelia*

A group of about 50 species of sturdy monopodial orchids found from Sri Lanka and India, across Southeast Asia to New Guinea and northeastern Australia. Erect-growing, with strap-like channeled leaves, in 2 ranks. Larger plants may branch at the base, and have numerous, very thick, cord-like roots. The inflorescences appear from the stem at the base of the leaf. They have showy long-lasting blooms, which come in a range of colors and combinations. What were previously known as the "terete-leafed vandas" have been transferred to the genus *Papilionanthe*, but in horticulture they continue to be known by their well-known, earlier name. This is one of the most important genera of plants for cut flower production in Thailand and Singapore. An extensive hybridizing program has developed using a handful of species, both within *Vanda* and in combinations with related genera. CULTIVATION: Vandas are readily grown in wooden baskets; most thrive in bright, humid, and intermediate to warm conditions, and are suited to tropical gardens and greenhouses in climates away from

the tropics. Best grown in pots using a coarse grade of pine bark as potting medium. The thick roots will often venture outside the confines of pot or basket; encourage this as the roots need unimpeded air circulation and must dry out quickly after watering. In the tropics many species and their hybrids bloom all year, peaking in spring and summer. Propagate from cuttings with at least 3 roots attached.

Vanda coerulea ★

♀ ☀/☁ ↔ 4–10 in (10–25 cm) ↕ 6–36 in (15–90 cm)

Mountainous species; India to China; one of the best known vandas. Erect spikes, often with over 12 blooms, in late summer to autumn. Large, flat, spectacular, pale to deep lilac-blue, tessellated flowers, 4 in (10 cm) across. Many improved clones in cultivation. Zones 9–11.

Vanda sanderiana

syn. *Euanthe sanderiana*

♀ ☀ ↔ 8–20 in (20–50 cm) ↕ 8–48 in (20–120 cm)

Large monopodial orchid; grows in forests on Mindanao in the Philippines; from sea level up to 1,640 ft (500 m); used extensively in hybrids. Upright inflorescence with up to 10 flowers, each 4 in (10 cm) wide, in autumn. Dorsal sepal and petals are faint violet-pink with chocolate brown spots near base. Lateral sepals are ochre-yellow with reddish brown veining. There is much variation in the coloring and several varieties have been described. Zones 11–12.

Vanda tricolor

♀ ☀/☁ ↔ 8–20 in (20–50 cm) ↕ 8–48 in (20–120 cm)

From Java, Indonesia; found on rocks or trees on fringes of lowland forest; distinctive and common species. Perfumed flowers, to 2½ in (6 cm) wide, white with dark reddish brown spots; lip purple, yellow and white patches at base. Blooms in autumn–winter. Zones 11–12.

Vanda Hybrids

♀ ☀/☁ ↔ 8–20 in (20–50 cm) ↕ 8–48 in (20–120 cm)

Thousands of *Vanda* hybrids have been created over the past century. Most breeding has been centered on 2 important and spectacular species, *V. coerulea* and *V. sanderiana* (syn. *Euanthe sanderiana*). *V. coerulea* is behind all the "blue" hybrids, many of which have darker tessellations throughout the bloom, and it has also made these hybrids more adaptable to cooler growing conditions. *V. sanderiana*

Stanhopea nigroviolacea

Vanda tricolor

has passed its large round flowers on to its progeny, and is responsible for many of the pink- and brown-flowered combinations. The albino form has also been used to produce many green and yellow hybrids. Individual blooms of the hybrid flowers vary in size from 1½–4 in (3.5–10 cm), and are produced all year round. **Bangkok Pink**, pinkish to purple blooms with fine spotting over flower; **Gordon Dillon**, round and very dark purple-black tessellated flowers; **Happy Smile**, mustard-colored blooms, prominently spotted with brown; **Marlie Dolera**, needs strong light to bloom well; **Robert's Delight**, pink-flowered; **Rothschildiana ★**, popular blue- to purple-flowered vanda, primary hybrid between *V. sanderiana* and *V. coerulea*; **Sansai Blue**, deep blue hybrid, with heavy influence from *V. coerulea*. Zones 11–12.

VANILLA

A genus of about 100 orchid species found throughout the wetter tropical regions of the world. They are unusual in having a vine-like growth habit, with adventitious roots being produced along nodes of the stem, adjacent to the succulent leaves. Many species start life as terrestrials before becoming epiphytic. Flowers are similar to the unrelated *Cattleya*, and can be quite showy, but generally only last a day. In heavy flowerings, fresh blooms are borne daily from short racemes. CULTIVATION: They need plenty of room to grow to their full potential. Commercially, they are often grown in pots with very long totems supporting the orchids' climbing habit, the roots adhering to the substrate. In private collections, they are often in hanging baskets, with many of the flexible stems manually turned back into the center of the plant. They need bright light and warm conditions, in a very humid environment, throughout the year. Propagate from cuttings.

Vanilla planifolia

VANILLA

♀ ☼ ↔ 1–10 ft (0.3–3 m) ↕ 1–10 ft (0.3–3 m)

Central and South America; vanilla essence extracted from seed capsules. Pale yellow-green flowers, 2½ in (6 cm), trumpet-like lip, in spring. Also a variegated leafed form in cultivation. Zones 11–12.

VUYLSTEKEARA

A trigeneric sympodial hybrid involving *Cochlioda*, *Miltonia*, and *Odontoglossum*. Generally, the crossing of *Odontodia* with *Miltonia* has formed these colorful hybrids. They produce long, erect to arching inflorescences of shapely blooms in a range of colors and patterns. CULTIVATION: *Vuylstekeara* orchids do not like their roots to dry out, so plant in sphagnum moss or a fine bark mix. They are suitable for intermediate to cool growing conditions, and need abundant water throughout the year and a part-shaded position. Give them a humid environment and plenty of air circulation. Propagate by division.

Vuylstekeara Hybrids

♀ ☼ ↔ 4–20 in (10–50 cm) ↕ 4–24 in (10–60 cm)

Members of the *Odontoglossum* alliance. Flowers range from 1½–5 in (3.5–12 cm) across petals, in spring–autumn. **Cambria ★**, popular hybrid, white and maroon blooms with yellow blotch on lip; **Ephyra**, raspberry-colored blooms with white edging to segments; **Everglades Promise**, showy pink and red blooms, large flared lip; **Linda Isler**, numerous claret blooms, white lip; **Memoria Mary Kavanaugh**, large purple flowers, a legacy of its parent *Miltonia spectabilis*. Zones 9–11.

Zygopetalum intermedium

ZYGOPETALUM

A small genus of about 16 hardy terrestrial and epiphytic sympodial orchids from South America. They have tall spikes of large, showy, long-lasting, and highly fragrant flowers. Many hybrids have been made, within both *Zygopetalum* and related genera, to produce compact plants and expand and intensify the color range of the blooms. CULTIVATION: Most may be grown in commercially available "orchid composts" (generally free draining but retain some moisture), or fine-grade pine bark. Epiphytic species prefer a mix with a high percentage of coarse bark. All like deep pots for their vigorous root system. Respond to frequent watering and feeding, and like to be moist all year, with increased watering and fertilizing spring–autumn while actively growing. They need high humidity and good air circulation, or leaf tips will dry off and foliage may spot. Propagate by division.

Zygopetalum intermedium

♀ ☼ ↔ 4–16 in (10–40 cm) ↕ 4–16 in (10–40 cm)

Brazil; similar to *Z. mackayi*. Up to 6 blooms, 3 in (8 cm) wide, on thick erect spikes, autumn–winter. Fleshy green petals and sepals blotched maroon-purple; lip, white with dark lilac veining. Zones 9–11.

Zygopetalum mackayi

♀ ☼ ↔ 4–16 in (10–40 cm) ↕ 4–16 in (10–40 cm)

From Brazil. Up to 10 blooms, 3 in (8 cm) wide, on thick erect spikes, autumn–winter. Fleshy green petals and sepals blotched with maroon-purple; fan-shaped lip, white with dark lilac veins. Zones 9–11.

Zygopetalum Hybrids

♀/✤ ☼ ↔ 4–16 in (10–40 cm) ↕ 4–16 in (10–40 cm)

Most hybrids have a heavy influence from *Z. mackayi*, and this has led to similarities between many of the crossings. The more compact plants have been obtained by the use of *Z. maxillare* as a parent; these may also bloom more than once a year. Flowers 2½–3 in (6–8 cm) across. **Alan Greatwood**, shapely and round dark brownish maroon blooms, distinctive greenish edge to petals and sepals, white lip, dark lilac veining; **Blanchetown**, light tan blooms, purple lip, dark striping; **Kiwi Dusk**, green blooms barred with maroon markings, contrasting white and deep lilac lip; and **Titanic**, robust, fragrant. Zones 9–11.

Ferns, Palms, and Cycads

Constituting one of the most primitive of plants, ferns—along with horsetails and club mosses—belong to a group of plants known as pteridophytes. Unlike most other vascular plants, ferns bear no flowers, fruit, or seeds, but instead reproduce by means of spores. Ferns grow in a variety of sizes, forms, and habits, but all ferns comprise three parts: a leaf (commonly called a frond), a rhizome or stem, and roots.

Although they look similar to each other, palms and cycads are actually quite different. Cycads are believed to have been prominent during the Jurassic period, and are more like conifers than palms (palms produce flowers, cycads do not). Over 180 species of cycads have been identified, and they are found in warm-temperate to tropical regions of the world. Palms are more numerous than cycads: there are about 2,300 species, mostly in the tropics and subtropics. Many are economically important, providing oils, fiber, waxes, food, drugs, and furniture (rattan).

Some ferns, palms, and cycads can be grown indoors, such as the Boston fern (*Nephrolepis exaltata* 'Bostoniensis') and *Cycas revoluta*. Other species and cultivars can be grown outdoors as single specimens or in small groups to enhance the garden with their wonderful textures and shapes.

Dicksonia antarctica, shown here in the wild in Tasmania, Australia, is an excellent plant for tubs, as long as the trunk is kept moist in hot dry weather.

Fern, Palm, and Cycad Finder

The following cultivation table features at-a-glance information for every species or hybrid with an individual entry in the Ferns, Palms, and Cycads chapter of this book. Simply find the plant you wish to know more about, and run your eye along the row to discover its height and spread, whether it is frost tolerant or not, the aspect it prefers, and more.

The type of plant is abbreviated to **F, P, C,** or **O:**
F – the plant is a fern.
P – the plant is a palm.
C – the plant is a cycad.
O – the plant is not technically a fern, palm, or cycad, but is used in the garden in the same way.

The climate(s) that each plant needs to thrive in the outdoors are given (some plants will grow in more than one climate), abbreviated to **C, W,** or **T:**

C – the plant prefers a cool climate.
W – the plant prefers a warm-temperate or subtropical climate.
T – the plant prefers a tropical climate.

The growth form of the plant is abbreviated to **C, R, Sc,** or **SS:**
C – the plant has a clumping habit.
R – the plant has a running rhizome.
Sc – the plant has a scrambling habit.
SS – the plant is single stemmed.

The growth rate of the plant is abbreviated to **F, M,** or **S:**
F – the plant grows at a fast rate.
M – the plant grows at a medium rate.
S – the plant grows at a slow rate.

Plant name	Height	Spread	Type	Climate	Growth form	Growth rate	Indoor use	Frost tolerant	Full sun	Half sun	Heavy shade
Adiantum aethiopicum	8–32 in (20–80 cm)	10–36 in (20–90 cm)	F	C/W	C/R	S	◆	◆		◆	◆
Adiantum capillus-veneris	12–24 in (30–60 cm)	12–24 in (30–60 cm)	F	W	R	S	◆	◆		◆	◆
Adiantum excisum	12–20 in (30–50 cm)	12–20 in (30–50 cm)	F	W/T	C/R	M				◆	◆
Adiantum hispidulum	12–20 in (30–50 cm)	12–20 in (30–50 cm)	F	W/T	C	M				◆	◆
Adiantum jordanii	12–24 in (30–60 cm)	12–24 in (30–60 cm)	F	W	C	M		◆		◆	◆
Adiantum pedatum	12–24 in (30–60 cm)	12–24 in (30–60 cm)	F	C/W	C	M	◆	◆		◆	◆
Adiantum peruvianum	32–40 in (80–100 cm)	32–40 in (80–100 cm)	F	W/T	R	S	◆			◆	◆
Adiantum raddianum	18–24 in (45–60 cm)	18–24 in (45–60 cm)	F	W/T	C	M	◆			◆	◆
Adiantum reniforme	2–8 in (5–20 cm)	2–8 in (5–20 cm)	F	W/T	R	S				◆	◆
Adiantum tenerum	12–36 in (30–90 cm)	12–36 in (30–90 cm)	F	W/T	R	M	◆			◆	◆
Adiantum venustum	8–32 in (20–80 cm)	12–48 in (30–120 cm)	F	C	R	S		◆			◆
Aiphanes caryotifolia	20 ft (6 m)	8 ft (2.4 m)	P	W/T	SS	M	◆			◆	
Anemia mexicana	20 in (50 cm)	24 in (60 cm)	F	W/T	R	M				◆	
Archontophoenix alexandrae	50 ft (15 m)	15 ft (4.5 m)	P	W/T	SS	F	◆		◆		
Archontophoenix cunninghamiana	60 ft (18 m)	15 ft (4.5 m)	P	W/T	SS	F	◆		◆		
Archontophoenix purpurea	80 ft (24 m)	15 ft (4.5 m)	P	W/T	SS	F			◆		
Areca catechu	50 ft (15 m)	12 ft (3.5 m)	P	W/T	SS	M				◆	
Areca triandra	10 ft (3 m)	8 ft (2.4 m)	P	W/T	SS	M				◆	
Arenga engleri	12 ft (3.5 m)	10 ft (3 m)	P	W/T	C	M				◆	
Arenga pinnata	60 ft (18 m)	40 ft (12 m)	P	W/T	SS	M				◆	
Arenga undulatifolia	20 ft (6 m)	15 ft (4.5 m)	P	W/T	C	M				◆	

Plant name	Height	Spread	Type	Climate	Growth form	Growth rate	Indoor use	Frost tolerant	Full sun	Half sun	Heavy shade
Asplenium bulbiferum	24–48 in (60–120 cm)	24–48 in (60–120 cm)	F	W	R	M	◆			◆	◆
Asplenium nidus	18–60 in (45–150 cm)	18–60 in (45–150 cm)	F	W/T	C	S	◆			◆	◆
Asplenium sagittatum	4–6 in (10–15 cm)	4–6 in (10–15 cm)	F	W	C	S		◆		◆	◆
Asplenium scolopendrium	8–24 in (20–60 cm)	8–24 in (20–60 cm)	F	C/W	C	S		◆		◆	◆
Athyrium filix-femina	2–5 ft (0.6–1.5 m)	3–7 ft (0.9–2 m)	F	C	R	S		◆		◆	◆
Athyrium niponicum	12–14 in (30–35 cm)	20–24 in (50–60 cm)	F	C	R	S		◆		◆	◆
Azolla filiculoides	¼–½ in (6–12 mm)	36 in (90 cm)	F	C	R	F	◆	◆	◆	◆	
Bismarckia nobilis	60 ft (18 m)	12 ft (3.5 m)	P	W/T	SS	M			◆		
Blechnum brasiliense	40–60 in (100–150 cm)	40–60 in (100–150 cm)	F	W	SS	M					◆
Blechnum gibbum	3–5 ft (0.9–1.5 m)	3–5 ft (0.9–1.5 m)	F	W	SS	M					◆
Blechnum nudum	24–30 in (60–75 cm)	18–30 in (45–75 cm)	F	W	SS	M					◆
Blechnum spicant	12–18 in (30–45 cm)	12–18 in (30–45 cm)	F	C/W	R	M		◆		◆	◆
Borassus flabellifer	60 ft (18 m)	15 ft (4.5 m)	P	W/T	SS	M			◆		
Bowenia spectabilis	5 ft (1.5 m)	5 ft (1.5 m)	C	W/T	R	M			◆		
Brahea armata	25 ft (8 m)	10 ft (3 m)	P	W	SS	M			◆		
Brahea brandegeei	40 ft (12 m)	15 ft (4.5 m)	P	W/T	SS	M			◆		
Brahea edulis	30 ft (9 m)	20 ft (6 m)	P	W/T	SS	M			◆		
Butia capitata	20 ft (6m)	15 ft (4.5 m)	P	W	SS	M		◆	◆		
Butia eriospatha	12 ft (3.5 m)	12 ft (3.5 m)	P	W	SS	M			◆		
Carpentaria acuminata	25–50 ft (8–15 m)	20–25 ft (6–8 m)	P	W/T	SS	F			◆		
Caryota mitis	20 ft (6 m)	10 ft (3 m)	P	W/T	C	F	◆		◆		
Caryota ochlandra	25 ft (8 m)	10 ft (3 m)	P	W/T	SS	F			◆		
Caryota urens	30 ft (9 m)	15 ft (4.5 m)	P	W/T	SS	M			◆		
Ceratozamia mexicana	3–7 ft (0.9–2 m)	4–8 ft (1.2–2.4 m)	C	W/T	SS	M				◆	
Chamaedorea ernesti-augusti	3 ft (0.9 m)	18 in (45 cm)	P	W/T	SS	M	◆			◆	
Chamaedorea microspadix	8 ft (2.4 m)	10 ft (3 m)	P	W/T	C	M	◆			◆	
Chamaedorea seifrizii	10 ft (3 m)	3 ft (0.9 m)	P	W/T	C	M	◆			◆	
Chamaerops humilis	15 ft (4.5 m)	12 ft (3.5 m)	P	W	C	M		◆	◆		
Cibotium schiedei	15 ft (4.5 m)	8 ft (2.4 m)	F	W	SS	M				◆	◆
Coccothrinax argentata	25 ft (8 m)	8 ft (2.4 m)	P	W/T	SS	M			◆		
Coccothrinax crinita	30 ft (9 m)	7 ft (2 m)	P	W/T	SS	M	◆		◆		
Coccothrinax miraguama	15 ft (4.5 m)	7 ft (2 m)	P	W/T	SS	M	◆		◆		
Cocos nucifera	100 ft (30 m)	10–20 ft (3–6 m)	P	T	SS	F			◆		

Plant name	Height	Spread	Type	Climate	Growth form	Growth rate	Indoor use	Frost tolerant	Full sun	Half sun	Heavy shade
Copernicia baileyana	40 ft (12 m)	10 ft (3 m)	P	W	SS	M				♦	♦
Copernicia prunifera	40 ft (12 m)	12 ft (3.5 m)	P	W/T	SS	M				♦	♦
Corypha umbraculifera	40–80 ft (12–24 m)	35–50 ft (10–15 m)	P	W/T	SS	M				♦	
Cyathea cooperi	20–40 ft (6–12 m)	20 ft (6 m)	F	W	SS	F					♦
Cyathea dealbata	30 ft (9 m)	20 ft (6 m)	F	W	SS	M		♦			♦
Cyathea dregei	15 ft (4.5 m)	10 ft (3 m)	F	W	SS	M		♦		♦	♦
Cycas circinalis	15 ft (4.5 m)	15 ft (4.5 m)	C	W/T	SS	S			♦		
Cycas media	15 ft (4.5 m)	10 ft (3 m)	C	W/T	SS	S			♦		
Cycas revoluta	10 ft (3 m)	6 ft (1.8 m)	C	W/T	SS	S	♦			♦	
Cyrtomium falcatum	24–36 in (60–90 cm)	24–36 in (60–90 cm)	F	C/W	C	F	♦	♦		♦	♦
Cyrtostachys renda	15–30 ft (4.5–9 m)	7–10 ft (2–3 m)	P	W/T	C	F				♦	
Davallia solida	12–18 in (30–45 cm)	24–36 in (60–90 cm)	F	W/T	C	M	♦				♦
Dicksonia antarctica	20 ft (6 m)	12 ft (3.5 m)	F	W	SS	M		♦		♦	♦
Dicksonia fibrosa	20 ft (6 m)	10 ft (3 m)	F	W	SS	M		♦		♦	♦
Dictyosperma album	60 ft (18 m)	20 ft (6 m)	P	W/T	SS	M			♦		
Dioon edule	6 ft (1.8 m)	5 ft (1.5 m)	C	W/T	SS	S				♦	♦
Dioon spinulosum	30 ft (9 m)	10 ft (3 m)	C	W/T	SS	S				♦	
Diplazium pycnocarpon	24–36 in (60–90 cm)	4 ft (1.2 m)	F	C	C	M		♦	♦	♦	
Doodia aspera	6 in (15 cm)	15 in (38 cm)	F	W	C	M	♦			♦	
Dryopteris cristata	18–30 in (45–75 cm)	36 in (90 cm)	F	C	C	M		♦			♦
Dryopteris erythrosora	24 in (60 cm)	16 in (40 cm)	F	C	C	M		♦			♦
Dryopteris filix-mas	48 in (120 cm)	24 in (60 cm)	F	C	C	M		♦		♦	
Dryopteris sieboldii	20 in (50 cm)	20 in (50 cm)	F	C/W	C	M		♦			♦
Dypsis decaryi	20 ft (6 m)	6 ft (1.8 m)	P	W/T	SS	M			♦		
Dypsis lutescens	20 ft (6 m)	6 ft (1.8 m)	P	W/T	C	M			♦		
Elaeis guineensis	60 ft (18 m)	12 ft (3.5 m)	P	W/T	SS	F			♦		
Encephalartos altensteinii	15 ft (4.5 m)	12 ft (3.5 m)	C	W	C	S			♦	♦	
Encephalartos horridus	3 ft (0.9 m)	3 ft (0.9 m)	C	W	SS	S			♦	♦	
Encephalartos villosus	10 ft (3 m)	20 ft (6 m)	C	W	C	S				♦	
Euterpe edulis	20–40 ft (6–12 m)	12–18 ft (3.5–5.5 m)	P	W/T	SS	F			♦		
Euterpe oleracea	20–60 ft (6–18 m)	12–18 ft (3.5–5.5 m)	P	W/T	C	F			♦		
Hemionitis arifolia	4–12 in (10–30 cm)	4–12 in (10–30 cm)	F	W	C	M					♦
Howea belmoreana	25 ft (8 m)	10 ft (3 m)	P	W	SS	M	♦			♦	

Plant name	Height	Spread	Type	Climate	Growth form	Growth rate	Indoor use	Frost tolerant	Full sun	Half sun	Heavy shade
Howea forsteriana	30–50 ft (9–15 m)	15 ft (4.5 m)	P	W	SS	M	◆		◆		
Johannesteijsmannia altifrons	15 ft (4.5 m)	10 ft (3 m)	P	W/T	SS	M					◆
Johannesteijsmannia magnifica	15 ft (4.5 m)	10 ft (3 m)	P	W/T	SS	M					◆
Jubaea chilensis	80 ft (24 m)	25 ft (8 m)	P	W	SS	M		◆	◆		
Latania loddigesii	25 ft (8 m)	12 ft (3.5 m)	P	W/T	SS	M			◆		
Latania verschaffeltii	35 ft (10 m)	15 ft (4.5 m)	P	W/T	SS	M			◆		
Lepidozamia hopei	20–70 ft (6–21 m)	8–15 ft (2.4–4.5 m)	C	W/T	SS	S				◆	◆
Lepidozamia peroffskyana	8–20 ft (2.4–6 m)	10–15 ft (3–4.5 m)	C	W/T	SS	S			◆		
Livistona australis	80 ft (24 m)	15 ft (4.5 m)	P	W	SS	M	◆		◆		
Livistona decipiens	50 ft (15 m)	8 ft (2.4 m)	P	W/T	SS	M			◆		
Livistona mariae	50–60 ft (15–18 m)	10 ft (3 m)	P	W	SS	M			◆		
Livistona rotundifolia	80 ft (24 m)	15 ft (4.5 m)	P	W/T	SS	M				◆	
Lycopodium clavatum	8–10 in (20–25 cm)	16–20 in (40–50 cm)	O	C	Sc	F		◆			◆
Lycopodium thyoides	6–18 in (15–45 cm)	18–36 in (45 –90 cm)	O	C/W	Sc	F				◆	
Macrozamia communis	3–8 ft (0.9–2.4 m)	7 ft (2 m)	C	W	SS	S				◆	
Macrozamia moorei	10–25 ft (3–8 m)	7 ft (2 m)	C	W	SS	S			◆		
Marsilea drummondii	6–12 in (15–30 cm)	7 ft (2 m)	F	W	R	F			◆		
Marsilea mutica	12–36 in (30–90 cm)	3–6 ft (0.9–1.8 m)	F	W	R	F			◆		
Matteuccia struthiopteris	36–60 in (90–150 cm)	18–30 in (45–75 cm)	F	C/W	R	F		◆		◆	
Microsorum grossum	24–36 in (60–90 cm)	24–36 in (60–90 cm)	F	W/T	R	M					◆
Microsorum punctatum	40 in (100 cm)	5 ft (1.5 m)	F	W/T	R	M					◆
Nephrolepis cordifolia	12–48 in (30–120 cm)	12–48 in (30–120 cm)	F	W/T	R	F	◆			◆	
Nephrolepis exaltata	36 in (90 cm)	36 in (90 cm)	F	W/T	R	F	◆				◆
Onoclea sensibilis	36 in (90 cm)	24 in (60 cm)	F	C	R	M		◆		◆	◆
Osmunda claytoniana	16–40 in (40–100 cm)	24–36 in (60–90 cm)	F	C	C	M		◆		◆	
Osmunda regalis	24–60 in (60–150 cm)	36 in (90 cm)	F	C/W	C	M		◆	◆	◆	◆
Pellaea falcata	6–9 in (15–22 cm)	6–9 in (15–22 cm)	F	C	R	M					◆
Pellaea rotundifolia	12–18 in (30–45 cm)	15–18 in (38–45 cm)	F	W/T	R	M	◆			◆	
Phlebodium aureum	24–36 in (60–90 cm)	24–36 in (60–90 cm)	F	W/T	R	M				◆	
Phoenix canariensis	70 ft (21 m)	30 ft (9 m)	P	W	SS	M			◆		
Phoenix reclinata	40 ft (12 m)	35 ft (10 m)	P	W	SS	M			◆		
Phoenix roebelenii	10 ft (3 m)	8 ft (2.4 m)	P	W/T	SS	M	◆		◆		
Platycerium bifurcatum	27–40 in (70–100 cm)	27–40 in (70–100 cm)	F	W	C	M	◆			◆	

Plant name	Height	Spread	Type	Climate	Growth form	Growth rate	Indoor use	Frost tolerant	Full sun	Half sun	Heavy shade
Platycerium veitchii	60 in (150 cm)	32 in (80 cm)	F	W	C	M	◆			◆	
Polypodium californicum	40 in (100 cm)	20 in (50 cm)	F	C/W	R	M		◆		◆	
Polypodium triseriale	16–24 in (40–60 cm)	16–24 in (40–60 cm)	F	W	R	M				◆	
Polypodium vulgare	10–12 in (25–30 cm)	10–12 in (25–30 cm)	F	C	C	M		◆		◆	
Polystichum acrostichoides	18–24 in (45–60 cm)	18–24 in (45–60 cm)	F	C	C	M				◆	
Polystichum aculeatum	18–24 in (45–60 cm)	18–24 in (45–60 cm)	F	C	C	M				◆	
Polystichum polyblepharon	48 in (120 cm)	48 in (120 cm)	F	C	C	M					◆
Polystichum setiferum	18–24 in (45–60 cm)	18–24 in (45–60 cm)	F	C	R	F		◆		◆	
Polystichum tsussimense	6–18 in (15–45 cm)	12–16 in (30–40 cm)	F	C	C	M		◆		◆	
Pritchardia hillebrandii	15–25 ft (4.5–8 m)	12–20 ft (3.5–6 m)	P	W/T	SS	M			◆		
Pritchardia pacifica	30 ft (9 m)	15 ft (4.5 m)	P	W/T	SS	M			◆		
Pritchardia thurstonii	25 ft (8 m)	12 ft (3.5 m)	P	W/T	SS	M			◆		
Pteridium aquilinum	2–8 ft (0.6–2.4 m)	30–60 ft (9–18 m)	F	C/W	R	F		◆	◆	◆	
Pteridium esculentum	10 ft (3 m)	60 ft (18 m)	F	C/W	R	F		◆	◆	◆	
Pteris argyraea	3–6 ft (0.9–1.8 m)	20–40 in (50–100 cm)	F	W/T	R	M	◆				◆
Pteris cretica	12–20 in (30–50 cm)	12–20 in (30–50 cm)	F	W/T	R	M	◆			◆	
Pteris ensiformis	8–12 in (20–30 cm)	8–12 in (20–30 cm)	F	W/T	R	M	◆			◆	
Pteris tricolor	5 ft (1.5 m)	3 ft (0.9 m)	F	W	R	M					◆
Pteris umbrosa	27–40 in (70–100 cm)	27–40 in (70–100 cm)	F	W	R	M					◆
Ptychosperma elegans	12–50 ft (3.5–15 m)	10–12 ft (3–3.5 m)	P	W	SS	F			◆		
Ptychosperma macarthurii	15–25 ft (4.5–8 m)	6–12 ft (1.8–3.5 m)	P	W	C	M				◆	
Rhapis excelsa	10 ft (3 m)	8–15 ft (2.4–4.5 m)	P	W/T	C	F	◆			◆	
Rhapis humilis	15 ft (4.5 m)	10 ft (3 m)	P	W/T	C	F	◆				◆
Rhopalostylis baueri	20 ft (6 m)	15 ft (4.5 m)	P	W	SS	S	◆				◆
Rhopalostylis sapida	20–35 ft (6–10 m)	10 ft (3 m)	P	W	SS	S	◆			◆	
Roystonea borinquena	50–60 ft (15–18 m)	15–20 ft (4.5–6 m)	P	W/T	SS	F			◆		
Roystonea oleracea	130 ft (40 m)	20 ft (6 m)	P	W/T	SS	M			◆		
Sabal bermudana	40 ft (12 m)	10 ft (3 m)	P	W	SS	M			◆		
Sabal causiarum	50 ft (15 m)	20 ft (6 m)	P	W/T	SS	M			◆		
Sabal mexicana	60 ft (18 m)	12 ft (3.5 m)	P	W/T	SS	M			◆		
Sabal minor	10 ft (3 m)	12 ft (3.5 m)	P	W/T	SS	M		◆	◆		
Sabal palmetto	80 ft (24 m)	15 ft (4.5 m)	P	W	SS	M		◆	◆		
Sabal uresana	25 ft (8 m)	10 ft (3 m)	P	W	SS	M		◆	◆		

Plant name	Height	Spread	Type	Climate	Growth form	Growth rate	Indoor use	Frost tolerant	Full sun	Half sun	Heavy shade
Sadleria cyatheoides	2–5 ft (0.6–1.5 m)	2–4 ft (0.6–1.2 m)	F	W/T	SS	M				◆	
Selaginella kraussiana	1 in (2.5 cm)	24–36 in (60–90 cm)	O	W	Sc	F	◆		◆	◆	
Selaginella martensii	6 in (15 cm)	8 in (20 cm)	O	W	Sc	M					◆
Selaginella uncinata	2 in (5 cm)	18–36 in (45–90 cm)	O	C/W	Sc	M		◆			◆
Serenoa repens	3–15 ft (0.9–4.5 m)	7 ft (2 m)	P	W	C	S		◆	◆		
Syagrus flexuosa	7–15 ft (2–4.5 m)	7–15 ft (2–4.5 m)	P	W/T	SS	M				◆	
Syagrus romanzoffiana	50 ft (15 m)	25 ft (8 m)	P	W/T	SS	M				◆	
Syagrus sancona	20–40 ft (6–12 m)	20 ft (6 m)	P	W/T	SS	M			◆		
Thrinax morrisii	35 ft (10 m)	10 ft (3 m)	P	W/T	SS	M				◆	
Thrinax parviflora	10–50 ft (3–15 m)	7 ft (2 m)	P	W/T	SS	M				◆	
Thrinax radiata	40 ft (12 m)	7 ft (2 m)	P	W/T	SS	M				◆	
Trachycarpus fortunei	35 ft (10 m)	12 ft (3.5 m)	P	W	SS	S		◆	◆		
Trachycarpus martianus	50 ft (15 m)	10 ft (3 m)	P	W	SS	S				◆	
Trachycarpus wagnerianus	10–20 ft (3–6 m)	8 ft (2.4 m)	P	W	SS	S				◆	
Veitchia arecina	35 ft (10 m)	20 ft (6 m)	P	W/T	SS	M			◆	◆	
Veitchia winin	50 ft (15 m)	10 ft (3 m)	P	W/T	SS	F				◆	
Verschaffeltia splendida	70 ft (21 m)	8 ft (2.4 m)	P	W/T	SS	M				◆	
Washingtonia filifera	50 ft (15 m)	25 ft (8 m)	P	W	SS	M				◆	
Woodsia × gracilis	4–10 in (10–25 cm)	12–20 in (30–50 cm)	F	C	R	M		◆		◆	
Woodsia ilvensis	4–10 in (10–25 cm)	12–20 in (30–50 cm)	F	C	R	M		◆		◆	
Woodwardia areolata	20–40 in (50–100 cm)	20–48 in (50–120 cm)	F	C/W	C	M		◆		◆	◆
Woodwardia fimbriata	3–7 ft (0.9–2 m)	3–7 ft (0.9–2 m)	F	W	C	M		◆		◆	◆
Woodwardia unigemmata	24–40 in (60–100 cm)	4–8 ft (1.2–2.4 m)	F	W/T	C	M				◆	◆
Zamia fairchildiana	8 ft (2.4 m)	5 ft (1.5 m)	C	W/T	SS	S					◆
Zamia furfuracea	3 ft (0.9 m)	7 ft (2 m)	C	W/T	SS	S				◆	
Zamia pumila	5 ft (1.5 m)	6 ft (1.8 m)	C	W/T	SS	S	◆			◆	

Adiantum capillus-veneris

Adiantum pedatum 'Imbricatum'

Adiantum reniforme

ADIANTUM

MAIDENHAIR FERN

Large genus of about 200 terrestrial fern species distributed world-wide; members of the maidenhair-fern (Adiantaceae) family. From the Greek *adiantos* (dry, unmoistened, or unwettable), because the leaflets appear to be waterproof. A wide range of frond colors: pink and red new fronds, changing to shades of green, including variegated types, on maturity. Pinnules are borne on thin, shiny, black or brown stalks, with oblong or fan-shaped leaflets.
CULTIVATION: Organically rich loams, kept moist but not soggy, with surface mulching in humid semi-shaded situations. Soil pH varies according to species. Protect from wind. Allow abundant light but shelter from hot sun. Propagate from spores or by division.

Adiantum aethiopicum

COMMON MAIDENHAIR FERN

☼/◑ ❄ ↔ 10–36 in (25–90 cm) ↑ 8–32 in (20–80 cm)
Widely distributed clumping fern from a range of climates in Africa, Australia, and New Zealand. Creeping rhizomes; clusters of spreading, pinnate, lacy, light green fronds on shiny black stalks. Zones 7–11.

Adiantum capillus-veneris

COMMON MAIDENHAIR, SOUTHERN MAIDENHAIR, TRUE MAIDENHAIR, VENUS MAIDEN-HAIR, VENUS-HAIR FERN, VENUS'S HAIR

☼/◑ ❄ ↔ 12–24 in (30–60 cm) ↑ 12–24 in (30–60 cm)
Robust wiry fern found worldwide in warm-temperate to tropical climates. Creeping rhizomes produce clusters of many fronds on circular black stalks. Deeply dissected triangular blades give a lacy appearance. Bronze pink new growth. Zones 8–11.

Adiantum excisum ★

CHILEAN MAIDENHAIR

☼/◑ ❄ ↔ 12–20 in (30–50 cm) ↑ 12–20 in (30–50 cm)
A small clump-forming fern from Chile, Panama, Mexico, and Bolivia, named for the deeply cut margins of its densely tufted fronds. Triangular blades, to 16 in (40 cm) long, have many short pinnules and wiry stalks. Needs neutral to alkaline soils. 'Rubrum', dark reddish brown fronds, new growth pale yellow. Zones 9–12.

Adiantum hispidulum

☼/◑ ❄ ↔ 12–20 in (30–50 cm) ↑ 12–20 in (30–50 cm)
ROUGH MAIDENHAIR FERN, ROSY MAIDENHAIR FERN, FIVE-FINGERED JACK
Small, clump-forming fern, native to Africa, southern Asia, Australia, and the South Pacific. Fronds have pinkish bronze new growth and overlapping pinnules. Creeping rhizomes. Young fronds initially red becoming light green, then dark green with maturity. Zones 9–12.

Adiantum jordanii

CALIFORNIAN MAIDENHAIR

☼ ◑ ❄ ↔ 12–24 in (30–60 cm) ↑ 12–24 in (30–60 cm)
Clump-forming fern from Mexico and west coast USA. Fronds have triangular pinnate blades of finely toothed pinnules. Flushes of new growth in early spring and again in autumn. Zones 8–10.

Adiantum pedatum

AMERICAN MAIDENHAIR FERN, EASTERN MAIDENHAIR, FIVE-FINGERED MAIDENHAIR FERN

◑ ❄ ↔ 12–24 in (30–60 cm) ↑ 12–24 in (30–60 cm)
A fern from temperate North America and East Asia. Bears pinnate fronds, with primary divisions to 12 in (30 cm) long and green triangular or oblong pinnules. Deciduous in cooler climates. *A. p.* subsp. *calderi*, small, clump-forming, upright form with bluish green fronds and small pinnules. *A. p.* var. *aleuticum*, deciduous and clump-forming, with pale green fronds, new fronds sometimes flushed pink. *A. p.* var. *subpumilum*, wind-tolerant dwarf variety, bluish green fronds and overlapping pinnules, yellowish green new growth. *A. p.* 'Imbricatum', crowded, stiffly erect, green fronds; 'Miss Sharples', golden green lobed fronds. Zones 4–9.

Adiantum peruvianum

PERUVIAN MAIDENHAIR FERN, SILVER DOLLAR MAIDENHAIR FERN

☼/◑ ❄ ↔ 32–40 in (80–100 cm) ↑ 32–40 in (80–100 cm)
From Ecuador, Peru, and Bolivia. Clusters of triangular, pinnate, green fronds borne on slender black stalks from a short-creeping to clump-forming rhizome. New growth is silvery rose in color with a metallic sheen. Zones 10–12.

Adiantum raddianum

DELTA MAIDENHAIR FERN

☼/◑ ❄ ↔ 18–24 in (45–60 cm) ↑ 18–24 in (45–60 cm)
A widely cultivated clump-forming fern native to tropical regions of Uruguay, Brazil, and Paraguay. Clusters of green pinnate fronds with triangular blades and wedge-shaped pinnules on purplish black stalks. This species has numerous cultivars, including 'Deflexum', a hardy more open form with black stems, triangular fronds; 'Elegans', hardy, triangular fronds, heart-shaped segments; 'Fritz Luth', triangular, bright green, erect fronds with overlapping segments; 'Gracillimum', pendulous divided fronds, pink new growth; 'Tinctum', triangular fronds and large, overlapping, wedge-shaped pinnules. Zones 10–12.

Adiantum reniforme

☼/◑ ⚬ ↔ 2–8 in (5–20 cm) ↕ 2–8 in (5–20 cm)

Unusual, small, colonizing maidenhair fern from Kenya, Tenerife, Madeira, and the Canary and Comoros Islands. Short-creeping rhizome. Tough, simple, undivided fronds are rounded to kidney-shaped, on wiry black stalks. Zones 10–12.

Adiantum tenerum

BRITTLE MAIDENHAIR FERN, FAN MAIDENHAIR FERN

☼/◑ ✿ ↔ 12–36 in (30–90 cm) ↕ 12–36 in (30–90 cm)

A species found growing in tropical to subtropical regions of southwestern USA, the West Indies, and Central America. It has a creeping rhizome and clusters of pinnate fronds with rounded or diamond-shaped blades, borne on glossy maroon-black stalks. 'Farleyense' features arching or drooping pinnate fronds, up to 36 in (90 cm) long, with large ruffled segments and sharp edges; 'Gloriosum Roseum' has arching or pendulous fronds with wavy segments and pink new growth; 'Japonicum' has fronds that reach 6–8 in (15–20 cm) long, with large, deeply lobed, overlapping pinnules on thin wiry stalks; and 'Lady M. Lyalle' produces pale green fronds that reach 12–24 in (30–60 cm) long, with large, deeply incised, fan-like segments. Zones 10–12.

Adiantum venustum

EVERGREEN MAIDENHAIR, HIMALAYAN MAIDENHAIR

☼/◑ ✽ ↔ 12–48 in (30–120 cm) ↕ 8–32 in (20–80 cm)

Native to high altitudes of Afghanistan, the Himalayas, India, and Canada. Deciduous in cooler climates. A creeping rhizome, fronds to 32 in (80 cm) long with triangular blades and toothed pinnules borne on stalks to 10 in (25 cm) long. Zones 4–9.

AIPHANES

Some beautiful palms belong to this tropical American genus of about 30 species from northern South America and the West Indies. Of the palm (Arecaceae) family, they are small to medium-sized feather-leafed palms of the rainforest undergrowth, armed with extremely sharp, needle-like, black spines that project from the trunk, frond stalks, and even leaflets. Leaflets widen toward their tips, which are truncated, toothed, and often frilled. Flowers are small and yellow or cream, in narrow panicles, followed by decorative, globular, bright red fruit.

CULTIVATION: The 3 to 4 species usually found in palm collections are easily grown outdoors in the tropics and warmer subtropics, in a sheltered position in partial shade and watered liberally in dry periods. Fertile well-drained soil is desirable. In cooler climates they require a heated conservatory or greenhouse, and can be kept in pots or tubs for many years before growing too large. Propagate these plants from seed after removing fruit flesh.

Aiphanes caryotifolia

RUFFLE PALM

☼ ✿ ↔ 8 ft (2.4 m) ↕ 20 ft (6 m)

Generally considered the most decorative species, native to Venezuela, Colombia, and Ecuador. Straight trunk, about 4 in (10 cm) across, with spines to 4 in (10 cm) long. Trunk crowned by a few elegantly arching fronds about 6 ft (1.8 m) long. Leaflets fresh green, in groups along whitish stalk, broadened apical edge strongly frilled, several radiating long teeth. Adult specimens produce short sprays of yellow flowers and brilliant red fruit. Zones 11–12.

ANEMIA

This genus of the comb-fern (Schizaeaceae) family contains over 100 species, occurring in tropical and warm-temperate regions of the Americas (most species), Africa, Madagascar, and India (one species). Its fronds arise from a creeping, hairy, fleshy stem. Frond blades are pinnate or pinnately compound, with the 2 lower segments only being fertile. Spore-bearing organs are borne in a single row on both sides of the leaflets.

CULTIVATION: Propagate these plants from spores or by division.

Anemia mexicana

syn. *Ornithopteris mexicana*

☼ ⚬ ↔ 24 in (60 cm) ↕ 20 in (50 cm)

Wiry, creeping, fleshy stem, covered with coarse blackish hairs, fronds scattered along it, stalks to 12 in (30 cm) long, blades to 10 in (25 cm) long by 6 in (15 cm) wide, lower pair of segments fertile, elongated, sterile segments in 4 to 6 pairs. Occurs on limestone cliffs, in canyons, and other limestone regions of Texas, USA, and northern Mexico. Spores in winter–spring. Zones 9–11.

ARCHONTOPHOENIX

Endemic to eastern Australia, this palm (Arecaceae) family genus consists of 6 species. They have a bare trunk topped by a crown-shaft of tightly furled frond bases. Each frond has many leaflets closely spaced in 2 regular rows; from base to tip the frond twists through 90 degrees so that near its outer end leaflets are almost vertical. Flowering branches emerge from the trunk below the crownshaft. Many, star-shaped, cream to pale mauve flowers on pendulous branchlets, and globular red fruit.

CULTIVATION: Popular ornamentals for frost-free climates, favored by landscapers for their fast early growth and complete shedding of old fronds. Although fairly sun hardy, they are shallow rooted and like well-mulched soil and much water in dry periods. Propagate from freshly fallen and cleaned seed. Protect young plants from strong sun.

Anemia mexicana

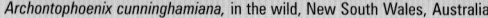

Archontophoenix cunninghamiana, in the wild, New South Wales, Australia

Archontophoenix purpurea

Archontophoenix alexandrae
ALEXANDRA PALM

☼ ≋ ↔ 15 ft (4.5 m) ↥ 50 ft (15 m)

From east coast of tropical Queensland, Australia, this species forms dense stands. Slightly bulbous pale gray trunk, plain green crownshaft, base has stepped rings. Fronds 8–10 ft (2.4–3 m) long, silvery white color beneath. Cream flowers. Zones 10–12.

Archontophoenix cunninghamiana
BANGALOW PALM, PICCABEEN PALM

☼ ≋ ↔ 15 ft (4.5 m) ↥ 60 ft (18 m)

Found growing from the Tropic of Capricorn to southern New South Wales, Australia. Grows mainly in moist forested gullies and stream banks. Similar to *A. alexandrae*, trunk less swollen, fronds droop more, with green undersides. Flowers pale mauve, appear from summer to autumn. Zones 10–11.

Archontophoenix purpurea
MOUNT LEWIS PALM

☼ ≋ ↔ 15 ft (4.5 m) ↥ 80 ft (24 m)

Recognized only recently, this species is from the high-rainfall mountains of far northern Queensland, Australia. Crownshaft is a dull purple-gray, new fronds are bronze. The large fruit grows to 1 in (25 mm) in diameter. Vigorous in cultivation. Zones 9–12.

ARECA

From the region between southern India and New Guinea, this palm (Arecaceae) genus of about 60 species is almost exclusively tropical. They are attractive small to medium-sized palms, mostly found in rainforest undergrowth. They vary in growth form with stems solitary or clustered from the base. Larger species have a

Areca triandra

well-developed crownshaft terminating the trunk. Flowering branches emerge from the top of the trunk just beneath the crownshaft. Flowers are small, mostly cream or yellow, on the branchlets in groups of 3. Red or yellow fruits are egg-shaped. CULTIVATION: Most *Areca* species thrive outdoors only in the wet tropics, though some from higher altitudes may grow in frost-free climates outside the tropics. They do best in sheltered situations with permanently moist soil. Larger species will tolerate strong sun; however, the smaller, more delicate ones need protection. In cooler climates theses plants require a greenhouse with high humidity. Propagate from fresh seed from which the flesh has been stripped away.

Areca catechu
BETEL PALM

☼ ✽ ↔ 12 ft (3.5 m) ↥ 50 ft (15 m)

Single-trunked palm, swollen green crownshaft. Arching feather-like fronds. Flowering branches, short, with stiff branchlets. Yellow to orange-red fruits, up to 3 in (8 cm) long. The chewing of betel nut is a widespread custom throughout the natural distribution region of this species. Zones 11–12.

Areca triandra

☼ ✽ ↔ 8 ft (2.4 m) ↥ 10 ft (3 m)

A species that occurs in mountain rainforest from eastern India to the Philippines. Produces a single-stemmed or multi-stemmed trunk, green, prominently ringed. Smooth green crownshafts, erect fronds with dark green leaflets. Panicles of cream flowers. Bright red fruits. Zones 11–12.

ARENGA

An interesting genus of the palm (Arecaceae) family, *Arenga* consists of about 20 species from tropical and subtropical East Asia to northeastern Australia and the Solomon Islands. Variable in size from diminutive palms of rainforest undergrowth to massive solitary trees. *A. pinnata* is a source of palm sugar. Many species have trunks sheathed in mats of blackish fibers. The fronds are variable. Flowering branches on single trunked species appear at the top of the fully grown trunk, followed by a succession of flowering branches down the trunk; after the lowest sets fruit the whole tree dies. The flowers, creamy yellow or orange, are highly perfumed. The fruits have a gelatinous flesh that is very irritating to the skin and mouth.

CULTIVATION: Arengas are vigorous palms that adapt well to cultivation. They do best in sheltered but sunny situations with ample soil moisture. All the multi-stemmed species will grow readily in pots in a conservatory and will take years to outgrow their containers. Propagate all species from seed, the clumping species may also be divided.

Arenga engleri
☼ ⚘ ↔ 10 ft (3 m) ↑ 12 ft (3.5 m)
Native to Taiwan and Japan's far southern Ryukyu Islands. Makes a dense clump. Fronds have regularly spaced leaflets with toothed edges. Orange flowers in summer. Cherry-sized fruits ripen from yellow to dark red in autumn. Zones 9–12.

Arenga pinnata
AREN, GOMUTI PALM, KABONG, SUGAR PALM
☼ ⚘ ↔ 40 ft (12 m) ↑ 60 ft (18 m)
From India or Myanmar. Always single-trunked; the trunk is covered in stiff blackish fibers. Fronds are plume-like. The first flowering branch is at 8 years, successive ones emerging over the next 3 to 5 years. Fruits ripen to blackish. Zones 10–12.

Arenga undulatifolia
syn. *Arenga ambong*
☼ ⚘ ↔ 15 ft (4.5 m) ↑ 20 ft (6 m)
A beautiful species from parts of Borneo and Sulawesi. Makes a clump of stems. Features large fronds that fan out gracefully. The short flowering branches are half-concealed among the frond bases. Fruits are the size of chicken eggs. Zones 11–12.

Asplenium sagittatum

Arenga undulatifolia

ASPLENIUM
SPLEENWORT
This genus of over 600 ferns, found in tropical and subtropical climates, belongs to the spleenwort (Aspleniaceae) family. Short rhizomes are covered with massed roots, hairs, and scales. The often leathery fronds grow mostly from a single crown, forming a fountain-like structure.

CULTIVATION: Plant them in freely draining organically rich soil in a moist, shady, humid spot; some can stand dry spells. Tropical species need frost protection. Apply slow-release and liquid fertilizers when growing. Propagate from spores or by detaching plantlets formed on fronds of some species.

Asplenium bulbiferum
HEN AND CHICKEN FERN, MOTHER SPLEENWORT
☼/☀ ⚘ ↔ 24–48 in (60–120 cm)
↑ 24–48 in (60–120 cm)
Terrestrial or epiphytic fern from New Zealand and Australia. Has a short-creeping to suberect rhizome and arching, membranous, pinnate fronds up to 48 in (120 cm) across. Flattened, grooved, green to brown stems, can reach up to 12 in (30 cm) long. Zones 9–11.

Asplenium nidus
BIRD'S-NEST FERN
☼/☀ ⚘ ↔ 18–60 in (45–150 cm) ↑ 18–60 in (45–150 cm)
This large fern has a wide distribution, ranging from East Africa through tropical Asia to northern Australia and the Pacific as far as Hawaii. Nest-like rosette of simple, erect, sword-shaped fronds to 5 ft (1.5 m) long. The leathery, glossy green fronds are held on short, scaly, black, suberect stems to 2 in (5 cm) long. Variable, with some lobed forms. *A. n.* var. *plicatum* has narrow, dark green, pleated, convoluted fronds. Zones 10–12.

Asplenium sagittatum
MULE'S FERN
☼/☀ ❄ ↔ 4–6 in (10–15 cm) ↑ 4–6 in (10–15 cm)
Native to the Mediterranean, this fern has simple or pinnate, glossy green, leathery fronds that can reach up to 6 in (15 cm) long on stems up to 6 in (15 cm) long. Zones 8–10.

Asplenium scolopendrium
syn. *Phyllitis scolopendrium*
HART'S TONGUE FERN, SCOLLIES
☼/☀ ❄ ↔ 8–24 in (20–60 cm) ↑ 8–24 in (20–60 cm)
A robust clump-forming fern, globally distributed through north temperate regions. Scaly rhizomes. Strap-like fronds, up to 24 in (60 cm) long, on short stems. Grows naturally on alkaline or acid soils but prefers lime in cultivation. Numerous cultivars, including 'Crispum Bolton's Nobile', with broad fronds up to 18 in (45 cm) long; 'Crispum Speciosum', with sharply tapered fronds sometimes with yellow stripes; 'Cristatum', fronds divided many times, each ending in a spreading crest; and 'Kaye's Lacerated', broad irregularly lobed fronds to 8 in (20 cm) long. Zones 4–10.

Athyrium niponicum var. pictum

Azolla filiculoides

ATHYRIUM

A member of the shield-fern family (Dryopteridaceae), this genus comprises more than 100 widely variable terrestrial fern species. They are from temperate to tropical regions, and feature short and erect to creeping rhizomes with scales entire to toothed, and brown to black in color. Fronds are leathery to membranous, often brittle. CULTIVATION: Most species in this genus prefer a well-drained, acidic, organically rich loam, with organic mulch applied, in shade or filtered sun. Tropical species are frost tender. Protect from wind, slugs, and snails. Maintain abundant moisture, including water sprayed on foliage in hot weather. Plants are easily propagated from spores or plantlets. Species with multiple crowns or creeping rhizomes can be divided.

Athyrium filix-femina
LADY FERN

☀/◐ ❊ ↔ 3–7 ft (0.9–2 m) ↑ 2–5 ft (0.6–1.5 m)

Graceful, easily grown, clumping fern native to northern temperate zones in India, China, Japan, North Africa, Canada, North America, Mexico, and Peru. Short-creeping to erect rhizomes. Spreading or arching pinnate fronds, to 3 ft (0.9 m) long, thin-textured and leathery. Smooth frond stalks are green to purple in color. Deciduous in colder regions. This species has over 300 cultivars, including 'Clarissima', a graceful uncrested fern, to 40 in (100 cm); 'Frizelliae' (tatting fern), with ball-shaped leaflets along the midrib; 'Glomeratum', with curious ball-like masses of leaflets on slender fronds; 'Magnificum Capitatum', frond alone crested, leaflets not crested; 'Minutissimum', a dwarf form with fronds 4–6 in (10–15 cm) long; 'Vernoniae', with crimson frond stalks, broadly triangular blades with strongly ruffled overlapping leaflets, ending in a tassel; and 'Victoriae', crested fronds, to 40 in (100 cm) tall, branched at base to form crosses. Zones 3–9.

Athyrium niponicum

☀/◐ ❊ ↔ 20–24 in (50–60 cm) ↑ 12–14 in (30–35 cm)

Fully frost-hardy fern from East Asia with a short-creeping reddish brown rhizome. Arching pinnate fronds with yellow-colored stems. *A. n.* var. *pictum* (Japanese painted fern) has new fronds metallic gray suffused with red or blue. *A. n.* 'Pictum Crested' (painted lady fern) features a purplish red midrib suffusing into a silver gray and aquamarine-green lamina. Zones 4–9.

AZOLLA
FAIRY MOSS, MOSQUITO FERN, WATER FERN

A genus of 8 species of floating aquatic ferns with a near-worldwide distribution. Allocated their own family, floating-fern (Azollaceae), these plants are quite unlike terrestrial ferns in appearance. Rather than having upright fronds, they carpet the water surface, forming new plants by division. Each plant has roots, a minute rhizome, and overlapping scales as foliage. Scales bright green if shaded, often red in full sun. In areas of hard frost they overwinter as submerged fragments. CULTIVATION: Think twice before introducing *Azolla* to a pond. It will soon cover the water surface, smothering more desirable plants. It is self-propagating and a small cluster dropped in the water will race away in warm weather.

Azolla filiculoides

☀/◐ ❊ ↔ 36 in (90 cm) ↑ ¼–½ in (6–12 mm)

Found in North and South America. Individual plantlets are of irregular shape, occasionally up to 4 in (10 cm) in length, massing to cover large areas. Purple-red in full sun. Zones 7–11.

BISMARCKIA

Endemic to Madagascar, this genus in the family Arecaceae has a single species, a fairly large fan palm with a solitary stout trunk topped by a crown of large fronds. These are roughly circular and divided to about half their depth into stiffly radiating segments. Male and female flowers in panicles on separate trees. Tiny male flowers on curving crimson spikes, female flowers on sparser yellowish spikes. Fruits are date-sized, with a single large seed. CULTIVATION: Widely grown in tropics and subtropics. Best with a distinct dry season, but tolerate cooler and moister regions if planted in a hot sunny spot. Propagate from fresh seed with the

Bismarckia nobilis

flesh stripped off; germination requires a container at least 12 in (30 cm) deep to accommodate the downward-growing cotyledon.

Bismarckia nobilis ★

syn. *Medemia nobilis*

☼ ⚘ ↔ 12 ft (3.5 m) ↑ 60 ft (18 m)

Attractive palm, trunk gray, slightly rough. Fronds large, pale bluish green, on a thick stalk about 6 ft (1.8 m) long, split into an inverted Y-shape at the base. Brown fruits. Zones 10–12.

BLECHNUM

A genus of 200 terrestrial or epiphytic ferns in the Blechnaceae family, most native to Australasia and Southeast Asia and from Mexico to southern South America. A single species, *B. spicant*, is widely distributed in cooler parts of the Northern Hemisphere. Erect or running fleshy stems covered in glossy brown scales. New fronds often red, bronze, or pink. Upright fronds, glossy and thick, pinnate or deeply and pinnately lobed, dark green in some species, lighter green in softer species. Fertile fronds, carrying continuous linear spore-bodies parallel to midrib, are narrower and more erect than spreading sterile fronds.

CULTIVATION: Mostly frost tender or half-hardy only; prefer slightly acidic, moist, humus-rich soil in a protected dense shade. Propagate from spores on constantly moist sphagnum moss.

Borassus flabellifer

Blechnum brasiliense

BRAZILIAN TREE FERN

☀ ⚘ ↔ 40–60 in (100–150 cm) ↑ 40–60 in (100–150 cm)

Vigorous tree fern from Brazil, Peru, Guatemala, and Ecuador. Frost tender. New spring growth is bronze-red. Old plants develop a stout erect trunk to 12 in (30 cm) tall, with radiating tussock of coarse crinkled fronds to 36 in (90 cm) long and 12 in (30 cm) wide with closely crowded leaflets. Remove the faded fronds regularly in order to maintain the plant's tidy appearance. 'Crispum' has slightly ruffled leaflet margins. Zones 9–11.

Blechnum gibbum ★

MINIATURE TREE FERN

☀ ⚘ ↔ 3–5 ft (0.9–1.5 m) ↑ 3–5 ft (0.9–1.5 m)

Vigorous fern from tropical and subtropical Pacific Islands. Erect, narrow, black, rooting trunk. Deeply divided, spreading sterile fronds, 3 ft (0.9 m) long, 12 in (30 cm) wide. Fertile fronds erect, numerous narrow leaflets, 4–6 in (10–15 cm) long. Zones 10–11.

Blechnum nudum

BLACK-STEM, FISHBONE WATER FERN

☀ ⚘ ↔ 18–30 in (45–75 cm) ↑ 24–30 in (60–75 cm)

Colonizing fern from southeastern Australia. Erect rhizome, can form sturdy slender trunk covered with black shiny leaf bases. Crown of sterile fronds, 16–40 in (40–100 cm) long. Erect fertile fronds, 8–27 in (20–70 cm) long, on short, glossy, black stalks. Tapering leaflets. 'Cristatum', 18 in (45 cm) tall, unusual and

rare crested form; 'Forcett Feather', compact form with leaflets deeply lobed, with an upright slightly arching habit, up to 24 in (60 cm) high and wide. Zones 8–10.

Blechnum spicant

DEER FERN, HARD FERN, LADDER FERN

☼/☀ ❄ ↔ 12–18 in (30–45 cm) ↑ 12–18 in (30–45 cm)

Low-growing tufted fern species from North America, Europe, and temperate Asia. Rhizome is short-creeping, erect, stout. Spreading, lance-shaped, leathery, dark-green sterile fronds, 6–8 in (15–20 cm) long, with up to 60 pairs of closely set leaflets. Fertile fronds are taller, up to 30 in (75 cm) long. 'Cristatum', a compact form reaching 4–8 in (10–20 cm) high, crested frond tips. Zones 5–9.

BORASSUS

A genus of massive fan palms in the family Arecaceae, *Borassus* consists of around 10 species ranging through tropical Africa and Asia as far east as New Guinea, growing mainly on open sandy plains and along river banks. The thick solitary trunks are generally covered in the remains of old frond stalks, forming a criss-crossing pattern. The fronds are divided into tapering segments that radiate stiffly or droop. Male and female flowers are borne on different trees; flowering branches bear small flowers on lateral branches. On the females large fruits with a fibrous husk develop. Some species have a wide range of uses, most notably as sources of palm sugar.

CULTIVATION: Successful cultivation requires a tropical climate. With access to groundwater, they will tolerate a long dry season, but they thrive in the wet tropics. Full sun is essential, and a deep, porous, well-drained soil is preferred. Propagate from seed only; when seeds sprout, plant out into individual containers.

Borassus flabellifer ★

LONTAR PALM, PALMYRA PALM

☼ ⚘ ↔ 15 ft (4.5 m) ↑ 60 ft (18 m)

Ranging from southern India and Sri Lanka to New Guinea and Indochina, similar in size to *B. aethiopum*. Fronds larger, to 10 ft (3 m) across; fruits larger, to 8 in (20 cm) across. Zones 11–12.

BOWENIA

This genus, belonging to the family Boweniaceae, is composed of 2 very similar species of cycads native to the forests of coastal northern Queensland, Australia. They have vigorous underground tubers and do not produce a trunk, instead sending up their branched fern-like "fronds" directly from the ground. The separate male and female cones also form at ground level and occur throughout much of the year.

CULTIVATION: These cycads prefer wet tropical conditions and revel in the dripping humidity of the rainforest. In temperate climates they need a heated greenhouse and do not readily adapt to normal indoor conditions and cultivation as house plants. Propagation is from seed or by dividing the rootstock.

Bowenia spectabilis

BYFIELD FERN

☼ ✦ ↔ 5 ft (1.5 m) ↑ 5 ft (1.5 m)

From coastal northern Queensland, Australia. Glossy, deep green, arching leaves, smooth-edged leaflets up to 4 in (10 cm) long. Male cones are dark green and cream. Female cones pineapple-shaped, yielding purple-green seeds. Zones 11–12.

BRAHEA

syn. *Erythea*

HESPER PALM

A genus of 12 species of attractive small to medium-sized fan palms in the family Arecaceae and from Mexico and Central America. They are usually grown for their striking appearance and beautiful foliage. Mostly from dry rocky habitats, in open woodland and low scrub, most species have a rough-surfaced single trunk topped by a compact crown of fronds. The flattened frond stalks are often edged with spines. Frond blades are fan-shaped. The flowering branches emerge from the frond bases, gracefully arching. White to yellowish flowers are tiny, crowded densely onto spike-like branchlets. Olive-shaped fruits ripen to blue-black; some are edible.

CULTIVATION: These sun-loving palms are very easily grown in most warm-temperate to subtropical climates, best where summers are hot and dry. Most will tolerate light frosts. They do best in well-drained moderately fertile soil with adequate subsoil moisture. Trim away the dead fronds. If left untrimmed the dead fronds form a thatch or "skirt" beneath the crown. Propagate from seed; early growth is often slow but may speed up after a trunk shows beneath the fronds.

Brahea armata ★

syn. *Erythea armata*

BLUE HESPER PALM, HESPER PALM

☼ ❄ ↔ 10 ft (3 m) ↑ 25 ft (8 m)

From the Baja California peninsula of western Mexico. Fronds stiff, pale blue-gray. Trunk stout. Flowering branches up to 15 ft (4.5 m) long, arching in a complete semicircle and held well clear of the foliage. Tiny cream flowers attract numerous insects. Zones 9–11.

Brahea brandegeei

syn. *Erythea brandegeei*

BRANDEGEE HESPER PALM, SAN JOSE HESPER PALM

☼ ❄ ↔ 15 ft (4.5 m) ↑ 40 ft (12 m)

A species found growing in steep canyons in southern Baja California, near San Jose del Cabo, Mexico. Trunk is brownish, slender, tapering upward. Fronds are pale green, drooping, partly hiding the flowering branches. It was collected in 1900 by the California botanist Brandegee. 'Elegans' (syn. *Erythea* 'Elegans'), a dwarf form, usually under 5 ft (1.5 m) tall. Zones 9–12.

Brahea edulis

syn. *Erythea edulis*

GUADALUPE PALM

☼ ❄ ↔ 20 ft (6 m) ↑ 30 ft (9 m)

A species from the remote Mexican island of Guadalupe, found growing in steep ravines running up from the seashore. Trunk is thick. Fronds are pale green with brownish woolly hairs. Shorter flowering branches thick, woolly, bearing greenish white flowers. Edible brown-black fruit. Zones 9–12.

BUTIA

BUTIA PALMS

This is a genus of small to medium-sized palms belonging to the family Arecaceae. The 8 species are native to subtropical and warm-temperate regions of eastern South America. They all have a large spindle-shaped bract around the flowering panicle in bud. Fronds arch from the trunk, consisting of 2 rows of thick narrow leaflets. The stout trunk is clothed by old frond stalks; when shed with age they leave a closely ringed gray surface. Sweet-scented cream to purplish flowers appear on stiff springy spikes; flowering branch bursts through a slit in the bract before the flowers open. The fruits are edible, and can be fermented to make a kind of wine.

CULTIVATION: Widely grown as landscape subjects in warm-temperate climates, they tolerate hot exposed environments. Deep-rooted, they tolerate dry topsoil, but are readily transplanted at any age. When trimming old fronds, cut bases at an even length to preserve the neat pattern on the trunk. Propagation is from seed, but germination may take some months.

Butia capitata ★

BUTIA PALM, JELLY PALM

☼ ❄ ↔ 15 ft (4.5 m) ↑ 20 ft (6 m)

From southern Brazil, Uruguay, and northern Argentina. Fronds recurving, grayish, to 10 ft (3 m) long. Large cream bracts, pale yellow to reddish flowers, in late spring to early summer. Fruits ripen in summer or autumn of the following year. Zones 8–11.

Brahea edulis

Butia capitata

Butia eriospatha

☼ ⚥ ↔ 12 ft (3.5 m) ↑ 12 ft (3.5 m)

From southern Brazil; similar to *B. capitata*. Outer surface of large bracts densely coated in brown woolly hairs, look like brown lambskin. Flowers reddish purple on the outside, in early summer. Zones 9–11.

CARPENTARIA *(see page 108)*

Carpentaria acuminata ★

CARPENTARIA PALM, THORA, YIRRGI YIRRGI

☼ ⚘ ↔ 20–25 ft (6–8 m) ↑ 25–50 ft (8–15 m)

Solitary fast-growing palm, with tall, narrow, erect, smooth, whitish gray trunk, 5–6 in (12–15 cm) across, ringed with scars and slightly enlarged at the base. It has a prominent crown of feathery pinnate leaves, up to 12 ft (3.5 m) long, with drooping tips. White flowers, oval bright scarlet fruit maturing in summer; the pulp irritates the skin. Australian Aboriginals eat the tender new growth or "cabbage." Zones 11–12.

CARYOTA

FISHTAIL PALM

Caryota consists of 12 species, in the palm (Arecaceae) family, ranging through tropical Asia. Most are single-stemmed; a few are multi-stemmed. Large bipinnate fronds divide into segments along either side of a midrib, with triangular or wedge-shaped leaflets, reminiscent of a fishtail. Flowering occurs at maximum stem height, the first flowering panicle bursts from the sheathing base of the topmost frond and bears flowers and fruit. Over several years panicles emerge from the stem in lower positions until at the base of the trunk, then with fruiting over, single stemmed plants die. Panicles have cream flowers crowded on drooping spikes. Pink to purple fruit follow. Sugary sap may be fermented for a sort of wine or beer. CULTIVATION: All are fine ornamental palms and most thrive equally well in frost-free climates, with adequate soil moisture. In hot climates growth is very fast, individual stems are short lived, becoming ragged and untidy with age. Propagation is from seed.

Caryota mitis ★

CLUSTER FISHTAIL PALM

☼ ⚥ ↔ 10 ft (3 m) ↑ 20 ft (6 m)

Widely cultivated species. Develops narrow clump of stems. Fronds, 6–10 ft (1.8–3 m) long, crowd together forming a luxuriant crown. Flowering panicles; a mass of scented cream flowers opening from green buds. Fruit dark red. Needs moist fertile soil. Zones 10–12.

Caryota ochlandra

CHINESE FISHTAIL PALM

☼ ⚥ ↔ 10 ft (3 m) ↑ 25 ft (8 m)

Native to southern China. Single-stemmed, trunk 6 in (15 cm) in diameter. Fronds along the trunk. Crowded, drooping, narrow leaflets. Flowering panicles 6 ft (1.8 m) high or more. Fruit deep red. Will survive light frosts. Zones 9–12.

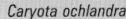

Caryota ochlandra

Ceratozamia mexicana

Caryota urens ★

FISHTAIL PALM, TODDY PALM

☼ ⚥ ↔ 15 ft (4.5 m) ↑ 30 ft (9 m)

A species cultivated in southern Asia as a source of sugar. Adapts to seasonally dry climates. Trunk 12 in (30 cm) in diameter, chalky white. Fronds with crowded, narrow, drooping leaflets. Flowering panicles 10 ft (3 m) long. Red fruit. Zones 10–12.

CERATOZAMIA

This genus of 9 to 16 palm-like cycads belongs to the zamia (Zamiaceae) family. The species are native to the mountains of Mexico, Belize, and Guatemala. Plants develop stout, rounded, and scarred trunks, with whorls of pinnate, erect or arching fronds. They produce cylindrical, dull green, female cones with single-spined scales; male cones are narrower, slightly felty, scaly, with 2 spines. Green or coppery new growth can be smooth or hairy. The genus is named from the Greek *ceras*, meaning horn, referring to pairs of horn-like spikes on the cones. CULTIVATION: Suitable for containers or the garden, plant in well-drained, mulched, slightly acid, humus-rich loam. Most prefer high humidity but gentle air movement and light to heavy shade; direct sun causes leaf damage. Protect the plants from frost and lightly fertilize in spring and summer. Propagate from freshly collected seed, which takes 6 to 12 months to germinate. Some species produce offsets and can be divided.

Ceratozamia mexicana

◐ ⚥ ↔ 4–8 ft (1.2–2.4 m) ↑ 3–7 ft (0.9–2 m)

A medium-sized cycad native to Mexico with a large, rounded, dark brown trunk. Young growth is light green and hairy. Develops a crown of 12 to 20 arching, erect or spreading, semi-glossy, dark green fronds, 5–8 ft (1.5–2.4 m) long, with up to 150 narrow leaflets, prickles on midribs and frond stalks. Bears erect brown male cones. The female cones are erect, cylindrical to barrel-shaped, and gray in color. Zones 9–12.

CHAMAEDOREA

Chamaedorea, in the family Arecaceae, is one of the larger genera of palms with over 100 species. They are attractive, small, understory palms which adapt to cultivation, especially as indoor plants. From tropical America, they include both clumping and single-stemmed palms. Fronds are either pinnate (feather palms) or undivided. Flowers are of different sexes on different plants, very small and fleshy, and borne on spikes. As small single-seeded fruits ripen, fruit color contrasts with that of the spike.

CULTIVATION: These tropical palms adapt well to frost-free warm-temperate climates. A few will tolerate light frosts. Some are quite sun-hardy in a humid climate, but most grow best in filtered light in a sheltered spot. Soil should be moderately fertile with a high organic content and the surface mulched with leaves. If grown indoors they need good light, though not direct sunlight. Feed them regularly in summer with a dilute high-nitrogen fertilizer. Propagate these plams from seed.

Chamaedorea ernesti-augusti

Chamaedorea ernesti-augusti

☀ ❄ ↔ 18 in (45 cm) ↑ 3 ft (0.9 m)

From southern Mexico to Honduras. Single-stemmed, wedge-shaped fronds, undivided, with a broad notch at the apex. The male plants have tiny red flowers, the females a spike of greenish flowers, turning bright orange. Small black fruit. Zones 10–12.

Chamaedorea microspadix

☀ ❄ ↔ 10 ft (3 m) ↑ 8 ft (2.4 m)

From southeastern Mexico. Clump of spreading, thin, bamboo-like stems. Fronds crowded, matt green broad leaflets. Flower panicles, females green, bearing bright scarlet fruits to ½ in (12 mm) in diameter. One of the most sun-hardy species. Zones 9–12.

Chamaedorea seifrizii

☀ ✦ ↔ 3 ft (0.9 m) ↑ 10 ft (3 m)

Native to Yucatan, Mexico. Multi-stemmed species, stiff ascending fronds, regularly spaced narrow leaflets. Short flowering branches emerge below the fronds; female plants bear pea-sized black fruit on orange spikes. Zones 11–12.

CHAMAEROPS

There is only a single, rather variable species in this genus of fan palms, part of the family Arecaceae, and native to far southern Europe, North Africa, and the eastern Mediterranean. Usually multi-stemmed, single-stemmed forms are known. The trunks of most wild plants are so short that the fronds appear to spring from the ground; however, in cultivation they may develop trunks of up to 15 ft (4.5 m) high. Fronds are small, divided into stiffly radiating segments; the stalks are armed with spines. The short flowering branches bear male and female flowers on different plants. Male flowers are yellow, conspicuous, and crowded onto flattened spikes. The females are sparser, a greenish color, and develop dull orange or tan fruits.

CULTIVATION: They need a temperate climate with warm summers, and will not thrive in the tropics. Plant in an open sunny spot in well-drained soil. Well suited to large pots or tubs for use in sunny conservatories or terraces. Propagation is normally from seed, large clumps can be divided with difficulty, if necessary.

Chamaerops humilis ★

MEDITERRANEAN FAN PALM

☀ ❄ ↔ 12 ft (3.5 m) ↑ 15 ft (4.5 m)

Fronds vary in size, color, and depth of division between segments. Forms with bluish foliage are sometimes found. *C. h.* var. *argentea* (syn. *C. h.* var. *cerifera*), stunning bluish foliage. Zones 8–10.

CIBOTIUM

This genus of 15 species of the tree fern (Dicksoniaceae) family, allied to *Dicksonia*, has a scattered distribution, occurring in Mexico, Central America, Hawaii, and parts of tropical and subtropical Asia. The trunk is often upright and tree-like, but in some species may grow horizontally before turning upward. Fronds are very finely divided and the crown and trunk are usually very fibrous and hairy.

CULTIVATION: Some species will tolerate light frosts, but most prefer moist warm-temperate to subtropical conditions. They should be planted in full shade or with shade from the hottest sun in constantly moist humus-enriched soil, and watered well in summer or during dry spells. Propagate them by removing basal shoots, from freshly cut lengths of trunk, or from spores.

Cibotium schiedei ★

MEXICAN TREE FERN

☀/☀ ❄ ↔ 8 ft (2.4 m) ↑ 15 ft (4.5 m)

Native to Mexico. Trunk covered with silky golden brown hairs. Mature fronds over 6 ft (1.8 m) long, light green, with bluish undersides. Side shoots develop into trunks, forming a clump. A species that tolerates light frosts. Zones 9–11.

Cibotium schiedei

Coccothrinax crinita

leaves, silvery and hairy beneath, and up to 6 ft (1.8 m) across, have 28 segments up to 24 in (60 cm) long, and short slender leaf stalks. Zones 10–12.

COCOS

This genus in the palm (Arecaceae) family contains just one species, found in coastal regions of all tropical seas worldwide, growing to a height of around 100 ft (30 m) in good conditions. The terminal head carries pinnate fronds. The 3-petalled flowers, seen only in the tropics, are produced in panicles from the leaf axils, followed by the coconuts, encased in thick fibrous husks. In tropical islands all parts of this tree are used: the trunks and fronds for building and weaving; the fiber for matting, rope, and soil-less composts; the flesh of the nut for food and drink; the endosperm for cosmetics; the oil for margarine and soap. The residue is used for cattle feed.
CULTIVATION: Coconuts can be grown successfully outdoors only in the tropics. In subtropical conditions they will not bear fruit. They grow best in coastal lowlands and on seashores. Coconuts will thrive if watered and fed moderately in the growing season. Grow in moist, well-drained, humus-rich soil in full sun. For container growing, provide an open mixture with coarse sand added.

Cocos nucifera
COCONUT PALM
☼ ⚶ ↔ 10–20 ft (3–6 m) ↑ 100 ft (30 m)
Large palm with a single trunk swollen at the base, often leaning away from the prevailing wind. Bright green pinnate fronds, up to 20 ft (6 m) long. Fragrant yellow flowers. Fruit covered with a thick husk, green ripening to yellow or orange-red. 'Malay Dwarf' ★, a widely grown strain, produces heavy crops of large golden-yellow nuts; 'Nino', a dwarf cultivar, will grow up to 10 ft (3 m); 'Panama Tall', a stately tall cultivar. Zone 12.

COPERNICIA
CARANDA PALM, WAX PALM
Native to tropical and subtropical regions of the West Indies and South America, this palm (Arecaceae) family genus consists of 24 or 25 species. They may be solitary or clumping, and may range from dwarf species to tall spectacular trees. The trunk, which may be covered with the bases of old fronds, or scarred, or occasionally bare, is often swollen at its base. The fan-like palmate fronds are stiff, deeply divided, and often spiny, the dead fronds remaining on the plant and creating a "petticoat" below the living fronds. All species have ornamental value, while one, *C. prunifera*, is grown commercially for the carnauba wax harvested from the leaves.
CULTIVATION: *Copernicia* species prefer an open sunny position in well-drained soil, although they will cope with half-sun. They are propagated from seed, which takes 3 to 10 months to germinate, according to species; however, seedling growth is slow.

COCCOTHRINAX
SILVER PALM, THATCH PALM
From tropical regions of the West Indies, Mexico, Honduras, the Bahamas, and Florida, USA, this genus in the palm (Arecaceae) family consists of 14 or more species. Fan-like palmate fronds have broad blades divided into long radiating segments that are glossy dark green above and silvery beneath. As the fronds die and fall away, they leave behind a layer of fibers that wear away, leaving a ringed trunk exposed. These palms are salt and wind tolerant.
CULTIVATION: Prefer an open, sunny, or part-protected spot in very well-drained soil, with adequate water in dry periods. Propagate from seed, which germinates within 2 to 6 months, depending on species.

Coccothrinax argentata ★
syns *Coccothrinax fragrans, C. jamaicensis, C. proctorii, C. readii*
FLORIDA SILVER PALM, SILVER PALM
☼ ⚶ ↔ 8 ft (2.4 m) ↑ 25 ft (8 m)
From Florida, USA, and the Bahamas. Solitary palm, smooth gray trunk. Small fan-like leaves, glossy light yellow-green above, silvery white below. Fragrant white flowers, purplish black fruits. Zones 10–12.

Coccothrinax crinita ★
OLD MAN PALM, THATCH PALM
☼ ⚶ ↔ 7 ft (2 m) ↑ 30 ft (9 m)
From tropical Cuba. Trunk 8 in (20 cm) wide; long, brown, woolly, fine fibers. Fan-like fronds, 6 ft (1.8 m) across, divided into segments, drooping blades, shiny green above, dull gray below. Zones 10–12.

Coccothrinax miraguama
syn. *Coccothrinax scoparia*
MIRAGUAMA
☼ ⚶ ↔ 7 ft (2 m) ↑ 15 ft (4.5 m)
Native of Cuba. Develops an elegant palm, trunk 6 in (15 cm) in diameter, covered in long fibers. The glossy, rigid, dark green

Copernicia baileyana ★

YAREY, YAREY HEMBRA

◐/◑ ❄ ↔ 10 ft (3 m) ↑ 40 ft (12 m)

An impressive palm, native to Cuba. Frond stalks to 4 ft (1.2 m) in length, covered with spines. Large crowded crown. Has huge, deeply segmented, bright green, fan-shaped fronds. Zones 10–12.

Copernicia prunifera ★

CARNAUBA

◐/◑ ❄ ↔ 12 ft (3.5 m) ↑ 40 ft (12 m)

From northeastern Brazil. Grown for its versatile wax. Large rounded crown, hard patterned trunk, lower portion covered in persistent leaf bases. Fan-like fronds divided into segments hang from deeply toothed leaf stalks. Zones 10–12.

CORYPHA

These tall erect members of the palm (Arecaceae) family have stout trunks and very large fan-shaped fronds. The around 6 species occur in tropical regions from Asia to Australia. After 30 to 50 years a mature palm produces a burst of millions of individual flowers at the top of the trunk; when the fruits that follow ripen, the whole palm dies. They make outstanding features for large gardens and parks, and in tropical countries the leaves, fruits, and stems have traditional uses.
CULTIVATION: In subtropical and tropical climates, grow these palms in well-drained organically rich soil with regular water during the warmer months. Propagate from fresh seed.

Corypha umbraculifera ★

TALIPOT PALM

◐ ✤ ↔ 35–50 ft (10–15 m) ↑ 40–80 ft (12–24 m)

From Sri Lanka and India. Giant palm with fan-shaped fronds to 17 ft (5 m) across. Spectacular inflorescences, 20–25 ft (6–8 m) long, the largest of any palm. Zones 11–12.

CYATHEA

Some 600 species of tree ferns with a wide distribution in the tropics and subtropics make up this genus, the second largest among the ferns. Some are among the largest of the tree-fern (Cyatheaceae) family, and can grow to as much as 50 ft (15 m) tall, rivaling the palms they resemble. Most species have a graceful habit, with large, soft, arching fronds atop a slender trunk. The old frond bases remain for some time but then fall to leave a trunk that though scarred may be almost smooth.
CULTIVATION: Species from furthest southern latitudes may survive temperatures as low as 10°F (−11.5°C), and even some tropical species may tolerate a very light frost. They prefer a constantly moist, humus-rich, fairly fertile soil. They also require atmospheric moisture and need misting and full shade in areas with low humidity or irregular rainfall. Propagation is from spores, or by removing the basal suckers that sometimes form around established plants of certain species.

Cyathea cooperi

SCALY TREE FERN, STRAW TREE FERN

☀ ❄ ↔ 20 ft (6 m) ↑ 20–40 ft (6–12 m)

A fast-growing fern from Australia. Chaffy straw-colored scales massed around frond bases. A weed in Hawaii. Zones 9–12.

Cyathea dealbata

SILVER TREE FERN

☀ ❄ ↔ 20 ft (6 m) ↑ 30 ft (9 m)

From New Zealand, this species is that country's sporting emblem. Large fern, fronds up to 12 ft (3.5 m) long. Distinctive, almost metallic, silvery white coloration on their undersides. Fronds soft, easily damaged by strong winds. Shelter is important. Zones 8–11.

Cyathea dregei

CAPE TREE FERN

◑/◐ ❄ ↔ 10 ft (3 m) ↑ 15 ft (4.5 m)

A South African species. The fronds arch downward, then turn up at the tips; relatively short, up to 6 ft (1.8 m) long, quite broad, with light colored undersides. A species that is surprisingly tolerant of both dry and cold conditions. Zones 8–11.

CYCAS

There are around 60 slow-growing woody-stemmed species in this genus of ancient plants in the cycad (Cycadaceae) family. They resemble palms but are not related. Almost all are from tropical and subtropical habitats. Long pinnate fronds are borne in annual flushes; some tropical species are leafless in the dry season. Male and female organs are found on separate plants; pollen in elongated cones at stem apex; seeds on leaf-like, often woolly scales, at first clustered at stem apex but left as "skirt" around stem after next flush of fronds emerges. A few species are garden grown.
CULTIVATION: Full sun and good drainage is required, but cycads can tolerate periods of drought. Propagate from seed or by removing and rooting dormant buds, which can be taken from the mature plant's trunk.

Cyathea cooperi, in the wild, Queensland, Australia

Cycas revoluta

Cycas circinalis ★
SAGO CYCAD, SAGO PALM

☼ ⚘ ↔ 15 ft (4.5 m) ↑ 15 ft (4.5 m)

A native of southern Asia, India, and the islands of the Pacific. Forms multiple, cylindrical, gray-brown trunks, crowned with bright green glossy fronds up to 10 ft (3 m) long, with a hooked midrib. Large shiny seeds, yellow and mahogany red. Zones 10–12.

Cycas media ★
NUT PALM, ZAMIA PALM

☼ ⚘ ↔ 10 ft (3 m) ↑ 15 ft (4.5 m)

Native of northern Australia. Develops a thick trunk, dark, clearly marked with triangular leaf-stem scars. Stiff dark green fronds, bright yellowish green when young, armed with yellow spines. Male cones yellowish brown. Female cones globular. Fruits ripen orange. Zones 10–12.

Cycas revoluta ★
JAPANESE SAGO CYCAD

☼ ⚘ ↔ 6 ft (1.8 m) ↑ 10 ft (3 m)

A Japanese species. Slow-growing, long-lived. Single, straight, cylindrical trunk, several trunks, or a branching trunk. Narrow stiff fronds, with narrow, dark, shiny leaflets. Attractive orange fruits in feathery husks. Good for indoors or for in sheltered courtyards. Zones 9–12.

CYRTOMIUM
This small genus of 15 to 20 fast-growing terrestrial or rock-inhabiting evergreen ferns from Hawaii, East Asia to South Africa, and Central to South America, is a member of the shield-fern (Dryopteridaceae) family. The plants produce erect densely scaly rhizomes. The broad, firm, pointed, pinnate fronds have pointed mostly sickle-shaped leaflets with smooth or irregular margins; fronds appear on short tufted stalks. The genus name

is derived from the Greek *kyrtoma,* meaning arch, and refers to veins that form arch-like patterns in some species.
CULTIVATION: These ferns are easily grown in light sandy soil or a mix that is kept moist to dry. Provide them with abundant water in summer, less in winter. They tolerate drier air than most ferns. They grow best in medium to high light, but keep them away from direct sunlight in summer. These plants propagate easily from spores in sandy peat in high humidity.

Cyrtomium falcatum
HOLLY FERN

☼/◐ ✽ ↔ 24–36 in (60–90 cm) ↑ 24–36 in (60–90 cm)

Medium-sized fern with erect rhizomes from India to East Asia, naturalized elsewhere in the Northern Hemisphere. Stems up to 16 in (40 cm) long, very dark green and glossy pinnate fronds, 8–24 in (20–60 cm) long, usually with 3 to 11 pairs of short-stalked, oval, thick, leathery leaflets, covered with reddish brown scales when young. 'Butterfieldii' (Butterfield holly fern), margins coarsely serrated; 'Cristatum' (syn. 'Mayi'), crested frond tips; 'Rochfordianum' (Rockford holly fern), segment margins deeply etched, like those of a holly leaf. Zones 6–11.

CYRTOSTACHYS
These 8 or 9 feathery leaved clump-forming palms from New Guinea, the Solomon Islands, Sumatra, Malaysia, and Borneo, are members of the palm (Arecaceae) family. They produce smooth, erect, ringed, often colorful stems with a vase-shaped crown of pinnate leaves on grooved stalks. The rigid leaflets are regularly spaced along a scaly midrib.
CULTIVATION: *Cyrtostachus* species are suited to container growth and do well in light shade when grown in the garden. They need regular watering. Most species are sensitive to cold. Propagate from freshly collected seed (which germinates in 2 weeks to 3 months, depending on species) or by division.

Cyrtostachys renda

Cyrtostachys renda ★
syn. *Cyrtostachys lakka*
LIPSTICK PALM, MAHARAJAH PALM, SEALING-WAX PALM

☼ ⚘ ↔ 7–10 ft (2–3 m)
↑ 15–30 ft (4.5–9 m)

Palm from the Malay Peninsula, Borneo, and Sumatra. The plants form thick clumps. Produce slender ringed stems, to 30 ft (9 m) long, and up to 10 stiff dark green leaves, up to 3–5 ft (0.9–1.5 m) long, with 50 to 100 leaflets, grayish blue underneath. Bears brilliant, glossy, scarlet crownshafts and leaf stalks. Green male and female flowers are borne on the same inflorescence. The oval black fruit contains oval seeds. 'Duvivierana' features a bright red crownshaft and stems; 'Orange Crownshaft' develops orange crownshafts and crowns of feathery leaves. Zones 11–12.

DAVALLIA

HARE'S FOOT FERN

A genus of about 40 semi-deciduous terrestrial or epiphytic ferns from warm-temperate, tropical, and subtropical regions that belong to the haresfoot-fern (Davalliaceae) family. Finely divided, triangular, lacy, shiny, pinnate fronds are borne on thick, long, creeping, branching, scaly rhizomes that run along the growing surface. Named for the resemblance of its furry, trailing, aerial rhizomes to animal paws.
CULTIVATION: These ferns are well suited to basket cultivation in warm humid spots protected from wind and frost. Grow in shade, in rich, moist, well-drained soil or a potting mix designed for epiphytic plants. Propagate from spores or by division of rhizomes.

Davallia solida

GIANT HARE'S FOOT, POLYNESIAN HARE'S FOOT
☀ ⚑ ↔ 24–36 in (60–90 cm)
↕ 12–18 in (30–45 cm)
Native to Malaysia, Australia, and the South Pacific islands. Fern with hairy, often aerial rhizomes. Tough, shiny, dark green, coarsely cut, bipinnate fronds, borne on scaly stalks. The leaflets have elliptical notched pinnules. *D. s.* var. *fejeensis* ★ produces more finely divided fronds, pendulous rhizomes, is suitable for basket cultivation; *D. s.* var. *pyxidata*, an eastern Australian variety with smaller fronds, hairless on the undersides; *D. s.* 'Ornata' bears broader pinnules with drooping tips; and 'Ruffled Ornata' produces broader ruffled pinnules. Zones 9–12.

DICKSONIA

This genus belonging to the family Dicksoniaceae of tree-ferns consists of around 30 species, occurring in the South Pacific, tropical America, and parts of Southeast Asia. The trunks are covered in the lower part by a dense mass of fibrous roots, and in the upper part by overlapping frond stalks, which persist after the fronds are shed with age. The fronds are large and arching, and

Dicksonia antarctica, in the wild, Tasmania, Australia

bipinnately divided into narrow, deeply lobed, parallel leaflets. Spore clusters on the undersides of the fronds are protected by a leaf cap, appearing as rows of tiny green balls along leaflet edges.
CULTIVATION: *Dicksonia* species are best grown in a moist well-drained soil in partial to full shade with protection from the wind. In cold climates, they grow best in greenhouses and conservatories. Propagation is usually from spores, or from offsets of the trunks. Some species transplant easily, or plants can even be re-established from the cut-off upper half of the trunk, as long as this is well covered by fibrous roots.

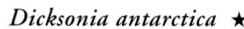
Dictyosperma album

Dicksonia antarctica ★

SOFT TREE FERN, TASMANIAN TREE FERN
☀/◐ ❄ ↔ 12 ft (3.5 m) ↕ 20 ft (6 m)
A native of southeastern Australia, from Tasmania north to Queensland, with attractive fronds, tripinnate. The trunk is a dark brown-black, densely fibrous, and upright. This species is an excellent plant for tubs. Shower the trunks to keep them moist in hot dry weather. Zones 8–10.

Dicksonia fibrosa

WHEKI-PONGA
☀/◐ ❄ ↔ 10 ft (3 m) ↕ 20 ft (6 m)
From New Zealand. An upright trunk, and brownish red, aerial fibrous rootlets. The fronds are dark green, 2- or 3-pinnate, the leaf stalks are hairy, and dark brown when mature. Grows best in a cool, moist, shaded environment. Zones 8–10.

DICTYOSPERMA

Although widely grown throughout the tropics for its ornamental value in landscaped gardens and as a container plant, this genus of one palm (family Arecaceae) is close to extinction in its native Mascarene Islands (Mauritius, Réunion, and Rodrigues) in the southern Indian Ocean. The arching pinnate leaves grow up to 10 ft (3 m) long. The large fragrant flowers are grouped in large clusters of 3s, with 1 female and 2 male blooms. Fruit are small, purplish black, bullet-shaped berries.
CULTIVATION: This palm can withstand strong winds, but is not drought tolerant and prefers high humidity in moist rich soils. It is best suited to warm coastal areas, in bright sunny situations. Propagate this attractive specimen plant from seed, which will take from 2 to 4 months to germinate.

Dictyosperma album ★

HURRICANE PALM, PRINCESS PALM
☼ ⚑ ↕ 60 ft (18 m) ↔ 20 ft (6 m)
An eye-catching tall palm with graceful crown, gray-ringed trunk, and swollen base. Feather-shaped fronds, with a yellow midrib; flowers are reddish. Attractive pot plant when young. *D. a.* var. *aureum*, prominent yellow stripe beneath the leaflets, indistinct veins; *D. a.* var. *conjugatum*, shorter with larger trunk, and long fringes hanging from the leaf tips. Zones 10–12.

DIOON

This genus of tree-like cycads belongs to the zamia (Zamiaceae) family, and is made up of 10 species found growing in Mexico and Central America. Palm-like in appearance, with upright trunks, ringed with the scars of old leaf bases, and frond-like leaves, their name is derived from the Greek and means "two eggs," a reference to their paired seeds. Cycads are ancient plants that do not bear true flowers, instead reproducing by means of pollen cones and seed cones, rather like conifers. The female or seed cones are often very large and woolly.
CULTIVATION: These plants are frost tender, and not tolerant of prolonged drought. *Dioon* species are best grown in moist, well-drained, humus-rich soil in a position in sun or partial shade. Water well during the warmer months. Restrict pruning to removing old trunks with untidy or dead foliage. Propagate from seed or by removing rooted offsets that develop at the base.

Dioon edule ★
MEXICAN FERN PALM
☼/◐ ❄ ↔ 5 ft (1.5 m) ↕ 6 ft (1.8 m)
This is a commonly cultivated species from Mexico. Fronds are upright, gray-green, blue-gray when young. The female cones contain edible seeds. Zones 10–12.

Dioon spinulosum ★
☼/◐ ❄ ↔ 10 ft (3 m) ↕ 30 ft (9 m)
From Mexico. Develops a slender trunk. Near-erect to arching fronds, woolly coating on emerging, wearing away with age. Sharp spines tip the aromatic dark green leaflets, which have a distinctive blue tint when young. Zones 10–12.

DIPLAZIUM

This genus of around 400 species of mostly tropical ferns, worldwide in their distribution, make up the majority of species in the family Athyriaceae. Some botanists have preferred to merge it with the genus *Athyrium*, in which case all species take that genus name. *Diplazium* species are ground-dwelling ferns with short or long rhizomes, sometimes forming a short erect trunk. The frond stalks are usually blackish and the fronds are broad and much divided; ultimate leaflets are toothed. On fertile fronds the dark spore-patches (sori) are linear and follow the veins; they are often arranged in a fan-like manner. In some species plantlets are produced on the frond tips.
CULTIVATION: In the wild these plants grow in moist soil, sometimes in the quite deep shade of the forest understory. They prefer very humid conditions and a spongy growing medium with a high organic content. Some of the species adapt easily to cultivation but others resent disturbance. Propagate these ferns from the spores or by division of the rhizomes.

Diplazium pycnocarpon
syn. *Athyrium pycnocarpon*
GLADE FERN, NARROW-LEAFED SPLEENWORT, SILVERY SPLEENWORT
☼/◐ ❄ ↔ 4 ft (1.2 m) ↕ 24–36 in (60–90 cm)
A species found growing from eastern Canada to southeastern USA. Deciduous fern that forms rosettes. The green arching

Dioon spinulosum

fronds are silvery, light green in spring, darkening in summer then turning russet before dying back. Zones 3–9.

DOODIA

HACK SAW FERN, RASP FERN
This genus of 12 species of very hardy and adaptable, medium-sized, terrestrial ferns from Sri Lanka to Polynesia, New Zealand, and Australia, is in the hard-fern (Blechnaceae) family. These long-lived ferns are closely related to *Blechnum* species. *Doodia* is known for its narrow, short, erect fronds; the fertile fronds are often taller than the sterile ones and with narrower leaflets. The new fronds have a distinctive red color that changes to different shades of green as they mature. The harsh leathery foliage can irritate sensitive skin.
CULTIVATION: *Doodia* species prefer acidic soils in a cool shady position, but they will also grow in dry rockery areas. Propagate them from spores; offspring may vary in color to parent plant. They are not fully hardy but will grow happily under glass.

Doodia aspera
PRICKLY RASP FERN
☼/◐ ❄ ↔ 15 in (38 cm) ↕ 6 in (15 cm)
A species from New Zealand, eastern Australia, and Norfolk Island, Australia. Tough, leathery upright fronds tend to arch. New foliage is red, which changes to mid-green as it matures. Tolerates sun but resents wet areas. Forms colonies. Zones 9–10.

DRYOPTERIS

BUCKLER FERN, SHIELD FERN, WOOD FERN

Part of the shield-fern (Dryopteridaceae) family, this genus is made up of about 200 species found in temperate forests, fields, and wet areas of the Northern Hemisphere. The genus contains the largest number of good ferns for ornamental gardening. The green foliage looks attractive with its upright arching fronds. These ferns work well when planted in mixed borders with most herbaceous plants. Many species have scaly tips to the fronds that can be dramatically beautiful in the spring as they begin to unravel. **CULTIVATION:** They are mostly deciduous but in mild areas will retain their foliage. This is an easy to cultivate, resilient fern group that will grow in poor dry soils, with little natural light. Propagate from spores as soon as they harden.

Dryopteris sieboldii

Dryopteris cristata

COMMON SHIELD FERN, CRESTED WOOD FERN, NARROW SWAMP FERN

☀ ❄ ↔ 36 in (90 cm) ↕ 18–30 in (45–75 cm)

From Europe and northern Asia and eastern North America. Erect fern with green, narrow, lance-shaped fronds with short, widely spaced, tilted leaflets. Spores held on undersides of fronds. Good in very damp areas. Will be evergreen in Zones 6 and 7. Zones 3–7.

Dryopteris erythrosora

AUTUMN FERN

☀ ❄ ↔ 16 in (40 cm) ↕ 24 in (60 cm)

From Asia. Shiny triangular fronds, rosy pink in spring, changing to bronze and eventually deep green as season progresses. Reliable, striking, and easy to grow. Usually deciduous. Zones 6–9.

Dryopteris filix-mas

MALE FERN

☀ ❄ ↔ 24 in (60 cm) ↕ 48 in (120 cm)

From Europe and North America. Mass of lance-shaped green fronds in spring. Spreads along the ground with rhizomes. Prefers part-shade and neutral to acid soil. Plant ceases growth in autumn, may become deciduous over winter. 'Barnesii', very tall and large, sparsely clothed, arching fronds, prefers a light dry soil, perfect in dry shade; 'Crispa', dwarf compact plant with sturdy, heavily crested, frilly fronds; 'Crispa Cristata', crested pale lime green, very frilly fronds; 'Cristata', foliage lightly crested, frond tips very frilly; 'Depauperata', compact fern with pretty, ruffled, dense, green foliage along each frond; **Grandiceps Group**, frond tips with heavy terminal crest, very vigorous, clumping; 'Grandiceps Wills', a striking plant, frond tips have large fluffy crests, vigorous and tolerant once established; 'Linearis Cristata', dwarf fern, dark green foliage, short narrow fronds, very tough. Zones 4–8.

Dryopteris sieboldii

JAPANESE WOOD FERN

☀ ❄ ↔ 20 in (50 cm) ↕ 20 in (50 cm)

A species found growing in Japan. Distinctive fern with glossy green palmate fronds. Broad lance-shaped leaves; each frond has 5 to 7 leaflets. Reliable once established. Zones 7–10.

DYPSIS

syns *Chrysalidocarpus, Neodypsis*

This genus of feather-leafed palms in the family Arecaceae consists of 140 species, all native to Madagascar except for 2 species on the Comoros Islands, and one on Pemba Island, Tanzania. Growth forms range from tiny undergrowth palms with pencil-thick stems and grass-like fronds, to quite massive palms that tower above the forest canopy. Stems solitary or clustered. Fronds are basically of feather type, some species have fronds that fork into two lobes; others a very few broad leaflets, and many plume-like fronds. Usually smooth crownshaft. Flowering panicles, below frond bases, bear small green, cream, or yellow (rarely red) flowers. Fruits are single-seeded drupes. **CULTIVATION:** Needs vary greatly; no species is frost tolerant. Some of the more robust species thrive outdoors and are very sun hardy; the more delicate species require shade and humidity. Most can be grown as indoor plants as long as light levels are not too low. Propagation is normally from seed, although the clumping *D. lutescens* can be divided.

Dypsis decaryi

syn. *Neodypsis decaryi*

THREE-CORNERED PALM, TRIANGLE PALM

☀ ❄ ↔ 6 ft (1.8 m) ↕ 20 ft (6 m)

From the far south of Madagascar. Fronds arranged in 3 vertical ranks, bluish gray, recurved tips. Sheaths and lower parts of the frond stalks are coated in rusty brown fur when young, ageing to gray. Develops a thick, closely ringed trunk. A species well-suited to growing in patio tubs and planter boxes. Zones 10–12.

Dypsis lutescens

syns *Areca lutescens, Chrysalidocarpus lutescens*

BUTTERFLY PALM, GOLDEN CANE PALM

☀ ❄ ↔ 6 ft (1.8 m) ↕ 20 ft (6 m)

From east coast of Madagascar. Forms compact clumps of yellow-green stems branching above ground, slender crownshaft. Fronds

Dypsis decaryi

Elaeis guineensis

recurved, stalks and midribs, yellow-orange. Branched flowering panicles, tiny yellow flowers. Oval yellow fruit. Zones 10–12.

ELAEIS
OIL PALM

This tropical palm genus (family Arecaceae) is made up of just 2 species, one is native to Central and South America and the other to Africa, where it occurs in open places, along streams and in swamps, and occasionally in savannah. They are large, single-stemmed plants with "feather" fronds. The large inflorescences appear year-round, with males and females separate but on the same plant. These palms fruit heavily. The seeds and pulp of the fruit contain large quantities of oils, which are used for many purposes, from soap, margarine, and candle manufacture to, in some tropical cities, car fuel.
CULTIVATION: Oil palms are ideal for tropical coastal areas, being salt tolerant; growth is slower in subtropical regions. They prefer a rich, moist, medium loam in a protected sunny position; keep the roots moist. Propagate from seed; crack open the hard shell of the large seed, or soak it in hot water, before germinating.

Elaeis guineensis
AFRICAN OIL PALM, MACAW FAT, OIL PALM
☼ ✿ ↔ 12 ft (3.5 m) ↑ 60 ft (18 m)
From tropical Africa. A large palm. Solid, erect, rough trunk is marked with scars. Shiny green fronds, up to 15 ft (4.5 m) long, forming a graceful spreading crown. Red flowers. Zones 11–12.

ENCEPHALARTOS

This African genus belonging to the zamia (Zamiaceae) family consists of around 100 species of slow-growing cycads, most of which come from southern Africa. There are both male and female plants. They prefer dry winters and summer rainfall. The pinnate fronds are often long and straight or arching, the leaflets are without a midrib and often spiny-toothed. Some develop a stout trunk, but suckering is common in those with underground cylindrical stems. The female plants have spectacular large seed cones with colorful fleshy seeds, maturing mostly in summer to autumn. Male pollen cones are usually smaller. The name comes from the Greek *en*, within, *cephale*, head, and *artos*, bread, referring to the starchy inner part of the trunk of some species, which is used as a staple food (sago) in some areas.
CULTIVATION: All species of *Encephalartos* require well-drained soil. Species with blue-toned leaves are generally more tolerant of full sun, dry conditions, and heat; those with softer green leaves do best in filtered shade, and with more regular watering. Propagate these cycads from seed or offsets.

Encephalartos altensteinii ★
PRICKLY CYCAD
☼/◑ ↔ 12 ft (3.5 m) ↑ 15 ft (4.5 m)
A species found growing in South Africa. A very slow-growing cycad. The trunk forms clumps from basal suckers. Stiff, glossy, green leaves; narrow leaflets with 1 to 3 prickles on each margin. Produces large yellow seed cones with red fruits. The trunks of the prickly cycad are a source of sago. Zones 10–11.

Encephalartos villosus

Encephalartos horridus
EASTERN CAPE BLUE CYCAD
☼/◑ ↔ 3 ft (0.9 m) ↑ 3 ft (0.9 m)
South African cycad. Stiff growth habit, blue-gray foliage. Most of the stem grows below ground. Fronds arching, to 3 ft (0.9 m) long; leaflets tipped with fierce spines. Cones a warm buff shade. Zones 9–11.

Encephalartos villosus ★
syns *Encephalartos villosus* f. *intermedia*, *E. niveo-lanuginosis*
☼ ↔ 20 ft (6 m) ↑ 10 ft (3 m)
Native to KwaZulu-Natal and the Cape region in South Africa, and to Swaziland. Occurring in scrubs and forests. No stem is above ground; distinguished by long, glossy, dark green leaves, to 10 ft (3 m), and its woolly crown. Leaflets narrow to lance-shaped, to 10 in (25 cm) long, margins with 1 to 3 teeth. Male cones are elongated ovate, yellow; female cones are ovate, also yellow, shorter and wider than the male. Red seeds. Zones 9–11.

EUTERPE
ASSAI PALM, MANACO

A genus of feather-leafed palms (family Arecaceae) with 7 species from tropical America, though up to 30 species have formerly been distinguished. Single-trunked or clustered, medium to large, with crowns of rather few pinnate fronds, their elongated basal sheaths forming a smooth crownshaft; leaflets droop gracefully, with finely tapering tips. The inflorescences appear in continuous succession from the trunk below the crownshaft; their branchlets have a dense covering of short soft hairs. The branchlets bear numerous small flowers in groups of one female flanked by two males. The smooth-coated, almost spherical, fruits contain a single seed. The vegetative buds, a single one terminating each trunk, are the principal source of palm-hearts, sometimes called "millionaire's salad" because their removal kills the trunk; but these palms are now grown rapidly in plantations and canned palm-hearts are sold quite cheaply.
CULTIVATION: Native to lowland rainforests and mountain forests and swamps. Fast growing, but because they need high humidity and temperatures they are really only suitable for tropical gardens, not for greenhouses in temperate regions. Propagate from seed.

Euterpe edulis ★

JUÇARA PALM, PALMITO, YAYIH

☼ ✤ ↔ 12–18 ft (3.5–5.5 m) ↑ 20–40 ft (6–12 m)

From coastal regions of Brazil and adjacent parts of Argentina and Paraguay. Slender, usually solitary, palm with a smooth green crownshaft. The finely divided fronds have 120 to 150 pendulous leaflets. Purple flowers are followed by clusters of small, round, dark purple fruit. It is generally agreed that *E. edulis* yields the best-tasting palm-hearts. Zones 11–12.

Euterpe oleracea

ASSAI PALM, AÇAÍ, MANAC, NAIDI, PINOT

☼ ✤ ↔ 12–18 ft (3.5–5.5 m) ↑ 20–60 ft (6–18 m)

A species found growing in the lower Amazon region of Brazil and far northern South America and west to Colombia. Clumping palm with several tall slender trunks and a crown of drooping feathery fronds, which emerge from a reddish crownshaft. The juicy blackish purple fruit is the basic ingredient of the sweet drink açaí, a staple of the Amazon's estuary region, and this species of palm also provides the major source of the palm-hearts used in the canning industry. Zones 11–12.

Euterpe edulis

HEMIONITIS

This genus of 7 species of evergreen ferns from the American tropics belongs to the maidenhair-fern (Adiantaceae) family. They have short, scaly, almost erect rhizomes and crowded, simple or pinnate, often hairy, rounded, heart-shaped or palm-shaped fronds. The fertile fronds are longer than the sterile fronds. The name *Hemionitis* comes from the Greek *hemionos,* meaning mule, referring to the plant's sterile fronds.
CULTIVATION: These fern species are suitable for container growth. They should be sheltered from full sun, and prefer a fibrous potting mix that is kept moist. Propagate them in spring to early summer from spores or plantlets arising from frond bases, or by dividing the rootball.

Hemionitis arifolia ★

HEART FERN, PIGGY-BACK FERN

☀ ♦ ↔ 4–12 in (10–30 cm) ↑ 4–12 in (10–30 cm)

A compact evergreen fern from India, Sri Lanka, Myanmar, Taiwan, and the Philippines. Produces wiry, rich brown to black, hairy stalks with plantlets forming at the bases. Simple, mid-green, triangular to heart-shaped fronds, rough to the touch, hairy and scaly underneath. Zones 10–11.

HOWEA

The 2 species in this genus of the palm (Arecaceae) family are natives of Lord Howe Island, off the coast of New South Wales, Australia. They are upright, single-trunked palms with lush heads of feather fronds. Flowerheads form near the base of the fronds and develop into red-green fruit.
CULTIVATION: Although quite frost tender, these palm species do not need high temperatures or bright light to grow well, so are

good house or conservatory plants. They will grow outdoors in frost-free gardens in any area that is not too hot and dry. They prefer a lightly shaded position with moist, humus-rich, well-drained soil. Propagation is from seed scarified before sowing and kept warm and moist until germination.

Howea belmoreana ★

BELMORE PALM, CURLY PALM, SENTRY PALM

☼ ♦ ↔ 10 ft (3 m) ↑ 25 ft (8 m)

The less commonly grown of the 2 species. A slender trunk ringed with the scar of old frond bases. Deep green fronds arch gracefully, and reach around 7 ft (2 m) long. Zones 10–11.

Howea forsteriana ★

KENTIA PALM, PARADISE PALM

☼ ♦ ↔ 15 ft (4.5 m) ↑ 30–50 ft (9–15 m)

Native to Lord Howe Island, also widely cultivated on nearby Norfolk Island for its seeds, for the nursery trade. Fronds up to 10 ft (3 m) long, usually held quite stiffly. Zones 10–11.

JOHANNESTEIJSMANNIA

JOEY PALM

This genus of 4 palms belonging to the family Arecaceae is endemic to tropical rainforests of southern Thailand, the Malay Peninsula, and Sumatra. Growing in the dense shade of the jungle canopy, a rosette of huge, simple, paddle-shaped fronds emerges from the very short, even subterranean trunk. These fronds collect litter and guide it to the center to cover the developing crown. The roots grow into the litter as it decays. Large

Johannesteijsmannia magnifica

fruits are covered with numerous corky warts. These magnificent palms are quite rare in the wild.
CULTIVATION: They are keenly sought by enthusiasts, and have been successfully grown in tropical and warm subtropical regions but need a moist well-shaded position. In colder areas they can be grown indoors in containers. Seed germinates readily if sown fresh. Joey palms display significant variation, even within individual species. Sow seed that comes from a specimen enjoying conditions similar to those where the palm will grow.

Johannesteijsmannia altifrons ★
☀ ⚘ ↔ 10 ft (3 m) ↕ 15 ft (4.5 m)
From Malay Peninsula and Sumatra. Huge paddle-shaped fronds. Simple, pleated, diamond-shaped leaves are used for thatching roofs in Malaysia. Crown has 20 fronds. The fruits are covered in corky warts. **Zones 11–12.**

Johannesteijsmannia magnifica
SILVER JOEY PALM
☀ ⚘ ↔ 10 ft (3 m) ↕ 15 ft (4.5 m)
From the rainforests of the central Malay Peninsula; rare in cultivation. Paddle-shaped fronds, to 8 ft (2.4 m) long, 4 ft (1.2 m) wide, with the underside covered in fine white hairs, giving them a silvery appearance. Fruits to 2 in (5 cm) wide, are covered with numerous corky warts. **Zones 11–12.**

JUBAEA
This genus contains a single species of palm, a member of the family Arecaceae and native to coastal areas of Chile, where wild populations have been greatly reduced by harvesting. Its tall stout trunk has a dense crown of leaves. The sugary sap is made locally into syrup or alcohol.
CULTIVATION: Tolerates short periods of light frost, but grow in a conservatory or greenhouse in cool climates. Plant in any reasonable soil in sun or filtered light and give plenty of water when young. Propagation is from fresh seed but germination is slow.

Jubaea chilensis
syn. *Jubaea spectabilis*
CHILEAN WINE PALM, COQUITO PALM
☀ ❄ ↔ 25 ft (8 m) ↕ 80 ft (24 m)
From Chile. Stout trunk, occasionally swollen in the middle. Dense crown; fronds to 15 ft (4.5 m) long, arching or rigid, pinnately arranged leaves. Long-stalked flowers are hidden within the leaves. Small, egg-shaped, edible yellow fruits, called coquito. **Zones 8–10.**

LATANIA
There are 3 species in this genus of the palm (Arecaceae) family, all endemic to the Mascarene Islands, east of Madagascar. Once more common in the drier parts of the islands' coastal regions, they are now rare owing to the clearing of land for agriculture. Each species is confined to one island. They are tall single-stemmed palms with large fan-shaped fronds. The male and female flowers are borne on separate plants, usually during the wet season. Although all 3 species are similar in general appearance, they differ in the coloration of the leaves.

Jubaea chilensis

Latania verschaffeltii

CULTIVATION: The young plants grow quite quickly, but they must be placed in full sun, in well-drained soil, and not exposed to frosts. Propagate from fresh seed, which can take approximately 4 months to germinate after sowing. Seed obtained from plants in cultivation, where there are 2 or 3 species growing near each other, can produce hybrids.

Latania loddigesii ★
BLUE LATAN PALM
☀ ⚘ ↔ 12 ft (3.5 m) ↕ 25 ft (8 m)
Native to Mauritius, the middle island of the Mascarene group. Blue-gray adult fronds with woolly white bases. Fronds over 15 ft (4.5 m) long. The flowers, on inflorescences to 6 ft (1.8 m), are borne in summer; male and female are similar in size. The fruit, round and fleshy, turns greenish brown when ripe. **Zones 10–12.**

Latania verschaffeltii ★
YELLOW LATAN PALM
☀ ⚘ ↔ 15 ft (4.5 m) ↕ 35 ft (10 m)
Native to the island of Rodrigues only. Dense white wool on the frond bases and stalks. Fronds green, not blue-gray. Leaf stalks and veins bright yellow to orange. **Zones 10–12.**

LEPIDOZAMIA
This genus of cycads in the zamia (Zamiaceae) family has only 2 living species; 2 others are known only from the fossil record. They occur in eastern Australia, growing in rainforest or similar sheltered environments near the coast. They are large plants with mostly unbranched, stout, erect, cylindrical trunks sheathed with old frond bases. The long fronds are pinnate and decorative; new fronds are produced in flushes. Male and female plants are separate; the cylindrical male cones are green and open spirally to release their pollen, while the larger and fatter female cones start out green but turn brown with age and contain mostly red seeds. Both male and female cones are possibly the largest among all cycad genera.
CULTIVATION: For outdoor cultivation plant in part-shade or filtered light in well-drained soil. The fronds tend to fade if exposed to too much sun. Indoors they require a well-lit position. Propagate from seed, which may take 1 or 2 years to germinate.

Lepidozamia hopei

WUNU

☀/☀ ❄ ↔ 8–15 ft (2.4–4.5 m) ↑ 20–70 ft (6–21 m)

Native to rainforests of northeastern Queensland; possibly the tallest of all cycads. Palm-like, with a smooth, pale yellow-brown, straight trunk, rarely branched. Fronds arching, pinnate; leaflets very glossy, dark green, to 1 in (25 mm) wide. Male cones to 18 in (45 cm) long, female cones to 24 in (60 cm) long. Zones 10–12.

Lepidozamia peroffskyana

SCALY ZAMIA

☀ ❄ ↔ 10–15 ft (3–4.5 m) ↑ 8–20 ft (2.4–6 m)

Extending from northeastern New South Wales into southeastern Queensland. Trunk rough, with diamond pattern of old corky frond bases. Fronds deep green, glossy; leaflets to ½ in (12 mm) wide. Male cones up to 30 in (75 cm) long, and female cones up to 36 in (90 cm) long. Zones 10–12.

LIVISTONA

A genus of some 30 species of medium and tall palms in the family Arecaceae. Found naturally in tropical and subtropical Australia and Southeast Asia in a wide range of habitats, from swamps and woodlands to inland gorges, often in extensive colonies. They have large fan-shaped fronds with long stalks armed with strong prickles. Cream to yellow flowers are borne in long-branched clusters among the foliage in winter or spring. The fruits are spherical to ovoid, usually blue-black, each containing a single seed enclosed in a thin oily flesh. CULTIVATION: These handsome fan palms make fine street trees or specimen plants for gardens. In cooler areas they may be grown in deep pots in an intermediate greenhouse or conservatory. One of the easiest of the palms to grow, they prefer a well-drained, neutral to acid, fertile soil but will adapt to a variety of soil types. They should be given a shady site when young. Propagate these palms from seed in spring or summer.

Lepidozamia hopei

Livistona australis ★

CABBAGE PALM, CABBAGE TREE PALM

☀ ❄ ↔ 15 ft (4.5 m) ↑ 80 ft (24 m)

A species found growing in low, moist, coastal regions of eastern Australia. Widely cultivated fan palm with dense crown of glossy fan-shaped fronds and a ringed gray to grayish brown trunk. Clusters of yellow to cream flowers are produced in late winter. Dull purple-black globular fruit follows. Zones 9–11.

Livistona decipiens

RIBBON FAN PALM, WEEPING CABBAGE PALM

☀ ❄ ↔ 8 ft (2.4 m) ↑ 50 ft (15 m)

Species from tropical and subtropical coastal Queensland. Tall attractive fan palm with a ringed brown trunk turning gray at maturity. Large glossy green fronds deeply divided into pendulous ribbon-like segments radiating in many planes; stalks strongly armed. Very small yellow flowers in spring. Fruit globular, glossy, black when ripe. Zones 10–12.

Livistona mariae

CENTRAL AUSTRALIAN CABBAGE PALM, RED-LEAFED PALM

☀ ❄ ↔ 10 ft (3 m) ↑ 50–60 ft (15–18 m)

From Palm Valley in central Australia's arid center; rare in the wild. Pale to dark gray trunk; rounded crown of shiny, gray-green, fan-shaped fronds. Creamy to greenish yellow flowers. Dark brown-black fruit. Zones 9–11.

Livistona rotundifolia ★

FOOTSTOOL PALM

☀ ❄ ↔ 15 ft (4.5 m) ↑ 80 ft (24 m)

A species native to eastern Indonesia, Malaysian Borneo, and the Philippines. Distinctive, large, glossy, circular fronds on the young plants give it its common name. Smooth, slender, gray trunk with a moderately dense crown. Produces yellow flowers. Scarlet fruit turning black when ripe. Zones 11–12.

LYCOPODIUM

CLUBMOSS

This genus of about 40 species, found in most parts of the world, gives its name to the clubmoss (Lycopodiaceae) family. Resembling mosses in their foliage, though mostly larger and more branched, they are traditionally treated as "fern-allies" but in fact are representatives of an unrelated and far more ancient group, some of them tree-like during the Carboniferous and Permian geological periods. Clubmosses today are evergreen perennials with aerial branches arising from creeping, often underground, rhizomes, or from long scrambling stems in the case of some tropical species. The leaves are tiny, densely clothing the stems or sometimes in 2 rows. Cone-like organs containing many

Livistona mariae, in the wild, Northern Territory, Australia

Lycopodium thyoides

Marsilea drummondii

small spore sacs terminate the branches. *Lycopodium* was formerly treated as a genus of about 400 species; however, the majority have now been split off into the genera *Huperzia* (including all the tropical epiphytic species) and *Lycopodiella*.

CULTIVATION: They are quite difficult to establish and maintain, and are rarely cultivated (in contrast to the epiphytic tassel-ferns in *Huperzia*, which are widely grown). Most likely to succeed in gritty acid soil kept permanently moist, and should be kept in a shaded position in high humidity. Propagate by division.

Lycopodium clavatum
GROUND PINE, RUNNING PINE

☀ ❄ ↔ 16–20 in (40–50 cm) ↑ 8–10 in (20–25 cm)
Widely distributed throughout temperate regions and in tropical highlands. Long trailing stems, with tiny, fine, needle-like leaves, to 4 mm long, crowded along them. Zones 2–9.

Lycopodium thyoides
syn. *Lycopodium complanatum* var. *validum*

☀ ❄ ↔ 18–36 in (45–90 cm) ↑ 6–18 in (15–45 cm)
From highlands of southern Mexico and Central and South America. Erect aerial stems arising from a long underground rhizome, with branches of 2 types: the sterile branches are spreading and repeatedly forked; fertile branches are erect and narrowly branched, with 4 to 8 long, thin, spore-bearing cones. Zones 9–10.

MACROZAMIA
This genus in the zamia (Zamiaceae) family contains around 38 species of cycads found in subtropical and warm-temperate Australia. Most grow in euca-lypt forests or woodlands, usually in poor soil. Some are palm-like with a usually unbranched stem forming a massive trunk above ground, others have the trunk below ground. The pinnate, spirally arranged, dark green to blue-green fronds are not as prickly as many other cycads. Male and female plants are separate, and both feature cones with scales that end in flattened spines. The large red or orange seeds were a traditional food of Aboriginal Australians. They are poisonous if eaten raw and must be carefully processed by being soaked, pounded, and baked. Various species have poisoned stock.

Macrozamia moorei

CULTIVATION: Best grown in well-drained sandy soil. The larger species, such as *M. moorei* and *M. riedlei*, prefer full sun, while the smaller species do best in shaded areas. Water regularly during the growing season. Propagate all species from fertile seed sown as soon as hardened.

Macrozamia communis ★
BURRAWANG

☀ ❄ ↔ 7 ft (2 m) ↑ 3–8 ft (0.9–2.4 m)
A cycad, native to New South Wales, Australia. Mostly underground trunk. Fronds grow to about 6 ft (1.8 m) long and have thick dull green leaflets. Female seeds have a bright red fleshy outer layer when mature, during summer months. Zones 9–11.

Macrozamia moorei ★
GIANT BURRAWANG, ZAMIA PALM

☀ ❄ ↔ 7 ft (2 m) ↑ 10–25 ft (3–8 m)
Tree-like cycad from central Queensland and northeastern New South Wales, Australia. Rounded crown of dull deep green to gray-green ridged fronds when mature. Large broadly cylindrical to barrel-shaped female cones, in summer. Zones 9–11.

MARSILEA
NARDOO, PEPPERWORT, WATER CLOVER

These attractive water plants come from tropical and temperate climates in Australia, Europe, Asia, and eastern USA. A genus of about 65 species of aquatic fern allies in the clover-fern (Marsileaceae) family, the plants have clover-shaped leaves that float on the water surface. Some species were dug up for their edible starchy sporocarps by Aboriginal Australians.

CULTIVATION: They can be grown in water up to 5 ft (1.5 m) deep in almost frost-free climates. May become weedy. Anchor them in the mud at the bottom of a pond or grow in a container. Propagate by division during cooler months.

Marsilea drummondii
COMMON NARDOO

☀ ❄ ↔ 7 ft (2 m) ↑ 6–12 in (15–30 cm)
An aquatic Australian plant found in all mainland states. Features a widely spreading rhizome and slender stems. Four-leafed clover-like leaves, pale to mid-green, grow up to 1¾ in (40 mm) long. Zones 9–11.

Marsilea mutica ★
BANDED NARDOO, NARDOO, WATER CLOVER

☀ ❄ ↔ 3–6 ft (0.9–1.8 m) ↑ 12–36 in (30–90 cm)
Perennial shallow-water floating fern from northern Australia and Southeast Asia. Weak, slender, spreading stems. The glossy olive green fronds have 4 wedge-shaped lobes with brown or light green zones, on stalks up to 36 in (90 cm) tall. Zones 9–11.

MATTEUCCIA

A member of the shield-fern (Dryopteridaceae) family, this genus contains 3 species of hardy deciduous ferns and is native to North America, Europe, and Asia. Fronds are tall, pinnate, with alternate leaflets in soft green. These elegant plants have an arching habit and are most at home in a waterside setting. They are easy to cultivate but have invasive underground stems.
CULTIVATION: Plant these ferns from autumn to spring in a slightly shaded, constantly moist spot, in lime-free soil that contains leaf mold. For best results, plant at least 48 in (120 cm) apart. Propagate by dividing the rhizomatous roots in autumn or winter.

Matteuccia struthiopteris
OSTRICH FERN, SHUTTLECOCK FERN
☀ ❀ ↔ 18–30 in (45–75 cm) ↑ 36–60 in (90–150 cm)
A fern from North America, East Asia, and Europe. Clumps of arching, leathery, pale green fronds. Dark brown spore-bearing fronds in the center of the clump, develop from summer to late winter and persist for up to a year. Zones 3–10.

MICROSORUM
syns *Microsorium, Phymatosorus*
This genus of 40 to 50 mostly epiphytic ferns from tropical and subtropical Africa, Asia, Australasia, and Polynesia belongs in the polypody (Polypodiaceae) family. The plants' surface-creeping or climbing rhizomes may be smooth or covered in scales and roots. Fronds arising from the rhizomes are stalked, simple or divided. The genus name is from the Greek *mikros*, meaning small, and *soros*, meaning mound, referring to the scattered spore bodies of most species.
CULTIVATION: These ferns prefer a position in full sun to half-shade in a moist, well-drained soil or fibrous mix. Propagate by division of rhizomes or from spores, from spring.

Microsorum grossum
syns *Microsorum grossum, M. scolopendrium*
☀ ⚘ ↔ 24–36 in (60–90 cm)
↑ 24–36 in (60–90 cm)
A medium-sized, normally epiphytic fern found growing in eastern Australia and Polynesia. Species widely used in the tropics as a ground cover. Has long-creeping rhizomes. Deeply lobed, leathery, triangular fronds, on short stalks are borne in summer. Spore bodies are located along the mid-ribs of the lobes. Zones 11–12.

Microsorum punctatum
syns *Microsorium punctatum, Polypodium-polycarpon*
CLIMBING BIRD'S NEST FERN
☀ ⚘ ↔ 5 ft (1.5 m) ↑ 40 in 100 cm)
Epiphytic fern found growing in tropical Africa, Asia, Australasia, and Polynesia. Has a dense ground-covering habit. Woody to fleshy, creeping, scaly, brownish rhizome. Long, simple, smooth, fleshy yet tough, pale to olive green, sword-shaped fronds appear in summer. Dot-like spore bodies. Zones 11–12.

Nephrolepis cordifolia

NEPHROLEPIS
BOSTON FERN, FISHBONE FERN, SWORD FERN
These ferns are found in the wild in many tropical areas such as Asia, Africa, Central America, and the West Indies. This genus of about 40 species belongs to the family Davalliaceae. They are terrestrial or epiphytic with short rhizomes and usually wiry spreading runners. The long tapering fronds bear varying numbers of alternating leaflets and may be erect, arching, or pendulous. Colonies become established quickly and some species are a weedy nuisance in warm countries.
CULTIVATION: These fern species are popular house plants in cool climates. Indoors they require bright filtered light and a humid atmosphere. In warm climates they are not fussy and are easily grown in part-shade or sun in reasonably moist soil, but they can become rampant. Propagate by division or from spores.

Microsorum punctatum

Nephrolepis cordifolia
ERECT SWORD FERN, LADDER FERN
☀ ⚘ ↔ 12–48 in (30–120 cm)
↑ 12–48 in (30–120 cm)
Native to tropics of the world. Erect or arching fronds, yellowish green to dark green. Blunt-ended, narrow, leathery leaflets. 'Duffii' (Duff's sword fern), dense fronds, often forked, crowded rounded leaflets; 'Kimberley Queen', tidier habit, tolerates more sun; and 'Plumosa', leaflets with lobed margins. Zones 10–12.

Nephrolepis exaltata
☀ ⚘ ↔ 36 in (90 cm) ↑ 36 in (90 cm)
A species native to the tropical regions of Africa, Asia, and the Americas. Tufted ferns with long, arching, pale lime green fronds, wavy-edged leaflets. 'Bostoniensis' (Boston fern) has broad lance-shaped fronds, pale lime green, fronds cascade as they mature; 'Bostoniensis Aurea' (golden Boston fern), lime green-gold fronds; 'Childsii', a hardy indoor plant, features broad pale green fronds that overlap each other; 'Hillii', fast-growing, with crested double fronds, a very adaptable cultivar; and 'Mini Ruffle', a miniature form with broad triangular-shaped fronds, has a definite lacy appearance. Zones 10–12.

ONOCLEA

BEAD FERN, SENSITIVE FERN

This genus contains a single species of deciduous fern that belongs to the shield-fern (Dryopteridaceae) family. It is native to eastern North America and eastern Asia where it grows in damp grassy or woodland areas. Fronds are pale green, often bronze-pink on opening, and sterile and fertile fronds are different in appearance. The common name of sensitive fern arises because the leaflets of the sterile fronds fold together in cold weather. The other common name refers to the bead-like leaflets of the fertile fronds. CULTIVATION: Grow in damp soil in part-shade. Suitable for waterside and woodland gardens. Can be an invasive plant where conditions suit. Propagate by division or from spores.

Onoclea sensibilis

◑/☀ ❄ ↔ 24 in (60 cm) ↕ 36 in (90 cm)

From eastern North America and eastern Asia. A spreading fern with triangular, pinnate, sterile fronds up to 36 in (90 cm) long. Fertile fronds, to 24 in (60 cm) long, are narrow with bead-like leaflets, and persist over winter. Zones 4–9.

OSMUNDA

This genus of about 10 species of tall, perennial, deciduous or evergreen, clump-forming ferns in the royal-fern (Osmundaceae) family is found in moist woods and shaded roadsides. Native to temperate and tropical areas in East Asia and North and South America, these deep-rooted ferns are attractive, rugged, and adaptable. In autumn, the green fronds turn a soft golden yellow. Fibrous dense roots may be used as a medium for growing epiphytes or orchids and are rich in nutrients. The unfurled young fronds (called croziers) are gathered in spring and are cooked as a delicacy called fiddleheads. CULTIVATION: Grow in partial shade in damp soil or at the water's edge. Top-dress in spring with rich compost and remove dead fronds. Propagate by division in autumn or sow spores when ripe. Plants may take some time to recover after dividing.

Osmunda claytoniana

INTERRUPTED FERN

☀ ❄ ↔ 24–36 in (60–90 cm) ↕ 16–40 in (40–100 cm)

Native to eastern North America. Deciduous fronds grow 24–48 in (60–120 cm) long. Stems round in cross-section, sometimes with fuzzy tufts. Fertile leaflets in the middle of the frond wither away, leaving a space or interruption, hence the common name. Zones 3–9.

Osmunda regalis

LOCUST FERN, ROYAL FERN

◐/☀ ❄ ↔ 36 in (90 cm) ↕ 24–60 in (60–150 cm)

From North, Central, and South America, Europe, and Asia. Large compound leaves. Broadly oval to oblong, bright green fronds make a dense rounded clump. Coppery

brown and bronze croziers, in spring. '**Purpurascens**', red to purplish fronds turn green in early summer; '**Cristata**', leathery green fronds, maturing to rich golden brown. Zones 3–10.

PELLAEA

CLIFF BRAKE

This is a genus of 80 small to medium-sized, rock-loving ferns belonging to the maidenhair-fern (Adiantaceae) family. Species are found growing mostly in tropical to warm-temperate regions. Plants have creeping or short rhizomes. The divided fronds are carried on dark or black stems, with small broad leaflets; spore-bodies are carried in bands along the frond margins. The genus is named from the Greek *pellos*, dusky, referring to the bluish gray leaves of some species. CULTIVATION: Cliff brakes prefer a rich, well-drained, slightly alkaline soil, in a partially or fully shaded protected position with high humidity. Propagate these ferns from spores or by division.

Pellaea falcata

syn. *Platyloma falcatum*

AUSTRALIAN CLIFF BRAKE, SICKLE FERN

☀ ▯ ↔ 6–9 in (15–22 cm) ↕ 6–9 in (15–22 cm)

Small, variable, terrestrial fern found naturally from temperate to subtropical areas from Australia, New Zealand, and some Pacific Islands. It features stout, creeping rhizomes and wiry, dark brown stems, 2–6 in (5–15 cm) long, covered with dark brown scales when young. The fishbone-like, shiny, leathery fronds can reach up to 18 in (45 cm) long. Sword-shaped leaflets grow up to 2 in (5 cm) long, and are a dull dark green above and a brownish color on the undersides. Zones 9–11.

Pellaea rotundifolia

ROUNDLEAF FERN

◐ ▯ ↔ 15–18 in (38–45 cm) ↕ 12–18 in (30–45 cm)

A fern found growing naturally in New Zealand and Australia, with creeping stout rhizomes. Narrowly oblong, dull dark green fronds can reach 6–12 in (15–30 cm) long, and have narrowly oblong to nearly circular, minutely serrated leaflets that are carried on stems up to 6 in (15 cm) tall. Stems of the roundleaf fern are covered with rust-colored scales. Zones 9–12.

Osmunda regalis

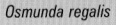

Osmunda regalis

PHLEBODIUM

This genus of 4 evergreen or semi-evergreen ferns belongs to the polypody (Polypodiaceae) family. Native to tropical America and the West Indies, they have thick, fleshy, creeping rhizomes sheathed with rust-colored to gold scales, and smooth, oval, divided fronds, leathery or papery in texture, on jointed stems. The genus name comes from the Greek *phlebodes,* meaning full of veins, and refers to the many veins on the fronds.

CULTIVATION: *Phlebodium* species like a rich, well-drained, moist soil in half-sun to shade, with regular watering and protection from frost. They are suited to cultivation in pots or in hanging baskets, and are propagated from spores or by division.

Phlebodium aureum
syn. *Polypodium aureum*
HARE'S FOOT FERN, RABBIT'S FOOT FERN

☀ ❦ ↔ 24–36 in (60–90 cm) ↕ 24–36 in (60–90 cm)

A widespread and variable evergreen epiphytic fern, found on palm trunks or tree limbs in tropical and subtropical regions of Mexico and the West Indies. Thick creeping rhizomes covered with golden yellow hairs. Deeply divided fronds, oval to triangular, up to 40 in (100 cm) long. Large narrow or strap-shaped leaflets vary in color from grayish green and silvery green to an intense powdery-looking blue-green, often with undulating margins. Leaflets turn purplish in cold weather. There are several cultivars with highly crested or wavy-edged fronds that are a metallic gray-blue in color, including: *P. a.* var. **areolatum**, erect, smooth, leathery fronds; '**Mandanum**', leaflets curved and wavy; '**Mayi**', ruffled and fringed leaflets. Zones 10–12.

PHOENIX

This genus in the palm (Arecaceae) family consists of around 17 species, mostly found growing in tropical and subtropical Africa, Madagascar, Canary Islands, Crete, and southern and western Asia. Solitary or clustered feather-leafed palms, with separate male and female plants, they have long pinnate leaves, with the lower leaflets on each frond reduced to stiff sharp spines. Panicles of small, 3-petalled, often yellow flowers are followed by yellow, orange, green, brown, or red to black fruits with one grooved seed. Some species produce dates and palm sugar.

CULTIVATION: Most *Phoenix* species do best when well-watered in productive soils, but they are fairly adaptable and will tolerate poorer drier soils in full sun as long as drainage is good. Propagate these useful palms from seed, or from suckers from suckering varieties. Remove old fronds carefully.

Phoenix canariensis ★
CANARY ISLAND DATE PALM

☀ ❧ ↔ 30 ft (9 m) ↕ 70 ft (21 m)

From the Canary Islands. Spreading crown, thick trunk covered in old frond base scars. Large, arching, green fronds up to 20 ft (6 m) long, sharply spined at the base. Cream to yellow flowers in drooping panicles, many orange fruits. Can be massive and set lots of seed; dispose of seeds carefully. Zones 9–11.

Phoenix reclinata
AFRICAN WILD DATE, SENEGAL DATE PALM

☀ ❧ ↔ 35 ft (10 m) ↕ 40 ft (12 m)

Palm from tropical Africa. Clustering habit; many slender trunks clothed with fibrous remains of old leaf stalks. Fronds up to 10 ft (3 m) long, with deep green leaflets, arranged irregularly, mostly in several planes. Small orange-red to black fruits. Zones 9–11.

Phoenix roebelenii ★
DWARF DATE PALM

☀ ❧ ↔ 8 ft (2.4 m) ↕ 10 ft (3 m)

A popular, elegant, small palm from Laos. Solitary rough trunk clothed with the remains of old frond stalks. Attractive, arching, deep green fronds, leaflets silvery beneath, lower leaflets reduced to sharp spines. Panicles of cream flowers followed by small, egg-shaped, black fruits. Zones 10–12.

PLATYCERIUM
syn. *Alcicornium*
ANTELOPE EARS, ELKHORN FERN, STAGHORN FERN

This genus is made up of about 18 evergreen, epiphytic ferns, members of the polypody (Polypodiaceae) family, widely spread throughout tropical areas. A short rhizome, concealed by the fronds, normally clasps the tree supporting the plant. Broad, flat, overlapping sterile fronds to 6 ft (1.8 m) long, without stems, become brown and papery with age. The erect or drooping, repeatedly forked fertile fronds grow on stems from the base of the sterile fronds, with spore-bodies underneath. The genus is named from the Greek *platys,* meaning broad, and *keras,* meaning a horn, referring to the branching habit of the fertile fronds.

CULTIVATION: These ferns are normally grown either on tree trunks or fastened to pieces of wood. They prefer warm, humid conditions in part-shade, in fibrous, peaty, and well-drained compost. Propagate them by division of suckers in spring or summer, or from spores during summer or early autumn.

Platycerium bifurcatum
COMMON STAGHORN FERN, ELKHORN FERN

☀ ❧ ↔ 27–40 in (70–100 cm) ↕ 27–40 in (70–100 cm)

A species found growing naturally in Southeast Asia, Polynesia, and northern Australia. Grayish green sterile fronds are erect,

Phlebodium aureum
var. *areolatum* 'Mandanum'

Phoenix canariensis

Platycerium veitchii

rounded, wavy and shallowly lobed, papery, stem-less, up to 24 in (60 cm) long. Fertile fronds are drooping, divided, up to 36 in (90 cm) long, with strap-like segments. *P. b.* var. *majus*, larger, greener, more leathery form. Zones 8–10.

Platycerium veitchii

SILVER ELKHORN FERN

☀ ⚘ ↔ 32 in (80 cm) ↑ 60 in (150 cm)
A native of northeastern Australia. Has stem-less, elliptical, brownish sterile fronds, to 18 in (45 cm) long, close together and forked into 2 strap-like lobes. Erect, spreading fertile fronds, that can reach up to 27 in (70 cm), divide into up to 3 twisted, triangular to linear lobes. Both frond types have a silvery appearance from the fine white hairs on the undersides. Zones 9–11.

POLYPODIUM

POLYPODY

This is a genus of about 75 deciduous, semi-evergreen or ever-green, epiphytic, rock-dwelling, or terrestrial ferns in the polypody (Polypodiaceae) family, from temperate regions of the Northern Hemisphere. They have stemmed, simple or divided fronds, with yellow spore-bodies on the backs of veins, and grow from creeping scaly rhizomes. The fronds dry up and fall in summer, but new fronds appear with autumn rain. The genus name comes from the Greek words *polys*, meaning many, and *pous*, meaning foot, refer-ring to the much-branching rhizomes.
CULTIVATION: Polypody prefer a fibrous, well-drained soil but will cope with heavy clay or gravel that is kept moist, particularly in winter, in a part-shade position. Propagate from spores in late summer, or by division of clumps or rhizomes in spring.

Polypodium californicum

CALIFORNIA POLYPODY

☀ ⚘ ↔ 20 in (50 cm) ↑ 40 in (100 cm)
This is a summer-deciduous, creeping, perennial fern that natu-rally inhabits moist rock crevices in California, USA. Arching,

deeply divided, oblong to triangular, green fronds, up to 12 in (30 cm) long and 6 in (15 cm) across, carried on straw-colored stems up to 8 in (20 cm) high. Zones 7–10.

Polypodium triseriale

ANGLE-VEIN FERN

☀ ⚘ ↔ 16–24 in (40–60 cm) ↑ 16–24 in (40–60 cm)
A species of fern from the West Indies, Central America, and northern South America. Herbaceous or leathery, divided fronds can reach up to 24 in (60 cm) long. The spreading, narrow, strap-shaped leaflets carried on lustrous, straw-colored to reddish brown stems up to 14 in (35 cm) long. Zones 9–10.

Polypodium triseriale

Polypodium vulgare

ADDER'S FERN, COMMON POLYPODY, GOLDEN MAIDENHAIR, WALL FERN

☀ ✳ ↔ 10–12 in (25–30 cm) ↑ 10–12 in (25–30 cm)
An evergreen fern, widely distributed throughout North America, Europe, Africa, and East Asia, suited to rock gardens. It grows from creeping, brownish, scarred rhizomes covered with copper-brown scales. Arching or erect, smooth, thinly tex-tured, sword-shaped to oval, leathery, herring-bone-like fronds, up to 12 in (30 cm) long, with closely set, horizontal or spreading segments carried on straw-colored stems. Zones 3–5.

POLYSTICHUM

HOLLY FERN, SWORD FERN

This genus consists of more than 175 ever-green, semi-evergreen, or deciduous terrestrial ferns, widely distributed throughout the world. Members of the shield-fern (Dryopteridaceae) family, they grow from stout, woody, densely scaly, erect or sprawling rhizomes. Tufted, thin to leathery fronds are divided pinnately to tripinnately into toothed leaflets with a tapered base, with rounded spore-bodies underneath, car-ried on straw-like, densely scaly stems. The genus is named from the Greek *polys*, meaning many, and *stichos*, meaning a row or file, a reference to the regular rows of spore.
CULTIVATION: These ferns prefer a position in partial shade and a moist well-drained soil with plenty of organic matter. Keep the plants tidy by removing dead fronds. Propagate by division in spring or from spores sown in summer.

Polystichum acrostichoides

CHRISTMAS FERN, DAGGER FERN

☀ ✳ ↔ 18–24 in (45–60 cm) ↑ 18–24 in (45–60 cm)
An evergreen fern from wooded slopes of North America. One of its common names reflects the resemblance of its leaf segments to Christmas stockings. Compact, sometimes branched rhizome covered with brownish orange scales, has long fibrous roots. The narrowly sword-shaped fronds, 8–30 in (20–75 cm) long, have 20 to 35 finely toothed, dark green leaflets per side; these have hair-like scales underneath and a densely scaly midrib. Native Americans used the rhizomes to make a tea to treat chills, fevers, pneumonia, and to induce vomiting. Zones 3–9.

Polystichum setiferum

Polystichum aculeatum

HARD SHIELD FERN, PRICKLY SHIELD FERN

☀ ❄ ↔ 18–24 in (45–60 cm) ↕ 18–24 in (45–60 cm)

Variable evergreen or semi-evergreen fern from Europe has rigid, sword-shaped, leathery fronds, 12–36 in (30–90 cm) long, with up to 50 toothed leaflets per side. Fronds are yellowish green in spring, maturing to dark glossy green, carried on short brown stems. **Densum Group**, densely massed fronds; '**Pulcherrimum**', sharply edged, delicate, dark green fronds. Zones 4–8.

Polystichum polyblepharon

HOLLY FERN, TASSEL FERN

☀ ❄ ↔ 48 in (120 cm) ↕ 48 in (120 cm)

An evergreen or semi-evergreen fern from South Korea and Japan. Narrowly oblong to oval, deep green, slightly lustrous fronds, which unfurl in a normal manner. They are clothed with white scales, then flip backward in a lax droop or tassel habit. They are 12–32 in (30–80 cm) long, have leaflets with oblong to oval, overlapping leaflets. The fronds are densely scaly on the underside, and are carried on stout brown stalks. Zones 5–9.

Polystichum setiferum

SOFT SHIELD FERN

☀ ❄ ↔ 18–24 in (45–60 cm) ↕ 18–24 in (45–60 cm)

Evergreen or semi-evergreen fern, from southern, western, and central Europe. Soft, sword-shaped, mid-green fronds, 12–48 in (30–120 cm) long, with up to 40 leaflets per side, carried on stalks that are covered with pale orange to brown scales. Bulbils form on frond midribs. **Cristatum Group**, crested, dark green, frilly fronds. **Divisilobum Group ★**, large, very frilly, light green fronds; group includes '**Divisilobum Densum**', delicate-looking fern; and '**Herrenhausen**', leathery, dark green fronds with pointed leaflets. **Plumosodivisilobum Group** with compact soft fronds, includes '**Plumosum Densum**', slightly smaller version with frilly lace-like fronds. '**Pulcherrimum Bevis**', elongated crested tips on ends of fronds; **Rotundatum Group**, fronds with rounded leaflets; and '**Wakeleyanum**', narrow fronds, with leaflets forming cross-pattern across midrib. Zones 5–9.

Polystichum tsussimense

syn. *Aspidium tsussimense*

KOREAN ROCK FERN, TSU-SHIMA HOLLY FERN

☀ ❄ ↔ 12–16 in (30–40 cm) ↕ 6–18 in (15–45 cm)

Clump-forming, evergreen or semi-evergreen fern, native to northeastern Asia, with thin, gently tapering, broadly sword-shaped to oval, dull green fronds, with distinctive black veining, 8–16 in (20–40 cm) long. Oval, finely toothed leaflets are carried on pale green to straw-colored stems covered with black to brown scales. Zones 6–9.

PRITCHARDIA

This is a genus of around 25 species of tropical fan palms, in the family Arecaceae, native to the Pacific Islands. They are grown for their impressive, large, flat fronds that are divided only about halfway to the midrib and have a neat pleated appearance. These palms, which may reach up to 70 ft (21 m) tall, have a smooth, slender, columnar trunk with grooved rings. They produce small, cream to orange, bell-shaped flowers in spikes or panicles at the base of the crown, usually in summer. These are followed by small dark brown to black fruits.

CULTIVATION: Frost tender, they need a warm humid climate and prefer humus-enriched well-drained soil in full sun with some protection from midday sun when young. Propagate from seed.

Pritchardia hillebrandii

LELO PALM, LOULOU

☀ ✦ ↔ 12–20 ft (3.5–6 m) ↕ 15–25 ft (4.5–8 m)

Solitary, unarmed fan palm from the Hawaiian Islands with fan-shaped, bluish green fronds with stiff leaflets with a waxy coating, carried on bluish green stems that are densely woolly underneath. Shiny, bluish black, spherical fruit. Zones 10–12.

Pritchardia pacifica ★

FIJI FAN PALM

☀ ✦ ↔ 15 ft (4.5 m) ↕ 30 ft (9 m)

Probably originally native to Tonga. Fan palm with very wide, lush, long-stemmed, pleated fronds, dense foliage head, rain-shedding skirt. Insignificant heads of yellow flowers. Fruit blackens when ripe. Zones 11–12.

Pritchardia thurstonii

Pritchardia thurstonii

☀ ✦ ↔ 12 ft (3.5 m) ↕ 25 ft (8 m)

Occurring in large colonies on one of the Fijian island groups. A slender palm with fan-shaped pleated leaves. Inflorescences to 8 ft (2.4 m) long hang below the leaves; bears yellow flowers. Dark red globular fruits. Zones 11–12.

PTERIDIUM

BRACKEN, BRAKE

This genus of the bracken (Dennstaedtiaceae) family occurs worldwide, except for arctic and arid regions. Botanists disagree about the number of species: some argue that all bracken plants fall within such a narrow range of variation that only one species (*P. aquilinum*) can be recognized, though divided into varieties;

others recognize a number of species, most with large geographical ranges that do not overlap. Fronds are tough, triangular, much-divided, arising from deeply buried, long-running, repeatedly branched rhizomes; one plant can form a patch 50 ft (15 m) or more across. Spores are borne in continuous bands along curled-under margins of frond segments, but reproduction from spores seems rare as plants spread so effectively by rhizomes. Fronds are frost-killed in autumn and new ones emerge in spring. Bracken is often seen as a weed because of its aggressive spread and difficulty of removal. Farmers dislike it because it smothers pastures and is toxic to livestock, but it is part of a healthy natural ecosystem and provides shelter to birds and other wildlife. Some hunter-gatherer societies eat the starchy rhizomes.

CULTIVATION: Deliberate cultivation of *Pteridium* species is rarely attempted; management of bracken is usually the requirement. It is resistant to many herbicides. The most successful removal method from grassed areas is continual cutting; this strategy eventually depletes its food reserves.

Pteridium aquilinum

☼/☀ ❋ ↔ 30–60 ft (9–18 m) ↑ 2–8 ft (0.6–2.4 m)
Common bracken of Europe, Asia, Africa, and temperate North America. Fronds hairy beneath to varying degrees, more so when young, bipinnate with primary divisions regularly spaced and evenly tapering, the secondary divisions deeply and fairly regularly lobed. *P. a.* var. *latiusculum* is the race from eastern North America, while *P. a.* var. *pubescens* is widespread in western North America. Zones 3–10.

Pteridium esculentum

syn. *Pteridium aquilinum* var. *esculentum*
☼/☀ ❋ ↔ 60 ft (18 m) ↑ 10 ft (3 m)
Common bracken of Australia, New Zealand, and some South Pacific islands. Fronds somewhat irregularly divided with thick but narrow segments, hairless except when young. Zones 8–11.

PTERIS

BRAKE, DISH FERN, TABLE FERN
This genus is made up of about 300 semi-evergreen or evergreen terrestrial ferns, native to tropical and subtropical regions and part of the brake (Pteridaceae) family. The plants have erect or creeping, scaly or hairy rhizomes and deciduous, arching, divided fronds on slender, erect, grooved stems. Spore-bodies are carried in hair-like structures along the frond margins. *Pteris* is the Greek word for fern, referring to the feathery fronds.

CULTIVATION: Brakes can grow in sun or shade, depending on the species, in moist peaty soil. Propagate these ground-dwellers by division in spring or from spores sown in summer.

Pteris argyraea

SILVER BRAKE
☀ ✂ ↔ 20–40 in (50–100 cm) ↑ 3–6 ft (0.9–1.8 m)
Evergreen fern native to the tropics. The erect or short-creeping rhizome is covered with papery brown scales. Green fronds with a broad, silvery white center line and narrow, oblong leaflets that grow 6–12 in (15–30 cm) long. Zones 10–12.

Pteris cretica

CRETAN BRAKE, RIBBON FERN
☀ ✂ ↔ 12–20 in (30–50 cm) ↑ 12–20 in (30–50 cm)
This evergreen or semi-evergreen fern is native to tropical regions of the Old World. It grows from slender, erect or short-creeping rhizomes. The fronds are oval or rounded, to 12 in (30 cm) long, with 1 to 5 pairs of simple or finger-like, forked, narrow, olive green leaflets, 4–8 in (10–20 cm) long, on slender, straw-colored stems. 'Albolineata' ★ has wider leaflets with a broad white stripe; 'Mayi' is up to 12 in (30 cm) high and has crested frond tips; and 'Wilsonii' has crested bright green fronds that give the plant a fan-like appearance. Zones 10–12.

Pteris ensiformis

syn. *Pteris crenata*
SWORD BRAKE
☀ ✂ ↔ 8–12 in (20–30 cm) ↑ 8–12 in (20–30 cm)
A slender fern found growing naturally from the Himalayas to Japan, the Philippines, Polynesia, and tropical Australia. It has dark green fronds, 6–12 in (15–30 cm) long, with slightly compound terminal leaflets and 4 to 5 pairs of lateral leaflets cut into 2- to 6-toothed oval lobes, grayish white around the midribs. 'Arguta', up to 20 in (50 cm) tall, features dark green fronds with central silvery white markings. Zones 10–12.

Pteridium esculentum, in the wild, New Caledonia

Pteris tricolor
PAINTED BRAKE

☀ ⊰ ↔ 3 ft (0.9 m) ↕ 5 ft (1.5 m)

Evergreen fern with broad, very glossy, triangular fronds divided into long, finger-like leaflets. Foliage emerges brilliant red, ages to copper or bronze, finally becoming dark green. The stems are a dark mahogany color. Zones 10–11.

Pteris umbrosa
JUNGLE BRAKE

☀ ⊰ ↔ 27–40 in (70–100 cm) ↕ 27–40 in (70–100 cm)

Evergreen fern forms dense clumps in sheltered positions in its native Australia, from a stout, creeping, brown, scaly rhizome. Erect dark green fronds, 12–20 in (30–50 cm) long, with narrow, finely toothed leaflets, 6 to 9 lateral leaflets per side. Zones 10–11.

Rhapis excelsa

PTYCHOSPERMA

These 30 solitary or clump-forming, feathery palms belong to the family Arecaceae and are native to northern Australia, New Guinea, the Solomon Islands, and Micronesia. They have slender, smooth, ringed trunks and distinct crownshafts. Gracefully curved, divided fronds have slender pointed leaflets, jagged or smooth-edged at the tips. Flowers are spirally arranged in groups of 3. The fruit is small, egg-shaped or elliptical, and sometimes beaked, containing a single furrowed seed. The genus is named from the Greek *ptychos*, wrinkled, and *sperma*, seed.

CULTIVATION: These palms need warmth and humidity, in a shaded position when young, in moist, well-drained and composted soil. Propagate from seed, which takes 6 to 12 weeks to germinate.

Ptychosperma elegans ★
syn. *Seaforthia elegans*
SEAFORTHIA PALM, SOLITAIRE PALM

☼ ✦ ↔ 10–12 ft (3–3.5 m) ↕ 12–50 ft (3.5–15 m)

A fast-growing palm found growing naturally in northeastern Australia. It has a gray, solitary trunk, and a woolly green crownshaft. There are relatively few, arching, bright green leaves, to 8 ft (2.4 m) long, and these have regularly arranged leaflets to 24 in (60 cm) long, toothed or notched at the tips. They are carried on long stems emerging from under the crownshaft. The large branching clusters of fragrant greenish white flowers are followed by large clusters of decorative, bright red, spherical to oval, berry-like fruit. Zones 10–11.

Ptychosperma macarthurii ★
syn. *Actinophloeus macarthurii*
MACARTHUR PALM

☀ ✦ ↔ 6–12 ft (1.8–3.5 m) ↕ 15–25 ft (4.5–8 m)

A densely clumping evergreen palm, native to New Guinea and northeastern Australia, common in tropical gardens. Develops a gray trunk, with a green woolly crownshaft. Small crown of dark green, arched fronds, reaching to 6 ft (1.8 m) long, with regularly

Ptychosperma macarthurii

arranged, broad leaflets with toothed tips. Branching sprays of yellowish flowers, produced on stems emerging from below the crownshaft, mostly during summer months, growing into long pendulous clusters of bright red fruits. Zones 10–11.

RHAPIS

This genus in the family Arecaceae consists of 12 species of small multi-stemmed palms found in the higher rainfall areas of subtropical and tropical regions of southern China as well as across Southeast Asia. They have a clumping habit, with bamboo-like stems and fan-shaped fronds that are deeply divided into finger-like segments. Rhapis palms are mostly dioecious, so both male and female plants are needed for seed production. Small, bowl-shaped, creamy yellow flowers are produced in panicles. The fruit is berry-like. Highly valued in horticulture, most species are long-lived landscape specimens in the garden; they are also used as a screen, or as tub or indoor plant.

CULTIVATION: Most members of the *Rhapis* genus are fairly adaptable plants, tolerating full sun to semi-shade and bright positions indoors. In full sun, some bleaching of the leaves may occur. Grow these palms in fertile well-drained soil protected from strong winds and frost. Humid conditions favor growth. Propagation is from seed, which can be somewhat slow, or by division.

Rhapis excelsa
LADY PALM, RHAPIS PALM

☀ ⊰ ↔ 8–15 ft (2.4–4.5 m) ↕ 10 ft (3 m)

Found growing naturally in southern China, this is one of the most popular species in the genus. A multi-stemmed fan palm. Slender stems are covered in brown interwoven fibers. Light green fronds, 5 to 8 stiff segments with blunt tips. Bowl-shaped cream flowers, throughout summer. Makes an excellent container plant. 'Variegata' features leaves with a white stripe. Zones 10–12.

Rhapis humilis

SLENDER LADY PALM

☀ ❄ ↔ 10 ft (3 m) ↕ 15 ft (4.5 m)

A native of southern China. Forms a spreading clump; numerous slender stems covered in interwoven brown fibers. Thin dark green fronds divided into many drooping segments with pointed tips. Propagate by division. Excellent indoor plant. Zones 10–12.

RHOPALOSTYLIS

This genus, in the family Arecaceae, contains just 2 species of palm. One is native to Norfolk Island and the Kermadec Islands, and the other, the world's most southerly growing palm, is found in New Zealand. They have pinnately divided fronds arising from the top of a solitary unarmed stem, which bears the scars of fallen leaves. Large heads of tiny flowers hang from below the prominent crownshaft. The red berries that follow are very showy. CULTIVATION: These palms are slow-growing and rather slow to flower. They should be given a shady and sheltered site to prevent damage to the fronds. They require a deep moist soil. In cool-temperate climates they make very good container plants for the greenhouse or conservatory. Propagation is from seed, which can be somewhat slow to germinate.

Rhopalostylis baueri

NORFOLK PALM

☀ ❄ ↔ 15 ft (4.5 m) ↕ 20 ft (6 m)

A native of Norfolk Island, with a subspecies in the Kermadec Islands. Arching deep green fronds, to 10 ft (3 m) long; ringed trunk. Flowerheads up to 24 in (60 cm) long, tiny white flowers, in late spring–summer. Large sprays of red berries. Zones 10–11.

Rhopalostylis sapida ★

NIKAU PALM

☀ ❄ ↔ 10 ft (3 m) ↕ 20–35 ft (6–10 m)

From New Zealand. Wider and lighter green fronds than those of *R. baueri*, arise almost erectly above bulbous crownshaft. Hanging flowerheads of tiny purplish pink flowers, in late spring–summer. Bright red fruits. Tree is 30 years old before flowering. Zones 9–11.

ROYSTONEA

ROYAL PALM

This genus in the family Arecaceae consists of about 10 species of single-stemmed palms, the majority from the humid tropical Caribbean Islands and surrounding coastal regions. These pinnate or feather-leafed palms have a prominent crownshaft. Many species have smooth gray-white trunks that may be swollen in the middle or base. Panicles of small, white, cup-shaped flowers appear from just below the crownshaft, followed by round, often deep purple berries. Most come from fertile low-lying forest areas near the sea, that are sometimes swampy. These palms make useful landscape subjects in the tropics and subtropics, where they are popularly used to line roads and paths or as specimen plantings. CULTIVATION: *Roystonea* palms will give the best results in a moist, well-drained, fertile soil in a position in full sun. They are moderately tolerant of seaside conditions. All species in the genus are self-pollinating, and can be propagated from seed.

Rhopalostylis baueri

Roystonea oleracea

Roystonea borinquena

syns *Oreodoxa borinquena*, *Roystonea hispaniolana*

PUERTO RICAN ROYAL PALM

☼ ❄ ↔ 15–20 ft (4.5–6 m) ↕ 50–60 ft (15–18 m)

A very fast growing palm from the West Indies. Grayish brown trunk, swollen above the middle, reaches about 24 in (60 cm) in diameter at the base. Develops a huge crown of arching, feathery, divided, bright green leaves, to 10 ft (3 m) long and 6 ft (1.8 m) across, with 2 crowded rows of leaflets with divided tips, up to 40 in (100 cm) long. Densely crowded clusters of yellow flowers emerge below the crownshaft, throughout summer. Pale brown oblong fruit, flat on one side. Zones 10–11.

Roystonea oleracea

CARIBBEAN ROYAL PALM

☼ ❄ ↔ 20 ft (6 m) ↕ 130 ft (40 m)

Occurs along Caribbean coast of South America and on Lesser Antilles islands of the West Indies. Grayish trunk swollen at the base, bright shiny green crownshaft, dark green fronds held in one plane, appear flat. Zones 11–12.

SABAL

PALMETTO

This genus in the palm (Arecaceae) family is made up of around 16 species found from southeastern USA to South America, the West Indies, and Bermuda. The plants mostly develop tall erect trunks, but some species are stemless; some have old frond bases remaining, others are clean. All species have fan-shaped fronds that are deeply divided. The small cream flowers are bisexual, and are borne in long sprays growing from between the leaves; they are followed by small berries. The leaves of some *Sabal* species are used for making baskets, hats, and matting; the trunks are used to produce furniture and wharf piles. Most palmetto palms are found growing in swampy areas in the subtropics and tropics. CULTIVATION: Most *Sabal* species are fairly adaptable palms that tolerate a range of soils, from wet to dry, as well as sandy; they even tolerate light frost. The best cultivation results, however, come from planting in a well-drained fertile soil in full sun, with adequate watering in the growth phase. Propagation is from seed.

Sabal causiarum

Sabal mexicana

Sadleria cyatheoides

Sabal bermudana

BERMUDA PALMETTO

☼ ✴ ↔ 10 ft (3 m) ↑ 40 ft (12 m)

A native of Bermuda, smaller in cultivation than the species. Fronds up to 10 ft (3 m) wide, 24 in (60 cm) segments, central section around 12 in (30 cm) wide, undivided. **Zones 10–11.**

Sabal causiarum

PUERTO RICO HAT PALM

☼ ✴ ↔ 20 ft (6 m) ↑ 50 ft (15 m)

From the West Indies islands of Anegada, Hispaniola, and Puerto Rico. Tall, stout, gray trunk. Heavy crown of bright green, sometimes dull blue-green, fan-like fronds to 10 ft (3 m) wide. White flowers in sprays. Small, spherical, black fruits. **Zones 9–12.**

Sabal mexicana

MEXICAN PALMETTO, OAXACA PALMETTO, RIO GRANDE PALMETTO

☼ ✴ ↔ 12 ft (3.5 m) ↑ 60 ft (18 m)

Adaptable species from Texas, USA, and Mexico. Thick trunk, crown of light green fronds. Blades have deeply divided thread-like filaments. Produces inflorescences of small, white, fragrant flowers. Large black fruits. **Zones 9–12.**

Sabal minor ★

DWARF PALMETTO, SCRUB PALMETTO

☼ ✴ ↔ 12 ft (3.5 m) ↑ 10 ft (3 m)

A species from southeastern USA. May form large clump of fronds at ground-level, or above-ground trunk. Large, stiff, blue-green fronds, narrow segments. Flower stalk grows from a clump, extending well above the foliage. **Zones 8–11.**

Sabal palmetto ★

CABBAGE PALM, PALMETTO

☼ ✴ ↔ 15 ft (4.5 m) ↑ 80 ft (24 m)

From southeastern USA. Mature trunk is bare. A large crown of twisted green to blue-green fan fronds, divided into segments, deeply lobed, thread-like filaments between. Inflorescences of small white flowers. Glossy brown to black fruits. **Zones 8–12.**

Sabal uresana

SONORAN PALMETTO

☼ ✴ ↔ 10 ft (3 m) ↑ 25 ft (8 m)

Eye-catching palm from Mexico. Large bluish green fan fronds, deeply divided into spreading segments; juvenile leaves bluer. Inflorescence as long as fronds. Brown fruits. **Zones 8–12.**

SADLERIA

This genus of 4 species of medium to large terrestrial ferns in the hard-fern (Blechnaceae) family is restricted to Hawaii, USA, and is generally found on lava in the wild. Stem is erect and trunk-like with age, with long, undivided scales. The fronds are pinnate, lobed, or bipinnate; the leaf stalks have at least one groove. The leaf segments are firm, veined, ovate to tongue-shaped, with a scalloped to smooth edge, slightly recurved, and hairless or with scales beneath. The spore-bodies form continuous lines along both sides of the midrib.

CULTIVATION: Grow these ferns in acid soils in frost-free humid sites, in shade, with no more than 6 hours of sun each day; keep moist year round. In temperate regions, grow under glass in a soil-less medium rich in crocks (although they are too big for all but the largest greenhouses). Propagate from spores.

Sadleria cyatheoides ★

☼ ✱ ↔ 2–4 ft (0.6–1.2 m) ↑ 2–5 ft (0.6–1.5 m)

A small tree fern, can form sizeable trunk with age. Emerging fronds pinkish red, becoming dark green and leathery. Leaflets have toothed margins. **Zones 10–12.**

SELAGINELLA

This genus in the spikemoss (Selaginellaceae) family consists of about 700 species of evergreen, creeping, ground-covering plants found in tropical and temperate regions right around the world.

Distinctive to the genus is the dainty fern-like foliage that covers the slightly hairy ground-hugging stems. The long creeping branches of spikemoss species can travel some distance over soil, shrubs, and rocky areas.

CULTIVATION: Cultivate these species in an open moist soil rich in humus. Spores form on the ends of leafy spikes, and can be harvested when ripe in order to propagate new plants. Alternatively, divide the rhizomes in summer or the rooted stems in spring.

Selaginella kraussiana
TRAILING SPIKEMOSS

☀/◑ ❄ ↔ 24–36 in (60–90 cm) ↑ 1 in (2.5 cm)

Perennial species from tropical and southern Africa. Trailing stems of bright green foliage; forms dense mats. Ideal for hanging baskets. 'Aurea', pale yellow to lime green foliage; 'Brownii', dense dark green to brown foliage, compact plant; 'Variegata', green foliage with creamy yellow streaks. Zones 10–11.

Selaginella martensii

☀ ❄ ↔ 8 in (20 cm), ↑ 6 in (15 cm)

A scrambling trailing perennial from Central America. Produces many-branched stems, and has glossy green leaves. Zones 10–11.

Selaginella uncinata
PEACOCK MOSS

☀ ❄ ↔ 18–36 in (45–90 cm) ↑ 2 in (5 cm)

Found growing naturally in China. Features delicate foliage with a trailing rooting system on its stems. Foliage has a distinctive gun-metal blue sheen. Zones 7–11.

SERENOA

This genus of palms in the family Arecaceae consists of a single species from southeastern USA, where it forms large colonies, particularly in coastal areas. It is short and has fan-shaped fronds. Branching flowerheads arise from within the foliage.

CULTIVATION: This adaptable palm grows in a range of soils and climates, including coastal areas, where it tolerates salt-laden winds. It does best in warm subtropical areas, and should be grown in a sunny situation. In cool climates it can be grown in pots in the greenhouse. Propagation is from seed.

Serenoa repens ★
SAW PALMETTO

☀ ❄ ↔ 7 ft (2 m) ↑ 3–15 ft (0.9–4.5 m)

Palm with a branching prostrate or subterranean trunk, forms dense clumps. Fan-shaped yellowish green to bluish and silvery green fronds are deeply divided into stiff segments, and borne on very thorny stalks. Produces fragrant cream flowers on branching woolly flowerheads. Zones 8–11.

SYAGRUS
syn. *Arecastrum*

This genus in the palm (Arecaceae) family consists of 32 species native to South America. Their fronds have a feathery appearance. Trunks may be single or clustered (some species are trunkless) and become smooth and ringed with age. Separate male and female flowers are produced in panicles on the same tree, followed by fibrous fleshy fruit. Some species are a source of palm kernel oil and wax. Most are suitable for growing in tropical and subtropical regions. *S. romanzoffiana* is suited to temperate areas. They may be grown as indoor plants but other palms from different genera are often better suited to indoor cultivation.

CULTIVATION: Most are adaptable and very hardy once established. They perform best in a well-drained moderately fertile soil with adequate watering and added fertilizer. They will tolerate seaside conditions and will grow in full sun to part-shade. Remove old fronds. Propagate from seed. These palms will transplant readily.

Syagrus flexuosa
ACUMA, PALMITO DO CAMPO

☀ ↗ ↔ 7–15 ft (2–4.5 m) ↑ 7–15 ft (2–4.5 m)

Solitary-trunked or clumping palm native to Brazil. A crown of arching gray fronds. Narrow leaflets arranged in groups of 2 to 4 along the stem. Flowering spikes borne within leaves. Zones 10–12.

Selaginella martensii

Serenoa repens

Syagrus romanzoffiana

Syagrus romanzoffiana ★

syns *Arecastrum romanzoffianum, Cocos plumosa*

COCOS PALM, QUEEN PALM

☀ ❄ ↔ 25 ft (8 m) ↑ 50 ft (15 m)

From Brazil. Gray trunk, thick head of deep green plume-like fronds to 15 ft (4.5 m). Cream flowers in panicles. Large heavy bunches of fat, orange, edible fruits highly favored by bats and insects. Zones 9–12.

Syagrus sancona

❄ ❄ ↔ 20 ft (6 m) ↑ 20–40 ft (6–12 m)

A rainforest palm native to South America. Single-trunked, with a graceful crown of arching fronds to 12 ft (3.5 m) long. Narrow leaflets arranged in groups of 2 to 4. Zones 10–12.

THRINAX

THATCH PALM

This genus, a member of the palm (Arecaceae) family, is made up of 7 species, the majority occurring in Florida, USA, the Caribbean Islands, Mexico, and Belize. Thatch palms are solitary-trunked fan palms with palmately lobed fronds on long unarmed stalks. The small flowers are cup-shaped and self-pollinating, borne in panicles from between the fronds and followed by fruit that is usually white. Members of this genus can be found growing in alkaline soils, from sea level to higher areas near the coast, including woodlands and mountain rainforests. They are very attractive palms, most being suited to tropical and subtropical regions although some are grown in warm-temperate zones. Thatch palms will make very handsome specimens or they can be used in garden bed plantings in combination with other species, or for tub planting.

CULTIVATION: They will give the best results when they are grown in well-drained soil in a warm sunny position that gives them protection from cold winds. In nature they grow in limestone soils. They are tolerant of salt winds. Propagation of these palms is from seed.

Thrinax morrisii

BRITTLE THATCH PALM, PEABERRY PALM

☀ ❄ ↔ 10 ft (3 m) ↑ 35 ft (10 m)

Small palm native to Cuba, the West Indies and Florida, USA. Smooth trunk swollen at base. Fan fronds blue-green, gray underside, small white dots. Arching panicles of tiny flowers, in summer. Clusters of small white fruit. Zones 11–12.

Thrinax parviflora

JAMAICAN FAN PALM, ROYAL PALMETTO

☀ ❄ ↔ 7 ft (2 m) ↑ 10–50 ft (3–15 m)

Variable small to medium palm from Jamaica. Green fan fronds, uneven surface. Fragrant cream to yellow flowers in panicles, in summer. Small white fruit. Zones 10–12.

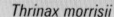
Thrinax morrisii

Thrinax parviflora

Thrinax radiata
FLORIDA THATCH PALM

☼ ⚘ ↔ 7 ft (2 m) ↑ 40 ft (12 m)

From the Caribbean to south Florida, USA. Fan fronds are deep green, on stalks with base clothed in fibers. Upright panicles of small, white, fragrant, summer flowers. White fruit. Zones 10–12.

TRACHYCARPUS
Originally found from southern China to the Himalayas, this is a genus of about 6 species grown for their attractive foliage and their cold tolerance. They are members of the palm (Arecaceae) family. The fan-shaped or circular fronds are up to 5 ft (1.5 m) across and divided almost to the base into stiff, narrow, pleated segments. Frond stalks are often armed with stout sharp teeth. The small fragrant flowers are followed by rounded or kidney-shaped dark purple or orange fruit. These palms are slow-growing and long-lived. They will make very good indoor plants in areas that experience severe frosts.

CULTIVATION: These palms will grow well in any well-drained soil that is reasonably fertile. They need plenty of water and do best in full sun or part-shade in a position that is sheltered from cold winds, especially when they are young. Potted specimens should be watered moderately during the growing season, much less in cooler weather. Propagate these species from fresh seed in spring.

Trachycarpus fortunei ★
CHINESE FAN PALM, CHINESE WINDMILL PALM, CHUSAN PALM

☼ ❄ ↔ 12 ft (3.5 m) ↑ 35 ft (10 m)

A widely cultivated cold-tolerant palm from northern Myanmar and central and eastern China. Slender trunk clothed in loose dark brown fibers and old frond bases. Deep green fan-shaped fronds are divided into many segments. Clusters of small yellow flowers, borne in summer. Bluish fruits. Zones 8–11.

Trachycarpus martianus ★
HIMALAYAN FAN PALM

☼ ⚘ ↔ 10 ft (3 m) ↑ 50 ft (15 m)

A slender-trunked species, native to northern India and Myanmar. Fiber on the trunk is confined to a region near the crown. Large fan fronds are dark green and evenly divided. Drooping yellow flowers appear in summer months. Black fruit. Zones 9–11.

Trachycarpus wagnerianus ★

☼ ⚘ ↔ 8 ft (2.4 m) ↑ 10–20 ft (3–6 m)

Known only in cultivation, this fan palm is probably a form of the far more commonly grown *T. fortunei*. Distinguished by its smaller and stiffer fronds and by the very tightly woven thatch that develops on its trunk. Zones 9–10.

VEITCHIA
This is a genus of 18 palms in the Arecaceae family, found growing naturally in Vanuatu, the Philippines, and Fiji. They develop

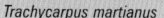

Trachycarpus martianus

Trachycarpus wagnerianus

single ringed trunks, conspicuous crownshafts, and long feather-like fronds. Flowers hang below the crownshaft; they are followed by clusters of red to orange-red fruit.

CULTIVATION: These palms are best suited to being grown in humid tropical areas, where they should be grown in a rich, moist but well-drained soil. Most species require a partly shaded situation when young, becoming more tolerant of sun as they mature. Some make good potted plants for the house or greenhouse in cool climates. Propagation of these species is from fresh seed.

Veitchia arecina

☼/◐ ⚶ ↔ 20 ft (6 m) ↑ 35 ft (10 m)

Native to coastal and lowland forests of Vanuatu. A palm with a slender gray trunk. Prominent whitish crownshaft is topped with a rather flat crown of finely divided fronds. Showy clusters of crimson fruit appear below the crownshaft. Zones 10–12.

Veitchia winin

◐ ⚶ ↔ 10 ft (3 m) ↑ 50 ft (15 m)

From Vanuatu. A relatively fast growing and flowering palm with a very slender trunk, pale green crownshaft, and stiff dark green arching fronds. Bears masses of white flowers. Fruit is bright red. Zones 10–12.

VERSCHAFFELTIA
A monotypic genus in the palm (Arecaceae) family, and native to the Seychelles. Plants are found growing naturally on steep slopes and in gorges, putting out aerial roots for extra anchorage. It is a single-stemmed spiny palm with smooth-edged leaves that are pinnately ribbed, with a prominently notched apex.

CULTIVATION: This interesting palm species is suitable for growing in humid tropical areas, where plants must be given shelter from strong winds. In cool climates, young plants can make interesting potted specimens for the house or greenhouse. Propagation of this palm is from fresh seed.

Veitchia winin

Verschaffeltia splendida

☼ ✣ ↔ 8 ft (2.4 m) ↑ 70 ft (21 m)

Trunk is ringed with long black spines, base has stilt-like aerial roots. Bright green leaves, undivided and pleated at first, later split and appear to be pinnate. Flowerheads arise within the leaves. Round fruits are olive green. Zones 10–12.

WASHINGTONIA

This genus in the palm (Arecaceae) family consists of 2 species from southwest USA and northwestern Mexico. These single-stemmed robust palms have fan leaves. The trunks are clothed in old leaf bases that hang like a skirt or petticoat. The leaves are deeply lobed with fibrous margins, while the small, bisexual, tube-shaped flowers can be creamy white or creamy apricot-pink, in slender hanging clusters among the leaves. The small fruits are drupes, and each contains a single seed. They come from desert areas where they obtain moisture from springs or streams, and can be seen cultivated in drier parts of tropical and subtropical regions as well as in temperate areas. They are useful for lining roadways and for planting in parklands.
CULTIVATION: These are very hardy and adaptable palms in a well-drained soil. They will tolerate full sun, exposed conditions and, once established, drought. Both species grow very tall, so a large garden is a must; dispose of seed carefully, to avoid unwanted proliferation. Decaying foliage can be a fire risk and it is wise to remove it. Propagation is from seed.

Washingtonia filifera ★

COTTON PALM, PETTICOAT PALM, WASHINGTONIA PALM

☼ ⚘ ↔ 25 ft (8 m) ↑ 50 ft (15 m)

Heavy, gray trunk clothed in old leaves. Long spiny leafstalks, gray-green leaves, with thread-like filaments. Panicles of creamy white flowers. Hard blackish drupes. Zones 9–11.

WOODSIA

Widespread in the northern temperate and tropical zones, this group of some 25 species of ferns belongs to the shield-fern (Dryopteridaceae) family. Most species develop short creeping rhizomes that are sometimes adapted for growing over rocks and in narrow crevices. The pinnate fronds, though not very finely divided, rarely grow more than about 16 in (40 cm) long. The

Washingtonia filifera

more northerly species may be deciduous or have greatly reduced fronds throughout the winter months. Many of the species have scaly red-brown stems and this coating can extend to the fronds, which tend to be slightly downy.
CULTIVATION: Those species of *Woodsia* that occur naturally on rocky outcrops, growing in crevices, will tolerate fairly sunny conditions; otherwise plant in half-sun or dappled light with moist, humus-rich soil. Water well during the growing season to encourage lush growth. Propagation is usually by division, which is easiest undertaken in early spring.

Woodsia × *gracilis*

LAWSON'S CLIFF FERN

◑ ❋ ↔ 12–20 in (30–50 cm) ↑ 4–10 in (10–25 cm)

This is a natural hybrid between the 2 species *W. alpina* and *W. ilvensis*. Features fronds up to 8 in (20 cm) long with red scaled stems, scaling sometimes occurring sparsely on fronds, which can have a leathery texture. Zones 4–9.

Woodsia ilvensis

FRAGRANT WOODSIA, RUSTY WOODSIA

◑ ❋ ↔ 12–20 in (30–50 cm) ↑ 4–10 in (10–25 cm)

A North American and Eurasian species often found growing in rock crevices. Fronds grow to 10 in (25 cm) long, often smaller, and have red-brown scales extending to the frond bases and sometimes quite vivid on the stems. Zones 1–9.

Woodsia × *gracilis*

WOODWARDIA

CHAIN FERN

A mainly North American and Asian genus of some 10 species of ferns of the hard-fern (Blechnaceae) family. The rhizomes may be short and stocky or elongated and creeping, sometimes forming short trunks. The fronds, which are usually long, gracefully arching, and borne in a crown, most often occur in distinctly different fertile (spore-bearing) and sterile forms. Frequently the sterile fronds are simple pinnate structures that are not further divided, though a few

Woodwardia fimbriata

Woodwardia unigemmata

species have feathery fronds. The fertile fronds tend to occur toward the center of the crown and are more erect, and often with conspicuous spore-bearing organs (sporangia).
CULTIVATION: They are best grown in humid woodland conditions with humus-rich soil that is well-drained but that remains moist throughout the year. Hardiness does vary considerably with the species. The hardier species are mainly deciduous. Propagation is mainly by division in early spring, though in suitable climates these ferns multiply freely from spores.

Woodwardia areolata

NETTED CHAIN FERN

☀/◑ ❄ ↔ 20–48 in (50–120 cm)
↕ 20–40 in (50–100 cm)
A tough deciduous species native to much of North America. Broad, simply divided pinnate sterile fronds up to 32 in (80 cm) long. Fertile fronds erect, slightly longer, with twisted segments often darkened by sporangia. Both of the frond forms feature dark stems. Zones 5–9.

Woodwardia fimbriata

GIANT CHAIN FERN

☀/◑ ❄ ↔ 3–7 ft (0.9–2 m)
↕ 3–7 ft (0.9–2 m)
An evergreen species from California and Arizona, USA. Fronds to 10 ft (3 m) long, frequently smaller. Sterile and fertile fronds do not differ greatly except for the obvious sporangia present on the undersides of fertile fronds. This is a species that may develop a short trunk with age. Zones 8–10.

Woodwardia unigemmata

☀/◑ ❄ ↔ 4–8 ft (1.2–2.4 m) ↕ 24–40 in (60–100 cm)
An evergreen species native to Southeast Asia and the Himalayas with broad, doubly divided fronds to nearly 4 ft (1.2 m) long. Young fronds often vivid red if they are exposed to sun. Fertile fronds do not differ greatly. Can produce new plantlets at frond tips. Zones 9–12.

ZAMIA

This genus in the zamia (Zamiaceae) family is made up of more than 55 species, most of which occur in South, Central, and

North America. All have pinnate leaves and cylindrical or tuber-like stems that are usually subterranean but may be above the ground. Plants are fern or palm-like in appearance, with the male and broader female cones borne on separate plants. Many species have highly toxic seeds. The spirally arranged arching leaves have mostly smooth leaflets, and the margins can be smooth-edged, toothed or bumpy, and spiny in some species. They come from a range of habitats. These plants make useful landscape subjects.

Zamia furfuracea

Most are best suited to tropical and subtropical regions that are free from frost.
CULTIVATION: Most are fairly adaptable in a well-drained soil. Tolerances vary; the understory types with softer lusher foliage usually are best in sheltered, more humid, semi-shaded positions, while the tougher-leafed species from more open habitats can usually tolerate more exposure and sun. Propagate from fresh seed.

Zamia fairchildiana ★

☀ ✦ ↔ 5 ft (1.5 m) ↕ 8 ft (2.4 m)
A species found growing in Costa Rica and western Panama. Attractive, with upright trunk. Leaves in whorls of 3 to 10, erect, thinly textured, papery green. Leaf stalk is densely prickly. Male cones are cream to yellow, female ones are yellowish green to light brown. Zones 11–12.

Zamia furfuracea ★

CARDBOARD PALM

☀ ✦ ↔ 7 ft (2 m) ↕ 3 ft (0.9 m)
Native to Mexico. Broad, hairy, stiff leaflets, attractive small to medium cycad, subterranean stem when young. Forms a mound of spreading leaves, olive green leathery leaflets, on spiny stalks. Cones are pink to red. An excellent tub plant. Zones 11–12.

Zamia pumila

GUAYIGA

☀ ✦ ↔ 6 ft (1.8 m) ↕ 5 ft (1.5 m)
From islands of the Caribbean. Bears short, many-branched, subterranean stems from which emerge 4 to 12 erect dark green leaves with smooth leaf stalks. Cones red to red-brown. Zones 10–12.

Index to Plant Names

Italicized page numbers refer to a photograph on the page, while plain page numbers indicate a reference in either the text or the tables.

Acknowledgments

Proofreading Puddingburn Publishing Services

Photographers David Banks, Chris Bell, Rob Blakers, Lorraine Blyth, Greg Bourke, Ken Brass, Geoff Bryant, Derek Butcher, Claver Carroll, Leigh Clapp, Mike Comb, David Austin Roses, Grant Dixon, Heather Donovan, e-garden Ltd, Bruce Elder, Katie Fallows, Derek Fells, Stuart Owen Fox, Richard Francis, Robert Gibson, William Grant, Denise Greig, Barry Griffith, Barry Grossman, Gil Hanly, Ivy Hansen, Dennis Harding, Jerry Harpur, Jack Hobbs, Neil Holmes, Paul Huntley, Richard I'Anson, Jason Ingram, Steve Johnson, David Keith Jones, Ionas Kaltenbach, Willie Kempen, Colin Kerr, Robert M. Knight, Carol Knoll, Albert Kuhnigk, Stan Lamond, Mike Langford, Gary Lewis, Geoff Longford, Stirling Macoboy, John McCann, David McGonigal, Richard McKenna, Ron Moon, Eberhard Morell, Barry Myers-Rice, Steve Newall, Connall Oosterbrock, Ron Parsons, Luke Pellatt, Larry Pitt, Craig Potton, Janet Price, Geof Prigge, Nick Rains, Christo Reid, Howard Rice, Jamie Robertson, Tony Rodd, Rolf Ulrich Roesler, Luke Saffigna, Don Skirrow, Raoul Slater, Michael Snedic, Peter Solness, Ken Stepnell, Warren Steptoe, Angus Stewart, Oliver Strewe, J. Peter Thoeming, David Titmuss, Wayne Turville, Georg Uebelhart, Ben-Erik van Wyk, Sharyn Vanderhorst, Kim Westerskov, Murray White, Vic Widman, Brent Wilson, Geoff Woods, Gary Yong Gee, Grant Young, James Young

Produced by Global Book Publishing Pty Ltd

Level 8, 15 Orion Road, Lane Cove, NSW 2066, Australia   Ph: (612) 9425 5800   Fax: (612) 9425 5804   Email: rightsmanager@globalpub.com.au
Photographs © Global Book Publishing Photo Library 2007   Text © Global Book Publishing Pty Ltd 2007